MODERN CONSTITUTIONAL LAW
CASES AND NOTES

Sixth Edition

By

Ronald D. Rotunda

The Albert E. Jenner, Jr. Professor of Law
University of Illinois

AMERICAN CASEBOOK SERIES®

WEST GROUP

ST. PAUL, MINN., 2000

American Casebook Series and the WP symbol are registered trademarks used herein under license.

ISBN 0–314–24652–5

TEXT IS PRINTED ON 10% POST CONSUMER RECYCLED PAPER

To Mark, Nora & Allen

*

Preface to the Sixth Edition

Much has changed over the years. When the first edition of this book was published, I was a young man in my 30s. Now I am a young man in my 50s. (Students will learn, as they get older, that one's perspective as to what is "old" changes with time.) One may think that all things tend towards entropy if they are used, and towards atrophy if they are not used. Well, law is different. Over time, law tends towards complexity. Constitutional Law is no exception to that principle.

Since the first edition, there has been relatively little change with respect to state powers under the dormant commerce clause, but the same cannot be said of federal powers in light of the commerce clause. *National League of Cities v. Usery* ushered in the rise of a new Tenth Amendment, followed by its fall (when the Court overruled *Usery*), followed by its partial resurrection with *New York v. United States* and cases within its wake. With the first edition, one speculated whether there were really any restrictions to federal power under the Commerce Clause. Now, with *United States v. Lopez*, we know that some limitations do exist. In fact, all nine justices agreed with that conclusion (although the four person dissent thought the law in question was within federal power).

Separation of Powers cases have also exploded since the first edition. Legislative veto, the Independent Counsel law, term limits for federal legislators, and the line item veto — for years these issues were mooted; now they are decided. The cases on state action have witnessed the creation of a new concept, the mirror image cases. The chapter on Equal Protection has seen the growth and later cut-backs in affirmative action. The Court has also reduced Congressional power to use the enforcement clauses of the Civil War Amendments. And the development in free speech law has been amazing, with the Court extending, for example, First Amendment protections to the Internet. The framers of our Constitution could not have anticipated the Internet. Indeed, few legal academics had heard of it when the first edition was published. But it is tribute to the genius of the framers that the magnificent protections of the Bill of Rights apply without regard to time. The number of cases dealing with religious freedom have also expanded, and the Court has been rethinking the issue of aid to private schools.

Yet, for all the changes, the basic organization of this book has not changed during the last twenty years. I like to think that this organizational stability is proof of my unusual prescience, but I think that another factor is more important. Changes in the law are inevitable, but these changes tend to be evolutionary. It is said that the judges do not own the law. They are merely its custodians, passing it down from one generation to the next. One of the important jobs of lawyers is to predict the law, and law is usually predictable because change is incremental. Even if one cannot predict a particular decision, one can predict the major arguments that both sides will use. Even if a particular decision is unanticipated, the arguments should be foreseen.

I express sincere thanks to my secretary, Ruth Manint, for her assistance in preparation of the manuscript, and to my colleague, John E. Nowak, for our many useful discussions on constitutional law. I am also indebted to the thoughtful suggestions of various law professors, law students, and others who have helped make this edition a better teaching tool. Finally, I appreciate the help of my research assistants over the last several years. The Stuart N. Greenberger Research Assistantship Fund has supplied funding for these research assistants.

A brief style note: for the main cases, the votes of all the justices are indicated, whether a justice's individual opinion is included or not. I have also deleted citations within cases without any special indication.

RONALD D. ROTUNDA
The Albert E. Jenner, Jr. Professor of Law

Champaign
April, 2000

Preface to the Fifth Edition

It is hard to believe that 16 years and four editions have passed since I wrote the Preface to the first edition of this book. The first edition was completed in Italy, where I was working on a project dealing with the efforts to create the European Union. Sixteen years ago, Western Europeans, as part of their long term effort to create a United States of Europe, wanted to examine the American experience with our unique federal structure. Since that first edition I have been privileged to travel to other countries—such as Cambodia and various countries of the former Soviet Bloc (Moldova, Ukraine, Romania, the Czech Republic). In each case, the new leaders of these countries also wanted to learn from the American experience. In fact, I began work on this edition last spring in Prague, where I was working with members of the Czech Bar and the Judiciary.

It is no coincidence that the newly emerging democracies, as well as Western Europe, often turn to the American constitutional experience. The countries of Europe and the far East are centuries older than the United States, but when it comes to constitution-building, we are the ones with the long tradition. It is well known that the United States Constitution is the oldest written constitution. What is less well known is that it is the oldest by far. Though there are nearly 200 written constitutions today, more than half were written after 1970. Only 15 constitutions were written prior to World War II, and only five were written prior to this century. Our constitution is the only one that was ratified in the Eighteenth Century. The second-oldest constitution is Norway's, and it dates only to 1815.

Our constitution does not appear to offer much when compared with the sweeping promises of the typical communist or socialist constitution. A recent Soviet constitution provided for the rights of "guaranteed work, health protection, [and] education." [1] Our Bill of Rights secures none of that. Yet, a half century after World War II, communism and its failed promises are in disarray, while democracy and a market economy are the wave of the future. As the modern author Salman Rushdie, has observed, the "people's spiritual needs, more than their material needs, have driven the commissars from power." [2] Our constitution gives no guarantee of food for the body but it offers food for the mind, by protecting freedom of

---

1. Konst. SSR ch. 7, art. 39–45 (1977, amended 1081).

2. Salman Rushdie, Is Nothing Sacred: The Herbert Read Memorial Lecture, Feb. 6, 1990, at 809. The spiritual head of Iran announced to the world in early 1989 that Rushdie must die because of his book, *Satan-ic Verses*, was, in the eyes of some Muslims, offensive. Since then, Rushdie went into hiding and several people who translated his book from English to other languages have been killed.

conscience. It protects the right to vote, so that people can choose a government that attends to material needs.

The organization of this edition is surprisingly similar to the organization of the first edition. That simple fact does not suggest that I have unusual prophetic powers, only that the law, including Constitutional Law, generally proceeds in logical steps. There is not the logic of Euclidian geometry, but there is a logic nonetheless.

The original edition was only 1025 pages long. This edition is only about 150 pages longer. The reason for the small increase is not that the Court has decided so little in the last 16 years, but rather that I have made a major effort to make sure that this edition is not too long, so that there can be adequate coverage of constitutional law within the confines of a typical law school class. But, the effort to put the book on a diet is not reached at the expense of thoroughness. It is better that students know a few things well, rather than to know very little about a lot of things.

I express sincere thanks to my secretary, Ruth Manint, for her assistance in preparation of the manuscript, and to my colleague, John E. Nowak, for our many useful discussions on constitutional law. I am also indebted to the thoughtful suggestions of various law professors, law students, and others who have helped make this edition a better teaching tool. Finally, I appreciate the help of my research assistants over the last several years. Funding has been made possible by the Stuart N. Greenberger Research Assistantship Fund.

A brief style note: for the main cases, the votes of all the justices are indicated, whether a justice's individual opinion is included or not. I have also deleted citations within cases without any special indication.

RONALD D. ROTUNDA
The Albert E. Jenner, Jr. Professor of Law

Champaign
January 1997

Preface to the Fourth Edition

It is said that as people become older, they tend to get a little fatter. So it is with books, as they move from one edition to the next. This book is now in its fourth edition, and I have tried to put it on a very strict diet. Unfortunately, Supreme Court decisions constitute the main diet of this book, and these decisions seem to be becoming longer and longer, with the law becoming more complex. The trick is to keep this book within managable size, without sacrificing completeness. With each new edition, this trick is getting a lot harder to perform.

Changes in the law have, of course, necessitated dropping some cases and adding others. Where the Supreme Court has shown particular interest in an area of law, or where an area seems more unsettled, I have focused more on the recent cases. See, for example, the Supreme Court's recent flurry of cases involving the public forum, § 10–3.3, and commercial speech, § 10–7. For most of the life of the Court, there has been a dearth of separation of powers cases. But not in recent years. Consequently, Chapter 5 has been expanded, with the addition, among others of *Bowsher v. Synar* (1986), invalidating portions of the Gramm-Rudman-Hollings Act, *Morrison v. Olson* (1988), upholding the Independent Counsel law, and *Mistretta v. United States* (1989), upholding the Sentencing Commission.

I have retained the basic pedagogical purposes of the first edition. The Preface to that edition, which explains my approach to the basic course in Constitutional Law, is reprinted after this one. This volume contains the more significant United States Supreme Court cases issued through June 1992, the end of the latest Court Term. More recent decisions will appear in the annual supplements, the first appearing in August, 1993. As before, in these annual cumulative supplements, I will seek to keep the number of excerpted cases to a minimum, rather than merely chronicle the work of the Court. These supplements will include only those new developments of particular note.

My students over the years, as well as several book reviews and colleagues who use this book in this school and elsewhere, have all caused me to rethink the structure and content of this casebook. I am also indebted to the various thoughtful suggestions of Professor Charles Alan Wright. I am grateful for these and other suggestions that have made this edition, I hope, not only more up-to-date than the previous edition but a better teaching tool.

I express sincere thanks to my secretary, Ruth Manint for her assistance in preparation of the manuscript, and Elaine Chin, the Stuart N. Greenberger Research Assistant.

A brief style note: for the main cases, the votes of all the justices are indicated, whether a justice's individual opinion is included or not. However, not all the votes of individual justices are included for the noted cases. Also, I have deleted citations within cases without any special indication.

R.D.R.

Champaign
January, 1993

*

Preface to the Third Edition

As in the first edition, I have intended to keep this book within manageable size, but without sacrificing completeness. The effort, unfortunately, has become more difficult over the years. The law is becoming more complex, and the opinions seem to be getting longer and longer. Changes in the law have, of course, necessitated dropping some cases and adding others. Where the Supreme Court has shown particular interest in an area of law, or where an area seems more unsettled, I have focused more on the recent cases. See, for example, the Supreme Court's recent flurry of cases involving the public forum cases, § 10–3.3, and commercial speech, § 10–7. For most of the life of the Court, there has been a dearth of separation of powers cases. But not in recent years. Consequently, Chapter 5 has been expanded, with the addition, among others of *Bowsher v. Synar* (1986) invalidating portions of the Gramm-Rudman-Hollings Act, and *Morrison v. Olson* (1988), upholding the Independent Counsel law.

I have retained the basic pedagogical purposes of the first edition. The Preface to that edition, which explains my approach to the basic course in Constitutional Law, is reprinted after this one. This volume contains the more significant United States Supreme Court cases issued through July 29, 1988, the end of the latest Court Term. More recent decisions will appear in the annual supplements, the first appearing in August, 1989. As before, in these annual cumulative supplements, I will seek to keep the number of excerpted cases to a minimum, rather than merely chronicle the work of the Court. These supplements will include only those new developments of particular note.

My students over the years, as well as several book reviews and colleagues who use this book in this school and elsewhere, have all caused me to rethink the structure and content of this casebook. For example, some professors have suggested that the casebook should include more information on commerce clause limitations on state and local taxing powers; therefore a textual note has been added as an appendix to the end of Chapter Three. I am also indebted to the various thoughtful suggestions of Professor Charles Alan Wright. I am grateful for these and other suggestions which have made this edition, I hope, not only more up-to-date than the previous edition but a better teaching tool.

I express sincere thanks to my secretary, Ruth Manint for her assistance in preparation of the manuscript.

A brief style note: for the main cases, the votes of all the justices are indicated, whether a justice's individual opinion is included or not. However, not all the votes of individual justices are included for the noted

cases. Also, I have deleted citations within cases without any special indication.

R.D.R.

Champaign
January, 1989

*

Preface to the Second Edition

This edition is a revision and update of the previous edition. It retains much of the same organization except that some of the complex procedural issues—which had been in Chapter One of the first edition—have been moved to a new Chapter Twelve, The Procedural Context of Constitutional Litigation.

As in the first edition, I have intended to keep this book within manageable size, but without sacrificing completeness. Changes in the law have, of course, necessitated dropping some cases and adding others. Where the Supreme Court has shown particular interest in an area of law, or where an area seems more unsettled, I have focused more on the recent cases. See, for example, the Supreme Court's recent interest in the state as market participant (Chapter 3, section 3–4); and the tenth amendment (Chapter 4, section 4–5). In other areas the Supreme Court has helped clarify the law, see for example its more complete definition of the public forum. See Chapter 10, section 10–3.3.

I have retained the basic pedagogical purposes of the first edition. The Preface to that edition, which explains my approach to the basic course in Constitutional Law, is reprinted immediately after this one. As in the first edition this volume contains the more significant United States Supreme Court cases issued through July 5, 1984, the end of the latest Court Term. I have also included in this volume the 1985 decision in *Garcia* which overruled *National League of Cities*. Other 1985 decisions will appear in the annual supplements. As before, I have sought to keep the number of excerpted cases to a minimum, rather than merely chronicle the work of the Court.

My students over the years, as well as several book reviews and colleagues who use this book in this school and elsewhere, have all caused me to rethink the structure and content of this casebook. For example, some professors have suggested that the casebook should include more information on commerce clause limitations on state and local taxing powers; therefore a textual note has been added as an appendix to the end of Chapter Three. I am also indebted to the various thoughtful suggestions of Professor Charles Alan Wright. I am grateful for these and other suggestions which have made this edition, I hope, not only more up-to-date than the previous edition but a better teaching tool.

I express sincere thanks to my secretary, Barbara Milazzo, for her assistance in preparation of the manuscript, and also to Marcia Williams and C. David Watson, third year law students at the University of Illinois, for their assistance.

Each year, at the end of the Supreme Court term, I will publish cumulative annual supplements, which will include only those new developments of particular importance.

R.D.R.

Champaign
January, 1985

*

Preface to the First Edition

I have intended this book to serve as a compact pedagogical tool introducing and exposing students to the underlying principles of constitutional law.[1] An understanding of these principles in the introductory constitutional law course is, I believe, much more important than simply acquiring knowledge of many intricate, rapidly changing, constitutional rules.[2] It is fair to say that in some areas only half of what a student learns in school today will be "law" by the time he or she graduates, and it is difficult to predict which half. Consequently it is of greater significance for a student to acquire from the case law a sound understanding of the basic principles. The student must also learn how to use these principles in developing an ability to analyze thoroughly the issues that will face the courts in the years ahead. Finally, he or she should have a sense of where the law is moving, because what the law ought to be influences what the law is and will be.

The goal of keeping this volume to a manageable size is not reached at the expense of thoroughness, for it is better to know a few things well than to know many things superficially. Thus I have sought to limit the size of the book in other ways. For example, the book treats sparingly certain areas that now are frequently taught as separate courses, such as state and local taxation and criminal procedure; it also restricts citations to and excerpts from secondary authority[3] in order to emphasize the case law; and it limits textual notes to a minimum in order to favor intensive coverage of a limited number of cases. Although this book is already substantially shorter than most of the other materials available, the teacher can further reduce its size by deciding to omit certain areas. Thus one may eliminate much of the first chapter on jurisdictional issues (or save these issues until the end of the course).

The coverage of this book focuses on those areas of constitutional law that are of basic and historical significance and those areas of contemporary interest that are likely to be of increasing importance in the years

---

1. Students interested in a research (as opposed to a teaching) tool can turn to J. Nowak, R. Rotunda, and J. Young, Constitutional Law (West Pub. Co. 1978) plus latest pocket part, or L. Tribe, American Constitutional Law (Foundation Press 1978). The organization of this casebook roughly follows the first of these texts, though I have made various organizational changes for pedagogical purposes.

2. Some imagine the law "as a big book of rules, and to know them may be the task of its apprentices. A third of a century ago the story used to be told at Harvard of the new law student who went to call on the dear

old lady in Brookline. 'Well, well,' she said, 'So you've been studying law for two weeks. How many laws have you learned?' " A. Sutherland, Prologue to an Introduction vii, viii, in An Introduction to Law: Selected Essays Reprinted from the Harvard Law Review (1965).

3. Thus, the book often omits secondary authority cited within an excerpted case. Also deleted are many internal case and statute citations within a case. Footnotes to cases are numbered as in the original. No special indication is made when footnotes, case law, and other authority are deleted within a case.

ahead. The emphasis is on *modern* constitutional law. Thus the text includes a rather extensive section on the treaty power, power over aliens, and similar foreign affairs problems. This section—as well as others, such as the zoning powers—also directs the student's attention to the civil liberties implications of the case law.

In determining which cases to excerpt, I have included not only the historical beacons, but also some of the lesser lights that help to provide thoughtful classroom discussion. For the same reason the book occasionally includes hypotheticals following some of the cases.[4] The case excerpts are usually quite lengthy to facilitate Socratic dialogue. Also, excessive editing makes it more difficult for a student to get a genuine feeling for the case: one who has had an opportunity to read an extensive excerpt of *Home Building & Loan Association v. Blaisdell* (1934) would not be surprised by the result of the more recent decision in *Allied Structural Steel v. Spannaus* (1978).

In preparing this book I have greatly profited from discussions with my colleagues at the University of Illinois who have read parts of the manuscript and offered helpful suggestions: Professors Francis Boyle, Daniel A. Farber, Mary Louise Fellows, Harry D. Krause, J. Steven Lawrence, Wayne R. LaFave, John E. Nowak, John E. Muench, Ralph Reisner, and J. Nelson Young. I am particularly indebted to John Nowak, for throughout this book are insights resulting from our many conversations on problems of constitutional law. I am grateful to former Dean John Cribbet and Dean Peter Hay, who offered encouragement, advice, and research support. Any errors that remain in the book are, of course, my responsibility. I would also like to thank the authors and publishers for permission to reprint excerpts of any copyrighted materials, and to thank Clarence Krantz and Steven Stevens, law students at the University of Illinois, for their careful cite checking and proof reading. My secretary, Diane Defeo, deserves special thanks for her assistance in preparation of the manuscript.

The cut off date for this book is October, 1980. Annual supplements will include only those new developments of particular importance, with the first supplement to appear in August, 1981.

RONALD D. ROTUNDA

Florence
January, 1981

---

4. Often these hypotheticals are followed by a case or other citation. The citation is intended for reference only, and the student should be able to discuss fully the issues (and often predict the result) on the basis of the prior reading, without examining the cited materials.

Summary of Contents

*

Table of Contents

―――――――

*

Table of Cases

The principal cases are in bold type. Cases cited or discussed in the text are roman type. References are to pages. Cases cited in principal cases and within other quoted materials are not included.

The United States Supreme Court, 2000

BACK ROW *(from left to right)*: Ruth Bader Ginsburg;
David H. Souter; Clarence Thomas; Stephen G. Breyer

FRONT ROW *(from left to right)*: Antonin Scalia; John Paul Stevens;
William H. Rehnquist; Sandra Day O'Connor; Anthony M. Kennedy

Reprinted with permission from the Collection, The Supreme Court Historical
Society.

*

The Justices of the Supreme Court

Chief Justice	Age at Appointment	President	Term of Service
John Jay	43	Washington	1789–1795
*John Rutledge	55	Washington	1795
Oliver Ellsworth	50	Washington	1796–1800
John Marshall	45	J. Adams	1801–1835
Roger B. Taney	58	Jackson	1836–1864
Salmon P. Chase	56	Lincoln	1864–1873
Morrison R. Waite	57	Grant	1874–1888
Melville W. Fuller	55	Cleveland	1888–1910
*Edward D. White	65	Taft	1910–1921
William H. Taft	63	Harding	1921–1930
*Charles E. Hughes	67	Hoover	1930–1941
*Harlan F. Stone	68	F.D. Roosevelt	1941–1946
Fred M. Vinson	56	Truman	1946–1953
Earl Warren	62	Eisenhower	1953–1969
Warren E. Burger	61	Nixon	1969–1986
*William H. Rehnquist	61	Reagan	1986–

Associate Justice	Age at Appointment	President	Term of Service
**John Rutledge	50	Washington	1789–1791
William Cushing	57	Washington	1789–1810
James Wilson	47	Washington	1789–1798
John Blair	57	Washington	1789–1796
James Iredell	38	Washington	1790–1799
Thomas Johnson	58	Washington	1791–1793
William Paterson	47	Washington	1793–1806
Samuel Chase	54	Washington	1796–1811
Bushrod Washington	36	J. Adams	1798–1829
Alfred Moore	44	J. Adams	1799–1804
William Johnson	32	Jefferson	1804–1834
Henry B. Livingston	49	Jefferson	1806–1823
Thomas Todd	42	Jefferson	1807–1826
Joseph Story	32	Madison	1811–1845
Gabriel Duval	58	Madison	1811–1835
Smith Thompson	55	Monroe	1823–1843
Robert Trimble	49	J.Q. Adams	1826–1828
John McLean	43	Jackson	1829–1861
Henry Baldwin	49	Jackson	1830–1844
James M. Wayne	45	Jackson	1835–1867

* Indicates was also an Associate Justice.   ** Indicates was also Chief Justice.

Associate Justice	Age at Appointment	President	Term of Service
Philip B. Barbour	52	Jackson	1836–1841
John Catron	51	Jackson	1837–1865
John McKinley	57	Van Buren	1837–1852
Peter V. Daniel	56	Van Buren	1841–1860
Samuel Nelson	52	Tyler	1845–1872
Levi Woodbury	56	Polk	1845–1851
Robert O. Grier	52	Polk	1846–1870
Benjamin Curtis	42	Fillmore	1851–1857
John A. Campbell	41	Pierce	1853–1861
Nathan Clifford	54	Buchanan	1858–1881
Noah H. Swayne	57	Lincoln	1862–1881
Samuel F. Miller	46	Lincoln	1862–1890
David Davis	47	Lincoln	1862–1877
Stephen J. Field	46	Lincoln	1863–1897
William Strong	61	Grant	1870–1880
Joseph P. Bradley	66	Grant	1870–1892
Ward Hunt	62	Grant	1872–1882
John M. Harlan	44	Hayes	1877–1911
William B. Woods	56	Hayes	1880–1887
Stanley Matthews	56	Garfield	1881–1889
Horace Gray	53	Arthur	1881–1902
Samuel Blatchford	62	Arthur	1882–1893
Lucius Q.C. Lamar	62	Cleveland	1888–1893
David J. Brewer	52	Harrison	1889–1910
Henry B. Brown	54	Harrison	1890–1906
George Shiras, Jr.	60	Harrison	1892–1903
Howell E. Jackson	60	Harrison	1893–1895
**Edward D. White	48	Cleveland	1894–1910
Rufus W. Peckham	57	Cleveland	1895–1909
Joseph McKenna	54	McKinley	1898–1925
Oliver W. Holmes, Jr.	61	T. Roosevelt	1902–1932
William R. Day	53	T. Roosevelt	1903–1922
William H. Moody	52	T. Roosevelt	1906–1910
Horace H. Lurton	65	Taft	1909–1914
**Charles E. Hughes	48	Taft	1910–1916
Willis Van Devanter	51	Taft	1910–1937
Joseph R. Lamar	53	Taft	1910–1916
Mahlon Pitney	54	Taft	1912–1922
James C. McReynolds	52	Wilson	1914–1941
Louis D. Brandeis	59	Wilson	1916–1939
John H. Clarke	58	Wilson	1916–1922
George Sutherland	60	Harding	1922–1938
Pierce Butler	56	Harding	1922–1939

** Indicates was also Chief Justice.

Associate Justice	Age at Appointment	President	Term of Service
Edward T. Sanford	57	Harding	1923–1930
**Harlan F. Stone	52	Coolidge	1925–1941
Owen J. Roberts	55	Hoover	1930–1945
Benjamin N. Cardozo	61	Hoover	1932–1938
Hugo L. Black	51	F.D. Roosevelt	1937–1971
Stanley F. Reed	53	F.D. Roosevelt	1938–1957
Felix Frankfurter	56	F.D. Roosevelt	1939–1962
William O. Douglas	40	F.D. Roosevelt	1939–1975
Frank Murphy	49	F.D. Roosevelt	1940–1949
James F. Byrnes	62	F.D. Roosevelt	1941–1942
Robert H. Jackson	49	F.D. Roosevelt	1941–1954
Wiley B. Rutledge	48	F.D. Roosevelt	1943–1949
Harold H. Burton	57	Truman	1945–1958
Tom C. Clark	49	Truman	1949–1967
Sherman Minton	58	Truman	1949–1956
John M. Harlan	55	Eisenhower	1955–1971
William J. Brennan	50	Eisenhower	1956–1990
Charles E. Whittaker	56	Eisenhower	1957–1962
Potter Stewart	43	Eisenhower	1958–1981
Byron R. White	44	Kennedy	1962–1993
Arthur J. Goldberg	54	Kennedy	1962–1965
Abe Fortas	55	L.B. Johnson	1965–1969
Thurgood Marshall	59	L.B. Johnson	1967–1991
Harry A. Blackmun	61	Nixon	1970–1994
Lewis F. Powell, Jr.	64	Nixon	1971–1987
**William H. Rehnquist	47	Nixon	1971–
John Paul Stevens	55	Ford	1975–
Sandra Day O'Connor	51	Reagan	1981–
Antonin Scalia	50	Reagan	1986–
Anthony M. Kennedy	51	Reagan	1988–
David H. Souter	51	Bush	1990–
Clarence Thomas	43	Bush	1991–
Ruth Bader Ginsburg	60	Clinton	1993–
Stephen G. Breyer	56	Clinton	1994–

** Indicates was also Chief Justice.

*

The Constitution of the United States *

1787 [1]

Preamble

We the People of the United States, in Order to form a more perfect Union, establish Justice, insure domestic Tranquility, provide for the

---

* Adapted, with permission, from United States Code Annotated, Constitution of the United States, Annotated (West Publishing Co. 1968).

1. In May, 1785, a committee of Congress made a report recommending an alteration in the Articles of Confederation, but no action was taken on it, and it was left to the State Legislatures to proceed in the matter. In January, 1786, the Legislature of Virginia passed a resolution providing for the appointment of five commissioners, who, or any three of them, should meet such commissioners as might be appointed in the other States of the Union, at a time and place to be agreed upon, to take into consideration the trade of the United States; to consider how far a uniform system in their commercial regulations may be necessary to their common interest and their permanent harmony; and to report to the several States such an act, relative to this great object, as, when ratified by them, will enable the United States in Congress effectually to provide for the same. The Virginia commissioners, after some correspondence, fixed the first Monday in September as the time, and the city of Annapolis as the place for the meeting, but only four other States were represented, viz.: Delaware, New York, New Jersey, and Pennsylvania; the commissioners appointed by Massachusetts, New Hampshire, North Carolina, and Rhode Island failed to attend. Under the circumstances of so partial a representation, the commissioners present agreed upon a report, (drawn by Mr. Hamilton of New York,) expressing their unanimous conviction that it might essentially tend to advance the interests of the Union if the States by which they were respectively delegated would concur, and use their endeavors to procure the concurrence of the other States, in the appointment of commissioners to meet at Philadelphia on the second Monday of May following, to take into consideration the situation of the United States; to devise such further provisions as should appear to them necessary to render the Constitution of the Federal Government adequate to the exigences of the Union; and to report such an act for that purpose to the United States in Congress assembled as, when agreed to by them, and afterwards confirmed by the Legislatures of every State, would effectually provide for the same.

Congress, on the 21st of February, 1787, adopted a resolution in favor of a convention, and the Legislatures of those States which had not already done so (with the exception of Rhode Island) promptly appointed delegates. On the 25th of May, seven States having convened, George Washington, of Virginia, was unanimously elected President, and the consideration of the proposed constitution was commenced. On the 17th of September, 1787, the Constitution as engrossed and agreed upon was signed by all the members present, except Mr. Gerry, of Massachusetts, and Messrs. Mason and Randolph, of Virginia. The president of the convention transmitted it to Congress, with a resolution stating how the proposed Federal Government should be put in operation, and an explanatory letter. Congress, on the 28th of September, 1787, directed the Constitution so framed, with the resolutions and letter concerning the same, to "be transmitted to the several Legislatures in order to be submitted to a convention of delegates chosen in each State by the people thereof, in conformity to the resolves of the convention."

On the 4th of March, 1789, the day which had been fixed for commencing the operations of Government under the new Constitution, it had been ratified by the conventions chosen in each State to consider it, as follows: Delaware, December 7, 1787; Pennsylvania, December 12, 1787; New Jersey, December 18, 1787; Georgia, January 2, 1788; Connecticut, January 9, 1788; Massachusetts, February 6, 1788; Maryland, April 28, 1788; South Carolina, May 23, 1788; New Hampshire, June 21, 1788; Virginia, June 26, 1788; and New York, July 26, 1788.

The President informed Congress, on the 28th of January, 1790, that North Carolina had ratified the Constitution November 21, 1789; and he informed Congress on the 1st

common defence, promote the general Welfare, and secure the Blessings of Liberty to ourselves and our Posterity, do ordain and establish this Constitution for the United States of America.

Article I

Section 1. All legislative Powers herein granted shall be vested in a Congress of the United States, which shall consist of a Senate and House of Representatives.

Section 2. [1] The House of Representatives shall be composed of Members chosen every second Year by the People of the several States, and the Electors in each State shall have the Qualifications requisite for Electors of the most numerous Branch of the State Legislature.

[2]   No Person shall be a Representative who shall not have attained to the Age of twenty five Years, and been seven Years a Citizen of the United States, and who shall not, when elected, be an Inhabitant of that State in which he shall be chosen.

[3]   [Representatives and direct Taxes shall be apportioned among the several States which may be included within this Union, according to their respective Numbers, which shall be determined by adding to the whole Number of free Persons, including those bound to Service for a Term of Years, and excluding Indians not taxed, three fifths of all other Persons.] The actual Enumeration shall be made within three Years after the first Meeting of the Congress of the United States, and within every subsequent Term of ten Years, in such Manner as they shall by Law direct. The Number of Representatives shall not exceed one for every thirty Thousand, but each State shall have at Least one Representative; and until such enumeration shall be made, the State of New Hampshire shall be entitled to chuse three, Massachusetts eight, Rhode Island and Providence Plantations one, Connecticut five, New York six, New Jersey four, Pennsylvania eight, Delaware one, Maryland six, Virginia ten, North Carolina five, South Carolina five, and Georgia three.

> **The clause of this paragraph inclosed in brackets was amended, as to the mode of apportionment of representatives among the several states, by the Fourteenth Amendment, § 2, and as to taxes on incomes without apportionment, by the Sixteenth Amendment.**

[4]   When vacancies happen in the Representation from any State, the Executive Authority thereof shall issue Writs of Election to fill such Vacancies.

[5]   The House of Representatives shall chuse their Speaker and other Officers; and shall have the sole Power of Impeachment.

Section 3. [1] [The Senate of the United States shall be composed of two Senators from each State, chosen by the Legislature thereof, for six Years; and each Senator shall have one Vote.]

of June, 1790, that Rhode Island had ratified the Constitution May 29, 1790. Vermont, in convention, ratified the Constitution January 10, 1791, and was on March 4, 1791, by an act of Congress approved February 18, 1791, "received and admitted into this Union as a new and entire member of the United States".

This paragraph and the clause of following paragraph inclosed in brackets were superseded by the Seventeenth Amendment.

[2] Immediately after they shall be assembled in Consequence of the first Election, they shall be divided as equally as may be into three Classes. The Seats of the Senators of the first Class shall be vacated at the Expiration of the Second Year, of the second Class at the Expiration of the fourth Year, and of the third Class at the Expiration of the sixth Year, so that one third may be chosen every second Year; [and if Vacancies happen by Resignation, or otherwise, during the Recess of the Legislature of any State, the Executive thereof may make temporary Appointments until the next Meeting of the Legislature, which shall then fill such Vacancies.]

See note to preceding paragraph of this section.

[3] No Person shall be a Senator who shall not have attained to the Age of thirty Years, and been nine Years a Citizen of the United States, and who shall not, when elected, be an Inhabitant of that State for which he shall be chosen.

[4] The Vice President of the United States shall be President of the Senate, but shall have no Vote, unless they be equally divided.

[5] The Senate shall chuse their other Officers, and also a President pro tempore, in the Absence of the Vice President, or when he shall exercise the Office of President of the United States.

[6] The Senate shall have the sole Power to try all Impeachments. When sitting for that Purpose, they shall be on Oath or Affirmation. When the President of the United States is tried, the Chief Justice shall preside: And no Person shall be convicted without the Concurrence of two thirds of the Members present.

[7] Judgment in Cases of Impeachment shall not extend further than to removal from Office, and disqualification to hold and enjoy any Office of honor, Trust, or Profit under the United States: but the Party convicted shall nevertheless be liable and subject to Indictment, Trial, Judgment, and Punishment, according to Law.

Section 4. [1] The Times, Places and Manner of holding Elections for Senators and Representatives, shall be prescribed in each State by the Legislature thereof; but the Congress may at any time by Law make or alter such Regulations, except as to the Places of chusing Senators.

[2] The Congress shall assemble at least once in every Year, and such Meeting shall be on the first Monday in December, unless they shall by Law appoint a different Day.

Section 5. [1] Each House shall be the Judge of the Elections, Returns, and Qualifications of its own Members, and a Majority of each shall constitute a Quorum to do Business; but a smaller Number may adjourn from day to day, and may be authorized to compel the Attendance of absent Members, in such Manner, and under such Penalties as each House may provide.

[2]   Each House may determine the Rules of its Proceedings, punish its Members for disorderly Behaviour, and, with the Concurrence of two thirds, expel a Member.

[3]   Each House shall keep a Journal of its Proceedings, and from time to time publish the same, excepting such Parts as may in their Judgment require Secrecy; and the Yeas and Nays of the Members of either House on any question shall, at the Desire of one fifth of those Present, be entered on the Journal.

[4]   Neither House, during the Session of Congress, shall, without the Consent of the other, adjourn for more than three days, nor to any other Place than that in which the two Houses shall be sitting.

Section 6. [1] The Senators and Representatives shall receive a Compensation for their Services, to be ascertained by Law, and paid out of the Treasury of the United States.   They shall in all Cases, except Treason, Felony and Breach of the Peace, be privileged from Arrest during their Attendance at the Session of their respective Houses, and in going to and returning from the same; and for any Speech or Debate in either House, they shall not be questioned in any other Place.

[2]   No Senator or Representative shall, during the Time for which he was elected, be appointed to any civil Office under the Authority of the United States, which shall have been created, or the Emoluments whereof shall have been increased during such time; and no Person holding any Office under the United States, shall be a Member of either House during his Continuance in Office.

Section 7. [1] All Bills for raising Revenue shall originate in the House of Representatives; but the Senate may propose or concur with Amendments as on other Bills.

[2]   Every Bill which shall have passed the House of Representatives and the Senate, shall, before it become a Law, be presented to the President of the United States; If he approve he shall sign it, but if not he shall return it, with his Objections to the House in which it shall have originated, who shall enter the Objections at large on their Journal, and proceed to reconsider it. If after such Reconsideration two thirds of that House shall agree to pass the Bill, it shall be sent together with the Objections, to the other House, by which it shall likewise be reconsidered, and if approved by two thirds of that House, it shall become a Law. But in all such Cases the Votes of both Houses shall be determined by Yeas and Nays, and the Names of the Persons voting for and against the Bill shall be entered on the Journal of each House respectively. If any Bill shall not be returned by the President within ten Days (Sundays excepted) after it shall have been presented to him, the Same shall be a Law, in like Manner as if he had signed it, unless the Congress by their Adjournment prevent its Return in which Case it shall not be a Law.

[3]   Every Order, Resolution, or Vote, to Which the Concurrence of the Senate and House of Representatives may be necessary (except on a question of Adjournment) shall be presented to the President of the United States; and before the Same shall take Effect, shall be approved by

him, or being disapproved by him, shall be repassed by two thirds of the Senate and House of Representatives, according to the Rules and Limitations prescribed in the Case of a Bill.

Section 8. [1] The Congress shall have Power to lay and collect Taxes, Duties, Imposts and Excises, to pay the Debts and provide for the common Defence and general Welfare of the United States; but all Duties, Imposts and Excises shall be uniform throughout the United States;

[2]   To borrow money on the credit of the United States;

[3]   To regulate Commerce with foreign Nations, and among the several States, and with the Indian Tribes;

[4]   To establish an uniform Rule of Naturalization, and uniform Laws on the subject of Bankruptcies throughout the United States;

[5]   To coin Money, regulate the Value thereof, and of foreign Coin, and fix the Standard of Weights and Measures;

[6]   To provide for the Punishment of counterfeiting the Securities and current Coin of the United States;

[7]   To Establish Post Offices and Post Roads;

[8]   To promote the Progress of Science and useful Arts, by securing for limited Times to Authors and Inventors the exclusive Right to their respective Writings and Discoveries;

[9]   To constitute Tribunals inferior to the supreme Court;

[10]   To define and punish Piracies and Felonies committed on the high Seas, and Offenses against the Law of Nations;

[11]   To declare War, grant Letters of Marque and Reprisal, and make Rules concerning Captures on Land and Water;

[12]   To raise and support Armies, but no Appropriation of Money to that Use shall be for a longer Term than two Years;

[13]   To provide and maintain a Navy;

[14]   To make Rules for the Government and Regulation of the land and naval Forces;

[15]   To provide for calling forth the Militia to execute the Laws of the Union, suppress Insurrections and repel Invasions;

[16]   To provide for organizing, arming, and disciplining, the Militia, and for governing such Part of them as may be employed in the Service of the United States, reserving to the States respectively, the Appointment of the Officers, and the Authority of training the Militia according to the discipline prescribed by Congress;

[17]   To exercise exclusive Legislation in all Cases whatsoever, over such District (not exceeding ten Miles square) as may, by Cession of particular States and the Acceptance of Congress, become the Seat of the Government of the United States, and to exercise like Authority over all Places purchased by the Consent of the Legislature of the State in which the Same shall be, for the Erection of Forts, Magazines, Arsenals, dock-Yards, and other needful Buildings;—And

[18]   To make all Laws which shall be necessary and proper for carrying into Execution the foregoing Powers, and all other Powers vested by this Constitution in the Government of the United States, or in any Department or Officer thereof.

Section 9. [1] The Migration or Importation of Such Persons as any of the States now existing shall think proper to admit, shall not be prohibited by the Congress prior to the Year one thousand eight hundred and eight, but a Tax or duty may be imposed on such Importation, not exceeding ten dollars for each Person.

[2]   The privilege of the Writ of Habeas Corpus shall not be suspended, unless when in Cases of Rebellion or Invasion the public Safety may require it.

[3]   No Bill of Attainder or ex post facto Law shall be passed.

[4]   No Capitation, or other direct, Tax shall be laid, unless in Proportion to the Census or Enumeration herein before directed to be taken.

[5]   No Tax or Duty shall be laid on Articles exported from any State.

[6]   No Preference shall be given by any Regulation of Commerce or Revenue to the Ports of one State over those of another: nor shall Vessels bound to, or from, one State be obliged to enter, clear, or pay Duties in another.

[7]   No money shall be drawn from the Treasury, but in Consequence of Appropriations made by Law; and a regular Statement and Account of the Receipts and Expenditures of all public Money shall be published from time to time.

[8]   No Title of Nobility shall be granted by the United States: And no Person holding any Office of Profit or Trust under them, shall, without the Consent of the Congress, accept of any present, Emolument, Office, or Title, of any kind whatever, from any King, Prince, or foreign State.

Section 10. [1] No State shall enter into any Treaty, Alliance, or Confederation; grant Letters of Marque and Reprisal; coin Money; emit Bills of Credit; make any Thing but gold and silver Coin a Tender in Payment of Debts; pass any Bill of Attainder, ex post facto Law, or Law impairing the Obligation of Contracts, or grant any Title of Nobility.

[2]   No State shall, without the Consent of the Congress, lay any Imposts or Duties on Imports or Exports, except what may be absolutely necessary for executing it's inspection Laws: and the net Produce of all Duties and Imposts, laid by any State on Imports or Exports, shall be for the Use of the Treasury of the United States; and all such Laws shall be subject to the Revision and Controul of the Congress.

[3]   No State shall, without the Consent of Congress, lay any Duty of Tonnage, keep Troops, or Ships of War in time of Peace, enter into any Agreement or Compact with another State, or with a foreign Power or en-

gage in War, unless actually invaded, or in such imminent Danger as will not admit of delay.

Article II

Section 1. [1] The executive Power shall be vested in a President of the United States of America. He shall hold his Office during the Term of four Years, and, together with the Vice President, chosen for the same Term, be elected, as follows:

[2] Each State shall appoint, in such Manner as the Legislature thereof may direct, a Number of Electors, equal to the whole Number of Senators and Representatives to which the State may be entitled in the Congress; but no Senator or Representative, or Person holding an Office of Trust or Profit under the United States, shall be appointed an Elector.

[3] [The Electors shall meet in their respective States, and vote by Ballot for two Persons, of whom one at least shall not be an Inhabitant of the same State with themselves. And they shall make a List of all the Persons voted for, and of the Number of Votes for each; which List they shall sign and certify, and transmit sealed to the Seat of the Government of the United States, directed to the President of the Senate. The President of the Senate shall, in the Presence of the Senate and House of Representatives, open all the Certificates, and the Votes shall then be counted. The Person having the greatest Number of Votes shall be the President, if such Number be a Majority of the whole Number of Electors appointed; and if there be more than one who have such Majority, and have an equal Number of Votes, then the House of Representatives shall immediately chuse by Ballot one of them for President; and if no Person have a Majority, then from the five highest on the List the said House shall in like Manner chuse the President. But in chusing the President, the Votes shall be taken by States, the Representation from each State having one Vote; A quorum for this Purpose shall consist of a Member or Members from two thirds of the States, and a Majority of all the States shall be necessary to a Choice. In every Case, after the Choice of the President, the Person having the greater Number of Votes of the Electors shall be the Vice President. But if there should remain two or more who have equal Votes, the Senate shall chuse from them by Ballot the Vice President.]

This paragraph, inclosed in brackets, was superseded by the Twelfth Amendment, post.

[4] The Congress may determine the Time of chusing the Electors, and the Day on which they shall give their Votes; which Day shall be the same throughout the United States.

[5] No person except a natural born Citizen, or a Citizen of the United States, at the time of the Adoption of this Constitution, shall be eligible to the Office of President; neither shall any Person be eligible to that Office who shall not have attained to the Age of thirty five Years, and been fourteen Years a Resident within the United States.

[6]   In case of the removal of the President from Office, or of his Death, Resignation or Inability to discharge the Powers and Duties of the said Office, the Same shall devolve on the Vice President and the Congress may by Law provide for the Case of Removal, Death, Resignation or Inability, both of the President and Vice President, declaring what Officer shall then act as President, and such Officer shall act accordingly, until the Disability be removed, or a President shall be elected.

[7]   The President shall, at stated Times, receive for his Services, a Compensation, which shall neither be increased nor diminished during the Period for which he shall have been elected, and he shall not receive within that Period any other Emolument from the United States, or any of them.

[8]   Before he enter on the Execution of his Office, he shall take the following Oath or Affirmation: "I do solemnly swear (or affirm) that I will faithfully execute the Office of President of the United States, and will to the best of my Ability, preserve, protect and defend the Constitution of the United States."

Section 2. [1] The President shall be Commander in Chief of the Army and Navy of the United States, and of the militia of the several States, when called into the actual Service of the United States; he may require the Opinion, in writing, of the principal Officer in each of the Executive Departments, upon any Subject relating to the Duties of their respective Offices and he shall have Power to grant Reprieves and Pardons for Offenses against the United States, except in Cases of Impeachment.

[2]   He shall have Power, by and with the Advice and Consent of the Senate, to make Treaties, provided two thirds of the Senators present concur; and he shall nominate, and by and with the Advice and Consent of the Senate, shall appoint Ambassadors, other public Ministers and Consuls, Judges of the supreme Court, and all other Officers of the United States, whose Appointments are not herein otherwise provided for, and which shall be established by Law; but the Congress may by Law vest the Appointment of such inferior Officers, as they think proper, in the President alone, in the Courts of Law, or in the Heads of Departments.

[3]   The President shall have Power to fill up all Vacancies that may happen during the Recess of the Senate, by granting Commissions which shall expire at the End of their next Session.

Section 3. He shall from time to time give to the Congress Information of the State of the Union, and recommend to their Consideration such Measures as he shall judge necessary and expedient; he may, on extraordinary Occasions, convene both Houses, or either of them, and in Case of Disagreement between them, with Respect to the Time of Adjournment, he may adjourn them to such Time as he shall think proper; he shall receive Ambassadors and other public Ministers; he shall take Care that the Laws be faithfully executed, and shall Commission all the Officers of the United States.

Section 4. The President, Vice President and all civil Officers of the United States, shall be removed from Office on Impeachment for, and Conviction of, Treason, Bribery, or other high Crimes and Misdemeanors.

Article III

Section 1. The judicial Power of the United States, shall be vested in one supreme Court, and in such inferior Courts as the Congress may from time to time ordain and establish. The Judges, both of the supreme and inferior Courts, shall hold their Offices during good Behaviour, and shall, at stated Times, receive for their Services a Compensation, which shall not be diminished during their Continuance in Office.

Section 2. [1] The judicial Power shall extend to all Cases, in Law and Equity, arising under this Constitution, the Laws of the United States, and Treaties made, or which shall be made, under their Authority;—to all Cases affecting Ambassadors, other public Ministers and Consuls;—to all Cases of admiralty and maritime Jurisdiction;—to Controversies to which the United States shall be a Party;—to Controversies between two or more States;—between a State and Citizens of another State;—between Citizens of different States;—between Citizens of the same State claiming Lands under the Grants of different States, and between a State, or the Citizens thereof, and foreign States, Citizens or Subjects.

[2] In all Cases affecting Ambassadors, other public Ministers and Consuls, and those in which a State shall be a Party, the supreme Court shall have original Jurisdiction. In all the other Cases before mentioned, the supreme Court shall have appellate Jurisdiction, both as to Law and Fact, with such Exceptions, and under such Regulations as the Congress shall make.

[3] The trial of all Crimes, except in Cases of Impeachment, shall be by Jury; and such Trial shall be held in the State where the said Crimes shall have been committed; but when not committed within any State, the Trial shall be at such Place or Places as the Congress may by Law have directed.

Section 3. [1] Treason against the United States, shall consist only in levying War against them, or, in adhering to their Enemies, giving them Aid and Comfort. No Person shall be convicted of Treason unless on the Testimony of two Witnesses to the same overt Act, or on Confession in open Court.

[2] The Congress shall have Power to declare the Punishment of Treason, but no Attainder of Treason shall work Corruption of Blood, or Forfeiture except during the Life of the Person attainted.

Article IV

Section 1. Full Faith and Credit shall be given in each State to the public Acts, Records, and judicial Proceedings of every other State. And the Congress may by general Laws prescribe the Manner in which such Acts, Records and Proceedings shall be proved, and the Effect thereof.

Section 2. [1] The Citizens of each State shall be entitled to all Privileges and Immunities of Citizens in the several States.

[2]   A Person charged in any State with Treason, Felony, or other Crime, who shall flee from Justice, and be found in another State, shall on demand of the executive Authority of the State from which he fled, be delivered up, to be removed to the State having Jurisdiction of the Crime.

[3]   No Person held to Service or Labour in one State, under the Laws thereof, escaping into another, shall, in Consequence of any Law or Regulation therein, be discharged from such Service or Labour, but shall be delivered up on Claim of the Party to whom such Service or Labour may be due.

Section 3. [1] New States may be admitted by the Congress into this Union; but no new State shall be formed or erected within the Jurisdiction of any other State; nor any State be formed by the Junction of two or more States, or Parts of States, without the Consent of the Legislatures of the States concerned as well as of the Congress.

[2]   The Congress shall have Power to dispose of and make all needful Rules and Regulations respecting the Territory or other Property belonging to the United States; and nothing in this Constitution shall be so construed as to Prejudice any Claims of the United States, or of any particular State.

Section 4. The United States shall guarantee to every State in this Union a Republican Form of Government, and shall protect each of them against Invasion; and on Application of the Legislature, or of the Executive (when the Legislature cannot be convened) against domestic Violence.

Article V

The Congress, whenever two thirds of both Houses shall deem it necessary, shall propose Amendments to this Constitution, or, on the Application of the Legislatures of two thirds of the several States, shall call a Convention for proposing Amendments, which, in either Case, shall be valid to all Intents and Purposes, as part of this Constitution, when ratified by the Legislatures of three fourths of the several States, or by Conventions in three fourths thereof, as the one or the other Mode of Ratification may be proposed by the Congress; Provided that no Amendment which may be made prior to the Year One thousand eight hundred and eight shall in any Manner affect the first and fourth Clauses in the Ninth Section of the first Article; and that no State, without its Consent, shall be deprived of its equal Suffrage in the Senate.

Article VI

[1]   All Debts contracted and Engagements entered into, before the Adoption of this Constitution, shall be as valid against the United States under this Constitution, as under the Confederation.

[2] This Constitution, and the Laws of the United States which shall be made in Pursuance thereof; and all Treaties made, or which shall be made, under the Authority of the United States, shall be the supreme Law of the Land; and the Judges in every State shall be bound thereby, any Thing in the Constitution or Laws of any State to the Contrary notwithstanding.

[3] The Senators and Representatives before mentioned, and the Members of the several State Legislatures, and all executive and judicial Officers, both of the United States and of the several States, shall be bound by Oath or Affirmation, to support this Constitution; but no religious Test shall ever be required as a Qualification to any Office or public Trust under the United States.

Article VII

The Ratification of the Conventions of nine States shall be sufficient for the Establishment of this Constitution between the States so ratifying the Same.

DONE in Convention by the Unanimous Consent of the States present the Seventeenth Day of September in the Year of Our Lord one thousand seven hundred and Eighty seven and of the Independence of the United States of America the Twelfth. IN WITNESS whereof We have hereunto subscribed our Names,

Go. WASHINGTON—
Presidt.
and deputy from
Virginia

New Hampshire

JOHN LANGDON   NICHOLAS
GILMAN

Massachusetts

NATHANIEL GORHAM   RUFUS KING

---

1. All of the Amendments except the 13th, 14th, 15th, and 16th, were not specifically assigned a number in the resolution proposing the Amendment. Brackets enclose the number for such Amendments. The 13th, 14th, 15th, and 16th Amendments were ratified by number and thus no brackets enclose such Amendment numbers.

2. The first ten amendments to the Constitution of the United States were proposed to the legislatures of the several States by the First Congress, on the 25th of September 1789. They were ratified by the following States, and the notifications of ratification by the governors thereof were successively communicated by the President to Congress: New Jersey, Novem-

ber 20, 1789; Maryland, December 19, 1789; North Carolina, December 22, 1789; South Carolina, January 19, 1790; New Hampshire, January 25, 1790; Delaware, January 28, 1790; Pennsylvania, March 10, 1790; New York, March 27, 1790; Rhode Island, June 15, 1790; Vermont, November 3, 1791, and Virginia, December 15, 1791. The legislatures of Connecticut, Georgia, and Massachusetts ratified them on April 19, 1939, March 24, 1939, and March 2, 1939, respectively.

Note: other amendments have also been ratified by states after the amendment has been announced as ratified; these other, after-the-fact ratifications are not usually noted in this appendix.

Connecticut

WM. SAML. JOHNSON   ROGER SHER-
MAN

New York

ALEXANDER HAMILTON

New Jersey

WIL: LIVINGSTON   WM. PATERSON
DAVID BREARLEY   JONA: DAYTON

Pennsylvania

B. FRANKLIN   THOS. FITZSI-
MONS
THOMAS MIFFLIN   JARED INGER-
SOLL
ROBT. MORRIS   JAMES WILSON
GEO. CLYMER   GOUV MORRIS

Delaware

GEO: READ   RICHARD BAS-
SETT
GUNNING BEDFORD jun   JACO: BROOM
JOHN DICKINSON

Maryland

JAMES MCHENRY   DANL. CARROLL
DAN OF ST THOS. JENIFER

Virginia

JOHN BLAIR   JAMES MADI-
SON, JR.

North Carolina

WM. BLOUNT   HU WILLIAMSON
RICHD. DOBBS SPAIGHT

South Carolina

J. RUTLEDGE   CHARLES
PINCKNEY
CHARLES COTESWORTH PINCKNEY   PIERCE BUTLER

Georgia

WILLIAM FEW   ABR BALDWIN
Attest   WILLIAM JACK-
SON

Secretary

ARTICLES IN ADDITION TO, AND AMENDMENT OF, THE CONSTI-
TUTION OF THE UNITED STATES OF AMERICA, PROPOSED
BY CONGRESS, AND RATIFIED BY THE LEGISLATURES OF

THE SEVERAL STATES PURSUANT TO THE FIFTH ARTICLE
OF THE ORIGINAL CONSTITUTION.[1]

Amendment [I] [1791] [2]

Congress shall make no law respecting an establishment of religion,
or prohibiting the free exercise thereof; or abridging the freedom of
speech, or of the press; or the right of the people peaceably to assemble,
and to petition the Government for a redress of grievances.

Amendment [II] [1791]

A well regulated Militia, being necessary to the security of a free
State, the right of the people to keep and bear Arms, shall not be infringed.

Amendment [III] [1791]

No Soldier shall, in time of peace be quartered in any house, without
the consent of the Owner, nor in time of war, but in a manner to be prescribed by law.

Amendment [IV] [1791]

The right of the people to be secure in their persons, houses, papers,
and effects, against unreasonable searches and seizures, shall not be violated, and no Warrants shall issue, but upon probable cause, supported by
Oath or affirmation, and particularly describing the place to be searched,
and the persons or things to be seized.

Amendment [V] [1791]

No person shall be held to answer for a capital, or otherwise infamous crime, unless on a presentment or indictment of a Grand Jury, except in cases arising in the land or naval forces, or in the Militia, when in
actual service in time of War or public danger; nor shall any person be
subject for the same offence to be twice put in jeopardy of life or limb; nor
shall be compelled in any criminal case to be a witness against himself,
nor be deprived of life, liberty, or property, without due process of law; nor
shall private property be taken for public use, without just compensation.

Amendment [VI] [1791]

In all criminal prosecutions, the accused shall enjoy the right to a
speedy and public trial, by an impartial jury of the State and district
wherein the crime shall have been committed, which district shall have
been previously ascertained by law, and to be informed of the nature and
cause of the accusation; to be confronted with the witnesses against him;
to have compulsory process for obtaining witnesses in his favor, and to
have the Assistance of Counsel for his defence.

Amendment [VII] [1791]

In Suits at common law, where the value in controversy shall exceed twenty dollars, the right of trial by jury shall be preserved, and no fact tried by jury, shall be otherwise re-examined in any Court of the United States, than according to the rules of the common law.

Amendment [VIII] [1791]

Excessive bail shall not be required, nor excessive fines imposed, nor cruel and unusual punishments inflicted.

Amendment [IX] [1791]

The enumeration in the Constitution, of certain rights, shall not be construed to deny or disparage others retained by the people.

Amendment [X] [1791]

The powers not delegated to the United States by the Constitution, nor prohibited by it to the States, are reserved to the States respectively, or to the people.

Amendment [XI] [1798]

The Judicial power of the United States shall not be construed to extend to any suit in law or equity, commenced or prosecuted against one of the United States by Citizens of another State, or by Citizens or Subjects of any Foreign State.

Historical Note

This amendment was proposed to the legislatures of the several States by the Third Congress, on the 5th September, 1794, and was declared in a message from the President to Congress, dated the 8th of January, 1798, to have been ratified by the legislatures of three-fourths of the States.

Amendment [XII] [1804]

The Electors shall meet in their respective states and vote by ballot for President and Vice-President, one of whom, at least, shall not be an inhabitant of the same state with themselves; they shall name in their ballots the person voted for as President, and in distinct ballots the person voted for as Vice-President, and they shall make distinct lists of all persons voted for as President, and of all persons voted for as Vice-President, and of the number of votes for each, which lists they shall sign and certify, and transmit sealed to the seat of the government of the United States, directed to the President of the Senate;—The President of the Senate shall, in the presence of the Senate and House of Representatives, open all the certificates and the votes shall then be counted;—The person having the greatest number of votes for President, shall be the President, if such number be a majority of the whole number of Electors appointed; and if no person have such majority, then from the persons having the highest numbers not exceeding three on the list of those voted for as President, the House of Representatives shall choose immediately, by ballot, the President. But in choosing the President, the votes shall be taken by states, the representation from each state having one vote; a quorum for this purpose shall consist of a member or members from two-thirds of the states, and a majority of all the states shall be necessary to a choice. And if the House of Representatives shall not choose a President whenever the right of choice shall devolve upon them before the fourth day of March next following, then the Vice-President shall act as President, as in the case of the death or other constitutional disability of the President.—The person having the greatest number of votes as Vice-President, shall be the Vice-President, if such number be a majority of the whole number of Electors appointed, and if no person have a majority, then from the two highest numbers on the list, the Senate shall choose the Vice-President; a quorum for the purpose shall consist of two-thirds of the whole number of Senators, and a majority of the whole number shall be necessary to a choice. But no person constitutionally ineligible to the office of President shall be eligible to that of Vice-President of the United States.

Historical Note

This amendment was proposed to the legislatures of the several States by the Eighth Congress, on the 12th of December, 1803, in lieu of the original third paragraph of the first section of the second article, and was declared in a proclamation of the Secretary of State, dated the 25th of September, 1804, to have been ratified by the legislatures of three-fourths of the States.

Amendment XIII [1865]

Section 1. Neither slavery nor involuntary servitude, except as a punishment for crime whereof the party shall have been duly convicted, shall exist within the United States, or any place subject to their jurisdiction.

Section 2. Congress shall have power to enforce this article by appropriate legislation.

Historical Note

This amendment was proposed to the legislatures of the several States by the Thirty-eighth Congress, on the 1st of February, 1865, and was declared, in a proclamation of the Secretary of State, dated the 18th of December, 1865, to have been ratified by the legislatures of twenty-seven of the thirty-six States, viz: Illinois, Rhode Island, Michigan, Maryland, New York, West Virginia, Maine, Kansas, Massachusetts, Pennsylvania, Virginia, Ohio, Missouri, Nevada, Indiana, Louisiana, Minnesota, Wisconsin, Vermont, Tennessee, Arkansas, Connecticut, New Hampshire, South Carolina, Alabama, North Carolina, and Georgia.

Amendment XIV [1868]

Section 1. All persons born or naturalized in the United States, and subject to the jurisdiction thereof, are citizens of the United States and of the State wherein they reside. No State shall make or enforce any law which shall abridge the privileges or immunities of citizens of the United States; nor shall any State deprive any person of life, liberty, or property, without due process of law; nor deny to any person within its jurisdiction the equal protection of the laws.

Section 2.   Representatives shall be apportioned among the several States according to their respective numbers, counting the whole number of persons in each State, excluding Indians not taxed. But when the right to vote at any election for the choice of electors for President and Vice President of the United States, Representatives in Congress, the Executive and Judicial officers of a State, or the members of the Legislature thereof, is denied to any of the male inhabitants of such State, being twenty-one years of age, and citizens of the United States, or in any way abridged, except for participation in rebellion, or other crime, the basis of representation therein shall be reduced in the proportion which the number of such male citizens shall bear to the whole number of male citizens twenty-one years of age in such State.

Section 3.   No person shall be a Senator or Representative in Congress, or elector of President and Vice President, or hold any office, civil or military, under the United States, or under any State, who having previously taken an oath, as a member of Congress, or as an officer of the United States, or as a member of any State legislature, or as an executive or judicial officer of any State, to support the Constitution of the United States, shall have engaged in insurrection or rebellion against the same, or given aid or comfort to the enemies thereof. But Congress may by a vote of two-thirds of each House, remove such disability.

Section 4.   The validity of the public debt of the United States, authorized by law, including debts incurred for payment of pensions and bounties for services in suppressing insurrection or rebellion, shall not be questioned. But neither the United States nor any State shall assume or pay any debt or obligation incurred in aid of insurrection or rebellion against the United States, or any claim for the loss or emancipation of any slave; but all such debts, obligations and claims shall be held illegal and void.

Section 5.   The Congress shall have power to enforce, by appropriate legislation, the provisions of this article.

Historical Note

This amendment was proposed to the legislatures of the several States by the Thirty-ninth Congress, on the 16th of June, 1866. On the 21st of July, 1868, Congress adopted and transmitted to the Department of State a concurrent resolution, declaring that "the legislatures of the States of Connecticut, Tennessee, New Jersey, Oregon, Vermont, New York, Ohio, Illinois, West Virginia, Kansas, Maine, Nevada, Missouri, Indiana, Minnesota, New Hampshire, Massachusetts, Nebraska, Iowa, Arkansas, Florida, North Carolina, Alabama, South Carolina, and Louisiana, being three-fourths and more of the several States of the Union, have ratified the fourteenth article of amendment to the Constitution of the United States, duly proposed by two-thirds of each House of the Thirty-ninth Congress: Therefore, Resolved, That said fourteenth article is hereby declared to be a part of the Constitution of the United States, and it shall be duly promulgated as such by the Secretary of State." The Secretary of State accordingly issued a proclamation, dated the 28th of July, 1868, declaring that the proposed fourteenth amendment had been ratified, in the manner hereafter mentioned by the legislatures of thirty of the thirty-six States, viz: Connecticut, June 30, 1866; New Hampshire, July 7, 1866; Tennessee, July 19, 1866; New Jersey, September 11, 1866, (and the legislature of the same State passed a resolution in April, 1868, to withdraw its consent to it); Oregon, September 19, 1866; Vermont, November 9, 1866; Georgia rejected it November 13, 1866, and ratified it July 21, 1868; North Carolina rejected it December 4, 1866, and ratified it July 4, 1868; South Carolina rejected it December 20, 1866, and ratified it July 9, 1868; New York ratified it January 10, 1867; Ohio ratified it January 11, 1867, (and the legislature of the same State passed a resolution in January, 1868, to withdraw its consent to it); Illinois ratified it January 15, 1867; West Virginia, January 16, 1867; Kansas, January 18, 1867; Maine, January 19, 1867; Nevada, January 22, 1867; Missouri, January 26, 1867; Indiana, January 29, 1867; Minnesota, February 1, 1867; Rhode Island, February 7, 1867; Wisconsin, February 13, 1867; Pennsylvania, February 13, 1867; Michigan, February 15, 1867; Massachusetts, March 20, 1867; Nebraska, June 15, 1867; Iowa, April 3, 1868; Arkansas, April 6, 1868; Florida, June 9, 1868; Louisiana, July 9, 1868; and Alabama, July 13, 1868. Georgia again ratified the amendment February 2, 1870. Texas rejected it November 1, 1866, and ratified it February 18, 1870. Virginia rejected it January 19, 1867, and ratified October 8, 1869. The amendment was rejected by Kentucky January 10, 1867; by Delaware February 8, 1867; by Maryland March 23, 1867.

Amendment XV [1870]

Section 1. The right of citizens of the United States to vote shall not be denied or abridged by the United States or by any State on account of race, color, or previous condition of servitude.

Section 2. The Congress shall have power to enforce this article by appropriate legislation.

Historical Note

This amendment was proposed to the legislatures of the several States by the Fortieth Congress, on the 27th of February, 1869, and was declared, in a proclamation of the Secretary of State, dated March 30, 1870, to have been ratified by the legislatures of twenty-nine of the thirty-seven States. The dates of these ratifications (arranged in the order of their reception at the Department of State) were: from North Carolina, March 5, 1869; West Virginia, March 3, 1869; Massachusetts, March 912, 1869; Wisconsin, March 9, 1869; Maine, March 12, 1869; Louisiana, March 5, 1869; Michigan, March 8, 1869; South Carolina, March 16, 1869; Pennsylvania, March 26, 1869; Arkansas, March 30, 1869; Connecticut, May 19, 1869; Florida, June 15, 1869; Illinois, March 5, 1869; Indiana, May 1314, 1869; New York, March 17April 14, 1869, (and the legislature of the same State passed a resolution January 5, 1870, to withdraw its consent to it); New Hampshire, July 7, 1869; Nevada, March 1, 1869; Vermont, October 21, 1869; Virginia, October 8, 1869; Missouri, January 10, 1870; Mississippi, January 1517, 1870; Ohio, January 27, 1870; Iowa, February 3, 1870; Kansas, January 1819, 1870; Minnesota, February 19, 1870; Rhode Island,

January 18, 1870; Nebraska, February 17, 1870; Texas, February 18, 1870. The State of Georgia also ratified the amendment February 2, 1870.

Amendment XVI [1913]

The Congress shall have power to lay and collect taxes on incomes, from whatever source derived, without apportionment among the several States, and without regard to any census or enumeration.

Historical Note

This Amendment was proposed to the legislatures of the several states by the Sixty-First Congress, on the 31st of July, 1909, and was declared, in a proclamation by the Secretary of State, dated the 25th of February, 1913, to have been ratified by the legislatures of the states of Alabama, Kentucky, South Carolina, Illinois, Mississippi, Oklahoma, Maryland, Georgia, Texas, Ohio, Idaho, Oregon, Washington, California, Montana, Indiana, Nevada, North Carolina, Nebraska, Kansas, Colorado, North Dakota, Michigan, Iowa, Missouri, Maine, Tennessee, Arkansas, Wisconsin, New York, South Dakota, Arizona, Minnesota, Louisiana, Delaware, and Wyoming, in all, thirty-six. The legislatures of New Jersey and New Mexico also passed resolutions ratifying the said proposed amendment.

Amendment [XVII] [1913]

[1]   The Senate of the United States shall be composed of two Senators from each State, elected by the people thereof, for six years; and each Senator shall have one vote. The electors in each State shall have the qualifications requisite for electors of the most numerous branch of the State legislatures.

[2]   When vacancies happen in the representation of any State in the Senate, the executive authority of such State shall issue writs of election to fill such vacancies: *Provided, that the legislature of any State may empower the executive thereof to make temporary appointments until the people fill the vacancies by election as the legislature may direct.*

[3]   This amendment shall not be so construed as to affect the election or term of any Senator chosen before it becomes valid as part of the Constitution.

Historical Note

This amendment was proposed to the legislatures of the several states by the Sixty-Second Congress, on the 16th of May, 1912, in lieu of the original first paragraph of section 3 of article I, and in lieu of so much of paragraph 2 of the same section as related to the filling of vacancies, and was declared, in a proclamation by the Secretary of State, dated the 31st of May, 1913, to have been ratified by the legislatures of the states of Massachusetts, Arizona, Minnesota, New York, Kansas, Oregon, North Carolina, California, Michigan, Idaho, West Virginia, Nebraska, Iowa, Montana, Texas, Washington, Wyoming, Colorado, Illinois, North Dakota, Nevada, Vermont, Maine, New Hampshire, Oklahoma, Ohio, South Dakota, Indiana, Missouri, New Mexico, New Jersey, Tennessee, Arkansas, Connecticut, Pennsylvania, and Wisconsin, said states constituting three-fourths of the whole number of states.

Amendment [XVIII] [1919]

Section 1.   After one year from the ratification of this article the manufacture, sale, or transportation of intoxicating liquors within, the importation thereof into, or the exportation thereof from the United States and all territory subject to the jurisdiction thereof for beverage purposes is hereby prohibited.

Section 2.   The Congress and the several States shall have concurrent power to enforce this article by appropriate legislation.

Section 3.   This article shall be inoperative unless it shall have been ratified as an amendment to the Constitution by the legislatures of the several States, as provided in the Constitution, within seven years from the date of the submission hereof to the States by the Congress.

Historical Note

This amendment was proposed to the legislatures of the several states by the Sixty-Fifth Congress, on the 19th day of December, 1917, and was declared, in a proclamation by the Acting Secretary of State, dated on the 29th day of January, 1919, to have been ratified by the legislatures of the states of Alabama, Arizona, California, Colorado, Delaware, Florida, Georgia, Idaho, Illinois, Indiana, Kansas, Kentucky, Louisiana, Maine, Maryland, Massachusetts, Michigan, Minnesota, Mississippi, Montana, Nebraska, New Hampshire, North Carolina, North Dakota, Ohio, Oklahoma, Oregon, South Dakota, South Carolina, Texas, Utah, Virginia, Washington, West Virginia, Wisconsin, and Wyoming.

Amendment [XIX] [1920]

[1]   The right of citizens of the United States to vote shall not be denied or abridged by the United States or by any State on account of sex.

[2]   Congress shall have power to enforce this article by appropriate legislation.

Historical Note

This amendment was proposed to the legislatures of the several states by the Sixty-Sixth Congress, on the 5th day of June, 1919, and was declared, in a proclamation by the Secretary of State, dated on the 26th day of August, 1920, to have been ratified by the legislatures of the states of Arizona, Arkansas, California, Colorado, Idaho, Illinois, Indiana, Iowa, Kansas, Kentucky, Maine, Massachusetts, Michigan, Minnesota, Missouri, Montana, Nebraska, Nevada, New Hampshire, New Jersey, New Mexico, North Dakota, New York, Ohio, Oklahoma, Oregon, Pennsylvania, Rhode Island, South Dakota, Tennessee, Texas, Utah, Washington, West Virginia, Wisconsin and Wyoming.

Amendment [XX] [1933]

Section 1.   The terms of the President and Vice President shall end at noon on the 20th day of January, and the terms of Senators and Representatives at noon on the 3d day of January, of the years in which such terms would have ended if this article had not been ratified; and the terms of their successors shall then begin.

Section 2.   The Congress shall assemble at least once in every year, and such meeting shall begin at noon on the 3d day of January, unless they shall by law appoint a different day.

Section 3.   If, at the time fixed for the beginning of the term of the President, the President elect shall have died, the Vice President elect shall become President. If the President shall not have been chosen before the time fixed for the beginning of his term, or if the President elect shall have failed to qualify, then the Vice President elect shall act as President until a President shall have qualified; and the Congress may by law provide for the case wherein neither a President elect nor a Vice President elect shall have qualified, declaring who shall then act as President, or the manner in which one who is to act shall be selected, and such person shall act accordingly until a President or Vice President shall have qualified.

Section 4.   The Congress may by law provide for the case of the death of any of the persons from whom the House of Representatives may choose a President whenever the right of choice shall have devolved upon them, and for the case of the death of any of the persons from whom the Senate may choose a Vice President whenever the right of choice shall have devolved upon them.

Section 5.   Sections 1 and 2 shall take effect on the 15th day of October following the ratification of this article.

Section 6.   This article shall be inoperative unless it shall have been ratified as an amendment to the Constitution by the legislatures of three-fourths of the several States within seven years from the date of its submission.

Historical Note

This amendment was proposed to the legislatures of the several states by the Seventy-Second Congress, on March 3, 1932, and was declared, in a proclamation by the Secretary of State, dated Feb. 6, 1933, to have been ratified by the legislatures of the states of Alabama, Arizona, Arkansas, California, Colorado, Connecticut, Delaware, Georgia, Idaho, Illinois, Indiana, Kansas, Kentucky, Louisiana, Maine, Massachusetts, Michigan, Minnesota, Mississippi, Missouri, Montana, Nebraska, New Jersey, New York, North Carolina, North Dakota, Ohio, Oklahoma, Pennsylvania, Rhode Island, South Carolina, South Dakota, Texas, Utah, Virginia, Washington, West Virginia, Wisconsin, and Wyoming.

Amendment [XXI] [1933]

Section 1.   The eighteenth article of amendment to the Constitution of the United States is hereby repealed.

Section 2.   The transportation or importation into any State, Territory, or possession of the United States for delivery or use therein of intoxicating liquors, in violation of the laws thereof, is hereby prohibited.

Section 3.   This article shall be inoperative unless it shall have been ratified as an amendment to the Constitution by conventions in the several States, as provided in the Constitution, within seven years from the date of the submission hereof to the States by the Congress.

Historical Note

This amendment was proposed to the several states by the Seventy-Second Congress, on Feb. 20, 1933, and was declared, in a proclamation by the Secretary of State, dated Dec. 5, 1933, to have been ratified by conventions in the States of Arizona, Alabama, Arkansas, California, Colorado, Connecticut, Delaware, Florida, Idaho, Illinois, Indiana, Iowa, Kentucky, Maryland, Massachusetts, Michigan, Minnesota, Missouri, Nevada, New Hampshire, New Jersey, New Mexico, New York, Ohio, Oregon, Pennsylvania, Rhode Island, Tennessee, Texas, Utah, Vermont, Virginia, Washington, West Virginia, Wisconsin and Wyoming.

Amendment [XXII] [1951]

Section 1. No person shall be elected to the office of the President more than twice, and no person who has held the office of President, or acted as President, for more than two years of a term to which some other person was elected President shall be elected to the office of President more than once. But this Article shall not apply to any person holding the office of President when this Article was proposed by the Congress, and shall not prevent any person who may be holding the office of President, or acting as President, during the term within which this Article becomes operative from holding the office of President or acting as President during the remainder of such term.

Section 2. This article shall be inoperative unless it shall have been ratified as an amendment to the Constitution by the legislatures of three-fourths of the several States within seven years from the date of its submission to the States by the Congress.

Historical Note

Proposal and Ratification. This amendment was proposed to the legislatures of the several States by the Eightieth Congress on Mar. 24, 1947 by House Joint Res. No. 27, and was declared by the Administrator of General Services on Mar. 1, 1951, to have been ratified. The legislatures ratified this Amendment on the following dates: Maine, Mar. 31, 1947; Michigan, Mar. 31, 1947; Iowa, Apr. 1, 1947; Kansas, Apr. 1, 1947; New Hampshire, Apr. 1, 1947; Delaware, Apr. 2, 1947; Illinois, Apr. 3, 1947; Oregon, Apr. 3, 1947; Colorado, Apr. 12, 1947; California, Apr. 15, 1947; New Jersey, Apr. 15, 1947; Vermont, Apr. 15, 1947; Ohio, Apr. 16, 1947; Wisconsin, Apr. 16, 1947; Pennsylvania, Apr. 29, 1947; Connecticut, May 21, 1947; Missouri, May 22, 1947; Nebraska, May 23, 1947; Virginia, Jan. 28, 1948; Mississippi, Feb. 12, 1948; New York, Mar. 9, 1948; South Dakota, Jan. 21, 1949; North Dakota, Feb. 25, 1949; Louisiana, May 17, 1950; Montana, Jan. 25, 1951; Indiana, Jan. 29, 1951; Idaho, Jan. 30, 1951; New Mexico, Feb. 12, 1951; Wyoming, Feb. 12, 1951; Arkansas, Feb. 15, 1951; Georgia, Feb. 17, 1951; Tennessee, Feb. 20, 1951; Texas, Feb. 22, 1951; Utah, Feb. 26, 1951; Nevada, Feb. 26, 1951; Minnesota, Feb. 27, 1951, and North Carolina, Feb. 28, 1951.

Subsequent to the proclamation, Amendment XXII was ratified by South Carolina on Mar. 13, 1951; Maryland, Mar. 14, 1951; Florida, Apr. 16, 1951, and Alabama, May 4, 1951.

Certification of Validity. Publication of the certifying statement of the Administrator of General Services that the Amendment had become valid was made on Mar. 1, 1951, F.R.Doc. 51–2940, 16 F.R. 2019.

Amendment [XXIII] [1961]

Section 1. The District constituting the seat of Government of the United States shall appoint in such manner as the Congress may direct:

A number of electors of President and Vice President equal to the whole number of Senators and Representatives in Congress to which the District would be entitled if it were a State, but in no event more than the least populous state; they shall be in addition to those appointed by the states, but they shall be considered, for the purposes of the election of President and Vice President, to be electors appointed by a state; and they shall meet in the District and perform such duties as provided by the twelfth article of amendment.

Section 2. The Congress shall have power to enforce this article by appropriate legislation.

Historical Note

Proposal and Ratification. This amendment was proposed by the Eighty-sixth Congress on June 16, 1960 and was declared by the Administrator of General Services on Apr. 3, 1961, to have been ratified.

The amendment was ratified by the following States: Hawaii, June 23, 1960; Massachusetts, Aug. 22, 1960; New Jersey, Dec. 19, 1960; New York, Jan. 17, 1961; California, Jan. 19, 1961; Oregon, Jan. 27, 1961; Maryland, Jan. 30, 1961; Idaho, Jan. 31, 1961; Maine, Jan. 31, 1961; Minnesota, Jan. 31, 1961; New Mexico, Feb. 1, 1961; Nevada, Feb. 2, 1961; Montana, Feb. 6, 1961; Colorado, Feb. 8, 1961; Washington, Feb. 9, 1961; West Virginia, Feb. 9, 1961; Alaska, Feb. 10, 1961; Wyoming, Feb. 13, 1961; South Dakota, Feb. 14, 1961; Delaware, Feb. 20, 1961; Utah, Feb. 21, 1961; Wisconsin, Feb. 21, 1961; Pennsylvania, Feb. 28, 1961; Indiana, Mar. 3, 1961; North Dakota, Mar. 3, 1961; Tennessee, Mar. 6, 1961; Michigan, Mar. 8, 1961; Connecticut, Mar. 9, 1961; Arizona, Mar. 10, 1961; Illinois, Mar. 14, 1961; Nebraska, Mar. 15, 1961; Vermont, Mar. 15, 1961; Iowa, Mar. 16, 1961; Missouri, Mar. 20, 1961; Oklahoma, Mar. 21, 1961; Rhode Island, Mar. 22, 1961; Kansas, Mar. 29, 1961; Ohio, Mar. 29, 1961, and New Hampshire, Mar. 30, 1961.

Certification of Validity. Publication of the certifying statement of the Administrator of General Services that the Amendment had become valid was made on Apr. 3, 1961, F.R.Doc. 61–3017, 26 F.R. 2808.

Amendment [XXIV] [1964]

Section 1. The right of citizens of the United States to vote in any primary or other election for President or Vice President, for electors for President or Vice President, or for Senator or Representative in Congress, shall not be denied or abridged by the United States or any State by reason of failure to pay any poll tax or other tax.

Section 2. The Congress shall have power to enforce this article by appropriate legislation.

Historical Note

Proposal and Ratification. This amendment was proposed by the Eighty-seventh Congress by Senate Joint Resolution No. 29, which was approved by the Senate on Mar. 27, 1962, and by the House of Representatives on Aug. 27, 1962. It was declared by the Administrator of General Services on Feb. 4, 1964, to have been ratified.

This amendment was ratified by the following States: Illinois, Nov. 14, 1962; New Jersey, Dec. 3, 1962; Oregon, Jan. 25, 1963; Montana, Jan. 28, 1963; West Virginia, Feb. 1, 1963; New York, Feb. 4, 1963; Maryland, Feb. 6, 1963; California, Feb. 7, 1963; Alaska, Feb. 11, 1963; Rhode Island, Feb. 14, 1963; Indiana, Feb. 19, 1963; Utah, Feb. 20, 1963; Michigan, Feb. 20, 1963; Colorado, Feb. 21, 1963; Ohio, Feb. 27, 1963; Minnesota, Feb. 27, 1963; New Mexico, Mar. 5, 1963; Hawaii, Mar. 6, 1963; North Dakota, Mar. 7, 1963; Idaho, Mar. 8, 1963; Washington, Mar. 14, 1963; Vermont, Mar. 15, 1963; Nevada, Mar. 19, 1963; Connecticut, Mar. 20, 1963; Tennessee, Mar. 21, 1963; Pennsylvania, Mar. 25, 1963; Wisconsin, Mar. 26, 1963; Kansas, Mar. 28, 1963; Massachusetts, Mar. 28, 1963; Nebraska, Apr. 4, 1963; Florida, Apr. 18, 1963; Iowa, Apr. 24, 1963; Delaware, May 1, 1963; Missouri, May 13, 1963; New Hampshire, June 12, 1963; Kentucky, June 27, 1963; Maine, Jan. 16, 1964; South Dakota, Jan. 23, 1964.

Certification of Validity. Publication of the certifying statement of the Administrator of General Services that the Amendment had become valid was made on Feb. 5, 1964, F.R.Doc. 64–1229, 29 F.R. 1715. President Johnson and the Administrator signed this certificate on Feb. 4, 1964.

Amendment [XXV] [1967]

Section 1. In the case of the removal of the President from office or of his death or resignation, the Vice President shall become President.

Section 2. Whenever there is a vacancy in the office of the Vice President, the President shall nominate a Vice President who shall take office upon confirmation by a majority vote of both Houses of Congress.

Section 3. Whenever the President transmits to the President pro tempore of the Senate and the Speaker of the House of Representatives his written declaration that he is unable to discharge the powers and duties of his office, and until he transmits to them a written declaration to the contrary, such powers and duties shall be discharged by the Vice President as Acting President.

Section 4. Whenever the Vice President and a majority of either the principal officers of the executive departments or of such other body as Congress may by law provide, transmit to the President pro tempore of the Senate and the Speaker of th e House of Representatives, their written declaration that the President is unable to discharge the powers and duties of his office, the Vice President shall immediately assume the powers and duties of the office as Acting President.

Thereafter, when the President transmits to the President pro tempore of the Senate and the Speaker of the House of Representatives his written declaration that no inability exists, he shall resume the powers and duties of his office unless the Vice President and a majority of either the principal officers of the executive department or of such other body as Congress may by law provide, transmit within four days to the President pro tempore of the Senate and the Speaker of the House of Representatives their written declaration that the President is unable to discharge the powers and duties of his office. Thereupon Congress shall decide the issue, assembling within forty-eight hours for that purpose if not in session. If the Congress, within twenty-one days after receipt of the latter written declaration, or, if Congress is not in session, within twenty-one days after Congress is required to assemble, determines by two-thirds vote of both Houses that the President is unable to discharge the powers and duties of his office, the Vice President shall continue to discharge the same as Acting President; otherwise, the President shall resume the powers and duties of his office.

Historical Note

Proposal and Ratification. This amendment was proposed by the Eighty-ninth Congress by Senate Joint Resolution No. 1, which was approved by the Senate on Feb. 19, 1965, and by the House of Representatives, in amended form, on Apr. 13, 1965. The House of Representatives agreed to a Conference Report on June 30, 1965, and the Senate agreed to the Conference Report on July 6, 1965. It was declared by the Administrator of General Services, on Feb. 23, 1967, to have been ratified.

This amendment was ratified by the following States: Nebraska, July 12, 1965; Wisconsin, July 13, 1965; Oklahoma, July 16, 1965; Massachusetts, Aug. 9, 1965; Pennsylvania, Aug. 18, 1965; Kentucky, Sept. 15, 1965; Arizona, Sept. 22, 1965; Michigan, Oct. 5, 1965; Indiana, Oct. 20, 1965; California, Oct. 21, 1965; Arkansas, Nov. 4, 1965; New Jersey, Nov. 29, 1965; Delaware, Dec. 7, 1965; Utah, Jan. 17, 1966; West Virginia, Jan. 20, 1966; Maine, Jan. 24, 1966; Rhode Island, Jan. 28, 1966; Colorado, Feb. 3, 1966; New Mexico, Feb. 3, 1966; Kansas, Feb. 8, 1966; Vermont, Feb. 10, 1966; Alaska, Feb. 18, 1966; Idaho, Mar. 2, 1966; Hawaii, Mar. 3, 1966; Virginia, Mar. 8, 1966; Mississippi, Mar. 10, 1966; New York, Mar. 14, 1966; Maryland, Mar. 23, 1966; Missouri, Mar. 30, 1966; New Hampshire, June 13, 1966; Louisiana, July 5, 1966; Tennessee, Jan. 12, 1967; Wyoming, Jan. 25, 1967; Washington, Jan. 26, 1967; Iowa, Jan. 26, 1967; Oregon, Feb. 2, 1967; Minnesota, Feb. 10, 1967; Nevada, Feb. 10, 1967; Connecticut, Feb. 14, 1967; Montana, Feb. 15, 1967; South Dakota, Mar. 6, 1967; Ohio, Mar. 7, 1967; Alabama, Mar. 14, 1967; North Carolina, Mar. 22, 1967; Illinois, Mar. 22, 1967; Texas, Apr. 25, 1967; Florida, May 25, 1967.

Certification of Validity. Publication of the certifying statement of the Administrator of General Services that the Amendment had become valid was made on Feb. 25, 1967, F.R.Doc. 67–2208, 32 F.R. 3287, and signed on July 23, 1967.

Amendment [XXVI] [1971]

Section 1. The right of citizens of the United States, who are eighteen years of age or older, to vote shall not be denied or abridged by the United States or by any State on account of age.

Section 2. The Congress shall have power to enforce this article by appropriate legislation.

Historical Note

Proposal and Ratification. This amendment was proposed by the Ninety-second Congress by Senate Joint Resolution No. 7, which was approved by the Senate on Mar. 10, 1971, and by the House of Representatives on Mar. 23, 1971. It was declared by the Administrator of General Services on July 5, 1971, to have been ratified.

This amendment was ratified by the following States: Connecticut, Mar. 23, 1971; Delaware, Mar. 23, 1971; Minnesota, Mar. 23, 1971; Tennessee, Mar. 23, 1971; Washington, Mar. 23, 1971; Hawaii, Mar. 24, 1971; Massachusetts, Mar. 24, 1971; Idaho, Mar. 30, 1971; Montana, Mar. 31, 1971; Arkansas, Apr. 1, 1971; Iowa, Apr. 1, 1971; Nebraska, Apr. 2, 1971; Kansas, Apr. 7, 1971; Michigan, Apr. 7, 1971; Indiana, Apr. 8, 1971; Maine, Apr. 9, 1971; Vermont, Apr. 16, 1971; California, Apr. 19, 1971; South Carolina, Apr. 28, 1971; West Virginia, Apr. 28, 1971; Pennsylvania, May 3, 1971; New Jersey, May 4, 1971; Texas, May 5, 1971; Maryland, May 6, 1971; New Hampshire, May 13, 1971; Arizona, May 17, 1971; Colorado, May 24, 1971; Louisiana, May 27, 1971; Rhode Island, May 27, 1971; New York, June 2, 1971; Oregon, June 5, 1971; Missouri, June 14, 1971; Wisconsin, June 18, 1971; Illinois, June 29, 1971; Alabama, June 30, 1971; Ohio, June 30, 1971; North Carolina, July 1, 1971; Oklahoma, July 1, 1971.

Certification of Validity. Publication of the certifying statement of the Administrator of General Services that the Amendment had become valid was made on July 7, 1971, F.R.Doc. 71–9691, 36 F.R. 12725, and signed on July 5, 1971.

Amendment [XXVII] [1992]

No law, varying the compensation for the services of the Senators and Representatives, shall take effect, until an election of Representatives shall have intervened.

Historical Note

Proposal and Ratification. This amendment was one of twelve that the first Congress proposed on September 25, 1789. Ten of these twelve became the first ten amendments, often called the Bill of Rights. A sufficient number of states did not ratify until 203 years later.

This amendment was ratified by the following States: Maryland, Dec. 19, 1789; North Carolina, Dec. 22, 1789; South Carolina, Jan. 19, 1790; Delaware, Jan. 28, 1790; Vermont, Nov. 3, 1791; Virginia, Dec. 15, 1791; Ohio, May 6, 1873; Wyoming, Mar. 3, 1978; Maine, Apr. 2, 1983; Colorado, Apr. 18, 1984; South Dakota, Feb. 21, 1985; New Hampshire, Mar. 7, 1985; Arizona, Apr. 3, 1985; Tennessee, May 23, 1985; Oklahoma, July 10, 1985; New Mexico, Feb. 14, 1986; Indiana, Feb. 24, 1986; Utah, Feb. 26, 1986; Arkansas, Mar. 5, 1987; Montana, Mar. 17, 1987; Connecticut, May 13, 1987; Wisconsin, June 30, 1987; Georgia, Feb. 2, 1988; West Virginia, Mar. 10, 1988; Louisiana, July 6, 1988; Iowa, Feb. 7, 1989; Idaho, Mar. 23, 1989; Nevada, Apr. 26, 1989; Alaska, May 5, 1989; Oregon, May 19, 1989; Minnesota, May 22, 1989; Texas, May 25, 1989; Kansas, Apr. 4, 1990; Florida, May 31, 1990; North Dakota, Mar. 25, 1991; Missouri, May 5, 1992; Alabama, May 5, 1992; Michigan, May 7, 1992; New Jersey, May 7, 1992; Illinois, May 12, 1992.

Certification of Validity. On May 13, 1992, the Archivist of the United States announced that he would accept this amendment as valid once he received formal notice pursuant to 1 U.S.C.A. § 106b.

*

MODERN
CONSTITUTIONAL LAW
CASES AND NOTES

Sixth Edition

*

Chapter 1

JUDICIAL REVIEW

1–1. THE ORIGINS

MARBURY v. MADISON
5 U.S. (1 Cranch) 137, 2 L.Ed. 60 (1803).

[In 1800 the Jeffersonians took control of the executive and legislative branches of the government from Adams' Federalist Party. Adams, who remained President until March 4, 1801,[1] responded to his defeat by seeking to maintain Federalist control of the judiciary through his appointment power. On January 20, 1801, he proposed his Secretary of State, John Marshall, as the new Chief Justice. Marshall took his judicial office in February, 1801, while continuing his position as Secretary of State until the end of President Adams' term.[2] In February, the Federalist Congress created more judgeships, and the Senate finished confirming Adams' appointees (the "midnight judges") on March 3d. Although William Marbury's commission as a Justice of the Peace in the District of Columbia had been signed and sealed, the Secretary of State had not delivered it by the time that Jefferson took office. Jefferson had no desire to correct this error, so Marbury asked the Supreme Court for a writ to compel Jefferson's Secretary of State, Madison, to hand over the commission. Marbury and others in his position went to the Supreme Court during the December term, 1801, and moved the Court for a rule requiring James Madison, Secretary of State, to show cause why a mandamus should not issue commanding him to cause to be delivered to them their commissions as justices of the peace in the District of Columbia. The Court issued the show cause order but the case was not then heard because Congress by statute had eliminated part of the Supreme Court's 1802 term. The case was not heard until the February, 1803 term. Marbury's attorney, in support of the jurisdiction of the

---

1. The terms of the President and Vice President now end at noon on the 20th day of January following the election. U.S. Const., Amend. XX, § 1.

2. See the excellent analysis in, William Van Alstyne, A Critical Guide to Marbury v. Madison, 1969 Duke L.J. 1; William A. Kaplin, The Concepts and Methods of Constitutional Law (1992).

1

Supreme Court, relied on section 13 of the Judiciary Act of 1789, which provided, in part, that: "the Supreme Court shall also have appellate jurisdiction from the circuit courts and courts of the several states, in the cases hereinafter specially provided for; and shall have power to issue writs of prohibition to the district courts, when proceeding as courts of admiralty and maritime jurisdiction; and writs of mandamus, in cases warranted by the principles and usages of law, to any courts appointed, or persons holding office, under the authority of the United States."]

[On February 24, 1803, CHIEF JUSTICE JOHN MARSHALL delivered the Opinion of the Court:]

At the last term on the affidavits then read and filed with the clerk, a rule was granted in this case, requiring the secretary of state to show cause why a mandamus should not issue, directing him to deliver to William Marbury his commission as a justice of the peace for the county of Washington, in the District of Columbia.

No cause has been shown, and the present motion is for a mandamus. The peculiar delicacy of this case, the novelty of some of its circumstances, and the real difficulty attending the points which occur in it, require a complete exposition of the principles on which the opinion to be given by the court is founded.

These principles have been, on the side of the applicant very ably argued at the bar. In rendering the opinion of the court, there will be some departure in form, though not in substance, from the points stated in that argument.

In the order in which the court has viewed this subject, the following questions have been considered and decided.

1st. Has the applicant a right to the commission he demands?

2d. If he has a right, and that right has been violated, do the laws of his country afford him a remedy?

3d. If they do afford him a remedy, is it a mandamus issuing from this court?

The first object of inquiry is,

1st. Has the applicant a right to the commission he demands? . . .

The last act to be done by the president is the signature of the commission. He has then acted on the advice and consent of the senate to his own nomination. The time for deliberation has then passed. He has decided. His judgment, on the advice and consent of the senate concurring with his nomination, has been made, and the officer is appointed. This appointment is evidenced by an open, unequivocal act; and being the last act required from the person making it, necessarily excludes the idea of its being, so far as respects the appointment, an inchoate and incomplete transaction. . . .

Mr. Marbury, then, since his commission was signed by the President, and sealed by the Secretary of State, was appointed; and as the law creating the office, gave the officer a right to hold for five years, independent of the executive, the appointment was not revocable, but vested in the officer legal rights, which are protected by the laws of his country.

To withhold his commission, therefore, is an act deemed by the court not warranted by law, but violative of a vested legal right.

This brings us to the second inquiry; which is,

2d. If he has a right, and that right has been violated, do the laws of this country afford him a remedy?

The very essence of civil liberty certainly consists in the right of every individual to claim the protection of the laws, whenever he receives an injury. One of the first duties of government is to afford that protection. In Great Britain the king himself is sued in the respectful form of a petition, and he never fails to comply with the judgment of his court....

The government of the United States has been emphatically termed a government of laws, and not of men. It will certainly cease to deserve this high appellation, if the laws furnish no remedy for the violation of a vested legal right.

If this obloquy is to be cast on the jurisprudence of our country, it must arise from the peculiar character of the case....

By the constitution of the United States, the President is invested with certain important political powers, in the exercise of which he is to use his own discretion, and is accountable only to his country in his political character and to his own conscience. To aid him in the performance of these duties, he is authorized to appoint certain officers, who act by his authority, and in conformity with his orders....

The conclusion from this reasoning is, that where the heads of departments are the political or confidential agents of the executive, merely to execute the will of the President, or rather to act in cases in which the executive possesses a constitutional or legal discretion, nothing can be more perfectly clear than that their acts are only politically examinable. But where a specific duty is assigned by law, and individual rights depend upon the performance of that duty, it seems equally clear that the individual who considers himself injured, has a right to resort to the laws of his country for a remedy....

It remains to be inquired whether,

3d. He is entitled to the remedy for which he applies. This depends on,

1st. The nature of the writ applied for; and,

2d. The power of this court.

1st. The nature of the writ....

1st. With respect to the officer to whom it would be directed. The intimate political relation subsisting between the President of the United

States and the heads of departments, necessarily renders any legal investigation of the acts of one of those high officers peculiarly irksome, as well as delicate; and excites some hesitation with respect to the propriety of entering into such investigation. Impressions are often received without much reflection or examination, and it is not wonderful that in such a case as this the assertion, by an individual, of his legal claims in a court of justice, to which claims it is the duty of that court to attend, should at first view be considered by some, as an attempt to intrude into the cabinet, and to intermeddle with the prerogatives of the executive.

It is scarcely necessary for the court to disclaim all pretensions to such jurisdiction. An extravagance, so absurd and excessive, could not have been entertained for a moment. The province of the court is, solely, to decide on the rights of individuals, not to inquire how the executive, or executive officers, perform duties in which they have a discretion. Questions in their nature political, or which are, by the constitution and laws, submitted to the executive, can never be made in this court.

But, if this be not such a question; if, so far from being an intrusion into the secrets of the cabinet, it respects a paper which, according to law, is upon record, and to a copy of which the law gives a right, on the payment of ten cents; if it be no intermeddling with a subject over which the executive can be considered as having exercised any control; what is there in the exalted station of the officer, which shall bar a citizen from asserting, in a court of justice, his legal rights? . . .

It is not by the office of the person to whom the writ is directed, but the nature of the thing to be done, that the propriety or impropriety of issuing a mandamus is to be determined. Where the head of a department acts in a case, in which executive discretion is to be exercised; in which he is the mere organ of executive will; it is again repeated, that any application to a court to control, in any respect, his conduct would be rejected without hesitation.

But where he is directed by law to do a certain act affecting the absolute rights of individuals, in the performance of which he is not placed under the particular direction of the President, and the performance of which the President cannot lawfully forbid, and therefore is never presumed to have forbidden; as for example, to record a commission, or a patent for land, which has received all the legal solemnities; or to give a copy of such record; in such cases, it is not perceived on what ground the courts of the country are further excused from the duty of giving judgment that right be done to an injured individual, than if the same services were to be performed by a person not the head of a department. . . .

This, then, is a plain case for a mandamus, either to deliver the commission, or a copy of it from the record; and it only remains to be inquired,

Whether it can issue from this court.

The act to establish the judicial courts of the United States authorizes the Supreme Court "to issue writs of mandamus in cases warranted by the principles and usages of law, to any courts appointed, or persons holding office, under the authority of the United States."

The Secretary of State, being a person holding an office under the authority of the United States, is precisely within the letter of the description, and if this court is not authorized to issue a writ of mandamus to such an officer, it must be because the law is unconstitutional, and therefore absolutely incapable of conferring the authority, and assigning the duties which its words purport to confer and assign.

The constitution vests the whole judicial power of the United States in one Supreme Court, and such inferior courts as congress shall, from time to time, ordain and establish. This power is expressly extended to all cases arising under the laws of the United States; and, consequently, in some form, may be exercised over the present case; because the right claimed is given by a law of the United States.

In the distribution of this power it is declared that "the Supreme Court shall have original jurisdiction in all cases affecting ambassadors, other public ministers and consuls, and those in which a state shall be a party. In all other cases, the Supreme Court shall have appellate jurisdiction."

It has been insisted, at the bar, that as the original grant of jurisdiction, to the Supreme and inferior courts, in general, and the clause, assigning original jurisdiction to the Supreme Court, contains no negative or restrictive words, the power remains to the legislature, to assign original jurisdiction to that court in other cases than those specified in the article which has been recited; provided those cases belong to the judicial power of the United States.

If it had been intended to leave it in the discretion of the legislature to apportion the judicial power between the Supreme and inferior courts according to the will of that body, it would certainly have been useless to have proceeded further than to have defined the judicial power, and the tribunals in which it should be vested. The subsequent part of the section is mere surplusage, is entirely without meaning, if such is to be the construction. If congress remains at liberty to give this court appellate jurisdiction, where the constitution has declared their jurisdiction shall be original; and original jurisdiction where the constitution has declared it shall be appellate; the distribution of jurisdiction, made in the constitution, is form without substance.

Affirmative words are often, in their operation, negative of other objects than those affirmed; and in this case, a negative or exclusive sense must be given to them, or they have no operation at all.

It cannot be presumed that any clause in the constitution is intended to be without effect; and, therefore, such a construction is inadmissible, unless the words require it. . . .

It is the essential criterion of appellate jurisdiction, that it revises and corrects the proceedings in a cause already instituted, and does not create that cause. Although, therefore, a mandamus may be directed to courts, yet to issue such a writ to an officer for the delivery of a paper, is in effect the same as to sustain an original action for that paper, and, therefore, seems not to belong to appellate, but to original jurisdiction. Neither is it necessary in such a case as this, to enable the court to exercise its appellate jurisdiction.

The authority, therefore, given to the Supreme Court, by the act establishing the judicial courts of the United States, to issue writs of mandamus to public officers, appears not to be warranted by the constitution; and it becomes necessary to inquire whether a jurisdiction so conferred can be exercised.

The question, whether an act, repugnant to the constitution, can become the law of the land, is a question deeply interesting to the United States; but, happily, not of an intricacy proportioned to its interest. It seems only necessary to recognize certain principles, supposed to have been long and well established, to decide it.

That the people have an original right to establish, for their future government, such principles, as, in their opinion, shall most conduce to their own happiness is the basis on which the whole American fabric has been erected. The exercise of this original right is a very great exertion; nor can it, nor ought it, to be frequently repeated. The principles, therefore, so established, are deemed fundamental. And as the authority from which they proceed is supreme, and can seldom act, they are designed to be permanent.

This original and supreme will organizes the government, and assigns to different departments their respective powers. It may either stop here, or establish certain limits not to be transcended by those departments.

The government of the United States is of the latter description. The powers of the legislature are defined and limited; and that those limits may not be mistaken, or forgotten, the constitution is written. To what purpose are powers limited, and to what purpose is that limitation committed to writing, if these limits may, at any time, be passed by those intended to be restrained? The distinction between a government with limited and unlimited powers is abolished, if those limits do not confine the persons on whom they are imposed, and if acts prohibited and acts allowed, are of equal obligation. It is a proposition too plain to be contested, that the constitution controls any legislative act repugnant to it; or, that the legislature may alter the constitution by an ordinary act.

Between these alternatives there is no middle ground. The constitution is either a superior paramount law, unchangeable by ordinary means, or it is on a level with ordinary legislative acts, and, like other acts, is alterable when the legislature shall please to alter it.

If the former part of the alternative be true, then a legislative act contrary to the constitution is not law: if the latter part be true, then written constitutions are absurd attempts, on the part of the people, to limit a power in its own nature illimitable.

Certainly all those who have framed written constitutions contemplate them as forming the fundamental and paramount law of the nation, and, consequently, the theory of every such government must be, that an act of the legislature, repugnant to the constitution, is void.

This theory is essentially attached to a written constitution, and, is consequently, to be considered, by this court, as one of the fundamental principles of our society. It is not therefore to be lost sight of in the further consideration of this subject.

If an act of the legislature, repugnant to the constitution, is void, does it, notwithstanding its invalidity, bind the courts, and oblige them to give it effect? Or, in other words, though it be not law, does it constitute a rule as operative as if it was a law? This would be to overthrow in fact what was established in theory; and would seem, at first view, an absurdity too gross to be insisted on. It shall, however, receive a more attentive consideration.

It is emphatically the province and duty of the judicial department to say what the law is. Those who apply the rule to particular cases, must of necessity expound and interpret that rule. If two laws conflict with each other, the courts must decide on the operation of each.

So if the law be in opposition to the constitution; if both the law and the constitution apply to a particular case, so that the court must either decide that case conformably to the law, disregarding the constitution; or conformably to the constitution, disregarding the law; the court must determine which of these conflicting rules governs the case. This is of the very essence of judicial duty.

If, then, the courts are to regard the constitution, and the constitution is superior to any ordinary act of the legislature, the constitution, and not such ordinary act, must govern the case to which they both apply.

Those, then, who controvert the principle that the constitution is to be considered, in court, as a paramount law, are reduced to the necessity of maintaining that courts must close their eyes on the constitution, and see only the law.

This doctrine would subvert the very foundation of all written constitutions. It would declare that an act which, according to the principles and theory of our government, is entirely void, is yet, in practice, completely obligatory. It would declare that if the legislature shall do what is expressly forbidden, such act, notwithstanding the express prohibition, is in reality effectual. It would be given to the legislature a practical and real omnipotence, with the same breath which professes to restrict their powers within narrow limits. It is prescribing limits, and declaring that those limits may be passed at pleasure.

That it thus reduces to nothing what we have deemed the greatest improvement on political institutions, a written constitution, would of itself be sufficient, in America, where written constitutions have been viewed with so much reverence, for rejecting the construction. But the peculiar expressions of the constitution of the United States furnish additional arguments in favour of its rejection.

The judicial power of the United States is extended to all cases arising under the constitution.

Could it be the intention of those who gave this power, to say that in using it the constitution should not be looked into? That a case arising under the constitution should be decided without examining the instrument under which it arises? This is too extravagant to be maintained.

In some cases, then, the constitution must be looked into by the judges. And if they can open it at all, what part of it are they forbidden to read or to obey?

There are many other parts of the constitution which serve to illustrate this subject.

It is declared that "no tax or duty shall be laid on articles exported from any state." Suppose a duty on the export of cotton, of tobacco, or of flour; and a suit instituted to recover it. Ought judgment to be rendered in such a case? Ought the judges to close their eyes on the constitution, and only see the law?

The constitution declares "that no bill of attainder or ex post facto law shall be passed."

If, however, such a bill should be passed, and a person should be prosecuted under it; must the court condemn to death those victims whom the constitution endeavors to preserve?

"No person," says the constitution, "shall be convicted of treason unless on the testimony of two witnesses to the same overt act, or on confession in open court." Here the language of the constitution is addressed especially to the courts. It prescribes, directly for them, a rule of evidence not to be departed from. If the legislature should change that rule, and declare one witness, or a confession out of court, sufficient for conviction, must the constitutional principle yield to the legislative act?

From these, and many other selections which might be made, it is apparent, that the framers of the constitution contemplated that instrument as a rule for the government of courts, as well as of the legislature.

Why otherwise does it direct the judges to take an oath to support it? This oath certainly applies in an especial manner, to their conduct in their official character. How immoral to impose it on them, if they were to be used as the instruments, and the knowing instruments, for violating what they swear to support!

The oath of office, too, imposed by the legislature, is completely demonstrative of the legislative opinion on this subject. It is in these words: "I do solemnly swear that I will administer justice without respect to persons, and do equal right to the poor and to the rich; and that I will faithfully and impartially discharge all the duties incumbent on me as _____, according to the best of my abilities and understanding agreeably to the constitution and laws of the United States."

Why does a judge swear to discharge his duties agreeably to the constitution of the United States, if that constitution forms no rule for his government? If it is closed upon him, and cannot be inspected by him? If such be the real state of things, this is worse than solemn mockery. To prescribe, or to take this oath, becomes equally a crime.

It is also not entirely unworthy of observation, that in declaring what shall be the supreme law of the land, the constitution itself is first mentioned; and not the laws of the United States generally, but those only which shall be made in pursuance of the constitution, have that rank.

Thus, the particular phraseology of the constitution of the United States confirms and strengthens the principle, supposed to be essential to all written constitutions, that a law repugnant to the constitution is void; and that courts, as well as other departments, are bound by that instrument.

The rule must be discharged.

COOPER v. AARON
358 U.S. 1, 78 S.Ct. 1401, 3 L.Ed.2d 5 (1958).

Opinion of the Court by THE CHIEF JUSTICE [WARREN], MR. JUSTICE BLACK, MR. JUSTICE FRANKFURTER, MR. JUSTICE DOUGLAS, MR. JUSTICE BURTON, MR. JUSTICE CLARK, MR. JUSTICE HARLAN, MR. JUSTICE BRENNAN, and MR. JUSTICE WHITTAKER.

As this case reaches us it raises questions of the highest importance to the maintenance of our federal system of government. It necessarily involves a claim by the Governor and Legislature of a State that there is no duty on state officials to obey federal court orders resting on this Court's considered interpretation of the United States Constitution. Specifically it involves actions by the Governor and Legislature of Arkansas upon the premise that they are not bound by our holding in *Brown v. Board of Education,* [§ 8–2.12, infra]. That holding was that the Fourteenth Amendment forbids States to use their governmental powers to bar children on racial grounds from attending schools where there is state participation through any arrangement, management, funds or property. We are urged to uphold a suspension of the Little Rock School Board's plan to do away with segregated public schools in Little Rock until state laws and efforts to upset and nullify our holding in *Brown v. Board of Education* have been further challenged and tested in the courts. We reject these contentions. . . .

Article VI of the Constitution makes the Constitution the "supreme Law of the Land." In 1803, Chief Justice Marshall, speaking for a unanimous Court, referring to the Constitution as "the fundamental and paramount law of the nation," declared in the notable case of *Marbury v. Madison,* that "It is emphatically the province and duty of the judicial department to say what the law is." This decision declared the basic principle that the federal judiciary is supreme in the exposition of the law of the Constitution, and that principle has ever since been respected by this Court and the Country as a permanent and indispensable feature of our constitutional system. It follows that the interpretation of the Fourteenth Amendment enunciated by this Court in the *Brown* case is the supreme law of the land, and Art. VI of the Constitution makes it of binding effect on the States "any Thing in the Constitution or Laws of any State to the Contrary notwithstanding." Every state legislator and executive and judicial officer is solemnly committed by oath taken pursuant to Art. VI, cl. 3, "to support this Constitution." Chief Justice Taney, speaking for a unanimous Court in 1859, said that this requirement reflected the framers' "anxiety to preserve it [the Constitution] in full force, in all its powers, and to guard against resistance to or evasion of its authority, on the part of a State.... " *Ableman v. Booth,* 21 How. 506, 524, 16 L.Ed. 169.

No state legislature or executive or judicial officer can war against the Constitution without violating his undertaking to support it. Chief Justice Marshall spoke for a unanimous Court in saying that: "If the legislatures of the several states may, at will, annul the judgments of the courts of the United States, and destroy the rights acquired under those judgments, the constitution itself becomes a solemn mockery.... " *United States v. Peters,* 5 Cranch 115, 136, 3 L.Ed. 53. A Governor who asserts a power to nullify a federal court order is similarly restrained. If he had such power, said Chief Justice Hughes, in 1932, also for a unanimous Court, "it is manifest that the fiat of a state Governor, and not the Constitution of the United States, would be the supreme law of the land; that the restrictions of the Federal Constitution upon the exercise of state power would be but impotent phrases.... " *Sterling v. Constantin,* 287 U.S. 378, 397–398, 53 S.Ct. 190, 195, 77 L.Ed. 375....

[A concurring opinion by FRANKFURTER, J., is omitted.]

THE FEDERALIST PAPERS, NO. 78, HAMILTON (1788)

... The complete independence of the courts of justice is peculiarly essential in a limited Constitution. By a limited Constitution, I understand one which contains certain specified exceptions to the legislative authority; such, for instance, as that it shall pass no bills of attainder, no *ex-post-facto* laws, and the like. Limitations of this kind can be preserved in practice no other way than through the medium of courts of justice, whose duty it must be to declare all acts contrary to the manifest tenor of the Constitution void. Without this, all the reservations of particular rights or privileges would amount to nothing.

Some perplexity respecting the rights of the courts to pronounce legislative acts void, because contrary to the constitution, has arisen from an imagination that the doctrine would imply a superiority of the judiciary to the legislative power. It is urged that the authority which can declare the acts of another void, must necessarily be superior to the one whose acts may be declared void.... The interpretation of the laws is the proper and peculiar province of the courts. A constitution is, in fact, and must be regarded by the judges, as a fundamental law. It therefore belongs to them to ascertain its meaning, as well as the meaning of any particular act proceeding from the legislative body. If there should happen to be an irreconcilable variance between the two that, which has the superior obligation and validity ought, of course, to be preferred; or, in other words, the Constitution ought to be preferred to the statute, the intention of the people to the intention of their agents....

It can be of no weight to say that the courts, on the pretense of a repugnancy, may substitute their own pleasure to the constitutional intentions of the legislature. This might as well happen in the case of two contradictory statutes; or it might as well happen in every adjudication upon any single statute. The courts must declare the sense of the law; and if they should be disposed to exercise WILL instead of JUDGMENT, the consequence would equally be the substitution of their pleasure to that of the legislative body. The observation, if it prove anything, would prove that there ought to be no judges distinct from that body....

Notes

1. Was Marshall's opinion in logical order? That is, should he have first discussed the question of jurisdiction? If Marshall had done that, would the remainder of his opinion have been necessary? Could President Jefferson or Secretary of State Madison refuse to obey Marshall's opinion?

2. Marshall's opinion invalidates section 13 of the Judiciary Act of 1789, enacted by the first Congress, many members of which had also been members of the Constitutional Convention of 1787. How likely is it that the framers of the Constitution would enact, two years later, a statute contrary to the Constitution? In upholding another clause of the same section 13, the Court later noted that it "was passed by the first Congress assembled under the Constitution, many of whose members had taken part in framing that instrument, and [that] is contemporaneous and weighty evidence of its true meaning." *Wisconsin v. Pelican Insurance Co.,* 127 U.S. 265, 297, 8 S.Ct. 1370, 1378, 32 L.Ed. 239 (1888).

Look carefully at section 13, reprinted at the end of the bracketed introduction to this opinion. Must section 13 be interpreted to grant the Supreme Court original jurisdiction to issue writs of mandamus? If a constitutional interpretation is possible, should Marshall have adopted it?

3. Could Marshall have avoided the constitutional issue by holding that the appointment was not vested until Marbury actually took office, or that the term of five years was not a minimum but a maximum? Cases since *Marbury* have upheld broader presidential powers over appointments than suggested by Marshall's dictum. E.g., *Myers v. United States,* 272 U.S. 52, 47

S.Ct. 21, 71 L.Ed. 160 (1926); *Humphrey's Ex'r v. United States,* 295 U.S. 602, 55 S.Ct. 869, 79 L.Ed. 1611 (1935); *United States v. Le Baron,* 60 U.S. (19 How.) 73, 15 L.Ed. 525 (1856). See Casebook, § 5–8.

4.   If the Constitution must be supreme over contrary law, why are the courts the final body to decide when a law is in fact contrary to the Constitution? Marshall explains that the judges take an oath to support the Constitution, but federal and state legislators, and executive and judicial officers are similarly bound by oath. U.S. Const., Art. VI, cl. 3. How can one branch of government, the Judiciary, be supreme over a coordinate branch, Congress?

Can democracy exist when the courts are not the final arbiters? In England, Parliament can change judicial decisions by statute. The French "have clung tenaciously to the idea that no judicial organ should be given the power to review statutes for conformity with a higher law. [U]ntil recently such control has been, at best, theoretical, and has always been entrusted to specifically political bodies." M. Cappelletti & W. Cohen, Comparative Constitutional Law 25 (1979). Although Swiss judges have the power to disregard the law of the cantons in conflict with the Swiss Federal Constitution, there is no judicial control over the constitutionality of federal laws, a limitation criticized by modern writers. Id. at 74.

Can democracy exist when the courts are final arbiters? Marshall says that our government is "a government of laws, and not of men." But judges are just as human as legislators. Is our government a government of judges? Charles Evans Hughes remarked in 1907: "We are under a Constitution, but the Constitution is what the judges say it is."[1] In 1930 Hughes became Chief Justice.

Is there a danger that the institution of judicial review will encourage the other branches of government to abdicate their responsibility to follow the Constitution? In 1935 President Roosevelt, by letter, urged a congressman to support a bill. The letter concluded: "I hope your committee will not permit doubts as to constitutionality, however reasonable, to block the suggested legislation."

Consider *Cooper v. Aaron,* supra. Are there any circumstances where a constitutional decision of the U.S. Supreme Court is not the supreme law of the land? If the Supreme Court upholds a statute, may the President later veto similar legislation on the grounds that it is unconstitutional? If the Supreme Court upholds a conviction and rejects a constitutional attack on the statute creating the offense, may the President pardon the offender on the grounds that the statute is unconstitutional? May the President instruct the Attorney General not to enforce a law he believes is unconstitutional? If the President so instructs, is he fulfilling his responsibility under Article II, § 3, to "take Care that the Laws be faithfully executed.... "? Would it have been proper in 1858, to attack, seek to nullify, or otherwise object to, *Dred Scott v. Sandford,* 60 U.S. (19 How.) 393, 15 L.Ed. 691 (1857)? That case declared unconstitutional the Missouri Compromise, which granted freedom

---

1.   Hughes, Speech before Elmira Chamber of Commerce in 1907, Addresses and   Papers, 133, 139 (1908).

to slaves in certain territories. *Dred Scott* was the next major case where the Court invalidated federal legislation.[2]

5.   It is sometimes argued that Marshall created the doctrine of judicial review out of whole cloth, that it sprung from his forehead like Pallas Athena from the forehead of Zeus. Others argue that the framers intended judicial review. Consider the following historical background.

In *Dr. Bonham's Case,* 8 Coke Rep. 118a (C.P.1610), Lord Chief Justice Edward Coke stated: "[W]hen an Act of Parliament is against common right and reason, or repugnant, or impossible to be performed, the common law will control it and adjudge such Act to be void." This statement "was the most controversial judicial dictum of Coke's life, due to be celebrated out of proportion to its real significance—one of those public statements which, as history progresses, men seize upon and interpret according to their need.... Actually, Coke based his decision on five points, not one. But it was the above clause which echoed down the centuries".[3]

The English Privy Counsel had the power to review acts of the colonies thought to be in violation of English law or their charters, and prior to *Marbury* some state courts purported to have the power of judicial review.[4] However, after *Marbury* Justice Gibson of the Pennsylvania Supreme Court attacked what he called the "professional dogma" of broad judicial review. In *Eakin v. Raub,* 12 S. & R. 330, 344–45 (Pa.1825), his separate opinion drew a distinction between state laws repugnant to the U.S. Constitution and state laws repugnant to a state constitution. He argued that the judiciary is bound to execute the latter but not the former, because the states have limited their sovereignty by joining the Union and subjecting themselves to the supremacy clause. As to a broad notion of judicial review, he argued: "[I]t is by no means clear, that to declare a law void which has been enacted according to the forms prescribed in the constitution is not a usurpation of legislative power.... If the judiciary will inquire into anything besides the form of enactment, where shall it stop? [N]o one will pretend that a judge would be justifiable in calling for the election returns, or scrutinizing the qualifications of those who composed the legislature. [T]he judiciary is not infallible; and an error by it would admit of no remedy but a more distinct expression of the public will, through the extraordinary medium of a convention; whereas, an error by the legislature admits of a remedy by an exertion of the same will, in the ordinary exercise of the right of suffrage.... " Gibson later changed his position because of acquiescence of the people and practical necessity. *Norris v. Clymer,* 2 Pa. 277, 281 (1845).

2.   As Professor Charles Alan Wright has pointed out, in *Hodgson v. Bowerbank,* 9 U.S. (5 Cranch) 303, 3 L.Ed. 108 (1809)—a case decided after *Marbury* and before *Dred Scott*—the Court ruled that § 11 of the Judiciary Act cannot constitutionally provide for federal jurisdiction in all suits simply because one of the parties is an alien, without regard to the citizenship of the other party. The Court rejected the argument presented that "[T]he judiciary act gives jurisdiction to the circuit courts in all suits in which an alien is a party." Chief Justice Marshall's curt response: "Turn to the article of the Constitution of the United States, for the statute cannot extend the jurisdiction beyond the limits of the Constitution." See, C. Wright, The Law of Federal Courts § 8, at 32 & n. 3 (5th ed. 1994).

3.   C. Bowen, The Lion and the Throne 315 (1957).

4.   See generally, J. Nowak & R. Rotunda, Constitutional Law 10–12 (West Group, 6th ed. 2000). See also, 1 R. Rotunda & J. Nowak, Treatise on Constitutional Law: Substance and Procedure §§ 1.1(g), 1.4 (West Group 3d ed. 1999).

What do you think of Justice Gibson's original distinction? Justice Holmes once said: "I do not think the United States would come to an end if we lost our power to declare an Act of Congress void. I do think the Union would be imperiled if we could not make that declaration as to the laws of the several States." Holmes, Collected Legal Papers 295–96 (1920).

The U.S. Supreme Court, before Marshall, purported to exercise the power of judicial review though no laws were ever invalidated. *Hayburn's Case,* 2 U.S. (2 Dall.) 408, 1 L.Ed. 436 (1792) concerned a statute empowering federal and state courts to determine the propriety and amount of pensions for disabled veterans of the Revolutionary War. The statute authorized the Secretary of War to review the court decision and transmit his opinion to Congress, which could, if it agreed, appropriate the necessary funds. The Circuit Court for the District of Pennsylvania refused to consider William Hayburn's application for a pension under the statute, and the Attorney General sought a writ of mandamus in the Supreme Court. Prior to the decision, Congress avoided a constitutional confrontation by amending the legislation to provide other relief for the pensioners, and the Supreme Court dismissed on grounds of mootness. In footnote (a) to the dismissal, however, the reporter noted some of the earliest thinking on the constitutional division between the legislative and judicial functions, quoting Chief Justice Jay and Justice Cushing as Circuit court Justices, holding that, because the duties under the original Act were not judicial, they could not perform them in their capacity as judges. The footnote in *Hayburn's Case* also cited letters to the President from two circuit courts concerning the same statute. In 1792 the Circuit Court for the District of Pennsylvania, consisting of Supreme Court Justices Wilson and Blair, and the Circuit Court for the District of North Carolina, including Justice Iredell, had written the President that no decision of any court of the United States could be subject to revision or suspension by the legislature because the Congress had no judicial power but impeachment.

In *Hollingsworth v. Virginia,* 3 U.S. (3 Dall.) 378, 381, & n.*, 1 L.Ed. 644 (1798), the Supreme Court refused to declare the 11th Amendment unconstitutional on the grounds that the President had not signed the resolution proposing the amendment to the states.

6. Does this historical background or the analysis in Federalist, No. 78, tell us how strictly the judiciary should scrutinize legislation challenged as unconstitutional? Recall that Marshall gave the example of a person convicted of treason under a statute that declares only one witness is necessary for conviction. The Constitution requires two witnesses, Act III, § cl. 1. Does that mean that the Court should only invalidate legislation clearly in conflict with the Constitution? Should (must) the Court, in cases of doubt, defer to the legislative judgment?

MARTIN v. HUNTER'S LESSEE
14 U.S. (1 Wheat.) 304, 4 L.Ed. 97 (1816).

[Before the Revolutionary War, Lord Fairfax had title to approximately 300,000 acres of Virginia land, known as Northern Neck. In 1779 the legislature of the Commonwealth of Virginia passed a law providing for forfeiture of property belonging to British subjects, who then were enemy aliens. This law provided a procedure for forfeiture known as an inquest of office. In 1782 the Virginia legislature passed another law declaring that Northern Neck was probably claimed by enemy aliens and was therefore forfeited. The procedure for forfeiture of such land pursuant to the Act of 1779 was not followed. Other legislation also specifically dealing with Northern Neck followed, and it was pursuant to one of these, the Act of 1785, that David Hunter claimed his land in Northern Neck.

[Meanwhile, the Revolutionary War had ended and the Treaty of 1783 with England had declared that there should be "no future confiscations" of land belonging to British subjects.

[David Hunter, in 1791, sued in the Virginia state courts to eject Lord Fairfax's heir, Denny Martin Fairfax, to whom Lord Fairfax willed the land. Hunter lost in the state trial court in 1794; in 1810 the Virginia Court of Appeals reversed the trial court. Pursuant to section 25 of the Judiciary Act of 1789, the case went to the U.S. Supreme Court. Chief Justice Marshall took no part in the case because he had personal interests in the case: he had contracted with Martin to purchase part of Northern Neck.

[Justice Story wrote the opinion for the Court reversing the Virginia Court of Appeals. In this opinion Story argued, among other things, that it was "admitted" that "no inquest of office was ever made pursuant to the acts on this subject at any time. And it would seem therefore to follow, upon common law reasoning, that the grant to the lessor of the original Plaintiff ... issued improvidently and erroneously, and passed nothing." *Fairfax's Devisee v. Hunter's Lessee,* 11 U.S. (7 Cranch) 603, 622, 3 L.Ed. 453 (1813). The Treaty thus protected the alien. Although Virginia could have secured title by an inquest of office, it had not done so before the operation of the Treaty.

[The case was then sent back to the Virginia Court of Appeals, which objected both to the fact that the U.S. Supreme Court reversed the Virginia Court, and to the tone of the Supreme Court mandate. The Virginia Court reprinted the mandate, which in part stated: "You therefore are commanded that such proceedings be had in said cause as according ... to said judgment and instructions of said Supreme Court ought to be had, the said writ of error notwithstanding." *Hunter v. Martin, Devisees of Fairfax,* 18 Va. (4 Munford) 1, 3 (1815).[1] The Virginia court refused to obey the mandate and held:

> The court is unanimously of opinion that the appellate power of the Supreme Court of the United States does not extend to this court under a sound construction of the constitution of the United States; that so much of the 25th section of the act of Congress, to establish

---

1. The tone of Supreme Court mandates has softened. Typically if a case is remanded, as to state courts, the mandate provides for "further proceedings not inconsistent with this opinion". As to lower federal courts the language is more assertive: such a remand provides for "further proceedings consistent with this opinion."

the judicial courts of the United States, as extends the appellate
jurisdiction of the Supreme Court to this court, is not in pursuance
of the constitution of the United States. That the writ of error in
this cause was improvidently allowed under the authority of that
act; that the proceedings thereon in the Supreme Court were coram
non judice in relation to this court, and that obedience to its
mandate be declined by the court.

[The case then went back to the U.S. Supreme Court.]

STORY, J., delivered the opinion of the court:

This is a writ of error from the Court of Appeals of Virginia, founded
upon the refusal of that court to obey the mandate of this court,
requiring the judgment rendered in this very cause, at February term,
1813, to be carried into due execution. . . .

The questions involved in this judgment are of great importance and
delicacy. Perhaps it is not too much to affirm that, upon their right
decision, rest some of the most solid principles which have hitherto been
supposed to sustain and protect the constitution itself. The great respect-
ability, too, of the court whose decisions we are called upon to review,
and the entire deference which we entertain for the learning and ability
of that court, add much to the difficulty of the task which has so
unwelcomely fallen upon us. It is, however, a source of consolation that
we have had the assistance of most able and learned arguments to aid
our inquiries; and that the opinion which is now to be pronounced has
been weighed with every solicitude to come to a correct result, and
matured after solemn deliberation.

Before proceeding to the principal questions, it may not be unfit to
dispose of some preliminary considerations which have grown out of the
arguments at the bar.

The constitution of the United States was ordained and established,
not by the states in their sovereign capacities, but emphatically, as the
preamble of the constitution declares, by "the people of the United
States." [I]t is perfectly clear that the sovereign powers vested in the
state governments, by their respective constitutions, remained unaltered
and unimpaired, except so far as they were granted to the government of
the United States. . . .

The constitution unavoidably deals in general language. It did not
suit the purposes of the people, in framing this great charter of our
liberties, to provide for minute specifications of its powers, or to declare
the means by which those powers should be carried into execution. It
was foreseen that this would be a perilous and difficult, if not an
impracticable, task. The instrument was not intended to provide merely
for the exigencies of a few years, but was to endure through a long lapse
of ages, the events of which were locked up in the inscrutable purposes
of Providence. . . . Hence its powers are expressed in general terms,
leaving to the legislature, from time to time, to adopt its own means to

effectuate legitimate objects, and to mold and model the exercise of its powers, as its own wisdom and the public interests should require....

This leads us to the consideration of the great question as to the nature and extent of the appellate jurisdiction of the United States.... The appellate power is not limited by the terms of the third article to any particular courts. The words are, "the judicial power (which includes appellate power) shall extend to all cases," etc., and "in all other cases before mentioned the Supreme Court shall have appellate jurisdiction." It is the case, then, and not the court, that gives the jurisdiction. If the judicial power extends to the case, it will be in vain to search in the letter of the constitution for any qualification as to the tribunal where it depends. It is incumbent, then, upon those who assert such a qualification to show its existence by necessary implication. If the text be clear and distinct, no restriction upon its plain and obvious import ought to be admitted, unless the inference be irresistible.

If the constitution meant to limit the appellate jurisdiction to cases pending in the courts of the United States, it would necessarily follow that the jurisdiction of these courts would, in all the cases enumerated in the constitution, be exclusive of state tribunals. How otherwise could the jurisdiction extend to all cases arising under the constitution, laws and treaties of the United States, or to all cases of admiralty and maritime jurisdiction? If some of these cases might be entertained by state tribunals, and no appellate jurisdiction as to them should exist, then the appellate power would not extend to all, but to some, cases. If state tribunals might exercise concurrent jurisdiction over all or some of the other classes of cases in the constitution without control, then the appellate jurisdiction of the United States might, as to such cases, have no real existence, contrary to the manifest intent of the constitution. Under such circumstances, to give effect to the judicial power, it must be construed to be exclusive; and this not only when the casus faederis should arise directly, but when it should arise, incidentally, in cases pending in state courts. This construction would abridge the jurisdiction of such courts far more than has been ever contemplated in any act of Congress.

On the other hand, if, as has been contended, a discretion be vested in Congress to establish, or not to establish, inferior courts at their own pleasure, and Congress should not establish such courts, the appellate jurisdiction of the Supreme Court would have nothing to act upon, unless it could act upon cases pending in the state courts. Under such circumstances it must be held that the appellate power would extend to state courts; for the constitution is peremptory that it shall extend to certain enumerated cases, which cases could exist in no other courts. Any other construction, upon this supposition, would involve this strange contradiction, that a discretionary power vested in Congress, and which they might rightfully omit to exercise, would defeat the absolute injunctions of the constitution in relation to the whole appellate power.

But it is plain that the framers of the constitution did contemplate that cases within the judicial cognizance of the United States not only might but would arise in the state courts, in the exercise of their ordinary jurisdiction. With this view the sixth article declares, that "this constitution, and the laws of the United States which shall be made in pursuance thereof, and all treaties made, or which shall be made, under the authority of the United States, shall be the supreme law of the land, and the judges in every state shall be bound thereby, anything in the constitution or laws of any state to the contrary notwithstanding." It is obvious that this obligation is imperative upon the state judges in their official, and not merely in their private, capacities. From the very nature of their judicial duties they would be called upon to pronounce the law applicable to the case in judgment. They were not to decide merely according to the laws or constitution of the state, but according to the constitution, laws and treaties of the United States—"the supreme law of the land."

A moment's consideration will show us the necessity and propriety of this provision in cases where the jurisdiction of the state courts is unquestionable. Suppose a contract for the payment of money is made between citizens of the same state, and performance thereof is sought in the courts of that state; no person can doubt that the jurisdiction completely and exclusively attaches, in the first instance, to such courts. Suppose at the trial the defendant sets up in his defense ... a state law, impairing the obligation of such contract, which law, if binding, would defeat the suit. The constitution of the United States has declared that no state shall ... pass a law impairing the obligation of contracts. If Congress shall not have passed a law providing for the removal of such a suit to the courts of the United States, must not the state court proceed to hear and determine it? Can a mere plea in defense be of itself a bar to further proceedings, so as to prohibit an inquiry into its truth or legal propriety, when no other tribunal exists to whom judicial cognizance of such cases is confided? Suppose an indictment for a crime in a state court, and the defendant should allege in his defense that the crime was created by an ex post facto act of the state, must not the state court, in the exercise of a jurisdiction which has already rightfully attached, have a right to pronounce on the validity and sufficiency of the defense? It would be extremely difficult, upon any legal principles, to give a negative answer to these inquiries. Innumerable instances of the same sort might be stated, in illustration of the position; and unless the state courts could sustain jurisdiction in such cases, this clause of the sixth article would be without meaning or effect, and public mischiefs, of a most enormous magnitude, would inevitably ensue.

It must, therefore, be conceded that the constitution not only contemplated, but meant to provide for cases within the scope of the judicial power of the United States, which might yet depend before state tribunals. It was foreseen that in the exercise of their ordinary jurisdiction, state courts would incidentally take cognizance of cases arising under the constitution, the laws and treaties of the United States. Yet to all these cases the judicial power, by the very terms of the constitution, is to extend. It cannot extend by original jurisdiction if that was already rightfully and exclusively attached in the state courts, which (as has been already shown) may occur; it must, therefore, extend by appellate jurisdiction, or not at all. It would seem to follow that the appellate power of the United States must, in such cases, extend to state tribunals; and if in such cases, there is no reason why it should not equally attach upon all others within the purview of the constitution. . . .

. . . The courts of the United States can, without question, revise the proceedings of the executive and legislative authorities of the states, and if they are found to be contrary to the constitution, may declare them to be of no legal validity. Surely the exercise of the same right over judicial tribunals is not a higher or more dangerous act of sovereign power.

Nor can such a right be deemed to impair the independence of state judges. It is assuming the very ground in controversy to assert that they possess an absolute independence of the United States. In respect to the powers granted to the United States, they are not independent; they are expressly bound to obedience by the letter of the constitution; and if they should unintentionally transcend their authority, or misconstrue the constitution, there is no more reason for giving their judgments an absolute and irresistible force than for giving it to the acts of the other co-ordinate departments of state sovereignty.

The argument urged from the possibility of the abuse of the revising power is equally unsatisfactory. It is always a doubtful course to argue against the use of existence of a power, from the possibility of its abuse. . . .

It is further argued that no great public mischief can result from a construction which shall limit the appellate power of the United States to cases in their own courts; first, because state judges are bound by an oath to support the constitution of the United States, and must be presumed to be men of learning and integrity; and, secondly, because Congress must have an unquestionable right to remove all cases within the scope of the judicial power from the state courts to the courts of the United States, at any time before final judgment, though not after final judgment. As to the first reason—admitting that the judges of the state courts are, and always will be, of as much learning, integrity, and wisdom, as those of the courts of the United States (which we very cheerfully admit), it does not aid the argument. It is manifest that the constitution has proceeded upon a theory of its own, and given or withheld powers according to the judgment of the American people, by whom it was adopted. We can only construe its powers, and cannot inquire into the policy or principles which induced the grant of them. The constitution has presumed (whether rightly or wrongly we do not inquire) that state attachments, state prejudices, state jealousies, and state interests, might sometimes obstruct, or control, or be supposed to obstruct or control, the regular administration of justice. . . .

This is not all. A motive of another kind, perfectly compatible, with the most sincere respect for state tribunals, might induce the grant of appellate power over their decisions. That motive is the importance, and even necessity of uniformity of decisions throughout the whole United States, upon all subjects within the purview of the constitution. Judges of equal learning and integrity, in different states, might differently interpret a statute, or a treaty of the United States, or even the constitution itself. . . .

There is an additional consideration, which is entitled to great weight. The constitution of the United States was designed for the common and equal benefit of all the people of the United States. The judicial power was granted for the same benign and salutary purposes. It was not to be exercised exclusively for the benefit of parties who might be plaintiffs, and would elect the national forum, but also for the protection of defendants who might be entitled to try their rights, or assert their privileges, before the same forum. Yet, if the construction contended for be correct, it will follow, that as the plaintiff may always elect the state court, the defendant, may be deprived of all the security which the constitution intended in aid of his rights. Such a state of things can in no respect be considered as giving equal rights. To obviate this difficulty, we are referred to the power which it is admitted Congress possess[es] to remove suits from state courts to the national courts; and this forms the second ground upon which the argument we are considering has been attempted to be sustained.

This power of removal is not to be found in express terms in any part of the constitution; if it be given, it is only given by implication, as a power necessary and proper to carry into effect some express power. The power of removal is certainly not, in strictness of language an exercise of original jurisdiction; it presupposes an exercise of original jurisdiction to have attached elsewhere. . . . If, then, the right of removal be included in the appellate jurisdiction, it is only because it is one mode of exercising that power, and as Congress is not limited by the constitution to any particular mode, or time of exercising it, it may authorize a removal either before or after judgment. The time, the process, and the manner, must be subject to its absolute legislative control. A writ of error is, indeed, but a process which removes the record of one court to the possession of another court, and enables the latter to inspect the proceedings, and give such judgment as its own opinion of the law and justice of the case may warrant. There is nothing in the nature of the process which forbids it from being applied by the legislature, to interlocutory as well as final judgments. . . . Nor, indeed, would the force of the arguments on either side materially vary if the right of removal were an exercise of original jurisdiction. It would equally trench upon the jurisdiction and independence of state tribunals.

The remedy, too, of removal of suits would be utterly inadequate to the purposes of the constitution, if it could act only on the parties, and not upon the state courts. . . . If state courts should deny the constitutionality of the authority to remove suits from their cognizance, in what manner could they be compelled to relinquish the jurisdiction? In respect to criminal cases, there would at once be an end of all control, and the state decisions would be paramount to the constitution; and though in civil suits the courts of the United States might act upon the parties, yet the state courts might act in the same way; and this conflict of jurisdictions would not only jeopardize private rights, but bring into imminent peril the public interests.

On the whole, the court are of opinion that the appellate power of the United States does extend to cases pending in the state courts; and that the 25th section of the judiciary act, which authorizes the exercise of this jurisdiction in the specified cases, by a writ of error, is supported by the letter and spirit of the constitution. We find no clause in that instrument which limits this power; and we dare not interpose a limitation where the people have not been disposed to create one.

Strong as this conclusion stands upon the general language of the constitution, it may still derive support from other sources. It is an historical fact that this exposition of the constitution, extending its appellate power to state courts, was, previous to its adoption, uniformly and publicly avowed by its friends, and admitted by its enemies, as the basis of their respective reasonings, both in and out of the state conventions. It is an historical fact that at the time when the judiciary act was submitted to the deliberations of the first Congress, composed, as it was, not only of men of great learning and ability, but of men who had acted a principal part in framing, supporting, or opposing that constitution, the same exposition was explicitly declared and admitted by the friends and by the opponents of that system. It is an historical fact that the Supreme Court of the United States have, from time to time, sustained this appellate jurisdiction in a great variety of cases, brought from the tribunals of many of the most important states in the Union, and that no state tribunal has ever breathed a judicial doubt on the subject, or declined to obey the mandate of the Supreme Court, until the present occasion. This weight of contemporaneous exposition by all parties, this acquiescence of enlightened state courts, and these judicial decisions of the Supreme Court through so long a period, do, as we think, place the doctrine upon a foundation of authority which cannot be shaken, without delivering over the subject to perpetual and irremediable doubts.

The next question which has been argued is, whether the case at bar be within the purview of the 25th section of the judiciary act, so that this court may rightfully sustain the present writ of error. This section, stripped of passages unimportant in this inquiry, enacts, in substance, that a final judgment or decree in any suit in the highest court of law or equity of a state, where is drawn in question the validity of a treaty or statute of, or an authority exercised under, the United States, and the decision is against their validity; or where is drawn in question the validity of a statute of, or an authority exercised under, any state, on the ground of their being repugnant to the constitution, treaties, or laws, of the United States, and the decision is in favor of such their validity; or of the constitution, or of a treaty or statute of, or commission held under, the United States, and the decision is against the title, right, privilege, or exemption, specially set up or claimed by either party under such clause of the said constitution, treaty, statute, or commission, may be re-examined and reversed or affirmed in the Supreme Court of the United States, upon a writ of error, in the same manner, and under the same regulations, and the writ shall have the same effect, as if the judgment or decree complained of had been rendered or passed in a circuit court, and the proceeding upon the reversal shall also be the same, except that the Supreme Court, instead of remanding the cause for a final decision, as before provided, may, at their discretion, if the cause shall have been once remanded before, proceed to a final decision of the same, and award execution. But no other error shall be assigned or regarded as a ground of reversal in any such case as aforesaid, than such as appears upon the face of the record, and immediately respects the before-mentioned question of validity or construction of the said constitution, treaties, statutes, commissions, or authorities in dispute.

That the present writ of error is founded upon a judgment of the court below, which drew in question and denied the validity of a statute of the United States, is incontrovertible, for it is apparent upon the face of the record.... But it is contended that the former judgment of this court was rendered upon a case not within the purview of this section of the judicial act, and that as it was pronounced by an incompetent jurisdiction, it was utterly void, and cannot be a sufficient foundation to sustain any subsequent proceedings. To this argument several answers may be given. In the first place, it is not admitted that, upon this writ of error, the former record is before us. The error now assigned is not in the former proceedings, but in the judgment rendered upon the mandate issued after the former judgment. The question now litigated is not upon the construction of a treaty, but upon the constitutionality of a statute of the United States, which is clearly within our jurisdiction....

In this case, however, from motives of a public nature, we are entirely willing to waive all objections, and to go back and re-examine the question of jurisdiction as it stood upon the record formerly in judgment. We have great confidence that our jurisdiction will, on a careful examination, stand confirmed as well upon principle as authority. It will be recollected that the action was an ejectment for a parcel of land in the Northern Neck, formerly belonging to Lord Fairfax. The original plaintiff claimed the land under a patent granted to him by the state of Virginia, in 1789, under a title supposed to be vested in that state by escheat or forfeiture. The original defendant claimed the land as devisee under the will of Lord Fairfax. [T]he title of the defendant was perfect and complete, if it was protected by the treaty of 1783....

The objection urged at the bar is, that this court cannot inquire into the title, but simply into the correctness of the construction put upon the treaty by the Court of Appeals; and that their judgment is not re-examinable here, unless it appear on the face of the record that some construction was put upon the treaty. If, therefore, that court might have decided the case upon the invalidity of the title ... independent of the treaty, there is an end of the appellate jurisdiction of this court. In support of this objection much stress is laid upon the last clause of the section, which declares that no other cause shall be regarded as a ground of reversal than such as appears on the face of the record and immediately respects the construction of the treaty, etc., in dispute.

If this be the true construction of the section, it will be wholly inadequate for the purposes which it professes to have in view, and may be evaded at pleasure.... What is the case for which the body of the section provides a remedy by writ of error? The answer must be in the words of the section, a suit where is drawn in question the construction of a treaty, and the decision is against *the title set up by the party*.... How, indeed, can it be possible to decide whether a title be within the protection of a treaty, until it is ascertained what that title is, and whether it have a legal validity? From the very necessity of the case, there must be a preliminary inquiry into the existence and structure of the title, before the court can construe the treaty in reference to that title. If the court below should decide that the title was bad, and, therefore, not protected by the treaty, must not this court have a power to decide the title to be good, and, therefore, protected by the treaty? Is not the treaty, in both instances, equally construed, and the title of the party, in reference to the treaty, equally ascertained and decided? ...

The restraining clause was manifestly intended for a very different purpose. It was foreseen that the parties might claim under various titles, and might assert various defenses, altogether independent of each other. The court might admit or reject evidence applicable to one particular title, and not to all, and in such cases it was the intention of Congress to limit what would otherwise have unquestionably attached to the court, the right of revising all the points involved in the cause. It therefore restrains this right to such errors as respect the questions specified in the section; and in this view, it has an appropriate sense, consistent with the preceding clauses. We are, therefore, satisfied, that, upon principle, the case was rightfully before us, and if the point were perfectly new, we should not hesitate to assert the jurisdiction....

We have not thought it incumbent on us to give any opinion upon the question, whether this court have authority to issue a writ of mandamus to the Court of Appeals to enforce the former judgments, as we do not think it necessarily involved in the decision of this cause.

It is the opinion of the whole court that the judgment of the Court of Appeals of Virginia, rendered on the mandate in this cause, be reversed, and the judgment of the District Court, held at Winchester, be, and the same is hereby affirmed.

JOHNSON, J. It will be observed in this case that the court disavows all intention to decide on the right to issue compulsory process to the state courts; thus leaving us, in my opinion, where the constitution and laws place us—supreme over persons and cases as far as our judicial powers extend, but not asserting any compulsory control over the state tribunals.

In this view I acquiesce in their opinion, but not altogether in the reasoning, or opinion, of my brother who delivered it. Few minds are accustomed to the same habit of thinking, and our conclusions are most satisfactory to ourselves when arrived at in our own way. . . .

Notes

1. The first case in which the Supreme Court held a state statute unconstitutional was in *Fletcher v. Peck,* 10 U.S. (6 Cranch) 87, 3 L.Ed. 162 (1810), but the case came to the Supreme Court from the U.S. circuit court for the district of Massachusetts, not from a state court. Marshall held that a Georgia state law impaired the obligation of contracts. After *Martin,* in *Cohens v. Virginia,* 19 U.S. (6 Wheat.) 264, 5 L.Ed. 257 (1821), the Court held that it also had jurisdiction under section 25 of the Judiciary Act to review state criminal proceedings. The Court, speaking again through Marshall, held that the eleventh amendment did not apply when suit was instituted by the state rather than by a noncitizen against a state, and that the fact that a state was a party to the suit was no objection to the Court's exercise of its jurisdiction.

2. There are two main issues in *Martin.* First, is section 25 of the Judiciary Act constitutional? Second, if it is, is the *Martin* case within section 25? As to the first issue, Story's argument may be divided into three sections.

First, he relies on the language of the Constitution, which extends the appellate power to all "cases." "It is the case, then, and not the court, that gives jurisdiction." Suppose an American citizen living in Great Britain claims exemption from some British taxes pursuant to a tax treaty between the United States and Great Britain. If the citizen sued or is sued in the British courts in a case raising as the only legal issue the interpretation of the treaty, does the U.S. Supreme Court have appellate jurisdiction over the House of Lords because it is the case and not the court that gives jurisdiction?

Next Story relied on a series of logical and policy arguments. Which of these arguments do you find compelling?

Finally, Story relies on the intent of the framers, historical practice, and the previous acquiescence of state courts. Do you find these historical arguments compelling? Federalist Papers No. 82, by Hamilton, argued: "[W]hat relation would subsist between the national and state courts in these instances of concurrent jurisdiction? I answer, an appeal would certainly lie from the latter, to the supreme court of the United States." Should Story have mentioned this fact? Note that the lengthy opinion excerpted above has a dearth of citations to authority.

Federalist Papers No. 82 also stated: "I perceive at present no impediment to the establishment of an appeal from the state courts, to the subordinate national tribunals. . . . " Does *Martin* support this conclusion?

3. Given that section 25 is constitutional, the second main issue is whether *Martin,* when it first was reviewed by the Supreme Court, was within section 25? What was the federal question? If the state court was right in concluding that the land was forfeited in 1782, *prior* to the Treaty of

1783, then was there any federal question regarding the operation of the Treaty? Is there any evidence that the Virginia Court or the U.S. Supreme Court disagreed about the interpretation of any treaty? Did the dispute merely involve an interpretation of state land law, i.e. was the forfeiture of property effectuated under state law prior to the date of the Treaty?

Story argues that section 25 should not be interpreted to allow a state to engage in an evasion of federal rights. Does he mean that federal courts may always look at state law de novo because sometimes there will be an evasion? Or does he mean that the federal court need not accept the state interpretation of the state's laws if in fact there has been an evasion?

If he means the former, are there any limits to federal court review of state law? Can the Supreme Court hear, on appeal from a state supreme court, a diversity of citizenship case because sometimes a state judge might be prejudiced against out of state residents?

If he means the latter, did he demonstrate that the state court evaded the federal treaty right? Can you develop such an argument?

4. Consider *Indiana ex rel. Anderson v. Brand,* 303 U.S. 95, 58 S.Ct. 443, 82 L.Ed. 685 (1938). Petitioner sued to keep her job as a public school teacher. Her contract for previous years had contained a clause incorporating the state's Teachers' Tenure Law, and she claimed that, by virtue of that act, she had a contract indefinite in duration that could be canceled only for specific causes. The state supreme court held for respondent and rested its decision on the grounds that the Teachers' Tenure Law had been repealed as to teachers in township schools and the repeal did not deprive the teacher of any vested property right nor impair the obligation of contracts. The Supreme Court said:

> As in most cases brought to this court under the contract clause of the Constitution, the question is as to the existence and nature of the contract and not as to the construction of the law which is supposed to impair it. . . . On such a question, one primarily of state law, we accord respectful consideration and great weight to the state's highest court but, in order that the constitutional mandate may not become a dead letter, we are bound to decide for ourselves whether a contract was made, what are its terms and conditions, and whether the state has, by later legislation, impaired its obligation. This involves an appraisal of the statutes of the State and the decisions of its courts. [W]e are of the opinion that the petitioner had a valid contract with the respondent, the obligation of which would be impaired by the termination of her employment. . . . The state courts in earlier cases so declared. The title of the act is couched in of contract. [The Court then discussed various state cases.]

> As the court below has not passed upon one of the grounds of demurrer which appears to involve no federal question, and may present a defense still open to the respondent, we reverse the judgment and remand the cause for further proceedings not inconsistent with this opinion.

When the case was remanded the state court upheld the demurrer on the ground that under state law the teacher's remedy of mandamus was inappropriate and that her rights must only be enforced by an action in her name. *State ex rel. Anderson v. Brand,* 214 Ind. 347, 13 N.E.2d 955 (1938). Could the Supreme Court have reviewed this decision?

Consider *Reich v. Collins,* 513 U.S. 106, 115 S.Ct. 547, 130 L.Ed.2d 454 (1994). Georgia imposed state income taxes on federal retirement benefits but not on state retirement benefits. In 1989, the Supreme Court declared unconstitutional such a discriminatory tax scheme. The following year, Reich, a retired federal military officer and Georgia taxpayer, sued in state court for a refund of taxes paid pursuant to this unconstitutional statute. The Georgia Supreme Court denied a refund, arguing that Reich only had a predeprivation remedy; he should have withheld the contested tax assessments and sued before paying them. The unanimous Court, in *Reich,* reversed. Due process allows a state to have an exclusively predeprivation remedy, as long as it is "clear and certain." Or, the state could provide an exclusively postdeprivation process, or a hybrid, or change the remedial scheme over time. "But what a State may *not* do, and what Georgia did here, is to reconfigure its scheme, unfairly, in *midcourse*—to 'bait and switch,' as some have described it." No prior Georgia Supreme Court cases had placed any limiting construction on the postdeprivation remedy.

In *Michigan v. Long,* 463 U.S. 1032, 103 S.Ct. 3469, 77 L.Ed.2d 1201 (1983), the Michigan Supreme Court ruled that it was unconstitutional to introduce certain evidence in a criminal case. The U.S. Supreme Court reversed, after O'Connor, J., for the Court, found jurisdiction:

> Before reaching the merits, we must consider Long's argument that we are without jurisdiction to decide this case because the decision below rests on an adequate and independent state ground. The court below referred twice to the state constitution in its opinion, but otherwise relied exclusively on federal law. Long argues that the Michigan courts have provided greater protection from searches and seizures under the state constitution than is afforded under the Fourth Amendment, and the references to the state constitution therefore establish an adequate and independent ground for the decision below.

> Respect for the independence of state courts, as well as avoidance of rendering advisory opinions, have been the cornerstones of this Court's refusal to decide cases where there is an adequate and independent state ground. It is precisely because of this respect for state courts, and this desire to avoid advisory opinions, that we do not wish to continue to decide issues of state law that go beyond the opinion that we review, or to require state courts to reconsider cases to clarify the grounds of their decisions. Accordingly, when, as in this case, a state court decision fairly appears to rest primarily on federal law, or to be interwoven with the federal law, and when the adequacy and independence of any possible state law ground is not clear from the face of the opinion, we will accept as the most reasonable explanation that the state court decided the case the way it did because it believed that federal law required it to do so. If a state court chooses merely to rely on federal precedents as it would on the precedents of all other jurisdictions, then it need only make clear by a plain statement in its judgment or opinion that the federal cases are being used only for the purpose of guidance, and do not themselves

compel the result that the court has reached. In this way, both justice and judicial administration will be greatly improved. If the state court decision indicates clearly and expressly that it is alternatively based on bona fide separate, adequate, and independent grounds, we, of course, will not undertake to review the decision.

This approach obviates in most instances the need to examine state law in order to decide the nature of the state court decision, and will at the same time avoid the danger of our rendering advisory opinions.[6] It also avoids the unsatisfactory and intrusive practice of requiring state courts to clarify their decisions to the satisfaction of this Court.... Our requirement of a "plain statement" that a decision rests upon adequate and independent state grounds does not in any way authorize the rendering of advisory opinions. Rather, in determining, as we must, whether we have jurisdiction to review a case that is alleged to rest on adequate and independent state grounds, we merely assume that there are no such grounds when it is not clear from the opinion itself that the state court relied upon an adequate and independent state ground and when it fairly appears that the state court rested its decision primarily on federal law.[8]

In dissent, Justice Stevens argued:

These are not cases in which an American citizen has been deprived of a right secured by the United States Constitution or a federal statute. Rather, they are cases in which a state court has upheld a citizen's assertion of a right, finding the citizen to be protected under both federal and state law. The complaining party is an officer of the state itself, who asks us to rule that the state court interpreted federal rights too broadly and "over-protected" the citizen. Such cases should not be of inherent concern to this Court.

What do you think of these two positions? Under Stevens' approach, would states be subject to phantom restrictions—i.e., restrictions imposed by state courts purportedly based on the U.S. Constitution, but contrary to the federal law applicable in any other jurisdiction—, virtually immune to change, that is, not subject to change by amending the state constitution, and not subject to change through U.S. Supreme Court review?

    5.   Consider the following:

• Assume that a state supreme court invalidates a state law as contrary to the state and federal guarantees of equal protection. Is there review in the U.S. Supreme Court?

6. There may be certain circumstances in which clarification is necessary or desirable, and we will not be foreclosed from taking the appropriate action.

8. ... In dissent, Justice Stevens proposes the novel view that this Court should never review a state court decision unless the Court wishes to vindicate a federal right that has been endangered. The rationale of the dissent is not restricted to cases where the decision is arguably supported by adequate and independent state grounds. Rather, Justice Stevens appears to believe that even if the decision below rests exclusively on federal grounds, this Court should not review the decision as long as there is no federal right that is endangered. ...

• Assume that the state invalidates a state law as contrary to the U.S. Constitution. May the U.S. Supreme Court review? If it reverses, may the state court then invalidate the law under the state constitution?

• If a state court invalidates a federal statute as contrary to both the state and federal constitutions, is there U.S. Supreme Court review?

• Assume that a state court holds that one of its laws retroactively changing the pension rights of its public employees does not take property without due process because the employees had no property right to their pension. May the U.S. Supreme Court review?

• Assume that defendant moves to dismiss a portion of plaintiff's cause of action because it is based on an allegedly unconstitutional statute. The state trial court refuses to grant the motion and the defendant files an interlocutory appeal. The state supreme court rules against defendant and remands for trial. Assume further that the case at this point cannot be reviewed by the U.S. Supreme Court because there is no final judgment. After trial, defendant then appeals again to the state supreme court, which refuses to reach the federal issue because of the procedural bar, "law of the case", caused by its decision in the earlier case. Is defendant foreclosed from review in the U.S. Supreme Court?

1–2. LIMITATIONS ON THE EXERCISE OF JUDICIAL REVIEW

1–2.1 *Statutory Jurisdiction of the Supreme Court, 28 U.S.C.A., Chapter 81*

§ 1251. Original jurisdiction

(a) The Supreme Court shall have original and exclusive jurisdiction of all controversies between two or more States.

(b) The Supreme Court shall have original but not exclusive jurisdiction of:

(1) All actions or proceedings to which ambassadors, other public ministers, consuls, or vice consuls of foreign states are parties;

(2) All controversies between the United States and a State;

(3) All actions or proceedings by a State against the citizens of another State or against aliens.

§ 1254. Courts of appeals; certiorari; certified questions

Cases in the courts of appeals may be reviewed by the Supreme Court by the following methods:

(1) By writ of certiorari granted upon the petition of any party to any civil or criminal case, before or after rendition of judgment or decree;

(2) By certification at any time by a court of appeals of any question of law in any civil or criminal case as to which instructions are desired, and upon such certification the Supreme Court may give

binding instructions or require the entire record to be sent up for decision of the entire matter in controversy.

§ 1257. State courts; certiorari

(a) Final judgments or decrees rendered by the highest court of a State in which a decision could be had, may be reviewed by the Supreme Court by writ of certiorari where the validity of a treaty or statute of the United States is drawn in question or where the validity of a statute of any State is drawn in question on the ground of its being repugnant to the Constitution, treaties, or laws of the United States, or where any title, right, privilege, or immunity is specially set up or claimed under the Constitution or the treaties or statutes of, or any commission held or authority exercised under, the United States.

(b) For the purposes of this section, the term "highest court of a State" includes the District of Columbia Court of Appeals.

Notes

1. Prior to September 30, 1978, section 1251(a) had read:

(a) The Supreme Court shall have original and exclusive jurisdiction of:

   (1) All controversies between two or more States.

   (2) All actions or proceedings against ambassadors or other public ministers of foreign states or their domestics or domestic servants, not inconsistent with the law of nations.

Do you think that this subsection was constitutional? Is the new subsection constitutional?

2. Prior to September, 1988, the law distinguished between cases where Supreme Court review of lower court decisions was mandatory (review by appeal) and cases where the review was discretionary (review by certiorari). Public Law 100–352 (June 27, 1988), 102 Stat. 662, changed all that. As the House Report explained, the "net effect of the bill is to convert the method of Supreme Court review to a discretionary, certiorari approach."

3. Is it necessary at all for Congress to enact a statute providing for the original jurisdiction of the Supreme Court? Or is Article III in this regard self-enforcing? The Court has often said that its original jurisdiction needs no enabling legislation. E.g., *Kentucky v. Dennison,* 65 U.S. (24 How.) 66, 98, 16 L.Ed. 717 (1861).

Could Congress require that cases within the Article III original jurisdiction be heard in a court other than the Supreme Court? *South Carolina v. Katzenbach,* 383 U.S. 301, 86 S.Ct. 803, 15 L.Ed.2d 769 (1966) upheld the Voting Rights Act of 1965. Section 14(b) Act provided that, if a state sought to be exempted from the Act or enjoin the enforcement of any of its provisions, it must bring its suit in the District of Columbia District Court. The majority held: "Congress might approximately limit litigation under this provision to a single court in the District of Columbia, pursuant to its constitutional power under Art. III, § 1, to 'ordain and establish' inferior tribunals." Justice Black in dissent said, if § 14(b) is an "attempt to limit the constitutionally created original jurisdiction of this Court, then I think that section is also unconstitutional."

South Carolina v. Katzenbach was itself an action brought in the Supreme Court's original jurisdiction. The Supreme Court accepted the case, notwithstanding section 14(b). How might the majority have been interpreting section 14(b)?

4. If a civil case is brought in the Supreme Court's original jurisdiction and the parties would be entitled to a jury trial if the case had been brought in lower federal court, would they be entitled to a jury trial before the Supreme Court? In our early history, such trials occurred. See *Georgia v. Brailsford,* 3 U.S. (3 Dall.) 1, 1 L.Ed. 483 (1794), an original case at law. Chief Justice Jay, for a unanimous Court, delivered the jury instructions in a debt action brought by Georgia, which had invoked the original jurisdiction because of procedural difficulties that occurred in earlier actions. What would be the vicinage of the jury? From what district would it be drawn?

5. *Illinois v. City of Milwaukee,* 406 U.S. 91, 93–94, 92 S.Ct. 1385, 1388, 31 L.Ed.2d 712 (1972):

> It has long been this Court's philosophy that "our original jurisdiction should be invoked sparingly." We construe 28 U.S.C.A. § 1251(a)(1), as we do Art. III, § 2, cl. 2, to honor our original jurisdiction but to make it obligatory only in appropriate cases. And the question of what is appropriate concerns, of course, the seriousness and dignity of the claim; yet beyond that it necessarily involves the availability of another forum where there is jurisdiction over the named parties, where the issues tendered may be litigated, and where appropriate relief may be had. We incline to a sparing use of our original jurisdiction so that our increasing duties with the appellate docket will not suffer.

1–2.2 Statutory Restrictions

EX PARTE McCARDLE
74 U.S. (7 Wall.) 506, 19 L.Ed. 264 (1869).

The case was this: ... Congress, on the 5th February, 1867, by "An act to amend an act to establish the judicial courts of the United States, approved September 24, 1789," provided that the several courts of the United States, and the several justices and judges of such courts, within their respective jurisdiction, in addition to the authority already conferred by law, should have power to grant writs of *habeas corpus* in all cases where any person may be restrained of his or her liberty in violation of the Constitution, or of any treaty or law of the United States. And that, from the final decision of any judge, justice, or court inferior to the Circuit Court, appeal might be taken to the Circuit Court of the United States for the district in which the cause was heard, and *from the judgment of the said Circuit Court to the Supreme Court of the United States.*

This statute being in force, one McCardle, alleging unlawful restraint by military force, preferred a petition in the court below, for the writ of *habeas corpus*.

The writ was issued, and a return was made by the military commander, admitting the restraint, but denying that it was unlawful.

It appeared that the petitioner was not in the military service of the United States, but was held in custody by military authority for trial before a military commission, upon charges founded upon the publication of articles alleged to be incendiary and libellous, in a newspaper of which he was editor. The custody was alleged to be under the authority of certain acts of Congress.

Upon the hearing, the petitioner was remanded to the military custody; but, upon his prayer, an appeal was allowed him to this court. . . . under the above-mentioned act of February 5, 1867.

A motion to dismiss this appeal was made at the last term, and, after argument, was denied.

Subsequently, on the 2d, 3d, 4th, and 9th March, [1868,] the case was argued very thoroughly and ably upon the merits, and was taken under advisement. While it was thus held, and before conference in regard to the decision proper to be made, an act was passed by Congress, returned with objections by the President, and, on the 27th March, repassed by the constitutional majority, the second section of which was as follows:

"*And be it further enacted,* That so much of the act approved February 5, 1867, entitled 'An act to amend an act to establish the judicial courts of the United States, approved September 24, 1789,' as authorized an appeal from the judgment of the Circuit Court to the Supreme Court of the United States, or the exercise of any such jurisdiction by said Supreme Court, on appeals which have been, or may hereafter be taken, be, and the same is hereby repealed."

The attention of the court was directed to this statute at the last term, but counsel having expressed a desire to be heard in argument upon its effect, and the Chief Justice being detained from his place here, by his duties in the Court of Impeachment, the cause was continued under advisement. Argument was now heard upon the effect of the repealing act.

Mr. Sharkey, for the appellant:

[T]his court is coexistent and co-ordinate with Congress, and must be able to exercise the whole judicial power of the United States, though Congress passed no act on the subject. The Judiciary Act of 1789 has been frequently changed. Suppose it were repealed. Would the court lose, wholly or at all, the power to pass on every case to which the judicial power of the United States extended? This act of March 27th, 1868, does take away the whole appellate power of this court in cases of *habeas corpus.* Can such results be produced? We submit that they cannot, and this court, then, we further submit, may still go on and pronounce judgment on the merits, as it would have done, had not the act of 27th March been passed....

Messrs. L. Trumbull and M.H. Carpenter, contra:

The Constitution gives to this court appellate jurisdiction in any case like the present one was, only with such exceptions and under such regulations as Congress makes....

The CHIEF JUSTICE [CHASE] delivered the opinion of the court.

The first question necessarily is that of jurisdiction; for, if the act of March 1868, takes away the jurisdiction defined by the act of February, 1867, it is useless, if not improper, to enter into any discussion of other questions.

It is quite true, as was argued by the counsel for the petitioner, that the appellate jurisdiction of this court is not derived from acts of Congress. It is, strictly speaking, conferred by the Constitution. But it is conferred "with such exceptions and under such regulations as Congress shall make."

It is unnecessary to consider whether, if Congress had made no exceptions and no regulations, this court might not have exercised general appellate jurisdiction under rules prescribed by itself. For among the earliest acts of the first Congress, at its first session, was the act of September 24th, 1789, to establish the judicial courts of the United States. That act provided for the organization of this court, and prescribed regulations for the exercise of its jurisdiction....

The principle that the affirmation of appellate jurisdiction implies the negation of all such jurisdiction not affirmed having been thus established, it was an almost necessary consequence that acts of Congress, providing for the exercise of jurisdiction, should come to be spoken of as acts granting jurisdiction, and not as acts making exceptions to the constitutional grant of it.

The exception to appellate jurisdiction in the case before us, however, is not an inference from the affirmation of other appellate jurisdiction. It is made in terms. The provision of the act of 1867, affirming the appellate jurisdiction of this court in cases of *habeas corpus* is expressly repealed. It is hardly possible to imagine a plainer instance of positive exception.

We are not at liberty to inquire into the motives of the legislature. We can only examine into its power under the Constitution; and the power to make exceptions to the appellate jurisdiction of this court is given by express words.

What, then, is the effect of the repealing act upon the case before us? We cannot doubt as to this. Without jurisdiction the court cannot proceed at all in any cause. Jurisdiction is power to declare the law, and when it ceases to exist, the only function remaining to the court is that of announcing the fact and dismissing the cause....

On the other hand, the general rule, supported by the best elementary writers, is, that "when an act of the legislature is repealed, it must be considered, except as to transactions past and closed, as if it never existed." [N]o judgment could be rendered in a suit after the repeal of the act under which it was brought and prosecuted.

It is quite clear, therefore, that this court cannot proceed to pronounce judgment in this case, for it has no longer jurisdiction of the appeal; and judicial duty is not less fitly performed by declining ungranted jurisdiction than in exercising firmly that which the Constitution and the laws confer.

Counsel seem to have supposed, if effect be given to the repealing act in question, that the whole appellate power of the court, in cases of *habeas corpus,* is denied. But this is an error. The act of 1868 does not except from that jurisdiction any cases but appeals from Circuit Courts under the act of 1867. It does not affect the jurisdiction which was previously exercised.

The appeal of the petitioner in this case must be

Dismissed for want of jurisdiction.

Notes

1.   Several months later, *Ex parte Yerger,* 75 U.S. (8 Wall.) 85, 19 L.Ed. 332 (1869) held that the statute of 1868, at issue in *McCardle,* did not prevent Yerger's review because he used the certiorari route, not affected by the 1868 repeal legislation. The Court concluded that the writs of habeas corpus and certiorari could revise the decision of the circuit court and free the prisoner from unlawful restraint. The Court never reached a decision on the merits challenging the Reconstruction Acts, however, because the case was mooted when the military authorities released Yerger from custody.

2.   How narrowly may *McCardle* be interpreted? May Congress in effect overrule *Marbury* by not providing for the Supreme Court's appellate and certiorari jurisdiction? By restricting the jurisdiction of the lower federal courts? Consider the following cases:

Martin v. Hunter's Lessee, [§ 1–1, supra] (Story, J., for the Court):

 ... The judicial power must, therefore, be vested in some court, by Congress; and to suppose that it was not an obligation binding on them, but might, at their pleasure, be omitted or declined, is to suppose that, under the sanction of the constitution they might defeat the constitution itself; a construction which would lead to such a result cannot be sound....

 If, then, it is the duty of Congress to vest the judicial power of the United States, it is a duty to vest the whole judicial power. The language, if imperative as to one part, is imperative as to all.... It would seem, therefore, to follow that Congress are bound to create some inferior courts, in which to vest all that jurisdiction which, under the constitution, is exclusively vested in the United States, and of which the Supreme Court cannot take original cognizance. They might establish one or more inferior courts; they might parcel out the jurisdiction among such courts, from time to time, at their own pleasure. But the whole judicial power of the United States should be, at all times, vested either in an original or appellate form, in some courts created under its authority.

White v. Fenner, 29 Fed.Cas. 1015 (No. 17,547)(C.C.R.I.1818)(Story, J., Circuit Justice):

This court has no jurisdiction, which is not given by statute.... The constitution declares, that it is mandatory to the legislature, that the judicial power of the United States shall extend to controversies "between citizens of different states"; and it is somewhat singular that the jurisdiction actually conferred on the courts of the United States should have stopped so far short of the constitutional extent.... The language of the act is so clear, that there is nothing on which to hang a doubt. Neither of the parties in this suit is a citizen of the state where the suit is brought. The suit must, therefore, be dismissed.

Sheldon v. Sill, 49 U.S. (8 How.) 441, 12 L.Ed. 1147 (1850)(Grier, J.):

The eleventh section of the Judiciary Act, which defines the jurisdiction of the Circuit Courts, restrains them from taking "cognizance of any suit to recover the contents of any promissory note or other chose in action, in favor of an assignee, unless a suit might have been prosecuted in such court to recover the contents, if no assignment had been made, except in cases of foreign bills of exchange." ... It has been alleged, that this restriction of the Judiciary Act, with regard to assignees of choses in action, is in conflict with this provision of the Constitution, and therefore void....

The Constitution has defined the limits of the judicial power of the United States, but has not prescribed how much of it shall be exercised by the Circuit Court; consequently, the statute which does prescribe the limits of their jurisdiction, cannot be in conflict with the Constitution, unless it confers powers not enumerated therein. Such has been the doctrine held by this court since its first establishment. To enumerate all the cases in which it has been either directly advanced or tacitly assumed would be tedious and unnecessary.

United States v. Klein, 80 U.S. (13 Wall.) 128, 20 L.Ed. 519 (1871). Klein sued in the Court of Claims under an 1863 statute that allowed the recovery of land captured or abandoned during the Civil War if the claimant could prove that he had not aided the rebellion. Relying on an earlier Supreme Court decision holding that a pardon proved conclusively that he had not assisted the rebellion, Klein won in the lower court. While the appeal was pending, Congress passed a statute providing that a presidential pardon would not support a claim for captured property; in fact, acceptance without disclaimer of a pardon for participation in the rebellion was to be conclusive evidence that the claimant had indeed aided the enemy; and, finally, when the Court of Claims based its judgment against the claimant on such a pardon, the Supreme Court would lack jurisdiction on appeal.

The Supreme Court invalidated the statute and its jurisdictional limitation. Chase, C.J., for the Court:

If [the statute] simply denied the right of appeal in a particular class of cases, there could be no doubt that it must be regarded as an exercise of the power of Congress to make "such exceptions from the appellate jurisdiction" as should seem to it expedient. But the language of the proviso shows plainly that it does not intend to withhold appellate jurisdiction except as a means to an end. Its great and controlling purpose is to deny pardons granted by the President the effect which this court had adjudged them to have. . . .

It seems to us that this is not an exercise of the acknowledged power of Congress to make exceptions and prescribe regulations to the appellate power. We must think that Congress has inadvertently passed the limit which separates the legislative from the judicial power.

3. RESTRICTING REMEDIES. *Lauf v. E.G. Shinner & Co.,* 303 U.S. 323, 58 S.Ct. 578, 82 L.Ed. 872 (1938)(Roberts, J., for the Court):

The District Court erred in granting an injunction in the absence of findings which the Norris–LaGuardia Act makes prerequisites to the exercise of jurisdiction. . . .

Section 7 declares that "no court of the United States shall have jurisdiction to issue a temporary or permanent injunction in any case involving or growing out of a labor dispute, as herein defined" except after a hearing of a described character, "and except after findings of fact by the court, to the effect (a) that unlawful acts have been threatened and will be committed unless restrained" or have been committed and will be continued unless restrained and that no injunction "shall be issued on account of any threat or unlawful act excepting against the person or persons, association, or organization making the threat or committing the unlawful act or actually authorizing or ratifying the same. . . . " By subsections (b) to (e) it is provided that relief shall not be granted unless the court finds that substantial and irreparable injury to complainants' property will follow; that as to each item of relief granted greater injury will be inflicted upon the complainant by denying the relief than will be inflicted upon defendants by granting it; that complainant has no adequate remedy at law; and that the public officers charged with the duty to protect complainants' property are unable or unwilling to provide adequate protection. There can be no question of the power of Congress thus to define and limit the jurisdiction of the inferior courts of the United States. The District Court made none of the required findings save as to irreparable injury and lack of remedy at law. It follows that in issuing the injunction it exceeded its jurisdiction.

4. TAKING AWAY CAUSES OF ACTION. In the mid–1940's the Supreme Court ruled that time spent by workers in previously noncompensable work, such as underground travel in iron ore mines, was part of the work week compensable under the Fair Labor Standards Act. Because this unexpected decision created immense retroactive liability for many businesses, Congress amended the statute to make such work noncompensable; section 2 of the Portal-to-Portal Act also withdrew the jurisdiction of the courts to hear cases that were presently pending or were to be brought under the old statute. That jurisdictional limitation, depriving plaintiffs of their right to recover

overtime pay, was upheld in several lower court decisions, including *Battaglia v. General Motors Corp.*, 169 F.2d 254 (2d Cir.), cert. denied 335 U.S. 887, 69 S.Ct. 236, 93 L.Ed. 425 (1948)(Chase, Circuit Judge):

> A few of the district court decisions sustaining section 2 of the Portal-to-Portal Act have done so on the ground that since jurisdiction of federal courts other than the Supreme Court is conferred by Congress, it may at the will of Congress be taken away in whole or in part. We think, however, that the exercise by Congress of its control over jurisdiction is subject to compliance with at least the requirements of the Fifth Amendment. [W]hile Congress has the undoubted power to give, withhold, and restrict the jurisdiction of courts other than the Supreme Court, it must not so exercise that power as to deprive any person of life, liberty, or property without due process of law or to take private property without just compensation.

The court held that the jurisdictional limitation was valid because it did not deprive plaintiffs of any vested rights.[1]

In contrast, consider *Plaut v. Spendthrift Farm, Inc.*, 514 U.S. 211, 115 S.Ct. 1447, 131 L.Ed.2d 328 (1995). On June 20, 1991, *Lampf, Pleva, Lipkind, Prupis & Petigrow v. Gilbertson*, 501 U.S. 350, 111 S.Ct. 2773, 115 L.Ed.2d 321 (1991) rejected many lower court cases and held that litigation based on § 10(b) of the Securities Exchange Act and SEC Rule 10b–5 must be commenced within one year after discovery of the facts constituting the violation and within three years after the violation. Following *Lampf*, the trial court dismissed petitioners' claims as untimely, there was no appeal, and the judgment became final after 30 days. In December of 1991, the President signed a law (§ 27A of the Securities Exchange Act) providing that, if any § 10(b) suit started before and dismissed as time barred after June 19, 1991—the day before *Lampf* was decided—would have been timely but for *Lampf*, then the case was to be reinstated if a motion to do so was made no later than 60 days after December 19, 1991. After § 27A was enacted, petitioners in this case filed a motion to reinstate their action previously dismissed with prejudice.

Scalia, J., for the Court, held that the law violated the separation of powers because it retroactively commanded federal courts to reopen *final* judgments, in violation of *Marbury v. Madison*. In no previous instance, said the Court, has Congress enacted retroactive legislation requiring an Article III court to set aside a final judgment. Article III gives federal courts "the power, not merely to rule on cases, but to *decide* them." (emphasis in original). "When a new law makes clear that it is retroactive, an appellate court must apply that law in reviewing judgments still on appeal that were rendered before the law was enacted, and must alter the outcome accordingly." However, there is "a distinction between judgments from which all appeals have been forgone or completed, and judgments that remain on

---

1. See, e.g., Hart, The Power of Congress to Limit the Jurisdiction of Federal Courts: An Exercise in Dialectic, 66 Harv. L.Rev. 1362 (1953); Van Alstyne, A Critical Guide to Ex Parte McCardle, 15 Ariz.L.Rev. 229 (1973); Rotunda, Congressional Power to Restrict the Jurisdiction of the Lower Federal Courts and the Problem of School Busing, 64 Georgetown L.J. 839 (1976); Clinton, A Mandatory View of Federal Court Jurisdiction: A Guided Quest for the Original Understanding of Article III, 132 U.Pa.L.Rev. 741 (1984).

appeal (or subject to being appealed). . . . " Section 27A is not like a law that provides that it applies "not only to proceedings brought after its enactment, but also to proceedings pending at the time, or brought after, the decision [in a particular case]." Such a law "says nothing about reopening final judgments. . . ."[1]

1–2.3 Advisory Opinions

MUSKRAT v. UNITED STATES
219 U.S. 346, 31 S.Ct. 250, 55 L.Ed. 246 (1911).

Mr. Justice Day delivered the opinion of the court.

These cases arise under an act of Congress undertaking to confer jurisdiction upon the Court of Claims, and upon this court on appeal, to determine the validity of certain acts of Congress hereinafter referred to. . . .

These proceedings were begun under the supposed authority of an act of Congress passed March 1, 1907 (a part of the Indian appropriation bill). As that legislation is important in this connection so much of the act as authorized the beginning of these suits is here inserted in full:

> That William Brown and Levi B. Gritts, on their own behalf and on behalf of all other Cherokee citizens, having like interests in the property allotted under the act of July first, nineteen hundred and two, entitled 'An act to provide for the allotment of lands of the Cherokee Nation, for the disposition of townsites therein, and for other purposes,' and David Muskrat and J. Henry Dick, on their own behalf, and on behalf of all Cherokee citizens enrolled as such for allotment as of September first, nineteen hundred and two, be, and they are hereby, authorized and empowered to institute their suits in the Court of Claims to determine the validity of any acts of Congress passed since the said act of July first, nineteen hundred and two, in so far as said acts, or any of them, attempt to increase or extend the restrictions upon alienation, encumbrance, or the right to

---

1. Compare, *Robertson v. Seattle Audubon Society,* 503 U.S. 429, 112 S.Ct. 1407, 118 L.Ed.2d 73 (1992). Environmentalists filed lawsuits challenging federal efforts to allow timber production from old-growth forests in the Pacific Northwest, claiming that the timber harvesting would injure the spotted owl, an endangered species. In 1990, in response to this ongoing litigation, Congress enacted "the Northwest Timber Compromise," which applied only for a certain period of time and only to 13 national forests in areas known to contain the spotted owl. Subsection (b)(6)(A) stated that "Congress hereby determines and directs that management [of certain forests] according to subsections (b)(3) and (b)(5) . . . is adequate consideration for the purpose of meeting the statutory requirements that are the basis for [the litigation in two cases]." The law identified these two pending cases by name and caption number.

Thomas, J., speaking for a unanimous Court, held that § (b)(6)(A) did not violate Article III; it only modified or compelled changes in preexisting law. The new law replaced the legal standards underlying these two cases. It did not direct any particular finding of fact or application of law to fact. Because § (b)(6)(A) did amend applicable law, the Court did not address the Court of Appeals' argument that *United States v. Klein* holds that a law violates Article III if it directs a decision in a pending case without amending the law.

lease the allotments of lands of Cherokee citizens, or to increase the number of persons entitled to share in the final distribution of lands and funds of the Cherokees beyond those enrolled for allotment as of September first, nineteen hundred and two, and provided for in the said act of July first, nineteen hundred and two.

And jurisdiction is hereby conferred upon the Court of Claims, with the right of appeal, by either party, to the Supreme Court of the United States, to hear, determine, and adjudicate each of said suits.

The suits brought hereunder shall be brought ... against the United States as a party defendant, and, for the speedy disposition of the questions involved, preference shall be given to the same by said courts, and by the Attorney General, who is hereby charged with the defense of said suits.

Upon the rendition of final judgment by the Court of Claims or the Supreme Court of the United States denying the validity of any portion of the said acts authorized to be brought into question, in either or both of said cases, the Court of Claims shall determine the amount to be paid the attorneys employed by the above-named parties in the prosecution thereof for services and expenses, and shall render judgment therefor, which shall be paid out of the funds in the United States Treasury belonging to the beneficiaries under the said act of July first, nineteen hundred and two.

This act is the authority for the maintenance of these two suits.

The first question in these cases, as in others, involves the jurisdiction of this court to entertain the proceeding, and that depends upon whether the jurisdiction conferred is within the power of Congress, having in view the limitations of the judicial power as established by the Constitution of the United States....

It will serve to elucidate the nature and extent of the judicial power thus conferred by the Constitution to note certain instances in which this court has had occasion to examine and define the same. As early as 1792, an act of Congress, March 23, 1792, was brought to the attention of this court, which undertook to provide for the settlement of claims of widows and orphans barred by the limitations theretofore established regulating claims to invalid pensions. The act was not construed by this court, but came under consideration before the then Chief Justice and another Justice of this court and the District Judge, and their conclusions are given in the margin of the report of *Hayburn's Case*, 2 U.S. (2 Dall.) 408, 1 L.Ed. 436 (1792). The act undertook to devolve upon the Circuit Court of the United States the duty of examining proofs, of determining what amount of the monthly pay would be equivalent to the disability ascertained, and to certify the same to the Secretary of War, who was to place the names of the applicants on the pension list of the United States in conformity thereto, unless he had cause to suspect imposition or mistake, in which event he might withhold the name of the applicant and report the same to Congress.

In the note to the report of the case in 2 Dall. it appeared that Chief Justice Jay, Mr. Justice Cushing and District Judge Duane unanimously agreed: . . .

> That neither the legislative nor the executive branches can constitutionally assign to the judicial any duties but such as are properly judicial, and to be performed in a judicial manner. That the duties assigned to the Circuit Courts, by this act, are not of that description. . . .

In 1793, by direction of the President, Secretary of State Jefferson addressed to the Justices of the Supreme Court a communication soliciting their views upon the question whether their advice to the executive would be available in the solution of important questions of the construction of treaties, laws of nations and laws of the land, which the Secretary said were often presented under circumstances which *do not give a cognizance of them to the tribunals of the country.* The answer to the question was postponed until the subsequent sitting of the Supreme Court, when Chief Justice Jay and his associates answered to President Washington that in consideration of the lines of separation drawn by the Constitution between the three departments of government, and being judges of a court of last resort, afforded strong arguments against the propriety of extrajudicially deciding the questions alluded to, and expressing the view that the power given by the Constitution to the President of calling on heads of departments for opinions "seems to have been purposely, as well as expressly, united to the executive departments." Correspondence & Public Papers of John Jay, vol. 3, p. 486. . . . It is therefore apparent that from its earliest history this court has consistently declined to exercise any powers other than those which are strictly judicial in their nature.

It therefore becomes necessary to inquire what is meant by the judicial power thus conferred by the Constitution upon this court and with the aid of appropriate legislation upon the inferior courts of the United States. . . .

As we have already seen by the express terms of the Constitution, the exercise of the judicial power is limited to "cases" and "controversies." Beyond this it does not extend, and unless it is asserted in a case or controversy within the meaning of the Constitution, the power to exercise it is nowhere conferred. . . .

Applying the principles thus long settled by the decisions of this court to the act of Congress undertaking to confer jurisdiction in this case, we find that William Brown and Levi B. Gritts, on their own behalf and on behalf of all other Cherokee citizens having like interest in the property allotted under the act of July 1, 1902, and David Muskrat and J. Henry Dick, for themselves and representatives of all Cherokee citizens enrolled as such for allotment as of September 1, 1902, are authorized and empowered to institute suits in the Court of Claims to determine the validity of acts of Congress passed since the act of July 1, 1902, in so far as the same attempt to increase or extend the restrictions upon alienation, encumbrance, or the right to lease the allotments of lands of Cherokee citizens, or to increase the number of persons entitled to share in the final distribution of lands and funds of the Cherokees beyond those enrolled for allotment as of September 1, 1902, and provided for in the said act of July 1, 1902.

The jurisdiction was given for that purpose first to the Court of Claims and then upon appeal to this court. That is, the object and purpose of the suit is wholly comprised in the determination of the constitutional validity of certain acts of Congress; and furthermore, in the last paragraph of the section, should a judgment be rendered in the Court of Claims or this court, denying the constitutional validity of such acts, then the amount of compensation to be paid to attorneys employed for the purpose of testing the constitutionality of the law is to be paid out of funds in the Treasury of the United States belonging to the beneficiaries, the act having previously provided that the United States should be made a party and the Attorney General be charged with the defense of the suits.

It is therefore evident that there is neither more nor less in this procedure than an attempt to provide for a judicial determination, final in this court, of the constitutional validity of an act of Congress. Is such a determination within the judicial power conferred by the Constitution, as the same has been interpreted and defined in the authoritative decisions to which we have referred? We think it is not. That judicial power, as we have seen, is the right to determine actual controversies arising between adverse litigants, duly instituted in courts of proper jurisdiction. The right to declare a law unconstitutional arises because an act of Congress relied upon by one or the other of such parties in determining their rights is in conflict with the fundamental law. The exercise of this, the most important and delicate duty of this court, is not given to it as a body with revisory power over the action of Congress, but because the rights of the litigants in justiciable controversies require the court to choose between the fundamental law and a law purporting to be enacted within constitutional authority, but in fact beyond the power delegated to the legislative branch of the Government. This attempt to obtain a judicial declaration of the validity of the act of Congress is not presented in a "case" or "controversy" to which, under the Constitution of the United States, the judicial power alone extends. It is true the United States is made a defendant to this action, but it has no interest adverse to the claimants. The object is not to assert a property right as against the Government, or to demand compensation for alleged wrongs because of action upon its part. The whole purpose of the law is to determine the constitutional validity of this class of legislation, in a suit not arising between parties concerning a property right necessarily involved in the decision in question, but in a proceeding against the Government in its sovereign capacity, and concerning which the only judgment required is to settle the doubtful character of the legislation in question. Such judgment will not conclude private parties, when actual litigation brings to the court the question of the constitutionality of such legislation. In a legal sense the judgment could not be executed, and amounts in fact to no more than an expression of opinion upon the validity of the acts in question. Confining the jurisdiction of this court within the limitations conferred by the Constitution, which the court has hitherto been careful to observe, and whose boundaries it has refused to transcend, we think the Congress, in the act of March 1, 1907, exceeded the limitations of legislative authority, so far as it required of this court action not judicial in its nature within the meaning of the Constitution.

Nor can it make any difference that the petitioners had brought suits in the Supreme Court of the District of Columbia to enjoin the Secretary of the Interior from carrying into effect the legislation subsequent to the act of July 1, 1902, which suits were pending when the jurisdictional act here involved was passed. The latter act must depend upon its own terms and be judged by the authority which it undertakes to confer. If such actions as are here attempted, to determine the validity of legislation, are sustained, the result will be that this court, instead of keeping within the limits of judicial power and deciding cases or controversies arising between opposing parties, as the Constitution intended it should, will be required to give opinions in the nature of advice concerning legislative action, a function never conferred upon it by the Constitution, and against the exercise of which this court has steadily set its face from the beginning.

The questions involved in this proceeding as to the validity of the legislation may arise in suits between individuals, and when they do and are properly brought before this court for consideration they, of course, must be determined in the exercise of its judicial functions. For the reasons we have stated, we are constrained to hold that these actions present no justiciable controversy within the authority of the court, acting within the limitations of the Constitution under which it was created. As Congress, in passing this act as a part of the plan involved, evidently intended to provide a review of the judgment of the Court of Claims in this court, as the constitutionality of important legislation is concerned, we think the act cannot be held to intend to confer jurisdiction on that court separately considered.

The judgments will be reversed and the cases remanded to the Court of Claims, with directions to dismiss the petition for want of jurisdiction.

Notes

1. What are the policy objections to advisory opinions by the federal courts? Which of these reasons—if any—apply to the facts in *Muskrat?*

2. The Court emphasizes that, under the statutory scheme, if the Court invalidates these acts, then the U.S. Treasury must pay the plaintiffs' attorney fees. Is anything wrong in that? Is the Court saying that if the Government pays attorneys fees of both plaintiffs and defendant, then the case is not within Article III? The Government pays the attorney fees of public defenders as well as the U.S. prosecutors.

In *United States v. Johnson,* 319 U.S. 302, 63 S.Ct. 1075, 87 L.Ed. 1413 (1943)(per curiam), a tenant protected by federal rent control sued the landlord, who won in the lower court by arguing that the rent control law and the regulations were unconstitutional. The United States intervened, defended the constitutionality of the statute, and appealed directly to the Supreme Court. On appeal the Government submitted plaintiff-tenant's affidavit showing that the plaintiff did not employ, pay, or even meet his attorney, had no knowledge of who paid the $15 filing fee, was assured by the defendant-landlord that the tenant would incur no expenses by bringing the suit, never read the complaint, and had no knowledge of the amount of judgment asked for until he read about it in the newspapers. The landlord's affidavit did not deny any of these allegations, and plaintiff-tenant filed no brief in the trial court. No false or fictitious facts were submitted to the lower court, so why should the Court refuse to decide it? The Supreme Court, holding that the suit was a friendly, collusive suit, vacated the judgment. "Even in a litigation where only private rights are involved, the judgment will not be allowed to stand where one of the parties has dominated the conduct of the suit by payment of fees of both."

Is the payment of attorney fees in *Muskrat* similar to the payment in *Johnson?*

3. One of the statutes under attack—restricting the Indians' right to alienate the land—was self-executing. How might the Indians test the constitutionality of this statute after *Muskrat?*

4. The other statute—increasing the number of Indians entitled to share in the final distribution of lands and funds of the Cherokees beyond those originally enrolled for allotment—was not self-executing: that is, the Secretaries of the Interior and Treasury had to add and approve the names of the new enrollees. In the third to the last paragraph of *Muskrat* the Court referred to a suit brought in the District of Columbia courts to enjoin the Secretaries of Interior and Treasury from carrying into effect this legislation. That case was *Gritts v. Fisher,* 224 U.S. 640, 32 S.Ct. 580, 56 L.Ed. 928 (1912). Gritts was also one of the plaintiffs in *Muskrat.* The Supreme Court ruled on the merits in *Gritts* that the plaintiffs had not shown that the acts increasing the number of enrollees deprived the original enrollees of property without due process.

Why could the Supreme Court in *Gritts* reach the merits when the year earlier it could not do so in *Muskrat?* The *Gritts* opinion did not even cite *Muskrat.*

5. How might you have drafted the jurisdictional statute in *Muskrat* to avoid the case or controversy problem?

6. At the time of the *Muskrat* decision the Court of Claims was not an Article III court. That is, Congress created that court pursuant to its legislative powers under Article I. As a "court" established under Article I it was not subject to the constraints of Article III. Its "judges" did not have lifetime tenure nor salary protection, nor was the court restricted by the case or controversy limitation. In fact, the Court of Claims was specifically authorized by statute to issue some advisory opinions to Congress. Later, Congress specifically provided for lifetime tenure and salary protections of Court of Claim judges; virtually limited the court's jurisdiction to Article III

business; and indicated its intent to treat the court as an Article III court. Only then, in *Glidden Co. v. Zdanok,* 370 U.S. 530, 82 S.Ct. 1459, 8 L.Ed.2d 671 (1962), did the Supreme Court declared the Court of Claims to be an Article III court. At the present time, Article I courts include the Court of Military Appeals (created pursuant to Congress' power under Article I to make rules for the regulation of the land and naval forces), the Tax Court (created pursuant to Congress' Article I tax powers), the District of Columbia courts (having jurisdiction roughly analogous to state courts and created pursuant to Congress' Article I power to govern the District), and some territorial courts (created pursuant to Congress' power to make all needful rules governing the territories).

Given the fact that the Court of Claims in 1911 was not subject to the restrictions of Article III, was it correct for the Supreme Court in *Muskrat* to invalidate all of the jurisdictional statute or should it have invalidated only that part which authorized an appeal to the U.S. Supreme Court?

7. Related to the *Muskrat* issue is the doctrine of feigned cases. E.g., *Moore v. Charlotte–Mecklenburg Board of Education,* 402 U.S. 47, 91 S.Ct. 1292, 28 L.Ed.2d 590 (1971)(per curiam) held: "At the hearing both parties argued to the three-judge court that the [state] anti-busing law was constitutional and urged that the order of the District Court adopting the Finger plan should be set aside. We are thus confronted with the anomaly that both litigants desire precisely the same result, namely a holding that the anti-busing plan is constitutional. There is, therefore, no case or controversy within the meaning of Art. III of the Constitution. *Muskrat v. United States.*"

However, the fact that the Government confesses error in a criminal case does not require the Court to agree. The public interest in reaching the proper result in a criminal case is entrusted to the courts as well as to the prosecutors. Also, "our judgments are precedents, and the proper administration of the criminal law cannot be left merely to the stipulation of the parties." *Young v. United States,* 315 U.S. 257, 62 S.Ct. 510, 86 L.Ed. 832 (1942).

8. THE ELEVENTH AMENDMENT. The Eleventh Amendment places some constitutional limitations on the exercise of judicial review by the federal courts. It was ratified in reaction to *Chisholm v. Georgia,* 2 U.S. (2 Dall.) 419, 1 L.Ed. 440 (1793), which had found federal jurisdiction of suits against a State for the payment of debt and past damages by noncitizens of that State. The Eleventh Amendment does not immunize the States from the restrictions of federal law but it does require that some types of suits against states be brought in State rather than federal court.[1]

---

1. The language of the Eleventh Amendment does not explicitly apply to suits against a State brought by its own citizens, but it is so interpreted. *Hans v. Louisiana,* 134 U.S. 1, 10 S.Ct. 504, 33 L.Ed. 842 (1890). However, the Amendment does not apply to the political subdivisions of the State, such as cities and school boards. The States may explicitly waive their Eleventh Amendment immunity.

In *Blatchford v. Native Village of Noatak,* 501 U.S. 775, 111 S.Ct. 2578, 115 L.Ed.2d 686 (1991), Scalia, J., for the Court, held that the Eleventh Amendment also bars Indian tribes from suing States in federal court. See J. Nowak & R. Rotunda, Constitutional Law 44–54 (5th ed. 1995); 1 R. Rotunda & J. Nowak, Treatise on Constitutional Law: Substance and Procedure § 2.12 (2d ed. 1992).

Ex parte Young, 209 U.S. 123, 28 S.Ct. 441, 52 L.Ed. 714 (1908) held the Eleventh Amendment did not bar an action in the federal courts seeking to enjoin a State Attorney General from enforcing a statute alleged to violate the Fourteenth Amendment. The Fourteenth Amendment can be used offensively as well as defensively by those whom it seeks to protect. When a State officer comes into conflict with Constitutional guarantees "he is in that case stripped of his official or representative capacity and is subject in his person to the consequences of his individual conduct." Thus the offending officer is not a representative of the State for Eleventh Amendment purposes; however, because he is acting under color of law, there is State action, for purposes of the Fourteenth Amendment.

The Eleventh Amendment also permits prospective injunctive relief to prevent Constitutional violations even though it will cost the State money to comply. *Milliken v. Bradley,* 433 U.S. 267, 97 S.Ct. 2749, 53 L.Ed.2d 745 (1977). Similarly, "damages against individual defendants are a permissible remedy in some circumstances notwithstanding the fact that they hold public office." *Scheuer v. Rhodes,* 416 U.S. 232, 94 S.Ct. 1683, 40 L.Ed.2d 90 (1974). But, if the suit is in essence for the recovery of *retroactive* money damages from the State treasury rather than the State official, the Amendment applies even though the State is not a named party. *Edelman v. Jordan,* 415 U.S. 651, 94 S.Ct. 1347, 39 L.Ed.2d 662 (1974)(improper for federal court to order State officials to release welfare benefits wrongfully withheld by the State because payment of State funds was a form of compensation).

Congress, however, by statute may create causes of action against the State even for retroactive damages when Congress enacts the statute pursuant to its power under § 5 of the Fourteenth Amendment. *Fitzpatrick v. Bitzer,* 427 U.S. 445, 96 S.Ct. 2666, 49 L.Ed.2d 614 (1976). See § 9–1 below. One of the purposes of the Fourteenth Amendment was to change the Constitution to give Congress more power over the States.[2]

But, Congress cannot constitutionally use the Commerce Clause to create private rights of action against the States and abrogate their Eleventh Amendment[3] immunity. The Eleventh Amendment prevents

---

2. But, it is not enough for Congress merely to invoke its § 5 powers. *E.g., College Savings Bank v. Florida Prepaid Postsecondary Education Expense Board,* 527 U.S. 666, 119 S.Ct. 2219, 144 L.Ed.2d 605 (1999) (5 to 4) (Scalia, J., for the Court); *Florida Prepaid Postsecondary Education Expense Board v. College Savings Bank,* 527 U.S. 627, 119 S.Ct. 2199, 144 L.Ed.2d 575 (1999) (5 to 4) (Rehnquist, J., for the Court). See § 9–1, below, which discusses these cases.

3. *Seminole Tribe v. Florida,* 517 U.S. 44, 116 S.Ct. 1114, 134 L.Ed.2d 252 (1996) overruling *Pennsylvania v. Union Gas Co.,* 491 U.S. 1, 109 S.Ct. 2273, 105 L.Ed.2d 1 (1989).

Alden v. Maine, 527 U.S. 706, 119 S.Ct. 2240, 144 L.Ed.2d 636 (1999) held (5 to 4) that Congress cannot use its authority under Article I to abrogate a State's immunity in that State's own courts. Plaintiffs sued Maine in Maine State Court claiming that it had violated the overtime provisions of the federal Fair Labor Standards Act. Kennedy, J., for the Court, concluded Congress' powers under Article I "do not include the power to subject nonconsenting States to private suits for damages in state courts. We decide as well that the State of Maine has not consented to suits for overtime pay and liquidated damages under the FLSA. On these premises we affirm the judgment sustaining dismissal of the suit."

Congress from using the Commerce Clause to authorize private parties to file suits in federal court against unconsenting States, whether the relief sought is prospective injunctive relief or retroactive monetary relief. The Commerce Clause does not restrict the reach of the subsequently-enacted Eleventh Amendment.

1–2.4 Political Questions

BAKER v. CARR

369 U.S. 186, 82 S.Ct. 691, 7 L.Ed.2d 663 (1962).

MR. JUSTICE BRENNAN delivered the opinion of the Court.

[Since 1901, the Tennessee legislature failed to enact any reapportionment of the state legislative districts, in spite of a state constitutional requirement for decennial reapportionment. Because of population growth and shifts, plaintiffs claimed that they and others similarly situated were denied the equal protection of the laws accorded them by the Fourteenth Amendment by virtue of the debasement of their votes, a claim which was dismissed by a three-judge federal court. Only 37% of the Tennessee voters elected 20 of the 33 Senators, and 40% of the voters elected 63 of the 99 members of the House. A single vote in Moore County, for example, was worth 19 votes in Hamilton County.

[The Supreme Court held that the district court had subject matter jurisdiction of the controversy; that plaintiffs had standing to sue the state's Secretary of State, Attorney General, members of the State Board of Elections, and similar individuals; and that it would not be necessary at this time to consider what remedy would be most appropriate if appellants prevail at the trial. The Court then turned to the question of whether the subject matter of the suit was justiciable, i.e., did it involve a political question.]

Alden went beyond the Eleventh Amendment: the "sovereign immunity of the States neither derives from nor is limited by the terms of the Eleventh Amendment." Instead, it is derived from, and is inherent in, the structure of the original constitution, and Congress does not have power under Article I to abrogate it. However, the state's constitutional privilege to assert its sovereign immunity in its own courts does not give a state the right to disregard the Constitution or a valid federal law. First, states may consent to suit in their own courts, just like the Federal Government does. In addition, this immunity belongs to the states, not to lesser entities such as municipalities. Moreover, plaintiffs can seek relief against state officers under *Ex parte Young* for injunctive or declaratory relief or for money damages when sued in their individual capacities. Also, the Federal Government could sue the States to enforce federal law: under the Constitution, "the States consented to suits brought by other States or by the Federal Government. A suit which is commenced and prosecuted against a State in the name of the United States by those who are entrusted with the constitutional duty to 'take Care that the Laws be faithfully executed,' differs in kind from the suit of an individual.... " And, "Congress may authorize private suits against nonconsenting States pursuant to its § 5 enforcement power."

Souter, J., filed a dissent, joined by Stevens, Ginsburg, & Breyer, JJ., arguing that the majority's conception of state sovereign immunity is neither true "to history nor to the structure of the Constitution," is "indefensible," and "probably [will be] fleeting."

IV

JUSTICIABILITY

[T]he mere fact that the suit seeks protection of a political right does not mean it presents a political question. Such an objection "is little more than a play upon words." Rather, it is argued that apportionment cases, whatever the actual wording of the complaint, can involve no federal constitutional right except one resting on the guaranty of a republican form of government [Article IV, § 4], and that complaints based on that clause have been held to present political questions which are nonjusticiable.

We hold that the claim pleaded here neither rests upon nor implicates the Guaranty Clause and that its justiciability is therefore not foreclosed by our decisions of cases involving that clause. [Review of a number of political question cases] reveals that in the Guaranty Clause cases and in the other "political question" cases, it is the relationship between the judiciary and the coordinate branches of the Federal Government, and not the federal judiciary's relationship to the States, which gives rise to the "political question."

We have said that "In determining whether a question falls within [the political question] category, the appropriateness under our system of government of attributing finality to the action of the political departments and also the lack of satisfactory criteria for a judicial determination are dominant considerations." The nonjusticiability of a political question is primarily a function of the separation of powers. Much confusion results from the capacity of the "political question" label to obscure the need for case-by-case inquiry.... To demonstrate this requires no less than to analyze representative cases and to infer from them the analytical threads that make up the political question doctrine. We shall then show that none of those threads catches this case.

Foreign relations: There are sweeping statements to the effect that all questions touching foreign relations are political questions.[31] Not only does resolution of such issues frequently turn on standards that defy judicial application, or involve the exercise of a discretion demonstrably committed to the executive or legislature; but many such questions uniquely demand single-voiced statement of the Government's views. Yet it is error to suppose that every case or controversy which touches foreign relations lies beyond judicial cognizance. Our cases in this field seem invariably to show a discriminating analysis of the particular question posed, in terms of the history of its management by the political branches, of its susceptibility to judicial handling in the light of its nature and posture in the specific case, and of the possible consequences of judicial action. For example, though a court will not ordinarily inquire

---

31. *E.g.,* "The conduct of the foreign relations of our Government is committed by the Constitution to the Executive and Legislative—'the political'—Departments of the Government, and the propriety of what may be done in the exercise of this political power is not subject to judicial inquiry or decision." *Oetjen v. Central Leather Co.,* 246 U.S. 297, 302, 38 S.Ct. 309, 311, 62 L.Ed. 726.

whether a treaty has been terminated, since on that question "governmental action ... must be regarded as of controlling importance," if there has been no conclusive "governmental action" then a court can construe a treaty and may find it provides the answer. Though a court will not undertake to construe a treaty in a manner inconsistent with a subsequent federal statute, no similar hesitancy obtains if the asserted clash is with state law.

While recognition of foreign governments so strongly defies judicial treatment that without executive recognition a foreign state has been called "a republic of whose existence we know nothing," and the judiciary ordinarily follows the executive as to which nation has sovereignty over disputed territory, once sovereignty over an area is politically determined and declared, courts may examine the resulting status and decide independently whether a statute applies to that area....

Dates of duration of hostilities: Though it has been stated broadly that "the power which declared the necessity is the power to declare its cessation, and what the cessation requires," here too analysis reveals isolable reasons for the presence of political questions, underlying this Court's refusal to review the political departments' determination of when or whether a war has ended. Dominant is the need for finality in the political determination, for emergency's nature demands "A prompt and unhesitating obedience," *Martin v. Mott,* 12 Wheat. 19, 30, 6 L.Ed. 537 (calling up of militia).... But deference rests on reason, not habit. The question in a particular case may not seriously implicate considerations of finality—e.g., a public program of importance (rent control) yet not central to the emergency effort. Further, clearly definable criteria for decision may be available. In such case the political question barrier falls away....

Validity of enactments: In *Coleman v. Miller,* [307 U.S. 433, 59 S.Ct. 972, 83 L.Ed. 1385,] this Court held that the questions of how long a proposed amendment to the Federal Constitution remained open to ratification, and what effect a prior rejection had on a subsequent ratification, were committed to congressional resolution and involved criteria of decision that necessarily escaped the judicial grasp. Similar considerations apply to the enacting process: "The respect due to coequal and independent departments," and the need for finality and certainty about the status of a statute contribute to judicial reluctance to inquire whether, as passed, it complied with all requisite formalities. But it is not true that courts will never delve into a legislature's records upon such a quest: If the enrolled statute lacks an effective date, a court will not hesitate to seek it in the legislative journals in order to preserve the enactment. *Gardner v. Collector,* 6 Wall. 499, 18 L.Ed. 890. The political question doctrine, a tool for maintenance of governmental order, will not be so applied as to promote only disorder.

The status of Indian tribes: This Court's deference to the political departments in determining whether Indians are recognized as a tribe, while it reflects familiar attributes of political questions, also has a unique element in that "the relation of the Indians to the United States is marked by peculiar and cardinal distinctions which exist no where else.... [The Indians are] domestic dependent nations ... in a state of pupilage. Their relation to the United States resembles that of a ward to his guardian." *Cherokee Nation v. Georgia,* 5 Pet. 1, 16, 17, 8 L.Ed. 25. Yet, here too, there is no blanket rule. While " 'It is for [Congress] ... , and not for the courts, to determine when the true interests of the Indian require his release from [the] condition of tutelage' ... , it is not meant by this that Congress may bring a community or body of people within the range of this power by arbitrarily calling them an Indian tribe.... " *United States v. Sandoval,* 231 U.S. 28, 46, 34 S.Ct. 1, 6, 58 L.Ed. 107....

It is apparent that several formulations which vary slightly according to the settings in which the questions arise may describe a political question, although each has one or more elements which identify it as essentially a function of the separation of powers. Prominent on the surface of any case held to involve a political question is found a textually demonstrable constitutional commitment of the issue to a coordinate political department; or a lack of judicially discoverable and manageable standards for resolving it; or the impossibility of deciding without an initial policy determination of a kind clearly for nonjudicial discretion; or the impossibility of a court's undertaking independent resolution without expressing lack of the respect due coordinate branches of government; or an unusual need for unquestioning adherence to a political decision already made; or the potentiality of embarrassment from multifarious pronouncements by various departments on one question.

Unless one of these formulations is inextricable from the case at bar, there should be no dismissal for nonjusticiability on the ground of a political question's presence. The doctrine of which we treat is one of "political questions," not one of "political cases." The courts cannot reject as "no law suit" a bona fide controversy as to whether some action denominated "political" exceeds constitutional authority. The cases we have reviewed show the necessity for discriminating inquiry into the precise facts and posture of the particular case, and the impossibility of resolution by any semantic cataloguing.

But it is argued that this case shares the characteristics of decisions that constitute a category not yet considered, cases concerning the Constitution's guaranty, in Art. IV, § 4, of a republican form of government. A conclusion as to whether the case at bar does present a political question cannot be confidently reached until we have considered those cases with special care. We shall discover that Guaranty Clause claims involve those elements which define a "political question," and for that reason and no other, they are nonjusticiable. [T]he nonjusticiability of such claims has nothing to do with their touching upon matters of state governmental organization.

Republican form of government: Luther v. Borden, 7 How. 1, 12
L.Ed. 581, though in form simply an action for damages for trespass was,
as Daniel Webster said in opening the argument for the defense, "an
unusual case." The defendants, admitting an otherwise tortious breaking
and entering, sought to justify their action on the ground that they were
agents of the established lawful government of Rhode Island, which
State was then under martial law to defend itself from active insurrection; that the plaintiff was engaged in that insurrection; and that they
entered under orders to arrest the plaintiff. The case arose "out of the
unfortunate political differences which agitated the people of Rhode
Island in 1841 and 1842," and which had resulted in a situation wherein
two groups laid competing claims to recognition as the lawful government. The plaintiff's right to recover depended upon which of the two
groups was entitled to such recognition; but the lower court's refusal to
receive evidence or hear argument on that issue, its charge to the jury
that the earlier established or "charter" government was lawful, and the
verdict for the defendants, were affirmed upon appeal to this Court....

Clearly, several factors were thought by the Court in *Luther* to make
the question there "political": the commitment to the other branches of
the decision as to which is the lawful state government; the unambiguous action by the President, in recognizing the charter government as
the lawful authority; the need for finality in the executive's decision; and
the lack of criteria by which a court could determine which form of
government was republican.[48]

But the only significance that *Luther* could have for our immediate
purposes is in its holding that the Guaranty Clause is not a repository of
judicially manageable standards which a court could utilize independently in order to identify a State's lawful government. The Court has since
refused to resort to the Guaranty Clause—which alone had been invoked
for the purpose—as the source of a constitutional standard for invalidating state action. See *Taylor & Marshall v. Beckham (No. 1),* 178 U.S.
548, 20 S.Ct. 890, 44 L.Ed. 1187 (claim that Kentucky's resolution of
contested gubernatorial election deprived voters of republican government held nonjusticiable); *Pacific States Tel. & T. Co. v. Oregon,* 223
U.S. 118, 32 S.Ct. 224, 56 L.Ed. 377 (claim that initiative and referendum negated republican government held nonjusticiable); *Kiernan v.
Portland,* 223 U.S. 151, 32 S.Ct. 231, 56 L.Ed. 386 (claim that municipal
charter amendment *per* municipal initiative and referendum negated
republican government held nonjusticiable)....

48. Even though the Court wrote of unrestrained legislative and executive authority under this Guaranty, thus making its
enforcement a political question, the Court
plainly implied that the political question
barrier was no absolute: "Unquestionably a
military government, established as the permanent government of the State, would not
be a republican government, and it would
be the duty of Congress to overthrow it."
Of course, it does not necessarily follow
that if Congress did not act, the Court
would. For while the judiciary might be able
to decide the limits of the meaning of "republican form," and thus the factor of lack
of criteria might fall away, there would
remain other possible barriers to decision
because of primary commitment to another
branch, which would have to be considered
in the particular fact setting presented....

Just as the Court has consistently held that a challenge to state action based on the Guaranty Clause presents no justiciable question so has it held, and for the same reasons, that challenges to congressional action on the ground of inconsistency with that clause present no justiciable question. In *Georgia v. Stanton,* 6 Wall. 50, 18 L.Ed. 721, the State sought by an original bill to enjoin execution of the Reconstruction Acts . . . Congress had clearly refused to recognize the republican character of the government of the suing State. It seemed to the Court that the only constitutional claim that could be presented was under the Guaranty Clause, and Congress having determined that the effects of the recent hostilities required extraordinary measures to restore governments of a republican form, this Court refused to interfere with Congress' action at the behest of a claimant relying on that very guaranty. . . . And it has pointed out that Congress is not required to establish republican government in the territories before they become States, and before they have attained a sufficient population to warrant a popularly elected legislature. *Downes v. Bidwell,* 182 U.S. 244, 278–279, 21 S.Ct. 770, 783–784, 45 L.Ed. 1088 (dictum).[53]

We come, finally, to the ultimate inquiry whether our precedents as to what constitutes a nonjusticiable "political question" bring the case before us under the umbrella of that doctrine. A natural beginning is to note whether any of the common characteristics which we have been able to identify and label descriptively are present. We find none: The question here is the consistency of state action with the Federal Constitution. We have no question decided, or to be decided, by a political branch of government coequal with this Court. Nor do we risk embarrassment of our government abroad, or grave disturbance at home if we take issue with Tennessee as to the constitutionality of her action here challenged. Nor need the appellants, in order to succeed in this action, ask the Court to enter upon policy determinations for which judicially manageable standards are lacking. Judicial standards under the Equal Protection Clause are well developed and familiar, and it has been open to courts since the enactment of the Fourteenth Amendment to determine, if on the particular facts they must, that a discrimination reflects *no* policy, but simply arbitrary and capricious action.

This case does, in one sense, involve the allocation of political power within a State, and the appellants might conceivably have added a claim under the Guaranty Clause. Of course, as we have seen, any reliance on that clause would be futile. But because any reliance on the Guaranty Clause could not have succeeded it does not follow that appellants may not be heard on the equal protection claim which in fact they tender.

53. On the other hand, the implication of the Guaranty Clause in a case concerning congressional action does not always preclude judicial action. It has been held that the clause gives Congress no power to impose restrictions upon a State's admission which would undercut the constitutional mandate that the States be on an equal footing. *Coyle v. Smith,* 221 U.S. 559, 31 S.Ct. 688, 55 L.Ed. 853. And in *Texas v. White,* 7 Wall. 700, 19 L.Ed. 227, although Congress had determined that the State's government was not republican in form, the State's standing to bring an original action in this Court was sustained.

True, it must be clear that the Fourteenth Amendment claim is not so enmeshed with those political question elements which render Guaranty Clause claims nonjusticiable as actually to present a political question itself. But we have found that not to be the case here. . . .

We conclude that the complaint's allegations of a denial of equal protection present a justiciable constitutional cause of action upon which appellants are entitled to a trial and a decision. The right asserted is within the reach of judicial protection under the Fourteenth Amendment.

The judgment of the District Court is reversed and the cause is remanded for further proceedings consistent with this opinion.

Reversed and remanded.

MR. JUSTICE WHITTAKER did not participate in the decision of this case.

MR. JUSTICE FRANKFURTER, whom MR. JUSTICE HARLAN, joins, dissenting.

. . . Disregard of inherent limits in the effective exercise of the Court's "judicial Power" not only presages the futility of judicial intervention in the essentially political conflict of forces by which the relation between population and representation has time out of mind been and now is determined. It may well impair the Court's position as the ultimate organ of "the supreme Law of the Land" in that vast range of legal problems, often strongly entangled in popular feeling, on which this Court must pronounce. The Court's authority—possessed of neither the purse nor the sword—ultimately rests on sustained public confidence in its moral sanction. Such feeling must be nourished by the Court's complete detachment, in fact and in appearance, from political entanglements and by abstention from injecting itself into the clash of political forces in political settlements.

A hypothetical claim resting on abstract assumptions is now for the first time made the basis for affording illusory relief for a particular evil. [T]he Court does not vouchsafe the lower courts—state and federal—guidelines for formulating specific, definite, wholly unprecedented remedies for the inevitable litigations that today's umbrageous disposition is bound to stimulate in connection with politically motivated reapportionments in so many States. . . .

[Concurring opinions of DOUGLAS, CLARK, & STEWART, JJ., & the dissenting opinion of HARLAN, J., joined by FRANKFURTER, J., are omitted.]

POWELL v. McCORMACK
395 U.S. 486, 89 S.Ct. 1944, 23 L.Ed.2d 491 (1969).

MR. CHIEF JUSTICE WARREN delivered the opinion of the Court.

[The House of Representatives of the 90th Congress "excluded", i.e., refused to seat, Adam Clayton Powell, who had been duly elected from his Congressional district. A House Select Committee was appointed to determine whether Powell met the standing qualifications of Art. I, § 2, clause 2 of which provides: "No Person shall be a representative who shall not have attained to the Age of twenty five years, and been seven years a Citizen of the United States, and who shall not, when elected, be an Inhabitant of that State in which he shall be chosen."

[The Committee also inquired whether he should be punished or expelled pursuant to Art. I, § 5. Clause 1 of that section provides: "Each House shall be the Judge of the Elections, Returns, and Qualifications of its own Members.... " Clause 2 adds that: "Each House may ... punish its Members for disorderly Behavior, and, with the Concurrence of two-thirds, expel a Member."

[Powell's attorneys argued that the standing requirements of Art. I, § 2, cl. 2 were the exclusive requirements for membership in the House and that punishment or expulsion pursuant to Art. I, § 5, cl. 2 was not possible until a member had first been seated. Consequently Powell would not testify before the Committee on any matters other than his eligibility under the standing qualifications of Art. I, § 2, cl. 2.

[The House Committee then issued a report that Powell met the standing qualifications of Art. I, § 2 but that he had asserted an unwarranted privilege and immunity from the processes of the courts of New York; that he had wrongfully diverted House funds for the use of others and himself; and that he had made false reports on expenditures of foreign currency to the Committee on House Administration. The Committee recommended that Powell be sworn and seated as a member of the 90th Congress but that he be censured by the House, fined $40,000 and be deprived of his seniority.

[A majority of the House rejected the motion to bring the Committee resolution to a vote, but amended it to call for the exclusion of Powell and a declaration that his seat was vacant. The Speaker of the House ruled that a simple majority was sufficient to pass the resolution if it were so amended. It was then amended and passed by a vote of 307 to 116.

[Both the district court and Court of Appeals decided against Powell. By the time the case reached the Supreme Court the 90th Congress had terminated and Powell was seated as a member of the 91st Congress. The majority of the Court rejected the argument that Powell's claim was now moot because they concluded that Powell's claim for back salary remained viable even though he had been seated by the 91st Congress.

[Next the Court rejected the argument that the Speech or Debate Clause of Art. I, § 6, cl. 1 barred Powell's suit. "Freedom of legislative activity and the purposes of the Speech or Debate Clause are fully protected if legislators are relieved of the burden of defending themselves." Thus, "though this action may be dismissed against the Congressmen, petitioners are entitled to maintain their action against House employees and to judicial review of the propriety of the decision to exclude petitioner Powell." The Court added by way of footnote that "we need not decide whether under the Speech or Debate Clause petitioners would be entitled to maintain this action solely against members of

Congress where no agents participated in the challenged action and no other remedy was available." The Court then turned to the question of justiciability.]

IV
Exclusion or Expulsion

The resolution excluding petitioner Powell was adopted by a vote in excess of two-thirds of the 434 Members of Congress—307 to 116. Article I, § 5, grants the House authority to expel a member "with the Concurrence of two thirds."[27] Respondents assert that the House may expel a member for any reason whatsoever and that, since a two-thirds vote was obtained, the procedure by which Powell was denied his seat in the 90th Congress should be regarded as an expulsion, not an exclusion.... Had the amendment [to exclude Powell] been regarded as an attempt to expel Powell, a two-thirds vote would have been constitutionally required. The Speaker ruled that the House was voting to exclude Powell, and we will not speculate what the result might have been if Powell had been seated and expulsion proceedings subsequently instituted.

Nor is the distinction between exclusion and expulsion merely one of form. The misconduct for which Powell was charged occurred prior to the convening of the 90th Congress. On several occasions the House has debated whether a member can be expelled for actions taken during a prior Congress and the House's own manual of procedure applicable in the 90th Congress states that "both Houses have distrusted their power to punish in such cases." ...

Finally, the proceedings which culminated in Powell's exclusion cast considerable doubt upon respondents' assumption that the two-thirds vote necessary to expel would have been mustered. These proceedings have been succinctly described by Congressman Eckhardt:

> ... as a practical matter, members who would not have denied Powell a seat if they were given the choice to punish him had to cast an aye vote or else record themselves as opposed to the only punishment that was likely to come before the House. Had the matter come up through the processes of expulsion, it appears that the two-thirds vote would have failed, and then members would have been able to apply a lesser penalty.[32]

We need express no opinion as to the accuracy of Congressman Eckhardt's prediction that expulsion proceedings would have produced a different result. However, the House's own views of the extent of its power to expel combined with the Congressman's analysis counsel that

---

27. Powell was "excluded" from the 90th Congress, i.e., he was not administered the oath of office and was prevented from taking his seat. If he had been allowed to take the oath and subsequently had been required to surrender his seat, the House's action would have constituted an "expulsion." Since we conclude that Powell was excluded from the 90th Congress, we ex-

press no view on what limitations may exist on Congress' power to expel or otherwise punish a member once he has been seated.

32. Eckhardt, The Adam Clayton Powell Case, 45 Texas L.Rev. 1205, 1209 (1967). The views of Congressman Eckhardt were echoed during the exclusion proceedings....

exclusion and expulsion are not fungible proceedings. The Speaker ruled that House Resolution No. 278 contemplated an exclusion proceeding. We must reject respondents' suggestion that we overrule the Speaker and hold that, although the House manifested an intent to exclude Powell, its action should be tested by whatever standards may govern an expulsion....

VI

JUSTICIABILITY

[W]e turn to the question whether the case is justiciable. Two determinations must be made in this regard. First, we must decide whether the claim presented and the relief sought are of the type which admit of judicial resolution. Second, we must determine whether the structure of the Federal Government renders the issue presented a "political question"—that is, a question which is not justiciable in federal court because of the separation of powers provided by the Constitution.

A.　General Considerations

... Respondents do maintain, however, that this case is not justiciable because, they assert, it is impossible for a federal court to "mold effective relief for resolving this case." Respondents emphasize that petitioners asked for coercive relief against the officers of the House, and, they contend, federal courts cannot issue mandamus or injunctions compelling officers or employees of the House to perform specific official acts. Respondents rely primarily on the Speech or Debate Clause to support this contention.

We need express no opinion about the appropriateness of coercive relief in this case, for petitioners sought a declaratory judgment, a form of relief the District Court could have issued....

B.　Political Question Doctrine

1.　Textually Demonstrable Constitutional Commitment....

Respondents' first contention is that this case presents a political question because under Art. I, § 5, there has been a "textually demonstrable constitutional commitment" to the House of the "adjudicatory power" to determine Powell's qualifications. Thus it is argued that the House, and the House alone, has power to determine who is qualified to be a member.

In order to determine whether there has been a textual commitment to a co-ordinate department of the Government, we must interpret the Constitution. In other words, we must first determine what power the Constitution confers upon the House through Art. I, § 5, before we can determine to what extent, if any, the exercise of that power is subject to judicial review. Respondents maintain that the House has broad power under § 5, and, they argue, the House may determine which are the qualifications necessary for membership. On the other hand, petitioners allege that the Constitution provides that an elected representative may be denied his seat only if the House finds he does not meet one of the standing qualifications expressly prescribed by the Constitution.

If examination of § 5 disclosed that the Constitution gives the House judicially unreviewable power to set qualifications for membership and to judge whether prospective members meet those qualifications, further review of the House determination might well be barred by the political question doctrine. On the other hand, if the Constitution gives the House power to judge only whether elected members possess the three standing qualifications set forth in the Constitution, further consideration would be necessary to determine whether any of the other formulations of the political question doctrine are "inextricable from the case at bar."[42] *Baker v. Carr.*

In other words, whether there is a "textually demonstrable constitutional commitment of the issue to a co-ordinate political department" of government and what is the scope of such commitment are questions we must resolve for the first time in this case. For, as we pointed out in *Baker v. Carr,* supra, "[d]eciding whether a matter has in any measure been committed by the Constitution to another branch of government, or whether the action of that branch exceeds whatever authority has been committed, is itself a delicate exercise in constitutional interpretation, and is a responsibility of this Court as ultimate interpreter of the Constitution."

In order to determine the scope of any "textual commitment" under Art. I, § 5, we necessarily must determine the meaning of the phrase to "be the Judge of the Qualifications of its own Members." Petitioners argue that the records of the debates during the Constitutional Convention; available commentary from the post-Convention, pre-ratification period; and early congressional applications of Art. I, § 5, support their construction of the section. Respondents insist, however, that a careful examination of the pre-Convention practices of the English Parliament and American colonial assemblies demonstrates that by 1787, a legislature's power to judge the qualifications of its members was generally understood to encompass exclusion or expulsion on the ground that an individual's character or past conduct rendered him unfit to serve. When the Constitution and the debates over its adoption are thus viewed in historical perspective, argue respondents, it becomes clear that the "qualifications" expressly set forth in the Constitution were not meant to limit the long-recognized legislative power to exclude or expel at will, but merely to establish "standing incapacities," which could be altered only by a constitutional amendment. Our examination of the relevant historical materials leads us to the conclusion that petitioners are correct and that the Constitution leaves the House[44] without authority to

---

42. Consistent with this interpretation, federal courts might still be barred by the political question doctrine from reviewing the House's factual determination that a member did not meet one of the standing qualifications. This is an issue not presented in this case and we express no view as to its resolution.

44. Since Art. I, § 5, cl. 1, applies to both Houses of Congress, the scope of the Senate's power to judge the qualifications of its members necessarily is identical to the

exclude any person, duly elected by his constituents, who meets all the requirements for membership expressly prescribed in the Constitution. [A lengthy analysis of the historical antecedents, including the English and colonial precedents, is omitted.] A fundamental principle of our representative democracy is, in Hamilton's words, "that the people should choose whom they please to govern them." 2 Elliot's Debates 257.

. . . Unquestionably, Congress has an interest in preserving its institutional integrity, but in most cases that interest can be sufficiently safeguarded by the exercise of its power to punish its members for disorderly behavior and, in extreme cases, to expel a member with the concurrence of two-thirds. In short, both the intention of the Framers, to the extent it can be determined, and an examination of the basic principles of our democratic system persuade us that the Constitution does not vest in the Congress a discretionary power to deny membership by a majority vote.

For these reasons, we have concluded that Art. I, § 5, is at most a "textually demonstrable commitment" to Congress to judge only the qualifications expressly set forth in the Constitution. Therefore, the "textual commitment" formulation of the political question doctrine does not bar federal courts from adjudicating petitioners' claims.

2. Other Considerations

Respondents' alternate contention is that the case presents a political question because judicial resolution of petitioners' claim would produce a "potentially embarrassing confrontation between coordinate branches" of the Federal Government. But, as our interpretation of Art. I, § 5, discloses, a determination of petitioner Powell's right to sit would require no more than an interpretation of the Constitution. Such a determination falls within the traditional role accorded courts to interpret the law, and does not involve a "lack of the respect due [a] coordinate [branch] of government," nor does it involve an "initial policy determination of a kind clearly for nonjudicial discretion." *Baker v. Carr.* Our system of government requires that federal courts on occasion interpret the Constitution in a manner at variance with the construction given the document by another branch. The alleged conflict that such an adjudication may cause cannot justify the courts' avoiding their constitutional responsibility.[86]

Nor are any of the other formulations of a political question "inextricable from the case at bar." *Baker v. Carr.* Petitioners seek a determination that the House was without power to exclude Powell from the 90th Congress, which, we have seen, requires an interpretation of the Constitution—a determination for which clearly there are "judicially . . . manageable standards." Finally, a judicial resolution of petitioners'

scope of the House's power, with the exception, of course, that Art. I, § 3, cl. 3, establishes different age and citizenship requirements for membership in the Senate.

86. In fact, the Court has noted that it is an "inadmissible suggestion" that action might be taken in disregard of a judicial determination. *McPherson v. Blacker,* 146 U.S. 1, 24, 13 S.Ct. 3, 6, 36 L.Ed. 869 (1892).

claim will not result in "multifarious pronouncements by various departments on one question." For, as we noted in *Baker v. Carr,* it is the responsibility of this Court to act as the ultimate interpreter of the Constitution. *Marbury v. Madison.* Thus, we conclude that petitioners' claim is not barred by the political question doctrine, and, having determined that the claim is otherwise generally justiciable, we hold that the case is justiciable. . . .

MR. JUSTICE DOUGLAS.

While I join the opinion of the Court, I add a few words. [I]f this were an expulsion case I would think that no justiciable controversy would be presented, the vote of the House being two-thirds or more. But it is not an expulsion case. Whether it could have been won as an expulsion case, no one knows. Expulsion for "misconduct" may well raise different questions, different considerations. . . .

MR. JUSTICE STEWART, dissenting.

I believe that events which have taken place since certiorari was granted in this case on November 18, 1968, have rendered it moot, and that the Court should therefore refrain from deciding the novel, difficult, and delicate constitutional questions which the case presented at its inception. . . .

Notes

1. Recall that Chief Justice Marshall stated in *Marbury v. Madison:* "The province of the court is, solely, to decide on the rights of individuals, not to inquire how the executive, or executive officers, perform duties in which they have a discretion. Questions in their nature political, or which are, by the constitution and laws, submitted to the executive, can never be made in this court."

What is the test for political questions in *Baker v. Carr,* supra? Given that test, should all claims under the "Republican Form of Government" clause be held to be political and nonjusticiable? Should it make any difference if Congress is using that clause as a source of power (as it did in the post Civil War Reconstruction)?

2. The majority in *Baker v. Carr* finds that there is an injury but does not tell us what the remedy might be. Justice Clark, in his concurring opinion, stated: "No one . . . contends that mathematical equality among voters is required by the Equal Protection Clause." 369 U.S. at 258, 82 S.Ct. at 732. Ultimately the Court mandated "one person, one vote." See § 8–3.21, infra.

3. Why is it necessary for the Court to explain that Powell was not expelled but excluded? Only a majority is needed for an exclusion and a two-thirds majority is needed for an expulsion. But over two-thirds voted against Powell, so what difference does it make what you call it?

Would the Court have heard the case if the House had first seated Powell? Compare the Douglas concurrence with the majority opinion at fn. 27.

4. Congressman Powell spent a lot of his free time on the island of Bimini in the Bahamas. Assume that the House had decided to exclude Powell because it determined that he was not really an inhabitant of New York, the state from which he was elected. Would the Court have heard the case then?

5. The majority says, at fn. 86, that it is an "inadmissible suggestion" that Congress might not obey the Court's order regarding Powell. Is that possibility not relevant? Should equity issue fruitless orders? Cf. *Lumley v. Wagner,* 1 De Gex, Macnaghten & Gordon 604 (Chancery 1852)(equity will not enforce a contract by an affirmative command ordering an opera singer to sing). *Powell,* in part VI(A), also found it important that petitioners sought declaratory relief. Is a declaratory judgment that is unenforceable really only an advisory opinion?

6. In *Gilligan v. Morgan,* 413 U.S. 1, 93 S.Ct. 2440, 37 L.Ed.2d 407 (1973), students at Kent State University sued for prospective injunctive relief against the Ohio National Guard. Plaintiffs wanted, "a judicial evaluation of the 'training, weaponry and orders' of the Ohio National Guard." Because plaintiffs sought "a broad call on judicial power to assume continuing regulatory jurisdiction over the activities of the Ohio National Guard" rather than a claim for damages for past injuries or an order "against some specified and imminently threatened unlawful action," the majority found the case nonjusticiable. Chief Justice Burger for the Court found that Art. I, § 8, cl. 16 vests in Congress the responsibility to prescribe discipline of the Militia, and that Congress has authorized the President to issue appropriate regulations. The majority argued that the requested relief "would necessarily draw the courts into a nonjusticiable political question over which we have no jurisdiction."[1]

In *Scheuer v. Rhodes,* 416 U.S. 232, 94 S.Ct. 1683, 40 L.Ed.2d 90 (1974), Chief Justice Burger, for a unanimous court, allowed the estates of three students to sue to collect damages against the Ohio National Guard, the Governor, and others for allegedly violating the students' civil rights. The Court specifically noted that *Gilligan* did not mandate a contrary result.

7. Should the question whether American involvement in an undeclared war is constitutional be justiciable?[2] What about an allegation that such a war violated a treaty signed by the United States?

8. To what extent should matters relating to the constitutional amendment process be considered political questions, immune from judicial review?

The principal case applying the political question doctrine to issues relating to amendments to the Constitution is *Coleman v. Miller,* 307 U.S. 433, 59 S.Ct. 972, 83 L.Ed. 1385 (1939), cited with approval in *Baker v. Carr.* Plaintiffs included members of the Kansas Senate, whose votes against ratification of a constitutional amendment to outlaw child labor had been

1. Four members of the Court dissented and argued that the case was moot. They did not discuss the political question issue.

2. The constitutionality of the Vietnam War was challenged in numerous cases but the Supreme Court never decided the issue.

See, e.g., *Mora v. McNamara,* 389 U.S. 934, 88 S.Ct. 282, 19 L.Ed.2d 287 (1967)(Stewart and Douglas, JJ., dissenting to denial of certiorari of case in which draftees sought to enjoin their shipment to Vietnam as unconstitutional).

overridden. They sued in state court to restrain the Kansas secretary of state from authenticating the ratifying resolution.

Petitioners argued that either a ratification or rejection of a proposed amendment cannot later be changed, but the Court held that the "question of the efficacy of ratifications by state legislatures, in the light of previous rejection or attempted withdrawal, should be regarded as a political question pertaining to the political departments, with the ultimate authority in the Congress in the exercise of its control over the promulgation of the adoption of the amendment." Congress, the Court said, could have enacted a statute relating to ratification after rejection (and rejection after ratification) but had not done so.

Finally, the petitioners argued that the proposed amendment could not be ratified because of the length of time—thirteen years—between its proposal and the Kansas ratification. The Court had held, in *Dillon v. Gloss,* 256 U.S. 368, 41 S.Ct. 510, 65 L.Ed. 994 (1921), that Congress may fix a reasonable time for ratification. But Congress had not done so. The Court recognized that it was inappropriate for the judiciary to weigh the economic, political, and social conditions to determine viability. The "decision by the Congress ... of the question whether the amendment had been adopted within a reasonable time would not be subject to review by the courts."[3]

On May 7, 1992, Michigan became the 38th state to ratify the 27th Amendment, which Madison had originally proposed 203 years earlier. It was first ratified by Maryland on December 19th, 1789. On May 18, 1992 the Archivist of the United States, after he received official notice of the ratification, declared the Amendment part of the Constitution, pursuant to his authority under 1 U.S.C.A. § 106b. See, 57 Federal Register 21187 (May 19, 1992). Various Congressional leaders were quoted as questioning the validity of the Amendment, but they backed off and both Houses of Congress passed resolutions declaring assent to the new Amendment.

When Congress proposed the Equal Rights Amendment in March, 1972, it placed no time limit for ratification in the text of the amendment, but rather placed a 7 year time limit in the resolution proposing the amendment. This period would have ended on March 22, 1979, but in October, 1978 the Congress enacted House Joint Resolution 638 extending the time limit by 3 years and 3 months. Was this extension subject to judicial review?[4]

9. In *United States v. Nixon,* § 5–6, infra, the Court held that a presidential decision not to respond to a subpoena in a criminal case was justiciable. And in *Goldwater v. Carter,* § 5–2, infra, a fragmented Court vacated the judgment of the Court of Appeals with directions to dismiss the complaint, which had charged that the President's termination of the treaty with Taiwan was unconstitutional. Several of the Justices thought that the question was nonjusticiable.

10. POLITICAL GERRYMANDERING. The Court has long prohibited drawing of political boundaries in order to invidiously fence out racial groups "so as

3. Butler, J., joined by McReynolds, J., dissented and would have held that more than a reasonable time had elapsed.

4. Compare Almond, Running Out of Time, 64 A.B.A.J. 1504 (1978)(opposing extension) with Rotunda, Running Out of Time, 64 A.B.A.J. 1507 (1978)(arguing that the issue was nonjusticiable).

to deprive them of their preexisting municipal vote."[5] Political gerrymandering raises different issues from such racial gerrymandering. At first, in several summary decisions, the Court affirmed lower court rulings that political gerrymandering equal protection challenges were nonjusticiable. E.g., *WMCA, Inc. v. Lomenzo,* 382 U.S. 4, 86 S.Ct. 24, 15 L.Ed.2d 2 (1965)(per curiam), summarily affirming 238 F.Supp. 916 (S.D.N.Y.1965). Later, *Gaffney v. Cummings,* 412 U.S. 735, 93 S.Ct. 2321, 37 L.Ed.2d 298 (1973) rejected a challenge to Connecticut's legislative apportionment because of partisan political structuring of the district lines: "We are quite unconvinced that the reapportionment plan offered by the three-member Board violated the Fourteenth Amendment because it attempted to reflect the relative strength of the parties in locating and defining election districts. It would be idle, we think, to contend that any political consideration taken into account in fashioning a reapportionment plan is sufficient to invalidate it."

Then, in *Davis v. Bandemer,* 478 U.S. 109, 106 S.Ct. 2797, 92 L.Ed.2d 85 (1986), Justice White, in a six to three decision, held that a suit challenging Indiana's 1981 state apportionment plan because it was alleged to have unconstitutionally diluted the votes of Indiana Democrats was justiciable under the Equal Protection Clause. The Democrats claimed that political gerrymandering was unconstitutional because it minimized their electoral strength. Justice White noted: "Over all the [Indiana State] House races statewide, Democratic candidates received 51.9% of the vote. Only 43 Democrats, however, were elected to the [100 member] House. Over all the [State] Senate races statewide, Democratic candidates received 53.1% of the vote. Thirteen (of 25) Democrats were elected [52%]." In two counties that had been divided into multi-member districts, Democratic candidates "drew 46.6% of the vote, but only 3 of 21 House seats were filled by Democrats."

Political gerrymandering, White said, is justiciable: the Court will not be deciding a matter "more properly decided by a coequal branch of or Government"; there "is no risk of foreign or domestic disturbance;" and, "we are not persuaded that there are no judicially discernible and manageable standards.... " The "mere fact" that "we may not now similarly perceive a likely arithmetic presumption in the instant context does not compel a conclusion that the claims presented here are non-justiciable. The one person, one vote principle had not yet been developed when *Baker* was decided." He admitted that the claims here do not concern districts of unequal size. Everyone has "the right to vote and to have his vote counted, and each elector may vote for and be represented by the same number of lawmakers."

Then he turned to the merits, and—on that question—he spoke not for the Court but for a plurality including Brennan, Marshall, and Blackmun, JJ. The White plurality rejected the lower court finding of unconstitutional gerrymandering and required a higher threshold for legal action.

5. *Gomillion v. Lightfoot,* 364 U.S. 339, 341, 81 S.Ct. 125, 127, 5 L.Ed.2d 110 (1960)(Frankfurter, J., for the Court, holding that a law altering the shape of the city of Tuskegee, Alabama from a square to an "uncouth" 28–sided figure in order to remove from the city all but four or five black voters, but not one single white resident, was unconstitutional discrimination against the blacks in violation of their Fifteenth Amendment right to vote).

"[U]nconstitutional discrimination occurs only when the electoral system is arranged in a manner that will consistently degrade a voter's or a group of voters' influence on the political process as a whole. [A]n equal protection violation may be found only where the electoral system substantially disadvantages certain groups in their opportunity to influence the political process effectively. [A] finding of unconstitutionality must be supported by evidence of continued frustration of the will of a majority of the voters or effective denial to a minority of the voters of a fair chance to influence the political process. . . . Inviting attack on minor departures from some supposed norm would too much embroil the judiciary in second-guessing the legislature. . . . We decline to take a major step toward that end. . . . "

O'Connor, J., joined by Burger, C.J., and Rehnquist, J., filed an opinion concurring in the judgment and objecting to the ruling on justiciability:

"[T]he partisan gerrymandering claims of major political parties raise a nonjusticiable political question that the judiciary should leave to the legislative branch as the Framers of the Constitution unquestionably intended. . . . If members of the major political parties are protected by the Equal Protection Clause from dilution of their voting strength, then members of every identifiable group that possesses distinctive interests and tends to vote on the basis of those interests should be able to bring similar claims. Federal courts will have no alternative but to attempt to recreate the complex process of legislative apportionment in the context of adversary litigation in order to reconcile the competing claims of political, religious, ethnic, racial, occupational, and socioeconomic groups. Even if there were some way of limiting such claims to organized political parties, the fact remains that the losing party or the losing group of legislators in every reapportionment will now be invited to fight the battle anew in federal court. . . . The right asserted in *Baker v. Carr* was an individual right to a vote whose weight was not arbitrarily subjected to 'debasement.' The rights asserted in this case are *group* rights to an equal share of political power and representation, and the 'arbitrary and capricious' standard discussed in *Baker v. Carr* cannot serve as the basis for recognizing such rights. . . . Furthermore, the Court fails to explain why a bipartisan gerrymander—which is what was approved in *Gaffney*—affects individuals any differently than a partisan gerrymander, which the Court makes vulnerable to constitutional challenge today."

Powell, J., joined by Stevens, J., agreed with White that the political gerrymandering was justiciable. However, they would have affirmed the lower court finding of a constitutional violation:

"Gerrymandering is 'the deliberate and arbitrary distortion of district boundaries and populations for partisan or personal political purposes.' [G]errymandering violates the Equal Protection Clause only when the redistricting plan serves 'no purpose other than to favor one segment—whether racial, ethnic, religious, economic, or political—that may occupy a position of strength at a particular time, or to disadvantage a politically weak segment of the community.'

"The term 'gerrymandering,' however, is also used loosely to describe the common practice of the party in power to choose the redistricting plan that gives it an advantage at the polls. [O]nly a sensitive and searching inquiry can distinguish gerrymandering in the 'loose' sense from gerrymandering that amounts to unconstitutional discrimination. . . . The concept of 'representation' necessarily applies to groups: groups of voters elect representatives, individual voters do not.

"[The] most basic flaw in the plurality's opinion is its failure to enunciate any standard that affords guidance to legislatures and courts. [The] factors that I believe properly should guide both legislators who redistrict and judges who test redistricting plans against constitutional challenges . . . are the shapes of voting districts and adherence to established political subdivision boundaries. Other relevant considerations include the nature of the legislative procedures by which the apportionment law was adopted and legislative history reflecting contemporaneous legislative goals."

NIXON v. UNITED STATES
506 U.S. 224, 113 S.Ct. 732, 122 L.Ed.2d 1 (1993).

CHIEF JUSTICE REHNQUIST delivered the opinion of the Court.

Petitioner Walter L. Nixon, Jr., asks this court to decide whether Senate Rule XI, which allows a committee of Senators to hear evidence against an individual who has been impeached and to report that evidence to the full Senate, violates the Impeachment Trial Clause, Art. I, § 3, cl. 6. That Clause provides that the "Senate shall have the sole Power to try all Impeachments." But before we reach the merits of such a claim, we must decide whether it is "justiciable," that is, whether it is a claim that may be resolved by the courts. We conclude that it is not.

Nixon, a former Chief Judge of the United States District Court for the Southern District of Mississippi, was convicted by a jury of two counts of making false statements before a federal grand jury and sentenced to prison. The grand jury investigation stemmed from reports that Nixon had accepted a gratuity from a Mississippi businessman in exchange for asking a local district attorney to halt the prosecution of the businessman's son. Because Nixon refused to resign from his office as a United States District Judge, he continued to collect his judicial salary while serving out his prison sentence. On May 10, 1989, the House of Representatives adopted three articles of impeachment for high crimes and misdemeanors. The first two articles charged Nixon with giving false testimony before the grand jury and the third article charged him with bringing disrepute on the Federal Judiciary.

After the House presented the articles to the Senate, the Senate voted to invoke its own Impeachment Rule XI, under which the presiding officer appoints a committee of Senators to "receive evidence and take testimony." Senate Impeachment Rule XI.[1] The Senate committee held

---

1. Specifically, Rule XI provides: "[I]n the trial of any impeachment the Pre-

four days of hearings, during which 10 witnesses, including Nixon, testified. Pursuant to Rule XI, the committee presented the full Senate with a complete transcript of the proceeding and a report stating the uncontested facts and summarizing the evidence on the contested facts. Nixon and the House impeachment managers submitted extensive final briefs to the full Senate and delivered arguments from the Senate floor during the three hours set aside for oral argument in front of that body. Nixon himself gave a personal appeal, and several Senators posed questions directly to both parties. The Senate voted by more than the constitutionally required two-thirds majority to convict Nixon on the first two articles. The presiding officer then entered judgment removing Nixon from his office as United States District Judge.

Nixon thereafter commenced the present suit, arguing that Senate Rule XI violates the constitutional grant of authority to the Senate to "try" all impeachments because it prohibits the whole Senate from taking part in the evidentiary hearings. Nixon sought a declaratory judgment that his impeachment conviction was void and that his judicial salary and privileges should be reinstated. The District Court held that his claim was nonjusticiable, and the Court of Appeals for the District of Columbia Circuit agreed.

[T]he concept of a textual commitment to a coordinate political department is not completely separate from the concept of a lack of judicially discoverable and manageable standards for resolving it; the lack of judicially manageable standards may strengthen the conclusion that there is a textually demonstrable commitment to a coordinate branch.

In this case, we must examine Art. I, § 3, cl. 6, to determine the scope of authority conferred upon the Senate by the Framers regarding impeachment. . . . The language and structure of this Clause are revealing. The first sentence is a grant of authority to the Senate, and the word "sole" indicates that this authority is reposed in the Senate and nowhere else. The next two sentences specify requirements to which the Senate proceedings shall conform: the Senate shall be on oath or

---

siding Officer of the Senate, if the Senate so orders, shall appoint a committee of Senators to receive evidence and take testimony at such times and places as the committee may determine, and for such purpose the committee so appointed and the chairman thereof, to be elected by the committee, shall (unless otherwise ordered by the Senate) exercise all the powers and functions conferred upon the Senate and the Presiding Officer of the Senate, respectively, under the rules of procedure and practice in the Senate when sitting on impeachment trials.

"Unless otherwise ordered by the Senate, the rules of procedure and practice in the Senate when sitting on impeachment trials shall govern the procedure and practice of the committee so appointed. The committee so appointed shall report to the Senate in writing a certified copy of the transcript of the proceedings and testimony had and given before such committee, and such report shall be received by the Senate and the evidence so received and the testimony so taken shall be considered to all intents and purposes, subject to the right of the Senate to determine competency, relevancy, and materiality, as having been received and taken before the Senate, but nothing herein shall prevent the Senate from sending for any witness and hearing his testimony in open Senate, or by order of the Senate having the entire trial in open Senate."

affirmation, a two-thirds vote is required to convict, and when the President is tried the Chief Justice shall preside.

Petitioner argues that the word "try" in the first sentence imposes by implication an additional requirement on the Senate in that the proceedings must be in the nature of a judicial trial. From there petitioner goes on to argue that this limitation precludes the Senate from delegating to a select committee the task of hearing the testimony of witnesses, as was done pursuant to Senate Rule XI. " '[T]ry' means more than simply 'vote on' or 'review' or 'judge.' In 1787 and today, trying a case means hearing the evidence, not scanning a cold record." Brief for Petitioner 25. Petitioner concludes from this that courts may review whether or not the Senate "tried" him before convicting him.

There are several difficulties with this position which lead us ultimately to reject it. The word "try," both in 1787 and later, has considerably broader meanings than those to which petitioner would limit it. Older dictionaries define try as "[t]o examine" or "[t]o examine as a judge." See 2 S. Johnson, A Dictionary of the English Language (1785). . . .

The conclusion that the use of the word "try" in the first sentence of the Impeachment Trial Clause lacks sufficient precision to afford any judicially manageable standard of review of the Senate's actions is fortified by the existence of the three very specific requirements that the Constitution does impose on the Senate when trying impeachments: the members must be under oath, a two-thirds vote is required to convict, and the Chief Justice presides when the President is tried. These limitations are quite precise, and their nature suggests that the Framers did not intend to impose additional limitations on the form of the Senate proceedings by the use of the word "try" in the first sentence.

Petitioner devotes only two pages in his brief to negating the significance of the word "sole" in the first sentence of Clause 6. . . . We think that the word "sole" is of considerable significance. Indeed, the word "sole" appears only one other time in the Constitution—with respect to the House of Representatives' "*sole* Power of Impeachment." Art. I, § 2, cl. 5 (emphasis added). The common sense meaning of the word "sole" is that the Senate alone shall have authority to determine whether an individual should be acquitted or convicted. The dictionary definition bears this out. . . .

Petitioner finally argues that even if significance be attributed to the word "sole" in the first sentence of the clause, the authority granted is to the Senate, and this means that "the Senate—not the courts, not a lay jury, not a Senate Committee—shall try impeachments." It would be possible to read the first sentence of the Clause this way, but it is not a natural reading. Petitioner's interpretation would bring into judicial purview not merely the sort of claim made by petitioner, but other similar claims based on the conclusion that the word "Senate" has imposed by implication limitations on procedures which the Senate might adopt. Such limitations would be inconsistent with the construction of the Clause as a whole, which, as we have noted, sets out three express limitations in separate sentences.

The history and contemporary understanding of the impeachment provisions support our reading of the constitutional language. The parties do not offer evidence of a single word in the history of the Constitutional Convention or in contemporary commentary that even alludes to the possibility of judicial review in the context of the impeachment powers. This silence is quite meaningful in light of the several explicit references to the availability of judicial review as a check on the Legislature's power with respect to bills of attainder, *ex post facto* laws, and statutes. See The Federalist No. 78, p. 524 (J. Cooke ed. 1961)("Limitations . . . can be preserved in practice no other way than through the medium of the courts of justice").

The Framers labored over the question of where the impeachment power should lie. Significantly, in at least two considered scenarios the power was placed with the Federal Judiciary. See 1 Farrand [The Records of the Federal Convention of 1787] 21–22 (Virginia Plan); *id.,* at 244 (New Jersey Plan). Indeed, Madison and the Committee of Detail proposed that the Supreme Court should have the power to determine impeachments. Despite these proposals, the Convention ultimately decided that the Senate would have "the sole Power to Try all Impeachments." According to Alexander Hamilton, the Senate was the "most fit depositary of this important trust" because its members are representatives of the people. See The Federalist No. 65. The Supreme Court was not the proper body because the Framers "doubted whether the members of that tribunal would, at all times, be endowed with so eminent a portion of fortitude as would be called for in the execution of so difficult a task" or whether the Court "would possess the degree of credit and authority" to carry out its judgment if it conflicted with the accusation brought by the Legislature—the people's representative. In addition, the Framers believed the Court was too small in number: "The awful discretion, which a court of impeachments must necessarily have, to doom to honor or to infamy the most confidential and the most distinguished characters of the community, forbids the commitment of the trust to a small number of persons."

There are two additional reasons why the Judiciary, and the Supreme Court in particular, were not chosen to have any role in impeachments. First, the Framers recognized that most likely there would be two sets of proceedings for individuals who commit impeachable offenses—the impeachment trial and a separate criminal trial. In fact, the Constitution explicitly provides for two separate proceedings. See Art. I, § 3, cl. 7. The Framers deliberately separated the two forums to avoid raising the specter of bias and to ensure independent judgments. . . . Certainly judicial review of the Senate's "trial" would introduce the same risk of bias as would participation in the trial itself.

Second, judicial review would be inconsistent with the Framers' insistence that our system be one of checks and balances. In our constitutional system, impeachment was designed to be the *only* check on the Judicial Branch by the Legislature. On the topic of judicial accountability, Hamilton wrote:

> "The precautions for their responsibility are comprised in the article respecting impeachments. They are liable to be impeached for malconduct by the house of representatives, and tried by the senate, and if convicted, may be dismissed from office and disqualified for holding any other. *This is the only provision on the point, which is consistent with the necessary independence of the judicial character, and is the only one which we find in our own constitution in respect to our own judges.*" *Id.*, No. 79 (emphasis added).

Judicial involvement in impeachment proceedings, even if only for purposes of judicial review, is counterintuitive because it would eviscerate the "important constitutional check" placed on the Judiciary by the Framers. Nixon's argument would place final reviewing authority with respect to impeachments in the hands of the same body that the impeachment process is meant to regulate.

Nevertheless, Nixon argues that judicial review is necessary in order to place a check on the Legislature. Nixon fears that if the Senate is given unreviewable authority to interpret the Impeachment Trial Clause, there is a grave risk that the Senate will usurp judicial power. The Framers anticipated this objection and created two constitutional safeguards to keep the Senate in check. The first safeguard is that the whole of the impeachment power is divided between the two legislative bodies, with the House given the right to accuse and the Senate given the right to judge.... The second safeguard is the two-thirds supermajority vote requirement. Hamilton explained that "[a]s the concurrence of two-thirds of the senate will be requisite to a condemnation, the security to innocence, from this additional circumstance, will be as complete as itself can desire."

In addition to the textual commitment argument, we are persuaded that the lack of finality and the difficulty of fashioning relief counsel against justiciability. [O]pening the door of judicial review to the procedures used by the Senate in trying impeachments would "expose the political life of the country to months, or perhaps years, of chaos." This lack of finality would manifest itself most dramatically if the President were impeached. The legitimacy of any successor, and hence his effectiveness, would be impaired severely, not merely while the judicial process was running its course, but during any retrial that a differently constituted Senate might conduct if its first judgment of conviction were invalidated. Equally uncertain is the question of what relief a court may give other than simply setting aside the judgment of conviction. Could it order the reinstatement of a convicted federal judge, or order Congress to create an additional judgeship if the seat had been filled in the interim?

Petitioner finally contends that a holding of nonjusticiability cannot be reconciled with our opinion in *Powell v. McCormack*. Our conclusion in *Powell* was based on the fixed meaning of "[q]ualifications" set forth in Art. I, § 2. The claim by the House that its power to "be the Judge of the Elections, Returns and Qualifications of its own Members" was a textual commitment of unreviewable authority was defeated by the existence of this separate provision specifying the only qualifications which might be imposed for House membership. The decision as to whether a member satisfied these qualifications *was* placed with the House, but the decision as to what these qualifications consisted of was not.

[W]e conclude, after exercising that delicate responsibility, that the word "try" in the Impeachment Clause does not provide an identifiable textual limit on the authority which is committed to the Senate.

For the foregoing reasons, the judgment of the Court of Appeals is

Affirmed.

JUSTICE STEVENS, concurring.

. . . Respect for a coordinate Branch of the Government forecloses any assumption that improbable hypotheticals like those mentioned by Justice White and Justice Souter will ever occur. Accordingly, the wise policy of judicial restraint, coupled with the potential anomalies associated with a contrary view, provide a sufficient justification for my agreement with the views of The Chief Justice.

JUSTICE WHITE, with whom JUSTICE BLACKMUN joins, concurring in the judgment.

Petitioner contends that the method by which the Senate convicted him on two articles of impeachment violates Art. I, § 3, cl. 6 of the Constitution, which mandates that the Senate "try" impeachments. The Court is of the view that the Constitution forbids us even to consider his contention. I find no such prohibition and would therefore reach the merits of the claim. I concur in the judgment because the Senate fulfilled its constitutional obligation to "try" petitioner.

. . . I would prefer not to announce an unreviewable discretion in the Senate to ignore completely the constitutional direction to "try" impeachment cases. When asked at oral argument whether that direction would be satisfied if, after a House vote to impeach, the Senate, without any procedure whatsoever, unanimously found the accused guilty of being "a bad guy," counsel for the United States answered that the Government's theory "leads me to answer that question yes." Especially in light of this advice from the Solicitor General, I would not issue an invitation to the Senate to find an excuse, in the name of other pressing business, to be dismissive of its critical role in the impeachment process. . . .

The majority finds a clear textual commitment in the Constitution's use of the word "sole" in the phrase "the Senate shall have the sole Power to try all impeachments." Art. I, § 3, cl. 6. . . . That the word "sole" is found only in the House and Senate Impeachment Clauses demonstrates that its purpose is to emphasize the distinct role of each in the impeachment process.... While the majority is thus right to interpret the term "sole" to indicate that the Senate ought to " 'functio[n] independently and without assistance or interference,' " it wrongly identifies the judiciary, rather than the House, as the source of potential interference with which the Framers were concerned when they employed the term "sole."

... Consider, by comparison [to "sole"], the treatment of Art. I, § 1, which grants "All legislative powers" to the House and Senate. As used in that context "all" is nearly synonymous with "sole"—both connote entire and exclusive authority. Yet the Court has never thought it would unduly interfere with the operation of the Legislative Branch to entertain difficult and important questions as to the extent of the legislative power. Quite the opposite, we have stated that the proper interpretation of the Clause falls within the province of the judiciary.

[T]he term "try" is hardly so elusive as the majority would have it. Were the Senate, for example, to adopt the practice of automatically entering a judgment of conviction whenever articles of impeachment were delivered from the House, it is quite clear that the Senate will have failed to "try" impeachments. Indeed in this respect, "try" presents no greater, and perhaps fewer, interpretive difficulties than some other constitutional standards that have been found amenable to familiar techniques of judicial construction, including, for example, "Commerce ... among the several States," Art. I, § 8, cl. 3, and "due process of law." ... [3]

The majority's conclusion that "try" is incapable of meaningful judicial construction is not without irony. One might think that if any class of concepts would fall within the definitional abilities of the judiciary, it would be that class having to do with procedural justice. Examination of the remaining question—whether proceedings in accordance with Senate Rule XI are compatible with the Impeachment Trial Clause—confirms this intuition.

Petitioner bears the rather substantial burden of demonstrating that, simply by employing the word "try," the Constitution prohibits the Senate from relying on a factfinding committee.... The fact that Art. III, § 2, cl. 3 specifically exempts impeachment trials from the jury requirement provides some evidence that the Framers were anxious not to have additional specific procedural requirements read into the term "try." Contemporaneous commentary further supports this view. Hamil-

3. The majority's *in terrorem* argument against justiciability—that judicial review of impeachments might cause national disruption and that the courts would be unable to fashion effective relief—merits only brief attention. In the typical instance, court review of impeachments would no more render the political system dysfunctional than has this litigation. The relief granted for unconstitutional impeachment trials would presumably be similar to the relief granted to other unfairly tried public employee-litigants. Finally, as applied to the special case of the President, the majority's argument merely points out that, were the Senate to convict the President without any kind of a trial, a constitutional crisis might well result. It hardly follows that the Court ought to refrain from upholding the Constitution in all impeachment cases. Nor does it follow that, in cases of Presidential impeachment, the Justices ought to abandon their Constitutional responsibilities because the Senate has precipitated a crisis.

ton, for example, stressed that . . . the proceedings not "be tied down to . . . strict rules, either in the delineation of the offence by the prosecutors, or in the construction of it by the Judges. . . . " The Federalist No. 65. . . .

It is also noteworthy that the delegation of fact-finding by judicial and quasi-judicial bodies was hardly unknown to the Framers. Jefferson, at least, was aware that the House of Lords sometimes delegated fact-finding in impeachment trials to committees and recommended use of the same to the Senate. . . . Particularly in light of the Constitution's grant to each House of the power to "determine the Rules of its Proceedings," see Art. I, § 5, cl. 2, the existence of legislative and judicial delegation strongly suggests that the Impeachment Trial Clause was not designed to prevent employment of a factfinding committee.

In short, textual and historical evidence reveals that the Impeachment Trial Clause was not meant to bind the hands of the Senate beyond establishing a set of minimal procedures. Without identifying the exact contours of these procedures, it is sufficient to say that the Senate's use of a factfinding committee under Rule XI is entirely compatible with the Constitution's command that the Senate "try all impeachments." Petitioner's challenge to his conviction must therefore fail.[4] . . .

JUSTICE SOUTER, concurring in the judgment.

. . . If the Senate were to act in a manner seriously threatening the integrity of its results, convicting, say, upon a coin-toss, or upon a summary determination that an officer of the United States was simply " 'a bad guy,' " judicial interference might well be appropriate. In such circumstances, the Senate's action might be so far beyond the scope of its constitutional authority, and the consequent impact on the Republic so great, as to merit a judicial response despite the prudential concerns that would ordinarily counsel silence. . . .

Notes

If the President, contesting his impeachment, claims that the allegations against him do not constitute "high crimes and misdemeanors, should that issue be subject to judicial review?" What if the President claims that the actions of the House or Senate were procedurally defective—e.g., his pleading of the Fifth Amendment was improperly found to be evidence of guilt; or that biased Senators did not recuse themselves; or other Senators only heard parts of the trial.

What if the President claims that, in the middle of the lengthy impeachment process, there was an intervening federal election, and the two Houses did not begin the process anew after the election? There was an intervening election between the House's impeachment of President Clinton and his trial and acquittal by the Senate. The President ultimately raised no legal motion based on this fact. In several instances the Senate has removed federal judges who were impeached by the House selected by the prior election.

---

4. . . . Justice Souter states that the Court ought not to entertain petitioner's constitutional claim because "[i]t seems fair to conclude," that the Senate tried him. . . . At best, this approach offers only the illusion of deference and respect by substituting impressionistic assessment for constitutional analysis.

Chapter 2

THE DOCTRINE OF IMPLIED POWERS

M'CULLOCH v. MARYLAND
17 U.S. (4 Wheat.) 316, 4 L.Ed. 579 (1819).

[In 1816 Congress incorporated the Second Bank of the United States. Maryland enacted a tax on any bank not chartered by the state, but branches of the Bank of the United States continued to operate and issue bank notes in Maryland, without payment of the tax; the federal government argued that since the Bank was a federal instrumentality it need not pay the state tax. The state responded that its tax was valid and that since the federal incorporation act was itself unconstitutional, the state statute did not interfere with any legitimate federal authority. Maryland sued the Bank's Baltimore cashier for the taxes and penalties. The state trial and appellate courts upheld the tax.]

MR. CHIEF JUSTICE MARSHALL delivered the opinion of the Court....

The first question made in the cause is, has Congress power to incorporate a bank? It has been truly said, that this can scarcely be considered as an open question, entirely unprejudiced by the former proceedings of the nation respecting it. The principle now contested was introduced at a very early period of our history, has been recognized by many successive legislatures, and has been acted upon by the judicial department, in cases of peculiar delicacy, as a law of undoubted obligation.

It will not be denied, that a bold and daring usurpation might be resisted, after an acquiescence still longer and more complete than this. But [the] power now contested was exercised by the first Congress elected under the present constitution. The bill for incorporating the bank of the United States did not steal upon an unsuspecting legislature, and pass unobserved. Its principle was completely understood, and was opposed with equal zeal and ability. After being resisted, first in the fair and open field of debate, and afterwards in the executive cabinet, with as much persevering talent as any measure has ever experienced, and being supported by arguments which convinced minds as pure and as intelligent as this country can boast, it became a law. The original act was permitted to expire; but a short experience of the embarrassments to which the refusal to revive it exposed the government, convinced those who were most prejudiced against the measure of its necessity, and induced the passage of the present law. It would require no ordinary share of intrepidity to assert that a measure adopted under these circumstances was a bold and plain usurpation, to which the constitution gave no countenance.

These observations belong to the cause; but they are not made under the impression that, were the question entirely new, the law would be found irreconcilable with the constitution.

In discussing this question, the counsel for the State of Maryland have deemed it of some importance, in the construction of the Constitution, to consider that instrument not as emanating from the people, but as the act of sovereign and independent states. The powers of the general government, it has been said, are delegated by the States, who alone are truly sovereign; and must be exercised in subordination to the States, who alone possess supreme domination.

It would be difficult to sustain this proposition. The Convention which framed the Constitution was, indeed, elected by the State legislatures. But the instrument, when it came from their hands was a mere proposal, without obligations, or pretensions to it. [This] instrument was submitted to the people. They acted upon it, in the only manner in which they can act safely, effectively, and wisely, on such a subject, by assembling in Convention [from which] the constitution derives its whole authority. The government proceeds directly from the people....

This government is acknowledged by all to be one of enumerated powers. The principle, that it can exercise only the powers granted to it ... is now universally admitted. But the question respecting the extent of the powers actually granted, is perpetually arising, and will probably continue to arise, as long as our system shall exist....

If any one proposition could command the universal assent of mankind, we might expect it would be this—that the government of the Union, though limited in its powers, is supreme within its sphere of action. This would seem to result necessarily from its nature. It is the government of all; its powers are delegated by all; it represents all, and acts for all. Though any one State may be willing to control its operations, no State is willing to allow others to control them. The nation, on those subjects on which it can act, must necessarily bind its component parts. But this question is not left to mere reason: the people have, in express terms, decided it, by saying, "this constitution, and the laws of the United States, which shall be made in pursuance thereof," "shall be the supreme law of the land," and by requiring that the members of the State legislatures, and the officers of the executive and judicial departments of the States, shall take the oath of fidelity to it....

Among the enumerated powers, we do not find that of establishing a bank or creating a corporation. But there is no phrase in the instrument which, like the articles of confederation, excludes incidental or implied powers; and which requires that everything granted shall be expressly and minutely described. Even the 10th amendment, which was framed for the purpose of quieting the excessive jealousies which had been excited, omits the word "expressly," and declares only that the powers "not delegated to the United States, nor prohibited to the States, are reserved to the States or to the people;" thus leaving the question, whether the particular power which may become the subject of contest has been delegated to the one government, or prohibited to the other, to depend on a fair construction of the whole instrument. The men who drew and adopted this amendment had experienced the embarrassments resulting from the insertion of this word in the articles of confederation, and probably omitted it to avoid those embarrassments. A constitution, to contain an accurate detail of all the subdivisions of which its great powers will admit, and of all the means by which they may be carried into execution, would partake of the prolixity of a legal code, and could scarcely be embraced by the human mind. It would probably never be understood by the public. Its nature, therefore, requires, that only its great outlines should be marked, its important objects designated, and the minor ingredients which compose those objects be deduced from the nature of the objects themselves. That this idea was entertained by the framers of the American constitution, is not only to be inferred from the nature of the instrument, but from the language. Why else were some of the limitations, found in the ninth section of the 1st article, introduced? It is also, in some degree, warranted by their having omitted to use any restrictive term which might prevent its receiving a fair and just interpretation. In considering this question, then, we must never forget, that it is *a constitution* we are expounding.

Although, among the enumerated powers of government, we do not find the word "bank" or "incorporation," we find the great powers to lay and collect taxes; to borrow money; to regulate commerce; to declare and conduct a war; and to raise and support armies and navies. The sword and the purse, all the external relations, and no inconsiderable portion of the industry of the nation, are entrusted to its government. It can never be pretended that these vast powers draw after them others of inferior importance, merely because they are inferior. Such an idea can never be advanced. But it may with great reason be contended, that a government, entrusted with such ample powers, on the due execution of which the happiness and prosperity of the nation so vitally depends, must also be entrusted with ample means for their execution. The power being given, it is the interest of the nation to facilitate its execution. It can never be their interest, and cannot be presumed to have been their intention, to clog and embarrass its execution by withholding the most appropriate means. Throughout this vast republic, from the St. Croix to the Gulf of Mexico, from the Atlantic to the Pacific, revenue is to be collected and expended, armies are to be marched and supported. The exigencies of the nation may require that the treasure raised in the north should be transported to the south, *that* raised in the east conveyed to the west, or that this order should be reversed. Is that construction of the constitution to be preferred which would render these operations difficult, hazardous, and expensive? Can we adopt that construction, (unless the words imperiously require it,) which would impute to the framers of that instrument, when granting these powers for the public good, the intention of impending their exercise by with-holding a choice of means? If, indeed, such be the mandate of the constitution, we have only to obey; but that instrument does not profess to enumerate the means by which the powers it confers may be executed; nor does it prohibit the creation of a corporation, if the existence of such a being be essential to the beneficial exercise of those powers. It is, then, the subject of fair inquiry, how far such means may be employed.

It is not denied, that the powers given to the government imply the ordinary means of execution. That, for example, of raising revenue, and applying it to national purposes, is admitted to imply the power of conveying money from place to place, as the exigencies of the nation may require, and of employing the usual means of conveyance. But it is denied that the government has its choice of means; or, that it may employ the most convenient means, if, to employ them, it be necessary to erect a corporation.

On what foundation does this argument rest? On this alone: The power of creating a corporation, is one appertaining to sovereignty, and is not expressly conferred on Congress. This is true. But all legislative powers appertain to sovereignty. . . .

The government which has a right to do an act, and has imposed on it the duty of performing that act, must, according to the dictates of reason, be allowed to select the means; and those who contend that it may not select any appropriate means, that one particular mode of effecting the object is excepted, take upon themselves the burden of establishing that exception.

. . . The power of creating a corporation, though appertaining to sovereignty, is not, like the power of making war, or levying taxes, or of regulating commerce, a great substantive and independent power, which cannot be implied as incidental to other powers, or used as a means of executing them. It is never the end for which other powers are exercised, but a means by which other objects are accomplished. No contributions are made to charity for the sake of an incorporation, but a corporation is created to administer the charity; no seminary of learning is instituted in order to be incorporated, but the corporate character is conferred to subserve the purposes of education. No city was ever built with the sole object of being incorporated, but is incorporated as affording the best means of being well governed. The power of creating a corporation is never used for its own sake, but for the purpose of effecting something else. No sufficient reason is, therefore, perceived, why it may not pass as incidental to those powers which are expressly given, if it be a direct mode of executing them.

But the constitution of the United States has not left the right of Congress to employ the necessary means, for the execution of the powers conferred on the government, to general reasoning. To its enumeration of powers is added that of making "all laws which shall be necessary and proper, for carrying into execution the foregoing powers, and all other powers vested by this constitution, in the government of the United States, or in any department thereof."

The counsel for the State of Maryland have urged various arguments, to prove that this clause, though in terms a grant of power, is not so in effect; but is really restrictive of the general right, which might otherwise be implied, of selecting means for executing the enumerated powers. In support of this proposition, they have found it necessary to contend, that this clause was inserted for the purpose of conferring on Congress the power of making laws. That, without it, doubts might be entertained, whether Congress could exercise its powers in the form of legislation.

But could this be the object for which it was inserted? ... After allowing each house to prescribe its own course of proceeding, after describing the manner in which a bill should become a law, would it have entered into the mind of a single member of the Convention, that an express power to make laws was necessary to enable the legislature to make them? That a legislature, endowed with legislative powers, can legislate, is a proposition too self-evident to have been questioned.

But the argument on which most reliance is placed, is drawn from the peculiar language of this clause. Congress is not empowered by it to make all laws, which may have relation to the powers conferred on the government, but such only as may be *"necessary and proper"* for carrying them into execution. The word *"necessary,"* is considered as controlling the whole sentence, and as limiting the right to pass laws for the execution of the granted powers, to such as are indispensable, and without which the power would be nugatory. That it excludes the choice of means, and leaves to Congress, in each case, that only which is most direct and simple.

Is it true, that this is the sense in which the word "necessary" is always used? Does it always import an absolute physical necessity, so strong, that one thing, to which another may be termed necessary, cannot exist without that other? ... To employ the means necessary to an end, is generally understood as employing any means calculated to produce the end, and not as being confined to those single means, without which the end would be entirely unattainable.... The word "necessary" ... has not a fixed character peculiar to itself. It admits of all degrees of comparison; and is often connected with other words, which increase or diminish the impression the mind receives of the urgency it imports. A thing may be necessary, very necessary, absolutely or indispensably necessary. To no mind would the same idea be conveyed, by these several phrases. This comment on the word is well illustrated, by the passage cited at the bar, from the 10th section of the 1st article of the constitution. It is, we think, impossible to compare the sentence which prohibits a State from laying "imposts, or duties on imports or exports, except what may be *absolutely* necessary for executing its inspection laws," with that which authorizes Congress "to make all laws which shall be necessary and proper for carrying into execution" the powers of the general government, without feeling a conviction that the convention understood itself to change materially the meaning of the word "necessary," by prefixing the word "absolutely." This word, then, like others, is used in various senses; and, in its construction, the subject, the context, the intention of the person using them, are all to be taken into view....

It must have been the intention of those who gave these powers, to insure, as far as human prudence could insure, their beneficial execution. This could not be done by confiding the choice of means to such narrow limits as not to leave it in the power of Congress to adopt any which might be appropriate, and which were conducive to the end. This provision is made in a constitution intended to endure for ages to come, and, consequently, to be adapted to the various *crises* of human affairs. To have prescribed the means by which government should, in all future time, execute its powers, would have been to change, entirely, the character of the instrument, and give it the properties of a legal code. It would have been an unwise attempt to provide, by immutable rules, for exigencies which, if foreseen at all, must have been seen dimly, and which can be best provided for as they occur.... If we apply this principle of construction to any of the powers of the government, we shall find it so pernicious in its operation that we shall be compelled to discard it....

So, with respect to the whole penal code of the United States: whence arises the power to punish in cases not prescribed by the constitution? All admit that the government may, legitimately, punish any violation of its laws; and yet, this is not among the enumerated powers of Congress. The right to enforce the observance of law, by punishing its infraction, might be denied with the more plausibility, because it is expressly given in some cases. Congress is empowered "to provide for the punishment of counterfeiting the securities and current coin of the United States," and "to define and punish piracies and felonies committed on the high seas, and offences against the law of nations." The several powers of Congress may exist, in a very imperfect state to be sure, but they may exist and be carried into execution, although no punishment should be inflicted in cases where the right to punish is not expressly given.

Take, for example, the power "to establish post offices and post roads." This power is executed by the single act of making the establishment. But, from this has been inferred the power and duty of carrying the mail along the post road, from one post office to another. And, from this implied power, has again been inferred the right to punish those who steal letters from the post office, or rob the mail. It may be said, with some plausibility, that the right to carry the mail, and to punish those who rob it, is not indispensably necessary to the establishment of a post office and post road. This right is indeed essential to the beneficial exercise of the power, but not indispensably necessary to its existence. . . .

In ascertaining the sense in which the word "necessary" is used in this clause of the constitution, we may derive some aid from that with which it is associated. Congress shall have power "to make all laws which shall be necessary and *proper* to carry into execution" the powers of the government. If the word "necessary" was used in that strict and rigorous sense for which the counsel for the State of Maryland contend, it would be an extraordinary departure from the usual course of the human mind, as exhibited in composition, to add a word, the only possible effect of which is to qualify that strict and rigorous meaning; to present to the mind the idea of some choice of means of legislation not strained and compressed within the narrow limits for which gentlemen contend.

But the argument which most conclusively demonstrates the error of the construction contended for by the counsel for the State of Maryland, is founded on the intention of the Convention, as manifested in the whole clause. To waste time and argument in proving that, without it, Congress might carry its powers into execution, would be not much less idle than to hold a lighted taper to the sun. . . . We think so for the following reasons:

1st. The clause is placed among the powers of Congress, not among the limitations on those powers.

2nd. Its terms purport to enlarge, not to diminish the powers vested in the government. It purports to be an additional power, not a restriction on those already granted. No reason has been, or can be assigned for thus concealing an intention to narrow the discretion of the national legislature under words which purport to enlarge it. The framers of the constitution wished its adoption, and well knew that it would be endangered by its strength, not by its weakness. . . .

The result of the most careful and attentive consideration bestowed upon this clause is, that if it does not enlarge, it cannot be construed to restrain the powers of Congress, or to impair the right of the legislature to exercise its best judgment in the selection of measures to carry into execution the constitutional powers of the government. If no other motive for its insertion can be suggested, a sufficient one is found in the desire to remove all doubts respecting the right to legislate on that vast mass of incidental powers which must be involved in the constitution, if that instrument be not a splendid bauble.

We admit, as all must admit, that the powers of the government are limited, and that its limits are not to be transcended. But we think the sound construction of the constitution must allow to the national legislature that discretion, with respect to the means by which the powers it confers are to be carried into execution, which will enable that body to perform the high duties assigned to it, in the manner most beneficial to the people. Let the end be legitimate, let it be within the scope of the constitution, and all means which are appropriate, which are plainly adapted to that end, which are not prohibited, but consist with the letter and spirit of the constitution, are constitutional.

That a corporation must be considered as a means not less usual, not of higher dignity, not more requiring a particular specification than other means, has been sufficiently proved. . . . Had it been intended to grant this power as one which should be distinct and independent, to be exercised in any case whatever, it would have found a place among the enumerated powers of the government. But being considered merely as a means, to be employed only for the purpose of carrying into execution the given powers, there could be no motive for particularly mentioning it . . . .

If a corporation may be employed indiscriminately with other means to carry into execution the powers of the government, no particular reason can be assigned for excluding the use of a bank, if required for its fiscal operations. To use one, must be within the discretion of Congress, if it be an appropriate mode of executing the powers of government. That it is a convenient, a useful, and essential instrument in the prosecution of its fiscal operations, is not now a subject of controversy . . . .

But, were its necessity less apparent, none can deny its being an appropriate measure; and if it is, the degree of its necessity, as has been very justly observed, is to be discussed in another place. Should Congress, in the execution of its powers, adopt measures which are prohibited by the constitution; or should Congress, under the pretext of executing its powers, pass laws for the accomplishment of objects not entrusted to the government; it would become the painful duty of this tribunal, should a case requiring such a decision come before it, to say that such an act was not the law of the land. But where the law is not prohibited, and is really calculated to effect any of the objects entrusted to the government, to undertake here to inquire into the degree of its necessity, would be to pass the line which circumscribes the judicial department, and to tread on legislative ground. This court disclaims all pretensions to such a power.

[T]he choice of means implies a right to choose a national bank in preference to State banks, and Congress alone can make the election . . . .

It being the opinion of the Court, that the act incorporating the bank is constitutional; and that the power of establishing a branch in the State of Maryland might be properly exercised by the bank itself, we proceed to inquire—

2. Whether the State of Maryland may, without violating the constitution, tax that branch? . . . [In this portion of the opinion, Marshall invalidated the state tax on the federal bank.]

We are unanimously of opinion, that the law passed by the legislature of Maryland, imposing a tax on the Bank of the United States, is unconstitutional and void....

Notes

1. The Supreme Court opinion in *McCulloch* has been called "by almost any reckoning the greatest decision John Marshall ever handed down—the one most important to the future of America, most influential in the Court's own doctrinal history, and most revealing of Marshall's unique talent for stately argument.... The Bank was viewed with special loathing by the states' rights advocates; any decision upholding its claim to exist and denying the state's claim to tax could be counted on to infuriate them.... On the other hand, it was clear to Marshall, as it has been to posterity, that a national government restricted in its powers by Maryland's narrow interpretation would be incapable of the great tasks that might lie before it." R.G. McCloskey, The American Supreme Court 66 (1960).

2. What are the historical arguments that Marshall develops to support his conclusion as to the meaning of the necessary and proper clause? The policy arguments? The arguments based on the language of the Constitution?

3. In 1803, by treaty with France, the United States purchased the Louisiana Territory, at a cost of about 2per acre, thereby securing free navigation of the Mississippi River and doubling the size of the nation. President Thomas Jefferson was an avowed strict constructionist—in fact, in 1791 Jefferson had advised President Washington that the bill incorporating the first Bank of the United States was unconstitutional, rejecting Hamilton's theory of implied powers. Consequently, after the purchase from Napoleon, Jefferson drafted a proposed Constitutional amendment empowering the Government to purchase territory. Jefferson's advisers opposed the idea because of the dangers of delaying the treaty; and Jefferson reluctantly agreed, hoping "that the good sense of our country will correct the evils of loose construction when it shall produce ill effects." Given Marshall's opinion in *McCulloch,* how would you justify federal power to purchase the Louisiana territory?

4. Agreeing with Jefferson in 1791 as to the lack of Constitutional power to incorporate a national bank, Madison unsuccessfully led the debate in Congress against Hamilton's proposal for the first Bank of the United States. Earlier, during "the Constitutional Convention Madison had proposed that Congress be empowered to 'grant charters of incorporation,' but the delegates had rejected his suggestion. In view of this action, he now believed that to assume that the power of incorporation could rightfully be implied either from the power to borrow money or from the 'necessary and proper' clause in Article I, Section 8, would be an unwarranted and dangerous precedent."[1] What could Marshall have said in response to Madison?

5. The second half of Marshall's opinion invalidated the state tax on the federally chartered bank, an instrumentality of the United States.

---

1. A. Kelly & W. Harbison, The American Constitution: Its Origins and Development 178 (4th ed. 1970).

Although the state tax was blatantly discriminatory (it did not apply at all to Maryland chartered banks), Marshall's opinion appeared to be based on broader grounds: "the power to tax involves the power to destroy." This dictum ushered in a broad doctrine of intergovernmental tax immunities—a doctrine that, unlike the first half of Marshall's opinion, has not stood the test of time. While the history and complexities of the intergovernmental tax immunity are normally considered in courses on state and local tax, we shall briefly note the basic contours of the doctrine.

It ought not be difficult to imply from our federal system of government that one sovereign may not by its laws attempt to destroy another sovereign or its instrumentalities. Thus Maryland by its tax laws may not discriminate against a Bank chartered by the United States Government. But Marshall did not appear to so limit his opinion; he said broadly that a state tax on the operations of an instrumentality of the United States, the Bank, is void. However the state could, said Marshall, impose a tax on the Bank's real property, "in common with the other real property within the State." If a nondiscriminatory property tax on property owned by a Bank chartered by the United States is valid, why is a nondiscriminatory tax on the operations of such a Bank invalid?

Congress, by statute, could invoke the necessary and proper clause to allow taxation of the operations of its instrumentalities, or to immunize the operations from even nondiscriminatory taxation. But no such statute existed in *McCulloch*. By way of illustration, 12 U.S.C.A. § 548 provides that states may levy nondiscriminatory taxes on national banks. For tax purposes, the statute provides that "a national bank shall be treated as a bank organized and existing under the laws of the State or other jurisdiction within which its principal office is located." See also *Carson v. Roane–Anderson Co.,* 342 U.S. 232, 72 S.Ct. 257, 96 L.Ed. 257 (1952)(federal government by statute can provide immunity from state taxation).

Marshall attempted to make his rigid tax immunity a one way street, because the "difference is that which always exists and always must exist, between the action of the whole on a part, and the action of a part on the whole. . . . " But this argument is not consistent with the fact that Marshall's holding was based on a theory of sovereignty. If a state cannot destroy federal sovereignty, then the federal government should not be able to destroy state sovereignty. Later cases thus made the immunity reciprocal and extended its application.

In the century following *McCulloch*, case law immunized from taxation secondary or derivative transactions relating to the performance of governmental functions. At its zenith the doctrine exempted the employees of the state and federal governments from income taxes imposed on the other. After all, an employee is an instrumentality of the employer, a tax on his salary is a tax on the instrumentality, and the power to tax is the power to destroy. *Dobbins v. Commissioners of Erie County,* 41 U.S. (16 Pet.) 435, 10 L.Ed. 1022 (1842)(state income tax on federal employee held unconstitutional); *Collector v. Day,* 78 U.S. (11 Wall.) 113, 20 L.Ed. 122 (1871)(federal income tax on state judge held unconstitutional).

Beginning in the 1930's, the Court, after realizing that whole areas of potential revenue would soon be immunized from any taxation, cut back on this doctrine. In the area of income taxes, the Court overruled prior cases and upheld the federal income tax imposed on the salaries of employees of the Port of New York Authority, *Helvering v. Gerhardt,* 304 U.S. 405, 58 S.Ct. 969, 82 L.Ed. 1427 (1938), and upheld a state income tax on an employee of a federal agency. *Graves v. New York ex rel. O'Keefe,* 306 U.S. 466, 59 S.Ct. 595, 83 L.Ed. 927 (1939). See also *Helvering v. Mountain Producers Corp.,* 303 U.S. 376, 58 S.Ct. 623, 82 L.Ed. 907 (1938)(no tax immunity to lessees of state or federal lands); *James v. Dravo Contracting Co.,* 302 U.S. 134, 58 S.Ct. 208, 82 L.Ed. 155 (1937)(no tax immunity as to state gross sales and income tax on the receipts derived by a contractor under a construction contract with the federal government).[2]

In the area of state sales and use taxes, the modern Court has held that such taxes are permissible if the *legal* incidence of the tax falls on one other than the federal government, regardless of where the economic burden may lie. Compare *Alabama v. King & Boozer,* 314 U.S. 1, 62 S.Ct. 43, 86 L.Ed. 3 (1941)(state sales tax on lumber purchased in the performance of a cost-plus contract with the federal government is valid, because the legal incidence was on the contractor, not the federal government), with *Kern–Limerick, Inc. v. Scurlock,* 347 U.S. 110, 74 S.Ct. 403, 98 L.Ed. 546 (1954)(state sales tax on tractors purchased to complete cost-plus contract with the federal government invalid because contract stated that the contractor acted as the agent of the federal government in buying the equipment).

It has long been held that property owned by the federal government is exempt from state and local property taxes, e.g., *Van Brocklin v. Anderson,* 117 U.S. 151, 6 S.Ct. 670, 29 L.Ed. 845 (1886). If the Government leases its property to private persons for business or personal use, a nondiscriminatory tax is permitted, e.g., *United States v. County of Fresno,* 429 U.S. 452, 97 S.Ct. 699, 50 L.Ed.2d 683 (1977).

For many years the Court has exempted federal obligations from state property taxes and the interest thereon from state income taxes. *Weston v. City Council of Charleston,* 27 U.S. (2 Pet.) 449, 7 L.Ed. 481 (1829); *Miller v. Milwaukee,* 272 U.S. 713, 47 S.Ct. 280, 71 L.Ed. 487 (1927). The Court similarly denied Congress the power to tax the interest on state or municipal bonds. *Pollock v. Farmers' Loan & Trust Co.,* 157 U.S. 429, 583–84, 15 S.Ct. 673, 690, 39 L.Ed. 759 (1895). Congress then codified these principles. In 1982, however, Congress removed the federal income tax exemption from interest earned on certain state and municipal bonds *unless* the bonds were issued in registered form: if the bonds were issued as bearer bonds, they would not be tax exempt. South Carolina, invoking the original jurisdiction of the Supreme Court, claimed that it violated the tenth amendment and

2. *Davis v. Michigan Department of Treasury,* 489 U.S. 803, 109 S.Ct. 1500, 103 L.Ed.2d 891 (1989) invalidated a Michigan income tax law that exempted from state taxation all retirement benefits paid by the state or its political subdivisions but levied an income tax on retirement benefits paid by other employers, including the Federal Government. The tax violated 4 U.S.C.A. § 111 (in which the United States consents to nondiscriminatory state taxation of fed-eral employees), and also violates the "principles of intergovernmental tax immunity by favoring retired state and local government employees over retired federal employees." Only Stevens, J., dissented. See also, *Barker v. Kansas,* 503 U.S. 594, 112 S.Ct. 1619, 118 L.Ed.2d 243 (1992), invalidating a Kansas income tax on federal military retirement benefits but not on the benefits received by state and local government employees.

principles of intergovernmental immunity for Congress to tax unregistered state and city bonds. In *South Carolina v. Baker,* 485 U.S. 505, 108 S.Ct. 1355, 99 L.Ed.2d 592 (1988), the Court rejected this challenge.

Justice Brennan, for the Court, overruled *Pollock*, and found no Constitutional violation because there was no evidence that Congress deprived South Carolina of "any right to participate in the national political process" or that Congress "singled out" South Carolina in a way that left it "politically isolated and powerless." In short: "the States can never tax the United States directly but can tax any private parties with whom it does business, even though the financial burden falls on the United States, as long as the tax does not discriminate against the United States or those with whom it deals.... The rule with respect to state tax immunity is essentially the same, except that at least some nondiscriminatory federal taxes can be collected directly from the States even though a parallel state tax could not be collected directly from the Federal Government."

Taxation that is destructive of state or federal sovereignty would still be held to violate the doctrine of intergovernmental immunity, but other governmental functions do not partake of any tax immunity. Thus, the federal government may tax state sales of mineral waters, *New York v. United States,* 326 U.S. 572, 66 S.Ct. 310, 90 L.Ed. 326 (1946), or municipally operated parks and beaches. *Wilmette Park District v. Campbell,* 338 U.S. 411, 70 S.Ct. 195, 94 L.Ed. 205 (1949)(federal admissions tax). The states do not have as broad a latitude in the taxation of federal activities. See, e.g., *United States v. State Tax Commission of Mississippi,* 421 U.S. 599, 95 S.Ct. 1872, 44 L.Ed.2d 404 (1975).

In general, Justice Holmes was vindicated when he said in, *Panhandle Oil Co. v. Mississippi ex rel. Knox,* 277 U.S. 218, 223, 48 S.Ct. 451, 453, 72 L.Ed. 857 (1928): "[T]he effect of certain dicta of Chief Justice Marshall ... were founded upon his often quoted proposition that the power to tax is the power to destroy. In those days it was not recognized as it is today that most of the distinctions of the law are distinctions of degree. If the state had any power it was assumed that they had all power, and that the necessary alternative was to deny it altogether. But this Court which so often has defeated the attempt to tax in certain ways can defeat an attempt to discriminate or otherwise go too far without wholly abolishing the tax. The power to tax is not the power to destroy while this Court sits." (Holmes, J., dissenting, joined by Brandeis & Stone, JJ.).[3]

---

3. *Panhandle* was overruled in *Alabama v. King & Boozer,* 314 U.S. 1, 62 S.Ct. 43, 86 L.Ed. 3 (1941). These issues are explored more fully in 1 R. Rotunda & J. Nowak, Treatise on Constitutional Law: Substance and Procedure §§ 13.1–13.11 (2d ed. 1992).

Chapter 3

STATE POWERS IN LIGHT OF THE COMMERCE CLAUSE

3-1. THE EARLY CASES

GIBBONS v. OGDEN
22 U.S. (9 Wheat.) 1, 6 L.Ed. 23 (1824).

[New York granted an exclusive license to operate a steamboat to Robert Livingston and Robert Fulton on all waters within the jurisdiction of that state. Livingston and Fulton assigned this license to Aaron Ogden, who sued to enjoin Gibbons from using any steamboats in navigating the waters within the territory of New York. Gibbons was running steamboats between New York City and Elizabethtown, New Jersey. Gibbons answered that the boats employed by him were duly enrolled and licensed to carry on the coasting trade under an Act of Congress passed Feb. 18, 1793. The state courts enjoined Gibbons, who appealed to the U.S. Supreme Court.]

Mr. [Daniel] Webster for the appellant [argued]:

By the law of New York, no one can navigate the bay of New York, the North River, the Sound, the lakes, or any of the waters of that state, by steam vessels, without a license from the grantees of New York, under penalty of forfeiture of the vessel. By the law of the neighboring states of Connecticut, no one can enter her waters with a steam vessel having such license. By the law of New Jersey, if any citizen of that state shall be restrained, under the New York law, from using steamboats between the ancient shores of New Jersey and New York, he shall be entitled to an action, for damages, in New Jersey, with treble costs against the party who thus restrains or impedes him under the law of New York! This act of New Jersey is called an act of retortion against the illegal and oppressive legislation of New York; and seems to be defended on those grounds of public law which justify reprisals between independent states.

It would hardly be contended that all these acts were consistent with the laws and constitution of the United States. If there were no power in the general government to control this extreme belligerent legislation of the states, the powers of the government were essentially deficient in a most important and interesting particular....

Mr. [Thomas] Oakley, for the respondent [answered]:

[T]he state has [with Congress] the concurrent power also to regulate and control [commerce] in all cases where its regulations do not actually conflict with those of Congress; ... if Congress deems such regulations to be injurious, it may control them by express provisions, operating directly upon the case....

MR. CHIEF JUSTICE MARSHALL delivered the opinion of the Court, and after stating the case, proceeded as follows:

The appellant contends that this decree is erroneous, because the laws which purport to give the exclusive privilege it sustains, are repugnant to the constitution and laws of the United States.

They are said to be repugnant:

1st. To that clause in the constitution which authorizes Congress to regulate commerce.

2d. To that which authorizes Congress to promote the progress of science and useful arts....

The words are: "Congress shall have power to regulate commerce with foreign nations, and among the several states, and with the Indian tribes."

The subject to be regulated is commerce; and our constitution being, as was aptly said at the bar, one of enumeration, and not of definition, to ascertain the extent of the power it becomes necessary to settle the meaning of the word. The counsel for the appellee would limit it to traffic, to buying and selling, or the interchange of commodities, and do not admit that it comprehends navigation. This would restrict a general term, applicable to many objects, to one of its significations. Commerce, undoubtedly, is traffic, but it is something more; it is intercourse. It describes the commercial intercourse between nations, and parts of nations, in all its branches, and is regulated by prescribing rules for carrying on that intercourse. The mind can scarcely conceive a system for regulating commerce between nations, which shall exclude all laws concerning navigation, which shall be silent on the admission of the vessels of the one nation into the ports of the other, and be confined to prescribing rules for the conduct of individuals, in the actual employment of buying and selling, or of barter.

If commerce does not include navigation, the government of the Union has no direct power over that subject, and can make no law prescribing what shall constitute American vessels, or requiring that they shall be navigated by American seamen. Yet this power has been exercised from the commencement of the government, has been exercised with the consent of all, and has been understood by all to be a commercial regulation. All America understands, and has uniformly understood, the word "commerce" to comprehend navigation. It was so understood, and must have been so understood, when the constitution was framed. The power over commerce, including navigation, was one of the primary objects for which the people of America adopted their government, and must have been contemplated in forming it. The convention must have used the word in that sense; because all have understood it in that sense, and the attempt to restrict it comes too late.

If the opinion that "commerce" as the word is used in the constitution, comprehends navigation also, requires any additional confirmation, that additional confirmation is, we think, furnished by the words of the instrument itself.... The 9th section of the 1st article declares that "no preference shall be given, by any regulation of commerce or revenue, to the ports of one state over those of another." This clause cannot be understood as applicable to those laws only which are passed for the purposes of revenue, because it is expressly applied to commercial regulations; and the most obvious preference which can be given to one port over another, in regulating commerce, relates to navigation. But the subsequent part of the sentence is still more explicit. It is, "nor shall vessels bound to or from one state, be obliged to enter, clear, or pay duties, in another." These words have a direct reference to navigation.

The universally acknowledged power of the government to impose embargoes, must also be considered as showing that all America is united in that construction which comprehends navigation in the word commerce.... The word used in the constitution, then, comprehends, and has been always understood to comprehend, navigation within its meaning; and a power to regulate navigation is as expressly granted as if that term had been added to the word "commerce."

To what commerce does this power extend? The constitution informs us, to commerce "with foreign nations, and among the several states, and with the Indian tribes."

It has, we believe, been universally admitted that these words comprehend every species of commercial intercourse between the United States and foreign nations. No sort of trade can be carried on between this country and any other, to which this power does not extend. It has been truly said, that commerce, as the word is used in the constitution, is a unit, every part of which is indicated by the term.

If this be the admitted meaning of the word, in its application to foreign nations, it must carry the same meaning throughout the sentence, and remain a unit, unless there be some plain intelligible cause which alters it.

The subject to which the power is next applied, is to commerce "among the several states." The word "among" means intermingled with. A thing which is among others, is intermingled with them. Commerce among the states cannot stop at the external boundary line of each state, but may be introduced into the interior. It is not intended to say that these words comprehend that commerce which is completely internal, which is carried on between man and man in a state, or between different parts of the same state, and which does not extend to or affect other states. Such a power would be inconvenient, and is certainly unnecessary.

Comprehensive as the word "among" is, it may very properly be restricted to that commerce which concerns more states than one. The phrase is not one which would probably have been selected to indicate the completely interior traffic of a state, because it is not an apt phrase for that purpose; and the enumeration of the particular classes of commerce to which the power was to be extended, would not have been made had the intention been to extend the power to every description. The enumeration presupposes something not enumerated; and that something, if we regard the language or the subject of the sentence, must be the exclusively internal commerce of a state. The genius and character of the whole government seem to be, that its action is to be applied to all the external concerns of the nation, and to those internal concerns which affect the states generally; but not to those which are completely within a particular state, which do not affect other states, and with which it is not necessary to interfere, for the purpose of executing some of the general powers of the government. The completely internal commerce of a state, then, may be considered as reserved for the state itself.

But, in regulating commerce with foreign nations, the power of Congress does not stop at the jurisdictional lines of the several states. It would be a very useless power if it could not pass those lines. The commerce of the United States with foreign nations, is that of the whole United States. Every district has a right to participate in it. The deep streams which penetrate our country in every direction, pass through the interior of almost every state in the Union, and furnish the means of exercising this right. If Congress has the power to regulate it, that power must be exercised whenever the subject exists. If it exists within the states, if a foreign voyage may commence or terminate at a port within a state, then the power of Congress may be exercised within a state. . . .

We are now arrived at the inquiry, What is this power? It is the power to regulate; that is, to prescribe the rule by which commerce is to be governed. This power, like all others vested in Congress, is complete in itself, may be exercised to its utmost extent, and acknowledges no limitations, other than are prescribed in the constitution. These are expressed in plain terms, and do not affect the questions which arise in this case, or which have been discussed at the bar. If, as has always been understood, the sovereignty of Congress, though limited to specified objects, is plenary as to those objects, the power over commerce with foreign nations, and among the several States, is vested in Congress as absolutely as it would be in a single government, having in its constitution the same restrictions on the exercise of the power as are found in the constitution of the United States. The wisdom and the discretion of Congress, their identity with the people, and the influence which their constituents possess at election, are, in this, as in many other instances, as that, for example, of declaring war, the sole restraints on which they have relied, to secure them from its abuse. They are the restraints on which the people must often rely solely, in all representative governments.

The power of Congress, then, comprehends navigation within the limits of every state in the Union; so far as that navigation may be, in any manner, connected with "commerce with foreign nations, or among the several states, or with the Indian tribes." It may, of consequence, pass the jurisdictional line of New York, and act upon the very waters to which the prohibition now under consideration applies.

But it has been urged with great earnestness, that although the power of Congress to regulate commerce with foreign nations, and among the several states, be co-extensive with the subject itself, and have no other limits than are prescribed in the constitution, yet the states may severally exercise the same power within their respective jurisdictions. In support of this argument, it is said that they possessed it as an inseparable attribute of sovereignty, before the formation of the constitution, and still retain it, except so far as they have surrendered it by that instrument; that this principle results from the nature of the government, and is secured by the tenth amendment; that an affirmative grant of power is not exclusive, unless in its own nature it be such that the continued exercise of it by the former possessor is inconsistent with the grant, and that this is not of that description.

The appellant, conceding these postulates, except the last, contends that full power to regulate a particular subject, implies the whole power, and leaves no residuum; that a grant of the whole is incompatible with the existence of a right in another to any part of it.

Both parties have appealed to the constitution, to legislative acts, and judicial decisions; and have drawn arguments from all these sources to support and illustrate the propositions they respectively maintain.

The grant of the power to lay and collect taxes is, like the power to regulate commerce, made in general terms, and has never been understood to interfere with the exercise of the same power by the states; and hence has been drawn an argument which has been applied to the question under consideration. But the two grants are not, it is conceived, similar in their terms or their nature. Although many of the powers formerly exercised by the states, are transferred to the government of the Union, yet the state governments remain, and constitute a most important part of our system. The power of taxation is indispensable to their existence, and is a power which in its own nature, is capable of residing in, and being exercised by, different authorities at the same time.... In imposing taxes for state purposes, they are not doing what Congress is empowered to do. Congress is not empowered to tax for those purposes which are within the exclusive province of the states. When, then, each government exercises the power of taxation, neither is exercising the power of the other. But, when a state proceeds to regulate commerce with foreign nations, or among the several states, it is exercising the very power that is granted to Congress, and is doing the very thing which Congress is authorized to do. There is no analogy, then, between the power of taxation and the power of regulating commerce.

In discussing the question, whether this power is still in the states, in the case under consideration, we may dismiss from it the inquiry, whether it is surrendered by the mere grant to Congress, or is retained until Congress shall exercise the power. We may dismiss that inquiry, because it has been exercised, and the regulations which Congress deemed it proper to make, are now in full operation. The sole question is, can a state regulate commerce with foreign nations and among the state, while Congress is regulating it? . . .

[T]he inspection laws [of Art. 1, § 10, cl. 2] are said to be regulations of commerce, and are certainly recognized in the constitution, as being passed in the exercise of a power remaining with the states. That inspection laws may have a remote and considerable influence on commerce, will not be denied; but that a power to regulate commerce is the source from which the right to pass them is derived, cannot be admitted. The objects of inspection laws is to improve the quality of articles produced by the labor of the country; to fit them for exportation; or it may be, for domestic use. They act upon the subject before it becomes an article of foreign commerce, or of commerce among the states, and prepare it for that purpose. They form a portion of that immense mass of legislation which embraces everything within the territory of a state not surrendered to the general government; all which can be most advantageously exercised by the states themselves. Inspection laws, quarantine laws, health laws of every description, as well as laws for regulating the internal commerce of a state, and those which respect turnpike-roads, ferries, etc., are component parts of this mass.

. . . If Congress license vessels to sail from one port to another, in the same State, the act is supposed to be, necessarily, incidental to the power expressly granted to Congress, and implies no claim of a direct power to regulate the purely internal commerce of a State, or to act directly on its system of police. So, if a State, in passing laws on subjects acknowledged to be within its control, and with a view to those subjects, shall adopt a measure of the same character with one which Congress may adopt, it does not derive its authority from the particular power which has been granted, but from some other, which remains with the State, and may be executed by the same means. All experience shows, that the same measures, or measures scarcely distinguishable from each other, may flow from distinct powers; but this does not prove that the powers themselves are identical. . . .

It has been contended by the counsel for the appellant, that, as the word "to regulate" implies in its nature, full power over the thing to be regulated, it excludes, necessarily, the action of all others that would perform the same operation on the same thing. That regulation is designed for the entire result, applying to those parts which remain as they were, as well as to those which are altered. It produces a uniform whole, which is as much disturbed and deranged by changing what the regulating power designs to leave untouched, as that on which it has operated.

There is great force in this argument, and the court is not satisfied that it has been refuted.

Since, however, in exercising the power of regulating their own purely internal affairs, whether of trading or police, the states may sometimes enact laws, the validity of which depends on their interfering with, and being contrary to, an act of Congress passed in pursuance of the constitution, the court will enter upon the inquiry, whether the laws of New York, as expounded by the highest tribunal of that state, have, in their application to this case, come into collision with an act of Congress, and deprived a citizen of a right to which that act entitles him. Should this collision exist, it will be immaterial whether those laws were passed in virtue of a concurrent power "to regulate commerce with foreign nations and among the several states," or in virtue of a power to regulate their domestic trade and police. In one case and the other, the acts of New York must yield to the law of Congress; and the decision sustaining the privilege they confer, against a right given by a law of the Union, must be erroneous.

. . . In the exercise of this power [over commerce] Congress has passed "an act for enrolling or licensing ships or vessels to be employed in the coasting trade and fisheries, and for regulating the same." The counsel for the respondent contend that this act does not give the right to sail from port to port, but confines itself to regulating a preexisting right, so far only as to confer certain privileges on enrolled and licensed vessels in its exercise.

It will at once occur, that, when a legislature attaches certain privileges and exemptions to the exercise of a right over which its control is absolute, the law must imply a power to exercise the right. The privileges are gone, if the right itself be annihilated. It would be contrary to all reason, and to the course of human affairs, to say that a state is unable to strip a vessel of the particular privileges attendant on the exercise of a right, and yet may annul the right itself; that the state of New York cannot prevent [a federally] enrolled and licensed vessel, proceeding from Elizabethtown, in New Jersey, to New York, from enjoying, in her course, and on her entrance into port, all the privileges conferred by the act of Congress; but can shut her up in her own port, and prohibit altogether her entering the waters and ports of another state. To the court it seems very clear, that the whole act on the subject of the coasting trade, according to those principles which govern the construction of statutes, implies, unequivocally, an authority to licensed vessels to carry on the coasting trade.

A coasting vessel employed in the transportation of passengers, is as much a portion of the American marine as one employed in the transportation of a cargo; and no reason is perceived why such vessel should be withdrawn from the regulating power of that government, which has been thought best fitted for the purpose generally. The provisions of the law respecting native seamen, and respecting ownership, are as applicable to vessels carrying men as to vessels carrying manufacturers; and no reason is perceived why the power over the subject should not be placed in the same hands. . . .

[The Court then decreed that "so much of the several laws of the State of New York, as prohibits vessels, licensed according to the laws of the United States, from navigating the waters of the State of New York, by means of fire or steam, is repugnant to the" United States Constitution and void, because these state laws conflicted with the privileges granted by the federal licensing law.]

MR. JUSTICE JOHNSON [concurring].

[The commerce] power must be exclusive; it can reside in but one potentate; and hence, the grant of this power [to Congress] carries with it the whole subject, leaving nothing for the State to act upon. . . . If there was any one object riding over every other in the adoption of the constitution, it was to keep the commercial intercourse among the States free from all invidious and partial restraints. And I cannot overcome the conviction, that if the [federal] licensing act was repealed to-morrow, the rights of the appellant to a reversal of the decision complained of, would be as strong as it is under this license. . . .

Notes

1. Does Marshall hold that the power of Congress in the area of interstate commerce is exclusive? Does he present arguments in favor of the exclusivity of the commerce power in Congress?

Does the Constitution itself grant to the states a "police power"? Professor (later Justice) Frankfurter said that the "police power" has "eluded attempts at definition." F. Frankfurter, The Commerce Clause under Marshall, Taney, & Waite 27 (1937). Is the term "police power" analytically helpful in deciding commerce clause questions?

Marshall concludes that the New York law is unconstitutional. Which constitutional provision justifies this conclusion?

2. Justice Johnson argues (1) that Congress' power over interstate commerce "must be exclusive" and (2) that "if the licensing act was repealed to-morrow, the rights of the appellant to a reversal of the decision complained of, would be as strong as it is under this license." In order to agree with Johnson's second statement, is it necessary to agree with the first?

3. This Court opinion striking the state monopoly resulted in increased competition and, not surprisingly, a substantial decrease in steamboat fares. 1 C. Warren, The Supreme Court in United States History 615 (Rev. ed. 1926).

4. In *Willson v. Black–Bird Creek Marsh Co.,* 27 U.S. (2 Pet.) 245, 7 L.Ed. 412 (1829) Delaware authorized the Black Bird Creek Marsh Co. to construct a dam across the creek. The defendants were the owners of a sloop that was regularly licensed and enrolled according to the federal navigation laws. The sloop broke the dam and plaintiffs sued for $20,000 damages. Defendants' attorney, Mr. Coxe, argued that if "Delaware has no right to

restrain particular vessels from using her navigable streams [and the Black Bird Creek was such a navigable stream, 'in the nature of a highway'], she cannot stop navigation of those streams." Mr. Wirt, for the plaintiffs below, responded:

> While the waters of the United States belong to the whole people of the nation, this creek continued subject to the power of the state in whose territory it rises. It is one of those sluggish reptile streams, that do not run but creep, and which, wherever it passes, spreads its venom, and destroys the health of all those who inhabit its marshes; and can it be asserted, that a law authorizing the erection of a dam, and the formation of banks which will draw off the pestilence, and give to those who have before suffered from disease, health and vigour, is unconstitutional?

Chief Justice Marshall, for a unanimous Court, held:

> We do not think that the act empowering the Black Bird Creek Marsh Company to place a dam across the creek, can, under all the circumstances of the case, be considered as repugnant to the power to regulate commerce in its dormant state, or as being in conflict with any law passed on the subject.

The New York statute in *Gibbons* resulted in keeping out Gibbons' boat, even though that boat was duly enrolled and licensed under federal law. The Delaware statute in *Willson* had the same result, yet that statute was not invalidated. Why? If the Delaware statute is justified by health and safety concerns, can New York argue that the purpose of its steamboat monopoly was to limit the number of steamboats to insure that those that are allowed to carry passengers are truly safe?

5. In a series of cases the Court divided on whether certain state laws flowed from the state police powers or from Congress' commerce powers. *Mayor, Aldermen and Commonalty of City of New York v. Miln,* 36 U.S. (11 Pet.) 102, 9 L.Ed. 648 (1837) upheld a report of information on out-of-state passengers arriving by ship in New York as an exercise of police power. Barbour, J., for the majority, said the police power included the power "to provide precautionary measures against the moral pestilence of paupers, vagabonds, and possibly convicts.... " Story, J., dissented because the act regulated interstate commerce. *The License Cases,* 46 U.S. (5 How.) 504, 12 L.Ed. 256 (1847)(consolidating three cases) upheld state laws that required licenses for the sale of liquor imported from out of state, but the Justices could not agree on the reasoning: Taney, C.J., wrote one opinion for the three cases; McLean, J., wrote three opinions for the three cases; Catron, J., wrote two opinions and Daniel, Woodbury, and Grier, JJ., wrote one opinion each. *The Passenger Cases* (Smith v. Turner), 48 U.S. (7 How.) 283, 12 L.Ed. 702 (1849) invalidated (5 to 4) state statutes taxing alien passengers arriving in those states' ports. Once again there was no majority opinion, and the Justices wrote eight separate opinions.

COOLEY v. BOARD OF WARDENS

53 U.S. (12 How.) 299, 13 L.Ed. 996 (1851).

MR. JUSTICE CURTIS delivered the opinion of the Court:

[The 29th section of the Act passed on March 2, 1803, by the Pennsylvania Legislature required, in general, that every ship entering or leaving the port of Philadelphia engage a local pilot or suffer monetary penalties. Cooley did not engage a pilot as required by the law, but claimed that he was exempt because the state law violated various constitutional provisions including Congress' power under the Commerce Clause.]

That the power to regulate commerce includes the regulation of navigation, we consider settled. And when we look to the nature of the service performed by pilots, to the relations which that service and its compensations bear to navigation between the several States, and between the ports of the United States, and foreign countries, we are brought to the conclusion, that the regulation of the qualifications of pilots, of the modes and times of offering and rendering their services, of the responsibilities which shall rest upon them, of the powers they shall possess, of the compensation they may demand, and of the penalties by which their rights and duties may be enforced, do constitute regulations of navigation, and consequently of commerce, within the just meaning of this clause of the Constitution.

The power to regulate navigation is the power to prescribe rules in conformity with which navigation must be carried on. It extends to the persons who conduct it, as well as to the instruments used. Accordingly, the first Congress assembled under the Constitution passed laws, requiring the masters of ships and vessels of the United States to be citizens of the United States, and established many rules for the government and regulation of officers and seamen. 1 Stat. at Large, 55, 131. These have been from time to time added to and changed, and we are not aware that their validity has been questioned.

. . . Conflicts between the laws of neighboring states, and discriminations favorable or adverse to commerce with particular foreign nations, might be created by state laws regulating pilotage, deeply affecting that equality of commercial rights, and that freedom from state interference, which those who formed the Constitution were so anxious to secure, and which the experience of more than half a century has taught us to value so highly. . . . The Act of 1789 contains a clear legislative exposition of the Constitution by the first Congress, to the effect that the power to regulate pilots was conferred on Congress by the Constitution. . . .

It becomes necessary, therefore, to consider whether this law of Pennsylvania, being a regulation of commerce, is valid.

The Act of Congress of the 7th of August, 1789, sec. 4, is as follows:

That all pilots in the bays, inlets, rivers, harbors, and ports of the United States, shall continue to be regulated in conformity with the existing laws of the States, respectively, wherein such pilots may be, or with such laws as the States may respectively hereafter enact for the purpose, until further legislative provision shall be made by Congress.

If the law of Pennsylvania, now in question, had been in existence at the date of this Act of Congress, we might hold it to have been adopted by Congress, and thus made a law of the United States, and so valid. Because this Act does, in effect, give the force of an Act of Congress, to the then existing state laws on this subject, so long as they should continue unrepealed by the State which enacted them.

But the law on which these actions are founded was not enacted till 1803. What effect, then, can be attributed to so much of the Act of 1789 as declares that pilots shall continue to be regulated in conformity "with such laws as the States may respectively hereafter enact for the purpose, until further legislative provision shall be made by Congress?"

If the States were divested of the power to legislate on this subject by the grant of the commercial power to Congress, it is plain this Act could not confer upon them power thus to legislate. If the Constitution excluded the States from making any law regulating commerce, certainly Congress cannot regrant, or in any manner reconvey to the States that power. And yet this Act of 1789 gives its sanction only to laws enacted by the States. This necessarily implies a constitutional power to legislate; for only a rule created by the sovereign power of a state acting in its legislative capacity, can be deemed a law, enacted by a state; and if the State has so limited its sovereign power that it no longer extends to a particular subject, manifestly it cannot, in any proper sense, be said to enact laws thereon. Entertaining these views we are brought directly and unavoidably to the consideration of the question, whether the grant of the commercial power to Congress, did per se deprive the States of all power to regulate pilots. This question has never been decided by this court, nor, in our judgment, has any case depending upon all the considerations which must govern this one, come before this court. The grant of commercial power to Congress does not contain any terms which expressly exclude the States from exercising an authority over its subject matter. If they are excluded it must be because the nature of the power, thus granted to Congress, requires that a similar authority should not exist in the States. If it were conceded on the one side, that the nature of this power, like that to legislate for the District of Columbia, is absolutely and totally repugnant to the existence of similar power in the States, probably no one would deny that the grant of the power to Congress, as effectually and perfectly excludes the States from all future legislation on the subject, as if express words had been used to exclude them. And on the other hand, if it were admitted that the existence of this power in Congress, like the power of taxation, is compatible with the existence of a similar power in the States, then it would be in conformity with the contemporary exposition of the Constitution (Federalist, No. 32), and with the judicial construction, given from time to time by this court, after the most deliberate consideration, to hold that the mere grant of such a power to Congress, did not imply a prohibition on the States to exercise the same power; that it is not the mere existence of such a power, but its exercise by Congress, which may be incompatible with the exercise of the same power by the States, and that the States may legislate in the absence of congressional regulations.

The diversities of opinion, therefore, which have existed on this subject, have arisen from the different views taken of the nature of this power. But when the nature of a power like this is spoken of, when it is said that the nature of the power requires that it should be exercised exclusively by Congress, it must be intended to refer to the subjects of that power, and to say they are of such a nature as to require exclusive legislation by Congress. Now, the power to regulate commerce, embraces a vast field, containing not only many, but exceedingly various subjects, quite unlike in their nature; some imperatively demanding a single uniform rule, operating equally on the commerce of the United States in every port; and some, like the subject now in question, as imperatively demanding that diversity, which alone can meet the local necessities of navigation.

Either absolutely to affirm, or deny, that the nature of this power requires exclusive legislation by Congress, is to lose sight of the nature of the subjects of this power, and to assert concerning all of them, what is really applicable but to a part. Whatever subjects of this power are in their nature national, or admit only of one uniform system, or plan of regulation, may justly be said to be of such a nature as to require exclusive legislation by Congress. That this cannot be affirmed of laws for the regulation of pilots and pilotage is plain. The Act of 1789 contains a clear and authoritative declaration by the first Congress, that the nature of this subject is such, that until Congress should find it necessary to exert its power, it should be left to the legislation of the States; that it is local and not national; that it is likely to be the best provided for, not by one system, or plan of regulations, but by as many as the legislative discretion of the several States should deem applicable to the local peculiarities of the ports within their limits.

Viewed in this light, so much of this Act of 1789 as declares that pilots shall continue to be regulated "by such laws as the States may respectively hereafter enact for that purpose," instead of being held to be inoperative, as an attempt to confer on the States a power to legislate, of which the Constitution had deprived them, is allowed an appropriate and important signification. It manifests the understanding of Congress, at the outset of the government, that the nature of this subject is not such as to require its exclusive legislation. The practice of the States, and of the national government, has been in conformity with this declaration, from the origin of the national government to this time; and the nature of the subject, when examined, is such as to leave no doubt of the superior fitness and propriety, not to say the absolute necessity, of different systems of regulation, drawn from local knowledge and experience, and conformed to local wants. How then, can we say, that by the mere grant of power to regulate commerce, the States are deprived of all the power to legislate on this subject, because from the nature of the power the legislation of Congress must be exclusive. This would be to affirm that the nature of the power is in any case, something different from the nature of the subject to which, in such case, the power extends, and that the nature of the power necessarily demands, in all cases, exclusive legislation by Congress, while the nature of one of the subjects of that power, not only does not require such exclusive legislation, but may be best provided for by many different systems enacted by the States, in conformity with the circumstances of the ports within their limits. In construing an instrument designed for the formation of a government, and in determining the extent of one of its important grants of power to legislate, we can make no such distinction between the nature of the power and the nature of the subject on which that power was intended practically to operate, nor consider the grant more extensive by affirming of the power, what is not true of its subject now in question.

It is the opinion of a majority of the court that the mere grant to Congress of the power to regulate commerce, did not deprive the States of power to regulate pilots, and that although Congress has legislated on this subject, its legislation manifests an intention, with a single exception, not to regulate this subject, but to leave its regulation to the several States. To these precise questions, which are all we are called on to decide, this opinion must be understood to be confined. It does not extend to the question what other subjects, under the commercial power, are within the exclusive control of Congress, or may be regulated by the States in the absence of all congressional legislation; nor to the general question how far any regulation of a subject by Congress may be deemed to operate as an exclusion of all legislation by the States upon the same subject. We decide the precise questions before us, upon what we deem sound principles, applicable to this particular subject in the state in which the legislation of Congress has left it. We go no farther.

We have not adverted to the practical consequences of holding that the States possess no power to legislate for the regulation of pilots, though in our apprehension these would be of the most serious importance. For more than sixty years this subject has been acted on by the States, and the systems of some of them created and of others essentially modified during that period. To hold that pilotage fees and penalties demanded and received during that time, have been illegally exacted, under color of void laws, would work an amount of mischief which a clear conviction of constitutional duty, if entertained, must force us to occasion, but which could be viewed by no just mind without deep regret. Nor would the mischief be limited to the past. If Congress were now to pass a law adopting the existing state laws, if enacted without authority, and in violation of the Constitution, it would seem to us to be a new and questionable mode of legislation.

If the grant of commercial power in the Constitution has deprived the States of all power to legislate for the regulation of pilots, if their laws on this subject are mere usurpations upon the exclusive power of the general government, and utterly void, it may be doubted whether Congress could, with propriety, recognize them as laws, and adopt them as its own acts; and how are the Legislatures of the States to proceed in the future, to watch over and amend these laws, as the progressive wants of a growing commerce will require, when the members of those Legislatures are made aware that they cannot legislate on this subject without violating the oaths they have taken to support the Constitution of the United States?

We are of the opinion that this state law was enacted by virtue of a power, residing in the State to legislate; that it is not in conflict with any law of Congress; that it does not interfere with any system which Congress has established by making regulations, or by intentionally leaving individuals to their own unrestricted action; that this law is therefore valid, and the judgment of the Supreme Court of Pennsylvania in each case must be affirmed.

MESSRS. JUSTICES MCLEAN and WAYNE dissented. MR. JUSTICE DANIEL, although he concurred in the judgment of the court, yet dissented from its reasoning.[1]

Notes

1. Justice Curtis' opinion for the Court created what has been called the Cooley Rule of Selected Exclusiveness. "This ingenious disengagement from the horns of the dilemma was not entirely satisfying to those, like [Chief Justice] Taney himself, who had argued for full concurrent state power in the commercial field, nor to those all-out nationalists, like Justice McLean, who had insisted that the states must leave commerce strictly alone. But neither localist nor nationalist could claim that the Court had wholly yielded to the other; each could justifiably feel that the announced doctrine in some part embodied his views." Robert McCloskey, The American Supreme Court 88 (1960).

2. *Henderson v. Mayor of City of New York,* 92 U.S. (2 Otto) 259, 23 L.Ed. 543 (1876) invalidated a state law requiring the shipmaster of every ship arriving in New York to pay a fee or give bond for every passenger. New York argued that the "act under consideration is not a regulation of commerce. It is a police regulation to protect the State from foreign paupers." Miller, J., for the Court answered: "Nothing is gained in the argument by calling it the police power. Very many statutes, when the authority on which their enactments rest is examined, may be referred to different

---

1. Justice McKinley, who was riding circuit, did not participate in this decision. The official reports do not indicate this fact because that was not the practice of the times. Curtis' correspondence shows that only eight justices participated in *Cooley.* John Frank, Justice Daniel Dissenting: A Biography of Peter V. Daniel, 1784–1860 (1964), at pp. 196, 197, 313 n. 26 (referring to letter from Curtis to George Ticknor), & 315 n. 8. Perhaps Chief Justice Taney joined the *Curtis* opinion because his vote was necessary to create a majority opinion of the Court. I am indebted to Professor Charles Alan Wright for bringing these facts to my attention.

sources of power, and supported equally well under any of them.... It must occur very often that the shading which marks the line between one class of legislation and another is ... not easily distinguishable. [W]henever the statute of a State invades the legislation which belongs exclusively to the Congress of the United States, it is void, no matter under what class of powers it may fall, or how closely allied to powers conceded to belong to the States."

3. In *Pennsylvania v. Wheeling & Belmont Bridge Co.,* 54 U.S. (13 How.) 518, 14 L.Ed. 249 (1852)(I), Pennsylvania sought an order abating a bridge over the Ohio River. Virginia had authorized construction of the bridge. The Court found that the bridge obstructed the navigation of the river and therefore ordered that it be elevated. Later that year, Congress passed a statute declaring that the bridge was a lawful structure in its present position and elevation, that it is a post road for the passage of the U.S. mails, and that vessels navigating on the river should not interfere with the elevation of the bridge. The Supreme Court held that the congressional statute was constitutional in *Pennsylvania v. Wheeling & Belmont Bridge Co.,* 59 U.S. (18 How.) 421, 15 L.Ed. 435 (1856)(II). McLean, J., who wrote the majority opinion in the first case dissented in the second. And Taney, C.J., who dissented in the first case joined the majority in the second.

Are the cases consistent? If the bridge is an unlawful obstruction of interstate navigation, how can a federal statute declaring the opposite be constitutional under the commerce clause? Can Congress, by statute, reverse a Supreme Court decision holding that a state law violated the commerce clause?

Leisy v. Hardin, 135 U.S. 100, 10 S.Ct. 681, 34 L.Ed. 128 (1890) applied the *Cooley* rule to invalidate an Iowa statute prohibiting the sale of intoxicating liquor as applied to imported liquor in the original package. The majority said that the out-of-state resident had a right to export beer into Iowa and sell it. Congress then enacted the Wilson Act, which provided that intoxicating liquors transported into any state are subject to the laws of that state "enacted in the exercise of its police power," and even though sold in the original package. The Court held this statute constitutional. *In re Rahrer,* 140 U.S. 545, 11 S.Ct. 865, 35 L.Ed. 572 (1891). Note that the federal statute had the effect of banning the liquor, which *Leisy* had held could not be banned. But *Cooley* said: "If the Constitution excluded the States from making any law regulating commerce, certainly Congress cannot regrant, or in any manner reconvey to the States that power."

4. Justice Curtis in *Cooley* said that Congress could adopt the past laws of a state but not delegate to the state the right to make such laws in the future. Why not?

Compare *United States v. Sharpnack,* 355 U.S. 286, 78 S.Ct. 291, 2 L.Ed.2d 282 (1958). In the Assimilative Crimes Act of 1948 Congress made applicable to federal enclaves (e.g., an Air Force Base) subsequently enacted criminal law of the state in which the enclave is situated. Sharpnack was charged with certain sex acts that were criminal under Texas law, where the Air Force Base was located, but not under federal law (except for the federal law incorporating by reference the state law subsequently enacted). Burton, J., for the Court, held:

Having the power to assimilate the state laws, Congress obviously has like power to renew such assimilation annually or daily in order to keep the laws in the enclaves current with those in the States. . . . Rather than being a delegation by Congress of its legislative authority to the States, it is a deliberate continuing adoption by Congress for federal enclaves of such unpre-empted offenses and punishments as shall have been already put in effect by the respective States for their own government.

Douglas, J., joined by Black, J., dissented: "[One] is entitled to the considered judgment of Congress whether the law applied to him fits the federal policy."

5. While the *Cooley* Rule of Selected Exclusiveness was an important analytical tool more useful than Marshall's origin of power test, it still left many problems unresolved. For example, what if a state pilotage law on its face or as applied discriminated against interstate commerce? What if it placed a great burden on interstate commerce arguably out of proportion to the alleged safety benefits? How does one determine which subjects are "in their nature national"? Which subjects are "local"?

Later decisions attempting to apply *Cooley,* invalidated state regulations that "directly" burdened interstate commerce, but not those that "indirectly" burdened such commerce. See, e.g., *Di Santo v. Pennsylvania,* 273 U.S. 34, 47 S.Ct. 267, 71 L.Ed. 524 (1927), holding that a state license law "directly" burdened interstate commerce. Justice Brandeis, joined by Justice Holmes, dissented and thought that the statute only burdened commerce "indirectly." Justice Stone, in his dissent, rejected these labels as conclusory and argued that a court should pragmatically consider "all the facts and circumstances, such as the nature of the regulation, its function, the character of the business involved and the actual flow of commerce [to reach] the conclusion that the regulation concerns interests peculiarly local and does not infringe the national interest in maintaining the freedom of commerce across state lines." See, Dowling, Interstate Commerce and State Power, 27 Va.L.Rev. 1 (1940). Consider Justice Stone's (and Professor Dowling's) position in light of the following modern cases.

3–2. TRANSPORTATION

SOUTH CAROLINA STATE HIGHWAY DEPARTMENT v. BARNWELL BROTHERS, INC.
303 U.S. 177, 58 S.Ct. 510, 82 L.Ed. 734 (1938).

MR. JUSTICE STONE delivered the opinion of the Court.

Act No. 259 of the General Assembly of South Carolina, of April 28, 1933, 38 Stat. 340, prohibits use on the state highways of motor trucks and "semi-trailer motor trucks" whose width exceeds 90 inches, and whose weight including load exceeds 20,000 pounds. . . . The trial court rested its decision that the statute unreasonably burdens interstate commerce, upon findings, not assailed here, that there is a large amount of motor truck traffic passing interstate in the southeastern part of the

United States, which would normally pass over the highways of South Carolina, but which will be barred from the state by the challenged restrictions if enforced, and upon its conclusion that, when viewed in the light of their effect upon interstate commerce, these restrictions are unreasonable.

To reach this conclusion the court weighed conflicting evidence and made its own determinations as to the weight and width of motor trucks commonly used in interstate traffic and the capacity of the specified highways of the state to accommodate such traffic without injury to them or danger to their users. It found that interstate carriage by motor trucks has become a national industry; that from 85 to 90% of the motor trucks used in interstate transportation are 96 inches wide and of a gross weight, when loaded, of more than ten tons; that only four other states prescribe a gross load weight as low as 20,000 pounds; and that the American Association of State Highway Officials and the National Conference on Street and Highway Safety in the Department of Commerce have recommended for adoption weight and width limitations in which weight is limited to axle loads of 16,000 to 18,000 pounds and width is limited to 96 inches. . . .

South Carolina has built its highways and owns and maintains them. It has received from the federal government, in aid of its highway improvements, money grants which have been expended upon the highways to which the injunction applies. But appellees do not challenge here the ruling of the district court that Congress has not undertaken to regulate the weight and size of motor vehicles in interstate motor traffic, and has left undisturbed whatever authority in that regard the states have retained under the Constitution.

While the constitutional grant to Congress of power to regulate interstate commerce has been held to operate of its own force to curtail state power in some measure,[2] it did not forestall all state action affecting interstate commerce. Ever since *Willson v. Black–Bird Creek Marsh Co.,* and *Cooley v. Board of Wardens,* it has been recognized that there are matters of local concern, the regulation of which unavoidably involves some regulation of interstate commerce but which, because of their local character and their number and diversity, may never be fully dealt with by Congress. . . . Few subjects of state regulation are so peculiarly of local concern as is the use of state highways. There are few, local regulation of which is so inseparable from a substantial effect on interstate commerce. Unlike the railroads, local highways are built,

---

2. State regulations affecting interstate commerce, whose purpose or effect is to gain for those within the state an advantage at the expense of those without, or to burden those out of the state without any corresponding advantage to those within, have been thought to impinge upon the constitutional prohibition even though Congress has not acted.

Underlying the stated rule has been the thought, often expressed in judicial opinion, that when the regulation is of such a character that its burden falls principally upon those without the state, legislative action is not likely to be subjected to those political restraints which are normally exerted on legislation where it affects adversely some interests within the state. See *Cooley v. Board of Wardens,* 13 L.Ed. 996.

owned and maintained by the state or its municipal subdivisions. The state has a primary and immediate concern in their safe and economical administration. The present regulations, or any others of like purpose, if they are to accomplish their end, must be applied alike to interstate and intrastate traffic both moving in large volume over the highways. The fact that they affect alike shippers in interstate and intrastate commerce in large number within as well as without the state is a safeguard against their abuse.... In the absence of [federal] legislation the judicial function, under the commerce clause ... , stops with the inquiry whether the state legislature in adopting regulations such as the present has acted within its province, and whether the means of regulation chosen are reasonably adapted to the end sought.

Here the first inquiry has already been resolved by our decisions that a state may impose non-discriminatory restrictions with respect to the character of motor vehicles moving in interstate commerce as a safety measure and as a means of securing the economical use of its highways. In resolving the second, courts do not sit as legislatures, either state or national. They cannot act as Congress does when, after weighing all the conflicting interests, state and national, it determines when and how much the state regulatory power shall yield to the larger interests of a national commerce. And in reviewing a state highway regulation where Congress has not acted, a court is not called upon, as are state legislatures, to determine what, in its judgment, is the most suitable restriction to be applied of those that are possible, or to choose that one which in its opinion is best adapted to all the diverse interests affected. When the action of a legislature is within the scope of its power, fairly debatable questions as to its reasonableness, wisdom and propriety are not for the determination of courts, but for the legislative body, on which rests the duty and responsibility of decision....

Since the adoption of one weight or width regulation, rather than another, is a legislative not a judicial choice, its constitutionality is not to be determined by weighing in the judicial scales the merits of the legislative choice and rejecting it if the weight of evidence presented in court appears to favor a different standard. Being a legislative judgment it is presumed to be supported by facts known to the legislature unless facts judicially known or proved preclude that possibility. Hence, in reviewing the present determination we examine the record, not to see whether the findings of the court below are supported by evidence, but to ascertain upon the whole record whether it is possible to say that the legislative choice is without rational basis. Not only does the record fail to exclude that possibility, but it shows affirmatively that there is adequate support for the legislative judgment....

There was testimony before the court to support its conclusion that the highways in question are capable of sustaining without injury a wheel load of 8,000 or 9,000 pounds. Much of this testimony appears to have been based on theoretical strength of concrete highways laid under ideal conditions, and none of it was based on an actual study of the highways of South Carolina or of the subgrade and other road building conditions which prevail there and which have a material bearing on the strength and durability of such highways. There is uncontradicted testimony that approximately 60% of the South Carolina standard paved highways in question were built without a longitudinal center joint which has since become standard practice. [O]wing to the distribution of the stresses on concrete roads when in use, those without a center joint have a tendency to develop irregular longitudinal cracks. . . .

. . . The present weight limitation was recommended by [a state] commission after a full consideration of relevant data, including a report by the state engineer who had constructed the concrete highways of the state and who advised a somewhat lower limitation as necessary for their preservation. The fact that many states have adopted a different standard is not persuasive. The conditions under which highways must be built in the several states, their construction and the demands made upon them, are not uniform. The road building art, as the record shows, is far from having attained a scientific certainty and precision, and scientific precision is not the criterion for the exercise of the constitutional regulatory power of the states. The legislature, being free to exercise its own judgment, is not bound by that of other legislatures. It would hardly be contended that if all the states had adopted a single standard none, in the light of its own experience and in the exercise of its judgment upon all the complex elements which enter into the problem, could change it.

Only a word need be said as to the width limitation. While a large part of the highways in question are from 18 to 20 feet in width, approximately 100 miles are only 16 feet wide. On all the use of a 96 inch truck leaves but a narrow margin for passing. On the road 16 feet wide it leaves none. The 90 inch limitation has been in force in South Carolina since 1920 and the concrete highways which it has built appear to be adapted to vehicles of that width. The record shows without contradiction that the use of heavy loaded trucks on the highways tends to force other traffic off the concrete surface onto the shoulders of the road adjoining its edges and to increase repair costs materially. [A]s the width of trucks is increased it obstructs the view of the highway, causing much inconvenience and increased hazard in its use. It plainly cannot be said that the width of trucks used on the highways in South Carolina is unrelated to their safety and cost of maintenance, or that a 90 inch width limitation adopted to safeguard the highways of the state, is not within the range of the permissible legislative choice.

The regulatory measures taken by South Carolina are within its legislative power. They do not infringe the Fourteenth Amendment, and the resulting burden on interstate commerce is not forbidden.

Reversed.

MR. JUSTICE CARDOZO and MR. JUSTICE REED took no part in the consideration or decision of this case.

SOUTHERN PACIFIC CO. v. ARIZONA

325 U.S. 761, 65 S.Ct. 1515, 89 L.Ed. 1915 (1945).

MR. CHIEF JUSTICE STONE delivered the opinion of the Court.

The Arizona Train Limit Law of May 16, 1912, Arizona Code Ann., 1939, § 69–119, makes it unlawful for any person or corporation to operate within the state a railroad train of more than fourteen passenger or seventy freight cars, and authorizes the state to recover a money penalty for each violation of the Act. The questions for decision are whether Congress has, by legislative enactment, restricted the power of the states to regulate the length of interstate trains as a safety measure and, if not, whether the statute contravenes the commerce clause of the Federal Constitution.

. . . We do not gain either from the Interstate Commerce Act's words or from the legislative history any hint that Congress in enacting them intended, apart from Interstate Commerce Commission action, to supersede state laws regulating train lengths. . . . We are therefore brought to appellant's principal contention, that the state statute contravenes the commerce clause of the Federal Constitution.

Although the commerce clause conferred on the national government power to regulate commerce, its possession of the power does not exclude all state power of regulation. Ever since *Willson v. Black–Bird Creek Marsh Co.,* and *Cooley v. Board of Wardens,* it has been recognized that, in the absence of conflicting legislation by Congress, there is a residuum of power in the state to make laws governing matters of local concern which nevertheless in some measure affect interstate commerce or even, to some extent, regulate it. [E]ver since *Gibbons v. Ogden,* the states have not been deemed to have authority to impede substantially the free flow of commerce from state to state, or to regulate those phases of the national commerce which, because of the need of national uniformity, demand that their regulation, if any, be prescribed by a single authority.[2] *Cooley v. Board of Wardens.* Whether or not this long-recognized distribution of power between the national and the state governments is predicated upon the implications of the commerce clause itself, *South Carolina Highway Dept. v. Barnwell Bro.,* or upon the presumed intention of Congress, where Congress has not spoken, *Leisy v. Hardin; In re Rahrer;* Dowling, Interstate Commerce and State Power, 27 Va.Law Rev. 1, the result is the same.

Congress has undoubted power to redefine the distribution of power over interstate commerce. It may either permit the states to regulate the commerce in a manner which would otherwise not be permissible, *In re Rahrer,* supra, or exclude state regulation even of matters of peculiarly

---

2. In applying this rule the Court has often recognized that to the extent that the burden of state regulation falls on interests outside the state, it is unlikely to be alleviated by the operation of those political restraints normally exerted when interests within the state are affected.

local concern which nevertheless affect interstate commerce. But in general Congress has left it to the courts to formulate the rules thus interpreting the commerce clause in its application, doubtless because it has appreciated the destructive consequences to the commerce of the nation if their protection were withdrawn, and has been aware that in their application state laws will not be invalidated without the support of relevant factual material which will "afford a sure basis" for an informed judgment. Meanwhile, Congress has accommodated its legislation, as have the states, to these rules as an established feature of our constitutional system. There has thus been left to the states wide scope for the regulation of matters of local state concern, even though it in some measure affects the commerce, provided it does not materially restrict the free flow of commerce across state lines, or interfere with it in matters with respect to which uniformity of regulation is of predominant national concern.

Hence the matters for ultimate determination here are the nature and extent of the burden which the state regulation of interstate trains, adopted as a safety measure, imposes on interstate commerce, and whether the relative weights of the state and national interests involved are such as to make inapplicable the rule, generally observed, that the free flow of interstate commerce and its freedom from local restraints in matters requiring uniformity of regulation are interests safeguarded by the commerce clause from state interference.

While this Court is not bound by the findings of the state court, and may determine for itself the facts of a case upon which an asserted federal right depends, the facts found by the state trial court showing the nature of the interstate commerce involved, and the effect upon it of the train limit law, are not seriously questioned.... The findings show that the operation of long trains, that is trains of more than fourteen passenger and more than seventy freight cars, is standard practice over the main lines of the railroads of the United States.... Outside of Arizona, where the length of trains is not restricted, appellant runs a substantial proportion of long trains. In 1939 on its comparable route for through traffic through Utah and Nevada from 66 to 85% of its freight trains were over seventy cars in length and over 43% of its passenger trains included more than fourteen passenger cars.

In Arizona, approximately 93% of the freight traffic and 95% of the passenger traffic is interstate. Because of the Train Limit Law appellant is required to haul over 30% more trains in Arizona than would otherwise have been necessary. The record shows a definite relationship between operating costs and the length of trains, the increase in length resulting in a reduction of operating costs per car. The additional cost of operation of trains complying with the Train Limit Law in Arizona amounts for the two railroads traversing that state to about $1,000,000 a year. The reduction in train lengths also impedes efficient operation. More locomotives and more manpower are required; the necessary conversion and reconversion of train lengths at terminals and the delay caused by breaking up and remaking long trains upon entering and leaving the state in order to comply with the law, delays the traffic and diminishes its volume moved in a given time, especially when traffic is heavy....

The unchallenged findings leave no doubt that the Arizona Train Limit Law imposes a serious burden on the interstate commerce conducted by appellant.... Compliance with a state statute limiting train lengths requires interstate trains of a length lawful in other states to be broken up and reconstituted as they enter each state according as it may impose varying limitations upon train lengths. The alternative is for the carrier to conform to the lowest train limit restriction of any of the states through which its trains pass, whose laws thus control the carriers' operations both within and without the regulating state....

At present the seventy freight car laws are enforced only in Arizona and Oklahoma, with a fourteen car passenger car limit in Arizona. The record here shows that the enforcement of the Arizona statute results in freight trains being broken up and reformed at the California border and in New Mexico, some distance from the Arizona line. Frequently it is not feasible to operate a newly assembled train from the New Mexico yard nearest to Arizona, with the result that the Arizona limitation governs the flow of traffic as far east as El Paso, Texas. For similar reasons the Arizona law often controls the length of passenger trains all the way from Los Angeles to El Paso.

If one state may regulate train lengths, so may all the others, and they need not prescribe the same maximum limitation. The practical effect of such regulation is to control train operations beyond the boundaries of the state exacting it because of the necessity of breaking up and reassembling long trains at the nearest terminal points before entering and after leaving the regulating state. The serious impediment to the free flow of commerce by the local regulation of train lengths and the practical necessity that such regulation, if any, must be prescribed by a single body having a nation-wide authority are apparent.

The trial court found that the Arizona law had no reasonable relation to safety, and made train operation more dangerous. Examination of the evidence and the detailed findings makes it clear that this conclusion was rested on facts found which indicate that such increased danger of accident and personal injury as may result from the greater length of trains is more than offset by the increase in the number of accidents resulting from the larger number of trains when train lengths are reduced. In considering the effect of the statute as a safety measure, therefore, the factor of controlling significance for present purposes is not whether there is basis for the conclusion of the Arizona Supreme Court that the increase in length of trains beyond the statutory maximum has an adverse effect upon safety of operation. The decisive question is whether in the circumstances the total effect of the law as a safety measure in reducing accidents and casualties is so slight or problematical as not to outweigh the national interest in keeping interstate commerce free from interferences which seriously impede it and subject it to local regulation which does not have a uniform effect on the interstate train journey which it interrupts.

The principal source of danger of accident from increased length of trains is the resulting increase of "slack action" of the train. Slack action is the amount of free movement of one car before it transmits its motion to an adjoining coupled car. [But] accidents due to slack action also occur in the operation of short trains. On comparison of the number of slack action accidents in Arizona with those in Nevada, where the length of trains is now unregulated, the trial court found that with substantially the same amount of traffic in each state the number of accidents was relatively the same in long as in short train operations. . . . Nor does it appear that slack action accidents occurring on passenger trains, whatever their length, are of sufficient severity to cause serious injury or damage.

As the trial court found, reduction of the length of trains also tends to increase the number of accidents because of the increase in the number of trains. . . . The number of accidents due to grade crossing collisions between trains and motor vehicles and pedestrians, and to collisions between trains, which are usually far more serious than those due to slack action, and accidents due to locomotive failures, in general vary with the number of trains. . . . Railroad statistics introduced into the record tend to show that this is the result of the application of the Arizona Train Limit Law to appellant, both with respect to all railroad casualties within the state and those affecting only trainmen whom the train limit law is supposed to protect. The accident rate in Arizona is much higher than on comparable lines elsewhere, where there is no regulation of length of trains. . . .

We think, as the trial court found, that the Arizona Train Limit Law, viewed as a safety measure, affords at most slight and dubious advantage, if any, over unregulated train lengths, because it results in an increase in the number of trains and train operations and the consequent increase in train accidents of a character generally more severe than those due to slack action. Its undoubted effect on the commerce is the regulation, without securing uniformity, of the length of trains operated in interstate commerce, which lack is itself a primary cause of preventing the free flow of commerce by delaying it and by substantially increasing its cost and impairing its efficiency. In these respects the case differs from those where a state, by regulatory measures affecting the commerce, has removed or reduced safety hazards without substantial interference with the interstate movement of trains. Such are measures abolishing the car stove, *New York, N.H. & H.R. Co. v. New York,* 165 U.S. 628, 17 S.Ct. 418, 41 L.Ed. 853, requiring locomotives to be supplied with electric headlights, *Atlantic Coast Line R. Co. v. Georgia,* 234 U.S. 280, 34 S.Ct. 829, 58 L.Ed. 1312; providing for full train crews, *Chicago, R.I. & P.R. Co. v. Arkansas,* 219 U.S. 453, 31 S.Ct. 275, 55 L.Ed. 290; and for the equipment of freight trains with cabooses, *Terminal Railroad Assn. v. Brotherhood,* supra.

The principle that, without controlling Congressional action, a state may not regulate interstate commerce so as substantially to affect its flow or deprive it of needed uniformity in its regulation is not to be avoided by "simply invoking the convenient apologetics of the police power," . . . . Here we conclude that the state does go too far. Its regulation of train lengths, admittedly obstructive to interstate train operation, and having a seriously adverse effect on transportation efficiency and economy, passes beyond what is plainly essential for safety since it does not appear that it will lessen rather than increase the danger of accident . . . .

Appellees especially rely on the full train crew cases, *Chicago, R.I. & P.R. Co. v. Arkansas,* supra; *St. Louis & I.M.R. Co. v. Arkansas,* supra; *Missouri Pacific R. Co. v. Norwood,* supra, and also on *South Carolina Highway Dept. v. Barnwell Bros.,* supra, as supporting the state's authority to regulate the length of interstate trains. While the full train crew laws undoubtedly placed an added financial burden on the railroads in order to serve a local interest, they did not obstruct interstate transportation or seriously impede it. They had no effects outside the state beyond those of picking up and setting down the extra employees at the state boundaries; they involved no wasted use of facilities or serious impairment of transportation efficiency, which are among the factors of controlling weight here. In sustaining those laws the Court considered the restriction a minimal burden on the commerce . . . .

South Carolina Highway Dept. v. Barnwell Bros., supra, was concerned with the power of the state to regulate the weight and width of motor cars passing interstate over its highways, a legislative field over which the state has a far more extensive control than over interstate railroads . . . . Regulations affecting the safety of [highway] use must be applied alike to intrastate and interstate traffic. The fact that they affect alike shippers in interstate and intrastate commerce in great numbers, within as well as without the state, is a safeguard against regulatory abuses. Their regulation is akin to quarantine measures, game laws, and like local regulations of rivers, harbors, piers, and docks, with respect to which the state has exceptional scope for the exercise of its regulatory power, and which, Congress not acting, have been sustained even though they materially interfere with interstate commerce.

The contrast between the present regulation and the full train crew laws in point of their effects on the commerce, and the like contrast with the highway safety regulations, in point of the nature of the subject of regulation and the state's interest in it, illustrate and emphasize the considerations which enter into a determination of the relative weights of state and national interests where state regulation affecting interstate commerce is attempted. Here examination of all the relevant factors makes it plain that the state interest is outweighed by the interest of the nation in an adequate, economical and efficient railway transportation service, which must prevail.

Reversed.

Mr. Justice Rutledge concurs in the result.

Mr. Justice Black, dissenting....

What the Court decides today is that it is unwise governmental policy to regulate the length of trains. I am therefore constrained to note my dissent....

[The dissenting opinion of Douglas, J., is omitted.]

Notes

1. Compare *Bibb v. Navajo Freight Lines, Inc.*, 359 U.S. 520, 79 S.Ct. 962, 3 L.Ed.2d 1003 (1959). An Illinois statute was unique in requiring the use of contour mudguards on trucks and trailers operated on Illinois highways. That statute conflicted with an Arkansas rule that forbade contour mudguards. At least 45 states made the straight, or conventional, mudguard legal. The trial court found that the contour mudguard was not safer than the straight mudguard and it also created new hazards. The costs and burdens of interstate trucks in adjusting to the Illinois statute were very great. The majority said:

> There is language [in *Barnwell*] which, read in isolation from such later decisions as *Southern Pacific Co. v. Arizona* ... would suggest that no showing of burden on interstate commerce is sufficient to invalidate local safety regulations in absence of some element of discrimination against interstate commerce. [However, like] any local law that conflicts with federal regulatory measures, state regulations that run afoul of the policy of free trade reflected in the Commerce Clause must also bow.
>
> This is one of those cases—few in number—where local safety measures that are nondiscriminatory place an unconstitutional burden on interstate commerce.... The conflict between the Arkansas regulation and the Illinois regulation also suggests that this regulation of mudguards is not one of those matters "admitting of diversity of treatment, according to the special requirements of local conditions".... [A] new safety device—out of line with the requirements of the other States—may be so compelling that the innovating State need not be the one to give way. But the present showing—balanced against the clear burden on commerce—is far too inconclusive to make this mudguard meet that test.

Does *Bibb*, in effect, reject *Southern Pacific's* distinction between it and *Barnwell?* Are the results of all three cases nevertheless consistent?

2. *Southern Pacific* invalidated state laws fixing maximum train lengths yet approved of earlier cases upholding state laws that set minimum train crew sizes, so called "full train crew laws." How do you distinguish these cases?

3. In *Southern Pacific* the majority said: "If one state may regulate train lengths, so may all the others, and they need not prescribe the same maximum limitation." *Huron Portland Cement Co. v. Detroit*, 362 U.S. 440, 80 S.Ct. 813, 4 L.Ed.2d 852 (1960) upheld the criminal provisions of Detroit's Smoke Abatement Code as applied to ships in interstate commerce while docked at the Detroit port. Federal regulation was extensive but

designed to deal with the safety of the ships, not the elimination of their pollution. The state statute was valid under the Commerce Clause. While the appellant argued "that other local governments might impose differing requirements as to air pollution, it has pointed to none." Should appellants have to wait until these differing requirements are enacted?

4. *Kassel v. Consolidated Freightways Corp.*, 450 U.S. 662, 101 S.Ct. 1309, 67 L.Ed.2d 580 (1981). While other midwest and western states permitted 65 foot double trailer trucks on its highways, Iowa restricted their length to 55 feet, subject to certain exceptions. For example, cities abutting the state line could enact a local ordinance to adopt the length limits of the adjoining state. The trial judge found that the 65 foot trailer trucks were as safe or safer than the shorter trucks and the state law substantially and impermissibly burdened interstate commerce. The Court of Appeals affirmed, noting that some of the statutory exemptions to Iowa's law disproportionately burdened out of state residents. The "border cities" exemption secured to these areas the benefits of larger trucks while the Iowa restriction discouraged larger trucks from using Iowa highways solely for interstate transit. Powell, joined by White, Blackmun, and Stevens, accepted this analysis and affirmed. Brennan, joined by Marshall, concurred in the judgment but concentrated more on Iowa's *motivation,* contending that Iowa's "actual rationale" was to discourage interstate traffic on Iowa's highways. The legislative history of Iowa's regulation, and the Governor's motivation as reflected in his veto message, indicated that Iowa's "actual purpose" was to "deflect some through traffic" from its highways. Since this purpose was protectionist in nature, the Commerce Clause prohibited it.

Should the Court focus more on objective factors or on the subjective motivations of the state legislature or Governor?

3–3. INCOMING COMMERCE

BALDWIN v. G.A.F. SEELIG, INC.
294 U.S. 511, 55 S.Ct. 497, 79 L.Ed. 1032 (1935).

MR. JUSTICE CARDOZO delivered the opinion of the Court. . . .

G.A.F. Seelig, Inc. is engaged in business as a milk dealer in the city of New York. It buys its milk, including cream, in Fair Haven, Vermont, from the Seelig Creamery Corporation, which in turn buys from the producers on the neighboring farms. The milk is transported to New York by rail in forty-quart cans, the daily shipment amounting to about 200 cans of milk and 20 cans of cream. Upon arrival in New York about 90% is sold to customers in the original cans, the buyers being chiefly hotels, restaurants and stores. About 10% is bottled in New York, and sold to customers in bottles. By concession, title passes from the Seelig Creamery to G.A.F. Seelig, Inc. at Fair Haven, Vermont. For convenience the one company will be referred to as the Creamery and the other as Seelig.

The New York Milk Control Act with the aid of regulations made thereunder has set up a system of minimum prices to be paid by dealers to producers. To keep the system unimpaired by competition from afar, the Act has a provision whereby the protective prices are extended to that part of the supply (about 30%) which comes from other states. The substance of the provision is that, so far as such a prohibition is permitted by the Constitution, there shall be no sale within the state of milk bought outside unless the price paid to the producers was one that would be lawful upon a like transaction within the state. . . .

Seelig buys its milk from the Creamery in Vermont at prices lower than the minimum payable to producers in New York. The Commissioner of Farms and Markets refuses to license the transaction of its business unless it signs an agreement to conform to the New York statute and regulations in the sale of the imported product. This the applicant declines to do. . . . This suit has been brought to restrain the enforcement of the Act in its application to the complainant, repugnancy being charged between its provisions when so applied and limitations imposed by the Constitution of the United States. A District Court of three judges has granted a final decree restraining the enforcement of the Act in so far as sales are made by the complainant while the milk is in the cans or other original packages in which it was brought into New York, but refusing an injunction as to milk taken out of the cans for bottling, and thereafter sold in bottles. . . . The case is here on cross-appeals.

First. An injunction was properly granted restraining the enforcement of the Act in its application to sales in the original packages.

New York has no power to project its legislation into Vermont by regulating the price to be paid in that state for milk acquired there. So much is not disputed. New York is equally without power to prohibit the introduction within her territory of milk of wholesome quality acquired in Vermont, whether at high prices or at low ones. This again is not disputed. Accepting those postulates, New York asserts her power to outlaw milk so introduced by prohibiting its sale thereafter if the price that has been paid for it to the farmers of Vermont is less than would be owing in like circumstances to farmers in New York. The importer in that view may keep his milk or drink it, but sell it he may not.

Such a power, if exerted, will set a barrier to traffic between one state and another as effective as if customs duties, equal to the price differential, had been laid upon the thing transported. Nice distinctions have been made at times between direct and indirect burdens. They are irrelevant when the avowed purpose of the obstruction, as well as its necessary tendency, is to suppress or mitigate the consequences of competition between the states. Such an obstruction is direct by the very terms of the hypothesis. We are reminded in the opinion below that a chief occasion of the commerce clauses was "the mutual jealousies and aggressions of the States, taking form in customs barriers and other economic retaliation." If New York, in order to promote the economic welfare of her farmers, may guard them against competition with the cheaper prices of Vermont, the door has been opened to rivalries and reprisals that were meant to be averted by subjecting commerce between the states to the power of the nation.

The argument is pressed upon us, however, that the end to be served by the Milk Control Act is something more than the economic welfare of the farmers or of any other class or classes. The end to be served is the maintenance of a regular and adequate supply of pure and wholesome milk, the supply being put in jeopardy when the farmers of the state are unable to earn a living income. Price security, we are told, is only a special form of sanitary security; the economic motive is secondary and subordinate; the state intervenes to make its inhabitants healthy, and not to make them rich. On that assumption we are asked to say that intervention will be upheld as a valid exercise by the state of its internal police power, though there is an incidental obstruction to commerce between one state and another. This would be to eat up the rule under the guise of an exception. Economic welfare is always related to health, for there can be no health if men are starving. Let such an exception be admitted, and all that a state will have to do in times of stress and strain is to say that its farmers and merchants and workmen must be protected against competition from without, lest they go upon the poor relief lists or perish altogether. To give entrance to that excuse would be to invite a speedy end of our national solidarity. The Constitution was framed under the dominion of a political philosophy less parochial in range. It was framed upon the theory that the peoples of the several states must sink or swim together, and that in the long run prosperity and salvation are in union and not division.

... We are told that farmers who are underpaid will be tempted to save the expense of sanitary precautions. [T]he evils springing from uncared for cattle must be remedied by measures of repression more direct and certain than the creation of a parity of prices between New York and other states. Appropriate certificates may be exacted from farmers in Vermont and elsewhere; milk may be excluded if necessary safeguards have been omitted; but commerce between the states is burdened unduly when one state regulates by indirection the prices to be paid to producers in another, in the faith that augmentation of prices will lift up the level of economic welfare, and that this will stimulate the observance of sanitary requirements in the preparation of the product. The next step would be to condition importation upon proof of a satisfactory wage scale in factory or shop, or even upon proof of the profits of the business. Whatever relation there may be between earnings and sanitation is too remote and indirect to justify obstructions to the normal flow of commerce in its movement between states.

... Subject to the paramount power of the Congress, a state may regulate the importation of unhealthy swine or cattle or decayed or noxious foods. Things such as these are not proper subjects of commerce, and there is no unreasonable interference when they are inspected and excluded. So a state may protect its inhabitants against the fraudulent substitution, by deceptive coloring or otherwise, of one article for another. It may give protection to travelers against the dangers of overcrowded highways. (*Bradley v. Public Utilities Commission*, 289 U.S. 92, 53 S.Ct. 577, 77 L.Ed. 1053) and protection to its residents against unnecessary noises.... None of these statutes ... approaches in drastic quality the statute here in controversy which would neutralize the economic consequences of free trade among the states.

Second. There was error in refusing an injunction to restrain the enforcement of the Act in its application to milk in bottles to be sold by the importer.

The test of the "original package," which came into our law with *Brown v. Maryland,* 12 Wheat. 419, 6 L.Ed. 678, is not inflexible and final for the transactions of interstate commerce, whatever may be its validity for commerce with other countries.... "A state tax upon merchandise brought in from another State, or upon its sales, whether in original packages or not, after it has reached its destination and is in a state of rest, is lawful only when the tax is not discriminating in its incidence against the merchandise because of its origin in another State." In brief, the test of the original package is not an ultimate principle. It is an illustration of a principle. It marks a convenient boundary and one sufficiently precise save in exceptional conditions. What is ultimate is the principle that one state in its dealings with another may not place itself in a position of economic isolation. Formulas and catchwords are subordinate to this overmastering requirement. Neither the power to tax nor the police power may be used by the state of destination with the aim and effect of establishing an economic barrier against competition with the products of another state or the labor of its residents. Restrictions so contrived are an unreasonable clog upon the mobility of commerce. They set up what is equivalent to a rampart of customs duties designed to neutralize advantages belonging to the place of origin. They are thus hostile in conception as well as burdensome in result. The form of the packages in such circumstances is immaterial, whether they are original or broken. The importer must be free from imposts framed for the very purpose of suppressing competition from without and leading inescapably to the suppression so intended....

The distinction is clear between a statute so designed and statutes of the type considered in *Leisy v. Hardin,* [§ 3–1, supra], to take one example out of many available. By the teaching of that decision intoxicating liquors are not subject to license or prohibition by the state of destination without congressional consent.[3] They become subject, however, to such laws when the packages are broken. There is little, if any, analogy between restrictions of that type and those in controversy here. In licensing or prohibiting the sale of intoxicating liquors a state does not attempt to neutralize economic advantages belonging to the place of origin. What it does is no more than to apply its domestic policy, rooted in its conceptions of morality and order, to property which for such a

---

3. The rule is different today under the   Twenty-first Amendment. Art. XXI, § 2.

purpose may fairly be deemed to have passed out of commerce and to be commingled in an absorbing mass . . . .

HENNEFORD v. SILAS MASON CO., INC.
300 U.S. 577, 57 S.Ct. 524, 81 L.Ed. 814 (1937).

Mr. Justice Cardozo delivered the opinion of the Court.

A statute of Washington taxing the use of chattels in that state is assailed in this suit as a violation of the commerce clause in so far as the tax is applicable to chattels purchased in another state and used in Washington thereafter.

Plaintiffs (appellees in this court) are engaged either as contractors or as subcontractors in the construction of the Grand Coulee Dam on the Columbia River. In the performance of that work they have brought into the state of Washington machinery, materials and supplies, such as locomotives, cars, conveyors, pumps, and trestle steel, which were bought at retail in other states. The cost of all the articles with transportation expenses added was $921,189.34. Defendants, the Tax Commission of Washington (appellants in this court) gave notice that plaintiffs had become subject through the use of this property to a tax of $18,423.78, two per cent of the cost, and made demand for payment. A District Court of three judges, adjudged the statute void upon its face and granted an interlocutory injunction, one judge dissenting. The case is here upon appeal.

Chapter 180 of the Laws of Washington for the year 1935, consisting of twenty titles, lays a multitude of excise taxes on occupations and activities. Only two of these taxes are important for the purposes of the case at hand, the "tax on retail sales," imposed by Title III, and the "compensating tax," imposed by Title IV on the privilege of use. Title III provides that after May 1, 1935, every retail sale in Washington, with a few enumerated exceptions, shall be subject to a tax of 2% of the selling price. Title IV, with the heading "compensating tax," provides that there shall be collected from every person in the state "a tax or excise for the privilege of using within this state any article of tangible personal property purchased subsequent to April 30, 1935," at the rate of 2% of the purchase price, including in such price the cost of transportation from the place where the article was purchased. If those provisions stood alone, they would mean that retail buyers within the state would have to pay a double tax, 2% upon the sale and 2% upon the use. Relief from such a burden is provided in another section which qualifies the use tax by allowing four exceptions. Only two of these exceptions (b and c) call for mention at this time. Subdivision (b) provides that the use tax shall not be laid unless the property has been bought at retail. Subdivision (c) provides that the tax shall not apply to the "use of any article of tangible personal property the sale or use of which has already been subjected to a tax equal to or in excess of that imposed by this title whether under the laws of this state or of some other state of the United States." If the rate of such other tax is less than 2%, the exemption is not to be complete, but in such circumstances the rate is to be measured by the difference.

The plan embodied in these provisions is neither hidden nor uncertain. A use tax is never payable where the user has acquired property by retail purchase in the state of Washington, except in the rare instances in which retail purchases in Washington are not subjected to a sales tax. On the other hand, a use tax is always payable where the user has acquired property by retail purchase in or from another state, unless he has paid a sales or use tax elsewhere before bringing it to Washington.... The practical effect of a system thus conditioned is readily perceived. One of its effects must be that retail sellers in Washington will be helped to compete upon terms of equality with retail dealers in other states who are exempt from a sales tax or any corresponding burden. Another effect, or at least another tendency, must be to avoid the likelihood of a drain upon the revenues of the state, buyers being no longer tempted to place their orders in other states in the effort to escape payment of the tax on local sales. Do these consequences which must have been foreseen, necessitate a holding that the tax upon the use is either a tax upon the operations of interstate commerce or a discrimination against such commerce obstructing or burdening it unlawfully?

1. The tax is not upon the operations of interstate commerce, but upon the privilege of use after commerce is at an end.

Things acquired or transported in interstate commerce may be subjected to a property tax, non-discriminatory in its operation, when they have become part of the common mass of property within the state of destination. This is so, indeed, though they are still in the original packages. For like reasons they may be subjected, when once they are at rest, to a non-discriminatory tax upon use or enjoyment. The privilege of use is only one attribute, among many, of the bundle of privileges that make up property or ownership.... Calling the tax an excise when it is laid solely upon the use does not make the power to impose it less, for anything the commerce clause has to say of its validity, than calling it a property tax and laying it on ownership....

2. The tax upon the use after the property is at rest is not so measured or conditioned as to hamper the transactions of interstate commerce or discriminate against them.

Equality is the theme that runs through all the sections of the statute. There shall be a tax upon the use, but subject to an offset if another use or sales tax has been paid for the same thing.... When the account is made up, the stranger from afar is subject to no greater burdens as a consequence of ownership than the dweller within the gates. The one pays upon one activity or incident, and the other upon another, but the sum is the same when the reckoning is closed. Equality exists when the chattel subjected to the use tax is bought in another state and then carried into Washington. It exists when the imported chattel is shipped from the state of origin under an order received directly from the state of destination. In each situation the burden borne by the owner is balanced by an equal burden where the sale is strictly local.... If the sales tax were abolished, the buyer in Washington would pay at once upon the use. He would have no longer an offsetting credit. While the sales tax is in force, he pays upon the sale, and pays at the same rate. For the owner who uses after buying from afar the effect is all one whether his competitor is taxable under one title or another. This common sense conclusion has ample precedent behind it....

Baldwin v. G.A.F. Seelig, Inc., is invoked by appellees as decisive of the controversy, but the case is far apart from this one. [New York] said in effect to farmers in Vermont: your milk cannot be sold by dealers to whom you ship it in New York unless you sell it to them in Vermont at a price determined here. What Washington is saying to sellers beyond her borders is something very different. In substance what she says is this: You may ship your goods in such amounts and at such prices as you please, but the goods when used in Washington after the transit is completed, will share an equal burden with goods that have been purchased here.

We are told that a tax upon the use, even though not unlawful by force of its effects alone, is vitiated by the motives that led to its adoption. These motives cause it to be stigmatized as equivalent to a protective tariff. But motives alone will seldom, if ever, invalidate a tax that apart from its motives would be recognized as lawful. Least of all will they be permitted to accomplish that result when equality and not preference is the end to be achieved. Catch words and labels, such as the words "protective tariff," are subject to the dangers that lurk in metaphors and symbols, and must be watched with circumspection lest they put us off our guard. A tariff, whether protective or for revenue, burdens the very act of importation, and if laid by a state upon its commerce with another is equally unlawful whether protection or revenue is the motive back of it. But a tax upon use, or, what is equivalent for present purposes, a tax upon property after importation is over, is not a clog upon the process of importation at all, any more than a tax upon the income or profits of a business. The contention would be futile that Washington in laying an ownership tax would be doing a wrong to nonresidents in allowing a credit for a sales tax already borne by the owner as a result of the same ownership.... Yet a word of caution should be added here to avoid the chance of misconception. We have not meant to imply by anything said in this opinion that allowance of a credit for other taxes paid to Washington made it mandatory that there should be a like allowance for taxes paid to other states. A state, for many purposes, is to be reckoned as a self-contained unit, which may frame its own system of burdens and exemptions without heeding systems elsewhere. If there are limits to that power, there is no need to mark them now. It will be time enough to mark them when a taxpayer paying in the state of origin is compelled to pay again in the state of destination. This statute by its framework avoids that possibility. The offsetting allowance has been conceded, whether the concession was necessary or not, and thus the system has been divested of any semblance of inequality or prejudice. A taxing act is not invalid because its exemptions are more generous than the state would have been free to make them by exerting the full measure of her power. . . .

The interlocutory injunction was erroneously granted, and the decree must be

Reversed.

Mr. Justice McReynolds and Mr. Justice Butler dissent.

Notes

1. Is Justice Cardozo's opinion in *Baldwin* consistent with Justice Cardozo's opinion in *Silas Mason?* New York's minimum price law puts its milk at a competitive disadvantage to Vermont milk. New York could not compensate for this disadvantage by attempting, in effect, to set a minimum price for the out of state milk. Washington's sales tax puts goods sold within the state at a competitive disadvantage compared to goods purchased out of state, which are not subject to Washington's sales tax. But Washington may set up a compensating use tax. "One of its effects," said Justice Cardozo in *Silas Mason,* "must be that retail sellers in Washington will be helped to compete upon terms of equality with retail dealers in other states who are exempt from a sales tax or any corresponding burden." Why may New York not use its milk pricing laws to help its producers compete upon terms of equality with milk produced in Vermont?

Suppose that New York attempts to help its in-state milk producers compete by giving them cash subsidies: each New York dairy farmer would receive several thousand dollars per year in cash. New York of course would not give this subsidy to Vermont farmers. New York farmers could now sell their milk for less than before because their overhead is, in effect, reduced by the state subsidy. Is this plan constitutional?

Suppose that New York now decides to pay the subsidy in the form of a tax advantage: New York dairy farmers, unlike other property owners in the state, would be exempt from paying property tax. Is this plan—motivated by a desire to give New York milk producers some economic assistance in spite of the *Baldwin* ruling—constitutional?

Consider *West Lynn Creamery, Inc. v. Healy,* 512 U.S. 186, 114 S.Ct. 2205, 129 L.Ed.2d 157 (1994). A Massachusetts milk pricing order imposed a tax on all fluid milk sold to Massachusetts retailers. (About two-thirds of the milk was produced out-of-state.) The state then distributed all of the money collected to Massachusetts dairy farmers only. Stevens, J., for the Court, invalidated the pricing order because it effectively discriminated against interstate commerce. Although the tax applied to all milk produced in Massachusetts, "its effect on Massachusetts producers is entirely (indeed more than) offset by the tax subsidy provided exclusively to Massachusetts dairy farmers. Like an ordinary tariff, the tax is thus effectively imposed only on out-of-state products." The fact that the tax rebate in this case goes to the milk farmers, even though the milk dealers paid the tax, reinforces the conclusion that the pricing order will favor the local farmers. Massachusetts violated the "cardinal principle" that it may not benefit in-state interests by burdening out-of-state competitors. The initial tax was nondiscriminatory, but it was coupled with a subsidy to one of the groups that paid the tax. The "state's political processes can no longer be relied upon to prevent legislative abuse, because one of the in-state interests which would otherwise lobby against the tax has been mollified by the subsidy."

In a footnote, the Court remarked that it had "never squarely confronted the constitutionality of subsidies, and we need not do so now." It noted that a pure subsidy to domestic industry funded out of general revenues would ordinarily impose no burden on interstate commerce, but general revenues did not fund the subsidy at issue here. "In addition, it is undisputed that States may try to attract business by creating an environment conducive to economic activity, as by maintaining good roads, sound public education, or low taxes."

2. Was the compensating use tax in *Silas Mason* discriminatory against out of state goods? Suppose a state had no sales tax. After *Silas Mason* could a state exact a 2% use tax on goods used in the state but purchased out of state and a 1% use tax on goods used in the state and purchased in the state?

3. At the end of *Silas Mason* Justice Cardozo said: "We have not meant to imply by anything said in this opinion that allowance of a credit for other taxes paid to Washington made it mandatory that there should be a like allowance for taxes paid to other states." Is Cardozo right? May Washington exact a use tax on all goods used within the state without giving any credit for another state's sales tax paid on goods purchased in that state? Suppose that Washington places a 2% sales tax on all goods purchased in Washington. It also places a 2% use tax on all goods used in Washington, except when the Washington state sales tax had previously been paid on the goods. There is no credit if the sales tax previously paid had been paid to another state. Does this taxing scheme discriminate against out of state goods? Is it constitutional?

4. Suppose New York forbids child labor within its boundaries. New York then finds that its producers are at a competitive disadvantage as to producers in a neighboring state that does not forbid child labor. May New York, after *Baldwin,* forbid the importation into New York of goods produced by child labor? If New York may not enact this law, what solution might New York seek?

5. THE 21ST AMENDMENT. In a footnote to *Baldwin,* Justice Cardozo referred to the effects on the commerce clause of the 21st Amendment. The Court has read this Amendment broadly to qualify the commerce clause. Thus, California may exact a $500 fee for the privilege of importing, into that state, beer from a sister state even though such a fee would have been unconstitutional, under the commerce clause, prior to the 21st Amendment. *State Board of Equalization v. Young's Market Co.,* 299 U.S. 59, 57 S.Ct. 77, 81 L.Ed. 38 (1936).

However it is an oversimplification to conclude that the 21st Amendment completely repealed the commerce clause as to the regulation of liquor. E.g., *California Retail Liquor Dealers Association v. Midcal Aluminum, Inc.,* 445 U.S. 97, 100 S.Ct. 937, 63 L.Ed.2d 233 (1980), where the Court invalidated a California wine-pricing statute as constituting resale price maintenance in violation of the Sherman Act. The Court said that although the 21st Amendment has given the state "wide latitude" in regulating liquor, that Amendment did not insulate the state law from a commerce clause challenge:

> [T]here is no bright line between federal and state powers over liquor. The Twenty-first Amendment grants the States virtually complete control over whether to permit importation or sale of liquor and how to structure the liquor distribution system. Although the States retain substantial discretion to establish other liquor regulations, those controls may be subject to the federal commerce power in appropriate situations. The competing state and federal interests can be reconciled only after careful scrutiny of those concerns in a "concrete case."

The statistics showing that the state interests in promoting temperance and protecting small licensees from the pricing policies of large retailers would be promoted little, if at all, by the resale price maintenance system. The national policy in favor of competition outweighs these "unsubstantiated state concerns."

The 21st Amendment does not seem to qualify the export/import clause, Art. 1, § 10, cl. 2. Thus Kentucky may not exact a tax on Scotch whisky because it violates the export/import clause, notwithstanding the language of the 21st Amendment. *Department of Revenue v. James B. Beam Distilling Co.,* 377 U.S. 341, 84 S.Ct. 1247, 12 L.Ed.2d 362 (1964).[1] Note that *Young's Market,* supra, upheld a similar tax on the importation of domestic beer.

The 21st Amendment does not negate an individual's civil rights protected by the Bill of Rights. Thus in *Craig v. Boren,* § 8–2.41, infra, when the Court held that there is unconstitutional sex discrimination that violates the equal protection clause when a state prohibits the sale of 3.2% beer to males under 21 and to females under 18, it noted:

> Once passing beyond consideration of the Commerce Clause, the relevance of the Twenty-first Amendment to other constitutional provisions becomes increasingly doubtful. [T]he Court has never recognized sufficient "strength" in the Amendment to defeat an otherwise established claim of invidious discrimination in violation of the Equal Protection Clause.

6. At the end of *Baldwin,* Justice Cardozo referred to the Original Package Doctrine. Today, in order to determine whether a state tax is constitutional, the primary question is whether the tax is discriminatory, both as to commerce clause problems, *Sonneborn Brothers v. Cureton,* 262 U.S. 506, 43 S.Ct. 643, 67 L.Ed. 1095 (1923), and export-import clause problems, *Michelin Tire Corp. v. Wages,* 423 U.S. 276, 96 S.Ct. 535, 46 L.Ed.2d 495 (1976). Whether the item's original package has been broken is not the real issue.

---

1. Justice Black, joined by Justice Goldberg, construed the 21st Amendment to allow the tax. Justice Black's dissent noted: "Although I was brought up to believe that Scotch whisky would need a tax preference to survive in competition with Kentucky bourbon, I never understood the Constitution to require a State to give such a preference. (My dissenting Brother asks me to say that this statement does not necessarily represent his views on the respective merits of Scotch and bourbon.)"

DEAN MILK CO. v. CITY OF MADISON
340 U.S. 349, 71 S.Ct. 295, 95 L.Ed. 329 (1951).

MR. JUSTICE CLARK delivered the opinion of the Court.

This appeal challenges the constitutional validity of ... an ordinance of the City of Madison, Wisconsin, regulating the sale of milk and milk products within the municipality's jurisdiction. One section in issue makes it unlawful to sell any milk as pasteurized unless it has been processed and bottled at an approved pasteurization plant within a radius of five miles from the central square of Madison.... Appellant is an Illinois corporation engaged in distributing milk and milk products in Illinois and Wisconsin....

The area defined by the ordinance with respect to milk sources encompasses practically all of Dane County and includes some 500 farms which supply milk for Madison. Within the five-mile area for pasteurization are plants of five processors, only three of which are engaged in the general wholesale and retail trade in Madison. Inspection of these farms and plants is scheduled once every thirty days and is performed by two municipal inspectors, one of whom is full-time. The courts below found that the ordinance in question promotes convenient, economical and efficient plant inspection.... Appellant was denied a license to sell its products within Madison solely because its pasteurization plants were more than five miles away. ·

It is conceded that the milk which appellant seeks to sell in Madison is supplied from farms and processed in plants licensed and inspected by public health authorities of Chicago, and is labeled "Grade A" under the Chicago ordinance which adopts the rating standards recommended by the United States Public Health Service.... However, Madison contends and we assume that in some particulars its ordinance is more rigorous than that of Chicago.

[There is no] objection to the avowed purpose of this enactment. We assume that difficulties in sanitary regulation of milk and milk products originating in remote areas may present a situation in which "upon a consideration of all the relevant facts and circumstances it appears that the matter is one which may appropriately be regulated in the interest of the safety, health and well-being of local communities.... " We also assume that since Congress has not spoken to the contrary, the subject matter of the ordinance lies within the sphere of state regulation even though interstate commerce may be affected.

But this regulation, like the provision invalidated in *Baldwin v. Seelig, Inc.,* in practical effect excludes from distribution in Madison wholesale milk produced and pasteurized in Illinois. In thus erecting an economic barrier protecting a major local industry against competition from without the State, Madison plainly discriminates against interstate commerce.[4] This it cannot do, even in the exercise of its unquestioned power to protect the health and safety of its people, if reasonable

---

4. It is immaterial that Wisconsin milk from outside the Madison area is subjected to the same proscription as that moving in interstate commerce. Cf. *Brimmer v. Rebman,* 138 U.S. 78, 82–83, 11 S.Ct. 213, 214, 34 L.Ed. 862.

nondiscriminatory alternatives, adequate to conserve legitimate local interests, are available. Cf. *Baldwin v. Seelig, Inc.,* supra. A different view, that the ordinance is valid simply because it professes to be a health measure, would mean that the Commerce Clause of itself imposes no limitations on state action other than those laid down by the Due Process Clause, save for the rare instance where a state artlessly discloses an avowed purpose to discriminate against interstate goods. Our issue then is whether the discrimination inherent in the Madison ordinance can be justified in view of the character of the local interests and the available methods of protecting them.

It appears that reasonable and adequate alternatives are available. If the City of Madison prefers to rely upon its own officials for inspection of distant milk sources, such inspection is readily open to it without hardship for it could charge the actual and reasonable cost of such inspection to the importing producers and processors. Moreover, appellee Health Commissioner of Madison testified that as proponent of the local milk ordinance he had submitted the provisions here in controversy and an alternative proposal based on § 11 of the Model Milk Ordinance recommended by the United States Public Health Service. The model provision imposes no geographical limitation on location of milk sources and processing plants but excludes from the municipality milk not produced and pasteurized conformably to standards as high as those enforced by the receiving city. In implementing such an ordinance, the importing city obtains milk ratings based on uniform standards and established by health authorities in the jurisdiction where production and processing occur. The receiving city may determine the extent of enforcement of sanitary standards in the exporting area by verifying the accuracy of safety ratings of specific plants or of the milkshed in the distant jurisdiction through the United States Public Health Service, which routinely and on request spot checks the local ratings. The Commissioner testified that Madison consumers "would be safeguarded adequately" under either proposal and that he had expressed no preference. . . .

To permit Madison to adopt a regulation not essential for the protection of local health interests and placing a discriminatory burden on interstate commerce would invite a multiplication of preferential trade areas destructive of the very purpose of the Commerce Clause. Under the circumstances here presented, the regulation must yield to the principle that "one state in its dealings with another may not place itself in a position of economic isolation." *Baldwin v. Seelig, Inc.,* supra.

For these reasons we conclude that the judgment below sustaining the five-mile provision as to pasteurization must be reversed. . . .

MR. JUSTICE BLACK, with whom MR. JUSTICE DOUGLAS and MR. JUSTICE MINTON concur, dissenting.

(1) This ordinance does not exclude wholesome milk coming from Illinois or anywhere else. It does require that all milk sold in Madison must be pasteurized within five miles of the center of the city. But there

was no finding in the state courts, nor evidence to justify a finding there or here, that appellant, Dean Milk Company, is unable to have its milk pasteurized within the defined geographical area.... Dean's personal preference to pasteurize in Illinois, not the ordinance, keeps Dean's milk out of Madison.

(2) Characterization of § 7.21 as a "discriminatory burden" on interstate commerce is merely a statement of the Court's result, which I think incorrect. The section does prohibit the sale of milk in Madison by interstate and intrastate producers who prefer to pasteurize over five miles distant from the city. But both state courts below found that § 7.21 represents a good-faith attempt to safeguard public health by making adequate sanitation inspections possible. While we are not bound by these findings, I do not understand the Court to overturn them. Therefore, the fact that § 7.21, like all health regulations, imposes some burden on trade, does not mean that it "discriminates" against interstate commerce.

(3) This health regulation should not be invalidated merely because the Court believes that alternative milk-inspection methods might insure the cleanliness and healthfulness of Dean's Illinois milk.... For while the "reasonable alternative" concept has been invoked to protect First Amendment rights, e.g., *Schneider v. State,* 308 U.S. 147, 162, 60 S.Ct. 146, 151, 84 L.Ed. 155, it has not heretofore been considered an appropriate weapon for striking down local health laws.... No case is cited, and I have found none, in which a bona fide health law was struck down on the ground that some other method of safeguarding health would be as good as, or better than, the one the Court was called on to review. In my view, to use this ground now elevates the right to traffic in commerce for profit above the power of the people to guard the purity of their daily diet of milk.

If, however, the principle announced today is to be followed, the Court should not strike down local health regulations unless satisfied beyond a reasonable doubt that the substitutes it proposes would not lower health standards. I do not think that the Court can so satisfy itself on the basis of its judicial knowledge. And the evidence in the record leads me to the conclusion that the substitute health measures suggested by the Court do not insure milk as safe as the Madison ordinance requires.

One of the Court's proposals is that Madison require milk processors to pay reasonable inspection fees at the milk supply "sources." Experience shows, however, that the fee method gives rise to prolonged litigation over the calculation and collection of the charges. E.g., *Sprout v. City of South Bend,* 277 U.S. 163, 48 S.Ct. 502, 72 L.Ed. 833.... The Court's second proposal is that Madison adopt § 11 of the "Model Milk Ordinance." The state courts made no findings as to the relative merits of this inspection ordinance and the one chosen by Madison. The evidence indicates to me that enforcement of the Madison law would assure a more healthful quality of milk than that which is entitled to use the label of "Grade A" under the Model Ordinance. Indeed, the United States Board of Public Health, which drafted the Model Ordinance, suggests that the provisions are "minimum" standards only. The Model Ordinance does not provide for continuous investigation of all pasteurization plants as does § 7.21 of the Madison ordinance. Under § 11, moreover, Madison would be required to depend on the Chicago inspection system since Dean's plants, and the farms supplying them with raw milk, are located in the Chicago milkshed. But there is direct and positive evidence in the record that milk produced under Chicago standards did not meet the Madison requirements. . . .

From what this record shows, and from what it fails to show, I do not think that either of the alternatives suggested by the Court would assure the people of Madison as pure a supply of milk as they receive under their own ordinance. On this record I would uphold the Madison law. At the very least, however, I would not invalidate it without giving the parties a chance to present evidence and get findings on the ultimate issues the Court thinks crucial—namely, the relative merits of the Madison ordinance and the alternatives suggested by the Court today.

Notes

1. Is Justice Clark right that the Madison ordinance substantially burdens interstate commerce, and that there are reasonable, nondiscriminatory alternatives to achieve Madison's health objectives? Is Justice Black correct that it was reasonable for the framers of the ordinance to reject each of Clark's alternatives as having their own disadvantages? Is Justice Clark really judging the wisdom of the relative merits of the different means of protecting public health? If so, should the Court engage in this active review?

2. Note that Madison's ordinance effectively insulated from competition not only milk imported from out of state but also milk imported from other parts of Wisconsin. The majority, in a footnote, said that this fact was immaterial, citing a case that simply repeats the conclusion. What reasons might support this conclusion?

3. Consider the following series of cases. Are they distinguishable?

Robbins v. Taxing District of Shelby County, 120 U.S. 489, 7 S.Ct. 592, 30 L.Ed. 694 (1887): The Court invalidated a Tennessee license tax (a flat fee) on "drummers," i.e., solicitors taking orders without a regular place of business in the taxing district. In contrast, "peddlers" are vendors who travel from place to place selling goods that they carry for that purpose. *Robbins* stated:

> It would not be difficult, however, to show that the tax authorized by the State of Tennessee in the present case is discriminative against the merchants and manufacturers of other States. They can only sell their goods in Memphis by the employment of drummers and by means of samples; whilst the merchants and manufacturers of Memphis, having regular licensed houses of business there, have no occasion for such agents; and if they had, they are not subject to any tax therefor. They are taxed for their licensed houses, it is true; but so, it is presumable,

are the merchants and manufacturers of other States in the places where they reside; and the tax on drummers operates greatly to their disadvantage in comparison to the merchants and manufacturers of Memphis. And such was undoubtedly one of its objects. This kind of taxation is usually imposed at the instance and solicitation of domestic dealers, as a means of protecting them from foreign competition.[1]

Breard v. Alexandria, 341 U.S. 622, 71 S.Ct. 920, 95 L.Ed. 1233 (1951) upheld a city ordinance (called a "Green River Ordinance") providing that peddlers and solicitors, before approaching a residence for the purpose of soliciting orders, are required to obtain the prior permission of the owners of the residences solicited. The majority noted that "[u]nwanted knocks on the door by day or night are a nuisance or worse to peace and quiet. The local retail merchant, too, has not been unmindful of the effective competition furnished by house-to-house selling in many lines." Though admitting that "[i]nterstate commerce itself knocks on the local door" the Court upheld the law. The particular vendor in this case solicited subscriptions for magazines. The Court distinguished an earlier decision, *Martin v. Struthers,* 319 U.S. 141, 63 S.Ct. 862, 87 L.Ed. 1313 (1943), which had invalidated, on First Amendment grounds, a city ordinance when applied to a person distributing free leaflets advertising a religious meeting.

The tax in *Robbins* only places a burden on interstate commerce. A Green River ordinance effectively prohibits it. Is *Breard* consistent with *Robbins?* With *Martin?*

Breard should be reconsidered after you have studied the new protection for so-called "commercial speech," § 10–6, infra.

4. *Great Atlantic & Pacific Tea Co., Inc. v. Cottrell,* 424 U.S. 366, 96 S.Ct. 923, 47 L.Ed.2d 55 (1976) unanimously invalidated a Mississippi law that provided that milk from another state may not be sold in Mississippi unless that other state accepts milk processed in Mississippi on a reciprocal basis. "The question presented by this case is whether Mississippi, consistently with the Commerce Clause ... may, pursuant to this regulation, constitutionally deny a Louisiana milk producer the right to sell in Mississippi milk satisfying Mississippi's health standards solely because the State of Louisiana has not signed a reciprocity agreement with the State of Mississippi as required by the regulation." Can you justify this decision?

Should it be unconstitutional for state *A* to refuse to admit out of state lawyers to practice unless that other state admits state *A* 's lawyers on a reciprocal basis?

5. *Chemical Waste Management, Inc. v. Hunt,* 504 U.S. 334, 112 S.Ct. 2009, 119 L.Ed.2d 121 (1992), used the commerce clause to invalidate an Alabama law that imposed a hazardous waste disposal fee on hazardous wastes generated outside of the state but disposed of at a commercial (i.e., private, non-state owned) facility within Alabama. The fee did not apply to waste originating from Alabama. The Court explained: "No state may attempt to isolate itself from a problem common to the several States by raising barriers to the free flow of interstate trade." The Court noted that

---

1. Contrast *Wagner v. City of Covington,* 251 U.S. 95, 40 S.Ct. 93, 64 L.Ed. 157 (1919)(flat license tax on peddlers constitutional).

prior cases upholding quarantine laws were inapplicable, because those laws did not discriminate against interstate commerce as such, but simply prevented traffic in noxious articles, whatever their origin.

Fort Gratiot Sanitary Landfill, Inc. v. Michigan Department of Natural Resources, 504 U.S. 353, 112 S.Ct. 2019, 119 L.Ed.2d 139 (1992), decided the same day, invalidated, under the commerce clause, a Michigan law that prohibited private landfill operators from accepting solid waste generated in another county, state, or country unless explicitly authorized by the receiving county. "Solid waste, even if it has no value, is an article of commerce." There is either a "sale" of garbage or a "purchase" of transportation and landfill disposal services. There is no logical reason why solid waste coming from outside the county should be treated differently from solid waste coming from within the county. The Court, citing *Dean Milk,* rejected the idea that Michigan's discrimination against interstate commerce should be excused because the Michigan law also discriminated against solid waste coming from other counties within Michigan. If a county excludes waste coming from other in-state counties (in addition to waste from out-of-state), that only affects the volume or extent of the restriction on commerce; it does not eliminate the discrimination against interstate commerce because of its interstate origin.

Oregon Waste Systems, Inc. v. Department of Environmental Quality, 511 U.S. 93, 114 S.Ct. 1345, 128 L.Ed.2d 13 (1994). Oregon imposed a $2.25 per ton surcharge on the in-state disposal of waste generated in other states, but only an 85per ton tax on the disposal of waste generated within the state of Oregon. Private landfill owners sued, and Thomas, J., for the Court, held that the tax was facially invalid under the dormant Commerce Clause. He rejected Oregon's argument that the differential surcharge was a "compensating fee," based on any added costs of disposing of waste from other states. "Respondents' failure to identify a specific charge on intrastate commerce equal to or exceeding the surcharge is fatal to their claim." The state's geographic distinction "patently discriminates against interstate commerce." However, "if out-of-state waste did impose higher costs on Oregon than in-state waste, Oregon could recover the increased cost through a differential charge on out-of-state waste, for then there would be 'a reason apart from its origin, why solid waste coming from outside the [State] should be treated differently.' " Rehnquist, C.J., joined by Blackmun, J., dissented.

C & A Carbone, Inc. v. Town of Clarkstown, 511 U.S. 383, 114 S.Ct. 1677, 128 L.Ed.2d 399 (1994). The town agreed with a private contractor that it would build a solid waste transfer station, operate it for five years, and then sell it to the town for $1. To make the deal attractive to the private contractor, the town enacted an ordinance that guaranteed a minimum waste flow to the waste transfer station: it required that all nonhazardous solid waste generated or brought into the town must be processed at the transfer station. By law, all recyclers, such as Carbone had to bring nonrecyclable waste to the transfer station and to pay an above-market tipping fee on waste that they had sorted.

Kennedy, J., for the Court, invalidated the ordinance. The law drives up the cost for out-of-state interests to dispose of the solid waste that they send to Carbone or any other local processor (except the favored one), and it deprives out-of-state business of access to the local market. The town may not use its regulatory power to favor one or more local businesses by prohibiting patronage of out of state competitors. Citing *Dean Milk,* the Court rejected the argument that the law was not discriminatory against interstate commerce because it also discriminated against in-state or other in-town processors. The protectionist law favored a single local business, eliminating competition in the waste-processing service. If the town were really concerned about health and safety, it could engage in nondiscriminatory alternatives, such as uniform safety regulations. The ordinance's purpose of generating revenue cannot justify discrimination against interstate commerce. "The Commerce Clause presumes a national market free from local legislation that discriminates in favor of local interests." O'Connor, J., concurred in the judgment. Souter, J., joined by Rehnquist, C.J. & Blackmun, J., dissented.

3–4. OUTGOING COMMERCE

H.P. HOOD & SONS v. DU MOND
336 U.S. 525, 69 S.Ct. 657, 93 L.Ed. 865 (1949).

MR. JUSTICE JACKSON delivered the opinion of the Court.

This case concerns the power of the State of New York to deny additional facilities to acquire and ship milk in interstate commerce where the grounds of denial are that such limitation upon interstate business will protect and advance local economic interests.

H.P. Hood & Sons, Inc., a Massachusetts corporation, has long distributed milk and its products to inhabitants of Boston. That city obtains about 90% of its fluid milk from states other than Massachusetts. Dairies located in New York State since about 1900 have been among the sources of Boston's supply, their contribution having varied but during the last ten years approximating 8%. The area in which Hood has been denied an additional license to make interstate purchases has been developed as a part of the Boston milkshed from which both the Hood Company and a competitor have shipped to Boston.

The state courts have held and it is conceded here that Hood's entire business in New York, present and proposed, is interstate commerce. This Hood has conducted for some time by means of three receiving depots, where it takes raw milk from farmers. The milk is not processed in New York but is weighed, tested and, if necessary, cooled and on the same day shipped as fluid milk to Boston. These existing plants have been operated under license from the State and are not in question here as the State has licensed Hood to continue them. The controversy concerns a proposed additional plant for the same kind of operation at Greenwich, New York.

Article 21 of the Agriculture and Markets Law of New York forbids a dealer to buy milk from producers unless licensed to do so by the Commissioner of Agriculture and Markets. For the license he must pay a substantial fee and furnish a bond to assure prompt payment to producers for milk. Under § 258, the Commissioner may not grant a license unless satisfied "that the applicant is qualified by character, experience, financial responsibility and equipment to properly conduct the proposed business." The Hood Company concededly has met all the foregoing tests and license for an additional plant was not denied for any failure to comply with these requirements. The Commissioner's denial was based on further provisions of this section which require him to be satisfied "that the issuance of the license will not tend to a destructive competition in a market already adequately served, and that the issuance of the license is in the public interest." . . .

The Commissioner found that Hood, if licensed at Greenwich, would permit its present suppliers at their option, to deliver at the new plant rather than the old ones and for a substantial number this would mean shorter hauls and savings in delivery costs. The new plant also would attract twenty to thirty producers, some of whose milk Hood anticipates will or may be diverted from other buyers. Other large milk distributors have plants within the general area and dealers serving Troy obtain milk in the locality. He found that Troy was inadequately supplied during the preceding short season.

In denying the application for expanded facilities, the Commissioner states his grounds as follows:

> . . . There is no evidence that any producer is without a market for his milk. There is no evidence that any producers not now delivering milk to applicant would receive any higher price, were they to deliver their milk to applicant's proposed plant. The issuance of a license to applicant which would permit it to operate an additional plant, would tend to a destructive competition in a market already adequately served, and would not be in the public interest. . . .

Pennsylvania enacted a law including provisions to protect producers which were very similar to those of this New York Act. A concern which operated a receiving plant in Pennsylvania from which it shipped milk to the New York City market challenged the Act upon grounds thus defined by this Court: "The respondent contends that the act, if construed to require it to obtain a license, to file a bond for the protection of producers, and to pay the farmers the prices prescribed by the Board, unconstitutionally regulates and burdens interstate commerce." *Milk Board v. Eisenberg Co.*, [noted below]. This Court, specifically limiting its judgment to the Act's provisions with respect to license, bond and regulation of prices to be paid to producers, considered their effect on interstate commerce "incidental and not forbidden by the Constitution, in the absence of regulation by Congress."

The present controversy begins where the *Eisenberg* decision left off. New York's regulations, designed to assure producers a fair price and a responsible purchaser, and consumers a sanitary and modernly equipped handler, are not challenged here but have been complied with. It is only additional restrictions, imposed for the avowed purpose and with the practical effect of curtailing the volume of interstate commerce to aid local economic interests, that are in question here, and no such measures were attempted or such ends sought to be served in the Act before the Court in the *Eisenberg* case.[9]

Our decision in a milk litigation most relevant to the present controversy deals with the converse of the present situation. *Baldwin v. Seelig,* [§ 3–3, supra].... [That case recognized that the] distinction between the power of the State to shelter its people from menaces to their health or safety and from fraud, even when those dangers emanate from interstate commerce, and its lack of power to retard, burden or constrict the flow of such commerce for their economic advantage, is one deeply rooted in both our history and our law.

... As most states serve their own interests best by sending their produce to market, the cases in which this Court has been obliged to deal with prohibitions or limitations by states upon exports of articles of commerce are not numerous. However, in a leading case, *West v. Kansas Natural Gas Co.,* 221 U.S. 229, 31 S.Ct. 564, 55 L.Ed. 716, the Court denied constitutional validity to a statute by which Oklahoma, by regulation of gas companies and pipe lines, sought to restrict the export of natural gas. The Court held that when a state recognizes an article to be a subject of commerce, it cannot prohibit it from being a subject of interstate commerce; that the right to engage in interstate commerce is not the gift of a state, and that a state cannot regulate or restrain it.

Later West Virginia, by act of the Legislature, undertook regulation of pipe-line companies intended to keep within West Virginia all natural gas there produced that might be required for local needs. This Court held that the State could not accord to its own consumers a preferred right of purchase over consumers in other states.... *Pennsylvania v. West Virginia,* 262 U.S. 553, at 597, 598.

In *Foster Packing Co. v. Haydel,* 278 U.S. 1, 49 S.Ct. 1, 73 L.Ed. 147, the Court cited these two cases as authority for this proposition that "A State is without power to prevent privately owned articles of trade from being shipped and sold in interstate commerce on the ground that they are required to satisfy local demands or because they are needed by the people of the State." [The Louisiana statute forbade the transportation beyond the State of shrimp taken in Louisiana waters until the shells and heads had been removed.] The Court also pointed out that "the purpose [of the statute there involved] is not to retain the shrimp for the use of the people of Louisiana; it is to favor the canning of the meat and the manufacture of bran in Louisiana.... " Thus ... the Court invalidated state enactments attempting to promote local interests at the expense of interstate commerce.

In *Parker v. Brown,* [noted below], California's restrictions on sales of raisins within the State to those who were there processing and packing them were attacked as invalid because approximately 95% of the

---

9. The Court said: "The Commonwealth [of Pennsylvania] does not essay to regulate or to restrain the shipment of the respondent's milk into New York.... "

crop would find its way into interstate commerce after processing and packing. However, the Court said: "... no case has gone so far as to hold that a state could not license or otherwise regulate the sale of articles within the state because the buyer, after processing and packing them, will, in the normal course of business, sell and ship them in interstate commerce.... The regulation is thus applied to transactions wholly intrastate before the raisins are ready for shipment in interstate commerce." This regulation of sale to local processors was distinguished from those which were held invalid in *Lemke v. Farmers' Grain Co. of Embden, N.D.,* 258 U.S. 50, 42 S.Ct. 244, 66 L.Ed. 458, and *Shafer v. Farmers' Grain Co. of Embden, N.D.,* 268 U.S. 189, 45 S.Ct. 481, 69 L.Ed. 909, because the regulation in the earlier cases was "of the business of those who purchased grain within the state for immediate shipment out of it." In those cases, the regulation was of interstate commerce itself. Another element in the *Parker* case which led the Court to sustain the California regulation was that it was one which the policy of Congress was to aid and encourage, and the Secretary of Agriculture had approved the State program by loans....

This principle that our economic unit is the Nation, which alone has the gamut of powers necessary to control of the economy, including the vital power of erecting customs barriers against foreign competition, has as its corollary that the states are not separable economic units.... The material success that has come to inhabitants of the states which make up this federal free trade unit has been the most impressive in the history of commerce, but the established interdependence of the states only emphasizes the necessity of protecting interstate movement of goods against local burdens and repressions. We need only consider the consequences if each of the few states that produce copper, lead, high-grade iron ore, timber, cotton, oil or gas should decree that industries located in that state shall have priority. What fantastic rivalries and dislocations and reprisals would ensue if such practices were begun! Or suppose that the field of discrimination and retaliation be industry. May Michigan provide that automobiles cannot be taken out of that State until local dealers' demands are fully met? Would she not have every argument in the favor of such a statute that can be offered in support of New York's limiting sales of milk for out-of-state shipment to protect the economic interests of her competing dealers and local consumers? Could Ohio then pounce upon the rubber-tire industry, on which she has a substantial grip, to retaliate for Michigan's auto monopoly?

Our system, fostered by the Commerce Clause, is that every farmer and every craftsman shall be encouraged to produce by the certainty that he will have free access to every market in the Nation, that no home embargoes will withhold his exports, and no foreign state will by customs duties or regulations exclude them. Likewise, every consumer may look to the free competition from every producing area in the Nation to protect him from exploitation by any. Such was the vision of the Founders; such has been the doctrine of this Court which has given it reality.

The State, however, insists that denial of the license for a new plant does not restrict or obstruct interstate commerce, because petitioner has been licensed at its other plants without condition or limitation as to the quantities it may purchase. Hence, it is said, all that has been denied petitioner is a local convenience—that of being able to buy and receive at Greenwich quantities of milk it is free to buy at Eagle Bridge and Salem. . . . But the argument also asks us to assume that the Commissioner's order will not operate in the way he found that it would as a reason for making it. He found that petitioner, at its new plant, would divert milk from the plants of some other large handlers in the vicinity, which plants "can handle more milk." This competition he did not approve. He also found it would tend to deprive local markets of needed supplies during the short season. In the face of affirmative findings that the proposed plant would increase petitioner's supply, we can hardly be asked to assume that denial of the license will not deny petitioner access to such added supplies. While the state power is applied in this case to limit expansion by a handler of milk who already has been allowed some purchasing facilities, the argument for doing so, if sustained, would be equally effective to exclude an entirely new foreign handler from coming into the State to purchase. . . .

Since the statute as applied violates the Commerce Clause and is not authorized by federal legislation pursuant to that Clause, it cannot stand. The judgment is reversed and the cause remanded for proceedings not inconsistent with this opinion.

It is so ordered.

Mr. Justice Black, dissenting. . . .

The language of this state Act is not discriminatory, the legislative history shows it was not so intended, and the commissioner has not administered it with a hostile eye. . . . The judicially directed march of the due process philosophy as an emancipator of business from regulation appeared arrested a few years ago. That appearance was illusory. That philosophy continues its march. The due process clause and commerce clause have been used like Siamese twins in a never-ending stream of challenges to government regulation. . . .

Mr. Justice Murphy joins in this opinion.

Mr. Justice Frankfurter, with whom Mr. Justice Rutledge joins, dissenting. . . .

As I see the central issue, therefore, it is whether the difference in degree between denying access to a market for failure to comply with sanitary or book-keeping regulations and denying it for the sake of preventing destructive competition from disrupting the market is great enough to justify a difference in result. . . .

Notes

1. What were the purposes of the New York law? Was the law discriminatory on its face? Justice Black in dissent makes the point that the

language of this Act was not discriminatory. The Court invalidated the New York statute "as applied", not "on its face." What does that mean?

Is Justice Black correct when he argues that the commerce clause is the emancipator of business from regulation? Does the majority opinion leave New York with alternative regulatory schemes to protect the local milk producers? Is there any distinction between a law invalidated on commerce clause grounds versus due process grounds?

2. Consider Justice Frankfurter's dissent. Is the denial of a license to enter a market in order to sell goods out of state different in degree, or in kind, from denial of a license for failure to comply with a sanitary or bookkeeping regulation? Does the difference between the two lie in the purpose for the denial of the license, or in the power of the applicant to remove the disability, or both?

3. *Milk Control Board v. Eisenberg Farm Products,* 306 U.S. 346, 59 S.Ct. 528, 83 L.Ed. 752 (1939), discussed in *Hood,* upheld a Pennsylvania law that required the licensing of milk dealers and fixed a minimum price paid to producers by the milk dealers, even to the extent it applied to a New York dealer purchasing milk for resale outside of Pennsylvania. Approximately 90% of the milk produced in Pennsylvania was consumed there. In *Parker v. Brown,* 317 U.S. 341, 63 S.Ct. 307, 87 L.Ed. 315 (1943) the Court upheld a California law that required all raisin producers in the state to deliver two-thirds of their crop to a marketing control committee, which could control the marketing of the crop so as to, in effect, fix the price. About 95% of the crop eventually would be marketed in interstate commerce. The declared purpose of the act was to "conserve the agricultural wealth of the State" and to "prevent economic waste in the marketing of agricultural products" of the state. The Court held the law did not violate the Sherman Act, the commerce clause, or other federal legislation; in fact, Congressional policy supported this state law and the Secretary of Agriculture had approved the State program by loans.

Are these cases distinguishable from *Hood?*

HUGHES v. OKLAHOMA
441 U.S. 322, 99 S.Ct. 1727, 60 L.Ed.2d 250 (1979).

MR. JUSTICE BRENNAN delivered the opinion of the Court.

The question presented for decision is whether Okl.Stat., Tit. 29, § 4–115(B) violates the Commerce Clause, insofar as it provides that "No person may transport or ship minnows for sale outside the state which were seined or procured within the waters of this state.... " Appellant William Hughes holds a Texas license to operate a commercial minnow business near Wichita Falls, Tex. An Oklahoma Game Ranger arrested him on a charge of violating § 4–115(B) by transporting from Oklahoma to Wichita Falls a load of natural minnows [i.e., not hatchery-bred] purchased from a minnow dealer licensed to do business in Oklahoma. Hughes' defense that § 4–115(B) was unconstitutional because it was repugnant to the Commerce Clause was rejected, and he was convicted and fined.... We reverse. *Geer v. Connecticut,* [161 U.S.

519, 16 S.Ct. 600, 40 L.Ed. 793 (1896),] on which the Court of Criminal Appeals relied, is overruled. . . .

Geer sustained against a Commerce Clause challenge a statute forbidding the transportation beyond the State of game birds that had been lawfully killed within the State. The decision rested on the holding that no interstate commerce was involved. This conclusion followed in turn from the view that the State had the power, as representative for its citizens, who "owned" in common all wild animals within the State, to control not only the *taking* of game but the *ownership* of game that had been lawfully reduced to possession. By virtue of this power, Connecticut could qualify the ownership of wild game taken within the State by, for example, prohibiting its removal from the State: "The common ownership imports the right to keep the property, if the sovereign so chooses, always within its jurisdiction for every purpose." . . .

MR. JUSTICE FIELD and the first MR. JUSTICE HARLAN dissented, rejecting as artificial and formalistic the Court's analysis of "ownership" and "commerce" in wild game. They would have affirmed the State's power to provide for the protection of wild game, but . . . "[w]hen an animal . . . is lawfully killed for the purposes of food or other uses of man, it becomes an article of commerce, and its use cannot be limited to the citizens of one state to the exclusion of citizens of another state." . . .

The case before us is the first in modern times to present facts essentially on all fours with *Geer*. We now conclude that challenges under the Commerce Clause to state regulations of wild animals should be considered according to the same general rule applied to state regulations of other natural resources, and therefore expressly overrule *Geer*. We thus bring our analytical framework into conformity with practical realities. Overruling *Geer* also eliminates the anomaly, created by the decisions distinguishing *Geer,* that statutes imposing the most extreme burdens on interstate commerce (essentially total embargoes) were the most immune from challenge. At the same time, the general rule we adopt in this case makes ample allowance for preserving, in ways not inconsistent with the Commerce Clause, the legitimate state concerns for conservation and protection of wild animals underlying the 19th century legal fiction of state ownership.

We turn then to the question whether the burden imposed on interstate commerce in wild game by § 4–115(B) is permissible under the general rule articulated in our precedents governing other types of commerce. Under that general rule we must inquire (1) whether the challenged statute regulates evenhandedly with only "incidental" effects on interstate commerce, or discriminates against interstate commerce either on its face or in practical effect; (2) whether the statute serves a legitimate local purpose; and, if so, (3) whether alternative means could promote this local purpose as well without discriminating against interstate commerce. . . .

Section 4–115(B) on its face discriminates against interstate commerce. It forbids the transportation of natural minnows out of the State for purposes of sale, and thus "overtly blocks the flow of interstate commerce at [the] State's borders." Such facial discrimination by itself may be a fatal defect, regardless of the State's purpose, because "the evil of protectionism can reside in legislative means as well as legislative ends." At a minimum such facial discrimination invokes the strictest scrutiny of any purported legitimate local purpose and of the absence of nondiscriminatory alternatives.

Oklahoma argues that § 4–115(B) serves a legitimate local purpose in that it is "readily apparent as a conservation measure." The State's interest in maintaining the ecological balance in state waters by avoiding the removal of inordinate numbers of minnows may well qualify as a legitimate local purpose. We consider the States' interests in conservation and protection of wild animals as legitimate local purposes similar to the States' interests in protecting the health and safety of their citizens. But the scope of legitimate state interests in "conservation" is narrower under this analysis than it was under *Geer*. A State may no longer "keep the property, if the sovereign so chooses, always within its jurisdiction for every purpose." The fiction of state ownership may no longer be used to force those outside the State to bear the full costs of "conserving" the wild animals within its borders when equally effective nondiscriminatory conservation measures are available.

Far from choosing the least discriminatory alternative, Oklahoma has chosen to "conserve" its minnows in the way that most overtly discriminates against interstate commerce. The State places no limits on the numbers of minnows that can be taken by licensed minnow dealers; nor does it limit in any way how these minnows may be disposed of within the State. Yet it forbids the transportation of any commercially significant number of natural minnows out of the State for sale. Section 4–115(B) is certainly not a "last ditch" attempt at conservation after nondiscriminatory alternatives have proven unfeasible. It is rather a choice of the most discriminatory means even though nondiscriminatory alternatives would seem likely to fulfill the State's purported legitimate local purpose more effectively.

We therefore hold that § 4–115(B) is repugnant to the Commerce Clause. The overruling of *Geer* does not leave the States powerless to protect and conserve wild animal life within their borders. Today's decision makes clear, however, that States may promote this legitimate purpose only in ways consistent with the basic principle that "our economic unit is the Nation," and that when a wild animal "becomes an article of commerce ... its use cannot be limited to the citizens of one State to the exclusion of citizens of another State." *Geer v. Connecticut, supra*, (Field, J., dissenting).

Reversed.

MR. JUSTICE REHNQUIST, with whom THE CHIEF JUSTICE [BURGER] joins, dissenting.

. . . This is not a case where a State's regulation permits residents to export naturally seined minnows but prohibits nonresidents from so doing. No person is allowed to export natural minnows for sale outside of Oklahoma; the statute is even-handed in its application. The State has not used its power to protect its own citizens from outside competition. . . .

Notes

1. Does *Hughes* invalidate the Oklahoma law on its face or as applied? Is the dissent correct that the Oklahoma law does not discriminate?

2. *Sporhase v. Nebraska,* 458 U.S. 941, 102 S.Ct. 3456, 73 L.Ed.2d 1254 (1982) held that water can be an article of commerce. The Court invalidated a state law that did not allow one to withdraw ground water from a well within Nebraska and transport it for use in another state unless "the state in which the water is to be used grants reciprocal rights to withdraw ground water from that state for use in the State of Nebraska."

3. *Maine v. Taylor,* 477 U.S. 131, 106 S.Ct. 2440, 91 L.Ed.2d 110 (1986) upheld the constitutionality of a law that prohibited the importation of live bait fish. The Court distinguished *Hughes v. Oklahoma* and upheld the evidentiary finding of the trial court that the Maine statute serves the legitimate local purpose of protecting local fish from certain types of parasites prevalent in out-of-state baitfish but not common to wild fish in Maine. Expert witnesses testified that it was a "physical impossibility" to inspect for commingled species because of the small size of baitfish and the large quantities in which they are shipped. Thus the statute serves a legitimate local purpose that could not be served as well by available nondiscriminatory means. Stevens, J., dissented, arguing that there "is something fishy about this case," and the state must demonstrate its ecological interests "with far greater specificity."

REEVES, INC. v. STAKE
447 U.S. 429, 100 S.Ct. 2271, 65 L.Ed.2d 244 (1980).

MR. JUSTICE BLACKMUN delivered the opinion of the Court.

The issue in this case is whether, consistent with the Commerce Clause, the State of South Dakota, in a time of shortage, may confine the sale of the cement it produces solely to its residents.

In 1919, South Dakota undertook plans to build a cement plant. The project, a product of the State's then prevailing Progressive political movement, was initiated in response to recent regional cement shortages that "interfered with and delayed both public and private enterprises," and that were "threatening the people of this state." . . . Over the years, buyers in no less than nine nearby States purchased cement from the State's plant. Between 1970 and 1977, some 40% of the plant's output went outside the State. . . .

As the 1978 construction season approached, difficulties at the plant slowed production. Meanwhile, a booming construction industry spurred demand for cement both regionally and nationally. The plant found itself unable to meet all orders. Faced with the same type of "serious cement shortage" that inspired the plant's construction, the Commission "reaffirmed its policy of supplying all South Dakota customers first and to honor all contract commitments, with the remaining volume allocated on a first come, first served basis." Reeves, which had no pre-existing long-term supply contract, was hit hard and quickly by this development.... Unable to find another supplier, Reeves was forced to cut production by 76% in mid-July.

[The Court of Appeals upheld the law, distinguished *Hughes v. Oklahoma,* and relied on *Hughes v. Alexandria Scrap Corp.,* 426 U.S. 794, 96 S.Ct. 2488, 49 L.Ed.2d 220 (1976)]. *Alexandria Scrap* concerned a Maryland program designed to remove abandoned automobiles from the State's roadways and junkyards. To encourage recycling, a "bounty" was offered for every Maryland-titled junk car converted into scrap. Processors located both in and outside Maryland were eligible to collect these subsidies. [A 1974] law imposed more exacting documentation requirements on out-of-state than in-state processors. By making it less remunerative for suppliers to transfer vehicles outside Maryland, the reform triggered a "precipitate decline in the number of bounty-eligible hulks supplied to appellee's [Virginia] plant from Maryland sources." Indeed, "[t]he practical effect was substantially the same as if Maryland had withdrawn altogether the availability of bounties on hulks delivered by unlicensed suppliers to licensed non-Maryland processors." ...

Alexandria Scrap did not involve "the kind of action with which the Commerce Clause is concerned." ... Having characterized Maryland as a market participant, rather than as a market regulator, the Court found no reason to "believe the Commerce Clause was intended to require independent justification for [the State's] action." The Court couched its holding in unmistakably broad terms. "Nothing in the purposes animating the Commerce Clause prohibits a State, in the absence of congressional action, from participating in the market and exercising the right to favor its own citizens over others."

The basic distinction drawn in *Alexandria Scrap* between States as market participants and States as market regulators makes good sense and sound law. As that case explains, the Commerce Clause responds principally to state taxes and regulatory measures impeding free private trade in the national marketplace. There is no indication of a constitutional plan to limit the ability of the States themselves to operate freely in the free market. The precedents comport with this distinction.

Restraint in this area is also counseled by considerations of state sovereignty, the role of each State " 'as the guardian and trustee for its people,' "and "the long recognized right of trader or manufacturer, engaged in an entirely private business, freely to exercise his own independent discretion as to parties with whom he will deal." Moreover, state proprietary activities may be, and often are, burdened with the same restrictions imposed on private market participants. Evenhandedness suggests that, when acting as proprietors, States should similarly share existing freedoms from federal constraints, including the inherent limits of the Commerce Clause. [A]s a rule, the adjustment of interests in this context is a task better suited for Congress than this Court.

South Dakota, as a seller of cement, unquestionably fits the "market participant" label more comfortably than a State acting to subsidize local scrap processors. Thus, the general rule of *Alexandria Scrap* plainly applies here. Petitioner argues, however, that the exemption for marketplace participation necessarily admits of exceptions. While conceding that possibility, we perceive in this case no sufficient reason to depart from the general rule.

. . . The State's refusal to sell to buyers other than South Dakotans is "protectionist" only in the sense that it limits benefits generated by a state program to those who fund the state treasury and whom the State was created to serve. Petitioner's argument apparently also would characterize as "protectionist" rules restricting to state residents the enjoyment of state educational institutions, energy generated by a state-run plant, police and fire protection, and agricultural improvement and business development programs. Such policies, while perhaps "protectionist" in a loose sense, reflect the essential and patently unobjectionable purpose of state government—to serve the citizens of the State.

Second, petitioner echoes the District Court's warning:

If a state in this union, were allowed to hoard its commodities or resources for the use of their own residents only, a drastic situation might evolve. For example, Pennsylvania or Wyoming might keep their coal, the northwest its timber, and the mining states their minerals. The result being that embargo may be retaliated by embargo and commerce would be halted at state lines.

This argument, although rooted in the core purpose of the Commerce Clause, does not fit the present facts. Cement is not a natural resource, like coal, timber, wild game, or minerals. Cf. *Hughes v. Oklahoma*. It is the end-product of a complex process whereby a costly physical plant and human labor act on raw materials. South Dakota has not sought to limit access to the State's limestone or other materials used to make cement. Nor has it restricted the ability of private firms or sister States to set up plants within its borders. . . .

Third, it is suggested that the South Dakota program is infirm because it places South Dakota suppliers of ready-mix concrete at a competitive advantage in the out-of-state market. [But] the competitive plight of out-of-state ready-mix suppliers cannot be laid solely at the feet of South Dakota. It is attributable as well to their own States' not providing or attracting alternative sources of supply and to the suppliers' own failure to guard against shortages by executing long-term supply contracts with the South Dakota plant.

In its last argument, petitioner urges that, had South Dakota not acted, free market forces would have generated an appropriate level of supply at free market prices for all buyers in the region. Having replaced free market forces, South Dakota should be forced to replicate how the free market would have operated under prevailing conditions. This argument appears to us to be simplistic and speculative.... Indeed, it is quite possible that petitioner would never have existed—far less operated successfully for 20 years—had it not been for South Dakota cement.

We conclude, then, that the arguments for invalidating South Dakota's resident-preference program are weak at best. Whatever residual force inheres in them is more than offset by countervailing considerations of policy and fairness. Reversal would discourage similar state projects, even though this project demonstrably has served the needs of state residents and has helped the entire region for more than a half century. Reversal also would rob South Dakota of the intended benefits of its foresight, risk, and industry. Under these circumstances, there is no reason to depart from the general rule of *Alexandria Scrap.*

The judgment of the United States Court of Appeals is affirmed.

It is so ordered.

MR. JUSTICE POWELL, with whom MR. JUSTICE BRENNAN, MR. JUSTICE WHITE, and MR. JUSTICE STEVENS join, dissenting.

The South Dakota Cement Commission has ordered that in times of shortage the state cement plant must turn away out-of-state customers until all orders from South Dakotans are filled. This policy represents precisely the kind of economic protectionism that the Commerce Clause was intended to prevent.[1] ...

This case presents a novel constitutional question. The Commerce Clause would bar legislation imposing on private parties the type of restraint on commerce adopted by South Dakota.[2] ...

Unlike the market subsidies at issue in *Alexandria Scrap,* the marketing policy of the South Dakota Cement Commission has cut off interstate trade. The State can raise such a bar when it enters the market to supply its own needs. In order to ensure an adequate supply of cement for public uses, the State can withhold from interstate commerce the cement needed for public projects. The State, however, has no parallel justification for favoring private, in-state customers over out-of-

---

1. By "protectionism," I refer to State policies designed to protect private economic interests within the State from the forces of the interstate market. I would exclude from this term policies relating to traditional governmental functions, such as education, and subsidy programs like the one at issue in *Hughes v. Alexandria Scrap Corp.*

2. The Court attempts to distinguish prior decisions that address the Commerce Clause limitations on a State's regulation of natural resource exploitation. E.g., *Hughes v. Oklahoma.* The Court contends that cement production, unlike the activities involved in those cases, "is the end-product of a complex process whereby a costly physical

plant and human labor act on raw materials." The Court's distinction fails in two respects. First, the principles articulated in the natural resources cases also have been applied in decisions involving agricultural production, notably milk processing. E.g., *H.P. Hood & Sons v. Du Mond.* More fundamentally, the Court's definition of cement production describes all sophisticated economic activity, including the exploitation of natural resources. The extraction of natural gas, for example, could hardly occur except through a "complex process whereby a costly physical plant and human labor act on raw materials." ...

state customers. In response to political concerns that likely would be inconsequential to a private cement producer, South Dakota has shut off its cement sales to customers beyond its borders. That discrimination constitutes a direct barrier to trade.... The effect on interstate trade is the same as if the state legislature had imposed the policy on private cement producers. The Commerce Clause prohibits this severe restraint on commerce....

Notes

1. *South–Central Timber Development, Inc. v. Wunnicke,* 467 U.S. 82, 104 S.Ct. 2237, 81 L.Ed.2d 71 (1984) invalidated an Alaskan law requiring that any purchasers of state-owned timber must engage in partial processing of the timber within Alaska before they could ship it out of state. Petitioner, an Alaskan corporation with no operating mill in that state, purchased the timber and shipped the unprocessed logs into foreign commerce. Alaska charged a "significantly lower price for the timber than it otherwise would" because of its in-state processing clause requirement. There was no majority opinion on the question of whether Alaska was a market participant or market regulator. White, J.'s plurality opinion, joined by Brennan, Blackmun, and Stevens, JJ., reasoned that Alaska participates in the timber market, but it also "imposes conditions downstream in the timber-processing market"—

> Alaska is not merely subsidizing local timber processing in an amount "roughly equal to the difference between the price the timber would fetch in the absence of such a requirement and the amount the state actually receives." If the State directly subsidized the timber-processing industry by such an amount, the purchaser would retain the option of taking advantage of the subsidy by processing timber in the State or foregoing the benefits of the subsidy and exporting unprocessed timber. Under the Alaska requirement, however, the choice is made for him: if he buys timber from the State he is not free to take the timber out of state prior to processing. [T]he limit of the market-participant doctrine must be that it allows a State to impose burdens on commerce within the market in which it is a participant, but allows it to do no further. The State may not impose conditions, whether by statute, regulation, or contract, that have a substantial regulatory effect outside of that particular market....
>
> There are sound reasons for distinguishing between a State's preferring its own residents in the initial disposition of goods when it is a market participant and a State's attachment of restrictions on dispositions subsequent to the goods coming to rest in private hands. First, simply as a matter of intuition a State market participant has a greater interest as a "private trader" in the immediate transaction than it has in what its purchaser does with the goods after the State no longer has an interest in them. The common law recognized such a notion in the doctrine of restraints on alienation. Similarly, the antitrust laws place limits on vertical restraints....
>
> Second, downstream restrictions have a greater regulatory effect than do limitations on the immediate transaction. Instead of merely

choosing its own trading partners, the State is attempting to govern the private, separate economic relationships of its trading partners; that is, it restricts the post-purchase activity of the purchaser, rather than merely the purchasing activity. [T]his restriction on private economic activity takes place after the completion of the parties' direct commercial obligations, rather than during the course of an ongoing commercial relationship in which the city retained a continuing proprietary interest in the subject of the contract. In sum, the State may not avail itself of the market-participant doctrine to immunize its downstream regulation of the timber-processing market in which it is not a participant.

Rehnquist, J., joined by O'Connor, J., dissented:

In my view, the line of distinction drawn in the plurality opinion between the State as market participant and the State as market regulator is both artificial and unconvincing.... Perhaps the State's actions do raise antitrust problems. But what the plurality overlooks is that the antitrust laws apply to a State only when it is acting as a market participant. When the State acts as a market regulator, it is immune from antitrust scrutiny.... Alaska is merely paying the buyer of the timber indirectly, by means of a reduced price, to hire Alaska residents to process the timber. Under existing precedent, the State could accomplish that same result in any number of ways. For example, the State could choose to sell its timber only to those companies that maintain active primary-processing plants in Alaska. *Reeves, Inc. v. Stake.* Or the State could directly subsidize the primary-processing industry within the State. *Hughes v. Alexandria Scrap Corp.* The State could even pay to have the logs processed and then enter the market only to sell processed logs. It seems to me unduly formalistic to conclude that the one path chosen by the State as best suited to promote its concerns is the path forbidden it by the Commerce Clause.

2. Compare *Wyoming v. Oklahoma*, 502 U.S. 437, 112 S.Ct. 789, 117 L.Ed.2d 1 (1992). The Court (6 to 3) invalidated Oklahoma legislation that required Oklahoma coal-fired electric generating plants (including privately owned plants) that were producing power for sale in Oklahoma to run a mixture of coal containing at least 10% Oklahoma-mined coal. Wyoming, using the Supreme Court's original jurisdiction, successfully challenged the Oklahoma rule as a violation of the dormant Commerce Clause.

3. *Camps Newfound/Owatonna, Inc. v. Town of Harrison*, 520 U.S. 564, 117 S.Ct. 1590, 137 L.Ed.2d 852 (1997). A nonprofit Maine corporation (financed by tuition, donations, and other revenues) operated a summer camp for children. Despite its nonprofit status, petitioner had to pay about $20,000 a year in real estate taxes because most of its campers (95%) were not Maine residents. Stevens, J., for the Court (5 to 4) held that an otherwise generally applicable state property tax violated the dormant commerce clause because its exemption for property owned by charitable institutions excluded organizations operated principally for the benefit of nonresidents. Maine can not tax "petitioner more heavily than other camp operators simply because its campers come principally from other States."

A real estate tax, like any other tax, may discriminate against interstate commerce. This tax encourages entities not to do business with nonresidents in order to avoid the discriminatory tax. In this context, the Maine statute "functionally serves as an export tariff that targets out-of-state consumers by taxing the businesses that principally serve them." The Maine law "facially discriminates against interstate commerce, and is all but *per se* invalid."

The fact that the camp is nonprofit does not change the analysis. The Court has held that the dormant commerce clause applies to activities undertaken without the intent of earning a profit. "Whether operated on a for-profit or nonprofit basis, they purchase goods and services in competitive markets, offer their facilities to a variety of patrons, and derive revenues from a variety of sources, some of which are local and some out of State."

Maine argued that its tax exemption should be viewed as either a legitimate discriminatory subsidy of only those charities that focus their activities on local concerns, or a governmental "purchase" of charitable services that falls within the "market participant" exemption. The majority rejected both arguments. Assuming a "direct subsidy benefitting only those nonprofits serving principally Maine residents would be permissible, our cases do not sanction a tax exemption serving similar ends." There are "constitutionally significant differences between subsidies and tax exemptions." States may grant subsidies funded from general tax revenues but not enact discriminatory taxes or discriminatory tax exemptions. Moreover, a tax program that has the purpose and effect of subsidizing a particular industry is not "the sort of direct state involvement in the market that falls within the market-participation doctrine."

Scalia, J., joined by Rehnquist, C.J., & Thomas & Ginsburg, JJ., dissented, arguing: "Maine's tax exemption, which excuses from taxation only that property used to relieve the State of its burden of caring for its residents, survives even our most demanding commerce-clause scrutiny." Thomas, J., joined by Scalia, J. (and in part by Rehnquist, C.J.), also filed a dissenting opinion. In the part joined by Rehnquist, Thomas said: "The negative commerce clause has no basis in the text of the Constitution, makes little sense, and has proved virtually unworkable in application."

3–5. PERSONAL MOBILITY

HICKLIN v. ORBECK
437 U.S. 518, 98 S.Ct. 2482, 57 L.Ed.2d 397 (1978).

Mr. Justice Brennan delivered the opinion of the Court.

In 1972, professedly for the purpose of reducing unemployment in the State, the Alaska Legislature passed an Act entitled "Local Hire Under State Leases." The key provision of "Alaska Hire," as the Act has come to be known, is the requirement that "all oil and gas leases, easements or right-of-way permits for oil or gas pipeline purposes, unitization agreements, or any renegotiation of any of the preceding to which the state is a party" contain a provision "requiring the employment of qualified Alaska residents" in preference to nonresidents. This employment preference is administered by providing persons meeting the statutory requirements for Alaskan residency with certificates of residence—"resident cards"—that can be presented to an employer covered by the Act as proof of residency. Appellants, individuals desirous of securing jobs covered by the Act but unable to qualify for the necessary resident cards, challenge Alaska Hire as violative of both the Privileges and Immunities Clause of Art. IV, § 2 and the Equal Protection Clause of the Fourteenth Amendment....

Appellants' principal challenge to Alaska Hire is made under the Privileges and Immunities Clause of Art. IV, § 2 [which] "establishes a norm of comity," that is to prevail among the States with respect to their treatment of each other's residents.[8] The purpose of the Clause, as described in *Paul v. Virginia,* 8 Wall. 168, 19 L.Ed. 357 (1868), is

> to place the citizens of each State upon the same footing with citizens of other States, so far as the advantages resulting from citizenship in those States are concerned. It relieves them from the disabilities of alienage in other States; it inhibits discriminating legislation against them by other States; it gives them the right of free ingress into other States, and egress from them; it insures to them in other States the same freedom possessed by the citizens of those States in the acquisition and enjoyment of property and in the pursuit of happiness; and it secures to them in other States the equal protection of their laws. It has been justly said that no provision in the Constitution has tended so strongly to constitute the citizens of the United States one people as this.

Appellants' appeal to the protection of the Clause is strongly supported by this Court's decisions holding violative of the Clause state discrimination against nonresidents seeking to ply their trade, practice their occupation, or pursue a common calling within the State. For example, in *Ward v. Maryland,* 12 Wall. 418, 20 L.Ed. 449 (1870), a Maryland statute regulating the sale of most goods in the city of Baltimore fell to the privileges and immunities challenge of a New Jersey resident against whom the law discriminated. The statute discriminated against nonresidents of Maryland in several ways: it required nonresident merchants to obtain licenses in order to practice their trade without requiring the same of certain similarly situated Maryland merchants; it charged nonresidents a higher license fee than those Maryland residents who were required to secure licenses; and it prohibited both resident and nonresident merchants from using nonresident salesmen, other than their regular employees, to sell their goods in the city. In holding that the statute violated the Privileges and Immunities Clause, the Court observed that "the clause plainly and unmistakably secures and protects the right of a citizen of one State to pass into any other State of the Union for the purpose of engaging in lawful commerce, trade, or business without molestation." ...

8. Although this Court has not always equated state residency with state citizenship, it is now established that the terms "citizen" and "resident" are "essentially interchangeable," for purposes of analysis of most cases under the Privileges and Immunities Clause of Art. IV, § 2.

Again *Toomer v. Witsell,* 334 U.S. 385, 68 S.Ct. 1156, 92 L.Ed. 1460 (1948), the leading modern exposition of the limitations the Clause places on a State's power to bias employment opportunities in favor of its own residents, invalidated a South Carolina statute that required nonresidents to pay a fee one hundred times greater than that paid by residents for a license to shrimp commercially in the three-mile maritime belt off the coast of that State. The Court reasoned that although the Privileges and Immunities Clause "does not preclude disparity of treatment in the many situations where there are perfectly valid independent reasons for it," "[i]t does bar discrimination against citizens of other States where there is no substantial reason for the discrimination beyond the mere fact that they are citizens of other States." A "substantial reason for the discrimination" would not exist, the Court explained, "unless there is something to indicate that noncitizens constitute a peculiar source of the evil at which the [discriminatory] statute is aimed." Moreover, even where the presence or activity of nonresidents causes or exacerbates the problem the State seeks to remedy, there must be a "reasonable relationship between the danger represented by noncitizens, as a class, and the ... discrimination practiced upon them." Toomer's analytical framework was confirmed in *Mullaney v. Anderson,* 342 U.S. 415, 72 S.Ct. 428, 96 L.Ed. 458 (1952), where it was applied to invalidate a scheme used by the Territory of Alaska for the licensing of commercial fishermen in territorial waters; under that scheme residents paid a license fee of only $5 while nonresidents were charged $50.

Even assuming that a State may validly attempt to alleviate its unemployment problem by requiring private employers within the State to discriminate against nonresidents—an assumption made at least dubious by *Ward*—it is clear that under the *Toomer* analysis reaffirmed in *Mullaney,* Alaska Hire's discrimination against nonresidents cannot withstand scrutiny under the Privileges and Immunities Clause. For although the statute may not violate the Clause if the State shows "something to indicate that noncitizens constitute a peculiar source of the evil at which the statute is aimed," ... certainly no showing was made on this record that nonresidents were "a peculiar source of the evil" Alaska Hire was enacted to remedy, namely Alaska's "uniquely high unemployment." ...

... Alaska contends that because the oil and gas that is the subject of Alaska Hire is *owned* by the State,[11] this ownership of itself is sufficient justification for the Act's discrimination against nonresidents, and takes the Act totally without the scope of the Privileges and Immunities Clause. [But] Alaska has little or no proprietary interest in much of the activity swept within the ambit of Alaska Hire; and the

11. At the time Alaska was admitted into the Union on January 3, 1959, 99% of all land within Alaska's borders was owned by the Federal Government. In becoming a State, Alaska was granted and became entitled to select approximately 103 million acres of those federal lands. Alaska Statehood, 72 Stat. 339, § 6, 48 U.S.C.A. preceding § 21. The selection process is not yet complete, but since 1959 large portions of land have been conveyed to the State, in fee, by the Federal Government. Full title to those lands and to the minerals on and below them is vested in the State.

connection of the State's oil and gas with much of the covered activity is sufficiently attenuated so that it cannot justifiably be the basis for requiring private employers to discriminate against nonresidents. The extensive reach of Alaska Hire is set out in Alaska Stat.Ann. § 38.40.050(a)(1977). That section provides:

> The provisions of this chapter apply to *all employment which is a result* of oil and gas leases, easements, leases or right-of-way permits *for oil or gas pipeline purposes,* unitization agreements or any renegotiation of any of the preceding to which the state is a party after July 7, 1972; however, the activity which generates the employment must take place inside the state and it must take place either on the property under the control of the person subject to this chapter *or be directly related to activity taking place on the property under his control* and the activity must be performed directly for the person subject to this chapter *or his contractor or a subcontractor of his contractor or a supplier of his contractor or subcontractor.* (Emphasis added.)

Under this provision, Alaska Hire extends to employers who have no connection whatsoever with the State's oil and gas, perform no work on state land, have no contractual relationship with the State, and receive no payment from the State. The Act goes so far as to reach suppliers who provide goods or services to subcontractors who, in turn, perform work for contractors despite the fact that none of these employers may themselves have direct dealings with the State's oil and gas or ever set foot on State land. Moreover, the Act's coverage is not limited to activities connected with the extraction of Alaska's oil and gas. It encompasses, as emphasized by the dissent below, "employment opportunities at refineries and in distribution systems utilizing oil and gas obtained under Alaska leases." ... In sum, the Act is an attempt to force virtually all businesses that benefit in some way from the economic ripple effect of Alaska's decision to develop her oil and gas resources to bias their employment practices in favor of the State's residents. We believe that Alaska's ownership of the oil and gas that is the subject matter of Alaska Hire simply constitutes insufficient justification for the pervasive discrimination against nonresidents that the Act mandates.

Although appellants raise no Commerce Clause challenge to the Act, the mutually reinforcing relationship between the Privileges and Immunities Clause of Art. IV and the Commerce Clause ... renders several Commerce decisions appropriate support for our conclusion. [These decisions] establish that the Commerce Clause circumscribes a State's ability to prefer its own citizens in the utilization of natural resources found within its borders, but destined for interstate commerce.... As Mr. Justice Cardozo observed in *Baldwin v. G.A.F. Seelig,* the Constitution "was framed upon the theory that the peoples of the several states must sink or swim together, and that in the long run prosperity and salvation are in union and not division."

Reversed.

Notes

1.   Assume that a state owns several thousand acres of land. To ease unemployment, the state grants unemployed residents, upon application, permission to farm a portion (up to 40 acres) of this land. The state charges no rental fee and denies any applications by nonresidents because they are nonresidents. Can this state system survive *Hicklin* or is it distinguishable?

2.   *Baldwin v. Fish and Game Commission of Montana,* 436 U.S. 371, 98 S.Ct. 1852, 56 L.Ed.2d 354 (1978) upheld a disparity between Montana residents and nonresidents in that state's hunting license system. Under this system if a nonresident wished to hunt only elk, he paid 25 times as much as the resident ($225 or $9). Other disparities also existed. About 75% of the elk were killed on federal lands. The law was challenged in part as a violation of the privileges and immunities clause of Article IV, section 2.

Justice Blackmun, for the majority, noted that the Privileges and Immunities Clause "was not isolated from the Commerce Clause." Both Clauses have their source in the Articles of Confederation, where the two concepts were together in the fourth Article. "Their separation may have been an assurance against an anticipated narrow reading of the Commerce Clause." He concluded, as to the privileges and immunities claim:

> Does the distinction made by Montana between residents and nonresidents in establishing access to elk hunting threaten a basic right in a way that offends the Privileges and Immunities Clause? Merely to ask the question seems to provide the answer. We repeat much of what already has been said above: Elk hunting by nonresidents in Montana is a recreation and a sport. In itself—wholly apart from license fees—it is costly and obviously available only to the wealthy nonresident or to the one so taken with the sport that he sacrifices other values in order to indulge in it and to enjoy what it offers. It is not a means to the nonresident's livelihood. The mastery of the animal and the trophy are the ends that are sought; appellants are not totally excluded from these. The elk supply, which has been entrusted to the care of the State by the people of Montana, is finite and must be carefully tended in order to be preserved.

> Appellants' interest in sharing this limited resource on more equal terms with Montana residents simply does not fall within the purview of the Privileges and Immunities Clause. Equality in access to Montana elk is not basic to the maintenance or well-being of the Union. Appellants do not—and cannot—contend that they are deprived of a means of a livelihood by the system or of access to any part of the State to which they may seek to travel. We do not decide the full range of activities that are sufficiently basic to the livelihood of the Nation that the States may not interfere with a nonresident's participation therein without similarly interfering with a resident's participation. Whatever rights or activities may be "fundamental" under the Privileges and Immunities Clause, we are persuaded, and hold, that elk hunting by nonresidents in Montana is not one of them.

Justice Brennan, who wrote the unanimous opinion in *Hicklin,* dissented in *Baldwin.* What was Blackmun's test in *Baldwin* to determine a violation of the Privileges and Immunities Clause? Is his test consistent with the result in *Hicklin?* What was Brennan's test in *Hicklin?* Is it consistent with the result in *Baldwin?* If *Baldwin* were brought again and challenged on commerce clause grounds, could it survive *Hughes?* Which group is most hurt economically by Montana's Elk regulations: in state or out of state residents?

3.   For case law challenging, on equal protection grounds, state powers affecting interstate mobility of persons, see *Shapiro v. Thompson,* § 8–3.31, infra.

UNITED BUILDING AND CONSTRUCTION TRADES COUNCIL OF CAMDEN COUNTY AND VICINITY v. MAYOR AND COUNCIL OF THE CITY OF CAMDEN

465 U.S. 208, 104 S.Ct. 1020, 79 L.Ed.2d 249 (1984).

JUSTICE REHNQUIST delivered the opinion of the Court.

A municipal ordinance of the city of Camden, New Jersey requires that at least 40% of the employees of contractors and subcontractors working on city construction projects be Camden residents. Appellant, the United Building and Construction Trades Council of Camden and Vicinity (the Council), challenges that ordinance as a violation of the Privileges and Immunities Clause, Article IV, § 2, of the United States Constitution. [T]he ordinance requires that on all construction projects funded by the city:

> The developer/contractor, in hiring for jobs, shall make every effort to employ persons residing within the City of Camden but, in no event, shall less than forty percent (40%) of the entire labor force be residents of the City of Camden.

The contractor is also obliged to ensure that any subcontractors working on such projects adhere to the same requirement.

. . . Since the Council filed its appeal, . . . , the Court decided *White v. Massachusetts Council of Const. Employers,* 460 U.S. 204, 103 S.Ct. 1042, 75 L.Ed.2d 1 (1983), which held that an executive order of the Mayor of Boston, requiring that at least 50% of all jobs on construction projects funded in whole or part by city funds be filled by bona fide city residents, was immune from scrutiny under the Commerce Clause because Boston was acting as a market participant rather than as a market regulator. In light of the decision in *White,* appellant has abandoned its Commerce Clause challenge to the Camden ordinance.

[T]he only question left for our consideration is whether the Camden ordinance, as now written, violates the Privileges and Immunities Clause. . . . The first argument can be quickly rejected. The fact that the ordinance in question is a municipal, rather than a state, law does not somehow place it outside the scope of the Privileges and Immunities Clause. [A] municipality is merely a political subdivision of the State from which its authority derives. . . .

The second argument merits more consideration. The New Jersey Supreme Court concluded that the Privileges and Immunities Clause does not apply to an ordinance that discriminates solely on the basis of *municipal* residency.... We cannot accept this argument. We have never read the Clause so literally as to apply it only to distinctions based on state citizenship. For example, in *Mullaney v. Anderson,* 342 U.S. 415, 419–420, 72 S.Ct. 428, 431–432, 96 L.Ed. 458 (1952), the Court held that the Alaska Territory had no more freedom to discriminate against those not residing in the Territory than did any State to favor its own citizens. And despite some initial uncertainty, it is now established that the terms "citizen" and "resident" are "essentially interchangeable," for purposes of analysis of most cases under the Privileges and Immunities Clause. A person who is not residing in a given State is *ipso facto* not residing in a city within that State. Thus, whether the exercise of a privilege is conditioned on state residency or on municipal residency he will just as surely be excluded.

Given the Camden ordinance, an out-of-state citizen who ventures into New Jersey will not enjoy the same privileges as the New Jersey citizen residing in Camden. It is true that New Jersey citizens not residing in Camden will be affected by the ordinance as well as out-of-state citizens. ...But New Jersey residents at least have a chance to remedy at the polls any discrimination against them. Out-of-state citizens have no similar opportunity, and they must "not be restricted to the uncertain remedies afforded by diplomatic processes and official retaliation."[9] We conclude that Camden's ordinance is not immune from constitutional review at the behest of out-of-state residents merely because some in-state residents are similarly disadvantaged.

Application of the Privileges and Immunities Clause to a particular instance of discrimination against out-of-state residents entails a two-step inquiry. As an initial matter, the court must decide whether the ordinance burdens one of those privileges and immunities protected by the Clause. *Baldwin v. Montana Fish and Game Comm'n.* Not all forms of discrimination against citizens of other States are constitutionally suspect.... Certainly, the pursuit of a common calling is one of the most fundamental of those privileges protected by the Clause. Many, if not most, of our cases expounding the Privileges and Immunities Clause have dealt with this basic and essential activity. Public employment,

9. [T]he dissent's proposed blanket exemption for all classifications that are less than state-wide would provide States with a simple means for evading the strictures of the Privileges and Immunities Clause. Suppose, for example, that California wanted to guarantee that all employees of contractors and subcontractors working on construction projects funded in whole or in part by state funds are state residents. Under the dissent's analysis, the California legislature need merely divide the State in half, providing one resident-hiring preference for Northern Californians on all such projects taking place in Northern California, and one for Southern Californians on all projects taking place in Southern California. State residents generally would benefit from the law at the expense of out-of-state residents; yet, the law would be immune from scrutiny under the Clause simply because it was not phrased in terms of *state* citizenship or residency. Such a formalistic construction would effectively write the Clause out of the Constitution.

however, is qualitatively different from employment in the private sector; it is a subspecies of the broader opportunity to pursue a common calling. We have held that there is no fundamental right to government employment for purposes of the Equal Protection Clause. Cf. *McCarthy v. Philadelphia Civil Service Comm'n,* 424 U.S. 645, 96 S.Ct. 1154, 47 L.Ed.2d 366 (1976)(per curiam)(rejecting equal protection challenge to municipal residency requirement for municipal workers). And in *White,* we held that for purposes of the Commerce Clause everyone employed on a city public works project is, "in a substantial if informal sense, 'working for the city.' "

It can certainly be argued that for purposes of the Privileges and Immunities Clause everyone affected by the Camden ordinance is also "working for the city" and, therefore, has no grounds for complaint when the city favors its own residents. But we decline to transfer mechanically into this context an analysis fashioned to fit the Commerce Clause.... When the State acts solely as a market participant, no conflict between state *regulation* and federal regulatory authority can arise. The Privileges and Immunities Clause, on the other hand, imposes a direct restraint on state action in the interests of interstate harmony. This concern with comity cuts across the market regulator-market participant distinction that is crucial under the Commerce Clause. It is discrimination against out-of-state residents on matters of fundamental concern which triggers the Clause, not regulation affecting interstate commerce. Thus, the fact that Camden is merely setting conditions on its expenditures for goods and services in the marketplace does not preclude the possibility that those conditions violate the Privileges and Immunities Clause:.... The fact that Camden is expending its own funds or funds it administers in accordance with the terms of a grant is certainly a factor—perhaps the crucial factor—to be considered in evaluating whether the statute's discrimination violates the Privileges and Immunities Clause. But it does not remove the Camden ordinance completely from the purview of the Clause.

In sum, Camden may, without fear of violating the Commerce Clause, pressure private employers engaged in public works projects funded in whole or in part by the city to hire city residents. But that same exercise of power to bias the employment decisions of private contractors and subcontractors against out-of-state residents may be called to account under the Privileges and Immunities Clause. A determination of whether a privilege is "fundamental" for purposes of that Clause does not depend on whether the employees of private contractors and subcontractors engaged in public works projects can or cannot be said to be "working for the city." The opportunity to seek employment with such private employers is "sufficiently basic to the livelihood of the Nation," as to fall within the purview of the Privileges and Immunities Clause even though the contractors and subcontractors are themselves engaged in projects funded in whole or part by the city.

The conclusion that Camden's ordinance discriminates against a protected privilege does not, of course, end the inquiry. We have stressed in prior cases that "[l]ike many other constitutional provisions, the privileges and immunities clause is not an absolute." It does not preclude discrimination against citizens of other States where there is a "substantial reason" for the difference in treatment. "[T]he inquiry in each case must be concerned with whether such reasons do exist and whether the degree of discrimination bears a close relation to them." As part of any justification offered for the discriminatory law, nonresidents must somehow be shown to "constitute a peculiar source of the evil at which the statute is aimed."

The city of Camden contends that its ordinance is necessary to counteract grave economic and social ills. Spiralling unemployment, a sharp decline in population, and a dramatic reduction in the number of businesses located in the city have eroded property values and depleted the city's tax base. The resident hiring preference is designed, the city contends, to increase the number of employed persons living in Camden and to arrest the "middle class flight" currently plaguing the city. The city also argues that all non-Camden residents employed on city public works projects, whether they reside in New Jersey or Pennsylvania, constitute a "source of the evil at which the statute is aimed." That is, they "live off" Camden without "living in" Camden. Camden contends that the scope of the discrimination practiced in the ordinance, with its municipal residency requirement, is carefully tailored to alleviate this evil without unreasonably harming nonresidents, who still have access to 60% of the available positions.

Every inquiry under the Privileges and Immunities Clause "must . . . be conducted with due regard for the principle that the states should have considerable leeway in analyzing local evils and in prescribing appropriate cures." This caution is particularly appropriate when a government body is merely setting conditions on the expenditure of funds it controls. The Alaska Hire statute at issue in *Hicklin v. Orbeck,* swept within its strictures not only contractors and subcontractors dealing directly with the State's oil and gas; it also covered suppliers who provided goods and services to those contractors and subcontractors. . . . No similar "ripple effect" appears to infect the Camden ordinance. It is limited in scope to employees working directly on city public works projects.

Nonetheless, we find it impossible to evaluate Camden's justification on the record as it now stands. No trial has ever been held in the case. No findings of fact have been made. The Supreme Court of New Jersey certified the case for direct appeal after the brief administrative proceedings that led to approval of the ordinance by the State Treasurer. It would not be appropriate for this Court either to make factual determinations as an initial matter or to take judicial notice of Camden's decay. We, therefore, deem it wise to remand the case to the New Jersey Supreme Court. That court may decide, consistent with state procedures, on the best method for making the necessary findings.

The judgment of the Supreme Court of New Jersey is reversed, and the case is remanded for proceedings not inconsistent with this opinion.

Reversed and Remanded.

[The dissenting opinion of BLACKMUN, J., is omitted.]

Notes

1. Does *United Building* apply to workers who are full time employees of the city, e.g., city firemen? Compare *McCarthy v. Philadelphia Civil Service Commission,* cited in *United Building* and also briefly noted in § 8–3.31, infra.

2. At the trial, what must Camden prove? Should the principle of *United Building* apply only in parts of the country? If, for example, New Jersey has a high unemployment problem, does that fact offer a special justification upholding the city's power to restrict employment on city projects to residents? If, in contrast, Delaware's unemployment problem were not as severe, should it be prohibited from implementing the Camden plan?

3. *Supreme Court of New Hampshire v. Piper,* 470 U.S. 274, 105 S.Ct. 1272, 84 L.Ed.2d 205 (1985) invalidated, under the Article IV privileges and immunities clause, a State Supreme Court Rule that excluded nonresidents from admission to the New Hampshire Bar even though they had passed the State's bar examination and intended to practice in New Hampshire. The Article IV clause "intended to create a national economic union." Although a state could provide for residency requirements that relate to it as a separate political community (like "the right to vote and the right to hold elective office"), a lawyer "is not an 'officer' of the State in any political sense." *Supreme Court of Virginia v. Friedman,* 487 U.S. 59, 108 S.Ct. 2260, 101 L.Ed.2d 56 (1988) reviewed a Virginia rule that permitted lawyers who was already admitted to practice in another state to be admitted to the Virginia bar on motion (i.e., without taking the Virginia bar examination) if they were permanent residents of Virginia. The Court (7 to 2) invalidated this condition and rejected the argument that the residency condition was valid because Virginia allowed the applicant the alternative of gaining admission, without regard to residency, by passing the bar examination. *Barnard v. Thorstenn,* 489 U.S. 546, 109 S.Ct. 1294, 103 L.Ed.2d 559 (1989), used the Privileges and Immunities Clause of Article IV to invalidate a requirement (imposed by the District Court of the Virgin Islands) that an otherwise qualified attorney must demonstrate that he or she has resided in the Virgin Islands for at least one year and that, if admitted, the attorney intends to continue to reside and practice in the Virgin Islands. The Court, noted that Congress made the Privileges and Immunities Clause applicable to the Virgin Islands by statute.

4. *Lunding v. New York Tax Appeals Tribunal,* 522 U.S. 287, 118 S.Ct. 766, 139 L.Ed.2d 717 (1998). O'Connor, J., for the Court, joined by Stevens, Scalia, Souter, Thomas, & Breyer, JJ., invalidated a New York statute that, in effect, denied nonresident taxpayers an income tax deduction for alimony paid to ex-spouses. New York argued that it taxes its residents on all of their income, regardless of the source, and therefore its residents should receive the benefit of a full deduction of such expenses; but nonresidents should not

be able to deduct their non-business expenses, *i.e.,* their "personal expenses," because such expenses are more appropriately allocated to the state of residence. New York argued that it may ignore personal deductions unconnected to the production of income in New York. However, New York's inability to could not tax the entire income of nonresidents does not justify discrimination. Under the Privileges and Immunities Clause, the constitutionality of one state's statutes affecting nonresidents cannot depend on the configuration of another state's statutes. That clause protects individuals who may migrate between states to live and work. Ginsburg, J., joined by Rehnquist, C.J., and Kennedy, J., dissented.

3–6. PREEMPTION

SILKWOOD v. KERR–McGEE CORP.
464 U.S. 238, 104 S.Ct. 615, 78 L.Ed.2d 443 (1984).

JUSTICE WHITE delivered the opinion of the Court. . . .

Karen Silkwood was a laboratory analyst for Kerr–McGee at its Cimmaron plant near Crescent, Oklahoma. The plant fabricated plutonium fuel pins for use as reactor fuel in nuclear power plants. Accordingly, the plant was subject to licensing and regulation by the Nuclear Regulatory Commission (NRC) pursuant to the Atomic Energy Act.

During a three-day period of November 1974, Silkwood was contaminated by plutonium from the Cimmaron plant. On November 5, Silkwood was grinding and polishing plutonium samples, utilizing glove boxes designed for that purpose. In accordance with established procedures, she checked her hands for contamination when she withdrew them from the glove box. When some contamination was detected, |s|he was immediately decontaminated, and at the end of her shift, the monitors detected no contamination. However, she was given urine and fecal kits and was instructed to collect samples in order to check for plutonium discharge.

The next day, Silkwood arrived at the plant and began doing paperwork in the laboratory. Upon leaving the laboratory, Silkwood monitored herself and again discovered surface contamination. Once again, she was decontaminated.

On the third day, November 7, Silkwood was monitored upon her arrival at the plant. High levels of contamination were detected. Four urine samples and one fecal sample submitted that morning were also highly contaminated. Suspecting that the contamination had spread to areas outside the plant, the company directed a decontamination squad to accompany Silkwood to her apartment. Silkwood's roommate, who was also an employee at the plant, was awakened and monitored. She was also contaminated, although to a lesser degree than Silkwood. The squad then monitored the apartment, finding contamination in several rooms, with especially high levels in the bathroom, the kitchen, and Silkwood's bedroom.

The contamination level in Silkwood's apartment was such that many of her personal belongings had to be destroyed. Silkwood herself was sent to the Los Alamos Scientific Laboratory to determine the extent of contamination in her vital body organs. She returned to work on November 13. That night, she was killed in an unrelated automobile accident.

Bill Silkwood, Karen's father, brought the present diversity action in his capacity as administrator of her estate. The action was based on common law tort principles under Oklahoma law and was designed to recover for the contamination injuries to Karen's person and property. Kerr–McGee stipulated that the plutonium which caused the contamination came from its plant, and the jury expressly rejected Kerr–McGee's allegation that Silkwood had intentionally removed the plutonium from the plant in an effort to embarrass the company. However, there were no other specific findings of fact with respect to the cause of the contamination.

During the course of the trial, evidence was presented which tended to show that Kerr–McGee did not always comply with NRC regulations. One Kerr–McGee witness conceded that the amount of plutonium which was unaccounted for during the period in question exceeded permissible limits. An NRC official testified that he did not feel that Kerr–McGee was conforming its conduct to the "as low as reasonably achievable" standard. There was also some evidence that the level of plutonium in Silkwood's apartment may have exceeded that permitted in an unrestricted area such as a residence.

However, there was also evidence that Kerr–McGee complied with most federal regulations. The NRC official testified that there were no serious personnel exposures at the plant and that Kerr–McGee did not exceed the regulatory requirements with respect to exposure levels that would result in significant health hazards. In addition, Kerr–McGee introduced the Commission's report on the investigation of the Silkwood incident in which the Commission determined that Kerr–McGee's only violation of regulations throughout the incident was its failure to maintain a record of the dates of two urine samples submitted by Silkwood.

[T]he [trial] court submitted the claims to the jury on alternative theories of strict liability and negligence. The court also instructed the jury with respect to punitive damages, explaining the standard by which Kerr–McGee's conduct was to be evaluated in determining whether such damages should be awarded:

[T]he jury may give damages for the sake of example and by way of punishment, if the jury finds the defendant or defendants have been guilty of oppression, fraud, or malice, actual or presumed. . . .

Exemplary damages are not limited to cases where there is direct evidence of fraud, malice or gross negligence. They may be allowed when there is evidence of such recklessness and wanton disregard of another's rights that malice and evil intent will be inferred. If a defendant is grossly and wantonly reckless in exposing others to dangers, the law holds him to have intended the natural consequences of his acts, and treats him as guilty of a willful wrong.

The jury returned a verdict in favor of Silkwood, finding actual damages of $505,000 ($500,000 for personal injuries and $5,000 for property damage) and punitive damages of $10,000,000. The trial court entered judgment against Kerr–McGee in that amount.

[The Tenth Circuit] first held that recovery for Silkwood's personal injuries was controlled exclusively by Oklahoma's workers' compensation law. It thus reversed the $500,000 judgment for those injuries. The court then affirmed the property damage portion of the award, holding that the workers' compensation law applied only to personal injuries and that Oklahoma law permitted an award under a theory of strict liability in the circumstances of this case. Finally, the court held that because of the federal statutes regulating the Kerr–McGee plant, "punitive damages may not be awarded in this case."

In reaching its conclusion with respect to the punitive damages award, the Court of Appeals adopted a broad preemption analysis. It concluded that "any state action that competes substantially with the AEC (NRC) in its regulation of radiation hazards associated with plants handling nuclear material" was impermissible. Because "[a] judicial award of exemplary damages under state law as punishment for bad practices or to deter future practices involving exposure to radiation is not less intrusive than direct legislative acts of the state," the court determined that such awards were preempted by federal law. Silkwood appealed, seeking review of the Court of Appeals' ruling with respect to the punitive damages award. . . .

As we recently observed in *Pacific Gas & Electric Co. v. State Energy Resources Conservation & Development Comm'n*, 461 U.S. 190, 103 S.Ct. 1713, 75 L.Ed.2d 752 (1983), state law can be preempted in either of two general ways. If Congress evidences an intent to occupy a given field, any state law falling within that field is preempted. If Congress has not entirely displaced state regulation over the matter in question, state law is still preempted to the extent it actually conflicts with federal law, that is, when it is impossible to comply with both state and federal law, or where the state law stands as an obstacle to the accomplishment of the full purposes and objectives of Congress. Kerr–McGee contends that the award in this case is invalid under either analysis. We consider each of these contentions in turn.

In *Pacific Gas & Electric*, an examination of the statutory scheme and legislative history of the Atomic Energy Act convinced us that "Congress ... intended that the federal government regulate the radiological safety aspects involved ... in the construction and operation of a nuclear plant." Thus, we concluded that "the federal government has occupied the entire field of nuclear safety concerns, except the limited powers expressly ceded to the states."

Kerr–McGee argues that our ruling in *Pacific Gas & Electric* is dispositive of the issue in this case. Noting that "regulation can be as effectively asserted through an award of damages as through some form of preventive relief," Kerr–McGee submits that because the state-authorized award of punitive damages in this case punishes and deters conduct related to radiation hazards, it falls within the prohibited field. However, a review of the same legislative history which prompted our holding in *Pacific Gas & Electric,* coupled with an examination of Congress' actions with respect to other portions of the Atomic Energy Act, convinces us that the preempted field does not extend as far as Kerr–McGee would have it. . . .

Congress' decision to prohibit the states from regulating the safety aspects of nuclear development was premised on its belief that the Commission was more qualified to determine what type of safety standards should be enacted in this complex area. As Congress was informed by the AEC, the 1959 legislation provided for continued federal control over the more hazardous materials because "the technical safety considerations are of such complexity that it is not likely that any State would be prepared to deal with them during the foreseeable future." If there were nothing more, this concern over the states' inability to formulate effective standards and the foreclosure of the states from conditioning the operation of nuclear plants on compliance with state-imposed safety standards arguably would disallow resort to state-law remedies by those suffering injuries from radiation in a nuclear plant. There is, however, ample evidence that Congress had no intention of forbidding the states from providing such remedies.

Indeed, there is no indication that Congress even seriously considered precluding the use of such remedies either when it enacted the Atomic Energy Act in 1954 and or when it amended it in 1959. This silence takes on added significance in light of Congress' failure to provide any federal remedy for persons injured by such conduct. It is difficult to believe that Congress would, without comment, remove all means of judicial recourse for those injured by illegal conduct.

More importantly, the only congressional discussion concerning the relationship between the Atomic Energy Act and state tort remedies indicates that Congress assumed that such remedies would be available. After the 1954 law was enacted, private companies contemplating entry into the nuclear industry expressed concern over potentially bankrupting state-law suits arising out of a nuclear incident. As a result, in 1957 Congress passed the Price–Anderson Act, an amendment to the Atomic Energy Act. That Act established an indemnification scheme under which operators of licensed nuclear facilities could be required to obtain up to $60 million in private financial protection against such suits. The government would then provide indemnification for the next $500 million of liability, and the resulting $560 million would be the limit of liability for any one nuclear incident.

Although the Price–Anderson Act does not apply to the present situation, the discussion preceding its enactment and subsequent amendment indicates that Congress assumed that persons injured by nuclear accidents were free to utilize existing state tort law remedies.... For example, the [Joint] Committee rejected a suggestion that it adopt a federal tort to replace existing state remedies, noting that such displacement of state remedies would engender great opposition....

Kerr–McGee focuses on the differences between compensatory and punitive damages awards and asserts that, at most, Congress intended to allow the former. This argument, however, is misdirected because our inquiry is not whether Congress expressly allowed punitive damages awards. Punitive damages have long been a part of traditional state tort law. As we noted above, Congress assumed that traditional principles of state tort law would apply with full force unless they were expressly supplanted. Thus, it is Kerr–McGee's burden to show that Congress intended to preclude such awards. Yet, the company is unable to point to anything in the legislative history or in the regulations that indicates that punitive damages were not to be allowed....

In sum, it is clear that in enacting and amending the Price–Anderson Act, Congress assumed that state-law remedies, in whatever form they might take, were available to those injured by nuclear incidents. This was so even though it was well aware of the NRC's exclusive authority to regulate safety matters. No doubt there is tension between the conclusion that safety regulation is the exclusive concern of the federal law and the conclusion that a state may nevertheless award damages based on its own law of liability. But as we understand what was done over the years in the legislation concerning nuclear energy, Congress intended to stand by both concepts and to tolerate whatever tension there was between them. We can do no less. It may be that the award of damages based on the state law of negligence or strict liability is regulatory in the sense that a nuclear plant will be threatened with damages liability if it does not conform to state standards, but that regulatory consequence was something that Congress was quite willing to accept.

We do not suggest that there could never be an instance in which the federal law would preempt the recovery of damages based on state law. But insofar as damages for radiation injuries are concerned, preemption should not be judged on the basis that the federal government has so completely occupied the field of safety that state remedies are foreclosed but on whether there is an irreconcilable conflict between the federal and state standards or whether the imposition of a state standard in a damages action would frustrate the objectives of the federal law. We perceive no such conflict or frustration in the circumstances of this case.

The United States, as amicus curiae, contends that the award of punitive damages in this case is preempted because it conflicts with the federal remedial scheme, noting that the NRC is authorized to impose civil penalties on licensees when federal standards have been violated. However, the award of punitive damages in the present case does not conflict with that scheme. Paying both federal fines and state-imposed punitive damages for the same incident would not appear to be physically impossible. Nor does exposure to punitive damages frustrate any purpose of the federal remedial scheme.... We conclude that the award of punitive damages in this case is not preempted by federal law....

JUSTICE BLACKMUN, with whom JUSTICE MARSHALL joins, dissenting.

... The Court acknowledges that Congress pre-empted state regulation of safety aspects of nuclear operations largely out of concern that States were without the technological expertise necessary to regulate them. Yet the Court concludes that Congress intended to allow a jury to impose substantial penalties upon a nuclear licensee for failure to follow what the jury regards as adequate safety procedures. The Court recognizes the paradox of its disposition, but blames the irrationality on Congress. Then, with humility, the Court explains that it is duty-bound to follow the dictates of Congress. But such institutional modesty cannot transfer the blame for the tension that today's decision injects into the regulation of nuclear power. The Court, in my view, tortures its earlier decisions and, more importantly, wreaks havoc with the regulatory structure that Congress carefully created....

The conduct that the jury's punitive damages award sought to regulate was the day-to-day safety procedures of nuclear licensees. There was no factual finding as to how the contamination of Karen Silkwood occurred; the trial judge expressly refused to give an instruction on intentional infliction, and the jury rejected Kerr–McGee's suggestion that Silkwood intentionally contaminated herself. It is abundantly clear, therefore, that the punitive damages award in this case deters a nuclear facility from operating in the same manner as Kerr–McGee. Authority for a State to do so, however, is precisely what the Court held to be preempted in *Pacific Gas*. Nuclear Regulatory Commission regulations covered virtually every aspect of the incident in which Silkwood was contaminated. The Atomic Energy Act provides a full enforcement arsenal—including criminal sanctions—to police compliance with federal standards.... The District Court nevertheless instructed the jury to fashion a fine to encourage Kerr–McGee and other nuclear licensees to meet in the future whatever safety standard the jury considered appropriate for plutonium.[5]

It is to be noted, of course, that the same preemption analysis produces the opposite conclusion when applied to an award of compensatory damages. It is true that the prospect of compensating victims of nuclear accidents will affect a licensee's safety calculus. Compensatory damages therefore have an indirect impact on daily operations of a nuclear facility.... The crucial distinction between compensatory and punitive damages is that the purpose of punitive damages is to regulate safety, whereas the purpose of compensatory damages is to compensate

---

5.   ... The jury was instructed further that compliance with federal standards was not a complete defense to the award of punitive damages:

"You are instructed, however, that you are not bound by these standards. Your duty is to determine what constitutes the exercise of reasonable care in handling plutonium, or the exercise of reckless and wanton conduct, in light of the physical characteristics of that material and the risks associated with it."

victims. Because the Federal Government does not regulate the compensation of victims, and because it is inconceivable that Congress intended to leave victims with no remedy at all, the preemption analysis established by *Pacific Gas* comfortably accommodates—indeed it compels—the conclusion that compensatory damages are not preempted whereas punitive damages are.

Differences in the means of calculating compensatory and punitive damages further distinguish the two, and highlight the fundamental incompatibility of punitive damages and federal standards. When a victim is determined to be eligible for a compensatory award, that award is calculated by reference to the victim's injury.... Punitive damages, in contrast, are calculated to compel adherence to a particular standard of safety—and it need not be a federal standard. In setting the punitive damages award in this case, the court instructed the jury to consider "the financial worth of the defendant" and award an "amount of exemplary damages ... consistent with the general purpose of such an award in deterring the defendant, and others like it, from committing similar acts in the future."

This preemption analysis eliminates the "tension" that the Court concedes its disposition creates. It remains faithful to the Federal Government's expressed desire to balance the conflict between promoting nuclear power and ensuring safe operation of nuclear plants. It preserves the ability of States to provide compensation to their citizens for injuries caused by radiation hazards. Finally, it avoids the anomaly of a jury's imposing a fine to regulate activity considered too complicated for state regulatory experts....

JUSTICE POWELL, with whom THE CHIEF JUSTICE [BURGER] and JUSTICE BLACKMUN join, dissenting....

Silkwood concedes that Congress did not refer to punitive damages in the text or legislative history of the 1954 Act or its subsequent amendments. The absence of an express reference appears plainly to bring state law of punitive damages within the sweeping preemption we found that Congress intended in *Pacific Gas and Electric Co.* Nevertheless, the Court today makes an exception to the rule announced only last term by refusing to find preemption unless the party arguing *for* preemption can find direct support in the statute, legislative history, or regulations. Where broad federal preemption has been found, the burden of proving an exception always should be on the party who wishes to rely on state law. The Court's decision today inexplicably shifts this burden to allow state law to prevail in the absence of a showing that Congress expressly had intended to preempt it....

Notes

1. Should a state law be preempted if it and federal law prohibit the same conduct but federal law provides for different or less severe sanctions?

What if the subject of the dual regulation can comply with both federal and state laws, but the laws are administered differently? For example, assume both state and federal law make it a crime to defraud the federal government. Under the federal administration, only the federal government could institute suit; under the state administration, either the state prosecutor, or any local prosecutor, or even a private citizen could file criminal charges, which would be made public and then referred to a grand jury. Should there be preemption of the state law?

2.   Powell's dissent in *Silkwood* approached the problem with a presumption favoring preemption. Who should have the burden of establishing preemption if Congressional intent is unclear? Should the Court be more or less active in striking down a state law as preempted than striking it down as a violation of the due process clause or similar constitutional clause?

3.   INTERSTATE COMPACTS. A useful method of federal-state cooperation is through the use of interstate compacts. See Article I, § 10, cl. 3, which allows a State to enter into "any Agreement or Compact with another State" if Congress consents. *Cuyler v. Adams,* 449 U.S. 433, 101 S.Ct. 703, 66 L.Ed.2d 641 (1981) held that "congressional consent transforms an interstate compact" into "a law of the United States." The Compact Clause *requires* congressional consent, the Court said, only if the agreement is directed to the formation of increased political power in the states that might encroach upon federal supremacy. The agreement in *Cuyler,* the Interstate Agreement on Retainers, and the Uniform Criminal Extradition Act, did not therefore require such consent, but it was "appropriate for consent," which "transforms the States' agreement into federal law." Thus, a "consequence of this metamorphosis is that, unless the compact to which Congress has consented is somehow unconstitutional, no court may order relief inconsistent with its express terms." *Texas v. New Mexico,* 462 U.S. 554, 103 S.Ct. 2558, 77 L.Ed.2d 1 (1983).

Appendix

AN INTRODUCTORY NOTE ON COMMERCE CLAUSE LIMITATIONS ON STATE TAXATION

Because the preceding materials have not focused on the commerce clause limitations on state taxing powers, the student might value a brief textual discussion of the main issues. This summary is admittedly general, and should not mask the fact that decisions scrutinizing state taxes under the commerce clause have been inconsistent, if not downright contrary. This confusion results primarily from attempting to balance two competing goals: keeping the stream of interstate commerce flowing and permitting states to extract, from interstate commerce, a fair share of the cost of government. In the past, commerce clause analysis of interstate taxation has been formalistic, focusing on such distinctions as whether the tax falls "directly" or "indirectly" on interstate commerce or whether it is on the "privilege" of conducting a business in interstate commerce.

The Supreme Court has shifted its focus to the practical consequences of the state tax upon the taxpayer and interstate commerce. *Complete Auto Transit, Inc. v. Brady,* 430 U.S. 274, 279, 97 S.Ct. 1076,

1079, 51 L.Ed.2d 326, 331 (1977) fashioned a four-part test from factors relied on in previous decisions. A state tax is permissible under the commerce clause if it [1] is "applied to an activity with a substantial nexus with the taxing State, [2] is fairly apportioned, [3] does not discriminate against interstate commerce, and [4] is fairly related to the services provided by the State."

Related to the scrutiny of state taxes under the commerce clause is the scrutiny of state taxes under the due process clause of the Fourteenth Amendment. Suits challenging state taxes have often relied on both clauses. Due process, which addresses a state's jurisdiction to tax an interstate business or activity, i.e., the territorial reach of a state's taxing power, requires some definite link, some "minimum connection," between the taxing state and the person, property or transaction taxed. There must also be "a rational relationship between the income attributed to that state and the intrastate values of the enterprise." *ASARCO Inc. v. Idaho State Tax Commission,* 458 U.S. 307, 328, 102 S.Ct. 3103, 3109, 73 L.Ed.2d 787, 795 (1982). The present commerce clause test makes a similar examination through its "substantial nexus" prong. However, commerce clause analysis goes one step beyond the due process focus by examining whether the state tax impermissibly burdens interstate commerce. Thus, even if the due process clause gives the state jurisdiction to tax, the commerce clause may require that the tax be fairly apportioned to prevent an undue burden on interstate commerce.

Although examination of state taxes is becoming more uniform after *Complete Auto,* the type of tax involved does affect the outcome. Let us review the major cases dealing with each type of tax.

Sales and Use Taxes. A "sales" tax is, as the name implies, a tax on the *sale* of property or services. A "use" tax is a tax on the *use* of goods within the state. See, *Henneford v. Silas Mason Co., Inc.,* Casebook § 3–3. A sales tax is one of the primary revenue producers for most states. The tax is usually charged to the buyer, with the seller acting as collection agent for the taxing state by adding the tax to the selling price.

Examination of sales taxes under the commerce clause has focused on the taxing state's relationship to the sale that is being taxed. The general rule is that only the state where the sale physically occurs may tax that transaction. For example, State *A's* imposition of a sales tax upon a sale made within its borders would be valid even though the purchaser ships the goods to State *B* immediately after the purchase, *International Harvester Co. v. Department of Treasury,* 322 U.S. 340, 64 S.Ct. 1019, 88 L.Ed. 1313 (1944); or even though the seller shipped the goods into State *A* from State *B* prior to the sale, *McGoldrick v. Berwind–White Coal Mining Co.,* 309 U.S. 33, 60 S.Ct. 388, 84 L.Ed. 565 (1940). State *A,* however, could not levy a sales tax upon goods purchased by one of its residents in State *B* and then shipped into State *A. McLeod v. J.E. Dilworth Co.,* 322 U.S. 327, 64 S.Ct. 1023, 88 L.Ed. 1304 (1944).

Oklahoma Tax Commission v. Jefferson Lines, Inc., 514 U.S. 175, 115 S.Ct. 1331, 131 L.Ed.2d 261 (1995) held that Oklahoma's sales tax on the full price of a bus ticket from Oklahoma to another state did not violate the dormant commerce clause and met all the criteria of *Complete Auto Transit*. In particular, the tax was internally consistent because, if every state were to impose a tax identical to Oklahoma's (a tax on ticket sales within the state for travel originating there), no sale would be subject to more than one state's tax. The tax was also externally consistent because the sale and partial delivery could not be duplicated as a taxable event in any other state. Like the sale of goods, the sale of services can ordinarily be treated as a single local state event. In this case, the tax falls on the buyer of services, who is no more subject to double taxation than the buyer of goods would be subject to double taxation.

Though a state cannot place a *sales* tax on out-of-state purchases by its residents, it may impose a *use* tax on the local buyer for the use or enjoyment of the goods within the state. The use tax supplements the state's sales tax revenues by taxing out-of-state purchases when those purchases are used within the taxing state. The use tax may also serve to protect local merchants from out-of-state competition offering lower prices because of a lower tax burden. Because the tax falls on a transaction (the use of the product) occurring within the taxing state, the use tax itself does not create any commerce clause problems.

The method of collection used, however, may raise commerce clause and due process problems. Because use taxes are imposed on the buyer, it is difficult for the taxing state to collect the taxes for some types of property. To avoid these difficulties, the taxing state often wishes to conscript the out-of-state seller (i.e., the mail order house) to collect the use tax by making the seller liable for any uncollected amounts. This conscription of the seller can violate due process and the commerce clause where the seller's relationship with the taxing state is insufficient to support the burden of collecting the tax.

Thus, the Court has invalidated imposition of a use tax collection duty where the out-of-state seller's only contacts with the taxing state were (1) radio and newspaper advertising that reached customers in the taxing state and attracted them to its store, and (2) occasional use of the taxing state's roads for deliveries to customers from that state. *Miller Brothers Co. v. Maryland*, 347 U.S. 340, 74 S.Ct. 535, 98 L.Ed. 744 (1954). There is also no use tax collection duty if the seller's only contacts with the taxing state were through the mails (e.g., mailing catalogues and making deliveries by mail or common carrier to customers in the taxing state). *National Bellas Hess v. Department of Revenue*, 386 U.S. 753, 87 S.Ct. 1389, 18 L.Ed.2d 505 (1967). However, *National Geographic Society v. California Board of Equalization*, 430 U.S. 551, 97 S.Ct. 1386, 51 L.Ed.2d 631 (1977) upheld the imposition of a use tax collection duty where the out-of-state seller maintained two offices in the taxing state, even though employees in these offices were engaged in activities unrelated to the mail order sales. These offices received the benefits and protections of state services. Although this case was decided a short time after *Complete Auto,* supra, the Court did not explicitly use its four-part test.

The *due process clause* (which requires "minimum contacts" with the taxing state) does not require that the mail order vendors have a physical presence in the state. However, the *commerce clause* requires that a vendor have a "substantial nexus" with the taxing state. A mail order vendor, whose only contacts with the taxing state are by mail or common carrier, lacks this "substantial nexus." Because only the commerce clause prohibits such taxes on mail order houses, Congress is "free to decide whether, when, and to what extent the States may burden interstate mail-order concerns with a duty to collect use taxes." *Quill Corporation v. North Dakota,* 504 U.S. 298, 112 S.Ct. 1904, 119 L.Ed.2d 91 (1992).

Severance Taxes. Severance taxes are imposed on the extraction of natural resources within a state's borders. In *Heisler v. Thomas Colliery Co.,* 260 U.S. 245, 43 S.Ct. 83, 67 L.Ed. 237 (1922)(coal mining), *Oliver Iron Mining Co. v. Lord,* 262 U.S. 172, 43 S.Ct. 526, 67 L.Ed. 929 (1923)(iron ore mining), and *Hope Natural Gas Co. v. Hall,* 274 U.S. 284, 47 S.Ct. 639, 71 L.Ed. 1049 (1927)(natural gas), the Court examined several severance taxes challenged as discriminating against interstate commerce and burdening interstate commerce. The Court rejected the charge of discrimination: although most of the natural resources left the state for consumption, there was no discrimination against interstate commerce because the tax had to be paid regardless of where the natural resources were consumed. The tax also did not unduly burden interstate commerce because the Court characterized the activities taxed as "local" in nature rather than a part of interstate commerce.

However, *Commonwealth Edison Co. v. Montana,* 453 U.S. 609, 101 S.Ct. 2946, 69 L.Ed.2d 884 (1981) recognized that the mining of coal for primarily out-of-state consumption was a part of interstate commerce. This case rejected the formalistic characterization analysis of *Heisler* and its progeny, scrutinized the severance tax under the *Complete Auto* test, but then came to the same conclusion as the earlier cases. The plaintiffs, four Montana Coal mining companies and eleven of their out-of-state utility company customers, argued that under the fourth prong of the *Complete Auto* test, the tax was not "fairly related to the services provided by the State." The Court responded that the evidence offered by the plaintiffs was unnecessary. Unlike scrutiny of user fees or taxes (i.e., specific charges for the use of state-provided facilities or services), which focus on whether the specific service justifies the charge, in this case the focus is on the state's general cost of providing service, because a general revenue tax is involved. Thus, services that benefit the taxed activity directly, like fire and police protection, would be considered as well as those services of indirect benefit, such as the maintenance of a trained workforce and the promotion of a civilized society. The tax did not discriminate against interstate commerce because it was levied on the extraction of all coal, not just on coal destined for use out of state.

Scrutiny of a state tax under the fourth prong of the *Complete Auto* test takes one step further the first prong requirement of a "substantial nexus" between the taxpayer and the state. The "fourth prong ... imposes the additional limitation that the *measure* of the tax must be reasonably related to the extent of the contact, since it is the activities or presence of the taxpayer in the State that may properly be made to bear a 'just share of the state tax burden.' "*Commonwealth Edison*, 453 U.S. at 626, 101 S.Ct. at 2958, 69 L.Ed.2d at 900 (emphasis in original). Because the tax is calculated as a percentage of the value of the coal extracted within the state, the measure was properly related to the taxpayer's presence in the state and therefore, to the services that the taxpayer received. The Court also noted that the question whether the tax rate itself is set at an appropriate level falls outside the scope of the fourth prong of *Complete Auto*.

Property Taxes. The analysis of these taxes under the commerce clause prior to *Complete Auto* differed depending on whether the tax fell on property being transported in interstate commerce or on property used in the transportation of interstate commerce. Scrutiny of both types, however, did utilize some of the factors present in current analysis and thus modern analysis should yield the same result.

For a tax on goods being transported in interstate commerce the Court focused on whether the goods were still in the stream of interstate commerce or had come to "rest" in the taxing state. In *Minnesota v. Blasius*, 290 U.S. 1, 54 S.Ct. 34, 78 L.Ed. 131 (1933), for example, the taxpayer was a livestock trader at the Minneapolis–St. Paul stockyards. There, he would purchase cattle that had been brought from other states, and hold the cattle until resold to purchasers who would then transport the cattle out of Minnesota. The taxpayer had purchased eleven head of cattle on April 30, 1929, and resold them on May 2, 1929. Minnesota assessed its yearly *ad valorem* property tax on all property within the state on May 1, 1929, including the taxpayer's cattle. The Court determined that the cattle "had come to rest" within the state and were therefore subject to the tax, a conclusion that should also be reached under the *Complete Auto* test. The continuous presence of property in the state satisfies the "substantial nexus" requirement of the first prong of the *Complete Auto* test. The tax was assessed on the regular tax day when Blasius owned and possessed the cattle; the property had come to rest, and thus a tax on such property would be fairly apportioned, satisfying the second prong of *Complete Auto*. The tax would also not discriminate against interstate commerce (the third prong) because it was an *ad valorem* property tax levied on all property in the state. And measuring the tax by the presence of property within the state would satisfy the fourth prong, requiring the tax to be fairly related to the services provided by the state.

When examining property taxes on instrumentalities of commerce, the Court, under the older case law, was quick to adopt a focus on the taxing state's relationship with the property and the taxpayer as one way of assuring that interstate commerce assumed its fair share of the cost of the state government. In *Braniff Airways, Inc. v. Nebraska State Board of Equalization,* 347 U.S. 590, 74 S.Ct. 757, 98 L.Ed. 967 (1954), Nebraska imposed an *ad valorem* property tax on Braniff's flight equipment. Braniff made 18 regularly scheduled stops in Nebraska to discharge and take on passengers, mail, freight and to refuel, but Braniff owned no other property in Nebraska, and rented depot space and other facilities as needed. The Court upheld the tax because "[h]abitual employment of property within the state" established a sufficient relationship with the state to justify the tax. Application of the *Complete Auto* test would probably render the same result today. When instrumentalities of commerce have a sufficient relationship with a state to be subject to that state's property tax, they have acquired a "tax situs" in that state. Such property can have a tax situs in more than one state, leading to multiple taxation, but such taxation of the instrumentalities of interstate commerce does not violate either the due process clause or the commerce clause if the tax is fairly apportioned on a mileage basis or other acceptable basis. *Union Tank Line v. Wright,* 249 U.S. 275, 39 S.Ct. 276, 63 L.Ed. 602 (1919). If property has not acquired a "tax situs" in any other state, then the state of the owner's domicile can impose its property tax at full value; no other jurisdiction could tax the property, so multiple taxation would not exist. *Central Railroad Co. v. Pennsylvania,* 370 U.S. 607, 82 S.Ct. 1297, 8 L.Ed.2d 720 (1962).

Income Taxes. *Northwestern States Portland Cement Co. v. Minnesota,* 358 U.S. 450, 79 S.Ct. 357, 3 L.Ed.2d 421 (1959) examined a state tax using an approach similar to the *Complete Auto* test. The Court held that "net income from the interstate operations of a foreign (out-of-state) corporation may be subjected to state taxation provided that the levy is not discriminatory and is properly apportioned to local activities within the state forming a sufficient nexus to support the same." The taxpayer was an Iowa corporation that solicited orders from Minnesota customers for its product through an office and five salesmen in Minnesota. Orders solicited were subject to acceptance in Iowa and deliveries were made by the taxpayer; no pickups by customers were permitted. Nearly half (48%) of the taxpayer's entire output was sold to Minnesota customers. Minnesota levied a tax on the net income of domestic and foreign corporations "whose business within the state consists exclusively of foreign commerce, interstate commerce, or both" and sought to impose it on Northwestern. The Court found that the presence of taxpayer's employees and sales office in the state provided a "sufficient nexus" with the state to tax the income generated by those employees.[1] The tax was not discriminatory because comparable taxes were imposed

---

1. Congress responded to this case by enacting 15 U.S.C.A. §§ 381–384, which, in general, prohibits a state income tax on out-of-state business when the business' only contacts with the taxing state are salesmen selling tangible personal property. Congress' major purpose was to define "sufficient nexus," and its definition "implicitly determine[d] that the state's interest in taxing business' activities below that limit was weaker than the national interest in promoting an open economy." *Heublein, Inc. v. South Carolina Tax Commission,* 409 U.S. 275, 280, 93 S.Ct. 483, 487, 34 L.Ed.2d 472, 478 (1972).

on domestic as well as foreign corporations and on those corporations engaged in intrastate as well as interstate commerce.

To calculate the amount of income attributable to the state, Minnesota used a three-factor apportionment formula. The factors were the ratios of: (1) taxpayer's sales assignable to the state to total sales, (2) taxpayer's tangible property within the state to total property owned, (3) taxpayer's in-state payroll to total payroll. The Court found this formula restricted the tax to that income derived from activities in the state and therefore was properly apportioned.

The rule developed in *Northwestern* is that "the entire net income of a corporation, generated by interstate as well as intrastate activities, may be fairly apportioned among the states for tax purposes by formulas utilizing in-state aspects of interstate affairs." Such taxation is permissible under the due process clause and the substantial nexus requirement of the commerce clause when there is a minimal connection between the intrastate activities and the taxing state and rational relationship between the intrastate values of the business and the income attributed to the state. *Mobil Oil Corp. v. Commissioner of Taxes,* 445 U.S. 425, 437, 100 S.Ct. 1223, 1231, 63 L.Ed.2d 510, 520 (1980); *Exxon Corp. v. Wisconsin Department of Revenue,* 447 U.S. 207, 219–20, 100 S.Ct. 2109, 2118, 65 L.Ed.2d 66, 79 (1980). The *Northwestern* rule has been extended to activities and income generated by international operations. *Container Corporation of America v. Franchise Tax Board,* 463 U.S. 159, 103 S.Ct. 2933, 77 L.Ed.2d 545 (1983).

The taxing state may apply its apportionment formula to the *entire net income* of a multistate business to attain a "rough approximation" of the income attributable to the intrastate activities and satisfy these requirements, if the business is considered "unitary." *Exxon,* 447 U.S. at 223, 100 S.Ct. at 2120, 65 L.Ed.2d at 81. A unitary business is an enterprise whose operations contribute to and depend upon each other for their success. The operations of such a business within the taxing state can provide a market or source of supply essential to the success of the out-of-state operations. The intrastate operations also benefit from functional integration, centralized management, and economies of scale arising from the operation of the business as a whole. The "unitary business principle" allows a state to apply its apportionment formula to tax a portion of the income from the corporation's separate divisions operating in other states rather than being restricted to only the activities physically occurring within its boundaries. The entire income of a unitary multistate business is included in the apportionment calculation when it "avails itself of the 'substantial privilege of carrying on business' within the State." *Exxon,* 447 U.S. at 220, 100 S.Ct. at 2118, 65 L.Ed.2d at 79.

To exclude income from the calculation, the taxpayer must prove that it was earned from activities unrelated to those conducted in the taxing state. This burden is difficult to sustain. In *Mobil,* the presence of marketing operations in the state justified the inclusion in Vermont's apportionment formula of dividend income from the taxpayer's subsidiaries, foreign and domestic, operating abroad, where their activities contributed to the taxpayer's petroleum enterprise. In *Exxon,* the interdependence of the taxpayer's exploration, production, and refining operations outside the state subjected the income from those operations to inclusion in Wisconsin's apportionment formula, although the taxpayer's functional accounting system treated each operation as separate.

However, the fact that a parent holds a significant financial interest in a subsidiary and thus has or could assert realistic control does not necessarily require that the parent apportion income derived from such subsidiaries. What is essential in applying the unitary principle is that the parent have centralization of management control over the business operations of the subsidiary. *ASARCO Inc. v. Idaho State Tax Commission,* 458 U.S. 307, 102 S.Ct. 3103, 73 L.Ed.2d 787 (1982); *F.W. Woolworth Co. v. Taxation and Revenue Department,* 458 U.S. 354, 102 S.Ct. 3128, 73 L.Ed.2d 819 (1982). In both of these cases the parent received intangibles (interest, dividends, or capital gains) from subsidiaries that (unlike the parent) did no business in the state, and were not vertically integrated with the parent.

How the apportionment of income is calculated, like the question of what income is included in the formula, are the subject of litigation. Recall in *Northwestern,* Minnesota had used a three-factor apportionment formula, which the Court upheld. In *Moorman Manufacturing Co. v. Bair,* 437 U.S. 267, 98 S.Ct. 2340, 57 L.Ed.2d 197 (1978), a taxpayer attacked Iowa's use of a single-factor apportionment formula based on sales within the state. Use of this formula allocated 50% more income to the state than would have the three-factor formula used by many other states. The taxpayer argued that the single-factor formula resulted in improper multiple taxation because Illinois, where the taxpayer manufactured its product and also made sales, used the three-factor formula, and thus included some of the same income already taxed in Iowa.

The majority upheld the Iowa formula, arguing that apportionment formulas are only rough approximations of income attributable to a particular state. Some overlap is to be expected and does not violate the commerce clause unless the taxpayer establishes by "clear and cogent evidence" that income attributed to the taxing state is, in fact, "out of all appropriate proportion to the business transacted" in the state. *Moorman,* 437 U.S. at 274, 98 S.Ct. at 2345, 57 L.Ed.2d at 205. The taxpayer failed to make such a showing. It did not establish that its Illinois operations (rather than the Iowa sales) created some of the profits attributed to Iowa. Without such evidence, dissimilar results between the two formulas did not establish multiple taxation.

Gross Receipts Taxes. A gross receipts tax can be more burdensome than a net income tax because it can be imposed when the business as a whole does not make a profit. In *Standard Pressed Steel Co. v. Washington Department of Revenue,* 419 U.S. 560, 95 S.Ct. 706, 42 L.Ed.2d 719 (1975), Washington imposed a business and occupation tax measured by gross receipts from sales that Standard had made to Boeing in that state. Standard's offices and manufacturing plants were located in other states. Boeing's orders and payments were accepted at the Standard home office. Standard shipped orders by common carrier. Standard employed only one person in the state, an engineer who consulted with Boeing about its anticipated needs and requirements for Standard's product and helped to alleviate any difficulties in the use of the product. The Court held that the activities of this lone employee provided a sufficient relationship between Washington and Standard to justify the tax under the due process and commerce clauses. The Court primarily focused on the importance of the employee to Standard's relationship with Boeing and only incidentally on Standard's relationship with the state.

A West Virginia gross receipts tax, on tangible property sold at wholesale in that state, unconstitutionally discriminated against interstate commerce because local manufacturers were exempt from that tax. Although local manufacturers had to pay a higher manufacturing tax, the gross receipts tax was not a compensating tax because manufacturing and wholesaling are not "substantially equivalent events." The manufacturing tax was not reduced when the West Virginia manufacturer sells its goods out of state, but the manufacturing tax was reduced when part of the manufacturing takes place out of state, demonstrating that the tax is on manufacturing and not a proxy for the gross receipts tax. *Armco Inc. v. Hardesty,* 467 U.S. 638, 104 S.Ct. 2620, 81 L.Ed.2d 540 (1984).

Business and Occupation Taxes. These are taxes imposed on the privilege of engaging in a business within a state. They can be assessed in several different ways.

In *Memphis Steam Laundry Cleaner, Inc. v. Stone,* 342 U.S. 389, 72 S.Ct. 424, 96 L.Ed. 436 (1952), Mississippi imposed a privilege tax on all laundries doing business in the state. Laundries licensed in the state paid a fixed fee depending on the size of the municipality in which they were located and $8 per laundry truck used. Laundries located in other states had to pay a fee of $50 per laundry truck used in the state. This disparity of treatment was discrimination against interstate commerce in violation of the commerce clause.

Complete Auto Transit v. Brady, 430 U.S. 274, 97 S.Ct. 1076, 51 L.Ed.2d 326 (1977), upheld a Mississippi privilege tax imposed on a Michigan corporation engaged in the transportation and delivery, to automobile dealers within the state, of cars that had been shipped from outside of Mississippi. The tax was measured as a percentage of the gross receipts collected from this activity. The Court recognized that the taxpayer's in-state activities were still a part of the stream of interstate commerce.

The Court had previously held that a state could not impose a tax on the privilege of engaging in interstate commerce regardless of how fairly the tax was apportioned. *Spector Motor Service, Inc. v. O'Connor,* 340

U.S. 602, 71 S.Ct. 508, 95 L.Ed. 573 (1951). *Complete Auto* overruled *Spector*, noting that there were no economic consequences that followed from the use of the phrase "privilege of engaging in interstate commerce" and continued focus on that phrase would place form over substance. Instead the Court used the four-factor test discussed above and upheld the tax.

The Court later applied the *Complete Auto* test to a privilege tax levied by Washington on stevedoring companies in the state. *Department of Revenue v. Association of Washington Stevedoring Companies,* 435 U.S. 734, 98 S.Ct. 1388, 55 L.Ed.2d 682 (1978). Stevedoring companies are engaged in the loading and unloading of ships engaged in interstate and foreign commerce. In two previous cases, *Puget Sound Stevedoring Co. v. Tax Commission,* 302 U.S. 90, 58 S.Ct. 72, 82 L.Ed. 68 (1937), and *Joseph v. Carter & Weekes Stevedoring Co.,* 330 U.S. 422, 67 S.Ct. 815, 91 L.Ed. 993 (1947), the Court had invalidated similar taxes because they applied "directly" to interstate commerce. The Court in this case rejected that artificial distinction, instead examined the economic consequences of the tax under *Complete Auto,* and upheld the tax.

Foreign Commerce. State taxes affecting foreign commerce must pass, as a threshold requirement, the same scrutiny as a tax on interstate commerce. If the tax passes that barrier, the next step is to analyze the tax under either the import-export clause (U.S. Const., Art. I, § 10, cl. 2) or the foreign commerce component of the commerce clause, depending on the property or activity involved.

Recall that at the end of the *Baldwin* case, § 3–3, Justice Cardozo referred to the Original Package Doctrine. That doctrine prohibited the taxation of any imported goods still in their "original package." Today, in order to determine whether a state tax is constitutional, the primary question is whether the tax is discriminatory, both as to commerce clause problems, *Sonneborn Brothers v. Cureton,* 262 U.S. 506, 43 S.Ct. 643, 67 L.Ed. 1095 (1923), and export-import clause problems, *Michelin Tire Corp. v. Wages,* 423 U.S. 276, 96 S.Ct. 535, 46 L.Ed.2d 495 (1976). Whether the item's original package has been broken is not the real issue.

Japan Line, Limited v. County of Los Angeles, 441 U.S. 434, 99 S.Ct. 1813, 60 L.Ed.2d 336 (1979) examined an apportioned state *ad valorem* property tax on foreign-owned instrumentalities of foreign commerce under the foreign commerce component of the commerce clause. The considerations underlying this area, besides the nexus, apportionment, and nondiscrimination questions of *Complete Auto,* are whether the tax creates substantial risk of international multiple taxation and whether the tax impairs federal uniformity in foreign commerce. In the area of foreign commerce the Court is more concerned with the possibility, rather than the actuality, of multiple taxation because the Court cannot require a foreign sovereign to apportion a tax. *Japan Line* invalidated the California *ad valorem* property tax on foreign owned instrumentalities of international commerce, i.e., cargo containers that were owned, based, and registered abroad, and used exclusively in international commerce. *Kraft General Foods, Inc. v. Iowa Department of Revenue and Finance,* 505 U.S. 71, 112 S.Ct. 2365, 120 L.Ed.2d 59 (1992) later held that an Iowa law that allowed corporations (in computing their Iowa business tax) to deduct dividends received from domestic subsidiaries but not foreign subsidiaries violated the foreign commerce clause.

Itel Containers International Corp. v. Huddleston, 507 U.S. 60, 113 S.Ct. 1095, 122 L.Ed.2d 421 (1993) upheld (8 to 1) Tennessee's sales tax on leases of containers owned by a domestic company for use exclusively in international shipping. Such a sales tax, as applied, does not violate the Commerce Clause, the Import–Export Clause, or the Supremacy Clause. It was not imposed on the importation or on imported goods, but rather on a business transaction occurring within the state. It did not draw revenue from the importation process, and thus did not violate the Import–Export Clause by diverting revenue from the federal government.

Barclays Bank PLC v. Franchise Tax Board of California, 512 U.S. 298, 114 S.Ct. 2268, 129 L.Ed.2d 244 (1994) upheld the constitutionality of California's "worldwide combined reporting" method of computing its corporate franchise tax as applied to domestic corporations with foreign parents, or to foreign corporations with either foreign parents or foreign subsidiaries. California first aggregated the worldwide income of all corporate entities that made up a unitary multinational business, and then taxed a percentage of that income equal to the average of the proportion of worldwide payroll, property, and sales located in California. The President had opposed this method, but the regulatory authority in this area is for Congress to exercise.

United States v. IBM, 517 U.S. 843, 116 S.Ct. 1793, 135 L.Ed.2d 124 (1996) held that the Export Clause, Art. I, § 9, cl. 5, prohibits the Federal Government from imposing a generally applicable, nondiscriminatory federal tax on goods in *export* transit. Cases decided under the dormant commerce clause or the Import–Export Clause (Art. I, § 10, cl. 2)—both of which limit *state* taxing power—do not govern the Export Clause. The dormant commerce only applies to *state* taxes that discriminate against interstate commerce, while the Export Clause denies Congress the power to tax exports at all.

Chapter 4

FEDERAL POWERS UNDER THE COMMERCE CLAUSE

4–1. THE PRE–1937 CASES

GIBBONS v. OGDEN
22 U.S. (9 Wheat.) 1, 6 L.Ed. 23 (1824).

[This case, together with the portion of CHIEF JUSTICE MARSHALL's opinion dealing with the scope of federal power under the Commerce Clause, appears at § 3–1.]

THE DANIEL BALL
77 U.S. (10 Wall.) 557, 19 L.Ed. 999 (1871).

[The Daniel Ball, a steamer, was navigating the Grand River and transporting merchandise and people between the cities of Grand Rapids and Grand Haven, all in the state of Michigan. Because the ship had neither been inspected for safety purposes nor licensed under the laws of the United States, the Government sued to recover a $500 fine. The district court dismissed the Government's action, but the circuit court reversed.]

MR. JUSTICE FIELD, after stating the case, delivered the opinion of the court, as follows:

Two questions are presented in this case for our determination.

First: Whether the steamer was at the time designated in the libel engaged in transporting merchandise and passengers on a navigable water of the United States within the meaning of the acts of Congress; and,

Second: Whether those acts are applicable to a steamer engaged as a common carrier between places in the same State, when a portion of the merchandise transported by her is destined to places in other States, or comes from places without the State, she not running in connection with

165

or in continuation of any line of steamers or other vessels, or any railway line leading to or from another State.

Upon the first of these questions we entertain no doubt.... Those rivers must be regarded as public navigable rivers in law which are navigable in fact. And they are navigable in fact when they are used, or are susceptible of being used, in their ordinary condition, as highways for commerce, over which trade and travel are or may be conducted in the customary modes of trade and travel on water. And they constitute navigable waters of the United States within the meaning of the acts of Congress, in contradistinction from the navigable waters of the States, when they form in their ordinary condition by themselves, or by uniting with other waters, a continued highway over which commerce is or may be carried on with other States or foreign countries in the customary modes in which such commerce is conducted by water.

But it is contended that the steamer Daniel Ball was only engaged in the internal commerce of the State of Michigan, and was not, therefore, required to be inspected or licensed, even if it be conceded that Grand River is a navigable water of the United States; and this brings us to the consideration of the second question presented.

There is undoubtedly an internal commerce which is subject to the control of the States.... In this case it is admitted that the steamer was engaged in shipping and transporting down Grand River, goods destined and marked for other States than Michigan, and in receiving and transporting up the river goods brought within the State from without its limits; but inasmuch as her agency in the transportation was entirely within the limits of the State, and she did not run in connection with, or in continuation of, any line of vessels or railway leading to other States, it is contended that she was engaged entirely in domestic commerce. But this conclusion does not follow. So far as she was employed in transporting goods destined for other States, or goods brought from without the limits of Michigan and destined to places within that State, she was engaged in commerce between the States, and however limited that commerce may have been, she was, so far as it went, subject to the legislation of Congress. She was employed as an instrument of that commerce; for whenever a commodity has begun to move as an article of trade from one State to another, commerce in that commodity between the States has commenced. The fact that several different and independent agencies are employed in transporting the commodity, some acting entirely in one State, and some acting through two or more States, does in no respect affect the character of the transaction. To the extent in which each agency acts in that transportation, it is subject to the regulation of Congress.

It is said that if the position here asserted be sustained, there is no such thing as the domestic trade of a State; that Congress may take the entire control of the commerce of the country, and extend its regulations to the railroads within a State on which grain or fruit is transported to a distant market. We answer that the present case relates to transportation on the navigable waters of the United States, and we are not called upon to express an opinion upon the power of Congress over interstate commerce when carried on by land transportation. And we answer further, that we are unable to draw any clear and distinct line between the authority of Congress to regulate an agency employed in commerce between the States, when that agency extends through two or more States, and when it is confined in its action entirely within the limits of a single State. If its authority does not extend to an agency in such commerce, when that agency is confined within the limits of a State, its entire authority over interstate commerce may be defeated. Several agencies combining, each taking up the commodity transported at the boundary line at one end of a State, and leaving it at the boundary line at the other end, the Federal jurisdiction would be entirely ousted, and the constitutional provision would become a dead letter.

We perceive no error in the record, and the decree of the Circuit Court must be

Affirmed.

UNITED STATES v. E.C. KNIGHT CO.
156 U.S. 1, 15 S.Ct. 249, 39 L.Ed. 325 (1895).

MR. CHIEF JUSTICE FULLER, after stating the case, delivered the opinion of the court.

By the purchase of the stock of the four Philadelphia refineries, with shares of its own stock, the American Sugar Refining Company acquired nearly complete control of the manufacture of refined sugar within the United States. The bill charged that the contracts under which these purchases were made constituted combinations in restraint of trade, and that in entering into them the defendants combined and conspired to restrain the trade and commerce in refined sugar among the several States and with foreign nations, contrary to the act of Congress of July 2, 1890.

The relief sought was the cancellation of the agreements under which the stock was transferred; the redelivery of the stock to the parties respectively; and an injunction against the further performance of the agreements and further violations of the act. . . .

In the view which we take of the case, we need not discuss whether because the tentacles which drew the outlying refineries into the dominant corporation were separately put out, therefore there was no combination to monopolize. . . .

The fundamental question is, whether conceding that the existence of a monopoly in manufacture is established by the evidence, that monopoly can be directly suppressed under the act of Congress in the mode attempted by this bill.

It cannot be denied that the power of a State to protect the lives, health, and property of its citizens, and to preserve good order and the public morals, "the power to govern men and things within the limits of its dominion," is a power originally and always belonging to the States, not surrendered by them to the general government, nor directly restrained by the Constitution of the United States, and essentially exclusive. The relief of the citizens of each State from the burden of monopoly and the evils resulting from the restraint of trade among such citizens was left with the States to deal with. . . .

The argument is that the power to control the manufacture of refined sugar is a monopoly over a necessary of life, to the enjoyment of which by a large part of the population of the United States interstate commerce is indispensable, and that, therefore, the general government in the exercise of the power to regulate commerce may repress such monopoly directly and set aside the instruments which have created it. But this argument cannot be confined to necessaries of life merely, and must include all articles of general consumption. Doubtless the power to control the manufacture of a given thing involves in a certain sense the control of its disposition, but this is a secondary and not the primary sense; and although the exercise of that power may result in bringing the operation of commerce into play, it does not control it, and affects it only incidentally and indirectly. Commerce succeeds to manufacture, and is not a part of it. The power to regulate commerce is the power to prescribe the rule by which commerce shall be governed, and is a power independent of the power to suppress monopoly. But it may operate in repression of monopoly whenever that comes within the rules by which commerce is governed or whenever the transaction is itself a monopoly of commerce.

It is vital that the independence of the commercial power and of the police power, and the delimitation between them, however sometimes perplexing, should always be recognized and observed, for while the one furnishes the strongest bond of union, the other is essential to the preservation of the autonomy of the States as required by our dual form of government; and acknowledged evils, however grave and urgent they may appear to be, had better be borne, than the risk be run, in the effort to suppress them, of more serious consequences by resort to expedients of even doubtful constitutionality.

It will be perceived how far-reaching the proposition is that the power of dealing with a monopoly directly may be exercised by the general government whenever interstate or international commerce may be ultimately affected. The regulation of commerce applies to the subjects of commerce and not to matters of internal police. Contracts to buy, sell, or exchange goods to be transported among the several States, the transportation and its instrumentalities, and articles bought, sold, or exchanged for the purposes of such transit among the States, or put in the way of transit, may be regulated, but this is because they form part of interstate trade or commerce. The fact that an article is manufactured for export to another State does not of itself make it an article of interstate commerce, and the intent of the manufacturer does not determine the time when the article or product passes from the control of the State and belongs to commerce. This was so ruled in *Coe v. Errol,* 116 U.S. 517, 6 Sup.Ct. 475, 29 L.Ed. 715 (1886).

[I]n *Kidd v. Pearson,* 128 U.S. 1, 20, 21, 22, 9 S.Ct. 6, 32 L.Ed. 346 (1888), where the question was discussed whether the right of a State to enact a statute prohibiting within its limits the manufacture of intoxicating liquors, except for certain purposes, could be overthrown by the fact that the manufacturer intended to export the liquors when made, it was held that the intent of the manufacturer did not determine the time when the article or product passed from the control of the State and belonged to commerce, and that, therefore, the statute, in omitting to except from its operation the manufacture of intoxicating liquors within the limits of the State for export, did not constitute an unauthorized interference with the right of Congress to regulate commerce....

In *Gibbons v. Ogden* and other cases often cited, the state laws, which were held inoperative, were instances of direct interference with, or regulations of, interstate or international commerce.... Contracts, combinations, or conspiracies to control domestic enterprise in manufacture, agriculture, mining, production in all its forms, or to raise or lower prices or wages, might unquestionably tend to restrain external as well as domestic trade, but the restraint would be an indirect result, however inevitable and whatever its extent, and such result would not necessarily determine the object of the contract, combination, or conspiracy.... Slight reflection will show that if the national power extends to all contracts and combinations in manufacture, agriculture, mining, and other productive industries, whose ultimate result may affect external commerce, comparatively little of business operations and affairs would be left for state control.

[T]he contracts and acts of the defendants related exclusively to the acquisition of the Philadelphia refineries and the business of sugar refining in Pennsylvania, and bore no direct relation to commerce between the States or with foreign nations. The object was manifestly private gain in the manufacture of the commodity, but not through the control of interstate or foreign commerce. It is true that the bill alleged that the products of these refineries were sold and distributed among the several States, and that all the companies were engaged in trade or commerce with the several States and with foreign nations; but this was no more than to say that trade and commerce served manufacture to fulfil its function. Sugar was refined for sale, and sales were probably made at Philadelphia for consumption, and undoubtedly for resale by the first purchasers throughout Pennsylvania and other States, and refined sugar was also forwarded by the companies to other States for sale. Nevertheless it does not follow that an attempt to monopolize, or the actual monopoly of, the manufacture was an attempt, whether executory or consummated, to monopolize commerce, even though, in order to dispose of the product, the instrumentality of commerce was necessarily invoked. [T]hat trade or commerce might be indirectly affected was not enough to entitle complainants to a decree....

[The dissenting opinion of HARLAN, J., is omitted.]

Notes

1. Is it relevant, in determining Congress' power over commerce, that in *Kidd v. Pearson,* relied on by Chief Justice Fuller in the majority opinion, the Court had upheld state power to prohibit an activity—the manufacture of intoxicating beverages within the state—even though the product was intended for export outside of the state?

In *Coe v. Errol,* also cited by the majority, the issue was whether certain logs cut in New Hampshire and hauled to a river town for out of state shipment could be taxed like other property in New Hampshire. The Court ruled that the owner's intent to export the logs and his partial preparation to do so did not exempt the logs from state taxation. Was Fuller's citation to *Coe* on point? Do the negative implications of the Commerce Clause limit Congress' affirmative power?

2. In *Northern Securities Co. v. United States,* 193 U.S. 197, 24 S.Ct. 436, 48 L.Ed. 679 (1904), Harlan, J., in a plurality opinion, stated:

[U]nder the leadership of defendants Hill and Morgan the stockholders of the Great Northern and Northern Pacific Railway corporations, having competing and substantially parallel lines from the Great Lakes and the Mississippi River to the Pacific Ocean at Puget Sound combined and conceived the scheme of organizing a corporation under the laws of New Jersey, which should *hold* the shares of the stock of the constituent companies, such shareholders, in lieu of their shares in those companies, to receive, upon an agreed basis of value, shares in the holding corporation.... Necessarily, also, the constituent companies ceased, under such a combination, to be in active competition for trade and commerce along their respective lines, and have become, practically, one powerful consolidated corporation, by the name of a holding corporation the principal, if not the sole, object for the formation of which was to carry out the purpose of the original combination under which competition between the constituent companies would cease.... The mere existence of such a combination and the power acquired by the holding company as its trustee, constitute a menace to, and a restraint upon, that freedom of commerce which Congress intended to recognize and protect, and which the public is entitled to have protected [under the Sherman Act].

Holmes, J., wrote a dissenting opinion concurred in by Fuller, C.J., and White & Peckham, JJ. Holmes said:

Great cases like hard cases make bad law. For great cases are called great, not by reason of their real importance in shaping the law of the future, but because of some accident of immediate overwhelming interest which appeals to the feelings and distorts the judgment. These immediate interests exercise a kind of hydraulic pressure which makes what previously was clear seem doubtful, and before which even well settled principles of law will bend. [I]t is clear that the mere fact of an indirect effect upon commerce not shown to be certain and very great, would not justify such a law. The point decided in *United States v. E.C. Knight Co.,* was that "the fact that trade or commerce might be indirectly affected was not enough to entitle complainants to a decree."

Commerce depends upon population, but Congress could not, on that ground, undertake to regulate marriage and divorce. If the act before us is to be carried out according to what seems to me the logic of the argument for the Government, which I do not believe that it will be, I can see no part of the conduct of life with which on similar principles Congress might not interfere.

In response to Holmes' dissent, President Teddy Roosevelt (who had appointed Holmes to the Court) said that he "could carve out of a banana a judge with more backbone than that."

3. In *Swift & Co. v. United States*, 196 U.S. 375, 25 S.Ct. 276, 49 L.Ed. 518 (1905), Justice Holmes, for a unanimous Court, upheld the constitutionality of the Sherman Act as applied to meat dealers throughout the United States:

[The Government's bill in equity] charges a combination of a dominant proportion of the dealers in fresh meat throughout the United States not to bid against each other in the live stock markets of the different States, to bid up prices for a few days in order to induce the cattle men to send their stock to the stock yards, to fix prices at which they will sell, and to that end to restrict shipments of meat when necessary, to establish a uniform rule of credit to dealers and to keep a black list, to make uniform and improper charges for cartage, and finally, to get less than lawful rates from the railroads to the exclusion of competitors.... Although the combination alleged embraces restraint and monopoly of trade within a single State, its effect upon commerce among the States is not accidental, secondary, remote or merely probable.... Therefore the case is not like *United States v. E.C. Knight Co.*, where the subject matter of the combination was manufacture and the direct object monopoly of manufacture within a State. However likely monopoly of commerce among the States in the article manufactured was to follow from the agreement it was not a necessary consequence nor a primary end. Here the subject matter is sales and the very point of the combination is to restrain and monopolize commerce among the States in respect of such sales. The two cases are near to each other, as sooner or later always must happen where lines are to be drawn, but the line between them is distinct.

[C]ommerce among the States is not a technical legal conception, but a practical one, drawn from the course of business. When cattle are sent for sale from a place in one State, with the expectation that they will end their transit, after purchase, in another, and when in effect they do so, with only the interruption necessary to find a purchaser at the stock yards, and when this is a typical, constantly recurring course, the current thus existing is a current of commerce among the States, and the purchase of the cattle is a part and incident of such commerce. What we say is true at least of such a purchase by residents in another State from that of the seller and of the cattle....

In *Stafford v. Wallace*, 258 U.S. 495, 42 S.Ct. 397, 66 L.Ed. 735 (1922), Chief Justice Taft, for the Court, elaborated on Holmes' metaphor:

The stockyards are not a place of rest or final destination. Thousands of head of live stock arrive daily by carload and trainload lots, and must be promptly sold and disposed of and moved out to give place to the constantly flowing traffic that presses behind. The stockyards are but a throat through which the current flows, and the transactions which occur therein are only incident to this current from the West to the East, and from one State to another.... The stockyards and the sales are necessary factors in the middle of this current of commerce....

The application of the commerce clause of the Constitution in the *Swift Case* was the result of the natural development of interstate commerce under modern conditions. It was the inevitable recognition of the great central fact that such streams of commerce from one part of the country to another which are ever flowing are in their very essence the commerce among the states and with foreign nations which historically it was one of the chief purposes of the Constitution to bring under national protection and control. This court declined to defeat this purpose ... and take it out of national regulation by a nice and technical inquiry into the non-interstate character of some of its necessary incidents and facilities when considered alone and without reference to their association with the movement of which they were an essential but subordinate part.

HOUSTON, EAST & WEST TEXAS RAILWAY v. UNITED STATES (THE SHREVEPORT CASE)

234 U.S. 342, 34 S.Ct. 833, 58 L.Ed. 1341 (1914).

MR. JUSTICE HUGHES delivered the opinion of the court.

These suits were brought in the Commerce Court by the Houston, East & West Texas Railway Company, and the Houston & Shreveport Railroad Company, and by the Texas & Pacific Railway Company, respectively, to set aside an order of the Interstate Commerce Commission, dated March 11, 1912, upon the ground that it exceeded the Commission's authority....

The gravamen of the complaint, said the Interstate Commerce Commission, was that the carriers made rates out of Dallas and other Texas points into eastern Texas which were much lower than those which they extended into Texas from Shreveport. The situation may be briefly described: Shreveport, Louisiana, is about 40 miles from the Texas state line, and 231 miles from Houston, Texas, on the line of the Houston, East & West Texas and Houston & Shreveport Companies (which are affiliated in interest); it is 189 miles from Dallas, Texas, on the line of the Texas & Pacific. Shreveport competes with both cities for the trade of the intervening territory. The rates on these lines from Dallas and Houston, respectively, eastward to intermediate points in Texas were much less, according to distance, than from Shreveport westward to the same points. It is undisputed that the difference was substantial and injuriously affected the commerce of Shreveport. It appeared, for example, that a rate of 60 cents carried first class traffic a distance of 160 miles to the eastward from Dallas, while the same rate would carry the same class of traffic only 55 miles into Texas from Shreveport.... In order to correct this discrimination [against Shreveport], the carriers were directed [by the I.C.C.] to desist from charging higher rates for the transportation of any commodity from Shreveport to Dallas and Houston, respectively, and intermediate points, than were contemporaneously charged for the carriage of such commodity from Dallas and Houston toward Shreveport for equal distances, as the Commission found that relation of rates to be reasonable....

... Manifestly the order might be complied with, and the discrimination avoided, either by reducing the interstate rates from Shreveport to the level of the competing intrastate rates, or by raising these intrastate rates to the level of the interstate rates, or by such reduction in the one case and increase in the other as would result in equality. But it is urged that, so far as the interstate rates were sustained by the Commission as reasonable, the Commission was without authority to compel their reduction in order to equalize them with the lower intrastate rates. The holding of the Commerce Court was that the order relieved the appellants from further obligation to observe the intrastate rates and that they were at liberty to comply with the Commission's requirements by increasing these rates sufficiently to remove the forbidden discrimination. The invalidity of the order in this aspect is challenged upon two grounds:

(1) That Congress is impotent to control the intrastate charges of an interstate carrier even to the extent necessary to prevent injurious discrimination against interstate traffic; and

(2) That, if it be assumed that Congress has this power, still it has not been exercised, and hence the action of the Commission exceeded the limits of the authority which has been conferred upon it.

First. It is unnecessary to repeat what has frequently been said by this court with respect to the complete and paramount character of the power confided to Congress to regulate commerce among the several States. It is of the essence of this power that, where it exists, it dominates. Interstate trade was not left to be destroyed or impeded by the rivalries of local governments.... The fact that carriers are instruments of intrastate commerce, as well as of interstate commerce, does not derogate from the complete and paramount authority of Congress over the latter or preclude the Federal power from being exerted to prevent the intrastate operations of such carriers from being made a means of injury to that which has been confided to Federal care. Wherever the interstate and intrastate transactions of carriers are so related that the government of the one involves the control of the other, it is Congress, and not the State, that is entitled to prescribe the final and dominant rule, for otherwise Congress would be denied the exercise of its constitutional authority and the State, and not the Nation, would be supreme within the national field.... Congress in the exercise of its paramount power may prevent the common instrumentalities of interstate and intrastate commercial intercourse from being used in their intrastate operations to the injury of interstate commerce. This is not to say that Congress possesses the authority to regulate the internal commerce of a State, as such, but that it does possess the power to foster and protect interstate commerce, and to take all measures necessary or appropriate to that end, although intrastate transactions of interstate carriers may thereby be controlled.

This principle is applicable here. We find no reason to doubt that Congress is entitled to keep the highway of interstate communication open to interstate traffic upon fair and equal terms. That an unjust discrimination in the rates of a common carrier, by which one person or locality is unduly favored as against another under substantially similar conditions of traffic, constitutes an evil is undeniable; and where this evil consists in the action of an interstate carrier in unreasonably discriminating against interstate traffic over its line, the authority of Congress to prevent it is equally clear. It is immaterial, so far as the protecting power of Congress is concerned, that the discrimination arises from intrastate rates as compared with interstate rates. The use of the instrument of interstate commerce in a discriminatory manner so as to inflict injury upon that commerce, or some part thereof, furnishes abundant ground for Federal intervention. Nor can the attempted exercise of state authority alter the matter, where Congress has acted, for a State may not authorize the carrier to do that which Congress is entitled to forbid and has forbidden.

[T]he power to deal with the relation between the two kinds of rates, as a relation, lies exclusively with Congress. It is manifest that the State cannot fix the relation of the carrier's interstate and intrastate charges without directly interfering with the former, unless it simply follows the standard set by Federal authority. . . .

It is also clear that, in removing the injurious discriminations against interstate traffic arising from the relation of intrastate to interstate rates, Congress is not bound to reduce the latter below what it may deem to be a proper standard fare to the carrier and to the public. Otherwise, it could prevent the injury to interstate commerce only by the sacrifice of its judgment as to interstate rates. Congress is entitled to maintain its own standard as to these rates and to forbid any discriminatory action by interstate carriers which will obstruct the freedom of movement of interstate traffic over their lines in accordance with the terms it establishes. . . .

Second. The remaining question is with regard to the scope of the power which Congress has granted to the Commission. [The Court concluded that Congress had in fact granted such power to the Commission.] . . .

In conclusion: Reading the order in the light of the report of the Commission, it does not appear that the Commission attempted to require the carriers to reduce their interstate rates out of Shreveport below what was found to be a reasonable charge for that service. So far as these interstate rates conformed to what was found to be reasonable by the Commission, the carriers are entitled to maintain them, and they are free to comply with the order by so adjusting the other rates, to which the order relates, as to remove the forbidden discrimination. But this result they are required to accomplish.

The decree of the Commerce Court is affirmed in each case.

Affirmed.

MR. JUSTICE LURTON and MR. JUSTICE PITNEY dissent.

Notes

A Wisconsin statute prescribed a maximum rate for rail passengers of 2a mile traveling intrastate. The I.C.C. prescribed rate for interstate passengers was 3.6a mile. The I.C.C. found that 3.6a mile was necessary to meet the net income requirement of the interstate railroad group, and that there was unjust discrimination against interstate commerce because of the lower state fares in intrastate commerce. Consequently, it ordered that the intrastate rates be raised, notwithstanding the state statute and even though such traffic was wholly within a state. Assuming that the I.C.C.'s order is within its statutory authority, is that statute constitutional? See *Railroad Commission of Wisconsin v. Chicago, Burlington & Quincy Railway Co.*, 257 U.S. 563, 42 S.Ct. 232, 66 L.Ed. 371 (1922)(Taft, C.J.).

LOTTERY CASE (CHAMPION v. AMES)
188 U.S. 321, 23 S.Ct. 321, 47 L.Ed. 492 (1903).

[The Government indicted appellant Champion for conspiracy to transport lottery tickets of the Pan–American Lottery Company in Paraguay, from Texas to California, in violation of "An act for the suppression of lottery traffic through national and interstate commerce. . . . "]

MR. JUSTICE HARLAN . . . delivered the opinion of the court.

The appellant insists that the carrying of lottery tickets from one State to another State by an express company engaged in carrying freight and packages from State to State, although such tickets may be contained in a box or package, does not constitute, and cannot by any act of Congress be legally made to constitute, *commerce* among the States. . . . [Our prior cases] show that commerce among the States embraces navigation, intercourse, communication, traffic, the transit of persons, and the transmission of messages by telegraph. . . .

It was said in argument that lottery tickets are not of any real or substantial value in themselves, and therefore are not subjects of commerce. If that were conceded to be the only legal tests as to what are to be deemed subjects of the commerce that may be regulated by Congress, we cannot accept as accurate the broad statement that such tickets are of no value. Upon their face they showed that the lottery company offered a large capital prize, to be paid to the holder of the ticket winning the prize at the drawing advertised to be held at Asuncion,

Paraguay.... Even if a holder did not draw a prize, the tickets, before the drawing, had a money value in the market among those who chose to sell or buy lottery tickets. In short, a lottery ticket is a subject of traffic, and is so designated in the act of 1895....

We are of opinion that lottery tickets are subjects of traffic and therefore are subjects of commerce, and the regulation of the carriage of such tickets from State to State, at least by independent carriers, is a regulation of commerce among the several States. But it is said that the statute in question does not regulate the carrying of lottery tickets from State to State, but by punishing those who cause them to be so carried Congress in effect prohibits such carrying; that in respect of the carrying from one State to another of articles or things that are, in fact, or according to usage in business, the subjects of commerce, the authority given Congress was not to *prohibit,* but only to *regulate.* This view was earnestly pressed at the bar by learned counsel, and must be examined.

... If lottery traffic, *carried on through interstate commerce,* is a matter of which Congress may take cognizance and over which its power may be exerted, can it be possible that it must tolerate the traffic, and simply regulate the manner in which it may be carried on? Or may not Congress, for the protection of the people of all the States, and under the power to regulate interstate commerce, devise such means, within the scope of the Constitution, and not prohibited by it, as will drive that traffic out of commerce among the States? ...

If a State, when considering legislation for the suppression of lotteries within its own limits, may properly take into view the evils that inhere in the raising of money, in that mode, why may not Congress, invested with the power to regulate commerce among the several States, provide that such commerce shall not be polluted by the carrying of lottery tickets from one State to another? ... If it be said that the act of 1895 is inconsistent with the Tenth Amendment, reserving to the States respectively or to the people the powers not delegated to the United States, the answer is that the power to regulate commerce among the States has been expressly delegated to Congress....

It is said, however, that if, in order to suppress lotteries carried on through interstate commerce, Congress may exclude lottery tickets from such commerce, that principle leads necessarily to the conclusion that Congress may arbitrarily exclude from commerce among the States any article, commodity or thing, of whatever kind or nature, or however useful or valuable, which it may choose, no matter with what motive.... It will be time enough to consider the constitutionality of such legislation when we must do so. The present case does not require the court to declare the full extent of the power that Congress may exercise in the regulation of commerce among the States. We may, however, repeat, in this connection, what the court has heretofore said, that the power of Congress to regulate commerce among the States, although plenary, cannot be deemed arbitrary, since it is subject to such limitations or restrictions as are prescribed by the Constitution. This power, therefore, may not be exercised so as to infringe rights secured or protected by that instrument. It would not be difficult to imagine legislation that would be justly liable to such an objection as that stated, and be hostile to the objects for the accomplishment of which Congress was invested with the general power to regulate commerce among the several States. But, as often said, the possible abuse of a power is not an argument against its existence. There is probably no governmental power that may not be exerted to the injury of the public. If what is done by Congress is manifestly in excess of the powers granted to it, then upon the courts will rest the duty of adjudging that its action is neither legal nor binding upon the people. . . .

Affirmed.

MR. CHIEF JUSTICE FULLER, with whom concur MR. JUSTICE BREWER, MR. JUSTICE SHIRAS and MR. JUSTICE PECKHAM, dissenting. . . .

. . . To hold that Congress has general police power would be to hold that it may accomplish objects not entrusted to the General Government, and to defeat the operation of the Tenth Amendment. . . .

If a lottery ticket is not an article of commerce, how can it become so when placed in an envelope or box or other covering, and transported by an express company? To say that the mere carrying of an article which is not an article of commerce in and of itself nevertheless becomes such the moment it is to be transported from one State to another, is to transform a non-commercial article into a commercial one simply because it is transported. I cannot conceive that any such result can properly follow.

It would be to say that everything is an article of commerce the moment it is taken to be transported from place to place, and of interstate commerce if from State to State. An invitation to dine, or to take a drive, or a note of introduction, all become articles of commerce under the ruling in this case, by being deposited with an express company for transportation. This in effect breaks down all the differences between that which is and that which is not, an article of commerce, and the necessary consequence is to take from the States all jurisdiction over the subject so far as interstate communication is concerned. It is a long step in the direction of wiping out all traces of state lines, and the creation of a centralized Government.

[Our view of the commerce clause] does not challenge the legislative power of a sovereign nation to exclude foreign persons or commodities or place an embargo, perhaps not permanent, upon foreign ships or manufactures. . . . There is no reservation of police powers or any other to a foreign nation or to an Indian tribe, and the scope of the power is not the same as that over interstate commerce. . . .

HAMMER v. DAGENHART (THE CHILD LABOR CASE)

247 U.S. 251, 38 S.Ct. 529, 62 L.Ed. 1101 (1918).

MR. JUSTICE DAY delivered the opinion of the court.

A bill was filed in the United States District Court for the Western District of North Carolina by a father in his own behalf and as next friend of his two minor sons, one under the age of fourteen years and the other between the ages of fourteen and sixteen years, employees in a cotton mill at Charlotte, North Carolina, to enjoin the enforcement of the act of Congress intended to prevent interstate commerce in the products of child labor. Act of Sept. 1, 1916.

The District Court held the act unconstitutional and entered a decree enjoining its enforcement. This appeal brings the case here.... The controlling question for decision is: Is it within the authority of Congress in regulating commerce among the States to prohibit the transportation in interstate commerce of manufactured goods, the product of a factor in which, within thirty days prior to their removal therefrom, children under the age of fourteen have been employed or permitted to work, or children between the ages of fourteen and sixteen years have been employed or permitted to work more than eight hours in any day, or more than six days in any week, or after the hour of seven o'clock P.M. or before the hour of 6 o'clock A.M.?

The power essential to the passage of this act, the Government contends, is found in the commerce clause of the Constitution which authorizes Congress to regulate commerce with foreign nations and among the States.... But it is insisted that adjudged cases in this court establish the doctrine that the power to regulate given to Congress incidentally includes the authority to prohibit the movement of ordinary commodities and therefore that the subject is not open for discussion. The cases demonstrate the contrary. They rest upon the character of the particular subjects dealt with and the fact that the scope of governmental authority, state or national, possessed over them is such that the authority to prohibit is as to them but the exertion of the power to regulate.

The first of these cases is *Champion v. Ames,* the so-called *Lottery Case,* in which it was held that Congress might pass a law having the effect to keep the channels of commerce free from use in the transportation of tickets used in the promotion of lottery schemes. In *Hipolite Egg Co. v. United States,* 220 U.S. 45, 31 S.Ct. 364, 55 L.Ed. 364, this court sustained the power of Congress to pass the Pure Food and Drug Act which prohibited the introduction into the States by means of interstate commerce of impure foods and drugs. In *Hoke v. United States,* 227 U.S. 308, 33 S.Ct. 281, 57 L.Ed. 523, this court sustained the constitutionality of the so-called "White Slave Traffic Act" whereby the transportation of a woman in interstate commerce for the purpose of prostitution was forbidden. In that case we said, having reference to the authority of Congress, under the regulatory power, to protect the channels of interstate commerce:

> If the facility of interstate transportation can be taken away from the demoralization of lotteries, the debasement of obscene literature, the contagion of diseased cattle or persons, the impurity of food and drugs, the like facility can be taken away from the systematic enticement to and the enslavement in prostitution and debauchery of women, and, more insistently, of girls.

In *Caminetti v. United States,* 242 U.S. 470, 37 S.Ct. 192, 61 L.Ed. 442, we held that Congress might prohibit the transportation of women in interstate commerce for the purposes of debauchery and kindred purposes. . . .

In each of these instances the use of interstate transportation was necessary to the accomplishment of harmful results. In other words, although the power over interstate transportation was to regulate, that could only be accomplished by prohibiting the use of the facilities of interstate commerce to effect the evil intended.

This element is wanting in the present case. The thing intended to be accomplished by this statute is the denial of the facilities of interstate commerce to those manufacturers in the States who employ children within the prohibited ages. The act in its effect does not regulate transportation among the States, but aims to standardize the ages at which children may be employed in mining and manufacturing within the States. The goods shipped are of themselves harmless. The act permits them to be freely shipped after thirty days from the time of their removal from the factory. When offered for shipment, and before transportation begins, the labor of their production is over, and the mere fact that they were intended for interstate commerce transportation does not make their production subject to federal control under the commerce power.

Over interstate transportation, or its incidents, the regulatory power of Congress is ample, but the production of articles, intended for interstate commerce, is a matter of local regulation. . . . *Coe v. Errol,* 116 U.S. 517, 6 Sup.Ct. 475, 29 L.Ed. 715. If it were otherwise, all manufacture intended for interstate shipment would be brought under federal control to the practical exclusion of the authority of the States, a result certainly not contemplated by the framers of the Constitution when they vested in Congress the authority to regulate commerce among the States. *Kidd v. Pearson,* 128 U.S. 1, 21, 9 Sup.Ct. 6, 10, 32 L.Ed. 346, 350.

It is further contended that the authority of Congress may be exerted to control interstate commerce in the shipment of child-made goods because of the effect of the circulation of such goods in other States where the evil of this class of labor has been recognized by local legislation, and the right to thus employ child labor has been more rigorously restrained than in the State of production. In other words, that the unfair competition, thus engendered, may be controlled by closing the channels of interstate commerce to manufacturers in those States where the local laws do not meet what Congress deems to be the more just standard of other States.

There is no power vested in Congress to require the States to exercise their police power so as to prevent possible unfair competition. Many causes may coöperate to give one State, by reason of local laws or conditions, an economic advantage over others. The Commerce Clause was not intended to give to Congress a general authority to equalize such conditions. In some of the States laws have been passed fixing minimum wages for women, in others the local law regulates the hours of labor of women in various employments. Business done in such States may be at an economic disadvantage when compared with States which have no such regulations; surely, this fact does not give Congress the power to deny transportation in interstate commerce to those who carry on business where the hours of labor and the rate of compensation for women have not been fixed by a standard in use in other States and approved by Congress.

The grant of power to Congress over the subject of interstate commerce was to enable it to regulate such commerce, and not to give it authority to control the States in their exercise of the police power over local trade and manufacture. The grant of authority over a purely federal matter was not intended to destroy the local power always existing and carefully reserved to the States in the Tenth Amendment to the Constitution. Police regulations relating to the internal trade and affairs of the States have been uniformly recognized as within such control. . . . We have neither authority nor disposition to question the motives of Congress in enacting this legislation. . . .

In our view the necessary effect of this act is, by means of a prohibition against the movement in interstate commerce of ordinary commercial commodities, to regulate the hours of labor of children in factories and mines within the States, a purely state authority. Thus the act in a two-fold sense is repugnant to the Constitution. It not only transcends the authority delegated to Congress over commerce but also exerts a power as to a purely local matter to which the federal authority does not extend. The far reaching result of upholding the act cannot be more plainly indicated than by pointing out that if Congress can thus regulate matters entrusted to local authority by prohibition of the movement of commodities in interstate commerce, all freedom of commerce will be at an end, and the power of the States over local matters may be eliminated, and thus our system of government be practically destroyed.

For these reasons we hold that this law exceeds the constitutional authority of Congress. It follows that the decree of the District Court must be

Affirmed.

Mr. Justice Holmes, dissenting. . . .

The first step in my argument is to make plain what no one is likely to dispute—that the statute in question is within the power expressly given to Congress if considered only as to its immediate effects and that if invalid it is so only upon some collateral ground. The statute confines itself to prohibiting the carriage of certain goods in interstate or foreign commerce. Congress is given power to regulate such commerce in unqualified terms. It would not be argued today that the power to regulate does not include the power to prohibit. Regulation means the prohibition of something, and when interstate commerce is the matter to be regulated I cannot doubt that the regulation may prohibit any part of such commerce that Congress sees fit to forbid. At all events it is established by the *Lottery Case* and others that have followed it that a law is not beyond the regulative power of Congress merely because it prohibits certain transportation out and out. *Champion v. Ames.* So I repeat that this statute in its immediate operation is clearly within the Congress's constitutional power.

The question then is narrowed to whether the exercise of its otherwise constitutional power by Congress can be pronounced unconstitutional because of its possible reaction upon the conduct of the States in a matter upon which I have admitted that they are free from direct control. I should have thought that that matter had been disposed of so fully as to leave no room for doubt. I should have thought that the most conspicuous decisions of this Court had made it clear that the power to regulate commerce and other constitutional powers could not be cut down or qualified by the fact that it might interfere with the carrying out of the domestic policy of any State. [N]otwithstanding *United States v. E.C. Knight Co.,* the Sherman Act has been made an instrument for the breaking up of combinations in restraint of trade and monopolies, using the power to regulate commerce as a foothold, but not proceeding because that commerce was the end actually in mind. The objection that the control of the States over production was interfered with was urged again and again but always in vain.

... It does not matter whether the supposed evil precedes or follows the transportation. It is enough that in the opinion of Congress the transportation encourages the evil. I may add that in the cases on the so-called White Slave Act it was established that the means adopted by Congress as convenient to the exercise of its power might have the character of police regulations. *Hoke v. United States,* 227 U.S. 308, 323, 33 S.Ct. 281, 57 L.Ed. 523; *Caminetti v. United States.* . . .

But I had thought that the propriety of the exercise of a power admitted to exist in some cases was for the consideration of Congress alone and that this Court always had disavowed the right to intrude its judgment upon questions of policy or morals. It is not for this Court to pronounce when prohibition is necessary to regulation if it ever may be necessary—to say that it is permissible as against strong drink but not as against the product of ruined lives.

The act does not meddle with anything belonging to the States. They may regulate their internal affairs and their domestic commerce as they like. But when they seek to send their products across the state line they are no longer within their rights. If there were no Constitution and no Congress their power to cross the line would depend upon their neighbors. Under the Constitution such commerce belongs not to the States but to Congress to regulate. It may carry out its views of public policy whatever indirect effect they may have upon the activities of the States. Instead of being encountered by a prohibitive tariff at her boundaries the State encounters the public policy of the United States which it is for Congress to express. The public policy of the United States is shaped with a view to the benefit of the nation as a whole. If, as has been the case within the memory of men still living, a State should take a different view of the propriety of sustaining a lottery from that which generally prevails, I cannot believe that the fact would require a different decision from that reached in *Champion v. Ames.* Yet in that case it would be said with quite as much force as in this that Congress was attempting to intermeddle with the State's domestic affairs. The national welfare as understood by Congress may require a different attitude within its sphere from that of some self-seeking State. It seems to me entirely constitutional for Congress to enforce its understanding by all the means at its command.

MR. JUSTICE MCKENNA, MR. JUSTICE BRANDEIS and MR. JUSTICE CLARKE concur in this opinion.

Notes

1. In *Caminetti v. United States,* 242 U.S. 470, 37 S.Ct. 192, 61 L.Ed. 442 (1917), cited by both the majority and dissent in the *Child Labor Case,* Day, J., for the Court, upheld the constitutionality of the White Slave Traffic Act as applied to Caminetti, who was charged with "assisting in obtaining transportation for a certain woman from Sacramento, California, to Reno, Nevada, in interstate commerce for the purpose of debauchery, and for an immoral purpose, to wit, that the aforesaid woman should be and become his mistress and concubine." Petitioner argued that the statute only reached "commercialized vice," that is, traffic in women for gain, but the Court disagreed: the "act has its constitutional sanction in the power of Congress over interstate commerce. The broad character of that authority was declared once [and] for all . . . in *Gibbons v. Odgen,* and has since been steadily adhered to and applied to a variety of new conditions as they have arisen."

2. Is the transportation in interstate commerce of goods manufactured by child labor a prelude to, or an encouragement of, any evil? For constitutional purposes, should it make a difference if the evil is a prelude or postlude?

Could a state prevent entry within its borders of goods from other states manufactured by child labor?

Is there any economic disincentive that might discourage a state from prohibiting the use of child labor to produce goods within its borders?

3. After this decision Congress tried to regulate child labor through the taxing power, but failed. See *The Child Labor Tax Case (Bailey v. Drexel Furniture Co.),* § 4–3, infra.

CARTER v. CARTER COAL CO.
298 U.S. 238, 56 S.Ct. 855, 80 L.Ed. 1160 (1936).

[The "Bituminous Coal Conservation Act of 1935" covered every producer of bituminous coal in the United States. It imposed a 15% tax on the sale price of coal at the mine, 90% of which was refundable if the producer filed with the National Bituminous Coal Commission (also set up by the Act) his acceptance of a Bituminous Coal Code, formulated by the Commission, which was also required to organize 23 coal district boards, which would fix minimum and maximum prices of coal at every coal mine in the United States, with such price variations as the coal boards deemed appropriate. As discussed more fully in the opinion, the labor provisions of the code provided for the setting of maximum daily and weekly hours and minimum wages after a vote by a set proportion of the producers and mine workers.

[Three suits were consolidated and after the trial court decisions the Supreme Court granted certiorari, bypassing the circuit courts.]

MR. JUSTICE SUTHERLAND delivered the opinion of the Court. . . .

The so-called excise tax of 15 *per centum* on the sale price of coal at the mine, or, in the case of captive coal the fair market value, with its drawback allowance of 13½%, is clearly not a tax but a penalty. . . . within the test laid down by this court in numerous cases. *Child Labor Tax Case,* [§ 4–3, infra]. . . . But it is not necessary to pursue the matter further. That the "tax" is in fact a penalty is not seriously in dispute. The position of the Government, as we understand it, is that the validity of the exaction does not rest upon the taxing power but upon the power of Congress to regulate interstate commerce; and that if the act in respect of the labor and price-fixing provisions be not upheld, the "tax" must fall with them. With that position we agree and confine our consideration accordingly.

. . . We first inquire, then—What is commerce? . . . That commodities produced or manufactured within a state are intended to be sold or transported outside the state does not render their production or manufacture subject to federal regulation under the commerce clause. As this court said in *Coe v. Errol,* 116 U.S. 517, 526, 6 S.Ct. 475, 29 L.Ed. 715, [718:] "Though intended for exportation, they may never be exported; the owner has a perfect right to change his mind; and until actually put in motion, for some place out of the State, or committed to the custody of a carrier for transportation to such place, why may they not be regarded as still remaining a part of the general mass of property in the State?" It is true that this was said in respect of a challenged power of the state to impose a tax; but the query is equally pertinent where the question, as here, is with regard to the power of regulation. The case was relied upon in *Kidd v. Pearson,* (128 U.S. 1, at page 26, 9 S.Ct. 6, 12, 32 L.Ed. 346 [352]) . . . "The police power of a State is as broad and plenary as its taxing power; and property within the State is subject to the operations of the former so long as it is within the regulating restrictions of the latter."

[Commerce] is the equivalent of the phrase "intercourse for the purposes of trade." Plainly, the incidents leading up to and culminating in the mining of coal do not constitute such intercourse. The employment of men, the fixing of their wages, hours of labor and working conditions, the bargaining in respect of these things—whether carried on separately or collectively—each and all constitute intercourse for the purposes of production, not of trade. The latter is a thing apart from the relation of employer and employee, which in all producing occupations is purely local in character. Extraction of coal from the mine is the aim and the completed result of local activities. Commerce in the coal mined is not brought into being by force of these activities, but by negotiations, agreements, and circumstances entirely apart from production. Mining brings the subject matter of commerce into existence. Commerce disposes of it.

[N]one of these essential antecedents of production constitutes a transaction in or forms any part of interstate commerce. *Schechter Corp. v. United States,* 295 U.S. 495, 55 S.Ct. 837, 79 L.Ed. 1570 (1935). Everything which moves in interstate commerce has had a local origin. Without local production somewhere, interstate commerce, as now carried on, would practically disappear. Nevertheless, the local character of mining, of manufacturing and of crop growing is a fact, and remains a fact, whatever may be done with the products. . . .

That the production of every commodity intended for interstate sale and transportation has some effect upon interstate commerce may be, if it has not already been, freely granted; and we are brought to the final and decisive inquiry, whether here that effect is direct, as the "preamble" [of the act] recites, or indirect. . . .

Whether the effect of a given activity or condition is direct or indirect is not always easy to determine. The word "direct" implies that the activity or condition invoked or blamed shall operate proximately— not mediately, remotely, or collaterally—to produce the effect. It connotes the absence of an efficient intervening agency or condition. And the extent of the effect bears no logical relation to its character. The distinction between a direct and an indirect effect turns, not upon the magnitude of either the cause or the effect, but entirely upon the manner in which the effect has been brought about. If the production by one man of a single ton of coal intended for interstate sale and shipment, and actually so sold and shipped, affects interstate commerce indirectly, the effect does not become direct by multiplying the tonnage, or increasing the number of men employed, or adding to the expense or complexities of the business, or by all combined. It is quite true that rules of law are sometimes qualified by considerations of degree, as the government argues. But the matter of degree has no bearing upon the question here, since that question is not—What is the *extent* of the local activity or condition, or the *extent* of the effect produced upon interstate commerce? but—What is the *relation* between the activity or condition and the effect?

. . . The relation of employer and employee is a local relation. At common law, it is one of the domestic relations. The wages are paid for the doing of local work. Working conditions are obviously local conditions. The employees are not engaged in or about commerce, but exclusively in producing a commodity. And the controversies and evils, which it is the object of the act to regulate and minimize, are local controversies and evils affecting local work undertaken to accomplish that local result. Such effect as they may have upon commerce, however extensive it may be, is secondary and indirect. An increase in the greatness of the effect adds to its importance. It does not alter its character.

[Turning to the labor relations section of the Act, it] delegates the power to fix maximum hours of labor to a part of the producers and the miners—namely, "the producers of more than two-thirds of the annual national tonnage production for the preceding calendar year" and "more than one-half of the mine workers employed"; and to producers of more than two-thirds of the district annual tonnage during the preceding calendar year and a majority of the miners, there is delegated the power to fix minimum wages for the district or group of districts. The effect, in respect of wages and hours, is to subject the dissentient minority, either of producers or miners or both, to the will of the stated majority, since, by refusing to submit, the minority at once incurs the hazard of enforcement of the drastic compulsory provisions of the act to which we have referred. To "accept," in these circumstances, is not to exercise a choice, but to surrender to force.

The power conferred upon the majority is, in effect, the power to regulate the affairs of an unwilling minority. This is legislative delegation in its most obnoxious form; for it is not even delegation to an official or an official body, presumptively disinterested, but to private persons whose interests may be and often are adverse to the interests of others in the same business. The record shows that the conditions of competition differ among the various localities. In some, coal dealers compete among themselves. In other localities, they also compete with the mechanical production of electrical energy and of natural gas. Some coal producers favor the code; others oppose it; and the record clearly indicates that this diversity of view arises from their conflicting and even antagonistic interests. The difference between producing coal and regulating its production is, of course, fundamental. The former is a private activity; the latter is necessarily a governmental function, since, in the very nature of things, one person may not be entrusted with the power to regulate the business of another, and especially of a competitor. And a statute which attempts to confer such power undertakes an intolerable and unconstitutional interference with personal liberty and private property. The delegation is so clearly arbitrary, and so clearly a denial of rights safeguarded by the due process clause of the Fifth Amendment, that it is unnecessary to do more than refer to decisions of this court which foreclose the question. *Schechter Corp. v. United States.*

Finally, we are brought to the price-fixing provisions of the code. The necessity of considering the question of their constitutionality will depend upon whether they are separable from the labor provisions so that they can stand independently. Section 15 of the act provides:

> If any provision of this Act, or the application thereof to any person or circumstances, is held invalid, the remainder of the Act and the application of such provisions to other persons or circumstances shall not be affected thereby.

[However, under the Act] wages, hours of labor, and working conditions are to be so adjusted as to effectuate the purposes of the act; and prices are to be so regulated as to *stabilize* wages, working conditions, and hours of labor which have been or are to be fixed under the labor provisions. The two are so woven together as to render the probability plain enough that uniform prices, in the opinion of Congress, could not be fairly fixed or effectively regulated, without also regulating these elements of labor which enter so largely into the cost of production.

These two sets of requirements are not like a collection of bricks, some of which may be taken away without disturbing the others, but rather are like the interwoven threads constituting the warp and woof of a fabric. . . . The price-fixing provisions of the code are thus disposed of without coming to the question of their constitutionality; but neither this disposition of the matter, nor anything we have said, is to be taken as indicating that the court is of opinion that these provisions, if separately enacted, could be sustained. . . .

[Thus the Court invalidated the entire Act. A separate opinion of HUGHES, C.J., agreed with the majority except he would not have invalidated the price fixing provisions of the act. CARDOZO, J., joined by BRANDEIS and STONE, JJ., would have upheld the Act's price fixing and would not have reached the other issues on the grounds of prematurity.]

Notes

1. *Railroad Retirement Board v. Alton Railroad Co.,* 295 U.S. 330, 55 S.Ct. 758, 79 L.Ed. 1468 (1935). Roberts, J., for the Court, invalidated the Railroad Retirement Act of 1934, which had established a compulsory retirement and pension system for all carriers subject to the Interstate Commerce Act. "There is provision for the creation of a fund to be deposited in the United States treasury (§§ 5, 8) and administered by a Board. . . . The retirement fund for payment of these pensions and for the expenses of administration of the system will arise from compulsory contributions from present and future employees and the carriers."

The Court held that the Act violated due process and was not, in purpose or effect, a regulation of interstate commerce. "There is no warrant for taking the property or money of one and transferring it to another without compensation, whether the object of the transfer be to build up the equipment of the transferee or to pension its employees." "[A] pension plan thus imposed is in no proper sense a regulation of the activity of interstate transportation. It is an attempt for social ends to impose by sheer fiat non-contractual incidents upon the relation of employer and employee, not as a rule or regulation of commerce and transportation between the States, but as a means of assuring a particular class of employees against old age dependency." Nor was the Government's reliance on previous court decisions sustaining the Safety Appliance Acts, the Employees' Liability Acts, hours-of-service laws, and others of analogous character relevant, for such laws "have a direct and intimate connection with the actual operation of the railroads."

Hughes C.J., joined by Brandeis, Stone, and Cardozo, JJ., dissented.

2. DELEGATION OF LEGISLATIVE POWER. *A.L.A. Schechter Poultry Corp. v. United States,* 295 U.S. 495, 55 S.Ct. 837, 79 L.Ed. 1570 (1935)(Hughes, C.J.). The Court, three weeks after the *Railroad Retirement Board* case, invalidated the National Industrial Recovery Act. The "live poultry code" was approved by the President as provided by the Act. The Code fixed the number of hours for workdays and prohibited practices said to constitute "unfair methods of competition." The NIRA was an unconstitutional, "sweeping" delegation of Congress' legislative powers to the President. The Act "supplies no standards for any trade, industry or activity. It does not undertake to prescribe rules of conduct to be applied to particular states of fact determined by appropriate administrative procedure. Instead of prescribing rules of conduct, it authorizes the making of codes to prescribe them." The President's discretion "is virtually unfettered." And, the slaughter of poultry was not interstate commerce. Although almost all poultry coming into New York was shipped from out of state, when the poultry reached New York, the interstate transaction ended.

Cardozo, J., joined by Stone, J., concurred: "Here, in the case before us, is an attempted delegation not confined to any single act nor to any class or group of acts identified or described by reference to a standard. Here in effect is a roving commission to inquire into evils and upon discovery correct them." Also, there is no power to regulate the "wages and hours of labor in the intrastate transactions that make up the defendants' business."

Is *Schechter* still good law? "Since *Schechter* no delegation has been held invalid, but none of them has had quite the imposing generality of the NIRA and the Court has been careful to distinguish it. The two most important cases uphold the agricultural licensing powers and the OPA war emergency powers."[1] Both of these decisions were after the 1937 Court Packing Plan, discussed below. The first case, *United States v. Rock Royal Co-operative,* 307 U.S. 533, 59 S.Ct. 993, 83 L.Ed. 1446 (1939), upheld the market control features of the new Agricultural Adjustment Act, which authorized the Secretary to prohibit "unfair methods of competition and unfair trade practices," and to protect the consumer by seeking to reach a certain level of prices "at as rapid a rate as the Secretary of Agriculture deems to be in the public interest and feasible in view of current consumptive demand."

---

1. Jaffe, An Essay on Delegation of Legislative Power: II, 47 Colum.L.Rev. 561, 578   (1947).

The second case, *Yakus v. United States,* 321 U.S. 414, 64 S.Ct. 660, 88 L.Ed. 834 (1944), upheld the powers of the Price Administrator to fix prices so that they, "in his judgment will be generally fair and equitable and will effectuate the purposes of this Act." The delegation was constitutional because the law "sufficiently marks the field within which the Administrator is to act so that it may be known whether he has kept within it in compliance with the legislative will."

Must delegation of legislative power to private groups or individuals always be unconstitutional? May the law provide that one in possession of a house has the discretionary power, backed up by the Sheriff, to exclude a third party from entering? May a state provide that lawyers or medical doctors should be regulated by committees of lawyers or medical doctors? May a state provide that no one may take its bar examination unless he or she has graduated from a law school accredited by the American Bar Association? Cf. *Wickard v. Filburn,* infra § 4–2, a post 1937, Court Packing Plan case.

3. THE COURT PACKING PLAN OF 1937. After the 1936 election (in which Franklin D. Roosevelt beat Alfred M. Landon by a large majority, winning every state except Maine and Vermont), F.D.R. turned his attention to the Supreme Court, which had, in a series of cases, and often by narrow majorities, sought to dismantle his New Deal Programs.[2] Various congressmen had proposed constitutional amendments, but Roosevelt chose a statutory solution.

Article III of the Constitution tells us very little about the make-up of the Court. The Constitution does not specify a salary (it protects it from diminution but does not require it to be raised);[3] it does not require the Justices to be lawyers; it says nothing about the terms of Court;[4] or the number of Justices on the Court. It is to the question of the number of Justices that Roosevelt turned. While the number had varied over the years, it had been set at nine Justices, including the Chief Justice, since the time of President U.S. Grant. F.D.R. proposed to increase that number.

Under his proposal, the President could appoint an additional federal judge or Justice for each one who had failed to retire within six months of reaching his 70th birthday. The maximum number of judges

2. "Month after month counsel for the Department of Justice dutifully presented their cases before a Court four of whose members seemed lost from the outset, hoping that this hostility would be restrained enough to allow the argument to proceed for the benefit of the uncommitted. The President's Court Plan, so startlingly if not shockingly crude in its assault on the independence of the judges, cannot be understood without an appreciation of the atmosphere in the courtroom, to which Government counsel had been subjected for four years and would have to expose themselves and their causes in the vital cases yet to be heard." Freund, Charles Evans Hughes as Chief Justice, 81 Harv.L.Rev. 4, 13 (1967).

3. In fact, Madison and Virginia proposed that the Constitution forbid any increase in salary into order to remove the possibility of affecting judicial independence by allowing justices to be tempted by increases. Because of the expectation that the cost of living might rise, this proposal was rejected.

4. The Jeffersonian Congress, for example, rescheduled the terms of Court so as to eliminate part of the 1802 Supreme Court term.

who might be appointed under the proposed legislation would be 50 and the total maximum membership on the Supreme Court level would be 15 Justices, a maximum that would be reached because six Justices were over 70 years old. The plan also included retirement benefits for the Justices. One must remember that the plan "was offered by a President who had just received an overwhelming popular vote of confidence and who had not yet been denied in Congress any of his important demands. Even the five or six judges who had provoked this threat must have slept rather uneasily for a few months."[5]

Roosevelt argued that new blood was needed on the Court and that the older Justices were less efficient, but the opposition saw this argument as disingenuous and immediately labeled it as a Court packing plan. The great majority of Congress, led by members of Roosevelt's own party, eventually defeated the proposal. Congress, however, did provide retirement benefits for Supreme Court Justices in a Judiciary Act passed in 1937, allowing conservative Justice Van Devanter to resign in May of 1937. Roosevelt appointed Senator Hugo Black, a staunch New Deal supporter, to replace him. Also during the fight over the proposal, the Supreme Court appeared to change its position and upheld the validity of several important items of New Deal and state economic legislation, as illustrated by the cases in the next section. Justice Roberts, in particular, appeared to leave the conservative bloc and join the liberal bloc. It was said that Roberts was "the switch in time that saved nine," although Roberts privately announced his vote in one case[6] in December, 1936— before the Court packing plan was unveiled.[7]

4–2. THE NEW DEAL COMMERCE CASES FROM 1937

NATIONAL LABOR RELATIONS BOARD v. JONES & LAUGHLIN STEEL CORP.
301 U.S. 1, 57 S.Ct. 615, 81 L.Ed. 893 (1937).

[The N.L.R.B. found that Jones & Laughlin Steel Corporation had violated the Act by engaging in an unfair labor practice affecting commerce in that it had discharged certain employees because of their union activity in order to discourage membership in the union. The Board

5. R. McCloskey, The American Supreme Court 169 (1960).

6. *West Coast Hotel v. Parrish*, 300 U.S. 379, 57 S.Ct. 578, 81 L.Ed. 703 (1937), upholding a state minimum wage law in a 5–4 vote. Felix Frankfurter, in his article entitled, Mr. Justice Roberts, 104 U.Pa. L.Rev. 311 (1955), rejected the argument that Roberts' had switched his position for cynical reasons. "It is one of the most ludicrous illustrations of the power of lazy repetition of uncritical talk that a judge with the character of Roberts should have attributed to him a change of judicial views out of deference to political considerations." In this article Frankfurter disclosed a memorandum that Roberts had given to him on November 9, 1945, after Roberts had resigned from the Bench. This memorandum explained how Roberts had changed his mind in the spring of 1936, before the court-packing plan was discussed. *Parrish* was the appropriate vehicle for Roberts to use to disclose his view, but publication of that case was delayed because of Justice Stone's illness.

7. 1 R. Rotunda & J. Nowak, Treatise on Constitutional Law: Substance and Procedure, § 2.7 (West Group, 3d ed. 1999).

ordered reinstatement, back pay, and other remedies, but the corporation refused to comply. The circuit court refused to enforce the order because it was, said the court, beyond the range of federal power.

[The Act stated that Congress found injury to commerce resulting from employers' rejection of collective bargaining and their denial of the employees' right to unionize. The Act further declared that the policy of the United States is to eliminate these causes of the obstruction to the free flow of commerce. The Act also set up the N.L.R.B., set forth the right of employees to unionize, defined unfair labor practices, laid down rules as to employee representation for collective bargaining, empowered the Board to prevent unfair labor practices, and prescribed the procedure to that end.]

Mr. Chief Justice Hughes delivered the opinion of the Court. . . .

The scope of the Act. The Act is challenged in its entirety as an attempt to regulate all industry, thus invading the reserved powers of the States over their local concerns. It is asserted that the references in the Act to interstate and foreign commerce are colorable at best; that the Act is not a true regulation of such commerce or of matters which directly affect it but on the contrary has the fundamental object of placing under the compulsory supervision of the federal government all industrial labor relations within the nation. [However, the Act's] grant of authority to the Board does not purport to extend to the relationship between all industrial employees and employers. Its terms do not impose collective bargaining upon all industry regardless of effects upon interstate or foreign commerce. It purports to reach only what may be deemed to burden or obstruct that commerce and, thus qualified, it must be construed as contemplating the exercise of control within constitutional bounds. It is a familiar principle that acts which directly burden or obstruct interstate or foreign commerce, or its free flow, are within the reach of the congressional power. Acts having that effect are not rendered immune because they grow out of labor disputes. It is the effect upon commerce, not the source of the injury, which is the criterion. . . .

The application of the Act to employees engaged in production.—The principle involved.—Respondent says that whatever may be said of employees engaged in interstate commerce, the industrial relations and activities in the manufacturing department of respondent's enterprise are not subject to federal regulation. The argument rests upon the proposition that manufacturing in itself is not commerce. *Schechter Corp. v. United States,* [§ 4–1, supra]; *Carter v. Carter Coal Co.,* [§ 4–1, supra].

The Government distinguishes these cases. The various parts of respondent's enterprise are described as interdependent and as thus involving "a great movement of iron ore, coal and limestone along well-defined paths to the steel mills, thence through them, and thence in the form of steel products into the consuming centers of the country—a definite and well-understood course of business." It is urged that these activities constitute a "stream" or "flow" of commerce, of which the

Aliquippa manufacturing plant is the focal point, and that industrial strife at that point would cripple the entire movement. Reference is made to our decision sustaining the Packers and Stockyards Act. *Stafford v. Wallace,* [§ 4–1, supra].

. . . The instances in which [the "stream of commerce"] metaphor has been used are but particular, and not exclusive, illustrations of the protective power which the Government invokes in support of the present Act. The congressional authority to protect interstate commerce from burdens and obstructions is not limited to transactions which can be deemed to be an essential part of a "flow" of interstate or foreign commerce. Burdens and obstructions may be due to injurious action springing from other sources. The fundamental principle is that the power to regulate commerce is the power to enact "all appropriate legislation" for "its protection and advancement" (*The Daniel Ball,* [§ 4–1, supra]); to adopt measures "to promote its growth and insure its safety"; "to foster, protect, control and restrain." That power is plenary and may be exerted to protect interstate commerce "no matter what the source of the dangers which threaten it." Although activities may be intrastate in character when separately considered, if they have such a close and substantial relation to interstate commerce that their control is essential or appropriate to protect that commerce from burdens and obstructions, Congress cannot be denied the power to exercise that control. Undoubtedly the scope of this power must be considered in the light of our dual system of government and may not be extended so as to embrace effects upon interstate commerce so indirect and remote that to embrace them, in view of our complex society, would effectually obliterate the distinction between what is national and what is local and create a completely centralized government. The question is necessarily one of degree. . . .

It is thus apparent that the fact that the employees here concerned were engaged in production is not determinative. The question remains as to the effect upon interstate commerce of the labor practice involved. In the *Schechter* case, supra, we found that the effect there was so remote as to be beyond the federal power. To find "immediacy or directness" there was to find it "almost anywhere," a result inconsistent with the maintenance of our federal system. In the *Carter* case, supra, the Court was of the opinion that the provisions of the statute relating to production were invalid upon several grounds,—that there was improper delegation of legislative power, and that the requirements not only went beyond any sustainable measure of protection of interstate commerce but were also inconsistent with due process. These cases are not controlling here.

Effects of the unfair labor practice in respondent's enterprise.— Giving full weight to respondent's contention with respect to a break in the complete continuity of the "stream of commerce" by reason of respondent's manufacturing operations, the fact remains that the stoppage of those operations by industrial strife would have a most serious effect upon interstate commerce. In view of respondent's far-flung activities, it is idle to say that the effect would be indirect or remote. It is obvious that it would be immediate and might be catastrophic. We are asked to shut our eyes to the plainest facts of our national life and to deal with the question of direct and indirect effects in an intellectual vacuum.... But with respect to the appropriateness of the recognition of self-organization and representation in the promotion of peace, the question is not essentially different in the case of employees in industries of such a character that interstate commerce is put in jeopardy from the case of employees of transportation companies. And of what avail is it to protect the facility of transportation, if interstate commerce is throttled with respect to the commodities to be transported! ...

The act has been criticized as one-sided in its application; that it subjects the employer to supervision and restraint and leaves untouched the abuses for which employees may be responsible; that it fails to provide a more comprehensive plan,—with better assurances of fairness to both sides and with increased chances of success in bringing about, if not compelling, equitable solutions of industrial disputes affecting interstate commerce. But we are dealing with the power of Congress, not with a particular policy or with the extent to which policy should go. We have frequently said that the legislative authority, exerted within its proper field, need not embrace all the evils within its reach. The Constitution does not forbid "cautious advance, step by step," in dealing with the evils which are exhibited in activities within the range of legislative power....

Reversed.

[The dissenting opinion of McReynolds, J., joined by Van Devanter, Sutherland, and Butler, JJ., is omitted].

UNITED STATES v. DARBY
312 U.S. 100, 61 S.Ct. 451, 85 L.Ed. 609 (1941).

Mr. Justice Stone delivered the opinion of the Court.

The two principal questions raised by the record in this case are, *first,* whether Congress has constitutional power to prohibit the shipment in interstate commerce of lumber manufactured by employees whose wages are less than a prescribed minimum or whose weekly hours of labor at that wage are greater than a prescribed maximum, and, *second,* whether it has power to prohibit the employment of workmen in the production of goods "for interstate commerce" at other than prescribed wages and hours. A subsidiary question is whether in connection with such prohibitions Congress can require the employer subject to them to keep records showing the hours worked each day and week by each of his employees including those engaged "in the production and manufacture of goods to-wit, lumber, for 'interstate commerce.'" ... The district court quashed the indictment in its entirety upon the broad grounds that the Act, which it interpreted as a regulation of manufacture within the states, is unconstitutional....

The prohibition of shipment of the proscribed goods in interstate commerce. . . .

While manufacture is not of itself interstate commerce, the shipment of manufactured goods interstate is such commerce and the prohibition of such shipment by Congress is indubitably a regulation of the commerce. The power to regulate commerce is the power "to prescribe the rule by which commerce is governed." *Gibbons v. Ogden,* [§ 3–1, supra]. It extends not only to those regulations which aid, foster and protect the commerce, but embraces those which prohibit it. It is conceded that the power of Congress to prohibit transportation in interstate commerce includes noxious articles, stolen articles, kidnapped persons, and articles such as intoxicating liquor or convict made goods, traffic in which is forbidden or restricted by the laws of the state of destination.

But it is said that the present prohibition falls within the scope of none of these categories; that while the prohibition is nominally a regulation of the commerce its motive or purpose is regulation of wages and hours of persons engaged in manufacture, the control of which has been reserved to the states and upon which Georgia and some of the states of destination have placed no restriction; that the effect of the present statute is not to exclude the proscribed articles from interstate commerce in aid of state regulation, but instead, under the guise of a regulation of interstate commerce, it undertakes to regulate wages and hours within the state contrary to the policy of the state which has elected to leave them unregulated. . . .

Such regulation is not a forbidden invasion of state power merely because either its motive or its consequence is to restrict the use of articles of commerce within the states of destination; and is not prohibited unless by other Constitutional provisions. It is no objection to the assertion of the power to regulate interstate commerce that its exercise is attended by the same incidents which attend the exercise of the police power of the states. . . . Whatever their motive and purpose, regulations of commerce which do not infringe some constitutional prohibition are within the plenary power conferred on Congress by the Commerce Clause. Subject only to that limitation, presently to be considered, we conclude that the prohibition of the shipment interstate of goods produced under the forbidden substandard labor conditions is within the constitutional authority of Congress.

In the more than a century which has elapsed since the decision of *Gibbons v. Ogden,* these principles of constitutional interpretation have been so long and repeatedly recognized by this Court as applicable to the Commerce Clause, that there would be little occasion for repeating them now were it not for the decision of this Court twenty-two years ago in *Hammer v. Dagenhart,* [§ 4–1, supra]. In that case it was held by a bare majority of the Court over the powerful and now classic dissent of Mr. Justice Holmes setting forth the fundamental issues involved, that Congress was without power to exclude the products of child labor from interstate commerce. The reasoning and conclusion of the Court's opinion there cannot be reconciled with the conclusion which we have reached, that the power of Congress under the Commerce Clause is plenary to exclude any article from interstate commerce subject only to the specific prohibitions of the Constitution.

Hammer v. Dagenhart has not been followed. The distinction on which the decision was rested that Congressional power to prohibit interstate commerce is limited to articles which in themselves have some harmful or deleterious property—a distinction which was novel when made and unsupported by any provision of the Constitution—has long since been abandoned. The thesis of the opinion that the motive of the prohibition or its effect to control in some measure the use or production within the states of the article thus excluded from the commerce can operate to deprive the regulation of its constitutional authority has long since ceased to have force. *Lottery Case,* [§ 4–1, supra]. And finally we have declared "The authority of the federal government over interstate commerce does not differ in extent or character from that retained by the states over intrastate commerce."

The conclusion is inescapable that *Hammer v. Dagenhart,* was a departure from the principles which have prevailed in the interpretation of the Commerce Clause both before and since the decision and that such vitality, as a precedent, as it then had has long since been exhausted. It should be and now is overruled.

Validity of the wage and hour requirements.... As the Government seeks to apply [§ 15(a)(2)] in the indictment, and as the court below construed the phrase "produced for interstate commerce," it embraces at least the case where an employer engaged, as is appellee, in the manufacture and shipment of goods in filling orders of extrastate customers, manufactures his product with the intent or expectation that according to the normal course of his business all or some part of it will be selected for shipment to those customers. Without attempting to define the precise limits of the phrase, we think the acts alleged in the indictment are within the sweep of the statute....

There remains the question whether such restriction on the production of goods for commerce is a permissible exercise of the commerce power. The power of Congress over interstate commerce is not confined to the regulation of commerce among the states. It extends to those activities intrastate which so affect interstate commerce or the exercise of the power of Congress over it as to make regulation of them appropriate means to the attainment of a legitimate end, and the exercise of the granted power of Congress to regulate interstate commerce. See *McCulloch v. Maryland.* [T]he power of Congress to regulate interstate commerce extends to the regulation through legislative action of activities intrastate which have a substantial effect on the commerce or the exercise of the Congressional power over it....

Congress, having by the present Act adopted the policy of excluding from interstate commerce all goods produced for the commerce which do not conform to the specified labor standards, it may choose the means reasonably adapted to the attainment of the permitted end, even though they involve control of intrastate activities. [Thus] Congress may require inspection and preventive treatment of all cattle in a disease infected area in order to prevent shipment in interstate commerce of some of the cattle without the treatment. *Thornton v. United States,* 271 U.S. 414, 46 S.Ct. 585, 70 L.Ed. 1013,.... And we have recently held that Congress in the exercise of its power to require inspection and grading of tobacco shipped in interstate commerce may compel such inspection and grading of all tobacco sold at local auction rooms from which a substantial part but not all of the tobacco sold is shipped in interstate commerce. *Currin v. Wallace,* [306 U.S. 1, 59 S.Ct. 379, 83 L.Ed. 441]....

The means adopted by § 15(a)(2) for the protection of interstate commerce by the suppression of the production of the condemned goods for interstate commerce is so related to the commerce and so affects it as to be within the reach of the commerce power. Congress, to attain its objective in the suppression of nationwide competition in interstate commerce by goods produced under substandard labor conditions, has made no distinction as to the volume or amount of shipments in the commerce or of production for commerce by any particular shipper or producer. It recognized that in present day industry, competition by a small part may affect the whole and that the total effect of the competition of many small producers may be great. The legislation aimed at a whole embraces all its parts.

So far as *Carter v. Carter Coal Co.,* [§ 4–1, supra], is inconsistent with this conclusion, its doctrine is limited in principle by the decisions under the Sherman Act and the National Labor Relations Act, which we have cited and which we follow.

Our conclusion is unaffected by the Tenth Amendment which ... states but a truism that all is retained which has not been surrendered. There is nothing in the history of its adoption to suggest that it was more than declaratory of the relationship between the national and state governments as it had been established by the Constitution before the amendment or that its purpose was other than to allay fears that the new national government might seek to exercise powers not granted, and that the states might not be able to exercise fully their reserved powers.

From the beginning and for many years the amendment has been construed as not depriving the national government of authority to resort to all means for the exercise of a granted power which are appropriate and plainly adapted to the permitted end....

Validity of the requirement of records of wages and hours.... Since, as we have held, Congress may require production for interstate commerce to conform to those conditions, it may require the employer, as a means of enforcing the valid law, to keep a record showing whether he has in fact complied with it. The requirement for records even of the intrastate transaction is an appropriate means to the legitimate end....

Reversed.

WICKARD v. FILBURN

317 U.S. 111, 63 S.Ct. 82, 87 L.Ed. 122 (1942).

Mr. Justice Jackson delivered the opinion of the Court. . . .

In July of 1940, pursuant to the Agricultural Adjustment Act of 1938, as then amended, there were established for the appellee's 1941 crop a wheat acreage allotment of 11.1 acres and a normal yield of 20.1 bushels of wheat an acre. He was given notice of such allotment in July of 1940, before the Fall planting of his 1941 crop of wheat, and again in July of 1941, before it was harvested. He sowed, however, 23 acres and harvested from his 11.9 acres of excess acreage 239 bushels, which under the terms of the Act as amended on May 26, 1941, constituted farm marketing excess, subject to a penalty of 49 cents a bushel, or $117.11 in all. The appellee has not paid the penalty and he has not postponed or avoided it by storing the excess under regulations of the Secretary of Agriculture, or by delivering it up to the Secretary. The Committee, therefore, refused him a marketing card, which was, under the terms of Regulations promulgated by the Secretary, necessary to protect a buyer from liability to the penalty and upon its protecting lien.

The general scheme of the Agricultural Adjustment Act of 1938 as related to wheat is to control the volume moving in interstate and foreign commerce in order to avoid surpluses and shortages and the consequent abnormally low or high wheat prices and obstructions to commerce. . . .

The Act further provides that whenever it appears that the total supply of wheat as of the beginning of any marketing year, beginning July 1, will exceed a normal year's domestic consumption and export by more than 35 per cent, the Secretary shall so proclaim not later than May 15 prior to the beginning of such marketing year; and that during the marketing year a compulsory national marketing quota shall be in effect with respect to the marketing of wheat. Between the issuance of the proclamation and June 10, the Secretary must, however, conduct a referendum of farmers who will be subject to the quota, to determine whether they favor or oppose it; and, if more than one-third of the farmers voting in the referendum do oppose, the Secretary must, prior to the effective date of the quota, by proclamation suspend its operation. . . .

Pursuant to the Act, the referendum of wheat growers was held on May 31, 1941. According to the required published statement of the Secretary of Agriculture, 81 per cent of those voting favored the marketing quota with 19 per cent opposed.

[The Court first held that a radio speech of the Secretary of Agriculture, advocating approval of the referendum—although alleged to be misleading—did not invalidate the referendum: to contend that a government official's failure "to meet judicial ideals of clarity, precision, and exhaustiveness" would invalidate a vote would imperil communications between administrators and the people.]

It is urged that under the Commerce Clause of the Constitution, Article I, § 8, clause 3, Congress does not possess the power it has in this instance sought to exercise. The question would merit little consideration since our decision in *United States v. Darby,* sustaining the federal power to regulate production of goods for commerce, except for the fact that this Act extends federal regulation to production not intended in any part for commerce but wholly for consumption on the farm. The Act includes a definition of "market" and its derivatives, so that as related to wheat, in addition to its conventional meaning, it also means to dispose of "by feeding (in any form) to poultry or livestock which, or the products of which, are sold, bartered, or exchanged, or to be so disposed of." Hence, marketing quotas not only embrace all that may be sold without penalty but also what may be consumed on the premises.... Even today, when [the commerce] power has been held to have great latitude, there is no decision of this Court that such activities may be regulated where no part of the product is intended for interstate commerce or intermingled with the subjects thereof. We believe that a review of the course of decision under the Commerce Clause will make plain, however, that questions of the power of Congress are not to be decided by reference to any formula which would give controlling force to nomenclature such as "production" and "indirect" and foreclose consideration of the actual effects of the activity in question upon interstate commerce.

... Except in regions of large-scale production, wheat is usually grown in rotation with other crops; for a nurse crop of grass seeding; and as a cover crop to prevent soil erosion and leaching. Some is sold, some kept for seed, and a percentage of the total production much larger than in areas of specialization is consumed on the farm and grown for such purpose. Such farmers, while growing some wheat, may even find the balance of their interest on the consumer's side.

The effect of consumption of home-grown wheat on interstate commerce is due to the fact that it constitutes the most variable factor in the disappearance of the wheat crop. Consumption on the farm where grown appears to vary in an amount greater than 20 per cent of average production. The total amount of wheat consumed as food varies but relatively little, and use as seed is relatively constant.

The maintenance by government regulation of a price for wheat undoubtedly can be accomplished as effectively by sustaining or increasing the demand as by limiting the supply. The effect of the statute before us is to restrict the amount which may be produced for market and the extent as well to which one may forestall resort to the market by producing to meet his own needs. That appellee's own contribution to the demand for wheat may be trivial by itself is not enough to remove him from the scope of federal regulation where, as here, his contribution, taken together with that of many others similarly situated, is far from trivial. *United States v. Darby,* supra.

It is well established by decisions of this Court that the power to regulate commerce includes the power to regulate the prices at which commodities in that commerce are dealt in and practices affecting such prices. One of the primary purposes of the Act in question was to increase the market price of wheat, and to that end to limit the volume thereof that could affect the market. It can hardly be denied that a factor of such volume and variability as home-consumed wheat would have a substantial influence on price and market conditions. This may arise because being in marketable condition such wheat overhangs the market and, if induced by rising prices, tends to flow into the market and check price increases. But if we assume that it is never marketed, it supplies a need of the man who grew it which would otherwise be reflected by purchases in the open market. Home-grown wheat in this sense competes with wheat in commerce. The stimulation of commerce is a use of the regulatory function quite as definitely as prohibitions or restrictions thereon. This record leaves us in no doubt that Congress may properly have considered that wheat consumed on the farm where grown, if wholly outside the scheme of regulation, would have a substantial effect in defeating and obstructing its purpose to stimulate trade therein at increased prices.

It is said, however, that this Act, forcing some farmers into the market to buy what they could provide for themselves, is an unfair promotion of the markets and prices of specializing wheat growers. It is of the essence of regulation that it lays a restraining hand on the self-interest of the regulated and that advantages from the regulation commonly fall to others. The conflicts of economic interest between the regulated and those who advantage by it are wisely left under our system to resolution by the Congress under its more flexible and responsible legislative process. Such conflicts rarely lend themselves to judicial determination. And with the wisdom, workability, or fairness, of the plan of regulation we have nothing to do.

[The Court then held that the Act did not violate due process and reversed the decision of the trial court, which had been in favor of the appellee. In the course of this discussion, the Court noted: "It is hardly lack of due process for the Government to regulate that which it subsidizes."]

Notes

1. After *Darby* and *Wickard,* what are the limits to the exercise of Congress' power under the commerce clause? One noted commentator stated: "[T]he possession of congressional power should not be confused with its exercise. Logically, Congress can regulate *every detail of almost every commercial transaction,* and as an incident of that regulation it can probably deal with the acquisition and ownership of property. It has not exercised its full power, at least partly because of concern for the balance of the federal system. . . . Whatever balance the Court might prefer to see struck between

state and nation, it must also remember that choosing the means of achieving permissible objectives is a legislative function. To that extent preserving the constitutional allocation of power between Court and Congress requires leaving to Congress the responsibility for the federal system."[1]

2.   Consider the following fact situations.

Defendant was criminally charged with violating a federal law regulating interstate commerce in that he forged and counterfeited a bill of lading purporting to represent goods received in Indiana for shipment to Ohio. He argued that the commerce clause could not reach his conduct because nothing moved in interstate commerce: the fictitious bill of lading did not relate to any shipment or contemplated shipment of goods. The district court agreed that there could be no commerce in nonexistent goods. Who should win? See *United States v. Ferger,* 250 U.S. 199, 39 S.Ct. 445, 63 L.Ed. 936 (1919).

The business of the Associated Press, a cooperative association of member newspapers, is the collection, assembly, and distribution of news. The Government charged that AP and others violated the Sherman Anti–Trust Act in that they set up a system of by-laws that prohibited AP members from selling news to non-members, and allowed each member to block non-member competitors from membership in AP. Is trade in "news" carried on among the states interstate commerce? See *Associated Press v. United States,* 326 U.S. 1, 65 S.Ct. 1416, 89 L.Ed. 2013 (1945).

The Government indicted an insurance association and its members for anti-trust violations in fixing noncompetitive premium rates on fire and other allied lines of insurance. The district court dismissed the indictment and held that the business of insurance is not commerce. The Government appealed. The Supreme Court said: "We may grant that a contract of insurance, considered as a thing apart from negotiation and execution, does not itself constitute interstate commerce." Also, the sales contracts are local in nature, but the business of insurance is conducted across state lines, with most of the large insurance companies located in the financial centers of the East. May the commerce clause reach such activity? See *United States v. South–Eastern Underwriters Association,* 322 U.S. 533, 64 S.Ct. 1162, 88 L.Ed. 1440 (1944).

The Government charged a retail druggist in Columbus, Georgia, with violating a section of the Food, Drug and Cosmetic Act of 1938, in that he had performed certain acts that resulted in sulfathiazole tablets being "misbranded" within the meaning of the act while the tablets were "held for sale after shipment in interstate commerce." A laboratory in Chicago shipped a number of bottles of these tablets to a consignee in Atlanta. The bottles were then properly labeled. The Columbus druggist bought one of these bottles, transferred it to Columbus, and held it for resale. On two occasions twelve tablets were removed from the properly labeled bottle, placed in a pill box, and sold to customers, without the appropriate label. The retail sales were made in Columbus nine months after the tablets had been shipped from Chicago to Atlanta. The circuit court reversed the

1. Cox, Foreword: Constitutional Adjudication and the Promotion of Human Rights, 80 Harv.L.Rev. 91, 118–19 (1966)(emphasis added).

conviction and the Government petitioned for certiorari. Who wins? *United States v. Sullivan,* 332 U.S. 689, 68 S.Ct. 331, 92 L.Ed. 297 (1948).

A married couple contracted to buy a home. To finance it, they needed a title examination, which only a member of the state bar could legally perform. None of the attorneys contacted would agree to perform the work for less than the minimum fee scheduled for lawyers published by the county bar and enforced by the state bar. The couple sued for damages and injunctive relief claiming that the minimum fee schedule violated the Sherman Act. The trial court enjoined the fee schedule but the circuit court reversed, holding that the activities of the bars did not have sufficient effect on interstate commerce to support Sherman Act jurisdiction, that title examination is generally a local service, and that (even if it is part of a transaction that crosses state lines) its effect on commerce is only "incidental." The Supreme Court accepted certiorari. On this issue, who wins? See *Goldfarb v. Virginia State Bar,* 421 U.S. 773, 95 S.Ct. 2004, 44 L.Ed.2d 572 (1975).

4–3. THE TAXING AND SPENDING POWER

CHILD LABOR TAX CASE (BAILEY v. DREXEL FURNITURE CO.)
259 U.S. 20, 42 S.Ct. 449, 66 L.Ed. 817 (1922).

MR. CHIEF JUSTICE TAFT delivered the opinion of the court.

This case presents the question of the constitutional validity of the Child Labor Tax Law. The plaintiff below, the Drexel Furniture Company, is engaged in the manufacture of furniture in the Western District of North Carolina. On September 20, 1921, it received a notice from Bailey, United States Collector of Internal Revenue for the District, that it had been assessed $6,312.79 for having during the taxable year 1919 employed and permitted to work in its factory a boy under fourteen years of age, thus incurring the tax of ten per cent. on its net profits for that year. The Company paid the tax under protest, and after rejection of its claim for a refund, brought this suit. . . .

The law is attacked on the ground that it is a regulation of the employment of child labor in the States—an exclusively state function under the Federal Constitution and within the reservations of the Tenth Amendment. It is defended on the ground that it is a mere excise tax levied by the Congress of the United States under its broad power of taxation conferred by § 8, Article I, of the Federal Constitution. We must construe the law and interpret the intent and meaning of Congress from the language of the act. The words are to be given their ordinary meaning unless the context shows that they are differently used. Does this law impose a tax with only that incidental restraint and regulation which a tax must inevitably involve? Or does it regulate by the use of the so-called tax as a penalty? If a tax, it is clearly an excise. If it were an excise on a commodity or other thing of value we might not be permitted under previous decisions of this court to infer solely from its heavy burden that the act intends a prohibition instead of a tax. But this act is more. It provides a heavy exaction for a departure from a detailed and specified course of conduct in business. That course of business is that employers shall employ in mines and quarries, children of an age greater than sixteen years; in mills and factories, children of an age greater than fourteen years, and shall prevent children of less than sixteen years in mills and factories from working more than eight hours a day or six days in the week. If an employer departs from this prescribed course of business, he is to pay to the Government one-tenth of his entire net income in the business for a full year. The amount is not to be proportioned in any degree to the extent or frequency of the departures, but is to be paid by the employer in full measure whether he employs five hundred children for a year, or employs only one for a day. Moreover, if he does not know the child is within the named age limit, he is not to pay; that is to say, it is only where he knowingly departs from the prescribed course that payment is to be exacted. Scienters are associated with penalties, not with taxes. The employer's factory is to be subject to inspection at any time not only by the taxing officers of the Treasury, the Department normally charged with the collection of taxes, but also by the Secretary of Labor and his subordinates whose normal function is the advancement and protection of the welfare of the workers. In the light of these features of the act, a court must be blind not to see that the so-called tax is imposed to stop the employment of children within the age limits prescribed. Its prohibitory and regulatory effect and purpose are palpable. All others can see and understand this. How can we properly shut our minds to it? . . .

Out of a proper respect for the acts of a coördinate branch of the Government, this court has gone far to sustain taxing acts as such, even though there has been ground for suspecting from the weight of the tax it was intended to destroy its subject. But, in the act before us, the presumption of validity cannot prevail, because the proof of the contrary is found on the very face of its provisions. Grant the validity of this law, and all that Congress would need to do, hereafter, in seeking to take over to its control any one of the great number of subjects of public interest, jurisdiction of which the States have never parted with, and which are reserved to them by the Tenth Amendment, would be to enact a detailed measure of complete regulation of the subject and enforce it by a so-called tax upon departures from it. To give such magic to the word "tax" would be to break down all constitutional limitation of the powers of Congress and completely wipe out the sovereignty of the States.

The difference between a tax and a penalty is sometimes difficult to define and yet the consequences of the distinction in the required method of their collection often are important. Where the sovereign enacting the law has power to impose both tax and penalty the difference between revenue production and mere regulation may be immaterial, but not so when one sovereign can impose a tax only, and the power of regulation rests in another. Taxes are occasionally imposed in the discretion of the legislature on proper subjects with the primary motive of obtaining revenue from them and with the incidental motive of discouraging them by making their continuance onerous. They do not lose their character as taxes because of the incidental motive. But there comes a time in the extension of the penalizing features of the so-called tax when it loses its character as such and becomes a mere penalty with the characteristics of regulation and punishment....

The case before us can not be distinguished from that of *Hammer v. Dagenhart,* [§ 4–1, supra].... In the case at the bar, Congress in the name of a tax which on the face of the act is a penalty seeks to do the same thing, and the effort must be equally futile....

But it is pressed upon us that this court has gone so far in sustaining taxing measures the effect or tendency of which was to accomplish purposes not directly within congressional power that we are bound by authority to maintain this law. The first of these is *Veazie Bank v. Fenno,* 8 Wall. 533, 19 L.Ed. 482. In that case, the validity of a law which increased a tax on the circulating notes of persons and state banks from one per centum to ten per centum was in question. [As] stated by the court: "It is insisted, however, that the tax in the case before us is excessive, and so excessive as to indicate a purpose on the part of Congress to destroy the franchise of the bank, and is, therefore, beyond the constitutional power of Congress."

To this the court answered:

> The first answer to this is that the judicial cannot prescribe to the legislative departments of the government limitations upon the exercise of its acknowledged powers. The power to tax may be exercised oppressively upon persons, but the responsibility of the legislature is not to the courts, but to the people by whom its members are elected. So if a particular tax bears heavily upon a corporation or a class of corporations, it cannot, for that reason only, be pronounced contrary to the Constitution.

It will be observed that the sole objection to the tax there was its excessive character. Nothing else appeared on the face of the act. It was an increase of a tax admittedly legal to a higher rate and that was all. There were no elaborate specifications on the face of the act, as here, indicating the purpose to regulate matters of state concern and jurisdiction through an exaction so applied as to give it the qualities of a penalty for violation of law rather than a tax.

It should be noted, too, that the court, speaking of the extent of the taxing power, used these cautionary words: "There are, indeed, certain virtual limitations, arising from the principles of the Constitution itself. It would undoubtedly be an abuse of the power if so exercised as to impair the separate existence and independent self-government of the States, or if exercised for ends inconsistent with the limited grants of power in the Constitution."

But more than this, what was charged to be the object of the excessive tax was within the congressional authority ... to secure a national medium or currency....

The next case is that of *McCray v. United States,* 195 U.S. 27, 24 S.Ct. 769, 49 L.Ed. 78. That, like the *Veazie Bank Case,* was the increase of an excise tax upon a subject properly taxable in which the taxpayers claimed that the tax had become invalid because the increase was excessive. It was a tax on oleomargarine, a substitute for butter. The tax on the white oleomargarine was one-quarter of a cent a pound, and on the yellow oleomargarine was first two cents and was then by the act in question increased to ten cents per pound. This court held that the discretion of Congress in the exercise of its constitutional powers to levy excise taxes could not be controlled or limited by the courts because the latter might deem the incidence of the tax oppressive or even destructive. It was the same principle as that applied in the *Veazie Bank Case.* This was that Congress in selecting its subjects for taxation might impose the burden where and as it would and that a motive disclosed in its selection to discourage sale or manufacture of an article by a higher tax than on some other did not invalidate the tax. In neither of these cases did the law objected to show on its face as does the law before us the detailed specifications of a regulation of a state concern and business with a heavy exaction to promote the efficacy of such regulation.

[Another] case is *United States v. Doremus,* 249 U.S. 86, 39 S.Ct. 214, 63 L.Ed. 493. That involved the validity of the Narcotic Drug Act, 38 Stat. 785, which imposed a special tax on the manufacture, importation and sale or gift of opium or coca leaves or their compounds or derivatives. It required every person subject to the special tax to register with the Collector of Internal Revenue his name and place of business and forbade him to sell except upon the written order of the person to whom the sale was made on a form prescribed by the Commissioner of Internal Revenue. The vendor was required to keep the order for two years, and the purchaser to keep a duplicate for the same time and both were to be subject to official inspection. Similar requirements were made as to sales upon prescriptions of a physician and as to the dispensing of such drugs directly to a patient by a physician. The validity of a special tax in the nature of an excise tax on the manufacture, importation and sale of such drugs was, of course, unquestioned. The provisions for subjecting the sale and distribution of the drugs to official supervision and inspection were held to have a reasonable relation to the enforcement of the tax and were therefore held valid.

The court said that the act could not be declared invalid just because another motive than taxation, not shown on the face of the act, might have contributed to its passage. This case does not militate against the conclusion we have reached in respect of the law now before us. The court, there, made manifest its view that the provisions of the so-called taxing act must be naturally and reasonably adapted to the collection of the tax and not solely to the achievement of some other purpose plainly within state power.

For the reasons given, we must hold the Child Labor Tax Law invalid and the judgment of the District Court is

Affirmed.

Mr. Justice Clarke dissents.

Notes

1. *United States v. Kahriger,* 345 U.S. 22, 73 S.Ct. 510, 97 L.Ed. 754 (1953) upheld the constitutionality of the occupational tax provisions of the Revenue Act of 1951, which taxed persons engaged in the business of accepting wagers, and required them to register with the Collector of Internal Revenue. Defendant argued that the tax violated the Tenth Amendment and his privilege against self-incrimination. As to the Tenth Amendment argument, the Court said:

> It is conceded that a federal excise tax does not cease to be valid merely because it discourages or deters the activities taxed. Nor is the tax invalid because the revenue obtained is negligible. Appellee, however, argues that the sole purpose of the statute is to penalize only illegal gambling in the states through the guise of a tax measure. As with the [other] excise taxes which we have held to be valid, the instant tax has a regulatory effect. But regardless of its regulatory effect, the wagering tax produces revenue. As such it surpasses both the narcotics and firearms taxes which we have found valid.
>
> It is axiomatic that the power of Congress to tax is extensive and sometimes falls with crushing effect on businesses deemed unessential or inimical to the public welfare, or where, as in dealings with narcotics, the collection of the tax also is difficult. As is well known, the constitutional restraints on taxing are few.... It is hard to understand why the power to tax should raise more doubts because of indirect effects than other federal powers.
>
> Penalty provisions in tax statutes added for breach of a regulation concerning activities in themselves subject only to state regulation have caused this Court to declare the enactments invalid. [A footnote at this point cited *The Child Labor Tax Case*]. Unless there are provisions extraneous to any tax need, courts are without authority to limit the exercise of the taxing power. All the provisions of this excise are adapted to the collection of a valid tax.

The Court went on to hold that the wagering tax also did not deny the Fifth Amendment's privilege against self-incrimination.

Justice Frankfurter, dissenting, noted:

> [T]o allow what otherwise is excluded from congressional authority to be brought within it by casting legislation in the form of a revenue measure could, as so significantly expounded in the *Child Labor Tax Case,* offer an easy way for the legislative imagination to control "any one of the great number of subjects of public interest, jurisdiction of which the States have never parted with ..." *Child Labor Tax Case,* at 38. I say "significantly" because Mr. Justice Holmes and two of the Justices who had joined his dissent in *Hammer v. Dagenhart,* McKenna and Brandeis, JJ., agreed with the opinion in the *Child Labor Tax Case.* Issues of such

gravity affecting the balance of powers within our federal system are not susceptible of comprehensive statement by smooth formulas such as that a tax is nonetheless a tax although it discourages the activities taxed, or that a tax may be imposed although it may effect ulterior ends. No such phrase, however fine and well-worn, enables one to decide the concrete case. [In this case] what was formally a means of raising revenue for the Federal Government was essentially an effort to check if not stamp out professional gambling.

In *Marchetti v. United States*, 390 U.S. 39, 88 S.Ct. 697, 19 L.Ed.2d 889 (1968), Harlan, J., for the Court, held that the petitioner's assertion of his Fifth Amendment privilege barred his prosecution for violating the federal occupational tax related to wagers. Paying the tax would have provided information incriminating to the petitioner in light of the various state and federal penalties imposed on wagering. The Court overruled *Kahriger* to the extent that it had failed to recognize such a privilege. A companion case, *Grosso v. United States*, 390 U.S. 62, 88 S.Ct. 709, 19 L.Ed.2d 906 (1968), invalidated the federal excise tax on wagering, also on Fifth Amendment grounds.

2. In *Atherton Mills v. Johnston*, 259 U.S. 13, 42 S.Ct. 422, 66 L.Ed. 814 (1922), the Court, per Taft, C.J., dismissed a case challenging the constitutionality of the child labor tax on the grounds of mootness: the person objecting to the tax turned sixteen. The Court had held *Atherton* for two terms without deciding it.

Professor Alexander Bickel—after examining an unpublished draft of *Atherton,* written by Brandeis in 1920 and circulated to the Justices but never published—concluded that Brandeis, in a case free of *Atherton's* jurisdictional difficulties, clearly would have upheld the child labor tax and perhaps in 1920 even a majority of the Court was so inclined. But Brandeis did not dissent when the issue actually came up on the merits in the *Child Labor Tax Case.* Bickel noted that Brandeis sometimes had suppressed dissents for tactical reasons. " 'Can't always dissent,' he said ... He also referred to Holmes' reluctance to dissent again after he had once had his say on a subject." Bickel surmised that it "might have seemed to Brandeis churlish, and a disservice in the long run to his effectiveness ... and to his future relations with the new Chief Justice, Taft, to turn around at this juncture and register a dissent."[1]

UNITED STATES v. BUTLER

297 U.S. 1, 56 S.Ct. 312, 80 L.Ed. 477 (1936).

[In the Agricultural Adjustment Act of 1933 Congress stated that "an economic emergency has arisen," causing a great reduction in the farmers' purchasing power and thereby obstructing "the normal currents of commerce." In order to raise the farmers' purchasing power, the Act sought to decrease the supply of farm products. Section 8 of the act

1. A. Bickel, The Unpublished Opinions of Mr. Justice Brandeis 3–4, 18–19 (1957). On the other hand, Spillenger, Reading the Judicial Canon: Alexander Bickel and the Book of Brandeis, 1 Journal of American History 125, 133–51 (June, 1992) casts doubt on Bickel's conclusion.

in effect provided that the Secretary of Agriculture "is not required, but is permitted, if in his uncontrolled judgment, the policy of the act will be so promoted, to make agreements with individual farmers for reduction of acreage or production [in return for rental or benefit payments] upon such terms as he may think fair and reasonable." "To obtain revenue for extraordinary expenses incurred by reason of the national emergency" the Act levied a processing tax "on the first domestic processing of the commodity, whether of domestic production or imported, and [this tax] shall be paid by the processor." § 9(a). The tax was set "at such rate as equals the difference between the current average farm price for the commodity and the fair exchange value," § 9(b), so that the farmer could achieve parity of purchasing power as compared with the designated "base period" for the particular commodity, § 2, usually 1909–1914.

[After the Secretary determined what the appropriate rental and benefit payments and processing and floor taxes on cotton should be, the United States presented its tax claim to the receivers of the Hoosac Mills Corp., who refused to pay. The district court found the taxes valid but the circuit court held them unconstitutional.]

MR. JUSTICE ROBERTS delivered the opinion of the Court....

The Government asserts that even if the respondents may question the propriety of the appropriation embodied in the statute their attack must fail because Article I, § 8 of the Constitution authorizes the contemplated expenditure of the funds raised by the tax. This contention presents the great and the controlling question in the case.... When an act of Congress is appropriately challenged in the courts as not conforming to the constitutional mandate the judicial branch of the Government has only one duty,—to lay the article of the Constitution which is invoked beside the statute which is challenged and to decide whether the latter squares with the former. [Only two clauses of Article 1, § 8] have any bearing upon the validity of the statute under review.

[Section 8, clause 3] endows the Congress with power "to regulate Commerce ... among the several States." Despite a reference in its first section to a burden upon, and an obstruction of the normal currents of commerce, the act under review does not purport to regulate transactions in interstate or foreign commerce. Its stated purpose is the control of agricultural production, a purely local activity, in an effort to raise the prices paid the farmer. Indeed, the Government does not attempt to uphold the validity of the act on the basis of the commerce clause, which, for the purpose of the present case, may be put aside as irrelevant.

The clause thought to authorize the legislation,—the first,—confers upon the Congress power "to lay and collect Taxes, Duties, Imposts and Excises, to pay the Debts and provide for the common Defence and general Welfare of the United States.... " It is not contended that this provision grants power to regulate agricultural production upon the theory that such legislation would promote the general welfare. The Government concedes that the phrase "to provide for the general welfare" qualifies the power "to lay and collect taxes." ... The necessary implication from the terms of the grant is that the public funds may be appropriated "to provide for the general welfare of the United States." . . .

Since the foundation of the Nation sharp differences of opinion have persisted as to the true interpretation of the phrase. Madison asserted it amounted to no more than a reference to the other powers enumerated in the subsequent clauses of the same section; that, as the United States is a government of limited and enumerated powers, the grant of power to tax and spend for the general national welfare must be confined to the enumerated legislative fields committed to the Congress. In this view the phrase is mere tautology, for taxation and appropriation are or may be necessary incidents of the exercise of any of the enumerated legislative powers. Hamilton, on the other hand, maintained the clause confers a power separate and distinct from those later enumerated, is not restricted in meaning by the grant of them, and Congress consequently has a substantive power to tax and to appropriate, limited only by the requirement that it shall be exercised to provide for the general welfare of the United States. Each contention has had the support of those whose views are entitled to weight. This court has noticed the question, but has never found it necessary to decide which is the true construction. Mr. Justice Story, in his Commentaries, espouses the Hamiltonian position. We shall not review the writings of public men and commentators or discuss the legislative practice. Study of all these leads us to conclude that the reading advocated by Mr. Justice Story is the correct one. While, therefore, the power to tax is not unlimited, its confines are set in the clause which confers it, and not in those of § 8 which bestow and define the legislative powers of the Congress. It results that the power of Congress to authorize expenditure of public moneys for public purposes is not limited by the direct grants of legislative power found in the Constitution.

But the adoption of the broader construction leaves the power to spend subject to limitations. . . . Hamilton . . . states that the purpose must be "general, and not local." Monroe, an advocate of Hamilton's doctrine, wrote: "Have Congress a right to raise and appropriate the money to any and to every purpose according to their will and pleasure? They certainly have not." Story says that if the tax be not proposed for the common defence or general welfare, but for other objects wholly extraneous, it would be wholly indefensible upon constitutional principles. And he makes it clear that the powers of taxation and appropriation extend only to matters of national, as distinguished from local welfare. . . .

We are not now required to ascertain the scope of the phrase "general welfare of the United States" or to determine whether an appropriation in aid of agriculture falls within it. Wholly apart from that question, another principle embedded in our Constitution prohibits the enforcement of the Agricultural Adjustment Act. The act invades the reserved rights of the states. It is a statutory plan to regulate and control agricultural production, a matter beyond the powers delegated to the federal government. The tax, the appropriation of the funds raised, and the direction for their disbursement, are but parts of the plan. They are but means to an unconstitutional end.

From the accepted doctrine that the United States is a government of delegated powers, it follows that those not expressly granted, or reasonably to be implied from such as are conferred, are reserved to the states or to the people. To forestall any suggestion to the contrary, the Tenth Amendment was adopted. The same proposition, otherwise stated, is that powers not granted are prohibited. None to regulate agricultural production is given, and therefore legislation by Congress for that purpose is forbidden....

If the taxing power may not be used as the instrument to enforce a regulation of matters of state concern with respect to which the Congress has no authority to interfere, may it, as in the present case, be employed to raise the money necessary to purchase a compliance which the Congress is powerless to command? The Government asserts that whatever might be said against the validity of the plan if compulsory, it is constitutionally sound because the end is accomplished by voluntary cooperation. There are two sufficient answers to the contention. The regulation is not in fact voluntary. The farmer, of course, may refuse to comply, but the price of such refusal is the loss of benefits. The amount offered is intended to be sufficient to exert pressure on him to agree to the proposed regulation. The power to confer or withhold unlimited benefits is the power to coerce or destroy.... But if the plan were one for purely voluntary co-operation it would stand no better so far as federal power is concerned. At best it is a scheme for purchasing with federal funds submission to federal regulation of a subject reserved to the states.

... There is an obvious difference between a statute stating the conditions upon which moneys shall be expended and one effective only upon assumption of a contractual obligation to submit to a regulation which otherwise could not be enforced. Many examples pointing the distinction might be cited. We are referred to appropriations in aid of education, and it is said that no one has doubted the power of Congress to stipulate the sort of education for which money shall be expended. But an appropriation to an educational institution which by its terms is to become available only if the beneficiary enters into a contract to teach doctrines subversive of the Constitution is clearly bad. An affirmance of the authority of Congress so to condition the expenditure of an appropriation would tend to nullify all constitutional limitations upon legislative power....

Congress has no power to enforce its commands on the farmer to the ends sought by the Agricultural Adjustment Act. It must follow that it may not indirectly accomplish those ends by taxing and spending to purchase compliance. The Constitution and the entire plan of our government negative any such use of the power to tax and to spend as the act undertakes to authorize. It does not help to declare that local conditions throughout the nation have created a situation of national concern; for this is but to say that whenever there is a widespread similarity of local conditions, Congress may ignore constitutional limitations upon its own powers and usurp those reserved to the states....

The judgment is

Affirmed.

MR. JUSTICE STONE, dissenting....

The constitutional power of Congress to levy an excise tax upon the processing of agricultural products is not questioned. The present levy is held invalid, not for any want of power in Congress to lay such a tax to defray public expenditures, including those for the general welfare, but because the use to which its proceeds are put is disapproved.

... The power of Congress to spend is inseparable from persuasion to action over which Congress has no legislative control. Congress may not command that the science of agriculture be taught in state universities. But if it would aid the teaching of that science by grants to state institutions, it is appropriate, if not necessary, that the grant be on the condition, incorporated in the Morrill Act, 12 Stat. 503, 26 Stat. 417, that it be used for the intended purpose. Similarly it would seem to be compliance with the Constitution, not violation of it, for the government to take and the university to give a contract that the grant would be so used....

The limitation now sanctioned must lead to absurd consequences. The government may give seeds to farmers, but may not condition the gift upon their being planted in places where they are most needed or even planted at all. The government may give money to the unemployed, but may not ask that those who get it shall give labor in return, or even use it to support their families. It may give money to sufferers from earthquake, fire, tornado, pestilence or flood, but may not impose conditions—health precautions designed to prevent the spread of disease, or induce the movement of population to safer or more sanitary areas. All that, because it is purchased regulation infringing state powers, must be left for the states, who are unable or unwilling to supply the necessary relief. The government may spend its money for vocational rehabilitation, 48 Stat. 389, but it may not, with the consent of all concerned, supervise the process which it undertakes to aid. It may spend its money for the suppression of the boll weevil, but may not compensate the farmers for suspending the growth of cotton in the infected areas. It may aid state reforestation and forest fire prevention agencies, 43 Stat. 653, but may not be permitted to supervise their conduct. It may support rural schools, 39 Stat. 929, 45 Stat. 1151, 48 Stat. 792, but may not condition its grant by the requirement that certain standards be maintained....

That the governmental power of the purse is a great one is not now for the first time announced.... The suggestion that it must now be curtailed by judicial fiat because it may be abused by unwise use hardly rises to the dignity of argument. So may judicial power be abused.... Courts are not the only agency of government that must be assumed to have capacity to govern....

Mr. Justice Brandeis and Mr. Justice Cardozo join in this opinion.

CHAS. C. STEWARD MACHINE CO. v. DAVIS
301 U.S. 548, 57 S.Ct. 883, 81 L.Ed. 1279 (1937).

Mr. Justice Cardozo delivered the opinion of the Court.

The validity of the tax imposed by the Social Security Act on employers of eight or more is here to be determined.

Petitioner, an Alabama corporation, paid a tax in accordance with the statute, filed a claim for refund with the Commissioner of Internal Revenue, and sued to recover the payment ($46.14), asserting a conflict between the statute and the Constitution of the United States....

The caption of Title IX is "Tax on Employers of Eight or More." Every employer (with stated exceptions) is to pay for each calendar year "an excise tax, with respect to having individuals in his employ," the tax to be measured by prescribed percentages of the total wages payable by the employer during the calendar year with respect to such employment.... The proceeds, when collected, go into the Treasury of the United States like internal-revenue collections generally. They are not earmarked in any way. In certain circumstances, however, credits are allowable. If the taxpayer has made contributions to an unemployment fund under a state law, he may credit such contributions against the federal tax, provided, however, that the total credit allowed to any taxpayer shall not exceed 90 per centum of the tax against which it is credited, and provided also that the state law shall have been certified to the Secretary of the Treasury by the Social Security Board as satisfying certain minimum criteria.... Some of the conditions thus attached to the allowance of a credit are designed to give assurance that the state unemployment compensation law shall be one in substance as well as name. Others are designed to give assurance that the contributions shall be protected against loss after payment to the state. To this last end there are provisions that before a state law shall have the approval of the Board it must direct that the contributions to the state fund be paid over immediately to the Secretary of the Treasury to the credit of the "Unemployment Trust Fund." [T]he Fund is to be held by the Secretary of the Treasury, who is to invest in government securities any portion not required in his judgment to meet current withdrawals. He is authorized and directed to pay out of the Fund to any competent state agency such sums as it may duly requisition from the amount standing to its credit.

Title III, which is also challenged as invalid, has the caption "Grants to States for Unemployment Compensation Administration." Under this title, certain sums of money are "authorized to be appropriated" for the purpose of assisting the states in the administration of their unemployment compensation laws. . . .

The assault on the statute proceeds on an extended front. . . .

First. The tax, which is described in the statute as an excise, is laid with uniformity throughout the United States as a duty, an impost or an excise upon the relation of employment. . . . The tax being an excise, its imposition must conform to the canon of uniformity. There has been no departure from this requirement. According to the settled doctrine the uniformity exacted is geographical, not intrinsic. . . .

Second. The excise is not invalid under the provisions of the Fifth Amendment by force of its exemptions. . . .

The classifications and exemptions directed by the statute now in controversy have support in considerations of policy and practical convenience that cannot be condemned as arbitrary. . . .

Third. The excise is not void as involving the coercion of the States in contravention of the Tenth Amendment or of restrictions implicit in our federal form of government.

The proceeds of the excise when collected are paid into the Treasury at Washington, and thereafter are subject to appropriation like public moneys generally. . . .

To draw the line intelligently between duress and inducement there is need to remind ourselves of facts as to the problem of unemployment that are now matters of common knowledge. The relevant statistics are gathered in the brief of counsel for the Government. Of the many available figures a few only will be mentioned. During the years 1929 to 1936, when the country was passing through a cyclical depression, the number of the unemployed mounted to unprecedented heights. Often the average was more than 10 million; at times a peak was attained of 16 million or more. Disaster to the breadwinner meant disaster to dependents. Accordingly the roll of the unemployed, itself formidable enough, was only a partial roll of the destitute or needy. The fact developed quickly that the states were unable to give the requisite relief. The problem had become national in area and dimensions. There was need of help from the nation if the people were not to starve. It is too late today for the argument to be heard with tolerance that in a crisis so extreme the use of the moneys of the nation to relieve the unemployed and their dependents is a use for any purpose narrower than the promotion of the general welfare. . . . The *parens patriae* has many reasons—fiscal and economic as well as social and moral—for planning to mitigate disasters that bring these burdens in their train.

In the presence of this urgent need for some remedial expedient, the question is to be answered whether the expedient adopted has overlept the bounds of power. The assailants of the statute say that its dominant end and aim is to drive the state legislatures under the whip of economic pressure into the enactment of unemployment compensation laws at the bidding of the central government. Supporters of the statute say that its operation is not constraint, but the creation of a larger freedom, the states and the nation joining in a cooperative endeavor to avert a common evil. Before Congress acted, unemployment compensation insurance was still, for the most part, a project and no more. Wisconsin was the pioneer. Her statute was adopted in 1931. At times bills for such insurance were introduced elsewhere, but they did not reach the stage of law. In 1935, four states (California, Massachusetts, New Hampshire and New York) passed unemployment laws on the eve of the adoption of the Social Security Act, and two others did likewise after the federal act and later in the year. [I]f states had been holding back before the passage of the federal law, inaction was not owing, for the most part, to the lack of sympathetic interest. Many held back through alarm lest, in laying such a toll upon their industries, they would place themselves in a position of economic disadvantage as compared with neighbors or competitors.[9] . . .

Who then is coerced through the operation of this statute? Not the taxpayer. He pays in fulfilment of the mandate of the local legislature. Not the state. Even now she does not offer a suggestion that in passing the unemployment law she was affected by duress. For all that appears she is satisfied with her choice, and would be sorely disappointed if it were now to be annulled. The difficulty with the petitioner's contention is that it confuses motive with coercion. "Every tax is in some measure regulatory. To some extent it interposes an economic impediment to the activity taxed as compared with others not taxed." In like manner every rebate from a tax when conditioned upon conduct is in some measure a temptation. But to hold that motive or temptation is equivalent to coercion is to plunge the law in endless difficulties. The outcome of such a doctrine is the acceptance of a philosophical determinism by which choice becomes impossible. Till now the law has been guided by a robust common sense which assumes the freedom of the will as a working hypothesis in the solution of its problems. The wisdom of the hypothesis has illustration in this case. Nothing in the case suggests the exertion of a power akin to undue influence, if we assume that such a concept can ever be applied with fitness to the relations between state and nation. Even on that assumption the location of the point at which pressure turns into compulsion, and ceases to be inducement, would be a question of degree,—at times, perhaps, of fact. The point had not been reached when Alabama made her choice. We cannot say that she was acting, not of her unfettered will, but under the strain of a persuasion equivalent to undue influence, when she chose to have relief administered under laws of her own making, by agents of her own selection, instead of under federal laws, administered by federal officers, with all the ensuing evils, at least to many minds, of federal patronage and power. There would be a strange irony, indeed, if her choice were now to be annulled on the basis of an assumed duress in the enactment of a statute which her

9. The attitude of Massachusetts is significant. Her act became a law August 12, 1935, two days before the federal act. Even so, she prescribed that its provisions should not become operative unless the federal bill became a law, or unless eleven [named] states . . . should impose on their employers burdens substantially equivalent. Her fear of competition is thus forcefully attested.

courts have accepted as a true expression of her will. We think the choice must stand.

In ruling as we do, we leave many questions open. We do not say that a tax is valid, when imposed by act of Congress, if it is laid upon the condition that a state may escape its operation through the adoption of a statute unrelated in subject matter to activities fairly within the scope of national policy and power. No such question is before us. In the tender of this credit Congress does not intrude upon fields foreign to its function. The purpose of its intervention, as we have shown, is to safeguard its own treasury and as an incident to that protection to place the states upon a footing of equal opportunity. Drains upon its own resources are to be checked; obstructions to the freedom of the states are to be leveled. It is one thing to impose a tax dependent upon the conduct of the taxpayers, or of the state in which they live, where the conduct to be stimulated or discouraged is unrelated to the fiscal need subserved by the tax in its normal operation, or to any other end legitimately national. The *Child Labor Tax Case,* [was] decided in the belief that the statutes there condemned were exposed to that reproach. It is quite another thing to say that a tax will be abated upon the doing of an act that will satisfy the fiscal need, the tax and the alternative being approximate equivalents. In such circumstances, if in no others, inducement or persuasion does not go beyond the bounds of power. We do not fix the outermost line. Enough for present purposes that wherever the line may be, this statute is within it. Definition more precise must abide the wisdom of the future. . . .

United States v. Butler, supra, is cited by petitioner as a decision to the contrary. . . . The decision was by a divided court, [and not] applicable to the situation here developed.

(a) The proceeds of the tax in controversy are not earmarked for a special group.

(b) The unemployment compensation law which is a condition of the credit has had the approval of the state and could not be a law without it.

(c) The condition is not linked to an irrevocable agreement, for the state at its pleasure may repeal its unemployment law, terminate the credit, and place itself where it was before the credit was accepted.

(d) The condition is not directed to the attainment of an unlawful end, but to an end, the relief of unemployment, for which nation and state may lawfully coöperate.

Fourth. The statute does not call for a surrender by the states of powers essential to their quasi-sovereign existence. . . .

A credit to taxpayers for payments made to a State under a state unemployment law will be manifestly futile in the absence of some assurance that the law leading to the credit is in truth what it professes to be. An unemployment law framed in such a way that the unemployed who look to it will be deprived of reasonable protection is one in name and nothing more. What is basic and essential may be assured by suitable conditions. The terms embodied in these sections are directed to that end. A wide range of judgment is given to the several states as to the particular type of statute to be spread upon their books. . . . What they may not do, if they would earn the credit, is to depart from those standards which in the judgment of Congress are to be ranked as fundamental. . . . In determining essentials Congress must have the benefit of a fair margin of discretion. One cannot say with reason that this margin has been exceeded, or that the basic standards have been determined in any arbitrary fashion. In the event that some particular condition shall be found to be too uncertain to be capable of enforcement, it may be severed from the others, and what is left will still be valid.

We are to keep in mind steadily that the conditions to be approved by the Board as the basis for a credit are not provisions of a contract, but terms of a statute, which may be altered or repealed. . . . By this we do not intimate that the conclusion would be different if a contract were discovered. Even sovereigns may contract without derogating from their sovereignty. . . .

The judgment is affirmed.

[The dissenting opinions of SUTHERLAND, J., joined by VAN DEVANTER, J., and of McREYNOLDS, J. and BUTLER, J., are omitted.]

Notes

1. In *Helvering v. Davis,* 301 U.S. 619, 57 S.Ct. 904, 81 L.Ed. 1307 (1937), decided the same day, Justice Cardozo rejected attacks on other provisions of the Social Security Act. Title VIII laid another excise on employers and also a special income tax on employees. Title II provided "for the payment of Old Age Benefits, and supplies the motive and occasion in the view of the assailants of the statute, for the levy of taxes imposed by Title VIII." The Court said:

> The conception of the spending power advocated by Hamilton and strongly reinforced by Story has prevailed, [yet] difficulties are left when the power is conceded. The line must still be drawn between one welfare and another, between particular and general. Where this shall be placed cannot be known through a formula in advance of the event. There is a middle ground or certainly a penumbra in which discretion is at large. The discretion, however, is not confined to the courts. The discretion belongs to Congress, unless the choice is clearly wrong, a display of arbitrary power, not an exercise of judgment. . . . Nor is the concept of the general welfare static. Needs that were narrow or parochial a century ago may be interwoven in our day with the well-being of the Nation. What is critical or urgent changes with the times.
>
> The purge of nation-wide calamity that began in 1929 has taught us many lessons. Not the least is the solidarity of interests that may once have seemed to be divided. . . . Congress did not improvise a judgment when it found that the award of old age benefits would be conducive to the general welfare. . . .

2. *Buckley v. Valeo,* 424 U.S. 1, 96 S.Ct. 612, 46 L.Ed.2d 659 (1976)(per curiam) upheld the constitutionality of the establishment of a Presidential Election Campaign Fund financed from general revenues against the charge, inter alia, that it was contrary to the general welfare. "Appellants' 'general welfare' contention erroneously treats the General Welfare Clause as a limitation upon congressional power. It is rather a grant of power, the scope of which is quite expansive, particularly in view of the enlargement of the power by the Necessary and Proper Clause. Congress has power to regulate Presidential elections and primaries; and public financing of Presidential Elections as a means to reform the electoral process was clearly a choice within the granted power. It is for Congress to decide which expenditures will promote the general welfare.... "

3. The Federal Hatch Act makes unlawful certain specified political activities of federal employees. Section 12(a) provides that "no officer or employee of any State or local agency whose principal employment is in connection with any activity which is financed in whole or in part by loans or grants made by the United States or by any Federal agency shall ... take any active part in political management or in political campaigns.... " In the case of a violation warranting removal of the employee, the Civil Service Commission is to notify the state or local agency and employee; if the state or local agency refuses to remove the employee (or, after removal, rehires him within 18 months), the federal agency is to withhold its loans or grants to the state or local agency in an amount equal to two years of compensation of the offending employee.

Oklahoma was ordered to remove France Paris, a member of the State Highway Commission and Chairman of the Oklahoma Democratic Central Committee. The state claimed that the alternative of complying with the order or losing federal highway grants was an unconstitutional attempt to regulate its internal affairs and invade its sovereignty. The parties agreed that the United States "is not concerned with and has no power to regulate local political activities as such of state officials." Was the Hatch Act, in this respect, valid pursuant to the spending power, including the power to fix the terms upon which money allotments to states shall be disbursed? See *Oklahoma v. United States Civil Service Commission,* 330 U.S. 127, 67 S.Ct. 544, 91 L.Ed. 794 (1947).

4. In *South Dakota v. Dole,* 483 U.S. 203, 107 S.Ct. 2793, 97 L.Ed.2d 171 (1987), the Court, per Rehnquist, C.J., upheld the power of Congress to withhold federal highway funds from states that allow the purchase or public possession of any alcoholic beverage by persons under twenty-one years of age. "Even if Congress might lack the power to impose a national minimum drinking age directly, we conclude that encouragement to state action found in [the federal law] is a valid use of the spending power." The "spending power is of course not unlimited," but the federal legislation did not pass those limits. First, the spending power must be in pursuit of the general welfare, which occurred here, "especially in light of the fact that 'the concept of welfare or the opposite is shaped by Congress.... ' " Second, if Congress desires to condition the state's receipt of funds, it "must do so unambiguously," so the states exercise their choice knowingly. That too existed here. Third "our cases have suggested (without significant elaboration) that conditions on federal grants might be illegitimate if they are unrelated 'to

the federal interest in particular national projects or programs.' " In this case "the condition imposed on Congress is directly related to one of the main purposes for which highway funds are expended—safe interstate travel." Finally, the Twenty-first Amendment is not an "independent constitutional bar" to the federal government's conditional grant of funds. The Court said that *United States v. Butler* "established that the constitutional limitations on Congress exercising its spending power are less exacting than those on its authority to regulate directly." It explained:

> "[T]he 'independent constitutional bar' limitation on the spending power is not, as petitioner suggests, a prohibition on the indirect achievement of objectives which Congress is not empowered to achieve directly. Instead, we think that ... the power may not be used to induce the States to engage in activities that would themselves be unconstitutional. Thus, for example, a grant of federal funds conditioned on invidiously discriminatory state action or the infliction of cruel and unusual punishment would be an illegitimate exercise of the Congress' broad spending power. But no such claim can be or is made here. Were South Dakota to succumb to the blandishments offered by Congress and raise its drinking age to 21, the State's action in so doing would not violate the constitutional rights of anyone.

> "Our decisions have recognized that in some circumstances the financial inducement offered by Congress might be so coercive as to pass the point at which pressure turns into compulsion. *Steward Machine Co. v. Davis.* Here, however, Congress has directed only that a State desiring to establish a minimum drinking age lower than 21 lose a relatively small percentage [5%] of certain federal highway funds. Petitioner contends that the coercive nature of this program is evident from the degree of success it has achieved. We cannot conclude, however, that a conditional grant of federal money of this sort is unconstitutional simply by reason of its success in achieving the congressional objective."

Brennan, J., dissented because he believed that the Twenty-first Amendment limited the spending power. O'Connor, J., the only other dissenter, argued that the federal law "is not a condition on spending reasonably related to the expenditure of federal funds and cannot be justified on that ground."

5. The reach of the spending power was illustrated when American satellites detected evidence that India was preparing for nuclear tests. Senator Glenn disclosed to surprised Indian officials that a 1994 law required the United States to cut off U.S. financial aid if such tests were conducted. India did not conduct the tests. Wall St. Journal, Jan. 5, 1996, at A1, col. 5.

6. Public Law 98–166, § 510, 97 Stat. at Large 1071, at 1102–03 (Nov. 28, 1983) forbade the use of any federal funds for any activity (other than Congressional testimony), "the purpose of which was to overturn or alter the per se prohibition on resale price maintenance in effect under Federal antitrust laws.... " The law was interpreted, and applied, to prohibit a Government attorney, during oral argument before the Supreme Court, from urging the Court to overturn the per se antitrust prohibition. Is such a law constitutional?

4–4. MODERN COMMERCE CLAUSE CASES

HEART OF ATLANTA MOTEL, INC. v. UNITED STATES

379 U.S. 241, 85 S.Ct. 348, 13 L.Ed.2d 258 (1964).

MR. JUSTICE CLARK delivered the opinion of the Court.

This is a declaratory judgment action attacking the constitutionality of Title II of the Civil Rights Act of 1964. A three-judge court, sustained the validity of the Act and issued a permanent injunction ... restraining appellant from continuing to violate the Act.... We affirm the judgment.

1. THE FACTUAL BACKGROUND AND CONTENTIONS OF THE PARTIES

The case comes here on admissions and stipulated facts. Appellant owns and operates the Heart of Atlanta Motel which has 216 rooms available to transient guests.... It is readily accessible to interstate highways 75 and 85 and state highways 23 and 41. Appellant solicits patronage from outside the State of Georgia through various national advertising media, including magazines of national circulation; it maintains over 50 billboards and highway signs within the State, soliciting patronage for the motel; it accepts convention trade from outside Georgia and approximately 75% of its registered guests are from out of State. Prior to passage of the Act the motel had followed a practice of refusing to rent rooms to Negroes, and it alleged that it intended to continue to do so. In an effort to perpetuate that policy this suit was filed.

The appellant contends that Congress in passing this Act exceeded its power to regulate commerce....

2. THE HISTORY OF THE ACT

Congress first evidenced its interest in civil rights legislation in the Civil Rights or Enforcement Act of April 9, 1866. There followed four Acts, with a fifth, the Civil Rights Act of March 1, 1875, culminating the series. In 1883 this Court struck down the public accommodations sections of the 1875 Act in the *Civil Rights Cases,* [§ 7–1, infra]. No major legislation in this field had been enacted by Congress for 82 years when the Civil Rights Act of 1957 became law. It was followed by the Civil Rights Act of 1960.... However, it was not until July 2, 1964, upon the recommendation of President Johnson, that the Civil Rights Act of 1964, here under attack, was finally passed....

3. TITLE II OF THE ACT

This Title is divided into seven sections beginning with § 201(a) which provides that:

> "All persons shall be entitled to the full and equal enjoyment of the goods, services, facilities, privileges, advantages, and accommodations of any place of public accommodation, as defined in this section, without discrimination or segregation on the ground of race, color, religion, or national origin."

There are listed in § 201(b) four classes of business establishments, each of which "serves the public" and "is a place of public accommodation" within the meaning of § 201(a) "if its operations affect commerce, or if discrimination or segregation by it is supported by State action." The covered establishments are:

"(1) any inn, hotel, motel, or other establishment which provides lodging to transient guests, other than an establishment located within a building which contains not more than five rooms for rent or hire and which is actually occupied by the proprietor of such establishment as his residence;

"(2) any restaurant, cafeteria . . . [not here involved];

"(3) any motion picture house . . . [not here involved];

"(4) any establishment . . . which is physically located within the premises of any establishment otherwise covered by this subsection, or . . . within the premises of which is physically located any such covered establishment . . . [not here involved]."

Section 201(c) defines the phrase "affect commerce" as applied to the above establishments. It first declares that "any inn, hotel, motel, or other establishment which provides lodging to transient guests" affects commerce *per se*. Restaurants, cafeterias, etc., in class two affect commerce only if they serve or offer to serve interstate travelers or if a substantial portion of the food which they serve or products which they sell have "moved in commerce." Motion picture houses and other places listed in class three affect commerce if they customarily present films, performances, etc., "which move in commerce." And the establishments listed in class four affect commerce if they are within, or include within their own premises, an establishment "the operations of which affect commerce." Private clubs are excepted under certain conditions. . . .

4. APPLICATION OF TITLE II TO HEART OF ATLANTA MOTEL

It is admitted that the operation of the motel brings it within the provisions of § 201(a) of the Act and that appellant refused to provide lodging for transient Negroes because of their race or color and that it intends to continue that policy unless restrained.

The sole question posed is, therefore, the constitutionality of the Civil Rights Act of 1964 as applied to these facts. The legislative history of the Act indicates that Congress based the Act on § 5 and the Equal Protection Clause of the Fourteenth Amendment as well as its power to regulate interstate commerce under Art. I, § 8, cl. 3, of the Constitution.

The Senate Commerce Committee made it quite clear that the fundamental object of Title II was to vindicate "the deprivation of personal dignity that surely accompanies denials of equal access to public establishments." At the same time, however, it noted that such an objective has been and could be readily achieved "by congressional action based on the commerce power of the Constitution." Our study of the legislative record, made in the light of prior cases, has brought us to the conclusion that Congress possessed ample power in this regard, and we have therefore not considered the other grounds relied upon. This is not to say that the remaining authority upon which it acted was not adequate, a question upon which we do not pass, but merely that since the commerce power is sufficient for our decision here we have considered it alone. . . .

5.   The Civil Rights Cases (1883), and their Application

In light of our ground for decision, it might be well at the outset to discuss the *Civil Rights Cases,* [§ 7–1, infra], which declared provisions of the Civil Rights Act of 1875 unconstitutional. We think that decision inapposite, and without precedential value in determining the constitutionality of the present Act. Unlike Title II of the present legislation, the 1875 Act broadly proscribed discrimination in "inns, public conveyances on land or water, theaters, and other places of public amusement," without limiting the categories of affected businesses to those impinging upon interstate commerce. . . .

6.   The Basis of Congressional Action

While the Act as adopted carried no congressional findings the record of its passage through each house is replete with evidence of the burdens that discrimination by race or color places upon interstate commerce. This testimony included the fact that our people have become increasingly mobile with millions of people of all races traveling from State to State; that Negroes in particular have been the subject of discrimination in transient accommodations, having to travel great distances to secure the same; that often they have been unable to obtain accommodations and have had to call upon friends to put them up overnight; and that these conditions had become so acute as to require the listing of available lodging for Negroes in a special guidebook which was itself "dramatic testimony to the difficulties" Negroes encounter in travel. These exclusionary practices were found to be nationwide, the Under Secretary of Commerce testifying that there is "no question that this discrimination in the North still exists to a large degree" and in the West and Midwest as well. This testimony indicated a qualitative as well as quantitative effect on interstate travel by Negroes. The former was the obvious impairment of the Negro traveler's pleasure and convenience that resulted when he continually was uncertain of finding lodging. As for the latter, there was evidence that this uncertainty stemming from racial discrimination had the effect of discouraging travel on the part of a substantial portion of the Negro community. . . . We shall not burden this opinion with further details since the voluminous testimony presents overwhelming evidence that discrimination by hotels and motels impedes interstate travel.

7.   The Power of Congress Over Interstate Travel

. . . In framing Title II of this Act Congress was also dealing with what it considered a moral problem. But that fact does not detract from the overwhelming evidence of the disruptive effect that racial discrimination has had on commercial intercourse. . . .

It is said that the operation of the motel here is of a purely local character. But, assuming this to be true, "[i]f it is interstate commerce that feels the pinch, it does not matter how local the operation which applies the squeeze." *United States v. Women's Sportswear Mfg. Ass'n,* 336 U.S. 460, 464, 69 S.Ct. 714, 716, 93 L.Ed. 805 (1949).... Thus the power of Congress to promote interstate commerce also includes the power to regulate the local incidents thereof, including local activities in both the States of origin and destination, which might have a substantial and harmful effect upon that commerce. One need only examine the evidence which we have discussed above to see that Congress may—as it has—prohibit racial discrimination by motels serving travelers, however "local" their operations may appear.

Nor does the Act deprive appellant of liberty or property under the Fifth Amendment. The commerce power invoked here by the Congress is a specific and plenary one authorized by the Constitution itself. The only questions are: (1) whether Congress had a rational basis for finding that racial discrimination by motels affected commerce, and (2) if it had such a basis, whether the means it selected to eliminate that evil are reasonable and appropriate. If they are, appellant has no "right" to select its guests as it sees fit, free from governmental regulation....

We, therefore, conclude that the action of the Congress in the adoption of the Act as applied here to a motel which concededly serves interstate travelers is within the power granted it by the Commerce Clause of the Constitution, as interpreted by this Court for 140 years. It may be argued that Congress could have pursued other methods to eliminate the obstructions it found in interstate commerce caused by racial discrimination. But this is a matter of policy that rests entirely with the Congress not with the courts. How obstructions in commerce may be removed—what means are to be employed—is within the sound and exclusive discretion of the Congress. It is subject only to one caveat—that the means chosen by it must be reasonably adapted to the end permitted by the Constitution. We cannot say that its choice here was not so adapted. The Constitution requires no more.

Affirmed.

MR. JUSTICE BLACK, concurring.

[T]he operations of both the motel and the restaurant here fall squarely within the measure Congress chose to adopt in the Act and deemed adequate to show a constitutionally prohibitable adverse effect on commerce. The choice of policy is of course within the exclusive power of Congress; but whether particular operations affect interstate commerce sufficiently to come under the constitutional power of Congress to regulate them is ultimately a judicial rather than a legislative question, and can be settled finally only by this Court. I agree that as applied to this motel and this restaurant the Act is a valid exercise of congressional power, in the case of the motel because the record amply demonstrates that its practice of discrimination tended directly to interfere with interstate travel, and in the case of the restaurant because Congress had ample basis for concluding that a widespread practice of racial discrimination by restaurants buying as substantial a quantity of goods shipped from other States as this restaurant buys could distort or impede interstate trade. . . .

[The concurring opinions of DOUGLAS and GOLDBERG, JJ., are omitted. Those opinions, as well as BLACK, J.'s also applied to *Katzenbach v. McClung,* infra.]

KATZENBACH v. McCLUNG
379 U.S. 294, 85 S.Ct. 377, 13 L.Ed.2d 290 (1964).

MR. JUSTICE CLARK delivered the opinion of the Court.

This case was argued with No. 515, *Heart of Atlanta Motel v. United States,* decided this date, in which we upheld the constitutional validity of Title II of the Civil Rights Act of 1964 against an attack by hotels, motels, and like establishments. This complaint for injunctive relief against appellants attacks the constitutionality of the Act as applied to a restaurant. The case was heard by a three-judge United States District Court and an injunction was issued restraining appellants from enforcing the Act against the restaurant. . . .

2. THE FACTS

Ollie's Barbecue is a family-owned restaurant in Birmingham, Alabama, specializing in barbecued meats and homemade pies, with a seating capacity of 220 customers. It is located on a state highway 11 blocks from an interstate one and a somewhat greater distance from railroad and bus stations. The restaurant caters to a family and white-collar trade with a take-out service for Negroes. It employs 36 persons, two-thirds of whom are Negroes.

In the 12 months preceding the passage of the Act, the restaurant purchased locally approximately $150,000 worth of food, $69,683 or 46% of which was meat that it bought from a local supplier who had procured it from outside the State. The District Court expressly found that a substantial portion of the food served in the restaurant had moved in interstate commerce. The restaurant has refused to serve Negroes in its dining accommodations since its original opening in 1927, and since July 2, 1964, it has been operating in violation of the Act. The court below concluded that if it were required to serve Negroes it would lose a substantial amount of business.

. . . There must be, [the district court] said, a close and substantial relation between local activities and interstate commerce which requires control of the former in the protection of the latter. The court concluded, however, that the Congress, rather than finding facts sufficient to meet this rule, had legislated a conclusive presumption that a restaurant affects interstate commerce if it serves or offers to serve interstate travelers or if a substantial portion of the food which it serves has moved in commerce. This, the court held, it could not do because there was no demonstrable connection between food purchased in interstate commerce and sold in a restaurant and the conclusion of Congress that discrimination in the restaurant would affect that commerce....

3. THE ACT AS APPLIED

... Ollie's Barbecue admits that it is covered by [the] provisions of the Act. The Government makes no contention that the discrimination at the restaurant was supported by the State of Alabama. There is no claim that interstate travelers frequented the restaurant. The sole question, therefore, narrows down to whether Title II, as applied to a restaurant annually receiving about $70,000 worth of food which has moved in commerce, is a valid exercise of the power of Congress. The Government has contended that Congress had ample basis upon which to find that racial discrimination at restaurants which receive from out of state a substantial portion of the food served does, in fact, impose commercial burdens of national magnitude upon interstate commerce. The appellees' major argument is directed to this premise. They urge that no such basis existed. It is to that question that we now turn.

4. THE CONGRESSIONAL HEARINGS

As we noted in *Heart of Atlanta Motel* both Houses of Congress conducted prolonged hearings on the Act. And, as we said there, while no formal findings were made, which of course are not necessary, it is well that we make mention of the testimony at these hearings the better to understand the problem before Congress and determine whether the Act is a reasonable and appropriate means toward its solution. The record is replete with testimony of the burdens placed on interstate commerce by racial discrimination in restaurants. A comparison of per capita spending by Negroes in restaurants, theaters, and like establishments indicated less spending, after discounting income differences, in areas where discrimination is widely practiced. This condition, which was especially aggravated in the South, was attributed in the testimony of the Under Secretary of Commerce to racial segregation. This diminutive spending springing from a refusal to serve Negroes and their total loss as customers has, regardless of the absence of direct evidence, a close connection to interstate commerce. The fewer customers a restaurant enjoys the less food it sells and consequently the less it buys. In addition, the Attorney General testified that this type of discrimination imposed "an artificial restriction on the market" and interfered with the flow of merchandise. In addition, there were many references to discriminatory situations causing wide unrest and having a depressant effect on general business conditions in the respective communities.

Moreover there was an impressive array of testimony that discrimination in restaurants had a direct and highly restrictive effect upon interstate travel by Negroes. This resulted, it was said, because discriminatory practices prevent Negroes from buying prepared food served on the premises while on a trip, except in isolated and unkempt restaurants and under most unsatisfactory and often unpleasant conditions. This obviously discourages travel and obstructs interstate commerce for one can hardly travel without eating. Likewise, it was said, that discrimination deterred professional, as well as skilled, people from moving into areas where such practices occurred and thereby caused industry to be reluctant to establish there. [T]he District Court was in error in concluding that there was no connection between discrimination and the movement of interstate commerce. [V]iewed in isolation, the volume of food purchased by Ollie's Barbecue from sources supplied from out of state was insignificant when compared with the total foodstuffs moving in commerce. But, as our late Brother Jackson said for the Court in *Wickard v. Filburn,* [§ 4–2, supra]:

> That appellee's own contribution to the demand for wheat may be trivial by itself is not enough to remove him from the scope of federal regulation where, as here, his contribution, taken together with that of many others similarly situated, is far from trivial.

5.   THE POWER OF CONGRESS TO REGULATE LOCAL ACTIVITIES . . .

The appellees . . . object to the omission of a provision for a case-by-case determination—judicial or administrative—that racial discrimination in a particular restaurant affects commerce. But Congress' action in framing this Act was not unprecedented. In *United States v. Darby,* [§ 4–2, supra], [the appellees argued], as do the appellees here, that the Act was invalid because it included no provision for an independent inquiry regarding the effect on commerce of substandard wages in a particular business. But the Court rejected the argument. . . . Here, as there, Congress has determined for itself that refusals of service to Negroes have imposed burdens both upon the interstate flow of food and upon the movement of products generally. Of course, the mere fact that Congress has said when particular activity shall be deemed to affect commerce does not preclude further examination by this Court. But where we find that the legislators, in light of the facts and testimony before them, have a rational basis for finding a chosen regulatory scheme necessary to the protection of commerce, our investigation is at an end. The only remaining question—one answered in the affirmative by the court below—is whether the particular restaurant either serves or offers to serve interstate travelers or serves food a substantial portion of which has moved in interstate commerce.

The appellees urge that Congress, in passing the Fair Labor Standards Act and the National Labor Relations Act, made specific findings which were embodied in those statutes. Here, of course, Congress has included no formal findings. But their absence is not fatal to the validity of the statute, see *United States v. Carolene Products Co.,* 304 U.S. 144, 152, 58 S.Ct. 778, 783, 82 L.Ed. 1234 (1938), for the evidence presented at the hearings fully indicated the nature and effect of the burdens on commerce which Congress meant to alleviate.

Confronted as we are with the facts laid before Congress, we must conclude that it had a rational basis for finding that racial discrimination in restaurants had a direct and adverse effect on the free flow of interstate commerce. Insofar as the sections of the Act here relevant are concerned, §§ 201(b)(2) and (c), Congress prohibited discrimination only in those establishments having a close tie to interstate commerce, i.e., those, like the McClungs', serving food that has come from out of the State. We think in so doing that Congress acted well within its power to protect and foster commerce in extending the coverage of Title II only to those restaurants offering to serve interstate travelers or serving food, a substantial portion of which has moved in interstate commerce....

The power of Congress in this field is broad and sweeping; where it keeps within its sphere and violates no express constitutional limitation it has been the rule of this Court, going back almost to the founding days of the Republic, not to interfere. The Civil Rights Act of 1964, as here applied, we find to be plainly appropriate in the resolution of what the Congress found to be a national commercial problem of the first magnitude. We find it in no violation of any express limitations of the Constitution and we therefore declare it valid.

The judgment is therefore

Reversed.

Notes

1. Is the reasoning in *Heart of Atlanta Motel v. United States* and *Katzenbach v. McClung* based on the commerce theory promulgated in the *Lottery Case,* § 4–1, supra, or in the *Shreveport* case, § 4–1, supra? Which rationale do you think is more persuasive?

2. *Perez v. United States,* 402 U.S. 146, 91 S.Ct. 1357, 28 L.Ed.2d 686 (1971). In Title II of the Consumer Credit Protection Act, 18 U.S.C.A. § 891 et seq., Congress stated that a large part of the income of organized crime "is generated by extortionate credit transaction," that "[a]mong the factors which have rendered past efforts at prosecution almost wholly ineffective has been the existence of exclusionary rules of evidence stricter than necessary for the protection of constitutional rights," that such transactions "are carried on to a substantial extent in interstate and foreign commerce and [e]ven where extortionate credit transactions are purely intrastate in character, they nevertheless directly affect interstate and foreign commerce."

The statute defined "extortionate credit transactions" as "the use or threat of the use of 'violence or other criminal means' in enforcement." Petitioner was convicted under this law, and there "was ample evidence showing petitioner was a 'loan shark' who used the threat of violence as a method of collection." Petitioner argued that Congress had no power to control the local activity of loan sharking without proof that the conduct affected interstate commerce. Justice Douglas, for the Court, upheld the statute:

> The Commerce Clause, reaches, in the main, three categories of problems. First, the use of channels of interstate or foreign commerce which Congress deems are being misused, as, for example, the shipment of stolen goods (18 U.S.C.A. §§ 2312–2315) or of persons who have been kidnaped (18 U.S.C.A. § 1201). Second, protection of the instrumentalities of interstate commerce, as, for example, the destruction of an aircraft (18 U.S.C.A. § 32), or persons or things in commerce, as, for example, thefts from interstate shipments (18 U.S.C.A. § 659). Third,

those activities affecting commerce. It is with this last category that we are here concerned.

... Petitioner is clearly *a member of the class* which engages in "extortionate credit transactions" as defined by Congress and the description of that class has the required definiteness. It was the "class of activities" test which we employed in *Atlanta Motel v. United States,* [and] *Katzenbach v. McClung*.... Where the *class of activities* is regulated and that *class* is within the reach of federal power, the courts have no power "to excise, as trivial, individual instances" of the class.

Extortionate credit transactions, though purely intrastate, may in the judgment of Congress affect interstate commerce. In an analogous situation, Mr. Justice Holmes, speaking for a unanimous Court, said: "[W]hen it is necessary in order to prevent an evil to make the law embrace more than the precise thing to be prevented it may do so." *Westfall v. United States,* 274 U.S. 256, 259, 47 S.Ct. 629, 71 L.Ed. 1036, 1037. In that case an officer of a state bank which was a member of the Federal Reserve System issued a fraudulent certificate of deposit and paid from the funds of the state bank. It was argued that there was no loss to the Reserve Bank. Mr. Justice Holmes replied, "But every fraud like the one before us weakens the member bank and therefore weakens the System." In the setting of the present case there is a tie-in between local loan sharks and interstate crime. The findings by Congress are quite adequate on that ground. [A] report ... submitted to the House on August 29, 1967 ... revealed that "organized crime takes over $350 million a year from America's poor through loan-sharking alone." ...

We have mentioned in detail the economic, financial, and social setting of the problem as revealed to Congress. We do so not to infer that Congress need make particularized findings in order to legislate. [L]oan sharking in its national setting is one way organized interstate crime holds its guns to the heads of the poor and the rich alike and syphons funds from numerous localities to finance its national operations.

Only Justice Stewart dissented:

[U]nder the statute before us a man can be convicted without any proof of interstate movement, of the use of the facilities of interstate commerce, or of facts showing that his conduct affected interstate commerce. I think the Framers of the Constitution never intended that the National Government might define as a crime and prosecute such wholly local activity through the enactment of federal criminal laws.

In order to sustain this law we would, in my view, have to be able at the least to say that Congress could rationally have concluded that loan sharking is an activity with interstate attributes that distinguish it in some substantial respect from other local crime. But it is not enough to say that loan sharking is a national problem, for all crime is a national problem. It is not enough to say that some loan sharking has interstate characteristics, for any crime may have an interstate setting. And the circumstance that loan sharking has an adverse impact on interstate business is not a distinguishing attribute, for interstate business suffers from almost all criminal activity, be it shoplifting or violence in the streets....

3. The Court, in *Heart of Atlanta Motel, McClung,* and *Perez,* emphasized that Congress need not make formal findings. Why not? A court normally would not uphold a rule of an administrative agency made without any findings. What is the justification for treating Congress differently?

4. FOOTNOTE 4 OF CAROLENE PRODUCTS. *Katzenbach v. McClung* cited and relied on *United States v. Carolene Products Co.,* 304 U.S. 144, 152, 58 S.Ct. 778, 783, 82 L.Ed. 1234 (1938). That case held that the "Filled Milk Act of 1923," which prohibits the shipment in interstate commerce of skimmed milk compounded with any fat or oil other than milk fat, so as to resemble milk or cream, was valid under the interstate commerce clause and did not infringe on the Fifth Amendment. Section 62 of the Act stated that filled milk is "injurious to the public health, and its sale constitutes a fraud upon the public." At the particular page that *McClung* cited (304 U.S. at 152), Stone, J., for the Court, stated:

> We may assume for present purposes that no pronouncement of a legislature can forestall attack upon the constitutionality of the prohibition which it enacts by applying opprobrious epithets to the prohibited act, and that a statute would deny due process which precluded the disproof in judicial proceedings of all facts which would show or tend to show that a statute depriving the suitor of life, liberty or property had a rational basis.

> But such we think is not the purpose or construction of the statutory characterization of filled milk as injurious to health and as a fraud upon the public. There is no need to consider it here as more than a declaration of the legislative findings deemed to support and justify the action taken as a constitutional exertion of the legislative power, aiding informed judicial review, as do the reports of legislative committees, by revealing the rationale of the legislation. Even in the absence of such aids the existence of facts supporting the legislative judgment is to be presumed, for regulatory legislation affecting ordinary commercial transactions is not to be pronounced unconstitutional unless in the light of the facts made known or generally assumed it is of such a character as to preclude the assumption that it rests upon some rational basis within the knowledge and experience of the legislators....

At the end of this last word, "legislators," Stone added footnote number 4, which said:

> There may be narrower scope for operation of the presumption of constitutionality when legislation appears on its face to be within a specific prohibition of the Constitution, such as those of the first ten amendments, which are deemed equally specific when held to be embraced within the Fourteenth. See *Stromberg v. California,* 283 U.S. 359, 369, 370, 51 S.Ct. 532, 535, 536, 75 L.Ed. 1117, 73 A.L.R. 1484; *Lovell v. Griffin,* 303 U.S. 444, 58 S.Ct. 666, 82 L.Ed. 949.

> It is unnecessary to consider now whether legislation which restricts those political processes which can ordinarily be expected to bring about repeal of undesirable legislation, is to be subjected to more

exacting judicial scrutiny under the general prohibitions of the Fourteenth Amendment than are most other types of legislation. On restrictions upon the right to vote, see *Nixon v. Herndon,* 273 U.S. 536, 47 S.Ct. 446, 71 L.Ed. 759; *Nixon v. Condon,* 286 U.S. 73, 52 S.Ct. 484, 76 L.Ed. 984, 88 A.L.R. 458; on restraints upon the dissemination of information, see *Near v. Minnesota,* 283 U.S. 697, 713–714, 718–720, 722, 51 S.Ct. 625, 630, 632, 633, 75 L.Ed. 1357; *Grosjean v. American Press Co.,* 297 U.S. 233, 56 S.Ct. 444, 80 L.Ed. 660; *Lovell v. Griffin,* supra; on interferences with political organizations, see *Stromberg v. California,* supra, 283 U.S. 359, 369, 51 S.Ct. 532, 535, 75 L.Ed. 1117, 73 A.L.R. 1484; *Fiske v. Kansas,* 274 U.S. 380, 47 S.Ct. 655, 71 L.Ed. 1108; *Whitney v. California,* 274 U.S. 357, 373–378, 47 S.Ct. 641, 647, 649, 71 L.Ed. 1095; *Herndon v. Lowry,* 301 U.S. 242, 57 S.Ct. 732, 81 L.Ed. 1066; and see Holmes, J., in *Gitlow v. New York,* 268 U.S. 652, 673, 45 S.Ct. 625, 69 L.Ed. 1138; as to prohibition of peaceable assembly, see *De Jonge v. Oregon,* 299 U.S. 353, 365, 57 S.Ct. 255, 260, 81 L.Ed. 278.

Nor need we enquire whether similar considerations enter into the review of statutes directed at particular religious, *Pierce v. Society of Sisters,* 268 U.S. 510, 45 S.Ct. 571, 69 L.Ed. 1070, 39 A.L.R. 468, or national, *Meyer v. Nebraska,* 262 U.S. 390, 43 S.Ct. 625, 67 L.Ed. 1042, 29 A.L.R. 1446; *Bartels v. Iowa,* 262 U.S. 404, 43 S.Ct. 628, 67 L.Ed. 1047; *Farrington v. Tokushige,* 273 U.S. 284, 47 S.Ct. 406, 71 L.Ed. 646, or racial minorities. *Nixon v. Herndon,* supra; *Nixon v. Condon,* supra: whether prejudice against discrete and insular minorities may be a special condition, which tends seriously to curtail the operation of those political processes ordinarily to be relied upon to protect minorities, and which may call for a correspondingly more searching judicial inquiry. Compare *McCulloch v. Maryland,* 4 Wheat. 316, 428, 4 L.Ed. 579; *South Carolina State Highway Department v. Barnwell Brothers,* 303 U.S. 177, 58 S.Ct. 510, 82 L.Ed. 734, decided February 14, 1938, note 2, and cases cited.

Given the great deference that the Court gives Congress in upholding the validity of laws under the Commerce Clause, how can the Court logically give less deference to Congress when its laws affect civil rights rather than property rights? Should the standard of review be a function of the right involved?

One should think about the issue raised in footnote 4 of *Carolene Products* not only at this juncture but throughout the course.

Cf. *Lynch v. Household Finance Corp.,* 405 U.S. 538, 92 S.Ct. 1113, 31 L.Ed.2d 424 (1972). Title 28, U.S.C.A. § 1343(3) gives the federal district courts original jurisdiction in an action to redress, under color of state law, any deprivation of any right, privilege, or immunity secured by the U.S. Constitution or by any Act of Congress providing for equal rights. In *Lynch* the Court, per Stewart, J., held that § 1343(3) does not distinguish between personal and property rights and therefore that § 1343(3) provides a federal forum to redress wrongful deprivations of property by persons acting under color of state law:

[T]he dichotomy between personal liberties and property rights is a false one. Property does not have rights. People have rights. The right to enjoy property without unlawful deprivation, no less than the right to speak or the right to travel, is in truth a "personal" right, whether the "property" in question be a welfare check, a home, or a savings account. In fact, a fundamental interdependence exists between the personal right to liberty and the personal right in property. Neither could have meaning without the other. That rights in property are basic civil rights has long been recognized. J. Locke, Of Civil Government 82–85 (1924); J. Adams, A Defence of the Constitutions of Government of the United States of America, in F. Coker, Democracy, Liberty, and Property 121–132 (1942); 1 W. Blackstone, Commentaries *138–140.

UNITED STATES v. LOPEZ
514 U.S. 549, 115 S.Ct. 1624, 131 L.Ed.2d 626 (1995).

CHIEF JUSTICE REHNQUIST delivered the opinion of the Court.

In the Gun–Free School Zones Act of 1990, Congress made it a federal offense "for any individual knowingly to possess a firearm at a place that the individual knows, or has reasonable cause to believe, is a school zone." 18 U.S.C. § 922(q)(1)(A). The Act neither regulates a commercial activity nor contains a requirement that the possession be connected in any way to interstate commerce. We hold that the Act exceeds the authority of Congress "[t]o regulate Commerce . . . among the several States. . . . "

On March 10, 1992, respondent, who was then a 12th-grade student, arrived at Edison High School in San Antonio, Texas, carrying a concealed .38 caliber handgun and five bullets. Acting upon an anonymous tip, school authorities confronted respondent, who admitted that he was carrying the weapon. He was arrested and charged under Texas law with firearm possession on school premises. The next day, the state charges were dismissed after federal agents charged respondent by complaint with violating the Gun–Free School Zones Act of 1990. 18 U.S.C. § 922(q)(1)(A).[10] . . .

On appeal, respondent challenged his conviction based on his claim that § 922(q) exceeded Congress' power to legislate under the Commerce Clause. The Court of Appeals for the Fifth Circuit agreed and reversed respondent's conviction. It held that, in light of what it characterized as insufficient congressional findings and legislative history, "section 922(q), in the full reach of its terms, is invalid as beyond the power of Congress under the Commerce Clause." [W]e now affirm. . . .

Jones & Laughlin Steel, Darby, and *Wickard* ushered in an era of Commerce Clause jurisprudence that greatly expanded the previously defined authority of Congress under that Clause. In part, this was a recognition of the great changes that had occurred in the way business was carried on in this country. Enterprises that had once been local or at most regional in nature had become national in scope. But the doctrinal

---

10. The term "school zone" is defined as "in, or on the grounds of, a public, parochial or private school" or "within a distance of 1,000 feet from the grounds of a public, parochial or private school." § 921(a)(25).

change also reflected a view that earlier Commerce Clause cases artificially had constrained the authority of Congress to regulate interstate commerce.

But even these modern-era precedents which have expanded congressional power under the Commerce Clause confirm that this power is subject to outer limits. In *Jones & Laughlin Steel,* the Court warned that the scope of the interstate commerce power "must be considered in the light of our dual system of government and may not be extended so as to embrace effects upon interstate commerce so indirect and remote that to embrace them, in view of our complex society, would effectively obliterate the distinction between what is national and what is local and create a completely centralized government." ... [11]

Consistent with this structure, we have identified three broad categories of activity that Congress may regulate under its commerce power. *Perez v. United States, supra.* First, Congress may regulate the use of the channels of interstate commerce. See, *e.g., Darby, Heart of Atlanta Motel.* Second, Congress is empowered to regulate and protect the instrumentalities of interstate commerce, or persons or things in interstate commerce, even though the threat may come only from intrastate activities. See, *e.g., Shreveport Rate Cases; Perez, supra....*

Finally, Congress' commerce authority includes the power to regulate those activities having a substantial relation to interstate commerce, *Jones & Laughlin Steel, i.e.,* those activities that substantially affect interstate commerce.

Within this final category, admittedly, our case law has not been clear whether an activity must "affect" or "substantially affect" interstate commerce in order to be within Congress' power to regulate it under the Commerce Clause. We conclude, consistent with the great weight of our case law, that the proper test requires an analysis of whether the regulated activity "substantially affects" interstate commerce.

We now turn to consider the power of Congress, in the light of this framework, to enact § 922(q). The first two categories of authority may be quickly disposed of: § 922(q) is not a regulation of the use of the channels of interstate commerce, nor is it an attempt to prohibit the interstate transportation of a commodity through the channels of commerce; nor can § 922(q) be justified as a regulation by which Congress has sought to protect an instrumentality of interstate commerce or a thing in interstate commerce. Thus, if § 922(q) is to be sustained, it must be under the third category as a regulation of an activity that substantially affects interstate commerce....

---

11. ... *Heart of Atlanta Motel, Inc.,* 379 U.S. at 273, 85 S.Ct. at 366 ("[W]hether particular operations affect interstate commerce sufficiently to come under the constitutional power of Congress to regulate them is ultimately a judicial rather than a legislative question, and can be settled finally only by this Court")(Black, J., concurring).

Even *Wickard,* which is perhaps the most far reaching example of Commerce Clause authority over intrastate activity, involved economic activity in a way that the possession of a gun in a school zone does not.... The Court said, in an opinion sustaining the application of the Act to Filburn's activity:

"... But if we assume that it is never marketed, it supplies a need of the man who grew it which would otherwise be reflected by purchases in the open market. Home-grown wheat in this sense competes with wheat in commerce."

Section 922(q) is a criminal statute that by its terms has nothing to do with "commerce" or any sort of economic enterprise, however broadly one might define those terms. Section 922(q) is not an essential part of a larger regulation of economic activity, in which the regulatory scheme could be undercut unless the intrastate activity were regulated. It cannot, therefore, be sustained under our cases upholding regulations of activities that arise out of or are connected with a commercial transaction, which viewed in the aggregate, substantially affects interstate commerce.

Second, § 922(q) contains no jurisdictional element which would ensure, through case-by-case inquiry, that the firearm possession in question affects interstate commerce. For example, in *United States v. Bass,* 404 U.S. 336, 92 S.Ct. 515, 30 L.Ed.2d 488 (1971), the Court interpreted former 18 U.S.C. § 1202(a), which made it a crime for a felon to "receiv[e], posses[s], or transpor[t] in commerce or affecting commerce ... any firearm." The Court interpreted the possession component of § 1202(a) to require an additional nexus to interstate commerce both because the statute was ambiguous and because "unless Congress conveys its purpose clearly, it will not be deemed to have significantly changed the federal-state balance." The *Bass* Court set aside the conviction because although the Government had demonstrated that Bass had possessed a firearm, it had failed "to show the requisite nexus with interstate commerce." The Court thus interpreted the statute to reserve the constitutional question whether Congress could regulate, without more, the "mere possession" of firearms....

Although as part of our independent evaluation of constitutionality under the Commerce Clause we of course consider legislative findings, and indeed even congressional committee findings, regarding effect on interstate commerce, the Government concedes that "[n]either the statute nor its legislative history contain[s] express congressional findings regarding the effects upon interstate commerce of gun possession in a school zone." We agree with the Government that Congress normally is not required to make formal findings as to the substantial burdens that an activity has on interstate commerce. But to the extent that congressional findings would enable us to evaluate the legislative judgment that the activity in question substantially affected interstate commerce, even though no such substantial effect was visible to the naked eye, they are lacking here.[4]

The Government argues that Congress has accumulated institutional expertise regarding the regulation of firearms through previous enactments. We agree, however, with the Fifth Circuit that importation of previous findings to justify § 922(q) is especially inappropriate here because the "prior federal enactments or Congressional findings [do not] speak to the subject matter of section 922(q) or its relationship to interstate commerce. Indeed, section 922(q) plows thoroughly new ground and represents a sharp break with the longstanding pattern of federal firearms legislation."

The Government's essential contention, *in fine,* is that we may determine here that § 922(q) is valid because possession of a firearm in a local school zone does indeed substantially affect interstate commerce. [T]he presence of guns in schools poses a substantial threat to the educational process by threatening the learning environment. A handicapped educational process, in turn, will result in a less productive citizenry. That, in turn, would have an adverse effect on the Nation's economic well-being. As a result, the Government argues that Congress could rationally have concluded that § 922(q) substantially affects interstate commerce. . . . The Government admits, under its "cost of crime" reasoning, that Congress could regulate not only all violent crime but all activities that might lead to violent crime, regardless of how tenuous they relate to interstate commerce. Similarly, under the Government's "national productivity" reasoning, Congress could regulate any activity that it found was related to the economic productivity of individual citizens: family law (including marriage, divorce, and child custody), for example. [I]f we were to accept the Government's arguments, we are hard-pressed to posit any activity by an individual that Congress is without power to regulate.

Although Justice Breyer argues that acceptance of the Government's rationales would not authorize a general federal police power, he is unable to identify any activity that the States may regulate but Congress may not. Justice Breyer posits that there might be some limitations on Congress' commerce power such as family law or certain aspects of education. These suggested limitations, when viewed in light of the dissent's expansive analysis, are devoid of substance.

Justice Breyer focuses, for the most part, on the threat that firearm possession in and near schools poses to the educational process and the potential economic consequences flowing from that threat. Specifically, the dissent reasons that (1) gun-related violence is a serious problem; (2) that problem, in turn, has an adverse effect on classroom learning; and

---

4. We note that on September 13, 1994, President Clinton signed into law the Violent Crime Control and Law Enforcement Act of 1994, Pub.L. 103–322, 108 Stat. 1796. Section 320904 of that Act, amends § 922(q) to include congressional findings regarding the effects of firearm possession in and around schools upon interstate and foreign commerce. The Government does not rely upon these subsequent findings as a substitute for the absence of findings in the first instance. . . .

(3) that adverse effect on classroom learning, in turn, represents a substantial threat to trade and commerce. This analysis would be equally applicable, if not more so, to subjects such as family law and direct regulation of education. . . .

Admittedly, a determination whether an intrastate activity is commercial or noncommercial may in some cases result in legal uncertainty. But, so long as Congress' authority is limited to those powers enumerated in the Constitution, and so long as those enumerated powers are interpreted as having judicially enforceable outer limits, congressional legislation under the Commerce Clause always will engender "legal uncertainty." . . . The Constitution mandates this uncertainty by withholding from Congress a plenary police power that would authorize enactment of every type of legislation. . . . In *Jones & Laughlin Steel,* we held that the question of congressional power under the Commerce Clause "is necessarily one of degree." . . .

These are not precise formulations, and in the nature of things they cannot be. But we think they point the way to a correct decision of this case. The possession of a gun in a local school zone is in no sense an economic activity that might, through repetition elsewhere, substantially affect any sort of interstate commerce. Respondent was a local student at a local school; there is no indication that he had recently moved in interstate commerce, and there is no requirement that his possession of the firearm have any concrete tie to interstate commerce.

To uphold the Government's contentions here, we would have to pile inference upon inference in a manner that would bid fair to convert congressional authority under the Commerce Clause to a general police power of the sort retained by the States. Admittedly, some of our prior cases have taken long steps down that road, giving great deference to congressional action. The broad language in these opinions has suggested the possibility of additional expansion, but we decline here to proceed any further. To do so would require us to conclude that the Constitution's enumeration of powers does not presuppose something not enumerated, and that there never will be a distinction between what is truly national and what is truly local. This we are unwilling to do.

For the foregoing reasons the judgment of the Court of Appeals is

Affirmed.

JUSTICE KENNEDY, with whom JUSTICE O'CONNOR joins, concurring. . . .

The statute now before us forecloses the States from experimenting and exercising their own judgment in an area to which States lay claim by right of history and expertise, and it does so by regulating an activity beyond the realm of commerce in the ordinary and usual sense of that term. The tendency of this statute to displace state regulation in areas of traditional state concern is evident from its territorial operation. There are over 100,000 elementary and secondary schools in the United States. Each of these now has an invisible federal zone extending 1,000 feet beyond the (often irregular) boundaries of the school property. In some communities no doubt it would be difficult to navigate without infringing on those zones. Yet throughout these areas, school officials would find their own programs for the prohibition of guns in danger of displacement by the federal authority unless the State chooses to enact a parallel rule. . . .

JUSTICE THOMAS, concurring.

. . . Although I join the majority, I write separately to observe that our case law has drifted far from the original understanding of the Commerce Clause. In a future case, we ought to temper our Commerce Clause jurisprudence in a manner that both makes sense of our more recent case law and is more faithful to the original understanding of that Clause.

We have said that Congress may regulate not only "Commerce . . . among the several states," but also anything that has a "substantial effect" on such commerce. This test, if taken to its logical extreme, would give Congress a "police power" over all aspects of American life. Unfortunately, we have never come to grips with this implication of our substantial effects formula. Although we have supposedly applied the substantial effects test for the past 60 years, we *always* have rejected readings of the Commerce Clause and the scope of federal power that would permit Congress to exercise a police power; our cases are quite clear that there are real limits to federal power. Indeed, on this crucial point, the majority and Justice Breyer agree in principle: the Federal Government has nothing approaching a police power. . . . At an appropriate juncture, I think we must modify our Commerce Clause jurisprudence. Today, it is easy enough to say that the Clause certainly does not empower Congress to ban gun possession within 1,000 feet of a school.

JUSTICE STEVENS, dissenting.

The welfare of our future "Commerce with foreign Nations, and among the several States," is vitally dependent on the character of the education of our children. . . . Congress has ample power to prohibit the possession of firearms in or near schools—just as it may protect the school environment from harms posed by controlled substances such as asbestos or alcohol. . . .

JUSTICE BREYER, with whom JUSTICE STEVENS, JUSTICE SOUTER, and JUSTICE GINSBURG join, dissenting.

The issue in this case is whether the Commerce Clause authorizes Congress to enact a statute that makes it a crime to possess a gun in, or near, a school. In my view, the statute falls well within the scope of the commerce power as this Court has understood that power over the last half-century. In reaching this conclusion, I apply three basic principles of Commerce Clause interpretation. First, the power to "regulate Commerce . . . among the several States," encompasses the power to regulate local activities insofar as they significantly affect interstate commerce.... I use the word "significant" because the word "substantial" implies a somewhat narrower power than recent precedent suggests....

Second, in determining whether a local activity will likely have a significant effect upon interstate commerce, a court must consider, not the effect of an individual act (a single instance of gun possession), but rather the cumulative effect of all similar instances (*i.e.,* the effect of all guns possessed in or near schools). See, *e.g., Wickard, supra....*

Third, the Constitution requires us to judge the connection between a regulated activity and interstate commerce, not directly, but at one remove. Courts must give Congress a degree of leeway in determining the existence of a significant factual connection between the regulated activity and interstate commerce—both because the Constitution delegates the commerce power directly to Congress and because the determination requires an empirical judgment of a kind that a legislature is more likely than a court to make with accuracy. The traditional words "rational basis" capture this leeway.... I recognize that we must judge this matter independently. "[S]imply because Congress may conclude that a particular activity substantially affects interstate commerce does not necessarily make it so."

... Congress could have found that gun-related violence near the classroom poses a serious economic threat (1) to consequently inadequately educated workers who must endure low paying jobs, and (2) to communities and businesses that might (in today's "information society") otherwise gain, from a well-educated work force, an important commercial advantage, of a kind that location near a railhead or harbor provided in the past. Congress might also have found these threats to be no different in kind from other threats that this Court has found within the commerce power, such as the threat that loan sharking poses to the "funds" of "numerous localities," *Perez v. United States,....*

To hold this statute constitutional is not to "obliterate" the "distinction of what is national and what is local," nor is it to hold that the Commerce Clause permits the Federal Government to "regulate any activity that it found was related to the economic productivity of individual citizens," to regulate "marriage, divorce, and child custody," or to regulate any and all aspects of education. For one thing, this statute is aimed at curbing a particularly acute threat to the educational process— the possession (and use) of life-threatening firearms in, or near, the classroom....

The majority's holding—that § 922 falls outside the scope of the Commerce Clause—creates three serious legal problems. First, the majority's holding runs contrary to modern Supreme Court cases that have upheld congressional actions despite connections to interstate or foreign commerce that are less significant than the effect of school violence.... The second legal problem the Court creates comes from its apparent belief that it can reconcile its holding with earlier cases by making a critical distinction between "commercial" and noncommercial "transaction[s]." ... The third legal problem created by the Court's holding is that it threatens legal uncertainty in an area of law that, until this case, seemed reasonably well settled....

[The dissenting opinion of SOUTER, J., is omitted.]

Notes

1.   The appellate court decision in *Lopez* noted that the federal law in question "makes it a federal offense to carry an unloaded firearm in an unlocked suitcase on a public sidewalk in front of one's residence, so long as that part of the sidewalk is within one thousand feet—two or three city blocks—of the boundary of the grounds of public or private school anywhere in the United States, regardless of whether it is during the school year or the school is in session." 2 F.3d 1342, 1346 n. 4 (5th Cir.1993).

Lopez did not overrule any prior case. Do you think that this case represents a watershed in commerce clause jurisprudence, or does it merely overturn a poorly drafted statute? Should this case come out differently if the Government proved that the defendant had purchased his gun from an out of state vendor?

2.   Less than a week after *Lopez,* the Court decided *United States v. Robertson,* 514 U.S. 669, 115 S.Ct. 1732, 131 L.Ed.2d 714 (1995)(per curiam). The Government prosecuted Juan Robertson for various narcotics offenses and for violating a provision of the Racketeer Influenced and Corrupt Organizations Act by investing proceeds of those unlawful activities in the "acquisition of any interest in, or the establishment or operations of, any enterprise which is engaged in, or the activities of which affect, interstate or foreign commerce." Robertson invested in a gold mine in Alaska. He was convicted on both the narcotics count and the RICO count, but the Ninth Circuit reversed the RICO count because the Government had failed to introduce sufficient evidence that the gold mine was "engaged in or affect[ed] interstate commerce." With no dissent, the Supreme Court reversed, and ruled that it was unnecessary to consider whether the activities of the gold mine "affected" interstate commerce, because the "affects" test is only necessary to "define the extent of Congress's power over purely *intra*state commercial activities that nonetheless have substantial *inter*state effects." In this case, there was proof of interstate commercial activity: money, workers, and goods crossed state lines. For example, Robertson purchased at least some mining equipment in California that was transported to Alaska. Robertson also transported $300,000 of gold (about 15% of the mine's total output) out of state. He sought workers from out of state and brought them to Alaska. Hence, under the statute the gold mine was an enterprise that was "engaged in ... interstate or foreign commerce." A corporation is engaged in such commerce "when it is itself 'directly engaged in the production, distribution, or acquisition of goods and services in interstate commerce.'"

4–5. MODERN TENTH AMENDMENT RESTRICTIONS ON THE COMMERCE POWER

NATIONAL LEAGUE OF CITIES v. USERY
426 U.S. 833, 96 S.Ct. 2465, 49 L.Ed.2d 245 (1976).

MR. JUSTICE REHNQUIST delivered the opinion of the Court.

Nearly 40 years ago Congress enacted the Fair Labor Standards Act [which was upheld] as a valid exercise of congressional authority under the commerce power in *United States v. Darby* [§ 4–2, supra].... The original Fair Labor Standards Act passed in 1938 specifically excluded the States and their political subdivisions from its coverage....

In a series of amendments beginning in 1961 Congress began to extend the provisions of the Fair Labor Standards Act to some types of public employees. The 1961 amendments to the Act extended its coverage to persons who were employed in "enterprises" engaged in commerce or in the production of goods for commerce. And in 1966, with the amendment of the definition of employers under the Act, the exemption heretofore extended to the States and their political subdivisions was removed with respect to employees of state hospitals, institutions, and schools. We nevertheless sustained the validity of the combined effect of these two amendments in *Maryland v. Wirtz*, 392 U.S. 183, 88 S.Ct. 2017, 20 L.Ed.2d 1020 (1968). [W]e have decided that the "far-reaching implications" of *Wirtz* should be overruled, and that the judgment of the District Court must be reversed....

... Appellants' essential contention is that the 1974 amendments to the Act, while undoubtedly within the scope of the Commerce Clause, encounter a ... constitutional barrier because they are to be applied directly to the States and subdivisions of States as employers.[12]

This Court has never doubted that there are limits upon the power of Congress to override state sovereignty, even when exercising its otherwise plenary powers to tax or to regulate commerce which are

---

12. Mr. Justice Brennan's dissent intimates that guarantees of individual liberties are the only sort of constitutional restrictions which this Court will enforce as against congressional action. It reasons that "Congress is constituted of representatives in both Senate and House *elected from the States*.... Decisions upon the extent of federal intervention under the Commerce Clause into the affairs of the States are in that sense decisions of the States themselves." Precisely what is meant by the phrase "are in that sense decisions of the States themselves" is not entirely clear from this language....

In *Myers v. United States*, 272 U.S. 52, 47 S.Ct. 21, 71 L.Ed. 160 (1926), the Court held that Congress could not by law limit the authority of the President to remove at will an officer of the Executive Branch appointed by him. In *Buckley v. Valeo*, 424 U.S. 1, 96 S.Ct. 612, 46 L.Ed.2d 659 (1976), the Court held that Congress could not constitutionally require that members of the Federal Elections Commission be appointed by officers of the House of Representatives and of the Senate, and that all such appointments had to be made by the President.... Just as the dissent contends that "the States are fully able to protect their own interests ... ," it could have been contended that the President, armed with the mandate of a national constituency and with the veto power, was able to protect *his* own interests. Nonetheless, in both cases the laws were held unconstitutional, because they trenched on the authority of the Executive Branch.

conferred by Art. I of the Constitution.... In *Fry* [*v. U.S.*, 421 U.S. 542, 95 S.Ct. 1792, 44 L.Ed.2d 363 (1975)], the Court recognized that an express declaration of this limitation is found in the Tenth Amendment:

> While the Tenth Amendment has been characterized as a "truism," stating merely that "all is retained which has not been surrendered," *United States v. Darby,* it is not without significance. The Amendment expressly declares the constitutional policy that Congress may not exercise power in a fashion that impairs the States' integrity or their ability to function effectively in a federal system.

In *New York v. United States,* 326 U.S. 572, 66 S.Ct. 310, 90 L.Ed. 326 (1946), Mr. Chief Justice Stone, speaking for four Members of an eight-Member Court in rejecting the proposition that Congress could impose taxes on the States so long as it did so in a nondiscriminatory manner, observed:

> A State may, like a private individual, own real property and receive income. But in view of our former decisions we could hardly say that a general non-discriminatory real estate tax (apportioned), or an income tax laid upon citizens and States alike could be constitutionally applied to the State's capitol, its State-house, its public school houses, public parks, or its revenues from taxes or school lands, even though all real property and all income of the citizen is taxed....

... It is one thing to recognize the authority of Congress to enact laws regulating individual businesses necessarily subject to the dual sovereignty of the government of the Nation and of the State in which they reside. It is quite another to uphold a similar exercise of congressional authority directed, not to private citizens, but to the States as States. We have repeatedly recognized that there are attributes of sovereignty attaching to every state government which may not be impaired by Congress, not because Congress may lack an affirmative grant of legislative authority to reach the matter, but because the Constitution prohibits it from exercising the authority in that manner.... One undoubted attribute of state sovereignty is the States' power to determine the wages which shall be paid to those whom they employ in order to carry out their governmental functions, what hours those persons will work, and what compensation will be provided where these employees may be called upon to work overtime. The question we must resolve here, then, is whether these determinations are " 'functions essential to separate and independent existence,' " so that Congress may not abrogate the States' otherwise plenary authority to make them.

In their complaint appellants advanced estimates of substantial costs which will be imposed upon them by the 1974 amendments. Since the District Court dismissed their complaint, we take its well-pleaded allegations as true.... Quite apart from the substantial costs imposed upon the States and their political subdivisions, the Act displaces state policies regarding the manner in which they will structure delivery of those governmental services which their citizens require. The Act, speaking directly to the States *qua* States, requires that they shall pay all but an extremely limited minority of their employees the minimum wage rates currently chosen by Congress. . . .

Our examination of the effect of the 1974 amendments, as sought to be extended to the States and their political subdivisions, satisfies us that both the minimum wage and the maximum hour provisions will impermissibly interfere with the integral governmental functions of these bodies. [The 1974 amendments will] significantly alter or displace the States' abilities to structure employer-employee relationships in such areas as fire prevention, police protection, sanitation, public health, and parks and recreation. These activities are typical of those performed by state and local governments in discharging their dual functions of administering the public law and furnishing public services.[16] Indeed, it is functions such as these which governments are created to provide, services such as these which the States have traditionally afforded their citizens. If Congress may withdraw from the States the authority to make those fundamental employment decisions upon which their systems for performance of these functions must rest, we think there would be little left of the States' " 'separate and independent existence.' " . . . We hold that insofar as the challenged amendments operate to directly displace the States' freedom to structure integral operations in areas of traditional governmental functions, they are not within the authority granted Congress by Art. I, § 8, cl. 3.[17]

One final matter requires our attention. Appellee has vigorously urged that we cannot, consistently with the Court's decisions in *Maryland v. Wirtz,* 392 U.S. 183, 88 S.Ct. 2017, 20 L.Ed.2d 1020 (1968), and *Fry* [*v. U.S.,* 421 U.S. 542, 95 S.Ct. 1792, 44 L.Ed.2d 363 (1975)], rule against him here. It is important to examine this contention so that it will be clear what we hold today, and what we do not.

With regard to *Fry,* we disagree with appellee. There the Court held that the Economic Stabilization Act of 1970 was constitutional as applied to temporarily freeze the wages of state and local government employees. The Court expressly noted that the degree of intrusion upon the protected area of state sovereignty was in that case even less than that worked by the amendments to the FLSA which were before the Court in *Wirtz.* The Court recognized that the Economic Stabilization Act was "an emergency measure to counter severe inflation that threatened the national economy."

We think our holding today quite consistent with *Fry.* The enactment at issue there was occasioned by an extremely serious problem which endangered the well-being of all the component parts of our

---

16. These examples are obviously not an exhaustive catalogue of the numerous line and support activities which are well within the area of traditional operations of state and local governments.

17. We express no view as to whether different results might obtain if Congress seeks to affect integral operations of state governments by exercising authority granted it under other sections of the Constitution such as the spending power, Art. I, § 8, cl. 1, or § 5 of the Fourteenth Amendment.

federal system and which only collective action by the National Government might forestall. The means selected were carefully drafted so as not to interfere with the States' freedom beyond a very limited, specific period of time. The effect of the across-the-board freeze authorized by that Act, moreover, displaced no state choices as to how governmental operations should be structured, nor did it force the States to remake such choices themselves. Instead, it merely required that the wage scales and employment relationships which the States themselves had chosen be maintained during the period of the emergency. Finally, the Economic Stabilization Act operated to reduce the pressures upon state budgets rather than increase them. These factors distinguish the statute in *Fry* from the provisions at issue here. The limits imposed upon the commerce power when Congress seeks to apply it to the States are not so inflexible as to preclude temporary enactments tailored to combat a national emergency....

With respect to the Court's decision in *Wirtz,* we reach a different conclusion. [W]e view of the conclusions expressed earlier in this opinion we do not believe the reasoning in *Wirtz* may any longer be regarded as authoritative.... [18] Congress may not exercise that power so as to force directly upon the States its choices as to how essential decisions regarding the conduct of integral governmental functions are to be made. We agree that such assertions of power, if unchecked, would indeed, as Mr. Justice Douglas cautioned in his dissent in *Wirtz,* allow "the National Government [to] devour the essentials of state sovereignty," and would therefore transgress the bounds of the authority granted Congress under the Commerce Clause. While there are obvious differences between the schools and hospitals involved in *Wirtz,* and the fire and police departments affected here, each provides an integral portion of those governmental services which the States and their political subdivisions have traditionally afforded their citizens. We are therefore persuaded that *Wirtz* must be overruled....

MR. JUSTICE BLACKMUN, concurring.

... Although I am not untroubled by certain possible implications of the Court's opinion—some of them suggested by the dissents—I do not read the opinion so despairingly as does my Brother Brennan. In my view, the result with respect to the statute under challenge here is necessarily correct. I may misinterpret the Court's opinion, but it seems to me that it adopts a balancing approach, and does not outlaw federal power in areas such as environmental protection, where the federal interest is demonstrably greater and where state facility compliance with imposed federal standards would be essential. With this understanding on my part of the Court's opinion, I join it.

---

18. The holding of *United States v. California,* [297 U.S. 175, 56 S.Ct. 421, 80 L.Ed. 567 (1936)] ... is quite consistent with our holding today. There California's activity to which the congressional command was directed was not in an area that the States have regarded as integral parts of their governmental activities. It was, on the contrary, the operation of a railroad engaged in "common carriage by rail in interstate commerce...." ...

Mr. Justice Brennan, with whom Mr. Justice White and Mr. Justice Marshall join, dissenting. . . .

My Brethren thus have today manufactured an abstraction without substance, founded neither in the words of the Constitution nor on precedent. An abstraction having such profoundly pernicious consequences is not made less so by characterizing the 1974 amendments as legislation directed against the "States *qua* States." . . . The reliance of my Brethren upon the Tenth Amendment as "an express declaration of [a state sovereignty] limitation," not only suggests that they overrule governing decisions of this Court that address this question but must astound scholars of the Constitution. . . .

. . . The only analysis even remotely resembling that adopted today is found in a line of opinions dealing with the Commerce Clause and the Tenth Amendment that ultimately provoked a constitutional crisis for the Court in the 1930's. E.g., *Carter v. Carter Coal Co.; United States v. Butler; Hammer v. Dagenhart* . . . My Brethren boldly assert that the decision as to wages and hours is an "undoubted attribute of state sovereignty," and then never say why. Indeed, they disclaim any reliance on the costs of compliance with the amendments in reaching today's result. . . .

Judicial restraint in this area merely recognizes that the political branches of our Government are structured to protect the interests of the States, as well as the Nation as a whole, and that the States are fully able to protect their own interests in the premises. Congress is constituted of representatives in both the Senate and House *elected from the States*. [T]he 1966 FSLA amendments are struck down and *Wirtz* is overruled on the basis of the conceptually unworkable essential-function test; and that the test is unworkable is demonstrated by my Brethren's inability to articulate any meaningful distinctions among state-operated railroads, see ante, n. 18, state-operated schools and hospitals, and state-operated police and fire departments.

We are left then with a catastrophic judicial body blow at Congress' power under the Commerce Clause. Even if Congress may nevertheless accomplish its objectives—for example, by conditioning grants of federal funds upon compliance with federal minimum wage and overtime standards—there is an ominous portent of disruption of our constitutional structure implicit in today's mischievous decision. I dissent.

Mr. Justice Stevens, dissenting. . . .

The Federal Government may, I believe, require the State to act impartially when it hires or fires the janitor, to withhold taxes from his paycheck, to observe safety regulations when he is performing his job, to forbid him from burning too much soft coal in the capitol furnace, from dumping untreated refuse in an adjacent waterway, from overloading a state-owned garbage truck, or from driving either the truck or the Governor's limousine over 55 miles an hour. Even though these and many other activities of the capitol janitor are activities of the State *qua* State, I have no doubt that they are subject to federal regulation. . . .

GARCIA v. SAN ANTONIO METROPOLITAN TRANSIT AUTHORITY

469 U.S. 528, 105 S.Ct. 1005, 83 L.Ed.2d 1016 (1985).

JUSTICE BLACKMUN delivered the opinion of the Court.

We revisit in these cases an issue raised in *National League of Cities v. Usery.* In that litigation, this Court, by a sharply divided vote, ruled that the Commerce Clause does not empower Congress to enforce the minimum-wage and overtime provisions of the Fair Labor Standards Act (FLSA) against the States "in areas of traditional governmental functions." Although *National League of Cities* supplied some examples of "traditional governmental functions," it did not offer a general explanation of how a "traditional" function is to be distinguished from a "nontraditional" one. Since then, federal and state courts have struggled with the task, thus imposed, of identifying a traditional function for purposes of state immunity under the Commerce Clause.

In the present cases, a Federal District Court concluded that municipal ownership and operation of a mass-transit system is a traditional governmental function and thus, under *National League of Cities,* is exempt from the obligations imposed by the FLSA. Faced with the identical question, three Federal Courts of Appeals and one state appellate court have reached the opposite conclusion.

Our examination of this "function" standard applied in these and other cases over the last eight years now persuades us that the attempt to draw the boundaries of state regulatory immunity in terms of "traditional governmental function" is not only unworkable but is inconsistent with established principles of federalism and, indeed, with those very federalism principles on which *National League of Cities* purported to rest. That case, accordingly, is overruled....

The present controversy concerns the extent to which [the San Antonio Metropolitan Transit Authority] SAMTA may be subjected to the minimum-wage and overtime requirements of the FLSA....

The prerequisites for governmental immunity under *National League of Cities* were summarized by this Court in *Hodel* [*v. Virginia Surface Mining & Reclamation Association, Inc.,* 452 U.S. 264, 101 S.Ct. 2352, 69 L.Ed.2d 1 (1981)]. Under that summary, four conditions must be satisfied before a state activity may be deemed immune from a particular federal regulation under the Commerce Clause. First, it is said that the federal statute at issue must regulate "the 'States as States.'" Second, the statute must "address matters that are indisputably 'attribute[s] of state sovereignty.'" Third, state compliance with the federal obligation must "directly impair [the States'] ability 'to structure integral operations in areas of traditional governmental functions.' 'Finally, the relation of state and federal interests must not be such that "the nature of the federal interest ... justifies state submission." ' "

The controversy in the present cases has focused on the third *Hodel* requirement—that the challenged federal statute trench on "traditional governmental functions." The District Court voiced a common concern: "Despite the abundance of adjectives, identifying which particular state functions are immune remains difficult." Just how troublesome the task has been is revealed by the results reached in other federal cases. Thus, [lower] courts have held that regulating ambulance services; licensing automobile drivers; operating a municipal airport; performing solid waste disposal; and operating a highway authority, are functions *protected* under *National League of Cities*. At the same time, [lower] courts have held that issuance of industrial development bonds; regulation of intrastate natural gas sales; regulation of traffic on public roads; regulation of air transportation; operation of a telephone system; leasing and sale of natural gas; operation of a mental health facility; and provision of in-house domestic services for the aged and handicapped, are *not* entitled to immunity. We find it difficult, if not impossible, to identify an organizing principle that places each of the cases in the first group on one side of a line and each of the cases in the second group on the other side. The constitutional distinction between licensing drivers and regulating traffic, for example, or between operating a highway authority and operating a mental health facility, is elusive at best.

Thus far, this Court itself has made little headway in defining the scope of the governmental functions deemed protected under *National League of Cities*. In that case the Court set forth examples of protected and unprotected functions, but provided no explanation of how those examples were identified. The only other case in which the Court has had occasion to address the problem is *Long Island....* We relied in large part there on "the *historical reality* that the operation of railroads is not among the functions *traditionally* performed by state and local governments," but we simultaneously disavowed "a static historical view of state functions generally immune from federal regulation." (first emphasis added; second emphasis in original). We held that the inquiry into a particular function's "traditional" nature was merely a means of determining whether the federal statute at issue unduly handicaps "basic state prerogatives," but we did not offer an explanation of what makes one state function a "basic prerogative" and another function not basic. Finally, having disclaimed a rigid reliance on the historical pedigree of state involvement in a particular area, we nonetheless found it appropriate to emphasize the extended historical record of *federal* involvement in the field of rail transportation.

... We rejected the possibility of making immunity turn on a purely historical standard of "tradition" in *Long Island,* and properly so. The most obvious defect of a historical approach to state immunity is that it prevents a court from accommodating changes in the historical functions of States, changes that have resulted in a number of once-private functions like education being assumed by the States and their subdivisions.[9] At the same time, the only apparent virtue of a rigorous historical standard, namely, its promise of a reasonably objective measure for state immunity, is illusory. Reliance on history as an organizing principle results in line-drawing of the most arbitrary sort; the genesis of state governmental functions stretches over a historical continuum from before the Revolution to the present, and courts would have to decide by fiat precisely how longstanding a pattern of state involvement had to be for federal regulatory authority to be defeated.[10]

A nonhistorical standard for selecting immune governmental functions is likely to be just as unworkable as is a historical standard. The goal of identifying "uniquely" governmental functions, for example, has been rejected by the Court in the field of government tort liability in part because the notion of a "uniquely" governmental function is unmanageable. Another possibility would be to confine immunity to "necessary" governmental services, that is, services that would be provided inadequately or not at all unless the government provided them. The set of services that fits into this category, however, may well be negligible. The fact that an unregulated market produces less of some service than a State deems desirable does not mean that the State itself must provide the service; in most if not all cases, the State can "contract out" by hiring private firms to provide the service or simply by providing subsidies to existing suppliers. It also is open to question how well equipped courts are to make this kind of determination about the workings of economic markets.

We believe, however, that there is a more fundamental problem at work here. . . . The problem is that neither the governmental/proprietary distinction nor any other that purports to separate out important governmental functions can be faithful to the role of federalism in a democratic society. The essence of our federal system is that within the realm of authority left open to them under the Constitution, the States must be equally free to engage in any activity that their citizens choose for the common weal, no matter how unorthodox or unnecessary anyone else—including the judiciary—deems state involvement to be. Any rule of state immunity that looks to the "traditional," "integral," or "necessary" nature of governmental functions inevitably invites an unelected federal judiciary to make decisions about which state policies it favors

---

9. Indeed, the "traditional" nature of a particular governmental function can be a matter of historical nearsightedness; today's self-evidently "traditional" function is often yesterday's suspect innovation. Thus, *National League of Cities* offered the provision of public parks and recreation as an example of a traditional governmental function. A scant 80 years earlier, however, in *Shoemaker v. United States,* 147 U.S. 282, 13 S.Ct. 361, 37 L.Ed. 170 (1893), the Court pointed out that city commons originally had been provided not for recreation but for grazing domestic animals "in common," and that "[i]n the memory of men now living, a proposition to take private property [by eminent domain] for a public park . . . would have been regarded as a novel exercise of legislative power."

10. For much the same reasons, the existence *vel non* of a tradition of *federal* involvement in a particular area does not provide an adequate standard for state immunity. Most of the Federal Government's current regulatory activity originated less than 50 years ago with the New Deal, and a good portion of it has developed within the past two decades. . . .

and which ones it dislikes. [T]he States cannot serve as laboratories for social and economic experiment, if they must pay an added price when they meet the changing needs of their citizenry by taking up functions that an earlier day and a different society left in private hands. . . .

We therefore now reject, as unsound in principle and unworkable in practice, a rule of state immunity from federal regulation that turns on a judicial appraisal of whether a particular governmental function is "integral" or "traditional." Any such rule leads to inconsistent results at the same time that it disserves principles of democratic self-governance, and it breeds inconsistency precisely because it is divorced from those principles. If there are to be limits on the Federal Government's power to interfere with state functions—as undoubtedly there are—we must look elsewhere to find them. We accordingly return to the underlying issue that confronted this Court in *National League of Cities*—the manner in which the Constitution insulates States from the reach of Congress' power under the Commerce Clause. . . . *National League of Cities* reflected the general conviction that the Constitution precludes "the National Government [from] devour[ing] the essentials of state sovereignty." . . .

The States unquestionably do "retai[n] a significant measure of sovereign authority." They do so, however, only to the extent that the Constitution has not divested them of their original powers and transferred those powers to the Federal Government. In the words of James Madison to the Members of the First Congress: "Interference with the power of the States was no constitutional criterion of the power of Congress. If the power was not given, Congress could not exercise it; if given, they might exercise it, although it should interfere with the laws, or even the Constitution of the States." 2 Annals of Cong. 1897 (1791). . . . With rare exceptions, like the guarantee, in Article IV, § 3, of state territorial integrity, the Constitution does not carve out express elements of state sovereignty that Congress may not employ its delegated powers to displace. . . .

. . . Apart from the limitation on federal authority inherent in the delegated nature of Congress' Article I powers, the principal means chosen by the Framers to ensure the role of the States in the federal system lies in the structure of the Federal Government itself. It is no novelty to observe that the composition of the Federal Government was designed in large part to protect the States from overreaching by Congress. The Framers thus gave the States a role in the selection both of the Executive and the Legislative Branches of the Federal Government. The States were vested with indirect influence over the House of Representatives and the Presidency by their control of electoral qualifications and their role in presidential elections. U.S. Const., Art. I, § 2, and Art. II, § 1. They were given more direct influence in the Senate, where each State received equal representation and each Senator was to be selected by the legislature of his State. Art. I, § 3. The significance attached to the States' equal representation in the Senate is underscored by the prohibition of any constitutional amendment divesting a State of equal representation without the State's consent. Art. V....

The effectiveness of the federal political process in preserving the States' interests is apparent even today in the course of federal legislation. [T]he States have been able to direct a substantial proportion of federal revenues into their own treasuries in the form of general and program-specific grants in aid....

We realize that changes in the structure of the Federal Government have taken place since 1789, not the least of which has been the substitution of popular election of Senators by the adoption of the Seventeenth Amendment in 1913, and that these changes may work to alter the influence of the States in the federal political process. Nonetheless, against this background, we are convinced that the fundamental limitation that the constitutional scheme imposes on the Commerce Clause to protect the "States as States" is one of process rather than one of result....

Insofar as the present cases are concerned, then, we need go no further than to state that we perceive nothing in the overtime and minimum-wage requirements of the FLSA, as applied to SAMTA, that is destructive of state sovereignty or violative of any constitutional provision. SAMTA faces nothing more than the same minimum-wage and overtime obligations that hundreds of thousands of other employers, public as well as private, have to meet....

Of course, we continue to recognize that the States occupy a special and specific position in our constitutional system and that the scope of Congress' authority under the Commerce Clause must reflect that position. But the principal and basic limit on the federal commerce power is that inherent in all congressional action—the built-in restraints that our system provides through state participation in federal governmental action. The political process ensures that laws that unduly burden the States will not be promulgated. In the factual setting of these cases the internal safeguards of the political process have performed as intended.

These cases do not require us to identify or define what affirmative limits the constitutional structure might impose on federal action affecting the States under the Commerce Clause. We note and accept Justice Frankfurter's observation in *New York v. United States*:

> "The process of Constitutional adjudication does not thrive on conjuring up horrible possibilities that never happen in the real world and devising doctrines sufficiently comprehensive in detail to cover the remotest contingency. Nor need we go beyond what is required for a reasoned disposition of the kind of controversy now before the Court." ...

We do not lightly overrule recent precedent. We have not hesitated, however, when it has become apparent that a prior decision has departed from a proper understanding of congressional power under the Commerce Clause. Due respect for the reach of congressional power within the federal system mandates that we do so now.

National League of Cities v. Usery, is overruled. The judgment of the District Court is reversed, and these cases are remanded to that court for further proceedings consistent with this opinion.

It is so ordered.

JUSTICE POWELL, with whom THE CHIEF JUSTICE [BURGER], JUSTICE REHNQUIST, and JUSTICE O'CONNOR join, dissenting.

... Despite some genuflecting in Court's opinion to the concept of federalism, today's decision effectively reduces the Tenth Amendment to meaningless rhetoric when Congress acts pursuant to the Commerce Clause....

The Court finds that the test of State immunity approved in *National League of Cities* and its progeny is unworkable and unsound in principle. In finding the test to be unworkable, the Court begins by mischaracterizing *National League of Cities* [which] adopted a familiar type of balancing test for determining whether Commerce Clause enactments transgress constitutional limitations imposed by the federal nature of our system of government. This omission is noteworthy, since the author of today's opinion joined *National League of Cities* and concurred separately to point out that the Court's opinion in that case "adopt[s] a balancing approach [that] does not outlaw federal power in areas ... where the federal interest is demonstrably greater and where state ... compliance with imposed federal standards would be essential." ...

Today's opinion does not explain how the States' role in the electoral process guarantees that particular exercises of the Commerce Clause power will not infringe on residual State sovereignty. Members of Congress are elected from the various States, but once in office they are members of the federal government.[8] ...

[The Tenth] Amendment states explicitly that "[t]he powers not delegated to the United States ... are reserved to the States." The Court recasts this language to say that the States retain their sovereign powers "only to the extent that the Constitution has not divested them of their original powers and transferred those powers to the Federal Government." This rephrasing is not a distinction without a difference; rather, it reflects the Court's unprecedented view that Congress is free under the Commerce Clause to assume a State's traditional sovereign power, and to do so without judicial review of its action....

JUSTICE O'CONNOR, with whom JUSTICE POWELL and JUSTICE REHNQUIST join, dissenting.

... The Framers perceived the interstate commerce power to be important but limited, and expected that it would be used primarily if

---

8. One can hardly imagine this Court saying that because Congress is composed of individuals, individual rights guaranteed by the Bill of Rights are amply protected by the political process. Yet, the position adopted today is indistinguishable in principle. The Tenth Amendment also is an essential part of the Bill of Rights.

not exclusively to remove interstate tariffs and to regulate maritime affairs and large-scale mercantile enterprise. [R]ecently the Federal Government has, with this Court's blessing, undertaken to tell the States the age at which they can retire their law enforcement officers, and the regulatory standards, procedures, and even the agenda which their utilities commissions must consider and follow. See *EEOC v. Wyoming,* 460 U.S. 226, 103 S.Ct. 1054, 75 L.Ed.2d 18 (1983); *FERC v. Mississippi,* 456 U.S. 742, 102 S.Ct. 2126, 72 L.Ed.2d 532 (1982). The political process has not protected against these encroachments on state activities, even though they directly impinge on a State's ability to make and enforce its laws. With the abandonment of *National League of Cities,* all that stands between the remaining essentials of state sovereignty and Congress is the latter's underdeveloped capacity for self-restraint....

JUSTICE REHNQUIST, dissenting.

... Justice Powell's reference to the "balancing test" approved in *National League of Cities* is not identical with the language in that case, which recognized that Congress could not act under its commerce power to infringe on certain fundamental aspects of state sovereignty that are essential to "the States' separate and independent existence." Nor is either test, or Justice O'Connor's suggested approach, precisely congruent with Justice Blackmun's views in 1976, when he spoke of a balancing approach which did not outlaw federal power in areas "where the federal interest is demonstrably greater." But under any one of these approaches the judgment in this case should be affirmed, and I do not think it incumbent on those of us in dissent to spell out further the fine points of a principle that will, I am confident, in time again command the support of a majority of this Court.

Notes

1. Responding to *Garcia,* Congress in November of 1985 enacted the Fair Labor Standards Amendments of 1985, authorizing states and their political subdivisions and interstate governmental agencies to provide compensatory time to their employees in lieu of overtime.

2. *Gregory v. Ashcroft,* 501 U.S. 452, 111 S.Ct. 2395, 115 L.Ed.2d 410 (1991) held that a provision of the Missouri Constitution that required state judges to retire at 70 did not violate either the equal protection clause or the Federal Age Discrimination in Employment Act. In the course of ruling on the federal claim, the majority per O'Connor, J. (joined by Rehnquist, C.J., & Scalia, Kennedy, & Souter, JJ.) stated that the authority of the people of the States to determine the qualifications of their most important government officials is "an authority that lies at 'the heart of representative government.' It is a power reserved to the States under the Tenth Amendment and guaranteed them by that provision of the Constitution under which the United States 'guarantee[s] to every state in this Union a Republican Form of Government.' U.S. Const., Art. IV, § 4." (internal citation and footnote omitted). White, J., joined by Stevens, J., filed a separate opinion that dissented on this point. Blackmun, J., joined by Marshall, J., filed a dissenting opinion that also disagreed with the majority.

NEW YORK v. UNITED STATES

505 U.S. 144, 112 S.Ct. 2408, 120 L.Ed.2d 120 (1992).

JUSTICE O'CONNOR delivered the opinion of the Court.

... In this case, we address the constitutionality of three provisions of the Low–Level Radioactive Waste Policy Amendments Act of 1985, Pub.L. 99–240, 99 Stat. 1842, 42 U.S.C. § 2021b *et seq.* The constitutional question is as old as the Constitution: It consists of discerning the proper division of authority between the Federal Government and the States. We conclude that while Congress has substantial power under the Constitution to encourage the States to provide for the disposal of the radioactive waste generated within their borders, the Constitution does not confer upon Congress the ability simply to compel the States to do so. We therefore find that only two of the Act's three provisions at issue are consistent with the Constitution's allocation of power to the Federal Government.

I

We live in a world full of low level radioactive waste. Radioactive material is present in luminous watch dials, smoke alarms, measurement devices, medical fluids, research materials, and the protective gear and construction materials used by workers at nuclear power plants. Low level radioactive waste is generated by the Government, by hospitals, by research institutions, and by various industries. The waste must be isolated from humans for long periods of time, often for hundreds of years. Millions of cubic feet of low level radioactive waste must be disposed of each year. [S]ince 1979 only three [low level radioactive] disposal sites—those in Nevada, Washington, and South Carolina—have been in operation. Waste generated in the rest of the country must be shipped to one of these three sites for disposal....

Faced with the possibility that the Nation would be left with no disposal sites for low level radioactive waste, Congress responded by enacting the Low–Level Radioactive Waste Policy Act. Relying largely on a report submitted by the National Governors' Association, Congress [in 1980] authorized States to enter into regional compacts that, once ratified by Congress, would have the authority beginning in 1986 to restrict the use of their disposal facilities to waste generated within member States. The 1980 Act included no penalties for States that failed to participate in this plan.

By 1985, only three approved regional compacts had operational disposal facilities; not surprisingly, these were the compacts formed around South Carolina, Nevada, and Washington, the three sited States. The following year, the 1980 Act would have given these three compacts the ability to exclude waste from nonmembers, and the remaining 31 States would have had no assured outlet for their low level radioactive waste. With this prospect looming, Congress once again took up the issue of waste disposal. The result was the legislation challenged here, the Low–Level Radioactive Waste Policy Amendments Act of 1985.

The 1985 Act was again based largely on a proposal submitted by the National Governors' Association. In broad outline, the Act embodies a compromise among the sited and unsited States. The sited States agreed to extend for seven years the period in which they would accept low level radioactive waste from other States. In exchange, the United States agreed to end their reliance on the sited States by 1992.

The mechanics of this compromise are intricate. [They provide] three types of incentives to encourage the States to comply with their statutory obligation to provide for the disposal of waste generated within their borders.

1. *Monetary incentives.* One quarter of the surcharges collected by the sited States must be transferred to an escrow account held by the Secretary of Energy. The Secretary then makes payments from this account to each State that has complied with a series of deadlines....

2. *Access incentives.* The second type of incentive involves the denial of access to disposal sites. States that fail to meet the July 1986 deadline may be charged twice the ordinary surcharge for the remainder of 1986 and may be denied access to disposal facilities thereafter....

3. *The take title provision.* The third type of incentive is the most severe. The Act provides:

> "If a State (or, where applicable, a compact region) in which low-level radioactive waste is generated is unable to provide for the disposal of all such waste generated within such State or compact region by January 1, 1996, each State in which such waste is generated, upon the request of the generator or owner of the waste, shall take title to the waste, be obligated to take possession of the waste, and shall be liable for all damages directly or indirectly incurred by such generator or owner as a consequence of the failure of the State to take possession of the waste as soon after January 1, 1996, as the generator or owner notifies the State that the waste is available for shipment."

These three incentives are the focus of petitioners' constitutional challenge. ...

New York, a State whose residents generate a relatively large share of the Nation's low level radioactive waste, did not join a regional compact. Instead, the State complied with the Act's requirements by enacting legislation providing for the siting and financing of a disposal facility in New York. The State has identified five potential sites, three in Allegany County and two in Cortland County. Residents of the two counties oppose the State's choice of location.

Petitioners—the State of New York and the two counties—filed this suit against the United States in 1990. [A]s the case stands before us, petitioners claim only that the Act is inconsistent with the Tenth Amendment and the Guarantee Clause.

II

... In some cases the Court has inquired whether an Act of Congress is authorized by one of the powers delegated to Congress in Article I of the Constitution. See, *e.g., McCulloch v. Maryland.* In other cases the Court has sought to determine whether an Act of Congress invades the province of state sovereignty reserved by the Tenth Amendment. See, *e.g., Garcia v. San Antonio Metropolitan Transit Authority.* In a case like this one, involving the division of authority between federal and state governments, the two inquiries are mirror images of each other. If a power is delegated to Congress in the Constitution, the Tenth Amendment expressly disclaims any reservation of that power to the States; if a power is an attribute of state sovereignty reserved by the Tenth Amendment, it is necessarily a power the Constitution has not conferred on Congress.

It is in this sense that the Tenth Amendment "states but a truism that all is retained which has not been surrendered." *United States v. Darby.* ... Congress exercises its conferred powers subject to the limitations contained in the Constitution. Thus, for example, under the Commerce Clause Congress may regulate publishers engaged in interstate commerce, but Congress is constrained in the exercise of that power by the First Amendment. The Tenth Amendment likewise restrains the power of Congress, but this limit is not derived from the text of the Tenth Amendment itself, which, as we have discussed, is essentially a tautology. Instead, the Tenth Amendment confirms that the power of the Federal Government is subject to limits that may, in a given instance, reserve power to the States. The Tenth Amendment thus directs us to determine, as in this case, whether an incident of state sovereignty is protected by a limitation on an Article I power....

Most of our recent cases interpreting the Tenth Amendment have concerned the authority of Congress to subject state governments to generally applicable laws. The Court's jurisprudence in this area has traveled an unsteady path. See *Maryland v. Wirtz* (1968)(state schools and hospitals are subject to Fair Labor Standards Act); *National League of Cities v. Usery* (1976)(overruling *Wirtz*)(state employers are *not* subject to Fair Labor Standards Act); *Garcia v. San Antonio Metropolitan Transit Authority* (1985)(overruling *National League of Cities*)(state employers are once again subject to Fair Labor Standards Act). This case presents no occasion to apply or revisit the holdings of any of these cases, as this is not a case in which Congress has subjected a State to the same legislation applicable to private parties.

This case instead concerns the circumstances under which Congress may use the States as implements of regulation; that is, whether Congress may direct or otherwise motivate the States to regulate in a particular field or a particular way.

[T]he Framers explicitly chose a Constitution that confers upon Congress the power to regulate individuals, not States. [E]ven where Congress has the authority under the Constitution to pass laws requiring or prohibiting certain acts, it lacks the power directly to compel the States to require or prohibit those acts. The allocation of power contained in the Commerce Clause, for example, authorizes Congress to regulate interstate commerce directly; it does not authorize Congress to regulate state governments' regulation of interstate commerce.

This is not to say that Congress lacks the ability to encourage a State to regulate in a particular way, or that Congress may not hold out incentives to the States as a method of influencing a State's policy choices. Our cases have identified a variety of methods, short of outright coercion, by which Congress may urge a State to adopt a legislative program consistent with federal interests. Two of these methods are of particular relevance here.

First, under Congress' spending power, "Congress may attach conditions on the receipt of federal funds." . . .

Second, where Congress has the authority to regulate private activity under the Commerce Clause, we have recognized Congress' power to offer States the choice of regulating that activity according to federal standards or having state law pre-empted by federal regulation. This arrangement, which has been termed "a program of cooperative federalism," is replicated in numerous federal statutory schemes. . . .

By either of these two methods, as by any other permissible method of encouraging a State to conform to federal policy choices, the residents of the State retain the ultimate decision as to whether or not the State will comply. If a State's citizens view federal policy as sufficiently contrary to local interests, they may elect to decline a federal grant. If state residents would prefer their government to devote its attention and resources to problems other than those deemed important by Congress, they may choose to have the Federal Government rather than the State bear the expense of a federally mandated regulatory program, and they may continue to supplement that program to the extent state law is not preempted. Where Congress encourages state regulation rather than compelling it, state governments remain responsive to the local electorate's preferences; state officials remain accountable to the people.

By contrast, where the Federal Government compels States to regulate, the accountability of both state and federal officials is diminished. If the citizens of New York, for example, do not consider that making provision for the disposal of radioactive waste is in their best interest, they may elect state officials who share their view. That view can always be preempted under the Supremacy Clause if is contrary to the national view, but in such a case it is the Federal Government that makes the decision in full view of the public, and it will be federal officials that suffer the consequences if the decision turns out to be detrimental or unpopular. But where the Federal Government directs the States to regulate, it may be state officials who will bear the brunt of public disapproval, while the federal officials who devised the regulatory program may remain insulated from the electoral ramifications of their decision. Accountability is thus diminished when, due to federal coercion, elected state officials cannot regulate in accordance with the views of the local electorate in matters not pre-empted by federal regulation.

With these principles in mind, we turn to the three challenged provisions of the Low–Level Radioactive Waste Policy Amendments Act of 1985.

III

... Construed as a whole, the Act comprises three sets of "incentives" for the States to provide for the disposal of low level radioactive waste generated within their borders. We consider each in turn....

A. The Act's first set of incentives, in which Congress has conditioned grants to the States upon the States' attainment of a series of milestones, is thus well within the authority of Congress under the Commerce and Spending Clauses. Because the first set of incentives is supported by affirmative constitutional grants of power to Congress, it is not inconsistent with the Tenth Amendment.

B. In the second set of incentives, Congress has authorized States and regional compacts with disposal sites gradually to increase the cost of access to the sites, and then to deny access altogether, to radioactive waste generated in States that do not meet federal deadlines. As a simple regulation, this provision would be within the power of Congress to authorize the States to discriminate against interstate commerce. Where federal regulation of private activity is within the scope of the Commerce Clause, we have recognized the ability of Congress to offer states the choice of regulating that activity according to federal standards or having state law pre-empted by federal regulation....

C. The take title provision is of a different character. This third so-called "incentive" offers States, as an alternative to regulating pursuant to Congress' direction, the option of taking title to and possession of the low level radioactive waste generated within their borders and becoming liable for all damages waste generators suffer as a result of the States' failure to do so promptly. In this provision, Congress has crossed the line distinguishing encouragement from coercion.

The take title provision offers state governments a "choice" of either accepting ownership of waste or regulating according to the instructions of Congress. Respondents do not claim that the Constitution would authorize Congress to impose either option as a freestanding requirement. On one hand, the Constitution would not permit Congress simply to transfer radioactive waste from generators to state governments. Such a forced transfer, standing alone, would in principle be no different than a congressionally compelled subsidy from state governments to radioactive waste producers. The same is true of the provision requiring the States to become liable for the generators' damages. Standing alone, this provision would be indistinguishable from an Act of Congress directing the States to assume the liabilities of certain state residents. Either type of federal action would "commandeer" state governments into the service of federal regulatory purposes, and would for this reason be inconsistent with the Constitution's division of authority between federal and state governments. On the other hand, the second alternative held out to state governments—regulating pursuant to Congress' direction—would, standing alone, present a simple command to state governments to implement legislation enacted by Congress. As we have seen, the Constitution does not empower Congress to subject state governments to this type of instruction.

Because an instruction to state governments to take title to waste, standing alone, would be beyond the authority of Congress, and because a direct order to regulate, standing alone, would also be beyond the authority of Congress, it follows that Congress lacks the power to offer the States a choice between the two. Unlike the first two sets of incentives, the take title incentive does not represent the conditional exercise of any congressional power enumerated in the Constitution. In this provision, Congress has not held out the threat of exercising its spending power or its commerce power; it has instead held out the threat, should the States not regulate according to one federal instruction, of simply forcing the States to submit to another federal instruction. A choice between two unconstitutionally coercive regulatory techniques is no choice at all. Either way, "the Act commandeers the legislative processes of the States by directly compelling them to enact and enforce a federal regulatory program," an outcome that has never been understood to lie within the authority conferred upon Congress by the Constitution.

Respondents emphasize the latitude given to the States to implement Congress' plan. The Act enables the States to regulate pursuant to Congress' instructions in any number of different ways. States may avoid taking title by contracting with sited regional compacts, by building a disposal site alone or as part of a compact, or by permitting private parties to build a disposal site. States that host sites may employ a wide range of designs and disposal methods, subject only to broad federal regulatory limits. This line of reasoning, however, only underscores the critical alternative a State lacks: A State may not decline to administer the federal program. No matter which path the State chooses, it must follow the direction of Congress.

The take title provision appears to be unique. No other federal statute has been cited which offers a state government no option other than that of implementing legislation enacted by Congress. Whether one views the take title provision as lying outside Congress' enumerated powers, or as infringing upon the core of state sovereignty reserved by the Tenth Amendment, the provision is inconsistent with the federal structure of our Government established by the Constitution.

IV

Respondents raise a number of objections to this understanding of the limits of Congress' power.

... First, the United States argues that the Constitution's prohibition of congressional directives to state governments can be overcome where the federal interest is sufficiently important to justify state submission. [W]hether or not a particularly strong federal interest enables Congress to bring state governments within the orbit of generally applicable *federal* regulation, no Member of the Court has ever suggested that such a federal interest would enable Congress to command a state government to enact *state* regulation. No matter how powerful the federal interest involved, the Constitution simply does not give Congress the authority to require the States to regulate. The Constitution instead gives Congress the authority to regulate matters directly and to pre-empt contrary state regulation. Where a federal interest is sufficiently strong to cause Congress to legislate, it must do so directly; it may not conscript state governments as its agents.

Second, the United States argues that the Constitution does, in some circumstances, permit federal directives to state governments. Various cases are cited for this proposition, but none support it. [A]ll involve congressional regulation of individuals, not congressional requirements that States regulate. Federal statutes enforceable in state courts do, in a sense, direct state judges to enforce them, but this sort of federal "direction" of state judges is mandated by the text of the Supremacy Clause. No comparable constitutional provision authorizes Congress to command state legislatures to legislate.

Additional cases cited by the United States discuss the power of federal *courts* to order state officials to comply with federal law. Again, however, the text of the Constitution plainly confers this authority on the federal courts, the "Judicial Power" of which "shall extend to all Cases, in Law and Equity, arising under this Constitution, [and] the Laws of the United States ... ; [and] to Controversies between two or more States; [and] between a State and Citizens of another State." U.S. Const., Art. III, § 2. The Constitution contains no analogous grant of authority to Congress. Moreover, the Supremacy Clause makes federal law paramount over the contrary positions of state officials; the power of federal courts to enforce federal law thus presupposes some authority to order state officials to comply. . . .

The sited State respondents focus their attention on the process by which the Act was formulated. . . . Respondents note that the Act embodies a bargain among the sited and unsited States, a compromise to which New York was a willing participant and from which New York has reaped much benefit. Respondents then pose what appears at first to be a troubling question: How can a federal statute be found an unconstitutional infringement of State sovereignty when state officials consented to the statute's enactment?

The answer follows from an understanding of the fundamental purpose served by our Government's federal structure. The Constitution does not protect the sovereignty of States for the benefit of the States or state governments as abstract political entities, or even for the benefit of the public officials governing the States. To the contrary, the Constitution divides authority between federal and state governments for the protection of individuals. State sovereignty is not just an end in itself: "Rather, federalism secures to citizens the liberties that derive from the diffusion of sovereign power." . . .

State officials thus cannot consent to the enlargement of the powers of Congress beyond those enumerated in the Constitution. Indeed, the facts of this case raise the possibility that powerful incentives might lead both federal and state officials to view departures from the federal structure to be in their personal interests. Most citizens recognize the need for radioactive waste disposal sites, but few want sites near their homes. As a result, while it would be well within the authority of either federal or state officials to choose where the disposal sites will be, it is likely to be in the political interest of each individual official to avoid being held accountable to the voters for the choice of location. If a federal official is faced with the alternatives of choosing a location or directing the States to do it, the official may well prefer the latter, as a means of shifting responsibility for the eventual decision. If a state official is faced with the same set of alternatives—choosing a location or having Congress direct the choice of a location—the state official may also prefer the latter, as it may permit the avoidance of personal responsibility. The interests of public officials thus may not coincide with the Constitution's intergovernmental allocation of authority. Where state officials purport to submit to the direction of Congress in this manner, federalism is hardly being advanced.

Nor does the State's prior support for the Act estop it from asserting the Act's unconstitutionality. While New York has received the benefit of the Act in the form of a few more years of access to disposal sites in other States, New York has never joined a regional radioactive waste compact. . . . That a party collaborated with others in seeking legislation has never been understood to estop the party from challenging that legislation in subsequent litigation.

V

Petitioners also contend that the Act is inconsistent with the Constitution's Guarantee Clause, which directs the United States to "guarantee to every State in this Union a Republican Form of Government." Because we have found the take title provision of the Act irreconcilable with the powers delegated to Congress by the Constitution and hence with the Tenth Amendment's reservation to the States of those powers not delegated to the Federal Government, we need only address the applicability of the Guarantee Clause to the Act's other two challenged provisions. . . . Even if we assume that petitioners' claim is justiciable, neither the monetary incentives provided by the Act nor the possibility that a State's waste producers may find themselves excluded from the disposal sites of another State can reasonably be said to deny any State a republican form of government. . . .

VI

[T]he take title provision may be severed without doing violence to the rest of the Act. . . .

... The judgment of the Court of Appeals is accordingly

Affirmed in part and reversed in part.

JUSTICE WHITE, with whom JUSTICE BLACKMUN and JUSTICE STEVENS join, concurring in part and dissenting in part.

The Court today affirms the constitutionality of two facets of the Low–Level Radioactive Waste Policy Amendments Act of 1985 (1985 Act).... I can only join Parts IIIA and IIIB, and I respectfully dissent from the rest of its opinion and the judgment reversing in part the judgment of the Court of Appeals.

... Unlike legislation that directs action from the Federal Government to the States, the 1980 and 1985 Acts reflected hard-fought agreements among States as referred by Congress. The distinction is key, and the Court's failure properly to characterize this legislation ultimately affects its analysis of the take title provision's constitutionality....

The State should be estopped from asserting the unconstitutionality of a provision that seeks merely to ensure that, after deriving substantial advantages from the 1985 Act, New York in fact must live up to its bargain by establishing an in-state low-level radioactive waste facility or assuming liability for its failure to act....

The Court's distinction between a federal statute's regulation of States and private parties for general purposes, as opposed to a regulation solely on the activities of States, is unsupported by our recent Tenth Amendment cases. In no case has the Court rested its holding on such a distinction. Moreover, the Court makes no effort to explain why this purported distinction should affect the analysis of Congress' power under general principles of federalism and the Tenth Amendment. The distinction, facilely thrown out, is not based on any defensible theory. Certainly one would be hard-pressed to read the spirited exchanges between the Court and dissenting Justices in *National League of Cities, supra,* and in *Garcia v. San Antonio Metropolitan Transit Authority, supra,* as having been based on the distinction now drawn by the Court. An incursion on state sovereignty hardly seems more constitutionally acceptable if the federal statute that "commands" specific action also applies to private parties. The alleged diminution in state authority over its own affairs is not any less because the federal mandate restricts the activities of private parties....

Though I disagree with the Court's conclusion that the take title provision is unconstitutional, I do not read its opinion to preclude Congress from adopting a similar measure through its powers under the Spending or Commerce Clauses. The Court makes clear that its objection is to the alleged "commandeer[ing]" quality of the take title provision. As its discussion of the surcharge and rebate incentives reveals, the spending power offers a means of enacting a take title provision under the Court's standards. Congress could, in other words, condition the payment of funds on the State's willingness to take title if it has not already provided a waste disposal facility. Under the scheme upheld in this case, for example, monies collected in the surcharge provision might be withheld or disbursed depending on a State's willingness to take title to or otherwise accept responsibility for the low-level radioactive waste generated in state after the statutory deadline for establishing its own waste disposal facility has passed.

Similarly, should a State fail to establish a waste disposal facility by the appointed deadline (under the statute as presently drafted, January 1, 1996), Congress has the power pursuant to the Commerce Clause to regulate directly the producers of the waste. Thus, as I read it, Congress could amend the statute to say that if a State fails to meet the January 1, 1996 deadline for achieving a means of waste disposal, and has not taken title to the waste, no low-level radioactive waste may be shipped out of the State of New York. [S]hould Congress amend the statute to meet the Court's objection and a State refuse to act, the National Legislature will have ensured at least a federal solution to the waste management problem . . . . .

JUSTICE STEVENS, concurring in part and dissenting in part.

Under the Articles of Confederation, the Federal Government had the power to issue commands to the States. Because that indirect exercise of federal power proved ineffective, the Framers of the Constitution empowered the Federal Government to exercise legislative authority directly over individuals within the States, even though that direct authority constituted a greater intrusion on State sovereignty. Nothing in that history suggests that the Federal Government may not also impose its will upon the several States as it did under the Articles. The Constitution enhanced, rather than diminished, the power of the Federal Government.

The notion that Congress does not have the power to issue "a simple command to state governments to implement legislation enacted by Congress," is incorrect and unsound. [T]he Federal Government directs state governments in many realms. The Government regulates state-operated railroads, state school systems, state prisons, state elections, and a host of other state functions. Similarly, there can be no doubt that, in time of war, Congress could either draft soldiers itself or command the States to supply their quotas of troops. I see no reason why Congress may not also command the States to enforce federal water and air quality standards or federal standards for the disposition of low-level radioactive wastes. . . .

Notes

1. Seventeen states, supporting New York's position, filed amicus briefs with the Supreme Court, even though prior to this decision, Congress had approved interstate Compacts governing 42 states. Can any of these 42 states properly seek to withdraw from their Compacts on the grounds that they granted their consents because of the threat of the "take-title" provision, which we now know is invalid?

2. Does the majority opinion, which called the Tenth Amendment a "tautology," use that Amendment to limit Congressional power, or is the majority relying on another provision?

Usery's rationale focused on the "substantial costs" that the 1974 Amendments to the Fair Labor Standards Act imposed on the states; it distinguished *Fry* (which had upheld a law that temporarily froze wages of state and local employees) as a decision that "operated to reduce the pressures upon state budgets rather than increase them." Does *New York v. United States* rely on this rationale?

3. One commentator suggests that the *New York* decision "casts a long shadow over both *Garcia* and federal regulation of state employees' wages and hours." The law invalidated in *New York* offered the state a choice "between designating waste-disposal sites or taking title to private producers' waste," an impermissible choice, said the Court, because the second option is "no different than a congressionally compelled subsidy from state governments to radioactive waste producers." But, "[f]ederal regulation of state employees' wages similarly could be viewed as a congressionally compelled subsidy from state governments to their employees."[1] What do you think?

PRINTZ v. UNITED STATES
521 U.S. 898, 117 S.Ct. 2365, 138 L.Ed.2d 914 (1997).

Justice Scalia delivered the opinion of the Court.

The question presented in these cases is whether certain interim provisions of the Brady Handgun Violence Prevention Act, Pub. L. 103–159 commanding state and local law enforcement officers to conduct background checks on prospective handgun purchasers and to perform certain related tasks, violate the Constitution.

I. The Gun Control Act of 1968 (GCA), 18 U.S.C.A. § 921 *et seq.*, establishes a detailed federal scheme governing the distribution of firearms. It prohibits firearms dealers from transferring handguns to any person under 21, not resident in the dealer's State, or prohibited by state or local law from purchasing or possessing firearms.... In 1993, Congress amended the GCA by enacting the Brady Act. The Act requires the Attorney General to establish a national instant background check system by November 30, 1998, and immediately puts in place certain interim provisions until that system becomes operative. Under the interim provisions, a firearms dealer who proposes to transfer a handgun must first: (1) receive from the transferee a statement (the Brady Form), containing the name, address and date of birth of the proposed transferee along with a sworn statement that the transferee is not among any of the classes of prohibited purchasers; (2) verify the identity of the transferee by examining an identification document; and (3) provide the "chief law enforcement officer" (CLEO) of the transferee's residence with notice of the contents (and a copy) of the Brady Form. With some exceptions, the dealer must then wait five business days before consum-

---

1. Merrit, Reviving State Sovereignty, Legal Times, July 27, 1992, at S28–S29.

mating the sale, unless the CLEO earlier notifies the dealer that he has no reason to believe the transfer would be illegal.

The Brady Act creates two significant alternatives to the foregoing scheme. A dealer may sell a handgun immediately if the purchaser possesses a state handgun permit issued after a background check, or if state law provides for an instant background check. In States that have not rendered one of these alternatives applicable to all gun purchasers, CLEOs are required to perform certain duties. When a CLEO receives the required notice of a proposed transfer from the firearms dealer, the CLEO must "make a reasonable effort to ascertain within 5 business days whether receipt or possession would be in violation of the law, including research in whatever State and local recordkeeping systems are available and in a national system designated by the Attorney General." The Act does not require the CLEO to take any particular action if he determines that a pending transaction would be unlawful; he may notify the firearms dealer to that effect, but is not required to do so. If, however, the CLEO notifies a gun dealer that a prospective purchaser is ineligible to receive a handgun, he must, upon request, provide the would-be purchaser with a written statement of the reasons for that determination. Moreover, if the CLEO does not discover any basis for objecting to the sale, he must destroy any records in his possession relating to the transfer, including his copy of the Brady Form. Under a separate provision of the GCA, any person who "knowingly violates [the Brady Act] shall be fined under this title, imprisoned for no more than 1 year, or both."

Petitioners Jay Printz and Richard Mack, the CLEOs for Ravalli County, Montana, and Graham County, Arizona, respectively, filed separate actions challenging the constitutionality of the Brady Act's interim provisions. In each case, the District Court held that the provision requiring CLEOs to perform background checks was unconstitutional, but concluded that that provision was severable from the remainder of the Act, effectively leaving a voluntary background-check system in place. A divided panel of the Court of Appeals for the Ninth Circuit reversed, finding none of the Brady Act's interim provisions to be unconstitutional.

II. [T]he Brady Act purports to direct state law enforcement officers to participate, albeit only temporarily, in the administration of a federally enacted regulatory scheme. Regulated firearms dealers are required to forward Brady Forms not to a federal officer or employee, but to the CLEOs, whose obligation to accept those forms is implicit in the duty imposed upon them to make "reasonable efforts" within five days to determine whether the sales reflected in the forms are lawful. While the CLEOs are subjected to no federal requirement that they prevent the sales determined to be unlawful (it is perhaps assumed that their state-law duties will require prevention or apprehension), they are empowered to grant, in effect, waivers of the federally prescribed 5–day waiting period for handgun purchases by notifying the gun dealers that they have no reason to believe the transactions would be illegal.

The petitioners here object to being pressed into federal service, and contend that congressional action compelling state officers to execute federal laws is unconstitutional. Because there is no constitutional text speaking to this precise question, the answer to the CLEOs' challenge must be sought in historical understanding and practice, in the structure of the Constitution, and in the jurisprudence of this Court. We treat those three sources, in that order, in this and the next two sections of this opinion.

Petitioners contend that compelled enlistment of state executive officers for the administration of federal programs is, until very recent years at least, unprecedented. The Government contends, to the contrary, that "the earliest Congresses enacted statutes that required the participation of state officials in the implementation of federal laws." [I]f, as petitioners contend, earlier Congresses avoided use of this highly attractive power, we would have reason to believe that the power was thought not to exist.

The Government observes that statutes enacted by the first Congresses required state courts to record applications for citizenship, to transmit abstracts of citizenship applications and other naturalization records to the Secretary of State, and to register aliens seeking naturalization and issue certificates of registry. It may well be, however, that these requirements applied only in States that authorized their courts to conduct naturalization proceedings. See *United States v. Jones,* 109 U. S. 513, 519–20, 3 S.Ct. 346, 27 L.Ed. 1015 (1883) (stating that these obligations were imposed "with the consent of the States" and "could not be enforced against the consent of the States").[2] Other statutes of that era apparently or at least arguably required state courts to perform functions unrelated to naturalization, such as resolving controversies between a captain and the crew of his ship concerning the seaworthiness of the vessel, hearing the claims of slave owners who had apprehended fugitive slaves and issuing certificates authorizing the slave's forced removal to the State from which he had fled, taking proof of the claims of Canadian refugees who had assisted the United States during the Revolutionary War, and ordering the deportation of alien enemies in times of war.

These early laws establish, at most, that the Constitution was originally understood to permit imposition of an obligation on state *judges* to enforce federal prescriptions, insofar as those prescriptions related to matters appropriate for the judicial power. That assumption was perhaps implicit in one of the provisions of the Constitution, and was explicit in another. In accord with the so-called Madisonian Compromise, Article III, § 1, established only a Supreme Court, and made the creation of lower federal courts optional with the Congress—even though it was obvious that the Supreme Court alone could not hear all federal

---

2. ... Our references throughout this opinion to "the dissent" are to the dissenting opinion of Justice Stevens, joined by Justice Ginsburg and Justice Breyer. The separate dissenting opinions of Justice Breyer and Justice Souter will be referred to as such.

cases throughout the United States. And the Supremacy Clause, Art. VI, cl. 2, announced that "the Laws of the United States ... shall be the supreme Law of the Land; and the Judges in every State shall be bound thereby." It is understandable why courts should have been viewed distinctively in this regard; unlike legislatures and executives, they applied the law of other sovereigns all the time. The principle underlying so-called "transitory" causes of action was that laws which operated elsewhere created obligations in justice that courts of the forum state would enforce. The Constitution itself, in the Full Faith and Credit Clause, Art. IV, § 1, generally required such enforcement with respect to obligations arising in other States.

For these reasons, we do not think the early statutes imposing obligations on state courts imply a power of Congress to impress the state executive into its service. Indeed, it can be argued that the numerousness of these statutes, contrasted with the utter lack of statutes imposing obligations on the States' executive (notwithstanding the attractiveness of that course to Congress), suggests an assumed *absence* of such power. The only early federal law the Government has brought to our attention that imposed duties on state executive officers is the Extradition Act of 1793, which required the "executive authority" of a State to cause the arrest and delivery of a fugitive from justice upon the request of the executive authority of the State from which the fugitive had fled. That was in direct implementation, however, of the Extradition Clause of the Constitution itself, see Art. IV, § 2.

Not only do the enactments of the early Congresses, as far as we are aware, contain no evidence of an assumption that the Federal Government may command the States' executive power in the absence of a particularized constitutional authorization, they contain some indication of precisely the opposite assumption. On September 23, 1789—the day before its proposal of the Bill of Rights—the First Congress enacted a law aimed at obtaining state assistance of the most rudimentary and necessary sort for the enforcement of the new Government's laws: the holding of federal prisoners in state jails at federal expense. Significantly, the law issued not a command to the States' executive, but a recommendation to their legislatures. Congress "recommended to the legislatures of the several States to pass laws, making it expressly the duty of the keepers of their gaols, to receive and safe keep therein all prisoners committed under the authority of the United States," and offered to pay 50 cents per month for each prisoner. [W]hen Georgia refused to comply with the request, Congress's only reaction was a law authorizing the marshal [in such circumstances] to rent a temporary jail until provision for a permanent one could be made.

In addition to early legislation, the Government also appeals to other sources we have usually regarded as indicative of the original understanding of the Constitution. It points to portions of The Federalist [but] none of these statements necessarily implies—what is the critical point here—that Congress could impose these responsibilities *without the consent of the States*. They appear to rest on the natural assumption that the States would consent to allowing their officials to assist the Federal Government. . . .

Another passage of The Federalist reads as follows:

"It merits particular attention . . . , that the laws of the Confederacy as to the *enumerated* and *legitimate* objects of its jurisdiction will become the SUPREME LAW of the land; to the observance of which all officers, legislative, executive, and judicial in each State will be bound by the sanctity of an oath. Thus, the legislatures, courts, and magistrates, of the respective members will be incorporated into the operations of the national government *as far as its just and constitutional authority extends;* and will be rendered auxiliary to the enforcement of its laws." The Federalist No. 27, at 177 (A. Hamilton) (emphasis in original).

The Government does not rely upon this passage, but Justice Souter . . . makes it the very foundation of his position; so we pause to examine it in some detail. Justice Souter finds "[t]he natural reading" of the phrases "will be incorporated into the operations of the national government" and "will be rendered auxiliary to the enforcement of its laws" to be that the National Government will have "authority . . . , when exercising an otherwise legitimate power (the commerce power, say), to require state 'auxiliaries' to take appropriate action." [One] problem with Justice Souter's reading is that it makes state *legislatures* subject to federal direction. (The passage in question, after all, does not include legislatures merely incidentally, as by referring to "all state officers"; it refers to legislatures *specifically* and *first of all*.) We have held, however, that state legislatures are *not* subject to federal direction. *New York v. United States* (1992).[5]

These problems are avoided, of course, if the calculatedly vague consequences the passage recites—"incorporated into the operations of the national government" and "rendered auxiliary to the enforcement of its laws"—are taken to refer to nothing more (or less) than the duty owed to the National Government, on the part of *all* state officials, to enact, enforce, and interpret state law in such fashion as not to obstruct the operation of federal law, and the attendant reality that all state actions constituting such obstruction, even legislative acts, are *ipso facto* invalid.

To complete the historical record, we must note that there is not only an absence of executive-commandeering statutes in the early Congresses, but there is an absence of them in our later history as well, at

---

5. Justice Souter seeks to avoid incompatibility with *New York* (a decision which he joined and purports to adhere to), by saying that the passage does not mean "any conceivable requirement may be imposed on any state official," and that "the essence of legislative power . . . is a discretion not subject to command," so that legislatures, at least, cannot be commanded. But then why were legislatures mentioned in the passage? It seems to us assuredly *not* a "natural reading" that being "rendered auxiliary to the enforcement of [the national government's] laws" means impressibility into federal service for "courts and magistrates" but something quite different for "legislatures." . . .

least until very recent years.... The Government cites the World War I selective draft law that authorized the President "to utilize the service of any or all departments and any or all officers or agents of the United States *and of the several States,* Territories, and the District of Columbia, and subdivisions thereof, in the execution of this Act," and made any person who refused to comply with the President's directions guilty of a misdemeanor. Act of May 18, 1917 (emphasis added). However, it is far from clear that the authorization "to utilize the service" of state officers was an authorization to *compel* the service of state officers. [I]n implementing the Act President Wilson did not commandeer the services of state officers, but instead requested the assistance of the States' governors, see Proclamation of May 18, 1917, 40 Stat. 1665 ("call[ing] upon the Governor of each of the several States . . . and all officers and agents of the several States . . . to perform certain duties"); Registration Regulations Prescribed by the President Under the Act of Congress Approved May 18, 1917, Part I, § 7 ("the governor [of each State] is *requested* to act under the regulations and rules prescribed by the President or under his direction") (emphasis added), obtained the consent of each of the governors, and left it to the governors to issue orders to their subordinate state officers. It is impressive that even with respect to a wartime measure the President should have been so solicitous of state independence.

The Government points to a number of federal statutes enacted within the past few decades that require the participation of state or local officials in implementing federal regulatory schemes. Some of these are connected to federal funding measures, and can perhaps be more accurately described as conditions upon the grant of federal funding than as mandates to the States; others, which require only the provision of information to the Federal Government, do not involve the precise issue before us here, which is the forced participation of the States' executive in the actual administration of a federal program....

III.   The constitutional practice we have examined above tends to negate the existence of the congressional power asserted here, but is not conclusive. We turn next to consideration of the structure of the Constitution, to see if we can discern among its "essential postulate[s]," a principle that controls the present cases....

The Framers' experience under the Articles of Confederation had persuaded them that using the States as the instruments of federal governance was both ineffectual and provocative of federal-state conflict. [T]he Framers rejected the concept of a central government that would act upon and through the States, and instead designed a system in which the state and federal governments would exercise concurrent authority over the people—who were, in Hamilton's words, "the only proper objects of government," The Federalist No. 15. We have set forth the historical record in more detail elsewhere, see *New York v. United States,* and need not repeat it here. It suffices to repeat the conclusion: "The

Framers explicitly chose a Constitution that confers upon Congress the power to regulate individuals, not States."[10]

We have thus far discussed the effect that federal control of state officers would have upon the first element of the "double security" alluded to by Madison: the division of power between State and Federal Governments. It would also have an effect upon the second element: the separation and equilibration of powers between the three branches of the Federal Government itself. The Constitution does not leave to speculation who is to administer the laws enacted by Congress; the President, it says, "shall take Care that the Laws be faithfully executed," Art. II, § 3, personally and through officers whom he appoints (save for such inferior officers as Congress may authorize to be appointed by the "Courts of Law" or by "the Heads of Departments" who are themselves presidential appointees), Art. II, § 2. The Brady Act effectively transfers this responsibility to thousands of CLEOs in the 50 States, who are left to implement the program without meaningful Presidential control (if indeed meaningful Presidential control is possible without the power to appoint and remove). The insistence of the Framers upon unity in the Federal Executive—to insure both vigor and accountability—is well known. That unity would be shattered, and the power of the President would be subject to reduction, if Congress could act as effectively without the President as with him, by simply requiring state officers to execute its laws.

The dissent of course resorts to the last, best hope of those who defend *ultra vires* congressional action, the Necessary and Proper Clause.... What destroys the dissent's Necessary and Proper Clause argument, however, is not the Tenth Amendment but the Necessary and Proper Clause itself. When a "La[w] ... for carrying into Execution" the Commerce Clause violates the principle of state sovereignty reflected in the various constitutional provisions we mentioned earlier, it is not a "La[w] ... *proper* for carrying into Execution the Commerce Clause," and is ... "merely [an] ac[t] of usurpation" which "deserve[s] to be treated as such." The Federalist No. 33 (A. Hamilton)....

[The Supremacy Clause] makes "Law of the Land" only "Laws of the United States which shall be made in Pursuance [of the Constitution]"; so the Supremacy Clause merely brings us back to the question discussed earlier, whether laws conscripting state officers violate state sovereignty and are thus not in accord with the Constitution.

IV. Finally, and most conclusively in the present litigation, we turn to the prior jurisprudence of this Court. Federal commandeering of

---

10. The dissent, reiterating Justice Stevens' dissent in *New York*, maintains that the Constitution merely *augmented* the preexisting power under the Articles to issue commands to the States with the additional power to make demands directly on individuals. That argument, however, was squarely rejected by the Court in *New York*, and with good reason. Many of Congress's powers under Art. I, § 8, were copied almost verbatim from the Articles of Confederation, indicating quite clearly that "[w]here the Constitution intends that our Congress enjoy a power once vested in the Continental Congress, it specifically grants it."

state governments is such a novel phenomenon that this Court's first experience with it did not occur until the 1970's, when the Environmental Protection Agency promulgated regulations requiring States to prescribe auto emissions testing, monitoring and retrofit programs, and to designate preferential bus and carpool lanes. The Courts of Appeals for the Fourth and Ninth Circuits invalidated the regulations on statutory grounds in order to avoid what they perceived to be grave constitutional issues; and the District of Columbia Circuit invalidated the regulations on both constitutional and statutory grounds. After we granted certiorari to review the statutory and constitutional validity of the regulations, the Government declined even to defend them, and instead rescinded some and conceded the invalidity of those that remained, leading us to vacate the opinions below and remand for consideration of mootness . . . . .

[I]n *New York v. United States* (1992) [we] held [that the Federal Government] "may not compel the States to enact or administer a federal regulatory program." The Government contends that *New York* is distinguishable on the following ground: unlike the "take title" provisions invalidated there, the background-check provision of the Brady Act does not require state legislative or executive officials to make policy, but instead issues a final directive to state CLEOs. It is permissible, the Government asserts, for Congress to command state or local officials to assist in the implementation of federal law so long as "Congress itself devises a clear legislative solution that regulates private conduct" and requires state or local officers to provide only "limited, non-policymaking help in enforcing that law." "[T]he constitutional line is crossed only when Congress compels the States to make law in their sovereign capacities."

. . . Executive action that has utterly no policymaking component is rare, particularly at an executive level as high as a jurisdiction's chief law-enforcement officer. Is it really true that there is no policymaking involved in deciding, for example, what "reasonable efforts" shall be expended to conduct a background check? . . .

Even assuming, moreover, that the Brady Act leaves no "policymaking" discretion with the States, we fail to see how that improves rather than worsens the intrusion upon state sovereignty. Preservation of the States as independent and autonomous political entities is arguably less undermined by requiring them to make policy in certain fields than . . . by "reduc[ing] [them] to puppets of a ventriloquist Congress." It is an essential attribute of the States' retained sovereignty that they remain independent and autonomous within their proper sphere of authority. It is no more compatible with this independence and autonomy that their officers be "dragooned" into administering federal law, than it would be compatible with the independence and autonomy of the United States that its officers be impressed into service for the execution of state laws . . . .

The Government also maintains that requiring state officers to perform discrete, ministerial tasks specified by Congress does not violate the principle of *New York* because it does not diminish the accountability of state or federal officials. This argument fails even on its own terms. By forcing state governments to absorb the financial burden of implementing a federal regulatory program, Members of Congress can take credit for "solving" problems without having to ask their constituents to pay for the solutions with higher federal taxes. And even when the States are not forced to absorb the costs of implementing a federal program, they are still put in the position of taking the blame for its burdensomeness and for its defects. Under the present law, for example, it will be the CLEO and not some federal official who stands between the gun purchaser and immediate possession of his gun. And it will likely be the CLEO, not some federal official, who will be blamed for any error (even one in the designated federal database) that causes a purchaser to be mistakenly rejected.

The dissent makes no attempt to defend the Government's basis for distinguishing *New York*, but instead advances what seems to us an even more implausible theory. The Brady Act, the dissent asserts, is different from the "take title" provisions invalidated in *New York* because the former is addressed to individuals—namely CLEOs—while the latter were directed to the State itself. That is certainly a difference, but it cannot be a constitutionally significant one. While the Brady Act is directed to "individuals," it is directed to them in their official capacities as state officers; it controls their actions, not as private citizens, but as the agents of the State.... To say that the Federal Government cannot control the State, but can control all of its officers, is to say nothing of significance [is] "empty formalistic reasoning of the highest order." By resorting to this, the dissent not so much distinguishes *New York* as disembowels it.

Finally, the Government puts forward a cluster of arguments that can be grouped under the heading: "The Brady Act serves very important purposes, is most efficiently administered by CLEOs during the interim period, and places a minimal and only temporary burden upon state officers." There is considerable disagreement over the extent of the burden, but we need not pause over that detail. Assuming *all* the mentioned factors were true, they might be relevant if we were evaluating whether the incidental application to the States of a federal law of general applicability excessively interfered with the functioning of state governments. But where, as here, it is the whole *object* of the law to direct the functioning of the state executive, and hence to compromise the structural framework of dual sovereignty, such a "balancing" analysis is inappropriate.[17] It is the very *principle* of separate state sovereignty that such a law offends, and no comparative assessment of the various

---

17. The dissent observes that "Congress could require private persons, such as hospital executives or school administrators, to provide arms merchants with relevant information about a prospective purchaser's fitness to own a weapon," and that "the burden on police officers [imposed by the Brady Act] would be permissible if a similar burden were also imposed on private parties with access to relevant data." That is undoubtedly true, but it does not advance the dissent's case. The Brady Act does not merely require CLEOs to report information in their private possession. It requires them to provide information that belongs to the State and is available to them only in

interests can overcome that fundamental defect. Cf. *Bowsher* [*v. Synar* (1986), Casebook, § 5–8] (declining to subject principle of separation of powers to a balancing test). [Thus we] conclude categorically, as we concluded categorically in *New York:* "The Federal Government may not compel the States to enact or administer a federal regulatory program." The mandatory obligation imposed on CLEOs to perform background checks on prospective handgun purchasers plainly runs afoul of that rule.

V. What we have said makes it clear enough that the central obligation imposed upon CLEOs by the interim provisions of the Brady Act—the obligation to "make a reasonable effort to ascertain within 5 business days whether receipt or possession [of a handgun] would be in violation of the law, including research in whatever State and local recordkeeping systems are available and in a national system designated by the Attorney General"—is unconstitutional. Extinguished with it, of course, is the duty implicit in the background-check requirement that the CLEO accept notice of the contents of, and a copy of, the completed Brady Form, which the firearms dealer is required to provide to him.

Petitioners also challenge, however, two other provisions of the Act: (1) the requirement that any CLEO "to whom a [Brady Form] is transmitted" destroy the form and any record containing information derived from it, and (2) the requirement that any CLEO who "determines that an individual is ineligible to receive a handgun" provide the would-be purchaser, upon request, a written statement of the reasons for that determination. With the background-check and implicit receipt-of-forms requirements invalidated, however, these provisions require no action whatsoever on the part of the CLEO. Quite obviously, the obligation to destroy all Brady Forms that he has received when he has received none, and the obligation to give reasons for a determination of ineligibility when he never makes a determination of ineligibility, are no obligations at all. These two provisions have conceivable application to a CLEO, in other words, only if he has chosen, voluntarily, to participate in administration of the federal scheme. The present petitioners are not in that position.[18] As to them, these last two challenged provisions are not unconstitutional, but simply inoperative.

There is involved in this Brady Act conundrum a severability question, which the parties have briefed and argued: whether firearms dealers in the jurisdictions at issue here, and in other jurisdictions, remain obliged to forward to the CLEO (even if he will not accept it) the requisite notice of the contents (and a copy) of the Brady Form; and to

their official capacity; and to conduct investigation in their official capacity, by examining databases and records that only state officials have access to. In other words, the suggestion that extension of this statute to private citizens would eliminate the constitutional problem posits the impossible.

18. We note, in this regard, that both CLEOs before us here assert that they are prohibited from taking on these federal responsibilities under state law. That assertion is clearly correct with regard to Montana law, which expressly enjoins any "county . . . or other local government unit" from "prohibit[ing] . . . or regulat[ing] the purchase, sale or other transfer (including delay in purchase, sale, or other transfer), ownership, [or] possession . . . of any . . . handgun." . . .

wait five business days before consummating the sale. These are important questions, but we have no business answering them in these cases. These provisions burden only firearms dealers and purchasers, and no plaintiff in either of those categories is before us here. We decline to speculate regarding the rights and obligations of parties not before the Court.

We held in *New York* that Congress cannot compel the States to enact or enforce a federal regulatory program. Today we hold that Congress cannot circumvent that prohibition by conscripting the State's officers directly. The Federal Government may neither issue directives requiring the States to address particular problems, nor command the States' officers, or those of their political subdivisions, to administer or enforce a federal regulatory program. It matters not whether policymaking is involved, and no case-by-case weighing of the burdens or benefits is necessary; such commands are fundamentally incompatible with our constitutional system of dual sovereignty. Accordingly, the judgment of the Court of Appeals for the Ninth Circuit is reversed.

It is so ordered.

JUSTICE O'CONNOR, concurring.

[T]he Court appropriately refrains from deciding whether other purely ministerial reporting requirements imposed by Congress on state and local authorities pursuant to its Commerce Clause powers are similarly invalid. See, *e.g.*, 42 U. S. C. § 5779(a) (requiring state and local law enforcement agencies to report cases of missing children to the Department of Justice). The provisions invalidated here, however, which directly compel state officials to administer a federal regulatory program, utterly fail to adhere to the design and structure of our constitutional scheme.

JUSTICE STEVENS, with whom JUSTICE SOUTER, JUSTICE GINSBURG, and JUSTICE BREYER join, dissenting.

When Congress exercises the powers delegated to it by the Constitution, it may impose affirmative obligations on executive and judicial officers of state and local governments as well as ordinary citizens. This conclusion is firmly supported by the text of the Constitution, the early history of the Nation, decisions of this Court, and a correct understanding of the basic structure of the Federal Government.

These cases do not implicate the more difficult questions associated with congressional coercion of state legislatures addressed in *New York United States* (1992). Nor need we consider the wisdom of relying on local officials rather than federal agents to carry out aspects of a federal program, or even the question whether such officials may be required to perform a federal function on a permanent basis. The question is whether Congress, acting on behalf of the people of the entire Nation, may require local law enforcement officers to perform certain duties during the interim needed for the development of a federal gun control program. It is remarkably similar to the . . . question whether Congress could impress state judges into federal service to entertain and decide cases that they would prefer to ignore.

Indeed, since the ultimate issue is one of power, we must consider its implications in times of national emergency. Matters such as the enlistment of air raid wardens, the administration of a military draft, the mass inoculation of children to forestall an epidemic, or perhaps the threat of an international terrorist, may require a national response before federal personnel can be made available to respond. . . .

The Brady Act was passed in response to what Congress described as an "epidemic of gun violence." The Act's legislative history notes that 15,377 Americans were murdered with firearms in 1992, and that 12,489 of these deaths were caused by handguns. . . . Between 1994 and 1996, approximately 6,600 firearm sales each month to potentially dangerous persons were prevented by Brady Act checks; over 70% of the rejected purchasers were convicted or indicted felons. Whether or not the evaluation reflected in the enactment of the Brady Act is correct as to the extent of the danger and the efficacy of the legislation, the congressional decision surely warrants more respect than it is accorded in today's unprecedented decision.

The text of the Constitution provides a sufficient basis for a correct disposition of this case. Article I, § 8, grants the Congress the power to regulate commerce among the States. [T]he additional grant of authority in that section of the Constitution "[t]o make all Laws which shall be necessary and proper for carrying into Execution the foregoing Powers" is surely adequate to support the temporary enlistment of local police officers in the process of identifying persons who should not be entrusted with the possession of handguns.

[The Tenth] Amendment provides no support for a rule that immunizes local officials from obligations that might be imposed on ordinary citizens. . . . [D]uring the debates concerning the ratification of the Constitution, it was assumed that state agents would act as tax collectors for the federal government. Opponents of the Constitution had repeatedly expressed fears that the new federal government's ability to impose taxes directly on the citizenry would result in an overbearing presence of federal tax collectors in the States. Federalists rejoined that this problem would not arise because, as Hamilton explained, "the United States . . . will make use of the State officers and State regulations for collecting" certain taxes. . . . [Federalist Papers], No. 45. The Court's response to this powerful historical evidence is weak. The majority suggests that "none of these statements necessarily implies . . . Congress could impose these responsibilities without the consent of the States." (emphasis omitted) . . . .

Recent developments demonstrate that the political safeguards protecting Our Federalism are effective. The majority expresses special concern that were its rule not adopted the Federal Government would be able to avail itself of the services of state government officials "at no cost to itself." But this specific problem of federal actions that have the effect of imposing so-called "unfunded mandates" on the States has been identified and meaningfully addressed by Congress in recent legislation. See Unfunded Mandates Reform Act of 1995.

... By limiting the ability of the Federal Government to enlist state officials in the implementation of its programs, the Court creates incentives for the National Government to aggrandize itself. In the name of State's rights, the majority would have the Federal Government create vast national bureaucracies to implement its policies. This is exactly the sort of thing that the early Federalists promised would not occur, in part as a result of the National Government's ability to rely on the magistracy of the states.

[T]he Court's reasoning contradicts *New York v. United States,* [which] squarely approved of cooperative federalism programs, designed at the national level but implemented principally by state governments. *New York* disapproved of a particular *method* of putting such programs into place, not the *existence* of federal programs implemented locally. Indeed, nothing in the majority's holding calls into question the three mechanisms for constructing such programs that *New York* expressly approved. Congress may require the States to implement its programs as a condition of federal spending, in order to avoid the threat of unilateral federal action in the area, or as a part of a program that affects States and private parties alike. ...

JUSTICE SOUTER, dissenting.

.... In deciding these cases, which I have found closer than I had anticipated, it is The Federalist that finally determines my position. ...Hamilton in No. 27 first notes that because the new Constitution would authorize the National Government to bind individuals directly through national law, it could "employ the ordinary magistracy of each [State] in the execution of its laws." Were he to stop here, he would not necessarily be speaking of anything beyond the possibility of cooperative arrangements by agreement. But he then ... states that "the Legislatures, Courts and Magistrates of the respective members will be incorporated into the operations of the national government, *as far as its just and constitutional authority extends;* and will be rendered auxiliary to the enforcement of its laws." The Federalist No. 27 (emphasis in original). The natural reading of this language is not merely that the officers of the various branches of state governments may be employed in the performance of national functions; Hamilton says that the state governmental machinery "will be incorporated" into the Nation's operation, and because the "auxiliary" status of the state officials will occur because they are "bound by the sanctity of an oath," I take him to mean that their auxiliary functions will be the products of their obligations thus undertaken to support federal law, not of their own, or the States', unfettered choices....

JUSTICE BREYER, with whom JUSTICE STEVENS joins, dissenting.

... The federal systems of Switzerland, Germany, and the European Union, for example, all provide that constituent states, not federal bureaucracies, will themselves implement many of the laws, rules, regulations, or decrees enacted by the central "federal" body....

[The opinion of Thomas, J., concurring, is omitted.]

Chapter 5

THE PRESIDENT AND CONGRESS

5–1. THE FOUNDATIONS OF THE FOREIGN AFFAIRS POW-ER

UNITED STATES v. CURTISS-WRIGHT EXPORT CORP.

299 U.S. 304, 57 S.Ct. 216, 81 L.Ed. 255 (1936).

MR. JUSTICE SUTHERLAND delivered the opinion of the Court.

On January 27, 1936, an indictment was returned in the court below, the first count of which charges that appellees, beginning with the 29th day of May, 1934, conspired to sell in the United States certain arms of war, namely fifteen machine guns, to Bolivia, a country then engaged in armed conflict in the Chaco, in violation of the Joint Resolution of Congress approved May 28, 1934, and the provisions of a proclamation issued on the same day by the President of the United States pursuant to authority conferred by § 1 of the resolution. In pursuance of the conspiracy, the commission of certain overt acts was alleged, details of which need not be stated. The Joint Resolution (c. 365, 48 Stat. 811) follows:

Resolved by the Senate and House of Representatives of the United States of America in Congress assembled, That if the President finds that the prohibition of the sale of arms and munitions of war in the United States to those countries now engaged in armed conflict in the Chaco may contribute to the reestablishment of peace between those countries, and if after consultation with the governments of other American Republics and with their coöperation, as well as that of such other governments as he may deem necessary, he makes proclamation to that effect, it shall be unlawful to sell, except under such limitations and exceptions as the President prescribes, any arms or munitions of war in any place in the United States to the countries now engaged in that armed conflict, or to any person, company, or association acting in the interest of either country, until otherwise ordered by the President or by Congress.

Sec. 2. Whoever sells any arms or munitions of war in violation of section 1 shall, on conviction, be punished by a fine not exceeding $10,000 or by imprisonment not exceeding two years, or both.

[President Roosevelt issued a proclamation prohibiting the sale of such arms and delegated to the Secretary of State the power to prescribe exceptions and limitations to the joint resolution which his proclamation made effective. 48 Stat. 1744. On November 14, 1935, the President revoked his proclamation "provided, however, that this action shall not have the effect of releasing or extinguishing any penalty, forfeiture or liability incurred under the aforesaid Proclamation."]

[A]ppellees urge that Congress abdicated its essential functions and delegated them to the Executive. Whether, if the Joint Resolution had related solely to internal affairs it would be open to the challenge that it constituted an unlawful delegation of legislative power to the Executive, we find it unnecessary to determine. The whole aim of the resolution is to affect a situation entirely external to the United States, and falling within the category of foreign affairs. The determination which we are called to make, therefore, is whether the Joint Resolution, as applied to that situation, is vulnerable to attack under the rule that forbids a delegation of the law-making power. In other words, assuming (but not deciding) that the challenged delegation, if it were confined to internal affairs, would be invalid, may it nevertheless be sustained on the ground that its exclusive aim is to afford a remedy for a hurtful condition within foreign territory?

It will contribute to the elucidation of the question if we first consider the differences between the powers of the federal government in respect of foreign or external affairs and those in respect of domestic or internal affairs. That there are differences between them, and that these differences are fundamental, may not be doubted.

The two classes of powers are different, both in respect of their origin and their nature. The broad statement that the federal government can exercise no powers except those specifically enumerated in the Constitution, and such implied powers as are necessary and proper to carry into effect the enumerated powers, is categorically true only in respect of our internal affairs. In that field, the primary purpose of the Constitution was to carve from the general mass of legislative powers *then possessed by the states* such portions as it was thought desirable to vest in the federal government, leaving those not included in the enumeration still in the states. *Carter v. Carter Coal Co.,* [§ 4–1, supra]. That this doctrine applies only to powers which the states had, is self evident. And since the states severally never possessed international powers, such powers could not have been carved from the mass of state powers but obviously were transmitted to the United States from some other source. During the colonial period, those powers were possessed exclusively by and were entirely under the control of the Crown. By the Declaration of Independence, "the Representatives of the United States of America" declared the United [not the several] Colonies to be free and independent states, and as such to have "full Power to levy War, conclude Peace, contract Alliances, establish Commerce and to do all other Acts and Things which Independent States may of right do."

As a result of the separation from Great Britain by the colonies acting as a unit, the powers of external sovereignty passed from the Crown not to the colonies severally, but to the colonies in their collective and corporate capacity as the United States of America. Even before the Declaration, the colonies were a unit in foreign affairs, acting through a common agency—namely the Continental Congress, composed of delegates from the thirteen colonies. That agency exercised the powers of war and peace, raised an army, created a navy, and finally adopted the Declaration of Independence. Rulers come and go; governments end and forms of government change; but sovereignty survives. A political society cannot endure without a supreme will somewhere. Sovereignty is never held in suspense. When, therefore, the external sovereignty of Great Britain in respect of the colonies ceased, it immediately passed to the Union. That fact was given practical application almost at once. The treaty of peace, made on September 23, 1783, was concluded between his Brittanic Majesty and the "United States of America." 8 Stat.—European Treaties—80.

The Union existed before the Constitution, which was ordained and established among other things to form "a more perfect Union." Prior to that event, it is clear that the Union, declared by the Articles of Confederation to be "perpetual," was the sole possessor of external sovereignty and in the Union it remained without change save in so far as the Constitution in express terms qualified its exercise. The Framers' Convention was called and exerted its powers upon the irrefutable postulate that though the states were several their people in respect of foreign affairs were one. In that convention, the entire absence of state power to deal with those affairs was thus forcefully stated by Rufus King:

> The states were not "sovereigns" in the sense contended for by some. They did not possess the peculiar features of sovereignty,— they could not make war, nor peace, nor alliances, nor treaties. Considering them as political beings, they were dumb, for they could not speak to any foreign sovereign whatever. They were deaf, for they could not hear any propositions from such sovereign. They had not even the organs or faculties of defence or offence, for they could not of themselves raise troops, or equip vessels, for war. 5 Elliott's Debates 212.

It results that the investment of the federal government with the powers of external sovereignty did not depend upon the affirmative grants of the Constitution. The powers to declare and wage war, to conclude peace, to make treaties, to maintain diplomatic relations with other sovereignties, if they had never been mentioned in the Constitution, would have vested in the federal government as necessary concomitants of nationality. Neither the Constitution nor the laws passed in pursuance of it have any force in foreign territory unless in respect of our own citizens; and operations of the nation in such territory must be governed by treaties, international understandings and compacts, and the principles of international law. As a member of the family of nations, the right and power of the United States in that field are equal to the right and power of the other members of the international family. Otherwise, the United States is not completely sovereign. The power to acquire territory by discovery and occupation (*Jones v. United States,* 137 U.S. 202, 212, 11 S.Ct. 80, 34 L.Ed. 691), the power to expel undesirable aliens (*Fong Yue Ting v. United States,* 149 U.S. 698, 705 et seq., 13 S.Ct. 1016, 37 L.Ed. 905), the power to make such international agreements as do not constitute treaties in the constitutional sense (*Altman & Co. v. United States,* 224 U.S. 583, 600, 601, 32 S.Ct. 593, 56 L.Ed. 894; Crandall, Treaties, Their Making and Enforcement, 2d ed., p. 102 and note 1), none of which is expressly affirmed by the Constitution, nevertheless exist as inherently inseparable from the conception of nationality. This the court recognized, and in each of the cases cited found the warrant for its conclusions not in the provisions of the Constitution, but in the law of nations....

Not only, as we have shown, is the federal power over external affairs in origin and essential character different from that over internal affairs, but participation in the exercise of the power is significantly limited. In this vast external realm, with its important, complicated, delicate and manifold problems, the President alone has the power to speak or listen as a representative of the nation. He *makes* treaties with the advice and consent of the Senate; but he alone negotiates. Into the field of negotiation the Senate cannot intrude; and Congress itself is powerless to invade it. As Marshall said in his great argument of March 7, 1800, in the House of Representatives, "The President is the sole organ of the nation in its external relations, and its sole representative with foreign nations." ...

It is important to bear in mind that we are here dealing not alone with an authority vested in the President by an exertion of legislative power, but with such an authority plus the very delicate, plenary and exclusive power of the President as the sole organ of the federal government in the field of international relations—a power which does not require as a basis for its exercise an act of Congress, but which, of course, like every other governmental power, must be exercised in subordination to the applicable provisions of the Constitution. It is quite apparent that if, in the maintenance of our international relations, embarrassment—perhaps serious embarrassment—is to be avoided and success for our aims achieved, congressional legislation which is to be made effective through negotiation and inquiry within the international field must often accord to the President a degree of discretion and freedom from statutory restriction which would not be admissible were domestic affairs alone involved. Moreover, he, not Congress, has the better opportunity of knowing the conditions which prevail in foreign countries, and especially is this true in time of war. He has his confidential sources of information. He has his agents in the form of diplomatic, consular and other officials. Secrecy in respect of information gathered by them may be highly necessary, and the premature disclosure of it productive of harmful results. Indeed, so clearly is this true that the first President refused to accede to a request to lay before the House of Representatives the instructions, correspondence and documents relating to the negotiation of the Jay Treaty—a refusal the wisdom of which was recognized by the House itself and has never since been doubted....

Practically every volume of the United States Statutes contains one or more acts or joint resolutions of Congress authorizing action by the President in respect of subjects affecting foreign relations, which either leave the exercise of the power to his unrestricted judgment, or provide a standard far more general than that which has always been considered requisite with regard to domestic affairs.... The result of holding that the joint resolution here under attack is void and unenforceable as constituting an unlawful delegation of legislative power would be to stamp this multitude of comparable acts and resolutions as likewise invalid. And while this court may not, and should not, hesitate to declare acts of Congress, however many times repeated, to be unconstitutional if beyond all rational doubt it finds them to be so, an impressive array of legislation such as we have just set forth, enacted by nearly every Congress from the beginning of our national existence to the present day, must be given unusual weight in the process of reaching a correct determination of the problem....

We deem it unnecessary to consider, *seriatim,* the several clauses which are said to evidence the unconstitutionality of the Joint Resolution as involving an unlawful delegation of legislative power. It is enough to summarize by saying that, both upon principle and in accordance with precedent, we conclude there is sufficient warrant for the broad discretion vested in the President to determine whether the enforcement of the statute will have a beneficial effect upon the reestablishment of peace in the affected countries; whether he shall make proclamation to bring the resolution into operation; whether and when the resolution shall cease to operate and to make proclamation accordingly; and to prescribe limitations and exceptions to which the enforcement of the resolution shall be subject....

The judgment of the court below must be reversed and the cause remanded for further proceedings in accordance with the foregoing opinion.

Reversed.

MR. JUSTICE MCREYNOLDS does not agree. He is of opinion that the court below reached the right conclusion and its judgment ought to be affirmed.

MR. JUSTICE STONE took no part in the consideration or decision of this case.

Notes

1.   Justice Sutherland assumed that the Congressional delegation of powers to the President would be invalid in the domestic sphere, but he upheld the delegation in the international sphere. He argued that the federal power over external affairs is different in origin from the power over domestic affairs. Consequently, the "broad statement that the federal government can exercise no powers except those specifically enumerated in the Constitution, and such implied powers as are necessary and proper to carry into effect the enumerated powers, is categorically true only in respect of our internal affairs." What does Sutherland mean? Do you agree?

If it was unnecessary for the Constitution to grant the power to declare war, make peace, make treaties, etc., why did the Constitution specifically mention such powers? Was it simply wordy? How might Sutherland have answered this concern?

Under Sutherland's theory, are there any limits to the assertion of presidential power in the international sphere? Normal delegation of powers doctrine, Sutherland says, does not apply. If the President's powers are not derived from the Constitution, can the Constitution limit their exercise? Is presidential power exercised in the international sphere limited by the Bill of Rights?

If one does not adopt the theory of the extra constitutional origin of the foreign affairs power, how can one explain the exercise of the power to acquire territory by discovery and occupation, the power to expel undesirable aliens, etc.?

2.   As to the historical accuracy of Sutherland's theory that the individual states never possessed international powers, see Van Tyne, Sovereignty in the American Revolution: An Historical Study, 12 Am.Hist.Rev. 529 (1906–07):

> However, dependent the [original thirteen] states might be upon each other for military strength to meet the assaults of England, facts, too numerous to be gainsaid, can be cited to show the opinion of state legislatures, state conventions, and individuals in the states as to the actual political independence and sovereignty of the state. To mere assertions in state constitutions that the state is independent and sovereign we need give little attention, but powers granted in constitutional conventions and acts of sovereignty done by state governments have greater importance. South Carolina specifically endowed its government with the power to make war, conclude a peace, enter into treaties, lay embargoes, and provide an army and navy. Other states specified some of these powers and implied the rest.

> That these powers were implied is proven by the exercise of them by the government established. Virginia ratified the treaty with France, and her diplomatic activity was so great that she established by law a clerkship of foreign correspondence. William Lee was sent to France by Governor Henry and was given power under the state seal to obtain arms or borrow money of "his most Christian Majesty." Franklin speaks of "three several states" negotiating with France for loans and naval and war supplies. He complains that they "seem to think it my duty . . .

to support and enforce their particular demands." In fact the states seem to have regarded the minister sent by Congress to be their particular minister as well as that of other states. Embargoes were laid and ports thrown open to the world by the enactments of state legislatures, sometimes at the suggestion of Congress, but often not. Patrick Henry, who had talked of all America being "thrown into one mass" and who was not a Virginian but an American—when he was seeking to increase the power of Virginia in the First Continental Congress, by securing proportional representation—this same eloquent Henry actively negotiated with Spain in 1778 for a loan and for the approval of Spain to the erection of a fort on Virginia's border, promising in return "the gratitude of this free and independent country, the trade in any or all of its valuable productions, and the friendship of its warlike inhabitants." The whole correspondence is in the tone of one not doubting the independence and sovereignty of his state.

. . . Congress organized a Continental navy, but nine of the thirteen states also fitted out navies of their own and they were able to tax their citizens for supporting the establishment, while Congress could only beg the states to support its navy. . . . As to privateering some of the states established state privateering, while some adopted the Continental system or adapted state laws to it.

3. Sutherland, in support of the distinction he drew as to the scope of presidential power in foreign as opposed to domestic affairs, also articulated several policy concerns (the need to speak with one voice to avoid embarrassment, the confidential information available to the President), and past historical practice (long, unbroken line of statutes delegating broad powers to the President in the area of foreign affairs). What do you think of these arguments?

4. Note that in *Curtiss–Wright* the President was acting in accordance with the will of Congress. Does *Curtiss–Wright* tell us anything about the scope of presidential power in the international sphere when the President is acting contrary to statute?

YOUNGSTOWN SHEET & TUBE CO. v. SAWYER
343 U.S. 579, 72 S.Ct. 863, 96 L.Ed. 1153 (1952).

MR. JUSTICE BLACK delivered the opinion of the Court.

We are asked to decide whether the President was acting within his constitutional power when he issued an order directing the Secretary of Commerce to take possession of and operate most of the Nation's steel mills. . . .

In the latter part of 1951, a dispute arose between the steel companies and their employees over terms and conditions that should be included in new collective bargaining agreements. Long-continued conferences failed to resolve the dispute. [Efforts of the Federal Mediation Service and the Federal Wage Stabilization Board resulted in no settlement.] On April 4, 1952, the Union gave notice of a nation-wide strike called to begin at 12:01 a.m. April 9. The indispensability of steel as a component of substantially all weapons and other war materials led the President to believe that the proposed work stoppage would immediately jeopardize our national defense [the Korean War effort] and that governmental seizure of the steel mills was necessary in order to assure the continued availability of steel. Reciting these considerations for his action, the President, a few hours before the strike was to begin, issued Executive Order 10340, [which] directed the Secretary of Commerce to take possession of most of the steel mills and keep them running. The Secretary immediately issued his own possessory orders, calling upon the presidents of the various seized companies to serve as operating managers for the United States. They were directed to carry on their activities in accordance with regulations and directions of the Secretary. The next morning the President sent a message to Congress reporting his action. Twelve days later he sent a second message. Congress has taken no action.

Obeying the Secretary's orders under protest, the companies brought proceedings against him in the District Court. Their complaints charged that the seizure was not authorized by an act of Congress or by any constitutional provisions. The District Court was asked to declare the orders of the President and the Secretary invalid and to issue preliminary and permanent injunctions restraining their enforcement. Opposing the motion for preliminary injunction, the United States asserted that a strike disrupting steel production for even a brief period would so endanger the well-being and safety of the Nation that the President had "inherent power" to do what he had done—power "supported by the Constitution, by historical precedent, and by court decisions." . . . Holding against the Government on all points, the District Court on April 30 issued a preliminary injunction. . . . On the same day the Court of Appeals stayed the District Court's injunction. Deeming it best that the issues raised be promptly decided by this Court, we granted certiorari on May 3 and set the cause for argument on May 12. . . .

The President's power, if any, to issue the order must stem either from an act of Congress or from the Constitution itself. There is no statute that expressly authorizes the President to take possession of property as he did here. Nor is there any act of Congress to which our attention has been directed from which such a power can fairly be implied. Indeed, we do not understand the Government to rely on statutory authorization for this seizure. There are two statutes which do authorize the President to take both personal and real property under certain conditions.[1] However, the Government admits that these conditions were not met and that the President's order was not rooted in either of the statutes. The Government refers to the seizure provisions of one of these statutes (§ 201(b) of the Defense Production Act) as "much too cumbersome, involved, and time-consuming for the crisis which was at hand."

1. The Selective Service Act of 1948, the   Defense Production Act of 1950.

Moreover, the use of the seizure technique to solve labor disputes in order to prevent work stoppages was not only unauthorized by any congressional enactment; prior to this controversy, Congress had refused to adopt that method of settling labor disputes. When the Taft–Hartley Act was under consideration in 1947, Congress rejected an amendment which would have authorized such governmental seizures in cases of emergency. Apparently it was thought that the technique of seizure, like that of compulsory arbitration, would interfere with the process of collective bargaining.

[I]t is not claimed that express constitutional language grants this power to the President. The contention is that presidential power should be implied from the aggregate of his powers under the Constitution. Particular reliance is placed on provisions in Article II which say that "The executive Power shall be vested in a President ...''; that "he shall take Care that the Laws be faithfully executed"; and that he "shall be Commander in Chief of the Army and Navy of the United States."

The order cannot properly be sustained as an exercise of the President's military power as Commander in Chief of the Armed Forces. The Government attempts to do so by citing a number of cases upholding broad powers in military commanders engaged in day-to-day fighting in a theater of war. Such cases need not concern us here. Even though "theater of war" be an expanding concept, we cannot with faithfulness to our constitutional system hold that the Commander in Chief of the Armed Forces has the ultimate power as such to take possession of private property in order to keep labor disputes from stopping production. This is a job for the Nation's lawmakers, not for its military authorities.

Nor can the seizure order be sustained because of the several constitutional provisions that grant executive power to the President. In the framework of our Constitution, the President's power to see that the laws are faithfully executed refutes the idea that he is to be a lawmaker. The Constitution limits his functions in the lawmaking process to the recommending of laws he thinks wise and the vetoing of laws he thinks bad. And the Constitution is neither silent nor equivocal about who shall make laws which the President is to execute. The first section of the first article says that "All legislative Powers herein granted shall be vested in a Congress of the United States.... " After granting many powers to the Congress, Article I goes on to provide that Congress may "make all Laws which shall be necessary and proper for carrying into Execution the foregoing Powers, and all other Powers vested by this Constitution in the Government of the United States, or in any Department or Officer thereof."

The President's order does not direct that a congressional policy be executed in a manner prescribed by Congress—it directs that a presidential policy be executed in a manner prescribed by the President.... The power of Congress to adopt such public policies as those proclaimed by the order is beyond question. It can authorize the taking of private property for public use. It can make laws regulating the relationships between employers and employees, prescribing rules designed to settle labor disputes, and fixing wages and working conditions in certain fields of our economy. The Constitution does not subject this lawmaking power of Congress to presidential or military supervision or control. . . .

The judgment of the District Court is

Affirmed.

MR. JUSTICE FRANKFURTER, concurring.

. . . Rigorous adherence to the narrow scope of the judicial function is especially demanded in controversies that arouse appeals to the Constitution. The attitude with which this Court must approach its duty when confronted with such issues is precisely the opposite of that normally manifested by the general public. So-called constitutional questions seem to exercise a mesmeric influence over the popular mind. This eagerness to settle—preferably forever—a specific problem on the basis of the broadest possible constitutional pronouncements may not unfairly be called one of our minor national traits. . . .

It is in this mood and with this perspective that the issue before the Court must be approached. We must therefore put to one side consideration of what powers the President would have had if there had been no legislation whatever bearing on the authority asserted by the seizure, or if the seizure had been only for a short, explicitly temporary period, to be terminated automatically unless Congressional approval were given. These and other questions, like or unlike, are not now here. I would exceed my authority were I to say anything about them.

The question before the Court comes in this setting. Congress has frequently—at least 16 times since 1916—specifically provided for executive seizure of production, transportation, communications, or storage facilities. In every case it has qualified this grant of power with limitations and safeguards. . . . The power to seize has uniformly been given only for a limited period or for a defined emergency, or has been repealed after a short period. . . . Previous seizure legislation had subjected the powers granted to the President to restrictions of varying degrees of stringency. Instead of giving him even limited powers, Congress in [the Labor Management Relations Act of] 1947 deemed it wise to require the President, upon failure of attempts to reach a voluntary settlement, to report to Congress if he deemed the power of seizure a needed shot for his locker. The President could not ignore the specific limitations of prior seizure statutes. No more could he act in disregard of the limitation put upon seizure by the 1947 Act. . . . Congress has expressed its will to withhold this power from the President as though it had said so in so many words. . . .

To be sure, the content of the three authorities of government is not to be derived from an abstract analysis. [A] systematic, unbroken, executive practice, long pursued to the knowledge of the Congress and never before questioned, engaged in by Presidents who have also sworn to uphold the Constitution, making as it were such exercise of power part of the structure of our government, may be treated as a gloss on "executive Power" vested in the President by § 1 of Art. II.

Such was the case of *United States v. Midwest Oil Co.,* 236 U.S. 459, 35 S.Ct. 309, 59 L.Ed. 673 [1915], [where the President] was dealing with the protection of property belonging to the United States. [L]ands which Congress had opened for entry were, over a period of 80 years and in 252 instances, and by Presidents learned and unlearned in the law, temporarily withdrawn from entry so as to enable Congress to deal with such withdrawals. No remotely comparable practice can be vouched for executive seizure of property at a time when this country was not at war, in the only constitutional way in which it can be at war. It would pursue the irrelevant to reopen the controversy over the constitutionality of some acts of Lincoln during the Civil War. See J.G. Randall, Constitutional Problems under Lincoln (Revised ed. 1951). Suffice it to say that he seized railroads in territory where armed hostilities had already interrupted the movement of troops to the beleaguered Capital, and his order was ratified by the Congress.... In this case, reliance on the powers that flow from declared war has been commendably disclaimed by the Solicitor General....

Mr. Justice Douglas, concurring.

There can be no doubt that the emergency which caused the President to seize these steel plants was one that bore heavily on the country. But the emergency did not create power; it merely marked an occasion when power should be exercised.... All executive power—from the reign of ancient kings to the rule of modern dictators—has the outward appearance of efficiency....

The President has no power to raise revenues. That power is in the Congress by Article I, Section 8 of the Constitution. The President might seize and the Congress by subsequent action might ratify the seizure. But until and unless Congress acted, no condemnation would be lawful. The branch of government that has the power to pay compensation for a seizure is the only one able to authorize a seizure or make lawful one that the President has effected. [This principle] squares with the theory of checks and balances expounded by Mr. Justice Black in the opinion of the Court in which I join....

Mr. Justice Jackson, concurring in the judgment and opinion of the Court.

... Just what our forefathers did envision, or would have envisioned had they foreseen modern conditions, must be divined from materials almost as enigmatic as the dreams Joseph was called upon to interpret for Pharaoh. A century and a half of partisan debate and scholarly speculation yields no net result but only supplies more or less apt quotations from respected sources on each side of any question. They largely cancel each other.[1] And court decisions are indecisive because of

---

1. A Hamilton may be matched against   a Madison. 7 The Works of Alexander Ham-

the judicial practice of dealing with the largest questions in the most narrow way. . . . Presidential powers are not fixed but fluctuate, depending upon their disjunction or conjunction with those of Congress. We may well begin by a somewhat over-simplified grouping of practical situations in which a President may doubt, or others may challenge, his powers, and by distinguishing roughly the legal consequences of this factor of relativity.

1. When the President acts pursuant to an express or implied authorization of Congress, his authority is at its maximum, for it includes all that he possesses in his own right plus all that Congress can delegate. In these circumstances, and in these only, may he be said (for what it may be worth) to personify the federal sovereignty. If his act is held unconstitutional under these circumstances, it usually means that the Federal Government as an undivided whole lacks power. A seizure executed by the President pursuant to an Act of Congress would be supported by the strongest of presumptions and the widest latitude of judicial interpretation, and the burden of persuasion would rest heavily upon any who might attack it.

2. When the President acts in absence of either a congressional grant or denial of authority, he can only rely upon his own independent powers, but there is a zone of twilight in which he and Congress may have concurrent authority, or in which its distribution is uncertain.[2] Therefore, congressional inertia, indifference or quiescence may sometimes, at least as a practical matter, enable, if not invite, measures on independent presidential responsibility. In this area, any actual test of power is likely to depend on the imperatives of events and contemporary imponderables rather than on abstract theories of law.

3. When the President takes measures incompatible with the expressed or implied will of Congress, his power is at its lowest ebb, for then he can rely upon his own constitutional powers minus any constitutional powers of Congress over the matter. Courts can sustain exclusive presidential control in such a case only by disabling the Congress from acting upon the subject. Presidential claim to a power at once so conclusive and preclusive must be scrutinized with caution, for what is at stake is the equilibrium established by our constitutional system.

Into which of these classifications does this executive seizure of the steel industry fit? It is eliminated from the first by admission, for it is conceded that no congressional authorization exists for this seizure. That takes away also the support of the many precedents and declarations which were made in relation, and must be confined, to this category.

ilton, 76–117; 1 Madison, Letters and Other Writings, 611–654. Professor Taft is counter-balanced by Theodore Roosevelt. Taft, Our Chief Magistrate and His Powers, 139–140; Theodore Roosevelt, Autobiography, 388–389. It even seems that President Taft cancels out Professor Taft. Compare his "Temporary Petroleum Withdrawal No. 5" of September 27, 1909, *United States v. Midwest Oil Co.*, 236 U.S. 459, 467, 468, 35 S.Ct. 309, 311, 59 L.Ed. 673, with his appraisal of executive power in "Our Chief Magistrate and His Powers" 139–140.

2. . . . Much of the Court's opinion [in *Curtiss-Wright*] is dictum. . . .

Can it then be defended under flexible tests available to the second category? It seems clearly eliminated from that class because Congress has not left seizure of private property an open field but has covered it by three statutory policies inconsistent with this seizure....

This leaves the current seizure to be justified only by the severe tests under the third grouping, where it can be supported only by any remainder of executive power after subtraction of such powers as Congress may have over the subject. In short, we can sustain the President only by holding that seizure of such strike-bound industries is within his domain and beyond control by Congress. Thus, this Court's first review of such seizures occurs under circumstances which leave presidential power most vulnerable to attack and in the least favorable of possible constitutional postures.

[One] clause on which the Government ... relies is that "The President shall be Commander in Chief of the Army and Navy of the United States.... " [T]he logic of an argument tendered at our bar [is] that the President having, on his own responsibility, sent American troops abroad [to fight the Korean War] derives from that act "affirmative power" to seize the means of producing a supply of steel for them. To quote [the Government's brief], "Perhaps the most forceful illustration of the scope of Presidential power in this connection is the fact that American troops in Korea, whose safety and effectiveness are so directly involved here, were sent to the field by an exercise of the President's constitutional powers." Thus, it is said, he has invested himself with "war powers."

I cannot foresee all that it might entail if the Court should indorse this argument. Nothing in our Constitution is plainer than that declaration of a war is entrusted only to Congress. Of course, a state of war may in fact exist without a formal declaration. But no doctrine that the Court could promulgate would seem to me more sinister and alarming than that a President whose conduct of foreign affairs is so largely uncontrolled, and often even is unknown, can vastly enlarge his mastery over the internal affairs of the country by his own commitment of the Nation's armed forces to some foreign venture. I do not, however, find it necessary or appropriate to consider the legal status of the Korean enterprise to discountenance argument based on it.

Assuming that we are in a war *de facto,* whether it is or is not a war *de jure,* does that empower the Commander in Chief to seize industries he thinks necessary to supply our army? The Constitution expressly places in Congress power "to raise and *support* Armies" and "to *provide* and *maintain* a Navy." (Emphasis supplied.) This certainly lays upon Congress primary responsibility for supplying the armed forces. [The President] has no monopoly of "war powers," whatever they are. While Congress cannot deprive the President of the command of the army and navy, only Congress can provide him an army or navy to command. It is also empowered to make rules for the "Government and Regulation of land and naval Forces," by which it may to some unknown extent impinge upon even command functions.

... We should not use this occasion to circumscribe, much less to contract, the lawful role of the President as Commander in Chief. I should indulge the widest latitude of interpretation to sustain his exclusive function to command the instruments of national force, at least when turned against the outside world for the security of our society. But, when it is turned inward, not because of rebellion but because of a lawful economic struggle between industry and labor, it should have no such indulgence. His command power is not such an absolute as might be implied from that office in a militaristic system but is subject to limitations consistent with a constitutional Republic whose law and policy-making branch is a representative Congress. The purpose of lodging dual titles in one man was to insure that the civilian would control the military, not to enable the military to subordinate the presidential office....

Mr. Justice Clark, concurring in the judgment of the Court.

[T]he Constitution does grant to the President extensive authority in times of grave and imperative national emergency. In fact, to my thinking, such a grant may well be necessary to the very existence of the Constitution itself. As Lincoln aptly said, "[is] it possible to lose the nation and yet preserve the Constitution?" In describing this authority I care not whether one calls it "residual," "inherent," "moral," "implied," "aggregate," "emergency," or otherwise. I am of the conviction that those who have had the gratifying experience of being the President's lawyer have used one or more of these adjectives only with the utmost of sincerity and the highest of purpose.

I conclude that where Congress has laid down specific procedures to deal with the type of crisis confronting the President, he must follow those procedures in meeting the crisis; but that in the absence of such action by Congress, the President's independent power to act depends upon the gravity of the situation confronting the nation. I cannot sustain the seizure in question because here.... Congress had prescribed methods to be followed by the President in meeting the emergency at hand....

[A separate opinion of Burton, J., concurring in both the opinion and judgment of the Court is omitted. Also omitted is the dissenting opinion of Vinson, C.J., joined by Reed & Minton, JJ.]

Notes

1. Note how quickly the Supreme Court can act if it really wants to. The district court entered its injunction on April 30, 1952. That same day the court of appeals stayed the action, and the Supreme Court granted certiorari on May 3d, bypassing the circuit court. Oral argument was May 12–13, and the case was decided on June 2d, with a series of opinions totaling approximately 130 pages in the U.S. Reports. Note also, while

President Truman was the real party in interest, the plaintiffs instead sued Sawyer, the Secretary of Commerce.

2. Justice Clark was the only member of the majority who did not join in the opinion of the Court. Why?

3. *Cunningham v. Neagle,* 135 U.S. 1, 10 S.Ct. 658, 34 L.Ed. 55 (1890). Neagle sued for habeas in federal court while he was a prisoner held in state custody for murder of one David Terry. The Attorney General had assigned Neagle, a U.S. deputy marshal, to protect Justice Field, whose life had been threatened. Neagle killed Terry because of "an anticipated attempt at violence on the part of Terry" against Field. The Court (with two dissents) authorized Neagle's release because he was a federal officer acting in line of duty. It was conceded that no statute authorized the President to assign a guard. The majority asked, rhetorically: "Is [the President's duty to faithfully execute the laws] limited to enforcement of acts of Congress or of treaties of the United States according to their *express terms,* or does it include the rights, duties and obligations growing out of the Constitution itself, our international relations, and all the protection implied by the nature of the government under the Constitution?"

How is *Neagle* different from *Youngstown?*

By statute Congress has authorized the President to supply Secret Service protection to Presidential candidates. During the 1976 presidential race, President Ford authorized the Secret Service to protect Senator Edward Kennedy, who insisted he was not a candidate and who did not run in any primaries, seek to obtain delegates, etc. Was the President's action authorized by *Neagle* or forbidden by *Youngstown?*

4. Does the Congressional refusal to authorize certain presidential powers necessarily imply that Congress wishes to preclude the President from exercising those powers? What if some Congressmen said, during the legislative debate, that they opposed the law as unnecessary, arguing that the President already has such inherent powers?

Assume that Congress passed a law forbidding the President to exercise a certain power. The President vetoed that law and Congress was unable to override the veto. How might those facts have affected the *Youngstown* case? How might Justice Jackson, with his twilight zone analysis, approach the problem? Or the other Justices?

5. THE WAR POWERS RESOLUTION. Only Congress can "declare" war, Art. I, § 8, cl. 11. But historically the President, at least within some limits, can "make" war. The original draft of this clause in fact did give Congress the power to "make" war, but the significance of this change in language is the subject of debate. Some of the framers wanted to make it clear that Congress could not conduct war and that the President could respond to sudden attacks.[1] Past Presidents have justified the power to engage in undeclared hostilities under theories of self-defense, protection of American neutrality and American nationals and property abroad, and fulfillment of collective security agreements (such as NATO), or congressional resolutions authoriz-

---

1. 1 Ronald D. Rotunda & John E. Nowak, Treatise on Constitutional Law: Substance and Procedure § 6.9 (West, 2d ed. 1992); John E. Nowak & Ronald D. Rotunda, Constitutional Law § 6.10 (West Hornbook Series, 5th ed. 1995).

ing or ratifying actions. In an effort to reassert more Congressional control over the war power, Congress enacted, over presidential veto, the War Powers Resolution, 50 U.S.C.A. §§ 1541 et seq. It provides that, if the President introduces U.S. forces into hostilities in the absence of a declaration of war, he must issue a report in writing to the Speaker of the House and President pro tempore of the Senate. Within 60 days thereafter, the President is supposed to terminate the use of such forces unless Congress has authorized the use of such force, extended the 60 day period, or is physically unable to meet because of an armed attack on the United States. The Joint Resolution concludes:

(d) Nothing in this joint resolution—

(1) is intended to alter the constitutional authority of the Congress or of the President, or the provisions of existing treaties; or

(2) shall be construed as granting any authority to the President with respect to the introduction of United States Armed Forces into hostilities or into situations wherein involvement in hostilities is clearly indicated by the circumstances which authority he would not have had in the absence of this joint resolution. . . .

5–2. TREATIES AND EXECUTIVE AGREEMENTS

MISSOURI v. HOLLAND
252 U.S. 416, 40 S.Ct. 382, 64 L.Ed. 641 (1920).

MR. JUSTICE HOLMES delivered the opinion of the court.

This is a bill in equity brought by the State of Missouri to prevent a game warden of the United States from attempting to enforce the Migratory Bird Treaty Act of July 3, 1918, and the regulations made by the Secretary of Agriculture in pursuance of the same. The ground of the bill is that the statute is an unconstitutional interference with the rights reserved to the States by the Tenth Amendment, and that the acts of the defendant done and threatened under that authority invade the sovereign right of the State and contravene its will manifested in statutes. The State also alleges a pecuniary interest, as owner of the wild birds within its borders and otherwise, admitted by the Government to be sufficient, but it is enough that the bill is a reasonable and proper means to assert the alleged quasi sovereign rights of a State. A motion to dismiss was sustained by the District Court on the ground that the act of Congress is constitutional. The State appeals.

On December 8, 1916, a treaty between the United States and Great Britain was proclaimed by the President. It recited that many species of birds in their annual migrations traversed certain parts of the United States and of Canada, that they were of great value as a source of food and in destroying insects injurious to vegetation, but were in danger of extermination through lack of adequate protection. It therefore provided for specified close seasons and protection in other forms, and agreed that the two powers would take or propose to their law-making bodies the necessary measures for carrying the treaty out. 39 Stat. 1702. The above mentioned Act of July 3, 1918, entitled an act to give effect to the convention, prohibited the killing, capturing or selling any of the migratory birds included in the terms of the treaty except as permitted by regulations compatible with those terms, to be made by the Secretary of Agriculture. Regulations were proclaimed on July 31, and October 25, 1918. It is unnecessary to go into any details, because, as we have said, the question raised is the general one whether the treaty and statute are void as an interference with the rights reserved to the States.

To answer this question it is not enough to refer to the Tenth Amendment, reserving the powers not delegated to the United States, because by Article II, § 2, the power to make treaties is delegated expressly, and by Article VI treaties made under the authority of the United States, along with the Constitution and laws of the United States made in pursuance thereof, are declared the supreme law of the land. If the treaty is valid there can be no dispute about the validity of the statute under Article I, § 8, as a necessary and proper means to execute the powers of the Government. The language of the Constitution as to the supremacy of treaties being general, the question before us is narrowed to an inquiry into the ground upon which the present supposed exception is placed.

It is said that a treaty cannot be valid if it infringes the Constitution, that there are limits, therefore, to the treaty-making power, and that one such limit is that what an act of Congress could not do unaided, in derogation of the powers reserved to the States, a treaty cannot do. An earlier act of Congress that attempted by itself and not in pursuance of a treaty to regulate the killing of migratory birds within the States had been held bad in the District Court. *United States v. Shauver,* 214 Fed. 154. *United States v. McCullagh,* 221 Fed. 288. Those decisions were supported by arguments that migratory birds were owned by the States in their sovereign capacity for the benefit of their people, and that under cases like *Geer v. Connecticut,* 161 U.S. 519, 16 Sup.Ct. 600, 40 L.Ed. 793, this control was one that Congress had no power to displace. The same argument is supposed to apply now with equal force.

Whether the two cases cited were decided rightly or not they cannot be accepted as a test of the treaty power. Acts of Congress are the supreme law of the land only when made in pursuance of the Constitution, while treaties are declared to be so when made under the authority of the United States. It is open to question whether the authority of the United States means more than the formal acts prescribed to make the convention. We do not mean to imply that there are no qualifications to the treaty-making power; but they must be ascertained in a different way. It is obvious that there may be matters of the sharpest exigency for the national well being that an act of Congress could not deal with but that a treaty followed by such an act could, and it is not lightly to be assumed that, in matters requiring national action, "a power which must belong to and somewhere reside in every civilized government" is not to be found. *Andrews v. Andrews,* 188 U.S. 14, 33, 23 S.Ct. 237, 47 L.Ed. 366. What was said in that case with regard to the powers of the

States applies with equal force to the powers of the nation in cases where the States individually are incompetent to act. We are not yet discussing the particular case before us but only are considering the validity of the test proposed. With regard to that we may add that when we are dealing with words that also are a constituent act, like the Constitution of the United States, we must realize that they have called into life a being the development of which could not have been foreseen completely by the most gifted of its begetters. It was enough for them to realize or to hope that they had created an organism; it has taken a century and has cost their successors much sweat and blood to prove that they created a nation. The case before us must be considered in the light of our whole experience and not merely in that of what was said a hundred years ago. The treaty in question does not contravene any prohibitory words to be found in the Constitution. The only question is whether it is forbidden by some invisible radiation from the general terms of the Tenth Amendment. We must consider what this country has become in deciding what that Amendment has reserved.

The State as we have intimated founds its claim of exclusive authority upon an assertion of title to migratory birds, an assertion that is embodied in statute. No doubt it is true that as between a State and its inhabitants the State may regulate the killing and sale of such birds, but it does not follow that its authority is exclusive of paramount powers. To put the claim of the State upon title is to lean upon a slender reed. Wild birds are not in the possession of anyone; and possession is the beginning of ownership. The whole foundation of the State's rights is the presence within their jurisdiction of birds that yesterday had not arrived, tomorrow may be in another State and in a week a thousand miles away. If we are to be accurate we cannot put the case of the State upon higher ground than that the treaty deals with creatures that for the moment are within the state borders, that it must be carried out by officers of the United States within the same territory, and that but for the treaty the State would be free to regulate this subject itself.

As most of the laws of the United States are carried out within the States and as many of them deal with matters which in the silence of such laws the State might regulate, such general grounds are not enough to support Missouri's claim. Valid treaties of course "are as binding within the territorial limits of the States as they are elsewhere throughout the dominion of the United States." No doubt the great body of private relations usually fall within the control of the State, but a treaty may override its power....

Here a national interest of very nearly the first magnitude is involved. It can be protected only by national action in concert with that of another power. The subject-matter is only transitorily within the State and has no permanent habitat therein. But for the treaty and the statute there soon might be no birds for any powers to deal with. We see nothing in the Constitution that compels the Government to sit by while a food supply is cut off and the protectors of our forests and our crops are destroyed. It is not sufficient to rely upon the States. The reliance is vain, and were it otherwise, the question is whether the United States is forbidden to act. We are of opinion that the treaty and statute must be upheld.

Decree affirmed.

MR. JUSTICE VAN DEVANTER and MR. JUSTICE PITNEY dissent.

Notes

1. Do any provisions of the Constitution limit the treaty power, or are treaties (unlike statutes) valid even if not made in pursuance to the Constitution?

DeGeofroy v. Riggs, 133 U.S. 258, 10 S.Ct. 295, 33 L.Ed. 642 (1890) upheld a treaty between the United States and France that allowed citizens of either country to inherit real or personal property from citizens of the other. State statutes had earlier prevented such inheritance. Field, J., for the Court said in dictum:

> That the treaty power of the United States extends to all proper subjects of negotiation between our government and the governments of other nations, is clear. It is also clear that the protection which should be afforded to the citizens of one country owning property in another, and the manner in which that property may be transferred, devised or inherited, are fitting subjects for such negotiation and of regulation by mutual stipulations between the two countries. . . . The treaty power, as expressed in the Constitution, is in terms unlimited except by those restraints which are found in that instrument against the action of the government or of its departments, and those arising from the nature of the government itself and of that of the States. It would not be contended that it extends so far as to authorize what the Constitution forbids, or a change in the character of the government or in that of one of the States, or a cession of any portion of the territory of the latter, without its consent. But with these exceptions, it is not perceived that there is any limit to the questions which can be adjusted touching any matter which is properly the subject of negotiation with a foreign country.

Cf. Restatement, Foreign Relations Law of the United States (Third) (A.L.I. 1986):

> Section 302, Comment c:

> *Subject matter of international agreements and "matters of international concern."* The Constitution refers to treaties and to other agreements or compacts with foreign powers (Article I, Section 10; Article II, Section 2; Article VI), but does not define such agreements or intimate any limitations as regards their purpose or subject matter. Contrary to what was once suggested, the Constitution does not require that an international agreement deal only with "matters of international concern." The references in the Constitution presumably incorporate the concept of treaty and other agreements in international law. International law knows no limitations on the purpose or subject matter of international agreements, other than that they may not conflict with a peremptory norm of international law. States may enter into an agreement on any

matter of concern to them, and international law does not look behind their motives or purposes in doing so. Thus, the United States may make an agreement on any subject suggested by its national interest in its relations with other nations.

If Canada and the United States sign a treaty requiring liquor stores located within fifty miles of either side of the border to be closed during certain hours, is that treaty constitutional under U.S. law? What about treaties relating to human rights? Is it constitutional for the United States to be party to an international convention banning slavery, or guaranteeing freedom of speech?

The Reporter's Note 2 to § 302 states:

It has sometimes been suggested that a treaty or other international agreement must deal with "a matter of international concern." That suggestion derived from a statement by Charles Evans Hughes. See 23 Proc.Am.Soc'y Int'l L. 194–96 (1929). . . . Hughes's statement may have implied only that an international agreement of the United States must be a bona fide agreement with another state, serving a foreign policy interest or purpose of the United States. That requirement may well be implied in the word "treaty" or "agreement" as used in international law and in the United States Constitution. See Comment c.

There is no principle either in international law or in American Constitutional Law that some subjects are intrinsically "domestic" and not permissible subjects for an international agreement.

Even Justice Field's assumption in *Riggs* that a treaty could not cede territory of a state without the latter's consent is debatable. If the United States lost a war, would a peace treaty ceding state territory be valid without that state's consent? The United States did cede territory in the settlement of the Northeast boundary and the 1842 treaty with Mexico, but the consents of the relevant states were in fact obtained, so the matter was never judicially tested.[1]

2. In *Missouri v. Holland*, the treaty provided that each of the two powers would propose to their law making bodies the necessary enactments to carry out the treaty. The treaty was thus "non-self-executing." It required implementing legislation by Congress before it could be enforced as law in the courts. If a treaty provided that the nationals of another country shall have the same rights to engage in business activities as U.S. nationals have, the treaty is "self-executing" and takes immediate effect as domestic law. To determine whether a treaty is self-executing the courts must interpret it, with the decision sometimes turning on nuances of grammar. Compare *Foster v. Neilson*, 27 U.S. (2 Pet.) 253, 7 L.Ed. 415 (1829)(treaty held not self-executing), with *United States v. Percheman*, 32 U.S. (7 Pet.) 51, 8 L.Ed. 604 (1833)(same treaty held self-executing after Court examined Spanish text of treaty).

3. THE BRICKER AMENDMENT. Because of the concern that treaties were not subject to the same constitutional restraints as federal statutory law, Senator Bricker led the effort in the early 1950's to enact the Bricker amendment to the Constitution, which provided that a treaty could become

---

1. See L. Henkin, Foreign Affairs and   the Constitution 395 (1972).

effective as internal law only through legislation that would be valid in the absence of a treaty. The proponents feared that a treaty could enlarge federal power over the states, and could be self-enforcing. A lower California state court had already held that a particular state land law was invalid because it conflicted with the United Nations Charter, which the court found to be self-executing. *Sei Fujii v. State,* 217 P.2d 481 (2d Dist.Cal.Ct.App. 1950). On appeal the Charter was found not to be self-executing but the state law was nonetheless invalidated on the basis of the Equal Protection Clause. 38 Cal.2d 718, 242 P.2d 617 (1952).

Opponents of the Bricker amendment argued that it would impair the foreign affairs power and that Bricker's fears were simply not well founded. The amendment was never approved. Much of the controversy over the Bricker amendment centered on the danger that the treaty power could override state law, but the framers may have intended that result. Would the framers have intended that the treaty power should also override the Bill of Rights or other specific constitutional limitations on executive or legislative powers? Is there anything in *Missouri v. Holland* that could support this conclusion?

4.   Assume that United States enters into a treaty with a foreign state. That state would cede territory to the United States in exchange for $7.2 million. The President signs the treaty with the advice and consent of the Senate. Could the treaty constitutionally provide that its ratification has the effect of appropriating the $7.2 million (without the House also voting to appropriate the money)? Restatement of the Law, Foreign Relations Law of the United States (Third) § 111, comment *I* (A.L.I.1986) says no, because the international agreement cannot "do what lies within the exclusive law-making power of Congress under the Constitution.".

WHITNEY v. ROBERTSON
124 U.S. 190, 8 S.Ct. 456, 31 L.Ed. 386 (1888).

Mr. Justice Field delivered the opinion of the court.

The plaintiffs are merchants, doing business in the city of New York, and in August, 1882, they imported a large quantity of "centrifugal and molasses sugars," the produce and manufacture of the island of San Domingo. These goods were similar in kind to sugars produced in the Hawaiian Islands, which are admitted free of duty under the treaty with the king of those islands, and the act of Congress, passed to carry the treaty into effect. They were duly entered at the custom house at the port of New York, the plaintiffs claiming that by the treaty with the Republic of San Domingo the goods should be admitted on the same terms, that is, free of duty, as similar articles, the produce and manufacture of the Hawaiian Islands. The defendant, who was, at the time collector of the port, refused to allow this claim, treated the goods as dutiable articles under the acts of Congress, and exacted duties on them to the amount of $21,936.

. . . The act of Congress under which the duties were collected authorized their exaction. It is of general application, making no exception in favor of goods of any country. It was passed after the treaty with the Dominican Republic, and, if there by any conflict between the stipulations of the treaty and the requirements of the law, the latter must control. A treaty is primarily a contract between two or more independent nations, and is so regarded by writers on public law. For the infraction of its provisions a remedy must be sought by the injured party through reclamations upon the other. When the stipulations are not self-executing they can only be enforced pursuant to legislation to carry them into effect, and such legislation is as much subject to modification and repeal by Congress as legislation upon any other subject. If the treaty contains stipulations which are self-executing, that is, require no legislation to make them operative, to that extent they have the force and effect of a legislative enactment. Congress may modify such provisions, so far as they bind the United States, or supersede them altogether. By the Constitution a treaty is placed on the same footing, and made of like obligation, with an act of legislation. Both are declared by that instrument to be the supreme law of the land, and no superior efficacy is given to either over the other. When the two relate to the same subject, the courts will always endeavor to construe them so as to give effect to both, if that can be done without violating the language of either; but if the two are inconsistent, the one last in date will control the other, provided always the stipulation of the treaty on the subject is self-executing. If the country with which the treaty is made is dissatisfied with the action of the legislative department, it may present its complaint to the executive head of the government, and take such other measures as it may deem essential for the protection of its interests. The courts can afford no redress. Whether the complaining nation has just cause of complaint, or our country was justified in its legislation, are not matters for judicial cognizance.... The duty of the courts is to construe and give effect to the latest expression of the sovereign will....

Notes

1. *Cook v. United States,* 288 U.S. 102, 53 S.Ct. 305, 77 L.Ed. 641 (1933). A statute enacted in 1922 authorized boarding vessels in certain circumstances to search and seize vessels suspected of smuggling intoxicating liquors into this country. A treaty of 1924 with Great Britain precluded searching British vessels in such circumstances. The Court invalidated the search as inconsistent with the treaty, although authorized by the statute.

Compare *Diggs v. Shultz,* 470 F.2d 461 (D.C.Cir.1972), cert. denied, 411 U.S. 931, 93 S.Ct. 1897, 36 L.Ed.2d 390 (1973). In 1966 the Security Council of the United Nations, with the affirmative vote of the United States, adopted a resolution directing member states to impose an embargo on trade with Southern Rhodesia. Pursuant to this resolution the President issued Executive Orders establishing criminal sanctions for violating the embargo. In 1971 Congress enacted the Byrd Amendment, which allowed the importation of certain materials from Southern Rhodesia. The Executive Branch then issued the appropriate import licenses. Plaintiffs sought declaratory and injunctive relief against this action. After finding the requisite standing, the court upheld the statute although it abrogated "one aspect of our treaty obligations under the U.N. Charter.... "

2. *The Chinese Exclusion Case (Chae Chan Ping v. U.S.),* 130 U.S. 581, 9 S.Ct. 623, 32 L.Ed. 1068 (1889). A Chinese laborer left the United States for a visit to China. While he was returning, Congress enacted a statute prohibiting Chinese laborers from entering the United States if they had departed before the act's enactment. The Chinese laborer claimed that the law of 1888 impaired a right vested under the treaty of 1880 and was therefore invalid because it conflicted with the treaty. Assuming such a conflict, which controls: the treaty or the statute?

Compare 21 Opinions of the Attorney General 347 (1896). A convention (treaty) between the United States and China in 1894 provided that certain Chinese who are resident in a British colony (Hong Kong) may be admitted into the United States upon production of a certificate from the British colonial government. A statute enacted in 1884 required, in such circumstances, that only the Chinese Government (and not the British authorities at Hong Kong) could issue a certificate. Assuming that the treaty is self-executing, should the United States accept the Hong Kong certificate?

3. Restatement, Foreign Relations Law of the United States (Revised), § 135(3)(A.L.I. Tent. Draft No. 1, 1980), provides: "The superseding of [a self-executing treaty] as domestic law of the United States by subsequent act of Congress does not relieve the United States of its international obligation or of the consequences of violation."

GOLDWATER v. CARTER
444 U.S. 996, 100 S.Ct. 533, 62 L.Ed.2d 428 (1979).

[President Carter gave unilateral notice of the termination of the mutual defense treaty to the Republic of China (Taiwan), to be effective on January 1, 1980, pursuant to the termination clause contained in the treaty allowing either party to terminate with one year's notice. The President also recognized the Peking Government rather than the Taiwan Government as the Government of China. Several senators, a former senator, and several members of the House sued for declaratory and injunctive relief claiming that the President may not terminate the treaty without legislative participation. The District Court held that the President's notice of termination was ineffective unless two-thirds of the Senate or a majority of both Houses approved. The Circuit Court reversed.]

The petition for a writ of certiorari is granted. The judgment of the Court of Appeals is vacated and the case is remanded to the District Court with directions to dismiss the complaint.

Mr. Justice Rehnquist, with whom The Chief Justice [Burger], Mr. Justice Stewart, and Mr. Justice Stevens join, concurring.

I am of the view that the basic question presented by the petitioners in this case is "political" and therefore nonjusticiable because it involves the authority of the President in the conduct of our country's foreign relations and the extent to which the Senate or the Congress is authorized to negate the action of the President. In *Coleman v. Miller,* 307 U.S. 433, 59 S.Ct. 972, 83 L.Ed. 1385 (1939), a case in which members of the Kansas Legislature brought an action attacking a vote of the State Senate in favor of the ratification of the Child Labor Amendment, Mr. Chief Justice Hughes wrote in what is referred to as the "Opinion of the Court":

> [T]he question of the efficacy of ratifications by state legislatures, in the light of previous rejection or attempted withdrawal, should be regarded as a political question pertaining to the political departments, with the ultimate authority in the Congress in the exercise of its control over the promulgation of the adoption of the Amendment.... Article V, speaking solely of ratification, contains no provision as to rejection....

... I believe it follows a fortiori from *Coleman* that the controversy in the instant case is a nonjusticiable political dispute that should be left for resolution by the Executive and Legislative Branches of the Government. Here, while the Constitution is express as to the manner in which the Senate shall participate in the ratification of a Treaty, it is silent as to that body's participation in the abrogation of a Treaty. In this respect the case is directly analogous to *Coleman,* supra.... In light of the absence of any constitutional provision governing the termination of a Treaty, and the fact that different termination procedures may be appropriate for different treaties (see, e.g., n. 1, infra), the instant case in my view also "must surely be controlled by political standards."

I think that the justifications for concluding that the question here is political in nature are even more compelling than in *Coleman* because it involves foreign relations—specifically a treaty commitment to use military force in the defense of a foreign government if attacked....

The present case differs in several important respects from *Youngstown Sheet & Tube Co. v. Sawyer,* cited by petitioners as authority both for reaching the merits of this dispute and for reversing the Court of Appeals. In *Youngstown* private litigants brought a suit contesting the President's authority under his war powers to seize the Nation's steel industry, an action of profound and demonstrable domestic impact. Here, by contrast, we are asked to settle a dispute between coequal branches of our government, each of which has resources available to protect and assert its interests, resources not available to private litigants outside the judicial forum.[1] Moreover, as in [*U.S. v. Curtiss–Wright Export*

---

1. As observed by Judge Wright in his concurring opinion below:

"Congress has initiated the termination of treaties by directing or requiring the President to give notice of termination, without any prior presidential request. Congress has annulled treaties without any presidential notice. It has conferred on the President the power to terminate a particular treaty, and it has enacted statutes practically nullifying the domestic effects of a treaty and thus caused the President to carry out termination.... Moreover, Congress has a variety of powerful tools for influencing foreign policy decisions that bear on treaty matters. Under Article I, Section 8 of the Constitution, it can regulate commerce with foreign nations, raise and support armies, and declare war. It has power over the appointment of ambassadors

Corp.], the effect of this action, as far as we can tell, is "entirely external to the United States, and [falls] within the category of foreign affairs." Finally, as already noted, the situation presented here is closely akin to that presented in *Coleman,* where the Constitution spoke only to the procedure for ratification of an amendment, not to its rejection....

MR. JUSTICE MARSHALL concurs in the result.

MR. JUSTICE POWELL, concurring.

Although I agree with the result reached by the Court, I would dismiss the complaint as not ripe for judicial review.... Prudential considerations persuade me that a dispute between Congress and the President is not ready for judicial review unless and until each branch has taken action asserting its constitutional authority. Differences between the President and the Congress are commonplace under our system. The differences should, and almost invariably do, turn on political rather than legal considerations. The Judicial Branch should not decide issues affecting the allocation of power between the President and Congress until the political branches reach a constitutional impasse. Otherwise, we would encourage small groups or even individual Members of Congress to seek judicial resolution of issues before the normal political process has the opportunity to resolve the conflict.

In this case ... Congress has taken no official action. In the present posture of this case, we do not know whether there ever will be an actual confrontation between the Legislative and Executive Branches. Although the Senate has considered a resolution declaring that Senate approval is necessary for the termination of any mutual defense treaty, no final vote has been taken on the resolution. Moreover, it is unclear whether the resolution would have retroactive effect. It cannot be said that either the Senate or the House has rejected the President's claim. If the Congress chooses not to confront the President, it is not our task to do so. I therefore concur in the dismissal of this case.

Mr. Justice Rehnquist suggests, however, that the issue presented by this case is a nonjusticiable political question which can never be considered by this Court. I cannot agree.... First, the existence of "a textually demonstrable constitutional commitment of the issue to a coordinate political branch," [*Baker v. Carr,* § 1–2.4, *supra*], turns on an examination of the constitutional provisions governing the exercise of the power in question. No constitutional provision explicitly confers upon the President the power to terminate treaties....

Second, there is no "lack of judicially discoverable and manageable standards for resolving" this case; nor is a decision impossible "without

and the funding of embassies and consulates. Congress thus retains a strong influence over the President's conduct in treaty matters. As our political history demonstrates, treaty creation and termination are complex phenomena rooted in the dynamic relationship between the two political branches of our government. We thus should decline the invitation to set in concrete a particular constitutionally acceptable arrangement by which the President and Congress are to share treaty termination."

an initial policy determination of a kind clearly for nonjudicial discretion." We are asked to decide whether the President may terminate a treaty under the Constitution without congressional approval. Resolution of the question may not be easy, but it only requires us to apply normal principles of interpretation to the constitutional provisions at issue. The present case involves neither review of the President's activities as Commander-in-Chief nor impermissible interference in the field of foreign affairs. Such a case would arise if we were asked to decide, for example, whether a treaty required the President to order troops into a foreign country.... This case "touches" foreign relations, but the question presented to us concerns only the constitutional division of power between Congress and the President.

A simple hypothetical demonstrates the confusion that I find inherent in Mr. Justice Rehnquist's concurring opinion. Assume that the President signed a mutual defense treaty with a foreign country and announced that it would go into effect despite its rejection by the Senate. Under Mr. Justice Rehnquist's analysis that situation would present a political question even though Art. II, § 2, clearly would resolve the dispute. Although the answer to the hypothetical case seems self-evident because it demands textual rather than interstitial analysis, the nature of the legal issue presented is no different from the issue presented in the case before us. In both cases, the Court would interpret the Constitution to decide whether congressional approval is necessary to give a Presidential decision on the validity of a treaty the force of law. Such an inquiry demands no special competence or information beyond the reach of the judiciary.

Finally, the political-question doctrine rests in part on prudential concerns calling for mutual respect among the three branches of government.... If this case were ripe for judicial review, none of these prudential considerations would be present. Interpretation of the Constitution does not imply lack of respect for a coordinate branch. If the President and the Congress had reached irreconcilable positions, final disposition of the question presented by this case would eliminate, rather than create, multiple constitutional interpretations.... If the Congress, by appropriate formal action, had challenged the President's authority to terminate the treaty with Taiwan, the resulting uncertainty could have serious consequences for our country. In that situation, it would be the duty of this Court to resolve the issue.

Mr. Justice Blackmun, with whom Mr. Justice White joins, dissenting in part.

In my view, the time factor and its importance are illusory; if the President does not have the power to terminate the Treaty (a substantial issue that we should address only after briefing and oral argument), the notice of intention to terminate surely has no legal effect. It is also indefensible, without further study, to pass on the issue of justiciability or on the issues of standing or ripeness. While I therefore join in the grant of the petition for certiorari, I would set the case for oral argument and give it the plenary consideration it so obviously deserves.

Mr. Justice Brennan, dissenting.

I respectfully dissent from the order directing the District Court to dismiss this case, and would affirm the judgment of the Court of Appeals insofar as it rests upon the President's well-established authority to recognize, and withdraw recognition from, foreign governments.

... Properly understood, the political question doctrine restrains courts from reviewing an exercise of foreign policy judgment by the coordinate political branch to which authority to make that judgment has been "constitutional[ly] commit[ted]." But the doctrine does not pertain when a court is faced with the antecedent question whether a particular branch has been constitutionally designated as the repository of political decisionmaking power. The issue of decisionmaking authority must be resolved as a matter of constitutional law, not political discretion; accordingly, it falls within the competence of the courts.

The constitutional question raised here is prudently answered in narrow terms. ...Our cases firmly establish that the Constitution commits to the President alone the power to recognize, and withdraw recognition from, foreign regimes. That mandate being clear, our judicial inquiry into the treaty rupture can go no further.

Notes

1.   While *Whitney v. Robertson,* considered the question of the effect of a treaty terminated by Congress, *Goldwater v. Carter* dealt with the question of treaty termination by the President alone. On this question, what is the disagreement between Brennan and Rehnquist? Do both opinions conclude that the President's authority to terminate the treaty with Taiwan may not be reviewed by the courts?

2.   Under Powell's theory, would the matter be ripe for review if the Senate passed a resolution declaring that its approval of the termination of the treaty was necessary? Or would the matter not be ripe until the President acted contrary to the resolution and refused to obey the treaty, i.e., refused to come to the defense of Taiwan? If the President refused to come to the aid of Taiwan with military force, could Congress force him to send troops? Could the Court order him to obey the treaty and send troops?

3.   Should the Court have instead dismissed the suit on the grounds that the plaintiffs lacked standing?

UNITED STATES v. PINK
315 U.S. 203, 62 S.Ct. 552, 86 L.Ed. 796 (1942).

Mr. Justice Douglas delivered the opinion of the Court.

This action was brought by the United States to recover the assets of the New York branch of the First Russian Insurance Co. which remained in the hands of respondent [the Superintendent of Insurance] after the payment of all domestic creditors. The material allegations of the complaint were, in brief, as follows:

The First Russian Insurance Co., organized under the laws of the former Empire of Russia, established a New York branch in 1907. It deposited with the Superintendent of Insurance, pursuant to the laws of New York, certain assets to secure payment of claims resulting from transactions of its New York branch. [I]n 1918 and 1919, the Russian Government nationalized the business of insurance and all of the property, wherever situated, of all Russian insurance companies (including the First Russian Insurance Co.), and discharged and cancelled all the debts of such companies and the rights of all shareholders in all such property. The New York branch of the First Russian Insurance Co. continued to do business in New York until 1925. At that time, respondent, pursuant to an order of the Supreme Court of New York, took possession of its assets for a determination and report upon the claims of the policyholders and creditors in the United States. Thereafter, all claims of domestic creditors, i.e., all claims arising out of the business of the New York branch, were paid by respondent, leaving a balance in his hands of more than $1,000,000. In 1931, the New York Court of Appeals directed respondent to dispose of that balance as follows: first, to pay claims of foreign creditors who had filed attachment prior to the commencement of the liquidation proceeding, and also such claims as were filed prior to the entry of the order on remittitur of that court; and second, to pay any surplus to a quorum of the board of directors of the company.... The major portion of the allowed claims, however, were not paid, a stay having been granted pending disposition of the claim of the United States. On November 16, 1933, the United States recognized the Union of Soviet Socialist Republics as the *de jure* Government of Russia and as an incident to that recognition accepted an assignment (known as the Litvinov Assignment) of certain claims. The Litvinov Assignment was in the form of a letter, dated November 16, 1933, to the President of the United States from Maxim Litvinov, People's Commissar for Foreign Affairs....

The New York Court of Appeals held in [*Moscow Fire Ins. Co. v. Bank of New York & Trust Co.,* 280 N.Y. 286, 20 N.E.2d 758 (1939)] that the Russian decrees in question had no extraterritorial effect. If that is true, it is decisive of the present controversy. For the United States acquired, under the Litvinov Assignment, only such rights as Russia had. If the Russian decrees left the New York assets of the Russian insurance companies unaffected, then Russia had nothing here to assign. But that question of foreign law is not to be determined exclusively by the state court. The claim of the United States based on the Litvinov Assignment raises a federal question. This Court will review or independently determine all questions on which a federal right is necessarily dependent.... We hold that, so far as its intended effect is concerned, the Russian decree embraced the New York assets of the First Russian Insurance Co.

The question of whether the decree should be given extraterritorial effect is, of course, a distinct matter. One primary issue raised in that connection is whether, under our constitutional system, New York law can be allowed to stand in the way. [New York case law is unequivocal, holding] that "under the law of this State such confiscatory decrees do not affect the property claimed here". . . .

It is one thing to hold, as was done in *Guaranty Trust Co. v. United States,* 304 U.S. page 142, 58 S.Ct. page 793, 82 L.Ed. 1224, that under the Litvinov Assignment the United States did not acquire "a right free of a preexisting infirmity," such as the running of the statute of limitations against the Russian Government, its assignor. Unlike the problem presented here, that holding in no way sanctions the asserted power of New York to deny enforcement of a claim under the Litvinov Assignment because of an overriding policy of the State which denies validity in New York of the Russian decrees on which the assigned claims rest. That power was denied New York in *United States v. Belmont,* 301 U.S. 324, 57 S.Ct. 758, 81 L.Ed. 1134 (1937). With one qualification, to be noted, the *Belmont* case is determinative of the present controversy. That case involved the right of the United States under the Litvinov Assignment to recover, from a custodian or stake-holder in New York, funds which had been nationalized and appropriated by the Russian decrees.

This Court, speaking through Mr. Justice Sutherland, held that the conduct of foreign relations is committed by the Constitution to the political departments of the Federal Government; that the propriety of the exercise of that power is not open to judicial inquiry; and that recognition of a foreign sovereign conclusively binds the courts and "is retroactive and validates all actions and conduct of the government so recognized from the commencement of its existence." It further held that recognition of the Soviet Government, the establishment of diplomatic relations with it, and the Litvinov Assignment were "all parts of one transaction, resulting in an international compact between the two governments." [I]t added: "The assignment and the agreements in connection therewith did not, as in the case of treaties, as that term is used in the treaty making clause of the Constitution (Art. II, § 2), require the advice and consent of the Senate." It held that the "external powers of the United States are to be exercised without regard to state laws or policies. The supremacy of a treaty in this respect has been recognized from the beginning." And it added that "all international compacts and agreements" are to be treated with similar dignity for the reason that "complete power over international affairs is in the national government and is not and cannot be subject to any curtailment or interference on the part of the several states." This Court did to stop to inquire whether in fact there was any policy of New York which enforcement of the Litvinov Assignment would infringe since "no state policy can prevail against the international compact here involved." . . .

The holding in the *Belmont* case is therefore determinative of the present controversy, unless the stake of the foreign creditors in this liquidation proceeding and the provision which New York has provided for their protection call for a different result.

The *Belmont* case forecloses any relief to the Russian corporation. For this Court held in that case: "... our Constitution, laws and policies have no extraterritorial operation, unless in respect of our own citizens.... What another country has done in the way of taking over property of its nationals, and especially of its corporations, is not a matter for judicial consideration here. Such nationals must look to their own government for any redress to which they may be entitled."

But it is urged that different considerations apply in case of the foreign creditors to whom the New York Court of Appeals ordered distribution of these funds. The argument is that their rights in these funds have vested by virtue of the New York decree; that to deprive them of the property would violate the Fifth Amendment which extends its protection to aliens as well as to citizens; and that the Litvinov Assignment cannot deprive New York of its power to administer the balance of the fund in accordance with its laws for the benefit of these creditors.

At the outset, it should be noted that, so far as appears, all creditors whose claims arose out of dealings with the New York branch have been paid.... The contest here is between the United States and creditors of the Russian corporation who, we assume, are not citizens of this country and whose claims did not arise out of transactions with the New York branch. The United States is seeking to protect not only claims which it holds but also claims of its nationals. Such claims did not arise out of transactions with this Russian corporation; they are, however, claims against Russia or its nationals. The existence of such claims and their non-payment had for years been one of the barriers to recognition of the Soviet regime by the Executive Department. The purpose of the discussions leading to the policy of recognition was to resolve "all questions outstanding" between the two nations. Settlement of all American claims against Russia was one method of removing some of the prior objections to recognition based on the Soviet policy of nationalization. The Litvinov Assignment was not only part and parcel of the new policy of recognition, it was also the method adopted by the Executive Department for alleviating in this country the rigors of nationalization. Congress tacitly recognized that policy....

If the President had the power to determine the policy which was to govern the question of recognition, then the Fifth Amendment does not stand in the way of giving full force and effect to the Litvinov Assignment. To be sure, aliens as well as citizens are entitled to the protection of the Fifth Amendment. A State is not precluded, however, by the Fourteenth Amendment from according priority to local creditors as against creditors who are nationals of foreign countries and whose claims arose abroad. By the same token, the Federal Government is not barred by the Fifth Amendment from securing for itself and our nationals priority against such creditors. And it matters not that the procedure adopted by the Federal Government is globular and involves a regrouping of assets. There is no Constitutional reason why this Government need act as the collection agent for nationals of other countries when it takes steps to protect itself or its own nationals on external debts. . . .

If the priority had been accorded American claims by treaty with Russia, there would be no doubt as to its validity. The same result obtains here. The powers of the President in the conduct of foreign relations included the power, without consent of the Senate, to determine the public policy of the United States with respect to the Russian nationalization decrees. "What government is to be regarded here as representative of a foreign sovereign state is a political rather than a judicial question, and is to be determined by the political department of the government." *Guaranty Trust Co. v. United States,* supra. That authority is not limited to a determination of the government to be recognized. It includes the power to determine the policy which is to govern the question of recognition. [T]he Litvinov Assignment was an international compact which did not require the participation of the Senate. . . . Recognition is not always absolute; it is sometimes conditional. Power to remove such obstacles to full recognition as settlement of claims of our nationals certainly is a modest implied power of the President who is the "sole organ of the federal government in the field of international relations." *United States v. Curtiss–Wright Corp.,* [§ 5–1, supra]. . . . Unless such a power exists, the power of recognition might be thwarted or seriously diluted. No such obstacle can be placed in the way of rehabilitation of relations between this country and another nation, unless the historic conception of the powers and responsibilities of the President in the conduct of foreign affairs is to be drastically revised. It was the judgment of the political department that full recognition of the Soviet Government required the settlement of all outstanding problems including the claims of our nationals. Recognition and the Litvinov Assignment were interdependent. We would usurp the executive function if we held that that decision was not final and conclusive in the courts. . . .

A treaty is a "Law of the Land" under the supremacy clause of the Constitution. Such international compacts and agreements as the Litvinov Assignment have a similar dignity. . . .

Enforcement of New York's policy as formulated by the *Moscow* case would collide with and subtract from the Federal policy, whether it was premised on the absence of extraterritorial effect of the Russian decrees, the conception of the New York branch as a distinct juristic personality, or disapproval by New York of the Russian program of nationalization. [T]he policies of the States become wholly irrelevant to the judicial inquiry when the United States, acting within its constitutional sphere, seeks enforcement of its foreign policy in the courts. . . . "In respect of all international negotiations and compacts, and in respect of our foreign relations generally, state lines disappear. As to such purposes the State of New York does not exist."

We hold that the right to the funds or property in question became vested in the Soviet Government as the successor to the First Russian

Insurance Co.; that this right has passed to the United States under the Litvinov Assignment; and that the United States is entitled to the property as against the corporation and the foreign creditors.

The judgment is reversed and the cause is remanded to the Supreme Court of New York for proceedings not inconsistent with this opinion.

Reversed.

MR. JUSTICE REED and MR. JUSTICE JACKSON did not participate in the consideration or decision of this case.

[The concurring opinion of FRANKFURTER, J. and the dissenting opinion of STONE, C.J., joined by ROBERTS, J., are omitted.]

Notes

1. No treaty is involved here. What is the source of the "law" that the Court is applying?

2. Under the Fifth Amendment, the United States may not simply confiscate the property of any person. How can the United States, by virtue of the Litvinov Assignment, take advantage of the fruits of the Russian confiscation?

3. Assume that, without benefit of a treaty, the President makes an agreement with Saudi Arabia, pursuant to which the United States will transfer a number of destroyers in exchange for the lease of areas for naval and air bases on Saudi territory. Is the executive agreement valid? See, Restatement of the Law (Second) Foreign Relations Law of the United States, § 121, illustration 2 (A.L.I.1965)(concluding yes, based on the President's powers as chief executive and commander-in-chief). Compare, Arrangement with Great Britain Respecting Naval and Air Bases, 54 Stat. 2405 (1940), 39 Ops.Atty.Gen. 484 (1940). See also, Restatement of the Law (Third), Foreign Relations Law of the United States, § 303(4)(A.L.I.1987).

4. Are valid executive agreements equal in all respects to valid treaties? Can a valid executive agreement override earlier enacted federal statutes?

United States v. Guy W. Capps, Inc., 204 F.2d 655 (4th Cir.1953). The court invalidated an executive agreement with Canada regulating that country's export of potatoes because the agreement conflicted with an earlier act of Congress, passed pursuant to Congress' power over foreign commerce. The Supreme Court affirmed, but on other grounds. 348 U.S. 296, 75 S.Ct. 326, 99 L.Ed. 329 (1955).

Contrast, L. Henkin, Foreign Affairs and the Constitution 186 (1972): "If one sees the Treaty Power as basically a Presidential power (albeit subject to check by the Senate) there is no compelling reason for giving less effect to agreements which he has authority to make without the Senate. If one accepts Presidential primacy in foreign affairs in relation to Congress, one might allow his agreements to prevail even in the face of earlier Congressional legislation. If one grants the President some legislative authority in foreign affairs—as in regard to sovereign immunity—one might grant it to him in this respect too."

5. See, Marcy, "SALT II Still Lives," New York Times, Jan. 29, 1980, at p. A20: "The Soviet invasion of Afghanistan has been described as dealing

the death blow to SALT II.... But surprise, surprise! SALT II is alive! According to the State Department, the principle of international law, shared by the United States and the Soviet Union, that is applicable is that 'a state should refrain from taking actions which would defeat the object and purpose of a treaty it has signed' until the treaty has been ratified and enters into force. Since last June, when SALT II was signed in Vienna by President Carter and Leonid I. Brezhnev, both the United States and the Soviet Union have been abiding by its terms."

Is it constitutional for the President to follow a treaty that the Senate has refused to ratify?

DAMES & MOORE v. REGAN
453 U.S. 654, 101 S.Ct. 2972, 69 L.Ed.2d 918 (1981).

JUSTICE REHNQUIST delivered the opinion of the Court.

The questions presented by this case touch fundamentally upon the manner in which our Republic is to be governed.... That dispute involves various Executive Orders and regulations by which the President nullified attachments and liens on Iranian assets in the United States, directed that these assets be transferred to Iran, and suspended claims against Iran that may be presented to an International Claims Tribunal. This action was taken in an effort to comply with an Executive Agreement between the United States and Iran. We granted certiorari before judgment in this case, and set an expedited briefing and argument schedule, because lower courts had reached conflicting conclusions on the validity of the President's actions and, as the Solicitor General informed us, unless the Government acted by July 19, 1981, Iran could consider the United States to be in breach of the Executive Agreement.

[W]e stress that the expeditious treatment of the issues involved by all of the courts which have considered the President's actions makes us acutely aware of the necessity to rest decision on the narrowest possible ground capable of deciding the case. *Ashwander v. TVA,* 297 U.S. 288, 347, 56 S.Ct. 466, 482, 80 L.Ed. 688 (1936)(Brandeis, J., concurring). This does not mean that reasoned analysis may give way to judicial fiat. It does mean that the statement of Justice Jackson—that we decide difficult cases presented to us by virtue of our commissions, not our competence—is especially true here. We attempt to lay down no general "guide-lines" covering other situations not involved here, and attempt to confine the opinion only to the very questions necessary to decision of the case.

I. On November 4, 1979, the American Embassy in Tehran was seized and our diplomatic personnel were captured and held hostage. In response to that crisis, President Carter, acting pursuant to the International Emergency Economic Powers Act, 50 U.S.C.A. §§ 1701–1706 (hereinafter "IEEPA"), declared a national emergency on November 14, 1979, and blocked the removal or transfer of "all property and interests in property of the Government of Iran, its instrumentalities and controlled entities and the Central Bank of Iran which are or become subject to the jurisdiction of the United States.... " Executive Order No. 12170. President Carter authorized the Secretary of the Treasury to promulgate regulations carrying out the blocking order....

On December 19, 1979, petitioner Dames & Moore filed suit in the United States District Court for the Central District of California against the Government of Iran, the Atomic Energy Organization of Iran, and a number of Iranian banks. [Petitioner claimed], however, that it was owed $3,436,694.30 plus interest for services performed under the contract [with the Atomic Energy Organization] prior to the date of termination. The District Court issued orders of attachment directed against property of the defendants, and the property of certain Iranian banks was then attached to secure any judgment that might be entered against them.

On January 20, 1981, the Americans held hostage were released by Iran pursuant to an Agreement entered into the day before and embodied in two Declarations of the Democratic and Popular Republic of Algeria. The Agreement stated that "it is the purpose of [the United States and Iran] ... to terminate all litigation as between the Government of each party and the nationals of the other, and to bring about the settlement and termination of all such claims through binding arbitration." [T]he Agreement called for the establishment of an Iran–United States Claims Tribunal which would arbitrate any claims not settled within 6 months. Awards of the Claims Tribunal are to be "final and binding" and "enforceable ... in the courts of any nation in accordance with its law." Under the Agreement, the United States is obligated:

> to terminate all legal proceedings in United States courts involving claims of United States persons and institutions against Iran and its state enterprises, to nullify all attachments and judgments obtained therein, to prohibit all further litigation based on such claims, and to bring about the termination of such claims through binding arbitration.

In addition, the United States must "act to bring about the transfer" by July 19, 1981, of all Iranian assets held in this country by American banks.... On January 19, 1981, President Carter issued a series of Executive Orders implementing the terms of the Agreement....

On February 24, 1981, President Reagan issued an Executive Order in which he "ratified" the January 19th Executive Orders. Moreover, he "suspended" all "claims which may be presented to the ... Tribunal" and provided that such claims "shall have no legal effect in any action now pending in any court of the United States." The suspension of any particular claim terminates if the Claims Tribunal determines that it has no jurisdiction over that claim; claims are discharged for all purposes when the Claims Tribunal either awards some recovery and that amount is paid, or determines that no recovery is due....

On April 28, 1981, petitioner filed this action in the District Court for declaratory and injunctive relief against the United States and the Secretary of the Treasury, seeking to prevent enforcement of the Executive Orders and Treasury Department regulations implementing the Agreement with Iran.... On May 28, 1981, the District Court denied petitioner's motion for a preliminary injunction and dismissed petitioner's complaint for failure to state a claim upon which relief could be granted....

II. The parties and the lower courts confronted with the instant questions have all agreed that much relevant analysis is contained in *Youngstown Sheet & Tube Co. v. Sawyer* ... Although we have in the past and do today find Justice Jackson's classification of executive actions into three general categories analytically useful, ... Justice Jackson himself recognized that his three categories represented "a somewhat over-simplified grouping," and it is doubtless the case that executive action in any particular instance falls, not neatly in one of three pigeon-holes, but rather at some point along a spectrum running from explicit congressional authorization to explicit congressional prohibition. This is particularly true as respects cases such as the one before us, involving responses to international crises the nature of which Congress can hardly have been expected to anticipate in any detail.

III. In nullifying post-November 14, 1979, attachments and directing those persons holding blocked Iranian funds and securities to transfer them to the Federal Reserve Bank of New York for ultimate transfer to Iran, President Carter cited five sources of express or inherent power. The Government, however, has principally relied on § 1702 of the IEEPA as authorization for these actions. Section 1702(a)(1) provides in part:

> At the times and to the extent specified in section 1701 of this title, the President may, under such regulations as he may prescribe, by means of instructions, licenses, or otherwise—
>
> (A) investigate, regulate, or prohibit—
>
> > (i) any transactions in foreign exchange,
> >
> > (ii) transfers of credit or payments between, by, through, or to any banking institution, to the extent that such transfers or payments involve any interest of any foreign country or a national thereof,
> >
> > (iii) the importing or exporting of currency or securities, and
>
> (B) investigate, regulate, direct and compel, nullify, void, prevent or prohibit, any acquisition, holding, withholding, use, transfer, withdrawal, transportation, importation or exportation of, or dealing in, or exercising any right, power or privilege with respect to, or transactions involving, any property in which any foreign country or a national thereof has any interest;
>
> by any person, or with respect to any property, subject to the jurisdiction of the United States.

The Government contends that the acts of "nullifying" the attachments and ordering the "transfer" of the frozen assets are specifically authorized by the plain language of the above statute.... According to petitioner, once the President instituted the November 14, 1979, blocking order, § 1702 authorized him "only to continue the freeze or to discontinue controls." We do not agree....

This Court has previously recognized that the congressional purpose in authorizing blocking orders is "to put control of foreign assets in the hands of the President...." Such orders permit the President to maintain the foreign assets at his disposal for use in negotiating the resolution of a declared national emergency. The frozen assets serve as a "bargaining chip" to be used by the President when dealing with a hostile country. Accordingly, it is difficult to accept petitioner's argument because the practical effect of it is to allow individual claimants throughout the country to minimize or wholly eliminate this "bargaining chip" through attachments, garnishments or similar encumbrances on property. Neither the purpose the statute was enacted to serve nor its plain language supports such a result.[6] ...

IV. Although we have concluded that the IEEPA constitutes specific congressional authorization to the President to nullify the attachments and order the transfer of Iranian assets, there remains the question of the President's authority to suspend claims pending in American courts. Such claims have, of course, an existence apart from the attachments which accompanied them. In terminating these claims through Executive Order No. 12294, the President purported to act under authority of both the IEEPA and 22 U.S.C.A. § 1732, the so-called "Hostage Act."

We conclude that although the IEEPA authorized the nullification of the attachments, it cannot be read to authorize the suspension of the claims. The claims of American citizens against Iran are not in themselves transactions involving Iranian property or efforts to exercise any rights with respect to such property. An *in personam* lawsuit, although it might eventually be reduced to judgment and that judgment might be executed upon, is an effort to establish liability and fix damages and does not focus on any particular property within the jurisdiction. The terms of the IEEPA therefore do not authorize the President to suspend claims in American courts. This is the view of all the courts which have considered the question.

The Hostage Act, passed in 1868, provides:

> Whenever it is made known to the President that any citizen of the United States has been unjustly deprived of his liberty by or

---

6. ... Our construction of petitioner's attachments as being "revocable," "contingent," and "in every sense subordinate to the President's power under the IEEPA," in effect answers petitioner's claim that even if the President has the authority to nullify the attachments and transfer the assets, the exercise of such would constitute an unconstitutional taking of property in violation of the Fifth Amendment absent just compensation. We conclude that because of the President's authority to prevent or condition attachments, and because of the orders he issued to this effect, petitioner did not acquire any "property" interest in its attachments of the sort that would support a constitutional claim for compensation.

under the authority of any foreign government, it shall be the duty of the President forthwith to demand of that government the reasons of such imprisonment; and if it appears to be wrongful and in violation of the rights of American citizenship, the President shall forthwith demand the release of such citizen, and if the release so demanded is unreasonably delayed or refused, the President shall use such means, not amounting to acts of war, as he may think necessary and proper to obtain or effectuate the release; and all the facts and proceedings relative thereto shall as soon as practicable be communicated by the President to Congress. 22 U.S.C.A. § 1732.

... The legislative history indicates that the Act was passed in response to a situation unlike the recent Iranian crisis. Congress in 1868 was concerned with the activity of certain countries refusing to recognize the citizenship of naturalized Americans traveling abroad, and repatriating such citizens against their will.... Although the Iranian hostage-taking violated international law and common decency, the hostages were not seized out of any refusal to recognize their American citizenship—they were seized precisely *because of* their American citizenship. The legislative history is also somewhat ambiguous on the question whether Congress contemplated presidential action such as that involved here or rather simply reprisals directed against the offending foreign country and *its* citizens.

Concluding that neither the IEEPA nor the Hostage Act constitutes specific authorization of the President's action suspending claims, however, is not to say that these statutory provisions are entirely irrelevant to the question of the validity of the President's action. We think both statutes highly relevant in the looser sense of indicating congressional acceptance of a broad scope for executive action in circumstances such as those presented in this case.... [T]he enactment of legislation closely related to the question of the President's authority in a particular case which evinces legislative intent to accord the President broad discretion may be considered to "invite" "measures on independent presidential responsibility." *Youngstown*, (Jackson, J., concurring). At least this is so where there is no contrary indication of legislative intent and when, as here, there is a history of congressional acquiescence in conduct of the sort engaged in by the President. It is to that history which we now turn.

Not infrequently in affairs between nations, outstanding claims by nationals of one country against the government of another country are "sources of friction" between the two sovereigns. *United States v. Pink.* [There is] a longstanding practice of settling such claims by executive agreement without the advice and consent of the Senate. Under such agreements, the President has agreed to renounce or extinguish claims of United States nationals against foreign governments in return for lump sum payments or the establishment of arbitration procedures. [T]he "United States has sometimes disposed of the claims of citizens without their consent, or even without consultation with them, usually without exclusive regard for their interests, as distinguished from those of the nation as a whole." Accord, The Restatement (Second) of the

Foreign Relations Law of the United States § 213 (1965)(President "may waive or settle a claim against a foreign state . . . even without the consent of the [injured] national"). It is clear that the practice of settling claims continues today. Since 1952, the President has entered into at least 10 binding settlements with foreign nations, including an $80 million settlement with the People's Republic of China.

Crucial to our decision today is the conclusion that Congress has implicitly approved the practice of claim settlement by executive agreement. This is best demonstrated by Congress' enactment of the International Claims Settlement Act of 1949, 22 U.S.C.A. § 1621 et seq., as amended (1980). The Act had two purposes: (1) to allocate to United States nationals funds received in the course of an executive claims settlement with Yugoslavia, and (2) to provide a procedure whereby funds resulting from future settlements could be distributed. . . .

In addition to congressional acquiescence in the President's power to settle claims, prior cases of this Court have also recognized that the President does have some measure of power to enter into executive agreements without obtaining the advice and consent of the Senate. [See] *United States v. Pink* . . . .

We . . . do not believe that the President has attempted to divest the federal courts of jurisdiction [in violation of Article III of the Constitution]. Executive Order No. 12294 purports only to "suspend" the claims, not divest the federal court of "jurisdiction." As we read the Executive Order, those claims not within the jurisdiction of the Claims Tribunal will "revive" and become judicially enforceable in United States courts. . . . The President has exercised the power, acquiesced in by Congress, to settle claims and, as such, has simply effected a change in the substantive law governing the lawsuit. . . . As Justice Frankfurter pointed out in *Youngstown,* "a systematic, unbroken executive practice, long pursued to the knowledge of Congress and never before questioned . . . may be treated as a gloss on 'Executive Power' vested in the President by § 1 of Art. II." . . .

Our conclusion is buttressed by the fact that the means chosen by the President to settle the claims of American nationals provided an alternate forum, the Claims Tribunal, which is capable of providing meaningful relief. [I]t is important to remember that we have already held that the President has the *statutory* authority to nullify attachments and to transfer the assets out of the country. The President's power to do so does not depend on his provision of a forum whereby claimants can recover on those claims. The fact that the President has provided such a forum here means that the claimants are receiving something in return for the suspension of their claims, namely, access to an international tribunal before which they may well recover something on their claims. Because there does appear to be a real "settlement" here, this case is more easily analogized to the more traditional claim settlement cases of the past.

Just as importantly, Congress has not disapproved of the action taken here. Though Congress has held hearings on the Iranian Agreement itself, Congress has not enacted legislation, or even passed a resolution, indicating its displeasure with the Agreement. Quite the contrary, the relevant Senate Committee has stated that the establishment of the Tribunal is "of vital importance to the United States." We are thus clearly not confronted with a situation in which Congress has in some way resisted the exercise of presidential authority.

Finally, we re-emphasize the narrowness of our decision. We do not decide that the President possesses plenary power to settle claims, even as against foreign governmental entities. . . . But where, as here, the settlement of claims has been determined to be a necessary incident to the resolution of a major foreign policy dispute between our country and another, and where, as here, we can conclude that Congress acquiesced in the President's action, we are not prepared to say that the President lacks the power to settle such claims.

V. We do not think it appropriate at the present time to address petitioner's contention that the suspension of claims, if authorized, would constitute a taking of property in violation of the Fifth Amendment to the United States Constitution in the absence of just compensation. Both petitioner and the Government concede that the question whether the suspension of the claims constitutes a taking is not ripe for review. However, this contention, and the possibility that the President's actions may effect a taking of petitioner's property, makes ripe for adjudication the question whether petitioner will have a remedy at law in the Court of Claims under the Tucker Act, 28 U.S.C.A. § 1491, in such an event. [T]o the extent petitioner believes it has suffered an unconstitutional taking by the suspension of the claims, we see no jurisdictional obstacle to an appropriate action in the United States Court of Claims under the Tucker Act.

The judgment of the District Court is accordingly affirmed, and the mandate shall issue forthwith.

JUSTICE STEVENS, concurring.

In my judgment the possibility that requiring this petitioner to prosecute its claim in another forum will constitute an unconstitutional "taking" is so remote that I would not address the jurisdictional question considered in Part V of the Court's opinion. However, I join the remainder of the opinion.

JUSTICE POWELL, concurring and dissenting in part.

I join the Court's opinion except its decision that the nullification of the attachments did not effect a taking of property interests giving rise to claims for just compensation. Ante, at n. 6. The nullification of attachments presents a separate question from whether the suspension and proposed settlement of claims against Iran may constitute a taking. I would leave both "taking" claims open for resolution on a case-by-case basis in actions before the Court of Claims. . . .

Notes

1. What constitutional limits, if any, might exist on the President's power to bargain with a foreign government to release American hostages? During the oral argument in *Dames & Moore,* the attorney representing Iran argued that the United States is under an obligation to support the hostage agreement and release the Iranian assets, and if the United States refused to transfer the assets, it would be liable. Justice Rehnquist asked: "What if the agreement had said no one in the U.S. should criticize the Ayatollah? Would the U.S. be liable?" The lawyer said yes. 49 U.S.L.W. 3961 (U.S. June 30, 1981). How would you respond?

2. Is it relevant whether or not International Law regards the hostage agreement as valid? One commentator—although arguing that United States should adhere to the agreement for political reasons—argued:

> Under general principles of international law, the United States government could denounce the agreements concluded between the United States, Algeria and Iran which led to the termination of the Iranian hostages crisis. According to Article 52 of the 1969 Vienna Convention on the Law of Treaties, a treaty is void if its conclusion was procured by the threat or use of force in violation of the principles of international law embodied in the United Nations Charter. Such a violation has already been definitely established to exist by the International Court of Justice in its 24 May 1980 Final Judgment in the *Case Concerning United States Diplomatic and Consular Staff in Teheran.* ... To deny the state the right to denounce an agreement concluded under duress would contravene the fundamental principle enunciated in Article 2(4) of the United Nations Charter that all states must refrain from the threat or use of force in their international relations. Boyle, Chicago Daily Law Bulletin, Feb. 12, 1981, at 1.

Are peace treaties often the product of force or the threat of force?

3. *Reid v. Covert,* 354 U.S. 1, 77 S.Ct. 1222, 1 L.Ed.2d 1148 (1957), after a rehearing, held that it was unconstitutional to try civilian dependents of Armed Forces servicemen by court martial in time of peace for capital offenses committed abroad. Executive agreements with Great Britain and Japan had authorized such military jurisdiction, but the Court declared those agreements unconstitutional. It was the first time that the Court invalidated an executive agreement. Justice Black's plurality opinion stated: "[W]e reject the idea that when the United States acts against citizens abroad it can do so free of the Bill of Rights. The United States is entirely a creature of the Constitution. Its power and authority have no other source. It can only act in accordance with all the limitations imposed by the Constitution.... There is nothing in *Missouri v. Holland* which is contrary to the position taken here. There the Court carefully noted that the treaty involved was not inconsistent with any specific provision of the Constitution. The Court was concerned with the Tenth Amendment.... To the extent that the United States can validly make treaties, the people and the States have delegated their power to the National Government and the Tenth Amendment is no barrier."

In *Kinsella v. United States ex rel. Singleton,* 361 U.S. 234, 80 S.Ct. 297, 4 L.Ed.2d 268 (1960), and companion cases decided the same day, the Court extended *Reid* so as to exclude from court martial jurisdiction, in time of peace, all capital or noncapital offenses committed by civilian dependents or civilian employees of the Armed Forces.

To what extent, if any, does *Reid* or *Dames & Moore* undercut the theory of *Curtiss–Wright,* § 5–1, supra, or the dictum in *Missouri v. Holland,* § 5–2, supra.

4. Approximately one month after the Court decided *Reid* it rendered its opinion in *Wilson v. Girard,* 354 U.S. 524, 77 S.Ct. 1409, 1 L.Ed.2d 1544 (1957)(per curiam). A U.S. soldier stationed in Japan caused the death of a Japanese woman. Japan indicted Girard after the United States notified Japan that Girard would be delivered to the Japanese authorities for trial. The United States turned over Girard pursuant to an administrative agreement, which had been authorized by a treaty with Japan. This agreement provided that the United States would have jurisdiction over offenses committed in Japan by members of the U.S. Armed Forces unless the United States waived its jurisdiction. The Court held that the waiver of qualified jurisdiction was constitutional.

Could the United States have waived its jurisdiction over someone like Mrs. Covert and turned her over to the British authorities if a treaty or executive agreement so provided? Once under British (or Japanese) jurisdiction, the U.S. Constitutional guarantees are, of course, inapplicable. So does Mrs. Covert have any cause to complain if she is court martialed by the U.S. Army instead?

5. Assume that the United States and Mexico agree by treaty to a transfer of prisoners, so that, under certain circumstances, Americans held in Mexican jails could elect to serve the remainder of their terms in U.S. prisons if both nations agreed. Assume that a prisoner is eligible only if: the offense for which he was convicted is generally punishable as a crime in the United States; the American prisoner waives any rights to challenge the Mexican conviction in an American court; and the time for direct appeal of the conviction has passed. Is this treaty valid? Should an American who is transferred nonetheless have a right to challenge his conviction and secure release under the writ of habeas corpus if the guarantees of the U.S. Constitution have not been followed by the Mexican authorities at his trial?

5–3. ADMISSION AND DEPORTATION OF ALIENS

GALVAN v. PRESS
347 U.S. 522, 74 S.Ct. 737, 98 L.Ed. 911 (1954).

MR. JUSTICE FRANKFURTER delivered the opinion of the Court.

Petitioner, an alien of Mexican birth, first entered the United States in 1918 and has since resided here with only occasional brief visits to his native country. In the course of two questionings, in March 1948, by the Immigration and Naturalization Service, he indicated that he had been a member of the Communist Party from 1944 to 1946. [In December 1950, petitioner had a de novo hearing. Shortly after it commenced, the examining officer lodged the additional charge that the petitioner, after entry to the United States, had been a member of the Communist Party, membership in which had been made a specific ground for deportation by the Internal Security Act of 1950. The Hearing Officer ordered him deported on that specific ground.] A petition for a writ of habeas corpus was denied by the District Court, and the dismissal was affirmed by the Court of Appeals for the Ninth Circuit.

[The Court, after a detailed discussion of the Act and its legislative history, concluded that the Act did not require support, or even demonstrated knowledge, of the Communist Party's advocacy of violence to be a prerequisite to deportation. "It is enough that the alien joined the Party, aware that he was joining an organization known as the Communist Party which operates as a distinct and active political organization, and that he did so of his own free will." The Court then concluded that, as construed, the Act did not violate due process.]

The power of Congress over the admission of aliens and their right to remain is necessarily very broad, touching as it does basic aspects of national sovereignty, more particularly our foreign relations and the national security. Nevertheless, considering what it means to deport an alien who legally became part of the American community, and the extent to which, since he is a "person," an alien has the same protection for his life, liberty and property under the Due Process Clause as is afforded to a citizen, deportation without permitting the alien to prove that he was unaware of the Communist Party's advocacy of violence strikes one with a sense of harsh incongruity. If due process bars Congress from enactments that shock the sense of fair play—which is the essence of due process—one is entitled to ask whether it is not beyond the power of Congress to deport an alien who was duped into joining the Communist Party, particularly when his conduct antedated the enactment of the legislation under which his deportation is sought. And this because deportation may, as this Court has said in *Ng Fung Ho v. White,* 259 U.S. 276, 284, 42 S.Ct. 492, 495, 66 L.Ed. 938, deprive a man "of all that makes life worth living"; and, as it has said in *Fong Haw Tan v. Phelan,* 333 U.S. 6, 10, 68 S.Ct. 374, 376, 92 L.Ed. 433, "deportation is a drastic measure and at times the equivalent of banishment or exile."

In light of the expansion of the concept of substantive due process as a limitation upon all powers of Congress, even the war power, much could be said for the view, were we writing on a clean slate, that the Due Process Clause qualifies the scope of political discretion heretofore recognized as belonging to Congress in regulating the entry and deportation of aliens. And since the intrinsic consequences of deportation are so close to punishment for crime, it might fairly be said also that the *ex post facto* Clause, even though applicable only to punitive legislation, should be applied to deportation.

But the slate is not clean. As to the extent of the power of Congress under review, there is not merely "a page of history," but a whole volume. Policies pertaining to the entry of aliens and their right to remain here are peculiarly concerned with the political conduct of government. In the enforcement of these policies, the Executive Branch of the Government must respect the procedural safeguards of due process. But that the formulation of these policies is entrusted exclusively to Congress has become about as firmly imbedded in the legislative and judicial tissues of our body politic as any aspect of our government. And whatever might have been said at an earlier date for applying the *ex post facto* Clause, it has been the unbroken rule of this Court that it has no application to deportation. We are not prepared to deem ourselves wiser or more sensitive to human rights than our predecessors....

Judgment affirmed.

MR. JUSTICE BLACK, with whom MR. JUSTICE DOUGLAS concurs, dissenting.

Petitioner has lived in this country thirty-six years, having come here from Mexico in 1918 when only seven years of age. He has an American wife to whom he has been married for twenty years, four children all born here, and a stepson who served this country as a paratrooper. Since 1940 petitioner has been a laborer at the Van Camp Sea Food Company in San Diego, California. In 1944 petitioner became a member of the Communist Party. Deciding that he no longer wanted to belong to that party, he got out sometime around 1946 or 1947. As pointed out in the Court's opinion, during the period of his membership the Communist Party functioned "as a distinct and active political organization." Party candidates appeared on California election ballots, and no federal law then frowned on Communist Party political activities. Now in 1954, however, petitioner is to be deported from this country solely because of his past lawful membership in that party. And this is to be done without proof or finding that petitioner knew that the party had any evil purposes or that he agreed with any such purposes that it might have had. On the contrary, there is strong evidence that he was a good, law-abiding man, a steady worker and a devoted husband and father loyal to this country and its form of government.

For joining a lawful political group years ago—an act which he had no possible reason to believe would subject him to the slightest penalty—petitioner now loses his job, his friends, his home, and maybe even his children, who must choose between their father and their native country. Perhaps a legislative act penalizing political activities legal when engaged in is not a bill of attainder. Conceivably an Act prescribing exile for prior innocent conduct does not violate the constitutional prohibition of *ex post facto* laws. It may be possible that this deportation order for engaging in political activities does not violate the First Amendment's clear ban against abridgment of political speech and assembly. Maybe it is not even a denial of due process and equal protection of the laws. I am unwilling to say, however, that despite these constitutional safeguards this man may be driven from our land because he joined a political party that California and the Nation then recognized as perfectly legal.

[A concurring opinion of REED, J., and a dissenting opinion of DOUGLAS, J., joined by BLACK, J., is omitted.]

FIALLO v. BELL

430 U.S. 787, 97 S.Ct. 1473, 52 L.Ed.2d 50 (1977).

MR. JUSTICE POWELL delivered the opinion of the Court.

This case brings before us a constitutional challenge to §§ 101(b)(1)(D) and 101(b)(2) of the Immigration and Nationality Act of 1952 (Act).

The Act grants special preference immigration status to aliens who qualify as the "children" or "parents" of United States citizens or lawful permanent residents. Under § 101(b)(1), a "child" is defined as an unmarried person under 21 years of age who is a legitimate or legitimated child, a stepchild, an adopted child, or an illegitimate child seeking preference by virtue of his relationship with his natural mother. The definition does not extend to an illegitimate child seeking preference by virtue of his relationship with his natural father. Moreover, under § 101(b)(2), a person qualifies as a "parent" for purposes of the Act solely on the basis of the person's relationship with a "child." As a result, the natural father of an illegitimate child who is either a United States citizen or permanent resident alien is not entitled to preferential treatment as a "parent."

The special preference immigration status provided for those who satisfy the statutory "parent-child" relationship depends on whether the immigrant's relative is a United States citizen or permanent resident alien. A United States citizen is allowed the entry of his "parent" or "child" without regard to *either* an applicable numerical quota *or* the labor certification requirement. On the other hand, a United States permanent resident alien is allowed the entry of the "parent" or "child" subject to numerical limitations but without regard to the labor certification requirement.

Appellants are three sets of unwed natural fathers and their illegitimate offspring who sought, either as an alien father or an alien child, a special immigration preference by virtue of a relationship to a citizen or resident alien child or parent. In each instance the applicant was informed that he was ineligible for an immigrant visa unless he qualified for admission under the general numerical limitations and, in the case of the alien parents, received the requisite labor certification.

Appellants filed this action ... challenging the constitutionality of §§ 101(b)(1) and 101(b)(2) of the Act under the First, Fifth, and Ninth Amendments. Appellants alleged that the statutory provisions (I) denied them equal protection by discriminating against natural fathers and their illegitimate children "on the basis of the father's marital status, the illegitimacy of the child and the sex of the parent without either compelling or rational justification"; (ii) denied them due process of law to the extent that there was established "an unwarranted conclusive presumption of the absence of strong psychological and economic ties between natural fathers and their children born out of wedlock and not legitimated"; and (iii) "seriously burden[ed] and infringe[d] upon the rights of natural fathers and their children, born out of wedlock and not legitimated, to mutual association, to privacy, to establish a home, to raise natural children and to be raised by the natural father." Appellants sought to enjoin permanently enforcement of the challenged statutory provisions to the extent that the statute precluded them from qualifying for the special preference accorded other "parents" and "children."

At the outset, it is important to underscore the limited scope of judicial inquiry into immigration legislation. This Court has repeatedly emphasized that "over no conceivable subject is the legislative power of Congress more complete than it is over" the admission of aliens. Our cases "have long recognized the power to expel or exclude aliens as a fundamental sovereign attribute exercised by the Government's political departments largely immune from judicial control." Our recent decisions have not departed from this long-established rule. Just last Term, for example, the Court had occasion to note that "the power over aliens is of a political character and therefore subject only to narrow judicial review." *Hampton v. Mow Sun Wong,* [§ 8–2.22, infra]; accord, *Mathews v. Diaz,* [§ 8–2.22, infra]. And we observed recently that in the exercise of its broad power over immigration and naturalization, "Congress regularly makes rules that would be unacceptable if applied to citizens."[4]

Appellants apparently do not challenge the need for special judicial deference to congressional policy choices in the immigration context,[5] but instead suggest that a "unique coalescing of factors" makes the instant case sufficiently unlike prior immigration cases to warrant more searching judicial scrutiny. Appellants first observe that since the statutory provisions were designed to reunite families wherever possible, the purpose of the statute was to afford rights not to aliens but to United States citizens and legal permanent residents. . . . Appellants suggest a second distinguishing factor. They argue that none of the prior immigration cases of this Court involved "double-barreled" discrimination based on sex and illegitimacy, infringed upon the due process rights of citizens and legal permanent residents, or implicated "the fundamental constitutional interests of United States citizens and permanent residents in a familial relationship." But this Court has resolved similar challenges to

---

4. Writing for the Court in *Galvan v. Press,* Mr. Justice Frankfurter noted that "much could be said for the view" that due process places some limitations on congressional power in the immigration area, "were we writing on a clean slate. But the slate is not clean. . . . "

We are no more inclined to reconsider this line of cases today than we were five years ago when we decided *Kleindienst v. Mandel,* 408 U.S. 753, 767, 92 S.Ct. 2576, 2584, 33 L.Ed.2d 683 (1972).

5. The appellees argue that the challenged sections of the Act, embodying as

they do "a substantive policy regulating the admission of aliens into the United States, [are] not an appropriate subject for judicial review." Our cases reflect acceptance of a limited judicial responsibility under the Constitution even with respect to the power of Congress to regulate the admission and exclusion of aliens, and there is no occasion to consider in this case whether there may be actions of the Congress with respect to aliens that are so essentially political in character as to be nonjusticiable.

immigration legislation based on other constitutional rights of citizens, and has rejected the suggestion that more searching judicial scrutiny is required. In *Kleindienst v. Mandel,* [408 U.S. 753, 92 S.Ct. 2576, 33 L.Ed.2d 683 (1972)], for example, United States citizens challenged the power of the Attorney General to deny a visa to an alien who, as a proponent of "the economic, international, and governmental doctrines of World communism," was ineligible to receive a visa under 8 U.S.C. § 1182(a)(28)(D) absent a waiver by the Attorney General. The citizen-appellees in that case conceded that Congress could prohibit entry of all aliens falling into the class defined by § 1182(a)(28)(D). They contended, however, that the Attorney General's statutory discretion to approve a waiver was limited by the Constitution and that their First Amendment rights were abridged by the denial of Mandel's request for a visa. The Court held that "when the Executive exercises this [delegated] power negatively on the basis of a facially legitimate and bona fide reason, the courts will neither look behind the exercise of that discretion, nor test it by balancing its justification against the First Amendment interests of those who seek personal communication with the applicant." We can see no reason to review the broad congressional policy choice at issue here under a more exacting standard than was applied in *Kleindienst v. Mandel,* a First Amendment case.

Finally, appellants characterize our prior immigration cases as involving foreign policy matters and congressional choices to exclude or expel groups of aliens that were "specifically and clearly perceived to pose a grave threat to the national security," "or to the general welfare of this country." We find no indication in our prior cases that the scope of judicial review is a function of the nature of the policy choice at issue. To the contrary, "[s]ince decisions in these matters may implicate our relations with foreign powers, and since a wide variety of classifications must be defined in the light of changing political and economic circumstances, such decisions are frequently of a character more appropriate to either the Legislature or the Executive than to the Judiciary," and "[t]he reasons that preclude judicial review of political questions also dictate a narrow standard of review of decisions made by the Congress or the President in the area of immigration and naturalization." *Mathews v. Diaz.* As Mr. Justice Frankfurter observed in his concurrence in *Harisiades v. Shaughnessy* [342 U.S. 580, 72 S.Ct. 512, 96 L.Ed. 586 (1952)]:

> The conditions of entry for every alien, the particular classes of aliens that shall be denied entry altogether, the basis for determining such classification, the right to terminate hospitality to aliens, the grounds, on which such determination shall be based, have been recognized as matters solely for the responsibility of the Congress and wholly outside the power of this Court to control. . . .

[The dissenting opinion of WHITE, J., and the dissenting opinion of MARSHALL, J., joined by BRENNAN, J., are omitted.]

Notes

1. *Flemming v. Nestor,* 363 U.S. 603, 80 S.Ct. 1367, 4 L.Ed.2d 1435 (1960). A section of the Social Security Act provided for the termination of old-age, survivor, and disability insurance payments of an alien deported after September 1, 1954, which was the date that this termination section was enacted. In 1955 Nestor, an alien, became eligible for old age benefits, but in 1956 he was deported because he had been a member of the Communist Party from 1933–1939. At that time (1933–1939) membership in the Communist Party was neither illegal nor a ground for deportation. From 1936 until 1956 Nestor made regular payments into the Social Security system. The district court held that Social Security Act's termination section deprived Nestor of an accrued property right to the Social Security benefits and was therefore unconstitutional.

The Supreme Court, per Harlan, J., reversed. The "right" to Social Security benefits is not any type of property right; the employees have no contractual interests. The Government simply taxes one group—workers— and pays the moneys received to another group—retired persons covered under the Act.

Nestor raised other claims: that he was punished without judicial trial; that the termination section amounted to a bill of attainder; that the law violated the ex post facto clause. All these claims were rejected because the Court found that deportation is "not punishment but an exercise of the plenary power of Congress to fix the conditions under which aliens are to be permitted to enter and remain in the country."

2. *United States ex rel. Knauff v. Shaughnessy,* 338 U.S. 537, 70 S.Ct. 309, 94 L.Ed. 317 (1950). The United States sought to exclude—without a hearing—the alien wife (war bride) of a American citizen solely upon a finding by the Attorney General that her admission would be prejudicial to the interests of the United States. The Court, per Minton, J., found that the Congressional statutory scheme authorized such action, and excluded judicial review. The citizen could not bring his wife into the country and could not find out why she was excluded. "Whatever the rule may be concerning deportation of persons who have gained entry into the United States, it is not within the province of any court, unless expressly authorized by law, to review the determination of the political branch of the Government to exclude a given alien.... Whatever the procedure authorized by Congress is, it is due process as far as an alien denied entry is concerned."

Shaughnessy v. United States ex rel. Mezei, 345 U.S. 206, 73 S.Ct. 625, 97 L.Ed. 956 (1953). Mezei, an alien immigrant was permanently excluded from the United States on security grounds. Because no other nation could take him, he was stranded on Ellis Island. The alien lawfully lived in the United States from 1923–1948 and then left for Hungary to visit his dying mother. On his return, armed with a visa issued by the American Consul in Budapest, he was denied entry on the "basis of information of a confidential nature, the disclosure of which would be prejudicial to the public interest." The Attorney General argued that his continued exclusion of the alien without a hearing was constitutional. The Supreme Court, per Clark, J., agreed: "It is true that aliens who have once passed through our gates, even illegally, may be expelled only after proceedings conforming to traditional notions of due process of law. But an alien on the threshold of initial entry stands on a different footing."[1]

Compare *Wong Yang Sung v. McGrath,* 339 U.S. 33, 70 S.Ct. 445, 94 L.Ed. 616 (1950). After an administrative hearing the immigration authorities sought to deport a Chinese citizen who had overstayed shore leave. He sought release in habeas contending that the hearing was not conducted in conformity with the procedural requirements of the Administrative Procedure Act. The Government argued that the A.P.A. was inapplicable. The Court, per Jackson, J., held that the A.P.A. applied: "But the difficulty with any argument premised on the proposition that the deportation statute does not require a hearing is that, without such hearing, there would be no constitutional authority for deportation. The constitutional requirement of procedural due process derives from the same source as Congress' power to legislate and, where applicable, permeates every valid enactment of that body. It was under compulsion of the Constitution that this Court long ago held that an antecedent deportation statute must provide a hearing at least for aliens who had not entered clandestinely and who had been here some time even if illegally."

3.   *Miller v. Albright,* 523 U.S. 420, 118 S.Ct. 1428, 140 L.Ed.2d 575 (1998). A Federal statute provided that a child born out of wedlock to an alien mother and American father must obtain formal proof of paternity before age 18 to acquire U.S. citizenship; in contrast, the illegitimate, foreign-born child of an alien father and an American mother, is an American citizen at birth. Petitioner was born in the Philippines, to an unwed Filipino mother and American father. After she was no longer a minor, a Texas court granted the father's paternity petition establishing the relationship. She then filed an application for citizenship, which was denied. Then she sued, claiming that the federal statute (requiring the paternity petition to be filed while she was a minor) violated the equal protection component of the Fifth Amendment because the statute contained no limitation on the time within which the child of a citizen *mother* may prove that she became a citizen at birth. The Court, with no majority opinion, rejected her claim.

Stevens, J., joined by Rehnquist, C.J., concluded that law constitutionally distinguished between the male and female parents of foreign born illegitimate children: unlike the situation involving the father, the "blood relationship to the birth mother is immediately obvious and is typically established by hospital records and birth certificates." The need for reliable proof of a "biological relationship between the potential citizen and its citizen parent is an important governmental objective."

O'Connor, J., joined by Kennedy, J., noted that the statute distinguishes on the basis of the sex of the parent, not the child. They argued that the petitioner should not have standing to raise the father's claim of sex discrimination (a claim that would be subject to heightened scrutiny, a scrutiny that the statute could not withstand). In contrast, petitioner's claim is subject only to rational basis scrutiny. Scalia, J., joined by Thomas, J., argued that the complaint should be dismissed because the Court does not

---

1.   A few months later, the Justice Department granted a parole to Mezei, "until his departure from the United States could be effected." Otherwise he would have faced indefinite detention. New York Times, Aug. 10, 1954, at 10 col. 2.

have the power to grant the requested relief: conferral of citizenship on a basis other than that prescribed by Congress. Petitioner was born outside of the United States so she can become a citizen only by statute, but no statute gives her citizenship.

Ginsburg, joined by Souter & Breyer, JJ., dissented, and Breyer, joined by Souter & Ginsburg, dissented. They argued that the statute unconstitutionally classified on the basis of sex.

4. Assuming that his actions are authorized by statute, could the President order the Immigration Service to emphasize and concentrate its resources on the deportation of illegal aliens from a particular country, e.g., Iran? Or might such an order constitute a violation of equal protection?

Could Congress change the immigration laws to place a quota, or ban, on the immigration into this country of aliens from Iran, whether seeking to come here for citizenship or for a temporary or permanent visit?

Could Congress, by statute, revoke the visas of all Iranian aliens who, prior to the statute, were lawfully resident?

Could Congress provide, by statute, that if any alien joins the Communist Party he must be deported? That if he criticizes the Federal Government he must be deported?

5–4. ACQUISITION AND LOSS OF CITIZENSHIP

AFROYIM v. RUSK

387 U.S. 253, 87 S.Ct. 1660, 18 L.Ed.2d 757 (1967).

Mr. Justice Black delivered the opinion of the Court.

Petitioner, born in Poland in 1893, immigrated to this country in 1912 and became a naturalized American citizen in 1926. He went to Israel in 1950, and in 1951 he voluntarily voted in an election for the Israeli Knesset, the legislative body of Israel. In 1960, when he applied for renewal of his United States passport, the Department of State refused to grant it on the sole ground that he had lost his American citizenship by virtue of § 401(e) of the Nationality Act of 1940 which provides that a United States citizen shall "lose" his citizenship if he votes "in a political election in a foreign state." Petitioner then brought this declaratory judgment action in federal district court alleging that § 401(e) violates both the Due Process Clause of the Fifth Amendment and § 1, cl. 1, of the Fourteenth Amendment which grants American citizenship to persons like petitioner. Because neither the Fourteenth Amendment nor any other provision of the Constitution expressly grants Congress the power to take away that citizenship once it has been acquired, petitioner contended that the only way he could lose his citizenship was by his own voluntary renunciation of it. Since the Government took the position that § 401(e) empowers it to terminate citizenship without the citizen's voluntary renunciation, petitioner argued that this section is prohibited by the Constitution. The District Court and the Court of Appeals, rejecting this argument, held that Congress has constitutional authority forcibly to take away citizenship for voting in a foreign country based on its implied power to regulate foreign affairs. Consequently, petitioner was held to have lost his American citizenship regardless of his intention not to give it up. This is precisely what this Court held in *Perez v. Brownell,* 356 U.S. 44, 78 S.Ct. 568, 2 L.Ed.2d 603.

The fundamental issue before this Court here, as it was in *Perez,* is whether Congress can consistently with the Fourteenth Amendment enact a law stripping an American of his citizenship which he has never voluntarily renounced or given up. The majority in *Perez* held that Congress could do this because withdrawal of citizenship is "reasonably calculated to effect the end that is within the power of Congress to achieve." That conclusion was reached by this chain of reasoning: Congress has an implied power to deal with foreign affairs as an indispensable attribute of sovereignty; this implied power, plus the Necessary and Proper Clause, empowers Congress to regulate voting by American citizens in foreign elections; involuntary expatriation is within the "ample scope" of "appropriate modes" Congress can adopt to effectuate its general regulatory power. Then, upon summarily concluding that "there is nothing in the ... Fourteenth Amendment to warrant drawing from it a restriction upon the power otherwise possessed by Congress to withdraw citizenship," the majority specifically rejected the "notion that the power of Congress to terminate citizenship depends upon the citizen's assent".

First we reject the idea expressed in *Perez* that, aside from the Fourteenth Amendment, Congress has any general power, express or implied, to take away an American citizen's citizenship without his assent. This power cannot, as *Perez* indicated, be sustained as an implied attribute of sovereignty possessed by all nations. Other nations are governed by their own constitutions, if any, and we can draw no support from theirs. In our country the people are sovereign and the Government cannot sever its relationship to the people by taking away their citizenship. Our Constitution governs us and we must never forget that our Constitution limits the Government to those powers specifically granted or those that are necessary and proper to carry out the specifically granted ones. The Constitution, of course, grants Congress no express power to strip people of their citizenship, whether in the exercise of the implied power to regulate foreign affairs or in the exercise of any specifically granted power. And even before the adoption of the Fourteenth Amendment, views were expressed in Congress and by this Court that under the Constitution the Government was granted no power, even under its express power to pass a uniform rule of naturalization, to determine what conduct should and should not result in the loss of citizenship.... In 1794 and 1797, many members of Congress still adhered to the English doctrine of perpetual allegiance and doubted whether a citizen could even voluntarily renounce his citizenship. By 1818, however, almost no one doubted the existence of the right of voluntary expatriation, but several judicial decisions had indicated that the right could not be exercised by the citizen without the consent of the

Federal Government in the form of enabling legislation. Therefore, a bill was introduced to provide that a person could voluntarily relinquish his citizenship by declaring such relinquishment in writing before a district court and then departing from the country. The opponents of the bill argued that Congress had no constitutional authority, either express or implied, under either the Naturalization Clause or the Necessary and Proper Clause, to provide that a certain act would constitute expatriation.... The bill was finally defeated. It is in this setting that six years later, in *Osborn v. Bank of the United States,* 9 Wheat. 738, 827, 6 L.Ed. 204, this Court, speaking through Chief Justice Marshall, declared in what appears to be a mature and well-considered dictum that Congress, once a person becomes a citizen, cannot deprive him of that status:

> [The naturalized citizen] becomes a member of the society, possessing all the rights of a native citizen, and standing, in the view of the constitution, on the footing of a native. The constitution does not authorize Congress to enlarge or abridge those rights. The simple power of the national Legislature, is to prescribe a uniform rule of naturalization [Art. I, § 8, cl. 4], and the exercise of this power exhausts it, so far as respects the individual.

Although these legislative and judicial statements may be regarded as inconclusive and must be considered in the historical context in which they were made,[15] any doubt as to whether prior to the passage of the Fourteenth Amendment Congress had the power to deprive a person against his will of citizenship once obtained should have been removed by the unequivocal terms of the Amendment itself. It provides its own constitutional rule in language calculated completely to control the status of citizenship: "All persons born or naturalized in the United States ... are citizens of the United States...." " There is no indication in these words of a fleeting citizenship, good at the moment it is acquired but subject to destruction by the Government at any time. Rather the Amendment can most reasonably be read as defining a citizenship which a citizen keeps unless he voluntarily relinquishes it. Once acquired, this Fourteenth Amendment citizenship was not to be shifted, canceled, or diluted at the will of the Federal Government, the States, or any other governmental unit.

It is true that the chief interest of the people in giving permanence and security to citizenship in the Fourteenth Amendment was the desire to protect Negroes. The *Dred Scott* decision, *Dred Scott v. Sandford,* 19 How. 393, 15 L.Ed. 691, had shortly before greatly disturbed many people about the status of Negro citizenship. [W]hen the Fourteenth Amendment passed the House without containing any definition of citizenship, the sponsors of the Amendment in the Senate insisted on inserting a constitutional definition and grant of citizenship. They ex-

---

15. The dissenting opinion here points to the fact that a Civil War Congress passed two Acts designed to deprive military deserters to the Southern side of the rights of citizenship. Measures of this kind passed in those days of emotional stress and hostility are by no means the most reliable criteria for determining what the Constitution means.

pressed fears that the citizenship so recently conferred on Negroes by the Civil Rights Act could be just as easily taken away from them by subsequent Congresses, and it was to provide an insuperable obstacle against every governmental effort to strip Negroes of their newly acquired citizenship that the first clause was added to the Fourteenth Amendment. . . .

This undeniable purpose of the Fourteenth Amendment to make citizenship of Negroes permanent and secure would be frustrated by holding that the Government can rob a citizen of his citizenship without his consent by simply proceeding to act under an implied general power to regulate foreign affairs or some other power generally granted. Though the framers of the Amendment were not particularly concerned with the problem of expatriation, it seems undeniable from the language they used that they wanted to put citizenship beyond the power of any governmental unit to destroy. In 1868, two years after the Fourteenth Amendment had been proposed, Congress specifically considered the subject of expatriation. Several bills were introduced to impose involuntary expatriation on citizens who committed certain acts. . . . The Act, as finally passed, merely recognized the "right of expatriation" as an inherent right of all people.

The entire legislative history of the 1868 Act makes it abundantly clear that there was a strong feeling in the Congress that the only way the citizenship it conferred could be lost was by the voluntary renunciation or abandonment by the citizen himself. And this was the unequivocal statement of the Court in the case of *United States v. Wong Kim Ark,* 169 U.S. 649, 18 S.Ct. 456, 42 L.Ed. 890 [1898]. The issues in that case were whether a person born in the United States to Chinese aliens was a citizen of the United States and whether, nevertheless, he could be excluded under the Chinese Exclusion Act, 22 Stat. 58. The Court first held that within the terms of the Fourteenth Amendment, Wong Kim Ark was a citizen of the United States, and then pointed out that though he might "renounce this citizenship, and become a citizen of . . . any other country," he had never done so. The Court then held that Congress could not do anything to abridge or affect his citizenship conferred by the Fourteenth Amendment. . . .

> Congress having no power to abridge the rights conferred by the Constitution upon those who have become naturalized citizens by virtue of acts of Congress, *a fortiori* no act . . . of Congress . . . can affect citizenship acquired as a birthright, by virtue of the Constitution itself. . . . The Fourteenth Amendment, while it leaves the power, where it was before, in Congress, to regulate naturalization, has conferred no authority upon Congress to restrict the effect of birth, declared by the Constitution to constitute a sufficient and complete right to citizenship.

To uphold Congress' power to take away a man's citizenship because he voted in a foreign election in violation of § 401(e) would be equivalent to holding that Congress has the power to "abridge," "affect," "restrict the effect of," and "take ... away" citizenship. Because the Fourteenth Amendment prevents Congress from doing any of these things, we agree with the CHIEF JUSTICE's dissent in the *Perez* case that the Government is without power to rob a citizen of his citizenship under § 401(e).[23]

Because the legislative history of the Fourteenth Amendment and of the expatriation proposals which preceded and followed it, like most other legislative history, contains many statements from which conflicting inferences can be drawn, our holding might be unwarranted if it rested entirely or principally upon that legislative history. But it does not. Our holding we think is the only one that can stand in view of the language and the purpose of the Fourteenth Amendment, and our construction of that Amendment, we believe, comports more nearly than *Perez* with the principles of liberty and equal justice to all that the entire Fourteenth Amendment was adopted to guarantee. Citizenship is no light trifle to be jeopardized any moment Congress decides to do so under the name of one of its general or implied grants of power. In some instances, loss of citizenship can mean that a man is left without the protection of citizenship in any country in the world—as a man without a country. Citizenship in this Nation is a part of a cooperative affair. Its citizenry is the country and the country is its citizenry. The very nature of our free government makes it completely incongruous to have a rule of law under which a group of citizens temporarily in office can deprive another group of citizens of their citizenship. We hold that the Fourteenth Amendment was designed to, and does, protect every citizen of this Nation against a congressional forcible destruction of his citizenship, whatever his creed, color, or race. Our holding does no more than to give to this citizen that which is his own, a constitutional right to remain a citizen in a free country unless he voluntarily relinquishes that citizenship.

Perez v. Brownell is overruled. The judgment is

Reversed.

MR. JUSTICE HARLAN, whom MR. JUSTICE CLARK, MR. JUSTICE STEWART, and MR. JUSTICE WHITE join, dissenting.

[The Court] declares that its result is bottomed upon the "language and the purpose" of the Citizenship Clause of the Fourteenth Amendment; in explanation, the Court offers only the terms of the clause itself, the contention that any other result would be "completely incongruous," and the essentially arcane observation that the "citizenry is the country and the country is its citizenry." [This Clause] neither denies nor provides to Congress any power of expatriation; its consequences are, for present purposes, exhausted by its declaration of the classes of individuals to whom citizenship initially attaches. Once obtained, citizenship is of

---

23. Of course, as The Chief Justice said in his dissent, 356 U.S., at 66, 78 S.Ct., at 580; naturalization unlawfully procured can be set aside. See, e.g., *Knauer v. United States,* 328 U.S. 654, 66 S.Ct. 1304, 90 L.Ed. 1500; *Baumgartner v. United States,* 322 U.S. 665, 64 S.Ct. 1240, 88 L.Ed. 1525; *Schneiderman v. United States,* 320 U.S. 118, 63 S.Ct. 1333, 87 L.Ed. 1796.

course protected from arbitrary withdrawal by the constraints placed around Congress' powers by the Constitution; it is not proper to create from the Citizenship Clause an additional, and entirely unwarranted, restriction upon legislative authority. The construction now placed on the Citizenship Clause rests, in the last analysis, simply on the Court's *ipse dixit*, evincing little more, it is quite apparent, than the present majority's own distaste for the expatriation power. . . .

ROGERS v. BELLEI

401 U.S. 815, 91 S.Ct. 1060, 28 L.Ed.2d 499 (1971).

MR. JUSTICE BLACKMUN delivered the opinion of the Court.

Under constitutional challenge here, primarily on Fifth Amendment due process grounds, but also on Fourteenth Amendment grounds, is § 301(b) of the Immigration and Nationality Act of June 27, 1952. Section 301(a) of the Act defines those persons who "shall be nationals and citizens of the United States at birth." Paragraph (7) of § 301(a) includes in that definition a person born abroad "of parents one of whom is an alien, and the other a citizen of the United States" who has met specified conditions of residence in this country. Section 301(b), however, provides that one who is a citizen at birth under § 301(a)(7) shall lose his citizenship unless, after age 14 and before age 28, he shall come to the United States and be physically present here continuously for at least five years. . . .

The facts are stipulated: The appellee, Aldo Mario Bellei (hereinafter the plaintiff), was born in Italy on December 22, 1939. He is now 31 years of age. The plaintiff's father has always been a citizen of Italy and never has acquired United States citizenship. The plaintiff's mother, however, . . . was a native-born United States citizen. She has retained that citizenship. . . . By Italian law the plaintiff acquired Italian citizenship upon his birth in Italy. He retains that citizenship. He also acquired United States citizenship at his birth under Rev.Stat. § 1993, [containing] a residence condition applicable to a child born abroad with one alien parent. . . . The plaintiff has come to the United States five different times. [The visits were several months each or less.] The plaintiff was warned in writing by United States authorities of the impact of § 301(b) when he was in this country in January 1963 and again in November of that year when he was in Italy. Sometime after February 11, 1964, he was orally advised by the American Embassy at Rome that he had lost his United States citizenship pursuant to § 301(b). In November 1966 he was so notified in writing by the American Consul in Rome when the plaintiff requested another American passport. . . .

The central fact, in our weighing of the plaintiff's claim to continuing and therefore current United States citizenship, is that he was born abroad. He was not born in the United States. He was not naturalized in the United States. And he has not been subject to the jurisdiction of the United States. All this being so, it seems indisputable that the first sentence of the Fourteenth Amendment has no application to plaintiff Bellei. He simply is not a Fourteenth–Amendment-first-sentence citizen. His posture contrasts with that of Mr. Afroyim, who was naturalized in the United States....

The plaintiff's claim thus must center in the statutory power of Congress and in the appropriate exercise of that power within the restrictions of any pertinent constitutional provisions other than the Fourteenth Amendment's first sentence. The reach of congressional power in this area is readily apparent.... This takes us, then, to the issue of the constitutionality of the exercise of that congressional power when it is used to impose the condition subsequent that confronted plaintiff Bellei. We conclude that its imposition is not unreasonable, arbitrary, or unlawful, and that it withstands the present constitutional challenge.

MR. JUSTICE BLACK, with whom MR. JUSTICE DOUGLAS and MR. JUSTICE MARSHALL join, dissenting....

The Constitution, written for the ages, cannot rise and fall with this Court's passing notions of what is "fair," or "reasonable," or "arbitrary." ... Speaking of [the Citizenship Clause of the Fourteenth Amendment], the Court held in *Afroyim* that no American can be deprived of his citizenship without his assent. Today, the Court overrules that holding....

[A dissenting opinion of BRENNAN, J., joined by DOUGLAS, J., is omitted.]

Notes

1.   Do you find it curious that neither the majority nor the dissent in *Afroyim* cited *United States v. Curtiss–Wright Export Corp.,* § 5–1? Would Justice Black attack or agree with the rationale of *Curtiss–Wright?*

Recall, from the previous section, the extreme deference the Court gives to Congress in matters relating to admission or deportation of aliens. Yet a majority of the Court in *Afroyim* gives virtually no deference to Congress in expatriation matters. How might the majority justify the distinction?

2.   *United States v. Wong Kim Ark,* 169 U.S. 649, 18 S.Ct. 456, 42 L.Ed. 890 (1898). In this case, discussed in *Afroyim,* the Court said: "The Fourteenth Amendment affirms the ancient and fundamental rule of citizenship by birth within the territory, in the allegiance and under the protection of the country, including all children here born of resident aliens, with the exceptions or qualifications (as old as the rule itself) of children of foreign sovereigns or their ministers, or born on foreign public ships, or of enemies within and during a hostile occupation of part of our territory, and with the single additional exception of children of members of the Indian tribes owing direct allegiance to their several tribes."

Chief Justice Fuller, joined by Justice Harlan, dissented: "[I object to the] proposition that a child born in this country of parents who were not citizens of the United States, and under the laws of their own country and of the United States could not become such ... is, from the moment of his birth a citizen of the United States, by virtue of the first clause of the Fourteenth Amendment, any act of Congress to the contrary notwithstanding."

Is a child born in the United States of parents who are illegal aliens a citizen of the United States? Could the United States deport the alien parents? Their child?

3.   Do you agree with Justice Black that *Bellei* overrules and rejects *Afroyim?*

4.   Mrs. Schneider, a German national by birth, came to this country as a small child with her parents and here acquired United States citizenship derivatively through her mother when her mother was naturalized in the United States. She remained here until she finished college, then went abroad for graduate work, was engaged to a German national, married in Germany, and stayed in residence there. She declared that she had no intention of returning to the United States. In 1959, the State Department denied her a passport on the ground that she had lost her United States citizenship under the specific provisions of § 352(a)(1) of the Immigration and Nationality Act, by continuous residence for three years in a foreign state of which she was formerly a national.

After *Afroyim* and *Bellei*, is the post naturalization residency requirement of section 352(a)(1) constitutional? See *Schneider v. Rusk,* 377 U.S. 163, 84 S.Ct. 1187, 12 L.Ed.2d 218 (1964).

5.   *Knauer v. United States,* 328 U.S. 654, 66 S.Ct. 1304, 90 L.Ed. 1500 (1946). The United States sought to revoke the naturalization of Knauer, a native of Germany, on the grounds that he had falsely represented that he was attached to the principles of the Constitution and that he had taken a false oath of allegiance. The Court, per Douglas, J., affirmed the revocation of citizenship after reviewing that evidence, both before and after naturalization, showing that Knauer was a "thorough-going Nazi" who falsely forswore allegiance to the German Reich.

Would this case come out the same way today?

5–5.   CONGRESSIONAL PRIVILEGE

AN INTRODUCTORY NOTE

In *Gravel v. United States,* 408 U.S. 606, 92 S.Ct. 2614, 33 L.Ed.2d 583 (1972), a federal grand jury investigated possible criminal conduct in connection with the release of the Pentagon Papers. Senator Gravel, on the night of June 29, 1971, convened a meeting of the Subcommittee on Buildings and Grounds of the Public Works Committee. He read extensively from a copy of the Pentagon Papers and placed the entire 47 volumes in the public record. One of Gravel's assistants, Leonard Rodberg, aided him in preparing for and conducting the meeting. The Court held:

We have no doubt that Senator Gravel may not be made to answer— either in terms of questions or in terms of defending himself from prosecution—for the events that occurred at the subcommittee meeting.... Even so, the United States strongly urges that because the Speech or Debate Clause confers a privilege only upon "Senators and Representatives," Rodberg himself has no valid claim to constitutional immunity from grand jury inquiry. In our view, ... for the purpose of construing the privilege a Member and his aide are to be "treated as one;" or, as the District Court put it: the "Speech or Debate Clause prohibits inquiry into things done by Dr. Rodberg as the Senator's agent or assistant which would have been legislative acts, and therefore privileged, if performed by the Senator personally." [The lower courts recognized] that it is literally impossible, in view of the complexities of the modern legislative process, with Congress almost constantly in session and matters of legislative concern constantly proliferating, for Members of Congress to perform their legislative tasks without the help of aides and assistants; that the day-to-day work of such aides is so critical to the Members' performance that they must be treated as the latter's alter egos; and that if they are not so recognized, the central role of the Speech or Debate Clause—to prevent intimidation of legislators by the Executive and accountability before a possibly hostile judiciary—will inevitably be diminished and frustrated....

We are convinced also that the Court of Appeals correctly determined that Senator Gravel's alleged arrangement with Beacon Press to publish the Pentagon Papers was not protected speech or debate within the meaning of Art. I, § 6, cl. 1, of the Constitution.... Here, private publication by Senator Gravel through the cooperation of Beacon Press was in no way essential to the deliberations of the Senate; nor does questioning as to private publication threaten the integrity or independence of the Senate by impermissibly exposing its deliberations to executive influence....

In *Doe v. McMillan*, 412 U.S. 306, 93 S.Ct. 2018, 36 L.Ed.2d 912 (1973), a House Special Select Subcommittee of the Committee on the District of Columbia submitted to the Speaker a Report on the Washington, D.C. public school system. Plaintiffs, under pseudonyms, sued the Committee members, the Superintendent of Documents and the Public Printer, and others alleging violations of their and their children's privacy rights by publication of lists of absentees, copies of test papers, and so on. The Report was printed and distributed by the Government Printing Office. Plaintiffs sought injunctive relief and compensatory and punitive damages. The Court held:

[T]he complaint in this case was barred by the Speech or Debate Clause insofar as it sought relief from the Congressmen–Committee members, from the Committee staff, from the consultant, or from the investigator, for introducing material at Committee hearings that identified particular individuals, for referring the report that included the material to the Speaker of the House, and for voting for publication of the report. Doubtless, also, a published report may, without losing Speech or Debate Clause protection, be distributed to and used for legislative purposes by Members of Congress, congressional committees, and institutional or individual legislative functionaries. [But those] such as the Superintendent of Documents or the Public Printer or legislative personnel, who participate in distribution of actionable material beyond the reasonable bounds of the legislative task, enjoy no speech or Debate Clause immunity. [O]ur conclusion, that general, public dissemination of materials otherwise actionable under local law is not protected by the Speech or Debate Clause, will [not] seriously undermine the informing function of Congress. To the extent that the Committee report is printed and internally distributed to Members of Congress under the protection of the Speech or Debate Clause, the work of Congress is in no way inhibited. Moreover, the internal distribution is public in the sense that materials internally circulated, unless sheltered by specific congressional order are available for inspection by the press and by the public. We only deal, in the present case, with general, public distribution beyond the halls of Congress and the establishments of its functionaries, and beyond the apparent needs of the "*due* functioning of the [legislative] process."

The majority merely dealt with the threshold question of immunity and did not decide whether, in the case before it, the limits of immunity for Congress' legitimate legislative needs had been exceeded. Nor did the Court consider the applicability of Article I, § 5, cl. 3, requiring each House to keep "a Journal of its Proceedings, and from time to time publish the same...."

In *Eastland v. U.S. Servicemen's Fund,* 421 U.S. 491, 95 S.Ct. 1813, 44 L.Ed.2d 324 (1975), the Servicemen's Fund sought to enjoin the issuance of a Congressional subpoena that directed a bank to produce bank records of the Fund. The Fund could not itself use the normal route and test the subpoena by resisting, risking contempt, and presenting its defenses to the criminal action, because the subpoena was directed to a third party, the bank. That third party, to avoid the possibility of contempt, would likely comply. The Fund feared that, if the identity of the donors were revealed, the Fund's contributions would decrease substantially, infringing on the organization's rights of association.

The Court held:

The power to investigate and to do so through compulsory process plainly falls within [the definition of "legitimate legislative" activities]. The issuance of a subpoena pursuant to an authorized investigation is similarly an indispensable ingredient of lawmaking.... The particular investigation at issue here is related to and in furtherance of a legitimate task of Congress. [T]he investigation upon which the Subcommittee had embarked concerned a subject on which "legislation could be had."

Consequently, the federal court could not enjoin issuance of the subpoena. However, if the subject of the subpoena resisted, any First Amendment or other defenses could be presented to the court, because "Congress [would then be] seeking the aid of the Judiciary to enforce its will" in the criminal prosecution for contempt.

UNITED STATES v. HELSTOSKI
442 U.S. 477, 99 S.Ct. 2432, 61 L.Ed.2d 12 (1979).

MR. CHIEF JUSTICE BURGER delivered the opinion of the Court.

We granted certiorari in this case to resolve important questions concerning the restrictions the Speech or Debate Clause places on the admissibility of evidence at a trial on charges that a former Member of the House had, while a Member, accepted money in return for promising to introduce and introducing private bills.

Respondent Helstoski is a former Member of the United States House of Representatives from New Jersey. In 1974, while Helstoski was a Member of the House, the Department of Justice began investigating reported political corruption, including allegations that aliens had paid money for the introduction of private bills which would suspend the application of the immigration laws so as to allow them to remain in this country. . . .

Helstoski testified as to his practices in introducing private immigration bills and he produced his files on numerous private bills. . . . Not until his ninth, and penultimate, appearance before a grand jury did Helstoski assert any privilege under the Speech or Debate Clause [when he] declined to produce a copy of an insert from the Congressional Record, saying "I consulted with my attorneys and based on the statement that was made on the floor, I don't have any right to be questioned at any other time or place as reference to statements made on the floor of Congress." Although that was the first instance which can even remotely be characterized as reliance upon the Speech or Debate Clause, Helstoski earlier had indicated an awareness of another aspect of the constitutional privileges afforded Congressmen. . . .

In June 1976, a grand jury returned a multiple-count indictment charging Helstoski and others with various criminal acts. . . . The District Judge . . . held that the Speech or Debate Clause did not require dismissal. He also ruled that the Government would not be allowed to offer evidence of the actual performance of any legislative acts. . . . The Government filed a timely appeal from the evidentiary ruling. . . .

[T]he Government contends that the Speech or Debate Clause does not bar the introduction of all evidence referring to legislative acts. It concedes that, absent a waiver, it may not introduce the bills themselves. But the Government argues that the Clause does not prohibit it from introducing evidence of discussions and correspondence which describe and refer to legislative acts if the discussions and correspondence did not occur during the legislative process. The Government contends that it seeks to introduce such evidence to show Helstoski's motive for taking money, not to show his motive for introducing the bills. Alternatively, the Government contends that Helstoski waived his protection under the Speech or Debate Clause when he voluntarily presented evidence to the grand juries. Volunteered evidence, the Government argues, is admissible at trial regardless of its content.

Finally, the Government argues, by enacting 18 U.S.C.A. § 201, Congress has shared its authority with the Executive and the Judiciary by express delegation authorizing the indictment and trial of Members who violate that section—in short an institutional decision to waive the privilege of the Clause.

The Court's holdings in *United States v. Johnson,* 383 U.S. 169, 86 S.Ct. 749, 15 L.Ed.2d 681 (1966), and *United States v. Brewster,* [408 U.S. 501, 92 S.Ct. 2531, 33 L.Ed.2d 507 (1972)] leave no doubt that evidence of a legislative act of a Member may not be introduced by the Government in a prosecution under § 201. . . .

In *Brewster,* we explained the holding of *Johnson* in this way:

> *Johnson* thus stands as a unanimous holding that a Member of Congress may be prosecuted under a criminal statute provided that the Government's case does not rely on legislative acts or the motivation for legislative acts. A legislative act has consistently been defined as an act generally done in Congress in relation to the business before it. In sum, the Speech or Debate Clause prohibits inquiry only into those things generally said or done in the House or the Senate in the performance of official duties and into the motivation for those acts.

The Government, however, argues that exclusion of references to past legislative acts will make prosecutions more difficult because such references are essential to show the motive for taking money. In addition, the Government argues that the exclusion of references to past acts is not logically consistent. In its view, if jurors are told of promises to perform legislative acts they will infer that the acts were performed, thereby calling the acts themselves into question.

We do not accept the Government's arguments; without doubt the exclusion of such evidence will make prosecutions more difficult. Indeed, the Speech or Debate Clause was designed to preclude prosecution of Members for legislative acts.[7] The Clause protects "against inquiry into

---

7. Mr. Justice Stevens suggests that our holding is broader than the Speech or Debate Clause requires. In his view, "it is illogical to adopt rules of evidence that will allow a Member of Congress effectively to immunize himself from conviction [for bribery] simply by inserting references to past legislative acts in all communications thus rendering all such evidence inadmissible." Nothing in our opinion, by any conceivable reading prohibits excising references to legislative acts, so that the remainder of the evidence would be admissible. This is a familiar process in the admission of documentary evidence. Of course a Member can use the Speech or Debate Clause as a shield against prosecution by the Executive Branch, but only for utterances within the scope of legislative acts as defined in our holdings. That is the clear purpose of the Clause. The Clause is also a shield for libel and beyond doubt it "has enabled reckless men to slander and even destroy others with impunity, but that was the conscious choice of the Framers." *United States v. Brewster.* Nothing in our holding today, however, immunizes a Member from punishment by the House or the Senate by

acts that occur in the regular course of the legislative process and into the motivation for those acts." It "precludes any showing of how [a legislator] acted, voted, or decided." Promises by a Member to perform an act in the future are not legislative acts. *Brewster* makes clear that the "compact" may be shown without impinging on the legislative function.

We therefore agree with the Court of Appeals that references to past legislative acts of a Member cannot be admitted without undermining the values protected by the Clause. . . .

MR. JUSTICE STEVENS misconstrues our holdings on the Speech or Debate Clause in urging, "The admissibility line should be based on the purpose of the offer rather than the specificity of the reference." The Speech or Debate Clause does not refer to the prosecutor's purpose in offering evidence. The Clause does not simply state, "No proof of a legislative act shall be *offered*"; the prohibition of the Clause is far broader. It provides that Members "shall not be *questioned* in any other Place." Indeed, as Mr. Justice Stevens recognizes, the admission of evidence of legislative acts "may reveal [to the jury] some information about the performance of legislative acts and the legislator's motivation in conducting official duties." Revealing information as to a legislative act—speaking or debating—to a jury would subject a Member to being "questioned" in a place other than the House or Senate, thereby violating the explicit prohibition of the Speech or Debate Clause.

As to what restrictions the Clause places on the admission of evidence, our concern is not with the "specificity" of the reference. Instead, our concern is whether there is mention of a legislative act. To effectuate the intent of the Clause, the Court has construed it to protect other "legislative acts" such as utterances in committee hearings and reports. E.g., *Doe v. McMillan*. But it is clear from the language of the Clause that protection extends only to an act that has already been performed. A promise to deliver a speech, to vote, or to solicit other votes at some future date is not "speech or debate." Likewise, a *promise* to introduce a bill is not a legislative act. Thus, in light of the strictures of *Johnson* and *Brewster*, the District Court order prohibiting the introduction of evidence "of the performance of a *past* legislative act" was redundant.

The Government argues that the prohibition of the introduction of evidence should not apply in this case because the protections of the Clause have been waived. The Government suggests two sources of waiver, (a) Helstoski's conduct and utterances, and (b) the enactment of § 201 by Congress. [W]e perceive no reason to decide whether an individual Member may waive the Speech or Debate Clause's protection against being prosecuted for a legislative act. Assuming that is possible, we hold that waiver can be found only after explicit and unequivocal renunciation of the protection. The ordinary rules for determining the appropriate standard of waiver do not apply in this setting. The Speech

disciplinary action including exclusion from   the Member's seat.

or Debate Clause was designed neither to assure fair trials nor to avoid coercion. Rather, its purpose was to preserve the constitutional structure of separate, coequal, and independent branches of government. The English and American history of the privilege suggest that any lesser standard would risk intrusion by the executive and the judiciary into the sphere of protected legislative activities. . . .

On the record before us, Helstoski's words and conduct cannot be seen as an explicit and unequivocal waiver of his immunity from prosecution for legislative acts—assuming such a waiver can be made. The exchanges between Helstoski and the various United States Attorneys indeed indicate a willingness to waive the protection of the Fifth Amendment; but the Speech or Debate Clause provides a separate, and distinct, protection which calls for at least as clear and unambiguous an expression of waiver. No such showing appears on this record.

[Section 201 makes it a criminal act for a public official corruptly to ask for or accept anything of value in return for being influenced in the performance of his or her official duties.] According to the Government, § 201 represents a collective decision to enlist the aid of the Executive Branch and the courts in the exercise of Congress' powers under Art. I, § 5, to discipline its Members. . . .

We recognize that an argument can be made from precedent and history that Congress, as a body, should not be free to strip individual Members of the protection guaranteed by the Clause from being "questioned" by the executive in the courts. . . . Assuming, *arguendo,* that the Congress could constitutionally waive the protection of the Clause for individual Members, such waiver could be shown only by an explicit and unequivocal expression. There is no evidence of such a waiver in the language or the legislative history of § 201 or any of its predecessors.

We conclude that there was neither individual nor institutional waiver and that the evidentiary barriers erected by the Speech or Debate Clause must stand. Accordingly, the judgment of the Court of Appeals is affirmed.

Affirmed.

MR. JUSTICE POWELL took no part in the consideration or decision of this case.

MR. JUSTICE STEVENS, with whom MR. JUSTICE STEWART joins, concurring in part and dissenting in part.

[T]he majority today does not read *Brewster* to foreclose the introduction of any evidence making reference to legislative acts. The Court holds that evidence referring only to acts to be performed in the future may be admitted into evidence. [I]t is equally true that the solicitation of a bribe which contains a self-laudatory reference to past performance is not itself a legislative act. Whether the legislator refers to past or to future performance, his statement will be probative of his intent in accepting payment and, in either event, may incidentally shed light on the performance and motivation of legislative acts. The proper remedy, in my judgment, is not automatic inadmissibility for past references and automatic admissibility for future references. Rather, drawing on the language of the Constitution itself, the test should require the trial court to analyze the purpose of the prosecutor's questioning. If the evidentiary references to legislative acts are merely incidental to a proper purpose, the judge should admit the evidence and instruct the jury as to its limited relevance. The Constitution mandates that legislative acts "shall not be questioned"; it does not say they shall not be mentioned....

Mr. Justice Brennan, dissenting.

While I have no quarrel with the Court's decision to limit the evidence which the Government may introduce at Helstoski's trial, I would go much further and order the dismissal of Helstoski's indictment altogether. [I] would hold that "a corrupt agreement to perform legislative acts, even if provable without reference to the acts themselves, may not be the subject of a general conspiracy prosecution."

HUTCHINSON v. PROXMIRE
443 U.S. 111, 99 S.Ct. 2675, 61 L.Ed.2d 411 (1979).

Mr. Chief Justice Burger delivered the opinion of the Court.

... Ronald Hutchinson, a research behavioral scientist, sued respondents, William Proxmire, a United States Senator, and his legislative assistant, Morton Schwartz, for defamation arising out of Proxmire's giving what he called his "Golden Fleece" award. The "award" went to federal agencies that had sponsored Hutchinson's research....

The bulk of Hutchinson's research was devoted to the study of emotional behavior. In particular, he sought an objective measure of aggression, concentrating upon the behavior patterns of certain animals, such as the clenching of jaws when they were exposed to various aggravating stressful stimuli. The National Aeronautics and Space Agency and the Navy were interested in the potential of this research for resolving problems associated with confining humans in close quarters for extended periods of time in space and undersea exploration.

The Golden Fleece Award to the agencies that had sponsored Hutchinson's research was based upon research done for Proxmire by Schwartz.... Schwartz helped to prepare a speech for Proxmire to present in the Senate on April 18, 1975; the text was then incorporated into an advance press release, with only the addition of introductory and concluding sentences. Copies were sent to a mailing list of 275 members of the news media throughout the United States and abroad.

Schwartz telephoned Hutchinson before releasing the speech to tell him of the award; Hutchinson protested that the release contained an inaccurate and incomplete summary of his research. Schwartz replied that he thought the summary was fair.

In the speech Proxmire described the federal grants for Hutchinson's research, concluding with the following comment.[3]

The funding of this nonsense makes me almost angry enough to scream and kick or even clench my jaws. It seems to me it is outrageous.

Dr. Hutchinson's studies should make the taxpayers as well as his monkeys grind their teeth. In fact, the good doctor has made a fortune from his monkeys and in the process made a monkey out of the American taxpayer.

It is time for the Federal Government to get out of this "monkey business." In view of the transparent worthlessness of Hutchinson's study of jaw-grinding and biting by angry or hard-drinking monkeys, it is time we put a stop to the bite Hutchinson and the bureaucrats who fund him have been taking of the taxpayer. 121 Cong.Rec. 10803 (1975).

In May 1975, Proxmire referred to his Golden Fleece Awards in a newsletter sent to about 100,000 people whose names were on a mailing list that included constituents in Wisconsin as well as persons in other states. [I]n 1975, Proxmire appeared on a television interview program where he referred to Hutchinson's research, though he did not mention Hutchinson by name. [In a 1976 newsletter] Proxmire summarized his Golden Fleece Awards of 1975. The letter did not mention Hutchinson's name . . .

After the award was announced, Schwartz, acting on behalf of Proxmire, contacted a number of the federal agencies that has sponsored the research. In his deposition he stated that he did not attempt to dissuade them from continuing to fund the research but merely discussed the subject. Hutchinson, by contrast, contends that these calls were intended to persuade the agencies to terminate his grants and contracts.

On April 16, 1976, Hutchinson filed this suit in United States District Court in Wisconsin. In Count I he alleges that as a result of the actions of Proxmire and Schwartz he has "suffered a loss of respect in his profession, has suffered injury to his feelings, has been humiliated, held up to public scorn, suffered extreme mental anguish and physical illness and pain to his person. Further, he has suffered a loss of income and ability to earn income in the future." Count II alleges that the respondents' conduct has interfered with Hutchinson's contractual relationships with supporters of his research. He later amended the complaint to add an allegation that his rights of privacy and peace and tranquility have been infringed. . . .

---

3. Proxmire is not certain that he actually delivered the speech on the Senate floor. He said that he might have merely inserted it into the Congressional Record. In light of that uncertainty, the question arises whether a nondelivered speech printed in the Congressional Record is covered by the Speech or Debate Clause. This Court has never passed on that question and neither the District Court nor the Court of Appeals seemed to think it was important. Nevertheless, we assume, without deciding, that a speech printed in the Congressional Record carries immunity under the Speech or Debate Clause as though delivered on the floor.

The Court of Appeals [held] that the Speech or Debate Clause protected the statements made in the press release and in the newsletters.... The follow-up telephone calls and the statements made by Proxmire on television and radio were not protected by the Speech or Debate Clause; they were, however, held by the Court of Appeals to be protected by the First Amendment.[10]

[T]he Court has given the [Speech or Debate] Clause a practical rather than a strictly literal reading which would limit the protection to utterances made within the four walls of either Chamber. Thus, we have held that committee hearings are protected, even if held outside the Chambers; committee reports are also protected. *Doe v. McMillan; Gravel v. United States;* Cf. *Coffin v. Coffin,* 4 Mass. 1, 27–28 (1808).

The gloss going beyond a strictly literal reading of the Clause has not, however, departed from the objective of protecting only legislative activities....

> Legislative acts are not all-encompassing. The heart of the Clause is speech or debate in either House. Insofar as the Clause is construed to reach other matters, *they must be an integral part of the deliberative and communicative processes* by which Members participate *in committee and House proceedings* with respect to the consideration and passage or rejection of proposed legislation or with respect to other matters which the Constitution places within the jurisdiction of either House. [C]ourts have extended the privilege to matters beyond pure speech or debate in either House, but "only when necessary to prevent indirect impairment of such deliberations." *Gravel v. United States* (emphasis added).

[N]othing in history or in the explicit language of the Clause suggests any intention to create an absolute privilege from liability or suit for defamatory statements made outside the Chamber.... Justice Story in his Commentaries, for example, explained that there was no immunity for republication of a speech first delivered in Congress....

We reach a similar conclusion here. A speech by Proxmire in the Senate would be wholly immune and would be available to other Members of Congress and the public in the Congressional Record. But neither the newsletters nor the press release was "essential to the deliberations of the Senate" and neither was part of the deliberative process.

Respondents, however, argue that newsletters and press releases are essential to the functioning of the Senate; without them, they assert, a Senator cannot have a significant impact on the other Senators. We may assume that a Member's published statements exert some influence on other votes in the Congress and therefore have a relationship to the legislative and deliberative process. But [we] are unable to discern any "conscious choice" [of the framers] to grant immunity for defamatory

---

10. ... Regardless of whether and to what extent the Speech or Debate Clause may protect calls to federal agencies seeking information, it does not protect attempts to influence the conduct of executive agencies or libelous comments made during the conversations.

statements scattered far and wide by mail, press, and the electronic media.

Respondents also argue that newsletters and press releases are privileged as part of the "informing function" of Congress. Advocates of a broad reading of the "informing function" sometimes tend to confuse two uses of the term "informing." In one sense, Congress informs itself collectively by way of hearings of its committees. It was in that sense that Woodrow Wilson used "informing" in a statement quoted by respondents. In reality, Wilson's statement related to congressional efforts to learn of the activities of the Executive Branch and administrative agencies; he did not include wide-ranging inquiries by individual Members on subjects of their choice. Moreover, Wilson's statement itself clearly implies a distinction between the *informing* function and the *legislative* function:

> Unless Congress have and use every means of acquainting itself with the acts and the disposition of the administrative agents of the government, the country must be helpless to learn how it is being served; and unless Congress both scrutinize these things and sift them by every form of discussion, the country must remain in embarrassing, crippling ignorance of the very affairs which it is most important that it should understand and direct. The informing function of Congress should be preferred even to its legislative function. [T]he only really self-governing people is that people which discusses and interrogates its administration. W. Wilson, Congressional Government 303 (1885).

It is in this narrower Wilsonian sense that this Court has employed "informing" in previous cases holding that congressional efforts to inform itself through committee hearings are part of the legislative function.

The other sense of the term, and the one relied upon by respondents, perceives it to be the duty of Members to tell the public about their activities. Valuable and desirable as it may be in broad terms, the transmittal of such information by individual Members in order to inform the public and other Members is not a part of the legislative function or the deliberations that make up the legislative process.[15] As a result, transmittal of such information by press releases and newsletters is not protected by the Speech or Debate Clause.

Doe v. McMillan, is not to the contrary. It dealt only with reports from congressional committees, and held that Members of Congress could not be held liable for voting to publish a report. Voting and preparing committee reports are the individual and collective expressions of opinion within the legislative process. As such, they are protected by

---

15. Provision for the use of the frank, 39 U.S.C.A. § 3210, does not alter our conclusion. Congress, by granting franking privileges, stationery allowances, and facilities to record speeches and statements for radio broadcast cannot expand the scope of the Speech or Debate Clause to render immune all that emanates via such helpful facilities.

the Speech or Debate Clause. Newsletters and press releases, by contrast, are primarily means of informing those outside the legislative forum; they represent the views and will of a single Member. It does not disparage either their value or their importance to hold that they are not entitled to the protection of the Speech or Debate Clause.

[The Court went on to hold that Hutchinson was not a "public figure" for purposes of *New York Times v. Sullivan,* § 10–8.1, infra, and that therefore he did not have to make a showing of *New York Times* "actual malice" to recover in his suit for defamation. The Court then remanded for further proceedings.]

MR. JUSTICE STEWART joins in all but footnote 10 of the Court's opinion. He cannot agree that the question whether a communication by a Congressman or a member of his staff with a federal agency is entitled to Speech or Debate Clause immunity depends upon whether the communication is defamatory. Because telephone calls to federal agency officials are a routine and essential part of the congressional oversight function, he believes such activity is protected by the Speech or Debate Clause.

MR. JUSTICE BRENNAN, dissenting.

[P]ublic criticism by legislators of unnecessary governmental expenditures, whatever its form, is a legislative act shielded by the Speech or Debate Clause. I would affirm the judgment below. . . .

5–6.　EXECUTIVE PRIVILEGE

UNITED STATES v. NIXON
418 U.S. 683, 94 S.Ct. 3090, 41 L.Ed.2d 1039 (1974).

MR. CHIEF JUSTICE BURGER delivered the opinion of the Court.

This litigation presents for review the denial of a motion, filed in the District Court on behalf of the President of the United States, in the case of *United States v. Mitchell,* to quash a third-party subpoena *duces tecum* issued by the United States District Court for the District of Columbia, pursuant to Fed.Rule Crim.Proc. 17(c). The subpoena directed the President to produce certain tape recordings and documents relating to his conversations with aides and advisers. The court rejected the President's claims of absolute executive privilege, of lack of jurisdiction, and of failure to satisfy the requirements of Rule 17(c). The President appealed to the Court of Appeals. We granted both the United States' petition for certiorari before judgment and also the President's cross-petition for certiorari before judgment[2] because of the public importance of the issues presented and the need for their prompt resolution.

2. The cross-petition in No. 73–1834 raised the issue whether the grand jury acted within its authority in naming the President as an unindicted coconspirator. Since we find resolution of this issue unnec-essary to resolution of the question whether the claim of privilege is to prevail, the cross-petition for certiorari is dismissed as improvidently granted. . . .

On March 1, 1974, a grand jury of the United States District Court for the District of Columbia returned an indictment charging seven named individuals[3] with various offenses, including conspiracy to defraud the United States and to obstruct justice. Although he was not designated as such in the indictment, the grand jury named the President, among others, as an unindicted coconspirator. On April 18, 1974, upon motion of the Special Prosecutor, see n. 8, infra, a subpoena *duces tecum* was issued pursuant to Rule 17(c) to the President by the United States District Court and made returnable on May 2, 1974. This subpoena required the production, in advance of the September 9 trial date, of certain tapes, memoranda, papers, transcripts, or other writings relating to certain precisely identified meetings between the President and others. The Special Prosecutor was able to fix the time, place, and persons present at these discussions because the White House daily logs and appointment records had been delivered to him. On April 30, the President publicly released edited transcripts of 43 conversations; portions of 20 conversations subject to subpoena in the present case were included. On May 1, 1974, the President's counsel filed a "special appearance" and a motion to quash the subpoena under Rule 17(c). This motion was accompanied by a formal claim of privilege....

In the District Court, the President's counsel argued that the court lacked jurisdiction to issue the subpoena because the matter was an intrabranch dispute between a subordinate and superior officer of the Executive Branch and hence not subject to judicial resolution.... He views the present dispute as essentially a "jurisdictional" dispute within the Executive Branch which he analogizes to a dispute between two congressional committees. Since the Executive Branch has exclusive authority and absolute discretion to decide whether to prosecute a case, *Confiscation Cases,* 7 Wall. 454, 19 L.Ed. 196 (1869); *United States v. Cox,* 342 F.2d 167, 171 (CA5), cert. denied sub nom. *Cox v. Hauberg,* 381 U.S. 935, 85 S.Ct. 1767, 14 L.Ed.2d 700 (1965), it is contended that a President's decision is final in determining what evidence is to be used in a given criminal case....

Our starting point is the nature of the proceeding for which the evidence is sought—here a pending criminal prosecution. It is a judicial proceeding in a federal court alleging violation of federal laws and is brought in the name of the United States as sovereign. Under the authority of Art. II, § 2, Congress has vested in the Attorney General the power to conduct the criminal litigation of the United States Government. It has also vested in him the power to appoint subordinate officers to assist him in the discharge of his duties. Acting pursuant to those statutes, the Attorney General has delegated the authority to represent the United States in these particular matters to a Special Prosecutor

---

3. The seven defendants were John N. Mitchell, H.R. Haldeman, John D. Ehrlichman, Charles W. Colson, Robert C. Mardian, Kenneth W. Parkinson, and Gordon Strachan. Each had occupied either a position of responsibility on the White House staff or a position with the Committee for the Re-election of the President. Colson entered a guilty plea on another charge and is no longer a defendant.

with unique authority and tenure.[8] The regulation gives the Special Prosecutor explicit power to contest the invocation of executive privilege in the process of seeking evidence deemed relevant to the performance of these specially delegated duties.

So long as this regulation is extant it has the force of law. In *United States ex rel. Accardi v. Shaughnessy,* 347 U.S. 260, 74 S.Ct. 499, 98 L.Ed. 681 (1954), regulations of the Attorney General delegated certain of his discretionary powers to the Board of Immigration Appeals and required that Board to exercise its own discretion on appeals in deportation cases. The Court held that so long as the Attorney General's regulations remained operative, he denied himself the authority to exercise the discretion delegated to the Board even though the original authority was his and he could reassert it by amending the regulations.

. . . Moreover, the delegation of authority to the Special Prosecutor in this case is not an ordinary delegation by the Attorney General to a subordinate officer: with the authorization of the President, the Acting Attorney General provided in the regulation that the Special Prosecutor was not to be removed without the "consensus" of eight designated leaders of Congress. N. 8, supra.

The demands of and the resistance to the subpoena present an obvious controversy in the ordinary sense, but that alone is not sufficient to meet constitutional standards. In the constitutional sense, controversy means more than disagreement and conflict; rather it means the kind of controversy courts traditionally resolve. Here at issue is the production or nonproduction of specified evidence deemed by the Special Prosecutor to be relevant and admissible in a pending criminal case. It is sought by one official of the Executive Branch within the scope of his express authority; it is resisted by the Chief Executive on the ground of his duty to preserve the confidentiality of the communications of the President.

---

8. The regulation issued by the Attorney General pursuant to his statutory authority, vests in the Special Prosecutor plenary authority to control the course of investigations and litigation related to "all offenses arising out of the 1972 Presidential Election for which the Special Prosecutor deems it necessary and appropriate to assume responsibility, allegations involving the President, members of the White House staff, or Presidential appointees, and any other matters which he consents to have assigned to him by the Attorney General." In particular, the Special Prosecutor was given full authority, *inter alia,* "to contest the assertion of 'Executive Privilege' . . . and handl[e] all aspects of any cases within his jurisdiction." The regulation then goes on to provide:

"In exercising this authority, the Special Prosecutor will have the greatest degree of independence that is consistent with the Attorney General's statutory accountability for all matters falling within the jurisdiction of the Department of Justice. The Attorney General will not countermand or interfere with the Special Prosecutor's decisions or actions. The Special Prosecutor will determine whether and to what extent he will inform or consult with the Attorney General about the conduct of his duties and responsibilities. In accordance with assurances given by the President to the Attorney General that the President will not exercise his Constitutional powers to effect the discharge of the Special Prosecutor or to limit the independence that he is hereby given, the Special Prosecutor will not be removed from his duties except for extraordinary improprieties on his part and without the President's first consulting the Majority and the Minority Leaders and Chairmen and ranking Minority Members of the Judiciary Committees of the Senate and House of Representatives and ascertaining that their consensus is in accord with his proposed action."

Whatever the correct answer on the merits, these issues are "of a type which are traditionally justiciable." ... Moreover, since the matter is one arising in the regular course of a federal criminal prosecution, it is within the traditional scope of Art. III power.

[W]e turn to the claim that the subpoena should be quashed because it demands "confidential conversations between a President and his close advisors that it would be inconsistent with the public interest to produce." The first contention is a broad claim that the separation of powers doctrine precludes judicial review of a President's claim of privilege. The second contention is that if he does not prevail on the claim of absolute privilege, the court should hold as a matter of constitutional law that the privilege prevails over the subpoena *duces tecum*....

No holding of the Court has defined the scope of judicial power specifically relating to the enforcement of a subpoena for confidential Presidential communications for use in a criminal prosecution, but other exercises of power by the Executive Branch and the Legislative Branch have been found invalid as in conflict with the Constitution. *Powell v. McCormack*, [§ 1–2.4, supra]; *Youngstown Sheet & Tube Co. v. Sawyer*, [§ 5–1, supra].... We therefore reaffirm that it is the province and duty of this Court "to say what the law is" with respect to the claim of privilege presented in this case. *Marbury v. Madison.*

In support of his claim of absolute privilege, the President's counsel urges two grounds, one of which is common to all governments and one of which is peculiar to our system of separation of powers. The first ground is the valid need for protection of communications between high Government officials and those who advise and assist them in the performance of their manifold duties; the importance of this confidentiality is too plain to require further discussion. Human experience teaches that those who expect public dissemination of their remarks may well temper candor with a concern for appearances and for their own interests to the detriment of the decisionmaking process. Whatever the nature of the privilege of confidentiality of Presidential communications in the exercise of Art. II powers, the privilege can be said to derive from the supremacy of each branch within its own assigned area of constitutional duties. Certain powers and privileges flow from the nature of enumerated powers;[16] the protection of the confidentiality of Presidential communications has similar constitutional underpinnings.

The second ground asserted by the President's counsel in support of the claim of absolute privilege rests on the doctrine of separation of powers. Here it is argued that the independence of the Executive Branch within its own sphere insulates a President from a judicial subpoena in

16. The Special Prosecutor argues that there is no provision in the Constitution for a Presidential privilege as to the President's communications corresponding to the privilege of Members of Congress under the Speech or Debate Clause. But the silence of the Constitution on this score is not dispositive. "The rule of constitutional interpretation announced in *McCulloch v. Maryland*, that that which was reasonably appropriate and relevant to the exercise of a granted power was to be considered as accompanying the grant, has been so universally applied that it suffices merely to state it."

an ongoing criminal prosecution, and thereby protects confidential Presidential communications.

However, neither the doctrine of separation of powers, nor the need for confidentiality of high-level communications, without more, can sustain an absolute, unqualified Presidential privilege of immunity from judicial process under all circumstances. The President's need for complete candor and objectivity from advisers calls for great deference from the courts. However, when the privilege depends solely on the broad, undifferentiated claim of public interest in the confidentiality of such conversations, a confrontation with other values arises. Absent a claim of need to protect military, diplomatic, or sensitive national security secrets, we find it difficult to accept the argument that even the very important interest in confidentiality of Presidential communications is significantly diminished by production of such material for *in camera* inspection with all the protection that a district court will be obliged to provide.... To read the Art. II powers of the President as providing an absolute privilege as against a subpoena essential to enforcement of criminal statutes on no more than a generalized claim of the public interest in confidentiality of nonmilitary and nondiplomatic discussions would upset the constitutional balance of "a workable government" and gravely impair the role of the courts under Art. III.

The expectation of a President to the confidentiality of his conversations and correspondence, like the claim of confidentiality of judicial deliberations, for example, has all the values to which we accord deference for the privacy of all citizens and, added to those values, is the necessity for protection of the public interest in candid, objective, and even blunt or harsh opinions in Presidential decisionmaking.... The privilege is fundamental to the operation of Government and inextricably rooted in the separation of powers under the Constitution. In *Nixon v. Sirica,* 159 U.S.App.D.C. 58, 487 F.2d 700 (1973), the Court of Appeals held that such Presidential communications are "presumptively privileged," and this position is accepted by both parties in the present litigation....

But this presumptive privilege must be considered in light of our historic commitment to the rule of law. This is nowhere more profoundly manifest than in our view that "the twofold aim [of criminal justice] is that guilt shall not escape or innocence suffer." ... To ensure that justice is done, it is imperative to the function of courts that compulsory process be available for the production of evidence needed either by the prosecution or by the defense.

[T]he Fifth Amendment to the Constitution provides that no man "shall be compelled in any criminal case to be a witness against himself." And, generally, an attorney or a priest may not be required to disclose what has been revealed in professional confidence. These and other interests are recognized in law by privileges against forced disclosure, established in the Constitution, by statute, or at common law. Whatever their origins, these exceptions to the demand for every man's evidence are not lightly created nor expansively construed, for they are in derogation of the search for truth.

In this case the President challenges a subpoena served on him as a third party requiring the production of materials for use in a criminal prosecution; he does so on the claim that he has a privilege against disclosure of confidential communications. He does not place his claim of privilege on the ground they are military or diplomatic secrets. As to these areas of Art. II duties the courts have traditionally shown the utmost deference to Presidential responsibilities.... No case of the Court, however, has extended this high degree of deference to a President's generalized interest in confidentiality. Nowhere in the Constitution, as we have noted earlier, is there any explicit reference to a privilege of confidentiality, yet to the extent this interest relates to the effective discharge of a President's powers, it is constitutionally based.

[W]e must weigh the importance of the general privilege of confidentiality of Presidential communications in performance of the President's responsibilities against the inroads of such a privilege on the fair administration of criminal justice.[19] The interest in preserving confidentiality is weighty indeed and entitled to great respect. However, we cannot conclude that advisers will be moved to temper the candor of their remarks by the infrequent occasions of disclosure because of the possibility that such conversations will be called for in the context of a criminal prosecution. On the other hand, the allowance of the privilege to withhold evidence that is demonstrably relevant in a criminal trial would cut deeply into the guarantee of due process of law and gravely impair the basic function of the courts....

We conclude that when the ground for asserting privilege as to subpoenaed materials sought for use in a criminal trial is based only on the generalized interest in confidentiality, it cannot prevail over the fundamental demands of due process of law in the fair administration of criminal justice. The generalized assertion of privilege must yield to the demonstrated, specific need for evidence in a pending criminal trial.

... If a President concludes that compliance with a subpoena would be injurious to the public interest he may properly, as was done here, invoke a claim of privilege on the return of the subpoena. Upon receiving a claim of privilege from the Chief Executive, it became the further duty of the District Court to treat the subpoenaed material as presumptively privileged and to require the Special Prosecutor to demonstrate that the Presidential material was "essential to the justice of the [pending criminal] case." *United States v. Burr.* Here the District Court treated the material as presumptively privileged, proceeded to find that the Special Prosecutor had made a sufficient showing to rebut the presump-

---

19. We are not here concerned with the balance between the President's generalized interest in confidentiality and the need for relevant evidence in civil litigation, nor with that between the confidentiality interest and congressional demands for information, nor with the President's interest in preserving state secrets. We address only the conflict between the President's assertion of a generalized privilege of confidentiality and the constitutional need for relevant evidence in criminal trials.

tion, and ordered an *in camera* examination of the subpoenaed material. On the basis of our examination of the record we are unable to conclude that the District Court erred in ordering the inspection. Accordingly we affirm the order of the District Court that subpoenaed materials be transmitted to that court. We now turn to the important question of the District Court's responsibilities in conducting the *in camera* examination of Presidential materials or communications delivered under the compulsion of the subpoena *duces tecum*.

. . . Statements that meet the test of admissibility and relevance must be isolated; all other material must be excised. At this stage the District Court is not limited to representations of the Special Prosecutor as to the evidence sought by the subpoena; the material will be available to the District Court. It is elementary that *in camera* inspection of evidence is always a procedure calling for scrupulous protection against any release or publication of material not found by the court, at that stage, probably admissible in evidence and relevant to the issues of the trial for which it is sought. That being true of an ordinary situation, it is obvious that the District Court has a very heavy responsibility to see to it that Presidential conversations, which are either not relevant or not admissible, are accorded that high degree of respect due the President of the United States. Mr. Chief Justice Marshall, sitting as a trial judge in the *Burr* case, supra, was extraordinarily careful to point out that "[i]n no case of this kind would a court be required to proceed against the President as against an ordinary individual." Marshall's statement cannot be read to mean in any sense that a President is above the law, but relates to the singularly unique role under Art. II of a President's communications and activities, related to the performance of duties under that Article. Moreover, a President's communications and activities encompass a vastly wider range of sensitive material than would be true of any "ordinary individual." It is therefore necessary[21] in the public interest to afford Presidential confidentiality the greatest protection consistent with the fair administration of justice. The need for confidentiality even as to idle conversations with associates in which casual reference might be made concerning political leaders within the country or foreign statesmen is too obvious to call for further treatment. . . .

Affirmed.

Mr. Justice Rehnquist took no part in the consideration or decision of these cases.

Notes

1.   Prior Presidential Subpoenas.

PRESIDENT THOMAS JEFFERSON. Prior to *United States v. Nixon*, perhaps the most famous case in which a President was required to give evidence was *United States v. Burr*, [25 F.Cas. 187 (No. 14,694) (C.C.Va.

---

21. When the subpoenaed material is delivered to the District Judge *in camera*, questions may arise as to the excising of parts, and it lies within the discretion of that court to seek the aid of the Special Prosecutor and the President's counsel for *in camera* consideration of the validity of particular excisions, whether the basis of excision is relevancy or admissibility or under such cases as *United States v. Reynolds*, 345 U.S. 1, 73 S.Ct. 528, 97 L.Ed. 727 (1953) or *C. & S. Air Lines v. Waterman S.S. Corp.*, 333 U.S. 103, 68 S.Ct. 431, 92 L.Ed. 568 (1948).

1807)], where Chief Justice Marshall, sitting on circuit during the treason trial of Aaron Burr, held the President was subject to subpoena.... Burr intended to obtain a letter from General James Wilkinson to President Jefferson on October 21, 1806, as well as documents containing instructions to the army and navy "to destroy" the "person and property" of Burr....

PRESIDENT JAMES MONROE. A virtually unknown case of a judicially upheld subpoena against a President involved President James Monroe. On January 3, 1818, Monroe became the second President to be served a subpoena while in office. He was summoned as a witness in behalf of the defendant in the court-martial case of Dr. William C. Barton. On two occasions, Dr. Barton had pressed President Monroe for a position at the Philadelphia naval hospital. Barton eventually received this appointment, leading one Dr. Thomas Harris, whom Barton replaced, to bring charges of "intrigue and misconduct" against Barton. Because Barton's meetings with the President were cited as contributing factors in the accusation, a summons was issued to the President. Secretary of State John Quincy Adams, on behalf of Monroe, solicited Attorney General Wirt's legal opinion on the matter. An unpublished, previously undiscovered, handwritten opinion of the Attorney General concluded that a subpoena *ad testificandum* could properly be issued to the President. Monroe indicated on the back of the summons that, because of official duties and his inability to leave "the seat of government," he would hold himself ready to give his testimony in the form of a deposition. He subsequently submitted answers to interrogatories forwarded by the court, a procedure apparently satisfactory to all parties, though his answers did not arrive until after the court had already dismissed the case.... [1]

2. The extent to which Jefferson actually complied with the Aaron Burr subpoena is a much mooted question, and the interpretation of the events following the subpoena are ambiguous. Jefferson withheld parts of the letter "as he thought it would be improper to produce" and Marshall apparently accepted this claim of privilege. The letter was not introduced into evidence.

Assume that Jefferson in fact refused to comply with the Marshall subpoena. Is that relevant?

3. The Court pointed out that on April 30, 1977, President Nixon publicly released edited transcripts of 43 conversations, including portions of 20 conversations subject to subpoena. Should the Court have found that the President "waived" his privilege by his partial disclosures?

4. Congress did not provide the Special Prosecutor any tenure protection by statute though some Congressmen urged that such action be taken;

1. Rotunda, Presidents and Ex-Presidents as Witnesses: A Brief Historical Footnote, 1975 U.Ill.L.Forum 1. See also, 1 R. Rotunda & Nowak, Treatise on Constitutional Law: Substance and Procedure §§ 7.1(a)–(d)(West Group, 3d ed. 1999) for discussion of other Presidential appearances.

he only had tenure by regulation, which provided he could not be removed without consensus of various congressional leaders. Could the President have mooted the controversy by having his Attorney General change the regulation to allow removal of the Special Prosecutor in the discretion of the Attorney General?

If a U.S. attorney sought to subpoena the President, would that dispute be intrabranch and not justiciable? Normally one party cannot control both sides of the litigation. Is that what happened in this case? Is that what would happen if a U.S. Attorney sought to enforce a subpoena?

5.   The Court, in finding "constitutional underpinnings" to the claim of executive privilege, quickly dismissed the argument that the constitutional silence as to the existence of the privilege was relevant. The Court, at n. 16, relied on the necessary and proper clause. Do you find the Court's argument persuasive?

6.   In determining that the President's assertion of executive privilege is not a political question, what test does the Court use? Is the Court saying that if the issues are of the type traditionally justiciable—here, the admissibility of evidence—then the matter is not political even if the alleged evidentiary privilege relates to executive privilege, national security, etc.?

Note that the Court quoted the language in *Marbury v. Madison,* that "[i]t is emphatically the province and duty of the judicial department to say what the law is." Do you find that language helpful? Should the Court also have quoted the following language from *Marbury:*

> The intimate political relation, subsisting between the president of the United States and the heads of departments, necessarily renders any legal investigation of the acts of one of those high officers peculiarly irksome, as well as delicate. [T]he assertion, by an individual, of his legal claims in a court of justice . . . should at first view be considered by some, as an attempt to intrude into the cabinet, and to intermeddle with the prerogatives of the executive. It is scarcely necessary for the court to disclaim all pretensions to such a jurisdiction. . . . The province of the courts is, solely, to decide on the rights of the individuals, not to inquire how the executive, or executive officers, perform duties in which they have a discretion. Questions, in their nature political, or which are, by the constitution and laws, submitted to the executive, can never be made in this court. But [this is] so far from being an intrusion into the secrets of the cabinet [because] it respects a paper, which, according to law, is upon record. . . .

7.   After this case, could President Nixon have protected the confidentiality of the tapes by claiming a need to protect national security secrets? Could President Nixon have protected the confidentiality of the tapes by pleading the Fifth Amendment?

8.   The Senate Select Committee on Presidential Campaign Activities (The Senate Watergate Committee) also sued to enforce its subpoena. The Committee argued in its briefs that the courts should not respect any assertion of executive privilege if there is probable cause that the conversations subpoenaed were made in furtherance of a crime. The Committee noted that other evidentiary privileges (other than the Fifth Amendment)—

e.g., the attorney-client privilege, the privilege of a juror as to jury deliberations—do not apply if the conversations were in furtherance of a crime.[2] The Select Committee's case never reached the Supreme Court but the D.C. Circuit rejected the claim. *Senate Select Committee on Presidential Campaign Activities v. Nixon,* 498 F.2d 725 (D.C.Cir.1974)(en banc), stating that the Committee, in the court's view, had not shown "sufficient need" for the tapes to fulfill its functions, but perhaps the House Impeachment Committee could make such a showing.

If the Supreme Court had adopted the Select Committee's test, would the Court have shown more or less judicial self-restraint? Would the Court have aggregated to itself a broader power under the Selected Committee's test as compared to the test it actually adopted?

NIXON v. ADMINISTRATOR OF GENERAL SERVICES
433 U.S. 425, 97 S.Ct. 2777, 53 L.Ed.2d 867 (1977).

MR. JUSTICE BRENNAN delivered the opinion of the Court.

Title I of Pub.L. 93–526, 88 Stat. 1695, note following 44 U.S.C.A. § 2107, the Presidential Recordings and Materials Preservation Act (hereafter Act), directs the Administrator of General Services, an official of the Executive Branch, to take custody of the Presidential papers and tape recordings of appellant, former President Richard M. Nixon, and promulgate regulations that (1) provide for the orderly processing and screening by Executive Branch archivists of such materials for the purpose of returning to appellant those that are personal and private in nature, and (2) determine the terms and conditions upon which public access may eventually be had to those materials that are retained. The question for decision is whether Title I is unconstitutional on its face as a violation of (1) the separation of powers; (2) Presidential privilege doctrines; (3) appellant's privacy interests; (4) appellant's First Amendment associational rights; or (5) the Bill of Attainder Clause. . . .

CLAIMS CONCERNING THE AUTONOMY OF THE EXECUTIVE BRANCH .

The Act was the product of joint action by the Congress and President Ford, who signed the bill into law. It is therefore urged by intervenor-appellees that, in this circumstance, the case does not truly present a controversy concerning the separation of powers, or a controversy concerning the Presidential privilege of confidentiality, because, it is argued, such claims may be asserted only by incumbents who are presently responsible to the American people for their action. We reject the argument that only an incumbent President may assert such claims and hold that appellant, as a former President, may also be heard to assert them. We further hold, however, that neither his separation-of-powers claim nor his claim of breach of constitutional privilege has merit. . . .

2. See, e.g., Federal Rules of Evidence, Proposed Rule 503(d)(1)(no attorney client privilege if conversation in furtherance of a crime or fraud); Proposed Rule 507 (no political vote privilege if vote cast illegally).

We reject at the outset appellant's argument that the Act's regulation of the disposition of Presidential materials within the Executive Branch constitutes, without more, a violation of the principle of separation of powers. Neither President Ford nor President Carter supports this claim. The Executive Branch became a party to the Act's regulation when President Ford signed the Act into law, and the administration of President Carter, acting through the Solicitor General, vigorously supports affirmance of the District Court's judgment sustaining its constitutionality. Moreover, the control over the materials remains in the Executive Branch. The Administrator of the General Services Administration, who must promulgate and administer the regulations that are the keystone of the statutory scheme, is himself an official of the Executive Branch, appointed by the President. The career archivists appointed to do the initial screening for the purpose of selecting out and returning to appellant his private and personal papers similarly are Executive Branch employees.

[I]n determining whether the Act disrupts the proper balance between the coordinate branches, the proper inquiry focuses on the extent to which it prevents the Executive Branch from accomplishing its constitutionally assigned functions. *United States v. Nixon.* Only where the potential for disruption is present must we then determine whether that impact is justified by an overriding need to promote objectives within the constitutional authority of Congress.

It is therefore highly relevant that the Act provides for custody of the materials in officials of the Executive Branch and that employees of that branch have access to the materials only "for lawful Government use, subject to the [Administrator's] regulations." § 102(d); 41 CFR §§ 105–63.205, 105–62.206, and 105–63.302 (1976). For it is clearly less intrusive to place custody and screening of the materials within the Executive Branch itself than to have Congress or some outside agency perform the screening function. While the materials may also be made available for use in judicial proceedings, this provision is expressly qualified by any rights, defense, or privileges that any person may invoke including, of course, a valid claim of executive privilege. Similarly, although some of the materials may eventually be made available for public access, the Act expressly recognizes the need both "to protect any party's opportunity to assert any legally or constitutionally based right or privilege," § 104(a)(5), and to return purely private materials to appellant, § 104(a)(7). These provisions plainly guard against disclosures barred by any defenses or privileges available to appellant or the Executive Branch. And appellant himself concedes that the Act "does not make the presidential materials available to the Congress—except insofar as Congressmen are members of the public and entitled to access when the public has it." The Executive Branch remains in full control of the Presidential materials, and the Act facially is designed to ensure that the materials can be released only when release is not barred by some applicable privilege inherent in that branch.

[T]here is abundant statutory precedent for the regulation and mandatory disclosure of documents in the possession of the Executive Branch. See, e.g., the Freedom of Information Act, 5 U.S.C.A. § 552; the Privacy Act of 1974, 5 U.S.C.A. § 552(a); the Government in the Sunshine Act, 5 U.S.C.A. § 552b; the Federal Records Act, 44 U.S.C.A. § 2101 et seq.; and a variety of other statutes, e.g., 13 U.S.C.A. §§ 8–9 (census data); 26 U.S.C.A. § 6103 (tax returns). Such regulation of material generated in the Executive Branch has never been considered invalid as an invasion of its autonomy.[8] Similar congressional power to regulate Executive Branch documents exists in this instance, a power that is augmented by the important interests that the Act seeks to attain.

Having concluded that the separation-of-powers principle is not necessarily violated by the Administrator's taking custody of and screening appellant's papers, we next consider appellant's more narrowly defined claim that the Presidential privilege shields these records from archival scrutiny. We start with what was established in *United States v. Nixon,* supra—that the privilege is a qualified one.... Unlike *United States v. Nixon,* in which appellant asserted a claim of absolute Presidential privilege against inquiry by the coordinate Judicial Branch, this case initially involves appellant's assertion of a privilege against the very Executive Branch in whose name the privilege is invoked. The nonfederal appellees rely on this apparent anomaly to contend that only an incumbent President can assert the privilege of the Presidency.

[W]e think that the Solicitor General states the sounder view, and we adopt it:

> "... The confidentiality necessary to this exchange cannot be measured by the few months or years between the submission of the information and the end of the President's tenure; the privilege is not for the benefit of the President as an individual, but for the benefit of the Republic. Therefore the privilege survives the individual President's tenure." Brief for Federal Appellees 33.

At the same time, however, the fact that neither President Ford nor President Carter supports appellant's claim detracts from the weight of his contention that the Act impermissibly intrudes into the executive function and the needs of the Executive Branch. This necessarily follows, for it must be presumed that the incumbent President is vitally concerned with and in the best position to assess the present and future needs of the Executive Branch, and to support invocation of the privilege accordingly.

[A]ny access will be governed by the guidelines of § 104, which direct the Administrator to take into account "the need to protect any party's opportunity to assert any ... constitutionally based right or

---

8. We see no reason to engage in the debate whether appellant has legal title to the materials. Such an inquiry is irrelevant for present purposes because § 105(c) as- sures appellant of just compensation if his economic interests are invaded, and, even if legal title is his, the materials are not thereby immune from regulation.

privilege," § 104(a)(5), and the need to return purely private materials to the appellant, § 104(a)(7). In view of these specific directions, there is no reason to believe that the restriction on public access ultimately established by regulation will not be adequate to preserve executive confidentiality. An absolute barrier to all outside disclosure is not practically or constitutionally necessary. [T]here has never been an expectation that the confidences of the Executive Office are absolute and unyielding. All former Presidents from President Hoover to President Johnson have deposited their papers in Presidential libraries (an example appellant has said he intended to follow) for governmental preservation and eventual disclosure. . . . The expectation of the confidentiality of executive communications thus has always been limited and subject to erosion over time after an administration leaves office.

We are thus left with the bare claim that the mere screening of the materials by the archivists will impermissibly interfere with candid communication of views by Presidential advisors. . . . The screening constitutes a very limited intrusion by personnel in the Executive Branch sensitive to executive concerns. These very personnel have performed the identical task in each of the Presidential libraries without any suggestion that such activity has in any way interfered with executive confidentiality. . . . Appellant has suggested no reason why review under the instant Act, rather than the Presidential Libraries Act, is significantly more likely to impair confidentiality, nor has he called into question the District Court's finding that the archivists' "record for discretion in handling confidential material is unblemished."

Moreover, adequate justifications are shown for this limited intrusion into executive confidentiality comparable to those held to justify the *in camera* inspection of the District Court sustained in *United States v. Nixon,* supra. . . . An incumbent President should not be dependent on happenstance or the whim of a prior President when he seeks access to records of past decisions that define or channel current governmental obligations. Nor should the American people's ability to reconstruct and come to terms with their history be truncated by an analysis of Presidential privilege that focuses only on the needs of the present. Congress can legitimately act to rectify the hit-or-miss approach that has characterized past attempts to protect these substantial interests by entrusting the materials to expert handling by trusted and disinterested professionals.

Other substantial public interests that led Congress to seek to preserve appellant's materials were the desire to restore public confidence in our political processes by preserving the materials as a source for facilitating a full airing of the events leading to appellant's resignation, and Congress' need to understand how those political processes had in fact operated in order to gauge the necessity for remedial legislation. Thus by preserving these materials, the Act may be thought to aid the legislative process and thus to be within the scope of Congress' broad investigative power, see, e.g., *Eastland v. United States Servicemen's Fund,* § 5–5, supra. . . .

In short, we conclude that the screening process contemplated by the Act will not constitute a more severe intrusion into Presidential confidentiality than the *in camera* inspection by the District Court approved in *United States v. Nixon*.... Appellant's right to assert the privilege is specifically preserved by the Act. The guideline provisions on their face are as broad as the privilege itself. If the broadly written protections of the Act should nevertheless prove inadequate to safeguard appellant's rights or to prevent usurpation of executive powers, there will be time enough to consider that problem in a specific factual context. For the present, we hold, in agreement with the District Court, that the Act on its face does not violate the Presidential privilege....

Finally, we address appellant's argument that the Act constitutes a bill of attainder proscribed by Art. I, § 9, of the Constitution. [I]n the present case, the Act's specificity—the fact that it refers to appellant by name—does not automatically offend the Bill of Attainder Clause. [A]ppellant constituted a legitimate class of one....

[The bill of attainder section is excerpted more fully infra, at § 6–4.]

[The concurring opinion of STEVENS, J., the opinions concurring in part and concurring in the judgment of WHITE, BLACKMUN, & POWELL, JJ., and the dissenting opinions of BURGER, C.J., & REHNQUIST, J., are omitted.]

Notes

1. Chief Justice Burger's dissent called the Court's holding "a grave repudiation of nearly 200 years of judicial precedent and historical practice." He noted: "No one has suggested that Congress will find its own 'core' functioning impaired by lack of the impounded papers, as we expressly found the judicial function would be impaired by lack of the materials subpoenaed in *United States v. Nixon*."

Nixon v. United States did not refer to any "core functions" of the three branches of government. Burger's original draft of that opinion did present a "core function" analysis, arguing that, because one of the "core functions" of the judiciary was ensuring that all evidence was available for a criminal trial, the President should comply with the subpoena. Various Justices, led by Justice Stewart, were concerned that a core functions formulation was too vague and expandable, allowing the possibility of "a defiant reinterpretation by the President." Finally, after several drafts and proposed drafts, the "core function" language was dropped. See Bob Woodward & Scott Armstrong, *The Brethren* 330–35, 337–38, 342–43 (1979).

2. Justice Rehnquist's dissent argued: "[T]oday's decision countenances the power of any future Congress to seize the official papers of an outgoing President as he leaves the inaugural stand. In so doing, it poses a real threat to the ability of future Presidents to receive candid advice and to give candid instructions. This result, so at odds with our previous case law on the separation of powers, will daily stand as a veritable sword of Damocles over every succeeding President and his advisors." Do you share that view?

3. Since *United States v. Nixon* found that executive privilege has "constitutional underpinnings," how can Congress effect that privilege by statute?

Is the Court holding that Congress can enact legislation governing presidential papers even though that office—unlike other executive offices, Department of Energy, Department of Education, etc.—is not a creature of Congress?

Is the Court holding that Congress' law can never be subject to constitutional challenge; *i.e.*, after this case, would former President Nixon have had any claim to attack a judgment of the Administrator making certain tapes public?

What test does the Court develop to determine if the Act is constitutional? Why does this Act meet that test?

4. If a former President can plead executive privilege, is that plea granted less deference than a plea by a sitting President? Why is it relevant that President Ford signed the disputed Act and that President Carter supported its constitutionality? Is the Court saying that only a sitting President has standing to invoke separation of powers principles? Is the Court saying that a test for a violation of separation of powers is whether or not the branch allegedly infringed upon objects? Is the Court saying that the case would have come out differently if the Act had been passed over a Presidential veto?

5. *Nixon v. Warner Communications, Inc.*, 435 U.S. 589, 98 S.Ct. 1306, 55 L.Ed.2d 570 (1978). The press sought to copy several Watergate tapes that had been introduced at trial. But the Court held that neither the guarantees of free speech nor public trial, nor any common law right of access gave the news organizations such rights. The opportunity to listen to the tapes at trial, to receive transcripts at trial, and to report what had been seen and heard satisfied any constitutional rights. The Court, per Powell, J., relied in particular on the view that the Presidential Recordings and Materials Preservation Act created an administrative procedure for public release of the tapes. Justice Stevens, dissenting, noted that the Act mandated public access and it "is therefore not surprising that petitioners responded to the Court's post-argument request for supplemental briefs by expressly disavowing any reliance on the Presidential Recordings Act.... For this Court now to rely on the Act as a basis for reversing the trial judge's considered judgment is ironic, to put it mildly."

6. THE PARDON POWER. An interesting clause separating Executive from Congressional powers is the pardoning power, Article II, § 2, cl. 1. See, e.g., *Ex parte Garland*, 71 U.S. (4 Wall.) 333, 18 L.Ed. 366 (1866):

> The power thus conferred is unlimited, with the exception [of cases of impeachment]. It extends to every offence known to the law, and may be exercised at any time after its commission, either before legal proceedings are taken, or during their pendency, or after conviction and judgment. This power of the President is not subject to legislative control. Congress can neither limit the effect of his pardon, nor exclude from its exercise any class of offenders....

... A pardon reaches both the punishment prescribed for the offence and the guilt of the offender; and when the pardon is full, it releases the punishment and blots out of existence the guilt, so that in the eye of the law the offender is as innocent as if he had never committed the offence. If granted before conviction, it prevents any of the penalties and disabilities consequent upon conviction from attaching; if granted after conviction, it removes the penalties and disabilities, and restores him to all his civil rights; it makes him, as it were, a new man, and gives him a new credit and capacity.

There is only this limitation to its operation: it does not restore offices forfeited, or property or interests vested in others in consequence of the conviction and judgment.

Congress may not limit the effects of a presidential pardon granted to a person because of his participation in the Civil War by requiring him, as a precondition to practicing law in the federal courts, to take an oath that he never had borne arms against the United States. To require that oath would restrict the effects of the pardon. *Ex parte Garland,* supra. See also, *United States v. Klein,* § 1–2.2, supra. The President may also attach conditions to a pardon. E.g., *Schick v. Reed,* 419 U.S. 256, 95 S.Ct. 379, 42 L.Ed.2d 430 (1974)(President may commute death sentence to life imprisonment without eligibility for parole, although such a condition was not authorized by statute). And no separation of powers principle precludes the pardoning power from extending not only to indictable crimes but to contempt of court. *Ex parte Grossman,* 267 U.S. 87, 45 S.Ct. 332, 69 L.Ed. 527 (1925).[1]

But a pardon cannot affect rights vested in others. "[I]f the proceeds [of forfeited property] have been paid into the treasury, the right to them has so far become vested in the United States that they can only be secured to the former owner of the property through an act of Congress. Moneys once in the treasury can only be withdrawn by an appropriation by law." *Knote v. United States,* 95 U.S. (5 Otto) 149, 24 L.Ed. 442 (1877). See Art. I, § 9, cl. 7. However if the property is not vested in another, it is restored by the pardon. *Illinois Central Railroad v. Bosworth,* 133 U.S. 92, 10 S.Ct. 231, 33 L.Ed. 550 (1890)(if legal disabilities that prevented person from exercising power on his "suspended fee" are removed by pardon, he is restored to the property that is not vested in others). The President's pardoning power also does not prevent Congress from enacting amnesty statutes. *The Laura,* 114 U.S. 411, 5 S.Ct. 881, 29 L.Ed. 147 (1885); *Brown v. Walker,* 161 U.S. 591, 16 S.Ct. 644, 40 L.Ed. 819 (1896).

NIXON v. FITZGERALD
457 U.S. 731, 102 S.Ct. 2690, 73 L.Ed.2d 349 (1982).

JUSTICE POWELL delivered the opinion of the Court.

The plaintiff in this lawsuit seeks relief in civil damages from a former President of the United States. The claim rests on actions

---

1. It has been argued that it would violate the separation of powers for the President to pardon an individual convicted of a nonstatutory contempt of Congress. E. Corwin, The President: Office and Powers, 414 n. 132 (4th Rev.Ed.1957). Cf. *Ex parte Grossman,* 267 U.S. 87, 121–22, 45 S.Ct. 332, 337, 69 L.Ed. 527 (1925). Nonstatutory, or common law, contempt of Congress is imposed directly by Congress sitting as a court. Under the statutory procedure, 2 U.S.C.A. § 192, the individual is indicted and tried before a federal court.

allegedly taken in the former President's official capacity during his tenure in office. The issue before us is the scope of the immunity possessed by the President of the United States.

In January 1970 the respondent A. Ernest Fitzgerald lost his job as a management analyst with the Department of the Air Force. [T]he Air Force characterized the action as taken to promote economy and efficiency in the armed forces. Respondent's discharge attracted unusual attention in Congress and in the press. Fitzgerald had attained national prominence approximately one year earlier, during the waning months of the presidency of Lyndon B. Johnson [when he] appeared before the Subcommittee on Economy in Government of the Joint Economic Committee of the United States Congress. To the evident embarrassment of his superiors in the Department of Defense, Fitzgerald testified that cost-overruns on the C–5A transport plane could approximate $2 billion. He also revealed that unexpected technical difficulties had arisen during the development of the aircraft.

Concerned that Fitzgerald might have suffered retaliation for his congressional testimony, the Subcommittee on Economy in Government convened public hearings on Fitzgerald's dismissal.... At a news conference on December 8, 1969, President Richard Nixon was queried about Fitzgerald's impending separation from government service. The President responded by promising to look into the matter. Shortly after the news conference the petitioner asked White House Chief of Staff H.R. Haldeman to arrange for Fitzgerald's assignment to another job within the Administration.... Fitzgerald's proposed reassignment encountered resistance within the Administration. In an internal memorandum of January 20, 1970, White House aide Alexander Butterfield reported to Haldeman that "Fitzgerald is no doubt a top-notch cost expert, but he must be given very low marks in loyalty; and after all, loyalty is the name of the game." Butterfield therefore recommended that "We should let him bleed, for a while at least." There is no evidence of White House efforts to reemploy Fitzgerald subsequent to the Butterfield memorandum.

Absent any offer of alternative federal employment, Fitzgerald complained to the Civil Service Commission.... After hearing over 4,000 pages of testimony, the Chief Examiner for the Civil Service Commission issued his decision in the Fitzgerald case on September 18, 1973 [holding] that Fitzgerald's dismissal had offended applicable civil service regulations [because] the departmental reorganization in which Fitzgerald lost his job, though purportedly implemented as an economy measure, was in fact motivated by "reasons purely personal to" respondent. As this was an impermissible basis for a reduction in force, the Examiner recommended Fitzgerald's reappointment to his old position or to a job of comparable authority. The Examiner, however, explicitly distinguished this narrow conclusion from a suggested finding that Fitzgerald had suffered retaliation for his testimony to Congress....

Following the Commission's decision, Fitzgerald filed a suit for damages in the United States District Court. [A district court order of March 26, 1980] held that Fitzgerald had stated triable causes of action under two federal statutes and the First Amendment to the Constitution.[20] The Court also ruled that petitioner was not entitled to claim absolute presidential immunity. . . .

This case now presents the claim that the President of the United States is shielded by absolute immunity from civil damages liability. . . .[27]

Applying the principles of our cases to claims of this kind, we hold that petitioner, as a former President of the United States, is entitled to absolute immunity from damages liability predicated on his official acts. We consider this immunity a functionally mandated incident of the President's unique office, rooted in the constitutional tradition of the separation of powers and supported by our history. Justice Story's analysis remains persuasive:

> "There are . . . incidental powers, belonging to the executive department, which are necessarily implied from the nature of the functions, which are confided to it. Among these, must necessarily be included the power to perform them. . . . The president cannot, therefore, be liable to arrest, imprisonment, or detention, while he is in the discharge of the duties of his office; and for this purpose his person must be deemed, in civil cases at least, to possess an official inviolability." J. Story, Commentaries on the Constitution of the United States, § 1563, at 418–419 (1833 ed.). . . .

In arguing that the President is entitled only to qualified immunity, the respondent relies on cases in which we have recognized immunity of this scope for governors and cabinet officers. E.g., *Butz v. Economou*, 438 U.S. 478, 98 S.Ct. 2894, 57 L.Ed.2d 895 [(1978)]; *Scheuer v. Rhodes*, 416 U.S. 232, 94 S.Ct. 1683, 40 L.Ed.2d 90 [(1974)]. We find these cases to be inapposite. The President's unique status under the Constitution distinguishes him from other executive officials.

Because of the singular importance of the President's duties, diversion of his energies by concern with private lawsuits would raise unique risks to the effective functioning of government. As is the case with prosecutors and judges—for whom absolute immunity now is established—a President must concern himself with matters likely to "arouse the most intense feelings." Yet, as our decisions have recognized, it is in precisely such cases that there exists the greatest public interest in providing an official "the maximum ability to deal fearlessly and impartially with" the duties of his office. This concern is compelling where the

---

20. . . . The correctness of the decision that a cause of action could be "implied" under these statutes is not currently before us. . . .

27. In the present case we therefore are presented only with "implied" causes of action, and we need not address directly the immunity question as it would arise if Congress expressly had created a damages action against the President of the United States. . . .

officeholder must make the most sensitive and far-reaching decisions entrusted to any official under our constitutional system.... In view of the visibility of his office and the effect of his actions on countless people, the President would be an easily identifiable target for suits for civil damages. Cognizance of this personal vulnerability frequently could distract a President from his public duties, to the detriment not only of the President and his office but also the Nation that the Presidency was designed to serve.... It is settled law that the separation-of-powers doctrine does not bar every exercise of jurisdiction over the President of the United States. See, e.g., *United States v. Nixon*; *United States v. Burr*, 25 F.Cas. 187, 191, 196 (No.14,694)(CC Va.1807); cf. *Youngstown Sheet & Tube Co. v. Sawyer* (1952).[36] But our cases also have established that a court, before exercising jurisdiction, must balance the constitutional weight of the interest to be served against the dangers of intrusion on the authority and functions of the Executive Branch. See *Nixon v. Administrator of General Services* (1977); *United States v. Nixon*. When judicial action is needed to serve broad public interests—as when the Court acts, not in derogation of the separation of powers, but to maintain their proper balance, cf. *Youngstown Sheet & Tube Co. v. Sawyer*, or to vindicate the public interest in an ongoing criminal prosecution, see *United States v. Nixon*—the exercise of jurisdiction has been held warranted. In the case of this merely private suit for damages based on a President's official acts, we hold it is not.

In defining the scope of an official's absolute privilege, this Court has recognized that the sphere of protected action must be related closely to the immunity's justifying purposes. Frequently our decisions have held that an official's absolute immunity should extend only to acts in performance of particular functions of his office. But the Court also has refused to draw functional lines finer than history and reason would support. In view of the special nature of the President's constitutional office and functions, we think it appropriate to recognize absolute Presidential immunity from damages liability for acts within the "outer perimeter" of his official responsibility.

Under the Constitution and laws of the United States the President has discretionary responsibilities in a broad variety of areas, many of them highly sensitive. In many cases it would be difficult to determine which of the President's innumerable "functions" encompassed a particular action. In this case, for example, respondent argues that he was dismissed in retaliation for his testimony to Congress—a violation of 5 U.S.C.A. § 7211 and 18 U.S.C.A. § 1505. The Air Force, however, has claimed that the underlying reorganization was undertaken to promote efficiency. Assuming that the petitioner Nixon ordered the reorganization in which respondent lost his job, an inquiry into the President's motives could not be avoided under the kind of "functional" theory asserted both by respondent and the dissent. Inquiries of this kind could be highly intrusive.... This construction would subject the President to

---

36. Although the President was not a party, the Court enjoined the Secretary of Commerce from executing a direct Presidential order.

trial on virtually every allegation that an action was unlawful, or was taken for a forbidden purpose. Adoption of this construction thus would deprive absolute immunity of its intended effect. It clearly is within the President's constitutional and statutory authority to prescribe the manner in which the Secretary will conduct the business of the Air Force. Because this mandate of office must include the authority to prescribe reorganizations and reductions in force, we conclude that petitioner's alleged wrongful acts lay well within the outer perimeter of his authority.

A rule of absolute immunity for the President will not leave the Nation without sufficient protection against misconduct on the part of the chief executive. There remains the constitutional remedy of impeachment. In addition, there are formal and informal checks on Presidential action that do not apply with equal force to other executive officials. The President is subjected to constant scrutiny by the press. Vigilant oversight by Congress also may serve to deter Presidential abuses of office, as well as to make credible the threat of impeachment. Other incentives to avoid misconduct may include a desire to earn re-election, the need to maintain prestige as an element of Presidential influence, and a President's traditional concern for his historical stature. The existence of alternative remedies and deterrents establishes that absolute immunity will not place the President "above the law." For the President, as for judges and prosecutors, absolute immunity merely precludes a particular private remedy for alleged misconduct in order to advance compelling public ends. . . .

CHIEF JUSTICE BURGER concurring.

I join the Court's opinion, but I write separately to underscore that the presidential immunity derives from and is mandated by the constitutional doctrine of separation of powers.

. . . The dissents are wide of the mark to the extent that they imply that the Court today recognizes sweeping immunity for a President for all acts. The Court does no such thing. The immunity is limited to civil damage claims. Moreover, a President, like Members of Congress, judges, prosecutors, or congressional aides—all having absolute immunity—are not immune for acts outside official duties. . . . [2] . . . When litigation

---

2. In their "parade of horribles" and lamentations, the dissents also wholly fail to acknowledge why the same perils they fear are not present in the absolute immunity the law has long recognized for numerous other officials. At least 75,000 public officers have absolute immunity from civil damage suits for acts within the scope of their official functions. The dissenting opinions manifest an astonishing blind side in pointing to that old reliable that "no man is above the law." The Court has had no difficulty expanding the absolute immunity of Members of Congress, and in granting derivative absolute immunity to numerous aides of Members. *United States v. Gravel,* [§ 5–5, supra].

We have since recognized absolute immunity for judges, *Stump v. Sparkman,* 435 U.S. 349, 98 S.Ct. 1099, 55 L.Ed.2d 331 (1978), and for prosecutors, *Imbler v. Pachtman,* 424 U.S. 409, 96 S.Ct. 984, 47 L.Ed.2d 128 (1976), yet the Constitution provides no hint that either judges, prosecutors or Congressional aides should be so protected. Absolute immunity for judges and prosecutors is seen to derive from the common law and public policy, which recognize the need to protect judges and prosecutors from harass-

processes are not tightly-controlled—and often they are not—they can be and are used as mechanisms of extortion. Ultimate vindication on the merits does not repair the damage.[5]

I fully agree that the constitutional concept of separation of independent co-equal powers dictates that a President be immune from civil damage actions based on acts within the scope of Executive authority while in office.[7] Far from placing a President above the law, the Court's holding places a President on essentially the same footing with judges and other officials whose absolute immunity we have recognized.

JUSTICE WHITE, with whom JUSTICE BRENNAN, JUSTICE MARSHALL, and JUSTICE BLACKMUN join, dissenting. . . .

Attaching absolute immunity to the office of the President, rather than to particular activities that the President might perform, places the President above the law. It is a reversion to the old notion that the King can do no wrong. . . . Taken at face value, the Court's position that as a matter of constitutional law the President is absolutely immune should mean that he is immune not only from damages actions but also from suits for injunctive relief, criminal prosecutions and, indeed, from any kind of judicial process. But there is no contention that the President is immune from criminal prosecution in the courts under the criminal laws enacted by Congress or by the states for that matter. Nor would such a claim be credible. The Constitution itself provides that impeachment shall not bar "Indictment, Trial, Judgment, and Punishment, according to Law." Art. I, § 2, cl. 7. Similarly, our cases indicate that immunity from damages actions carries no protection from criminal prosecution.

Neither can there be a serious claim that the separation of powers doctrine insulates presidential action from judicial review or insulates the President from judicial process. No argument is made here that the President, whatever his liability for money damages, is not subject to the courts' injunctive powers. [N]either subjecting presidential actions to a judicial determination of their constitutionality, nor subjecting the President to judicial process violates the separation of powers doctrine. Similarly, neither has been held to be sufficiently intrusive to justify a judicially declared rule of immunity. With respect to intrusion by the judicial process itself on Executive functions, subjecting the President to

ment. The potential danger to the citizenry from the malice of thousands of prosecutors and judges is at once more pervasive and less open to constant, public scrutiny than the actions of a President.

5. . . . In this case Fitzgerald received substantial relief through the route provided by Congress: the Civil Service Commission ordered him reinstated with backpay. Similarly situated persons are therefore not without an adequate remedy. In addition, respondent Fitzgerald has also received a settlement of $142,000 [from Nixon]. It can hardly be said he has had no remedy. [footnote repositioned.]

7. In footnote 27, ante, the Court suggests that "we need not address directly" whether Congress could create a damages action against a President. However, the Court's holding, in my view, effectively resolves that issue; once it is established that the Constitution confers absolute immunity, as the Court holds today, legislative action cannot alter that result. Nothing in the Court's opinion is to be read as suggesting that a Constitutional holding of this Court can be legislatively overruled or modified.

private claims for money damages involves no more than this. If there is a separation of powers problem here, it must be found in the nature of the *remedy* and not in the *process* involved....

[The dissenting opinion of BLACKMUN, J., joined by BRENNAN and MARSHALL, JJ., is omitted.]

Notes

1.   The same day that the Court decided this case it decided, *Harlow v. Fitzgerald.* Powell again wrote the opinion of the Court, which all the other members joined, except Chief Justice Burger, who wrote the sole dissent. Fitzgerald had sued not only Nixon but White House aides Harlow and Butterfield, claiming that they had participated in a conspiracy to violate his constitutional and statutory rights.

The Court refused to extend the President's absolute immunity to his chief aides. "For executive officials in general, qualified immunity represents the norm." Executive officials do not derive any absolute immunity from the President, unless the function that they are performing demands such immunity. The official claiming absolute immunity has the burden to demonstrate that the responsibilities of his office embrace such a sensitive function that he requires a total shield from liability and that he was performing such a function for which liability is asserted. Some Presidential "alter egos" could make such a showing. For example, "a derivative claim to Presidential immunity would be strongest in such 'central' Presidential domains as foreign policy and national security, in which the President could not discharge his singularly vital mandate without delegating functions nearly as sensitive as his own."

The earlier case law had stated that qualified immunity would not be available if the official *"knew or reasonably should have known"* that his actions would violate the plaintiff's constitutional rights *"or if he took the action with malicious intention* to cause a deprivation of constitutional rights or other injury...." (emphasis by the Court). Because this subjective element made it difficult for the trial courts to weed out insubstantial claims, the Court fashioned a new rule:

> Reliance on the objective reasonableness of an official's conduct, as measured by reference to clearly established law, should avoid excessive disruption of government and permit the resolution of many insubstantial claims on summary judgment. On summary judgment, the judge appropriately may determine, not only the currently applicable law, but whether that law was clearly established at the time an action occurred. If the law at that time was not clearly established, an official could not reasonably be expected to anticipate subsequent legal developments, nor could he fairly be said to "know" that the law forbade conduct not previously identified as unlawful. Until this threshold immunity question is resolved, discovery should not be allowed. If the law was clearly established, the immunity defense ordinarily should fail, since a reasonably competent public official should know the law governing his conduct. Nevertheless, if the official pleading the defense claims extraordinary circumstances and can prove that he neither knew nor should have known of the relevant legal standard, the defense should be sustained.

But again, the defense would turn primarily on objective factors. [B]are allegations of malice should not suffice to subject government officials either to the costs of trial or to the burdens of broad-reaching discovery. We therefore hold that government officials performing discretionary functions generally are shielded from liability for civil damages insofar as their conduct does not violate clearly established statutory or constitutional rights of which a reasonable person would have known.

Chief Justice Burger's dissent would have given absolute immunity for the President's "alter ego" or "elbow aides" because these personal aides work more closely with the President on a daily basis than Cabinet officials or other executive officials do.

2. *Mitchell v. Forsyth,* 472 U.S. 511, 105 S.Ct. 2806, 86 L.Ed.2d 411 (1985), was a suit for damages against former Attorney General John Mitchell because, in 1970, he had authorized a warrantless wiretap on the grounds of a domestic threat to the national security. Over one year later, in 1971, in a different case, the Supreme Court ruled that such wiretaps violated the Fourth Amendment. When Forsyth learned of the wiretap against him, he filed suit against Mitchell for damages. The Supreme Court ruled that Mitchell was not entitled to absolute prosecutorial immunity because the purpose of the wiretap (as Mitchell himself insisted) was not to further a criminal investigation but only to gather intelligence for national security purposes. However, Mitchell was entitled to qualified immunity, and—because it was not "clearly established" that warrantless national security wiretaps were unconstitutional in 1970—he was entitled to summary judgment.

CLINTON v. JONES
520 U.S. 681, 117 S.Ct. 1636, 137 L.Ed.2d 945 (1997).

JUSTICE STEVENS delivered the opinion of the Court.

This case raises a constitutional and a prudential question concerning the Office of the President of the United States. Respondent, a private citizen, seeks to recover damages from the current occupant of that office based on actions allegedly taken before his term began. The President submits that in all but the most exceptional cases the Constitution requires federal courts to defer such litigation until his term ends and that, in any event, respect for the office warrants such a stay. Despite the force of the arguments supporting the President's submissions, we conclude that they must be rejected.

Petitioner, William Jefferson Clinton, was elected to the Presidency in 1992, and re-elected in 1996. His term of office expires on January 20, 2001. In 1991 he was the Governor of the State of Arkansas. Respondent, Paula Corbin Jones, is a resident of California. In 1991 she lived in Arkansas, and was an employee of the Arkansas Industrial Development Commission.

On May 6, 1994, she commenced this action in the United States District Court for the Eastern District of Arkansas by filing a complaint naming petitioner and Danny Ferguson, a former Arkansas State Police officer, as defendants. The complaint alleges two federal claims, and two state law claims over which the federal court has jurisdiction because of the diverse citizenship of the parties. As the case comes to us, we are required to assume the truth of the detailed—but as yet untested—factual allegations in the complaint.

Those allegations principally describe events that are said to have occurred on the afternoon of May 8, 1991, during an official conference held at the Excelsior Hotel in Little Rock, Arkansas. The Governor delivered a speech at the conference; respondent—working as a state employee—staffed the registration desk. She alleges that Ferguson persuaded her to leave her desk and to visit the Governor in a business suite at the hotel, where he made "abhorrent"[2] sexual advances that she vehemently rejected. She further claims that her superiors at work subsequently dealt with her in a hostile and rude manner, and changed her duties to punish her for rejecting those advances. Finally, she alleges that after petitioner was elected President, Ferguson defamed her by making a statement to a reporter that implied she had accepted petitioner's alleged overtures, and that various persons authorized to speak for the President publicly branded her a liar by denying that the incident had occurred.

Respondent seeks actual damages of $75,000, and punitive damages of $100,000. Her complaint contains four counts. The first charges that petitioner, acting under color of state law, deprived her of rights protected by the Constitution, in violation of 42 U.S.C.A. § 1983. The second charges that petitioner and Ferguson engaged in a conspiracy to violate her federal rights, also actionable under federal law. See 42 U.S.C.A. § 1985. The third is a state common law claim for intentional infliction of emotional distress, grounded primarily on the incident at the hotel. The fourth count, also based on state law, is for defamation, embracing both the comments allegedly made to the press by Ferguson and the statements of petitioner's agents. Inasmuch as the legal sufficiency of the claims has not yet been challenged, we assume, without deciding, that each of the four counts states a cause of action as a matter of law. With the exception of the last charge, which arguably may involve conduct within the outer perimeter of the President's official responsibilities, it is perfectly clear that the alleged misconduct of petitioner was unrelated to any of his official duties as President of the United States and, indeed, occurred before he was elected to that office.

[The trial judge denied] a motion to dismiss on grounds of Presidential immunity, [but] ruled that discovery in the case could go forward, but ordered any trial stayed until the end of petitioner's Presidency.... Relying in part on the fact that respondent had failed to bring her complaint until two days before the 3–year period of limitations expired, she concluded that the public interest in avoiding litigation that might hamper the President in conducting the duties of his office outweighed any demonstrated need for an immediate trial. [T]he Court of Appeals

---

2.   Complaint ¶ 26.

affirmed the denial of the motion to dismiss, but because it regarded the order postponing the trial until the President leaves office as the "functional equivalent" of a grant of temporary immunity, it reversed that order. . . .

[W]e have often stressed the importance of avoiding the premature adjudication of constitutional questions. [It is therefore] appropriate to identify two important constitutional issues not encompassed within the questions presented by the petition for certiorari that we need not address today.

First, [i]f this case were being heard in a state forum, instead of advancing a separation of powers argument, petitioner would presumably rely on federalism and comity concerns,[13] as well as the interest in protecting federal officials from possible local prejudice that underlies the authority to remove certain cases brought against federal officers from a state to a federal court. Whether those concerns would present a more compelling case for immunity is a question that is not before us.

Second, our decision rejecting the immunity claim and allowing the case to proceed does not require us to confront the question whether a court may compel the attendance of the President at any specific time or place. We assume that the testimony of the President, both for discovery and for use at trial, may be taken at the White House at a time that will accommodate his busy schedule, and that, if a trial is held, there would be no necessity for the President to attend in person, though he could elect to do so.[14]

Petitioner's principal submission—that "in all but the most exceptional cases" the Constitution affords the President temporary immunity from civil damages litigation arising out of events that occurred before he took office—cannot be sustained on the basis of precedent.

Only three sitting Presidents have been defendants in civil litigation involving their actions prior to taking office. Complaints against Theodore Roosevelt and Harry Truman had been dismissed before they took office; the dismissals were affirmed after their respective inaugurations.[15] Two companion cases arising out of an automobile accident were filed against John F. Kennedy in 1960 during the Presidential campaign.[16] After taking office, he unsuccessfully argued that his status as Commander in Chief gave him a right to a stay under the Soldiers' and Sailors' Civil Relief Act of 1940. The motion for a stay was denied by the

---

13. Because the Supremacy Clause makes federal law "the supreme Law of the Land," any direct control by a state court over the President, who has principal responsibility to ensure that those laws are "faithfully executed," Art. II, § 3, may implicate concerns that are quite different from the interbranch separation of powers questions addressed here.

14. Although Presidents have responded to written interrogatories, given deposi-

tions, and provided videotaped trial testimony, no sitting President has ever testified, or been ordered to testify, in open court.

15. See *People ex rel. Hurley v. Roosevelt*, 179 N.Y. 544, 71 N.E. 1137 (1904); *DeVault v. Truman*, 354 Mo. 1193, 194 S.W.2d 29 (1946).

16. See *Bailey v. Kennedy*, No. 757,200 (Cal.Super.Ct. 1960); *Hills v. Kennedy*, No. 757,201 (Cal.Super.Ct. 1960).

District Court, and the matter was settled out of court. Thus, none of those cases sheds any light on the constitutional issue before us.

The principal rationale for affording certain public servants immunity from suits for money damages arising out of their official acts is inapplicable to unofficial conduct. In cases involving prosecutors, legislators, and judges we have repeatedly explained that the immunity serves the public interest in enabling such officials to perform their designated functions effectively without fear that a particular decision may give rise to personal liability.... *Fitzgerald*. Our central concern was to avoid rendering the President "unduly cautious in the discharge of his official duties."[19]

This reasoning provides no support for an immunity for *unofficial* conduct. As we explained in *Nixon v. Fitzgerald*, "the sphere of protected action must be related closely to the immunity's justifying purposes." Because of the President's broad responsibilities, we recognized in that case an immunity from damages claims arising out of official acts extending to the "outer perimeter of his authority." But we have never suggested that the President, or any other official, has an immunity that extends beyond the scope of any action taken in an official capacity. See *id.* (Burger, C. J., concurring) (noting that "a President, like Members of Congress, judges, prosecutors, or congressional aides—all having absolute immunity—are not immune for acts outside official duties").

Moreover, when defining the scope of an immunity for acts clearly taken *within* an official capacity, we have applied a functional approach. "Frequently our decisions have held that an official's absolute immunity should extend only to acts in performance of particular functions of his office." *Fitzgerald*. Hence, for example, a judge's absolute immunity does not extend to actions performed in a purely administrative capacity. See *Forrester v. White*, 484 U. S. 219, 229–30, 108 S.Ct. 538, 545–46, 98 L.Ed.2d 555 (1988). As our opinions have made clear, immunities are grounded in "the nature of the function performed, not the identity of the actor who performed it."

Petitioner's effort to construct an immunity from suit for unofficial acts grounded purely in the identity of his office is unsupported by precedent.

We are also unpersuaded by the evidence from the historical record to which petitioner has called our attention. He points to a comment by Thomas Jefferson protesting the subpoena *duces tecum* Chief Justice Marshall directed to him in the Burr trial, a statement in the diaries

---

19. Petitioner draws our attention to *dicta* in *Fitzgerald*, which he suggests are helpful to his cause. We noted there that "[b]ecause of the singular importance of the President's duties, diversion of his energies by concern with private lawsuits would raise unique risks to the effective functioning of government," and suggested further that "[c]ognizance of ... personal vulnerability frequently could distract a President from his public duties." [H]owever, it is clear that our dominant concern was with the diversion of the President's attention during the decisionmaking process caused by needless worry as to the possibility of damages actions stemming from any particular official decision. Moreover, *Fitzgerald* did not present the issue raised in this case because that decision involved claims against a *former* President.

kept by Senator William Maclay of the first Senate debates, in which then Vice–President John Adams and Senator Oliver Ellsworth are recorded as having said that "the President personally [is] not . . . subject to any process whatever," lest it be "put . . . in the power of a common Justice to exercise any Authority over him and Stop the Whole Machine of Government," and to a quotation from Justice Story's Commentaries on the Constitution. None of these sources sheds much light on the question at hand.[23]

Respondent, in turn, has called our attention to conflicting historical evidence. Speaking in favor of the Constitution's adoption at the Pennsylvania Convention, James Wilson—who had participated in the Philadelphia Convention at which the document was drafted—explained that, although the President "is placed [on] high," "not a single privilege is annexed to his character; far from being above the laws, he is amenable to them in his private character as a citizen, and in his public character by impeachment." This description is consistent with both the doctrine of presidential immunity as set forth in *Fitzgerald*, and rejection of the immunity claim in this case. With respect to acts taken in his "public character"—that is official acts—the President may be disciplined principally by impeachment, not by private lawsuits for damages. But he is otherwise subject to the laws for his purely private acts. . . .

Petitioner's strongest argument supporting his immunity claim is based on the text and structure of the Constitution. [P]etitioner contends that he occupies a unique office with powers and responsibilities so vast and important that the public interest demands that he devote his undivided time and attention to his public duties. He submits that—given the nature of the office—the doctrine of separation of powers places limits on the authority of the Federal Judiciary to interfere with the Executive Branch that would be transgressed by allowing this action to proceed.

---

23. Jefferson's argument provides little support for respondent's position. [T]he prerogative Jefferson claimed was denied him by the Chief Justice in the very decision Jefferson was protesting, and this Court has subsequently reaffirmed that holding. See *United States v. Nixon* (1974). The statements supporting a similar proposition recorded in Senator Maclay's diary are inconclusive of the issue before us here for the same reason. In addition, this material is hardly proof of the unequivocal common understanding at the time of the founding. Immediately after mentioning the positions of Adams and Ellsworth, Maclay went on to point out in his diary that he virulently disagreed with them, concluding that his opponents' view "[s]hows clearly how amazingly fond of the old leven many People are."

Finally, Justice Story's comments in his constitutional law treatise provide no sub-

stantial support for respondent's position. Story wrote that because the President's "incidental powers" must include "the power to perform [his duties], without any obstruction," he "cannot, therefore, be liable to arrest, imprisonment, or detention, while he is in the discharge of the duties of his office; and *for this purpose* his person must be deemed, in civil cases at least, to possess an official inviolability." 3 Story, Commentaries on the Constitution § 1563 (emphasis added). Story said only that "*an* official inviolability,"(emphasis added), was necessary to preserve the President's ability to perform the functions of the office; he did not specify the dimensions of the necessary immunity. While we have held that an immunity from suits grounded on official acts is necessary to serve this purpose, see *Fitzgerald*, it does not follow that the broad immunity from *all* civil damages suits that petitioner seeks is also necessary.

We have no dispute with the initial premise of the argument. [W]hile we suspect that even in our modern era there remains some truth to Chief Justice Marshall's suggestion that the duties of the Presidency are not entirely "unremitting," *United States v. Burr*, 25 F. Cas. 30, 34 (C.C.D.Va.1807), we accept the initial premise of the Executive's argument. It does not follow, however, that separation of powers principles would be violated by allowing this action to proceed. [I]n this case there is no suggestion that the Federal Judiciary is being asked to perform any function that might in some way be described as "executive." Respondent is merely asking the courts to exercise their core Article III jurisdiction to decide cases and controversies. Whatever the outcome of this case, there is no possibility that the decision will curtail the scope of the official powers of the Executive Branch. The litigation of questions that relate entirely to the unofficial conduct of the individual who happens to be the President poses no perceptible risk of misallocation of either judicial power or executive power.

[P]etitioner contends that this particular case—as well as the potential additional litigation that an affirmance of the Court of Appeals judgment might spawn—may impose an unacceptable burden on the President's time and energy, and thereby impair the effective performance of his office.

Petitioner's predictive judgment finds little support in either history or the relatively narrow compass of the issues raised in this particular case. [I]n the more than 200–year history of the Republic, only three sitting Presidents have been subjected to suits for their private actions. If the past is any indicator, it seems unlikely that a deluge of such litigation will ever engulf the Presidency. As for the case at hand, if properly managed by the District Court, it appears to us highly unlikely to occupy any substantial amount of petitioner's time.

Of greater significance, petitioner errs by presuming that interactions between the Judicial Branch and the Executive, even quite burdensome interactions, necessarily rise to the level of constitutionally forbidden impairment of the Executive's ability to perform its constitutionally mandated functions. As Madison explained, separation of powers does not mean that the branches "ought to have no *partial agency* in, or no *controul* over the acts of each other."[37] The fact that a federal court's exercise of its traditional Article III jurisdiction may significantly burden the time and attention of the Chief Executive is not sufficient to establish a violation of the Constitution. Two long-settled propositions, first announced by Chief Justice Marshall, support that conclusion.

First, we have long held that when the President takes official action, the Court has the authority to determine whether he has acted within the law. Perhaps the most dramatic example of such a case is our holding that President Truman exceeded his constitutional authority when he issued an order directing the Secretary of Commerce to take possession of and operate most of the Nation's steel mills in order to

37.   The Federalist No. 47 (J. Cooke ed.   1961) (emphasis in original).

avert a national catastrophe. *Youngstown Sheet & Tube Co. v. Sawyer.* Despite the serious impact of that decision on the ability of the Executive Branch to accomplish its assigned mission, and the substantial time that the President must necessarily have devoted to the matter as a result of judicial involvement, we exercised our Article III jurisdiction to decide whether his official conduct conformed to the law. Our holding was an application of the principle established in *Marbury v. Madison,* that "[i]t is emphatically the province and duty of the judicial department to say what the law is."

Second, it is also settled that the President is subject to judicial process in appropriate circumstances. Although Thomas Jefferson apparently thought otherwise, Chief Justice Marshall, when presiding in the treason trial of Aaron Burr, ruled that a subpoena *duces tecum* could be directed to the President. *United States v. Burr* (CC Va. 1807). We unequivocally and emphatically endorsed Marshall's position when we held that President Nixon was obligated to comply with a subpoena commanding him to produce certain tape recordings of his conversations with his aides. *United States v. Nixon* (1974). . . .

Sitting Presidents have responded to court orders to provide testimony and other information with sufficient frequency that such interactions between the Judicial and Executive Branches can scarcely be thought a novelty. President Monroe responded to written interrogatories, see Rotunda, Presidents and Ex–Presidents as Witnesses: A Brief Historical Footnote, 1975 U. Ill. Law Forum 1, 5–6; President Nixon—as noted above—produced tapes in response to a subpoena *duces tecum,* see *United States v. Nixon;* President Ford complied with an order to give a deposition in a criminal trial, *United States v. Fromme,* 405 F. Supp. 578 (E.D.Cal.1975); and President Clinton has twice given videotaped testimony in criminal proceedings, see *United States v. McDougal,* 934 F. Supp. 296 (E.D.Ark.1996); *United States v. Branscum,* No., LRP–CR–96–49 (E.D. Ark., June 7, 1996). Moreover, sitting Presidents have also voluntarily complied with judicial requests for testimony. President Grant gave a lengthy deposition in a criminal case under such circumstances, 1 R. Rotunda & J. Nowak, Treatise on Constitutional Law § 7.1 (2d ed. 1992), and President Carter similarly gave videotaped testimony for use at a criminal trial, *ibid.*

"[T]he separation-of-powers doctrine does not bar every exercise of jurisdiction over the President of the United States." *Fitzgerald.* If the Judiciary may severely burden the Executive Branch by reviewing the legality of the President's official conduct, and if it may direct appropriate process to the President himself, it must follow that the federal courts have power to determine the legality of his unofficial conduct. The burden on the President's time and energy that is a mere by-product of such review surely cannot be considered as onerous as the direct burden imposed by judicial review and the occasional invalidation of his official actions. We therefore hold that the doctrine of separation of powers does not require federal courts to stay all private actions against the President until he leaves office.

The reasons for rejecting such a categorical rule apply as well to a rule that would require a stay "in all but the most exceptional cases." *Brief for Petitioner I.* [I]f the Framers of the Constitution had thought it necessary to protect the President from the burdens of private litigation, we think it far more likely that they would have adopted a categorical rule than a rule that required the President to litigate the question whether a specific case belonged in the "exceptional case" subcategory. [T]he question whether a specific case should receive exceptional treatment is more appropriately the subject of the exercise of judicial discretion than an interpretation of the Constitution. Accordingly, we turn to the question whether the District Court's decision to stay the trial until after petitioner leaves office was an abuse of discretion. . . .

Strictly speaking the stay was not the functional equivalent of the constitutional immunity that petitioner claimed, because the District Court ordered discovery to proceed. Moreover, a stay of either the trial or discovery might be justified by considerations that do not require the recognition of any constitutional immunity. The District Court has broad discretion to stay proceedings as an incident to its power to control its own docket. As we have explained, "[e]specially in cases of extraordinary public moment, [a plaintiff] may be required to submit to delay not immoderate in extent and not oppressive in its consequences if the public welfare or convenience will thereby be promoted." Although we have rejected the argument that the potential burdens on the President violate separation of powers principles, those burdens are appropriate matters for the District Court to evaluate in its management of the case. The high respect that is owed to the office of the Chief Executive, though not justifying a rule of categorical immunity, is a matter that should inform the conduct of the entire proceeding, including the timing and scope of discovery.[40]

Nevertheless, we are persuaded that it was an abuse of discretion for the District Court to defer the trial until after the President leaves office. Such a lengthy and categorical stay takes no account whatever of the respondent's interest in bringing the case to trial. The complaint was filed within the statutory limitations period—albeit near the end of that period—and delaying trial would increase the danger of prejudice resulting from the loss of evidence, including the inability of witnesses to recall specific facts, or the possible death of a party.

The . . . District Court may have given undue weight to the concern that a trial might generate unrelated civil actions that could conceivably hamper the President in conducting the duties of his office. If and when that should occur, the court's discretion would permit it to manage those actions in such fashion (including deferral of trial) that interference with

---

40. Although these claims are in fact analytically distinct, the District Court does not appear to have drawn that distinction. Rather than basing its decision on particular factual findings that might have buttressed an exercise of discretion, the District Court instead suggested that a discretionary stay was supported by the *legal conclusion* that such a stay was required by *Fitzgerald.* . . .

the President's duties would not occur. But no such impingement upon the President's conduct of his office was shown here.

We add a final comment on two matters that are discussed at length in the briefs: the risk that our decision will generate a large volume of politically motivated harassing and frivolous litigation, and the danger that national security concerns might prevent the President from explaining a legitimate need for a continuance.

We are not persuaded that either of these risks is serious. Most frivolous and vexatious litigation is terminated at the pleading stage or on summary judgment, with little if any personal involvement by the defendant. Moreover, the availability of sanctions provides a significant deterrent to litigation directed at the President in his unofficial capacity for purposes of political gain or harassment. . . .Several Presidents, including petitioner, have given testimony without jeopardizing the Nation's security. In short, we have confidence in the ability of our federal judges to deal with both of these concerns.

If Congress deems it appropriate to afford the President stronger protection, it may respond with appropriate legislation. As petitioner notes in his brief, Congress has enacted more than one statute providing for the deferral of civil litigation to accommodate important public interests. See, *e.g.*, Soldiers' and Sailors' Civil Relief Act of 1940, 50 U.S.C.A. App. §§ 501–525 (provisions governing, *inter alia*, tolling or stay of civil claims by or against military personnel during course of active duty). If the Constitution embodied the rule that the President advocates, Congress, of course, could not repeal it. But our holding today raises no barrier to a statutory response to these concerns.

The Federal District Court has jurisdiction to decide this case. Like every other citizen who properly invokes that jurisdiction, respondent has a right to an orderly disposition of her claims. Accordingly, the judgment of the Court of Appeals is affirmed.

It is so ordered.

JUSTICE BREYER, concurring in the judgment.

. . . To obtain a postponement the President must "bea[r] the burden of establishing its need." In my view, however, once the President sets forth and explains a conflict between judicial proceeding and public duties, the matter changes. At that point, the Constitution permits a judge to schedule a trial in an ordinary civil damages action (where postponement normally is possible without overwhelming damage to a plaintiff) only within the constraints of a constitutional principle—a principle that forbids a federal judge in such a case to interfere with the President's discharge of his public duties. . . .Yet, I agree with the majority that there is no automatic temporary immunity and that the President should have to provide the District Court with a reasoned explanation of why the immunity is needed; and I also agree that, in the absence of that explanation, the court's postponement of the trial date was premature. For those reasons, I concur in the result.

Notes

1. Jones' complaint was unusually specific.* If the complaint were more vague, should the decision have come out any differently?

2. After this decision, and shortly before the date scheduled for trial, the trial judge granted President Clinton's motion for summary judgement on the merits. Plaintiffs filed an appeal. After oral argument in the Eight Circuit but before any decision, President Clinton settled the case for $850,000. Later, the trial judge held President Clinton in civil contempt of court for lying in his civil deposition. *Jones v. Clinton*, 36 F.Supp.2d 1118 (E.D.Ark.1999). The court found: "the President's deposition testimony [in the *Jones* case] regarding whether he had ever been alone with Ms. Lewinsky [a White House intern] was intentionally false, and his statements regarding whether he had ever engaged in sexual relations with Ms. Lewinsky likewise were intentionally false, notwithstanding tortured definitions and interpretations of the term 'sexual relations.'" 36 F.Supp.2d at 1130 (footnote omitted). The President then paid $90,686 in civil contempt fines. Earlier, for events arising out of this lawsuit, the House of Representatives impeached President Clinton but the Senate refused to remove him from office.

3. In *Forrester v. White*, 484 U.S. 219, 108 S.Ct. 538, 98 L.Ed.2d 555 (1988), cited in the Court's opinion, a judge demoted and fired a probation worker, allegedly because of her sex, in violation of the Equal Protection Clause. The Court ruled that the judge was not acting as a judge but as an employer, so there was no absolute immunity. The Court acknowledged the difficulties in drawing a line between "truly judicial acts, for which immunity is appropriate, and acts that simply happen to have been done by judges." Administrative decisions, which judges may on occasion be assigned by law to perform, are not judicial acts, "even though they may be essential to the very functioning of the courts." For example, there is no judicial immunity for a judge who "had been charged in a criminal indictment with discriminating on the basis of race in selecting trial jurors for the county's courts."

5–7. THE LEGISLATIVE VETO

IMMIGRATION AND NATURALIZATION SERVICE v. CHADHA
462 U.S. 919, 103 S.Ct. 2764, 77 L.Ed.2d 317 (1983).

CHIEF JUSTICE BURGER delivered the opinion of the Court.

We granted certiorari [to consider] a challenge to the constitutionali-

---

* The Jones Complaint, ¶¶ 18–22, alleged:

"18. Clinton then took Jones' hand and pulled her toward him, so that their bodies were in close proximity.

"19. Jones removed her hand from his and retreated several feet.

"20. However, Clinton approached Jones again. He said: 'I love the way your hair flows down your back' and 'I love your curves.' While saying these things, Clinton put his hand on Plaintiff's leg and started sliding it toward the hem of Plaintiff's cu-

lottes. Clinton also bent down to attempt to kiss Jones on the neck.

"21. Jones exclaimed, 'What are you doing?' and escaped from Clinton's physical proximity by walking away from him. . . . Clinton asked Jones: 'Are you married?' She responded that she had a regular boyfriend. Clinton then approached the sofa and as he sat down he lowered his trousers and underwear exposing his erect penis and asked Jones to 'kiss it.'

"22. There were distinguishing characteristics in Clinton's genital area that were obvious to Jones."

ty of the provision in § 244(c)(2) of the Immigration and Nationality Act, 8 U.S.C.A. § 1254(c)(2), authorizing one House of Congress, by resolution, to invalidate the decision of the Executive Branch, pursuant to authority delegated by Congress to the Attorney General of the United States, to allow a particular deportable alien to remain in the United States.

Chadha is an East Indian who was born in Kenya and holds a British passport. He was lawfully admitted to the United States in 1966 on a nonimmigrant student visa. His visa expired on June 30, 1972. [At the deportation hearing in 1974] Chadha conceded that he was deportable for overstaying his visa and the hearing was adjourned to enable him to file an application for suspension of deportation under § 244(a)(1) of the Act, 8 U.S.C.A. § 1254(a)(1).... The immigration judge found that Chadha met the requirements of § 244(a)(1): he had resided continuously in the United States for over seven years, was of good moral character, and would suffer "extreme hardship" if deported. Pursuant to § 244(c)(1) of the Act, 8 U.S.C.A. § 1254(c)(1), the immigration judge suspended Chadha's deportation and a report of the suspension was transmitted to Congress....

Once the Attorney General's recommendation for suspension of Chadha's deportation was conveyed to Congress, Congress had the power under § 244(c)(2) of the Act, 8 U.S.C.A. § 1254(c)(2), to veto the Attorney General's determination that Chadha should not be deported. Section 244(c)(2) provides:

> (2) In the case of an alien specified in paragraph (1) of subsection (a) of this subsection—

> if during the session of the Congress at which a case is reported, or prior to the close of the session of the Congress next following the session at which a case is reported, either the Senate or the House of Representatives passes a resolution stating in substance that it does not favor the suspension of such deportation, the Attorney General shall thereupon deport such alien or authorize the alien's voluntary departure at his own expense under the order of deportation in the manner provided by law. If, within the time above specified, neither the Senate nor the House of Representatives shall pass such a resolution, the Attorney General shall cancel deportation proceedings.

The June 25, 1974 order of the immigration judge suspending Chadha's deportation remained outstanding as a valid order for a year and a half. For reasons not disclosed by the record, Congress did not exercise the veto authority reserved to it under § 244(c)(2) until the first session of the 94th Congress. This was the final session in which Congress, pursuant to § 244(c)(2), could act to veto the Attorney General's determination that Chadha should not be deported. The session ended on December 19, 1975. Absent Congressional action, Chadha's deportation proceedings would have been cancelled after this date and his status adjusted to that of a permanent resident alien. See 8 U.S.C.A. § 1254(d).

On December 12, 1975, Representative Eilberg, Chairman of the Judiciary Subcommittee on Immigration, Citizenship, and International Law, introduced a resolution opposing "the granting of permanent residence in the United States to [six] aliens", including Chadha.... The resolution had not been printed and was not made available to other Members of the House prior to or at the time it was voted on. So far as the record before us shows, the House consideration of the resolution was based on Representative Eilberg's statement from the floor that "[i]t was the feeling of the committee, after reviewing 340 cases, that the aliens contained in the resolution [Chadha and five others] did not meet these statutory requirements, particularly as it relates to hardship; and it is the opinion of the committee that their deportation should not be suspended." The resolution was passed without debate or recorded vote. Since the House action was pursuant to § 244(c)(2), the resolution was not treated as an Article I legislative act; it was not submitted to the Senate or presented to the President for his action.

[Chadha appealed to the Board of Immigration Appeals and then sought review in the Ninth Circuit, which] held that the House was without constitutional authority to order Chadha's deportation; accordingly it directed the Attorney General "to cease and desist from taking any steps to deport this alien based upon the resolution enacted by the House of Representatives." The essence of its holding was that § 244(c)(2) violates the constitutional doctrine of separation of powers. We granted certiorari ... and we now affirm.

[T]he fact that a given law or procedure is efficient, convenient, and useful in facilitating functions of government, standing alone, will not save it if it is contrary to the Constitution.** Convenience and efficiency are not the primary objectives—or the hallmarks—of democratic government*** and our inquiry is sharpened rather than blunted by the fact

---

** Without the provision for one-House veto, Congress would presumably retain the power, during the time allotted in § 244(c)(2), to enact a law, in accordance with the requirements of Article I of the Constitution, mandating a particular alien's deportation, unless, of course, other constitutional principles place substantive limitations on such action. Cf. Attorney General Jackson's attack on H.R. 9766, 76th Cong., 3d Sess. (1940), a bill to require the Attorney General to deport an individual alien.... See n. 17, infra. [Footnote Repositioned.]

*** Without the one-House veto, § 244 resembles the "report and wait" provision approved by the Court in *Sibbach v. Wilson,* 312 U.S. 1, 61 S.Ct. 422, 85 L.Ed. 479 (1941). The statute examined in *Sibbach* provided that the newly promulgated Federal Rules of Civil Procedure "shall not take effect until they shall have been reported to Congress by the Attorney General at the beginning of a regular session thereof and until after the close of such session." This statute did *not* provide that Congress could unilaterally veto the Federal Rules. Rather, it gave Congress the opportunity to review the Rules before they became effective and to pass legislation barring their effectiveness if the Rules were found objectionable. This technique was used by Congress when it acted in 1973 to stay, and ultimately to revise, the proposed Rules of Evidence. [Footnote Repositioned.]

that Congressional veto provisions are appearing with increasing frequency in statutes which delegate authority to executive and independent agencies. "Since 1932, when the first veto provision was enacted into law, 295 congressional veto-type procedures have been inserted in 196 different statutes as follows: from 1932 to 1939, five statutes were affected; from 1940–49, nineteen statutes; between 1950–59, thirty-four statutes; and from 1960–69, forty-nine. From the year 1970 through 1975, at least one hundred sixty-three such provisions were included in eighty-nine laws."

JUSTICE WHITE undertakes to make a case for the proposition that the one-House veto is a useful "political invention," and we need not challenge that assertion. We can even concede this utilitarian argument although the long range political wisdom of this "invention" is arguable. [W]e find that the purposes underlying the Presentment Clauses, Art. I, § 7, cls. 2, 3, and the bicameral requirement of Art. I, § 1 and § 7, cl. 2, guide our resolution of the important question presented in this case. The very structure of the articles delegating and separating powers under Arts. I, II, and III exemplify the concept of separation of powers and we now turn to Art. I.

The Presentment Clauses. The records of the Constitutional Convention reveal that the requirement that all legislation be presented to the President before becoming law was uniformly accepted by the Framers. Presentment to the President and the Presidential veto were considered so imperative that the draftsmen took special plans to assure that these requirements could not be circumvented.... The President's role in the lawmaking process also reflects the Framers' careful efforts to check whatever propensity a particular Congress might have to enact oppressive, improvident, or ill-considered measures....

Bicameralism. The bicameral requirement of Art. I, §§ 1, 7 was of scarcely less concern to the Framers than was the Presidential veto and indeed the two concepts are interdependent. By providing that no law could take effect without the concurrence of the prescribed majority of the Members of both Houses, the Framers reemphasized their belief, already remarked upon in connection with the Presentment Clauses, that legislation should not be enacted unless it has been carefully and fully considered by the Nation's elected officials....

... Not every action taken by either House is subject to the bicameralism and presentment requirements of Art. I. Whether actions taken by either House are, in law and fact, an exercise of legislative power depends not on their form but upon "whether they contain matter which is properly to be regarded as legislative in its character and effect." S.Rep. No. 1335, 54th Cong., 2d Sess., 8 (1897).

Examination of the action taken here by one House pursuant to § 244(c)(2) reveals that it was essentially legislative in purpose and effect. In purporting to exercise power defined in Art. I, § 8, cl. 4 to "establish an uniform Rule of Naturalization," the House took action that had the purpose and effect of altering the legal rights, duties and relations of persons, including the Attorney General, Executive Branch officials and Chadha, all outside the legislative branch. Section 244(c)(2) purports to authorize one House of Congress to require the Attorney General to deport an individual alien whose deportation otherwise would be cancelled under § 244. The one-House veto operated in this case to overrule the Attorney General and mandate Chadha's deportation; absent the House action, Chadha would remain in the United States. Congress has *acted* and its action has altered Chadha's status.

The legislative character of the one-House veto in this case is confirmed by the character of the Congressional action it supplants. Neither the House of Representatives nor the Senate contends that, absent the veto provision in § 244(c)(2), either of them, or both of them acting together, could effectively require the Attorney General to deport an alien once the Attorney General, in the exercise of legislatively delegated authority,* had determined the alien should remain in the United States. Without the challenged provision in § 244(c)(2), this could have been achieved, if at all, only by legislation requiring deportation.** Similarly, a veto by one House of Congress under § 244(c)(2) cannot be justified as an attempt at amending the standards set out in § 244(a)(1), or as a repeal of § 244 as applied to Chadha. Amendment and repeal of statutes, no less than enactment, must conform with Art. I.

The nature of the decision implemented by the one-House veto in this case further manifests its legislative character. After long experience with the clumsy, time consuming private bill procedure, Congress made a deliberate choice to delegate to the Executive Branch, and specifically to the Attorney General, the authority to allow deportable aliens to remain in this country in certain specified circumstances. It is not

---

* Congress protests that affirming the Court of Appeals in this case will sanction "lawmaking by the Attorney General.... Why is the Attorney General exempt from submitting his proposed changes in the law to the full bicameral process?" To be sure, some administrative agency action—rule making, for example—may resemble "lawmaking." ... When the Attorney General performs his duties pursuant to § 244, he does not exercise "legislative" power. The bicameral process is not necessary as a check on the Executive's administration of the laws because his administrative activity cannot reach beyond the limits of the statute that created it—a statute duly enacted pursuant to Art. I, §§ 1, 7. The constitutionality of the Attorney General's execution of the authority delegated to him by § 244 involves only a question of delegation doctrine. The courts, when a case or controversy arises, can always "ascertain whether the will of Congress has been obeyed," and can enforce adherence to statutory standards. It is clear, therefore, that the Attorney General acts in his presumptively Art. II capacity when he administers the Immi-

gration and Nationality Act. Executive action under legislatively delegated authority that might resemble "legislative" action in some respects is not subject to the approval of both Houses of Congress and the President for the reason that the Constitution does not so require. That kind of Executive action is always subject to check by the terms of the legislation that authorized it; and if that authority is exceeded it is open to judicial review as well as the power of Congress to modify or revoke the authority entirely. A one-House veto is clearly legislative in both character and effect and is not so checked; the need for the check provided by Art. I, §§ 1, 7 is therefore clear. Congress' authority to delegate portions of its power to administrative agencies provides no support for the argument that Congress can constitutionally control administration of the laws by way of a Congressional veto.

** We express no opinion as to whether such legislation would violate any constitutional provision. See note 8, supra.

disputed that this choice to delegate authority is precisely the kind of decision that can be implemented only in accordance with the procedures set out in Art. I. Disagreement with the Attorney General's decision on Chadha's deportation—that is, Congress' decision to deport Chadha—no less than Congress' original choice to delegate to the Attorney General the authority to make that decision, involves determinations of policy that Congress can implement in only one way: bicameral passage followed by presentment to the President. Congress must abide by its delegation of authority until that delegation is legislatively altered or revoked.

Finally, we see that when the Framers intended to authorize either House of Congress to act alone and outside of its prescribed bicameral legislative role, they narrowly and precisely defined the procedure for such action. There are but four provisions in the Constitution, explicit and unambiguous, by which one House may act alone with the unreviewable force of law, not subject to the President's veto:

(a) The House of Representatives alone was given the power to initiate impeachments. Art. I, § 2, cl. 6;

(b) The Senate alone was given the power to conduct trials following impeachment on charges initiated by the House and to convict following trial. Art. I, § 3, cl. 5;

(c) The Senate alone was given final unreviewable power to approve or to disapprove presidential appointments. Art. II, § 2, cl. 2;

(d) The Senate alone was given unreviewable power to ratify treaties negotiated by the President. Art. II, § 2, cl. 2.

Clearly, when the Draftsmen sought to confer special powers on one House, independent of the other House, or of the President, they did so in explicit, unambiguous terms . . . .

We hold that the Congressional veto provision in § 244(c)(2) is severable from the Act and that it is unconstitutional. Accordingly, the judgment of the Court of Appeals is

Affirmed.

JUSTICE POWELL, concurring in the judgment.

The Court's decision, based on the Presentment Clauses, Art. I, § 7, cls. 2 and 3, apparently will invalidate every use of the legislative veto. The breadth of this holding gives one pause. . . . In my view, the case may be decided on a narrower ground. When Congress finds that a particular person does not satisfy the statutory criteria for permanent residence in this country it has assumed a judicial function in violation of the principle of separation of powers. Accordingly, I concur in the judgment . . . .

JUSTICE WHITE, dissenting . . . .

The prominence of the legislative veto mechanism in our contemporary political system and its importance to Congress can hardly be overstated. It has become a central means by which Congress secures the accountability of executive and independent agencies. Without the legislative veto, Congress is faced with a Hobson's choice: either to refrain from delegating the necessary authority, leaving itself with a hopeless task of writing laws with the requisite specificity to cover endless special circumstances across the entire policy landscape, or in the alternative, to abdicate its lawmaking function to the executive branch and independent agencies. To choose the former leaves major national problems unresolved; to opt for the latter risks unaccountable policymaking by those not elected to fill that role. Accordingly, over the past five decades, the legislative veto has been placed in nearly 200 statutes. The device is known in every field of governmental concern: reorganization, budgets, foreign affairs, war powers, and regulation of trade, safety, energy, the environment and the economy....

For all these reasons, the apparent sweep of the Court's decision today is regrettable. The Court's Article I analysis appears to invalidate all legislative vetoes irrespective of form or subject.... If the veto devices so flagrantly disregarded the requirements of Article I as the Court today suggests, I find it incomprehensible that Congress, whose members are bound by oath to uphold the Constitution, would have placed these mechanisms in nearly 200 separate laws over a period of 50 years.

... We should not find the lack of a specific constitutional authorization for the legislative veto surprising, and I would not infer disapproval of the mechanism from its absence. From the summer of 1787 to the present the government of the United States has become an endeavor far beyond the contemplation of the Framers. Only within the last half century has the complexity and size of the Federal Government's responsibilities grown so greatly that the Congress must rely on the legislative veto as the most effective if not the only means to insure their role as the nation's lawmakers. But the wisdom of the Framers was to anticipate that the nation would grow and new problems of governance would require different solutions. Accordingly, our Federal Government was intentionally chartered with the flexibility to respond to contemporary needs without losing sight of fundamental democratic principles....

... The power to exercise a legislative veto is not the power to write new law without bicameral approval or presidential consideration. The veto must be authorized by statute and may only negative what an Executive department or independent agency has proposed. On its face, the legislative veto no more allows one House of Congress to make law than does the presidential veto confer such power upon the President.... If Congress may delegate lawmaking power to independent and executive agencies, it is most difficult to understand Article I as forbidding Congress from also reserving a check on legislative power for itself. Absent the veto, the agencies receiving delegations of legislative or quasi-legislative power may issue regulations having the force of law without bicameral approval and without the President's signature. It is thus not apparent why the reservation of a veto over the exercise of that legislative power must be subject to a more exacting test. In both cases, it is enough that the initial statutory authorizations comply with the Article I requirements.

... In *Currin v. Wallace,* 306 U.S. 1, 59 S.Ct. 379, 83 L.Ed. 441 (1939), the statute provided that restrictions upon the production or marketing of agricultural commodities was to become effective only upon the favorable vote by a prescribed majority of the affected farmers. *United States v. Rock Royal Co-operative,* 307 U.S. 533, 577, 59 S.Ct. 993, 1014, 83 L.Ed. 1446 (1939), upheld an act which gave producers of specified commodities the right to veto marketing orders issued by the Secretary of Agriculture. [T]he Court's decision today suggests that Congress may place a "veto" power over suspensions of deportation in private hands or in the hands of an independent agency, but is forbidden from reserving such authority for itself. . . .

... The Attorney General's suspension of deportation is equivalent to a proposal for legislation. The nature of the Attorney General's role as recommendatory is not altered because § 244 provides for congressional action through disapproval rather than by ratification. In comparison to private bills, which must be initiated in the Congress and which allow a Presidential veto to be overridden by a two-thirds majority in both Houses of Congress, § 244 augments rather than reduces the executive branch's authority. So understood, congressional review does not undermine, as the Court of Appeals thought, the "weight and dignity" that attends the decisions of the Executive Branch. . . .

I do not suggest that all legislative vetoes are necessarily consistent with separation of powers principles. A legislative check on an inherently executive function, for example that of initiating prosecutions, poses an entirely different question. But the legislative veto device here—and in many other settings—is far from an instance of legislative tyranny over the Executive. It is a necessary check on the unavoidably expanding power of the agencies, both executive and independent, as they engage in exercising authority delegated by Congress. . . .

[The dissenting opinion of REHNQUIST, J., joined by WHITE, J., is omitted.]

5–8. THE LINE–ITEM VETO

CLINTON v. CITY OF NEW YORK
524 U.S. 417, 118 S.Ct. 2091, 141 L.Ed.2d 393 (1998).

Justice STEVENS delivered the opinion of the Court.

[*Raines v. Byrd* (1997), § 12.43, held that Members of Congress did not have standing to maintain a constitutional challenge to the Line Item Veto Act (Act), 2 U.S.C. § 691 et seq., because they had not alleged a sufficiently concrete injury. Less than two months later, President Clinton exercised his authority under that Act by canceling § 4722(c) of the Balanced Budget Act of 1997, which waived the Federal Government's statutory right to recoupment of as much as $2.6 billion in taxes that the State of New York had levied against Medicaid providers. He also canceled § 968 of the Taxpayer Relief Act of 1997, which permitted the owners of certain food refiners and processors to defer recognition of capital gains if they sold their stock to eligible farmers' cooperatives. Appellees, claiming they had been injured, filed separate actions against the President and other officials challenging the cancellations. The District Court consolidated the suits, found that at least one of the plaintiffs in each suit had standing, and held that the Act's cancellation procedures violate the Presentment Clause, Art. I, § 7, cl. 2. Stevens, J., for the Court, allowed expedited review pursuant to the Line Item Veto Act, and ruled that appellees have standing to challenge the Act's constitutionality. Then he turned to the merits.]

The Line Item Veto Act gives the President the power to "cancel in whole" three types of provisions that have been signed into law: "(1) any dollar amount of discretionary budget authority; (2) any item of new direct spending; or (3) any limited tax benefit." 2 U.S.C. § 691(a). It is undisputed that the New York case involves an "item of new direct spending" and that the Snake River case involves a "limited tax benefit" as those terms are defined in the Act. It is also undisputed that each of those provisions had been signed into law pursuant to Article I, § 7, of the Constitution before it was canceled.

The Act requires the President to adhere to precise procedures whenever he exercises his cancellation authority. In identifying items for cancellation he must consider the legislative history, the purposes, and other relevant information about the items. He must determine, with respect to each cancellation, that it will "(i) reduce the Federal budget deficit; (ii) not impair any essential Government functions; and (iii) not harm the national interest." Moreover, he must transmit a special message to Congress notifying it of each cancellation within five calendar days (excluding Sundays) after the enactment of the canceled provision. . . .

A cancellation takes effect upon receipt by Congress of the special message from the President. See § 691b(a). If, however, a "disapproval bill" pertaining to a special message is enacted into law, the cancellations set forth in that message become "null and void." The Act sets forth a detailed expedited procedure for the consideration of a "disapproval bill," but no such bill was passed for either of the cancellations involved in these cases. A majority vote of both Houses is sufficient to enact a disapproval bill. The Act does not grant the President the authority to cancel a disapproval bill, but he does, of course, retain his constitutional authority to veto such a bill.

The effect of a cancellation is plainly stated in § 691(e), which defines the principal terms used in the Act. [T]he cancellation prevents the item "from having legal force or effect." . . . In both legal and practical effect, the President has amended two Acts of Congress by repealing a portion of each. "[R]epeal of statutes, no less than enactment, must conform with Art. I." *INS v. Chadha.* ... There are important differences between the President's "return" of a bill pursuant to Article I, § 7, and the exercise of the President's cancellation authority pursuant to the Line Item Veto Act. The constitutional return takes place before the bill becomes law; the statutory cancellation occurs after the bill becomes law. The constitutional return is of the entire bill; the statutory cancellation is of only a part. Although the Constitution expressly authorizes the President to play a role in the process of enacting statutes, it is silent on the subject of unilateral Presidential action that either repeals or amends parts of duly enacted statutes.

There are powerful reasons for construing constitutional silence on this profoundly important issue as equivalent to an express prohibition. The procedures governing the enactment of statutes set forth in the text of Article I were the product of the great debates and compromises that produced the Constitution itself. ...Our first President understood the text of the Presentment Clause as requiring that he either "approve all the parts of a Bill, or reject it in toto." What has emerged in these cases from the President's exercise of his statutory cancellation powers, however, are truncated versions of two bills that passed both Houses of Congress. They are not the product of the "finely wrought" procedure that the Framers designed. ...

The Government advances two related arguments to support its position that despite the unambiguous provisions of the Act, cancellations do not amend or repeal properly enacted statutes in violation of the Presentment Clause. First, relying primarily on *Field v. Clark*, 143 U.S. 649, 12 S.Ct. 495, 36 L.Ed. 294 (1892), the Government contends that the cancellations were merely exercises of discretionary authority granted to the President by the Balanced Budget Act and the Taxpayer Relief Act read in light of the previously enacted Line Item Veto Act. Second, the Government submits that the substance of the authority to cancel tax and spending items "is, in practical effect, no more and no less than the power to 'decline to spend' specified sums of money, or to 'decline to implement' specified tax measures." Neither argument is persuasive.

In *Field v. Clark*, the Court upheld the constitutionality of the Tariff Act of 1890. That statute contained a "free list" of almost 300 specific articles that were exempted from import duties "unless otherwise specially provided for in this act." Section 3 was a special provision that directed the President to suspend that exemption for sugar, molasses, coffee, tea, and hides "whenever, and so often" as he should be satisfied that any country producing and exporting those products imposed duties on the agricultural products of the United States that he deemed to be "reciprocally unequal and unreasonable ..." The section then specified the duties to be imposed on those products during any such suspension.

[There are] three critical differences between the power to suspend the exemption from import duties and the power to cancel portions of a duly enacted statute. First, the exercise of the suspension power was contingent upon a condition that did not exist when the Tariff Act was passed: the imposition of "reciprocally unequal and unreasonable" import duties by other countries. In contrast, the exercise of the cancellation power within five days after the enactment of the Balanced Budget and Tax Reform Acts necessarily was based on the same conditions that Congress evaluated when it passed those statutes. Second, under the Tariff Act, when the President determined that the contingency had arisen, he had a duty to suspend; in contrast, while it is true that the President was required by the Act to make three determinations before he canceled a provision, those determinations did not qualify his discretion to cancel or not to cancel. Finally, whenever the President suspended an exemption under the Tariff Act, he was executing the policy that Congress had embodied in the statute. In contrast, whenever the President cancels an item of new direct spending or a limited tax benefit he is rejecting the policy judgment made by Congress and relying on his own policy judgment. Thus, the conclusion in *Field v. Clark* that the suspensions mandated by the Tariff Act were not exercises of legislative power does not undermine our opinion that cancellations pursuant to the Line Item Veto Act are the functional equivalent of partial repeals of Acts of Congress that fail to satisfy Article I, § 7.

The Government's reliance upon other tariff and import statutes, discussed in *Field*, that contain provisions similar to the one challenged in *Field* is unavailing for the same reasons. [These] statutes all relate to foreign trade, and this Court has recognized that in the foreign affairs arena, the President has "a degree of discretion and freedom from statutory restriction which would not be admissible were domestic affairs alone involved." *United States v. Curtiss–Wright Export Corp.* (1936). ... The Line Item Veto Act authorizes the President himself to effect the repeal of laws, for his own policy reasons, without observing the procedures set out in Article I, § 7. The fact that Congress intended such a result is of no moment. Although Congress presumably anticipated that the President might cancel some of the items in the Balanced Budget Act and in the Taxpayer Relief Act, Congress cannot alter the procedures set out in Article I, § 7, without amending the Constitution.[40]

Neither are we persuaded by the Government's contention that the President's authority to cancel new direct spending and tax benefit items is no greater than his traditional authority to decline to spend appropriated funds. ... Congress has given the Executive broad discretion over

---

40. The Government argues that the Rules Enabling Act, 28 U.S.C. § 2072(b), permits this Court to "repeal" prior laws without violating Article I, § 7. Section 2072(b) provides that this Court may promulgate rules of procedure for the lower federal courts and that "[a]ll laws in conflict with such rules shall be of no further force or effect after such rules have taken effect." See *Sibbach v. Wilson & Co.*, 312 U.S. 1, 10, 61 S.Ct. 422, 425, 85 L.Ed. 479 (1941) (stating that the procedural rules that this Court promulgates, "if they are within the authority granted by Congress, repeal" a prior inconsistent procedural statute). In enacting § 2072(b), however, Congress expressly provided that laws inconsistent with the procedural rules promulgated by this Court would automatically be repealed upon the enactment of new rules in order to create a uniform system of rules for Article III courts. As in the tariff statutes, Congress itself made the decision to repeal prior rules upon the occurrence of a particular event—here, the promulgation of procedural rules by this Court.

the expenditure of appropriated funds. For example, the First Congress appropriated "sum[s] not exceeding" specified amounts to be spent on various Government operations. See, e.g., Act of Sept. 29, 1789. [Then, and] in later years, the President was given wide discretion with respect to both the amounts to be spent and how the money would be allocated among different functions. It is argued that the Line Item Veto Act merely confers comparable discretionary authority over the expenditure of appropriated funds. The critical difference between this statute and all of its predecessors, however, is that unlike any of them, this Act gives the President the unilateral power to change the text of duly enacted statutes. None of the Act's predecessors could even arguably have been construed to authorize such a change.

Although they are implicit in what we have already written, the profound importance of these cases makes it appropriate to emphasize three points.

First, we express no opinion about the wisdom of the procedures authorized by the Line Item Veto Act.

Second, although appellees challenge the validity of the Act on alternative grounds, the only issue we address concerns the "finely wrought" procedure commanded by the Constitution. [B]ecause we conclude that the Act's cancellation provisions violate Article I, § 7, of the Constitution, we find it unnecessary to consider the District Court's alternative holding that the Act "impermissibly disrupts the balance of powers among the three branches of government."

Third, our decision rests on the narrow ground that the procedures authorized by the Line Item Veto Act are not authorized by the Constitution. . . .

Justice KENNEDY, concurring. . . .

I write to respond to my colleague Justice BREYER, who observes that the statute does not threaten the liberties of individual citizens, a point on which I disagree. . . . Liberty is always at stake when one or more of the branches seek to transgress the separation of powers. . . . That a congressional cession of power is voluntary does not make it innocuous. [O]ne Congress cannot yield up its own powers, much less those of other Congresses to follow. . . .

Justice SCALIA, with whom Justice O'CONNOR joins, and with whom Justice BREYER joins as to Part III, concurring in part and dissenting in part.

. . . In my view, the Snake River appellees lack standing to challenge the President's cancellation of the "limited tax benefit," and the constitutionality of that action should not be addressed. I think the New York appellees have standing to challenge the President's cancellation of an "item of new direct spending" [Parts I & II, relating to standing, are omitted.]

III. . . . The Presentment Clause requires, in relevant part, that "[e]very Bill which shall have passed the House of Representatives and the Senate, shall, before it becomes a Law, be presented to the President of the United States; If he approve he shall sign it, but if not he shall return it," U.S. Const., Art. I, § 7, cl. 2. There is no question that enactment of the Balanced Budget Act complied with these requirements: the House and Senate passed the bill, and the President signed it into law. It was only *after* the requirements of the Presentment Clause had been satisfied that the President exercised his authority under the Line Item Veto Act to cancel the spending item. Thus, the Court's problem with the Act is not that it authorizes the President to veto parts of a bill and sign others into law, but rather that it authorizes him to "cancel"—prevent from "having legal force or effect"—certain parts of duly enacted statutes.

Article I, § 7 of the Constitution obviously prevents the President from cancelling a law that Congress has not authorized him to cancel. Such action cannot possibly be considered part of his execution of the law, and if it is legislative action, as the Court observes, " 'repeal of statutes, no less than enactment, must conform with Art. I.' "But that is not this case. . . . In 1809, Congress passed a law authorizing the President to cancel trade restrictions against Great Britain and France if either revoked edicts directed at the United States. Joseph Story regarded the conferral of that authority as entirely unremarkable in *The Orono*, 18 F. Cas. 830, No. 10,585, (CCD Mass. 1812). The Tariff Act of 1890 authorized the President to "suspend, by proclamation to that effect" certain of its provisions if he determined that other countries were imposing "reciprocally unequal and unreasonable" duties. This Court upheld the constitutionality of that Act in *Field v. Clark*, reciting the history since 1798 of statutes conferring upon the President the power to, inter alia, "discontinue the prohibitions and restraints hereby enacted and declared," "suspend the operation of the aforesaid act," and "declare the provisions of this act to be inoperative."

As much as the Court goes on about Art. I, § 7, therefore, that provision does not demand the result the Court reaches. It no more categorically prohibits the Executive *reduction* of congressional dispositions in the course of implementing statutes that authorize such reduction, than it categorically prohibits the Executive *augmentation* of congressional dispositions in the course of implementing statutes that authorize such augmentation—generally known as substantive rulemaking. There are, to be sure, limits upon the former just as there are limits upon the latter—and I am prepared to acknowledge that the limits upon the former may be much more severe. Those limits are established, however, not by some categorical prohibition of Art. I, § 7, which our cases conclusively disprove, but by what has come to be known as the doctrine of unconstitutional delegation of legislative authority: When authorized Executive reduction or augmentation is allowed to go too far, it usurps the nondelegable function of Congress and violates the separation of powers.

It is this doctrine, and not the Presentment Clause, that was discussed in the *Field* opinion, and it is this doctrine, and not the

Presentment Clause, that is the issue presented by the statute before us here. That is why the Court is correct to distinguish prior authorizations of Executive cancellation, such as the one involved in *Field*, on the ground that they were contingent upon an Executive finding of fact, and on the ground that they related to the field of foreign affairs, an area where the President has a special "degree of discretion and freedom," These distinctions have nothing to do with whether the details of Art. I, § 7 have been complied with, but everything to do with whether the authorizations went too far by transferring to the Executive a degree of political, law-making power that our traditions demand be retained by the Legislative Branch.

I turn, then, to the crux of the matter: whether Congress's authorizing the President to cancel an item of spending gives him a power that our history and traditions show must reside exclusively in the Legislative Branch. I may note, to begin with, that the Line Item Veto Act is not the first statute to authorize the President to "cancel" spending items. In *Bowsher v. Synar* (1986), we addressed the constitutionality of the Balanced Budget and Emergency Deficit Control Act of 1985, 2 U.S.C. § 901 et seq., which required the President, if the federal budget deficit exceeded a certain amount, to issue a "sequestration" order mandating spending reductions specified by the Comptroller General. § 902. The effect of sequestration was that "amounts sequestered ... shall be *permanently cancelled*," § 902(a)(4) (emphasis added). We held that the Act was unconstitutional, not because it impermissibly gave the Executive legislative power, but because it gave the Comptroller General, an officer of the Legislative Branch over whom Congress retained removal power, "the ultimate authority to determine the budget cuts to be made," "functions ... *plainly entailing execution of the law in constitutional terms*." (emphasis added). The President's discretion under the Line Item Veto Act is certainly broader than the Comptroller General's discretion was under the 1985 Act, but it is no broader than the discretion traditionally granted the President in his execution of spending laws.

Insofar as the degree of political, "law-making" power conferred upon the Executive is concerned, there is not a dime's worth of difference between Congress's authorizing the President to *cancel* a spending item, and Congress's authorizing money to be spent on a particular item at the President's discretion. And the latter has been done since the Founding of the Nation. From 1789–1791, the First Congress made lump-sum appropriations for the entire Government—"sum[s] not exceeding" specified amounts for broad purposes. Act of Sept. 29, 1789. From a very early date Congress also made permissive individual appropriations, leaving the decision whether to spend the money to the President's unfettered discretion. In 1803, it appropriated $50,000 for the President to build "not exceeding fifteen gun boats, to be armed, manned and fitted out, and employed for such purposes as in his opinion the public service may require," Act of Feb. 28, 1803. President Jefferson reported that "[t]he sum of fifty thousand dollars appropriated by

Congress for providing gun boats remains unexpended. The favorable and peaceable turn of affairs on the Mississippi rendered an immediate execution of that law unnecessary." Examples of appropriations committed to the discretion of the President abound in our history. . . .

Certain Presidents have claimed Executive authority to withhold appropriated funds even absent an express conferral of discretion to do so. In 1876, for example, President Grant reported to Congress that he would not spend money appropriated for certain harbor and river improvements, because "[u]nder no circumstances [would he] allow expenditures upon works not clearly national," and in his view, the appropriations were for "works of purely private or local interest, in no sense national." President Franklin D. Roosevelt impounded funds appropriated for a flood control reservoir and levee in Oklahoma. President Truman ordered the impoundment of hundreds of millions of dollars that had been appropriated for military aircraft. President Nixon, the Mahatma Ghandi of all impounders, asserted at a press conference in 1973 that his "constitutional right" to impound appropriated funds was "absolutely clear." Our decision two years later in *Train v. City of New York*, 420 U.S. 35, 95 S.Ct. 839, 43 L.Ed.2d 1 (1975), proved him wrong, but it implicitly confirmed that Congress may confer discretion upon the executive to withhold appropriated funds, even funds appropriated for a specific purpose. The statute at issue in *Train* authorized spending "not to exceed" specified sums for certain projects, and directed that such "[s]ums authorized to be appropriated . . . shall be allotted" by the Administrator of the Environmental Protection Agency. Upon enactment of this statute, the President directed the Administrator to allot no more than a certain part of the amount authorized. This Court held, as a matter of statutory interpretation, that the statute did not grant the Executive discretion to withhold the funds, but required allotment of the full amount authorized.

The short of the matter is this: Had the Line Item Veto Act authorized the President to "decline to spend" any item of spending contained in the Balanced Budget Act of 1997, there is not the slightest doubt that authorization would have been constitutional. What the Line Item Veto Act does instead—authorizing the President to "cancel" an item of spending—is technically different. But the technical difference does *not* relate to the technicalities of the Presentment Clause, which have been fully complied with; and the doctrine of unconstitutional delegation, which *is* at issue here, is preeminently *not* a doctrine of technicalities. The title of the Line Item Veto Act, which was perhaps designed to simplify for public comprehension, or perhaps merely to comply with the terms of a campaign pledge, has succeeded in faking out the Supreme Court. The President's action it authorizes in fact is not a line-item veto and thus does not offend Art. I, § 7; and insofar as the substance of that action is concerned, it is no different from what Congress has permitted the President to do since the formation of the Union. . . .

Justice BREYER, with whom Justice O'CONNOR and Justice SCALIA join as to Part III, dissenting.

I. I agree with the Court that the parties have standing, but I do not agree with its ultimate conclusion. In my view the Line Item Veto Act does not violate any specific textual constitutional command, nor does it violate any implicit Separation of Powers principle. Consequently, I believe that the Act is constitutional. . . .

III. The Court believes that the Act violates the literal text of the Constitution. A simple syllogism captures its basic reasoning:

> Major Premise: The Constitution sets forth an exclusive method for enacting, repealing, or amending laws.

> Minor Premise: The Act authorizes the President to "repea[l] or amen[d]" laws in a different way, namely by announcing a cancellation of a portion of a previously enacted law.

> Conclusion: The Act is inconsistent with the Constitution.

I find this syllogism unconvincing, however, because its Minor Premise is faulty. When the President "canceled" the two appropriation measures now before us, he did not *repeal* any law nor did he *amend* any law. He simply *followed* the law, leaving the statutes, as they are literally written, intact.

To understand why one cannot say, *literally speaking*, that the President has repealed or amended any law, imagine how the provisions of law before us might have been, but were not, written. Imagine that the canceled New York health care tax provision at issue here, had instead said the following:

> Section One. Taxes . . . that were collected by the State of New York from a health care provider before June 1, 1997 and for which a waiver of provisions [requiring payment] have been sought . . . are deemed to be permissible health care related taxes . . . *provided however that the President may prevent the just-mentioned provision from having legal force or effect if he determines x, y and z.* (Assume x, y and z to be the same determinations required by the Line Item Veto Act).

Whatever a person might say, or think, about the constitutionality of this imaginary law, there is one thing the English language would prevent one from saying. One could not say that a President who "prevent[s]" the deeming language from "having legal force or effect," see 2 U.S.C. § 691e(4)(B), has either *repealed* or *amended* this particular hypothetical statute. Rather, the President has *followed* that law to the letter. He has exercised the power it explicitly delegates to him. He has executed the law, not repealed it.

It could make no significant difference to this linguistic point were the italicized proviso to appear, not as part of what I have called Section One, but, instead, at the bottom of the statute page, say referenced by an asterisk, with a statement that it applies to every spending provision in the act next to which a similar asterisk appears. And that being so, it could make no difference if that proviso appeared, instead, in a different, earlier-enacted law, along with legal language that makes it applicable to every future spending provision picked out according to a specified formula. See, e.g., 1 U.S.C. § 1 (in *"any* Act of Congress" singular words include plural, and vice versa) (emphasis added).

But, of course, this last-mentioned possibility is this very case. [T]he President has not "repealed" or "amended" anything. He has simply executed a power conferred upon him by Congress, which power is contained in laws that were enacted in compliance with the exclusive method set forth in the Constitution. See *Field v. Clark* (1892) (President's power to raise tariff rates *"was a part of the law itself, as it left the hands of Congress "*(emphasis added)).

. . . This is not the first time that Congress has delegated to the President or to others this kind of power—a contingent power to deny effect to certain statutory language. See, e.g., Pub.L. 95–384, § 13(a) ("Section 620(x) of the Foreign Assistance Act of 1961 *shall be of no further force and effect* upon the President's determination and certification to the Congress that the resumption of full military cooperation with Turkey is in the national interest of the United States and [other criteria]") (emphasis added); 28 U.S.C. § 2072 (Supreme Court is authorized to promulgate rules of practice and procedure in federal courts, and "[a]ll laws in conflict with such rules *shall be of no further force and effect"*) (emphasis added); 41 U.S.C. § 405b (subsection (a) requires the Office of Federal Procurement Policy to issue "[g]overnment-wide regulations" setting forth a variety of conflict of interest standards, but subsection (e) says that "if the President determine[s]" that the regulations "would have a significantly adverse effect on the accomplishment of the mission" of government agencies, "the requirement [to promulgate] the regulations . . . *shall be null and void"*) (emphasis added); Gramm–Rudman–Hollings Act, § 252(a)(4), 99 Stat. 1074 (authorizing the President to issue a "final order" that has the effect of *"permanently cancell[ing] "*sequestered amounts in spending statutes in order to achieve budget compliance) (emphasis added); Pub.L. 104–208, 110 Stat. 3009–695 ("Public Law 89–732 [dealing with immigration from Cuba] *is repealed* . . . upon a determination by the President . . . that a democratically elected government in Cuba is in power") (emphasis added); Pub.L. 99–498, § 701, 100 Stat. 1532 (amending § 758 of the Higher Education Act of 1965) (Secretary of Education "may" sell common stock in an educational loan corporation; if the Secretary decides to sell stock, and "if the Student Loan Marketing Association acquires from the Secretary" over 50 percent of the voting stock, "section 754 [governing composition of the Board of Directors] *shall be of no further force or effect"*) (emphasis added); Pub.L. 104–134, § 2901(c), 110 Stat. 1321–160 (President is "authorized to suspend the provisions of the [preceding] proviso" which suspension may last for *entire* effective period of proviso, if he determines suspension is "appropriate based upon the public interest in sound environmental management . . . [or] the protection of national or locally-affected interests, or protection of any cultural, biological or historic resources"). . . .

IV. Because I disagree with the Court's holding of literal violation, I must consider whether the Act nonetheless violates Separation of Powers principles—principles that arise out of the Constitution's vesting of the "executive Power" in "a President," and "[a]ll legislative Powers" in "a Congress." There are three relevant Separation of Powers questions here: (1) Has Congress given the President the wrong kind of power, i.e., "non-Executive" power? (2) Has Congress given the President the power to "encroach" upon Congress' own constitutionally reserved territory? (3) Has Congress given the President too much power, violating the doctrine of "nondelegation?" These three limitations help assure "adequate control by the citizen's representatives in Congress," upon which Justice KENNEDY properly insists. And with respect to this Act, the answer to all these questions is "no." . . .

[O]ne cannot say that the Act "encroaches" upon Congress' power, when Congress retained the power to insert, by simple majority, into any future appropriations bill, into any section of any such bill, or into any phrase of any section, a provision that says the Act will not apply. See 2 U.S.C. § 691f(c)(1) (1994 ed., Supp. II). And it is Congress that drafts and enacts the appropriations statutes that are subject to the Act in the first place—and thereby defines the outer limits of the President's cancellation authority. Thus *this* Act is not the sort of delegation "without . . . sufficient check" that concerns Justice KENNEDY. (concurring opinion). Indeed, the President acts only in response to, and on the terms set by, the Congress. . . .

Notes

In some situations, Congress authorizes and appropriates funds for various programs but the President impounds—*i.e.,* refuses to spend— the money. Supporters of the President's power to impound funds sometimes claim an "inherent" presidential power to refuse to spend appropriations, such as where the expenditure of funds might violate a constitutional provision. Proponents also claim a statutory authority to impound usually claimed to derive from general statutes, such as the public debt ceiling. It is argued that where increased federal spending could threaten the goals of other statutes designed to restrict expenditures, the President, who is bound by the Constitution to faithfully execute *all* of the laws of the United States, must have the ability to withhold funds to resolve conflicting statutory duties. In 1838 *Kendall v. United States ex rel. Stokes*, 37 U.S. (12 Pet.) 524, 9 L.Ed. 1181 (1838) held that, when Congress has *expressly directed* that sums be spent, the President has no constitutional power not to spend them. In that case, Congress had passed a private act ordering the Postmaster General to pay petitioner Kendall for services rendered.

Train v. New York, 420 U.S. 35, 95 S.Ct. 839, 43 L.Ed.2d 1 (1975) reaffirmed the principle that, if the statute is explicit, the Court will not permit the Executive Branch to impound (refuse to spend) the money. In that case, the Administrator of the Environmental Protection Agency refused to allot six billion dollars during fiscal years 1973 and 1974 under the Water Pollution Control Act. The Court found that the allotment provisions in the Act were mandatory, and rejected the argument that the law gave total discretion to the Administrator. But *Train* steered clear of broader constitutional issues on impoundment. If Congress does not make such an explicit command to spend appropriated funds, *Train* appeared to agree (or, at least, it assumed) that the President could impound the funds. If statutes give the President discretion to spend, no case has rejected a Presidential power to impound.

So, instead of giving the President a line item veto, assume that Congress, by statute, authorized the President to impound funds. Is that a simple way of getting around *Clinton v. City of New York?*

There a some differences between an impoundment authority and a line item veto power. When the President vetoes a spending bill, Congress can override that veto. In contrast, when the President impounds funds, no action is sent back for Congress to override. In addition, the impoundment power is greater because the President can continuously adjust the dollars impounded during the life of the expenditure. An item veto gives the President only one shot to stop the item. The power to impound is greater than the power to cast a veto or item veto.

5–9. APPOINTMENT AND REMOVAL POWER

BOWSHER v. SYNAR
478 U.S. 714, 106 S.Ct. 3181, 92 L.Ed.2d 583 (1986).

CHIEF JUSTICE BURGER delivered the opinion of the Court.

The question presented by these appeals is whether the assignment by Congress to the Comptroller General of the United States of certain functions under the Balanced Budget and Emergency Deficit Control Act of 1985 violates the doctrine of separation of powers.

On December 12, 1985, the President signed into law the Balanced Budget and Emergency Deficit Control Act of 1985, popularly known as the "Gramm–Rudman–Hollings Act." The purpose of the Act is to eliminate the federal budget deficit. To that end, the Act sets a "maximum deficit amount" for federal spending for each of fiscal years 1986 through 1991. The size of that maximum deficit amount progressively reduces to zero in fiscal year 1991. If in any fiscal year the federal budget deficit exceeds the maximum deficit amount by more than a specified sum, the Act requires across-the-board cuts in federal spending to reach the targeted deficit level, with half of the cuts made to defense programs and the other half made to non-defense programs. The Act exempts certain priority programs from these cuts.

These "automatic" reductions are accomplished through a rather complicated procedure, spelled out in § 251, the so-called "reporting provisions" of the Act. Each year, the Directors of the Office of Management and Budget (OMB) and the Congressional Budget Office (CBO) independently estimate the amount of the federal budget deficit for the upcoming fiscal year. If that deficit exceeds the maximum targeted deficit amount for that fiscal year by more than a specified amount, the Directors of OMB and CBO independently calculate, on a program-by-program basis, the budget reductions necessary to ensure that the deficit does not exceed the maximum deficit amount. The Act then requires the Directors to report jointly their deficit estimates and budget reduction calculations to the Comptroller General.

The Comptroller General, after reviewing the Directors' report, then reports his conclusions to the President. The President in turn must issue a "sequestration" order mandating the spending reductions specified by the Comptroller General. There follows a period during which Congress may by legislation reduce spending to obviate, in whole or in part, the need for the sequestration order. If such reductions are not enacted, the sequestration order becomes effective and the spending reductions included in that order are made.

Anticipating constitutional challenge to these procedures, the Act also contains a "fallback" deficit reduction process to take effect "[i]n the event that any of the reporting procedures described in section 251 are invalidated." Under these provisions, the report prepared by the Directors of OMB and the CBO is submitted directly to a specially-created Temporary Joint Committee on Deficit Reduction, which must report in five days to both Houses a joint resolution setting forth the content of the Directors' report. Congress then must vote on the resolution under special rules, which render amendments out of order. If the resolution is passed and signed by the President, it then serves as the basis for a Presidential sequestration order....

A three-judge District Court, appointed pursuant to 2 U.S.C.A. § 922(a)(5)(Supp.1986), invalidated the reporting provisions. *Synar v. United States,* 626 F.Supp. 1374 (D.D.C.1986)(Scalia, Johnson, Gasch, JJ.)....

A threshold issue is whether the Members of Congress, members of the National Treasury Employees Union, or the Union itself have standing to challenge the constitutionality of the Act in question. It is clear that members of the Union, one of whom is an appellee here, will sustain injury by not receiving a scheduled increase in benefits. This is sufficient to confer standing under § 274(a)(2) and Article III. We therefore need not consider the standing issue as to the Union or Members of Congress. Accordingly, we turn to the merits of the case....

The Constitution does not contemplate an active role for Congress in the supervision of officers charged with the execution of the laws it enacts. The President appoints "Officers of the United States" with the "Advice and Consent of the Senate.... " Article II, § 2. Once the appointment has been made and confirmed, however, the Constitution explicitly provides for removal of Officers of the United States by Congress only upon impeachment by the House of Representatives and conviction by the Senate. An impeachment by the House and trial by the Senate can rest only on "Treason, Bribery or other high Crimes and Misdemeanors." Article II, § 4. A direct congressional role in the removal of officers charged with the execution of the laws beyond this limited one is inconsistent with separation of powers.

This was made clear in debate in the First Congress in 1789. When Congress considered an amendment to a bill establishing the Department of Foreign Affairs, the debate centered around whether the Congress "should recognize and declare the power of the President under the Constitution to remove the Secretary of Foreign Affairs without the advice and consent of the Senate." James Madison urged rejection of a congressional role in the removal of Executive Branch officers, other than by impeachment.... Madison's position ultimately prevailed, and a congressional role in the removal process was rejected. This "Decision of 1789" provides "contemporaneous and weighty evidence" of the Constitution's meaning since many of the Members of the first Congress "had taken part in framing that instrument."

This Court first directly addressed this issue in *Myers v. United States,* 272 U.S. 52, 47 S.Ct. 21, 71 L.Ed. 160 (1925). At issue in *Myers* was a statute providing that certain postmasters could be removed only "by and with the advice and consent of the Senate." The President removed one such postmaster without Senate approval, and a lawsuit ensued. Chief Justice Taft, writing for the Court, declared the statute unconstitutional on the ground that for Congress to "draw to itself, or to either branch of it, the power to remove or the right to participate in the exercise of that power ... would be ... to infringe the constitutional principle of the separation of governmental powers."

A decade later, in *Humphrey's Executor v. United States,* 295 U.S. 602, 55 S.Ct. 869, 79 L.Ed. 1611 (1935), relied upon heavily by appellants, a Federal Trade Commissioner who had been removed by the President sought back pay. *Humphrey's Executor* involved an issue not presented either in the *Myers* case or in this case—i.e. the power of Congress to limit the President's powers of removal of a Federal Trade Commissioner.[4] The relevant statute permitted removal "by the President," but only "for inefficiency, neglect of duty, or malfeasance in office." Justice Sutherland, speaking for the Court, upheld the statute,

---

4. Appellants therefore are wide of the mark in arguing that an affirmance in this case requires casting doubt on the status of "independent" agencies because no issues involving such agencies are presented here. The statutes establishing independent agencies typically specify either that the agency members are removable by the President for specified causes, see, e.g., 15 U.S.C. § 41 (members of the Federal Trade Commission may be removed by the President "for inefficiency, neglect of duty, or malfeasance in office"), or else do not specify a removal procedure, see, e.g., 2 U.S.C. § 437c (Federal Election Commission). This case involves nothing like these statutes, but rather a statute that provides for direct Congressional involvement over the decision to remove the Comptroller General. Appellants have referred us to no independent agency whose members are removable by the Congress for certain causes short of impeachable offenses, as is the Comptroller General.

holding that "illimitable power of removal is not possessed by the President [with respect to Federal Trade Commissioners]." The Court distinguished *Myers,* reaffirming its holding that congressional participation in the removal of executive officers is unconstitutional.... The Court reached a similar result in *Wiener v. United States,* 357 U.S. 349, 78 S.Ct. 1275, 2 L.Ed.2d 1377 (1958), concluding that, under *Humphrey's Executor,* the President did not have unrestrained removal authority over a member of the War Crimes Commission.

In light of these precedents, we conclude that Congress cannot reserve for itself the power of removal of an officer charged with the execution of the laws except by impeachment. To permit the execution of the laws to be vested in an officer answerable only to Congress would, in practical terms, reserve in Congress control over the execution of the laws. As the District Court observed, "Once an officer is appointed, it is only the authority that can remove him, and not the authority that appointed him, that he must fear and, in the performance of his functions, obey." The structure of the Constitution does not permit Congress to execute the laws; it follows that Congress cannot grant to an officer under its control what it does not possess.

Our decision in *INS v. Chadha,* supports this conclusion.... To permit an officer controlled by Congress to execute the laws would be, in essence, to permit a congressional veto. Congress could simply remove, or threaten to remove, an officer for executing the laws in any fashion found to be unsatisfactory to Congress. This kind of congressional control over the execution of the laws, *Chadha* makes clear, is constitutionally impermissible....

Appellants urge that the Comptroller General performs his duties independently and is not subservient to Congress. We agree with the District Court that this contention does not bear close scrutiny.

The critical factor lies in the provisions of the statute defining the Comptroller General's office relating to removability.[5] Although the Comptroller General is nominated by the President from a list of three individuals recommended by the Speaker of the House of Representatives and the President pro tempore of the Senate, see 31 U.S.C. § 703(a)(2), and confirmed by the Senate, he is removable only at the initiative of Congress. He may be removed not only by impeachment but also by Joint Resolution of Congress "at any time" resting on any one of the following bases:

"(i) permanent disability;

"(ii) inefficiency;

"(iii) neglect of duty;

---

5. We reject appellants' argument that consideration of the effect of a removal provision is not "ripe" until that provision is actually used. As the District Court concluded, "it is the Comptroller General's presumed desire to avoid removal by pleasing Congress, which creates the here-and-now subservience to another branch that raises separation-of-powers problems." The Impeachment Clause of the Constitution can hardly be thought to be undermined because of non-use.

"(iv) malfeasance; or

"(v) a felony or conduct involving moral turpitude."

31 U.S.C. § 703(e)(1)B.[7]

[T]he dissent is simply in error to suggest that the political realities reveal that the Comptroller General is free from influence by Congress. . . . Comptroller General Warren, who had been a member of Congress for 15 years before being appointed Comptroller General, testified that: "[A]lthough heading a great agency, it is an agency of the Congress, and *I am an agent of the Congress.*" And, in one conflict during Comptroller General McCarl's tenure, he asserted his independence of the Executive Branch, stating: "Congress . . . is . . . the only authority to which there lies an appeal from the decision of this office. . . . "

Against this background, we see no escape from the conclusion that, because Congress had retained removal authority over the Comptroller General, he may not be entrusted with executive powers. The remaining question is whether the Comptroller General has been assigned such powers in the Balanced Budget and Emergency Deficit Control Act of 1985.

The primary responsibility of the Comptroller General under the instant Act is the preparation of a "report." This report must contain detailed estimates of projected federal revenues and expenditures. The report must also specify the reductions, if any, necessary to reduce the deficit to the target for the appropriate fiscal year. The reductions must be set forth on a program-by-program basis.

In preparing the report, the Comptroller General is to have "due regard" for the estimates and reductions set forth in a joint report submitted to him by the Director of CBO and the Director of OMB, the President's fiscal and budgetary advisor. However, the Act plainly contemplates that the Comptroller General will exercise his independent judgment and evaluation with respect to those estimates. The Act also provides that the Comptroller General's report "shall explain fully any differences between the contents of such report and the report of the Directors."

Appellants suggest that the duties assigned to the Comptroller General in the Act are essentially ministerial and mechanical so that their performance does not constitute "execution of the law" in a

---

7. Although the President could veto such a joint resolution, the veto could be overriden by a two-thirds vote of both Houses of Congress. Thus, the Comptroller General could be removed in the face of Presidential opposition. Like the District Court, we therefore read the removal provision as authorizing removal by Congress alone.

This provision was included, as one Congressman explained in urging passage of the Act, because Congress "felt that [the Comptroller General] should be brought under the sole control of Congress, so that Congress at the moment when it found he was inefficient and was not carrying on the duties of his office as he should and as the Congress expected, could remove him without the long, tedious process of a trial by impeachment." 61 Cong.Rec. 1081 (1921).

meaningful sense. On the contrary, we view these functions as plainly entailing execution of the law in constitutional terms. Interpreting a law enacted by Congress to implement the legislative mandate is the very essence of "execution" of the law. Under § 251, the Comptroller General must exercise judgment concerning facts that affect the application of the Act. He must also interpret the provisions of the Act to determine precisely what budgetary calculations are required. Decisions of that kind are typically made by officers charged with executing a statute.

The executive nature of the Comptroller General's functions under the Act is revealed in § 252(a)(3) which gives the Comptroller General the ultimate authority to determine the budget cuts to be made. Indeed, the Comptroller General commands the President himself to carry out, without the slightest variation (with exceptions not relevant to the constitutional issues presented), the directive of the Comptroller General as to the budget reductions:

> "The [Presidential] order *must provide* for reductions in the manner specified in section 251(a)(3), *must incorporate* the provisions of the [Comptroller General's] report submitted under section 251(b), and *must be consistent with such report in all respects.* The President *may not modify or recalculate any of the estimates, determinations, specifications, bases, amounts, or percentages* set forth in the report submitted under section 251(b) in determining the reductions to be specified in the order with respect to programs, projects, and activities, or with respect to budget activities, within an account.... " § 252(a)(3)(emphasis added).

Congress of course initially determined the content of the Balanced Budget and Emergency Deficit Control Act; and undoubtedly the content of the Act determines the nature of the executive duty. However, as *Chadha* makes clear, once Congress makes its choice in enacting legislation, its participation ends. Congress can thereafter control the execution of its enactment only indirectly—by passing new legislation. By placing the responsibility for execution of the Balanced Budget and Emergency Deficit Control Act in the hands of an officer who is subject to removal only by itself, Congress in effect has retained control over the execution of the Act and has intruded into the executive function. The Constitution does not permit such intrusion.

We now turn to the final issue of remedy. Appellants urge that rather than striking down § 251 and invalidating the significant power Congress vested in the Comptroller General to meet a national fiscal emergency, we should take the lesser course of nullifying the statutory provisions of the 1921 Act that authorizes Congress to remove the Comptroller General. [A]ppellant's argument would require this Court to undertake a weighing of the importance Congress attached to the removal provisions in the Budget and Accounting Act of 1921 as well as in other subsequent enactments against the importance it placed on the Balanced Budget and Emergency Deficit Control Act of 1985. Fortunately this is a thicket we need not enter. The language of the Balanced

Budget and Emergency Deficit Control Act itself settles the issue. In § 274(f), Congress has explicitly provided "fallback" provisions in the Act that take effect "[i]n the event . . . *any* of the reporting procedures described in section 251 are invalidated." The fallback provisions are " 'fully operative as a law.' " . . . Indeed, striking the removal provisions would lead to a statute that Congress would probably have refused to adopt. . . . Accordingly, rather than perform the type of creative and imaginative statutory surgery urged by appellants, our holding simply permits the fallback provisions to come into play. . . .

Our judgment is stayed for a period not to exceed 60 days to permit Congress to implement the fallback provisions.

Justice Stevens, with whom Justice Marshall joins, concurring in the judgment.

. . . It is not the dormant, carefully circumscribed congressional removal power that represents the primary constitutional evil. Nor do I agree with the conclusion of both the majority and the dissent that the analysis depends on a labeling of the functions assigned to the Comptroller General as "executive powers." Rather, I am convinced that the Comptroller General must be characterized as an agent of Congress because of his longstanding statutory responsibilities; that the powers assigned to him under the Gramm–Rudman–Hollings Act require him to make policy that will bind the Nation; and that, when Congress, or a component or an agent of Congress, seeks to make policy that will bind the Nation, it must follow the procedures mandated by Article I of the Constitution—through passage by both Houses and presentment to the President. In short, Congress may not exercise its fundamental power to formulate national policy by delegating that power to one of its two Houses, to a legislative committee, or to an individual agent of the Congress such as the Speaker of the House of Representatives, the Sergeant at Arms of the Senate, or the Director of the Congressional Budget Office. *INS v. Chadha.* That principle, I believe, is applicable to the Comptroller General. . . .

The powers delegated to the Comptroller General by § 251 of the Act before us today have a . . . chameleon-like quality. The District Court persuasively explained why they may be appropriately characterized as executive powers. But, when that delegation is held invalid, the "fallback provision" provides that the report that would otherwise be issued by the Comptroller General shall be issued by Congress itself. In the event that the resolution is enacted, the congressional report will have the same legal consequences as if it had been issued by the Comptroller General. In that event, moreover, surely no one would suggest that Congress had acted in any capacity other than "legislative." Since the District Court expressly recognized the validity of what it described as the " 'fallback' deficit reduction process," it obviously did not doubt the constitutionality of the performance by Congress of the functions delegated to the Comptroller General. . . .

Justice White, dissenting.

The Court, acting in the name of separation of powers, takes upon itself to strike down the Gramm–Rudman–Hollings Act, one of the most novel and far-reaching legislative responses to a national crisis since the New Deal. The basis of the Court's action is a solitary provision of another statute that was passed over sixty years ago and has lain dormant since that time. I cannot concur in the Court's action....

It is evident (and nothing in the Court's opinion is to the contrary) that the powers exercised by the Comptroller General under the Gramm–Rudman Act are not such that vesting them in an officer not subject to removal at will by the President would in itself improperly interfere with Presidential powers. Determining the level of spending by the Federal Government is not by nature a function central either to the exercise of the President's enumerated powers or to his general duty to ensure execution of the laws; rather, appropriating funds is a peculiarly legislative function, and one expressly committed to Congress by Art. I, § 9, which provides that "[n]o Money shall be drawn from the Treasury, but in Consequence of Appropriations made by Law." In enacting Gramm–Rudman, Congress has chosen to exercise this legislative power to establish the level of federal spending by providing a detailed set of criteria for reducing expenditures below the level of appropriations in the event that certain conditions are met. Delegating the execution of this legislation—that is, the power to apply the Act's criteria and make the required calculations—to an officer independent of the President's will does not deprive the President of any power that he would otherwise have or that is essential to the performance of the duties of his office. Rather, the result of such a delegation, from the standpoint of the President, is no different from the result of more traditional forms of appropriation: under either system, the level of funds available to the Executive branch to carry out its duties is not within the President's discretionary control. To be sure, if the budget-cutting mechanism required the responsible officer to exercise a great deal of policymaking discretion, one might argue that having created such broad discretion Congress had some obligation based upon Art. II to vest it in the Chief Executive or his agents. In Gramm–Rudman, however, Congress has done no such thing; instead, it has created a precise and articulated set of criteria designed to minimize the degree of policy choice exercised by the officer executing the statute and to ensure that the relative spending priorities established by Congress in the appropriations it passes into law remain unaltered. Given that the exercise of policy choice by the officer executing the statute would be inimical to Congress' goal in enacting "automatic" budget-cutting measures, it is eminently reasonable and proper for Congress to vest the budget-cutting authority in an officer who is to the greatest degree possible nonpartisan and independent of the President and his political agenda and who therefore may be relied upon not to allow his calculations to be colored by political considerations....

[T]he Court overlooks or deliberately ignores the decisive difference between the congressional removal provision and the legislative veto struck down in *Chadha:* under the Budget and Accounting Act, Congress may remove the Comptroller only through a joint resolution, which by definition must be passed by both Houses and signed by the President. In other words, a removal of the Comptroller under the statute *satisfies the requirements of bicameralism and presentment laid down in Chadha.* The majority's citation of *Chadha* for the proposition that Congress may only control the acts of officers of the United States "by passing new legislation," in no sense casts doubt on the legitimacy of the removal provision, for that provision allows Congress to effect removal only through action that constitutes legislation as defined in *Chadha....* Indeed, *Chadha* expressly recognizes that while congressional meddling with administration of the laws outside of the legislative process is impermissible, congressional control over executive officers exercised through the legislative process is valid. Thus, if the existence of a statute permitting removal of the Comptroller through joint resolution (that is, through the legislative process) renders his exercise of executive powers unconstitutional, it is for reasons having virtually nothing to do with *Chadha....*

The practical result of the removal provision is not to render the Comptroller unduly dependent upon or subservient to Congress, but to render him one of the most independent officers in the entire federal establishment. Those who have studied the office agree that the procedural and substantive limits on the power of Congress and the President to remove the Comptroller make dislodging him against his will practically impossible. [O]f the six Comptrollers who have served since 1921, none has been threatened with, much less subjected to, removal. [T]he threat to separation of powers conjured up by the majority is wholly chimerical. [T]he role of this Court should be limited to determining whether the Act so alters the balance of authority among the branches of government as to pose a genuine threat to the basic division between the lawmaking power and the power to execute the law. Because I see no such threat, I cannot join the Court in striking down the Act.

I dissent.

JUSTICE BLACKMUN, dissenting.

... Any incompatibility, I feel, should be cured by refusing to allow congressional removal—if it ever is attempted—and not by striking down the central provisions of the Deficit Control Act. However wise or foolish it may be, that statute unquestionably ranks among the most important federal enactments of the past several decades. I cannot see the sense of invalidating legislation of this magnitude in order to preserve a cumbersome, 65–year–old removal power that has never been exercised and appears to have been all but forgotten until this litigation.

... The legislative history of the Deficit Control Act contains no mention of the 1921 statute, and both Houses of Congress have argued in this Court that, if necessary, the removal provision should be invalidated rather than § 251. To the extent that the absence of express fallback provisions in the 1921 statute signifies anything, it [would] appear to signify only that, if the removal provision were invalidated, Congress preferred simply that the remainder of the statute should remain in effect without alteration....

Notes

After *Bowsher,* Congress amended the Act, P. L. 100–119, 101 Stat. 754 (Sept. 20, 1987), title I, § 102(a), amending, inter alia, 2 U.S.C.A. §§ 252(a)(1) & (a)(2), so that a presidential sequestration order would be triggered automatically by a report from the Director of the Office of Management and Budget. The OMB Director's report would give due regard to a report issued earlier by the Director of the Congressional Budget Office. There is no role for the Comptroller General in the preparation and issuance of sequestration reports. President Reagan, in signing the law, stated [23 Weekly Compilation of Presidential Documents 1091 (Oct. 5, 1987)]:

> I wish to make clear my understanding that sections 252(a)(1) and (2) of the amended Act—which direct the President to issue an order "in strict accordance" with the report submitted by the Office of Management and Budget—do not preclude me or future Presidents from exercising our authority to supervise the execution of the law by overseeing and directing the Director of OMB in the preparation and, if necessary, revision of his reports. If this provision were interpreted otherwise so as to require the President to follow the orders of a subordinate, it would plainly constitute an unconstitutional infringement of the President's authority as head of a unitary Executive branch.

MORRISON v. OLSON

487 U.S. 654, 108 S.Ct. 2597, 101 L.Ed.2d 569 (1988).

CHIEF JUSTICE REHNQUIST delivered the opinion of the Court.

This case presents us with a challenge to the independent counsel provisions of the Ethics in Government Act of 1978, 28 U.S.C.A. §§ 49, 591 et seq. We hold today that these provisions of the Act do not violate the Appointments Clause of the Constitution, Art. II, § 2, cl. 2, or the limitations of Article III, nor do they impermissibly interfere with the President's authority under Article II in violation of the constitutional principle of separation of powers.

Briefly stated, Title VI of the Ethics of Government Act (Title VI or the Act), 28 U.S.C.A. §§ 591–599, allows for the appointment of an "independent counsel" to investigate and, if appropriate, prosecute certain high ranking government officials for violations of federal criminal laws. The Act requires the Attorney General, upon receipt of information that he determines is "sufficient to constitute grounds to investigate whether any person [covered by the Act] may have violated any Federal criminal law," to conduct a preliminary investigation of the matter. When the Attorney General has completed this investigation, or 90 days has elapsed, he is required to report to a special court (the Special Division) created by the Act "for the purpose of appointing independent counsels." 28 U.S.C.A. § 49. If the Attorney General determines that "there are no reasonable grounds to believe that further investigation is warranted," then he must notify the Special Division of this result. In such a case, "the division of the court shall have no power to appoint an independent counsel." If, however, the Attorney General has determined that there are "reasonable grounds to believe that further investigation or prosecution is warranted," then he "shall apply to the division of the court for the appointment of an independent counsel." The Attorney General's application to the court "shall contain sufficient information to assist the [court] in selecting an independent counsel and in defining that independent counsel's prosecutorial jurisdiction." Upon receiving this application, the Special Division "shall appoint an appropriate independent counsel and shall define that independent counsel's prosecutorial jurisdiction."

With respect to all matters within the independent counsel's jurisdiction, the Act grants the counsel "full power and independent authority to exercise all investigative and prosecutorial functions and powers of the Department of Justice, the Attorney General, and any other officer or employee of the Department of Justice." ... The counsel may appoint employees, may request and obtain assistance from the Department of Justice, and may accept referral of matters from the Attorney General if the matter falls within the counsel's jurisdiction as defined by the Special Division. The Act also states that an independent counsel "shall, except where not possible, comply with the written or other established policies of the Department of Justice respecting enforcement of the criminal laws." In addition, whenever a matter has been referred to an independent counsel under the Act, the Attorney General and the Justice Department are required to suspend all investigations and proceedings regarding the matter. An independent counsel has "full authority to dismiss matters within [his] prosecutorial jurisdiction without conducting an investigation or at any subsequent time before prosecution, if to do so would be consistent" with Department of Justice policy.

Two statutory provisions govern the length of an independent counsel's tenure in office. The first defines the procedure for removing an independent counsel. Section 596(a)(1) provides:

> "An independent counsel appointed under this chapter may be removed from office, other than by impeachment and conviction, only by the personal action of the Attorney General and only for good cause, physical disability, mental incapacity, or any other condition that substantially impairs the performance of such independent counsel's duties."

If an independent counsel is removed pursuant to this section, the Attorney General is required to submit a report to both the Special Division and the Judiciary Committees of the Senate and the House "specifying the facts found and the ultimate grounds for such removal." Under the current version of the Act, an independent counsel can obtain judicial review of the Attorney General's action by filing a civil action in the United States District Court for the District of Columbia. Members of the Special Division "may not hear or determine any such civil action or any appeal of a decision in any such civil action." The reviewing court is authorized to grant reinstatement or "other appropriate relief."

The other provision governing the tenure of the independent counsel defines the procedures for "terminating" the counsel's office. Under § 596(b)(1), the office of an independent counsel terminates when he notifies the Attorney General that he has completed or substantially completed any investigations or prosecutions undertaken pursuant to the Act. In addition, the Special Division, acting either on its own or on the suggestion of the Attorney General, may terminate the office of an independent counsel at any time if it finds that "the investigation of all matters within the prosecutorial jurisdiction of such independent counsel . . . have been completed or so substantially completed that it would be appropriate for the Department of Justice to complete such investigations and prosecutions."

Finally, the Act provides for Congressional oversight of the activities of independent counsels. An independent counsel may from time to time send Congress statements or reports on his activities. The "appropriate committees of the Congress" are given oversight jurisdiction in regard to the official conduct of an independent counsel, and the counsel is required by the Act to cooperate with Congress in the exercise of this jurisdiction. The counsel is required to inform the House of Representatives of "substantial and credible information which [the counsel] receives . . . that may constitute grounds for an impeachment." In addition, the Act gives certain Congressional Committee Members the power to "request in writing that the Attorney General apply for the appointment of an independent counsel." The Attorney General is required to respond to this request within a specified time but is not required to accede to the request.

The proceedings in this case provide an example of how the Act works in practice. [In 1982 the President ordered the Administrator of the Environmental Protection Agency to invoke executive privilege and withhold certain subpoenaed documents from two House subcommittees because the documents contained "enforcement sensitive information." In response, the House voted to hold the Administrator in contempt; the United States and the Administrator then sued the House. After the trial court urged the parties to compromise, the conflict apparently ended when the Administrator offered the House committees limited access to the contested documents. The next year, in 1984, the House Judiciary Committee began a 2½ year investigation into the Justice Department's role in the EPA's refusal to turn over the documents. That investigation produced a 3,000 page report that the Committee issued over the dissent of all but one of its minority party members. The report suggested that appellee Olson (then Assistant Attorney General for the Office of Legal Counsel) had given false and misleading testimony to the subcommittee and that appellees Schmults (then Deputy Attorney General) and Dinkins (then Assistant Attorney General for the Land and Resources Division) had wrongfully withheld certain documents from the Committee thus obstructing its investigation. The Chairman of the Judiciary Committee forwarded a copy of this report to the Attorney General with a formal request that he seek appointment of an independent counsel. The Attorney General, after a preliminary investigation (and after concluding that both Schmults and Dinkins lack criminal intent to obstruct the Committee's investigation), applied to the Special Division for the appointment of an independent counsel solely with respect to Olson. In January, 1987, after Morrison (the independent counsel) asked the Special Division to refer to her the allegations against Schmults and Dinkins, the Special Division ruled that it had no authority to review the Attorney General's decision not to seek appointment of an independent counsel for Schmults and Dinkins but that its original grant of jurisdiction was broad enough to inquire whether Olson may have conspired with others, including Schmults and Dinkins, to obstruct the Committee's investigation. Appellant Morrison then caused the grand jury to issue subpoenas on the appellees, who moved to quash them on the ground that the independent counsel provisions of the Act were unconstitutional. The district court upheld the constitutionality of the Act, and a divided Court of Appeals reversed.] Appellant then sought review by this Court, and we noted probable jurisdiction. We now reverse....

The Appointments Clause of Article II reads as follows:

"[The President] shall nominate, and by and with the Advice and Consent of the Senate, shall appoint Ambassadors, other public Ministers and Consuls, Judges of the supreme Court, and all other Officers of the United States, whose Appointments are not herein otherwise provided for, and which shall be established by Law: but the Congress may by Law vest the Appointment of such inferior Officers, as they think proper, in the President alone, in the Courts of Law, or in the Heads of Departments." U.S. Const., Art. II, § 2, cl. 2.

... The initial question is, accordingly, whether appellant is an "inferior" or a "principal" officer. If she is the latter, as the Court of Appeals concluded, then the Act is in violation of the Appointments Clause.

The line between "inferior" and "principal" officers is one that is far from clear, and the Framers provided little guidance into where it should be drawn. We need not attempt here to decide exactly where the line falls between the two types of officers, because in our view appellant clearly falls on the "inferior officer" side of that line. Several factors lead to this conclusion.

First, appellant is subject to removal by a higher Executive Branch official. Although appellant may not be "subordinate" to the Attorney General (and the President) insofar as she possesses a degree of independent discretion to exercise the powers delegated to her under the Act, the fact that she can be removed by the Attorney General indicates that she is to some degree "inferior" in rank and authority. Second, appellant is empowered by the Act to perform only certain, limited duties. An independent counsel's role is restricted primarily to investigation and, if appropriate, prosecution for certain federal crimes. Admittedly, the Act delegates to appellant "full power and independent authority to exercise all investigative and prosecutorial functions and powers of the Department of Justice," but this grant of authority does not include any authority to formulate policy for the Government or the Executive Branch, nor does it give appellant any administrative duties outside of those necessary to operate her office. The Act specifically provides that in policy matters appellant is to comply to the extent possible with the policies of the Department.

Third, appellant's office is limited in jurisdiction. Not only is the Act itself restricted in applicability to certain federal officials suspected of certain serious federal crimes, but an independent counsel can only act within the scope of the jurisdiction that has been granted by the Special Division pursuant to a request by the Attorney General. Finally, appellant's office is limited in tenure. There is concededly no time limit on the appointment of a particular counsel. Nonetheless, the office of independent counsel is "temporary" in the sense that an independent counsel is appointed essentially to accomplish a single task, and when that task is over the officer is terminated, either by the counsel herself or by action of the Special Division. . . .

This conclusion is consistent with our few previous decisions that considered the question of whether a particular government official is a "principal" or an "inferior" officer. . . . In *Ex parte Siebold,* 100 (10 Otto) U.S. 371, 25 L.Ed. 717 (1880), the Court found that federal "supervisor[s] of elections," who were charged with various duties involving oversight of local congressional elections, were inferior officers for purposes of the Clause. In *Go–Bart Importing Co. v. United States,* 282 U.S. 344, 352–53, 51 S.Ct. 153, 156, 75 L.Ed. 374 (1931), we held that "United States commissioners are inferior officers." These commissioners had various judicial and prosecutorial powers, including the power to arrest and imprison for trial, to issue warrants, and to institute prosecutions under "laws relating to the elective franchise and civil rights." All of this is consistent with our reference in *United States v. Nixon,* 418 U.S. 683, 694, 696, 94 S.Ct. 3090, 3100, 3102, 41 L.Ed.2d 1039 (1974), to the office of Watergate Special Prosecutor—whose authority was similar to that of appellant—as a "subordinate officer."

This does not, however, end our inquiry under the Appointments Clause. Appellees argue that even if appellant is an "inferior" officer, the Clause does not empower Congress to place the power to appoint such an officer outside the Executive Branch. [T]he language of this "excepting clause" [in the Appointments Clause] admits of no limitation on interbranch appointments. Indeed, the inclusion of "as they think proper" seems clearly to give Congress significant discretion to determine whether it is "proper" to vest the appointment of, for example, executive officials in the "courts of Law." . . .

We do not mean to say that Congress' power to provide for interbranch appointments of "inferior officers" is unlimited. In addition to separation of powers concerns, which would arise if such provisions for appointment had the potential to impair the constitutional functions assigned to one of the branches, *Siebold* itself suggested that Congress' decision to vest the appointment power in the courts would be improper if there was some "incongruity" between the functions normally performed by the courts and the performance of their duty to appoint. 100 U.S., at 398 ("the duty to appoint inferior officers, when required thereto by law, is a constitutional duty of the courts; and in the present case there is no such incongruity in the duty required as to excuse the courts from its performance, or to render their acts void"). In this case, however, we do not think it impermissible for Congress to vest the power to appoint independent counsels in a specially created federal court. We thus disagree with the Court of Appeals' conclusion that there is an inherent incongruity about a court having the power to appoint prosecutorial officers.[13] We have recognized that courts may appoint private attorneys to act as prosecutor for judicial contempt judgments. See *Young v. United States ex rel. Vuitton et Fils S.A.,* 481 U.S. 787, 107 S.Ct. 2124, 95 L.Ed.2d 740 (1987). In *Go–Bart Importing Co. v. United States,* we approved court appointment of United States commissioners, who exercised certain limited prosecutorial powers. In *Siebold,* as well, we indicated that judicial appointment of federal marshals, who are "executive officer[s]," would not be inappropriate. Lower courts have also upheld interim judicial appointments of United States Attorneys, see *United States v. Solomon,* 216 F.Supp. 835 (S.D.N.Y.1963), and Congress itself has vested the power to make these interim appointments in the district courts, see 28 U.S.C.A. § 546(d). Congress of course was concerned when it created the office of independent counsel with the conflicts of interest that could arise in situations when the Executive Branch is called upon to investigate its own high-ranking officers. If it were to remove the appointing authority from the Executive Branch, the most logical place to put it was in the Judicial Branch. In the light of the Act's provision making the judges of the Special Division ineligible to participate in any matters relating to an independent counsel they have appointed, we do not think that appointment of the independent counsels by the court runs afoul of the constitutional limitation on "incongruous" interbranch appointments.

Appellees next contend that the powers vested in the Special Division by the Act conflict with Article III of the Constitution. [O]nce it is accepted that the Appointments Clause gives Congress the power to vest the appointment of officials such as the independent counsel in the "courts of Law," there can be no Article III objection to the Special Division's exercise of that power, as the power itself derives from the Appointments Clause, a source of authority for judicial action that is

---

13. Indeed, in light of judicial experience with prosecutors in criminal cases, it could be said that courts are especially well qualified to appoint prosecutors. This is not a case in which judges are given power to appoint an officer in an area in which they have no special knowledge or expertise, as in, for example, a statute authorizing the courts to appoint officials in the Department of Agriculture or the Federal Energy Regulatory Commission.

independent of Article III. Appellees contend, however, that the Division's Appointments Clause powers do not encompass the power to define the independent counsel's jurisdiction. We disagree. In our view, Congress' power under the Clause to vest the "Appointment" of inferior officers in the courts may, in certain circumstances, allow Congress to give the courts some discretion in defining the nature and scope of the appointed official's authority. Particularly when, as here, Congress creates a temporary "office" the nature and duties of which will by necessity vary with the factual circumstances giving rise to the need for an appointment in the first place, it may vest the power to define the scope of the office in the court as an incident to the appointment of the officer pursuant to the Appointments Clause. This said, we do not think that Congress may give the Division *unlimited* discretion to determine the independent counsel's jurisdiction. In order for the Division's definition of the counsel's jurisdiction to be truly "incidental" to its power to appoint, the jurisdiction that the court decides upon must be demonstrably related to the factual circumstances that gave rise to the Attorney General's investigation and request for the appointment of the independent counsel in the particular case.

The Act also vests in the Special Division various powers and duties in relation to the independent counsel that, because they do not involve appointing the counsel or defining her jurisdiction, cannot be said to derive from the Division's Appointments Clause authority. These duties include granting extensions for the Attorney General's preliminary investigation; receiving the report of the Attorney General at the conclusion of his preliminary investigation; referring matters to the counsel upon request,[18] receiving reports from the counsel regarding expenses incurred; receiving a report from the Attorney General following the removal of an independent counsel; granting attorney's fees upon request to individuals who were investigated but not indicted by an independent counsel; receiving a final report from the counsel; deciding whether to release the counsel's final report to Congress or the public and determining whether any protective orders should be issued; and terminating an independent counsel when his task is completed.

Leaving aside for the moment the Division's power to terminate an independent counsel, we do not think that Article III absolutely prevents Congress from vesting these other miscellaneous powers in the Special Division pursuant to the Act. [Some] provisions of the Act do require the court to exercise some judgment and discretion, but the powers granted by these provisions are themselves essentially ministerial. The Act simply does not give the Division the power to "supervise" the independent counsel in the exercise of her investigative or prosecutorial authority. And, the functions that the Special Division is empowered to perform

---

18. In our view, this provision does not empower the court to expand the original scope of the counsel's jurisdiction; that may be done only upon request of the Attorney General pursuant to § 593(c)(2). At most, § 594(e) authorizes the court simply to refer matters that are "relate[d] to the independent counsel's prosecutorial jurisdiction" as already defined.

are not inherently "Executive"; indeed, they are directly analogous to functions that federal judges perform in other contexts, such as deciding whether to allow disclosure of matters occurring before a grand jury, deciding to extend a grand jury investigation, or awarding attorney's fees.

We are more doubtful about the Special Division's power to terminate the office of the independent counsel pursuant to § 596(b)(2). As appellees suggest, the power to terminate, especially when exercised by the Division on its own motion, is "administrative" to the extent that it requires the Special Division to monitor the progress of proceedings of the independent counsel and come to a decision as to whether the counsel's job is "completed." It also is not a power that could be considered typically "judicial," as it has few analogues among the court's more traditional powers. Nonetheless, we do not, as did the Court of Appeals, view this provision as a significant judicial encroachment upon executive power or upon the prosecutorial discretion of the independent counsel.

... The termination provisions of the Act do not give the Special Division anything approaching the power to remove the counsel while an investigation or court proceeding is still underway—this power is vested solely in the Attorney General. As we see it, "termination" may occur only when the duties of the counsel are truly "completed" or "so substantially completed" that there remains no need for any continuing action by the independent counsel. It is basically a device for removing from the public payroll an independent counsel who has served her purpose, but is unwilling to acknowledge the fact. So construed, the Special Division's power to terminate does not pose a sufficient threat of judicial intrusion into matters that are more properly within the Executive's authority to require that the Act be invalidated as inconsistent with Article III.

Nor do we believe, as appellees contend, that the Special Division's exercise of the various powers specifically granted to it under the Act poses any threat to the "impartial and independent federal adjudication of claims within the judicial power of the United States." We reach this conclusion for two reasons. First, the Act as it currently stands gives the Special Division itself no power to review any of the actions of the independent counsel or any of the actions of the Attorney General with regard to the counsel. Accordingly, there is no risk of partisan or biased adjudication of claims regarding the independent counsel by that court. Second, the Act prevents members of the Special Division from participating in "*any* judicial proceeding concerning a matter which involves such independent counsel while such independent counsel is serving in that office or which involves the exercise of such independent counsel's official duties, regardless of whether such independent counsel is still serving in that office." 28 U.S.C. § 49(f)(emphasis added); see also § 596(a)(3)(preventing members of the Special Division from participating in review of the Attorney General's decision to remove an independent counsel). We think both the special court and its judges are sufficiently isolated by these statutory provisions from the review of the activities of the independent counsel so as to avoid any taint of the independence of the judiciary such as would render the Act invalid under Article III.

We emphasize, nevertheless, that the Special Division has no authority to take any action or undertake any duties that are not specifically authorized by the Act. The gradual expansion of the authority of the Special Division might in another context be a bureaucratic success story, but it would be one that would have serious constitutional ramifications. The record in other cases involving independent counsels indicate that the Special Division has at times given advisory opinions or issued orders that are not directly authorized by the Act. Two examples of this were cited by the Court of Appeals, which noted that the Special Division issued "orders" that ostensibly exempted the independent counsel from conflict of interest laws. In another case, the Division reportedly ordered that a counsel postpone an investigation into certain allegations until the completion of related state criminal proceedings. The propriety of the Special Division's actions in these instances is not before us as such, but we nonetheless think it appropriate to point out not only that there is no authorization for such actions in the Act itself, but that the division's exercise of unauthorized powers risks the transgression of the constitutional limitations of Article III that we have just discussed.

We now turn to consider whether the Act is invalid under the constitutional principle of separation of powers. Two related issues must be addressed: The first is whether the provision of the Act restricting the Attorney General's power to remove the independent counsel to only those instances in which he can show "good cause," taken by itself, impermissibly interferes with the President's exercise of his constitutionally appointed functions. The second is whether, taken as a whole, the Act violates the separation of powers by reducing the President's ability to control the prosecutorial powers wielded by the independent counsel.

Two Terms ago we had occasion to consider whether it was consistent with the separation of powers for Congress to pass a statute that authorized a government official who is removable only by Congress to participate in what we found to be "executive powers." *Bowsher v. Synar.* We held in *Bowsher* that "Congress cannot reserve for itself the power of removal of an officer charged with the execution of the laws except by impeachment." A primary antecedent for this ruling was our 1925 decision in *Myers v. United States,* 272 U.S. 52, 47 S.Ct. 21, 71 L.Ed. 160 (1926) [that invalidated] a federal statute by which certain postmasters of the United States could be removed by the President only "by and with the advice and consent of the Senate." . . .

Unlike both *Bowsher* and *Myers,* this case does not involve an attempt by Congress itself to gain a role in the removal of executive officials other than its established powers of impeachment and conviction. The Act instead puts the removal power squarely in the hands of the Executive Branch; an independent counsel may be removed from office, "only by the personal action of the Attorney General, and only for good cause." There is no requirement of congressional approval of the Attorney General's removal decision, though the decision is subject to judicial review. § 596(a)(3). In our view, the removal provisions of the Act make this case more analogous to *Humphrey's Executor v. United States,* 295 U.S. 602, 55 S.Ct. 869, 79 L.Ed. 1611 (1935), and *Wiener v. United States,* 357 U.S. 349, 78 S.Ct. 1275 (1958), than to *Myers* or *Bowsher.*

In *Humphrey's Executor,* the issue was whether a statute restricting the President's power to remove the commissioners of the Federal Trade Commission only for "inefficiency, neglect of duty, or malfeasance in office" was consistent with the Constitution. We stated that whether Congress can "condition the [President's power of removal] by fixing a definite term and precluding a removal except for cause, will depend upon the character of the office." ... At least in regard to "quasi-legislative" and "quasi-judicial" agencies such as the FTC, "[t]he authority of Congress, in creating [such] agencies, to require them to act in discharge of their duties independently of executive control ... includes, as an appropriate incident, power to fix the period during which they shall continue in office, and to forbid their removal except for cause in the meantime." ...

Similarly, in *Wiener* we considered whether the President had unfettered discretion to remove a member of the War Claims Commission, which had been established by Congress in the War Claims Act of 1948, 62 Stat. 1240. The Commission's function was to receive and adjudicate certain claims for compensation from those who had suffered personal injury or property damage at the hands of the enemy during World War II. Commissioners were appointed by the President, with the advice and consent of the Senate, but the statute made no provision for the removal of officers, perhaps because the Commission itself was to have a limited existence. As in *Humphrey's Executor,* however, the Commissioners were entrusted by Congress with adjudicatory powers that were to be exercised free from executive control.... Accordingly, we rejected the President's attempt to remove a Commissioner "merely because he wanted his own appointees on [the] Commission," stating that "no such power is given to the President directly by the Constitution, and none is impliedly conferred upon him by statute." ...

We undoubtedly did rely on the terms "quasi-legislative" and "quasi-judicial" to distinguish the officials involved in *Humphrey's Executor* and *Wiener* from those in *Myers,* but our present considered view is that the determination of whether the Constitution allows Congress to impose a "good cause"-type restriction on the President's power to remove an official cannot be made to turn on whether or not that official is classified as "purely executive." The analysis contained in our removal cases is designed not to define rigid categories of those officials who may or may not be removed at will by the President, but to ensure that Congress does not interfere with the President's exercise of the "executive power" and his constitutionally appointed duty to "take care that the laws be faithfully executed" under Article II. *Myers* was undoubtedly correct in its holding, and in its broader suggestion that there are some "purely executive" officials who must be removable by the President at will if he is to be able to accomplish his constitutional role.... At the other end of the spectrum from *Myers,* the characterization of the agencies in *Humphrey's Executor* and *Wiener* as "quasi-legislative" or "quasi-judicial" in large part reflected our judgment that it was not essential to the President's proper execution of his Article II powers that these agencies be headed up by individuals who were removable at will. We do not mean to suggest that an analysis of the functions served by the officials at issue is irrelevant. But the real question is whether the removal restrictions are of such a nature that they impede the President's ability to perform his constitutional duty, and the functions of the officials in question must be analyzed in that light.

Considering for the moment the "good cause" removal provision in isolation from the other parts of the Act at issue in this case, we cannot say that the imposition of a "good cause" standard for removal by itself unduly trammels on executive authority. There is no real dispute that the functions performed by the independent counsel are "executive" in the sense that they are law enforcement functions that typically have been undertaken by officials within the Executive Branch. [H]owever, the independent counsel is an inferior officer under the Appointments Clause, with limited jurisdiction and tenure and lacking policymaking or significant administrative authority. Although the counsel exercises no small amount of discretion and judgment in deciding how to carry out her duties under the Act, we simply do not see how the President's need to control the exercise of that discretion is so central to the functioning of the Executive Branch as to require as a matter of constitutional law that the counsel be terminable at will by the President.

Nor do we think that the "good cause" removal provision at issue here impermissibly burdens the President's power to control or supervise the independent counsel, as an executive official, in the execution of her duties under the Act. [T]he congressional determination to limit the removal power of the Attorney General was essential, in the view of Congress, to establish the necessary independence of the office. We do not think that this limitation as it presently stands sufficiently deprives the President of control over the independent counsel to interfere impermissibly with his constitutional obligation to ensure the faithful execution of the laws.

The final question to be addressed is whether the Act, taken as a whole, violates the principle of separation of powers by unduly interfering with the role of the Executive Branch. [W]e have never held that the Constitution requires that the three Branches of Government "operate with absolute independence." *United States v. Nixon;* see also *Nixon v. Administrator of General Services....*

We observe first that this case does not involve an attempt by Congress to increase its own powers at the expense of the Executive

Branch. Unlike some of our previous cases, most recently *Bowsher v. Synar,* ... Congress retained for itself no powers of control or supervision over an independent counsel. The Act does empower certain members of Congress to request the Attorney General to apply for the appointment of an independent counsel, but the Attorney General has no duty to comply with the request, although he must respond within a certain time limit. Other than that, Congress' role under the Act is limited to receiving reports or other information and oversight of the independent counsel's activities, § 595(a), functions that we have recognized generally as being incidental to the legislative function of Congress.

Similarly, we do not think that the Act works any *judicial* usurpation of properly executive functions. [U]nder the Act the Special Division has no power to appoint an independent counsel *sua sponte;* it may only do so upon the specific request of the Attorney General, and the courts are specifically prevented from reviewing the Attorney General's decision not to seek appointment. In addition, once the court has appointed a counsel and defined her jurisdiction, it has no power to supervise or control the activities of the counsel. ... The Act does give a federal court the power to review the Attorney General's decision to remove an independent counsel, but in our view this is a function that is well within the traditional power of the judiciary.

Finally, we do not think that the Act "impermissibly undermine[s]" the powers of the Executive Branch, or "disrupts the proper balance between the coordinate branches [by] prevent[ing] the Executive Branch from accomplishing its constitutionally assigned functions," *Nixon v. Administrator of General Services,* supra. It is undeniable that the Act reduces the amount of control or supervision that the Attorney General and, through him, the President exercises over the investigation and prosecution of a certain class of alleged criminal activity. The Attorney General is not allowed to appoint the individual of his choice; he does not determine the counsel's jurisdiction; and his power to remove a counsel is limited. [But], the Attorney General retains the power to remove the counsel for "good cause," a power that we have already concluded provides the Executive with substantial ability to ensure that the laws are "faithfully executed" by an independent counsel. No independent counsel may be appointed without a specific request by the Attorney General, and the Attorney General's decision not to request appointment if he finds "no reasonable grounds to believe that further investigation is warranted" is committed to his unreviewable discretion. The Act thus gives the Executive a degree of control over the power to initiate an investigation by the independent counsel. In addition, the jurisdiction of the independent counsel is defined with reference to the facts submitted by the Attorney General, and once a counsel is appointed, the Act requires that the counsel abide by Justice Department policy unless it is not "possible" to do so. Notwithstanding the fact that the counsel is to some degree "independent" and free from Executive supervision to a greater extent than other federal prosecutors, in our view these features of the Act give the Executive Branch sufficient control over the independent counsel to ensure that the President is able to perform his constitutionally assigned duties . . . .

JUSTICE KENNEDY took no part in the consideration or decision of this case.

JUSTICE SCALIA, dissenting.

"[T]he great security," wrote Madison, "against a gradual concentration of the several powers in the same department consists in giving to those who administer each department the necessary constitutional means and personal motives to resist encroachments of the others. The provision for defense must in this, as in all other cases, be made commensurate to the danger of attack." Federalist No. 51. Madison continued:

> "But it is not possible to give to each department an equal power of self-defense. In republican government, the legislative authority necessarily predominates. The remedy for this inconveniency is to divide the legislature into different branches; and to render them, by different modes of election and different principles of action, as little connected with each other as the nature of their common functions and their common dependence on the society will admit. . . . As the weight of the legislative authority requires that it should be thus divided, the weakness of the executive may require, on the other hand, that it should be fortified."

The major "fortification" provided, of course, was the veto power. But in addition to providing fortification, the founders conspicuously and very consciously declined to sap the executive's strength in the same way they had weakened the legislature: by dividing the executive power. Proposals to have multiple executives, or a council of advisors with separate authority were rejected . . . .

That is what this suit is about. Power. . . . Frequently an issue of this sort will come before the Court clad, so to speak, in sheep's clothing: the potential of the asserted principle to effect important change in the equilibrium of power is not immediately evident, and must be discerned by a careful and perceptive analysis. But this wolf comes as a wolf.

. . . Although the Court's opinion asserts that the Attorney General had "no duty to comply with the [congressional] request," that is not entirely accurate. He had a duty to comply unless he could conclude that there were "no reasonable grounds to believe," not that prosecution was warranted, but merely that *"further investigation"* was warranted, 28 U.S.C.A. § 592(b)(1)(emphasis added), after a 90–day investigation in which he was prohibited from using such routine investigative techniques as grand juries, plea bargaining, grants of immunity or even subpoenas, see § 592(a)(2). The Court also makes much of the fact that "the courts are specifically prevented from reviewing the Attorney General's decision not to seek appointment, § 592(f)." Yes, but *Congress* is not prevented from reviewing it. The context of this statute is acrid with the smell of threatened impeachment. Where, as here, a request for appointment of an independent counsel has come from the Judiciary Committee of either House of Congress, the Attorney General must, if he decides not to seek appointment, explain to that Committee why. See also 28 U.S.C.A. § 595(c)(independent counsel must report to the House of Representatives information "that may constitute grounds for an impeachment").

Thus, by the application of this statute in the present case, Congress has effectively compelled a criminal investigation of a high-level appointee of the President in connection with his actions arising out of a bitter power dispute between the President and the Legislative Branch. . . .

Art. II, § 1, cl. 1 of the Constitution provides: "The executive Power shall be vested in a President of the United States." [T]his does not mean *some of* the executive power, but *all of* the executive power. It seems to me, therefore, that the decision of the Court of Appeals invalidating the present statute must be upheld on fundamental separation-of-powers principles if the following two questions are answered affirmatively: (1) Is the conduct of a criminal prosecution (and of an investigation to decide whether to prosecute) the exercise of purely executive power? (2) Does the statute deprive the President of the United States of exclusive control over the exercise of that power? Surprising to say, the Court appears to concede an affirmative answer to both questions, but seeks to avoid the inevitable conclusion that since the statute vests some purely executive power in a person who is not the President of the United States it is void.

[T]he Court points out that the President, through his Attorney General, has at least *some* control. That concession is alone enough to invalidate the statute, but I cannot refrain from pointing out that the Court greatly exaggerates the extent of that "some" presidential control. "Most importan[t]" among these controls, the Court asserts, is the Attorney General's "power to remove the counsel for 'good cause.' "This is somewhat like referring to shackles as an effective means of locomotion.

[T]he Court points out that the Act directs the independent counsel to abide by general Justice Department policy, except when not "possible." The exception alone shows this to be an empty promise. Even without that, however, one would be hard put to come up with many investigative or prosecutorial "policies" (other than those imposed by the Constitution or by Congress through law) that are absolute. Almost all investigative and prosecutorial decisions—including the ultimate decision whether, after a technical violation of the law has been found, prosecution is warranted—involve the balancing of innumerable legal and practical considerations. Indeed, even political considerations (in the nonpartisan sense) must be considered, as exemplified by the recent decision of an independent counsel to subpoena the former Ambassador of Canada, producing considerable tension in our relations with that country. Another preeminently political decision is whether getting a conviction in a particular case is worth the disclosure of national security information that would be necessary. The Justice Department and our intelligence agencies are often in disagreement on this point, and the Justice Department does not always win. The present Act even goes so far as specifically to take the resolution of that dispute away from the President and give it to the independent counsel. In sum, the balancing of various legal, practical and political considerations, none of which is absolute, is the very essence of prosecutorial discretion. To take this away is to remove the core of the prosecutorial function, and not merely "some" presidential control. . . .

Is it unthinkable that the President should have such exclusive power, even when alleged crimes by him or his close associates are at issue? No more so than that Congress should have the exclusive power of legislation, even when what is at issue is its own exemption from the burdens of certain laws. No more so than that this Court should have the exclusive power to pronounce the final decision on justiciable cases and controversies, even those pertaining to the constitutionality of a statute reducing the salaries of the Justices. A system of separate and coordinate powers necessarily involves an acceptance of exclusive power that can theoretically be abused. . . . The checks against any Branch's abuse of its exclusive powers are twofold: First, retaliation by one of the other Branch's use of *its* exclusive powers: Congress, for example, can impeach the Executive who willfully fails to enforce the laws; the Executive can decline to prosecute under unconstitutional statutes; and the courts can dismiss malicious prosecutions: Second, and ultimately, there is the political check that the people will replace those in the political branches (the branches more "dangerous to the political rights of the Constitution," Federalist No. 78, p. 465) who are guilty of abuse. Political pressures produced special prosecutors—for Teapot Dome and for Watergate, for example—long before this statute created the independent counsel. See Act of Feb. 8, 1924, ch. 16, 43 Stat. 5–6.

The Court has, nonetheless, replaced the clear constitutional prescription that the executive power belongs to the President with a "balancing test." What are the standards to determine how the balance is to be struck, that is, how much removal of presidential power is too much? [The Court] simply *announces,* with no analysis, that the ability to control the decision whether to investigate and prosecute the President's closest advisors, and indeed the President himself, is not "so central to the functioning of the Executive Branch" as to be constitutionally required to be within the President's control. Apparently that is so because we say it is so. . . .

[I]n the 10 years since the institution of the independent counsel was established by law, there have been nine highly publicized investigations, a source of constant political damage to two administrations. That they could not remotely be described as merely the application of "normal" investigatory and prosecutory standards is demonstrated by, in addition to the language of the statute ("no reasonable grounds to believe"), the following facts: Congress appropriates approximately $50 million annually for general legal activities, salaries and expenses of the Criminal Division of the Department of Justice. . . . By comparison, between May 1986 and August 1987, four independent counsel (not all of whom were operating for that entire period of time) spent almost $5 million (one-tenth of the amount annually appropriated to the entire Criminal Division), spending almost $1 million in the month of August 1987 alone. For fiscal year 1989, the Department of Justice has requested $52 million for the entire Criminal Division, DOJ Budget Request 285, and $7 million to support the activities of independent counsel. . . .

[T]he Court does not attempt to "decide exactly" what establishes the line between principal and "inferior" officers, but is confident that, whatever the line may be, appellant "clearly falls on the 'inferior officer' side" of it. The Court gives three reasons: *First*, she "is subject to removal by a higher Executive branch official," namely the Attorney General. *Second*, she is "empowered by the Act to perform only certain, limited duties." *Third*, her office is "limited in jurisdiction" and "limited in tenure."

The first of these lends no support to the view that appellant is an inferior officer. Appellant is removable only for "good cause" or physical or mental incapacity. By contrast, most (if not all) *principal* officers in the Executive Branch may be removed by the President *at will*. I fail to see how the fact that appellant is more difficult to remove than most principal officers helps to establish that she is an inferior officer. . . .

The second reason offered by the Court—that appellant performs only certain, limited duties—may be relevant to whether she is an inferior officer, but it mischaracterizes the extent of her powers. As the Court states: "Admittedly, the Act delegates to appellant [the] *'full power and independent authority to exercise all investigative and prosecutorial functions and powers of the Department of Justice.'* ". . . . Court seeks to brush this away by asserting that the independent counsel's power does not include any authority to "formulate policy for the Government or the Executive Branch." But the same could be said for all officers of the Government, with the single exception of the President. All of them only formulate policy within their respective spheres of responsibility. . . .

The final set of reasons given by the Court for why the independent counsel clearly is an inferior officer emphasizes the limited nature of her jurisdiction and tenure. Taking the latter first, I find nothing unusually limited about the independent counsel's tenure. To the contrary, unlike most high-ranking Executive Branch officials, she continues to serve until she (or the Special Division) decides that her work is substantially completed. . . . As to the scope of her jurisdiction, there can be no doubt that is small (though far from unimportant). But within it she exercises more than the full power of the Attorney General. The Ambassador to Luxembourg is not anything less than a principal officer, simply because Luxembourg is small. And the federal judge who sits in a small district is not for that reason "inferior in rank and authority." . . .

The independent counsel is not even subordinate to the President. The Court essentially admits as much, noting that "appellant may not be 'subordinate' to the Attorney General (and the President) insofar as she possesses a degree of independent discretion to exercise the powers delegated to her under the Act." In fact, there is no doubt about it. . . .

Because appellant is not subordinate to another officer, she is not an "inferior" officer and her appointment other than by the President with the advice and consent of the Senate is unconstitutional. . . .

There is of course no provision in the Constitution stating who may remove executive officers, except the provisions for removal by impeachment. Before the present decision it was established, however, (1) that the President's power to remove principal officers who exercise purely executive powers could not be restricted, see *Myers v. United States,* and (2) that his power to remove inferior officers who exercise purely executive powers, and whose appointment Congress had removed from the usual procedure of presidential appointment with Senate consent, could be restricted, at least where the appointment had been made by an officer of the Executive Branch, see ibid.[4] . . .

Since our 1935 decision in *Humphrey's Executor v. United States*—which was considered by many at the time the product of an activist, anti-New Deal court bent on reducing the power of President Franklin Roosevelt—it has been established that the line of permissible restriction upon removal of principal officers lies at the point at which the powers exercised by those officers are no longer purely executive. Thus, removal restrictions have been generally regarded as lawful for so-called "independent regulatory agencies," such as the Federal Trade Commission, which engage substantially in what has been called the "quasi-legislative activity" of rulemaking, and for members of Article I courts, such as the Court of Military Appeals, who engage in the "quasi-judicial" function of adjudication. . . . By contrast, "our present considered view" is simply that *any* Executive officer's removal can be restricted, so long as the President remains "able to accomplish his constitutional role."

There are now no lines. If the removal of a prosecutor, the virtual embodiment of the power to "take care that the laws be faithfully executed," can be restricted, what officer's removal cannot? . . . What about a special Assistant Secretary of State, with responsibility for one very narrow area of foreign policy, who would not only have to be

---

4. The Court misunderstands my opinion to say that "every officer of the United States exercising any part of [the executive] power must serve at the pleasure of the President and be removable by him at will." Of course, as my discussion here demonstrates, that has never been the law and I do not assert otherwise. What I *do* assert—and what the Constitution seems plainly to prescribe—is that the President must have control over all exercises of the executive power. That requires that he have plenary power to remove principal officers such as the independent counsel, but it does not require that he have plenary power to remove inferior officers. Since the latter are, as I have described, subordinate to, i.e., subject to the supervision of, principal officers who (being removable at will) have the President's complete confidence, it is enough—at least if they have been appointed by the President or by a principal officer—that they be removable *for cause,* which would include, of course, the failure to accept supervision. . . .

confirmed by the Senate but could also be removed only pursuant to certain carefully designed restrictions? Could this possibly render the President "[un]able to accomplish his constitutional role"? . . .

Only someone who has worked in the field of law enforcement can fully appreciate the vast power and the immense discretion that are placed in the hands of a prosecutor with respect to the objects of his investigation. Justice Robert Jackson, when he was Attorney General under President Franklin Roosevelt, described it in a memorable speech to United States Attorneys, as follows:

"There is a most important reason why the prosecutor should have, as nearly as possible, a detached and impartial view of all groups in his community. Law enforcement is not automatic. It isn't blind. One of the greatest difficulties of the position of prosecutor is that he must pick his cases, because no prosecutor can even investigate all of the cases in which he receives complaints. . . .

"If the prosecutor is obliged to choose his case, it follows that he can choose his defendants. Therein is the most dangerous power of the prosecutor: that he will pick people that he thinks he should get, rather than cases that need to be prosecuted. With the law books filled with a great assortment of crimes, a prosecutor stands a fair chance of finding at least a technical violation of some act on the part of almost anyone. In such a case, it is not a question of discovering the commission of a crime and then looking for the man who has committed it, it is a question of picking the man and then searching the law books, or putting investigators to work, to pin some offense on him. It is in this realm—in which the prosecutor picks some person whom he dislikes or desires to embarrass, or selects some group of unpopular persons and then looks for an offense, that the greatest danger of abuse of prosecuting power lies. It is here that law enforcement becomes personal, and the real crime becomes that of being unpopular with the predominant or governing group, being attached to the wrong political views, or being personally obnoxious to or in the way of the prosecutor himself." R. Jackson, The Federal Prosecutor, Address Delivered at the Second Annual Conference of United States Attorneys, April 1, 1940.

[A] similar list of horribles could be attributed to an ordinary Justice Department prosecution—a vindictive prosecutor, an antagonistic staff, etc. But the difference is the difference that the Founders envisioned when they established a single Chief Executive accountable to the people: the blame can be assigned to someone who can be punished. . . .

Notes

1. Shortly after the decision in *Morrison v. Olson* (and after a 28 month investigation), Independent Counsel Alexia Morrison dropped the case against Theodore B. Olson.

2. *Young v. United States ex rel. Vuitton et Fils S.A.*, 481 U.S. 787, 107 S.Ct. 2124, 95 L.Ed.2d 740 (1987) held that federal courts have "inherent authority" to appoint a *private attorney* to prosecute a contempt of court order. The Judiciary must have "a means to vindicate its own authority without complete dependence on other branches." The petitioners had been found guilty of violating an injunction prohibiting infringement of the respondent's trademark. However the trial court erred in appointing as the prosecutor the counsel for the interested party in the underlying civil trademark litigation, thus creating a conflict of interest between the public prosecutor's duty to seek justice, not merely to convict, and the private attorney's duty of zealous representation of the private client.

3. After the Independent Counsel statute expired, Congress reenacted it at the urging of President Clinton and Attorney General Reno. Attorney General Reno then appointed several Independent Counsel to investigate various Cabinet officials and also President Clinton himself, in connection with charges involving a real estate deal known as "Whitewater," and later expanded to include allegations involving misuse of FBI files, abuses of the White House Travel Office, and alleged perjury and obstruction in connection with an affair with a White House intern. In 1999, Congress allowed the Independent Counsel law to expire again. Both President Clinton and Independent Counsel Kenneth Starr urged that the law not be reenacted. In his Congressional testimony, Judge Starr said that the law was "constitutionally dubious," and: "If politicization and the loss of public confidence are inevitable, then we should leave the full responsibility where our laws and traditions place it, on the Attorney General."

4. *Edmond v. United States*, 520 U.S. 651, 117 S.Ct. 1573, 137 L.Ed.2d 917 (1997). Scalia, J., for the Court, held that Congress constitutionally may authorize the Secretary of Transportation to appoint civilian members to the Coast Guard Court of Criminal Appeals. These military judges are inferior officers whom the head of a Department (the Secretary of Transportation) may appoint. *Morrison v. Olson* did not purport to set forth "a definitive test" to determine whether an office is "inferior" for purposes of the appointments clause.

> Generally speaking, the term "inferior officer" connotes a relationship with some higher ranking officer or officers below the President: whether one is an "inferior" officer depends on whether he has a superior. It is not enough that other officers may be identified who formally maintain a higher rank, or possess responsibility of a greater magnitude. If that were the intention, the Constitution might have used the phrase "lesser officer." Rather, in the context of a clause designed to preserve political accountability relative to important government assignments, we think it evident that "inferior officers" are officers whose work is directed and supervised at some level by others who were appointed by presidential nomination with the advice and consent of the Senate.

The Judge Advocate General cannot attempt to influence the outcome of individual proceedings by threat of removal or otherwise, but he does exercise administrative oversight over this court; he is charged with prescribing uniform rules of procedure, and he may remove a judge "from his judicial assignment without cause." He cannot reverse the court's decisions, but another Executive Branch entity (the Court of Appeals for the Armed Forces) can do that. It is "significant" that "the judges of the Court of Criminal Appeals have no power to render a final decision on behalf of the United States unless permitted to do so by other executive officers."

MISTRETTA v. UNITED STATES
488 U.S. 361, 109 S.Ct. 647, 102 L.Ed.2d 714 (1989).

JUSTICE BLACKMUN delivered the opinion of the Court.

In this litigation, we granted certiorari before judgment in the United States Court of Appeals for the Eighth Circuit in order to consider the constitutionality of the Sentencing Guidelines promulgated by the United States Sentencing Commission. The Commission is a body created under the Sentencing Reform Act of 1984. . . .

For almost a century, the Federal Government employed in criminal cases a system of indeterminate sentencing. [U]nder the indeterminate-sentence system, Congress defined the maximum, the judge imposed a sentence within the statutory range (which it usually could replace with probation), and the Executive Branch's parole official eventually determined the actual duration of imprisonment. Serious disparities in sentences, however, were common. Rehabilitation as a sound penological theory came to be questioned and, in any event, was regarded by some as an unattainable goal for most cases. . . .

The Act, as adopted, revised the old sentencing process in several ways:

1. It rejects imprisonment as a means of promoting rehabilitation, and it states that punishment should serve retributive, educational, deterrent, and incapacitative goals.

2. It consolidates the power that had been exercised by the sentencing judge and the Parole Commission to decide what punishment an offender should suffer. This is done by creating the United States Sentencing Commission, directing that Commission to devise guidelines to be used for sentencing, and prospectively abolishing the Parole Commission.

3. It makes all sentences basically determinate. A prisoner is to be released at the completion of his sentence reduced only by any credit earned by good behavior while in custody.

4. It makes the Sentencing Commission's guidelines binding on the courts, although it preserves for the judge the discretion to depart from the guideline applicable to a particular case if the judge finds an aggravating or mitigating factor present that the Commission did not adequately consider when formulating guidelines. The Act also requires the court to state its reasons for the sentence imposed and to give "the specific reason" for imposing a sentence different from that described in the guideline.

5. It authorizes limited appellate review of the sentence. It permits a defendant to appeal a sentence that is above the defined range, and it permits the Government to appeal a sentence that is below that range. It also permits either side to appeal an incorrect application of the guideline....

The Commission is established "as an independent commission in the judicial branch of the United States." § 991(a). It has seven voting members (one of whom is the Chairman) appointed by the President "by and with the advice and consent of the Senate." "At least three of the members shall be Federal judges selected after considering a list of six judges recommended to the President by the Judicial Conference of the United States." *Ibid.* No more than four members of the Commission shall be members of the same political party. The Attorney General, or his designee, is an ex officio non-voting member. The Chairman and other members of the Commission are subject to removal by the President "only for neglect of duty or malfeasance in office or for other good cause shown." Except for initial staggering of terms, a voting member serves for six years and may not serve more than two full terms.

In addition to the duty the Commission has to promulgate determinative-sentence guidelines, it is under an obligation periodically to "review and revise" the guidelines. It is to "consult with authorities on, and individual and institutional representatives of, various aspects of the Federal criminal justice system." It must report to Congress "any amendments of the guidelines." It is to make recommendations to Congress whether the grades or maximum penalties should be modified. It must submit to Congress at least annually an analysis of the operation of the guidelines. It is to issue "general policy statements" regarding their application. And it has the power to "establish general policies ... as are necessary to carry out the purposes" of the legislation; to "monitor the performance of probation officers" with respect to the guidelines, § 995(a)(9); to "devise and conduct periodic training programs of instruction in sentencing techniques for judicial and probation personnel" and others, § 995(a)(18); and to "perform such other functions as are required to permit Federal courts to meet their responsibilities" as to sentencing, § 995(a)(22)....

On Dec. 10, 1987, John M. Mistretta (petitioner) and another were indicted in the United States District Court for the Western District of Missouri on three counts centering in a cocaine sale. Mistretta moved to have the promulgated Guidelines ruled unconstitutional on the grounds that the Sentencing Commission was constituted in violation of the established doctrine of separation of powers, and that Congress delegated excessive authority to the Commission to structure the Guidelines....

Petitioner argues that in delegating the power to promulgate sentencing guidelines for every federal criminal offense to an independent Sentencing Commission, Congress has granted the Commission excessive legislative discretion in violation of the constitutionally based nondelegation doctrine. We do not agree. . . . So long as Congress "shall lay down by legislative act an intelligible principle to which the person or body authorized to [exercise the delegated authority] is directed to conform, such legislative action is not a forbidden delegation of legislative power."

[W]e harbor no doubt that Congress' delegation of authority to the Sentencing Commission is sufficiently specific and detailed to meet constitutional requirements. . . . We cannot dispute petitioner's contention that the Commission enjoys significant discretion in formulating guidelines. The Commission does have discretionary authority to determine the relative severity of federal crimes and to assess the relative weight of the offender characteristics that Congress listed for the Commission to consider. The Commission also has significant discretion to determine which crimes have been punished too leniently, and which too severely. § 994(m). Congress has called upon the Commission to exercise its judgment about which types of crimes and which types of criminals are to be considered similar for the purposes of sentencing.[11] . . .

Developing proportionate penalties for hundreds of different crimes by a virtually limitless array of offenders is precisely the sort of intricate, labor-intensive task for which delegation to an expert body is especially appropriate. Although Congress has delegated significant discretion to the Commission to draw judgments from its analysis of existing sentencing practice and alternative sentencing models, "Congress is not confined to that method of executing its policy which involves the least possible delegation of discretion to administrative officers." *Yakus v. United States.* We have no doubt that in the hands of the Commission "the criteria which Congress has supplied are wholly adequate for carrying out the general policy and purpose" of the Act.

Having determined that Congress has set forth sufficient standards for the exercise of the Commission's delegated authority, we turn to Mistretta's claim that the Act violates the constitutional principle of separation of powers.

[P]etitioner claims that in delegating to an independent agency within the Judicial Branch the power to promulgate sentencing guidelines, Congress unconstitutionally has required the Branch, and individual Article III judges, to exercise not only their judicial authority, but legislative authority—the making of sentencing policy—as well. Such rulemaking authority, petitioner contends, may be exercised by Con-

---

11. Petitioner argues that the excessive breadth of Congress' delegation to the Commission is particularly apparent in the Commission's considering whether to "reinstate" the death penalty for some or all of those crimes for which capital punishment is still authorized in the Federal Criminal Code. . . . We assume, without deciding, that the Commission was assigned the power to effectuate the death penalty provisions of the Criminal Code. That the Commission may have this authority (but has not exercised it) does not affect our analysis. Congress did not authorize the Commission to enact a federal death penalty for any offense. As for every other offense within the Commission's jurisdiction, the Commission could include the death penalty within the guidelines only if that punishment was authorized in the first instance by Congress and only if such inclusion comported with the substantial guidance Congress gave the Commission in fulfilling its assignments. Justice Brennan does not join this footnote.

gress, or delegated by Congress to the Executive, but may not be delegated to or exercised by the Judiciary. . . .

LOCATION OF THE COMMISSION

The Sentencing Commission unquestionably is a peculiar institution within the framework of our Government. Although placed by the Act in the Judicial Branch, it is not a court and does not exercise judicial power. Rather, the Commission is an "independent" body comprised of seven voting members including at least three federal judges, entrusted by Congress with the primary task of promulgating sentencing guidelines. Our constitutional principles of separated powers are not violated, however, by mere anomaly or innovation. Setting to one side, for the moment, the question whether the composition of the Sentencing Commission violates the separation of powers, we observe that Congress' decision to create an independent rulemaking body to promulgate sentencing guidelines and to locate that body within the Judicial Branch is not unconstitutional unless Congress has vested in the Commission powers that are more appropriately performed by the other Branches or that undermine the integrity of the Judiciary.

According to express provision of Article III, the judicial power of the United States is limited to "Cases" and "Controversies." See *Muskrat v. United States.* In implementing this limited grant of power, we have refused to issue advisory opinions or to resolve disputes that are not justiciable. . . . Nonetheless, we have recognized significant exceptions to this general rule and have approved the assumption of some nonadjudicatory activities by the Judicial Branch. In keeping with Justice Jackson's *Youngstown* admonition that the separation of powers contemplates the integration of dispersed powers into a workable government, we have recognized the constitutionality of a "twilight area" in which the activities of the separate Branches merge. . . .

That judicial rulemaking, at least with respect to some subjects, falls within this twilight area is no longer an issue for dispute. None of our cases indicate that rulemaking *per se* is a function that may not be performed by an entity within the Judicial Branch, either because rulemaking is inherently nonjudicial or because it is a function exclusively committed to the Executive Branch.[14] On the contrary, we specifically

---

14.   . . . Although in *INS v. Chadha,* we characterized rulemaking as "Executive action" not governed by the Presentment Clauses, we did so as part of our effort to distinguish the rulemaking of administrative agencies from "lawmaking" by Congress which is subject to the presentment requirements of Article I. 462 U.S., at 953, n. 16, 103 S.Ct., at 2785, n. 16. Plainly, this reference to rulemaking as an executive function was not intended to undermine our recognition in previous cases and in over 150 years of practice that rulemaking pursuant to a legislative delegation is not the exclusive prerogative of the Executive.

On the contrary, rulemaking power originates in the Legislative Branch and becomes an executive function only when delegated by the Legislature to the Executive Branch.

[S]ince Congress has empowered the President to appoint and remove Commission members, the President's relationship to the Commission is functionally no different from what it would have been had Congress not located the Commission in the Judicial Branch. Indeed, since the Act grants ex officio membership on the Commission to the Attorney General or his des-

have held that Congress, in some circumstances, may confer rulemaking authority on the Judicial Branch. In *Sibbach v. Wilson & Co.,* 312 U.S. 1, 61 S.Ct. 422, 85 L.Ed. 479 (1941), we upheld a challenge to certain rules promulgated under the Rules Enabling Act of 1934 which conferred upon the Judiciary the power to promulgate federal rules of civil procedure.... Pursuant to this power to delegate rulemaking authority to the Judicial Branch, Congress expressly has authorized this Court to establish rules for the conduct of its own business and to prescribe rules of procedure for lower federal courts in bankruptcy cases, in other civil cases, and in criminal cases, and to revise the federal rules of evidence.

Our approach to other nonadjudicatory activities that Congress has vested either in federal courts or in auxiliary bodies within the Judicial Branch has been identical to our approach to judicial rulemaking: consistent with the separation of powers, Congress may delegate to the Judicial Branch nonadjudicatory functions that do not trench upon the prerogatives of another Branch and that are appropriate to the central mission of the Judiciary.... Though not the subject of constitutional challenge, by established practice, we have recognized Congress' power to create the Judicial Conference of the United States, and the Rules Advisory Committees that it oversees, and the Administrative Office of the United States Courts whose myriad responsibilities include the administration of the entire probation service.[15] These entities, some of which are comprised of judges, others of judges and nonjudges, still others of nonjudges only, do not exercise judicial power in the constitutional sense of deciding cases and controversies, but they share the common purpose of providing for the fair and efficient fulfillment of responsibilities that are properly the province of the Judiciary. Thus, although the judicial power of the United States is limited by express provision of Article III to "Cases" and "Controversies," we have never held, and have clearly disavowed in practice, that the Constitution prohibits Congress from assigning to courts or auxiliary bodies within the Judicial Branch administrative or rulemaking duties that, in the words of Chief Justice Marshall, are "necessary and proper.... for carrying into execution all the judgments which the judicial department has the power to pronounce." *Wayman v. Southard,* 10 Wheat., at 21 [1825]. Because of their close relation to the central mission of the Judicial Branch, such extrajudicial activities are consonant with the

ignee, the Executive Branch's involvement in the Commission is greater than in other independent agencies, such as the Securities and Exchange Commission, not located in the Judicial Branch.

15. The Judicial Conference of the United States is charged with "promot[ing] uniformity of management procedures and the expeditious conduct of court business," in part by "a continuous study of the operation and effect of the general rules of practice and procedure" and recommending changes "to promote simplicity in procedure, fairness in administration, the just determination of litigation, and the elimination of unjustifiable expense and delay." 28 U.S.C. § 331 (1982 ed. and Supp. IV). Similarly, the Administrative Office of the United States Courts handles the administrative and personnel matters of the courts, matters essential to the effective and efficient operation of the judicial system. § 604 (1982 ed. and Supp. IV). Congress also has established the Federal Judicial Center which studies improvements in judicial administration. §§ 620–628 (1982 ed. and Supp. IV).

integrity of the Branch and are not more appropriate for another Branch.

... That Congress should vest such rulemaking in the Judicial Branch, far from being "incongruous" or vesting within the Judiciary responsibilities that more appropriately belong to another Branch, simply acknowledges the role that the Judiciary always has played, and continues to play, in sentencing.[17] [T]he Commission's functions, like this Court's function in promulgating procedural rules, are clearly attendant to a central element of the historically acknowledged mission of the Judicial Branch....

We agree with petitioner that the nature of the Commission's rulemaking power is not strictly analogous to this Court's rulemaking power under the enabling acts. Although we are loathe to enter the logical morass of distinguishing between substantive and procedural rules, and although we have recognized that the Federal Rules of Civil Procedure regulate matters "falling within the uncertain area between substance and procedure, [and] are rationally capable of classification as either," *Hanna v. Plumer,* 380 U.S., at 472, 85 S.Ct., at 1144, we recognize that the task of promulgating rules regulating practice and pleading before federal courts does not involve the degree of political judgment integral to the Commission's formulation of sentencing guidelines.[18] ...

We do not believe, however, that the significantly political nature of the Commission's work renders unconstitutional its placement within the Judicial Branch. Our separation-of-powers analysis does not turn on the labelling of an activity as "substantive" as opposed to "procedural," or "political" as opposed to "judicial." Rather, our inquiry is focused on the "unique aspects of the congressional plan at issue and its practical consequences in light of the larger concerns that underlie Article III." In this case, the "practical consequences" of locating the Commission within the Judicial Branch pose no threat of undermining the integrity of the Judicial Branch or of expanding the powers of the Judiciary beyond constitutional bounds by uniting within the Branch the political or quasi-legislative power of the Commission with the judicial power of the courts.

First, although the Commission is located in the Judicial Branch, its powers are not united with the powers of the Judiciary in a way that has

---

17. Indeed, had Congress decided to confer responsibility for promulgating sentencing guidelines on the Executive Branch, we might face the constitutional questions whether Congress unconstitutionally had assigned judicial responsibilities to the executive or unconstitutionally had united the power to prosecute and the power to sentence within one Branch. The Justice Department testified before the Senate to this very effect: "If guidelines were to be promulgated by an agency outside the judicial branch, it might be viewed as an encroachment on the sentencing function...."

18. Under its mandate, the Commission must make judgments about the relative importance of such considerations as the "circumstances under which the offense was committed," the "community view of the gravity of the offense," and the "deterrent effect a particular sentence may have on the commission of the offense by others." 28 U.S.C. § 994(c)(2), (4), (6).

meaning for separation-of-powers analysis. Whatever constitutional problems might arise if the powers of the Commission were vested in a court, the Commission is not a court, does not exercise judicial power, and is not controlled by or accountable to members of the Judicial Branch. The Commission, on which members of the Judiciary may be a minority, is an independent agency in every relevant sense. In contrast to a court's exercising judicial power, the Commission is fully accountable to Congress, which can revoke or amend any or all of the Guidelines as it sees fit either within the 180–day waiting period. In contrast to a court, the Commission's members are subject to the President's limited powers of removal. In contrast to a court, its rulemaking is subject to the notice and comment requirements of the Administrative Procedure Act. [B]ecause Congress vested the power to promulgate sentencing guidelines in an independent agency, not a court, there can be no serious argument that Congress combined legislative and judicial power within the Judicial Branch.[20]

Second, although the Commission wields rulemaking power and not the adjudicatory power exercised by individual judges when passing sentence, the placement of the Sentencing Commission in the Judicial Branch has not increased the Branch's authority. Prior to the passage of the Act, the Judicial Branch, as an aggregate, decided precisely the questions assigned to the Commission: what sentence is appropriate to what criminal conduct under what circumstances. [I]n placing the Commission in the Judicial Branch, Congress cannot be said to have aggrandized the authority of that Branch or to have deprived the Executive Branch of a power it once possessed. Indeed, because the Guidelines have the effect of promoting sentencing within a narrower range than was previously applied, the power of the Judicial Branch is, if anything, somewhat diminished by the Act. And, since Congress did not unconstitutionally delegate its own authority, the Act does not unconstitutionally diminish Congress' authority. Thus, although Congress has authorized the Commission to exercise a greater degree of political judgment than has been exercised in the past by any one entity within the Judicial Branch, in the unique context of sentencing, this authorization does nothing to upset the balance of power among the Branches. . . .

---

20. We express no opinion about whether, under the principles of separation of powers, Congress may confer on a court rulemaking authority such as that exercised by the Sentencing Commission. . . . We note, however, that the constitutional calculus is different for considering nonadjudicatory activities performed by bodies that exercise judicial power and enjoy the constitutionally mandated autonomy of courts from what it is for considering the nonadjudicatory activities of independent nonadjudicatory agencies that Congress merely has located within the Judicial Branch pursuant to its powers under the Necessary and Proper Clause. We make no attempt here to define the nonadjudicatory duties that are appropriate for auxiliary bodies within the Judicial Branch, but not for courts. Nonetheless, it is clear to us that an independent agency located within the Judicial Branch may undertake without constitutional consequences policy judgments pursuant to a legitimate congressional delegation of authority that, if undertaken by a court, might be incongruous to or destructive of the central adjudicatory mission of the Branch. In this sense, the issue we face here is different from the issue we faced in *Morrison v. Olson,* where we considered the constitutionality of the nonadjudicatory functions assigned to the "Special Division" court created by the Ethics in Government Act of 1978. . . .

Nor do the Guidelines, though substantive, involve a degree of political authority inappropriate for a nonpolitical branch. Although the Guidelines are intended to have substantive effects on public behavior (as do the rules of procedure), they do not bind or regulate the primary conduct of the public or vest in the Judicial Branch the legislative responsibility for establishing minimum and maximum penalties for every crime. They do no more than fetter the discretion of sentencing judges to do what they have done for generations—impose sentences within the broad limits established by Congress. . . .

COMPOSITION OF THE COMMISSION

We now turn to petitioner's claim that Congress' decision to require at least three federal judges to serve on the Commission and to require those judges to share their authority with nonjudges undermines the integrity of the Judicial Branch. . . . We find Congress' requirement of judicial service somewhat troublesome, but we do not believe that the Act impermissibly interferes with the functioning of the Judiciary.

The text of the Constitution contains no prohibition against the service of active federal judges on independent commissions such as that established by the Act. The Constitution does include an Incompatibility Clause applicable to national legislators [U.S. Const., Art. I, § 6, cl. 2]. No comparable restriction applies to judges, and we find it at least inferentially meaningful that at the Constitutional Convention two prohibitions against plural officeholding by members of the judiciary were proposed, but did not reach the floor of the Convention for a vote.

Our inferential reading that the Constitution does not prohibit Article III judges from undertaking extrajudicial duties finds support in the historical practice of the Founders after ratification. . . . The first Chief Justice, John Jay, served simultaneously as Chief Justice and as Ambassador to England, where he negotiated the treaty that bears his name. Oliver Ellsworth served simultaneously as Chief Justice and as Minister to France. While he was Chief Justice, John Marshall served briefly as Secretary of State and was a member of the Sinking Fund Commission with responsibility for refunding the Revolutionary War debt. All these appointments were made by the President with the "Advice and Consent" of the Senate. . . . Charles Warren, in his history of this Court, reports that the Senate specifically rejected by a vote of 18–8 a resolution proposed during the debate over Jay's nomination to the effect that such extrajudicial service was "contrary to the spirit of the Constitution." This contemporaneous practice by the Founders themselves is significant evidence that the constitutional principle of separation of powers does not absolutely prohibit extrajudicial service.

Subsequent history, moreover, reveals a frequent and continuing, albeit controversial, practice of extrajudicial service. In 1877, five Justices served on the Election Commission that resolved the hotly contested Presidential election of 1876, where Samuel J. Tilden and Rutherford B. Hayes were the contenders. Justices Nelson, Fuller, Brewer, Hughes, Day, Roberts, and Van Devanter served on various arbitral commissions.

Justice Roberts was a member of the commission organized to investigate the attack on Pearl Harbor. Justice Jackson was one of the prosecutors at the Nuremberg trials; and Chief Justice Warren presided over the commission investigating the assassination of President Kennedy. Such service has been no less a practice among lower court federal judges. While these extrajudicial activities spawned spirited discussion and frequent criticism, and although some of the judges who undertook these duties sometimes did so with reservation and may have looked back on their service with regret, "traditional ways of conducting government ... give meaning" to the Constitution. *Youngstown Sheet & Tube Co. v. Sawyer* (concurring opinion). . . .

In light of the foregoing history and precedent, we conclude that the principle of separation of powers does not absolutely prohibit Article III judges from serving on commissions such as that created by the Act. The judges serve on the Sentencing Commission not pursuant to their status and authority as Article III judges, but solely because of their appointment by the President as the Act directs. Such power as these judges wield as Commissioners is not judicial power; it is administrative power derived from the enabling legislation. Just as the nonjudicial members of the Commission act as administrators, bringing their experience and wisdom to bear on the problems of sentencing disparity, so too the judges, uniquely qualified on the subject of sentencing, assume a wholly administrative role upon entering into the deliberations of the Commission. In other words, the Constitution, at least as a *per se* matter, does not forbid judges from wearing two hats; it merely forbids them from wearing both hats at the same time. This is not to suggest, of course, that every kind of extrajudicial service under every circumstance necessarily accords with the Constitution. . . . The ultimate inquiry remains whether a particular extrajudicial assignment undermines the integrity of the Judicial Branch. . . .

In our view, petitioner significantly overstates the mandatory nature of Congress' directive that at least three members of the Commission shall be federal judges, as well as the effect of this service on the practical operation of the Judicial Branch. Service on the Commission by any particular judge is voluntary. . . . That federal judges participate in the promulgation of guidelines does not affect their or other judges' ability impartially to adjudicate sentencing issues. Cf. *Mississippi Publishing Corp. v. Murphree,* 326 U.S. 438, 66 S.Ct. 242, 90 L.Ed. 185 (1946)(that this Court promulgated the Federal Rules of Civil Procedure did not foreclose its consideration of challenges to their validity). . . .

Although it is a judgment that is not without difficulty, we conclude that the participation of federal judges on the Sentencing Commission does not threaten, either in fact or in appearance, the impartiality of the Judicial Branch. We are drawn to this conclusion by one paramount consideration: that the Sentencing Commission is devoted exclusively to the development of rules to rationalize a process that has been and will continue to be performed exclusively by the Judicial Branch. In our view,

this is an essentially neutral endeavor and one in which judicial participation is peculiarly appropriate. . . .

Finally, we reject petitioner's argument that the mixed nature of the
Commission violates the Constitution by requiring Article III judges to
share judicial power with nonjudges. As noted earlier, the Commission is
not a court and exercises no judicial power. Thus, the Act does not vest
Article III power in nonjudges or require Article III judges to share their
power with nonjudges.

PRESIDENTIAL CONTROL

The Act empowers the President to appoint all seven members of
the Commission with the advice and consent of the Senate. The Act
further provides that the President shall make his choice of judicial
appointees to the Commission after considering a list of six judges
recommended by the Judicial Conference of the United States. The Act
also grants the President authority to remove members of the Commission, although "only for neglect of duty or malfeasance in office or for
other good cause shown." 28 U.S.C. § 991(a).

Mistretta argues that this power of Presidential appointment and
removal prevents the Judicial Branch from performing its constitutionally assigned functions. See *Nixon v. Administrator of General Services.*

The notion that the President's power to appoint federal judges to
the Commission somehow gives him influence over the Judicial Branch
or prevents, even potentially, the Judicial Branch from performing its
constitutionally assigned functions is fanciful. We have never considered
it incompatible with the functioning of the Judicial Branch that the
President has the power to elevate federal judges from one level to
another or to tempt judges away from the bench with Executive Branch
positions. The mere fact that the President within his appointment
portfolio has positions that may be attractive to federal judges does not,
of itself, corrupt the integrity of the Judiciary. . . .

The President's removal power over Commission members poses a
similarly negligible threat to judicial independence. The Act does not,
and could not under the Constitution, authorize the President to remove,
or in any way diminish the status of Article III judges, as judges. Even if
removed from the Commission, a federal judge appointed to the Commission would continue, absent impeachment, to enjoy tenure "during good
Behavior" and a full judicial salary. U.S. Const., Art. III, § 1.[32] [W]e see
no risk that the President's limited removal power will compromise the
impartiality of Article III judges serving on the Commission and, consequently, no risk that the Act's removal provision will prevent the

---

32. . . . Concededly, since Commission
members receive a salary equal to that of a
court of appeals judge, 28 U.S.C. § 992(c),
district court judges appointed to the Commission receive an increase in salary. We do
not address the hypothetical constitutional
question whether, under the Compensation
Clause of Article III, a district judge removed from the Commission must continue
to be paid the higher salary.

Judicial Branch from performing its constitutionally assigned function of fairly adjudicating cases and controversies.[35]

... The Constitution's structural protections do not prohibit Congress from delegating to an expert body located within the Judicial Branch the intricate task of formulating sentencing guidelines consistent with such significant statutory direction as is present here. Nor does our system of checked and balanced authority prohibit Congress from calling upon the accumulated wisdom and experience of the Judicial Branch in creating policy on a matter uniquely within the ken of judges. Accordingly, we hold that the Act is constitutional. ...

JUSTICE SCALIA, dissenting.

While the products of the Sentencing Commission's labors have been given the modest name "Guidelines," they have the force and effect of laws, prescribing the sentences criminal defendants are to receive. A judge who disregards them will be reversed, 18 U.S.C. § 3742. I dissent from today's decision because I can find no place within our constitutional system for an agency created by Congress to exercise no governmental power other than the making of laws.

There is no doubt that the Sentencing Commission has established significant, legally binding prescriptions governing application of governmental power against private individuals—indeed, application of the ultimate governmental power, short of capital punishment.[1] [T]he decisions made by the Commission are far from technical, but are heavily laden (or ought to be) with value judgments and policy assessments. This fact is sharply reflected in the Commission's product, as described by the dissenting Commissioner:

> "Under the guidelines, the judge could give the same sentence for abusive sexual contact that puts the child in fear as for unlawfully entering or remaining in the United States. Similarly, the guidelines permit equivalent sentences for the following pairs of offenses: drug trafficking and a violation of the Wild Free–Roaming Horses and Burros Act; arson with a destructive device and failure to surrender a cancelled naturalization certificate; ..."

---

35. [W]e hold here no more than that Congress may vest in the President the power to remove for good cause an Article III judge from a nonadjudicatory independent agency placed within the Judicial Branch. Because an Article III judge serving on a nonadjudicatory commission is not exercising judicial power, and because such limited removal power gives the President no control over judicatory functions, interbranch removal authority under these limited circumstances poses no threat to the balance of power among the Branches. Our paramount concern in *Bowsher* that Congress was accreting to itself the power to control the functions of another Branch is not implicated by a removal provision, like the one at issue here, which provides no control in one Branch over the constitutionally assigned mission of another Branch.

1. It is even arguable that the Commission has authority to establish guidelines and procedures for imposing the death penalty, thus reinstituting that sanction under federal statutes for which (by reason of our recent decisions) it has been thought unusable because of constitutionally inadequate procedures. The Justice Department believes such authority exists, and has encouraged the Commission to exercise it.

[I agree] with the Court's rejection of petitioner's contention that the doctrine of unconstitutional delegation of legislative authority has been violated because of the lack of intelligible, congressionally prescribed standards to guide the Commission. Precisely because the scope of delegation is largely uncontrollable by the courts, we must be particularly rigorous in preserving the Constitution's structural restrictions that deter excessive delegation. The major one, it seems to me, is that the power to make law cannot be exercised by anyone other than Congress, except in conjunction with the lawful exercise of executive or judicial power.

The whole theory of *lawful* congressional "delegation" is not that Congress is sometimes too busy or too divided and can therefore assign its responsibility of making law to someone else; but rather that a certain degree of discretion, and thus of law-making, *inheres* in most executive or judicial action, and it is up to Congress, by the relative specificity or generality of its statutory commands, to determine—up to a point—how small or how large that degree shall be. Thus, the courts could be given the power to say precisely what constitutes a "restraint of trade," see *Standard Oil Co. of New Jersey v. United States,* 221 U.S. 1, 31 S.Ct. 502, 55 L.Ed. 619 (1911), or to adopt rules of procedure, see *Sibbach v. Wilson & Co.,* 312 U.S. 1, 22, 61 S.Ct. 422, 429, 85 L.Ed. 479 (1941), or to prescribe by rule the manner in which their officers shall execute their judgments, *Wayman v. Southard,* 10 Wheat. 1, 45, 6 L.Ed. 253 (1825), because that "lawmaking" was ancillary to their exercise of judicial powers. And the Executive could be given the power to adopt policies and rules specifying in detail what radio and television licenses will be in the "public interest, convenience or necessity," because that was ancillary to exercise of its executive powers in granting and policing licenses and making a "fair and equitable allocation" of the electromagnetic spectrum.[2] Or to take examples closer to the case before us: Trial judges could be given the power to determine what factors justify a greater or lesser sentence within the statutorily prescribed limits because that was ancillary to their exercise of the judicial power of pronouncing sentence upon individual defendants. And the President, through the Parole Commission subject to his appointment and removal, could be given the power to issue Guidelines specifying when parole would be available, because that was ancillary to the President's exercise of the executive power to hold and release federal prisoners....

In the present case, however, a pure delegation of legislative power is precisely what we have before us. It is irrelevant whether the standards are adequate, because they are not standards related to the exercise of executive or judicial powers; they are, plainly and simply, standards for further legislation. [T]he Commission neither exercises

---

2. An executive agency can, of course, be created with no power other than the making of rules, as long as that agency is subject to the control of the President and the President has executive authority related to the rulemaking. In such circumstances, the rulemaking is ultimately ancillary to the President's executive powers.

any executive power on its own, nor is subject to the control of the President who does. . . .

By reason of today's decision, I anticipate that Congress will find delegation of its lawmaking powers much more attractive in the future. If rulemaking can be entirely unrelated to the exercise of judicial or executive powers, I foresee all manner of "expert" bodies, insulated from the political process, to which Congress will delegate various portions of its lawmaking responsibility. How tempting to create an expert Medical Commission (mostly MDs, with perhaps a few PhDs in moral philosophy) to dispose of such thorny, "no-win" political issues as the withholding of life-support systems in federally funded hospitals, or the use of fetal tissue for research. This is an undemocratic precedent that we set—not because of the scope of the delegated power, but because its recipient is not one of the three Branches of Government. The only governmental power the Commission possesses is the power to make law; and it is not the Congress.

. . . It is already a leap from the proposition that a person who is not the President may exercise executive powers to the proposition we accepted in *Morrison* that a person who is *neither* the President *nor* is subject to the President's control may exercise executive powers. But with respect to the exercise of judicial powers (the business of the Judicial Branch) the platform for such a leap does not even exist. For unlike executive power, judicial and legislative powers have never been thought delegable. A judge may not leave the decision to his law clerk, or to a master. See *United States v. Raddatz,* 447 U.S. 667, 683, 100 S.Ct. 2406, 2416, 65 L.Ed.2d 424 (1980). Senators and Members of the House may not send delegates to consider and vote upon bills in their place. Thus, however well established may be the "independent agencies" of the Executive Branch, here we have an anomaly beyond equal: an independent agency exercising governmental power on behalf of a Branch where all governmental power is supposed to be exercised personally by the judges of courts.[3]

. . . If an "independent agency" such as this can be given the power to fix sentences previously exercised by district courts, I must assume that a similar agency can be given the powers to adopt Rules of Procedure and Rules of Evidence previously exercised by this Court. The bases for distinction would be thin indeed. . . . I think the Court errs, in other words, not so much because it mistakes the degree of commingling, but because it fails to recognize that this case is not about commingling,

---

3. There are of course agencies within the Judicial Branch (because they operate under the control of courts or judges) which are not themselves courts, see, *e.g.,* 28 U.S.C. § 601 *et seq.* (Administrative Office of the United States Courts), just as there are agencies within the Legislative Branch (because they operate under the control of Congress) which are not themselves Sena- tors or Representatives, see, *e.g.,* 31 U.S.C. § 701 *et seq.* (General Accounting Office). But these agencies, unlike the Sentencing Commission, exercise no governmental pow- ers, that is, they establish and determine neither private rights nor the prerogatives of the other Branches. They merely assist the courts and the Congress in *their* exer- cise of judicial and legislative powers.

but about the creation of a new branch altogether, a sort of junior-varsity Congress. . . .

Notes

1.   One commentator on *Mistretta* has argued that the appointment of federal judges to the Sentencing Commission violates the "case or controversy" requirement. Judges impose sentences in the context of "live, individualized cases." But the Commission "promulgates binding, generalized guidelines, much as a legislature would. [C]ould anyone imagine that a law directing the federal judiciary to promulgate binding regulations enforcing the First Amendment right of free speech could survive examination under the 'case or controversy' requirement, on the ground that the judiciary has traditionally developed the substance of First Amendment law in the context of live cases? Yet the court's reasoning in upholding the Sentencing Commission effectively amounts to the same type of questionable logic."[1] What do you think?

2.   *Metropolitan Washington Airports Authority v. Citizens for the Abatement of Aircraft Noise, Inc.,* 501 U.S. 252, 111 S.Ct. 2298, 115 L.Ed.2d 236 (1991). An Act of Congress transferred operating control of Washington National Airport and Dulles International Airport to the Metropolitan Washington Airports Authority (MWAA), an entity created by a compact between Virginia and the District of Columbia. Local residents objected to the noise, safety, and pollution of National Airport's flight paths over densely populated areas. Congress did not want this new entity to respond to complaints by shifting any significant air traffic from National Airport (conveniently located close to downtown Washington) to Dulles (in a rural area miles from downtown). Thus, Congress authorized the transfer of control to MWAA *on the condition* that MWAA create a "Board of Review," composed of nine Members of Congress who serve on Congressional committees with jurisdiction over transportation issues. The Board of Review could veto any decisions made by MWAA's Board of Directors, thus safe-guarding Congressional interests.

Stevens, J., for the Court, held that the Board of Review violated the separation-of-powers.[1] The statute stated that Members of Congress serve "in their individual capacities, as representatives of the users of the airports," but the Court, relying on *Mistretta,* concluded that separation-of-powers analysis does not turn on the label of an activity. The Act of Congress did not require the appointed Members to be users of the airports, though they were required to have congressional responsibilities for air transportation regulation. The Act also gave Congress "substantial power" over the appointment and removal of its Members who would serve on this Board. If the Board's power is executive, then, pursuant to *Bowsher v.*

---

1.   Redish, Judges Don't Belong on Sentencing Commission, Wall St.J., Feb. 14, 1989, at A16, col. 5 (Midwest ed.).

1.   A footnote Court explained that because "we invalidate the Board of Review under basic separation-of-powers principles, we need not address respondents' claim that Members of Congress serve in violation of the Incompatibility and Ineligibility Clauses" (Art. I, § 6), or the Appointments Clause, Art. II, § 2, cl. 2. White, J., joined by Rehnquist, C.J. & Marshall, J., dissented, objecting that the "Court strikes down yet another innovative and otherwise lawful governmental experiment, in the name of separation of powers."

Synar, "the Constitution does not permit an agent of Congress to exercise it." Alternatively, if the power is legislative, then, under *INS v. Chadha,* the Board of Review is invalid because Congress may exercise legislative power only "in conformity with the bicameralism and presentment requirements of Art. I, § 7."

5–10. TERM LIMITS ON U.S. SENATORS AND REPRESENTATIVES

U.S. TERM LIMITS, INC. v. THORNTON
514 U.S. 779, 115 S.Ct. 1842, 131 L.Ed.2d 881 (1995).

JUSTICE STEVENS delivered the opinion of the Court.

The Constitution sets forth qualifications for membership in the Congress of the United States. Article I, § 2, cl. 2, which applies to the House of Representatives, provides:

"No Person shall be a Representative who shall not have attained to the Age of twenty five Years, and been seven Years a Citizen of the United States, and who shall not, when elected, be an Inhabitant of that State in which he shall be chosen."

Article I, § 3, cl. 3, which applies to the Senate, similarly provides:

"No Person shall be a Senator who shall not have attained to the Age of thirty Years, and been nine Years a Citizen of the United States, and who shall not, when elected, be an Inhabitant of that State for which he shall be chosen."

Today's cases present a challenge to an amendment to the Arkansas State Constitution that prohibits the name of an otherwise-eligible candidate for Congress from appearing on the general election ballot if that candidate has already served three terms in the House of Representatives or two terms in the Senate. The Arkansas Supreme Court held that the amendment violates the Federal Constitution. We agree with that holding. Such a state-imposed restriction is contrary to the "fundamental principle of our representative democracy," embodied in the Constitution, that "the people should choose whom they please to govern them." *Powell v. McCormack,* 395 U.S. 486, 547, 89 S.Ct. 1944, 1977, 23 L.Ed.2d 491 (1969)(1969)(internal quotation marks omitted). Allowing individual States to adopt their own qualifications for congressional service would be inconsistent with the Framers' vision of a uniform National Legislature representing the people of the United States. If the qualifications set forth in the text of the Constitution are to be changed, that text must be amended.

I. At the general election on November 3, 1992, the voters of Arkansas adopted Amendment 73 to their State Constitution. Proposed as a "Term Limitation Amendment," its preamble stated:

"The people of Arkansas find and declare that elected officials who remain in office too long become preoccupied with reelection and ignore their duties as representatives of the people. Entrenched incumbency has reduced voter participation and has led to an electoral system that is less free, less competitive, and less representative than the system established by the Founding Fathers. Therefore, the people of Arkansas, exercising their reserved powers, herein limit the terms of the elected officials.''

The limitations in Amendment 73 apply to three categories of elected officials. Section 1 [limits elected official in the executive branch of state government to 4–year terms. Section 2 limits members of the Arkansas House to three 2–year terms and members of the Arkansas Senate to two 4–year terms. The Arkansas Supreme Court upheld the term limits on members of the executive branch and legislative branch of the state government; those sections of Amendment 73 were not before the U.S. Supreme Court.] Section 3, the provision at issue in these cases, applies to the Arkansas Congressional Delegation. It provides:

> "(a) Any person having been elected to three or more terms as a member of the United States House of Representatives from Arkansas shall not be certified as a candidate and shall not be eligible to have his/her name placed on the ballot for election to the United States House of Representatives from Arkansas.

> "(b) Any person having been elected to two or more terms as a member of the United States Senate from Arkansas shall not be certified as a candidate and shall not be eligible to have his/her name placed on the ballot for election to the United States Senate from Arkansas."

Amendment 73 states that it is self-executing and shall apply to all persons seeking election after January 1, 1993.

II. [T]he constitutionality of Amendment 73 depends critically on the resolution of two distinct issues. The first is whether the Constitution forbids States from adding to or altering the qualifications specifically enumerated in the Constitution. The second is, if the Constitution does so forbid, whether the fact that Amendment 73 is formulated as a ballot access restriction rather than as an outright disqualification is of constitutional significance. Our resolution of these issues draws upon our prior resolution of a related but distinct issue: whether Congress has the power to add to or alter the qualifications of its Members.

Twenty-six years ago, in *Powell v. McCormack,* we reviewed the history and text of the Qualifications Clauses in a case involving an attempted exclusion of a duly elected Member of Congress. The principal issue was whether the power granted to each House in Art. I, § 5, to judge the "Qualifications of its own Members" includes the power to impose qualifications other than those set forth in the text of the Constitution. [W]e held that it does not. [*Powell*] establishes two important propositions: first, that the "relevant historical materials" compel the conclusion that, at least with respect to qualifications imposed by Congress, the Framers intended the qualifications listed in the Constitution to be exclusive; and second, that that conclusion is equally compelled by an understanding of the "fundamental principle of our representative democracy ... 'that the people should choose whom they please to govern them.' " ...

III. Our reaffirmation of *Powell* does not necessarily resolve the specific questions presented in these cases. ... Petitioners argue that the Constitution contains no express prohibition against state-added qualifications, and that Amendment 73 is therefore an appropriate exercise of a State's reserved power to place additional restrictions on the choices that its own voters may make. We disagree for two independent reasons. First, we conclude that the power to add qualifications is not within the "original powers" of the States, and thus is not reserved to the States by the Tenth Amendment. Second, even if States possessed some original power in this area, we conclude that the Framers intended the Constitution to be the exclusive source of qualifications for members of Congress, and that the Framers thereby "divested" States of any power to add qualifications. ...

Source of the Power

Contrary to petitioners' assertions, the power to add qualifications is not part of the original powers of sovereignty that the Tenth Amendment reserved to the States. Petitioners' Tenth Amendment argument misconceives the nature of the right at issue because that Amendment could only "reserve" that which existed before. As Justice Story recognized, "... No state can say, that it has reserved, what it never possessed." 1 Story [Commentaries on the Constitution] § 627.

Justice Story's position thus echoes that of Chief Justice Marshall in *McCulloch v. Maryland,* 4 Wheat. 316 (1819). In *McCulloch,* the Court rejected the argument that the Constitution's silence on the subject of state power to tax corporations chartered by Congress implies that the States have "reserved" power to tax such federal instrumentalities. As Chief Justice Marshall pointed out, an "original right to tax" such federal entities "never existed, and the question whether it has been surrendered, cannot arise." In language that presaged Justice Story's argument, Chief Justice Marshall concluded: "This opinion does not deprive the States of any resources which they originally possessed."

With respect to setting qualifications for service in Congress, no such right existed before the Constitution was ratified. ... Art. I, § 5, cl. 1 provides: "Each House shall be the Judge of the Elections, Returns and Qualifications of its own Members." The text of the Constitution thus gives the representatives of all the people the final say in judging the qualifications of the representatives of any one State. For this reason, the dissent falters when it states that "the people of Georgia have no say over whom the people of Massachusetts select to represent them in Congress."

Two other sections of the Constitution further support our view of the Framers' vision. First, consistent with Story's view, the Constitution provides that the salaries of representatives should "be ascertained by Law, and paid out of the Treasury of the United States," Art. I, § 6, rather than by individual States. The salary provisions reflect the view that representatives owe their allegiance to the people, and not to States. Second, the provisions governing elections reveal the Framers' understanding that powers over the election of federal officers had to be delegated to, rather than reserved by, the States. It is surely no coincidence that the context of federal elections provides one of the few areas in which the Constitution expressly requires action by the States, namely that "[t]he Times, Places and Manner of holding Elections for Senators and Representatives, shall be prescribed in each State by the legislature thereof." This duty parallels the duty under Article II that "Each State shall appoint, in such Manner as the Legislature thereof may direct, a Number of Electors." Art. II, § 1, cl. 2. These Clauses are express delegations of power to the States to act with respect to federal elections.

[A]ny state power to set the qualifications for membership in Congress must derive not from the reserved powers of state sovereignty, but rather from the delegated powers of national sovereignty. In the absence of any constitutional delegation to the States of power to add qualifications to those enumerated in the Constitution, such a power does not exist.

The Preclusion of State Power

Even if we believed that States possessed as part of their original powers some control over congressional qualifications, the text and structure of the Constitution, the relevant historical materials, and, most importantly, the "basic principles of our democratic system" all demonstrate that the Qualifications Clauses were intended to preclude the States from exercising any such power and to fix as exclusive the qualifications in the Constitution. . . .

The Convention and Ratification Debates

The available affirmative evidence indicates the Framers' intent that States have no role in the setting of qualifications. In Federalist Paper No. 52, dealing with the House of Representatives, Madison addressed the "qualifications of the electors and the elected." . . . Madison then explicitly contrasted the state control over the qualifications of electors with the lack of state control over the qualifications of the elected:

"The qualifications of the elected, being less carefully and properly defined by the State constitutions, and being at the same time more susceptible of uniformity, have been very properly considered and regulated by the convention. A representative of the United States must be of the age of twenty-five years; must have been seven years a citizen of the United States; must, at the time of his election be an inhabitant of the State he is to represent; and, during the time of his service must be in no office under the United States. Under these reasonable limitations, the door of this part of the federal government is open to merit of every description, whether native or adoptive, whether young or old, and without regard to poverty or wealth, or to any particular profession of religious faith."

Madison emphasized this same idea in Federalist 57. . . .

We also find compelling the complete absence in the ratification debates of any assertion that States had the power to add qualifications. In those debates, the question whether to require term limits, or "rotation," was a major source of controversy. The draft of the Constitution that was submitted for ratification contained no provision for rotation. . . . Even proponents of ratification expressed concern about the "abandonment in every instance of the necessity of rotation in office."[24] . . . [N]owhere in the extensive ratification debates have we found any statement by either a proponent or an opponent of rotation that the draft constitution would permit States to require rotation for the representatives of their own citizens. . . .

Democratic Principles

. . . Permitting individual States to formulate diverse qualifications for their representatives would result in a patchwork of state qualifications, undermining the uniformity and the national character that the Framers envisioned and sought to ensure. Such a patchwork would also sever the direct link that the Framers found so critical between the National Government and the people of the United States.[32]

State Practice

Petitioners [argue] that the practice of the States immediately after the adoption of the Constitution demonstrates their understanding that they possessed such power. One may properly question the extent to which the States' own practice is a reliable indicator of the contours of restrictions that the Constitution imposed on States, especially when no court has ever upheld a state-imposed qualification of any sort. But petitioners' argument is unpersuasive even on its own terms. At the time of the Convention, "[a]lmost all the State Constitutions required members of their Legislatures to possess considerable property." Despite this near uniformity, only one State, Virginia, placed similar restrictions on members of Congress, requiring that a representative be, inter alia, a "freeholder." Just 15 years after imposing a property qualification, Virginia replaced that requirement with a provision requiring that

---

24. 4 Letter of December 20, 1787 from Thomas Jefferson to James Madison. In 1814, in another private letter, Jefferson expressed the opinion that the States had not abandoned the power to impose term limits. See Letter of Jan. 31, 1814 to Joseph C. Cabell. Though he noted that his reasoning on the matter "appears to me to be sound," he went on to note:

"but, on so recent a change of view, caution requires us not to be too confident, and that we admit this to be one of the doubtful questions on which honest men may differ with the purest of motives; and the more

readily, as we find we have differed from ourselves on it."

The text of Jefferson's response clearly belies the dissent's suggestion that Jefferson "himself did not entertain serious doubts of its correctness."

32. There is little significance to the fact that Amendment 73 was adopted by a popular vote, rather than as an act of the state legislature. . . . This is proper, because the voters of Arkansas, in adopting Amendment 73, were acting as citizens of the State of Arkansas, and not as citizens of the National Government. . . .

representatives be only "qualified according to the constitution of the United States." ...

The contemporaneous state practice with respect to term limits is similar. At the time of the Convention, States widely supported term limits in at least some circumstances. The Articles of Confederation contained a provision for term limits.... Despite this widespread support, no State sought to impose any term limits on its own federal representatives....

IV. Petitioners argue that, even if States may not add qualifications, Amendment 73 is constitutional because it is not such a qualification, and because Amendment 73 is a permissible exercise of state power to regulate the "Times, Places and Manner of Holding Elections." We reject these contentions.

Unlike §§ 1 and 2 of Amendment 73, which create absolute bars to service for long-term incumbents running for state office, § 3 merely provides that certain Senators and Representatives shall not be certified as candidates and shall not have their names appear on the ballot. They may run as write-in candidates and, if elected, they may serve. Petitioners contend that only a legal bar to service creates an impermissible qualification, and that Amendment 73 is therefore consistent with the Constitution.

Petitioners support their restrictive definition of qualifications with language from *Storer v. Brown,* 415 U.S. 724, 94 S.Ct. 1274, 39 L.Ed.2d 714 (1974), in which we faced a constitutional challenge to provisions of the California Elections Code that regulated the procedures by which both independent candidates and candidates affiliated with qualified political parties could obtain ballot position in general elections. The Code required candidates affiliated with a qualified party to win a primary election, and required independents to make timely filing of nomination papers signed by at least 5% of the entire vote cast in the last general election. The Code also denied ballot position to independents who had voted in the most recent primary election or who had registered their affiliation with a qualified party during the previous year.

In *Storer,* we rejected the argument that the challenged procedures created additional qualifications as "wholly without merit." We noted that petitioners "would not have been disqualified had they been nominated at a party primary or by an adequately supported independent petition and then elected at the general election." We concluded that the California Code "no more establishes an additional requirement for the office of Representative than the requirement that the candidate win the primary to secure a place on the general ballot or otherwise demonstrate substantial community support." Petitioners maintain that, under *Storer,* Amendment 73 is not a qualification....

In our view, Amendment 73 is an indirect attempt to accomplish what the Constitution prohibits Arkansas from accomplishing directly. As the plurality opinion of the Arkansas Supreme Court recognized,

Amendment 73 is an "effort to dress eligibility to stand for Congress in ballot access clothing," because the "intent and the effect of Amendment 73 are to disqualify congressional incumbents from further service." We must, of course, accept the State Court's view of the purpose of its own law: we are thus authoritatively informed that the sole purpose of § 3 of Amendment 73 was to attempt to achieve a result that is forbidden by the Federal Constitution. Indeed, it cannot be seriously contended that the intent behind Amendment 73 is other than to prevent the election of incumbents. The preamble of Amendment 73 states explicitly: "[T]he people of Arkansas ... herein limit the terms of elected officials." ...

Petitioners do, however, contest the Arkansas Supreme Court's conclusion that the Amendment has the same practical effect as an absolute bar. They argue that the possibility of a write-in campaign creates a real possibility for victory, especially for an entrenched incumbent. One may reasonably question the merits of that contention. [E]ven if petitioners are correct that incumbents may occasionally win reelection as write-in candidates, there is no denying that the ballot restrictions will make it significantly more difficult for the barred candidate to win the election. In our view, an amendment with the avowed purpose and obvious effect of evading the requirements of the Qualifications Clauses by handicapping a class of candidates cannot stand. ...

Petitioners make the related argument that Amendment 73 merely regulates the "Manner" of elections, and that the Amendment is therefore a permissible exercise of state power under Article I, § 4, cl. 1 (the Elections Clause) to regulate the "Times, Places and Manner" of elections. We cannot agree.

A necessary consequence of petitioners' argument is that Congress itself would have the power to "make or alter" a measure such as Amendment 73. Art. I, § 4, cl. 1. That the Framers would have approved of such a result is unfathomable. As our decision in *Powell* and our discussion above make clear, the Framers were particularly concerned that a grant to Congress of the authority to set its own qualifications would lead inevitably to congressional self-aggrandizement and the upsetting of the delicate constitutional balance. ...

Moreover, petitioners' broad construction of the Elections Clause is fundamentally inconsistent with the Framers' view of that Clause. The Framers intended the Elections Clause to grant States authority to create procedural regulations, not to provide States with license to exclude classes of candidates from federal office. ...

Our cases interpreting state power under the Elections Clause reflect the same understanding. ... For example, in *Storer v. Brown,* the case on which petitioners place principal reliance, we upheld the validity of certain provisions of the California Election Code. In so doing, we emphasized the States' interest in having orderly, fair, and honest elections "rather than chaos." We also recognized the "States' strong interest in maintaining the integrity of the political process by preventing interparty raiding," and explained that the specific requirements applicable to independents were "expressive of a general state policy aimed at maintaining the integrity of the various routes to the ballot." In other cases, we have approved the States' interests in avoiding "voter confusion, ballot overcrowding, or the presence of frivolous candidacies," in "seeking to assure that elections are operated equitably and efficiently," and in "guard[ing] against irregularity and error in the tabulation of votes." In short, we have approved of state regulations designed to ensure that elections are " 'fair and honest and . . . [that] some sort of order, rather than chaos, . . . accompan[ies] the democratic processes.' "

The provisions at issue in *Storer* and our other Elections Clause cases were thus constitutional because they regulated election *procedures* and did not even arguably impose any substantive qualification rendering a class of potential candidates ineligible for ballot position. [C]ases upholding state regulations of election procedures thus provide little support for the contention that a state-imposed ballot access restriction is constitutional when it is undertaken for the twin goals of disadvantaging a particular class of candidates and evading the dictates of the Qualifications Clauses.[48]

[The dissent challenges] the assertion that the Arkansas amendment has the likely effect of creating a qualification, and suggesting that the true intent of Amendment 73 was not to evade the Qualifications Clause but rather to simply "level the playing field." Neither of these objections has merit.

As to the first, it is simply irrelevant to our holding today. As we note above, our prior cases strongly suggest that write-in candidates will have only a slim chance of success, and the Arkansas plurality agreed. However, we expressly do not rest on this Court's prior observations regarding write-in candidates. Instead, we hold that a state amendment is unconstitutional when it has the likely effect of handicapping a class of candidates and has the sole purpose of creating additional qualifications indirectly. Thus, the dissent's discussion of the evidence concerning the possibility that a popular incumbent will win a write-in election is simply beside the point.

As to the second argument, we find wholly unpersuasive the dissent's suggestion that Amendment 73 was designed merely to "level the playing field." [I]t is obvious that the sole purpose of Amendment 73 was to limit the terms of elected officials, both State and federal, and that Amendment 73, therefore, may not stand. . . .

---

48. Nor does *Clements v. Fashing*, 457 U.S. 957, 102 S.Ct. 2836, 73 L.Ed.2d 508 (1982) support petitioners. In *Clements*, the Court rejected First and Fourteenth Amendment challenges to Texas' so-called "resign-to-run" provision. That provision treated an elected state official's declaration of candidacy for another elected office as an automatic resignation from the office then held. We noted that the regulation was a permissible attempt to regulate state office-holders. See *id.*, at 972 ("Appellees are elected state officeholders who contest restrictions on partisan political activity.")(emphasis deleted); *id.*, at 974, n. 1 (Stevens, J., concurring in part and concurring in judgment)("The fact that appellees hold state office is sufficient to justify a restriction on their ability to run for other office that is not imposed on the public generally"). . . .

The judgment is affirmed.

It is so ordered.

JUSTICE THOMAS, with whom THE CHIEF JUSTICE [REHNQUIST], JUSTICE O'CONNOR, and JUSTICE SCALIA join, dissenting.

It is ironic that the Court bases today's decision on the right of the people to "choose whom they please to govern them." Under our Constitution, there is only one State whose people have the right to "choose whom they please" to represent Arkansas in Congress. The Court holds, however, that neither the elected legislature of that State nor the people themselves (acting by ballot initiative) may prescribe any qualifications for those representatives. The majority therefore defends the right of the people of Arkansas to "choose whom they please to govern them" by invalidating a provision that won nearly 60% of the votes cast in a direct election and that carried every congressional district in the State.

I dissent. Nothing in the Constitution deprives the people of each State of the power to prescribe eligibility requirements for the candidates who seek to represent them in Congress. The Constitution is simply silent on this question. And where the Constitution is silent, it raises no bar to action by the States or the people.

I

Because the majority fundamentally misunderstands the notion of "reserved" powers, I start with some first principles. Contrary to the majority's suggestion, the people of the States need not point to any affirmative grant of power in the Constitution in order to prescribe qualifications for their representatives in Congress, or to authorize their elected state legislators to do so. . . .

When they adopted the Federal Constitution, of course, the people of each State surrendered some of their authority to the United States (and hence to entities accountable to the people of other States as well as to themselves). They affirmatively deprived their States of certain powers, see, *e.g.,* Art. I, § 10, and they affirmatively conferred certain powers upon the Federal Government, see, *e.g.,* Art. I, § 8. Because the people of the several States are the only true source of power, however, the Federal Government enjoys no authority beyond what the Constitution confers: the Federal Government's powers are limited and enumerated.
. . .

In each State, the remainder of the people's powers—"[t]he powers not delegated to the United States by the Constitution, nor prohibited by it to the States," Amdt. 10—are either delegated to the state government or retained by the people. The Federal Constitution does not specify which of these two possibilities obtains; it is up to the various state constitutions to declare which powers the people of each State have delegated to their state government. As far as the Federal Constitution is concerned, then, the States can exercise all powers that the Constitution does not withhold from them. The Federal Government and the States thus face different default rules: where the Constitution is silent about the exercise of a particular power—that is, where the Constitution does not speak either expressly or by necessary implication—the Federal Government lacks that power and the States enjoy it. . . .

Any ambiguity in the Tenth Amendment's use of the phrase "the people" is cleared up by the body of the Constitution itself. Article I begins by providing that the Congress of the United States enjoys "[a]ll legislative Powers herein granted," § 1, and goes on to give a careful enumeration of Congress' powers, § 8. It then concludes by enumerating certain powers that are *prohibited* to the States. The import of this structure is the same as the import of the Tenth Amendment: if we are to invalidate Arkansas' Amendment 73, we must point to something in the Federal Constitution that deprives the people of Arkansas of the power to enact such measures.

The majority disagrees that it bears this burden. [It] begins by announcing an enormous and untenable limitation on the principle expressed by the Tenth Amendment. [Its] essential logic is that the state governments could not "reserve" any powers that they did not control at the time the Constitution was drafted. But it was not the state governments that were doing the reserving. The Constitution derives its authority instead from the consent of *the people* of the States. Given the fundamental principle that all governmental powers stem from the people of the States, it would simply be incoherent to assert that the people of the States could not reserve any powers that they had not previously controlled.

The Tenth Amendment's use of the word "reserved" does not help the majority's position. If someone says that the power to use a particular facility is reserved to some group, he is not saying anything about whether that group has previously used the facility. . . .

[Unlike *Garcia v. San Antonio Metropolitan Transit Authority* (1985), the] question raised by the present case, however, is not whether any principle of state sovereignty implicit in the Tenth Amendment bars congressional action that Article I appears to authorize, but rather whether Article I bars state action that it does not appear to forbid. The principle necessary to answer this question is express on the Tenth Amendment's face: unless the Federal Constitution affirmatively prohibits an action by the States or the people, it raises no bar to such action.

The majority also seeks support for its view of the Tenth Amendment in *McCulloch v. Maryland*. But this effort is misplaced. *McCulloch* did make clear that a power need not be "expressly" delegated to the United States or prohibited to the States in order to fall outside the Tenth Amendment's reservation; delegations and prohibitions can also arise by necessary implication. True to the text of the Tenth Amendment, however, *McCulloch* indicated that all powers as to which the Constitution does not speak (whether expressly or by necessary implication) are "reserved" to the state level. Thus, in its only discussion of the Tenth Amendment, *McCulloch* observed that the Amendment "leav[es] the question, whether the particular power which may become the subject of contest has been delegated to the one government, or prohibited to the other, to depend on a fair construction of the whole [Constitution]." *McCulloch* did not qualify this observation by indicating that the question also turned on whether the States had enjoyed the power before the framing. To the contrary, *McCulloch* seemed to assume that the people had "conferred on the general government the power contained in the constitution, and on the States the whole residuum of power." *Id.* . . . .

For the past 175 years, *McCulloch* has been understood to rest on the proposition that the Constitution affirmatively barred Maryland from imposing its tax on the Bank's operations. . . . For the majority, however, *McCulloch* apparently turned on the fact that before the Constitution was adopted, the States had possessed no power to tax the instrumentalities of the governmental institutions that the Constitution created. This understanding of *McCulloch* makes most of Chief Justice Marshall's opinion irrelevant; according to the majority, there was no need to inquire into whether federal law deprived Maryland of the power in question, because the power could not fall into the category of "reserved" powers anyway.

Despite the majority's citation of *Garcia* and *McCulloch,* the only true support for its view of the Tenth Amendment comes from Joseph Story's 1833 treatise on constitutional law. See 2 J. Story, Commentaries on the Constitution of the United States §§ 623–628. Justice Story was a brilliant and accomplished man, and one cannot casually dismiss his views. On the other hand, he was not a member of the Founding generation, and his Commentaries on the Constitution were written a half century after the framing. Rather than representing the original understanding of the Constitution, they represent only his own understanding. . . .

The majority also sketches out what may be an alternative (and narrower) argument. Again citing Story, the majority suggests that it would be inconsistent with the notion of "national sovereignty" for the States or the people of the States to have any reserved powers over the selection of Members of Congress. [W]hile the majority is correct that the Framers expected the selection process to create a "direct link" between members of the House of Representatives and the people, the link was between the Representatives from each State and the people of that State; the people of Georgia have no say over whom the people of Massachusetts select to represent them in Congress. This arrangement must baffle the majority, whose understanding of Congress would surely fit more comfortably within a system of nationwide elections. . . .

The majority seeks support from the Constitution's specification that Members of Congress "shall receive a Compensation for their Services, to be ascertained by Law, and paid out of the Treasury of the United States." Art. I, § 6, cl. 1. [T]hat Members of Congress draw a federal salary once they have assembled hardly means that the people of the States lack reserved powers over the selection of their representatives. . . . Madison specifically indicated that even with the compensation provision in place, the individual States still enjoyed the reserved power to supplement the federal salary. . . .

In fact, the Constitution's treatment of Presidential elections actively contradicts the majority's position. While the individual States have no "reserved" power to set qualifications for the office of President, we have long understood that they do have the power (as far as the Federal Constitution is concerned) to set qualifications for their Presidential electors—the delegates that each State selects to represent it in the electoral college that actually chooses the Nation's chief executive. [Art. II, § 1, cl. 2] Even respondents do not dispute that the States may establish qualifications for their delegates to the electoral college, as long as those qualifications pass muster under other constitutional provisions (primarily the First and Fourteenth Amendments). As the majority cannot argue that the Constitution affirmatively grants this power, the power must be one that is "reserved" to the States. It necessarily follows that the majority's understanding of the Tenth Amendment is incorrect, for the position of Presidential elector surely " 'spring[s] out of the existence of the national government.' "

In a final effort to deny that the people of the States enjoy "reserved" powers over the selection of their representatives in Congress, the majority suggests that the Constitution expressly delegates to the States certain powers over congressional elections. Such delegations of power, the majority argues, would be superfluous if the people of the States enjoyed reserved powers in this area.

Only one constitutional provision—the Times, Places and Manner Clause of Article I, § 4—even arguably supports the majority's suggestion. [H]owever, this Clause does not delegate any authority to the States. Instead, it simply imposes a duty upon them. The majority gets it exactly right: by specifying that the state legislatures "shall" prescribe the details necessary to hold congressional elections, the Clause "expressly requires action by the States." This command meshes with one of the principal purposes of Congress' "make or alter" power: to ensure that the States hold congressional elections in the first place, so that Congress continues to exist. . . . Constitutional provisions that impose affirmative duties on the States are hardly inconsistent with the notion of reserved powers.

Of course, the second part of the Times, Places and Manner Clause does grant a power rather than impose a duty. As its contrasting uses of the words "shall" and "may" confirm, however, the Clause grants power exclusively to Congress, not to the States. If the Clause did not exist at all, the States would still be able to prescribe the times, places, and manner of holding congressional elections; the deletion of the provision would simply deprive Congress of the power to override these state regulations. . . .

II

I take it to be established, then, that the people of Arkansas do enjoy "reserved" powers over the selection of their representatives in Congress. [W]e may not override the decision of the people of Arkansas unless something in the Federal Constitution deprives them of the power to enact such measures. The majority settles on "the Qualifications Clauses" as the constitutional provisions that Amendment 73 violates....

A. The provisions that are generally known as the Qualifications Clauses [Art. I, § 2, cl. 2 and Art. I, § 3, cl. 3] merely establish *minimum* qualifications. They are quite different from an *exclusive* formulation, such as the following:

> "Every Person who shall have attained to the age of twenty five Years, and been seven Years a Citizen of the United States, and who shall, when elected, be an Inhabitant of that State in which he shall be chosen, shall be eligible to be a Representative."

At least on their face, then, the Qualifications Clauses do nothing to prohibit the people of a State from establishing additional eligibility requirements for their own representatives.

Joseph Story thought that such a prohibition was nonetheless implicit in the constitutional list of qualifications, because "[f]rom the very nature of such a provision, the affirmation of these qualifications would seem to imply a negative of all others." 2 Commentaries on the Constitution of the United States § 624 (1833). This argument rests on the maxim *expressio unius est exclusio alterius*....

[However, at] most, the specification of certain nationwide disqualifications in the Constitution implies the negation of other *nationwide* disqualifications; it does not imply that individual States or their people are barred from adopting their own disqualifications on a state-by-state basis. Thus, the one delegate to the Philadelphia Convention who voiced anything approaching Story's argument said only that a recital of qualifications in the Constitution would imply that *Congress* lacked any qualification-setting power. See 2 Farrand 123 (remarks of John Dickinson).

The Qualifications Clauses do prevent the individual States from abolishing all eligibility requirements for Congress.... If the people of a State decide that they would like their representatives to possess additional qualifications, however, they have done nothing to frustrate the policy behind the Qualifications Clauses. Anyone who possesses all of the constitutional qualifications, plus some qualifications required by state law, still has all of the federal qualifications. [T]he Constitution gives the people of other States no basis to complain if the people of Arkansas elect a freshman representative in preference to a long-term incumbent. That being the case, it is hard to see why the rights of the people of other States have been violated when the people of Arkansas decide to enact a more general disqualification of long-term incumbents. Such a disqualification certainly is subject to scrutiny under other constitutional provisions, such as the First and Fourteenth Amendments. But as long as the candidate whom they send to Congress meets the constitutional age, citizenship, and inhabitancy requirements, the people of Arkansas have not violated the Qualifications Clauses. . . .

As for the majority's related assertion that the Framers intended qualification requirements to be uniform, this is a conclusion, not an argument. Indeed, it is a conclusion that the Qualifications Clauses themselves contradict. At the time of the framing, and for some years thereafter, the Clauses' citizenship requirements incorporated laws that varied from State to State. Thus, the Qualifications Clauses themselves made it possible that a person would be qualified to represent State *A* in Congress even though a similarly situated person would not be qualified to represent State *B*. . . . The very first contested-election case in the House of Representatives, which involved the citizenship of a would-be Congressman from South Carolina, illustrates this principle. As Representative James Madison told his colleagues, "I take it to be a clear point, that we are to be guided, in our decision, by the laws and constitution of South Carolina, so far as they can guide us; and where the laws do not expressly guide us, we must be guided by principles of a general nature. . . . "

[N]either the text nor the apparent purpose of the Qualifications Clauses does anything to refute Thomas Jefferson's elegant legal analysis:

> "Had the Constitution been silent, nobody can doubt but that the right to prescribe all the qualifications and disqualifications of those they would send to represent them, would have belonged to the State. So also the Constitution might have prescribed the whole, and excluded all others. It seems to have preferred the middle way. It has exercised the power in part, by declaring some disqualifications. . . . But it does not declare, itself, that the member shall not be a lunatic, a pauper, a convict of treason, of murder, of felony, or other infamous crime, or a non-resident of his district; nor does it prohibit to the State the power of declaring these, or any other disqualifications which its particular circumstances may call for; and these may be different in different States. Of course, then, by the tenth amendment, the power is reserved to the State." Letter to Joseph C. Cabell (Jan. 31, 1814), in 14 Writings of Thomas Jefferson 82–83 (A. Lipscomb ed. 1904).[14]

B. Although the Qualifications Clauses neither state nor imply the prohibition that it finds in them, the majority infers from the Framers' "democratic principles" that the Clauses must have been generally

---

14. The majority notes Jefferson's concession that state power to supplement the Qualifications Clauses was "one of the doubtful questions on which honest men may differ with the purest motives." See *ante,* n. 24. But while Jefferson cautioned against impugning the motives of people who might disagree with his position, his use of the phrase "[o]f course" suggests that he himself did not entertain serious doubts of its correctness.

understood to preclude the people of the States and their state legislatures from prescribing any additional qualifications for their representatives in Congress. But the majority's evidence on this point establishes only two more modest propositions: (1) the Framers did not want the Federal Constitution itself to impose a broad set of disqualifications for congressional office, and (2) the Framers did not want the Federal Congress to be able to supplement the few disqualifications that the Constitution does set forth. The logical conclusion is simply that the Framers did not want the people of the States and their state legislatures to be constrained by too many qualifications imposed at the national level. The evidence does not support the majority's more sweeping conclusion that the Framers intended to bar the people of the States and their state legislatures from adopting additional eligibility requirements to help narrow their own choices.

I agree with the majority that Congress has no power to prescribe qualifications for its own Members. [N]othing in the Constitution grants Congress this power. In the absence of such a grant, Congress may not act. But deciding whether the Constitution denies the qualification-setting power to the States and the people of the States requires a fundamentally different legal analysis.

Despite the majority's claims to the contrary, this explanation for Congress' incapacity to supplement the Qualifications Clauses is perfectly consistent with the reasoning of *Powell v. McCormack* (1969). [T]he critical question in *Powell* was whether § 5 conferred a qualification-setting power—not whether the Qualifications Clauses took it away....

The fact that the Framers did not grant a qualification-setting power to Congress does not imply that they wanted to bar its exercise at the state level. One reason why the Framers decided not to let Congress prescribe the qualifications of its own members was that incumbents could have used this power to perpetuate themselves or their ilk in office. As Madison pointed out at the Philadelphia Convention, Members of Congress would have an obvious conflict of interest if they could determine who may run against them. 2 Farrand 250. But neither the people of the States nor the state legislatures would labor under the same conflict of interest when prescribing qualifications for Members of Congress, and so the Framers would have had to use a different calculus in determining whether to deprive them of this power.

... The majority never identifies the democratic principles that would have been violated if a state legislature, in the days before the Constitution was amended to provide for the direct election of Senators, had imposed some limits of its own on the field of candidates that it would consider for appointment.[16] Likewise, the majority does not explain why democratic principles forbid the people of a State from

---

16. Oregon, for instance, pioneered a system in which the state legislature bound itself to appoint the candidates chosen in a state-wide vote of the people. See Hills, A Defense of State Constitutional Limits on Federal Congressional Terms, 53 U.Pitt.L.Rev. 97, 108 (1991). The majority is in the uncomfortable position of suggesting that this system violated "democratic principles."

adopting additional eligibility requirements to help narrow their choices among candidates seeking to represent them in the House of Representatives. . . .

In seeking ratification of the Constitution, James Madison did assert that "[u]nder these reasonable limitations [set out in the House Qualifications Clause], the door of this part of the federal government is open to merit of every description. . . . " The Federalist No. 52, at 326. [T]here is no reason to interpret these statements as anything more than claims that the Constitution itself imposes relatively few disqualifications for congressional office. . . .

C. In addition to its arguments about democratic principles, the majority asserts that more specific historical evidence supports its view that the Framers did not intend to permit supplementation of the Qualifications Clauses. But when one focuses on the distinction between congressional power to add qualifications for congressional office and the power of the people or their state legislatures to add such qualifications, one realizes that this assertion has little basis. [*Powell v. McCormack*] has no bearing on the question now before the Court. As the majority ultimately concedes, it does not establish "the Framers' intent that the qualifications in the Constitution be fixed and exclusive;" it shows only that the Framers did not intend Congress to be able to enact qualifications laws. . . .

To the extent that the records from the Philadelphia Convention itself shed light on this case, they tend to hurt the majority's case. The only evidence that directly bears on the question now before the Court comes from the Committee of Detail, a five-member body that the Convention charged with the crucial task of drafting a Constitution to reflect the decisions that the Convention had reached during its first two months of work. . . . The Qualifications Clause for the House of Delegates [what became the House of Representatives] originally read as follows: "The qualifications of a delegate shall be the age of twenty five years at least, and citizenship: *and any person possessing these qualifications may be elected except* [blank space]." (emphasis added). The drafter(s) of this language apparently contemplated that the Committee might want to insert some exceptions to the exclusivity provision. But rather than simply deleting the word "except"—as it might have done if it had decided to have no exceptions at all to the exclusivity provision— the Committee deleted the exclusivity provision itself. In the document that has come down to us, all the words after the colon are crossed out.

The majority speculates that the exclusivity provision may have been deleted as superfluous. But the same draft that contained the exclusivity language in the House Qualifications Clause contained no such language in the Senate Qualifications Clause. Thus, the draft appears to reflect a deliberate judgment to distinguish between the House qualifications and the Senate qualifications, and to make only the former exclusive. If so, then the deletion of the exclusivity provision indicates that the Committee expected neither list of qualifications to be exclusive. . . .

In discussing the ratification period, the majority stresses two principal data. One of these pieces of evidence is no evidence at all—literally. The majority devotes considerable space to the fact that the recorded ratification debates do not contain any affirmative statement that the States can supplement the constitutional qualifications. . . . The majority reasons that delegates at several of the ratifying conventions attacked the Constitution for failing to require Members of Congress to rotate out of office.[23] . . . But the majority's argument cuts both ways. The recorded ratification debates also contain no affirmative statement that the States *cannot* supplement the constitutional qualifications. . . . If the Federal Constitution had been understood to deprive the States of this significant power, one might well have expected its opponents to seize on this point in arguing against ratification. . . .

If one concedes that the absence of relevant records from the ratification debates is not strong evidence for either side, then the majority's only significant piece of evidence from the ratification period is Federalist No. 52. [H]owever, this essay simply does not talk about "the lack of state control over the qualifications of the elected," whether "explicitly" or otherwise. [W]hile Madison did say that the qualifications of the elected were "more susceptible of uniformity" than the qualifications of electors, he did not say that the Constitution prescribes anything but uniform minimum qualifications for congressmen. That, after all, is more than it does for congressional electors.

Nor do I see any reason to infer from Federalist No. 52 that the Framers intended to deprive the States of the power to add to these minimum qualifications. [T]he constitutional text supports the contrary inference. [A]t the time of the framing some States also imposed religious qualifications on state legislators. The Framers evidently did not want States to impose such qualifications on federal legislators, for the Constitution specifically provides that "no religious Test shall ever be required as a Qualification to any Office or public Trust under the United States." Art. VI, cl. 3. Both the context and the plain language of the Clause show that it bars the States as well as the Federal Government from imposing religious disqualifications on federal offices. But the only reason for extending the Clause to the States would be to protect Senators and Representatives from state-imposed religious qualifications. . . . If the *expressio unius* maxim cuts in any direction in this case, then, it undermines the majority's position: the Framers' prohibition on state-imposed religious disqualifications for Members of Congress suggests that other types of state-imposed disqualifications are permissible.

23. . . . Just as individual States could extend the vote to women before the adoption of the Nineteenth Amendment, could prohibit poll taxes before the adoption of the Twenty-fourth Amendment, and could lower the voting age before the adoption of the Twenty-sixth Amendment, so the Framers' decision not to impose a nationwide limit on congressional terms did not itself bar States from adopting limits of their own.

See Rotunda, Rethinking Term Limits for Federal Legislators in Light of the Structure of the Constitution, 73 Ore.L.Rev. 561, 574 (1994).

More than a century ago, this Court was asked to invalidate a Michigan election law because it called for Presidential electors to be elected on a district-by-district basis rather than being chosen by "the State" as a whole. See Art. II, § 1, cl. 2. Conceding that the Constitution might be ambiguous on this score, the Court asserted that "where there is ambiguity or doubt, or where two views may well be entertained, contemporaneous and subsequent practical construction[s] are entitled to the greatest weight." *McPherson v. Blacker*, 146 U.S. 1, 13 S.Ct. 3, 36 L.Ed. 869 (1892). The Court then described the district-based selection processes used in 2 of the 10 States that participated in the first presidential election in 1788, 3 of the 15 States that participated in 1792, and 5 of the 16 States that participated in 1796. Though acknowledging that in subsequent years "most of the States adopted the general ticket system," the Court nonetheless found this history "decisive" proof of the constitutionality of the district method. Thus, the Court resolved its doubts in favor of the state law, "the contemporaneous practical exposition of the Constitution being too strong and obstinate to be shaken.... "

Here too, state practice immediately after the ratification of the Constitution refutes the majority's suggestion that the Qualifications Clauses were commonly understood as being exclusive. Five States supplemented the constitutional disqualifications in their very first election laws, and the surviving records suggest that the legislatures of these States considered and rejected the interpretation of the Constitution that the majority adopts today.

[Moreover], while the Constitution merely requires representatives to be inhabitants of their State, the legislatures of five of the seven States that divided themselves into districts for House elections added that representatives also had to be inhabitants of the district that elected them. Three of these States adopted durational residency requirements too, insisting that representatives have resided within their districts for at least a year (or, in one case, three years) before being elected....

III

It is radical enough for the majority to hold that the Constitution implicitly precludes the people of the States from prescribing any eligibility requirements for the congressional candidates who seek their votes. This holding, after all, does not stop with negating the term limits that many States have seen fit to impose on their Senators and Representatives. Today's decision also means that no State may disqualify congressional candidates whom a court has found to be mentally incompetent, see, *e.g.*, Fla.Stat. §§ 97.041(2), 99.021(1)(a)(1991), who are currently in prison, see, *e.g.*, Ill.Comp.Stat.Ann., ch. 10, §§ 5/3–5, 5/7–10, 5/10–5 (1993 and West Supp.1995), or who have past vote-fraud convictions, see, *e.g.*, Ga.Code Ann. §§ 21–2–2(25), 21–2–8 (1993 and Supp.1994). Likewise, after today's decision, the people of each State must leave open the possibility that they will trust someone with their vote in Congress even though they do not trust him with *a* vote in the election for Congress. See, *e.g.*, R.I.Gen.Laws § 17–14–1.2 (1988)(restricting candidacy to people "qualified to vote").

In order to invalidate § 3 of Amendment 73, however, the majority must go farther. The bulk of the majority's analysis—like Part II of my dissent—addresses the issues that would be raised if Arkansas had prescribed "genuine, unadulterated, undiluted term limits." See Rotunda, 73 Ore.L.Rev., at 570. But as the parties have agreed, Amendment 73 does not actually create this kind of disqualification. It does not say that covered candidates may not serve any more terms in Congress if reelected, and it does not indirectly achieve the same result by barring those candidates from seeking reelection. It says only that if they are to win reelection, they must do so by write-in votes.

One might think that this is a distinction without a difference. As the majority notes, "[t]he uncontested data submitted to the Arkansas Supreme Court" show that write-in candidates have won only six congressional elections in this century. But while the data's accuracy is indeed "uncontested," petitioners filed an equally uncontested affidavit challenging the data's relevance. As political science professor James S. Fay swore to the Arkansas Supreme Court, "[m]ost write-in candidacies in the past have been waged by fringe candidates, with little public support and extremely low name identification." To the best of Professor Fay's knowledge, in modern times only two incumbent Congressmen have ever sought reelection as write-in candidates. One of them was Dale Alford of Arkansas, who had first entered the House of Representatives by winning 51% of the vote as a write-in candidate in 1958; Alford then waged a write-in campaign for reelection in 1960, winning a landslide 83% of the vote against an opponent who enjoyed a place on the ballot. The other incumbent write-in candidate was Philip J. Philbin of Massachusetts, who—despite losing his party primary and thus his spot on the ballot—won 27% of the vote in his unsuccessful write-in candidacy. According to Professor Fay, these results—coupled with other examples of successful write-in campaigns, such as Ross Perot's victory in North Dakota's 1992 Democratic presidential primary—"demonstrate that when a write-in candidate is well-known and well-funded, it is quite possible for him or her to win an election."

[T]he majority emphasizes another purported conclusion of the Arkansas Supreme Court. As the majority notes, the plurality below asserted that "[t]he intent" of Amendment 73 was "to disqualify congressional incumbents from further service." . . . I am not sure why the intent behind a law should affect our analysis under the Qualifications Clauses. The majority nonetheless thinks it clear that the goal of § 3 is "to prevent the election of incumbents." In reaching this conclusion at the summary-judgment stage, however, the majority has given short shrift to petitioners' contrary claim. . . . One of petitioners' central arguments is that congressionally conferred advantages have artificially inflated the pre-existing electoral chances of the covered candidates, and that Amendment 73 is merely designed to level the playing field on which challengers compete with them.

To understand this argument requires some background. Current federal law (enacted, of course, by congressional incumbents) confers numerous advantages on incumbents, and these advantages are widely thought to make it "significantly more difficult" for challengers to defeat them. For instance, federal law gives incumbents enormous advantages in building name recognition and good will in their home districts. See, *e.g.,* 39 U.S.C. § 3210 (permitting Members of Congress to send "franked" mail free of charge); 2 U.S.C. §§ 61–1, 72a, 332 (permitting Members to have sizable taxpayer-funded staffs); 2 U.S.C. § 123b (establishing the House Recording Studio and the Senate Recording and Photographic Studios). At the same time that incumbent Members of Congress enjoy these in-kind benefits, Congress imposes spending and contribution limits in congressional campaigns that "can prevent challengers from spending more . . . to overcome their disadvantage in name recognition." Many observers believe that the campaign-finance laws also give incumbents an "enormous fund-raising edge" over their challengers by giving a large financing role to entities with incentives to curry favor with incumbents. In addition, the internal rules of Congress put a substantial premium on seniority, with the result that each Member's already plentiful opportunities to distribute benefits to his constituents increase with the length of his tenure. In this manner, Congress effectively "fines" the electorate for voting against incumbents.

Cynics see no accident in any of this. . . . Even in the November 1994 elections, which are widely considered to have effected the most sweeping change in Congress in recent memory, 90 percent of the incumbents who sought reelection to the House were successful, and nearly half of the losers were completing only their first terms. Only 2 of the 26 Senate incumbents seeking reelection were defeated, and one of them had been elected for the first time in a special election only a few years earlier.

The voters of Arkansas evidently believe that incumbents would not enjoy such overwhelming success if electoral contests were truly fair— that is, if the government did not put its thumb on either side of the scale. The majority offers no reason to question the accuracy of this belief. [P]etitioners portray § 3 of Amendment 73 as an effort at the state level to offset the electoral advantages that congressional incumbents have conferred upon themselves at the federal level. . . .

I do not mean to suggest that States have unbridled power to handicap particular classes of candidates, even when those candidates enjoy federally conferred advantages that may threaten to skew the electoral process. But laws that allegedly have the purpose and effect of handicapping a particular class of candidates traditionally are reviewed under the First and Fourteenth Amendments rather than the Qualifications Clauses. Compare *Storer v. Brown* (undertaking a lengthy First and Fourteenth Amendment analysis of a California rule that denied ballot access to any independent candidate for Congress who had not severed his ties to a political party at least one year prior to the immediately preceding primary election, or 17 months before the general election) with *id.*, n. 16 (dismissing as "wholly without merit" the notion that this rule might violate the Qualifications Clauses). Term-limit measures have tended to survive such review without difficulty. See, *e.g., Moore v. McCartney*, 425 U.S. 946, 96 S.Ct. 1689, 48 L.Ed.2d 190 (1976)(dismissing an appeal on the ground that limits on the terms of state officeholders do not even raise a substantial federal question under the First and Fourteenth Amendments).

To analyze such laws under the Qualifications Clauses may open up whole new vistas for courts. If it is true that "the current congressional campaign finance system ... has created an electoral system so stacked against challengers that in many elections voters have no real choices," are the Federal Election Campaign Act Amendments of 1974 unconstitutional under (of all things) the Qualifications Clauses? .... The majority's opinion may not go so far, although it does not itself suggest any principled stopping point. No matter how narrowly construed, however, today's decision reads the Qualifications Clauses to impose substantial implicit prohibitions on the States and the people of the States.... Rather, I would read the Qualifications Clauses to do no more than what they say. I respectfully dissent.

[The opinion of Kennedy, J., concurring, is omitted.]

Notes

1. After the decision, Ray Thornton, the Arkansas legislator who was the respondent in this case, announced that he would retire next year, after having served six years in the House. "The people of Arkansas," he declared, "have said term limits are desired, and I will honor that."

2. If Justice Stevens had agreed with Justice Thomas on the meaning and relevance of the Tenth Amendment, would Stevens have been obligated to come out differently, or could Stevens have still ruled that state-imposed term limits are unconstitutional? Recall that Thomas says that "a power need not be 'expressly' delegated to the United States or prohibited to the States in order to fall outside the Tenth Amendment's reservation.... " Does not Thomas accept the concept of implied powers?

3. In *Storer v. Brown*, 415 U.S. 724, 94 S.Ct. 1274, 39 L.Ed.2d 714 (1974), discussed by both the majority and dissent in *Thornton*, a California law forbade ballot access on various grounds. One of the grounds, § 6830(d), denied ballot access to an independent candidate for elective office if he had registered his affiliation with a political party within one year prior to the immediately preceding primary election. Therefore, two candidates who had been registered Democrats within a year prior to the 1972 primary could not get on the ballot to run as independents for Congress. The law, which imposes "a substantial barrier" against independent candidates, "furthers the State's interest in the stability of its political system." The majority (6 to 3) upheld this section and rejected the claim that § 6830(d) established an additional qualification for office: "The non-affiliation requirement no more

establishes an additional requirement for the office of Representative than the requirement that the candidate win the primary to secure a place on the general ballot or otherwise demonstrate substantial community support." Also, "the independent candidate who cannot qualify for the ballot may nevertheless resort to the write-in alternative. . . . "

4. Assume that a state is divided into 10 districts. Would it be unconstitutional for a state to require that all candidates for U.S. Representative run by district and that they all be *residents* of the district in which they run?

If there is no district residency requirement, is there still a "qualification" for office if the state requires that the candidates run and win by district? In other words, assume that in district #1, Candidate *A* wins because she has 100 more votes than Candidate *B*. However, assume further that Candidate *B* has more votes than any of the other candidates in the other nine districts. Perhaps, in the other districts, there was low voter turnout, or third party candidates. Candidate *B* does not win a seat because—even though she received the second highest vote total in all 10 districts (even though she received more votes than any other candidate except one)—she did not receive the votes in the right district. Is this district requirement a "qualification" for office?

5. The Arkansas law is written as a ballot access law, not as a permanent disqualification from office. During oral argument, counsel for the respondents agreed with Justice Scalia that the Arkansas law is not a "qualification." When asked by Justice Stevens whether the respondents conceded that the ballot access is not a qualification, he answered, "Yes," to which Stevens responded: "That's a major concession." 63 U.S. Law Week, at 3453 (U.S. Dec. 13, 1994). Consequently, at the end of Stevens' opinion, he did not simply invalidate the Arkansas law. First, he had to show that it was really a term limit law.

If another state enacted a ballot access restriction like the kind imposed by Arkansas, could a lower court uphold the restriction if the court finds that its *intent* is not to impose absolute term limits but only to level the playing field, reduce the incentive for gerrymandered districts, respond to the incumbent's advantage in campaign fund raising and name recognition, etc.?

What if the other state enacted a ballot access restriction that (unlike the Arkansas law) was not permanent. For example, the law would provide that a candidate for Senator could be on the ballot no more than two times out of every three. This restriction on ballot access, like the ballot access restriction in *Storer v. Brown,* is not a lifetime restriction. Souter, in oral argument, distinguished *Storer* on that basis. Is this ballot access procedure similar to the scheme upheld in *Storer?*

Alternatively, may a state provide (in an effort to level the playing field) that, if an incumbent Representative runs more than a given number of times in a row, then that candidate can remain on the ballot, *but* the Representative's political party must also nominate another candidate to run for the same office. For example, if Representative Jane Doe, a Republican, would seek yet another term, her name could appear on the ballot as the nominee of the Republican Party, but only if the Republican Party nominated another person who would also carry the Republican Party label.

After *Thornton,* Senator Hank Brown (R., Colo.) proposed a bill to define the residency requirement. It said that Representatives or Senators are not inhabitants of their state if they are not physically present there for half the year for 12 years in a row. Would such a law be constitutional?

6.   If the Court had held that states could impose term limits on federal legislators, would that have meant that they could impose term limits on the President? Or (since voters can only vote directly for electors, not for the President) would that mean that states could impose term limits on people running as Presidential electors?

Chapter 6

DUE PROCESS

6–1. SUBSTANTIVE ECONOMIC DUE PROCESS

SLAUGHTER–HOUSE CASES (BUTCHERS' BENEV. ASS'N v. CRESCENT CITY LIVE–STOCK LANDING AND SLAUGHTER–HOUSE CO.)

83 U.S. (16 Wall.) 36, 21 L.Ed. 394 (1873).

[Louisiana enacted a statute in 1869 that made it illegal to slaughter animals in New Orleans except "that the 'Crescent City Stock Landing and Slaughter–House Company' may establish *themselves* at any point or place" as provided in the act. Other butchers sued to enjoin the state created monopoly, lost in the state courts, and appealed to the Supreme Court. Under the Act, butchers could still slaughter, but they had to do it at the Slaughter–House Co. and pay it reasonable compensation for such use of the slaughter house.]

MR. JUSTICE MILLER . . . delivered the opinion of the Court. . . .

Unless, . . . the exclusive privilege granted by this charter to the corporation, is beyond the power of the legislature of the Louisiana, there can be no just exception to the validity of the statute. . . . The plaintiffs in error accepting this issue, allege that the statute is a violation of the Constitution of the United States in these several particulars:

That it creates an involuntary servitude forbidden by the thirteenth article of amendment;

That it abridges the privileges and immunities of citizens of the United States;

That it denies to the plaintiffs the equal protection of the laws; and,

That it deprives them of their property without due process of law; contrary to the provisions of the first section of the fourteenth article of amendment.

This court is thus called upon for the first time to give construction to these articles.

451

[In light of] events, almost too recent to be called history, but which are familiar to us all; and on the most casual examination of the language of [the 13th, 14th, and 15th] amendments, no one can fail to be impressed with the one pervading purpose found in them all, lying at the foundation of each, and without which none of them would have been even suggested; we mean the freedom of the slave race, the security and firm establishment of that freedom, and the protection of the newly-made freeman and citizen from the oppressions of those who had formerly exercised unlimited dominion over him. It is true that only the fifteenth amendment, in terms, mentions the negro by speaking of his color and his slavery. But it is just as true that each of the other articles was addressed to the grievances of that race, and designed to remedy them as the fifteenth.

We do not say that no one else but the negro can share in this protection. Both the language and spirit of these articles are to have their fair and just weight in any question of construction. Undoubtedly while negro slavery alone was in the mind of the Congress which proposed the thirteenth article, it forbids any other kind of slavery, now or hereafter. If Mexican peonage or the Chinese coolie labor system shall develop slavery of the Mexican or Chinese race within our territory, this amendment may safely be trusted to make it void. And so if other rights are assailed by the States, which properly and necessarily fall within the protection of these articles, that protection will apply, though the party interested may not be of African descent. . . .

The first section of the fourteenth article, to which our attention is more specially invited, opens with a definition of citizenship—not only citizenship of the United States, but citizenship of the States. No such definition was previously found in the Constitution. . . . [In the first sentence of the first section of the Fourteenth Amendment] the distinction between citizenship of the United States and citizenship of a State is clearly recognized and established. Not only may a man be a citizen of the United States without being a citizen of a State, but an important element is necessary to convert the former into the latter. He must reside within the State to make him a citizen of it, but it is only necessary that he should be born or naturalized in the United States to be a citizen of the Union.

It is quite clear, then, that there is a citizenship of the United States, and a citizenship of a State, which are distinct from each other, and which depend upon different characteristics or circumstances in the individual. We think this distinction and its explicit recognition in this amendment of great weight in this argument, because the next paragraph of this same section, which is the one mainly relied on by the plaintiffs in error, speaks only of privileges and immunities of citizens of the United States, and does not speak of those of citizens of the several States. The argument, however, in favor of the plaintiffs rests wholly on the assumption that the citizenship is the same, and the privileges and immunities guaranteed by the clause are the same.

The language is, "No State shall make or enforce any law which shall abridge the privileges or immunities of citizens of *the United States.*" It is a little remarkable, if this clause was intended as a protection to the citizen of a State against the legislative power of his own State, that the word citizen of the State should be left out when it is so carefully used, and used in contradistinction to citizens of the United States, in the very sentence which precedes it. It is too clear for argument that the change in phraseology was adopted understandingly and with a purpose.

Of the privileges and immunities of the citizen of the United States, and of the privileges and immunities of the citizen of the State, . . . it is only the former which are placed by this clause under the protection of the Federal Constitution, and that the latter, whatever they may be, are not intended to have any additional protection by this paragraph of the amendment. . . .

[Article IV, § 2 provides:] "The citizens of each State shall be entitled to all the privileges and immunities of citizens of the several States." . . . Fortunately, we are not without judicial construction of this clause of the Constitution. The first and the leading case on the subject is that of *Corfield v. Coryell,* decided by Mr. Justice Washington in the Circuit Court for the District of Pennsylvania in 1823.

"The inquiry," he says, "is, what are the privileges and immunities of citizens of the several States? We feel no hesitation in confining these expressions to those privileges and immunities which are *fundamental;* which belong of right to the citizens of all free governments, and which have at all times been enjoyed by citizens of the several States which compose this Union, from the time of their becoming free, independent, and sovereign. What these fundamental principles are, it would be more tedious than difficult to enumerate. They may all, however, be comprehended under the following general heads: protection by the government, with the right to acquire and possess property of every kind, and to pursue and obtain happiness and safety, subject, nevertheless, to such restraints as the government may prescribe for the general good of the whole."

[Article IV, § 2 of the Constitution] did not create those rights, which it called privileges and immunities of citizens of the States. It threw around them in that clause no security for the citizen of the State in which they were claimed or exercised. Nor did it profess to control the power of the State governments over the rights of its own citizens. Its sole purpose was to declare to the several States, that whatever those rights, as you grant or establish them to your own citizens, or as you limit or qualify, or impose restrictions on their exercise, the same, neither more nor less, shall be the measure of the rights of citizens of other States within your jurisdiction.

It would be the vainest show of learning to attempt to prove by citations of authority, that up to the adoption of the recent amendments, no claim or pretense was set up that those rights depended on the

Federal government for their existence or protection, beyond the very few express limitations which the Federal Constitution imposed upon the States—such, for instance, as the prohibition against ex post facto laws, bills of attainder, and laws impairing the obligation of contracts. But with the exception of these and a few other restrictions, the entire domain of the privileges and immunities of citizens of the States, as above defined, lay within the constitutional and legislative power of the States, and without that of the Federal government. Was it the purpose of the fourteenth amendment, by the simple declaration that no State should make or enforce any law which shall abridge the privileges and immunities of *citizens of the United States,* to transfer the security and protection of all the civil rights which we have mentioned, from the States to the Federal government? And where it is declared that Congress shall have the power to enforce that article, was it intended to bring within the power of Congress the entire domain of civil rights heretofore belonging exclusively to the States?

All this and more must follow, if the proposition of the plaintiffs in error be sound. For not only are these rights subject to the control of Congress whenever in its discretion any of them are supposed to be abridged by State legislation, but that body may also pass laws in advance, limiting and restricting the exercise of legislative power by the States, in their most ordinary and usual functions, as in its judgment it may think proper on all such subjects. [S]uch a construction followed by the reversal of the judgments of the Supreme Court of Louisiana in these cases, would constitute this court a perpetual censor upon all legislation of the States, on the civil rights of their own citizens, with authority to nullify such as it did not approve as consistent with those rights, as they existed at the time of the adoption of this amendment. . . .

Having shown that the privileges and immunities relied on in the argument are those which belong to citizens of the States as such, and that they are left to the State governments for security and protection, and not by this article placed under the special care of the Federal government, we may hold ourselves excused from defining the privileges and immunities of citizens of the United States which no State can abridge, until some case involving those privileges may make it necessary to do so. But lest it should be said that no such privileges and immunities are to be found if those we have been considering are excluded, we venture to suggest some which owe their existence to the Federal government, its National character, its Constitution, or its laws.

One of these is well described in the case of *Crandall v. Nevada,* [73 U.S. (6 Wall.) 35, 18 L.Ed. 745 (1867)]. It is said to be the right of the citizen of this great country, protected by implied guarantees of its Constitution, "to come to the seat of government to assert any claim he may have upon that government, to transact any business he may have with it, to seek its protection, to share its offices, to engage in administering its functions. He has the right of free access to its seaports, through which all operations of foreign commerce are conducted, to the subtreasuries, land offices, and courts of justice in the several States."

Another privilege of a citizen of the United States is to demand the care and protection of the Federal government over his life, liberty, and property when on the high seas or within the jurisdiction of a foreign government. Of this there can be no doubt, nor that the right depends upon his character as a citizen of the United States. The right to peaceably assemble and petition for redress of grievances, the privilege of the writ of *habeas corpus,* are rights of the citizen guaranteed by the Federal Constitution. The right to use the navigable waters of the United States, however they may penetrate the territory of the several States, all rights secured to our citizens by treaties with foreign nations are dependent upon citizenship of the United States, and not citizenship of a State. . . .

The argument has not been much pressed in these cases that the defendant's charter deprives the plaintiffs of their property without due process of law, or that it denies to them the equal protection of the law. . . . [U]nder no construction of [the due process clause] that we have ever seen, or any that we deem admissible, can the restraint imposed by the State of Louisiana upon the exercise of their trade by the butchers of New Orleans be held to be a deprivation of property within the meaning of that provision. The existence of laws in the States where the newly emancipated negroes resided, which discriminated with gross injustice and hardship against them as a class, was the evil to be remedied by [the equal protection] clause, and by it such laws are forbidden.

If, however, the States did not conform their laws to its requirements, then by the fifth section of the article of amendment Congress was authorized to enforce it by suitable legislation. We doubt very much whether any action of a State not directed by way of discrimination against the negroes as a class, or on account of their race, will ever be held to come within the purview of this provision. It is so clearly a provision for that race and that emergency, that a strong case would be necessary for its application to any other. But as it is a State that is to be dealt with, and not alone the validity of its laws, we may safely leave that matter until Congress shall have exercised its power, or some case of State oppression, by denial of equal justice in its courts, shall have claimed a decision at our hands. We find no such case in the one before us, and do not deem it necessary to go over the argument again, as it may have relation to this particular clause of the amendment.

The judgments of the Supreme Court of Louisiana in these cases are

Affirmed.

Mr. Justice Field, dissenting:

[If the Fourteenth Amendment] only refers, as held by the majority of the court in their opinion, to such privileges and immunities as were before its adoption specially designated in the Constitution or necessarily implied as belonging to citizens of the United States, it was a vain and idle enactment, which accomplished nothing, and most unnecessarily excited Congress and the people on its passage. . . . But if the amendment refers to the natural and inalienable rights which belong to all citizens, the inhibition has a profound significance and consequence.

What, then, are the privileges and immunities which are secured against abridgment by State legislation? In the first section of the Civil Rights Act Congress has given its interpretation to these terms, or at least has stated some of the rights which, in its judgment, these terms include; it has there declared that they include the right "to make and enforce contracts, to sue, be parties and give evidence, to inherit, purchase, lease, sell, hold, and convey real and personal property, and to full and equal benefit of all laws and proceedings for the security of person and property." That act, it is true, was passed before the fourteenth amendment, but the amendment was adopted ... to obviate objections to legislation of a similar character, extending the protection of the National government over the common rights of all citizens of the United States. Accordingly, after its ratification, Congress re-enacted the act under the belief that whatever doubts may have previously existed of its validity, they were removed by the amendment.

... The privileges and immunities designated are those *which of right belong to the citizens of all free governments*. Clearly among these must be placed the right to pursue a lawful employment in a lawful manner, without other restraint than such as equally affects all persons. [G]rants of exclusive privileges, such as is made by the act in question, are opposed to the whole theory of free government, and it requires no aid from any bill of rights to render them void. That only is a free government, in the American sense of the term, under which the inalienable right of every citizen to pursue his happiness is unrestrained, except by just, equal, and impartial laws.

I am authorized by THE CHIEF JUSTICE [CHASE], MR. JUSTICE SWAYNE, and MR. JUSTICE BRADLEY, to state that they concur with me in this dissenting opinion.

MR. JUSTICE BRADLEY, also dissenting:

... The granting of monopolies, or exclusive privileges to individuals or corporations, is an invasion of the right of others to choose a lawful calling, and an infringement of personal liberty. It was so felt by the English nation as far back as the reigns of Elizabeth and James.... In my view, a law which prohibits a large class of citizens from adopting a lawful employment, or from following a lawful employment previously adopted, does deprive them of liberty as well as property, without due process of law. Their right of choice is a portion of their liberty; their occupation is their property. Such a law also deprives those citizens of the equal protection of the laws, contrary to the last clause of the section....

[A dissenting opinion of SWAYNE, J., is omitted.]

Notes

1. Until 1999, the Supreme Court only once used the privileges or immunities clause of the Fourteenth Amendment, in a majority opinion to

invalidate state legislation. Within five years, that decision was overruled. *Colgate v. Harvey,* 296 U.S. 404, 56 S.Ct. 252, 80 L.Ed. 299 (1935), overruled, *Madden v. Kentucky,* 309 U.S. 83, 60 S.Ct. 406, 84 L.Ed. 590 (1940): "We think it quite clear that the right to carry out an incident to a trade, business or calling such as the deposit of money in banks is not a privilege of national citizenship.... *Colgate v. Harvey* must be and is overruled." The Court then upheld a Kentucky ad valorem tax. Note that *Madden,* unlike *Colgate,* was decided after the Court Packing Plan, discussed in § 4–1.

Given *Slaughter-House*'s definition of "privileges or immunities," are you surprised that the clause has been infrequently used?

This changed in 1999. In *Saenz v. Roe,* 526 U.S. 489, 119 S.Ct. 1518, 143 L.Ed.2d 689 (1999), California limited the maximum welfare benefits to newly arrived residents (those who resided in California for less than 12 months) to the amount that would have been payed by the state of the family's prior residence. Stevens, J., for the Court (7 to 2), discussed the "right of travel" cases in § 8–3.31, below, and invalidated the law, relying on the privileges and immunities clause of the Fourteenth Amendment:

> "What is at issue in this case, then, is ... the right of the newly arrived citizen to the same privileges and immunities enjoyed by other citizens of the same State. That right is protected not only by the new arrival's status as a state citizen, but also by her status as a citizen of the United States. That additional source of protection is plainly identified in the opening words of the Fourteenth Amendment...." (footnote omitted).

The Court then invalidated the law because "those travelers who elect to become permanent residents," have the "right to be treated like other citizens of that State."

Rehnquist, C.J., dissenting, joined by Thomas, J., said:

> "The Court today breathes new life into the previously dormant Privileges or Immunities Clause of the Fourteenth Amendment—a Clause relied upon by this Court in only one other decision, *Colgate v. Harvey* (1935), overruled five years later by *Madden v. Kentucky* (1940). It uses this Clause to strike down what I believe is a reasonable measure falling under the head of a 'good-faith residency requirement.' Because I do not think any provision of the Constitution—and surely not a provision relied upon for only the second time since its enactment 130 years ago—requires this result, I dissent."

Thomas, J., joined by Rehnquist, C.J., also filed a dissent where he said that he "would be open to reevaluating [the Privileges and Immunities Clause's] meaning in an appropriate case. Before invoking the Clause, however, we should endeavor to understand what the framers of the Fourteenth Amendment thought that it meant."

2. *Munn v. Illinois,* 94 U.S. (4 Otto) 113, 24 L.Ed. 77 (1876) upheld an Illinois law that fixed the maximum charges for the storage of grain at warehouses in Chicago and certain other places where the grain was sold in bulk. The Court reasoned that the due process clause protects private property, but "when private property is 'affected with a public interest, it ceases to be *juris privati only*.' ... When, therefore, one devotes his property

to a use in which the public has an interest, he, in effect, grants to the public an interest in that use, and must submit to be controlled by the public for the common good, to the extent of the interest he has thus created." The negative implication of this reasoning was made clearer when the Court added, by way of dictum: "[T]he legislature has no control over [a private] contract." Field, J., again dissented.

Then, *Santa Clara County v. Southern Pacific Railway,* 118 U.S. 394, 6 S.Ct. 1132, 30 L.Ed. 118 (1886) held that corporations are "persons" within the meaning of the Fourteenth Amendment.

Mugler v. Kansas, 123 U.S. 623, 8 S.Ct. 273, 31 L.Ed. 205 (1887) upheld a state law prohibiting the manufacture and sale of alcohol. In dictum the Court said: "There are, of necessity, limits beyond which legislation cannot rightfully go.... If, therefore, a statute purporting to have been enacted to protect the public health, the public morals, or the public safety, has no real or substantial relation to those objects, or is a palpable invasion of rights secured by the fundamental law, it is the duty of the courts to so adjudge, and thereby give effect to the Constitution."

In *Chicago, Milwaukee & St. Paul Railway Co. v. Minnesota,* 134 U.S. 418, 10 S.Ct. 462, 33 L.Ed. 970 (1890), a statute empowered a state commission to set "equal and reasonable" rates for rail transport of property. However, the state court had interpreted the statute to make these rates conclusive, with no judicial inquiry; the statute also did not provide for any summons or notice to, or hearing for, the railroad before the commission set the rates. Because of this procedural defect the Court invalidated the law: "It deprives the company of its right to a judicial investigation by due process of law, under the forms and with the machinery provided by the wisdom of successive ages for the investigation judicially of the truth of a matter in controversy, and substitutes therefore, as an absolute finality, the action of a railroad commission...." The dissent complained that the majority's decision "practically overrules *Munn v. Illinois.*"

Allgeyer v. Louisiana, 165 U.S. 578, 17 S.Ct. 427, 41 L.Ed. 832 (1897) invalidated a statute prohibiting anyone in the state from dealing with marine insurance companies that had not complied in all respects with Louisiana law. In this case, no business was done in the state; the contract was made and would be performed outside the state's jurisdiction. The fact that the defendant-insured mailed a letter to the out of state insurance company was insufficient to support Louisiana's assertion of extraterritorial jurisdiction. The Court, per Peckham, J., added by way of dictum: "The liberty mentioned in [the fourteenth] amendment [embraces] the right to the citizen to be free in the enjoyment of all his faculties; to be free to use them in all lawful ways; to live and work where he will; to earn his livelihood by any lawful calling; to pursue any livelihood or avocation, and for that purpose to enter into all contracts which may be proper, necessary and essential to carrying out to a successful conclusion the purposes above mentioned."

Holden v. Hardy, 169 U.S. 366, 18 S.Ct. 383, 42 L.Ed. 780 (1898) upheld a state law prohibiting workers in underground mines and smelters from working more than eight hours a day except in cases of emergency. The

Court justified the law in light of the special health problems of such workers and the unequal bargaining power of the parties.

LOCHNER v. NEW YORK

198 U.S. 45, 25 S.Ct. 539, 49 L.Ed. 937 (1905).

Mr. Justice Peckham, . . . delivered the opinion of the Court.

The indictment, it will be seen, charges that the plaintiff in error violated . . . the labor law of the State of New York, in that he wrongfully and unlawfully required and permitted an employé working for him to work more than sixty hours in one week. . . .

The statute necessarily interferes with the right of contract between the employer and employés, concerning the number of hours in which the latter may labor in the bakery of the employer. The general right to make a contract in relation to his business is part of the liberty of the individual protected by the Fourteenth Amendment of the Federal Constitution. *Allgeyer v. Louisiana.* Under that provision no State can deprive any person of life, liberty or property without due process of law. The right to purchase or to sell labor is part of the liberty protected by this amendment, unless there are circumstances which exclude the right. There are, however, certain powers, existing in the sovereignty of each State in the Union, somewhat vaguely termed police powers, the exact description and limitation of which have not been attempted by the courts. Those powers, broadly stated and without, at present, any attempt at a more specific limitation, relate to the safety, health, morals and general welfare of the public. Both property and liberty are held on such reasonable conditions as may be imposed by the governing power of the State in the exercise of those powers, and with such conditions the Fourteenth Amendment was not designed to interfere. *Mulger v. Kansas*. . . .

This court has recognized the existence and upheld the exercise of the police powers of the States in many cases which might fairly be considered as border ones. . . . Among the later cases where the state law has been upheld by this court is that of *Holden v. Hardy*. . . . It was held that the kind of employment, mining, smelting, etc., and the character of the employés in such kinds of labor, were such as to make it reasonable and proper for the State to [limit the workers to eight hours per day]. It will be observed that, even with regard to that class of labor, the Utah statute provided for cases of emergency wherein the provisions of the statute would not apply. The statute now before this court has no emergency clause in it, and, if the statute is valid, there are no circumstances and no emergencies under which the slightest violation of the provisions of the act would be innocent. There is nothing in *Holden v. Hardy* which covers the case now before us. . . .

It must, of course, be conceded that there is a limit to the valid exercise of the police power by the State. There is no dispute concerning this general proposition. Otherwise the Fourteenth Amendment would have no efficacy.... In every case that comes before this court, there-fore, where legislation of this character is concerned and where the protection of the Federal Constitution is sought, the question necessarily arises: Is this a fair, reasonable and appropriate exercise of the police power of the State, or is it an unreasonable, unnecessary and arbitrary interference with the right of the individual to his personal liberty or to enter into those contracts in relation to labor which may seem to him appropriate or necessary for the support of himself and his family? Of course the liberty of contract relating to labor includes both parties to it. The one has as much right to purchase as the other to sell labor.

This is not a question of substituting the judgment of the court for that of the legislature. If the act be within the power of the State it is valid, although the judgment of the court might be totally opposed to the enactment of such a law. But the question would still remain: Is it within the police power of the State? and that question must be an-swered by the court.

The question whether this act is valid as a labor law, pure and simple, may be dismissed in a few words. There is no reasonable ground for interfering with the liberty of person or the right of free contract, by determining the hours of labor, in the occupation of a baker. There is no contention that bakers as a class are not equal in intelligence and capacity to men in other trades or manual occupations, or that they are not able to assert their rights and care for themselves without the protecting arm of the State, interfering with their independence of judgment and of action. They are in no sense wards of the State. Viewed in the light of a purely labor law, with no reference whatever to the question of health, we think that a law like the one before us involves neither the safety, the morals nor the welfare of the public, and that the interest of the public is not in the slightest degree affected by such an act. The law must be upheld, if at all, as a law pertaining to the health of the individual engaged in the occupation of a baker. It does not affect any other portion of the public than those who are engaged in that occupation. Clean and wholesome bread does not depend upon whether the baker works but ten hours per day or only sixty hours a week. The limitation of the hours of labor does not come within the police power on that ground....

We think the limit of the police power has been reached and passed in this case. There is, in our judgment, no reasonable foundation for holding this is to be necessary or appropriate as a health law to safeguard the public health or the health of the individuals who are following the trade of a baker. If this statute be valid, and if, therefore, a proper case is made out in which to deny the right of an individual, *sui juris,* as employer or employé, to make contracts for the labor of the latter under the protection of the provisions of the Federal Constitution, there would seem to be no length to which legislation of this nature might not go....

We think that there can be no fair doubt that the trade of a baker, in and of itself, is not an unhealthy one to that degree which would authorize the legislature to interfere with the right to labor, and with the right of free contract on the part of the individual, either as employer or employé. In looking through statistics regarding all trades and occupations, it may be true that the trade of a baker does not appear to be as healthy as some other trades, and is also vastly more healthy than still others. To the common understanding the trade of a baker has never been regarded as an unhealthy one. Very likely physicians would not recommend the exercise of that or of any other trade as a remedy for ill health. Some occupations are more healthy than others but we think there are none which might not come under the power of the legislature to supervise and control the hours of working therein, if the mere fact that the occupation is not absolutely and perfectly healthy is to confer that right upon the legislative department of the Government. It might be safely affirmed that almost all occupations more or less affect the health. There must be more than the mere fact of the possible existence of some small amount of unhealthiness to warrant legislative interference with liberty. It is unfortunately true that labor, even in any department, may possibly carry with it the seeds of unhealthiness. But are we all, on that account, at the mercy of legislative majorities? A printer, a tinsmith, a locksmith, a carpenter, a cabinetmaker, a dry goods clerk, a bank's, a lawyer's or a physician's clerk, or a clerk in almost any kind of business, would all come under the power of the legislature, on this assumption. No trade, no occupation, no mode of earning one's living, could escape this all-pervading power, and the acts of the legislature in limiting the hours of labor in all employments would be valid, although such limitation might seriously cripple the ability of the laborer to support himself and his family. . . .

It is also urged . . . that it is to the interest of the State that its population should be strong and robust, and therefore any legislation which may be said to tend to make people healthy must be valid as health laws, enacted under the police power. If this be a valid argument and a justification for this kind of legislation, it follows that the protection of the Federal Constitution from undue interference with liberty of person and freedom of contract is visionary, wherever the law is sought to be justified as a valid exercise of the police power. Scarcely any law but might find shelter under such assumptions, and conduct, properly so called, as well as contract, would come under the restrictive sway of the legislature. Not only the hours of employés, but the hours of employers, could be regulated, and doctors, lawyers, scientists, all professional men, as well as athletes and artisans, could be forbidden to fatigue their brains and bodies by prolonged hours of exercise, lest the fighting strength of the State be impaired. We mention these extreme cases because the contention is extreme. We do not believe in the soundness of the views which uphold this law. On the contrary, [t]he act is not, within any fair meaning of the term, a health law, but is an illegal interference with the rights of individuals, both employers and employés, to make contracts regarding labor upon such terms as they may think best, or which they may agree upon with the other parties to such contracts. Statutes of the nature of that under review, limiting the hours in which grown and intelligent men may labor to earn their living, are mere meddlesome interferences with the rights of the individual. . . .

It is impossible for us to shut our eyes to the fact that many of the laws of this character, while passed under what is claimed to be the police power for the purpose of protecting the public health or welfare, are, in reality, passed from other motives. . . . It seems to us that the real object and purpose were simply to regulate the hours of labor between the master and his employés (all being men, *sui juris*), in a private business, not dangerous in any degree to morals or in any real and substantial degree, to the health of the employés. Under such circumstances the freedom of master and employé to contract with each other in relation to their employment, and in defining the same, cannot be prohibited or interfered with, without violating the Federal Constitution. . . .

Reversed.

MR. JUSTICE HARLAN, with whom MR. JUSTICE WHITE and MR. JUSTICE DAY concurred, dissenting.

. . . It is enough for the determination of this case, and it is enough for this court to know, that the question is one about which there is room for debate and for an honest difference of opinion. There are many reasons of a weighty, substantial character, based upon the experience of mankind, in support of the theory that, all things considered, more than ten hours' steady work each day, from week to week, in a bakery or confectionery establishment, may endanger the health, and shorten the lives of the workmen, thereby diminishing their physical and mental capacity to serve the State, and to provide for those dependent upon them. If such reasons exist that ought to be the end of this case. . . .

MR. JUSTICE HOLMES dissenting. . . .

This case is decided upon an economic theory which a large part of the country does not entertain. If it were a question whether I agreed with that theory, I should desire to study it further and long before making up my mind. But I do not conceive that to be my duty, because I strongly believe that my agreement or disagreement has nothing to do with the right of a majority to embody their opinions in law. It is settled by various decisions of this court that state constitutions and state laws may regulate life in many ways which we as legislators might think as injudicious or if you like as tyrannical as this, and which equally with this interfere with the liberty to contract. Sunday laws and usury laws are ancient examples. A more modern one is the prohibition of lotteries. The liberty of the citizen to do as he likes so long as he does not interfere with the liberty of others to do the same, which has been a shibboleth for some well-known writers, is interfered with by school laws, by the Post Office, by every state or municipal institution which takes his money for purposes thought desirable, whether he likes it or not. The Fourteenth

Amendment does not enact Mr. Herbert Spencer's Social Statics. The other day we sustained the Massachusetts vaccination law. *Jacobson v. Massachusetts,* 197 U.S. 11, 25 S.Ct. 358, 49 L.Ed. 643. United States and state statutes and decisions cutting down the liberty to contract by way of combination are familiar to this court. *Northern Securities Co. v. United States,* 193 U.S. 197, 48 L.Ed. 679, 24 S.Ct. 436. Two years ago we upheld the prohibition of sales of stock on margins or for future delivery in the constitution of California. *Otis v. Parker,* 187 U.S. 606, 47 L.Ed. 323, 23 S.Ct. 168. The decision sustaining an eight hour law for miners is still recent. *Holden v. Hardy,* 169 U.S. 366, 42 L.Ed. 780, 18 S.Ct. 383. Some of these laws embody convictions or prejudices which judges are likely to share. Some may not. But a constitution is not intended to embody a particular economic theory, whether of paternalism and the organic relation of the citizen to the State or of *laissez faire.* It is made for people of fundamentally differing views, and the accident of our finding certain opinions natural and familiar or novel and even shocking ought not to conclude our judgment upon the question whether statutes embodying them conflict with the Constitution of the United States.

General propositions do not decide concrete cases.... Every opinion tends to become a law. I think that the word liberty in the Fourteenth Amendment is perverted when it is held to prevent the natural outcome of a dominant opinion, unless it can be said that a rational and fair man necessarily would admit that the statute proposed would infringe fundamental principles as they have been understood by the traditions of our people and our law. It does not need research to show that no such sweeping condemnation can be passed upon the statute before us. A reasonable man might think it a proper measure on the score of health. Men whom I certainly could not pronounce unreasonable would uphold it as a first instalment of a general regulation of the hours of work....

Notes

1. *Muller v. Oregon,* 208 U.S. 412, 28 S.Ct. 324, 52 L.Ed. 551 (1908). Oregon law forbade females employed in any mechanical establishment, or factory, or laundry from working more than ten hours a day. Petitioner was convicted of violating the statute. Relying on *Lochner,* she argued to the Supreme Court that the statute violated the Fourteenth Amendment. Brewer, J., for a unanimous Court, upheld the law, based on the following reasoning:

> In patent cases counsel are apt to open the argument with a discussion of the state of the art. It may not be amiss, in the present case, before examining the constitutional question, to notice the course of legislation as well as expressions of opinion from other than judicial sources. In the brief filed by Mr. Louis D. Brandeis, for the defendant in error, is a very copious collection of all these matters, an epitome of which is found in the margin.[1] ...

1. The following legislation of the States   impose restrictions in some form or another

The legislation and opinions referred to in the margin may not be, technically speaking, authorities, and in them is little or no discussion of the constitutional question presented to us for determination, yet they are significant of a widespread belief that woman's physical structure, and the functions she performs in consequence thereof, justify special legislation restricting or qualifying the conditions under which she should be permitted to toil. Constitutional questions, it is true, are not settled by even a consensus of present public opinion, for it is the peculiar value of a written constitution that it places in unchanging form limitations upon legislative action, and thus gives a permanence and stability to popular government which otherwise would be lacking. At the same time, when a question of fact is debated and debatable, and the extent to which a special constitutional limitation goes is affected by the truth in respect to that fact, a widespread and long continued belief concerning it is worthy of consideration. We take judicial cognizance of all matters of general knowledge. . . .

That woman's physical structure and the performance of maternal functions place her at a disadvantage in the struggle for subsistence is obvious. This is especially true when the burdens of motherhood are upon her. [A]s healthy mothers are essential to vigorous offspring, the physical wellbeing of woman becomes an object of public interest and care in order to preserve the strength and vigor of the race. . . .

upon the hours of labor that may be required of women: Massachusetts: chap. 221, 1874, Rev.Laws 1902, chap. 106, § 24; Rhode Island: 1885, Acts and Resolves 1902, chap. 994, p. 73; Louisiana: § 4, Act 43, p. 55, Laws of 1886, Rev.Laws 1904, vol. 1, p. 989; Connecticut: 1887, Gen.Stat. revision 1902, § 4691; Maine: chap. 139, 1887, Rev.Stat.1903, chap. 40, § 48, p. 401; New Hampshire: 1887, Laws 1907, chap. 94, p. 95; Maryland: chap. 455, 1888, Pub.Gen. Laws 1903, art. 100, § 1; Virginia: p. 150, 1889–1890, Code 1904, tit. 51A, chap. 178A, § 3657b; Pennsylvania: No. 26, p. 30, 1897, Laws 1905, No. 226, p. 352; New York: Laws 1899, § 1, chap. 560, p. 752, Laws 1907, chap. 507, § 77, subdiv. 3, p. 1078; Nebraska: 1899, Comp.Stat.1905, § 7955, p. 1986; Washington: Stat.1901, chap. 68, § 1, p. 118; Colorado: Acts 1903, chap. 138, § 3, p. 310; New Jersey: 1892, Gen.Stat.1895, p. 2350, §§ 66, 67; Oklahoma: 1890, Rev.Stat. 1903, chap. 25, art. 58, § 729; North Dakota: 1877, Rev.Code 1905, § 9440; South Dakota: 1877, Rev.Code (Penal Code, § 764), p. 1185; Wisconsin: § 1, chap. 83, Laws of 1867, Code 1898, § 1728; South Carolina: Acts 1907, No. 233, p. 487.

In foreign legislation Mr. Brandeis calls attention to these statutes: Great Britain: Factories Act of 1844, chap. 15, pp. 161, 171; Factory and Workshop Act of 1901, chap. 22, pp. 60, 71; and see 1 Edw. VII, chap. 22. France, 1848; Act Nov. 2, 1892, and March 30, 1900. Switzerland, Canton of Glarus, 1848; Federal Law 1877, art. 2, § 1. Austria, 1855; Acts 1897, art. 96a, §§ 1–3. Holland, 1889; art. 5, § 1. Italy, June 19, 1902, art. 7. Germany, Laws 1891.

Then follow extracts from over ninety reports of committees, bureaus of statistics, commissioners of hygiene, inspectors of factories, both in this country and in Europe, to the effect that long hours of labor are dangerous for women, primarily because of their special physical organization. The matter is discussed in these reports in different aspects, but all agree as to the danger. It would of course take too much space to give these reports in detail. Following them are extracts from similar reports discussing the general benefits of short hours from an economic aspect of the question. In many of these reports individual instances are given tending to support the general conclusion. Perhaps the general scope and character of all these reports may be summed up in what an inspector for Hanover says: The reasons for the reduction of the working day to ten hours—(a) the physical organization of women, (b) her maternal functions, (c) the rearing and education of the children, (d) the maintenance of the home—are all so important and so far reaching that the need for such reduction need hardly be discussed.

For these reasons, and without questioning in any respect the decision in *Lochner v. New York,* we are of the opinion that it cannot be adjudged that the act in question is in conflict with the Federal Constitution, so far as it respects the work of a female in a laundry, and the judgment of the Supreme Court of Oregon is Affirmed.

Is *Muller* consistent with *Lochner?*

2. *Bunting v. Oregon,* 243 U.S. 426, 37 S.Ct. 435, 61 L.Ed. 830 (1917). Petitioner was convicted of violating an Oregon statute prohibiting the employment of anyone in a mill, factory, or manufacturing establishment more than ten hours in one day except for watchmen and employees when engaged in making necessary repairs or in case of emergency. The employee, however, could work up to thirteen hours a day if the employer paid time and a-half for the extra hours. McKenna, J., for the Court, upheld the law:

> There is a contention made that the law, even regarded as regulating hours of service, is not either necessary or useful "for preservation of the health of employés in mills, factories and manufacturing establishments". The record contains no facts to support the contention, and against it is the judgment of the legislature and the [state] Supreme Court, which said: "In view of the well-known fact that the custom in our industries does not sanction a longer service than 10 hours per day, it cannot be held, as a matter of law, that the legislative requirement is unreasonable or arbitrary as to hours of labor. Statistics show that the average daily working time among working-men in different countries is, in Australia, 8 hours; in Great Britain, 9; in the United States, 9¾; in Denmark, 9¾; in Norway, 10; Sweden, France, and Switzerland, 10½; Germany, 10¼; Belgium, Italy, and Austria, 11; and in Russia, 12 hours."

White, C.J., & Van Devanter & McReynolds, JJ., dissented without opinion. Brandeis, J., appointed to the Court in 1916, took no part in the consideration and decision of the case. The majority did not even cite *Lochner.* Is *Bunting* consistent with *Lochner?*

3. *Adkins v. Children's Hospital,* 261 U.S. 525, 43 S.Ct. 394, 67 L.Ed. 785 (1923). A congressional statute set minimum wages for women and children in Washington, D.C. A hospital and a woman hotel worker sued to enjoin the act. The lower courts enjoined the act, and the Supreme Court, per Sutherland, J., affirmed:

> There is, of course, no such thing as absolute freedom of contract. It is subject to a great variety of restraints. But freedom of contract is, nevertheless, the general rule and restraint the exception; and the exercise of legislative authority to abridge it can be justified only by the existence of exceptional circumstances.... A law forbidding work to continue beyond a given number of hours leaves the parties free to contract about wages and thereby equalize whatever additional burdens may be imposed upon the employer as a result of the restrictions as to hours, by an adjustment in respect of the amount of wages....

> [This] is not a law dealing with any business charged with a public interest or with public work, or to meet and tide over a temporary emergency. It has nothing to do with the character, methods or periods

of wage payments. It does not prescribe hours of labor or conditions under which labor is to be done. It is not for the protection of persons under legal disability or for the prevention of fraud. It is simply and exclusively a price-fixing law, confined to adult women (for we are not now considering the provisions relating to minors), who are legally as capable of contracting for themselves as men . . . .

We are asked, upon the one hand, to consider the fact that several States have adopted similar statutes, and we are invited, upon the other hand, to give weight to the fact that three times as many States, presumably as well informed and as anxious to promote the health and morals of their people, have refrained from enacting such legislation. We have also been furnished with a large number of printed opinions approving the policy of the minimum wage, and our own reading has disclosed a large number to the contrary. These are all proper enough for the consideration of the lawmaking bodies, . . . but they reflect no legitimate light upon the question of its validity, and that is what we are called upon to decide. The elucidation of that question cannot be aided by counting heads . . . .

Brandeis, J., took no part in the consideration or decision, but Taft, C.J., joined by Sanford, J., dissented:

[T]he opinion herein does not overrule the *Bunting Case* in express terms, and therefore I assume that the conclusion in this case rests on the distinction between a minimum of wages and a maximum of hours in the limiting of liberty to contract. I regret to be at variance with the Court as to the substance of this distinction. In absolute freedom of contract the one term is as important as the other, for both enter equally into the consideration given and received, a restriction as to one is not any greater in essence than the other, and is of the same kind. One is the multiplier and the other the multiplicand.

Holmes, J., also dissented, noting:

The earlier decisions upon the same words in the Fourteenth Amendment [that are in the Fifth] began within our memory and went no farther than an unpretentious assertion of the liberty to follow the ordinary callings. Later that innocuous generality was expanded into the dogma, Liberty of Contract. Contract is not specially mentioned in the text that we have to construe. It is merely an example of doing what you want to do, embodied in the word liberty. But pretty much all law consists in forbidding men to do some things that they want to do, and contract is no more exempt from law than other acts.

NEBBIA v. NEW YORK

291 U.S. 502, 54 S.Ct. 505, 78 L.Ed. 940 (1934).

MR. JUSTICE ROBERTS delivered the opinion of the Court.

The Legislature of New York established, by Chapter 158 of the Laws of 1933, a Milk Control Board with power, among other things, to "fix minimum and maximum . . . retail prices to be charged by . . . stores to consumers for consumption off the premises where sold." The Board fixed nine cents as the price to be charged by a store for a quart of milk. Nebbia, the proprietor of a grocery store in Rochester, sold two quarts and a five cent loaf of bread for eighteen cents; and was convicted for violating the Board's order. At his trial he asserted the statute and order contravene the equal protection clause and the due process clause of the Fourteenth Amendment, and renewed the contention in successive appeals to the county court and the Court of Appeals. Both overruled his claim and affirmed the conviction.

The question for decision is whether the Federal Constitution prohibits a state from so fixing the selling price of milk. We first inquire as to the occasion for the legislation and its history.

During 1932 the prices received by farmers for milk were much below the cost of production. The decline in prices during 1931 and 1932 was much greater than that of prices generally. The situation of the families of dairy producers had become desperate and called for state aid similar to that afforded the unemployed, if conditions should not improve.

[A state legislative committee concluded that the] fluid milk industry is affected by factors of instability peculiar to itself which call for special methods of control. Under the best practicable adjustment of supply to demand the industry must carry a surplus of about 20 per cent., because milk, an essential food, must be available as demanded by consumers every day in the year, and demand and supply vary from day to day and according to the season; but milk is perishable and cannot be stored. Close adjustment of supply to demand is hindered by several factors difficult to control. Thus surplus milk presents a serious problem, as the prices which can be realized for it for other uses are much less than those obtainable for milk sold for consumption in fluid form or as cream. . . . The fact that the larger distributors find it necessary to carry large quantities of surplus milk, while the smaller distributors do not, leads to price-cutting and other forms of destructive competition. Smaller distributors, who take no responsibility for the surplus, by purchasing their milk at the blended prices (i.e., an average between the price paid the producer for milk for sale as fluid milk, and the lower surplus milk price paid by the larger organizations) can undersell the larger distributors. Indulgence in this price-cutting often compels the larger dealer to cut the price, to his own and the producer's detriment. . . .

[A] serious question is whether, in the light of the conditions disclosed, the enforcement of § 312(e) denied the appellant the due process secured to him by the Fourteenth Amendment. . . .

The Fifth Amendment, in the field of federal activity, and the Fourteenth, as respects state action, do not prohibit governmental regulation for the public welfare. They merely condition the exertion of the admitted power, by securing that the end shall be accomplished by methods consistent with due process. And the guaranty of due process, as has often been held, demands only that the law shall not be unreasonable, arbitrary or capricious, and that the means selected shall have a real and substantial relation to the object sought to be attained. It results that a regulation valid for one sort of business, or in given circumstances, may be invalid for another sort, or for the same business under other circumstances, because the reasonableness of each regulation depends upon the relevant facts.

The milk industry in New York has been the subject of long-standing and drastic regulation in the public interest. The legislative investigation of 1932 was persuasive of the fact that for this and other reasons unrestricted competition aggravated existing evils, and the normal law of supply and demand was insufficient to correct maladjustments detrimental to the community.... In the order of which complaint is made the Milk Control Board fixed a price of ten cents per quart for sales by a distributor to a consumer, and nine cents by a store to a consumer, thus recognizing the lower costs of the store, and endeavoring to establish a differential which would be just to both. In the light of the facts the order appears not to be unreasonable or arbitrary, or without relation to the purpose to prevent ruthless competition from destroying the wholesale price structure on which the farmer depends for his livelihood, and the community for an assured supply of milk.

But we are told that ... the public control of rates or prices is *per se* unreasonable and unconstitutional, save as applied to businesses affected with a public interest; that a business so affected is one in which property is devoted to an enterprise of a sort which the public itself might appropriately undertake, or one whose owner relies on a public grant or franchise for the right to conduct the business, or in which he is bound to serve all who apply; in short, such as is commonly called a public utility; or a business in its nature a monopoly. The milk industry, it is said, possesses none of these characteristics, and, therefore, not being affected with a public interest, its charges may not be controlled by the state. Upon the soundness of this contention the appellant's case against the statute depends.

We may as well say at once that the dairy industry is not, in the accepted sense of the phrase, a public utility.... It is clear that there is no closed class or category of businesses affected with a public interest, and the function of courts in the application of the Fifth and Fourteenth Amendments is to determine in each case whether circumstances vindicate the challenged regulation as a reasonable exertion of governmental authority or condemn it as arbitrary or discriminatory. The phrase "affected with a public interest" can, in the nature of things, mean no more than that an industry, for adequate reason, is subject to control for the public good.... So far as the requirement of due process is concerned, and in the absence of other constitutional restriction, a state is free to adopt whatever economic policy may reasonably be deemed to promote public welfare, and to enforce that policy by legislation adapted to its purpose. The courts are without authority either to declare such policy, or, when it is declared by the legislature, to override it. If the laws passed are seen to have a reasonable relation to a proper legislative purpose, and are neither arbitrary nor discriminatory, the requirements of due process are satisfied, and judicial determination to that effect renders a court *functus officio.* "Whether the free operation of the normal laws of competition is a wise and wholesome rule for trade and commerce is an economic question which this court need not consider or determine." ... Price control, like any other form of regulation, is unconstitutional only if arbitrary, discriminatory, or demonstrably irrelevant to the policy the legislature is free to adopt, and hence an unnecessary and unwarranted interference with individual liberty.

Tested by these considerations we find no basis in the due process clause of the Fourteenth Amendment for condemning the provisions of the Agriculture and Markets Law here drawn into question.

The judgment is

Affirmed.

Separate Opinion of MR. JUSTICE MCREYNOLDS.

... Of the assailed statute the Court of Appeals says— ... "With the wisdom of the legislature we have naught to do." ... But plainly, I think, this Court must have regard to the wisdom of enactment.... The judgment of the court below should be reversed. MR. JUSTICE VAN DEVANTER, MR. JUSTICE SUTHERLAND, and MR. JUSTICE BUTLER authorize me to say that they concur in this opinion.

Notes

1. *West Coast Hotel v. Parrish,* 300 U.S. 379, 57 S.Ct. 578, 81 L.Ed. 703 (1937). Washington State established a minimum wage law for women and minors. The state supreme court, reversing the trial court, sustained the constitutionality of the statute and appellant sought relief based on *Adkins v. Children's Hospital.* Hughes, C.J., for the Court, upheld the statute:

> In each case the violation alleged by those attacking minimum wage regulation for women is deprivation of freedom of contract. What is this freedom? The Constitution does not speak of freedom of contract. It speaks of liberty and prohibits the deprivation of liberty without due process of law. In prohibiting that deprivation the Constitution does not recognize an absolute and uncontrollable liberty. [R]egulation which is reasonable in relation to its subject and is adopted in the interests of the community is due process....

> There is an additional and compelling consideration which recent economic experience has brought into a strong light. The exploitation of a class of workers who are in an unequal position with respect to bargaining power and are thus relatively defenceless against the denial of a living wage is not only detrimental to their health and well being but casts a direct burden for their support upon the community.... While in the instant case no factual brief has been presented, there is no reason to doubt that the State of Washington has encountered the same social problem that is present elsewhere. [T]he case of *Adkins v. Children's Hospital,* supra, should be, and it is, overruled....

Sutherland, J., joined by Van Devanter, McReynolds, & Butler, JJ., dissented.

Note that *Parrish* was a post Court Packing plan decision.[1]

2. *United States v. Darby,* 312 U.S. 100, 125, 61 S.Ct. 451, 462, 85 L.Ed. 609 (1941), excerpted more fully at § 4–2, supra, validated a federal law fixing the minimum wage and maximum hours of workers in interstate commerce. The due process discussion took only about one-half page in the U.S. Reports: "Since our decision on *West Coast Hotel v. Parrish,* it is no longer open to question that the fixing of a minimum wage is within the legislative power and that the base fact of its exercise is not a denial of due process under the Fifth more than under the Fourteenth Amendment. Nor is it any longer open to question that it is within the legislative power to fix maximum hours. Similarly, the statute is not objectionable because applied alike to both men and women."

3. *Ferguson v. Skrupa,* 372 U.S. 726, 83 S.Ct. 1028, 10 L.Ed.2d 93 (1963). A federal district court enjoined, as violating due process, a Kansas statute making it a misdemeanor to engage "in the business of debt adjusting" except as incident to the practice of law. Black, J., for the Court, reversed.

> The doctrine that prevailed in *Lochner* and like cases—that due process authorizes courts to hold laws unconstitutional when they believe the legislature has acted unwisely—has long since been discarded. We have returned to the original constitutional proposition that courts do not substitute their social and economic beliefs for the judgment of legislative bodies, who are elected to pass laws.... Whether the legislature takes for its textbook Adam Smith, Herbert Spencer, Lord Keynes, or some other is no concern of ours. The Kansas debt adjusting statute may be wise or unwise. But relief, if any be needed, lies not with us but with the body constituted to pass laws for the State of Kansas.

There were no dissents. Harlan, J., concurred in the judgment "on the grounds that this state measure bears a rational relation to a constitutionally permissible objective."

4. An often quoted test to judge the validity of economic regulation is found in *United States v. Carolene Products Co.,* 304 U.S. 144, 58 S.Ct. 778, 82 L.Ed. 1234 (1938), excerpted (with the Court's famous footnote 4) at § 4–4: "[T]he existence of facts supporting the legislative judgment is to be presumed, for regulatory legislation affecting ordinary commercial transactions is not to be pronounced unconstitutional unless in the light of the facts made known or generally assumed it is of such a character as to preclude the assumption that it rests upon some rational basis within the knowledge and experience of the legislators."

6–2. A NOTE ON THE INCORPORATION OF THE BILL OF RIGHTS

Prior to the Civil War, Supreme Court decisions did not focus on the due process clause, for Chief Justice Marshall had held in 1833 that the Bill of Rights did not apply to the states. *Barron v. Mayor and City*

---

1. The Court Packing Plan is discussed   at the end of § 4–1.

Council of City of Baltimore, 32 U.S. (7 Pet.) 243, 8 L.Ed. 672 (1833). Only a few substantive limitations in the body of the Constitution applied to the states, e.g., the prohibitions against bills of attainder, ex post facto laws, and impairments of contracts. See Art. I, § 10, cl. 1. As far as federal legislation was concerned, the Court did not then exercise active review.

After the Civil War, the Court's attention shifted. The Fourteenth Amendment, now part of the Constitution, contained due process language virtually identical to the Fifth's, except that it applied to the states. In addition to "process" or procedure, the Court gave this clause a substantive component. We have already seen the rise and fall of substantive economic due process from the *Slaughter–House Cases* to *Lochner* to *Nebbia.* The due process clause has also been used in the selective incorporation of the substantive limitations of the Bill of Rights. Although due process, after 1937, has had little impact over purely economic regulation of business, some Justices and commentators have accused the Court of using that clause to return to *Lochner*-type reasoning in its treatment of due process in civil rights cases. Justice White, dissenting in *Moore v. East Cleveland,* 431 U.S. 494, 97 S.Ct. 1932, 52 L.Ed.2d 531 (1977), succinctly summarized the development:

> The emphasis of the Due Process Clause is on "process." As Mr. Justice Harlan once observed, it has been "ably and insistently argued in response to what were felt to be abuses by this Court of its reviewing power," that the Due Process Clause should be limited "to a guarantee of procedural fairness." *Poe v. Ullman,* 367 U.S. 497, 540, 81 S.Ct. 1752, 1775, 6 L.Ed.2d 989 (1961)(dissenting opinion). These arguments had seemed "persuasive" to Justices Brandeis and Holmes, *Whitney v. California,* 274 U.S. 357, 373, 47 S.Ct. 641, 647, 71 L.Ed. 1095 (1927), but they recognized that the Due Process Clause, by virtue of case-to-case "judicial inclusion and exclusion," *Davidson v. New Orleans,* 96 U.S. 97, 104, 24 L.Ed. 616 (1878), had been construed to proscribe matters of substance, as well as inadequate procedures, and to protect from invasion by the States "all fundamental rights comprised within the term liberty." *Whitney v. California,* supra, 274 U.S., at 373, 47 S.Ct., at 647.

> Mr. Justice Black also recognized that the Fourteenth Amendment had substantive as well as procedural content. But believing that its reach should not extend beyond the specific provisions of the Bill of Rights, see *Adamson v. California,* 332 U.S. 46, 68, 67 S.Ct. 1672, 1683, 91 L.Ed. 1903 (1947)(dissenting opinion), he never embraced the idea that the Due Process Clause empowered the courts to strike down merely unreasonable or arbitrary legislation, nor did he accept Mr. Justice Harlan's consistent view. See *Griswold v. Connecticut,* 381 U.S. 479, 507, 85 S.Ct. 1678, 1694, 14 L.Ed.2d 510 (1965)(Black, J., dissenting), and id., at 499, 85 S.Ct., at 1689 (Harlan, J., concurring in judgment). Writing at length in dissent in *Poe v. Ullman,* supra, at 543, Mr. Justice Harlan stated the essence of his position as follows:

"This 'liberty' is not a series of isolated points pricked out in terms of the taking of property; the freedom of speech, press, and religion; the right to keep and bear arms; the freedom from unreasonable searches and seizures; and so on. It is a rational continuum which, broadly speaking, includes a freedom from all substantial arbitrary impositions and purposeless restraints, see *Allgeyer v. State of Louisiana*, 165 U.S. 578, 17 S.Ct. 427, 41 L.Ed. 832; *Holden v. Hardy*, 169 U.S. 366, 18 S.Ct. 383, 42 L.Ed. 780; *Booth v. Illinois*, 184 U.S. 425, 22 S.Ct. 425, 46 L.Ed. 623; *Nebbia v. New York*, 291 U.S. 502, 54 S.Ct. 505, 78 L.Ed. 940; *Skinner v. Oklahoma*, 316 U.S. 535, 544, 62 S.Ct. 1110, 1114, 86 L.Ed. 1655 (concurring opinion); *Schware v. Board of Bar Examiners*, 353 U.S. 232, 77 S.Ct. 752, 1 L.Ed.2d 796, and which also recognizes, what a reasonable and sensitive judgment must, that certain interests require particularly careful scrutiny of the state needs asserted to justify their abridgment. Cf. *Skinner v. Oklahoma*, supra; *Bolling v. Sharpe* [347 U.S. 497 (1954)]".

This construction was far too open ended for Mr. Justice Black. For him, *Meyer v. Nebraska*, 262 U.S. 390, 43 S.Ct. 625, 67 L.Ed. 1042 (1923),[1] and *Pierce v. Society of Sisters*, 268 U.S. 510, 45 S.Ct. 571, 69 L.Ed. 1070 (1925),[2] as substantive due process cases, were as suspect as *Lochner v. New York*, 198 U.S. 45, 25 S.Ct. 539, 49 L.Ed. 937 (1905), *Coppage v. Kansas*, 236 U.S. 1, 35 S.Ct. 240, 59 L.Ed. 441 (1915), and *Adkins v. Children's Hospital*, 261 U.S. 525, 43 S.Ct. 394, 67 L.Ed. 785 (1923). In his view, *Ferguson v. Skrupa*, 372 U.S. 726, 83 S.Ct. 1028, 10 L.Ed.2d 93 (1963), should have finally disposed of them all. But neither *Meyer* nor *Pierce* has been overruled, and recently there have been decisions of the same genre— *Roe v. Wade*, 410 U.S. 113, 93 S.Ct. 705, 35 L.Ed.2d 147 (1973);[3] *Loving v. Virginia*, 388 U.S. 1, 87 S.Ct. 1817, 18 L.Ed.2d 1010 (1967);[4] *Griswold v. Connecticut*,[5] supra; and *Eisenstadt v. Baird*,[6] 405 U.S. 438, 92 S.Ct. 1029, 31 L.Ed.2d 349 (1972). Not all of these

1. *Meyer* declared unconstitutional, under the due process clause a state law prohibiting the teaching of any subject to any person in any language other than English, in public and private schools. The statute also forbade teaching foreign languages in grade school. Meyer had been convicted of teaching the subject of reading in the German language. McReynolds, J., delivered the opinion for the Court. [Footnote by editor].

2. In *Pierce* the Court, again through McReynolds, J., invalidated a state law that prohibited private or parochial schools and required that normal children between 8 and 16 who have not completed the eighth grade to attend only public schools. The Court found that the statute unreasonably interfered with the "liberty" of parents and the "property" of the schools. [Footnote by editor].

3. *Roe* invalidated much antiabortion legislation. See § 8–3.43, infra. [Footnote by editor].

4. *Loving* invalidated a state antimiscegenation law. See § 8–3.5, infra. [Footnote by editor].

5. *Griswold* invalidated a state law prohibiting the use of contraceptives by married couples. See § 8–3.42, infra. [Footnote by editor].

6. *Eisenstadt* invalidated a state statute that prohibited distribution of contraceptives to unmarried persons. See § 8–3.42, infra. [Footnote by editor].

decisions purport to rest on substantive due process grounds, compare *Roe v. Wade,* supra, 410 U.S., at 152–153, 93 S.Ct., at 726–727, with *Eisenstadt v. Baird,* supra, 410 U.S., at 453–454, 92 S.Ct., at 1038–1039, but all represented substantial reinterpretations of the Constitution.

––––––––

The Court has thus used the due process clause to fashion nontextual rights, most notably what is often called a right to "privacy."[7] It has also used the clause to incorporate some, but not all, of the substantive limitations of the Bill of Rights, and to apply those limitations to the states by virtue of the due process clause of the Fourteenth Amendment. The modern test to determine whether a guarantee of the Bill of Rights also applies to the states is whether the clause in question "is fundamental to the American scheme of justice...." *Duncan v. Louisiana,* 391 U.S. 145, 149, 88 S.Ct. 1444, 20 L.Ed.2d 491 (1968). Under the modern view, once a right is incorporated, it is applied to limit the states in the same way that it is applied to limit the Federal Government, e.g., *Malloy v. Hogan,* 378 U.S. 1, 84 S.Ct. 1489, 12 L.Ed.2d 653 (1964), though there have been a minority of Justices who have argued that the incorporated rights should be applied less strictly against the states. E.g.; *Roth v. United States,* 354 U.S. 476, 496, 77 S.Ct. 1304, 1315, 1 L.Ed.2d 1498 (1957)(Harlan, J., concurring and dissenting); *Johnson v. Louisiana,* 406 U.S. 356, 366, 92 S.Ct. 1620, 1635, 32 L.Ed.2d 152 (1972)(Powell, J., concurring).

The incorporated rights are as follows:

The Court has incorporated all of the First Amendment, *Cantwell v. Connecticut,* 310 U.S. 296, 60 S.Ct. 900, 84 L.Ed. 1213 (1940)(free exercise); *Everson v. Board of Education,* 330 U.S. 1, 67 S.Ct. 504, 91 L.Ed. 711 (1947)(establishment); *Gitlow v. New York,* 268 U.S. 652, 666, 45 S.Ct. 625, 630, 69 L.Ed. 1138 (1925)(speech and press); *De Jonge v. Oregon,* 299 U.S. 353, 57 S.Ct. 255, 81 L.Ed. 278 (1937)(assembly and petition).

The Second Amendment has not been held to be applicable to the states, *Presser v. Illinois,* 116 U.S. 252, 265, 6 S.Ct. 580, 584, 29 L.Ed. 615 (1886).

The Third Amendment has not been the subject of any litigation in the Supreme Court.

The Fourth Amendment has been incorporated, *Wolf v. Colorado,* 338 U.S. 25, 69 S.Ct. 1359, 93 L.Ed. 1782 (1949).

The Fifth Amendment's guarantee of a grand jury has not been applied to the states, *Hurtado v. California,* 110 U.S. 516, 4 S.Ct. 292, 28

7. Some of the privacy cases, because of their close relationship to the equal protec- tion clause, are excerpted below in § 8–3.4.

L.Ed. 232 (1884), but the other guarantees of that Amendment are incorporated, *Benton v. Maryland,* 395 U.S. 784, 89 S.Ct. 2056, 23 L.Ed.2d 707 (1969)(double jeopardy); *Malloy v. Hogan,* 378 U.S. 1, 84 S.Ct. 1489, 12 L.Ed.2d 653 (1964)(self-incrimination); *Chicago, Burlington & Quincy Railway Co. v. Chicago,* 166 U.S. 226, 17 S.Ct. 581, 41 L.Ed. 979 (1897)(just compensation).

The SIXTH AMENDMENT protections are also applied to the states, *Klopfer v. North Carolina,* 386 U.S. 213, 87 S.Ct. 988, 18 L.Ed.2d 1 (1967)(speedy trial); *In re Oliver,* 333 U.S. 257, 68 S.Ct. 499, 92 L.Ed. 682 (1948)(public trial and notice of charges); *Irvin v. Dowd,* 366 U.S. 717, 81 S.Ct. 1639, 6 L.Ed.2d 751 (1961)(impartial jury); *Duncan v. Louisiana,* 391 U.S. 145, 88 S.Ct. 1444, 20 L.Ed.2d 491 (1968)(jury trial); *Pointer v. Texas,* 380 U.S. 400, 85 S.Ct. 1065, 13 L.Ed.2d 923 (1965)(confrontation); *Washington v. Texas,* 388 U.S. 14, 87 S.Ct. 1920, 18 L.Ed.2d 1019 (1967)(compulsory process); *Gideon v. Wainwright,* 372 U.S. 335, 83 S.Ct. 792, 9 L.Ed.2d 799 (1963)(counsel).

The SEVENTH AMENDMENT right to jury trial in suits at common law with over $20 in controversy is not applicable to the states. *Minneapolis & St. Louis Railway Co. v. Bombolis,* 241 U.S. 211, 36 S.Ct. 595, 60 L.Ed. 961 (1916).

Most, and perhaps all, of the EIGHTH AMENDMENT is incorporated. *Robinson v. California,* 370 U.S. 660, 82 S.Ct. 1417, 8 L.Ed.2d 758 (1962)(cruel and unusual punishment); Cf. *Schilb v. Kuebel,* 404 U.S. 357, 365, 92 S.Ct. 479, 484, 30 L.Ed.2d 502 (1971)("the Eighth Amendment's proscription of excessive bail has been assumed to have application to the States through the Fourteenth Amendment"). There are no cases directly on point on the excessive fine guarantee. Cf. *Tate v. Short,* 401 U.S. 395, 91 S.Ct. 668, 28 L.Ed.2d 130 (1971)(equal protection clause of Fourteenth Amendment used to protect indigents subject to fine).

The NINTH AMENDMENT has not been held to be applicable to the states, cf. *Griswold v. Connecticut,* 381 U.S. 479, 492, 85 S.Ct. 1678, 1686, 14 L.Ed.2d 510 (1965)(Goldberg, J., joined by Warren, C.J., and Brennan, J., concurring: "I do not mean to imply that the Ninth Amendment is applied against the States by the Fourteenth.")

The TENTH AMENDMENT does not apply to the states by its own language.

6–3. THE NEW PROCEDURAL DUE PROCESS

AN INTRODUCTORY NOTE ON THE NEW PROCEDURAL DUE PROCESS

For many years the Court held that the Government was not subject to the procedural due process guarantees unless it sought to deprive someone of a right rather than a privilege. When a state policeman objected that he was being fired because of his political activities, Judge (later Justice) Holmes simply stated: "The petitioner may have a constitutional right to talk politics, but he has no constitutional right to be a policeman."[1] Unfortunately, the Court never developed adequate tests to determine what is a "right" versus a "privilege," so the labels were merely conclusory.[2]

In 1970, in *Goldberg v. Kelly,* excerpted at § 6–3.2, infra, the Court turned down a new road when it recognized statutory entitlements—"welfare benefits"—as "property" deserving of procedural due process. At first it was difficult to determine where this road might lead (which is why the cases will not be discussed in chronological order), but now it appears that the Court engages in a two-step analysis. First, is something "life," "liberty," or "property" ?[3] If it is, the Government cannot deprive a person of it unless the Government offers procedural due process. Thus the next question is: what process is due? Under this second issue is a subsidiary one: *when* is the process due, *i.e.,* before or after the termination of benefits?

This area of the law in particular has exploded in recent years and procedural due process questions must now be considered in various law school courses such as creditors' rights (e.g., attachment of property), administrative law (e.g., agency termination of benefits), criminal law (e.g., revocation of parole), and other areas. Here, you will at least be introduced to a few of the more significant cases and issues in this area.

6–3.1 Defining "Liberty" and "Property"

BOARD OF REGENTS v. ROTH
408 U.S. 564, 92 S.Ct. 2701, 33 L.Ed.2d 548 (1972).

[In 1968 Roth was hired for one year as an assistant professor at Wisconsin State University—Oshkosh. At the end of the year he was told that he would not be rehired for the next academic year. Under Wisconsin statutes, a tenured teacher was entitled to continued employment "during efficiency and good behavior" but state law left the decision whether to rehire a nontenured teacher like Roth "to the unfettered discretion of university officials." A tenured teacher could not be discharged except for cause, upon written charges, and pursuant to certain procedures. A nontenured teacher has somewhat similar protection but only *during* his one year term. There was no real protection for a nontenured teacher who was simply not rehired at the end of the contract. Under the Rules promulgated by the Board of Regents, no reason need be given for nonretention and there were no review or appeals. Roth sued, claiming that the failure to rehire him violated his

1. *McAuliffe v. Mayor of New Bedford,* 155 Mass. 216, 220, 29 N.E. 517 (1892).

2. See generally, Van Alstyne, The Demise of the Right–Privilege Distinction in Constitutional Law, 81 Harv.L.Rev. 1439 (1968).

3. Because only governmental action is subject to Fifth and Fourteenth Amendment safeguards, the Court must first determine that such state action exists. In some cases whether or not there exists the requisite state action will be the controlling question: that issue will not be discussed at this point but in Chapter 7, infra.

substantive rights (he alleged a violation of free speech in that the true reason for the decision not to rehire was to punish him for certain statements critical of the University), and procedural rights (he alleged that the failure of the university to provide him with notice and hearing prior to the decision on nonretention violated his procedural rights). Only the question as to whether Roth was deprived of liberty or property was before the Court.]

MR. JUSTICE STEWART delivered the opinion of the Court....

The requirements of procedural due process apply only to the deprivation of interests encompassed by the Fourteenth Amendment's protection of liberty and property. When protected interests are implicated, the right to some kind of prior hearing is paramount. But the range of interests protected by procedural due process is not infinite.

The District Court decided that procedural due process guarantees apply in this case by assessing and balancing the weights of the particular interests involved.... And a weighing process has long been a part of any determination of the *form* of hearing required in particular situations by procedural due process. But, to determine whether due process requirements apply in the first place, we must look not to the "weight" but to the *nature* of the interest at stake. We must look to see if the interest is within the Fourteenth Amendment's protection of liberty and property.

[O]n the record before us, all that clearly appears is that the respondent was not rehired for one year at one university. It stretches the concept too far to suggest that a person is deprived of "liberty" when he simply is not rehired in one job but remains as free as before to seek another.

The Fourteenth Amendment's procedural protection of property is a safeguard of the security of interests that a person has already acquired in specific benefits. These interests—property interests—may take many forms.... To have a property interest in a benefit, a person clearly must have more than an abstract need or desire for it. He must have more than a unilateral expectation of it. He must, instead, have a legitimate claim of entitlement to it. It is a purpose of the ancient institution of property to protect those claims upon which people rely in their daily lives, reliance that must not be arbitrarily undermined. It is a purpose of the constitutional right to a hearing to provide an opportunity for a person to vindicate those claims.

Property interests, of course, are not created by the Constitution. Rather, they are created and their dimensions are defined by existing rules or understandings that stem from an independent source such as state law—rules or understandings that secure certain benefits and that support claims of entitlement to those benefits. Thus, the welfare recipients in *Goldberg v. Kelly,* [§ 6–3.2, infra], had a claim of entitlement to welfare payments that was grounded in the statute defining eligibility for them....

Just as the welfare recipients' "property" interest in welfare payments was created and defined by statutory terms, so the respondent's "property" interest in employment at Wisconsin State University—Oshkosh was created and defined by the terms of his appointment. Those terms secured his interest in employment up to June 30, 1969. But the important fact in this case is that they specifically provided that the respondent's employment was to terminate on June 30. They did not provide for contract renewal absent "sufficient cause." Indeed, they made no provision for renewal whatsoever.

Thus, the terms of the respondent's appointment secured absolutely no interest in re-employment for the next year. They supported absolutely no possible claim of entitlement to re-employment. Nor, significantly, was there any state statute or University rule or policy that secured his interest in re-employment or that created any legitimate claim to it. In these circumstances, the respondent surely had an abstract concern in being rehired, but he did not have a *property* interest sufficient to require the University authorities to give him a hearing when they declined to renew his contract of employment. . . .

We must conclude that the summary judgment for the respondent should not have been granted, since the respondent has not shown that he was deprived of liberty or property protected by the Fourteenth Amendment. The judgment of the Court of Appeals, accordingly, is reversed and the case is remanded for further proceedings consistent with this opinion.

It is so ordered.

MR. JUSTICE POWELL took no part in the decision of this case.

MR. JUSTICE MARSHALL, dissenting. . . .

In my view, every citizen who applies for a government job is entitled to it unless the government can establish some reason for denying the employment. This is the "property" right that I believe is protected by the Fourteenth Amendment and that cannot be denied "without due process of law." And it is also liberty—liberty to work—which is the "very essence of the personal freedom and opportunity" secured by the Fourteenth Amendment.

This Court has often had occasion to note that the denial of public employment is a serious blow to any citizen. Thus, when an application for public employment is denied or the contract of a government employee is not renewed, the government must say why, for it is only when the reasons underlying government action are known that citizens feel secure and protected against arbitrary government action. Employment is one of the greatest, if not the greatest, benefits that governments offer in modern-day life. When something as valuable as the opportunity to work is at stake, the government may not reward some citizens and not others without demonstrating that its actions are fair and equitable. And it is procedural due process that is our fundamental guarantee of fairness, our protection against arbitrary, capricious, and unreasonable government action....

[A concurring opinion of BURGER, C.J., & dissenting opinions of DOUGLAS & BRENNAN, JJ., are omitted.]

PERRY v. SINDERMANN
408 U.S. 593, 92 S.Ct. 2694, 33 L.Ed.2d 570 (1972).

MR. JUSTICE STEWART delivered the opinion of the Court.

From 1959 to 1969 the respondent, Robert Sindermann, was a teacher in the state college system of the State of Texas. After teaching for two years at the University of Texas and for four years at San Antonio Junior College, he became a professor of Government and Social Science at Odessa Junior College in 1965. He was employed at the college for four successive years, under a series of one-year contracts. He was successful enough to be appointed, for a time, the cochairman of his department.

During the 1968–1969 academic year, however, controversy arose between the respondent and the college administration. The respondent was elected president of the Texas Junior College Teachers Association. In this capacity, he left his teaching duties on several occasions to testify before committees of the Texas Legislature, and he became involved in public disagreements with the policies of the college's Board of Regents. In particular, he aligned himself with a group advocating the elevation of the college to four-year status—a change opposed by the Regents. And, on one occasion, a newspaper advertisement appeared over his name that was highly critical of the Regents.

Finally, in May 1969, the respondent's one-year employment contract terminated and the Board of Regents voted not to offer him a new contract for the next academic year. The Regents issued a press release setting forth allegations of the respondent's insubordination. But they provided him no official statement of the reasons for the nonrenewal of his contract. And they allowed him no opportunity for a hearing to challenge the basis of the nonrenewal.

... We granted a writ of certiorari, and we have considered this case along with *Board of Regents v. Roth*. The first question presented is whether the respondent's lack of a contractual or tenure right to re-employment, taken alone, defeats his claim that the nonrenewal of his contract violated the First and Fourteenth Amendments. We hold that it does not.

For at least a quarter-century, this Court has made clear that even though a person has no "right" to a valuable governmental benefit and even though the government may deny him the benefit for any number of reasons, there are some reasons upon which the government may not rely. It may not deny a benefit to a person on a basis that infringes his constitutionally protected interests—especially, his interest in freedom of speech. For if the government could deny a benefit to a person because of his constitutionally protected speech or associations, his exercise of those freedoms would in effect be penalized and inhibited. This would allow the government to "produce a result which [it] could not command directly." Such interference with constitutional rights is impermissible.... For this reason we hold that the grant of summary judgment against the respondent, without full exploration of this issue, was improper.

The respondent's lack of formal contractual or tenure security in continued employment at Odessa Junior College, though irrelevant to his free speech claim, is highly relevant to his procedural due process claim. But it may not be entirely dispositive.

... As in *Roth,* the mere showing that he was not rehired in one particular job, without more, did not amount to a showing of a loss of liberty. Nor did it amount to a showing of a loss of property. But the respondent's allegations—which we must construe most favorably to the respondent at this stage of the litigation—do raise a genuine issue as to his interest in continued employment at Odessa Junior College. He alleged that this interest, though not secured by a formal contractual tenure provision, was secured by a no less binding understanding fostered by the college administration. In particular, the respondent alleged that the college had a *de facto* tenure program, and that he had tenure under that program. He claimed that he and others legitimately relied upon an unusual provision that had been in the college's official Faculty Guide for many years:

> *Teacher Tenure:* Odessa College has no tenure system. The Administration of the College wishes the faculty member to feel that he has permanent tenure as long as his teaching services are satisfactory and as long as he displays a cooperative attitude toward his co-workers and his superiors, and as long as he is happy in his work.

Moreover, the respondent claimed legitimate reliance upon guidelines promulgated by the Coordinating Board of the Texas College and University System that provided that a person, like himself, who had been employed as a teacher in the state college and university system for seven years or more has some form of job tenure. Thus, the respondent offered to prove that a teacher with his long period of service at this particular State College had no less a "property" interest in continued employment than a formally tenured teacher at other colleges, and had no less a procedural due process right to a statement of reasons and a hearing before college officials upon their decision not to retain him.

We have made clear in *Roth,* supra, that "property" interests subject to procedural due process protection are not limited by a few rigid, technical forms. Rather, "property" denotes a broad range of interests that are secured by "existing rules or understandings." A person's interest in a benefit is a "property" interest for due process purposes if there are such rules or mutually explicit understandings that support his claim of entitlement to the benefit and that he may invoke at a hearing.

A written contract with an explicit tenure provision clearly is evidence of a formal understanding that supports a teacher's claim of entitlement to continued employment unless sufficient "cause" is shown. Yet absence of such an explicit contractual provision may not always foreclose the possibility that a teacher has a "property" interest in re-employment. For example, the law of contracts in most, if not all, jurisdictions long has employed a process by which agreements, though not formalized in writing, may be "implied." 3 A. Corbin on Contracts §§ 561–572A (1960). Explicit contractual provisions may be supplemented by other agreements implied from "the promisor's words and conduct in the light of the surrounding circumstances." Id., at § 562. And, "[t]he meaning of [the promisor's] words and acts is found by relating them to the usage of the past." Ibid.

A teacher, like the respondent, who has held his position for a number of years, might be able to show from the circumstances of this service—and from other relevant facts—that he has a legitimate claim of entitlement to job tenure. [T]here may be an unwritten "common law" in a particular university that certain employees shall have the equivalent of tenure. This is particularly likely in a college or university, like Odessa Junior College, that has no explicit tenure system even for senior members of its faculty, but that nonetheless may have created such a system in practice.

In this case, the respondent has alleged the existence of rules and understandings, promulgated and fostered by state officials, that may justify his legitimate claim of entitlement to continued employment absent "sufficient cause." We disagree with the Court of Appeals insofar as it held that a mere subjective "expectancy" is protected by procedural due process, but we agree that the respondent must be given an opportunity to prove the legitimacy of his claim of such entitlement in light of "the policies and practices of the institution." Proof of such a property interest would not, of course, entitle him to reinstatement. But such proof would obligate college officials to grant a hearing at his request, where he could be informed of the grounds for his nonretention and challenge their sufficiency.

Therefore, while we do not wholly agree with the opinion of the Court of Appeals, its judgment remanding this case to the District Court is

Affirmed.

MR. JUSTICE POWELL took no part in the decision of this case.

[A concurring opinion of BURGER, C.J., an opinion dissenting in part, of BRENNAN, J., joined by DOUGLAS, J., and an opinion dissenting in part, of MARSHALL, J., are omitted.]

Notes

1. *Wisconsin v. Constantineau,* 400 U.S. 433, 91 S.Ct. 507, 27 L.Ed.2d 515 (1971). Pursuant to a state statute the police chief of Hartford, without notice or hearing to Constantineau, posted a notice in retail liquor outlets in

Hartford forbidding the sale or gift of liquor to Constantineau for one year. The Court, per Douglas, J., held that the statute did not meet the requirements of due process: "Where a person's good name, reputation, honor, or integrity is at stake because of what the government is doing to him, notice and an opportunity to be heard are essential." Under the Wisconsin Act, a person subject to a "posting" was given no process at all. "This appellee was not afforded a chance to defend herself. She may have been the victim of an official's caprice. Only when the whole proceedings leading to the pinning of an unsavory label on a person are aired can oppressive results be prevented."

Compare *Paul v. Davis,* 424 U.S. 693, 96 S.Ct. 1155, 47 L.Ed.2d 405 (1976). Police officials circulated a flyer to Louisville merchants accusing Davis of being an "active shoplifter." Though charges had been brought against him, they had been dropped, and he had never been convicted of that offense. He sued for damages and injunctive relief claiming that state action had deprived him of a liberty interest because the designation inhibited him "from entering business establishments for fear of being suspected of shoplifting and possibly apprehended, and would seriously impair his future employment opportunities." The Court, per Rehnquist, J., found no liberty or property interest at stake:

> We think that the [language in *Constantineau*], "because of, what the government is doing to him," referred to the fact that the governmental action taken in that case deprived the individual of a right previously held under state law—the right to purchase or obtain liquor in common with the rest of the citizenry. "Posting," therefore, significantly altered her status as a matter of state law, and it was that alteration of legal status which, combined with the injury resulting from the defamation, justified the invocation of procedural safeguards. The "stigma" resulting from the defamatory character of the posting was doubtless an important factor in evaluating the extent of harm worked by that act, but we do not think that such defamation, standing alone, deprived Constantineau of any "liberty" protected by the procedural guarantees of the Fourteenth Amendment. [In the present case,] Kentucky law does not extend to respondent any legal guarantee of present enjoyment of reputation which has been altered as a result of petitioners' actions. Rather his interest in reputation is simply one of a number which the state may protect against by virtue of its tort law, providing a forum for vindication of those interests by means of damages actions. Any harm or injury to that interest, even where as here inflicted by an officer of the State, does not result in a deprivation of any "liberty" or "property" recognized by state or federal law, nor has it worked any change of respondent's status as theretofore recognized under the State's laws. For these reasons we hold that the interest in reputation asserted in this case is neither "liberty" nor "property" guaranteed against state deprivation without due process of law.

Brennan, J., joined by Marshall, J., dissented, arguing that "the Court by mere fiat and with no analysis wholly excludes personal interest in reputation from the ambit of 'life, liberty, or property' under the Fifth and Fourteenth Amendments, thus rendering due process concerns *never* applicable to the official stigmatization, however arbitrary, of an individual. . . . The potential of today's decision is frightening for a free people."

2. *Leis v. Flynt*, 439 U.S. 438, 99 S.Ct. 698, 58 L.Ed.2d 717 (1979)(per curiam). A state trial judge denied respondents' motion to allow out-of-state counsel permission to represent Flynt *pro hac vice*. The Circuit Court held that the lawyer could not be denied that permission "without a meaningful hearing, the application of a reasonably clear legal standard and the statement of a rational basis for exclusion." The Supreme Court, without hearing oral argument, reversed:

> A claim of entitlement under state law, to be enforceable, must be derived from statute or legal rule or through a mutually explicit understanding. The record here is devoid of any indication that an out-of-state lawyer may claim such an entitlement in Ohio, where the rules of the Ohio Supreme Court expressly consign the authority to approve a *pro hac vice* appearance to the discretion of the trial judge. Even if, as the Court of Appeals believed, respondents . . . had reasonable expectations of professional service they have not shown the requisite *mutual* understanding that they would be permitted to represent their clients in any particular case in the Ohio courts. . . . There simply was no deprivation here of some right previously held under state law.

3. *Kentucky Department of Corrections v. Thompson*, 490 U.S. 454, 109 S.Ct. 1904, 104 L.Ed.2d 506 (1989) held that Kentucky prison regulations do not give state inmates a liberty interest in receiving certain visitors. If the due process clause itself does not directly guarantee the liberty, then the state may create a protected liberty interest "by placing substantive limitations on official discretion." Normally the state reaches this result by limiting official decisionmaking and "by mandating the outcome to be reached upon a finding that the relevant criteria have been met." However, if the administrator has "unfettered" discretion, there is no state-created liberty interest. These regulations lack "the requisite relevant mandatory language." For example, they provide that the "administrative staff reserves the right to allow or disallow visits." And visitors "*may* be excluded if they fall within one of the described categories, but they need not be. Nor need visitors fall within one of the described categories in order to be excluded."

Sandin v. Conner,, 515 U.S. 472, 115 S.Ct. 2293, 132 L.Ed.2d 418 (1995). Rehnquist, C.J., for the Court (5 to 4) found no liberty interest, and hence no deprivation of procedural due process, when Hawaiian prison officials refused to allow a prisoner the right to present witnesses during a disciplinary hearing; after the hearing the prisoner was sentenced to segregation for misconduct. A court, when interpreting a law defining rights and remedies for the general public, normally looks to the language of the law, but it is "a good deal less sensible" to do so "in the case of a prison regulation primarily designed to guide correctional officials in the administration of a prison." When courts comb prison regulations in search of mandatory language, they create disincentives for states to codify prison management procedures, and they involve the court in the day-to-day management of prisons. Hence, courts should look to the nature of the deprivation rather than looking merely at the language in the regulation. In the context of prisoners, state-created liberty interests "will generally be limited to freedom from restraint which, while not exceeding the sentence in such an unexpected manner as to give rise to protection by the Due Process Clause of its own force, nonetheless imposes atypical and significant hardship on the inmate in relation to the ordinary incidents of prison life."

Applying this test, the Court concluded that the defendant's discipline in segregated confinement did not present the atypical, significant deprivation where a state might conceivably create a liberty interest. His "concededly punitive" confinement generally mirrored conditions imposed on inmates in protective custody. Inmates in the general prison population at that prison often faced "lockdown" time, and the state expunged the defendant's disciplinary record after 9 months. Therefore neither Hawaiian prison regulations nor the Due Process Clause created a liberty interest that would impose procedural protections.

4. *DeShaney v. Winnebago County Department of Social Services,* 489 U.S. 189, 109 S.Ct. 998, 103 L.Ed.2d 249 (1989). Joshua DeShaney, a four year old boy beaten by his father over a period of time, was finally injured so severely that he fell into a life-threatening coma, became retarded, and was expected to spend the rest of his life confined in an institution for the profoundly retarded. DeShaney sued social workers and other local officials who had received repeated complaints and had reason to believe that his father was subjecting him to child abuse, but did not remove him from his father's custody. One social worker's reaction to the news of the most recent incident was, "I just knew the phone would ring some day and Joshua would be dead."

Petitioner complained that the respondents' failure to act deprived him of liberty in violation of the due process clause of the Fourteenth Amendment. Rehnquist, C.J., for the Court (6 to 3) disagreed. "[N]othing in the language of the Due Process Clause itself requires the State to protect the life, liberty, and property of its citizens against invasion by private actors. The Clause is phrased as a limitation on the State's power to act, not as a guarantee of certain minimal levels of safety and security." The Court declined to consider an argument, not raised below, that "Wisconsin child protection statutes gave to Joshua an 'entitlement' to receive protective services in accordance with the terms of the statute, an entitlement which would enjoy due process protection against state deprivation under our decision in *Board of Regents v. Roth.*"

6–3.2   *Determining What Process is Due*

GOLDBERG v. KELLY
397 U.S. 254, 90 S.Ct. 1011, 25 L.Ed.2d 287 (1970).

M R. J USTICE B RENNAN delivered the opinion of the Court.

The question for decision is whether a State that terminates public assistance payments to a particular recipient without affording him the opportunity for an evidentiary hearing prior to termination denies the recipient procedural due process in violation of the Due Process Clause of the Fourteenth Amendment....

The constitutional issue to be decided ... is the narrow one whether the Due Process Clause requires that the recipient be afforded an evidentiary hearing *before* the termination of benefits. The District Court held that only a pre-termination evidentiary hearing would satisfy the constitutional command, and rejected the argument of the state and city officials that the combination of the post-termination "fair hearing" with the informal pre-termination review disposed of all due process claims. The court said: "While post-termination review is relevant, there is one overpowering fact which controls here. By hypothesis, a welfare recipient is destitute, without funds or assets. . . . Suffice it to say that to cut off a welfare recipient in the face of . . . 'brutal need' without a prior hearing of some sort is unconscionable, unless overwhelming considerations justify it." . . .

Appellant does not contend that procedural due process is not applicable to the termination of welfare benefits. Such benefits are a matter of statutory entitlement for persons qualified to receive them.[8] Their termination involves state action that adjudicates important rights. The constitutional challenge cannot be answered by an argument that public assistance benefits are "a 'privilege' and not a 'right.' "Relevant constitutional restraints apply as much to the withdrawal of public assistance benefits as to disqualification for unemployment compensation; or to denial of a tax exemption; or to discharge from public employment. The extent to which procedural due process must be afforded the recipient is influenced by the extent to which he may be "condemned to suffer grievous loss," and depends upon whether the recipient's interest in avoiding that loss outweighs the governmental interest in summary adjudication. . . .

It is true, of course, that some governmental benefits may be administratively terminated without affording the recipient a pre-termination evidentiary hearing.[10] [But] when welfare is discontinued, only a

---

8. It may be realistic today to regard welfare entitlements as more like "property" than a "gratuity." Much of the existing wealth in this country takes the form of rights that do not fall within traditional commonlaw concepts of property. It has been aptly noted that

"[s]ociety today is built around entitlement. The automobile dealer has his franchise, the doctor and lawyer their professional licenses, the worker his union membership, contract, and pension rights. . . . Many of the most important of these entitlements now flow from government: subsidies to farmers and businessmen, routes for airlines and channels for television stations; long term contracts for defense, space, and education; social security pensions for individuals. Such sources of security, whether private or public, are no longer regarded as luxuries or gratuities. . . . It is only the poor whose entitlements, although recognized by public policy, have not been effectively enforced." Reich, Individual Rights and Social Wel-

fare: The Emerging Legal Issues, 74 Yale L.J. 1245, 1255 (1965). See also Reich, The New Property, 73 Yale L.J. 733 (1964).

10. One Court of Appeals has stated: "In a wide variety of situations, it has long been recognized that where harm to the public is threatened, and the private interest infringed is reasonably deemed to be of less importance, an official body can take summary action pending a later hearing." *R.A. Holman & Co. v. SEC,* 299 F.2d 127, 131, cert. denied, 370 U.S. 911, 82 S.Ct. 1257, 8 L.Ed.2d 404 (1962)(suspension of exemption from stock registration requirement). See also, for example, *Ewing v. Mytinger & Casselberry, Inc.,* 339 U.S. 594, 70 S.Ct. 870, 94 L.Ed. 1088 (1950)(seizure of mislabeled vitamin product). In *Cafeteria & Restaurant Workers Union v. McElroy,* [367 U.S. at 896, 81 S.Ct. at 1749 (1961)], summary dismissal of a public employee was upheld because "[i]n [its] proprietary military capacity, the Federal Government . . .

pre-termination evidentiary hearing provides the recipient with procedural due process. For qualified recipients, welfare provides the means to obtain essential food, clothing, housing, and medical care. Thus the crucial factor in this context—a factor not present in the case of the blacklisted government contractor, the discharged government employee, the taxpayer denied a tax exemption, or virtually anyone else whose governmental entitlements are ended—is that termination of aid pending resolution of a controversy over eligibility may deprive an *eligible* recipient of the very means by which to live while he waits. Since he lacks independent resources, his situation becomes immediately desperate. His need to concentrate upon finding the means for daily subsistence, in turn, adversely affects his ability to seek redress from the welfare bureaucracy.

Moreover, important governmental interests are promoted by affording recipients a pre-termination evidentiary hearing. [Public assistance] is not mere charity, but a means to "promote the general Welfare, and secure the Blessings of Liberty to ourselves and our Posterity." The same governmental interests that counsel the provision of welfare, counsel as well its uninterrupted provision to those eligible to receive it; pre-termination evidentiary hearings are indispensable to that end.

Appellant does not challenge the force of these considerations but argues that they are outweighed by countervailing governmental interests in conserving fiscal and administrative resources. These interests, the argument goes, justify the delay of any evidentiary hearing until after discontinuance of the grants. Summary adjudication protects the public fisc by stopping payments promptly upon discovery of reason to believe that a recipient is no longer eligible. Since most terminations are accepted without challenge, summary adjudication also conserves both the fisc and administrative time and energy by reducing the number of evidentiary hearings actually held.

[T]hese governmental interests are not overriding in the welfare context. The requirement of a prior hearing doubtless involves some greater expense, and the benefits paid to ineligible recipients pending decision at the hearing probably cannot be recouped, since these recipients are likely to be judgment-proof. But the State is not without weapons to minimize these increased costs. Much of the drain on fiscal and administrative resources can be reduced by developing procedures for prompt pre-termination hearings and by skillful use of personnel and facilities. Indeed, the very provision for a post-termination evidentiary hearing in New York's Home Relief program is itself cogent evidence that the State recognizes the primacy of the public interest in correct eligibility determinations and therefore in the provision of procedural safeguards. Thus, the interest of the eligible recipient in uninterrupted receipt of public assistance, coupled with the State's interest that his payments not be erroneously terminated, clearly outweighs the State's

has traditionally exercised unfettered control," and because the case involved the Government's "dispatch of its own internal affairs."

competing concern to prevent any increase in its fiscal and administrative burdens. . . .

[T]he pre-termination hearing need not take the form of a judicial or quasi-judicial trial. We bear in mind that the statutory "fair hearing" will provide the recipient with a full administrative review. Accordingly, the pre-termination hearing has one function only: to produce an initial determination of the validity of the welfare department's grounds for discontinuance of payments in order to protect a recipient against an erroneous termination of his benefits. Thus, a complete record and a comprehensive opinion, which would serve primarily to facilitate judicial review and to guide future decisions, need not be provided at the pre-termination stage. . . . We wish to add that we, no less than the dissenters, recognize the importance of not imposing upon the States or the Federal Government in this developing field of law any procedural requirements beyond those demanded by rudimentary due process.

"The fundamental requisite of due process of law is the opportunity to be heard." The hearing must be "at a meaningful time and in a meaningful manner." In the present context these principles require that a recipient have timely and adequate notice detailing the reasons for a proposed termination, and an effective opportunity to defend by confronting any adverse witnesses and by presenting his own arguments and evidence orally. These rights are important in cases such as those before us, where recipients have challenged proposed terminations as resting on incorrect or misleading factual premises or on misapplication of rules or policies to the facts of particular cases.

We are not prepared to say that the seven-day notice currently provided by New York City is constitutionally insufficient *per se,* although there may be cases where fairness would require that a longer time be given. Nor do we see any constitutional deficiency in the content or form of the notice. New York employs both a letter and a personal conference with a caseworker to inform a recipient of the precise questions raised about his continued eligibility. Evidently the recipient is told the legal and factual bases for the Department's doubts. This combination is probably the most effective method of communicating with recipients.

The city's procedures presently do not permit recipients to appear personally with or without counsel before the official who finally determines continued eligibility. Thus a recipient is not permitted to present evidence to that official orally, or to confront or cross-examine adverse witnesses. These omissions are fatal to the constitutional adequacy of the procedures.

The opportunity to be heard must be tailored to the capacities and circumstances of those who are to be heard. It is not enough that a welfare recipient may present his position to the decision maker in writing or secondhand through his caseworker. Written submissions are an unrealistic option for most recipients, who lack the educational attainment necessary to write effectively and who cannot obtain professional assistance. Moreover, written submissions do not afford the flexibility of oral presentations; they do not permit the recipient to mold his argument to the issues the decision maker appears to regard as important. Particularly where credibility and veracity are at issue, as they must be in many termination proceedings, written submissions are a wholly unsatisfactory basis for decision. . . . Therefore a recipient must be allowed to state his position orally. Informal procedures will suffice; in this context due process does not require a particular order of proof or mode of offering evidence.

In almost every setting where important decisions turn on questions of fact, due process requires an opportunity to confront and cross-examine adverse witnesses. . . . Welfare recipients must therefore be given an opportunity to confront and cross-examine the witnesses relied on by the department. "The right to be heard would be, in many cases, of little avail if it did not comprehend the right to be heard by counsel." We do not say that counsel must be provided at the pre-termination hearing, but only that the recipient must be allowed to retain an attorney if he so desires. Counsel can help delineate the issues, present the factual contentions in an orderly manner, conduct cross-examination, and generally safeguard the interests of the recipient. We do not anticipate that this assistance will unduly prolong or otherwise encumber the hearing. . . .

Finally, the decision maker's conclusion as to a recipient's eligibility must rest solely on the legal rules and evidence adduced at the hearing. To demonstrate compliance with this elementary requirement, the decision maker should state the reasons for his determination and indicate the evidence he relied on, though his statement need not amount to a full opinion or even formal findings of fact and conclusions of law. And, of course, an impartial decision maker is essential. We agree with the District Court that prior involvement in some aspects of a case will not necessarily bar a welfare official from acting as a decision maker. He should not, however, have participated in making the determination under review.

Affirmed.

Mr. Justice Black, dissenting.

In the last half century the United States, along with many, perhaps most, other nations of the world, has moved far toward becoming a welfare state, that is, a nation that for one reason or another taxes its most affluent people to help support, feed, clothe, and shelter its less fortunate citizens. The result is that today more than nine million men, women, and children in the United States receive some kind of state or federally financed public assistance in the form of allowances or gratuities, generally paid them periodically, usually by the week, month, or quarter. Since these gratuities are paid on the basis of need, the list of recipients is not static, and some people go off the lists and others are added from time to time. These ever-changing lists put a constant administrative burden on government and it certainly could not have reasonably anticipated that this burden would include the additional procedural expense imposed by the Court today. . . .

The more than a million names on the relief rolls in New York, and the more than nine million names on the rolls of all the 50 States were not put there at random. The names are there because state welfare officials believed that those people were eligible for assistance. Probably in the officials' haste to make out the lists many names were put there erroneously in order to alleviate immediate suffering, and undoubtedly some people are drawing relief who are not entitled under the law to do so. Doubtless some draw relief checks from time to time who know they are not eligible, either because they are not actually in need or for some other reason. Many of those who thus draw undeserved gratuities are without sufficient property to enable the government to collect back from them any money they wrongfully receive. But the Court today holds that it would violate the Due Process Clause of the Fourteenth Amendment to stop paying those people weekly or monthly allowances unless the government first affords them a full "evidentiary hearing" even though welfare officials are persuaded that the recipients are not rightfully entitled to receive a penny under the law. In other words, although some recipients might be on the lists for payment wholly because of deliberate fraud on their part, the Court holds that the government is helpless and must continue, until after an evidentiary hearing, to pay money that it does not owe, never has owed, and never could owe. I do not believe there is any provision in our Constitution that should thus paralyze the government's efforts to protect itself against making payments to people who are not entitled to them. . . . It somewhat strains credulity to say that the government's promise of charity to an individual is property belonging to that individual when the government denies that the individual is honestly entitled to receive such a payment.

I would have little, if any, objection to the majority's decision in this case if it were written as the report of the House Committee on Education and Labor, but as an opinion ostensibly resting on the language of the Constitution I find it woefully deficient. . . . The majority [weighs] "the recipient's interest in avoiding" the termination of welfare benefits against "the governmental interest in summary adjudication." Today's balancing act requires a "pre-termination evidentiary hearing," yet there is nothing that indicates what tomorrow's balance will be. [I]t is obvious that today's result does not depend on the language of the Constitution itself or the principles of other decisions, but solely on the collective judgment of the majority as to what would be a fair and humane procedure in this case. . . .

The Court apparently feels that this decision will benefit the poor and needy. In my judgment the eventual result will be just the opposite. While today's decision requires only an administrative, evidentiary hearing, the inevitable logic of the approach taken will lead to constitutionally imposed, time-consuming delays of a full adversary process of administrative and judicial review. . . . Thus the end result of today's decision may well be that the government, once it decides to give welfare benefits, cannot reverse that decision until the recipient has had the benefits of full administrative and judicial review, including, of course, the opportunity to present his case to this Court. Since this process will usually entail a delay of several years, the inevitable result of such a constitutionally imposed burden will be that the government will not put a claimant on the rolls initially until it has made an exhaustive investigation to determine his eligibility. While this Court will perhaps have insured that no needy person will be taken off the rolls without a full "due process" proceeding, it will also have insured that many will never get on the rolls, or at least that they will remain destitute during the lengthy proceedings followed to determine initial eligibility. . . .

[The dissenting opinions of BURGER, C.J., joined by BLACK, J., and of STEWART, J., are omitted.]

MATHEWS v. ELDRIDGE
424 U.S. 319, 96 S.Ct. 893, 47 L.Ed.2d 18 (1976).

MR. JUSTICE POWELL delivered the opinion of the Court.

The issue in this case is whether the Due Process Clause of the Fifth Amendment requires that prior to the termination of Social Security disability benefit payments the recipient be afforded an opportunity for an evidentiary hearing.

Cash benefits are provided to workers during periods in which they are completely disabled under the disability insurance benefits program created by the 1956 amendments to Title II of the Social Security Act. Respondent Eldridge was first awarded benefits in June 1968. In March 1972, he received a questionnaire from the state agency charged with monitoring his medical condition. Eldridge completed the questionnaire, indicating that his condition had not improved and identifying the medical sources, including physicians, from whom he had received treatment recently. The state agency then obtained reports from his physician and a psychiatric consultant. After considering these reports and other information in his file the agency informed Eldridge by letter that it had made a tentative determination that his disability had ceased in May 1972. The letter included a statement of reasons for the proposed termination of benefits, and advised Eldridge that he might request reasonable time in which to obtain and submit additional information pertaining to his condition.

In his written response, Eldridge disputed one characterization of his medical condition and indicated that the agency already had enough evidence to establish his disability. The state agency then made its final determination that he had ceased to be disabled in May 1972. This determination was accepted by the Social Security Administration (SSA), which notified Eldridge in July that his benefits would terminate after that month. The notification also advised him of his right to seek reconsideration by the state agency of this initial determination within six months.

Instead of requesting reconsideration Eldridge commenced this action challenging the constitutional validity of the administrative procedures established by the Secretary of Health, Education, and Welfare for assessing whether there exists a continuing disability. He sought an immediate reinstatement of benefits pending a hearing on the issue of his disability.... The Secretary does not contend that procedural due process is inapplicable to terminations of Social Security disability benefits [but] contends that the existing administrative procedures ... provide all the process that is constitutionally due before a recipient can be deprived of that interest.... Eldridge agrees that the review procedures available to a claimant before the initial determination of ineligibility becomes final would be adequate if disability benefits were not terminated until after the evidentiary hearing stage of the administrative process. The dispute centers upon what process is due prior to the initial termination of benefits, pending review.

... In only one case, *Goldberg v. Kelly,* has the Court held that a hearing closely approximating a judicial trial is necessary. In other cases requiring some type of pretermination hearing as a matter of constitutional right the Court has spoken sparingly about the requisite procedures.... These decisions underscore the truism that " '[d]ue process,' unlike some legal rules, is not a technical conception with a fixed content unrelated to time, place and circumstances." "[D]ue process is flexible and calls for such procedural protections as the particular situation demands." Accordingly, resolution of the issue whether the administrative procedures provided here are constitutionally sufficient requires analysis of the governmental and private interests that are affected. More precisely, our prior decisions indicate that identification of the specific dictates of due process generally requires consideration of three distinct factors: First, the private interest that will be affected by the official action; second, the risk of an erroneous deprivation of such interest through the procedures used, and the probable value, if any, of additional or substitute procedural safeguards; and finally, the Government's interest, including the function involved and the fiscal and administrative burdens that the additional or substitute procedural requirement would entail....

Despite the elaborate character of the administrative procedures provided by the Secretary, the courts below held them to be constitutionally inadequate, concluding that due process requires an evidentiary hearing prior to termination. In light of the private and governmental interests at stake here and the nature of the existing procedures, we think this was error.

Since a recipient whose benefits are terminated is awarded full retroactive relief if he ultimately prevails, his sole interest is in the uninterrupted receipt of this source of income pending final administrative decision on his claim. His potential injury is thus similar in nature to that of the welfare recipient in *Goldberg*. . . .

Only in *Goldberg* has the Court held that due process requires an evidentiary hearing prior to a temporary deprivation. It was emphasized there that welfare assistance is given to persons on the very margin of subsistence. . . . Eligibility for disability benefits, in contrast, is not based upon financial need. Indeed, it is wholly unrelated to the worker's income or support from many other sources, such as earnings of other family members, workmen's compensation awards, tort claims awards, savings, private insurance, public or private pensions, veterans' benefits, food stamps, public assistance, or the "many other important programs, both public and private, which contain provisions for disability payments affecting a substantial portion of the work force. . . ."

As *Goldberg* illustrates, the degree of potential deprivation that may be created by a particular decision is a factor to be considered in assessing the validity of any administrative decisionmaking process. The potential deprivation here is generally likely to be less than in *Goldberg*, although the degree of difference can be overstated. . . .

As we recognized last Term, "the possible length of wrongful deprivation of . . . benefits [also] is an important factor in assessing the impact of official action on the private interests." The Secretary concedes that the delay between a request for a hearing before an administrative law judge and a decision on the claim is currently between 10 and 11 months. Since a terminated recipient must first obtain a reconsideration decision as a prerequisite to invoking his right to an evidentiary hearing, the delay between the actual cutoff of benefits and final decision after a hearing exceeds one year.

In view of the torpidity of this administrative review process, and the typically modest resources of the family unit of the physically disabled worker, the hardship imposed upon the erroneously terminated disability recipient may be significant. Still, the disabled worker's need is likely to be less than that of a welfare recipient. In addition to the possibility of access to private resources, other forms of government assistance will become available where the termination of disability benefits places a worker or his family below the subsistence level. In view of these potential sources of temporary income, there is less reason here than in *Goldberg* to depart from the ordinary principle, established by our decisions, that something less than an evidentiary hearing is sufficient prior to adverse administrative action.

An additional factor to be considered here is the fairness and reliability of the existing pretermination procedures, and the probable value, if any, of additional procedural safeguards. Central to the evaluation of any administrative process is the nature of the relevant inquiry. In order to remain eligible for benefits the disabled worker must demonstrate by means of "medically acceptable clinical and laboratory diagnostic techniques," 42 U.S.C.A. § 423(d)(3), that he is unable "to engage in any substantial gainful activity by reason of any *medically determinable* physical or mental impairment...." § 423(d)(1)(A)(emphasis supplied). In short, a medical assessment of the worker's physical or mental condition is required. This is a more sharply focused and easily documented decision than the typical determination of welfare entitlement. In the latter case, a wide variety of information may be deemed relevant, and issues of witness credibility and veracity often are critical to the decisionmaking process. *Goldberg* noted that in such circumstances "written submissions are a wholly unsatisfactory basis for decision."

By contrast, the decision whether to discontinue disability benefits will turn, in most cases, upon "routine, standard, and unbiased medical reports by physician specialists," concerning a subject whom they have personally examined.... To be sure, credibility and veracity may be a factor in the ultimate disability assessment in some cases. But procedural due process rules are shaped by the risk of error inherent in the truthfinding process as applied to the generality of cases, not the rare exceptions. The potential value of an evidentiary hearing, or even oral presentation to the decisionmaker, is substantially less in this context than in *Goldberg*.

The decision in *Goldberg* also was based on the Court's conclusion that written submissions were an inadequate substitute for oral presentation because they did not provide an effective means for the recipient to communicate his case to the decisionmaker. [Here, in contrast, the] detailed questionnaire which the state agency periodically sends the recipient identifies with particularity the information relevant to the entitlement decision, and the recipient is invited to obtain assistance from the local SSA office in completing the questionnaire. More importantly, the information critical to the entitlement decision usually is derived from medical sources, such as the treating physician. Such sources are likely to be able to communicate more effectively through written documents than are welfare recipients or the lay witnesses supporting their cause. The conclusions of physicians often are supported by X-rays and the results of clinical or laboratory tests, information typically more amenable to written than to oral presentation.

A further safeguard against mistake is the policy of allowing the disability recipient's representative full access to all information relied upon by the state agency. In addition, prior to the cutoff of benefits the agency informs the recipient of its tentative assessment, the reasons therefor, and provides a summary of the evidence that it considers most relevant. Opportunity is then afforded the recipient to submit additional evidence or arguments, enabling him to challenge directly the accuracy of information in his file as well as the correctness of the agency's tentative conclusions. These procedures, again as contrasted with those before the Court in *Goldberg,* enable the recipient to "mold" his argument to respond to the precise issues which the decisionmaker regards as crucial.

Despite these carefully structured procedures, *amici* point to the significant reversal rate for appealed cases as clear evidence that the current process is inadequate. Depending upon the base selected and the line of analysis followed, the relevant reversal rates urged by the contending parties vary from a high of 58.6% for appealed reconsideration decisions to an overall reversal rate of only 3.3%. Bare statistics rarely provide a satisfactory measure of the fairness of a decisionmaking process. Their adequacy is especially suspect here since the administrative review system is operated on an open-file basis. A recipient may always submit new evidence, and such submissions may result in additional medical examinations. Such fresh examinations were held in approximately 30% to 40% of the appealed cases in fiscal 1973, either at the reconsideration or evidentiary hearing stage of the administrative process. In this context, the value of reversal rate statistics as one means of evaluating the adequacy of the pretermination process is diminished. Thus, although we view such information as relevant, it is certainly not controlling in this case.

In striking the appropriate due process balance the final factor to be assessed is the public interest. This includes the administrative burden and other societal costs that would be associated with requiring, as a matter of constitutional right, an evidentiary hearing upon demand in all cases prior to the termination of disability benefits. The most visible burden would be the incremental cost resulting from the increased number of hearings and the expense of providing benefits to ineligible recipients pending decision. [T]hat full benefits would continue until after such hearings would assure the exhaustion in most cases of this attractive option. Nor would the theoretical right of the Secretary to recover undeserved benefits result, as a practical matter, in any substantial offset to the added outlay of public funds. [E]xperience with the constitutionalizing of government procedures suggests that the ultimate additional cost in terms of money and administrative burden would not be insubstantial.

Financial cost alone is not a controlling weight in determining whether due process requires a particular procedural safeguard prior to some administrative decision. But the Government's interest, and hence that of the public, in conserving scarce fiscal and administrative resources is a factor that must be weighed. [T]he cost of protecting those whom the preliminary administrative process has identified as likely to be found undeserving may in the end come out of the pockets of the deserving since resources available for any particular program of social welfare are not unlimited.

But more is implicated in cases of this type than ad hoc weighing of fiscal and administrative burdens against the interests of a particular category of claimants. The ultimate balance involves a determination as to when, under our constitutional system, judicial-type procedures must be imposed upon administrative action to assure fairness. [D]ifferences in the origin and function of administrative agencies "preclude wholesale transplantation of the rules of procedure, trial, and review which have evolved from the history and experience of courts." The judicial model of an evidentiary hearing is neither a required, nor even the most effective, method of decisionmaking in all circumstances. The essence of due process is the requirement that "a person in jeopardy of serious loss [be given] notice of the case against him and opportunity to meet it." All that is necessary is that the procedures be tailored, in light of the decision to be made, to "the capacities and circumstances of those who are to be heard," *Goldberg v. Kelly,* to insure that they are given a meaningful opportunity to present their case. In assessing what process is due in this case, substantial weight must be given to the good-faith judgments of the individuals charged by Congress with the administration of social welfare programs that the procedures they have provided assure fair consideration of the entitlement claims of individuals. This is especially so where, as here, the prescribed procedures not only provide the claimant with an effective process for asserting his claim prior to any administrative action, but also assure a right to an evidentiary hearing, as well as to subsequent judicial review, before the denial of his claim becomes final.

We conclude that an evidentiary hearing is not required prior to the termination of disability benefits and that the present administrative procedures fully comport with due process.

The judgment of the Court of Appeals is

Reversed.

MR. JUSTICE STEVENS took no part in the consideration or decision of this case.

MR. JUSTICE BRENNAN, with whom MR. JUSTICE MARSHALL, concurs, dissenting.

[T]he very legislative determination to provide disability benefits, without any prerequisite determination of need in fact, presumes a need by the recipient which is not this Court's function to denigrate. Indeed, in the present case, it is indicated that because disability benefits were terminated there was a foreclosure upon the Eldridge home and the family's furniture was repossessed, forcing Eldridge, his wife, and their children to sleep in one bed. Finally, it is also no argument that a worker, who has been placed in the untenable position of having been denied disability benefits, may still seek other forms of public assistance.

Notes

1. In terms of procedural safeguards, exactly what did *Goldberg v. Kelly* give to Kelly that *Mathews v. Eldridge* did not give to Eldridge? Why?

2. *Sniadach v. Family Finance Corp.,* 395 U.S. 337, 89 S.Ct. 1820, 23 L.Ed.2d 349 (1969). Petitioner claimed that the Wisconsin statutory garnishment procedure violated due process because it gave no notice or opportunity to be heard before the *in rem* seizure of her wages: "[T]he clerk of the court issues the summons at the request of the creditor's lawyer; and it is the latter who by serving the garnishee sets in motion the machinery whereby the wages are frozen. They may, it is true, be unfrozen if the trial of the main suit is ever had and the wage earner wins on the merits. But in the interim the wage earner is deprived of his enjoyment of earned wages

without any opportunity to be heard and to tender any defense he may have, whether it be fraud or otherwise."

Douglas, J., for the Court invalidated the law. Although recognizing that such "summary procedure may well meet the requirements of due process in extraordinary situations," the Court noted that, because prejudgment garnishment may impose tremendous hardship on the wage earner and gives the creditor "enormous" leverage, the general rule is that there must be notice and prior hearing before garnishment.

Fuentes v. Shevin, 407 U.S. 67, 92 S.Ct. 1983, 32 L.Ed.2d 556 (1972). State statutes provided for the issuance of writs ordering state agents to seize a person's possessions, simply upon the *ex parte* application of any person who claimed a right to them and posted a security bond. The writ was issued by the court clerk without judicial supervision. The statutes did not give the possessor of the property any notice or opportunity to challenge the seizure at any prior hearing. The Court, per Stewart, J., invalidated the statutes because they did not require an opportunity for a hearing before the state authorized the seizure. "[N]o later hearing and no damage award can undo the fact that the arbitrary taking that was subject to the right of procedural due process has already occurred." The Court found no clear waiver of procedural rights in the conditional sales contract and did "not concern [itself] with the involuntariness or unintelligence of a waiver when the contractual language relied upon does not, on its face, even amount to a waiver."

White, J., joined by Burger, C.J., & Blackmun, J., dissented: "The Court's rhetoric is seductive, but in end analysis, the result it reaches will have little impact and represents no more than ideological tinkering with state law. It would appear that creditors could withstand attack under today's opinion simply by making clear in the controlling credit instruments that they may retake possession without a hearing, or, for that matter, without resort to judicial process at all.... None of this seems worth the candle to me."

Mitchell v. W.T. Grant Co., 416 U.S. 600, 94 S.Ct. 1895, 40 L.Ed.2d 406 (1974). A Louisiana trial judge ordered the sequestration of personal property on the application of a creditor who had made an installment sale of the goods to petitioner and whose affidavit asserted delinquency and prayed for sequestration to enforce a vendor's lien under state law. The Court, per White, J., held that the sequestration did not violate due process, even though the judge had ordered it *ex parte,* without prior notice or opportunity for hearing.

Not only the purchaser but also the seller had an interest in the property because state law provided the seller with a vendor's lien to secure the unpaid balance of the purchase price. In *Sniadach,* in contrast, the suing creditor had no prior interest in the property attached. The Court also distinguished *Fuentes.* "A writ of sequestration is available to forestall waste or alienation of the property, but [unlike the statutes involved in *Fuentes*] conclusory claims of ownership on lien will not suffice under the Louisiana statute.... Moreover, ... the requisite showing must be made to a judge, and judicial authorization obtained. Mitchell was not at the unsupervised mercy of the creditor and court functionaries. [This judicial control] is one of the measures adopted by the State to minimize the risk that the *ex parte* procedure will lead to a wrongful taking." In addition, the statute entitled the debtor immediately to seek dissolution of the writ, which the court will order unless the creditor proves the grounds upon which the writ was issued, the existence of the debt, the lien, and delinquency. If the creditor does not meet his proof the court may order return of the property and assess damages in favor of the debtor, including attorney's fees. The Court concluded, it "must be sensitive to the possible consequences ... of invalidating this state statute. Doing so might not increase private violence, but self-help repossession could easily lessen protections for the debtor."

Powell, J., concurred and argued that *Fuentes* was really overruled. Stewart, J., joined by Douglas & Marshall, JJ., dissented, complaining that *Fuentes* had in effect been overruled. Brennan, J., also dissented.

North Georgia Finishing, Inc. v. Di–Chem, Inc., 419 U.S. 601, 95 S.Ct. 719, 42 L.Ed.2d 751 (1975). The Court, per White, J., invalidated a Georgia statute permitting garnishment of bank accounts. "Here, a bank account, surely a form of property, was impounded and, absent a bond, put totally beyond use during the pendency of the litigation on the alleged debt, all by a writ of garnishment issued by a court clerk without notice or opportunity for an early hearing and without participation by a judicial officer.... The Georgia garnishment statute has none of the saving characteristics of the Louisiana statute" in *W.T. Grant.* The fact that the case did not involve a consumer's household necessities but garnishment of a corporation's sizable bank account, was immaterial because "the probability of irreparable injury in the latter case is sufficiently great so that some procedures are necessary to guard against the risk of initial error."

It should also be noted that *North Georgia,* like *Sniadach* but unlike *W.T. Grant,* did not involve the installment sale or chattel mortgage situation: the creditor in *North Georgia* had no prior interest in the property attached.

Stewart, J., concurred, pleased that his "report of the demise of *Fuentes v. Shevin* seems to have been greatly exaggerated." Powell, J., concurred in the judgment; Blackmun, J., joined by Rehnquist, J., dissented.

United States v. James Daniel Good Real Property, 510 U.S. 43, 114 S.Ct. 492, 126 L.Ed.2d 490 (1993), held that the Government, in the absence of exigent circumstances, could not seize real property used in drug transactions without preseizure notice and a meaningful opportunity for a hearing. The Due Process Clause (and not solely the Fourth Amendment) controls this case because the Government is not seizing property to preserve evidence of criminal wrongdoing but to assert ownership and control over the property. Applying *Mathews v. Eldridge,* the Court rejected the argument that any pressing need justifies *ex parte* seizure: real property, unlike a boat or car, cannot abscond. The "court's jurisdiction can be preserved without prior seizure ... simply by posting notice on the property and leaving a copy of the process with the occupant."

3. *Goss v. Lopez,* 419 U.S. 565, 95 S.Ct. 729, 42 L.Ed.2d 725 (1975). High school students claimed a violation of due process for the state school to suspend students, without a hearing, for up to 10 days. The Court, per White, J., found that, under state law, appellees "plainly had legitimate

claims of entitlement to a public education." While the state statute "permits school principals to suspend students for up to 10 days ... suspensions may not be imposed without any grounds whatsoever. All the schools had their own rules specifying the grounds for expulsion or suspension. Having chosen to extend the right to an education to people of appellee' class generally, Ohio may not withdraw that right on grounds of misconduct absent fundamentally fair procedures to determine whether the misconduct has occurred."

The student must be given oral or written notice of the charges against him and, if he denies them, an explanation of the evidence the authorities have and an opportunity to present his side of the story as a precaution against unfair or mistaken findings of misconduct. However, there need be no delay between the time notice is given and the hearing, and there can be special circumstances where prior notice and hearing cannot be required.

Ingraham v. Wright, 430 U.S. 651, 97 S.Ct. 1401, 51 L.Ed.2d 711 (1977). Junior high students claimed that the use of corporal punishment in public schools violated their constitutional rights. Powell, J., for the Court, held first that the Eighth Amendment is inapplicable because the cruel and unusual punishment clause was designed to protect those convicted of crime. Turning to the due process question he held that "liberty" encompasses freedom from bodily restraint and punishment. "It is fundamental that the state cannot hold and physically punish an individual except in accordance with due process of law. This constitutionally protected liberty interest is at stake in this case. There is, of course, a *de minimis* level of imposition with which the Constitution is not concerned. But at least where school authorities, acting under color of state law, deliberately decide to punish a child for misconduct by restraining the child and inflicting appreciable physical pain, we hold that the Fourteenth Amendment liberty interests are implicated."

The majority went on to hold that the process that was due was satisfied by the state's preservation of common law constraints and remedies. "Were it not for the common-law privilege permitting teachers to inflict reasonable corporal punishment on children in their care, and the availability of the traditional remedies for abuse, the case for requiring advance procedural safeguards would be strong indeed." The *pre* suspension hearing required in *Goss* was distinguished because "this case does not involve the state-created property interest in public education. The purpose of corporal punishment is to correct a child's behavior without interrupting his education. That corporal punishment may, in a rare case, have the unintended effect of temporarily removing a child from school affords no basis for concluding that the practice itself deprives students of property protected by the Fourteenth Amendment."[1]

White, J., joined by Brennan, Marshall, & Stevens, JJ., dissented, arguing both that the Eighth Amendment was applicable and that more process was due because the after-the-fact tort remedy provided "*no process*" before the infliction of the punishment. Stevens, J., also wrote a dissenting opinion.

---

1. See, e.g., *Board of Curators v. Horowitz,* 435 U.S. 78, 98 S.Ct. 948, 55 L.Ed.2d 124 (1978)(student dismissals for academic, as opposed to disciplinary, cause do not necessitate a hearing before the school's decisionmaking body).

Parham v. J.R., 442 U.S. 584, 99 S.Ct. 2493, 61 L.Ed.2d 101 (1979) determined the process that is due a minor whose parent (or guardian) was seeking to commit the child to a state mental health facility. A neutral factfinder, who need not be trained in law but could be a staff physician, should evaluate independently the child's mental and emotional condition and need for treatment to determine whether the statutory requirements for admission are satisfied. That inquiry must carefully probe the child's background, use all available sources, and include an interview with the child. The child's continuing need for commitment must be reviewed periodically by a similarly independent procedure. It is not necessary for the deciding physician to conduct a formal or quasi-formal hearing, for "due process is not violated by use of informal, traditional medical investigative techniques."

4. *Bell v. Burson,* 402 U.S. 535, 91 S.Ct. 1586, 29 L.Ed.2d 90 (1971) held that due process applies to deprivation of a driver's license. The Court invalidated a Georgia law requiring suspension of the license and motor vehicle registration of an uninsured driver involved in an accident unless he posts security to cover the amount of damages claimed by the aggrieved accident victim or unless he presents a notarized release from liability plus proof of future financial responsibility. "If the statute barred licenses to all motorists who did not post security or carry liability insurance, the statute would not, under our cases, violate the Fourteenth Amendment." But in the context of Georgia's "fault-oriented scheme," there must be a prior hearing limited to the determination of whether there is a reasonable possibility of judgments in the amounts claimed being rendered against the licensee.

In light of *Burson* consider this problem. Under Illinois law, the Secretary of State issued regulations providing for automatic suspension or revocation of a driving license after conviction of three moving traffic offenses within 12 months. The Secretary assigned "points" for various types of driving offenses and the sanction after three moving violations is a function of how many points that the driver has accumulated. After suspension or revocation the Secretary must immediately provide written notice and schedule a full evidentiary hearing if requested, but no prior hearing is required. The only issue before the Court was one of timing: must the hearing occur prior to the deprivation? Is *Burson* distinguishable? See *Dixon v. Love,* 431 U.S. 105, 97 S.Ct. 1723, 52 L.Ed.2d 172 (1977).

Congress legislatively mandated a substantive change in the eligibility requirements of the federal food stamp program, which caused reduction of benefits in varying amounts or a termination in benefits for families with income close to the border between eligibility and ineligibility. Plaintiffs claimed that they have "a constitutional right to advance notice of the amendment's specific impact on their entitlement to food stamps before the statutory change could be implemented by reducing or terminating their benefits." What result? *Atkins v. Parker,* 472 U.S. 115, 105 S.Ct. 2520, 86 L.Ed.2d 81 (1985).

5. *Mount Healthy City School District Board of Education v. Doyle,* 429 U.S. 274, 97 S.Ct. 568, 50 L.Ed.2d 471 (1977). An untenured teacher claimed that the Board's refusal to renew his contract violated his First Amendment rights, applied to the states through the Fourteenth. He said that he had

been fired because of various activities protected as free speech. Rehnquist, J., for the unanimous Court held:

> Doyle's claims under the First and Fourteenth Amendments are not defeated by the fact that he did not have tenure. Even though he could have been discharged for no reason whatever, and had no constitutional right to a hearing prior to the decision not to rehire him, *Board of Regents v. Roth,* he may nonetheless establish a claim to reinstatement if the decision not to rehire him was made by reason of his exercise of constitutionally protected First Amendment freedoms. *Perry v. Sindermann.*

After Doyle showed that his protected speech was a "motivating factor" in the decision not to hire him, the trial court "should have gone on to determine whether the Board had shown by a preponderance of the evidence that it would have reached the same decision as to respondent's reemployment even in the absence of the protected speech."

In *Roth* and *Perry* the Court made clear that if the state teacher were tenured, there must be a *prior* hearing before the teacher is deprived of his "property." But Doyle's trial on his free speech deprivation claim would occur *after* the Board's refusal to renew his contract. He could not, merely by making a free speech claim, require the Board to rehire him pending suit. Why the difference in timing?

6. *Walters v. National Association of Radiation Survivors,* 473 U.S. 305, 105 S.Ct. 3180, 87 L.Ed.2d 220 (1985) upheld the constitutionality of 38 U.S.C.A. § 3404(c), which limits to only $10 the fee that may be paid to an attorney or agent who represents a claimant seeking Veterans benefits for a service-connected death or disability. The veterans suffered no due process violation. Applying the *Mathews v. Eldridge* analysis, the Court gave "great weight" to the governmental interest in administering benefits in an informal, nonadversarial way, so that the claimant could receive the award without dividing it with the attorney. "It would take an extraordinarily strong showing of probability of error under the present system—and the probability that the presence of attorneys would sharply diminish that possibility—to warrant a holding that the fee limitation denies claimants due process of law." The record made no such showing.

7. PUNITIVE DAMAGES. *Honda Motor Co., Ltd. v. Oberg,* 512 U.S. 415, 114 S.Ct. 2331, 129 L.Ed.2d 336 (1994). Stevens, J., for the Court, held that a provision of the Oregon Constitution prohibiting judicial review of the amount of punitive damages awarded by a jury "unless the court can affirmatively say there is no evidence to support the verdict," violates due process. Under the unique Oregon law, if the defendant's only basis for relief is the *amount* of punitive damages the jury awarded, there is no procedure for reducing or setting aside that award, even if the award is "admittedly excessive."

> "Punitive damages pose an acute danger of arbitrary deprivation of property. [But] Oregon has removed [the] safeguard [of judicial review] without providing any substitute procedure. [W]e hold that Oregon's denial of judicial review of the size of punitive damage awards violates the Due Process Clause of the Fourteenth Amendment."

In a footnote the Court did not answer "the more difficult question of what standard of review is constitutionally required." There may not be much practical difference, said the Court, between review that focuses on "passion and prejudice," or "gross excessiveness," or a verdict "against the great weight of the evidence." All of these may be rough equivalents of the standard of whether "no rational trier of fact could have" reached the same verdict.

Scalia, J., concurred. Ginsburg, J., joined by Rehnquist, C.J., dissented, arguing that Oregon's procedures were adequate.

BMW of North America, Inc. v. Gore, 517 U.S. 559, 116 S.Ct. 1589, 134 L.Ed.2d 809 (1996). The paint surface of a new, $40,000 BMW car, had been damaged, probably by acid rain, when the car was shipped from Germany. BMW repaired the damage for $601. Because its policy was not to disclose repairs costing less than 3% of the cost of the car, it did not disclose the repair to the purchaser. When the purchaser discovered the repair nine months later, he sued, claiming that the nondisclosure was fraud. The jury awarded $4,000 in compensatory damages (for the alleged decrease in the value of the car) and $4 million in punitive damages. The Alabama supreme court cut the punitive damage award to $2 million. Stevens, J., for the Court (5 to 4), for the first time held that a punitive damage award was "grossly excessive" and in violation of due process. He refused to draw any bright line, and said that courts should consider three factors in determining whether punitive damage awards were reasonable: the degree of reprehensibility of the defendant's conduct (here, the damage was purely economic; the presale repainting did not affect the car's performance, safety, or appearance); the ratio between the punitive award and the actual harm (here, 500 to 1); and the difference between the punitive award and civil or criminal sanctions imposed for comparable misconduct (Alabama's maximum fine for deceptive trade practices was $2,000). Stevens cautioned state courts not to impose economic sanctions on violators of its laws with the intent of changing the tortfeasors' lawful conduct in other states. The Court remanded to the Alabama court to apply the new rule.

Breyer, J., joined by O'Connor & Souter, JJ., filed a concurring opinion. Scalia, J., joined by Thomas, JJ., dissented, arguing that the due process clause did not impose substantive guarantees against an "unreasonable" punitive damage award. Ginsburg, J., joined by Rehnquist, C.J., also dissented, and objected to "unnecessary intrusion into an area dominantly of state concern."

CLEVELAND BOARD OF EDUCATION
v. LOUDERMILL
470 U.S. 532, 105 S.Ct. 1487, 84 L.Ed.2d 494 (1985).

JUSTICE WHITE delivered the opinion of the Court.

In these cases we consider what pretermination process must be accorded a public employee who can be discharged only for cause.

In 1979 the Cleveland Board of Education, petitioner in No. 83–1362, hired respondent James Loudermill as a security guard. On his job application, Loudermill stated that he had never been convicted of a felony. Eleven months later, as part of a routine examination of his employment records, the Board discovered that in fact Loudermill had been convicted of grand larceny in 1968. By letter dated November 3, 1980, the Board's Business Manager informed Loudermill that he had been dismissed because of his dishonesty in filling out the employment application. Loudermill was not afforded an opportunity to respond to the charge of dishonesty or to challenge his dismissal. On November 13, the Board adopted a resolution officially approving the discharge.

Under Ohio law, Loudermill was a "classified civil servant." Such employees can be terminated only for cause, and may obtain administrative review if discharged. Pursuant to this provision, Loudermill filed an appeal with the Cleveland Civil Service Commission on November 12. The Commission appointed a referee, who held a hearing on January 29, 1981. Loudermill argued that he had thought that his 1968 larceny conviction was for a misdemeanor rather than a felony. The referee recommended reinstatement. On July 20, 1981, the full Commission heard argument and orally announced that it would uphold the dismissal. . . .

Although the Commission's decision was subject to judicial review in the state courts, Loudermill instead brought the present suit in the Federal District Court for the Northern District of Ohio. The complaint alleged that § 124.34 was unconstitutional on its face because it did not provide the employee an opportunity to respond to the charges against him prior to removal. As a result, discharged employees were deprived of liberty and property without due process. The complaint also alleged that the provision was unconstitutional as applied because discharged employees were not given sufficiently prompt post-removal hearings.

[T]he District Court dismissed for failure to state a claim on which relief could be granted. It held that because the very statute that created the property right in continued employment also specified the procedures for discharge, and because those procedures were followed, Loudermill was, by definition, afforded all the process due. The post-termination hearing also adequately protected Loudermill's liberty interests. Finally, the District Court concluded that, in light of the Commission's crowded docket, the delay in processing Loudermill's administrative appeal was constitutionally acceptable. The other case before us arises on similar facts and followed a similar course. . . .

Property interests are not created by the Constitution, "they are created and their dimensions are defined by existing rules or understandings that stem from an independent source such as state law. . . ." The Ohio statute plainly creates such an interest. Respondents were "classified civil service employees," entitled to retain their positions "during good behavior and efficient service," who could not be dismissed "except . . . for . . . misfeasance, malfeasance, or nonfeasance in office." The statute plainly supports the conclusion, reached by both lower courts, that respondents possessed property rights in continued employment. . . .

[T]he argument accepted by the District Court, has its genesis in the plurality opinion in *Arnett v. Kennedy,* 416 U.S. 134, 94 S.Ct. 1633, 40 L.Ed.2d 15 (1974). *Arnett* involved a challenge by a former federal employee to the procedures by which he was dismissed. The plurality reasoned that where the legislation conferring the substantive right also sets out the procedural mechanism for enforcing that right, the two cannot be separated:

> "[W]here the grant of a substantive right is inextricably intertwined with the limitations on the procedures which are to be employed in determining that right, a litigant in the position of appellee must take the bitter with the sweet."

This view garnered three votes in *Arnett,* but was specifically rejected by the other six Justices. Since then, this theory has at times seemed to gather some additional support.

[T]he "bitter with the sweet" approach misconceives the constitutional guarantee. If a clearer holding is needed, we provide it today. The point is straightforward: the Due Process Clause provides that certain substantive rights—life, liberty, and property—cannot be deprived except pursuant to constitutionally adequate procedures. The categories of substance and procedure are distinct. Were the rule otherwise, the Clause would be reduced to a mere tautology. "Property" cannot be defined by the procedures provided for its deprivation any more than can life or liberty. The right to due process "is conferred, not by legislative grace, but by constitutional guarantee. While the legislature may elect not to confer a property interest in [public] employment, it may not constitutionally authorize the deprivation of such an interest, once conferred, without appropriate procedural safeguards." In short, once it is determined that the Due Process Clause applies, "the question remains what process is due." The answer to that question is not to be found in the Ohio statute.

An essential principle of due process is that a deprivation of life, liberty, or property "be preceded by notice and opportunity for hearing appropriate to the nature of the case." We have described "the root requirement" of the Due Process Clause as being "that an individual be given an opportunity for a hearing *before* he is deprived of any significant property interest."[7] This principle requires "some kind of a hearing" prior to the discharge of an employee who has a constitutionally protected property interest in his employment. . . . Even decisions finding no constitutional violation in termination procedures have relied on the existence of some pretermination opportunity to respond. For example, in *Arnett* six Justices found constitutional minima satisfied where

7. There are, of course, some situations in which a post-deprivation hearing will satisfy due process requirements. See *Ewing v. Mytinger & Casselberry, Inc.,* 339 U.S. 594, 70 S.Ct. 870, 94 L.Ed. 1088 (1950); *North American Cold Storage Co. v. Chicago,* 211 U.S. 306, 29 S.Ct. 101, 53 L.Ed. 195 (1908).

the employee had access to the material upon which the charge was based and could respond orally and in writing and present rebuttal affidavits. See also *Barry v. Barchi,* 443 U.S. 55, 65, 99 S.Ct. 2642, 2649, 61 L.Ed.2d 365 (1979)(no due process violation where horse trainer whose license was suspended "was given more than one opportunity to present his side of the story").

The need for some form of pretermination hearing, recognized in these cases, is evident from a balancing of the competing interests at stake. These are the private interest in retaining employment, the governmental interest in the expeditious removal of unsatisfactory employees and the avoidance of administrative burdens, and the risk of an erroneous termination. See *Mathews v. Eldridge.*

First, the significance of the private interest in retaining employment cannot be gainsaid. . . . Second, some opportunity for the employee to present his side of the case is recurringly of obvious value in reaching an accurate decision. . . . Even where the facts are clear, the appropriateness or necessity of the discharge may not be; in such cases, the only meaningful opportunity to invoke the discretion of the decisionmaker is likely to be before the termination takes effect.[8] . . .

The governmental interest in immediate termination does not outweigh these interests. [A]ffording the employee an opportunity to respond prior to termination would impose neither a significant administrative burden nor intolerable delays. Furthermore, the employer shares the employee's interest in avoiding disruption and erroneous decisions; and until the matter is settled, the employer would continue to receive the benefit of the employee's labors. It is preferable to keep a qualified employee on than to train a new one. A governmental employer also has an interest in keeping citizens usefully employed rather than taking the possibly erroneous and counter-productive step of forcing its employees onto the welfare rolls. Finally, in those situations where the employer perceives a significant hazard in keeping the employee on the job, it can avoid the problem by suspending with pay.

The foregoing considerations indicate that the pretermination "hearing," though necessary, need not be elaborate. . . . In general, "something less" than a full evidentiary hearing is sufficient prior to adverse administrative action. Under state law, respondents were later entitled to a full administrative hearing and judicial review. The only question is what steps were required before the termination took effect.

In only one case, *Goldberg v. Kelly,* has the Court required a full adversarial evidentiary hearing prior to adverse governmental action. However, as the *Goldberg* Court itself pointed out, that case presented significantly different considerations than are present in the context of public employment. Here, the pretermination hearing need not defini-

---

8. This is not to say that where state conduct is entirely discretionary the Due Process Clause is brought into play. Nor is it to say that a person can insist on a hearing in order to argue that the decisionmaker should be lenient and depart from legal requirements. . . .

tively resolve the propriety of the discharge. It should be an initial check against mistaken decisions—essentially, a determination of whether there are reasonable grounds to believe that the charges against the employee are true and support the proposed action.

The essential requirements of due process, and all that respondents seek or the Court of Appeals required, are notice and an opportunity to respond. The opportunity to present reasons, either in person or in writing, why proposed action should not be taken is a fundamental due process requirement. The tenured public employee is entitled to oral or written notice of the charges against him, an explanation of the employer's evidence, and an opportunity to present his side of the story. To require more than this prior to termination would intrude to an unwarranted extent on the government's interest in quickly removing an unsatisfactory employee.

Our holding rests in part on the provisions in Ohio law for a full post-termination hearing. In his cross-petition Loudermill asserts, as a separate constitutional violation, that his administrative proceedings took too long. The Court of Appeals held otherwise, and we agree. The Due Process Clause requires provision of a hearing "at a meaningful time." At some point, a delay in the post-termination hearing would become a constitutional violation. In the present case, however, the complaint merely recites the course of proceedings and concludes that the denial of a "speedy resolution" violated due process. This reveals nothing about the delay except that it stemmed in part from the thoroughness of the procedures. A 9–month adjudication is not, of course, unconstitutionally lengthy per se. Yet Loudermill offers no indication that his wait was unreasonably prolonged other than the fact that it took nine months. . . .

We conclude that all the process that is due is provided by a pretermination opportunity to respond, coupled with post-termination administrative procedures as provided by the Ohio statute. Because respondents allege in their complaints that they had no chance to respond, the District Court erred in dismissing for failure to state a claim. The judgment of the Court of Appeals is affirmed, and the case is remanded for further proceedings consistent with this opinion.

So ordered.

JUSTICE MARSHALL, concurring in part and concurring in the judgment.

. . . I continue to believe that *before the decision is made to terminate an employee's wages,* the employee is entitled to an opportunity to test the strength of the evidence "by confronting and cross-examining adverse witnesses and by presenting witnesses on his own behalf, whenever there are substantial disputes in testimonial evidence." Because the Court suggests that even in this situation due process requires no more than notice and an opportunity to be heard before wages are cut off, I am not able to join the Court's opinion in its entirety. . . .

JUSTICE BRENNAN, concurring in part and dissenting in part.

. . . In holding that Loudermill's administrative proceedings did not take too long, the Court plainly does *not* state a flat rule that nine-month delays in deciding discharge appeals will pass constitutional scrutiny as a matter of course. . . .

JUSTICE REHNQUIST, dissenting.

. . . We ought to recognize the totality of the State's definition of the property right in question, and not merely seize upon one of several paragraphs in a unitary statute to proclaim that in that paragraph the State has inexorably conferred upon a civil service employee something which it is powerless under the United States Constitution to qualify in the next paragraph of the statute. This practice ignores our duty under *Roth* to rely on state law as the source of property interests for purposes of applying the Due Process Clause of the Fourteenth Amendment. . . .

Having concluded by this somewhat tortured reasoning that Ohio has created a property right in the respondents in this case, the Court naturally proceeds to inquire what process is "due" before the respondents may be divested of that right. This customary "balancing" . . . is simply an *ad hoc* weighing which depends to a great extent upon how the Court subjectively views the underlying interests at stake. The results in previous cases and in this case have been quite unpredictable. . . . The results from today's balance certainly do not jibe with the result in *Goldberg* or *Mathews v. Eldridge*. . . .

Notes

1. *Federal Deposit Insurance Corp. v. Mallen,* 486 U.S. 230, 108 S.Ct. 1780, 100 L.Ed.2d 265 (1988) unanimously upheld a federal law that authorized the FDIC to suspend a bank officer of a federally insured bank if it found that the officer had been charged for a crime involving dishonesty or breach of trust punishable by a term in excess of one year, and that the officer's continued employment "[might] pose a threat to the interests of the bank's depositors or [might] threaten to impair public confidence in the bank. . . . " The statute gave the suspended official a right to demonstrate (at a *post*-suspension hearing) that his or her continued service would not pose a threat to the interests of the depositors or impair public confidence in the bank. The statute required the FDIC to hold a hearing within 30 days of a written request and render a decision within 60 days of the hearing. In this case the president of an Illinois bank had been indicted for conspiracy to commit mail fraud.

The Court agreed that the bank president's interest in continuing his job was a property right, but the indicted bank official did not have a right to a pre-suspension hearing, given the congressional finding that a prompt suspension was necessary to maintain public confidence in the banking system and that the charge was not baseless: "A grand jury had determined that there was probable cause to believe that appellee had committed a felony." The post-suspension procedure was also constitutional, for it was reasonable for Congress to determine that it might take 30 days to prepare for the hearing and up to 60 more days to reach a decision that might involve complex issues. Finally, it was constitutional to give the hearing officer the discretion whether to accept oral testimony. "There is no inexorable requirement that oral testimony must be heard in every administrative proceeding in which it is tendered," because the testimony might be cumulative or otherwise unnecessary.

2. *Gilbert v. Homar*, 520 U.S. 924 117 S.Ct. 1807, 138 L.Ed.2d 120 (1997). On August 26, 1992, state police arrested and charged with a drug felony a tenured state employee [a policeman employed at East Stroudsburg University (ESU), a state university]. ESU officials then suspended him immediately, without pay, pending their own investigation. The criminal charges were dismissed on September 1, but his suspension remained in effect. On September 18, 1992, he was given the opportunity to tell his side of the story to ESU officials. He was later demoted to groundskeeper and sued, claiming that the failure to provide him with notice and hearing before suspending him without pay violated due process.

The Third Circuit accepted this argument, relying on the dictum in *Loudermill* that, "in those situations where the employer perceives a significant hazard in keeping the employee on the job, it can avoid the problem by suspending him *with* pay." (emphasis added). However, Scalia, J., for a unanimous Court, reversed. Where "a State must act quickly, or where it would be impractical to provide predeprivation process, postdeprivation process satisfies the requirement of the Due Process Clause."

The Court then applied the three-part test of *Mathews v. Eldridge*. First, respondent has a private interest in the uninterrupted receipt of his paycheck, but, "unlike the employee in *Loudermill,* who faced *termination*, respondent only faced a *temporary suspension* without pay." If there is a sufficiently prompt post-suspension hearing, the lost income is relatively insubstantial compared with termination. Second, consider the risk of erroneous deprivation and the likely value of additional procedures. The purpose of a pretermination hearing is to determine if there are reasonable grounds to believe that the charges are true; the purpose of any "pre*suspension* hearing would be to assure that there are reasonable grounds to support the suspension without pay. That has already been assured by the arrest and the filing of charges." Third, the state's interest in immediately suspending employees who occupy positions of "great public trust and high public visibility, such as police officers" is "significant." While the state could have given the respondent a paid leave, "the government does not have to give an employee charged with a felony a paid leave at taxpayer expense." While the employer has discretion not to suspend, there is no constitutional obligation for the state to provide a pre*suspension* hearing where the employee seeks to invoke that discretion. The Court then remanded to determine if respondent received "an adequately prompt *post*-suspension hearing."

6–4. BILLS OF ATTAINDER

AN INTRODUCTORY NOTE

Comparatively few cases have relied on the bill of attainder clauses of Art. I, § 9, cl. 3, & § 10, cl. 1. In two post-Civil War cases the Court invalidated state and federal laws as bills of attainder. In *Cummings v.*

Missouri, 71 U.S. (4 Wall.) 277, 18 L.Ed. 356 (1866) the state constitution provided that one could not engage in certain professions unless he first swore that he had not taken any part in the rebellion against the United States. Cummings, a priest, was convicted of engaging in the ministry without taking the oath. In the companion case, *Ex parte Garland,* 71 U.S. (4 Wall.) 333, 18 L.Ed. 366 (1866), a lawyer sought permission to practice although he could not take a similar oath required by a federal statute. The Court, in two 5 to 4 opinions, invalidated the oaths on the ground, among others that the laws were legislative acts inflicting "punishment" within the meaning of the bills of attainder clauses, on a specific group of lawyers and ministers—those who had upheld the rebellion and hence could not truthfully take the oath.

The next important case was *United States v. Lovett,* 328 U.S. 303, 66 S.Ct. 1073, 90 L.Ed. 1252 (1946). Congress enacted a law providing that no salary could be paid to three named individuals. The Court said that it was necessary to understand "the circumstances leading to" the passage of the law. Congressman Dies, in a speech on the floor of the House, charged 39 government employees as "crackpot, radical bureaucrats". A proposed amendment to an appropriations bill was then introduced that would deny compensation to these named individuals. The Dies charges were referred to as "indictments" and investigated by the Appropriations subcommittee. After hearings and many references in the legislative history to one's "day in court," the need for a report of the "investigations," and "findings", the subcommittee concluded that the three named individuals were guilty of "subversive activities." The Court invalidated the statute as a bill of attainder. "[C]utting off the pay of certain named individuals found guilty of disloyalty makes it no less galling or effective than if it had been done by Act which designated the conduct as criminal." The Court, in broad language, stated:

> [L]egislative acts, no matter what their form, that apply either to named individuals or to easily ascertainable members of a group in such a way as to inflict punishment on them without a judicial trial are bills of attainder prohibited by the Constitution.

Garner v. Board of Public Works, 341 U.S. 716, 71 S.Ct. 909, 95 L.Ed. 1317 (1951) refused to invalidate a municipal ordinance that required city employees to take an oath that, for five years previously, they had not taught or advocated the overthrow by force of the state and federal governments.[1] The Court held the oath requirement, passed in 1948, only served to implement an amendment to the city Charter, passed in 1941, which had barred from public service anyone who, after 1941, taught or advocated the violent overthrow of the Government. The

---

1. The city ordinance also required every employee to execute an affidavit "stating whether or not he is or ever was a member of the Communist Party of the United States of America or of the Communist Political Association, and if he is or was such a member, stating the dates when he became, and the periods during which he was, such a member...." The Court upheld the affidavit requirement because "past loyalty may have a reasonable relationship to present and future trust." The Court noted, however, that: "Not before us is the question whether the city may determine that an employee's disclosure of such political affiliation justifies his discharge."

majority distinguished *Lovett* as a case where the law had not declared "general and prospectively operative standards of qualification and eligibility for public employment." The majority assumed that scienter was implicit in each clause of the oath and rejected First Amendment and other challenges.

In *United States v. Brown,* 381 U.S. 437, 85 S.Ct. 1707, 14 L.Ed.2d 484 (1965), the pendulum swung the other way and the Court invalidated a federal law making it a crime for a member of the Communist Party to be a union official. The defendant was convicted although the Government neither charged nor proved that he had advocated or suggested illegal activity by the union or had proposed a political strike. The Court said:

> Congress undoubtedly possesses power under the Commerce Clause to enact legislation designed to keep from positions affecting interstate commerce persons who may use such positions to bring about political strikes. In § 504, however, Congress has exceeded the authority granted it by the Constitution. The statute does not set forth a generally applicable rule decreeing that any person who commits certain acts or possesses certain characteristics (acts and characteristics which, in Congress' view, make them likely to initiate political strikes) shall not hold union office, and leave to courts and juries the job of deciding what persons have committed the specified acts or possess the specified characteristics. Instead, it designates in no uncertain terms the persons who cannot hold union office without incurring criminal liability—members of the Communist Party.

After *Brown,* the next significant case was *Nixon v. Administrator of General Services.* In reading this case consider what should be the test to determine whether a law in fact inflicts "punishment" within the meaning of the bill of attainder clause; to what extent should the Court engage in a subjective examination of congressional "motive" or a more objective examination of the "purpose" of the law.

NIXON v. ADMINISTRATOR OF GENERAL SERVICES
433 U.S. 425, 97 S.Ct. 2777, 53 L.Ed.2d 867 (1977).

[This case and its factual background are more fully excerpted at § 5–6, supra. Former President Nixon objected to the constitutionality of the Presidential Recordings and Materials Preservation Act, which directed the Administrator of the General Services Administration to take custody of his papers and other materials, including tapes, to promulgate regulations to govern eventual public access to some of the materials, and to screen the materials, all pursuant to various statutory guidelines. Because the Act applied only to one named individual, former President Nixon, appellant argued that the law was a bill of attainder.]

MR. JUSTICE BRENNAN delivered the opinion of the Court. . . .

BILL OF ATTAINDER CLAUSE

Finally, we address appellant's argument that the Act constitutes a bill of attainder proscribed by Art. I, § 9, of the Constitution.[30] His argument is that Congress acted on the premise that he had engaged in " 'misconduct,' "was an " 'unreliable custodian' "of his own documents, and generally was deserving of a *legislative judgment* of blameworthiness." Thus, he argues, the Act is pervaded with the key features of a bill of attainder: a law that legislatively determines guilt and inflicts punishment upon an identifiable individual without provision of the protections of a judicial trial. See *United States v. Brown; United States v. Lovett; Ex parte Garland; Cummings v. Missouri.*

[A]ppellant argues that *Brown* establishes that the Constitution is offended whenever a law imposes undesired consequences on an individual or on a class that is not defined at a proper level of generality.... His view would cripple the very process of legislating, for any individual or group that is made the subject of adverse legislation can complain that the lawmakers could and should have defined the relevant affected class at a greater level of generality.[31] [The Bill of Attainder clause] surely was not intended to serve as a variant of the equal protection doctrine, invalidating every Act of Congress or the States that legislatively burdens some persons or groups but not all other plausible individuals.[34] In short, while the Bill of Attainder Clause serves as an important "bulwark against tyranny," *United States v. Brown,* it does not do so by limiting Congress to the choice of legislating for the universe, or legislating only benefits, or not legislating at all.

Thus, in the present case, the Act's specificity—the fact that it refers to appellant by name—does not automatically offend the Bill of Attainder Clause. Indeed, viewed in context, the focus of the enactment can be fairly and rationally understood. It is true that Title I deals exclusively with appellant's papers. But Title II casts a wider net by establishing a special commission to study and recommend appropriate legislation regarding the preservation of the records of future Presidents and all other federal officials. In this light, Congress' action to preserve

---

30. Article I, § 9, applicable to Congress, provides that "[n]o Bill of Attainder or ex post facto Law shall be passed," and Art. I, § 10, applicable to the States, provides that "[n]o State shall ... pass any Bill of Attainder, ex post facto Law...." The linking of bills of attainder and *ex post facto* laws is explained by the fact that a legislative denunciation and condemnation of an individual often acted to impose retroactive punishment.

31. In this case, for example, appellant faults the Act for taking custody of his papers but not those of other Presidents. But even a congressional definition of the class consisting of all Presidents would have been vulnerable to the claim of being overly specific, since the definition might more generally include all members of the Executive Branch, or all members of the Government, or all in possession of Presidential papers, or all in possession of Government papers. This does not dispose of appellant's contention that the Act focuses upon him with the requisite degree of specificity for a bill of attainder, but it demonstrates that simple reference to the breadth of the Act's focus cannot be determinative of the reach of the Bill of Attainder Clause as a limitation upon legislative action that disadvantages a person or group.

34. *Brown* recognized this by making clear that conflict-of-interest laws, which inevitably prohibit conduct on the part of designated individuals or classes of individuals, do not contravene the bill of attainder guarantee. *Brown* specifically noted the validity of § 32 of the Banking Act of 1933, which disqualified identifiable members of a group—officers and employees of underwriting organizations—from serving as officers of Federal Reserve banks....

only appellant's records is easily explained by the fact that at the time of the Act's passage, only his materials demanded immediate attention. [H]e alone had entered into a depository agreement, the Nixon–Sampson agreement, which by its terms called for the destruction of certain of the materials. Indeed, as the federal appellees argue, "appellant's depository agreement ... created an imminent danger that the tape recordings would be destroyed if appellant, who had contracted phlebitis, were to die." In short, appellant constituted a legitimate class of one, and this provides a basis for Congress' decision to proceed with dispatch with respect to his materials while accepting the status of his predecessors' papers and ordering the further consideration of generalized standards to govern his successors.

Moreover, even if the specificity element were deemed to be satisfied here, the Bill of Attainder Clause would not automatically be implicated. Forbidden legislative punishment is not involved merely because the Act imposes burdensome consequences. Rather, we must inquire further whether Congress, by lodging appellant's materials in the custody of the General Services Administration pending their screening by Government archivists and the promulgation of further regulations, "inflict[ed] punishment" within the constitutional proscription against bills of attainder. . . .

In England a bill of attainder originally connoted a parliamentary Act sentencing a named individual or identifiable members of a group to death. Article I, § 9, however, also proscribes enactments originally characterized as bills of pains and penalties, that is, legislative Acts inflicting punishment other than execution. Generally addressed to persons considered disloyal to the Crown or State, "pains and penalties" historically consisted of a wide array of punishments: commonly included were imprisonment, banishment, and the punitive confiscation of property by the sovereign. Our country's own experience with bills of attainder resulted in the addition of another sanction to the list of impermissible legislative punishments: a legislative enactment barring designated individuals or groups from participation in specified employments or vocations, a mode of punishment commonly employed against those legislatively branded as disloyal. See, e.g., *Cummings v. Missouri,* (barring clergymen from ministry in the absence of subscribing to a loyalty oath); *United States v. Lovett,* (barring named individuals from Government employment); *United States v. Brown,* (barring Communist Party members from offices in labor unions).

Needless to say, appellant cannot claim to have suffered any of these forbidden deprivations at the hands of the Congress. While it is true that Congress ordered the General Services Administration to retain control over records that appellant claims as his property, § 105 of the Act makes provision for an award by the District Court of "just compensation." This undercuts even a colorable contention that the Government has punitively confiscated appellant's property, for the "owner [thereby] is to be put in the same position monetarily as he would have occupied if his property had not been taken." Thus, no feature of the challenged Act falls within the historical meaning of legislative punishment.

But our inquiry is not ended by the determination that the Act imposes no punishment traditionally judged to be prohibited by the Bill of Attainder Clause. Our treatment of the scope of the Clause has never precluded the possibility that new burdens and deprivations might be legislatively fashioned that are inconsistent with the bill of attainder guarantee. The Court, therefore, often has looked beyond mere historical experience and has applied a functional test of the existence of punishment, analyzing whether the law under challenge, viewed in terms of the type and severity of burdens imposed, reasonably can be said to further nonpunitive legislative purposes. Where such legitimate legislative purposes do not appear, it is reasonable to conclude that punishment of individuals disadvantaged by the enactment was the purpose of the decisionmakers.

Application of the functional approach to this case leads to rejection of appellant's argument that the Act rests upon a congressional determination of his blameworthiness and a desire to punish him. [L]egitimate justifications for passage of the Act are readily apparent. First, in the face of the Nixon–Sampson agreement which expressly contemplated the destruction of some of appellant's materials, Congress stressed the need to preserve "[i]nformation included in the materials of former President Nixon [that] is needed to complete the prosecutions of Watergate-related crimes." H.R.Rep. No. 93–1507, p. 2 (1974). Second, again referring to the Nixon–Sampson agreement, Congress expressed its desire to safeguard the "public interest in gaining appropriate access to materials of the Nixon Presidency which are of general historical significance. The information in these materials will be of great value to the political health and vitality of the United States." ... Evaluated in terms of these asserted purposes, the law plainly must be held to be an act of nonpunitive legislative policymaking....

A third recognized test of punishment is strictly a motivational one: inquiring whether the legislative record evinces a congressional intent to punish. See, e.g., *United States v. Lovett*.... First, both Senate and House Committee Reports, in formally explaining their reasons for urging passage of the Act, expressed no interest in punishing or penalizing appellant. [I]t seems clear that the actions of both Houses of Congress were predominantly precipitated by a resolve to undo the recently negotiated Nixon–Sampson agreement, the terms of which departed from the practice of former Presidents in that they expressly contemplated the destruction of certain Presidential materials.... The relevant Committee Reports thus cast no aspersions on appellant's personal conduct and contain no condemnation of his behavior as meriting the infliction of punishment. Rather, they focus almost exclusively on the meaning and effect of an agreement recently announced by the General Services Administration which most Members of Congress perceived to be inconsistent with the public interest.

Nor do the floor debates on the measure suggest that Congress was intent on encroaching on the judicial function of punishing an individual for blameworthy offenses. When one of the opponents of the legislation, mischaracterizing the safeguards embodied in the bill, stated that it is "one which partakes of the characteristics of a bill of attainder ... ," (Sen. Hruska), a key sponsor of the measure responded by expressly denying any intention of determining appellant's blameworthiness or imposing punitive sanctions:

> This bill does not contain a word to the effect that Mr. Nixon is guilty of any violation of the law. It does not inflict any punishment on him. So it has no more relation to a bill of attainder ... than my style of pulchritude is to be compared to that of the Queen of Sheba. (Sen. Ervin).

In this respect, the Act stands in marked contrast to that invalidated in *United States v. Lovett*.... We, of course, do not suggest that such a formal legislative announcement of moral blameworthiness or punishment is necessary to an unlawful bill of attainder. But the decided absence from the legislative history of any congressional sentiments expressive of this purpose is probative of nonpunitive intentions....

One final consideration should be mentioned in light of the unique posture of this controversy. In determining whether a legislature sought to inflict punishment on an individual, it is often useful to inquire into the existence of less burdensome alternatives by which that legislature (here Congress) could have achieved its legitimate nonpunitive objectives. Today, in framing his challenge to the Act, appellant contends that such an alternative was readily available:

> If Congress had provided that the Attorney General or the Administrator of General Services could institute a civil suit in an appropriate federal court to enjoin disposition ... of presidential historical materials ... by any person who could be shown to be an "unreliable custodian" or who had "engaged in misconduct" or who "would violate a criminal prohibition," the statute would have left to judicial determination, after a fair proceeding, the factual allegations regarding Mr. Nixon's blameworthiness. Brief for Appellant 137.

We have no doubt that Congress might have selected this course. It very well may be, however, that Congress chose not to do so on the view that a full-fledged judicial inquiry into appellant's conduct and reliability would be no less punitive and intrusive than the solution actually adopted. For Congress doubtless was well aware that just three months earlier, appellant had resisted efforts to subject himself and his records to the scrutiny of the Judicial Branch, *United States v. Nixon*, [§ 5–6, supra], a position apparently maintained to this day. A rational and fairminded Congress, therefore, might well have decided that the carefully tailored law that it enacted would be less objectionable to appellant than the alternative that he today appears to endorse....

Mr. Justice Stevens, concurring.

... The opinion of the Court leaves unmentioned the two facts which I consider decisive in this regard. Appellant resigned his office under unique circumstances and accepted a pardon for any offenses committed while in office. By so doing, he placed himself in a different class from all other Presidents.... If I did not consider it appropriate to take judicial notice of those facts, I would be unwilling to uphold the power of Congress to enact special legislation directed only at one former President at a time when his popularity was at its nadir. For even when it deals with Presidents or former Presidents, the legislative focus should be upon "the calling" rather than "the person." In short, in my view, this case will not be a precedent for future legislation which relates, not to the Office of President, but just to one of its occupants....

[STEWART, MARSHALL, STEVENS, POWELL, & BLACKMUN, JJ. all joined the portion of the Court's opinion dealing with the bill of attainder issue. WHITE, J., concurred in the result as to that issue. The separate concurring opinions of WHITE, BLACKMUN, & POWELL, JJ. and the dissenting opinion of REHNQUIST, J., and BURGER, C.J., are omitted.]

6–5. IMPAIRMENT OF CONTRACTS

HOME BUILDING & LOAN ASSOCIATION
v. BLAISDELL

290 U.S. 398, 54 S.Ct. 231, 78 L.Ed. 413 (1934).

[In 1933, during the Great Depression, Minnesota adopted a Mortgage Moratorium Law, which provided that, during the emergency declared to exist, relief may be had through authorized judicial proceedings with respect to mortgage foreclosures and execution sales of real estate, in the form of postponement of sales and extensions of periods of redemption. The law provided that it was to remain in effect "only during the continuance of the emergency and in no event beyond May 1, 1935." The courts could not extend the period of redemption or postpone the sale beyond that date. Under the particular provision of the Act before the Court in *Blaisdell,* the state courts, subject to the Act's limitation, were authorized to extend the period of redemption from foreclosure sales, provided that the court entered an order determining the reasonable value of the income on the property, or, if the property has no income, its reasonable rental value, and requiring the mortgagor to pay all or a reasonable part of such income or rental value for, or toward, the payment of taxes, insurance, interest, mortgage or judgment indebtedness in the manner fixed by the court. Blaisdell invoked the statute and secured a judicial order extending the period of redemption from a foreclosure sale. Because of the extension, the mortgagee was unable to obtain possession and convey title in fee as it would have been able to do had the statute not been enacted.]

MR. CHIEF JUSTICE HUGHES delivered the opinion of the Court.

... The statute does not impair the integrity of the mortgage indebtedness. The obligation for interest remains. The statute does not affect the validity of the sale or the right of a mortgagee-purchaser to title in fee, or his right to obtain a deficiency judgment, if the mortgagor fails to redeem within the prescribed period. Aside from the extension of time, the other conditions of redemption are unaltered.... While the mortgagee-purchaser is debarred from actual possession, he has, so far as rental value is concerned, the equivalent of possession during the extended period.

In determining whether the provision for this temporary and conditional relief exceeds the power of the State by reason of the clause in the Federal Constitution prohibiting impairment of the obligations of contracts, we must consider the relation of emergency to constitutional power, the historical setting of the contract clause, the development of the jurisprudence of this Court in the construction of that clause, and the principles of construction which we may consider to be established.

Emergency does not create power. Emergency does not increase granted power or remove or diminish the restrictions imposed upon power granted or reserved.... While emergency does not create power, emergency may furnish the occasion for the exercise of power. "Although an emergency may not call into life a power which has never lived, nevertheless emergency may afford a reason for the exertion of a living power already enjoyed." ... When the provisions of the Constitution, in grant or restriction, are specific, so particularized as not to admit of construction, no question is presented. Thus, emergency would not permit a State to have more than two Senators in the Congress.... But where constitutional grants and limitations of power are set forth in general clauses, which afford a broad outline, the process of construction is essential to fill in the details. That is true of the contract clause....

In the construction of the contract clause, the debates in the Constitutional Convention are of little aid. But the reasons which led to the adoption of that clause, and of the other prohibitions of Section 10 of Article I, are not left in doubt and have frequently been described with eloquent emphasis. The widespread distress following the revolutionary period, and the plight of debtors, had called forth in the States an ignoble array of legislative schemes for the defeat of creditors and the invasion of contractual obligations. Legislative interferences had been so numerous and extreme that the confidence essential to prosperous trade had been undermined and the utter destruction of credit was threatened....

To ascertain the scope of the constitutional prohibition we examine the course of judicial decisions in its application. These put it beyond question that the prohibition is not an absolute one and is not to be read with literal exactness like a mathematical formula.... The obligation of a contract is "the law which binds the parties to perform their agreement." *Sturges v. Crowninshield,* 4 Wheat. 122, 197, 4 L.Ed. 529. This Court has said that "the laws which subsist at the time and place of the making of a contract, and where it is to be performed, enter into and form a part of it, as if they were expressly referred to or incorporated in its terms...." But this broad language cannot be taken without qualification. Chief Justice Marshall pointed out the distinction between obligation and remedy. *Sturges v. Crowninshield,* supra. Said he: "The distinction between the obligation of a contract, and the remedy given by the legislature to enforce that obligation, has been taken at the bar, and exists in the nature of things. Without impairing the obligation of the contract, the remedy may certainly be modified as the wisdom of the nation shall direct." ... And Chief Justice Waite, ... in *Antoni v. Greenhow,* 107 U.S. 769, 775, 2 S.Ct. 91, 96, 27 L.Ed. 468, added: "In all such cases the question becomes, therefore, one of reasonableness, and of that the legislature is primarily the judge."

The obligations of a contract are impaired by a law which renders them invalid, or releases or extinguishes them and impairment, as above noted, has been predicated of laws which without destroying contracts derogate from substantial contractual rights. In *Sturges v. Crowninshield,* a state insolvent law, which discharged the debtor from liability was held to be invalid as applied to contracts in existence when the law was passed.... But in *Penniman's Case,* 103 U.S. 714, 720, 26 L.Ed. 602, the Court decided that a statute abolishing imprisonment for debt did not, within the meaning of the Constitution, impair the obligation of contracts previously made; and the Court said: "The general doctrine of this court on this subject may be thus stated: In modes of proceeding and forms to enforce the contract the legislature has the control, and may enlarge, limit or alter them, provided it does not deny a remedy or so embarrass it with conditions or restrictions as seriously to impair the value of the right." ...

Not only is the constitutional provision qualified by the measure of control which the State retains over remedial processes, but the State also continues to possess authority to safeguard the vital interests of its people.... [N]ot only are existing laws read into contracts in order to fix obligations as between the parties, but the reservation of essential attributes of sovereign power is also read into contracts as a postulate of the legal order....

While the charters of private corporations constitute contracts, a grant of exclusive privilege is not to be implied as against the State. *Charles River Bridge v. Warren Bridge,* 11 Pet. 420, 9 L.Ed. 773. And all contracts are subject to the right of eminent domain. *West River Bridge v. Dix,* 6 How. 507, 12 L.Ed. 535. The reservation of this necessary authority of the State is deemed to be a part of the contract....

The legislature cannot "bargain away the public health or the public morals." Thus, the constitutional provision against the impairment of contracts was held not to be violated by an amendment of the state constitution which put an end to a lottery theretofore authorized by the legislature. *Stone v. Mississippi,* 101 U.S. 814, 819, 25 L.Ed. 1079. The lottery was a valid enterprise when established under express state authority, but the legislature in the public interest could put a stop to it.

A similar rule has been applied to the control by the State of the sale of intoxicating liquors....

Undoubtedly, whatever is reserved of state power must be consistent with the fair intent of the constitutional limitation of that power. The reserved power cannot be construed so as to destroy the limitation, nor is the limitation to be construed to destroy the reserved power in its essential aspects. They must be construed in harmony with each other. This principle precludes a construction which would permit the State to adopt as its policy the repudiation of debts or the destruction of contracts or the denial of means to enforce them. But it does not follow that conditions may not arise in which a temporary restraint of enforcement may be consistent with the spirit and purpose of the constitutional provision and thus be found to be within the range of the reserved power of the State to protect the vital interests of the community....

It is no answer to say that this public need was not apprehended a century ago, or to insist that what the provision of the Constitution meant to the vision of that day it must mean to the vision of our time. If by the statement that what the Constitution meant at the time of its adoption it means to-day, it is intended to say that the great clauses of the Constitution must be confined to the interpretation which the framers, with the conditions and outlook of their time, would have placed upon them, the statement carries its own refutation. It was to guard against such a narrow conception that Chief Justice Marshall uttered the memorable warning—"We must never forget that it is *a constitution* we are expounding" (*McCulloch v. Maryland*)—"a constitution intended to endure for ages to come, and consequently, to be adapted to the various *crises* of human affairs." ...

Applying the criteria established by our decisions we conclude:

1. An emergency existed in Minnesota which furnished a proper occasion for the exercise of the reserved power of the State to protect the vital interests of the community....

2. The legislation was addressed to a legitimate end, that is, the legislation was not for the mere advantage of particular individuals but for the protection of a basic interest of society.

3. In view of the nature of the contracts in question—mortgages of unquestionable validity—the relief afforded and justified by the emergency, in order not to contravene the constitutional provision, could only be of a character appropriate to that emergency and could be granted only upon reasonable conditions.

4. The conditions upon which the period of redemption is extended do not appear to be unreasonable....

In the absence of legislation, courts of equity have exercised jurisdiction in suits for the foreclosure of mortgages to fix the time and terms of sale and to refuse to confirm sales upon equitable grounds where they were found to be unfair or inadequacy of price was so gross as to shock the conscience. The "equity of redemption" is the creature of equity....

5. The legislation is temporary in operation. It is limited to the exigency which called it forth. . . .

[A dissenting opinion of SUTHERLAND, J., joined by VAN DEVANTER, MCREYNOLDS, & BUTLER, JJ., is omitted.]

ALLIED STRUCTURAL STEEL CO. v. SPANNAUS
438 U.S. 234, 98 S.Ct. 2716, 57 L.Ed.2d 727 (1978).

MR. JUSTICE STEWART delivered the opinion of the Court.

The issue in this case is whether the application of Minnesota's Private Pension Benefits Protection Act to the appellant violates the Contract Clause of the United States Constitution.

In 1974 appellant Allied Structural Steel Co. (company), a corporation with its principal place of business in Illinois, maintained an office in Minnesota with 30 employees. Under the company's general pension plan, adopted in 1963 and qualified as a single-employer plan under § 401 of the Internal Revenue Code,[2] salaried employees were covered as follows: At age 65 an employee was entitled to retire and receive a monthly pension generally computed by multiplying 1% of his average monthly earnings by the total number of his years of employment with the company. Thus, an employee aged 65 or more could retire without satisfying any particular length-of-service requirement, but the size of his pension would reflect the length of his service with the company. . . . Those employees who quit or were discharged before age 65 without fulfilling [certain] conditions did not acquire any pension rights.

The company was the sole contributor to the pension trust fund, and each year it made contributions to the fund based on actuarial predictions of eventual payout needs. Although those contributions once made were irrevocable, in the sense that they remained part of the pension trust fund, the plan neither required the company to make specific contributions nor imposed any sanction on it for failing to contribute adequately to the fund.

The company not only retained a virtually unrestricted right to amend the plan in whole or in part, but was also free to terminate the plan and distribute the trust assets at any time and for any reason. In the event of a termination, the assets of the fund were to go, first, to meet the plan's obligation to those employees already retired and receiving pensions; second, to those eligible for retirement; and finally, if any balance remained, to the other employees covered under the plan whose pension rights had not yet vested. Employees within each of these categories were assured payment only to the extent of the pension assets. . . . The plan also specifically advised employees that neither its existence nor any of its terms were to be understood as implying any

2. The plan was not the result of a collective-bargaining agreement, and no such agreement is at issue in this case.

assurance that employees could not be dismissed from their employment with the company at any time.

In sum, an employee who did not die, did not quit, and was not discharged before meeting one of the requirements of the plan would receive a fixed pension at age 65 if the company remained in business and elected to continue the pension plan in essentially its existing form.

On April 9, 1974, Minnesota enacted the law here in question, the Private Pension Benefits Protection Act. Under the Act, a private employer of 100 employees or more—at least one of whom was a Minnesota resident—who provided pension benefits under a plan meeting the qualifications of § 401 of the Internal Revenue Code, was subject to a "pension funding charge" if he either terminated the plan or closed a Minnesota office. The charge was assessed if the pension funds were not sufficient to cover full pensions for all employees who had worked at least 10 years. The Act required the employer to satisfy the deficiency by purchasing deferred annuities, payable to the employees at their normal retirement age. A separate provision specified that periods of employment prior to the effective date of the Act were to be included in the 10–year employment criterion.

During the summer of 1974 the company began closing its Minnesota office. On July 31, it discharged 11 of its 30 Minnesota employees, and the following month it notified the Minnesota Commissioner of Labor and Industry, as required by the Act, that it was terminating an office in the State. At least nine of the discharged employees did not have any vested pension rights under the company's plan, but had worked for the company for 10 years or more and thus qualified as pension obligees of the company under the law that Minnesota had enacted a few months earlier. On August 18, the State notified the company that it owed a pension funding charge of approximately $185,000 under the provisions of the Private Pension Benefits Protection Act.

The company brought suit in a Federal District Court asking for injunctive and declaratory relief. It claimed that the Act unconstitutionally impaired its contractual obligations to its employees under its pension agreement. . . .

Although it was perhaps the strongest single constitutional check on state legislation during our early years as a Nation, the Contract Clause receded into comparative desuetude with the adoption of the Fourteenth Amendment, and particularly with the development of the large body of jurisprudence under the Due Process Clause of that Amendment in modern constitutional history.[12] Nonetheless, the Contract Clause remains part of the Constitution. It is not a dead letter. And its basic

---

12. Indeed, at least one commentator has suggested that "the results might be the same if the contract clause were dropped out of the Constitution, and the challenged statutes all judged as reasonable or unreasonable deprivations of property." Hale, The Supreme Court and the Contract Clause: III, 57 Harv.L.Rev. 852, 890–891 (1944).

contours are brought into focus by several of this Court's 20th century decisions.

First of all, it is to be accepted as a commonplace that the Contract Clause does not operate to obliterate the police power of the States.... If the Contract Clause is to retain any meaning at all, however, it must be understood to impose *some* limits upon the power of a State to abridge existing contractual relationships, even in the exercise of its otherwise legitimate police power. The existence and nature of those limits were clearly indicated in a series of cases in this Court arising from the efforts of the States to deal with the unprecedented emergencies brought on by the severe economic depression of the early 1930's.

In *Home Building & Loan Assn. v. Blaisdell,* ... the Court clearly implied that if the Minnesota moratorium legislation had not possessed the characteristics attributed to it by the Court, it would have been invalid under the Contract Clause of the Constitution.[13] These implications were given concrete force in three cases that followed closely in *Blaisdell's* wake.

In *W.B. Worthen Co. v. Thomas,* 292 U.S. 426, 54 S.Ct. 816, 78 L.Ed. 1344, the Court dealt with an Arkansas law that exempted the proceeds of a life insurance policy from collection by the beneficiary's judgment creditors. Stressing the retroactive effect of the state law, the Court held that it was invalid under the Contract Clause, since it was not precisely and reasonably designed to meet a grave temporary emergency in the interest of the general welfare. In *W.B. Worthen Co. v. Kavanaugh,* 295 U.S. 56, 55 S.Ct. 555, 79 L.Ed. 1298, the Court was confronted with another Arkansas law that diluted the rights and remedies of mortgage bondholders. The Court held the law invalid under the Contract Clause. "Even when the public welfare is invoked as an excuse," Mr. Justice Cardozo wrote for the Court, the security of a mortgage cannot be cut down "without moderation or reason or in a spirit of oppression." And finally, in *Treigle v. Acme Homestead Assn.,* 297 U.S. 189, 56 S.Ct. 408, 80 L.Ed. 575, the Court held invalid under the Contract Clause a Louisiana law that modified the existing withdrawal rights of the members of a building and loan association. "Such an interference with the right of contract," said the Court, "cannot be justified by saying that in the public interest the operations of building associations may be controlled and regulated, or that in the same interest their charters may be amended."

The most recent Contract Clause case in this Court was *United States Trust Co. v. New Jersey,* 431 U.S. 1, 97 S.Ct. 1505, 52 L.Ed.2d 92 (1977).[14] In that case the Court again recognized that although the

---

13. In *Veix v. Sixth Ward Building & Loan Assn.,* 310 U.S. 32, 38, 60 S.Ct. 792, 795, 84 L.Ed. 1061, the Court took into account still another consideration in upholding a state law against a Contract Clause attack: the petitioner had "pur- chased into an enterprise already regulated in the particular to which he now objects."

14. See also *El Paso v. Simmons,* 379 U.S. 497, 85 S.Ct. 577, 13 L.Ed.2d 446. There the Court held that a Texas law shortening the time within which a default-

absolute language of the Clause must leave room for "the 'essential attributes of sovereign power,' ... necessarily reserved by the States to safeguard the welfare of their citizens," that power has limits when its exercise effects substantial modifications of private contracts. Despite the customary deference courts give to state laws directed to social and economic problems, "[l]egislation adjusting the rights and responsibilities of contracting parties must be upon reasonable conditions and of a character appropriate to the public purpose justifying its adoption." Evaluating with particular scrutiny a modification of a contract to which the State itself was a party, the Court in that case held that legislative alteration of the rights and remedies of Port Authority bondholders violated the Contract Clause because the legislation was neither necessary nor reasonable.[15]

In applying these principles to the present case, the first inquiry must be whether the state law has, in fact, operated as a substantial impairment of a contractual relationship.[16] The severity of the impairment measures the height of the hurdle the state legislation must clear. Minimal alteration of contractual obligations may end the inquiry at its first stage. Severe impairment, on the other hand, will push the inquiry to a careful examination of the nature and purpose of the state legislation. . . .

Here, [the company] had no reason to anticipate that its employees' pension rights could become vested except in accordance with the terms of the plan. It relied heavily, and reasonably, on this legitimate contractual expectation in calculating its annual contributions to the pension fund. The effect of Minnesota's Private Pension Benefits Protection Act on this contractual obligation was severe. . . .

Not only did the state law thus retroactively modify the compensation that the company had agreed to pay its employees from 1963 to 1974, but it did so by changing the company's obligations in an area where the element of reliance was vital—the funding of a pension plan. [T]he statute in question here nullifies express terms of the company's contractual obligations and imposes a completely unexpected liability in potentially disabling amounts. There is not even any provision for

---

ed land claim could be reinstated did not violate the Contract Clause. "We do not believe that it can seriously be contended that the buyer was substantially induced to enter into these contracts on the basis of a defeasible right to reinstatement . . . or that he interpreted that right to be of everlasting effect. . . ."

15. The Court indicated that impairments of a State's own contracts would face more stringent examination under the Contract Clause than would laws regulating contractual relationships between private parties, although it was careful to add that "private contracts are not subject to unlimited modification under the police power."

16. The novel construction of the Contract Clause expressed in the dissenting opinion is wholly contrary to the decisions of this Court. The narrow view that the Clause forbids only state laws that diminish the duties of a contractual obligor and not laws that increase them, a view arguably suggested by *Satterlee v. Matthewson*, 2 Pet. 380, 7 L.Ed. 458, has since been expressly repudiated. Moreover, in any bilateral contract the diminution of duties on one side effectively increases the duties on the other. . . .

gradual applicability or grace periods. Compare the Employee Retirement Income Security Act of 1974 (ERISA). [Also, this] legislation ... was not enacted to deal with a situation remotely approaching the broad and desperate emergency economic conditions of the early 1930's—conditions of which the Court in *Blaisdell* took judicial notice.[24] ...

This Minnesota law simply does not possess the attributes of those state laws that in the past have survived challenge under the Contract Clause of the Constitution. The law was not even purportedly enacted to deal with a broad, generalized economic or social problem. It did not operate in an area already subject to state regulation at the time the company's contractual obligations were originally undertaken, but invaded an area never before subject to regulation by the State.[25] It did not effect simply a temporary alteration of the contractual relationships of those within its coverage, but worked a severe, permanent, and immediate change in those relationships—irrevocably and retroactively. And its narrow aim was leveled, not at every Minnesota employer, not even at every Minnesota employer who left the State, but only at those who had in the past been sufficiently enlightened as voluntarily to agree to establish pension plans for their employees.

[W]e do hold that if the Contract Clause means anything at all, it means that Minnesota could not constitutionally do what it tried to do to the company in this case.

The judgment of the District Court is reversed.

It is so ordered.

MR. JUSTICE BLACKMUN took no part in the consideration or decision of this case.

MR. JUSTICE BRENNAN, with whom MR. JUSTICE WHITE and MR. JUSTICE MARSHALL join, dissenting.

... The Act does not relieve either the employer or his employees of any existing contract obligation. Rather, the Act simply creates an additional, supplemental duty of the employer, no different in kind from myriad duties created by a wide variety of legislative measures which defeat settled expectations but which have nonetheless been sustained by this Court. For this reason, the Minnesota Act, in my view, does not implicate the Contract Clause in any way. The basic fallacy of today's decision is its mistaken view that the Contract Clause protects all contract-based expectations, including that of an employer that his obligations to his employees will not be legislatively enlarged beyond those explicitly provided in his pension plan.

... Although the debates in the Constitutional Convention and the subsequent public discussion of the Constitution are not particularly enlightening in determining the scope of the Clause, they support the

---

24. This is not to suggest that only an emergency of great magnitude can constitutionally justify a state law impairing the obligations of contracts.

25. See n. 13, supra.

view that the sole evil at which the Contract Clause was directed was the theretofore rampant state legislative interference with the ability of creditors to obtain the payment or security provided for by contract. The Framers regarded the Contract Clause as simply an adjunct to the currency provisions of Art. I, § 10, which operated primarily to bar legislation depriving creditors of the payment of the full value of their loans. The Clause was thus intended by the Framers to be applicable only to laws which altered the obligations of contracts by effectively relieving one party of the obligation to perform a contract duty.

The terms of the Contract Clause negate any basis for its interpretation as protecting all contract-based expectations from unjustifiable interference. It applies, as confirmed by consistent judicial interpretations, only to *state legislative* Acts. Its inapplicability to impairments by state judicial acts or by national legislation belies interpretation of the Clause as intended broadly to make all contract expectations inviolable.... Decisions over the past 50 years have developed a coherent, unified interpretation of all the constitutional provisions that may protect economic expectations and these decisions have recognized a broad latitude in States to effect even severe interference with existing economic values when reasonably necessary to promote the general welfare....

Notes

1. *United States Trust Co. v. New Jersey,* 431 U.S. 1, 97 S.Ct. 1505, 52 L.Ed.2d 92 (1977), cited in *Spannaus,* involved a *public* contract, and therefore "complete deference to a legislative assessment of reasonableness and necessity is not appropriate because the State's self-interest is at stake."[1] The Port Authority of New York and New Jersey was established in 1921 by a bistate compact consented to by Congress. In 1962 it was proposed that the Port Authority take over the Hudson & Manhattan R.R., but the bondholders were concerned that takeovers of deficit-ridden railroads would impair the Authority's ability to meet its bond obligations. A New Jersey Senate committee concluded that the solution to this concern was "[l]imiting by a constitutionally protected statutory covenant with Port Authority bondholders the extent to which Port Authority revenues and reserves pledged to such bondholders can in the future be applied to the deficits of possible future Port Authority passenger railroad facilities beyond the original Hudson & Manhattan Railroad system." Hence a statutory covenant of 1962 resulted between the two states and "the holders of any affected bonds," authorizing the Authority to acquire and operate the Railroad (and

---

1. When Congress or the state legislature enacts a law, the presumption (unless there is "some clear indication" to the contrary) is that the law was not intended to grant private, contractual, vested rights but merely was intended to declare a policy to be followed until the legislature decides otherwise. *National Railroad Passenger Corp. v. Atchison, T. & S.F. Ry. Co.,* 470 U.S. 451, 105 S.Ct. 1441, 84 L.Ed.2d 432 (1985)(no impairment of private contractual rights between Amtrak and various railroads when federal law required private railroads, which had terminated their passenger railroad obligations, to reimburse Amtrak for the private railroad employees' continued discount travel privileges on Amtrak; the reimbursement was set at rates in excess of the incremental costs of the passes).

also to construct and operate the World Trade Center). In return, the state and the Authority agreed that revenues and reserves securing the bonds would not be depleted by operation of deficit-producing passenger railroads beyond certain "permitted deficits." In 1974, in order to allow the Authority to fund additional mass transit, both states repealed the 1962 covenant retroactively. Plaintiff bondholder sued claiming an impairment of contracts. The Court (4 to 3)[2] found an impairment.

The Court noted the prior case law holding that "the police power and the power of eminent domain were among those that could not be 'contracted away,' but the State could bind itself in the future exercise of its taxing and spending powers. Such formalistic distinctions perhaps cannot be dispositive, but they contain an important element of truth. Whatever the propriety of a State's binding itself to a future course of conduct in other contexts, the power to enter into effective financial arrangements cannot be questioned."

Are *Blaisdell* and *Spannaus* consistent? Do *Spannaus* and *United States Trust* lead us back down the road to *Lochner,* § 6–1, supra? Under *Spannaus* could the State protect the pension rights of workers in the state by any other means, such as resort to its taxing and spending powers? Did the State have such alternatives open to it in *United States Trust?*

2. If the federal government passed the same type of law enacted in *Spannaus* or *United States Trust,* should the Court come out any differently as to its validity? With footnote 12 of *Spannaus* contrast *Pension Benefit Guaranty Corp. v. R.A. Gray & Co.,* 467 U.S. 717, 104 S.Ct. 2709, 81 L.Ed.2d 601 (1984), where Brennan, J., wrote for a unanimous Court that the Fifth Amendment's due process clause was not violated by the retroactive aspects of the Multiemployer Pension Act Amendments Act of 1980 (MPAA). This Act, signed into law on Sept. 26, 1980, was passed because an earlier law enacted in 1976—the Employee Retirement Income Security Act (ERISA) referred to in *Spannaus*—did not adequately protect pension plans from the effects of employer withdrawal. MPAA was retroactive to April 29, 1980. (Congress first considered MPAA on February 27, 1979.) MPAA required an employer withdrawing from a multiemployer pension plan to pay the employers' proportionate share of the plan's unfunded vested benefit. One of the problems of ERISA was that it encouraged employer withdrawals. The retroactive feature of MPAA reflected Congress' concern "that employers would have an even greater incentive to withdraw if they knew that legislation to impose more burdensome liability on withdrawing employers was being considered." The Court upheld the law as rational and said (at footnote 6) that cases like *Spannaus* do not "control judicial review of retroactive federal legislation affecting economic benefits and burdens." The Court said that the standards under the Due Process Clause are "less searching:"

> [I]t is suggested that we apply constitutional principles that have been developed under the Contract Clause when reviewing this federal legislation. We have never held, however, that the principles embodied in the

---

2. Stewart, J. took no part in the decision; Powell, J. took no part in either the consideration or decision. Burger, C.J., filed a short concurring opinion, and Brennan, J., joined by White & Marshall, JJ., dissented.

Fifth Amendment's Due Process Clause are coextensive with prohibitions existing against state impairment of preexisting contracts. Indeed, ... we have contrasted the limitations imposed on States by the Contract Clause with the less searching standards imposed on economic legislation by the Due Process Clauses. [R]etrospective civil legislation may offend due process if it is "particularly 'harsh and oppressive,' "[but] that standard does not differ from the prohibition against arbitrary and irrational legislation. . . .

3. Presently the U.S. Government exempts from its income tax the interest received on municipal bonds. Consequently people purchase the bonds at lower interest rates than they would otherwise accept. Some states also exempt from their state income tax the interest from their own bonds. Would it violate the contract clause for a state to pass a new law taxing the interest from its own bonds and applying that law retroactively to interest from bonds purchased before the enactment of the new law?

Assume that it is constitutional for the U.S. Government to pass a new law taxing interest from state bonds. Would it be constitutional for Congress to apply that law retroactively to state bonds purchased before the date of the new law?

Presently the U.S. Government provides by statute that the interest from U.S. bonds are exempt from state (but not federal) income tax. Would it be constitutional for the U.S. Government to enact a new law allowing the states to tax the interest from U.S. bonds and applying the law retroactively to U.S. bonds purchased before the effective date of the law?

6–6.   THE TAKING OF PROPERTY

6–6.1 Taking By Possession

UNITED STATES v. CAUSBY
328 U.S. 256, 66 S.Ct. 1062, 90 L.Ed. 1206 (1946).

MR. JUSTICE DOUGLAS delivered the opinion of the Court.

This is a case of first impression. The problem presented is whether respondents' property was taken, within the meaning of the Fifth Amendment, by frequent and regular flights of army and navy aircraft over respondents' land at low altitudes. The Court of Claims held that there was a taking and entered judgment for respondents, one judge dissenting. . . .

Respondents own 2.8 acres near an airport outside of Greensboro, North Carolina. It has on it a dwelling house, and also various outbuildings which were mainly used for raising chickens. The end of the airport's northwest-southeast runway is 2,220 feet from respondents' barn and 2,275 feet from their house. The path of glide to this runway passes directly over the property—which is 100 feet wide and 1,200 feet long. The 30 to 1 safe glide angle[1] approved by the Civil Aeronautics

---

1.   A 30 to 1 glide angle means one foot of elevation or descent for every 30 feet of horizontal distance.

Authority passes over this property at 83 feet, which is 67 feet above the house, 63 feet above the barn and 18 feet above the highest tree. The use by the United States of this airport is pursuant to a lease executed in May, 1942, for a term commencing June 1, 1942 and ending June 30, 1942, with a provision for renewals until June 30, 1967, or six months after the end of the national emergency, whichever is the earlier.

Various aircraft of the United States use this airport—bombers, transports and fighters. . . . They come close enough at times to appear barely to miss the tops of the trees and at times so close to the tops of the trees as to blow the old leaves off. The noise is startling. And at night the glare from the planes brightly lights up the place. As a result of the noise, respondents had to give up their chicken business. As many as six to ten of their chickens were killed in one day by flying into the walls from fright. The total chickens lost in that manner was about 150. Production also fell off. The result was the destruction of the use of the property as a commercial chicken farm. Respondents are frequently deprived of their sleep and the family has become nervous and frightened. Although there have been no airplane accidents on respondents' property, there have been several accidents near the airport and close to respondents' place. [The Court of Claims] held that the United States had taken an easement over the property on June 1, 1942, and that the value of the property destroyed and the easement taken was $2,000. . . .

It is ancient doctrine that at common law ownership of the land extended to the periphery of the universe—*Cujus est solum ejus est usque ad coelum.* But that doctrine has no place in the modern world. The air is a public highway, as Congress has declared. Were that not true, every transcontinental flight would subject the operator to countless trespass suits. Common sense revolts at the idea. To recognize such private claims to the airspace would clog these highways, seriously interfere with their control and development in the public interest, and transfer into private ownership that to which only the public has a just claim.

But that general principle does not control the present case. For the United States conceded on oral argument that if the flights over respondents' property rendered it uninhabitable, there would be a taking compensable under the Fifth Amendment. It is the owner's loss, not the taker's gain, which is the measure of the value of the property taken. . . . If, by reason of the frequency and altitude of the flights, respondents could not use this land for any purpose, their loss would be complete. It would be as complete as if the United States had entered upon the surface of the land and taken exclusive possession of it.

We agree that in those circumstances there would be a taking. . . . It would not be a case of incidental damages arising from a legalized nuisance such as was involved in *Richards v. Washington Terminal Co.,* 233 U.S. 546, 34 S.Ct. 654, 58 L.Ed. 1088. In that case, property owners whose lands adjoined a railroad line were denied recovery for damages resulting from the noise, vibrations, smoke and the like, incidental to the operations of the trains. In the supposed case, the line of flight is over the land. And the land is appropriated as directly and completely as if it were used for the runways themselves.

There is no material difference between the supposed case and the present one, except that here enjoyment and use of the land are not completely destroyed. But that does not seem to us to be controlling. The path of glide for airplanes might reduce a valuable factory site to grazing land, an orchard to a vegetable patch, a residential section to a wheat field. Some value would remain. But the use of the airspace immediately above the land would limit the utility of the land and cause a diminution in its value....

The fact that the path of glide taken by the planes was that approved by the Civil Aeronautics Authority does not change the result. The navigable airspace which Congress has placed in the public domain is "airspace above the minimum safe altitudes of flight prescribed by the Civil Aeronautics Authority." 49 U.S.C.A. § 180. If that agency prescribed 83 feet as the minimum safe altitude, then we would have presented the question of the validity of the regulation. But nothing of the sort has been done. The path of glide governs the method of operating—of landing or taking off. The altitude required for that operation is not the minimum safe altitude of flight which is the downward reach of the navigable airspace. The minimum prescribed by the Authority is 500 feet during the day and 1,000 feet at night for air carriers, and from 300 to 1,000 feet for other aircraft, depending on the type of plane and the character of the terrain. Hence, the flights in question were not within the navigable airspace which Congress placed within the public domain. If any airspace needed for landing or taking off were included, flights which were so close to the land as to render it uninhabitable would be immune. But the United States concedes, as we have said, that in that event there would be a taking. Thus, it is apparent that the path of glide is not the minimum safe altitude of flight within the meaning of the statute. The Civil Aeronautics Authority has, of course, the power to prescribe air traffic rules. But Congress has defined navigable airspace only in terms of one of them—the minimum safe altitudes of flight.

We have said that the airspace is a public highway. Yet it is obvious that if the landowner is to have full enjoyment of the land, he must have exclusive control of the immediate reaches of the enveloping atmosphere. Otherwise buildings could not be erected, trees could not be planted, and even fences could not be run. The principle is recognized when the law gives a remedy in case overhanging structures are erected on adjoining land. The landowner owns at least as much of the space above the ground as he can occupy or use in connection with the land. The fact that he does not occupy it in a physical sense—by the erection of buildings and the like—is not material. [T]he flight of airplanes, which skim the surface but do not touch it, is as much an appropriation of the use of the land as a more conventional entry upon it. We would not doubt that, if the United States erected an elevated railway over respondents' land at the precise altitude where its planes now fly, there would be a partial taking, even though none of the supports of the structure rested on the land....

The airplane is part of the modern environment of life, and the inconveniences which it causes are normally not compensable under the Fifth Amendment. The airspace, apart from the immediate reaches above the land, is part of the public domain. We need not determine at this time what those precise limits are. Flights over private land are not a taking, unless they are so low and so frequent as to be a direct and immediate interference with the enjoyment and use of the land. We need not speculate on that phase of the present case. For the findings of the Court of Claims plainly establish that there was a diminution in value of the property and that the frequent, low-level flights were the direct and immediate cause. We agree with the Court of Claims that a servitude has been imposed upon the land.... Since on this record it is not clear whether the easement taken is a permanent or a temporary one, it would be premature for us to consider whether the amount of the award made by the Court of Claims was proper.

The judgment is reversed and the cause is remanded to the Court of Claims so that it may make the necessary findings in conformity with this opinion.

Reversed.

Mr. Justice Jackson took no part in the consideration or decision of this case.

Mr. Justice Black, dissenting.

[T]he allegation of noise and glare resulting in damages, constitutes at best an action in tort where there might be recovery if the noise and light constituted a nuisance, a violation of a statute, or were the result of negligence.[2] ... The concept of taking property as used in the Constitution has heretofore never been given so sweeping a meaning. The Court's opinion presents no case where a man who makes noise or shines light onto his neighbor's property has been ejected from that property for wrongfully taking possession of it. Nor would anyone take seriously a claim that noisy automobiles passing on a highway are taking wrongful possession of the homes located thereon, or that a city elevated train which greatly interferes with the sleep of those who live next to it wrongfully takes their property.... The future adjustment of the rights and remedies of property owners, which might be found necessary

---

2. As to the damage to chickens, Judge Madden, dissenting from this judgment against the Government, said, "When railroads were new, cattle in fields in sight and hearing of the trains were alarmed, thinking that the great moving objects would turn aside and harm them. Horses ran away at the sight and sound of a train or a threshing machine engine. The farmer's chickens have to get over being alarmed at the incredible racket of the tractor starting up suddenly in the shed adjoining the chicken house. These sights and noises are a part of our world, and airplanes are now and will be to a greater degree, likewise a part of it. These disturbances should not be treated as torts, in the case of the airplane, any more than they are so treated in the case of the railroad or public highway." 104 Ct.Cls. 342, 358.

because of the flight of planes at safe altitudes, should, especially in view of the imminent expansion of air navigation, be left where I think the Constitution left it, with Congress. . . .

MR. JUSTICE BURTON joins in this dissent.

Notes

1. After *Causby,* Congress redefined "navigable airspace" to mean "airspace above the minimum altitudes of flight prescribed by regulations issued under this chapter, and *shall include* airspace needed to insure safety in *take-off and landing of aircraft.*" 72 Stat. 739 (emphasis added). The approach area to the northeast runway of a county airport, as designed by the county and approved by the Civil Aeronautics Administration (C.A.A.), passed over petitioner's residence, which was 3250 feet from the end of the runway. Given the approved glide area, there was a clearance of 11.36 feet between the bottom of the glide angle and petitioner's chimney. "The airlines that use the airport are lessees of respondent; and the leases give them, among other things, the right 'to land' and 'take-off.' No flights were in violation of the regulations of the C.A.A.; nor were any flights lower than necessary for a safe landing or take-off."

During almost continuous daily flights, often several minutes apart, "it was often impossible for people in the house to converse or to talk on the telephone. The plaintiff and members of his household . . . were frequently unable to sleep even with ear plugs and sleeping pills; they would frequently be awakened by the flight and the noise of the planes; the windows of their home would frequently rattle and at times plaster fell down from the walls and ceilings; their health was affected and impaired, and they sometimes were compelled to sleep elsewhere."

Plaintiff argued that the county had taken an air easement over his property for which it must pay just compensation. The state supreme court ruled for the defendants. How should the U.S. Supreme Court decide? See *Griggs v. Allegheny County,* 369 U.S. 84, 82 S.Ct. 531, 7 L.Ed.2d 585 (1962).

2. MILITARY ACTIONS. *National Board of YMCA v. United States,* 395 U.S. 85, 89 S.Ct. 1511, 23 L.Ed.2d 117 (1969). The petitioners' buildings were next to each other on the Atlantic side of the Panama Canal Zone, at its boundary with the Republic of Panama. A riot began, members of the mob entered these buildings, began looting, and started a fire. U.S. troops entered the buildings, ejected the rioters, and moved back outside the building. The commanding officer moved his troops inside the buildings to protect his men from the sniper fire. The buildings remained under siege, subject to a barrage of Molotov cocktails, and set to flame. After several days, the mob dispersed. Petitioners sought compensation for the considerable damage done by the rioters after the troops entered the building. The Court, per Brennan, J., denied such relief:

> Ordinarily, of course, governmental occupation of private property de- prives the private owner of his use of the property, and it is this deprivation for which the Constitution requires compensation. [But in] the instant case, the physical occupation by the troops did not deprive petitioners of any use of their buildings. At the time the troops entered, the riot was already well under way, and petitioners' buildings were

already under heavy attack. Throughout the period of occupation, the buildings could not have been used by petitioners in any way. Thus petitioners could only claim compensation for the increased damage by rioters resulting from the presence of troops. But such a claim would not seem to depend on whether the troops were positioned in the buildings. Troops standing just outside a building could as well cause increased damage by rioters to that building as troops positioned inside. [T]he temporary, unplanned occupation of petitioners' buildings in the course of battle does not constitute direct and substantial enough government involvement to warrant compensation under the Fifth Amendment. We have no occasion to decide whether compensation might be required where the Government in some fashion not present here makes private property a particular target for destruction by private parties.

Stewart, J., concurred, with the understanding that if U.S. "military forces should use a building for their own purposes—as a defense bastion or command post, for example—it seems to me this would be a Fifth Amendment taking, even though the owner himself were not actually deprived of any personal use of the building." Harlan, J., concurred in the result: if the troops had simply retreated from the riot area, then the rioters would have subjected the buildings to greater damage. Black, J., joined by Douglas, J., dissented: whenever "the Government determines that one person's property—whatever it may be—is essential to the war effort and appropriates it for the common good, the public purse, rather than the individual, should bear the loss."

3. Forfeiture of Property Used in a Crime. *Bennis v. Michigan,* 516 U.S. 442, 116 S.Ct. 994, 134 L.Ed.2d 68 (1996). Petitioner was joint owner, with her husband, of a car, in which her husband engaged in illegal sex with a prostitute. The trial judge declared the car forfeit as a public nuisance (it was the instrumentality of a crime). Although petitioner lacked knowledge of her husband's activity, the judge, exercising his equitable discretion, allowed no offset for her interest. The judge took into account that the couple owned a second car; although the judge could order the payment of one-half of the sale proceeds, after deduction of costs, to the innocent co-title holder, he declined to do so because of the age and value of the car (an 11–year old car recently purchased for $600).

Rehnquist, C.J., for the Court (5 to 4) found, under these facts (including the trial court's remedial discretion), no violation of due process or the taking of property clause. A "long and unbroken line of cases holds that an owner's interest in property may be forfeited by reason of the use to which the property is put even though the owner did not know that it was to be put to such use." This car was not stolen from the petitioner, and it "facilitated and was used in criminal activity." To the dissent's argument that this line of cases "would justify the confiscation of an ocean liner just because one of its passengers sinned while on board," the Court simply said: when "such application shall be made it will be time enough to pronounce it." Stevens, J. (joined by Souter & Breyer, JJ.) & Kennedy, J., filed dissenting opinions.

4. *Kaiser Aetna v. United States,* 444 U.S. 164, 100 S.Ct. 383, 62 L.Ed.2d 332 (1979). A privately owned pond was separated from navigable waters by a barrier beach and used for aquatic agriculture. The owner

invested substantial money to make various improvements in the pond. The Federal Government contended "that as a result of one of these improvements, the pond's connection to the navigable water in a manner approved by the Corps of Engineers, the owner has somehow lost one of the most essential sticks in the bundle of rights that are commonly characterized as property—the right to exclude others." The Ninth Circuit ruled that when the owner converted the pond into a marina and connected it to the bay, it became subject to a "navigational servitude" and the public thus acquired a right of access. The Supreme Court, per Rehnquist, J., reversed:

> We have not the slightest doubt that the Government could have refused to allow such dredging on the ground that it would have impaired navigation in the bay, or could have conditioned its approval of the dredging on petitioners' agreement to comply with various measures that it deemed appropriate for the promotion of navigation. But what petitioners now have is a body of water that was private property under Hawaiian law, linked to navigable water by a channel dredged by them with the consent of the respondent. While the consent of individual officials representing the United States cannot "estop" the United States, it can lead to the fruition of a number of expectancies embodied in the concept of "property,"—expectancies that, if sufficiently important, the Government must condemn and pay for before it takes over the management of the landowner's property. [T]he "right to exclude," so universally held to be a fundamental element of the property right, falls within this category of interests that the Government cannot take without compensation. This is not a case in which the Government is exercising its regulatory power in a manner that will cause an insubstantial devaluation of petitioners' private property; rather, the imposition of the navigational servitude in this context will result in an actual physical invasion of the privately owned marina.

Contrast *PruneYard Shopping Center v. Robins,* 447 U.S. 74, 100 S.Ct. 2035, 64 L.Ed.2d 741 (1980). The California Supreme Court had held that the California Constitution protected speech and petitioning, reasonably exercised, in shopping centers, even if privately owned. The U.S. Supreme Court, per Rehnquist, J., held that, although the U.S. Constitution does not afford such free speech rights, a state may interpret its own Constitution more expansively. This California interpretation did not infringe the appellants' Constitutional property rights or any other federal guarantees.

> There is nothing to suggest that preventing appellants from prohibiting this sort of activity will unreasonably impair the value or use of their property as a shopping center. The PruneYard is a large commercial complex ... open to the public at large [and, under the California ruling,] the PruneYard may restrict expressive activity by adopting time, place and manner regulations that will minimize any interference with its commercial functions. Appellees were orderly, and they limited their activity to the common areas of the shopping center. [T]he fact that they may have "physically invaded" appellants' property cannot be viewed as determinative. This case is quite different from *Kaiser Aetna v. United States* [where the] marina was open only to fee-paying members, and the fees were paid in part "to maintain the privacy and security of the pond."

Nollan v. California Coastal Commission, 483 U.S. 825, 107 S.Ct. 3141, 97 L.Ed.2d 677 (1987) held (5 to 4) that it was a "taking" when the California Coastal Commission granted a permit to the Nollans to replace their small beachfront bungalow with a larger house *on the condition that* they allow the public an easement to pass across the Nollans' beach (which was located between two public beaches). Scalia, J., for the Court, noted that an outright, uncompensated, permanent, public access easement would violate the Takings Clause. In order for the Commission to condition a rebuilding permit on the Nollans' granting such an access-easement, the condition must substantially further governmental purposes that would justify the denial of the permit; in order for the condition to constitute regulation and not a taking, the condition substituted for the prohibition must further the same governmental purposes as the justification for denying the permit and prohibiting the use. In this case the access-easement condition was not a proper exercise of land use regulation because the condition does not further a public purpose related to the permit requirement. Stevens, J., in dissent complained that the vagueness of the majority's test will leave land-use planners guessing about how the court will react to subsequent cases.

Dolan v. City of Tigard, 512 U.S. 374, 114 S.Ct. 2309, 129 L.Ed.2d 304 (1994) considered the required degree of connection between what the city imposes as a condition of obtaining a building permit, and the projected impact of the proposed development. The City of Tigard agreed to grant a building permit to petitioner to expand her store and pave her gravel parking lot on the condition that she dedicate a portion of her property for flood control (for a public greenway along a creek, to minimize flooding exacerbated by her proposed increase in paved surfaces) and for traffic improvements (about 10% of her property for a pedestrian-bicycle path to relieve traffic congestion, which might be increased because of her development). Petitioner argued that this condition was an unconstitutional, uncompensated taking.

Rehnquist, C.J., for the Court, agreed that the state or city has a broad power over land use planning because zoning rules are applied generally. However, here the city made an "adjudicative decision to condition" the granting of a building permit "for an individual parcel." Moreover, the condition imposed was not merely a restriction on her use of the land but a requirement that she deed part of the property to the city. *Nollan* requires an "essential nexus" between the legitimate state interests and the permit condition. The city's legitimate purposes (flooding prevention and reduced traffic congestion) met this requirement. Then, the Court turned to the question left open in *Nollan,* the connection required between proposed development and the city's conditions:

> "We think a term such as 'rough proportionality' best encapsulates what we hold to be the requirement of the Fifth Amendment. No precise mathematical calculation is required, but the city must make some sort of individualized determination that the required dedication is related both in nature and extent to the impact of the proposed development." (footnote omitted).

The Court justified placing the burden on the city: when courts evaluate "most generally applicable zoning regulations, the burden properly rests on the party challenging the regulation to prove that it constitutes an arbitrary regulation of property rights. Here, in contrast, the city made an adjudicative decision to condition petitioner's application for a building permit on an individual parcel. In this situation, the burden properly rests on the city."

5. *Yee v. City of Escondido,* 503 U.S. 519, 112 S.Ct. 1522, 118 L.Ed.2d 153 (1992). Mobile home park owners complained that a local rent control ordinance, when coupled with the California Mobilehome Residency Law, amounted to physical occupation of their property, entitling them to just compensation. The state Mobilehome law provided that, when a tenant sells his mobile home, the new owner can continue to rent land on which the mobile home sits. The mobile home park owner may terminate the mobile home owner's tenancy only for nonpayment of rent or if the park owner changes the use of the land. The City of Escondido imposed rent control on mobile home rents. The Court, per O'Connor, J., ruled that there was no physical occupation of the mobile home park owners' property. "The government effects a physical taking only where it *requires* the landowner to submit to the physical occupation of his land." The park owners have voluntarily rented their land to mobile home owners, and neither the state nor the city require the mobile home park owners to continue to rent the land as a mobile home park. Whether the city ordinance was a violation of substantive due process or constituted a *regulatory* taking was not before the Court.

6–6.2 *Taking By Regulation*

VILLAGE OF BELLE TERRE v. BORAAS
416 U.S. 1, 94 S.Ct. 1536, 39 L.Ed.2d 797 (1974).

Mr. Justice Douglas delivered the opinion of the Court.

Belle Terre is a village on Long Island's north shore of about 220 homes inhabited by 700 people. Its total land area is less than one square mile. It has restricted land use to one-family dwellings excluding lodging houses, boarding houses, fraternity houses, or multiple-dwelling houses. The word "family" as used in the ordinance means, "[o]ne or more persons related by blood, adoption, or marriage, living and cooking together as a single housekeeping unit, exclusive of household servants. A number of persons but not exceeding two (2) living and cooking together as a single housekeeping unit though not related by blood, adoption, or marriage shall be deemed to constitute a family."

Appellees the Dickmans are owners of a house in the village and leased it in December 1971 for a term of 18 months to Michael Truman. Later Bruce Boraas became a colessee. Then Anne Parish moved into the house along with three others. These six are students at nearby State University at Stony Brook and none is related to the other by blood, adoption, or marriage. When the village served the Dickmans with an "Order to Remedy Violations" of the ordinance, the owners plus three tenants thereupon brought this action under 42 U.S.C. § 1983 for an injunction and a judgment declaring the ordinance unconstitutional. The

District Court held the ordinance constitutional, and the Court of Appeals reversed, one judge dissenting. The case is here by appeal.

This case brings to this Court a different phase of local zoning regulations from those we have previously reviewed. *Village of Euclid v. Ambler Realty Co.*, 272 U.S. 365, 47 S.Ct. 114, 71 L.Ed. 303, involved a zoning ordinance classifying land use in a given area into six categories.... Heights of buildings were prescribed for each zone; also, the size of land areas required for each kind of use was specified. The land in litigation was vacant and being held for industrial development; and evidence was introduced showing that under the restricted-use ordinance the land would be greatly reduced in value. The claim was that the landowner was being deprived of liberty and property without due process within the meaning of the Fourteenth Amendment.

The Court sustained the zoning ordinance under the police power of the State, saying that the line "which in this field separates the legitimate from the illegitimate assumption of power is not capable of precise delimitation. It varies with circumstances and conditions." ... The Court listed as considerations bearing on the constitutionality of zoning ordinances the danger of fire or collapse of buildings, the evils of overcrowding people, and the possibility that "offensive trades, industries, and structures" might "create nuisance" to residential sections. But even those historic police power problems need not loom large or actually be existent in a given case. For the exclusion of "all industrial establishments" does not mean that "only offensive or dangerous industries will be excluded." That fact does not invalidate the ordinance; the Court held: "The inclusion of a reasonable margin to insure effective enforcement [may be justified because] in some fields, the bad fades into the good by such insensible degrees that the two are not capable of being readily distinguished and separated in terms of legislation."

The main thrust of the case in the mind of the Court was in the exclusion of industries and apartments, and as respects that it commented on the desire to keep residential areas free of "disturbing noises"; "increased traffic"; the hazard of "moving and parked automobiles"; the "depriving children of the privilege of quiet and open spaces for play, enjoyed by those in more favored localities." The ordinance was sanctioned because the validity of the legislative classification was "fairly debatable" and therefore could not be said to be wholly arbitrary.

Our decision in *Berman v. Parker*, 348 U.S. 26, 75 S.Ct. 98, 99 L.Ed. 27, sustained a land-use project in the District of Columbia against a landowner's claim that the taking violated the Due Process Clause and the Just Compensation Clause of the Fifth Amendment. The essence of the argument against the law was, while taking property for ridding an area of slums was permissible, taking it "merely to develop a better balanced, more attractive community" was not. We refused to limit the concept of public welfare that may be enhanced by zoning regulations. We said:

Miserable and disreputable housing conditions may do more than spread disease and crime and immorality. They may also suffocate the spirit by reducing the people who live there to the status of cattle. They may indeed make living an almost insufferable burden. They may also be an ugly sore, a blight on the community which robs it of charm, which makes it a place from which men turn. The misery of housing may despoil a community as an open sewer may ruin a river.

We do not sit to determine whether a particular housing project is or is not desirable. The concept of the public welfare is broad and inclusive.... The values it represents are spiritual as well as physical, aesthetic as well as monetary. It is within the power of the legislature to determine that the community should be beautiful as well as healthy, spacious as well as clean, well-balanced as well as carefully patrolled.

... We deal with economic and social legislation where legislatures have historically drawn lines which we respect against the charge of violation of the Equal Protection Clause if the law be " 'reasonable, not arbitrary' "and bears "a rational relationship to a [permissible] state objective."

It is said, however, that if two unmarried people can constitute a "family," there is no reason why three or four may not. But every line drawn by a legislature leaves some out that might well have been included. That exercise of discretion, however, is a legislative, not a judicial, function....

Mr. Justice Marshall, dissenting....

Had the owners alone brought this suit alleging that the restrictive ordinance deprived them of their property or was an irrational legislative classification, I would agree that the ordinance would have to be sustained....

My disagreement with the Court today is based upon my view that the ordinance in this case unnecessarily burdens appellees' First Amendment freedom of association and their constitutionally guaranteed right to privacy.... The instant ordinance discriminates on the basis of ... a personal lifestyle choice as to household companions. It permits any number of persons related by blood or marriage, be it two or twenty, to live in a single household, but it limits to two the number of unrelated persons bound by profession, love, friendship, religious or political affiliation, or mere economics who can occupy a single home. Belle Terre imposes upon those who deviate from the community norm in their choice of living companions significantly greater restrictions than are applied to residential groups who are related by blood or marriage, and compose the established order within the community. The village has, in effect, acted to fence out those individuals whose choice of lifestyle differs from that of its current residents.

This is not a case where the Court is being asked to nullify a township's sincere efforts to maintain its residential character by preventing the operation of rooming houses, fraternity houses, or other commercial or high-density residential uses. Unquestionably, a town is free to restrict such uses.... This ordinance, however, limits the density of occupancy of only those homes occupied by unrelated persons. It thus reaches beyond control of the use of land or the density of population, and undertakes to regulate the way people choose to associate with each other within the privacy of their own homes....

[The dissenting opinion of BRENNAN, J., contending that a case or controversy no longer exists, is omitted.]

Notes

1. Justice Marshall's dissent notes: "Had the owners alone brought this suit alleging that the restrictive ordinance deprived them of their property or was an irrational classification, I would agree that the ordinance would have to be sustained." Why? Would Marshall subject all zoning ordinances to the same degree of scrutiny, whether attacked on First or Fifth Amendment grounds? Would Justice Douglas?

In *Moore v. City of East Cleveland,* 431 U.S. 494, 97 S.Ct. 1932, 52 L.Ed.2d 531 (1977), a fragmented Court invalidated a housing ordinance that limited the occupancy of a dwelling unit to members of a single family, but defined "family" narrowly, so that Mrs. Moore could not live with her two grandsons, who were first cousins rather than brothers. Powell, J., joined by Brennan, Marshall, & Blackmun, JJ., announced the judgment of the Court and invalidated the ordinance on substantive due process grounds. *Belle Terre,* he argued, did not govern the case because that ordinance only affected *"unrelated* individuals." Powell acknowledged that, as "the history of the *Lochner* era demonstrates, there is reason for concern lest the only limits to such judicial intervention become the predilections of those who happen at the time to be Members of this Court." But that history only counsels caution; "it does not counsel abandonment...." The Court, he said, should respect "the teachings of history" in order to find "[a]ppropriate limits on substantive due process." The Constitution, he argued, "protects the sanctity of the family precisely because the institution of the family is deeply rooted in this Nation's history and tradition."

Stevens, J., concurred in the judgment; Brennan, J., joined by Marshall, J., concurred; Stewart J., joined by Rehnquist, J., dissented (and noted that the appellant did not request a variance from the zoning laws although she could have done so); White, J. & Burger, C.J., filed dissenting opinions.

2. Although some state courts, relying on the state constitution, have been active in invalidating zoning rules as uncompensated takings, economic attacks on zoning regulations have not fared as well in the federal courts when attacked under the U.S. Constitution. Consider *Penn Central Transportation Co. v. New York,* 438 U.S. 104, 98 S.Ct. 2646, 57 L.Ed.2d 631 (1978). Justice Brennan, for the Court, summarized the basic issue:

The question presented is whether a city may, as part of a comprehensive program to preserve historic landmarks and historic districts, place restrictions on the development of individual historic landmarks—in addition to those imposed by applicable zoning ordinances—without effecting a "taking" requiring the payment of "just compensation." Specifically, we must decide whether the application of New York City's Landmarks Preservation Law to the parcel of land occupied by Grand Central Terminal has "taken" its owners' property in violation of the Fifth and Fourteenth Amendments.

Under the law, the Landmark Preservation Commission could designate certain property as a "landmark." If such designation was upheld after judicial review, the landmark was subject to various restrictions, such as requiring that any proposed alterations to the building's external appearance have the prior approval of the Commission. Penn Central claimed that the Commission's refusal to allow it to build a multistory office building above the Grand Central Terminal was an unconstitutional "taking". The state court upheld the law, inter alia, on the grounds that it provided that Penn Central could transfer the development rights above the Terminal to numerous sites in the vicinity of the Terminal, that these transferable rights were valuable, and may constitute fair compensation for the loss of the development rights above the terminal.

The Supreme Court affirmed, but did not decide whether the transferable development rights constituted "just compensation".[1] Rather it held that no "taking" had occurred:

> [T]his Court, quite simply, has been unable to develop any "set formula" for determining when "justice and fairness" require that economic injuries caused by public action be compensated by the government, rather than remain disproportionately concentrated on a few persons.... In engaging in these essentially ad hoc, factual inquiries, the Court's decisions have identified several factors that have particular significance. The economic impact of the regulation on the claimant and, particularly, the extent to which the regulation has interfered with distinct investment-backed expectations are, of course, relevant considerations. So, too, is the character of the governmental action. A "taking" may more readily be found when the interference with property can be characterized as a physical invasion by government, see e.g., *United States v. Causby,* than when interference arises from some public program adjusting the benefits and burdens of economic life to promote the common good. [I]n instances in which a state tribunal reasonably concluded that "the health, safety, morals, or general welfare" would be promoted by prohibiting particular contemplated uses of land, this Court has upheld land-use regulations that destroyed or adversely affected recognized real property interests. Zoning laws are, of course, the classic example, which have been viewed as permissible governmental action even when prohibiting the most beneficial use of the property.

---

1. Rehnquist, J., joined by Burger, C.J. and Stevens, J., dissented: "While neighboring landowners are free to use their land and 'air rights' in any way consistent with the broad boundaries of New York zoning, Penn Central, absent the permission of appellees, must forever maintain its property in its present state. The property has been thus subjected to a nonconsensual servitude not borne by any neighboring or similar properties. Appellees have thus destroyed—in a literal sense, 'taken'—substantial property rights of Penn Central...."

Zoning laws generally do not affect existing uses of real property, but "taking" challenges have also been held to be without merit in a wide variety of situations when the challenged governmental actions prohibited a beneficial use to which individual parcels had previously been devoted and thus caused substantial individualized harm. *Miller v. Schoene,* 276 U.S. 272, 48 S.Ct. 246, 72 L.Ed. 568 (1928), is illustrative. In that case, a state entomologist, acting pursuant to a state statute, ordered the claimants to cut down a large number of ornamental red cedar trees because they produced cedar rust fatal to apple trees cultivated nearby. Although the statute provided for recovery of any expense incurred in removing the cedars, and permitted claimants to use the felled trees, it did not provide compensation for the value of the standing trees or for the resulting decrease in market value of the properties as a whole. A unanimous Court held that this latter omission did not render the statute invalid. The Court held that the State might properly make "a choice between the preservation of one class of property and that of the other" and since the apple industry was important in the State involved, concluded that the State had not exceeded "its constitutional powers by deciding upon the destruction of one class of property [without compensation] in order to save another which, in the judgment of the legislature, is of greater value to the public."

Again, *Hadacheck v. Sebastian,* 239 U.S. 394, 36 S.Ct. 143, 60 L.Ed. 348 (1915), upheld a law prohibiting the claimant from continuing his otherwise lawful business of operating a brickyard in a particular physical community on the ground that the legislature had reasonably concluded that the presence of the brickyard was inconsistent with neighboring uses. . . .

Pennsylvania Coal Co. v. Mahon, 260 U.S. 393, 43 S.Ct. 158, 67 L.Ed. 322 (1922), is the leading case for the proposition that a state statute that substantially furthers important public policies may so frustrate distinct investment-backed expectations as to amount to a "taking." There the claimant had sold the surface rights to particular parcels of property, but expressly reserved the right to remove the coal thereunder. A Pennsylvania statute, enacted after the transactions, forbade any mining of coal that caused the subsidence of any house, unless the house was the property of the owner of the underlying coal and was more than 150 feet from the improved property of another. Because the statute made it commercially impracticable to mine the coal, and thus had nearly the same effect as the complete destruction of rights claimant had reserved from the owners of the surface land, the Court held that the statute was invalid as effecting a "taking" without just compensation.

In *Hadacheck v. Sebastian,* cited in *Penn Central,* supra, the land was worth about $800,000 if used for brick-making purposes but not more than $60,000 for residential or any other purposes. The ordinance made it illegal to establish or operate a brickyard within the city limits. At the time that Petitioner purchased the land (because of the bed of clay) it was outside the city limits and no one thought that the city would annex the territory and apply its ordinance. During the last seven years the land had been used as a brickyard without complaint. The ordinance did not prohibit the removal of the brick clay but did prohibit its manufacture into bricks in that locality. It provided no compensation. A unanimous Court upheld the law: "There must be progress, and if in its march private interests are in the way they must yield to the good of the community."

Hadacheck has been called a "classic" example of some of "the most violently offensive decisions not to compensate.... It would be no less erratic for society to explain to a homeowner, as it bulldozed his house out of the way of a new public school or pumping station, that he should have realized from the beginning that congestion would necessitate these facilities." To those who argue that the brickmaker should internalize the benefits and costs of his operation by purchasing enough of the surrounding land to buffer adjacent buildings from the impact of his brickworks, one might ask whether this rule applies only to brickmakers, or to homebuilders as well. "[Why] is it not incumbent on the homebuilder to acquire a buffer zone—enough surrounding land to insulate himself from the effects of any brickworks which an owner of adjacent land may choose to build...." Michelman, Property, Utility, and Fairness: Comments on the Ethical Foundations of "Just Compensation" Law, 80 Harv.L.Rev. 1165, 1237, 1242–43 (1967).

In *Lucas v. South Carolina Coastal Council,* 505 U.S. 1003, 112 S.Ct. 2886, 120 L.Ed.2d 798 (1992), Lucas bought two residential beach front lots (about 300 feet from the shore) for nearly $1 million. He planned to build two single family residences, like the owners of the immediately adjacent property had already done. Two years later, before he was able to build, South Carolina enacted legislation that required that land like his be left substantially in its natural state. The law, which provided no compensation, prohibited the erection of any new permanent habitable structures, but did not require Lucas' neighbors to tear down their houses. The state trial court found that the law made his parcels "valueless" and deprived him of "any reasonable economic use" of the land. The judge awarded $1.2 million compensation for this regulatory "taking" of property. The state supreme court reversed, because the state law had declared, in a conclusory fashion, that improvement of the beach front property was inconsistent with the public interest.

Scalia, J., for the Court (6 to 3), reversed and remanded. He quoted the "oft-cited maxim" that, "while property may be regulated to a certain extent, if regulation goes too far, it will be recognized as a taking." Thus, if a regulation denies "all economically beneficial or productive use of land," there is a "taking" because there is the economic equivalent of physical appropriation. However—

> [T]he owner of a lake bed, for example, would not be entitled to compensation when he is denied the requisite permit to engage in a landfilling operation that would have the effect of flooding others' land. Nor the corporate owner of a nuclear generating plant, when it is directed to remove all improvements from its land upon discovery that the plant sits astride an earthquake fault. Such regulatory action may well have the effect of eliminating the land's only economically productive use, but it does not proscribe a productive use that was previously

permissible under relevant property and nuisance principles. The use of these properties for what are now expressly prohibited purposes was always unlawful.... When, however, a regulation that declares "off-limits" all economically productive or beneficial uses of land goes beyond what the relevant background principles would dictate, compensation must be paid to sustain it.

Stevens, J., in dissent, criticized the "deprivation of all economically beneficial use" rule as "wholly arbitrary:" the "landowner whose property is diminished in value 95% recovers nothing," while the landowner suffering a complete elimination of value "recovers the land's full value." Scalia, in a footnote, replied that Stevens' assumption (that a landowner whose deprivation is one step short of complete is not entitled to compensation) is wrong. "Such an owner might not be able to claim the benefit of our categorical formulation," but " '[t]he economic impact of the regulation on the claimant and ... the extent to which the regulation has interfered with distinct investment-backed expectations' are keenly relevant to takings analysis generally."

Blackmun, J., also dissenting, argued that the state trial court's finding that Lucas' property had lost all economic value was "almost certainly erroneous," because Lucas still "enjoy other attributes of ownership" such as "the right to exclude others," the right to sell the property, the right to picnic on the property, "camp in a tent, or live on the property in a movable trailer." Blackmun did not mention it, but Lucas, as the technical owner, also had the "right" to pay property tax and be liable in tort for injuries involving the property.

3. *Andrus v. Allard*, 444 U.S. 51, 100 S.Ct. 318, 62 L.Ed.2d 210 (1979). Regulations issued pursuant to the Eagle Protection Act and the Migratory Bird Treaty Act prohibited commercial transactions in parts of certain birds, even though the birds had been legally killed before the birds had come under the protection of the Acts. Appellees were engaged in the trade of Indian artifacts, some of which were partly composed of the feathers of currently protected birds, but these artifacts existed before the statutory protections had come into force. The Court upheld the regulations and rejected appellees' claim that their property was "taken" without just compensation. The regulations—

> do not compel the surrender of the artifacts, and there is no physical invasion or restraint upon them. Rather, a significant restriction has been imposed on one means of disposing of the artifacts. But the denial of one traditional property right does not always amount to a taking. At least where an owner possesses a full "bundle" of property rights, the destruction of one "strand" of the bundle is not a taking, because the aggregate must be viewed in its entirety. In this case, it is crucial that appellees retain the rights to possess and transport their property, and to donate or devise the protected birds. [L]oss of future profits— unaccompanied by any physical property restriction—provides a slender reed upon which to rest a takings claim.

4. *Phillips v. Washington Legal Foundation*, 524 U.S. 156, 118 S.Ct. 1925, 141 L.Ed.2d 174 (1998). Texas, 48 other states, and the District of Columbia have adopted an Interest on Lawyers' Trust Fund Accounts

("IOLTA") program. Under IOLTA, certain client trust funds held by a lawyer in connection with the practice of law (typically funds nominal in amount or held for a short period of time, considered without regard to the funds of other clients) are deposited in bank accounts. IOLTA seeks to use the interest that these funds generate to finance state projects, such as legal services for low-income individuals. The question before the Court was narrow: whether the interest was "property" of the lawyer or client for purposes of the Takings Clause. Rehnquist, C.J., for the Court (5 to 4), held such interest on a client's funds is property of the client even if the relevant bank charges would mean the client could never spend it. For example, the Court said, rental income would be the property of the owner of a building even if collecting the rent cost more than the tenant had paid. The general rule is that "interest follows principal." Because the questions had not been decided below, the Court remanded on the issue whether the IOLTA program constituted an unconstitutional taking of the clients' property and what, if any, compensation might be due.

Souter, J. (joined by Breyer, Stevens, & Ginsburg, JJ.) and Breyer, J. (joined by Stevens, Souter, & Ginsburg, JJ.) filed dissenting opinions. They argued that it was meaningless to talk of "taking" or calling "property" an asset that had no practical value to the client. Under pre-existing federal law, the client's principal could not generate interest (because federal law prohibits for-profit corporations and partnerships from earning interest on demand deposits unless the interest is earned in an IOLTA account).

5. *Eastern Enterprises v. Apfel,* 524 U.S. 498 118 S.Ct. 2131, 141 L.Ed.2d 451(1998) considered the constitutionality of the Coal Industry Health Benefit Act of 1992 ("1992 Coal Act"). Various factors (an increase in benefits for retired miners, an increase in eligible recipients, the decline in coal production, the increase in health care cost) caused financial problems for the 1950 and 1974 Health Benefit Plans for coal miners. Congress enacted the 1992 Coal Act, which imposed on Eastern the obligation for over 1,000 retired miners who had worked for the company before 1966. Eastern had left the coal business in 1965. Eastern claimed that this retroactive liability constituted an unconstitutional taking of property and a violation of due process.

O'Connor, J., joined by Rehnquist, C.J. & Scalia & Thomas, JJ., concluded that the 1992 Coal Act, as applied to Eastern Enterprises, effects an unconstitutional taking of property because it placed a severe, disproportionate, and an extremely retroactive burden on a former coal operator. The Court must evaluate the Act's "justice and fairness," taking into account (1) the economic impact of the regulation, (2) its interference with reasonable investor backed expectations, and (3) the character of the governmental action. In general, Congress has considerable leeway to enact economic legislation that affects contractual commitments between private parties, and it may impose retroactive liability to some degree, particularly when it is confine to "short and limited periods required by the practicalities of producing national legislation."

However, the 1992 Coal Act imposed severe liability ($50 to $100 million dollars) on a limited class of parties that could not have anticipated their liability, which was substantiality disproportionate to the parties' experience.

When Eastern was in the coal business, the benefits to miners were far less extensive than under even the 1974 law, were not vested, and were fully subject to alteration or termination. The 1992 Coal Act retroactively imposed liability on Eastern for its activities between 1946 and 1965. The Coal Act is unlike the Black Lung Benefits Act of 1972, which spread the cost of employment-related disabilities to those who profited from the fruits of the employees' labor. Congress's solution was also unusual in that it singled out certain employers for substantial burdens, based on their conduct far in the past, unrelated to any commitment that the employers made or to any injury that they may have caused. Thomas, J., also filed a concurring opinion.

Kennedy, J., concurring in the judgment and dissenting in part (he disagreed with the plurality's takings analysis), concluded the application of the Coal Act was "arbitrary" and violated substantive economic due process. He argued that due process protection for property should incorporate a settled tradition against retroactive laws of great severity.

Stevens, J. (joined by Souter, Ginsburg, & Breyer, JJ.), and Breyer, J. (joined by Stevens, Souter, & Ginsburg, JJ.) each filed dissents. Stevens argued that there was "an implicit understanding" that the coal operators would provide the miners with lifetime health benefits. Breyer argued that it is not "fundamentally unfair" to make Eastern Enterprises pay the health care costs of retired miners who had worked for Eastern prior to 1965.

Chapter 7

STATE ACTION

7–1. INTRODUCTION

THE CIVIL RIGHTS CASES
(UNITED STATES v. STANLEY;
UNITED STATES v. RYAN;
UNITED STATES v. NICHOLS;
UNITED STATES v. SINGLETON;
ROBINSON v. MEMPHIS
& CHARLESTON RY. CO.)

109 U.S. 3, 3 S.Ct. 18, 27 L.Ed. 835 (1883).

These cases were all founded on the first and second sections of the Act of Congress, known as the Civil Rights Act, passed March 1st, 1875, entitled "An Act to protect all citizens in their civil and legal rights." Two of the cases, those against Stanley and Nichols, were indictments for denying to persons of color the accommodations and privileges of an inn or hotel; two of them, those against Ryan and Singleton, were, one on information, the other an indictment, for denying to individuals the privileges and accommodations of a theater, the information against Ryan being for refusing a colored person a seat in the dress circle of Maguire's theater in San Francisco; and the indictment against Singleton was for denying to another person, whose color was not stated, the full enjoyment of the accommodations of the theater known as the Grand Opera House in New York, "said denial not being made for any reasons by law applicable to citizens of every race and color, and regardless of any previous condition of servitude." The case of Robinson and wife against the Memphis & Charleston R.R. Company was an action brought in the Circuit Court of the United States for the Western District of Tennessee, to recover the penalty of five hundred dollars given by the second section of the act; and the gravamen was the refusal by the conductor of the railroad company to allow the wife to ride in the ladies' car, for the reason, as stated in one of the counts, that she was a person of African descent. . . .

542

Mr. Justice Bradley delivered the opinion of the Court. After stating the facts in the above language he continued:

It is obvious that the primary and important question in all the cases is the constitutionality of the law: for if the law is unconstitutional none of the prosecutions can stand.

The sections of the law referred to provide as follows:

Sec. 1. That all persons within the jurisdiction of the United States shall be entitled to the full and equal enjoyment of the accommodations, advantages, facilities, and privileges of inns, public conveyances on land or water, theaters, and other places of public amusement; subject only to the conditions and limitations established by law, and applicable alike to citizens of every race and color, regardless of any previous condition of servitude.

Sec. 2. That any person who shall violate the foregoing section ... shall for every such offence forfeit and pay the sum of five hundred dollars to the person aggrieved thereby, to be recovered in an action of debt, with full costs; and shall also, for every such offence, be deemed guilty of a misdemeanor, and, upon conviction thereof, shall be fined not less than five hundred nor more than one thousand dollars, or shall be imprisoned not less than thirty days nor more than one year ...

Has Congress constitutional power to make such a law? Of course, no one will contend that the power to pass it was contained in the Constitution before the adoption of the last three amendments. The power is sought, first, in the Fourteenth Amendment, and the views and arguments of distinguished Senators, advanced whilst the law was under consideration, claiming authority to pass it by virtue of that amendment, are the principal arguments adduced in favor of the power.

[Under the Fourteenth Amendment, it] is State action of a particular character that is prohibited. Individual invasion of individual rights is not the subject-matter of the amendment. It has a deeper and broader scope. It nullifies and makes void all State legislation, and State action of every kind, which impairs the privileges and immunities of citizens of the United States, or which injures them in life, liberty or property without due process of law, or which denies to any of them the equal protection of the laws. It not only does this, but, in order that the national will, thus declared, may not be a mere *brutum fulmen,* the last section of the amendment invests Congress with power to enforce it by appropriate legislation. To enforce what? To enforce the prohibition. To adopt appropriate legislation for correcting the effects of such prohibited State laws and State acts, and thus to render them effectually null, void, and innocuous. This is the legislative power conferred upon Congress, and this is the whole of it.... And so in the present case, until some State law has been passed, or some State action through its officers or agents has been taken, adverse to the rights of citizens sought to be protected by the Fourteenth Amendment, no legislation of the United States under said amendment, nor any proceeding under such legislation, can be called into activity: for the prohibitions of the amendment are against State laws and acts done under State authority. . . .

If this legislation is appropriate for enforcing the prohibitions of the amendment, it is difficult to see where it is to stop. Why may not Congress with equal show of authority enact a code of laws for the enforcement and vindication of all rights of life, liberty, and property? If it is supposable that the States may deprive persons of life, liberty, and property without due process of law (and the amendment itself does suppose this), why should not Congress proceed at once to prescribe due process of law for the protection of every one of these fundamental rights, in every possible case, as well as to prescribe equal privileges in inns, public conveyances, and theaters? The truth is, that the implication of a power to legislate in this manner is based upon the assumption that if the States are forbidden to legislate or act in a particular way on a particular subject, and power is conferred upon Congress to enforce the prohibition, this gives Congress power to legislate generally upon that subject, and not merely power to provide modes of redress against such State legislation or action. The assumption is certainly unsound. It is repugnant to the Tenth Amendment of the Constitution. . . .

In this connection it is proper to state that civil rights, such as are guaranteed by the Constitution against State aggression, cannot be impaired by the wrongful acts of individuals, unsupported by State authority in the shape of laws, customs, or judicial or executive proceedings. . . .

Of course, these remarks do not apply to those cases in which Congress is clothed with direct and plenary powers of legislation over the whole subject, accompanied with an express or implied denial of such power to the States, as in the regulation of commerce with foreign nations, among the several States, and with the Indian tribes, the coining of money. [I]t is clear that the law in question cannot be sustained by any grant of legislative power made to Congress by the Fourteenth Amendment. . . . Whether the law would be a valid one as applied to the Territories and the District is not a question for consideration in the cases before us: they all being cases arising within the limits of States. And whether Congress, in the exercise of its power to regulate commerce amongst the several States, might or might not pass a law regulating rights in public conveyances passing from one State to another, is also a question which is not now before us, as the sections in question are not conceived in any such view.

But the power of Congress to adopt direct and primary, as distinguished from corrective legislation, on the subject in hand, is sought, in the second place, from the Thirteenth Amendment. . . . By its own unaided force and effect it abolished slavery, and established universal freedom. Still, legislation may be necessary and proper to meet all the various cases and circumstances to be affected by it, and to prescribe proper modes of redress for its violation in letter or spirit. And such legislation may be primary and direct in its character; for the amendment is not a mere prohibition of State laws establishing or upholding slavery, but an absolute declaration that slavery or involuntary servitude shall not exist in any part of the United States.

It is true, that slavery cannot exist without law, any more than property in lands and goods can exist without law: and, therefore, the Thirteenth Amendment may be regarded as nullifying all State laws which establish or uphold slavery. But it has a reflex character also, establishing and decreeing universal civil and political freedom throughout the United States; and it is assumed, that the power vested in Congress to enforce the article by appropriate legislation, clothes Congress with power to pass all laws necessary and proper for abolishing all badges and incidents of slavery in the United States: and upon this assumption it is claimed, that this is sufficient authority for declaring by law that all persons shall have equal accommodations and privileges in all inns, public conveyances, and places of amusement; the argument being, that the denial of such equal accommodations and privileges is, in itself, a subjection to a species of servitude within the meaning of the amendment. Conceding the major proposition to be true, that Congress has a right to enact all necessary and proper laws for the obliteration and prevention of slavery with all its badges and incidents, is the minor proposition also true, that the denial to any person of admission to the accommodations and privileges of an inn, a public conveyance, or a theater, does subject that person to any form of servitude, or tend to fasten upon him any badge of slavery? . . .

The long existence of African slavery in this country gave us very distinct notions of what it was, and what were its necessary incidents. . . . Congress, as we have seen, by the Civil Rights Bill of 1866, passed in view of the Thirteenth Amendment, before the Fourteenth was adopted, undertook to wipe out these burdens and disabilities, the necessary incidents of slavery, constituting its substance and visible form; and to secure to all citizens of every race and color, and without regard to previous servitude, those fundamental rights which are the essence of civil freedom, namely, the same right to make and enforce contracts, to sue, be parties, give evidence, and to inherit, purchase, lease, sell and convey property, as is enjoyed by white citizens. Whether this legislation was fully authorized by the Thirteenth Amendment alone, without the support which it afterward received from the Fourteenth Amendment, after the adoption of which it was re-enacted with some additions, it is not necessary to inquire. It is referred to for the purpose of showing that at that time (in 1866) Congress did not assume, under the authority given by the Thirteenth Amendment, to adjust what may be called the social rights of men and races in the community; but only to declare and vindicate those fundamental rights which appertain to the essence of citizenship, and the enjoyment or deprivation of which constitutes the essential distinction between freedom and slavery. . . .

The only question under the present head, therefore, is, whether the refusal to any persons of the accommodations of an inn, or a public conveyance, or a place of public amusement, by an individual, and without any sanction or support from any State law or regulation, does inflict upon such persons any manner of servitude, or form of slavery, as those terms are understood in this country? [S]uch an act of refusal has nothing to do with slavery or involuntary servitude, and that if it is violative of any right of the party, his redress is to be sought under the laws of the State; or if those laws are adverse to his rights and do not protect him, his remedy will be found in the corrective legislation which Congress has adopted, or may adopt, for counteracting the effect of State laws, or State action, prohibited by the Fourteenth Amendment. It would be running the slavery argument into the ground to make it apply to every act of discrimination which a person may see fit to make as to the guests he will entertain, or as to the people he will take into his coach or cab or car, or admit to his concert or theater, or deal with in other matters of intercourse or business. Innkeepers and public carriers, by the laws of all the States, so far as we are aware, are bound, to the extent of their facilities, to furnish proper accommodation to all unobjectionable persons who in good faith apply for them. If the laws themselves make any unjust discrimination, amenable to the prohibitions of the Fourteenth Amendment, Congress has full power to afford a remedy under that amendment and in accordance with it.

When a man has emerged from slavery, and by the aid of beneficent legislation has shaken off the inseparable concomitants of that state, there must be some stage in the progress of his elevation when he takes the rank of a mere citizen, and ceases to be the special favorite of the laws, and when his rights as a citizen, or a man, are to be protected in the ordinary modes by which other men's rights are protected. There were thousands of free colored people in this country before the abolition of slavery, enjoying all the essential rights of life, liberty and property the same as white citizens; yet no one, at that time, thought that it was any invasion of his personal status as a freeman because he was not admitted to all the privileges enjoyed by white citizens, or because he was subjected to discriminations in the enjoyment of accommodations in inns, public conveyances and places of amusement. Mere discriminations on account of race or color were not regarded as badges of slavery.

[Thus,] the first and second sections of the act of Congress of March 1st, 1875, entitled "An Act to protect all citizens in their civil and legal rights," are unconstitutional and void, and that judgment should be rendered upon the several indictments in those cases accordingly.

And it is so ordered.

MR. JUSTICE HARLAN dissenting.

The opinion in these cases proceeds, it seems to me, upon grounds entirely too narrow and artificial. I cannot resist the conclusion that the substance and spirit of the recent amendments of the Constitution have been sacrificed by a subtle and ingenious verbal criticism.

[T]here are burdens and disabilities which constitute badges of slavery and servitude, and ... such discrimination practised by corporations and individuals in the exercise of their public or quasi-public functions is a badge of servitude the imposition of which Congress may prevent under its power, by appropriate legislation, to enforce the Thirteenth Amendment; and, consequently, without reference to its enlarged power under the Fourteenth Amendment, the act of March 1, 1875, is not, in my judgment, repugnant to the Constitution.

It remains now to consider these cases with reference to the power Congress has possessed since the adoption of the Fourteenth Amendment.... The assumption that this amendment consists wholly of prohibitions upon State laws and State proceedings in hostility to its provisions, is unauthorized by its language.... because the power of Congress is not restricted to the enforcement of prohibitions upon State laws or State action. It is, in terms distinct and positive, to enforce "the *provisions of this article*" of amendment; not simply those of a prohibitive character, but the provisions—*all* of the provisions—affirmative and prohibitive, of the amendment....

But what was secured to colored citizens of the United States—as between them and their respective States—by the national grant to them of State citizenship? ... There is one, if there be no other—exemption from race discrimination in respect of any civil right belonging to citizens of the white race in the same State. That, surely, is their constitutional privilege when within the jurisdiction of other States. And such must be their constitutional right, in their own State, unless the recent amendments be splendid baubles, thrown out to delude those who deserved fair and generous treatment at the hands of the nation. Citizenship in this country necessarily imports at least equality of civil rights among citizens of every race in the same State.

[Even] if it were conceded that the power of Congress could not be brought into activity until the rights specified in the act of 1875 had been abridged or denied by some State law or State action, I maintain that the decision of the court is erroneous. There has been adverse State action.... In every material sense applicable to the practical enforcement of the Fourteenth Amendment, railroad corporations, keepers of inns, and managers of places of public amusement are agents or instrumentalities of the State, because they are charged with duties to the public, and are amenable, in respect of their duties and functions, to governmental regulation. [A] denial, by these instrumentalities of the State, to the citizen, because of his race, of that equality of civil rights secured to him by law, is a denial by the State, within the meaning of the Fourteenth Amendment. If it be not, then that race is left, in respect of the civil rights in question, practically at the mercy of corporations and individuals wielding power under the States....

The court, in its opinion, reserves the question whether Congress, in the exercise of its power to regulate commerce amongst the several States, might or might not pass a law regulating rights in public conveyances passing from one State to another.... Might not the act of 1875 be maintained in that case, as applicable at least to commerce between the States, notwithstanding it does not, upon its face, profess to have been passed in pursuance of the power of Congress to regulate commerce? Has it ever been held that the judiciary should overturn a statute, because the legislative department did not accurately recite therein the particular provision of the Constitution authorizing its enactment? We have often enforced municipal bonds in aid of railroad subscriptions, where they failed to recite the statute authorizing their issue, but recited one which did not sustain their validity. The inquiry in such cases has been, was there, in any statute, authority for the execution of the bonds? . . .

Notes

Bell v. Maryland, 378 U.S. 226, 84 S.Ct. 1814, 12 L.Ed.2d 822 (1964). Twelve black students entered a restaurant and sought service. When an employee asked them to leave solely because of their race, they refused, and were convicted of criminal trespass. After the state courts affirmed the conviction, the Baltimore and Maryland enacted laws making it unlawful for restaurants to deny service because of race. The Court, per Brennan, J., then remanded the case so that the state court could consider whether to nullify the convictions in view of the change in state law, which apparently would apply to this case, pending at the time of the supervening legislation. Goldberg, J.'s concurrence, joined by Warren, C.J., and in part by Douglas, J., considered the historical background of the *Civil Rights Cases:*

> [In the *Civil Rights Cases,* Justice Bradley stated]: "Innkeepers and public carriers, by the laws of all the States, so far as we are aware, are bound, to the extent of their facilities, to furnish proper accommodation to all unobjectionable persons who in good faith apply for them."

> This assumption, whatever its validity at the time of the 1883 decision, has proved to be unfounded. Although reconstruction ended in 1877, six years before the *Civil Rights Cases,* there was little immediate action in the South to establish segregation, in law or in fact, in places of public accommodation.[26] This benevolent, or perhaps passive, attitude endured about a decade and then in the late 1880's States began to enact laws mandating unequal treatment in public places. Finally, three-quarters of a century later, after this Court declared such legislative action invalid, some States began to utilize and make available their common law to sanction similar discriminatory treatment.

> A State applying its statutory or common law to deny rather than protect the right of access to public accommodations has clearly made the assumption of the opinion in the *Civil Rights Cases* inapplicable and has, as the author of that opinion would himself have recognized, denied the constitutionally intended equal protection. Indeed, in light of the assumption so explicitly stated in the *Civil Rights Cases,* it is significant that Mr. Justice Bradley, who spoke for the Court had earlier in

26. "Woodward, The Strange Career of Jim Crow (1955), 15–26, points out that segregation in its modern and pervasive form is a relatively recent phenomenon. Although the speed of the movement varied, it was not until 1904, for example, that Maryland, the respondent in this case, extended Jim Crow legislation to railroad coaches and other common carriers. In the 1870's Negroes in Baltimore, Maryland, successfully challenged attempts to segregate transit facilities."

correspondence with Circuit Judge Woods expressed the view that the Fourteenth Amendment "not only prohibits the making or enforcing of laws which shall abridge the privileges of the citizen; but prohibits the states from denying to all persons within its jurisdiction the equal protection of the laws." [H]e concluded that: "Denying includes inaction as well as action. And denying the equal protection of the laws includes the omission to protect, as well as the omission to pass laws for protection." These views are fully consonant with this Court's recognition that state conduct which might be described as "inaction" can nevertheless constitute responsible "state action" within the meaning of the Fourteenth Amendment.

7–2. THE PUBLIC FUNCTION

MARSH v. ALABAMA
326 U.S. 501, 66 S.Ct. 276, 90 L.Ed. 265 (1946).

MR. JUSTICE BLACK delivered the opinion of the Court.

In this case we are asked to decide whether a State, consistently with the First and Fourteenth Amendments, can impose criminal punishment on a person who undertakes to distribute religious literature on the premises of a company-owned town contrary to the wishes of the town's management. The town, a suburb of Mobile, Alabama, known as Chickasaw, is owned by the Gulf Shipbuilding Corporation. Except for that it has all the characteristics of any other American town. The property consists of residential buildings, streets, a system of sewers, a sewage disposal plant and a "business block" on which business places are situated. A deputy of the Mobile County Sheriff, paid by the company, serves as the town's policeman. Merchants and service establishments have rented the stores and business places on the business block and the United States uses one of the places as a post office from which six carriers deliver mail to the people of Chickasaw and the adjacent area. The town and the surrounding neighborhood, which can not be distinguished from the Gulf property by anyone not familiar with the property lines, are thickly settled, and according to all indications the residents use the business block as their regular shopping center. To do so, they now, as they have for many years, make use of a company-owned paved street and sidewalk located alongside the store fronts in order to enter and leave the stores and the post office. Intersecting company-owned roads at each end of the business block lead into a four-lane public highway which runs parallel to the business block at a distance of thirty feet. There is nothing to stop highway traffic from coming onto the business block and upon arrival a traveler may make free use of the facilities available there. In short the town and its shopping district are accessible to and freely used by the public in general and there is nothing to distinguish them from any other town and shopping center except the fact that the title to the property belongs to a private corporation.

Appellant, a Jehovah's Witness, came onto the sidewalk we have just described, stood near the post office and undertook to distribute religious literature. In the stores the corporation had posted a notice which read as follows: "This Is Private Property, and Without Written Permission, No Street, or House Vendor, Agent or Solicitation of Any Kind Will Be Permitted." Appellant was warned that she could not distribute the literature without a permit and told that no permit would be issued to her. She protested that the company rule could not be constitutionally applied so as to prohibit her from distributing religious writings. When she was asked to leave the sidewalk and Chickasaw she declined. The deputy sheriff arrested her and she was charged [and convicted] in the state court with violating Title 14, § 426 of the 1940 Alabama Code which makes it a crime to enter or remain on the premises of another after having been warned not to do so. . . .

Had the title to Chickasaw belonged not to a private but to a municipal corporation and had appellant been arrested for violating a municipal ordinance rather than a ruling by those appointed by the corporation to manage a company town it would have been clear that appellant's conviction must be reversed. [H]ad the people of Chickasaw owned all the homes, and all the stores, and all the streets, and all the sidewalks, all those owners together could not have set up a municipal government with sufficient power to pass an ordinance completely barring the distribution of religious literature. Our question then narrows down to this: Can those people who live in or come to Chickasaw be denied freedom of press and religion simply because a single company has legal title to all the town? For it is the State's contention that the mere fact that all the property interests in the town are held by a single company is enough to give that company power, enforceable by a state statute, to abridge these freedoms.

We do not agree that the corporation's property interests settle the question. The State urges in effect that the corporation's right to control the inhabitants of Chickasaw is coextensive with the right of a homeowner to regulate the conduct of his guests. We cannot accept that contention. Ownership does not always mean absolute dominion. The more an owner, for his advantage, opens up his property for use by the public in general, the more do his rights become circumscribed by the statutory and constitutional rights of those who use it. Thus, the owners of privately held bridges, ferries, turnpikes and railroads may not operate them as freely as a farmer does his farm. Since these facilities are built and operated primarily to benefit the public and since their operation is essentially a public function, it is subject to state regulation. . . .

We do not think it makes any significant constitutional difference as to the relationship between the rights of the owner and those of the public that here the State, instead of permitting the corporation to operate a highway, permitted it to use its property as a town, operate a "business block" in the town and a street and sidewalk on that business block. Whether a corporation or a municipality owns or possesses the town the public in either case has an identical interest in the functioning of the community in such manner that the channels of communication remain free. As we have heretofore stated, the town of Chickasaw does not function differently from any other town. The "business block" serves as the community shopping center and is freely accessible and open to the people in the area and those passing through. The managers appointed by the corporation cannot curtail the liberty of press and religion of these people consistently with the purposes of the Constitutional guarantees, and a state statute, as the one here involved, which enforces such action by criminally punishing those who attempt to distribute religious literature clearly violates the First and Fourteenth Amendments to the Constitution.

Many people in the United States live in company-owned towns.[5] These people, just as residents of municipalities, are free citizens of their State and country. Just as all other citizens they must make decisions which affect the welfare of community and nation. To act as good citizens they must be informed. In order to enable them to be properly informed their information must be uncensored. There is no more reason for depriving these people of the liberties guaranteed by the First and Fourteenth Amendments than there is for curtailing these freedoms with respect to any other citizen.

When we balance the Constitutional rights of owners of property against those of the people to enjoy freedom of press and religion, as we must here, we remain mindful of the fact that the latter occupy a preferred position. . . . In our view the circumstance that the property rights to the premises where the deprivation of liberty, here involved, took place, were held by others than the public, is not sufficient to justify the State's permitting a corporation to govern a community of citizens so as to restrict their fundamental liberties and the enforcement of such restraint by the application of a state statute. Insofar as the State has attempted to impose criminal punishment on appellant for undertaking to distribute religious literature in a company town, its action cannot stand. The case is reversed and the cause remanded for further proceedings not inconsistent with this opinion.

Reversed and remanded.

MR. JUSTICE JACKSON took no part in the consideration or decision of this case.

MR. JUSTICE FRANKFURTER, concurring.

. . . Title to property as defined by State law controls property relations; it cannot control issues of civil liberties which arise precisely because a company town is a town as well as a congeries of property relations. And similarly the technical distinctions on which a finding of

---

5. In the bituminous coal industry alone, approximately one-half of the miners in the United States lived in company-owned houses in the period from 1922–23. The percentage varied from 9 per cent in Illinois and Indiana and 64 per cent in Kentucky, to almost 80 per cent in West Virginia. . . .

"trespass" so often depends are too tenuous to control decision regarding the scope of the vital liberties guaranteed by the Constitution. . . .

MR. JUSTICE REED, dissenting. . . .

. . . The rights of the owner, which the Constitution protects as well as the right of free speech, are not outweighed by the interests of the trespasser, even though he trespasses in behalf of religion or free speech. . . . Appellant . . . was free to engage in such practices on the public highways, without becoming a trespasser on the company's property.

THE CHIEF JUSTICE [STONE] and MR. JUSTICE BURTON join in this dissent.

HUDGENS v. NATIONAL LABOR RELATIONS BOARD

424 U.S. 507, 96 S.Ct. 1029, 47 L.Ed.2d 196 (1976).

MR. JUSTICE STEWART delivered the opinion of the Court.

A group of labor union members who engaged in peaceful primary picketing within the confines of a privately owned shopping center were threatened by an agent of the owner with arrest for criminal trespass if they did not depart. . . .

The petitioner, Scott Hudgens, is the owner of the North DeKalb Shopping Center, located in suburban Atlanta, Ga. The center consists of a single large building with an enclosed mall. Surrounding the building is a parking area which can accommodate 2,640 automobiles. The shopping center houses 60 retail stores leased to various businesses. One of the lessees is the Butler Shoe Co. Most of the stores, including Butler's, can be entered only from the interior mall.

In January 1971, warehouse employees of the Butler Shoe Co. went on strike to protest the company's failure to agree to demands made by their union in contract negotiations. The strikers decided to picket not only Butler's warehouse but its nine retail stores in the Atlanta area as well, including the store in the North DeKalb Shopping Center. . . . The general manager of the shopping center informed the employees that they could not picket within the mall or on the parking lot and threatened them with arrest if they did not leave. . . .

The union subsequently filed with the Board an unfair labor practice charge against Hudgens. . . . In the present posture of the case the most basic question is whether the respective rights and liabilities of the parties are to be decided under the criteria of the National Labor Relations Act alone, under a First Amendment standard, or under some combination of the two. It is to that question, accordingly, that we now turn.

It is, of course, a commonplace that the constitutional guarantee of free speech is a guarantee only against abridgment by government, federal or state. . . . This elementary proposition is little more than a truism. But even truisms are not always unexceptionably true, and an exception to this one was recognized almost 30 years ago in *Marsh v. Alabama*. . . .

It was the *Marsh* case that in 1968 provided the foundation for the Court's decision in *Amalgamated Food Employees Union v. Logan Valley Plaza*, 391 U.S. 308, 88 S.Ct. 1601, 20 L.Ed.2d 603. That case involved peaceful [labor] picketing within a large shopping center near Altoona, Pa. . . . The Court's opinion then reviewed the *Marsh* case in detail, emphasized the similarities between the business block in Chickasaw, Ala., and the Logan Valley shopping center, and unambiguously concluded: "The shopping center here is clearly the functional equivalent of the business district of Chickasaw involved in *Marsh*." Upon the basis of that conclusion, the Court held that the First and Fourteenth Amendments required reversal of the judgment of the Pennsylvania Supreme Court.

There were three dissenting opinions in the *Logan Valley* case, one of them by the author of the Court's opinion in *Marsh*, Mr. Justice Black. His disagreement with the Court's reasoning was total:

> In affirming petitioners' contentions the majority opinion relies on *Marsh v. Alabama*, supra, and holds that respondents' property has been transformed to some type of public property. But *Marsh* was never intended to apply to this kind of situation. *Marsh* dealt with the very special situation of a company-owned town, complete with streets, alleys, sewers, stores, residences, and everything else that goes to make a town . . . I can find very little resemblance between the shopping center involved in this case and Chickasaw, Alabama. There are no homes, there is no sewage disposal plant, there is not even a post office on this private property which the Court now considers the equivalent of a "town." The question is, Under what circumstances can private property be treated as though it were public? The answer that *Marsh* gives is when that property has taken on *all* the attributes of a town, i.e., "residential buildings, streets, a system of sewers, a sewage disposal plant and a 'business block' on which business places are situated." I can find nothing in *Marsh* which indicates that if one of these features is present, e.g., a business district, this is sufficient for the Court to confiscate a part of an owner's private property and give its use to people who want to picket on it.

> To hold that store owners are compelled by law to supply picketing areas for pickets to drive store customers away is to create a court-made law wholly disregarding the constitutional basis on which private ownership of property rests in this country. . . .

Four years later the Court had occasion to reconsider the *Logan Valley* doctrine in *Lloyd Corp. v. Tanner*, 407 U.S. 551, 92 S.Ct. 2219, 33 L.Ed.2d 131. That case involved a shopping center covering some 50 acres in downtown Portland, Ore. On a November day in 1968 five young people entered the mall of the shopping center and distributed handbills protesting the then ongoing American military operations in Vietnam. Security guards told them to leave, and they did so, "to avoid arrest." They subsequently brought suit in a Federal District Court, seeking declaratory and injunctive relief. The trial court ruled in their favor, holding that the distribution of handbills on the shopping center's property was protected by the First and Fourteenth Amendments. The Court of Appeals for the Ninth Circuit affirmed the judgment, expressly relying on this Court's *Marsh* and *Logan Valley* decisions. This Court reversed the judgment of the Court of Appeals.

The Court in its *Lloyd* opinion did not say that it was overruling the *Logan Valley* decision. Indeed, a substantial portion of the Court's opinion in *Lloyd* was devoted to pointing out the differences between the two cases, noting particularly that, in contrast to the handbilling in *Lloyd,* the picketing in *Logan Valley* had been specifically directed to a store in the shopping center and the pickets had had no other reasonable opportunity to reach their intended audience.[5] But the fact is that the reasoning of the Court's opinion in *Lloyd* cannot be squared with the reasoning of the Court's opinion in *Logan Valley.*

It matters not that some Members of the Court may continue to believe that the *Logan Valley* case was rightly decided. Our institutional duty is to follow until changed the law as it now is, not as some Members of the Court might wish it to be. And in the performance of that duty we make clear now, if it was not clear before, that the rationale of *Logan Valley* did not survive the Court's decision in the *Lloyd* case. Not only did the *Lloyd* opinion incorporate lengthy excerpts from two of the dissenting opinions in *Logan Valley,* the ultimate holding in *Lloyd* amounted to a total rejection of the holding in *Logan Valley. . . .*

If a large self-contained shopping center *is* the functional equivalent of a municipality, as *Logan Valley* held, then the First and Fourteenth Amendments would not permit control of speech within such a center to depend upon the speech's content. For while a municipality may constitutionally impose reasonable time, place, and manner regulations on the use of its streets and sidewalks for First Amendment purposes, and may even forbid altogether such use of some of its facilities, what a municipality may *not* do under the First and Fourteenth Amendments is to discriminate in the regulation of expression on the basis of the content of that expression. . . . It conversely follows, therefore, that if the respondents in the *Lloyd* case did not have a First Amendment right to enter that shopping center to distribute handbills concerning Vietnam, then

---

5. Insofar as the two shopping centers differed as such, the one in *Lloyd* more closely resembled the business section in Chickasaw, Ala.:

"The principal differences between the two centers are that the Lloyd Center is larger than Logan Valley, that Lloyd Center contains more commercial facilities, that Lloyd Center contains a range of professional and nonprofessional services that were

not found in Logan Valley, and that Lloyd Center is much more intertwined with public streets than Logan Valley. Also, as in *Marsh, supra,* Lloyd's private police are given full police power by the city of Portland, even though they are hired, fired, controlled, and paid by the owners of the Center. This was not true in *Logan Valley.*" 407 U.S., at 575 (Marshall, J., dissenting).

the pickets in the present case did not have a First Amendment right to enter this shopping center for the purpose of advertising their strike against the Butler Shoe Co.

We conclude, in short, that under the present state of the law the constitutional guarantee of free expression has no part to play in a case such as this. From what has been said it follows that the rights and liabilities of the parties in this case are dependent exclusively upon the National Labor Relations Act. [Therefore] the judgment is vacated and the case is remanded to the Court of Appeals with directions to remand to the National Labor Relations Board, so that the case may be there considered under the statutory criteria of the National Labor Relations Act alone.

It is so ordered.

Mr. Justice Stevens took no part in the consideration or decision of this case.

Mr. Justice Marshall, with whom Mr. Justice Brennan joins, dissenting. . . .

In *Logan Valley* we recognized what the Court today refuses to recognize—that the owner of the modern shopping center complex, by dedicating his property to public use as a business district, to some extent displaces the "State" from control of historical First Amendment forums, and may acquire a virtual monopoly of places suitable for effective communication. The roadways, parking lots, and walkways of the modern shopping center may be as essential for effective speech as the streets and sidewalks in the municipal or company-owned town. I simply cannot reconcile the Court's denial of any role for the First Amendment in the shopping center with *Marsh's* recognition of a full role for the First Amendment on the streets and sidewalks of the company-owned town. . . .

In *Marsh,* the private entity had displaced the "state" from control of all the places to which the public had historically enjoyed access for First Amendment purposes, and the First Amendment was accordingly held fully applicable to the private entity's conduct. The shopping center owner, on the other hand, controls only a portion of such places, leaving other traditional public forums available to the citizen. But the shopping center owner may nevertheless control all places essential for the effective undertaking of some speech-related activities—namely, those related to the activities of the shopping center. As for those activities, then, the First Amendment ought to have application under the reasoning of *Marsh* and that was precisely the state of the law after *Lloyd*. . . .

[The opinion of Powell, J., joined by Burger, C.J., concurring, and of White, J., concurring in the result, are omitted.]

AN INTRODUCTORY NOTE ON THE WHITE PRIMARY CASES

Nixon v. Herndon, 273 U.S. 536, 47 S.Ct. 446, 71 L.Ed. 759 (1927) invalidated, under the Equal Protection Clause of the Fourteenth Amendment, a Texas law that expressly excluded blacks from voting in the state Democratic Primary. That same year Texas responded by enacting a statute providing that every political party in the state, through its Executive Committee, shall have the power, subject to some restrictions, to determine who would be qualified to vote or otherwise participate in the political party. The Democratic Party's State Executive Committee then adopted a resolution excluding blacks from its primaries.

The Court also invalidated this statute. "Whatever inherent power a State political party has to determine the content of its membership resides in the state convention." The statute changed that. "To this [executive] committee the statute here in controversy has attempted to confide authority to determine of its own motion the requisites of party membership and in so doing to speak for the party as a whole.... Whatever power of exclusion has been exercised by the members of the committee has come to them, therefore, not as delegates of the party, but as delegates of the State." Thus, there was state action and the statute violated equal protection *Nixon v. Condon,* 286 U.S. 73, 52 S.Ct. 484, 76 L.Ed. 984 (1932).

In response, on May 24, 1932, the State Democratic Convention adopted a resolution allowing only whites to be party members. A state official then refused to issue a ballot in the Democratic Party primary to petitioner because of his color. The Court held that because the state convention had declared the voter qualifications, the convention's actions were not state action. *Grovey v. Townsend,* 295 U.S. 45, 55 S.Ct. 622, 79 L.Ed. 1292 (1935).

The Court overruled *Grovey* less than a decade later in *Smith v. Allwright,* 321 U.S. 649, 64 S.Ct. 757, 88 L.Ed. 987 (1944), a case also arising in Texas. Between *Grovey* and *Smith* the Court had decided *United States v. Classic,* 313 U.S. 299, 61 S.Ct. 1031, 85 L.Ed. 1368 (1941), holding that Art. I, § 4, cl. 1, authorized Congress to regulate primary as well as general elections to choose representatives in Congress, where the primary is by law made an integral part of the election machinery. The *Smith* Court said that *Classic* was a "recognition of the place of the primary in the electoral scheme, [which] makes clear that state delegation to a party of the power to fix the qualifications of primary elections is delegation of a state function that may make the party's action the action of the state.... If the State requires a certain electoral procedure, prescribes a general election ballot made up of party nominees so chosen and limits the choice of the electorate in general elections for state offices, practically speaking, to those whose names appear on such a ballot, it endorses, adopts and enforces the discrimination against Negroes, practiced by a party entrusted by Texas law with the determination of the qualifications of participants in the primary. This is state action within the meaning of the Fifteenth Amendment."

Roberts, J., the author of *Grovey,* dissented, protesting: "the instant decision, overruling that announced about nine years ago, tends to bring adjudications of this tribunal into the same class as a restricted railroad ticket, good for this day and train only."

TERRY v. ADAMS

345 U.S. 461, 73 S.Ct. 809, 97 L.Ed. 1152 (1953).

MR. JUSTICE BLACK announced the judgment of the Court and an opinion in which MR. JUSTICE DOUGLAS and MR. JUSTICE BURTON join.

. . . This case raises questions concerning the constitutional power of a Texas county political organization called the Jaybird Democratic Association or Jaybird Party to exclude Negroes from its primaries on racial grounds. The Jaybirds deny that their racial exclusions violate the Fifteenth Amendment. They contend that the Amendment applies only to elections or primaries held under state regulation, that their association is not regulated by the state at all, and that it is not a political party but a self-governing voluntary club. The District Court held the Jaybird racial discriminations invalid and entered judgment accordingly. The Court of Appeals reversed. . . .

There was evidence that: The Jaybird Association or Party was organized in 1889. Its membership was then and always has been limited to white people; they are automatically members if their names appear on the official list of county voters. It has been run like other political parties with an executive committee named from the county's voting precincts. Expenses of the party are paid by the assessment of candidates for office in its primaries. Candidates for county offices submit their names to the Jaybird Committee in accordance with the normal practice followed by regular political parties all over the country. Advertisements and posters proclaim that these candidates are running subject to the action of the Jaybird primary. While there is no legal compulsion on successful Jaybird candidates to enter Democratic primaries, they have nearly always done so and with few exceptions since 1889 have run and won without opposition in the Democratic primaries and the general elections that followed. Thus the party has been the dominant political group in the county since organization, having endorsed every county-wide official elected since 1889.

It is apparent that Jaybird activities follow a plan purposefully designed to exclude Negroes from voting and at the same time to escape the Fifteenth Amendment's command that the right of citizens to vote shall neither be denied nor abridged on account of race. These were the admitted party purposes according to the following testimony of the Jaybird's president: . . . .

Q. And then one of the purposes of your organization is for the specific purpose of excluding negroes from voting, isn't it?

A. Yes. . . .

It is significant that precisely the same qualifications as those prescribed by Texas entitling electors to vote at county-operated primaries are adopted as the sole qualifications entitling electors to vote at the county-wide Jaybird primaries with a single proviso—Negroes are excluded. Everyone concedes that such a proviso in the county-operated primaries would be unconstitutional. The Jaybird Party thus brings into being and holds precisely the kind of election, that the Fifteenth Amendment seeks to prevent. When it produces the equivalent of the prohibited election, the damage has been done.

For a state to permit such a duplication of its election processes is to permit a flagrant abuse of those processes to defeat the purposes of the Fifteenth Amendment. The use of the county-operated primary to ratify the result of the prohibited election merely compounds the offense. It violates the Fifteenth Amendment for a state, by such circumvention, to permit within its borders the use of any device that produces an equivalent of the prohibited election.

The only election that has counted in this Texas county for more than fifty years has been that held by the Jaybirds from which Negroes were excluded. The Democratic primary and the general election have become no more than the perfunctory ratifiers of the choice that has already been made in Jaybird elections from which Negroes have been excluded. It is immaterial that the state does not control that part of this elective process which it leaves for the Jaybirds to manage. The Jaybird primary has become an integral part, indeed the only effective part, of the elective process that determines who shall rule and govern in the county. The effect of the whole procedure, Jaybird primary plus Democratic primary plus general election, is to do precisely that which the Fifteenth Amendment forbids—strip Negroes of every vestige of influence in selecting the officials who control the local county matters that intimately touch the daily lives of citizens.

We reverse the Court of Appeals' judgment reversing that of the District Court. We affirm the District Court's holding that the combined Jaybird–Democratic-general election machinery has deprived these petitioners of their right to vote on account of their race and color. The case is remanded to the District Court to enter such orders and decrees as are necessary and proper under the jurisdiction it has retained under 28 U.S.C. § 2202. In exercising this jurisdiction, the Court is left free to hold hearings to consider and determine what provisions are essential to afford Negro citizens of Fort Bend County full protection from future discriminatory Jaybird–Democratic-general election practices which deprive citizens of voting rights because of their color.

Reversed and remanded.

MR. JUSTICE FRANKFURTER.

. . . The application of the prohibition of the Fifteenth Amendment to "any State" is translated by legal jargon to read "State action." This phrase gives rise to a false direction in that it implies some impressive machinery or deliberative conduct normally associated with what orators call a sovereign state. The vital requirement is State responsibility—that somewhere, somehow, to some extent, there be an infusion of conduct by officials, panoplied with State power, into any scheme by which colored citizens are denied voting rights merely because they are colored.

As the action of the entire white voting community, the Jaybird primary is as a practical matter the instrument of those few in this small county who are politically active—the officials of the local Democratic party and, we may assume, the elected officials of the county. As a matter of practical politics, those charged by State law with the duty of assuring all eligible voters an opportunity to participate in the selection of candidates at the primary—the county election officials who are normally leaders in their communities—participate by voting in the Jaybird primary. They join the white voting community in proceeding with elaborate formality, in almost all respects parallel to the procedures dictated by Texas law for the primary itself, to express their preferences in a wholly successful effort to withdraw significance from the State-prescribed primary, to subvert the operation of what is formally the law of the State for primaries in this county. . . .

It does not follow, however, that the relief granted below was proper. Since the vice of this situation is not that the Jaybird primary itself is the primary discriminatorily conducted under State law but is that the determination there made becomes, in fact, the determination in the Democratic primary by virtue of the participation and acquiescence of State authorities, a federal court cannot require that petitioners be allowed to vote in the Jaybird primary. The evil here is that the State, through the action and abdication of those whom it has clothed with authority, has permitted white voters to go through a procedure which predetermines the legally devised primary. To say that Negroes should be allowed to vote in the Jaybird primary would be to say that the State is under a duty to see to it that Negroes may vote in that primary. We cannot tell the State that it must participate in and regulate this primary; we cannot tell the State what machinery it will use. But a court of equity can free the lawful political agency from the combination that subverts its capacity to function. What must be done is that this county be rid of the means by which the unlawful "usage," in this case asserts itself.

Mr. Justice Clark, with whom The Chief Justice [Vinson], Mr. Justice Reed, and Mr. Justice Jackson join, concurring.

. . . Significantly, since 1889 the winners of the Jaybird Democratic Association balloting, with but a single exception shown by this record,[13]

---

13. In 1944, Mr. Charles Schultz emerged victorious from the Jaybird balloting and was indorsed as its candidate for County Judge. In the July Democratic primary, Schultz triumphed by a vote of 2,025 to 1 for Mr. Mike Dornak. Schultz held office for two terms until 1948. In that year, in accord with a Jaybird Association rule prohibiting more than two consecutive terms in office, Mr. Baker received the Jay-ran unopposed and invariably won in the Democratic July primary and the subsequent general elections for county-wide office.

Quite evidently the Jaybird Democratic Association operates as an auxiliary of the local Democratic Party organization, selecting its nominees and using its machinery for carrying out an admitted design of destroying the weight and effect of Negro ballots in Fort Bend County. To be sure, the Democratic primary and the general election are nominally open to the colored elector. But his must be an empty vote cast after the real decisions are made. And because the Jaybird-indorsed nominee meets no opposition in the Democratic primary, the Negro minority's vote is nullified at the sole stage of the local political process where the bargaining and interplay of rival political forces would make it count. . . .

MR. JUSTICE MINTON, dissenting.

. . . Apparently so far [the Jaybirds] have succeeded in convincing the voters of this County in most instances that their supported candidates should win. This seems to differ very little from situations common in many other places far north of the Mason–Dixon line, such as areas where a candidate must obtain the approval of a religious group. In other localities, candidates are carefully selected by both parties to give proper weight to Jew, Protestant and Catholic, and certain posts are considered the sole possession of certain ethnic groups. The propriety of these practices is something the courts sensibly have left to the good or bad judgment of the electorate. It must be recognized that elections and other public business are influenced by all sorts of pressures from carefully organized groups. We have pressure from labor unions, from the National Association of Manufacturers, from the Silver Shirts, from the National Association for the Advancement of Colored People, from the Ku Klux Klan and others. Far from the activities of these groups being properly labeled as state action, under either the Fourteenth or the Fifteenth Amendment, they are to be considered as attempts to influence or obtain state action.

The courts do not normally pass upon these pressure groups, whether their causes are good or bad, highly successful or only so-so. It is difficult for me to see how this Jaybird Association is anything but such a pressure group. [It] differs little from the situation in many parts of the "Bible Belt" where a church stamp of approval or that of the Anti–Saloon League must be put on any candidate who does not want to lose the election.

Notes

Cousins v. Wigoda, 419 U.S. 477, 95 S.Ct. 541, 42 L.Ed.2d 595 (1975), arose out of a 1972 credentials challenge to Mayor Daley's Illinois delegation

bird indorsement for the county judgeship. Schultz, however, insisted on running in the Democratic primary; he lost out to Baker by a vote of 2,209 to 803. The record reveals, however, that the Jaybird-indorsed candidates for *precinct* office were not quite as consistently successful.

to the Democratic National Convention. Before the National Convention's Credentials Committee, the Cousins delegates challenged the Daley delegates on the grounds that the latter had been elected, in the March, 1972 state primary, in violation of Party guidelines. The Convention seated the Cousins delegation, but the Daley delegates obtained an injunction from the Illinois Circuit Court enjoining the Cousins delegates from acting as delegates to the Convention. Then the state court held the Cousins delegates in contempt.

The Supreme Court reversed, finding that the asserted state interests were insufficient to justify the abridgement of the exercise of the constitutionally protected rights of association of the Cousins delegates and the National Democratic Party. "Whatever the case of actions presenting claims that the Party's delegate selection procedures are not exercised within the confines of the Constitution—and no such claims are made here—this is a case where 'the convention itself [was] the proper forum for determining intra-party disputes as to which delegates should be seated.' "

In the course of the opinion of the Court, Justice Brennan added the following footnote:

4. We emphasize that [there] are not before us in this case, and we intimate no views upon the merits of, such questions as:

(1) whether the decisions of a national political party in the area of delegate selection constitute state or governmental action, and, if so, whether or to what extent principles of the political question doctrine counsel against judicial intervention. Respondents concede, and we agree, that "[i]n the context of the instant case, it is not necessary to determine whether Convention action is 'state action'.... " See *Lynch v. Torquato,* 343 F.2d 370 (C.A.3 1965). See also the Texas White Primary Cases, *Nixon v. Herndon,* 273 U.S. 536, 47 S.Ct. 446, 71 L.Ed. 759 (1927); *Nixon v. Condon,* 286 U.S. 73, 52 S.Ct. 484, 76 L.Ed. 984 (1932); *Smith v. Allwright,* 321 U.S. 649, 64 S.Ct. 757, 88 L.Ed. 987 (1944); *Terry v. Adams,* 345 U.S. 461, 73 S.Ct. 809, 97 L.Ed. 1152 (1953). For the differing views of commentators, see Chambers & Rotunda, Reform of Presidential Nominating Conventions, 56 Va.L.Rev. 179 (1970); Note, Constitutional Safeguards in the Selection of Delegates to Presidential Nominating Conventions, 78 Yale L.J. 1228 (1969).

(2) whether national political parties are subject to the principles of the reapportionment decisions, or other constitutional restraints, in their methods of delegate selection and allocation. Compare *Bode v. National Democratic Party,* 452 F.2d 1302 (1971), with *Irish v. Democratic–Farmer–Labor Party,* 399 F.2d 119 (C.A.8 1968); and see *Gray v. Sanders,* 372 U.S. 368, 378 n. 10, 83 S.Ct. 801, 9 L.Ed.2d 821 (1963)....

(3) whether or to what extent national political parties and their nominating conventions are regulable by, or only by, Congress. See *Newberry v. United States,* 256 U.S. 232, 275, 41 S.Ct. 469, 65 L.Ed. 913 (1921)(Pitney, J., dissenting).

Rehnquist, J., joined by Burger, C.J., & Stewart, J., concurred in the result and objected to this footnote:

Footnote 4 of the Court's opinion disclaims any intimation of views on the following questions.... But immediately following the disclaimer, the Court proceeds to cite numerous opinions of courts of appeals and district courts, as well as law review commentaries, which to the unsophisticated mind might seem to portend an answer to each of these questions.

How would you answer these questions? Are the Democratic and Republican National Conventions performing a public function? For what purposes might they constitute state action?

7–3. COURT ENFORCEMENT OF PRIVATE AGREEMENTS

SHELLEY v. KRAEMER
334 U.S. 1, 68 S.Ct. 836, 92 L.Ed. 1161 (1948).

Mr. Chief Justice Vinson delivered the opinion of the Court.

These cases present for our consideration questions relating to the validity of court enforcement of private agreements, generally described as restrictive covenants, which have as their purpose the exclusion of persons of designated race or color from the ownership or occupancy of real property. Basic constitutional issues of obvious importance have been raised. . . .

On August 11, 1945, pursuant to a contract of sale, petitioners Shelley, who are Negroes, for valuable consideration received from one Fitzgerald a warranty deed to the parcel in question. The trial court found that petitioners had no actual knowledge of the restrictive agreement at the time of the purchase.

On October 9, 1945, respondents, as owners of other property subject to the terms of the restrictive covenant, brought suit in the Circuit Court of the city of St. Louis praying that petitioners Shelley be restrained from taking possession of the property and that judgment be entered divesting title out of petitioners Shelley and revesting title in the immediate grantor or in such other person as the court should direct. The trial court denied the requested relief on the ground that the restrictive agreement, upon which respondents based their action, had never become final and complete because it was the intention of the parties to that agreement that it was not to become effective until signed by all property owners in the district, and signatures of all the owners had never been obtained. The Supreme Court of Missouri sitting *en banc* held the agreement effective and concluded that enforcement of its provisions violated no rights guaranteed to petitioners by the Federal Constitution. At the time the court rendered its decision, petitioners were occupying the property in question.

[R]estrictions on the right of occupancy of the sort sought to be created by the private agreements in these cases could not be squared with the requirements of the Fourteenth Amendment if imposed by state statute or local ordinance. We do not understand respondents to urge the contrary. In the case of *Buchanan v. Warley,* [245 U.S. 60, 38 S.Ct. 16, 62 L.Ed. 149 (1917)], a unanimous Court declared unconstitutional the provisions of a city ordinance which denied to colored persons the right to occupy houses in blocks in which the greater number of houses were occupied by white persons, and imposed similar restrictions on white persons with respect to blocks in which the greater number of houses were occupied by colored persons. During the course of the opinion in that case, this Court stated: "The Fourteenth Amendment and these statutes enacted in furtherance of its purpose operate to qualify and entitle a colored man to acquire property without state legislation discriminating against him solely because of color." . . .

But the present cases, unlike those just discussed, do not involve action by state legislatures or city councils. . . . Since the decision of this Court in the *Civil Rights Cases,* [§ 7–1, supra] the principle has become firmly embedded in our constitutional law that the action inhibited by the first section of the Fourteenth Amendment is only such action as may fairly be said to be that of the States. That Amendment erects no shield against merely private conduct, however discriminatory or wrongful. We conclude, therefore, that the restrictive agreements standing alone cannot be regarded as violative of any rights guaranteed to petitioners by the Fourteenth Amendment. So long as the purposes of those agreements are effectuated by voluntary adherence to their terms, it would appear clear that there has been no action by the State and the provisions of the Amendment have not been violated.

But here there was more. These are cases in which the purposes of the agreements were secured only by judicial enforcement by state courts of the restrictive terms of the agreements. . . . We have no doubt that there has been state action in these cases in the full and complete sense of the phrase. The undisputed facts disclose that petitioners were willing purchasers of properties upon which they desired to establish homes. The owners of the properties were willing sellers; and contracts of sale were accordingly consummated. It is clear that but for the active intervention of the state courts, supported by the full panoply of state power, petitioners would have been free to occupy the properties in question without restraint.

These are not cases, as has been suggested, in which the States have merely abstained from action, leaving private individuals free to impose such discriminations as they see fit. Rather, these are cases in which the States have made available to such individuals the full coercive power of government to deny to petitioners, on the grounds of race or color, the enjoyment of property rights in premises which petitioners are willing and financially able to acquire and which the grantors are willing to sell. The difference between judicial enforcement and nonenforcement of the restrictive covenants is the difference to petitioners between being denied rights of property available to other members of the community and being accorded full enjoyment of those rights on an equal footing.

The enforcement of the restrictive agreements by the state courts in these cases was directed pursuant to the common-law policy of the States as formulated by those courts in earlier decisions. [J]udicial action is not immunized from the operation of the Fourteenth Amendment simply because it is taken pursuant to the state's common-law policy. Nor is the Amendment ineffective simply because the particular pattern of discrimination, which the State has enforced, was defined initially by the terms of a private agreement. State action, as that phrase is understood for the purposes of the Fourteenth Amendment, refers to exertions of state power in all forms. And when the effect of that action is to deny rights subject to the protection of the Fourteenth Amendment, it is the obligation of this Court to enforce the constitutional commands.

We hold that in granting judicial enforcement of the restrictive agreements in these cases, the States have denied petitioners the equal protection of the laws and that, therefore, the action of the state courts cannot stand. We have noted that freedom from discrimination by the States in the enjoyment of property rights was among the basic objectives sought to be effectuated by the framers of the Fourteenth Amendment. That such discrimination has occurred in these cases is clear. Because of the race or color of these petitioners they have been denied rights of ownership or occupancy enjoyed as a matter of course by other citizens of different race or color....

Respondents urge, however, that since the state courts stand ready to enforce restrictive covenants excluding white persons from the ownership or occupancy of property covered by such agreements, enforcement of covenants excluding colored persons may not be deemed a denial of equal protection of the laws to the colored persons who are thereby affected.[28] This contention does not bear scrutiny.... The rights created by the first section of the Fourteenth Amendment are, by its terms, guaranteed to the individual. The rights established are personal rights. It is, therefore, no answer to these petitioners to say that the courts may also be induced to deny white persons rights of ownership and occupancy on grounds of race or color. Equal protection of the laws is not achieved through indiscriminate imposition of inequalities....

Reversed.

MR. JUSTICE REED, MR. JUSTICE JACKSON, and MR. JUSTICE RUTLEDGE took no part in the consideration or decision of these cases.

Notes

1. Is the Court saying that restrictive covenants are like zoning laws and thus constitute a "public function"? Or is the case be based on another theory?

Assume that a white homeowner tells a prospective black purchaser that he would sell his house to the black but for his color. The black then sues to force a sale and the court holds that, under the common law rule, the white can refuse to sell his fee simple to a person because of his color or for any

---

28. It should be observed that the restrictions relating to residential occupancy contained in ordinances involved in the *Buchanan* [case], cited supra, and declared by this Court to be inconsistent with the requirements of the Fourteenth Amendment, applied equally to white persons and Negroes.

other reason. Assuming that no state or federal statutes are involved, is *Shelley* applicable, or distinguishable?

Assume that a person dies, leaving his entire estate to his local church. If the court probates the will, is that state action within the meaning of *Shelley* (thus raising First Amendment Establishment of Religion problems)?

2. *Barrows v. Jackson,* 346 U.S. 249, 73 S.Ct. 1031, 97 L.Ed. 1586 (1953) held that racially restrictive covenants not only were unenforceable in equity—as *Shelley* had held—but were unenforceable at law. Petitioners had sued respondent, a white, for damages for selling her home to non-Caucasians, in violation of a restrictive covenant.

EVANS v. NEWTON
382 U.S. 296, 86 S.Ct. 486, 15 L.Ed.2d 373 (1966).

Mr. Justice Douglas delivered the opinion of the Court.

In 1911 United States Senator Augustus O. Bacon executed a will that devised to the Mayor and Council of the City of Macon, Georgia, a tract of land which, after the death of the Senator's wife and daughters, was to be used as "a park and pleasure ground" for white people only, the Senator stating in the will that while he had only the kindest feeling for the Negroes he was of the opinion that "in their social relations the two races (white and negro) should be forever separate." The will provided that the park should be under the control of a Board of Managers of seven persons, all of whom were to be white. The city kept the park segregated for some years but in time let Negroes use it, taking the position that the park was a public facility which it could not constitutionally manage and maintain on a segregated basis.

Thereupon, individual members of the Board of Managers of the park brought this suit in a state court against the City of Macon and the trustees of certain residuary beneficiaries of Senator Bacon's estate, asking that the city be removed as trustee and that the court appoint new trustees, to whom title to the park would be transferred. The city answered, alleging it could not legally enforce racial segregation in the park. The other defendants admitted the allegation and requested that the city be removed as trustee....

The Georgia court accepted the resignation of the city as trustee and appointed three individuals as new trustees, finding it unnecessary to pass on the other claims of the heirs. On appeal by the Negro intervenors, the Supreme Court of Georgia affirmed, holding that Senator Bacon had the right to give and bequeath his property to a limited class, that charitable trusts are subject to supervision of a court of equity, and that the power to appoint new trustees so that the purpose of the trust would not fail was clear. The case is here on a writ of certiorari.

There are two complementary principles to be reconciled in this case. One is the right of the individual to pick his own associates so as to express his preferences and dislikes, and to fashion his private life by joining such clubs and groups as he chooses. The other is the constitutional ban in the Equal Protection Clause of the Fourteenth Amendment against state-sponsored racial inequality, which of course bars a city from acting as trustee under a private will that serves the racial segregation cause. *Pennsylvania v. Board of Trusts,* 353 U.S. 230, 77 S.Ct. 806, 1 L.Ed.2d 792. A private golf club, however, restricted to either Negro or white membership is one expression of freedom of association. But a municipal golf course that serves only one race is state activity indicating a preference on a matter as to which the State must be neutral. What is "private" action and what is "state" action is not always easy to determine. . . . If a testator wanted to leave a school or center for the use of one race only and in no way implicated the State in the supervision, control, or management of that facility, we assume *arguendo* that no constitutional difficulty would be encountered.

This park, however, is in a different posture. For years it was an integral part of the City of Macon's activities. From the pleadings we assume it was swept, manicured, watered, patrolled, and maintained by the city as a public facility for whites only, as well as granted tax exemption under Ga.Code Ann. § 92–201. The momentum it acquired as a public facility is certainly not dissipated *ipso facto* by the appointment of "private" trustees. So far as this record shows, there has been no change in municipal maintenance and concern over this facility. Whether these public characteristics will in time be dissipated is wholly conjectural. If the municipality remains entwined in the management or control of the park, it remains subject to the restraints of the Fourteenth Amendment. . . . We only hold that where the tradition of municipal control had become firmly established, we cannot take judicial notice that the mere substitution of trustees instantly transferred this park from the public to the private sector.

This conclusion is buttressed by the nature of the service rendered the community by a park. The service rendered even by a private park of this character is municipal in nature. It is open to every white person, there being no selective element other than race. Golf clubs, social centers, luncheon clubs, . . . and other like organizations in the private sector are often racially oriented. A park, on the other hand, is more like a fire department or police department that traditionally serves the community. Mass recreation through the use of parks is plainly in the public domain, and state courts that aid private parties to perform that public function on a segregated basis implicate the State in conduct proscribed by the Fourteenth Amendment. . . . Under the circumstances of this case, we cannot but conclude that the public character of this park requires that it be treated as a public institution subject to the command of the Fourteenth Amendment, regardless of who now has title under state law. . . .

Reversed.

MR. JUSTICE WHITE.

. . . Whether the successor trustees may themselves operate the park on a segregated basis is the question. The majority holds that they may not. I agree, but for different reasons.... I would ... hold that the racial condition in the trust may not be given effect by the new trustees because, in my view, it is incurably tainted by discriminatory state legislation validating such a condition under state law. The state legislation to which I refer is §§ 69–504 and 69–505 of the Georgia Code, which were adopted in 1905, just six years before Senator Bacon's will was executed. Sections 69–504 and 69–505 make lawful charitable trusts "dedicated in perpetuity to the public use as a park, pleasure ground, or for other public purpose" and provide that "the use of said park, pleasure ground, or other property so conveyed to said municipality [may] be limited to the white race only, or to white women and children only, or to the colored race only, or to colored women and children only, or to any other race, or to the women and children of any other race only.... " [I]f the validity of the racial condition in Senator Bacon's trust would have been in doubt but for the 1905 statute and if the statute removed such doubt only for racial restrictions, leaving the validity of nonracial restrictions still in question, the absence of coercive language in the legislation would not prevent application of the Fourteenth Amendment. For such a statute would depart from a policy of strict neutrality in matters of private discrimination by enlisting the State's assistance only in aid of racial discrimination....

[The opinions of BLACK, J., dissenting, and of HARLAN, J., joined by STEWART, J., dissenting, are omitted.]

EVANS v. ABNEY
396 U.S. 435, 90 S.Ct. 628, 24 L.Ed.2d 634 (1970).

MR. JUSTICE BLACK delivered the opinion of the Court.

... As a result of our earlier decision in this case ... the Supreme Court of Georgia ruled that Senator Bacon's intention to provide a park for whites only had become impossible to fulfill and that accordingly the trust had failed and the parkland and other trust property had reverted by operation of Georgia law to the heirs of the Senator....

When a city park is destroyed because the Constitution requires it to be integrated, there is reason for everyone to be disheartened.... Here, however, the action of the Georgia Supreme Court declaring the Baconsfield trust terminated presents no violation of constitutionally protected rights, and any harshness that may have resulted from the state court's decision can be attributed solely to its intention to effectuate as nearly as possible the explicit terms of Senator Bacon's will.

Petitioners first argue that the action of the Georgia court violates the United States Constitution in that it imposes a drastic "penalty," the "forfeiture" of the park, merely because of the city's compliance with the constitutional mandate expressed by this Court in *Evans v. Newton.* Of course, *Evans v. Newton,* did not speak to the problem of whether Baconsfield should or could continue to operate as a park; it held only that its continued operation as a park had to be without racial discrimination.... We think, however, that the will of Senator Bacon and Georgia law provide all the justification necessary for imposing such a "penalty." The construction of wills is essentially a state-law question, and in this case the Georgia Supreme Court, as we read its opinion, interpreted Senator Bacon's will as embodying a preference for termination of the park rather than its integration. Given this, the Georgia court had no alternative under its relevant trust laws, which are long standing and neutral with regard to race, but to end the Baconsfield trust and return the property to the Senator's heirs.

... In the case at bar there is not the slightest indication that any of the Georgia judges involved were motivated by racial animus or discriminatory intent of any sort in construing and enforcing Senator Bacon's will.... Similarly, the situation presented in this case is also easily distinguishable from that presented in *Shelley v. Kraemer,* where we held unconstitutional state judicial action which had affirmatively enforced a private scheme of discrimination against Negroes. Here the effect of the Georgia decision eliminated all discrimination against Negroes in the park by eliminating the park itself, and the termination of the park was a loss shared equally by the white and Negro citizens of Macon since both races would have enjoyed a constitutional right of equal access to the park's facilities had it continued.... The only choice the Georgia courts either had or exercised in this regard was their judicial judgment in construing Bacon's will to determine his intent, and the Constitution imposes no requirement upon the Georgia courts to approach Bacon's will any differently than they would approach any will creating any charitable trust of any kind....

[O]ur holding today reaffirms the traditional role of the States in determining whether or not to apply their *cy pres* doctrines to particular trusts.... More fundamentally, however, the loss of charitable trusts such as Baconsfield is part of the price we pay for permitting deceased persons to exercise a continuing control over assets owned by them at death. This aspect of freedom of testation, like most things, has its advantages and disadvantages. The responsibility of this Court, however, is to construe and enforce the Constitution and laws of the land as they are and not to legislate social policy on the basis of our own personal inclinations....

The judgment is

Affirmed.

MR. JUSTICE MARSHALL took no part in the consideration or decision of this case.

MR. JUSTICE DOUGLAS, dissenting.

[P]utting the property in the hands of the heirs will not necessarily achieve the racial segregation that Bacon desired. We deal with city real estate. If a theater is erected, Negroes cannot be excluded. If a restaurant is opened, Negroes must be served. If office or housing structures are erected, Negro tenants must be eligible. If a church is erected, mixed marriage ceremonies may be performed. If a court undertook to attach a racial-use condition to the property once it became "private," that would be an unconstitutional covenant or condition. Bacon's basic desire can be realized only by the repeal of the Fourteenth Amendment. So the fact is that in the vicissitudes of time there is no constitutional way to assure that this property will not serve the needs of Negroes. . . .

MR. JUSTICE BRENNAN, dissenting.

. . . *Shelley v. Kraemer,* stands at least for the proposition that where parties of different races are willing to deal with one another a state court cannot keep them from doing so by enforcing a privately devised racial restriction. Nothing in the record suggests that after our decision in *Evans v. Newton,* supra, the City of Macon retracted its previous willingness to manage Baconsfield on a nonsegregated basis, or that the white beneficiaries of Senator Bacon's generosity were unwilling to share it with Negroes, rather than have the park revert to his heirs. Indeed, although it may be that the city would have preferred to keep the park segregated, the record suggests that, given the impossibility of that goal, the city wanted to keep the park open. . . . Thus, so far as the record shows, this is a case of a state court's enforcement of a racial restriction to prevent willing parties from dealing with one another. The decision of the Georgia courts thus, under *Shelley v. Kraemer,* constitutes state action denying equal protection.

Notes

1. Could Douglas have written his opinion differently in *Evans v. Newton* so that he would have avoided the result in *Evans v. Abney*?

Assume that a racially restrictive covenant in a residential housing development provides that, if the property is ever sold to a black, the land *automatically* reverts to the remaining white homeowners. Does *Shelley* prohibit that result? Is *Evans v. Abney* distinguishable?

2. THE SIT-IN CASES. During the early 1960's the Supreme Court heard several cases in which blacks were convicted under state criminal trespass or disturbing the peace laws when they sat in the "white-only" section of various lunch counters and restaurants and refused to move after having been ordered to do so by the agent of the establishment. Neither state nor federal laws at the time required the restaurants to serve blacks. The Supreme Court managed to reverse these convictions on narrow grounds without a Court majority ever adopting any broad state action theories.

Garner v. Louisiana, 368 U.S. 157, 82 S.Ct. 248, 7 L.Ed.2d 207 (1961), for example, reversed the convictions (under a state disturbing the peace statute) of those who had engaged in a sit-in, because the record was "totally devoid of evidentiary support" that petitioners caused any disturbance of the peace.

Peterson v. Greenville, 373 U.S. 244, 83 S.Ct. 1119, 10 L.Ed.2d 323 (1963) reversed the trespass conviction of blacks who had engaged in a lunch counter sit-in. The store manager asked the blacks to leave because integrated service was "contrary to local customs" and in violation of a city ordinance. "[T]hese convictions cannot stand, even assuming, as respondent contends, that the manager would have acted as he did independently of the existence of the ordinance. [The state cannot save the convictions] by attempting to separate the mental urges of the discriminators."

Lombard v. Louisiana, 373 U.S. 267, 83 S.Ct. 1122, 10 L.Ed.2d 338 (1963), decided the same day, reversed the trespass convictions of three blacks and one white who had sat in a privately owned restaurant that served only whites. The case involved no statutes or ordinances but the Police Superintendent and the Mayor had previously announced publicly that—in the words of the Mayor—"no additional sit-in demonstrations ... will be permitted.... " The Court held that, because of the officials' pronouncements, "the city must be treated exactly as if it had an ordinance prohibiting such conduct ... The official command here was to direct continuance of segregated services in restaurants.... " Douglas, J., concurring, would have decided on broader grounds. Relying on *Shelley v. Kraemer* he argued that there was state action when the state judiciary "put criminal sanctions behind racial discrimination in public places."

Congress, under its commerce power, enacted the Civil Rights Act of 1964, 78 Stat. 241, which precluded such trespass prosecutions by creating substantive rights.[1] In *Hamm v. Rock Hill,* 379 U.S. 306, 85 S.Ct. 384, 13 L.Ed.2d 300 (1964) the Court applied that law to convictions rendered but not finalized before the law's passage. The Court followed the old common law rule of statutory construction that: "if subsequent to the judgment and before the decision of the appellate court, a law intervenes and positively changes the rule which governs, the law must be obeyed. [T]he court must decide according to existing laws, and if it be necessary to set aside a judgment, rightful when rendered, but which cannot be affirmed but in violation of law, the judgment must be set aside," quoting Marshall, C.J., in *United States v. The Peggy,* 5 U.S. (1 Cranch) 103, 110, 2 L.Ed. 49 (1801). *Hamm* noted: "The great purpose of the civil rights legislation was to obliterate the effect of a distressing chapter in our history."[2]

7–4. SYMBIOTIC AND FINANCIAL RELATIONSHIPS

BURTON v. WILMINGTON PARKING AUTHORITY
365 U.S. 715, 81 S.Ct. 856, 6 L.Ed.2d 45 (1961).

MR. JUSTICE CLARK delivered the opinion of the Court.

In this action for declaratory and injunctive relief it is admitted that the Eagle Coffee Shoppe, Inc., a restaurant located within an off-street automobile parking building in Wilmington, Delaware, has refused to serve appellant food or drink solely because he is a Negro. The parking building is owned and operated by the Wilmington Parking Authority, an agency of the State of Delaware, and the restaurant is the Authority's lessee. Appellant claims that such refusal abridges his rights under the

---

1. See *Heart of Atlanta Motel, Inc. v. United States,* § 4–4, and *Katzenbach v. McClung,* § 4–4, both decided the same day as *Hamm.*

2. Note that this statute applied to convictions and trespasses that had occurred *prior* to the law's enactment. How does that affect interstate commerce?

Equal Protection Clause of the Fourteenth Amendment to the United States Constitution. The Supreme Court of Delaware has held that Eagle was acting in "a purely private capacity" under its lease; that its action was not that of the Authority and was not, therefore, state action within the contemplation of the prohibitions contained in that Amendment. It also held that under 24 Del.Code, § 1501,[1] Eagle was a restaurant, not an inn, and that as such it "is not required [under Delaware law] to serve any and all persons entering its place of business." . . .

The Authority was created by the City of Wilmington pursuant to 22 Del.Code, §§ 501–515. It is "a public body corporate and politic, exercising public powers of the State as an agency thereof." § 504. Its statutory purpose is to provide adequate parking facilities for the convenience of the public and thereby relieve the "parking crisis, which threatens the welfare of the community. . . . " [It] has no power to pledge the credit of the State of Delaware but may issue its own revenue bonds which are tax exempt. Any and all property owned or used by the Authority is likewise exempt from state taxation.

The first project undertaken by the Authority was the erection of a parking facility on Ninth Street in downtown Wilmington. [T]he Authority was advised by its retained experts that the anticipated revenue from the parking of cars and proceeds from sale of its bonds would not be sufficient to finance the construction costs of the facility. Moreover, the bonds were not expected to be marketable if payable solely out of parking revenues. To secure additional capital needed for its "debt-service" requirements, and thereby to make bond financing practicable, the Authority decided it was necessary to enter long-term leases with responsible tenants for commercial use of some of the space available in the projected "garage building." The public was invited to bid for these leases.

In April 1957 such a private lease, for 20 years and renewable for another 10 years, was made with Eagle Coffee Shoppe, Inc., for use as a "restaurant, dining room, banquet hall, cocktail lounge and bar and for no other use and purpose." The multi-level space of the building which was let to Eagle, although "within the exterior walls of the structure, has no marked public entrance leading from the parking portion of the facility into the restaurant proper . . . [whose main entrance] is located on Ninth Street." In its lease the Authority covenanted to complete construction expeditiously, including completion of "the decorative finishing of the leased premises and utilities therefor, without cost to Lessee". . . . Eagle spent some $220,000 to make the space suitable for its operation and, to the extent such improvements were so attached to

---

1. The statute provides that: "No keeper of an inn, tavern, hotel, or restaurant, or other place of public entertainment or refreshment of travelers, guests, or customers shall be obliged, by law, to furnish entertainment or refreshment to persons whose reception or entertainment by him would be offensive to the major part of his customers, and would injure his business. As used in this section, 'customers' includes all who have occasion for entertainment or refreshment."

realty as to become part thereof, Eagle to the same extent enjoys the Authority's tax exemption.

The Authority further agreed to furnish heat for Eagle's premises, gas service for the boiler room, and to make, at its own expense, all necessary structural repairs, all repairs to exterior surfaces except store fronts and any repairs caused by lessee's own act or neglect. The Authority retained the right to place any directional signs on the exterior of the let space which would not interfere with or obscure Eagle's display signs. Agreeing to pay an annual rental of $28,700, Eagle covenanted to "occupy and use the leased premises in accordance with all applicable laws, statutes, ordinances and rules and regulations of any federal, state or municipal authority." Its lease, however, contains no requirement that its restaurant services be made available to the general public on a nondiscriminatory basis, in spite of the fact that the Authority has power to adopt rules and regulations respecting the use of its facilities except any as would impair the security of its bondholders.

Other portions of the structure were leased to other tenants, including a bookstore, a retail jeweler, and a food store. Upon completion of the building, the Authority located at appropriate places thereon official signs indicating the public character of the building, and flew from mastheads on the roof both the state and national flags.

In August 1958 appellant parked his car in the building and walked around to enter the restaurant by its front door on Ninth Street. Having entered and sought service, he was refused it. Thereafter he filed this declaratory judgment action in the Court of Chancery.

. . . Because the virtue of the right to equal protection of the laws could lie only in the breadth of its application, its constitutional assurance was reserved in terms whose imprecision was necessary if the right were to be enjoyed in the variety of individual-state relationships which the Amendment was designed to embrace. For the same reason, to fashion and apply a precise formula for recognition of state responsibility under the Equal Protection Clause is an "impossible task" which "This Court has never attempted." Only by sifting facts and weighing circumstances can the nonobvious involvement of the State in private conduct be attributed its true significance. . . .

The land and building were publicly owned. As an entity, the building was dedicated to "public uses" in performance of the Authority's "essential governmental functions." 22 Del.Code, §§ 501, 514. The costs of land acquisition, construction, and maintenance are defrayed entirely from donations by the City of Wilmington, from loans and revenue bonds and from the proceeds of rentals and parking services out of which the loans and bonds were payable. Assuming that the distinction would be significant, the commercially leased areas were not surplus state property, but constituted a physically and financially integral and, indeed, indispensable part of the State's plan to operate its project as a self-sustaining unit. Upkeep and maintenance of the building, including necessary repairs, were responsibilities of the Authority and were payable out of public funds. It cannot be doubted that the peculiar relationship of the restaurant to the parking facility in which it is located confers on each an incidental variety of mutual benefits. Guests of the restaurant are afforded a convenient place to park their automobiles, even if they cannot enter the restaurant directly from the parking area. Similarly, its convenience for diners may well provide additional demand for the Authority's parking facilities. Should any improvements effected in the leasehold by Eagle become part of the realty, there is no possibility of increased taxes being passed on to it since the fee is held by a tax-exempt government agency. Neither can it be ignored, especially in view of Eagle's affirmative allegation that for it to serve Negroes would injure its business, that profits earned by discrimination not only contribute to, but also are indispensable elements in, the financial success of a governmental agency.

Addition of all these activities, obligations and responsibilities of the Authority, the benefits mutually conferred, together with the obvious fact that the restaurant is operated as an integral part of a public building devoted to a public parking service, indicates that degree of state participation and involvement in discriminatory action which it was the design of the Fourteenth Amendment to condemn. It is irony amounting to grave injustice that in one part of a single building, erected and maintained with public funds by an agency of the State to serve a public purpose, all persons have equal rights, while in another portion, also serving the public, a Negro is a second-class citizen, offensive because of his race, without rights and unentitled to service, but at the same time fully enjoys equal access to nearby restaurants in wholly privately owned buildings. As the Chancellor pointed out, in its lease with Eagle the Authority could have affirmatively required Eagle to discharge the responsibilities under the Fourteenth Amendment imposed upon the private enterprise as a consequence of state participation. But no State may effectively abdicate its responsibilities by either ignoring them or by merely failing to discharge them whatever the motive may be.... By its inaction, the Authority, and through it the State, has not only made itself a party to the refusal of service, but has elected to place its power, property and prestige behind the admitted discrimination. The State has so far insinuated itself into a position of interdependence with Eagle that it must be recognized as a joint participant in the challenged activity, which, on that account, cannot be considered to have been so "purely private" as to fall without the scope of the Fourteenth Amendment.

Because readily applicable formulae may not be fashioned, the conclusions drawn from the facts and circumstances of this record are by no means declared as universal truths on the basis of which every state leasing agreement is to be tested. Owing to the very "largeness" of government, a multitude of relationships might appear to some to fall within the Amendment's embrace, but that, it must be remembered, can be determined only in the framework of the peculiar facts or circumstances present. Therefore respondents' prophecy of nigh universal application of a constitutional precept so peculiarly dependent for its invocation upon appropriate facts fails to take into account "Differences in circumstances [that] beget appropriate differences in law". Specifically defining the limits of our inquiry, what we hold today is that when a State leases public property in the manner and for the purpose shown to have been the case here, the proscriptions of the Fourteenth Amendment must be complied with by the lessee as certainly as though they were binding covenants written into the agreement itself.

The judgment of the Supreme Court of Delaware is reversed and the cause remanded for further proceedings consistent with this opinion.

Reversed and remanded.

MR. JUSTICE STEWART, concurring.

I agree that the judgment must be reversed, but I reach that conclusion by a route much more direct than the one traveled by the Court. In upholding Eagle's right to deny service to the appellant solely because of his race, the Supreme Court of Delaware relied upon a statute of that State which permits the proprietor of a restaurant to refuse to serve "persons whose reception or entertainment by him would be offensive to the major part of his customers.... " There is no suggestion in the record that the appellant as an individual was such a person. The highest court of Delaware has thus construed this legislative enactment as authorizing discriminatory classification based exclusively on color. Such a law seems to me clearly violative of the Fourteenth Amendment. I think therefore, that the appeal was properly taken, and that the statute, as authoritatively construed by the Supreme Court of Delaware, is constitutionally invalid.

MR. JUSTICE HARLAN, whom MR. JUSTICE WHITTAKER joins, dissenting.

The Court's opinion, by a process of first undiscriminatingly throwing together various factual bits and pieces and then undermining the resulting structure by an equally vague disclaimer, seems to me to leave completely at sea just what it is in this record that satisfies the requirement of "state action." ...

[The dissenting opinion of FRANKFURTER, J., is omitted.]

Notes

1. *Norwood v. Harrison*, 413 U.S. 455, 93 S.Ct. 2804, 37 L.Ed.2d 723 (1973) prohibited Mississippi from supplying textbooks to students attending racially discriminatory private schools. The State lent free textbooks to all students in the State under a program that dated back to 1940:

This Court has consistently affirmed decisions enjoining state tuition grants to students attending racially discriminatory private schools. A textbook lending program is not legally distinguishable from the forms of state assistance foreclosed by the prior cases. Free textbooks, like tuition grants directed to private school students, are a form of financial assistance inuring to the benefit of the private schools themselves.... Textbooks are a basic educational tool and, like tuition grants, they are provided only in connection with schools; they are to be distinguished from generalized services government might provide to schools in common with others. Moreover, the textbooks provided to private school students by the State in this case are a form of assistance readily available from sources entirely independent of the State—unlike, for example, "such necessities of life as electricity, water, and police and fire protection." [T]he Constitution does not permit the State to aid discrimination even when there is no precise casual relationship between state financial aid to a private school and the continued well-being of that school. A State may not grant the type of tangible financial aid here involved if that aid has a significant tendency to facilitate, reinforce, and support private discrimination. . . .

[*Everson v. Board of Education,* 330 U.S. 1, 67 S.Ct. 504, 91 L.Ed. 711 (1947)] held that the Establishment Clause of the First Amendment did not prohibit New Jersey from "spending tax-raised funds to pay the bus fares of parochial school pupils as a part of a general program under which it pays the fares of pupils attending public and other schools." [*Board of Education v.*] *Allen,* 392 U.S. 236, 88 S.Ct. 1923, 20 L.Ed.2d 1060 (1968)], following *Everson,* sustained a New York law requiring school textbooks to be lent free of charge to all students, including those in attendance at parochial schools, in specified grades. Neither *Allen* nor *Everson* is dispositive of the issue before us in this case. [T]he transcendent value of free religious exercise in our constitutional scheme leaves room for "play in the joints" to the extent of cautiously delineated secular governmental assistance to religious schools, despite the fact that such assistance touches on the conflicting values of the Establishment Clause by indirectly benefitting the religious schools and their sponsors. In contrast, although the Constitution does not proscribe private bias, it places no value on discrimination as it does on the values inherent in the Free Exercise Clause. Invidious private discrimination may be characterized as a form of exercising freedom of association protected by the First Amendment, but it has never been accorded affirmative constitutional protections. . . .

2.　*Rendell–Baker v. Kohn,* 457 U.S. 830, 102 S.Ct. 2764, 73 L.Ed.2d 418 (1982) held that state action was not involved when a private school (with income derived primarily from public sources, and regulated by public authorities) discharged certain employees. The state had contracted with a private institution to deal with students with drug problems or other special needs. Because of a dispute the school director fired Rendell–Baker and several other teachers, allegedly in violation of free speech and procedural due process. Burger, C.J., for the Court, argued that the fact that the school received in recent years between 90%, and 99% of its operating budget from various state and federal agencies did not make the school's discharge decisions acts of the state. Many private corporations also contract with government to build roads, submarines, and dams. "Acts of such private contractors do not become acts of the government by reason of their significant or even total engagement in performing public contracts."

Second, although the State extensively regulated the school in matters concerning record keeping and student-teacher ratios, the decisions to discharge petitioners was not required or even influenced by the regulations, which showed "relatively little interest" in personnel matters. Third, the private group was not performing a public function; although the State intends to provide education for maladjusted students at public expense, this legislative policy choice does not make such services "the exclusive province" of the state.

Fourth, there is no "symbiotic relationship" between the school and the state similar to that which existed between the restaurant and the state in *Burton*. The State "profited from the restaurant's discriminatory conduct" but in this case the "school's fiscal relationship with the State is not different from that of many contractors performing services for the government." Finally, there is no evidence that the State "has attempted to avoid its constitutional duties by a sham arrangement which attempts to disguise provision of public services as acts of private parties."

White, J., concurred in the judgment: "For me, the critical factor is the absence of any allegation that the employment decision was itself based upon some rule of conduct or policy put forth by the State. '[I]n contrast to the extensive regulation of the school generally, the various regulators showed relatively little interest in the school's personnel matters. The employment decision remains, therefore, a private decision not fairly attributable to the state.' "

Only Marshall, J., joined by Brennan, J., dissented, arguing that the school is "an arm of the state." "Although shipbuilders and dambuilders, like the school, may be dependent on government funds, they are not so closely supervised by the government. And unlike most private contractors, the school is performing a statutory duty of the State." The dissent also stated that, because the majority focused on the fact that the acts in this case are personnel decisions, it "would apparently concede that actions directly affecting the students could be treated as under color of law.... " Do you agree?

No opinion discussed *Norwood v. Harrison*. Can you distinguish it?

3.   On the same day that it decided *Rendell–Baker*, the Court decided *Blum v. Yaretsky*, 457 U.S. 991, 102 S.Ct. 2777, 73 L.Ed.2d 534 (1982). Rehnquist, J., wrote the opinion of the Court and, again, Brennan, J., joined by Marshall, J., filed the only dissents. The State reimbursed nursing homes for the reasonable cost of the health care services. To assure that the services are medically necessary, federal regulations required that each home establish a utilization review committee (URC) of physicians who should periodically determine if the patient should remain in the facility or be transferred to a more or less intensive level of care. Medicaid patients residing in private nursing homes challenged decisions to discharge or transfer them without notice or an opportunity to be heard. The Court only ruled on the power of nursing homes and the patients' attending physicians to decide independently to initiate transfers. The majority concluded that there was no state action. The State is not responsible for decisions to discharge or transfer "particular patients" because they "ultimately turn on medical judgments made by private parties according to professional standards that are not established by the State." The regulations impose a range of penalties on nursing homes that fail to transfer or discharge patients whose continued stay there is inappropriate, but these regulations them-

selves "do not dictate the decision to discharge or transfer in a particular case." Also the State's adjustments in Medicaid benefit levels in response to the decisions to discharge or transfer a patient does not constitute approval or enforcement of that decision.

White, J., concurring in the judgment, said that for state action to exist, the "respondents must show that the transfer or discharge is made on the basis of some rule or decision for which the state is responsible. It is not enough to show that the state takes certain actions in response to this private decision. The rule of decision implicated in the actions at issue here appears to be nothing more than a medical judgment. This is the clear import of the majority's conclusion that the 'decisions ultimately turn on medical judgments made by private parties according to professional standards that are not established by the State,' with which I agree."

Polk County v. Dodson, 454 U.S. 312, 102 S.Ct. 445, 70 L.Ed.2d 509 (1981) held that a public defender performing a lawyer's traditional functions as counsel to defendant in a criminal case is not a state actor merely because she is paid by the state; her relationship with her client is "identical to that existing between any other lawyer and client." By contrast, a public defender making hiring and firing decisions on behalf of the State is a state actor. *Branti v. Finkel,* § 10–9.3, infra.

4. *Lebron v. National Railroad Passenger Corp.,* 513 U.S. 374, 115 S.Ct. 961, 130 L.Ed.2d 902 (1995). An artist sued Amtrak (the National Railroad Passenger Corp.), claiming that its rejection of the artist's lease of billboard space because of its political content violated the First Amendment. Scalia, J., for the Court, held that Amtrak is a governmental agency or instrumentality for Constitutional purposes. Although Amtrak's authorizing statute declares that it is not "an agency or establishment of the United States Government," that statute decides Amtrak's status as a governmental entity only for matters within the control of Congress, such as whether it is subject to statutes that impose obligations or confer powers on governmental entities (e.g., the Administrative Procedure Act), or whether Congress deprives it of sovereign immunity from suit. Congress cannot exempt Amtrak from the restrictions of the First Amendment any more than Congress could declare by statute that the FBI is exempt from the Fourth Amendment. When the Government "creates a corporation by special law, for the furtherance of governmental objectives, and retains for itself permanent authority to appoint a majority of the directors of that corporation, the corporation is part of the Government for purposes of the First Amendment." The Court then remanded to decide the plaintiff's free speech claim.

7–5. LICENSING

MOOSE LODGE NO. 107 v. IRVIS
407 U.S. 163, 92 S.Ct. 1965, 32 L.Ed.2d 627 (1972).

MR. JUSTICE REHNQUIST delivered the opinion of the Court....

The District Court in its opinion found that "a Caucasian member in good standing brought plaintiff, a Negro, to the [Moose] Lodge's dining room and bar as his guest and requested service of food and beverages. The Lodge through its employees refused service to plaintiff solely because he is a Negro." It is undisputed that each local Moose Lodge is bound by the constitution and general bylaws of the Supreme Lodge, the latter of which contain a provision limiting membership in the lodges to white male Caucasians. The District Court in this connection found that "[t]he lodges accordingly maintain a policy and practice of restricting membership to the Caucasian race and permitting members to bring only Caucasian guests on lodge premises, particularly to the dining room and bar." . . .

Appellee, while conceding the right of private clubs to choose members upon a discriminatory basis, asserts that the licensing of Moose Lodge to serve liquor by the Pennsylvania Liquor Control Board amounts to such state involvement with the club's activities as to make its discriminatory practices forbidden by the Equal Protection Clause of the Fourteenth Amendment. The relief sought and obtained by appellee in the District Court was an injunction forbidding the licensing by the liquor authority of Moose Lodge until it ceased its discriminatory practices. . . .

Here there is nothing approaching the symbiotic relationship between lessor and lessee that was present in *Burton,* [§ 7–4, supra]. . . . Far from apparently holding itself out as a place of public accommodation, Moose Lodge quite ostentatiously proclaims the fact that it is not open to the public at large. Nor is it located and operated in such surroundings that although private in name, it discharges a function or performs a service that would otherwise in all likelihood be performed by the State. In short, while Eagle was a public restaurant in a public building, Moose Lodge is a private social club in a private building.

With the exception hereafter noted, the Pennsylvania Liquor Control Board plays absolutely no part in establishing or enforcing the membership or guest policies of the club that it licenses to serve liquor. There is no suggestion in this record that Pennsylvania law, either as written or as applied, discriminates against minority groups either in their right to apply for club licenses themselves or in their right to purchase and be served liquor in places of public accommodation. The only effect that the state licensing of Moose Lodge to serve liquor can be said to have on the right of any other Pennsylvanian to buy or be served liquor on premises other than those of Moose Lodge is that for some purposes club licenses are counted in the maximum number of licenses that may be issued in a given municipality. Basically each municipality has a quota of one retail license for each 1,500 inhabitants. Licenses issued to hotels, municipal golf courses, and airport restaurants are not counted in this quota, nor are club licenses until the maximum number of retail licenses is reached. Beyond that point, neither additional retail licenses nor additional club licenses may be issued so long as the number of issued and outstanding retail licenses remains at or above the statutory maximum.

The District Court was at pains to point out in its opinion what it considered to be the "pervasive" nature of the regulation of private clubs by the Pennsylvania Liquor Control Board. However detailed this type of regulation may be in some particulars, it cannot be said to in any way foster or encourage racial discrimination. Nor can it be said to make the State in any realistic sense a partner or even a joint venturer in the club's enterprise. The limited effect of the prohibition against obtaining additional club licenses when the maximum number of retail licenses allotted to a municipality has been issued, when considered together with the availability of liquor from hotel, restaurant, and retail licensees, falls far short of conferring upon club licensees a monopoly in the dispensing of liquor in any given municipality or in the State as a whole. We therefore hold that, with the exception hereafter noted, the operation of the regulatory scheme enforced by the Pennsylvania Liquor Control Board does not sufficiently implicate the State in the discriminatory guest policies of Moose Lodge to make the latter "state action" within the ambit of the Equal Protection Clause of the Fourteenth Amendment.

The District Court found that the regulations of the Liquor Control Board adopted pursuant to statute affirmatively require that "[e]very club licensee shall adhere to all of the provisions of its Constitution and By–Laws." ... Even though the Liquor Control Board regulation in question is neutral in its terms, the result of its application in a case where the constitution and bylaws of a club required racial discrimination would be to invoke the sanctions of the State to enforce a concededly discriminatory private rule. State action, for purposes of the Equal Protection Clause, may emanate from rulings of administrative and regulatory agencies as well as from legislative or judicial action. *Shelley v. Kraemer,* makes it clear that the application of state sanctions to enforce such a rule would violate the Fourteenth Amendment. Although the record before us is not as clear as one would like, appellant has not persuaded us that the District Court should have denied any and all relief.

Appellee was entitled to a decree enjoining the enforcement of § 113.09 of the regulations promulgated by the Pennsylvania Liquor Control Board insofar as that regulation requires compliance by Moose Lodge with provisions of its constitution and bylaws containing racially discriminatory provisions. He was entitled to no more. The judgment of the District Court is reversed, and the cause remanded with instructions to enter a decree in conformity with this opinion.

Reversed and remanded.

Mr. Justice Douglas, with whom Mr. Justice Marshall joins, dissenting.

... Liquor licenses in Pennsylvania, unlike driver's licenses, or marriage licenses, are not freely available to those who meet racially neutral qualifications. There is a complex quota system, which the majority accurately describes. What the majority neglects to say is that the quota for Harrisburg, where Moose Lodge No. 107 is located, has been full for many years. No more club licenses may be issued in that city. This state-enforced scarcity of licenses restricts the ability of blacks to obtain liquor, for liquor is commercially available *only* at private clubs for a significant portion of each week. Access by blacks to places that serve liquor is further limited by the fact that the state quota is filled. A group desiring to form a nondiscriminatory club which would serve blacks must purchase a license held by an existing club, which can exact a monopoly price for the transfer. The availability of such a license is speculative at best, however, for, as Moose Lodge itself concedes, without a liquor license a fraternal organization would be hard pressed to survive.

Thus, the State of Pennsylvania is putting the weight of its liquor license, concededly a valued and important adjunct to a private club, behind racial discrimination. . . .

MR. JUSTICE BRENNAN, with whom MR. JUSTICE MARSHALL joins, dissenting.

When Moose Lodge obtained its liquor license, the State of Pennsylvania became an active participant in the operation of the Lodge bar. Liquor licensing laws are only incidentally revenue measures; they are primarily pervasive regulatory schemes under which the State dictates and continually supervises virtually every detail of the operation of the licensee's business. Very few, if any, other licensed businesses experience such complete state involvement. Yet the Court holds that such involvement does not constitute "state action". . . .

JACKSON v. METROPOLITAN EDISON CO.

419 U.S. 345, 95 S.Ct. 449, 42 L.Ed.2d 477 (1974).

MR. JUSTICE REHNQUIST delivered the opinion of the Court.

Respondent Metropolitan Edison Co. is a privately owned and operated Pennsylvania corporation which holds a certificate of public convenience issued by the Pennsylvania Public Utility Commission empowering it to deliver electricity to a service area which includes the city of York, Pa. As a condition of holding its certificate, it is subject to extensive regulation by the Commission. Under a provision of its general tariff filed with the Commission, it has the right to discontinue service to any customer on reasonable notice of nonpayment of bills.

[After Metropolitan terminated petitioner's service, she sued claiming] that under state law she had an entitlement to reasonably continuous electrical service to her home and that Metropolitan's termination of her service for alleged nonpayment, action allowed by a provision of its general tariff filed with the Commission, constituted "state action" depriving her of property in violation of the Fourteenth Amendment's guarantee of due process of law. . . .

Petitioner advances a series of contentions which, in her view, lead to the conclusion that this case should fall on the *Burton* side [§ 7–4,] supra of the line drawn in the *Civil Rights Cases,* [§ 7–1,] supra rather than on the *Moose Lodge* side of that line. We find none of them persuasive. Petitioner first argues that "state action" is present because of the monopoly status allegedly conferred upon Metropolitan by the State of Pennsylvania. [A]lthough certain monopoly aspects were presented in *Moose Lodge No. 107,* supra, we found that the Lodge's action was not subject to the provisions of the Fourteenth Amendment....

Petitioner next urges that state action is present because respondent provides an essential public service required to be supplied on a reasonably continuous basis by Pa.Stat.Ann., Tit. 66, § 1171 (1959), and hence performs a "public function." We have, of course, found state action present in the exercise by a private entity of powers traditionally exclusively reserved to the State. See, e.g., *Terry v. Adams,* (election); *Marsh v. Alabama,* (company town); *Evans v. Newton,* (municipal park). If we were dealing with the exercise by Metropolitan of some power delegated to it by the State which is traditionally associated with sovereignty, such as eminent domain, our case would be quite a different one....

Perhaps in recognition of the fact that the supplying of utility service is not traditionally the exclusive prerogative of the State, petitioner invites the expansion of the doctrine of this limited line of cases into a broad principle that all businesses "affected with the public interest" are state actors in all their actions. We decline the invitation.... Doctors, optometrists, lawyers, Metropolitan, and [an] upstate New York grocery selling a quart of milk are all in regulated businesses, providing arguably essential goods and services, "affected with a public interest." We do not believe that such a status converts their every action, absent more, into that of the State.

We also reject the notion that Metropolitan's termination is state action because the State "has specifically authorized and approved" the termination practice. In the instant case, Metropolitan filed with the Public Utility Commission a general tariff—a provision of which states Metropolitan's right to terminate service for nonpayment. This provision has appeared in Metropolitan's previously filed tariffs for many years and has never been the subject of a hearing or other scrutiny by the Commission.... The nature of governmental regulation of private utilities is such that a utility may frequently be required by the state regulatory scheme to obtain approval for practices a business regulated in less detail would be free to institute without any approval from a regulatory body. Approval by a state utility commission of such a request from a regulated utility, where the commission has not put its own weight on the side of the proposed practice by ordering it, does not transmute a practice initiated by the utility and approved by the commission into "state action." At most, the Commission's failure to overturn this practice amounted to no more than a determination that a Pennsylvania utility was authorized to employ such a practice if it so desired. Respondent's exercise of the choice allowed by state law where the initiative comes from it and not from the State, does not make its action in doing so "state action" for purposes of the Fourteenth Amendment.

We also find absent in the instant case the symbiotic relationship presented in *Burton v. Wilmington Parking Authority*, ... Metropolitan is a privately owned corporation, and it does not lease its facilities from the State of Pennsylvania. It alone is responsible for the provision of power to its customers. In common with all corporations of the State it pays taxes to the State, and it is subject to a form of extensive regulation by the State in a way that most other business enterprises are not. But this was likewise true of the appellant club in *Moose Lodge No. 107 v. Irvis,* supra . . . .

All of petitioner's arguments taken together show no more than that Metropolitan was a heavily regulated, privately owned utility, enjoying at least a partial monopoly in the providing of electrical service within its territory, and that it elected to terminate service to petitioner in a manner which the Pennsylvania Public Utility Commission found permissible under state law. Under our decision this is not sufficient to connect the State of Pennsylvania with respondent's action so as to make the latter's conduct attributable to the State for purposes of the Fourteenth Amendment. . . .

MR. JUSTICE MARSHALL, dissenting . . . .

What is perhaps most troubling about the Court's opinion is that it would appear to apply to a broad range of claimed constitutional violations by the company. The Court has not adopted the notion, accepted elsewhere, that different standards should apply to state-action analysis when different constitutional claims are presented. Thus, the majority's analysis would seemingly apply as well to a company that refused to extend service to Negroes, welfare recipients, or any other group that the company preferred, for its own reasons, not to serve. I cannot believe that this Court would hold that the State's involvement with the utility company was not sufficient to impose upon the company an obligation to meet the constitutional mandate of nondiscrimination. Yet nothing in the analysis of the majority opinion suggests otherwise. I dissent.

[The dissenting opinions of DOUGLAS, J., & BRENNAN, J., are omitted.]

7–6. STATE NONFINANCIAL FACILITATION OF PRIVATE ACTS

REITMAN v. MULKEY
387 U.S. 369, 87 S.Ct. 1627, 18 L.Ed.2d 830 (1967).

MR. JUSTICE WHITE delivered the opinion of the Court.

The question here is whether Art. I, § 26, of the California Constitution denies "to any person . . . the equal protection of the laws" within the meaning of the Fourteenth Amendment of the Constitution of the United States. Section 26 of Art. I, an initiated measure submitted to the people as Proposition 14 in a statewide ballot in 1964, provides in part as follows:

Neither the State nor any subdivision or agency thereof shall deny, limit or abridge, directly or indirectly, the right of any person, who is willing or desires to sell, lease or rent any part or all of his real property, to decline to sell, lease or rent such property to such person or persons as he, in his absolute discretion, chooses.

The real property covered by § 26 is limited to residential property and contains an exception for state-owned real estate.

[T]he Mulkeys, who are husband and wife and respondents here, sued alleging that petitioners had refused to rent them an apartment solely on account of their race. An injunction and damages were demanded. Petitioners moved for summary judgment. [The California Supreme Court] held that Art. I, § 26, was invalid as denying the equal protection of the laws guaranteed by the Fourteenth Amendment. . . .

We affirm the judgments of the California Supreme Court. We first turn to the opinion of that court in *Reitman,* which quite properly undertook to examine the constitutionality of § 26 in terms of its "immediate objective," its "ultimate effect" and its "historical context and the conditions existing prior to its enactment." Judgments such as these we have frequently undertaken ourselves. But here the California Supreme Court has addressed itself to these matters and we should give careful consideration to its views because they concern the purpose, scope, and operative effect of a provision of the California Constitution.

First, the court considered whether § 26 was concerned at all with private discriminations in residential housing. This involved a review of past efforts by the California Legislature to regulate such discriminations. The Unruh Act, on which respondents based their cases, was passed in 1959. The Hawkins Act, followed and prohibited discriminations in publicly assisted housing. [I]n 1963, came the Rumford Fair Housing Act, superseding the Hawkins Act and prohibiting racial discriminations in the sale or rental of any private dwelling containing more than four units. . . .

It was against this background that Proposition 14 was enacted. Its immediate design and intent, the California court said, were "to overturn state laws that bore on the right of private sellers and lessors to discriminate," the Unruh and Rumford Acts, and "to forestall future state action that might circumscribe this right." This aim was successfully achieved: the adoption of Proposition 14 "generally nullifies both the Rumford and Unruh Acts as they apply to the housing market," and establishes "a purported constitutional right to *privately* discriminate on grounds which admittedly would be unavailable under the Fourteenth Amendment *should state action* be involved."

Second, the court conceded that the State was permitted a neutral position with respect to private racial discriminations and that the State was not bound by the Federal Constitution to forbid them. But, because a significant state involvement in private discriminations could amount to unconstitutional state action, *Burton v. Wilmington Parking Authority,* the court deemed it necessary to determine whether Proposition 14 invalidly involved the State in racial discriminations in the housing market. Its conclusion was that it did.

[I]t concluded that a prohibited state involvement could be found "even where the state can be charged with only encouraging," rather than commanding discrimination. Also of particular interest to the court was Mr. Justice Stewart's concurrence in *Burton v. Wilmington Parking Authority,* where it was said that the Delaware courts had construed an existing Delaware statute as "authorizing" racial discrimination in restaurants and that the statute was therefore invalid. To the California court "[t]he instant case presents an undeniably analogous situation" wherein the State had taken affirmative action designed to make private discriminations legally possible. Section 26 was said to have changed the situation from one in which discrimination was restricted "to one wherein it is encouraged, within the meaning of the cited decisions"; § 26 was legislative action "which authorized private discrimination" and made the State "at least a partner in the instant act of discrimination.... " The court could "conceive of no other purpose for an application of section 26 aside from authorizing the perpetration of a purported private discrimination.... " The judgment of the California court was that § 26 unconstitutionally involves the State in racial discriminations and is therefore invalid under the Fourteenth Amendment.

There is no sound reason for rejecting this judgment. Petitioners contend that the California court has misconstrued the Fourteenth Amendment since the repeal of any statute prohibiting racial discrimination, which is constitutionally permissible, may be said to "authorize" and "encourage" discrimination because it makes legally permissible that which was formerly proscribed. But, as we understand the California court, it did not posit a constitutional violation on the mere repeal of the Unruh and Rumford Acts. It did not read either our cases or the Fourteenth Amendment as establishing an automatic constitutional barrier to the repeal of an existing law prohibiting racial discriminations in housing; nor did the court rule that a State may never put in statutory form an existing policy of neutrality with respect to private discriminations. What the court below did was first to reject the notion that the State was required to have a statute prohibiting racial discriminations in housing. Second, it held the intent of § 26 was to authorize private racial discriminations in the housing market, to repeal the Unruh and Rumford Acts and to create a constitutional right to discriminate on racial grounds in the sale and leasing of real property. Hence, the court dealt with § 26 as though it expressly authorized and constitutionalized the private right to discriminate. Third, the court assessed the ultimate impact of § 26 in the California environment and concluded that the section would encourage and significantly involve the State in private racial discrimination contrary to the Fourteenth Amendment.

The California court could very reasonably conclude that § 26 would and did have wider impact than a mere repeal of existing statutes.... The right to discriminate, including the right to discriminate on racial grounds, was now embodied in the State's basic charter, immune from legislative, executive, or judicial regulation at any level of the state government. Those practicing racial discriminations need no longer rely solely on their personal choice. They could now invoke express constitutional authority, free from censure or interference of any kind from official sources. . . . Here the California court, armed as it was with the knowledge of the facts and circumstances concerning the passage and potential impact of § 26, and familiar with the milieu in which that provision would operate, has determined that the provision would involve the State in private racial discriminations to an unconstitutional degree. We accept this holding of the California court. . . .

Affirmed.

Mr. Justice Douglas, concurring. . . .

Zoning is a state and municipal function. When the State leaves that function to private agencies or institutions which are licensees and which practice racial discrimination and zone our cities into white and black belts or white and black ghettoes, it suffers a governmental function to be performed under private auspices in a way the State itself may not act. The present case is therefore kin to *Terry v. Adams*, [§ 7–2, supra], ...

Mr. Justice Harlan, whom Mr. Justice Black, Mr. Justice Clark, and Mr. Justice Stewart join, dissenting.

[A]ll that has happened is that California has effected a *pro tanto* repeal of its prior statutes forbidding private discrimination. This runs no more afoul of the Fourteenth Amendment than would have California's failure to pass any such antidiscrimination statutes in the first instance. The fact that such repeal was also accompanied by a constitutional prohibition against future enactment of such laws by the California Legislature cannot well be thought to affect, from a federal constitutional standpoint, the validity of what California has done. The Fourteenth Amendment does not reach such state constitutional action any more than it does a simple legislative repeal of legislation forbidding private discrimination.

[T]he grounds which prompt legislators or state voters to repeal a law do not determine its constitutional validity. That question is decided by what the law does, not by what those who voted for it wanted it to do, and it must not be forgotten that the Fourteenth Amendment does not compel a State to put or keep any particular law about race on its books. The Amendment only forbids a State to pass or keep in effect laws discriminating on account of race. California has not done this. The only "factual" matter relied on by the majority of the California Supreme Court was the context in which Proposition 14 was adopted. . . . This, of course, is nothing but a legal conclusion as to federal constitutional law, the California Supreme Court not having relied in any way upon the State Constitution. . . .

There is no question that the adoption of § 26, repealing the former state antidiscrimination laws and prohibiting the enactment of such state laws in the future, constituted "state action" within the meaning of the Fourteenth Amendment. The only issue is whether this provision impermissibly deprives any person of equal protection of the laws.... The denial of equal protection emerges only from the conclusion reached by the Court that the implementation of a new policy of governmental neutrality, embodied in a constitutional provision and replacing a former policy of antidiscrimination, has the effect of lending encouragement to those who wish to discriminate. In the context of the actual facts of the case, this conclusion appears to me to state only a truism: people who want to discriminate but were previously forbidden to do so by state law are now left free because the State has chosen to have no law on the subject at all. Obviously whenever there is a change in the law it will have resulted from the concerted activity of those who desire the change, and its enactment will allow those supporting the legislation to pursue their private goals.

A moment of thought will reveal the far-reaching possibilities of the Court's new doctrine, which I am sure the Court does not intend. Every act of private discrimination is either forbidden by state law or permitted by it. There can be little doubt that such permissiveness—whether by express constitutional or statutory provision, or implicit in the common law—to some extent "encourages" those who wish to discriminate to do so. Under this theory "state action" in the form of laws that do nothing more than passively permit private discrimination could be said to tinge *all* private discrimination with the taint of unconstitutional state encouragement....

I think that this decision is not only constitutionally unsound, but in its practical potentialities short-sighted. Opponents of state antidiscrimination statutes are now in a position to argue that such legislation should be defeated because, if enacted, it may be unrepealable.

Notes

1. *Hunter v. Erickson,* 393 U.S. 385, 89 S.Ct. 557, 21 L.Ed.2d 616 (1969). White, J., for the Court, concluded that section 137 of the Akron City Charter violated the equal protection clause:

> The question in this case is whether the City of Akron, Ohio, has denied a Negro citizen, Nellie Hunter, the equal protection of its laws by amending the city charter to prevent the city council from implementing any ordinance dealing with racial, religious, or ancestral discrimination in housing without the approval of the majority of the voters of Akron.... Akron argues that this case is unlike *Reitman v. Mulkey,* in that here the city charter declares no right to discriminate in housing, authorizes and encourages no housing discrimination, and places no ban on the enactment of fair housing ordinances. But we need not rest on *Reitman* to decide this case. Here, unlike *Reitman,* there was an explicitly racial classification treating racial housing matters differently from other racial and housing matters.

By adding § 137 to its Chapter the City of Akron ... drew a distinction between those groups who sought the law's protection against racial, religious, or ancestral discriminations in the sale and rental of real estate and those who sought to regulate real property transactions in the pursuit of other ends. Those who sought, or would benefit from, most ordinances regulating the real property market remained subject to the general rule: the ordinance would become effective 30 days after passage by the City Council, or immediately if passed as an emergency measure, and would be subject to referendum only if 10% of the electors so requested by filing a proper and timely petition. Passage by the Council sufficed unless the electors themselves invoked the general referendum provisions of the city charter. But for those who sought protection against racial bias, the approval of the City Council was not enough. A referendum was required by charter at a general or regular election, without any provision for use of the expedited special election ordinarily available. The Akron charter obviously made it substantially more difficult to secure enactment of ordinances subject to § 137. Only laws to end housing discrimination based on "race, color, religion, national origin or ancestry" must run § 137's gauntlet....

2. *James v. Valtierra,* 402 U.S. 137, 91 S.Ct. 1331, 28 L.Ed.2d 678 (1971). Black, J., for the Court, upheld Article XXXIV of the California state constitution, which provided that no low-rent housing project should be developed, constructed, or acquired by a state public body until the project was approved by a majority of those voting at a community election. A three-judge district court had held that the Article denied plaintiffs (who were eligible for low-cost public housing) the equal protection of the laws:

> Unlike the Akron referendum provision it cannot be said that California's Article XXXIV rests on distinctions based on race. The Article requires referendum approval for any low-rent public housing project, not only for projects which will be occupied by a racial minority. And the record here would not support any claim that a law seemingly neutral on its face is in fact aimed at a racial minority. The present case could be affirmed only by extending *Hunter,* and this we decline to do.

> California's entire history demonstrates the repeated use of referendums to give citizens a voice on questions of public policy ... and referendums have been a commonplace occurrence in the State's active political life. Provisions for referendums demonstrate devotion to democracy, not to bias, discrimination, or prejudice. Nonetheless, appellees contend that Article XXXIV denies them equal protection because it demands a mandatory referendum while many other referendums only take place upon citizen initiative. They suggest that the mandatory nature of the Article XXXIV referendum constitutes unconstitutional discrimination because it hampers persons desiring public housing from achieving their objective when no such roadblock faces other groups seeking to influence other public decisions to their advantage. But of course a lawmaking procedure that "disadvantages" a particular group does not always deny equal protection. Under any such holding, presumably a State would not be able to require referendums on any subject unless referendums were required on all, because they would always

disadvantage some group. And this Court would be required to analyze governmental structures to determine whether a gubernatorial veto provision or a filibuster rule is likely to "disadvantage" any of the diverse and shifting groups that make up the American people.

Furthermore, an examination of California law reveals that persons advocating low-income housing have not been singled out for mandatory referendums while no other group must face that obstacle. Mandatory referendums are required for approval of state constitutional amendments, for the issuance of general obligation long-term bonds by local governments, and for certain municipal territorial annexations. . . .

Marshall, J., joined by Brennan and Blackmun, JJ., dissented, arguing that the mandatory referendum unfairly singled out low-income persons, and that classifications on the basis of poverty should be "suspect" and judged as harshly as classifications on the basis of race.[1]

3.   Do *Hunter* and *James* shed any light on the rationale in *Reitman?* How would you rationalize *Reitman?*

4.   Consider *Anderson v. Martin,* 375 U.S. 399, 84 S.Ct. 454, 11 L.Ed.2d 430 (1964): "Louisiana Revised Statutes § 18:1174.1 provides that in all primary, general or special elections, the nomination papers and ballots shall designate the race of candidates for elective office. The question involved in this appeal is whether this requirement violates the Equal Protection and Due Process Clauses of the Fourteenth Amendment or the Fifteenth Amendment. . . . A three-judge United States District Court . . . upheld the constitutionality of the statute by a 2–to–1 vote. . . . In the abstract, Louisiana imposes no restriction upon anyone's candidacy nor upon an elector's choice in the casting of his ballot. . . . "

How should the Supreme Court rule? Given that a citizen can cast his vote for whomever he chooses and for whatever reason he pleases, is this Louisiana statute neutral or does it involve prohibited state action?

WASHINGTON v. SEATTLE SCHOOL DISTRICT NO. 1

458 U.S. 457, 102 S.Ct. 3187, 73 L.Ed.2d 896 (1982).

JUSTICE BLACKMUN delivered the opinion of the Court.

[Approximately 37% of the school children in the Seattle School District are minorities: black, Asian, American Indian, or Hispanic. To reduce the problem of racially imbalanced schools created by segregated housing patterns the School Board, since 1963, implemented various plans, such as voluntary transfers from neighborhood schools. In March 1978 the Board enacted the "Seattle Plan," which makes extensive use of mandatory busing and other forms of mandatory student reassignments to achieve racial integration. This Seattle Plan, like the earlier one, is not required by the U.S. Constitution. An organization called

---

1. For case law on the question of poverty as not involving a suspect class, see   § 8–2.5.

Citizens for Voluntary Integration Committee (CiVIC) opposed the Seattle Plan.] CiVIC drafted a statewide initiative designed to terminate the use of mandatory busing for purposes of racial integration. This proposal, known as Initiative 350, provided that "no school board ... shall directly or indirectly require any student to attend a school other than the school which is geographically nearest or next nearest the student's place of residence ... and which offers the course of study pursued by such student.... " The initiative then set out, however, a number of broad exceptions to this requirement, [e.g.,] a student may be assigned beyond his neighborhood school if he "requires special education, care or guidance".... The initiative envisioned busing for racial purposes in only one circumstance: it did not purport to "prevent any court of competent jurisdiction from adjudicating constitutional issues relating to the public schools."

Its proponents placed Initiative 350 on the Washington ballot for the November 1978 general election. During the ensuing campaign, the District Court concluded, the leadership of CiVIC "acted legally and responsibly," and did not address "its appeals to the racial biases of the voters." At the same time, however, the court's findings demonstrate that the initiative was directed solely at desegregative busing in general, and at the Seattle Plan in particular. Thus, "[e]xcept for the assignment of students to effect racial balancing, the drafters of Initiative 350 attempted to preserve to school districts the maximum flexibility in the assignment of students," and "[e]xcept for racially-balancing purposes" the initiative "permits local school districts to assign students other than to their nearest or next nearest schools for most, if not all, of the major reasons for which students are at present assigned to schools other than their nearest nor next nearest schools." In campaigning for the measure, CiVIC officials accurately represented that its passage would result in "no loss of school district flexibility other than in busing for desegregation purposes," and it is evident that the campaign focused almost exclusively on the wisdom of "forced busing" for integration.

[The lower courts invalidated Initiative 350.] As Justice Harlan noted while concurring in the Court's opinion in *Hunter* [*v. Erickson*, 393 U.S. 385, 89 S.Ct. 557, 21 L.Ed.2d 616 (1969)], laws structuring political institutions or allocating political power according to "neutral principles"—such as the executive veto, or the typically burdensome requirements for amending state constitutions—are not subject to equal protection attack, though they may "make it more difficult for minorities to achieve favorable legislation." Because such laws make it more difficult for *every* group in the community to enact comparable laws, they "provid[e] a just framework within which the diverse political groups in our society may fairly compete." Thus, the political majority may generally restructure the political process to place obstacles in the path of everyone seeking to secure the benefits of governmental action. But a different analysis is required when the State allocates governmental power non-neutrally, by explicitly using the *racial* nature of a decision to determine the decisionmaking process. State action of this kind, the

Court said, "places *special* burdens on racial minorities within the governmental process," (emphasis added), thereby "making it *more* difficult for certain racial and religious minorities [than for other members of the community] to achieve legislation that is in their interest." (emphasis added)(Harlan, J., concurring). Such a structuring of the political process, the Court said, was "no more permissible than [is] denying [members of a racial minority] the vote, on an equal basis with others."

. . . In our view, Initiative 350 must fall because it does "not attemp[t] to allocate governmental power on the basis of any general principle." *Hunter v. Erickson* (Harlan, J., concurring). Instead, it uses the racial nature of an issue to define the governmental decisionmaking structure, and thus imposes substantial and unique burdens on racial minorities.

[D]espite its facial neutrality there is little doubt that the initiative was effectively drawn for racial purposes. Neither the initiative's sponsors, nor the District Court, nor the Court of Appeals had any difficulty perceiving the racial nature of the issue settled by Initiative 350. . . . It undoubtedly is true, as the United States suggests, that the proponents of mandatory integration cannot be classified by race: Negroes and whites may be counted among both the supporters and the opponents of Initiative 350. And it should be equally clear that white as well as Negro children benefit from exposure to "ethnic and racial diversity in the classroom."[15] But neither of these factors serves to distinguish *Hunter,* for we may fairly assume that members of the racial majority both favored and benefited from Akron's fair housing ordinance. In any event, our cases suggest that desegregation of the public schools, like the Akron open housing ordinance, at bottom inures primarily to the benefit of the minority, and is designed for that purpose. . . .

We are also satisfied that the practical effect of Initiative 350 is to work a reallocation of power of the kind condemned in *Hunter*. The initiative removes the authority to address a racial problem—and only a racial problem—from the existing decisionmaking body, in such a way as to burden minority interests. Those favoring the elimination of *de facto* school segregation now must seek relief from the state legislature, or from the statewide electorate. Yet authority over all other student assignment decisions, as well as over most other areas of educational policy, remains vested in the local school board. Indeed, by specifically exempting from Initiative 350's proscriptions most non-racial reasons for assigning students away from their neighborhood schools, the initiative expressly requires those championing school integration to surmount a considerably higher hurdle than persons seeking comparable legislative action. . . .

15. Appellants and the United States do not challenge the propriety of race-conscious student assignments for the purpose of achieving integration, even absent a finding of prior *de jure* segregation. We therefore do not specifically pass on that issue.

The state appellants and the United States, in response to this line of analysis, argue that Initiative 350 has not worked *any* reallocation of power. They note that the State necessarily retains plenary authority over Washington's system of education, and therefore they suggest that the initiative amounts to nothing more than an unexceptional example of a State's intervention in its own school system. [But] when the political process or the decisionmaking mechanism used to *address* racially conscious legislation—and only such legislation—is singled out for peculiar and disadvantageous treatment, the governmental action plainly "rests on 'distinctions based on race.' "[29] . . .

JUSTICE POWELL, with whom the CHIEF JUSTICE [BURGER], JUSTICE REHNQUIST, and JUSTICE O'CONNOR join, dissenting. . . .

In the absence of a constitutional violation, no decision of this Court compels a school district to adopt or maintain a mandatory busing program for racial integration. Accordingly, the Court does not hold that the adoption of a neighborhood school policy by *local* school districts would be unconstitutional. Rather, it holds that the adoption of such a policy at the *State* level—rather than at the local level—violates the Equal Protection Clause of the Fourteenth Amendment.

[W]e have never held, or even intimated, that absent a federal constitutional violation, a State *must* choose to treat persons differently on the basis of race. In the absence of a federal constitutional violation requiring race-specific remedies, a policy of strict racial neutrality by a State would violate no federal constitutional principle. In particular, a neighborhood school policy and a decision *not* to assign students on the basis of their race, does not offend the Fourteenth Amendment.[6] . . . Yet this Court holds that neither the legislature or the people of the State of Washington could alter what the District had decided. The Court argues that the people of Washington by Initiative 350 created a racial classification, and yet must agree that identical action by the Seattle School District itself would have created no such classification. This is not an easy argument to answer because it seems to make no sense. . . .

Hunter, therefore, is simply irrelevant. It is the *Court* that by its decision today disrupts the normal course of State government.[14] Under

29. Thus we do not hold, as the dissent implies, that the State's attempt to repeal a desegregation program creates a racial classification, while "identical action" by the Seattle School Board does not. It is the State's race-conscious restructuring of its decision-making process that is impermissible, not the simple repeal of the Seattle Plan.

6. Indeed, in the absence of a finding of segregation by the School District, mandatory busing on the basis of race raises constitutional difficulties of its own. Extensive pupil transportation may threaten liberty or privacy interests. Moreover, when a State or school board assigns students on the basis of their race, it acts on the basis of a racial classification, and we have consistently held that "[a] racial classification, regardless of purported motivation is presumptively invalid and can be upheld only upon an extraordinary justification."

14. The Court's decision intrudes deeply into normal State decisionmaking. Under its holding the people of the State of Washington apparently are forever barred from developing a different policy on mandatory busing where a School District previously has adopted one of its own. This principle would not seem limited to the question of mandatory busing. Thus, if the admissions committee of a State law school developed

its unprecedented theory of a vested constitutional right to local decisionmaking, the State apparently is now forever barred from addressing the perplexing problems of how best to educate fairly *all* children in a multiracial society where, as in this case, the local school board has acted first. . . .

CRAWFORD v. BOARD OF EDUCATION
458 U.S. 527, 102 S.Ct. 3211, 73 L.Ed.2d 948 (1982).

JUSTICE POWELL delivered the opinion of the Court.

An amendment to the California Constitution provides that state courts shall not order mandatory pupil assignment or transportation unless a federal court would do so to remedy a violation of the Equal Protection Clause of the Fourteenth Amendment of the United States Constitution. The question for our decision is whether this provision is itself in violation of the Fourteenth Amendment.

[In 1976 the California Supreme Court ruled] that under the California Constitution "state school boards . . . bear a constitutional obligation to take reasonable steps to alleviate segregation in the public schools, whether the segregation be de facto or de jure in origin." . . . In November 1979 the voters of the State of California ratified Proposition I, an amendment to the Due Process and Equal Protection Clauses of the State Constitution. Proposition I conforms the power of state courts to order busing to that exercised by the federal courts under the Fourteenth Amendment:

> [N]o court of this state may impose upon the State of California or any public entity, board, or official any obligation or responsibility with respect to the use of pupil school assignment or pupil transportation, (1) except to remedy a specific violation by such party that would also constitute a violation of the Equal Protection Clause of the 14th Amendment to the United States Constitution, and (2) unless a federal court would be permitted under federal decisional law to impose that obligation or responsibility upon such party to remedy the specific violation of the Equal Protection Clause. . . .

[The California Court of Appeals upheld the constitutionality of Proposition I.]

[We reject] the contention that once a State chooses to do "more" than the Fourteenth Amendment requires, it may never recede. . . . It would be paradoxical to conclude that by adopting the Equal Protection Clause of the Fourteenth Amendment, the voters of the State thereby had violated it. Moreover, even after Proposition I, the California Constitution still imposes a greater duty of desegregation than does the Federal

an affirmative action plan that came under fire, the Court apparently would find it unconstitutional for any higher authority to intervene unless that authority traditionally dictated admissions policies. As a constitutional matter, the Dean of the Law School, the faculty of the University as a whole, the University President, the Chancellor of the University System, and the Board of Regents might be powerless to intervene despite their greater authority under State law. . . .

Constitution. The state courts of California continue to have an obligation under state law to order segregated school districts to use voluntary desegregation techniques, whether or not there has been a finding of intentional segregation. The school districts themselves retain a state law obligation to take reasonably feasible steps to desegregate, and they remain free to adopt reassignment and busing plans to effectuate desegregation.[12] ...

We would agree that if Proposition I employed a racial classification it would be unconstitutional unless necessary to further a compelling state interest.... But Proposition I does not embody a racial classification. It neither says nor implies that persons are to be treated differently on account of their race. It simply forbids state courts from ordering pupil school assignment or transportation in the absence of a Fourteenth Amendment violation. The benefit it seeks to confer—neighborhood schooling—is made available regardless of race in the discretion of school boards....

Nor can it be said that Proposition I distorts the political process for racial reasons or that it allocates governmental or judicial power on the basis of a discriminatory principle. [It is] constitutional for the people of the State to determine that the standard of the Fourteenth Amendment was more appropriate for California courts to apply in desegregation cases than the standard repealed by Proposition I.

[W]e see no reason to challenge the [state] Court of Appeal's conclusion that the voters of the State were not motivated by a discriminatory purpose. In this case the Proposition was approved by an overwhelming majority of the electorate. It received support from members of all races.[33] The purposes of the Proposition are stated in its text and are legitimate, nondiscriminatory objectives. In these circumstances, we will not dispute the judgment of the Court of Appeal or impugn the motives of the State's electorate.

Accordingly the judgment of the California Court of Appeal is

Affirmed.

JUSTICE BLACKMUN with whom JUSTICE BRENNAN joins, concurring.

While I join the opinion of the Court, I write separately to address what I believe are the critical distinctions between this case and *Washington v. Seattle School District No. 1.* ...

State courts do not create the rights they enforce; those rights originate elsewhere—in the state legislature, in the State's political subdivisions, or in the state constitution itself. When one of those rights is repealed, and therefore is rendered unenforceable in the courts, that

---

12. [T]he Proposition would not bar state court enforcement of state *statutes* requiring busing for desegregation or for any other purpose.

33. Proposition I received support from 73.9% of the voters in Los Angeles county which has a "minority" population—including persons of Spanish origin—of over 50%. By contrast, the Proposition received its smallest percentage of the vote in Humboldt and Marin counties which are nearly all-white in composition.

action hardly can be said to restructure the State's decisionmaking mechanism. [T]he people of California—the same "entity" that put in place the state constitution, and created the enforceable obligation to desegregate—have made the desegregation obligation judicially unenforceable. . . .

JUSTICE MARSHALL, dissenting.

. . . I fail to see how a fundamental redefinition of the governmental decisionmaking structure with respect to the same racial issue can be unconstitutional when the state seeks to remove the authority from local school boards, yet constitutional when the state attempts to achieve the same result by limiting the power of its courts. . . .

Notes

A Colorado state constitutional amendment did not allow state and local governments to enact laws prohibiting discrimination against homosexuals because of their homosexuality. *Romer v. Evans*, 517 U.S. 620, 116 S.Ct. 1620, 134 L.Ed.2d 855 (1996), in § 8–3.44, declared that amendment unconstitutional. The Court did not purport to rely on *Reitman v. Mulkey* and related cases.

FLAGG BROTHERS, INC. v. BROOKS
436 U.S. 149, 98 S.Ct. 1729, 56 L.Ed.2d 185 (1978).

MR. JUSTICE REHNQUIST delivered the opinion of the Court.

The question presented by this litigation is whether a warehouseman's proposed sale of goods entrusted to him for storage, as permitted by New York Uniform Commercial Code § 7–210 is an action properly attributable to the State of New York. . . . According to her complaint, the allegations of which we must accept as true, respondent Shirley Brooks and her family were evicted from their apartment in Mount Vernon, N.Y., on June 13, 1973. The city marshal arranged for Brooks' possessions to be stored by petitioner Flagg Brothers, Inc., in its warehouse. Brooks was informed of the cost of moving and storage, and she instructed the workmen to proceed, although she found the price too high. On August 25, 1973, after a series of disputes over the validity of the charges being claimed by petitioner Flagg Brothers, Brooks received a letter demanding that her account be brought up to date within 10 days "or your furniture will be sold." A series of subsequent letters from respondent and her attorneys produced no satisfaction.

Brooks [later joined by another plaintiff] thereupon initiated this class action in the District Court under 42 U.S.C.A. § 1983, seeking damages, an injunction against the threatened sale of her belongings, and the declaration that such a sale pursuant to § 7–210 would violate the Due Process and Equal Protection Clauses of the Fourteenth Amendment. [R]espondents allege that Flagg Brothers has deprived them of their right, secured by the Fourteenth Amendment to be free from state deprivations of property without due process of law. Thus, they must establish not only that Flagg Brothers acted under color of the challenged statute, but also that its actions are properly attributable to the State of New York.

It must be noted that respondents have named no public officials as defendants in this action. The city marshal, who supervised their evictions, was dismissed from the case by the consent of all the parties. This total absence of overt official involvement plainly distinguishes this case from earlier decisions imposing procedural restrictions on creditors' remedies.... Thus, the only issue presented by this case is whether Flagg Brothers' action may fairly be attributed to the State of New York. We conclude that it may not.

Respondents' primary contention is that New York has delegated to Flagg Brothers a power "traditionally exclusively reserved to the State." They argue that the resolution of private disputes is a traditional function of civil government, and that the State in § 7–210 has delegated this function to Flagg Brothers. [However, while] many functions have been traditionally performed by governments, very few have been "exclusively reserved to the State."

One such area has been elections.... A second line of cases under the public-function doctrine originated with *Marsh v. Alabama*. Just as the Texas Democratic Party in *Smith* and the Jaybird Democratic Association in *Terry* effectively performed the entire public function of selecting public officials, so too the Gulf Shipbuilding Corp. performed all the necessary municipal functions in the town of Chickasaw, Ala., which it owned....

These two branches of the public-function doctrine have in common the feature of exclusivity. Although the elections held by the Democratic Party and its affiliates were the only meaningful elections in Texas, and the streets owned by the Gulf Shipbuilding Corp. were the only streets in Chickasaw, the proposed sale by Flagg Brothers under § 7–210 is not the only means of resolving this purely private dispute. Respondent Brooks has never alleged that state law barred her from seeking a waiver of Flagg Brothers' right to sell her goods at the time she authorized their storage. Presumably, respondent Jones, who alleges that she never authorized the storage of her goods, could have sought to replevy her goods at any time under state law. The challenged statute itself provides a damages remedy against the warehouseman for violations of its provisions. This system of rights and remedies, recognizing the traditional place of private arrangements in ordering relationships in the commercial world,[9] can hardly be said to have delegated to Flagg Brothers an exclusive prerogative of the sovereign....

[T]here are a number of state and municipal functions not covered by our election cases or governed by the reasoning of *Marsh* which have been administered with a greater degree of exclusivity by States and municipalities than has the function of so-called "dispute resolution."

---

9. Unlike the parade of horribles suggested by our Brother Stevens in dissent, this case does not involve state authorization of private breach of the peace.

Among these are such functions as education, fire and police protection, and tax collection.[14] We express no view as to the extent, if any, to which a city or State might be free to delegate to private parties the performance of such functions and thereby avoid the strictures of the Fourteenth Amendment. The mere recitation of these possible permutations and combinations of factual situations suffices to caution us that their resolution should abide the necessity of deciding them.

Respondents further urge that Flagg Brothers' proposed action is properly attributable to the State because the State has authorized and encouraged it in enacting § 7–210. Our cases state "that a State is responsible for the . . . act of a private party when the State, by its law, has compelled the act." This Court, however, has never held that a State's mere acquiescence in a private action converts that action into that of the State. . . . If New York had no commercial statutes at all, its courts would still be faced with the decision whether to prohibit or to permit the sort of sale threatened here the first time an aggrieved bailor came before them for relief. A judicial decision to deny relief would be no less an "authorization" or "encouragement" of that sale than the legislature's decision embodied in this statute. . . . If the mere denial of judicial relief is considered sufficient encouragement to make the State responsible for those private acts, all private deprivations of property would be converted into public acts whenever the State, for whatever reason, denies relief sought by the putative property owner. . . .

Here, the State of New York has not compelled the sale of a bailor's goods, but has merely announced the circumstances under which its courts will not interfere with a private sale. Indeed, the crux of respondents' complaint is not that the State *has* acted, but that it has *refused* to act. This statutory refusal to act is no different in principle from an ordinary statute of limitations whereby the State declines to provide a remedy for private deprivations of property after the passage of a given period of time.

We conclude that the allegations of these complaints do not establish a violation of these respondents' Fourteenth Amendments rights by either respondent Flagg Brothers or the State of New York. . . .

Mr. Justice Brennan took no part in the consideration or decision of these cases.

Mr. Justice Stevens, with whom Mr. Justice White and Mr. Justice Marshall join, dissenting. . . .

In determining that New York's statute cannot be scrutinized under the Due Process Clause, the Court reasons that the warehouseman's proposed sale is solely private action because the state statute "*permits*

---

14. [T]his Court has never considered the private exercise of traditional police functions. In *Griffin v. Maryland,* 378 U.S. 130, 84 S.Ct. 1770, 12 L.Ed.2d 754 (1964), the State contended that the deputy sheriff in question had acted only as a private security employee, but this Court specifically found that he "purported to exercise the authority of a deputy sheriff." *Griffin* thus sheds no light on the constitutional status of private police forces, and we express no opinion here.

but does not compel" the sale, (emphasis added), and because the warehouseman has not been delegated a power "*exclusively* reserved to the State," (emphasis added). Under this approach a State could enact laws authorizing private citizens to use self-help in countless situations without any possibility of federal challenge. A state statute could authorize the warehouseman to retain all proceeds of the lien sale, even if they far exceeded the amount of the alleged debt; it could authorize finance companies to enter private homes to repossess merchandise; or indeed, it could authorize "any person with sufficient physical power," to acquire and sell the property of his weaker neighbor. An attempt to challenge the validity of any such outrageous statute would be defeated by the reasoning the Court uses today: The Court's rationale would characterize action pursuant to such a statute as purely private action, which the State permits but does not compel, in an area not exclusively reserved to the State. . . .

[The dissenting opinion of MARSHALL, J., is omitted.]

Notes

1. *Lugar v. Edmondson Oil Co., Inc.*, 457 U.S. 922, 102 S.Ct. 2744, 73 L.Ed.2d 482 (1982) distinguished *Flagg Brothers* and found state action (5 to 4). Edmondson sued Lugar for a debt in Virginia state court. Under state law, Edmondson also secured a prejudgment writ of attachment after alleging (in an ex parte petition to the clerk of the state court) that Lugar was disposing or might dispose of his property to defeat his creditors. The county sheriff then executed the writ. After the levy there was a hearing on the propriety of the attachment, and the state judge ordered the attachment dismissed because Edmondson had failed to prove its allegations. However Edmondson still won the debt action and some of Lugar's property was sold to pay the debt. Lugar then sued Edmondson, claiming that it had deprived him of property (by the writ of attachment) without procedural due process of law, first, because it misused Virginia procedure, and, second, because the Virginia procedure itself (providing for an attachment after an ex parte petition) was unconstitutional.

Justice White, for the Court, articulated the basic test to determine when the deprivation of a federal right may be fairly attributed to the state:

> First, the deprivation must be caused by the exercise of some right or privilege created by the state or by a rule of conduct imposed by the state or by a person for whom the state is responsible. . . . Second, the party charged with the deprivation must be a person who may fairly be said to be a state actor. This may be because he is a state official, because he has acted together with or has obtained significant aid from state officials, or because his conduct is otherwise chargeable to the state. Without a limit such as this, private partners could face constitutional litigation whenever they seek to rely on some state rule governing their interactions with the community surrounding them.

For example in *Flagg Brothers* the state was responsible for the section of the New York Commercial Code subject to challenge, but the warehouseman who acted pursuant to this statute was a private party. Something more was needed. What would convert the private party into a state actor "might vary with the circumstances."

Edmondson's alleged private *mis*use of the state statute could not be attributed to the state, but the procedural scheme that the statute created was state action. Similarly a private party's joint participation with state officials in the seizure of private property makes that private party a state actor. This case, unlike *Flagg Brothers,* involved state action because the sheriff attached property on the ex parte application of Edmondson. Thus, there was a cause of action for damages for alleged violation of procedural due process.

2. *American Manufacturers Mutual Insurance Co. v. Sullivan,* , 526 U.S. 40, 119 S.Ct. 977, 143 L.Ed.2d 130 (1999). The Pennsylvania workers' compensation system provided that an employer or insurer may withhold payments for disputed medical treatment pending an independent review that decides if the treatment is "reasonable and necessary." Rehnquist, C.J., for the Court, held that a *private* insurer's decision to withhold payment for disputed medical treatment is not "state action" for purposes of the Fourteenth Amendment.

The private insurer's decision to withhold payment of benefits pending this "utilization review" is not "fairly attributable" to the state under *Lugar* because the state did not "significantly encourage" or "authorize" the private insurers' actions. The state's decision could be seen as state inaction, because it in effect restored to the insurers an option (which they historically exercised before the adoption of the worker's compensation law) to defer payment of a bill until it was substantiated. There is no state action when private entities take action that has the mere approval or acquiescence of the state.

In addition, the private insurers are not exercising powers that traditionally belong to the state, because the state is not obligated by its statutory or constitutional scheme to provide medical treatment or workers' compensation benefits to injured workers. Instead Pennsylvania's law imposes that obligation on employers.

The Court also held that there was no deprivation of "property" without due process because the state law does not entitle the worker to payment of *all* medical services once the employer's initial liability is established. Instead, the entitlement is only for "reasonable" and "necessary" medical treatment. In other words, the claimants do not have a property interest in being paid for medical treatments *prior* to a determination that they are reasonable and necessary.

EDMONSON v. LEESVILLE CONCRETE CO., INC.
500 U.S. 614, 111 S.Ct. 2077, 114 L.Ed.2d 660 (1991).

JUSTICE KENNEDY delivered the opinion of the Court.

We must decide in the case before us whether a private litigant in a civil case may use peremptory challenges to exclude jurors on account of their race. Recognizing the impropriety of racial bias in the courtroom, we hold the race-based exclusion violates the equal protection rights of the challenged jurors.

[Edmonson sued Leesville Concrete Co. for negligent personal injury. Leesville used two of its three peremptory challenges authorized by statute to remove black persons from the prospective jury. Edmonson, who is black, asked the trial court to require Leesville to articulate a race-neutral explanation for the peremptory challenges. The trial court refused, ruling that *Batson v. Kentucky,* § 8–2.11 (which held that it violated equal protection for state officials to use peremptory challenges to strike blacks from the jury) does not apply in civil proceedings. A jury of 11 whites and one black then ruled for Edmonson, assessing total damages of $90,000, but awarding him only $18,000 because of his contributory negligence.]

That an act violates the Constitution when committed by a government official, however, does not answer the question whether the same act offends constitutional guarantees if committed by a private litigant or his attorney.... We begin our discussion within the framework for state action analysis set forth in *Lugar [v. Edmondson Oil Co.].* There we considered the state action question in the context of a due process challenge to a State's procedure allowing private parties to obtain prejudgment attachments. We asked first whether the claimed constitutional deprivation resulted from the exercise of a right or privilege having its source in state authority, and second, whether the private party charged with the deprivation could be described in all fairness as a state actor.

There can be no question that the first part of the *Lugar* inquiry is satisfied here. By their very nature, peremptory challenges have no significance outside a court of law. Their sole purpose is to permit litigants to assist the government in the selection of an impartial trier of fact.... Peremptory challenges are permitted only when the government, by statute or decisional law, deems it appropriate to allow parties to exclude a given number of persons who otherwise would satisfy the requirements for service on the petit jury....

Given that the statutory authorization [28 U.S.C.A. § 1870] for the challenges exercised in this case is clear, the remainder of our state action analysis centers around the second part of the *Lugar* test, whether a private litigant in all fairness must be deemed a government actor in the use of peremptory challenges. Although we have recognized that this aspect of the analysis is often a factbound inquiry, our cases disclose certain principles of general application. [I]t is relevant to examine the following: the extent to which the actor relies on governmental assistance and benefits, *Burton v. Wilmington Parking Authority,* whether the actor is performing a traditional governmental function, see *Terry v. Adams; Marsh v. Alabama;* and whether the injury caused is aggravated in a unique way by the incidents of governmental authority, see *Shelley v. Kraemer.* Based on our application of these three principles to the circumstances here, we hold that the exercise of peremptory challenges by the defendant in the District Court was pursuant to a course of state action.

Although private use of state-sanctioned private remedies or procedures does not rise, by itself, to the level of state action, our cases have found state action when private parties make extensive use of state procedures with "the overt, significant assistance of state officials." It cannot be disputed that, without the overt, significant participation of the government, the peremptory challenge system, as well as the jury trial system of which it is a part, simply could not exist. [A] private party could not exercise its peremptory challenges absent the overt, significant assistance of the court.... By enforcing a discriminatory peremptory challenge, the court "has not only made itself a party to the [biased act], but has elected to place its power, property and prestige behind the [alleged] discrimination." *Burton v. Wilmington Parking Authority.* In so doing, the government has "create[d] the legal framework governing the [challenged] conduct," and in a significant way has involved itself with invidious discrimination.

[W]e next consider whether the action in question involves the performance of a traditional function of the government. A traditional function of government is evident here. The peremptory challenge is used in selecting an entity that is a quintessential governmental body, having no attributes of a private actor. The jury exercises the power of the court and of the government that confers the court's jurisdiction. [I]n all jurisdictions a true verdict will be incorporated in a judgment enforceable by the court. These are traditional functions of government, not of a select, private group beyond the reach of the Constitution. If a government confers on a private body the power to choose the government's employees or officials, the private body will be bound by the constitutional mandate of race-neutrality. *Rendell–Baker v. Kohn.* At least a plurality of the Court recognized this principle in *Terry v. Adams* [§ 7–2]....

The principle that the selection of state officials, other than through election by all qualified voters, may constitute state action applies with even greater force in the context of jury selection through the use of peremptory challenges. Though the motive of a peremptory challenge may be to protect a private interest, the objective of jury selection proceedings is to determine representation on a governmental body. Were it not for peremptory challenges, there would be no question that the entire process of determining who will serve on the jury constitutes state action. The fact that the government delegates some portion of this power to private litigants does not change the governmental character of the power exercised. The delegation of authority that in *Terry* occurred without the aid of legislation occurs here through explicit statutory authorization.

We find respondent's reliance on *Polk County v. Dodson* [§ 7–4] unavailing. In that case, we held that a public defender is not a state actor in his general representation of a criminal defendant, even though he may be in his performance of other official duties. While recognizing the employment relation between the public defender and the government, we noted that the relation is otherwise adversarial in nature.

...In the ordinary context of civil litigation in which the government is not a party, an adversarial relation does not exist between the government and a private litigant. In the jury selection process, the government and private litigants work for the same end. Just as a government employee was deemed a private actor because of his purpose and functions in *Dodson,* so here a private entity becomes a government actor for the limited purpose of using peremptories during jury selection. The selection of jurors represents a unique governmental function delegated to private litigants by the government and attributable to the government for purposes of invoking constitutional protections against discrimination by reason of race....

In the case before us, the parties do not act pursuant to any contractual relation with the government. Here, as in most civil cases, the initial decision whether to sue at all, the selection of counsel, and any number of ensuing tactical choices in the course of discovery and trial may be without the requisite governmental character to be deemed state action. That cannot be said of the exercise of peremptory challenges, however; when private litigants participate in the selection of jurors, they serve an important function within the government and act with its substantial assistance. If peremptory challenges based on race were permitted, persons could be required by summons to be put at risk of open and public discrimination as a condition of their participation in the justice system. The injury to excluded jurors would be the direct result of governmental delegation and participation.

Finally, we note that the injury caused by the discrimination is made more severe because the government permits it to occur within the courthouse itself. Few places are a more real expression of the constitutional authority of the government than a courtroom, where the law itself unfolds.

[We also conclude that] an opposing litigant may raise the excluded person's rights on his or her behalf [because] persons excluded from jury service will be unable to protect their own rights applies with equal force in a civil trial....

It remains to consider whether a prima facie case of racial discrimination has been established in the case before us, requiring Leesville to offer race-neutral explanations for its peremptory challenges. In *Batson,* we held that determining whether a prima facie case has been established requires consideration of all relevant circumstances, including whether there has been a pattern of strikes against members of a particular race. The same approach applies in the civil context, and we leave it to the trial courts in the first instance to develop evidentiary rules for implementing our decision.

The judgment is reversed, and the case is remanded for further proceedings consistent with our opinion.

It is so ordered.

JUSTICE O'CONNOR, with whom THE CHIEF JUSTICE [REHNQUIST] and JUSTICE SCALIA join, dissenting.

The Court concludes that the action of a private attorney exercising a peremptory challenge is attributable to the government and therefore may compose a constitutional violation. This conclusion is based on little more than that the challenge occurs in the course of a trial. Not everything that happens in a courtroom is state action.... The government erects the platform; it does not thereby become responsible for all that occurs upon it. As much as we would like to eliminate completely from the courtroom the specter of racial discrimination, the Constitution does not sweep that broadly. Because I believe that a peremptory strike by a private litigant is fundamentally a matter of private choice and not state action, I dissent....

The peremptory challenge "allow[s] parties," in this case *private* parties, to exclude potential jurors. It is the nature of a peremptory that its exercise is left wholly within the discretion of the litigant.... By allowing the litigant to strike jurors for even the most subtle of discerned biases, the peremptory challenge fosters both the perception and reality of an impartial jury. In both criminal and civil trials, the peremptory challenge is a mechanism for the exercise of *private* choice in the pursuit of fairness. The peremptory is, by design, an enclave of private action in a government-managed proceeding.

The Court amasses much ostensible evidence of the Federal Government's "overt, significant participation" in the peremptory process. Most of this evidence is irrelevant to the issue at hand. ...All of this activity, as well as the trial judge's control over *voir dire,* are merely prerequisites to the use of a peremptory challenge; they do not constitute participation *in* the challenge. That these actions may be necessary to a peremptory challenge—in the sense that there could be no such challenge without a venire from which to select—no more makes the challenge state action than the building of roads and provision of public transportation makes state action of riding on a bus.

The entirety of the Government's actual participation in the peremptory process boils down to a single fact: "When a lawyer exercises a peremptory challenge, the judge advises the juror he or she has been excused." The alleged state action here is a far cry from that the Court found, for example, in *Shelley v. Kraemer* [where the] coercive power of the State was necessary in order to enforce the private choice of those who had created the covenants: "[B]ut for the active intervention of the state courts, supported by the full panoply of state power, petitioners would have been free to occupy the properties in question without restraint." Moreover, the courts in *Shelley* were asked to enforce a facially discriminatory contract. In contrast, peremptory challenges are "exercised without a reason stated [and] without inquiry." A judge does not "significantly encourage" discrimination by the mere act of excusing a juror in response to an unexplained request. [Also, the state courts in *Shelley* used coercive force to impose conformance on parties who did not wish to discriminate. "Enforcement of peremptory challenges, on the other hand, does not compel anyone to discriminate; the discrimination is wholly a matter of private choice....

The Court relies also on *Burton v. Wilmington Parking Authority.* But the decision in that case depended on the perceived symbiotic relationship between a restaurant and the state parking authority from whom it leased space in a public building. [T]he government's involvement in the use of peremptory challenges falls far short of "interdependence" or "joint participation." Whatever the continuing vitality of *Burton* beyond its facts, see *Jackson v. Metropolitan Edison Co.,* it does not support the Court's conclusion here.

Jackson is a more appropriate analogy to this case. Metropolitan Edison terminated Jackson's electrical service under authority granted it by the State, pursuant to a procedure approved by the state utility commission. Nonetheless, we held that Jackson could not challenge the termination procedure on due process grounds. The termination was not state action because the State had done nothing to encourage the particular termination practice. . . . To the same effect is *Flagg Bros., Inc. v. Brooks* . . . .

"The essential nature of the peremptory challenge is that it is one exercised without a reason stated, without inquiry and without being subject to the court's control." The government neither encourages nor approves such challenges. Accordingly, there is no "overt, significant participation" by the government. The Court errs also when it concludes that the exercise of a peremptory challenge is a traditional government function. [T]he "tradition" is one of unguided private choice. . . .

JUSTICE SCALIA, dissenting. . . .

The concrete benefits of the Court's newly discovered constitutional rule are problematic. It will not necessarily be a net help rather than hindrance to minority litigants in obtaining racially diverse juries. In criminal cases, *Batson v. Kentucky,* already prevents the *prosecution* from using race-based strikes. The effect of today's decision (which logically must apply to criminal prosecutions) will be to prevent the *defendant* from doing so—so that the minority defendant can no longer seek to prevent an all-white jury, or to seat as many jurors of his own race as possible. . . . *Both* sides have peremptory challenges [in civil cases], and they are sometimes used to *assure* rather than to *prevent* a racially diverse jury.

The concrete costs of today's decision, on the other hand, are not at all doubtful; and they are enormous. We have now added to the duties of already-submerged state and federal trial courts the obligation to assure that race is not included among the other factors (sex, age, religion, political views, economic status) used by private parties in exercising their peremptory challenges. . . . Thus, yet another complexity is added to an increasingly Byzantine system of justice that devotes more and more of its energy to sideshows and less and less to the merits of the case. . . .

Notes

1. Justice Kennedy argued that one reason there was state action was because "an adversarial relation does not exist between the government and

a private litigant. In the jury selection process, the government and private litigants work for the same end." Relying on this distinction, the Georgia Supreme Court ruled that a criminal defendant may use racially discriminatory peremptory challenges, because the criminal defendant and the government are in an adversarial relation. In *Georgia v. McCollum,* 505 U.S. 42, 112 S.Ct. 2348, 120 L.Ed.2d 33 (1992), Blackmun, J., for the Court, dismissed this argument: "the fact that a defendant exercises a peremptory challenge to further his interest in acquittal does not conflict with a finding of state action." The Court then held that the Constitution prohibits a criminal defendant from engaging in purposeful racial discrimination when exercising peremptory challenges. Blackmun also stated: "But there is a distinction between exercising a peremptory challenge to discriminate invidiously against jurors on account of race and exercising a peremptory challenge to remove an individual juror who harbors racial prejudice." O'Connor, J. and Scalia, J., each filed dissenting opinions. O'Connor objected to the majority "spinning out a theory that defendants and their lawyers transmogrify from government adversaries into state actors when they exercise a peremptory challenge, and then change back to perform other defense functions."

2. *J.E.B. v. Alabama,* 511 U.S. 127, 114 S.Ct. 1419, 128 L.Ed.2d 89 (1994) held (6 to 3) that the Equal Protection Clause prohibits discrimination in jury selection on the basis of sex, or "on the assumption that an individual will be biased in a particular case for no reason other than the fact that the person happens to be a woman or happens to be a man." The Court then remanded a case where an all-female jury found the putative father to be the father of the child; the state had used 9 of its 10 peremptory strikes to remove male jurors.

7–7. "MIRROR IMAGE" CASES

NATIONAL COLLEGIATE ATHLETIC ASSOCIATION v. TARKANIAN
488 U.S. 179, 109 S.Ct. 454, 102 L.Ed.2d 469 (1988).

JUSTICE STEVENS delivered the opinion of the Court.

When he became head basketball coach at University of Nevada, Las Vegas (UNLV) in 1973, Jerry Tarkanian inherited a team with a mediocre 14–14 record. App. 188, 205. Four years later the team won 29 out of 32 games and placed third in the championship tournament sponsored by the National Collegiate Athletic Association (NCAA), to which UNLV belongs.

Yet in September 1977 UNLV informed Tarkanian that it was going to suspend him. [T]he impetus was a report by the NCAA detailing 38 violations of NCAA rules by UNLV personnel, including 10 involving Tarkanian. The NCAA had placed the University's basketball team on probation for two years and ordered UNLV to show cause why the NCAA should not impose further penalties unless UNLV severed all ties during the probation between its intercollegiate athletic program and Tarkanian.

Facing demotion and a drastic cut in pay, Tarkanian brought suit in Nevada state court, alleging that he had been deprived of his Fourteenth Amendment due process rights in violation of 42 U.S.C. § 1983. Ultimately Tarkanian obtained injunctive relief and an award of attorney's fees against both UNLV and the NCAA. NCAA's liability may be upheld only if its participation in the events that led to Tarkanian's suspension constituted "state action" prohibited by the Fourteenth Amendment ... We granted certiorari to review the Nevada Supreme Court's holding that the NCAA engaged in state action when it conducted its investigation and recommended that Tarkanian be disciplined. We now reverse....

UNLV is a branch of the University of Nevada, a state-funded institution. [T]he executives of UNLV unquestionably act under color of state law.

The NCAA is an unincorporated association of approximately 960 members, including virtually all public and private universities and four-year colleges conducting major athletic programs in the United States. Basic policies of the NCAA are determined by the members at annual conventions. Between conventions, the Association is governed by its Council, which appoints various committees to implement specific programs.

One of the NCAA's fundamental policies "is to maintain intercollegiate athletics as an integral part of the educational program and the athlete as an integral part of the student body, and by so doing, retain a clear line of demarcation between college athletics and professional sports." It has therefore adopted rules, which it calls "legislation," governing the conduct of the intercollegiate athletic programs of its members. This NCAA legislation applies to a variety of issues, such as academic standards for eligibility, admissions, financial aid, and the recruiting of student athletes. By joining the NCAA, each member agrees to abide by and to enforce such rules.

The NCAA's bylaws provide that its enforcement program shall be administered by a Committee on Infractions. [T]he Committee may order a member institution to show cause why that member should not suffer further penalties unless it imposes a prescribed discipline on an employee; it is not authorized, however, to sanction a member institution's employees directly....

During its investigation of UNLV, the Committee on Infractions included three law professors, a mathematics professor, and the dean of a graduate school. Four of them were on the faculties of state institutions; one represented a private university....

The Committee proposed a series of sanctions against UNLV, including a two-year period of probation during which its basketball team could not participate in post-season games or appear on television. The Committee also requested UNLV to show cause why additional penalties should not be imposed against UNLV if it failed to discipline Tarkanian by removing him completely from the University's intercollegiate athletic program during the probation period. [T]he Council on August 25, 1977 unanimously approved the Committee's investigation and hearing process and adopted all its recommendations.

[The UNLV vice president] advised the president that he had three options:

> "1. Reject the sanction requiring us to disassociate Coach Tarkanian from the athletic program and take the risk of still heavier sanctions, *e.g.,* possible extra years of probation.

> "2. Recognize the University's delegation to the NCAA of the power to act as ultimate arbiter of these matters, thus reassigning Mr. Tarkanian from his present position—though tenured and without adequate notice—even while believing that the NCAA was wrong.

> "3. Pull out of the NCAA completely on the grounds that you will not execute what you hold to be their unjust judgments."

[T]he president accepted the second option and notified Tarkanian [who] filed an action in Nevada state court for declaratory and injunctive relief against UNLV and [eventually, against the NCAA. After various procedural maneuvers and lengthy delays,] the trial judge conducted a two-week bench trial and resolved the issues in Tarkanian's favor. The court concluded that NCAA's conduct constituted state action for jurisdictional and constitutional purposes, and that its decision was arbitrary and capricious. It reaffirmed its earlier injunction barring UNLV from disciplining Tarkanian or otherwise enforcing the Confidential Report. Additionally, it enjoined the NCAA from conducting "any further proceedings against the University," from enforcing its show-cause order, and from taking any other action against the University that had been recommended in the Confidential Report. [T]he Nevada trial court [also] awarded Tarkanian attorney's fees of almost $196,000, 90% of which was to be paid by the NCAA. The NCAA appealed both the injunction and the fee order. Not surprisingly, UNLV, which had scored a total victory except for its obligation to pay a fraction of Tarkanian's fees, did not appeal. [Subject to some modifications, the Nevada Supreme Court affirmed.]

In the typical case raising a state action issue, a private party has taken the decisive step that caused the harm to the plaintiff, and the question is whether the State was sufficiently involved to treat that decisive conduct as state action. [I]n the usual case we ask whether the State provided a mantle of authority that enhanced the power of the harm-causing individual actor.

This case uniquely mirrors the traditional state action case. Here the final act challenged by Tarkanian—his suspension—was committed by UNLV. A state university without question is a state actor. When it decides to impose a serious disciplinary sanction upon one of its tenured employees, it must comply with the terms of the Due Process Clause of the Fourteenth Amendment to the Federal Constitution. Thus when

UNLV notified Tarkanian that he was being separated from all relations with the University's basketball program, it acted under color of state law within the meaning of 42 U.S.C. § 1983.

The mirror image presented in this case requires us to step through an analytical looking glass to resolve it. Clearly UNLV's conduct was influenced by the rules and recommendations of the NCAA, the private party. But it was UNLV, the state entity, that actually suspended Tarkanian. Thus the question is not whether UNLV participated to a critical extent in the NCAA's activities, but whether UNLV's actions in compliance with the NCAA rules and recommendations turned the NCAA's conduct into state action.

[T]he NCAA's several hundred other public and private member institutions each similarly affected those policies. Those institutions, the vast majority of which were located in States other than Nevada, did not act under color of Nevada law. It necessarily follows that the source of the legislation adopted by the NCAA is not Nevada but the collective membership, speaking through an organization that is independent of any particular State.[13]

State action nonetheless might lie if UNLV, by embracing the NCAA's rules, transformed them into state rules and the NCAA into a state actor. UNLV engaged in state action when it adopted the NCAA's rules to govern its own behavior, but that would be true even if UNLV had taken no part in the promulgation of those rules.... UNLV retained the authority to withdraw from the NCAA and establish its own standards.... Neither UNLV's decision to adopt the NCAA's standards nor its minor role in their formulation is a sufficient reason for concluding that the NCAA was acting under color of Nevada law when it promulgated standards governing athlete recruitment, eligibility, and academic performance.

Tarkanian further asserts that the NCAA's investigation, enforcement proceedings, and consequent recommendations constituted state action because they resulted from a delegation of power by UNLV.... It is, of course, true that a state may delegate authority to a private party and thereby make that party a state actor. Thus, we recently held that a private physician who had contracted with a state prison to attend to the inmates' medical needs was a state actor. *West v. Atkins,* 487 U.S. 42, 108 S.Ct. 2250, 101 L.Ed.2d 40 (1988). But UNLV delegated no power to the NCAA to take specific action against any University employee. The commitment by UNLV to adhere to NCAA enforcement procedures was enforceable only by sanctions that the NCAA might impose on UNLV itself.

---

13. The situation would, of course, be different if the membership consisted entirely of institutions located within the same State, many of them public institutions created by the same sovereign. The dissent apparently agrees that the NCAA was not acting under color of state law in its relationships with private universities, which constitute the bulk of its membership. See *post,* at n. 2.

Indeed, the notion that UNLV's promise to cooperate in the NCAA enforcement proceedings was tantamount to a partnership agreement or the transfer of certain University powers to the NCAA is belied by the history of this case. It is quite obvious that UNLV used its best efforts to retain its winning coach—a goal diametrically opposed to the NCAA's interest in ascertaining the truth of its investigators' reports. During the several years that the NCAA investigated the alleged violations, the NCAA and UNLV acted much more like adversaries than like partners engaged in a dispassionate search for the truth. The NCAA cannot be regarded as an agent of UNLV for purposes of that proceeding. It is more correctly characterized as an agent of its remaining members which, as competitors of UNLV, had an interest in the effective and evenhanded enforcement of NCAA's recruitment standards. Just as a state-compensated public defender acts in a private capacity when she represents a private client in a conflict against the State, *Polk County v. Dodson,* 454 U.S. 312, 320, 102 S.Ct. 445, 450, 70 L.Ed.2d 509 (1981), the NCAA is properly viewed as a private actor at odds with the State when it represents the interests of its entire membership in an investigation of one public university.[16]

The NCAA enjoyed no governmental powers to facilitate its investigation.[17] It had no power to subpoena witnesses, to impose contempt sanctions, or to assert sovereign authority over any individual. Its greatest authority was to threaten sanctions against UNLV, with the ultimate sanction being expulsion of the University from membership. [T]he NCAA did not—indeed, could not—directly discipline Tarkanian or any other state university employee.... UNLV could have retained Tarkanian and risked additional sanctions, perhaps even expulsion from the NCAA, or it could have withdrawn voluntarily from the Association.

Finally, Tarkanian argues that the power of the NCAA is so great that the UNLV had no practical alternative to compliance with its

---

16. Tarkanian argues that UNLV and the NCAA were "joint participants" in state action. He would draw support from *Burton v. Wilmington Parking Authority,* .... In the case before us the state and private parties' relevant interests do not coincide, as they did in *Burton;* rather, they have clashed throughout the investigation, the attempt to discipline Tarkanian, and this litigation. UNLV and the NCAA were antagonists, not joint participants, and the NCAA may not be deemed a state actor on this ground.

17. In *Dennis v. Sparks,* 449 U.S. 24, 101 S.Ct. 183, 66 L.Ed.2d 185 (1980), on which the dissent relies, the parties had entered into a corrupt agreement to perform a judicial act. As we explained:

"[H]ere the allegations were that an official act of the defendant judge was the product of a corrupt conspiracy involving bribery of the judge. Under these allegations, the private parties conspiring with the judge were acting under color of state law; and it is of no consequence in this respect that the judge himself is immune from damages liability. Immunity does not change the character of the judge's action or that of his co-conspirators. Indeed, his immunity is dependent on the challenged conduct being an official judicial act within his statutory jurisdiction, broadly construed.... " *Id.,* at 28–29, 101 S.Ct., at 186–187 (footnote and citations omitted).

In this case there is no suggestion of any impropriety respecting the agreement between the NCAA and UNLV.... Cf. *Adickes v. Kress & Co.,* 398 U.S. 144, 149–150 & n. 5, 90 S.Ct. 1598, 1603–1604 & n. 5, 26 L.Ed.2d 142 (1970)(private restaurant that denied plaintiff service in violation of federal law would be liable as state actor upon proof that it conspired with police officer to deprive plaintiff of her constitutional rights).

demands. We are not at all sure this is true,[19] but even if we assume that a private monopolist can impose its will on a state agency by a threatened refusal to deal with it, it does not follow that such a private party is therefore acting under color of state law. Cf. *Jackson* [*v. Metropolitan Edison Co.*, § 7–5] (State's conferral of monopoly status does not convert private party into state actor).

In final analysis the question is whether "the conduct allegedly causing the deprivation of a federal right [can] be fairly attributable to the State." It would be ironic indeed to conclude that the NCAA's imposition of sanctions against UNLV—sanctions that UNLV and its counsel, including the Attorney General of Nevada, steadfastly opposed during protracted adversary proceedings—is fairly attributable to the State of Nevada. It would be more appropriate to conclude that UNLV has conducted its athletic program under color of the policies adopted by the NCAA, rather than that those policies were developed and enforced under color of Nevada law.

The judgment of the Nevada Supreme Court is reversed and the case is remanded to that court for further proceedings not inconsistent with this opinion.

It is so ordered.

JUSTICE WHITE, with whom JUSTICE BRENNAN, JUSTICE MARSHALL, and JUSTICE O'CONNOR join, dissenting.

All agree that UNLV, a public university, is a state actor, and that the suspension of Jerry Tarkanian, a public employee, was state action. The question here is whether the NCAA acted jointly with UNLV in suspending Tarkanian and thereby also became a state actor. I would hold that it did.

[T]he situation presented by this case is not unknown to us and certainly is not unique. In both *Adickes v. S.H. Kress & Co.*, 398 U.S. 144, 90 S.Ct. 1598, 26 L.Ed.2d 142 (1970), and *Dennis v. Sparks*, 449 U.S. 24, 101 S.Ct. 183, 66 L.Ed.2d 185 (1980), we faced the question of whether private parties could be held to be state actors in cases in which the final or decisive act was carried out by a state official. In both cases we held that the private parties could be found to be state actors, if they were "jointly engaged with state officials in the challenged action."

The facts of *Dennis* are illustrative. In *Dennis,* a state trial judge enjoined the production of minerals from oil leases owned by the plaintiff. The injunction was later dissolved on appeal as having been issued illegally. The plaintiff then filed suit under 42 U.S.C. § 1983, alleging that the judge had conspired with the party seeking the original injunction—a private corporation—the sole owner of the corporation, and the two sureties on the injunction bond to deprive the plaintiff of due process by corruptly issuing the injunction. We held unanimously

---

19. [T]hat UNLV's options were unpalatable does not mean that they were nonexistent.

that under the facts as alleged the private parties were state actors because they were "willful participant[s] in joint action with the State or its agents." See also *Adickes, supra* (plaintiff entitled to relief under § 1983 against private party if she can prove that private party and police officer "reached an understanding" to cause her arrest on impermissible grounds).

On the facts of the present case, the NCAA acted jointly with UNLV in suspending Tarkanian. First, Tarkanian was suspended for violations of NCAA rules, which UNLV embraced in its agreement with the NCAA. . . . Second, the NCAA and UNLV also agreed that the NCAA would conduct the hearings concerning violations of its rules. . . . As a result of this agreement, the NCAA conducted the very hearings the Nevada Supreme Court held to have violated Tarkanian's right to procedural due process. Third, the NCAA and UNLV agreed that the findings of fact made by the NCAA at the hearings it conducted would be binding on UNLV.

[I]t was the NCAA's findings that Tarkanian had violated NCAA rules, made at NCAA-conducted hearings, all of which were agreed to by UNLV in its membership agreement with the NCAA, that resulted in Tarkanian's suspension by UNLV. On these facts, the NCAA was "jointly engaged with [UNLV] officials in the challenged action," and therefore was a state actor. See *Dennis, supra.*

[T]he majority relies on the fact that the NCAA did not have any power to take action directly against Tarkanian as indicating that the NCAA was not a state actor. But the same was true in *Dennis:* the private parties did not have any power to issue an injunction against the plaintiff. Only the trial judge, using his authority granted under state law, could impose the injunction. Next, the majority points out that UNLV was free to withdraw from the NCAA at any time. . . . But of course the trial judge in *Dennis* could have withdrawn from his agreement at any time as well. . . .

Finally, the majority relies extensively on the fact that the NCAA and UNLV were adversaries throughout the proceedings before the NCAA. [T]his opportunity for opposition, provided for by the terms of the membership agreement between UNLV and the NCAA, does not undercut the agreement itself. Surely our decision in *Dennis* would not have been different had the private parties permitted the trial judge to seek to persuade them that he should not grant the injunction before finally holding the judge to his agreement with them to do so. The key there, as with any conspiracy, is that ultimately the parties agreed to take the action. . . .

Notes

1. If the University of Nevada, Las Vegas (UNLV) had joined the NCAA in its appeal of both the injunction and the attorney's fee order (see footnotes 16, 17, supra), or had announced that it wanted to root out any

possible NCAA violations as much as the NCAA did, would that make the NCAA actions "state action"?

2. UNLV did not appeal the trial court judgment barring it from adopting the NCAA proposed discipline against Tarkanian, and was not a party to the United States Supreme Court decision. What happens next? If UNLV does not discipline Tarkanian, may the NCAA discipline UNLV? If the NCAA does seek to discipline UNLV, can the Nevada state courts enjoin the NCAA from interfering with the state injunction against UNLV?

3. In the wake of *Tarkanian*, some states considered legislation requiring that the NCAA provide more procedural due process in its investigations. Commentators criticized the NCAA on antitrust grounds, claiming that universities, in collusion with professional teams, created a monopoly to stifle competition for labor by setting players' salaries at roughly zero. By "acting as de facto farm clubs for the pros, universities have forced most young men, irrespective of their mental abilities, to attend college in order to play pro basketball and football. An inner-city kid with significant baseball talent can sign with a club when he leaves high school. A similar youth whose sport is basketball or football has to get accepted by and attend a college. Thus, scandal is inevitable. Universities, like members of any cartel, have an incentive to cheat; they hope to attract top athletics and keep in school kids who have neither an aptitude nor interest in higher education. [F]inancial benefits offered under the table to lure a top basketball or football player are precisely the sort provided openly to a stand-out baseball or hockey player. It is an unfair cartel agreement, not morality, that is violated. [T]he NCAA is about money, not student athletics." Bandow, The Real NCAA Scandal, Wall St. Jrl., June 21, 1991, at A12, col. 4–6.

Chapter 8

EQUAL PROTECTION

8–1. TRADITIONAL EQUAL PROTECTION

RAILWAY EXPRESS AGENCY, INC. v. NEW YORK
336 U.S. 106, 69 S.Ct. 463, 93 L.Ed. 533 (1949).

MR. JUSTICE DOUGLAS delivered the opinion of the Court.

Section 124 of the Traffic Regulations of the City of New York promulgated by the Police Commissioner provides:

> No person shall operate, or cause to be operated, in or upon any street an advertising vehicle; provided that nothing herein contained shall prevent the putting of business notices upon business delivery vehicles, so long as such vehicles are engaged in the usual business or regular work of the owner and not used merely or mainly for advertising.

Appellant is engaged in a nation-wide express business. It operates about 1,900 trucks in New York City and sells the space on the exterior sides of these trucks for advertising. That advertising is for the most part unconnected with its own business. It was convicted in the magistrate's court and fined....

The Court of Special Sessions concluded that advertising on vehicles using the streets of New York City constitutes a distraction to vehicle drivers and to pedestrians alike and therefore affects the safety of the public in the use of the streets. We do not sit to weigh evidence on the due process issue in order to determine whether the regulation is sound or appropriate; nor is it our function to pass judgment on its wisdom....

The question of equal protection of the laws is pressed more strenuously on us. It is pointed out that the regulation draws the line between advertisements of products sold by the owner of the truck and general advertisements. It is argued that unequal treatment on the basis of such a distinction is not justified by the aim and purpose of the regulation. It is said, for example, that one of appellant's trucks carrying the advertise-

612

ment of a commercial house would not cause any greater distraction of pedestrians and vehicle drivers than if the commercial house carried the same advertisement on its own truck. Yet the regulation allows the latter to do what the former is forbidden from doing. It is therefore contended that the classification which the regulation makes has no relation to the traffic problem since a violation turns not on what kind of advertisements are carried on trucks but on whose trucks they are carried.

That, however, is a superficial way of analyzing the problem, even if we assume that it is premised on the correct construction of the regulation. The local authorities may well have concluded that those who advertise their own wares on their trucks do not present the same traffic problem in view of the nature or extent of the advertising which they use. It would take a degree of omniscience which we lack to say that such is not the case. If that judgment is correct, the advertising displays that are exempt have less incidence on traffic than those of appellants.

We cannot say that that judgment is not an allowable one. Yet if it is, the classification has relation to the purpose for which it is made and does not contain the kind of discrimination against which the Equal Protection Clause affords protection. It is by such practical considerations based on experience rather than by theoretical inconsistencies that the question of equal protection is to be answered. And the fact that New York City sees fit to eliminate from traffic this kind of distraction but does not touch what may be even greater ones in a different category, such as the vivid displays on Times Square, is immaterial. It is no requirement of equal protection that all evils of the same genus be eradicated or none at all....

Affirmed.

MR. JUSTICE RUTLEDGE acquiesces in the Court's opinion and judgment, *dubitante* on the question of equal protection of the laws.

MR. JUSTICE JACKSON, concurring.

There are two clauses of the Fourteenth Amendment which this Court may invoke to invalidate ordinances by which municipal governments seek to solve their local problems. One says that no state shall "deprive any person of life, liberty, or property, without due process of law." The other declares that no state shall "deny to any person within its jurisdiction the equal protection of the laws."

My philosophy as to the relative readiness with which we should resort to these two clauses is almost diametrically opposed to the philosophy which prevails on this Court.... The burden should rest heavily upon one who would persuade us to use the due process clause to strike down a substantive law or ordinance. Even its provident use against municipal regulations frequently disables all government—state, municipal and federal—from dealing with the conduct in question because the requirement of due process is also applicable to State and Federal Governments. Invalidation of a statute or an ordinance on due process grounds leaves ungoverned and ungovernable conduct which many people find objectionable.

Invocation of the equal protection clause, on the other hand, does not disable any governmental body from dealing with the subject at hand. It merely means that the prohibition or regulation must have a broader impact. I regard it as a salutary doctrine that cities, states and the Federal Government must exercise their powers so as not to discriminate between their inhabitants except upon some reasonable differentiation fairly related to the object of regulation. This equality is not merely abstract justice. The framers of the Constitution knew, and we should not forget today, that there is no more effective practical guaranty against arbitrary and unreasonable government than to require that the principles of law which officials would impose upon a minority must be imposed generally. Conversely, nothing opens the door to arbitrary action so effectively as to allow those officials to pick and choose only a few to whom they will apply legislation and thus to escape the political retribution that might be visited upon them if larger numbers were affected. Courts can take no better measure to assure that laws will be just than to require that laws be equal in operation....

In this case, if the City of New York should assume that display of any advertising on vehicles tends and intends to distract the attention of persons using the highways and to increase the dangers of its traffic, I should think it fully within its constitutional powers to forbid it all.... Instead of such general regulation of advertising, however, the City seeks to reduce the hazard only by saying that while some may, others may not exhibit such appeals. The same display, for example, advertising cigarettes, which this appellant is forbidden to carry on its trucks, may be carried on the trucks of a cigarette dealer and might on the trucks of this appellant if it dealt in cigarettes. And almost an identical advertisement, certainly one of equal size, shape, color and appearance, may be carried by this appellant if it proclaims its own offer to transport cigarettes. But it may not be carried so long as the message is not its own but a cigarette dealer's offer to sell the same cigarettes....

As a matter of principle and in view of my attitude toward the equal protection clause, I do not think differences of treatment under law should be approved on classification because of differences unrelated to the legislative purpose. The equal protection clause ceases to assure either equality or protection if it is avoided by any conceivable difference that can be pointed out between those bound and those left free....

The question in my mind comes to this. Where individuals contribute to an evil or danger in the same way and to the same degree, may those who do so for hire be prohibited, while those who do so for their own commercial ends but not for hire be allowed to continue? I think the answer has to be that the hireling may be put in a class by himself and may be dealt with differently than those who act on their own. But this is not merely because such a discrimination will enable the lawmaker to diminish the evil. That might be done by many classifications, which I should think wholly unsustainable. It is rather because there is a real difference between doing in self-interest and doing for hire, so that it is one thing to tolerate action from those who act on their own and it is another thing to permit the same action to be promoted for a price....

Notes

1. *Morey v. Doud,* 354 U.S. 457, 77 S.Ct. 1344, 1 L.Ed.2d 1485 (1957). The Illinois Community Currency Exchange Act required that any firm selling or issuing money orders in the State must secure a license and submit to state regulation. However the statute exempted from its coverage American Express Company money orders. The Court, per Burton, J., invalidated the law as a violation of equal protection. The Court found that the purpose of the Act was to afford the public continuing protection but the "discrimination in favor of the American Express Company does not conform to this purpose." Although American Express "is a responsible institution operating on a worldwide basis," its exemption from regulation will continue (unless the statute is amended) "whether or not the American Express Company retains its present characteristics." And competitors will be subject to the Act even if they are or become substantially identical to American Express. The Court reasoned that the statute created a closed class and, like those statutes giving an economic advantage to those engaged in a business as of a certain arbitrary date, it was a violation of equal protection.

Black, J., and Frankfurter, J., joined by Harlan, J., dissented.

City of New Orleans v. Dukes, 427 U.S. 297, 96 S.Ct. 2513, 49 L.Ed.2d 511 (1976)(per curiam). A New Orleans ordinance prohibited vendors selling foodstuffs from pushcarts in the Vieux Carre, French Quarter, unless the vendors had continuously operated the same business there for eight or more years prior to January 1, 1972. The Court of Appeals invalidated the legislation and the Supreme Court reversed:

> The record makes abundantly clear that the amended ordinance, including the "grandfather provision," is solely an economic regulation aimed at enhancing the vital role of the French Quarter's tourist-oriented charm in the economy of New Orleans. When local economic regulation is challenged solely as violating the Equal Protection Clause, this Court consistently defers to legislative determinations as to the desirability of particular statutory discriminations. Unless a classification trammels fundamental personal rights or is drawn upon inherently suspect distinctions such as race, religion, or alienage, our decisions presume the constitutionality of the statutory discriminations and require only that the classification challenged be rationally related to a legitimate state interest. States are accorded wide latitude in the regulation of their local economies under their police powers, and rational distinctions may be made with substantially less than mathematical exactitude. Legislatures may implement their program step by step, in such economic areas, adopting regulations that only partially ameliorate a perceived evil and deferring complete elimination of the evil to future regulations....

Nevertheless, relying on *Morey v. Doud,* as its "chief guide," the Court of Appeals held that even though the exemption of the two vendors was rationally related to legitimate city interests on the basis of facts extant when the ordinance was amended, the "grandfather clause" still could not stand because "the hypothesis that a present eight year veteran of the pushcart hot dog market in the Vieux Carre will continue to operate in a manner more consistent with the traditions of the Quarter than would any other operator is without foundation." ... *Morey v. Doud* ... was a needlessly intrusive judicial infringement on the State's legislative powers, and we have concluded that the equal protection analysis employed in that opinion should no longer be followed. *Morey* was the only case in the last half century to invalidate a wholly economic regulation solely on equal protection grounds, and we are now satisfied that the decision was erroneous. *Morey* is, as appellee and the Court of Appeals properly recognized, essentially indistinguishable from this case, but the decision so far departs from proper equal protection analysis in cases of exclusively economic regulation that it should be and it is, overruled.

2. The Court frequently cites *Lindsley v. Natural Carbonic Gas Co.,* 220 U.S. 61, 31 S.Ct. 337, 55 L.Ed. 369 (1911) as setting the proper test to determine the constitutionality of laws challenged under traditional, economic equal protection:

1. The equal protection clause of the Fourteenth Amendment does not take from the State the power to classify in the adoption of police laws, but admits of the exercise of a wide scope of discretion in that regard, and avoids what is done only when it is without any reasonable basis and therefore is purely arbitrary. 2. A classification having some reasonable basis does not offend against that clause merely because it is not made with mathematical nicety or because in practice it results in some inequality. 3. When the classification in such a law is called in question, if any state of facts reasonably can be conceived that would sustain it, the existence of that state of facts at the time the law was enacted must be assumed. 4. One who assails the classification in such a law must carry the burden of showing that it does not rest upon any reasonable basis, but is essentially arbitrary.

3. In *Metropolitan Life Insurance Co. v. Ward,* 470 U.S. 869, 105 S.Ct. 1676, 84 L.Ed.2d 751 (1985), the Court (5 to 4) surprised many observers by using the Equal Protection Clause to invalidate an Alabama statute that taxed out-of-state insurance companies at a higher rate than domestic insurance companies. All out-of-state insurance companies paid a tax ranging from 2% to 4% (depending on various conditions) on their gross premiums received from business conducted in Alabama. All domestic companies paid a flat 1% tax. A federal statute, the McCarran–Ferguson Act, exempts the insurance industry from Commerce Clause restrictions, so the Court did not invalidate the discriminatory tax on that ground. Instead, Justice Powell, for the Court, turned to the Equal Protection Clause.

Alabama justified its tax on the grounds that its purpose is to promote "the business of its domestic insurers *in Alabama* by penalizing foreign insurers who also want to do business in the State." (emphasis in original).

This purpose "is purely and completely discriminatory, designed only to favor domestic industry within the State, no matter what the cost to foreign corporations also seeking to do business there." The Equal Protection Clause was intended to prevent this "very sort of parochial discrimination."

A second purpose of the tax discrimination, the lower court found, was to encourage investment in Alabama and in its governmental securities. (By investing in specified Alabama assets and securities, a foreign company could reduce, but not eliminate, the differential on tax rates.) This purpose, the majority said, was also not legitimate "when furthered by discrimination." In footnote 10 the Court said:

> "This case does not involve or question, as the dissent suggests, the broad authority of a State to promote and regulate its own economy. We hold only that such regulation may not be accompanied by imposing discriminatorily higher taxes on nonresident corporations solely because they are nonresidents."

The Court then remanded so that the lower court could rule on the "legitimacy" of other alleged purposes.

Justice O'Connor, joined by Brennan, Marshall, and Rehnquist, JJ., dissented. It was "astonishing." and "[m]ost troubling" that the majority "discovers in the Equal Protection Clause an implied prohibition against classifications whose purpose is to give the 'home team' an advantage over interstate competitors even where Congress has authorized such advantages." It is dangerous to use the Equal Protection Clause to prohibit barriers to interstate business irrespective of the Commerce Clause. "The Commerce Clause is a flexible tool of economic policy that Congress may use as it sees fit, letting it lie dormant or invoking it to limit as well as promote the free flow of commerce. Doctrines of equal protection are constitutional limits that constrain the acts of federal and state legislatures alike." Sometimes, Congress approves "parochial favoritism." The majority, however, has placed the Equal Protection Clause "as an independent barrier if courts should determine that either Congress or a State has ventured the 'wrong' direction down what has become, by judicial fiat, the one-way street of the Commerce Clause."

Later that same term, in *Northeast Bancorp, Inc. v. Board of Governors,* 472 U.S. 159, 105 S.Ct. 2545, 86 L.Ed.2d 112 (1985), the Court found no violation of the Equal Protection Clause when Massachusetts enacted a law providing that an out-of-state bank could acquire an in-state bank only if the out-of-state bank had its principal place of business in one of the other New England States and that other State accorded equivalent reciprocal privileges to the banks of Massachusetts. Connecticut had a similar law. There was no dormant Commerce Clause problem because Congress had authorized regional bank acquisitions as provided for in the Massachusetts and Connecticut laws. The Court, with no dissents, distinguished *Metropolitan Life* as a case that had held that—

> "encouraging the formation of new domestic insurance companies within a State and encouraging capital investment in the State's assets and governmental securities were not, standing alone, legitimate state purposes which could permissibly be furthered by discriminating against out-of-state corporations in favor of local corporations. [T]he States in

question—Massachusetts and Connecticut—are not favoring local corporations at the expense of out-of-state corporations. They are favoring out-of-state corporations domiciled within the New England region over out-of-state corporations from other parts of the country, and to this extent their laws may be said to 'discriminate' against the latter."

The Court specifically referred to footnote 10 of *Metropolitan Life,* and concluded that, under the "traditional rational basis" test, the Massachusetts and Connecticut statutes were valid because of the desire to favor "widely dispersed control of banking." The laws combined "the beneficial effect of increasing the number of banking competitors with the need to preserve a close relationship between those in the community who need credit and those who provide credit."

4. *Allegheny Pittsburgh Coal Co. v. County Commission of Webster County, West Virginia,* 488 U.S. 336, 109 S.Ct. 633, 102 L.Ed.2d 688 (1989) unanimously held that a West Virginia county's tax assessments on real property violated the equal protection clause. The tax assessor valued the petitioner's real property on the basis of its recent purchase price, but made only minor modifications in the assessments of land that had not recently been sold, with the result of gross disparities in the assessed value of generally comparable land. A state "may divide different kinds of property into classes and assign to each class a different tax burden so long as those divisions and burdens are reasonable.... But West Virginia has not drawn such a distinction. Its Constitution and laws provide that all property of the kind held by petitioners shall be taxed as a rate uniform throughout the state according to its estimated market value." Petitioners have been subjected to "intentional systematic undervaluation by state officials" of comparable neighboring property in the same county. Their property has been assessed at about 8 to 35 times more than comparable neighboring property, and after more than a decade there has been little change. If "general adjustments are accurate enough over a short period of time to equalize the differences in proportion between the assessments of a class of property holders, the Equal Protection Clause is satisfied." But here, the County's adjustment policy would require more than 500 years to equalize the assessments.

In a footnote the Court added: "We need not and do not decide today whether the Webster County assessment method would stand on a different footing if it were the law of a State, generally applied, instead of the aberrational enforcement policy it appears to be." The Court noted that California had adopted such a policy of reassessing only for inflation or when the property is transferred or there is construction on it. The California system is based on the belief that the state "should not tax unrealized paper gains in the value of the property." Subsequently, *Nordlinger v. Hahn,* 505 U.S. 1, 112 S.Ct. 2326, 120 L.Ed.2d 1 (1992) held that this California property tax scheme was rational and did not violate the equal protection clause. Only Stevens, J., dissented.

FCC v. Beach Communications, Inc., 508 U.S. 307, 113 S.Ct. 2096, 124 L.Ed.2d 211 (1993). When Congress regulated the cable TV industry, it drew a distinction between facilities that serve separately owned and managed buildings versus those that serve one or more buildings under common ownership or management. The statute exempted from regulation cable facilities that fell in the latter category, if they provided services without using public rights-of-way. The D.C. Circuit held that this distinction was irrational, and therefore violated the implied equal protection component of the Fifth Amendment. The Supreme Court, without any dissents, reversed.

Thomas, J., for the Court emphasized that in "areas of social and economic policy, a statutory classification that neither proceeds along suspect lines nor infringes fundamental constitutional rights must be upheld against equal protection challenge if there is any reasonably conceivable state of facts that could provide a rational basis for the classification." "[B]ecause we never require a legislature to articulate its reasons for enacting a statute, it is entirely irrelevant for constitutional purposes whether the conceived reason for the challenged distinction actually motivated the legislature." The legislature's choice "may be based on rational speculation unsupported by evidence or empirical data." Particularly where the legislature engages in line drawing, there will be cases where persons with "an almost equally strong claim to favored treatment" are placed on different sides of the line. In this case it is "plausible" for Congress to assume that systems under common ownership "would typically be limited in size or would share some other attribute" such that regulations were not needed.

8–2. SUSPECT CLASSES AND OTHER CLASSIFICATIONS

8–2.1 Race

8–2.11 The Beginnings

STRAUDER v. WEST VIRGINIA
100 U.S. (10 Otto) 303, 25 L.Ed. 664 (1879).

MR. JUSTICE STRONG delivered the opinion of the court.

The plaintiff in error, a colored man was indicted for murder in the Circuit Court of Ohio County, in West Virginia, on the 20th of October, 1874, and upon trial was convicted and sentenced. [I]t is now, in substance, averred that at the trial in the State court the defendant (now plaintiff in error) was denied rights to which he was entitled under the Constitution and laws of the United States [because under state law blacks are ineligible to serve on the grand or petit jury.]

[The question] is not whether a colored man, when an indictment has been preferred against him, has a right to a grand or a petit jury composed in whole or in part of persons of his own race or color, but it is whether, in the composition or selection of jurors by whom he is to be indicted or tried, all persons of his race or color may be excluded by law, solely because of their race or color, so that by no possibility can any colored man sit upon the jury.

[The Fourteenth Amendment] is one of a series of constitutional provisions having a common purpose; namely, securing to a race recently emancipated, a race that through many generations had been held in slavery, all the civil rights that the superior race enjoy.... It was designed to assure to the colored race the enjoyment of all the civil rights that under the law are enjoyed by white persons, and to give to that race the protection of the general government, in that enjoyment, whenever it should be denied by the States. It not only gave citizenship and the privileges of citizenship to persons of color, but it denied to any State the power to withhold from them the equal protection of the laws.... What is this but declaring that the law in the States shall be the same for the black as for the white; that all persons, whether colored or white, shall stand equal before the laws of the States, and, in regard to the colored race, for whose protection the amendment was primarily designed, that no discrimination shall be made against them by law because of their color? The words of the amendment, it is true, are prohibitory, but they contain a necessary implication of a positive immunity, or right, most valuable to the colored race,—the right to exemption from unfriendly legislation against them distinctively as colored,—exemption from legal discriminations, implying inferiority in civil society, lessening the security of their enjoyment of the rights which others enjoy, and discriminations which are steps towards reducing them to the condition of a subject race.

That the West Virginia statute respecting juries—the statute that controlled the selection of the grand and petit jury in the case of the plaintiff in error—is such a discrimination ought not to be doubted. Nor would it be if the persons excluded by it were white men.... Nor if a law should be passed excluding all naturalized Celtic Irishmen, would there be any doubt of its inconsistency with the spirit of the amendment. The very fact that colored people are singled out and expressly denied by a statute all right to participate in the administration of the law, as jurors, because of their color, though they are citizens, and may be in other respects fully qualified, is practically a brand upon them, affixed by the law, an assertion of their inferiority, and a stimulant to that race prejudice which is an impediment to securing to individuals of the race that equal justice which the law aims to secure to all others....

We do not say that within the limits from which it is not excluded by the amendment a State may not prescribe the qualifications of its jurors, and in so doing make discriminations. It may confine the selection to males, to freeholders, to citizens, to persons within certain ages, or to persons having educational qualifications. We do not believe the Fourteenth Amendment was ever intended to prohibit this. Looking at its history, it is clear it had no such purpose. Its aim was against discrimination because of race or color.... It is not easy to comprehend how it can be said that while every white man is entitled to a trial by a jury selected from persons of his own race or color, or, rather, selected without discrimination against his color, and a negro is not, the latter is equally protected by the law with the former....

The judgment of the Supreme Court of West Virginia will be reversed, and the case remitted with instructions to reverse the judgment of the Circuit Court of Ohio county; and it is

So ordered.

[The dissenting opinion of FIELD, J., joined by CLIFFORD, J., is omitted.]

Notes

1. *Batson v. Kentucky,* 476 U.S. 79, 106 S.Ct. 1712, 90 L.Ed.2d 69 (1986) overturned *Swain v. Alabama,* 380 U.S. 202, 85 S.Ct. 824, 13 L.Ed.2d 759 (1965), to the extent that it had held that the Constitution does not require any inquiry into a prosecutor's reasons for using peremptory challenges to strike blacks from the jury panel in the criminal trial of black defendants. Under *Batson,* the defendant must show that he is a member of a cognizable racial group, and that the prosecutor exercised his peremptory challenges to remove from the panel members of the defendant's race. The judge should look at all the facts (e.g., the prosecutor's questions during *voir dire*) in order to decide if the prosecutor's use of peremptory challenges created a prima facie case of racial discrimination against black jurors. The prosecutor must then offer a "neutral explanation for challenging black jurors." This explanation "need not rise to the level justifying exercise of a challenge for cause." The Equal Protection Clause "forbids the States to strike black veniremen on the assumption that they will be biased in a particular case simply because the defendant is black."

2. In *Powers v. Ohio,* 499 U.S. 400, 111 S.Ct. 1364, 113 L.Ed.2d 411 (1991), Kennedy, J., for the Court, held that, under the equal protection clause, a criminal defendant may object to race-based exclusions of jurors effectuated through peremptory challenges whether or not defendant and the excluded jurors share the same race. The white defendant, on trial for aggravated murder and other offenses, objected to the state's use of peremptory challenges to remove seven black venire persons from the jury. Excluding jurors "solely by reason of their race" deprives them of a significant opportunity to participate in civil life, and throws doubt on the integrity of the judicial process and the fairness of the criminal proceeding. The Court concluded that this criminal defendant has suffered "cognizable injury" and has standing to raise the third-party equal protection claims of the jurors.

Scalia, J., joined by Rehnquist, C.J., dissented, arguing that no one excluded jurors "of *his* [the white defendant's] race, and thus did not deprive *him* [the white defendant] of the equal protection of the laws." (emphasis added).

Subsequently, in *Hernandez v. New York,* 500 U.S. 352, 111 S.Ct. 1859, 114 L.Ed.2d 395 (1991), a divided Court, with no majority opinion, concluded that an appellate court should accept (unless it is clearly erroneous) a trial court's conclusion that a prosecutor's exercise of peremptory strikes did not amount to intentional racial discrimination. The prosecutor explained that he struck two Latino venirepersons not in an effort to exclude Latinos but because their demeanor and responses to voir dire convinced him that they would have difficulty accepting the interpreter's translation of Spanish into English.

3. *J.E.B. v. Alabama,* 511 U.S. 127, 114 S.Ct. 1419, 128 L.Ed.2d 89 (1994) held that sex, like race, "is an unconstitutional proxy for juror competence and impartiality." The Court reversed the case of a putative

father whom the state had sued for child support. The state used 9 of its 10 peremptory strikes to remove male jurors, and the all-female jury then ruled against the defendant. Like race-based *Batson* claims, a party alleging sex discrimination must make a prima facie showing of intentional discrimination before the party exercising the challenge must explain the basis for the strike. If an explanation is required, it "need not rise to the level of a 'for cause' challenge." The explanation must be on a juror characteristic other than sex, and must not be pretextual.*

YICK WO v. HOPKINS
118 U.S. 356, 6 S.Ct. 1064, 30 L.Ed. 220 (1886).

[San Francisco ordinances, enacted in 1880, vested in the board of supervisors the discretion to grant or withhold their consent to the use of wooden buildings as laundries. There were no such restrictions on stone or brick buildings. Petitioner, a native of China and a subject of the Emperor, sought a writ of habeas corpus after he was imprisoned for violating the ordinances. He had been engaged in the laundry business on the same premises for 22 years and the board of fire wardens and the health officer had inspected his facilities and found all arrangements to be proper. The city claimed the purpose of the ordinances was to protect the public against the danger of fire, though no such purpose appeared on the face of the statute.

[Of the 320 laundries in the city, Chinese owned and operated about 240; approximately 310 were constructed of wood, the same material used for 90% of the houses in the city. The board had denied the application of all the Chinese (approximately 200) who had applied for licenses, all of whom had occupied and used the houses for laundries for more than 20 years. With one exception the board had granted the applications of all the nonChinese who had applied, about 80.]

Mr. Justice Matthews delivered the opinion of the Court.

[The ordinances] seem intended to confer, and actually do confer, not a discretion to be exercised upon a consideration of the circumstances of each case, but a naked and arbitrary power to give or withhold consent, not only as to places, but as to persons. So that, if an applicant for such consent, being in every way a competent and qualified person, and having complied with every reasonable condition demanded by any public interest, should, failing to obtain the requisite consent of the supervisors to the prosecution of his business, apply for redress by the judicial process[,] it would be a sufficient answer for them to say that the law had conferred upon them authority to withhold their assent, without reason and without responsibility. The power given to them is not confided to their discretion in the legal sense of that term, but is granted to their mere will. It is purely arbitrary, and acknowledges neither guidance nor restraint.... The ordinance, therefore, also differs from the not unusual case, where discretion is lodged by law in public officers

---

* Blackmun, J., wrote the opinion of the Court. Rehnquist, C.J., filed a dissenting opinion; Scalia, J., joined by Rehnquist, C.J. & Thomas, J., filed a dissenting opinion.

or bodies to grant or withhold licenses to keep taverns, or places for the sale of spirituous liquors, and the like, when one of the conditions is that the applicant shall be a fit person for the exercise of the privilege, because in such cases the fact of fitness is submitted to the judgment of the officer, and calls for the exercise of a discretion of a judicial nature.

The rights of the petitioners, as affected by the proceedings of which they complain, are not less, because they are aliens and subjects of the Emperor of China.... The Fourteenth Amendment to the Constitution is not confined to the protection of citizens....

When we consider the nature and the theory of our institutions of government, the principles upon which they are supposed to rest, and review the history of their development, we are constrained to conclude that they do not mean to leave room for the play and action of purely personal and arbitrary power.... For, the very idea that one man may be compelled to hold his life, or the means of living, or any material right essential to the enjoyment of life, at the mere will of another, seems to be intolerable in any country where freedom prevails, as being the essence of slavery itself.

There are many illustrations that might be given of this truth, which would make manifest that it was self-evident in the light of our system of jurisprudence. The case of the political franchise of voting is one. Though not regarded strictly as a natural right, but as a privilege merely conceded by society according to its will, under certain conditions, nevertheless it is regarded as a fundamental political right, because preservative of all rights.

... In the present cases we are not obliged to reason from the probable to the actual.... For the cases present the ordinances in actual operation, and the facts shown establish an administration directed so exclusively against a particular class of persons as to warrant and require the conclusion, that, whatever may have been the intent of the ordinances as adopted, they are applied by the public authorities charged with their administration, and thus representing the State itself, with a mind so unequal and oppressive as to amount to a practical denial by the State of that equal protection of the laws which is secured to the petitioners, as to all other persons, by the broad and benign provisions of the Fourteenth Amendment to the Constitution of the United States. Though the law itself be fair on its face and impartial in appearance, yet, if it is applied and administered by public authority with an evil eye and an unequal hand, so as practically to make unjust and illegal discriminations between persons in similar circumstances, material to their rights, the denial of equal justice is still within the prohibition of the Constitution....

The present cases, as shown by the facts disclosed in the record, are within this class. It appears that both petitioners have complied with every requisite, deemed by the law or by the public officers charged with its administration, necessary for the protection of neighboring property from fire, or as a precaution against injury to the public health. No reason whatever, except the will of the supervisors, is assigned why they should not be permitted to carry on, in the accustomed manner, their harmless and useful occupation, on which they depend for a livelihood. And while this consent of the supervisors is withheld from them and from two hundred others who have also petitioned, all of whom happen to be Chinese subjects, eighty others, not Chinese subjects, are permitted to carry on the same business under similar conditions. The fact of this discrimination is admitted. No reason for it is shown, and the conclusion cannot be resisted, that no reason for it exists except hostility to the race and nationality to which the petitioners belong, and which in the eye of the law is not justified. The discrimination is, therefore, illegal, and the public administration which enforces it is a denial of the equal protection of the laws and a violation of the Fourteenth Amendment of the Constitution. The imprisonment of the petitioners is, therefore, illegal, and they must be discharged. [The cases of Yick Wo and Wo Lee are] remanded, each to the proper court, with directions to discharge the petitioners from custody and imprisonment.

PLESSY v. FERGUSON

163 U.S. 537, 16 S.Ct. 1138, 41 L.Ed. 256 (1896).

MR. JUSTICE BROWN, after stating the case, delivered the opinion of the Court.

This case turns upon the constitutionality of an act of the General Assembly of the State of Louisiana, passed in 1890, providing for separate [but equal] railway carriages for the white and colored races. . . .

The petition for the writ of prohibition averred that petitioner was seven eighths Caucasian and one eighth African blood; that the mixture of colored blood was not discernible in him, and that he was entitled to every right, privilege and immunity secured to citizens of the United States of the white race; and that, upon such theory, he took possession of a vacant seat in a coach where passengers of the white race were accommodated, and was ordered by the conductor to vacate said coach and take a seat in another assigned to persons of the colored race, and having refused to comply with such demand he was forcibly ejected with the aid of a police officer, and imprisoned in the parish jail to answer a charge of having violated the above act. . . .

The object of the [fourteenth] amendment was undoubtedly to enforce the absolute equality of the two races before the law, but in the nature of things it could not have been intended to abolish distinctions based upon color, or to enforce social, as distinguished from political, equality, or a commingling of the two races upon terms unsatisfactory to either. Laws permitting, and even requiring, their separation in places where they are liable to be brought into contact do not necessarily imply the inferiority of either race to the other, and have been generally, if not universally, recognized as within the competency of the state legislatures in the exercise of their police power. The most common instance of this is connected with the establishment of separate schools for white and colored children, which has been held to be a valid exercise of the legislative power even by courts of States where the political rights of the colored race have been longest and most earnestly enforced. . . .

We consider the underlying fallacy of the plaintiff's argument to consist in the assumption that the enforced separation of the two races stamps the colored race with a badge of inferiority. If this be so, it is not by reason of anything found in the act, but solely because the colored race chooses to put that construction upon it. The argument necessarily assumes that if . . . the colored race should become the dominant power in the state legislature, and should enact a law in precisely similar terms, it would thereby relegate the white race to an inferior position. We imagine that the white race, at least, would not acquiesce in this assumption. The argument also assumes that social prejudices may be overcome by legislation, and that equal rights cannot be secured to the negro except by an enforced commingling of the two races. We cannot accept this proposition. If the two races are to meet upon terms of social equality, it must be the result of natural affinities, a mutual appreciation of each other's merits and a voluntary consent of individuals. . . .

MR. JUSTICE HARLAN dissenting.

[I]f this statute of Louisiana is consistent with the personal liberty of citizens, why may not the State require the separation in railroad coaches of native and naturalized citizens of the United States, or of Protestants and Roman Catholics? . . .

The white race deems itself to be the dominant race in this country. And so it is, in prestige, in achievements, in education, in wealth and in power. So, I doubt not, it will continue to be for all time, if it remains true to its great heritage and holds fast to the principles of constitutional liberty. But in view of the Constitution, in the eye of the law, there is in this country no superior, dominant, ruling class of citizens. There is no caste here. Our Constitution is color-blind, and neither knows nor tolerates classes among citizens. In respect of civil rights, all citizens are equal before the law. The humblest is the peer of the most powerful. The law regards man as man, and takes no account of his surroundings or of his color when his civil rights as guaranteed by the supreme law of the land are involved. It is, therefore, to be regretted that this high tribunal, the final expositor of the fundamental law of the land, has reached the conclusion that it is competent for a State to regulate the enjoyment by citizens of their civil rights solely upon the basis of race.

. . . Sixty millions of whites are in no danger from the presence here of eight millions of blacks. The destinies of the two races, in this country, are indissolubly linked together, and the interests of both require that the common government of all shall not permit the seeds of race hate to be planted under the sanction of law. What can more certainly arouse race hate, what more certainly create and perpetuate a feeling of distrust between these races, than state enactments, which, in fact, proceed on the ground that colored citizens are so inferior and degraded that they cannot be allowed to sit in public coaches occupied by white citizens? That, as all will admit, is the real meaning of such legislation as was enacted in Louisiana....

MR. JUSTICE BREWER did not hear the argument or participate in the decision of this case.

8–2.12 The Brown Decisions

BROWN v. BOARD OF EDUCATION
347 U.S. 483, 74 S.Ct. 686, 98 L.Ed. 873 (1954).

MR. CHIEF JUSTICE WARREN delivered the opinion of the Court.

These cases come to us from the States of Kansas, South Carolina, Virginia, and Delaware. They are premised on different facts and different local conditions, but a common legal question justifies their consideration together in this consolidated opinion.

In each of the cases, minors of the Negro race, through their legal representatives, seek the aid of the courts in obtaining admission to the public schools of their community on a nonsegregated basis. In each instance, they had been denied admission to schools attended by white children under laws requiring or permitting segregation according to race. This segregation was alleged to deprive the plaintiffs of the equal protection of the laws under the Fourteenth Amendment. In each of the cases other than the Delaware case, a three-judge federal district court denied relief to the plaintiffs on the so-called "separate but equal" doctrine announced by this Court in *Plessy v. Ferguson*. Under that doctrine, equality of treatment is accorded when the races are provided substantially equal facilities, even though these facilities be separate. In the Delaware case, the Supreme Court of Delaware adhered to that doctrine, but ordered that the plaintiffs be admitted to the white schools because of their superiority to the Negro schools.

The plaintiffs contend that segregated public schools are not "equal" and cannot be made "equal," and that hence they are deprived of the equal protection of the laws. Because of the obvious importance of the question presented, the Court took jurisdiction. Argument was heard in the 1952 Term, and reargument was heard this Term on certain questions propounded by the Court.

Reargument was largely devoted to the circumstances surrounding the adoption of the Fourteenth Amendment in 1868. It covered exhaustively consideration of the Amendment in Congress, ratification by the states, then existing practices in racial segregation, and the views of proponents and opponents of the Amendment. This discussion and our own investigation convince us that, although these sources cast some light, it is not enough to resolve the problem with which we are faced. At best, they are inconclusive. The most avid proponents of the post-War Amendments undoubtedly intended them to remove all legal distinctions among "all persons born or naturalized in the United States." Their opponents, just as certainly, were antagonistic to both the letter and the spirit of the Amendments and wished them to have the most limited effect. What others in Congress and the state legislatures had in mind cannot be determined with any degree of certainty.

An additional reason for the inconclusive nature of the Amendment's history, with respect to segregated schools, is the status of public education at that time. In the South, the movement toward free common schools, supported by general taxation, had not yet taken hold. Education of white children was largely in the hands of private groups. Education of Negroes was almost nonexistent, and practically all of the race were illiterate. In fact, any education of Negroes was forbidden by law in some states. Today, in contrast, many Negroes have achieved outstanding success in the arts and sciences as well as in the business and professional world. It is true that public school education at the time of the Amendment had advanced further in the North, but the effect of the Amendment on Northern States was generally ignored in the congressional debates. Even in the North, the conditions of public education did not approximate those existing today. The curriculum was usually rudimentary; ungraded schools were common in rural areas; the school term was but three months a year in many states; and compulsory school attendance was virtually unknown. As a consequence, it is not surprising that there should be so little in the history of the Fourteenth Amendment relating to its intended effect on public education.

In the first cases in this Court construing the Fourteenth Amendment, decided shortly after its adoption, the Court interpreted it as proscribing all state-imposed discriminations against the Negro race. The doctrine of "separate but equal" did not make its appearance in this Court until 1896 in the case of *Plessy v. Ferguson,* involving not education but transportation. American courts have since labored with the doctrine for over half a century. In this Court, there have been six cases involving the "separate but equal" doctrine in the field of public education. In *Cumming v. County Board of Education,* 175 U.S. 528, 20 S.Ct. 197, 44 L.Ed. 262, and *Gong Lum v. Rice,* 275 U.S. 78, 48 S.Ct. 91, 72 L.Ed. 172, the validity of the doctrine itself was not challenged. In more recent cases, all on the graduate school level, inequality was found in that specific benefits enjoyed by white students were denied to Negro students of the same educational qualifications. *Missouri ex rel. Gaines v. Canada,* 305 U.S. 337, 59 S.Ct. 232, 83 L.Ed. 208; *Sipuel v. Oklahoma,* 332 U.S. 631, 68 S.Ct. 299, 92 L.Ed. 247; *Sweatt v. Painter,* 339 U.S. 629, 70 S.Ct. 848, 94 L.Ed. 1114; *McLaurin v. Oklahoma State Regents,* 339 U.S. 637, 70 S.Ct. 851, 94 L.Ed. 1149. In none of these cases was it necessary to re-examine the doctrine to grant relief to the Negro plaintiff. And in *Sweatt v. Painter,* the Court expressly reserved decision on the question whether *Plessy v. Ferguson* should be held inapplicable to public education.

In the instant cases, that question is directly presented. Here, unlike *Sweatt v. Painter,* there are findings below that the Negro and white schools involved have been equalized, or are being equalized, with respect to buildings, curricula, qualifications and salaries of teachers, and other "tangible" factors. Our decision, therefore, cannot turn on merely a comparison of these tangible factors in the Negro and white schools involved in each of the cases. We must look instead to the effect of segregation itself on public education.

In approaching this problem, we cannot turn the clock back to 1868 when the Amendment was adopted, or even to 1896 when *Plessy v. Ferguson* was written. We must consider public education in the light of its full development and its present place in American life throughout the Nation. Only in this way can it be determined if segregation in public schools deprives these plaintiffs of the equal protection of the laws.

Today, education is perhaps the most important function of state and local governments. Compulsory school attendance laws and the great expenditures for education both demonstrate our recognition of the importance of education to our democratic society. It is required in the performance of our most basic public responsibilities, even service in the armed forces. It is the very foundation of good citizenship. Today it is a principal instrument in awakening the child to cultural values, in preparing him for later professional training, and in helping him to adjust normally to his environment. In these days, it is doubtful that any child may reasonably be expected to succeed in life if he is denied the opportunity of an education. Such an opportunity, where the state has undertaken to provide it, is a right which must be made available to all on equal terms.

We come then to the question presented: Does segregation of children in public schools solely on the basis of race, even though the physical facilities and other "tangible" factors may be equal, deprive the children of the minority group of equal educational opportunities? We believe that it does.

In *Sweatt v. Painter,* supra, in finding that a segregated law school for Negroes could not provide them equal educational opportunities, this Court relied in large part on "those qualities which are incapable of objective measurement but which make for greatness in a law school." In *McLaurin v. Oklahoma State Regents,* supra, the Court, in requiring that a Negro admitted to a white graduate school be treated like all other students, again resorted to intangible considerations: "... his ability to study, to engage in discussions and exchange views with other students, and, in general, to learn his profession." Such considerations apply with added force to children in grade and high schools. To separate them from others of similar age and qualifications solely because of their race generates a feeling of inferiority as to their status in the community that may affect their hearts and minds in a way unlikely ever to be undone. The effect of this separation on their educational opportunities was well stated by a finding in the Kansas case by a court which nevertheless felt compelled to rule against the Negro plaintiffs:

> Segregation of white and colored children in public schools has a detrimental effect upon the colored children. The impact is greater

when it has the sanction of the law; for the policy of separating the races is usually interpreted as denoting the inferiority of the negro group. A sense of inferiority affects the motivation of a child to learn. Segregation with the sanction of law, therefore, has a tendency to [retard] the educational and mental development of negro children and to deprive them of some of the benefits they would receive in a racial[ly] integrated school system.

Whatever may have been the extent of psychological knowledge at the time of *Plessy v. Ferguson,* this finding is amply supported by modern authority.[11] Any language in *Plessy v. Ferguson* contrary to this finding is rejected.

We conclude that in the field of public education the doctrine of "separate but equal" has no place. Separate educational facilities are inherently unequal. Therefore, we hold that the plaintiffs and others similarly situated for whom the actions have been brought are, by reason of the segregation complained of, deprived of the equal protection of the laws guaranteed by the Fourteenth Amendment. This disposition makes unnecessary any discussion whether such segregation also violates the Due Process Clause of the Fourteenth Amendment.

Because these are class actions, because of the wide applicability of this decision, and because of the great variety of local conditions, the formulation of decrees in these cases presents problems of considerable complexity. On reargument, the consideration of appropriate relief was necessarily subordinated to the primary question—the constitutionality of segregation in public education. We have now announced that such segregation is a denial of the equal protection of the laws. In order that we may have the full assistance of the parties in formulating decrees, the cases will be restored to the docket, and the parties are requested to present further argument on Questions 4 and 5 previously propounded by the Court for the reargument this Term. The Attorney General of the United States is again invited to participate. The Attorneys General of the states requiring or permitting segregation in public education will also be permitted to appear as *amici curiae* upon request to do so by September 15, 1954, and submission of briefs by October 1, 1954.

It is so ordered.

BOLLING v. SHARPE
347 U.S. 497, 74 S.Ct. 693, 98 L.Ed. 884 (1954).

MR. CHIEF JUSTICE WARREN delivered the opinion of the Court.

This case challenges the validity of segregation in the public schools of the District of Columbia. The petitioners, minors of the Negro race,

11. K.B. Clark, Effect of Prejudice and Discrimination on Personality Development (Midcentury White House Conference on Children and Youth, 1950); Witmer and Kotinsky, Personality in the Making (1952), c. VI; Deutscher and Chein, The Psychological Effects of Enforced Segregation: A Survey of Social Science Opinion, 26 J.Psychol. 259 (1948); Chein, What are the Psychological Effects of Segregation Under Conditions of Equal Facilities?, 3 Int.J.Opinion and Attitude Res. 229 (1949); Brameld, Educational Costs, in Discrimination and National Welfare (MacIver, ed., 1949), 44–48; Frazier, The Negro in the United States (1949), 674–681. And see generally Myrdal, An American Dilemma (1944).

allege that such segregation deprives them of due process of law under the Fifth Amendment. . . .

We have this day held that the Equal Protection Clause of the Fourteenth Amendment prohibits the states from maintaining racially segregated public schools. The legal problem in the District of Columbia is somewhat different, however. The Fifth Amendment, which is applicable in the District of Columbia, does not contain an equal protection clause as does the Fourteenth Amendment which applies only to the states. But the concepts of equal protection and due process, both stemming from our American ideal of fairness, are not mutually exclusive. The "equal protection of the laws" is a more explicit safeguard of prohibited unfairness than "due process of law," and, therefore, we do not imply that the two are always interchangeable phrases. But, as this Court has recognized, discrimination may be so unjustifiable as to be violative of due process.

Classifications based solely upon race must be scrutinized with particular care, since they are contrary to our traditions and hence constitutionally suspect.[3] As long ago as 1896, this Court declared the principle "that the Constitution of the United States, in its present form, forbids, so far as civil and political rights are concerned, discrimination by the General Government, or by the States, against any citizen because of his race."[4] . . .

Although the Court has not assumed to define "liberty" with any great precision, that term is not confined to mere freedom from bodily restraint. Liberty under law extends to the full range of conduct which the individual is free to pursue, and it cannot be restricted except for a proper governmental objective. Segregation in public education is not reasonably related to any proper governmental objective, and thus it imposes on Negro children of the District of Columbia a burden that constitutes an arbitrary deprivation of their liberty in violation of the Due Process Clause.

In view of our decision that the Constitution prohibits the states from maintaining racially segregated public schools, it would be unthinkable that the same Constitution would impose a lesser duty on the Federal Government. We hold that racial segregation in the public schools of the District of Columbia is a denial of the due process of law guaranteed by the Fifth Amendment to the Constitution.

For the reasons set out in *Brown v. Board of Education*, this case will be restored to the docket for reargument on Questions 4 and 5 previously propounded by the Court.

---

3. *Korematsu v. United States*, 323 U.S. 214, 216, 65 S.Ct. 193, 194, 89 L.Ed. 194; *Hirabayashi v. United States*, 320 U.S. 81, 100, 63 S.Ct. 1375, 1385, 87 L.Ed. 1774.

4. *Gibson v. Mississippi*, 162 U.S. 565, 591, 16 S.Ct. 904, 910, 40 L.Ed. 1075. Cf. *Steele v. Louisville & Nashville R. Co.*, 323 U.S. 192, 198–199, 65 S.Ct. 226, 230, 89 L.Ed. 173.

It is so ordered.

Notes

1.   Consider footnote 11 of the *Brown* opinion. If K.B. Clark were to change his mind, should the Court change its legal results? Does *Brown* rest on empirical studies subject to change, or on something else?

Should a white person have standing to sue to integrate a black (or a white) school?

2.   Following *Brown* the Court applied that case to a host of other activities outside of the field of education. All were short per curiam opinions or orders, some without citation and others merely citing *Brown*. E.g., *Muir v. Louisville Park Theatrical Association,* 347 U.S. 971, 74 S.Ct. 783, 98 L.Ed. 1112 (1954)(per curiam)(amphitheater in city park); *Mayor and City Council of Baltimore v. Dawson,* 350 U.S. 877, 76 S.Ct. 133, 100 L.Ed. 774 (1955)(per curiam)(public beaches and bathhouses); *Holmes v. City of Atlanta,* 350 U.S. 879, 76 S.Ct. 141, 100 L.Ed. 776 (1955)(per curiam)(municipal golf courses); *Gayle v. Browder,* 352 U.S. 903, 77 S.Ct. 145, 1 L.Ed.2d 114 (1956)(per curiam)(municipal buses); *New Orleans City Park Improvement Association v. Detiege,* 358 U.S. 54, 79 S.Ct. 99, 3 L.Ed.2d 46 (1958)(per curiam)(public parks and golf courses); *State Athletic Commission v. Dorsey,* 359 U.S. 533, 79 S.Ct. 1137, 3 L.Ed.2d 1028 (1959)(per curiam)(athletic contests); *Turner v. City of Memphis,* 369 U.S. 350, 82 S.Ct. 805, 7 L.Ed.2d 762 (1962)(per curiam)(municipal airport restaurants); *Johnson v. Virginia,* 373 U.S. 61, 83 S.Ct. 1053, 10 L.Ed.2d 195 (1963)(per curiam)(courtroom seating); and *Schiro v. Bynum,* 375 U.S. 395, 84 S.Ct. 452, 11 L.Ed.2d 412 (1964)(per curiam)(municipal auditoriums).

3.   In *Korematsu* and *Hirabayashi,* cited in *Bolling* in footnote 3, the Court, relying on the war powers, upheld racial classifications involving curfews and relocations imposed on Japanese–Americans shortly after the Japanese attack on Pearl Harbor. In *Korematsu,* Justices Roberts, Murphy, and Jackson each filed vigorous dissents. Black, J., for the Court, in upholding the law, did say that racial classifications are "immediately suspect," and—although not invalid per se—must be subjected to "the most rigid scrutiny." Internment of Japanese–Americans did not end until more than a year after Japan had surrendered.

BROWN v. BOARD OF EDUCATION
349 U.S. 294, 75 S.Ct. 753, 99 L.Ed. 1083 (1955).

Mr. Chief Justice Warren delivered the opinion of the Court.

These cases were decided on May 17, 1954. The opinions of that date, declaring the fundamental principle that racial discrimination in public education is unconstitutional, are incorporated herein by reference. All provisions of federal, state, or local law requiring or permitting such discrimination must yield to this principle. There remains for consideration the manner in which relief is to be accorded.

Because these cases arose under different local conditions and their disposition will involve a variety of local problems, we requested further argument on the question of relief.[2] In view of the nationwide importance of the decision, we invited the Attorney General of the United States and the Attorneys General of all states requiring or permitting racial discrimination in public education to present their views on that question. The parties, the United States, and the States of Florida, North Carolina, Arkansas, Oklahoma, Maryland, and Texas filed briefs and participated in the oral argument.

These presentations were informative and helpful to the Court in its consideration of the complexities arising from the transition to a system of public education freed of racial discrimination. The presentations also demonstrated that substantial steps to eliminate racial discrimination in public schools have already been taken, not only in some of the communities in which these cases arose, but in some of the states appearing as *amici curiae,* and in other states as well. Substantial progress has been made in the District of Columbia and in the communities in Kansas and Delaware involved in this litigation. The defendants in the cases coming to us from South Carolina and Virginia are awaiting the decision of this Court concerning relief.

Full implementation of these constitutional principles may require solution of varied local school problems. School authorities have the primary responsibility for elucidating, assessing, and solving these problems; courts will have to consider whether the action of school authorities constitutes good faith implementation of the governing constitutional principles. Because of their proximity to local conditions and the possible need for further hearings, the courts which originally heard these cases can best perform this judicial appraisal. Accordingly, we believe it appropriate to remand the cases to those courts.

In fashioning and effectuating the decrees, the courts will be guided by equitable principles. Traditionally, equity has been characterized by a practical flexibility in shaping its remedies and by a facility for adjusting and reconciling public and private needs. These cases call for the exercise

2. Further argument was requested on the following questions previously propounded by the Court:

"4. Assuming it is decided that segregation in public schools violates the Fourteenth Amendment

"(*a*) would a decree necessarily follow providing that, within the limits set by normal geographic school districting, Negro children should forthwith be admitted to schools of their choice, or

"(*b*) may this Court, in the exercise of its equity powers, permit an effective gradual adjustment to be brought about from existing segregated systems to a system not based on color distinctions?

"5. On the assumption on which questions 4(*a*) and (*b*) are based, and assuming further that this Court will exercise its eq-

uity powers to the end described in question 4(*b*),

"(*a*) should this Court formulate detailed decrees in these cases;

"(*b*) if so, what specific issues should the decrees reach;

"(*c*) should this Court appoint a special master to hear evidence with a view to recommending specific terms for such decrees;

"(*d*) should this Court remand to the courts of first instance with directions to frame decrees in these cases, and if so what general directions should the decrees of this Court include and what procedures should the courts of first instance follow in arriving at the specific terms of more detailed decrees?"

of these traditional attributes of equity power. At stake is the personal interest of the plaintiffs in admission to public schools as soon as practicable on a nondiscriminatory basis. To effectuate this interest may call for elimination of a variety of obstacles in making the transition to school systems operated in accordance with the constitutional principles set forth in our May 17, 1954, decision. Courts of equity may properly take into account the public interest in the elimination of such obstacles in a systematic and effective manner. But it should go without saying that the vitality of these constitutional principles cannot be allowed to yield simply because of disagreement with them.

While giving weight to these public and private considerations, the courts will require that the defendants make a prompt and reasonable start toward full compliance with our May 17, 1954, ruling. Once such a start has been made, the courts may find that additional time is necessary to carry out the ruling in an effective manner. The burden rests upon the defendants to establish that such time is necessary in the public interest and is consistent with good faith compliance at the earliest practicable date. To that end, the courts may consider problems related to administration, arising from the physical condition of the school plant, the school transportation system, personnel, revision of school districts and attendance areas into compact units to achieve a system of determining admission to the public schools on a nonracial basis, and revision of local laws and regulations which may be necessary in solving the foregoing problems. They will also consider the adequacy of any plans the defendants may propose to meet these problems and to effectuate a transition to a racially nondiscriminatory school system. During this period of transition, the courts will retain jurisdiction of these cases.

The judgments below, except that in the Delaware case, are accordingly reversed and the cases are remanded to the District Courts to take such proceedings and enter such orders and decrees consistent with this opinion as are necessary and proper to admit to public schools on a racially nondiscriminatory basis with all deliberate speed the parties to these cases. The judgment in the Delaware case—ordering the immediate admission of the plaintiffs to schools previously attended only by white children—is affirmed on the basis of the principles stated in our May 17, 1954, opinion, but the case is remanded to the Supreme Court of Delaware for such further proceedings as that Court may deem necessary in light of this opinion.

It is so ordered.

Notes

1. THE "ALL DELIBERATE SPEED" DOCTRINE. *Brown II* was not the first case that invoked the "all deliberate speed" language.[1] Yet it was the first

---

1. See *Virginia v. West Virginia*, 222 U.S. 17, 19–20, 32 S.Ct. 4, 5–6, 56 L.Ed. 71 (1911)(Holmes, J.): "A question like the present should be disposed of without undue delay. But a State cannot be expected to move with the celerity of a private busi-

case to invoke it in a civil liberties context. How can the Court hold that a State is depriving blacks of equal protection of the law and, yet, still allow the state to continue the deprivation for a time? When the Court later invalidated state laws forbidding the sale of birth control pills, see § 8–3.42, such laws were declared unenforceable at once. The state did not have the option of eliminating such laws with all deliberate speed. Should the Court in *Brown II* simply have declared unenforceable all state or local laws requiring segregation in education?[2]

2. IMPLEMENTING BROWN II. *Cooper v. Aaron* (excerpted supra § 1–1). In this 1958 case Arkansas state authorities actively obstructed a school board's court approved desegregation plan. Among other things the Governor had called on the national guard, which forcibly prevented 9 black children from entering the previously all white Little Rock high school. The President dispatched federal troops to effectuate the admission of the students and control the large crowds of demonstrators. The school board later asked for a two and one-half year postponement of the desegregation plan "because of extreme public hostility," engendered largely by the Governor and other state officials. The district court granted the delay, but the court of appeals reversed and the Supreme Court affirmed the appellate decision. "The constitutional rights of respondents are not to be sacrificed or yielded to the violence of the Governor and Legislature," and "law and order are not here preserved by depriving the Negro children of their constitutional rights." The district court, when it considered all the factors to determine "deliberate speed" should have excluded "hostility to racial desegregation."

Goss v. Board of Education, 373 U.S. 683, 83 S.Ct. 1405, 10 L.Ed.2d 632 (1963) invalidated a portion of a desegregation plan that allowed a student to transfer from a school in which he was a member of a racial minority to a school where he was in the racial majority. Over nine years had passed since *Brown I* and thus "the context in which we must interpret and apply this language ['all deliberate speed'] has been significantly altered."

ness man; it is enough if it proceeds, in the language of the English Chancery, with all deliberate speed." See also, *Radio Station WOW v. Johnson,* 326 U.S. 120, 132, 65 S.Ct. 1475, 1482, 89 L.Ed. 569 (1945)(Frankfurter, J.): "We think that State power is amply respected if it is qualified merely to the extent of requiring it to withhold execution of that portion of its decree requiring retransfer of the physical properties until steps are ordered to be taken, with all deliberate speed, to enable the [Federal Communications] Commission to deal with new applications in connection with the station." Cf. *The Hound of Heaven,* 1 The Works of Francis Thompson 107 (1913): "But with unhurrying chase,/and unperturbed pace,/Deliberate speed, majestic instancy.... "

2. See B. Schwartz, Super Chief: Earl Warren and His Supreme Court—A Judicial Biography 124 (Unabridged ed. 1983): "In his later years, Warren concluded that he had been sold a bill of goods when Frankfurter induced him to use the phrase. It would have been better, he came to believe, to have ordered desegregation forthwith. By then, however, Black's prediction of the 'glacial' pace of desegregation had proved, if anything, over optimistic. The Justices had, to be sure, not expected enthusiastic compliance by the South. But the extent of opposition was something that had not been foreseen. Looking back, Warren, at least, felt that much of the defiance could have been avoided if the South had not been led to believe that 'deliberate speed' would countenance indefinite delay. When a comparable problem arose in 1964 in connection with enforcement of the 'one man-one vote' principle in legislative apportionments, the Chief did not hesitate to urge immediate enforcement, regardless of the problems in individual states in adapting to the new rule." One of the first things Warren did, when he arrived at the Supreme Court, was to end separate restrooms for blacks. Id. at 127.

Griffin v. County School Board of Prince Edward County, 377 U.S. 218, 84 S.Ct. 1226, 12 L.Ed.2d 256 (1964), had been one of the cases that *Brown II* had remanded for further relief. Virginia responded in various ways, such as cutting off state funds to public schools where whites and blacks attended together, closing such schools, paying tuition grants to children in nonsectarian private schools, and extending state retirement benefits to teachers in newly created private schools. After the state court invalidated the laws cutting off state funds and closing mixed schools, the state adopted other tactics such as a new tuition grant program, and a repeal of the compulsory attendance laws. The Supervisors of Prince Edward County then responded to a court desegregation order by refusing to levy any school taxes for the 1959–1960 school year. The public schools in that county were closed. Meanwhile a private school for white children opened, supported primarily by state and county tuition grants. The county also provided property tax credits for contributions to any "nonprofit, nonsectarian private school." Blacks were without formal schooling from 1959 to 1963.

The Supreme Court affirmed the district court's order enjoining the county from paying tuition grants or giving tax credits so long as public schools remained closed. Moreover, the district court, "may, if necessary to prevent further racial discrimination, require the Supervisors to exercise the power that is theirs to levy taxes to raise funds adequate to reopen, operate, and maintain without racial discrimination a public school system in Prince Edward County like that operated in other counties in Virginia." The Court added: "An order of this kind is within the court's power if required to assure these petitioners that their constitutional rights will no longer be denied them. The time for mere 'deliberate speed' has run out, and that phrase can no longer justify denying these Prince Edward County school children their constitutional rights to an education equal to that afforded by the public schools in other parts of Virginia."

Some states responded to *Brown II* by instituting desegregation at a pace of one grade a year. After *Griffin* the Court invalidated such plans as too slow, *Rogers v. Paul,* 382 U.S. 198, 86 S.Ct. 358, 15 L.Ed.2d 265 (1965). Other states responded with a "freedom-of-choice" plan, allowing a pupil to choose his own public school. *Green v. New Kent County School Board,* 391 U.S. 430, 88 S.Ct. 1689, 20 L.Ed.2d 716 (1968) invalidated such a plan. Given the long history of segregation it was insufficient for the Board merely to open its white school to blacks and its black school to whites. Under *Brown II,* school boards "such as the respondent then operating state-controlled dual systems were . . . clearly charged with the affirmative duty to take whatever steps might be necessary to convert to a unitary system in which racial discrimination would be eliminated root and branch."

The Court did not invalidate all freedom of choice plans, but found that, given the history of this school, the plan was unacceptable. "The burden on a school board today is to come forward with a plan that promises realistically to work, and promises realistically to work *now*." (emphasis in original). The plan must promise "meaningful and immediate progress towards disestablishing state-imposed segregation." The black school enrolled 85% of all the black children but not one white. Other plans, such as zoning, must be used if they are a "speedier" means of converting to a unitary school system.

The Board must fashion steps "to convert promptly to a system without a 'white' school and a 'Negro' school, but just schools."

Carter v. West Feliciana Parish School Board, 396 U.S. 290, 90 S.Ct. 608, 24 L.Ed.2d 477 (1970)(per curiam) reversed a Fifth Circuit opinion that had allowed a one-semester delay in the implementation of a desegregation order that had been issued in the middle of the school year. Two members of the Court thought that the time between a finding of noncompliance and the effect of the remedy, including any judicial review, should not exceed eight weeks. Four others thought that even that delay was too long.

In *Swann v. Charlotte–Mecklenburg Board of Education,* 402 U.S. 1, 91 S.Ct. 1267, 28 L.Ed.2d 554 (1971) the Supreme Court, per Burger, C.J., examined the broad range of judicial alternatives to eliminate the last vestiges of a school system long segregated by law. Given a past history of segregation, if it is possible to identify a white or a black school "simply by reference to the racial composition of teachers and staff, the quality of school buildings and equipment, or the organization of sports activities, a *prima facie* case of violation of substantive constitutional rights under the Equal Protection Clause is shown." The first remedial responsibility is to eliminate any invidious racial distinctions. With respect to transportation, supporting personnel, extracurricular activities, maintenance of buildings, and the distribution of equipment, the corrective action is straightforward.

As for teachers, in order to achieve a plan that "promises realistically to work *now*" the district court need not be required to be colorblind in assigning teachers, given a past history of legal segregation.

As for the construction of new schools and the closing of old ones, these choices have been used as a "potent weapon" to create or maintain segregated schools, e.g., by closing schools as they become racially mixed and by building new schools in white suburban areas farthest from black population centers. Such choices are evidence of the existence of legally imposed school segregation and the district court has the responsibility to assure that future school construction and abandonment do not perpetuate or reestablish a dual school system.

Then the Court turned to the assignment of students:

- *Racial balance.* The district court, said *Swann,* may not require as a substantive constitutional right any particular degree of racial balance. Every school need not always reflect the racial composition of the school system as a whole. Yet the district court did not err when it sought a 71–29 ratio of white to black in each school, reflecting the fact that the pupils of the school system of 107 schools were approximately 71% white and 29% black. Under the circumstances of this case the "limited use made of mathematical ratios" was within the court's equitable discretion. "Awareness of the racial composition of the whole school system is likely to be a useful starting point in shaping a remedy to correct past constitutional violations."

- *One-race schools.* The existence of a school primarily or totally of one race in a school system is not evidence of segregation imposed by law. But there is a presumption against such schools, if the district has a history of such segregation. The school system converting to a unitary system has "the burden of showing that such school assignments are genuinely nondiscriminatory" and not the product of present or past discrimination. Also, an optional majority-to-minority transfer provision is a "useful part of every desegregation plan."

• *Remedial altering of attendance zones.* "[O]ne of the principal tools employed by school planners and by courts to break up the dual school system has been a frank—and sometimes—drastic gerrymandering of school districts and attendance zones. An additional step was pairing, 'clustering,' or 'grouping' to accomplish the transfer of Negro students out of formerly segregated Negro schools and transfer of white students to formerly all-Negro schools." Often these zones "are neither compact nor contiguous; indeed they may be on opposite ends of the city. As an interim corrective measure, this cannot be said to be beyond the broad remedial powers of a court." In this area the Supreme Court will rely "on the informed judgment of the district courts in the first instance and on courts of appeals."

• *Transportation of students.* "Bus transportation has been an integral part of the public education system for years [and the] importance of bus transportation as a normal and accepted tool of educational policy is readily discernible in this and the companion case. [W]e find no basis for holding that the local school authorities may not be required to employ bus transportation as one tool of desegregation. Desegregation plans cannot be limited to the walk-in school. An objection to transportation of students may have validity when the time or distance of travel is so great as to either risk the health of the children or significantly impinge on the educational process."

The following year the Court further broadened lower court powers in two cases decided the same day, *Wright v. Council of the City of Emporia,* 407 U.S. 451, 92 S.Ct. 2196, 33 L.Ed.2d 51 (1972) and *United States v. Scotland Neck City Board of Education,* 407 U.S. 484, 92 S.Ct. 2214, 33 L.Ed.2d 75 (1972). The first case was a 5 to 4 opinion; the four dissenters in the first case concurred in the result in the second. In both cases the Court upheld lower court orders enjoining, under the facts of those cases, state or local officials from carving out a new school district from an existing one when the district had not yet completed the process of dismantling a system of legally enforced school segregation, and the creation of the new districts would have the effect of hindering the process of desegregation.

In *Emporia,* the Court said: "Only when it became clear—15 years after our decision in *Brown I*—that segregation in the county system was finally to be abolished, did Emporia attempt to take its children out of the county system. Under these circumstances, the power of the District Court to enjoin Emporia's withdrawal from that system need not rest upon an independent constitutional violation." In *Scotland Neck,* the respondents' primary argument in support of carving out a new school district from an old one "was that separation of the Scotland Neck schools from those of Halifax County was necessary to avoid 'white flight' by Scotland Neck residents into private schools that would follow complete dismantling of the dual school system. [W]hile this development may be cause for deep concern to the respondents, it cannot ... be accepted as a reason for achieving anything less than complete uprooting of the dual public school system."[1]

3. LIFTING DESEGREGATION DECREES. *Board of Education of Oklahoma City Public Schools v. Dowell,* 498 U.S. 237, 111 S.Ct. 630, 112 L.Ed.2d 715 (1991). As more and more schools became integrated, young black children had to be bused further from their inner-city homes to outlying areas. In *Dowell,* the school board wanted to implement a student assignment system that would increase parental involvement and reduce busing burdens on young black children. Under this student reassignment system, 11 of 64 elementary schools would be greater than 90% black, 22 would be greater than 90% white plus other minorities, and 31 would be racially mixed. The district court found that the school district was no longer a "dual" school system but had achieved "unitary" status, that the integrated school board (a majority of whom were black) had done nothing for 25 years to promote segregation, and that present residential segregation was the result of private decision making and economics and was too attenuated to be a vestige of former school segregation.

Rehnquist, C.J., for the Court (5 to 3, with Souter, J., not participating) ruled that a school district desegregation decree is not intended to operate in perpetuity, and that the lower court should dissolve the decree if it determines that the school district "was being operated in compliance with the commands of the Equal Protection Clause" and "that it was unlikely that the school board would return to its former ways.... " Federal supervision of school districts to remedy past discrimination is intended to be temporary. The Court remanded. Marshall, J., joined by Blackmun & Stevens, JJ. dissented, arguing that formerly *de jure* segregated school districts must take all feasible steps "to *eliminate* racially identifiable schools." (emphasis in original).

Freeman v. Pitts, 503 U.S. 467, 112 S.Ct. 1430, 118 L.Ed.2d 108 (1992). The district court ruled that the DeKalb County School System, in Georgia, had achieved unitary status in some but not all respects. Thus the district court relinquished remedial control as to those aspects where unitary status had been achieved (student attendance and three other categories), but retained supervisory authority only for those aspects where the school system was not in full compliance. The Eleventh Circuit reversed and held that the district court should retain full remedial authority until the school system achieves unitary status in all categories at the same time. The Supreme Court, with no dissents, agreed with the district court. The "district court may determine that it will not order further remedies in the area of student assignments" if the school district shows that "racial imbalance is not traceable, in a proximate way, to constitutional violations." Resegregation that is a product not of state action but of private choices does

---

1. Cf. *Palmore v. Sidoti,* 466 U.S. 429, 104 S.Ct. 1879, 80 L.Ed.2d 421 (1984), holding that if a state court divests a natural mother of custody of her infant because of remarriage to a person of a different race, there is a violation of equal protection. The state court had referred to the child's peer pressures and social stigmatization: "The

Constitution cannot control such prejudices but neither can it tolerate them.... 'Public officials sworn to uphold the Constitution may not avoid a constitutional duty by bowing to the hypothetical effects of private racial prejudice that they assume to be both widely and deeply held.' "

not have constitutional implications. "As the *de jure* violation becomes more remote in time and these demographic changes intervene, it becomes less likely that a current racial imbalance in a school district is a vestige of the prior *de jure* system. The causal link is even more attenuated if the school system has demonstrated its good faith."

4. UNIVERSITIES. *United States v. Fordice,* 505 U.S. 717, 112 S.Ct. 2727, 120 L.Ed.2d 575 (1992). Mississippi, after resisting desegregation efforts for years, decided to grant different "missions" to various state universities. Three historically white universities were designated "comprehensive" universities; the sole urban university (historically black) was designated an "urban" university; and the rest (including both historically black and historically white universities) were designated as "regional." By the mid–1980's 71% of the state's black students attended the historically black universities, while 99% of the state's white students attended the historically white universities.

Various state decisions, such as its admission policies, helped perpetuate this present discrimination. In 1964 the state required that students seeking to attend the historically white universities must achieve a higher ACT minimum composite score than those seeking to attend the historically black institutions. The state initially imposed this requirement (which had a disproportionate impact on black students) "for a discriminatory purpose," although it now said that it kept the policy to help insure that students are better prepared.

The district court (which ruled in favor of Mississippi) found that there was "unnecessary duplication" of nonessential or noncore programs. The "whole notion of 'separate but equal' required the duplicative programs in two sets of schools," and the "present unnecessary duplication is a continuation of that practice." Also, Mississippi's scheme of institutional mission classification helped perpetuate the former *de jure* system because only historically white institutions were classified as "comprehensive," entitling them to more funds, the most advanced programs, and the widest range of curricular functions. Finally, the state continued to operate all 8 universities, even though some schools are only 20 to 35 miles apart. Simply closing one or more schools would decrease the discriminatory effects of the present system.

The Court agreed that *Green v. New Kent County* did not apply because a state university system is "quite different" from an elementary or secondary school system: different universities are not fungible; students, as a matter of choice, decide whether to attend universities; and the state historically has not assigned students to particular institutions. However, that "does not mean that a race-neutral admissions policy cures the constitutional violation of a dual system." Mississippi could not meet its burden to prove that it has met its affirmative obligation to dismantle its prior *de jure* segregated *university* system merely by adopting a race-neutral admissions policy and offering students the freedom to choose which state higher education facility they wished to attend; Mississippi does not meet its burden *if* it perpetuates policies traceable to its prior dual system that continue to have segregated effects (by influencing student enrollment decisions or by fostering segregation in other facets of the university system) "and such policies are without sound educational justification and can be practicably eliminated. . . . '' White, J., for the Court remanded for appropriate findings.

Thomas, J., filed a separate concurring opinion noting that the standard the Court is applying to higher education is different than the one applied in *Green v. New Kent County School Board* because "it does not compel the elimination of all observed racial imbalance. [Thus] it portends neither the destruction of historically black colleges nor the severing of those institutions from their distinctive histories and traditions." Although "a State is not constitutionally *required* to maintain its historically black institutions as such, I do not understand our opinion to hold that a State is *forbidden* from doing so. It would be ironic, to say the least, if the institutions that sustained blacks during segregation were themselves destroyed in an effort to combat its vestiges."

8–2.13 Desegregation in the North, the De Facto/De Jure Distinction, and Problems of Purpose, Motive, and Effect

KEYES v. SCHOOL DISTRICT NO. 1
413 U.S. 189, 93 S.Ct. 2686, 37 L.Ed.2d 548 (1973).

MR. JUSTICE BRENNAN delivered the opinion of the Court.

This school desegregation case concerns the Denver, Colorado, school system. That system has never been operated under a constitutional or statutory provision that mandated or permitted racial segregation in public education. . . . There were in 1969, 119 schools with 96,580 pupils in the school system. . . . The District Court found that by the construction of a new, relatively small elementary school, Barrett, in the middle of the Negro community west of Park Hill, by the gerrymandering of student attendance zones, by the use of so-called "optional zones," and by the excessive use of mobile classroom units, among other things, the respondent School Board had engaged over almost a decade after 1960 in an unconstitutional policy of deliberate racial segregation with respect to the Park Hill schools. The court therefore ordered the Board to desegregate those schools through the implementation of the three rescinded resolutions.

Segregation in Denver schools is not limited, however, to the schools in the Park Hill area, and not satisfied with their success in obtaining relief for Park Hill, petitioners pressed their prayer that the District Court order desegregation of all segregated schools in the city of Denver, particularly the heavily segregated schools in the core city area. But that court concluded that its finding of a purposeful and systematic program of racial segregation affecting thousands of students in the Park Hill area did not, in itself, impose on the School Board an affirmative duty to eliminate segregation throughout the school district. Instead, the court fractioned the district and held that petitioners had to make a fresh showing of *de jure* segregation in each area of the city for which they sought relief. Moreover, the District Court held that its finding of intentional segregation in Park Hill was not in any sense material to the question of segregative intent in other areas of the city. Under this restrictive approach, the District Court concluded that petitioners' evidence of intentionally discriminatory School Board action in areas of the district other than Park Hill was insufficient to "dictate the conclusion that this is *de jure* segregation which calls for an all-out effort to desegregate. It is more like *de facto* segregation, with respect to which the rule is that the court cannot order desegregation in order to provide a better balance."

[First,] the District Court erred in separating Negroes and Hispanos for purposes of defining a "segregated" school. We have held that Hispanos constitute an identifiable class for purposes of the Fourteenth Amendment.... In fact, the District Court itself recognized that "[o]ne of the things which the Hispano has in common with the Negro is economic and cultural deprivation and discrimination." ...

... We have never suggested that plaintiffs in school desegregation cases must bear the burden of proving the elements of *de jure* segregation as to each and every school or each and every student within the school system. [W]here plaintiffs prove that the school authorities have carried out a systematic program of segregation affecting a substantial portion of the students, schools, teachers, and facilities within the school system, it is only common sense to conclude that there exists a predicate for a finding of the existence of a dual school system. Several considerations support this conclusion. First, it is obvious that a practice of concentrating Negroes in certain schools by structuring attendance zones or designating "feeder" schools on the basis of race has the reciprocal effect of keeping other nearby schools predominantly white. Similarly, the practice of building a school—such as the Barrett Elementary School in this case—to a certain size and in a certain location, "with conscious knowledge that it would be a segregated school," has a substantial reciprocal effect on the racial composition of other nearby schools. So also, the use of mobile classrooms, the drafting of student transfer policies, the transportation of students, and the assignment of faculty and staff, on racially identifiable bases, have the clear effect of earmarking schools according to their racial composition, and this, in turn, together with the elements of student assignment and school construction, may have a profound reciprocal effect on the racial composition of residential neighborhoods within a metropolitan area, thereby causing further racial concentration within the schools....

In short, common sense dictates the conclusion that racially inspired school board actions have an impact beyond the particular schools that are the subjects of those actions. This is not to say, of course, that there can never be a case in which the geographical structure of, or the natural boundaries within, a school district may have the effect of dividing the district into separate, identifiable and unrelated units. Such a determination is essentially a question of fact to be resolved by the trial court in the first instance, but such cases must be rare. In the absence of such a determination, proof of state-imposed segregation in a substantial portion of the district will suffice to support a finding by the trial court of the existence of a dual system. Of course, where that finding is made, as in cases involving statutory dual systems, the school authorities have an affirmative duty "to effectuate a transition to a racially nondiscriminatory school system." . . .

[W]here as here, the case involves one school board, a finding of intentional segregation on its part in one portion of a school system is highly relevant to the issue of the board's intent with respect to other segregated schools in the system. This is merely an application of the well-settled evidentiary principle that "the prior doing of other similar acts, whether clearly a part of a scheme or not, is useful as reducing the possibility that the act in question was done with innocent intent." 2 J. Wigmore, Evidence 200 (3d ed. 1940). . . .

Applying these principles in the special context of school desegregation cases, we hold that a finding of intentionally segregative school board actions in a meaningful portion of a school system, as in this case, creates a presumption that other segregated schooling within the system is not adventitious. It establishes, in other words, a prima facie case of unlawful segregative design on the part of school authorities, and shifts to those authorities the burden of proving that other segregated schools within the system are not also the result of intentionally segregative actions. This is true even if it is determined that different areas of the school district should be viewed independently of each other because, even in that situation, there is high probability that where school authorities have effectuated an intentionally segregative policy in a meaningful portion of the school system, similar impermissible considerations have motivated their actions in other areas of the system. We emphasize that the differentiating factor between *de jure* segregation and so-called *de facto* segregation . . . is *purpose* or *intent* to segregate. [If] an intentionally segregative policy is practiced in a meaningful or significant segment of a school system, as in this case, the school authorities cannot be heard to argue that plaintiffs have proved only "isolated and individual" unlawfully segregative actions. . . .

In discharging that burden, it is not enough, of course, that the school authorities rely upon some allegedly logical, racially neutral explanation for their actions. Their burden is to adduce proof sufficient to support a finding that segregative intent was not among the factors that motivated their actions. The courts below attributed much significance to the fact that many of the Board's actions in the core city area antedated our decision in *Brown*. We reject any suggestion that remoteness in time has any relevance to the issue of intent. If the actions of school authorities were to any degree motivated by segregative intent and the segregation resulting from those actions continues to exist, the fact of remoteness in time certainly does not make those actions any less "intentional."

This is not to say, however, that the prima facie case may not be met by evidence supporting a finding that a lesser degree of segregated schooling in the core city area would not have resulted even if the Board had not acted as it did. [However, a] close examination is required before concluding that the connection does not exist. Intentional school segregation in the past may have been a factor in creating a natural environment for the growth of further segregation. Thus, if respondent School Board cannot disprove segregative intent, it can rebut the prima facie case only by showing that its past segregative acts did not create or contribute to the current segregated condition of the core city schools.

The respondent School Board invoked at trial its "neighborhood school policy" as explaining racial and ethnic concentrations within the core city schools, arguing that since the core city area population had long been Negro and Hispano, the concentrations were necessarily the result of residential patterns and not of purposefully segregative policies. We have no occasion to consider in this case whether a "neighborhood school policy" of itself will justify racial or ethnic concentrations in the absence of a finding that school authorities have committed acts constituting *de jure* segregation. It is enough that we hold that the mere assertion of such a policy is not dispositive where, as in this case, the school authorities have been found to have practiced *de jure* segregation in a meaningful portion of the school system by techniques that indicate that the "neighborhood school" concept has not been maintained free of manipulation. . . .

MR. CHIEF JUSTICE BURGER concurs in the result.

MR. JUSTICE WHITE took no part in the decision of this case.

MR. JUSTICE DOUGLAS.

While I join the opinion of the Court, I agree with my Brother Powell that there is, for the purposes of the Equal Protection Clause of the Fourteenth Amendment as applied to the school cases, no difference between *de facto* and *de jure* segregation. The school board is a state agency and the lines that it draws, the locations it selects for school sites, the allocation it makes of students, the budgets it prepares are state action for Fourteenth Amendment purposes. . . .

MR. JUSTICE POWELL concurring in part and dissenting in part.

. . . Unwilling and footdragging as the process was in most places, substantial progress toward achieving integration has been made in Southern States. No comparable progress has been made in many nonsouthern cities with large minority populations primarily because of the *de facto/de jure* distinction nurtured by the courts and accepted complacently by many of the same voices which denounced the evils of segregated schools in the South. But if our national concern is for those who attend such schools, rather than for perpetuating a legalism rooted in history rather than present reality, we must recognize that the evil of operating separate schools is no less in Denver than in Atlanta. . . . I would not, however, perpetuate the *de jure/de facto* distinction nor would I leave to petitioners the initial tortuous effort of identifying "segregative acts" and deducing "segregative intent." I would hold, quite simply, that where segregated public schools exist within a school district to a substantial degree, there is a prima facie case that the duly constituted public authorities (I will usually refer to them collectively as the "school board") are sufficiently responsible to warrant imposing upon them a nationally applicable burden to demonstrate they nevertheless are operating a genuinely integrated school system. [T]he facts deemed necessary to establish *de jure* discrimination present problems of subjective intent which the courts cannot fairly resolve. . . .

MR. JUSTICE REHNQUIST, dissenting.

[I]n the absence of a statute requiring segregation, there must necessarily be the sort of factual inquiry which was unnecessary in those jurisdictions where racial mixing in the schools was forbidden by law. Underlying the Court's entire opinion is its apparent thesis that a district judge is at least permitted to find that if a single attendance zone between two individual schools in the large metropolitan district is found by him to have been "gerrymandered," the school district is guilty of operating a "dual" school system, and is apparently a candidate for what is in practice a federal receivership. [U]nless the Equal Protection Clause of the Fourteenth Amendment now be held to embody a principle of "taint," found in some primitive legal systems but discarded centuries ago in ours, such a result can only be described as the product of judicial fiat. . . .

Notes

1. The Court often shows great deference to lower court findings that a *de jure* segregated school system exists. E.g., *Columbus Board of Education v. Penick,* 443 U.S. 449, 99 S.Ct. 2941, 61 L.Ed.2d 666 (1979) and *Dayton Board of Education v. Brinkman,* 443 U.S. 526, 99 S.Ct. 2971, 61 L.Ed.2d 720 (1979). The district court and the appellate court in *Penick* concluded that "[w]hile the Columbus school system's dual black-white character was not mandated by state law as of 1954, the record certainly shows intentional segregation by the Columbus Board." The Supreme Court, 7 to 2, affirmed. In *Brinkman,* the district court had dismissed the complaint but the appellate court reversed and found de jure segregation in the school system. In a 5 to 4 vote the Supreme Court again affirmed the appellate court. In *Penick,* Justice White for the Court noted: "The dissenters in this case claim a better grasp of the historical and ultimate facts than the two courts below had. But on the issue of whether there was a dual school system in Columbus, Ohio, in 1954, on the record before us we are much more impressed by the views of the judges who have lived with the case over the years. Also, our dissenting Brothers' suggestion that this Court should play a special oversight role in reviewing the factual determinations of the lower courts in school desegregation cases asserts an omnipotence and omniscience that we do not have and should not claim."

Rehnquist, J., joined by Powell, J., dissented in both cases: "The lower courts' methodology would all but eliminate the distinction between *de facto* and *de jure* segregation and render all school systems captives of a remote and ambiguous past." Powell asserted that the "Court indulges the courts below in their stringing together a chain of 'presumptions,' not one of which is close enough to reality to be reasonable. This chain leads inexorably to the remarkable conclusion that the absence of integration found to exist in a high percentage of the 241 schools in Columbus and Dayton was caused entirely by intentional violations of the Fourteenth Amendment by the school boards of these two cities."

2. INTERDISTRICT REMEDIES. *Milliken v. Bradley,* 418 U.S. 717, 94 S.Ct. 3112, 41 L.Ed.2d 1069 (1974) was the first case on the Supreme Court level to consider a court ordered desegregation plan involving more than one school district in order to remedy *de jure* segregation found to exist in one district. The lower court, after finding *de jure* segregation in the City of Detroit, directed defendants to submit desegregation plans encompassing a three county metropolitan area of 85 school districts not parties to the action. The district court designated 53 of these districts plus Detroit as the "desegregation area," and held that the acts of the Detroit Board of Education, as a subordinate entity of the state, were attributable to the state, thus creating vicarious liability. Over the dissents of four Justices the Court, per Burger, C.J., reversed:

> The [district] court's analytical starting point was its conclusion that school district lines are no more than arbitrary lines on a map drawn "for political convenience." Boundary lines may be bridged where there has been a constitutional violation calling for interdistrict relief, but the notion that school district lines may be casually ignored or treated as a mere administrative convenience is contrary to the history of public education in our country. No single tradition in public education is more deeply rooted than local control over the operation of schools; local autonomy has long been thought essential both to the maintenance of community concern and support for public schools and to quality of the educational process. [T]he scope of the remedy is determined by the nature and extent of the constitutional violation. Before the boundaries of separate and autonomous school districts may be set aside by consolidating the separate units for remedial purposes or by imposing a cross-district remedy, it must first be shown that there has been a constitutional violation within one district that produces a significant segregative effect in another district. Specifically, it must be shown that racially discriminatory acts of the state or local school districts, or of a single school district have been a substantial cause of interdistrict segregation. Thus an interdistrict remedy might be in order where the racially discriminatory acts of one or more school districts caused racial segregation in an adjacent district, or where district lines have been deliberately drawn on the basis of race. In such circumstances an interdistrict remedy would be appropriate to eliminate the interdistrict segregation directly caused by the constitutional violation. Conversely, without an interdistrict violation and interdistrict effect, there is no constitutional wrong calling for an interdistrict remedy.

> The record before us, voluminous as it is, contains evidence of *de jure* segregated conditions only in the Detroit schools.... To approve the remedy ordered by the court would impose on the outlying districts, not shown to have committed any constitutional violation, a wholly impermissible remedy based on a standard not hinted at in *Brown I* and *II* or any holding of this Court.... The constitutional right of the Negro respondents residing in Detroit is to attend a unitary school system in

that district. Unless petitioners drew the district lines in a discriminatory fashion, or arranged for white students residing in the Detroit District to attend schools in Oakland and Macomb Counties, they were under no constitutional duty to make provisions for Negro students to do so.

Contrast, *Hills v. Gautreaux,* 425 U.S. 284, 96 S.Ct. 1538, 47 L.Ed.2d 792 (1976). The lower court found that the U.S. Department of Housing and Urban Development, by financial and other assistance to the Chicago Housing Authority, had aided in discrimination in connection with the selection of sites for public housing in Chicago, causing racially segregated housing. The appellate court ordered metropolitan area relief not limited to the geographic boundary of Chicago. The Supreme Court affirmed.

> The critical distinction between HUD and the suburban school districts in *Milliken* is that HUD has been found to have violated the Constitution. [U]nlike the desegregation remedy found erroneous in *Milliken,* a judicial order directing relief will not necessarily entail coercion of uninvolved governmental units, because both CHA and HUD have authority to operate outside the Chicago city limits. [In] contrast to the desegregation order in [*Milliken*], a metropolitan area relief order directed to HUD would not consolidate or in any way restructure local governmental units.

Missouri v. Jenkins, 515 U.S. 70, 115 S.Ct. 2038, 132 L.Ed.2d 63 (1995). Rehnquist, C.J., for the Court (5 to 4), reversed lower court orders that increased salaries for virtually all instructional and noninstructional staff within the Kansas City, Missouri School District (KCMSD) and required the state to continue to fund remedial "quality education" programs because student achievement levels were still "at or below national norms at many grade levels." The trial court, dismissed as "irrelevant" the state's argument that the present conditions of the facilities were not traceable to unlawful segregation, and candidly acknowledged that it had urged the school district planners "to dream." Consequently, the annual desegregation costs approached $200 million, exceeding the annual cost per pupil of any other school district in Missouri. The court-ordered remedial plan resulted in high schools with green houses and vivariums; Model United Nations wired for language translation, 2,000 square foot planetarium, broadcast capable radio and television studios, etc.

The trial court found only an intra-district violation, but designed a plan to attract nonminority students from outside the KCMSD schools. This "inter district goal is beyond the scope of the intra district violation." A court may not devise a remedy "to accomplish indirectly what it admittedly lacks the remedial authority to mandate directly: the interdistrict transfer of students." The district court's findings that segregation led to "white flight" were inconsistent internally with the record. The Court emphasized that its ruling was fully consistent with *Milliken* and *Gautreaux.* It was also error for the lower court to require continued funding of elaborate education programs because student achievement levels were still "at or below national norms at many grade levels." That is not the correct test. Instead the court should decide whether "the reduction in achievement by minority students attributed to prior *de jure* segregation has been remedied to the extent practicable."

O'Connor, J., & Thomas, J., each filed a concurring opinion. Thomas, J., noted:

> It never ceases to amaze me that the courts are so willing to assume that anything that is predominantly black must be inferior.... Without a basis in any real finding of intentional government action, the District Court's imposition of liability upon the State of Missouri improperly rests upon a theory that racial imbalances are unconstitutional.... This position appears to rest upon the idea that any school that is black is inferior, and that blacks cannot succeed without the benefit of the company of whites.

> The District Court's willingness to adopt such stereotypes stemmed from a misreading of our earliest school desegregation case. In *Brown v. Board of Education* (1954)(*Brown I*), [the Court] did not say that "racially isolated" schools were inherently inferior; the harm that it identified was tied purely to *de jure* segregation, not *de facto* segregation. Indeed, *Brown I* itself did not need to rely upon any psychological or social-science research in order to announce the simple, yet fundamental truth that the Government cannot discriminate among its citizens on the basis of race. As the Court's unanimous opinion indicated: "[I]n the field of public education the doctrine of 'separate but equal' has no place. Separate educational facilities are inherently unequal." At the heart of this interpretation of the Equal Protection Clause lies the principle that the Government must treat citizens as individuals, and not as members of racial, ethnic or religious groups. It is for this reason that we must subject all racial classifications to the strictest of scrutiny, which (aside from two decisions rendered in the midst of wartime, see *Hirabayashi v. United States* (1943); *Korematsu v. United States* (1944)) has proven automatically fatal.

> Segregation was not unconstitutional because it might have caused psychological feelings of inferiority. Public school systems that separated blacks and provided them with superior educational resources—making blacks "feel" superior to whites sent to lesser schools—would violate the Fourteenth Amendment, whether or not the white students felt stigmatized, just as do school systems in which the positions of the races are reversed. Psychological injury or benefit is irrelevant to the question whether state actors have engaged in intentional discrimination—the critical inquiry for ascertaining violations of the Equal Protection Clause
> . . . . .

> Regardless of the relative quality of the schools, segregation violated the Constitution because the State classified students based on their race. Of course, segregation additionally harmed black students by relegating them to schools with substandard facilities and resources. But neutral policies, such as local school assignments, do not offend the Constitution when individual private choices concerning work or residence produce schools with high black populations. The Constitution does not prevent individuals from choosing to live together, to work

together, or to send their children to school together, so long as the State does not interfere with their choices on the basis of race.

Souter, J., joined by Stevens, Ginsburg, & Breyer, JJ., filed a dissenting opinion, and Ginsburg, J., also filed a dissenting opinion.

WASHINGTON v. DAVIS
426 U.S. 229, 96 S.Ct. 2040, 48 L.Ed.2d 597 (1976).

MR. JUSTICE WHITE delivered the opinion of the Court.

This case involves the validity of a qualifying test administered to applicants for positions as police officers in the District of Columbia Metropolitan Police Department. The test was sustained by the District Court but invalidated by the Court of Appeals. We are in agreement with the District Court and hence reverse the judgment of the Court of Appeals.

[The test, known as "Test 21," is used generally throughout the federal service and was developed by the Civil Service Commission to test "verbal ability, vocabulary, reading and comprehension." The Court of Appeals declared] that lack of discriminatory intent in designing and administering Test 21 was irrelevant; the critical fact was rather that a far greater proportion of blacks—four times as many—failed the test than did whites. This disproportionate impact, standing alone and without regard to whether it indicated a discriminatory purpose, was held sufficient to establish a constitutional violation, absent proof by petitioners that the test was an adequate measure of job performance in addition to being an indicator of probable success in the training program, a burden which the court ruled petitioners had failed to discharge. That the Department had made substantial efforts to recruit blacks was held beside the point....

The central purpose of the Equal Protection Clause of the Fourteenth Amendment is the prevention of official conduct discriminating on the basis of race. It is also true that the Due Process Clause of the Fifth Amendment contains an equal protection component prohibiting the United States from invidiously discriminating between individuals or groups. *Bolling v. Sharpe,* [§ 8–2.12, supra]. But our cases have not embraced the proposition that a law or other official act, without regard to whether it reflects a racially discriminatory purpose, is unconstitutional *solely* because it has a racially disproportionate impact.

... "The differentiating factor between *de jure* segregation and so-called *de facto* segregation ... is *purpose* or *intent* to segregate." ... This is not to say that the necessary discriminatory racial purpose must be express or appear on the face of the statute, or that a law's disproportionate impact is irrelevant in cases involving Constitution-based claims of racial discrimination. A statute, otherwise neutral on its face, must not be applied so as invidiously to discriminate on the basis of race. *Yick Wo v. Hopkins.*

[A]n invidious discriminatory purpose may often be inferred from the totality of the relevant facts, including the fact, if it is true, that the law bears more heavily on one race than another. It is also not infrequently true that the discriminatory impact—in the jury cases for example, the total or seriously disproportionate exclusion of Negroes from jury venires—may for all practical purposes demonstrate unconstitutionality because in various circumstances the discrimination is very difficult to explain on nonracial grounds. Nevertheless, we have not held that a law, neutral on its face and serving ends otherwise within the power of government to pursue, is invalid under the Equal Protection Clause simply because it may affect a greater proportion of one race than of another. Disproportionate impact is not irrelevant, but it is not the sole touchstone of an invidious racial discrimination forbidden by the Constitution. Standing alone, it does not trigger the rule, that racial classifications are to be subjected to the strictest scrutiny and are justifiable only by the weightiest of considerations. . . .

As an initial matter, we have difficulty understanding how a law establishing a racially neutral qualification for employment is nevertheless racially discriminatory and denies "any person . . . equal protection of the laws" simply because a greater proportion of Negroes fail to qualify than members of other racial or ethnic groups. . . . Test 21, which is administered generally to prospective Government employees, concededly seeks to ascertain whether those who take it have acquired a particular level of verbal skill; and it is untenable that the Constitution prevents the Government from seeking modestly to upgrade the communicative abilities of its employees rather than to be satisfied with some lower level of competence, particularly where the job requires special ability to communicate orally and in writing. Respondents, as Negroes, could no more successfully claim that the test denied them equal protection than could white applicants who also failed. The conclusion would not be different in the face of proof that more Negroes than whites had been disqualified by Test 21. . . .

Nor on the facts of the case before us would the disproportionate impact of Test 21 warrant the conclusion that it is a purposeful device to discriminate against Negroes and hence an infringement of the constitutional rights of respondents as well as other black applicants. As we have said, the test is neutral on its face and rationally may be said to serve a purpose the Government is constitutionally empowered to pursue. Even agreeing with the District Court that the differential racial effect of Test 21 called for further inquiry, we think the District Court correctly held that the affirmative efforts of the Metropolitan Police Department to recruit black officers, the changing racial composition of the recruit classes and of the force in general, and the relationship of the test to the training program negated any inference that the Department discriminated on the basis of race or that "a police officer qualifies on the color of his skin rather than ability."

Under Title VII, Congress provided that when hiring and promotion practices disqualifying substantially disproportionate numbers of blacks are challenged, discriminatory purpose need not be proved, and that it is an insufficient response to demonstrate some rational basis for the challenged practices. It is necessary, in addition, that they be "validated" in terms of job performance in any one of several ways, perhaps by ascertaining the minimum skill, ability, or potential necessary for the position at issue and determining whether the qualifying tests are appropriate for the selection of qualified applicants for the job in question. However this process proceeds, it involves a more probing judicial review of, and less deference to, the seemingly reasonable acts of administrators and executives than is appropriate under the Constitution where special racial impact, without discriminatory purpose, is claimed. We are not disposed to adopt this more rigorous standard for the purposes of applying the Fifth and the Fourteenth Amendments in cases such as this.

A rule that a statute designed to serve neutral ends is nevertheless invalid, absent compelling justification, if in practice it benefits or burdens one race more than another would be far reaching and would raise serious questions about, and perhaps invalidate, a whole range of tax, welfare, public service, regulatory, and licensing statutes that may be more burdensome to the poor and to the average black than to the more affluent white. Given that rule, such consequences would perhaps be likely to follow. However, in our view, extension of the rule beyond those areas where it is already applicable by reason of statute, such as in the field of public employment, should await legislative prescription....

[The Court also found no applicable statutory violations].

Mr. Justice Stevens, concurring....

Frequently the most probative evidence of intent will be objective evidence of what actually happened rather than evidence describing the subjective state of mind of the actor. For normally the actor is presumed to have intended the natural consequences of his deeds. This is particularly true in the case of governmental action which is frequently the product of compromise, of collective decisionmaking, and of mixed motivation. It is unrealistic, on the one hand, to require the victim of alleged discrimination to uncover the actual subjective intent of the decisionmaker or, conversely, to invalidate otherwise legitimate action simply because an improper motive affected the deliberation of a participant in the decisional process. A law conscripting clerics should not be invalidated because an atheist voted for it.... On the other hand, when the disproportion is as dramatic as in *Yick Wo v. Hopkins,* it really does not matter whether the standard is phrased in terms of purpose or effect.

My agreement ... rests on a ground narrower than the Court describes. I do not rely at all on the evidence of good-faith efforts to recruit black police officers. In my judgment, neither those efforts nor the subjective good faith of the District administration, would save Test 21 if it were otherwise invalid. There are two reasons why I am convinced that the challenge to Test 21 is insufficient. First, the test serves the neutral and legitimate purpose of requiring all applicants to meet a uniform minimum standard of literacy. . . . Second, the same test is used throughout the federal service. The applicants for employment in the District of Columbia Police Department represent such a small fraction of the total number of persons who have taken the test that their experience is of minimal probative value in assessing the neutrality of the test itself. That evidence, without more, is not sufficient to overcome the presumption that a test which is this widely used by the Federal Government is in fact neutral in its effect as well as its "purpose" as that term is used in constitutional adjudication. . . .

[The dissenting opinion of BRENNAN, J., joined by MARSHALL, J. is omitted. They dissented on the statutory issue. STEWART, J. joined the opinion of the Court only as to the constitutional issue.]

VILLAGE OF ARLINGTON HEIGHTS
v. METROPOLITAN HOUSING
DEVELOPMENT CORP.
429 U.S. 252, 97 S.Ct. 555, 50 L.Ed.2d 450 (1977).

MR. JUSTICE POWELL delivered the opinion of the Court.

In 1971 respondent Metropolitan Housing Development Corporation (MHDC) applied to petitioner, the Village of Arlington Heights, Ill., for the rezoning of a 15–acre parcel from single-family to multiple-family classification. Using federal financial assistance, MHDC planned to build 190 clustered townhouse units for low-and moderate-income tenants. The Village denied the rezoning request. MHDC, [sued, alleging] that the denial was racially discriminatory and that it violated, *inter alia,* the Fourteenth Amendment. . . .

[Opponents of rezoning stressed] two arguments. First, the area always had been zoned single-family, and the neighboring citizens had built or purchased there in reliance on that classification. Rezoning threatened to cause a measurable drop in property value for neighboring sites. Second, the Village's apartment policy, adopted by the Village Board in 1962 and amended in 1970, called for R–5 zoning primarily to serve as a buffer between single-family development and land uses thought incompatible, such as commercial or manufacturing districts. Lincoln Green did not meet this requirement, as it adjoined no commercial or manufacturing district.

[T]he Court of Appeals ruled that the denial of rezoning must be examined in light of its "historical context and ultimate effect." Northwest Cook County was enjoying rapid growth in employment opportunities and population, but it continued to exhibit a high degree of residential segregation. The court held that Arlington Heights could not simply ignore this problem. Indeed, it found that the Village had been "exploiting" the situation by allowing itself to become a nearly all-white community. The Village had no other current plans for building low-and moderate-income housing, and no other R–5 parcels in the Village were available to MHDC at an economically feasible price.

Against this background, the Court of Appeals ruled that the denial of the Lincoln Green proposal had racially discriminatory effects and could be tolerated only if it served compelling interests. Neither the buffer policy nor the desire to protect property values met this exacting standard. The court therefore concluded that the denial violated the Equal Protection Clause of the Fourteenth Amendment....

Our decision last Term in *Washington v. Davis,* made it clear that official action will not be held unconstitutional solely because it results in a racially disproportionate impact.... *Davis* does not require a plaintiff to prove that the challenged action rested solely on racially discriminatory purposes. Rarely can it be said that a legislature or administrative body operating under a broad mandate made a decision motivated solely by a single concern, or even that a particular purpose was the "dominant" or "primary" one. In fact, it is because legislators and administrators are properly concerned with balancing numerous competing considerations that courts refrain from reviewing the merits of their decisions, absent a showing of arbitrariness or irrationality. But racial discrimination is not just another competing consideration. When there is a proof that a discriminatory purpose has been a motivating factor in the decision, this judicial deference is no longer justified.

Determining whether invidious discriminatory purpose was a motivating factor demands a sensitive inquiry into such circumstantial and direct evidence of intent as may be available. The impact of the official action—whether it "bears more heavily on one race than another," *Washington v. Davis,* supra—may provide an important starting point. Sometimes a clear pattern, unexplainable on grounds other than race, emerges from the effect of the state action even when the governing legislation appears neutral on its face. *Yick Wo v. Hopkins.* ... But such cases are rare. Absent a pattern as stark as that in *Yick Wo,* impact alone is not determinative, and the Court must look to other evidence.

The historical background of the decision is one evidentiary source, particularly if it reveals a series of official actions taken for invidious purposes. The specific sequence of events leading up to the challenged decision also may shed some light on the decisionmaker's purposes. For example, if the property involved here always had been zoned R–5 but suddenly was changed to R–3 when the town learned of MHDC's plans to erect integrated housing, we would have a far different case. Departures from the normal procedural sequence also might afford evidence that improper purposes are playing a role. Substantive departures too may be relevant, particularly if the factors usually considered important by the decisionmaker strongly favor a decision contrary to the one reached.

The legislative or administrative history may be highly relevant, especially where there are contemporary statements by members of the decision-making body, minutes of its meetings, or reports. In some extraordinary instances the members might be called to the stand at trial to testify concerning the purpose of the official action, although even then such testimony frequently will be barred by privilege. 8 J. Wigmore, Evidence § 2371 (McNaughton rev. ed. 1961).[18]

. . . The impact of the Village's decision does arguably bear more heavily on racial minorities. Minorities constitute 18% of the Chicago area population, and 40% of the income groups said to be eligible for Lincoln Green. But there is little about the sequence of events leading up to the decision that would spark suspicion. The area around the Viatorian property has been zoned R–3 since 1959, the year when Arlington Heights first adopted a zoning map. Single-family homes surround the 80–acre site, and the Village is undeniably committed to single-family homes as its dominant residential land use. The rezoning request progressed according to the usual procedures. The Plan Commission even scheduled two additional hearings, at least in part to accommodate MHDC and permit it to supplement its presentation with answers to questions generated at the first hearing.

The statements by the Plan Commission and Village Board members, as reflected in the official minutes, focused almost exclusively on the zoning aspects of the MHDC petition, and the zoning factors on which they relied are not novel criteria in the Village's rezoning decisions. There is no reason to doubt that there has been reliance by some neighboring property owners on the maintenance of single-family zoning in the vicinity. The Village originally adopted its buffer policy long before MHDC entered the picture and has applied the policy too consistently for us to infer discriminatory purpose from its application in this case. Finally, MHDC called one member of the Village Board to the stand at trial. Nothing in her testimony supports an inference of invidious purpose.

In sum, the evidence does not warrant overturning the concurrent findings of both courts below. Respondents simply failed to carry their burden of proving that discriminatory purpose was a motivating factor in the Village's decision.[21] This conclusion ends the constitutional inquiry. The Court of Appeals' further finding that the Village's decision carried a discriminatory "ultimate effect" is without independent constitutional significance. . . .

---

18. This Court has recognized, ever since *Fletcher v. Peck*, 6 Cranch 87, 130–131, 3 L.Ed. 162 (1810), that judicial inquiries into legislative or executive motivation represent a substantial intrusion into the workings of other branches of government. Placing a decisionmaker on the stand is therefore "usually to be avoided." *Citizens to Preserve Overton Park v. Volpe*, 401 U.S. 402, 420, 91 S.Ct. 814, 825, 28 L.Ed.2d 136 (1971). The problems involved have prompted a good deal of scholarly commentary.

21. Proof that the decision by the Village was motivated in part by a racially discriminatory purpose would not necessarily have required invalidation of the challenged decision. Such proof would, however, have shifted to the Village the burden of establishing that the same decision would have resulted even had the impermissible purpose not been considered. If this were established, the complaining party in a case of this kind no longer fairly could attribute the injury complained of to improper consideration of a discriminatory purpose. In such circumstances, there would be no justification for judicial interference with the challenged decision. But in this case respondents failed to make the required threshold showing.

MR. JUSTICE STEVENS took no part in the consideration or decision of this case.

[The opinion of MARSHALL, J., joined by BRENNAN, J., concurring in part and dissenting in part, and the dissenting opinion of WHITE, J., are omitted.]

Notes

1. In *City of Mobile v. Bolden,* 446 U.S. 55, 100 S.Ct. 1490, 64 L.Ed.2d 47 (1980), a divided Court with no majority opinion refused to require Mobile, Alabama (a city governed by a Commission of three members elected at-large) to dismantle its at-large system of government. Black voters had brought a class action arguing that the practice of electing the City Commissioners at-large unfairly diluted their voting strength in violation of the Fourteenth and Fifteenth Amendments. Stewart, J., joined by Burger, C.J., Powell and Rehnquist, JJ., concluded that the plaintiffs had not proven "purposeful discrimination" and hence there could be no violation of the Fourteenth or Fifteenth Amendments. While no black had been elected to the city commission, blacks "register and vote in Mobile 'without hindrance' "and "there are no official obstacles" in the way of blacks who wish to become candidates for election to the commission. The "right to equal participation in the electoral process does not protect any 'political group,' however defined, from electoral defeat." The trial court had relied on the "substantial history of official racial discrimination in Alabama. But past discrimination cannot, in the manner of original sin, condemn governmental action that is not itself unlawful."

2. *Rogers v. Lodge,* 458 U.S. 613, 102 S.Ct. 3272, 73 L.Ed.2d 1012 (1982) upheld a trial court ruling that the at-large system of voting in a Georgia county violated the Fourteenth Amendment rights of blacks because it was "maintained for invidious purposes" even though it was racially neutral when adopted. Therefore the trial court divided the county into five districts for purposes of electing County Commissioners. The majority ruled that the trial court's findings supported the ultimate finding of intentional discrimination necessary under *Mobile v. Bolden.*

Stevens, J., in dissent, warned: "in the long run constitutional adjudication that is premised on a case-by-case appraisal of the subjective intent of local decisionmakers cannot possibly satisfy the requirement of impartial administration of the law that is embodied in the Equal Protection Clause of the Fourteenth Amendment."

3. In *Hunter v. Underwood,* 471 U.S. 222, 105 S.Ct. 1916, 85 L.Ed.2d 222 (1985), Justice Rehnquist, for a unanimous Court, invalidated § 182 of the Alabama Constitution of 1901, which provided for the disenfranchisement of persons convicted of "any crime . . . involving moral turpitude." In the particular case, two voters (one black, and one white) were blocked from the voter rolls because they had each been convicted of the misdemeanor of presenting a worthless check. The trial court had refused to invalidate § 182, but the Court of Appeals reversed.

Although § 182 was racially neutral on its face, the Court of Appeals had found (and the Supreme Court agreed) that the evidence of its discriminatory impact was "indisputable." In 1903, the law had disenfranchised about ten times as many blacks as whites. Even in modern times, blacks were "at least 1.7 times as likely as whites to suffer" the loss of the vote. Rehnquist then said:

> Presented with a neutral state law that produces disproportionate effects along racial lines, the Court of Appeals was correct in applying the approach of *Arlington Heights* to determine whether the law violates the Equal Protection Clause of the Fourteenth Amendment: "[O]fficial action will not be held unconstitutional solely because it results in a racially disproportionate impact.... Proof of racially discriminatory intent or purpose is required to show a violation of the Equal Protection Clause." See *Washington v. Davis*. Once racial discrimination is shown to have been a "substantial" or "motivating" factor behind enactment of the law, the burden shifts to the law's defenders to demonstrate that the law would have been enacted without this factor.

Rehnquist acknowledged that proving motivation "is often a problematic undertaking," which is especially difficult when we look at a multimember body "the size of the Alabama Constitutional Convention of 1901." However, the evidence of a racially discriminatory intent in this case was clear. "The delegates to the all-white convention were not secretive about their purpose." In fact, neither the District Court (which rejected the plaintiffs' claim) nor the appellants (defending the Alabama law) seriously disputed "the claim that this zeal for white supremacy ran rampant at the convention." The district court was "clearly erroneous" in refusing to conclude that racial discrimination was not a "substantial" or "motivating" factor behind § 182. Even if the "real purpose behind § 182 was to disenfranchise poor whites as well as blacks," this additional purpose does not make insignificant the purpose to discriminate against blacks, and that purpose was a "but-for" motivation for the enactment of § 182. The Court affirmed the Court of Appeals and held that § 182 violated the Equal Protection Clause.[2]

8–2.14　Reverse Discrimination

REGENTS OF THE UNIVERSITY OF CALIFORNIA v. BAKKE

438 U.S. 265, 98 S.Ct. 2733, 57 L.Ed.2d 750 (1978).

Mr. Justice Powell announced the judgment of the Court.

This case presents a challenge to the special admissions program of the petitioner, the Medical School of the University of California at Davis, which is designed to assure the admission of a specified number of students from certain minority groups. The Superior Court of California sustained respondent's challenge, holding that petitioner's program violated the California Constitution, Title VI of the Civil Rights Act of 1964, and the Equal Protection Clause of the Fourteenth Amendment. The court enjoined petitioner from considering respondent's race or the race

---

2. The Court also held that the "other crime" provision in § 2 of the Fourteenth Amendment "was not designed to permit the purposeful facial discrimination attend-ing the enactment and operation of § 182 which otherwise violated § 1 of the Fourteenth Amendment."

of any other applicant in making admissions decisions. It refused, however, to order respondent's admission to the Medical School, holding that he had not carried his burden of proving that he would have been admitted but for the constitutional and statutory violations. The Supreme Court of California affirmed those portions of the trial court's judgment declaring the special admissions program unlawful and enjoining petitioner from considering the race of any applicant. It modified that portion of the judgment denying respondent's requested injunction and directed the trial court to order his admission.

For the reasons stated in the following opinion, I believe that so much of the judgment of the California court as holds petitioner's special admissions program unlawful and directs that respondent be admitted to the Medical School must be affirmed. For the reasons expressed in a separate opinion, my Brothers THE CHIEF JUSTICE [BURGER], MR. JUSTICE STEWART, MR. JUSTICE REHNQUIST, and MR. JUSTICE STEVENS concur in this judgment. I also conclude for the reasons stated in the following opinion that the portion of the court's judgment enjoining petitioner from according any consideration to race in its admissions process must be reversed. For reasons expressed in separate opinions, my Brothers MR. JUSTICE BRENNAN, MR. JUSTICE WHITE, MR. JUSTICE MARSHALL, and MR. JUSTICE BLACKMUN concur in this judgment.

Affirmed in part and reversed in part.

I*

The Medical School of the University of California at Davis opened in 1968 with an entering class of 50 students. In 1971, the size of the entering class was increased to 100 students, a level at which it remains. No admissions program for disadvantaged or minority students existed when the school opened, and the first class contained three Asians but no blacks, no Mexican–Americans, and no American Indians. Over the next two years, the faculty devised a special admissions program to increase the representation of "disadvantaged" students in each medical school class.

The special admissions program operated with a separate committee, a majority of whom were members of minority groups. On the 1973 application form, candidates were asked to indicate whether they wished to be considered as "economically and/or educationally disadvantaged" applicants; on the 1974 form the question was whether they wished to be considered as members of a "minority group," which the Medical School apparently viewed as "Blacks," "Chicanos," "Asians," and "American Indians." If these questions were answered affirmatively, the application was forwarded to the special admissions committee. No formal definition of "disadvantaged" was ever produced, but the chairman of the special committee screened each application to see whether it reflected economic or educational deprivation. [S]pecial candidates did not have to meet the

---

* Mr. Justice Brennan, Mr. Justice White, Mr. Justice Marshall, and Mr. Justice Blackmun join Parts I and V–C of this opinion. Mr. Justice White also joins Part III–A of this opinion.

2.5 grade point average cutoff applied to regular applicants. . . . While the overall class size was still 50, the prescribed number was 8; in 1973 and 1974, when the class size had doubled to 100, the prescribed number of special admissions also doubled, to 16. . . . Although disadvantaged whites applied to the special program in large numbers, none received an offer of admission through that process. Indeed, in 1974, at least, the special committee explicitly considered only "disadvantaged" special applicants who were members of one of the designated minority groups.

Allan Bakke is a white male who applied to the Davis Medical School in both 1973 and 1974. [In 1973 Bakke's application came late in the year causing his rejection. After his rejection Bakke wrote the Associate Dean protesting the special admissions program. In 1974 his faculty interviewer by coincidence was the Associate Dean, who gave Bakke the lowest of his six ratings. Again he was rejected and he filed suit. The California Supreme Court, relying only on the Equal Protection Clause, ordered the University to demonstrate that Bakke would not have been admitted even in the absence of the special admissions program. After the University conceded its inability to carry that burden, the court ordered Bakke admitted.] . . .

II

A. . . . We assume, only for the purposes of this case, that respondent has a right of action under Title VI.

B. The language of § 601, 78 Stat. 252, like that of the Equal Protection Clause, is majestic in its sweep:

> No person in the United States shall, on the ground of race, color, or national origin, be excluded from participation in, be denied the benefits of, or be subjected to discrimination under any program or activity receiving Federal financial assistance.

. . . Examination of the voluminous legislative history of Title VI reveals a congressional intent to halt federal funding of entities that violate a prohibition of racial discrimination similar to that of the Constitution. Although isolated statements of various legislators, taken out of context, can be marshaled in support of the proposition that § 601 enacted a purely colorblind scheme, without regard to the reach of the Equal Protection Clause, these comments must be read against the background of both the problem that Congress was addressing and the broader view of the statute that emerges from a full examination of the legislative debates. . . . In view of the clear legislative intent, Title VI must be held to proscribe only those racial classifications that would violate the Equal Protection Clause or the Fifth Amendment.

III

A. [T]he parties fight a sharp preliminary action over the proper characterization of the special admissions program. Petitioner prefers to view it as establishing a "goal" of minority representation in the Medical School. Respondent, echoing the courts below, labels it a racial quota. This semantic distinction is beside the point: The special admissions program is undeniably a classification based on race and ethnic background. To the extent that there existed a pool of at least minimally qualified minority applicants to fill the 16 special admissions seats, white applicants could compete only for 84 seats in the entering class, rather than the 100 open to minority applicants. Whether this limitation is described as a quota or a goal, it is a line drawn on the basis of race and ethnic status.

. . . The guarantee of equal protection cannot mean one thing when applied to one individual and something else when applied to a person of another color. If both are not accorded the same protection, then it is not equal. Nevertheless, petitioner argues that the court below erred in applying strict scrutiny to the special admissions program because white males, such as respondent, are not a "discrete and insular minority" requiring extraordinary protection from the majoritarian political process. This rationale, however, has never been invoked in our decisions as a prerequisite to subjecting racial or ethnic distinctions to strict scrutiny. . . . These characteristics may be relevant in deciding whether or not to add new types of classifications to the list of "suspect" categories or whether a particular classification survives close examination. Racial and ethnic classifications, however, are subject to stringent examination without regard to these additional characteristics. . . . Racial and ethnic distinctions of any sort are inherently suspect and thus call for the most exacting judicial examination.

B. Petitioner urges us to adopt for the first time a more restrictive view of the Equal Protection Clause and hold that discrimination against members of the white "majority" cannot be suspect if its purpose can be characterized as "benign."[34] The clock of our liberties, however, cannot be turned back to 1868. It is far too late to argue that the guarantee of equal protection to *all* persons permits the recognition of special wards entitled to a degree of protection greater than that accorded others.[35]

. . .

---

34. In the view of Mr. Justice Brennan [et al.], the pliable notion of "stigma" is the crucial element in analyzing racial classifications. The Equal Protection Clause is not framed in terms of "stigma." Certainly the word has no clearly defined constitutional meaning. It reflects a subjective judgment that is standardless. *All* state-imposed classifications that rearrange burdens and benefits on the basis of race are likely to be viewed with deep resentment by the individuals burdened. [They] are likely to find little comfort in the notion that the deprivation they are asked to endure is merely the price of membership in the dominant majority and that its imposition is inspired by the supposedly benign purpose of aiding others. One should not lightly dismiss the inherent unfairness of, and the perception of mistreatment that accompanies, a system of allocating benefits and privileges on the basis of skin color and ethnic origin. Moreover, Mr. Justice Brennan [et al.], offer no principle for deciding whether preferential classifications reflect a benign remedial purpose or a malevolent stigmatic classification, since they are willing in this case to accept mere *post hoc* declarations by an isolated state entity—a medical school faculty—unadorned by particularized findings of past discrimination, to establish such a remedial purpose.

35. Professor Bickel noted the self-contradiction of that view:

"The lesson of the great decisions of the Supreme Court and the lesson of contemporary history have been the same for at least a generation: discrimination on the basis of race is illegal, immoral, unconstitutional, inherently wrong, and destructive of democratic society. Now this is to be unlearned and we are told that this is not a matter of

Once the artificial line of a "two-class theory" of the Fourteenth Amendment is put aside, the difficulties entailed in varying the level of judicial review according to a perceived "preferred" status of a particular racial or ethnic minority are intractable. The concepts of "majority" and "minority" necessarily reflect temporary arrangements and political judgments. As observed above, the white "majority" itself is composed of various minority groups, most of which can lay claim to a history of prior discrimination at the hands of the State and private individuals. Not all of these groups can receive preferential treatment and corresponding judicial tolerance of distinctions drawn in terms of race and nationality, for then the only "majority" left would be a new minority of white Anglo–Saxon Protestants. There is no principled basis for deciding which groups would merit "heightened judicial solicitude" and which would not.[36] Courts would be asked to evaluate the extent of the prejudice and consequent harm suffered by various minority groups. Those whose societal injury is thought to exceed some arbitrary level of tolerability then would be entitled to preferential classifications at the expense of individuals belonging to other groups. Those classifications would be free from exacting judicial scrutiny. As these preferences began to have their desired effect, and the consequences of past discrimination were undone, new judicial rankings would be necessary. The kind of variable sociological and political analysis necessary to produce such rankings simply does not lie within the judicial competence—even if they otherwise were politically feasible and socially desirable.

Moreover, there are serious problems of justice connected with the idea of preference itself. First, it may not always be clear that a so-called preference is in fact benign. Courts may be asked to validate burdens imposed upon individual members of a particular group in order to advance the group's general interest. Nothing in the Constitution supports the notion that individuals may be asked to suffer otherwise impermissible burdens in order to enhance the societal standing of their ethnic groups. Second, preferential programs may only reinforce common stereotypes holding that certain groups are unable to achieve

---

fundamental principle but only a matter of whose ox is gored. Those for whom racial equality was demanded are to be more equal than others. Having found support in the Constitution for equality, they now claim support for inequality under the same Constitution." A. Bickel, The Morality of Consent 133 (1975).

36. [Justice Brennan et al.] would require as a justification for a program such as petitioner's, only two findings: (I) that there has been some form of discrimination against the preferred minority groups by "society at large," (it being conceded that petitioner had no history of discrimination), and (ii) that "there is reason to believe" that the disparate impact sought to be rectified by the program is the "product" of such discrimination....

The breadth of this hypothesis is unprecedented in our constitutional system. [The second step] involves a speculative leap: but for this discrimination by society at large, Bakke "would have failed to qualify for admission" because Negro applicants— nothing is said about Asians,—would have made better scores. Not one word in the record supports this conclusion.... [I]f it may be concluded *on this record* that each of the minority groups preferred by the petitioner's special program is entitled to the benefit of the presumption, it would seem difficult to determine that any of the dozens of minority groups that have suffered "societal discrimination" cannot also claim it, in any area of social intercourse.

success without special protection based on a factor having no relationship to individual worth. Third, there is a measure of inequity in forcing
innocent persons in respondent's position to bear the burdens of redressing grievances not of their making.

By hitching the meaning of the Equal Protection Clause to these
transitory considerations, we would be holding, as a constitutional principle, that judicial scrutiny of classifications touching on racial and
ethnic background may vary with the ebb and flow of political
forces....

C. Petitioner contends that on several occasions this Court has
approved preferential classifications without applying the most exacting
scrutiny. Most of the cases upon which petitioner relies are drawn from
three areas: school desegregation, employment discrimination, and sex
discrimination. Each of the cases cited presented a situation materially
different from the facts of this case.

The school desegregation cases are inapposite. Each involved remedies for clearly determined constitutional violations. E.g., *Swann v.
Charlotte–Mecklenburg Board of Education.* Racial classifications thus
were designed as remedies for the vindication of constitutional entitlement. Moreover, the scope of the remedies was not permitted to exceed
the extent of the violations. Here, there was no judicial determination of
constitutional violation as a predicate for the formulation of a remedial
classification.

The employment discrimination cases also do not advance petitioner's cause. For example, in *Franks v. Bowman Transportation Co.,* 424
U.S. 747, 96 S.Ct. 1251, 47 L.Ed.2d 444 (1976), we approved a retroactive award of seniority to a class of Negro truckdrivers who had been the
victims of discrimination—not just by society at large, but by the
respondent in that case. While this relief imposed some burdens on other
employees, it was held necessary " 'to make [the victims] whole for
injuries suffered on account of unlawful employment discrimination.' "
... Such preferences also have been upheld where a legislative or
administrative body charged with the responsibility made determinations of past discrimination by the industries affected, and fashioned
remedies deemed appropriate to rectify the discrimination. But we have
never approved preferential classifications in the absence of proved
constitutional or statutory violations.[41]

Nor is petitioner's view as to the applicable standard supported by
the fact that gender-based classifications are not subjected to this level of
scrutiny. Gender-based distinctions are less likely to create the analytical
and practical problems present in preferential programs premised on

41. [W]e are not here presented with an
occasion to review legislation by Congress
pursuant to its powers under § 2 of the
Thirteenth Amendment and § 5 of the
Fourteenth Amendment to remedy the effects of prior discrimination. *Katzenbach v.
Morgan* [§ 9–1, infra]; *Jones v. Alfred H.*
Mayer Co. [§ 9–2, infra]. We have previously recognized the special competence of
Congress to make findings with respect to
the effects of identified past discrimination
and its discretionary authority to take appropriate remedial measures.

racial or ethnic criteria. With respect to gender there are only two possible classifications. The incidence of the burdens imposed by preferential classifications is clear. There are no rival groups which can claim that they, too, are entitled to preferential treatment. Classwide questions as to the group suffering previous injury and groups which fairly can be burdened are relatively manageable for reviewing courts. [T]he perception of racial classifications as inherently odious stems from a lengthy and tragic history that gender-based classifications do not share. In sum, the Court has never viewed such classification as inherently suspect or as comparable to racial or ethnic classifications for the purpose of equal protection analysis. . . .

IV

We have held that in "order to justify the use of a suspect classification, a State must show that its purpose or interest is both constitutionally permissible and substantial, and that its use of the classification is 'necessary . . . to the accomplishment' of its purpose or the safeguarding of its interest." The special admissions program purports to serve the purposes of: (I) "reducing the historic deficit of traditionally disfavored minorities in medical schools and in the medical profession;" (ii) countering the effects of societal discrimination; (iii) increasing the number of physicians who will practice in communities currently underserved; and (iv) obtaining the educational benefits that flow from an ethnically diverse student body. It is necessary to decide which, if any, of these purposes is substantial enough to support the use of a suspect classification.

If petitioner's purpose is to assure within its student body some specified percentage of a particular group merely because of its race or ethnic origin, such a preferential purpose must be rejected not as insubstantial but as facially invalid. Preferring members of any one group for no reason other than race or ethnic origin is discrimination for its own sake. This the Constitution forbids.

. . . We have never approved a classification that aids persons perceived as members of relatively victimized groups at the expense of other innocent individuals in the absence of judicial, legislative, or administrative findings of constitutional or statutory violations. . . . Petitioner does not purport to have made, and is in no position to make, such findings. Its broad mission is education, not the formulation of any legislative policy or the adjudication of particular claims of illegality. For reasons similar to those stated in Part III of this opinion, isolated segments of our vast governmental structures are not competent to make those decisions, at least in the absence of legislative mandates and legislatively determined criteria.[45]

45. For example, the University is unable to explain its selection of only the four favored groups—Negroes, Mexican-Americans, American Indians and Asians—for preferential treatment. The inclusion of the last group is especially curious in light of the substantial numbers of Asians admitted through the regular admissions process.

. . . Petitioner simply has not carried its burden of demonstrating that it must prefer members of particular ethnic groups over all other individuals in order to promote better health-care delivery to deprived citizens. Indeed, petitioner has not shown that its preferential classification is likely to have any significant effect on the problem.

The fourth goal asserted by petitioner is the attainment of a diverse student body. This clearly is a constitutionally permissible goal for an institution of higher education. Academic freedom, though not a specifically enumerated constitutional right, long has been viewed as a special concern of the First Amendment. The freedom of a university to make its own judgments as to education includes the selection of its student body. . . . Thus, in arguing that its universities must be accorded the right to select those students who will contribute the most to the "robust exchange of ideas," petitioner invokes a countervailing constitutional interest, that of the First Amendment. In this light, petitioner must be viewed as seeking to achieve a goal that is of paramount importance in the fulfillment of its mission.

. . . Physicians serve a heterogeneous population. . . . Ethnic diversity, however, is only one element in a range of factors a university properly may consider in attaining the goal of a heterogeneous student body. Although a university must have wide discretion in making the sensitive judgments as to who should be admitted, constitutional limitations protecting individual rights may not be disregarded. . . . As the interest of diversity is compelling in the context of a university's admissions program, the question remains whether the program's racial classification is necessary to promote this interest.

V

A. It may be assumed that the reservation of a specified number of seats in each class for individuals from the preferred ethnic groups would contribute to the attainment of considerable ethnic diversity in the student body. But petitioner's argument that this is the only effective means of serving the interest of diversity is seriously flawed. . . . The diversity that furthers a compelling state interest encompasses a far broader array of qualifications and characteristics of which racial or ethnic origin is but a single though important element. Petitioner's special admissions program, focused *solely* on ethnic diversity, would hinder rather than further attainment of genuine diversity.

Nor would the state interest in genuine diversity be served by expanding petitioner's two-track system into a multitrack program with a prescribed number of seats set aside for each identifiable category of applicants. Indeed, it is inconceivable that a university would thus pursue the logic of petitioner's two-track program to the illogical end of insulating each category of applicants with certain desired qualifications from competition with all other applicants. The experience of other university admissions programs, which take race into account in achieving the educational diversity valued by the First Amendment, demonstrates that the assignment of a fixed number of places to a minority group is not a necessary means toward that end. An illuminating example is found in the Harvard College program:

> In recent years Harvard College has expanded the concept of diversity to include students from disadvantaged economic, racial and ethnic groups. [T]his new definition of diversity has meant that race has been a factor in some admission decisions. When the Committee on Admissions reviews the large middle group of applicants who are "admissible" and deemed capable of doing good work in their courses, the race of an applicant may tip the balance in his favor just as geographic origin or a life spent on a farm may tip the balance in other candidates' cases. A farm boy from Idaho can bring something to Harvard College that a Bostonian cannot offer. Similarly, a black student can usually bring something that a white person cannot offer. [The] awareness [of the necessity of including more than a token number of black students] does not mean that the Committee sets a minimum number of blacks or of people from west of the Mississippi who are to be admitted....

In such an admissions program, race or ethnic background may be deemed a "plus" in a particular applicant's file, yet it does not insulate the individual from comparison with all other candidates for the available seats. The file of a particular black applicant may be examined for his potential contribution to diversity without the factor of race being decisive when compared, for example, with that of an applicant identified as an Italian–American if the latter is thought to exhibit qualities more likely to promote beneficial educational pluralism. Such qualities could include exceptional personal talents, unique work or service experience, leadership potential, maturity, demonstrated compassion, a history of overcoming disadvantage, ability to communicate with the poor, or other qualifications deemed important....

This kind of program treats each applicant as an individual in the admissions process. The applicant who loses out on the last available seat to another candidate receiving a "plus" on the basis of ethnic background will not have been foreclosed from all consideration for that seat simply because he was not the right color or had the wrong surname. It would mean only that his combined qualifications, which may have included similar nonobjective factors, did not outweigh those of the other applicant. His qualifications would have been weighed fairly and competitively, and he would have not basis to complain of unequal treatment under the Fourteenth Amendment.[52]

It has been suggested that an admissions program which considers race only as one factor is simply a subtle and more sophisticated—but no less effective—means of according racial preference than the Davis program. A facial intent to discriminate, however, is evident in petition-

---

52. The denial to respondent of this right to individualized consideration without regard to his race is the principal evil of petitioner's special admissions program. Nowhere in the opinion of Mr. Justice Brennan, Mr. Justice White, Mr. Justice Marshall, and Mr. Justice Blackmun is this denial even addressed.

er's preference program and not denied in this case. No such facial infirmity exists in an admissions program where race or ethnic background is simply one element—to be weighed fairly against other elements—in the selection process. [A] court would not assume that a university, professing to employ a facially nondiscriminatory admissions policy, would operate it as a cover for the functional equivalent of a quota system. In short, good faith would be presumed in the absence of a showing to the contrary in the manner permitted by our cases. See, e.g., *Arlington Heights v. Metropolitan Housing Dev. Corp.,* [§ 8–2.13, supra]; *Washington v. Davis* [§ 8–2.13, supra].

B. In summary, it is evident that the Davis special admissions program involves the use of an explicit racial classification never before countenanced by this Court. It tells applicants who are not Negro, Asian, or Chicano that they are totally excluded from a specific percentage of the seats in an entering class. No matter how strong their qualifications, quantitative and extracurricular, including their own potential for contribution to educational diversity, they are never afforded the chance to compete with applicants from the preferred groups for the special admissions seats. At the same time, the preferred applicants have the opportunity to compete for every seat in the class.

The fatal flaw in petitioner's preferential program is its disregard of individual rights as guaranteed by the Fourteenth Amendment. *Shelley v. Kraemer,* [§ 7–3, supra]. [W]hen a State's distribution of benefits or imposition of burdens hinges on ancestry or the color of a person's skin or ancestry, that individual is entitled to a demonstration that the challenged classification is necessary to promote a substantial state interest. Petitioner has failed to carry this burden. For this reason, that portion of the California court's judgment holding petitioner's special admissions program invalid under the Fourteenth Amendment must be affirmed.

C. In enjoining petitioner from ever considering the race of any applicant, however, the courts below failed to recognize that the State has a substantial interest that legitimately may be served by a properly devised admissions program involving the competitive consideration of race and ethnic origin. For this reason, so much of the California court's judgment as enjoins petitioner from any consideration of the race of any applicant must be reversed.

VI

With respect to respondent's entitlement to an injunction directing his admission to the Medical School, petitioner has conceded that it could not carry its burden of proving that, but for the existence of its unlawful special admissions program, respondent still would not have been admitted. Hence, respondent is entitled to the injunction, and that portion of the judgment must be affirmed.

Opinion of MR. JUSTICE BRENNAN, MR. JUSTICE WHITE, MR. JUSTICE MARSHALL, and MR. JUSTICE BLACKMUN, concurring in the judgment in part and dissenting in part.

[The multiple opinions in this case should not] mask the central meaning of today's opinions: Government may take race into account when it acts not to demean or insult any racial group, but to remedy disadvantages cast on minorities by past racial prejudice, at least when appropriate findings have been made by judicial, legislative, or administrative bodies with competence to act in this area. . . .

[W]e cannot . . . let color blindness become myopia which masks the reality that many "created equal" have been treated within our lifetimes as inferior both by the law and by their fellow citizens. . . . The assertion of human equality is closely associated with the proposition that differences in color or creed, birth or status, are neither significant nor relevant to the way in which persons should be treated. Nonetheless, the position that such factors must be "constitutionally an irrelevance," *Edwards v. California,* 314 U.S. 160, 185, 62 S.Ct. 164, 172, 86 L.Ed. 119 (1941)(Jackson, J., concurring), summed up by the shorthand phrase "[o]ur Constitution is color-blind," *Plessy v. Ferguson,* (Harlan, J., dissenting), has never been adopted by this Court as the proper meaning of the Equal Protection Clause. Indeed, we have expressly rejected this proposition on a number of occasions.

Our cases have always implied that an "overriding statutory purpose," could be found that would justify racial classifications. See, e.g., *Korematsu v. United States,* [§ 8–2.12, supra]; *Hirabayashi v. United States,* [§ 8–2.12, supra]. . . . We conclude, therefore, that racial classifications are not *per se* invalid under the Fourteenth Amendment. Accordingly, we turn to the problem of articulating what our role should be in reviewing state action that expressly classifies by race.

Respondent argues that racial classifications are always suspect and, consequently, that this Court should weigh the importance of the objectives served by Davis' special admissions program to see if they are compelling. [But] whites as a class [do not] have any of the "traditional indicia of suspectness: the class is not saddled with such disabilities, or subjected to such a history of purposeful unequal treatment, or relegated to such a position of political powerlessness as to command extraordinary protection from the majoritarian political process." Moreover, if the University's representations are credited, this is not a case where racial classifications are "irrelevant and therefore prohibited." Nor has anyone suggested that the University's purposes contravene the cardinal principle that racial classifications that stigmatize—because they are drawn on the presumption that one race is inferior to another or because they put the weight of government behind racial hatred and separatism—are invalid without more.[33]

[B]ecause of the significant risk that racial classifications established for ostensibly benign purposes can be misused, causing effects not unlike those created by invidious classifications, it is inappropriate to inquire only whether there is any conceivable basis that might sustain such a

---

33. Indeed, even in *Plessy v. Ferguson* the Court recognized that a classification by race that presumed one race to be inferior to another would have to be condemned.

classification. Instead, to justify such a classification an important and articulated purpose for its use must be shown. In addition, any statute must be stricken that stigmatizes any group or that singles out those least well represented in the political process to bear the brunt of a benign program. Thus, our review under the Fourteenth Amendment should be strict—not " 'strict' in theory and fatal in fact," because it is stigma that causes fatality—but strict and searching nonetheless.

Davis' articulated purpose of remedying the effects of past societal discrimination is, under our cases, sufficiently important to justify the use of race-conscious admissions programs where there is a sound basis for concluding that minority underrepresentation is substantial and chronic, and that the handicap of past discrimination is impeding access of minorities to the Medical School.

[A] requirement of a judicial determination of a constitutional or statutory violation as a predicate for race-conscious remedial actions would ... undermine efforts to achieve voluntary compliance with the requirements of law....

Certainly, on the basis of the undisputed factual submissions before this Court, Davis had a sound basis for believing that the problem of under-representation of minorities was substantial and chronic and that the problem was attributable to handicaps imposed on minority applicants by past and present racial discrimination. Until at least 1973, the practice of medicine in this country was, in fact, if not in law, largely the prerogative of whites. In 1950, for example, while Negroes constituted 10% of the total population, Negro physicians constituted only 2.2% of the total number of physicians. The overwhelming majority of these, moreover, were educated in two predominantly Negro medical schools, Howard and Meharry. By 1970, the gap between the proportion of Negroes in medicine and their proportion in the population had widened: The number of Negroes employed in medicine remained frozen at 2.2% while the Negro population had increased to 11.1%. The number of Negro admittees to predominantly white medical schools, moreover, had declined in absolute numbers during the years 1955 to 1964....

The second prong of our test—whether the Davis program stigmatizes any discrete group or individual and whether race is reasonably used in light of the program's objectives—is clearly satisfied by the Davis program. It is not even claimed that Davis' program in any way operates to stigmatize or single out any discrete and insular, or even any identifiable, nonminority group. Nor will harm comparable to that imposed upon racial minorities by exclusion or separation on grounds of race be the likely result of the program.... True, whites are excluded from participation in the special admissions program, but this fact only operates to reduce the number of whites to be admitted in the regular admissions program in order to permit admission of a reasonable percentage—less than their proportion of the California population—of otherwise underrepresented qualified minority applicants.

Nor was Bakke in any sense stamped as inferior by the Medical School's rejection of him. Indeed, it is conceded by all that he satisfied those criteria regarded by the school as generally relevant to academic performance better than most of the minority members who were admitted. . . .

In addition, there is simply no evidence that the Davis program discriminates intentionally or unintentionally against any minority group which it purports to benefit. The program does not establish a quota in the invidious sense of a ceiling on the number of minority applicants to be admitted. Nor can the program reasonably be regarded as stigmatizing the program's beneficiaries or their race as inferior. . . . Once admitted, these students must satisfy the same degree requirements as regularly admitted students. . . .

[First, with] respect to any factor (such as poverty or family educational background) that may be used as a substitute for race as an indicator of past discrimination, whites greatly outnumber racial minorities simply because whites make up a far larger percentage of the total population and therefore far outnumber minorities in absolute terms at every socioeconomic level. For example, of a class of recent medical school applicants from families with less than $10,000 income, at least 71% were white. Of all 1970 families headed by a person *not* a high school graduate which included related children under 18, 80% were white and 20% were racial minorities. Moreover, while race is positively correlated with differences in GPA and MCAT scores, economic disadvantage is not. Thus, it appears that economically disadvantaged whites do not score less well than economically advantaged whites, while economically advantaged blacks score less well than do disadvantaged whites. These statistics graphically illustrate that the University's purpose to integrate its classes by compensating for past discrimination could not be achieved by a general preference for the economically disadvantaged or the children of parents of limited education unless such groups were to make up the entire class.

Second, the Davis admissions program does not simply equate minority status with disadvantage. Rather, Davis considers on an individual basis each applicant's personal history to determine whether he or she has likely been disadvantaged by racial discrimination. . . . True, the procedure by which disadvantage is detected is informal, but we have never insisted that educators conduct their affairs through adjudicatory proceedings, and such insistence here is misplaced. . . .

Finally, Davis' special admissions program cannot be said to violate the Constitution simply because it has set aside a predetermined number of places for qualified minority applicants rather than using minority status as a positive factor to be considered in evaluating the applications of disadvantaged minority applicants. For purposes of constitutional adjudication, there is no difference between the two approaches. . . . That the Harvard approach does not also make public the extent of the preference and the precise workings of the system while the Davis program employs a specific, openly stated number, does not condemn the latter plan for purposes of Fourteenth Amendment adjudication....

MR. JUSTICE MARSHALL....

Three hundred and fifty years ago, the Negro was dragged to this country in chains to be sold into slavery. Uprooted from his homeland and thrust into bondage for forced labor, the slave was deprived of all legal rights. It was unlawful to teach him to read; he could be sold away from his family and friends at the whim of his master; and killing or maiming him was not a crime. The system of slavery brutalized and dehumanized both master and slave....

The position of the Negro today in America is the tragic but inevitable consequence of centuries of unequal treatment. Measured by any benchmark of comfort or achievement, meaningful equality remains a distant dream for the Negro. A Negro child today has a life expectancy which is shorter by more than five years than that of a white child. The Negro child's mother is over three times more likely to die of complications in childbirth, and the infant mortality rate for Negroes is nearly twice that for whites. The median income of the Negro family is only 60% that of the median of a white family, and the percentage of Negroes who live in families with incomes below the poverty line is nearly four times greater than that of whites. When the Negro child reaches working age, he finds that America offers him significantly less than it offers his white counterpart. For Negro adults, the unemployment rate is twice that of whites, and the unemployment rate for Negro teenagers is nearly three times that of white teenagers. A Negro male who completes four years of college can expect a median annual income of merely $110 more than a white male who has only a high school diploma. Although Negroes represent 11.5% of the population, they are only 1.2% of the lawyers and judges, 2% of the physicians, 2.3% of the dentists, 1.1% of the engineers and 2.6% of the college and university professors....

[A]fter several hundred years of class-based discrimination against Negroes, the Court is unwilling to hold that a class-based remedy for that discrimination is permissible. [D]ifferences in the experience of the Negro make it difficult for me to accept that Negroes cannot be afforded greater protection under the Fourteenth Amendment where it is necessary to remedy the effects of past discrimination....

MR. JUSTICE BLACKMUN....

It is somewhat ironic to have us so deeply disturbed over a program where race is an element of consciousness, and yet to be aware of the fact, as we are, that institutions of higher learning, albeit more on the undergraduate than the graduate level, have given conceded preferences up to a point to those possessed of athletic skills, to the children of alumni, to the affluent who may bestow their largess on the institutions, and to those having connections with celebrities, the famous, and the powerful....

In order to get beyond racism, we must first take account of race. There is no other way. And in order to treat some persons equally, we must treat them differently.

MR. JUSTICE STEVENS, with whom THE CHIEF JUSTICE [BURGER], MR. JUSTICE STEWART, and MR. JUSTICE REHNQUIST join, concurring in the judgment in part and dissenting in part.

It is always important at the outset to focus precisely on the controversy before the Court.[1] ... Section 601 of the Civil Rights Act of 1964 provides:

> No person in the United States shall, on the ground of race, color, or national origin, be excluded from participation in, be denied the benefits of, or be subjected to discrimination under any program or activity receiving Federal financial assistance.

... The plain language of the statute therefore requires affirmance of the judgment below. A different result cannot be justified unless that language misstates the actual intent of the Congress that enacted the statute or the statute is not enforceable in a private action. Neither conclusion is warranted.... In the words of the House Report, Title VI stands for "the general principle that *no person* ... be excluded from participation ... on the ground of race, color, or national origin under any program or activity receiving Federal financial assistance." H.R.Rep. No. 914, pt. 1, 88th Cong., 1st Sess., 25 (1963)(emphasis added). This same broad view of Title VI and § 601 was echoed throughout the congressional debate and was stressed by every one of the major spokesmen for the Act. [T]he proponents of Title VI assumed that the Constitution itself required a colorblind standard on the part of government, but that does not mean that the legislation only codifies an existing constitutional prohibition....

[The separate opinion of WHITE, J., is omitted.]

Notes

1. The Harvard Plan, to which Justice Powell refers in *Bakke*, had interesting origins. In 1922 President A. Lawrence Lowell of Harvard, supported by bigoted alumni, called for a quota system to limit the number of Jews attending Harvard. (By that time the proportion had reached 22%.) The Harvard Overseers and faculty formally rejected the proposal, so Lowell "imposed a limit of 1,000 students in each incoming class and then urged his admissions officials to seek a broad geographical distribution—that is, to accept more students from Southern and Western states where comparatively few Jews lived. By the time Lowell retired in 1933, the proportion of Jews had shrunk to 10%."[1]

---

1. Four Members of the Court have undertaken to announce the legal and constitutional effect of this Court's judgment. See opinion of Justices Brennan, White, Marshall, and Blackmun. It is hardly necessary to state that only a majority can speak for the Court or determine what is the "central meaning" of any judgment of the Court.

1. Time Magazine, Sept. 18, 1986, at 65. In 1988, Harvard denied that it used quotas to limit Asian–Americans. Harvard acknowledged that Asian–Americans (both ap-

In 1992, the Department of Education's Office of Civil Rights found that Boalt Hall, the University of California's law school at Berkeley, had been violating *Bakke* ever since 1978. The challenged procedures called for a "goal" of 8%–10% African–Americans, 8%–10% Hispanic–Americans; 5%–7% Asian–Americans; and 1% Native–Americans. Pursuant to these procedures, which excluded a large number of highly qualified Asian–Americans, Boalt Hall "segregated the applicant pools: minority students competed only with applicants from their own racial background. The school covered shortfalls of minority students by pulling applicants off equally segregated waiting lists." Until 1989 it explicitly informed applicants about their status on these lists by stating, e.g., "You are presently in the bottom half of the Asian waiting list."[2] Boalt Hall, while not admitting guilt, agreed to change its procedures.

2. In the term after *Bakke,* the Supreme Court decided an issue reserved in *Bakke.* The Court, per Stevens, J., implied a private right of action for violation of Title VI of the Civil Rights Act. *Cannon v. University of Chicago,* 441 U.S. 677, 99 S.Ct. 1946, 60 L.Ed.2d 560 (1979). White, Blackmun, and Powell, JJ., dissented.

3. *Fullilove v. Klutznick,* 448 U.S. 448, 100 S.Ct. 2758, 65 L.Ed.2d 902 (1980). A very fragmented Court, with no majority opinion, rejected a challenge, on its face, to the federal minority business enterprise (MBE) "set-aside" program of the Public Works Employment Act of 1977. The law required that (unless there was an administrative waiver) at least 10% of federal funds granted for local public works projects must be set aside to be used by state or local grantees to purchase business or supplies by "minority business enterprises," which were defined as at least 50% owned by "minority" group members, who in turn were defined as "citizens of the United States who are Negroes, Spanish-speaking, Orientals, Indians, Eskimos, and Aleuts." Burger, C.J., joined by White & Powell, JJ., upheld the law; Marshall, J., joined by Brennan & Blackmun, JJ., concurred in the judgment. Stewart, J., joined by Rehnquist, J., dissented, arguing, "Our Constitution is color-blind," and even "good faith racial discrimination" is bad.

Stevens, J.'s dissent argued that the statute was not "narrowly tailored" because it raised many questions ["why were these six racial classifications and no others, included;" "what percentage of Oriental blood" is required; are "businesses formed just to take advantage of the preference eligible"] that Congress failed to answer in a "responsible way." There was only a brief discussion of the law on the Senate and House floor, and "virtually no debate." Moreover, "the very attempt to define with precision a beneficiary's qualifying racial characteristics is repugnant to our constitutional ideals." If "the National Government is to make a serious effort to define racial classes by criteria that can be administered objectively, it must study precedents

plicants and admitted students) typically scored about 40 points higher than any other group on the combined SAT verbal and mathematics test, and that over the last ten years, there has been a 3.7% difference between the admission rate at Harvard and Radcliffe for Asian–Americans and whites. However, Harvard said, the difference in admission rates is not the result of a quota: although "Asian–Americans are slightly stronger than whites on academic criteria, they are slightly less strong on extracurricular criteria." In addition, fewer Asian–Americans were children of alums. Harvard Statement on Asian–American Admissions (Jan. 1988).

2. Greve, The Newest Move in Law Schools' Quota Game, Wall St. Jrl., Oct. 5, 1992, at A12, col. 3–6.

such as the First Regulation to the Reichs Citizenship Law of November 14, 1935.''

In *Wygant v. Jackson Board of Education,* 476 U.S. 267, 106 S.Ct. 1842, 90 L.Ed.2d 260 (1986), a divided Court, again with no majority opinion, invalidated a provision in a collective bargaining agreement that required the school board, if laying off teachers, to lay off the least senior first, except that at no time would there be a greater percentage of minority personnel laid off than the current percentage of minority personnel employed at the time of the layoff. Nonminority school teachers brought suit claiming that they were laid off because of their race in violation of Equal Protection. Powell, J., announced the judgment of the Court and delivered an opinion that Burger, C.J., & Rehnquist, J., joined and O'Connor, J., joined in part. Powell said:

> [T]he role model theory employed by the District Court has no logical stopping point. [It] actually could be used to escape the obligation to remedy such practices by justifying the small percentage of black teachers by reference to the small percentage of black students. [T]he idea that black students are better off with black teachers could lead to the very system the Court rejected in *Brown v. Board of Education.*

Stevens, J. dissented. Marshall, J., joined by Brennan & Blackmun, JJ., also dissented:

> The Board's goal of preserving minority proportions could have been achieved, perhaps, in a different way. For example, if layoffs had been determined by lottery, the ultimate effect would have been retention of current racial percentages. A random system, however, would place every teacher in equal jeopardy, working a much greater upheaval of the seniority hierarchy than that occasioned by Article XII; it is not at all a less restrictive means of achieving the Board's goal.

O'Connor, J., concurred in part and in the judgment; White, J., concurred in the judgment.

In *Richmond v. J.A. Croson Co.,* 488 U.S. 469, 109 S.Ct. 706, 102 L.Ed.2d 854 (1989), the Court invalidated a Minority Business Enterprises (MBEs) set-aside program adopted by the City Council of Richmond, Virginia. The law, patterned after the federal law, required prime contractors (other than minority-owned prime contractors) to whom the city awarded construction contracts, to subcontract at least 30% of the dollar amount of such contracts to one or more (MBEs), defined as a business at least 51% owned by "[c]itizens of the United States, who are Blacks, Spanish-speaking, Orientals, Indians, Eskimos, or Aleuts." O'Connor, J., (in a portion of her opinion that attracted a majority of the Court) said:

> [In *Fullilove*] Congress was exercising its power under § 5 of the Fourteenth Amendment in making a finding that past discrimination would cause federal funds to be distributed in a manner which reinforced prior patterns of discrimination. While the States and their subdivisions may take remedial action when they possess evidence that their own spending practices are exacerbating a pattern of prior discrimination, they must identify that discrimination, public or private, with some specificity before they may use race-conscious relief. If all a state

or local government need do is find a congressional report on the subject to enact a set-aside program, the constraints of the Equal Protection Clause will, in effect, have been rendered a nullity. [N]one of the evidence presented by the city points to any identified discrimination in the Richmond construction industry. We, therefore, hold that the city has failed to demonstrate a compelling interest in apportioning public contracting opportunities on the basis of race. To accept Richmond's claim that past societal discrimination alone can serve as the basis for rigid racial preferences would be to open the door to competing claims for "remedial relief" for every disadvantaged group. . . .

The foregoing analysis applies only to the inclusion of blacks within the Richmond set-aside program. There is *absolutely no evidence* of past discrimination against Spanish-speaking, Oriental, Indian, Eskimo, or Aleut persons in any aspect of the Richmond construction industry. . . . It may well be that Richmond has never had an Aleut or Eskimo citizen. The random inclusion of racial groups that, as a practical matter, may never have suffered from discrimination in the construction industry in Richmond, suggests that perhaps the city's purpose was not in fact to remedy past discrimination. . . .

Kennedy, J., concurring in part and in the judgment, said: "The process by which a law that is an equal protection violation when enacted by a State becomes transformed to an equal protection guarantee when enacted by Congress poses a difficult proposition for me; but as it is not before us, any reconsideration of that issue must await some further case." Scalia, J., concurring in the judgment, agreed with the Court's "conclusion that strict scrutiny must be applied to all governmental classification by race, whether or not its asserted purpose is 'remedial' or 'benign.' "He added: "At least where state or local action is at issue, only a social emergency rising to the level of imminent danger to life and limb—for example, a prison race riot, requiring temporary segregation of inmates—can justify an exception to the principle embodied in the Fourteenth Amendment that '[o]ur Constitution is color-blind, and neither knows nor tolerates classes among citizens,' *Plessy v. Ferguson* (Harlan, J., dissenting)."

Marshall, J., joined by Brennan & Blackmun JJ., dissented:

It is a welcome symbol of racial progress when the former capital of the Confederacy acts forthrightly to confront the effects of racial discrimination in its midst. [The Constitution does not] prevent Richmond, Virginia, from allocating a portion of its contracting dollars for businesses owned or controlled by members of minority groups. Indeed, Richmond's set-aside program is indistinguishable in all meaningful respects from—and in fact was patterned upon—the federal set-aside plan which this Court upheld in *Fullilove v. Klutznick*. [T]oday's decision marks a deliberate and giant step backward in this Court's affirmative action jurisprudence.

In *Metro Broadcasting, Inc. v. Federal Communications Commission*, 497 U.S. 547, 110 S.Ct. 2997, 111 L.Ed.2d 445 (1990), Brennan, J., for the Court (5 to 4), held that a federal affirmative action program and certain minority preference policies of the Federal Communications Commission did not violate the equal protection component of the Fifth Amendment. "The policies in question are (1) a program awarding an enhancement for minority ownership in comparative proceedings for new licenses, and (2) the minority 'distress sale' program, which permits a limited category of existing radio and television broadcast stations to be transferred only to minority-controlled firms." Even if these racial preferences were not " 'remedial' in the sense of being designed to compensate victims of past governmental or societal discrimination," they are "constitutionally permissible to the extent that they serve important governmental objectives within the power of Congress and are substantially related to achievement of those objectives." Congress wanted to promote minority participation in the broadcast industry. "It is of overriding significance in these cases that the FCC's minority ownership programs have been specifically approved—indeed, mandated—by Congress." Stevens, J., filed a concurring opinion.

Kennedy, J., joined by Scalia, J., dissented: "[A]fter a century of judicial opinions we interpret the Constitution to do no more than move us from 'separate but equal' to 'unequal but benign.' " O'Connor, J., joined by Rehnquist, C.J. & Scalia & Kennedy, JJ., dissented:

> At the heart of the Constitution's guarantee of equal protection lies the simple command that the Government must treat citizens "as *individuals,* not 'as simply components of a racial, religious, sexual or national class.' " ... The Court's emphasis on "benign racial classifications" suggests confidence in its ability to distinguish good from harmful governmental uses of racial criteria. History should teach greater humility.

Five years later, *Adarand* overruled *Metro Broadcasting*:

ADARAND CONSTRUCTORS, INC. v. PENA
515 U.S. 200, 115 S.Ct. 2097, 132 L.Ed.2d 158 (1995).

JUSTICE O'CONNOR announced the judgment of the Court and delivered an opinion with respect to Parts I, II, III–A, III–B, III–D, and IV, which is for the Court except insofar as it might be inconsistent with the views expressed in JUSTICE SCALIA's concurrence, and an opinion with respect to Part III–C in which JUSTICE KENNEDY joins.

Petitioner Adarand Constructors, Inc., claims that the Federal Government's practice of giving general contractors on government projects a financial incentive to hire subcontractors controlled by "socially and economically disadvantaged individuals," and in particular, the Government's use of race-based presumptions in identifying such individuals, violates the equal protection component of the Fifth Amendment's Due Process Clause. The Court of Appeals rejected Adarand's claim. We conclude, however, that courts should analyze cases of this kind under a different standard of review than the one the Court of Appeals applied. We therefore vacate the Court of Appeals' judgment and remand the case for further proceedings.

I.

In 1989, the Central Federal Lands Highway Division (CFLHD), which is part of the United States Department of Transportation (DOT), awarded the prime contract for a highway construction project in Colorado to Mountain Gravel & Construction Company. Mountain Gravel then solicited bids from subcontractors for the guardrail portion of the contract. Adarand, a Colorado-based highway construction company specializing in guardrail work, submitted the low bid. Gonzales Construction Company also submitted a bid.

The prime contract's terms provide that Mountain Gravel would receive additional compensation if it hired subcontractors certified as small businesses controlled by "socially and economically disadvantaged individuals." Gonzales is certified as such a business; Adarand is not. Mountain Gravel awarded the subcontract to Gonzales, despite Adarand's low bid, and Mountain Gravel's Chief Estimator has submitted an affidavit stating that Mountain Gravel would have accepted Adarand's bid, had it not been for the additional payment it received by hiring Gonzales instead. Federal law requires that a subcontracting clause similar to the one used here must appear in most federal agency contracts, and it also requires the clause to state that "[t]he contractor shall presume that socially and economically disadvantaged individuals include Black Americans, Hispanic Americans, Native Americans, Asian Pacific Americans, and other minorities, or any other individual found to be disadvantaged by the [Small Business] Administration pursuant to section 8(a) of the Small Business Act." Adarand claims that the presumption set forth in that statute discriminates on the basis of race in violation of the Federal Government's Fifth Amendment obligation not to deny anyone equal protection of the laws.

[The federal District Court granted the Government's motion for summary judgment. The Court of Appeals for the Tenth Circuit affirmed.] It understood our decision in *Fullilove v. Klutznick* (1980), to have adopted "a lenient standard, resembling intermediate scrutiny, in assessing" the constitutionality of federal race-based action. Applying that "lenient standard," as further developed in *Metro Broadcasting, Inc. v. FCC* (1990), the Court of Appeals upheld the use of subcontractor compensation clauses. We granted certiorari.

II.

Adarand, in addition to its general prayer for "such other and further relief as to the Court seems just and equitable," specifically seeks declaratory and injunctive relief against any *future* use of subcontractor compensation clauses. [W]e must consider whether Adarand has standing to seek forward-looking relief. [To determine if] future use of subcontractor compensation clauses will cause Adarand "imminent" injury, [we] must ask whether Adarand has made an adequate showing that sometime in the relatively near future it will bid on another government contract that offers financial incentives to a prime contractor for hiring disadvantaged subcontractors. We conclude that Adarand has satisfied this requirement. Adarand's general manager said in a deposition that his company bids on every guardrail project in Colorado. . . .

III.

The Government urges that "[t]he Subcontracting Compensation Clause program is ... a program based on *disadvantage,* not on race," and thus that it is subject only to "the most relaxed judicial scrutiny." To the extent that the statutes and regulations involved in this case are race neutral, we agree. The Government concedes, however, that "the race-based rebuttable presumption used in some certification determinations under the Subcontracting Compensation Clause" is subject to some heightened level of scrutiny. The parties disagree as to what that level should be. (We note, incidentally, that this case concerns only classifications based explicitly on race, and presents none of the additional difficulties posed by laws that, although facially race neutral, result in racially disproportionate impact and are motivated by a racially discriminatory purpose. See generally *Arlington Heights v. Metropolitan Housing Development Corp.; Washington v. Davis.*)

Adarand's claim arises under the Fifth Amendment to the Constitution, which provides that "No person shall ... be deprived of life, liberty, or property, without due process of law." Although this Court has always understood that Clause to provide some measure of protection against *arbitrary* treatment by the Federal Government, it is not as explicit a guarantee of *equal* treatment as the Fourteenth Amendment, which provides that "No *State* shall ... deny to any person within its jurisdiction the equal protection of the laws" (emphasis added). Our cases have accorded varying degrees of significance to the difference in the language of those two Clauses. We think it necessary to revisit the issue here.

A. [*Bolling v. Sharpe* (1954)] concerned school desegregation, but its reasoning was not so limited. [It] reiterated " 'that the Constitution of the United States, in its present form, forbids, so far as civil and political rights are concerned, discrimination *by the General Government, or by the States,* against any citizen because of his race.' " The Court's application of that general principle to the case before it, and the resulting imposition on the Federal Government of an obligation equivalent to that of the States, followed as a matter of course....

B. ... The Court's failure to produce a majority opinion in *Bakke, Fullilove,* and *Wygant* left unresolved the proper analysis for remedial race-based governmental action.... The Court resolved the issue, at least in part, in 1989. *Richmond v. J.A. Croson Co.* (1989), concerned a city's determination that 30% of its contracting work should go to minority-owned businesses. A majority of the Court in *Croson* held that "the standard of review under the Equal Protection Clause is not dependent on the race of those burdened or benefited by a particular classification," and that the single standard of review for racial classifications should be "strict scrutiny." ... With *Croson,* the Court finally agreed that the Fourteenth Amendment requires strict scrutiny of all race-based action by state and local governments. But *Croson* of course had no occasion to declare what standard of review the Fifth Amendment requires for such action taken by the Federal Government. *Croson* observed simply that the Court's "treatment of an exercise of congressional power in *Fullilove* cannot be dispositive here," because *Croson's* facts did not implicate Congress' broad power under § 5 of the Fourteenth Amendment.

Despite lingering uncertainty in the details, however, the Court's cases through *Croson* had established three general propositions with respect to governmental racial classifications. First, skepticism: " '[a]ny preference based on racial or ethnic criteria must necessarily receive a most searching examination,' " *Wygant* (plurality opinion of Powell, J.). Second, consistency: "the standard of review under the Equal Protection Clause is not dependent on the race of those burdened or benefited by a particular classification," *Croson* (plurality opinion). And third, congruence: "[e]qual protection analysis in the Fifth Amendment area is the same as that under the Fourteenth Amendment," *Bolling v. Sharpe.* Taken together, these three propositions lead to the conclusion that any person, of whatever race, has the right to demand that any governmental actor subject to the Constitution justify any racial classification subjecting that person to unequal treatment under the strictest judicial scrutiny. . . .

A year [after *Croson*], however, the Court took a surprising turn. *Metro Broadcasting, Inc. v. FCC* (1990), involved a Fifth Amendment challenge to two race-based policies of the Federal Communications Commission. In *Metro Broadcasting,* the Court repudiated the long-held notion that "it would be unthinkable that the same Constitution would impose a lesser duty on the Federal Government" than it does on a State to afford equal protection of the laws, *Bolling.* It did so by holding that "benign" federal racial classifications need only satisfy intermediate scrutiny, even though *Croson* had recently concluded that such classifications enacted by a State must satisfy strict scrutiny. "[B]enign" federal racial classifications, the Court said, "—even if those measures are not 'remedial' in the sense of being designed to compensate victims of past governmental or societal discrimination—are constitutionally permissible to the extent that they serve *important* governmental objectives within the power of Congress and are *substantially related* to achievement of those objectives." *Metro Broadcasting* (emphasis added). The Court did not explain how to tell whether a racial classification should be deemed "benign," other than to express "confiden[ce] that an 'examination of the legislative scheme and its history' will separate benign measures from other types of racial classifications."

Applying this test, the Court first noted that the FCC policies at issue did not serve as a remedy for past discrimination. Proceeding on the assumption that the policies were nonetheless "benign," it concluded that they served the "important governmental objective" of "enhancing broadcast diversity," and that they were "substantially related" to that objective. It therefore upheld the policies.

By adopting intermediate scrutiny as the standard of review for congressionally mandated "benign" racial classifications, *Metro Broadcasting* departed from prior cases in two significant respects. First, it turned its back on *Croson's* explanation of why strict scrutiny of all governmental racial classifications is essential:

> "Absent searching judicial inquiry into the justification for such race-based measures, there is simply no way of determining what classifications are 'benign' or 'remedial' and what classifications are in fact motivated by illegitimate notions of racial inferiority or simple racial politics. [T]he purpose of strict scrutiny is to 'smoke out' illegitimate uses of race by assuring that the legislative body is pursuing a goal important enough to warrant use of a highly suspect tool. The test also ensures that the means chosen 'fit' this compelling goal so closely that there is little or no possibility that the motive for the classification was illegitimate racial prejudice or stereotype." *Croson* (plurality opinion of O'Connor, J.).

We adhere to that view today, despite the surface appeal of holding "benign" racial classifications to a lower standard, because "it may not always be clear that a so-called preference is in fact benign," *Bakke* (opinion of Powell, J.). "[M]ore than good motives should be required when government seeks to allocate its resources by way of an explicit racial classification system." Days, Fullilove, 96 Yale L.J. 453, 485 (1987).

Second, *Metro Broadcasting* squarely rejected one of the three propositions established by the Court's earlier equal protection cases, namely, congruence between the standards applicable to federal and state racial classifications, and in so doing also undermined the other two—skepticism of all racial classifications, and consistency of treatment irrespective of the race of the burdened or benefited group. Under *Metro Broadcasting,* certain racial classifications ("benign" ones enacted by the Federal Government) should be treated less skeptically than others; and the race of the benefited group is critical to the determination of which standard of review to apply. *Metro Broadcasting* was thus a significant departure from much of what had come before it.

The three propositions undermined by *Metro Broadcasting* all derive from the basic principle that the Fifth and Fourteenth Amendments to the Constitution protect *persons,* not *groups*. It follows from that principle that all governmental action based on race—a *group* classification long recognized as "in most circumstances irrelevant and therefore prohibited"—should be subjected to detailed judicial inquiry to ensure that the *personal* right to equal protection of the laws has not been infringed. These ideas have long been central to this Court's understanding of equal protection, and holding "benign" state and federal racial classifications to different standards does not square with them. "[A] free people whose institutions are founded upon the doctrine of equality," should tolerate no retreat from the principle that government may treat people differently because of their race only for the most compelling reasons. Accordingly, we hold today that all racial classifications, imposed by whatever federal, state, or local governmental actor, must be analyzed by a reviewing court under strict scrutiny. In other words, such classifications are constitutional only if they are narrowly tailored measures that further compelling governmental interests. To the extent that *Metro Broadcasting* is inconsistent with that holding, it is overruled....

Justice Stevens concurs in our view that courts should take a skeptical view of all governmental racial classifications.... The point of carefully examining the interest asserted by the government in support of a racial classification, and the evidence offered to show that the classification is needed, is precisely to distinguish legitimate from illegitimate uses of race in governmental decisionmaking.... And Justice Stevens himself has already explained in his dissent in *Fullilove* why "good intentions" alone are not enough to sustain a supposedly "benign" racial classification: "[E]ven though it is not the actual predicate for this legislation, a statute of this kind inevitably is perceived by many as resting on an assumption that those who are granted this special preference are less qualified in some respect that is identified purely by their race. Because that perception—*especially when fostered by the Congress of the United States*—can only exacerbate rather than reduce racial prejudice, it will delay the time when race will become a truly irrelevant, or at least insignificant, factor. *Unless Congress clearly articulates the need and basis* for a racial classification, *and also tailors the classification to its justification,* the Court should not uphold this kind of statute." *Fullilove, supra* (dissenting opinion)(emphasis added; footnote omitted); see also *id.,* ("Racial classifications are simply too pernicious to permit any but the most exact connection between justification and classification"); *Croson, supra* (Stevens, J., concurring in part and concurring in judgment)("Although [the legislation at issue] stigmatizes the disadvantaged class with the unproven charge of past racial discrimination, it actually imposes a greater stigma on its supposed beneficiaries"); but cf. *post* (Stevens, J., dissenting)....

Justice Stevens also claims that we have ignored any difference between federal and state legislatures. But requiring that Congress, like the States, enact racial classifications only when doing so is necessary to further a "compelling interest" does not contravene any principle of appropriate respect for a co-equal Branch of the Government. It is true that various Members of this Court have taken different views of the authority § 5 of the Fourteenth Amendment confers upon Congress to deal with the problem of racial discrimination, and the extent to which courts should defer to Congress' exercise of that authority. We need not, and do not, address these differences today....

C.   ... It is worth pointing out the difference between the applications of *stare decisis* in this case and in *Planned Parenthood of Southeastern Pa. v. Casey* (1992) [§ 8–3.43; *Casey* refused to overrule *Roe v. Wade,* § 8–3.43. *Roe* created a right to abortion in certain instances.]. *Casey* explained how considerations of *stare decisis* inform the decision whether to overrule a long-established precedent that has become integrated into the fabric of the law. [S]uch precedent is likely to have engendered substantial reliance, as was true in *Casey* itself, *id.* ("[F]or two decades of economic and social developments, people have organized intimate relationships and made choices that define their views of themselves and their places in society, in reliance on the availability of abortion in the event that contraception should fail"). But in this case, as we have explained, we do not face a precedent of that kind, because *Metro Broadcasting* itself *departed* from our prior cases—and did so quite recently. By refusing to follow *Metro Broadcasting,* then, we do not depart from the fabric of the law; we restore it. [R]eliance on a case that has recently departed from precedent is likely to be minimal, particularly where, as here, the rule set forth in that case is unlikely to affect primary conduct in any event. . . .

D. Our action today makes explicit [that] federal racial classifications, like those of a State, must serve a compelling governmental interest, and must be narrowly tailored to further that interest. [T]o the extent (if any) that *Fullilove* held federal racial classifications to be subject to a less rigorous standard, it is no longer controlling. But we need not decide today whether the program upheld in *Fullilove* would survive strict scrutiny as our more recent cases have defined it. . . . We think that requiring strict scrutiny is the best way to ensure that courts will consistently give racial classifications that kind of detailed examination, both as to ends and as to means.

. . . Finally, we wish to dispel the notion that strict scrutiny is "strict in theory, but fatal in fact." The unhappy persistence of both the practice and the lingering effects of racial discrimination against minority groups in this country is an unfortunate reality, and government is not disqualified from acting in response to it. As recently as 1987, for example, every Justice of this Court agreed that the Alabama Department of Public Safety's "pervasive, systematic, and obstinate discriminatory conduct" justified a narrowly tailored race-based remedy. See *United States v. Paradise,* 480 U.S. 149, 107 S.Ct. 1053, 94 L.Ed.2d 203 (1987) [noted below]. When race-based action is necessary to further a compelling interest, such action is within constitutional constraints if it satisfies the "narrow tailoring" test this Court has set out in previous cases.

IV.

Because our decision today alters the playing field in some important respects, we think it best to remand the case to the lower courts for further consideration in light of the principles we have announced. . . . The Court of Appeals did not decide the question whether the interests served by the use of subcontractor compensation clauses are properly described as "compelling." It also did not address the question of narrow tailoring in terms of our strict scrutiny cases, by asking, for example, whether there was "any consideration of the use of race-neutral means to increase minority business participation" in government contracting, *Croson, supra,* or whether the program was appropriately limited such that it "will not last longer than the discriminatory effects it is designed to eliminate." [Furthermore], unresolved questions remain concerning the details of the complex regulatory regimes implicated by the use of subcontractor compensation clauses. . . .

It is so ordered.

JUSTICE SCALIA, concurring in part and concurring in the judgment.

I join the opinion of the Court, except Part III–C, and except insofar as it may be inconsistent with the following: In my view, government can never have a "compelling interest" in discriminating on the basis of race in order to "make up" for past racial discrimination in the opposite direction. Individuals who have been wronged by unlawful racial discrimination should be made whole; but under our Constitution there can be no such thing as either a creditor or a debtor race. That concept is alien to the Constitution's focus upon the individual, see Amdt. 14, § 1 ("[N]or shall any State . . . deny *to any person*" the equal protection of the laws)(emphasis added), and its rejection of dispositions based on race, see Amdt. 15, § 1 (prohibiting abridgment of the right to vote "on account of race") or based on blood, see Art. III, § 3 ("[N]o Attainder of Treason shall work Corruption of Blood"); Art. I, § 9 ("No Title of Nobility shall be granted by the United States"). To pursue the concept of racial entitlement—even for the most admirable and benign of purposes—is to reinforce and preserve for future mischief the way of thinking that produced race slavery, race privilege and race hatred. In the eyes of government, we are just one race here. It is American.

It is unlikely, if not impossible, that the challenged program would survive under this understanding of strict scrutiny, but I am content to leave that to be decided on remand.

JUSTICE THOMAS, concurring in part and concurring in the judgment.

I agree with the majority's conclusion that strict scrutiny applies to *all* government classifications based on race. I write separately, however, to express my disagreement with the premise underlying Justice Stevens' and Justice Ginsburg's dissents: that there is a racial paternalism exception to the principle of equal protection. I believe that there is a "moral [and] constitutional equivalence," *post* (Stevens, J., dissenting), between laws designed to subjugate a race and those that distribute benefits on the basis of race in order to foster some current notion of equality. Government cannot make us equal; it can only recognize, respect, and protect us as equal before the law.

That these programs may have been motivated, in part, by good intentions cannot provide refuge from the principle that under our Constitution, the government may not make distinctions on the basis of race. . . . These programs not only raise grave constitutional questions, they also undermine the moral basis of the equal protection principle. Purchased at the price of immeasurable human suffering, the equal protection principle reflects our Nation's understanding that such classifications ultimately have a destructive impact on the individual and our society. [R]acial paternalism and its unintended consequences can be as poisonous and pernicious as any other form of discrimination. So-called "benign" discrimination teaches many that because of chronic and apparently immutable handicaps, minorities cannot compete with them without their patronizing indulgence. Inevitably, such programs engender attitudes of superiority or, alternatively, provoke resentment among those who believe that they have been wronged by the government's use of race. These programs stamp minorities with a badge of inferiority and may cause them to develop dependencies or to adopt an attitude that they are "entitled" to preferences. Indeed, Justice Stevens once recognized the real harms stemming from seemingly "benign" discrimination. See *Fullilove v. Klutznick* (Stevens, J., dissenting)(noting that "remedial" race legislation "is perceived by many as resting on an assumption that those who are granted this special preference are less qualified in some respect that is identified purely by their race").

In my mind, government-sponsored racial discrimination based on benign prejudice is just as noxious as discrimination inspired by malicious prejudice.[1] In each instance, it is racial discrimination, plain and simple.

JUSTICE STEVENS, with whom JUSTICE GINSBURG joins, dissenting. . . .

The Court's concept of "consistency" assumes that there is no significant difference between a decision by the majority to impose a special burden on the members of a minority race and a decision by the majority to provide a benefit to certain members of that minority notwithstanding its incidental burden on some members of the majority. In my opinion that assumption is untenable. . . . Invidious discrimination is an engine of oppression, subjugating a disfavored group to enhance or maintain the power of the majority. Remedial race-based preferences reflect the opposite impulse: a desire to foster equality in society. No sensible conception of the Government's constitutional obligation to "govern impartially," should ignore this distinction. . . .

The Court's explanation for treating dissimilar race-based decisions as though they were equally objectionable is a supposed inability to differentiate between "invidious" and "benign" discrimination. But the term "affirmative action" is common and well understood. Its presence in everyday parlance shows that people understand the difference between good intentions and bad. As with any legal concept, some cases may be difficult to classify,[4] but our equal protection jurisprudence has identified a critical difference between state action that imposes burdens on a disfavored few and state action that benefits the few "in spite of" its adverse effects on the many. . . .

---

1. It should be obvious that every racial classification helps, in a narrow sense, some races and hurts others. As to the races benefited, the classification could surely be called "benign." Accordingly, whether a law relying upon racial taxonomy is "benign" or "malign," either turns on " 'whose ox is gored,' "or on distinctions found only in the eye of the beholder.

4. For example, in *Richmond v. J.A. Croson Co.* (1989), a majority of the members of the city council that enacted the race-based set-aside were of the same race as its beneficiaries.

Moreover, the Court may find that its new "consistency" approach to race-based classifications is difficult to square with its insistence upon rigidly separate categories for discrimination against different classes of individuals. For example, as the law currently stands, the Court will apply "intermediate scrutiny" to cases of invidious gender discrimination and "strict scrutiny" to cases of invidious race discrimination, while applying the same standard for benign classifications as for invidious ones. If this remains the law, then today's lecture about "consistency" will produce the anomalous result that the Government can more easily enact affirmative-action programs to remedy discrimination against women than it can enact affirmative-action programs to remedy discrimination against African Americans—even though the primary purpose of the Equal Protection Clause was to end discrimination against the former slaves. . . .

The Court's concept of "congruence" assumes that there is no significant difference between a decision by the Congress of the United States to adopt an affirmative-action program and such a decision by a State or a municipality. In my opinion that assumption is untenable. It ignores important practical and legal differences between federal and state or local decisionmakers. [There is a] special "institutional competence" of our National Legislature. [Also] federal affirmative-action programs represent the will of our entire Nation's elected representatives, whereas a state or local program may have an impact on nonresident entities who played no part in the decision to enact it. . . .

In the programs challenged in this case, Congress has acted both with respect to private individuals and, as in *Fullilove,* with respect to the States themselves. When Congress does this, it draws its power directly from § 5 of the Fourteenth Amendment. . . . Congressional deliberations about a matter as important as affirmative action should be accorded far greater deference than those of a State or municipality. . . .

JUSTICE SOUTER, with whom JUSTICE GINSBURG and JUSTICE BREYER join, dissenting. . . .

In assessing the degree to which today's holding portends a departure from past practice, it is also worth noting that nothing in today's opinion implies any view of Congress's § 5 power and the deference due its exercise that differs from the views expressed by the *Fullilove* plurality. The Court simply notes the observation in *Croson* "that the Court's 'treatment of an exercise of congressional power in *Fullilove* cannot be dispositive here,' because *Croson*'s facts did not implicate Congress' broad power under § 5 of the Fourteenth Amendment," and explains that there is disagreement among today's majority about the extent of the § 5. There is therefore no reason to treat the opinion as affecting one way or another the views of § 5 power. . . . Thus, today's decision should leave § 5 exactly where it is as the source of an interest of the national government sufficiently important to satisfy the corresponding requirement of the strict scrutiny test. . . .

Notes

1. The article on *Fullilove* that the majority cited in section III(B) was written by Drew Days (Professor at Yale when he wrote the article), who was the U.S. Solicitor General who argued this case.

In *United States v. Paradise,* 480 U.S. 149, 107 S.Ct. 1053, 94 L.Ed.2d 203 (1987), which the majority cites as an example of permissible affirmative action, the trial court had found, in 1972, that the Alabama Department of Public Safety has systematically excluded blacks from employment as state troopers in violation of the Fourteenth Amendment. By 1979, 5 years after the trial court had ordered the Department to refrain from employment discrimination, including promotions, there still were no blacks who had attained the upper ranks of the department. After various consent decrees, it was not until 1983 that the department agreed to promote 4 blacks to corporal (among 15 new corporals). The trial court then ordered that, "for a period of time," at least 50% of those promoted to corporal must be black, if qualified black candidates were available. The trial court also imposed a 50% promotional requirement in the other upper ranks, but only if (1) there were qualified black candidates available, *and if* (3) a particular rank were less than 25% black, *and if* (3) the Department had not developed and implemented a promotion plan that did not have adverse impact for the relevant rank. Pursuant to this order, the Department promoted 8 blacks and 8 whites, and also submitted its proposed corporal and sergeant promotional procedures for corporal and sergeant. The trial court then suspended the 50% requirement.

The Supreme Court, with no majority, affirmed the one-for-one promotional requirement. O'Connor, J., filed a dissent, joined by Scalia, J. and Rehnquist, C.J., arguing that the trial court's action was not narrowly tailored. (White, J., also dissented on similar grounds.) The dissent argued that the "one-for-one promotion quota used in this case far exceeded the percentage of blacks in the trooper force, and there is no evidence in the record that such an extreme quota was necessary to eradicate the effects of the Department's delay." The plurality argued that the one-for-one promotion, when compared to the 25% minority labor pool, was not arbitrary, because the 50% figure was not the goal but merely determines the speed at which the 25% goal would be achieved. The dissent objected that this argument has no logical stopping point: "even a 100% quota could be defended on the ground that it merely 'determined how quickly the Department progressed toward' some ultimate goal." The dissent claimed that the real, "*in terrorem* purpose" of the trial court order "cannot survive strict scrutiny."

2. After the decision in *Richmond v. J.A. Croson Co.,* discussed in *Adarand Constructors,* about 50 of the approximately 200 affirmative action plans of state and local governments were voluntarily dropped. Lower court decisions eliminated approximately another dozen plans. In Richmond, the percentage of the city's construction contracts dropped from more than 30% to the low single digits.[1]

---

1. Barrett & Frisby, "Affirmative–Action Advocates Seeking Lessons from States to Help Preserve Federal Programs," Wall

3.   Perhaps a typical beneficiary of the a Small Business Administration Program that steers government contracts to "socially and economically disadvantaged" people is someone like Ms. Santos Garza. She bought a "nearly defunct" security company from a white businessman, whom she married a year later. He became one of her 375 employees. Because she is of Mexican descent, when she bought the company, she became eligible for the SBA program and was automatically presumed to be socially disadvantaged. She denied that she was fronting for her husband. By 1995, about 75% of her contracts came to her from the SBA program. Her company had annual revenues of over $10 million, and she lived in a $350,000 house. Critics of the program argue that it is unfair to give favored treatment and government contracts to people already in the middle class; others respond that it would be "senseless" to give the help to poorer people, who are "almost certain to fail." Ms. Garza says that she is "sick and tired" of minorities who complain that they are too poor. "Work and you won't be poor," she said. She also defended affirmative action: "I never would have made it from a tiny company—four people—to where I am today without the set-asides."[2]

4.   There has been controversies as to whether one is a member of a minority group. In 1988, two white Irish–Americans were dismissed from the Boston Fire Department after officials discovered that they had represented themselves as black when they joined the department a decade earlier. In 1990, the San Francisco Civil Service Commission ruled that one firefighter was an Italian–American masquerading as a Mexican–American, and thus was ineligible for an affirmative action program. The firefighter, whose father was born in Italy, claimed that his mother's birth certificate was lost, but he produced her baptismal certificate stating that she was born in Mexico, although baptized in California. The Civil Service ruled that she was born in California. Some San Francisco Hispanic firefighters then proposed creation of a 12 member panel of Hispanic firefighters to rule on ethnicity. They also argued that people of Spanish descent should be disqualified as Hispanics for affirmative action. Meanwhile, a blond, blue-eyed 5–year old was admitted to a very desirable kindergarten because her parents described her as "nonwhite" in the application form. The assistant superintendent for integration responded: "But you have to accept what the parent says because there are a lot of mixed marriages. We're not an investigatory agency."[7]

5.   After *Adarand*, will it be easier for the Federal Government to justify affirmative action for women (using a middle tier analysis) than for racial minorities (using strict scrutiny)? Keep this question in mind when you consider the issue in § 8–2.43. Also keep in mind the references to section 5 of the Fourteenth Amendment, which is considered in § 9–2.

St.Jrl., June 14, 1995, at A16, col. 2 (midwest ed.).

2. Barrett, "Successful, Affluent but Still 'Disadvantaged' "Wall St.J., June 13, 1995, at B1, col. 3–6.

7. Fortune, Jan. 28, 1991, at 107, col. 3. McCoy, Taking Advantage, Wall St. Jrl., Feb. 12, 1991, at A1, col. 1 & A5, col. 1–3; Fortune, Jan. 14, 1991, at 111, col. 3.

8–2.2 *Alienage*

8–2.21 State Power

AMBACH v. NORWICK

441 U.S. 68, 99 S.Ct. 1589, 60 L.Ed.2d 49 (1979).

MR. JUSTICE POWELL delivered the opinion of the Court.

This case presents the question whether a State, consistently with the Equal Protection Clause of the Fourteenth Amendment, may refuse to employ as elementary and secondary school teachers aliens who are eligible for United States citizenship but who refuse to seek naturalization. . . .

The decisions of this Court regarding the permissibility of statutory classifications involving aliens have not formed an unwavering line over the years. State regulation of the employment of aliens long has been subject to constitutional constraints. In *Yick Wo v. Hopkins,* the Court struck down an ordinance which was applied to prevent aliens from running laundries, and in *Truax v. Raich,* 239 U.S. 33, 36 S.Ct. 7, 60 L.Ed. 131 (1915), a [state] law requiring at least 80% of the employees of certain businesses to be citizens was held to be an unconstitutional infringement of an alien's "right to work for a living in the common occupations of the community . . .". At the same time, however, the Court also has recognized a greater degree of latitude for the States when aliens were sought to be excluded from public employment. At the time *Truax* was decided, the governing doctrine permitted States to exclude aliens from various activities when the restriction pertained to "the regulation or distribution of the public domain, or of the common property or resources of the people of the State. . . . " Hence, as part of a larger authority to forbid aliens from owning land, *Terrace v. Thompson,* 263 U.S. 197, 44 S.Ct. 15, 68 L.Ed. 255 (1923); harvesting wildlife, *McCready v. Virginia,* 4 Otto 391, 94 U.S. 391, 24 L.Ed. 248 (1877); or maintaining an inherently dangerous enterprise, *Ohio ex rel. Clarke v. Deckebach,* 274 U.S. 392, 47 S.Ct. 630, 71 L.Ed. 1115 (1927), States permissibly could exclude aliens from working on public construction projects, *Crane v. New York,* 239 U.S. 195, 36 S.Ct. 85, 60 L.Ed. 218 (1915), and, it appears, from engaging in any form of public employment at all, see *Truax,* supra.

Over time, the Court's decisions gradually have restricted the activities from which States are free to exclude aliens. The first sign that the Court would question the constitutionality of discrimination against aliens even in areas affected with a "public interest" appeared in *Oyama v. California,* 332 U.S. 633, 68 S.Ct. 269, 92 L.Ed. 249 (1948). The Court there held that statutory presumptions designed to discourage evasion of California's ban on alien landholding discriminated against the citizen children of aliens. The same Term, the Court held that the "ownership" a State exercises over fish found in its territorial waters "is inadequate to justify California in excluding any or all aliens who are lawful residents of the State from making a living by fishing in the ocean off its shores while permitting all others to do so." *Takahashi v. Fish & Game Comm'n,* 334 U.S. 410, 421, 68 S.Ct. 1138, 1144, 92 L.Ed. 1478 (1948). This process of withdrawal from the former doctrine culminated in *Graham v. Richardson,* [403 U.S. 365, 91 S.Ct. 1848, 29 L.Ed.2d 534 (1971)], which for the first time treated classifications based on alienage as "inherently suspect and subject to close judicial scrutiny." Applying *Graham,* this Court has held invalid statutes that prevented aliens from entering a State's classified civil service, *Sugarman v. Dougall,* 413 U.S. 634, 93 S.Ct. 2842, 37 L.Ed.2d 853 (1973), practicing law, *In re Griffiths,* 413 U.S. 717, 93 S.Ct. 2851, 37 L.Ed.2d 910 (1973), working as an engineer, *Examining Board v. Flores de Otero,* 426 U.S. 572, 96 S.Ct. 2264, 49 L.Ed.2d 65 (1976), and receiving state educational benefits, *Nyquist v. Mauclet,* 432 U.S. 1, 97 S.Ct. 2120, 53 L.Ed.2d 63 (1977).

Although our more recent decisions have departed substantially from the public-interest doctrine of *Truax's* day, they have not abandoned the general principle that some state functions are so bound up with the operation of the State as a governmental entity as to permit the exclusion from those functions of all persons who have not become part of the process of self-government. In *Sugarman,* we recognized that a State could, "in an appropriately defined class of positions, require citizenship as a qualification for office." We went on to observe:

> Such power inheres in the State by virtue of its obligation, already noted above, 'to preserve the basic conception of a political community'.... And this power and responsibility of the State applies, not only to the qualifications of voters, but also to persons holding state elective or important nonelective executive, legislative, and judicial positions, for officers who participate directly in the formulation, execution, or review of broad public policy perform functions that go to the heart of representative government.

The exclusion of aliens from such governmental positions would not invite as demanding scrutiny from this Court.

Applying the rational-basis standard, we held last Term that New York could exclude aliens from the ranks of its police force. *Foley v. Connelie,* 435 U.S. 291, 98 S.Ct. 1067, 55 L.Ed.2d 287 (1978). Because the police function fulfilled "a most fundamental obligation of government to its constituency" and by necessity cloaked policemen with substantial discretionary powers, we viewed the police force as being one of those appropriately defined classes of positions for which a citizenship requirement could be imposed. Accordingly, the State was required to justify its classification only "by a showing of some rational relationship between the interest sought to be protected and the limiting classification."

The rule for governmental functions, which is an exception to the general standard applicable to classifications based on alienage, rests on important principles inherent in the Constitution. The distinction between citizens and aliens, though ordinarily irrelevant to private activity, is fundamental to the definition and government of a State. [A]n oath of allegiance or similar ceremony cannot substitute for the unequivocal legal bond citizenship represents. It is because of this special significance of citizenship that governmental entities, when exercising the functions of government have wider latitude in limiting the participation of noncitizens.

In determining whether, for purposes of equal protection analysis, teaching in public schools constitutes a governmental function, we look to the role of public education and to the degree of responsibility and discretion teachers possess in fulfilling that role. See *Foley v. Connelie,* supra. Each of these considerations supports the conclusion that public school teachers may be regarded as performing a task "that go[es] to the heart of representative government." *Sugarman v. Dougall,* supra.[6]

Public education, like the police function, "fulfills a most fundamental obligation of government to its constituency." The importance of public schools in the preparation of individuals for participation as citizens, and in the preservation of the values on which our society rests, long has been recognized by our decisions.... Other authorities have perceived public schools as an "assimilative force" by which diverse and conflicting elements in our society are brought together on a broad but common ground.... This influence [of the teacher] is crucial to the continued good health of a democracy.

Furthermore, it is clear that all public school teachers, and not just those responsible for teaching the courses most directly related to government, history, and civic duties, should help fulfill the broader function of the public school system. Teachers, regardless of their specialty, may be called upon to teach other subjects, including those expressly dedicated to political and social subjects. More importantly, a State properly may regard all teachers as having an obligation to promote civic virtues and understanding in their classes, regardless of the subject taught. Certainly a State also may take account of a teacher's function as an example for students, which exists independently of particular classroom subjects. In light of the foregoing considerations, we think it clear that public school teachers come well within the "governmental function" principle recognized in *Sugarman* and *Foley.* Accordingly, the Constitution requires only that a citizenship requirement applicable to teaching in the public schools bear a rational relationship to a legitimate state interest.

---

6. [T]he dissent on the one hand depreciates the importance of New York's citizenship requirement because it is not applied to private school teachers, and on the other hand argues that the role teachers perform in our society is no more significant than that filled by attorneys. This misses the point of *Foley* and *Sugarman.* New York's citizenship requirement is limited to a governmental function because it applies only to teachers employed by and acting as agents of the State. The Connecticut statute held unconstitutional in *In re Griffiths,* 413 U.S. 717, 93 S.Ct. 2851, 37 L.Ed.2d 910 (1973), by contrast, applied to all attorneys, most of whom do not work for the government. The exclusion of aliens from access to the bar implicated the right to pursue a chosen occupation, not access to public employment....

As the legitimacy of the State's interest in furthering the educational goals outlined above is undoubted, it remains only to consider whether § 3001(3) bears a rational relationship to this interest. The restriction is carefully framed to serve its purpose, as it bars from teaching only those aliens who have demonstrated their unwillingness to obtain United States citizenship. Appellees, and aliens similarly situated, in effect have chosen to classify themselves....

MR. JUSTICE BLACKMUN, with whom MR. JUSTICE BRENNAN, MR. JUSTICE MARSHALL, and MR. JUSTICE STEVENS join, dissenting.

Once again the Court is asked to rule upon the constitutionality of one of New York's many statutes that impose a requirement of citizenship upon a person before that person may earn his living in a specified occupation.[1] These New York statutes, for the most part, have their origin in the frantic and overreactive days of the First World War when attitudes of parochialism and fear of the foreigner were the order of the day.... It seems constitutionally absurd, to say the least, that in these lower levels of public education a Frenchman may not teach French or, indeed, an Englishwoman may not teach the grammar of the English language.... I perceive a number of difficulties along the easy road the Court takes to this conclusion:

First, the New York statutory structure itself refutes the argument. Section 3001(3), the very statute at issue here, provides for exceptions with respect to alien teachers "employed pursuant to regulations adopted by the commissioner of education permitting such employment." ... Also, New York is unconcerned with any citizenship qualification for teachers in the private schools of the State, even though the record indicates that about 18% of the pupils at the elementary and secondary levels attend private schools. The education of those pupils seems not to be inculcated with something less than what is desirable for citizenship and what the Court calls an influence "crucial to the continued good health of a democracy." ... And the stark fact that the State permits some aliens to sit on certain local school boards, reveals how shallow and indistinct is New York's line of demarcation between citizenship and noncitizenship....

Second, the New York statute is all-inclusive in its disqualifying provisions.... It is "neither narrowly confined nor precise in its application," nor limited to the accomplishment of substantial state interests. *Sugarman v. Dougall.*

Third, the New York classification is irrational. Is it better to employ a poor citizen teacher than an excellent resident alien teacher? . . .

Fourth, it is logically impossible to differentiate between this case concerning teachers and *In re Griffiths* concerning attorneys. If a resi-

---

1. ... Among [such statutes still in effect] are those relating to the occupations of inspector, certified shorthand reporter, funeral director, masseur, physical therapist, and animal technician.

dent alien *may not* constitutionally be barred from taking a state bar examination and thereby becoming qualified to practice law in the courts of a State, how is one to comprehend why a resident alien *may* constitutionally be barred from teaching in the elementary and secondary levels of a State's public schools? . . .

PLYLER v. DOE
457 U.S. 202, 102 S.Ct. 2382, 72 L.Ed.2d 786 (1982).

JUSTICE BRENNAN delivered the opinion of the Court.

The question presented by these cases is whether, consistent with the Equal Protection Clause of the Fourteenth Amendment, Texas may deny to undocumented school-age children the free public education that it provides to children who are citizens of the United States or legally admitted aliens. . . .

In May 1975, the Texas legislature revised its education laws to withhold from local school districts any state funds for the education of children who were not "legally admitted" into the United States. The 1975 revision also authorized local school districts to deny enrollment in their public schools to children not "legally admitted" to the country. These cases involve constitutional challenges to those provisions. . . .

The Fourteenth Amendment provides that "No State shall . . . deprive any person of life, liberty, or property, without due process of law; nor deny to *any person within its jurisdiction* the equal protection of the laws." Appellants argue at the outset that undocumented aliens, because of their immigration status, are not "persons within the jurisdiction" of the State of Texas, and that they therefore have no right to the equal protection of Texas law. We reject this argument. Whatever his status under the immigration laws, an alien is surely a "person" in any ordinary sense of that term. . . . That a person's initial entry into a State, or into the United States, was unlawful, and that he may for that reason be expelled, cannot negate the simple fact of his presence within the State's territorial perimeter. [H]e is subject to the full range of obligations imposed by the State's civil and criminal laws. And until he leaves the jurisdiction—either voluntarily, or involuntarily in accordance with the Constitution and laws of the United States—he is entitled to the equal protection of the laws that a State may choose to establish. . . .

Sheer incapability or lax enforcement of the laws barring entry into this country, coupled with the failure to establish an effective bar to the employment of undocumented aliens, has resulted in the creation of a substantial "shadow population" of illegal migrants—numbering in the millions—within our borders. This situation raises the specter of a permanent caste of undocumented resident aliens, encouraged by some to remain here as a source of cheap labor, but nevertheless denied the benefits that our society makes available to citizens and lawful residents. The existence of such an underclass presents most difficult problems for a Nation that prides itself on adherence to principles of equality under law.[19]

The children who are plaintiffs in these cases are special members of this underclass. Persuasive arguments support the view that a State may withhold its beneficence from those whose very presence within the United States is the product of their own unlawful conduct. These arguments do not apply with the same force to classifications imposing disabilities on the minor *children* of such illegal entrants. At the least, those who elect to enter our territory by stealth and in violation of our law should be prepared to bear the consequences, including, but not limited to, deportation. But the children of those illegal entrants are not comparably situated. [T]he children who are plaintiffs in these cases "can affect neither their parents' conduct nor their own status." Even if the State found it expedient to control the conduct of adults by acting against their children, legislation directing the onus of a parent's misconduct against his children does not comport with fundamental conceptions of justice. "[N]o child is responsible for his birth and penalizing the . . . child is an ineffectual—as well as unjust—way of deterring the parent."

Of course, undocumented status is not irrelevant to any proper legislative goal. Nor is undocumented status an absolutely immutable characteristic since it is the product of conscious, indeed unlawful, action. But § 21.031 is directed against children, and imposes its discriminatory burden on the basis of a legal characteristic over which children can have little control. It is thus difficult to conceive of a rational justification for penalizing these children for their presence within the United States. Yet that appears to be precisely the effect of § 21.031.

Public education is not a "right" granted to individuals by the Constitution. But neither is it merely some governmental "benefit" indistinguishable from other forms of social welfare legislation. Both the importance of education in maintaining our basic institutions, and the lasting impact of its deprivation on the life of the child, mark the distinction. [There are] significant social costs borne by our Nation when select groups are denied the means to absorb the values and skills upon which our social order rests. . . .

---

19. We reject the claim that "illegal aliens" are a "suspect class." . . . Unlike most of the classifications that we have recognized as suspect, entry into this class, by virtue of entry into this country, is the product of voluntary action. Indeed, entry into the class is itself a crime. In addition, it could hardly be suggested that undocumented status is a "constitutional irrelevancy." With respect to the actions of the federal government, alienage classifications may be intimately related to the conduct of foreign policy, to the federal prerogative to control access to the United States, and to the plenary federal power to determine who has sufficiently manifested his allegiance to become a citizen of the Nation. No State may independently exercise a like power. But if the Federal Government has by uniform rule prescribed what it believes to be appropriate standards for the treatment of an alien subclass, the States may, of course, follow the federal direction.

These well-settled principles allow us to determine the proper level of deference to be afforded § 21.031. [M]ore is involved in this case than the abstract question whether § 21.031 discriminates against a suspect class, or whether education is a fundamental right. Section 21.031 imposes a lifetime hardship on a discrete class of children not accountable for their disabling status. The stigma of illiteracy will mark them for the rest of their lives. By denying these children a basic education, we deny them the ability to live within the structure of our civic institutions, and foreclose any realistic possibility that they will contribute in even the smallest way to the progress of our Nation. In determining the rationality of § 21.031, we may appropriately take into account its costs to the Nation and to the innocent children who are its victims. In light of these countervailing costs, the discrimination contained in § 21.031 can hardly be considered rational unless it furthers some substantial goal of the State. . . .

But we are unable to find in the congressional immigration scheme any statement of policy that might weigh significantly in arriving at an equal protection balance concerning the State's authority to deprive these children of an education. . . . The State does not claim that the conservation of state educational resources was ever a congressional concern in restricting immigration. More importantly, . . . an illegal entrant might be granted federal permission to continue to reside in this country, or even to become a citizen. In light of the discretionary federal power to grant relief from deportation, a State cannot realistically determine that any particular undocumented child will in fact be deported until after deportation proceedings have been completed. It would of course be most difficult for the State to justify a denial of education to a child enjoying an inchoate federal permission to remain.

We are reluctant to impute to Congress the intention to withhold from these children, for so long as they are present in this country through no fault of their own, access to a basic education. In other contexts, undocumented status, coupled with some articulable federal policy, might enhance State authority with respect to the treatment of undocumented aliens. But in the area of special constitutional sensitivity presented by this case, and in the absence of any contrary indication fairly discernible in the present legislative record, we perceive no national policy that supports the State in denying these children an elementary education. . . .

Appellants argue that the classification at issue furthers an interest in the "preservation of the state's limited resources for the education of its lawful residents."[22] [But] a concern for preservation of resources standing alone can hardly justify the classification used in allocating

---

22. Appellant School District sought at oral argument to characterize the alienage classification contained in § 21.031 as simply a test of residence. [I]llegal entry into the country would not, under traditional criteria, bar a person from obtaining domicile within a State. Appellants have not shown that the families of undocumented children do not comply with the established standards by which the State historically tests residence. . . .

those resources. [W]e discern three colorable state interests that might support § 21.031.

First, appellants appear to suggest that the State may seek to protect the State from an influx of illegal immigrants. [However], the available evidence suggests that illegal aliens underutilize public services, while contributing their labor to the local economy and tax money to the State fisc. The dominant incentive for illegal entry into the State of Texas is the availability of employment; few if any illegal immigrants come to this country, or presumably to the State of Texas, in order to avail themselves of a free education. . . .

Second . . . appellants suggest that undocumented children are appropriately singled out for exclusion because of the special burdens they impose on the State's ability to provide high quality public education. [E]ven if improvement in the quality of education were a likely result of barring some *number* of children from the schools of the State, the State must support its selection of *this* group as the appropriate target for exclusion. In terms of educational cost and need, however, undocumented children are "basically indistinguishable" from legally resident alien children.

Finally, appellants suggest that undocumented children are appropriately singled out because their unlawful presence within the United States renders them less likely than other children to remain within the boundaries of the State, and to put their education to productive social or political use within the State. Even assuming that such an interest is legitimate, it is an interest that is most difficult to quantify. The State has no assurance that any child, citizen or not, will employ the education provided by the State within the confines of the State's borders. . . .

If the State is to deny a discrete group of innocent children the free public education that it offers to other children residing within its borders, that denial must be justified by a showing that it furthers some substantial state interest. No such showing was made here. Accordingly, the judgment of the Court of Appeals in each of these cases is

Affirmed.

JUSTICE POWELL, concurring.

[T]he exclusion[4] of appellee's class[5] of children from state-provided education is a type of punitive discrimination based on status that is impermissible under the Equal Protection Clause. [I]t hardly can be argued rationally that anyone benefits from the creation within our borders of a subclass of illiterate persons many of whom will remain in

---

4. . . . Of course a school district may require that illegal alien children, like any other children, actually reside in the school district before admitting them to the schools. A requirement of *de facto* residency, uniformly applied, would not violate any principle of equal protection. [footnote repositioned].

5. . . . A different case would be presented in the unlikely event that a minor, old enough to be responsible for illegal entry and yet still of school age, entered this country illegally on his own volition.

the State, adding to the problems and costs of both State and National Governments attendant upon unemployment, welfare and crime.

CHIEF JUSTICE BURGER, with whom JUSTICE WHITE, JUSTICE REHNQUIST, and JUSTICE O'CONNOR join, dissenting.

Were it our business to set the Nation's social policy, I would agree without hesitation that it is senseless for an enlightened society to deprive any children—including illegal aliens—of an elementary education. I fully agree that it would be folly—and wrong—to tolerate creation of a segment of society made up of illiterate persons, many having a limited or no command of our language. However, the Constitution does not constitute us as "Platonic Guardians" nor does it vest in this Court the authority to strike down laws because they do not meet our standards of desirable social policy, "wisdom," or "common sense."
. . .

I have no quarrel with the conclusion that the Equal Protection Clause of the Fourteenth Amendment *applies* to aliens who, after their illegal entry into this country, are indeed physically "within the jurisdiction" of a State. [But the] Equal Protection Clause does not mandate identical treatment of different categories of persons.

The dispositive issue in these cases, simply put, is whether, for purposes of allocating its finite resources, a State has a legitimate reason to differentiate between persons who are lawfully within the State and those who are unlawfully there. The distinction the State of Texas has drawn—based not only upon its own legitimate interests but on classifications established by the federal government in its immigration laws and policies—is not unconstitutional.... Yet by patching together bits and pieces of what might be termed quasi-suspect-class and quasi-fundamental-rights analysis, the Court spins out a theory custom-tailored to the facts of these cases. In the end, we are told little more than that the level of scrutiny employed to strike down the Texas law applies only when illegal alien children are deprived of a public education.[3] If ever a court was guilty of an unabashedly result-oriented approach, this case is a prime example.

The Court first suggests that these illegal alien children, although not a suspect class, are entitled to special solicitude under the Equal Protection Clause because they lack "control" over or "responsibility" for their unlawful entry into this country. Similarly, the Court appears to take the position that § 21.031 is presumptively "irrational" because it has the effect of imposing "penalties" on "innocent" children.[4] Howev-

---

3. The Court implies, for example, that the Fourteenth Amendment would not require a State to provide welfare benefits to illegal aliens.

4. Both the opinion of the Court and Justice Powell's concurrence imply that appellees are being "penalized" because their *parents* are illegal entrants. However, Texas has classified appellees on the basis of *their* *own* illegal status, not that of their parents. Children born in this country to illegal alien parents, including some of appellees' siblings, are not excluded from the Texas schools. Nor does Texas discriminate against appellees because of their Mexican origin or citizenship. Texas provides a free public education to countless thousands of

er, the Equal Protection Clause does not preclude legislators from classifying among persons on the basis of factors and characteristics over which individuals may be said to lack "control." Indeed, in some circumstances persons generally, and children in particular, may have little control over or responsibility for such things as their ill-health, need for public assistance, or place of residence. Yet a state legislature is not barred from considering, for example, relevant differences between the mentally-healthy and the mentally-ill, or between the residents of different counties, simply because these may be factors unrelated to individual choice or to any "wrongdoing." The Equal Protection Clause . . . it is not an all-encompassing "equalizer" designed to eradicate every distinction for which persons are not "responsible." The Court does not presume to suggest that appellees' purported lack of culpability for their illegal status prevents them from being deported or otherwise "penalized" under federal law. Yet would deportation be any less a "penalty" than denial of privileges provided to legal residents?[6] . . .

The second strand of the Court's analysis rests on the premise that, although public education is not a constitutionally-guaranteed right, "neither is it merely some governmental 'benefit' indistinguishable from other forms of social welfare legislation." . . . Is the Court suggesting that education is more "fundamental" than food, shelter, or medical care?

Once it is conceded—as the Court does—that illegal aliens are not a suspect class, and that education is not a fundamental right, our inquiry should focus on and be limited to whether the legislative classification at issue bears a rational relationship to a legitimate state purpose. [I]t simply is not "irrational" for a State to conclude that it does not have the same responsibility to provide benefits for persons whose very presence in the State and this country is illegal as it does to provide for persons lawfully present. By definition, illegal aliens have no right whatever to be here, and the State may reasonably, and constitutionally, elect not to provide them with governmental services at the expense of those who are lawfully in the State.[11] . . .

It is significant that the federal government has seen fit to exclude illegal aliens from numerous social welfare programs, such as the food stamp program, 7 U.S.C.A. § 2015(f) and 7 CFR § 273.4 (1981), the old age assistance, aid to families with dependent children, aid to the blind, aid to the permanently and totally disabled, and supplemental security income programs, 45 CFR § 233.50 (1981), the medicare hospital insurance benefits program, 42 U.S.C.A. § 1395i–2 and 42 CFR

Mexican immigrants who are lawfully in this country.

6. Indeed, even children of illegal alien parents born in the United States can be said to be "penalized" when their parents are deported.

11. The Court suggests that the State's classification is improper because "[a]n ille-

gal entrant might be granted federal permission to continue to reside in this country, or even to become a citizen." However, once an illegal alien is given federal permission to remain, he is no longer subject to exclusion from the tuition-free public schools under § 21.031. . . .

§ 405.205(b)(1981), and the medicaid hospital insurance benefits for the aged and disabled program, 42 U.S.C.A. § 1395o and 42 CFR § 405.103(a)(4)(1981). Although these exclusions do not conclusively demonstrate the constitutionality of the State's use of the same classification for comparable purposes, at the very least they tend to support the rationality of excluding illegal alien residents of a State from such programs so as to preserve the State's finite revenues for the benefit of lawful residents.

The Court maintains—as if this were the issue—that "barring undocumented children from local schools would not necessarily improve the quality of education provided in those schools." However, the legitimacy of barring illegal aliens from programs such as medicare or medicaid does not depend on a showing that the barrier would "improve the quality" of medical care given to persons lawfully entitled to participate in such programs. . . .

[The concurring opinions of MARSHALL, J., and BLACKMUN, J., are omitted.]

Notes

1. The University of Maryland, a State institution, charges lower tuition and fees for students who are domiciled within the State. U.S. citizens and immigrant aliens may obtain such in-state status upon a showing of domicile but nonimmigrant aliens, even if domiciled in that State, are ineligible for such status. Insofar as this policy applied to nonimmigrant aliens who held G–4 visas, it was challenged, and in *Toll v. Moreno*, 458 U.S. 1, 102 S.Ct. 2977, 73 L.Ed.2d 563 (1982) the Court invalidated this policy under the Supremacy Clause. First, Congress has allowed G–4 aliens to establish domicile in the United States. Second, federal law exempts such aliens from federal (and in many cases, state and local) taxes on the salaries that they receive from certain international organizations; the University's policy of charging higher tuition in an effort to recoup its losses from taxes frustrates the federal policy of exemption. Therefore the University policy to deny in-state tuition to G–4 aliens solely because of that status violated the Supremacy Clause.

The Court did not decide this case on Equal Protection grounds. Would that have been a preferential ground? Should the Court have decided the other alien cases on Supremacy Clause grounds?

2. *Martinez v. Bynum*, 461 U.S. 321, 103 S.Ct. 1838, 75 L.Ed.2d 879 (1983), upheld a Texas statute that allowed school districts to deny tuition free admission to its public schools to minors who live apart from their parents, guardians, or other persons having lawful control of them, if their presence in the school district is "for the primary purpose of attending the public free schools." The minor in this case was a U.S. citizen by birth, whose parents were Mexican citizens living in Mexico. Over only the dissent of Justice Marshall, the Court stated:

A bona fide residence requirement, appropriately defined and uniformly applied, furthers the substantial state interest in assuring that services provided for its residents are enjoyed only by residents. Such a requirement with respect to attendance in public free schools does not violate the Equal Protection Clause of the Fourteenth Amendment. It does not burden or penalize the constitutional right of interstate travel, for any person is free to move to a State and to establish residence there. A bona fide residence requirement simply requires that the person *does* establish residence before demanding the services that are restricted to residents.

3. In *Kadrmas v. Dickinson Public Schools,* 487 U.S. 450, 108 S.Ct. 2481, 101 L.Ed.2d 399 (1988), the Court (5 to 4) upheld the constitutionality of a state statute that permitted some public school districts to charge a user fee for bus transportation. This fee could not exceed the district's estimated cost of providing the service. The majority held that there was a rational basis for the statutory classification, which was not subject to strict scrutiny. The appellants argued that *Plyler v. Doe* required the Court to subject the state law to "heightened" scrutiny, as in cases where the Court has reviewed discriminatory classifications based on sex or illegitimacy. The majority said:

> We have not extended this holding [in *Plyler*] beyond the "unique circumstances" that provoked its "unique confluence of theories and rationales" Nor do we think that the case before us today is governed by the holding in *Plyler*. Unlike the children in that case, Sarita Kadrmas has not been penalized by the government for illegal conduct by her parents. . . . Nor do we see any reason to suppose that this user fee will "promot[e] the creation and perpetuation of a sub-class of illiterates within our boundaries, surely adding to the problems and costs of unemployment, welfare, and crime."

8–2.22 Federal Power

MATHEWS v. DIAZ
426 U.S. 67, 96 S.Ct. 1883, 48 L.Ed.2d 478 (1976).

MR. JUSTICE STEVENS delivered the opinion of the Court.

The question presented by the Secretary's appeal is whether Congress may condition an alien's eligibility for participation in a federal medical insurance program on continuous residence in the United States for a five-year period and admission for permanent residence. The District Court held that the first condition was unconstitutional and that it could not be severed from the second. Since we conclude that both conditions are constitutional, we reverse. . . .

There are literally millions of aliens within the jurisdiction of the United States. The Fifth Amendment, as well as the Fourteenth Amendment, protects every one of these persons from deprivation of life, liberty, or property without due process of law. Even one whose presence in this country is unlawful, involuntary, or transitory is entitled to that constitutional protection.

The fact that all persons, aliens and citizens alike, are protected by the Due Process Clause does not lead to the further conclusion that all aliens are entitled to enjoy all the advantages of citizenship or, indeed, to the conclusion that all aliens must be placed in a single homogeneous legal classification. For a host of constitutional and statutory provisions rest on the premise that a legitimate distinction between citizens and aliens may justify attributes and benefits for one class not accorded to the other; and the class of aliens is itself a heterogeneous multitude of persons with a wide-ranging variety of ties to this country.

In the exercise of its broad power over naturalization and immigration, Congress regularly makes rules that would be unacceptable if applied to citizens. The exclusion of aliens and the reservation of the power to deport have no permissible counterpart in the Federal Government's power to regulate the conduct of its own citizenry. The fact that an Act of Congress treats aliens differently from citizens does not in itself imply that such disparate treatment is "invidious."

In particular, the fact that Congress has provided some welfare benefits for citizens does not require it to provide like benefits for *all aliens.* Neither the overnight visitor, the unfriendly agent of a hostile foreign power, the resident diplomat, nor the illegal entrant, can advance even a colorable constitutional claim to a share in the bounty that a conscientious sovereign makes available to its own citizens and *some* of its guests. The decision to share that bounty with our guests may take into account the character of the relationship between the alien and this country: Congress may decide that as the alien's tie grows stronger, so does the strength of his claim to an equal share of that munificence.

The real question presented by this case is not whether discrimination between citizens and aliens is permissible; rather, it is whether the statutory discrimination *within* the class of aliens—allowing benefits to some aliens but not to others—is permissible. We turn to that question.

[T]he responsibility for regulating the relationship between the United States and our alien visitors has been committed to the political branches of the Federal Government.... Any rule of constitutional law that would inhibit the flexibility of the political branches of government to respond to changing world conditions should be adopted only with the greatest caution. The reasons that preclude judicial review of political questions also dictate a narrow standard of review of decisions made by the Congress or the President in the area of immigration and naturalization. [I]t is unquestionably reasonable for Congress to make an alien's eligibility depend on both the character and the duration of his residence. Since neither requirement is wholly irrational, this case essentially involves nothing more than a claim that it would have been more reasonable for Congress to select somewhat different requirements of the same kind....

Graham v. Richardson, 403 U.S. 365, 91 S.Ct. 1848, 29 L.Ed.2d 534 [1971], provides the strongest support for appellees' position. That case holds that state statutes that deny welfare benefits to resident aliens, or to aliens not meeting a requirement of durational residence within the United States, violate the Equal Protection Clause of the Fourteenth Amendment and encroach upon the exclusive federal power over the entrance and residence of aliens. Of course, the latter ground of decision actually supports our holding today that it is the business of the political branches of the Federal Government, rather than that of either the States or the Federal Judiciary, to regulate the conditions of entry and residence of aliens. The equal protection analysis also involves significantly different considerations because it concerns the relationship between aliens and the States rather than between aliens and the Federal Government.

Insofar as state welfare policy is concerned, there is little, if any, basis for treating persons who are citizens of another State differently from persons who are citizens of another country. Both groups are noncitizens as far as the State's interests in administering its welfare programs are concerned. Thus, a division by a State of the category of persons who are not citizens of that State into subcategories of United States citizens and aliens has no apparent justification, whereas, a comparable classification by the Federal Government is a routine and normally legitimate part of its business. Furthermore, whereas the Constitution inhibits every State's power to restrict travel across its own borders, Congress is explicitly empowered to exercise that type of control over travel across the borders of the United States. [I]t is not "political hypocrisy" to recognize that the Fourteenth Amendment's limits on state powers are substantially different from the constitutional provisions applicable to the federal power over immigration and naturalization. . . .

We hold that § 1395o(2)(B) has not deprived appellees of liberty or property without due process of law.

The judgment of the District Court is

Reversed.

Notes

1. In *Hampton v. Mow Sun Wong*, 426 U.S. 88, 96 S.Ct. 1895, 48 L.Ed.2d 495 (1976), decided the same day as *Diaz*, Stevens, J., again wrote the opinion of the Court. But, unlike the unanimous opinion in *Diaz, Mow Sun Wong* drew four dissents.

Five lawful, permanently residing aliens challenged the constitutionality of U.S. Civil Service regulations barring resident aliens from employment in the federal competitive civil service. Earlier, in *Sugarman v. Dougall*, 413 U.S. 634, 93 S.Ct. 2842, 37 L.Ed.2d 853 (1973), the Court had invalidated a state law excluding aliens from permanent positions in all of the state's competitive civil service. The Court had found that the law was not carefully tailored to serve substantial state interests. The Court in *Mow Sun Wong* reaffirmed that the "concept of equal justice under law is served by the Fifth Amendment's guarantee of due process, as well as by the Equal Protection Clause of the Fourteenth Amendment." However, "although both Amendments require the same type of analysis," the "two protections are not always coextensive." Hence the analysis required more than a simple extension of *Sugarman*, because "overriding national interests may provide a justification for a citizenship requirement in the federal service even though an identical requirement may not be enforced by a State."

The U.S. Civil Service broad employment prohibition, the Court acknowledged, could serve various interests: giving the President a bargaining chip in seeking reciprocal concessions in his negotiations with foreign powers; giving aliens an incentive to qualify for naturalization; and avoiding the administrative effort of classifying those sensitive positions which should only be held by citizens. However, "due process requires that there be a legitimate basis for presuming that the rule was actually intended to serve" such an overriding national interest. Such a presumption would be appropriate "if the [prohibition on alien employment] were expressly mandated by Congress, or the President," or by an agency that had responsibility for fostering or protecting that interest.

The Civil Service Commission had no such responsibility for foreign affairs, treaty negotiation, or naturalization policies. Since Congress had not delegated to the Civil Service the authority to make such policy judgments regarding aliens, and the President and Congress had not mandated such restrictions themselves, the Court invalidated the U.S. Civil Service rule because it had the same impact as the aggregate impact of the state rules invalidated in Sugarman. The Court reached this conclusion after assuming, without deciding, that Congress or the President could exclude all aliens from the civil service.

Three months after *Mow Sun Wong*, President Ford issued an executive order barring, with certain exceptions, noncitizens from employment in the federal civil service. Executive Order 11935, 41 Fed.Reg. 37301 (Sept. 2, 1976), 5 C.F.R., Part 7, § 7.4. On remand the district court upheld the constitutionality of the executive order. *Mow Sun Wong v. Hampton*, 435 F.Supp. 37, 42–46 (N.D.Cal.1977).

2. *Reno v. Flores*, 507 U.S. 292, 113 S.Ct. 1439, 123 L.Ed.2d 1 (1993) rejected (7 to 2) constitutional challenges to a regulation of the Immigration and Nationalization Service (INS) governing release of detained alien juveniles, holding that the regulation permitting detained juvenile aliens to be released only to their parents, close relatives, or legal guardians (except in unusual and compelling circumstances) does not facially violate procedural or substantive due process or the Fifth Amendment. The Court, relying on *Mathews v. Diaz*, concluded that "the responsibility for regulating the relationship between the United States and our alien visitors has been committed to the political branches of the Federal Government." The Court rejected the argument that there was unconstitutional disparate treatment in violation of the equal protection component of the Fifth Amendment: one law allowed the release of alien juveniles to close relatives or legal guardians but detained all others; in contrast, another law released *non-alien* juveniles to unrelated adults [e.g., the director of a shelter-care facility] pending federal delinquency proceedings, (see 18 U.S.C.A. § 5034), but detained unaccompanied *alien* juveniles pending deportation proceedings. The Court responded:

> "The tradition of reposing custody in close relatives and legal guardians is in our view sufficient to support the former distinction; and the difference between citizens and aliens is adequate to support the latter."

8–2.3 Illegitimacy

LALLI v. LALLI

439 U.S. 259, 99 S.Ct. 518, 58 L.Ed.2d 503 (1978).

Mr. Justice Powell announced the judgment of the Court and delivered an opinion, in which The Chief Justice [Burger] and Mr. Justice Stewart join.

This case presents a challenge to the constitutionality of § 4–1.2 of New York's Estates, Powers, and Trusts Law, which requires illegitimate children who would inherit from their fathers by intestate succession to provide a particular form of proof of paternity. Legitimate children are not subject to the same requirement.

Appellant Robert Lalli claims to be the illegitimate son of Mario Lalli who died intestate on January 7, 1973, in the State of New York. Appellant's mother, who died in 1968, never was married to Mario. [Robert and his sister Maureen claimed that they were entitled to inherit from Mario as his children although they had not complied] with § 4–1.2, which provides in part:

> An illegitimate child is the legitimate child of his father so that he and his issue inherit from his father if a court of competent jurisdiction has, during the lifetime of the father, made an order of filiation declaring paternity in a proceeding instituted during the pregnancy of the mother or within two years from the birth of the child.

Appellant conceded that he had not obtained an order of filiation during his putative father's lifetime. [But he] tendered certain evidence of his relationship with Mario Lalli, including a notarized document in which Lalli, in consenting to appellant's marriage, referred to him as "my son," and several affidavits by persons who stated that Lalli had acknowledged openly and often that Robert and Maureen were his children. . . .

We begin our analysis with *Trimble* [*v. Gordon,* 430 U.S. 762, 97 S.Ct. 1459, 52 L.Ed.2d 31 (1977)]. At issue in that case was the constitutionality of an Illinois statute providing that a child born out of wedlock could inherit from his intestate father only if the father had "acknowledged" the child and the child had been legitimated by the intermarriage of the parents. The appellant in *Trimble* was a child born out of wedlock whose father had neither acknowledged her nor married her mother. He had, however, been found to be her father in a judicial decree ordering him to contribute to her support. When the father died intestate, the child was excluded as a distributee because the statutory requirements for inheritance had not been met.

We concluded that the Illinois statute discriminated against illegitimate children in a manner prohibited by the Equal Protection Clause. Although ... classifications based on illegitimacy are not subject to "strict scrutiny," they nevertheless are invalid under the Fourteenth

Amendment if they are not substantially related to permissible state interests. Upon examination, we found that the Illinois law failed that test.

Two state interests were proposed which the statute was said to foster: the encouragement of legitimate family relationships and the maintenance of an accurate and efficient method of disposing of an intestate decedent's property.... We again rejected the argument that "persons will shun illicit relations because the offspring may not one day reap the benefits" that would accrue to them were they legitimate. *Weber v. Aetna Casualty & Surety Co.,* 406 U.S. 164, 92 S.Ct. 1400, 31 L.Ed.2d 768 (1972). The statute therefore was not defensible as an incentive to enter legitimate family relationships.

Illinois' interest in safeguarding the orderly disposition of property at death was more relevant to the statutory classification.... An important aspect of that framework is a response to the often difficult problem of proving the paternity of illegitimate children and the related danger of spurious claims against intestate estates. These difficulties, we said, "might justify a more demanding standard for illegitimate children claiming under their fathers' estates than that required either for illegitimate children claiming under their mothers' estates or for legitimate children generally." *Trimble,* supra.

The Illinois statute, however, was constitutionally flawed because, by insisting upon not only an acknowledgment by the father, but also the marriage of the parents, it excluded "at least some significant categories of illegitimate children of intestate men [whose] inheritance rights can be recognized without jeopardizing the orderly settlement of estates or the dependability of titles to property passing under intestacy laws." We concluded that the Equal Protection Clause required that a statute placing exceptional burdens on illegitimate children in the furtherance of proper state objectives must be more " 'carefully tuned to alternative considerations,' " than was true of the broad disqualification in the Illinois law....

At the outset we observe that § 4–1.2 is different in important respects from the statutory provision overturned in *Trimble....* As illustrated by the facts in *Trimble,* even a judicial declaration of paternity was insufficient to permit inheritance. Under § 4–1.2, by contrast, the marital status of the parents is irrelevant. The single requirement at issue here is an evidentiary one—that the paternity of the father be declared in a judicial proceeding sometime before his death.[5] The child need not have been legitimated in order to inherit from his father. Had

---

5. Section 4–1.2 requires not only that the order of filiation be made during the lifetime of the father, but that the proceeding in which it is sought be commenced "during the pregnancy of the mother or within two years from the birth of the child." ... As the New York Court of Appeals has not passed upon the constitutionality of the two-year limitation, that question is not before us. Our decision today therefore sustains § 4–1.2 under the Equal Protection Clause only with respect to its requirement that a judicial order of filiation be issued during the lifetime of the father of an illegitimate child.

the appellant in *Trimble* been governed by § 4–1.2, she would have been a distributee of her father's estate.

A related difference between the two provisions pertains to the state interests said to be served by them. The Illinois law was defended, in part, as a means of encouraging legitimate family relationships. No such justification has been offered in support of § 4–1.2. The Court of Appeals disclaimed that the purpose of the statute, "even in small part, was to discourage illegitimacy, to mold human conduct or to set societal norms." The absence in § 4–1.2 of any requirement that the parents intermarry or otherwise legitimate a child born out of wedlock and our review of the legislative history of the statute confirm this view.

Our inquiry, therefore, is focused narrowly. We are asked to decide whether the discrete procedural demands that § 4–1.2 places on illegitimate children bear an evident and substantial relation to the particular state interests this statute is designed to serve.

The primary state goal underlying the challenged aspects of § 4–1.2 is to provide for the just and orderly disposition of property at death.[6] ... This interest is directly implicated in paternal inheritance by illegitimate children because of the peculiar problems of proof that are involved. Establishing maternity is seldom difficult. As one New York Surrogate's Court has observed: "[T]he birth of the child is a recorded or registered event usually taking place in the presence of others. In most cases the child remains with the mother and for a time is necessarily reared by her. That the child is the child of a particular woman is rarely difficult to prove." Proof of paternity, by contrast, frequently is difficult when the father is not part of a formal family unit. "The putative father often goes his way unconscious of the birth of a child. Even if conscious, he is very often totally unconcerned because of the absence of any ties to the mother. Indeed the mother may not know *who* is responsible for her pregnancy." ...

Even where an individual claiming to be the illegitimate child of a deceased man makes himself known, the difficulties facing an estate are likely to persist. Because of the particular problems of proof, spurious claims may be difficult to expose. The [New York] Commission therefore sought to protect "innocent adults and those rightfully interested in their estates from fraudulent claims of heirship and harassing litigation instituted by those seeking to establish themselves as illegitimate heirs."

As the State's interests are substantial, we now consider the means adopted by New York to further these interests. In order to avoid the problems described above, the commission recommended a requirement designed to ensure the accurate resolution of claims of paternity and to minimize the potential for disruption of estate administration. Accuracy is enhanced by placing paternity disputes in a judicial forum during the

---

6. The presence in this case of the State's interest in the orderly disposition of a decedent's property at death distinguishes it from others in which that justification for an illegitimacy-based classification was absent. E.g., *Weber v. Aetna Casualty & Surety Co.*

lifetime of the father.... In addition, requiring that the order be issued during the father's lifetime permits a man to defend his reputation against "unjust accusations in paternity claims," which was a secondary purpose of § 4–1.2....

Appellant contends that § 4–1.2, like the statute at issue in *Trimble,* excludes "significant categories of illegitimate children" who could be allowed to inherit "without jeopardizing the orderly settlement" of their intestate fathers' estates. He urges that those in his position—"known" illegitimate children who, despite the absence of an order of filiation obtained during their fathers' lifetimes, can present convincing proof of paternity—cannot rationally be denied inheritance as they pose none of the risks § 4–1.2 was intended to minimize.

We do not question that there will be some illegitimate children who would be able to establish their relationship to their deceased fathers without serious disruption of the administration of estates and that, as applied to such individuals, § 4–1.2 appears to operate unfairly. But few statutory classifications are entirely free from the criticism that they sometimes produce inequitable results. Our inquiry under the Equal Protection Clause does not focus on the abstract "fairness" of a state law, but on whether the statute's relation to the state interests it is intended to promote is so tenuous that it lacks the rationality contemplated by the Fourteenth Amendment.

The Illinois statute in *Trimble* was constitutionally unacceptable because it effected a total statutory disinheritance of children born out of wedlock who were not legitimated by the subsequent marriage of their parents. The reach of the statute was far in excess of its justifiable purposes. Section 4–1.2 does not share this defect. Inheritance is barred only where there has been a failure to secure evidence of paternity during the father's lifetime in the manner prescribed by the State. This is not a requirement that inevitably disqualifies an unnecessarily large number of children born out of wedlock.

The New York courts have interpreted § 4–1.2 liberally and in such a way as to enhance its utility to both father and child without sacrificing its strength as a procedural prophylactic. For example, a father of illegitimate children who is willing to acknowledge paternity can waive his defenses in a paternity proceeding, or even institute such a proceeding himself.[10] [T]he courts have excused "technical" failures by illegitimate children to comply with the statute in order to prevent unnecessary injustice....

As the history of § 4–1.2 clearly illustrates, the New York Legislature desired to "grant to illegitimates *in so far as practicable* rights of inheritance on a par with those enjoyed by legitimate children," Commission Report 265 (emphasis added), while protecting the important state interests we have described. Section 4–1.2 represents a carefully

---

10. In addition to making intestate succession possible, of course, a father is always free to provide for his illegitimate child by will.

considered legislative judgment as to how this balance best could be achieved.

Even if, as Mr. Justice Brennan believes, § 4–1.2 could have been written somewhat more equitably, it is not the function of a court "to hypothesize independently on the desirability or feasibility of any possible alternative[s]" to the statutory scheme formulated by New York. "These matters of practical judgment and empirical calculation are for [the State] ... In the end, the precise accuracy of [the State's] calculations is not a matter of specialized judicial competence; and we have no basis to question their detail beyond the evident consistency and substantiality."[11]

We conclude that the requirement imposed by § 4–1.2 on illegitimate children who would inherit from their fathers is substantially related to the important state interests the statute is intended to promote. We therefore find no violation of the Equal Protection Clause.

The judgment of the New York Court of Appeals is

Affirmed.

For the reasons stated in his dissent in *Trimble v. Gordon,* 430 U.S. 762, 777, 97 S.Ct. 1459, 52 L.Ed.2d 31 (1977), Mr. Justice Rehnquist concurs in the judgment of affirmance.

Mr. Justice Blackmun, concurring in the judgment....

I would overrule *Trimble,* but the Court refrains from doing so on the theory that the result in *Trimble,* is justified because of the peculiarities of the Illinois Probate Act there under consideration. This, of course, is an explanation, but, for me, it is an unconvincing one. I therefore must regard *Trimble* as a derelict, explainable only because of the overtones of its appealing facts, and offering little precedent for constitutional analysis of State intestate succession laws. If *Trimble* is not a derelict, the corresponding statutes of other States will be of questionable validity until this Court passes on them, one by one ...

Mr. Justice Brennan, with whom Mr. Justice White, Mr. Justice Marshall, and Mr. Justice Stevens join, dissenting.

Trimble v. Gordon, 430 U.S. 762, 97 S.Ct. 1459, 52 L.Ed.2d 31 (1977), declares that the state interest in the accurate and efficient determination of paternity can be adequately served by requiring the illegitimate child to offer into evidence a "formal acknowledgment of paternity." Id., at 772 n. 14, 97 S.Ct. at 1466. The New York statute is inconsistent with this command. Under the New York scheme, an

---

11. ... Mario Lalli's signature to [a "Certificate of Consent" required by New York for the marriage of a minor] was acknowledged by a notary public, but the certificate contains no oath or affirmation as to the truth of its contents.... The important state interests of safeguarding the accurate and orderly disposition of property at death, emphasized in *Trimble* and reiterated in our opinion today, could be frustrated easily if there were a constitutional rule that any notarized but unsworn statement identifying an individual as a "child" must be accepted as adequate proof of paternity regardless of the context in which the statement was made.

illegitimate child may inherit intestate only if there has been a judicial finding of paternity during the lifetime of the father.

The present case illustrates the injustice of the departure from *Trimble* worked by today's decision sustaining the New York rule. All interested parties concede that Robert Lalli is the son of Mario Lalli. Mario Lalli supported Robert during his son's youth. Mario Lalli formally acknowledged Robert Lalli as his son. Yet, for want of a judicial order of filiation entered during Mario's lifetime, Robert Lalli is denied his intestate share of his father's estate. [T]he fear that unknown illegitimates might assert belated claims hardly justifies cutting off the rights of known illegitimates such as Robert Lalli. . . .

[The concurring opinion of STEWART, J., is omitted.]

Notes

1. *Pickett v. Brown,* 462 U.S. 1, 103 S.Ct. 2199, 76 L.Ed.2d 372 (1983) unanimously invalidated a Tennessee law requiring that certain paternity and support actions be filed within two years after the child's birth. The state's interest in preventing stale claims is becoming "more attenuated as scientific advances in blood testing have alleviated the problem of proof surrounding paternity actions."

2. *Weber v. Aetna Casualty & Surety Co.,* 406 U.S. 164, 92 S.Ct. 1400, 31 L.Ed.2d 768 (1972) invalidated a Louisiana law that denied to dependent, unacknowledged, illegitimate children a right to recover benefits under Louisiana's workmen's compensation law for the death of their biological father on an equal footing with the father's dependent legitimate children. Under the state law, the biological father could not have acknowledged his illegitimate children even if he had desired to do so: the state prohibited acknowledgment of children if the parents were incapable of contracting marriage at the time of conception; in this case the biological father could not marry the mother because he remained married to his first wife. "The burdens of illegitimacy, already weighty, became doubly so when neither parent nor child can legally lighten them." The state's interest in problems of proof was not served by this statute: "By limiting recovery to dependents of the deceased, Louisiana substantially lessens the possible problems of locating illegitimate children and of determining uncertain claims of parenthood." Finally, the state's interest in legitimate family relationships is not served by the statute: "no child is responsible for his birth and penalizing the illegitimate child is an ineffective—as well as an unjust—way of deterring the parent."

Justice Rehnquist was the sole dissent:

All legislation involves classification and line drawing of one kind or another. When this Court expands the traditional "reasonable basis" standard for judgment under the Equal Protection Clause into a search for "legitimate" state interests that the legislation may "promote," and "for fundamental personal rights" that it might "endanger," it is doing nothing less than passing policy judgments upon the acts of every state legislature in the country.

3. *Clark v. Jeter*, 486 U.S. 456, 108 S.Ct. 1910, 100 L.Ed.2d 465 (1988) invalidated, as a violation of equal protection, a Pennsylvania law that ordinarily required an illegitimate child to establish paternity within six years of the illegitimate child's birth, while a legitimate child could seek support from his or her parents at any time. The unanimous Court was persuaded that the six-year statute of limitations was not substantially related to Pennsylvania's interest in avoiding stale or fraudulent claims because in some other cases it places no limit on when the paternity issue may be litigated (e.g., at any time, under the intestacy statute, if there is "clear and convincing evidence that the man was the father of the child"), and because "increasingly sophisticated tests for genetic markers permit the exclusion of over 99% of those who might be accused of paternity, regardless of the age of the child."

In the course of this opinion, the Court *unanimously* agreed on the proper "intermediate scrutiny" test to be used when examining state legislation challenged under the Equal Protection Clause:

> In considering whether state legislation violates the Equal Protection Clause of the Fourteenth Amendment, U.S. Const., Amdt. 14, § 1, we apply different levels of scrutiny to different types of classifications. At a minimum, a statutory classification must be rationally related to a legitimate governmental purpose. Classifications based on race or national origin, and classifications affecting fundamental rights, are given the most exacting scrutiny. Between these extremes of rational basis review and strict scrutiny lies a level of intermediate scrutiny, which generally has been applied to discriminatory classifications based on sex or illegitimacy.

> To withstand intermediate scrutiny, a statutory classification must be substantially related to an important governmental objective.

8–2.4 Sex

8–2.41 Introduction

FRONTIERO v. RICHARDSON
411 U.S. 677, 93 S.Ct. 1764, 36 L.Ed.2d 583 (1973).

Mr. Justice Brennan announced the judgment of the Court and an opinion in which Mr. Justice Douglas, Mr. Justice White, and Mr. Justice Marshall join.

The question before us concerns the right of a female member of the uniformed services to claim her spouse as a "dependent" for the purposes of obtaining increased quarters allowances and medical and dental benefits under 37 U.S.C.A. §§ 401, 403, and 10 U.S.C.A. §§ 1072, 1076, on an equal footing with male members. Under these statutes, a serviceman may claim his wife as a "dependent" without regard to whether she is in fact dependent upon him for any part of her support. A servicewoman, on the other hand, may not claim her husband as a "dependent" under these programs unless he is in fact dependent upon her for over one-half of his support. Thus, the question for decision is whether this difference in treatment constitutes an unconstitutional discrimination against servicewomen in violation of the Due Process Clause of the Fifth Amendment.

Although the legislative history of these statutes sheds virtually no light on the purposes underlying the differential treatment accorded male and female members, a majority of the three-judge District Court surmised that Congress might reasonably have concluded that, since the husband in our society is generally the "breadwinner" in the family—and the wife typically the "dependent" partner—"it would be more economical to require married female members claiming husbands to prove actual dependency than to extend the presumption of dependency to such members." Indeed, given the fact that approximately 99% of all members of the uniformed services are male, the District Court speculated that such differential treatment might conceivably lead to a "considerable saving of administrative expense and manpower."

At the outset, appellants contend that classifications based upon sex, like classifications based upon race, alienage, and national origin, are inherently suspect and must therefore be subjected to close judicial scrutiny. We agree and, indeed, find at least implicit support for such an approach in our unanimous decision only last Term in *Reed v. Reed,* 404 U.S. 71, 92 S.Ct. 251, 30 L.Ed.2d 225 (1971).

In *Reed,* the Court considered the constitutionality of an Idaho statute providing that, when two individuals are otherwise equally entitled to appointment as administrator of an estate, the male applicant must be preferred to the female. Appellant, the mother of the deceased, and appellee, the father, filed competing petitions for appointment as administrator of their son's estate. Since the parties, as parents of the deceased, were members of the same entitlement class, the statutory preference was invoked and the father's petition was therefore granted. Appellant claimed that this statute, by giving a mandatory preference to males over females without regard to their individual qualifications, violated the Equal Protection Clause of the Fourteenth Amendment.

The Court noted that the Idaho statute "provides that different treatment be accorded to the applicants on the basis of their sex; it thus establishes a classification subject to scrutiny under the Equal Protection Clause." Under "traditional" equal protection analysis, a legislative classification must be sustained unless it is "patently arbitrary" and bears no rational relationship to a legitimate governmental interest.

In an effort to meet this standard, appellee contended that the statutory scheme was a reasonable measure designed to reduce the workload on probate courts by eliminating one class of contests. Moreover, appellee argued that the mandatory preference for male applicants was in itself reasonable since "men [are] as a rule more conversant with business affairs than . . . women."

Despite these contentions, however, the Court held the statutory preference for male applicants unconstitutional. In reaching this result, the Court implicitly rejected appellee's apparently rational explanation of the statutory scheme, and concluded that, by ignoring the individual qualifications of particular applicants, the challenged statute provided "dissimilar treatment for men and women who are ... similarly situated." The Court therefore held that, even though the State's interest in achieving administrative efficiency "is not without some legitimacy," "[t]o give a mandatory preference to members of either sex over members of the other, merely to accomplish the elimination of hearings on the merits, is to make the very kind of arbitrary legislative choice forbidden by the [Constitution].... " This departure from "traditional" rational-basis analysis with respect to sex-based classifications is clearly justified.

There can be no doubt that our Nation has had a long and unfortunate history of sex discrimination. Traditionally, such discrimination was rationalized by an attitude of "romantic paternalism" which, in practical effect, put women, not on a pedestal, but in a cage. Indeed, this paternalistic attitude became so firmly rooted in our national consciousness that, 100 years ago, a distinguished Member of this Court was able to proclaim:

> "Man is, or should be, woman's protector and defender. The natural and proper timidity and delicacy which belongs to the female sex evidently unfits it for many of the occupations of civil life.... The paramount destiny and mission of woman are to fulfil the noble and benign offices of wife and mother. This is the law of the Creator." *Bradwell v. State,* 16 Wall. 130, 141, 21 L.Ed. 442 (1873)(Bradley, J., concurring).

As a result of notions such as these, our statute books gradually became laden with gross, stereotyped distinctions between the sexes and, indeed, throughout much of the 19th century the position of women in our society was, in many respects, comparable to that of blacks under the pre-Civil War slave codes. Neither slaves nor women could hold office, serve on juries, or bring suit in their own names, and married women traditionally were denied the legal capacity to hold or convey property or to serve as legal guardians of their own children. And although blacks were guaranteed the right to vote in 1870, women were denied even that right—which is itself "preservative of other basic civil and political rights"—until adoption of the Nineteenth Amendment half a century later.

It is true, of course, that the position of women in America has improved markedly in recent decades. Nevertheless, it can hardly be doubted that, in part because of the high visibility of the sex characteristic, women still face pervasive, although at times more subtle, discrimination in our educational institutions, in the job market and perhaps most conspicuously, in the political arena.

Moreover, since sex, like race and national origin, is an immutable characteristic determined solely by the accident of birth, the imposition of special disabilities upon the members of a particular sex because of their sex would seem to violate "the basic concept of our system that

legal burdens should bear some relationship to individual responsibility
..." *Weber v. Aetna Casualty & Surety Co.* And what differentiates sex
from such nonsuspect statuses as intelligence or physical disability, and
aligns it with the recognized suspect criteria, is that the sex characteristic frequently bears no relation to ability to perform or contribute to
society. As a result, statutory distinctions between the sexes often have
the effect of invidiously relegating the entire class of females to inferior
legal status without regard to the actual capabilities of its individual
members.

[W]e can only conclude that classifications based upon sex, like
classifications based upon race, alienage, or national origin, are inherently suspect, and must therefore be subjected to strict judicial scrutiny.
Applying the analysis mandated by that stricter standard of review, it is
clear that the statutory scheme now before us is constitutionally invalid.

[T]he Government concedes that the differential treatment accorded
men and women under these statutes serves no purpose other than mere
"administrative convenience." In essence, the Government maintains
that, as an empirical matter, wives in our society frequently are dependent upon their husbands, while husbands rarely are dependent upon
their wives. Thus, the Government argues that Congress might reasonably have concluded that it would be both cheaper and easier simply
conclusively to presume that wives of male members are financially
dependent upon their husbands, while burdening female members with
the task of establishing dependency in fact.[22]

The Government offers no concrete evidence, however, tending to
support its view that such differential treatment in fact saves the
Government any money. In order to satisfy the demands of strict judicial
scrutiny, the Government must demonstrate, for example, that it is
actually cheaper to grant increased benefits with respect to *all* male
members, than it is to determine which male members are in fact
entitled to such benefits and to grant increased benefits only to those
members whose wives actually meet the dependency requirement....

In any case, our prior decisions make clear that, although efficacious
administration of governmental programs is not without some importance, "the Constitution recognizes higher values than speed and efficiency." And when we enter the realm of "strict judicial scrutiny," there
can be no doubt that "administrative convenience" is not a shibboleth,
the mere recitation of which dictates constitutionality.... We therefore
conclude that, by according differential treatment to male and female
members of the uniformed services for the sole purpose of achieving
administrative convenience, the challenged statutes violate the Due
Process Clause of the Fifth Amendment insofar as they require a female
member to prove the dependency of her husband.

---

22. It should be noted that these statutes are not in any sense designed to rectify the effects of past discrimination against women. On the contrary, these statutes seize upon a group—women—who have historically suffered discrimination in employment, and rely on the effects of this past discrimination as a justification for heaping on additional economic disadvantages.

Reversed.

MR. JUSTICE STEWART concurs in the judgment, agreeing that the statutes before us work an invidious discrimination in violation of the Constitution. *Reed v. Reed.*

MR. JUSTICE REHNQUIST dissents for the reasons stated by Judge Rives in his opinion for the District Court.

MR. JUSTICE POWELL, with whom THE CHIEF JUSTICE [BURGER] and MR. JUSTICE BLACKMUN join, concurring in the judgment.

. . . It is unnecessary for the Court in this case to characterize sex as a suspect classification, with all of the far-reaching implications of such a holding. *Reed v. Reed,* which abundantly supports our decision today, did not add sex to the narrowly limited group of classifications which are inherently suspect. In my view, we can and should decide this case on the authority of *Reed* and reserve for the future any expansion of its rationale.

There is another, and I find compelling, reason for deferring a general categorizing of sex classifications as invoking the strictest test of judicial scrutiny. The Equal Rights Amendment, which if adopted will resolve the substance of this precise question, has been approved by the Congress and submitted for ratification by the States. If this Amendment is duly adopted, it will represent the will of the people accomplished in the manner prescribed by the Constitution. By acting prematurely and unnecessarily, as I view it, the Court has assumed a decisional responsibility at the very time when state legislatures, functioning within the traditional democratic process, are debating the proposed Amendment. It seems to me that this reaching out to pre-empt by judicial action a major political decision which is currently in process of resolution does not reflect appropriate respect for duly prescribed legislative processes. . . .

CRAIG v. BOREN
429 U.S. 190, 97 S.Ct. 451, 50 L.Ed.2d 397 (1976).

MR. JUSTICE BRENNAN delivered the opinion of the Court.

The interaction of two sections of an Oklahoma statute prohibits the sale of "nonintoxicating" 3.2% beer to males under the age of 21 and to females under the age of 18. The question to be decided is whether such a gender-based differential constitutes a denial to males 18–20 years of age of the equal protection of the laws in violation of the Fourteenth Amendment. . . .

Analysis may appropriately begin with the reminder that *Reed [v. Reed,* 404 U.S. 71, 92 S.Ct. 251, 30 L.Ed.2d 225 (1971)] emphasized that statutory classifications that distinguish between males and females are "subject to scrutiny under the Equal Protection Clause." To withstand constitutional challenge, previous cases establish that classifications by gender must serve important governmental objectives and must be substantially related to achievement of those objectives. . . .

Reed v. Reed has also provided the underpinning for decisions that have invalidated statutes employing gender as an inaccurate proxy for other, more germane bases of classification. Hence, "archaic and over-broad" generalizations, concerning the financial position of servicewom-en, *Frontiero v. Richardson,* supra, and working women, could not justify use of a gender line in determining eligibility for certain governmental entitlements. Similarly, increasingly outdated misconceptions concerning the role of females in the home rather than in the "marketplace and world of ideas" were rejected as loose-fitting characterizations incapable of supporting state statutory schemes that were premised upon their accuracy. In light of the weak congruence between gender and the characteristic or trait that gender purported to represent, it was neces-sary that the legislatures choose either to realign their substantive laws in a gender-neutral fashion, or to adopt procedures for identifying those instances where the sex-centered generalization actually comported with fact.

In this case, too, "*Reed,* we feel, is controlling. . . . " We turn then to the question whether, under *Reed,* the difference between males and females with respect to the purchase of 3.2% beer warrants the differen-tial in age drawn by the Oklahoma statute. We conclude that it does not. . . . We accept for purposes of discussion the District Court's identi-fication of the objective underlying §§ 241 and 245 as the enhancement of traffic safety. Clearly, the protection of public health and safety represents an important function of state and local governments. Howev-er, appellees' statistics in our view cannot support the conclusion that the gender-based distinction closely serves to achieve that objective and therefore the distinction cannot under *Reed* withstand equal protection challenge.

The appellees introduced a variety of statistical surveys. First, an analysis of arrest statistics for 1973 demonstrated that 18—20–year–old male arrests for "driving under the influence" and "drunkenness" substantially exceeded female arrests for that same age period.[8] Similar-ly, youths aged 17–21 were found to be overrepresented among those killed or injured in traffic accidents, with males again numerically exceeding females in this regard. . . .

Even were this statistical evidence accepted as accurate, it neverthe-less offers only a weak answer to the equal protection question presented here. The most focused and relevant of the statistical surveys, arrests of 18–20–year–olds for alcohol-related driving offenses, exemplifies the ulti-mate unpersuasiveness of this evidentiary record. Viewed in terms of the correlation between sex and the actual activity that Oklahoma seeks to regulate—driving while under the influence of alcohol—the statistics broadly establish that .18% of females and 2% of males in that age group

8.   . . . Even if we assume that a legisla-ture may rely on such arrest data in some situations, these figures do not offer sup-port for a differential age line, for the dis-proportionate arrests of males persisted at older ages; indeed, in the case of arrests for drunkenness, the figures for all ages indi-cated "even more male involvement in such arrests at later ages."

were arrested for that offense. While such a disparity is not trivial in a statistical sense, it hardly can form the basis for employment of a gender line as a classifying device. Certainly if maleness is to serve as a proxy for drinking and driving, a correlation of 2% must be considered an unduly tenuous "fit." Indeed, prior cases have consistently rejected the use of sex as a decisionmaking factor even though the statutes in question certainly rested on far more predictive empirical relationships than this. . . .

There is no reason to belabor this line of analysis. It is unrealistic to expect either members of the judiciary or state officials to be well versed in the rigors of experimental or statistical technique. But this merely illustrates that proving broad sociological propositions by statistics is a dubious business, and one that inevitably is in tension with the normative philosophy that underlies the Equal Protection Clause. Suffice to say that the showing offered by the appellees does not satisfy us that sex represents a legitimate, accurate proxy for the regulation of drinking and driving. In fact, when it is further recognized that Oklahoma's statute prohibits only the selling of 3.2% beer to young males and not their drinking the beverage once acquired (even after purchase by their 18—20–year–old female companions), the relationship between gender and traffic safety becomes far too tenuous to satisfy *Reed's* requirement that the gender-based difference be substantially related to achievement of the statutory objective.

We hold, therefore, that under *Reed,* Oklahoma's 3.2% beer statute invidiously discriminates against males 18–20 years of age.

Appellees argue, however, that §§ 241 and 245 enforce state policies concerning the sale and distribution of alcohol and by force of the Twenty-first Amendment should therefore be held to withstand the equal protection challenge. . . . Once passing beyond consideration of the Commerce Clause, the relevance of the Twenty-first Amendment to other constitutional provisions becomes increasingly doubtful. [S]ocial science studies that have uncovered quantifiable differences in drinking tendencies dividing along both racial and ethnic lines strongly suggest the need for application of the Equal Protection Clause in preventing discriminatory treatment that almost certainly would be perceived as invidious.[22] In sum, the principles embodied in the Equal Protection Clause are not to be rendered inapplicable by statistically measured but loose-fitting generalities concerning the drinking tendencies of aggregate groups. We thus hold that the operation of the Twenty-first Amendment does not alter the application of equal protection standards that otherwise govern this case.

We conclude that the gender-based differential contained in Okla. Stat., Tit. 37, § 245 constitutes a denial of the equal protection of the

---

22. Thus, if statistics were to govern the permissibility of state alcohol regulation without regard to the Equal Protection Clause as a limiting principle, it might follow that States could freely favor Jews and Italian Catholics at the expense of all other Americans, since available studies regularly demonstrate that the former two groups exhibit the lowest rates of problem drinking. . . .

laws to males aged 18–20 and reverse the judgment of the District Court.[24]

It is so ordered.

Mr. Justice Powell, concurring.

[T]his gender-based classification does not bear a fair and substantial relation to the object of the legislation.[1]

Mr. Justice Stevens, concurring.

There is only one Equal Protection Clause. It requires every State to govern impartially. It does not direct the courts to apply one standard of review in some cases and a different standard in other cases. Whatever criticism may be leveled at a judicial opinion implying that there are at least three such standards applies with the same force to a double standard.

I am inclined to believe that what has become known as the two-tiered analysis of equal protection claims does not describe a completely logical method of deciding cases, but rather is a method the Court has employed to explain decisions that actually apply a single standard in a reasonably consistent fashion. . . .

. . . The classification is not totally irrational. . . . But even assuming some such slight benefit, it does not seem to me that an insult to all of the young men of the State can be justified by visiting the sins of the 2% on the 98%.

Mr. Justice Rehnquist, dissenting.

The Court's disposition of this case is objectionable on two grounds. First is its conclusion that *men* challenging a gender-based statute which treats them less favorably than women may invoke a more stringent standard of judicial review than pertains to most other types of classifications. Second is the Court's enunciation of this standard, without citation to any source, as being that "classifications by gender must serve *important* governmental objectives and must be *substantially* related to achievement of those objectives." Ante (emphasis added). The only redeeming feature of the Court's opinion, to my mind, is that it apparently signals a retreat by those who joined the plurality opinion in *Frontiero v. Richardson,* from their view that sex is a "suspect" classifi-

---

24. [T]he Oklahoma Legislature is free to redefine any cutoff age for the purchase and sale of 3.2% beer that it may choose, provided that the redefinition operates in a gender-neutral fashion.

1. As is evident from our opinions, the Court has had difficulty in agreeing upon a standard of equal protection analysis that can be applied consistently to the wide variety of legislative classifications. There are valid reasons for dissatisfaction with the "two-tier" approach that has been prominent in the Court's decisions in the past decade. Although viewed by many as a re-

sult-oriented substitute for more critical analysis, that approach—with its narrowly limited "upper-tier"—now has substantial precedential support. As has been true of *Reed* and its progeny, our decision today will be viewed by some as a "middle-tier" approach. [C]andor compels the recognition that the relatively deferential "rational basis" standard of review normally applied takes on a sharper focus when we address a gender-based classification. So much is clear from our recent cases. [footnote repositioned.]

cation for purposes of equal protection analysis. I think the Oklahoma statute challenged here need pass only the "rational basis" equal protection analysis and I believe that it is constitutional under that analysis. . . .

The Court's conclusion that a law which treats males less favorably than females "must serve important governmental objectives and must be substantially related to achievement of those objectives" apparently comes out of thin air. The Equal Protection Clause contains no such language, and none of our previous cases adopt that standard. . . . Both of the phrases used are so diaphanous and elastic as to invite subjective judicial preferences or prejudices relating to particular types of legislation, masquerading as judgments whether such legislation is directed at "important" objectives or, whether the relationship to those objectives is "substantial" enough. [T]he Judicial Branch is probably in no worse position than the Legislative or Executive Branches to determine if there is *any* rational relationship between a classification and the purpose which it might be thought to serve. But the introduction of the adverb "substantially" requires courts to make subjective judgments as to operational effects, for which neither their expertise nor their access to data fits them. And even if we manage to avoid both confusion and the mirroring of our own preferences in the development of this new doctrine, the thousands of judges in other courts who must interpret the Equal Protection Clause may not be so fortunate.

[The opinions of BLACKMUN, J., concurring in part, of STEWART, J., concurring in the judgment, and of BURGER, C.J., dissenting, are omitted.]

Notes

1. *Geduldig v. Aiello,* 417 U.S. 484, 94 S.Ct. 2485, 41 L.Ed.2d 256 (1974). The issue before the Court was whether the State of California's disability insurance program invidiously discriminated against women by not paying insurance benefits for disability that accompanies normal pregnancy and childbirth. The State intended the program to be self-supporting by the covered employees, and it chose a contribution rate "to maintain the solvency of the program" and "to permit low-income employees to participate with minimal personal sacrifice." If the state were to pay disability benefits for normal pregnancy and delivery, the increased costs to the program would be substantial.

The Court held (over the dissents of Brennan, Douglas, & Marshall, JJ.) that the state insurance program did not violate equal protection. "There is no risk from which men are protected and women are not. Likewise, there is no risk from which women are protected and men are not." This case thus is "a far cry" from cases like *Reed v. Reed* and *Frontiero v. Richardson*. The California insurance program does not exclude anyone from benefit eligibility because of sex but merely removes one physical condition—pregnancy— from the list of compensable disabilities. "While it is true that only women can become pregnant, it does not follow that every legislative classification concerning pregnancy is a sex-based classification. . . . " Unless the discrimination based on pregnancy is a mere "pretext designed to effect an invidious discrimination against the members of one sex or the other," lawmakers are constitutionally free to make such distinctions "on any reasonable basis." The California program "divides potential recipients into two groups— pregnant women and nonpregnant persons. While the first group is exclusively female, the second includes members of both sexes. The fiscal and actuarial benefits of the program thus accrue to members of both sexes."

Two years later the Court found that such pregnancy distinctions in disability benefit plans did not constitute sex discrimination for purposes of Title VII of the Civil Rights Act of 1964. *General Electric Co. v. Gilbert,* 429 U.S. 125, 97 S.Ct. 401, 50 L.Ed.2d 343 (1976). In 1978 Congress reversed that result by amending the statute.

2. THE PROPOSED EQUAL RIGHTS AMENDMENT. Congress submitted the E.R.A. to the states for ratification on March 22, 1972. Not enough states voted to ratify the E.R.A., which provided:

> *Section* 1. Equality of rights under the law shall not be denied or abridged by the United States or by any State on account of sex.

> *Section* 2. The Congress shall have the power to enforce, by appropriate legislation, the provisions of this article.

> *Section* 3. This amendment shall take effect two years after the date of ratification.

3. THE MERGING OF SEX AND ILLEGITIMACY CLASSIFICATIONS. In *Caban v. Mohammed,* 441 U.S. 380, 99 S.Ct. 1760, 60 L.Ed.2d 297 (1979) the Court (5 to 4), per Powell, J., invalidated under the Equal Protection Clause a section of New York law that allowed an unwed mother, subject to some exceptions, to block the adoption of her child simply by withholding consent. The unwed father had no similar power. He could stop the adoption only by showing that the best interests of the child would not permit the child's adoption by the petitioning couple.

The appellant was the father of the illegitimate children. He lived with them and the unwed mother for a number of years and contributed to the support of the family. Then the mother left with her children and took up residence with another man whom she later married. This couple sought to adopt the illegitimate children and cut off appellant's parental rights. The Court found that the classification was sex-based. In order to be upheld it "must serve important governmental objectives and must be substantially related to achievement of those objectives." In concluding that the law did not meet this test the Court first rejected the assumption that maternal and paternal roles are invariably different at every stage of a child's development. Nor did the state's interest in promoting the adoption of illegitimate children justify the law, for there is no reason to believe that unwed fathers as a class would be more likely to object to the adoption of their children than unwed mothers.

Unwed fathers may be difficult to locate and identify at birth, but this case did not involve such facts. "In those cases where the father never has come forward to participate in the rearing of his child, nothing in the Equal Protection Clause precludes the State from withholding from him the privilege of vetoing the adoption of that child." But "where the father has established a substantial relationship with the child and has admitted his paternity, a State should have no difficulty in identifying the father even of children born out of wedlock. Thus no showing has been made that the different treatment afforded unmarried fathers and unmarried mothers under § 111 bears a substantial relationship to the proclaimed interest of the State in promoting the adoption of illegitimate children." The Court concluded that section 111 "is another example of 'overbroad generalizations' in gender-based classifications."[1]

Stevens, J., joined by Burger, C.J., and Rehnquist, J., dissented. Only "the mother carries the child; it is she who has the constitutional right to decide whether to bear it or not. In many cases, only the mother knows who sired the child, and it will often be within her power to withhold that fact, and even the fact of her pregnancy, from that person. If during pregnancy the mother should marry a different partner, the child will be legitimate when born, and the natural father may never even know that his 'rights' have been affected." Stewart, J., also dissented. To facilitate adoptions "the consent of only one parent should ordinarily be required for adoption of a child born out of wedlock. The mother has been chosen as the parent whose consent is indispensable. A different choice would defy common sense."

Parham v. Hughes, 441 U.S. 347, 99 S.Ct. 1742, 60 L.Ed.2d 269 (1979) was decided the same day. It was also a 5 to 4 decision, but the sex classification was upheld and there was no majority opinion. Stewart, J. (joined by Burger, C.J., & Rehnquist & Stevens, JJ.) wrote a plurality opinion upholding a Georgia law allowing the mother of an illegitimate child to sue for the wrongful death of that child but not allowing the father to sue for wrongful death unless he had legitimated the child. The state law did "not reflect any overbroad generalizations about men as a class, but rather the reality that in Georgia only a father can by unilateral action legitimate an illegitimate child." The statute distinguished "between fathers who have legitimated their children and those who have not." Nor were the illegitimacy cases relevant because the statute did not pass out differing burdens or benefits to legitimates and illegitimates; it simply denied the biological father "the right to sue for his illegitimate child's wrongful death." The statutory scheme supports the state's interest in avoiding fraudulent claims of paternity in wrongful death actions.

Powell, J., concurred in the judgment. Georgia law allowed the father to lift his burden by a simple court proceeding: he could petition the court to legitimate his child. At this proceeding, the mother could either support or rebut the father's paternity claim. In contrast, the father in *Caban* could lift his statutory burden only by marrying the mother, which "often is tanta-

---

1. *Lehr v. Robertson,* 463 U.S. 248, 103 S.Ct. 2985, 77 L.Ed.2d 614 (1983) upheld a New York law that failed to give the putative father any notice and opportunity to be heard prior to an adoption order. The putative father had never developed any significant relationship with the child: he never supported her and rarely saw the child in the two years since her birth; he did not file, with the "putative father registry," his intent to claim paternity to any child born out of wedlock; had he done so, he would have been entitled to receive notice of any adoption proceeding for that child. "When an unwed father demonstrates a full commitment to the responsibilities of parenthood ... his interest in personal contact with the child acquires substantial protection, [b]ut the mere existence of a biological link does not merit equivalent constitutional protection."

mount to a total exclusion of fathers, as marriage is possible only with the consent of the mother."

White, J., joined by Brennan, Marshall, & Blackmun, JJ., dissented. Georgia law, they argued, required unmarried fathers, but not unmarried mothers, to have pursued the statutory legitimization procedure in order later to bring an action for wrongful death. "That only fathers *may* resort to the legitimization process cannot dissolve the sex discrimination in *requiring* them to."

4. In *Michael M. v. Superior Court,* 450 U.S. 464, 101 S.Ct. 1200, 67 L.Ed.2d 437 (1981), the Court, without a majority opinion, held California's "statutory rape" law did not violate equal protection even though the statute made men alone criminally liable for illegal intercourse, which the law defined as intercourse "with a female not the wife of the perpetrator, where the female is under the age of 18 years." Michael M. was 17½ and had intercourse with a female also under 18.

Justice Rehnquist, for the plurality, noted, first, that the purpose of the statute, as offered by the state and as accepted by the California Supreme Court, was legitimate: to prevent illegitimate teenage pregnancies. "Moreover, the risk of pregnancy itself constitutes a substantial deterrence to young females. No similar natural sanctions deter males. A criminal sanction imposed solely on males thus serves to roughly 'equalize' the deterrents on the sexes." A sex-neutral statute could frustrate the state's interest in effective enforcement because "a female is surely less likely to report violations of the statute if she herself would be subject to criminal prosecution."

Justice Stewart, concurring, emphasized "the substantial physical risks for prepubescent females that are not shared by their male counterparts." Empirical evidence showed that sexual abuse of young females is a more serious problem than sexual abuse of young males.

Justice Brennan, joined by White and Marshall, JJ., dissenting, argued that the California statute is not substantially related to the achievement of the asserted goal of preventing teenage pregnancies. The experience of other jurisdictions does not support "the plurality's conclusion that a gender-neutral statutory rape law 'may well be incapable of enforcement.' [T]he laws of Arizona, Florida, and Illinois permit prosecution of both minor females and minor males for engaging in mutual sexual conduct." Even if a sex-neutral statute would be more difficult to enforce, "the State has still not shown that those enforcement problems would make such a statute less effective than a gender-based statute in deterring minor females from engaging in sexual intercourse." This dissent said that the California Supreme Court had engaged in "sexual stereotyping," when it stated: "The Legislature is well within its power in imposing criminal sanctions against males, alone, because they are the *only* persons who may physiologically cause the result which the law properly seeks to avoid. (emphasis in original)."

5. The Military Draft. *Rostker v. Goldberg,* 453 U.S. 57, 101 S.Ct. 2646, 69 L.Ed.2d 478 (1981) upheld (6–3) a provision of the Military Selective

Service Act that authorized the President to require the registration of males but not females. Rehnquist, J., for the Court, emphasized that the "case arises in the context of Congress' authority over national defense and military affairs, and perhaps in no other area has the Court accorded Congress greater deference." Also, this case is "quite different" from many prior sex-based discrimination cases because, "Congress did not act unthinkingly or reflexively ... The question of registering women for the draft not only received considerable national attention and was the subject of wide-ranging public debate, but also was extensively considered by Congress in hearings, floor debate, and in committee."

Congress determined that, if a draft took place, the need would be for combat troops. "The purpose of registration, therefore, was to prepare for a draft of *combat troops*. Women as a group, however, unlike men as a group, are not eligible for combat. The restrictions on the participation of women in combat in the Navy and Air Force are statutory.... The Army and Marine Corps preclude the use of women in combat as a matter of established policy." And the appellees elected not to challenge the constitutionality of these restrictions against women in combat.

Thus, the Court concluded: "Men and women, because of the combat restrictions on women, are simply not similarly situated for purposes of a draft or registration for a draft. Congress' decision to authorize the registration of only men, therefore, does not violate the Due Process Clause. The exemption of women from registration is not only sufficiently but closely related to Congress' purpose in authorizing registration. The fact that Congress and the Executive have decided that women should not serve in combat fully justifies Congress in not authorizing their registration, since the purpose of registration is to develop a pool of potential combat troops."

Marshall, J., joined by Brennan, J., dissented: "[T]he majority concludes that women may be excluded from registration because they will not be needed in the event of a draft. This analysis, however, focuses on the wrong question. The relevant inquiry under the *Craig v. Boren* test is not whether a *gender-neutral* classification would substantially advance important governmental interests. Rather, the question is whether the gender based classification is itself substantially related to the achievement of the asserted governmental interest. Thus, the Government's task in this case is to demonstrate that excluding women from registration substantially furthers the goal of preparing for a draft of combat troops. [T]he Government makes no claim that preparing for a draft of combat troops cannot be accomplished just as effectively by *registering* both men and women but *drafting* only men if only men turn out to be needed. Nor can the Government argue that this alternative entails the additional cost and administrative inconvenience of registering women. This Court has repeatedly stated that the administrative convenience of employing a gender classification is not an adequate constitutional justification under the *Craig v. Boren* test." White, J., joined by Brennan, J., also filed a dissenting opinion.

8–2.42 The De Facto/De Jure Distinction

PERSONNEL ADMINISTRATOR OF MASSACHUSETTS v. FEENEY

442 U.S. 256, 99 S.Ct. 2282, 60 L.Ed.2d 870 (1979).

MR. JUSTICE STEWART delivered the opinion of the Court.

This case presents a challenge to the constitutionality of the Massachusetts veterans' preference statute, Mass.Gen.Laws Ann., ch. 31, § 23, on the ground that it discriminates against women in violation of the Equal Protection Clause of the Fourteenth Amendment. Under ch. 31, § 23, all veterans who qualify for state civil service positions must be considered for appointment ahead of any qualifying nonveterans. The preference operates overwhelmingly to the advantage of males. . . .

The Federal Government and virtually all of the States grant some sort of hiring preference to veterans. The Massachusetts preference, which is loosely termed an "absolute lifetime" preference, is among the most generous. It applies to all positions in the State's classified civil service, which constitute approximately 60% of the public jobs in the State. . . .

The veterans' hiring preference in Massachusetts, as in other jurisdictions, has traditionally been justified as a measure designed to reward veterans for the sacrifice of military service, to ease the transition from military to civilian life, to encourage patriotic service, and to attract loyal and well-disciplined people to civil service occupations. [It operates to benefit] an overwhelmingly male class. This is attributable in some measure to the variety of federal statutes, regulations, and policies that have restricted the number of women who could enlist in the United States Armed Forces, and largely to the simple fact that women have never been subjected to a military draft. When this litigation was commenced, then, over 98% of the veterans in Massachusetts were male; only 1.8% were female. And over one-quarter of the Massachusetts population were veterans. . . .

Classifications based upon gender, not unlike those based upon race, have traditionally been the touchstone for pervasive and often subtle discrimination. This Court's recent cases teach that such classifications must bear a close and substantial relationship to important governmental objectives, *Craig v. Boren* [§ 8–2.41, supra]. [A]ny state law overtly or covertly designed to prefer males over females in public employment would require an exceedingly persuasive justification to withstand a constitutional challenge under the Equal Protection Clause of the Fourteenth Amendment. . . .

When a statute gender-neutral on its face is challenged on the ground that its effects upon women are disproportionably adverse, a twofold inquiry is thus appropriate. The first question is whether the statutory classification is indeed neutral in the sense that it is not gender-based. If the classification itself, covert or overt, is not based upon gender, the second question is whether the adverse effect reflects invidious gender-based discrimination. See *Arlington Heights v. Metropolitan Housing Dev. Corp.* [§ 8–2.13, supra]. In this second inquiry, impact provides an "important starting point," but purposeful discrimination is "the condition that offends the Constitution."

[A]ppellee has conceded that ch. 31, § 23, is neutral on its face. She has also acknowledged that state hiring preferences for veterans are not *per se* invalid, for she has limited her challenge to the absolute lifetime preference that Massachusetts provides to veterans. The District Court made two central findings that are relevant here: first, that ch. 31, § 23, serves legitimate and worthy purposes; second, that the absolute preference was not established for the purpose of discriminating against women. The appellee has thus acknowledged and the District Court has thus found that the distinction between veterans and nonveterans drawn by ch. 31, § 23, is not a pretext for gender discrimination. The appellee's concession and the District Court's finding are clearly correct.

If the impact of this statute could not be plausibly explained on a neutral ground, impact itself would signal that the real classification made by the law was in fact not neutral. See *Washington v. Davis* [§ 8–2.13, supra]; *Arlington Heights v. Metropolitan Housing Dev. Corp.* But there can be but one answer to the question whether this veteran preference excludes significant numbers of women from preferred state jobs because they are women or because they are nonveterans. Apart from the fact that the definition of "veterans" in the statute has always been neutral as to gender and that Massachusetts has consistently defined veteran status in a way that has been inclusive of women who have served in the military, this is not a law that can plausibly be explained only as a gender-based classification. Indeed, it is not a law that can rationally be explained on that ground. Veteran status is not uniquely male. Although few women benefit from the preference, the nonveteran class is not substantially all female. To the contrary, significant numbers of nonveterans are men, and all nonveterans—male as well as female—are placed at a disadvantage. Too many men are affected by ch. 31, § 23, to permit the inference that the statute is but a pretext for preferring men over women.

Moreover, as the District Court implicitly found, the purposes of the statute provide the surest explanation for its impact. Just as there are cases in which impact alone can unmask an invidious classification, cf. *Yick Wo v. Hopkins,* there are others, in which—notwithstanding impact—the legitimate noninvidious purposes of a law cannot be missed. This is one. The distinction made by ch. 31, § 23, is, as it seems to be, quite simply between veterans and nonveterans, not between men and women.

The dispositive question, then, is whether the appellee has shown that a gender-based discriminatory purpose has, at least in some measure, shaped the Massachusetts veterans' preference legislation. [First, she claims that the nature of the preference is] demonstrably gender-biased in the sense that it favors a status reserved under federal military policy primarily to men. . . .

The contention that this veterans' preference is "inherently nonneutral" or "gender-biased" presumes that the State, by favoring veterans, intentionally incorporated into its public employment policies the panoply of sex-based and assertedly discriminatory federal laws that have prevented all but a handful of women from becoming veterans. There are two serious difficulties with this argument. First, it is wholly at odds with the District Court's central finding that Massachusetts has not offered a preference to veterans for the purpose of discriminating against women. Second, it cannot be reconciled with the assumption made by both the appellee and the District Court that a more limited hiring preference for veterans could be sustained. Taken together, these difficulties are fatal. . . .

To be sure, this case is unusual in that it involves a law that by design is not neutral. The law overtly prefers veterans as such. [I]t does not purport to define a job-related characteristic. To the contrary, it confers upon a specifically described group—perceived to be particularly deserving—a competitive headstart. But the District Court found, and the appellee has not disputed, that this legislative choice was legitimate. The basic distinction between veterans and nonveterans, having been found not gender-based, and the goals of the preference having been found worthy, ch. 31 must be analyzed as is any other neutral law that casts a greater burden upon women as a group than upon men as a group. The enlistment policies of the Armed Services may well have discriminated on the basis of sex. But the history of discrimination against women in the military is not on trial in this case.

The appellee's ultimate argument rests upon the presumption, common to the criminal and civil law, that a person intends the natural and foreseeable consequences of his voluntary actions. . . . "Discriminatory purpose," however, implies more than intent as volition or intent as awareness of consequences.[24] It implies that the decisionmaker, in this case a state legislature, selected or reaffirmed a particular course of action at least in part "because of," not merely "in spite of," its adverse effects upon an identifiable group.[25] Yet nothing in the record demon-

---

24. Proof of discriminatory intent must necessarily usually rely on objective factors, several of which were outlined in *Arlington Heights v. Metropolitan Housing Dev. Corp.* The inquiry is practical. What a legislature or any official entity is "up to" may be plain from the results its actions achieve, or the results they avoid. Often it is made clear from what has been called, in a different context, "the give and take of the situation."

25. This is not to say that the inevitability or foreseeability of consequences of a neutral rule has no bearing upon the existence of discriminatory intent. Certainly,

when the adverse consequences of a law upon an identifiable group are as inevitable as the gender-based consequences of ch. 31, § 23, a strong inference that the adverse effects were desired can reasonably be drawn. But in this inquiry—made as it is under the Constitution—an inference is a working tool, not a synonym for proof. When as here, the impact is essentially an unavoidable consequence of a legislative policy that has in itself always been deemed to be legitimate, and when, as here, the statutory history and all of the available evidence affirmatively demonstrate the op-

strates that this preference for veterans was originally devised or subsequently re-enacted because it would accomplish the collateral goal of keeping women in a stereotypic and predefined place in the Massachusetts Civil Service....

The judgment is reversed, and the case is remanded for further proceedings consistent with this opinion.

It is so ordered.

MR. JUSTICE MARSHALL, with whom MR. JUSTICE BRENNAN joins, dissenting.

... Because less than 2% of the women in Massachusetts are veterans, the absolute preference formula has rendered desirable state civil service employment an almost exclusively male prerogative. [T]his consequence follows foreseeably, indeed inexorably, from the long history of policies severely limiting women's participation in the military.[1]

Appellants here advance three interests in support of the absolute preference system.... With respect to the first interest, facilitating veterans' transition to civilian status, the statute is plainly overinclusive. By conferring a permanent preference, the legislation allows veterans to invoke their advantage repeatedly, without regard to their date of discharge....

Nor is the Commonwealth's second asserted interest, encouraging military service, a plausible justification for this legislative scheme. In its original and subsequent re-enactments, the statute extended benefits retroactively to veterans who had served during a prior specified period. [Also, the law] bestows benefits on men drafted as well as those who volunteered.

Finally, the Commonwealth's third interest, rewarding veterans, does not "adequately justify the salient features" of this preference system. Where a particular statutory scheme visits substantial hardship on a class long subject to discrimination, the legislation cannot be sustained unless " 'carefully tuned to alternative considerations.' " Here, there are a wide variety of less discriminatory means by which Massachusetts could effect its compensatory purposes. For example, a point preference system, such as that maintained by many States and the Federal Government, or an absolute preference for a limited duration, would reward veterans without excluding all qualified women from upper level civil service positions.... Unlike [tax abatements, educational subsidies, and special programs for needy veterans] and similar benefits, the costs of which are distributed across the taxpaying public generally, the Massachusetts statute exacts a substantial price from a discrete group of individuals who have long been subject to employment discrimination....

posite, the inference simply fails to ripen into proof.

1. [U]nlike the employment examination in *Washington v. Davis,* which the Court found to be demonstrably job related, the Massachusetts preference statute incorporates the results of sex-based military policies irrelevant to women's current fitness for civilian public employment.

[The concurring opinion of STEVENS, J., joined by WHITE, J., is omitted.]

8–2.43 Reverse Discrimination

MISSISSIPPI UNIVERSITY FOR WOMEN v. HOGAN
458 U.S. 718, 102 S.Ct. 3331, 73 L.Ed.2d 1090 (1982).

JUSTICE O'CONNOR delivered the opinion of the Court.

This case presents the narrow issue of whether a state statute that excludes males from enrolling in a state-supported professional nursing school violates the Equal Protection Clause of the Fourteenth Amendment. The facts are not in dispute. In 1884, the Mississippi legislature created the Mississippi Industrial Institute and College for the Education of White Girls of the State of Mississippi, [now called the] Mississippi University for Women (MUW), [which] has from its inception limited its enrollment to women.[1] In 1971, MUW established a School of Nursing. . . .

Respondent, Joe Hogan, is a registered nurse but does not hold a baccalaureate degree in nursing. Since 1979, he has worked as a nursing supervisor in a medical center in Columbus, the city in which MUW is located. In 1979, Hogan applied for admission to the MUW School of Nursing's baccalaureate program. Although he was otherwise qualified, he was denied admission to the School of Nursing solely because of his sex. School officials informed him that he could audit the courses in which he was interested, but could not enroll for credit. Hogan filed an action in the United States District Court for the Northern District of Mississippi, [seeking] injunctive and declaratory relief, as well as compensatory damages. . . . We granted certiorari, and now affirm the judgment of the Court of Appeals.[7]

We begin our analysis aided by several firmly-established principles. Because the challenged policy expressly discriminates among applicants on the basis of gender, it is subject to scrutiny under the Equal Protection Clause of the Fourteenth Amendment. That this statute discriminates against males rather than against females does not exempt it from scrutiny or reduce the standard of review.[8] Our decisions also

1. . . . Mississippi maintains no other single-sex public university or college. Thus, we are not faced with the question of whether States can provide "separate but equal" undergraduate institutions for males and females.

7. [B]ecause we review judgments, not statements in opinions, we decline to address the question of whether MUW's admissions policy, as applied to males seeking admission to schools other than the School of Nursing, violates the Fourteenth Amendment.

8. Without question, MUW's admissions policy worked to Hogan's disadvantage. Although Hogan could have attended classes and received credit in one of Mississippi's state-supported coeducational nursing programs, none of which was located in Columbus, he could attend only by driving a considerable distance from his home. A similarly situated female would not have been required to choose between foregoing credit and bearing that inconvenience. Moreover, since many students enrolled in the School of Nursing hold full-time jobs, Hogan's female colleagues had available an

establish that the party seeking to uphold a statute that classifies individuals on the basis of their gender must carry the burden of showing an "exceedingly persuasive justification" for the classification. [T]he classification [must serve] "important governmental objectives and that the discriminatory means employed" are "substantially related to the achievement of those objectives."

Although the test for determining the validity of a gender-based classification is straightforward, it must be applied free of fixed notions concerning the roles and abilities of males and females. Care must be taken in ascertaining whether the statutory objective itself reflects archaic and stereotypic notions.... If the State's objective is legitimate and important, we next determine whether the requisite direct, substantial relationship between objective and means is present....

The State's primary justification for maintaining the single-sex admissions policy of MUW's School of Nursing is that it compensates for discrimination against women and, therefore, constitutes educational affirmative action. As applied to the School of Nursing, we find the State's argument unpersuasive.

In limited circumstances, a gender-based classification favoring one sex can be justified if it intentionally and directly assists members of the sex that is disproportionately burdened. [But] "the mere recitation of a benign, compensatory purpose is not an automatic shield which protects against any inquiry into the actual purposes underlying a statutory scheme." ...

It is readily apparent that a State can evoke a compensatory purpose to justify an otherwise discriminatory classification only if members of the gender benefited by the classification actually suffer a disadvantage related to the classification. We considered such a situation in *Califano v. Webster,* 430 U.S. 313, 97 S.Ct. 1192, 51 L.Ed.2d 360 (1977), which involved a challenge to a statutory classification that allowed women to eliminate more low-earning years than men for purposes of computing Social Security retirement benefits. Although the effect of the classification was to allow women higher monthly benefits than were available to men with the same earning history, we upheld the statutory scheme, noting that it took into account that women "as such have been unfairly hindered from earning as much as men" and "work[ed] directly to remedy" the resulting economic disparity.

A similar pattern of discrimination against women influenced our decision in *Schlesinger v. Ballard* [419 U.S. 498, 95 S.Ct. 572, 42 L.Ed.2d 610 (1975)]. There, we considered a federal statute that granted female Naval officers a 13–year tenure of commissioned service before mandatory discharge, but accorded male officers only a 9–year tenure. We recognized that, because women were barred from combat duty, they had had fewer opportunities for promotion than had their male counterparts.

opportunity, not open to Hogan, to obtain credit for additional training. The policy of denying males the right to obtain credit toward a baccalaureate degree thus imposed upon Hogan "a burden he would not bear were he female."

By allowing women an additional four years to reach a particular rank before subjecting them to mandatory discharge, the statute directly compensated for other statutory barriers to advancement.

In sharp contrast, Mississippi has made no showing that women lacked opportunities to obtain training in the field of nursing or to attain positions of leadership in that field when the MUW School of Nursing opened its door or that women currently are deprived of such opportunities. In fact, in 1970, the year before the School of Nursing's first class enrolled, women earned 94 percent of the nursing baccalaureate degrees conferred in Mississippi and 98.6 percent of the degrees earned nationwide. . . .

Rather than compensate for discriminatory barriers faced by women, MUW's policy of excluding males from admission to the School of Nursing tends to perpetuate the stereotyped view of nursing as an exclusively woman's job. By assuring that Mississippi allots more openings in its state-supported nursing schools to women than it does to men, MUW's admissions policy lends credibility to the old view that women, not men, should become nurses, and makes the assumption that nursing is a field for women a self-fulfilling prophecy. Thus, we conclude that, although the State recited a "benign, compensatory purpose," it failed to establish that the alleged objective is the actual purpose underlying the discriminatory classification.[16]

The policy is invalid also because it fails the second part of the equal protection test, for the State has made no showing that the gender-based classification is substantially and directly related to its proposed compensatory objective. To the contrary, MUW's policy of permitting men to attend classes as auditors fatally undermines its claim that women, at least those in the School of Nursing, are adversely affected by the presence of men. . . .

Thus, considering both the asserted interest and the relationship between the interest and the methods used by the State, we conclude that the State has fallen far short of establishing the "exceedingly persuasive justification" needed to sustain the gender-based classification. Accordingly, we hold that MUW's policy of denying males the right

---

16. Even were we to assume that discrimination against women affects their opportunity to obtain an education or to obtain leadership roles in nursing, the challenged policy nonetheless would be invalid, for the State has failed to establish that the legislature intended the single-sex policy to compensate for any perceived discrimination. Cf. *Califano v. Webster,* 430 U.S. 313, 318, 97 S.Ct. 1192, 51 L.Ed.2d 360 (1977)(legislative history of the compensatory statute revealed that Congress "directly addressed the justification for differing treatment of men and women" and "purposely enacted the more favorable treatment for female wage earners . . ."). The State has provided no evidence whatever that the Mississippi Legislature has ever attempted to justify its differing treatment of men and women seeking nurses' training. Indeed, the only statement of legislative purpose is that in § 37–117–3 of the Mississippi Code, a statement that relies upon the very sort of archaic and overbroad generalizations about women that we have found insufficient to justify a gender-based classification. E.g., *Orr v. Orr,* 440 U.S. 268, 99 S.Ct. 1102, 59 L.Ed.2d 306 (1979).

to enroll for credit in its School of Nursing violates the Equal Protection Clause of the Fourteenth Amendment.[17]

In an additional attempt to justify its exclusion of men from MUW's School of Nursing, the State [relies on] § 901(a) in Title IX of the Educational Amendments of 1972, 20 U.S.C.A. § 1681(a). Although § 901(a) prohibits gender discrimination in education programs that receive federal financial assistance, subsection 5 exempts the admissions policies of under-graduate institutions "that traditionally and continually from [their] establishment [have] had a policy of admitting only students of one sex" from the general prohibition. Arguing that Congress enacted Title IX in furtherance of its power to enforce the Fourteenth Amendment, a power granted by § 5 of that Amendment, the State would have us conclude that § 1681(a)(5) is but "a congressional limitation upon the broad prohibitions of the Equal Protection Clause of the Fourteenth Amendment."

The argument requires little comment. Initially, it is far from clear that Congress intended, through § 1681(a)(5), to exempt MUW from any constitutional obligation. Rather, Congress apparently intended, at most, to exempt MUW from the requirements of Title IX. Even if Congress envisioned a constitutional exemption, the State's argument would fail. Section 5 of the Fourteenth Amendment gives Congress broad power indeed to enforce the command of the Amendment and "to secure to all persons the enjoyment of perfect equality of civil rights and the equal protection of the laws against State denial or invasion.... " Congress' power under § 5, however, "is limited to adopting measures to enforce the guarantees of the Amendment; § 5 grants Congress no power to restrict, abrogate, or dilute these guarantees." *Katzenbach v. Morgan*, [§ 9–1, infra]. Although we give deference to congressional decisions and classifications, neither Congress nor a State can validate a law that denies the rights guaranteed by the Fourteenth Amendment....

CHIEF JUSTICE BURGER, dissenting.

I agree generally with JUSTICE POWELL's dissenting opinion. I write separately, however, to emphasize that the Court's holding today is limited to the context of a professional nursing school. Since the Court's opinion relies heavily on its finding that women have traditionally dominated the nursing profession, it suggests that a State might well be justified in maintaining, for example, the option of an all-women's business school or liberal arts program.

JUSTICE BLACKMUN, dissenting....

17. Justice Powell's dissent suggests that a second objective is served by the gender-based classification in that Mississippi has elected to provide women a choice of educational environments. Since any gender-based classification provides one class a benefit or choice not available to the other class, however, that argument begs the question. The issue is not whether the benefited class profits from the classification, but whether the State's decision to confer a benefit only upon one class by means of a discriminatory classification is substantially related to achieving a legitimate and substantial goal.

[This] ruling, it seems to me, places in constitutional jeopardy any state-supported educational institution that confines its student body in any area to members of one sex, even though the State elsewhere provides an equivalent program to the complaining applicant. The Court's reasoning does not stop with the School of Nursing of the Mississippi University for Women. I hope that we do not lose all values that some think are worthwhile (and are not based on differences of race or religion) and relegate ourselves to needless conformity....

JUSTICE POWELL, with whom JUSTICE REHNQUIST joins, dissenting.

[Respondent is not] significantly disadvantaged by MUW's all-female tradition. His constitutional complaint is based upon a single asserted harm: that he must *travel* to attend the state-supported nursing schools that concededly are available to him. The Court characterizes this injury as one of "inconvenience." Ante, at n. 8. [T]here is, of course, no constitutional right to attend a state-supported university in one's home town. Thus the Court, to redress respondent's injury of inconvenience, must rest its invalidation of MUW's single-sex program on a mode of "sexual stereotype" reasoning that has no application whatever to the respondent or to the "wrong" of which he complains. At best this is anomalous. And ultimately the anomaly reveals legal error—that of applying a heightened equal protection standard, developed in cases of genuine sexual stereotyping, to a narrowly utilized state classification that provides an *additional* choice for women. Moreover, I believe that Mississippi's educational system should be upheld in this case even if this inappropriate method of analysis is applied.

Coeducation, historically, is a novel educational theory.... The Carnegie Commission on Higher Education has reported that it "favor[s] the continuation of colleges for women. They provide an element of diversity ... and [an environment in which women] generally ... speak up more in their classes, ... hold more positions of leadership on campus, ... and have more role models and mentors among women teachers and administrators." ... The Equal Protection Clause was never intended to be applied to this kind of case.[18]

Notes

United States v. Virginia, , 518 U.S. 515, 116 S.Ct. 2264, 135 L.Ed.2d 735 (1996). The Virginia Military Institute (VMI) was a single-sex male college operated by the Commonwealth of Virginia. The United States sued VMI, claiming that its male-only policy violated equal protection. The

---

18. ... The Court holds today that they have deprived Hogan of constitutional rights because MUW is adjudged guilty of sex discrimination.... I see no principled way—in light of the Court's rationale—to reach a different result with respect to other MUW schools and departments. But given the Court's insistence that its decision applies only to the School of Nursing, it is my view that the Board and officials of MUW may continue to operate the remainder of the University on a single-sex basis without fear of personal liability. The standard of such liability is whether the conduct of the official "violate[s] clearly established statutory or constitutional rights of which a reasonable person would have known". The Court today leaves in doubt the reach of its decision.

District Court ruled in favor of VMI, but the Fourth Circuit reversed and ordered Virginia to remedy the constitutional violation. Virginia proposed to establish what it called a parallel program for women (called the Virginia Women's Institute for Leadership, or VWIL) to be located at a private liberal arts college for women. The district court affirmed, as did the Fourth Circuit, after finding that the VMI and VWIL students would receive "substantially comparable" benefits, although even the Fourth Circuit acknowledged that the VWIL degree lacked the prestige and historical benefit of the VMI degree.

Ginsburg, J., for the Court, reversed and held that equal protection precluded Virginia from reserving exclusively to men the unique educational opportunities that VMI affords. Virginia argued that its offering of an option for single-sex education fostered diversity in education, but the Court responded that, when the state offers benign justifications for categorical exclusions of types of people, those justifications must describe the state's actual purposes and not be merely rationalizations for its actions. Virginia did not demonstrate that VMI's all-male policy was established or maintained for the purpose of diversifying educational opportunities within the state. Virginia also argued that its all-male policy was necessary to VMI's mission of producing "citizen-soldiers" by using an "adversative method" of training (involving physical and mental discipline and loss of privacy). The Court agreed that the admission of women into VMI would require accommodations, primarily in terms of arranging housing assignments (to give "each sex privacy from the other sex in living arrangements") and changing physical training programs for female cadets (because of "physiological differences between male and female individuals"). But VMI's goal of creating citizen-soldiers and its implementing methodology is not inherently unsuitable to women. VMI could not exclude all women from a program from which some were qualified. VWIL's creation did not cure the constitutional violation because it was unequal in both tangible and intangible factors (e.g., curricular choices, faculty stature, funding, prestige, alumni support and influence) and did not afford females the pressures, hazards, and psychological bonding characteristic of VMI's adversative training. The Court assumed that "most women would not choose VMI's adversative method," but, "the question is whether the State can constitutionally deny to women who have the will and capacity, the training and attendant opportunities that VMI uniquely affords".

In a footnote, the Court said: "We do not question the State's prerogative evenhandedly to support diverse educational opportunities. We address specifically and only an educational opportunity recognized by the District Court and the Court of Appeals as 'unique.'" The Court then quoted footnote 1 of *Mississippi University for Women,* which said: "we are not faced with the question of whether States can provide 'separate but equal' undergraduate institutions for males and females."

Rehnquist, C.J., filed an opinion concurring in the judgment. In the course of the majority opinion, the Court had said that parties defending sex-based government action "must demonstrate an 'exceedingly persuasive justification' for that action." Rehnquist expressed concern that the Court was introducing "an element of uncertainty respecting the appropriate test." (The majority, however, did not purport to create a more difficult test for sex-based classifications, and used identical language in *Mississippi University for Women*.) While Rehnquist agreed that the creation of VWIL was an inadequate remedy, he also argued that a sufficient remedy would exist if Virginia demonstrated that "its interest in educating men in a single-sex environment is matched by its interest in educating women in a single-sex institution." The two institutions need not have to have the "same number of PhD's, similar SAT scores, or comparable athletic fields." One "could be strong in computer sciences, the other could be strong in liberal arts." It would be enough if the "two institutions offered the same quality of education and were of the same overall caliber."

Thomas, J., took no part in the consideration or decision of the case. Scalia, J., filed the only dissent. He criticized the Court for writing into the Constitution "the smug assurances" of the present age, and noted that the Court provided no example of a program "that would pass muster under its reasoning today: not even, for example, a football or wrestling program. On the Court's theory, any woman ready, willing, and physically able to participate in such a program would, as a constitutional matter, be entitled to do so."

In *Norwood v. Harrison* (1973) [§ 7–4] the Court held that it would be unconstitutional for the state to provide financial support (the state allowed the students to borrow free textbooks) to assist racially discriminatory private schools. Would it be constitutional for the Federal or State Governments to provide financial assistance to private single-sex universities? In dissent, Justice Scalia argued: "The only hope for state-assisted single-sex private schools is that the Court will not apply in the future the principles of law it has applied today. That is a substantial hope, I am happy and ashamed to say. [D]oes not the Court positively invite private colleges to rely upon our ad-hocery by assuring them this case is 'unique'? I would not advise the foundation of any new single-sex college (especially an all-male one) with the expectation of being allowed to receive any government support; but it is too soon to abandon in despair those single-sex colleges already in existence. It will certainly be possible for this Court to write a future opinion that ignores the broad principles of law set forth today, and that characterizes as utterly dispositive the opinion's perceptions that VMI was a uniquely prestigious all-male institution, conceived in chauvinism, etc., etc. I will not join that opinion."

8–2.5 Wealth and Age

DANDRIDGE v. WILLIAMS
397 U.S. 471, 90 S.Ct. 1153, 25 L.Ed.2d 491 (1970).

MR. JUSTICE STEWART delivered the opinion of the Court.

This case involves the validity of a method used by Maryland, in the administration of an aspect of its public welfare program, to reconcile the demands of its needy citizens with the finite resources available to meet those demands. Like every other State in the Union, Maryland participates in the Federal Aid to Families With Dependent Children (AFDC) program, which originated with the Social Security Act of 1935. . . .

The operation of the Maryland welfare system is not complex.... It computes the standard of need for each eligible family based on the number of children in the family and the circumstances under which the family lives. In general, the standard of need increases with each additional person in the household, but the increments become proportionately smaller. The regulation here in issue imposes upon the grant that any single family may receive an upper limit of $250 per month in certain counties and Baltimore City, and of $240 per month elsewhere in the State. The appellees all have large families, so that their standards of need as computed by the State substantially exceed the maximum grants that they actually receive under the regulation. The appellees urged in the District Court that the maximum grant limitation operates to discriminate against them merely because of the size of their families, in violation of the Equal Protection Clause of the Fourteenth Amendment....

... The regulation can be clearly justified, Maryland argues, in terms of legitimate state interests in encouraging gainful employment, in maintaining an equitable balance in economic status as between welfare families and those supported by a wage-earner, in providing incentives for family planning, and in allocating available public funds in such a way as fully to meet the needs of the largest possible number of families. The District Court, while apparently recognizing the validity of at least some of these state concerns, nonetheless held that the regulation "is invalid on its face for overreaching," that it violates the Equal Protection Clause "[b]ecause it cuts too broad a swath on an indiscriminate basis as applied to the entire group of AFDC eligibles to which it purports to apply...."

If this were a case involving government action claimed to violate the First Amendment guarantee of free speech, a finding of "overreaching" would be significant and might be crucial. For when otherwise valid governmental regulation sweeps so broadly as to impinge upon activity protected by the First Amendment, its very overbreadth may make it unconstitutional. But the concept of "overreaching" has no place in this case. For here we deal with state regulation in the social and economic field, not affecting freedoms guaranteed by the Bill of Rights, and claimed to violate the Fourteenth Amendment only because the regulation results in some disparity in grants of welfare payments to the largest AFDC families. For this Court to approve the invalidation of state economic or social regulation as "overreaching" would be far too reminiscent of an era when the Court thought the Fourteenth Amendment gave it power to strike down state laws "because they may be unwise, improvident, or out of harmony with a particular school of thought." *Williamson v. Lee Optical Co.,* 348 U.S. 483, 488, 75 S.Ct. 461, 464, 99 L.Ed. 563. That era long ago passed into history. *Ferguson v. Skrupa,* [§ 6–1, supra].

In the area of economics and social welfare, a State does not violate the Equal Protection Clause merely because the classifications made by its laws are imperfect. If the classification has some "reasonable basis," it does not offend the Constitution simply because the classification "is not made with mathematical nicety or because in practice it results in some inequality." *Lindsley v. Natural Carbonic Gas Co.,* [§ 8–1, supra]. "The problems of government are practical ones and may justify, if they do not require, rough accommodations—illogical, it may be, and unscientific." "A statutory discrimination will not be set aside if any state of facts reasonably may be conceived to justify it."

To be sure, the cases cited, and many others enunciating this fundamental standard under the Equal Protection Clause, have in the main involved state regulation of business or industry. The administration of public welfare assistance, by contrast, involves the most basic economic needs of impoverished human beings. We recognize the dramatically real factual difference between the cited cases and this one, but we can find no basis for applying a different constitutional standard. It is a standard that has consistently been applied to state legislation restricting the availability of employment opportunities. And it is a standard that is true to the principle that the Fourteenth Amendment gives the federal courts no power to impose upon the States their views of what constitutes wise economic or social policy.

Under this long-established meaning of the Equal Protection Clause, it is clear that the Maryland maximum grant regulation is constitutionally valid. We need not explore all the reasons that the State advances in justification of the regulation. It is enough that a solid foundation for the regulation can be found in the State's legitimate interest in encouraging employment and in avoiding discrimination between welfare families and the families of the working poor. By combining a limit on the recipient's grant with permission to retain money earned, without reduction in the amount of the grant, Maryland provides an incentive to seek gainful employment. And by keying the maximum family AFDC grants to the minimum wage a steadily employed head of a household receives, the State maintains some semblance of an equitable balance between families on welfare and those supported by an employed breadwinner.

It is true that in some AFDC families there may be no person who is employable. It is also true that with respect to AFDC families whose determined standard of need is below the regulatory maximum, and who therefore receive grants equal to the determined standard, the employment incentive is absent. But the Equal Protection Clause does not require that a State must choose between attacking every aspect of a problem or not attacking the problem at all. *Lindsley v. Natural Carbonic Gas Co.* It is enough that the State's action be rationally based and free from invidious discrimination. The regulation before us meets that test.

We do not decide today that the Maryland regulation is wise, that it best fulfills the relevant social and economic objectives that Maryland might ideally espouse, or that a more just and humane system could not be devised. Conflicting claims of morality and intelligence are raised by opponents and proponents of almost every measure, certainly including the one before us. But the intractable economic, social, and even philosophical problems presented by public welfare assistance programs are not the business of this Court. The Constitution may impose certain procedural safeguards upon systems of welfare administration, *Goldberg v. Kelly,* [§ 6–3.2, supra]. But the Constitution does not empower this Court to second-guess state officials charged with the difficult responsibility of allocating limited public welfare funds among the myriad of potential recipients.

The judgment is reversed.

[The concurring opinions of BLACK, J., joined by BURGER, C.J., and of HARLAN, J., and the dissenting opinion of MARSHALL, J., joined by BRENNAN, J., are omitted.]

SAN ANTONIO INDEPENDENT SCHOOL DISTRICT v. RODRIGUEZ
411 U.S. 1, 93 S.Ct. 1278, 36 L.Ed.2d 16 (1973).

MR. JUSTICE POWELL delivered the opinion of the Court.

This suit attacking the Texas system of financing public education was initiated by Mexican–American parents whose children attend the elementary and secondary schools in the Edgewood Independent School District, an urban school district in San Antonio, Texas....

The school district in which appellees reside, the Edgewood Independent School District, has been compared throughout this litigation with the Alamo Heights Independent School District. This comparison between the least and most affluent districts in the San Antonio area serves to illustrate the manner in which the dual system of finance operates and to indicate the extent to which substantial disparities exist despite the State's impressive progress in recent years. Edgewood is one of seven public school districts in the metropolitan area. Approximately 22,000 students are enrolled in its 25 elementary and secondary schools. The district is situated in the core-city sector of San Antonio in a residential neighborhood that has little commercial or industrial property. The residents are predominantly of Mexican–American descent: approximately 90% of the student population is Mexican–American and over 6% is Negro. The average assessed property value per pupil is $5,960—the lowest in the metropolitan area—and the median family income ($4,686) is also the lowest. At an equalized tax rate of $1.05 per $100 of assessed property—the highest in the metropolitan area—the district contributed $26 to the education of each child for the 1967–1968 school year above its Local Fund Assignment for the Minimum Foundation Program. The Foundation Program contributed $222 per pupil for a state-local total of $248. Federal funds added another $108 for a total of $356 per pupil.

Alamo Heights is the most affluent school district in San Antonio. Its six schools, housing approximately 5,000 students, are situated in a residential community quite unlike the Edgewood District. The school population is predominantly "Anglo," having only 18% Mexican–Americans and less than 1% Negroes. The assessed property value per pupil exceeds $49,000, and the median family income is $8,001. In 1967–1968 the local tax rate of $.85 per $100 of valuation yielded $333 per pupil over and above its contribution to the Foundation Program. Coupled with the $225 provided from that Program, the district was able to supply $558 per student. Supplemented by a $36 per-pupil grant from federal sources, Alamo Heights spent $594 per pupil.[35]

[Such substantial disparities] led the District Court to conclude that Texas' dual system of public school financing violated the Equal Protection Clause. The District Court held that the Texas system discriminates on the basis of wealth in the manner in which education is provided for its people. Finding that wealth is a "suspect" classification and that education is a "fundamental" interest, the District Court held that the Texas system could be sustained only if the State could show that it was premised upon some compelling state interest. On this issue the court concluded that "[n]ot only are defendants unable to demonstrate compelling state interests ... they fail even to establish a reasonable basis for these classifications."

... First, in support of their charge that the system discriminates against the "poor," ... there is reason to believe that the poorest families are not necessarily clustered in the poorest property districts. [A] Connecticut study found, not surprisingly, that the poor were clustered around commercial and industrial areas—those same areas that provide the most attractive sources of property tax income for school districts....

Second, ... lack of personal resources has not occasioned an absolute deprivation of the desired benefit. The argument here is not that the children in districts having relatively low assessable property values are receiving no public education; rather, it is that they are receiving a poorer quality education than that available to children in districts having more assessable wealth. Apart from the unsettled and disputed question whether the quality of education may be determined by the amount of money expended for it, a sufficient answer to appellees' argument is that, at least where wealth is involved, the Equal Protection Clause does not require absolute equality or precisely equal advantages....[60] ...

35. ... Higher salaries are guaranteed to teachers having more years of experience and possessing more advance degrees. Therefore, Alamo Heights, which has a greater percentage of experienced personnel with advanced degrees, receives more state support.... [footnote repositioned.]

60. An educational financing system might be hypothesized, however, in which the analogy to the wealth discrimination cases would be considerably closer. If elementary and secondary education were made available by the State only to those able to pay a tuition assessed against each pupil, there would be a clearly defined class of "poor" people—definable in terms of their inability to pay the prescribed sum—who would be absolutely precluded from receiving an education. That case would present a far more compelling set of circumstances for judicial assistance than the case before us today. After all, Texas has undertaken to do a good deal more than provide an education to those who can afford it. It has provided what it considers to be an adequate base education for all children and

This brings us, then, to the third way in which the classification scheme might be defined—*district* wealth discrimination. Since the only correlation indicated by the evidence is between district property wealth and expenditures, it may be argued that discrimination might be found without regard to the individual income characteristics of district residents.... The system of alleged discrimination and the class it defines have none of the traditional indicia of suspectness: the class is not saddled with such disabilities, or subjected to such a history of purposeful unequal treatment, or relegated to such a position of political powerlessness as to command extraordinary protection from the majoritarian political process.

We thus conclude that the Texas system does not operate to the peculiar disadvantage of any suspect class. [Appellees] also assert that the State's system impermissibly interferes with the exercise of a "fundamental" right and that accordingly the prior decisions of this Court require the application of the strict standard of judicial review....

In *Brown v. Board of Education,* [§ 8–2.12, supra], a unanimous Court recognized that "education is perhaps the most important function of state and local governments." What was said there in the context of racial discrimination has lost none of its vitality with the passage of time.... But the importance of a service performed by the State does not determine whether it must be regarded as fundamental for purposes of examination under the Equal Protection Clause. [T]he key to discovering whether education is "fundamental" is not to be found in comparisons of the relative societal significance of education as opposed to subsistence or housing. Nor is it to be found by weighing whether education is as important as the right to travel. Rather, the answer lies in assessing whether there is a right to education explicitly or implicitly guaranteed by the Constitution.

Education, of course, is not among the rights afforded explicit protection under our Federal Constitution. Nor do we find any basis for saying it is implicitly so protected. [Appellees] insist that education is itself a fundamental personal right because it is essential to the effective exercise of First Amendment freedoms and to intelligent utilization of the right to vote. [A]ppellees urge that the right to speak is meaningless unless the speaker is capable of articulating his thoughts intelligently and persuasively.... Exercise of the franchise, it is contended, cannot be divorced from the educational foundation of the voter.... Yet we have never presumed to possess either the ability or the authority to guarantee to the citizenry the most *effective* speech or the most *informed* electoral choice. That these may be desirable goals of a system of freedom of expression and of a representative form of government is not to be doubted. These are indeed goals to be pursued by a people whose thoughts and beliefs are freed from governmental interference. But they

---

has attempted, though imperfectly, to ameliorate by state funding and by the local assessment program the disparities in local tax resources.

are not values to be implemented by judicial intrusion into otherwise legitimate state activities. . . .

Furthermore, the logical limitations on appellees' nexus theory are difficult to perceive. How, for instance, is education to be distinguished from the significant personal interests in the basics of decent food and shelter? Empirical examination might well buttress an assumption that the ill-fed, ill-clothed, and ill-housed are among the most ineffective participants in the political process, and that they derive the least enjoyment from the benefits of the First Amendment. If so, appellees' thesis would cast serious doubt on the authority of *Dandridge v. Williams*, ...

We need not rest our decision, however, solely on the inappropriateness of the strict-scrutiny test. A century of Supreme Court adjudication under the Equal Protection Clause affirmatively supports the application of the traditional standard of review, which requires only that the State's system be shown to bear some rational relationship to legitimate state purposes. . . .We have here nothing less than a direct attack on the way in which Texas has chosen to raise and disburse state and local tax revenues. We are asked to condemn the State's judgment in conferring on political subdivisions the power to tax local property to supply revenues for local interests. In so doing, appellees would have the Court intrude in an area in which it has traditionally deferred to state legislatures. . . . Education, perhaps even more than welfare assistance, presents a myriad of "intractable economic, social, and even philosophical problems." *Dandridge v. Williams* . . . .

In sum, to the extent that the Texas system of school financing results in unequal expenditures between children who happen to reside in different districts, we cannot say that such disparities are the product of a system that is so irrational as to be invidiously discriminatory. . . .

MR. JUSTICE MARSHALL, with whom MR. JUSTICE DOUGLAS concurs, dissenting. . . .

To begin, I must once more voice my disagreement with the Court's rigidified approach to equal protection analysis. See *Dandridge v. Williams* (dissenting opinion). The Court apparently seeks to establish today that equal protection cases fall into one of two neat categories which dictate the appropriate standard of review—strict scrutiny or mere rationality. But this Court's decisions in the field of equal protection defy such easy categorization. A principled reading of what this Court has done reveals that it has applied a spectrum of standards in reviewing discrimination allegedly violative of the Equal Protection Clause. This spectrum clearly comprehends variations in the degree of care with which the Court will scrutinize particular classifications, depending, I believe, on the constitutional and societal importance of the interest adversely affected and the recognized invidiousness of the basis upon which the particular classification is drawn. [I]t will not do to suggest that the "answer" to whether an interest is fundamental for purposes of equal protection analysis is *always* determined by whether that interest "is a right ... explicitly or implicitly guaranteed by the Constitution." ...

The majority is, of course, correct when it suggests that the process of determining which interests are fundamental is a difficult one. But I do not think the problem is insurmountable. And I certainly do not accept the view that the process need necessarily degenerate into an unprincipled, subjective "picking-and-choosing" between various interests or that it must involve this Court in creating "substantive constitutional rights in the name of guaranteeing equal protection of the laws." Although not all fundamental interests are constitutionally guaranteed, the determination of which interests are fundamental should be firmly rooted in the text of the Constitution. The task in every case should be to determine the extent to which constitutionally guaranteed rights are dependent on interests not mentioned in the Constitution. As the nexus between the specific constitutional guarantee and the nonconstitutional interest draws closer, the nonconstitutional interest becomes more fundamental and the degree of judicial scrutiny applied when the interest is infringed on a discriminatory basis must be adjusted accordingly....

[I]t seems to me inescapably clear that this Court has consistently adjusted the care with which it will review state discrimination in light of the constitutional significance of the interests affected and the invidiousness of the particular classification.... The majority suggests, however, that a variable standard of review would give this Court the appearance of a "superlegislature." I cannot agree. Such an approach seems to me a part of the guarantees of our Constitution and of the historic experiences with oppression of and discrimination against discrete, powerless minorities which underlie that document. In truth, the Court itself will be open to the criticism raised by the majority so long as it continues on its present course of effectively selecting in private which cases will be afforded special consideration without acknowledging the true basis of its action....

The only justification offered by appellants to sustain the discrimination in educational opportunity caused by the Texas financing scheme is local educational control.... In Texas, statewide laws regulate in fact the most minute details of local public education. [E]ven even if we accept Texas' general dedication to local control in educational matters, it is difficult to find any evidence of such dedication with respect to fiscal matters....

[The opinions of STEWART, J., concurring, and WHITE, J., joined by DOUGLAS and BRENNAN, JJ., dissenting, are omitted.]

Notes

1. In *Papasan v. Allain,* 478 U.S. 265, 106 S.Ct. 2932, 92 L.Ed.2d 209 (1986), the Court, per White, J., held that a cause of action was stated by an allegation that unequal distribution of funds for education were not rationally related to a legitimate state interest. The Court said that *Rodriguez* held that "funding disparities resulting from differences in local taxes were

acceptable because [they were] related to the state goal of allowing a measure of effective local control over school funding levels. *Rodriguez* did not, however, purport to validate all funding decisions. It held merely that the variations that resulted from allowing local control over local property tax funding of the public schools were constitutionally permissible in that case." *Papasan* said that plaintiffs would have to prove that the differential treatment was not rationally related to a legitimate state interest. Justice Powell, joined by Chief Justice Burger and Justice Rehnquist, objected and concluded that the attack on the system of financing public schools in Mississippi should be foreclosed by *Rodriguez.*

2. AGE DISCRIMINATION. State law forced Robert Murgia, an officer in the uniformed Massachusetts State Police, to retire at age 50. Given that service in the police can be arduous, the state required such uniformed officers to pass a comprehensive physical examination biennially until age 40. After that, the officers had to pass a more rigorous examination annually. Murgia had passed such an examination four months before he was forced to retire. Because there was no dispute that he had excellent physical and mental health and that he was capable of performing his duties, he challenged the mandatory retirement law as denying him equal protection. The Supreme Court rejected the challenge, over the dissent of Marshall, J. *Massachusetts Board of Retirement v. Murgia,* 427 U.S. 307, 96 S.Ct. 2562, 49 L.Ed.2d 520 (1976)(per curiam).

Citing *Dandridge v. Williams* and *San Antonio Independent School District v. Rodriguez,* the Court first stated that the right of governmental employment is not *per se* fundamental. The Court went on to explain:

> Nor does the class of uniformed state police officers over 50 constitute a suspect class for purposes of equal protection analysis. *Rodriguez,* observed that a suspect class is one saddled with such disabilities, or subjected to such a history of purposeful unequal treatment, or relegated to such a position of political powerlessness as to command extraordinary protection from the majoritarian political process. While the treatment of the aged in this Nation has not been wholly free of discrimination, such persons, unlike, say, those who have been discriminated against on the basis of race or national origin, have not experienced a history of purposeful unequal treatment or been subjected to unique disabilities on the basis of stereotyped characteristics not truly indicative of their abilities. The class subject to the compulsory retirement feature of the Massachusetts statute consists of uniformed state police officers over the age of 50. It cannot be said to discriminate only against the elderly. Rather, it draws the line at a certain age in middle life. But even old age does not define a discrete and insular group, *United States v. Carolene Products Co.,* [§ 4–4, supra], in need of "extraordinary protection from the majoritarian political process." Instead, it marks a stage that each of us will reach if we live out our normal span. Even if the statute could be said to impose a penalty upon a class defined as the aged, it would not impose a distinction sufficiently akin to those classifications that we have found suspect to call for strict judicial scrutiny.

The purpose of the state retirement law is to assure physical preparedness of its uniformed police; physical ability declines with age; and 50 years marks a cut off that is not irrational. "That the State chooses not to determine fitness more precisely through individualized testing after age 50 is not to say that the objective of assuring physical fitness is not rationally furthered by a maximum-age limitation. It is only to say that with regard to the interest of all concerned, the State perhaps has not chosen the best means to accomplish this purpose."[1]

Gregory v. Ashcroft, 501 U.S. 452, 111 S.Ct. 2395, 115 L.Ed.2d 410 (1991). O'Connor, J., for the Court, ruled that a provision of the Missouri Constitution requiring appointed state judges to retire at age 70 violates neither the federal Age Discrimination in Employment Act, nor the Equal Protection Clause. It is rational to conclude that the threat of deterioration is sufficiently great and the alternatives for removal sufficiently inadequate that they will require all judges to retire at age 70.

3. IRREBUTTABLE PRESUMPTIONS. In a few cases, primarily in the 1970's, the Court invalidated various laws on the grounds that they established irrebuttable presumptions, thereby denying a litigant procedural due process by not providing an opportunity to be heard and refute the presumption. Thus in *Cleveland Board of Education v. LaFleur,* 414 U.S. 632, 94 S.Ct. 791, 39 L.Ed.2d 52 (1974) the Court, per Stewart, J., invalidated public school board mandatory maternity leave rules that required pregnant teachers to quit their job without pay several months before giving birth. The teacher on maternity leave was not promised reemployment after the birth of her child, though she was given priority. Stewart reasoned that the rules "amount to a conclusive presumption that every pregnant teacher who reaches the fifth or sixth month of pregnancy is physically incapable of continuing. There is no individualized determination by the teacher's doctor—or the school board's—as to any particular teacher's ability to continue at her job. The rules contain an irrebuttable presumption of physical incompetency, and that presumption applies even when the medical evidence as to an individual woman's physical status might be wholly to the contrary." A conclusive presumption that is not necessarily nor universally true "is violative of the Due Process Clause."

Powell, J., concurred in the result but not the reasoning, arguing that such laws should be analyzed under equal protection. All laws classify on the basis of factual and other assumptions and the real question is whether that classification is proper, not whether the state has granted an individualized hearing.

---

1. *Lyng v. Castillo,* 477 U.S. 635, 106 S.Ct. 2727, 91 L.Ed.2d 527 (1986) upheld the statutory definition of "household" in the Federal Food Stamp Program. Parents, children, and siblings living together are generally treated as a single household, while more distant relatives or groups of unrelated people living together are not, unless they also customarily purchase food and prepare meals together. The definition is rational: it makes it more difficult for individuals to manipulate the rules to obtain greater benefits. Relying on *Murgia* the Court rejected any equal protection challenge. It was error to judge the statutory definition under heightened scrutiny. "Close relatives are not a 'suspect' or 'quasi-suspect' class." Nor does the statutory classification " 'directly and substantially' interfere with family living arrangements and thereby burden a fundamental right."

Rehnquist, J., joined by Burger, C.J., dissented, objecting to Justice Stewart's "enlist[ing] the Court in another quixotic engagement in his apparently unending war on irrebuttable presumptions." Hundreds of years ago the shift from judgments made on an *ad hoc* basis by the King's representatives to relatively uniform rules enacted by a law making body was thought "to have been a significant step forward in the achievement of a civilized society."

Under Stewart's analysis, what of laws that set a minimum age to contract a valid marriage, to drink liquor, or to drive a car?

Most commentators attacked the irrebuttable presumption analysis, and the Court seems to have ended it with *Weinberger v. Salfi,* 422 U.S. 749, 95 S.Ct. 2457, 45 L.Ed.2d 522 (1975), upholding, under the Social Security Act, eligibility classifications of surviving spouses and stepchildren based on the duration of their relationship to the deceased wage earner. Justice Rehnquist wrote the majority opinion and concluded that there is "no basis for our requiring individualized determinations when Congress can rationally conclude not only that generalized rules are appropriate to its purposes and concerns, but also that the difficulties of individual determinations outweigh the marginal increments in the precise effectuation of congressional concern which they might be expected to produce."

Since *Weinberger* the irrebuttable presumption doctrine, while not officially entombed, seems to have died quietly. Note how *Murgia* simply ignored the doctrine.

4. THE MENTALLY RETARDED. *City of Cleburne v. Cleburne Living Center,* 473 U.S. 432, 105 S.Ct. 3249, 87 L.Ed.2d 313 (1985) rejected (6 to 3) any intermediate standard of review for the mentally retarded, but then held that the denial by Cleburne, Texas, of a special use permit under its zoning laws to a group home for the mentally retarded was unconstitutional under the Equal Protection Clause because it was "irrational." The city would have permitted the group home if it were not for the mentally retarded. The city did not require a special use permit for fraternity houses, boarding houses, nursing homes for convalescents, etc.

The Court acknowledged that legislation "singling out the retarded for special treatment reflects the real and undeniable differences between the retarded and others." But, said the Court, differences regarding the mentally retarded as a group "are largely irrelevant" unless the Home in this case threatens "legitimate interests of the city in a way that other permitted uses such as boarding houses and hospitals do not." The Court invalidated the ordinance as applied because it said that there was no rational basis to believe that this Home for the mentally retarded posed "any special threat to the city's legitimate interest." "[M]ere negative attitudes, or fear, unsubstantiated by factors which are properly cognizable in a zoning proceeding, are not permissible bases for treating a home for the mentally retarded differently from apartment houses, multiple dwellings and the like." The Home was also across the street from a high school, and the city was concerned that the high school students might harass the residents of the Home but "the school itself is attended by about 30 mentally retarded students, and denying a permit based on such vague, undifferentiated fears is" improper. The city claimed concern because the Home would be on a 500 year flood plain, but this objection did not explain why only the Home had to obtain a special use permit, and other uses—such as boarding houses—did not. The city was also concerned about the number of the people in the Home, and the size of the Home. But if the Home were used for any other purpose, such as a nursing home, this density restriction would not apply.[2]

Heller v. Doe, 509 U.S. 312, 113 S.Ct. 2637, 125 L.Ed.2d 257 (1993). Kentucky's involuntary commitment procedure allows mentally *retarded* individuals to be institutionalized if there is "clear and convincing" evidence of their retardation. However, the state may commit mentally *ill* individuals only upon proof "beyond a reasonable doubt." The Court, per Kennedy, J., held that this distinction is rational and thus does not violate the equal protection clause. The two conditions are different: it is easier to diagnose mental illness; it is easier to determine, in the case of mental retardation, whether the subject is dangerous to self or others; and the prevailing ways of treating mental retardation are less invasive than those relating to mental illness. It is also rational (and therefore constitutional) for the state to allow close relatives to participate in involuntary commitment proceedings of the mentally retarded but not the mentally ill because mental retardation appears in one's development period where relatives or guardians are likely to have intimate knowledge of the subject's abilities, while mental illness may manifest itself after minority. Also, relatives and guardians may provide useful information without increasing the risk of erroneous commitment of retarded persons, and thus there is also no violation of the due process clause.

Souter, J., joined by Blackmun & Stevens, JJ., dissented, arguing that Kentucky's different procedures to institutionalize the mentally ill and the mentally retarded are "not supported by any rational justification," and thus violate the Constitution. In Part I, Souter argued that the Court should inquire into the State's proffered justifications, and examine "the distinction in treatment in light of the purposes put forward to support it." In Part II of this dissent, which O'Connor, J., joined, he agreed that there are "obviously" differences between mental retardation and mental illness, but the differences do not "rationally" justify Kentucky's disparate treatment.

5. *Dandridge, Rodriguez,* and *Murgia* raise the issue not only if the classification is "suspect" but also whether it affects a "fundamental right." The question of how to determine what are "fundamental rights," and what is the standard to be used in judging a law establishing classifications that affect fundamental rights is the subject of the next section.

---

2. Stevens, J., joined by Burger, C.J. concurred, but objected to the three-tier basis of review, and reaffirmed the analysis presented in Justice Stevens' concurring opinion in *Craig v. Boren,* § 8–2.41. Marshall, J., joined by Brennan & Blackmun, JJ., concurred in the judgment in part and dissented in part. They would have applied an intermediate standard of review, and believed that the majority opinion really applied that standard but "masquerad[ed]" in the language of the rational basis test. They would have invalidated the ordinance on its face.

8–3.   FUNDAMENTAL RIGHTS

8–3.1   Access to the Courts

GRIFFIN v. ILLINOIS

351 U.S. 12, 76 S.Ct. 585, 100 L.Ed. 891 (1956).

MR. JUSTICE BLACK announced the judgment of the Court and an opinion in which THE CHIEF JUSTICE [WARREN], MR. JUSTICE DOUGLAS, and MR. JUSTICE CLARK join.

Illinois law provides that "Writs of error in all criminal cases are writs of right and shall be issued of course." The question presented here is whether Illinois may, consistent with the Due Process and Equal Protection Clauses of the Fourteenth Amendment, administer this statute so as to deny adequate appellate review to the poor while granting such review to all others.

[Petitioners, convicted of armed robbery, moved in trial court that a stenographic transcript of the proceedings be furnished them without pay because they were too poor to pay the necessary fees. Without such a transcript it is often impossible to prepare a bill of exceptions in order to get full appellate review by a writ of error. Under the Illinois Post–Conviction Hearing Act] indigents may obtain a free transcript to obtain appellate review of constitutional questions but not of other alleged trial errors such as admissibility and sufficiency of evidence. In their Post–Conviction proceeding petitioners alleged that there were manifest non-constitutional errors in the trial which entitled them to have their convictions set aside on appeal and that the only impediment to full appellate review was their lack of funds to buy a transcript. These allegations have not been denied. . . .

Providing equal justice for poor and rich, weak and powerful alike is an age-old problem. . . . In this tradition, our own constitutional guaranties of due process and equal protection both call for procedures in criminal trials which allow no invidious discriminations between persons and different groups of persons. Both equal protection and due process emphasize the central aim of our entire judicial system—all people charged with crime must, so far as the law is concerned, "stand on an equality before the bar of justice in every American court."

Surely no one would contend that either a State or the Federal Government could constitutionally provide that defendants unable to pay court costs in advance should be denied the right to plead not guilty or to defend themselves in court. Such a law would make the constitutional promise of a fair trial a worthless thing. Notice, the right to be heard, and the right to counsel would under such circumstances be meaningless promises to the poor. In criminal trials a State can no more discriminate on account of poverty than on account of religion, race, or color. Plainly the ability to pay costs in advance bears no rational relationship to a defendant's guilt or innocence and could not be used as an excuse to deprive a defendant of a fair trial. . . .

There is no meaningful distinction between a rule which would deny the poor the right to defend themselves in a trial court and one which effectively denies the poor an adequate appellate review accorded to all who have money enough to pay the costs in advance. It is true that a State is not required by the Federal Constitution to provide appellate courts or a right to appellate review at all. See, e.g., *McKane v. Durston,* 153 U.S. 684, 687–688, 14 S.Ct. 913, 914–915, 38 L.Ed. 867 [(1894)]. But that is not to say that a State that does grant appellate review can do so in a way that discriminates against some convicted defendants on account of their poverty. Appellate review has now become an integral part of the Illinois trial system for finally adjudicating the guilt or innocence of a defendant. Consequently at all stages of the proceedings the Due Process and Equal Protection Clauses protect persons like petitioners from invidious discriminations.

All of the States now provide some method of appeal from criminal convictions, recognizing the importance of appellate review to a correct adjudication of guilt or innocence. Statistics show that a substantial proportion of criminal convictions are reversed by state appellate courts. Thus to deny adequate review to the poor means that many of them may lose their life, liberty or property because of unjust convictions which appellate courts would set aside. Many States have recognized this and provided aid for convicted defendants who have a right to appeal and need a transcript but are unable to pay for it. A few have not. Such a denial is a misfit in a country dedicated to affording equal justice to all and special privileges to none in the administration of its criminal law. There can be no equal justice where the kind of trial a man gets depends on the amount of money he has. Destitute defendants must be afforded as adequate appellate review as defendants who have money enough to buy transcripts.

The Illinois Supreme Court denied these petitioners relief under the Post–Conviction Act because of its holding that no constitutional rights were violated. In view of our holding to the contrary the State Supreme Court may decide that petitioners are now entitled to a transcript, as the State's brief suggests. We do not hold, however, that Illinois must purchase a stenographer's transcript in every case where a defendant cannot buy it. The Supreme Court may find other means of affording adequate and effective appellate review to indigent defendants. For example, it may be that bystanders' bills of exceptions or other methods of reporting trial proceedings could be used in some cases. The Illinois Supreme Court appears to have broad power to promulgate rules of procedure and appellate practice. We are confident that the State will provide corrective rules to meet the problem which this case lays bare.

The judgment of the Supreme Court of Illinois is vacated and the cause is remanded to that court for further action not inconsistent with the foregoing paragraph. MR. JUSTICE FRANKFURTER joins in this disposition of the case.

Vacated and remanded.

[The opinions of FRANKFURTER, J., concurring in the judgment, of BURTON & MINTON, JJ., joined by REED & HARLAN, JJ., dissenting, and of HARLAN, J., dissenting, are omitted].

DOUGLAS v. CALIFORNIA
372 U.S. 353, 83 S.Ct. 814, 9 L.Ed.2d 811 (1963).

MR. JUSTICE DOUGLAS delivered the opinion of the Court.

... The record shows that petitioners requested, and were denied, the assistance of counsel on appeal, even though it plainly appeared they were indigents. In denying petitioners' requests, the California District Court of Appeal stated that it had "gone through" the record and had come to the conclusion that "no good whatever could be served by appointment of counsel." ... In *Griffin v. Illinois,* we held that a State may not grant appellate review in such a way as to discriminate against some convicted defendants on account of their poverty. There the right to a free transcript on appeal was in issue. Here the issue is whether or not an indigent shall be denied the assistance of counsel on appeal. In either case the evil is the same: discrimination against the indigent. For there can be no equal justice where the kind of an appeal a man enjoys "depends on the amount of money he has."

In spite of California's forward treatment of indigents, under its present practice the type of an appeal a person is afforded in the District Court of Appeal hinges upon whether or not he can pay for the assistance of counsel. If he can the appellate court passes on the merits of his case only after having the full benefit of written briefs and oral argument by counsel. If he cannot the appellate court is forced to prejudge the merits before it can even determine whether counsel should be provided. At this stage in the proceedings only the barren record speaks for the indigent, and, unless the printed pages show that an injustice has been committed, he is forced to go without a champion on appeal. Any real chance he may have had of showing that his appeal has hidden merit is deprived him when the court decides on an *ex parte* examination of the record that the assistance of counsel is not required.

We are not here concerned with problems that might arise from the denial of counsel for the preparation of a petition for discretionary or mandatory review beyond the stage in the appellate process at which the claims have once been presented by a lawyer and passed upon by an appellate court. We are dealing only with the *first appeal,* granted as a matter of right to rich and poor alike (Cal.Penal Code §§ 1235, 1237), from a criminal conviction. [I]t is appropriate to observe that a State can, consistently with the Fourteenth Amendment, provide for differences so long as the result does not amount to a denial of due process or an "invidious discrimination." [W]here the merits of *the one and only appeal* an indigent has as of right are decided without benefit of counsel, we think an unconstitutional line has been drawn between rich and poor.

When an indigent is forced to run this gantlet of a preliminary showing of merit, the right to appeal does not comport with fair procedure.... The present case, where counsel was denied petitioners on appeal, shows that the discrimination is not between "possibly good and obviously bad cases," but between cases where the rich man can require the court to listen to argument of counsel before deciding on the merits, but a poor man cannot. There is lacking that equality demanded by the Fourteenth Amendment where the rich man, who appeals as of right, enjoys the benefit of counsel's examination into the record, research of the law, and marshalling of arguments on his behalf, while the indigent, already burdened by a preliminary determination that his case is without merit, is forced to shift for himself. The indigent, where the record is unclear or the errors are hidden, has only the right to a meaningless ritual, while the rich man has a meaningful appeal.

We vacate the judgment of the District Court of Appeal and remand the case to that court for further proceedings not inconsistent with this opinion.

It is so ordered.

[The opinions of CLARK, J., dissenting, and of HARLAN, J., joined by STEWART, J., dissenting, are omitted].

Notes

1.   On the same day that the Court decided *Douglas,* it held, in *Gideon v. Wainwright,* 372 U.S. 335, 83 S.Ct. 792, 9 L.Ed.2d 799 (1963), that the state must provide the assistance of counsel to indigent criminal defendants at any critical stage of the proceedings prior to appeal. However, *Gideon* relied on the Sixth Amendment's right to counsel. In other cases, the Court has used the *Griffin–Douglas* Equal Protection analysis to find rights for indigent defendants not within the Sixth Amendment. For example, the state must waive transcript fees for appeal even if the case does not involve the incarceration of the defendant. *Mayer v. Chicago,* 404 U.S. 189, 92 S.Ct. 410, 30 L.Ed.2d 372 (1971); the state may not require indigents to pay filing fees to have access to appellate courts, *Burns v. Ohio,* 360 U.S. 252, 79 S.Ct. 1164, 3 L.Ed.2d 1209 (1959), or to post-conviction proceedings following appeals, *Smith v. Bennett,* 365 U.S. 708, 81 S.Ct. 895, 6 L.Ed.2d 39 (1961). If an indigent defendant makes a preliminary showing that his sanity at the time of the crime is likely to be a significant factor at trial, due process requires the State to provide a psychiatrist's assistance. *Ake v. Oklahoma,* 470 U.S. 68, 105 S.Ct. 1087, 84 L.Ed.2d 53 (1985). However the state need not provide counsel to indigent defendants in discretionary appeals or collateral attack proceedings after their first appeal as of right. *Ross v. Moffitt,* 417 U.S. 600, 94 S.Ct. 2437, 41 L.Ed.2d 341 (1974).

The state also may not imprison an indigent beyond the maximum term specified by statute because of his or her failure to pay a fine. *Williams v. Illinois,* 399 U.S. 235, 90 S.Ct. 2018, 26 L.Ed.2d 586 (1970)(trial court, pursuant to statute, directed defendant to serve the maximum term of one year and then work off, at the rate of $5 per day, the $500 fine and $5 costs levied against him; held, violation of equal protection). If the state provides only for fines for certain offenses, it cannot imprison indigents who are unable to pay. *Tate v. Short,* 401 U.S. 395, 91 S.Ct. 668, 28 L.Ed.2d 130 (1971)(trial court had ordered, pursuant to statute, defendant with accumulated traffic fines of $425 be imprisoned to work off the fine at a rate of $5 per day; held, violation of equal protection); *Bearden v. Georgia,* 461 U.S. 660, 103 S.Ct. 2064, 76 L.Ed.2d 221 (1983)(under Fourteenth Amendment court may not automatically revoke probation because defendant could not pay his fine, without first determining that defendant had not made sufficient bona fide efforts to pay, or that there did not exist adequate alternative forms of punishment, such as extending the time for making payments, reducing the fine, or directing the performance of some form of labor or public service in lieu of the fine).

2.　*Johnson v. Avery,* 393 U.S. 483, 89 S.Ct. 747, 21 L.Ed.2d 718 (1969) invalidated a regulation prohibiting prisoners from assisting each other in filing habeas corpus applications and other legal actions. See also *Wolff v. McDonnell,* 418 U.S. 539, 94 S.Ct. 2963, 41 L.Ed.2d 935 (1974)(extending *Avery* to civil rights actions).

In *Bounds v. Smith,* 430 U.S. 817, 97 S.Ct. 1491, 52 L.Ed.2d 72 (1977) the Court, relying on these cases and the *Griffin–Douglas* reasoning, held that states "must protect the rights of prisoners to access to the courts by providing them with law libraries or alternative sources of legal knowledge." Dissenting in *Bounds,* Burger, C.J., argued that the Court "leaves us unenlightened as to the source of the 'right of access to the courts' which it perceives or of the requirement that States 'foot the bill' for assuring such access for prisoners who want to act as legal researchers and brief writers."

3.　CIVIL ACTIONS. Welfare recipients challenged, as applied to them, state requirements for payment of court fees and costs for service of process that restricted their access to the courts in actions for divorce. The Court, per Harlan, J., invalidated the requirements. "Our conclusion is that, given the basic position of the marriage relationship in this society's hierarchy of values and the concomitant state monopolization of the means for legally dissolving this relationship, due process does prohibit a State from denying, solely because of inability to pay, access to its courts to individuals who seek judicial dissolution of their marriages." *Boddie v. Connecticut,* 401 U.S. 371, 91 S.Ct. 780, 28 L.Ed.2d 113 (1971). Justice Douglas, concurring in the result, argued that the case should be decided upon the principles developed in the line of cases marked by *Griffin v. Illinois,* rather than the Court's due process rationale.

In *United States v. Kras,* 409 U.S. 434, 93 S.Ct. 631, 34 L.Ed.2d 626 (1973) the Court (5 to 4) upheld provisions in the Bankruptcy Act imposing fees as a condition to a discharge in voluntary bankruptcy. Blackmun, J., for the Court distinguished *Boddie.* First, that case involved marriage, an interest of basic importance to our society; second, the state monopolized the means of legally dissolving it. Bankruptcy, in contrast, "is not the only method available to a debtor for the adjustment of his legal relationship with his creditors." He might be able to adjust his debts by negotiated agreement with his creditors. Bankruptcy itself involved no fundamental right or suspect class, and the fee requirement is a rational means of making the bankruptcy system self-sustaining.

In *Ortwein v. Schwab,* 410 U.S. 656, 93 S.Ct. 1172, 35 L.Ed.2d 572 (1973)(per curiam), the Court (5 to 4) upheld an Oregon appellate filing fee of $25 as applied to indigents seeking to appeal an adverse welfare decision reducing their benefits. The Court said that the sought-after increase in welfare benefits is not a fundamental right; each of the appellants had received an agency hearing; and the payment of welfare to the poor is in the area of economics and social welfare where the Equal Protection Clause is satisfied by a showing of rationality.

Little v. Streater, 452 U.S. 1, 101 S.Ct. 2202, 68 L.Ed.2d 627 (1981). A Connecticut statute provided that, in paternity actions, the cost of blood grouping tests is to be borne by the party requesting them. Under the circumstances of this case, Burger, C.J., for a unanimous Court, held that the statute violated Due Process. Because the mother's child received public assistance, state law compelled the mother to disclose the father and institute a paternity action. The state was a party to this action and would be the recipient of the court ordered support payments. Under the state law—

> the defendant in a paternity suit is placed at a distinct disadvantage in that his testimony alone is insufficient to overcome the plaintiff's prima facie case. Among the most probative additional evidence the defendant might offer are the results of blood grouping tests [because of their recognized capacity to exclude a high percentage of falsely accused putative fathers], but if he is indigent, the State essentially denies him that reliable scientific proof by requiring that he bear its cost.

Thus, the state's monetary interest was not sufficient to overcome the important private interests. "Without aid in obtaining blood test evidence in a paternity case, an indigent defendant, who faces the state as an adversary and who must overcome the evidentiary burden Connecticut imposes, lacks 'a meaningful opportunity to be heard.' *Boddie v. Connecticut.*"

M.L.B. v. S.L.J., 519 U.S. 102, 117 S.Ct. 555, 136 L.Ed.2d 473 (1996). The father of two minor children sued to terminate his divorced wife's parental rights to their biological children. The Mississippi trial court granted this termination decree, and the biological mother sought to appeal. That appeal was conditioned on her prepayment of record preparation fees estimated at $2,353.36. She could not afford these fees, so she sought leave to appeal *in forma pauperis,* a motion that the state court denied. Ginsburg, J., for the Court acknowledged that the Constitution grants no right to appellate review, but once a state grants a right, it may not "bolt the door to equal justice" (quoting Frankfurter, J., concurring in *Griffin*). The Court reviewed earlier cases and concluded that most decisions rested on an equal protection rationale because "due process does not independently require that the State provide a right to appeal." Decrees terminating forever parental rights are a "unique kind of deprivation" and are different from most other civil actions. M.L.B. is defending against the state's destruction of her family bonds. Consequently, her case is not like *Ortwein* or *Kras* and is more like *Boddie*: given the fundamental interest at stake, Mississippi may not refuse to pay for M.L.B.'s transcript on appeal. Kennedy, J., concurring in the judgment, would have decided the case exclusively on due process grounds. Thomas, J., dissented, joined by Scalia, J., and, in part, by Rehnquist, C.J.

8–3.2 Voting

8–3.21 Apportionment

REYNOLDS v. SIMS
377 U.S. 533, 84 S.Ct. 1362, 12 L.Ed.2d 506 (1964).

[Alabama plaintiffs, suing various state and political party officials charged with duties in connection with state elections, claimed that the malapportioned state legislature violated the Equal Protection Clause. Because the last reapportionment of the state legislature was based on the 1900 census, and the population growth had been uneven, plaintiffs claimed serious discrimination in the allocation of legislative representation. After the Supreme Court found such a claim justiciable, *Baker v. Carr,* § 1–2.4, supra, the district court held that the inequality of existing representation violated Equal Protection and that the proposed state legislative reapportionment was inadequate. It ordered a temporary reapportionment plan for the 1962 election, and retained jurisdiction.]

MR. CHIEF JUSTICE WARREN delivered the opinion of the Court....

In *Gray v. Sanders,* 372 U.S. 368, 83 S.Ct. 801, 9 L.Ed.2d 821, we held that the Georgia county unit system, applicable in statewide primary elections, was unconstitutional since it resulted in a dilution of the weight of the votes of certain Georgia voters merely because of where they resided. After indicating that the Fifteenth and Nineteenth Amendments prohibit a State from overweighting or diluting votes on the basis of race or sex, we stated:

> How then can one person be given twice or ten times the voting power of another person in a statewide election merely because he lives in a rural area or because he lives in the smallest rural county? Once the geographical unit for which a representative is to be chosen is designated, all who participate in the election are to have an equal vote—whatever their race, whatever their sex, whatever their occupation, whatever their income, and wherever their home may be in that geographical unit. This is required by the Equal Protection Clause of the Fourteenth Amendment. The concept of 'we the people' under the Constitution visualizes no preferred class of voters but equality among those who meet the basic qualifications. The idea that every voter is equal to every other voter in his State, when he casts his ballot in favor of one of several competing candidates, underlies many of our decisions.

Continuing, we stated that "there is no indication in the Constitution that homesite or occupation affords a permissible basis for distinguishing between qualified voters within the State." And, finally, we concluded: "The conception of political equality from the Declaration of Independence, to Lincoln's Gettysburg Address, to the Fifteenth, Seventeenth, and Nineteenth Amendments can mean only one thing—one person, one vote." . . .

In *Wesberry v. Sanders,* 376 U.S. 1, 84 S.Ct. 526, 11 L.Ed.2d 481, decided earlier this Term, we held that attacks on the constitutionality of congressional districting plans enacted by state legislatures do not present nonjusticiable questions and should not be dismissed generally for "want of equity." We determined that the constitutional test for the validity of congressional districting schemes was one of substantial equality of population among the various districts established by a state legislature for the election of members of the Federal House of Representatives.

In that case we decided that an apportionment of congressional seats which "contracts the value of some votes and expands that of others" is unconstitutional, since "the Federal Constitution intends that when qualified voters elect members of Congress each vote be given as much weight as any other vote. . . . " We concluded that the constitutional prescription for election of members of the House of Representatives "by the People," construed in its historical context, "means that as nearly as is practicable one man's vote in a congressional election is to be worth as much as another's." . . . [U.S. Const., Art. I, § 2, cl. 1].

Gray and *Wesberry* are of course not dispositive of or directly controlling on our decision in these cases involving state legislative apportionment controversies. Admittedly, those decisions, in which we held that, in statewide and in congressional elections, one person's vote must be counted equally with those of all other voters in a State, were based on different constitutional considerations and were addressed to rather distinct problems. But neither are they wholly inapposite. *Gray,* though not determinative here since involving the weighting of votes in statewide elections, established the basic principle of equality among voters within a State, and held that voters cannot be classified, constitutionally, on the basis of where they live, at least with respect to voting in statewide elections. And our decision in *Wesberry* was of course grounded on that language of the Constitution which prescribes that members of the Federal House of Representatives are to be chosen "by the People," while attacks on state legislative apportionment schemes, such as that involved in the instant cases, are principally based on the Equal Protection Clause of the Fourteenth Amendment. . . .

A predominant consideration in determining whether a State's legislative apportionment scheme constitutes an invidious discrimination violative of rights asserted under the Equal Protection Clause is that the rights allegedly impaired are individual and personal in nature. . . . Undoubtedly, the right of suffrage is a fundamental matter in a free and democratic society. Especially since the right to exercise the franchise in a free and unimpaired manner is preservative of other basic civil and political rights, any alleged infringement of the right of citizens to vote must be carefully and meticulously scrutinized. Almost a century ago, in *Yick Wo v. Hopkins,* [§ 8–2.11, supra], the Court referred to "the political franchise of voting'' as ''a fundamental political right, because preservative of all rights.''

Legislators represent people, not trees or acres. Legislators are elected by voters, not farms or cities or economic interests. As long as ours is a representative form of government, and our legislatures are those instruments of government elected directly by and directly representative of the people, the right to elect legislators in a free and unimpaired fashion is a bedrock of our political system. It could hardly be gainsaid that a constitutional claim had been asserted by an allegation that certain otherwise qualified voters had been entirely prohibited from voting for members of their state legislature. And, if a State should provide that the votes of citizens in one part of the State should be given two times, or five times, or 10 times the weight of votes of citizens in another part of the State, it could hardly be contended that the right to vote of those residing in the disfavored areas had not been effectively diluted.... Of course, the effect of state legislative districting schemes which give the same number of representatives to unequal numbers of constituents is identical. Overweighting and overvaluation of the votes of those living here has the certain effect of dilution and undervaluation of the votes of those living there....

Logically, in a society ostensibly grounded on representative government, it would seem reasonable that a majority of the people of a State could elect a majority of that State's legislators. [T]he concept of equal protection has been traditionally viewed as requiring the uniform treatment of persons standing in the same relation to the governmental action questioned or challenged. With respect to the allocation of legislative representation, all voters, as citizens of a State, stand in the same relation regardless of where they live. Any suggested criteria for the differentiation of citizens are insufficient to justify any discrimination, as to the weight of their votes, unless relevant to the permissible purposes of legislative apportionment. Since the achieving of fair and effective representation for all citizens is concededly the basic aim of legislative apportionment, we conclude that the Equal Protection Clause guarantees the opportunity for equal participation by all voters in the election of state legislators. Diluting the weight of votes because of place of residence impairs basic constitutional rights under the Fourteenth Amendment just as much as invidious discriminations based upon factors such as race.... Our constitutional system amply provides for the protection of minorities by means other than giving them majority control of state legislatures. And the democratic ideals of equality and majority rule, which have served this Nation so well in the past, are hardly of any less significance for the present and the future.

We are told that the matter of apportioning representation in a state legislature is a complex and many-faceted one. We are advised that States can rationally consider factors other than population in apportioning legislative representation. We are admonished not to restrict the power of the States to impose differing views as to political philosophy on their citizens. We are cautioned about the dangers of entering into political thickets and mathematical quagmires. Our answer is this: a denial of constitutionally protected rights demands judicial protection; our oath and our office require no less of us.... Population is, of necessity, the starting point for consideration and the controlling criterion for judgment in legislative apportionment controversies....

We hold that, as a basic constitutional standard, the Equal Protection Clause requires that the seats in both houses of a bicameral state legislature must be apportioned on a population basis. Simply stated, an individual's right to vote for state legislators is unconstitutionally impaired when its weight is in a substantial fashion diluted when compared with votes of citizens living in other parts of the State.... Much has been written since our decision in *Baker v. Carr* about the applicability of the so-called federal analogy to state legislative apportionment arrangements. [T]he federal analogy [is] inapposite and irrelevant to state legislative districting schemes. Attempted reliance on the federal analogy appears often to be little more than an after-the-fact rationalization offered in defense of maladjusted state apportionment arrangements. The original constitutions of 36 of our States provided that representation in both houses of the state legislatures would be based completely, or predominantly, on population. And the Founding Fathers clearly had no intention of establishing a pattern or model for the apportionment of seats in state legislatures when the system of representation in the Federal Congress was adopted. Demonstrative of this is the fact that the Northwest Ordinance, adopted in the same year, 1787, as the Federal Constitution, provided for the apportionment of seats in territorial legislatures solely on the basis of population.

The system of representation in the two Houses of the Federal Congress is one ingrained in our Constitution, as part of the law of the land. It is one conceived out of compromise and [arises] from unique historical circumstances. [T]he Equal Protection Clause requires both houses of a state legislature to be apportioned on a population basis. The right of a citizen to equal representation and to have his vote weighted equally with those of all other citizens in the election of members of one house of a bicameral state legislature would amount to little if States could effectively submerge the equal-population principle in the apportionment of seats in the other house....

We do not believe that the concept of bicameralism is rendered anachronistic and meaningless when the predominant basis of representation in the two state legislative bodies is required to be the same—population.... One body could be composed of single-member districts while the other could have at least some multimember districts. The length of terms of the legislators in the separate bodies could differ. The numerical size of the two bodies could be made to differ, even significantly, and the geographical size of districts ... could also be made to differ. [A]pportionment in one house could be arranged so as to balance off minor inequities in the representation of certain areas in the other house....

By holding that as a federal constitutional requisite both houses of a state legislature must be apportioned on a population basis, we mean that the Equal Protection Clause requires that a State make an honest and good faith effort to construct districts, in both houses of its legislature, as nearly of equal population as is practicable. We realize that it is a practical impossibility to arrange legislative districts so that each one has an identical number of residents, or citizens, or voters. Mathematical exactness or precision is hardly a workable constitutional requirement. . . . Since, almost invariably, there is a significantly larger number of seats in state legislative bodies to be distributed within a State than congressional seats, it may be feasible to use political subdivision lines to a greater extent in establishing state legislative districts than in congressional districting while still affording adequate representation to all parts of the State. To do so would be constitutionally valid, so long as the resulting apportionment was one based substantially on population and the equal-population principle was not diluted in any significant way. Somewhat more flexibility may therefore be constitutionally permissible with respect to state legislative apportionment than in congressional districting. . . . A State may legitimately desire to maintain the integrity of various political subdivisions, insofar as possible, and provide for compact districts of contiguous territory in designing a legislative apportionment scheme. . . .

History indicates, however, that many States have deviated, to a greater or lesser degree, from the equal-population principle in the apportionment of seats in at least one house of their legislatures. So long as the divergences from a strict population standard are based on legitimate considerations incident to the effectuation of a rational state policy, some deviations from the equal-population principle are constitutionally permissible with respect to the apportionment of seats in either or both of the two houses of a bicameral state legislature. But neither history alone, nor economic or other sorts of group interests, are permissible factors in attempting to justify disparities from population-based representation. Citizens, not history or economic interests, cast votes. Considerations of area alone provide an insufficient justification for deviations from the equal-population principle. Again, people, not land or trees or pastures, vote. Modern developments and improvements in transportation and communications make rather hollow, in the mid–1960's, most claims that deviations from population-based representation can validly be based solely on geographical considerations. Arguments for allowing such deviations in order to insure effective representation for sparsely settled areas and to prevent legislative districts from becoming so large that the availability of access of citizens to their representatives is impaired are today, for the most part, unconvincing.

A consideration that appears to be of more substance in justifying some deviations from population-based representation in state legislatures is that of insuring some voice to political subdivisions, as political subdivisions. . . . But if, even as a result of a clearly rational state policy of according some legislative representation to political subdivisions, population is submerged as the controlling consideration in the apportionment of seats in the particular legislative body, then the right of all of the State's citizens to cast an effective and adequately weighted vote would be unconstitutionally impaired. . . .

That the Equal Protection Clause requires that both houses of a state legislature be apportioned on a population basis does not mean that States cannot adopt some reasonable plan for periodic revision of their apportionment schemes. Decennial reapportionment appears to be a rational approach to readjustment of legislative representation in order to take into account population shifts and growth. [W]e do not mean to intimate that more frequent reapportionment would not be constitutionally permissible or practically desirable. But if reapportionment were accomplished with less frequency, it would assuredly be constitutionally suspect. . . .

We do not consider here the difficult question of the proper remedial devices which federal courts should utilize in state legislative apportionment cases. Remedial techniques in this new and developing area of the law will probably often differ with the circumstances of the challenged apportionment and a variety of local conditions. It is enough to say now that, once a State's legislative apportionment scheme has been found to be unconstitutional, it would be the unusual case in which a court would be justified in not taking appropriate action to insure that no further elections are conducted under the invalid plan. However, under certain circumstances, such as where an impending election is imminent and a State's election machinery is already in progress, equitable considerations might justify a court in withholding the granting of immediately effective relief in a legislative apportionment case, even though the existing apportionment scheme was found invalid. In awarding or withholding immediate relief, a court is entitled to and should consider the proximity of a forthcoming election and the mechanics and complexities of state election laws, and should act and rely upon general equitable principles. With respect to the timing of relief, a court can reasonably endeavor to avoid a disruption of the election process which might result from requiring precipitate changes that could make unreasonable or embarrassing demands on a State in adjusting to the requirements of the court's decree. . . .

. . . Since the District Court evinced its realization that its ordered reapportionment could not be sustained as the basis for conducting the 1966 election of Alabama legislators, and avowedly intends to take some further action should the reapportioned Alabama Legislature fail to enact a constitutionally valid, permanent apportionment scheme in the interim, we affirm the judgment below and remand the cases for further proceedings consistent with the views stated in this opinion.

It is so ordered.

MR. JUSTICE HARLAN, dissenting.

. . . Stripped of aphorisms, the Court's argument boils down to the assertion that appellees' right to vote has been invidiously "debased" or "diluted" by systems of apportionment which entitle them to vote for fewer legislators than other voters, an assertion which is tied to the Equal Protection Clause only by the constitutionally frail tautology that "equal" means "equal."

. . . Whatever one might take to be the application to these cases of the Equal Protection Clause if it stood alone, I am unable to understand the Court's utter disregard of the second section [of the Fourteenth Amendment] which expressly recognizes the States' power to deny "or in any way" abridge the right of their inhabitants to vote for "the members of the [State] Legislature," and its express provision of a remedy for such denial or abridgment. The comprehensive scope of the second section and its particular reference to the state legislatures preclude the suggestion that the first section was intended to have the result reached by the Court today. If indeed the words of the Fourteenth Amendment speak for themselves, as the majority's disregard of history seems to imply, they speak as clearly as may be against the construction which the majority puts on them. [U]nless one takes the highly implausible view that the Fourteenth Amendment controls methods of apportionment but leaves the right to vote itself unprotected, the conclusion is inescapable that the Court has, for purposes of these cases, relegated the Fifteenth and Nineteenth Amendments to the same limbo of constitutional anachronisms to which the second section of the Fourteenth Amendment has been assigned. . . .

Although the Court—necessarily, as I believe—provides only generalities in elaboration of its main thesis, its opinion nevertheless fully demonstrates how far removed these problems are from fields of judicial competence. Recognizing that "indiscriminate districting" is an invitation to "partisan gerrymandering," the Court nevertheless excludes virtually every basis for the formation of electoral districts other than "indiscriminate districting." In one or another of today's opinions, the Court declares it unconstitutional for a State to give effective consideration to any of the following in establishing legislative districts:

(1) history;

(2) "economic or other sorts of group interests";

(3) area;

(4) geographical considerations;

(5) a desire "to insure effective representation for sparsely settled areas";

(6) "availability of access of citizens to their representatives";

(7) theories of bicameralism (except those approved by the Court);

(8) occupation;

(9) "an attempt to balance urban and rural power."

(10) the preference of a majority of voters in the State.

So far as presently appears, the *only* factor which a State may consider, apart from numbers, is political subdivisions. But even "a clearly rational state policy" recognizing this factor is unconstitutional if "population is submerged as the controlling consideration.... " ...

These decisions also cut deeply into the fabric of our federalism. [N]o thinking person can fail to recognize that the aftermath of these cases, however desirable it may be thought in itself, will have been achieved at the cost of a radical alteration in the relationship between the States and the Federal Government, more particularly the Federal Judiciary. Only one who has an overbearing impatience with the federal system and its political processes will believe that that cost was not too high or was inevitable.

Finally, these decisions give support to a current mistaken view of the Constitution and the constitutional function of this Court. This view, in a nutshell, is that every major social ill in this country can find its cure in some constitutional "principle," and that this Court should "take the lead" in promoting reform when other branches of government fail to act. The Constitution is not a panacea for every blot upon the public welfare, nor should this Court, ordained as a judicial body, be thought of as a general haven for reform movements. [W]hen, in the name of constitutional interpretation, the Court *adds* something to the Constitution that was deliberately excluded from it, the Court in reality substitutes its view of what should be so for the amending process....

[The opinion of CLARK, J., concurring in the affirmance, and the separate opinion of STEWART, J., are omitted].

Notes

1. WHEN MALAPPORTIONMENT IS DESIRED BY A MAJORITY OF THE VOTERS. On the same day that it decided *Reynolds*, the Court decided five other cases, from Colorado, Delaware, Maryland, New York, and Virginia. Of particular interest is *Lucas v. Forty–Fourth General Assembly of Colorado,* 377 U.S. 713, 84 S.Ct. 1459, 12 L.Ed.2d 632 (1964). During the lower court litigation Colorado voters adopted, by a wide margin, a state constitutional amendment (No. 7) providing for the apportionment of the state house of representatives on the basis of population and the state senate on the basis of population *and* a variety of other factors. The voters also rejected, likewise by a wide margin, an amendment (No. 8) apportioning both houses on a population basis. A majority of the voters in every county of the State voted in favor of No. 7 and against No. 8. However, "[a]n individual's constitutionally protected right to cast an equally weighted vote cannot be denied even by a vote of a majority of a State's electorate, if the apportionment scheme adopted by the voters fails to measure up to the requirements of the Equal Protection Clause. [T]hat an apportionment plan is adopted in a popular referendum is insufficient to sustain its constitutionality or to induce a court of equity to refuse to act.... A citizen's constitutional rights can hardly be infringed because a majority of the people choose that it be. [T]hat a challenged legislative apportionment plan was approved by the electorate is without federal constitutional significance, if the scheme adopted fails to satisfy the

basic requirements of the Equal Protection Clause, as delineated in our opinion in *Reynolds v. Sims*."

2. APPLICABILITY OF REYNOLDS TO OTHER GOVERNMENTAL UNITS. After several false starts the Court finally settled on a test to determine when *Reynolds* applies to local governmental units. *Reynolds* applies if the officials are selected by popular vote: "[A]s a general rule, whenever a state or local government decides to select persons by popular election to perform governmental functions, the Equal Protection Clause of the Fourteenth Amendment requires that each qualified voter must be given an equal opportunity to participate in that election, and when members of an elected body are chosen from separate districts, each district must be established on a basis that will insure, so far as is practicable, that equal numbers of voters can vote for proportionally equal numbers of officials. It is of course possible that there might be some case in which a State elects certain functionaries whose duties are so far removed from normal governmental activities and so disproportionately affect different groups that a popular election in compliance with *Reynolds* might not be required.... " *Hadley v. Junior College District,* 397 U.S. 50, 90 S.Ct. 791, 25 L.Ed.2d 45 (1970)(*Reynolds* applicable to trustees of junior college district selected by popular vote).

Fortson v. Morris, 385 U.S. 231, 87 S.Ct. 446, 17 L.Ed.2d 330 (1966) held that *Reynolds* was not applicable when the state constitution requires the General Assembly to select the Governor in a situation where, after two primaries and one general election, no candidate had received a majority of the popular votes cast. Because the popular election had failed to produce a majority candidate, the state may provide for a new election where the state legislators are the voters.

Reynolds does not prohibit the state from setting up residential districts (of unequal population) within a county and requiring that each official elected by the entire county reside in a different district. The districts are merely the basis for residence of the candidates, not for voting or representation. Although the candidate must reside in a certain portion of the county, he or she is elected by and represents the entire county. *Dallas County v. Reese,* 421 U.S. 477, 95 S.Ct. 1706, 44 L.Ed.2d 312 (1975)(per curiam).

3. MATHEMATICAL PRECISION. Recall that *Reynolds* said that "[s]omewhat more flexibility" may be permissible with respect to state legislative apportionment than in congressional districting. Also, the Court based *Reynolds* on the Equal Protection guarantee while it based *Wesberry* on Article 1, § 2, cl. 1, providing that U.S. Representatives shall be chosen "by the People." The Court, in subsequent cases, has been more tolerant of slight malapportionment in elections for state office than it has been for elections to Congress.

Karcher v. Daggett, 462 U.S. 725, 103 S.Ct. 2653, 77 L.Ed.2d 133 (1983) held (5 to 4) that Art. I, § 2, permits only those limited population variances that are unavoidable despite a good faith effort to achieve absolute equality, or for which special justification is shown. The maximum population difference between the smallest and the largest district in New Jersey was 3,674 people or only .6984% of the average district. However, the New Jersey legislature had rejected another plan with a maximum population difference of 2,375 or .4514%. Even though the maximum deviation in New Jersey was less than the predictable undercount in available census data, the legislature should use the best actual census data available. There is no *de minimis* level that does not need special justification. "[A]bsolute population equality" is the "paramount objective of apportionment" in the case of congressional districts. Because New Jersey did not prove that the minor (but real) statistical disparity was unavoidable and did not prove that the deviations were necessary to achieve a legitimate state objective (e.g., "making districts compact, respecting municipal boundaries, preserving the cores of prior districts, and avoiding contests between incumbent Representatives"), then the plan failed.

Contrast *Mahan v. Howell,* 410 U.S. 315, 93 S.Ct. 979, 35 L.Ed.2d 320 (1973), modified 411 U.S. 922, 93 S.Ct. 1475, 36 L.Ed.2d 316 (1973), which involved apportionment of the Virginia Senate and House of Delegates. The ideal district in Virginia would have 46,485 persons per delegate. The districts varied from an overrepresentation of 6.8% to an underrepresentation of 9.6%, for a "total percentage derivation" of 16.4%. The Court found that the desire of the General Assembly to maintain the integrity of traditional county and city boundaries justified this total percentage deviation of 16.4%. In *Connor v. Finch,* 431 U.S. 407, 97 S.Ct. 1828, 52 L.Ed.2d 465 (1977) the Court did not accept a reapportionment plan of 16.5% in the Mississippi Senate and 19.3% in the House. Unlike *Mahan,* where the legislature's plan produced the minimum deviations while keeping intact political boundaries, another plan would have cut across fewer county boundaries and have a smaller percentage deviation.

Smaller deviations do not even require special justification. *White v. Regester,* 412 U.S. 755, 93 S.Ct. 2332, 37 L.Ed.2d 314 (1973)(9.9% deviation allowed in election for Texas House of Representatives).

4. EXTRAORDINARY AND CONCURRENT MAJORITIES. *Gordon v. Lance,* 403 U.S. 1, 91 S.Ct. 1889, 29 L.Ed.2d 273 (1971) upheld a state law requiring a 60% voter approval before a political subdivision could incur bonded indebtedness. In dictum, it upheld supermajorities for votes within the legislature and also state requirements that a given issue be approved by a majority of all registered voters. However it intimated "no view" on the constitutionality of requiring unanimity, or giving a veto power to a small group, or requiring extraordinary majorities in an election for public office.

Town of Lockport v. Citizens for Community Action at the Local Level, Inc., 430 U.S. 259, 97 S.Ct. 1047, 51 L.Ed.2d 313 (1977) upheld a state law providing that a new county charter could go into effect only if it was approved by a referendum election by separate majorities of those who lived in the cities and in the counties outside of the cities. In some counties the city voters outnumbered the voters outside of the city, and in other counties the city voters were in the minority. New county charters often affect both city and county operations because they transfer functions between the city and county. Given the different interests of the two groups and the lack of invidiousness, the Court upheld the concurrent majority requirement.[1]

---

1. For a more complete discussion of the ramifications of *Reynolds,* see 3 R. Rotunda & J. Nowak, Treatise on Constitutional Law: Substance and Procedure § 18.36 (2d ed. 1992); J. Nowak & R. Rotunda, Constitutional Law § 14.36 (5th ed. 1995). On Political Gerrymandering, see *Davis v. Ban-*

5. THE CENSUS. *United States Department of Commerce v. Montana,* 503 U.S. 442, 112 S.Ct. 1415, 118 L.Ed.2d 87 (1992). Montana challenged a federal statute (enacted in 1941) that determined the number of representatives to which each state is entitled after each decennial census. Article I, § 2, cl. 3 provides that each state shall have at least one representative and that the number of representatives must not exceed one for every 30,000 persons. In addition, implicit in the text of the Constitution and supported by continuous historical practice is the requirement that congressional districts not cross state lines.

From the very beginning of our history, the application of Article I, § 2, cl. 3 has resulted in fractional remainders: the fractional portion of the number that results when the state's total population is divided by the population of the ideal district must either be ignored, or rounded to one whole Representative, because states can only be represented by a whole number of legislators. Over the years, Congress has tried various plans to deal with this problem. In 1941 Congress enacted a statute that uses a method called the "equal portions" method. Montana objected because its use after the 1990 census resulted in reducing its House delegation from two representatives to one. Justice Stevens, speaking for a unanimous Court, rejected Montana's claims. "The constitutional framework that generated the need for compromise in the apportionment process must also delegate to Congress a measure of discretion that is broader than that accorded to the States in the much easier task of determining district sizes within State borders." Congress' "apparently good-faith choice of a method of apportionment of Representatives among the several States 'according to their numbers' commands far more deference than a state districting decision that is capable of being reviewed under a relatively rigid mathematical standard."

Later that term, *Franklin v. Massachusetts,* 505 U.S. 788, 112 S.Ct. 2767, 120 L.Ed.2d 636 (1992) rejected Massachusetts' challenge to the method used for counting federal employees serving overseas. The allocation of approximately one million overseas military personnel to the state designated in their personnel files as their "home of record" resulted in the shift of a representative from Massachusetts to Washington. A three-judge federal court in Massachusetts held that the decision to allocate military personnel serving overseas to their "home of record" was unconstitutional. A portion of Justice O'Connor's opinion, which was an opinion for the Court, concluded that the Secretary's allocation of overseas federal employees to their home states is consistent with the constitutional language.[2]

---

demer, 478 U.S. 109, 106 S.Ct. 2797, 92 L.Ed.2d 85 (1986), § 1–2.4, supra.

2. Part III of O'Connor's opinion, joined by Rehnquist, C.J. & White & Thomas, JJ., concluded that Massachusetts had standing to object to the decision to include overseas federal employees. She did not decide whether the court could order injunctive relief against the President because she determined that declaratory relief against the Secretary of Commerce would supply adequate relief. Scalia, J., in his separate opinion, concurring in part and in the judgment,

was the only justice specifically objecting to standing: "Unless the other branches are to be entirely subordinated to the Judiciary, we cannot direct the President to take a specified executive act or the Congress to perform particular legislative duties. [W]e cannot remedy appellees' asserted injury without ordering declaratory or injunctive relief against appellant President Bush, and since we have no power to do that, I believe appellees' constitutional claims should be dismissed."

Wisconsin v. City of New York, 517 U.S. 1, 116 S.Ct. 1091, 134 L.Ed.2d 167 (1996). For the 1990 Census, the Secretary of Commerce decided that an "actual enumeration" would best be achieved by not using any statistical adjustment, including one that had been designed to correct an undercount in the initial enumeration. Rehnquist, C.J., for the unanimous Court, held that the Secretary's decision was not subject to heightened scrutiny under *Wesberry v. Sanders* and conformed to constitutional and statutory safeguards. Art. I, § 2, cl. 3, vests Congress with "virtually unlimited discretion" in conducting the census, and the Secretary acted rationally under the law. With respect to the argument that the census undercounted some people, the Court asked, in a footnote: "One might wonder how the Census Bureau is able to determine whether there is an undercount and its size?·After all, if the *actual* population of the United States is known, then the conduct of the census would seem wholly redundant."

8–3.22 Poll Taxes

HARPER v. VIRGINIA STATE BOARD OF ELECTIONS
383 U.S. 663, 86 S.Ct. 1079, 16 L.Ed.2d 169 (1966).

MR. JUSTICE DOUGLAS delivered the opinion of the Court.

These are suits by Virginia residents to have declared unconstitutional Virginia's poll tax.[1]

While the right to vote in federal elections is conferred by Art. I, § 2, of the Constitution, the right to vote in state elections is nowhere expressly mentioned. It is argued that the right to vote in state elections is implicit, particularly by reason of the First Amendment and that it may not constitutionally be conditioned upon the payment of a tax or fee. We do not stop to canvass the relation between voting and political expression. For it is enough to say that once the franchise is granted to the electorate, lines may not be drawn which are inconsistent with the Equal Protection Clause of the Fourteenth Amendment. That is to say, the right of suffrage "is subject to the imposition of state standards which are not discriminatory and which do not contravene any restriction that Congress, acting pursuant to its constitutional powers, has imposed." *Lassiter v. Northampton County Board of Elections,* 360 U.S. 45, 51, 79 S.Ct. 985, 3 L.Ed.2d 1072. We were speaking there of a state literacy test which we sustained, warning that the result would be different if a literacy test, fair on its face, were used to discriminate against a class. But the *Lassiter* case does not govern the result here, because, unlike a poll tax, the "ability to read and write ... has some relation to standards designed to promote intelligent use of the ballot."

We conclude that a State violates the Equal Protection Clause of the Fourteenth Amendment whenever it makes the affluence of the voter or

---

1. Section 173 of Virginia's Constitution directs the General Assembly to levy an annual poll tax not exceeding $1.50 on every resident of the State 21 years of age and over (with exceptions not relevant here).... Section 18 of the Constitution includes payment of poll taxes as a precondition for voting....

payment of any fee an electoral standard. Voter qualifications have no relation to wealth nor to paying or not paying this or any other tax.... Long ago in *Yick Wo v. Hopkins,* [§ 8–2.11, supra], the Court referred to "the political franchise of voting" as a "fundamental political right, because preservative of all rights." Recently in *Reynolds v. Sims,* we said, "Undoubtedly, the right of suffrage is a fundamental matter in a free and democratic society." ...

We say the same whether the citizen, otherwise qualified to vote, has $1.50 in his pocket or nothing at all, pays the fee or fails to pay it. The principle that denies the State the right to dilute a citizen's vote on account of his economic status or other such factors by analogy bars a system which excludes those unable to pay a fee to vote or who fail to pay.

It is argued that a State may exact fees from citizens for many different kinds of licenses; that if it can demand from all an equal fee for a driver's license, it can demand from all an equal poll tax for voting. But we must remember that the interest of the State, when it comes to voting, is limited to the power to fix qualifications. Wealth, like race, creed, or color, is not germane to one's ability to participate intelligently in the electoral process. Lines drawn on the basis of wealth or property, like those of race are traditionally disfavored. *Griffin v. Illinois,* [§ 8–3.1, supra]; *Douglas v. California,* [§ 8–3.1, supra]. To introduce wealth or payment of a fee as a measure of a voter's qualifications is to introduce a capricious or irrelevant factor. The degree of the discrimination is irrelevant. In this context—that is, as a condition of obtaining a ballot— the requirement of fee paying causes an "invidious" discrimination that runs afoul of the Equal Protection Clause. Levy "by the poll," as stated in *Breedlove v. Suttles,* [302 U.S. 277, 58 S.Ct. 205, 82 L.Ed. 252 (1937)] is an old familiar form of taxation; and we say nothing to impair its validity so long as it is not made a condition to the exercise of the franchise. *Breedlove v. Suttles* sanctioned its use as "a prerequisite of voting." To that extent the *Breedlove* case is overruled.

We agree, of course, with MR. JUSTICE HOLMES that the Due Process Clause of the Fourteenth Amendment "does not enact Mr. Herbert Spencer's Social Statics" (*Lochner v. New York,* [§ 6–1, supra]). Likewise, the Equal Protection Clause is not shackled to the political theory of a particular era. In determining what lines are unconstitutionally discriminatory, we have never been confined to historic notions of equality, any more than we have restricted due process to a fixed catalogue of what was at a given time deemed to be the limits of fundamental rights. Notions of what constitutes equal treatment for purposes of the Equal Protection Clause *do* change.... Our conclusion, like that in *Reynolds v. Sims,* is founded not on what we think governmental policy should be, but on what the Equal Protection Clause requires.

We have long been mindful that where fundamental rights and liberties are asserted under the Equal Protection Clause, classifications which might invade or restrain them must be closely scrutinized and carefully confined. Those principles apply here. For to repeat, wealth or fee paying has, in our view, no relation to voting qualifications; the right to vote is too precious, too fundamental to be so burdened or conditioned.

Reversed.

MR. JUSTICE BLACK, dissenting. . . .

It should be pointed out at once that the Court's decision is to no extent based on a finding that the Virginia law as written or as applied is being used as a device or mechanism to deny Negro citizens of Virginia the right to vote on account of their color. . . . All voting laws treat some persons differently from others in some respects. Some bar a person from voting who is under 21 years of age; others bar those under 18. Some bar convicted felons or the insane, and some have attached a freehold or other property qualification for voting. . . . State poll tax legislation can "reasonably," "rationally" and without an "invidious" or evil purpose to injure anyone be found to rest on a number of state policies including (1) the State's desire to collect its revenue, and (2) its belief that voters who pay a poll tax will be interested in furthering the State's welfare when they vote. Certainly it is rational to believe that people may be more likely to pay taxes if payment is a prerequisite to voting. [The Court] seems to be using the old "natural-law-due-process formula" to justify striking down state laws as violations of the Equal Protection Clause. . . .

MR. JUSTICE HARLAN, whom MR. JUSTICE STEWART joins, dissenting.

The final demise of state poll taxes, already totally proscribed by the Twenty–Fourth Amendment with respect to federal elections and abolished by the States themselves in all but four States with respect to state elections, is perhaps in itself not of great moment. But the fact that the *coup de grace* has been administered by this Court instead of being left to the affected States or to the federal political process should be a matter of continuing concern to all interested in maintaining the proper role of this tribunal under our scheme of government. . . .

8–3.23 Property Qualifications

HILL v. STONE

421 U.S. 289, 95 S.Ct. 1637, 44 L.Ed.2d 172 (1975).

MR. JUSTICE MARSHALL delivered the opinion of the Court.

[Texas provides for] a "dual box election procedure" to be used in all the State's local bond elections. Under this procedure, all persons owning taxable property rendered[1] for taxation voted in one box, and all other registered voters cast their ballots in a separate box. The results in

---

1. To "render" property for taxation means to list it with the tax assessor-collec-   tor of the taxing district in question. . . . [Footnote repositioned]

both boxes were tabulated, and the bond issue would be deemed to have passed only if it was approved by a majority vote both in the "renderers' box" and in the aggregate of both boxes. . . .

On April 11, 1972, the city of Fort Worth conducted a tax bond election, using the dual-box system to authorize the sale of bonds to . . . build a city library. Since the state eligibility restrictions had previously been construed to require only that the prospective voter render some property for taxation, even if he did not actually pay any tax on the property, all those who signed an affidavit indicating that they had rendered some property were permitted to vote in the "renders' box." Of the 29,000 voters who participated in the bond election, approximately 24,000 voted as renderers and 5,000 as nonrenderers. . . . Although the library bonds were approved by a majority of all the voters, they were defeated in the renderers' box, and were therefore deemed not to have been authorized. The appellees, three of whom had voted as nonrenderers, then filed this action in the United States District Court for the Northern District of Texas, claiming that the partial disfranchisement of persons not rendering property for taxation denied them equal protection of the laws. . . .

In *Kramer v. Union Free School District No. 15,* 395 U.S. 621, 89 S.Ct. 1886, 23 L.Ed.2d 583 (1969), we held that in an election of general interest, restrictions on the franchise other than residence, age, and citizenship must promote a compelling state interest in order to survive constitutional attack. The appellant in *Kramer* challenged a New York statute that limited eligibility to vote in local school board elections to persons who owned or leased taxable real property in the school district, or who had children enrolled in the public schools. We expressed no opinion in *Kramer* whether a State might in some circumstances limit the franchise to those "primarily interested" in the election,[5] but we held that the New York statute had impermissibly excluded many persons with a distinct and direct interest in the decisions of the school board, while at the same time including others with no substantial interest in school affairs. The fact that the school district was supported by a property tax did not mean that only those subject to direct assessment felt the effects of the tax burden, and the inclusion of parents would not exhaust the class of persons interested in the conduct of local school affairs.

In *Cipriano v. City of Houma,* 395 U.S. 701, 89 S.Ct. 1897, 23 L.Ed.2d 647 (1969), decided the same day, we invalidated a Louisiana statute limiting the franchise in local revenue bond elections to the

---

5. We answered that question in *Salyer Land Co. v. Tulare Lake Basin Water District,* 410 U.S. 719, 93 S.Ct. 1224, 35 L.Ed.2d 659 (1973). In that case, we held that a water district created for the purpose of acquiring, storing, and distributing water for agricultural purposes could constitutionally have a board of directors selected in an election in which votes were allocated according to the assessed value of each voter's land. Because of its "special limited purpose and . . . the disproportionate effect of its activities on landowners as a group," the Court held that the water district election was of sufficient "special interest" to a single group that the franchise could constitutionally be denied to others.

"property taxpayers" of the district. As in *Kramer,* the city had failed to prove that under its classification all those excluded from voting were in fact substantially less interested or affected than those permitted to vote. The bonds in *Cipriano* were intended to finance extension and improvement of the city's utility system. We pointed out that the operation of a utility system affects property owners and nonproperty owners alike, and since those not included among the eligible voters often use the utility services, they might well feel the effect of outstanding revenue bonds through the utility rates they would be required to pay.

The next Term, in *City of Phoenix v. Kolodziejski,* [399 U.S. 204, 90 S.Ct. 1990, 26 L.Ed.2d 523 (1970)] we ruled unconstitutional a similar restriction of the franchise to real property taxpayers in a general obligation bond issue. The interests of property owners and nonproperty owners in a general obligation bond issue, we held, were not sufficiently disparate to justify excluding those owning no real property. The residents of the city, whether property owners or not, had a common interest in the facilities that the bond issue would make available, and they would all be substantially affected by the outcome of the election, both in terms of the benefits provided and the obligations incurred.... :

> Property taxes may be paid initially by property owners, but a significant part of the ultimate burden of each year's tax on rental property will very likely be borne by the tenant rather than the landlord since ... the landlord will treat the property tax as a business expense and normally will be able to pass all or a large part of this cost on to the tenants in the form of higher rent.

In addition, we noted that property taxes on commercial property would normally be treated as a cost of doing business and would "be reflected in the prices of goods and services purchased by nonproperty owners and property owners alike."

The basic principle expressed in these cases is that as long as the election in question is not one of special interest, any classification restricting the franchise on grounds other than residence, age, and citizenship cannot stand unless the district or State can demonstrate that the classification serves a compelling state interest.

The appellant's claim that the Fort Worth election was one of special interest and thus outside the principles of the *Kramer* case runs afoul of our decision in *City of Phoenix v. Kolodziejski,* supra....

In making the alternative contentions that the "rendering requirement" creates no real "classification," or that the classification created should be upheld as being reasonable, the appellant misconceives the rationale of *Kramer* and its successors. Appellant argues that since all property is required to be rendered for taxation, and since anyone can vote in a bond election if he renders any property, no matter how little, the Texas scheme does not discriminate on the basis of wealth or property. Our cases, however, have not held or intimated that only property-based classifications are suspect; in an election of general interest, restrictions on the franchise of any character must meet a stringent test of justification. The Texas scheme creates a classification based on rendering, and it in effect disfranchises those who have not rendered their property for taxation in the year of the bond election. Mere reasonableness will therefore not suffice to sustain the classification created in this case.

... Quite apart from the general interest of the library bond election, the appellant's contention that the rendering requirement imposes no real impediment to participation itself undercuts the claim that it serves the purpose of protecting those who will bear the burden of the debt obligations. If anyone can become eligible to vote by rendering property of even negligible value, the rendering requirement can hardly be said to select voters according to the magnitude of their prospective liability for the city's indebtedness.[8]

The appellee city officials argue that the rendering qualification furthers another state interest: it encourages prospective voters to render their property and thereby helps enforce the State's tax laws. This argument is difficult to credit. The use of the franchise to compel compliance with other, independent state objectives is questionable in any context. It seems particularly dubious here, since under the State's construction of the rendering requirement, an individual will be given the right to vote if he renders any property at all, no matter how trivial. Those rendering solely to earn the right to vote in bond elections may well render property of minimal value, in order to qualify for voting without imposing upon themselves a substantial tax liability. The rendering requirement thus seems unlikely to have any significant impact on the asserted state policy of encouraging each person to render all of his property....

In order to avoid the possibility of upsetting previous bond elections in the State, ... we hold that the District Court's ruling should apply only to those bond authorization elections that were not final on the date of the District Court's judgment. As to other jurisdictions that may have restrictive voting classifications similar to those in Texas, we hold that our decision should not apply where the authorization to issue the securities is legally complete as of the date of this decision.

Affirmed.

MR. JUSTICE DOUGLAS took no part in the consideration or decision of this case.

[The dissenting opinion of REHNQUIST, J., joined by BURGER, C.J., and STEWART, J., is omitted.]

---

8. This argument is similar to the one made by the State of Georgia in defense of its "freeholder" requirement for membership on county boards of education. *Turner v. Fouche*, 396 U.S. 346, 363–364, 90 S.Ct. 532, 542, 24 L.Ed.2d 567 (1970). The State there claimed that the freeholder require- ment imposed no real burden, since a candidate would qualify if he owned even a single square inch of land. We concluded that if that was the case it was difficult to conceive that the requirement served any rational state interest whatsoever.

Notes

Quinn v. Millsap, 491 U.S. 95, 109 S.Ct. 2324, 105 L.Ed.2d 74 (1989) unanimously invalidated, under the Equal Protection Clause, a provision of the Missouri Constitution that required appointment to the "board of freeholders" (a board that drafts a reorganization plan for city and county government to be submitted to the voters for approval) be limited to real property owners. The Court rejected the Missouri Supreme Court's argument that the Equal Protection Clause "has no relevancy" because the board "exercises no general governmental powers." Membership on the board is a form of public service, and the "Equal Protection Clause protects appellants' right to be considered for appointment to the board without the burden of 'invidiously discriminatory disqualifications.' 'Otherwise the Equal Protection Clause would be inapplicable "even to a requirement that all members of the board be white males." ' "

8–3.24 Access to the Ballot

ILLINOIS STATE BOARD OF ELECTIONS
v. SOCIALIST WORKERS PARTY
440 U.S. 173, 99 S.Ct. 983, 59 L.Ed.2d 230 (1979).

MR. JUSTICE MARSHALL delivered the opinion of the Court.

Under the Illinois Election Code, new political parties and independent candidates must obtain the signatures of 25,000 qualified voters in order to appear on the ballot in statewide elections. However, a different standard applies in elections for offices of political subdivisions of the State. The minimum number of signatures required for those elections is 5% of the number of persons who voted at the previous election for offices of the particular subdivision. In the city of Chicago, application of this standard has produced the incongruous result that a new party or an independent candidate needs substantially more signatures to gain access to the ballot than a similarly situated party or candidate for statewide office. The question before us is whether this discrepancy violates the Equal Protection Clause of the Fourteenth Amendment....

In determining whether the Illinois signature requirements for new parties and independent candidates as applied in the city of Chicago violate the Equal Protection Clause, we must examine the character of the classification in question, the importance of the individual interests at stake, and the state interests asserted in support of the classification. *Kramer v. Union School Dist.,* 395 U.S. 621, 626, 89 S.Ct. 1886, 1889, 23 L.Ed.2d 583 (1969); *Williams v. Rhodes,* 393 U.S. 23, 30, 89 S.Ct. 5, 10, 21 L.Ed.2d 24 (1968).

The provisions of the Illinois Election Code at issue incorporate a geographic classification. For purposes of setting the minimum-signature requirements, the Code distinguishes state candidates, political parties, and the voters supporting each, from city candidates, parties, and voters. In 1977, an independent candidate or a new political party in Chicago, a city with approximately 718,937 voters eligible to sign nominating petitions for the mayoral election in 1977, had to secure over 10,000 more signatures on nominating petitions than an independent candidate or new party in state elections, who had a pool of approximately 4.5 million eligible voters from which to obtain signatures. That the distinction between state and city elections undoubtedly is valid for some purposes does not resolve whether it is valid as applied here.

Restrictions on access to the ballot burden two distinct and fundamental rights, "the right of individuals to associate for the advancement of political beliefs, and the right of qualified voters, regardless of their political persuasion, to cast their votes effectively." *Williams v. Rhodes,* supra. The freedom to associate as a political party, a right we have recognized as fundamental, see 393 U.S., at 30–31, has diminished practical value if the party can be kept off the ballot. Access restrictions also implicate the right to vote because absent recourse to referendums, "voters can assert their preferences only through candidates or parties or both." *Lubin v. Panish,* 415 U.S. 709, 716, 94 S.Ct. 1315, 1320, 39 L.Ed.2d 702 (1974). By limiting the choices available to voters, the State impairs the voters' ability to express their political preferences. And for reasons too self-evident to warrant amplification here, we have often reiterated that voting is of the most fundamental significance under our constitutional structure.

When such vital individual rights are at stake, a State must establish that its classification is necessary to serve a compelling interest. To be sure, the Court has previously acknowledged that States have a legitimate interest in regulating the number of candidates on the ballot. In *Lubin v. Panish,* supra, we observed:

> A procedure inviting or permitting every citizen to present himself to the voters on the ballot without some means of measuring the seriousness of the candidate's desire and motivation would make rational voter choices more difficult because of the size of the ballot and hence would tend to impede the electoral process.... The means of testing the seriousness of a given candidacy may be open to debate; the fundamental importance of ballots of reasonable size limited to serious candidates with some prospects of public support is not. Similarly, in *Bullock v. Carter,* 405 U.S. 134, 145, 92 S.Ct. 849, 857, 31 L.Ed.2d 92 (1972)(footnote omitted), the Court expressed concern for the States' need to assure that the winner of an election "is the choice of a majority, or at least a strong plurality, of those voting, without the expense and burden of runoff elections." Consequently, we have upheld properly drawn statutes that require a preliminary showing of a "significant modicum of support" before a candidate or party may appear on the ballot.

However, our previous opinions have also emphasized that "even when pursuing a legitimate interest, a State may not choose means that unnecessarily restrict constitutionally protected liberty," and we have required that States adopt the least drastic means to achieve their ends. This requirement is particularly important where restrictions on access to the ballot are involved. The States' interest in screening out frivolous candidates must be considered in light of the significant role that third parties have played in the political development of the Nation. Abolitionists, Progressives, and Populists have undeniably had influence, if not always electoral success. As the records of such parties demonstrate, an election campaign is a means of disseminating ideas as well as attaining political office. Overbroad restrictions on ballot access jeopardize this form of political expression.

The signature requirements for independent candidates and new political parties seeking offices in Chicago are plainly not the least restrictive means of protecting the State's objectives. The Illinois Legislature has determined that its interest in avoiding overloaded ballots in statewide elections is served by the 25,000–signature requirement. Yet appellant has advanced no reason, much less a compelling one, why the State needs a more stringent requirement for Chicago. At oral argument, appellant explained that the signature provisions for statewide elections originally reflected a different approach than those for elections in political subdivisions. Not only were independent candidates and new political parties in state elections required to obtain 25,000 signatures, but those signatures also had to meet standards pertaining to geographic distribution. By comparison, candidates and parties in city elections had only to obtain signatures from a flat percentage of the qualified voters. In *Moore v. Ogilvie,* 394 U.S. 814, 89 S.Ct. 1493, 23 L.Ed.2d 1 (1969), this Court struck down on equal protection grounds Illinois' requirement that the nominating petition of a candidate for statewide office include the signatures of at least 200 qualified voters from at least 50 counties. Following *Moore,* the Court of Appeals for the Seventh Circuit invalidated a provision in the amended statute which specified that no more than 13,000 signatures on a new party's petition for statewide elections could come from any one county. Thus, appellant noted, the invalidation of the geographic constraints has tied the requirements for both city and state candidates solely to a population standard, giving rise to the anomaly at issue here.

Although this account may explain the anomaly, appellant still has suggested no reasons that justify its continuation. Historical accident, without more, cannot constitute a compelling state interest. We therefore hold that the Illinois Election Code is unconstitutional insofar as it requires independent candidates and new political parties to obtain more than 25,000 signatures in Chicago....

The Chief Justice [Burger] concurs in the judgment.

Mr. Justice Blackmun, concurring.

Although I join the Court's opinion and its strict-scrutiny approach for election cases, I add these comments to record purposefully, and perhaps somewhat belatedly, my unrelieved discomfort with what seems to be a continuing tendency in this Court to use as tests such easy phrases as "compelling [state] interest" and "least drastic [or restrictive] means." I have never been able fully to appreciate just what a "compelling state interest" is. If it means "convincingly controlling," or "incapable of being overcome" upon any balancing process, then, of course, the test merely announces an inevitable result, and the test is no test at all. And, for me, "least drastic means" is a slippery slope and also the signal of the result the Court has chosen to reach. A judge would be unimaginative indeed if he could not come up with something a little less "drastic" or a little less "restrictive" in almost any situation, and thereby enable himself to vote to strike legislation down. This is reminiscent of the Court's indulgence, a few decades ago, in substantive due process in the economic area as a means of nullification.

I feel, therefore, and have always felt, that these phrases are really not very helpful for constitutional analysis.... Apart from their use, however, the result the Court reaches here is the correct one. It is with these reservations that I join the Court's opinion.

[The opinions of STEVENS, J., concurring in part and concurring in the judgment, and REHNQUIST, J., concurring in the judgment, are omitted.]

Notes

1. *Williams v. Rhodes,* 393 U.S. 23, 89 S.Ct. 5, 21 L.Ed.2d 24 (1968). Ohio's election laws made it "virtually impossible for a new political party, even though it has hundreds of thousands of members," to be placed on the state ballot to choose presidential electors. For example, a new party had to meet an early deadline for filing petitions signed by qualified voters totaling 15% of the number of ballots cast in the last preceding gubernatorial election and elect, at a primary election (conforming to detailed standards), delegates and alternates to a national convention. The state also abolished write-in votes. However, the established parties (i.e., the Democrats and Republicans) only had to have obtained 10% of the votes in the last gubernatorial election in order to be placed on the ballot. Because the right to vote and to associate were implicated, the Court found no "compelling state interest" to justify such burdens on minor parties. The interest in promoting a two party system is not legitimate because the old parties should have no monopoly and thereby preclude new parties from competing in ideas and governmental policies. The legitimate goal of preventing ballot confusion could be met with much lower ballot access requirements.

Contrast, *Jenness v. Fortson,* 403 U.S. 431, 91 S.Ct. 1970, 29 L.Ed.2d 554 (1971). Georgia provided that a political party whose candidate received at least 20% of the vote for the last gubernatorial or presidential election would have the candidate's name printed on the general election ballot, but a non-party candidate had to secure the signatures of 5% of the total number of electors eligible to vote in the last election for the office the candidate is seeking in order to have his name printed on the ballot. Georgia, however, allowed write-in votes; had no unreasonably long filing deadline; did not require of new parties an elaborate primary election; and allowed independent candidates to run without party affiliation. The Court held the 5% requirement was a reasonable way of serving the state's interest in preventing ballot confusion.

2.   The Court invalidated filing fee requirements as a prerequisite to ballot access as applied to indigents in *Bullock v. Carter,* 405 U.S. 134, 92 S.Ct. 849, 31 L.Ed.2d 92 (1972)(filing fees from $1000 to $8900) and *Lubin v. Panish,* 415 U.S. 709, 94 S.Ct. 1315, 39 L.Ed.2d 702 (1974)(filing fee of 2% of annual salary of office sought). Filing fees do not test the genuineness of a candidacy or the extent of his voter support, because a wealthy but frivolous candidate can write a check and a serious but impecunious candidate may be prevented from running. *Lubin* concluded: "Selection of candidates solely on the basis of ability to pay a fixed fee without providing any alternative means is not reasonably necessary to the accomplishment of the State's legitimate election interests."

8–3.3 *Travel*

8–3.31 *Interstate Travel*

SHAPIRO v. THOMPSON
394 U.S. 618, 89 S.Ct. 1322, 22 L.Ed.2d 600 (1969).

MR. JUSTICE BRENNAN delivered the opinion of the Court.

These three appeals were restored to the calendar for reargument. Each is an appeal from a decision of a three-judge District Court holding unconstitutional a State or District of Columbia statutory provision which denies welfare assistance to residents of the State or District who have not resided within their jurisdictions for at least one year immediately preceding their applications for such assistance. We affirm the judgments of the District Courts in the three cases. . . .

There is no dispute that the effect of the waiting-period requirement in each case is to create two classes of needy resident families indistinguishable from each other except that one is composed of residents who have resided a year or more, and the second of residents who have resided less than a year, in the jurisdiction. On the basis of this sole difference the first class is granted and the second class is denied welfare aid upon which may depend the ability of the families to obtain the very means to subsist—food, shelter, and other necessities of life. In each case, the District Court found that appellees met the test for residence in their jurisdictions, as well as all other eligibility requirements except the requirement of residence for a full year prior to their applications. On reargument, appellees' central contention is that the statutory prohibition of benefits to residents of less than a year creates a classification which constitutes an invidious discrimination denying them equal protection of the laws. We agree. The interests which appellants assert are promoted by the classification either may not constitutionally be promoted by government or are not compelling governmental interests.

Primarily, appellants justify the waiting-period requirement as a protective device to preserve the fiscal integrity of state public assistance programs. It is asserted that people who require welfare assistance during their first year of residence in a State are likely to become continuing burdens on state welfare programs. [I]f such people can be deterred from entering the jurisdiction by denying them welfare benefits during the first year, state programs to assist long-time residents will not be impaired by a substantial influx of indigent newcomers....

We do not doubt that the one-year waiting-period device is well suited to discourage the influx of poor families in need of assistance.... But the purpose of inhibiting migration by needy persons into the State is constitutionally impermissible. This Court long ago recognized that the nature of our Federal Union and our constitutional concepts of personal liberty unite to require that all citizens be free to travel throughout the length and breadth of our land uninhibited by statutes, rules, or regulations which unreasonably burden or restrict this movement.... We have no occasion to ascribe the source of this right to travel interstate to a particular constitutional provision.[8] It suffices that, as MR. JUSTICE STEWART said for the Court in *United States v. Guest,* 383 U.S. 745, 757–758, 86 S.Ct. 1170, 16 L.Ed.2d 239, 249 (1966):

> The constitutional right to travel from one State to another ... occupies a position fundamental to the concept of our Federal Union. It is a right that has been firmly established and repeatedly recognized. [T]he right finds no explicit mention in the Constitution. The reason, it has been suggested, is that a right so elementary was conceived from the beginning to be a necessary concomitant of the stronger Union the Constitution created. In any event, freedom to travel throughout the United States has long been recognized as a basic right under the Constitution.

Thus, the purpose of deterring the in-migration of indigents cannot serve as justification for the classification created by the one-year waiting period, since that purpose is constitutionally impermissible.

Alternatively, appellants argue that even if it is impermissible for a State to attempt to deter the entry of all indigents, the challenged classification may be justified as a permissible state attempt to discourage those indigents who would enter the State solely to obtain larger benefits. [But] a State may no more try to fence out those indigents who seek higher welfare benefits than it may try to fence out indigents generally. Implicit in any such distinction is the notion that indigents

---

8. In *Corfield v. Coryell,* 6 Fed.Cas. pp. 546, 552 (No. 3230)(C.C.E.D.Pa.1825), *Paul v. Virginia,* 8 Wall. (75 U.S.) 168, 180, 19 L.Ed. 357 (1869), and *Ward v. Maryland,* 12 Wall. (79 U.S.) 418, 430, 20 L.Ed. 449 (1871), the right to travel interstate was grounded upon the Privileges and Immunities Clause of Art. IV, § 2. See also *Slaughter–House Cases,* 16 Wall. 36, 79, 21 L.Ed. 394 (1873); *Twining v. New Jersey,* 211 U.S. 78, 97, 29 S.Ct. 14, 18, 53 L.Ed. 97 (1908). In *Edwards v. California,* 314 U.S. 160, 181, 183–185, 62 S.Ct. 164, 170, 171–172, 86 L.Ed. 119 (1941)(Douglas and Jackson, JJ., concurring), and *Twining v. New Jersey,* supra, reliance was placed on the Privileges [or] Immunities Clause of the

Fourteenth Amendment. See also *Crandall v. Nevada,* 6 Wall. (73 U.S.) 35 (1868). In *Edwards v. California,* supra, and the *Passenger Cases,* 7 How. 283 (1849), a Commerce Clause approach was employed.

See also *Kent v. Dulles,* 357 U.S. 116, 125, 78 S.Ct. 1113, 1118, 2 L.Ed.2d 1204 (1958); *Aptheker v. Secretary of State,* 378 U.S. 500, 505–506, 84 S.Ct. 1659, 1663, 12 L.Ed.2d 992 (1964); *Zemel v. Rusk,* 381 U.S. 1, 14, 85 S.Ct. 1271, 1279, 14 L.Ed.2d 179 (1965), where the freedom of Americans to travel outside the country was grounded upon the Due Process Clause of the Fifth Amendment.

who enter a State with the hope of securing higher welfare benefits are somehow less deserving than indigents who do not take this consideration into account. But we do not perceive why a mother who is seeking to make a new life for herself and her children should be regarded as less deserving because she considers, among other factors, the level of a State's public assistance. Surely such a mother is no less deserving than a mother who moves into a particular State in order to take advantage of its better educational facilities.

Appellants argue further that the challenged classification may be sustained as an attempt to distinguish between new and old residents on the basis of the contribution they have made to the community through the payment of taxes. [T]his reasoning would logically permit the State to bar new residents from schools, parks, and libraries or deprive them of police and fire protection. Indeed it would permit the State to apportion all benefits and services according to the past tax contributions of its citizens. The Equal Protection Clause prohibits such an apportionment of state services.[10]

We recognize that a State has a valid interest in preserving the fiscal integrity of its programs. It may legitimately attempt to limit its expenditures, whether for public assistance, public education, or any other program. But a State may not accomplish such a purpose by invidious distinctions between classes of its citizens. It could not, for example, reduce expenditures for education by barring indigent children from its schools. Similarly, in the cases before us, appellants must do more than show that denying welfare benefits to new residents saves money. The saving of welfare costs cannot justify an otherwise invidious classification. . . .

Appellants next advance as justification certain administrative and related governmental objectives allegedly served by the waiting-period requirement. They argue that the requirement (1) facilitates the planning of the welfare budget; (2) provides an objective test of residency; (3) minimizes the opportunity for recipients fraudulently to receive payments from more than one jurisdiction; and (4) encourages early entry of new residents into the labor force.

At the outset, we reject appellants' argument that a mere showing of a rational relationship between the waiting period and these four admittedly permissible state objectives will suffice to justify the classification. The waiting-period provision denies welfare benefits to otherwise eligible applicants solely because they have recently moved into the jurisdiction. But in moving from State to State or to the District of Columbia appellees were exercising a constitutional right, and any classification which serves to penalize the exercise of that right, unless shown to be necessary to promote a *compelling* governmental interest, is unconstitutional.

10. We are not dealing here with state insurance programs which may legitimately tie the amount of benefits to the individual's contributions.

The argument that the waiting-period requirement facilitates budget predictability is wholly unfounded. The records in all three cases are utterly devoid of evidence that either State or the District of Columbia in fact uses the one-year requirement as a means to predict the number of people who will require assistance in the budget year. . . .

The argument that the waiting period serves as an administratively efficient rule of thumb for determining residency similarly will not withstand scrutiny. The residence requirement and the one-year waiting-period requirement are distinct and independent prerequisites for assistance under these three statutes, and the facts relevant to the determination of each are directly examined by the welfare authorities. Before granting an application, the welfare authorities investigate the applicant's employment, housing, and family situation and in the course of the inquiry necessarily learn the facts upon which to determine whether the applicant is a resident.

Similarly, there is no need for a State to use the one-year waiting period as a safeguard against fraudulent receipt of benefits; for less drastic means are available, and are employed, to minimize that hazard. Of course, a State has a valid interest in preventing fraud by any applicant, whether a newcomer or a long-time resident. . . . Since double payments can be prevented by a letter or a telephone call, it is unreasonable to accomplish this objective by the blunderbuss method of denying assistance to all indigent newcomers for an entire year.

Pennsylvania suggests that the one-year waiting period is justified as a means of encouraging new residents to join the labor force promptly. But this logic would also require a similar waiting period for long-term residents of the State. A state purpose to encourage employment provides no rational basis for imposing a one-year waiting-period restriction on new residents only.

We conclude therefore that appellants in these cases do not use and have no need to use the one-year requirement for the governmental purposes suggested. Thus, even under traditional equal protection tests a classification of welfare applicants according to whether they have lived in the State for one year would seem irrational and unconstitutional. But, of course, the traditional criteria do not apply in these cases. Since the classification here touches on the fundamental right of interstate movement, its constitutionality must be judged by the stricter standard of whether it promotes a *compelling* state interest. Under this standard, the waiting-period requirement clearly violates the Equal Protection Clause.[21]

Connecticut and Pennsylvania argue, however, that the constitutional challenge to the waiting-period requirements must fail because Con-

---

21. We imply no view of the validity of waiting-period *or* residence requirements determining eligibility to vote, eligibility for tuition-free education, to obtain a license to practice a profession, to hunt or fish, and so forth. Such requirements may promote compelling state interests on the one hand, or, on the other, may not be penalties upon the exercise of the constitutional right of interstate travel.

gress expressly approved the imposition of the requirement by the States as part of the jointly funded AFDC program, 42 U.S.C.A. § 602(b). . . . Congress may not authorize the States to violate the Equal Protection Clause. . . .

The waiting-period requirement in the District of Columbia Code involved in No. 33 is also unconstitutional even though it was adopted by Congress as an exercise of federal power. For the reasons we have stated in invalidating the Pennsylvania and Connecticut provisions, the District of Columbia provision is also invalid—the Due Process Clause of the Fifth Amendment prohibits Congress from denying public assistance to poor persons otherwise eligible solely on the ground that they have not been residents of the District of Columbia for one year at the time their applications are filed.

Accordingly, the judgments in Nos. 9, 33 and 34 are

Affirmed.

MR. CHIEF JUSTICE WARREN, with whom MR. JUSTICE BLACK joins, dissenting.

. . . Appellees insist that a congressionally mandated residence requirement would violate their right to travel. The import of their contention is that Congress, even under its "plenary" power to control interstate commerce, is constitutionally prohibited from imposing residence requirements. I reach a contrary conclusion for I am convinced that the extent of the burden on interstate travel when compared with the justification for its imposition requires the Court to uphold this exertion of federal power. . . . Our cases require only that Congress have a rational basis for finding that a chosen regulatory scheme is necessary to the furtherance of interstate commerce. See, e.g., *Katzenbach v. McClung,* [§ 4–4, supra]; *Wickard v. Filburn,* [§ 4–2, supra]. Certainly, a congressional finding that residence requirements allowed each State to concentrate its resources upon new and increased programs of rehabilitation ultimately resulting in an enhanced flow of commerce as the economic condition of welfare recipients progressively improved is rational and would justify imposition of residence requirements under the Commerce Clause. . . .

MR. JUSTICE HARLAN, dissenting. . . .

The "compelling interest" doctrine, which today is articulated more explicitly than ever before, constitutes an increasingly significant exception to the long-established rule that a statute does not deny equal protection if it is rationally related to a legitimate governmental objective. . . . Today's decision, it seems to me, reflects to an unusual degree the current notion that this Court possesses a peculiar wisdom all its own whose capacity to lead this Nation out of its present troubles is contained only by the limits of judicial ingenuity in contriving new constitutional principles to meet each problem as it arises. . . . I consider it particularly unfortunate that this judicial roadblock to the powers of Congress in this field should occur at the very threshold of the current discussions regarding the "federalizing" of these aspects of welfare relief.

[The opinion of STEWART, J., concurring, is omitted.]

Notes

1. MEDICAL CARE. *Memorial Hosp. v. Maricopa County,* 415 U.S. 250, 94 S.Ct. 1076, 39 L.Ed.2d 306 (1974) invalidated an Arizona statute requiring a one year residence in a county as a condition to receiving nonemergency hospitalization or medical care at the county's expense. The county argued that, unlike *Shapiro,* its durational residency requirement penalizes not interstate but intrastate travel. The Court found it unnecessary to decide whether to draw a constitutional distinction between interstate and intrastate travel because the appellant seeking free medical care "has been effectively penalized for his interstate migration, although this was accomplished under the guise of a county residence requirement. What would be unconstitutional if done directly by the State can no more readily be accomplished by a county at the State's direction."

Under *Shapiro* the denial of the basic "necessities of life" is an impermissible penalty on the right to travel; medical care is also "a basic necessity of life" to an indigent. "Governmental privileges or benefits necessary to basic sustenance have often been viewed as being of greater constitutional significance than less essential forms of governmental entitlements. It would be odd, indeed, to find that the State of Arizona was required to afford [the appellant] welfare assistance to keep him from the discomfort of inadequate housing or the pangs of hunger but could deny him the medical care to relieve him from the wheezing and gasping for breath that attend his [chronic asthmatic and bronchial illness]."

2. TUITION PAYMENTS. Many state universities charge lower tuition for in-state residents. The Court upheld a University of Minnesota regulation providing that no student could qualify as a resident for tuition purposes unless he had been, for at least one year immediately prior, a bona fide domiciliary of the state. *Starns v. Malkerson,* 326 F.Supp. 234 (D.Minn. 1970), affirmed summarily without opinion 401 U.S. 985, 91 S.Ct. 1231, 28 L.Ed.2d 527 (1971). A permanent bar, however is impermissible, *Vlandis v. Kline,* 412 U.S. 441, 93 S.Ct. 2230, 37 L.Ed.2d 63 (1973) (Connecticut law providing that out of state residents, as defined in the Act, will never be treated as residents for tuition purposes is invalid). One cannot equal the value of higher education with the "necessities of life," such as food, clothing, and shelter. "*Shapiro involved the immediate and pressing need for preservation of life and health* [but the] durational residence requirement for attendance at publicly financed institutions of higher learning [does] not involve similar risks." 326 F.Supp. at 238, quoted with approval in *Memorial Hospital,* supra, 415 U.S. at 260 n. 15, 94 S.Ct., at 1083 n. 15, 39 L.Ed.2d 306 (emphasis added by Supreme Court).

3. VOTING. *Dunn v. Blumstein,* 405 U.S. 330, 92 S.Ct. 995, 31 L.Ed.2d 274 (1972) invalidated a Tennessee law requiring a voter to be a resident of the state for one year and of the county for three months before he could vote. The state can restrict the vote to bona fide state residents, but appellee was a bona fide resident of the state and county when he attempted to

register. Appellee objected to the additional durational residency requirement. The interests penalized two fundamental rights, the right to travel
and to vote, but the lengthy durational requirement did not serve any
compelling state interest. The state's interest in preventing voter fraud was
valid, but could be served by a shorter waiting period. "It is sufficient to
note here that 30 days appears to be an ample period of time for the State to
complete whatever administrative tasks are necessary to prevent fraud—and
a year, or three months, too much."

Marston v. Lewis, 410 U.S. 679, 93 S.Ct. 1211, 35 L.Ed.2d 627
(1973)(per curiam)(50 day durational voter residency requirement and 50
day voter registration requirement upheld because the record showed that
such time was necessary to permit preparation of accurate voter lists).

4. CANDIDACY. State laws often require that candidates for elective office
meet durational residency requirements.[1] The Supreme Court has not dealt
with this issue in detail, but it has summarily affirmed lower court rulings
upholding such durational residency requirements. E.g., *Chimento v. Stark,*
353 F.Supp. 1211 (D.N.H.)(three judge court), affirmed summarily, without
opinion 414 U.S. 802, 94 S.Ct. 125, 38 L.Ed.2d 39 (1973)(7 year durational
residency requirement for candidates for Governor).

5. CONTINUING RESIDENCY. *McCarthy v. Philadelphia Civil Service Commission,* 424 U.S. 645, 96 S.Ct. 1154, 47 L.Ed.2d 366 (1976)(per curiam)
upheld a city ordinance requiring city employees to be residents of the city.
Shapiro, Dunn, and *Memorial Hospital* did not question "the validity of a
condition placed on municipal employment that a person be a resident *at the
time* of his application. In this case appellant claims a constitutional right to
be employed by the city of Philadelphia *while* he is living elsewhere. There is
no support in our cases for such a claim. We have previously differentiated
between a requirement of continuing residency and a requirement of a prior
residency of a given duration." (emphasis in original).

6. DIVORCE. *Sosna v. Iowa,* 419 U.S. 393, 95 S.Ct. 553, 42 L.Ed.2d 532
(1975) upheld an Iowa law providing, in general, that unless the respondent
is a resident of the state, the petitioner in a divorce action must be a resident
of the state for one year prior to the filing of the petition. The Court noted
that domestic relations is an area long regarded as "an exclusive province of
the States." Also, Iowa's requirement only delayed, but did not deny,
petitioner's access to the courts. And the justification for the law did not lie
merely on budgetary considerations or administrative convenience but rather on the State's interest "in avoiding officious intermeddling in matters in
which another State has a paramount interest and in minimizing the
susceptibility of its own decrees to collateral attack."

7. DEPARTURE OF IN-STATE CRIMINALS. Georgia law provided that a parent
who wilfully and voluntarily abandoned his or her child was guilty of a
misdemeanor, but those parents who commit that offense within Georgia
and thereafter leave the state are guilty of a felony. *Jones v. Helms,* 452 U.S.
412, 101 S.Ct. 2434, 69 L.Ed.2d 118 (1981) upheld the constitutionality of

---

1. Cf. U.S. Const., Art. 1, § 2, cl. 2 (Representative must be U.S. citizen for 7
years); § 3, cl. 3 (Senator must be U.S.
citizen for 9 years); Art. II, § 1, cl. 5 (President must be a U.S. resident for 14 years
and a natural born U.S. citizen or a citizen
at the time of the adoption of the Constitution).

this law against a challenge that it violated the right to travel and the Equal Protection Clause. Previous cases invalidating state laws imposed a burden on the right to travel by citizens whose right had not been qualified in any way. But here "appellee's criminal conduct within the State of Georgia necessarily qualified his right thereafter freely to travel interstate." Georgia did not seek to justify different treatment of old versus new residents, nor residents versus nonresidents. It did not simply penalize someone for leaving the state. Because the "departure aggravates the consequences of conduct that is otherwise punishable, the State may treat the entire sequence of events, from the initial offense to departure from the State, as more serious than its separate components." The statute did not violate Equal Protection, so the state need not demonstrate that the statute's purposes could be furthered by less restrictive means.

ZOBEL v. WILLIAMS
457 U.S. 55, 102 S.Ct. 2309, 72 L.Ed.2d 672 (1982).

CHIEF JUSTICE BURGER delivered the opinion of the Court. . . .

The 1967 discovery of large oil reserves on state-owned land in the Prudhoe Bay area of Alaska resulted in a windfall to the State. The State, which had a total budget of $124 million in 1969, before the oil revenues began to flow into the state coffers, received $3.7 billion in petroleum revenues during the 1981 fiscal year. . . . Alaska in 1976 adopted a constitutional amendment establishing the Permanent Fund into which the State must deposit at least 25% of its mineral income each year. . . . In 1980, the legislature enacted a dividend program to distribute annually a portion of the Fund's earnings directly to the State's adult residents. Under the plan, each citizen 18 years of age or older receives one dividend unit for each year of residency subsequent to 1959, the first year of statehood. The statute fixed the value of each dividend unit at $50 for the 1979 fiscal year; a one-year resident thus would receive one unit, or $50, while a resident of Alaska since it became a State in 1959 would receive 21 units, or $1,050. The value of a dividend unit will vary each year depending on the income of the Permanent Fund and the amount of that income the State allocates for other purposes. The State now estimates that the 1985 fiscal year dividend will be nearly four times as large as that for 1979.

Appellants, residents of Alaska since 1978, brought this suit in 1980 challenging the dividend distribution plan as violative of their right to equal protection guarantees and their constitutional right to migrate to Alaska, to establish residency there and thereafter to enjoy the full rights of Alaska citizenship on the same terms as all other citizens of the State. [The] Alaska Supreme Court . . . upheld the statute.

The Alaska dividend distribution law is quite unlike the durational residency requirements we examined in [e.g.] *Shapiro v. Thompson*. Those cases involved laws which required new residents to reside in the State a fixed minimum period to be eligible for certain benefits available on an equal basis to all other residents. The asserted purpose of the durational residency requirements was to assure that only persons who had established *bona fide* residence received rights and benefits provided for residents.

The Alaska statute does not impose any threshold waiting period on those seeking dividend benefits; persons with less than a full year of residency are entitled to share in the distribution. Nor does the statute purport to establish a test of the *bona fides* of state residence. Instead, the dividend statute creates fixed, permanent distinctions between an ever increasing number of perpetual classes of concededly *bona fide* residents, based on how long they have been in the State....[5]

When a State distributes benefits unequally, the distinctions it makes are subject to scrutiny under the Equal Protection Clause of the Fourteenth Amendment. Generally, a law will survive that scrutiny if the distinction it makes rationally furthers a legitimate state purpose. Some particularly invidious distinctions are subject to more rigorous scrutiny. Appellants claim that the distinctions made by the Alaska law should be subjected to the higher level of scrutiny applied to the durational residency requirements in *Shapiro v. Thompson,* supra and *Memorial Hospital v. Maricopa County,* supra. The State, on the other hand, asserts that the law need only meet the minimum rationality test. In any event, if the statutory scheme cannot pass even the minimal test proposed by the State, we need not decide whether any enhanced scrutiny is called for.

[T]he first two state objectives—creating a financial incentive for individuals to establish and maintain Alaska residence, and assuring prudent management of the Permanent Fund and the State's natural and mineral resources—are not rationally related to the distinctions Alaska seeks to make between newer residents and those who have been in the State since 1959. [T]he State's interest is not in any way served by granting greater dividends to persons for their residency during the 21 years prior to the enactment. Nor does the State's purpose of furthering the prudent management of the Permanent Fund and the state's resources support retrospective application of its plan to the date of statehood.... The State similarly argues that equal per capita distribution would encourage rapacious development of natural resources. Even if we assume that the state interest is served by increasing the dividend for each year of residency beginning with the date of enactment, is it rationally served by granting greater dividends in varying amounts to those who resided in Alaska during the 21 years prior to enactment? We think not.

The last of the State's objectives—to reward citizens for past contributions—alone was relied upon by the Alaska Supreme Court to support the retrospective application of the law to 1959. However, that objective

---

5. ... The statute does not involve the kind of discrimination which the Privileges and Immunities Clause of Art. IV was designed to prevent. That Clause "was designed to insure to a citizen of State A who ventures into State B the same privileges which the citizens of State B enjoy." The Clause is thus not applicable to this case.

is not a legitimate state purpose. A similar "past contributions" argument was made and rejected in *Shapiro v. Thompson,* supra....

If the States can make the amount of a cash dividend depend on length of residence, what would preclude varying university tuition on a sliding scale based on years of residence—or even limiting access to finite public facilities, eligibility for student loans, for civil service jobs, or for government contracts by length of domicile? Could States impose different taxes based on length of residence? Alaska's reasoning could open the door to state apportionment of other rights, benefits and services according to length of residency. It would permit the states to divide citizens into expanding numbers of permanent classes. Such a result would be clearly impermissible.

We need not consider whether the State could enact the dividend program prospectively only. Invalidation of a portion of a statute does not necessarily render the whole invalid unless it is evident that the legislature would not have enacted the legislation without the invalid portion. Here, we need not speculate as to the intent of the Alaska legislature; the legislation expressly provides that invalidation of any portion of the statute renders the whole invalid.... However, it is of course for the Alaska courts to pass on the severability clause of the statute.

Reversed and Remanded.

JUSTICE BRENNAN, with whom JUSTICE MARSHALL, JUSTICE BLACKMUN, and JUSTICE POWELL join, concurring....

[I]f each State were free to reward its citizens incrementally for their years of residence, so that a citizen leaving one State would thereby forfeit his accrued seniority, only to have to begin building such seniority again in his new State of residence, then the mobility so essential to the economic progress of our Nation, and so commonly accepted as a fundamental aspect of our social order, would not long survive. [T]he Alaska plan discriminates against the recently naturalized citizen, in favor of the Alaska citizen of longer duration; it discriminates against the eighteen year old native resident, in favor of all residents of longer duration. If the Alaska plan were limited to discriminations such as these, and did not purport to apply to migrants from sister States, interstate travel would not be noticeably burdened—yet those discriminations would surely be constitutionally suspect.

... To be sure, allegiance and attachment may be rationally measured by length of residence—length of residence may, for example, be used to test the *bona fides* of citizenship—and allegiance and attachment may bear some rational relationship to a very limited number of legitimate state purposes. Cf. *Chimento v. Stark,* 353 F.Supp. 1211 (D.N.H.)(three-judge court), aff'd summarily, without opinion, 414 U.S. 802, 94 S.Ct. 125, 38 L.Ed.2d 39 (1973), (seven year citizenship requirement to run for governor); U.S. Const., art. I, § 2, cl. 2, § 3, cl. 3; art. II, § 1, cl. 4. But those instances in which length of residence could provide a legitimate basis for distinguishing one citizen from another are rare. . . .

JUSTICE O'CONNOR, concurring in the judgment. . . .

. . . Stripped to its essentials, the plan denies non-Alaskans settling in the State the same privileges afforded longer-term residents. The Privileges and Immunities Clause of Article IV, which guarantees "[t]he Citizens of each State . . . all Privileges and Immunities of Citizens in the several States," addresses just this type of discrimination. Accordingly, I would measure Alaska's scheme against the principles implementing the Privileges and Immunities Clause. In addition to resolving the particular problems raised by Alaska's scheme, this analysis supplies a needed foundation for many of the "right to travel" claims discussed in the Court's prior opinions. . . . The circumstance that some of the disfavored citizens already live in Alaska does not negate the fact that "the citizen of State A who ventures into [Alaska]" to establish a home labors under a continuous disability.

JUSTICE REHNQUIST, dissenting.

Alaska's dividend distribution scheme represents one State's effort to apportion unique economic benefits among its citizens. Although the wealth received from the oil deposits of Prudhoe Bay may be quite unlike the economic resources enjoyed by most States, Alaska's distribution of that wealth is in substance no different from any other State's allocation of economic benefits. The distribution scheme being in the nature of economic regulation, I am at a loss to see the rationality behind the Court's invalidation of it as a denial of equal protection. This Court has long held that state economic regulations are presumptively valid, and violate the Fourteenth Amendment only in the rarest of circumstances. [T]he illegitimacy of a State's recognizing the past contributions of its citizens has been established by the Court only in certain cases considering an infringement of the right to travel,[1] and the majority itself rightly declines to apply the strict scrutiny analysis of those right-to-travel cases. . . .

Notes

1. Following this decision, Alaska enacted a $420 million plan designed to give every Alaskan with at least six months residency by October 15, 1982, a one time check for $1,000 each. In subsequent years smaller amounts would be distributed equally to all Alaskans. Distributing this money has its problems. The Alaskan supervisor in charge of distributing the money complained: "People were so much nicer when we were asking them for money. Now that we are giving it away, they get so rude." The state has received "hundreds of possibly fraudulent applications" creating "a paperwork nightmare." One anonymous caller told state officials that he had

---

1. The Court relies upon *Shapiro v. Thompson* in holding that Alaska may not justify its dividend distribution scheme by a desire to reward its citizens for their past contributions. In *Shapiro*, however, the Court found that the classification at issue "touche[d] on the fundamental right of interstate movement" and therefore could be justified only if it promoted a "*compelling state interest*." (emphasis in original). . . .

sent in a bogus request for state money and then dared the officials to catch him. State officials are also concerned about the state's image in the rest of the United States. References to the "blue-eyed Arabs of the North" might make it much easier for outside politicians to impose new federal taxes on Alaskan oil. Wall St. Jrl., Sept. 13, 1982, at 23 (midwest ed.).

2. *Hooper v. Bernalillo County Assessor,* 472 U.S. 612, 105 S.Ct. 2862, 86 L.Ed.2d 487 (1985). In 1981 the New Mexico legislature enacted legislation granting *annual* property tax exemptions to any honorably discharged Vietnam veteran who was on active duty at least 90 days and who was a New Mexico resident before May 8, 1976. Chief Justice Burger, for the Court, invalidated the statute under the authority of *Zobel.* "When a State distributes benefits unequally, the distinctions it makes are subject to scrutiny under the Equal Protection Clause of the Fourteenth Amendment." Appellants argued for the level of scrutiny used in *Shapiro v. Thompson,* while appellees argued for the minimum rational basis scrutiny. The Court did not decide this dispute, for it found that the statute lacked minimum rationality.

The Court said "The New Mexico statute, by singling previous residents for the tax exemption, rewards only those citizens for their past contributions towards our nation's military effort in Vietnam. *Zobel* teaches that such an objective is 'not a legitimate state purpose.'" (The dissent of Stevens, J., joined by Rehnquist and O'Connor, JJ., found this statement "remarkable." The dissent argued that *"Zobel* surely did not imply that past contributions to the nation's military effort would not justify a special reward.... "). The majority concluded that *"Zobel* made clear that the Constitution will not tolerate a state benefit program that creates fixed, permanent distinctions ... between ... classes of concededly bona fide residents, based on how long they have been in the State." (quoting *Zobel*).

Justice Stevens' dissent argued: "If New Mexico had awarded gold medallions to all of its resident veterans on May 1, 1976, I believe it would be absurd for a veteran arriving in the State in 1981 to claim that he or she had a constitutional right either to a comparable medal or to have all other medal recipients return them to the State." Can you respond to Justice Stevens' argument?

Attorney General of New York v. Soto–Lopez, 476 U.S. 898, 106 S.Ct. 2317, 90 L.Ed.2d 899 (1986). The Court, with no majority opinion, invalidated a New York State statute that provided a preference in civil service opportunities to resident veterans who were New York residents at the time they had entered military service.

3. *Saenz v. Roe,* 526 U.S. 489, 119 S.Ct. 1518, 143 L.Ed.2d 689 (1999). California limited the maximum welfare benefits it would pay to newly arrived residents (those who resided in the state for less than 12 months) to the amount that the state of the family's prior residence would have paid. Stevens, J., for the Court (7 to 2), discussed the "right of travel" cases in this section and then invalidated the law, relying on the privileges and immunities clause of the Fourteenth Amendment. He said:

"The 'right to travel' discussed in our cases embraces at least three different components. It protects the right of a citizen of one State to enter and to leave another State, the right to be treated as a welcome visitor rather than an unfriendly alien when temporarily present in the second State, and, for those travelers who elect to become permanent residents, the right to be treated like other citizens of that State."

The Court "need not identify the source" of the first component in the text of the Constitution. The source of the second component is the "Privileges and Immunities Clause of Article IV, and the source of the third component is 'plainly identified in the opening words of the Fourteenth Amendment,' stating: 'No State shall make or enforce any law which shall abridge the privileges or immunities of citizens of the United States.' "

The Court then invalidated the California law. "Neither mere rationality nor some intermediate standard of review should be used to judge the constitutionality of a state rule that discriminates against some of its citizens because they have been domiciled in the State for less than a year." The state cannot justify the law to deter welfare applicants from migrating to California because California cannot fence out the indigent. The state's fiscal justification is invalid because the state cannot accomplish this purpose by the discriminatory means that it has chosen. Finally, congressional approval of this durational residency requirement does not justify the law because Congress may not authorize the states to violate the Fourteenth Amendment. Rehnquist, C.J., joined by Thomas, J., dissenting, noted that the Court "breathes new life into the previously dormant Privileges and Immunities Clause of the Fourteenth Amendment."

8–3.32 Foreign Travel

HAIG v. AGEE

453 U.S. 280, 101 S.Ct. 2766, 69 L.Ed.2d 640 (1981).

Chief Justice Burger delivered the opinion of the Court.

The question presented is whether the President, acting through the Secretary of State, has authority to revoke a passport on the ground that the holder's activities in foreign countries are causing or are likely to cause serious damage to the national security or foreign policy of the United States.

Philip Agee, an American citizen, currently resides in West Germany. From 1957 to 1968, he was employed by the Central Intelligence Agency. He held key positions in the division of the Agency that is responsible for covert intelligence gathering in foreign countries.... In 1974, Agee called a press conference in London to announce his "campaign to fight the United States CIA wherever it is operating." ... The record reveals that [his] identifications [of CIA agents] divulge classified information, violate Agee's express contract not to make any public statements about Agency matters without prior clearance by the Agency, have prejudiced the ability of the United States to obtain intelligence, and have been followed by episodes of violence against the persons and organizations identified.[7]

In December 1979, the Secretary of State revoked Agee's passport and delivered an explanatory notice to Agee in West Germany. The notice states in part:

> The Department's action is predicated upon a determination made by the Secretary under the provisions of [22 C.F.R.] Section 51.70(b)(4) that your activities abroad are causing or are likely to cause serious damage to the national security or the foreign policy of the United States. The reasons for the Secretary's determination are, in summary, as follows: Since the early 1970's it has been your stated intention to conduct a continuous campaign to disrupt the intelligence operations of the United States. In carrying out that campaign you have traveled in various countries (including, among others, Mexico, the United Kingdom, Denmark, Jamaica, Cuba, and Germany), and your activities in those countries have caused serious damage to the national security and foreign policy of the United States. Your stated intention to continue such activities threatens additional damage of the same kind.

The notice also advised Agee of his right to an administrative hearing and offered to hold such a hearing in West Germany on 5 days' notice.

Agee at once filed suit against the Secretary. He alleged that the regulation invoked by the Secretary has not been authorized by Congress and is invalid; that the regulation is impermissibly overbroad; that the revocation prior to a hearing violated his Fifth Amendment right to procedural due process; and that the revocation violated a Fifth Amendment liberty interest in a right to travel and a First Amendment right to criticize government policies.... For purposes of [his summary judgment] motion, Agee conceded the Government's factual averments and its claim that his activities were causing or were likely to cause serious damage to the national security or foreign policy of the United States. The District Court held that the regulation exceeded the statutory powers of the Secretary under the Passport Act of 1926, granted summary judgment for Agee, and ordered the Secretary to restore his passport.

A divided panel of the Court of Appeals affirmed. It held that the Secretary was required to show that Congress had authorized the

---

7. In July 1974, two days after a Jamaica press conference at which Agee's principal collaborator identified Richard Kinsman as CIA Chief of Station in Jamaica, Kinsman's house was strafed with automatic gunfire. Four days after the same press conference, three men approached the Jamaica home of another man similarly identified as an Agency officer. Police challenged the men and gunfire was exchanged. In December 1975, Richard Welch was murdered in Greece after the publication of an article in an English-language newspaper in Athens naming Welch as CIA Chief of Station. In January 1981, two American officials of the American Institute for Free Labor Development, previously identified as a CIA front by Agee and discussed extensively in Agee's book *Inside the Company: CIA Diary*, were assassinated in El Salvador. The Government does not assert that Agee has specifically incited anyone to commit murder. However, affidavits of the CIA's Deputy Director for Operations set out and support his judgment that Agee's purported identifications are "thinly-veiled invitations to violence."

regulation either by an express delegation or by implied approval of a "substantial and consistent" administrative practice, *Zemel v. Rusk,* 381 U.S. 1, 12, 85 S.Ct. 1271, 14 L.Ed.2d 179 (1965). The court found no express statutory authority for the revocation. It perceived only one other case of actual passport revocation under the regulation since it was promulgated and only five other instances prior to that in which passports were actually denied "even arguably for national security or foreign policy reasons." . . . The court also regarded it as material that most of the Government's authorities dealt with powers of the Executive Branch "during time of war or national emergency" or with respect to persons "engaged in criminal conduct."[15]

We granted certiorari, and stayed the judgment of the Court of Appeals until our disposition of the case on the grant of certiorari.[16] The principal question before us is whether the statute authorizes the action of the Secretary pursuant to the policy announced by the challenged regulation.

Although the historical background that we develop later is important, we begin with the language of the statute. The Passport Act of 1926 provides in pertinent part:

"The Secretary of State may grant and issue passports, and cause passports to be granted, issued, and verified in foreign countries by diplomatic representatives of the United States . . . under such rules as the President shall designate and prescribe for and on behalf of the United States, and no other person shall grant, issue, or verify such passports."

This language is unchanged since its original enactment in 1926. The Passport Act does not in so many words confer upon the Secretary a power to revoke a passport. Nor, for that matter, does it expressly authorize denials of passport applications. Neither, however, does any statute expressly limit those powers. It is beyond dispute that the Secretary has the power to deny a passport for reasons not specified in the statutes. For example, in *Kent v. Dulles,* 357 U.S. 116, 78 S.Ct. 1113, 2 L.Ed.2d 1204 (1958), the Court recognized congressional acquiescence in Executive policies of refusing passports to applicants "participating in illegal conduct, trying to escape the toils of the law, promoting passport frauds, or otherwise engaging in conduct which would violate the laws of the United States."* In *Zemel,* the Court held that "the weightiest considerations of national security" authorized the Secretary to restrict travel to Cuba at the time of the Cuban missile crisis. Agee concedes that

---

15. The Court of Appeals stressed that Agee had not been indicted. In dicta, the court expressed approval of 22 CFR § 51.70(a)(1)(1980), which provides for withholding of a passport if the applicant is the subject of an outstanding federal felony warrant.

16. The Government represents that Agee's passport has been cancelled and that the Secretary has provided Agee with iden-

tification papers permitting him to return to the United States. The regulations at issue contain an exception for "direct return to the United States."

* [Ed. Note: *Kent,* without reaching the Constitutional issues, held that Congress had not authorized the Secretary of State to deny passports to persons who were Communist Party members.]

if the Secretary may deny a passport application for a certain reason, he may revoke a passport on the same ground.

Particularly in light of the "broad rule-making authority granted in the [1926] Act," a consistent administrative construction of that statute must be followed by the courts "unless there are compelling indications that it is wrong." This is especially so in the areas of foreign policy and national security, where congressional silence is not to be equated with congressional disapproval.... Matters intimately related to foreign policy and national security are rarely proper subjects for judicial intervention....

The history of passport controls since the earliest days of the Republic shows congressional recognition of Executive authority to withhold passports on the basis of substantial reasons of national security and foreign policy. Prior to 1856, when there was no statute on the subject, the common perception was that the issuance of a passport was committed to the sole discretion of the Executive and that the Executive would exercise this power in the interests of the national security and foreign policy of the United States.... The President and the Secretary of State consistently construed the 1856 Act to preserve their authority to withhold passports on national security and foreign policy grounds.... The Executive construed the 1926 Act to work no change in prior practice and specifically interpreted it to authorize denial of a passport on grounds of national security or foreign policy.... Despite the longstanding and officially promulgated view that the Executive had the power to withhold passports for reasons of national security and foreign policy, Congress in 1978, "though it once again enacted legislation relating to passports, left completely untouched the broad rulemaking authority granted in the earlier Act." *Zemel.*

Agee argues that the only way the Executive can establish implicit congressional approval is by proof of longstanding and consistent *enforcement* of the claimed power: that is, by showing that many passports were revoked on national security and foreign policy grounds. For this proposition, he relies on *Kent....*

The Secretary has construed and applied his regulations consistently, and it would be anomalous to fault the Government because there were so few occasions to exercise the announced policy and practice. Although a pattern of actual enforcement is one indicator of Executive policy, it suffices that the Executive has "openly asserted" the power at issue. *Kent* is not to the contrary. There, it was shown that the claimed governmental policy had not been enforced consistently....

The *Kent* Court had no occasion to consider whether the Executive had the power to revoke the passport of an individual whose *conduct* is damaging the national security and foreign policy of the United States. *Kent* involved denials of passports solely on the basis of political beliefs entitled to First Amendment protection. See *Aptheker v. Secretary of State,* 378 U.S. 500, 84 S.Ct. 1659, 12 L.Ed.2d 992 (1964).... The protection accorded beliefs standing alone is very different from the protection accorded conduct. Thus, in *Aptheker v. Secretary of State,* the Court held that a statute [a provision of the Subversive Control Act of 1950,] which, like the policy at issue in *Kent,* denied passports to Communists solely on the basis of political beliefs unconstitutionally "establishes an irrebuttable presumption that individuals who are members of the specified organizations will, if given passports, engage in activities inimical to the security of the United States." The Court recognized that the legitimacy of the objective of safeguarding our national security is "obvious and unarguable." The Court explained that the statute at issue was not the least restrictive alternative available: "The prohibition against travel is supported only by a tenuous relationship between the bare fact of organizational membership and the activity Congress sought to proscribe."

Beliefs and speech are only part of Agee's "campaign to fight the United States CIA." In that sense, this case contrasts markedly with the facts in *Kent* and *Aptheker.*[57] No presumptions, rebuttable or otherwise, are involved, for Agee's conduct in foreign countries presents a serious danger to American officials abroad and serious danger to the national security. We hold that the policy announced in the challenged regulations is "sufficiently substantial and consistent" to compel the conclusion that Congress has approved it. See *Zemel,* 381 U.S. at 12, 85 S.Ct. at 1279, 14 L.Ed.2d at 188.

Agee also attacks the Secretary's action on three constitutional grounds: first, that the revocation of his passport impermissibly burdens his freedom to travel; second, that the action was intended to penalize his exercise of free speech and deter his criticism of government policies and practices; and third, that failure to accord him a prerevocation hearing violated his Fifth Amendment right to procedural due process. In light of the express language of the passport regulations, which permits their application only in cases involving likelihood of "serious damage" to national security or foreign policy, these claims are without merit.

Revocation of a passport undeniably curtails travel, but the freedom to travel abroad with a "letter of introduction" in the form of a passport issued by the sovereign is subordinate to national security and foreign policy considerations; as such, it is subject to reasonable governmental regulation. The Court has made it plain that the *freedom* to travel outside the United States must be distinguished from the *right* to travel within the United States. [T]his Court has often pointed out the crucial difference between the freedom to travel internationally and the right of interstate travel.

---

57. The same is true of *Dayton v. Dulles,* 357 U.S. 144, 78 S.Ct. 1127, 2 L.Ed.2d 1221 (1958), the companion case to *Kent.* In *Dayton,* the Secretary refused to issue a passport to a physicist who sought to go to India to engage in experimental research. [T]he Secretary's "Decision and Findings" showed "only a denial of a passport for reasons which we have today held to be impermissible," citing *Kent.* The "Decision and Findings," set out in the Appendix to the Court's opinion, does not cite a single instance of Dayton's conduct, as distinguished from mere support for "the Communist movement" or association with known Communists.

The constitutional right of interstate travel is virtually unqualified. By contrast the "right" of international travel has been considered to be no more than an aspect of the "liberty" protected by the Due Process Clause of the Fifth Amendment. As such this "right," the Court has held, can be regulated within the bounds of due process. (Citations omitted.) *Califano v. Torres,* 435 U.S. 1, 4 n. 6, 98 S.Ct. 906, 908 n. 6, 55 L.Ed.2d 65.

Protection of the foreign policy of the United States is a governmental interest of great importance, since foreign policy and national security considerations cannot neatly be compartmentalized.

Measures to protect the secrecy of our Government's foreign intelligence operations plainly serve these interests.... Not only has Agee jeopardized the security of the United States, but he has endangered the interests of countries other than the United States—thereby creating serious problems for American foreign relations and foreign policy. Restricting Agee's foreign travel, although perhaps not certain to prevent all of Agee's harmful activities, is the only avenue open to the Government to limit these activities.

Assuming *arguendo* that First Amendment protections reach beyond our national boundaries, Agee's First Amendment claim has no foundation.... To the extent the revocation of his passport operates to inhibit Agee, "it is an inhibition of *action*," rather than of speech. Agee is as free to criticize the United States Government as he was when he held a passport—always subject, of course, to express limits on certain rights by virtue of his contract with the Government.

On this record, the Government is not required to hold a prerevocation hearing.... [W]hen there is a substantial likelihood of "serious damage" to national security or foreign policy as a result of a passport holder's activities in foreign countries, the Government may take action to ensure that the holder may not exploit the sponsorship of his travels by the United States.... The Constitution's due process guarantees call for no more than what has been accorded here: a statement of reasons and an opportunity for a prompt postrevocation hearing.

We reverse the judgment of the Court of Appeals and remand for further proceedings consistent with this opinion.

Reversed and remanded.

JUSTICE BLACKMUN, concurring.

There is some force, I feel, in JUSTICE BRENNAN's observations, that today's decision cannot be reconciled fully with all the reasoning of *Zemel v. Rusk* and, particularly, of *Kent v. Dulles,* and that the Court is cutting back somewhat upon the opinions in those cases *sub silentio*. I would have preferred to have the Court disavow forthrightly the aspects of *Zemel* and *Kent* that may suggest that evidence of a longstanding Executive policy or construction in this area is not probative of the issue of congressional authorization. Nonetheless, believing this is what the Court in effect has done, I join its opinion.

JUSTICE BRENNAN, with whom JUSTICE MARSHALL joins, dissenting.

[C]learly neither *Zemel* nor *Kent* holds that a longstanding Executive *policy* or *construction* is sufficient proof that Congress has implicitly authorized the Secretary's action. The cases hold that an administrative *practice* must be demonstrated; in fact *Kent* unequivocally states that mere *construction* by the Executive—no matter how longstanding and consistent—is *not* sufficient. The passage in *Kent* is worthy of full quotation:

> Under the 1926 Act and its predecessor a large body of precedents grew up which repeat over and again that the issuance of passports is "a discretionary act" on the part of the Secretary of State. The scholars, the courts, the Chief Executive, and the Attorneys General, all so said. This long-continued *executive construction* should be enough, it is said, to warrant the inference that Congress adopted it. But the key to that problem, as we shall see, is in the manner in which the Secretary's discretion was *exercised,* not in the *bare fact that he had discretion. Kent v. Dulles.*

The Court's requirement in *Kent* of evidence of the Executive's *exercise* of discretion as opposed to its possession of discretion may best be understood as a preference for the strongest proof that Congress knew of and acquiesced in that authority. The presence of sensitive constitutional questions in the passport revocation context cautions against applying the normal rule that administrative constructions in cases of statutory construction are to be given great weight. Only when Congress had maintained its silence in the face of a consistent and substantial pattern of actual passport denials or revocations—where the parties will presumably object loudly, perhaps through legal action, to the Secretary's exercise of discretion—can this Court be sure that Congress is aware of the Secretary's actions and has implicitly approved that exercise of discretion. [T]his case is a prime example of the adage that "bad facts make bad law." Philip Agee is hardly a model representative of our Nation. And the Executive Branch has attempted to use one of the only means at its disposal, revocation of a passport, to stop respondent's damaging statements. But just as the Constitution protects both popular and unpopular speech, it likewise protects both popular and unpopular travelers. And it is important to remember that this decision applies not only to Philip Agee, whose activities could be perceived as harming the national security, but also to other citizens who may merely disagree with Government foreign policy and express their views.[9] . . .

9. An excerpt from the Government's portion of the oral argument is particularly revealing:

"QUESTION: General McCree, supposing a person right now were to apply for a passport to go to Salvador, and when asked the purpose of his journey, to say, to denounce the United States policy in Salvador in supporting the junta. And the Secretary of State says, I just will not issue a passport for that purpose. Do you think that he can consistently do that in the light of our previous cases?

"SOLICITOR GENERAL McCREE: I would say, yes, he can. Because we have to vest these—The President of the United States and the Secretary of State working under him are charged with conducting the foreign policy of the Nation, and the freedom

Notes

1. *Califano v. Aznavorian,* 439 U.S. 170, 99 S.Ct. 471, 58 L.Ed.2d 435 (1978) upheld a federal statute that provided that certain federal benefits may not be paid for any month that the recipient spends entirely outside of the United States. The Court, without a dissent, rejected the argument that the federal law placed an unconstitutional burden on the right of international travel. While the right of interstate travel "is virtually unqualified," the " 'right' of international travel has been considered to be no more than an aspect of the 'liberty' protected by the Due Process Clause of the Fifth Amendment." Unless the Congressional limitation is "wholly irrational, it is constitutional in spite of its incidental effect on international travel."

2. *Regan v. Wald,* 468 U.S. 222, 104 S.Ct. 3026, 82 L.Ed.2d 171 (1984) upheld the constitutionality of regulations restricting certain travel to Cuba. The regulations did not permit general tourist or business travel but allowed certain types of travel, such as "official visits, news gathering, professional research, and visits to close relatives." Like *Zemel* (and unlike *Kent* or *Aptheker*), no citizen was denied a passport because of his political beliefs or associations, or any other characteristic peculiar to the plaintiff but rather because of foreign policy considerations affecting all citizens.

Plaintiffs argued that there was no emergency at the present time, but Rehnquist, J., for the Court explained that the holding in *Zemel* "was not tied to the Court's independent foreign policy analysis. Matters relating 'to the conduct of foreign relations ... are so exclusively entrusted to the political branches of governments as to be largely immune from judicial inquiry or interference.' [T]here is an adequate basis under the Due Process Clause of the Fifth Amendment to sustain the President's decision to curtail the flow of hard currency to Cuba—currency that could then be used in support of Cuban adventurism—by restricting travel."

8–3.4 Privacy and Sexual Autonomy

8–3.41 Sterilization

SKINNER v. OKLAHOMA EX REL. WILLIAMSON
316 U.S. 535, 62 S.Ct. 1110, 86 L.Ed. 1655 (1942).

Mr. Justice Douglas delivered the opinion of the Court.

This case touches a sensitive and important area of human rights. Oklahoma deprives certain individuals of a right which is basic to the perpetuation of a race—the right to have offspring. Oklahoma has decreed the enforcement of its law against petitioner, overruling his claim that it violated the Fourteenth Amendment. Because that decision raised grave and substantial constitutional questions, we granted the petition for certiorari.

The statute involved is Oklahoma's Habitual Criminal Sterilization Act. That Act defines an "habitual criminal" as a person who, having

of speech that we enjoy domestically may be different from that that we can exercise in this context."

The reach of the Secretary's discretion is potentially staggering.

been convicted two or more times for crimes "amounting to felonies involving moral turpitude," either in an Oklahoma court or in a court of any other State, is thereafter convicted of such a felony in Oklahoma and is sentenced to a term of imprisonment in an Oklahoma penal institution. Machinery is provided for the institution by the Attorney General of a proceeding against such a person in the Oklahoma courts for a judgment that such person shall be rendered sexually sterile. Notice, an opportunity to be heard, and the right to a jury trial are provided. The issues triable in such a proceeding are narrow and confined. If the court or jury finds that the defendant is an "habitual criminal" and that he "may be rendered sexually sterile without detriment to his or her general health," then the court "shall render judgment to the effect that said defendant be rendered sexually sterile" by the operation of vasectomy in case of a male, and of salpingectomy in case of a female. Only one other provision of the Act is material here, and that is § 195, which provides that "offenses arising out of the violation of the prohibitory laws, revenue acts, embezzlement, or political offenses, shall not come or be considered within the terms of this Act."

Petitioner was convicted in 1926 of the crime of stealing chickens, and was sentenced to the Oklahoma State Reformatory. In 1929 he was convicted of the crime of robbery with firearms, and was sentenced to the reformatory. In 1934 he was convicted again of robbery with firearms, and was sentenced to the penitentiary. He was confined there in 1935 when the Act was passed. In 1936 the Attorney General instituted proceedings against him. . . .

[This law fails] to meet the requirements of the equal protection clause of the Fourteenth Amendment. We do not stop to point out all of the inequalities in this Act. A few examples will suffice. In Oklahoma, grand larceny is a felony. Larceny is grand larceny when the property taken exceeds $20 in value. Embezzlement is punishable "in the manner prescribed for feloniously stealing property of the value of that embezzled." Hence, he who embezzles property worth more than $20 is guilty of a felony. A clerk who appropriates over $20 from his employer's till and a stranger who steals the same amount are thus both guilty of felonies. If the latter repeats his act and is convicted three times, he may be sterilized. But the clerk is not subject to the pains and penalties of the Act no matter how large his embezzlements nor how frequent his convictions. . . .

It was stated in *Buck v. Bell,* [274 U.S. 200, 47 S.Ct. 584, 71 L.Ed. 1000 (1927)], that the claim that state legislation violates the equal protection clause of the Fourteenth Amendment is "the usual last resort of constitutional arguments." Under our constitutional system the States in determining the reach and scope of particular legislation need not provide "abstract symmetry." [A] State is not constrained in the exercise of its police power to ignore experience which marks a class of offenders or a family of offenses for special treatment. Nor is it prevented by the equal protection clause from confining "its restrictions to those classes of cases where the need is deemed to be clearest." . . .

But the instant legislation runs afoul of the equal protection clause, though we give Oklahoma that large deference which the rule of the foregoing cases requires. We are dealing here with legislation which involves one of the basic civil rights of man. Marriage and procreation are fundamental to the very existence and survival of the race. The power to sterilize, if exercised, may have subtle, far-reaching and devastating effects. In evil or reckless hands it can cause races or types which are inimical to the dominant group to wither and disappear. There is no redemption for the individual whom the law touches. Any experiment which the State conducts is to his irreparable injury. He is forever deprived of a basic liberty. We mention these matters not to reexamine the scope of the police power of the States. We advert to them merely in emphasis of our view that strict scrutiny of the classification which a State makes in a sterilization law is essential, lest unwittingly, or otherwise, invidious discriminations are made against groups or types of individuals in violation of the constitutional guaranty of just and equal laws.... Sterilization of those who have thrice committed grand larceny, with immunity for those who are embezzlers, is a clear, pointed, unmistakable discrimination. Oklahoma makes no attempt to say that he who commits larceny by trespass or trick or fraud has biologically inheritable traits which he who commits embezzlement lacks. Oklahoma's line between larceny by fraud and embezzlement is determined, as we have noted, "with reference to the time when the fraudulent intent to convert the property to the taker's own use" arises. We have not the slightest basis for inferring that that line has any significance in eugenics, nor that the inheritability of criminal traits follows the neat legal distinctions which the law has marked between those two offenses. In terms of fines and imprisonment, the crimes of larceny and embezzlement rate the same under the Oklahoma code. Only when it comes to sterilization are the pains and penalties of the law different. The equal protection clause would indeed be a formula of empty words if such conspicuously artificial lines could be drawn.... If such a classification were permitted, the technical common law concept of a "trespass" based on distinctions which are "very largely dependent upon history for explanation" could readily become a rule of human genetics....

Reversed.

Mr. Chief Justice Stone, concurring:

I concur in the result, but I am not persuaded that we are aided in reaching it by recourse to the equal protection clause. If Oklahoma may resort generally to the sterilization of criminals on the assumption that their propensities are transmissible to future generations by inheritance, I seriously doubt that the equal protection clause requires it to apply the measure to all criminals in the first instance, or to none.

Moreover, if we must presume that the legislature knows—what science has been unable to ascertain—that the criminal tendencies of any class of habitual offenders are transmissible regardless of the varying mental characteristics of its individuals, I should suppose that we must likewise presume that the legislature, in its wisdom, knows that the criminal tendencies of some classes of offenders are more likely to be transmitted than those of others. And so I think the real question we have to consider is not one of equal protection, but whether the whole-sale condemnation of a class to such an invasion of personal liberty, without opportunity to any individual to show that his is not the type of case which would justify resort to it, satisfies the demands of due process.

... Although petitioner here was given a hearing to ascertain whether sterilization would be detrimental to his health, he was given none to discover whether his criminal tendencies are of an inheritable type. Undoubtedly a state may, after appropriate inquiry, constitutional-ly interfere with the personal liberty of the individual to prevent the transmission by inheritance of his socially injurious tendencies. *Buck v. Bell.* But until now we have not been called upon to say that it may do so without giving him a hearing and opportunity to challenge the existence as to him of the only facts which could justify so drastic a measure....

[The concurring opinion of JACKSON, J., is omitted.]

Notes

In *Buck v. Bell,* 274 U.S. 200, 47 S.Ct. 584, 71 L.Ed. 1000 (1927), cited in *Skinner,* the Court upheld the constitutionality of a Virginia statute that provided for the sterilization of "mental defectives" in state institutions after a finding by a hearing board that the mental defective "is the probable potential parent of socially inadequate offspring, likewise afflicted, that she may be sexually sterilized without detriment to her general health and that her welfare and that of society will be promoted by her sterilization." Justice Holmes, for the Court, said:

> We have seen more than once that the public welfare may call upon the best citizens for their lives. It would be strange if it could not call upon those who already sap the strength of the State for these lesser sacri-fices, often not felt to be such by those concerned, in order to prevent our being swamped with incompetence. It is better for all the world, if instead of waiting to execute degenerate offspring for crime, or to let them starve for their imbecility, society can prevent those who are manifestly unfit from continuing their kind. The principle that sustains compulsory vaccination is broad enough to cover cutting the Fallopian tubes. *Jacobson v. Massachusetts*, 197 U.S. 11, 25 S.Ct. 358, 49 L.Ed. 643 (1905). Three generations of imbeciles are enough.

Justice Butler filed, without opinion, the only dissent.

8–3.42 Contraception

GRISWOLD v. CONNECTICUT
381 U.S. 479, 85 S.Ct. 1678, 14 L.Ed.2d 510 (1965).

MR. JUSTICE DOUGLAS delivered the opinion of the Court.

Appellant Griswold is Executive Director of the Planned Parenthood League of Connecticut. Appellant Buxton is a licensed physician and a professor at the Yale Medical School who served as Medical Director for the League at its Center in New Haven—a center open and operating from November 1 to November 10, 1961, when appellants were arrested.

They gave information, instruction, and medical advice to *married persons* as to the means of preventing conception. They examined the wife and prescribed the best contraceptive device or material for her use. Fees were usually charged, although some couples were serviced free. [A Connecticut statute provides that it is a crime, punishable by a fine and imprisonment of up to one year, to use "any drug, medicinal article or instrument for the purpose of preventing conception;" another statute punishes an accessory as though he were a principal. Appellants were found guilty as accessories and fined $100 each.]

We think that appellants have standing to raise the constitutional rights of the married people with whom they had a professional relationship. [T]he accessory should have standing to assert that the offense which he is charged with assisting is not, or cannot constitutionally be, a crime. . . .

Coming to the merits, we are met with a wide range of questions that implicate the Due Process Clause of the Fourteenth Amendment. Overtones of some arguments suggest that *Lochner v. New York,* [§ 6–1, supra], should be our guide. But we decline that invitation. . . . We do not sit as a super-legislature to determine the wisdom, need, and propriety of laws that touch economic problems, business affairs, or social conditions. This law, however, operates directly on an intimate relation of husband and wife and their physician's role in one aspect of that relation. . . .

By *Pierce v. Society of Sisters,* [268 U.S. 510, 45 S.Ct. 571, 69 L.Ed. 1070 (1925)], the right to educate one's children as one chooses is made applicable to the States by the force of the First and Fourteenth Amendments. By *Meyer v. Nebraska,* [262 U.S. 390, 43 S.Ct. 625, 67 L.Ed. 1042 (1923)], the same dignity is given the right to study the German language in a private school. In other words, the State may not, consistent with the spirit of the First Amendment, contract the spectrum of available knowledge. . . . Without those peripheral rights the specific rights would be less secure. And so we reaffirm the principle of the *Pierce* and the *Meyer* cases. In *NAACP v. Alabama,* 357 U.S. 449, 462, 78 S.Ct. 1163, 1172, we protected the "freedom to associate and privacy in one's associations," noting that freedom of association was a peripheral First Amendment right. Disclosure of membership lists of a constitutionally valid association, we held, was invalid "as entailing the likelihood of a substantial restraint upon the exercise by petitioner's members of their right to freedom of association." In other words, the First Amendment has a penumbra where privacy is protected from governmental intrusion. . . .

The foregoing cases suggest that specific guarantees in the Bill of Rights have penumbras, formed by emanations from those guarantees that help give them life and substance. Various guarantees create zones of privacy. The right of association contained in the penumbra of the First Amendment is one, as we have seen. The Third Amendment in its prohibition against the quartering of soldiers "in any house" in time of peace without the consent of the owner is another facet of that privacy. The Fourth Amendment explicitly affirms the "right of the people to be secure in their persons, houses, papers, and effects, against unreasonable searches and seizures." The Fifth Amendment in its Self–Incrimination Clause enables the citizen to create a zone of privacy which government may not force him to surrender to his detriment. The Ninth Amendment provides: "The enumeration in the Constitution, of certain rights, shall not be construed to deny or disparage others retained by the people." ... We have had many controversies over these penumbral rights of "privacy and repose." See, e.g., *Skinner v. Oklahoma*. These cases bear witness that the right of privacy which presses for recognition here is a legitimate one.

The present case, then, concerns a relationship lying within the zone of privacy created by several fundamental constitutional guarantees. And it concerns a law which, in forbidding the *use* of contraceptives rather than regulating their manufacture or sale, seeks to achieve its goals by means having a maximum destructive impact upon that relationship. Such a law cannot stand in light of the familiar principle, so often applied by this Court, that a "governmental purpose to control or prevent activities constitutionally subject to state regulation may not be achieved by means which sweep unnecessarily broadly and thereby invade the area of protected freedoms." *NAACP v. Alabama*. Would we allow the police to search the sacred precincts of marital bedrooms for telltale signs of the use of contraceptives? The very idea is repulsive to the notions of privacy surrounding the marriage relationship.

We deal with a right of privacy older than the Bill of Rights—older than our political parties, older than our school system. Marriage is a coming together for better or for worse, hopefully enduring, and intimate to the degree of being sacred. It is an association that promotes a way of life, not causes; a harmony in living, not political faiths; a bilateral loyalty, not commercial or social projects. Yet it is an association for as noble a purpose as any involved in our prior decisions.

Reversed.

MR. JUSTICE GOLDBERG, whom THE CHIEF JUSTICE [WARREN] and MR. JUSTICE BRENNAN join, concurring.

... In reaching the conclusion that the right of marital privacy is protected, as being within the protected penumbra of specific guarantees of the Bill of Rights, the Court refers to the Ninth Amendment. I add these words to emphasize the relevance of that Amendment to the Court's holding.... This Court, in a series of decisions, has held that the Fourteenth Amendment absorbs and applies to the States those specifics of the first eight amendments which express fundamental personal rights. The language and history of the Ninth Amendment reveal that the Framers of the Constitution believed that there are additional fundamental rights, protected from governmental infringement, which exist alongside those fundamental rights specifically mentioned in the first eight constitutional amendments.... The Amendment is almost entirely the work of James Madison. It was introduced in Congress by him and passed the House and Senate with little or no debate and virtually no change in language. It was proffered to quiet expressed fears that a bill of specifically enumerated rights could not be sufficiently broad to cover all essential rights and that the specific mention of certain rights would be interpreted as a denial that others were protected....

While this Court has had little occasion to interpret the Ninth Amendment, "[i]t cannot be presumed that any clause in the constitution is intended to be without effect." *Marbury v. Madison*. ... To hold that a right so basic and fundamental and so deep-rooted in our society as the right of privacy in marriage may be infringed because that right is not guaranteed in so many words by the first eight amendments to the Constitution is to ignore the Ninth Amendment and to give it no effect whatsoever. [A] judicial construction that this fundamental right is not protected by the Constitution because it is not mentioned in explicit terms by one of the first eight amendments or elsewhere in the Constitution would violate the Ninth Amendment, which specifically states that "[t]he enumeration in the Constitution, of certain rights, shall not be *construed* to deny or disparage others retained by the people." (Emphasis added.)

A dissenting opinion suggests that my interpretation of the Ninth Amendment somehow "broaden[s] the powers of this Court." [But] I do not mean to imply that the Ninth Amendment is applied against the States by the Fourteenth. Nor do I mean to state that the Ninth Amendment constitutes an independent source of rights protected from infringement by either the States or the Federal Government. Rather, the Ninth Amendment shows a belief of the Constitution's authors that fundamental rights exist that are not expressly enumerated in the first eight amendments and an intent that the list of rights included there not be deemed exhaustive.... I do not see how this broadens the authority of the Court; rather it serves to support what this Court has been doing in protecting fundamental rights.

Nor am I turning somersaults with history in arguing that the Ninth Amendment is relevant in a case dealing with a *State's* infringement of a fundamental right. While the Ninth Amendment—and indeed the entire Bill of Rights—originally concerned restrictions upon *federal* power, the subsequently enacted Fourteenth Amendment prohibits the States as well from abridging fundamental personal liberties. And, the Ninth Amendment, in indicating that not all such liberties are specifically mentioned in the first eight amendments, is surely relevant in showing the existence of other fundamental personal rights, now protected from state, as well as federal, infringement. In sum, the Ninth Amendment simply lends strong support to the view that the "liberty" protected by the Fifth and Fourteenth Amendments from infringement by the Federal Government or the States is not restricted to rights specifically mentioned in the first eight amendments.

In determining which rights are fundamental, judges are not left at large to decide cases in light of their personal and private notions. Rather, they must look to the "traditions and [collective] conscience of our people" to determine whether a principle is "so rooted [there] . . . as to be ranked as fundamental." . . . "Liberty" also "gains content from the emanations of . . . specific [constitutional] guarantees" and "from experience with the requirements of a free society." *Poe v. Ullman,* 367 U.S. 497, 517, 81 S.Ct. 1752, 1763, 6 L.Ed.2d 989 (dissenting opinion of MR. JUSTICE DOUGLAS).[7]

I agree fully with the Court that, applying these tests, the right of privacy is a fundamental personal right, emanating "from the totality of the constitutional scheme under which we live." . . . The Connecticut statutes here involved deal with a particularly important and sensitive area of privacy—that of the marital relation and the marital home. . . .

I agree with MR. JUSTICE HARLAN's statement in his dissenting opinion in *Poe v. Ullman,* 367 U.S. 497, 551–552, 81 S.Ct. 1752, 1781: "Certainly the safeguarding of the home does not follow merely from the sanctity of property rights. The home derives its pre-eminence as the seat of family life. And the integrity of that life is something so fundamental that it has been found to draw to its protection the principles of more than one explicitly granted Constitutional right. . . . Of this whole 'private realm of family life' it is difficult to imagine what is more private or more intimate than a husband and wife's marital relations." . . .

The logic of the dissents would sanction federal or state legislation that seems to me even more plainly unconstitutional than the statute before us. Surely the Government, absent a showing of a compelling subordinating state interest, could not decree that all husbands and wives must be sterilized after two children have been born to them. Yet by their reasoning such an invasion of marital privacy would not be subject to constitutional challenge because, while it might be "silly," no provision of the Constitution specifically prevents the Government from curtailing the marital right to bear children and raise a family. While it may shock some of my Brethren that the Court today holds that the Constitution protects the right of marital privacy, in my view it is far more shocking to believe that the personal liberty guaranteed by the Constitution does not include protection against such totalitarian limitation of family size, which is at complete variance with our constitutional concepts. Yet, if upon a showing of a slender basis of rationality, a law outlawing voluntary birth control by married persons is valid, then, by the same reasoning, a law requiring compulsory birth control also would seem to be valid. In my view, however, both types of law would

7. In light of the tests enunciated in these cases it cannot be said that a judge's responsibility to determine whether a right is basic and fundamental in this sense vests him with unrestricted personal discretion. . . .

unjustifiably intrude upon rights of marital privacy which are constitutionally protected. . . .

Although the Connecticut birth-control law obviously encroaches upon a fundamental personal liberty, the State does not show that the law serves any "subordinating [state] interest which is compelling" or that it is "necessary . . . to the accomplishment of a permissible state policy." The State, at most, argues that there is some rational relation between this statute and what is admittedly a legitimate subject of state concern—the discouraging of extra-marital relations. . . . The rationality of this justification is dubious, particularly in light of the admitted widespread availability to all persons in the State of Connecticut, unmarried as well as married, of birth-control devices for the prevention of disease, as distinguished from the prevention of conception. . . . The State of Connecticut does have statutes, the constitutionality of which is beyond doubt, which prohibit adultery and fornication. These statutes demonstrate that means for achieving the same basic purpose of protecting marital fidelity are available to Connecticut without the need to "invade the area of protected freedoms."

Finally, it should be said of the Court's holding today that it in no way interferes with a State's proper regulation of sexual promiscuity or misconduct. As my Brother Harlan so well stated in his dissenting opinion in *Poe v. Ullman,* supra, 367 U.S. at 553, 81 S.Ct. at 1782:

> Adultery, homosexuality and the like are sexual intimacies which the State forbids . . . but the intimacy of husband and wife is necessarily an essential and accepted feature of the institution of marriage, an institution which the State not only must allow, but which always and in every age it has fostered and protected. It is one thing when the State exerts its power either to forbid extra-marital sexuality . . . or to say who may marry, but it is quite another when, having acknowledged a marriage and the intimacies inherent in it, it undertakes to regulate by means of the criminal law the details of that intimacy. . . .

MR. JUSTICE HARLAN, concurring in the judgment. . . .

In my view, the proper constitutional inquiry in this case is whether this Connecticut statute infringes the Due Process Clause of the Fourteenth Amendment because the enactment violates basic values "implicit in the concept of ordered liberty," *Palko v. Connecticut,* 302 U.S. 319, 325, 58 S.Ct. 149, 152, 82 L.Ed. 288. For reasons stated at length in my dissenting opinion in *Poe v. Ullman,* supra, I believe that it does. While the relevant inquiry may be aided by resort to one or more of the provisions of the Bill of Rights, it is not dependent on them or any of their radiations. The Due Process Clause of the Fourteenth Amendment stands, in my opinion, on its own bottom. . . .

While I could not more heartily agree that judicial "self restraint" is an indispensable ingredient of sound constitutional adjudication, I do submit that the formula suggested [by the dissent] for achieving it is more hollow than real. "Specific" provisions of the Constitution, no less than "due process," lend themselves as readily to "personal" interpretations by judges whose constitutional outlook is simply to keep the Constitution in supposed "tune with the times". Need one go further than to recall last Term's reapportionment cases, *Wesberry v. Sanders,* 376 U.S. 1, 84 S.Ct. 526, 11 L.Ed.2d 481 and *Reynolds v. Sims,* [§ 8–3.21, supra], where a majority of the Court "interpreted" "by the People" (Art. I, § 2) and "equal protection" (Amdt. 14) to command "one person, one vote," an interpretation that was made in the face of irrefutable and still unanswered history to the contrary?

Judicial self-restraint will not, I suggest, be brought about in the "due process" area by the historically unfounded incorporation formula long advanced by my Brother Black, and now in part espoused by my Brother Stewart. It will be achieved in this area, as in other constitutional areas, only by continual insistence upon respect for the teachings of history, solid recognition of the basic values that underlie our society, and wise appreciation of the great roles that the doctrines of federalism and separation of powers have played in establishing and preserving American freedoms. . . .

Mr. Justice White, concurring in the judgment.

[S]tatutes regulating sensitive areas of liberty do, under the cases of this Court, require "strict scrutiny," *Skinner v. Oklahoma,* and "must be viewed in the light of less drastic means for achieving the same basic purpose." [N]othing in this record justif[ies] the sweeping scope of this statute, with its telling effect on the freedoms of married persons, and therefore conclude that it deprives such persons of liberty without due process of law.

Mr. Justice Black, with whom Mr. Justice Stewart joins, dissenting. . . .

The Court talks about a constitutional "right of privacy" as though there is some constitutional provision or provisions forbidding any law ever to be passed which might abridge the "privacy" of individuals. But there is not. There are, of course, guarantees in certain specific constitutional provisions which are designed in part to protect privacy at certain times and places with respect to certain activities. Such, for example, is the Fourth Amendment's guarantee against "unreasonable searches and seizures." But I think it belittles that Amendment to talk about it as though it protects nothing but "privacy." To treat it that way is to give it a niggardly interpretation, not the kind of liberal reading I think any Bill of Rights provision should be given. The average man would very likely not have his feelings soothed any more by having his property seized openly than by having it seized privately and by stealth. He simply wants his property left alone. And a person can be just as much, if not more, irritated, annoyed and injured by an unceremonious public arrest by a policeman as he is by a seizure in the privacy of his office or home.

One of the most effective ways of diluting or expanding a constitutionally guaranteed right is to substitute for the crucial word or words of a constitutional guarantee another word or words, more or less flexible and more or less restricted in meaning. This fact is well illustrated by the use of the term "right of privacy" as a comprehensive substitute for the Fourth Amendment's guarantee against "unreasonable searches and seizures." ... I like my privacy as well as the next one, but I am nevertheless compelled to admit that government has a right to invade it unless prohibited by some specific constitutional provision. For these reasons I cannot agree with the Court's judgment and the reasons it gives for holding this Connecticut law unconstitutional....

The due process argument which my Brothers HARLAN and WHITE adopt here is based, as their opinions indicate, on the premise that this Court is vested with power to invalidate all state laws that it considers to be arbitrary, capricious, unreasonable, or oppressive, or on this Court's belief that a particular state law under scrutiny has no "rational or justifying" purpose, or is offensive to a "sense of fairness and justice." If these formulas based on "natural justice," or others which mean the same thing, are to prevail, they require judges to determine what is or is not constitutional on the basis of their own appraisal of what laws are unwise or unnecessary. The power to make such decisions is of course that of a legislative body....

Of the cases on which my Brothers WHITE and GOLDBERG rely so heavily, undoubtedly the reasoning of two of them supports their result here—as would that of a number of others which they do not bother to name, e.g., *Lochner v. New York*.... The two they do cite and quote from, *Meyer v. Nebraska,* and *Pierce v. Society of Sisters,* were both decided in opinions by MR. JUSTICE McREYNOLDS which elaborated the same natural law due process philosophy found in *Lochner v. New York,* supra, one of the cases on which he relied in *Meyer,* along with such other long-discredited decisions as, e.g., *Adkins v. Children's Hospital....* [7]

My Brother GOLDBERG has adopted the recent discovery that the Ninth Amendment as well as the Due Process Clause can be used by this Court as authority to strike down all state legislation which this Court thinks violates "fundamental principles of liberty and justice," or is contrary to the "traditions and [collective] conscience of our people." He also states, without proof satisfactory to me, that in making decisions on this basis judges will not consider "their personal and private notions." One may ask how they can avoid considering them. Our Court certainly has no machinery with which to take a Gallup Poll. And the scientific miracles of this age have not yet produced a gadget which the Court can use to determine what traditions are rooted in the "[collective] conscience of our people." [The Ninth] Amendment was passed, not to broaden the powers of this Court or any other department of "the

7. In *Meyer,* in the very same sentence quoted in part by my Brethren in which he asserted that the Due Process Clause gave an abstract and inviolable right "to marry, establish a home and bring up children," Mr. Justice McReynolds also asserted the heretofore discredited doctrine that the Due Process Clause prevented States from interfering with "the right of the individual to contract."

General Government," but, as every student of history knows, to assure the people that the Constitution in all its provisions was intended to limit the Federal Government to the powers granted expressly or by necessary implication. [F]or a period of a century and a half no serious suggestion was ever made that the Ninth Amendment, enacted to protect state powers against federal invasion, could be used as a weapon of federal power to prevent state legislatures from passing laws they consider appropriate to govern local affairs.

The Due Process Clause with an "arbitrary and capricious" or "shocking to the conscience" formula was liberally used by this Court to strike down economic legislation in the early decades of this century, threatening, many people thought, the tranquility and stability of the Nation. See, e.g., *Lochner v. New York.* That formula based on subjective considerations of "natural justice," is no less dangerous when used to enforce this Court's views about personal rights than those about economic rights. I had thought that we had laid that formula, as a means for striking down state legislation, to rest once and for all in cases like *West Coast Hotel Co. v. Parrish,* [§ 6–1, supra]....

MR. JUSTICE STEWART, whom MR. JUSTICE BLACK joins, dissenting.

Since 1879 Connecticut has had on its books a law which forbids the use of contraceptives by anyone. I think this is an uncommonly silly law.... But we are not asked in this case to say whether we think this law is unwise, or even asinine. We are asked to hold that it violates the United States Constitution. And that I cannot do.... It is the essence of judicial duty to subordinate our own personal views, our own ideas of what legislation is wise and what is not. If, as I should surely hope, the law before us does not reflect the standards of the people of Connecticut, the people of Connecticut can freely exercise their true Ninth and Tenth Amendment rights to persuade their elected representatives to repeal it. That is the constitutional way to take this law off the books.[8]

Notes

1. *Eisenstadt v. Baird,* 405 U.S. 438, 92 S.Ct. 1029, 31 L.Ed.2d 349 (1972) invalidated a Massachusetts law that made it a crime to sell or distribute any contraceptive drug or device; however, physicians could administer or prescribe contraceptives for *married* persons and pharmacists could fill prescriptions for contraceptives for *married* persons. Under the statutory scheme, single persons could not obtain contraceptives from anyone to prevent pregnancy, but married or single persons could obtain contraceptives from anyone to prevent, not pregnancy, but the spread of disease. Brennan, J., for the Court invalidated the statute:

> If under *Griswold* the distribution of contraceptives to married persons cannot be prohibited, a ban on distribution to unmarried persons would be equally impermissible. It is true that in *Griswold* the right of privacy in question inhered in the marital relationship. Yet the marital couple is

8. The Connecticut House of Representatives recently passed a bill (House Bill No. 2462) repealing the birth control law. The State Senate has apparently not yet acted on the measure, and today is relieved of that responsibility by the Court.

not an independent entity with a mind and heart of its own, but an association of two individuals each with a separate intellectual and emotional makeup. If the right of privacy means anything, it is the right of the *individual,* married or single, to be free from unwarranted governmental intrusion into matters so fundamentally affecting a person as the decision whether to bear or beget a child. On the other hand, if *Griswold* is no bar to a prohibition on the distribution of contraceptives, the State could not, consistently with the Equal Protection Clause, outlaw distribution to unmarried but not to married persons. In each case the evil, as perceived by the State, would be identical, and the underinclusion would be invidious.... We hold that by providing dissimilar treatment for married and unmarried persons who are similarly situated, Massachusetts General Laws Ann., c. 272, §§ 21 and 21A, violate the Equal Protection Clause.

2. *Carey v. Population Services Int'l,* 431 U.S. 678, 97 S.Ct. 2010, 52 L.Ed.2d 675 (1977) invalidated, insofar as it applied to nonprescription contraceptives, a New York law making it a crime: (1) for any person to sell or distribute any contraceptive to a minor under the age of 16; (2) for anyone other than a licensed pharmacist to distribute contraceptives to persons 16 or older; and (3) for anyone, including licensed pharmacists, to advertise or display contraceptives. Relying on *Griswold,* and *Eisenstadt,* the Court invalidated the prohibition on the distribution of nonprescription contraceptives to adults except through licensed physicians. It also invalidated the restrictions on advertising as a violation of free speech. However, there was no opinion for the Court invalidating the New York law as it applied to the distribution of nonprescription contraceptives to those under 16.

Brennan, J., joined by Stewart, Marshall, and Blackmun, JJ., argued that the state may not affect the privacy interests even of minors unless the restrictions serve significant state interests. White, J., concurred because the state did not demonstrate that the state law would measurably deter early sexual activity. Powell, J., objected to "subjecting restrictions on the sexual activity of the young to heightened judicial review," but agreed to invalidate the law because it infringed on the privacy interests of married females between 14 and 16 (a 14 year old female could marry in New York with the consent of her parents and a family court judge), and it interfered with the parents' authority over their children (the law prohibited even parents from distributing contraceptives to their children). He emphasized that the states "have broad latitude to legislate with respect to adolescents" and he would allow the state to encourage minors to seek the advice of their parents before engaging in sexual intercourse. Stevens, J., believed that the statute violated due process by forcing minors who engage in sexual activities to bear children. Burger, C.J., and Rehnquist, J., dissented.

3. MARRIAGE AS A FUNDAMENTAL RIGHT. *Loving v. Virginia,* 388 U.S. 1, 87 S.Ct. 1817, 18 L.Ed.2d 1010 (1967) invalidated a Virginia law that made it a crime for whites to marry nonwhites. (The Virginia statute made an exception for the "descendants of John Rolfe and Pocahontas.") Warren, C.J., for the Court, held that antimiscegenation law violated Equal Protection. "There can be no doubt that restricting the freedom to marry solely because of racial classifications violates the central meaning of the Equal Protection Clause." Warren went on to hold that this law also violated Due Process.

"The freedom to marry has long been recognized as one of the vital personal rights essential to the orderly pursuit of happiness by free men. Marriage is one of the 'basic civil rights of man,' fundamental to our very existence and survival. *Skinner v. Oklahoma.* To deny this fundamental freedom on so unsupportable a basis as the racial classifications embodied in these statutes, classifications so directly subversive of the principle of equality at the heart of the Fourteenth Amendment, is surely to deprive all the State's citizens of liberty without due process of law." Stewart, J. concurred in the judgment of the Court because of his belief that "it is simply not possible for a state law to be valid under our Constitution which makes the criminality of an act depend upon the race of the actor."

In *Zablocki v. Redhail,* 434 U.S. 374, 98 S.Ct. 673, 54 L.Ed.2d 618 (1978), Marshall, J., for the Court, relied on *Loving* to invalidate a Wisconsin law that required that any Wisconsin resident "having minor issue not in his custody and which he is under obligation to support by any court order or judgment" could not marry without first obtaining a court order granting permission. The Wisconsin court, in turn, could not grant permission unless the marriage applicant submitted proof of compliance with any support obligation and demonstrated that the children covered by the support order were not likely thereafter to become public charges. Marshall reasoned that because marriage is a fundamental right, a statutory classification that "significantly interferes" with its exercise must fall unless "it is supported by sufficiently important state interests and is closely tailored to effectuate only those interests." The "collection device" rationale is not narrowly tailored. It provides no money to the applicant's prior children if the applicant is unable to meet the statutory requirements; the state has more direct means of collecting the money, such as civil contempt proceedings; the law does not limit new financial commitments other than those arising out of the contemplated marriage; and the new spouse may improve the applicant's financial situation.

The Court distinguished *Califano v. Jobst,* 434 U.S. 47, 98 S.Ct. 95, 54 L.Ed.2d 228 (1977), which had upheld provisions of the Social Security Act that affected the freedom to marry. That Act provided for termination of a dependent child's benefits upon marriage to an individual not entitled to benefits under the law. In *Jobst,* a permanently disabled individual had his benefits terminated because he married an equally disabled woman who was not a beneficiary under the Act. Although the Social Security Act thus imposed a financial disincentive to marriage, *Zablocki* explained that it "placed no direct legal obstacle" to the marriage. Stevens, J., concurring in the judgment, argued that a "classification based on marital status is fundamentally different from a classification which determines who may lawfully enter into the marriage relationship." He would distinguish laws "prohibiting marriage to a child, a close relative, or a person afflicted with venereal disease . . . . "

Turner v. Safley, 482 U.S. 78, 107 S.Ct. 2254, 96 L.Ed.2d 64 (1987), invalidated a prison regulation that, in effect, permitted a prison inmate to marry only when there is already a pregnancy or the birth of an illegitimate child. *Zablocki* applied to prison inmates, the Court said, but even under a reasonable relationship test this marriage regulation would not withstand scrutiny. There is no reason to believe, for example, that the marriage prohibition prevented love triangles: "surely in [a] prison housing both male and female prisoners [as in this case], inmate rivalries are as likely to develop without a formal marriage ceremony as with one." The Court distinguished a case that prohibited marriages of inmates sentenced to life imprisonment because there was not the same expectation that the marriage "ultimately will be fully consummated," and "denial of the [marriage] right was part of the punishment for crime."

8–3.43 Abortion

ROE v. WADE
410 U.S. 113, 93 S.Ct. 705, 35 L.Ed.2d 147 (1973).

Mr. Justice Blackmun delivered the opinion of the Court.

This Texas federal appeal and its Georgia companion, *Doe v. Bolton,* [410 U.S. 179, 93 S.Ct. 739, 35 L.Ed.2d 201,] present constitutional challenges to state criminal abortion legislation. We forthwith acknowledge our awareness of the sensitive and emotional nature of the abortion controversy, of the vigorous opposing views, even among physicians, and of the deep and seemingly absolute convictions that the subject inspires.... In addition, population growth, pollution, poverty, and racial overtones tend to complicate and not to simplify the problem....

The Texas statutes that concern us here ... make it a crime to "procure an abortion," as therein defined, or to attempt one, except with respect to "an abortion procured or attempted by medical advice for the purpose of saving the life of the mother." Similar statutes are in existence in a majority of the States....

Jane Roe. Despite the use of the pseudonym, no suggestion is made that Roe is a fictitious person. For purposes of her case, we accept as true, and as established, her existence; her pregnant state, as of the inception of her suit in March 1970 and as late as May 21 of that year when she filed an alias affidavit with the District Court; and her inability to obtain a legal abortion in Texas....

The appellee notes, however, that the record does not disclose that Roe was pregnant at the time of the District Court hearing on May 22, 1970, or on the following June 17 when the court's opinion and judgment were filed. And he suggests that Roe's case must now be moot because she and all other members of her class are no longer subject to any 1970 pregnancy.

The usual rule in federal cases is that an actual controversy must exist at stages of appellate or certiorari review, and not simply at the date the action is initiated. But when, as here, pregnancy is a significant fact in the litigation, the normal 266–day human gestation period is so short that the pregnancy will come to term before the usual appellate process is complete. If that termination makes a case moot, pregnancy litigation seldom will survive much beyond the trial stage, and appellate review will be effectively denied. Our law should not be that rigid.

Pregnancy often comes more than once to the same woman, and in the general population, if man is to survive, it will always be with us. Pregnancy provides a classic justification for a conclusion of nonmootness. It truly could be "capable of repetition, yet evading review." We, therefore, agree with the District Court that Jane Roe had standing to undertake this litigation, that she presented a justiciable controversy, and that the termination of her 1970 pregnancy has not rendered her case moot. . . .

The principal thrust of appellant's attack on the Texas statutes is that they improperly invade a right, said to be possessed by the pregnant woman, to choose to terminate her pregnancy. Appellant would discover this right in the concept of personal "liberty" embodied in the Fourteenth Amendment's Due Process Clause; or in personal, marital, familial, and sexual privacy said to be protected by the Bill of Rights or its penumbras, see *Griswold v. Connecticut,* or among those rights reserved to the people by the Ninth Amendment, *Griswold v. Connecticut,* (Goldberg, J., concurring). Before addressing this claim, we feel it desirable briefly to survey, in several aspects, the history of abortion, for such insight as that history may afford us, and then to examine the state purposes and interests behind the criminal abortion laws.

It perhaps is not generally appreciated that the restrictive criminal abortion laws in effect in a majority of States today are of relatively recent vintage. Those laws, generally proscribing abortion or its attempt at any time during pregnancy except when necessary to preserve the pregnant woman's life, are not of ancient or even of common-law origin. Instead, they derive from statutory changes effected, for the most part, in the latter half of the 19th century.

[In a lengthy historical section the Court noted, inter alia, that at the time of the Persian Empire criminal abortions were severely punished, but "abortion was practiced in Greek times as well as in the Roman Era, and that 'it was resorted to without scruple,' "notwithstanding the Hippocratic Oath forbidding abortions. At common law "abortion performed *before* 'quickening'—the first recognizable movement of the fetus *in utero,* appearing usually from the 16th to the 18th week of pregnancy—was not an indictable offense." After quickening it was either a felony or a lesser crime.]

Three reasons have been advanced to explain historically the enactment of criminal abortion laws in the 19th century and to justify their continued existence. It has been argued occasionally that these laws were the product of a Victorian social concern to discourage illicit sexual conduct. Texas, however, does not advance this justification in the present case, and it appears that no court or commentator has taken the argument seriously. . . .

A second reason is concerned with abortion as a medical procedure. When most criminal abortion laws were first enacted, the procedure was a hazardous one for the woman. . . . Appellants and various *amici* refer to medical data indicating that abortion in early pregnancy, that is, prior to the end of the first trimester, although not without its risk, is now relatively safe. Mortality rates for women undergoing early abortions, where the procedure is legal, appear to be as low as or lower than the rates for normal childbirth. Consequently, any interest of the State in protecting the woman from an inherently hazardous procedure, except when it would be equally dangerous for her to forgo it, has largely disappeared. Of course, important state interests in the areas of health and medical standards do remain. The State has a legitimate interest in seeing to it that abortion, like any other medical procedure, is performed under circumstances that insure maximum safety for the patient. This interest obviously extends at least to the performing physician and his staff, to the facilities involved, to the availability of after-care, and to adequate provision for any complication or emergency that might arise. The prevalence of high mortality rates at illegal "abortion mills" strengthens, rather than weakens, the State's interest in regulating the conditions under which abortions are performed. Moreover, the risk to the woman increases as her pregnancy continues. Thus, the State retains a definite interest in protecting the woman's own health and safety when an abortion is proposed at a late stage of pregnancy.

The third reason is the State's interest—some phrase it in terms of duty—in protecting prenatal life. Some of the argument for this justification rests on the theory that a new human life is present from the moment of conception. The State's interest and general obligation to protect life then extends, it is argued, to prenatal life. Only when the life of the pregnant mother herself is at stake, balanced against the life she carries within her, should the interest of the embryo or fetus not prevail. Logically, of course, a legitimate state interest in this area need not stand or fall on acceptance of the belief that life begins at conception or at some other point prior to live birth. In assessing the State's interest, recognition may be given to the less rigid claim that as long as at least *potential* life is involved, the State may assert interests beyond the protection of the pregnant woman alone. . . .

The Constitution does not explicitly mention any right of privacy. In a line of decisions, however, . . . the Court has recognized that a right of personal privacy, or a guarantee of certain areas or zones of privacy, does exist under the Constitution. . . . These decisions make it clear that only personal rights that can be deemed "fundamental" or "implicit in the concept of ordered liberty," *Palko v. Connecticut,* 302 U.S. 319, 325, 58 S.Ct. 149, 152, 82 L.Ed. 288 (1937), are included in this guarantee of personal privacy. They also make it clear that the right has some extension to activities relating to marriage, *Loving v. Virginia,* [§ 8–3.42]; procreation, *Skinner v. Oklahoma,* [§ 8–3.41]; contraception, *Eisenstadt v. Baird,* [§ 8–3.42]; family relationships, *Prince v. Massachusetts,* 321 U.S. 158, 166, 64 S.Ct. 438, 442, 88 L.Ed. 645 (1944); and child rearing and education, *Pierce v. Society of Sisters,* 268 U.S. 510, 535, 45 S.Ct. 571, 573, 69 L.Ed. 1070 (1925), *Meyer v. Nebraska,* [262 U.S. 390, 43 S.Ct. 625, 67 L.Ed. 1042 (1923)].

This right of privacy, whether it be founded in the Fourteenth Amendment's concept of personal liberty and restrictions upon state action, as we feel it is, or, as the District Court determined, in the Ninth Amendment's reservation of rights to the people, is broad enough to encompass a woman's decision whether or not to terminate her pregnancy. The detriment that the State would impose upon the pregnant woman by denying this choice altogether is apparent. Specific and direct harm medically diagnosable even in early pregnancy may be involved. Maternity, or additional offspring, may force upon the woman a distressful life and future. Psychological harm may be imminent. Mental and physical health may be taxed by child care. There is also the distress, for all concerned, associated with the unwanted child, and there is the problem of bringing a child into a family already unable, psychologically and otherwise, to care for it. In other cases, as in this one, the additional difficulties and continuing stigma of unwed motherhood may be involved. All these are factors the woman and her responsible physician necessarily will consider in consultation.

On the basis of elements such as these, appellant and some *amici* argue that the woman's right is absolute and that she is entitled to terminate her pregnancy at whatever time, in whatever way, and for whatever reason she alone chooses. With this we do not agree. [A] State may properly assert important interests in safeguarding health, in maintaining medical standards, and in protecting potential life. At some point in pregnancy, these respective interests become sufficiently compelling to sustain regulation of the factors that govern the abortion decision. The privacy right involved, therefore, cannot be said to be absolute. In fact, it is not clear to us that the claim asserted by some *amici* that one has an unlimited right to do with one's body as one pleases bears a close relationship to the right of privacy previously articulated in the Court's decisions. The Court has refused to recognize an unlimited right of this kind in the past. *Jacobson v. Massachusetts,* 197 U.S. 11, 25 S.Ct. 358, 49 L.Ed. 643 (1905)(vaccination); *Buck v. Bell,* 274 U.S. 200, 47 S.Ct. 584, 71 L.Ed. 1000 (1927)(sterilization).

We, therefore, conclude that the right of personal privacy includes the abortion decision, but that this right is not unqualified and must be considered against important state interests in regulation.... Where certain "fundamental rights" are involved, the Court has held that regulation limiting these rights may be justified only by a "compelling state interest," *Kramer v. Union Free School District,* 395 U.S. 621, 89 S.Ct. 1886, 23 L.Ed.2d 583 (1969), and that legislative enactments must be narrowly drawn to express only the legitimate state interests at stake. *Griswold v. Connecticut....*

The appellee and certain *amici* argue that the fetus is a "person" within the language and meaning of the Fourteenth Amendment. In support of this, they outline at length and in detail the well-known facts of fetal development. If this suggestion of personhood is established, the appellant's case, of course, collapses, for the fetus' right to life would then be guaranteed specifically by the Amendment. The appellant conceded as much on reargument. On the other hand, the appellee conceded on reargument that no case could be cited that holds that a fetus is a person within the meaning of the Fourteenth Amendment.

The Constitution does not define ''person'' in so many words. Section 1 of the Fourteenth Amendment contains three references to ''person.'' The first, in defining ''citizens,'' speaks of ''persons born or naturalized in the United States.'' The word also appears both in the Due Process Clause and in the Equal Protection Clause. ''Person'' is used in other places in the Constitution: in the listing of qualifications for Representatives and Senators, Art. I, § 2, cl. 2, and § 3, cl. 3; in the Apportionment Clause, Art. I, § 2, cl. 3;[53] in the Migration and Importation provision, Art. I, § 9, cl. 1; in the Emolument Clause, Art. I, § 9, cl. 8; in the Electors provisions, Art. II, § 1, cl. 2, and the superseded cl. 3; in the provision outlining qualifications for the office of President, Art. II, § 1, cl. 5; in the Extradition provisions, Art. IV, § 2, cl. 2, and the superseded Fugitive Slave Clause 3; and in the Fifth, Twelfth, and Twenty-second Amendments, as well as in §§ 2 and 3 of the Fourteenth Amendment. But in nearly all these instances, the use of the word is such that it has application only postnatally. None indicates, with any assurance, that it has any possible pre-natal application.

All this, together with our observation, supra, that throughout the major portion of the 19th century prevailing legal abortion practices were far freer than they are today, persuades us that the word ''person,'' as used in the Fourteenth Amendment, does not include the unborn....

The pregnant woman cannot be isolated in her privacy. She carries an embryo and, later, a fetus, if one accepts the medical definitions of the developing young in the human uterus. The situation therefore is inherently different from marital intimacy....

Texas urges that, apart from the Fourteenth Amendment, life begins at conception and is present throughout pregnancy, and that, therefore, the State has a compelling interest in protecting that life from and after conception. We need not resolve the difficult question of when life begins. When those trained in the respective disciplines of medicine, philosophy, and theology are unable to arrive at any consensus, the judiciary, at this point in the development of man's knowledge, is not in a position to speculate as to the answer.

It should be sufficient to note briefly the wide divergence of thinking on this most sensitive and difficult question. There has always been strong support for the view that life does not begin until live birth. This was the belief of the Stoics. [T]he common law found greater significance in quickening. Physicians and their scientific colleagues have regarded that event with less interest and have tended to focus either upon conception, upon live birth, or upon the interim point at which the fetus becomes ''viable,'' that is, potentially able to live outside the mother's

---

53. We are not aware that in the taking of any census under this clause, a fetus has ever been counted.

womb, albeit with artificial aid. Viability is usually placed at about seven months (28 weeks) but may occur earlier, even at 24 weeks. . . .

In view of all this, we do not agree that, by adopting one theory of life, Texas may override the rights of the pregnant woman that are at stake. We repeat, however, that the State does have an important and legitimate interest in preserving and protecting the health of the pregnant woman, whether she be a resident of the State or a nonresident who seeks medical consultation and treatment there, and that it has still *another* important and legitimate interest in protecting the potentiality of human life. These interests are separate and distinct. Each grows in substantiality as the woman approaches term and, at a point during pregnancy, each becomes "compelling."

With respect to the State's important and legitimate interest in the health of the mother, the "compelling" point, in the light of present medical knowledge, is at approximately the end of the first trimester. This is so because of the now-established medical fact that until the end of the first trimester mortality in abortion may be less than mortality in normal childbirth. It follows that, from and after this point, a State may regulate the abortion procedure to the extent that the regulation reasonably relates to the preservation and protection of maternal health. Examples of permissible state regulation in this area are requirements as to the qualifications of the person who is to perform the abortion; as to the licensure of that person; as to the facility in which the procedure is to be performed, that is, whether it must be a hospital or may be a clinic or some other place of less-than-hospital status; as to the licensing of the facility; and the like.

This means, on the other hand, that, for the period of pregnancy prior to this "compelling" point, the attending physician, in consultation with his patient, is free to determine, without regulation by the State, that, in his medical judgment, the patient's pregnancy should be terminated. If that decision is reached, the judgment may be effectuated by an abortion free of interference by the State.

With respect to the State's important and legitimate interest in potential life, the "compelling" point is at viability. This is so because the fetus then presumably has the capability of meaningful life outside the mother's womb. State regulation protective of fetal life after viability thus has both logical and biological justifications. If the State is interested in protecting fetal life after viability, it may go so far as to proscribe abortion during that period, except when it is necessary to preserve the life or health of the mother.

Measured against these standards, Art. 1196 of the Texas Penal Code, in restricting legal abortions to those "procured or attempted by medical advice for the purpose of saving the life of the mother," sweeps too broadly. The statute makes no distinction between abortions performed early in pregnancy and those performed later, and it limits to a single reason, "saving" the mother's life, the legal justification for the procedure. The statute, therefore, cannot survive the constitutional attack made upon it here. . . .

MR. CHIEF JUSTICE BURGER, concurring. . . .

I do not read the Court's holdings today as having the sweeping consequences attributed to them by the dissenting Justices. . . . Plainly, the Court today rejects any claim that the Constitution requires abortions on demand.

MR. JUSTICE REHNQUIST, dissenting.

. . . I have difficulty in concluding, as the Court does, that the right of "privacy" is involved in this case. . . . A transaction resulting in an operation such as this is not "private" in the ordinary usage of that word. Nor is the "privacy" that the Court finds here even a distant relative of the freedom from searches and seizures protected by the Fourth Amendment to the Constitution, which the Court has referred to as embodying a right to privacy.

If the Court means by the term "privacy" no more than that the claim of a person to be free from unwanted state regulation of consensual transactions may be a form of "liberty" protected by the Fourteenth Amendment, there is no doubt that similar claims have been upheld in our earlier decisions on the basis of that liberty. . . . But that liberty is not guaranteed absolutely against deprivation, only against deprivation without due process of law. The test traditionally applied in the area of social and economic legislation is whether or not a law such as that challenged has a rational relation to a valid state objective. *Williamson v. Lee Optical Co.*, 348 U.S. 483, 491, 75 S.Ct. 461, 466, 99 L.Ed. 563 (1955). The Due Process Clause of the Fourteenth Amendment undoubtedly does place a limit, albeit a broad one, on legislative power to enact laws such as this. If the Texas statute were to prohibit an abortion even where the mother's life is in jeopardy, I have little doubt that such a statute would lack a rational relation to a valid state objective under the test stated in *Williamson*.

[Also] the Court adds a new wrinkle to [the "compelling state interest"] test by transposing it from the legal considerations associated with the Equal Protection Clause of the Fourteenth Amendment to this case arising under the Due Process Clause of the Fourteenth Amendment. Unless I misapprehend the consequences of this transplanting of the "compelling state interest test," the Court's opinion will accomplish the seemingly impossible feat of leaving this area of the law more confused than it found it.

While the Court's opinion quotes from the dissent of MR. JUSTICE HOLMES in *Lochner v. New York,* the result it reaches is more closely attuned to the majority opinion of MR. JUSTICE PECKHAM in that case. . . . The decision here to break pregnancy into three distinct terms and to outline the permissible restrictions the State may impose in each one, for example, partakes more of judicial legislation than it does of a determination of the intent of the drafters of the Fourteenth Amendment. . . .

MR. JUSTICE WHITE, with whom MR. JUSTICE REHNQUIST joins, dissenting.

. . . The common claim before us is that for any [reason], or for no reason at all, and without asserting or claiming any threat to life or health, any woman is entitled to an abortion at her request if she is able to find a medical advisor willing to undertake the procedure. . . . With all due respect, I dissent. I find nothing in the language or history of the Constitution to support the Court's judgment. . . . In a sensitive area such as this, involving as it does issues over which reasonable men may easily and heatedly differ, I cannot accept the Court's exercise of its clear power of choice by interposing a constitutional barrier to state efforts to protect human life and by investing mothers and doctors with the constitutionally protected right to exterminate it. This issue, for the most part, should be left with the people and to the political processes the people have devised to govern their affairs. . . .

[The concurring opinions of DOUGLAS and STEWART, JJ. are omitted.]

Notes

1. *Doe v. Bolton,* 410 U.S. 179, 93 S.Ct. 739, 35 L.Ed.2d 201 (1973), the companion case to *Roe,* upheld a provision in Georgia law allowing the physician to perform an abortion only if it "is necessary," based "upon his best clinical judgment." This law was not unduly vague, said the Court, because the physician may exercise his judgment in light of all the attendant circumstances. The Court, however, invalidated three procedural demands of the Georgia law: "(1) that the abortion be performed in a hospital accredited by the Joint Commission on Accreditation of Hospitals (J.C.A.H.); (2) that the procedure be approved by the hospital staff abortion committee; and (3) that the performing physician's judgment be confirmed by the independent examinations of the patient by two other licensed physicians."

The Court argued that the accreditation requirement was invalid because it did not apply to nonabortion surgery, the state did not show that only J.C.A.H. hospitals could meet its interest in protecting the patient, and the hospital requirement failed to exclude the first trimester of pregnancy. The other two procedural restrictions also did not withstand scrutiny for they similarly did not apply to other types of surgery, restricted the patient's rights, and were unsupported by her health needs. "If a physician is licensed by the State, he is recognized by the State as capable of exercising acceptable clinical judgment." Hence the State cannot require that the performing physician's judgment be confirmed by other physicians.

Georgia had a requirement that the woman requesting an abortion swear that she is a bona fide legal resident of Georgia. Although there was no durational residency requirement, the Court invalidated that provision under the Privileges and Immunities Clause of Article IV, section 2, cl. 1 because the Georgia rule "is not based on any policy of preserving state-supported facilities for Georgia residents, for the bar also applies to private hospitals and to privately retained physicians. There is no intimation, either, that Georgia facilities are utilized to capacity in caring for Georgia residents."

Two years later, *Connecticut v. Menillo,* 423 U.S. 9, 96 S.Ct. 170, 46 L.Ed.2d 152 (1975)(per curiam) held that a Connecticut law making it a crime for "any person" to attempt an abortion was constitutional as applied to an attempted abortion performed by a someone other than a licensed physician. This restriction was constitutional, even during the first trimester. The Court, in a very brief opinion, simply stated that *"Roe* teaches that a State cannot restrict a decision by a woman, with the advice of her physician, to terminate her pregnancy during the first trimester . . . . " Thus, prosecution of a *non*physician for performing an abortion infringes "upon no realm of personal privacy secured by the Constitution against state interference." There were no dissents.

Subsequently, the Court said that "neither the legislature nor the courts" can define viability objectively, either in terms of weeks of gestation, or fetal weight, or any other single factor, because the judgment of the doctor must control. "Viability is reached when, in the judgment of the attending physician on the particular facts of the case before him, there is a reasonable likelihood of the fetus' sustained survival outside the womb, with or without artificial support." *Colautti v. Franklin,* 439 U.S. 379, 99 S.Ct. 675, 58 L.Ed.2d 596 (1979)(6 to 3).

Is *Roe v. Wade* a woman's rights case, or a doctor's rights case?

2. Later cases considered myriad other issues that appeared in the wake of *Roe v. Wade.* For example, *Planned Parenthood of Central Missouri v. Danforth,* 428 U.S. 52, 96 S.Ct. 2831, 49 L.Ed.2d 788 (1976) upheld a requirement that a woman seeking an abortion in the first trimester give her consent in writing. This case also upheld various record-keeping requirements because the information was treated confidentially and might be useful in protecting maternal health, but these requirements "perhaps [were] approaching impermissible [constitutional] limits" as applied to the first trimester. A divided Court invalidated a requirement of spousal consent if the woman is married (or parental consent for an unmarried woman under 18) unless a doctor certifies that the abortion is necessary to preserve the mother's life. First, the state cannot delegate to a spouse a veto power that the state itself cannot exercise; secondly, the parental interests do not outweigh the privacy rights "of the competent minor mature enough to have become pregnant." Not considered was the extent to which the state could require spousal or parental *notification* (as opposed to spousal or parental *consent*).

In *Ohio v. Akron Center for Reproductive Health,* 497 U.S. 502, 110 S.Ct. 2972, 111 L.Ed.2d 405 (1990), a divided Court upheld an Ohio law that prohibited an unmarried, unemancipated woman under 18 from securing an abortion unless either one parent has consented in writing, or the physician has given notice to one parent or guardian, or the court has approved the abortion (based on a finding that the woman is sufficiently mature to bypass parental notice or that the parent has abused her, or that notice is not in her best interests), or the court has provided constructive authorization by inaction. Kennedy, J.'s plurality opinion, joined by Rehnquist, C.J., & White & Scalia, JJ., said that a woman's abortion decision embraces "her own destiny and personal dignity, and the origins of the other human life that lie within the embryo." Blackmun, J., joined by Brennan & Marshall, JJ., dissenting, referred to this portion of Kennedy's opinion as "hyperbole that can have but one result: to further incite an American press, public, and pulpit already inflamed. . . . "

Planned Parenthood of Central Missouri, supra, also struck down a section of a law that forbade the use of saline amniocentesis (the insertion of saline into the amniotic sac, a procedure—unlike some other procedures— that will destroy the fetus) as a method of abortion after the first trimester because the law, the Court said, was not necessary to maternal health. Even though the prostaglandin method was safer for the mother, it was not widely available, and saline abortions were "an accepted medical procedure." White, J., dissenting (joined by Burger, C.J. & Rehnquist J.) noted that the trial below showed that the saline method was "far less safe a method" for the woman. In fact, the Chief of Obstetrics at Yale had testified that "physicians should be liable for malpractice if they chose saline over prostaglandin. . . ." The Court did not reach the constitutionality of another provision of the Missouri law, which declared that an infant who survived an attempted abortion not performed to save the mother's life or health was an abandoned ward of the state, and the mother and a consenting father were deprived of parental rights.

Akron v. Akron Center for Reproductive Health, Inc., 462 U.S. 416, 103 S.Ct. 2481, 76 L.Ed.2d 687 (1983) invalidated a requirement that second trimester abortions be performed in a hospital because recent medical evidence showed that they could be performed safely and with less expense on an outpatient basis in appropriate nonhospital facilities. The majority also held that the state's interest in maternal health did not justify a law requiring that the attending physician orally inform the woman of various matters such as the "development of her fetus," the "date of possible viability," the "physical and emotional complications that may result from an abortion," and the availability of agencies that might provide assistance with respect to "birth control, adoption, and childbirth." "[M]uch of the information required is designed not to inform the woman's consent but rather to persuade her to withhold it altogether." To assure informed consent the state should only describe "the general subject matter relevant to informed consent." The majority struck a provision requiring the doctor to give the woman information "which in his own medical judgment is relevant to her decision" whether to abort, because it "is unreasonable for a State to insist that only a physician is competent to provide the information and counseling relevant to informed consent." *Akron* also invalidated a requirement that a woman wait 24 hours before consenting to an abortion because there was no evidence that this waiting period would make the abortion safer.

Akron produced an interesting dissent from O'Connor, J., joined by White & Rehnquist, JJ. She objected to—

> "an analytical framework that varies according to the 'stages' of pregnancy, where those stages, and their concomitant standards of review, differ according to the level of medical technology available when a particular challenge to state regulation occurs. . . . The *Roe* framework, then, is clearly on a collision course with itself. As the medical risks of various abortion procedures decrease, the point at which the State may

regulate for reasons of maternal health is moved further forward to actual childbirth. As medical science becomes better able to provide for the separate existence of the fetus, the point of viability is moved further back toward conception. [P]*otential* life is no less potential in the first weeks of pregnancy than it is at viability or afterward. . . . Although the Court refused to 'resolve the difficult question of when life begins,' the Court chose the point of viability—when the fetus is *capable* of life independent of its mother—to permit the complete proscription of abortion. The choice of viability as the point at which the state interest in *potential* life becomes compelling is no less arbitrary than choosing any point before viability or any point afterward. Accordingly, I believe that the State's interest in protecting potential human life exists throughout the pregnancy."

Powell. J. replied that the Court should "adher[e] to *stare decisis*," and "the dissenting opinion rejects the basic premise of *Roe* and its progeny."

Blackmun, J., for the Court in *Thornburgh v. American College of Obstetricians and Gynecologists,* 476 U.S. 747, 106 S.Ct. 2169, 90 L.Ed.2d 779 (1986) invalidated a Pennsylvania law that imposed various requirements on abortion: e.g., a requirement that the physician advise the woman that medical assistance may be available and that the father is responsible for financial assistance to support the child ("poorly disguised elements of discouragement for the abortion decision"); the requirement that the physician inform the woman of all particular medical risks of abortion ("intrudes upon the physician's exercise of proper professional judgment"); various reporting requirements (the reports of the woman's age, race, marital status, and number of prior pregnancies "go well beyond the health-related interests"); and a provision requiring presence of a second physician to be present during an abortion performed when viability is possible, with the second physician taking all reasonable steps to preserve the child's life and health (the legislature failed to provide "a medical-emergency exception"). Burger, C.J., dissented: "[E]very member of the *Roe* Court rejected the idea of abortion on demand." White, J., joined by Rehnquist, J., dissented, objected to the majority's "linguistic nit-picking" and called for *Roe*'s overruling. A separate dissent by O'Connor, J. (joined by Rehnquist, J.) argued: "This Court's abortion decisions have already worked a major distortion in the Court's constitutional jurisprudence," but because "Pennsylvania has not asked the Court to reconsider or overrule *Roe v. Wade,* I do not address that question."

3. FINANCIAL ASSISTANCE. In *Maher v. Roe,* 432 U.S. 464, 97 S.Ct. 2376, 53 L.Ed.2d 484 (1977), Powell, J., for a divided Court (6 to 3), held that the equal protection clause did not require a state to pay the expenses incident to nontherapeutic (i.e., not medically necessary) abortions for indigent women simply because it had made the decision to pay the expenses incident to childbirth. The majority said that *Roe* did not prevent a state from making "a value judgment favoring childbirth over abortion and . . . implement[ing] that judgment by the allocation of public funds." Brennan, Blackmun, & Marshall, JJ., each filed dissenting opinions.

Subsequently, *Harris v. McRae,* 448 U.S. 297, 100 S.Ct. 2671, 65 L.Ed.2d 784 (1980), (5 to 4), upheld the Hyde Amendment, which permitted federal funding of the costs associated with child birth, but prohibited the use of federal funds to reimburse the cost of abortions under the Medicaid program except under certain specified circumstances (e.g., when the life of the mother would be endangered if the fetus were carried to term; for victims of rape or incest who promptly reported to a law enforcement or public health agency). Although the Hyde Amendment withheld funding for some medically necessary abortions, the Court upheld its constitutionality: "whether the freedom of a woman to choose to terminate her pregnancy for health reasons lies at the core or the periphery of the due process liberty recognized in *Wade,* it simply does not follow that a woman's freedom of choice carries with it a constitutional entitlement to the financial resources to avail herself of the full range of protected choices." The Court found no violation of the equal protection component of the fifth amendment.

Brennan, J., joined by Marshall & Blackmun, J., dissented: "abortion and childbirth, when stripped of the sensitive moral arguments surrounding the abortion controversy, are simply two alternative medical methods of dealing with pregnancy.... By funding all the expenses associated with childbirth and none of the expenses incurred in terminating pregnancy, the government literally makes an offer that the indigent woman cannot afford to refuse." Marshall, Stevens, & Blackmun, JJ. also filed dissenting opinions.

In *Webster v. Reproductive Health Services,* 492 U.S. 490, 109 S.Ct. 3040, 106 L.Ed.2d 410 (1989), a fragmented Court upheld various provisions of a Missouri statute. In a part of Rehnquist, C.J.'s opinion that attracted a majority, the Court upheld the provision that prohibited public employees (within the scope of their employment) from performing or assisting an abortion not necessary to save the life of the mother. The Court also upheld a section that provided that no public facility could be used to perform or assist an abortion not necessary to save the life of the mother. "[T]he State need not commit any resources to facilitating abortions, even if it can turn a profit by doing so." The Court also refused to invalidate the law's preamble although it declared that the "life of each human being begins at conception." The "preamble does not by its terms regulate abortion or any other aspect of appellees's medical practice."

Blackmun, J., joined by Brennan & Marshall, JJ., concurred in part and dissented in part. Stevens, J., also concurred in part and dissented in part, and argued that the state has "no interest in protecting the newly fertilized egg from physical pain or mental anguish," because, he asserted, "the capacity for such suffering does not yet exist."

Rust v. Sullivan, 500 U.S. 173, 111 S.Ct. 1759, 114 L.Ed.2d 233 (1991)(Rehnquist, C.J., for the Court) rejected a facial challenge to regulations of the Department of Health and Human Services that limited the ability of recipients (if they accept funding pursuant to Title X of the Public Health Service Act) to engage in abortion-related activities. Title X provided federal funding for family-planning services, and stated: "None of the funds appropriated under this subchapter shall be used in programs where abortion is a method of family planning." The Title X funds should support only "preventive family planning services, population research, infertility services, and other related medical, informational, and educational activities." The regulations limited Title X to "preconceptual counseling, education, and general reproductive health care," and excluded "pregnancy care (including obstetric or prenatal care)." The Title X project was "expressly prohibited from referring a pregnant woman to an abortion provider, even upon specific request." A permissible response to such an inquiry would be that "the project does not consider abortion an appropriate method of family planning and therefore does not counsel or refer for abortion." These regulations were popularly referred to as the "gag rule."

Rehnquist emphasized that Title X is limited to *preconceptual* services, and does not offer or furnish *any* "services related to childbirth." If a Title X project refers a pregnant client for prenatal or social services, it is forbidden to "steer" clients to providers who offer abortion as a method of family planning. Because Title X projects may not engage in abortion activities while engaging in Title X work, they must be organized so that they are "physically and financially separate" from prohibited abortion activities. The doctor's ability to provide, and the woman's right to receive, abortion information remained unfettered outside the context of the Title X project.

Relying on *Harris v. McRae*, the Court did not accept the argument that the government's unequal subsidization violated the Constitution. It "strains logic" to find that the "mere decision to exclude abortion-related services from a federally funded *pre-conceptual* family planning program is unconstitutional." (emphasis in original). The Court rejected the argument that the regulations violated the first amendment because they prohibited discussion about abortion as a lawful option. (The free speech aspect of the case is considered in § 10–3.4.) And it rejected plaintiffs claim that the regulations would not permit a Title X project to refer to a provider of abortions or abortion-related services a woman whose pregnancy places her life in imminent peril: "Abortion counseling as a 'method of family planning' is prohibited, and it does not seem that a medically necessitated abortion in such circumstances would be the equivalent of its use as a 'method of family planning.'"

Blackmun, J., joined by Marshall, J. & in part by Stevens, J., dissented. By "suppressing medically pertinent information and injecting a restrictive ideological message unrelated to considerations of maternal health, the Government" violated the Fifth Amendment. Stevens, J. also filed a dissenting opinion. O'Connor, J. filed a dissenting opinion arguing that the statute did not authorize the regulations.

PLANNED PARENTHOOD OF SOUTHEASTERN PENNSYLVANIA v. CASEY
505 U.S. 833, 112 S.Ct. 2791, 120 L.Ed.2d 674 (1992).

JUSTICE O'CONNOR, JUSTICE KENNEDY, and JUSTICE SOUTER announced the judgment of the Court and delivered the opinion of the Court with respect to Parts I, II, III, V–A, V–C, and VI, an opinion with respect to Part V–E, in which JUSTICE STEVENS joins, and an opinion with respect to Parts IV, V–B, and V–D.[1]

---

1. Ed. note: The various slip opinions in this case totaled 177 pages. Only a small portion is excerpted here.

I.   Liberty finds no refuge in a jurisprudence of doubt.... At issue in these cases are five provisions of the Pennsylvania Abortion Control Act of 1982 as amended in 1988 and 1989.... The Act requires that a woman seeking an abortion give her informed consent prior to the abortion procedure, and specifies that she be provided with certain information at least 24 hours before the abortion is performed. For a minor to obtain an abortion, the Act requires the informed consent of one of her parents, but provides for a judicial bypass option if the minor does not wish to or cannot obtain a parent's consent. Another provision of the Act requires that, unless certain exceptions apply, a married woman seeking an abortion must sign a statement indicating that she has notified her husband of her intended abortion. The Act exempts compliance with these three requirements in the event of a "medical emergency," which is defined in § 3203 of the Act. In addition to the above provisions regulating the performance of abortions, the Act imposes certain reporting requirements on facilities that provide abortion services.

[The District Court held all these provisions unconstitutional, but the Third Circuit upheld all the regulations except for the husband notification requirement.]

After considering the fundamental constitutional questions resolved by *Roe,* principles of institutional integrity, and the rule of *stare decisis,* we are led to conclude this: the essential holding of *Roe v. Wade* should be retained and once again reaffirmed.

It must be stated at the outset and with clarity that *Roe*'s essential holding, the holding we reaffirm, has three parts. First is a recognition of the right of the woman to choose to have an abortion before viability and to obtain it without undue interference from the State. Before viability, the State's interests are not strong enough to support a prohibition of abortion or the imposition of a substantial obstacle to the woman's effective right to elect the procedure. Second is a confirmation of the State's power to restrict abortions after fetal viability, if the law contains exceptions for pregnancies which endanger a woman's life or health. And third is the principle that the State has legitimate interests from the outset of the pregnancy in protecting the health of the woman and the life of the fetus that may become a child. These principles do not contradict one another; and we adhere to each.

II.   Constitutional protection of the woman's decision to terminate her pregnancy derives from the Due Process Clause of the Fourteenth Amendment. It declares that no State shall "deprive any person of life, liberty, or property, without due process of law." The controlling word in the case before us is "liberty." ...

Neither the Bill of Rights nor the specific practices of States at the time of the adoption of the Fourteenth Amendment marks the outer limits of the substantive sphere of liberty which the Fourteenth Amendment protects. See U.S. Const., Amend. 9.... In *Griswold* [*v. Connecticut*] we held that the Constitution does not permit a State to forbid a married couple to use contraceptives. That same freedom was later guaranteed, under the Equal Protection Clause, for unmarried couples. See *Eisenstadt v. Baird* (1972). Constitutional protection was extended to the sale and distribution of contraceptives in *Carey v. Population Services International* [1977]. It is settled now, as it was when the Court heard arguments in *Roe v. Wade,* that the Constitution places limits on a State's right to interfere with a person's most basic decisions about family and parenthood, as well as bodily integrity.

The inescapable fact is that adjudication of substantive due process claims may call upon the Court in interpreting the Constitution to exercise that same capacity which by tradition courts always have exercised: reasoned judgment. Its boundaries are not susceptible of expression as a simple rule. That does not mean we are free to invalidate state policy choices with which we disagree; yet neither does it permit us to shrink from the duties of our office....

Men and women of good conscience can disagree, and we suppose some always shall disagree, about the profound moral and spiritual implications of terminating a pregnancy, even in its earliest stage. Some of us as individuals find abortion offensive to our most basic principles of morality, but that cannot control our decision. Our obligation is to define the liberty of all, not to mandate our own moral code. The underlying constitutional issue is whether the State can resolve these philosophic questions in such a definitive way that a woman lacks all choice in the matter, except perhaps in those rare circumstances in which the pregnancy is itself a danger to her own life or health, or is the result of rape or incest.

It is conventional constitutional doctrine that where reasonable people disagree the government can adopt one position or the other. That theorem, however, assumes a state of affairs in which the choice does not intrude upon a protected liberty....

Our law affords constitutional protection to personal decisions relating to marriage, procreation, contraception, family relationships, child rearing, and education.... These matters, involving the most intimate and personal choices a person may make in a lifetime, choices central to personal dignity and autonomy, are central to the liberty protected by the Fourteenth Amendment. At the heart of liberty is the right to define one's own concept of existence, of meaning, of the universe, and of the mystery of human life. Beliefs about these matters could not define the attributes of personhood were they formed under compulsion of the State.

These considerations begin our analysis of the woman's interest in terminating her pregnancy but cannot end it, for this reason: though the abortion decision may originate within the zone of conscience and belief, it is more than a philosophic exercise. Abortion is a unique act. It is an act fraught with consequences for others: for the woman who must live with the implications of her decision; for the persons who perform and assist in the procedure; for the spouse, family, and society which must confront the knowledge that these procedures exist, procedures some deem nothing short of an act of violence against innocent human life; and, depending on one's beliefs, for the life or potential life that is aborted. Though abortion is conduct, it does not follow that the State is entitled to proscribe it in all instances. That is because the liberty of the woman is at stake in a sense unique to the human condition and so unique to the law. The mother who carries a child to full term is subject to anxieties, to physical constraints, to pain that only she must bear.... Her suffering is too intimate and personal for the State to insist, without more, upon its own vision of the woman's role, however dominant that vision has been in the course of our history and our culture. The destiny of the woman must be shaped to a large extent on her own conception of her spiritual imperatives and her place in society.

[I]n some critical respects the abortion decision is of the same character as the decision to use contraception, to which *Griswold v. Connecticut, Eisenstadt v. Baird,* and *Carey v. Population Services International* afford constitutional protection. We have no doubt as to the correctness of those decisions. They support the reasoning in *Roe* relating to the woman's liberty because they involve personal decisions concerning not only the meaning of procreation but also human responsibility and respect for it.... *Roe* was, of course, an extension of those cases and, as the decision itself indicated, the separate States could act in some degree to further their own legitimate interests in protecting prenatal life. [T]he reservations any of us may have in reaffirming the central holding of *Roe* are outweighed by the explication of individual liberty we have given combined with the force of *stare decisis*. We turn now to that doctrine.

III. ... Although *Roe* has engendered opposition, it has in no sense proven "unworkable," representing as it does a simple limitation beyond which a state law is unenforceable. ...

[F]or two decades of economic and social developments, people have organized intimate relationships and made choices that define their views of themselves and their places in society, in reliance on the availability of abortion in the event that contraception should fail. The ability of women to participate equally in the economic and social life of the Nation has been facilitated by their ability to control their reproductive lives. The Constitution serves human values, and while the effect of reliance on *Roe* cannot be exactly measured, neither can the certain cost of overruling *Roe* for people who have ordered their thinking and living around that case be dismissed.

No evolution of legal principle has left *Roe's* doctrinal footings weaker than they were in 1973. No development of constitutional law since the case was decided has implicitly and explicitly left *Roe* behind as a mere survivor of obsolete constitutional thinking. [O]ne could classify *Roe* as *sui generis*. If the case is so viewed, then there clearly has been no erosion of its central determination....

Nor will courts building upon *Roe* be likely to hand down erroneous decisions as a consequence. Even on the assumption that the central holding of *Roe* was in error, that error would go only to the strength of the state interest in fetal protection, not to the recognition afforded by the Constitution to the woman's liberty. The latter aspect of the decision fits comfortably within the framework of the Court's prior decisions including *Skinner v. Oklahoma ex rel. Williamson,* (1942), *Griswold, supra, Loving v. Virginia,* (1967), and *Eisenstadt v. Baird,* (1972), the holdings of which are "not a series of isolated points," but mark a "rational continuum." . . .

The soundness of this prong of the *Roe* analysis is apparent from a consideration of the alternative. If indeed the woman's interest in deciding whether to bear and beget a child had not been recognized as in *Roe,* the State might as readily restrict a woman's right to choose to carry a pregnancy to term as to terminate it, to further asserted state interests in population control, or eugenics, for example. Yet *Roe* has been sensibly relied upon to counter any such suggestions. *E.g., Arnold v. Board of Education of Escambia County, Ala.,* 880 F.2d 305, 311 (C.A.11 1989)(relying upon *Roe* and concluding that government officials violate the Constitution by coercing a minor to have an abortion); *Avery v. County of Burke,* 660 F.2d 111, 115 (C.A.4 1981)(county agency inducing teenage girl to undergo unwanted sterilization on the basis of misrepresentation that she had sickle cell trait); see also *In re Quinlan,* 70 N.J. 10, 355 A.2d 647, cert. denied *sub nom. Garger v. New Jersey,* 429 U.S. 922, 97 S.Ct. 319, 50 L.Ed.2d 289 (1976)(relying on *Roe* in finding a right to terminate medical treatment). In any event, because *Roe*'s scope is confined by the fact of its concern with postconception potential life, a concern otherwise likely to be implicated only by some forms of contraception protected independently under *Griswold* and later cases, any error in *Roe* is unlikely to have serious ramifications in future cases.

We have seen how time has overtaken some of *Roe*'s factual assumptions: advances in maternal health care allow for abortions safe to the mother later in pregnancy than was true in 1973, and advances in neonatal care have advanced viability to a point somewhat earlier. But these facts go only to the scheme of time limits on the realization of competing interests, and the divergences from the factual premises of 1973 have no bearing on the validity of *Roe*'s central holding, that viability marks the earliest point at which the State's interest in fetal life is constitutionally adequate to justify a legislative ban on nontherapeutic abortions. The soundness or unsoundness of that constitutional judgment in no sense turns on whether viability occurs at approximately 28 weeks, as was usual at the time of *Roe,* at 23 to 24 weeks, as it sometimes does today, or at some moment even slightly earlier in pregnancy, as it may if fetal respiratory capacity can somehow be enhanced in the future. Whenever it may occur, the attainment of viability may continue to serve as the critical fact, just as it has done since *Roe* was decided; which is to say that no change in *Roe*'s factual underpinning has left its central holding obsolete, and none supports an argument for overruling it . . . .

In a less significant case, *stare decisis* analysis could, and would, stop at the point we have reached. But the sustained and widespread debate *Roe* has provoked calls for some comparison between that case and others of comparable dimension that have responded to national controversies and taken on the impress of the controversies addressed. Only two such decisional lines from the past century present themselves for examination, and in each instance the result reached by the Court accorded with the principles we apply today.

The first example is that line of cases identified with *Lochner v. New York,* (1905), which imposed substantive limitations on legislation limiting economic autonomy in favor of health and welfare regulation, adopting, in Justice Holmes' view, the theory of *laissez-faire . . . . West Coast Hotel Co. v. Parrish,* (1937), signalled the demise of *Lochner* by overruling *Adkins.* In the meantime, the Depression had come and, with it, the lesson that seemed unmistakable to most people by 1937, that the interpretation of contractual freedom protected in *Adkins* rested on fundamentally false factual assumptions about the capacity of a relatively unregulated market to satisfy minimal levels of human welfare . . . .

The second comparison that 20th century history invites is with the cases employing the separate-but-equal rule for applying the Fourteenth Amendment's equal protection guarantee. They began with *Plessy v. Ferguson* (1896), holding that legislatively mandated racial segregation in public transportation works no denial of equal protection, rejecting the argument that racial separation enforced by the legal machinery of American society treats the black race as inferior. The *Plessy* Court considered "the underlying fallacy of the plaintiff's argument to consist in the assumption that the enforced separation of the two races stamps the colored race with a badge of inferiority. If this be so, it is not by reason of anything found in the act, but solely because the colored race chooses to put that construction upon it." Whether, as a matter of historical fact, the Justices in the *Plessy* majority believed this or not, this understanding of the implication of segregation was the stated justification for the Court's opinion. But this understanding of the facts and the rule it was stated to justify were repudiated in *Brown v. Board of Education,* (1954) . . . .

The Court in *Brown* addressed these facts of life by observing that whatever may have been the understanding in *Plessy*'s time of the power of segregation to stigmatize those who were segregated with a "badge of inferiority," it was clear by 1954 that legally sanctioned segregation had just such an effect, to the point that racially separate public educational facilities were deemed inherently unequal. Society's understanding of the facts upon which a constitutional ruling was sought in 1954 was thus fundamentally different from the basis claimed for the decision in 1896. While we think *Plessy* was wrong the day it was decided, we must also recognize that the *Plessy* Court's explanation for its decision was so clearly at odds with the facts apparent to the Court in 1954 that the decision to reexamine *Plessy* was on this ground alone not only justified but required.

... Because neither the factual underpinnings of *Roe*'s central holding nor our understanding of it has changed (and because no other indication of weakened precedent has been shown) the Court could not pretend to be reexamining the prior law with any justification beyond a present doctrinal disposition to come out differently from the Court of 1973. To overrule prior law for no other reason than that would run counter to the view repeated in our cases, that a decision to overrule should rest on some special reason over and above the belief that a prior case was wrongly decided.

... Despite the variety of reasons that may inform and justify a decision to overrule, we cannot forget that such a decision is usually perceived (and perceived correctly) as, at the least, a statement that a prior decision was wrong. There is a limit to the amount of error that can plausibly be imputed to prior courts. If that limit should be exceeded, disturbance of prior rulings would be taken as evidence that justifiable reexamination of principle had given way to drives for particular results in the short term. The legitimacy of the Court would fade with the frequency of its vacillation.

[Also, when] Court decides a case in such a way as to resolve the sort of intensely divisive controversy reflected in *Roe* and those rare, comparable cases, its decision has a dimension that the resolution of the normal case does not carry. It is the dimension present whenever the Court's interpretation of the Constitution calls the contending sides of a national controversy to end their national division by accepting a common mandate rooted in the Constitution.

The Court is not asked to do this very often, having thus addressed the Nation only twice in our lifetime, in the decisions of *Brown* and *Roe*. But when the Court does act in this way, its decision requires an equally rare precedential force to counter the inevitable efforts to overturn it and to thwart its implementation. [T]o overrule under fire in the absence of the most compelling reason to reexamine a watershed decision would subvert the Court's legitimacy beyond any serious question. . . .

IV. [T]he point where much criticism has been directed at *Roe* [is] a criticism that always inheres when the Court draws a specific rule from what in the Constitution is but a general standard. [T]he urgent claims of the woman to retain the ultimate control over her destiny and her body, claims implicit in the meaning of liberty, require us to perform that function. Liberty must not be extinguished for want of a line that is clear. And it falls to us to give some real substance to the woman's liberty to determine whether to carry her pregnancy to full term.

We conclude the line should be drawn at viability, so that before that time the woman has a right to choose to terminate her pregnancy.

We adhere to this principle for two reasons. First, as we have said, is the doctrine of *stare decisis*....

The second reason is that the concept of viability, as we noted in *Roe,* is the time at which there is a realistic possibility of maintaining and nourishing a life outside the womb, so that the independent existence of the second life can in reason and all fairness be the object of state protection that now overrides the rights of the woman....

On the other side of the equation is the interest of the State in the protection of potential life. [I]t must be remembered that *Roe v. Wade* speaks with clarity in establishing not only the woman's liberty but also the State's "important and legitimate interest in potential life." That portion of the decision in *Roe* has been given too little acknowledgement and implementation by the Court in its subsequent cases.... *Roe* established a trimester framework to govern abortion regulations.... A framework of this rigidity was unnecessary and in its later interpretation sometimes contradicted the State's permissible exercise of its powers.

Though the woman has a right to choose to terminate or continue her pregnancy before viability, it does not at all follow that the State is prohibited from taking steps to ensure that this choice is thoughtful and informed. Even in the earliest stages of pregnancy, the State may enact rules and regulations designed to encourage her to know that there are philosophic and social arguments of great weight that can be brought to bear in favor of continuing the pregnancy to full term and that there are procedures and institutions to allow adoption of unwanted children as well as a certain degree of state assistance if the mother chooses to raise the child herself. " '[T]he Constitution does not forbid a State or city, pursuant to democratic processes, from expressing a preference for normal childbirth.' " It follows that States are free to enact laws to provide a reasonable framework for a woman to make a decision that has such profound and lasting meaning. This, too, we find consistent with *Roe*'s central premises, and indeed the inevitable consequence of our holding that the State has an interest in protecting the life of the unborn.

We reject the trimester framework, which we do not consider to be part of the essential holding of *Roe.*

... Numerous forms of state regulation might have the incidental effect of increasing the cost or decreasing the availability of medical care, whether for abortion or any other medical procedure. The fact that a law which serves a valid purpose, one not designed to strike at the right itself, has the incidental effect of making it more difficult or more expensive to procure an abortion cannot be enough to invalidate it. Only where state regulation imposes an undue burden on a woman's ability to make this decision does the power of the State reach into the heart of the liberty protected by the Due Process Clause....

The very notion that the State has a substantial interest in potential life leads to the conclusion that not all regulations must be deemed unwarranted. Not all burdens on the right to decide whether to terminate a pregnancy will be undue. In our view, the undue burden standard is the appropriate means of reconciling the State's interest with the woman's constitutionally protected liberty.... A finding of an undue burden is a shorthand for the conclusion that a state regulation has the purpose or effect of placing a substantial obstacle in the path of a woman seeking an abortion of a nonviable fetus.... Unless it has that effect on her right of choice, a state measure designed to persuade her to choose childbirth over abortion will be upheld if reasonably related to that goal. Regulations designed to foster the health of a woman seeking an abortion are valid if they do not constitute an undue burden.

Even when jurists reason from shared premises, some disagreement is inevitable. That is to be expected in the application of any legal standard which must accommodate life's complexity. We do not expect it to be otherwise with respect to the undue burden standard. We give this summary:

(a) To protect the central right recognized by *Roe v. Wade* while at the same time accommodating the State's profound interest in potential life, we will employ the undue burden analysis as explained in this opinion. An undue burden exists, and therefore a provision of law is invalid, if its purpose or effect is to place a substantial obstacle in the path of a woman seeking an abortion before the fetus attains viability.

(b) We reject the rigid trimester framework of *Roe v. Wade.* To promote the State's profound interest in potential life, throughout pregnancy the State may take measures to ensure that the woman's choice is informed, and measures designed to advance this interest will not be invalidated as long as their purpose is to persuade the woman to choose childbirth over abortion. These measures must not be an undue burden on the right.

(c) As with any medical procedure, the State may enact regulations to further the health or safety of a woman seeking an abortion. Unnecessary health regulations that have the purpose or effect of presenting a substantial obstacle to a woman seeking an abortion impose an undue burden on the right.

(d) Our adoption of the undue burden analysis does not disturb the central holding of *Roe v. Wade,* and we reaffirm that holding. Regardless of whether exceptions are made for particular circumstances, a State may not prohibit any woman from making the ultimate decision to terminate her pregnancy before viability.

(e) We also reaffirm *Roe*'s holding that "subsequent to viability, the State in promoting its interest in the potentiality of human life may, if it chooses, regulate, and even proscribe, abortion except where it is necessary, in appropriate medical judgment, for the preservation of the life or health of the mother."

These principles control our assessment of the Pennsylvania statute, and we now turn to the issue of the validity of its challenged provisions.

V.   ... **A.** Because it is central to the operation of various other requirements, we begin with the statute's definition of medical emergency. Under the statute, a medical emergency is

"[t]hat condition which, on the basis of the physician's good faith clinical judgment, so complicates the medical condition of a pregnant woman as to necessitate the immediate abortion of her pregnancy to avert her death or for which a delay will create serious risk of substantial and irreversible impairment of a major bodily function." 18 Pa.Cons.Stat. (1990). § 3203.

Petitioners argue that the definition is too narrow, contending that it forecloses the possibility of an immediate abortion despite some significant health risks. If the contention were correct, we would be required to invalidate the restrictive operation of the provision, for the essential holding of *Roe* forbids a State from interfering with a woman's choice to undergo an abortion procedure if continuing her pregnancy would constitute a threat to her health.

The District Court found that there were three serious conditions which would not be covered by the statute: preeclampsia, inevitable abortion, and premature ruptured membrane.... While the definition could be interpreted in an unconstitutional manner, the Court of Appeals construed the phrase "serious risk" to include those circumstances. [We] conclude that, as construed by the Court of Appeals, the medical emergency definition imposes no undue burden on a woman's abortion right.

B.   We next consider the informed consent requirement. Except in a medical emergency, the statute requires that at least 24 hours before performing an abortion a physician inform the woman of the nature of the procedure, the health risks of the abortion and of childbirth, and the "probable gestational age of the unborn child." The physician or a qualified nonphysician must inform the woman of the availability of printed materials published by the State describing the fetus and providing information about medical assistance for childbirth, information about child support from the father, and a list of agencies which provide adoption and other services as alternatives to abortion. An abortion may not be performed unless the woman certifies in writing that she has been informed of the availability of these printed materials and has been provided them if she chooses to view them....

To the extent *Akron I* and *Thornburgh* find a constitutional violation when the government requires, as it does here, the giving of truthful, nonmisleading information about the nature of the procedure, the attendant health risks and those of childbirth, and the "probable gestational age" of the fetus, those cases go too far, are inconsistent with *Roe*'s acknowledgment of an important interest in potential life, and are overruled....

We also see no reason why the State may not require doctors to inform a woman seeking an abortion of the availability of materials relating to the consequences to the fetus, even when those consequences have no direct relation to her health. An example illustrates the point. We would think it constitutional for the State to require that in order for there to be informed consent to a kidney transplant operation the recipient must be supplied with information about risks to the donor as well as risks to himself or herself. . . .

Whatever constitutional status the doctor-patient relation may have as a general matter, in the present context it is derivative of the woman's position. The doctor-patient relation does not underlie or override the two more general rights under which the abortion right is justified: the right to make family decisions and the right to physical autonomy. On its own, the doctor-patient relation here is entitled to the same solicitude it receives in other contexts. Thus, a requirement that a doctor give a woman certain information as part of obtaining her consent to an abortion is, for constitutional purposes, no different from a requirement that a doctor give certain specific information about any medical procedure.

All that is left of petitioners' argument is an asserted First Amendment right of a physician not to provide information about the risks of abortion, and childbirth, in a manner mandated by the State. To be sure, the physician's First Amendment rights not to speak are implicated, but only as part of the practice of medicine, subject to reasonable licensing and regulation by the State. We see no constitutional infirmity in the requirement that the physician provide the information mandated by the State here.

The Pennsylvania statute also requires us to reconsider the holding in *Akron I* that the State may not require that a physician, as opposed to a qualified assistant, provide information relevant to a woman's informed consent. Since there is no evidence on this record that requiring a doctor to give the information as provided by the statute would amount in practical terms to a substantial obstacle to a woman seeking an abortion, we conclude that it is not an undue burden. . . .

Our analysis of Pennsylvania's 24–hour waiting period between the provision of the information deemed necessary to informed consent and the performance of an abortion under the undue burden standard requires us to reconsider the premise behind the decision in *Akron I* invalidating a parallel requirement. In *Akron I* we said: "Nor are we convinced that the State's legitimate concern that the woman's decision be informed is reasonably served by requiring a 24–hour delay as a matter of course." We consider that conclusion to be wrong. The idea that important decisions will be more informed and deliberate if they follow some period of reflection does not strike us as unreasonable, particularly where the statute directs that important information become part of the background of the decision. The statute, as construed by the Court of Appeals, permits avoidance of the waiting period in the event of a medical emergency and the record evidence shows that in the vast majority of cases, a 24–hour delay does not create any appreciable health risk. In theory, at least, the waiting period is a reasonable measure to implement the State's interest in protecting the life of the unborn, a measure that does not amount to an undue burden.

Whether the mandatory 24–hour waiting period is nonetheless invalid because in practice it is a substantial obstacle to a woman's choice to terminate her pregnancy is a closer question. [T]he District Court found that for those women who have the fewest financial resources, those who must travel long distances, and those who have difficulty explaining their whereabouts to husbands, employers, or others, the 24–hour waiting period will be "particularly burdensome." [T]he District Court concluded that the waiting period does not further the state "interest in maternal health" and "infringes the physician's discretion to exercise sound medical judgment." Yet, as we have stated, under the undue burden standard a State is permitted to enact persuasive measures which favor childbirth over abortion, even if those measures do not further a health interest. And while the waiting period does limit a physician's discretion, that is not, standing alone, a reason to invalidate it. In light of the construction given the statute's definition of medical emergency by the Court of Appeals, and the District Court's findings, we cannot say that the waiting period imposes a real health risk.

We also disagree with the District Court's conclusion that the "particularly burdensome" effects of the waiting period on some women require its invalidation. A particular burden is not of necessity a substantial obstacle. Whether a burden falls on a particular group is a distinct inquiry from whether it is a substantial obstacle even as to the women in that group. And the District Court did not conclude that the waiting period is such an obstacle even for the women who are most burdened by it. Hence, on the record before us, and in the context of this facial challenge, we are not convinced that the 24–hour waiting period constitutes an undue burden. . . .

C. Section 3209 of Pennsylvania's abortion law provides, except in cases of medical emergency, that no physician shall perform an abortion on a married woman without receiving a signed statement from the woman that she has notified her spouse that she is about to undergo an abortion. The woman has the option of providing an alternative signed statement certifying that her husband is not the man who impregnated her; that her husband could not be located; that the pregnancy is the result of spousal sexual assault which she has reported; or that the woman believes that notifying her husband will cause him or someone else to inflict bodily injury upon her. A physician who performs an abortion on a married woman without receiving the appropriate signed statement will have his or her license revoked, and is liable to the husband for damages. . . .

The American Medical Association (AMA) has published a summary of the recent research in this field, which indicates that in an average 12–month period in this country, approximately two million women are the victims of severe assaults by their male partners. [T]he District Court's findings reinforce what common sense would suggest. In well-functioning marriages, spouses discuss important intimate decisions such as whether to bear a child. But there are millions of women in this country who are the victims of regular physical and psychological abuse at the hands of their husbands. Should these women become pregnant, they may have very good reasons for not wishing to inform their husbands of their decision to obtain an abortion. Many may have justifiable fears of physical abuse, but may be no less fearful of the consequences of reporting prior abuse to the Commonwealth of Pennsylvania. Many may have a reasonable fear that notifying their husbands will provoke further instances of child abuse; these women are not exempt from § 3209's notification requirement. Many may fear devastating forms of psychological abuse from their husbands, including verbal harassment, threats of future violence, the destruction of possessions, physical confinement to the home, the withdrawal of financial support, or the disclosure of the abortion to family and friends. These methods of psychological abuse may act as even more of a deterrent to notification than the possibility of physical violence, but women who are the victims of the abuse are not exempt from § 3209's notification requirement. [V]ictims of spousal sexual assault are extremely reluctant to report the abuse to the government; hence, a great many spousal rape victims will not be exempt from the notification requirement imposed by § 3209. The spousal notification requirement is thus likely to prevent a significant number of women from obtaining an abortion. . . .

Respondents attempt to avoid the conclusion that § 3209 is invalid by pointing out that it imposes almost no burden at all for the vast majority of women seeking abortions. They begin by noting that only about 20 percent of the women who obtain abortions are married. They then note that of these women about 95 percent notify their husbands of their own volition. Thus, respondents argue, the effects of § 3209 are felt by only one percent of the women who obtain abortions. Respondents argue that since some of these women will be able to notify their husbands without adverse consequences or will qualify for one of the exceptions, the statute affects fewer than one percent of women seeking abortions. For this reason, it is asserted, the statute cannot be invalid on its face. We disagree with respondents' basic method of analysis.

The analysis does not end with the one percent of women upon whom the statute operates; it begins there. Legislation is measured for consistency with the Constitution by its impact on those whose conduct it affects. . . . The proper focus of constitutional inquiry is the group for whom the law is a restriction, not the group for whom the law is irrelevant. [For] a large fraction of the cases in which § 3209 is relevant, it will operate as a substantial obstacle to a woman's choice to undergo an abortion. It is an undue burden, and therefore invalid.

This conclusion is in no way inconsistent with our decisions upholding parental notification or consent requirements. Those enactments, and our judgment that they are constitutional, are based on the quite reasonable assumption that minors will benefit from consultation with their parents and that children will often not realize that their parents have their best interests at heart. We cannot adopt a parallel assumption about adult women....

D. We next consider the parental consent provision. Except in a medical emergency, an unemancipated young woman under 18 may not obtain an abortion unless she and one of her parents (or guardian) provides informed consent as defined above. If neither a parent nor a guardian provides consent, a court may authorize the performance of an abortion upon a determination that the young woman is mature and capable of giving informed consent and has in fact given her informed consent, or that an abortion would be in her best interests.

We have been over most of this ground before. Our cases establish, and we reaffirm today, that a State may require a minor seeking an abortion to obtain the consent of a parent or guardian, provided that there is an adequate judicial bypass procedure. Under these precedents, in our view, the one-parent consent requirement and judicial bypass procedure are constitutional....

E. Under the recordkeeping and reporting requirements of the statute, every facility which performs abortions is required to file a report stating its name and address as well as the name and address of any related entity, such as a controlling or subsidiary organization. In the case of state-funded institutions, the information becomes public.

For each abortion performed, a report must be filed identifying: the physician (and the second physician where required); the facility; the referring physician or agency; the woman's age; the number of prior pregnancies and prior abortions she has had; gestational age; the type of abortion procedure; the date of the abortion; whether there were any pre-existing medical conditions which would complicate pregnancy; medical complications with the abortion; where applicable, the basis for the determination that the abortion was medically necessary; the weight of the aborted fetus; and whether the woman was married, and if so, whether notice was provided or the basis for the failure to give notice. Every abortion facility must also file quarterly reports showing the number of abortions performed broken down by trimester. In all events, the identity of each woman who has had an abortion remains confidential.

In *Danforth,* we held that recordkeeping and reporting provisions "that are reasonably directed to the preservation of maternal health and that properly respect a patient's confidentiality and privacy are permissible." We think that under this standard, all the provisions at issue here except that relating to spousal notice are constitutional. Although they do not relate to the State's interest in informing the woman's choice, they do relate to health. The collection of information with respect to actual patients is a vital element of medical research, and so it cannot be said that the requirements serve no purpose other than to make abortions more difficult. Nor do we find that the requirements impose a substantial obstacle to a woman's choice. At most they might increase the cost of some abortions by a slight amount. While at some point increased cost could become a substantial obstacle, there is no such showing on the record before us.

Subsection (12) of the reporting provision requires the reporting of, among other things, a married woman's "reason for failure to provide notice" to her husband. This provision in effect requires women, as a condition of obtaining an abortion, to provide the Commonwealth with the precise information we have already recognized that many women have pressing reasons not to reveal. Like the spousal notice requirement itself, this provision places an undue burden on a woman's choice, and must be invalidated for that reason. . . .

JUSTICE STEVENS, concurring in part and dissenting in part. . . .

In my opinion, . . . §§ 3205(a)(2)(I)–(iii) of the Pennsylvania statute are unconstitutional. Those sections require a physician or counselor to provide the woman with a range of materials clearly designed to persuade her to choose not to undergo the abortion. [A] correct application of the "undue burden" standard leads to the same conclusion concerning the constitutionality of these requirements. A state-imposed burden on the exercise of a constitutional right is measured both by its effects and by its character: A burden may be "undue" either because the burden is too severe or because it lacks a legitimate, rational justification. The 24–hour delay requirement fails both parts of this test. . . . The counseling provisions are similarly infirm. . . .

JUSTICE BLACKMUN, concurring in part, concurring in the judgment in part, and dissenting in part.

I join parts I, II, III, V–A, V–C, and VI of the joint opinion of JUSTICES O'CONNOR, KENNEDY, and SOUTER. [W]hile I believe that the joint opinion errs in failing to invalidate the other regulations, I am pleased that the joint opinion has not ruled out the possibility that these regulations may be shown to impose an unconstitutional burden. The joint opinion makes clear that its specific holdings are based on the insufficiency of the record before it. I am confident that in the future evidence will be produced to show that "in a large fraction of the cases in which [these regulations are] relevant, [they] will operate as a substantial obstacle to a woman's choice to undergo an abortion." . . .

In one sense, the Court's approach is worlds apart from that of The Chief Justice and Justice Scalia. And yet, in another sense, the distance between the two approaches is short—the distance is but a single vote. I am 83 years old. I cannot remain on this Court forever, and when I do step down, the confirmation process for my successor well may focus on the issue before us today. That, I regret, may be exactly where the choice between the two worlds will be made.

CHIEF JUSTICE REHNQUIST, with whom JUSTICE WHITE, JUSTICE SCALIA, and JUSTICE THOMAS join, concurring in the judgment in part and dissenting in part.

The joint opinion, following its newly-minted variation on *stare decisis*, retains the outer shell of *Roe v. Wade*, but beats a wholesale retreat from the substance of that case. We believe that *Roe* was wrongly decided, and that it can and should be overruled consistently with our traditional approach to *stare decisis* in constitutional cases. We would adopt the approach of the plurality in *Webster v. Reproductive Health Services,* and uphold the challenged provisions of the Pennsylvania statute in their entirety.

. . . Unlike marriage, procreation and contraception, abortion "involves the purposeful termination of potential life." *Harris v. McRae,* (1980). The abortion decision must therefore "be recognized as *sui generis,* different in kind from the others that the Court has protected under the rubric of personal or family privacy and autonomy." *Thornburgh v. American College of Obstetricians and Gynecologists, supra* (White, J., dissenting). One cannot ignore the fact that a woman is not isolated in her pregnancy, and that the decision to abort necessarily involves the destruction of a fetus. To look "at the act which is assertedly the subject of a liberty interest in isolation from its effect upon other people [is] like inquiring whether there is a liberty interest in firing a gun where the case at hand happens to involve its discharge into another person's body."

Nor do the historical traditions of the American people support the view that the right to terminate one's pregnancy is "fundamental." The common law which we inherited from England made abortion after "quickening" an offense. At the time of the adoption of the Fourteenth Amendment, statutory prohibitions or restrictions on abortion were commonplace; in 1868, at least 28 of the then–37 States and 8 Territories had statutes banning or limiting abortion. By the turn of the century virtually every State had a law prohibiting or restricting abortion on its books. By the middle of the present century, a liberalization trend had set in. But 21 of the restrictive abortion laws in effect in 1868 were still in effect in 1973 when *Roe* was decided, and an overwhelming majority of the States prohibited abortion unless necessary to preserve the life or health of the mother. On this record, it can scarcely be said that any deeply rooted tradition of relatively unrestricted abortion in our history supported the classification of the right to abortion as "fundamental" under the Due Process Clause of the Fourteenth Amendment. . . .

The joint opinion of Justices O'Connor, Kennedy, and Souter cannot bring itself to say that *Roe* was correct as an original matter, but the authors are of the view that "the immediate question is not the soundness of *Roe's* resolution of the issue, but the precedential force that must be accorded to its holding." Instead of claiming that *Roe* was correct as a matter of original constitutional interpretation, the opinion therefore contains an elaborate discussion of *stare decisis.* This discussion of the principle of *stare decisis* appears to be almost entirely dicta, because the joint opinion does not apply that principle in dealing with *Roe. Roe* decided that a woman had a fundamental right to an abortion. The joint opinion rejects that view. *Roe* decided that abortion regulations were to be subjected to "strict scrutiny" and could be justified only in the light of "compelling state interests." The joint opinion rejects that view. *Roe* analyzed abortion regulation under a rigid trimester framework, a framework which has guided this Court's decisionmaking for 19 years. The joint opinion rejects that framework. . . .

The joint opinion discusses several *stare decisis* factors which, it asserts, point toward retaining a portion of *Roe.* Two of these factors are that the main "factual underpinning" of *Roe* has remained the same, and that its doctrinal foundation is no weaker now than it was in 1973. [S]urely there is no requirement, in considering whether to depart from *stare decisis* in a constitutional case, that a decision be more wrong now than it was at the time it was rendered. If that were true, the most outlandish constitutional decision could survive forever, based simply on the fact that it was no more outlandish later than it was when originally rendered.

Nor does the joint opinion faithfully follow this alleged requirement. The opinion frankly concludes that *Roe* and its progeny were wrong in failing to recognize that the State's interests in maternal health and in the protection of unborn human life exist throughout pregnancy. But there is no indication that these components of *Roe* are any more incorrect at this juncture than they were at its inception.

The joint opinion also points to the reliance interests involved in this context in its effort to explain why precedent must be followed for precedent's sake. . . . But, as the joint opinion apparently agrees, any traditional notion of reliance is not applicable here. The Court today cuts back on the protection afforded by *Roe,* and no one claims that this action defeats any reliance interest in the disavowed trimester framework. Similarly, reliance interests would not be diminished were the Court to go further and acknowledge the full error of *Roe,* as "reproductive planning could take virtually immediate account of" this action.

The joint opinion thus turns to what can only be described as an unconventional—and unconvincing—notion of reliance, a view based on the surmise that the availability of abortion since *Roe* has led to "two decades of economic and social developments" that would be undercut if the error of *Roe* were recognized. The joint opinion's assertion of this fact is undeveloped and totally conclusory. In fact, one can not be sure to what economic and social developments the opinion is referring. Surely it is dubious to suggest that women have reached their "places in society" in reliance upon *Roe,* rather than as a result of their determination to obtain higher education and compete with men in the job market, and of society's increasing recognition of their ability to fill positions that were previously thought to be reserved only for men.

In the end, having failed to put forth any evidence to prove any true reliance, the joint opinion's argument is based solely on generalized assertions about the national psyche, on a belief that the people of this country have grown accustomed to the *Roe* decision over the last 19 years and have "ordered their thinking and living around" it. As an initial matter, one might inquire how the joint opinion can view the "central holding" of *Roe* as so deeply rooted in our constitutional culture, when it so casually uproots and disposes of that same decision's trimester framework. Furthermore, at various points in the past, the same could have been said about this Court's erroneous decisions that the Constitution allowed "separate but equal" treatment of minorities, or that "liberty" under the Due Process Clause protected "freedom of contract." The "separate but equal" doctrine lasted 58 years after *Plessy,* and *Lochner's* protection of contractual freedom lasted 32 years. However, the simple fact that a generation or more had grown used to these major decisions did not prevent the Court from correcting its errors in those cases, nor should it prevent us from correctly interpreting the Constitution here.

Apparently realizing that conventional *stare decisis* principles do not support its position, the joint opinion advances a belief that retaining a portion of *Roe* is necessary to protect the "legitimacy" of this Court. [T]he joint opinion goes on to state that when the Court "resolve[s] the sort of intensely divisive controversy reflected in *Roe* and those rare, comparable cases," its decision is exempt from reconsideration under established principles of *stare decisis* in constitutional cases. This is so, the joint opinion contends, because in those "intensely divisive" cases the Court has "call[ed] the contending sides of a national controversy to end their national division by accepting a common mandate rooted in the Constitution," and must therefore take special care not to be perceived as "surrender[ing] to political pressure" and continued opposition. This is a truly novel principle, one which is contrary to both the Court's historical practice and to the Court's traditional willingness to tolerate criticism of its opinions. Under this principle, when the Court has ruled on a divisive issue, it is apparently prevented from overruling that decision for the sole reason that it was incorrect, *unless opposition to the original decision has died away.*

[B]ecause the Court's duty is to ignore public opinion and criticism on issues that come before it, its members are in perhaps the worst position to judge whether a decision divides the Nation deeply enough to justify such uncommon protection. Although many of the Court's decisions divide the populace to a large degree, we have not previously on that account shied away from applying normal rules of *stare decisis* when urged to reconsider earlier decisions. Over the past 21 years, for example, the Court has overruled in whole or in part 34 of its previous constitutional decisions. . . . Public protests should not alter the normal application of *stare decisis,* lest perfectly lawful protest activity be penalized by the Court itself.

Taking the joint opinion on its own terms, we doubt that its distinction between *Roe,* on the one hand, and *Plessy* and *Lochner,* on the other, withstands analysis. The joint opinion acknowledges that the Court improved its stature by overruling *Plessy* in *Brown* on a deeply divisive issue. And our decision in *West Coast Hotel,* which overruled *Adkins v. Children's Hospital, supra,* and *Lochner,* was rendered at a time when Congress was considering President Franklin Roosevelt's proposal to "reorganize" this Court and enable him to name six additional Justices in the event that any member of the Court over the age of 70 did not elect to retire. It is difficult to imagine a situation in which the Court would face more intense opposition to a prior ruling than it did at that time, and, under the general principle proclaimed in the joint opinion, the Court seemingly should have responded to this opposition by stubbornly refusing to reexamine the *Lochner* rationale, lest it lose legitimacy by appearing to "overrule under fire."

The joint opinion ... asserts that the Court could justifiably overrule its decision in *Lochner* only because the Depression had convinced "most people" that constitutional protection of contractual freedom contributed to an economy that failed to protect the welfare of all. Surely the joint opinion does not mean to suggest that people saw this Court's failure to uphold minimum wage statutes as the cause of the Great Depression! In any event, the *Lochner* Court did not base its rule upon the policy judgment that an unregulated market was fundamental to a stable economy; it simply believed, erroneously, that "liberty" under the Due Process Clause protected the "right to make a contract." *Lochner v. New York*. Nor is it the case that the people of this Nation only discovered the dangers of extreme laissez faire economics because of the Depression. State laws regulating maximum hours and minimum wages were in existence well before that time....

When the Court finally recognized its error in *West Coast Hotel*, it did not engage in the *post hoc* rationalization that *Lochner* had been based on an economic view that had fallen into disfavor, and that it therefore should be overruled. Chief Justice Hughes in his opinion for the Court simply recognized what Justice Holmes had previously recognized in his *Lochner* dissent, that "[t]he Constitution does not speak of freedom of contract." *West Coast Hotel Co. v. Parrish*.

The joint opinion also agrees that the Court acted properly in rejecting the doctrine of "separate but equal" in *Brown*. In fact, the opinion lauds *Brown* in comparing it to *Roe*. This is strange, in that under the opinion's "legitimacy" principle the Court would seemingly have been forced to adhere to its erroneous decision in *Plessy* because of its "intensely divisive" character. To us, adherence to *Roe* today under the guise of "legitimacy" would seem to resemble more closely adherence to *Plessy* on the same ground. Fortunately, the Court did not choose that option in *Brown,* and instead frankly repudiated *Plessy*. The joint opinion concludes that such repudiation was justified only because of newly discovered evidence that segregation had the effect of treating one race as inferior to another. But it can hardly be argued that this was not urged upon those who decided *Plessy,* as Justice Harlan observed in his dissent that the law at issue "puts the brand of servitude and degradation upon a large class of our fellow-citizens, our equals before the law." *Plessy v. Ferguson* (Harlan, J., dissenting). It is clear that the same arguments made before the Court in *Brown* were made in *Plessy* as well. The Court in *Brown* simply recognized, as Justice Harlan had recognized beforehand, that the Fourteenth Amendment does not permit racial segregation. The rule of *Brown* is not tied to popular opinion about the evils of segregation; it is a judgment that the Equal Protection Clause does not permit racial segregation, no matter whether the public might come to believe that it is beneficial. On that ground it stands, and on that ground alone the Court was justified in properly concluding that the *Plessy* Court had erred.

... In assuming that the Court is perceived as "surrender[ing] to political pressure" when it overrules a controversial decision, the joint opinion forgets that there are two sides to any controversy. ...The decision in *Roe* has engendered large demonstrations, including repeated marches on this Court and on Congress, both in opposition to and in support of that opinion. A decision either way on *Roe* can therefore be perceived as favoring one group or the other. But this perceived dilemma arises only if one assumes, as the joint opinion does, that the Court should make its decisions with a view toward speculative public perceptions. If one assumes instead, as the Court surely did in both *Brown* and *West Coast Hotel,* that the Court's legitimacy is enhanced by faithful interpretation of the Constitution irrespective of public opposition, such self-engendered difficulties may be put to one side....

The end result of the joint opinion's paeans of praise for legitimacy is the enunciation of a brand new standard for evaluating state regulation of a woman's right to abortion—the "undue burden" standard. As indicated above, *Roe v. Wade* adopted a "fundamental right" standard under which state regulations could survive only if they met the requirement of "strict scrutiny." While we disagree with that standard, it at least had a recognized basis in constitutional law at the time *Roe* was decided. The same cannot be said for the "undue burden" standard, which is created largely out of whole cloth by the authors of the joint opinion. It is a standard which even today does not command the support of a majority of this Court. And it will not, we believe, result in the sort of "simple limitation," easily applied, which the joint opinion anticipates. In sum, it is a standard which is not built to last.

... Because the undue burden standard is plucked from nowhere, the question of what is a "substantial obstacle" to abortion will undoubtedly engender a variety of conflicting views. For example, in the very matter before us now, the authors of the joint opinion would uphold Pennsylvania's 24–hour waiting period, concluding that a "particular burden" on some women is not a substantial obstacle. But the authors would at the same time strike down Pennsylvania's spousal notice provision, after finding that in a "large fraction" of cases the provision will be a substantial obstacle. And, while the authors conclude that the informed consent provisions do not constitute an "undue burden," Justice Stevens would hold that they do.

Furthermore, while striking down the spousal *notice* regulation, the joint opinion would uphold a parental *consent* restriction that certainly places very substantial obstacles in the path of a minor's abortion choice. The joint opinion is forthright in admitting that it draws this distinction based on a policy judgment that parents will have the best interests of their children at heart, while the same is not necessarily true of husbands as to their wives. This may or may not be a correct judgment, but it is quintessentially a legislative one. The "undue burden" inquiry does not in any way supply the distinction between parental consent and spousal consent which the joint opinion adopts. Despite the efforts of the joint opinion, the undue burden standard presents nothing more workable than the trimester framework which it discards today. Under the guise of the Constitution, this Court will still impart its own preferences on the States in the form of a complex abortion code.

The sum of the joint opinion's labors in the name of *stare decisis* and "legitimacy" is this: *Roe v. Wade* stands as a sort of judicial Potemkin Village, which may be pointed out to passers by as a monument to the importance of adhering to precedent. But behind the facade, an entirely new method of analysis, without any roots in constitutional law, is imported to decide the constitutionality of state laws regulating abortion. Neither *stare decisis* nor "legitimacy" are truly served by such an effort.

We have stated above our belief that the Constitution does not subject state abortion regulations to heightened scrutiny. Accordingly, we think that the correct analysis is that set forth by the plurality opinion in *Webster*. A woman's interest in having an abortion is a form of liberty protected by the Due Process Clause, but States may regulate abortion procedures in ways rationally related to a legitimate state interest. With this rule in mind, we examine each of the challenged provisions.

Section 3205 of the Act imposes certain requirements related to the informed consent of a woman seeking an abortion.... We conclude that this provision of the statute is rationally related to the State's interest in assuring that a woman's consent to an abortion be a fully informed decision.... For the same reason, we do not feel bound to follow this Court's previous holding that a State's 24–hour mandatory waiting period is unconstitutional. See *Akron v. Akron Center for Reproductive Health* ....

Section 3209 of the Act contains the spousal notification provision. ...We first emphasize that Pennsylvania has not imposed a spousal *consent* requirement of the type the Court struck down in *Planned Parenthood of Central Mo. v. Danforth*. [T]his case involves a much less intrusive requirement of spousal *notification,* not consent. [P]etitioners argue, many notified husbands will prevent abortions through physical force, psychological coercion, and other types of threats. But Pennsylvania has incorporated exceptions in the notice provision in an attempt to deal with these problems.... Furthermore, because this is a facial challenge to the Act, it is insufficient for petitioners to show that the notification provision "might operate unconstitutionally under some conceivable set of circumstances." Thus, it is not enough for petitioners to show that, in some "worst-case" circumstances, the notice provision will operate as a grant of veto power to husbands. Because they are making a facial challenge to the provision, they must "show that no set of circumstances exists under which the [provision] would be valid." This they have failed to do.

The question before us is therefore whether the spousal notification requirement rationally furthers any legitimate state interests. We conclude that it does.... As Judge Alito observed in his dissent below, "[t]he Pennsylvania legislature could have rationally believed that some married women are initially inclined to obtain an abortion without their husbands' knowledge because of perceived problems—such as economic constraints, future plans, or the husbands' previously expressed opposition—that may be obviated by discussion prior to the abortion." ...

JUSTICE SCALIA, with whom THE CHIEF JUSTICE, JUSTICE WHITE, and JUSTICE THOMAS join, concurring in the judgment in part and dissenting in part.

My views on this matter are unchanged from those I set forth in my separate opinions in *Webster v. Reproductive Health Services,* (1989)(Scalia, J., concurring in part and concurring in judgment), and *Ohio v. Akron Center for Reproductive Health,* (1990)(*Akron II*)(Scalia, J., concurring). The States may, if they wish, permit abortion-on-demand, but the Constitution does not *require* them to do so. The permissibility of abortion, and the limitations upon it, are to be resolved like most important questions in our democracy: by citizens trying to persuade one another and then voting. As the Court acknowledges, "where reasonable people disagree the government can adopt one position or the other." The Court is correct in adding the qualification that this "assumes a state of affairs in which the choice does not intrude upon a protected liberty,"—but the crucial part of that qualification is the penultimate word. A State's choice between two positions on which reasonable people can disagree is constitutional even when (as is often the case) it intrudes upon a "liberty" in the absolute sense. Laws against bigamy, for example—which entire societies of reasonable people disagree with—intrude upon men and women's liberty to marry and live with one another. But bigamy happens not to be a liberty specially "protected" by the Constitution.

That is, quite simply, the issue in this case: not whether the power of a woman to abort her unborn child is a "liberty" in the absolute sense; or even whether it is a liberty of great importance to many women. Of course it is both. The issue is whether it is a liberty protected by the Constitution of the United States. I am sure it is not. I reach that conclusion not because of anything so exalted as my views concerning the "concept of existence, of meaning, of the universe, and of the mystery of human life." Rather, I reach it for the same reason I reach the conclusion that bigamy is not constitutionally protected—because of two simple facts: (1) the Constitution says absolutely nothing about it, and (2) the longstanding traditions of American society have permitted it to be legally proscribed.[1] . . .

Beyond that brief summary of the essence of my position, I will not swell the United States Reports with repetition of what I have said before; and applying the rational basis test, I would uphold the Pennsylvania statute in its entirety. I must, however, respond to a few of the more outrageous arguments in today's opinion. . . .

"The inescapable fact is that adjudication of substantive due process claims may call upon the Court in interpreting the Constitution to exercise that same capacity which by tradition courts always have exercised: reasoned judgment."

Assuming that the question before us is to be resolved at such a level of philosophical abstraction, in such isolation from the traditions of American society, as by simply applying "reasoned judgment," I do not see how that could possibly have produced the answer the Court arrived at in *Roe v. Wade.* Today's opinion describes the methodology of *Roe,* quite accurately, as weighing against the woman's interest the State's " 'important and legitimate interest in protecting the potentiality of human life.' " But "reasoned judgment" does not begin by begging the question, as *Roe* and subsequent cases unquestionably did by assuming that what the State is protecting is the mere "potentiality of human life." The whole argument of abortion opponents is that what the Court calls the fetus and what others call the unborn child *is a human life.* Thus, whatever answer *Roe* came up with after conducting its "balancing" is bound to be wrong, unless it is correct that the human fetus is in some critical sense merely potentially human. There is of course no way to determine that as a legal matter; it is in fact a value judgment. Some societies have considered newborn children not yet human, or the incompetent elderly no longer so. . . .

The emptiness of the "reasoned judgment" that produced *Roe* is displayed in plain view by the fact that, after more than 19 years of effort by some of the brightest (and most determined) legal minds in the country, after more than 10 cases upholding abortion rights in this Court, and after dozens upon dozens of *amicus* briefs submitted in this and other cases, the best the Court can do to explain how it is that the word "liberty" *must* be thought to include the right to destroy human

---

1. The Court's suggestion, *ante,* that adherence to tradition would require us to uphold laws against interracial marriage is entirely wrong. Any tradition in that case was contradicted *by a text*—an Equal Protection Clause that explicitly establishes racial equality as a constitutional value. See *Loving v. Virginia* (1967). The enterprise launched in *Roe,* by contrast, sought to *establish*—in the teeth of a clear, contrary tradition—a value found nowhere in the constitutional text.

There is, of course, no comparable tradition barring recognition of a "liberty inter-

est" in carrying one's child to term free from state efforts to kill it. For that reason, it does not follow that the Constitution does not protect childbirth simply because it does not protect abortion. The Court's contention, that the only way to protect childbirth is to protect abortion shows the utter bankruptcy of constitutional analysis deprived of tradition as a validating factor. It drives one to say that the only way to protect the right to eat is to acknowledge the constitutional right to starve oneself to death.

fetuses is to rattle off a collection of adjectives that simply decorate a
value judgment and conceal a political choice.... But it is obvious to
anyone applying "reasoned judgment" that the same adjectives can be
applied to many forms of conduct that this Court (including one of the
Justices in today's majority, see *Bowers v. Hardwick,* (1986)) has held
are *not* entitled to constitutional protection—because, like abortion, they
are forms of conduct that have long been criminalized in American
society. Those adjectives might be applied, for example, to homosexual
sodomy, polygamy, adult incest, and suicide, all of which are equally
"intimate" and "deep[ly] personal" decisions involving "personal autonomy and bodily integrity," and all of which can constitutionally be
proscribed because it is our unquestionable constitutional tradition that
they are proscribable. It is not reasoned judgment that supports the
Court's decision; only personal predilection. Justice Curtis's warning is
as timely today as it was 135 years ago:

> "[W]hen a strict interpretation of the Constitution, according to the
> fixed rules which govern the interpretation of laws, is abandoned,
> and the theoretical opinions of individuals are allowed to control its
> meaning, we have no longer a Constitution; we are under the
> government of individual men, who for the time being have power to
> declare what the Constitution is, according to their own views of
> what it ought to mean." *Dred Scott v. Sandford* (1857)(Curtis, J.,
> dissenting).

"Liberty finds no refuge in a jurisprudence of doubt."

One might have feared to encounter this august and sonorous
phrase in an opinion defending the real *Roe v. Wade,* rather than the
revised version fabricated today by the authors of the joint opinion. The
shortcomings of *Roe* did not include lack of clarity: Virtually all regulation of abortion before the third trimester was invalid. But to come
across this phrase in the joint opinion—which calls upon federal district
judges to apply an "undue burden" standard as doubtful in application
as it is unprincipled in origin—is really more than one should have to
bear....

The joint opinion explains that a state regulation imposes an "undue burden" if it "has the purpose or effect of placing a substantial
obstacle in the path of a woman seeking an abortion of a nonviable
fetus." An obstacle is "substantial," we are told, if it is "calculated[,]
[not] to inform the woman's free choice, [but to] hinder it." This latter
statement cannot possibly mean what it says. *Any* regulation of abortion
that is intended to advance what the joint opinion concedes is the State's
"substantial" interest in protecting unborn life will be "calculated [to]
hinder" a decision to have an abortion. It thus seems more accurate to
say that the joint opinion would uphold abortion regulations only if they
do not *unduly* hinder the woman's decision. That, of course, brings us
right back to square one: Defining an "undue burden" as an "undue
hindrance" (or a "substantial obstacle") hardly "clarifies" the test.
Consciously or not, the joint opinion's verbal shell game will conceal raw

judicial policy choices concerning what is "appropriate" abortion legislation.

. . . . Reason finds no refuge in this jurisprudence of confusion.

"While we appreciate the weight of the arguments . . . that _Roe_ should be overruled, the reservations any of us may have in reaffirming the central holding of _Roe_ are outweighed by the explication of individual liberty we have given combined with the force of _stare decisis_."

The Court's reliance upon _stare decisis_ can best be described as contrived. It insists upon the necessity of adhering not to all of _Roe_, but only to what it calls the "central holding." It seems to me that _stare decisis_ ought to be applied even to the doctrine of _stare decisis_, and I confess never to have heard of this new, keep-what-you-want-and-throw-away-the-rest version. . . .

I am certainly not in a good position to dispute that the Court _has saved_ the "central holding" of _Roe_, since to do that effectively I would have to know what the Court has saved, which in turn would require me to understand (as I do not) what the "undue burden" test means. [But] I have always thought . . . that the arbitrary trimester framework, which the Court today discards, was quite as central to _Roe_ as the arbitrary viability test, which the Court today retains. It seems particularly ungrateful to carve the trimester framework out of the core of _Roe_, since its very rigidity (in sharp contrast to the utter indeterminability of the "undue burden" test) is probably the only reason the Court is able to say, in urging _stare decisis_, that _Roe_ "has in no sense proven 'unworkable.' " . . . I thought I might note, however, that the following portions of _Roe_ have not been saved:

• Under _Roe_, requiring that a woman seeking an abortion be provided truthful information about abortion before giving informed written consent is unconstitutional, if the information is designed to influence her choice, _Thornburgh; Akron I_. Under the joint opinion's "undue burden" regime (as applied today, at least) such a requirement is constitutional.

• Under _Roe_, requiring that information be provided by a doctor, rather than by nonphysician counselors, is unconstitutional, _Akron I_. Under the "undue burden" regime (as applied today, at least) it is not.

• Under _Roe_, requiring a 24–hour waiting period between the time the woman gives her informed consent and the time of the abortion is unconstitutional, _Akron I, supra_. Under the "undue burden" regime (as applied today, at least) it is not.

• Under _Roe_, requiring detailed reports that include demographic data about each woman who seeks an abortion and various information about each abortion is unconstitutional, _Thornburgh, supra_. Under the "undue burden" regime (as applied today, at least) it generally is not.

"Where, in the performance of its judicial duties, the Court decides a case in such a way as to resolve the sort of intensely

divisive controversy reflected in *Roe* ..., its decision has a dimension that the resolution of the normal case does not carry. It is the dimension present whenever the Court's interpretation of the Constitution calls the contending sides of a national controversy to end their national division by accepting a common mandate rooted in the Constitution."

The Court's description of the place of *Roe* in the social history of the United States is unrecognizable. Not only did *Roe* not, as the Court suggests, *resolve* the deeply divisive issue of abortion; it did more than anything else to nourish it, by elevating it to the national level where it is infinitely more difficult to resolve. National politics were not plagued by abortion protests, national abortion lobbying, or abortion marches on Congress, before *Roe v. Wade* was decided. Profound disagreement existed among our citizens over the issue—as it does over other issues, such as the death penalty—but that disagreement was being worked out at the state level. As with many other issues, the division of sentiment within each State was not as closely balanced as it was among the population of the Nation as a whole, meaning not only that more people would be satisfied with the results of state-by-state resolution, but also that those results would be more stable. Pre–*Roe,* moreover, political compromise was possible.

Roe's mandate for abortion-on-demand destroyed the compromises of the past, rendered compromise impossible for the future, and required the entire issue to be resolved uniformly, at the national level. At the same time, *Roe* created a vast new class of abortion consumers and abortion proponents by eliminating the moral opprobrium that had attached to the act. ("If the Constitution *guarantees* abortion, how can it be bad?"—not an accurate line of thought, but a natural one.) [T]o portray *Roe* as the statesmanlike "settlement" of a divisive issue, a jurisprudential Peace of Westphalia that is worth preserving, is nothing less than Orwellian. *Roe* fanned into life an issue that has inflamed our national politics in general, and has obscured with its smoke the selection of Justices to this Court in particular, ever since. And by keeping us in the abortion-umpiring business, it is the perpetuation of that disruption, rather than of any *pax Roeana,* that the Court's new majority decrees.

"[T]o overrule under fire ... would subvert the Court's legitimacy....

"To all those who will be ... tested by following, the Court implicitly undertakes to remain steadfast.... The promise of constancy, once given, binds its maker for as long as the power to stand by the decision survives and ... the commitment [is not] obsolete....

"[The American people's] belief in themselves as ... a people [who aspire to live according to the rule of law] is not readily separable from their understanding of the Court invested with the authority to decide their constitutional cases and speak

before all others for their constitutional ideals. If the Court's legitimacy should be undermined, then, so would the country be in its very ability to see itself through its constitutional ideals."

The Imperial Judiciary lives. It is instructive to compare this Nietzschean vision of us unelected, life-tenured judges—leading a Volk who will be "tested by following," and whose very "belief in themselves" is mystically bound up in their "understanding" of a Court that "speak[s] before all others for their constitutional ideals"—with the somewhat more modest role envisioned for these lawyers by the Founders.

> "The judiciary . . . can take no active resolution whatever. It may truly be said to have neither FORCE nor WILL but merely judgment. . . . " *The Federalist* No. 78.

. . . I am appalled by, the Court's suggestion that the decision whether to stand by an erroneous constitutional decision must be strongly influenced—*against* overruling, no less—by the substantial and continuing public opposition the decision has generated. The Court's judgment that any other course would "subvert the Court's legitimacy" must be another consequence of reading the error-filled history book that described the deeply divided country brought together by *Roe.* In my history-book, the Court was covered with dishonor and deprived of legitimacy by *Dred Scott v. Sandford* (1857), an erroneous (and widely opposed) opinion that it did not abandon, rather than by *West Coast Hotel Co. v. Parrish* (1937), which produced the famous "switch in time" from the Court's erroneous (and widely opposed) constitutional opposition to the social measures of the New Deal. (. . . *Dred Scott* was "very possibly the first application of substantive due process in the Supreme Court, the original precedent for *Lochner v. New York* and *Roe v. Wade.*" D. Currie, The Constitution in the Supreme Court 271 (1985)(footnotes omitted).)

[T]he notion that the Court must adhere to a decision for as long as the decision faces "great opposition" and the Court is "under fire" acquires a character of almost czarist arrogance. We are offended by these marchers who descend upon us, every year on the anniversary of *Roe,* to protest our saying that the Constitution requires what our society has never thought the Constitution requires. These people who refuse to be "tested by following" must be taught a lesson. We have no Cossacks, but at least we can stubbornly refuse to abandon an erroneous opinion that we might otherwise change—to show how little they intimidate us.

Of course, as The Chief Justice points out, we have been subjected to what the Court calls "political pressure" by *both* sides of this issue. Maybe today's decision *not* to overrule *Roe* will be seen as buckling to pressure from *that* direction. . . .

What makes all this relevant to the bothersome application of "political pressure" against the Court are the twin facts that the American people love democracy and the American people are not fools. As long as this Court thought (and the people thought) that we Justices were doing essentially lawyers' work up here—reading text and discerning our society's traditional understanding of that text—the public pretty much left us alone. Texts and traditions are facts to study, not convictions to demonstrate about. But if in reality our process of constitutional adjudication consists primarily of making *value judgments* . . . then a free and intelligent people's attitude towards us can be expected to be (*ought* to be) quite different. The people know that their value judgments are quite as good as those taught in any law school—maybe better. If, indeed, the "liberties" protected by the Constitution are, as the Court says, undefined and unbounded, then the people *should* demonstrate, to protest that we do not implement *their* values instead of *ours*. [C]onfirmation hearings for new Justices *should* deteriorate into question-and-answer sessions in which Senators go through a list of their constituents' most favored and most disfavored alleged constitutional rights, and seek the nominee's commitment to support or oppose them. Value judgments, after all, should be voted on, not dictated; and if our Constitution has somehow accidently committed them to the Supreme Court, at least we can have a sort of plebiscite each time a new nominee to that body is put forward. Justice Blackmun not only regards this prospect with equanimity, he solicits it. . . .

There is a poignant aspect to today's opinion. Its length, and what might be called its epic tone, suggest that its authors believe they are bringing to an end a troublesome era in the history of our Nation and of our Court. "It is the dimension" of authority, they say, to "cal[l] the contending sides of national controversy to end their national division by accepting a common mandate rooted in the Constitution."

It is no more realistic for us in this case, than it was for [Chief Justice Taney] in [*Dred Scott v. Sandford* (1857)] to think that an issue of the sort they both involved—an issue involving life and death, freedom and subjugation—can be "speedily and finally settled" by the Supreme Court, as President James Buchanan in his inaugural address said the issue of slavery in the territories would be. Quite to the contrary, by foreclosing all democratic outlet for the deep passions this issue arouses, by banishing the issue from the political forum that gives all participants, even the losers, the satisfaction of a fair hearing and an honest fight, by continuing the imposition of a rigid national rule instead of allowing for regional differences, the Court merely prolongs and intensifies the anguish.

We should get out of this area, where we have no right to be, and where we do neither ourselves nor the country any good by remaining.

Notes

1. *Fargo Women's Health Organization v. Schafer*, 507 U.S. 1013, 113 S.Ct. 1668, 123 L.Ed.2d 285 (1993). The district court rejected applicants' facial challenge to an abortion law on the grounds that they were unable to show that under no set of circumstances would the challenged provisions be valid. The Eighth Circuit denied the applicants' motion for a stay and injunction pending appeal, so the applicants asked for similar relief from the

Supreme Court, which denied it. O'Connor, J., joined by Souter, J., concurred in the denial and filed a brief opinion stating that "our denial of relief should not be viewed as signaling agreement with the lower courts' reasoning." When *Casey* invalidated Pennsylvania's "spousal-notice provisions, we did not require petitioners to show that the provision would be invalid in all circumstances. Rather, we made clear that a law restricting abortions constitutes an undue burden, and hence is invalid, if, 'in a large fraction of the cases in which [the law] is relevant, it will operate as a substantial obstacle to a woman's choice to undergo an abortion.'" The lower courts, O'Connor argued, should have applied this test. Blackmun & Stevens, JJ., filed no opinion and simply voted to grant the application for a stay and injunction pending appeal.

2. *Mazurek v. Armstrong*, 520 U.S. 968, 117 S.Ct. 1865, 138 L.Ed.2d 162 (1997) (per curiam). Plaintiffs sought to enjoin a Montana law that only allowed licensed physicians to perform abortions. Similar rules exist in 40 other states. The trial court refused a preliminary injunction, but the Ninth ruled that the physician-only requirement was invalid because its purpose was to create a "substantial obstacle" to a woman seeking an abortion and that the plaintiffs had established a "fair chance of success on the merits." The Supreme Court reversed; the plaintiffs were unlikely prevail on the claim that the Montana restriction imposed an "undue burden" on the woman's right to choose an abortion. The majority referred to *Connecticut v. Menillo* (1975), supra, which had held that "prosecutions for abortions conducted by nonphysicians infringe upon no realm of personal privacy secured by the Constitution against state interference." The district court had discussed this case, but it was not "so much as cited by the Court of Appeals." Stevens, J., joined by Ginsburg & Breyer, JJ., dissented on that grounds that the case was not of "sufficient importance" to grant certiorari.

3. Some state courts are allowing wrongful death actions brought by non-viable fetuses. (Some fetuses as young as 20 weeks are now viable.) In the typical case, the pregnant woman suffers a miscarriage because of an accident (e.g., tainted food) and then sues for wrongful death on behalf of the fetus. Some abortion rights groups oppose this trend in the law: "Recognition of the [nonviable] fetus as an individual person is a back-door way to undermine the rights guaranteed" by *Roe v. Wade*, said Kathryn Kolbert, of the Center for Reproductive Law and Policy, a group advocating abortion rights. Charlotte Snead, of West Virginians for Life, replied that the women-plaintiffs in these cases "were robbed of their choice." Without the injury, "there would've been a normal child."* What do you think?

8–3.44 Homosexuality

BOWERS v. HARDWICK
478 U.S. 186, 106 S.Ct. 2841, 92 L.Ed.2d 140 (1986).

JUSTICE WHITE delivered the opinion of the Court.

In August 1982, respondent was charged with violating the Georgia statute criminalizing sodomy by committing that act with another adult

---

* Frances A. McMorris, Courts are Giving New Rights to Fetuses, Wall St. Jrl., Sept. 4, 1996, at B1, col. 4, 5 & B2 at col. 4 (midwest ed.).

male in the bedroom of respondent's home.[1] After a preliminary hearing, the District Attorney decided not to present the matter to the grand jury unless further evidence developed.

Respondent then brought suit in the Federal District Court, challenging the constitutionality of the statute insofar as it criminalized consensual sodomy.[2] He asserted that he was a practicing homosexual, that the Georgia sodomy statute, as administered by the defendants, placed him in imminent danger of arrest, and that the statute for several reasons violates the Federal Constitution. The District Court granted the defendants' motion to dismiss for failure to state a claim [but a] divided panel of the Court of Appeals for the Eleventh Circuit [held] that the Georgia statute violated respondent's fundamental rights because his homosexual activity is a private and intimate association that is beyond the reach of state regulation by reason of the Ninth Amendment and the Due Process Clause of the Fourteenth Amendment.... We agree with the State that the Court of Appeals erred, and hence reverse its judgment.

This case does not require a judgment on whether laws against sodomy between consenting adults in general, or between homosexuals in particular, are wise or desirable. It raises no question about the right or propriety of state legislative decisions to repeal their laws that criminalize homosexual sodomy, or of state court decisions invalidating those laws on state constitutional grounds. The issue presented is whether the Federal Constitution confers a fundamental right upon homosexuals to engage in sodomy and hence invalidates the laws of the many States that still make such conduct illegal and have done so for a very long time. The case also calls for some judgment about the limits of the Court's role in carrying out its constitutional mandate.

We first register our disagreement with the Court of Appeals and with respondent that the Court's prior cases have construed the Constitution to confer a right of privacy that extends to homosexual sodomy and for all intents and purposes have decided this case. The reach of this line of cases was sketched in *Carey v. Population Services International.* *Pierce v. Society of Sisters,* [§ 6–2], and *Meyer v. Nebraska,* [§ 6–2], were

---

1. Ga.Code Ann. § 16–6–2 (1984) provides, in pertinent part, as follows:

"(a) A person commits the offense of sodomy when he performs or submits to any sexual act involving the sex organs of one person and the mouth or anus of another....

"(b) A person convicted of the offense of sodomy shall be punished by imprisonment for not less than one nor more than 20 years.... "

2. John and Mary Doe were also plaintiffs in the action. They alleged that they wished to engage in sexual activity proscribed by § 16–6–2 in the privacy of their home, and that they had been "chilled and deterred" from engaging in such activity by

both the existence of the statute and Hardwick's arrest. The District Court held, however, that because they had neither sustained, nor were in immediate danger of sustaining, any direct injury from the enforcement of the statute, they did not have proper standing to maintain the action. [T]he Does do not challenge that holding in this Court.

The only claim properly before the Court, therefore, is Hardwick's challenge to the Georgia statute as applied to consensual homosexual sodomy. We express no opinion on the constitutionality of the Georgia statute as applied to other acts of sodomy.

described as dealing with child rearing and education; ... *Skinner v. Oklahoma ex rel. Williamson,* with procreation; *Loving v. Virginia,* [§ 8–3.5], with marriage; *Griswold v. Connecticut,* and *Eisenstadt v. Baird,* with contraception; and *Roe v. Wade,* with abortion. The latter three cases were interpreted as construing the Due Process Clause of the Fourteenth Amendment to confer a fundamental individual right to decide whether or not to beget or bear a child. *Carey v. Population Services International.*

Accepting the decisions in these cases and the above description of them, we think it evident that none of the rights announced in those cases bears any resemblance to the claimed constitutional right of homosexuals to engage in acts of sodomy that is asserted in this case. No connection between family, marriage, or procreation on the one hand and homosexual activity on the other has been demonstrated, either by the Court of Appeals or by respondent. Moreover, any claim that these cases nevertheless stand for the proposition that any kind of private sexual conduct between consenting adults is constitutionally insulated from state proscription is unsupportable. Indeed, the Court's opinion in *Carey* twice asserted that the privacy right, which the *Griswold* line of cases found to be one of the protections provided by the Due Process Clause, did not reach so far.

Precedent aside, however, respondent would have us announce, as the Court of Appeals did, a fundamental right to engage in homosexual sodomy. This we are quite unwilling to do.... Striving to assure itself and the public that announcing rights not readily identifiable in the Constitution's text involves much more than the imposition of the Justices' own choice of values on the States and the Federal Government, the Court has sought to identify the nature of the rights qualifying for heightened judicial protection. In *Palko v. Connecticut,* 302 U.S. 319, 325, 326, 58 S.Ct. 149, 152, 82 L.Ed. 288 (1937), it was said that this category includes those fundamental liberties that are "implicit in the concept of ordered liberty," such that "neither liberty nor justice would exist if [they] were sacrificed." A different description of fundamental liberties appeared in *Moore v. East Cleveland,* [§ 6–6.2] (opinion of Powell, J.), where they are characterized as those liberties that are "deeply rooted in this Nation's history and tradition." See also *Griswold v. Connecticut.*

It is obvious to us that neither of these formulations would extend a fundamental right to homosexuals to engage in acts of consensual sodomy. Proscriptions against that conduct have ancient roots. Sodomy was a criminal offense at common law and was forbidden by the laws of the original thirteen States when they ratified the Bill of Rights. In 1868, when the Fourteenth Amendment was ratified, all but 5 of the 37 States in the Union had criminal sodomy laws. In fact, until 1961, all 50 States outlawed sodomy, and today, 24 States and the District of Columbia continue to provide criminal penalties for sodomy performed in private and between consenting adults. Against this background, to claim that a right to engage in such conduct is "deeply rooted in this

Nation's history and tradition" or "implicit in the concept of ordered liberty" is, at best, facetious.

Nor are we inclined to take a more expansive view of our authority to discover new fundamental rights imbedded in the Due Process Clause. The Court is most vulnerable and comes nearest to illegitimacy when it deals with judge-made constitutional law having little or no cognizable roots in the language or design of the Constitution. That this is so was painfully demonstrated by the face-off between the Executive and the Court in the 1930's, which resulted in the repudiation of much of the substantive gloss that the Court had placed on the Due Process Clause of the Fifth and Fourteenth Amendments. There should be, therefore, great resistance to expand the substantive reach of those Clauses, particularly if it requires redefining the category of rights deemed to be fundamental. Otherwise, the Judiciary necessarily takes to itself further authority to govern the country without express constitutional authority. The claimed right pressed on us today falls far short of overcoming this resistance.

Respondent, however, asserts that the results should be different where the homosexual conduct occurs in the privacy of the home. He relies on *Stanley v. Georgia,* [§ 10–12.1], where the Court held that the First Amendment prevents conviction for possessing and reading obscene material in the privacy of his home: "If the First Amendment means anything, it means that a State has no business telling a man, sitting alone in his house, what books he may read or what films he may watch."

Stanley did protect conduct that would not have been protected outside the home, and it partially prevented the enforcement of state obscenity laws; but the decision was firmly grounded in the First Amendment. The right pressed upon us here has no similar support in the text of the Constitution, and it does not qualify for recognition under the prevailing principles for construing the Fourteenth Amendment. Its limits are also difficult to discern. Plainly enough, otherwise illegal conduct is not always immunized whenever it occurs in the home. Victimless crimes, such as the possession and use of illegal drugs do not escape the law where they are committed at home. *Stanley* itself recognized that its holding offered no protection for the possession in the home of drugs, firearms, or stolen goods. And if respondent's submission is limited to the voluntary sexual conduct between consenting adults, it would be difficult, except by fiat, to limit the claimed right to homosexual conduct while leaving exposed to prosecution adultery, incest, and other sexual crimes even though they are committed in the home. We are unwilling to start down that road.

Even if the conduct at issue here is not a fundamental right, respondent asserts that there must be a rational basis for the law and that there is none in this case other than the presumed belief of a majority of the electorate in Georgia that homosexual sodomy is immoral and unacceptable. This is said to be an inadequate rationale to support the law. The law, however, is constantly based on notions of morality, and if all laws representing essentially moral choices are to be invalidated under the Due Process Clause, the courts will be very busy indeed. Even respondent makes no such claim, but insists that majority sentiments about the morality of homosexuality should be declared inadequate. We do not agree, and are unpersuaded that the sodomy laws of some 25 States should be invalidated on this basis.[8]

Accordingly, the judgment of the Court of Appeals is reversed.

CHIEF JUSTICE BURGER, concurring.

[In constitutional terms there is no such thing as a fundamental right to commit homosexual sodomy. [T]he proscriptions against sodomy have very "ancient roots." Decisions of individuals relating to homosexual conduct have been subject to state intervention throughout the history of Western Civilization. Condemnation of those practices is firmly rooted in Judaeo–Christian moral and ethical standards. Homosexual sodomy was a capital crime under Roman law. During the English Reformation when powers of the ecclesiastical courts were transferred to the King's Courts, the first English statute criminalizing sodomy was passed. Blackstone described "the infamous crime against nature" as an offense of "deeper malignity" than rape, a heinous act "the very mention of which is a disgrace to human nature," and "a crime not fit to be named." The common law of England, including its prohibition of sodomy, became the received law of Georgia and the other Colonies. In 1816 the Georgia Legislature passed the statute at issue here, and that statute has been continuously in force in one form or another since that time. To hold that the act of homosexual sodomy is somehow protected as a fundamental right would be to cast aside millennia of moral teaching. . . .]

JUSTICE POWELL, concurring.

I join the opinion of the Court. I agree with the Court that there is no fundamental right—i.e., no substantive right under the Due Process Clause—such as that claimed by respondent, and found to exist by the Court of Appeals. This is not to suggest, however, that respondent may not be protected by the Eighth Amendment of the Constitution. The Georgia statute at issue in this case authorizes a court to imprison a person for up to 20 years for a single private, consensual act of sodomy. In my view, a prison sentence for such conduct—certainly a sentence of long duration—would create a serious Eighth Amendment issue. Under the Georgia statute a single act of sodomy, even in the private setting of a home, is a felony comparable in terms of the possible sentence imposed to serious felonies such as aggravated battery, first degree arson, and robbery.

In this case, however, respondent has not been tried, much less convicted and sentenced.[2] Moreover, respondent has not raised the

---

8. Respondent does not defend the judgment below based on the Ninth Amendment, the Equal Protection Clause or the Eighth Amendment.

2. [P]rior to the complaint against re-

Eighth Amendment issue below. For these reasons this constitutional argument is not before us.

JUSTICE BLACKMUN, with whom JUSTICE BRENNAN, JUSTICE MARSHALL, and JUSTICE STEVENS, join, dissenting.

This case is no more about "a fundamental right to engage in homosexual sodomy," as the Court purports to declare, than *Katz v. United States,* 389 U.S. 347, 88 S.Ct. 507, 19 L.Ed.2d 576 (1967), was about a fundamental right to place interstate bets from a telephone booth. Rather, this case is about "the most comprehensive of rights and the right most valued by civilized men," namely, "the right to be let alone." *Olmstead v. United States,* 277 U.S. 438, 478, 48 S.Ct. 564, 572, 72 L.Ed. 944 (1928)(Brandeis, J., dissenting).

[T]he fact that the moral judgments expressed by statutes like § 16–6–2 may be "natural and familiar ... ought not to conclude our judgment upon the question whether statutes embodying them conflict with the Constitution of the United States." *Roe v. Wade,* quoting *Lochner v. New York,* (Holmes, J., dissenting). Like Justice Holmes, I believe that "[i]t is revolting to have no better reason for a rule of law than that so it was laid down in the time of Henry IV. It is still more revolting if the grounds upon which it was laid down have vanished long since, and the rule simply persists from blind imitation of the past." Holmes, The Path of the Law, 10 Harv.L.Rev. 457, 469 (1897). [W]e must analyze respondent's claim in the light of the values that underlie the constitutional right to privacy. ...

First, the Court's almost obsessive focus on homosexual activity is particularly hard to justify in light of the broad language Georgia has used. Unlike the Court, the Georgia Legislature has not proceeded on the assumption that homosexuals are so different from other citizens that their lives may be controlled in a way that would not be tolerated if it limited the choices of those other citizens.... The sex or status of the persons who engage in the act is irrelevant as a matter of state law. In fact, to the extent I can discern a legislative purpose for Georgia's 1968 enactment of § 16–6–2, that purpose seems to have been to broaden the coverage of the law to reach heterosexual as well as homosexual activity. I therefore see no basis for the Court's decision to treat this case as an "as applied" challenge to § 16–6–2, see n. 2, or for Georgia's attempt, both in its brief and at oral argument, to defend § 16–6–2 solely on the grounds that it prohibits homosexual activity. Michael Hardwick's standing may rest in significant part on Georgia's apparent willingness to enforce against homosexuals a law it seems not to have any desire to enforce against heterosexuals. But his claim that § 16–6–2 involves an

spondent Hardwick, there had been no reported decision involving prosecution for private homosexual sodomy under this statute for several decades. [This] history of nonenforcement suggests the moribund character today of laws criminalizing this type of private, consensual conduct. Some 26 states have repealed similar statutes. [F]or the reasons stated by the Court, I cannot say that conduct condemned for hundreds of years has now become a fundamental right.

unconstitutional intrusion into his privacy and his right of intimate association does not depend in any way on his sexual orientation.

Second, I disagree with the Court's refusal to consider whether § 16–6–2 runs afoul of the Eighth or Ninth Amendments or the Equal Protection Clause of the Fourteenth Amendment. Ante, n. 8. Respondent's complaint expressly invoked the Ninth Amendment, and he relied heavily before this Court on *Griswold v. Connecticut,* which identifies that Amendment as one of the specific constitutional provisions giving "life and substance" to our understanding of privacy. More importantly, the procedural posture of the case requires that we affirm the Court of Appeals' judgment if there is *any* ground on which respondent may be entitled to relief. This case is before us on petitioner's motion to dismiss for failure to state a claim. ... I need not reach either the Eighth Amendment or the Equal Protection Clause issues because I believe that Hardwick has stated a cognizable claim that § 16–6–2 interferes with constitutionally protected interests in privacy and freedom of intimate association. But neither the Eighth Amendment nor the Equal Protection Clause is so clearly irrelevant that a claim resting on either provision should be peremptorily dismissed. The Court's cramped reading of the issue before it makes for a short opinion, but it does little to make for a persuasive one.

"Our cases long have recognized that the Constitution embodies a promise that a certain private sphere of individual liberty will be kept largely beyond the reach of government." *Thornburgh v. American Coll. of Obst. & Gyn.* In construing the right to privacy, the Court has proceeded along two somewhat distinct, albeit complementary, lines. First, it has recognized a privacy interest with reference to certain *decisions* that are properly for the individual to make. E.g., *Roe v. Wade.* Second, it has recognized a privacy interest with reference to certain *places* without regard for the particular activities in which the individuals who occupy them are engaged. The case before us implicates both the decisional and the spatial aspects of the right to privacy....

The behavior for which Hardwick faces prosecution occurred in his own home, a place to which the Fourth Amendment attaches special significance. The Court's treatment of this aspect of the case is symptomatic of its overall refusal to consider the broad principles that have informed our treatment of privacy in specific cases.... "The right of the people to be secure in their ... houses," expressly guaranteed by the Fourth Amendment, is perhaps the most "textual" of the various constitutional provisions that inform our understanding of the right to privacy, and thus I cannot agree with the Court's statement that "[t]he right pressed upon us here has no ... support in the text of the Constitution." Indeed, the right of an individual to conduct intimate relationships in the intimacy of his or her own home seems to me to be the heart of the Constitution's protection of privacy. ...

First, petitioner asserts that the acts made criminal by the statute may have serious adverse consequences for "the general public health and welfare," such as spreading communicable diseases or fostering other criminal activity. Inasmuch as this case was dismissed by the District Court on the pleadings, it is not surprising that the record before us is barren of any evidence to support petitioner's claim. In light of the state of the record, I see no justification for the Court's attempt to equate the private, consensual sexual activity at issue here with the "possession in the home of drugs, firearms, or stolen goods," to which *Stanley* refused to extend its protection. None of the behavior so mentioned in *Stanley* can properly be viewed as "[v]ictimless:" drugs and weapons are inherently dangerous, and for property to be "stolen," someone must have been wrongfully deprived of it. Nothing in the record before the Court provides any justification for finding the activity forbidden by § 16–6–2 to be physically dangerous, either to the persons engaged in it or to others.[4] . . .

The assertion that "traditional Judeo–Christian values proscribe" the conduct involved cannot provide an adequate justification for § 16–6–2. . . . The legitimacy of secular legislation depends instead on whether the State can advance some justification for its law beyond its conformity to religious doctrine. . . . Statutes banning public sexual activity are entirely consistent with protecting the individual's liberty interest in decisions concerning sexual relations: the same recognition that those decisions are intensely private which justifies protecting them from governmental interference can justify protecting individuals from unwilling exposure to the sexual activities of others. But the mere fact that intimate behavior may be punished when it takes place in public cannot dictate how States can regulate intimate behavior that occurs in intimate places.[7] . . .

JUSTICE STEVENS, with whom JUSTICE BRENNAN and JUSTICE MARSHALL join, dissenting.

Like the statute that is challenged in this case, the rationale of the Court's opinion applies equally to the prohibited conduct regardless of whether the parties who engage in it are married or unmarried, or are of the same or different sexes.

---

4. [A] court could find simple, analytically sound distinctions between certain private, consensual sexual conduct, on the one hand, and adultery and incest (the only two vaguely specific "sexual crimes" to which the majority points), on the other. For example, marriage, in addition to its spiritual aspects, is a civil contract that entitles the contracting parties to a variety of governmentally provided benefits. A State might define the contractual commitment necessary to become eligible for these benefits to include a commitment of fidelity and then punish individuals for breaching that contract. Moreover, a State might conclude that adultery is likely to injure third persons, in particular, spouses and children of persons who engage in extramarital af-

fairs. With respect to incest, a court might well agree with respondent that the nature of familial relationships renders true consent to incestuous activity sufficiently problematical that a blanket prohibition of such activity is warranted. Notably, the Court makes no effort to explain why it has chosen to group private, consensual homosexual activity with adultery and incest rather than with private, consensual heterosexual activity by unmarried persons or, indeed, with oral or anal sex within marriage.

7. . . . If the law is not invalid, then the police *can* invade the home to enforce it, provided, of course, that they obtain a determination of probable cause from a neutral magistrate. . . .

Society has every right to encourage its individual members to follow particular traditions in expressing affection for one another and in gratifying their personal desires. It, of course, may prohibit an individual from imposing his will on another to satisfy his own selfish interests. It also may prevent an individual from interfering with, or violating, a legally sanctioned and protected relationship, such as marriage. And it may explain the relative advantages and disadvantages of different forms of intimate expression. But when individual married couples are isolated from observation by others, the way in which they voluntarily choose to conduct their intimate relations is a matter for them—not the State—to decide.[10] The essential "liberty" that animated the development of the law in cases like *Griswold, Eisenstadt,* and *Carey* surely embraces the right to engage in nonreproductive, sexual conduct that others may consider offensive or immoral. Paradoxical as it may seem, our prior cases thus establish that a State may not prohibit sodomy within "the sacred precincts of marital bedrooms," *Griswold,* indeed, between unmarried heterosexual adults. *Eisenstadt*....

ROMER v. EVANS

517 U.S. 620, 116 S.Ct. 1620, 134 L.Ed.2d 855 (1996).

JUSTICE KENNEDY delivered the opinion of the Court....

I.

The enactment challenged in this case is an amendment to the Constitution of the State of Colorado, adopted in a 1992 statewide referendum. The parties and the state courts refer to it as "Amendment 2," its designation when submitted to the voters. The impetus for the amendment and the contentious campaign that preceded its adoption came in large part from ordinances that had been passed in various Colorado municipalities. For example, the cities of Aspen and Boulder and the City and County of Denver each had enacted ordinances [that protected] persons discriminated against by reason of their sexual orientation. Amendment 2 repeals these ordinances to the extent they prohibit discrimination on the basis of "homosexual, lesbian or bisexual orientation, conduct, practices or relationships." Colo. Const., Art. II, § 30b.

Yet Amendment 2, in explicit terms, does more than repeal or rescind these provisions. It prohibits all legislative, executive or judicial action at any level of state or local government designed to protect the named class, a class we shall refer to as homosexual persons or gays and lesbians. The amendment reads:

"No Protected Status Based on Homosexual, Lesbian, or Bisexual Orientation. Neither the State of Colorado, through any of its

---

10. Indeed, the Georgia Attorney General concedes that Georgia's statute would be unconstitutional if applied to a married couple. See Tr. of Oral Arg. (stating that application of the statute to a married couple "would be unconstitutional" because of the "right of marital privacy as identified by the Court in *Griswold*"). Significantly, Georgia passed the current statute three years after the Court's decision in *Griswold.*

branches or departments, nor any of its agencies, political subdivisions, municipalities or school districts, shall enact, adopt or enforce any statute, regulation, ordinance or policy whereby homosexual, lesbian or bisexual orientation, conduct, practices or relationships shall constitute or otherwise be the basis of or entitle any person or class of persons to have or claim any minority status, quota preferences, protected status or claim of discrimination. This Section of the Constitution shall be in all respects self-executing.''

[T]he State Supreme Court held that Amendment 2 was subject to strict scrutiny under the Fourteenth Amendment because it infringed the fundamental right of gays and lesbians to participate in the political process. *Evans v. Romer*, 854 P.2d 1270 (Colo.1993)(*Evans* I). To reach this conclusion, the state court relied on our voting rights cases, e.g., *Reynolds v. Sims*, 377 U.S. 533, 84 S.Ct. 1362, 12 L.Ed.2d 506 (1964), and on our precedents involving discriminatory restructuring of governmental decisionmaking, see, e.g., *Hunter v. Erickson*, 393 U.S. 385, 89 S.Ct. 557, 21 L.Ed.2d 616 (1969); *Reitman v. Mulkey*, 387 U.S. 369, 87 S.Ct. 1627, 18 L.Ed.2d 830 (1967); *Washington v. Seattle School Dist. No. 1*, 458 U.S. 457, 102 S.Ct. 3187, 73 L.Ed.2d 896 (1982). On remand, the State advanced various arguments in an effort to show that Amendment 2 was narrowly tailored to serve compelling interests, but the trial court found none sufficient. It enjoined enforcement of Amendment 2, and the Supreme Court of Colorado, in a second opinion, affirmed the ruling. *Evans v. Romer*, 882 P.2d 1335 (Colo.1994)(*Evans* II). We granted certiorari and now affirm the judgment, but on a rationale different from that adopted by the State Supreme Court.

II.

The State's principal argument in defense of Amendment 2 is that it puts gays and lesbians in the same position as all other persons. So, the State says, the measure does no more than deny homosexuals special rights. This reading of the amendment's language is implausible. We rely not upon our own interpretation of the amendment but upon the authoritative construction of Colorado's Supreme Court.... The critical discussion of the amendment, set out in *Evans* I, is as follows:

"The immediate objective of Amendment 2 is, at a minimum, to repeal existing statutes, regulations, ordinances, and policies of state and local entities that barred discrimination based on sexual orientation.

"The 'ultimate effect' of Amendment 2 is to prohibit any governmental entity from adopting similar, or more protective statutes, regulations, ordinances, or policies in the future unless the state constitution is first amended to permit such measures."

Sweeping and comprehensive is the change in legal status effected by this law. So much is evident from the ordinances that the Colorado Supreme Court declared would be void by operation of Amendment 2. Homosexuals, by state decree, are put in a solitary class with respect to transactions and relations in both the private and governmental spheres.

The amendment withdraws from homosexuals, but no others, specific legal protection from the injuries caused by discrimination, and it forbids reinstatement of these laws and policies.

[Colorado's state and local laws] have set forth an extensive catalogue of traits which cannot be the basis for discrimination, including age, military status, marital status, pregnancy, parenthood, custody of a minor child, political affiliation, physical or mental disability of an individual or of his or her associates—and, in recent times, sexual orientation.... Amendment 2 bars homosexuals from securing protection against the injuries that these public-accommodations laws address. That in itself is a severe consequence, but there is more. Amendment 2, in addition, nullifies specific legal protections for this targeted class in all transactions in housing, sale of real estate, insurance, health and welfare services, private education, and employment.

Not confined to the private sphere, Amendment 2 also operates to repeal and forbid all laws or policies providing specific protection for gays or lesbians from discrimination by every level of Colorado government. The State Supreme Court cited two examples of protections in the governmental sphere that are now rescinded and may not be reintroduced. The first is Colorado Executive Order D0035 (1990), which forbids employment discrimination against " 'all state employees, classified and exempt' on the basis of sexual orientation." Also repealed, and now forbidden, are "various provisions prohibiting discrimination based on sexual orientation at state colleges." The repeal of these measures and the prohibition against their future reenactment demonstrates that Amendment 2 has the same force and effect in Colorado's governmental sector as it does elsewhere and that it applies to policies as well as ordinary legislation.

Amendment 2's reach may not be limited to specific laws passed for the benefit of gays and lesbians. It is a fair, if not necessary, inference from the broad language of the amendment that it deprives gays and lesbians even of the protection of general laws and policies that prohibit arbitrary discrimination in governmental and private settings.... The state court did not decide whether the amendment has this effect, however, and neither need we. [E]ven if, as we doubt, homosexuals could find some safe harbor in laws of general application, we cannot accept the view that Amendment 2's prohibition on specific legal protections does no more than deprive homosexuals of special rights. To the contrary, the amendment imposes a special disability upon those persons alone. Homosexuals are forbidden the safeguards that others enjoy or may seek without constraint. They can obtain specific protection against discrimination only by enlisting the citizenry of Colorado to amend the state constitution or perhaps, on the State's view, by trying to pass helpful laws of general applicability. This is so no matter how local or discrete the harm, no matter how public and widespread the injury....

III.

The Fourteenth Amendment's promise that no person shall be denied the equal protection of the laws must co-exist with the practical necessity that most legislation classifies for one purpose or another, with resulting disadvantage to various groups or persons. We have attempted to reconcile the principle with the reality by stating that, if a law neither burdens a fundamental right nor targets a suspect class, we will uphold the legislative classification so long as it bears a rational relation to some legitimate end.

Amendment 2 fails, indeed defies, even this conventional inquiry. First, the amendment has the peculiar property of imposing a broad and undifferentiated disability on a single named group, an exceptional and, as we shall explain, invalid form of legislation. Second, its sheer breadth is so discontinuous with the reasons offered for it that the amendment seems inexplicable by anything but animus toward the class that it affects; it lacks a rational relationship to legitimate state interests.

Amendment 2 confounds this normal process of judicial review. It is at once too narrow and too broad. It identifies persons by a single trait and then denies them protection across the board. The resulting disqualification of a class of persons from the right to seek specific protection from the law is unprecedented in our jurisprudence. . . .

It is not within our constitutional tradition to enact laws of this sort. Central both to the idea of the rule of law and to our own Constitution's guarantee of equal protection is the principle that government and each of its parts remain open on impartial terms to all who seek its assistance. . . . A law declaring that in general it shall be more difficult for one group of citizens than for all others to seek aid from the government is itself a denial of equal protection of the laws in the most literal sense.

Davis v. Beason, 133 U.S. 333, 10 S.Ct. 299, 33 L.Ed. 637 (1890), not cited by the parties but relied upon by the dissent, is not evidence that Amendment 2 is within our constitutional tradition, and any reliance upon it as authority for sustaining the amendment is misplaced. In *Davis*, the Court approved an Idaho territorial statute denying Mormons, polygamists, and advocates of polygamy the right to vote and to hold office because, as the Court construed the statute, it "simply excludes from the privilege of voting, or of holding any office of honor, trust or profit, those who have been convicted of certain offences, and those who advocate a practical resistance to the laws of the Territory and justify and approve the commission of crimes forbidden by it." To the extent Davis held that persons advocating a certain practice may be denied the right to vote, it is no longer good law. To the extent it held that the groups designated in the statute may be deprived of the right to vote because of their status, its ruling could not stand without surviving strict scrutiny, a most doubtful outcome. To the extent Davis held that a convicted felon may be denied the right to vote, its holding is not implicated by our decision and is unexceptionable.

A second and related point is that laws of the kind now before us raise the inevitable inference that the disadvantage imposed is born of animosity toward the class of persons affected. Even laws enacted for broad and ambitious purposes often can be explained by reference to legitimate public policies which justify the incidental disadvantages they impose on certain persons. Amendment 2, however, in making a general announcement that gays and lesbians shall not have any particular protections from the law, inflicts on them immediate, continuing, and real injuries that outrun and belie any legitimate justifications that may be claimed for it. We conclude that, in addition to the far-reaching deficiencies of Amendment 2 that we have noted, the principles it offends, in another sense, are conventional and venerable; a law must bear a rational relationship to a legitimate governmental purpose, and Amendment 2 does not.

The primary rationale the State offers for Amendment 2 is respect for other citizens' freedom of association, and in particular the liberties of landlords or employers who have personal or religious objections to homosexuality. Colorado also cites its interest in conserving resources to fight discrimination against other groups. The breadth of the Amendment is so far removed from these particular justifications that we find it impossible to credit them. We cannot say that Amendment 2 is directed to any identifiable legitimate purpose or discrete objective. It is a status-based enactment divorced from any factual context from which we could discern a relationship to legitimate state interests; it is a classification of persons undertaken for its own sake, something the Equal Protection Clause does not permit.

We must conclude that Amendment 2 classifies homosexuals not to further a proper legislative end but to make them unequal to everyone else. This Colorado cannot do. A State cannot so deem a class of persons a stranger to its laws. Amendment 2 violates the Equal Protection Clause, and the judgment of the Supreme Court of Colorado is affirmed.

It is so ordered.

JUSTICE SCALIA, with whom the CHIEF JUSTICE [REHNQUIST] and JUSTICE THOMAS join, dissenting.

The Court has mistaken a Kulturkampf for a fit of spite. The constitutional amendment before us here is not the manifestation of a " 'bare . . . desire to harm' " homosexuals, but is rather a modest attempt by seemingly tolerant Coloradans to preserve traditional sexual mores against the efforts of a politically powerful minority to revise those mores through use of the laws. That objective, and the means chosen to achieve it, are not only unimpeachable under any constitutional doctrine hitherto pronounced (hence the opinion's heavy reliance upon principles of righteousness rather than judicial holdings); they have been specifically approved by the Congress of the United States and by this Court.

In holding that homosexuality cannot be singled out for disfavorable treatment, the Court contradicts a decision, unchallenged here, pronounced only 10 years ago, see *Bowers v. Hardwick* (1986), and places the prestige of this institution behind the proposition that opposition to homosexuality is as reprehensible as racial or religious bias. Whether it is or not is *precisely* the cultural debate that gave rise to the Colorado constitutional amendment (and to the preferential laws against which the amendment was directed). Since the Constitution of the United States says nothing about this subject, it is left to be resolved by normal democratic means, including the democratic adoption of provisions in state constitutions. This Court has no business imposing upon all Americans the resolution favored by the elite class from which the Members of this institution are selected, pronouncing that "animosity" toward homosexuality, is evil. I vigorously dissent.

Let me first discuss Part II of the Court's opinion, its longest section, which is devoted to rejecting the State's arguments that Amendment 2 "puts gays and lesbians in the same position as all other persons," and "does no more than deny homosexuals special rights." The Court concludes that this reading of Amendment 2's language is "implausible" under the "authoritative construction" given Amendment 2 by the Supreme Court of Colorado. [However, in] *Evans v. Romer*, 882 P.2d 1335, 1346 n. 9 (1994), the Colorado court stated:

> "... *Amendment 2 is not intended to have any effect on this legislation, but seeks only to prevent the adoption of antidiscrimination laws intended to protect gays, lesbians, and bisexuals.*" (emphasis added).

The Court utterly fails to distinguish this portion of the Colorado court's opinion.... This analysis, which is fully in accord with (indeed, follows inescapably from) the text of the constitutional provision, lays to rest such horribles, raised in the course of oral argument, as the prospect that assaults upon homosexuals could not be prosecuted. The amendment prohibits special treatment of homosexuals, and nothing more. It would not affect, for example, a requirement of state law that pensions be paid to all retiring state employees with a certain length of service; homosexual employees, as well as others, would be entitled to that benefit. But it would prevent the State or any municipality from making death-benefit payments to the "life partner" of a homosexual when it does not make such payments to the long-time roommate of a nonhomosexual employee....

Despite all of its hand-wringing about the potential effect of Amendment 2 on general antidiscrimination laws, the Court's opinion ultimately does not dispute all this, but assumes it to be true. The only denial of equal treatment it contends homosexuals have suffered is this: They may not obtain *preferential* treatment without amending the state constitution. That is to say, the principle underlying the Court's opinion is that one who is accorded equal treatment under the laws, but cannot as readily as others obtain *preferential* treatment under the laws, has been denied equal protection of the laws. If merely stating this alleged "equal protection" violation does not suffice to refute it, our constitutional jurisprudence has achieved terminal silliness.

The central thesis of the Court's reasoning is that any group is denied equal protection when, to obtain advantage (or, presumably, to avoid disadvantage), it must have recourse to a more general and hence more difficult level of political decisionmaking than others. [I]t seems to me most unlikely that any multilevel democracy can function under such a principle. For *whenever* a disadvantage is imposed, or conferral of a benefit is prohibited, at one of the higher levels of democratic decision-making (*i.e.*, by the state legislature rather than local government, or by the people at large in the state constitution rather than the legislature), the affected group has (under this theory) been denied equal protection. To take the simplest of examples, consider a state law prohibiting the award of municipal contracts to relatives of mayors or city councilmen. Once such a law is passed, the group composed of such relatives must, in order to get the benefit of city contracts, persuade the state legislature—unlike all other citizens, who need only persuade the municipality. It is ridiculous to consider this a denial of equal protection, which is why the Court's theory is unheard-of.

The Court might reply that the example I have given is *not* a denial of equal protection only because the same "rational basis" (avoidance of corruption) which renders constitutional the substantive discrimination against relatives (i.e., the fact that they alone cannot obtain city contracts) also automatically suffices to sustain what might be called the electoral-procedural discrimination against them (i.e., the fact that they must go to the state level to get this changed). This is of course a perfectly reasonable response, and would explain why "electoral-procedural discrimination" has not hitherto been heard of: a law that is valid in its substance is automatically valid in its level of enactment. But the Court cannot afford to make this argument [because] there is no doubt of a rational basis for the substance of the prohibition at issue here. The Court's entire novel theory rests upon the proposition that there is something special—something that cannot be justified by normal "rational basis" analysis—in making a disadvantaged group (or a nonpreferred group) resort to a higher decisionmaking level. That proposition finds no support in law or logic.

I turn next to whether there was a legitimate rational basis for the substance of the constitutional amendment—for the prohibition of special protection for homosexuals.[1] It is unsurprising that the Court avoids discussion of this question, since the answer is so obviously yes. The case most relevant to the issue before us today is not even mentioned in the Court's opinion: In *Bowers v. Hardwick*, we held that the Constitution does not prohibit what virtually all States had done from the founding of the Republic until very recent years—making homosexual conduct a crime. [The] Respondents' briefs did not urge overruling *Bowers*, and at oral argument respondents' counsel expressly disavowed any intent to seek such overruling. If it is constitutionally permissible for a State to

---

1. The Court evidently agrees that "rational basis"—the normal test for compliance with the Equal Protection Clause—is the governing standard. The trial court rejected respondents' argument that homosexuals constitute a "suspect" or "quasi-suspect" class, and respondents elected not to appeal that ruling to the Supreme Court of Colorado. And the Court implicitly rejects the Supreme Court of Colorado's holding that Amendment 2 infringes upon a "fundamental right" of "independently identifiable class[es]" to "participate equally in the political process."

make homosexual conduct criminal, surely it is constitutionally permissible for a State to enact other laws merely *disfavoring* homosexual conduct. ("[T]here can hardly be more palpable discrimination against a class than making the conduct that defines the class criminal." *Padula v. Webster*, 822 F.2d 97, 103 (1987).) And *a fortiori* it is constitutionally permissible for a State to adopt a provision *not even* disfavoring homosexual conduct, but merely prohibiting all levels of state government from bestowing *special protections* upon homosexual conduct. Respondents (who, unlike the Court, cannot afford the luxury of ignoring inconvenient precedent) counter *Bowers* with the argument that a greater-includes-the-lesser rationale cannot justify Amendment 2's application to individuals who do not engage in homosexual acts, but are merely of homosexual "orientation." Some courts of appeals have concluded that, with respect to laws of this sort at least, that is a distinction without a difference. The Supreme Court of Colorado itself appears to be of this view. See 882 P.2d, at 1349–1350 ("Amendment 2 targets this class of persons based on four characteristics: sexual orientation; conduct; practices; and relationships. Each characteristic provides a potentially different way of identifying that class of persons who are gay, lesbian, or bisexual. These four characteristics are not truly severable from one another because each provides nothing more than a different way of identifying *the same class of persons*")(emphasis added).

But assuming that, in Amendment 2, a person of homosexual "orientation" is someone who does not engage in homosexual conduct but merely has a tendency or desire to do so, *Bowers* still suffices to establish a rational basis for the provision. If it is rational to criminalize the conduct, surely it is rational to deny special favor and protection to those with a self-avowed tendency or desire to engage in the conduct. Indeed, where criminal sanctions are not involved, homosexual "orientation" is an acceptable stand-in for homosexual conduct. A State "does not violate the Equal Protection Clause merely because the classifications made by its laws are imperfect," *Dandridge v. Williams* (1970). [J]ust as a mandatory retirement age of 50 for police officers does not violate equal protection even though it prematurely ends the careers of many policemen over 50 who still have the capacity to do the job, see *Massachusetts Bd. of Retirement v. Murgia* (1976)(*per curiam*), Amendment 2 is not constitutionally invalid simply because it could have been drawn more precisely so as to withdraw special antidiscrimination protections only from those of homosexual "orientation" who actually engage in homosexual conduct. As Justice KENNEDY wrote, when he was on the Court of Appeals, in a case involving discharge of homosexuals from the Navy: "Nearly any statute which classifies people may be irrational as applied in particular cases. Discharge of the particular plaintiffs before us would be rational, under minimal scrutiny, not because their particular cases present the dangers which justify Navy policy, but instead because the general policy of discharging all homosexuals is rational." *Beller v. Middendorf*, 632 F.2d 788, 808–809, n. 20 (C.A.9 1980)(citation omitted).

Moreover, even if the provision regarding homosexual "orientation" *were* invalid, respondents' challenge to Amendment 2—which is a facial challenge—must fail. "A facial challenge to a legislative Act is, of course, the most difficult challenge to mount successfully, since the challenger must establish that no set of circumstances exists under which the Act would be valid." It would not be enough for respondents to establish (if they could) that Amendment 2 is unconstitutional as applied to those of homosexual "orientation"; since, under *Bowers*, Amendment 2 is unquestionably constitutional as applied to those who engage in homosexual conduct, the facial challenge cannot succeed. Some individuals of homosexual "orientation" who do not engage in homosexual acts might successfully bring an as-applied challenge to Amendment 2, but so far as the record indicates, none of the respondents is such a person.

[What Colorado] has done is not only unprohibited, but eminently reasonable, with close, congressionally approved precedent in earlier constitutional practice. First, as to its eminent reasonableness. The Court's opinion contains grim, disapproving hints that Coloradans have been guilty of "animus" or "animosity" toward homosexuality, as though that has been established as Unamerican. Of course it is our moral heritage that one should not hate any human being or class of human beings. But I had thought that one could consider certain conduct reprehensible—murder, for example, or polygamy, or cruelty to animals—and could exhibit even "animus" toward such conduct. Surely that is the only sort of "animus" at issue here: moral disapproval of homosexual conduct, the same sort of moral disapproval that produced the centuries-old criminal laws that we held constitutional in *Bowers*. The Colorado amendment does not, to speak entirely precisely, prohibit giving favored status to people who are *homosexuals*; they can be favored for many reasons—for example, because they are senior citizens or members of racial minorities. But it prohibits giving them favored status *because of their homosexual conduct*—that is, it prohibits favored status *for homosexuality*.

But though Coloradans are, as I say, *entitled* to be hostile toward homosexual conduct, the fact is that the degree of hostility reflected by Amendment 2 is the smallest conceivable. The Court's portrayal of Coloradans as a society fallen victim to pointless, hate-filled "gay-bashing" is so false as to be comical. Colorado not only is one of the 25 States that have repealed their antisodomy laws, but was among the first to do so. But the society that eliminates criminal punishment for homosexual acts does not necessarily abandon the view that homosexuality is morally wrong and socially harmful; often, abolition simply reflects the view that enforcement of such criminal laws involves unseemly intrusion into the intimate lives of citizens.

[B]ecause those who engage in homosexual conduct tend to reside in disproportionate numbers in certain communities, and of course care about homosexual-rights issues much more ardently than the public at large, they possess political power much greater than their numbers, both locally and statewide. [Amendment 2] sought to counter both the geographic concentration and the disproportionate political power of homosexuals by (1) resolving the controversy at the statewide level, and (2) making the election a single-issue contest for both sides. It put directly, to all the citizens of the State, the question: Should homosexuality be given special protection? They answered no. The Court today asserts that this most democratic of procedures is unconstitutional. Lacking any cases to establish that facially absurd proposition, it simply asserts that it must be unconstitutional, because it has never happened before.

> "It is not within our constitutional tradition to enact laws of this sort. Central both to the idea of the rule of law and to our own Constitution's guarantee of equal protection is the principle that government and each of its parts remain open on impartial terms to all who seek its assistance."

[T]his is proved false every time a state law prohibiting or disfavoring certain conduct is passed, because such a law prevents the adversely affected group—whether drug addicts, or smokers, or gun owners, or motorcyclists—from changing the policy thus established in "each of [the] parts" of the State. What the Court says is even demonstrably false at the constitutional level. The Eighteenth Amendment to the Federal Constitution, for example, deprived those who drank alcohol not only of the power to alter the policy of prohibition *locally* or through *state legislation*, but even of the power to alter it through *state constitutional amendment* or *federal legislation*. [T]here is a much closer analogy, one that involves precisely the effort by the majority of citizens to preserve its view of sexual morality statewide, against the efforts of a geographically concentrated and politically powerful minority to undermine it. The constitutions of the States of Arizona, Idaho, New Mexico, Oklahoma, and Utah *to this day* contain provisions stating that polygamy is "forever prohibited." Polygamists, and those who have a polygamous "orientation," have been "singled out" by these provisions for much more severe treatment than merely denial of favored status; and that treatment can only be changed by achieving amendment of the state constitutions. The Court's disposition today suggests that these provisions are unconstitutional, and that polygamy must be permitted in these States on a state-legislated, or perhaps even local-option, basis—unless, of course, polygamists for some reason have fewer constitutional rights than homosexuals.

[The Court] has approved a territorial statutory provision that went even further, depriving polygamists of the ability even to achieve a constitutional amendment, by depriving them of the power to vote. In *Davis v. Beason*, 133 U.S. 333, 10 S.Ct. 299, 33 L.Ed. 637 (1890), Justice Field wrote for a unanimous Court:

> "In our judgment, § 501 of the Revised Statutes of Idaho Territory, which provides that 'no person ... who is a bigamist or polygamist or who teaches, advises, counsels, or encourages any person or persons to become bigamists or polygamists ... is permitted to vote

at any election, or to hold any position or office of honor, trust, or profit within this Territory,' *is not open to any constitutional or legal objection.*" (emphasis added).

To the extent, if any, that this opinion permits the imposition of adverse consequences upon mere abstract advocacy of polygamy, it has of course been overruled by later cases. But the proposition that polygamy can be criminalized, and those engaging in that crime deprived of the vote, remains good law. See *Richardson v. Ramirez*, 418 U.S. 24, 53, 94 S.Ct. 2655, 2670, 41 L.Ed.2d 551 (1974). *Beason* rejected the argument that "such discrimination is a denial of the equal protection of the laws."... [3]

This Court cited *Beason* with approval as recently as 1993, in an opinion authored by the same Justice who writes for the Court today. That opinion said: "[A]dverse impact will not always lead to a finding of impermissible targeting. For example, a social harm may have been a legitimate concern of government for reasons quite apart from discrimination.... See, e.g., ... *Davis v. Beason.*" *Church of Lukumi Babalu Aye, Inc. v. Hialeah*, 508 U.S. 520, 535, 113 S.Ct. 2217, 2228, 124 L.Ed.2d 472 (1993). It remains to be explained how § 501 of the Idaho Revised Statutes was not an "impermissible targeting" of polygamists, but (the much more mild) Amendment 2 is an "impermissible targeting" of homosexuals. Has the Court concluded that the perceived social harm of polygamy is a "legitimate concern of government," and the perceived social harm of homosexuality is not?

I strongly suspect that the answer to the last question is yes, which leads me to the last point I wish to make: The Court [engages in] stern disapproval of "animosity" towards homosexuality.... I would not myself indulge in such official praise for heterosexual monogamy, because I think it no business of the courts (as opposed to the political branches) to take sides in this culture war....

When the Court takes sides in the culture wars, it tends to be with the knights rather than the villeins—and more specifically with the Templars, reflecting the views and values of the lawyer class from which the Court's Members are drawn. How that class feels about homosexuality will be evident to anyone who wishes to interview job applicants at

---

3. The Court labors mightily to get around *Beason*, see but cannot escape the central fact that this Court found the statute at issue—which went much further than Amendment 2, denying polygamists not merely special treatment but the right to *vote*—"not open to any constitutional or legal objection," rejecting the appellant's argument (much like the argument of respondents today) that the statute impermissibly "single[d] him out." The Court [argues] that "[t]o the extent [*Beason*] held that the groups designated in the statute may be deprived of the right to vote because of their status, its ruling could not stand without surviving strict scrutiny, a most doubtful outcome." But if that is so, it is only because we have declared the right *to vote* to be a "fundamental political right," deprivation of which triggers strict scrutiny. Amendment 2, of course, does not deny the fundamental right to vote, and the Court rejects the Colorado court's view that there exists a fundamental right to participate in the political process. Strict scrutiny is thus not in play here. Finally, the Court's suggestion that § 501 of the Revised Statutes of Idaho, and Amendment 2, deny rights on account of "status" (rather than conduct) opens up a broader debate involving the significance of *Bowers* to this case, a debate which the Court is otherwise unwilling to join.

virtually any of the Nation's law schools. The interviewer may refuse to offer a job because the applicant is a Republican; because he is an adulterer; because he went to the wrong prep school or belongs to the wrong country club; because he eats snails; because he is a womanizer; because she wears real-animal fur; or even because he hates the Chicago Cubs. But if the interviewer should wish not to be an associate or partner of an applicant because he disapproves of the applicant's homosexuality, then he will have violated the pledge which the Association of American Law Schools requires all its member-schools to exact from job interviewers: "assurance of the employer's willingness" to hire homosexuals.... I dissent.

Notes

1. The majority never cited *Bowers*. How would you distinguish the case?

2. After this case, is the military's "don't ask, don't tell" policy constitutional? Under this policy, the military does not ask recruits if they are homosexual, but will dismiss homosexuals from the service if they announce (or practice) their homosexuality.

3. Would a state law that prohibited the state government or local government from discriminating, for or against, anyone based on age or sexual orientation be constitutional?

4. Assume that a state enacts a law prohibiting the state, or private individuals, from discriminating (on the basis of age) against people over 50 years of age. Later, the state repeals that law. Is that repeal constitutional? Assume next that the state repeals the law and also enacts a state constitutional amendment taking away from state or local governments the power to reenact legislation prohibiting such age discrimination. Is that state constitutional amendment valid under the U.S. Constitution?

8–3.5 A Right to Die?

CRUZAN v. DIRECTOR, MISSOURI DEPARTMENT OF HEALTH
497 U.S. 261, 110 S.Ct. 2841, 111 L.Ed.2d 224 (1990).

CHIEF JUSTICE REHNQUIST delivered the opinion of the Court.

Petitioner Nancy Beth Cruzan was rendered incompetent as a result of severe injuries sustained during an automobile accident. Co-petitioners Lester and Joyce Cruzan, Nancy's parents and co-guardians, sought a court order directing the withdrawal of their daughter's artificial feeding and hydration equipment after it became apparent that she had virtually no chance of recovering her cognitive faculties. The Supreme Court of Missouri held that because there was no clear and convincing evidence of Nancy's desire to have life-sustaining treatment withdrawn under such circumstances, her parents lacked authority to effectuate such a request. We granted certiorari, and now affirm.

On the night of January 11, 1983, Nancy Cruzan lost control of her car as she traveled down Elm Road in Jasper County, Missouri. The vehicle overturned, and Cruzan was discovered lying face down in a ditch without detectable respiratory or cardiac function. Paramedics were able to restore her breathing and heartbeat at the accident site, and she was transported to a hospital in an unconscious state. An attending neurosurgeon diagnosed her as having sustained probable cerebral contusions compounded by significant anoxia (lack of oxygen). The Missouri trial court in this case found that permanent brain damage generally results after 6 minutes in an anoxic state; it is estimated that Cruzan was deprived of oxygen from 12 to 14 minutes.... In order to ease feeding and further the recovery, surgeons implanted a gastrostomy feeding and hydration tube in Cruzan with the consent of her then husband. Subsequent rehabilitative efforts proved unavailing. She now lies in a Missouri state hospital in what is commonly referred to as a persistent vegetative state: generally, a condition in which a person exhibits motor reflexes but evinces no indications of significant cognitive function.[1] The State of Missouri is bearing the cost of her care.

After it had become apparent that Nancy Cruzan had virtually no chance of regaining her mental faculties her parents asked hospital employees to terminate the artificial nutrition and hydration procedures. All agree that such a removal would cause her death. The employees refused to honor the request without court approval. The parents then sought and received authorization from the state trial court for termination. The court found that a person in Nancy's condition had a fundamental right under the State and Federal Constitutions to refuse or direct the withdrawal of "death prolonging procedures." The court also found that Nancy's "expressed thoughts at age twenty-five in somewhat serious conversation with a housemate friend that if sick or injured she would not wish to continue her life unless she could live at least halfway normally suggests that given her present condition she would not wish to continue on with her nutrition and hydration."

The Supreme Court of Missouri reversed by a divided vote. The court recognized a right to refuse treatment embodied in the common-law doctrine of informed consent, but expressed skepticism about the application of that doctrine in the circumstances of this case. The court also declined to read a broad right of privacy into the State Constitution which would "support the right of a person to refuse medical treatment in every circumstance," and expressed doubt as to whether such a right

---

1. The State Supreme Court, adopting much of the trial court's findings, described Nancy Cruzan's medical condition as follows:

"... (1) [H]er respiration and circulation are not artificially maintained and are within the normal limits of a thirty-year-old female; (2) she is oblivious to her environment except for reflective responses to sound and perhaps painful stimuli; ... (7) she has no cognitive or reflexive ability to swallow food or water to maintain her daily essential needs and ... she will never recover her ability to swallow sufficient [sic] to satisfy her needs. [She] is diagnosed as in a persistent vegetative state. She is not dead. She is not terminally ill. Medical experts testified that she could live another thirty years." ...

existed under the United States Constitution. It then decided that the Missouri Living Will statute embodied a state policy strongly favoring the preservation of life. The court found that Cruzan's statements to her roommate regarding her desire to live or die under certain conditions were "unreliable for the purpose of determining her intent," "and thus insufficient to support the co-guardians claim to exercise substituted judgment on Nancy's behalf." It rejected the argument that Cruzan's parents were entitled to order the termination of her medical treatment, concluding that "no person can assume that choice for an incompetent in the absence of the formalities required under Missouri's Living Will statutes or the clear and convincing, inherently reliable evidence absent here." The court also expressed its view that "[b]road policy questions bearing on life and death are more properly addressed by representative assemblies" than judicial bodies.

We granted certiorari to consider the question of whether Cruzan has a right under the United States Constitution which would require the hospital to withdraw life-sustaining treatment from her under these circumstances.

[T]he common-law doctrine of informed consent is viewed as generally encompassing the right of a competent individual to refuse medical treatment. Beyond that, these decisions demonstrate both similarity and diversity in their approach to decision of what all agree is a perplexing question with unusually strong moral and ethical overtones. State courts have available to them for decision a number of sources—state constitutions, statutes, and common law—which are not available to us. In this Court, the question is simply and starkly whether the United States Constitution prohibits Missouri from choosing the rule of decision which it did. This is the first case in which we have been squarely presented with the issue of whether the United States Constitution grants what is in common parlance referred to as a "right to die." [I]n deciding "a question of such magnitude and importance ... it is the [better] part of wisdom not to attempt, by any general statement, to cover every possible phase of the subject."

The Fourteenth Amendment provides that no State shall "deprive any person of life, liberty, or property, without due process of law." The principle that a competent person has a constitutionally protected liberty interest in refusing unwanted medical treatment may be inferred from our prior decisions. In *Jacobson v. Massachusetts,* 197 U.S. 11, 24–30 (1905), for instance, the Court balanced an individual's liberty interest in declining an unwanted smallpox vaccine against the State's interest in preventing disease. Decisions prior to the incorporation of the Fourth Amendment into the Fourteenth Amendment analyzed searches and seizures involving the body under the Due Process Clause and were thought to implicate substantial liberty interests....

But determining that a person has a "liberty interest" under the Due Process Clause does not end the inquiry,[7] "whether respondent's

7. Although many state courts have   held that a right to refuse treatment is

constitutional rights have been violated must be determined by balancing his liberty interests against the relevant state interests."

Petitioners insist that under the general holdings of our cases, the forced administration of life-sustaining medical treatment, and even of artificially-delivered food and water essential to life, would implicate a competent person's liberty interest. Although we think the logic of the cases discussed above would embrace such a liberty interest, the dramatic consequences involved in refusal of such treatment would inform the inquiry as to whether the deprivation of that interest is constitutionally permissible. But for purposes of this case, we assume that the United States Constitution would grant a competent person a constitutionally protected right to refuse lifesaving hydration and nutrition.

Petitioners go on to assert that an incompetent person should possess the same right in this respect as is possessed by a competent person. They rely primarily on our decisions in *Parham v. J.R.,* [442 U.S. 584 (1979)], and *Youngberg v. Romeo,* 457 U.S. 307 (1982). In *Parham,* we held that a mentally disturbed minor child had a liberty interest in "not being confined unnecessarily for medical treatment," but we certainly did not intimate that such a minor child, after commitment, would have a liberty interest in refusing treatment. In *Youngberg,* we held that a seriously retarded adult had a liberty interest in safety and freedom from bodily restraint. *Youngberg,* however, did not deal with decisions to administer or withhold medical treatment.

The difficulty with petitioners' claim is that in a sense it begs the question: an incompetent person is not able to make an informed and voluntary choice to exercise a hypothetical right to refuse treatment or any other right. Such a "right" must be exercised for her, if at all, by some sort of surrogate. Here, Missouri has in effect recognized that under certain circumstances a surrogate may act for the patient in electing to have hydration and nutrition withdrawn in such a way as to cause death, but it has established a procedural safeguard to assure that the action of the surrogate conforms as best it may to the wishes expressed by the patient while competent. Missouri requires that evidence of the incompetent's wishes as to the withdrawal of treatment be proved by clear and convincing evidence. The question, then, is whether the United States Constitution forbids the establishment of this procedural requirement by the State. We hold that it does not.

Whether or not Missouri's clear and convincing evidence requirement comports with the United States Constitution depends in part on what interests the State may properly seek to protect in this situation. Missouri relies on its interest in the protection and preservation of human life, and there can be no gainsaying this interest. As a general matter, the States—indeed, all civilized nations—demonstrate their commitment to life by treating homicide as serious crime. Moreover, the

encompassed by a generalized constitutional right of privacy, we have never so held. We believe this issue is more properly analyzed in terms of a Fourteenth Amendment liberty interest. See *Bowers v. Hardwick.*

majority of States in this country have laws imposing criminal penalties on one who assists another to commit suicide. We do not think a State is required to remain neutral in the face of an informed and voluntary decision by a physically-able adult to starve to death.

But in the context presented here, a State has more particular interests at stake. The choice between life and death is a deeply personal decision of obvious and overwhelming finality. We believe Missouri may legitimately seek to safeguard the personal element of this choice through the imposition of heightened evidentiary requirements. It cannot be disputed that the Due Process Clause protects an interest in life as well as an interest in refusing life-sustaining medical treatment. Not all incompetent patients will have loved ones available to serve as surrogate decisionmakers. And even where family members are present, "[t]here will, of course, be some unfortunate situations in which family members will not act to protect a patient." A State is entitled to guard against potential abuses in such situations. Similarly, a State is entitled to consider that a judicial proceeding to make a determination regarding an incompetent's wishes may very well not be an adversarial one, with the added guarantee of accurate factfinding that the adversary process brings with it. Finally, we think a State may properly decline to make judgments about the "quality" of life that a particular individual may enjoy, and simply assert an unqualified interest in the preservation of human life to be weighed against the constitutionally protected interests of the individual.

In our view, Missouri has permissibly sought to advance these interests through the adoption of a "clear and convincing" standard of proof to govern such proceedings.... An erroneous decision not to terminate results in a maintenance of the status quo; the possibility of subsequent developments such as advancements in medical science, the discovery of new evidence regarding the patient's intent, changes in the law, or simply the unexpected death of the patient despite the administration of life-sustaining treatment, at least create the potential that a wrong decision will eventually be corrected or its impact mitigated. An erroneous decision to withdraw life-sustaining treatment, however, is not susceptible of correction. [W]e conclude that a State may apply a clear and convincing evidence standard in proceedings where a guardian seeks to discontinue nutrition and hydration of a person diagnosed to be in a persistent vegetative state....

The Supreme Court of Missouri held that in this case the testimony adduced at trial did not amount to clear and convincing proof of the patient's desire to have hydration and nutrition withdrawn.... The testimony adduced at trial consisted primarily of Nancy Cruzan's statements made to a housemate about a year before her accident that she would not want to live should she face life as a "vegetable," and other observations to the same effect. The observations did not deal in terms with withdrawal of medical treatment or of hydration and nutrition. We cannot say that the Supreme Court of Missouri committed constitutional error in reaching the conclusion that it did.

Petitioners alternatively contend that Missouri must accept the "substituted judgment" of close family members even in the absence of substantial proof that their views reflect the views of the patient. [I]n *Parham,* where the patient was a minor, we also *upheld* the constitutionality of a state scheme in which parents made certain decisions for mentally ill minors. Here again petitioners would seek to turn a decision which allowed a State to rely on family decisionmaking into a constitutional requirement that the State recognize such decisionmaking. But constitutional law does not work that way.

No doubt is engendered by anything in this record but that Nancy Cruzan's mother and father are loving and caring parents. If the State were required by the United States Constitution to repose a right of "substituted judgment" with anyone, the Cruzans would surely qualify. But we do not think the Due Process Clause requires the State to repose judgment on these matters with anyone but the patient herself. Close family members may have a strong feeling—a feeling not at all ignoble or unworthy, but not entirely disinterested, either—that they do not wish to witness the continuation of the life of a loved one which they regard as hopeless, meaningless, and even degrading. But there is no automatic assurance that the view of close family members will necessarily be the same as the patient's would have been had she been confronted with the prospect of her situation while competent. All of the reasons previously discussed for allowing Missouri to require clear and convincing evidence of the patient's wishes lead us to conclude that the State may choose to defer only to those wishes, rather than confide the decision to close family members.[12]

The judgment of the Supreme Court of Missouri is

Affirmed.

Justice O'Connor, concurring.

[T]he Court does not today decide the issue whether a State must also give effect to the decisions of a surrogate decisionmaker. See *ante,* n. 12. In my view, such a duty may well be constitutionally required to protect the patient's liberty interest in refusing medical treatment....

Justice Scalia, concurring.

The various opinions in this case portray quite clearly the difficult, indeed agonizing, questions that are presented by the constantly increasing power of science to keep the human body alive for longer than any reasonable person would want to inhabit it. The States have begun to grapple with these problems through legislation. I am concerned, from

---

12. We are not faced in this case with the question of whether a State might be required to defer to the decision of a surrogate if competent and probative evidence established that the patient herself had expressed a desire that the decision to terminate life-sustaining treatment be made for her by that individual.

.... The differences between the choice made *by* a competent person to refuse medical treatment, and the choice made *for* an incompetent person by someone else to refuse medical treatment, are so obviously different that the State is warranted in establishing rigorous procedures for the latter class of cases which do not apply to the former class.

the tenor of today's opinions, that we are poised to confuse that enterprise as successfully as we have confused the enterprise of legislating concerning abortion—requiring it to be conducted against a background of federal constitutional imperatives that are unknown because they are being newly crafted from Term to Term. That would be a great misfortune.

While I agree with the Court's analysis today, and therefore join in its opinion, I would have preferred that we announce, clearly and promptly, that the federal courts have no business in this field; that American law has always accorded the State the power to prevent, by force if necessary, suicide—including suicide by refusing to take appropriate measures necessary to preserve one's life; that the point at which life becomes "worthless," and the point at which the means necessary to preserve it become "extraordinary" or "inappropriate," are neither set forth in the Constitution nor known to the nine Justices of this Court any better than they are known to nine people picked at random from the Kansas City telephone directory; and hence, that even when it *is* demonstrated by clear and convincing evidence that a patient no longer wishes certain measures to be taken to preserve her life, it is up to the citizens of Missouri to decide, through their elected representatives, whether that wish will be honored. It is quite impossible (because the Constitution says nothing about the matter) that those citizens will decide upon a line less lawful than the one we would choose; and it is unlikely (because we know no more about "life-and-death" than they do) that they will decide upon a line less reasonable.

The text of the Due Process Clause does not protect individuals against deprivations of liberty *simpliciter*. It protects them against deprivations of liberty "without due process of law." To determine that such a deprivation would not occur if Nancy Cruzan were forced to take nourishment against her will, it is unnecessary to reopen the historically recurrent debate over whether "due process" includes substantive restrictions. It is at least true that no "substantive due process" claim can be maintained unless the claimant demonstrates that the State has deprived him of a right historically and traditionally protected against State interference. *Bowers v. Hardwick,* 478 U.S. 186, 192 (1986). That cannot possibly be established here.

At common law in England, a suicide—defined as one who "deliberately puts an end to his own existence, or commits any unlawful malicious act, the consequence of which is his own death," 4 W. Blackstone, Commentaries * 189—was criminally liable. . . .

Petitioners rely on three distinctions to separate Nancy Cruzan's case from ordinary suicide: (1) that she is permanently incapacitated and in pain; (2) that she would bring on her death not by any affirmative act but by merely declining treatment that provides nourishment; and (3) that preventing her from effectuating her presumed wish to die requires violation of her bodily integrity. None of these suffices. Suicide was not excused even when committed "to avoid those ills which [persons] had not the fortitude to endure.'' 4 Blackstone, *supra,* at * 189. ''The life of those to whom life has become a burden—of those who are hopelessly diseased or fatally wounded—nay, even the lives of criminals condemned to death, are under the protection of the law, equally as the lives of those who are in the full tide of life's enjoyment and anxious to continue to live.'' *Blackburn v. State,* 23 Ohio St. 146, 163 (1873). Thus, a man who prepared a poison, and placed it within reach of his wife, ''to put an end to her suffering'' from a terminal illness was convicted of murder, *People v. Roberts,* 211 Mich. 187, 178 N.W. 690, 693 (1920)....

The second asserted distinction—suggested by the recent cases canvassed by the Court concerning the right to refuse treatment, relies on the dichotomy between action and inaction. Suicide, it is said, consists of an affirmative act to end one's life; refusing treatment is not an affirmative act ''causing'' death, but merely a passive acceptance of the natural process of dying. I readily acknowledge that the distinction between action and inaction has some bearing upon the legislative judgment of what ought to be prevented as suicide—though even there it would seem to me unreasonable to draw the line precisely between action and inaction, rather than between various forms of inaction. It would not make much sense to say that one may not kill oneself by walking into the sea, but may sit on the beach until submerged by the incoming tide; or that one may not intentionally lock oneself into a cold storage locker, but may refrain from coming indoors when the temperature drops below freezing. Even as a legislative matter, in other words, the intelligent line does not fall between action and inaction but between those forms of inaction that consist of abstaining from ''ordinary'' care and those that consist of abstaining from ''excessive'' or ''heroic'' measures. Unlike action *vs.* inaction, that is not a line to be discerned by logic or legal analysis, and we should not pretend that it is.

But to return to the principal point for present purposes: the irrelevance of the action-inaction distinction. Starving oneself to death is no different from putting a gun to one's temple as far as the common-law definition of suicide is concerned; the cause of death in both cases is the suicide's conscious decision to ''pu[t] an end to his own existence.'' 4 Blackstone, *supra,* at * 189. [T]he early cases considering the claimed right to refuse medical treatment dismissed as specious the nice distinction between ''passively submitting to death and actively seeking it. The distinction may be merely verbal, as it would be if an adult sought death by starvation instead of a drug. If the State may interrupt one mode of self-destruction, it may with equal authority interfere with the other.''

The third asserted basis of distinction—that frustrating Nancy Cruzan's wish to die in the present case requires interference with her bodily integrity—is likewise inadequate, because such interference is impermissible only if one begs the question whether her refusal to undergo the treatment on her own is suicide. It has always been lawful not only for the State, but even for private citizens, to interfere with bodily integrity to prevent a felony. That general rule has of course been applied to suicide. At common law, even a private person's use of force to prevent suicide was privileged. It is not even reasonable, much less required by the Constitution, to maintain that although the State has the right to prevent a person from slashing his wrists it does not have the power to apply physical force to prevent him from doing so, nor the power, should he succeed, to apply, coercively if necessary, medical measures to stop the flow of blood. . . .

. . . Suppose that Nancy Cruzan were in precisely the condition she is in today, except that she could be fed and digest food and water *without* artificial assistance. How is the State's "interest" in keeping her alive thereby increased, or her interest in deciding whether she wants to continue living reduced? It seems to me, in other words, that Justice Brennan's position ultimately rests upon the proposition that it is none of the State's business if a person wants to commit suicide. . . . This is a view that some societies have held, and that our States are free to adopt if they wish. But it is not a view imposed by our constitutional traditions, in which the power of the State to prohibit suicide is unquestionable.

What I have said above is not meant to suggest that I would think it desirable, if we were sure that Nancy Cruzan wanted to die, to keep her alive by the means at issue here. I assert only that the Constitution has nothing to say about the subject. To raise up a constitutional right here we would have to create out of nothing (for it exists neither in text nor tradition) some constitutional principle whereby, although the State may insist that an individual come in out of the cold and eat food, it may not insist that he take medicine; and although it may pump his stomach empty of poison he has ingested, it may not fill his stomach with food he has failed to ingest. Are there, then, no reasonable and humane limits that ought not to be exceeded in requiring an individual to preserve his own life? There obviously are, but they are not set forth in the Due Process Clause. What assures us that those limits will not be exceeded is the same constitutional guarantee that is the source of most of our protection—what protects us, for example, from being assessed a tax of 100% of our income above the subsistence level, from being forbidden to drive cars, or from being required to send our children to school for 10 hours a day, none of which horribles is categorically prohibited by the Constitution. Our salvation is the Equal Protection Clause, which requires the democratic majority to accept for themselves and their loved ones what they impose on you and me. This Court need not, and has no authority to, inject itself into every field of human activity where irrationality and oppression may theoretically occur, and if it tries to do so it will destroy itself.

JUSTICE BRENNAN, with whom JUSTICE MARSHALL and JUSTICE BLACKMUN join, dissenting.

. . . Because I believe that Nancy Cruzan has a fundamental right to be free of unwanted artificial nutrition and hydration, which right is not outweighed by any interests of the State, and because I find that the improperly biased procedural obstacles imposed by the Missouri Supreme Court impermissibly burden that right, I respectfully dissent. Nancy Cruzan is entitled to choose to die with dignity....

[I]f a competent person has a liberty interest to be free of unwanted medical treatment, as both the majority and Justice O'Connor concede, it must be fundamental. ...The right to be free from unwanted medical attention is a right to evaluate the potential benefit of treatment and its possible consequences according to one's own values and to make a personal decision whether to subject oneself to the intrusion. For a patient like Nancy Cruzan, the sole benefit of medical treatment is being kept metabolically alive. Neither artificial nutrition nor any other form of medical treatment available today can cure or in any way ameliorate her condition. Irreversibly vegetative patients are devoid of thought, emotion and sensation; they are permanently and completely unconscious....

Although the right to be free of unwanted medical intervention, like other constitutionally protected interests, may not be absolute,[12] no State interest could outweigh the rights of an individual in Nancy Cruzan's position. Whatever a State's possible interests in mandating life-support treatment under other circumstances, there is no good to be obtained here by Missouri's insistence that Nancy Cruzan remain on life-support systems if it is indeed her wish not to do so. ... The only State interest asserted here is a general interest in the preservation of life. But the State has no legitimate general interest in someone's life, completely abstracted from the interest of the person living that life, that could outweigh the person's choice to avoid medical treatment....

... Missouri may constitutionally impose only those procedural requirements that serve to enhance the accuracy of a determination of Nancy Cruzan's wishes or are at least consistent with an accurate determination. The Missouri "safeguard" that the Court upholds today does not meet that standard. The determination needed in this context is whether the incompetent person would choose to live in a persistent vegetative state on life-support or to avoid this medical treatment. Missouri's rule of decision imposes a markedly asymmetrical evidentiary burden. Only evidence of specific statements of treatment choice made by the patient when competent is admissible to support a finding that the patient, now in a persistent vegetative state, would wish to avoid further medical treatment. Moreover, this evidence must be clear and convincing. No proof is required to support a finding that the incompetent person would wish to continue treatment....

JUSTICE STEVENS, dissenting.

... Missouri's intrusion upon these fundamental liberties must, at a minimum, bear a reasonable relationship to a legitimate state end. Missouri asserts that its policy is related to a state interest in the protection of life. In my view, however, it is an effort to define life,

---

12. See *Jacobson v. Massachusetts,* 197 U.S. 11, 26–27 (1905)(upholding a Massachusetts law imposing fines or imprisonment on those refusing to be vaccinated as "of paramount necessity" to that State's fight against a smallpox epidemic).

rather than to protect it, that is the heart of Missouri's policy. Missouri insists, without regard to Nancy Cruzan's own interests, upon equating her life with the biological persistence of her bodily functions.... Even laws against suicide presuppose that those inclined to take their own lives have *some* interest in living, and, indeed, that the depressed people whose lives are preserved may later be thankful for the State's intervention. Likewise, decisions that address the "quality of life" of incompetent, but conscious, patients rest upon the recognition that these patients have *some* interest in continuing their lives, even if that interest pales in some eyes when measured against interests in dignity or comfort. Not so here. Contrary to the Court's suggestion, Missouri's protection of life in a form abstracted from the living is not commonplace; it is aberrant....

Notes

The lower court hear more evidence and decided that the Cruzan family had met the clear and convincing standard. Nancy Cruzan died December 26, 1990, 12 days after a court ordered (at her parents' request) that a feeding tube implanted in her stomach be removed.

WASHINGTON v. GLUCKSBERG
521 U.S. 702, 117 S.Ct. 2258, 138 L.Ed.2d 772 (1997).

CHIEF JUSTICE REHNQUIST delivered the opinion of the Court.

The question presented in this case is whether Washington's prohibition against "caus[ing]" or "aid[ing]" a suicide offends the Fourteenth Amendment to the United States Constitution. We hold that it does not.

It has always been a crime to assist a suicide in the State of Washington. ... Today, Washington law provides: "A person is guilty of promoting a suicide attempt when he knowingly causes or aids another person to attempt suicide." Wash. Rev. Code 9A.36.060(1) (1994). "Promoting a suicide attempt" is a felony, punishable by up to five years imprisonment and up to a $10,000 fine. At the same time, Washington's Natural Death Act, enacted in 1979, states that the "withholding or withdrawal of life-sustaining treatment" at a patient's direction "shall not, for any purpose, constitute a suicide."[13]

Petitioners in this case are the State of Washington and its Attorney General. [Respondent-physicians] occasionally treat terminally ill, suffering patients, and declare that they would assist these patients in ending their lives if not for Washington's assisted-suicide ban. [Respondents]

---

13. Under Washington's Natural Death Act, "adult persons have the fundamental right to control the decisions relating to the rendering of their own health care, including the decision to have life-sustaining treatment withheld or withdrawn in instances of a terminal condition or permanent unconscious condition." [Any] "adult person may execute a directive directing the withholding or withdrawal of life-sustaining treatment in a terminal condition or permanent unconscious condition," § 70.122.030, and a physician who, in accordance with such a directive, participates in the withholding or withdrawal of life-sustaining treatment is immune from civil, criminal, or professional liability.

asserted "the existence of a liberty interest protected by the Fourteenth Amendment which extends to a personal choice by a mentally competent, terminally ill adult to commit physician-assisted suicide." Relying primarily on *Planned Parenthood v. Casey* (1992), and *Cruzan v. Director, Missouri Dept. of Health* (1990) the District Court agreed, and concluded that Washington's assisted-suicide ban is unconstitutional because it "places an undue burden on the exercise of [that] constitutionally protected liberty interest." The District Court also decided that the Washington statute violated the Equal Protection Clause's requirement that " 'all persons similarly situated . . . be treated alike.' "

[The] Ninth Circuit [en banc] affirmed the District Court. [T]he court held that the State's assisted-suicide ban was unconstitutional "as applied to terminally ill competent adults who wish to hasten their deaths with medication prescribed by their physicians." The court did not reach the District Court's equal-protection holding. We granted certiorari, and now reverse.

I. We begin, as we do in all due-process cases, by examining our Nation's history, legal traditions, and practices. [F]or over 700 years, the Anglo–American common-law tradition has punished or otherwise disapproved of both suicide and assisting suicide. [T]he prohibitions against assisting suicide never contained exceptions for those who were near death. Rather, "[t]he life of those to whom life ha[d] become a burden—of those who [were] hopelessly diseased or fatally wounded—nay, even the lives of criminals condemned to death, [were] under the protection of law, equally as the lives of those who [were] in the full tide of life's enjoyment, and anxious to continue to live." *Blackburn v. State*, 23 Ohio St. 146, 163 (1872). . . .

Though deeply rooted, the States' assisted-suicide bans have in recent years been reexamined and, generally, reaffirmed. Because of advances in medicine and technology, Americans today are increasingly likely to die in institutions, from chronic illnesses. Public concern and democratic action are therefore sharply focused on how best to protect dignity and independence at the end of life, with the result that there have been many significant changes in state laws and in the attitudes these laws reflect. Many States, for example, now permit "living wills," surrogate health-care decisionmaking, and the withdrawal or refusal of life-sustaining medical treatment. See *Vacco v. Quill, post*; *People v. Kevorkian*, 447 Mich. 436, 478–80, and nn. 53–56, 527 N. W. 2d 714, 731–32, and nn. 53–56 (1994). At the same time, however, voters and legislators continue for the most part to reaffirm their States' prohibitions on assisting suicide. [O]n April 30, 1997, President Clinton signed the Federal Assisted Suicide Funding Restriction Act of 1997, which prohibits the use of federal funds in support of physician-assisted suicide.

Thus, the States are currently engaged in serious, thoughtful examinations of physician-assisted suicide and other similar issues. For example, New York State's Task Force on Life and the Law—an ongoing, blue-ribbon commission composed of doctors, ethicists, lawyers, religious leaders, and interested laymen—... unanimously concluded that "[l]e-galizing assisted suicide and euthanasia would pose profound risks to many individuals who are ill and vulnerable.... [T]he potential dangers of this dramatic change in public policy would outweigh any benefit that might be achieved." ...

II. The Due Process Clause guarantees more than fair process, and the "liberty" it protects includes more than the absence of physical restraint. [It includes, e.g.,] the rights to marry, *Loving v. Virginia* (1967); to have children, *Skinner v. Oklahoma ex rel. Williamson* (1942); to direct the education and upbringing of one's children, *Meyer v. Nebraska* (1923); *Pierce v. Society of Sisters* (1925); to marital privacy, *Griswold v. Connecticut* (1965); to use contraception, *Eisenstadt v. Baird* (1972); to bodily integrity, *Rochin v. California*, 342 U. S. 165, 72 S.Ct. 205, 96 L.Ed. 183 (1952), and to abortion, *Planned Parenthood v. Casey*. We have also assumed, and strongly suggested, that the Due Process Clause protects the traditional right to refuse unwanted lifesaving medical treatment. *Cruzan.*

But we "ha[ve] always been reluctant to expand the concept of substantive due process because guideposts for responsible decisionmaking in this unchartered area are scarce and open-ended." By extending constitutional protection to an asserted right or liberty interest, we, to a great extent, place the matter outside the arena of public debate and legislative action. We must therefore "exercise the utmost care ... ," lest the liberty protected by the Due Process Clause be subtly transformed into the policy preferences of the members of this Court.

Our established method of substantive-due-process analysis has two primary features: First, we have regularly observed that the Due Process Clause specially protects those fundamental rights and liberties which are, objectively, "deeply rooted in this Nation's history and tradition," and "implicit in the concept of ordered liberty," such that "neither liberty nor justice would exist if they were sacrificed," *Palko v. Connecticut* (1937). Second, we have required in substantive-due-process cases a "careful description" of the asserted fundamental liberty interest. *Cruzan....*

[T]he development of this Court's substantive-due-process jurisprudence, described briefly above, has been a process whereby the outlines of the "liberty" specially protected by the Fourteenth Amendment—never fully clarified, to be sure, and perhaps not capable of being fully clarified—have at least been carefully refined by concrete examples involving fundamental rights found to be deeply rooted in our legal tradition. This approach tends to rein in the subjective elements that are necessarily present in due-process judicial review. In addition, by establishing a threshold requirement—that a challenged state action implicate a fundamental right—before requiring more than a reasonable relation to a legitimate state interest to justify the action, it avoids the need for complex balancing of competing interests in every case.

[*Cruzan* assumed] "that the United States Constitution would grant a competent person a constitutionally protected right to refuse lifesaving hydration and nutrition." We concluded that, notwithstanding this right, the Constitution permitted Missouri to require clear and convincing evidence of an incompetent patient's wishes concerning the withdrawal of life-sustaining treatment.

[The Ninth Circuit] concluded that "*Cruzan*, by recognizing a liberty interest that includes the refusal of artificial provision of life-sustaining food and water, necessarily recognize[d] a liberty interest in hastening one's own death." The right assumed in *Cruzan*, however, was not simply deduced from abstract concepts of personal autonomy. Given the common-law rule that forced medication was a battery, and the long legal tradition protecting the decision to refuse unwanted medical treatment, our assumption was entirely consistent with this Nation's history and constitutional traditions. The decision to commit suicide with the assistance of another may be just as personal and profound as the decision to refuse unwanted medical treatment, but it has never enjoyed similar legal protection. Indeed, the two acts are widely and reasonably regarded as quite distinct. See *Quill v. Vacco, post.* In *Cruzan* itself, we recognized that most States outlawed assisted suicide—and even more do today—and we certainly gave no intimation that the right to refuse unwanted medical treatment could be somehow transmuted into a right to assistance in committing suicide.

Respondents also rely on *Casey.* ... The Court of Appeals, like the District Court, found *Casey* " 'highly instructive' " and " 'almost prescriptive' " for determining " 'what liberty interest may inhere in a terminally ill person's choice to commit suicide' ":

> "Like the decision of whether or not to have an abortion, the decision how and when to die is one of 'the most intimate and personal choices a person may make in a lifetime,' a choice 'central to personal dignity and autonomy.' "

... That many of the rights and liberties protected by the Due Process Clause sound in personal autonomy does not warrant the sweeping conclusion that any and all important, intimate, and personal decisions are so protected, and *Casey* did not suggest otherwise.

The history of the law's treatment of assisted suicide in this country has been and continues to be one of the rejection of nearly all efforts to permit it. That being the case, our decisions lead us to conclude that the asserted "right" to assistance in committing suicide is not a fundamental liberty interest protected by the Due Process Clause. The Constitution also requires, however, that Washington's assisted-suicide ban be rationally related to legitimate government interests. This requirement is unquestionably met here. As the court below recognized,[20] Washington's assisted-suicide ban implicates a number of state interests.

---

20. The court identified and discussed six state interests: (1) preserving life; (2) preventing suicide; (3) avoiding the involvement of third parties and use of arbitrary,

First, Washington has an "unqualified interest in the preservation of human life." *Cruzan*. The State's prohibition on assisted suicide, like all homicide laws, both reflects and advances its commitment to this interest. Model Penal Code § 210.5, Comment 5, at 100 ("[T]he interests in the sanctity of life that are represented by the criminal homicide laws are threatened by one who expresses a willingness to participate in taking the life of another").[22] [T]he States "may properly decline to make judgments about the 'quality' of life that a particular individual may enjoy," *Cruzan*. This remains true, as *Cruzan* makes clear, even for those who are near death. . . .

Those who attempt suicide—terminally ill or not—often suffer from depression or other mental disorders. See New York Task Force (more than 95% of those who commit suicide had a major psychiatric illness at the time of death; among the terminally ill, uncontrolled pain is a "risk factor" because it contributes to depression); *cf.* Back, Wallace, Starks, & Pearlman, Physician–Assisted Suicide and Euthanasia in Washington State, 275 JAMA 919, 924 (1996) ("[I]ntolerable physical symptoms are not the reason most patients request physician-assisted suicide or euthanasia"). [M]any people who request physician-assisted suicide withdraw that request if their depression and pain are treated. H. Hendin, Seduced by Death: Doctors, Patients and the Dutch Cure 24–25 (1997) (suicidal, terminally ill patients "usually respond well to treatment for depressive illness and pain medication and are then grateful to be alive"). The New York Task Force, however, expressed its concern that, because depression is difficult to diagnose, physicians and medical professionals often fail to respond adequately to seriously ill patients' needs. Thus, legal physician-assisted suicide could make it more difficult for the State to protect depressed or mentally ill persons, or those who are suffering from untreated pain, from suicidal impulses.

The State also has an interest in protecting the integrity and ethics of the medical profession. [T]he American Medical Association, like many other medical and physicians' groups, has concluded that "[p]hysician-assisted suicide is fundamentally incompatible with the physician's role as healer." American Medical Association, Code of Ethics § 2.211 (1994); see Council on Ethical and Judicial Affairs, Decisions Near the End of Life, 267 JAMA 2229, 2233 (1992) ("[T]he societal risks of involving physicians in medical interventions to cause patients' deaths is too great").

Next, the State has an interest in protecting vulnerable groups— including the poor, the elderly, and disabled persons—from abuse, ne-

unfair, or undue influence; (4) protecting family members and loved ones; (5) protecting the integrity of the medical profession; and (6) avoiding future movement toward euthanasia and other abuses.

22. "[N]early all states expressly disapprove of suicide and assisted suicide either in statutes dealing with durable powers of attorney in health-care situations, or in 'living will' statutes. In addition, all states provide for the involuntary commitment of persons who may harm themselves as the result of mental illness, and a number of states allow the use of nondeadly force to thwart suicide attempts." *People v. Kevorkian*.

glect, and mistakes. The Court of Appeals dismissed the State's concern that disadvantaged persons might be pressured into physician-assisted suicide as "ludicrous on its face." [But] the New York Task Force warned that "[l]egalizing physician-assisted suicide would pose profound risks to many individuals who are ill and vulnerable.... The risk of harm is greatest for the many individuals in our society whose autonomy and well-being are already compromised by poverty, lack of access to good medical care, advanced age, or membership in a stigmatized social group." New York Task Force 120; see *Compassion in Dying*, 49 F.3d at 593 ("[A]n insidious bias against the handicapped—again coupled with a cost-saving mentality—makes them especially in need of Washington's statutory protection"). If physician-assisted suicide were permitted, many might resort to it to spare their families the substantial financial burden of end-of-life health-care costs.

The State's interest here goes beyond protecting the vulnerable from coercion; it extends to protecting disabled and terminally ill people from prejudice, negative and inaccurate stereotypes, and "societal indifference." The State's assisted-suicide ban reflects and reinforces its policy that the lives of terminally ill, disabled, and elderly people must be no less valued than the lives of the young and healthy, and that a seriously disabled person's suicidal impulses should be interpreted and treated the same way as anyone else's. See New York Task Force 101–102; Physician–Assisted Suicide and Euthanasia in the Netherlands: A Report of Chairman Charles T. Canady, at 9, 20 (discussing prejudice toward the disabled and the negative messages euthanasia and assisted suicide send to handicapped patients).

Finally, the State may fear that permitting assisted suicide will start it down the path to voluntary and perhaps even involuntary euthanasia. The Court of Appeals struck down Washington's assisted-suicide ban only "as applied to competent, terminally ill adults who wish to hasten their deaths by obtaining medication prescribed by their doctors." Washington insists, however, that the impact of the court's decision will not and cannot be so limited. If suicide is protected as a matter of constitutional right, it is argued, "every man and woman in the United States must enjoy it." The Court of Appeals' decision, and its expansive reasoning, provide ample support for the State's concerns. The court noted, for example, that the "decision of a duly appointed surrogate decision maker is for all legal purposes the decision of the patient himself;" that "in some instances, the patient may be unable to self-administer the drugs and ... administration by the physician ... may be the only way the patient may be able to receive them;" and that not only physicians, but also family members and loved ones, will inevitably participate in assisting suicide. [W]hat is couched as a limited right to "physician-assisted suicide" is likely, in effect, a much broader license, which could prove extremely difficult to police and contain. Washington's ban on assisting suicide prevents such erosion.

This concern is further supported by evidence about the practice of euthanasia in the Netherlands. The Dutch government's own study revealed that in 1990, there were 2,300 cases of voluntary euthanasia (defined as "the deliberate termination of another's life at his request"), 400 cases of assisted suicide, and more than 1,000 cases of euthanasia without an explicit request. In addition to these latter 1,000 cases, the study found an additional 4,941 cases where physicians administered lethal morphine overdoses without the patients' explicit consent. This study suggests that, despite the existence of various reporting procedures, euthanasia in the Netherlands has not been limited to competent, terminally ill adults who are enduring physical suffering, and that regulation of the practice may not have prevented abuses in cases involving vulnerable persons, including severely disabled neonates and elderly persons suffering from dementia. The New York Task Force, citing the Dutch experience, observed that "assisted suicide and euthanasia are closely linked," and concluded that the "risk of ... abuse is neither speculative nor distant." Washington, like most other States, reasonably ensures against this risk by banning, rather than regulating, assisting suicide.

We need not weigh exactly the relative strengths of these various interests. They are unquestionably important and legitimate, and Washington's ban on assisted suicide is at least reasonably related to their promotion and protection. We therefore hold that [this state law] does not violate the Fourteenth Amendment, either on its face or "as applied to competent, terminally ill adults who wish to hasten their deaths by obtaining medication prescribed by their doctors."[24] ...

It is so ordered.

[EDITOR'S NOTE: On the same day, the Court also decided *Vacco v. Quill*. In both cases Rehnquist, C.J., delivered the opinion of the Court, joined by O'Connor, Scalia, Kennedy, & Thomas, JJ. O'Connor, J., filed a concurring opinion, joined by Ginsburg & Breyer, JJ., in part. Stevens, J., Souter, J., Ginsburg, JJ., also filed opinions concurring in the result. These separate opinions follow *Vacco*.]

VACCO v. QUILL
521 U.S. 793, 117 S.Ct. 2293, 138 L.Ed.2d 834 (1997).

CHIEF JUSTICE REHNQUIST delivered the opinion of the Court.

In New York, as in most States, it is a crime to aid another to commit or attempt suicide, but patients may refuse even lifesaving

---

24. Justice Stevens states that "the Court does conceive of respondents' claim as a facial challenge—addressing not the application of the statute to a particular set of plaintiffs before it, but the constitutionality of the statute's categorical prohibition.... "*Post* (opinion concurring in judgment). We emphasize that we today reject the Court of Appeals' specific holding that the statute is unconstitutional "as applied" to a particular class. Justice Stevens agrees with this holding, but would not "foreclose the possibility that an individual plaintiff seeking to hasten her death, or a doctor whose assistance was sought, could prevail in a more particularized challenge." Our opinion does not absolutely foreclose such a claim. However, given our holding that the Due Process Clause of the Fourteenth Amendment does not provide heightened protection to the asserted liberty interest in ending one's life with a physician's assistance, such a claim would have to be quite different from the ones advanced by respondents here.

medical treatment. The question presented by this case is whether New York's prohibition on assisting suicide therefore violates the Equal Protection Clause of the Fourteenth Amendment. We hold that it does not.

[Respondents are New York physicians who] assert that although it would be "consistent with the standards of [their] medical practice[s]" to prescribe lethal medication for "mentally competent, terminally ill patients" who are suffering great pain and desire a doctor's help in taking their own lives, they are deterred from doing so by New York's ban on assisting suicide. Respondents, and three gravely ill patients who have since died,[4] sued the State's Attorney General in the United States District Court. They urged that because New York permits a competent person to refuse life-sustaining medical treatment, and because the refusal of such treatment is "essentially the same thing" as physician-assisted suicide, New York's assisted-suicide ban violates the Equal Protection Clause.

The District Court disagreed: "[I]t is hardly unreasonable or irrational for the State to recognize a difference between allowing nature to take its course, even in the most severe situations, and intentionally using an artificial death-producing device." The court noted New York's "obvious legitimate interests in preserving life, and in protecting vulnerable persons," and concluded that "[u]nder the United States Constitution and the federal system it establishes, the resolution of this issue is left to the normal democratic processes within the State."

The Court of Appeals for the Second Circuit reversed [arguing that] "New York law does not treat equally all competent persons who are in the final stages of fatal illness and wish to hasten their deaths," because "those in the final stages of terminal illness who are on life-support systems are allowed to hasten their deaths by directing the removal of such systems; but those who are similarly situated, except for the previous attachment of life-sustaining equipment, are not allowed to hasten death by self-administering prescribed drugs." In the court's view, "[t]he ending of life by [the withdrawal of life-support systems] is *nothing more nor less than assisted suicide*." (emphasis added). . . .

The Equal Protection Clause . . . creates no substantive rights. Instead, it embodies a general rule that States must treat like cases alike but may treat unlike cases accordingly. If a legislative classification or distinction "neither burdens a fundamental right nor targets a suspect class, we will uphold [it] so long as it bears a rational relation to some legitimate end."

New York's statutes outlawing assisting suicide affect and address matters of profound significance to all New Yorkers alike. They neither infringe fundamental rights nor involve suspect classifications. *Washing-*

---

4. These three patients stated that they had no chance of recovery, faced the "prospect of progressive loss of bodily function and integrity and increasing pain and suffering," and desired medical assistance in ending their lives.

ton v. Glucksberg, ante. These laws are therefore entitled to a "strong presumption of validity."

On their faces, neither New York's ban on assisting suicide nor its statutes permitting patients to refuse medical treatment treat anyone differently than anyone else or draw any distinctions between persons. *Everyone*, regardless of physical condition, is entitled, if competent, to refuse unwanted lifesaving medical treatment; *no one* is permitted to assist a suicide. Generally speaking, laws that apply evenhandedly to all "unquestionably comply" with the Equal Protection Clause.

. . . Unlike the Court of Appeals, we think the distinction between assisting suicide and withdrawing life-sustaining treatment, a distinction widely recognized and endorsed in the medical profession[6] and in our legal traditions, is both important and logical; it is certainly rational. "When the basic classification is rationally based, uneven effects upon particular groups within a class are ordinarily of no constitutional concern".

The distinction comports with fundamental legal principles of causation and intent. First, when a patient refuses life-sustaining medical treatment, he dies from an underlying fatal disease or pathology; but if a patient ingests lethal medication prescribed by a physician, he is killed by that medication.

Furthermore, a physician who withdraws, or honors a patient's refusal to begin, life-sustaining medical treatment purposefully intends, or may so intend, only to respect his patient's wishes and "to cease doing useless and futile or degrading things to the patient when [the patient] no longer stands to benefit from them." The same is true when a doctor provides aggressive palliative care; in some cases, painkilling drugs may hasten a patient's death, but the physician's purpose and intent is, or may be, only to ease his patient's pain. A doctor who assists a suicide, however, "must, necessarily and indubitably, intend primarily that the patient be made dead." Similarly, a patient who commits suicide with a doctor's aid necessarily has the specific intent to end his or her own life, while a patient who refuses or discontinues treatment might not. See, *e.g., Matter of Conroy, supra* (patients who refuse life-sustaining treatment "may not harbor a specific intent to die" and may instead "fervently wish to live, but to do so free of unwanted medical technology, surgery, or drugs").

The law has long used actors' intent or purpose to distinguish between two acts that may have the same result. See, *e.g., United States v. Bailey*, 444 U. S. 394, 403–406 (1980) ("[T]he . . . common law of homicide often distinguishes . . . between a person who knows that another person will be killed as the result of his conduct and a person who acts with the specific purpose of taking another's life"). Put differently, the law distinguishes actions taken "because of" a given end from

6. The American Medical Association emphasizes the "fundamental difference between refusing life-sustaining treatment and demanding a life-ending treatment." . . .

actions taken "in spite of" their unintended but foreseen consequences. *Compassion in Dying v. Washington*, 79 F. 3d 790, 858 (C.A.9 1996) (Kleinfeld, J., dissenting) ("When General Eisenhower ordered American soldiers onto the beaches of Normandy, he knew that he was sending many American soldiers to certain death.... His purpose, though, was to ... liberate Europe from the Nazis").

Given these general principles, it is not surprising that many courts, including New York courts, have carefully distinguished refusing life-sustaining treatment from suicide. See, *e.g.*, *Fosmire v. Nicoleau*, 75 N. Y. 2d 218, 227, and n. 2, 551 N. E. 2d 77, 82, and n. 2 (1990) ("[M]erely declining medical ... care is not considered a suicidal act").[7] In fact, the first state-court decision explicitly to authorize withdrawing lifesaving treatment noted the "real distinction between the self-infliction of deadly harm and a self-determination against artificial life support." *In re Quinlan*, 70 N. J. 10, 43, 52, and n. 9, 355 A. 2d 647, 665, 670, and n. 9, cert. denied *sub nom. Garger v. New Jersey*, 429 U. S. 922 (1976). ...

Similarly, the overwhelming majority of state legislatures have drawn a clear line between assisting suicide and withdrawing or permitting the refusal of unwanted lifesaving medical treatment by prohibiting the former and permitting the latter. [E]ven as the States move to protect and promote patients' dignity at the end of life, they remain opposed to physician-assisted suicide. ...

This Court has also recognized, at least implicitly, the distinction between letting a patient die and making that patient die. In *Cruzan v. Director, Mo. Dept. of Health* (1990), ... our assumption of a right to refuse treatment was grounded not, as the Court of Appeals supposed, on the proposition that patients have a general and abstract "right to hasten death," but on well established, traditional rights to bodily integrity and freedom from unwanted touching, *Cruzan* (O'Connor, J., concurring). In fact, we observed that "the majority of States in this country have laws imposing criminal penalties on one who assists another to commit suicide." *Cruzan* therefore provides no support for the notion that refusing life-sustaining medical treatment is "nothing more nor less than suicide." [Thus] we disagree with respondents' claim that the distinction between refusing lifesaving medical treatment and assisted suicide is "arbitrary" and "irrational."[11] ... By permitting

---

7. Thus, the Second Circuit erred in reading New York law as creating a "right to hasten death"; instead, the authorities cited by the court recognize a right to refuse treatment, and nowhere equate the exercise of this right with suicide. [*See*] *Rivers v. Katz*, 67 N. Y. 2d 485, 495, 495 N. E. 2d 337, 343 (1986) (right to refuse antipsychotic medication is not absolute, and may be limited when "the patient presents a danger to himself").

11. Respondents also argue that the State irrationally distinguishes between

physician-assisted suicide and "terminal sedation," a process respondents characterize as "induc[ing] barbiturate coma and then starv[ing] the person to death." Petitioners insist, however, that " '[a]lthough proponents of physician-assisted suicide and euthanasia contend that terminal sedation is covert physician-assisted suicide or euthanasia, the concept of sedating pharmacotherapy is based on informed consent and the principle of double effect.' "Reply Brief for Petitioners 12. Just as a State may prohibit assisting suicide while permitting patients to refuse unwanted lifesaving

everyone to refuse unwanted medical treatment while prohibiting anyone from assisting a suicide, New York law follows a longstanding and rational distinction.

New York's reasons for recognizing and acting on this distinction—including prohibiting intentional killing and preserving life; preventing suicide; maintaining physicians' role as their patients' healers; protecting vulnerable people from indifference, prejudice, and psychological and financial pressure to end their lives; and avoiding a possible slide towards euthanasia—are discussed in greater detail in our opinion in *Glucksberg, ante.* These valid and important public interests easily satisfy the constitutional requirement that a legislative classification bear a rational relation to some legitimate end.[12]

The judgment of the Court of Appeals is reversed.

It is so ordered.

Justice O'Connor, concurring.*

. . . . I join the Court's opinions because I agree that there is no generalized right to "commit suicide." But respondents urge us to address the narrower question whether a mentally competent person who is experiencing great suffering has a constitutionally cognizable interest in controlling the circumstances of his or her imminent death. I see no need to reach that question in the context of the facial challenges to the New York and Washington laws at issue here. The parties and *amici* agree that in these States a patient who is suffering from a terminal illness and who is experiencing great pain has no legal barriers to obtaining medication, from qualified physicians, to alleviate that suffering, even to the point of causing unconsciousness and hastening death. [T]he State's interests in protecting those who are not truly competent or facing imminent death, or those whose decisions to hasten death would not truly be voluntary, are sufficiently weighty to justify a prohibition against physician-assisted suicide.

Every one of us at some point may be affected by our own or a family member's terminal illness. There is no reason to think the democratic process will not strike the proper balance between the interests of terminally ill, mentally competent individuals who would

---

treatment, it may permit palliative care related to that refusal, which may have the foreseen but unintended "double effect" of hastening the patient's death. See New York Task Force, When Death is Sought, *supra* ("It is widely recognized that the provision of pain medication is ethically and professionally acceptable even when the treatment may hasten the patient's death, if the medication is intended to alleviate pain and severe discomfort, not to cause death").

12. Justice Stevens observes that our holding today "does not foreclose the possi-

bility that some applications of the New York statute may impose an intolerable intrusion on the patient's freedom." (concurring opinion). This is true, but, as we observe in *Glucksberg*, a particular plaintiff hoping to show that New York's assisted-suicide ban was unconstitutional in his particular case would need to present different and considerably stronger arguments than those advanced by respondents here.

* Justice Ginsburg concurs in the Court's judgments substantially for the reasons stated in this opinion. Justice Breyer joins this opinion except insofar as it joins the opinions of the Court.

seek to end their suffering and the State's interests in protecting those who might seek to end life mistakenly or under pressure. . . .

JUSTICE STEVENS, concurring in the judgments . . . . .

Today, the Court decides that Washington's statute prohibiting assisted suicide is not invalid "on its face," that is to say, in all or most cases in which it might be applied. That holding, however, does not foreclose the possibility that some applications of the statute might well be invalid.

. . . The value to others of a person's life is far too precious to allow the individual to claim a constitutional entitlement to complete autonomy in making a decision to end that life. Thus, I fully agree with the Court that the "liberty" protected by the Due Process Clause does not include a categorical "right to commit suicide which itself includes a right to assistance in doing so."

[A] decision upholding a general statutory prohibition of assisted suicide does not mean that every possible application of the statute would be valid. A State, like Washington, that has authorized the death penalty and thereby has concluded that the sanctity of human life does not require that it always be preserved, must acknowledge that there are situations in which an interest in hastening death is legitimate. Indeed, . . . I am also convinced that there are times when it is entitled to constitutional protection.

[T]he American Medical Association unequivocally endorses the practice of terminal sedation—the administration of sufficient dosages of pain-killing medication to terminally ill patients to protect them from excruciating pain even when it is clear that the time of death will be advanced. The purpose of terminal sedation is to ease the suffering of the patient and comply with her wishes, and the actual cause of death is the administration of heavy doses of lethal sedatives. This same intent and causation may exist when a doctor complies with a patient's request for lethal medication to hasten her death.

[S]ome applications of the New York statute may impose an intolerable intrusion on the patient's freedom. [T]he so-called "unqualified interest in the preservation of human life," is not itself sufficient to outweigh the interest in liberty that may justify the only possible means of preserving a dying patient's dignity and alleviating her intolerable suffering.

JUSTICE SOUTER, concurring in the judgment. . . .

The analogies between the abortion cases and this one are several. Even though the State has a legitimate interest in discouraging abortion, see *Casey* (joint opinion of O'Connor, Kennedy, and Souter, JJ.), the Court recognized a woman's right to a physician's counsel and care. Like the decision to commit suicide, the decision to abort potential life can be made irresponsibly and under the influence of others, and yet the Court has held in the abortion cases that physicians are fit assistants. Without physician assistance in abortion, the woman's right would have too often amounted to nothing more than a right to self-mutilation, and without a physician to assist in the suicide of the dying, the patient's right will often be confined to crude methods of causing death, most shocking and painful to the decedent's survivors. . . .

[W]hichever way the Court might rule today, events could overtake its assumptions, as experimentation in some jurisdictions confirmed or discredited the concerns about progression from assisted suicide to euthanasia. Legislatures, on the other hand, have superior opportunities to obtain the facts necessary for a judgment about the present controversy. Not only do they have more flexible mechanisms for factfinding than the Judiciary, but their mechanisms include the power to experiment, moving forward and pulling back as facts emerge within their own jurisdictions. . . .

I do not decide here what the significance might be of legislative foot-dragging in ascertaining the facts going to the State's argument that the right in question could not be confined as claimed . . . . The Court should accordingly stay its hand to allow reasonable legislative consideration. While I do not decide for all time that respondents' claim should not be recognized, I acknowledge the legislative institutional competence as the better one to deal with that claim at this time.

> [EDITOR'S NOTE: Justice Souter, concurring in the judgment in *Vacco*, wrote that the "reasons that lead me to conclude in *Glucksberg* that the prohibition on assisted suicide is not arbitrary under the due process standard also support the distinction between assistance to suicide, which is banned, and practices such as termination of artificial life support and death-hastening pain medication, which are permitted."]

JUSTICE GINSBURG, concurring in the judgments.

I concur in the Court's judgments in these cases substantially for the reasons stated by Justice O'Connor in her concurring opinion.

JUSTICE BREYER, concurring in the judgments.

I [join] Justice O'Connor's . . . separate opinion, except insofar as it joins the majority. . . . I shall briefly explain how I differ from the Court. [T]he laws of New York and of Washington do not prohibit doctors from providing patients with drugs sufficient to control pain despite the risk that those drugs themselves will kill. . . . Were the legal circumstances different—for example, were state law to prevent the provision of palliative care, including the administration of drugs as needed to avoid pain at the end of life—then the law's impact upon serious and otherwise unavoidable physical pain (accompanying death) would be more directly at issue. And as Justice O'Connor suggests, the Court might have to revisit its conclusions in these cases.

Chapter 9

CONGRESSIONAL ENFORCEMENT
OF CIVIL RIGHTS

9-1. THE FOURTEENTH AMENDMENT

KATZENBACH v. MORGAN
384 U.S. 641, 86 S.Ct. 1717, 16 L.Ed.2d 828 (1966).

Mr. Justice Brennan delivered the opinion of the Court.

These cases concern the constitutionality of § 4(e) of the Voting Rights Act of 1965. That law, in the respects pertinent in these cases, provides that no person who has successfully completed the sixth primary grade in a public school in, or a private school accredited by, the Commonwealth of Puerto Rico in which the language of instruction was other than English shall be denied the right to vote in any election because of his inability to read or write English. Appellees, registered voters in New York City, brought this suit to challenge the constitutionality of § 4(e) insofar as it *pro tanto* prohibits the enforcement of the election laws of New York requiring an ability to read and write English as a condition of voting. [A]ppellees attack § 4(e) insofar as it would enable [many New York City residents who come from Puerto Rico] to vote.... We hold that, in the application challenged in these cases, § 4(e) is a proper exercise of the powers granted to Congress by § 5 of the Fourteenth Amendment and that by force of the Supremacy Clause, Article VI, the New York English literacy requirement cannot be enforced to the extent that it is inconsistent with § 4(e)....

The Attorney General of the State of New York argues that an exercise of congressional power under § 5 of the Fourteenth Amendment that prohibits the enforcement of a state law can only be sustained if the judicial branch determines that the state law is prohibited by the provisions of the Amendment that Congress sought to enforce.... We disagree. Neither the language nor history of § 5 supports such a construction. As was said with regard to § 5 in *Ex parte Com. of Virginia,* 100 U.S. 339, 345, 25 L.Ed. 676 [1880], "It is the power of Congress which has been enlarged. Congress is authorized to *enforce* the prohibitions by appropriate legislation. Some legislation is contemplated to make the amendments fully effective." A construction of § 5 that would require a judicial determination that the enforcement of the state law precluded by Congress violated the Amendment, as a condition of sustaining the congressional enactment, would depreciate both congressional resourcefulness and congressional responsibility for implementing the Amendment. It would confine the legislative power in this context to the insignificant role of abrogating only those state laws that the judicial branch was prepared to adjudge unconstitutional, or of merely informing the judgment of the judiciary by particularizing the "majestic generalities" of § 1 of the Amendment.

Thus our task in this case is not to determine whether the New York English literacy requirement, as applied to deny the right to vote to a person who successfully completed the sixth grade in a Puerto Rican school, violates the Equal Protection Clause. Accordingly, our decision in *Lassiter v. Northampton County Bd. of Elections,* 360 U.S. 45, 79 S.Ct. 985, 3 L.Ed.2d 1072 [1959], sustaining the North Carolina English literacy requirement as not in all circumstances prohibited by the first sections of the Fourteenth and Fifteenth Amendments, is inapposite. *Lassiter* did not present the question before us here: Without regard to whether the judiciary would find that the Equal Protection Clause itself nullifies New York's English literacy requirement as so applied, could Congress prohibit the enforcement of the state law by legislating under § 5 of the Fourteenth Amendment? In answering this question, our task is limited to determining whether such legislation is, as required by § 5, appropriate legislation to enforce the Equal Protection Clause.

By including § 5 the draftsmen sought to grant to Congress, by a specific provision applicable to the Fourteenth Amendment, the same broad powers expressed in the Necessary and Proper Clause, Art. I, § 8, cl. 18. The classic formulation of the reach of those powers was established by Chief Justice Marshall in *McCulloch v. Maryland. Ex parte State of Virginia,* 100 U.S., at 345–346, 25 L.Ed. 676, decided 12 years after the adoption of the Fourteenth Amendment, held that congressional power under § 5 had this same broad scope.... Thus the *McCulloch v. Maryland* standard is the measure of what constitutes "appropriate legislation" under § 5 of the Fourteenth Amendment. Correctly viewed, § 5 is a positive grant of legislative power authorizing Congress to exercise its discretion in determining whether and what legislation is needed to secure the guarantees of the Fourteenth Amendment....[10]

---

10. Contrary to the suggestion of the dissent, § 5 does not grant Congress power to exercise discretion in the other direction and to enact "statutes so as in effect to dilute equal protection and due process decisions of this Court." We emphasize that Congress' power under § 5 is limited to adopting measures to enforce the guarantees of the Amendment; § 5 grants Congress no power to restrict, abrogate, or dilute these guarantees. Thus, for example, an enactment authorizing the States to establish racially segregated systems of education would not be—as required by § 5—a measure "to enforce" the Equal Protection Clause since that clause of its own force prohibits such state laws.

There can be no doubt that § 4(e) may be regarded as an enactment to enforce the Equal Protection Clause. Congress explicitly declared that it enacted § 4(e) "to secure the rights under the fourteenth amendment of persons educated in American-flag schools in which the predominant classroom language was other than English." ... More specifically, § 4(e) may be viewed as a measure to secure for the Puerto Rican community residing in New York nondiscriminatory treatment by government—both in the imposition of voting qualifications and the provision or administration of governmental services, such as public schools, public housing and law enforcement.

Section 4(e) may be readily seen as "plainly adapted" to furthering these aims of the Equal Protection Clause. The practical effect of § 4(e) is to prohibit New York from denying the right to vote to large segments of its Puerto Rican community. Congress has thus prohibited the State from denying to that community the right that is "preservative of all rights." This enhanced political power will be helpful in gaining nondiscriminatory treatment in public services for the entire Puerto Rican community.[11] ... It was for Congress, as the branch that made this judgment, to assess and weigh the various conflicting considerations— the risk or pervasiveness of the discrimination in governmental services, the effectiveness of eliminating the state restriction on the right to vote as a means of dealing with the evil, the adequacy or availability of alternative remedies, and the nature and significance of the state interests that would be affected by the nullification of the English literacy requirement as applied to residents who have successfully completed the sixth grade in a Puerto Rican school. It is not for us to review the congressional resolution of these factors. It is enough that we be able to perceive a basis upon which the Congress might resolve the conflict as it did. There plainly was such a basis to support § 4(e) in the application in question in this case. Any contrary conclusion would require us to be blind to the realities familiar to the legislators.

The result is no different if we confine our inquiry to the question whether § 4(e) was merely legislation aimed at the elimination of an invidious discrimination in establishing voter qualifications. We are told that New York's English literacy requirement originated in the desire to provide an incentive for non-English speaking immigrants to learn the English language and in order to assure the intelligent exercise of the franchise. Yet Congress might well have questioned, in light of the many exemptions provided,[13] and some evidence suggesting that prejudice

11. Cf. *James Everard's Breweries v. Day,* [265 U.S. 545, 44 S.Ct. 628, 68 L.Ed. 1174], which held that, under the Enforcement Clause of the Eighteenth Amendment, Congress could prohibit the prescription of intoxicating malt liquor for medicinal purposes even though the Amendment itself only prohibited the manufacture and sale of intoxicating liquors for beverage purposes. Cf. also the settled principle applied in the *Shreveport Case (Houston, E. & W.T.R. Co. v. United States),* [§ 4–1, supra], and ex-pressed in *United States v. Darby,* [§ 4–2, supra], that the power of Congress to regulate interstate commerce "extends to those activities intrastate which so affect interstate commerce or the exercise of the power of Congress over it as to make regulation of them appropriate means to the attainment of a legitimate end.... "

13. The principal exemption complained of is that for persons who had been eligible to vote before January 1, 1922.

played a prominent role in the enactment of the requirement, whether these were actually the interests being served. Congress might have also questioned whether denial of a right deemed so precious and fundamental in our society was a necessary or appropriate means of encouraging persons to learn English, or of furthering the goal of an intelligent exercise of the franchise. Finally, Congress might well have concluded that as a means of furthering the intelligent exercise of the franchise, an ability to read or understand Spanish is as effective as ability to read English for those to whom Spanish-language newspapers and Spanish-language radio and television programs are available to inform them of election issues and governmental affairs. Since Congress undertook to legislate so as to preclude the enforcement of the state law, and did so in the context of a general appraisal of literacy requirements for voting, to which it brought a specially informed legislative competence, it was Congress' prerogative to weigh these competing considerations. Here again, it is enough that we perceive a basis upon which Congress might predicate a judgment that the application of New York's English literacy requirement to deny the right to vote to a person with a sixth grade education in Puerto Rican schools in which the language of instruction was other than English constituted an invidious discrimination in violation of the Equal Protection Clause.

There remains the question whether the congressional remedies adopted in § 4(e) constitute means which are not prohibited by, but are consistent "with the letter and spirit of the constitution." The only respect in which appellees contend that § 4(e) fails in this regard is that the section itself works an invidious discrimination in violation of the Fifth Amendment by prohibiting the enforcement of the English literacy requirement only for those educated in American-flag schools (schools located within United States jurisdiction) in which the language of instruction was other than English, and not for those educated in schools beyond the territorial limits of the United States in which the language of instruction was also other than English. This is not a complaint that Congress, in enacting § 4(e), has unconstitutionally denied or diluted anyone's right to vote but rather that Congress violated the Constitution by not extending the relief effected in § 4(e) to those educated in non-American-flag schools.

[W]e are guided by the familiar principles that a "statute is not invalid under the Constitution because it might have gone farther than it did," that a legislature need not "strike at all evils at the same time," and that "reform may take one step at a time, addressing itself to the phase of the problem which seems most acute to the legislative mind."

Guided by these principles, we are satisfied that appellees' challenge to this limitation in § 4(e) is without merit. [T]he congressional choice to limit the relief effected in § 4(e) may, for example, reflect Congress' greater familiarity with the quality of instruction in American-flag schools.... We hold only that the limitation on relief effected in § 4(e) does not constitute a forbidden discrimination since these factors might well have been the basis for the decision of Congress to go "no farther than it did." We therefore conclude that § 4(e), in the application challenged in this case, is appropriate legislation to enforce the Equal Protection Clause and that the judgment of the District Court must be and hereby is

Reversed.

MR. JUSTICE DOUGLAS joins the Court's opinion except for the discussion of the question whether the congressional remedies adopted in § 4(e) constitute means which are not prohibited by, but are consistent with "the letter and spirit of the constitution." On that question, he reserves judgment until such time as it is presented by a member of the class against which that particular discrimination is directed.

MR. JUSTICE HARLAN, whom MR. JUSTICE STEWART joins, dissenting. . . .

When recognized state violations of federal constitutional standards have occurred, Congress is of course empowered by § 5 to take appropriate remedial measures to redress and prevent the wrongs. But it is a judicial question whether the condition with which Congress has thus sought to deal is in truth an infringement of the Constitution, something that is the necessary prerequisite to bringing the § 5 power into play at all. Thus, in *Ex parte Virginia,* supra, involving a federal statute making it a federal crime to disqualify anyone from jury service because of race, the Court first held as a matter of constitutional law that "the Fourteenth Amendment secures, among other civil rights, to colored men, when charged with criminal offences against a State, an impartial jury trial, by jurors indifferently selected or chosen without discrimination against such jurors because of their color." Only then did the Court hold that to enforce this prohibition upon state discrimination, Congress could enact a criminal statute of the type under consideration. . . .

Section 4(e), however, presents a significantly different type of congressional enactment. The question here is not whether the statute is appropriate remedial legislation to cure an established violation of a constitutional command, but whether there has in fact been an infringement of that constitutional command, that is, whether a particular state practice or, as here, a statute is so arbitrary or irrational as to offend the command of the Equal Protection Clause of the Fourteenth Amendment. That question is one for the judicial branch ultimately to determine. Were the rule otherwise, Congress would be able to qualify this Court's constitutional decisions under the Fourteenth and Fifteenth Amendments, let alone those under other provisions of the Constitution, by resorting to congressional power under the Necessary and Proper Clause. In view of this Court's holding in *Lassiter,* supra, that an English literacy test is a permissible exercise of state supervision over its franchise, I do not think it is open to Congress to limit the effect of that decision as it has undertaken to do by § 4(e). In effect the Court reads § 5 of the Fourteenth Amendment as giving Congress the power to define the *substantive* scope of the Amendment. If that indeed be the true reach of § 5, then I do not see why Congress should not be able as well to exercise its § 5 "discretion" by enacting statutes so as in effect to dilute equal protection and due process decisions of this Court. In all such cases there is room for reasonable men to differ as to whether or not a denial of equal protection or due process has occurred, and the final decision is one of judgment. Until today this judgment has always been one for the judiciary to resolve.

I do not mean to suggest in what has been said that a legislative judgment of the type incorporated in § 4(e) is without any force whatsoever. Decisions on questions of equal protection and due process are based not on abstract logic, but on empirical foundations. To the extent "legislative facts" are relevant to a judicial determination, Congress is well equipped to investigate them, and such determinations are of course entitled to due respect.... But no such factual data provide a legislative record supporting § 4(e)[9] by way of showing that Spanish-speaking citizens are fully as capable of making informed decisions in a New York election as are English-speaking citizens....

Notes

1. In *Oregon v. Mitchell*, 400 U.S. 112, 91 S.Ct. 260, 27 L.Ed.2d 272 (1970), a fragmented Court upheld various provisions of the Voting Rights Act Amendments of 1970. The Court found that it was constitutional for Congress to abolish literacy tests as requisite to vote, to abolish state durational residency requirements in presidential elections, and to enfranchise 18–year olds in federal (but not state) elections. However, a majority of the Court, using different rationales,[1] invalidated § 302, which set the age of 18 for voters in state and local elections. Stewart, J.'s separate opinion argued:

> "*Katzenbach v. Morgan* does not hold that Congress has the power to determine what are and what are not 'compelling state interests' for equal protection purposes. [That] Court upheld the statute on two grounds: that Congress could conclude that enhancing the political power of the Puerto Rican community by conferring the right to vote was an appropriate means of remedying discriminatory treatment in public services; and that Congress could conclude that the New York statute was tainted by the impermissible purpose of denying the right to vote to Puerto Ricans, an undoubted invidious discrimination under the Equal Protection Clause. [But the] state laws that § 302 invalidates do not invidiously discriminate against any discrete and insular minority. Unlike the statute considered in *Morgan*, § 302 is valid only if Congress has the power not only to provide the means of eradicating situations

9. There were no committee hearings or reports referring to this section, which was introduced from the floor during debate on the full Voting Rights Act.

1. Black, J., relied on Article I, § 4 of the Constitution to conclude that Congress can regulate national (but not local) elections. Harlan, J., concurring in part and dissenting in part, relied on the history of the 14th Amendment to conclude that "no part of the legislation now under review can be upheld as a legitimate exercise of congressional power under that Amendment." Dissenting from this argument was Douglas, J., who read Congress' § 5 power broadly and argued that Harlan's history of the 14th Amendment was "irrelevant to the present problem." Brennan, White, & Marshall, JJ. in a separate opinion, also "would uphold § 302 as a valid exercise congressional power under § 5 of the Fourteenth Amendment."

that amount to a violation of the Equal Protection Clause, but also to determine as a matter of substantive constitutional law what situations fall within the ambit of the clause and what state interests are 'compelling.' "[2]

The following year, the states ratified the 26th Amendment, guaranteeing that votes of citizens 18 years of age or older may not be abridged by the United States or any State on account of age.

2. In *United States v. Guest,* 383 U.S. 745, 86 S.Ct. 1170, 16 L.Ed.2d 239 (1966), a majority of the justices, in different opinions, expressed the view, in dictum, that section 5 of the Fourteenth Amendment authorizes Congress to enact laws punishing conspiracies to interfere with the exercise of Fourteenth Amendment rights, whether or not state officers or others acting under color of law are implicated in the conspiracies. After *Katzenbach v. Morgan* and *Oregon v. Mitchell* is the *Guest* dictum now the law?

CITY OF BOERNE v. FLORES
521 U.S. 507, 117 S.Ct. 2157, 138 L.Ed.2d 624 (1997).

JUSTICE KENNEDY delivered the opinion of the Court.*

A decision by local zoning authorities to deny a church a building permit was challenged under the Religious Freedom Restoration Act of 1993 (RFRA), 42 U. S. C.A. § 2000bb *et seq.* The case calls into question the authority of Congress to enact RFRA. We conclude the statute exceeds Congress' power.

I

[St. Peter Catholic Church, built in 1923, in the city of Boerne, Texas, seats about 230 worshippers, a number too small for its growing parish. The church planned alterations to enlarge the building. A few months later, but the Boerne City Council passed an ordinance authorizing the city's Historic Landmark Commission to prepare a preservation plan with proposed historic landmarks and districts. Under the ordinance, the Commission must preapprove construction affecting historic landmarks or buildings in a historic district. The Archbishop applied for a building permit, but the city authorities, relying on the ordinance and the designation of a historic district (which, they argued, included the church), denied the application. The Archbishop brought this suit challenging the permit denial. The Archbishop relied upon RFRA as one basis for relief from the refusal to issue the permit. The District Court concluded that by enacting RFRA Congress exceeded the scope of its enforcement power under § 5 of the Fourteenth Amendment. The Fifth Circuit reversed.] We granted certiorari, and now reverse.

---

2. Stewart, J., concurring in part and dissenting in part, was joined by Burger, C.J. & Blackmun, J. Cf. *Mississippi University for Women v. Hogan,* § 8–2.43, which rejects the argument that Congress could use section 5 of the Fourteenth Amendment to authorize sex discrimination.

* Justice Scalia joins all but Part III–A–1 of this opinion.

II

Congress enacted RFRA in direct response to the Court's decision in *Employment Div., Dept. of Human Resources of Ore. v. Smith* (1990) [§ 11–3]. There we considered a Free Exercise Clause claim brought by members of the Native American Church who were denied unemployment benefits when they lost their jobs because they had used peyote. Their practice was to ingest peyote for sacramental purposes, and they challenged an Oregon statute of general applicability which made use of the drug criminal. In evaluating the claim, we declined to apply the balancing test set forth in *Sherbert v. Verner* (1963)[§ 11–3], under which we would have asked whether Oregon's prohibition substantially burdened a religious practice and, if it did, whether the burden was justified by a compelling government interest. [Applying] the *Sherbert* test, the *Smith* decision explained, would have produced an anomaly in the law, a constitutional right to ignore neutral laws of general applicability. The anomaly would have been accentuated, the Court reasoned, by the difficulty of determining whether a particular practice was central to an individual's religion. We explained, moreover, that it "is not within the judicial ken to question the centrality of particular beliefs or practices to a faith, or the validity of particular litigants' interpretations of those creeds." . . .

The *Smith* decision acknowledged the Court had employed the *Sherbert* test in considering free exercise challenges to state unemployment compensation rules on three occasions where the balance had tipped in favor of the individual. Those cases, the Court explained, stand for "the proposition that where the State has in place a system of individual exemptions, it may not refuse to extend that system to cases of religious hardship without compelling reason." By contrast, where a general prohibition, such as Oregon's, is at issue, "the sounder approach, and the approach in accord with the vast majority of our precedents, is to hold the test inapplicable to [free exercise] challenges." *Smith* held that neutral, generally applicable laws may be applied to religious practices even when not supported by a compelling governmental interest.

Four Members of the Court disagreed. They argued the law placed a substantial burden on the Native American Church members so that it could be upheld only if the law served a compelling state interest and was narrowly tailored to achieve that end. Justice O'Connor concluded Oregon had satisfied the test, while Justice Blackmun, joined by Justice Brennan and Justice Marshall, could see no compelling interest justifying the law's application to the members.

These points of constitutional interpretation were debated by Members of Congress in hearings and floor debates. Many criticized the Court's reasoning, and this disagreement resulted in the passage of RFRA. Congress announced:

"(1) [T]he framers of the Constitution, recognizing free exercise of religion as an unalienable right, secured its protection in the First Amendment to the Constitution;

"(2) laws 'neutral' toward religion may burden religious exercise as surely as laws intended to interfere with religious exercise;

"(3) governments should not substantially burden religious exercise without compelling justification;

"(4) in *Employment Division v. Smith* (1990), the Supreme Court virtually eliminated the requirement that the government justify burdens on religious exercise imposed by laws neutral toward religion; and

"(5) the compelling interest test as set forth in prior Federal court rulings is a workable test for striking sensible balances between religious liberty and competing prior governmental interests." 42 U. S. C. § 2000bb(a).

The Act's stated purposes are:

"(1) to restore the compelling interest test as set forth in *Sherbert v. Verner* (1963) and to guarantee its application in all cases where free exercise of religion is substantially burdened; and

"(2) to provide a claim or defense to persons whose religious exercise is substantially burdened by government."

RFRA prohibits "[g]overnment" from "substantially burden[ing]" a person's exercise of religion even if the burden results from a rule of general applicability unless the government can demonstrate the burden "(1) is in furtherance of a compelling governmental interest; and (2) is the least restrictive means of furthering that compelling governmental interest." The Act's mandate applies to any "branch, department, agency, instrumentality, and official (or other person acting under color of law) of the United States," as well as to any "State, or ... subdivision of a State." ...

III

A

... Congress relied on its Fourteenth Amendment enforcement power in enacting the most far reaching and substantial of RFRA's provisions, those which impose its requirements on the States.... [R]espondent contends, with support from the United States as *amicus*, that RFRA is permissible enforcement legislation. Congress, it is said, is only protecting by legislation one of the liberties guaranteed by the Fourteenth Amendment's Due Process Clause, the free exercise of religion, beyond what is necessary under *Smith*. ...

All must acknowledge that § 5 is "a positive grant of legislative power" to Congress, *Katzenbach v. Morgan* (1966).... Legislation which deters or remedies constitutional violations can fall within the sweep of Congress' enforcement power even if in the process it prohibits conduct which is not itself unconstitutional and intrudes into "legislative spheres of autonomy previously reserved to the States."

It is also true, however, that "[a]s broad as the congressional enforcement power is, it is not unlimited." *Oregon v. Mitchell* (opinion of Black, J.). In assessing the breadth of § 5's enforcement power, we begin with its text. Congress has been given the power "to enforce" the "provisions of this article." We agree with respondent, of course, that Congress can enact legislation under § 5 enforcing the constitutional right to the free exercise of religion. The "provisions of this article," to which § 5 refers, include the Due Process Clause of the Fourteenth Amendment [which incorporates the Free Exercise Clause].

Congress' power under § 5, however, extends only to "enforc[ing]" the provisions of the Fourteenth Amendment. The Court has described this power as "remedial," *South Carolina v. Katzenbach* (1966) [§ 9–3]. The design of the Amendment and the text of § 5 are inconsistent with the suggestion that Congress has the power to decree the substance of the Fourteenth Amendment's restrictions on the States. Legislation which alters the meaning of the Free Exercise Clause cannot be said to be enforcing the Clause. Congress does not enforce a constitutional right by changing what the right is. It has been given the power "to enforce," not the power to determine what constitutes a constitutional violation. Were it not so, what Congress would be enforcing would no longer be, in any meaningful sense, the "provisions of [the Fourteenth Amendment]."

While the line between measures that remedy or prevent unconstitutional actions and measures that make a substantive change in the governing law is not easy to discern, and Congress must have wide latitude in determining where it lies, the distinction exists and must be observed. There must be a congruence and proportionality between the injury to be prevented or remedied and the means adopted to that end. Lacking such a connection, legislation may become substantive in operation and effect. History and our case law support drawing the distinction, one apparent from the text of the Amendment.

1. The Fourteenth Amendment's history confirms the remedial, rather than substantive, nature of the Enforcement Clause. The Joint Committee on Reconstruction of the 39th Congress began drafting what would become the Fourteenth Amendment in January 1866.... In February, Republican Representative John Bingham of Ohio reported the following draft amendment to the House of Representatives on behalf of the Joint Committee:

> "The Congress shall have power to make all laws which shall be necessary and proper to secure to the citizens of each State all privileges and immunities of citizens in the several States, and to all persons in the several States equal protection in the rights of life, liberty, and property." Cong. Globe, 39th Cong., 1st Sess., 1034 (1866).

The proposal encountered immediate opposition, which continued through three days of debate. Members of Congress from across the political spectrum criticized the Amendment, and the criticisms had a common theme: The proposed Amendment gave Congress too much legislative power at the expense of the existing constitutional structure.... The revised Amendment proposal did not raise the concerns expressed earlier regarding broad congressional power to prescribe uniform national laws with respect to life, liberty, and property. [T]he new measure passed both Houses and was ratified in July 1868 as the Fourteenth Amendment. [It] confers substantive rights against the States which, like the provisions of the Bill of Rights, are self-executing. The power to interpret the Constitution in a case or controversy remains in the Judiciary.

2. The remedial and preventive nature of Congress' enforcement power, and the limitation inherent in the power, were confirmed in our earliest cases on the Fourteenth Amendment. In the *Civil Rights Cases* (1883) [§ 7–1], the Court invalidated sections of the Civil Rights Act of 1875 which prescribed criminal penalties for denying to any person "the full enjoyment of" public accommodations and conveyances, on the grounds that it exceeded Congress' power by seeking to regulate private conduct. The Enforcement Clause, the Court said, did not authorize Congress to pass "general legislation upon the rights of the citizen, but corrective legislation; that is, such as may be necessary and proper for counteracting such laws as the States may adopt or enforce, and which, by the amendment, they are prohibited from making or enforcing.... "

. . .

Recent cases have continued to revolve around the question of whether § 5 legislation can be considered remedial. [T]he Court continued to acknowledge the necessity of using strong remedial and preventive measures to respond to the widespread and persisting deprivation of constitutional rights resulting from this country's history of racial discrimination. See *Oregon v. Mitchell* ("In enacting the literacy test ban ... Congress had before it a long history of the discriminatory use of literacy tests to disfranchise voters on account of their race") (opinion of Black, J.); *id.* (Literacy tests "have been used at times as a discriminatory weapon against some minorities, not only Negroes but Americans of Mexican ancestry, and American Indians") (opinion of Douglas, J.); *id.* ("Congress could have determined that racial prejudice is prevalent throughout the Nation, and that literacy tests unduly lend themselves to discriminatory application, either conscious or unconscious") (opinion of Harlan, J.); *id.*, ("[T]here is no question but that Congress could legitimately have concluded that the use of literacy tests anywhere within the United States has the inevitable effect of denying the vote to members of racial minorities whose inability to pass such tests is the direct consequence of previous governmental discrimination in education") (opinion of Brennan, J.); *id.* ("[N]ationwide [suspension of literacy tests] may be reasonably thought appropriate when Congress acts against an evil such as racial discrimination which in varying degrees manifests itself in every part of the country") (opinion of Stewart, J.); *Morgan*, (Congress had a factual basis to conclude that New

York's literacy requirement "constituted an invidious discrimination in violation of the Equal Protection Clause").

3. Any suggestion that Congress has a substantive, non-remedial power under the Fourteenth Amendment is not supported by our case law. In *Oregon v. Mitchell*, a majority of the Court concluded Congress had exceeded its enforcement powers by enacting legislation lowering the minimum age of voters from 21 to 18 in state and local elections. The five Members of the Court who reached this conclusion explained that the legislation intruded into an area reserved by the Constitution to the States. Four of these five were explicit in rejecting the position that § 5 endowed Congress with the power to establish the meaning of constitutional provisions. Justice Black's rejection of this position might be inferred from his disagreement with Congress' interpretation of the Equal Protection Clause.

There is language in our opinion in *Katzenbach v. Morgan* (1966) which could be interpreted as acknowledging a power in Congress to enact legislation that expands the rights contained in § 1 of the Fourteenth Amendment. This is not a necessary interpretation, however, or even the best one.... The Court provided two related rationales for its conclusion that § 4(e) could "be viewed as a measure to secure for the Puerto Rican community residing in New York nondiscriminatory treatment by government." Under the first rationale, Congress could prohibit New York from denying the right to vote to large segments of its Puerto Rican community, in order to give Puerto Ricans "enhanced political power" that would be "helpful in gaining nondiscriminatory treatment in public services for the entire Puerto Rican community." Section 4(e) thus could be justified as a remedial measure to deal with "discrimination in governmental services." The second rationale, an alternative holding, did not address discrimination in the provision of public services but "discrimination in establishing voter qualifications." The Court perceived a factual basis on which Congress could have concluded that New York's literacy requirement "constituted an invidious discrimination in violation of the Equal Protection Clause." Both rationales for upholding § 4(e) rested on unconstitutional discrimination by New York and Congress' reasonable attempt to combat it. As Justice Stewart explained in *Oregon v. Mitchell*, interpreting *Morgan* to give Congress the power to interpret the Constitution "would require an enormous extension of that decision's rationale."

If Congress could define its own powers by altering the Fourteenth Amendment's meaning, no longer would the Constitution be "superior paramount law, unchangeable by ordinary means." It would be "on a level with ordinary legislative acts, and, like other acts, ... alterable when the legislature shall please to alter it." *Marbury v. Madison*. Under this approach, it is difficult to conceive of a principle that would limit congressional power. See Van Alstyne, The Failure of the Religious Freedom Restoration Act under Section 5 of the Fourteenth Amendment, 46 Duke L. J. 291, 292–303 (1996). ...

We now turn to consider whether RFRA can be considered enforcement legislation under § 5 of the Fourteenth Amendment.

B

Respondent contends that RFRA is a proper exercise of Congress' remedial or preventive power. The Act, it is said, is a reasonable means of protecting the free exercise of religion as defined by *Smith*. It prevents and remedies laws which are enacted with the unconstitutional object of targeting religious beliefs and practices. To avoid the difficulty of proving such violations, it is said, Congress can simply invalidate any law which imposes a substantial burden on a religious practice unless it is justified by a compelling interest and is the least restrictive means of accomplishing that interest. If Congress can prohibit laws with discriminatory effects in order to prevent racial discrimination in violation of the Equal Protection Clause, then it can do the same, respondent argues, to promote religious liberty.

While preventive rules are sometimes appropriate remedial measures, there must be a congruence between the means used and the ends to be achieved. The appropriateness of remedial measures must be considered in light of the evil presented. Strong measures appropriate to address one harm may be an unwarranted response to another, lesser one.

A comparison between RFRA and the Voting Rights Act is instructive. In contrast to the record which confronted Congress and the judiciary in the voting rights cases, RFRA's legislative record lacks examples of modern instances of generally applicable laws passed because of religious bigotry. The history of persecution in this country detailed in the hearings mentions no episodes occurring in the past 40 years. See, *e.g.,* Religious Freedom Restoration Act of 1991, Hearings on H. R. 2797 before the Subcommittee on Civil and Constitutional Rights of the House Committee on the Judiciary, 102d Cong., 2d Sess., 331–334 (1993). Rather, the emphasis of the hearings was on laws of general applicability which place incidental burdens on religion. Much of the discussion centered upon anecdotal evidence of autopsies performed on Jewish individuals and Hmong immigrants in violation of their religious beliefs, and on zoning regulations and historic preservation laws (like the one at issue here), which as an incident of their normal operation, have adverse effects on churches and synagogues. It is difficult to maintain that they are examples of legislation enacted or enforced due to animus or hostility to the burdened religious practices or that they indicate some widespread pattern of religious discrimination in this country. Congress' concern was with the incidental burdens imposed, not the object or purpose of the legislation. This lack of support in the legislative record, however, is not RFRA's most serious shortcoming. Judicial deference, in most cases, is based not on the state of the legislative record Congress compiles but "on due regard for the decision of the body constitutionally appointed to decide." *Oregon v. Mitchell* (opinion of Harlan, J.). As a general matter, it is for Congress to determine the method by which it will reach a decision.

Regardless of the state of the legislative record, RFRA cannot be considered remedial, preventive legislation, if those terms are to have any meaning. RFRA is so out of proportion to a supposed remedial or preventive object that it cannot be understood as responsive to, or designed to prevent, unconstitutional behavior. It appears, instead, to attempt a substantive change in constitutional protections. Preventive measures prohibiting certain types of laws may be appropriate when there is reason to believe that many of the laws affected by the congressional enactment have a significant likelihood of being unconstitutional. Remedial legislation under § 5 "should be adapted to the mischief and wrong which the [Fourteenth] [A]mendment was intended to provide against." *Civil Rights Cases*.

RFRA is not so confined. Sweeping coverage ensures its intrusion at every level of government, displacing laws and prohibiting official actions of almost every description and regardless of subject matter. RFRA's restrictions apply to every agency and official of the Federal, State, and local Governments. 42 U.S.C.A. § 2000bb–2(1). RFRA applies to all federal and state law, statutory or otherwise, whether adopted before or after its enactment. RFRA has no termination date or termination mechanism. Any law is subject to challenge at any time by any individual who alleges a substantial burden on his or her free exercise of religion.

The reach and scope of RFRA distinguish it from other measures passed under Congress' enforcement power, even in the area of voting rights. In *South Carolina v. Katzenbach*, the challenged provisions were confined to those regions of the country where voting discrimination had been most flagrant, and affected a discrete class of state laws, *i.e.*, state voting laws. Furthermore, to ensure that the reach of the Voting Rights Act was limited to those cases in which constitutional violations were most likely (in order to reduce the possibility of overbreadth), the coverage under the Act would terminate "at the behest of States and political subdivisions in which the danger of substantial voting discrimination has not materialized during the preceding five years." The provisions restricting and banning literacy tests, upheld in *Katzenbach v. Morgan* (1966), and *Oregon v. Mitchell*, (1970), attacked a particular type of voting qualification, one with a long history as a "notorious means to deny and abridge voting rights on racial grounds." ... This is not to say, of course, that § 5 legislation requires termination dates, geographic restrictions or egregious predicates. Where, however, a congressional enactment pervasively prohibits constitutional state action in an effort to remedy or to prevent unconstitutional state action, limitations of this kind tend to ensure Congress' means are proportionate to ends legitimate under § 5.

The stringent test RFRA demands of state laws reflects a lack of proportionality or congruence between the means adopted and the legitimate end to be achieved. If an objector can show a substantial burden on his free exercise, the State must demonstrate a compelling governmental interest and show that the law is the least restrictive means of furthering its interest. Claims that a law substantially burdens someone's exercise of religion will often be difficult to contest. See *Smith* ("What principle of law or logic can be brought to bear to contradict a believer's assertion that a particular act is 'central' to his personal faith?"). Requiring a State to demonstrate a compelling interest and show that it has adopted the least restrictive means of achieving that interest is the most demanding test known to constitutional law.... Laws valid under *Smith* would fall under RFRA without regard to whether they had the object of stifling or punishing free exercise. ...

[RFRA's substantial burden test] is not even a discriminatory effects or disparate impact test. It is a reality of the modern regulatory state that numerous state laws, such as the zoning regulations at issue here, impose a substantial burden on a large class of individuals. When the exercise of religion has been burdened in an incidental way by a law of general application, it does not follow that the persons affected have been burdened any more than other citizens, let alone burdened because of their religious beliefs. In addition, the Act imposes in every case a least restrictive means requirement—a requirement that was not used in the pre-*Smith* jurisprudence RFRA purported to codify—which also indicates that the legislation is broader than is appropriate if the goal is to prevent and remedy constitutional violations.

[C]ourts retain the power, as they have since *Marbury v. Madison*, to determine if Congress has exceeded its authority under the Constitution. Broad as the power of Congress is under the Enforcement Clause of the Fourteenth Amendment, RFRA contradicts vital principles necessary to maintain separation of powers and the federal balance. The judgment of the Court of Appeals sustaining the Act's constitutionality is reversed.

It is so ordered.

Notes

1. Stevens, J., filed a concurring opinion. Scalia, J., joined by Stevens, J., filed an opinion concurring in the judgment. Souter, J., filed a dissent arguing that, because the Court did not order reargument on whether *Smith* should be overruled, he would dismiss certiorari as having been improvidently granted; thus he dissented from the Court's disposition of the case. O'Connor, J., filed a dissent joined in part by Breyer, J. In the part that Breyer joined, O'Connor argued that the *Smith* decision should be overruled. Breyer, J., filed a dissent that agreed with O'Connor that *Smith* should be overruled; he did not find it necessary to reach the question of Congressional power under § 5 of the Fourteenth Amendment. In the part of the O'Connor dissent that Breyer did not join, O'Connor said:

[I]f I agreed with the Court's standard in *Smith,* I would join the opinion. As the Court's careful and thorough historical analysis shows, Congress lacks the "power to decree the *substance* of the Fourteenth Amendment's restrictions on the States."

2. RFRA, by its terms, "applies to all Federal and State law, and the implementation of that law." Does this decision invalidate RFRA as to both federal and state laws or only as to state laws?

3. In two cases, decided the same day, the Court reaffirmed that § 5 of the Fourteenth Amendment gives Congress the power to create causes of action against the state to enforce the Fourteenth Amendment, but found the power not properly exercised.

In *College Savings Bank v. Florida Prepaid Postsecondary Education Expense Board,* 527 U.S. 666, 119 S.Ct. 2219, 144 L.Ed.2d 605 (1999) (5 to 4) (Scalia, J., for the Court), plaintiff sued Florida for false and misleading advertising under the Federal Trademark Act of 1946 (the Lanham Act). The Trademark Remedy Clarification Act ("TRCA") subjected states to suit. The plaintiff argued that Congress' abrogation of sovereign immunity in the TRCA was valid on the grounds that it enforced the Fourteenth Amendment's guarantee that a state will not deprive anyone of property without due process. The Court rejected that argument.

Laws enacted pursuant to § 5 must be for the purpose of remedying or preventing constitutional violations. There is no taking of property because there is no property right to be free from a business competitor's false advertising about its own product nor a right to be secure in one's business interests. First, the hallmark of a constitutionally protected property interest is the right to exclude others. The Lanham Act's false-advertising provisions bear no relationship to any right to exclude. The Lahham Act's provisions dealing with infringement of trademarks may well be "property" because the owner can exclude others from using them, but Lanham Act's false-advertising provisions bear no relationship to any right to exclude. Second, while a business's assets are property, and any state taking of those assets is a "deprivation," there is no decision of this Court or any other that recognizes "a property right in freedom from a competitor's false advertising about its own products."

The Court then held that Florida did not impliedly waive its sovereign immunity by engaging in activities in interstate commerce, thus overruling *Parden v. Terminal Ry. Co. of Alabama State Docks Dept.,* 377 U.S. 184, 84 S.Ct. 1207, 12 L.Ed.2d 233 (1964)(which found an implied waiver).

Breyer, J., joined by Stevens, Souter, & Ginsburg, JJ., dissented and would follow *Parden*: "When a State engages in ordinary commercial ventures, it acts like a private person, outside the area of its 'core' responsibilities, and in a way unlikely to prove essential to the fulfillment of a basic governmental obligation." Stevens, J., also filed a dissenting opinion.

In *Florida Prepaid Postsecondary Education Expense Board v. College Savings Bank,* 527 U.S. 627, 119 S.Ct. 2199, 144 L.Ed.2d 575 (1999) (5 to 4) (Rehnquist, J., for the Court), Congress enacted a statute expressly abrogating the states' sovereign immunity for patent violations. College Savings Bank sued the Florida State Board for patent infringement, arguing that Congress has exercised its powers under § 5 of the Fourteenth Amendment to protect the due process property guarantees of a patent holder. Rehnquist, C.J., for the Court, agreed that Congress can abrogate a state's sovereign immunity using its § 5 power and that patents are property. However, because Congress' enforcement power is remedial, Congress must tailor its legislative scheme to remedying or preventing the conduct that violates the Fourteenth Amendment. That was not done in this case:

> [A] State's infringement of a patent, though interfering with a patent owner's right to exclude others, does not by itself violate the Constitution. Instead, only where the State provides no remedy, or only inadequate remedies, to injured patent owners for its infringement of their patent could a deprivation of property without due process result.... Congress, however, barely considered the availability of state remedies for patent infringement and hence whether the States' conduct might have amounted to a constitutional violation under the Fourteenth Amendment. It did hear a limited amount of testimony to the effect that the remedies available in some States were uncertain. ... The primary point made by these witnesses, however, was not that state remedies were constitutionally inadequate, but rather that they were less convenient than federal remedies. [T]he evidence before Congress suggested that most state infringement was innocent or at worst negligent. Such negligent conduct, however, does not violate the Due Process Clause of the Fourteenth Amendment.
>
> The legislative record thus suggests that the Patent Remedy Act does not respond to a history of "widespread and persisting deprivation of constitutional rights" of the sort Congress has faced in enacting proper prophylactic § 5 legislation. *City of Boerne.* ... Congress did nothing to limit the coverage of the Act to cases involving arguable constitutional violations, such as where a State refuses to offer any state-court remedy for patent owners whose patents it had infringed. Nor did it make any attempt to confine the reach of the Act by limiting the remedy to certain types of infringement, such as nonnegligent infringement or infringement authorized pursuant to state policy; or providing for suits only against States with questionable remedies or a high incidence of infringement.
>
> The majority concluded that the statute's apparent aim was to provide a uniform remedy for patent infringement and to place States on the same footing as private parties. While these are proper Article I concerns, only the Fourteenth Amendment and not Article I authorizes Congress to abrogate state immunity from suit.

Stevens, J., joined by Souter, Ginsburg, & Breyer, JJ., dissented, arguing that the law was an appropriate exercise of Congress' power under § 5 of the Fourteenth Amendment to prevent state deprivations of property without due process of law.

9–2.   THE THIRTEENTH AMENDMENT

JONES v. ALFRED H. MAYER CO.
392 U.S. 409, 88 S.Ct. 2186, 20 L.Ed.2d 1189 (1968).

Mr. Justice Stewart delivered the opinion of the Court.

In this case we are called upon to determine the scope and the constitutionality of an Act of Congress, 42 U.S.C.A. § 1982, which provides that:

All citizens of the United States shall have the same right, in every State and Territory, as is enjoyed by white citizens thereof to inherit, purchase, lease, sell, hold, and convey real and personal property.

On September 2, 1965, the petitioners filed a complaint in the District Court for the Eastern District of Missouri, alleging that the respondents had refused to sell them a home in the Paddock Woods community of St. Louis County for the sole reason that petitioner Joseph Lee Jones is a Negro. Relying in part upon § 1982, the petitioners sought injunctive and other relief.... For the reasons that follow, we reverse the judgment of the Court of Appeals. We hold that § 1982 bars *all* racial discrimination, private as well as public, in the sale or rental of property, and that the statute, thus construed, is a valid exercise of the power of Congress to enforce the Thirteenth Amendment.*

At the outset, it is important to make clear precisely what this case does *not* involve. Whatever else it may be, 42 U.S.C.A. § 1982 is not a comprehensive open housing law. In sharp contrast to the Fair Housing Title (Title VIII) of the Civil Rights Act of 1968, the statute in this case deals only with racial discrimination and does not address itself to discrimination on grounds of religion or national origin. It does not deal specifically with discrimination in the provision of services or facilities in connection with the sale or rental of a dwelling. It does not prohibit advertising or other representations that indicate discriminatory preferences. It does not refer explicitly to discrimination in financing arrangements or in the provision of brokerage services. It does not empower a federal administrative agency to assist aggrieved parties. It makes no provision for intervention by the Attorney General....

We begin with the language of the statute itself. In plain and unambiguous terms, § 1982 grants to all citizens, without regard to race or color, "the same right" to purchase and lease property "as is enjoyed by white citizens." As the Court of Appeals in this case evidently recognized, that right can be impaired as effectively by "those who place property on the market" as by the State itself. [W]henever property "is placed on the market for whites only, whites have a right denied to Negroes." ... On its face, therefore, § 1982 appears to prohibit *all* discrimination against Negroes in the sale or rental of property—discrimination by private owners as well as discrimination by public authorities. [R]espondents argue that Congress cannot possibly have intended any such result. Our examination of the relevant history, however, persuades us that Congress meant exactly what it said.

In its original form, 42 U.S.C.A. § 1982 was part of § 1 of the Civil Rights Act of 1866. [I]f § 1 had been intended to grant nothing more than an immunity from *governmental* interference, then much of § 2

---

* Because we have concluded that the discrimination alleged in the petitioners' complaint violated a federal statute that Congress had the power to enact under the Thirteenth Amendment, we find it unnecessary to decide whether that discrimination also violated the Equal Protection Clause of the Fourteenth Amendment.

would have made no sense at all.** For that section, which provided fines and prison terms for certain individuals who deprived others of rights "secured or protected" by § 1, was carefully drafted to exempt private violations of § 1 from the criminal sanctions it imposed. There would, of course, have been no private violations to exempt if the only "right" granted by § 1 had been a right to be free of discrimination by public officials. Hence the structure of the 1866 Act, as well as its language, points to the conclusion urged by the petitioners in this case— that § 1 was meant to prohibit *all* racially motivated deprivations of the rights enumerated in the statute, although only those deprivations perpetrated "under color of law" were to be criminally punishable under § 2. [T]he same Congress that wanted to do away with the Black Codes *also* had before it an imposing body of evidence pointing to the mistreatment of Negroes by private individuals and unofficial groups, mistreatment unrelated to any hostile state legislation.... The congressional debates are replete with references to private injustices against Negroes—references to white employers who refused to pay their Negro workers, white planters who agreed among themselves not to hire freed slaves without the permission of their former masters, white citizens who assaulted Negroes or who combined to drive them out of their communities....

President Andrew Johnson vetoed the Act on March 27, and in the brief congressional debate that followed, his supporters characterized its reach in all-embracing terms. One stressed the fact that § 1 would confer "the right ... to purchase ... real estate ... without any qualification and without any restriction whatever ..." Another predicted, as a corollary, that the Act would preclude preferential treatment for white persons in the rental of hotel rooms and in the sale of church pews. Those observations elicited no reply. On April 6 the Senate, and on April 9 the House, overrode the President's veto by the requisite majorities, and the Civil Rights Act of 1866 became law....

The remaining question is whether Congress has power under the Constitution to do what § 1982 purports to do: to prohibit all racial discrimination, private and public, in the sale and rental of property. Our starting point is the Thirteenth Amendment, for it was pursuant to that constitutional provision that Congress originally enacted what is now § 1982....

As its text reveals, the Thirteenth Amendment "is not a mere prohibition of State laws establishing or upholding slavery, but an

---

** Section 2 provided:

"That any person who, *under color of any law, statute, ordinance, regulation, or custom,* shall subject, or cause to be subjected, any inhabitant of any State or Territory to the deprivation of any right secured or protected by this act, or to different punishment, pains, or penalties on account of such person having at any time been held in a condition of slavery or involuntary servitude, except as a punishment for crime whereof the party shall have been duly convicted, or by reason of his color or race, than is prescribed for the punishment of white persons, shall be deemed guilty of a misdemeanor, and, on conviction, shall be punished by fine not exceeding one thousand dollars, or imprisonment not exceeding one year, or both, in the discretion of the court." (Emphasis added.) ...

absolute declaration that slavery or involuntary servitude shall not exist in any part of the United States." *Civil Rights Cases,* [§ 7–1, supra]. It has never been doubted, therefore, "that the power vested in Congress to enforce the article by appropriate legislation," ibid., includes the power to enact laws "direct and primary, operating upon the acts of individuals, whether sanctioned by State legislation or not." Id.

. . . Does the authority of Congress to enforce the Thirteenth Amendment "by appropriate legislation" include the power to eliminate all racial barriers to the acquisition of real and personal property? We think the answer to that question is plainly yes. "By its own unaided force and effect," the Thirteenth Amendment "abolished slavery, and established universal freedom." *Civil Rights Cases.* Whether or not the Amendment *itself* did any more than that—a question not involved in this case—it is at least clear that the Enabling Clause of that Amendment empowered Congress to do much more. For that clause clothed "Congress with power to pass *all laws necessary and proper for abolishing all badges and incidents of slavery in the United States.*" Ibid. (Emphasis added.)

. . . Senator Trumbull of Illinois, the Chairman of the Judiciary Committee, had brought the Thirteenth Amendment to the floor of the Senate in 1864. In defending the constitutionality of the 1866 Act, he argued . . .

> . . . I have no doubt that under this provision . . . we may destroy all these discriminations in civil rights against the black man; and if we cannot, our constitutional amendment amounts to nothing. It was for that purpose that the second clause of that amendment was adopted, which says that Congress shall have authority, by appropriate legislation, to carry into effect the article prohibiting slavery. Who is to decide what that appropriate legislation is to be? The Congress of the United States; and it is for Congress to adopt such appropriate legislation as it may think proper, so that it be a means to accomplish the end.

Surely Senator Trumbull was right. Surely Congress has the power under the Thirteenth Amendment rationally to determine what are the badges and the incidents of slavery, and the authority to translate that determination into effective legislation. Nor can we say that the determination Congress has made is an irrational one. For this Court recognized long ago that, whatever else they may have encompassed, the badges and incidents of slavery—its "burdens and disabilities"—included restraints upon "those fundamental rights which are the essence of civil freedom, namely, the same right . . . to inherit, purchase, lease, sell and convey property, as is enjoyed by white citizens." *Civil Rights Cases.* Just as the Black Codes, enacted after the Civil War to restrict the free exercise of those rights, were substitutes for the slave system, so the exclusion of Negroes from white communities became a substitute for the Black Codes. And when racial discrimination herds men into ghettos and makes their ability to buy property turn on the color of their skin, then it too is a relic of slavery.

Negro citizens, North and South, who saw in the Thirteenth Amendment a promise of freedom—freedom to "go and come at pleasure" and to "buy and sell when they please"—would be left with "a mere paper guarantee" if Congress were powerless to assure that a dollar in the hands of a Negro will purchase the same thing as a dollar in the hands of a white man. At the very least, the freedom that Congress is empowered to secure under the Thirteenth Amendment includes the freedom to buy whatever a white man can buy, the right to live wherever a white man can live. If Congress cannot say that being a free man means at least this much, then the Thirteenth Amendment made a promise the Nation cannot keep. . . .

Mr. Justice Harlan, whom Mr. Justice White joins, dissenting.

. . . The Court finds it "plain and unambiguous," that [§ 1982] forbids purely private as well as state-authorized discrimination. With all respect, I do not find it so. For me, there is an inherent ambiguity in the term "right," as used in § 1982. The "right" referred to may either be a right to equal status under the law, in which case the statute operates only against state-sanctioned discrimination, or it may be an "absolute" right enforceable against private individuals. To me, the words of the statute, taken alone, suggest the former interpretation, not the latter.

[After a lengthy historical discussion, Harlan concluded that] the most which can be said with assurance about the intended impact of the 1866 Civil Rights Act upon purely private discrimination is that the Act probably was envisioned by most members of Congress as prohibiting official, community-sanctioned discrimination in the South, engaged in pursuant to local "customs" which in the recent time of slavery probably were embodied in laws or regulations. Acts done under the color of such "customs" were, of course, said by the Court in the *Civil Rights Cases,* to constitute "state action" prohibited by the Fourteenth Amendment. Adoption of a "state action" construction of the Civil Rights Act would therefore have the additional merit of bringing its interpretation into line with that of the Fourteenth Amendment, which this Court has consistently held to reach only "state action."

[Moreover] I have concluded that this is one of those rare instances in which an event which occurs after the hearing of argument so diminishes a case's public significance, when viewed in light of the difficulty of the questions presented, as to justify this Court in dismissing the writ as improvidently granted.

The occurrence to which I refer is the recent enactment of the Civil Rights Act of 1968. Title VIII of that Act contains comprehensive "fair housing" provisions, which by the terms of § 803 will become applicable on January 1, 1969, to persons who, like the petitioners, attempt to buy houses from developers. . . . The political process now having taken hold again in this very field, I am at a loss to understand why the Court should have deemed it appropriate or, in the circumstances of this case, necessary to proceed with such precipitate and insecure strides. I am not dissuaded from my view by the circumstance that ... the 1968 Act apparently will not entitle these petitioners to the relief which they seek. For the certiorari jurisdiction was not conferred upon this Court ... "for the benefit of the particular litigants," but to decide issues, "the settlement of which is of importance to the public as distinguished from ... the parties." I deem it far more important that this Court should avoid, if possible, the decision of constitutional and unusually difficult statutory questions than that we fulfill the expectations of every litigant who appears before us. . . .

For these reasons, I would dismiss the writ of certiorari as improvidently granted.

[The concurring opinion of DOUGLAS, J., is omitted.]

RUNYON v. McCRARY

427 U.S. 160, 96 S.Ct. 2586, 49 L.Ed.2d 415 (1976).

MR. JUSTICE STEWART delivered the opinion of the Court.

The principal issue presented by these consolidated cases is whether a federal law, namely 42 U.S.C.A. § 1981, prohibits private schools from excluding qualified children solely because they are Negroes.

The respondents in No. 75–62, Michael McCrary and Colin Gonzales, are Negro children. By their parents, they filed a class action against the petitioners in No. 75–62, Russell and Katheryne Runyon, who are the proprietors of Bobbe's School in Arlington, Va. Their complaint alleged that they had been prevented from attending the school because of the petitioners' policy of denying admission to Negroes, in violation of 42 U.S.C.A. § 1981.[1] They sought declaratory and injunctive relief and damages. On the same day Colin Gonzales, the respondent in No. 75–66, filed a similar complaint by his parents against the petitioner in No. 75–66, Fairfax–Brewster School, Inc., located in Fairfax County, Va. y(4)27

The suits were consolidated for trial. The findings ... were as follows. Bobbe's School opened in 1958 and [t]he Fairfax–Brewster School commenced operations in 1955. . . . Neither school has ever accepted a Negro child for any of its programs. In response to a mailed brochure addressed "resident" and an advertisement in the "Yellow Pages" of the telephone directory, Mr. and Mrs. Gonzales telephoned and then visited the Fairfax–Brewster School in May 1969. After the visit, they submitted an application for Colin's admission to the day camp. The school responded with a form letter, which stated that the

---

1. Title 42 U.S.C.A. § 1981 provides:

"All persons within the jurisdiction of the United States shall have the same right in every State and Territory to make and enforce contracts, to sue, be parties, give evidence, and to the full and equal benefit of all laws and proceedings for the security of persons and property as is enjoyed by white citizens, and shall be subject to like punishment, pains, penalties, taxes, licenses, and exactions of every kind, and to no other."

school was "unable to accommodate [Colin's] application." Mr. Gonzales telephoned the school. Fairfax–Brewster's Chairman of the Board explained that the reason for Colin's rejection was that the school was not integrated. Mr. Gonzales then telephoned Bobbe's School, from which the family had also received in the mail a brochure addressed to "resident." In response to a question concerning that school's admissions policies, he was told that only members of the Caucasian race were accepted. In August 1972, Mrs. McCrary telephoned Bobbe's School in response to an advertisement in the telephone book. She inquired about nursery school facilities for her son, Michael. She also asked if the school was integrated. The answer was no.

Upon these facts, the District Court found that the Fairfax–Brewster School had rejected Colin Gonzales' application on account of his race and that Bobbe's School had denied both children admission on racial grounds. The court held that 42 U.S.C.A. § 1981 makes illegal the schools' racially discriminatory admissions policies. It therefore enjoined Fairfax–Brewster School and Bobbe's School and the member schools of the Southern Independent School Association from discriminating against applicants for admission on the basis of race....

It is worth noting at the outset some of the questions that these cases do not present. They do not present any question of the right of a private social organization to limit its membership on racial or any other grounds.* They do not present any question of the right of a private school to limit its student body to boys, to girls, or to adherents of a particular religious faith, since 42 U.S.C.A. § 1981 is in no way addressed to such categories of selectivity. They do not even present the application of § 1981 to private sectarian schools that practice *racial exclusion* on religious grounds. Rather, these cases present only two basic questions: whether § 1981 prohibits private, commercially operated, nonsectarian schools from denying admission to prospective students because they are Negroes, and, if so, whether that federal law is constitutional as so applied.

It is now well established that § 1 of the Civil Rights Act of 1866, 14 Stat. 27, 42 U.S.C.A. § 1981, prohibits racial discrimination in the making and enforcement of private contracts. *Jones v. Alfred H. Mayer Co.* [T]hat holding necessarily implied that the portion of § 1 of the 1866 Act presently codified as 42 U.S.C.A. § 1981 likewise reaches purely private acts of racial discrimination. [Thus] a Negro's § 1 right to "make and enforce contracts" is violated if a private offeror refuses to extend to a Negro, solely because he is a Negro, the same opportunity to enter into contracts as he extends to white offerees....

It is apparent that the racial exclusion practiced by the Fairfax–Brewster School and Bobbe's Private School amounts to a classic violation of § 1981.... The educational services of Bobbe's School and the Fairfax–Brewster School were advertised and offered to members of the

* See generally *Moose Lodge No. 107 v. Irvis* [§ 7–5, supra].

general public. But neither school offered services on an equal basis to white and nonwhite students....

The question remains whether § 1981, as applied, violates constitutionally protected rights of free association and privacy, or a parent's right to direct the education of his children.

1. Freedom of Association

In *NAACP v. Alabama,* 357 U.S. 449, 78 S.Ct. 1163, 2 L.Ed.2d 1488 and similar decisions, the Court has recognized a First Amendment right "to engage in association for the advancement of beliefs and ideas...." [I]t may be assumed that parents have a First Amendment right to send their children to educational institutions that promote the belief that racial segregation is desirable, and that the children have an equal right to attend such institutions. But it does not follow that the *practice* of excluding racial minorities from such institutions is also protected by the same principle. "[T]he Constitution ... places no value on discrimination," and while "[i]nvidious private discrimination may be characterized as a form of exercising freedom of association protected by the First Amendment ... it has never been accorded affirmative constitutional protections...." In any event, as the Court of Appeals noted, "there is no showing that discontinuance of [the] discriminatory admission practices would inhibit in any way the teaching in these schools of any ideas or dogma."

2. Parental Rights

In *Meyer v. Nebraska,* 262 U.S. 390, 43 S.Ct. 625, 67 L.Ed. 1042, the Court held that the liberty protected by the Due Process Clause of the Fourteenth Amendment includes the right "to acquire useful knowledge, to marry, establish a home and bring up children," and, concomitantly, the right to send one's children to a private school that offers specialized training—in that case, instruction in the German language. In *Pierce v. Society of Sisters,* 268 U.S. 510, 45 S.Ct. 571, 69 L.Ed. 1070, the Court applied "the doctrine of *Meyer v. Nebraska,*" to hold unconstitutional an Oregon law requiring the parent, guardian, or other person having custody of a child between 8 and 16 years of age to send that child to public school on pain of criminal liability. [T]he present application of § 1981 infringes no parental right recognized in *Meyer* [or] *Pierce....* No challenge is made to the petitioner schools' right to operate or the right of parents to send their children to a particular private school rather than a public school. Nor do these cases involve a challenge to the subject matter which is taught at any private school. Thus, the Fairfax–Brewster School and Bobbe's School and members of the intervenor association remain presumptively free to inculcate whatever values and standards they deem desirable. *Meyer* and its progeny entitle them to no more.

3. The Right of Privacy

The Court has held that in some situations the Constitution confers a right of privacy. [W]hile parents have a constitutional right to send their children to private schools and a constitutional right to select private schools that offer specialized instruction, they have no constitutional right to provide their children with private school education unfettered by reasonable government regulation. Section 1981, as applied to the conduct at issue here, constitutes an exercise of federal legislative power under § 2 of the Thirteenth Amendment fully consistent with *Meyer, Pierce,* and the cases that followed in their wake. . . .

Mr. Justice Powell, concurring.

If the slate were clean I might well be inclined to agree with Mr. Justice White. . . .

. . . In certain personal contractual relationships . . . such as those where the offeror selects those with whom he desires to bargain on an individualized basis, or where the contract is the foundation of a close association (such as, for example, that between an employer and a private tutor, babysitter, or housekeeper), there is reason to assume that, although the choice made by the offeror is selective, it reflects "a purpose of exclusiveness" other than the desire to bar members of the Negro race. Such a purpose, certainly in most cases, would invoke associational rights long respected.

The case presented on the record before us does not involve this type of personal contractual relationship. . . . The schools extended a public offer open, on its face, to any child meeting certain minimum qualifications who chose to accept. They advertised in the "Yellow Pages" of the telephone directories and engaged extensively in general mail solicitations to attract students. The schools are operated strictly on a commercial basis, and one fairly could construe their opened invitations as offers that matured into binding contracts when accepted by those who met the academic, financial, and other racially neutral specified conditions as to qualifications for entrance. There is no reason to assume that the schools had any special reason for exercising an option of personal choice among those who responded to their public offers. A small kindergarten or music class, operated on the basis of personal invitations extended to a limited number of preidentified students, for example, would present a far different case.

I do not suggest that a "bright line" can be drawn that easily separates the type of contract offer within the reach of § 1981 from the type without. [But some principles] are clear: § 1981, as interpreted by our prior decisions, does reach certain acts of racial discrimination that are "private" in the sense that they involve no *state* action. But choices, including those involved in entering into a contract, that are "private" in the sense that they are not part of a commercial relationship offered generally or widely, and that reflect the selectivity exercised by an individual entering into a personal relationship, certainly were never intended to be restricted by the 19th century Civil Rights Acts. The open offer to the public generally involved in the cases before us is simply not a "private" contract in this sense. Accordingly, I join the opinion of the Court.

MR. JUSTICE STEVENS, concurring.

... Were we writing on a clean slate, I would therefore vote to reverse. But *Jones* has been decided and is now an important part of the fabric of our law....

MR. JUSTICE WHITE, with whom MR. JUSTICE REHNQUIST joins, dissenting.

... Whites had at the time when § 1981 was first enacted, and have (with a few exceptions mentioned below), no right to make a contract with an unwilling private person, no matter what that person's motivation for refusing to contract. [It] always has been central to the very concept of a "contract" that there be "assent by the parties who form the contract to the terms thereof".... What is conferred by 42 U.S.C.A. § 1981 is the *right*—which was enjoyed by whites—"to make contracts" with other willing parties and to "enforce" those contracts in court. Section 1981 would thus invalidate any state statute or court-made rule of law which would have the effect of disabling Negroes or any other class of persons from making contracts or enforcing contractual obligations or otherwise giving less weight to their obligations than is given to contractual obligations running to whites. The statute by its terms [offers] no cause of action by respondent students against petitioner schools based on the latter's racially motivated decision not to contract with them.

... As the associational or contractual relationships become more private, the pressures to hold § 1981 inapplicable to them will increase. Imaginative judicial construction of the word "contract" is foreseeable; Thirteenth Amendment limitations on Congress' power to ban "badges and incidents of slavery" may be discovered; the doctrine of the right to association may be bent to cover a given situation. In any event, courts will be called upon to balance sensitive policy considerations against each other—considerations which have never been addressed by any Congress—all under the guise of "construing" a statute. This is a task appropriate for the Legislature, not for the Judiciary.

[T]his Court's construction of § 1982 in *Jones v. Alfred H. Mayer Co.,* does not require me to construe § 1981 in a similar manner. The former is a Thirteenth Amendment statute under which the Congress may and did seek to reach private conduct, at least with respect to sales of real estate. The latter is a Fourteenth Amendment statute under which the Congress may and did reach only state action....

Notes

1. In *Griffin v. Breckenridge,* 403 U.S. 88, 91 S.Ct. 1790, 29 L.Ed.2d 338 (1971) certain blacks brought a cause of action for compensatory and punitive damages against defendants who mistakenly believed that one R.G. Grady was a civil rights worker. The defendants allegedly stopped Grady's car and assaulted and beat the passengers in order to prevent them from enjoying equal protection of the laws, "including but not limited to their rights to freedom of speech, movement, association and assembly.... " The

Court held that 42 U.S.C.A. § 1985(3)[1] reached such activity (although the conspiracy did not involve any color of law) and was constitutional: "The constitutional shoals that would lie in the path of interpreting § 1985(3) as a general federal tort law can be avoided by giving full effect to the congressional purpose—by requiring, as an element of the cause of action, the kind of invidiously discriminatory motivation stressed by the sponsors. . . . The language requiring intent to deprive of *equal* protection, or *equal* privileges and immunities means that there must be some racial or perhaps otherwise class-based, invidiously discriminatory animus behind the conspirators' action. . . . Congress was wholly within its powers under § 2 of the Thirteenth Amendment in creating a statutory cause of action for Negro citizens who have been the victims of conspiratorial racially discriminatory private action aimed at depriving them of the basic rights that the law secures to all free men."* The Court also relied on the right of interstate travel as a premise for justifying federal jurisdiction.

2. *McDonald v. Santa Fe Trail Transportation Co.,* 427 U.S. 273, 96 S.Ct. 2574, 49 L.Ed.2d 493 (1976) was decided the same day as *Runyon.* The employer discharged two white employees, the petitioners, for theft of its property but it did not discharge a black employee similarly charged. The Court, per Marshall, J., held that petitioners stated a claim under 42 U.S.C.A. § 1981.

> [O]ur examination of the language and history of § 1981 convinces us that § 1981 is applicable to racial discrimination in private employment against white persons. [W]e cannot accept the view that the terms of § 1981 exclude its application to racial discrimination against white persons. On the contrary, the statute explicitly applies to *"all* persons" (emphasis added) including white persons. [T]he phrase "as is enjoyed by white citizens" . . . simply [emphasizes] "the racial character of the rights being protected. . . . "

1. 42 U.S.C.A. § 1985(3), in its entirety, provides as follows:

"(3) Depriving persons of rights or privileges

If two or more persons in any State or Territory conspire or go in disguise on the highway or on the premises of another, for the purpose of depriving, either directly or indirectly, any person or class of persons of the equal protection of the laws, or of equal privileges and immunities under the laws; or for the purpose of preventing or hindering the constituted authorities of any State or Territory from giving or securing to all persons within such State or Territory the equal protection of the laws; or if two or more persons conspire to prevent by force, intimidation, or threat, any citizen who is lawfully entitled to vote, from giving his support or advocacy in a legal manner, toward or in favor of the election of any lawfully qualified person as an elector for President or Vice President, or as a Member of Congress of the United States; or to injure any citizen in person or property on account of such support or advocacy; in any case of conspiracy set forth in this section, if one or more persons engaged therein do, or cause to be done, any act in furtherance of the object of such conspiracy, whereby another is injured in his person or property, or deprived of having and exercising any right or privilege of a citizen of the United States, the party so injured or deprived may have an action for the recovery of damages occasioned by such injury or deprivation, against any one or more of the conspirators."

* Contrast, *United Brotherhood of Carpenters & Joiners v. Scott,* 463 U.S. 825, 103 S.Ct. 3352, 77 L.Ed.2d 1049 (1983)("an alleged conspiracy to infringe First Amendment rights is not a violation of § 1985(3) unless it is proved that the state is involved in the conspiracy or that the aim of the conspiracy is to influence the activity of the state.").

White, J., joined by Rehnquist, J., dissented, referred to the *McDonald* holding in combination with the *Runyon* holding, and argued: "Thus, under the majority's construction of § 1981 in this case, a former slaveowner was given a cause of action against his former slave if the former slave refused to work for him on the ground that he was a white man. It is inconceivable that Congress ever intended such a result."

The entire Court also agreed that Title VII of the Civil Rights Act of 1964 prohibits racial discrimination in private employment against whites on the same terms as racial discrimination against nonwhites.[3]

3. *United Steelworkers of America AFL–CIO–CLC v. Weber,* 443 U.S. 193, 99 S.Ct. 2721, 61 L.Ed.2d 480 (1979). In *McDonald* the Court said, in footnote 8, that it was not considering the permissibility of an affirmative action program, whether judicially prompted or otherwise required. In *Weber* the Court, per Brennan, J., held that Title VII did not forbid private employers and unions from voluntarily agreeing on bona fide affirmative action plans that accord racial preferences. "[T]he adoption of the Kaiser—USWA plan for the Gramercy plant falls within the area of discretion left by Title VII to the private sector voluntarily to adopt affirmative action plans designed to eliminate conspicuous racial imbalance in traditionally segregated job categories."

4. *General Building Contractors Association v. Pennsylvania,* 458 U.S. 375, 102 S.Ct. 3141, 73 L.Ed.2d 835 (1982) held (over the dissents of Marshall and Brennan, JJ.) that proof of intentional discrimination is necessary for liability to be imposed under § 1981. Mere proof of disparate racial impact is not enough: "§ 1981, like the Equal Protection Clause, can be violated only by purposeful discrimination." Absent such intent, there can be no vicarious liability; nor can there be any substantial injunctive relief against a party not found to have violated anyone's substantive rights.

5. After *Runyon* could Congress constitutionally enact a statute, pursuant to its authority under the Thirteenth Amendment, giving to all persons the same right to make and enforce contracts, etc. "as is enjoyed by male citizens"?

6. On November 21, 1991, Congress amended § 1981 to read as follows:

§ 1981. Equal rights under the law

(a) Statement of equal rights

All persons within the jurisdiction of the United States shall have the same right in every State and Territory to make and enforce

---

3. *Saint Francis College v. Al–Khazraji,* 481 U.S. 604, 107 S.Ct. 2022, 95 L.Ed.2d 582 (1987) held that the legislative history of § 1981 indicated that "Congress intended to protect from discrimination identifiable classes of persons who are subject to intentional discrimination solely because of their ancestry or ethnic characteristics." Such groups could include Finns, Gypsies, Hebrews, Arabs, Germans, Italians, etc. "If respondent [a U.S. citizen born in Iraq] on remand can prove that he was subjected to intentional discrimination based on the fact that he was born an Arab, rather than solely on the place or nation of his origin, or his religion, he will have made out a case under § 1981." Accord, *Shaare Tefila Congregation v. Cobb,* 481 U.S. 615, 107 S.Ct. 2019, 95 L.Ed.2d 594 (1987)(relying on *Al–Khazraji,* the Court concluded that, under § 1982, "Jews and Arabs were among the people [at the time § 1982 was adopted] considered to be distinct races and hence within the protection of the statute.").

contracts, to sue, be parties, give evidence, and to the full and equal benefit of all laws and proceedings for the security of persons and property as is enjoyed by white citizens, and shall be subject to like punishment, pains, penalties, taxes, licenses, and exactions of every kind, and to no other.

(b) Definition

For purposes of this section, the term "make and enforce contracts" includes the making, performance, modification, and termination of contracts, and the enjoyment of all benefits, privileges, terms, and conditions of the contractual relationship.

(c) Protection against impairment

The rights protected by this section are protected against impairment by nongovernmental discrimination and impairment under color of State law.

(As amended Pub.L. 102–166, Title I, § 101, Nov. 21, 1991, 105 Stat. 1071.)

9–3. THE FIFTEENTH AMENDMENT

SOUTH CAROLINA v. KATZENBACH
383 U.S. 301, 86 S.Ct. 803, 15 L.Ed.2d 769 (1966).

MR. CHIEF JUSTICE WARREN delivered the opinion of the Court.

By leave of the Court, South Carolina has filed a bill of complaint, seeking a declaration that selected provisions of the Voting Rights Act of 1965 violate the Federal Constitution, and asking for an injunction against enforcement of these provisions by the Attorney General. Original jurisdiction is founded on the presence of a controversy between a State and a citizen of another State under Art. III, § 2, of the Constitution. Because no issues of fact were raised in the complaint, and because of South Carolina's desire to obtain a ruling prior to its primary elections in June 1966, we dispensed with appointment of a special master and expedited our hearing of the case.

The constitutional propriety of the Voting Rights Act of 1965 must be judged with reference to the historical experience which it reflects.... The heart of the Act is a complex scheme of stringent remedies aimed at areas where voting discrimination has been most flagrant. Section 4(a)-(d) lays down a formula defining the States and political subdivisions to which these new remedies apply. The first of the remedies, contained in § 4(a), is the suspension of literacy tests and similar voting qualifications for a period of five years from the last occurrence of substantial voting discrimination. Section 5 prescribes a second remedy, the suspension of all new voting regulations pending review by federal authorities to determine whether their use would perpetuate voting discrimination. The third remedy, covered in §§ 6(b), 7, 9, and 13(a), is the assignment of federal examiners on certification by the Attorney General to list qualified applicants who are thereafter entitled to vote in all elections. . . .

These provisions of the Voting Rights Act of 1965 are challenged on the fundamental ground that they exceed the powers of Congress and encroach on an area reserved to the States by the Constitution. South Carolina and certain of the *amici curiae* also attack specific sections of the Act for more particular reasons. . . . Some of these contentions may be dismissed at the outset. The word "person" in the context of the Due Process Clause of the Fifth Amendment cannot, by any reasonable mode of interpretation, be expanded to encompass the States of the Union, and to our knowledge this has never been done by any court. Likewise, courts have consistently regarded the Bill of Attainder Clause of Article I and the principle of the separation of powers only as protections for individual persons and private groups, those who are peculiarly vulnerable to nonjudicial determinations of guilt. Nor does a State have standing as the parent of its citizens to invoke these constitutional provisions against the Federal Government, the ultimate *parens patriae* of every American citizen. The objections to the Act which are raised under these provisions may therefore be considered only as additional aspects of the basic question presented by the case: Has Congress exercised its powers under the Fifteenth Amendment in an appropriate manner with relation to the States?

The ground rules for resolving this question are clear. . . . As against the reserved powers of the States, Congress [under the Fifteenth Amendment] may use any rational means to effectuate the constitutional prohibition of racial discrimination in voting.

[Section] 2 of the Fifteenth Amendment expressly declares that "Congress shall have power to enforce this article by appropriate legislation." . . . The basic test to be applied in a case involving § 2 of the Fifteenth Amendment is the same as in all cases concerning the express powers of Congress with relation to the reserved powers of the States. Chief Justice Marshall laid down the classic formulation, 50 years before the Fifteenth Amendment was ratified [in] *McCulloch v. Maryland.* The Court has subsequently echoed his language in describing each of the Civil War Amendments. . . .

Congress exercised its authority under the Fifteenth Amendment in an inventive manner when it enacted the Voting Rights Act of 1965. First: The measure prescribes remedies for voting discrimination which go into effect without any need for prior adjudication. This was clearly a legitimate response to the problem, for which there is ample precedent under other constitutional provisions. See *Katzenbach v. McClung,* [§ 4–4, supra]. Congress had found that case-by-case litigation was inadequate to combat widespread and persistent discrimination in voting, because of the inordinate amount of time and energy required to overcome the obstructionist tactics invariably encountered in these lawsuits. . . .

Second: The Act intentionally confines these remedies to a small number of States and political subdivisions which in most instances were familiar to Congress by name. This, too, was a permissible method of dealing with the problem. . . . The doctrine of the equality of States, invoked by South Carolina, does not bar this approach, for that doctrine applies only to the terms upon which States are admitted to the Union, and not to the remedies for local evils which have subsequently appeared. See *Coyle v. Smith,* 221 U.S. 559, 31 S.Ct. 688, 55 L.Ed. 853, and cases cited therein.

COVERAGE FORMULA

We now consider the related question of whether the specific States and political subdivisions within § 4(b) of the Act were an appropriate target for the new remedies. South Carolina contends that the coverage formula is awkwardly designed in a number of respects and that it disregards various local conditions which have nothing to do with racial discrimination. These arguments, however, are largely beside the point. . . . The areas . . . , for which there was evidence of actual voting discrimination, share two characteristics incorporated by Congress into the coverage formula: the use of tests and devices for voter registration, and a voting rate in the 1964 presidential election at least 12 points below the national average. Tests and devices are relevant to voting discrimination because of their long history as a tool for perpetrating the evil; a low voting rate is pertinent for the obvious reason that widespread disenfranchisement must inevitably affect the number of actual voters. Accordingly, the coverage formula is rational in both practice and theory. It was therefore permissible to impose the new remedies on the few remaining States and political subdivisions covered by the formula, at least in the absence of proof that they have been free of substantial voting discrimination in recent years. Congress is clearly not bound by the rules relating to statutory presumptions in criminal cases when it prescribes civil remedies against other organs of government under § 2 of the Fifteenth Amendment.

It is irrelevant that the coverage formula excludes certain localities which do not employ voting tests and devices but for which there is evidence of voting discrimination by other means. . . . Legislation need not deal with all phases of a problem in the same way, so long as the distinctions drawn have some basis in practical experience. There are no States or political subdivisions exempted from coverage under § 4(b) in which the record reveals recent racial discrimination involving tests and devices. This fact confirms the rationality of the formula.

Acknowledging the possibility of overbreadth, the Act provides for termination of special statutory coverage at the behest of States and political subdivisions in which the danger of substantial voting discrimination has not materialized during the preceding five years. Despite South Carolina's argument to the contrary, Congress might appropriately limit litigation under this provision to a single court in the District of Columbia, pursuant to its constitutional power under Art. III, § 1, to "ordain and establish" inferior federal tribunals. . . .

South Carolina contends that these termination procedures are a nullity because they impose an impossible burden of proof upon States and political subdivisions entitled to relief. [H]owever, an area need do no more than submit affidavits from voting officials, asserting that they have not been guilty of racial discrimination through the use of tests and devices during the past five years, and then refute whatever evidence to the contrary may be adduced by the Federal Government. Section 4(d) further assures that an area need not disprove each isolated instance of voting discrimination in order to obtain relief in the termination proceedings. The burden of proof is therefore quite bearable, particularly since the relevant facts relating to the conduct of voting officials are peculiarly within the knowledge of the States and political subdivisions themselves.

The Act bars direct judicial review of the findings by the Attorney General and the Director of the Census which trigger application of the coverage formula. [But] the findings not subject to review consist of objective statistical determinations by the Census Bureau and a routine analysis of state statutes by the Justice Department. These functions are unlikely to arouse any plausible dispute, as South Carolina apparently concedes. In the event that the formula is improperly applied, the area affected can always go into court and obtain termination of coverage under § 4(b), provided of course that it has not been guilty of voting discrimination in recent years. This procedure serves as a partial substitute for direct judicial review.

SUSPENSION OF TESTS

. . . The Act suspends literacy tests and similar devices for a period of five years from the last occurrence of substantial voting discrimination. . . . States and political subdivisions which had been allowing white illiterates to vote for years could not sincerely complain about "dilution" of their electorates through the registration of Negro illiterates. Congress knew that continuance of the tests and devices in use at the present time, no matter how fairly administered in the future, would freeze the effect of past discrimination in favor of unqualified white registrants. Congress permissibly rejected the alternative of requiring a complete re-registration of all voters, believing that this would be too harsh on many whites who had enjoyed the franchise for their entire adult lives.

REVIEW OF NEW RULES

The Act suspends new voting regulations pending scrutiny by federal authorities to determine whether their use would violate the Fifteenth Amendment. This may have been an uncommon exercise of congressional power, as South Carolina contends, but the Court has recognized that exceptional conditions can justify legislative measures not otherwise appropriate. . . . Nor has Congress authorized the District Court to issue advisory opinions, in violation of the principles of Article III invoked by Georgia as *amicus curiae*. The Act automatically suspends the operation of voting regulations enacted after November 1, 1964, and furnishes mechanisms for enforcing the suspension. A State or political subdivision wishing to make use of a recent amendment to its voting laws therefore has a concrete and immediate "controversy" with the Federal Government. An appropriate remedy is a judicial determination that continued suspension of the new rule is unnecessary to vindicate rights guaranteed by the Fifteenth Amendment.

FEDERAL EXAMINERS

The Act authorizes the appointment of federal examiners to list qualified applicants who are thereafter entitled to vote, subject to an expeditious challenge procedure. This was clearly an appropriate response to the problem, closely related to remedies authorized in prior cases. In many of the political subdivisions covered by § 4(b) of the Act, voting officials have persistently employed a variety of procedural tactics to deny Negroes the franchise, often in direct defiance or evasion of federal court decrees. Congress realized that merely to suspend voting rules which have been misused or are subject to misuse might leave this localized evil undisturbed. As for the briskness of the challenge procedure, Congress knew that in some of the areas affected, challenges had been persistently employed to harass registered Negroes....

In recognition of the fact that there were political subdivisions covered by § 4(b) of the Act in which the appointment of federal examiners might be unnecessary, Congress assigned the Attorney General the task of determining the localities to which examiners should be sent.... Section 6(b) sets adequate standards to guide the exercise of his discretion, by directing him to calculate the registration ratio of non-whites to whites, and to weigh evidence of good-faith efforts to avoid possible voting discrimination. At the same time, the special termination procedures of § 13(a) provide indirect judicial review for the political subdivisions affected, assuring the withdrawal of federal examiners from areas where they are clearly not needed.

... We here hold that the portions of the Voting Rights Act properly before us are a valid means for carrying out the commands of the Fifteenth Amendment. Hopefully, millions of non-white Americans will now be able to participate for the first time on an equal basis in the government under which they live.... The bill of complaint is

Dismissed.

MR. JUSTICE BLACK, concurring and dissenting.

I agree with substantially all of the Court's opinion sustaining the power of Congress under § 2 of the Fifteenth Amendment to suspend state literacy tests and similar voting qualifications and to authorize the Attorney General to secure the appointment of federal examiners to register qualified voters in various sections of the country.... I dissent from its holding that every part of § 5 of the Act is constitutional. Section 4(a), to which § 5 is linked, suspends for five years all literacy tests and similar devices in those States coming within the formula of § 4(b). Section 5 goes on to provide that a State covered by § 4(b) can in no way amend its constitution or laws relating to voting without first trying to persuade the Attorney General of the United States or the Federal District Court for the District of Columbia that the new proposed laws do not have the purpose and will not have the effect of denying the right to vote to citizens on account of their race or color. I think this section is unconstitutional on at least two grounds.

(a) The Constitution gives federal courts jurisdiction over cases and controversies only. [I]t is hard for me to believe that a justiciable controversy can arise in the constitutional sense from a desire by the United States Government or some of its officials to determine in advance what legislative provisions a State may enact or what constitutional amendments it may adopt. [If there is a] a case or controversy, [then] the most appropriate judicial forum for settling these important questions is this Court acting under its original Art. III, § 2, jurisdiction to try cases in which a State is a party.[1] At least a trial in this Court would treat the States with the dignity to which they should be entitled as constituent members of our Federal Union. . . .

(b) My second and more basic objection to § 5 is that Congress has here exercised its power under § 2 of the Fifteenth Amendment through the adoption of means that conflict with the most basic principles of the Constitution. [T]he States [should] have power to pass laws and amend their constitutions without first sending their officials hundreds of miles away to beg federal authorities to approve them. Moreover, it seems to me that § 5 which gives federal officials power to veto state laws they do not like is in direct conflict with the clear command of our Constitution that "The United States shall guarantee to every State in this Union a Republican Form of Government." [T]he inevitable effect of any such law . . . is to create the impression that the State or States treated in this way are little more than conquered provinces. . . .

Notes

1. *Gomillion v. Lightfoot,* 364 U.S. 339, 81 S.Ct. 125, 5 L.Ed.2d 110 (1960). The Alabama legislature enacted a law that redefined the boundaries of the City Tuskegee, altering its shape from a square to an "uncouth" and "strangely irregular" twenty-eight-sided figure, with the result of removing from the city's boundaries all (except four to five) of its 400 black voters but not one single white voter or resident. The plaintiffs claimed that Act 140 was "a device to disenfranchise Negro citizens." The lower courts held that there was no cause of action, but Frankfurter, J., for the Court, reversed. The allegations are "a mathematical demonstration that the legislation is solely concerned with segregating white and colored voters," in violation of the Fifteenth Amendment. Whittaker, J., concurring, argued that the decision should be rested on the Equal Protection Clause of the Fourteenth Amendment.

1. If § 14(b) of the Act by stating that no court other than the District Court for the District of Columbia shall issue a judgment under § 5 is an attempt to limit the constitutionally created original jurisdiction of this Court, then I think that section is also unconstitutional.

Chart Showing Tuskegee, Alabama, Before and After Act 140

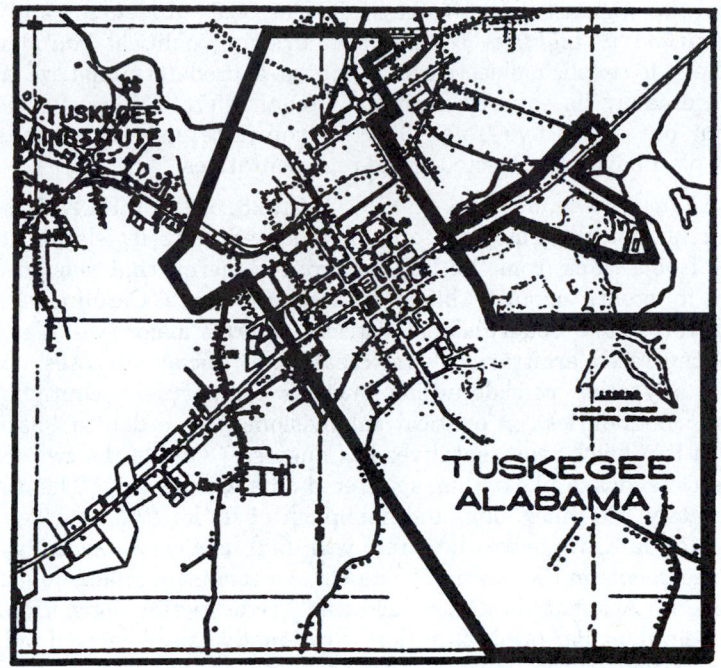

The entire area of the square comprised the City prior to Act 140. The irregular black-bordered figure within the square represents the post-enactment city.

2. *United Jewish Organizations of Williamsburgh, Inc. v. Carey,* 430 U.S. 144, 97 S.Ct. 996, 51 L.Ed.2d 229 (1977). Certain counties in New York became subject to §§ 4 and 5 of the Voting Rights Act of 1965 because a literacy test was used in 1968 and fewer than 50% of the voting age residents there had voted in the 1968 Presidential election. The Justice Department claimed that there were not enough nonwhite voters in most of the nonwhite districts. To raise the nonwhite majority from 61% to 65% (which was the Department of Justice figure), and thereby obtain Justice Department approval to its redistricting, the state transferred part of an Hasidic Jewish community to an adjoining district. Hasidic Jews sued, claiming that the dilution of the vote of Hasidic Jewish community violated the Fourteenth Amendment. The Court, with no majority opinion, rejected that argument. White, J., joined by Stevens & Rehnquist, JJ., found no violation because the plan "represented no racial slur or stigma with respect to whites or any other race." Brennan, J., found no violation because the classification was

not motivated by "racial animus." Stewart, J., joined by Powell, J., concurred in the judgment because there was no showing of "purposeful discrimination against white voters." Burger, C.J., dissented, and argued that *Gomillion v. Lightfoot* teaches that drawing political boundary lines "with the sole, explicit objective of reaching a predetermined racial result cannot ordinarily be squared with the Constitution." Moreover, he noted that "four out of the five 'safe' (65% +) nonwhite districts established by the 1974 plan have since elected white representatives."*

3. *Shaw v. Reno*, 509 U.S. 630, 113 S.Ct. 2816, 125 L.Ed.2d 511 (1993). O'Connor, J., for the Court (5 to 4), invalidated state legislation (enacted because of objections from the U.S. Attorney General) that was specifically designed to create majority black districts in North Carolina. Plaintiffs complained that two Congressional districts, where a majority of black voters were concentrated arbitrarily, were created for racial purposes, "without regard to any other considerations, such as compactness, contiguousness, geographic boundaries, or political subdivisions," in order to "assure the election of two black representatives in Congress." One of the two majority-black districts looked like a "bug splattered on a windshield." The other was approximately 160 miles long, and, for much of its length, no wider than a highway. If you drove down the street with both car doors open, "you'd kill most of the people in the district." The U.S. Government relied on § 2 of the Voting Rights Act, but the Court held that "redistricting legislation that is so extremely irregular on its face that it rationally can be viewed only as an effort to segregate the races for purposes of voting without regard for traditional districting principles and without compelling justification" states a cause of action under the equal protection clause. Compactness, contiguity, and respect for political boundaries are not constitutionally required, but they "are objective factors that may serve to defeat a claim that a district has been gerrymandered on racial grounds." If people are widely separated by geographic and political boundaries but placed together because of the color of their skin, there is "an uncomfortable resemblance to political apartheid." Therefore, an allegation that legislation, race-neutral on its face, cannot "rationally be understood as anything other than an effort to separate voters into different districts on the basis of race, and that the separation lacks sufficient justification" states a cause of action under the Equal Protection Clause. The Court remanded for further proceedings. White, J., joined by Blackmun & Stevens, JJ., and Blackmun, J., Stevens, J., and Souter, J., each filed dissenting opinions.

MILLER v. JOHNSON
515 U.S. 900, 115 S.Ct. 2475, 132 L.Ed.2d 762 (1995).

JUSTICE KENNEDY delivered the opinion of the Court.

The constitutionality of Georgia's congressional redistricting plan is at issue here. In *Shaw v. Reno* (1993), we held that a plaintiff states a claim under the Equal Protection Clause by alleging that a state redistricting plan, on its face, has no rational explanation save as an effort to separate voters on the basis of race. The question we now decide is

* On motivation in racial cases, see also,   § 8–2.13.

whether Georgia's new Eleventh District gives rise to a valid equal protection claim under the principles announced in *Shaw,* and, if so, whether it can be sustained nonetheless as narrowly tailored to serve a compelling governmental interest.

In 1965, the Attorney General designated Georgia a covered jurisdiction under § 4(b) of the Voting Rights Act. In consequence, § 5 of the Act requires Georgia to obtain either administrative preclearance by the Attorney General or approval by the United States District Court for the District of Columbia of any change in a "standard, practice, or procedure with respect to voting" made after November 1, 1964. The preclearance mechanism applies to congressional redistricting plans, and requires that the proposed change "not have the purpose and will not have the effect of denying or abridging the right to vote on account of race or color." "[T]he purpose of § 5 has always been to insure that no voting-procedure changes would be made that would lead to a retrogression in the position of racial minorities with respect to their effective exercise of the electoral franchise."

Between 1980 and 1990, one of Georgia's 10 congressional districts was a majority-black district, that is, a majority of the district's voters were black. The 1990 Decennial Census indicated that Georgia's population of 6,478,216 persons, 27% of whom are black, entitled it to an additional eleventh congressional seat, prompting Georgia's General Assembly to redraw the State's congressional districts. Both the House and the Senate adopted redistricting guidelines which, among other things, required single-member districts of equal population, contiguous geography, nondilution of minority voting strength, fidelity to precinct lines where possible, and compliance with §§ 2 and 5 of the Act. Only after these requirements were met did the guidelines permit drafters to consider other ends, such as maintaining the integrity of political subdivisions, preserving the core of existing districts, and avoiding contests between incumbents.

[The General Assembly's first plan] contained two majority-minority districts, the Fifth and Eleventh, and an additional district, the Second, in which blacks comprised just over 35% of the voting age population. Despite the plan's increase in the number of majority-black districts from one to two and the absence of any evidence of an intent to discriminate against minority voters, the Department of Justice refused preclearance on January 21, 1992. The Department's objection letter noted a concern that Georgia had created only two majority-minority districts, and that the proposed plan did not "recognize" certain minority populations by placing them in a majority-black district.

The General Assembly returned to the drawing board. A new plan was enacted and submitted for preclearance. This second attempt assigned the black population in Central Georgia's Baldwin County to the Eleventh District and increased the black populations in the Eleventh, Fifth and Second Districts. The Justice Department refused preclearance again, relying on alternative plans proposing three majority-minority districts. One of the alternative schemes relied on by the Department was the so-called "max-black" plan, drafted by the American Civil Liberties Union (ACLU) for the General Assembly's black caucus....

Twice spurned, the General Assembly set out to create three majority-minority districts to gain preclearance. Using the ACLU's "max-black" plan as its benchmark, the General Assembly enacted a plan that

> "bore all the signs of [the Justice Department's] involvement: The black population of Meriwether County was gouged out of the Third District and attached to the Second District by the narrowest of land bridges; Effingham and Chatham Counties were split to make way for the Savannah extension, which itself split the City of Savannah; and the plan as a whole split 26 counties, 23 more than the existing congressional districts."

... The Almanac of American Politics has this to say about the Eleventh District: "Geographically, it is a monstrosity, stretching from Atlanta to Savannah. Its core is the plantation country in the center of the state, lightly populated, but heavily black. It links by narrow corridors the black neighborhoods in Augusta, Savannah and southern DeKalb County." Georgia's plan included three majority-black districts, though, and received Justice Department preclearance on April 2, 1992.

Elections were held under the new congressional redistricting plan on November 4, 1992, and black candidates were elected to Congress from all three majority-black districts. On January 13, 1994, appellees, five white voters from the Eleventh District, filed this action against various state officials.... As residents of the challenged Eleventh District, all appellees had standing. *United States v. Hays* (1995) [discussed in the *Notes*]. Their suit alleged that Georgia's Eleventh District was a racial gerrymander and so a violation of the Equal Protection Clause as interpreted in *Shaw v. Reno*....

A majority of the District Court panel [found] that the "evidence of the General Assembly's intent to racially gerrymander the Eleventh District is overwhelming, and practically stipulated by the parties involved," the District Court held that race was the predominant, overriding factor in drawing the Eleventh District. Appellants do not take issue with the court's factual finding of this racial motivation. Rather, they contend that evidence of a legislature's deliberate classification of voters on the basis of race cannot alone suffice to state a claim under *Shaw*. They argue that, regardless of the legislature's purposes, a plaintiff must demonstrate that a district's shape is so bizarre that it is unexplainable other than on the basis of race, and that appellees failed to make that showing here. Appellants' conception of the constitutional violation misapprehends our holding in *Shaw* and the Equal Protection precedent upon which *Shaw* relied.

Shaw recognized a claim "analytically distinct" from a vote dilution claim. Whereas a vote dilution claim alleges that the State has enacted a particular voting scheme as a purposeful device "to minimize or cancel out the voting potential of racial or ethnic minorities," an action disadvantaging voters of a particular race, the essence of the equal protection claim recognized in *Shaw* is that the State has used race as a basis for separating voters into districts. Just as the State may not, absent extraordinary justification, segregate citizens on the basis of race in its public parks, buses, golf courses, beaches, and schools, so did we recognize in *Shaw* that it may not separate its citizens into different voting districts on the basis of race. The idea is a simple one: "At the heart of the Constitution's guarantee of equal protection lies the simple command that the Government must treat citizens 'as individuals, not "as simply components of a racial, religious, sexual or national class." ' " *Metro Broadcasting, Inc. v. FCC* (1990)(O'Connor, J., dissenting). When the State assigns voters on the basis of race, it engages in the offensive and demeaning assumption that voters of a particular race, because of their race, "think alike, share the same political interests, and will prefer the same candidates at the polls."

Our observation in *Shaw* of the consequences of racial stereotyping was not meant to suggest that a district must be bizarre on its face before there is a constitutional violation.... Our circumspect approach and narrow holding in *Shaw* did not erect an artificial rule barring accepted equal protection analysis in other redistricting cases. Shape is relevant not because bizarreness is a necessary element of the constitutional wrong or a threshold requirement of proof, but because it may be persuasive circumstantial evidence that race for its own sake, and not other districting principles, was the legislature's dominant and controlling rationale in drawing its district lines. The logical implication, as courts applying *Shaw* have recognized, is that parties may rely on evidence other than bizarreness to establish race-based districting.

[O]utside the districting context, statutes are subject to strict scrutiny under the Equal Protection Clause not just when they contain express racial classifications, but also when, though race neutral on their face, they are motivated by a racial purpose or object. In the rare case, where the effect of government action is a pattern " 'unexplainable on grounds other than race,' " "[t]he evidentiary inquiry is . . . relatively easy." *Arlington Heights, supra.* As early as *Yick Wo v. Hopkins* (1886), the Court recognized that a laundry permit ordinance was administered in a deliberate way to exclude all Chinese from the laundry business; and in *Gomillion v. Lightfoot* (1960), the Court concluded that the redrawing of Tuskegee, Alabama's municipal boundaries left no doubt that the plan was designed to exclude blacks. Even in those cases, however, it was the presumed racial purpose of state action, not its stark manifestation, that was the constitutional violation. Patterns of discrimination as conspicuous as these are rare, and are not a necessary predicate to a violation of the Equal Protection Clause. In the absence of a pattern as stark as those in *Yick Wo* or *Gomillion,* "impact alone is not determinative, and the Court must look to other evidence" of race-based decisionmaking. *Arlington Heights....*

Appellants and some of their *amici* argue that the Equal Protection Clause's general proscription on race-based decisionmaking does not obtain in the districting context because redistricting by definition involves racial considerations. Underlying their argument are the very stereotypical assumptions the Equal Protection Clause forbids. It is true that redistricting in most cases will implicate a political calculus in which various interests compete for recognition, but it does not follow from this that individuals of the same race share a single political interest. The view that they do is "based on the demeaning notion that members of the defined racial groups ascribe to certain 'minority views' that must be different from those of other citizens," the precise use of race as a proxy the Constitution prohibits. Nor can the argument that districting cases are excepted from standard equal protection precepts be resuscitated by *United Jewish Organizations of Williamsburgh, Inc. v. Carey* (1977), where the Court addressed a claim that New York violated the Constitution by splitting a Hasidic Jewish community in order to include additional majority-minority districts. As we explained in *Shaw*, a majority of the Justices in *UJO* construed the complaint as stating a vote dilution claim, so their analysis does not apply to a claim that the State has separated voters on the basis of race. To the extent any of the opinions in that "highly fractured decision," can be interpreted as suggesting that a State's assignment of voters on the basis of race would be subject to anything but our strictest scrutiny, those views ought not be deemed controlling.

In sum, we make clear that parties alleging that a State has assigned voters on the basis of race are neither confined in their proof to evidence regarding the district's geometry and makeup nor required to make a threshold showing of bizarreness. Today's case requires us further to consider the requirements of the proof necessary to sustain this equal protection challenge.

Federal court review of districting legislation represents a serious intrusion on the most vital of local functions. It is well settled that "reapportionment is primarily the duty and responsibility of the State." Electoral districting is a most difficult subject for legislatures, and so the States must have discretion to exercise the political judgment necessary to balance competing interests. Although race-based decisionmaking is inherently suspect, until a claimant makes a showing sufficient to support that allegation the good faith of a state legislature must be presumed. The courts, in assessing the sufficiency of a challenge to a districting plan, must be sensitive to the complex interplay of forces that enter a legislature's redistricting calculus. Redistricting legislatures will, for example, almost always be aware of racial demographics; but it does not follow that race predominates in the redistricting process. The distinction between being aware of racial considerations and being motivated by them may be difficult to make. This evidentiary difficulty, together with the sensitive nature of redistricting and the presumption of good faith that must be accorded legislative enactments, requires courts to exercise extraordinary caution in adjudicating claims that a state has drawn district lines on the basis of race. The plaintiff's burden is to show, either through circumstantial evidence of a district's shape and demographics or more direct evidence going to legislative purpose, that race was the predominant factor motivating the legislature's decision to place a significant number of voters within or without a particular district. To make this showing, a plaintiff must prove that the legislature subordinated traditional race-neutral districting principles, including but not limited to compactness, contiguity, respect for political subdivisions or communities defined by actual shared interests, to racial considerations. Where these or other race-neutral considerations are the basis for redistricting legislation, and are not subordinated to race, a state can "defeat a claim that a district has been gerrymandered on racial lines." These principles inform the plaintiff's burden of proof at trial. Of course, courts must also recognize these principles, and the intrusive potential of judicial intervention into the legislative realm, when assessing under the Federal Rules of Civil Procedure the adequacy of a plaintiff's showing at the various stages of litigation and determining whether to permit discovery or trial to proceed.

In our view, the District Court applied the correct analysis, and its finding that race was the predominant factor motivating the drawing of the Eleventh District was not clearly erroneous. The court found it was "exceedingly obvious" from the shape of the Eleventh District, together with the relevant racial demographics, that the drawing of narrow land bridges to incorporate within the District outlying appendages containing nearly 80% of the district's total black population was a deliberate attempt to bring black populations into the district. Although by comparison with other districts the geometric shape of the Eleventh District may not seem bizarre on its face, when its shape is considered in conjunction with its racial and population densities, the story of racial gerrymandering seen by the District Court becomes much clearer. Although this evidence is quite compelling, we need not determine whether it was, standing alone, sufficient to establish a *Shaw* claim that the Eleventh District is unexplainable other than by race. The District Court had before it considerable additional evidence showing that the General Assembly was motivated by a predominant, overriding desire to assign black populations to the Eleventh District and thereby permit the creation of a third majority-black district in the Second.... On this record, we fail to see how the District Court could have reached any conclusion other than that race was the predominant factor in drawing Georgia's Eleventh District; and in any event we conclude the court's finding is not clearly erroneous.... Although a legislature's compliance with "traditional districting principles such as compactness, contiguity, and respect for political subdivisions" may well suffice to refute a claim of racial gerrymandering, appellants cannot make such a refutation where, as here, those factors were subordinated to racial objectives.... Race was, as the District Court found, the predominant, overriding factor explaining the General Assembly's decision to attach to the Eleventh District various appendages containing dense majority-black populations. As a result, Georgia's congressional redistricting plan cannot be upheld unless it satisfies strict scrutiny, our most rigorous and exacting standard of constitutional review.

To satisfy strict scrutiny, the State must demonstrate that its districting legislation is narrowly tailored to achieve a compelling interest. There is a "significant state interest in eradicating the effects of past racial discrimination." The State does not argue, however, that it created the Eleventh District to remedy past discrimination, and with good reason: there is little doubt that the State's true interest in designing the Eleventh District was creating a third majority-black district to satisfy the Justice Department's preclearance demands. Whether or not in some cases compliance with the Voting Rights Act, standing alone, can provide a compelling interest independent of any interest in remedying past discrimination, it cannot do so here. [C]ompliance with federal antidiscrimination laws cannot justify race-based districting where the challenged district was not reasonably necessary under a constitutional reading and application of those laws. The congressional plan challenged here was not required by the Voting Rights Act under a correct reading of the statute. . . .

We do not accept the contention that the State has a compelling interest in complying with whatever preclearance mandates the Justice Department issues. When a state governmental entity seeks to justify race-based remedies to cure the effects of past discrimination, we do not accept the government's mere assertion that the remedial action is required. Rather, we insist on a strong basis in evidence of the harm being remedied. "The history of racial classifications in this country suggests that blind judicial deference to legislative or executive pronouncements of necessity has no place in equal protection analysis." Our presumptive skepticism of all racial classifications, prohibits us as well from accepting on its face the Justice Department's conclusion that racial districting is necessary under the Voting Rights Act. Where a State relies on the Department's determination that race-based districting is necessary to comply with the Voting Rights Act, the judiciary retains an independent obligation in adjudicating consequent equal protection challenges to ensure that the State's actions are narrowly tailored to achieve a compelling interest. Were we to accept the Justice Department's objection itself as a compelling interest adequate to insulate racial districting from constitutional review, we would be surrendering to the Executive Branch our role in enforcing the constitutional limits on race-based official action. We may not do so. . . .

Georgia's drawing of the Eleventh District was not required under the Act because there was no reasonable basis to believe that Georgia's earlier enacted plans violated § 5. Wherever a plan is "ameliorative," a term we have used to describe plans increasing the number of majority-minority districts, it "cannot violate § 5 unless the new apportionment itself so discriminates on the basis of race or color as to violate the Constitution." Georgia's first and second proposed plans increased the number of majority-black districts from 1 out of 10 (10%) to 2 out of 11 (18.18%). These plans were "ameliorative" and could not have violated

§ 5's non-retrogression principle.... "[A]meliorative changes, even if they fall short of what might be accomplished in terms of increasing minority representation, cannot be found to violate section 5 unless they so discriminate on the basis of race or color as to violate the Constitution." Days, Section 5 and the Role of the Justice Department, in B. Grofman & C. Davidson, Controversies in Minority Voting 56 (1992). [Though] the State has the burden to prove a nondiscriminatory purpose under § 5, Georgia's Attorney General provided a detailed explanation for the State's initial decision not to enact the max-black plan. The District Court accepted this explanation, and found an absence of any discriminatory intent. The State's policy of adhering to other districting principles instead of creating as many majority-minority districts as possible does not support an inference that the plan "so discriminates on the basis of race or color as to violate the Constitution," and thus cannot provide any basis under § 5 for the Justice Department's objection.

Instead of grounding its objections on evidence of a discriminatory purpose, it would appear the Government was driven by its policy of maximizing majority-black districts.... In utilizing § 5 to require States to create majority-minority districts wherever possible, the Department of Justice expanded its authority under the statute beyond what Congress intended and we have upheld.

Section 5 was directed at preventing a particular set of invidious practices which had the effect of "undo[ing] or defeat[ing] the rights recently won by nonwhite voters." As we explained in *Beer v. United States* (1976),

> " 'Section 5 was a response to a common practice in some jurisdictions of staying one step ahead of the federal courts by passing new discriminatory voting laws as soon as the old ones had been struck down. That practice had been possible because each new law remained in effect until the Justice Department or private plaintiffs were able to sustain the burden of proving that the new law, too, was discriminatory.... Congress therefore decided, as the Supreme Court held it could, "to shift the advantage of time and inertia from the perpetrators of the evil to its victim," by "freezing election procedures in the covered areas unless the changes can be shown to be nondiscriminatory." 425 U.S., at 140 (quoting H.R.Rep. No. 94–196, pp. 57–58 (1975)(footnotes omitted)).

"[T]he purpose of § 5 has always been to insure that no voting-procedure changes would be made that would lead to a retrogression in the position of racial minorities with respect to their effective exercise of the electoral franchise." The Justice Department's maximization policy seems quite far removed from this purpose. We are especially reluctant to conclude that § 5 justifies that policy given the serious constitutional concerns it raises. In *South Carolina v. Katzenbach* (1966), we upheld § 5 as a necessary and constitutional response to some states' "extraordinary stratagem[s] of contriving new rules of various kinds for the sole purpose of perpetuating voting discrimination in the face of adverse federal court decrees." But our belief in *Katzenbach* that the federalism costs exacted by § 5 preclearance could be justified by those extraordinary circumstances does not mean they can be justified in the circumstances of this case. And the Justice Department's implicit command that States engage in presumptively unconstitutional race-based districting brings the Voting Rights Act, once upheld as a proper exercise of Congress' authority under § 2 of the Fifteenth Amendment, *Katzenbach,* into tension with the Fourteenth Amendment. As we recalled in *Katzenbach* itself, Congress' exercise of its Fifteenth Amendment authority even when otherwise proper still must " 'consist with the letter and spirit of the constitution.' "We need not, however, resolve these troubling and difficult constitutional questions today. There is no indication Congress intended such a far-reaching application of § 5, so we reject the Justice Department's interpretation of the statute and avoid the constitutional problems that interpretation raises.

The Voting Rights Act, and its grant of authority to the federal courts to uncover official efforts to abridge minorities' right to vote, has been of vital importance in eradicating invidious discrimination from the electoral process and enhancing the legitimacy of our political institutions. Only if our political system and our society cleanse themselves of that discrimination will all members of the polity share an equal opportunity to gain public office regardless of race. As a Nation we share both the obligation and the aspiration of working toward this end. The end is neither assured nor well served, however, by carving electorates into racial blocs. "If our society is to continue to progress as a multiracial democracy, it must recognize that the automatic invocation of race stereotypes retards that progress and causes continued hurt and injury." It takes a shortsighted and unauthorized view of the Voting Rights Act to invoke that statute, which has played a decisive role in redressing some of our worst forms of discrimination, to demand the very racial stereotyping the Fourteenth Amendment forbids.

The judgment of the District Court is affirmed, and the case is remanded for further proceedings consistent with this decision.

It is so ordered.

Justice O'Connor, concurring.

I understand the threshold standard the Court adopts—"that the legislature subordinated traditional race-neutral districting principles ... to racial considerations"—to be a demanding one.... Application of the Court's standard does not throw into doubt the vast majority of the Nation's 435 congressional districts, where presumably the States have drawn the boundaries in accordance with their customary districting principles. That is so even though race may well have been considered in the redistricting process. But application of the Court's standard helps achieve *Shaw*'s basic objective of making extreme instances of gerrymandering subject to meaningful judicial review. I therefore join the Court's opinion.

Justice Stevens, dissenting.

... I cannot see how respondents in these cases could assert the injury the Court attributes to them. Respondents, plaintiffs below, are white voters in Georgia's Eleventh Congressional District. The Court's conclusion that they have standing to maintain a *Shaw* claim appears to rest on a theory that their placement in the Eleventh District caused them " 'representational harms.' " The *Shaw* Court explained the concept of "representational harms" as follows: "When a district obviously is created solely to effectuate the perceived common interests of one racial group, elected officials are more likely to believe that their primary obligation is to represent only the members of that group, rather than their constituency as a whole." Although the *Shaw* Court attributed representational harms solely to a message sent by the legislature's action, those harms can only come about if the message is received—that is, first, if all or most black voters support the same candidate, and, second, if the successful candidate ignores the interests of her white constituents. Respondents' standing, in other words, ultimately depends on the very premise the Court purports to abhor: that voters of a particular race " 'think alike, share the same political interests, and will prefer the same candidates at the polls.' " This generalization, as the Court recognizes, is "offensive and demeaning." ...

Equally distressing is the Court's equation of traditional gerrymanders, designed to maintain or enhance a dominant group's power, with a dominant group's decision to share its power with a previously underrepresented group.... I do not see how a districting plan that favors a politically weak group can violate equal protection....

Justice Ginsburg, with whom Justices Stevens and Breyer join, and with whom Justice Souter joins except as to Part III–B, dissenting....

To accommodate the reality of ethnic bonds, legislatures have long drawn voting districts along ethnic lines. Our Nation's cities are full of districts identified by their ethnic character—Chinese, Irish, Italian, Jewish, Polish, Russian, for example. The creation of ethnic districts reflecting felt identity is not ordinarily viewed as offensive or demeaning to those included in the delineation.... Until now, no constitutional infirmity has been seen in districting Irish or Italian voters together, for example, so long as the delineation does not abandon familiar apportionment practices. If Chinese–Americans and Russian–Americans may seek and secure group recognition in the delineation of voting districts, then African–Americans should not be dissimilarly treated. Otherwise, in the name of equal protection, we would shut out "the very minority group whose history in the United States gave birth to the Equal Protection Clause."

Part III–B

Under the Court's approach, judicial review of the same intensity, *i.e.*, strict scrutiny, is in order once it is determined that an apportionment is predominantly motivated by race. It matters not at all, in this new regime, whether the apportionment dilutes or enhances minority voting strength. ... Special circumstances justify vigilant judicial inspection to protect minority voters—circumstances that do not apply to majority voters. . . . Cf. *United States v. Carolene Products Co.,* 304 U.S. 144, 153, n. 4 (1938)(referring to the "more searching judicial inquiry" that may properly attend classifications adversely affecting "discrete and insular minorities"). The majority, by definition, encounters no such blockage. White voters in Georgia do not lack means to exert strong pressure on their state legislators. . . .

Notes

1.   Georgia's 11th District at issue in *Miller*:

2.   *United States v. Hays,* 515 U.S. 737, 115 S.Ct. 2431, 132 L.Ed.2d 635 (1995) was decided the same day as *Miller*. Plaintiffs claimed that Louisiana's congressional redistricting plan, called Act I, was an unconstitutional racial gerrymander in violation of the equal protection clause. Their claim's primary focus was on District 4, a "majority-minority district," that is, a district in which a majority of the population is a member of a specific minority group. However, the plaintiffs lived in District 5.

O'Connor, J., for the Court, held that plaintiffs lacked standing. To have standing, a plaintiff must demonstrate "individualized harm," not a generalized grievance. So, the Court rejected the claim that everyone in the state has standing. The Court admitted that the burden of showing "individualized harm" may not be easily met in the racial gerrymandering context because it is often "difficult to discern why a particular citizen was put in one district or another." However, the Court argued, if a district is created solely to effectuate the perceived common interests of a particular racial group, then elected officials are more likely to represent the members of that group rather than their constituency as a whole. Therefore, a plaintiff who resides in the racially gerrymandered district has standing, but one who does not reside there, does not suffer these special harms, and must present "specific evidence" that he has personally suffered special injury. Assume that the state creates a misshapen district that excludes all blacks. Assume, further, that no whites within the district object. Does that mean that the racial gerrymandering is immune from challenge based on lack of standing?

The plaintiffs in *Gomillion v. Lightfoot* (1960), noted supra, were black citizens of Alabama who had been, prior to its redistricting, residents of the City of Tuskegee. Though, they were not residents of the redefined City, the Court did not suggest that there was any problem with their standing. Should they be denied standing?

3. Democrats "largely support redrawn districts that can be won by black candidates. But isolating black voters in new districts also helps the GOP in the old districts. Dozens of Republicans now have safer districts or can mount serious challenges on what had been solid Democratic turf.... A total of 23 Southern districts with white Democratic incumbents lost black constituents after redistricting. Democrats also were hurt in the region's GOP districts, which lost an average of 43% of their black voters."[1]

4. *Shaw v. Hunt,* 517 U.S. 899, 116 S.Ct. 1894, 135 L.Ed.2d 207 (1996), on remand from *Shaw v. Reno* (1993). Rehnquist, C.J., for the Court, agreed with the unanimous lower court finding that the "serpentine" districting was deliberately drawn to produce one or more districts of a certain racial composition. The trial court also held (2 to 1) that the redistricting plan was "narrowly tailored to further the State's compelling interests in complying with §§ 2 and 5 of the Voting Rights Act." On this issue, the Court, reversed, and held that the "bizarre-looking" majority-black district violated the equal protection clause. First, the asserted state interest in eliminating the effects of past discrimination is not a compelling interest because that claimed interest did not actually precipitate the use of race in this redistricting plan. Second, creating an additional majority-black district was not required under a correct reading of § 5. (The Court did not reach the question whether compliance with the Voting Rights Act, § 5 was, on its own, a compelling state interest). Third, the racial gerrymandering was not a narrowly tailored remedy to comply with § 2 of the Act because the minority group was not geographically compact: § 2 only targets vote-dilution to individuals in a particular area. Stevens, J., filed a dissenting opinion joined in part by Ginsburg & Breyer, JJ. Souter, J., filed a dissenting opinion also joined in part by Ginsburg & Breyer, JJ.

5. *Abrams v. Johnson,* 521 U.S. 74, 117 S.Ct. 1925, 138 L.Ed.2d 285 (1997). This case is an appeal from the trial court's rulings after the remand in *Miller v. Johnson* (1995). The three-judge district court had deferred to the Georgia legislature to draw up a new plan, but when the legislature could not reach agreement, the court drew up its own plan, containing only one majority-black district, in the Atlanta area. The district court found that Georgia did not have a black population of sufficient concentration to allow creation of a second majority-black district, and said that creation of this second district would require it to "subordinate Georgia's traditional districting policies and consider race predominately, to the exclusion of both constitutional norms and common sense." Its plan split no counties outside of Atlanta, did not mix urban and rural areas, and did not use districts with strange geographic shapes. Other proposals that the court rejected would have created two (or three) majority-black districts, but they had other problems, *e.g.,* they split counties, had shapes similar to the plan that had

---

1. Frisby, "Florida Race Shows How Democrats Were Hurt by Effort to Create   Black–Dominated Districts," Wall St. Jrl., Oct. 25, 1994, at A20 (midwest ed.).

earlier been found to be unconstitutional, and so forth. (A "plan jointly sponsored by John Lewis, a black Democrat member of the U.S. House of Representatives from Georgia, and Newt Gingrich, a white Republican member" contained two majority-black districts.) The appellants and the United States appealed, arguing that the district court plan did not adequately take into account the interests of Georgia's black population.

Kennedy, J., for the Court (joined by Rehnquist, C.J., and O'Connor, Scalia, & Thomas, JJ.), held that district court's plan was not unconstitutional and did not violate the Voting Rights Act of 1965. There was "ample evidence" to support the district court's conclusions that it could not draw "the second majority-black district without allowing that one consideration to predominate over other traditional and neutral districting principles, principles which were a valid expression of legislative policy."

Breyer, J., (joined by Stevens, Souter, & Ginsburg, JJ.) filed a dissenting opinion, arguing that the district court should not have departed from the intention of the Georgia legislature favoring creation of two such districts.

Lawyer v. Department of Justice, 521 U.S. 567, 117 S.Ct. 2186, 138 L.Ed.2d 669 (1997) involved a reapportionment of a Florida Senate district. The Court accepted the three-judge federal district court finding that the plan did not subordinate traditional districting principles to race as "not clearly erroneous." The particular redrawn district was located entirely in the Tampa Bay area with an end-to-end distance no greater than most Florida Senate districts. Its shape "does not stand out as different from numerous other Florida House and Senate districts." The district does cross a body of water and covers portions of three counties, but these features were common characteristics of Florida's legislative districts, a product of the state's geography and of the fact that 40 Senate districts cover 67 counties. The district has 36.2% black voting age population, which is "significantly higher" than the overall percentage of black voters in that area, but "we have never suggested that the percentage of black residents in a district may not exceed the percentage of black residents in any of the counties from which the district is created, and have never recognized similar racial composition of different political districts as being necessary to avoid an inference of racial gerrymandering in any one of them."

Souter, J., wrote the opinion of the Court (joined by Rehnquist, C.J., and Stevens, Ginsburg, & Breyer, JJ.). Scalia, J., dissented (joined by O'Connor, Kennedy, & Thomas, JJ.) The dissent did not reach the constitutionality of the court-drawn district but argued that the district court should first have offered the Florida legislature a more reasonable opportunity to craft its own solution.

Chapter 10

FREEDOM OF SPEECH

10–1. ADVOCACY OF ILLEGAL CONDUCT

SCHENCK v. UNITED STATES
249 U.S. 47, 39 S.Ct. 247, 63 L.Ed. 470 (1919).

Mr. Justice Holmes delivered the opinion of the court.

[Defendants were convicted of] a conspiracy to violate the Espionage Act of June 15, 1917, by causing and attempting to cause insubordination, & c., in the military and naval forces of the United States, and to obstruct the recruiting and enlistment service of the United States, when the United States was at war with the German Empire, to-wit, that the defendants wilfully conspired to have printed and circulated to men who had been called and accepted for military service under the Act of May 18, 1917, a document set forth and alleged to be calculated to cause such insubordination and obstruction. . . . It denied the power to send our citizens away to foreign shores to shoot up the people of other lands, and added that words could not express the condemnation such cold-blooded ruthlessness deserves, & c., & c., winding up "You must do your share to maintain, support and uphold the rights of the people of this country." Of course the document would not have been sent unless it had been intended to have some effect, and we do not see what effect it could be expected to have upon persons subject to the draft except to influence them to obstruct the carrying of it out. The defendants do not deny that the jury might find against them on this point.

But it is said, suppose that that was the tendency of this circular, it is protected by the First Amendment to the Constitution. Two of the strongest expressions are said to be quoted respectively from well-known public men. It well may be that the prohibition of laws abridging the freedom of speech is not confined to previous restraints, although to prevent them may have been the main purpose, as intimated in *Patterson v. Colorado*, 205 U.S. 454, 462, 27 S.Ct. 556, 51 L.Ed. 879. We admit that in many places and in ordinary times the defendants in saying all that was said in the circular would have been within their constitutional rights. But the character of every act depends upon the circumstances in which it is done. The most stringent protection of free speech would not protect a man in falsely shouting fire in a theatre and causing a panic. It does not even protect a man from an injunction against uttering words that may have all the effect of force. *Gompers v. Buck's Stove & Range Co.,* 221 U.S. 418, 439, 31 S.Ct. 492, 55 L.Ed. 797. The question in every case is whether the words used are used in such circumstances and are of such a nature as to create a clear and present danger that they will bring about the substantive evils that Congress has a right to prevent. It is a question of proximity and degree. When a nation is at war many things that might be said in time of peace are such a hindrance to its effort that their utterance will not be endured so long as men fight and that no Court could regard them as protected by any constitutional right. It seems to be admitted that if an actual obstruction of the recruiting service were proved, liability for words that produced that effect might be enforced. The statute of 1917 in § 4 punishes conspiracies to obstruct as well as actual obstruction. If the act, (speaking, or circulating a paper,) its tendency and the intent with which it is done are the same, we perceive no ground for saying that success alone warrants making the act a crime. . . .

Judgments affirmed.

ABRAMS v. UNITED STATES
250 U.S. 616, 40 S.Ct. 17, 63 L.Ed. 1173 (1919).

[Defendants were convicted of conspiring to violate the Espionage Act, and the Supreme Court, through Justice Clarke affirmed. The claim that the Espionage Act conflicts with the First Amendment "is sufficiently discussed and definitely negatived in *Schenck v. U.S.* . . ."]

MR. JUSTICE HOLMES dissenting.

This indictment is founded wholly upon the publication of two leaflets. . . . The first of these leaflets says that the President's cowardly silence about the intervention in Russia reveals the hypocrisy of the plutocratic gang in Washington. It intimates that "German militarism combined with allied capitalism to crush the Russian revolution"—goes on that the tyrants of the world fight each other until they see a common enemy—working class enlightenment. . . . The other leaflet, headed "Workers—Wake Up," with abusive language says that America together with the Allies will march for Russia to help the Czecko–Slovaks in their struggle against the Bolsheviki, and that this time the hypocrites shall not fool the Russian emigrants and friends of Russia in America. . . .

In this case sentences of twenty years imprisonment have been imposed for the publishing of two leaflets that I believe the defendants had as much right to publish as the Government has to publish the Constitution of the United States now vainly invoked by them. Even if I am technically wrong and enough can be squeezed from these poor and puny anonymities to turn the color of legal litmus paper; I will add, even if what I think the necessary intent were shown; the most nominal punishment seems to me all that possibly could be inflicted, unless the defendants are to be made to suffer not for what the indictment alleges but for the creed that they avow—a creed that I believe to be the creed of ignorance and immaturity when honestly held, as I see no reason to doubt that it was held here, but which, although made the subject of examination at the trial, no one has a right even to consider in dealing with the charges before the Court.

Persecution for the expression of opinions seems to me perfectly logical. If you have no doubt of your premises or your power and want a certain result with all your heart you naturally express your wishes in law and sweep away all opposition. To allow opposition by speech seems to indicate that you think the speech impotent, as when a man says that he has squared the circle, or that you do not care whole-heartedly for the result, or that you doubt either your power or your premises. But when men have realized that time has upset many fighting faiths, they may come to believe even more than they believe the very foundations of their own conduct that the ultimate good desired is better reached by free trade in ideas—that the best test of truth is the power of the thought to get itself accepted in the competition of the market, and that truth is the only ground upon which their wishes safely can be carried out. That at any rate is the theory of our Constitution. It is an experiment, as all life is an experiment. Every year if not every day we have to wager our salvation upon some prophecy based upon imperfect knowledge. While that experiment is part of our system I think that we should be eternally vigilant against attempts to check the expression of opinions that we loathe and believe to be fraught with death, unless they so imminently threaten immediate interference with the lawful and pressing purposes of the law that an immediate check is required to save the country. I wholly disagree with the argument of the Government that the First Amendment left the common law as to seditious libel in force. History seems to me against the notion. I had conceived that the United States through many years had shown its repentance for the Sedition Act of 1798, by repaying fines that it imposed. Only the emergency that makes it immediately dangerous to leave the correction of evil counsels to time warrants making any exception to the sweeping command, "Congress shall make no law ... abridging the freedom of speech." Of course I am speaking only of expressions of opinion and exhortations, which were all that were uttered here, but I regret that I cannot put into more impressive words my belief that in their conviction upon this indictment the defendants were deprived of their rights under the Constitution of the United States.

MR. JUSTICE BRANDEIS concurs with the foregoing opinion.

GITLOW v. NEW YORK

268 U.S. 652, 45 S.Ct. 625, 69 L.Ed. 1138 (1925).

[New York law made it a felony to advocate "by word of mouth or writing" the doctrine of criminal anarchy, "that organized government should be overthrown by force or violence ... or by any unlawful means." Defendants were convicted for publishing a radical manifesto which urged revolutionary Socialism to use "mass industrial revolts to broaden the strike, make it general and militant, and develop it into mass political strikes and revolutionary mass action for the annihilation of the parliamentary state."]

MR. JUSTICE SANFORD delivered the opinion of the Court....

For present purposes we may and do assume that freedom of speech and of the press—which are protected by the First Amendment from abridgment by Congress—are among the fundamental personal rights and "liberties" protected by the due process clause of the Fourteenth Amendment from impairment by the States....

By enacting the present statute the State has determined, through its legislative body, that utterances advocating the overthrow of organized government by force, violence and unlawful means, are so inimical to the general welfare and involve such danger of substantive evil that they may be penalized in the exercise of its police power. That determination must be given great weight. Every presumption is to be indulged in favor of the validity of the statute.... That utterances inciting to the overthrow of organized government by unlawful means, present a sufficient danger of substantive evil to bring their punishment within the range of legislative discretion, is clear. Such utterances, by their very nature, involve danger to the public peace and to the security of the State. They threaten breaches of the peace and ultimate revolution. And the immediate danger is none the less real and substantial, because the effect of a given utterance cannot be accurately foreseen. The State cannot reasonably be required to measure the danger from every such utterance in the nice balance of a jeweler's scale. A single revolutionary spark may kindle a fire that, smouldering for a time, may burst into a sweeping and destructive conflagration. It cannot be said that the State is acting arbitrarily or unreasonably when in the exercise of its judgment as to the measures necessary to protect the public peace and safety, it seeks to extinguish the spark without waiting until it has enkindled the flame or blazed into the conflagration....

It is clear that the question in such cases is entirely different from that involved in those cases where the statute merely prohibits certain acts involving the danger of substantive evil, without any reference to language itself, and it is sought to apply its provisions to language used by the defendant for the purpose of bringing about the prohibited results.... And the general statement in the *Schenck Case* that the "question in every case is whether the words are used in such circumstances and are of such a nature as to create a clear and present danger that they will bring about the substantive evils,"—upon which great reliance is placed in the defendant's argument—was manifestly intended, as shown by the context, to apply only in cases of this class, and has no application to those like the present, where the legislative body itself has previously determined the danger of substantive evil arising from utterances of a specified character....

And finding, for the reasons stated, that the statute is not in itself unconstitutional, and that it has not been applied in the present case in derogation of any constitutional right, the judgment of the Court of Appeals is

Affirmed.

MR. JUSTICE HOLMES, dissenting.

MR. JUSTICE BRANDEIS and I are of opinion that this judgment should be reversed.... I think that the criterion sanctioned by the full Court in *Schenck v. United States,* applies.... If what I think the correct test is applied, it is manifest that there was no present danger of an attempt to overthrow the government by force on the part of the admittedly small minority who shared the defendant's views. It is said that this manifesto was more than a theory, that it was an incitement. Every idea is an incitement. It offers itself for belief and if believed it is acted on unless some other belief outweighs it or some failure of energy stifles the movement at its birth. The only difference between the expression of an opinion and an incitement in the narrower sense is the speaker's enthusiasm for the result. Eloquence may set fire to reason. But whatever may be thought of the redundant discourse before us it had no chance of starting a present conflagration. If in the long run the beliefs expressed in proletarian dictatorship are destined to be accepted by the dominant forces of the community, the only meaning of free speech is that they should be given their chance and have their way.

If the publication of this document had been laid as an attempt to induce an uprising against government at once and not at some indefinite time in the future it would have presented a different question. The object would have been one with which the law might deal, subject to the doubt whether there was any danger that the publication could produce any result, or in other words, whether it was not futile and too remote from possible consequences. But the indictment alleges the publication and nothing more.

WHITNEY v. CALIFORNIA
274 U.S. 357, 47 S.Ct. 641, 71 L.Ed. 1095 (1927).

[Whitney was convicted of violating the California law against criminal syndicalism. SANFORD, J., for the Court, affirmed.]

MR. JUSTICE BRANDEIS, concurring.

Miss Whitney was convicted of the felony of assisting in organizing, in the year 1919, the Communist Labor Party of California, of being a member of it, and of assembling with it. These acts are held to constitute a crime, because the party was formed to teach criminal syndicalism. The statute which made these acts a crime restricted the right of free speech and of assembly theretofore existing. The claim is that the statute, as applied, denied to Miss Whitney the liberty guaranteed by the Fourteenth Amendment.

The felony which the statute created is a crime very unlike the old felony of conspiracy or the old misdemeanor of unlawful assembly. The mere act of assisting in forming a society for teaching syndicalism, of becoming a member of it, or of assembling with others for that purpose is given the dynamic quality of crime. There is guilt although the society may not contemplate immediate promulgation of the doctrine. Thus the accused is to be punished, not for contempt, incitement or conspiracy, but for a step in preparation, which, if it threatens the public order at all, does so only remotely. The novelty in the prohibition introduced is that the statute aims, not at the practice of criminal syndicalism, nor even directly at the preaching of it, but at association with those who propose to preach it.

Despite arguments to the contrary which had seemed to me persuasive, it is settled that the due process clause of the Fourteenth Amendment applies to matters of substantive law as well as to matters of procedure. Thus all fundamental rights comprised within the term liberty are protected by the Federal Constitution from invasion by the States. The right of free speech, the right to teach and the right of assembly are, of course, fundamental rights. These may not be denied or abridged. But, although the rights of free speech and assembly are fundamental, they are not in their nature absolute. Their exercise is subject to restriction, if the particular restriction proposed is required in order to protect the State from destruction or from serious injury, political, economic or moral. That the necessity which is essential to a valid restriction does not exist unless speech would produce, or is intended to produce, a clear and imminent danger of some substantive evil which the State constitutionally may seek to prevent has been settled. See *Schenck v. United States.*

It is said to be the function of the legislature to determine whether at a particular time and under the particular circumstances the formation of, or assembly with, a society organized to advocate criminal syndicalism constitutes a clear and present danger of substantive evil; and that by enacting the law here in question the legislature of California determined that question in the affirmative. Compare *Gitlow v. New York.* But where a statute is valid only in case certain conditions exist, the enactment of the statute cannot alone establish the facts which are essential to its validity. . . .

This Court has not yet fixed the standard by which to determine when a danger shall be deemed clear; how remote the danger may be and yet be deemed present; and what degree of evil shall be deemed sufficiently substantial to justify resort to abridgement of free speech and assembly as the means of protection. To reach sound conclusions on these matters, we must bear in mind why a State is, ordinarily, denied the power to prohibit dissemination of social, economic and political doctrine which a vast majority of its citizens believes to be false and fraught with evil consequence.

Those who won our independence believed that the final end of the State was to make men free to develop their faculties; and that in its government the deliberative forces should prevail over the arbitrary. They valued liberty both as an end and as a means. They believed liberty to be the secret of happiness and courage to be the secret of liberty. They believed that freedom to think as you will and to speak as you think are means indispensable to the discovery and spread of political truth; that without free speech and assembly discussion would be futile; that with them, discussion affords ordinarily adequate protection against the dissemination of noxious doctrine; that the greatest menace to freedom is an inert people; that public discussion is a political duty; and that this should be a fundamental principle of the American government.[1] They recognized the risks to which all human institutions are subject. But they knew that order cannot be secured merely through fear of punishment for its infraction; that it is hazardous to discourage thought, hope and imagination; that fear breeds repression; that repression breeds hate; that hate menaces stable government; that the path of safety lies in the opportunity to discuss freely supposed grievances and proposed remedies; and that the fitting remedy for evil counsels is good ones. Believing in the power of reason as applied through public discussion, they eschewed silence coerced by law—the argument of force in its worst form. Recognizing the occasional tyrannies of governing majorities, they amended the Constitution so that free speech and assembly should be guaranteed.

Fear of serious injury cannot alone justify suppression of free speech and assembly. Men feared witches and burnt women. It is the function of speech to free men from the bondage of irrational fears. To justify suppression of free speech there must be reasonable ground to fear that serious evil will result if free speech is practiced. There must be reasonable ground to believe that the danger apprehended is imminent. There must be reasonable ground to believe that the evil to be prevented is a serious one. Every denunciation of existing law tends in some measure to increase the probability that there will be violation of it. Condonation of a breach enhances the probability. Expressions of approval add to the probability. Propagation of the criminal state of mind by teaching syndicalism increases it. Advocacy of law-breaking heightens it still

---

1. Compare Thomas Jefferson: "We have nothing to fear from the demoralizing reasonings of some, if others are left free to demonstrate their errors and especially when the law stands ready to punish the first criminal act produced by the false reasonings; these are safer corrections than the conscience of the judge." Quoted by Charles A. Beard, The Nation, July 7, 1926, vol. 123, p. 8. Also in first Inaugural Address: "If there be any among us who would wish to dissolve this union or change its republican form, let them stand undisturbed as monuments of the safety with which error of opinion may be tolerated where reason is left free to combat it."

further. But even advocacy of violation, however reprehensible morally, is not a justification for denying free speech where the advocacy falls short of incitement and there is nothing to indicate that the advocacy would be immediately acted on. The wide difference between advocacy and incitement, between preparation and attempt, between assembling and conspiracy, must be borne in mind. In order to support a finding of clear and present danger it must be shown either that immediate serious violence was to be expected or was advocated, or that the past conduct furnished reason to believe that such advocacy was then contemplated.

... If there be time to expose through discussion the falsehood and fallacies, to avert the evil by the processes of education, the remedy to be applied is more speech, not enforced silence. Only an emergency can justify repression. Such must be the rule if authority is to be reconciled with freedom. Such, in my opinion, is the command of the Constitution. It is therefore always open to Americans to challenge a law abridging free speech and assembly by showing that there was no emergency justifying it.

Moreover, even imminent danger cannot justify resort to prohibition of these functions essential to effective democracy, unless the evil apprehended is relatively serious. Prohibition of free speech and assembly is a measure so stringent that it would be inappropriate as the means for averting a relatively trivial harm to society. A police measure may be unconstitutional merely because the remedy, although effective as means of protection, is unduly harsh or oppressive. Thus, a State might, in the exercise of its police power, make any trespass upon the land of another a crime, regardless of the results or of the intent or purpose of the trespasser. It might, also, punish an attempt, a conspiracy, or an incitement to commit the trespass. But it is hardly conceivable that this Court would hold constitutional a statute which punished as a felony the mere voluntary assembly with a society formed to teach that pedestrians had the moral right to cross unenclosed, unposted, waste lands and to advocate their doing so, even if there was imminent danger that advocacy would lead to a trespass. The fact that speech is likely to result in some violence or in destruction of property is not enough to justify its suppression. There must be the probability of serious injury to the State. Among free men, the deterrents ordinarily to be applied to prevent crime are education and punishment for violations of the law, not abridgment of the rights of free speech and assembly....

Whether in 1919, when Miss Whitney did the things complained of, there was in California such clear and present danger of serious evil, might have been made the important issue in the case. She might have required that the issue be determined either by the court or the jury. She claimed below that the statute as applied to her violated the Federal Constitution; but she did not claim that it was void because there was no clear and present danger of serious evil, nor did she request that the existence of these conditions of a valid measure thus restricting the rights of free speech and assembly be passed upon by the court or a jury.... Under these circumstances the judgment of the state court cannot be disturbed. . . . This is a writ of error to a state court. Because we may not enquire into the errors now alleged, I concur in affirming the judgment of the state court.

MR. JUSTICE HOLMES joins in this opinion.

Notes

1. *Dennis v. United States,* 341 U.S. 494, 71 S.Ct. 857, 95 L.Ed. 1137 (1951) upheld the defendants' conviction for violation of the Smith Act. The indictment charged the defendants with "wilfully and knowingly conspiring to advocate and teach the duty and necessity of overthrowing and destroying the Government of the United States by force and violence."

Said Chief Justice Vinson, who wrote the plurality opinion: "Obviously, the words ['clear and present danger'] cannot mean that before the Government may act, it must wait until the *putsch* is about to be executed, the plans have been laid and the signal awaited. If Government is aware that a group aiming at its overthrow is attempting to indoctrinate its members and to commit them to a course whereby they will strike when the leaders feel the circumstances permit, action by the Government is required. . . . In the instant case the trial judge charged the jury that they could not convict unless they found that petitioners intended to overthrow the Government 'as speedily as circumstances would permit.' " This does not mean, and could not properly mean, that they would not strike until there was certainty of success. What was meant was that the revolutionists would strike when they thought the time was ripe. We must therefore reject the contention that success or probability of success is the criterion." Any attempt to overthrow the Government by force, "even though doomed from the outset because of inadequate numbers or power of the revolutionists, is a sufficient evil for Congress to prevent." Vinson then quoted from and adopted the rephrasing, by the appellate court, of the clear and present danger test: "Chief Judge Learned Hand, writing for the majority below, interpreted the phrase as follows: 'In each case [courts] must ask whether the gravity of the "evil," discounted by its improbability, justifies such invasion of free speech as is necessary to avoid the danger.' We adopt this statement of the rule."

Vinson also agreed with the court below that the requisite danger existed. "The mere fact that from the period 1945 to 1948 petitioners' activities did not result in an attempt to overthrow the Government by force and violence is of course no answer to the fact that there was a group that was ready to make the attempt. . . . It is the existence of the conspiracy which creates the danger. If the ingredients to the reaction are present, we cannot bind the Government to wait until the catalyst is added."

Frankfurter, J., concurring, argued that the ascendancy of the Communist doctrine was a matter of common knowledge that "would amply justify a legislature in concluding that recruitment of additional members for the Party would create a substantial danger to national security." Frankfurter thought that in *Gitlow v. New York,* supra, it would require "excessive tolerance of the legislative judgment to suppose that the *Gitlow* publication in the circumstances could justify serious concern. In contrast, there is ample justification for a legislative judgment that the conspiracy now before us is a substantial threat to national order and security."

2. *Yates v. United States,* 354 U.S. 298, 77 S.Ct. 1064, 1 L.Ed.2d 1356 (1957) reversed and remanded the convictions of petitioners convicted of conspiring "to advocate and teach the duty and necessity of overthrowing the Government of the United States by force and violence. . . . " Harlan, J., for the majority, stated that the Court was "faced with the question whether the Smith Act prohibits advocacy and teaching of forcible overthrow as an abstract principle, divorced from any effort to instigate action to that end, so long as such advocacy or teaching is engaged in with evil intent. We hold that it does not."

The lower courts had misconceived *Dennis.* "The essence of the *Dennis* holding was that indoctrination of a group in preparation for future violent action, as well as exhortation to immediate action, by advocacy found to be directed to 'action for the accomplishment' of forcible overthrow, to violence as 'a rule or principle of action,' and employing 'language of incitement' is not constitutionally protected when the group is of sufficient size and cohesiveness, is sufficiently oriented towards action, and other circumstances are such as reasonably to justify apprehension that action will occur. This is quite a different thing from the view of the District Court here that mere doctrinal justification of forcible overthrow, if engaged in with the intent to accomplish overthrow, is punishable *per se* under the Smith Act. That sort of advocacy, even though uttered with the hope that it may ultimately lead to violent revolution, is too remote from concrete action to be regarded as the kind of indoctrination preparatory to action which was condemned in *Dennis.* . . . The essential distinction is that those to whom the advocacy is addressed must be urged to *do* something, now or in the future, rather than merely to *believe* in something."

BRANDENBURG v. OHIO
395 U.S. 444, 89 S.Ct. 1827, 23 L.Ed.2d 430 (1969).

PER CURIAM.

The appellant, a leader of a Ku Klux Klan group, was convicted under the Ohio Criminal Syndicalism statute for "advocat[ing] . . . the duty, necessity, or propriety of crime, sabotage, violence, or unlawful methods of terrorism as a means of accomplishing industrial or political reform" and for "voluntarily assembl[ing] with any society, group, or assemblage of persons formed to teach or advocate the doctrines of criminal syndicalism." He was fined $1,000 and sentenced to one to 10 years' imprisonment. . . . We reverse.

The record shows that a man, identified at trial as the appellant, telephoned an announcer-reporter on the staff of a Cincinnati television station and invited him to come to a Ku Klux Klan "rally" to be held at a farm in Hamilton County. With the cooperation of the organizers, the reporter and a cameraman attended the meeting and filmed the events. Portions of the films were later broadcast on the local station and on a national network. . . .

One film showed 12 hooded figures, some of whom carried firearms. They were gathered around a large wooden cross, which they burned. No one was present other than the participants and the newsmen who made the film. Most of the words uttered during the scene were incomprehensible when the film was projected, but scattered phrases could be understood that were derogatory of Negroes and, in one instance, of Jews. Another scene on the same film showed the appellant, in Klan regalia, making a speech. The speech, in full, was as follows:

> This is an organizers' meeting. We have had quite a few members here today which are—we have hundreds, hundreds of members throughout the State of Ohio. I can quote from a newspaper clipping from the Columbus, Ohio Dispatch, five weeks ago Sunday morning. The Klan has more members in the State of Ohio than does any other organization. We're not a revengent organization, but if our President, our Congress, our Supreme Court, continues to suppress the white, Caucasian race, it's possible that there might have to be some revengeance taken. We are marching on Congress July the Fourth, four hundred thousand strong. From there we are dividing into two groups, one group to march on St. Augustine, Florida, the other group to march into Mississippi. Thank you.

The second film showed six hooded figures one of whom, later identified as the appellant, repeated a speech very similar to that recorded on the first film. The reference to the possibility of "revengeance" was omitted, and one sentence was added: "Personally, I believe the nigger should be returned to Africa, the Jew returned to Israel." Though some of the figures in the films carried weapons, the speaker did not.

The Ohio Criminal Syndicalism Statute was enacted in 1919. From 1917 to 1920, identical or quite similar laws were adopted by 20 States and two territories. In 1927, this Court sustained the constitutionality of California's Criminal Syndicalism Act, Cal.Penal Code §§ 11400–11402, the text of which is quite similar to that of the laws of Ohio. *Whitney v. California.* The Court upheld the statute on the ground that, without more, "advocating" violent means to effect political and economic change involves such danger to the security of the State that the State may outlaw it. But *Whitney* has been thoroughly discredited by later decisions. See *Dennis v. United States.* These later decisions have fashioned the principle that the constitutional guarantees of free speech and free press do not permit a State to forbid or proscribe advocacy of the use of force or of law violation except where such advocacy is directed to inciting or producing imminent lawless action and is likely to incite or produce such action.[2] As we said in *Noto v. United States,* 367 U.S. 290,

---

2. It was on the theory that the Smith Act, 54 Stat. 670, 18 U.S.C.A. § 2385, embodied such a principle and that it had been applied only in conformity with it that this Court sustained the Act's constitutionality. *Dennis v. United States,* 341 U.S. 494, 71 S.Ct. 857, 95 L.Ed. 1137 (1951). That this was the basis for *Dennis* was emphasized in *Yates v. United States,* 354 U.S. 298, 320–324, 77 S.Ct. 1064, 1077–1079, 1 L.Ed.2d 1356 (1957), in which the Court overturned convictions for advocacy of the forcible overthrow of the Government under the Smith Act, because the trial judge's instruc-

297–298, 81 S.Ct. 1517, 1520–1521, 6 L.Ed.2d 836 (1961), "the mere abstract teaching … of the moral propriety or even moral necessity for a resort to force and violence, is not the same as preparing a group for violent action and steeling it to such action." A statute which fails to draw this distinction impermissibly intrudes upon the freedoms guaranteed by the First and Fourteenth Amendments. It sweeps within its condemnation speech which our Constitution has immunized from governmental control. . . .

Accordingly, we are here confronted with a statute which, by its own words and as applied, purports to punish mere advocacy and to forbid, on pain of criminal punishment, assembly with others merely to advocate the described type of action. Such a statute falls within the condemnation of the First and Fourteenth Amendments. The contrary teaching of *Whitney v. California,* supra, cannot be supported, and that decision is therefore overruled.

Reversed.

MR. JUSTICE BLACK, concurring.

I agree with the views expressed by MR. JUSTICE DOUGLAS in his concurring opinion in this case that the "clear and present danger" doctrine should have no place in the interpretation of the First Amendment. I join the Court's opinion, which, as I understand it, simply cites *Dennis v. United States,* but does not indicate any agreement on the Court's part with the "clear and present danger" doctrine on which *Dennis* purported to rely.

[The concurring opinion of DOUGLAS, J., is omitted.]

HESS v. INDIANA
414 U.S. 105, 94 S.Ct. 326, 38 L.Ed.2d 303 (1973).

PER CURIAM.

Gregory Hess appeals from his conviction in the Indiana courts for violating the State's disorderly conduct statute. . . .

The events leading to Hess' conviction began with an antiwar demonstration on the campus of Indiana University. In the course of the demonstration, approximately 100 to 150 of the demonstrators moved onto a public street and blocked the passage of vehicles. When the demonstrators did not respond to verbal directions from the sheriff to clear the street, the sheriff and his deputies began walking up the street, and the demonstrators in their path moved to the curbs on either side, joining a large number of spectators who had gathered. Hess was standing off the street as the sheriff passed him. The sheriff heard Hess utter the word "fuck" in what he later described as a loud voice and immediately arrested him on the disorderly conduct charge. It was later

tions had allowed conviction for mere advo-   forcible action.
cacy, unrelated to its tendency to produce

stipulated that what appellant had said was "We'll take the fucking street later," or "We'll take the fucking street again." Two witnesses who were in the immediate vicinity testified, apparently without contradiction, that they heard Hess' words and witnessed his arrest. They indicated that Hess did not appear to be exhorting the crowd to go back into the street, that he was facing the crowd and not the street when he uttered the statement, that his statement did not appear to be addressed to any particular person or group, and that his tone, although loud, was no louder than that of the other people in the area. . . .

The Indiana Supreme Court placed primary reliance on the trial court's finding that Hess' statement "was intended to incite further lawless action on the part of the crowd in the vicinity of appellant and was likely to produce such action." At best, however, the statement could be taken as counsel for present moderation; at worst, it amounted to nothing more than advocacy of illegal action at some indefinite future time. This is not sufficient to permit the State to punish Hess' speech. Under our decisions, "the constitutional guarantees of free speech and free press do not permit a State to forbid or proscribe advocacy of the use of force or of law violation except where such advocacy is directed to inciting or producing *imminent* lawless action and is likely to incite or produce such action." *Brandenburg v. Ohio,* 395 U.S. 444, 447, 89 S.Ct. 1827, 1829, 23 L.Ed.2d 430 (1969). (Emphasis added.) Since the uncontroverted evidence showed that Hess' statement was not directed to any person or group of persons, it cannot be said that he was advocating, in the normal sense, any action. And since there was no evidence, or rational inference from the import of the language, that his words were intended to produce, and likely to produce, *imminent* disorder, those words could not be punished by the State on the ground that they had "a 'tendency to lead to violence.' "

Accordingly, the motion to proceed *in forma pauperis* is granted and the judgment of the Supreme Court of Indiana is reversed.

MR. JUSTICE REHNQUIST, with whom THE CHIEF JUSTICE [BURGER] and MR. JUSTICE BLACKMUN join, dissenting.

[C]ertain facts are clearly established. Appellant was arrested during the course of an antiwar demonstration conducted at Indiana University in May 1970. The demonstration was of sufficient size and vigor to require the summoning of police, and both the Sheriff's Department and the Bloomington Police Department were asked to help university officials and police remove demonstrators blocking doorways to a campus building. At the time the sheriff arrived, "approximately 200–300 persons" were assembled at that particular building.

The doorways eventually were cleared of demonstrators, in the process, two students were placed under arrest. This action did not go unnoticed by the demonstrators. As the stipulation notes, "[i]n apparent response to these arrests, about 100–150 of the persons who had gathered as spectators went into Indiana Avenue in front of Bryan Hall and in front of the patrol car in which the two arrestees had been placed."

Thus, by contrast to the majority's somewhat antiseptic description of this massing as being "[i]n the course of the demonstration," the demonstrators' presence in the street was not part of the normal "course of the demonstration" but could reasonably be construed as an attempt to intimidate and impede the arresting officers. Furthermore, as the stipulation also notes, the demonstrators "did not respond to verbal directions" from the sheriff to clear the street. Thus, the sheriff and his deputies found it necessary to disperse demonstrators by walking up the street directly into their path. Only at that point did the demonstrators move to the curbs.

... Surely the sentence "We'll take the fucking street later (or again)" is susceptible of characterization as an exhortation, particularly when uttered in a loud voice while facing a crowd. The opinions of two defense witnesses cannot be considered *proof* to the contrary, since the trial court was perfectly free to reject this testimony if it so desired. Perhaps, as these witnesses and the majority opinion seem to suggest, appellant was simply expressing his views to the world at large, but that is surely not the only rational explanation. ...

The simple explanation for the result in this case is that the majority has interpreted the evidence differently from the courts below. In doing so, however, I believe the Court has exceeded the proper scope of our review. Rather than considering the "evidence" in the light most favorable to the appellee and resolving credibility questions against the appellant, as many of our cases have required, the Court has instead fashioned its own version of events from a paper record, some "uncontroverted evidence," and a large measure of conjecture. Since this is not the traditional function of any appellate court, and is surely not a wise or proper use of the authority of this Court, I dissent.

10–2. PRIOR RESTRAINT

NEW YORK TIMES CO. v. UNITED STATES
403 U.S. 713, 91 S.Ct. 2140, 29 L.Ed.2d 822 (1971).

[On June 13th, 1971 the Sunday *New York Times* published the first installment of what became popularly known as the Pentagon Papers, based on a 47 volume top secret study of the American involvement in the Vietnam War. Commissioned by Secretary of Defense Robert S. McNamara in 1967, the documentary history covered the American interest in the Indochinese area from World War II to May 1968, when the Paris peace talks began.[1] (It was later learned that Daniel Ellsberg, a

---

1. The Pentagon's secret history showed:

"• That the Kennedy Administration, though ultimately spared from major escalation decisions by the death of its leader, transformed a policy of 'limited-risk gamble,' which it inherited, into a 'broad com-

mitment' that left President Johnson with a choice between more war and withdrawal.

"• That the Johnson Administration, though the President was reluctant and hesitant to take the final decisions, intensified the covert warfare against North Vietnam and began planning in the spring of

former Pentagon official, had engaged in an unauthorized disclosure—a "leak"—of the documents.)

[After the *Times'* third installment, on Tuesday, Attorney General John Mitchell secured a temporary restraining order in the Southern District of New York on the grounds that the massive leak endangered national security. A few days later, on June 18, the *Washington Post* began to publish parts of the secret report, and the Government once again sought a restraining order. Both district courts, after a hearing, denied an injunction. The Second Circuit remanded for further proceedings but the D.C. Circuit affirmed its district court. The Supreme Court granted certiorari in both cases, with Black, Douglas, Brennan, and Marshall, JJ., dissenting. They would have denied certiorari and lifted any restraints imposed on the *Times* and *Post*. Certiorari was granted on June 25th, the case was set for oral argument on June 26th at 11:00 A.M., and the Supreme Court opinion was issued on June 30th.]

PER CURIAM.

We granted certiorari in these cases in which the United States seeks to enjoin the New York Times and the Washington Post from publishing the contents of a classified study entitled "History of U.S. Decision–Making Process on Viet Nam Policy."

"Any system of prior restraints of expression comes to this Court bearing a heavy presumption against its constitutional validity." *Bantam Books, Inc. v. Sullivan,* 372 U.S. 58, 70, 83 S.Ct. 631, 639, 9 L.Ed.2d 584 (1963); see also *Near v. Minnesota ex rel. Olson,* [noted infra]. The Government "thus carries a heavy burden of showing justification for the imposition of such a restraint." *Organization for a Better Austin v. Keefe,* 402 U.S. 415, 419, 91 S.Ct. 1575, 1578, 29 L.Ed.2d 1 (1971). The District Court for the Southern District of New York in the *New York Times* case and the District Court for the District of Columbia and the Court of Appeals for the District of Columbia Circuit in the *Washington Post* case held that the Government had not met that burden. We agree.

The judgment of the Court of Appeals for the District of Columbia Circuit is therefore affirmed. The order of the Court of Appeals for the Second Circuit is reversed and the case is remanded with directions to enter a judgment affirming the judgment of the District Court for the Southern District of New York. The stays entered June 25, 1971, by the Court are vacated. The judgments shall issue forthwith.

So ordered.

MR. JUSTICE BLACK, with whom MR. JUSTICE DOUGLAS joins, concurring.

1964 to wage overt war, a full year before it publicly revealed the depth of its involvement and its fear of defeat.

"• That this campaign of growing clandestine military pressure through 1964 and the expanding program of bombing North Vietnam in 1965 were begun despite the judgment of the Government's intelligence community that the measures would not cause Hanoi to cease its support of the Vietcong insurgency in the South, and that the bombing was deemed militarily ineffective within a few months."

The Pentagon Papers, As Published by the New York Times, Based on The Investigative Reporting of Neil Sheehan at xi (1971).

I adhere to the view that the Government's case against the Washington Post should have been dismissed and that the injunction against the New York Times should have been vacated without oral argument when the cases were first presented to this Court. I believe that every moment's continuance of the injunctions against these newspapers amounts to a flagrant, indefensible, and continuing violation of the First Amendment. Furthermore, after oral argument, I agree completely that we must affirm the judgment of the Court of Appeals for the District of Columbia Circuit and reverse the judgment of the Court of Appeals for the Second Circuit for the reasons stated by my Brothers Douglas and Brennan. In my view it is unfortunate that some of my Brethren are apparently willing to hold that the publication of news may sometimes be enjoined. Such a holding would make a shambles of the First Amendment. . . .

In the First Amendment the Founding Fathers gave the free press the protection it must have to fulfill its essential role in our democracy. The press was to serve the governed, not the governors. The Government's power to censor the press was abolished so that the press would remain forever free to censure the Government. The press was protected so that it could bare the secrets of government and inform the people. Only a free and unrestrained press can effectively expose deception in government. And paramount among the responsibilities of a free press is the duty to prevent any part of the government from deceiving the people and sending them off to distant lands to die of foreign fevers and foreign shot and shell. In my view, far from deserving condemnation for their courageous reporting, the New York Times, the Washington Post, and other newspapers should be commended for serving the purpose that the Founding Fathers saw so clearly. In revealing the workings of government that led to the Vietnam war, the newspapers nobly did precisely that which the Founders hoped and trusted they would do.

[W]e are asked to hold that despite the First Amendment's emphatic command, the Executive Branch, the Congress, and the Judiciary can make laws enjoining publication of current news and abridging freedom of the press in the name of "national security." The Government does not even attempt to rely on any act of Congress. Instead it makes the bold and dangerously far-reaching contention that the courts should take it upon themselves to "make" a law abridging freedom of the press in the name of equity, presidential power and national security, even when the representatives of the people in Congress have adhered to the command of the First Amendment and refused to make such a law. To find that the President has "inherent power" to halt the publication of news by resort to the courts would wipe out the First Amendment and destroy the fundamental liberty and security of the very people the Government hopes to make "secure." No one can read the history of the adoption of the First Amendment without being convinced beyond any doubt that it was injunctions like those sought here that Madison and his collaborators intended to outlaw in this Nation for all time.

The word "security" is a broad, vague generality whose contours should not be invoked to abrogate the fundamental law embodied in the First Amendment. The guarding of military and diplomatic secrets at the expense of informed representative government provides no real security for our Republic. The Framers of the First Amendment, fully aware of both the need to defend a new nation and the abuses of the English and Colonial governments, sought to give this new society strength and security by providing that freedom of speech, press, religion, and assembly should not be abridged. . . .

MR. JUSTICE DOUGLAS, with whom MR. JUSTICE BLACK joins, concurring. . . .

The power to wage war is "the power to wage war successfully." But the war power stems from a declaration of war. The Constitution by Art. I, § 8, gives Congress, not the President, power "[t]o declare War." Nowhere are presidential wars authorized. We need not decide therefore what leveling effect the war power of Congress might have.

These disclosures[3] may have a serious impact. But that is no basis for sanctioning a previous restraint on the press. . . .

The Government says that it has inherent powers to go into court and obtain an injunction to protect the national interest, which in this case is alleged to be national security. *Near v. Minnesota ex rel. Olson,* 283 U.S. 697, 51 S.Ct. 625, 75 L.Ed. 1357, repudiated that expansive doctrine in no uncertain terms. The dominant purpose of the First Amendment was to prohibit the widespread practice of governmental suppression of embarrassing information. It is common knowledge that the First Amendment was adopted against the widespread use of the common law of seditious libel to punish the dissemination of material that is embarrassing to the powers-that-be. . . .

MR. JUSTICE BRENNAN, concurring.

I write separately in these cases only to emphasize what should be apparent: that our judgments in the present cases may not be taken to indicate the propriety, in the future, of issuing temporary stays and restraining orders to block the publication of material sought to be suppressed by the Government. So far as I can determine, never before has the United States sought to enjoin a newspaper from publishing information in its possession. . . .

The error that has pervaded these cases from the outset was the granting of any injunctive relief whatsoever, interim or otherwise. The entire thrust of the Government's claim throughout these cases has been that publication of the material sought to be enjoined "could," or "might," or "may" prejudice the national interest in various ways. But

---

3. There are numerous sets of this material in existence and they apparently are not under any controlled custody. Moreover, the President has sent a set to the Congress. We start then with a case where there already is rather wide distribution of the material that is destined for publicity, not secrecy. I have gone over the material listed in the *in camera* brief of the United States. It is all history, not future events. None of it is more recent than 1968.

the First Amendment tolerates absolutely no prior judicial restraints of the press predicated upon surmise or conjecture that untoward consequences may result.[1] Our cases, it is true, have indicated that there is a single, extremely narrow class of cases in which the First Amendment's ban on prior judicial restraint may be overridden. Our cases have thus far indicated that such cases may arise only when the Nation "is at war," *Schenck v. United States*, [§ 10–1, supra], during which times "[n]o one would question but that a government might prevent actual obstruction to its recruiting service or the publication of the sailing dates of transports or the number and location of troops." *Near v. Minnesota ex rel. Olson....* "[T]he chief purpose of [the First Amendment's] guaranty [is] to prevent previous restraints upon publication." *Near v. Minnesota ex rel. Olson.* Thus, only governmental allegation and proof that publication must inevitably, directly, and immediately cause the occurrence of an event kindred to imperiling the safety of a transport already at sea can support even the issuance of an interim restraining order. In no event may mere conclusions be sufficient: for if the Executive Branch seeks judicial aid in preventing publication, it must inevitably submit the basis upon which that aid is sought to scrutiny by the judiciary. And therefore, every restraint issued in this case, whatever its form, has violated the First Amendment—and not less so because that restraint was justified as necessary to afford the courts an opportunity to examine the claim more thoroughly. Unless and until the Government has clearly made out its case, the First Amendment commands that no injunction may issue.

MR. JUSTICE STEWART, with whom MR. JUSTICE WHITE joins, concurring.

... We are asked, quite simply, to prevent the publication by two newspapers of material that the Executive Branch insists should not, in the national interest, be published. I am convinced that the Executive is correct with respect to some of the documents involved. But I cannot say that disclosure of any of them will surely result in direct, immediate, and irreparable damage to our Nation or its people. That being so, there can under the First Amendment be but one judicial resolution of the issues before us. I join the judgments of the Court.

MR. JUSTICE WHITE, with whom MR. JUSTICE STEWART joins, concurring.

I concur in today's judgments, but only because of the concededly extraordinary protection against prior restraints enjoyed by the press under our constitutional system. I do not say that in no circumstances

---

1. *Freedman v. Maryland*, [§ 10–12.4, infra], and similar cases regarding temporary restraints of allegedly obscene materials are not in point. For those cases rest upon the proposition that "obscenity is not protected by the freedoms of speech and press." Here there is no question but that the material sought to be suppressed is within the protection of the First Amendment; the only question is whether, notwithstanding that fact, its publication may be enjoined for a time because of the presence of an overwhelming national interest. Similarly, copyright cases have no pertinence here: the Government is not asserting an interest in the particular form of words chosen in the documents, but is seeking to suppress the ideas expressed therein. And the copyright laws, of course, protect only the form of expression and not the ideas expressed.

would the First Amendment permit an injunction against publishing information about government plans or operations.[1] Nor, after examining the materials the Government characterizes as the most sensitive and destructive, can I deny that revelation of these documents will do substantial damage to public interests. Indeed, I am confident that their disclosure will have that result. But I nevertheless agree that the United States has not satisfied the very heavy burden that it must meet to warrant an injunction against publication in these cases, at least in the absence of express and appropriately limited congressional authorization for prior restraints in circumstances such as these.

The Government's position is simply stated: The responsibility of the Executive for the conduct of the foreign affairs and for the security of the Nation is so basic that the President is entitled to an injunction against publication of a newspaper story whenever he can convince a court that the information to be revealed threatens "grave and irreparable" injury to the public interest; and the injunction should issue whether or not the material to be published is classified, whether or not publication would be lawful under relevant criminal statutes enacted by Congress, and regardless of the circumstances by which the newspaper came into possession of the information.

. . . If the United States were to have judgment under such a standard in these cases, our decision would be of little guidance to other courts in other cases, for the material at issue here would not be available from the Court's opinion or from public records, nor would it be published by the press. Indeed, even today where we hold that the United States has not met its burden, the material remains sealed in court records and it is properly not discussed in today's opinions. Moreover, because the material poses substantial dangers to national interests and because of the hazards of criminal sanctions, a responsible press may choose never to publish the more sensitive materials. To sustain the Government in these cases would start the courts down a long and hazardous road that I am not willing to travel, at least without congressional guidance and direction.

---

1. The congress has authorized a strain of prior restraints against private parties in certain instances. The National Labor Relations Board routinely issues cease-and-desist orders against employers who it finds have threatened or coerced employees in the exercise of protected rights. See 29 U.S.C.A. § 160(c). Similarly, the Federal Trade Commission is empowered to impose cease-and-desist orders against unfair methods of competition. 15 U.S.C.A. § 45(b). Such orders can, and quite often do, restrict what may be spoken or written under certain circumstances. See, e.g., *NLRB v. Gissel Packing Co.*, 395 U.S. 575, 616–620, 89 S.Ct. 1918, 1941–1943, 23 L.Ed.2d 547 (1969). [N]o one denies that a newspaper can properly be enjoined from publishing the copyrighted works of another. See *L.A. Westermann Co. v. Dispatch Co.*, 249 U.S. 100, 39 S.Ct. 194, 63 L.Ed. 499 (1919). Newspapers do themselves rely from time to time on the copyright as a means of protecting their accounts of important events. However, those enjoined under the statutes relating to the National Labor Relations Board and the Federal Trade Commission are private parties, not the press; and when the press is enjoined under the copyright laws the complainant is a private copyright holder enforcing a private right. These situations are quite distinct from the Government's request for an injunction against publishing information about the affairs of government, a request admittedly not based on any statute.

[H]ere, publication has already begun and a substantial part of the threatened damage has already occurred. The fact of a massive breakdown in security is known, access to the documents by many unauthorized people is undeniable, and the efficacy of equitable relief against these or other newspapers to avert anticipated damage is doubtful at best.

What is more, terminating the ban on publication of the relatively few sensitive documents the Government now seeks to suppress does not mean that the law either requires or invites newspapers or others to publish them or that they will be immune from criminal action if they do. . . .

The Criminal Code contains numerous provisions potentially relevant to these cases. Section 797 makes it a crime to publish certain photographs or drawings of military installations. Section 798, also in precise language, proscribes knowing and willful publication of any classified information concerning the cryptographic systems or communication intelligence activities of the United States as well as any information obtained from communication intelligence operations. If any of the material here at issue is of this nature, the newspapers are presumably now on full notice of the position of the United States and must face the consequences if they publish. I would have no difficulty in sustaining convictions under these sections on facts that would not justify the intervention of equity and the imposition of a prior restraint.

. . . I am not, of course, saying that either of these newspapers has yet committed a crime or that either would commit a crime if it published all the material now in its possession. That matter must await resolution in the context of a criminal proceeding if one is instituted by the United States. In that event, the issue of guilt or innocence would be determined by procedures and standards quite different from those that have purported to govern these injunctive proceedings.

Mr. Justice Marshall, concurring.

. . . The Constitution provides that Congress shall make laws, the President execute laws, and courts interpret laws. *Youngstown Sheet & Tube Co. v. Sawyer,* [§ 5–1, supra]. It did not provide for government by injunction in which the courts and the Executive Branch can "make law" without regard to the action of Congress. . . .

On at least two occasions Congress has refused to enact legislation that would have made the conduct engaged in here unlawful and given the President the power that he seeks in this case. In 1917 during the debate over the original Espionage Act, still the basic provisions of § 793, Congress rejected a proposal to give the President in time of war or threat of war authority to directly prohibit by proclamation the publication of information relating to national defense that might be useful to the enemy. . . . In 1957 the United States Commission on Government Security found that "[a]irplane journals, scientific periodicals, and even the daily newspaper have featured articles containing information and other data which should have been deleted in whole or in part for security reasons." [T]he Commission proposed that "Congress enact legislation making it a crime for any person willfully to disclose without proper authorization, for any purpose whatever, information classified 'secret' or 'top secret,' knowing, or having reasonable grounds to believe, such information to have been so classified." [The proposal] was rejected.

MR. CHIEF JUSTICE BURGER, dissenting.

... An issue of this importance should be tried and heard in a judicial atmosphere conducive to thoughtful, reflective deliberation, especially when haste, in terms of hours, is unwarranted in light of the long period the Times, by its own choice, deferred publication.[1] ...

Would it have been unreasonable, since the newspaper could anticipate the Government's objections to release of secret material, to give the Government an opportunity to review the entire collection and determine whether agreement could be reached on publication? Stolen or not, if security was not in fact jeopardized, much of the material could no doubt have been declassified, since it spans a period ending in 1968. [T]he newspapers and Government might well have narrowed the area of disagreement as to what was and was not publishable, leaving the remainder to be resolved in orderly litigation, if necessary. To me it is hardly believable that a newspaper long regarded as a great institution in American life would fail to perform one of the basic and simple duties of every citizen with respect to the discovery or possession of stolen property or secret government documents. That duty, I had thought—perhaps naively—was to report forthwith, to responsible public officers. This duty rests on taxi drivers, Justices, and the New York Times. The course followed by the Times, whether so calculated or not, removed any possibility of orderly litigation of the issues. If the action of the judges up to now has been correct, that result is sheer happenstance.... I would direct that the District Court on remand give priority to the *Times* case to the exclusion of all other business of that court but I would not set arbitrary deadlines....

MR. JUSTICE HARLAN, with whom THE CHIEF JUSTICE [BURGER] and MR. JUSTICE BLACKMUN join, dissenting.

... With all respect, I consider that the Court has been almost irresponsibly feverish in dealing with these cases. Both the Court of Appeals for the Second Circuit and the Court of Appeals for the District of Columbia Circuit rendered judgment on June 23. The New York Times' petition for certiorari, its motion for accelerated consideration thereof, and its application for interim relief were filed in this Court on June 24 at about 11 a.m. The application of the United States for interim relief in the *Post* case was also filed here on June 24 at about 7:15 p.m. This Court's order setting a hearing before us on June 26 at 11 a.m., a course which I joined only to avoid the possibility of even more

---

1. [T]he Times conducted its analysis of the 47 volumes of Government documents over a period of several months and did so with a degree of security that a government might envy....

peremptory action by the Court, was issued less than 24 hours before. The record in the *Post* case was filed with the Clerk shortly before 1 p.m. on June 25; the record in the *Times* case did not arrive until 7 or 8 o'clock that same night. The briefs of the parties were received less than two hours before argument on June 26.

This frenzied train of events took place in the name of the presumption against prior restraints created by the First Amendment. Due regard for the extraordinarily important and difficult questions involved in these litigations should have led the Court to shun such a precipitate timetable. In order to decide the merits of these cases properly, some or all of the following questions should have been faced:

1. Whether the Attorney General is authorized to bring these suits in the name of the United States. This question involves as well the construction and validity of a singularly opaque statute—the Espionage Act, 18 U.S.C.A. § 793(e).

2. Whether the First Amendment permits the federal courts to enjoin publication of stories which would present a serious threat to national security. See *Near v. Minnesota ex rel. Olson,* 283 U.S. 697, 716, 51 S.Ct. 625, 631, 75 L.Ed. 1357 (1931)(dictum).

3. Whether the threat to publish highly secret documents is of itself a sufficient implication of national security to justify an injunction on the theory that regardless of the contents of the documents harm enough results simply from the demonstration of such a breach of secrecy.

4. Whether the unauthorized disclosure of any of these particular documents would seriously impair the national security.

5. What weight should be given to the opinion of high officers in the Executive Branch of the Government with respect to questions 3 and 4.

6. Whether the newspapers are entitled to retain and use the documents notwithstanding the seemingly uncontested facts that the documents, or the originals of which they are duplicates, were purloined from the Government's possession and that the newspapers received them with knowledge that they had been feloniously acquired.

7. Whether the threatened harm to the national security or the Government's possessory interest in the documents justifies the issuance of an injunction against publication in light of—

a. The strong First Amendment policy against prior restraints on publication;

b. The doctrine against enjoining conduct in violation of criminal statutes; and

c. The extent to which the materials at issue have apparently already been otherwise disseminated.

These are difficult questions of fact, of law, and of judgment; the potential consequences of erroneous decision are enormous. The time which has been available to us, to the lower courts, and to the parties has been wholly inadequate for giving these cases the kind of consideration they deserve....

Forced as I am to reach the merits of these cases, I dissent from the opinion and judgments of the Court.... Even if there is some room for the judiciary to override the executive determination, it is plain that the scope of review must be exceedingly narrow. I can see no indication in the opinions of either the District Court or the Court of Appeals in the *Post* litigation that the conclusions of the Executive were given even the deference owing to an administrative agency, much less that owing to a co-equal branch of the Government operating within the field of its constitutional prerogative....

Mr. Justice Blackmun, dissenting.

... Judge Wilkey, dissenting in the District of Columbia case, after a review of only the affidavits before his court (the basic papers had not then been made available by either party), concluded that there were a number of examples of documents that, if in the possession of the Post, and if published, "could clearly result in great harm to the nation," and he defined "harm" to mean "the death of soldiers, the destruction of alliances, the greatly increased difficulty of negotiation with our enemies, the inability of our diplomats to negotiate.... " I, for one, have now been able to give at least some cursory study not only to the affidavits, but to the material itself. I regret to say that from this examination I fear that Judge Wilkey's statements have possible foundation. I therefore share his concern. I hope that damage has not already been done. If, however, damage has been done, and if, with the Court's action today, these newspapers proceed to publish the critical documents and there results therefrom "the death of soldiers, the destruction of alliances, the greatly increased difficulty of negotiation with our enemies, the inability of our diplomats to negotiate," to which list I might add the factors of prolongation of the war and of further delay in the freeing of United States prisoners, then the Nation's people will know where the responsibility for these sad consequences rests.

Notes

1. *Near v. Minnesota ex rel. Olson*, 283 U.S. 697, 51 S.Ct. 625, 75 L.Ed. 1357 (1931). In this case, cited several times in the *New York Times* case, the Court, speaking through Hughes, C.J., invalidated a state law allowing a state court to abate, as a public nuisance, a "malicious, scandalous and defamatory newspaper magazine or other periodical."[1] The Court said: "If

---

1. The dissent of Butler, J., joined by Van Devanter, McReynolds, & Sutherland, JJ., included long excerpts from the newspaper, a brief portion of which follows:

"Practically every vendor of vile hooch, every owner of a moonshine still, every snake-faced gangster and embryonic yegg in the Twin Cities is a JEW.... I simply state a fact when I say that ninety percent of the crimes committed against society in this city are committed by Jew gangsters.... It is Jew, Jew, Jew.... I am launching no attack against the Jewish people AS A RACE. I am merely calling attention to a FACT.... Up to the present we have been merely tapping on the window. Very soon

we cut through mere details of procedure, the operation and effect of the statute in substance is that public authorities may bring the owner or publisher of a newspaper or periodical before a judge upon a charge of conducting a business of publishing scandalous and defamatory matter—in particular that the matter consists of charges against public officers of official dereliction—and unless the owner or publisher is able and disposed to bring competent evidence to satisfy the judge that the charges are true and published with good motives and for justifiable ends, his newspaper or periodical is suppressed and further publication is made punishable as a contempt. This is the essence of censorship. [I]t has generally, if not universally, considered that it is the chief purpose of the [speech] guaranty to prevent previous restraints upon publication."

The Court added, by way of dictum, that "the protection even as to previous restraint is not absolutely unlimited. But the limitation has been recognized only in exceptional cases ... No one would question but that a government might prevent actual obstruction to its recruiting service or the publication of the sailing dates of transports or the number and location of troops."

2. The Government never brought criminal charges against any newspaper for printing the Pentagon Papers, but it did prosecute Daniel Ellsberg. The trial judge directed a verdict of acquittal because of various prosecution improprieties. On the question of the constitutionality of a criminal prosecution against a newspaper for publishing secret information leaked to it, see *Landmark Communications, Inc. v. Virginia,* 435 U.S. 829, 98 S.Ct. 1535, 56 L.Ed.2d 1 (1978). Burger, C.J., for the Court, explained that the issue to be decided was—

> whether the First Amendment permits the criminal punishment of third persons who are strangers to the inquiry, including the news media, for divulging or publishing truthful information regarding confidential proceedings of the Judicial Inquiry and Review Commission. We are not here concerned with the possible applicability of the statute to one who secures the information by illegal means and thereafter divulges it. We do not have before us any constitutional challenge to a State's power to keep the Commission's proceedings confidential or to punish participants for breach of this mandate. Nor does Landmark argue for any constitutionally compelled right of access for the press to those proceedings.

Although confidentiality promotes the effectiveness of the judicial inquiry—

> the publication Virginia seeks to punish under its statute lies near the core of the First Amendment, and the Commonwealth's interests advanced by the imposition of criminal sanctions are insufficient to justify the actual and potential encroachments on freedom of speech and of the press which follow therefrom.

There were no dissents. Stewart, J., concurring in the judgment, said: "Though government may deny access to information and punish its theft, government may not prohibit or punish the publication of that information

we shall start smashing glass." 283 U.S. at   724–27 n. 1.

once it falls into the hands of the press, unless the need for secrecy is manifestly overwhelming.''

In *Smith v. Daily Mail Publishing Co.*, 443 U.S. 97, 99 S.Ct. 2667, 61 L.Ed.2d 399 (1979), the Court, again speaking through Burger, C.J., invalidated a state statute that made it a crime for a newspaper to publish, without the written approval of the juvenile court, the name of any youth charged as a juvenile offender. The papers had lawfully secured the information ''simply by asking various witnesses, the police and an assistant prosecuting attorney who were at the school.'' Whether one views the statute ''as a prior restraint or as a penal sanction for publishing lawfully obtained, truthful information is not dispositive because even the latter action requires the highest form of state interest to sustain its validity. [S]tate action to punish the publication of truthful information seldom can satisfy constitutional standards.''

Cox Broadcasting Corp. v. Cohn, 420 U.S. 469, 95 S.Ct. 1029, 43 L.Ed.2d 328 (1975)(excerpted at § 10–8.2) held that the state, even in a right to privacy action, may not impose sanctions on the accurate publication of the name of a rape victim obtained from public records open to public inspection. *Butterworth v. Smith*, 494 U.S. 624, 110 S.Ct. 1376, 108 L.Ed.2d 572 (1990) invalidated a Florida statute that prohibited (with certain limited exceptions) a grand jury witness from disclosing testimony that he gave to the grand jury, even after the grand jury term had ended. A Florida news reporter wanted to publish his experiences in dealing with the grand jury. The unanimous Court found that the state's interest in preserving grand jury secrecy is either not served by, or is insufficient, to warrant prohibiting truthful speech on matters of public concern.

SNEPP v. UNITED STATES
444 U.S. 507, 100 S.Ct. 763, 62 L.Ed.2d 704 (1980).

P ER C URIAM . . . .

Based on his experiences as a CIA agent, Snepp published a book about certain CIA activities in South Vietnam. Snepp published the account without submitting it to the Agency for prepublication review. As an express condition of his employment with the CIA in 1968, however, Snepp had executed an agreement promising that he would ''not . . . publish . . . any information or material relating to the Agency, its activities or intelligence activities generally, either during or after the term of [his] employment . . . without specific prior approval of the Agency.'' The promise was an integral part of Snepp's concurrent undertaking ''not to disclose any classified information relating to the Agency without proper authorization.'' Thus, Snepp had pledged not to divulge *classified* information and not to publish *any* information without prepublication clearance. The Government brought this suit to enforce Snepp's agreement. It sought a declaration that Snepp had breached the contract, an injunction requiring Snepp to submit future writings for prepublication review, and an order imposing a constructive trust for the Government's benefit on all profits that Snepp might earn from publishing the book in violation of his fiduciary obligations to the Agency.[2]

The District Court found that Snepp had "willfully, deliberately and surreptitiously breached his position of trust with the CIA and the [1968] secrecy agreement" by publishing his book without submitting it for prepublication review. The court also found that Snepp deliberately misled CIA officials into believing that he would submit the book for prepublication clearance. Finally, the court determined as a fact that publication of the book had "caused the United States irreparable harm and loss." The District Court therefore enjoined future breaches of Snepp's agreement and imposed a constructive trust on Snepp's profits.

The Court of Appeals accepted the findings of the District Court and agreed that Snepp had breached a valid contract.[3] It specifically affirmed the finding that Snepp's failure to submit his manuscript for prepublication review had inflicted "irreparable harm" on intelligence activities vital to our national security. Thus, the court upheld the injunction against future violations of Snepp's prepublication obligation. The court, however, concluded that the record did not support imposition of a constructive trust. The conclusion rested on the court's perception that Snepp had a First Amendment right to publish unclassified information and the Government's concession—for the purposes of this litigation— that Snepp's book divulged no classified intelligence.[4] In other words, the court thought that Snepp's fiduciary obligation extended only to preserving the confidentiality of classified material. It therefore limited recovery to nominal damages and to the possibility of punitive damages if the Government—in a jury trial—could prove tortious conduct. . . .

---

2. At the time of suit, Snepp already had received about $60,000 in advance payments. His contract with his publisher provides for royalties and other potential profits.

3. . . . In his petition for certiorari, Snepp relies primarily on the claim that his agreement is unenforceable as a prior restraint on protected speech.

When Snepp accepted employment with the CIA, he voluntarily signed the agreement that expressly obligated him to submit any proposed publication for prior review. He does not claim that he executed this agreement under duress. Indeed, he voluntarily reaffirmed his obligation when he left the Agency. We agree with the Court of Appeals that Snepp's agreement is an "entirely appropriate" exercise of the CIA Director's statutory mandate to "protec[t] intelligence sources and methods from unauthorized disclosure," 50 U.S.C.A. § 403(d)(3). Moreover, this Court's cases make clear that—even in the absence of an express agreement—the CIA could have acted to protect substantial government interests by imposing reasonable restrictions on employee activities that in other contexts might be protected by the First Amendment. The Government has a compelling interest in protecting both the secrecy of information important to our national security and the appearance of confidentiality so essential to the effective operation of our foreign intelligence service. The agreement that Snepp signed is a reasonable means for protecting this vital interest.

4. The Government's concession distinguished this case from *United States v. Marchetti*, 466 F.2d 1309 (CA4), cert. denied, 409 U.S. 1063, 93 S.Ct. 553, 34 L.Ed.2d 516 (1972). There, the Government claimed that a former CIA employee intended to violate his agreement not to publish any *classified* information. *Marchetti* therefore did not consider the appropriate remedy for the breach of an agreement to submit all material for prepublication review. By relying on *Marchetti* in this case, the Court of Appeals overlooked the difference between Snepp's breach and the violation at issue in *Marchetti*.

Whether Snepp violated his trust does not depend upon whether his book actually contained classified information. The Government does not deny—as a general principle—Snepp's right to publish unclassified information. Nor does it contend—at this stage of the litigation—that Snepp's book contains classified material. The Government simply claims that, in light of the special trust reposed in him and the agreement that he signed, Snepp should have given the CIA an opportunity to determine whether the material he proposed to publish would compromise classified information or sources. Neither of the Government's concessions undercuts its claim that Snepp's failure to submit to prepublication review was a breach of his trust.

Both the District Court and the Court of Appeals found that a former intelligence agent's publication of unreviewed material relating to intelligence activities can be detrimental to vital national interests even if the published information is unclassified. When a former agent relies on his own judgment about what information is detrimental, he may reveal information that the CIA—with its broader understanding of what may expose classified information and confidential sources—could have identified as harmful.... Admiral Turner, Director of the CIA, testified without contradiction that Snepp's book and others like it have seriously impaired the effectiveness of American intelligence operations. "Over the last six to nine months," he said,

> we have had a number of sources discontinue work with us. We have had more sources tell us that they are very nervous about continuing work with us. We have had very strong complaints from a number of foreign intelligence services with whom we conduct liaison, who have questioned whether they should continue exchanging information with us, for fear it will not remain secret. I cannot estimate to you how many potential sources or liaison arrangements have never germinated because people were unwilling to enter into business with us.[8]

In view of this and other evidence in the record, both the District Court and the Court of Appeals recognized that Snepp's breach of his explicit obligation to submit his material—classified or not—for prepublication clearance has irreparably harmed the United States Government.

The decision of the Court of Appeals denies the Government the most appropriate remedy for Snepp's acknowledged wrong. Indeed, as a practical matter, the decision may well leave the Government with no reliable deterrent against similar breaches of security. No one disputes that the actual damages attributable to a publication such as Snepp's

---

8. ... The dissent argues that the Court is allowing the CIA to "censor" its employees' publications. Snepp's contract, however, requires no more than a clearance procedure subject to judicial review. If Snepp, in compliance with his contract, had submitted his manuscript for review and the Agency had found it to contain sensitive material, presumably—if one accepts Snepp's present assertion of good intentions—an effort would have been made to eliminate harmful disclosures. Absent agreement in this respect, the Agency would have borne the burden of seeking an injunction against publication.

generally are unquantifiable. Nominal damages are a hollow alternative, certain to deter no one. The punitive damages recoverable after a jury trial are speculative and unusual. Even if recovered, they may bear no relation to either the Government's irreparable loss or Snepp's unjust gain.... Proof of the tortious conduct necessary to sustain an award of punitive damages might force the Government to disclose some of the very confidences that Snepp promised to protect....

A constructive trust, on the other hand, protects both the Government and the former agent from unwarranted risks. This remedy is the natural and customary consequence of a breach of trust. It deals fairly with both parties by conforming relief to the dimensions of the wrong. If the agent secures prepublication clearance, he can publish with no fear of liability. If the agent publishes unreviewed material in violation of his fiduciary and contractual obligation, the trust remedy simply requires him to disgorge the benefits of his faithlessness.... We therefore reverse the judgment of the Court of Appeals in so far as it refused to impose a constructive trust on Snepp's profits, and we remand the case to the Court of Appeals for reinstatement of the full judgment of the District Court.

So ordered.

Mr. Justice Stevens, with whom Mr. Justice Brennan and Mr. Justice Marshall join, dissenting....

In this case Snepp admittedly breached his duty to submit the manuscript of his book, *Decent Interval,* to the CIA for prepublication review. However, the Government has conceded that the book contains no classified, nonpublic material. Thus, by definition, the interest in confidentiality that Snepp's contract was designed to protect has not been compromised. Nevertheless, the Court today grants the Government unprecedented and drastic relief in the form of a constructive trust over the profits derived by Snepp from the sale of the book....

The rule of law the Court announces today is not supported by statute, by the contract, or by the common law. Although Congress has enacted a number of criminal statutes punishing the unauthorized dissemination of certain types of classified information, it has not seen fit to authorize the constructive trust remedy the Court creates today. Nor does either of the contracts Snepp signed with the agency provide for any such remedy in the event of a breach.[4] ...

The Court has not persuaded me that a rule of reason analysis should not be applied to Snepp's covenant to submit to prepublication review. Like an ordinary employer, the CIA has a vital interest in protecting certain types of information; at the same time, the CIA employee has a countervailing interest in preserving a wide range of

---

4. In both his original employment agreement and the termination agreement Snepp acknowledged the criminal penalties that might attach to any publication of classified information. In his employment agreement he also agreed that a breach of the agreement would be cause for termination of his employment. No other remedies were mentioned in either agreement.

work opportunities (including work as an author) and in protecting his First Amendment rights. The public interest lies in a proper accommodation that will preserve the intelligence mission of the agency while not abridging the free flow of unclassified information. When the Government seeks to enforce a harsh restriction on the employee's freedom,[9] despite its admission that the interest the agreement was designed to protect—the confidentiality of classified information—has not been compromised, an equity court might well be persuaded that the case is not one in which the covenant should be enforced.

But even assuming that Snepp's covenant to submit to prepublication review should be enforced, the constructive trust imposed by the Court is not an appropriate remedy. If an employee has used his employer's confidential information for his own personal profit, a constructive trust over those profits is obviously an appropriate remedy because the profits are the direct result of the breach. But Snepp admittedly did not use confidential information in his book; nor were the profits from his book in any sense a product of his failure to submit the book for prepublication review. For, even if Snepp had submitted the book to the agency for prepublication review, the Government's censorship authority would surely have been limited to the excision of classified material. In this case, then, it would have been obliged to clear the book for publication in precisely the same form as it now stands. Thus, Snepp has not gained any profits as a result of his breach; the Government, rather than Snepp, will be unjustly enriched if he is required to disgorge profits attributable entirely to his own legitimate activity.

Despite the fact that Snepp has not caused the Government the type of harm that would ordinarily be remedied by the imposition of a constructive trust, the Court attempts to justify a constructive trust remedy on the ground that the Government has suffered *some* harm.... Admiral Stansfield Turner['s] truncated testimony does not explain, however, whether these unidentified "other" books actually contained classified information. If so, it is difficult to believe that the publication of a book like Snepp's which does not reveal classified information, has significantly weakened the agency's position. Nor does it explain whether the unidentified foreign agencies who have stopped cooperating with the CIA have done so because of a legitimate fear that secrets will be revealed or because they merely disagree with our Government's classification policies....

The uninhibited character of today's exercise in lawmaking is highlighted by the Court's disregard to two venerable principles that favor a more conservative approach to this case.

First, for centuries the English-speaking judiciary refused to grant equitable relief unless the plaintiff could show that his remedy at law

---

9. The covenant imposes a serious prior restraint on Snepp's ability to speak freely, and is of indefinite duration and scope—factors that would make most similar covenants unenforceable. See, e.g., *E.L. Conwell* & *Co. v. Gutberlet,* 429 F.2d 527, 528 (C.A.4 1970)(holding void under Maryland law a covenant with no durational or geographical limitation).

was inadequate. Without waiting for an opportunity to appraise the adequacy of the punitive damage remedy in this case, the Court has jumped to the conclusion that equitable relief is necessary.

Second, and of greater importance, the Court seems unaware of the fact that its drastic new remedy has been fashioned to enforce a species of prior restraint on a citizen's right to criticize his government.[17] Inherent in this prior restraint is the risk that the reviewing agency will misuse its authority to delay the publication of a critical work or to persuade an author to modify the contents of his work beyond the demands of secrecy. The character of the covenant as a prior restraint on free speech surely imposes an especially heavy burden on the censor to justify the remedy it seeks. It would take more than the Court has written to persuade me that that burden has been met.

I respectfully dissent.

Notes

1. "Frank W. Snepp III was one of the last Americans to be evacuated by helicopter from the roof of the U.S. embassy in Saigon in the frantic hours before the city's fall on April 30, 1975. Snepp, then 31 and a senior analyst for the Central Intelligence Agency, with 4½ years experience in Viet Nam, thought the agency's withdrawal planning had been shockingly inept, particularly in that hundreds of local CIA collaborators were simply left behind to meet whatever fate awaited them. After he returned to Washington, where he was awarded the agency's Medal of Merit, he quit to write *Decent Interval,* a critical account of the CIA's performance during South Viet Nam's final days, published in 1977. [W]hen the CIA demanded to see his manuscript, Snepp refused. He maintained that he was obliged to submit only classified or nonpublic information.... The agency, which has been troubled by the spy-and-tell books of another former agent, Philip Agee, decided to take Snepp to court to show that the secrecy pledge was not to be trifled with. [M]any experts say, [the *Snepp* decision] could prompt many more agencies to adopt secrecy agreements (at present, the CIA, the FBI and the Defense Intelligence Agency insist on prepublication review, while several other departments and agencies require certain employees not to disclose confidential information)." Time Magazine, Mar. 3, 1980, at 48.

2. Stansfield Turner, the CIA Director who had pressed the litigation against Snepp, later had trouble with CIA censors who required him to delete portions of a book that he was writing on the secret intelligence business. Snepp commented, "Nobody can delight in the spectacle of a fellow citizen struggling against the rigors of official censorship, but this

---

17. The mere fact that the agency has the authority to review the text of a critical book in search of classified information before it is published is bound to have an inhibiting effect on the author's writing. Moreover, the right to delay publication until the review is completed is itself a form of prior restraint that would not be tolerated in other contexts. See, e.g., *New York Times Co. v. United States.* In view of the national interest in maintaining an effective intelligence service, I am not prepared to say that the restraint is necessarily intolerable in this context. I am, however, prepared to say that, certiorari having been granted, the issue surely should not be resolved in the absence of full briefing and argument.

time 'round, I really feel like the guy who says, 'I told you so.' Washington Post," May 20, 1983, at p. A10, col. 1–2.

10–3. TIME, PLACE, AND MANNER RESTRICTIONS AND THE PUBLIC FORUM

10–3.1 The Procedural Context

WALKER v. CITY OF BIRMINGHAM
388 U.S. 307, 87 S.Ct. 1824, 18 L.Ed.2d 1210 (1967).

MR. JUSTICE STEWART delivered the opinion of the Court.

On Wednesday, April 10, 1963, officials of Birmingham, Alabama, filed a bill of complaint in a state circuit court asking for injunctive relief against 139 individuals and two organizations.... The circuit judge granted a temporary injunction as prayed in the bill, enjoining the petitioners from, among other things, participating in or encouraging mass street parades or mass processions without a permit as required by a Birmingham ordinance.[1]

Five of the eight petitioners were served with copies of the writ early the next morning. Several hours later four of them held a press conference. There a statement was distributed, declaring their intention to disobey the injunction because it was "raw tyranny under the guise of maintaining law and order." ... That night a meeting took place at which one of the petitioners announced that "[i]njunction or no injunction we are going to march tomorrow." The next afternoon, Good Friday, a large crowd gathered.... Some of the crowd followed the marchers and spilled out into the street. At least three of the petitioners participated in this march. Meetings sponsored by some of the petitioners were held that night and the following night, where calls for volunteers to "walk" and go to jail were made. On Easter Sunday, April 14, a crowd of between 1,500 and 2,000 people congregated in the midafternoon in the vicinity of Seventh Avenue and Eleventh Street North in Birmingham. One of the petitioners was seen organizing members of the crowd in formation. A group of about 50, headed by three other petitioners, started down the sidewalk two abreast. At least one other petitioner was among the marchers. Some 300 or 400 people from among the onlookers followed in a crowd that occupied the entire width of the street and overflowed onto the sidewalks. Violence occurred. Members of the crowd threw rocks that injured a newspaperman and damaged a police motorcycle.

---

1. ... The Birmingham parade ordinance, § 1159 of the Birmingham City Code, provides that:

"It shall be unlawful to organize or hold, or to assist in organizing or holding, or to take part or participate in, any parade or procession or other public demonstration on the streets or other public ways of the city, unless a permit therefor has been secured from the commission.

"... The commission shall grant a written permit ... unless in its judgment the public welfare, peace, safety, health, decency require that it be refused...."

The next day the city officials who had requested the injunction applied to the state circuit court for an order to show cause why the petitioners should not be held in contempt for violating it. At the ensuing hearing the petitioners sought to attack the constitutionality of the injunction on the ground that it was vague and overbroad, and restrained free speech. They also sought to attack the Birmingham parade ordinance upon similar grounds, and upon the further ground that the ordinance had previously been administered in an arbitrary and discriminatory manner.

The circuit court refused to consider any of the contentions [holding] that the only issues before it were whether it had jurisdiction to issue the temporary injunction, and whether thereafter the petitioners had knowingly violated it. [T]he court found against the petitioners, and imposed upon each of them a sentence of five days in jail and a $50 fine, in accord with an Alabama statute. The Supreme Court of Alabama affirmed. . . .

Without question the state court that issued the injunction had, as a court of equity, jurisdiction over the petitioners and over the subject matter of the controversy. And this is not a case where the injunction was transparently invalid or had only a frivolous pretense to validity. We have consistently recognized the strong interest of state and local governments in regulating the use of their streets and other public places. *Cox v. State of New Hampshire,* 312 U.S. 569, 61 S.Ct. 762, 85 L.Ed. 1049; *Poulos v. State of New Hampshire,* 345 U.S. 395, 73 S.Ct. 760, 97 L.Ed. 1105. When protest takes the form of mass demonstrations, parades, or picketing on public streets and sidewalks, the free passage of traffic and the prevention of public disorder and violence become important objects of legitimate state concern. . . .

The generality of the language contained in the Birmingham parade ordinance upon which the injunction was based would unquestionably raise substantial constitutional issues concerning some of its provisions. *Schneider v. State of New Jersey,* 308 U.S. 147, 60 S.Ct. 146, 84 L.Ed. 155; *Saia v. People of State of New York,* 334 U.S. 558, 68 S.Ct. 1148, 92 L.Ed. 1574; *Kunz v. People of State of New York,* 340 U.S. 290, 71 S.Ct. 312, 95 L.Ed. 280. The petitioners, however, did not even attempt to apply to the Alabama courts for an authoritative construction of the ordinance. Had they done so, those courts might have given the licensing authority granted in the ordinance a narrow and precise scope, as did the New Hampshire courts in *Cox v. State of New Hampshire* and *Poulos v. State of New Hampshire.* Here, just as in *Cox* and *Poulos,* it could not be assumed that this ordinance was void on its face.

The breadth and vagueness of the injunction itself would also unquestionably be subject to substantial constitutional question. But the way to raise that question was to apply to the Alabama courts to have the injunction modified or dissolved. The injunction in all events clearly prohibited mass parading without a permit, and the evidence shows that the petitioners fully understood that prohibition when they violated it.

The petitioners also claim that they were free to disobey the injunction because the parade ordinance on which it was based had been administered in the past in an arbitrary and discriminatory fashion. In support of this claim they sought to introduce evidence that, a few days before the injunction issued, requests for permits to picket had been made to a member of the city commission. One request had been rudely rebuffed.[9] . . . Assuming the truth of this proffered evidence, it does not follow that the parade ordinance was void on its face. The petitioners, moreover, did not apply for a permit either to the commission itself or to any commissioner after the injunction issued. Had they done so, and had the permit been refused, it is clear that their claim of arbitrary or discriminatory administration of the ordinance would have been considered by the state circuit court upon a motion to dissolve the injunction.

This case would arise in quite a different constitutional posture if the petitioners, before disobeying the injunction, had challenged it in the Alabama courts, and had been met with delay or frustration of their constitutional claims. But there is no showing that such would have been the fate of a timely motion to modify or dissolve the injunction. There was an interim of two days between the issuance of the injunction and the Good Friday march. The petitioners give absolutely no explanation of why they did not make some application to the state court during that period. The injunction had issued *ex parte;* if the court had been presented with the petitioners' contentions, it might well have dissolved or at least modified its order in some respects. If it had not done so, Alabama procedure would have provided for an expedited process of appellate review. It cannot be presumed that the Alabama courts would have ignored the petitioners' constitutional claims. . . .

The rule of law upon which the Alabama courts relied in this case was one firmly established by previous precedents. We do not deal here, therefore, with a situation where a state court has followed a regular past practice of entertaining claims in a given procedural mode, and without notice has abandoned that practice to the detriment of a litigant who finds his claim foreclosed by a novel procedural bar. This is not a case where a procedural requirement has been sprung upon an unwary litigant when prior practice did not give him fair notice of its existence. . . .

These precedents clearly put the petitioners on notice that they could not bypass orderly judicial review of the injunction before disobeying it. Any claim that they were entrapped or misled is wholly unfounded, a conclusion confirmed by evidence in the record showing that when the petitioners deliberately violated the injunction they expected to go to jail.

---

9. Mrs. Lola Hendricks, *not* a petitioner in this case, testified that on April 3: "... I asked Commissioner Connor for the permit, and asked if he could issue the permit, or other persons who would refer me to, persons who would issue a permit. He said, 'No, you will not get a permit in Birmingham, Alabama to picket. I will picket you over to the City Jail,' and he repeated that twice."

The rule of law that Alabama followed in this case reflects a belief that in the fair administration of justice no man can be judge in his own case, however exalted his station, however righteous his motives, and irrespective of his race, color, politics, or religion. This Court cannot hold that the petitioners were constitutionally free to ignore all the procedures of the law and carry their battle to the streets. One may sympathize with the petitioners' impatient commitment to their cause. But respect for judicial process is a small price to pay for the civilizing hand of law, which alone can give abiding meaning to constitutional freedom.

Affirmed.

MR. CHIEF JUSTICE WARREN, with whom MR. JUSTICE BRENNAN and MR. JUSTICE FORTAS join, dissenting.

Petitioners in this case contend that they were convicted under an ordinance that is unconstitutional on its face because it submits their First and Fourteenth Amendment rights to free speech and peaceful assembly to the unfettered discretion of local officials. They further contend that the ordinance was unconstitutionally applied to them because the local officials used their discretion to prohibit peaceful demonstrations by a group whose political viewpoint the officials opposed. The Court does not dispute these contentions, but holds that petitioners may nonetheless be convicted and sent to jail because the patently unconstitutional ordinance was copied into an injunction—issued *ex parte* without prior notice or hearing on the request of the Commissioner of Public Safety—forbidding all persons having notice of the injunction to violate the ordinance without any limitation of time. I dissent because I do not believe that the fundamental protections of the Constitution were meant to be so easily evaded, or that "the civilizing hand of law" would be hampered in the slightest by enforcing the First Amendment in this case. . . .

These facts lend no support to the court's charges that petitioners were presuming to act as judges in their own case, or that they had a disregard for the judicial process. They did not flee the jurisdiction or refuse to appear in the Alabama courts. Having violated the injunction, they promptly submitted themselves to the courts to test the constitutionality of the injunction and the ordinance it parroted. They were in essentially the same position as persons who challenge the constitutionality of a statute by violating it, and then defend the ensuing criminal prosecution on constitutional grounds. It has never been thought that violation of a statute indicated such a disrespect for the legislature that the violator always must be punished even if the statute was unconstitutional. On the contrary, some cases have required that persons seeking to challenge the constitutionality of a statute first violate it to establish their standing to sue. Indeed, it shows no disrespect for law to violate a statute on the ground that it is unconstitutional and then to submit one's case to the courts with the willingness to accept the penalty if the statute is held to be valid. . . .

I do not believe that giving this Court's seal of approval to such a gross misuse of the judicial process is likely to lead to greater respect for the law any more than it is likely to lead to greater protection for First Amendment freedoms. The *ex parte* temporary injunction has a long and odious history in this country, and its susceptibility to misuse is all too apparent from the facts of the case. . . .

MR. JUSTICE DOUGLAS, with whom THE CHIEF JUSTICE [WARREN], MR. JUSTICE BRENNAN, and MR. JUSTICE FORTAS concur, dissenting. . . .

The right to defy an unconstitutional statute is basic in our scheme. Even when an ordinance requires a permit to make a speech, to deliver a sermon, to picket, to parade, or to assemble, it need not be honored when it is invalid on its face. *Lovell v. City of Griffin,* 303 U.S. 444, 452–453, 58 S.Ct. 666, 669, 82 L.Ed. 949; *Thornhill v. State of Alabama,* 310 U.S. 88, 97, 60 S.Ct. 736, 741–742, 84 L.Ed. 1093.

By like reason, where a permit has been arbitrarily denied, one need not pursue the long and expensive route to this Court to obtain a remedy. The reason is the same in both cases. For if a person must pursue his judicial remedy before he may speak, parade, or assemble, the occasion when protest is desired or needed will have become history and any later speech, parade, or assembly will be futile or pointless. . . . An ordinance—unconstitutional on its face or patently unconstitutional as applied—is not made sacred by an unconstitutional injunction that enforces it. . . .

[The dissenting opinion of BRENNAN, J., joined by WARREN, C.J. & DOUGLAS & FORTAS, JJ. is omitted.]

Notes

Forsyth County v. Nationalist Movement, 505 U.S. 123, 112 S.Ct. 2395, 120 L.Ed.2d 101 (1992). A Georgia county ordinance required a permit for a demonstration on public property. If the cost of protecting participants exceeded the usual and normal costs of law enforcement, this ordinance demanded a fee to cover the cost of protecting the participants in the demonstration, up to a maximum fee of $1,000. Respondents, who proposed to demonstrate against the Martin Luther King, Jr. federal holiday sued, objecting to the fee.

The Court, speaking through Blackmun, J., held that an ordinance that permits a government official to vary the cost of a permit to reflect the estimated cost of maintaining public order is unconstitutional on its face. The ordinance left the decision of how much to charge, or whether to charge anything, to the unbridled discretion of the government official, who was not required to rely on objective standards or provide any explanation. The ordinance was also content-based, because it required the government official, in order to access accurately the cost of security, to examine the content of the message, determine what the public response to that message would be, and then judge the number of police necessary to meet that response. Thus people expressing views unpopular with bottle-throwers, might have to pay more for their permit. The listeners' "reaction to speech is not a content-neutral basis for regulation." The $1,000 cap, or a lower cap could not save the ordinance. "A tax based on the content of speech does not become more constitutional because it is a small tax."

Rehnquist, C.J., joined by White, Scalia, & Thomas, JJ., dissented, arguing that the Constitution permits parade license fees of more than a nominal amount. The dissent did not reach the issue of whether the ordinance places too much discretion in the county official.

SHUTTLESWORTH v. CITY OF BIRMINGHAM
394 U.S. 147, 89 S.Ct. 935, 22 L.Ed.2d 162 (1969).

MR. JUSTICE STEWART delivered the opinion of the Court.

The petitioner stands convicted for violating an ordinance of Birmingham, Alabama, making it an offense to participate in any "parade or procession or other public demonstration" without first obtaining a permit from the City Commission. The question before us is whether that conviction can be squared with the Constitution of the United States.

On the afternoon of April 12, Good Friday, 1963, 52 people, all Negroes, were led out of a Birmingham church by three Negro ministers, one of whom was the petitioner, Fred L. Shuttlesworth. . . .

At the end of four blocks the marchers were stopped by the Birmingham police, and were arrested for violating § 1159 of the General Code of Birmingham. [This same march and the same section of the Birmingham Code was the subject of the Court's opinion in *Walker v. City of Birmingham,* supra.] . . . .

The petitioner was convicted for violation of § 1159 and was sentenced to 90 days' imprisonment at hard labor and an additional 48 days at hard labor in default of payment of a $75 fine and $24 costs. [The state Supreme Court] giving the language of § 1159 [quoted in footnote 1 of *Walker*] an extraordinarily narrow construction, reversed the judgment of the Court of Appeals and reinstated the conviction. We granted certiorari to consider the petitioner's constitutional claims.

There can be no doubt that the Birmingham ordinance, as it was written, conferred upon the City Commission virtually unbridled and absolute power to prohibit any "parade," "procession," or "demonstration" on the city's streets or public ways. For in deciding whether or not to withhold a permit, the members of the Commission were to be guided only by their own ideas of "public welfare, peace, safety, health, decency, good order, morals or convenience." This ordinance as it was written, therefore, fell squarely within the ambit of the many decisions of this Court over the last 30 years, holding that a law subjecting the exercise of First Amendment freedoms to the prior restraint of a license, without narrow, objective, and definite standards to guide the licensing authority, is unconstitutional. "It is settled by a long line of recent decisions of this Court that an ordinance which, like this one, makes the peaceful enjoyment of freedoms which the Constitution guarantees contingent upon the uncontrolled will of an official—as by requiring a permit or license which may be granted or withheld in the discretion of such official—is an unconstitutional censorship or prior restraint upon the enjoyment of those freedoms." And our decisions have made clear that a person faced with such an unconstitutional licensing law may ignore it and engage with impunity in the exercise of the right of free expression for which the law purports to require a license. "The Constitution can hardly be thought to deny to one subjected to the restraints of such an ordinance the right to attack its constitutionality, because he has not yielded to its demands."

It is argued, however, that what was involved here was not "pure speech," but the use of public streets and sidewalks, over which a municipality must rightfully exercise a great deal of control in the interest of traffic regulation and public safety. That, of course, is true. We have emphasized before this that "the First and Fourteenth Amendments [do not] afford the same kind of freedom to those who would communicate ideas by conduct such as patrolling, marching, and picketing on streets and highways, as these amendments afford to those who communicate ideas by pure speech." *Cox v. Louisiana,* 379 U.S. 536, 555, 85 S.Ct. 453, 464, 13 L.Ed.2d 471. "Governmental authorities have the duty and responsibility to keep their streets open and available for movement."

But our decisions have also made clear that picketing and parading may nonetheless constitute methods of expression, entitled to First Amendment protection. "Wherever the title of streets and parks may rest, they have immemorially been held in trust for the use of the public and, time out of mind, have been used for purposes of assembly, communicating thoughts between citizens, and discussing public questions. Such use of the streets and public places has, from ancient times, been a part of the privileges, immunities, rights, and liberties of citizens. The privilege of a citizen of the United States to use the streets and parks for communication of views on national questions may be regulated in the interest of all; it is not absolute, but relative, and must be exercised in subordination to the general comfort and convenience, and in consonance with peace and good order; but it must not, in the guise of regulation, be abridged or denied." *Hague v. C.I.O.,* 307 U.S. 496, 515–516, 59 S.Ct. 954, 964, 83 L.Ed. 1423 (opinion of MR. JUSTICE ROBERTS, joined by MR. JUSTICE BLACK).

Accordingly, "[a]lthough this Court has recognized that a statute may be enacted which prevents serious interference with normal usage of streets and parks, ... we have consistently condemned licensing systems which vest in an administrative official discretion to grant or withhold a permit upon broad criteria unrelated to proper regulation of public places." Even when the use of its public streets and sidewalks is involved, therefore, a municipality may not empower its licensing officials to roam essentially at will, dispensing or withholding permission to speak, assemble, picket, or parade, according to their own opinions regarding the potential effect of the activity in question on the "welfare," "decency," or "morals" of the community.

Understandably, under these settled principles, the Alabama Court of Appeals was unable to reach any conclusion other than that § 1159 was unconstitutional. The terms of the Birmingham ordinance clearly gave the City Commission extensive authority to issue or refuse to issue parade permits on the basis of broad criteria entirely unrelated to legitimate municipal regulation of the public streets and sidewalks.

It is said, however, that no matter how constitutionally invalid the Birmingham ordinance may have been as it was written, nonetheless the authoritative construction that has now been given it by the Supreme Court of Alabama has so modified and narrowed its terms as to render it constitutionally acceptable. It is true that in affirming the petitioner's conviction in the present case, the Supreme Court of Alabama performed a remarkable job of plastic surgery upon the face of the ordinance. The court stated that when § 1159 provided that the City Commission could withhold a permit whenever "in its judgment the public welfare, peace, safety, health, decency, good order, morals or convenience require," the ordinance really meant something quite different:

> ... We also hold that under § 1159 the Commission is without authority to act in an arbitrary manner or with unfettered discretion in regard to the issuance of permits. Its discretion must be exercised with uniformity of method of treatment upon the facts of each application, free from improper or inappropriate considerations and from unfair discrimination. A systematic, consistent and just order of treatment with reference to the convenience of public use of the streets and sidewalks must be followed. Applications for permits to parade must be granted if, after an investigation it is found that the convenience of the public in the use of the streets or sidewalks would not thereby be unduly disturbed.

In transforming § 1159 into an ordinance authorizing no more than the objective and even-handed regulation of traffic on Birmingham's streets and public ways, the Supreme Court of Alabama made a commendable effort to give the legislation "a field of operation within constitutional limits." We may assume that this exercise was successful, and that the ordinance as now authoritatively construed would pass constitutional muster. It does not follow, however, that the severely narrowing construction put upon the ordinance by the Alabama Supreme Court in November of 1967 necessarily serves to restore constitutional validity to a conviction that occurred in 1963 under the ordinance as it was written....

In *Cox* [*v. New Hampshire,* 312 U.S. 569, 61 S.Ct. 762, 85 L.Ed. 1049] the Court found that control of the streets had not been exerted unconstitutionally. There the Court was dealing with a parade-permit statute that was silent as to the criteria governing the granting of permits. In affirming the appellants' convictions for parading without a permit, the New Hampshire Supreme Court had construed the statute to require the issuance of a permit to anybody who applied, subject only to the power of the licensing authority to specify the "time, place and manner" of the parade in order to accommodate competing demands for public use of the streets. . . .

In the present case we are confronted with quite a different situation. In April of 1963 the ordinance that was on the books in Birmingham contained language that affirmatively conferred upon the members of the Commission absolute power to refuse a parade permit whenever they thought "the public welfare, peace, safety, health, decency, good order, morals or convenience require that it be refused." It would have taken extraordinary clairvoyance for anyone to perceive that this language meant what the Supreme Court of Alabama was destined to find that it meant more than four years later; and, with First Amendment rights hanging in the balance, we would hesitate long before assuming that either the members of the Commission or the petitioner possessed any such clairvoyance at the time of the Good Friday march.

But we need not deal in assumptions. For, as the respondent in this case has reminded us, in assessing the constitutional claims of the petitioner, "[i]t is less than realistic to ignore the surrounding relevant circumstances. These include not only facts developed in the Record in this case, but also those shown in the opinions in the related case of *Walker v. City of Birmingham.*" The petitioner here was one of the petitioners in the *Walker* case, in which, just two Terms ago, we had before us a record showing many of the "surrounding relevant circumstances" of the Good Friday march. As the respondent suggests, we may properly take judicial notice of the record in that litigation between the same parties who are now before us.

Uncontradicted testimony was offered in *Walker* to show that over a week before the Good Friday march petitioner Shuttlesworth sent a representative to apply for a parade permit. She went to the City Hall and asked "to see the person or persons in charge to issue permits, permits for parading, picketing, and demonstrating." She was directed to Commissioner Connor, who denied her request in no uncertain terms. "He said, 'No, you will not get a permit in Birmingham, Alabama to picket. I will picket you over to the City Jail,' and he repeated that twice." . . .

These "surrounding relevant circumstances" make it indisputably clear, we think, that in April of 1963—at least with respect to this petitioner and his organization—the city authorities thought the ordinance meant exactly what it said. . . .

This case, therefore, is a far cry from *Cox v. New Hampshire,* where it could be said that there was nothing to show "that the statute has been administered otherwise than in the . . . manner which the state court has construed it to require." Here, by contrast, it is evident that the ordinance was administered so as in the words of Chief Justice Hughes, "to deny or unwarrantedly abridge the right of assembly and the opportunities for the communication of thought . . . immemorially associated with resort to public places." The judgment is

Reversed.

Mr. Justice Black concurs in the result.

Mr. Justice Marshall took no part in the consideration or decision of this case.

[The concurring opinion of Harlan, J., is omitted.]

10–3.2 Protection of the Public From Fraud and Annoyance

SECRETARY OF STATE OF MARYLAND
v. JOSEPH H. MUNSON, INC.
467 U.S. 947, 104 S.Ct. 2839, 81 L.Ed.2d 786 (1984).

Justice Blackmun delivered the opinion of the Court.

In *Village of Schaumburg v. Citizens for a Better Environment,* 444 U.S. 620, 100 S.Ct. 826, 63 L.Ed.2d 73 (1980), this Court, with one dissenting vote, concluded that a municipal ordinance prohibiting the solicitation of contributions by a charitable organization that did not use at least 75% of its receipts for "charitable purposes" was unconstitutionally overbroad in violation of the First and Fourteenth Amendments. The issue in the present case is whether a Maryland statute with a like percentage limitation, but with provisions that render it more "flexible" than the *Schaumburg* ordinance, can withstand constitutional attack. . . .

Joseph H. Munson Co., Inc. (Munson), an Indiana corporation, instituted this action in the Circuit Court for Anne Arundel County, Md., seeking declaratory and injunctive relief against the Secretary of State of Maryland (Secretary). Munson is a professional for-profit fundraiser in the business of promoting fundraising events and giving advice to customers on how those events should be conducted. Its Maryland customers include various chapters of the Fraternal Order of Police (FOP).

Section 103A et seq., Art. 41, Md.Ann.Code (1982), concern charitable organizations. Section 103D prohibits such an organization, in connection with any fundraising activity, from paying or agreeing to pay as expenses more than 25% of the amount raised. Munson in its complaint alleged that it regularly charges an FOP chapter an amount in excess of 25% of the gross raised for the event it promotes. Munson also alleged that the Secretary had informed it that Munson was subject to § 103D and would be prosecuted if it failed to comply with the provisions of that statute. . . .

The Court in *Schaumburg* determined first that charitable solicitations are so intertwined with speech that they are entitled to the protections of the First Amendment:

> Prior authorities, therefore, clearly establish that charitable appeals for funds, on the street or door to door, involve a variety of speech interests—communication of information, the dissemination and propagation of views and ideas, and the advocacy of causes—

that are within the protection of the First Amendment. Soliciting financial support is undoubtedly subject to reasonable regulation but the latter must be undertaken with due regard for the reality that solicitation is characteristically intertwined with informative and perhaps persuasive speech seeking support for particular causes or for particular views on economic, political, or social issues, and for the reality that without solicitation the flow of such information and advocacy would likely cease.

Because the percentage limitation restricted the ways in which charities might engage in solicitation activity, the Court concluded that it was a "direct and substantial limitation on protected activity that cannot be sustained unless it serves a sufficiently strong, subordinating interest that the Village is entitled to protect." In addition, in order to be valid, the limitation would have to be a "narrowly drawn regulatio[n] designed to serve [the] interes[t] without unnecessarily interfering with First Amendment freedoms."

Although the Court in *Schaumburg* recognized that the Village had legitimate interests in protecting the public from fraud, crime, and undue annoyance, it rejected the limitation because it was not a precisely tailored means of accommodating those interests.... The justification for the limitation was an assumption that any organization using more than 25% of its receipts on fundraising, salaries, and overhead was not charitable, but was a commercial, for-profit enterprise. Any such enterprise that represented itself as a charity thus was fraudulent.

The flaw in the Village's assumption, as the Court recognized, was that there is no necessary connection between fraud and high solicitation and administrative costs. A number of other factors may result in high costs; the most important of these is that charities often are combining solicitation with dissemination of information, discussion, and advocacy of public issues, an activity clearly protected by the First Amendment and as to which the Village had asserted no legitimate interest in prohibiting. In light of the fact that the interest in protecting against fraud can be accommodated by measures less intrusive than a direct prohibition on solicitation,[9] the Court concluded that the limitation was insufficiently related to the governmental interests asserted to justify its interference with protected speech.[10]

Schaumburg left open the primary question now before this Court—whether the constitutional deficiencies in a percentage limitation on funds expended in solicitation are remedies by the possibility of an administrative waiver of the limitation for a charity that can demon-

---

9. The Court noted, for instance, that the Village could punish fraud directly and could require disclosure of the finances of a charitable organization so that a member of the public could make an informed decision about whether to contribute.

10. The Court also found little connection between the percentage limitation and

the protection of public safety or residential privacy. Both goals were better furthered by provisions addressed directly to the asserted interest—such as a prohibition on the use of convicted felons as solicitors and a provision allowing homeowners to post signs barring solicitors from their property.

strate financial necessity. [Section 103D] directs the Secretary of State to "issue rules and regulations to permit a charitable organization to pay or agree to pay for expenses in connection with a fundraising activity more than 25% of its total gross income in those instances where the 25% limitation would effectively prevent the charitable organization from raising contributions." Having now considered the question left open in *Schaumburg,* however, we conclude that the waiver provision does not save the statute.

The [state] Court of Appeals concluded that the exception in § 103D was "extremely narrow," being confined to instances "where the 25% limitation would effectively prevent the charitable organization from raising contributions," and of no avail to an organization whose high fundraising costs were attributable to legitimate policy decisions about how to use its funds, rather than to inability to raise funds. Under the Court of Appeals' interpretation, the Secretary has no discretion to determine that reasons other than financial necessity warrant a waiver. The statute does not help the charity whose solicitation costs are high because it chooses, as was stipulated here, to disseminate information as a part of its fundraising. Thus, the organizations that were of primary concern to the Court in *Schaumburg,* those whose high costs were due to " 'information dissemination, discussion, and advocacy of public issues,' "remain barred by the statute from carrying on those protected First Amendment activities.[12]

The Secretary urges that even though there may remain charities whose First Amendment activity is limited by the statute, we should not strike down the statute on its face because, with the waiver provision, it no longer is "substantially overbroad." We are not persuaded.

"Substantial overbreadth" is a criterion the Court has invoked to avoid striking down a statute on its face simply because of the possibility that it might be applied in an unconstitutional manner. It is appropriate in cases where, despite some possibly impermissible application, the " 'remainder of the statute . . . covers a whole range of easily identifiable and constitutionally proscribable . . . conduct. . . . ' " In such a case, the

---

12. The Secretary disagrees with the Court of Appeals' interpretation of the scope of her discretion. She urges that she has discretion to grant a waiver "whenever necessary" and that she has done so "in an extremely liberal manner, with special care shown for the rights of advocacy groups." We have no reason to second guess the Court of Appeals' interpretation of its own state law. But even if the Secretary were correct, . . . we would find the statute only slightly less troubling. Our cases make clear that a statute that requires such a "license" for the dissemination of ideas is inherently suspect. By placing discretion in the hands of an official to grant or deny a license, such a statute creates a threat of

censorship that by its very existence chills free speech. Under the Secretary's interpretation, charities whose First Amendment rights are abridged by the fundraising limitation simply would have traded a direct prohibition on their activity for a licensing scheme that, if it is available to them at all, is available only at the unguided discretion of the Secretary of State. Particularly where the percentage limitation itself is so poorly suited to accomplishing the State's goal, and where there are alternative means to serve the same purpose, there is little justification for straining to salvage the statute by invoking the possibility of official dispensation to engage in protected activity.

Court has required a litigant to demonstrate that the statute "as applied" to him is unconstitutional.

This is not such a case. Here there is no core of easily identifiable and constitutionally proscribable conduct that the statute prohibits. While there no doubt are organizations that have high fundraising costs not due to protected First Amendment activity and that, therefore, should not be heard to complain that their activities are prohibited, this statute cannot distinguish those organizations from charities that have high costs due to protected First Amendment activities. The flaw in the statute is not simply that it includes within its sweep some impermissible applications, but that in all its applications, it operates on a fundamentally mistaken premise that high solicitation costs are an accurate measure of fraud....

Where, as here, a statute imposes a direct restriction on protected First Amendment activity,[16] and where the defect in the statute is that the means chosen to accomplish the State's objectives are too imprecise, so that in all its applications the statute creates an unnecessary risk of chilling free speech, the statute is properly subject to facial attack. The possibility of a waiver may decrease the number of impermissible applications of the statute, but it does nothing to remedy the statute's fundamental defect. We conclude that, regardless of the waiver provision, *Schaumburg* requires that the percentage limitation in the Maryland statute be rejected....

We agree with the Court of Appeals of Maryland that § 103D is unconstitutionally overbroad. The judgment of that court therefore is affirmed.

It is so ordered.

JUSTICE REHNQUIST, with whom THE CHIEF JUSTICE [BURGER], JUSTICE POWELL, and JUSTICE O'CONNOR join, dissenting.

[O]n the authority of [*Schaumburg*], the Court strikes down a markedly different Maryland statute, whose primary and legitimate

---

16. The dissenters' suggestion that, because the Maryland statute regulates only the economic relationship between charities and professional fundraisers, it is not a direct restriction on the charities' First Amendment activity is perplexing. Any restriction on the amount of money a charity can pay to a third party as a fundraising expense could be labelled "economic regulation." The fact that paid solicitors are used to disseminate information did not alter the *Schaumburg* Court's conclusion that a limitation on the amount a charity can spend in fundraising activity is a direct restriction on the charity's First Amendment rights. Whatever the State's purpose in enacting the statute, the fact remains that the percentage limitation is a direct restriction on the amount of money a charity can spend on fundraising activity.

For similar reasons, it is the dissent that "simply misses the point" when it urges that there is an element of "fraud" in a professional fundraiser's soliciting money for a charity if a high proportion of those funds are expended in fundraising. [T]he charity's "purpose" may include public education. It is no more fraudulent for a charity to pay a professional fundraiser to engage in legitimate public educational activity than it is for the charity to engage in that activity itself. And concerns about unscrupulous professional fundraisers, like concerns about fraudulent charities, can and are accommodated directly, through disclosure and registration requirements and penalties for fraudulent conduct.

effect is to prohibit professional fundraisers from charging charities a fee of more than 25% of the amount raised. The Court, invoking the doctrine of "overbreadth," reaches this result not at the behest of any affected charity, but at the behest of a professional fundraising organization. Believing that in this case the overbreadth doctrine is not merely "strong medicine," *Broadrick v. Oklahoma,* 413 U.S. 601, 613, 93 S.Ct. 2908, 2916, 37 L.Ed.2d 830, 841 (1973), but "bad medicine," I dissent.

... When a litigant challenges the constitutionality of a statute, he challenges the statute's application to him. He claims, for example, that his activities, which the statute seeks to regulate, are protected by the First Amendment. If he prevails, the Court invalidates the statute, not *in toto,* but only as applied to those activities. The law is refined by preventing improper applications on a case-by-case basis. In the meantime, the interests underlying the law can still be served by its enforcement within constitutional bounds. A successful overbreadth challenge, on the other hand, suspends enforcement of a statute entirely. The interests underlying the law, however substantial, are simply negated until the statute is either rewritten by the legislature or "reinterpreted" by an authorized court to serve those interests more narrowly. The litigant is permitted to raise the rights of third parties not before the court in order to forestall even legitimate applications of the law....

One might as a matter of original inquiry question whether an overbreadth challenge should ever be allowed, given that the Declaratory Judgment Act and the availability of preliminary injunctive relief will usually permit a litigant to discover the scope of constitutional protection afforded his activity without subjecting himself to criminal prosecution. [O]ur cases at least indicate that the doctrine is to be used sparingly....

As to Munson and other professional fundraisers who were not themselves engaged in speech activities, § 103D, read in conjunction with § 103F, is merely an economic regulation controlling the fees the firm is permitted to charge. A similar regulation governing, for example, the fees charged by an employment agency would be judged and approved under the minimum rationality standard traditionally applied to economic regulations. Of course, a ceiling on the fees charged by professional fundraisers may have an incidental and indirect impact on protected expression—as would, for example, a ceiling placed on the fees charged by literary agents—in that marginal producers could be forced out of the market. In other words, price controls might tend to make these services less available, much as rent control is thought to make rental housing less available. But such an indirect and incidental impact on expression is not sufficient to subject such regulation to strict First Amendment scrutiny. Otherwise, national forest legislation would be equally suspect as tending to raise the price and limit the quantity of paper.

Even if limitations on the fees charged by professional fundraisers were subjected to heightened scrutiny, however, those limitations serve a number of legitimate and substantial governmental interests. They insure that funds solicited from the public for a charitable purpose will not be excessively diverted to private pecuniary gain. In the process, they encourage the public to give by allowing the public to give with confidence that money designed for a charity will be spent on charitable purposes. [E]ven if a fundraiser were to fully disclose to every donor that half of the money collected would be used for "expenses," so that there could be no question of "fraud" in the common law sense of that word, the State's interest is not an end. [The] law protects the charities themselves from being overcharged by unscrupulous professional fundraisers.

The Court, therefore, is simply mistaken when it claims that "there is no core of easily identifiable and constitutionally proscribable conduct that the statute prohibits." The rates charged by professional fundraisers are in fact both "easily identifiable" and "constitutionally proscribable." If Maryland's statute regulated only the rates charged by professional fundraisers to charitable organizations, this would be an easy case. The statute would be clearly constitutional.

But of course the statute also applies to solicitation expenses other than those spent on professional fundraisers. To that extent, therefore, the statute directly regulates the solicitation activities of charities and is subject to more intense scrutiny. Even as applied directly to charities, however, the statute serves legitimate objectives in so far as it regulates fundraising costs not attributable to public education or advocacy. Again, donor confidence is enhanced by such a regulation, and the intended objects of the public's bounty are benefited.... In baldly claiming that advocacy organizations "remain barred by the statute from carrying on those protected First Amendment activities," the Court simply ignores or slights some crucial differences between this statute and the ordinance at issue in *Schaumburg*.

First of all, administrative and overhead costs that are not attributable to fundraising are not included in the 25% calculation of § 103D(a). Thus, the salaries of researchers, policy makers and technical support staff, as well as general overhead expenses, do not count as fundraising costs.... Second, § 103D(b) specifically excludes from the definition of fundraising costs many of the costs associated with combined advocacy and fundraising activities.... Thus, unlike the ordinance in *Schaumburg*, the costs of receptions, picnics and other social events at which advocacy organizations seek converts are not included in the fundraising calculus. Nor are costs associated with printing and mailing advocacy literature. Again, the statute is more carefully designed to accommodate the protected expression of such organizations. Sections 103D(a) and (b) together largely eliminate the concerns of *Schaumburg*.

Third, § 103D(a) directs the Secretary to "issue rules and regulations to permit a charitable organization to pay or agree to pay for expenses in connection with a fund-raising activity more than 25% of its total gross income in those instances where the 25% limitation would effectively prevent the charitable organization from raising contributions." The Maryland Court of Appeals has said that this waiver provision is "extremely narrow," but it should still suffice to alleviate the Court's concern that "unpopular" charities will be precluded from soliciting. A charity unable to meet the 25% limit due to the unpopularity of its cause would clearly be entitled to a statutory exemption.

Finally, even for those activities which mingle fundraising and advocacy, but do not fall within the exceptions of § 103D(b), § 103D(a) appears to call for a *pro rata* allocation of expenses into those expenses attributable to the fundraising portion of the activity and those attributable to the advocacy portion.... If such a *pro rata* allocation is required by the statute, then expenses associated with door-to-door solicitation by a member of the organization, which involves advocacy and education as well as an appeal for financial support, could not be charged entirely to fundraising.[5] If that is correct, the statute is not overbroad at all. Expenses associated with advocacy and public education would be completely excluded from the fundraising calculus. The crucial point is that we can't know precisely how such activities will be accommodated unless we first give Maryland a chance to face the question in concrete situations.

It would be foolish to claim that these four statutory safeguards will ensure that the statute will never be applied in such a way as to improperly inhibit the protected expression of any advocacy organization. No statute bears an absolute guarantee that it will always be applied within constitutional bounds; consequently, no such guarantee can be demanded. The question before the Court, we must remember, is whether the likely overbreadth of the statute is *substantial* in relation to its legitimate sweep....

[The concurring opinion of Stevens, J. is omitted.]

Notes

1. The Foreign Agents Registration Act defined the term "political propaganda" to include any communication that is reasonably adapted to, or intended to influence the recipient within the United States with reference to "the policies of a foreign country or foreign political party." When the agent of a foreign principal disseminated this "political propaganda" the law required that he or she make a disclosure statement to the recipients. This disclosure included the agent's identity, the identity of the principal for whom the agent was acting, a statement that a report describing the materials is registered with the Department of Justice, and a statement that such registration "does not indicate approval of the contents of this material

---

5. [O]ne of the Secretary's regulations provides that any public education activity which includes "an appeal, specific or implied, for financial support, shall be fully allocated to fund-raising expenses." But that regulation is not necessarily consistent with the statutory scheme. It has yet to be tested and we therefore do not know if it would be upheld by the Maryland courts. At any rate, possible constitutional failings in the regulations passed pursuant to a statute do not form a basis for holding the statute itself unconstitutional. A far less drastic solution would be, in an appropriate case, to strike down the regulation.

by the United States Government." The term "political propaganda" did not appear in the disclosure form that had to be filed, but it was used in the Act. This registration requirement "is comprehensive, applied equally to agents of friendly, neutral, and unfriendly governments." It included all advocacy materials even if completely accurate.

Barry Keene, a member of the California State Senate, wanted to exhibit three films (discussing acid rain and nuclear war) distributed by the National Film Board of Canada, a registered agent of the Government of Canada. Keene did "not want the Department of Justice and the public to regard him as the disseminator of foreign political propaganda. . . ." The district court ruled "that Congress violated the First Amendment by using the term 'political propaganda' as the statutory name for the regulated category of expression." The Supreme Court reversed, in *Meese v. Keene,* 481 U.S. 465, 107 S.Ct. 1862, 95 L.Ed.2d 415 (1987).[1]

The Court, although recognizing that "political propaganda" has a pejorative connotation, concluded that Congress simply required labeling information to identify its foreign origin. The law did not prohibit Keene or others from explaining to prospective viewers (before, during, or after the film's viewing, or in a separate context) that "Canada's interest in the consequences of nuclear war and acid rain does not necessarily undermine the integrity or the persuasiveness of its advocacy."

2. *Riley v. National Federation of the Blind of North Carolina, Inc.,* 487 U.S. 781, 108 S.Ct. 2667, 101 L.Ed.2d 669 (1988) involved the North Carolina Charitable Solicitations Act, which had a three tier schedule to define a prima facie reasonable fee that a professional fund raiser may charge: (1) a fee of up to 20% of the receipts was deemed reasonable; (2) a fee from 20% to 35% was deemed unreasonable if the solicitation "did not involve the dissemination of information, discussion, or advocacy related to public issues as directed by the [charity]"; (3) a fee in excess of 35% was presumed unreasonable unless the solicitation involved dissemination or advocacy on public issues directed by the charity, or because otherwise the charity's ability to raise money or communicate would be significantly diminished. Brennan, J., for the Court invalidated this three tier system as burdening free speech and not narrowly tailored to prevent fraud.

The North Carolina law also required professional fund raisers to disclose to potential donors the percentage of charitable funds (collected during the previous 12 months in that state) that were actually turned over to the charity. The Court invalidated this provision as well, as a content based regulation because mandating speech necessarily alters the speech's content. Freedom of speech includes the freedom of what not to say. The state's interest in informing donors was neither narrowly tailored nor weighty enough.

Finally, the Court invalidated North Carolina's licensing requirement for professional fund raisers. Even assuming that North Carolina could

---

1. The constitutionality of the underlying registration requirements of the Foreign Agents Registration Act were not at issue. Blackmun, J., joined by Brennan & Marshall, JJ., dissented. They objected to the government's "disparagement" of Keene's speech. "The Act mandates disclosure, not direct censorship, but the underlying goal was to control the spread of propaganda by foreign agents."

license professional fund raisers, the regulation must provide that the licensor, in a brief period, will either issue the license or go to court. The North Carolina law permitted a delay with no limit.

Justice Scalia joined in all of the opinion except for footnote 11, where the majority said: "However, nothing in this opinion should be taken to suggest that the State may not require a fund raiser to disclose unambiguously his or her professional status." Scalia argued, where "core First Amendment speech is at issue, the State can assess liability for specific instances of deliberate deception, but it cannot impose a prophylactic rule requiring disclosure even when deliberate statements are not made."

Chief Justice Rehnquist's dissent, joined by O'Connor, J. noted that North Carolina had revised its statute to attempt to comply with *Munson:* "Yet the Court obdurately refuses to allow the various States which have legislated in this area to distinguish between . . . incidental fund raising . . . and the entirely commercial activities of people whose job is, simply put, figuring out how to raise money for charities."

3. *Ward v. Rock Against Racism,* 491 U.S. 781, 109 S.Ct. 2746, 105 L.Ed.2d 661 (1989) upheld city regulations designed to limit excessively amplified music at the Naumberg Acoustic Bandshell in New York City's Central Park to protect those who used a quiet, recreational area of the Park called the Sheep Meadow, and also to protect residences in the Central Park West area. In the past, in response to numerous complaints, the city would monitor the volume and request that it be lowered when limits were exceeded. After two citations were issued to Rock Against Racism (an unincorporated association dedicated to promote "antiracist views") the city eventually turned off the power during one of their concerts, but the audience became "abusive and disruptive." Then the city considered establishing a fixed decibel limit, but abandoned that idea when it learned that the impact on listeners varies in response to factors like change in air temperature, audience size, and so forth. Next the city rejected employing a sound technician to operate the equipment of whomever was using the Bandshell because the city technician might have difficulty satisfying the needs of the musicians while operating unfamiliar equipment. Instead, the city concluded that it would furnish high quality sound equipment and retain an independent, experienced sound technician for all performances at the Bandshell. The respondents, sued seeking damages and a declaration that the guidelines were invalid on their face. The hearings showed that the performers who used the city's sound system (ranging from opera to salsa to reggae) "were uniformly pleased with the quality of the sound provided."

The Court of Appeals had held that the guideline was not the "least intrusive upon the freedom of expression as is reasonably necessary to achieve a legitimate purpose of the regulation." However, the Supreme Court, per Kennedy, J., rejected the facial challenge to these city noise regulations. The sound amplification rules did not authorize the city to vary the sound quality "based on the message being delivered by performers." The Court reaffirmed that time, place, and manner regulations "must be narrowly tailored to serve the government's legitimate content-neutral interests but that it need not be the least-restrictive means of doing so. Rather, the requirement of narrow tailoring is satisfied 'so long as the . . . regulation promotes a substantial government interest that would be achieved less effectively absent the regulation.' "Marshall, J., joined by Brennan & Stevens, JJ., dissented, arguing that New York City's sound amplification guidelines were not narrowly tailored to serve its interest in regulating loud noise. The Government's interest in avoiding loud sounds cannot justify its total control over sound equipment, "any more than its interest in avoiding litter could justify a ban on handbill distribution." In both cases, the government can pursue its legitimate goals less intrusively by directly punishing the evil—"the persons responsible for excessive sounds and the persons who litter."

4. ANONYMITY. *McIntyre v. Ohio Elections Commission,* 514 U.S. 334, 115 S.Ct. 1511, 131 L.Ed.2d 426 (1995). An Ohio statute prohibited the distribution of anonymous campaign literature. Margaret McIntyre was fined $100 because she distributed leaflets (objecting to a proposed school tax levy) identifying her only as "concerned parents and taxpayers." The Ohio Supreme Court rejected her first amendment challenge, arguing that the law served to identify those who engage in fraud, libel, and false advertising. Stevens, J., for the Court, reversed and invalidated the statute.

An author is generally free to decide to be anonymous, for the decision to exclude her name, like other editorial decisions, is an aspect of free speech. She may be motivated by fear of economic, official, or social reprisal, or merely a desire to preserve her privacy, or have her speech evaluated without regard to its authorship. The Ohio law is limited to writings designed to influence an election ("core political speech") and so must be subjected to "exacting scrutiny." This law has "no language limiting its application to fraudulent, false, or libelous statements." It regulates speech based on its content (when its purpose is to influence an election). In this case, the name of the private author, probably unknown to the recipient of the handbill, adds "little, if anything, to the reader's ability to evaluate the document's message." The state, in short, may not seek "to punish fraud indirectly, by indiscriminately outlawing a category of speech, based on its content, with no necessary relationship to the danger sought to be prevented."

Buckley v. American Constitutional Law Foundation, Inc., 525 U.S. 182, 119 S.Ct. 636, 142 L.Ed.2d 599 (1999). Plaintiffs challenged various state restrictions on Colorado's initiative and referendum petition process. Ginsburg, J., for the Court, said that there is "no litmus paper test" to separate valid ballot access provisions from restrictions that violate free speech, and thus the Court must make "hard judgments" This narrowly drafted opinion considered three restraints that placed on the ballot-initiative process. First, only registered voters could circulate the initiative petitions. Second, the circulators had to wear an identification badge bearing their names. Third, the law required proponents of an initiative to report the names and addresses of all circulators who were paid to circulate the petitions and the amount paid to each of them.

The Court invalidated all three restrictions. The state laws, which limited the pool of potential circulators and deprived them of anonymity at the moment they sought to communicate their message to voters, were not justified by administrative efficiency or detection of fraud. For example,

Colorado's interest in enabling the public to identify and the state to apprehend any petition circulators who engage in misconduct is taken care of by another state requirement that circulators disclose their names and addresses on affidavits submitted with each petition section.

10–3.3 Defining the Public Forum

PERRY EDUCATION ASSOCIATION v. PERRY LOCAL EDUCATORS' ASSOCIATION
460 U.S. 37, 103 S.Ct. 948, 74 L.Ed.2d 794 (1983).

JUSTICE WHITE delivered the opinion of the Court.

Perry Education Association is the duly elected exclusive bargaining representative for the teachers of the Metropolitan School District of Perry Township, Indiana. A collective bargaining agreement with the Board of Education provided that Perry Education Association, but no other union, would have access to the interschool mail system and teacher mailboxes in the Perry Township schools. The issue in this case is whether the denial of similar access to the Perry Local Educators' Association, a rival teacher group, violates the First and Fourteenth Amendments.

The Metropolitan School District of Perry Township, Indiana, operates a public school system of thirteen separate schools. Each school building contains a set of mailboxes for the teachers. Interschool delivery by school employees permits messages to be delivered rapidly to teachers in the district. The primary function of this internal mail system is to transmit official messages among the teachers and between the teachers and the school administration. In addition, teachers use the system to send personal messages and individual school building principals have allowed delivery of messages from various private organizations.[2]

Prior to 1977, both the Perry Education Association (PEA) and the Perry Local Educators' Association (PLEA) represented teachers in the school district and apparently had equal access to the interschool mail system. In 1977, PLEA challenged PEA's status as *de facto* bargaining representative for the Perry Township teachers by filing an election petition with the Indiana Education Employment Relations Board (Board). PEA won the election and was certified as the exclusive representative, as provided by Indiana law.

The Board permits a school district to provide access to communication facilities to the union selected for the discharge of the exclusive representative duties of representing the bargaining unit and its individual members without having to provide equal access to rival unions. Following the election, PEA and the school district negotiated a labor contract in which the school board gave PEA "access to teachers'

---

2. Local parochial schools, church groups, YMCAs, and Cub Scout units have used the system. The record does not indicate whether any requests for use have been denied, nor does it reveal whether permission must separately be sought for every message that a group wishes delivered to the teachers.

mailboxes in which to insert material" and the right to use the inter-school mail delivery system to the extent that the school district incurred no extra expense by such use. The labor agreement noted that these access rights were being accorded to PEA "acting as the representative of the teachers" and went on to stipulate that these access rights shall not be granted to any other "school employee organization"—a term of art defined by Indiana law to mean "any organization which has school employees as members and one of whose primary purposes is representing school employees in dealing with their employer." The PEA contract with these provisions was renewed in 1980 and is presently in force.

The exclusive access policy applies only to use of the mailboxes and school mail system. PLEA is not prevented from using other school facilities to communicate with teachers. PLEA may post notices on school bulletin boards; may hold meetings on school property after school hours; and may, with approval of the building principals, make announcements on the public address system. Of course, PLEA also may communicate with teachers by word of mouth, telephone, or the United States mail. Moreover, under Indiana law, the preferential access of the bargaining agent may continue only while its status as exclusive representative is insulated from challenge. While a representation contest is in progress, unions must be afforded equal access to such communication facilities.

[Plaintiffs] sought injunctive and declaratory relief and damages. [The Seventh Circuit] held that once the school district "opens its internal mail system to PEA but denies it to PLEA, it violates both the Equal Protection Clause and the First Amendment." It acknowledged that PEA had "legal duties to the teachers that PLEA does not have" but reasoned that "without an independent reason why equal access for other labor groups and individual teachers is undesirable, the special duties of the incumbent do not justify opening the system to the incumbent alone."

... There is no question that constitutional interests are implicated by denying PLEA use of the interschool mail system.... But this is not to say that the First Amendment requires equivalent access to all parts of a school building in which some form of communicative activity occurs.... The existence of a right of access to public property and the standard by which limitations upon such a right must be evaluated differ depending on the character of the property at issue.

In places which by long tradition or by government fiat have been devoted to assembly and debate, the rights of the state to limit expressive activity are sharply circumscribed. At one end of the spectrum are streets and parks which "have immemorially been held in trust for the use of the public, and, time out of mind, have been used for purposes of assembly, communicating thoughts between citizens, and discussing public questions." In these quintessential public forums, the government may not prohibit all communicative activity. For the state to enforce a content-based exclusion it must show that its regulation is necessary to serve a compelling state interest and that it is narrowly drawn to achieve that end. *Carey v. Brown,* 447 U.S. 455, 461, 100 S.Ct. 2286, 2290, 65 L.Ed.2d 263 (1980). The state may also enforce regulations of the time, place, and manner of expression which are content-neutral, are narrowly tailored to serve a significant government interest, and leave open ample alternative channels of communication. *United States Postal Service v. Council of Greenburgh,* [noted infra].

A second category consists of public property which the state has opened for use by the public as a place for expressive activity. The Constitution forbids a state to enforce certain exclusions from a forum generally open to the public even if it was not required to create the forum in the first place. *Widmar v. Vincent,* 454 U.S. 263, 102 S.Ct. 269, 70 L.Ed.2d 440 (1981)(university meeting facilities).[7] Although a state is not required to indefinitely retain the open character of the facility, as long as it does so it is bound by the same standards as apply in a traditional public forum. Reasonable time, place and manner regulations are permissible, and a content-based prohibition must be narrowly drawn to effectuate a compelling state interest.

Public property which is not by tradition or designation a forum for public communication is governed by different standards. We have recognized that the "First Amendment does not guarantee access to property simply because it is owned or controlled by the government." *United States Postal Service v. Greenburgh Civic Ass'n,* supra. In addition to time, place, and manner regulations, the state may reserve the forum for its intended purposes, communicative or otherwise, as long as the regulation on speech is reasonable and not an effort to suppress expression merely because public officials oppose the speaker's view. As we have stated on several occasions, "the State, no less than a private owner of property, has power to preserve the property under its control for the use to which it is lawfully dedicated."

The school mail facilities at issue here fall within this third category. The Court of Appeals recognized that Perry School District's interschool mail system is not a traditional public forum: "We do not hold that a school's internal mail system is a public forum in the sense that a school board may not close it to all but official business if it chooses." On this point the parties agree. Nor do the parties dispute that, as the District Court observed, the "normal and intended function [of the school mail facilities] is to facilitate internal communication of school related matters to teachers." The internal mail system, at least by policy, is not held open to the general public. It is instead PLEA's position that the school mail facilities have become a "limited public forum" from which it may not be excluded because of the periodic use of the system by private nonschool connected groups, and PLEA's own unrestricted access to the system prior to PEA's certification as exclusive representative.

7. A public forum may be created for a limited purpose such as use by certain groups, e.g., *Widmar v. Vincent* (student groups), or for the discussion of certain subjects, e.g., *City of Madison Joint School District v. Wisconsin Employment Relations Comm'n,* 429 U.S. 167, 97 S.Ct. 421, 50 L.Ed.2d 376 (1976)(school board business).

Neither of these arguments is persuasive. The use of the internal school mail by groups not affiliated with the schools is no doubt a relevant consideration. If by policy or by practice the Perry School District has opened its mail system for indiscriminate use by the general public, then PLEA could justifiably argue a public forum has been created. This, however, is not the case. As the case comes before us, there is no indication in the record that the school mailboxes and interschool delivery system are open for use by the general public. Permission to use the system to communicate with teachers must be secured from the individual building principal. There is no court finding or evidence in the record which demonstrates that this permission has been granted as a matter of course to all who seek to distribute material. We can only conclude that the schools do allow some outside organizations such as the YMCA, Cub Scouts, and other civic and church organizations to use the facilities. This type of selective access does not transform government property into a public forum. In *Greer v. Spock,* 424 U.S., at 838 n. 10, 96 S.Ct., at 1217 n. 10, the fact that other civilian speakers and entertainers had sometimes been invited to appear at Fort Dix did not convert the military base into a public forum. And in *Lehman v. Shaker Heights,* [noted infra], a plurality of the Court concluded that a city transit system's rental of space in its vehicles for commercial advertising did not require it to accept partisan political advertising.

Moreover, even if we assume that by granting access to the Cub Scouts, YMCAs, and parochial schools, the school district has created a "limited" public forum, the constitutional right of access would in any event extend only to other entities of similar character. While the school mail facilities thus might be a forum generally open for use by the Girl Scouts, the local boys' club and other organizations that engage in activities of interest and educational relevance to students, they would not as a consequence be open to an organization such as PLEA, which is concerned with the terms and conditions of teacher employment.

PLEA also points to its ability to use the school mailboxes and delivery system on an equal footing with PEA prior to the collective bargaining agreement signed in 1978. Its argument appears to be that the access policy in effect at that time converted the school mail facilities into a limited public forum generally open for use by employee organizations, and that once this occurred, exclusions of employee organizations thereafter must be judged by the constitutional standard applicable to public forums. The fallacy in the argument is that it is not the forum, but PLEA itself, which has changed. Prior to 1977, there was no exclusive representative for the Perry school district teachers. PEA and PLEA each represented its own members. Therefore the school district's policy of allowing both organizations to use the school mail facilities simply reflected the fact that both unions represented the teachers and had legitimate reasons for use of the system. PLEA's previous access was consistent with the school district's preservation of the facilities for school-related business, and did not constitute creation of a public forum in any broader sense.

Because the school mail system is not a public forum, the School District had no "constitutional obligation per se to let any organization use the school mail boxes." In the Court of Appeals' view, however, the access policy adopted by the Perry schools favors a particular viewpoint, that of the PEA, on labor relations, and consequently must be strictly scrutinized regardless of whether a public forum is involved. There is, however, no indication that the school board intended to discourage one viewpoint and advance another. We believe it is more accurate to characterize the access policy as based on the *status* of the respective unions rather than their views. Implicit in the concept of the nonpublic forum is the right to make distinctions in access on the basis of subject matter and speaker identity. These distinctions may be impermissible in a public forum but are inherent and inescapable in the process of limiting a nonpublic forum to activities compatible with the intended purpose of the property. The touchstone for evaluating these distinctions is whether they are reasonable in light of the purpose which the forum at issue serves.

The differential access provided PEA and PLEA is reasonable because it is wholly consistent with the district's legitimate interest in "preserv[ing] the property ... for the use to which it is lawfully dedicated." Use of school mail facilities enables PEA to perform effectively its obligations as exclusive representative of *all* Perry Township teachers. Conversely, PLEA does not have any official responsibility in connection with the school district and need not be entitled to the same rights of access to school mailboxes. . . . Moreover, exclusion of the rival union may reasonably be considered a means of insuring labor-peace within the schools. The policy "serves to prevent the District's schools from becoming a battlefield for inter-union squabbles."

The Court of Appeals accorded little or no weight to PEA's special responsibilities. In its view these responsibilities, while justifying PEA's access, did not justify denying equal access to PLEA. The Court of Appeals would have been correct if a public forum were involved here. But the internal mail system is not a public forum. As we have already stressed, when government property is not dedicated to open communication the government may—without further justification—restrict use to those who participate in the forum's official business.

Finally, the reasonableness of the limitations on PLEA's access to the school mail system is also supported by the substantial alternative channels that remain open for union-teacher communication to take place. These means range from bulletin boards to meeting facilities to the United States mail. During election periods, PLEA is assured of equal access to all modes of communication. There is no showing here that PLEA's ability to communicate with teachers is seriously impinged by the restricted access to the internal mail system. The variety and type of alternative modes of access present here compare favorably with those in other nonpublic forum cases where we have upheld restrictions on access.

The Court of Appeals also held that the differential access provided the rival unions constituted impermissible content discrimination in violation of the Equal Protection Clause of the Fourteenth Amendment. We have rejected this contention when cast as a First Amendment argument, and it fares no better in equal protection garb. As we have explained above, PLEA did not have a First Amendment or other right of access to the interschool mail system. The grant of such access to PEA, therefore, does not burden a fundamental right of the PLEA. Thus, the decision to grant such privileges to the PEA need not be tested by the strict scrutiny applied when government action impinges upon a fundamental right protected by the Constitution. The school district's policy need only rationally further a legitimate state purpose. That purpose is clearly found in the special responsibilities of an exclusive bargaining representative.

The Seventh Circuit and PLEA rely on *Police Department of Chicago v. Mosley,* 408 U.S. 92, 92 S.Ct. 2286, 33 L.Ed.2d 212 (1972) and *Carey v. Brown,* 447 U.S. 455, 100 S.Ct. 2286, 65 L.Ed.2d 263 (1980). In *Mosley* and *Carey,* we struck down prohibitions on peaceful picketing in a public forum. In *Mosley,* the City of Chicago permitted peaceful picketing on the subject of a school's labor-management dispute, but prohibited other picketing in the immediate vicinity of the school. In *Carey,* the challenged state statute barred all picketing of residences and dwellings except the peaceful picketing of a place of employment involved in a labor dispute. In both cases, we found the distinction between classes of speech violative of the Equal Protection Clause. The key to those decisions, however, was the presence of a public forum. In a public forum, by definition, all parties have a constitutional right of access and the state must demonstrate compelling reasons for restricting access to a single class of speakers, a single viewpoint, or a single subject.

When speakers and subjects are similarly situated, the state may not pick and choose. Conversely on government property that has not been made a public forum, not all speech is equally situated, and the state may draw distinctions which relate to the special purpose for which the property is used. As we have explained above, for a school mail facility, the difference in status between the exclusive bargaining representative and its rival is such a distinction.

The Court of Appeals invalidated the limited privileges PEA negotiated as the bargaining voice of the Perry Township teachers by misapplying our cases that have dealt with the rights of free expression on streets, parks and other fora generally open for assembly and debate. Virtually every other court to consider this type of exclusive access policy has upheld it as constitutional, and today, so do we. The judgment of the Court of Appeals is

Reversed.

JUSTICE BRENNAN, with whom JUSTICE MARSHALL, JUSTICE POWELL, and JUSTICE STEVENS join, dissenting. . . .

The Court fundamentally misperceives the essence of the respondents' claims and misunderstands the thrust of the Court of Appeals' well-reasoned opinion. This case does not involve an "absolute access" claim. It involves an "equal access" claim. As such it does not turn on whether the internal school mail system is a "public forum." In focusing on the public forum issue, the Court disregards the First Amendment's central proscription against censorship, in the form of viewpoint discrimination, in any forum, public or nonpublic.

The First Amendment's prohibition against government discrimination among viewpoints on particular issues falling within the realm of protected speech has been noted extensively in the opinions of this Court. In *Niemotko v. Maryland,* 340 U.S. 268, 71 S.Ct. 325, 95 L.Ed. 267 (1951), two Jehovah's Witnesses were denied access to a public park to give Bible talks. Members of other religious organizations had been granted access to the park for purposes related to religion. The Court found that the denial of access was based on public officials' disagreement with the Jehovah's Witnesses' views, and held it invalid. During the course of its opinion, the Court stated: "The right to equal protection of the laws, in the exercise of those freedoms of speech and religion protected by the First and Fourteenth Amendments, has a firmer foundation than the whims or personal opinions of a local governing body." . . .

City of Madison Joint School District v. Wisconsin Employment Relations Commission, [429 U.S. 167, 97 S.Ct. 421, 50 L.Ed.2d 376 (1976)], considered the question of whether a state may constitutionally require a board of education to prohibit teachers other than union representatives from speaking at public meetings about matters relating to pending collective bargaining negotiations. The board had been found guilty of a prohibited labor practice for permitting a teacher to speak who opposed one of the proposals advanced by the union in contract negotiations. The board was ordered to cease and desist from permitting employees, other than union representatives, to appear and to speak at board meetings on matters subject to collective bargaining. We held this order invalid. During the course of our opinion we stated: "Whatever its duties as an employer, when the board sits in public meetings to conduct public business and hear the views of citizens, it may not be required to discriminate between speakers on the basis of their employment, or the content of their speech."

There is another line of cases, closely related to those implicating the prohibition against viewpoint discrimination, that have addressed the First Amendment principle of subject matter, or content, neutrality. Generally, the concept of content neutrality prohibits the government from choosing the subjects that are appropriate for public discussion. The content neutrality cases frequently refer to the prohibition against viewpoint discrimination and both concepts have their roots in the First

Amendment's bar against censorship. But unlike the viewpoint discrimination concept, which is used to strike down government restrictions on speech by particular speakers, the content neutrality principle is invoked when the government has imposed restrictions on speech related to an entire subject area. The content neutrality principle can be seen as an outgrowth of the core First Amendment prohibition against viewpoint discrimination.

We have invoked the prohibition against content discrimination to invalidate government restrictions on access to public forums. We also have relied on this prohibition to strike down restrictions on access to a limited public forum. Finally, we have applied the doctrine of content neutrality to government regulation of protected speech in cases in which no restriction of access to public property was involved.

Admittedly, this Court has not always required content neutrality in restrictions on access to government property. We upheld content-based exclusions in *Lehman v. City of Shaker Heights,* [noted infra], in *Greer v. Spock,* 424 U.S. 828, 96 S.Ct. 1211, 47 L.Ed.2d 505 (1976), and in *Jones v. North Carolina Prisoners' Union,* 433 U.S. 119, 97 S.Ct. 2532, 53 L.Ed.2d 629 (1977). All three cases involved an unusual forum, which was found to be nonpublic, and the speech was determined for a variety of reasons to be incompatible with the forum. These cases provide some support for the notion that the government is permitted to exclude certain subjects from discussion in nonpublic forums.[3] They provide no support, however, for the notion that government, once it has opened up government property for discussion of specific subjects, may discriminate among viewpoints on those topics. Although *Greer, Lehman,* and *Jones* permitted content-based restrictions, none of the cases involved viewpoint discrimination. All of the restrictions were viewpoint-neutral. We expressly noted in *Greer* that the exclusion was "objectively and even-handedly applied.... "[4]

Once the government permits discussion of certain subject matter, it may not impose restrictions that discriminate among viewpoints on those subjects whether a nonpublic forum is involved or not.[5] ... We

---

3. There are several factors suggesting that these decisions are narrow and of limited importance. First, the forums involved were unusual. A military base was involved in *Greer v. Spock,* advertising space on a city transit system in *Lehman v. City of Shaker Heights,* and a prison in *Jones v. North Carolina Prisoners' Union.* Moreover, the speech involved was arguably incompatible with each forum, especially in *Greer,* which involved speeches and demonstrations of a partisan political nature on a military base, and in *Jones,* which involved labor union organizational activities in a prison....

4. In his concurring opinion in *Greer v. Spock,* supra, Justice Powell noted the absence of any viewpoint discrimination in the

regulations and stated that the military authorities would be barred from discriminating among viewpoints on political issues....

5. This is not to suggest that a government may not close a nonpublic forum altogether or limit access to the forum to those involved in the "official business" of the agency. Restrictions of this type are consistent with the government's right "to preserve the property under its control for the use to which it is lawfully dedicated." Limiting access to a nonpublic government forum to those involved in the "official business" of the agency also protects the government's interest, *qua* government, in speaking clearly and definitively.

have never held that government may allow discussion of a subject and then discriminate among viewpoints on that particular topic, even if the government for certain reasons may entirely exclude discussion of the subject from the forum. In this context, the greater power does not include the lesser because for First Amendment purposes exercise of the lesser power is more threatening to core values. Viewpoint discrimination is censorship in its purest form and government regulation that discriminates among viewpoints threatens the continued vitality of "free speech."

Against this background, it is clear that the Court's approach to this case is flawed. By focusing on whether the interschool mail system is a public forum, the Court disregards the independent First Amendment protection afforded by the prohibition against viewpoint discrimination. This case does not involve a claim of an absolute right of access to the forum to discuss any subject whatever. If it did, public forum analysis might be relevant. This case involves a claim of equal access to discuss a subject that the board has approved for discussion in the forum. In essence, the respondents are not asserting a right of access at all; they are asserting a right to be free from discrimination. The critical inquiry, therefore, is whether the board's grant of exclusive access to the petitioner amounts to prohibited viewpoint discrimination. . . .

On a practical level, the only reason for the petitioner to seek an exclusive access policy is to deny its rivals access to an effective channel of communication. No other group is explicitly denied access to the mail system. In fact, as the Court points out, many other groups have been granted access to the system. Apparently, access is denied to the respondents because of the likelihood of their expressing points of view different from the petitioner's on a range of subjects. The very argument the petitioner advances in support of the policy, the need to preserve labor peace, also indicates that the access policy is not viewpoint-neutral.

In short, the exclusive access policy discriminates against the respondents based on their viewpoint. The board has agreed to amplify the speech of the petitioner, while repressing the speech of the respondents based on the respondents' point of view. This sort of discrimination amounts to censorship and infringes the First Amendment rights of the respondents. . . . While the board may have a legitimate interest in granting the petitioner access to the system it has no legitimate interest in making that access exclusive by denying access to the respondents. . . .

The petitioner also argues, and the Court agrees, that the exclusive access policy is justified by the state's interest in preserving labor peace. As the Court of Appeals found, there is no evidence on this record that granting access to the respondents would result in labor instability. In addition, there is no reason to assume that the respondents' messages would be any more likely to cause labor discord when received by members of the majority union than the petitioner's messages would when received by the respondents. . . .

Although the state's interest in preserving labor peace in the schools in order to prevent disruption is unquestionably substantial, merely articulating the interest is not enough to sustain the exclusive access policy in this case. There must be some showing that the asserted interest is advanced by the policy. In the absence of such a showing, the exclusive access policy must fall. . . .

Notes

1. FAIRGROUNDS. *Heffron v. International Society for Krishna Conscious-ness, Inc.,* 452 U.S. 640, 101 S.Ct. 2559, 69 L.Ed.2d 298 (1981) upheld the power of Minnesota to require a religious organization desiring to distribute and sell religious literature and solicit donations at a state fair to do so only at an assigned booth within the fairgrounds. These booths were rented to anyone on a first come, first serve basis. The state fair rule applied to all enterprises, whether nonprofit, charitable, or commercial. It also allowed anyone to engage in face to face discussions with fair visitors anywhere on the fairgrounds. The Krishna Society argued that one of its religious rituals, "Sankirtan," required its members to distribute and sell religious literature and solicit donations.

The Court upheld the rule as a reasonable time, place, and manner regulation, justified without reference to the content of the speech. The method of allocating rental space was nondiscriminatory. The rule served a significant government interest because of the state's special need to maintain the orderly movement of the crowd, given the large number of exhibitors and visitors attending the fair. Unlike a city street, which is "a place where people may enjoy the open air or the company of friends and neighbors in a relaxed environment," a state fair "is a temporary event attracting great numbers of visitors who come to the event for a short period to see and experience the host of exhibits and attractions at the fair. The flow of the crowd and demands of safety are more pressing in the context of the fair." Less restrictive alternatives, such as penalizing disorder and disruption, would probably not work because any exemption applied to the Krishna Society would have to apply to a large number of other groups, including religious, social, political, charitable, and perhaps even commercial organizations. "[F]or present purposes," religious organizations do not "enjoy rights to communicate, distribute, and solicit on the fairgrounds superior to those of other organizations having social, political, or other ideological messages to proselytize."

2. PICKETING. *United States v. Grace,* 461 U.S. 171, 103 S.Ct. 1702, 75 L.Ed.2d 736 (1983). Section 13k of 40 U.S.C.A. prohibited the "display [of] any flag, banner, or device designed or adapted to bring into public notice any party, organization, or movement" in the U.S. Supreme Court building and on its "grounds," which were defined to include the public sidewalks surrounding the Supreme Court building. The Court held that, to the extent section 13k applied to the public sidewalks surrounding the Supreme Court building, it was unconstitutional. Banning the specified conduct on these sidewalks is no more necessary to judicial tranquility "than on any other sidewalks in the city." In contrast to the public sidewalks, the actual Supreme Court building and grounds (although publicly owned) have "not been traditionally held open for the use of the public for expressive activi-

ties." This property "is not transformed into a 'public forum' merely because the public is permitted to freely enter and leave the grounds at practically all times and the public is admitted to the building during specified hours."

Boos v. Barry, 485 U.S. 312, 108 S.Ct. 1157, 99 L.Ed.2d 333 (1988). The first part of a federal statute, called the "display clause," prohibited the display of any sign within 500 feet of a foreign embassy if that sign tends to bring the foreign government into "public odium" or "public disrepute." It applied only to signs, not the spoken word. The Court invalidated that provision as a content-based restriction on political speech in the public forum. The Government argued that the law served a compelling state interest—our international law obligation to shield diplomats from speech that offends their dignity. Even assuming that such an interest was compelling—and the Court said that it was "not persuaded" that differences between American citizens (who must tolerate "insulting and even outrageous speech") and foreign officials "require us to deviate from these principles here"—the law was not "narrowly tailored" to serve that interest. A significantly less restrictive alternative would be a statute prohibiting anyone from attempting to intimidate, obstruct, or harass a foreign official. Indeed, Congress had already enacted such a statute for the rest of the country.

The Court upheld the second portion of the statute, the "congregation clause," which prohibited three or more people from congregating within 500 feet of the embassy if the congregation is directed at the embassy and if the people refuse to disperse after having been ordered to do so by the police. The lower court had narrowly interpreted the statute to allow the police to order dispersal "only when the police reasonably believe that a threat to the security or peace of the embassy is present." As interpreted, the statute was not impermissibly vague.

In *Frisby v. Schultz,* 487 U.S. 474, 108 S.Ct. 2495, 101 L.Ed.2d 420 (1988), a divided Court, speaking through O'Connor, J., rejected a facial challenge to an ordinance completely banning picketing "before or about" any residence. Persons opposed to abortion picketed on a public street in front of the residence of a doctor who performed abortions. The picketing, though generally orderly and peaceful, generated controversy and the town responded by enacting a broad ban, making it "unlawful for any person to engage in picketing before or about the residence or dwelling of any individual in the Town of Brookfield."

The Supreme Court interpreted the ordinance narrowly, as prohibiting "only picketing focused on," and taking place "solely in front of a particular residence." In contrast, marching through residential neighborhoods "or even walking a route in front of an entire block of houses, is not prohibited by this ordinance." Although a residential public street is "the archetype of a traditional public forum," the state's interest in protecting residential privacy and the unwilling listener was important. "The type of focused picketing prohibited by the Brookfield ordinance is fundamentally different from more generally directed means of communication that may not be completely banned in residential areas," such as handbilling, solicitation, or marching. This picketing "is narrowly directed at the household, not the public." Even "if some such picketers have a broader communicative purpose, their activity nonetheless inherently and offensively intrudes on residential privacy." The Court emphasized that it was only rejecting a facial challenge to the law. Specific applications of the law—"for example, a particular resident's use of his or her home as a place of business or public meeting, or to picketers present at a particular home by invitation of the resident—may present somewhat different questions."

Brennan, J., joined by Marshall, J., dissented, and would allow the Government to regulate the number of residential picketers, the hours during which the picketing could take place, and the noise level of the picketing, but would not allow the Government to ban residential picketing in its entirety. Stevens, J., also dissented. He believed that the ordinance was overbroad, because its language covered picketing to willing and indifferent recipients. For example, the ordinance would literally prohibit a fifth grader from carrying a sign in front of a residence that simply said, "Get well Charlie—Our team needs you."

3. CHARITABLE SOLICITATION ON GOVERNMENT PROPERTY. *Cornelius v. NAACP Legal Defense and Educational Fund, Inc.*, 473 U.S. 788, 105 S.Ct. 3439, 87 L.Ed.2d 567 (1985). The Combined Federal Campaign (CFC) is a charity drive directed at federal employees during working hours. An Executive Order limited participation to tax-exempt, nonprofit charitable agencies providing direct health and welfare services to individuals or their families. The Order specifically excluded legal defense and political advocacy organizations. The Court (4 to 3) (Marshall and Powell did not participate) upheld the constitutionality of the Executive Order.

Charitable solicitation is a form of free speech, and the relevant forum is the CFC, not the federal workplace, because the respondents only seek access to a particular means of communication, the CFC. The CFC is a nonpublic forum because neither the Government's practice nor policy suggested any intent to convert the CFC into a public forum open to all tax-exempt organizations. The charitable organizations need permission to solicit, and while "the record does not show how many organizations have been denied permission throughout the 24–year history of CFC, there is no evidence suggesting that the granting of the requisite permission is merely ministerial."

Control "over access to a nonpublic forum can be based on subject matter and speaker identity so long as the distinctions drawn are reasonable in light of the purpose served by the forum and are viewpoint neutral." It was reasonable for the Government to conclude that money given directly for food and shelter to the needy is more beneficial than money given for litigation, and the restrictions on access avoided the appearance of government favoritism with particular viewpoints. The Court remanded to determine whether the Government impermissibly excluded the respondents from the CFC because it disagreed with their viewpoints.

Blackmun, J., joined by Brennan, J., dissented, accepted *Perry*, but argued: "Rather than taking the nature of the property into account in balancing the First Amendment interests of the speaker and society's interest in freedom of speech against the interests served by reserving the property to its normal use, the Court simply labels the property and dispenses with the balancing." Stevens, J. also dissented, questioning whether the *Perry* analysis was "particularly helpful," because none of the advocacy organizations would receive any CFC donations unless the employees specifically designated such an organization.

In *Arkansas Educational Television Commission v. Forbes*, 523 U.S. 666, 118 S.Ct. 1633, 140 L.Ed.2d 875 (1998), the Court elaborated on the criteria of a "nonpublic forum." Designated public fora, in contrast to traditional public fora, like the streets and parks, are created by "purposeful governmental action," to make the property "generally available." A "designated public forum is not created when the government allows selective access for individual speakers rather than general access for a class of speakers." If a university makes its meeting facilities "generally open" to registered student groups, it would create a designated public forum. "General access" indicates that "the property is a designated public forum," while "selective access" indicates "the property is a nonpublic forum." "The *Cornelius* distinction between general and selective access furthers First Amendment interests. By recognizing the distinction, we encourage the government to open its property to some expressive activity in cases where, if faced with an all-or-nothing choice, it might not open the property at all."

4.   SCHOOL ASSEMBLIES. *Bethel School District No. 403 v. Fraser*, 478 U.S. 675, 106 S.Ct. 3159, 92 L.Ed.2d 549 (1986) upheld (7 to 2) a broad power of school authorities to discipline a student for delivering at the school assembly a speech that promoted a student government candidate by using "pervasive sexual innuendo," e.g., by describing his candidate as "a man who is firm—he's firm in his pants, he's firm in his shirt, his character is firm—but most of all, his belief in you, the students of Bethel, is firm." The school suspended the 17 year old student for two days. The audience of about 600 students included students 14 years old or older. Some responded to the speech with hooting and yelling; others responded "by gestures [that] graphically simulated the sexual activities pointedly alluded to in respondent's speech."

Burger, C.J., for the Court, said: "Surely it is a highly appropriate function of public school education to prohibit the use of vulgar and offensive terms in public discourse." Burger called the speech "obscene," and said that it "was plainly offensive to both teachers and students," was "acutely insulting to teen-age girl students," and "could well be seriously damaging to its less mature audience, many of whom were only 14 years old and on the threshold of awareness of human sexuality." The penalties imposed in this case also "were unrelated to any political viewpoint." Brennan, J., concurred in the judgment, arguing that the speech was no more obscene "than the bulk of programs currently on prime-time television or in the local cinema," but it may be punished as "disruptive."

Marshall, J., dissented, noting that the lower courts had concluded that the Board of Education had not shown any disruption of the educational process. Stevens, J., also dissented. The student "should not be disciplined for speaking frankly in a school assembly if he had no reason to anticipate punitive consequences." The speaker was in a better position to determine whether his audience would be offended "than is a group of judges who are at least two generations, and 3,000 miles away from the scene of the crime."

5. SCHOOL NEWSPAPERS. *Hazelwood School District v. Kuhlmeier,* 484 U.S. 260, 108 S.Ct. 562, 98 L.Ed.2d 592 (1988)(5–3) held that educators may exercise broad editorial control over the contents of a high school newspaper produced as part of the school's journalism curriculum.[1] There was no first amendment violation when the principal did not allow the school-sponsored newspaper to publish two articles, one dealing with student pregnancy and the other dealing with the impact of divorce on students. The principal was concerned that it might be easy to identify the pregnant students from the story and that the references to sexual activity and birth control were inappropriate for some of the younger students. He also believed that the second article should not be published unless the person criticized had the opportunity to defend himself.

Under *Perry,* the school newspaper was not a public forum because the school authorities did not open it for indiscriminate use by the general public: the students publishing the newspaper received grades and academic credit; the newspaper was produced as part of a class; the journalism teacher exercised a great deal of authority over the newspaper, such as the power to assign story ideas and edit stories; the principal reviewed each issue prior to publication; and the school subsidized the school newspaper's annual budget. This case concerns "educators' authority over school-sponsored publications, theatrical productions, and other expressive activities that students, parents, and members of the public might reasonably perceive to bear the imprimatur of the school." These activities may be considered part of the school curriculum, even if they do not occur in a traditional classroom setting, "so long as they are supervised by faculty members and designed to impart particular knowledge or skills to student participants and audiences." A school, in its capacity as publisher of a school newspaper or producer of a school play, may "disassociate itself" from speech that is "ungrammatical, poorly written, inadequately researched, biased or prejudiced, vulgar or profane, or unsuitable for immature audiences." Educators may exercise editorial control over the style and content of student speech "in school-sponsored activities so long as their actions are reasonably related to legitimate pedagogical concerns." There is a violation of free speech only when the censorship of the school-sponsored activity "has no valid educational purpose".

6. POLLING PLACES. A Tennessee law (like the law of many other jurisdictions) prohibited the solicitation of votes and the display or distribution of campaign materials within 100 feet of the entrance to a polling place. The Tennessee Supreme Court held that the law violated the first and fourteenth amendments, but the Supreme Court, with no majority opinion, reversed. *Burson v. Freeman,* 504 U.S. 191, 112 S.Ct. 1846, 119 L.Ed.2d 5 (1992). Blackmun, J., joined by Rehnquist, C.J. & White & Kennedy, JJ., agreed that the law, on its face, was a content-based restriction on speech in a public forum, and must be subjected to exacting scrutiny, but it was constitutional because it served a compelling state interest: to prevent voter intimidation and election fraud. "The only way to preserve the secrecy of the ballot is to limit access to the area around the voter." The next question is

---

1. In a footnote the Court stated: "We need not now decide whether the same degree of deference is appropriate with respect to school-sponsored expressive activities at the college and university level."

"*how large* a restricted zone is permissible or sufficiently tailored." The plurality rejected the argument that the 100 foot boundary was not narrowly tailored. Admittedly, the state had no empirical proof, but "it is difficult to make specific findings about the effects of a voting regulation." The Tennessee Supreme Court had required that the boundary be reduced to 25 feet, but it takes only about 15 seconds to walk the 75 additional feet. The plurality concluded that a 100 foot boundary is on the constitutional side of the line. It is the rare case where "we have held that a law survives strict scrutiny. This, however, is such a rare case."

Scalia, J., concurring in the judgment, argued that, if the category of "traditional public forum" is to be an analytical tool rather than a conclusory label, "it must remain faithful to its name and derive its content from *tradition*." The area around the polling booth, by tradition, was not a public forum. He saw the law as a reasonable, viewpoint-neutral regulation of a nonpublic forum. Kennedy, J. concurred. Stevens, J., joined by O'Connor & Souter, JJ., dissented, arguing that the evidence that Tennessee introduced at trial to justify the 100 foot campaign-free zone was "exceptionally thin."

INTERNATIONAL SOCIETY FOR KRISHNA CONSCIOUSNESS, INC. v. LEE
505 U.S. 672, 112 S.Ct. 2701, 120 L.Ed.2d 541 (1992).

CHIEF JUSTICE REHNQUIST delivered the opinion of the Court.

In this case we consider whether an airport terminal operated by a public authority is a public forum and whether a regulation prohibiting solicitation in the interior of an airport terminal violates the First Amendment.

The relevant facts in this case are not in dispute. Petitioner International Society for Krishna Consciousness, Inc. (ISKCON) is a not-for-profit religious corporation whose members perform a ritual known as *sankirtan*. The ritual consists of " 'going into public places, disseminating religious literature and soliciting funds to support the religion.' "The primary purpose of this ritual is raising funds for the movement. . . .

The airports [that the Port Authority own and operate] are funded by user fees and operated to make a regulated profit. Most space at the three airports is leased to commercial airlines, which bear primary responsibility for the leasehold. The Port Authority retains control over unleased portions, including La Guardia's Central Terminal Building, portions of Kennedy's International Arrivals Building, and Newark's North Terminal Building (we refer to these areas collectively as the "terminals"). The terminals are generally accessible to the general public and contain various commercial establishments such as restaurants, snack stands, bars, newsstands, and stores of various types. Virtually all who visit the terminals do so for purposes related to air travel. These visitors principally include passengers, those meeting or seeing off passengers, flight crews, and terminal employees.

The Port Authority has adopted a regulation forbidding within the terminals the repetitive solicitation of money or distribution of literature. The regulation states:

"1. The following conduct is prohibited within the interior areas of buildings or structures at an air terminal if conducted by a person to or with passers-by in a continuous or repetitive manner:

"(a) The sale or distribution of any merchandise, including but not limited to jewelry, food stuffs, candles, flowers, badges and clothing.

"(b) The sale or distribution of flyers, brochures, pamphlets, books or any other printed or written material.

"(c) Solicitation and receipt of funds."

The regulation governs only the terminals; The Port Authority permits solicitation and distribution on the sidewalks outside the terminal buildings. The regulation effectively prohibits petitioner from performing *sankirtan* in the terminals.

The Court of Appeals affirmed in part and reversed in part. [A] divided panel concluded that the terminals are not public fora. As a result, the restrictions were required only to satisfy a standard of reasonableness. The Court of Appeals then concluded that, presented with the issue, this Court would find that the ban on solicitation was reasonable, but the ban on distribution was not....[3]

... Where the government is acting as a proprietor, managing its internal operations, rather than acting as lawmaker with the power to regulate or license, its action will not be subjected to the heightened review to which its actions as a lawmaker may be subject. Thus, we have upheld a ban on political advertisements in city-operated transit vehicles, *Lehman v. City of Shaker Heights,* even though the city permitted other types of advertising on those vehicles. Similarly, we have permitted a school district to limit access to an internal mail system used to communicate with teachers employed by the district. *Perry Education Assn. v. Perry Local Educators' Ass'n.*

[A] traditional public forum is property that has as "a principal purpose ... the free exchange of ideas." Moreover, consistent with the notion that the government—like other property owners—"has power to preserve the property under its control for the use to which it is lawfully dedicated," the government does not create a public forum by inaction. Nor is a public forum created "whenever members of the public are permitted freely to visit a place owned or operated by the Government." The decision to create a public forum must instead be made "by intentionally opening a nontraditional forum for public discourse." Finally, we have recognized that the location of property also has bearing because separation from acknowledged public areas may serve to indicate that the separated property is a special enclave, subject to greater restriction.

These precedents foreclose the conclusion that airport terminals are public fora. Reflecting the general growth of the air travel industry,

---

3. We deal here only with ISKCON's petition raising the permissibility of solicitation. Respondent's cross-petition concerning the leafletting ban is disposed of in the companion case, *Lee v. International Society for Krishna Consciousness, Inc.*

airport terminals have only recently achieved their contemporary size and character. But given the lateness with which the modern air terminal has made its appearance, it hardly qualifies for the description of having "immemorially . . . time out of mind" been held in the public trust and used for purposes of expressive activity. Moreover, even within the rather short history of air transport, it is only "[i]n recent years [that] it has become a common practice for various religious and non-profit organizations to use commercial airports as a forum for the distribution of literature, the solicitation of funds, the proselytizing of new members, and other similar activities." Thus, the tradition of airport activity does not demonstrate that airports have historically been made available for speech activity. Nor can we say that these particular terminals, or airport terminals generally, have been intentionally opened by their operators to such activity; the frequent and continuing litigation evidencing the operators' objections belies any such claim. In short, there can be no argument that society's time-tested judgment, expressed through acquiescence in a continuing practice, has resolved the issue in petitioner's favor.

Petitioner attempts to circumvent the history and practice governing airport activity by pointing our attention to the variety of speech activity that it claims historically occurred at various "transportation nodes" such as rail stations, bus stations, wharves, and Ellis Island. Even if we were inclined to accept petitioner's historical account describing speech activity at these locations, an account respondent contests, we think that such evidence is of little import for two reasons. First, much of the evidence is irrelevant to *public* fora analysis, because sites such as bus and rail terminals traditionally have had *private* ownership. The development of privately owned parks that ban speech activity would not change the public fora status of publicly held parks. But the reverse is also true. The practices of privately held transportation centers do not bear on the government's regulatory authority over a publicly owned airport.

Second, the relevant unit for our inquiry is an airport, not "transportation nodes" generally. When new methods of transportation develop, new methods for accommodating that transportation are also likely to be needed. And with each new step, it therefore will be a new inquiry whether the transportation necessities are compatible with various kinds of expressive activity. To make a category of "transportation nodes," therefore, would unjustifiably elide what may prove to be critical differences of which we should rightfully take account. The "security magnet," for example, is an airport commonplace that lacks a counterpart in bus terminals and train stations. And public access to air terminals is also not infrequently restricted—just last year the Federal Aviation Administration required airports for a 4–month period to limit access to areas normally publicly accessible. To blithely equate airports with other transportation centers, therefore, would be a mistake.

The differences among such facilities are unsurprising since, as the Court of Appeals noted, airports are commercial establishments funded by users fees and designed to make a regulated profit, and where nearly all who visit do so for some travel related purpose. As commercial enterprises, airports must provide services attractive to the marketplace. In light of this, it cannot fairly be said that an airport terminal has a principal purpose "promoting the free exchange of ideas." To the contrary, the record demonstrates that Port Authority management considers the purpose of the terminals to be the facilitation of passenger air travel, not the promotion of expression. . . .

The restrictions here challenged, therefore, need only satisfy a requirement of reasonableness. [T]he restriction " 'need only be *reasonable; it need not be the most reasonable or the only reasonable limitation.'* "We have no doubt that under this standard the prohibition on solicitation passes muster.

We have on many prior occasions noted the disruptive effect that solicitation may have on business. "Solicitation requires action by those who would respond: The individual solicited must decide whether or not to contribute (which itself might involve reading the solicitor's literature or hearing his pitch), and then, having decided to do so, reach for a wallet, search it for money, write a check, or produce a credit card." Passengers who wish to avoid the solicitor may have to alter their path, slowing both themselves and those around them. The result is that the normal flow of traffic is impeded. This is especially so in an airport, where "air travelers, who are often weighted down by cumbersome baggage . . . may be hurrying to catch a plane or to arrange ground transportation." Delays may be particularly costly in this setting, as a flight missed by only a few minutes can result in hours worth of subsequent inconvenience.

In addition, face-to-face solicitation presents risks of duress that are an appropriate target of regulation. The skillful, and unprincipled, solicitor can target the most vulnerable, including those accompanying children or those suffering physical impairment and who cannot easily avoid the solicitation. The unsavory solicitor can also commit fraud through concealment of his affiliation or through deliberate efforts to shortchange those who agree to purchase. Compounding this problem is the fact that, in an airport, the targets of such activity frequently are on tight schedules. This in turn makes such visitors unlikely to stop and formally complain to airport authorities. As a result, the airport faces considerable difficulty in achieving its legitimate interest in monitoring solicitation activity to assure that travelers are not interfered with unduly.

The Port Authority has concluded that its interest in monitoring the activities can best be accomplished by limiting solicitation and distribution to the sidewalk areas outside the terminals. This sidewalk area is frequented by an overwhelming percentage of airport users. [I]t would be odd to conclude that the Port Authority's terminal regulation is unreasonable despite the Port Authority having otherwise assured access to an area universally traveled.

The inconveniences to passengers and the burdens on Port Authority officials flowing from solicitation activity may seem small, but viewed against the fact that "pedestrian congestion is one of the greatest problems facing the three terminals," the Port Authority could reasonably worry that even such incremental effects would prove quite disruptive. Moreover, "the justification for the Rule should not be measured by the disorder that would result from granting an exemption solely to ISKCON." For if petitioner is given access, so too must other groups. "Obviously, there would be a much larger threat to the State's interest in crowd control if all other religious, nonreligious, and noncommercial organizations could likewise move freely." As a result, we conclude that the solicitation ban is reasonable.

For the foregoing reasons, the judgment of the Court of Appeals sustaining the ban on solicitation in Port Authority terminals is

Affirmed.

JUSTICE O'CONNOR, concurring in No. 91–155 and concurring in the judgment in No. 91–339.

In the decision below, the Court of Appeals upheld a ban on solicitation of funds within the airport terminals operated by the Port Authority of New York and New Jersey, but struck down a ban on the repetitive distribution of printed or written material within the terminals. I would affirm both parts of that judgment.

[T]he "special attributes" and "surrounding circumstances" of the airports operated by the Port Authority are determinative. Not only has the Port Authority chosen *not* to limit access to the airports under its control, it has created a huge complex open to travelers and nontravelers alike. The airports house restaurants, cafeterias, snack bars, coffee shops, cocktail lounges, post offices, banks, telegraph offices, clothing shops, drug stores, food stores, nurseries, barber shops, currency exchanges, art exhibits, commercial advertising displays, bookstores, newsstands, dental offices and private clubs. The International Arrivals Building at JFK Airport even has two branches of Bloomingdale's.

. . . In my view, the Port Authority is operating a shopping mall as well as an airport. The reasonableness inquiry, therefore, is not whether the restrictions on speech are "consistent with . . . preserving the property" for air travel, *Perry, supra,* but whether they are reasonably related to maintaining the multipurpose environment that the Port Authority has deliberately created.

Applying that standard, I agree with the Court in No. 91–155 that the ban on solicitation is reasonable. Face-to-face solicitation is incompatible with the airport's functioning in a way that the other, permitted activities are not. . . .

In my view, however, the regulation banning leafletting—or, in the Port Authority's words, the "continuous or repetitive . . . distribution of . . . printed or written material"—cannot be upheld as reasonable on this record. I therefore concur in the judgment in No. 91–339 striking down that prohibition. While the difficulties posed by solicitation in a nonpublic forum are sufficiently obvious that its regulation may "rin[g] of common-sense," the same is not necessarily true of leafletting. To the contrary, we have expressly noted that leafletting does not entail the same kinds of problems presented by face-to-face solicitation. Specifically, "[o]ne need not ponder the contents of a leaflet or pamphlet in order mechanically to take it out of someone's hand.... 'The distribution of literature does not require that the recipient stop in order to receive the message the speaker wishes to convey; instead the recipient is free to read the message at a later time.'" With the possible exception of avoiding litter, it is difficult to point to any problems intrinsic to the act of leafletting that would make it naturally incompatible with a large, multipurpose forum such as those at issue here.... Moreover, the Port Authority has not offered any justifications or record evidence to support its ban on the distribution of pamphlets alone. Its argument is focused instead on the problems created when literature is distributed in conjunction with a solicitation plea....

Of course, it is still open for the Port Authority to promulgate regulations of the time, place, and manner of leafletting which are "content-neutral, narrowly tailored to serve a significant government interest, and leave open ample alternative channels of communication." For example, during the many years that this litigation has been in progress, the Port Authority has not banned *sankirtan* completely from JFK International Airport, but has restricted it to a relatively uncongested part of the airport terminals, the same part that houses the airport chapel. In my view, that regulation meets the standards we have applied to time, place, and manner restrictions of protected expression.

I would affirm the judgment of the Court of Appeals in both No. 91–155 and No. 91–339.

JUSTICE KENNEDY, with whom JUSTICE BLACKMUN, JUSTICE STEVENS, and JUSTICE SOUTER join as to Part I, concurring in the judgment.

While I concur in the judgment affirming in this case, my analysis differs in substantial respects from that of the Court. In my view the airport corridors and shopping areas outside of the passenger security zones, areas operated by the Port Authority, are public forums, and speech in those places is entitled to protection against all government regulation inconsistent with public forum principles. The Port Authority's blanket prohibition on the distribution or sale of literature cannot meet those stringent standards, and I agree it is invalid under the First and Fourteenth Amendments. The Port Authority's rule disallowing in-person solicitation of money for immediate payment, however, is in my view a narrow and valid regulation of the time, place, and manner of protected speech in this forum, or else is a valid regulation of the nonspeech element of expressive conduct. I would sustain the Port Authority's ban on solicitation and receipt of funds.

I.   ... The Court's analysis rests on an inaccurate view of history. The notion that traditional public forums are property which have public discourse as their principal purpose is a most doubtful fiction. The types of property that we have recognized as the quintessential public forums are streets, parks, and sidewalks. It would seem apparent that the principal purpose of streets and sidewalks, like airports, is to facilitate transportation, not public discourse, and we have recognized as much. Similarly, the purpose for the creation of public parks may be as much for beauty and open space as for discourse. Thus under the Court's analysis, even the quintessential public forums would appear to lack the necessary elements of what the Court defines as a public forum.

The effect of the Court's narrow view of the first category of public forums is compounded by its description of the second purported category, the so-called "designated" forum. The requirements for such a designation are so stringent that I cannot be certain whether the category has any content left at all. In any event, it seems evident that under the Court's analysis today few if any types of property other than those already recognized as public forums will be accorded that status.

The Court's answer to these objections appears to be a recourse to history as justifying its recognition of streets, parks, and sidewalks, but apparently no other types of government property, as traditional public forums. . . .

One of the places left in our mobile society that is suitable for discourse is a metropolitan airport. It is of particular importance to recognize that such spaces are public forums because in these days an airport is one of the few government-owned spaces where many persons have extensive contact with other members of the public. Given that private spaces of similar character are not subject to the dictates of the First Amendment, it is critical that we preserve these areas for protected speech. In my view, our public forum doctrine must recognize this reality, and allow the creation of public forums which do not fit within the narrow tradition of streets, sidewalks, and parks. We have allowed flexibility in our doctrine to meet changing technologies in other areas of constitutional interpretation, and I believe we must do the same with the First Amendment.

II. It is my view, however, that the Port Authority's ban on the "solicitation and receipt of funds" within its airport terminals should be upheld under the standards applicable to speech regulations in public forums. The regulation may be upheld as either a reasonable time, place, and manner restriction, or as a regulation directed at the nonspeech element of expressive conduct. The two standards have considerable overlap in a case like this one. . . .

I am in full agreement with the statement of the Court that solicitation is a form of protected speech. If the Port Authority's solicitation regulation prohibited all speech which requested the contribution of funds, I would conclude that it was a direct, content-based restriction of speech in clear violation of the First Amendment. The Authority's regulation does not prohibit all solicitation, however; it prohibits the "solicitation and receipt of funds." I do not understand this regulation to prohibit all speech that solicits funds. It reaches only personal solicitations for immediate payment of money. Otherwise, the "receipt of funds" phrase would be written out of the provision. The regulation does not cover, for example, the distribution of preaddressed envelopes along with a plea to contribute money to the distributor or his organization. As I understand the restriction it is directed only at the physical exchange of money, which is an element of conduct interwoven with otherwise expressive solicitation. In other words, the regulation permits expression that solicits funds, but limits the manner of that expression to forms other than the immediate receipt of money.

So viewed, I believe the Port Authority's rule survives our test for speech restrictions in the public forum. In-person solicitation of funds, when combined with immediate receipt of that money, creates a risk of fraud and duress which is well recognized, and which is different in kind from other forms of expression or conduct. Travelers who are unfamiliar with the airport, perhaps even unfamiliar with this country, its customs and its language, are an easy prey for the money solicitor. I agree in full with the Court's discussion of these dangers. . . .

Because the Port Authority's solicitation ban is directed at these abusive practices and not at any particular message, idea, or form of speech, the regulation is a content-neutral rule serving a significant government interest. . . .

Much of what I have said about the solicitation of funds may seem to apply to the sale of literature, but the differences between the two activities are of sufficient significance to require they be distinguished for constitutional purposes. The Port Authority's flat ban on the distribution or sale of printed material must, in my view, fall in its entirety. The application of our time, place, and manner test to the ban on sales leads to a result quite different from the solicitation ban. For one, the government interest in regulating the sales of literature is not as powerful as in the case of solicitation. The danger of a fraud arising from such sales is much more limited than from pure solicitation, because in the case of a sale the nature of the exchange tends to be clearer to both parties. Also, the Port Authority's sale regulation is not as narrowly drawn as the solicitation rule, since it does not specify the receipt of money as a critical element of a violation. And perhaps most important, the flat ban on sales of literature leaves open fewer alternative channels of communication than the Port Authority's more limited prohibition on the solicitation and receipt of funds. Given the practicalities and ad hoc nature of much expressive activity in the public forum, sales of literature must be completed in one transaction to be workable. Attempting to collect money at another time or place is a far less plausible option in the context of a sale than when soliciting donations, because the literature sought to be sold will under normal circumstances be distributed within the forum. These distinctions have been recognized by the National Park Service, which permits the sale or distribution of literature, while prohibiting solicitation. Thus the Port Authority's regulation allows no practical means for advocates and organizations to sell literature within the public forums which are its airports.

Against all of this must be balanced the great need, recognized by our precedents, to give the sale of literature full First Amendment protection. We have long recognized that to prohibit distribution of literature for the mere reason that it is sold would leave organizations seeking to spread their message without funds to operate. "It should be remembered that the pamphlets of Thomas Paine were not distributed free of charge." . . .

JUSTICE SOUTER, with whom JUSTICE BLACKMUN and JUSTICE STEVENS join, concurring in the judgment in No. 91–339 and dissenting in No. 91–155.

I join in Part I of Justice Kennedy's opinion and the judgment of affirmance in No. 91–339. I agree with Justice Kennedy's view of the rule that should determine what is a public forum and with his conclusion that the public areas of the airports at issue here qualify as such. . . .

From the Court's conclusion in No. 91–155, however, sustaining the total ban on solicitation of money for immediate payment, I respectfully dissent. "We have held the solicitation of money by charities to be fully protected as the dissemination of ideas. See *Secretary of State of Maryland v. Joseph H. Munson Co.* (1984). It is axiomatic that, although fraudulent misrepresentation of facts can be regulated, the dissemination of ideas cannot be regulated to prevent it from being unfair or unreasonable." *Riley v. National Federation of Blind of N.C., Inc.* (1988)(Scalia, J., concurring in part and concurring in judgment)(some citations omitted).

As Justice Kennedy's opinion indicates, the respondent comes closest to justifying the restriction as one furthering the government's interest in preventing coercion and fraud. The claim to be preventing coercion is weak to start with. While a solicitor can be insistent, a pedestrian on the street or airport concourse can simply walk away or walk on. . . .

Notes

Lee v. International Society for Krishna Consciousness, Inc., 505 U.S. 830, 112 S.Ct. 2709, 120 L.Ed.2d 669 (1992)(per curiam), the companion case to this case, held, in a brief opinion, that the ban on distribution of literature in the Port Authority airport terminals was invalid under the first amendment. Rehnquist, C.J., joined by White, Scalia & Thomas, JJ., dissented:

[A] differential ban that permits leafletting but prohibits solicitation, while giving the impression of permitting the Port Authority at least half of what it seeks, may in fact prove for the Port Authority to be a much more Pyrrhic victory. Under the regime that is today sustained, the Port Authority is obliged to permit leafletting. But monitoring leafletting activity in order to ensure that it is *only* leafletting that occurs, and not also soliciting, may prove little less burdensome than the monitoring that would be required if solicitation were permitted. At a minimum, therefore, I think it remains open whether at some future date the Port Authority may be able to reimpose a complete ban, having developed evidence that enforcement of a differential ban is overly burdensome. Until now it has had no reason or means to do this, since it is only today that such a requirement has been announced.

10–3.4 Government Subsidization of Speech

RUST v. SULLIVAN
500 U.S. 173, 111 S.Ct. 1759, 114 L.Ed.2d 233 (1991).

[Regulations of the U.S. Department of Health and Human Services limited the ability of recipients who accepted funding pursuant to Title X of the Public Health Service Act to engage in abortion related activities. The law provides federal funds for family-planning services (such as preventive family planning, preconceptual counseling, population research, infertility services) but stated that "[n]one of the funds appropriated under this subchapter shall be used in programs where abortion is a method of family planning." The regulations provided that Title X funds should not be used for "pregnancy care (including obstetric or prenatal care)" and expressly prohibited a Title X project "from referring a pregnant woman to an abortion provider, even upon specific request." A permissible response to such a request would be: "the project does not consider abortion an appropriate method of family planning and therefore does not counsel or refer for abortion." Petitioners attacked these regulations on their face. The abortion aspects of this case are referred to in § 8–3.4.]

CHIEF JUSTICE REHNQUIST delivered the opinion of the Court. . . .

Petitioners contend that the regulations violate the First Amendment by impermissibly discriminating based on viewpoint because they prohibit "all discussion about abortion as a lawful option—including counseling, referral, and the provision of neutral and accurate information about ending a pregnancy—while compelling the clinic or counselor to provide information that promotes continuing a pregnancy to term." [P]etitioners also assert that while the Government may place certain conditions on the receipt of federal subsidies, it may not "discriminate invidiously in its subsidies in such a way as to 'ai[m] at the suppression of dangerous ideas.' "*Regan,* [noted below].

There is no question but that the statutory prohibition contained in § 1008 is constitutional. In *Maher v. Roe,* we upheld a state welfare regulation under which Medicaid recipients received payments for services related to childbirth, but not for nontherapeutic abortions. The Court rejected the claim that this unequal subsidization worked a violation of the Constitution. We held that the government may "make a value judgment favoring childbirth over abortion, and . . . implement that judgment by the allocation of public funds." Here the Government is exercising the authority it possesses to subsidize family planning services which will lead to conception and child birth, and declining to "promote or encourage abortion." The Government can, without violating the Constitution, selectively fund a program to encourage certain activities it believes to be in the public interest, without at the same time funding an alternate program which seeks to deal with the problem in another way. In so doing, the Government has not discriminated on the basis of viewpoint; it has merely chosen to fund one activity to the exclusion of the other. "[A] legislature's decision not to subsidize the exercise of a fundamental right does not infringe the right." *Regan.* "A refusal to fund protected activity, without more, cannot be equated with the imposition of a 'penalty' on that activity." "There is a basic difference between direct state interference with a protected activity and state encouragement of an alternative activity consonant with legislative policy."

The challenged regulations implement the statutory prohibition by prohibiting counseling, referral, and the provision of information regarding abortion as a method of family planning. They are designed to ensure that the limits of the federal program are observed. The Title X program is designed not for prenatal care, but to encourage family planning. A doctor who wished to offer prenatal care to a project patient who became pregnant could properly be prohibited from doing so because such service is outside the scope of the federally funded program. The regulations prohibiting abortion counseling and referral are of the same ilk; "no funds appropriated for the project may be used in programs where abortion is a method of family planning," and a doctor employed by the project may be prohibited in the course of his project duties from counseling abortion or referring for abortion. This is not a case of the Government "suppressing a dangerous idea," but of a prohibition on a project grantee or its employees from engaging in activities outside of its scope.

To hold that the Government unconstitutionally discriminates on the basis of viewpoint when it chooses to fund a program dedicated to advance certain permissible goals, because the program in advancing those goals necessarily discourages alternate goals, would render numerous government programs constitutionally suspect. When Congress established a National Endowment for Democracy to encourage other countries to adopt democratic principles, 22 U.S.C.A. § 4411(b), it was not constitutionally required to fund a program to encourage competing lines of political philosophy such as Communism and Fascism. Petitioners' assertions ultimately boil down to the position that if the government chooses to subsidize one protected right, it must subsidize analogous counterpart rights. But the Court has soundly rejected that proposition. *Regan.* Within far broader limits than petitioners are willing to concede, when the government appropriates public funds to establish a program it is entitled to define the limits of that program.

We believe that petitioners' reliance upon our decision in *Arkansas Writers' Project, Inc. v. Ragland,* 481 U.S. 221, 107 S.Ct. 1722, 95 L.Ed.2d 209 (1987), is misplaced. That case involved a state sales tax which discriminated between magazines on the basis of their content. Relying on this fact, and on the fact that the tax "targets a small group within the press," ... the Court held the tax invalid. But we have here not the case of a general law singling out a disfavored group on the basis of speech content, but a case of the Government refusing to fund activities, including speech, which are specifically excluded from the scope of the project funded.

Petitioners rely heavily on their claim that the regulations would not, in the circumstance of a medical emergency, permit a Title X project to refer a woman whose pregnancy places her life in imminent peril to a provider of abortions or abortion-related services. This case, of course, involves only a facial challenge to the regulations, and we do not have before us any application by the Secretary to a specific fact situation. On their face, we do not read the regulations to bar abortion referral or counseling in such circumstances. Abortion counseling as a "method of family planning" is prohibited, and it does not seem that a medically necessitated abortion in such circumstances would be the equivalent of its use as a "method of family planning." Neither § 1008 nor the specific restrictions of the regulations would apply. Moreover, the regulations themselves contemplate that a Title X project would be permitted to engage in otherwise prohibited abortion-related activity in such circumstances. Section 59.8(a)(2) provides a specific exemption for emergency care and requires Title X recipients "to refer the client immediately to an appropriate provider of emergency medical services." Section 59.5(b)(1) also requires Title X projects to provide "necessary referral to other medical facilities when medically indicated."

Petitioners also contend that the restrictions on the subsidization of abortion-related speech contained in the regulations are impermissible because they condition the receipt of a benefit, in this case Title X funding, on the relinquishment of a constitutional right, the right to engage in abortion advocacy and counseling.

[However] the government is not denying a benefit to anyone, but is instead simply insisting that public funds be spent for the purposes for which they were authorized. The Secretary's regulations do not force the Title X grantee to give up abortion-related speech; they merely require that the grantee keep such activities separate and distinct from Title X activities. Title X expressly distinguishes between a Title X *grantee* and a Title X *project*. The grantee, which normally is a health care organization, may receive funds from a variety of sources for a variety of purposes. The grantee receives Title X funds, however, for the specific and limited purpose of establishing and operating a Title X project. The regulations govern the scope of the Title X *project's* activities, and leave the grantee unfettered in its other activities. The Title X *grantee* can continue to perform abortions, provide abortion-related services, and engage in abortion advocacy; it simply is required to conduct those activities through programs that are separate and independent from the project that receives Title X funds....

Similarly, in *Regan* we held that Congress could, in the exercise of its spending power, reasonably refuse to subsidize the lobbying activities of tax-exempt charitable organizations by prohibiting such organizations from using tax-deductible contributions to support their lobbying efforts.... The condition that federal funds will be used only to further the purposes of a grant does not violate constitutional rights. "Congress could, for example, grant funds to an organization dedicated to combating teenage drug abuse, but condition the grant by providing that none of the money received from Congress should be used to lobby state legislatures."

By requiring that the Title X grantee engage in abortion-related activity separately from activity receiving federal funding, Congress has, consistent with our teachings in *League of Women Voters* and *Regan,* not denied it the right to engage in abortion-related activities. Congress has merely refused to fund such activities out of the public fisc, and the Secretary has simply required a certain degree of separation from the Title X project in order to ensure the integrity of the federally funded program.

The same principles apply to petitioners' claim that the regulations abridge the free speech rights of the grantee's staff. Individuals who are voluntarily employed for a Title X project must perform their duties in accordance with the regulation's restrictions on abortion counseling and referral. The employees remain free, however, to pursue abortion-related activities when they are not acting under the auspices of the Title X project. The regulations, which govern solely the scope of the Title X project's activities, do not in any way restrict the activities of those persons acting as private individuals. The employees' freedom of expression is limited during the time that they actually work for the project; but this limitation is a consequence of their decision to accept employment in a project, the scope of which is permissibly restricted by the funding authority.[5]

---

5. Petitioners also contend that the regulations violate the First Amendment by penalizing speech funded with non-Title X monies. They argue that since Title X requires that grant recipients contribute to the financing of Title X projects through the use of matching funds and grant-related income, the regulation's restrictions on abortion counseling and advocacy penalize privately funded speech.

We find this argument flawed for several reasons. First, Title X subsidies are just that, subsidies. The recipient is in no way compelled to operate a Title X project; to avoid the force of the regulations, it can simply decline the subsidy. By accepting Title X funds, a recipient voluntarily consents to any restrictions placed on any matching funds or grant-related income. Potential grant recipients can choose between accepting Title X funds—subject to the Government's conditions that they provide matching funds and forgo abortion counseling and referral in the Title X project—or declining the subsidy and financing their own unsubsidized program. We have never held that the Government violates the First Amendment simply by offering that choice. Second, the Secretary's regulations apply only to Title X programs. A recipient is therefore able to "limi[t] the use of its federal funds to [Title X] activities." It is in no way "barred from using even wholly private funds to finance" its pro-abortion activities outside the Title X program. The regulations are limited to Title X funds; the recipient remains free to use private, non-Title X funds to finance abortion-related activities.

This is not to suggest that funding by the Government, even when coupled with the freedom of the fund recipients to speak outside the scope of the Government-funded project, is invariably sufficient to justify government control over the content of expression. For example, this Court has recognized that the existence of a Government "subsidy," in the form of Government-owned property, does not justify the restriction of speech in areas that have "been traditionally open to the public for expressive activity," or have been "expressly dedicated to speech activity." *Perry Education Assn. v. Perry Local Educators' Assn.* Similarly, we have recognized that the university is a traditional sphere of free expression so fundamental to the functioning of our society that the Government's ability to control speech within that sphere by means of conditions attached to the expenditure of Government funds is restricted by the vagueness and overbreadth doctrines of the First Amendment. It could be argued by analogy that traditional relationships such as that between doctor and patient should enjoy protection under the First Amendment from government regulation, even when subsidized by the Government. We need not resolve that question here, however, because the Title X program regulations do not significantly impinge upon the doctor-patient relationship. Nothing in them requires a doctor to represent as his own any opinion that he does not in fact hold. Nor is the doctor-patient relationship established by the Title X program sufficiently all-encompassing so as to justify an expectation on the part of the patient of comprehensive medical advice. The program does not provide post-conception medical care, and therefore a doctor's silence with regard to abortion cannot reasonably be thought to mislead a client into thinking that the doctor does not consider abortion an appropriate option for her. The doctor is always free to make clear that advice regarding abortion is simply beyond the scope of the program. In these circumstances, the general rule that the Government may choose not to subsidize speech applies with full force....

JUSTICE BLACKMUN, with whom JUSTICE MARSHALL joins, and with whom Justice Stevens joins as to Parts II and III, dissenting.[1] ...

II.   ... Until today, the Court never has upheld viewpoint-based suppression of speech simply because that suppression was a condition upon the acceptance of public funds. Whatever may be the Government's power to condition the receipt of its largess upon the relinquishment of constitutional rights, it surely does not extend to a condition that suppresses the recipient's cherished freedom of speech based solely upon the content or viewpoint of that speech.... Title X grantees may provide counseling and referral regarding any of a wide range of family planning and other topics, save abortion....

The Regulations are also clearly viewpoint-based. While suppressing speech favorable to abortion with one hand, the Secretary compels anti-abortion speech with the other. For example, the Department of Health

---

1. Part III is excerpted at § 8–3.4. O'Connor, J. joined Part I of this dissent, which avoided the constitutional issue by construing the statute to preclude the regulations at issue. O'Connor and Stevens also each wrote separate dissenting opinions.

and Human Services' own description of the Regulations makes plain that "Title X projects are *required* to facilitate access to prenatal care and social services, including adoption services, that might be needed by the pregnant client to promote her well-being and that of her child, while making it abundantly clear that the project is not permitted to promote abortion by facilitating access to abortion through the referral process." 53 Fed.Reg. 2927 (1988)(emphasis added). . . .

The Regulations pertaining to "advocacy" are even more explicitly viewpoint-based. These provide: "A Title X project may not *encourage, promote or advocate* abortion as a method of family planning." § 59.10 (emphasis added). They explain: "This requirement prohibits actions to *assist* women to obtain abortions or *increase* the availability or accessibility of abortion for family planning purposes." § 59.10(a) (emphasis added). The Regulations do not, however, proscribe or even regulate anti-abortion advocacy. These are clearly restrictions aimed at the suppression of "dangerous ideas."

Remarkably, the majority concludes that "the Government has not discriminated on the basis of viewpoint; it has merely chosen to fund one activity to the exclusion of another." But the majority's claim that the Regulations merely limit a Title X project's speech to preventive or preconceptional services, rings hollow in light of the broad range of non-preventive services that the Regulations authorize Title X projects to provide.[2] By refusing to fund those family-planning projects that advocate abortion *because* they advocate abortion, the Government plainly has targeted a particular viewpoint. . . .

The majority's reliance upon *Regan* in this connection is also misplaced. That case stands for the proposition that government has no obligation to subsidize a private party's efforts to petition the legislature regarding its views. Thus, if the challenged Regulations were confined to non-ideological limitations upon the use of Title X funds for lobbying activities, there would exist no violation of the First Amendment. . . .

. . . The Government's articulated interest in distorting the doctor/patient dialogue—ensuring that federal funds are not spent for a purpose outside the scope of the program—falls far short of that necessary to justify the suppression of truthful information and professional medical opinion regarding constitutionally protected conduct. Moreover, the offending Regulation is not narrowly tailored to serve this interest. For example, the governmental interest at stake could be served by imposing rigorous bookkeeping standards to ensure financial separation or adopting content-neutral rules for the balanced dissemination of family-planning and health information. . . .

2. In addition to requiring referral for prenatal care and adoption services, the Regulations permit general health services such as physical examinations, screening for breast cancer, treatment of gynecological problems, and treatment for sexually transmitted diseases. 53 Fed.Reg. 2927 (1988). None of the latter are strictly preventive, preconceptional services.

Notes

1. *Regan v. Taxation With Representation of Washington,* 461 U.S. 540, 103 S.Ct. 1997, 76 L.Ed.2d 129 (1983), although not a public forum case, provides an interesting example of the use of equal protection/free speech analysis. A unanimous Court upheld a provision of the Internal Revenue Code that allowed taxpayers to deduct contributions to nonprofit organizations only if "no substantial part" of their activities involved "carrying on propaganda, or otherwise attempting to influence legislation." The granting of deductions, the Court recognized, is a form of subsidy. Congress may properly choose not "to subsidize lobbying as extensively as it chose to subsidize other activities that nonprofit organizations undertake to promote the public welfare." No law prohibited any organization's right to receive nondeductible contributions (or deductible ones to support its nonlobbying activity). "We again reject the 'notion that First Amendment rights are somehow not fully realized unless they are subsidized by the State.'"

Congress also could make an exception to its own laws and allow the deductibility of contributions to veterans organizations even though they are permitted to lobby. This distinction is rational because of the policy of providing advantages to veterans due to their past contributions. A "legislative decision not to subsidize the exercise of a fundamental right does not infringe that right, and thus is not subject to strict scrutiny." For example, Congress could "grant funds to an organization dedicated to combatting teenage drug abuse, but condition the grant by providing that none of the money received from Congress should be used to lobby state legislatures. [At the same time it could] also enact a statute providing public money for an organization dedicated to combatting teenage alcohol abuse and impose no conditions against using funds obtained from Congress for lobbying."[1]

2. *Leathers v. Medlock,* 499 U.S. 439, 111 S.Ct. 1438, 113 L.Ed.2d 494 (1991), citing *Regan,* rejected a first amendment challenge to an Arkansas sales tax that excluded or exempted the print media but not cable television or cable and satellite services. The tax was of general applicability, covering all tangible personal property and a broad range of services. Thus, it did not single out the press and did not threaten to suppress the expression of particular ideas and viewpoints. In addition, the Arkansas tax did not target a small group of speakers. There was no evidence that Arkansas had targeted cable television "in a purposeful attempt" to interfere with free speech. Finally, it did not discriminate on the basis of the content of the taxpayer's speech. "[D]ifferential taxation of speakers, even members of the press, does not implicate the First Amendment unless the tax is directed at, or presents the danger of suppressing, particular ideas." The Court remanded so that the state court could pass on the petitioners' equal protection arguments.[2]

3. *Simon & Schuster, Inc. v. Members of New York State Crime Victims Board,* 502 U.S. 105, 112 S.Ct. 501, 116 L.Ed.2d 476 (1991) relied on *Regan*

---

1. For an application of the content-based speech rules in a religious setting, see § 11–2.2.

2. Marshall, J., joined by Blackmun, J., dissented because they "believe that the First Amendment prohibits the State from singling out a particular information medium for heavier tax burdens than are borne by like-situated media."

and *Leathers* to invalidate New York's "Son of Sam" statute, which required accused or "convicted" criminal's income from works describing his crime be deposited in an escrow account; these funds were then made available to victims of crime and the criminal's creditors. The statute treated as "convicted" any person who admitted to a crime even if that person had not been prosecuted. The Court ruled that the law singled out and placed a financial burden on speech on a particular subject and thus is "presumptively inconsistent with the First Amendment. . . . " In order for the state to justify such differential treatment, the regulation must be "necessary to serve a compelling state interest and [be] narrowly drawn to achieve that end." The state has a compelling interest in compensating victims from the fruits of crimes, but the statute was not narrowly tailored to achieve that objective. The law is "significantly overinclusive" because it applies to works on any subject, provided that the author expresses thoughts or recollections about a crime, however tangentially. Thus, it would apply to the *Confessions of Saint Augustine,* where the author deplored his "past foulness," including the theft of pears from a neighbor's vineyard. Similarly, it would cover *The Autobiography of Malcolm X,* which described crimes committed before Malcolm X became a public figure. The Court explicitly did not comment on the statutes of other jurisdictions designed to serve similar purposes.

Blackmun, J. and Kennedy, J., each filed separate opinions concurring in the judgment. Kennedy argued that it is "both unnecessary and incorrect to ask whether the State can show that the statute 'is necessary to serve a compelling state interest and is narrowly drawn to achieve that end.' " The Court should only consider the "straightforward question whether the State may enact a burdensome restriction of speech based on content only, apart from any considerations of time, place, and manner or the use of the public forum."

NATIONAL ENDOWMENT FOR THE ARTS v. FINLEY

524 U.S. 569, 118 S.Ct. 2168, 141 L.Ed.2d 500 (1998).

Justice O'CONNOR delivered the opinion of the Court.*

The National Foundation on the Arts and Humanities Act, as amended in 1990, requires the Chairperson of the National Endowment for the Arts (NEA) to ensure that "artistic excellence and artistic merit are the criteria by which [grant] applications are judged, taking into consideration general standards of decency and respect for the diverse beliefs and values of the American public." 20 U.S.C. § 954(d)(1). In this case, we review the Court of Appeals' determination that § 954(d)(1), on its face, impermissibly discriminates on the basis of viewpoint and is void for vagueness under the First and Fifth Amendments. We conclude that § 954(d)(1) is facially valid, as it neither inherently interferes with First Amendment rights nor violates constitutional vagueness principles.

---

* Editor's Note: O'CONNOR, J., delivered the opinion of the Court, in which REHNQUIST, C.J., and STEVENS, KENNEDY, and BREYER, JJ., joined, and in which GINSBURG, J., joined except for Part II–B. SCALIA, J., filed an opinion concurring in the judgment, in which THOMAS, J., joined. SOUTER, J., filed a dissenting opinion.

I.   ... Applications for NEA funding are initially reviewed by advisory panels composed of experts in the relevant field of the arts. Under the 1990 Amendments to the enabling statute, those panels must reflect "diverse artistic and cultural points of view" and include "wide geographic, ethnic, and minority representation," as well as "lay individuals who are knowledgeable about the arts." §§ 959(c)(1)-(2). The panels report to the 26–member National Council on the Arts (Council), which, in turn, advises the NEA Chairperson. The Chairperson has the ultimate authority to award grants but may not approve an application as to which the Council has made a negative recommendation.

Since 1965, the NEA has distributed over three billion dollars in grants to individuals and organizations, [and] only a handful of the agency's roughly 100,000 awards have generated formal complaints about misapplied funds or abuse of the public's trust. Two provocative works, however, prompted public controversy in 1989 ... The Institute of Contemporary Art at the University of Pennsylvania had used $30,000 of [NEA money] to fund a 1989 retrospective of photographer Robert Mapplethorpe's work. The exhibit, entitled *The Perfect Moment*, included homoerotic photographs that several Members of Congress condemned as pornographic. Members also denounced artist Andres Serrano's work *Piss Christ*, a photograph of a crucifix immersed in urine. Serrano had been awarded a $15,000 grant from the Southeast Center for Contemporary Art, an organization that received NEA support.

When considering the NEA's appropriations for fiscal year 1990, Congress reacted to the controversy surrounding the Mapplethorpe and Serrano photographs by eliminating $45,000 from the agency's budget, the precise amount contributed to the two exhibits by NEA grant recipients.... Ultimately, Congress adopted the Williams/Coleman Amendment, a bipartisan compromise between Members opposing any funding restrictions and those favoring some guidance to the agency. In relevant part, the Amendment became § 954(d)(1), which directs the Chairperson, in establishing procedures to judge the artistic merit of grant applications, to "tak[e] into consideration general standards of decency and respect for the diverse beliefs and values of the American public."

The NEA has not promulgated any official interpretation of the provision, but in December 1990, the Council unanimously adopted a resolution to implement § 954(d)(1) merely by ensuring that the members of the advisory panels that conduct the initial review of grant applications represent geographic, ethnic, and aesthetic diversity. John Frohnmayer, then Chairperson of the NEA, also declared that he would "count on [the] procedures" ensuring diverse membership on the peer review panels to fulfill Congress' mandate.

The four individual respondents in this case, Karen Finley, John Fleck, Holly Hughes, and Tim Miller, are performance artists who applied for NEA grants before § 954(d)(1) was enacted. An advisory panel recommended approval of respondents' projects, [but a] majority of the Council subsequently recommended disapproval, and in June 1990, the NEA informed respondents that they had been denied funding. Respondents filed suit, alleging that the NEA had violated their First Amendment rights by rejecting the applications on political grounds....

The District Court denied the NEA's motion for judgment on the pleadings, and, after discovery, the NEA agreed to settle the individual respondents' statutory and as-applied constitutional claims by paying the artists the amount of the vetoed grants, damages, and attorney's fees. The District Court then granted summary judgment in favor of respondents on their facial constitutional challenge to § 954(d)(1) and enjoined enforcement of the provision [and a] divided panel of the Court of Appeals affirmed the District Court's ruling.

II. A. Respondents raise a facial constitutional challenge to § 954(d)(1), and consequently they confront "a heavy burden" in advancing their claim. *Rust v. Sullivan*. Facial invalidation "is, manifestly, strong medicine" that "has been employed by the Court sparingly and only as a last resort." ...

Respondents argue that the provision is a paradigmatic example of viewpoint discrimination because it rejects any artistic speech that either fails to respect mainstream values or offends standards of decency. The premise of respondents' claim is that § 954(d)(1) constrains the agency's ability to fund certain categories of artistic expression. The NEA, however, reads the provision as merely hortatory [and] agency asserts that it has adequately implemented § 954(d)(1) merely by ensuring the representation of various backgrounds and points of view on the advisory panels that analyze grant applications. ...We do not decide whether the NEA's view—that the formulation of diverse advisory panels is sufficient to comply with Congress' command—is in fact a reasonable reading of the statute. It is clear, however, that the text of § 954(d)(1) imposes no categorical requirement. The advisory language stands in sharp contrast to congressional efforts to prohibit the funding of certain classes of speech. When Congress has in fact intended to affirmatively constrain the NEA's grant-making authority, it has done so in no uncertain terms. See § 954(d)(2) ("[O]bscenity is without artistic merit, is not protected speech, and shall not be funded"). ...

That § 954(d)(1) admonishes the NEA merely to take "decency and respect" into consideration, and that the legislation was aimed at reforming procedures rather than precluding speech, undercut respondents' argument that the provision inevitably will be utilized as a tool for invidious viewpoint discrimination. [W]e do not perceive a realistic danger that § 954(d)(1) will compromise First Amendment values. ...

Respondents' claim that the provision is facially unconstitutional may be reduced to the argument that the criteria in § 954(d)(1) are sufficiently subjective that the agency could utilize them to engage in viewpoint discrimination. [I]t seems unlikely that this provision will introduce any greater element of selectivity than the determination of "artistic excellence" itself. ...Any content-based considerations that may be taken into account in the grant-making process are a consequence of the nature of arts funding. [I]t would be "impossible to have a highly selective grant program without denying money to a large amount of constitutionally protected expression." The "very assumption" of the NEA is that grants will be awarded according to the "artistic worth of competing applications," and absolute neutrality is simply "inconceivable."

Respondent's reliance on our decision in *Rosenberger v. Rector and Visitors of Univ. of Va.*, 515 U.S. 819, 115 S.Ct. 2510, 132 L.Ed.2d 700 (1995) [§ 11–2.2]is therefore misplaced. In *Rosenberger*, a public university declined to authorize disbursements from its Student Activities Fund to finance the printing of a Christian student newspaper. We held that by subsidizing the Student Activities Fund, the University had created a limited public forum, from which it impermissibly excluded all publications with religious editorial viewpoints. . . . In the context of arts funding, in contrast to many other subsidies, the Government does not indiscriminately "encourage a diversity of views from private speakers." The NEA's mandate is to make aesthetic judgments, and the inherently content-based "excellence" threshold for NEA support sets it apart from the subsidy at issue in *Rosenberger*–which was available to all student organizations that were " 'related to the educational purpose of the University,' "—and from comparably objective decisions on allocating public benefits, such as access to a school auditorium or a municipal theater, or the second class mailing privileges available to " 'all newspapers and other periodical publications.' "

[W]e have no occasion here to address an as-applied challenge in a situation where the denial of a grant may be shown to be the product of invidious viewpoint discrimination. If the NEA were to leverage its power to award subsidies on the basis of subjective criteria into a penalty on disfavored viewpoints, then we would confront a different case. We have stated that, even in the provision of subsidies, the Government may not "ai[m] at the suppression of dangerous ideas," *Regan v. Taxation With Representation of Washington*, supra, and if a subsidy were "manipulated" to have a "coercive effect," then relief could be appropriate. . . . Unless and until § 954(d)(1) is applied in a manner that raises concern about the suppression of disfavored viewpoints, however, we uphold the constitutionality of the provision.

B. Finally, although the First Amendment certainly has application in the subsidy context, we note that the Government may allocate competitive funding according to criteria that would be impermissible were direct regulation of speech or a criminal penalty at stake. So long as legislation does not infringe on other constitutionally protected rights, Congress has wide latitude to set spending priorities. See *Regan v. Taxation with Representation of Wash.* In the 1990 Amendments . . . Congress modified the declaration of purpose in the NEA's enabling act to provide . . . that "[p]ublic funds . . . must ultimately serve public purposes the Congress defines." And as we held in *Rust*, Congress may "selectively fund a program to encourage certain activities it believes to be in the public interest, without at the same time funding an alternative program which seeks to deal with the problem in another way." In doing so, "the Government has not discriminated on the basis of viewpoint; it has merely chosen to fund one activity to the exclusion of the other."

III. The lower courts also erred in invalidating § 954(d)(1) as unconstitutionally vague. Under the First and Fifth Amendments, speakers are protected from arbitrary and discriminatory enforcement of vague standards. The terms of the provision are undeniably opaque, and if they appeared in a criminal statute or regulatory scheme, they could raise substantial vagueness concerns. It is unlikely, however, that speakers will be compelled to steer too far clear of any "forbidden area" in the context of grants of this nature. [W]hen the Government is acting as patron rather than as sovereign, the consequences of imprecision are not constitutionally severe.

In the context of selective subsidies, it is not always feasible for Congress to legislate with clarity. Indeed, if this statute is unconstitutionally vague, then so too are all government programs awarding scholarships and grants on the basis of subjective criteria such as "excellence." See, e.g., 2 U.S.C. § 802 (establishing the Congressional Award Program to "promote initiative, achievement, and excellence among youths in the areas of public service, personal development, and physical and expedition fitness"). Section 954(d)(1) merely adds some imprecise considerations to an already subjective selection process. It does not, on its face, impermissibly infringe on First or Fifth Amendment rights. Accordingly, the judgment of the Court of Appeals is reversed and the case is remanded for further proceedings consistent with this opinion.

It is so ordered.

Justice SCALIA, with whom Justice THOMAS joins, concurring in the judgment.

"The operation was a success, but the patient died." What such a procedure is to medicine, the Court's opinion in this case is to law. It sustains the constitutionality of 20 U.S.C. § 954(d)(1) by gutting it. The most avid congressional opponents of the provision could not have asked for more. I write separately because, unlike the Court, I think that § 954(d)(1) must be evaluated as written, rather than as distorted by the agency it was meant to control. By its terms, it establishes content-and-viewpoint-based criteria upon which grant applications are to be evaluated. And that is perfectly constitutional.

I. THE STATUTE MEANS WHAT IT SAYS

Section 954(d)(1) provides [that]:

> "(1) artistic excellence and artistic merit are the criteria by which applications are judged, taking into consideration general standards of decency and respect for the diverse beliefs and values of the American public."

... The application reviewers must take into account "general standards of decency" and "respect for the diverse beliefs and values of the American public" when evaluating artistic excellence and merit. One can regard this as either suggesting that decency and respect are elements of what Congress regards as artistic excellence and merit, or as suggesting that decency and respect are factors to be taken into account *in addition to* artistic excellence and merit. But either way, it is entirely, 100% clear that decency and respect are to be taken into account in evaluating applications. This is so apparent that I am at a loss to understand what the Court has in mind (other than the gutting of the statute) when it speculates that the statute is merely "advisory." ...

I agree with the Court that § 954(d)(1) "imposes no categorical requirement," in the sense that it does not require the denial of all applications that violate general standards of decency or exhibit disrespect for the diverse beliefs and values of Americans. But [to] the extent a particular applicant exhibits disrespect for the diverse beliefs and values of the American public or fails to comport with general standards of decency, the likelihood that he will receive a grant diminishes. [T]he decisionmaker, all else being equal, will favor applications that display decency and respect, and disfavor applications that do not.

... It is evident in the legislative history that § 954(d)(1) was prompted by, and directed at, the public funding of such offensive productions as Serrano's "Piss Christ," the portrayal of a crucifix immersed in urine, and Mapplethorpe's show of lurid homoerotic photographs. Thus, even if one strays beyond the plain text it is perfectly clear that the statute was meant to disfavor—that is, to discriminate against—such productions. Not to ban their funding absolutely, to be sure (though as I shall discuss, that also would not have been unconstitutional); but to make their funding more difficult. [This] law unquestionably disfavors—discriminates against—indecency and disrespect for the diverse beliefs and values of the American people. I turn, then, to whether such viewpoint discrimination violates the Constitution.

II. WHAT THE STATUTE SAYS IS CONSTITUTIONAL

... With the enactment of § 954(d)(1), Congress did not abridge the speech of those who disdain the beliefs and values of the American public, nor did it abridge indecent speech. Those who wish to create indecent and disrespectful art are as unconstrained now as they were before the enactment of this statute. *Avant-garde* artists such as respondents remain entirely free to *epater les bourgeois*;[2] they are merely

2. Which they do quite well. The *oeuvres d'art* for which the four individual plaintiffs in this case sought funding have been described as follows:

"Finley's controversial show, 'We Keep Our Victims Ready,' contains three segments. In the second segment, Finley visually recounts a sexual assault by stripping to the waist and smearing chocolate on her breasts and by using profanity to describe the assault. Holly Hughes' monologue 'World Without End' is a somewhat graphic recollection of the artist's realization of her lesbianism and reminiscence of her mother's sexuality. John Fleck, in his stage performance 'Blessed Are All the Little Fishes,' confronts alcoholism and Catholicism. During the course of the per-

deprived of the additional satisfaction of having the bourgeoisie taxed to pay for it. It is preposterous to equate the denial of taxpayer subsidy with measures " 'aimed at the suppression of dangerous ideas.' "*Regan v. Taxation with Representation of Wash*....

One might contend, I suppose, that a threat of rejection by the only available source of free money would constitute coercion and hence "abridgment" within the meaning of the First Amendment. I would not agree with such a contention, which would make the NEA the mandatory patron of all art too indecent, too disrespectful, or even too *kitsch* to attract private support. But even if one accepts the contention, it would have no application here. The NEA is far from the sole source of funding for art—even indecent, disrespectful, or just plain bad art. Accordingly, the Government may earmark NEA funds for projects it deems to be in the public interest without thereby abridging speech.

Section 954(d)(1) is no more discriminatory, and no less constitutional, than virtually every other piece of funding legislation enacted by Congress. "The Government can, without violating the Constitution, selectively fund a program to encourage certain activities it believes to be in the public interest, without at the same time funding an alternative program.... "*Rust v. Sullivan*. [W]hen Congress chose to establish the National Endowment for Democracy it was not constitutionally required to fund programs encouraging competing philosophies of government—an example of funding discrimination that cuts much closer than this one to the core of *political* speech which is the primary concern of the First Amendment. It takes a particularly high degree of chutzpah for the NEA to contradict this proposition, since the agency itself discriminates—and is required by law to discriminate—in favor of artistic (as opposed to scientific, or political, or theological) expression. ...[3]

The nub of the difference between me and the Court is that I regard the distinction between "abridging" speech and funding it as a fundamental divide, on this side of which the First Amendment is inapplicable.

. . .

Finally, what is true of the First Amendment is also true of the constitutional rule against vague legislation: it has no application to funding. Insofar as it bears upon First Amendment concerns, the vagueness doctrine addresses the problems that arise from government regulation of expressive conduct, not government grant programs. In the former context, vagueness produces an abridgment of lawful speech; in the latter it produces, at worst, a waste of money. [I]f the vagueness

---

formance, Fleck appears dressed as a mermaid, urinates on the stage and creates an altar out of a toilet bowl by putting a photograph of Jesus Christ on the lid. Tim Miller derives his performance 'Some Golden States' from childhood experiences, from his life as a homosexual, and from the constant threat of AIDS. Miller uses vegetables in his performances to represent sexual symbols."

3. I suppose it would be unconstitutional for the government to give money to an organization devoted to the promotion of candidates nominated by the Republican party—but it would be just as unconstitutional for the government itself to promote candidates nominated by the Republican party, and I do not think that that unconstitutionality has anything to do with the First Amendment. [footnote repositioned]

doctrine were applicable, the agency charged with making grants under a statutory standard of "artistic excellence"—and which has itself thought that standard met by everything from the playing of Beethoven to a depiction of a crucifix immersed in urine—would be of more dubious constitutional validity than the "decency" and "respect" limitations that respondents (who demand to be judged on the same strict standard of "artistic excellence") have the humorlessness to call too vague.

[T]he Court notes with satisfaction that "only a handful of the agency's roughly 100,000 awards have generated formal complaints." The Congress that felt it necessary to enact § 954(d)(1) evidently thought it much *more* noteworthy that *any* money exacted from American taxpayers had been used to produce a crucifix immersed in urine, or a display of homoerotic photographs. . . . Instead of banning the funding of such productions absolutely, which I think would have been entirely constitutional, Congress took the lesser step of requiring them to be disfavored in the evaluation of grant applications. The Court's opinion today renders even that lesser step a nullity. For that reason, I concur only in the judgment.

Justice SOUTER, dissenting.

The question here is whether the italicized segment of this statute is unconstitutional on its face: "artistic excellence and artistic merit are the criteria by which applications [for grants from the National Endowment for the Arts] are judged, *taking into consideration general standards of decency and respect for the diverse beliefs and values of the American public.*" 20 U.S.C. § 954(d) (emphasis added). It is.

The decency and respect proviso mandates viewpoint-based decisions in the disbursement of government subsidies, and the Government has wholly failed to explain why the statute should be afforded an exemption from the fundamental rule of the First Amendment that viewpoint discrimination in the exercise of public authority over expressive activity is unconstitutional. . . .

[A] statute disfavoring speech that fails to respect America's "diverse beliefs and values" is the very model of viewpoint discrimination. . . . What if the statute required a panel to apply criteria "taking into consideration the centrality of Christianity to the American cultural experience," or "taking into consideration whether the artist is a communist," or "taking into consideration the political message conveyed by the art," or even "taking into consideration the superiority of the white race"? Would the Court hold these considerations facially constitutional, merely because the statute had no requirement to give them any particular, much less controlling, weight? . . .

. . . The Government calls attention to the roles of government-as-speaker and government-as-buyer, in which the government is of course entitled to engage in viewpoint discrimination: if the Food and Drug Administration launches an advertising campaign on the subject of smoking, it may condemn the habit without also having to show a cowboy taking a puff on the opposite page; and if the Secretary of

Defense wishes to buy a portrait to decorate the Pentagon, he is free to prefer George Washington over George the Third.

The Government freely admits, however, that it neither speaks through the expression subsidized by the NEA, nor buys anything for itself with its NEA grants. On the contrary, ... the Government acts as a patron, financially underwriting the production of art by private artists and impresarios for independent consumption. Accordingly, the Government would have us liberate government-as-patron from First Amendment strictures not by placing it squarely within the categories of government-as-buyer or government-as-speaker, but by recognizing a new category by analogy to those accepted ones. ...

The NEA ... is a subsidy scheme created to encourage expression of a diversity of views from private speakers. ... So long as Congress chooses to subsidize expressive endeavors at large, it has no business requiring the NEA to turn down funding applications of artists and exhibitors who devote their "freedom of thought, imagination, and inquiry" to defying our tastes, our beliefs, or our values. ...[17] ...

Notes

1. The NEA, like Congress, acts on behalf of the Government. Constitutionally, may the NEA decide not to use taxpayers' money to subsidize art that many taxpayers find offensive? If the NEA decided to subsidize some film-making, must it subsidize some movies that are NC18 (no children under age 18)? Or, may the NEA decide that, because all taxpayers are paying for the subsidy, the objects of the NEA's largess should be able to be viewed all taxpayers (i.e., G-rated)?

2. Consider Justice Souter's dissent. If Congress amended the NEA statute to provide that the NEA is *not* "a subsidy scheme created to encourage expression of a diversity of views from private speakers" would Justice Souter change the result of his dissent? If Congress ordered the NEA not to subsidize art that is racist towards blacks and other minority groups (or not to subsidize art that "mocks God"), would that be unconstitutional viewpoint discrimination for Justice Souter?

10–3.5 Injunctions and the Public Forum

MADSEN v. WOMEN'S HEALTH CENTER, INC.
512 U.S. 753, 114 S.Ct. 2516, 129 L.Ed.2d 593 (1994).

CHIEF JUSTICE REHNQUIST delivered the opinion of the Court.

Petitioners challenge the constitutionality of an injunction entered by a Florida state court which prohibits antiabortion protestors from demonstrating in certain places and in various ways outside of a health

---

17. I agree with the Court that § 954(d) is not unconstitutionally vague. Any chilling that results from imprecision in the drafting of standards (such as "artistic excellence and artistic merit") by which the government awards scarce grants and scholarships is an inevitable and permissible consequence of distributing prizes on the basis of criteria dealing with a subject that defies exactness. ...

clinic that performs abortions. We hold that the establishment of a 36–foot buffer zone on a public street from which demonstrators are excluded passes muster under the First Amendment, but that several other provisions of the injunction do not.

I.   Respondents operate abortion clinics throughout central Florida. Petitioners and other groups and individuals are engaged in activities near the site of one such clinic in Melbourne, Florida. They picketed and demonstrated where the public street gives access to the clinic. In September 1992, a Florida state court permanently enjoined petitioners from blocking or interfering with public access to the clinic, and from physically abusing persons entering or leaving the clinic. Six months later, [the trial court] issued a broader injunction, which is challenged here.

The court found that, despite the initial injunction, protesters continued to impede access to the clinic by congregating on the paved portion of the street—Dixie Way—leading up to the clinic, and by marching in front of the clinic's driveways. It found that as vehicles heading toward the clinic slowed to allow the protesters to move out of the way, "sidewalk counselors" would approach and attempt to give the vehicle's occupants antiabortion literature. The number of people congregating varied from a handful to 400, and the noise varied from singing and chanting to the use of loudspeakers and bullhorns.

The protests, the court found, took their toll on the clinic's patients. A clinic doctor testified that, as a result of having to run such a gauntlet to enter the clinic, the patients "manifested a higher level of anxiety and hypertension causing those patients to need a higher level of sedation to undergo the surgical procedures, thereby increasing the risk associated with such procedures." The noise produced by the protestors could be heard within the clinic, causing stress in the patients both during surgical procedures and while recuperating in the recovery rooms. And those patients who turned away because of the crowd to return at a later date, the doctor testified, increased their health risks by reason of the delay.

. . . Petitioners picketed in front of clinic employees' residences; shouted at passersby; rang the doorbells of neighbors and provided literature identifying the particular clinic employee as a "baby killer." Occasionally, the protestors would confront minor children of clinic employees who were home alone. [The state court] therefore amended its prior order, enjoining a broader array of activities. The amended injunction prohibits petitioners[1] from engaging in the following acts:

"(1) At all times on all days, from entering the premises and property of the Aware Woman Center for Choice [the Melbourne clinic]. . . .

---

1. In addition to petitioners, the state court's order was directed at "Operation Rescue, Operation Rescue America, Operation Goliath, their officers, agents, members, employees and servants, and . . . Bruce Cadle, Pat Mahoney, Randall Terry, . . . and all persons acting in concert or participation with them, or on their behalf."

"(2) At all times on all days, from blocking, impeding, inhibiting, or in any other manner obstructing or interfering with access to, ingress into and egress from any building or parking lot of the Clinic.

"(3) At all times on all days, from congregating, picketing, patrolling, demonstrating or entering that portion of public right-of-way or private property within [36] feet of the property line of the Clinic. . . . An exception to the 36 foot buffer zone is the area immediately adjacent to the Clinic on the east. . . . The [petitioners] must remain at least [5] feet from the Clinic's east line. Another exception to the 36 foot buffer zone relates to the record title owners of the property to the north and west of the Clinic. The prohibition against entry into the 36 foot buffer zones does not apply to such persons and their invitees. The other prohibitions contained herein do apply, if such owners and their invitees are acting in concert with the [petitioners].

"(4) During the hours of 7:30 a.m. through noon, on Mondays through Saturdays, during surgical procedures and recovery periods, from singing, chanting, whistling, shouting, yelling, use of bullhorns, auto horns, sound amplification equipment or other sounds or images observable to or within earshot of the patients inside the Clinic.

"(5) At all times on all days, in an area within [300] feet of the Clinic, from physically approaching any person seeking the services of the Clinic unless such person indicates a desire to communicate by approaching or by inquiring of the [petitioners].

"(6) At all times on all days, from approaching, congregating, picketing, patrolling, demonstrating or using bullhorns or other sound amplification equipment within [300] feet of the residence of any of the [respondents'] employees, staff, owners or agents, or blocking or attempting to block, barricade, or in any other manner, temporarily or otherwise, obstruct the entrances, exits or driveways of the residences of any of the [respondents'] employees, staff, owners or agents. The [petitioners] and those acting in concert with them are prohibited from inhibiting or impeding or attempting to impede, temporarily or otherwise, the free ingress or egress of persons to any street that provides the sole access to the street on which those residences are located.

"(7) At all times on all days, from physically abusing, grabbing, intimidating, harassing, touching, pushing, shoving, crowding or assaulting persons entering or leaving, working at or using services at the [respondents'] Clinic or trying to gain access to, or leave, any of the homes of owners, staff or patients of the Clinic.

"(8) At all times on all days, from harassing, intimidating or physically abusing, assaulting or threatening any present or former doctor, health care professional, or other staff member, employee or volunteer who assists in providing services at the [respondents'] Clinic.

"(9) At all times on all days, from encouraging, inciting, or securing other persons to commit any of the prohibited acts listed herein."

The Florida Supreme Court upheld the constitutionality of the trial court's amended injunction. That court recognized that the forum at issue, which consists of public streets, sidewalks, and rights-of-way, is a traditional public forum [but it] determined that the restrictions are content neutral, and it accordingly refused to apply the heightened scrutiny dictated by *Perry Education Assn. v. Perry Local Educators' Assn.* (1983)(To enforce a content-based exclusion the State must show that its regulation is necessary to serve a compelling state interest and that it is narrowly drawn to achieve that end). Instead, the court [determined] whether the restrictions are "narrowly tailored to serve a significant government interest, and leave open ample alternative channels of communication." It concluded that they were.

[T]he United States Court of Appeals for the Eleventh Circuit heard a separate challenge to the same injunction. [It] struck down the injunction [stating] that the asserted interests in public safety and order were already protected by other applicable laws and that these interests could be protected adequately without infringing upon the First Amendment rights of others. The Court of Appeals found the injunction to be content based and neither necessary to serve a compelling state interest nor narrowly drawn to achieve that end. We granted certiorari to resolve the conflict. . . .

II.   We begin by addressing petitioners' contention that the state court's order, because it is an injunction that restricts only the speech of antiabortion protesters, is necessarily content or viewpoint based. . . . We disagree. To accept petitioners' claim would be to classify virtually every injunction as content or viewpoint based. An injunction, by its very nature, applies only to a particular group (or individuals) and regulates the activities, and perhaps the speech, of that group. It does so, however, because of the group's past actions in the context of a specific dispute between real parties. . . .

The fact that the injunction in the present case did not prohibit activities of those demonstrating in favor of abortion is justly attributable to the lack of any similar demonstrations by those in favor of abortion, and of any consequent request that their demonstrations be regulated by injunction. There is no suggestion in this record that Florida law would not equally restrain similar conduct directed at a target having nothing to do with abortion; none of the restrictions imposed by the court were directed at the contents of petitioner's message.

Our principal inquiry in determining content neutrality is whether the government has adopted a regulation of speech "without reference to the content of the regulated speech." [T]he state court imposed restrictions on petitioners incidental to their antiabortion message because they repeatedly violated the court's original order. That petitioners all share the same viewpoint regarding abortion does not in itself demonstrate that some invidious content-or viewpoint-based purpose motivated the issuance of the order. It suggests only that those in the group *whose conduct* violated the court's order happen to share the same opinion regarding abortions being performed at the clinic. In short, the fact that the injunction covered people with a particular viewpoint does not itself render the injunction content or viewpoint based.[2] Accordingly, the injunction issued in this case does not demand the level of heightened scrutiny set forth in *Perry Education Assn.* And we proceed to discuss the standard which does govern.

III. If this were a content-neutral, generally applicable statute, instead of an injunctive order, its constitutionality would be assessed under the standard set forth in *Ward v. Rock Against Racism* (1989) [§ 10–3.2], and similar cases. Given that the forum around the clinic is a traditional public forum, we would determine whether the time, place, and manner regulations were "narrowly tailored to serve a significant governmental interest."

There are obvious differences, however, between an injunction and a generally applicable ordinance. Ordinances represent a legislative choice regarding the promotion of particular societal interests. Injunctions, by contrast, are remedies imposed for violations (or threatened violations) of a legislative or judicial decree. Injunctions also carry greater risks of censorship and discriminatory application than do general ordinances. "[T]here is no more effective practical guaranty against arbitrary and unreasonable government than to require that the principles of law which officials would impose upon a minority must be imposed generally." *Railway Express Agency, Inc. v. New York* (1949). Injunctions, of course, have some advantages over generally applicable statutes in that they can be tailored by a trial judge to afford more precise relief than a statute where a violation of the law has already occurred.

We believe that these differences require a somewhat more stringent application of general First Amendment principles in this context.[3] [W]hen evaluating a content-neutral injunction, we think that our standard time, place, and manner analysis is not sufficiently rigorous. We must ask instead whether the challenged provisions of the injunction

---

2. We also decline to adopt the prior restraint analysis urged by petitioners. Prior restraints do often take the form of injunctions. See, *e.g., New York Times Co. v. United States* (1971)(refusing to enjoin publications of the "Pentagon Papers") ... Not all injunctions which may incidentally affect expression, however, are "prior restraints" in the sense that that term was used in *New York Times.* Here petitioners are not prevented from expressing their message in any one of several different ways; they are simply prohibited from expressing it within the 36–foot buffer zone. Moreover, the injunction was issued not because of the content of petitioners' expression, as was the case in *New York Times Co.,* but because of their prior unlawful conduct.

3. Under general equity principles, an injunction issues only if there is a showing that the defendant has violated, or imminently will violate, some provision of statutory or common law, and that there is a "cognizable danger of recurrent violation."

burden no more speech than necessary to serve a significant government interest.

Both Justice Stevens and Justice Scalia disagree with the standard we announce, for policy reasons. Justice Stevens believes that "injunctive relief should be judged by a more lenient standard than legislation," because injunctions are imposed on individuals or groups who have engaged in illegal activity. Justice Scalia, by contrast, believes that content-neutral injunctions are "*at least* as deserving of strict scrutiny as a statutory, content-based restriction," [because] injunctions, even though they might not "attack content *as content*," may be used to suppress particular ideas; that individual judges should not be trusted to impose injunctions in this context; and that an injunction is procedurally more difficult to challenge than a statute. We believe that consideration of *all* of the differences and similarities between statutes and injunctions supports, as a matter of policy, the standard we apply here. [We also] do not believe that this injunction constitutes a prior restraint, and we therefore believe that the "heavy presumption" against its constitutionality does not obtain here. See n. 2, *supra* . . . .

The Florida Supreme Court concluded that numerous significant government interests are protected by the injunction. It noted that the State has a strong interest in protecting a woman's freedom to seek lawful medical or counseling services in connection with her pregnancy. The State also has a strong interest in ensuring the public safety and order . . . . In addition, the court believed that the State's strong interest in residential privacy, acknowledged in *Frisby v. Schultz*, applied by analogy to medical privacy. [T]argeted picketing of a hospital or clinic threatens not only the psychological, but the physical well-being of the patient held "captive" by medical circumstance. We agree with the Supreme Court of Florida that the combination of these governmental interests is quite sufficient to justify an appropriately tailored injunction to protect them. We now examine each contested provision of the injunction to see if it burdens more speech than necessary to accomplish its goal.[5]

A.

1. We begin with the 36–foot buffer zone. The state court prohibited petitioners from "congregating, picketing, patrolling, demonstrating or entering" any portion of the public right-of-way or private property within 36 feet of the property line of the clinic as a way of ensuring access to the clinic. This speech-free buffer zone requires that petitioners move to the other side of Dixie Way and away from the driveway of the clinic . . . . The buffer zone also applies to private property to the north

---

5. Petitioners do not challenge the first two provisions of the state court's 1993 order. The provisions composed what had been the state court's 1992 permanent injunction and they chiefly addressed blocking, impeding, and inhibiting access to the clinic and its parking lot. Nor do petitioners challenge the restrictions in paragraphs 7, 8, and 9, which prohibit them from harassing and physically abusing clinic doctors, staff, and patients trying to gain access to the clinic or their homes.

and west of the clinic property. We examine each portion of the buffer zone separately.

We have noted a distinction between the type of focused picketing banned from the buffer zone and the type of generally disseminated communication that cannot be completely banned in public places, such as handbilling and solicitation. See *Frisby, supra.*... Here the picketing is directed primarily at patients and staff of the clinic.

The 36–foot buffer zone protecting the entrances to the clinic and the parking lot is a means of protecting unfettered ingress to and egress from the clinic, and ensuring that petitioners do not block traffic on Dixie Way. The state court seems to have had few other options to protect access given the narrow confines around the clinic. As the Florida Supreme Court noted, Dixie Way is only 21 feet wide in the area of the clinic. The state court was convinced that allowing the petitioners to remain on the clinic's sidewalk and driveway was not a viable option in view of the failure of the first injunction to protect access. And allowing the petitioners to stand in the middle of Dixie Way would obviously block vehicular traffic.

The need for a complete buffer zone near the clinic entrances and driveway may be debatable, but some deference must be given to the state court's familiarity with the facts and the background of the dispute between the parties even under our heightened review. Moreover, one of petitioners' witnesses during the evidentiary hearing before the state court conceded that the buffer zone was narrow enough to place petitioners at a distance of no greater than 10 to 12 feet from cars approaching and leaving the clinic. Protesters standing across the narrow street from the clinic can still be seen and heard from the clinic parking lots. ... The failure of the first order to accomplish its purpose may be taken into consideration in evaluating the constitutionality of the broader order. On balance, we hold that the 36–foot buffer zone around the clinic entrances and driveway burdens no more speech than necessary to accomplish the governmental interest at stake.

Justice Scalia's dissent argues that a videotape made of demonstrations at the clinic represents "what one must presume to be the worst of the activity justifying the injunction." This seems to us a gratuitous assumption. The videotape was indeed introduced by respondents, presumably because they thought it supported their request for the second injunction. [P]etitioners themselves studiously refrained from challenging the factual basis for the injunction both in the state courts and here. Before the Florida Supreme Court, petitioners states that "... The sole question presented by this appeal is a question of law, and for purposes of this appeal [petitioners] are assuming, *arguendo,* that a factual basis exists to grant injunctive relief." Petitioners argued against including the factual record as an appendix in the Florida Supreme Court, and never certified a full record. We must therefore judge this case on the assumption that the evidence and testimony presented to the state court supported its findings that the presence of protesters standing, marching, and demonstrating near the clinic's entrance interfered with ingress to and egress from the clinic despite the issuance of the earlier injunction.

2. The inclusion of private property on the back and side of the clinic in the 36–foot buffer zone raises different concerns. The accepted purpose of the buffer zone is to protect access to the clinic and to facilitate the orderly flow of traffic on Dixie Way. [N]othing in the record indicates that petitioners' activities on the private property have obstructed access to the clinic. Nor was evidence presented that protestors located on the private property blocked vehicular traffic on Dixie Way. Absent evidence that petitioners standing on the private property have obstructed access to the clinic, blocked vehicular traffic, or otherwise unlawfully interfered with the clinic's operation, this portion of the buffer zone fails to serve the significant government interests relied on by the Florida Supreme Court. We hold that on the record before us the 36–foot buffer zone as applied to the private property to the north and west of the clinic burdens more speech than necessary to protect access to the clinic.

B.

In response to high noise levels outside the clinic, the state court restrained the petitioners from "singing, chanting, whistling, shouting, yelling, use of bullhorns, auto horns, sound amplification equipment or other sounds or images observable to or within earshot of the patients inside the [c]linic" during the hours of 7:30 a.m. through noon on Mondays through Saturdays.... Noise control is particularly important around hospitals and medical facilities during surgery and recovery periods.... We hold that the limited noise restrictions imposed by the state court order burden no more speech than necessary to ensure the health and well-being of the patients at the clinic. The First Amendment does not demand that patients at a medical facility undertake Herculean efforts to escape the cacophony of political protests. ...

C.

The same, however, cannot be said for the "images observable" provision of the state court's order. Clearly, threats to patients or their families, however communicated, are proscribable under the First Amendment. But rather than prohibiting the display of signs that could be interpreted as threats or veiled threats, the state court issued a blanket ban on all "images observable." This broad prohibition on all "images observable" burdens more speech than necessary to achieve the purpose of limiting threats to clinic patients or their families. [I]f the blanket ban on "images observable" was intended to reduce the level of anxiety and hypertension suffered by the patients inside the clinic, it would still fail. The only plausible reason a patient would be bothered by "images observable" inside the clinic would be if the patient found the expression contained in such images disagreeable. But it is much easier for the clinic to pull its curtains than for a patient to stop up her ears, and no more is required to avoid seeing placards through the windows of the clinic. This provision of the injunction violates the First Amendment.

D.

The state court ordered that petitioners refrain from physically approaching any person seeking services of the clinic "unless such person indicates a desire to communicate" in an area within 300 feet of the clinic. The state court was attempting to prevent clinic patients and staff from being "stalked" or "shadowed" by the petitioners as they approached the clinic.... But it is difficult, indeed, to justify a prohibition on *all* uninvited approaches of persons seeking the services of the clinic, regardless of how peaceful the contact may be, without burdening more speech than necessary to prevent intimidation and to ensure access to the clinic. Absent evidence that the protesters' speech is independently proscribable (*i.e.*, "fighting words" or threats), or is so infused with violence as to be indistinguishable from a threat of physical harm, this provision cannot stand. "[I]n public debate our own citizens must tolerate insulting, and even outrageous, speech in order to provide adequate breathing space to the freedoms protected by the First Amendment." The "consent" requirement alone invalidates this provision; it burdens more speech than is necessary to prevent intimidation and to ensure access to the clinic.[6]

E.

The final substantive regulation challenged by petitioners relates to a prohibition against picketing, demonstrating, or using sound amplification equipment within 300 feet of the residences of clinic staff. The prohibition also covers impeding access to streets that provide the sole access to streets on which those residences are located. The same analysis applies to the use of sound amplification equipment here as that discussed above: the government may simply demand that petitioners turn down the volume if the protests overwhelm the neighborhood....

But the 300–foot zone around the residences in this case is much larger than the zone provided for in the ordinance which we approved in *Frisby* [§ 10–3.3]. The ordinance at issue there ... was limited to "focused picketing taking place solely in front of a particular residence." By contrast, the 300–foot zone would ban "[g]eneral marching through residential neighborhoods, or even walking a route in front of an entire block of houses." The record before us does not contain sufficient justification for this broad a ban on picketing; it appears that a limitation on the time, duration of picketing, and number of pickets outside a smaller zone could have accomplished the desired result.

IV. Petitioners also challenge the state court's order as being vague and overbroad. They object to the portion of the injunction making it applicable to those acting "in concert" with the named parties.

***

6. We need not decide whether the "images observable" and "no-approach" provisions are content based.

But petitioners themselves are named parties in the order, and they therefore lack standing to challenge a portion of the order applying to persons who are not parties. Nor is that phrase subject, at the behest of petitioners, to a challenge for "overbreadth"; the phrase itself does not prohibit any conduct, but is simply directed at unnamed parties who might later be found to be acting "in concert" with the named parties. As such, the case is governed by our holding in *Regal Knitwear Co. v. NLRB,* 324 U.S. 9, 14, 65 S.Ct. 478, 481, 89 L.Ed. 661 (1945). There a party subject to an injunction argued that the order was invalid because of a provision that it applied to "successors and assigns" of the enjoined party. Noting that the party pressing the claim was not a successor or assign, we characterized the matter as "an abstract controversy over the use of these words."

Petitioners also contend that the "in concert" provision of the injunction impermissibly limits their freedom of association guaranteed by the First Amendment. But petitioners are not enjoined from associating with others or from joining with them to express a particular viewpoint. The freedom of association protected by the First Amendment does not extend to joining with others for the purpose of depriving third parties of their lawful rights.

V. In sum, we uphold the noise restrictions and the 36–foot buffer zone around the clinic entrances and driveway because they burden no more speech than necessary to eliminate the unlawful conduct targeted by the state court's injunction. We strike down as unconstitutional the 36–foot buffer zone as applied to the private property to the north and west of the clinic, the "images observable" provision, the 300–foot no-approach zone around the clinic, and the 300–foot buffer zone around the residences, because these provisions sweep more broadly than necessary to accomplish the permissible goals of the injunction. Accordingly, the judgment of the Florida Supreme Court is

Affirmed in part, and reversed in part.

Justice Scalia, with whom Justice Kennedy and Justice Thomas join, concurring in the judgment in part and dissenting in part.

The judgment in today's case has an appearance of moderation and Solomonic wisdom, upholding as it does some portions of the injunction while disallowing others. That appearance is deceptive. The entire injunction in this case departs so far from the established course of our jurisprudence that in any other context it would have been regarded as a candidate for summary reversal. But the context here is abortion. A long time ago, in dissent from another abortion-related case, Justice O'Connor, joined by then-Justice Rehnquist, wrote: "This Court's abortion decisions have already worked a major distortion in the Court's constitutional jurisprudence. . . . " Today the ad hoc nullification machine claims its latest, greatest, and most surprising victim: the First Amendment.

Because I believe that the judicial creation of a 36–foot zone in which only a particular group, which had broken no law, cannot exercise its rights of speech, assembly, and association, and the judicial enactment of a noise prohibition, applicable to that group and that group alone, are profoundly at odds with our First Amendment precedents and traditions, I dissent.

I. The record of this case contains a videotape, with running caption of time and date, displaying what one must presume to be the worst of the activity justifying the injunction issued by Judge McGregor and partially approved today by this Court. The tape was edited down (from approximately 6 to 8 hours of footage to ½ hour) by Ruth Arick, a management consultant employed by the clinic and by the Feminist Majority Foundation. Anyone seriously interested in what this case was about must view that tape. [A lengthy description is omitted; parts of it include the following:] At one point, Randall Terry arrives and the press converge upon him, apparently in Dixie Way itself. A sign is held near his head reading "Randall Terry Sucks." Terry appears to be speaking to the press and at one point tears pages from a notebook of some kind. Through all of this, abortion opponents and abortion-rights supporters appear to be inches from one another on each side of the south border of the property. They exchange words, but at no time is there any violence or even any discernible jostling or physical contact between these political opponents. . . . The videotape and the rest of the record, including the trial court's findings, show that a great many forms of expression and conduct occurred in the vicinity of the clinic. These include singing, chanting, praying, shouting, the playing of music both from the clinic and from handheld boom boxes, speeches, peaceful picketing, communication of familiar political messages, handbilling, persuasive speech directed at opposing groups on the issue of abortion, efforts to persuade individuals not to have abortions, personal testimony, interviews with the press, and media efforts to report on the protest. What the videotape, the rest of the record, and the trial court's findings do not contain is any suggestion of violence near the clinic, nor do they establish any attempt to prevent entry or exit.

II. [The Court] creates, brand-new for this abortion-related case, an additional standard that is (supposedly) "somewhat more stringent," than intermediate scrutiny, yet not as "rigorous," as strict scrutiny. The Court does not give this new standard a name, but perhaps we could call it intermediate-intermediate scrutiny. The difference between it and intermediate scrutiny (which the Court acknowledges is inappropriate for injunctive restrictions on speech) is frankly too subtle for me to describe, so I must simply recite it: whereas intermediate scrutiny requires that the restriction be "narrowly tailored to serve a significant government interest," the new standard requires that the restriction "burden no more speech than necessary to serve a significant government interest."

[A] restriction upon speech imposed by injunction (whether nominally content based or nominally content neutral) is *at least* as deserving of strict scrutiny as a statutory, content-based restriction. That is so for several reasons: The danger of content-based statutory restrictions upon speech is that they may be designed and used precisely to suppress the ideas in question rather than to achieve any other proper governmental aim. But that same danger exists with injunctions. [Here, the] injunction was sought against a single-issue advocacy group by persons and organizations with a business or social interest in suppressing that group's point of view. The second reason speech-restricting injunctions are at least as deserving of strict scrutiny is obvious enough: they are the product of individual judges rather than of legislatures—and often of judges who have been chagrined by prior disobedience of their orders. The right to free speech should not lightly be placed within the control of a single man or woman. And the third reason is that the injunction is a much more powerful weapon than a statute, and so should be subjected to greater safeguards. Normally, when injunctions are enforced through contempt proceedings, only the defense of factual innocence is available. The collateral bar rule of *Walker v. Birmingham* (1967) eliminates the defense that the injunction itself was unconstitutional. . . .

Finally, though I believe speech-restricting injunctions are dangerous enough to warrant strict scrutiny even when they are not technically content based, I think the injunction in the present case was content based (indeed, viewpoint based) to boot. The Court claims that it was directed, not at those who *spoke* certain things (anti-abortion sentiments), but at those who *did* certain things (violated the earlier injunction). If that were true, then the injunction's residual coverage of "all persons acting in concert or participation with [the named individuals and organizations], or on their behalf" would not include those who merely entertained the same beliefs and wished to express the same views as the named defendants. But the construction given to the injunction by the issuing judge, which is entitled to great weight, is to the contrary: all those who wish to express the same views as the named defendants are deemed to be "acting in concert or participation." Following issuance of the amended injunction, a number of persons were arrested for walking within the 36–foot speech-free zone. At an April 12, 1993, hearing before the trial judge who issued the injunction, the following exchanges occurred:

> MR. LACY: "I was wondering how we can—why we were arrested and confined as being in concert with these people that we don't know, when other people weren't, that were in that same buffer zone, and it was kind of selective as to who was picked and who was arrested and who was obtained for the same buffer zone in the same public injunction."

> THE COURT: "Mr. Lacy, I understand that those on the other side of the issue [abortion-rights supporters] were also in the area. If you are referring to them, the Injunction did not pertain to those on the other side of the issue, because *the word in concert with means in concert with those who had taken a certain position in respect to the clinic, adverse to the clinic. If you are saying that is the selective basis that the pro-choice were not arrested when pro-life was arrested, that's the basis of the selection* . . . . " Tr. 104–105 (Appearance Hearings Held Before Judge McGregor (emphasis added)).

III.   ... According to the Court, the state court imposed the later injunction's "restrictions on petitioner[s'] ... antiabortion message because they repeatedly violated the court's original order." Surprisingly, the Court accepts this reason as valid, without asking whether the court's findings of fact support it—whether, that is, the acts of which the petitioners stood convicted *were* violations of the original injunction.

The Court simply takes this on faith—even though violation of the original injunction is an essential part of the reasoning whereby it approves portions of the amended injunction, even though petitioners denied any violation of the original injunction, even though the utter lack of proper basis for the other challenged portions of the injunction hardly inspires confidence that the lower courts knew what they were doing, and even though close examination of the factual basis for essential conclusions is the usual practice in First Amendment cases....

[The original injunction] prohibited the doing (or urging) of *only three things:* 1) "physically abusing persons entering, leaving, working or using any services" of the abortion clinic (there is no allegation of that); 2) "trespassing on [or] sitting in" the abortion clinic (there is no allegation of that); and 3) "blocking, impeding or obstructing ingress into or egress from" the abortion clinic. Only the last of these has any conceivable application here, and it seems to me that it must reasonably be read to refer to *intentionally* blocking, impeding or obstructing, and *not* to such temporary obstruction as may be the normal and incidental consequence of other protest activity....

I almost forgot to address the facts showing prior violation of law (including judicial order) with respect to the other portion of the injunction the Court upholds: the no-noise-within-earshot-of-patients provision. That is perhaps because, amazingly, neither the Florida courts *nor this Court* makes the slightest attempt to link that provision to prior violations of law. The relevant portion of the Court's opinion, Part II–B, simply reasons that hospital patients should not have to be bothered with noise, from political protests or anything else (which is certainly true), and that therefore the noise restrictions could be imposed *by injunction* (which is certainly false). Since such a law is reasonable, in other words, it can be enacted by a single man to bind only a single class of social protesters. The pro-abortion demonstrators who were often making (if respondents' videotape is accurate) *more* noise than the petitioners, can continue to shout their chants at their opponents exiled across the street to their hearts' content....

... Nor is it relevant to my point that "petitioners themselves studiously refrained from challenging the factual basis for the injunction." I accept the facts as the Florida court found them; I deny that those facts support its *conclusion* ... that the original injunction had been violated. The Court concludes its response as follows:

"We must therefore judge this case on the assumption that the evidence and testimony presented to the state court supported its findings that the presence of protesters standing, marching, and demonstrating near the clinic's entrance interfered with ingress to and egress from the clinic despite the issuance of the earlier injunction.''

But a finding that they "interfered with ingress and egress ... *despite* the ... earlier injunction" is not enough. The earlier injunction did not, and could not, prohibit all "interference"—for example, the minor interference incidentally produced by lawful picketing and leafleting. What the Court needs, and cannot come up with, is a finding that the petitioners interfered *in a manner prohibited by the earlier injunction.* A conclusion that they "block[ed], imped[ed] or obstruct[ed] ingress ... or egress" (the terminology of the original injunction) within the only fair, and indeed the only permissible, meaning of that phrase cannot be supported by the facts found. . . .

Finally, I turn to the Court's application of the second part of its test: whether the provisions of the injunction "burden no more speech than necessary" to serve the significant interest protected. [T]he Court could have (for the first time) ordered the demonstrators to stay out of the street (the original injunction did not remotely require that). It could have limited the number of demonstrators permitted on the clinic side of Dixie Way. And it could have forbidden the pickets to walk on the driveways. The Court's only response to these options is that "[t]he state court was convinced that [they would not work] in view of the failure of the first injunction to protect access." But must we accept that conclusion as valid—when the original injunction contained no command (or at the very least no *clear* command) that had been disobeyed, and contained nothing even *related* to staying out of the street? If the "burden no more speech than necessary" requirement can be avoided by merely opining that (for some reason) no lesser restriction than *this* one will be obeyed, it is not much of a requirement at all.

[T]he Court has left a powerful loaded weapon lying about today. What we have decided seems to be, and will be reported by the media as, an abortion case. But it will go down in the lawbooks, it will be cited, as a free-speech injunction case—and the damage its novel principles produce will be considerable. The proposition that injunctions against speech are subject to a standard indistinguishable from (unless perhaps more lenient in its application than) the "intermediate scrutiny" standard we have used for "time, place, and manner" legislative restrictions; the notion that injunctions against speech need not be closely tied to any violation of law, but may simply implement sound social policy; and the practice of accepting trial-court conclusions permitting injunctions without considering whether those conclusions are supported by any findings of fact—these latest by-products of our abortion jurisprudence ought to give all friends of liberty great concern. For these reasons, I dissent from that portion of the judgment upholding parts of the injunction.

Justice Stevens, concurring in part and dissenting in part.

[I]njunctive relief should be judged by a more lenient standard than legislation. [L]egislation is imposed on an entire community, regardless of individual culpability. By contrast, injunctions apply solely to an individual or a limited group of individuals who, by engaging in illegal conduct, have been judicially deprived of some liberty—the normal consequence of illegal activity. [A] statute prohibiting demonstrations within 36 feet of an abortion clinic would probably violate the First Amendment, but an injunction directed at a limited group of persons who have engaged in unlawful conduct in a similar zone might well be constitutional. [We should give] appropriate deference to the judge's unique familiarity with the facts.

[The opinion of SOUTER, J., concurring, is omitted.]

Notes

1. *Schenck v. Pro–Choice Network of Western New York,* 519 U.S. 357, 117 S.Ct. 855, 137 L.Ed.2d 1 (1997). Plaintiffs, including an abortion clinic, secured an injunction against petitioners and others from hindering access to the abortion clinic. Rehnquist, C.J., for the Court, finding many factual similarities between this case and *Madsen,* applied that case to determine if the injunction burdened "more speech than necessary to serve a significant governmental interest."

First, the *"floating buffer zone"*—which banned "demonstrating" within fifteen feet of "any person or vehicle seeking access to or leaving" the clinic—violated the First Amendment and cannot be sustained "on this record." The Court ruled (8 to 1) that this portion of the injunction was too broad as to location (public sidewalks) and the type of speech prevented ("communicating a message from a normal conversational distance or handing leaflets to persons entering or leaving the clinics"). The Court acknowledged that it had "before us a record that shows physically abusive conduct, harassment of the police that hampered law enforcement, and the tendency of even peaceful conversations to devolve into aggressive and sometimes violent conduct." *Madsen* illustrates that a record of abusive conduct may make a prohibition on classic speech in limited parts of the public sidewalk permissible. However, the Court "need not decide whether the governmental interests involved would ever justify some sort of zone of separation between individuals entering the clinics and protestors, measured by the distance between the two. We hold here that because this broad prohibition on speech 'floats,' it cannot be sustained on this record."

The 15–foot floating buffer zone around vehicles restricted the speech of those "who simply line the sidewalk or curb in an effort to chant, shout, or hold signs peacefully." A more limited (and fixed) buffer that simply kept protestors from driveways and parking lot entrances would have been sufficient. There is no "generalized 'right to be left alone' on the public street or sidewalk." The anti-abortion protested had engaged in "aggressive techniques," such as "jostling, grabbing, pushing, and shoving women," and " 'in-your-face' yelling." People must tolerate "insulting, and even outrageous speech" to provide adequate "breathing space" for the First Amendment. The 15–foot separation made it difficult for protestors to communicate with people entering or leaving the clinic, because some of the sidewalks were only 17–feet wide. If the protestors tried to stay 15–feet behind the person, they are faced with the problem of avoiding people entering or leaving the clinic and walking the opposite direction.

The Court also found constitutional (6 to 3) the trial court's imposition of a *"fixed buffer zone"*—which banned "demonstrating" within fifteen feet of "doorways or doorway entrances, parking lot entrances, driveways and driveway entrances" of the clinic.

This injunction was necessary to preserve "public safety." Even though the plaintiffs here and in *Madsen* never pleaded a "threat to public safety," that does not preclude the trial court from relying on this ground. The evidence showed that protestors "effectively blocked or hindered people from entering and exiting" the clinic doorways, and harassed local police "verbally and by mail," which made it far from certain that the police would be able to effectively counteract protestors who blocked doorways.

The defendants "stipulated that 'physical blocking' could be enjoined," but challenged the rest of the injunction, including the ban on "demonstrating" within the fixed buffer zone, which also banned "peaceful, nonobstructive demonstrations on public sidewalks or rights of way." But the Court ruled that the trial judge "was entitled to conclude" that some of the defendants who were allowed within the fixed buffer would "not merely engage in stationary, nonobstructive demonstrations" but would continue to "aggressively follow and crowd individuals right up to the clinic door and then refuse to move" or would "impede or block the progress of cars." The district court "was entitled to conclude on this record that the only feasible way to shield individuals within the fixed buffer zone from unprotected conduct" is to "keep the entire area clear of defendant protestors."

The Court rejected the argument that the court should have first tried a non-speech injunction or that the injunction's term "demonstrators" is vague. Also, the Court said that the injunction is not content-based simply because it allows a patient to terminate a protestor's right to speak when the patient disagrees with the message being conveyed. The abortion counselors remain free to espouse their message outside the 15–foot buffer zone, and the limit on their freedom to speak this message within the zone is a "result of their own previous harassment and intimidation of patients."

Scalia, J., joined by Kennedy & Thomas, JJ., concurring in part and dissenting in part, would have invalidated the entire injunction. The dissent said that the majority allows a trial judge to issue a decree even if it is not necessary to protect the plaintiff if the majority thinks that it was necessary to protect the public interest. "Every private suit makes the district judge a sort of one-man Committee of Public Safety." The Court, said the dissent, approved the injunction not on the basis of what the trial court found but on the basis of what the trial court might have found. In this case, said the dissent, "no cause of action related to obstruction of access was properly found to support the injunction."

Breyer, J., concurring in part and dissenting in part, would have upheld the injunction in its entirety . .

2. Assume a period before federal and state laws made it illegal for private lunch counters to discriminate on the basis of race in serving

customers. Protestors might target a segregated diner and hinder lunch counter patrons from entering the establishment (sometimes by yelling at patrons, chanting, entering the premises and sitting at lunch counters but ordering no or very little food). Supporters of the lunch counter might fight with the protestors. If local police were unable to counteract these demonstrators, could a federal or state court enjoin such activities by civil rights protestors?

3. Some celebrities have successfully sought injunctions against "paparazzi" (photographers who follow celebrities and frequently take pictures in an annoying way). One court ordered a paparazzi to stay 25 feet away from Jacqueline Kennedy Onassis when she traveled in public. Is this type of floating buffer zone now unconstitutional? Are paparazzi engaged in First Amendment activities? If so, are these injunctions always unconstitutional?

Under what circumstances, if any, might a court be able to enjoin (or a statute prohibit) aggressive street beggars, *i.e.*, people who follow others on the public sidewalks, asking for hand-outs, yelling, cursing, pushing, shoving, and engaging in "in-your-face" conduct?

10–4. FIGHTING WORDS AND HOSTILE AUDIENCES

COHEN v. CALIFORNIA
403 U.S. 15, 91 S.Ct. 1780, 29 L.Ed.2d 284 (1971).

MR. JUSTICE HARLAN delivered the opinion of the Court.

This case may seem at first blush too inconsequential to find its way into our books, but the issue it presents is of no small constitutional significance. Appellant Paul Robert Cohen was convicted in the Los Angeles Municipal Court of violating that part of California Penal Code § 415 which prohibits "maliciously and willfully disturb[ing] the peace or quiet of any neighborhood or person ... by ... offensive conduct...." He was given 30 days' imprisonment. The facts upon which his conviction rests are detailed in the opinion of the Court of Appeal of California, Second Appellate District, as follows:

> On April 26, 1968, the defendant was observed in the Los Angeles County Courthouse in the corridor outside of division 20 of the municipal court wearing a jacket bearing the words "Fuck the Draft" which were plainly visible. There were women and children present in the corridor. The defendant was arrested. The defendant testified that he wore the jacket knowing that the words were on the jacket as a means of informing the public of the depth of his feelings against the Vietnam War and the draft.

> The defendant did not engage in, nor threaten to engage in, nor did anyone as the result of his conduct in fact commit or threaten to commit any act of violence. The defendant did not make any loud or unusual noise, nor was there any evidence that he uttered any sound prior to his arrest.

In affirming the conviction the Court of Appeal held that "offensive conduct" means "behavior which has a tendency to provoke *others* to acts of violence or to in turn disturb the peace," and that the State had proved this element because, on the facts of this case, "[i]t was certainly reasonably foreseeable that such conduct might cause others to rise up to commit a violent act against the person of the defendant or attempt to forcibly remove his jacket." ...

In order to lay hands on the precise issue which this case involves, it is useful first to canvass various matters which this record does *not* present.

The conviction quite clearly rests upon the asserted offensiveness of the *words* Cohen used to convey his message to the public. The only "conduct" which the State sought to punish is the fact of communication.... Further, the State certainly lacks power to punish Cohen for the underlying content of the message the inscription conveyed. At least so long as there is no showing of an intent to incite disobedience to or disruption of the draft, Cohen could not, consistently with the First and Fourteenth Amendments, be punished for asserting the evident position on the inutility or immorality of the draft his jacket reflected.

Appellant's conviction, then, rests squarely upon his exercise of the "freedom of speech" protected from arbitrary governmental interference by the Constitution and can be justified, if at all, only as a valid regulation of the manner in which he exercised that freedom, not as a permissible prohibition on the substantive message it conveys.... In this vein, too, however, we think it important to note that several issues typically associated with such problems are not presented here.

In the first place, Cohen was tried under a statute applicable throughout the entire State. Any attempt to support this conviction on the ground that the statute seeks to preserve an appropriately decorous atmosphere in the courthouse where Cohen was arrested must fail....

In the second place, as it comes to us, this case cannot be said to fall within those relatively few categories of instances where prior decisions have established the power of government to deal more comprehensively with certain forms of individual expression simply upon a showing that such a form was employed. This is not, for example, an obscenity case. Whatever else may be necessary to give rise to the States' broader power to prohibit obscene expression, such expression must be, in some significant way, erotic....

This Court has also held that the States are free to ban the simple use, without a demonstration of additional justifying circumstances, of so-called "fighting words," those personally abusive epithets which, when addressed to the ordinary citizen, are, as a matter of common knowledge, inherently likely to provoke violent reaction. *Chaplinsky v. New Hampshire,* [noted infra]. While the four-letter word displayed by Cohen in relation to the draft is not uncommonly employed in a personally provocative fashion, in this instance it was clearly not "directed to the person of the hearer." No individual actually or likely to be present could reasonably have regarded the words on appellant's jacket as a direct personal insult. Nor do we have here an instance of the exercise of the State's police power to prevent a speaker from intentionally provoking a given group to hostile reaction. Cf. *Feiner v. New York,* [noted infra]; *Terminiello v. Chicago,* [noted infra]. There is, as noted above, no showing that anyone who saw Cohen was in fact violently aroused or that appellant intended such a result.

Finally, in arguments before this Court much has been made of the claim that Cohen's distasteful mode of expression was thrust upon unwilling or unsuspecting viewers, and that the State might therefore legitimately act as it did in order to protect the sensitive from otherwise unavoidable exposure to appellant's crude form of protest. Of course, the mere presumed presence of unwitting listeners or viewers does not serve automatically to justify curtailing all speech capable of giving offense. While this Court has recognized that government may properly act in many situations to prohibit intrusion into the privacy of the home of unwelcome views and ideas which cannot be totally banned from the public dialogue, e.g., *Rowan v. United States Post Office Dept.,* 397 U.S. 728, 90 S.Ct. 1484, 25 L.Ed.2d 736 (1970), we have at the same time consistently stressed that "we are often 'captives' outside the sanctuary of the home and subject to objectionable speech." Id. The ability of government, consonant with the Constitution, to shut off discourse solely to protect others from hearing it is, in other words, dependent upon a showing that substantial privacy interests are being invaded in an essentially intolerable manner. Any broader view of this authority would effectively empower a majority to silence dissidents simply as a matter of personal predilections.

In this regard, persons confronted with Cohen's jacket were in a quite different posture than, say, those subjected to the raucous emissions of sound trucks blaring outside their residences. Those in the Los Angeles courthouse could effectively avoid further bombardment of their sensibilities simply by averting their eyes. And, while it may be that one has a more substantial claim to a recognizable privacy interest when walking through a courthouse corridor than, for example, strolling through Central Park, surely it is nothing like the interest in being free from unwanted expression in the confines of one's own home. Given the subtlety and complexity of the factors involved, if Cohen's "speech" was otherwise entitled to constitutional protection, we do not think the fact that some unwilling "listeners" in a public building may have been briefly exposed to it can serve to justify this breach of the peace conviction where, as here, there was no evidence that persons powerless to avoid appellant's conduct did in fact object to it, and where that portion of the statute upon which Cohen's conviction rests evinces no concern, either on its face or as construed by the California courts, with the special plight of the captive auditor, but, instead, indiscriminately sweeps within its prohibitions all "offensive conduct" that disturbs "any neighborhood or person."

Against this background, the issue flushed by this case stands out in bold relief. It is whether California can excise, as "offensive conduct," one particular scurrilous epithet from the public discourse, either upon the theory of the court below that its use is inherently likely to cause violent reaction or upon a more general assertion that the States, acting as guardians of public morality, may properly remove this offensive word from the public vocabulary.

The rationale of the California court is plainly untenable. At most it reflects an "undifferentiated fear or apprehension of disturbance [which] is not enough to overcome the right to freedom of expression." We have been shown no evidence that substantial numbers of citizens are standing ready to strike out physically at whoever may assault their sensibilities with execrations like that uttered by Cohen. There may be some persons about with such lawless and violent proclivities, but that is an insufficient base upon which to erect, consistently with constitutional values, a governmental power to force persons who wish to ventilate their dissident views into avoiding particular forms of expression. The argument amounts to little more than the self-defeating proposition that to avoid physical censorship of one who has not sought to provoke such a response by a hypothetical coterie of the violent and lawless, the States may more appropriately effectuate that censorship themselves.

Admittedly, it is not so obvious that the First and Fourteenth Amendment must be taken to disable the States from punishing public utterance of this unseemly expletive in order to maintain what they regard as a suitable level of discourse within the body politic. We think, however, that examination and reflection will reveal the shortcomings of a contrary viewpoint. . . .

To many, the immediate consequence of this freedom may often appear to be only verbal tumult, discord, and even offensive utterance. These are, however, within established limits, in truth necessary side effects of the broader enduring values which the process of open debate permits us to achieve. That the air may at times seem filled with verbal cacophony is, in this sense not a sign of weakness but of strength. We cannot lose sight of the fact that, in what otherwise might seem a trifling and annoying instance of individual distasteful abuse of a privilege, these fundamental societal values are truly implicated.

[T]he principle contended for by the State seems inherently boundless. How is one to distinguish this from any other offensive word? Surely the State has no right to cleanse public debate to the point where it is grammatically palatable to the most squeamish among us. Yet no readily ascertainable general principle exists for stopping short of that result were we to affirm the judgment below. For, while the particular four-letter word being litigated here is perhaps more distasteful than most others of its genre, it is nevertheless often true that one man's vulgarity is another's lyric. Indeed, we think it is largely because governmental officials cannot make principled distinctions in this area that the Constitution leave matters of taste and style so largely to the individual.

Additionally, we cannot overlook the fact, because it is well illustrated by the episode involved here, that much linguistic expression serves a dual communicative function: it conveys not only ideas capable of relatively precise, detached explication, but otherwise inexpressible emotions as well. In fact, words are often chosen as much for their emotive as their cognitive force. We cannot sanction the view that the Constitution, while solicitous of the cognitive content of individual speech, has little or no regard for that emotive function which, practically speaking, may often be the more important element of the overall message sought to be communicated. . . .

Finally, and in the same vein, we cannot indulge the facile assumption that one can forbid particular words without also running a substantial risk of suppressing ideas in the process. Indeed, governments might soon seize upon the censorship of particular words as a convenient guise for banning the expression of unpopular views. We have been able as noted above, to discern little social benefit that might result from running the risk of opening the door to such grave results.

It is, in sum, our judgment that, absent a more particularized and compelling reason for its actions, the State may not, consistently with the First and Fourteenth Amendments, make the simple public display here involved of this single four-letter expletive a criminal offense. Because that is the only arguably sustainable rationale for the conviction here at issue, the judgment below must be

Reversed.

[The dissenting opinion of BLACKMUN, J., joined by BURGER, C.J., and BLACK, J., and joined in part by WHITE, J., is omitted.]

Notes

1. Three of the cases cited and relied on in *Cohen* are of particular interest. First, *Chaplinsky v. New Hampshire,* 315 U.S. 568, 62 S.Ct. 766, 86 L.Ed. 1031 (1942). Chaplinsky, encountering the city fire marshal, addressed him as a "God damned racketeer and a damned fascist." The Court upheld his conviction under a narrowly drawn state statute banning face-to-face words "having a direct tendency to cause acts of violence by the person to whom, individually, the remark is addressed." The test, said the Court, "is what men of common intelligence would understand would be words likely to cause an average addressee to fight."

In *Terminiello v. Chicago,* 337 U.S. 1, 69 S.Ct. 894, 93 L.Ed. 1131 (1949) the Court invalidated a breach of the peace conviction of Terminiello for denouncing Jews and others, including the turbulent and angry crowd outside the auditorium where he was speaking. The trial judge had instructed the jury to convict if the speech "stirs the public to anger, invites dispute, brings about a condition of unrest, or creates a disturbance, or if it molests the inhabitants in the enjoyment of peace and quiet by arousing alarm." The Court reversed the conviction without reaching the question of whether the speech constituted "fighting words." The jury instruction was in error. "[A] function of free speech under our system of government is to invite dispute," and do the other things explicitly forbidden by the jury instruction. A conviction "resting on any of those grounds [relied on in the jury instruction] may not stand."

Feiner v. New York, 340 U.S. 315, 71 S.Ct. 303, 95 L.Ed. 295 (1951) upheld the disorderly conduct conviction of Feiner, who was speaking on a street corner attacking among others, President Truman as a "bum", and the American Legion as the "Nazi Gestapo." Some in the crowd were hostile and others favored Feiner. After he had spoken for about a half hour urging blacks to "rise up in arms," the police arrested him and led him away in an effort to prevent violent reaction. "It is one thing to say that the police cannot be used as an instrument of suppression of unpopular views, and another to say that, when as here the speaker passes the bounds of argument or persuasion and undertakes incitement to riot, they are powerless to prevent a breach of the peace."

2. After *Cohen* the Court has generally overturned similar convictions on the grounds, often used in First Amendment cases, that the state statute was overbroad or too vague. *Gooding v. Wilson,* 405 U.S. 518, 92 S.Ct. 1103, 31 L.Ed.2d 408 (1972) is an illustrative case. When police officers were attempting to restore order to a public building Wilson said to one: "White son of a bitch, I'll kill you," and to another: "You son of a bitch, if you ever put your hands on me again, I'll cut you all to pieces." The Georgia statute prohibited "opprobrious or abusive language tending to cause a breach of the peace." The majority found, after examining Georgia law, that the state standard allowed juries to determine guilt as "measured by common understanding and practice," a phrase not necessarily limited to "fighting words."

3. *Collin v. Smith,* 578 F.2d 1197 (7th Cir.1978), cert. denied 439 U.S. 916, 99 S.Ct. 291, 58 L.Ed.2d 264 (1978). The members of the National Socialist Party of America, clothed with the swastika and other symbols of the Nazis, were planning to march in front of the Village Hall in Skokie, a Chicago suburb with a large Jewish population, including several thousand survivors of the Nazi holocaust. The court invalidated various attempts to forbid the march, including an ordinance No. 77–5–N–995 (hereinafter "995") prohibiting the dissemination of any materials promoting and inciting racial hatred. The court said in part:

> It is said that the proposed march is not speech, or even speech plus, but rather an invasion, intensely menacing no matter how peacefully conducted. The Village's expert psychiatric witness, in fact, testified that the effect of the march would be much the same regardless of whether uniforms and swastikas were displayed, due to the intrusion of self-proclaimed Nazis into what he characterized as predominately Jewish turf. There is room under the First Amendment for the government to protect targeted listeners from offensive speech, but only when the speaker intrudes on the privacy of the home, or a captive audience cannot practically avoid exposure.... This case does not involve intrusion into people's homes. There *need be* no captive audience, as Village residents may, if they wish, simply avoid the Village Hall for thirty minutes on a Sunday afternoon, which no doubt would be their normal course of conduct on a day when the Village Hall was not open in the regular course of business. Absent such intrusion or captivity, there is no justifiable substantial privacy interest to save 995 from constitutional infirmity, when it attempts, by fiat, to declare the entire Village, at all times, a privacy zone that may be sanitized from the offensiveness of Nazi ideology and symbols.

[The ordinance also] suffers from substantial overbreadth [because] it could conceivably be applied to criminalize dissemination of *The Merchant of Venice* or a vigorous discussion of the merits of reverse racial discrimination in Skokie. [Though the ordinance may be] fatally vague as well, because it turns in part on subjective reactions to prohibited conduct, we do not deem it necessary to rest our decision on that ground.

R.A.V. v. CITY OF ST. PAUL
505 U.S. 377, 112 S.Ct. 2538, 120 L.Ed.2d 305 (1992).

JUSTICE SCALIA delivered the opinion of the Court.

In the predawn hours of June 21, 1990, petitioner and several other teenagers allegedly assembled a crudely-made cross by taping together broken chair legs. They then allegedly burned the cross inside the fenced yard of a black family that lived across the street from the house where petitioner was staying. Although this conduct could have been punished under any of a number of laws,[1] one of the two provisions under which respondent city of St. Paul chose to charge petitioner (then a juvenile) was the St. Paul Bias–Motivated Crime Ordinance, which provides:

"Whoever places on public or private property a symbol, object, appellation, characterization or graffiti, including, but not limited to, a burning cross or Nazi swastika, which one knows or has reasonable grounds to know arouses anger, alarm or resentment in others on the basis of race, color, creed, religion or gender commits disorderly conduct and shall be guilty of a misdemeanor."

Petitioner moved to dismiss this count on the ground that the St. Paul ordinance was substantially overbroad and impermissibly content-based and therefore facially invalid under the First Amendment.[2] The trial court granted this motion, but the Minnesota Supreme Court reversed. That court rejected petitioner's overbreadth claim because, as construed in prior Minnesota cases, the modifying phrase "arouses anger, alarm or resentment in others" limited the reach of the ordinance to conduct that amounts to "fighting words," i.e., "conduct that itself inflicts injury or tends to incite immediate violence ... ," *In re Welfare of R.A.V.,* (Minn.1991)(citing *Chaplinsky v. New Hampshire* (1942)), and therefore the ordinance reached only expression "that the first amendment does not protect." The court also concluded that the ordinance was not impermissibly content-based because, in its view, "the ordinance is a narrowly tailored means toward accomplishing the compelling govern-

1. The conduct might have violated Minnesota statutes carrying significant penalties. See, e.g., Minn.Stat. § 609.713(1)(1987)(providing for up to five years in prison for terroristic threats); § 609.563 (arson)(providing for up to five years and a $10,000 fine, depending on the value of the property intended to be damaged); § 606.595 (Supp.1992)(criminal dam-

age to property)(providing for up to one year and a $3,000 fine, depending upon the extent of the damage to the property).

2. Petitioner has also been charged, in Count I of the delinquency petition, with a violation of Minn.Stat. § 609.2231(4)(Supp.1990)(racially motivated assaults). Petitioner did not challenge this count.

mental interest in protecting the community against bias-motivated threats to public safety and order." ...

I. In construing the St. Paul ordinance, we are bound by the construction given to it by the Minnesota court. Accordingly, we accept the Minnesota Supreme Court's authoritative statement that the ordinance reaches only those expressions that constitute "fighting words" within the meaning of *Chaplinsky*. Petitioner and his amici urge us to modify the scope of the *Chaplinsky* formulation, thereby invalidating the ordinance as "substantially overbroad." We find it unnecessary to consider this issue. Assuming, arguendo, that all of the expression reached by the ordinance is proscribable under the "fighting words" doctrine, we nonetheless conclude that the ordinance is facially unconstitutional in that it prohibits otherwise permitted speech solely on the basis of the subjects the speech addresses....

We have sometimes said that [some] categories of expression are "not within the area of constitutionally protected speech," *Roth*, supra; *Beauharnais,* supra; *Chaplinsky,* supra, or that the "protection of the First Amendment does not extend" to them. Such statements must be taken in context, however, and are no more literally true than is the occasionally repeated shorthand characterizing obscenity "as not being speech at all." What they mean is that these areas of speech can, consistently with the First Amendment, be regulated *because of their constitutionally proscribable content* (obscenity, defamation, etc.)—not that they are categories of speech entirely invisible to the Constitution, so that they may be made the vehicles for content discrimination unrelated to their distinctively proscribable content. Thus, the government may proscribe libel; but it may not make the further content discrimination of proscribing only libel critical of the government. We recently acknowledged this distinction in *[New York] v. Ferber,* [§ 10–12.1] where, in upholding New York's child pornography law, we expressly recognized that there was no "question here of censoring a particular literary theme.... " ...

Our cases surely do not establish the proposition that the First Amendment imposes no obstacle whatsoever to regulation of particular instances of such proscribable expression, so that the government "may regulate [them] freely," post (White, J., concurring in judgment). That would mean that a city council could enact an ordinance prohibiting only those legally obscene works that contain criticism of the city government or, indeed, that do not include endorsement of the city government. Such a simplistic, all-or-nothing-at-all approach to First Amendment protection is at odds with common sense and with our jurisprudence as well.[4] It

---

4. Justice White concedes that a city council cannot prohibit only those legally obscene works that contain criticism of the city government, but asserts that to be the consequence, not of the First Amendment, but of the Equal Protection Clause. Such content-based discrimination would not, he asserts, "be rationally related to a legitimate government interest." But of course the only *reason* that government interest is not a "legitimate" one is that it violates the First Amendment. This Court itself has occasionally fused the First Amendment into the Equal Protection Clause in this fashion,

is not true that "fighting words" have at most a *"de minimis"* expressive content, or that their content is in *all respects* "worthless and undeserving of constitutional protection"; sometimes they are quite expressive indeed. We have not said that they constitute *"no part of the expression of ideas,"* but only that they constitute "no *essential* part of any exposition of ideas." *Chaplinsky* (emphasis added).

The proposition that a particular instance of speech can be proscribable on the basis of one feature (e.g., obscenity) but not on the basis of another (e.g., opposition to the city government) is commonplace, and has found application in many contexts. We have long held, for example, that nonverbal expressive activity can be banned because of the action it entails, but not because of the ideas it expresses—so that burning a flag in violation of an ordinance against outdoor fires could be punishable, whereas burning a flag in violation of an ordinance against dishonoring the flag is not. *[Texas v.] Johnson* [§ 10–10]; *United States v. O'Brien,* [§ 10–10]. Similarly, we have upheld reasonable "time, place, or manner" restrictions, but only if they are "justified without reference to the content of the regulated speech." And just as the power to proscribe particular speech on the basis of a noncontent element (e.g., noise) does not entail the power to proscribe the same speech on the basis of a content element; so also, the power to proscribe it on the basis of *one* content element (e.g., obscenity) does not entail the power to proscribe it on the basis of *other* content elements.

In other words, the exclusion of "fighting words" from the scope of the First Amendment simply means that, for purposes of that Amendment, the unprotected features of the words are, despite their verbal character, essentially a "nonspeech" element of communication. Fighting words are thus analogous to a noisy sound truck: Each is, as Justice Frankfurter recognized, a "mode of speech;" both can be used to convey an idea; but neither has, in and of itself, a claim upon the First Amendment. As with the sound truck, however, so also with fighting words: The government may not regulate use based on hostility—or favoritism—towards the underlying message expressed. Compare *Frisby v. Schultz,* [§ 10.33] (upholding, against facial challenge, a content-neutral ban on targeted residential picketing) with *Carey v. Brown,*

but at least with the acknowledgment (which Justice White cannot afford to make) that the First Amendment underlies its analysis. See *Police Dept. of Chicago v. Mosley,* 408 U.S. 92, 95, 92 S.Ct. 2286, 2289–2290, 33 L.Ed.2d 212 (1972)(ordinance prohibiting only nonlabor picketing violated the Equal Protection Clause because there was no "appropriate governmental interest" supporting the distinction inasmuch as "the First Amendment means that government has no power to restrict expression because of its message, its ideas, its subject matter, or its content").

Justice Stevens seeks to avoid the point by dismissing the notion of obscene anti-government speech as "fantastical," apparently believing that any reference to politics prevents a finding of obscenity. Unfortunately for the purveyors of obscenity, that is obviously false. A shockingly hard core pornographic movie that contains a model sporting a political tattoo can be found, *"taken as a whole* [to] lack serious literary, artistic, political, or scientific value," *Miller v. California,* 413 U.S. 15, 24, 93 S.Ct. 2607, 2614–2615, 37 L.Ed.2d 419 (1973)(emphasis added).... And of course the concept of racist fighting words is, unfortunately, anything but a "highly speculative hypothetical."

[§ 10.3.3] (invalidating a ban on residential picketing that exempted labor picketing).

The concurrences describe us as setting forth a new First Amendment principle that prohibition of constitutionally proscribable speech cannot be "underinclusive," (White, J., concurring in judgment)—a First Amendment "absolutism" whereby "within a particular proscribable category of expression, . . . a government must either proscribe *all* speech or no speech at all," (Stevens, J., concurring in judgment). That easy target is of the concurrences' own invention. In our view, the First Amendment imposes not an "underinclusiveness" limitation but a "content discrimination" limitation upon a State's prohibition of proscribable speech. There is no problem whatever, for example, with a State's prohibiting obscenity (and other forms of proscribable expression) only in certain media or markets, for although that prohibition would be "underinclusive," it would not discriminate on the basis of content.

Even the prohibition against content discrimination that we assert the First Amendment requires is not absolute. It applies differently in the context of proscribable speech than in the area of fully protected speech. The rationale of the general prohibition, after all, is that content discrimination "raises the specter that the Government may effectively drive certain ideas or viewpoints from the marketplace." But content discrimination among various instances of a class of proscribable speech often does not pose this threat.

When the basis for the content discrimination consists entirely of the very reason the entire class of speech at issue is proscribable, no significant danger of idea or viewpoint discrimination exists. Such a reason, having been adjudged neutral enough to support exclusion of the entire class of speech from First Amendment protection, is also neutral enough to form the basis of distinction within the class. To illustrate: A State might choose to prohibit only that obscenity which is the most patently offensive *in its prurience*—i.e., that which involves the most lascivious displays of sexual activity. But it may not prohibit, for example, only that obscenity which includes offensive *political* messages. And the Federal Government can criminalize only those threats of violence that are directed against the President, see 18 U.S.C. § 871—since the reasons why threats of violence are outside the First Amendment (protecting individuals from the fear of violence, from the disruption that fear engenders, and from the possibility that the threatened violence will occur) have special force when applied to the person of the President. See *Watts v. United States*, 394 U.S. 705, 707, 89 S.Ct. 1399, 1401, 22 L.Ed.2d 664 (1969)(upholding the facial validity of § 871 because of the "overwhelming interest in protecting the safety of [the] Chief Executive and in allowing him to perform his duties without interference from threats of physical violence"). But the Federal Government may not criminalize only those threats against the President that mention his policy on aid to inner cities. And to take a final example (one mentioned by Justice Stevens), a State may choose to regulate price advertising in one industry but not in others, because the risk of fraud (one of the characteristics of commercial speech that justifies depriving it of full First Amendment protection) is in its view greater there. But a State may not prohibit only that commercial advertising that depicts men in a demeaning fashion.

Another valid basis for according differential treatment to even a content-defined subclass of proscribable speech is that the subclass happens to be associated with particular "secondary effects" of the speech, so that the regulation is *"justified* without reference to the content of the ... speech," *Renton v. Playtime Theatres, Inc.,* 475 U.S. 41, 48, 106 S.Ct. 925, 929, 89 L.Ed.2d 29 (1986); see also *Young v. American Mini Theatres, Inc.,* 427 U.S. 50, 71, n. 34, 96 S.Ct. 2440, 2453 n. 34, 49 L.Ed.2d 310 (1976)(plurality). A State could, for example, permit all obscene live performances except those involving minors. Moreover, since words can in some circumstances violate laws directed not against speech but against conduct (a law against treason, for example, is violated by telling the enemy the nation's defense secrets), a particular content-based subcategory of a proscribable class of speech can be swept up incidentally within the reach of a statute directed at conduct rather than speech. Thus, for example, sexually derogatory "fighting words," among other words, may produce a violation of Title VII's general prohibition against sexual discrimination in employment practices, 42 U.S.C. § 2000e–2; 29 CFR § 1604.11 (1991). See also 18 U.S.C. § 242; 42 U.S.C. §§ 1981, 1982. Where the government does not target conduct on the basis of its expressive content, acts are not shielded from regulation merely because they express a discriminatory idea or philosophy.

[T]o validate [selective restrictions on speech] (where totally proscribable speech is at issue) it may not even be necessary to identify any particular "neutral" basis, so long as the nature of the content discrimination is such that there is no realistic possibility that official suppression of ideas is afoot. (We cannot think of any First Amendment interest that would stand in the way of a State's prohibiting only those obscene motion pictures with blue-eyed actresses.) Save for that limitation, the regulation of "fighting words," like the regulation of noisy speech, may address some offensive instances and leave other, equally offensive, instances alone.

II. Applying these principles to the St. Paul ordinance, we conclude that, even as narrowly construed by the Minnesota Supreme Court, the ordinance is facially unconstitutional. Although the phrase in the ordinance, "arouses anger, alarm or resentment in others," has been limited by the Minnesota Supreme Court's construction to reach only those symbols or displays that amount to "fighting words," the remaining, unmodified terms make clear that the ordinance applies only to "fighting words" that insult, or provoke violence, "on the basis of race, color, creed, religion or gender." Displays containing abusive invective, no matter how vicious or severe, are permissible unless they are addressed to one of the specified disfavored topics. Those who wish to use "fighting words" in connection with other ideas—to express hostility, for example, on the basis of political affiliation, union membership, or homosexuality—are not covered. The First Amendment does not permit St. Paul to impose special prohibitions on those speakers who express views on disfavored subjects.

In its practical operation, moreover, the ordinance goes even beyond mere content discrimination, to actual viewpoint discrimination. Displays containing some words—odious racial epithets, for example—would be prohibited to proponents of all views. But "fighting words" that do not themselves invoke race, color, creed, religion, or gender—aspersions upon a person's mother, for example—would seemingly be usable *ad libitum* in the placards of those arguing *in favor* of racial, color, etc. tolerance and equality, but could not be used by that speaker's opponents. One could hold up a sign saying, for example, that all "anti-Catholic bigots" are misbegotten; but not that all "papists" are, for that would insult and provoke violence "on the basis of religion." St. Paul has no such authority to license one side of a debate to fight freestyle, while requiring the other to follow Marquis of Queensberry Rules.

What we have here, it must be emphasized, is not a prohibition of fighting words that are directed at certain persons or groups (which would be *facially* valid if it met the requirements of the Equal Protection Clause); but rather, a prohibition of fighting words that contain (as the Minnesota Supreme Court repeatedly emphasized) messages of "bias-motivated" hatred and in particular, as applied to this case, messages "based on virulent notions of racial supremacy." 464 N.W.2d, at 508, 511. One must wholeheartedly agree with the Minnesota Supreme Court that "it is the responsibility, even the obligation, of diverse communities to confront such notions in whatever form they appear," ibid., but the manner of that confrontation cannot consist of selective limitations upon speech. St. Paul's brief asserts that a general "fighting words" law would not meet the city's needs because only a content-specific measure can communicate to minority groups that the "group hatred" aspect of such speech "is not condoned by the majority." Brief for Respondent 25. The point of the First Amendment is that majority preferences must be expressed in some fashion other than silencing speech on the basis of its content.

. . . St. Paul concedes in its brief that the ordinance applies only to "racial, religious, or gender-specific symbols" such as "a burning cross, Nazi swastika or other instrumentality of like import." [T]he reason why fighting words are categorically excluded from the protection of the First Amendment is not that their content communicates any particular idea, but that their content embodies a particularly intolerable (and socially unnecessary) *mode* of expressing *whatever* idea the speaker wishes to convey. St. Paul has not singled out an especially offensive mode of expression—it has not, for example, selected for prohibition only those fighting words that communicate ideas in a threatening (as opposed to a merely obnoxious) manner. Rather, it has proscribed fighting words of whatever manner that communicate messages of racial, gender, or religious intolerance. Selectivity of this sort creates the possibility that the city is seeking to handicap the expression of particular ideas. That possibility would alone be enough to render the ordinance presumptively invalid, but St. Paul's comments and concessions in this case elevate the possibility to a certainty[7]....

Finally, St. Paul and its *amici* ... assert that the ordinance helps to ensure the basic human rights of members of groups that have historically been subjected to discrimination, including the right of such group members to live in peace where they wish. We do not doubt that these interests are compelling, and that the ordinance can be said to promote them.... The dispositive question in this case, therefore, is whether content discrimination is reasonably necessary to achieve St. Paul's compelling interests; it plainly is not. An ordinance not limited to the favored topics, for example, would have precisely the same beneficial effect. In fact the only interest distinctively served by the content limitation is that of displaying the city council's special hostility towards the particular biases thus singled out. That is precisely what the First Amendment forbids. The politicians of St. Paul are entitled to express that hostility—but not through the means of imposing unique limitations upon speakers who (however benightedly) disagree.

Let there be no mistake about our belief that burning a cross in someone's front yard is reprehensible. But St. Paul has sufficient means at its disposal to prevent such behavior without adding the First Amendment to the fire.

The judgment of the Minnesota Supreme Court is reversed, and the case is remanded for proceedings not inconsistent with this opinion.

It is so ordered.

JUSTICE WHITE, with whom JUSTICE BLACKMUN and JUSTICE O'CONNOR join, and with whom JUSTICE STEVENS joins except as to Part I(A), concurring in the judgment....

This case could easily be decided within the contours of established First Amendment law by holding, as petitioner argues, that the St. Paul ordinance is fatally overbroad because it criminalizes not only unprotected expression but expression protected by the First Amendment. Instead, "finding it unnecessary" to consider the questions upon which we granted review, the Court holds the ordinance facially unconstitutional on a ground that was never presented to the Minnesota Supreme Court, a ground that has not been briefed by the parties before this Court, a ground that requires serious departures from the teaching of prior cases....

I. [T]he Court announces that earlier Courts did not mean their repeated statements that certain categories of expression are "not within

---

7. St. Paul has not argued in this case that the ordinance merely regulates that subclass of fighting words which is most likely to provoke a violent response. But even if one assumes (as appears unlikely) that the categories selected may be so de-scribed, that would not justify selective regulation under a "secondary effects" theory. [I]t is clear that the St. Paul ordinance regulates on the basis of the "primary" effect of the speech—i.e., its persuasive (or repellant) force. [footnote repositioned]

the area of constitutionally protected speech." *Roth,* supra. See ante, citing *Chaplinsky.* The present Court submits that such clear statements "must be taken in context" and are not "literally true." . . . Should the government want to criminalize certain fighting words, the Court now requires it to criminalize all fighting words.

. . . It is inconsistent to hold that the government may proscribe an entire category of speech because the content of that speech is evil, but that the government may not treat a subset of that category differently without violating the First Amendment; the content of the subset is by definition worthless and undeserving of constitutional protection.

The majority's observation that fighting words are "quite expressive indeed," is no answer. Fighting words are not a means of exchanging views, rallying supporters, or registering a protest; they are directed against individuals to provoke violence or to inflict injury. Therefore, a ban on all fighting words or on a subset of the fighting words category would restrict only the social evil of hate speech, without creating the danger of driving viewpoints from the marketplace.

Therefore, the Court's insistence on inventing its brand of First Amendment underinclusiveness puzzles me. The overbreadth doctrine has the redeeming virtue of attempting to avoid the chilling of protected expression, but the Court's new "underbreadth" creation serves no desirable function. Instead, it permits, indeed invites, the continuation of expressive conduct that in this case is evil and worthless in First Amendment terms, until the city of St. Paul cures the underbreadth by adding to its ordinance a catch-all phrase such as "and all other fighting words that may constitutionally be subject to this ordinance."

Any contribution of this holding to First Amendment jurisprudence is surely a negative one, since it necessarily signals that expressions of violence, such as the message of intimidation and racial hatred conveyed by burning a cross on someone's lawn, are of sufficient value to outweigh the social interest in order and morality that has traditionally placed such fighting words outside the First Amendment.[4] Indeed, by characterizing fighting words as a form of "debate," the majority legitimates hate speech as a form of public discussion. . . .

In a second break with precedent, the Court refuses to sustain the ordinance even though it would survive under the strict scrutiny applicable to other protected expression. Assuming, arguendo, that the St. Paul ordinance is a content-based regulation of protected expression, it nevertheless would pass First Amendment review under settled law upon a showing that the regulation "is necessary to serve a compelling state interest and is narrowly drawn to achieve that end." . . . Under the majority's view, a narrowly drawn, content-based ordinance could never

---

4. This does not suggest, of course, that cross burning is always unprotected. Burning a cross at a political rally would almost certainly be protected expression. Cf. *Brandenburg v. Ohio,* [Section 10–1] (1969). But in such a context, the cross burning could not be characterized as a "direct personal insult or an invitation to exchange fisticuffs," to which the fighting words doctrine applies.

pass constitutional muster if the object of that legislation could be accomplished by banning a wider category of speech. This appears to be a general renunciation of strict scrutiny review, a fundamental tool of First Amendment analysis. . . .

Although the First Amendment does not apply to categories of unprotected speech, such as fighting words, the Equal Protection Clause requires that the regulation of unprotected speech be rationally related to a legitimate government interest. A defamation statute that drew distinctions on the basis of political affiliation or "an ordinance prohibiting only those legally obscene works that contain criticism of the city government," would unquestionably fail rational basis review.

Turning to the St. Paul ordinance and assuming arguendo, as the majority does, that the ordinance is not constitutionally overbroad (but see Part II, infra), there is no question that it would pass equal protection review. The ordinance proscribes a subset of "fighting words," those that injure "on the basis of race, color, creed, religion or gender." This selective regulation reflects the City's judgment that harms based on race, color, creed, religion, or gender are more pressing public concerns than the harms caused by other fighting words. In light of our Nation's long and painful experience with discrimination, this determination is plainly reasonable. Indeed, as the majority concedes, the interest is compelling.

The Court has patched up its argument with an apparently nonexhaustive list of ad hoc exceptions, in what can be viewed either as an attempt to confine the effects of its decision to the facts of this case, or as an effort to anticipate some of the questions that will arise from its radical revision of First Amendment law.

For instance, if the majority were to give general application to the rule on which it decides this case, today's decision would call into question the constitutionality of the statute making it illegal to threaten the life of the President. Surely, this statute, by singling out certain threats, incorporates a content-based distinction; it indicates that the Government especially disfavors threats against the President as opposed to threats against all others. But because the Government could prohibit all threats and not just those directed against the President, under the Court's theory, the compelling reasons justifying the enactment of special legislation to safeguard the President would be irrelevant, and the statute would fail First Amendment review.

To save the statute, the majority has engrafted the following exception onto its newly announced First Amendment rule: Content-based distinctions may be drawn within an unprotected category of speech if the basis for the distinctions is "the very reason the entire class of speech at issue is proscribable." Thus, the argument goes, the statute making it illegal to threaten the life of the President is constitutional, "since the reasons why threats of violence are outside the First Amendment (protecting individuals from the fear of violence, from the disruption that fear engenders, and from the possibility that the threatened violence will occur) have special force when applied to the person of the President."

The exception swallows the majority's rule. Certainly, it should apply to the St. Paul ordinance, since "the reasons why [fighting words] are outside the First Amendment ... have special force when applied to [groups that have historically been subjected to discrimination]." ...

As its second exception, the Court posits that certain content-based regulations will survive under the new regime if the regulated subclass "happens to be associated with particular 'secondary effects' of the speech ... ," which the majority treats as encompassing instances in which "words can ... violate laws directed not against speech but against conduct ..." Again, there is a simple explanation for the Court's eagerness to craft an exception to its new First Amendment rule: Under the general rule the Court applies in this case, Title VII hostile work environment claims would suddenly be unconstitutional.

Title VII makes it unlawful to discriminate "because of [an] individual's race, color, religion, sex, or national origin," and the regulations covering hostile workplace claims forbid "sexual harassment," which includes "unwelcome sexual advances, requests for sexual favors, and other verbal or physical conduct of a sexual nature" which creates "an intimidating, hostile, or offensive working environment." 29 CFR § 1604.11(a)(1991). The regulation does not prohibit workplace harassment generally; it focuses on what the majority would characterize as the "disfavored topic" of sexual harassment. In this way, Title VII is similar to the St. Paul ordinance that the majority condemns because it "imposes special prohibitions on those speakers who express views on disfavored subjects." Under the broad principle the Court uses to decide the present case, hostile work environment claims based on sexual harassment should fail First Amendment review; because a general ban on harassment in the workplace would cover the problem of sexual harassment, any attempt to proscribe the subcategory of sexually harassing expression would violate the First Amendment.

Hence, the majority's second exception, which the Court indicates would insulate a Title VII hostile work environment claim from an underinclusiveness challenge because "sexually derogatory 'fighting words' ... may produce a violation of Title VII's general prohibition against sexual discrimination in employment practices." But application of this exception to a hostile work environment claim does not hold up under close examination.

First, the hostile work environment regulation is not keyed to the presence or absence of an economic *quid pro quo,* but to the impact of the speech on the victimized worker. Consequently, the regulation would no more fall within a secondary effects exception than does the St. Paul ordinance. Second, the majority's focus on the statute's general prohibition on discrimination glosses over the language of the specific regulation governing hostile working environment, which reaches beyond any "incidental" effect on speech. If the relationship between the broader statute and specific regulation is sufficient to bring the Title VII regulation within [the majority's exception], then all St. Paul need do to bring its ordinance within this exception is to add some prefatory language concerning discrimination generally.

As the third exception to the Court's theory for deciding this case, the majority concocts a catchall exclusion to protect against unforeseen problems, a concern that is heightened here given the lack of briefing on the majority's decisional theory. This final exception would apply in cases in which "there is no realistic possibility that official suppression of ideas is afoot." As I have demonstrated, this case does not concern the official suppression of ideas. The majority discards this notion out-of-hand. . . .

II. Although I disagree with the Court's analysis, I do agree with its conclusion: The St. Paul ordinance is unconstitutional. However, I would decide the case on overbreadth grounds. [T]he ordinance is invalid on its face. Although the ordinance as construed reaches categories of speech that are constitutionally unprotected, it also criminalizes a substantial amount of expression that—however repugnant—is shielded by the First Amendment. . . .

[T]he Minnesota court was far from clear in identifying the "injuries" inflicted by the expression that St. Paul sought to regulate. [That court] (tracking the language of the ordinance) that "the ordinance censors only those displays that one knows or should know will create anger, alarm or resentment based on racial, ethnic, gender or religious bias." I therefore understand the court to have ruled that St. Paul may constitutionally prohibit expression that "by its very utterance" causes "anger, alarm or resentment." Our fighting words cases have made clear, however, that such generalized reactions are not sufficient to strip expression of its constitutional protection. The mere fact that expressive activity causes hurt feelings, offense, or resentment does not render the expression unprotected. . . .

JUSTICE BLACKMUN, concurring in the judgment.

[T]here is the possibility that this case will not significantly alter First Amendment jurisprudence, but, instead, will be regarded as an aberration—a case where the Court manipulated doctrine to strike down an ordinance whose premise it opposed, namely, that racial threats and verbal assaults are of greater harm than other fighting words. I fear that the Court has been distracted from its proper mission by the temptation to decide the issue over "politically correct speech" and "cultural diversity," neither of which is presented here. If this is the meaning of today's opinion, it is perhaps even more regrettable. . . .

I concur in the judgment, however, because I agree with Justice White that this particular ordinance reaches beyond fighting words to speech protected by the First Amendment.

JUSTICE STEVENS, with whom JUSTICE WHITE and JUSTICE BLACKMUN join as to Part I, concurring in the judgment.

[W]hile I agree that the St. Paul ordinance is unconstitutionally overbroad for the reasons stated in Part II of Justice White's opinion, I write separately to suggest how the allure of absolute principles has skewed the analysis of both the majority and concurring opinions.

I.   ... It is not, the Court rules, that certain "categories" of expression are "unprotected," but rather that certain "elements" of expression are wholly "proscribable." [T]hough the act may be regulated because it contains a proscribable element, it may not be regulated on the basis of another (nonproscribable) element it also contains. Thus, obscene antigovernment speech may be regulated because it is obscene, but not because it is antigovernment. It is this revision of the categorical approach that allows the Court to assume that the St. Paul ordinance proscribes only fighting words, while at the same time concluding that the ordinance is invalid because it imposes a content-based regulation on expressive activity.

As an initial matter, the Court's revision of the categorical approach seems to me something of an adventure in a doctrinal wonderland, for the concept of "obscene antigovernment" speech is fantastical.... If expression is antigovernment, it does not "lack serious ... political ... value" and cannot be obscene....

I am, however, even more troubled by the second step of the Court's analysis—namely, its conclusion that the St. Paul ordinance is an unconstitutional content-based regulation of speech. Drawing on broadly worded dicta, the Court establishes a near-absolute ban on content-based regulations of expression and holds that the First Amendment prohibits the regulation of fighting words by subject matter. Thus, while the Court rejects the "all-or-nothing-at-all" nature of the categorical approach, it promptly embraces an absolutism of its own: within a particular "proscribable" category of expression, the Court holds, a government must either proscribe all speech or no speech at all.[1] ...

... In broadest terms, our entire First Amendment jurisprudence creates a regime based on the content of speech. The scope of the First Amendment is determined by the content of expressive activity: Although the First Amendment broadly protects "speech," it does not protect the right to "fix prices, breach contracts, make false warranties, place bets with bookies, threaten, [or] extort." ...

Core political speech occupies the highest, most protected position; commercial speech and nonobscene, sexually explicit speech are regarded as a sort of second-class expression; obscenity and fighting words receive

---

1. The Court disputes this characterization because it has crafted two exceptions, one for "certain media or markets" and the other for content discrimination based upon "the very reason that the entire class of speech at issue is proscribable." These exceptions are, at best, ill-defined. The Court does not tell us whether, with respect to the former, fighting words such as cross-burning could be proscribed only in certain neighborhoods where the threat of violence is particularly severe, or whether, with respect to the second category, fighting words that create a particular risk of harm (such as a race riot) would be proscribable. The hypothetical and illusory category of these two exceptions persuades me that either my description of the Court's analysis is accurate or that the Court does not in fact mean much of what it says in its opinion.

the least protection of all. Assuming that the Court is correct that this last class of speech is not wholly "unprotected," it certainly does not follow that fighting words and obscenity receive the same sort of protection afforded core political speech. Yet in ruling that proscribable speech cannot be regulated based on subject matter, the Court does just that. Perversely, this gives fighting words greater protection than is afforded commercial speech. If Congress can prohibit false advertising directed at airline passengers without also prohibiting false advertising directed at bus passengers and if a city can prohibit political advertisements in its buses while allowing other advertisements, it is ironic to hold that a city cannot regulate fighting words based on "race, color, creed, religion or gender" while leaving unregulated fighting words based on "union membership or homosexuality." The Court today turns First Amendment law on its head: Communication that was once entirely unprotected (and that still can be wholly proscribed) is now entitled to greater protection than commercial speech—and possibly greater protection than core political speech.

Perhaps because the Court recognizes these perversities, it quickly offers some ad hoc limitations on its newly extended prohibition on content-based regulations. First, the Court states that a content-based regulation is valid "when the content discrimination is based upon the very reason the entire class of speech ... is proscribable." In a pivotal passage, the Court writes

"the Federal Government can criminalize only those physical threats that are directed against the President, see 18 U.S.C. § 871—since the reasons why threats of violence are outside the First Amendment (protecting individuals from the fear of violence, from the disruption that fear engenders, and from the possibility that the threatened violence will occur) have special force when applied to the ... President."

As I understand this opaque passage, Congress may choose from the set of unprotected speech (all threats) to proscribe only a subset (threats against the President) because those threats are particularly likely to cause "fear of violence," "disruption," and actual "violence."

Precisely this same reasoning, however, compels the conclusion that St. Paul's ordinance is constitutional. Just as Congress may determine that threats against the President entail more severe consequences than other threats, so St. Paul's City Council may determine that threats based on the target's race, religion, or gender cause more severe harm to both the target and to society than other threats. This latter judgment— that harms caused by racial, religious, and gender-based invective are qualitatively different from that caused by other fighting words—seems to me eminently reasonable and realistic....

II. Although I agree with much of Justice White's analysis, I do not join Part I–A of his opinion because I have reservations about the "categorical approach" to the First Amendment....

III. As the foregoing suggests, I disagree with both the Court's and part of Justice White's analysis of the constitutionality [of the] St. Paul ordinance. Unlike the Court, I do not believe that all content-based regulations are equally infirm and presumptively invalid; unlike Justice White, I do not believe that fighting words are wholly unprotected by the First Amendment. . . .

The Court writes:

"One could hold up a sign saying, for example, that 'all anti-Catholic bigots' are misbegotten; but not that all 'papists' are, for that would insult and provoke violence 'on the basis of religion.' "

This may be true, but it hardly proves the Court's point. The Court's reasoning is asymmetrical. The response to a sign saying that "all [religious] bigots are misbegotten" is a sign saying that "all advocates of religious tolerance are misbegotten." Assuming such signs could be fighting words (which seems to me extremely unlikely), neither sign would be banned by the ordinance for the attacks were not "based on . . . religion" but rather on one's beliefs about tolerance. Conversely (and again assuming such signs are fighting words), just as the ordinance would prohibit a Muslim from hoisting a sign claiming that all Catholics were misbegotten, so the ordinance would bar a Catholic from hoisting a similar sign attacking Muslims.

The St. Paul ordinance is evenhanded. In a battle between advocates of tolerance and advocates of intolerance, the ordinance does not prevent either side from hurling fighting words at the other on the basis of their conflicting ideas, but it does bar both sides from hurling such words on the basis of the target's "race, color, creed, religion or gender." To extend the Court's pugilistic metaphor, the St. Paul ordinance simply bans punches "below the belt"—by either party. It does not, therefore, favor one side of any debate. . . .

In sum, the St. Paul ordinance (as construed by the Court) regulates expressive activity that is wholly proscribable and does so not on the basis of viewpoint, but rather in recognition of the different harms caused by such activity. Taken together, these several considerations persuade me that the St. Paul ordinance is not an unconstitutional content-based regulation of speech. Thus, were the ordinance not over-broad, I would vote to uphold it.

WISCONSIN v. MITCHELL
508 U.S. 476, 113 S.Ct. 2194, 124 L.Ed.2d 436 (1993).

CHIEF JUSTICE REHNQUIST delivered the opinion of the Court.

Respondent Todd Mitchell's sentence for aggravated battery was enhanced because he intentionally selected his victim on account of the victim's race. The question presented in this case is whether this penalty enhancement is prohibited by the First and Fourteenth Amendments. We hold that it is not.

On the evening of October 7, 1989, a group of young black men and boys, including Mitchell, gathered at an apartment complex in Kenosha, Wisconsin. Several members of the group discussed a scene from the motion picture "Mississippi Burning," in which a white man beat a young black boy who was praying. The group moved outside and Mitchell asked them: " 'Do you all feel hyped up to move on some white people?' " Shortly thereafter, a young white boy approached the group on the opposite side of the street where they were standing. As the boy walked by, Mitchell said: " 'You all want to fuck somebody up? There goes a white boy; go get him.' "Mitchell counted to three and pointed in the boy's direction. The group ran towards the boy, beat him severely, and stole his tennis shoes. The boy was rendered unconscious and remained in a coma for four days.

After a jury trial in the Circuit Court for Kenosha County, Mitchell was convicted of aggravated battery. That offense ordinarily carries a maximum sentence of two years' imprisonment. But because the jury found that Mitchell had intentionally selected his victim because of the boy's race, the maximum sentence for Mitchell's offense was increased to seven years under [Wisconsin Statute] § 939.645. That provision enhances the maximum penalty for an offense whenever the defendant "[i]ntentionally selects the person against whom the crime . . . is committed . . . because of the race, religion, color, disability, sexual orientation, national origin or ancestry of that person. . . ." The Circuit Court sentenced Mitchell to four years' imprisonment for the aggravated battery. [The Wisconsin] Supreme Court held that the statute "violates the First Amendment directly by punishing what the legislature has deemed to be offensive thought." It rejected the State's contention "that the statute punishes only the 'conduct' of intentional selection of a victim." According to the court, "[t]he statute punishes the 'because of' aspect of the defendant's selection, the *reason* the defendant selected the victim, the *motive* behind the selection." (emphasis in original). And under *R.A.V. v. St. Paul*, "the Wisconsin legislature cannot criminalize bigoted thought with which it disagrees."

The Supreme Court also held that the penalty-enhancement statute was unconstitutionally overbroad. It reasoned that, in order to prove that a defendant intentionally selected his victim because of the victim's protected status, the State would often have to introduce evidence of the defendant's prior speech, such as racial epithets he may have uttered before the commission of the offense. This evidentiary use of protected speech, the court thought, would have a "chilling effect" on those who feared the possibility of prosecution for offenses subject to penalty enhancement. Finally, the court distinguished antidiscrimination laws, which have long been held constitutional, on the ground that the Wisconsin statute punishes the "subjective mental process" of selecting a victim because of his protected status, whereas antidiscrimination laws prohibit "objective acts of discrimination." . . . We reverse.

Mitchell argues that we are bound by the Wisconsin Supreme Court's conclusion that the statute punishes bigoted thought and not conduct. There is no doubt that we are bound by a state court's construction of a state statute.... But here the Wisconsin Supreme Court did not, strictly speaking, construe the Wisconsin statute in the sense of defining the meaning of a particular statutory word or phrase. Rather, it merely characterized the "practical effect" of the statute for First Amendment purposes. See 169 Wis.2d, at 166–167, 485 N.W.2d, at 813 ("Merely because the statute refers in a literal sense to the intentional 'conduct' of selecting, does not mean the court must turn a blind eye to the intent and practical effect of the law—punishment of motive or thought"). This assessment does not bind us. Once any ambiguities as to the meaning of the statute are resolved, we may form our own judgment as to its operative effect.

The State argues that the statute does not punish bigoted thought, as the Supreme Court of Wisconsin said, but instead punishes only conduct. While this argument is literally correct, it does not dispose of Mitchell's First Amendment challenge. [U]nder the Wisconsin statute the same criminal conduct may be more heavily punished if the victim is selected because of his race or other protected status than if no such motive obtained. Thus, although the statute punishes criminal conduct, it enhances the maximum penalty for conduct motivated by a discriminatory point of view more severely than the same conduct engaged in for some other reason or for no reason at all. Because the only reason for the enhancement is the defendant's discriminatory motive for selecting his victim, Mitchell argues (and the Wisconsin Supreme Court held) that the statute violates the First Amendment by punishing offenders' bigoted beliefs.

Traditionally, sentencing judges have considered a wide variety of factors in addition to evidence bearing on guilt in determining what sentence to impose on a convicted defendant. The defendant's motive for committing the offense is one important factor. See 1 W. LaFave & A. Scott, Substantive Criminal Law § 3.6(b), p. 324 (1986)("Motives are most relevant when the trial judge sets the defendant's sentence, and it is not uncommon for a defendant to receive a minimum sentence because he was acting with good motives, or a rather high sentence because of his bad motives"); cf. *Tison v. Arizona*, 481 U.S. 137, 156, 107 S.Ct. 1676, 95 L.Ed.2d 127 (1987)("Deeply ingrained in our legal tradition is the idea that the more purposeful is the criminal conduct, the more serious is the offense, and, therefore, the more severely it ought to be punished"). Thus, in many States the commission of a murder, or other capital offense, for pecuniary gain is a separate aggravating circumstance under the capital-sentencing statute.

But it is equally true that a defendant's abstract beliefs, however obnoxious to most people, may not be taken into consideration by a sentencing judge. *Dawson v. Delaware*, 503 U.S. 159, 112 S.Ct. 1093, 117 L.Ed.2d 309 (1992). In *Dawson*, the State introduced evidence at a capital-sentencing hearing that the defendant was a member of a white supremacist prison gang. Because "the evidence proved nothing more than [the defendant's] abstract beliefs," we held that its admission violated the defendant's First Amendment rights. In so holding, however, we emphasized that "the Constitution does not erect a *per se* barrier to the admission of evidence concerning one's beliefs and associations at sentencing simply because those beliefs and associations are protected by the First Amendment." Thus, in *Barclay v. Florida,* 463 U.S. 939, 103 S.Ct. 3418, 77 L.Ed.2d 1134 (1983)(plurality opinion), we allowed the sentencing judge to take into account the defendant's racial animus towards his victim. The evidence in that case showed that the defendant's membership in the Black Liberation Army and desire to provoke a "race war" were related to the murder of a white man for which he was convicted. Because "the elements of racial hatred in [the] murder" were relevant to several aggravating factors, we held that the trial judge permissibly took this evidence into account in sentencing the defendant to death. . . .

Mitchell argues that the Wisconsin penalty-enhancement statute is invalid because it punishes the defendant's discriminatory motive, or reason, for acting. But motive plays the same role under the Wisconsin statute as it does under federal and state antidiscrimination laws, which we have previously upheld against constitutional challenge. *Runyon v. McCrary,* [§ 9–2]. Title VII, for example, makes it unlawful for an employer to discriminate against an employee *"because of* such individual's race, color, religion, sex, or national origin." 42 U.S.C. § 2000e–2(a)(1)(emphasis added). [M]ore recently, in *R.A.V. v. St. Paul,* we cited Title VII (as well as 18 U.S.C. § 242 and 42 U.S.C. §§ 1981 and 1982) as an example of a permissible content-neutral regulation of conduct. Nothing in our decision last Term in *R.A.V.* compels a different result here. [W]hereas the ordinance struck down in *R.A.V.* was explicitly directed at expression (*i.e.,* "speech" or "messages") the statute in this case is aimed at conduct unprotected by the First Amendment.

Moreover, the Wisconsin statute singles out for enhancement bias-inspired conduct because this conduct is thought to inflict greater individual and societal harm. [A]ccording to the State and its *amici,* bias-motivated crimes are more likely to provoke retaliatory crimes, inflict distinct emotional harms on their victims, and incite community unrest. The State's desire to redress these perceived harms provides an adequate explanation for its penalty-enhancement provision over and above mere disagreement with offenders' beliefs or biases. As Blackstone said long ago, "it is but reasonable that among crimes of different natures those should be most severely punished, which are the most destructive of the public safety and happiness." 4 W. Blackstone, Commentaries * 16.

Finally, there remains to be considered Mitchell's argument that the Wisconsin statute is unconstitutionally overbroad because of its "chilling effect" on free speech. Mitchell argues (and the Wisconsin Supreme Court agreed) that the statute is "overbroad" because evidence of the defendant's prior speech or associations may be used to prove that the defendant intentionally selected his victim on account of the victim's protected status. Consequently, the argument goes, the statute impermissibly chills free expression with respect to such matters by those concerned about the possibility of enhanced sentences if they should in the future commit a criminal offense covered by the statute. We find no merit in this contention.

The sort of chill envisioned here is far more attenuated and unlikely than that contemplated in traditional "overbreadth" cases. We must conjure up a vision of a Wisconsin citizen suppressing his unpopular bigoted opinions for fear that if he later commits an offense covered by the statute, these opinions will be offered at trial to establish that he selected his victim on account of the victim's protected status, thus qualifying him for penalty-enhancement. To stay within the realm of rationality, we must surely put to one side minor misdemeanor offenses covered by the statute, such as negligent operation of a motor vehicle, for it is difficult, if not impossible, to conceive of a situation where such offenses would be racially motivated. We are left, then, with the prospect of a citizen suppressing his bigoted beliefs for fear that evidence of such beliefs will be introduced against him at trial if he commits a more serious offense against person or property. This is simply too speculative a hypothesis to support Mitchell's overbreadth claim.

The First Amendment, moreover, does not prohibit the evidentiary use of speech to establish the elements of a crime or to prove motive or intent. Evidence of a defendant's previous declarations or statements is commonly admitted in criminal trials subject to evidentiary rules dealing with relevancy, reliability, and the like. Nearly half a century ago, in *Haupt v. United States,* 330 U.S. 631, 67 S.Ct. 874, 91 L.Ed. 1145 (1947), we rejected a contention similar to that advanced by Mitchell here. Haupt was tried for the offense of treason, which, as defined by the Constitution (Art. III, § 3), may depend very much on proof of motive. To prove that the acts in question were committed out of "adherence to the enemy" rather than "parental solicitude," the Government introduced evidence of conversations that had taken place long prior to the indictment, some of which consisted of statements showing Haupt's sympathy with Germany and Hitler and hostility towards the United States. We rejected Haupt's argument that this evidence was improperly admitted. While "[s]uch testimony is to be scrutinized with care to be certain the statements are not expressions of mere lawful and permissible difference of opinion with our own government or quite proper appreciation of the land of birth," we held that "these statements . . . clearly were admissible on the question of intent and adherence to the enemy." See also *Price Waterhouse v. Hopkins,* 490 U.S. 228, 251–252, 109 S.Ct. 1775, 1791, 104 L.Ed.2d 268 (1989)(plurality opinion)(allowing evidentiary use of defendant's speech in evaluating Title VII discrimination claim).

For the foregoing reasons, we hold that Mitchell's First Amendment rights were not violated by the application of the Wisconsin penalty-enhancement provision in sentencing him. The judgment of the Supreme Court of Wisconsin is therefore reversed, and the case is remanded for further proceedings not inconsistent with this opinion.

It is so ordered.

10–5. SPECIAL PROBLEMS OF THE BROADCAST MEDIA

MIAMI HERALD PUB. CO. v. TORNILLO
418 U.S. 241, 94 S.Ct. 2831, 41 L.Ed.2d 730 (1974).

MR. CHIEF JUSTICE BURGER delivered the opinion of the Court.

The issue in this case is whether a state statute granting a political candidate a right to equal space to reply to criticism and attacks on his record by a newspaper violates the guarantees of a free press.

In the fall of 1972, appellee, Executive Director of the Classroom Teachers Association, apparently a teachers' collective-bargaining agent, was a candidate for the Florida House of Representatives. On September 20, 1972, and again on September 29, 1972, appellant printed editorials critical of appellee's candidacy.[1] In response to these editorials appellee demanded that appellant print verbatim his replies, defending the role of the Classroom Teachers Association and the organization's accomplishments for the citizens of Dade County. Appellant declined to print the appellee's replies, and appellee brought suit ... premised on Florida Statute § 104.38 (1973), a "right of reply" statute which provides that if a candidate for nomination or election is assailed regarding his personal character or official record by any newspaper, the candidate has the right to demand that the newspaper print, free of cost to the candidate, any reply the candidate may make to the newspaper's charges. The reply must appear in as conspicuous a place and in the same kind of type as the charges which prompted the reply, provided it does not take up more space than the charges. Failure to comply with the statute constitutes a first-degree misdemeanor....

The appellee and supporting advocates of an enforceable right of access to the press vigorously argue that government has an obligation to ensure that a wide variety of views reach the public.... It is urged that at the time the First Amendment to the Constitution was ratified in 1791 as part of our Bill of Rights the press was broadly representative of the people it was serving. While many of the newspapers were intensely partisan and narrow in their views, the press collectively presented a broad range of opinions to readers. Entry into publishing was inexpensive; pamphlets and books provided meaningful alternatives to the

---

1. ... the text of the September 29, 1972, editorial is as follows:

"FROM the people who brought you this—the teacher strike of '68—come now instructions on how to vote for responsible government, i.e., ... for Pat Tornillo. The tracts and blurbs and bumper stickers pile up daily in teachers' school mailboxes amidst continuing pouts that the School Board should be delivering all this at your expense. [Tornillo] has been kicking the public shin to call attention to his shake-down statesmanship. He and whichever acerbic prexy is in alleged office have always felt their private ventures so chock-full of public weal that we should leap at the chance to nab the tab, be it half the Glorious Leader's salary or the dues check-off or anything else except perhaps mileage on the staff hydrofoil. Give him public office, says Pat, and he will no doubt live by the Golden Rule. Our translation reads that as more gold and more rule."

organized press for the expression of unpopular ideas and often treated events and expressed views not covered by conventional newspapers. A true marketplace of ideas existed in which there was relatively easy access to the channels of communication.

Access advocates submit that [the] elimination of competing newspapers in most of our large cities, and the concentration of control of media that results from the only newspaper's being owned by the same interests which own a television station and a radio station, are important components of this trend toward concentration of control of outlets to inform the public. The result of these vast changes has been to place in a few hands the power to inform the American people and shape public opinion.... But the same economic factors which have caused the disappearance of vast numbers of metropolitan newspapers, have made entry into the marketplace of ideas served by the print media almost impossible. It is urged that the claim of newspapers to be "surrogates for the public" carries with it a concomitant fiduciary obligation to account for that stewardship. From this premise it is reasoned that the only effective way to insure fairness and accuracy and to provide for some accountability is for government to take affirmative action. The First Amendment interest of the public in being informed is said to be in peril because the "marketplace of ideas" is today a monopoly controlled by the owners of the market. Proponents of enforced access to the press take comfort from language in several of this Court's decisions which suggests that the First Amendment acts as a sword as well as a shield, that it imposes obligations on the owners of the press in addition to protecting the press from government regulation.

... A responsible press is an undoubtedly desirable goal, but press responsibility is not mandated by the Constitution and like many other virtues it cannot be legislated. Appellee's argument that the Florida statute does not amount to a restriction of appellant's right to speak because "the statute in question here has not prevented the *Miami Herald* from saying anything it wished" begs the core question.... The Florida statute operates as a command in the same sense as a statute or regulation forbidding appellant to publish specified matter. Governmental restraint on publishing need not fall into familiar or traditional patterns to be subject to constitutional limitations on governmental powers. The Florida statute exacts a penalty on the basis of the content of a newspaper. The first phase of the penalty resulting from the compelled printing of a reply is exacted in terms of the cost in printing and composing time and materials and in taking up space that could be devoted to other material the newspaper may have preferred to print. It is correct, as appellee contends, that a newspaper is not subject to the finite technological limitations of time that confront a broadcaster but it is not correct to say that, as an economic reality, a newspaper can proceed to infinite expansion of its column space to accommodate the replies that a government agency determines or a statute commands the readers should have available.

Faced with the penalties that would accrue to any newspaper that published news or commentary arguably within the reach of the right-of-access statute, editors might well conclude that the safe course is to avoid controversy. Therefore, under the operation of the Florida statute, political and electoral coverage would be blunted or reduced. . . .

Even if a newspaper would face no additional costs to comply with a compulsory access law and would not be forced to forgo publication of news or opinion by the inclusion of a reply, the Florida statute fails to clear the barriers of the First Amendment because of its intrusion into the function of editors. A newspaper is more than a passive receptacle or conduit for news, comment, and advertising. The choice of material to go into a newspaper, and the decisions made as to limitations on the size and content of the paper, and treatment of public issues and public officials—whether fair or unfair—constitute the exercise of editorial control and judgment. It has yet to be demonstrated how governmental regulation of this crucial process can be exercised consistent with First Amendment guarantees of a free press as they have evolved to this time. Accordingly, the judgment of the Supreme Court of Florida is reversed.

It is so ordered.

MR. JUSTICE BRENNAN, with whom MR. JUSTICE REHNQUIST joins, concurring.

I understand it, addresses only "right of reply" statutes and implies no view upon the constitutionality of "retraction" statutes affording plaintiffs able to prove defamatory falsehoods a statutory action to require publication of a retraction.

[The concurring opinion of WHITE, J., is omitted.]

Notes

1. *Pacific Gas & Electric Co. v. Public Utilities Commission,* 475 U.S. 1, 106 S.Ct. 903, 89 L.Ed.2d 1 (1986). A fragmented Court, with no majority opinion, held that the California Public Utilities Commission may not require a privately owned utility company to include (in its billing envelopes) speech of a third party (in this case, a private group called TURN, "Toward Utility Rate Normalization") with which the utility disagreed. Justice Powell's plurality opinion, joined by Burger, C.J., and Brennan and O'Connor, JJ., concluded that the utility's newsletter is "no different from a small newspaper." Its stories ranged from energy-savings tips to wildlife conservation to billings to recipes. The Utility Commission may not force access to the utility's newsletter TURN. Because the Utility Commission concluded that the public would benefit "more from exposure to a variety of views", it had concluded that TURN should be allowed to use the "extra space" in the billing envelope four times a year. The "extra space" was defined as the space remaining in the billing envelope after the monthly bill and required legal notices up to the total envelope weight so as not to result in any additional postage. The Commission had ruled that the ratepayers owned this extra space, but "expressly declined to hold that under California law appellant's customers own the entire billing envelopes and everything contained therein." The "Commission's access order thus clearly requires

appellant to use *its* property as a vehicle for spreading a message with which it disagrees." (emphasis in original).

2. COMPELLED SUBSIDIZATION OF ADVERTISING. *Glickman v. Wileman Brothers & Elliott, Inc.*, 521 U.S. 457, 117 S.Ct. 2130, 138 L.Ed.2d 585 (1997). The Secretary of Agriculture, pursuant to statute, issued various orders that imposed assessments to cover the cost of generic advertising of California nectarines, plums, and peaches. (E.g., "California Summer Fruits" are "wholesome, delicious, and attractive to discerning shoppers.") Those who paid the assessments (growers, handlers, and processors of California tree fruits) claimed that their forced subsidization of this generic advertising violated their free speech.

Stevens, J., for the Court (with O'Connor, Kennedy, Ginsburg, & Breyer, JJ.), rejected these challenges, arguing that these marketing orders are a form of economic regulation that has displaced competition in certain markets. The marketing orders must be approved by affected producers who market at least at least two-thirds of the volume of the commodity. This advertising serves the producers' and handlers' common interest in selling particular products.

The Court concluded that compelling the respondents to fund this advertising was an economic question for Congress, rather than a First Amendment issue for the Court.

> "First, the marketing orders impose no restraint on the freedom of any producer to communicate any message to any audience. Second, they do not compel any person to engage in any actual or symbolic speech. Third, they do not compel the producers to endorse or to finance any political or ideological views. Indeed, since all of the respondents are engaged in the business of marketing California nectarines, plums, and peaches, it is fair to presume that they agree with the central message of the speech that is generated by the generic program. Thus, none of our First Amendment jurisprudence provides any support for the suggestion that the promotional regulations should be scrutinized under a different standard than that applicable to the other anticompetitive features of the marketing orders."

There is a free speech right not to be compelled to contribute to an organization "whose expressive activities conflict with one's 'freedom of belief.' "For example, the state can compel union members to pay dues to support activities related to collective bargaining, because those costs are germane to an otherwise lawful regulatory program, but the state cannot compel union members to make contributions for political purposes unrelated to collective bargaining. In this case the assessments are germane to the regulatory program and requiring respondents to pay them cannot be said "to engender any crisis of conscience."

Souter, J., joined by Rehnquist, C.J., & Scalia, J., (& Thomas, J., in part), dissented, arguing that compelled subsidization of speech should only be lawful if the government can prove that it has "a substantial interest," the regulation "directly advances that interest," and it is "narrowly tailored." The program challenged here fails all three prongs. Thomas, J. (joined by Scalia, J., in part) argued that it is incongruous for the majority to suggest that the forced subsidization of this advertising does not violate the First Amendment while a law that forbade voluntary contributions would.

FEDERAL COMMUNICATIONS COMMISSION
v. LEAGUE OF WOMEN VOTERS
468 U.S. 364, 104 S.Ct. 3106, 82 L.Ed.2d 278 (1984).

JUSTICE BRENNAN delivered the opinion of the Court.

Moved to action by a widely felt need to sponsor independent sources of broadcast programming as an alternative to commercial broadcasting, Congress set out in 1967 to support and promote the development of noncommercial, educational broadcasting stations. A keystone of Congress' program was the Public Broadcasting Act of 1967, 47 U.S.C.A. § 390 et seq., which established the Corporation for Public Broadcasting, a nonprofit corporation authorized to disburse federal funds to noncommercial television and radio stations in support of station operations and educational programming. Section 399 of that Act, as amended by the Public Broadcasting Amendments Act of 1981, forbids any "noncommercial educational broadcasting station which receives a grant from the Corporation" to "engage in editorializing." 47 U.S.C.A. § 399. In this case, we are called upon to decide whether Congress, by imposing that restriction, has passed a "law ... abridging the freedom of speech, or of the press" in violation of the First Amendment of the Constitution.... While the suit was pending before the District Court, Congress amended § 399 by confining the ban on editorializing to noncommercial stations that receive Corporation grants and by separately prohibiting all noncommercial stations from making political endorsements, irrespective of whether they receive federal funds. Subsequently, appellees amended their complaint to reflect this change, challenging only the ban on editorializing....

The fundamental principles that guide our evaluation of broadcast regulation are by now well established. First, we have long recognized that Congress, acting pursuant to the Commerce Clause, has power to regulate the use of this scarce and valuable national resource. The distinctive feature of Congress' efforts in this area has been to ensure through the regulatory oversight of the FCC that only those who satisfy the "public interest, convenience and necessity" are granted a license to use radio and television broadcast frequencies. 47 U.S.C.A. § 309(a).[11]

Second, Congress may, in the exercise of this power, seek to assure that the public receives through this medium a balanced presentation of information on issues of public importance that otherwise might not be

---

11. The prevailing rationale for broadcast regulation based on spectrum scarcity has come under increasing criticism in recent years. Critics, including the incumbent Chairman of the FCC, charge that with the advent of cable and satellite television technology, communities now have access to such a wide variety of stations that the scarcity doctrine is obsolete. We are not prepared, however, to reconsider our long-standing approach without some signal from Congress or the FCC that technological developments have advanced so far that some revision of the system of broadcast regulation may be required.

addressed if control of the medium were left entirely in the hands of those who own and operate broadcasting stations. Although such governmental regulation has never been allowed with respect to the print media, *Miami Herald Publishing Co. v. Tornillo,* we have recognized that "differences in the characteristics of new media justify differences in the First Amendment standards applied to them." *Red Lion Broadcasting Co. v. FCC,* 395 U.S. 367, 386, 89 S.Ct. 1794, 1805, 23 L.Ed.2d 371, 387 (1969). The fundamental distinguishing characteristic of the new medium of broadcasting that, in our view, has required some adjustment in First Amendment analysis is that "[b]roadcasting frequencies are a scarce resource [that] must be portioned out among applicants." *Columbia Broadcasting System, Inc. v. Democratic National Committee,* 412 U.S. 94, 101, 93 S.Ct. 2080, 2086, 36 L.Ed.2d 772, 783 (1973). Thus, our cases have taught that, given spectrum scarcity, those who are granted a license to broadcast must serve in a sense as fiduciaries for the public by presenting "those views and voices which are representative of his community and which would otherwise, by necessity, be barred from the airwaves." *Red Lion,* supra. As we observed in that case, because "[i]t is the purpose of the First Amendment to preserve an uninhibited marketplace of ideas in which truth will ultimately prevail, . . . the right of the public to receive suitable access to social, political, esthetic, moral and other ideas and experiences [through the medium of broadcasting] is crucial here [and it] may not constitutionally be abridged either by the Congress or the FCC."

Finally, although the government's interest in ensuring balanced coverage of public issues is plainly both important and substantial, we have, at the same time, made clear that broadcasters are engaged in a vital and independent form of communicative activity. As a result, the First Amendment must inform and give shape to the manner in which Congress exercises its regulatory power in this area. Unlike common carriers, broadcasters are "entitled under the First Amendment to exercise 'the widest journalistic freedom consistent with their public [duties].'" *Columbia Broadcasting System, Inc. v. FCC,* 453 U.S. 367, 395, 101 S.Ct. 2813, 2829, 69 L.Ed.2d 706, 728 (1981)(quoting *Columbia Broadcasting System, Inc. v. Democratic National Committee,* supra). Indeed, if the public's interest in receiving a balanced presentation of views is to be fully served, we must necessarily rely in large part upon the editorial initiative and judgment of the broadcasters who bear the public trust.

Our prior cases illustrate these principles. In *Red Lion,* for example, we upheld the FCC's "fairness doctrine"—which requires broadcasters to provide adequate coverage of public issues and to ensure that this coverage fairly and accurately reflects the opposing views—because the doctrine advanced the substantial governmental interest in ensuring balanced presentations of views in this limited medium and yet posed no threat that a "broadcaster [would be denied permission] to carry a particular program or to publish his own views.''[12] Similarly, in *Columbia Broadcasting System, Inc. v. FCC,* supra, the Court upheld the right of access for federal candidates imposed by § 312(a)(7) of the Communications Act both because that provision ''makes a significant contribution to freedom of expression by enhancing the ability of candidates to present, and the public to receive, information necessary for the effective operation of the democratic process,'' and because it defined a sufficiently *''limited* right of 'reasonable' access'' so that ''the discretion of broadcasters to present their views on any issue or to carry any particular type of programming'' was not impaired. (emphasis in original). Finally, in *Columbia Broadcasting System, Inc. v. Democratic National Committee,* supra, the Court affirmed the FCC's refusal to require broadcast licensees to accept all paid political advertisements. Although it was argued that such a requirement would serve the public's First Amendment interest in receiving additional views on public issues, the Court rejected this approach, finding that such a requirement would tend to transform broadcasters into common carriers and would intrude unnecessarily upon the editorial discretion of broadcasters. The FCC's ruling, therefore, helped to advance the important purposes of the Communications Act, grounded in the First Amendment, of preserving the right of broadcasters to exercise ''the widest journalistic freedom consistent with [their] public obligations,'' and of guarding against ''the risk of an enlargement of Government control over the content of broadcast discussion of public issues.''[13]

Thus, although the broadcasting industry plainly operates under restraints not imposed upon other media, the thrust of these restrictions has generally been to secure the public's First Amendment interest in

12. We note that the FCC, observing that ''[i]f any substantial possibility exists that the [fairness doctrine] rules have impeded, rather than furthered, First Amendment objectives, repeal may be warranted on that ground alone,'' has tentatively concluded that the rules, by effectively chilling speech, do not serve the public interest, and has therefore proposed to repeal them. Notice of Proposed Rulemaking In re Repeal or Modification of the Personal Attack and Political Editorial Rules, 48 Fed.Reg. 28295, 28298, 28301 (June 21, 1983). Of course, the Commission may, in the exercise of its discretion, decide to modify or abandon these rules, and we express no view on the legality of either course. As we recognized in *Red Lion,* however, were it to be shown by the Commission that the fairness doctrine ''has the effect of reducing rather than enhancing'' speech, we would then be forced to reconsider the constitutional basis of our decision in that case.

13. This Court's decision in *FCC v. Pacifica Foundation,* 438 U.S. 726, 98 S.Ct. 3026, 57 L.Ed.2d 1073 (1978), upholding an exercise of the Commission's authority to regulate broadcasts containing ''indecent'' [but not constitutionally ''obscene''] language as applied to a particular afternoon broadcast of a George Carlin monologue, is consistent with the approach taken in our other broadcast cases. There, the Court focused on certain physical characteristics of broadcasting—specifically, that the medium's uniquely pervasive presence renders impossible any prior warning for those listeners who may be offended by indecent language, and, second, that the ease with which children may gain access to the medium, especially during daytime hours, creates a substantial risk that they may be exposed to such offensive expression without parental supervision.... In this case, by contrast, we are faced not with indecent expression, but rather with expression that is at the core of First Amendment protections, and no claim is made by the Government that the expression of editorial opinion by noncommercial stations will create a substantial ''nuisance'' of the kind addressed in *FCC v. Pacifica Foundation.*

receiving a balanced presentation of views on diverse matters of public concern. As a result of these restrictions, of course, the absolute freedom to advocate one's own positions without also presenting opposing viewpoints—a freedom enjoyed, for example, by newspaper publishers and soapbox orators—is denied to broadcasters. But, as our cases attest, these restrictions have been upheld only when we were satisfied that the restriction is narrowly tailored to further a substantial governmental interest, such as ensuring adequate and balanced coverage of public issues. Making that judgment requires a critical examination of the interests of the public and broadcasters in light of the particular circumstances of each case. E.g., *FCC v. Pacifica Foundation,* supra.

We turn now to consider whether the restraint imposed by § 399 satisfies the requirements established by our prior cases for permissible broadcast regulation. Before assessing the government's proffered justifications for the statute, however, two central features of the ban against editorializing must be examined, since they help to illuminate the importance of the First Amendment interests at stake in this case.

First, the restriction imposed by § 399 is specifically directed at a form of speech—namely, the expression of editorial opinion—that lies at the heart of First Amendment protection.... Second, the scope of § 399's ban is defined solely on the basis of the content of the suppressed speech. [I]n enacting § 399 Congress appears to have sought to limit discussion of controversial topics and thus to shape the agenda for public debate.

In seeking to defend the prohibition on editorializing imposed by § 399, the Government urges that the statute was aimed at preventing two principal threats to the overall success of the Public Broadcasting Act of 1967. According to this argument, the ban was necessary, first, to protect noncommercial educational broadcasting stations from being coerced, as a result of federal financing, into becoming vehicles for government propagandizing or the objects of governmental influence; and, second, to keep these stations from becoming convenient targets for capture by private interest groups wishing to express their own partisan viewpoints.[16] By seeking to safeguard the public's right to a balanced presentation of public issues through the prevention of either govern-

---

16. The Government also contends that § 399 is intended to prevent the use of taxpayer monies to promote private views with which taxpayers may disagree. [V]irtually every congressional appropriation will to some extent involve a use of public money as to which some taxpayers may object. Nevertheless, this does not mean that those taxpayers have a constitutionally protected right to enjoin such expenditures. Nor can this interest be invoked to justify a congressional decision to suppress speech. [T]his is not a case in which an individual taxpayer is forced in his daily life to identify with particular views expressed by educational broadcasting stations. Even if this were a serious interest, it is belied by the underinclusiveness of § 399. The Government concedes—indeed it insists—that all sorts of controversial speech are subsidized by the 1967 Act, and yet out of all of this potentially objectionable speech, only the expression of editorial opinion by local stations is selected for suppression. If angry taxpayers were really the central, animating concern of Congress when it passed the 1967 Act, then § 399 does not go far enough in suppressing controversial speech in this medium. That the provision is so unrelated to this asserted purpose suggests that the Government's interest is not substantial.

mental or private bias, these objectives are, of course, broadly consistent with the goals identified in our earlier broadcast regulation cases. But, in sharp contrast to the restrictions upheld in *Red Lion* or in *Columbia Broadcasting System, Inc. v. FCC,* which left room for editorial discretion and simply required broadcast editors to grant others access to the microphone, § 399 directly prohibits the broadcaster from speaking out on public issues even in a balanced and fair manner. The Government insists, however, that the hazards posed in the "special" circumstances of noncommercial educational broadcasting are so great that § 399 is an indispensable means of preserving the public's First Amendment interests. We disagree.

[A]n examination of both the overall legislative scheme established by the 1967 Act and the character of public broadcasting demonstrates that the interest asserted by the Government is not substantially advanced by § 399. First, to the extent that federal financial support creates a risk that stations will lose their independence through the bewitching power of governmental largesse, the elaborate structure established by the Public Broadcasting Act already operates to insulate local stations from governmental interference. Congress not only mandated that the new Corporation for Public Broadcasting would have a private, bipartisan structure, see §§ 396(c)-(f), but also imposed a variety of important limitations on its powers. The Corporation was prohibited from owning or operating any station, § 396(g)(3), it was required to adhere strictly to a standard of "objectivity and balance" in disbursing federal funds to local stations, § 396(g)(1)(A), and it was prohibited from contributing to or otherwise supporting any candidate for office, § 396(f)(3)....

Even if these statutory protections were thought insufficient to the task, however, suppressing the particular category of speech restricted by § 399 is simply not likely, given the character of the public broadcasting system, to reduce substantially the risk that the Federal Government will seek to influence or put pressure on local stations. An underlying supposition of the Government's argument in this regard is that individual noncommercial stations are likely to speak so forcefully on particular issues that Congress, the ultimate source of the stations' Federal funding, will be tempted to retaliate against these individual stations by restricting appropriations for all of public broadcasting. But, as the District Court recognized, the character of public broadcasting suggests that such a risk is speculative at best. There are literally hundreds of public radio and television stations in communities scattered throughout the United States and its territories. Given that central fact, it seems reasonable to infer that the editorial voices of these stations will prove to be as distinctive, varied, and idiosyncratic as the various communities they represent. More importantly, the editorial focus of any particular station can fairly be expected to focus largely on issues affecting only its community. Accordingly, absent some showing by the Government to the contrary, the risk that local editorializing will place all of public broadcasting in jeopardy is not sufficiently pressing to warrant § 399's broad suppression of speech.

Indeed, what is far more likely than local station editorials to pose the kinds of dangers hypothesized by the Government are the wide variety of programs addressing controversial issues produced, often with substantial CPB funding, for national distribution to local stations. Such programs truly have the potential to reach a large audience and, because of the critical commentary they contain, to have the kind of genuine national impact that might trigger a congressional response or kindle governmental resentment. The ban imposed by § 399, however, instead, leveled solely at the expression of editorial opinion by local station management, a form of expression that is far more likely to be aimed at a smaller local audience, to have less national impact, and to be confined to local issues. . . .

Furthermore, the manifest imprecision of the ban imposed by § 399 reveals that its proscription is not sufficiently tailored to the harms it seeks to prevent to justify its substantial interference with broadcasters' speech. Section 399 includes within its grip a potentially infinite variety of speech, most of which would not be related in any way to governmental affairs, political candidacies or elections. [T]he Government never explains how, say, an editorial by local station management urging improvements in a town's parks or museums will so infuriate Congress or other Federal officials that the future of public broadcasting will be imperiled unless such editorials are suppressed. Nor is it explained how the suppression of editorials alone serves to reduce the risk of governmental retaliation and interference when it is clear that station management is fully able to broadcast controversial views so long as such views are not labelled as its own.

The Government appears to recognize these flaws in § 399, because it focuses instead on the suggestion that the source of governmental influence may well be state and local governments, many of which have established public broadcasting commissions that own and operate local noncommercial educational stations. . . . The Government's argument, however, proves too much. First, § 399's ban applies to the many private noncommercial community organizations that own and operate stations that are not controlled in any way by state or local government. Second, the legislative history of the Public Broadcasting Act clearly indicates that Congress was concerned with "assur[ing] complete freedom from any *Federal Government influence.*"

[A]lthough Congress was clearly aware in 1967 that many noncommercial educational stations were owned by state and local governments, it did not hesitate to extend Federal assistance to such stations, it imposed no special requirements to restrict state or local control over these stations, and, indeed, it ensured through the structure of the Act that these stations would be as insulated from Federal interference as the wholly private stations.[24]

24.   ... Whether a prohibition on edito-   rializing restricted to the licensees of State

Finally, although the Government certainly has a substantial interest in ensuring that the audiences of noncommercial stations will not be led to think that the broadcaster's editorials reflect the official view of the government, this interest can be fully satisfied by less restrictive means that are readily available. To address this important concern, Congress could simply require public broadcasting stations to broadcast a disclaimer every time they editorialize which would state that the editorial represents only the view of the station's management and does not in any way represent the views of the Federal Government or any of the station's other sources of funding.

In sum, § 399's broad ban on all editorializing by every station that receives CPB funds far exceeds what is necessary to protect against the risk of governmental interference or to prevent the public from assuming that editorials by public broadcasting stations represent the official view of government. The regulation impermissibly sweeps within its prohibition a wide range of speech by wholly private stations on topics that do not take a directly partisan stand or that have nothing whatever to do with federal, state or local government.

Assuming that the Government's second asserted interest in preventing noncommercial stations from becoming a "privileged outlet for the political and ideological opinions of station owners and management," is legitimate, the substantiality of this asserted interest is dubious. The patent over-and underinclusiveness of § 399's ban "undermines the likelihood of a genuine [governmental] interest" in preventing private groups from propagating their own views via public broadcasting. . . .

In short, § 399 does not prevent the use of noncommercial stations for the presentation of partisan views on controversial matters; instead, it merely bars a station from specifically communicating such views on its own behalf or on behalf of its management. If the vigorous expression of controversial opinions is, as the Government assures us, affirmatively encouraged by the Act, and if local licensees are permitted under the Act to exercise editorial control over the selection of programs, controversial or otherwise, that are aired on their stations, then § 399 accomplishes only one thing—the suppression of editorial speech by station management. It does virtually nothing, however, to reduce the risk that public stations will serve solely as outlets for expression of narrow partisan views. [T]he "sacrifice [of] First Amendment protections for so speculative a gain is not warranted. . . . "

Finally, the public's interest in preventing public broadcasting stations from becoming forums for lopsided presentations of narrow partisan positions is already secured by a variety of other regulatory means that intrude far less drastically upon the "journalistic freedom" of noncommercial broadcasters. The requirements of the FCC's fairness

and local governmental entities would pass constitutional muster is a question we need not decide.

doctrine, for instance, which apply to commercial and noncommercial stations alike, ensure that such editorializing would maintain a reasonably balanced and fair presentation of controversial issues.... The solution to this problem offered by § 399, however, is precisely the opposite of the remedy prescribed by the FCC and endorsed by the Court in *Red Lion*. Rather than requiring noncommercial broadcasters who express editorial opinions on controversial subjects to permit *more speech* on such subjects to ensure that the public's First Amendment interest in receiving a balanced account of the issue is met, § 399 simply silences all editorial speech by such broadcasters. Since the breadth of § 399 extends so far beyond what is necessary to accomplish the goals identified by the Government, it fails to satisfy the First Amendment standards that we have applied in this area.

We therefore hold that even if some of the hazards at which § 399 was aimed are sufficiently substantial, the restriction is not crafted with sufficient precision to remedy those dangers that may exist to justify the significant abridgement of speech worked by the provision's broad ban on editorializing. The statute is not narrowly tailored to address any of the government's suggested goals. Moreover, the public's "paramount right" to be fully and broadly informed on matters of public importance through the medium of noncommercial educational broadcasting is not well served by the restriction, for its effect is plainly to diminish rather than augment "the volume and quality of coverage" of controversial issues. Nor do we see any reason to deny noncommercial broadcasters the right to address matters of public concern on the basis of merely speculative fears of adverse public or governmental reactions to such speech.

Although the Government did not present the argument in any form to the District Court, it now seeks belatedly to justify § 399 on the basis of Congress' Spending Power. Relying upon our recent decision in *Regan v. Taxation With Representation*, 461 U.S. 540, 103 S.Ct. 1997, 76 L.Ed.2d 129 (1983) [excerpted § 10–3.4, supra], the Government argues that by prohibiting noncommercial educational stations that receive CPB grants from editorializing, Congress has, in the proper exercise of its Spending Power, simply determined that it "will not subsidize public broadcasting station editorials." In *Taxation With Representation*, the Court found that Congress could, in the exercise of its Spending Power, reasonably refuse to subsidize the lobbying activities of tax-exempt charitable organizations by prohibiting such organizations from using tax-deductible contributions to support their lobbying efforts. In so holding, however, we explained that such organizations remained free "to receive tax-deductible contributions to support non-lobbying activit[ies]." Thus, a charitable organization could create, under § 501(c)(3) of the Internal Revenue Code, an affiliate to conduct its non-lobbying activities using tax-deductible contributions, and, at the same time, establish, under § 501(c)(4), a separate affiliate to pursue its lobbying efforts without such contributions. Given that statutory alternative, the Court concluded that "Congress has not infringed any First Amendment rights or regulated any First Amendment activity; [it] has simply chosen not to pay for TWR's lobbying."

In this case, however, unlike the situation faced by the charitable organization in *Taxation With Representation,* a noncommercial educational station that receives only 1% of its overall income from CPB grants is barred absolutely from all editorializing. Therefore, in contrast to the appellee in *Taxation With Representation,* such a station is not able to segregate its activities according to the source of its funding. The station has no way of limiting the use of its Federal funds to all non-editorializing activities, and, more importantly, it is barred from using even wholly private funds to finance its editorial activity.

Of course, if Congress were to adopt a revised version of § 399 that permitted noncommercial educational broadcasting stations to establish "affiliate" organizations which could then use the station's facilities to editorialize with non-federal funds, such a statutory mechanism would plainly be valid under the reasoning of *Taxation With Representation*. . . . But in the absence of such authority, we must reject the Government's contention that our decision in *Taxation With Representation* is controlling here.[27]

In conclusion, we emphasize that our disposition of this case rests upon a narrow proposition. We do not hold that the Congress or the FCC are without power to regulate the content, timing, or character of speech by noncommercial educational broadcasting stations. Rather, we hold only that the specific interests sought to be advanced by § 399's ban on editorializing are either not sufficiently substantial or are not served in a sufficiently limited manner to justify the substantial abridgement of important journalistic freedoms which the First Amendment jealously protects. Accordingly, the judgment of the District Court is

Affirmed.

JUSTICE REHNQUIST, with whom THE CHIEF JUSTICE [BURGER] and JUSTICE WHITE join, dissenting.

All but three paragraphs of the Court's lengthy opinion in this case are devoted to the development of a scenario in which the government appears as the "Big Bad Wolf," and appellee Pacifica [the owner of several noncommercial broadcasting stations] as "Little Red Riding Hood." . . . Perhaps a more appropriate analogy than that of Little Red Riding Hood and the Big Bad Wolf is that of Faust and Mephistopheles; Pacifica, well aware of § 399's condition on its receipt of public money, nonetheless accepted the public money and now seeks to avoid the conditions which Congress legitimately has attached to receipt of that funding. . . .

---

27. . . . Justice Rehnquist's reliance upon *Oklahoma v. United States Civil Service Commission,* [§ 4–3, supra], is also misplaced. [I]t was only in the context of rejecting Oklahoma's Tenth Amendment claim that the Court used the language cited by the dissent. [T]he Court never intimated in *Oklahoma v. CSC* that the mere presence of government funds was a sufficient reason to uphold the Hatch Act's restrictions on employee freedoms on the basis of relaxed First Amendment standards.

The Court's three-paragraph discussion of why § 399, repeatedly reexamined and retained by Congress, violates the First Amendment is to me utterly unpersuasive. Congress has rationally determined that the bulk of the taxpayers whose monies provide the funds for grants by the CPB would prefer not to see the management of local educational stations promulgate its own private views on the air at taxpayer expense. Accordingly Congress simply has decided not to subsidize stations which engage in that activity. Last term, in *Regan v. Taxation With Representation,* we upheld a provision of the Internal Revenue Code which deprives an otherwise eligible organization of its tax-exempt status and its right to receive tax-deductible contributions if it engages in lobbying. [T]he Court today seeks to avoid the thrust of that opinion by pointing out that a public broadcasting station is barred from editorializing with its non-federal funds even though it may receive only a minor fraction of its income from CPB grants....

But to me there is no distinction between § 399 and the statute which we upheld in *Oklahoma v. United States Civil Service Commission* [§ 4–3, supra]. Section 12(a) of the Hatch Act totally prohibits any local or state employee who is employed in any activity which receives partial or total financing from the United States from taking part in any political activities. One might just as readily denounce such congressional action as prohibiting employees of a state or local government receiving even a minor fraction of that government's income from federal assistance from exercising their First Amendment right to speak. But not surprisingly this Court upheld the Hatch Act provision in *Oklahoma v. United States Civil Service Commission,* supra, succinctly stating: "While the United States is not concerned with, and has no power to regulate, local political activities as such of state officials, it does have power to fix the terms upon which its money allotments to states shall be disbursed."[1]

The Court seems to believe that Congress actually subsidizes editorializing only if a station uses federal money specifically to cover the expenses that the Court believes can be isolated as editorializing expenses. But to me the Court's approach ignores economic reality. CPB's unrestricted grants are used for salaries, training, equipment, promotion, etc.—financial expenditures which benefit all aspects of a station's programming, including management's editorials. Given the impossibility of compartmentalizing programming expenses in any meaningful way, it seems clear to me that the only effective means for preventing the use of public monies to subsidize the airing of management's views is for Congress to ban a subsidized station from all on-the-air editorializing....

---

1. The Court takes pains to show that the argument rejected in *United States Civil Service Commission* was a Tenth Amendment argument. Without belaboring the point, in my view a fair reading of the opinion is that the Court used the quoted language in that case to refer to a First Amendment argument similar to this one, as well as to a Tenth Amendment argument.

This is not to say that the government may attach *any* condition to its largess; it is only to say that when the government is simply exercising its power to allocate its own public funds, we need only find that the condition imposed has a rational relationship to Congress' purpose in providing the subsidy and that it is not primarily "aimed at the suppression of dangerous ideas." In this case Congress' prohibition is directly related to its purpose in providing subsidies for public broadcasting, and it is plainly rational for Congress to have determined that taxpayer monies should not be used to subsidize management's views or to pay for management's exercise of partisan politics. Indeed, it is entirely rational for Congress to have wished to avoid the appearance of government sponsorship of a particular view or a particular political candidate. Furthermore, Congress' prohibition is strictly neutral. In no sense can it be said that Congress has prohibited only editorial views of one particular ideological bent. Nor has it prevented public stations from airing programs, documentaries, interviews, etc. dealing with controversial subjects, so long as management itself does not expressly endorse a particular viewpoint. And Congress has not prevented station management from communicating its own views on those subjects through any medium other than subsidized public broadcasting.

For the foregoing reasons I find this case entirely different from the so-called "unconstitutional condition" cases, wherein the Court has stated that the government "may not deny a benefit to a person on a basis that infringes his constitutionally protected interests—especially his interest in freedom of speech." In those cases the suppressed speech was not content-neutral in the same sense as here, and in those cases, there is at best only a strained argument that the legislative purpose of the condition imposed was to avoid *subsidizing* the prohibited speech. *Speiser v. Randall,* [357 U.S. 513, 78 S.Ct. 1332, 2 L.Ed.2d 1460 (1958)], is illustrative of the difference. In that case California's decision to deny its property tax exemption to veterans who would not declare that they would not work to overthrow the government was plainly directed at suppressing what California regarded as speech of a dangerous content. And the condition imposed was so unrelated to the benefit to be conferred that it is difficult to argue that California's property tax exemption actually subsidized the dangerous speech. . . .

Justice White: Believing that the editorializing and candidate endorsement proscription stand or fall together and being confident that Congress may condition use of its funds on abstaining from political endorsements, I join Justice Rehnquist's dissenting opinion.

Justice Stevens, dissenting.

The court jester who mocks the King must choose his words with great care. An artist is likely to paint a flattering portrait of his patron. The child who wants a new toy does not preface his request with a comment on how fat his mother is. Newspaper publishers have been known to listen to their advertising managers. Elected officials may remember how their elections were financed. By enacting the statutory provision that the Court invalidates today, a sophisticated group of legislators expressed a concern about the potential impact of government funds on pervasive and powerful organs of mass communication. One need not have heard the raucous voice of Adolph Hitler over Radio Berlin to appreciate the importance of that concern....

The statute does not violate the fundamental principle that the citizen's right to speak may not be conditioned upon the sovereign's agreement with what the speaker intends to say. On the contrary, the statute was enacted in order to protect that very principle—to avoid the risk that some speakers will be rewarded or penalized for saying things that appeal to—or are offensive to—the sovereign.[7] The interests the statute is designed to protect are interests that underlie the First Amendment itself.

In my judgment the interest in keeping the Federal Government out of the propaganda arena is of overriding importance. That interest is of special importance in the field of electronic communication, not only because that medium is so powerful and persuasive, but also because it is the one form of communication that is licensed by the Federal Government. When the Government already has great potential power over the electronic media, it is surely legitimate to enact statutory safeguards to make sure that it does not cross the threshold that separates neutral regulation from the subsidy of partisan opinion....[10] ...

Notes

1. In *FCC v. Pacifica Foundation,* 438 U.S. 726, 98 S.Ct. 3026, 57 L.Ed.2d 1073 (1978)(distinguished in *FCC v. League of Women Voters*) the Court (5 to 4), with no majority, upheld the power of the FCC to regulate a radio broadcast that was "indecent but not obscene." An FM station broadcast a 12 minute monologue, entitled, "Filthy Words," by George Carlin, a satirist. Carlin had delivered the broadcast before a live audience in a California theater, and the FM station broadcast the recording at 2 p.m., on Tuesday, October 30, 1973. A motorist who heard the broadcast while driving with his young son complained to the FCC, which ruled that the broadcast was prohibited by 18 U.S.C.A. § 1464, a criminal statute prohibiting "obscene, indecent, or profane language by means of radio communica-

7. [T]he statute will also protect the listener's interest in not having his tax payments used to finance the advocacy of causes he opposes.... The Court briefly observes that the taxpayers do not have a constitutionally protected right to enjoin such expenditures and then leaps to the conclusion that given the fact that the funding scheme itself is not unconstitutional, this interest cannot be used to support the statute at issue here. Ante at n. 16. The conclusion manifestly does not follow from the premise, and this interest is plainly legitimate and significant.

10. The majority argues that the Government's concededly substantial interest in ensuring that audiences of educational stations will not perceive the station to be a government propaganda organ can be fully satisfied by requiring such stations to broadcast a disclaimer each time they editorialize stating that the editorial "does not in any way represent the views of the Federal Government...." This solution would be laughable were it not so Orwellian: the answer to the fact that there is a real danger that the editorials are really government propaganda is for the government to require the station to tell the audience that it is not propaganda at all!

tion." The FCC issued a declaratory order, and imposed no formal sanctions, but it stated that if subsequent complaints were received it would decide whether to utilize the available sanctions, including a license revocation. The FCC wanted to "channel" the broadcast to times of the day when children were most likely not present in the audience.

Stevens, J.'s plurality opinion emphasized "the narrowness" of the holding. It did not involve a two-way conversation between a cab driver and a dispatcher, or a telecast of an Elizabethan comedy. "We have not decided that an occasional expletive in either setting would justify any sanction or, indeed, that this broadcast would justify a criminal prosecution. The Commission's decision rested entirely on a nuisance rationale under which context is all-important." Relevant factors that Stevens mentioned included the time of day, the content of the program, and the possible differences between radio, television, and closed-circuit transmissions. Powell, J., joined by Blackmun, J., argued that the FCC's power is justified by "the unique characteristics of the broadcast media, combined with society's right to protect its children from speech generally agreed to be inappropriate for their years, and with the interest of unwilling adults in not being assaulted by such offensive speech in their homes."

Brennan, J., joined by Marshall, J., dissented: "Because the Carlin monologue is obviously not an erotic appeal to the prurient interests of children, the Court, for the first time, allows the government to prevent minors from gaining access to materials that are not obscene, and are therefore protected as to them. [I]t has the anomalous subsidiary effect, at least in the radio context at issue here, of making completely unavailable to adults material which may not constitutionally be kept even from children."[1]

2. *Red Lion,* as noted in *FCC v. League of Women Voters,* upheld the "fairness doctrine." FCC policy promoted the fairness doctrine since 1949, but after a lower court ruled that it was not an Act of Congress and the FCC could repeal it, Congress passed a statute to make the rule permanent.

---

1. The Appendix to the Opinion of the Court, 438 U.S. 751 through 755, reprinted the entire verbatim transcript of the "Filthy Words" broadcast. In part the monologue stated:

"Aruba-du, ruba-tu, ruba-tu. I was thinking about the curse words and the swear words, the cuss words and the words that you can't say, that you're not supposed to say all the time.... A guy who used to be in Washington knew that his phone was tapped, used to answer, 'Fuck Hoover, yes, go ahead.' (laughter) Okay, I was thinking one night about the words you couldn't say on the public, ah, airwaves. [B]astard you can say, and hell and damn so I have to figure out which ones you couldn't and ever and it came down to seven but the list is open to amendment, and in fact, has been changed, uh, by now, ha, a lot of people pointed things out to me, and I noticed some myself. The original seven words were, shit, piss, fuck, cunt, cocksucker, motherfucker, and tits. Those are the ones that will curve your spine, grow hair on your hands and (laughter) maybe, even bring us, God help us, peace without honor (laughter) um, and a bourbon. (laughter) ... I found three more words that had to be put on the list of words you could never say on television, and they were fart, turd and twat, those three. (laughter) ... Even in a Walt Disney movie, you can say, We're going to snatch that pussy and put him in a box and bring him on the airplane. (murmur, laughter) Everybody loves it. The twat stands alone, man, as it should. And two-way words. Ah, ass is okay providing you're riding into town on a religious feast day. (laughter) You can't say, up your *ass.* (laughter) You can say, stuff it! (murmur) There are certain things you can say its weird but you can just come so close. Before I cut, I, uh, want to, ah, thank you for listening to my words, man, fellow, uh space travelers. Thank you man for tonight and thank you also. (clapping, whistling)"

President Reagan, in June, 1987, vetoed the legislation as unconstitutional. His veto message said: "This type of content-based regulation by the federal government is, in my judgment, antagonistic to the freedom of expression guaranteed" by the Constitution.

3. PUBLIC TELEVISION'S EXCLUSION OF INDEPENDENT CANDIDATE FROM TELE-VISED CANDIDATE DEBATE. *Arkansas Educational Television Commission v. Forbes*, 523 U.S. 666, 118 S.Ct. 1633, 140 L.Ed.2d 875 (1998). A state-owned public television broadcaster (AETC) sponsored a debate between the two major party candidates for the 1992 election in the Third Congressional District in Arkansas. AETC denied Ralph P. Forbes (a third-party candidate with little popular support) permission to participate in the debate. Forbes sued, claiming that the First Amendment gave him a right to participate in the debate. Kennedy, J., for the Court, held (6 to 3) that the televised debate was a nonpublic forum from which the broadcaster could exclude a candidate in the reasonable, viewpoint-neutral exercise of its journalistic discretion. The jury made express findings that AETC's decision to exclude Forbes had not been influenced by political pressure or disagreement with his views.

In general, Kennedy explained, the public forum doctrine should not be transplanted to public television broadcasting because any broad right of access is antithetical to the discretion that stations must exercise to fulfill their journalistic and statutory obligations, "and the nature of editorial discretion counsels against subjecting broadcasters to claims of viewpoint discrimination." Even principled exclusions "rooted in sound journalistic judgment can often be characterized as viewpoint-based." Just like universities select one commencement speaker, a broadcaster will, by nature, facilitate the expression of some viewpoints over others. If the judiciary required pre-established criteria for access, "it would risk implicating the courts in judgments that should be left to the exercise of journalistic discretion."*

As a general matter, public broadcasting should not be scrutinized under the public forum doctrine, but candidate debates "present the narrow exception to the rule" for two reasons. First, unlike a political talk show (where the host can express partisan ideas and limit discussion to them), a debate is designed to be a forum for the candidates' political speech. Second, these debates are "of exceptional significance in the electoral process." Nonetheless, the candidate debate was "a nonpublic forum, from which AETC would exclude Forbes in the reasonable, viewpoint-neutral exercise of its journalistic discretion." Under the First Amendment, "the exclusion of a speaker from a nonpublic forum must not be based on the speaker's viewpoint and must otherwise be reasonable in light of the purpose of the property." AETC met these requirements.

The Court added, while the First Amendment does not, of its own force, impose neutral rules for access to public broadcasting, this "is not to say

---

* Stevens, J., joined by Souter & Ginsburg, JJ., dissented. These justices agreed that a state-owned television network does not have the obligation to allow every candidate access to the political debates that it sponsors, but that AETC acted unconstitutionally because this particular decision was ad hoc, and—whether it was based on "newsworthiness," as argued in the Supreme Court, or "political viability," as argued in the Court of Appeals—it was made by the staff without "pre-established, objective criteria."

that the First Amendment would bar the legislative imposition of neutral rules for access to public broadcasting."

4. *Denver Area Educational Telecommunications Consortium, Inc. v. FCC,* 518 U.S. 727, 116 S.Ct. 2374, 135 L.Ed.2d 888 (1996). Plaintiffs challenged three sections of a federal law designed to regulate cable television broadcasting of "patently offensive" sex-related material. The very fragmented Court invalidated two provisions and upheld one provision. Breyer, J., announced the Judgment of the Court and delivered the Opinion of the Court with respect to Part III (in which Stevens, O'Connor, Kennedy, Souter, & Ginsburg, JJ., joined).*

A *leased cable channel* is a channel that federal law requires a cable system operator to reserve for commercial lease by unaffiliated third parties. SECTION 10(B) required cable system operators to segregate "patently offensive" sex-related material that appears on leased channel (but not on other channels) to a separate channel, to block that channel, to unblock that channel within 30 days of a subscriber's written request, and to reblock it within 30 days of a subscriber's written request. Breyer, J., for the Court, invalidated this provision under the First Amendment. The delays of up to 30 days would require subscribers to engage in significant advanced planning, and the writing would adversely affect viewers who fear for their reputations if the list were inadvertently made public. Congress used less restrictive means to deal with non-leased cable channels, and there is no explanation for the difference in treatment.

SECTION 10(A) of the law permitted (but did-not require) cable system operators to prohibit "patently offensive" or "indecent" programming transmitted over leased channels. Between 1984 and 1992, other law prohibited cable system operators from exercising editorial control. Breyer (joined by Stevens, O'Connor, & Souter) upheld this provision, in a ruling described as narrow. The Court should not impose "a rigid single standard, good now and for all future media and purposes," which may "straightjacket" the Government's ability to respond to serious problems.

SECTION 10(C) permitted a cable operator to prevent transmission of "patently offensive" programming on public access channels. A *public access channel* is channel capacity that cable operators agreed to reserve for public, governmental, and educational access as part of the consideration that municipalities obtained in exchange for awarding a cable franchise. Breyer (joined by Stevens & Souter) ruled that this section, unlike § 10(A), is unconstitutional. Cable operators did not historically exercise editorial control over these channels, and therefore § 10(C), unlike § 10(A), "does not restore to cable operators editorial rights that they once had, and the countervailing First Amendment interest is nonexistent, or at least diminished."

---

* He also delivered an Opinion with respect to Parts I, II, & V (which Stevens, O'Connor & Souter, JJ., joined), & an Opinion with respect to Parts IV & VI (which Stevens & Souter, JJ., joined). Stevens, J., & Souter, J., filed concurring opinions. O'Connor, J., filed an Opinion concurring in part & dissenting in part. Kennedy, J., filed an Opinion concurring in part, concurring in the judgment in part, & dissenting in part (which Ginsburg, J., joined). Thomas, J., filed an Opinion concurring in the judgment in part & dissenting in part (which Rehnquist, C.J., & Scalia, J., joined).

Kennedy, J. (joined by Ginsburg, J.), joined in the opinion of the Court invalidating § 10(B), but would invalidate the other two sections as well. "Sections 10(A) and (C) disadvantage nonobscene, indecent programming, a protected category of expression." Sections 10(A) and (C) apply to access channels, each of which is a "designated public forum," which the government has opened to the public for expressive activity. Kennedy also criticized the plurality's narrow focus:

"The plurality opinion, insofar as it upholds § 10(A) of the 1992 Cable Act, is adrift. When confronted with a threat to free speech in the context of an emerging technology, we ought to have the discipline to analyze the case by reference to existing elaborations of constant First Amendment principles. . . . Rather than undertake this task, however, the plurality just declares that, all things considered, § 10(A) seems fine."

Thomas, J. (joined by Rehnquist, C.J. & Scalia, J.) concurred in the judgment in part and dissented in part. He would uphold all three sections: "cable operators are generally entitled to much the same First Amendment protection as the print media." Like a "free-lance writer seeking a paper in which to publish newspaper editorials, a programmer is protected in searching for an outlet for cable programming, but has no free-standing First Amendment right to have that programming transmitted. Cf. *Miami Herald Publishing Co. v. Tornillo.*" While viewers have a general right to see what a willing operator transmits, they have "no right to force an unwilling operator to speak."

"None of the petitioners in these cases are cable operators; they are all cable viewers or access programmers or their representative organizations. It is not intuitively obvious that the First Amendment protects the interests petitioners assert, and neither petitioners nor the plurality have adequately explained the source or justification of those asserted rights."

5. *Turner Broadcasting System, Inc. v. FCC,* 512 U.S. 622, 114 S.Ct. 2445, 129 L.Ed.2d 497 (1994). In 1992, Congress enacted the Cable Television and Consumer Protection and Competition Act. Sections 4 and 5 required cable television systems to devote a portion of their channels to the transmission of local broadcast stations, in order to aid broadcast television. Cable operators sued, claiming that these "must-carry" provisions violated the first amendment.

First, the Court ruled that it should not use the less rigorous standard of review reserved for broadcast regulation because the problems of broadcast scarcity and signal interference does not apply to cable. But strict scrutiny should not apply to the must-carry rules because they are content-neutral: the Congressional purpose was not to control content but to "ensure that broadcast television will retain a large enough potential audience to earn necessary advertising revenue."

The Court chose "the intermediate level of scrutiny": a content-neutral regulation will be sustained if "it furthers an important or substantial governmental interest" unrelated to the suppression of free expression, and if the incidental restriction on alleged First Amendment freedoms "is no greater than is essential to the furtherance of that interest." The regulation need not be the least speech-restrictive means of advancing the Government's interests. Rather, "narrow tailoring" is satisfied "if the regulation promotes a substantial government interest that would be achieved less effectively absent the regulation."

The Court remanded for further proceedings, and in 1997, this case came back to the Court in *Turner Broadcasting System, Inc. v. Federal Communications Commission,* 520 U.S. 180, 117 S.Ct. 1174, 137 L.Ed.2d 369 (1997). Justice Kennedy, for the Court, decided the two questions left open during the first appeal: first, whether the record now supports Congress' predictive judgment that the must-carry provisions further important governmental interests, and second, whether the provisions do not burden substantially more speech than necessary to further those interests. The Court answered both questions affirmatively, and concluded that the must-carry provisions are consistent with the First Amendment.

Congress did not believe that broadcast television would disappear in its entirety without must-carry, but that without it, "significant numbers of broadcast stations will be refused carriage on cable systems," and those "broadcast stations denied carriage will either deteriorate to a substantial degree or fail altogether." The Court acknowledged that the factual record developed below "also contains evidence to support a contrary conclusion." For example, "only 31 broadcast stations actually went dark during the period without must-carry (one of which failed after a tornado destroyed its transmitter), and during the same period some 263 new stations signed on the air." However—the question is" not whether Congress, as an objective matter, was correct to determine must-carry is necessary to prevent a substantial number of broadcast stations from losing cable carriage and suffering significant financial hardship. Rather, the question is whether the legislative conclusion was reasonable and supported by substantial evidence in the record before Congress. ... We are not at liberty to substitute our judgment for the reasonable conclusion of a legislative body."

Stevens, J., filed a concurring opinion. Breyer, J., concurred in part and rejected the majority's anticompetitive analysis. Instead, he relied on "the statute's other objectives, namely '(1) preserving the benefits of free, over-the-air local broadcast television,' and '(2) promoting the widespread dissemination of information from a multiplicity of sources.' Whether or not the statute does or does not sensibly compensate for some significant market defect, it undoubtedly seeks to provide over-the-air viewers who *lack* cable with a rich mix of over-the-air programming by guaranteeing the over-the-air stations that provide such programming with the extra dollars that an additional cable audience will generate."

O'Connor, J., joined by Scalia, Thomas, & Ginsburg, JJ., dissented:

[P]romoting fair competition is a legitimate and substantial Government goal. But the Court nowhere examines whether the breadth of the must-carry provisions comports with a goal of preventing anticompetitive harms. Instead, in the course of its inquiry into whether the must-carry provisions are "narrowly tailored," the principal opinion simply assumes that most adverse carriage decisions are anticompetitively motivated, and that must-carry is therefore a measured response to a problem of anticompetitive behavior. We ordinarily do not substitute unstated and untested assumptions for our independent evaluation of the facts bearing upon an issue of constitutional law. Perhaps because of the difficulty of defending the must-carry provisions as a measured response to anticompetitive behavior, the Court asserts an "independent" interest in preserving a "multiplicity" of broadcast programming sources.

[But neither] the principal opinion nor the partial concurrence ever explains what kind of conduct, apart from anticompetitive conduct, threatens the "multiplicity" of broadcast programming sources. Indeed, the only justification advanced by the parties for furthering this interest is heavily content based. It is undisputed that the broadcast stations protected by must-carry are the "marginal" stations within a given market; the record on remand reveals that any broader threat to the broadcast system was entirely mythical.... Must-carry is thus justified as a way of preserving viewers' access to a Spanish or Chinese language station or of preventing an independent station from adopting a home-shopping format. Undoubtedly, such goals are reasonable and important, and the stations in question may well be worthwhile targets of Government subsidies. But appellees' characterization of must-carry as a means of protecting these stations, like the Court's explicit concern for promoting "community self-expression" and the "local origination of broadcast programming," reveals a content-based preference for broadcast programming. This justification of the regulatory scheme is, in my view, wholly at odds with the *Turner* Court's premise that must-carry is a means of preserving "access to free television programming—*whatever its content*" (emphasis added)....

10–6.   THE PRESS AND THE CRIMINAL JUSTICE SYSTEM

10–6.1 Protection of Confidential Sources

BRANZBURG v. HAYES
408 U.S. 665, 92 S.Ct. 2646, 33 L.Ed.2d 626 (1972).

Opinion of the Court by MR. JUSTICE WHITE, announced by THE CHIEF JUSTICE [BURGER]....

On November 15, 1969, the Courier–Journal carried a story under petitioner's by-line describing in detail his observations of two young residents of Jefferson County synthesizing hashish from marihuana, an activity which, they asserted earned them about $5,000 in three weeks. The article included a photograph of a pair of hands working above a laboratory table on which was a substance identified by the caption as hashish. The article stated that petitioner had promised not to reveal the identity of the two hashish makers. Petitioner was shortly subpoenaed by the Jefferson County grand jury; he appeared, but refused to identify the individuals he had seen possessing marihuana or the persons he had seen making hashish from marihuana. A state trial court judge ordered petitioner to answer these questions. [Other cases consolidated herein have a similar factual background.] ...

Petitioners Branzburg and Pappas and respondent Caldwell press First Amendment claims that may be simply put: that to gather news it is often necessary to agree either not to identify the source of information published or to publish only part of the facts revealed, or both; that if the reporter is nevertheless forced to reveal these confidences to a grand jury, the source so identified and other confidential sources of other reporters will be measurably deterred from furnishing publishable information, all to the detriment of the free flow of information protected by the First Amendment. Although the newsmen in these cases do not claim an absolute privilege against official interrogation in all circumstances, they assert that the reporter should not be forced either to appear or to testify before a grand jury or at trial until and unless sufficient grounds are shown for believing that the reporter possesses information relevant to a crime the grand jury is investigating, that the information the reporter has is unavailable from other sources, and that the need for the information is sufficiently compelling to override the claimed invasion of First Amendment interests occasioned by the disclosure....

We do not question the significance of free speech, press, or assembly to the country's welfare. Nor is it suggested that news gathering does not qualify for First Amendment protection; without some protection for seeking out the news, freedom of the press could be eviscerated. But these cases involve no intrusions upon speech or assembly, no prior restraint or restriction on what the press may publish, and no express or implied command that the press publish what it prefers to withhold. No exaction or tax for the privilege of publishing, and no penalty, civil or criminal, related to the content of published material is at issue here. The use of confidential sources by the press is not forbidden or restricted; reporters remain free to seek news from any source by means within the law. No attempt is made to require the press to publish its sources of information or indiscriminately to disclose them on request....

It is clear that the First Amendment does not invalidate every incidental burdening of the press that may result from the enforcement of civil or criminal statutes of general applicability. [O]therwise valid laws serving substantial public interests may be enforced against the press as against others, despite the possible burden that may be imposed. The Court has emphasized that "[t]he publisher of a newspaper has no special immunity from the application of general laws. He has no special privilege to invade the rights and liberties of others." *Associated Press v. NLRB,* 301 U.S. 103, 132–133, 57 S.Ct. 650, 656, 81 L.Ed. 953 (1937). It was there held that the Associated Press, a news-gathering and disseminating organization, was not exempt from the requirements of the National Labor Relations Act. "[T]he right to speak and publish does not carry with it the unrestrained right to gather information." ...

It is thus not surprising that the great weight of authority is that newsmen are not exempt from the normal duty of appearing before a grand jury and answering questions relevant to a criminal investigation. At common law, courts consistently refused to recognize the existence of any privilege authorizing a newsman to refuse to reveal confidential information to a grand jury. [T]he grand jury's authority to subpoena witnesses is not only historic, but essential to its task. Although the powers of the grand jury are not unlimited and are subject to the supervision of a judge, the long-standing principle that "the public ... has a right to every man's evidence," except for those persons protected by a constitutional, common law, or statutory privilege, is particularly applicable to grand jury proceedings.

A number of States have provided newsmen a statutory privilege of varying breadth, but the majority have not done so, and none has been provided by federal statute. Until now the only testimonial privilege for unofficial witnesses that is rooted in the Federal Constitution is the Fifth Amendment privilege against compelled self-incrimination. We are asked to create another by interpreting the First Amendment to grant newsmen a testimonial privilege that other citizens do not enjoy. This we decline to do. Fair and effective law enforcement aimed at providing security for the person and property of the individual is a fundamental function of government, and the grand jury plays an important, constitutionally mandated role in this process. On the records now before us, we perceive no basis for holding that the public interest in law enforcement and in ensuring effective grand jury proceedings is insufficient to override the consequential, but uncertain, burden on news gathering that is said to result from insisting that reporters, like other citizens, respond to relevant questions put to them in the course of a valid grand jury investigation or criminal trial....

Thus, we cannot seriously entertain the notion that the First Amendment protects a newsman's agreement to conceal the criminal conduct of his source, or evidence thereof, on the theory that it is better to write about crime than to do something about it. Insofar as any reporter in these cases undertook not to reveal or testify about the crime he witnessed, his claim of privilege under the First Amendment presents no substantial question. The crimes of news sources are no less reprehensible and threatening to the public interest when witnessed by a reporter than when they are not....

Accepting the fact, however, that an undetermined number of informants not themselves implicated in crime will nevertheless, for whatever reason, refuse to talk to newsmen if they fear identification by a reporter in an official investigation, we cannot accept the argument that the public interest in possible future news about crime from undisclosed, unverified sources must take precedence over the public interest in pursuing and prosecuting those crimes reported to the press by informants and in thus deterring the commission of such crimes in the future....

We are admonished that refusal to provide a First Amendment reporter's privilege will undermine the freedom of the press to collect and disseminate news. But this is not the lesson history teaches us.... From the beginning of our country the press has operated without constitutional protection for press informants, and the press has flourished. The existing constitutional rules have not been a serious obstacle to either the development or retention of confidential news sources by the press. [T]he investigation of crime by the grand jury implements a fundamental governmental role of securing the safety of the person and property of the citizen, and it appears to us that calling reporters to give testimony in the manner and for the reasons that other citizens are called "bears a reasonable relationship to the achievement of the governmental purpose asserted as its justification." . . .

Similar considerations dispose of the reporters' claims that preliminary to requiring their grand jury appearance, the State must show that a crime has been committed and that they possess relevant information not available from other sources, for only the grand jury itself can make this determination. The role of the grand jury as an important instrument of effective law enforcement necessarily includes an investigatory function with respect to determining whether a crime has been committed and who committed it. . . .

The privilege claimed here is conditional, not absolute; given the suggested preliminary showings and compelling need, the reporter would be required to testify. Presumably, such a rule would reduce the instances in which reporters could be required to appear, but predicting in advance when and in what circumstances they could be compelled to do so would be difficult. Such a rule would also have implications for the issuance of compulsory process to reporters at civil and criminal trials and at legislative hearings. If newsmen's confidential sources are as sensitive as they are claimed to be, the prospect of being unmasked whenever a judge determines the situation justifies it is hardly a satisfactory solution to the problem. For them, it would appear that only an absolute privilege would suffice.

We are unwilling to embark the judiciary on a long and difficult journey to such an uncertain destination. The administration of a constitutional newsman's privilege would present practical and conceptual difficulties of a high order. Sooner or later, it would be necessary to define those categories of newsmen who qualified for the privilege, a questionable procedure in light of the traditional doctrine that liberty of the press is the right of the lonely pamphleteer who uses carbon paper or a mimeograph just as much as of the large metropolitan publisher who utilizes the latest photocomposition methods. . . . The informative function asserted by representatives of the organized press in the present cases is also performed by lecturers, political pollsters, novelists, academic researchers, and dramatists. Almost any author may quite accurately assert that he is contributing to the flow of information to the public, that he relies on confidential sources of information, and that these sources will be silenced if he is forced to make disclosures before a grand jury.

At the federal level, Congress has freedom to determine whether a statutory newsman's privilege is necessary and desirable and to fashion standards and rules as narrow or broad as deemed necessary to deal with the evil discerned and, equally important, to refashion those rules as experience from time to time may dictate. There is also merit in leaving state legislatures free, within First Amendment limits, to fashion their own standards in light of the conditions and problems with respect to the relations between law enforcement officials and press in their own areas. It goes without saying, of course, that we are powerless to bar state courts from responding in their own way and construing their own constitutions so as to recognize a newsman's privilege, either qualified or absolute.

In addition, there is much force in the pragmatic view that the press has at its disposal powerful mechanisms of communication and is far from helpless to protect itself from harassment or substantial harm. Furthermore, if what the newsmen urged in these cases is true—that law enforcement cannot hope to gain and may suffer from subpoenaing newsmen before grand juries—prosecutors will be loath to risk so much for so little. Thus, at the federal level the Attorney General has already fashioned a set of rules for federal officials in connection with subpoenaing members of the press to testify before grand juries or at criminal trials. . . .

Finally, as we have earlier indicated, news gathering is not without its First Amendment protections, and grand jury investigations if instituted or conducted other than in good faith, would pose wholly different issues for resolution under the First Amendment. Official harassment of the press undertaken not for purposes of law enforcement but to disrupt a reporter's relationship with his news sources would have no justification. Grand juries are subject to judicial control and subpoenas to motions to quash. We do not expect courts will forget that grand juries must operate within the limits of the First Amendment as well as the Fifth. . . .

MR. JUSTICE POWELL, concurring.

I add this brief statement to emphasize what seems to me to be the limited nature of the Court's holding. The Court does not hold that newsmen, subpoenaed to testify before a grand jury, are without constitutional rights with respect to the gathering of news or in safeguarding their sources. Certainly, we do not hold, as suggested in Mr. Justice Stewart's dissenting opinion, that state and federal authorities are free to "annex" the news media as "an investigative arm of government." The solicitude repeatedly shown by this Court for First Amendment freedoms should be sufficient assurance against any such effort, even if one seriously believed that the media—properly free and untrammeled in the fullest sense of these terms—were not able to protect themselves.

As indicated in the concluding portion of the opinion, the Court states that no harassment of newsmen will be tolerated. If a newsman believes that the grand jury investigation is not being conducted in good faith he is not without remedy. Indeed, if the newsman is called upon to give information bearing only a remote and tenuous relationship to the subject of the investigation, or if he has some other reason to believe that his testimony implicates confidential source relationships without a legitimate need of law enforcement, he will have access to the court on a motion to quash and an appropriate protective order may be entered....

MR. JUSTICE STEWART, with whom MR. JUSTICE BRENNAN and MR. JUSTICE MARSHALL join, dissenting.

... While Mr. Justice Powell's enigmatic concurring opinion gives some hope of a more flexible view in the future, the Court in these cases holds that a newsman has no First Amendment right to protect his sources when called before a grand jury. The Court thus invites state and federal authorities to undermine the historic independence of the press by attempting to annex the journalistic profession as an investigative arm of government. Not only will this decision impair performance of the press' constitutionally protected functions, but it will, I am convinced, in the long run harm rather than help the administration of justice....

A corollary of the right to publish must be the right to gather news.... It is obvious that informants are necessary to the news-gathering process as we know it today. If it is to perform its constitutional mission, the press must do far more than merely print public statements or publish prepared handouts.... It is equally obvious that the promise of confidentiality may be a necessary prerequisite to a productive relationship between a newsman and his informants....

Accordingly, when a reporter is asked to appear before a grand jury and reveal confidences, I would hold that the government must (1) show that there is probable cause to believe that the newsman has information that is clearly relevant to a specific probable violation of law; (2) demonstrate that the information sought cannot be obtained by alternative means less destructive of First Amendment rights; and (3) demonstrate a compelling and overriding interest in the information. [B]efore the government's burden to make such a showing were triggered, the reporter would have to move to quash the subpoena, asserting the basis on which he considered the particular relationship a confidential one....

[The dissenting opinion of DOUGLAS, J., is omitted.]

Notes

Cohen v. Cowles Media Co., 501 U.S. 663, 111 S.Ct. 2513, 115 L.Ed.2d 586 (1991). Cohen, associated with one party's political campaign, gave court records concerning another party's candidate for Lieutenant Governor to reporters after receiving a promise of confidentiality. The court records showed that the candidate, in 1969, was charged with three counts of unlawful assembly, and in 1970 was convicted of petit theft (later vacated). The newspapers' editorial staffs did not keep this promise and published Cohen's name; Cohen was then fired from his job. He sued for damages in state court on a breach of promise theory, and won, but the state supreme court reversed, ruling that the First Amendment barred a cause of action. White, J., for the Court, joined by Rehnquist, C.J., & Stevens, Scalia &

Kennedy, JJ., reversed, holding that the First Amendment did not bar a cause of action. It was permissible for the state to apply a law of general applicability, such as a law of promissory estoppel, that does not target or single out the press. The majority then remanded so that the state court could determine whether promissory estoppel had been established under state law and whether the state constitution shielded the press.*

On remand, the Minnesota Supreme Court reinstated a $200,000 damage award. From 1988 to the early part of 1992, about six cases similar to Mr. Cohen's law suit were filed by various parties claiming that news publications breached a promise of confidentiality.

ZURCHER v. STANFORD DAILY
436 U.S. 547, 98 S.Ct. 1970, 56 L.Ed.2d 525 (1978).

MR. JUSTICE WHITE delivered the opinion of the Court. . . .

Late in the day on Friday, April 9, 1971, officers of the Palo Alto Police Department and of the Santa Clara County Sheriff's Department responded to a call from the director of the Stanford University Hospital requesting the removal of a large group of demonstrators who had seized the hospital's administrative offices and occupied them since the previous afternoon. . . . The police chose to force their way in at the west end of the corridor. [A] group of demonstrators emerged through the doors at the east end and, armed with sticks and clubs, attacked the group of nine police officers stationed there. One officer was knocked to the floor and struck repeatedly on the head; another suffered a broken shoulder. All nine were injured. . . .

On Sunday, April 11, a special edition of the Stanford Daily (Daily), a student newspaper published at Stanford University, carried articles and photographs devoted to the hospital protest and the violent clash between demonstrators and police. The photographs carried the byline of a Daily staff member and indicated that he had been at the east end of the hospital hallway where he could have photographed the assault on the nine officers. The next day, the Santa Clara County District Attorney's Office secured a warrant from the Municipal Court for an immediate search of the Daily's offices for negatives, film, and pictures showing the events and occurrences at the hospital on the evening of April 9. . . . The warrant affidavit contained no allegation or indication that members of the Daily staff were in any way involved in unlawful acts at the hospital.

The search pursuant to the warrant was conducted later that day by four police officers and took place in the presence of some members of the Daily staff. The Daily's photographic laboratories, filing cabinets,

---

* Blackmun, J., joined by Marshall & Souter, JJ., dissented, arguing this fact situation did not involve holding the press to a law of general applicability involving commercial activities, but rather a law making the press liable based on the content of the publication. Souter, J., joined by Marshall, Blackmun, & O'Connor, JJ., also dissented, but distinguished other cases where liability might be more appropriate in their view, such as where the injured party is a more private party.

desks, and wastepaper baskets were searched. Locked drawers and rooms were not opened. The officers apparently had opportunity to read notes and correspondence during the search; but, contrary to claims of the staff, the officers denied that they had exceeded the limits of the warrant. They had not been advised by the staff that the areas they were searching contained confidential materials. The search revealed only the photographs that had already been published on April 11, and no materials were removed from the Daily's office.

A month later the Daily and various members of its staff, respondents here, brought a civil action in the United States District Court for the Northern District of California.... [The district court granted declaratory relief and the circuit court affirmed. The Supreme Court reversed. First, it rejected the district court's proposed rule, which would forbid the issuance of a warrant to search for materials in possession of one not suspected of crime unless there is probable cause to believe, based on facts presented in a sworn affidavit, that a subpoena *duces tecum* would be impracticable and that the possessor of the objects sought would disregard a court order not to remove or destroy them. The Supreme Court then turned to the First Amendment claim.]

The District Court held, and respondents assert here, that whatever may be true of third-party searches generally, where the third party is a newspaper, there are additional factors derived from the First Amendment that justify a nearly *per se* rule forbidding the search warrant and permitting only the subpoena *duces tecum*.... First, searches will be physically disruptive to such an extent that timely publication will be impeded. Second, confidential sources of information will dry up, and the press will also lose opportunities to cover various events because of fears of the participants that press files will be readily available to the authorities. Third, reporters will be deterred from recording and preserving their recollections for future use if such information is subject to seizure. Fourth, the processing of news and its dissemination will be chilled by the prospects that searches will disclose internal editorial deliberations. Fifth, the press will resort to self-censorship to conceal its possession of information of potential interest to the police.

... Where the materials sought to be seized may be protected by the First Amendment, the requirements of the Fourth Amendment must be applied with "scrupulous exactitude." ... Hence, in *Stanford v. Texas,* 379 U.S. 476, 85 S.Ct. 506, 13 L.Ed.2d 431 (1965), the Court invalidated a warrant authorizing the search of a private home for all books, records, and other materials relating to the Communist Party, on the ground that whether or not the warrant would have been sufficient in other contexts, it authorized the searchers to rummage among and make judgments about books and papers and was the functional equivalent of a general warrant, one of the principal targets of the Fourth Amendment. Where presumptively protected materials are sought to be seized, the warrant requirement should be administered to leave as little as possible to the discretion or whim of the officer in the field.

Similarly, where seizure is sought of allegedly obscene materials, the judgment of the arresting officer alone is insufficient to justify issuance of a search warrant or a seizure without a warrant incident to arrest. The procedure for determining probable cause must afford an opportunity for the judicial officer to "focus searchingly on the question of obscenity." *Marcus v. Search Warrant,* 367 U.S. 717, 81 S.Ct. 1708, 6 L.Ed.2d 1127 (1961).

... Aware of the long struggle between Crown and press and desiring to curb unjustified official intrusions, the Framers took the enormously important step of subjecting searches to the test of reasonableness and to the general rule requiring search warrants issued by neutral magistrates. They nevertheless did not forbid warrants where the press was involved, did not require special showings that subpoenas would be impractical, and did not insist that the owner of the place to be searched, if connected with the press, must be shown to be implicated in the offense being investigated.... Properly administered, the preconditions for a warrant—probable cause, specificity with respect to the place to be searched and the things to be seized, and overall reasonableness— should afford sufficient protection against the harms that are assertedly threatened by warrants for searching newspaper offices.

There is no reason to believe, for example, that magistrates cannot guard against searches of the type, scope, and intrusiveness that would actually interfere with the timely publication of a newspaper. Nor, if the requirements of specificity and reasonableness are properly applied, policed, and observed, will there be any occasion or opportunity for officers to rummage at large in newspaper files or to intrude into or to deter normal editorial and publication decisions. The warrant issued in this case authorized nothing of this sort. Nor are we convinced, any more than we were in *Branzburg v. Hayes,* that confidential sources will disappear and that the press will suppress news because of fears of warranted searches. Whatever incremental effect there may be in this regard if search warrants, as well as subpoenas, are permissible in proper circumstances, it does not make a constitutional difference in our judgment.

The fact is that respondents and *amici* have pointed to only a very few instances in the entire United States since 1971 involving the issuance of warrants for searching newspaper premises. This reality hardly suggests abuse; and if abuse occurs there will be time enough to deal with it. Furthermore, the press is not only an important, critical, and valuable asset to society, but it is not easily intimidated—nor should it be....

We note finally that if the evidence sought by warrant is sufficiently connected with the crime to satisfy the probable-cause requirement, it will very likely be sufficiently relevant to justify a subpoena and to withstand a motion to quash. Further, Fifth Amendment and state shield-law objections that might be asserted in opposition to compliance with a subpoena are largely irrelevant to determining the legality of a search warrant under the Fourth Amendment. Of course, the Fourth Amendment does not prevent or advise against legislative or executive efforts to establish nonconstitutional protections against possible abuses of the search warrant procedure, but we decline to reinterpret the Amendment to impose a general constitutional barrier against warrants to search newspaper premises, to require resort to subpoenas as a general rule, or to demand prior notice and hearing in connection with the issuance of search warrants. . . .

MR. JUSTICE BRENNAN took no part in the consideration or decision of these cases.

MR. JUSTICE POWELL, concurring.

[Justice Stewart's dissenting opinion] would read into the Fourth Amendment, as a new and *per se* exception, the rule that any search of an entity protected by the Press Clause of the First Amendment is unreasonable so long as a subpoena could be used as a substitute procedure. Even aside from the difficulties involved in deciding on a case-by-case basis whether a subpoena can serve as an adequate substitute,* I agree with the Court that there is no constitutional basis for such a reading. . . .

MR. JUSTICE STEWART, with whom MR. JUSTICE MARSHALL joins, dissenting.

[In addition to the physical disruption of the operation of the newspaper] there is another and more serious burden on a free press imposed by an unannounced police search of a newspaper office: the possibility of disclosure of information received from confidential sources, or of the identity of the sources themselves. Protection of those sources is necessary to ensure that the press can fulfill its constitutionally designated function of informing the public, because important information can often be obtained only by an assurance that the source will not be revealed. *Branzburg v. Hayes* (dissenting opinion). . . .

A search warrant allows police officers to ransack the files of a newspaper, reading each and every document until they have found the one named in the warrant, while a subpoena would permit the newspaper itself to produce only the specific documents requested. A search, unlike a subpoena, will therefore lead to the needless exposure of confidential information completely unrelated to the purpose of the investigation. The knowledge that police officers can make an unan-

---

* For example, respondents had announced a policy of destroying any photographs that might aid prosecution of protesters. App. 118, 152–153. Use of a subpoena, as proposed by the dissent would be of no utility in face of a policy of destroying evidence. And unless the policy were publicly announced, it probably would be difficult to show the impracticality of a subpoena as opposed to a search warrant. . . .

While the existence of this policy was not before the magistrate at the time of the warrant's issuance, it illustrates the possible dangers of creating separate standards for the press alone.

nounced raid on a newsroom is thus bound to have a deterrent effect on the availability of confidential news sources. The end result, wholly inimical to the First Amendment, will be a diminishing flow of potentially important information to the public. . . .

[The dissenting opinion of STEVENS, J., is omitted.]

Notes

Congress responded to *Zurcher* by enacting *The Privacy Protection Act of 1980*, codified at 42 U.S.C.A. §§ 2000aa through 2000aa–12. The Act applies to any government officer or employee, state or federal. Such persons, in connection with the investigation or prosecution of a criminal offense, may not search for or seize any work product (i.e., materials, including mental impressions, prepared in anticipation of communicating such materials to the public, other than materials that are the fruits or instrumentalities of a crime) if such materials are possessed by a person reasonably believed to have a purpose to disseminate to the public by a public communication (such as newspaper, book, or broadcast) that is in, or affecting, interstate or foreign commerce. These restrictions on the search or seizure power are not applicable if the materials relate to the national defense, classified information or restricted data, or if there is reason to believe that immediate seizure is necessary to prevent death or serious bodily injury. Similar restrictions apply to search or seizure of documentary materials (i.e., materials upon which information is recorded, such as written or printed materials or photographs, but excluding the fruits or instrumentalities of a crime) possessed by a person in connection with a purpose to disseminate to the public a newspaper, book, broadcast or similar form of public communication in or affecting interstate or foreign commerce. These restrictions are also subject to certain exceptions. For example, the seizure of documentary materials is usually not prohibited if there is reasonable cause to believe that the person possessing the materials has committed or is committing a criminal offense to which the materials relate, or immediate seizure is necessary to prevent death or serious bodily harm, or giving notice would result in destruction, alteration, or concealment of the materials. This portion of the Act also does not apply to national defense, classified information, or restricted data. The entire Act is inapplicable to border searchers.

A person subjected to a search or seizure unlawful under this Act has a civil cause of action for damages against the United States or a State (if the latter has waived its sovereign immunity under the Constitution) and against the State employee or officer (if the State has not waived its sovereign immunity). The damages shall be actual damages but not less than liquidated damages of $1000 plus reasonable attorneys' fees and costs. "Evidence otherwise admissible in a proceeding shall not be excluded on the basis of a violation of this Act."

Would *The Privacy Protection Act of 1980* change the result in *Zurcher* given the facts of that case?

10–6.2 Fair Trial and Free Press

NEBRASKA PRESS ASSOCIATION v. STUART
427 U.S. 539, 96 S.Ct. 2791, 49 L.Ed.2d 683 (1976).

Mr. Chief Justice Burger delivered the opinion of the Court.

The respondent State District Judge entered an order restraining the petitioners from publishing or broadcasting accounts of confessions or admissions made by the accused or facts "strongly implicative" of the accused in a widely reported murder of six persons. We granted certiorari to decide whether the entry of such an order on the showing made before the state court violated the constitutional guarantee of freedom of the press. . . .

In *Sheppard v. Maxwell*, 384 U.S. 333, 86 S.Ct. 1507, 16 L.Ed.2d 600 (1966), the Court focused sharply on the impact of pretrial publicity and a trial court's duty to protect the defendant's constitutional right to a fair trial. With only Mr. Justice Black dissenting, and he without opinion, the Court ordered a new trial for the petitioner, even though the first trial had occurred 12 years before. Beyond doubt the press had shown no responsible concern for the constitutional guarantee of a fair trial; the community from which the jury was drawn had been inundated by publicity hostile to the defendant. But the trial judge "did not fulfill his duty to protect [the defendant] from the inherently prejudicial publicity which saturated the community and to control disruptive influences in the courtroom." The Court noted that "unfair and prejudicial news comment on pending trials has become increasingly prevalent," and issued a strong warning:

> Due process requires that the accused receive a trial by an impartial jury free from outside influences. Given the pervasiveness of modern communications and the difficulty of effacing prejudicial publicity from the minds of the jurors, *the trial courts must take strong measures to ensure that the balance is never weighed against the accused* . . . . Of course, there is nothing that proscribes the press from reporting events that transpire in the courtroom. But where there is a reasonable likelihood that prejudicial news prior to trial will prevent a fair trial, the judge should *continue the case* until the threat abates, *or transfer it* to another county not so permeated with publicity. In addition, *sequestration of the jury* was something the judge should have raised *sua sponte* with counsel. If publicity during the proceedings threatens the fairness of the trial, a new trial should be ordered. But we must remember that reversals are but palliatives; the cure lies in those remedial measures that will prevent the prejudice at its inception. The courts must take such steps by rule and regulation that will protect their processes from prejudicial outside interferences. *Neither prosecutors, counsel for defense, the accused, witnesses, court staff nor enforcement officers coming under the jurisdiction of the court should be permitted to frustrate its function.* Collaboration between counsel and the press as to informa-

tion affecting the fairness of a criminal trial is not only subject to regulation, but is highly censurable and worthy of disciplinary measures. (emphasis added).

[In *Sheppard,* a] new trial followed, in which the accused was acquitted.

... None of our decided cases on prior restraint involved restrictive orders entered to protect a defendant's right to a fair and impartial jury, but the opinions on prior restraint have a common thread relevant to this case.... The thread running through all these cases is that prior restraints on speech and publication are the most serious and the least tolerable infringement on First Amendment rights. A criminal penalty or a judgment in a defamation case is subject to the whole panoply of protections afforded by deferring the impact of the judgment until all avenues of appellate review have been exhausted. Only after judgment has become final, correct or otherwise, does the law's sanction become fully operative. A prior restraint, by contrast and by definition, has an immediate and irreversible sanction. If it can be said that a threat of criminal or civil sanctions after publication "chills" speech, prior restraint "freezes" it at least for the time. The damage can be particularly great when the prior restraint falls upon the communication of news and commentary on current events....

The authors of the Bill of Rights did not undertake to assign priorities as between First Amendment and Sixth Amendment rights, ranking one as superior to the other. [I]t is not for us to rewrite the Constitution by undertaking what they declined to do. It is unnecessary, after nearly two centuries, to establish a priority applicable in all circumstances. Yet it is nonetheless clear that the barriers to prior restraint remain high unless we are to abandon what the Court has said for nearly a quarter of our national existence and implied throughout all of it.

We turn now to the record in this case to determine whether, as Learned Hand put it, "the gravity of the 'evil,' discounted by its improbability, justifies such invasion of free speech as is necessary to avoid the danger." *United States v. Dennis,* [§ 10–1, supra]. To do so, we must examine the evidence before the trial judge when the order was entered to determine (a) the nature and extent of pretrial news coverage; (b) whether other measures would be likely to mitigate the effects of unrestrained pretrial publicity; and (c) how effectively a restraining order would operate to prevent the threatened danger. The precise terms of the restraining order are also important. We must then consider whether the record supports the entry of a prior restraint on publication, one of the most extraordinary remedies known to our jurisprudence.

A. ... Our review of the pretrial record persuades us that the trial judge was justified in concluding that there would be intense and pervasive pretrial publicity concerning this case. He could also reasonably conclude, based on common human experience, that publicity might impair the defendant's right to a fair trial.

B. ... We have [also] examined this record to determine the probable efficacy of the measures short of prior restraint on the press and speech. There is no finding that alternative measures [discussed in *Sheppard v. Maxwell,* supra] would not have protected Simants' [the defendant's] rights, and the Nebraska Supreme Court did no more than imply that such measures might not be adequate. Moreover, the record is lacking in evidence to support such a finding.

C. We must also assess the probable efficacy of prior restraint on publication as a workable method of protecting Simants' right to a fair trial, and we cannot ignore the reality of the problems of managing and enforcing pretrial restraining orders. [T]he events disclosed by the record took place in a community of 850 people. It is reasonable to assume that, without any news accounts being printed or broadcast, rumors would travel swiftly by word of mouth. One can only speculate on the accuracy of such reports, given the generative propensities of rumors; they could well be more damaging than reasonably accurate news accounts. But plainly a whole community cannot be restrained from discussing a subject intimately affecting life within it. Given these practical problems, it is far from clear that prior restraint on publication would have protected Simants' rights.

D. Finally, another feature of this case leads us to conclude that the restrictive order entered here is not supportable. At the outset the County Court entered a very broad restrictive order, the terms of which are not before us; it then held a preliminary hearing open to the public and the press. There was testimony concerning at least two incriminating statements made by Simants to private persons; the statement— evidently a confession—that he gave to law enforcement officials was also introduced. The State District Court's later order was entered after this public hearing and, as modified by the Nebraska Supreme Court, enjoined reporting of (1) "[c]onfessions or admissions against interest made by the accused to law enforcement officials"; (2) "[c]onfessions or admissions against interest, oral or written, if any, made by the accused to third parties, excepting any statements, if any, made by the accused to representatives of the news media"; and (3) all "[o]ther information strongly implicative of the accused as the perpetrator of the slayings."

To the extent that his order prohibited the reporting of evidence adduced at the open preliminary hearing, it plainly violated settled principles: "[T]here is nothing that proscribes the press from reporting events that transpire in the courtroom." *Sheppard v. Maxwell.* [O]nce a public hearing had been held, what transpired there could not be subject to prior restraint.

The third prohibition of the order was defective in another respect as well. As part of a final order, entered after plenary review, this prohibition regarding "implicative" information is too vague and too broad to survive the scrutiny we have given to restraints on First Amendment rights. The third phase of the order entered falls outside permissible limits....

Of necessity our holding is confined to the record before us. But our conclusion is not simply a result of assessing the adequacy of the showing made in this case; it results in part from the problems inherent in meeting the heavy burden of demonstrating, in advance of trial, that without prior restraint a fair trial will be denied. The practical problems of managing and enforcing restrictive orders will always be present. In this sense, the record now before us is illustrative rather than exceptional. It is significant that when this Court has reversed a state conviction because of prejudicial publicity, it has carefully noted that some course of action short of prior restraint would have made a critical difference. However difficult it may be, we need not rule out the possibility of showing the kind of threat to fair trial rights that would possess the requisite degree of certainty to justify restraint. This Court has frequently denied that First Amendment rights are absolute and has consistently rejected the proposition that a prior restraint can never be employed....

MR. JUSTICE WHITE, concurring.

[F]or the reasons which the Court itself canvasses there is grave doubt in my mind whether orders with respect to the press such as were entered in this case would ever be justifiable....

MR. JUSTICE BRENNAN, with whom MR. JUSTICE STEWART and MR. JUSTICE MARSHALL join, concurring in the judgment.

... The right to a fair trial by a jury of one's peers is unquestionably one of the most precious and sacred safeguards enshrined in the Bill of Rights. I would hold, however, that resort to prior restraints on the freedom of the press is a constitutionally impermissible method for enforcing that right; judges have at their disposal a broad spectrum of devices for ensuring that fundamental fairness is accorded the accused without necessitating so drastic an incursion on the equally fundamental and salutary constitutional mandate that discussion of public affairs in a free society cannot depend on the preliminary grace of judicial censors....

[The concurring opinion of POWELL, J., and the opinion of STEVENS, J., concurring in the judgment, are omitted.]

Notes

1. Contrast *Seattle Times Co. v. Rhinehart,* 467 U.S. 20, 104 S.Ct. 2199, 81 L.Ed.2d 17 (1984), a civil case. A unanimous Court upheld a state court's protective order that prohibited a newspaper (a defendant in a libel case) from publishing pre-trial discovery information in advance of trial regarding the plaintiff's financial affairs and names and addresses of donors, clients, or members of the plaintiff's religious group. The newspaper could not use the information in any way except where necessary to prepare for and try the case. The protective order did not apply to information gained by means other than the discovery process. Discovery rules are a matter of "legislative grace," and a "litigant has no First Amendment right of access to information made available only for purposes of trying his suit." A

protective order "prohibiting dissemination of discovered information before trial is not the kind of classic prior restraint that requires exacting First Amendment scrutiny." Thus, if a protective order is entered on a showing of good cause, is limited to the context of pretrial civil discovery, and does not restrict the dissemination of information if gained from other sources, it does not offend the First Amendment.

2. *Gentile v. State Bar of Nevada,* 501 U.S. 1030, 111 S.Ct. 2720, 115 L.Ed.2d 888 (1991). Attorney Gentile held a press conference a few hours after Nevada indicted his client on criminal charges. Gentile made a brief prepared statement and declined to answer reporters' questions seeking more detailed comments. Six months later a jury acquitted Gentile's client of all counts. Then the State Bar of Nevada filed a complaint against Gentile for allegedly violating Nevada Supreme Court Rule 177, governing pretrial publicity. This ethics Rule was almost identical to the ABA Model Rules of Professional Conduct, Rule 3.6 (which the ABA later amended to take *Gentile* into account). The state supreme court imposed a private reprimand for Mr. Gentile. On appeal, a very fragmented U.S. Supreme Court reversed.

Nevada Rule 177(1) prohibited an attorney from making "an extrajudicial statement that a reasonable person would expect to be disseminated by means of public communication if the lawyer knows or reasonably should know that it will have a substantial likelihood of materially prejudicing an adjudicative proceeding." Rule 177(2) then listed a number of statements (e.g., the expected testimony of a witness, or the credibility, reputation, or criminal record of a party) that are "ordinarily ... likely" to result in material prejudice. Rule 177(3) provided a "safe harbor," listing statements that can be made (e.g., the general nature of the claim or defense, information contained in a public record) "notwithstanding" the previous two sections. Kennedy, J., announced the judgment of the Court, and delivered the opinion of the Court with respect to Parts III and VI; Rehnquist, C.J. delivered the opinion of the Court with respect to Parts I and II.

Kennedy, J., for the Court, held that—as interpreted by the state court—Rule 177 is void for vagueness. Moreover, Rule 177(3)(a safe-harbor provision) misled petitioner by its use of the word "notwithstanding," which led him into thinking that he could give his press conference without fear of discipline, even if he knows or reasonably should know that his statement will have a substantial likelihood of materially prejudicing an adjudicative proceeding. Even though Gentile studied the ethics rules and made "a conscious effort" to comply (he gave only a brief opening statement, and declined to answer reporters' questions seeking more detailed comments), he was still found in violation, demonstrating that Rule 177 created a "trap for the wary as well as the unwary."

Part I of Kennedy, J.'s opinion (joined by Marshall, Blackmun, & Stevens, JJ.), noted:

> "[O]ne central point must dominate the analysis: this case involves classic political speech. The State Bar of Nevada reprimanded petitioner for his assertion, supported by a brief sketch of his client's defense, that the State sought the indictment and conviction of an innocent man as a 'scapegoat,' and had not 'been honest enough to indict the people who did it; the police department, crooked cops.' At issue here is the

constitutionality of a ban on political speech critical of the government and its officials.''

In Parts I and II, Rehnquist, C.J. for the Court (joined by White, O'Connor, Scalia, & Souter, JJ.), concluded that Nevada's "substantial likelihood of material prejudice" test—a test used by most other states as well—satisfied the First Amendment when used to restrict the speech of lawyers representing clients in pending cases, even though it is less protective of speech interests than the test used to regulate the press during pending proceeding in *Nebraska Press Association v. Stuart*. He rejected petitioner's argument that Nevada must demonstrate a "clear and present danger" of "actual prejudice or imminent threat" before any discipline may be imposed on a lawyer who "initiates a press conference such as occurred here." Rehnquist concluded that states, seeking to assure fair trials before impartial jurors, have substantial interest in preventing lawyers, officers of the court, from imposing costs, such as a change in venue, on the judicial system and on the litigants. Moreover, this restraint on lawyers' speech is "narrowly tailored" because it applies only to speech substantially likely to have a materially prejudicial effect, is viewpoint neutral, and merely postponed a lawyer's speech until after the trial.

RICHMOND NEWSPAPERS, INC. v. VIRGINIA
448 U.S. 555, 100 S.Ct. 2814, 65 L.Ed.2d 973 (1980).

MR. CHIEF JUSTICE BURGER announced the judgment of the Court and delivered an opinion in which MR. JUSTICE WHITE and MR. JUSTICE STEVENS joined.

The narrow question presented in this case is whether the right of the public and press to attend criminal trials is guaranteed under the United States Constitution. . . .

We begin consideration of this case by noting that the precise issue presented here has not previously been before this Court for decision. In *Gannett Co., Inc. v. DePasquale,* 443 U.S. 368, 99 S.Ct. 2898, 61 L.Ed.2d 608 (1979), the Court was not required to decide whether a right of access to *trials,* as distinguished from hearings on *pre*trial motions, was constitutionally guaranteed. The Court held that the Sixth Amendment's guarantee to the accused of a public trial gave neither the public nor the press an enforceable right of access to a *pre*trial suppression hearing. . . . Moreover, the Court did not decide whether the First and Fourteenth Amendments guarantee a right of the public to attend trials; nor did the dissenting opinion reach this issue. . . . But here for the first time the Court is asked to decide whether a criminal trial itself may be closed to the public upon the unopposed request of a defendant, without any demonstration that closure is required to protect the defendant's superior right to a fair trial, or that some other overriding consideration requires closure. . . .

We have found nothing to suggest that the presumptive openness of the trial, which English courts were later to call "one of the essential qualities of a court of justice," was not also an attribute of the judicial systems of colonial America. In Virginia, for example, such records as there are of early criminal trials indicate that they were open, and nothing to the contrary has been cited.... Both Hale in the 17th century and Blackstone in the 18th saw the importance of openness to the proper functioning of a trial; it gave assurance that the proceedings were conducted fairly to all concerned, and it discouraged perjury, the misconduct of participants, and decisions based on secret bias or partiality.... The early history of open trials in part reflects the widespread acknowledgement, long before there were behavioral scientists, that public trials had significant community therapeutic value. Even without such experts to frame the concept in words, people sensed from experience and observation that, especially in the administration of criminal justice, the means used to achieve justice must have the support derived from public acceptance of both the process and its results....

The First Amendment, in conjunction with the Fourteenth, prohibits governments from "abridging the freedom of speech, or of the press; or the right of the people peaceably to assemble, and to petition the Government for a redress of grievances." These expressly guaranteed freedoms share a common core purpose of assuring freedom of communication on matters relating to the functioning of government. Plainly it would be difficult to single out any aspect of government of higher concern and importance to the people than the manner in which criminal trials are conducted; ... What this means in the context of trials is that the First Amendment guarantees of speech and press, standing alone, prohibit government from summarily closing courtroom doors which had long been open to the public at the time that amendment was adopted....

It is not crucial whether we describe this right to attend criminal trials to hear, see, and communicate observations concerning them as a "right of access," or a "right to gather information," for we have recognized that "without some protection for seeking out the news, freedom of the press could be eviscerated." *Branzburg v. Hayes,* [§ 10–6.1, supra]. The explicit, guaranteed rights to speak and to publish concerning what takes place at a trial would lose much meaning if access to observe the trial could, as it was here, be foreclosed arbitrarily.

We hold that the right to attend criminal trials* is implicit in the guarantees of the First Amendment; without the freedom to attend such trials, which people have exercised for centuries, important aspects of freedom of speech and "of the press could be eviscerated." *Branzburg.*

Having concluded there was a guaranteed right of the public under the First and Fourteenth Amendments to attend the trial of Stevenson's case, we return to the closure order challenged by appellants. [A]lthough the Sixth Amendment guarantees the accused a right to a public trial, it does not give a right to a private trial. Despite the fact that this was the

---

* Whether the public has a right to attend trials of civil cases is a question not raised by this case, but we note that historically both civil and criminal trials have been presumptively open.

fourth trial of the accused, the trial judge made no findings to support closure; no inquiry was made as to whether alternative solutions would have met the need to ensure fairness; there was no recognition of any right under the Constitution for the public or press to attend the trial. In contrast to the pretrial proceeding dealt with in *Gannett,* there exist in the context of the trial itself various tested alternatives to satisfy the constitutional demands of fairness. See, *e.g., Nebraska Press Association v. Stuart.* There was no suggestion that any problems with witnesses could not have been dealt with by their exclusion from the courtroom or their sequestration during the trial. Nor is there anything to indicate that sequestration of the jurors would not have guarded against their being subjected to any improper information. All of the alternatives admittedly present difficulties for trial courts, but none of the factors relied on here was beyond the realm of the manageable. Absent an overriding interest articulated in findings, the trial of a criminal case must be open to the public.** Accordingly, the judgment under review is reversed.

Reversed.

MR. JUSTICE POWELL took no part in the consideration or decision of this case.

MR. JUSTICE STEVENS, concurring.

This is a watershed case. Until today the Court has accorded virtually absolute protection to the dissemination of information or ideas, but never before has it squarely held that the acquisition of newsworthy matter is entitled to any constitutional protection whatsoever. An additional word of emphasis is therefore appropriate. [F]or the first time, the Court unequivocally holds that an arbitrary interference with access to important information is an abridgement of the freedoms of speech and of the press protected by the First Amendment....

MR. JUSTICE BLACKMUN concurring in the judgment....

It is gratifying, first, to see the Court now looking to and relying upon legal history in determining the fundamental public character of the criminal trial.... It is gratifying, second, to see the Court wash away at least some of the graffiti that marred the prevailing opinions in *Gannett. ...*

** We have no occasion here to define the circumstances in which all or parts of a criminal trial may be closed to the public, but our holding today does not mean that the First Amendment rights of the public and representatives of the press are absolute. Just as a government may impose reasonable time, place, and manner restrictions upon the use of its streets in the interest of such objectives as the free flow of traffic, so may a trial judge, in the interest of the fair administration of justice, impose reasonable limitations on access to a trial.... It is far more important that trials be conducted in a quiet and orderly setting than it is to preserve that atmosphere on city streets. Moreover, since courtrooms have limited capacity, there may be occasions when not every person who wishes to attend can be accommodated. In such situations, reasonable restrictions on general access are traditionally imposed, including preferential seating for media representatives.

The Court's ultimate ruling in *Gannett,* with such clarification as is provided by the opinions in this case today, apparently is now to the effect that there is no *Sixth* Amendment right on the part of the public—or the press—to an open hearing on a motion to suppress. I, of course, continue to believe that *Gannett* was in error, [and] that the right to a public trial is to be found where the Constitution explicitly placed it—in the Sixth Amendment. . . .

[The opinion of BRENNAN, J., joined by MARSHALL, J., concurring in the judgment; the concurring opinion of WHITE, J., and the dissent of REHNQUIST, J., are omitted.]

Notes

1. *Globe Newspaper Co. v. Superior Court,* 457 U.S. 596, 102 S.Ct. 2613, 73 L.Ed.2d 248 (1982) involved a statute that *required* trial judges to exclude the press and general public from the courtroom during the testimony of the victim in cases involving certain specified sexual offenses. The Court invalidated the law (which required no particularized determinations in individual cases), but left open the possibility that under appropriate circumstances and in individual cases the trial court could exclude the press and public during the testimony of minor victims of sex crimes. The Court, per Brennan, J., explained that under *Richmond Newspapers* the First Amendment, as applied to the states, grants to the press and general public "a right of access to *criminal trials*" (emphasis in original). States may deny access only if denial serves "a compelling governmental interest, and is narrowly tailored to serve that interest." The judge should consider the minor victim's wishes regarding disclosure, as well as the victim's age and maturity, the interests of relatives, the nature of the crime, and so on. In the present case the defendant objected to closure, the state made no motion for closure, and the victims might have been willing to testify without closure.

Burger, C.J., joined by Rehnquist, J., dissented and objected to the paradox that the Court decision "denies the victim the kind of protection routinely given to juveniles who commit crimes."

2. *Press–Enterprise Co. v. Superior Court* [*Press–Enterprise I*], 464 U.S. 501, 104 S.Ct. 819, 78 L.Ed.2d 629 (1984) held that the First Amendment guarantee of open criminal trials also mandated open voir dire examination of potential jurors. The trial involved the rape and murder of a teenage girl. Generalized interests in protecting the accused's right to a fair trial and the prospective jurors' right to privacy did not overcome the presumption of openness. That presumption may be overcome "only by an overriding interest based on findings that closure is essential to preserve higher values and is narrowly tailored to serve that interest. The interest is to be articulated along with findings specific enough that a reviewing court can determine whether the closure order was properly entered."*

---

* *Press–Enterprise Co. v. Superior Court* [*Press–Enterprise II*], 478 U.S. 1, 106 S.Ct. 2735, 92 L.Ed.2d 1 (1986). The Court, per Burger, C.J., held that there was a First Amendment right of access to transcripts of a preliminary hearing of the type conducted in California. The State and Press–Enterprise Company moved to release a preliminary hearing transcript but the trial court denied the motion. Unlike a Grand Jury proceeding, there has been "a tradition of accessibility" to this type of public hearing,

3. *Waller v. Georgia,* 467 U.S. 39, 104 S.Ct. 2210, 81 L.Ed.2d 31 (1984) unanimously held that the Sixth Amendment right to public trial extends to pretrial suppression hearings that had been closed to the public over the objection of the defendant. The Court did not find it necessary to discuss the First Amendment claim, but held that, nonetheless, the tests of *Press–Enterprise* must be met. In *Waller* closure was far more extensive than necessary to protect any privacy interests involved. The remedy for this constitutional violation is not inevitably a new trial, but rather a new suppression hearing. "A new trial need be held only if a new, public suppression hearing results in the suppression of material evidence not suppressed at the first trial, or in some other material change in the positions of the parties."

CHANDLER v. FLORIDA

449 U.S. 560, 101 S.Ct. 802, 66 L.Ed.2d 740 (1981).

CHIEF JUSTICE BURGER delivered the opinion of the Court.

The question presented on this appeal is whether, consistent with constitutional guarantees, a state may provide for radio, television, and still photographic coverage of a criminal trial for public broadcast, notwithstanding the objection of the accused.

Over the past 50 years, some criminal cases characterized as "sensational" have been subjected to extensive coverage by news media, sometimes seriously interfering with the conduct of the proceedings and creating a setting wholly inappropriate for the administration of justice. Judges, lawyers, and others soon became concerned, and in 1937, after study, the American Bar Association House of Delegates adopted Judicial Canon 35, declaring that all photographic and broadcast coverage of courtroom proceedings should be prohibited. In 1952, the House of Delegates amended Canon 35 to proscribe television coverage as well.... In Florida, the rule was embodied in Canon 3A(7) of the Florida Code of Judicial Conduct.

[Florida, after a pilot program, changed its Canon 3A(7) to allow electronic media and still photography coverage of public judicial proceedings in the state appellate and trial courts, without the consent of the parties.] The Florida court was of the view that because of the

and this hearing "is often the final and most important step in the criminal proceeding." Therefore the court cannot close these proceedings "unless specific, on the record findings are made demonstrating that 'closure is essential to preserve higher values and is narrowly tailored to serve that interest,' "citing *Press–Enterprise I.* Accord, *El Vocero de Puerto Rico (Caribbean International News Corp.) v. Puerto Rico,* 508 U.S. 147, 113 S.Ct. 2004, 124 L.Ed.2d 60 (1993)(per curiam). The Court, without dissent, held that Puerto Rico's requirement of a private preliminary hearing (similar to the private hearing involved in *Press–Enter-* *prise II*) violates the First Amendment. The concern that publicity will prejudice the accused's right to a fair trial is a concern that courts must address on a case-by-case basis, not on the basis of a general requirement of a private hearing. Puerto Rican tradition and experience does not justify a closed hearing because one should not look to the experience or practice of any particular jurisdiction but to the experience of the type or kind of hearing throughout the United States. The "established and widespread tradition of open preliminary hearings among the States was canvassed in *Press–Enterprise* and is controlling here."

significant effect of the courts on the day-to-day lives of the citizenry, it was essential that the people have confidence in the process. It felt that broadcast coverage of trials would contribute to wider public acceptance and understanding of decisions....

The implementing guidelines specify in detail the kind of electronic equipment to be used and the manner of its use. For example, no more than one television camera and only one camera technician are allowed. Existing recording systems used by court reporters are used by broadcasters for audio pickup. Where more than one broadcast news organization seeks to cover a trial, the media must pool coverage. No artificial lighting is allowed. The equipment is positioned in a fixed location, and it may not be moved during trial. Videotaping equipment must be remote from the courtroom. Film, videotape, and lenses may not be changed while the court is in session. No audio recording of conferences between lawyers, between parties and counsel, or at the bench is permitted. The judge has sole and plenary discretion to exclude coverage of certain witnesses, and the jury may not be filmed. The judge has discretionary power to forbid coverage whenever satisfied that coverage may have a deleterious effect on the paramount right of the defendant to a fair trial. The Florida Supreme Court has the right to revise these rules as experience dictates, or indeed to bar all broadcast coverage of photography in courtrooms.

In July 1977, appellants were charged with conspiracy to commit burglary, grand larceny, and possession of burglary tools. The counts covered breaking and entering a well-known Miami Beach restaurant. The details of the alleged criminal conduct are not relevant to the issue before us, but several aspects of the case distinguish it from a routine burglary. At the time of their arrest, appellants were Miami Beach policemen. The State's principal witness was John Sion, an amateur radio operator who, by sheer chance, had overheard and recorded conversations between the appellants over their police walkie-talkie radios during the burglary. Not surprisingly, these novel factors attracted the attention of the media....

After several additional fruitless attempts by the appellants to prevent electronic coverage of the trial, the jury was selected. [After trial, the] jury returned a guilty verdict on all counts. Appellants moved for a new trial, claiming that because of the television coverage, they had been denied a fair and impartial trial. No evidence of specific prejudice was tendered. The Florida District Court of Appeal affirmed the convictions....

At the outset, it is important to note that in promulgating the revised Canon 3A(7), the Florida Supreme Court pointedly rejected any state or federal constitutional right of access on the part of photographers or the broadcast media to televise or electronically record and thereafter disseminate court proceedings.... The Florida Supreme Court predicated the revised Canon 3A(7) upon its supervisory authority over the Florida courts, and not upon any constitutional imperative.

Hence, we have before us only the limited question of the Florida Supreme Court's authority to promulgate the canon for the trial of cases in Florida courts. . . .

Appellants rely chiefly on *Estes v. Texas,* 381 U.S. 532, 85 S.Ct. 1628, 14 L.Ed.2d 543 (1965), and CHIEF JUSTICE WARREN's separate concurring opinion in that case. They argue that the televising of criminal trials is inherently a denial of due process, and they read *Estes* as announcing a *per se* constitutional rule to that effect. . . . JUSTICE HARLAN provided the fifth vote necessary in support of the judgment. In a separate opinion, he pointedly limited his concurrence: "I concur in the opinion of the Court, subject, however, to the reservations and only to the extent indicated in this opinion." (HARLAN, J. concurring). A careful analysis of JUSTICE HARLAN's opinion is therefore fundamental to an understanding of the ultimate holding of *Estes.*

JUSTICE HARLAN began by observing that the question of the constitutional permissibility of televised trials was one fraught with unusual difficulty. . . .

> In the context of a trial of intense public interest, there is certainly a strong possibility that the timid or reluctant witness, for whom a court appearance even at its traditional best is a harrowing affair, will become more timid or reluctant when he finds that he will also be appearing before a "hidden audience" of unknown but large dimensions. There is certainly a strong possibility that the "cocky" witness having a thirst for the limelight will become more "cocky" under the influence of television. And who can say that the juror who is gratified by having being chosen for a front-line case, an ambitious prosecutor, a publicity-minded defense attorney, and even a conscientious judge will not stray, albeit unconsciously, from doing what "comes naturally" into pluming themselves for a satisfactory television "performance"?

JUSTICE HARLAN faced squarely the reality that these possibilities carry "grave potentialities for distorting the integrity of the judicial process," and that, although such distortions may produce no telltale signs, "their effects may be far more pervasive and deleterious than the physical disruptions which all would concede would vitiate a conviction." The "countervailing factors" alluded to by JUSTICE HARLAN were, as here, the educational and informational value to the public. JUSTICE STEWART, joined by JUSTICES BLACK, BRENNAN, and WHITE in dissent, concluded that no prejudice had been shown and that Estes' Fourteenth Amendment rights had not been violated.

[I]t is fair to say that JUSTICE HARLAN viewed the holding as limited to the proposition that "*what was done in this case* infringed the fundamental right to a fair trial assured by the Due Process Clause of the Fourteenth Amendment." (emphasis added). [W]e conclude that *Estes* is not to be read as announcing a constitutional rule barring still photographic, radio and television coverage in all cases and under all circumstances. . . .

An absolute constitutional ban on broadcast coverage of trials cannot be justified simply because there is a danger that, in some cases, prejudicial broadcast accounts of pretrial and trial events may impair the ability of jurors to decide the issue of guilt or innocence uninfluenced by extraneous matter. The risk of juror prejudice in some cases does not justify an absolute ban on news coverage of trials by the printed media; so also the risk of such prejudice does not warrant an absolute constitutional ban on all broadcast coverage. A case attracts a high level of public attention because of its intrinsic interest to the public and the manner of reporting the event. The risk of juror prejudice is present in any publication of a trial, but the appropriate safeguard against such prejudice is the defendant's right to demonstrate that the media's coverage of his case—be it printed or broadcast—compromised the ability of the particular jury that heard the case to adjudicate fairly.

As we noted earlier, the concurring opinions in *Estes* expressed concern that the very presence of media cameras and recording devices at a trial inescapably gives rise to an adverse psychological impact on the participants in the trial.... Not unimportant to the position asserted by Florida and other states is the change in television technology since 1962, when Estes was tried. It is urged, and some empirical data are presented, that many of the negative factors found in *Estes*—cumbersome equipment, cables, distracting lighting, numerous camera technicians—are less substantial factors today than they were at that time.

It is also significant that safeguards have been built into the experimental programs in state courts, and into the Florida program, to avoid some of the most egregious problems envisioned by the six opinions in the *Estes* case. Florida admonishes its courts to take special pains to protect certain witnesses—for example, children, victims of sex crimes, some informants, and even the very timid witness or party— from the glare of publicity and the tensions of being "on camera."

The Florida guidelines place on trial judges positive obligations to be on guard to protect the fundamental right of the accused to a fair trial. The Florida statute, being one of the few permitting broadcast coverage of criminal trials over the objection of the accused, raises problems not present in the statutes of other states. Inherent in electronic coverage of a trial is the risk that the very awareness by the accused of the coverage and the contemplated broadcast may adversely affect the conduct of the participants and the fairness of the trial, yet leave no evidence of how the conduct or the trial's fairness was affected. Given this danger, it is significant that Florida requires that objections of the accused to coverage be heard and considered on the record by the trial court. In addition to providing a record for appellate review, a pretrial hearing enables a defendant to advance the basis of his objection to broadcast coverage and allows the trial court to define the steps necessary to minimize or eliminate the risks of prejudice to the accused. Experiments such as the one presented here may well increase the number of appeals by adding a new basis for claims to reverse, but this is a risk Florida has chosen to take after preliminary experimentation. Here, the record does not indicate that appellants requested an evidentiary hearing to show adverse impact or injury. Nor does the record reveal anything more than generalized allegations of prejudice. . . .

Whatever may be the "mischievous potentialities [of broadcast coverage] for intruding upon the detached atmosphere which should always surround the judicial process," *Estes v. Texas,* at present no one has been able to present empirical data sufficient to establish that the mere presence of the broadcast media inherently has an adverse effect on that process. The appellants have offered nothing to demonstrate that their trial was subtly tainted by broadcast coverage—let alone that all broadcast trials would be so tainted. . . .

Although not essential to our holding, we note that at *voir dire,* the jurors were asked if the presence of the camera would in any way compromise their ability to consider the case. Each answered that the camera would not prevent him from considering the case solely on the merits. The trial court instructed the jurors not to watch television accounts of the trial, and the appellants do not contend that any juror violated this instruction. The appellants have offered no evidence that any participant in this case was affected by the presence of cameras. In short, there is no showing that the trial was compromised by television coverage, as was the case in *Estes.*

. . . Nothing of the "Roman circus" or "Yankee Stadium" atmosphere, as in *Estes,* prevailed here, however, nor have appellants attempted to show that the unsequestered jury was exposed to "sensational" coverage, in the sense of *Estes* or of *Sheppard v. Maxwell,* 384 U.S. 333, 86 S.Ct. 1507, 16 L.Ed.2d 600 (1966). Absent a showing of prejudice of constitutional dimensions to these defendants, there is no reason for this Court either to endorse or to invalidate Florida's experiment.

In this setting, because this Court has no supervisory authority over state courts, our review is confined to whether there is a constitutional violation. We hold that the Constitution does not prohibit a state from experimenting with the program authorized by revised Canon 3A(7).

Affirmed.

Justice Stevens took no part in the decision of this case.

[The opinions of Stewart, J., concurring in the result, and of White, J., concurring in the judgment, are omitted.]

10–7. COMMERCIAL SPEECH

CENTRAL HUDSON GAS & ELECTRIC CORP. v. PUBLIC SERVICE COMMISSION
447 U.S. 557, 100 S.Ct. 2343, 65 L.Ed.2d 341 (1980).

Mr. Justice Powell delivered the opinion of the Court.

This case presents the question whether a regulation of the Public Service Commission of the State of New York violates the First and

Fourteenth Amendments because it completely bans promotional advertising by an electrical utility.

In December 1973, the Commission, appellee here, ordered electric utilities in New York State to cease all advertising that "promot[es] the use of electricity." ... The Commission declared all promotional advertising contrary to the national policy of conserving energy. It acknowledged that the ban is not a perfect vehicle for conserving energy.... Still, the Commission adopted the restriction because it was deemed likely to "result in some dampening of unnecessary growth" in energy consumption. The Commission's order explicitly permitted "informational" advertising designed to encourage "*shifts* of consumption" from peak demand times to periods of low electricity demand. Informational advertising would not seek to increase aggregate consumption, but would invite a leveling of demand throughout any given 24–hour period....

The Commission's order restricts only commercial speech, that is, expression related solely to the economic interests of the speaker and its audience. *Virginia Pharmacy Board v. Virginia Citizens Consumer Council* [noted infra]; *Bates v. State Bar of Arizona* [noted infra]. The First Amendment, as applied to the States through the Fourteenth Amendment, protects commercial speech from unwarranted governmental regulation. Commercial expression not only serves the economic interest of the speaker, but also assists consumers and furthers the societal interest in the fullest possible dissemination of information. In applying the First Amendment to this area, we have rejected the "highly paternalistic" view that government has complete power to suppress or regulate commercial speech. "[P]eople will perceive their own best interests if only they are well enough informed, and ... the best means to that end is to open the channels of communication rather than to close them.... " See *Linmark Associates, Inc. v. Willingboro* [noted infra]. Even when advertising communicates only an incomplete version of the relevant facts, the First Amendment presumes that some accurate information is better than no information at all.

Nevertheless, our decisions have recognized "the 'commonsense' distinction between speech proposing a commercial transaction, which occurs in an area traditionally subject to government regulation, and other varieties of speech." *Ohralik v. Ohio State Bar Assn.* [noted infra]. The Constitution therefore accords a lesser protection to commercial speech than to other constitutionally guaranteed expression. The protection available for particular commercial expression turns on the nature both of the expression and of the governmental interests served by its regulation.

The First Amendment's concern for commercial speech is based on the informational function of advertising. Consequently, there can be no constitutional objection to the suppression of commercial messages that do not accurately inform the public about lawful activity. The government may ban forms of communication more likely to deceive the public than to inform it, *Friedman v. Rogers* [noted infra], or commercial speech related to illegal activity, *Pittsburgh Press Co. v. Human Relations Comm'n,* 413 U.S. 376, 388, 93 S.Ct. 2553, 2560, 37 L.Ed.2d 669 (1973).* If the communication is neither misleading nor related to unlawful activity, the government's power is more circumscribed. . . .**

In commercial speech cases, then, a four-part analysis has developed. At the outset, we must determine whether the expression is protected by the First Amendment. For commercial speech to come within that provision, it at least must concern lawful activity and not be misleading. Next, we ask whether the asserted governmental interest is substantial. If both inquiries yield positive answers, we must determine whether the regulation directly advances the governmental interest asserted, and whether it is not more extensive than is necessary to serve that interest.

The Commission does not claim that the expression at issue either is inaccurate or relates to unlawful activity. Yet [because] appellant holds a monopoly over the sale of electricity in its service area, the state court suggested that the Commission's order restricts no commercial speech of any worth. . . . This reasoning falls short of establishing that appellant's advertising is not commercial speech protected by the First Amendment. . . . Even in monopoly markets, the suppression of advertising reduces the information available for consumer decisions and thereby defeats the purpose of the First Amendment. . . .

The Commission offers two state interests as justifications for the ban on promotional advertising. The first concerns energy conservation. Any increase in demand for electricity—during peak or off-peak periods—means greater consumption of energy. [N]o one can doubt the importance of energy conservation. Plainly, therefore, the state interest asserted is substantial. The Commission also argues that promotional advertising will aggravate inequities caused by the failure to base the utilities' rates on marginal cost. [P]romotion of off-peak consumption also would increase consumption during peak periods. If peak demand were to rise, the absence of marginal cost rates would mean that the rates charged for the additional power would not reflect the true costs of expanding production. Instead, the extra costs would be borne by all consumers through higher overall rates. Without promotional advertising, the Commission stated, this inequitable turn of events would be less

---

* In most other contexts, the First Amendment prohibits regulation based on the content of the message. Two features of commercial speech permit regulation of its content. First, commercial speakers have extensive knowledge of both the market and their products. Thus, they are well situated to evaluate the accuracy of their messages and the lawfulness of the underlying activity. In addition, commercial speech, the offspring of economic self-interest, is a hardy breed of expression that is not "particularly susceptible to being crushed by overbroad regulation."

** We review with special care regulations that entirely suppress commercial speech in order to pursue a nonspeech-related policy. In those circumstances, a ban on speech could screen from public view the underlying governmental policy. Indeed, in recent years this Court has not approved a blanket ban on commercial speech unless the expression itself was flawed in some way, either because it was deceptive or related to unlawful activity.

likely to occur.... The State's concern that rates be fair and efficient represents a clear and substantial governmental interest.

Next, we focus on the relationship between the State's interests and the advertising ban. Under this criterion, the Commission's laudable concern over the equity and efficiency of appellant's rates does not provide a constitutionally adequate reason for restricting protected speech. The link between the advertising prohibition and appellant's rate structure is, at most, tenuous. The impact of promotional advertising on the equity of appellant's rates is highly speculative....

In contrast, the State's interest in energy conservation is directly advanced by the Commission order at issue here. There is an immediate connection between advertising and demand for electricity. Central Hudson would not contest the advertising ban unless it believed that promotion would increase its sales. [However, the] Commission's order prevents appellant from promoting electric services that would reduce energy use by diverting demand from less efficient sources, or that would consume roughly the same amount of energy as do alternative sources. In neither situation would the utility's advertising endanger conservation or mislead the public. To the extent that the Commission's order suppresses speech that in no way impairs the State's interest in energy conservation, the Commission's order violates the First and Fourteenth Amendments and must be invalidated.

The Commission also has not demonstrated that its interest in conservation cannot be protected adequately by more limited regulation of appellant's commercial expression. To further its policy of conservation, the Commission could attempt to restrict the format and content of Central Hudson's advertising. It might, for example, require that the advertisements include information about the relative efficiency and expense of the offered service, both under current conditions and for the foreseeable future. In the absence of a showing that more limited speech regulation would be ineffective, we cannot approve the complete suppression of Central Hudson's advertising....

Mr. Justice Blackmun, with whom Mr. Justice Brennan joins, concurring in the judgment.

I agree with the Court that the Public Service Commission's ban on promotional advertising of electricity by public utilities is inconsistent with the First and Fourteenth Amendments. I concur only in the Court's judgment, however, because I believe the test now evolved and applied by the Court is not consistent with our prior cases and does not provide adequate protection for truthful, nonmisleading, noncoercive commercial speech.

The Court asserts that "a four-part analysis has developed" from our decisions concerning commercial speech.... I agree with the Court that this level of intermediate scrutiny is appropriate for a restraint on commercial speech designed to protect consumers from misleading or coercive speech, or a regulation related to the time, place, or manner of commercial speech. I do not agree, however, that the Court's four-part test is the proper one to be applied when a State seeks to suppress information about a product in order to manipulate a private economic decision that the State cannot or has not regulated or outlawed directly. . . .

I seriously doubt whether suppression of information concerning the availability and price of a legally offered product is ever a permissible way for the State to "dampen" demand for or use of the product. Even though "commercial" speech is involved, such a regulatory measure strikes at the heart of the First Amendment. This is because it is a covert attempt by the State to manipulate the choices of its citizens, not by persuasion or direct regulation, but by depriving the public of the information needed to make a free choice. As the Court recognizes, the State's policy choices are insulated from the visibility and scrutiny that direct regulation would entail and the conduct of citizens is molded by the information that government chooses to give them. Ante, at n. 9. See Rotunda, The Commercial Speech Doctrine in the Supreme Court, 1976 U. of Ill. Law Forum 1080, 1080–1083 (1976). If the First Amendment guarantee means anything, it means that, absent clear and present danger, government has no power to restrict expression because of the effect its message is likely to have on the public. . . .

It appears that the Court would permit the State to ban all direct advertising of air conditioning, assuming that a more limited restriction on such advertising would not effectively deter the public from cooling its homes. In my view, our cases do not support this type of suppression. If a governmental unit believes that use or over-use of air conditioning is a serious problem, it must attack that problem directly, by prohibiting air conditioning or regulating thermostat levels. . . .

MR. JUSTICE STEVENS, with whom MR. JUSTICE BRENNAN joins, concurring in the judgment.

[O]ne of the two definitions the Court uses in addressing that issue is too broad and the other may be somewhat too narrow. The Court first describes commercial speech as "expression related solely to the economic interests of the speaker and its audience." Although it is not entirely clear whether this definition uses the subject matter of the speech or the motivation of the speaker as the limiting factor, it seems clear to me that it encompasses speech that is entitled to the maximum protection afforded by the First Amendment. Neither a labor leader's exhortation to strike, nor an economist's dissertation on the money supply, should receive any lesser protection because the subject matter concerns only the economic interests of the audience. Nor should the economic motivation of a speaker qualify his constitutional protection; even Shakespeare may have been motivated by the prospect of pecuniary reward. Thus, the Court's first definition of commercial speech is unquestionably too broad.

The Court's second definition refers to "speech proposing a commercial transaction." A salesman's solicitation, a broker's offer, and a manufacturer's publication of a price list or the terms of his standard warranty would unquestionably fit within this concept. Presumably, the definition is intended to encompass advertising that advises possible buyers of the availability of specific products at specific prices and describes the advantages of purchasing such items.... I am persuaded that it should not include the entire range of communication that is embraced within the term "promotional advertising." ...

The justification for the regulation is nothing more than the expressed fear that the audience may find the utility's message persuasive. [I]f the perceived harm associated with greater electrical usage is not sufficiently serious to justify direct regulation, surely it does not constitute the kind of clear and present danger that can justify the suppression of speech. [I concur] because I do not consider this to be a "commercial speech" case....

[The opinion of BRENNAN, J. concurring in the judgment, and the dissenting opinion of REHNQUIST, J., are omitted.]

Notes

1. On the same day that it decided *Central Hudson,* the Court held, in *Consolidated Edison Co. of New York, Inc. v. Public Service Commission of New York,* 447 U.S. 530, 100 S.Ct. 2326, 65 L.Ed.2d 319 (1980) that the First Amendment, as incorporated by the Fourteenth, is violated by an order of the Public Service Commission of New York that prohibited the inclusion in monthly electric bills of inserts discussing controversial issues of public policy.

First National Bank v. Bellotti, 435 U.S. 765, 98 S.Ct. 1407, 55 L.Ed.2d 707 (1978) invalidated a Massachusetts criminal statute that forbade corporations from spending money to influence the vote on referendums. The state court had held that the First Amendment rights of a corporation are limited to issues that materially affect its business, property, or assets. The banks in this case wanted to publicize their views against a proposed state constitutional amendment that would have allowed the legislature to impose a graduated personal income tax. The Supreme Court said:

> The inherent worth of the speech in terms of its capacity for informing the public does not depend upon the identity of its source, whether corporation, association, union, or individual ... A commercial advertisement is constitutionally protected not so much because it pertains to the seller's business as because it furthers the societal interest in the "free flow of commercial information."

2. ADVERTISING REGARDING ABORTION, CONTRACEPTION, AND DRUGS. *Bigelow v. Virginia,* 421 U.S. 809, 95 S.Ct. 2222, 44 L.Ed.2d 600 (1975) held that Virginia could not constitutionally punish the publisher of a newspaper for printing an abortion referral agency's paid advertisement that promoted the agency's services and contained information about the availability of abortions.

One year later, *Virginia Pharmacy Board v. Virginia Citizens Consumer Council,* 425 U.S. 748, 96 S.Ct. 1817, 48 L.Ed.2d 346 (1976) held that Virginia's ban on pharmacists' advertising prescription drug prices also violated free speech. The choice "between the dangers of suppressing information and the dangers of its misuse if it is freely available" is a choice "that the First Amendment makes for us." Only Justice Rehnquist dissented. Blackmun, J., for the Court, said:

> "Virginia is free to require whatever professional standards it wishes of its pharmacists; it may subsidize them or protect them from competition in other ways. But it may not do so by keeping the public in ignorance of the entirely lawful terms that competing pharmacists are offering. In this sense, the justifications Virginia has offered for suppressing the flow of prescription drug price information, far from persuading us that the flow is not protected by the First Amendment, have reinforced our view that it is. We so hold."

Carey v. Population Services International, 431 U.S. 678, 97 S.Ct. 2010, 52 L.Ed.2d 675 (1977) invalidated a New York law that made it a crime for anyone, including licensed pharmacists, to advertise or display contraceptives. That the advertisements might be offensive "to some does not justify its suppression." Nor is the law justified on the theory that open advertising would legitimize sexual activity by young people because the advertisements could not be characterized as "directed to inciting or producing imminent lawless action and ... likely to incite or produce such action," within the meaning of *Brandenburg v. Ohio,* § 10–1, supra. See also *Bolger v. Youngs Drug Products Corp.,* 463 U.S. 60, 103 S.Ct. 2875, 77 L.Ed.2d 469 (1983)(Mail advertisements for contraceptives are commercial speech protected by the First Amendment; federal law prohibiting the making of unsolicited advertisements, as applied to appellee's mailings, is unconstitutional).

3. LAWYER ADVERTISING. In 1977 the Supreme Court invalidated state regulations forbidding attorneys from advertising the prices at which certain routine services will be performed. *Bates v. State Bar of Arizona,* 433 U.S. 350, 97 S.Ct. 2691, 53 L.Ed.2d 810 (1977).* The Court did not address "the peculiar problems associated with advertising claims relating to the *quality* of legal services. Such claims are not susceptible to precise measurement or verification and, under some circumstances, might well be deceptive or misleading to the public, or even false." Nor did the Court consider "in-person solicitation of clients—at the hospital room or accident site, or in any other situation that breeds undue influence—by attorneys or their agents or 'runners.' "

This second issue was later considered in two companion cases, *In re Primus,* 436 U.S. 412, 98 S.Ct. 1893, 56 L.Ed.2d 417 (1978), and *Ohralik v. Ohio State Bar Association,* 436 U.S. 447, 98 S.Ct. 1912, 56 L.Ed.2d 444 (1978). *Primus* concluded that the state could not constitutionally discipline a lawyer (assisting the ACLU), for advising a prospective client—who had been sterilized as a condition of the continued receipt of medical assistance under the Medicaid program—that a lawsuit might be appropriate. A letter also informed the prospective client of the ACLU's offer of free representa-

---

* The Court, although invalidating the restrictions on attorney advertising, did not apply the overbreadth doctrine. Because overbreadth is "strong medicine," which "has been employed ... sparingly and only as a last resort, we decline to apply it to professional advertising, a context where it is not necessary to further its intended objective." The Court argued that, since such "advertising is linked to commercial well-being, it seems unlikely that such speech is particularly susceptible to being crushed by overbroad regulation."

tion. Primus' solicitation on behalf of a nonprofit organization (which litigated as a form of political expression) could only be regulated where actual harm is shown in the particular case. In contrast, *Ohralik* held that, in the facts of that case, the state could discipline a lawyer for soliciting clients in person, for pecuniary gain, because the circumstances were likely to result in misleading, deceptive, and overbearing conduct, which the state can prevent, without showing harm in a given case. The lawyer in that case solicited an auto accident victim in a hospital where she lay in traction and sought out another victim on the day she left the hospital. He urged both to employ him, used a concealed tape recorder to assure evidence of the assent to representation, and refused to withdraw when asked to do so.

It is difficult to predict the outcome of cases lying between the two extremes represented by these two fact situations. Marshall, J., concurring, offered a more precise test. He would allow "benign" solicitation even though commercially motivated—that is, "solicitation by advice and information that is truthful and that is present in a noncoercive, nondeceitful, and dignified manner to a potential client who is emotionally and physically capable of making a rational decision either to accept or reject the representation. . . ."

Matter of R.M.J., 455 U.S. 191, 102 S.Ct. 929, 71 L.Ed.2d 64 (1982) unanimously invalidated various restrictions on lawyer advertising. The state supreme court had reprimanded R.M.J. because he deviated from the precise listing of areas of practice included in the state's Rule 4 governing lawyer advertising. For example, his advertisement listed "real estate" instead of "property," and he listed "contracts," although Rule 4 did not list that latter term at all. The state did not show that R.M.J.'s listing was deceptive and could show no substantial interest that this restriction promoted. Similarly the Court invalidated a rule prohibiting a lawyer from identifying the jurisdictions where he is licensed to practice law.* Finally the Court invalidated a rule that prohibited mailing cards (which announced the opening of his office) to persons other than "lawyers, former clients, personal friends and relatives." The silent record did not justify the reason for the absolute prohibition. Even if a reason existed, the state could use less restrictive means, such as requiring that a copy of any mailings be filed with the state.

Zauderer v. Office of Disciplinary Counsel, 471 U.S. 626, 105 S.Ct. 2265, 85 L.Ed.2d 652 (1985) held that the state may not discipline an attorney who solicits business by running newspaper advertisements containing nondeceptive illustrations, offering to represent women who had suffered injury from the Dalkon Shield Intrauterine Device, and offering legal advice, such as the advice that claims may not yet be time barred. The legal advice was not false or deceptive.

However, *Zauderer* held that the state could discipline an attorney for failure to include in his advertisements some information reasonably necessary to make his advertisement not misleading. The lawyer advertised that "if there is no recovery, no legal fees are owed by our clients," but failed to

---

* R.M.J. also emphasized in large boldface type that he was a member of the U.S. Supreme Court bar, a "relatively uninfor- mative fact." But the record did not show that it was misleading.

disclose that "the clients might be liable for significant litigation costs even if their lawsuits were unsuccessful.... " There are "material differences between disclosure requirements and outright prohibitions of speech." The former prohibits no speech and the lawyer's "constitutionally protected interest in *not* providing any particular factual information in his advertising is minimal." (emphasis in original). So long as the disclosure requirements are "reasonably related to the State's interest in preventing deception of consumers," and not "unduly burdensome," there is no first amendment violation. It was not necessary for the state to demonstrate that the disclosure requirements are the "least restrictive means" to serve the state's purposes. Nor is a disclosure requirement invalid if it is underinclusive, i.e., "if it does not get at all facets of the problem it is designed to ameliorate." Usually, governments are entitled to attack problems piecemeal, unless "their policies implicate rights so fundamental that strict scrutiny must be applied."

In *Shapero v. Kentucky Bar Association,* 486 U.S. 466, 108 S.Ct. 1916, 100 L.Ed.2d 475 (1988) the Court (6 to 3) invalidated, as a violation of free speech, state prohibitions against attorneys sending truthful, non-deceptive letters to potential clients known to face particular legal problems (i.e., targeted, direct-mail advertising). The Court noted that targeted mailing is merely a more efficient form of mass mailing. Brennan, J., in a plurality opinion, went on to conclude that petitioner's particular letter was not misleading merely because it engaged in the liberal use of underscored, upper case letters—e.g., "Call NOW, don't wait"; "it is FREE, there is NO charge for calling." Nor was the letter misleading because it contained assertions that stated no objective fact ("It may surprise you what I may be able to do for you").

White & Stevens, JJ., dissented from this plurality opinion because they believed that the issue of whether the petitioner's particular letter was misleading should be decided by the state courts in the first instance. O'Connor, J., joined by Rehnquist, C.J. & Scalia, J., filed a dissenting opinion. They wanted to reexamine the entire line of attorney-advertising cases.**

Peel v. Attorney Registration and Disciplinary Commission of Illinois, 496 U.S. 91, 110 S.Ct. 2281, 110 L.Ed.2d 83 (1990). Because Illinois did not

---

** Contrast, *Edenfield v. Fane,* 507 U.S. 761, 113 S.Ct. 1792, 123 L.Ed.2d 543 (1993), which invalidated (8 to 1, with only O'Connor, J., dissenting) a Florida ban on in-person, uninvited, direct *face-to-face* or telephone contact by Certified Public Accountants soliciting business in the business context. As applied, the Florida ban on CPA solicitation in the business context violated free speech. The CPA soliciting business intends to communicate truthful, non-deceptive information proposing a lawful commercial transaction. This law need only be reasonably tailored to serve a substantial state interest. Yet, it failed even this intermediate standard of review because the state offered no studies or even anecdotal evidence that personal solicitation by CPAs creates dangers of fraud, overreaching, or compromised independence. The Court said that *Ohralik*'s "narrow holding" depended on "certain 'unique' features of in-person solicitation by lawyers." The CPA, unlike a lawyer, is not trained in the art of persuasion; the prospective clients, unlike "the young accident victim in *Ohralik*," are "sophisticated experienced business executives;" there is no pressure to retain the CPA on the spot. Even after *Ohralik,* the state must prove that the preventative measures that it proposes will contribute "in a material way" to relieving a "serious" problem.

permit an attorney to hold himself out as "certified" or a "specialist" except for patent, trademark, and admiralty lawyers, the Illinois Supreme Court censured Peel, whose letterhead stated that he was certified as a civil trial specialist by the National Board of Trial Advocacy (NBTA), a bona fide private group that has developed a set of objective and demanding standards and procedures for periodic certification of lawyers with experience and competence in trial work. The U.S. Supreme Court (5 to 4, with no majority opinion) reversed. Stevens, J., joined by Brennan, Blackmun, & Kennedy, JJ., explained that the issue was whether "a lawyer has a constitutional right, under the standards applicable to commercial speech, to advertise his or her certification as a trial specialist by NBTA." The facts on Peel's letterhead were both true and verifiable. Though Peel's claim was facially accurate, Illinois argued that Peel's letterhead implied a higher quality or ability than noncertified lawyers. But Illinois had confused "the distinction between statements of opinion or quality and statements of objective facts that may support an inference of quality." Peel's statement of certification by a private group, the NBTA, has no more potential to mislead than an attorney advertising that he is admitted to practice before the U.S. Supreme Court, a statement that *Matter of R.M.J.* found constitutionally protected. Thus, Peel's letterhead was neither actually nor inherently nor potentially misleading. If the state believes that statements of private certification might be potentially misleading, the state could require a disclaimer about the certifying organization or the standards of a specialty.

Ibanez v. Florida Department of Business and Professional Regulation, Board of Accountancy, 512 U.S. 136, 114 S.Ct. 2084, 129 L.Ed.2d 118 (1994). Ginsburg, J., for the unanimous Court, held that it violated free speech when the Florida Board of Accountancy reprimanded Silvia Ibanez, an attorney, because she truthfully stated in her legal advertising that she was also a Certified Public Accountant (CPA). The state Board of Accountancy had licensed her as a CPA. "[W]e cannot imagine how consumers could be misled by her truthful representation" that she is a CPA.

The Court, 7 to 2 (O'Connor, J., joined by Rehnquist, C.J. dissented), also rejected sanctions based on the fact that Ms. Ibanez had truthfully stated that she was a Certified Financial Planner (CFP). A bona fide private organization had certified her as a CFP. A Florida rule prohibited the use of "specialist" unless accompanied by an elaborate disclaimer, "in the immediate proximity of the statement that implies formal recognition as a specialist," that states that "the recognizing agency is not affiliated with or sanctioned by the state or federal government," and that sets out the requirements for recognition, "including, but not limited to, education, experience[,] and testing." The Board failed to show any harm that is "potentially real, not purely hypothetical," and the detail required on the disclaimer would effectively rule out use of the designation on a business card, letterhead, or yellow pages listing. "We have never sustained restrictions on constitutionally protected speech based on a record so bare as the one on which the Board relies here."

4. TRADE NAMES. *Friedman v. Rogers,* 440 U.S. 1, 99 S.Ct. 887, 59 L.Ed.2d 100 (1979) upheld a Texas law that prohibited the practice of optometry under a trade name. The Court argued that the trade names could be misleading:

A trade name is, however, a significantly different form of commercial speech from that considered in *Virginia Pharmacy* and *Bates*. [W]e are concerned with a form of commercial speech that has no intrinsic meaning. A trade name conveys no information about the price and nature of the services offered by an optometrist until it acquires meaning over a period of time by associations formed in the minds of the public between the name and some standard of price or quality. Because these ill-defined associations of trade names with price and quality information can be manipulated by the users of trade names, there is a significant possibility that trade names will be used to mislead the public. The possibilities for deception are numerous. The trade name of an optometrical practice can remain unchanged despite changes in the staff of optometrists upon whose skill and care the public depends when it patronizes the practice. Thus, the public may be attracted by a trade name that reflects the reputation of an optometrist no longer associated with the practice [or an optometrist may] assume a new trade name if negligence or misconduct casts a shadow over the old one. ... The use of a trade name also facilitates the advertising essential to large-scale commercial practices with numerous branch offices, conduct the State rationally may wish to discourage while not prohibiting commercial optometrical practice altogether.

Blackmun, J., joined by Marshall, J. dissented:

Because a trade name has no intrinsic meaning, it cannot by itself be deceptive. A trade name will deceive only if it is used in a misleading context. [A]bsent some other regulatory justification, a State may not prohibit the dissemination of truthful commercial information. By disclosing his individual name along with his trade name, the commercial optometrist acts in the spirit of our First Amendment jurisprudence, where traditionally "the remedy to be applied is more speech, not enforced silence."

5. OUTDOOR ADVERTISING. In *Linmark Associates, Inc. v. Township of Willingboro,* 431 U.S. 85, 97 S.Ct. 1614, 52 L.Ed.2d 155 (1977) the Court, per Marshall, J., invalidated a township ordinance that prohibited the posting of "For Sale" or "Sold" signs. The purpose of the prohibition was to stem the flight of white homeowners from a racially integrated community. The township did not ban all lawn signs, nor all lawn signs of a particular size; rather, it prohibited particular signs because of their content, "because it fears their 'primary' effect—that they will cause those receiving the information to act on it." In order to promote integrated housing, Willingboro could "give widespread publicity—through 'Not For Sale' signs or other methods— to the number of whites remaining in Willingboro. And it surely can endeavor to create inducements to retain individuals who are considering selling their homes."

In *Metromedia, Inc. v. City of San Diego,* 453 U.S. 490, 101 S.Ct. 2882, 69 L.Ed.2d 800 (1981), the Court, with no majority opinion, invalidated a San Diego ordinance that imposed substantial prohibitions on outdoor advertising displays. The ordinance stated that its purpose was to eliminate distracting signs and improve the city's appearance. It permitted "onsite" commercial advertising (a sign advertising goods or services available on the property where the sign is located) but forbade all other commercial advertising and all noncommercial advertising using fixed structure signs unless they were within one of twelve specified exceptions (e.g., commemorative historical plaques; religious signs; for sale signs; temporary political campaign signs).

Justice White's plurality opinion, joined by Stewart, Marshall & Powell, JJ., concluded that the ordinance was unconstitutional on its face. The general ban on noncommercial advertising was not valid: the use of onsite billboards to carry commercial messages related to the commercial use of the premises is allowed, while "the use of otherwise identical billboards to carry noncommercial messages is generally prohibited. The city does not explain how or why noncommercial billboards located in places where commercial billboards are permitted would be more threatening to safe driving or would detract more from the beauty of the city." Also because the ordinance's various exceptions allow some noncommercial messages on billboards throughout the city, the city must allow other noncommercial messages throughout the city.

Justice Brennan, joined by Blackmun, J., concluded that, as a "practical" matter, the San Diego ordinance was a total ban on billboards, whether commercial or noncommercial, and that San Diego could not show that a total ban "directly furthered" a "sufficiently substantial governmental interest." These justices doubted whether San Diego or any large city could meet the burden they proposed. In dictum they said that the federal government should be able to demonstrate that "billboards could be entirely banned in Yellowstone National Park, where their very existence would so obviously be inconsistent with the surrounding landscape." Brennan left open the question of the constitutionality of the federal Highway Beautification Act of 1965, 23 U.S.C.A. § 131. Compare *Railway Express Agency, Inc. v. New York,* § 8–1.

Contrast *Los Angeles City Council v. Taxpayers for Vincent,* 466 U.S. 789, 104 S.Ct. 2118, 80 L.Ed.2d 772 (1984). A 6 to 3 majority upheld a city ordinance that prohibited the posting of signs on public property. Taxpayers for Vincent, a group supporting a candidate for election to the city council, attached signs supporting Vincent to utility poles. City employees removed them along with other signs, most of which were commercial in nature. The Court, relying on *Metromedia,* emphasized that the ordinance was a content neutral prohibition justified by the city's aesthetic interests in avoiding visual clutter. Also, utility poles are not a public forum, and, if the city had created an exception for appellees' political speech and not other types of speech, it might create "a risk of engaging in constitutionally forbidden content discrimination." Brennan, J., joined by Marshall & Blackmun, JJ., dissented: Los Angeles must demonstrate that its goal of eliminating visual clutter "in a serious and comprehensive manner." And, "it might be difficult for Los Angeles to make the type of showing which I have suggested."

City of Ladue v. Gilleo, 512 U.S. 43, 114 S.Ct. 2038, 129 L.Ed.2d 36 (1994). The unanimous Court invalidated a city ordinance that banned most residential signs. The law allowed small residential signs advertising that the property is for sale, signs for churches and schools, commercial signs in commercially zoned districts, etc. It did not allow Margaret Gilleo to display an 8.5 by 11 inch sign in her window, which stated: "For Peace in the Gulf." Gilleo opposed the Persian Gulf War. The City justified the ordinance as an effort to prevent "ugliness, visual blight and clutter," because signs "tarnish the natural beauty of the landscape," etc.

The Court assumed that the ordinance was viewpoint and content-neutral and that the various exemptions in the ordinance reflected legitimate differences among the side effects of various kinds of signs. The law was invalid, not because of its exemptions (that is, not because the law discriminated on the basis of the content of speech), but because it simply prohibited too much speech. Even content-neutral restrictions are invalid if they unduly limit one's ability to engage in free expression:

> Ladue has almost completely foreclosed a venerable means of communication that is both unique and important. It has totally foreclosed that medium to political, religious, or personal messages. [R]esidential signs play an important part in political campaigns, during which they are displayed to signal the resident's support for particular candidates, parties, or causes.... Although prohibitions foreclosing entire media may be completely free of content or viewpoint discrimination, the danger they pose to the freedom of speech is readily apparent—by eliminating a common means of speaking, such measures can suppress too much speech.... Precisely because of their location, such signs provide information about the identity of the "speaker."

The Court said different considerations might apply to signs (whether political or otherwise) that residents displayed for a fee, or off-site commercial advertisements on residential property.

6. THE "LEAST RESTRICTIVE MEANS" TEST. *Board of Trustees of the State University of New York v. Fox,* 492 U.S. 469, 109 S.Ct. 3028, 106 L.Ed.2d 388 (1989). The State University of New York (SUNY) had a rule (Resolution 66–156) prohibiting private commercial enterprises from operating in SUNY facilities. The Resolution was applied to prohibit students in their dormitories from hosting Tupperware-type parties demonstrating and selling housewares of the American Future System, Inc. (AFS). Justice Scalia, for the Court, concluded that the student AFS parties were commercial speech because they " 'propose a commercial transaction,' which is the test for identifying commercial speech." Although these Tupperware-type parties touch on other subjects, such as how to run an efficient home, that fact does not put them in the category of fully protected speech.

The Court ruled that it was error to apply the "least restrictive means" test to commercial speech cases. Cases like *Central Hudson* do not require that government restrictions on commercial speech be "absolutely the least severe that will achieve the desired end." Rather, there must be only a "reasonable" fit—a "fit that is not necessarily perfect"—between the governmental ends and the means chosen to accomplish those ends. So long as the means are "narrowly tailored" to achieve the desired objectives, it is for the government decisionmakers to judge what manner of regulation may best be employed. The government, however, has the burden to show that its goal is "substantial" and that "the cost [has been] carefully calculated." The Court added: "We reject the contention that the test we have described is overly permissive. It is far different, of course, from the 'rational basis' test used for Fourteenth Amendment equal protection analysis.''

The case was remanded to consider other challenges to Resolution 156. The Resolution reached other conduct that consisted of speech for profit (such as private tutoring, legal advice, and medical consultation). ''While these examples consist of speech for a profit, they do not consist of speech that *proposes* a commercial transaction, which is what defines commercial speech.''

7. *City of Cincinnati v. Discovery Network, Inc.,* 507 U.S. 410, 113 S.Ct. 1505, 123 L.Ed.2d 99 (1993). Cincinnati refused to allow the respondents to distribute commercial publications (such as free magazines advertising real estate) through the use of free standing newsracks on the city sidewalks. The city called these commercial publications ''commercial handbills'' and argued that the purpose of its prohibition was to make the sidewalks more attractive and promote safer streets (e.g., people might trip over the newsracks). However, while the city sought to remove the 62 newsracks distributing commercial publications, it did not apply its prohibition to newsracks (numbering about 1,500 to 2,000) that sold *newspapers* (defined as publications published daily or weekly and *primarily* covering or commenting on current events).

Applying *Central Hudson* and *Fox,* the Court (6 to 3) invalidated the city's ban. The city has a valid concern with the aggregate number of newsracks on the streets, but not with their contents, because each newsrack, whether it contains ''newspapers'' or ''commercial handbills'' is equally unattractive. There is no basis of distinction between ''newspapers'' and ''handbills'' that is relevant to any interest that the city has asserted. Even if it is assumed that the city could ban all newsracks on public property, that would not justify the discriminatory ban (based on the content of the newsracks) that the city imposed.

Blackmun, J., concurring, argued that ''the analysis set forth in *Central Hudson* and refined in *Fox* affords insufficient protection for truthful, noncoercive commercial speech concerning lawful activities.'' Intermediate scrutiny is appropriate for time, place, or manner restrictions (without regard to content) or when the restraint on commercial speech is designed to protect the consumer from misleading or coercive speech, but not when the restriction ''suppresses truthful commercial speech to serve some other government purpose.'' He urged the Court to abandon *Central Hudson's* analysis entirely in favor of giving ''full protection for truthful, noncoercive commercial speech about lawful activities.''

POSADAS DE PUERTO RICO ASSOCIATES v. TOURISM CO. OF PUERTO RICO
478 U.S. 328, 106 S.Ct. 2968, 92 L.Ed.2d 266 (1986).

JUSTICE REHNQUIST delivered the opinion of the Court.

In this case we address the facial constitutionality of a Puerto Rico statute and regulations restricting advertising of casino gambling aimed at the residents of Puerto Rico.... Appellant sought a declaratory judgment that the statute and regulations, both facially and as applied by the Tourism Company, impermissibly suppressed commercial speech in violation of the First Amendment and the equal protection and due process guarantees of the United States Constitution.* ...

In 1948, the Puerto Rico Legislature legalized certain forms of casino gambling [but] also provided that "[n]o gambling room shall be permitted to advertise or otherwise offer their facilities to the public of Puerto Rico." ... Appellee Tourism Company of Puerto Rico, a public corporation, assumed the regulatory powers.... Regulation 76a–1(7), as amended in 1971, provides in pertinent part:

> "No concessionaire, nor his agent or employee is authorized to advertise the gambling parlors to the public in Puerto Rico. The advertising of our games of chance is hereby authorized through newspapers, magazines, radio, television and other publicity media outside Puerto Rico subject to the prior editing and approval by the Tourism Development Company of the advertisement to be submitted in draft to the Company." 15 R. & R.P.R. § 76a–1(7) (1972).

... On February 16, 1979, the Tourism Company issued to all casino franchise holders a memorandum setting forth the following interpretation of the advertising restrictions:

> "This prohibition includes the use of the word 'casino' in matchbooks, lighters, envelopes, inter-office and/or external correspondence, invoices, napkins, brochures, menus, elevators, glasses, plates, lobbies, banners, flyers, paper holders, pencils, telephone books, directories, bulletin boards or in any hotel dependency or object which may be accessible to the public in Puerto Rico."

Pursuant to this administrative interpretation, the Tourism Company assessed additional fines against appellant....

Appellant then filed a declaratory judgment action against the Tourism Company in the Superior Court of Puerto Rico, San Juan Section, seeking a declaration that the Act and implementing regulations, both facially and as applied by the Tourism Company, violated appellant's commercial speech rights under the United States Constitution.... After a trial, the Superior Court held that "[t]he administrative interpretation and application has been capricious, arbitrary, erroneous and unreasonable, and has produced absurd results which are contrary to law." The court therefore determined that it must "override the regulatory deficiency to save the constitutionality of the statute." ... The court also issued the following narrowing construction of Regulation 76a–1(7):

---

* We have held that Puerto Rico is subject to the First Amendment Speech Clause, *Balzac v. Porto Rico,* 258 U.S. 298, 314, 42 S.Ct. 343, 349, 66 L.Ed. 627 (1922), the Due Process Clause of either the Fifth or the Fourteenth Amendment, *Calero–Toledo v. Pearson Yacht Leasing Co.,* 416 U.S. 663, 668–669, n. 5, 94 S.Ct. 2080, 2084–2085, n. 5, 40 L.Ed.2d 452 (1974), and the equal protection guarantee of either the Fifth or the Fourteenth Amendment, *Examining Board v. Flores de Otero,* 426 U.S. 572, 599–601, 96 S.Ct. 2264, 2279–2281, 49 L.Ed.2d 65 (1976).

"Advertisements of the casinos in Puerto Rico are prohibited in the local publicity media addressed to inviting the residents of Puerto Rico to visit the casinos. . . .

"We hereby allow, within the jurisdiction of Puerto Rico, advertising by the casinos addressed to tourists, provided they do not invite the residents of Puerto Rico to visit the casino, even though said announcements may incidentally reach the hands of a resident. . . .

"We hereby authorize advertising in the mass communication media of the country, where the trade name of the hotel is used even though it may contain a reference to the casino provided that the word casino is never used alone nor specified. Among the announcements allowed, by way of illustration, are the use of the trade name with which the hotel is identified for the promotion of special vacation packages and activities at the hotel, in invitations, 'billboards,' bulletins and programs or activities sponsored by the hotel. . . .

"Since a *clausus* enumeration of this regulation is unforeseeable, any other situation or incident relating to the legal restriction must be measured in light of the public policy of promoting tourism. If the object of the advertisement is the tourist, it passes legal scrutiny."

The court entered judgment declaring that appellant's constitutional rights had been violated by the Tourism Company's past application of the advertising restrictions, but that the restrictions were not facially unconstitutional and could be sustained, as "modified by the guidelines issued by this Court on this date." The Supreme Court of Puerto Rico dismissed appellant's appeal of the Superior Court's decision on the ground that it "d[id] not present a substantial constitutional question." . . .

. . . Under *Central Hudson,* commercial speech receives a limited form of First Amendment protection so long as it concerns a lawful activity and is not misleading or fraudulent. Once it is determined that the First Amendment applies to the particular kind of commercial speech at issue, then the speech may be restricted only if the government's interest in doing so is substantial, the restrictions directly advance the government's asserted interest, and the restrictions are no more extensive than necessary to serve that interest.

The particular kind of commercial speech at issue here, namely, advertising of casino gambling aimed at the residents of Puerto Rico, concerns a lawful activity and is not misleading or fraudulent, at least in the abstract. We must therefore proceed to the three remaining steps of the *Central Hudson* analysis in order to determine whether Puerto Rico's advertising restrictions run afoul of the First Amendment. The first of these three steps involves an assessment of the strength of the government's interest in restricting the speech. . . . The Tourism Company's brief before this Court explains the legislature's belief that "[e]xcessive casino gambling among local residents . . . would produce serious harmful effects on the health, safety and welfare of the Puerto Rican citizens, such as the disruption of moral and cultural patterns, the increase in local crime, the fostering of prostitution, the development of corruption, and the infiltration of organized crime." These are some of the very same concerns, of course, that have motivated the vast majority of the 50 States to prohibit casino gambling. We have no difficulty in concluding that the Puerto Rico Legislature's interest in the health, safety, and welfare of its citizens constitutes a "substantial" governmental interest....

The last two steps of the *Central Hudson* analysis basically involve a consideration of the "fit" between the legislature's ends and the means chosen to accomplish those ends. Step three asks the question whether the challenged restrictions on commercial speech "directly advance" the government's asserted interest. In the instant case, the answer to this question is clearly "yes." The Puerto Rico Legislature obviously believed, when it enacted the advertising restrictions at issue here, that advertising of casino gambling aimed at the residents of Puerto Rico would serve to increase the demand for the product advertised. We think the legislature's belief is a reasonable one, and the fact that appellant has chosen to litigate this case all the way to this Court indicates that appellant shares the legislature's view....

Appellant argues, however, that the challenged advertising restrictions are underinclusive because other kinds of gambling such as horse racing, cockfighting, and the lottery may be advertised to the residents of Puerto Rico. Appellant's argument is misplaced for two reasons. First, whether other kinds of gambling are advertised in Puerto Rico or not, the restrictions on advertising of casino gambling "directly advance" the legislature's interest in reducing demand for games of chance.... Second, the legislature's interest, as previously identified, is not necessarily to reduce demand for all games of chance, but to reduce demand for casino gambling. According to the Superior Court, horse racing, cockfighting, "picas," or small games of chance at fiestas, and the lottery "have been traditionally part of the Puerto Rican's roots," so that "the legislator could have been more flexible than in authorizing more sophisticated games which are not so widely sponsored by the people." In other words, the legislature felt that for Puerto Ricans the risks associated with casino gambling were significantly greater than those associated with the more traditional kinds of gambling in Puerto Rico. In our view, the legislature's separate classification of casino gambling, for purposes of the advertising ban, satisfies the third step of the *Central Hudson* analysis.

We also think it clear beyond peradventure that the challenged statute and regulations satisfy the fourth and last step of the *Central Hudson* analysis, namely, whether the restrictions on commercial speech are no more extensive than necessary to serve the government's interest. The narrowing constructions of the advertising restrictions announced by the Superior Court ensure that the restrictions will not affect advertising of casino gambling aimed at tourists, but will apply only to such advertising when aimed at the residents of Puerto Rico. Appellant contends, however, that the First Amendment requires the Puerto Rico Legislature to reduce demand for casino gambling among the residents of Puerto Rico not by suppressing commercial speech that might *encourage* such gambling, but by promulgating additional speech designed to *discourage* it. We reject this contention. We think it is up to the legislature to decide whether or not such a "counterspeech" policy would be as effective in reducing the demand for casino gambling as a restriction on advertising.... We therefore hold that the Supreme Court of Puerto Rico properly rejected appellant's First Amendment claim.

Appellant argues, however, that the challenged advertising restrictions are constitutionally defective under our decisions in *Carey v. Population Services Int'l,* 431 U.S. 678, 97 S.Ct. 2010, 52 L.Ed.2d 675 (1977), and *Bigelow v. Virginia,* 421 U.S. 809, 95 S.Ct. 2222, 44 L.Ed.2d 600 (1975). In *Carey,* this Court struck down a ban on any "advertisement or display" of contraceptives, and in *Bigelow,* we reversed a criminal conviction based on the advertisement of an abortion clinic. We think appellant's argument ignores a crucial distinction between the *Carey* and *Bigelow* decisions and the instant case. In *Carey* and *Bigelow,* the underlying conduct that was the subject of the advertising restrictions was constitutionally protected and could not have been prohibited by the State. Here, on the other hand, the Puerto Rico Legislature surely could have prohibited casino gambling by the residents of Puerto Rico altogether. In our view, the greater power to completely ban casino gambling necessarily includes the lesser power to ban advertising of casino gambling, and *Carey* and *Bigelow* are hence inapposite.... It would just as surely be a strange constitutional doctrine which would concede to the legislature the authority to totally ban a product or activity, but deny to the legislature the authority to forbid the stimulation of demand for the product or activity through advertising on behalf of those who would profit from such increased demand. Legislative regulation of products or activities deemed harmful, such as cigarettes, alcoholic beverages, and prostitution, has varied from outright prohibition on the one hand, see, e.g., Cal.Penal Code Ann. § 647(b)(West Supp.1986)(prohibiting soliciting or engaging in act of prostitution), to legalization of the product or activity with restrictions on stimulation of its demand on the other hand, see, e.g., Nev.Rev.Stat. §§ 244.345(1), (8)(1986)(authorizing licensing of houses of prostitution except in counties with more than 250,000 population), §§ 201.430, 201.440 (prohibiting advertising of houses of prostitution "[i]n any public theater, on the public streets of any city or town, or on any public highway," or "in [a] place of business").* To rule out the latter,

---

* See also 15 U.S.C. § 1335 (prohibiting cigarette advertising "on any medium of electronic communication subject to the jurisdiction of the Federal Communications Commission"), upheld in *Capital Broadcasting Co. v. Mitchell,* 333 F.Supp. 582 (1971), aff'd [without opinion], 405 U.S. 1000, 92 S.Ct. 1289, 31 L.Ed.2d 472 (1972); Miss.Code Ann. § 67–1–85 (Supp.1985)(prohibiting most forms of liquor sign advertising), upheld in *Dunagin v. City of Oxford, Miss.,* [718 F.2d 738 (5th Cir.1983)(en banc)].

intermediate kind of response would require more than we find in the First Amendment.

Appellant's final argument in opposition to the advertising restrictions is that they are unconstitutionally vague.... Even assuming that appellant's argument has merit with respect to the bare statutory language, however, we have already noted that we are bound by the Superior Court's narrowing construction of the statute. Viewed in light of that construction, and particularly with the interpretive assistance of the implementing regulations as modified by the Superior Court, we do not find the statute unconstitutionally vague.

For the foregoing reasons, the decision of the Supreme Court of Puerto Rico that, as construed by the Superior Court, § 8 of the Games of Chance Act of 1948 and the implementing regulations do not facially violate the First Amendment or the due process or equal protection guarantees of the Constitution, is affirmed.**

It is so ordered.

JUSTICE BRENNAN, with whom JUSTICE MARSHALL and JUSTICE BLACKMUN join, dissenting....

I see no reason why commercial speech should be afforded less protection than other types of speech where, as here, the government seeks to suppress commercial speech in order to deprive consumers of accurate information concerning lawful activity. [N]o differences between commercial and other kinds of speech justify protecting commercial speech less extensively where, as here, the government seeks to manipulate private behavior by depriving citizens of truthful information concerning lawful activities....

While tipping its hat to [strict scrutiny] standards, the Court does little more than defer to what it perceives to be the determination by Puerto Rico's legislature that a ban on casino advertising aimed at residents is reasonable. The Court totally ignores the fact that commercial speech is entitled to substantial First Amendment protection, giving the government unprecedented authority to eviscerate constitutionally protected expression.

... Neither the statute on its face nor the legislative history indicates that the Puerto Rico Legislature thought that serious harm would result if residents were allowed to engage in casino gambling; indeed, the available evidence suggests exactly the opposite. Puerto Rico has legalized gambling casinos, and permits its residents to patronize them. Thus, the Puerto Rico legislature has determined that permitting residents to engage in casino gambling will not produce the "serious harmful effects" that have led a majority of States to ban such activity. Residents of Puerto Rico are also permitted to engage in a variety of

---

** Justice Stevens claims that the Superior Court's narrowing construction creates an impermissible "prior restraint" on protected speech, because that court required the submission of certain casino advertising to appellee for its prior approval. This argument was not raised by appellant either below or in this Court, and we therefore express no view on [it].

other gambling activities—including horse racing, "picas", dog racing, cockfighting, and the Puerto Rico lottery—all of which are allowed to advertise freely to residents. Indeed, it is surely not farfetched to suppose that the legislature chose to restrict casino advertising not because of the "evils" of casino gambling, but because it preferred that Puerto Ricans spend their gambling dollars on the Puerto Rico lottery. In any event, in light of the legislature's determination that serious harm will *not* result if residents are permitted and *encouraged* to gamble, I do not see how Puerto Rico's interest in discouraging its residents from engaging in casino gambling can be characterized as "substantial," even if the legislature had actually asserted such an interest which, of course, it has not. Cf. *Capital Cities Cable, Inc. v. Crisp,* 467 U.S. 691, 715, 104 S.Ct. 2694, 2709, 81 L.Ed.2d 580 (1984)(Oklahoma's selective regulation of liquor advertising "suggests limits on the substantiality of the interests it asserts") [state regulations invalidated on preemption grounds].

The Court nevertheless sustains Puerto Rico's advertising ban because the legislature *could* have determined that casino gambling would seriously harm the health, safety, and welfare of the Puerto Rican citizens.*** This reasoning is contrary to this Court's long established First Amendment jurisprudence. When the government seeks to place restrictions upon commercial speech, a court may not, as the Court implies today, simply speculate about valid reasons that the government might have for enacting such restrictions. Rather, the government ultimately bears the burden of justifying the challenged regulation, and it is incumbent upon the government to *prove* that the interests it seeks to further are real and substantial.

[E]ven assuming that an advertising ban would effectively reduce residents' patronage of gambling casinos, it is not clear how it would directly advance Puerto Rico's interest in controlling the "serious harmful effects" the Court associates with casino gambling. In particular, it is unclear whether banning casino advertising aimed at residents would affect local crime, prostitution, the development of corruption, or the infiltration of organized crime. Because Puerto Rico actively promotes its casinos to tourists, these problems are likely to persist whether or not residents are also encouraged to gamble. Absent some showing that a ban on advertising aimed only at residents will directly advance Puerto Rico's interest in controlling the harmful effects allegedly associated with casino gambling, Puerto Rico may not constitutionally restrict protected expression in that way.

Finally, appellee has failed to show that Puerto Rico's interest in controlling the harmful effects allegedly associated with casino gambling "cannot be protected adequately by more limited regulation of appel-

---

*** ... A majority of States have chosen not to legalize casino gambling, and we have never suggested that this might be unconstitutional. However, having decided to legalize casino gambling, Puerto Rico's decision to ban truthful speech concerning entirely lawful activity raises serious First Amendment problems. Thus, the "constitutional doctrine" which bans Puerto Rico from banning advertisements concerning lawful casino gambling is not so strange a restraint—it is called the First Amendment.

lant's commercial expression." *Central Hudson,* supra. Rather than suppressing constitutionally protected expression, Puerto Rico could seek directly to address the specific harms thought to be associated with casino gambling. Thus, Puerto Rico could continue carefully to monitor casino operations to guard against "the development of corruption, and the infiltration of organized crime." It could vigorously enforce its criminal statutes to combat "the increase in local crime [and] the fostering of prostitution." It could establish limits on the level of permissible betting, or promulgate additional speech designed to discourage casino gambling among residents.... In this case, nothing suggests that the Puerto Rico Legislature ever considered the efficacy of measures other than suppressing protected expression. More importantly, there has been no showing that alternative measures would inadequately safeguard the Commonwealth's interest in controlling the harmful effects allegedly associated with casino gambling. Under these circumstances, Puerto Rico's ban on advertising clearly violates the First Amendment.

The Court believes that Puerto Rico constitutionally may prevent its residents from obtaining truthful commercial speech concerning otherwise lawful activity because of the effect it fears this information will have. However, "[i]t is precisely this kind of choice between the dangers of suppressing information, and the dangers of its misuse if it is freely available, that the First Amendment makes for us." *Virginia Pharmacy Board.* "[T]he people in our democracy are entrusted with the responsibility for judging and evaluating the relative merits of conflicting arguments." *First National Bank v. Bellotti....* I would hold that Puerto Rico may not suppress the dissemination of truthful information about entirely lawful activity merely to keep its residents ignorant. The Court, however, would allow Puerto Rico to do just that, thus dramatically shrinking the scope of First Amendment protection available to commercial speech, and giving government officials unprecedented authority to eviscerate constitutionally protected expression. I respectfully dissent.

Justice Stevens, with whom Justice Marshall and Justice Blackmun join, dissenting.

The Court concludes that "the greater power to completely ban casino gambling necessarily includes the lesser power to ban advertising of casino gambling." Whether a State may ban all advertising of an activity that it permits but could prohibit—such as gambling, prostitution, or the consumption of marijuana or liquor—is an elegant question of constitutional law. It is not, however, appropriate to address that question in this case because Puerto Rico's rather bizarre restraints on speech are so plainly forbidden by the First Amendment.

Puerto Rico does not simply "ban advertising of casino gambling." Rather, Puerto Rico blatantly discriminates in its punishment of speech depending on the publication, audience, and words employed. Moreover, the prohibitions, as now construed by the Puerto Rico courts, establish a regime of prior restraint and articulate a standard that is hopelessly vague and unpredictable. . . .

With respect to the audience, the newly construed regulations plainly discriminate in terms of the intended listener or reader. Casino advertising must be "addressed to tourists." It must not "invite the residents of Puerto Rico to visit the casino." The regulation thus poses what might be viewed as a reverse Privileges and Immunities problem: Puerto Rico's residents are singled out for disfavored treatment in comparison to all other Americans.* But nothing so fancy is required to recognize the obvious First Amendment problem in this kind of audience discrimination. I cannot imagine that this Court would uphold an Illinois regulation that forbade advertising "addressed" to Illinois residents while allowing the same advertiser to communicate his message to visitors and commuters; we should be no more willing to uphold a Puerto Rico regulation that forbids advertising "addressed" to Puerto Rico residents. . . .

With respect to prior restraint, the Superior Court's opinion establishes a regime of censorship. In a section of the opinion that the majority fails to include, the court explained:

> "We hereby authorize the publicity of the casinos in newspapers, magazines, radio, television or any other publicity media, of our games of chance in the exterior *with the previous approval of the Tourism Company* regarding the text of said ad, which must be submitted in draft to the Company. . . . " (emphasis added).

A more obvious form of prior restraint is difficult to imagine. . . .

Notes

1. During oral argument the counsel for Puerto Rico said that a casino could advertise in a Spanish language daily with ninety-nine percent local circulation so long as the "advertising is addressed to tourists and not to residents."

2. Consider the principle presented in *Posadas*, that "the greater power to completely ban casino gambling necessarily includes the lesser power to ban advertising of casino gambling." What about the advertising restriction invalidated in *Central Hudson*? No one has a constitutional right to waste electricity. New York, in *Central Hudson*, could have simply banned the use of all electric hair dryers, or all energy inefficient heat pumps, or all electric toothbrushes. Yet *Central Hudson* teaches us that New York could not, under the first amendment, prohibit advertising that promotes the wasteful (but lawful) use of electricity. If New York cannot constitutionally dampen New Yorkers' demand for electricity by prohibiting promotional advertising, can Puerto Rico dampen Puerto Rican demand for casino advertising by prohibiting promotional advertising?

---

* Perhaps, since Puerto Rico somewhat ambivalently regards a gambling casino as a good thing for the local proprietor and an evil for the local patrons, the ban on local advertising might be viewed as a form of protection against the poison that Puerto Rico uses to attract strangers into its web. If too much speech about the poison were permitted, local residents might not only partake of it but also decide to prohibit it.

Perhaps one might argue that the gambling in *Posadas* is really different from the energy waste in *Central Hudson,* because gambling can be harmful and energy waste is not. The Court did not draw this distinction, perhaps because *Virginia Pharmacy,* which it cited, had foreclosed it. That case held that it was unconstitutional for the state to restrict advertising promoting *prescription* drugs. Prescription drugs can be harmful. That's why they are not freely available. Indeed, the harm from prescription drugs is much more certain than the assumptions the Court made regarding the supposed unique harm flowing to Puerto Ricans who engage in lawful casino gambling.

We have all seen advertisements that say something like: "Are you feeling down? Have a headache? Try Excedrin." After *Virginia Pharmacy* a pharmacist has a constitutional right to run an advertisement that says: "Feeling blue? Ask your doctor to prescribe Valium. And when he does, buy it here. We're cheaper." If a pharmacist has a constitutional right to promote (push) Valium, why does *Posadas* draw a very different line when dealing with advertising of casino gambling directed to Puerto Ricans?

3. *United States v. Edge Broadcasting Co.,* 509 U.S. 418, 113 S.Ct. 2696, 125 L.Ed.2d 345 (1993). Edge Broadcasting is a radio station licensed in North Carolina, where lotteries are illegal. Over 90% of Edge Broadcasting's listeners lived in Virginia, which sponsored a lottery. The radio station, on the border between the two states, wanted to broadcast Virginia lottery advertisements, but Federal statutes prohibited broadcasting lottery advertising into a state that did not allow lotteries (although it allowed such broadcasting by a broadcaster licensed by a state that sponsored a lottery, even if its signal reached a state where lotteries were illegal). The Court held that, as applied to Edge, the law did not violate the First Amendment.

White, J., for the Court, specifically did not consider the Government's argument that *Central Hudson* was inapplicable because the "greater power" to prohibit "vices" such as gambling "necessarily includes the lesser power" to ban advertisements about them. Applying the four-part test of *Central Hudson,* the Court then upheld the law. First, the majority assumed that Edge would broadcast nonmisleading information about the Virginia lottery, a legal activity, and second, the federal government has a substantial interest in supporting the policies of nonlottery states while not interfering with the policies of lottery states. The third and fourth factors under *Central Hudson* basically required the court to consider the fit "between the legislature's ends and the means chosen to accomplish those ends." The majority announced, without elaboration, that Congress "might have continued to ban all radio or television lottery advertisements, even by stations in States that have legalized lotteries." The congressional interest of balancing the interests of the antigambling policy of states like North Carolina, while not unduly interfering with the lotteries sponsored by states like Virginia "is the substantial governmental interest that satisfies *Central Hudson,*" and "is also the interest that is directly served by applying the statutory restriction to all stations in North Carolina" even if, as applied to respondent, "there were only marginal advancement of that interest."

Applying the fourth prong of *Central Hudson,* the majority argued that the regulations were not more extensive than necessary to serve the governmental interest because, as in *Posadas,* the fit, while "not necessarily perfect," was "reasonable." If the respondent's broadcast signals reached a portion of the North Carolina audience, then "this would be in derogation of the substantial federal interest in supporting North Carolina's laws making lotteries illegal." The lower courts were in error in concluding that the statutory restrictions, as applied to the respondent, were ineffectual in that 11% of Edge Broadcasting's audience (the North Carolina residents) also listened to Virginia radio and television ads and read Virginia newspapers, all of which carried the lottery ads: "Even if all of the residents of Edge's North Carolina service area listened to lottery ads from Virginia stations, it would still be true that 11% of radio listening time in that area would be free of such material."

Stevens, J., joined by Blackmun, J., dissented. "[S]uppressing truthful advertising regarding a neighboring State's lottery, an activity which is, of course, perfectly legal, is a patently unconstitutional means of effectuating the Government's asserted interest in protecting the policies of nonlottery States. Indeed, I had thought that we had so held almost two decades ago [in] *Bigelow v. Virginia.*"

Rubin v. Coors Brewing Co., 514 U.S. 476, 115 S.Ct. 1585, 131 L.Ed.2d 532 (1995) invalidated a federal law that prohibited beer labels from displaying alcohol content unless state law required disclosure of alcohol content. Thomas, J., for the Court, applying *Central Hudson,* found that the commercial speech concerned a lawful activity and was not misleading. Next, he rejected the Government argument that the federal labeling law served a substantial interest (supporting state laws that banned display of alcohol content). "Unlike the situation in *Edge Broadcasting,* the policies of some States do not prevent neighboring States from pursuing their own alcohol related policies within their respective borders." States could directly ban disclosure of alcohol content, "subject, of course, to the same First Amendment restrictions that apply to the Federal Government."

The federal law did not "directly and materially advance" the interest in preventing "strength wars" among brewers because of its "overall irrationality." For example, the federal law allowed disclosure of alcohol content on the labels of wine and hard liquor, and even compelled disclosure for wines of more than 14% alcohol. The law also allows brewers to signal high alcohol content by using the term "malt liquor." The labeling ban was also not sufficiently tailored to its goal. Instead of restricting speech, the Government, e.g., could directly limit the alcohol content of beer. The majority refused to rely on the argument raised in *Posadas,* that the "greater power to completely ban" a product "includes the lesser power to ban advertising of" that product; the Court suggested that this argument was dictum.

44 Liquormart, Inc. v. Rhode Island, 517 U.S. 484, 116 S.Ct. 1495, 134 L.Ed.2d 711 (1996) invalidated a state law banning advertisements of accurate information about retail liquor prices except at the point of sale. The Court was fragmented as to its reasoning, but no Justice dissented. Part of Justice Stevens' opinion was the opinion the Court and part was a plurality opinion. Stevens, J., joined by Kennedy, Souter, & Ginsburg, JJ., argued that the state could promote temperance by higher taxes on liquor or educational campaigns, without restricting any speech. "The First Amendment directs us to be especially skeptical of regulations that seek to keep people in the dark for what the government perceives to be their own good." Thomas, J., concurring in the judgment and in parts of the Opinion of the Court, argued that when "the government's asserted interest is to keep legal users of a product or service ignorant in order to manipulate their choices in the marketplace, the balancing test adopted" of *Central Hudson Gas* should not be applied. "Rather, such an 'interest' is *per se* illegitimate and can no more justify regulation of 'commercial' speech than it can justify regulation of 'noncommercial' speech."

Greater New Orleans Broadcasting Association, Inc. v. United States, 527 U.S. 173, 119 S.Ct. 1923, 144 L.Ed.2d 161 (1999). In *Edge Broadcasting,* § 1304 of title 18 was used to bar advertising of Virginia's lottery by a broadcaster located in North Carolina, where lotteries were illegal. In contrast, in this case, the Court, used the four-part *Central Hudson* test and held that § 1304 may not constitutionally be applied to forbid advertisements of private casino gambling broadcast by petitioners' radio and television stations located in Louisiana, where such gambling is legal. The petitioners wanted to broadcast promotional advertising for gaming available at private casinos located in both Louisiana and Mississippi. Under some circumstances, broadcast signals might also be heard in neighboring Texas and Arkansas, where private casino gambling is unlawful. Justice Stevens, who dissented in *Posadas*, wrote the opinion for the Court. He noted that the Court of Appeals, which the Supreme Court reversed, had relied on *Posadas*, but otherwise he did not discuss that case.

The federal law, in this case, cannot satisfy the third and fourth prongs of *Central Hudson*. First, the Court said, citing *Rubin v. Coors Brewing Co.* that the Government's argument (limiting advertising will lessen gambling's social costs by limiting demand) is specious because § 1304 and its regulations are so riddled by exemptions and inconsistencies that the Government cannot hope to exonerate it. For example, the law prohibits broadcasters from carrying advertising about privately operated commercial casinos regardless of the station's or casino's location, but exempts advertising of state-owned casinos, certain occasional commercial casino gambling, and tribal casinos even if the broadcaster is located in, or broadcasts to, a jurisdiction with strict anti-gambling policies. Any differences between non-Indian and Indian businesses do not "justify abridging non-Indians' freedom of speech more severely than the freedom of their tribal competitors. For the power to prohibit or to regulate particular conduct does not necessarily include the power to prohibit or regulate speech about that conduct." Nor can the federal policy be justified as "assisting" states with their policies disfavoring private casinos. Even if these state policies were more coherent than federal policies, § 1304 sacrifices an "intolerable amount of truthful speech about lawful conduct" compared to the social ills that one could reasonably hope such a ban to eliminate.

Rehnquist, C.J., filed a concurring opinion, and Thomas, J., filed an opinion concurring in the judgment, reaffirming his position in *44 Liquormart* that, under the First Amendment, the Government should not be able "to keep legal users of a product or service ignorant in order to manipulate their choices in the marketplace."

FLORIDA BAR v. WENT FOR IT, INC.
515 U.S. 618, 115 S.Ct. 2371, 132 L.Ed.2d 541 (1995).

JUSTICE O'CONNOR delivered the opinion of the Court.

Rules of the Florida Bar prohibit personal injury lawyers from sending targeted direct-mail solicitations to victims and their relatives for 30 days following an accident or disaster. This case asks us to consider whether such rules violate the First and Fourteenth Amendments of the Constitution. We hold that in the circumstances presented here, they do not.

[In 1990, the Florida Supreme Court adopted two rules] at issue in this case. Rule 4–7.4(b)(1) provides that "[a] lawyer shall not send, or knowingly permit to be sent, . . . a written communication to a prospective client for the purpose of obtaining professional employment if: (A) the written communication concerns an action for personal injury or wrongful death or otherwise relates to an accident or disaster involving the person to whom the communication is addressed or a relative of that person, unless the accident or disaster occurred more than 30 days prior to the mailing of the communication." Rule 4–7.8(a) states that "[a] lawyer shall not accept referrals from a lawyer referral service unless the service: (1) engages in no communication with the public and in no direct contact with prospective clients in a manner that would violate the Rules of Professional Conduct if the communication or contact were made by the lawyer." Together, these rules create a brief 30–day blackout period after an accident during which lawyers may not, directly or indirectly, single out accident victims or their relatives in order to solicit their business.

In March 1992, G. Stewart McHenry and his wholly owned lawyer referral service, Went For It, Inc., filed this action for declaratory and injunctive relief in the United States District Court for the Middle District of Florida challenging Rules 4.7–4(b)(1) and 4.7–8 as violative of the First and Fourteenth Amendments to the Constitution. . . .

[W]e engage in "intermediate" scrutiny of restrictions on commercial speech, analyzing them under the framework set forth in *Central Hudson Gas & Electric Corp. v. Public Service Comm'n of N.Y.* (1980). Under *Central Hudson,* the government may freely regulate commercial speech that concerns unlawful activity or is misleading. Commercial speech that falls into neither of those categories, like the advertising at issue here, may be regulated if the government satisfies a test consisting of three related prongs: first, the government must assert a substantial interest in support of its regulation; second, the government must demonstrate that the restriction on commercial speech directly and materially advances that interest; and third, the regulation must be " 'narrowly drawn.' "

"Unlike rational basis review, the *Central Hudson* standard does not permit us to supplant the precise interests put forward by the State with other suppositions." *Edenfield v. Fane* (1993). The Florida Bar asserts that it has a substantial interest in protecting the privacy and tranquility of personal injury victims and their loved ones against intrusive, unsolicited contact by lawyers.* ... The regulation [is also] an effort to protect the flagging reputations of Florida lawyers by preventing them from engaging in conduct that, the Bar maintains, " 'is universally regarded as deplorable and beneath common decency because of its intrusion upon the special vulnerability and private grief of victims or their families.' " We have little trouble crediting the Bar's interest as substantial [because] "the protection of potential clients' privacy is a substantial state interest." See *Edenfield*.

Under *Central Hudson*'s second prong, the State must demonstrate that the challenged regulation "advances the Government's interest 'in a direct and material way.' " That burden, we have explained, " 'is not satisfied by mere speculation and conjecture; rather, a governmental body seeking to sustain a restriction on commercial speech must demonstrate that the harms it recites are real and that its restriction will in fact alleviate them to a material degree.' " In *Edenfield,* the Court invalidated a Florida ban on in-person solicitation by certified public accountants (CPAs). ...Finding nothing in the record to substantiate the State's allegations of harm, we invalidated the regulation.

The direct-mail solicitation regulation before us does not suffer from such infirmities. The Florida Bar submitted a 106–page summary of its 2–year study of lawyer advertising and solicitation to the District Court. That summary contains data—both statistical and anecdotal—supporting the Bar's contentions that the Florida public views direct-mail solicitations in the immediate wake of accidents as an intrusion on privacy that reflects poorly upon the profession.... Fifty-four percent of the general population surveyed said that contacting persons concerning accidents or similar events is a violation of privacy.... Significantly, 27% of direct-mail recipients reported that their regard for the legal profession and for the judicial process as a whole was "lower" as a result of receiving the direct mail.

The anecdotal record mustered by the Bar is noteworthy for its breadth and detail. With titles like "Scavenger Lawyers" (The Miami Herald, Sept. 29, 1987) and "Solicitors Out of Bounds" (St. Petersburg Times, Oct. 26, 1987), newspaper editorial pages in Florida have burgeoned with criticism of Florida lawyers who send targeted direct mail to victims shortly after accidents....

In light of this showing—which respondents at no time refuted, save by the conclusory assertion that the rule lacked "any factual basis,"—we conclude that the Bar has satisfied the second prong of the *Central Hudson* test. In dissent, Justice Kennedy complains that we have before us few indications of the sample size or selection procedures employed by

* At prior stages of this litigation, the Bar asserted a different interest, in addition to that urged now, in protecting people against undue influence and overreaching. Because the Bar does not press this interest before us, we do not consider it....

Magid Associates (a nationally renowned consulting firm) and no copies of the actual surveys employed. [W]e do not read our case law to require that empirical data come to us accompanied by a surfeit of background information. [W]e are satisfied that the ban on direct-mail solicitation in the immediate aftermath of accidents, unlike the rule at issue in *Edenfield,* targets a concrete, nonspeculative harm.

In reaching a contrary conclusion, the Court of Appeals determined that this case was governed squarely by *Shapero v. Kentucky Bar Assn.* (1988). Making no mention of the Bar's study, the court concluded that " 'a targeted letter [does not] invade the recipient's privacy any more than does a substantively identical letter mailed at large. The invasion, if any, occurs when the lawyer discovers the recipient's legal affairs, not when he confronts the recipient with the discovery.' "In many cases, the Court of Appeals explained, "this invasion of privacy will involve no more than reading the newspaper."

While some of *Shapero*'s language might be read to support the Court of Appeals' interpretation, *Shapero* differs in several fundamental respects from the case before us. First and foremost, *Shapero*'s treatment of privacy was casual. Contrary to the dissent's suggestions, the State in *Shapero* did not seek to justify its regulation as a measure undertaken to prevent lawyers' invasions of privacy interests. Rather, the State focused exclusively on the special dangers of overreaching inhering in targeted solicitations. Second, in contrast to this case, *Shapero* dealt with a broad ban on *all* direct-mail solicitations, whatever the time frame and whoever the recipient. Finally, the State in *Shapero* assembled no evidence attempting to demonstrate any actual harm caused by targeted direct mail. . . .

[In this case, the] intrusion targeted by the Bar's regulation stems not from the fact that a lawyer has learned about an accident or disaster (as the Court of Appeals notes, in many instances a lawyer need only read the newspaper to glean this information), but from the lawyer's confrontation of victims or relatives with such information, while wounds are still open, in order to solicit their business. In this respect, an untargeted letter mailed to society at large is different in kind from a targeted solicitation; the untargeted letter involves no willful or knowing affront to or invasion of the tranquility of bereaved or injured individuals and simply does not cause the same kind of reputational harm to the profession unearthed by the Florida Bar's study.

Nor do we find *Bolger v. Youngs Drug Products Corp.* (1983), dispositive of the issue, despite any superficial resemblance. In *Bolger,* we rejected the Federal Government's paternalistic effort to ban potentially "offensive" and "intrusive" direct-mail advertisements for contraceptives. [But] the harm targeted by the Florida Bar cannot be eliminated by a brief journey to the trash can. The purpose of the 30–day targeted direct-mail ban is to forestall the outrage and irritation with the state-licensed legal profession that the practice of direct solicitation only days after accidents has engendered. The Bar is concerned not with citizens' "offense" in the abstract, but with the demonstrable detrimental effects that such "offense" has on the profession it regulates....

Passing to *Central Hudson*'s third prong, we examine the relationship between the Florida Bar's interests and the means chosen to serve them. See *Board of Trustees of State University of N.Y. v. Fox*. With respect to this prong, the differences between commercial speech and noncommercial speech are manifest. In *Fox*, we made clear that the "least restrictive means" test has no role in the commercial speech context. "What our decisions require," instead, [is a fit] that is not necessarily perfect, but reasonable....

Respondents levy a great deal of criticism, [which] may be parsed into two components. First, the rule does not distinguish between victims in terms of the severity of their injuries. According to respondents, the rule is unconstitutionally overinclusive insofar as it bans targeted mailings even to citizens whose injuries or grief are relatively minor. Second, the rule may prevent citizens from learning about their legal options, particularly at a time when other actors—opposing counsel and insurance adjusters—may be clamoring for victims' attentions. Any benefit arising from the Bar's regulation, respondents implicitly contend, is outweighed by these costs.

We are not persuaded by respondents' allegations of constitutional infirmity. We find little deficiency in the ban's failure to distinguish among injured Floridians by the severity of their pain or the intensity of their grief.... Unlike respondents, we do not see "numerous and obvious less-burdensome alternatives" to Florida's short temporal ban....

Respondents' second point would have force if the Bar's rule were not limited to a brief period and if there were not many other ways for injured Floridians to learn about the availability of legal representation during that time. Our lawyer advertising cases have afforded lawyers a great deal of leeway to devise innovative ways to attract new business. Florida permits lawyers to advertise on prime-time television and radio as well as in newspapers and other media. They may rent space on billboards. They may send untargeted letters to the general population, or to discrete segments thereof. There are, of course, pages upon pages devoted to lawyers in the Yellow Pages of Florida telephone directories.... These ample alternative channels for receipt of information about the availability of legal representation during the 30–day period following accidents may explain why, despite the ample evidence, testimony, and commentary submitted by those favoring (as well as opposing) unrestricted direct-mail solicitation, respondents have not pointed to—and we have not independently found—a single example of an individual case in which immediate solicitation helped to avoid, or failure to solicit within 30 days brought about, the harms that concern the dissent. In fact, the record contains considerable empirical survey information suggesting that Floridians have little difficulty finding lawyers when they need one. ...

The judgment of the Court of Appeals, accordingly, is *reversed.*

JUSTICE KENNEDY, with whom JUSTICE STEVENS, JUSTICE SOUTER, and JUSTICE GINSBURG join, dissenting.

Attorneys who communicate their willingness to assist potential clients are engaged in speech protected by the First and Fourteenth Amendments. That principle has been understood since *Bates v. State Bar of Arizona.* The Court today undercuts this guarantee in an important class of cases and unsettles leading First Amendment precedents, at the expense of those victims most in need of legal assistance. With all respect for the Court, in my view its solicitude for the privacy of victims and its concern for our profession are misplaced and self-defeating, even upon the Court's own premises.

I take it to be uncontroverted that when an accident results in death or injury, it is often urgent at once to investigate the occurrence, identify witnesses, and preserve evidence. Vital interests in speech and expression are, therefore, at stake when by law an attorney cannot direct a letter to the victim or the family explaining this simple fact and offering competent legal assistance. Meanwhile, represented and better informed parties, or parties who have been solicited in ways more sophisticated and indirect, may be at work. Indeed, these parties, either themselves or by their attorneys, investigators, and adjusters, are free to contact the unrepresented persons to gather evidence or offer settlement. This scheme makes little sense. As is often true when the law makes little sense, it is not first principles but their interpretation and application that have gone awry. [W]hat is at stake is the suppression of information and knowledge that transcends the financial self-interests of the speaker.

[T]he first of the *Central Hudson* factors to be considered is whether the interest the State pursues in enacting the speech restriction is a substantial one. The State says two different interests meet this standard. The first is the interest "in protecting the personal privacy and tranquility" of the victim and his or her family. . . . The problem the Court confronts, and cannot overcome, is our recent decision in *Shapero v. Kentucky Bar Assn.* (1988). [W]e made an explicit distinction between direct in-person solicitations and direct mail solicitations. *Shapero,* like this case, involved a direct mail solicitation, and there the State recited its fears of "overreaching and undue influence." We found, however, no such dangers presented by direct mail advertising. "[A] letter, like a printed advertisement (but unlike a lawyer), can readily be put in a drawer to be considered later, ignored, or discarded." . . .

To avoid the controlling effect of *Shapero* in the case before us, the Court seeks to declare that a different privacy interest is implicated. As it sees the matter, the substantial concern is that victims or their families will be offended by receiving a solicitation during their grief and trauma. But we do not allow restrictions on speech to be justified on the ground that the expression might offend the listener. On the contrary, we have said that these "are classically not justifications validating the suppression of expression protected by the First Amendment." *Carey v.*

Population Services International (1977). And in *Zauderer v. Office of Disciplinary Counsel of Supreme Court of Ohio* (1985), where we struck down a ban on attorney advertising, we held that "the mere possibility that some members of the population might find advertising . . . offensive cannot justify suppressing it. The same must hold true for advertising that some members of the bar might find beneath their dignity."

We have applied this principle to direct mail cases as well as with respect to general advertising, noting that the right to use the mails is protected by the First Amendment. See *Bolger v. Youngs Drug Products Corp.* (1983)(Rehnquist, J., concurring). In *Bolger,* we held that a statute designed to "shiel[d] recipients of mail from materials that they are likely to find offensive" furthered an interest of "little weight," noting that "we have consistently held that the fact that protected speech may be offensive to some does not justify its suppression." It is only where an audience is captive that we will assure its protection from some offensive speech. The occupants of a household receiving mailings are not a captive audience, and the asserted interest in preventing their offense should be no more controlling here than in our prior cases. All the recipient of objectional mailings need do is to take "the 'short, though regular, journey from mail box to trash can.'" As we have observed, this is "an acceptable burden, at least so far as the Constitution is concerned." If these cases forbidding restrictions on speech that might be offensive are to be overruled, the Court should say so.

In the face of these difficulties of logic and precedent, the State and the opinion of the Court turn to a second interest: protecting the reputation and dignity of the legal profession. The argument is, it seems fair to say, that all are demeaned by the crass behavior of a few. The argument takes a further step in the *amicus* brief filed by the Association of Trial Lawyers of America. There it is said that disrespect for the profession from this sort of solicitation (but presumably from no other sort of solicitation) results in lower jury verdicts. [But] direct solicitation may serve vital purposes and promote the administration of justice, and to the extent the bar seeks to protect lawyers' reputations by preventing them from engaging in speech some deem offensive, the State is doing nothing more (as *amicus* the Association of Trial Lawyers of America is at least candid enough to admit) than manipulating the public's opinion by suppressing speech that informs us how the legal system works. . . . This, of course, is censorship pure and simple; and censorship is antithetical to the first principles of free expression.

Even were the interests asserted substantial, the regulation here fails the second part of the *Central Hudson* test, which requires that the dangers the State seeks to eliminate be real and that a speech restriction or ban advance that asserted State interest in a direct and material way. [W]hat the State has offered falls well short of demonstrating that the harms it is trying to redress are real, let alone that the regulation directly and materially advances the State's interests. . . . There is no description of the statistical universe or scientific framework that permits any productive use of the information the so-called Summary of

Record contains. The majority describes this anecdotal matter as "noteworthy for its breadth and detail," but when examined, it is noteworthy for its incompetence. The selective synopses of unvalidated studies deal, for the most part, with television advertising and phone book listings, and not direct mail solicitations.... The most generous reading of this document permits identification of 34 pages on which direct mail solicitation is arguably discussed. Of these, only two are even a synopsis of a study of the attitudes of Floridians towards such solicitations. The bulk of the remaining pages include comments by lawyers about direct mail (some of them favorable), excerpts from citizen complaints about such solicitation, and a few excerpts from newspaper articles on the topic. Our cases require something more than a few pages of self-serving and unsupported statements by the State to demonstrate that a regulation directly and materially advances the elimination of a real harm when the State seeks to suppress truthful and nondeceptive speech.

It is telling that the essential thrust of all the material adduced to justify the State's interest is devoted to the reputational concerns of the Bar. It is not at all clear that this regulation advances the interest of protecting persons who are suffering trauma and grief, and we are cited to no material in the record for that claim. Indeed, when asked at oral argument what a "typical injured plaintiff get[s] in the mail," the Bar's lawyer replied: "That's not in the record ... and I don't know the answer to that question." Having declared that the privacy interest is one both substantial and served by the regulation, the Court ought not to be excused from justifying its conclusion.

[P]rompt legal representation is essential where death or injury results from accidents. The only seeming justification for the State's restriction is the one the Court itself offers, which is that attorneys can and do resort to other ways of communicating important legal information to potential clients. Quite aside from the latent protectionism for the established bar that the argument discloses, it fails for the more fundamental reason that it concedes the necessity for the very representation the attorneys solicit and the State seeks to ban. The accident victims who are prejudiced to vindicate the State's purported desire for more dignity in the legal profession will be the very persons who most need legal advice, for they are the victims who, because they lack education, linguistic ability, or familiarity with the legal system, are unable to seek out legal services.

[T]he Court neglects the fact that this problem is largely self-policing: Potential clients will not hire lawyers who offend them. And even if a person enters into a contract with an attorney and later regrets it, Florida, like some other States, allows clients to rescind certain contracts with attorneys within a stated time after they are executed. The State's restriction deprives accident victims of information which may be critical to their right to make a claim for compensation for injuries. The telephone book and general advertisements may serve this purpose in part; but the direct solicitation ban will fall on those who most need legal representation: for those with minor injuries, the victims too ill-informed to know an attorney may be interested in their cases; for those with serious injuries, the victims too ill-informed to know that time is of the essence if counsel is to assemble evidence and warn them not to enter into settlement negotiations or evidentiary discussions with investigators for opposing parties. ...The very fact that some 280,000 direct mail solicitations are sent to accident victims and their survivors in Florida each year is some indication of the efficacy of this device....

It is most ironic that, for the first time since *Bates v. State Bar of Arizona,* the Court now orders a major retreat from the constitutional guarantees for commercial speech in order to shield its own profession from public criticism. Obscuring the financial aspect of the legal profession from public discussion through direct mail solicitation, at the expense of the least sophisticated members of society, is not a laudable constitutional goal. There is no authority for the proposition that the Constitution permits the State to promote the public image of the legal profession by suppressing information about the profession's business aspects....

Notes

1. Newspapers reported that Justice Breyer was the crucial fifth vote in *Went for It,* and that Justice O'Connor went out of her way to accommodate his views. Therefore, in one particular paragraph she emphasized that lawyers have alternatives to attract accident victims: lawyers may "send untargeted letters to the general population, or to discrete segments thereof."* What do you think of this distinction? Is the Court saying that the first amendment gives lawyers the right to send out general mailings, but lawyers may not send out letters targeted to people most likely to need their services? Should the first amendment allow the mailing of advertisements only if the mailing is done in an inefficient manner?

2. The Florida rule at issue in this case only applied if the targeted letter is sent "to a prospective client." Hence the rule did not govern contact by defense attorneys at all, who remained free to contact tort victims and urge them not to sue and to accept a settlement. Why should this rule make the distinction between targeted mailing by plaintiff-lawyers and targeted mailing (or even personal visits) by defense-lawyers? For 30 days, are accident victims fair game for defense lawyers?

3. The majority emphasized that some recipients of the targeted mailing sent within 30 days of an accident did not like to receive such letters. Should we not expect that those people who do not like to hire lawyers who send such letters will not do so, while those people who find the letters useful will hire the lawyers. If most people do not like the letters, lawyers who send them will learn not to waste their money on them. However, under the Florida rule, a client may find that he or she has hired the type of lawyer who (but for the Florida rule) would have sent such targeted mailings. Therefore, by keeping people in the dark, the Florida rule takes away from

* Paul Barrett, "Split Court Lets States Curb Ambulance Chasers," Wall St. Jrl., June 22, 1995, at B1, col. 6, B10, col. 4 (midwest ed.)

clients the right to refuse to hire a lawyer who would send this type of targeted mail.

4. The ABA has engaged in extensive study of legal advertising and its affects on the public perception of lawyers. ABA COMMISSION ON ADVERTISING, LAWYER ADVERTISING AT THE CROSSROADS (1995). It could not replicate what Florida purported to find. In fact, the ABA study showed one remarkable steady correlation: if a state bar association, in preparation for a judicial challenge, sponsors a study linking the public perception of lawyers with advertising or targeted mail, only then does the study find a negative relationship. The actual Florida study threw out some results and did not consider others. Even then, Floridians were nearly evenly divided between those who opposed targeted mail and those who actually wanted to receive it. Most people, it turns out, have their perception of lawyers shaped not by advertising or mailings but by reading and watching fictionalized portrayals of lawyers. When people were asked to name the lawyer they most admire, frequently cited names were Perry Mason and Matlock. Matlock is more widely admired than Hillary Rodham Clinton.**

10–8. DEFAMATION AND PRIVACY

10–8.1 Defamation

NEW YORK TIMES CO. v. SULLIVAN
376 U.S. 254, 84 S.Ct. 710, 11 L.Ed.2d 686 (1964).

MR. JUSTICE BRENNAN delivered the opinion of the Court.

We are required in this case to determine for the first time the extent to which the constitutional protections for speech and press limit a State's power to award damages in a libel action brought by a public official against critics of his official conduct.

Respondent L.B. Sullivan is one of the three elected Commissioners of the City of Montgomery, Alabama. He testified that he was "Commissioner of Public Affairs and the duties are supervision of the Police Department, Fire Department, Department of Cemetery and Department of Scales." He brought this civil libel action against the four individual petitioners, who are Negroes and Alabama clergymen, and against petitioner the New York Times Company, a New York corporation which publishes the New York Times, a daily newspaper. A jury in the Circuit Court of Montgomery County awarded him damages of $500,000, the full amount claimed, against all the petitioners, and the Supreme Court of Alabama affirmed.

Respondent's complaint alleged that he had been libeled by statements in a full-page advertisement that was carried in the New York Times on March 29, 1960. [The advertisement appealed for funds and described certain events.] ... Of the 10 paragraphs of text in the

** See, William E. Hornsby, Jr. & Kurt Schimmel, Regulating Lawyer Advertising: Public Images and the Irresistible Aristote- lian Impulse, 9 Georgetown J. of Legal Ethics 325 (1996).

advertisement, the third and a portion of the sixth were the basis of respondent's claim of libel. They read as follows:

Third paragraph:

In Montgomery, Alabama, after students sang "My Country, 'Tis of Thee" on the State Capitol steps, their leaders were expelled from school, and truckloads of police armed with shotguns and tear-gas ringed the Alabama State College Campus. When the entire student body protested to state authorities by refusing to re-register, their dining hall was padlocked in an attempt to starve them into submission.

Sixth paragraph:

Again and again the Southern violators have answered Dr. King's peaceful protests with intimidation and violence. They have bombed his home almost killing his wife and child. They have assaulted his person. They have arrested him seven times—for "speeding", "loitering" and similar "offenses." And now they have charged him with "perjury"—a *felony* under which they could imprison him for *ten years* . . . .

Although neither of these statements mentions respondent by name, he contended that the word "police" in the third paragraph referred to him as the Montgomery Commissioner who supervised the Police Department, so that he was being accused of "ringing" the campus with police. He further claimed that the paragraph would be read as imputing to the police, and hence to him, the padlocking of the dining hall in order to starve the students into submission. As to the sixth paragraph, he contended that since arrests are ordinarily made by the police, the statement "They have arrested [Dr. King] seven times" would be read as referring to him. . . .

It is uncontroverted that some of the statements contained in the two paragraphs were not accurate descriptions of events which occurred in Montgomery. [For example, although] Negro students staged a demonstration on the State Capitol steps, they sang the National Anthem and not "My Country, 'Tis of Thee." Dr. King had not been arrested seven times, but only four; and although he claimed to have been assaulted some years earlier in connection with his arrest for loitering outside a courtroom, one of the officers who made the arrest denied that there was such an assault. . . .

Under Alabama law as applied in this case, a publication is "libelous per se" if the words "tend to injure a person . . . in his reputation" or to "bring [him] into public contempt"; the trial court stated that the standard was met if the words are such as to "injure him in his public office, or impute misconduct to him in his office, or want of official integrity, or want of fidelity to a public trust . . ." The jury must find that the words were published "of and concerning" the plaintiff, but where the plaintiff is a public official his place in the governmental hierarchy is sufficient evidence to support a finding that his reputation has been affected by statements that reflect upon the agency of which he is in charge. Once "libel per se" has been established, the defendant has no defense as to stated facts unless he can persuade the jury that they were true in all their particulars.... Unless he can discharge the burden of proving truth, general damages are presumed, and may be awarded without proof of pecuniary injury. A showing of actual malice is apparently a prerequisite to recovery of punitive damages, and the defendant may in any event forestall a punitive award by a retraction meeting the statutory requirements. Good motives and belief in truth do not negate an inference of malice, but are relevant only in mitigation of punitive damages if the jury chooses to accord them weight.

The question before us is whether this rule of liability, as applied to an action brought by a public official against critics of his official conduct, abridges the freedom of speech and of the press that is guaranteed by the First and Fourteenth Amendments....

The general proposition that freedom of expression upon public questions is secured by the First Amendment has long been settled by our decisions. The constitutional safeguard, we have said, "was fashioned to assure unfettered interchange of ideas for the bringing about of political and social changes desired by the people." ... The First Amendment, said Judge Learned Hand, "presupposes that right conclusions are more likely to be gathered out of a multitude of tongues, than through any kind of authoritative selection. To many this is, and always will be, folly; but we have staked upon it our all." *United States v. Associated Press,* 52 F.Supp. 362, 372 (S.D.N.Y.1943)....

Thus we consider this case against the background of a profound national commitment to the principle that debate on public issues should be uninhibited, robust, and wide-open, and that it may well include vehement, caustic, and sometimes unpleasantly sharp attacks on government and public officials. The present advertisement, as an expression of grievance and protest on one of the major public issues of our time, would seem clearly to qualify for the constitutional protection. The question is whether it forfeits that protection by the falsity of some of its factual statements and by its alleged defamation of respondent. [It is recognized that] erroneous statement is inevitable in free debate, and that it must be protected if the freedoms of expression are to have the "breathing space" that they "need ... to survive." ...

Injury to official reputation affords no more warrant for repressing speech that would otherwise be free than does factual error. Where judicial officers are involved, this Court has held that concern for the dignity and reputation of the courts does not justify the punishment as criminal contempt of criticism of the judge or his decision.... If judges are to be treated as "men of fortitude, able to thrive in a hardy climate," surely the same must be true of other government officials, such as elected city commissioners. Criticism of their official conduct does not lose its constitutional protection merely because it is effective criticism and hence diminishes their official reputations.

If neither factual error nor defamatory content suffices to remove the constitutional shield from criticism of official conduct, the combination of the two elements is no less inadequate. This is the lesson to be drawn from the great controversy over the Sedition Act of 1798, 1 Stat. 596, which first crystallized a national awareness of the central meaning of the First Amendment. That statute made it a crime, punishable by a $5,000 fine and five years in prison, "if any person shall write, print, utter or publish ... any false, scandalous and malicious writing or writings against the government of the United States, or either house of the Congress ... , or the President ... , with intent to defame ... or to bring them, or either of them, into contempt or disrepute; or to excite against them, or either or any of them, the hatred of the good people of the United States." The Act allowed the defendant the defense of truth, and provided that the jury were to be judges both of the law and the facts. Despite these qualifications, the Act was vigorously condemned as unconstitutional in an attack joined in by Jefferson and Madison....

Although the Sedition Act was never tested in this Court, the attack upon its validity has carried the day in the court of history. Fines levied in its prosecution were repaid by Act of Congress on the ground that it was unconstitutional. Calhoun, reporting to the Senate on February 4, 1836, assumed that its invalidity was a matter "which no one now doubts." Jefferson, as President, pardoned those who had been convicted and sentenced under the Act and remitted their fines, stating: "I discharged every person under punishment or prosecution under the sedition law, because I considered, and now consider, that law to be a nullity, as absolute and as palpable as if Congress had ordered us to fall down and worship a golden image." The invalidity of the Act has also been assumed by Justices of this Court. See Holmes, J., dissenting and joined by Brandeis, J., in *Abrams v. United States,* [§ 10–1, supra]; Jackson, J., dissenting in *Beauharnais v. Illinois,* 343 U.S. 250, 288–289, 72 S.Ct. 725, 96 L.Ed. 919; Douglas, The Right of the People (1958), p. 47. These views reflect a broad consensus that the Act, because of the restraint it imposed upon criticism of government and public officials, was inconsistent with the First Amendment....

What a State may not constitutionally bring about by means of a criminal statute is likewise beyond the reach of its civil law of libel. The fear of damage awards under a rule such as that invoked by the Alabama courts here may be markedly more inhibiting than the fear of prosecution under a criminal statute. Alabama, for example, has a criminal libel law.... Presumably a person charged with violation of this statute enjoys ordinary criminal-law safeguards such as the requirements of an indictment and of proof beyond a reasonable doubt. These safeguards are not available to the defendant in a civil action. The judgment awarded in this case—without the need for any proof of actual pecuniary loss—was one thousand times greater than the maximum fine provided by the Alabama criminal statute, and one hundred times greater than that provided by the Sedition Act. And since there is no double-jeopardy limitation applicable to civil lawsuits, this is not the only judgment that may be awarded against petitioners for the same publication. Whether or not a newspaper can survive a succession of such judgments, the pall of fear and timidity imposed upon those who would give voice to public criticism is an atmosphere in which the First Amendment freedoms cannot survive. Plainly the Alabama law of civil libel is "a form of regulation that creates hazards to protected freedoms markedly greater than those that attend reliance upon the criminal law."

The state rule of law is not saved by its allowance of the defense of truth. . . . A rule compelling the critic of official conduct to guarantee the truth of all his factual assertions—and to do so on pain of libel judgments virtually unlimited in amount—leads to a comparable "self-censorship." Allowance of the defense of truth, with the burden of proving it on the defendant, does not mean that only false speech will be deterred. . . . Under such a rule, would-be critics of official conduct may be deterred from voicing their criticism, even though it is believed to be true and even though it is in fact true, because of doubt whether it can be provided in court or fear of the expense of having to do so. They tend to make only statements which "steer far wider of the unlawful zone." The rule thus dampens the vigor and limits the variety of public debate. It is inconsistent with the First and Fourteenth Amendments.

The constitutional guarantees require, we think, a federal rule that prohibits a public official from recovering damages for a defamatory falsehood relating to his official conduct unless he proves that the statement was made with "actual malice"—that is, with knowledge that it was false or with reckless disregard of whether it was false or not. . . .

We hold today that the Constitution delimits a State's power to award damages for libel in actions brought by public officials against critics of their official conduct. Since this is such an action,* the rule requiring proof of actual malice is applicable. While Alabama law apparently requires proof of actual malice for an award of punitive damages, where general damages are concerned malice is "presumed." Such a presumption is inconsistent with the federal rule. "The power to create presumptions is not a means of escape from constitutional restrictions." . . . Since the trial judge did not instruct the jury to differentiate between general and punitive damages, it may be that the verdict was wholly an award of one or the other. But it is impossible to know, in view of the general verdict returned. Because of this uncertainty, the judgment must be reversed and the case remanded.

Since respondent may seek a new trial, we deem that considerations of effective judicial administration require us to review the evidence in the present record to determine whether it could constitutionally support a judgment for respondent. This Court's duty is not limited to the elaboration of constitutional principles; we must also in proper cases

---

* We have no occasion here to determine how far down into the lower ranks of government employees the "public official" designation would extend for purposes of this rule, or otherwise to specify categories of persons who would or would not be included. . . .

review the evidence to make certain that those principles have been constitutionally applied. This is such a case, particularly since the question is one of alleged trespass across "the line between speech unconditionally guaranteed and speech which may legitimately be regulated." ...

Applying these standards, we consider that the proof presented to show actual malice lacks the convincing clarity which the constitutional standard demands, and hence that it would not constitutionally sustain the judgment for respondent under the proper rule of law. The case of the individual petitioners requires little discussion. Even assuming that they could constitutionally be found to have authorized the use of their names on the advertisement, there was no evidence whatever that they were aware of any erroneous statements or were in any way reckless in that regard. The judgment against them is thus without constitutional support.

As to the Times, we similarly conclude that the facts do not support a finding of actual malice. [T]here is evidence that the Times published the advertisement without checking its accuracy against the news stories in the Times' own files. The mere presence of the stories in the files does not, of course, establish that the Times "knew" the advertisement was false, since the state of mind required for actual malice would have to be brought home to the persons in the Times' organization having responsibility for the publication of the advertisement.... We think the evidence against the Times supports at most a finding of negligence in failing to discover the misstatements, and is constitutionally insufficient to show the recklessness that is required for a finding of actual malice....

[The concurring opinion of BLACK, J., joined by DOUGLAS, J., and the opinion of GOLDBERG, J., joined by DOUGLAS, J., concurring in the result, are omitted.]

Notes

1. PUBLIC OFFICIALS AND THE AREAS OF PUBLIC COMMENT. *Rosenblatt v. Baer,* 383 U.S. 75, 86 S.Ct. 669, 15 L.Ed.2d 597 (1966), applied the New York Times malice test to a defamation action brought by the Supervisor of the Belknap County Recreation Area, a ski resort. The Belknap County Commissioners, an elected group, employed the Supervisor. After the Supervisor was discharged, a local newspaper column could be read as attacking the former Supervisor. The Court rejected the idea that the definition of "public official" should be supplied by reference to state law:

> the "public official" designation applies at the very least to those among the hierarchy of government employees who have, or appear to the public to have, substantial responsibility for or control over the conduct of government affairs.... Where a position in government has such apparent importance that the public has an independent interest in the qualifications and performance of the person who holds it, beyond the general public interest in the qualifications and performance of all employees ... the New York Times malice standards apply.

By way of footnote the Court rejected the suggestion that its test might apply to a night watchman accused of stealing state secrets. "The employee's position must be one which would invite public scrutiny and discussion of the person holding it, entirely apart from the scrutiny and discussion occasioned by the particular charges in the controversy."

Monitor Patriot Co. v. Roy, 401 U.S. 265, 91 S.Ct. 621, 28 L.Ed.2d 35 (1971) held that the New York Times rule was also intended to apply to *candidates* for public office.

Garrison v. Louisiana, 379 U.S. 64, 85 S.Ct. 209, 13 L.Ed.2d 125 (1964) reversed a conviction for criminal libel of a man who had charged that certain state court judges were inefficient, took excessive vacations, opposed official investigations of vice, and were possibly subject to racketeer influences. "The New York Times rule is not rendered inapplicable because an official's private reputation, as well as his public reputation, is harmed. The public official rule protects the paramount public interest in a free flow of information to the people concerning public officials, their servants. To this end, anything which might touch on an official's fitness for office is relevant." In *Monitor Patriot Co. v. Roy,* supra, the Court added: "The principal activity of a candidate in our political system, his 'office', so to speak, consists in putting before the voters every conceivable aspect of his public and private life that he thinks may lead the electorate to gain a good impression of him."

2. PUBLIC FIGURES. *Curtis Publishing Co. v. Butts,* 388 U.S. 130, 87 S.Ct. 1975, 18 L.Ed.2d 1094 (1967) extended New York Times to apply to "public figures". Butts, at the time of the alleged defamation, was the athletic director of the University of Georgia. In a companion case, *Associated Press v. Walker,* the Court applied *New York Times* to Walker, a private citizen accused of leading a violent crowd against federal marshals enforcing a court's desegregation decree. He was a former Army general and "a man of some political prominence." Chief Justice Warren's concurrence explained that public figures are those "who do not hold public office at the moment [but] are nevertheless intimately involved in the resolution of important public questions or, by reason of their fame, shape events in areas of concern to society at large."

3. In *Herbert v. Lando,* 441 U.S. 153, 99 S.Ct. 1635, 60 L.Ed.2d 115 (1979) the media defendants in a libel action urged the Court to create a special First Amendment privilege for the Press to use when sued for libel: "we are urged to hold for the first time that when a member of the press is alleged to have circulated damaging falsehoods and is sued for injury to the plaintiff's reputation, the plaintiff is barred from inquiring into the editorial processes of those responsible for the publication, even though the inquiry would produce evidence material to the proof of a critical element of his cause of action." The Court refused because *"New York Times* and its progeny made it essential to proving liability that the plaintiff focus on the conduct and state of mind of the defendant." Therefore, "the thoughts and editorial processes of the alleged defamer" are open to examination.

4. JURISDICTION. *Keeton v. Hustler Magazine, Inc.,* 465 U.S. 770, 104 S.Ct. 1473, 79 L.Ed.2d 790 (1984) held, with no dissent, that the defendant's regular circulation of magazines in New Hampshire allows that state to assert jurisdiction in a libel action based on the contents of the magazine. Plaintiff was not a resident of New Hampshire, but sued there because the statutes of limitations in every jurisdiction except New Hampshire had run on Plaintiff's cause of action. New Hampshire, like most states, followed the "single publication rule," which allowed a successful plaintiff to collect damages caused in *all* states even though most of her injuries had been sustained outside of New Hampshire. *Calder v. Jones,* 465 U.S. 783, 104 S.Ct. 1482, 79 L.Ed.2d 804 (1984), decided the same day, refused to add any special free speech considerations on top of the ordinary "sufficient contacts" requirements of due process: "[T]he potential chill on protected First Amendment activity stemming from libel and defamation actions is already taken into account in the constitutional limitations on the substantive law governing such suits. To reintroduce those concepts at the jurisdictional stage would be a form of double counting."

5.   SCOPE OF REVIEW. *Bose Corp. v. Consumers Union of the United States, Inc.,* 466 U.S. 485, 104 S.Ct. 1949, 80 L.Ed.2d 502 (1984) Court held that, in a libel case, because of first amendment concerns, the appellate court is not limited to the "clearly erroneous" standard in reviewing the trial judge's factual conclusions in order to determine whether a news organization acted with actual malice. The appellate court must perform an independent review.*

Anderson v. Liberty Lobby, Inc., 477 U.S. 242, 106 S.Ct. 2505, 91 L.Ed.2d 202 (1986) held that, in a New York Times libel action, a court, when a ruling on defendant's summary judgment motion, must determine whether the evidence presented could support a reasonable jury finding that plaintiff has demonstrated New York Times malice with "convincing clarity." Thus the Court, per White, J., held that a district court acted properly when it granted summary judgment to Jack Anderson and others who were sued because they published articles describing various respondents (including Willis Carto, the founder of Liberty Lobby, Inc., a self-styled citizens lobby) as neo-Nazi, anti-Semitic, and racist. Anderson submitted an affidavit by the author of the two articles in question. The affidavit said that the reporter had spent a substantial amount of time researching the articles and that the facts were obtained from a wide variety of sources. He detailed the sources for the statements alleged to be libelous. The reporter said he believed and still believes the truth of the statements made. The respondents argued that several sources were patently unreliable and that the petitioners had failed to adequately verify their information. Because a summary judgment motion is similar to a directed verdict motion, plaintiff must show more than a mere "scintilla" of evidence: "there must be evidence on which the jury could reasonably find for the plaintiff." While the defendant has the burden to show no genuine issue of fact, the plaintiff—in order to survive the summary judgment motion—must present affirmative evidence to support a jury

---

* A study of 112 libel appeals over a 10 year period showed that media defendants were quite successful on appeal because of the requirement of an independent appellate review. Only 28.3% of the damage awards made it through the appeal process undisturbed; 41.3% of the libel verdicts against media defendants were reversed entirely; 14.1% were reversed in part, with new trials ordered; in 16.3% of the libel verdicts against media defendants, the courts of appeal upheld the verdicts but threw out or reduced the damages. Milo Geylelin, Libel Defendants Fare Well on Appeal, Research Finds, Wall St.Jrl., May 31, 1994, at B10, col. 1 (midwest ed.)

verdict. "This is true even where the evidence is likely to be within the possession of the defendant, as long as the plaintiff has held a full opportunity to conduct discovery."

Harte–Hanks Communications Inc. v. Connaughton, 491 U.S. 657, 109 S.Ct. 2678, 105 L.Ed.2d 562 (1989) upheld, with no dissents, a $200,000 libel verdict ($5,000 compensatory and $195,000 punitive damages) in favor of an unsuccessful candidate for judge and against a local newspaper that supported the reelection of the incumbent. This case was the first in 22 years where the Supreme Court upheld a damage award against the news media in a case filed by a public figure. Respondent alleged that the newspaper published a defamatory, false story, with *New York Times* "malice." Stevens, J., for the Court, ruled that "a public figure plaintiff must prove more than an extreme departure from professional standards and that a newspaper's motive in publishing a story—whether to promote an opponent's candidacy or to increase its circulation—cannot provide a sufficient basis for finding actual malice." "Reckless disregard" means that the defendant has a "high degree of awareness of ... probable falsity" or has "entertained serious doubts as to the truth of his publication." The Court then carefully examined the testimony and concluded that there was "clear and convincing proof" supporting the jury finding of "actual malice." The reviewing court "must consider the factual record in full," although "credibility determinations are reviewed under the clearly erroneous standard" because the fact finders could observe the demeanor of the witnesses. In affirming the damage award, the Court considered the trial court's instructions, the jury's answers to three special interrogatories, and the facts not in dispute.

6. THE PETITION CLAUSE. *McDonald v. Smith,* 472 U.S. 479, 105 S.Ct. 2787, 86 L.Ed.2d 384 (1985) held that the Petition Clause of the First Amendment does not give a defendant in a libel action absolute immunity. The plaintiff had charged defendant with knowingly sending false and libelous letters to President Reagan and others in order to undermine the chances of plaintiff being appointed U.S. Attorney. The Petition Clause does not require state libel law to expand the qualified privilege already afforded by *New York Times v. Sullivan.*

7. EMOTIONAL DISTRESS. *Hustler Magazine v. Falwell,* 485 U.S. 46, 108 S.Ct. 876, 99 L.Ed.2d 41 (1988). *Hustler Magazine* published a parody of a Compari Liqueur advertisement, entitled, "Jerry Falwell talks about his first time." Actual Compari advertisements included interviews with famous personalities about the "first time" they tried Compari, with the sexual double entendre of the "first time." The parody resembled a Compari advertisement and included an alleged interview with Jerry Falwell, a nationally known minister, host of a nationally syndicated television show, and commentator on public affairs. Neither party disputed that Jerry Falwell was a public figure. In the parody, Jerry Falwell stated that his "first time" was during a drunken incestuous meeting with his mother in an outhouse. The bottom of the page contained the disclaimer: "Fiction; Ad and Personality Parody." Jerry Falwell filed suit and, while that case was pending, *Hustler* reprinted the parody. The jury awarded $100,000 in actual damages and $50,000 in punitive damages.

The Court held that a public figure or public official may not recover for the tort of intentional infliction of emotional distress without showing that the publication at issue contains a "false statement of fact which was made with 'actual malice,' i.e., with knowledge that the statement was false or with reckless disregard as to whether or not it was true." The plaintiff did not meet this test because the jury found that the *Hustler* parody could not reasonably be understood as describing actual facts about the plaintiff or actual events in which he participated. "Were we to hold otherwise, there can be little doubt that political cartoonists and satirists would be subjected to damages awards without any showing that their work falsely defamed its subject." The Court conceded that political cartoons are to the politician about as welcome as a bee sting. For example, early cartoons portrayed George Washington as an ass.*

8. FABRICATED QUOTATIONS. *Masson v. New Yorker Magazine, Inc.*, 501 U.S. 496, 111 S.Ct. 2419, 115 L.Ed.2d 447 (1991). A public figure sued for libel, claiming that an author (in the course of writing a very unflattering portrait of him) used quotation marks, with knowledge of their inaccuracy, to attribute to him comments that he had not made. The Court, per Kennedy, J., ruled that the attributed quotations had the degrees of falsity required to prove a state of mind of deliberate or reckless falsification (that is, *New York Times* "malice"), so that the plaintiff could defeat a motion for summary judgment and go to trial on the merits. The Court considered six purported quotations, yet "in each instance no identical statement appears in more than 40 hours of taped interviews." The plaintiff claimed that defendant fabricated five passages, and omitted a crucial portion of the sixth, rendering it misleading.

Justice Kennedy said: "In general, quotation marks around a passage indicate to the reader that the passage reproduces the speaker's words verbatim." However, "quotations do not always convey that the speaker actually said or wrote the quoted material." For example, an acknowledgment that "the work is so-called docudrama or historical fiction, or that it recreates conversations from memory, not from recordings, might indicate that the quotations should not be interpreted as the actual statements of the speaker to whom they are attributed."

However, the Court rejected the Ninth Circuit's view that an altered quotation is protected "so long as it is a 'rational interpretation' of an actual statement...." The Court also rejected plaintiff's argument that "any alteration beyond correction of grammar or syntax by itself proves falsity" for *New York Times* malice:

> "If an author alters a speaker's words but effects no material change in meaning, including any meaning conveyed by the manner or fact of expression, the speaker suffers no injury to reputation that is compensable as a defamation. [A] deliberate alteration of the words uttered by a plaintiff does not equate with knowledge of falsity for purposes of *New York Times Co. v. Sullivan* and *Gertz v. Robert Welch, Inc.,* unless the alteration results in a material change in the meaning of the words

---

* There were no dissents. Justice White concurred in the judgment: *"New York Times v. Sullivan* has little to do with this case, for here the jury found that the ad contained no assertion of fact."

conveyed by the statement. The use of quotations to attribute words not in fact spoken bears in a most important way on that inquiry, but it is not dispositive in every case."

White, J., joined by Scalia, J., dissented to this section: "the Court states that deliberate misquotation does not amount to *New York Times* malice unless it results in a material change in the meaning conveyed by the statement. This ignores the fact that under *New York Times*, reporting a known falsehood—here the knowingly false attribution—is sufficient proof of malice. The falsehood, apparently, must be substantial; the reporter may lie a little, but not too much."

GERTZ v. ROBERT WELCH, INC.
418 U.S. 323, 94 S.Ct. 2997, 41 L.Ed.2d 789 (1974).

[Elmer Gertz, a Chicago lawyer, was retained by a family in a civil action suing one Nuccio, a police officer, for killing one of its members. The state ultimately obtained Nuccio's conviction for murder in the second degree. An article in *The American Opinion*, published by the John Birch Society, claimed that the prosecution of Nuccio was part of the Communist campaign against the police and that Gertz was a "Leninist", a "Communist-fronter", and so on. The article contained serious inaccuracies.]

MR. JUSTICE POWELL delivered the opinion of the Court....

The principal issue in this case is whether a newspaper or broadcaster that publishes defamatory falsehoods about an individual who is neither a public official nor a public figure may claim a constitutional privilege against liability for the injury inflicted by those statements. The Court considered this question on the rather different set of facts presented in *Rosenbloom v. Metromedia, Inc.*, 403 U.S. 29, 91 S.Ct. 1811, 29 L.Ed.2d 296 (1971). Rosenbloom, a distributor of nudist magazines, was arrested for selling allegedly obscene material while making a delivery to a retail dealer. The police obtained a warrant and seized his entire inventory of 3,000 books and magazines. He sought and obtained an injunction prohibiting further police interference with his business. He then sued a local radio station for failing to note in two of its newscasts that the 3,000 items seized were only "reportedly" or "allegedly" obscene and for broadcasting references to "the smut literature racket" and to "girlie-book peddlers" in its coverage of the court proceeding for injunctive relief. He obtained a judgment against the radio station, but the Court of Appeals for the Third Circuit held the *New York Times* privilege applicable to the broadcast and reversed.

This Court affirmed the decision below, but no majority could agree on a controlling rationale.... Mr. Justice Brennan's conclusion for the *Rosenbloom* plurality [was] that "all discussion and communication involving matters of public or general concern," warrant the protection from liability for defamation accorded by the rule originally enunciated in *New York Times Co. v. Sullivan....* He abjured the suggested distinction between public officials and public figures on the one hand

and private individuals on the other. He focused instead on society's interest in learning about certain issues: "If a matter is a subject of public or general interest, it cannot suddenly become less so merely because a private individual is involved, or because in some sense the individual did not 'voluntarily' choose to become involved." Thus, under the plurality opinion, a private citizen involuntarily associated with a matter of general interest has no recourse for injury to his reputation unless he can satisfy the demanding requirements of the *New York Times* test. . . .

. . . The first remedy of any victim of defamation is self-help—using available opportunities to contradict the lie or correct the error and thereby to minimize its adverse impact on reputation. Public officials and public figures usually enjoy significantly greater access to the channels of effective communication and hence have a more realistic opportunity to counteract false statements than private individuals normally enjoy. Private individuals are therefore more vulnerable to injury, and the state interest in protecting them is correspondingly greater.

More important than the likelihood that private individuals will lack effective opportunities for rebuttal, there is a compelling normative consideration underlying the distinction between public and private defamation plaintiffs. An individual who decides to seek governmental office must accept certain necessary consequences of that involvement in public affairs. He runs the risk of closer public scrutiny than might otherwise be the case. . . . Those classed as public figures stand in a similar position. Hypothetically, it may be possible for someone to become a public figure through no purposeful action of his own, but the instances of truly involuntary public figures must be exceedingly rare. For the most part those who attain this status have assumed roles of special prominence in the affairs of society. Some occupy positions of such persuasive power and influence that they are deemed public figures for all purposes. More commonly, those classed as public figures have thrust themselves to the forefront of particular public controversies in order to influence the resolution of the issues involved. In either event, they invite attention and comment.

Even if the foregoing generalities do not obtain in every instance, the communications media are entitled to act on the assumption that public officials and public figures have voluntarily exposed themselves to increased risk of injury from defamatory falsehood concerning them. No such assumption is justified with respect to a private individual. He has not accepted public office or assumed an "influential role in ordering society." *Curtis Publishing Co. v. Butts,* 388 U.S., at 164, 87 S.Ct., at 1996 (Warren, C.J., concurring in result). He has relinquished no part of his interest in the protection of his own good name, and consequently he has a more compelling call on the courts for redress of injury inflicted by defamatory falsehood. Thus, private individuals are not only more vulnerable to injury than public officials and public figures; they are also more deserving of recovery.

For these reasons we conclude that the States should retain substantial latitude in their efforts to enforce a legal remedy for defamatory falsehood injurious to the reputation of a private individual. The extension of the *New York Times* test proposed by the *Rosenbloom* plurality would abridge this legitimate state interest to a degree that we find unacceptable....

We hold that, so long as they do not impose liability without fault, the States may define for themselves the appropriate standard of liability for a publisher or broadcaster of defamatory falsehood injurious to a private individual. This approach provides a more equitable boundary between the competing concerns involved here. It recognizes the strength of the legitimate state interest in compensating private individuals for wrongful injury to reputation, yet shields the press and broadcast media from the rigors of strict liability for defamation. At least this conclusion obtains where, as here, the substance of the defamatory statement "makes substantial danger to reputation apparent." This phrase places in perspective the conclusion we announce today. Our inquiry would involve considerations somewhat different from those discussed above if a State purported to condition civil liability on a factual misstatement whose content did not warn a reasonably prudent editor or broadcaster of its defamatory potential. Such a case is not now before us, and we intimate no view as to its proper resolution.

Our accommodation of the competing values at stake in defamation suits by private individuals allows the States to impose liability on the publisher or broadcaster of defamatory falsehood on a less demanding showing than that required by *New York Times*. This conclusion is not based on a belief that the considerations which prompted the adoption of the *New York Times* privilege for defamation of public officials and its extension to public figures are wholly inapplicable to the context of private individuals. Rather, we endorse this approach in recognition of the strong and legitimate state interest in compensating private individuals for injury to reputation. But this countervailing state interest extends no further than compensation for actual injury. For the reasons stated below, we hold that the States may not permit recovery of presumed or punitive damages, at least when liability is not based on a showing of knowledge of falsity or reckless disregard for the truth.

The common law of defamation is an oddity of tort law, for it allows recovery of purportedly compensatory damages without evidence of actual loss. Under the traditional rules pertaining to actions for libel, the existence of injury is presumed from the fact of publication. Juries may award substantial sums as compensation for supposed damage to reputation without any proof that such harm actually occurred. The largely uncontrolled discretion of juries to award damages where there is no loss unnecessarily compounds the potential of any system of liability for defamatory falsehood to inhibit the vigorous exercise of First Amendment freedoms. Additionally, the doctrine of presumed damages invites juries to punish unpopular opinion rather than to compensate individuals for injury sustained by the publication of a false fact. More to the point, the States have no substantial interest in securing for plaintiffs such as this petitioner gratuitous awards of money damages far in excess of any actual injury.

We would not, of course, invalidate state law simply because we doubt its wisdom, but here we are attempting to reconcile state law with a competing interest grounded in the constitutional command of the First Amendment. It is therefore appropriate to require that state remedies for defamatory falsehood reach no farther than is necessary to protect the legitimate interest involved. It is necessary to restrict defamation plaintiffs who do not prove knowledge of falsity or reckless disregard for the truth to compensation for actual injury. We need not define "actual injury," as trial courts have wide experience in framing appropriate jury instructions in tort actions. Suffice it to say that actual injury is not limited to out-of-pocket loss. Indeed, the more customary types of actual harm inflicted by defamatory falsehood include impairment of reputation and standing in the community, personal humiliation, and mental anguish and suffering. Of course, juries must be limited by appropriate instructions, and all awards must be supported by competent evidence concerning the injury, although there need be no evidence which assigns an actual dollar value to the injury.

We also find no justification for allowing awards of punitive damages against publishers and broadcasters held liable under state-defined standards of liability for defamation. In most jurisdictions jury discretion over the amounts awarded is limited only by the gentle rule that they not be excessive. Consequently, juries assess punitive damages in wholly unpredictable amounts bearing no necessary relation to the actual harm caused. And they remain free to use their discretion selectively to punish expressions of unpopular views. Like the doctrine of presumed damages, jury discretion to award punitive damages unnecessarily exacerbates the danger of media self-censorship, but, unlike the former rule, punitive damages are wholly irrelevant to the state interest that justifies a negligence standard for private defamation actions. They are not compensation for injury. Instead, they are private fines levied by civil juries to punish reprehensible conduct and to deter its future occurrence. In short, the private defamation plaintiff who establishes liability under a less demanding standard than that stated by *New York Times* may recover only such damages as are sufficient to compensate him for actual injury.

Notwithstanding our refusal to extend the *New York Times* privilege to defamation of private individuals, respondent contends that we should affirm the judgment below on the ground that petitioner is either a public official or a public figure. There is little basis for the former assertion. Several years prior to the present incident, petitioner had served briefly on housing committees appointed by the mayor of Chicago, but at the time of publication he had never held any remunerative governmental position. Respondent admits this but argues that petitioner's appearance at the coroner's inquest rendered him a "de facto public official." Our cases recognize no such concept. Respondent's suggestion would sweep all lawyers under the *New York Times* rule as officers of the court and distort the plain meaning of the "public official" category beyond all recognition. We decline to follow it.

Respondent's characterization of petitioner as a public figure raises a different question. That designation may rest on either of two alternative bases. In some instances an individual may achieve such pervasive fame or notoriety that he becomes a public figure for all purposes and in all contexts. More commonly, an individual voluntarily injects himself or is drawn into a particular public controversy and thereby becomes a public figure for a limited range of issues. In either case such persons assume special prominence in the resolution of public questions.

Petitioner has long been active in community and professional affairs. He has served as an officer of local civic groups and of various professional organizations, and he has published several books and articles on legal subjects. Although petitioner was consequently well known in some circles, he had achieved no general fame or notoriety in the community. None of the prospective jurors called at the trial had ever heard of petitioner prior to this litigation, and respondent offered no proof that this response was atypical of the local population. We would not lightly assume that a citizen's participation in community and professional affairs rendered him a public figure for all purposes. Absent clear evidence of general fame or notoriety in the community, and pervasive involvement in the affairs of society, an individual should not be deemed a public personality for all aspects of his life. It is preferable to reduce the public-figure question to a more meaningful context by looking to the nature and extent of an individual's participation in the particular controversy giving rise to the defamation.

In this context it is plain that petitioner was not a public figure. He played a minimal role at the coroner's inquest, and his participation related solely to his representation of a private client. He took no part in the criminal prosecution of Officer Nuccio. Moreover, he never discussed either the criminal or civil litigation with the press and was never quoted as having done so. He plainly did not thrust himself into the vortex of this public issue, nor did he engage the public's attention in an attempt to influence its outcome. We are persuaded that the trial court did not err in refusing to characterize petitioner as a public figure for the purpose of this litigation.

We therefore conclude that the *New York Times* standard is inapplicable to this case and that the trial court erred in entering judgment for respondent. Because the jury was allowed to impose liability without fault and was permitted to presume damages without proof of injury, a new trial is necessary. We reverse and remand for further proceedings in accord with this opinion.

It is so ordered.

[The concurring opinion of BLACKMUN, J., and the dissenting opinions of BURGER, C.J., DOUGLAS, BRENNAN, and WHITE, JJ., are omitted.]

Notes

Time, Inc. v. Firestone, 424 U.S. 448, 96 S.Ct. 958, 47 L.Ed.2d 154 (1976), held that Mrs. Mary Alice Firestone was not a public figure, so *Gertz* set out the constitutional limitations in her libel suit against Time Magazine for incorrectly reporting the trial of her divorce from Russell Firestone, "the scion of one of America's wealthier industrial families." However, Justice Marshall's dissent pointed out that Mrs. Firestone was prominent in Palm Beach society, and her "appearances in the press were evidently frequent enough to warrant her subscribing to a press-clipping service." When she brought her suit she had "reason to know of the likely public interest in the proceedings." In fact, Mrs. Firestone held several press conferences in the course of the proceedings.

Nonetheless, the Court, speaking through Rehnquist, J., held that she was not a public figure. She "did not assume any role of especial prominence in the affairs of society, other than perhaps Palm Beach society, and she did not thrust herself to the forefront of any particular public controversy in order to influence the resolution of the issues involved in it." Her press conferences were merely an attempt to satisfy inquiring reporters, not an attempt to affect the outcome of the trial. "Dissolution of a marriage through judicial proceedings is not the sort of 'public controversy' referred to in *Gertz,* even though the marital difficulties of extremely wealthy individuals may be of interest to some portions of the reading public." The Court also rejected Time's "claim for automatic extension of the *New York Times* privilege to all reports of judicial proceedings."

DUN & BRADSTREET, INC. v. GREENMOSS BUILDERS, INC.

472 U.S. 749, 105 S.Ct. 2939, 86 L.Ed.2d 593 (1985).

JUSTICE POWELL announced the judgment of the Court and delivered an opinion, in which JUSTICE REHNQUIST and JUSTICE O'CONNOR joined.

In *Gertz v. Robert Welch, Inc.,* 418 U.S. 323, 94 S.Ct. 2997, 41 L.Ed.2d 789 (1974), we held that the First Amendment restricted the damages that a private individual could obtain from a publisher for a libel that involved a matter of public concern. More specifically, we held that in these circumstances the First Amendment prohibited awards of presumed and punitive damages for false and defamatory statements unless the plaintiff shows "actual malice," that is, knowledge of falsity or reckless disregard for the truth. The question presented in this case is whether this rule of *Gertz* applies when the false and defamatory statements do not involve matters of public concern.

Petitioner Dun & Bradstreet, a credit reporting agency, provides subscribers with financial and related information about businesses. All the information is confidential; under the terms of the subscription agreement the subscribers may not reveal it to anyone else. On July 26, 1976, petitioner sent a report to five subscribers indicating that respondent, a construction contractor, had filed a voluntary petition for bankruptcy. This report was false and grossly misrepresented respondent's assets and liabilities. That same day, while discussing the possibility of future financing with its bank, respondent's president was told that the bank had received the defamatory report. He immediately called petitioner's regional office, explained the error, and asked for a correction. In addition, he requested the names of the firms that had received the false report in order to assure them that the company was solvent. Petitioner promised to look into the matter but refused to divulge the names of those who had received the report.

After determining that its report was indeed false, petitioner issued a corrective notice on or about August 3, 1976 to the five subscribers who had received the initial report. The notice stated that one of respondent's former employees, not respondent itself, had filed for bankruptcy and that respondent "continued in business as usual." Respondent told petitioner that it was dissatisfied with the notice and it again asked for a list of subscribers who had seen the initial report. Again petitioner refused to divulge their names.

Respondent then brought this defamation action in Vermont state court. It alleged that the false report had injured its reputation and sought both compensatory and punitive damages. The trial established that the error in petitioner's report had been caused when one of its employees, a seventeen year old high school student paid to review Vermont bankruptcy pleadings, had inadvertently attributed to respondent a bankruptcy petition filed by one of respondent's former employees. Although petitioner's representative testified that it was routine practice to check the accuracy of such reports with the businesses themselves, it did not try to verify the information about respondent before reporting it.

After trial, the jury returned a verdict in favor of respondent and awarded $50,000 in compensatory or presumed damages and $300,000 in punitive damages. Petitioner moved for a new trial. It argued that in *Gertz v. Robert Welch, Inc.,* this Court had ruled broadly "that the States may not permit recovery of presumed or punitive damages, at least when liability is not based on a showing of knowledge of falsity or reckless disregard for the truth," and it argued that the judge's instructions in this case permitted the jury to award such damages on a lesser showing. . . .

In *Gertz,* we held that the fact that expression concerned a public issue did not by itself entitle the libel defendant to the constitutional protections of *New York Times. . . .* In libel actions brought by private persons we found the competing interests different. [W]e held that a State could not allow recovery of presumed and punitive damages absent a showing of "actual malice." Nothing in our opinion, however, indicated that this same balance would be struck regardless of the type of speech involved.

We have never considered whether the *Gertz* balance obtains when the defamatory statements involve no issue of public concern. To make this determination, we must employ the approach approved in *Gertz* and balance the State's interest in compensating private individuals for injury to their reputation against the First Amendment interest in protecting this type of expression. This state interest is identical to the one weighed in *Gertz.* There we found that it was "strong and legitimate." ... The First Amendment interest, on the other hand, is less important than the one weighed in *Gertz.* We have long recognized that not all speech is of equal First Amendment importance. It is speech on " 'matters of public concern' "that is "at the heart of the First Amendment's protection." ... In contrast, speech on matters of purely private concern is of less First Amendment concern....

While such speech is not totally unprotected by the First Amendment, its protections are less stringent. In *Gertz,* we found that the state interest in awarding presumed and punitive damages was not "substantial" in view of their effect on speech at the core of First Amendment concern. This interest, however, *is* "substantial" relative to the incidental effect these remedies may have on speech of significantly less constitutional interest. The rationale of the common law rules has been the experience and judgment of history that "proof of actual damage will be impossible in a great many cases where, from the character of the defamatory words and the circumstances of publication, it is all but certain that serious harm, has resulted in fact." W. Prosser, Law of Torts § 112, p. 765 (4th ed. 1971).... In light of the reduced constitutional value of speech involving no matters of public concern, we hold that the state interest adequately supports awards of presumed and punitive damages—even absent a showing of "actual malice."

The only remaining issue is whether petitioner's credit report involved a matter of public concern. In a related context, we have held that "[w]hether ... speech addresses a matter of public concern must be determined by [the expression's] content, form, and context ... as revealed by the whole record." These factors indicate that petitioner's credit report concerns no public issue.* It was speech solely in the individual interest of the speaker and its specific business audience. This particular interest warrants no special protection when—as in this case—the speech is wholly false and clearly damaging to the victim's business reputation. Moreover, since the credit report was made available to only five subscribers, who, under the terms of the subscription agreement, could not disseminate it further, it cannot be said that the report involves any "strong interest in the free flow of commercial information." There is simply no credible argument that this type of credit reporting requires special protection to ensure that "debate on public issues [will] be uninhibited, robust, and wide-open."

---

* The dissent suggests that our holding today leaves all credit reporting subject to reduced First Amendment protection. This is incorrect. The protection to be accorded a particular credit report depends on whether the report's "content, form, and context" indicate that it concerns a public matter. We also do not hold, as the dissent suggests we do, that the report is subject to reduced constitutional protection because it constitutes economic or commercial speech. We discuss such speech, along with advertising, only to show how many of the same concerns that argue in favor of reduced constitutional protection in those areas apply here as well.

In addition, the speech here, like advertising, is hardy and unlikely to be deterred by incidental state regulation. It is solely motivated by the desire for profit, which, we have noted, is a force less likely to be deterred than others. Arguably, the reporting here was also more objectively verifiable than speech deserving of greater protection. In any case, the market provides a powerful incentive to a credit reporting agency to be accurate, since false credit reporting is of no use to creditors. Thus, any incremental "chilling" effect of libel suits would be of decreased significance.

We conclude that permitting recovery of presumed and punitive damages in defamation cases absent a showing of "actual malice" does not violate the First Amendment when the defamatory statements do not involve matters of public concern. Accordingly, we affirm the judgment of the Vermont Supreme Court.

It is so ordered.

CHIEF JUSTICE BURGER, concurring in the judgment....

I continue to believe ... that *Gertz* was ill-conceived, and therefore agree with Justice White that *Gertz* should be overruled. ...

JUSTICE WHITE, concurring in the judgment....

I joined the judgment and opinion in *New York Times*. I also joined later decisions extending the *New York Times* standard to other situations. But I came to have increasing doubts about the soundness of the Court's approach and about some of the assumptions underlying it.... I dissented in *Gertz,* asserting that the common-law remedies should be retained for private plaintiffs. I remain convinced that *Gertz* was erroneously decided. I have also become convinced that the Court struck an improvident balance in the *New York Times* case between the public's interest in being fully informed about public officials and public affairs and the competing interest of those who have been defamed in vindicating their reputation. [I]n *New York Times* cases, the public official's complaint will be dismissed unless he alleges and makes out a jury case of a knowing or reckless falsehood. Absent such proof, there will be no jury verdict or judgment of any kind in his favor, even if the challenged publication is admittedly false. The lie will stand, and the public continue to be misinformed about public matters. This will recurringly happen because the putative plaintiff's burden is so exceedingly difficult to satisfy and can be discharged only by expensive litigation....* ...

In *New York Times,* instead of escalating the plaintiff's burden of proof to an almost impossible level, we could have achieved our stated goal by limiting the recoverable damages to a level that would not unduly threaten the press. Punitive damages might have been scrutinized ... or perhaps even entirely forbidden. Presumed damages to

---

* If the plaintiff succeeds in proving a jury case of malice, it may be that the jury will be asked to bring in separate verdicts on falsity and malice. In that event, there could be a verdict in favor of the plaintiff on falsity, but against him on malice. There would be no judgment in his favor, but the verdict on falsity would be a public one and would tend to set the record right and clear the plaintiff's name....

reputation might have been prohibited, or limited, as in *Gertz.* Had that course been taken and the common-law standard of liability been retained, the defamed public official, upon proving falsity, could at least have had a judgment to that effect. His reputation would then be vindicated; and to the extent possible, the misinformation circulated would have been countered. He might have also recovered a modest amount, enough perhaps to pay his litigation expenses. At the very least, the public official should not have been required to satisfy the actual malice standard where he sought no damages but only to clear his name. In this way, both First Amendment and reputational interests would have been far better served. . . .

It is interesting that Justice Powell declines to follow the *Gertz* approach in this case. I had thought that the decision in *Gertz* was intended to reach cases that involve any false statements of fact injurious to reputation, whether the statement is made privately or publicly and whether or not it implicates a matter of public importance. Justice Powell, however, distinguishes *Gertz* as a case that involved a matter of public concern, an element absent here. Wisely, in my view, Justice Powell does not rest his application of a different rule here on a distinction drawn between media and non-media defendants. On that issue, I agree with Justice Brennan that the First Amendment gives no more protection to the press in defamation suits than it does to others exercising their freedom of speech. None of our cases affords such a distinction; to the contrary, the Court has rejected it at every turn.* It should be rejected again, particularly in this context, since it makes no sense to give the most protection to those publishers who reach the most readers and therefore pollute the channels of communication with the most misinformation and do the most damage to private reputation. If *Gertz* is to be distinguished from this case, on the ground that it applies only where the allegedly false publication deals with a matter of general or public importance, then where the false publication does not deal with such a matter, the common-law rules would apply whether the defendant is a member of the media or other public disseminator or a non-media individual publishing privately. Although Justice Powell speaks only of the inapplicability of the *Gertz* rule with respect to presumed and punitive damages, it must be that the *Gertz* requirement of some kind of fault on the part of the defendant is also inapplicable in cases such as this.

As I have said, I dissented in *Gertz,* and I doubt that the decision in that case has made any measurable contribution to First Amendment or reputational values since its announcement. Nor am I sure that it has saved the press a great deal of money. Like the *New York Times* decision, the burden that plaintiffs must meet invites long and complicated discovery involving detailed investigation of the workings of the press, how a news story is developed, and the state of mind of the reporter and publisher. That kind of litigation is very expensive. I

* . . . From its inception, without discussing the issue, we have applied the rule of *New York Times* to non-media defendants. . . .

suspect that the press would be no worse off financially if the common-law rules were to apply and if the judiciary was careful to insist that damages awards be kept within bounds. A legislative solution to the damages problem would also be appropriate. Moreover, since libel plaintiffs are very likely more interested in clearing their names than in damages, I doubt that limiting recoveries would deter or be unfair to them. In any event, I cannot assume that the press, as successful and powerful as it is, will be intimidated into withholding news that by decent journalistic standards it believes to be true. . . .

JUSTICE BRENNAN, with whom JUSTICE MARSHALL, JUSTICE BLACKMUN and JUSTICE STEVENS join, dissenting.

[A]lthough protection of the type of expression at issue [credit reporting] is admittedly not the "central meaning of the First Amendment," *Gertz* makes clear that the First Amendment nonetheless requires restraints on presumed and punitive damage awards for this expression. The lack of consensus in approach to these idiosyncratic facts should not, however, obscure the solid allegiance the principles of *New York Times v. Sullivan* continue to command in the jurisprudence of this Court.

[T]he Court in *Rosenbloom v. Metromedia, Inc.,* 403 U.S. 29, 91 S.Ct. 1811, 29 L.Ed.2d 296 (1971), and *Gertz v. Robert Welch, Inc.,* focused largely on defining the circumstances under which protection of the central First Amendment value of robust debate of *public issues* should mandate plaintiffs to show actual malice to obtain a judgment and actual damages; the Court settled on a rule requiring actual malice as a prerequisite to recovery only in suits brought by public officials or public figures. We have also recognized, however, that the First Amendment requires significant protection from defamation law's chill for a range of expression far broader than simply speech about pure political issues. . . . The ready availability and unconstrained application of presumed and punitive damages in libel actions is too blunt a regulatory instrument to satisfy this First Amendment principle, even when the alleged libel does not implicate directly the type of speech at issue in *New York Times v. Sullivan.* Justice Harlan made precisely this point in *Rosenbloom:*

> At a minimum, *even in the purely private libel area,* I think the First Amendment should be construed to limit the imposition of punitive damages to those situations in which actual malice is proved. This is the typical standard employed in assessing anyone's liability for punitive damages where the underlying aim of the law is to compensate for harm actually caused, . . . and no conceivable state interest could justify imposing a harsher standard on the exercise of *those freedoms that are given explicit protection by the First Amendment.* (dissenting opinion)(emphasis added).

Justice Harlan's perception formed the cornerstone of the Court's analysis in *Gertz.* . . . The only question presented is whether a jury award of presumed and punitive damages based on less than a showing of actual malice is constitutionally permissible. *Gertz* provides a forthright negative answer. To preserve the jury verdict in this case, therefore, the opinions of Justice Powell and Justice White have cut away the protective mantle of *Gertz*. . . . * Even accepting the notion that a distinction can and should be drawn between matters of public concern and matters of purely private concern, however, the analyses presented by both Justice Powell and Justice White fail on their own terms. Both, by virtue of what they hold in this case, propose an impoverished definition of "matters of public concern" that is irreconcilable with First Amendment principles. The credit reporting at issue here surely involves a subject matter of sufficient public concern to require the comprehensive protections of *Gertz*. Were this speech appropriately characterized as a matter of only private concern, moreover, the elimination of the *Gertz* restrictions on presumed and punitive damages would still violate basic First Amendment requirements.

The five Members of the Court voting to affirm the damage award in this case have provided almost no guidance as to what constitutes a protected "matter of public concern." Justice White offers nothing at all, but his opinion does indicate that the distinction turns on solely the subject matter of the expression and not on the extent or conditions of dissemination of that expression. Justice Powell adumbrates a rationale that would appear to focus primarily on subject matter. The opinion relies on the fact that the speech at issue was "solely in the individual interest of the speaker and its *business* audience," (emphasis added). Analogizing explicitly to advertising, the opinion also states that credit reporting is "hardy" and "solely motivated by the desire for profit." These two strains of analysis suggest that Justice Powell is excluding the subject matter of credit reports from "matters of public concern" because the speech is predominantly in the realm of matters of economic concern.

In evaluating the subject matter of expression, this Court has consistently rejected the argument that speech is entitled to diminished First Amendment protection simply because it concerns economic matters or is in the economic interest of the speaker or the audience. . . . More importantly, an announcement of the bankruptcy of a local company is information of potentially great concern to residents of the community where the company is located; . . . such a bankruptcy "in a single factory may have economic repercussions for a whole region." And knowledge about solvency and the effect and prevalence of bankruptcy certainly would inform citizen opinions about questions of economic regulation. It is difficult to suggest that a bankruptcy is not a subject matter of public concern when federal law requires invocation of judicial mechanisms to effectuate it and makes the fact of the bankruptcy a matter of public record. . . .

* One searches *Gertz* in vain for a single word to support the proposition that limits on presumed and punitive damages obtained only when speech involved matters of public concern. *Gertz* could not have been grounded in such a premise. Distrust of placing in the courts the power to decide what speech was of public concern was precisely the rationale *Gertz* offered for rejecting the *Rosenbloom* plurality approach. . . .

The credit reports of Dun & Bradstreet bear few of the earmarks of commercial speech that might be entitled to somewhat less rigorous protection. In *every* case in which we have permitted more extensive state regulation on the basis of a commercial speech rationale the speech being regulated was pure advertising—an offer to buy or sell goods and services or encouraging such buying and selling. Credit reports are not commercial advertisements for a good or service or a proposal to buy or sell such a product. We have been extremely chary about extending the "commercial speech" doctrine beyond this narrowly circumscribed category of advertising because often vitally important speech will be uttered to advance economic interests and because the profit motive making such speech hardy dissipates rapidly when the speech is not advertising....

Even if Justice Powell's characterization of the credit reporting at issue here were accepted in its entirety, ... this does not justify the elimination of restrictions on presumed and punitive damages. State efforts to regulate commercial speech in the form of advertising must abide by the requirement that the regulatory means chosen be narrowly tailored so as to avoid any unnecessary chilling of protected expression.*
... *Gertz* held that in a defamation action punitive damages, designed to chill and not to compensate, were *"wholly irrelevant"* to furtherance of any valid state interest....

Notes

1. *Philadelphia Newspapers, Inc. v. Hepps,* 475 U.S. 767, 106 S.Ct. 1558, 89 L.Ed.2d 783 (1986) held (5 to 4) that: "where a newspaper publishes speech of public concern, a private-figure plaintiff cannot recover damages without also showing that the statements at issue are false." There can be no common law presumption that defamatory speech is false. The private-figure plaintiff must show that the defendant was at fault and that the speech was false.

Justice O'Connor for the majority shed some light on the meaning of *Dun & Bradstreet.* First, is the plaintiff a public figure; second, is the speech "of public concern?" If the answer to both questions is yes, the libel plaintiff must surmount the very high barrier of *New York Times v. Sullivan,* and prove scienter as well as falsity. If the answer to the first question is no, but the answer to the second is yes, *Gertz* applies, and the plaintiff must prove at least negligence and falsity in order to recover actual damages. If the answer

---

* Indeed Justice Powell has chosen a particularly inapt set of facts as a basis for urging a return to the common law. Though the individual's interest in reputation is certainly at the core of notions of human dignity, the reputational interest at stake here is that of a corporation. Similarly, that this speech is solely commercial in nature undercuts the argument that presumed damages should be unrestrained in actions like this one because actual harm will be difficult to prove. If the credit report is viewed as commercial expression, proving that actual damages occurred is relatively easy. For instance, an alleged libel concerning a bank's customer may cause the bank to lower the credit limit or raise the interest rate charged that customer. The commercial context does not increase the need for presumed damages, but if anything [it] reduces the need to presume harm. At worst the commercial damages caused by such action should be no more difficult to ascertain than many other traditional elements of tort damages.

to both questions is no, then the Constitution does "not necessarily force any change in at least some of the features of the common-law landscape."

Hepps throws little light on the definition of a "matter of public concern." In that case a series of newspaper articles contained the theme that the plaintiffs (private figures) had links to organized crime and that those links influenced the state's governmental processes. Speech concerning the political process, announced the Court, was of public concern.

O'Connor, joined only by Marshall and Powell, stated in a footnote that they were reserving the question of whether the rule the Court announced applied to nonmedia defendants. Brennan's concurrence, joined by Blackmun, specifically noted that there should be no distinction between media and nonmedia defendants. Stevens, joined by Burger, C.J., and White and Rehnquist, JJ., dissented, and called the majority's results "pernicious."

2. FACT VERSUS OPINION. In *Milkovich v. Lorain Journal Co.,* 497 U.S. 1, 110 S.Ct. 2695, 111 L.Ed.2d 1 (1990), the Court, per Rehnquist, C.J., rejected any artificial dichotomy between "opinion" and "fact." There is no "wholesale defamation exemption for anything that might be labeled 'opinion.' "A newspaper columnist had written an article implying that a local high school wrestling coach lied under oath in a judicial proceeding about an altercation involving his team at a home wrestling match. The article, for example, said that "[A]nyone who attended the meet ... knows in his heart that Milkovich and Scott lied at the hearing after each having given his solemn oath to tell the truth."

The *Hepps* decision, said the Court, "ensures that a statement of opinion relating to matters of public concern which does not contain a provably false factual connotation will receive full constitutional protection." For example, the statement—"I think that Mayor Jones lied"—is really no different than the statement—"Jones is a liar." Both statements may be proved to be false because the speaker did not really think that Jones lied, but said it anyway or, because Jones had not really lied. On the other hand, the statement—"In my opinion Mayor Jones shows his abysmal ignorance by accepting the teachings of Marx and Lenin"—is not actionable because "it is a statement of opinion relating to matters of public concern which does not contain a provably false factual connotation.... " The "issue of falsity relates to the *defamatory* facts implied by a statement." Similarly, vigorous epithet (calling a real estate developer's negotiating position "blackmail") is not actionable when the reasonable reader perceived the words as mere rhetorical hyperbole.

> [W]here a statement of "opinion" on a matter of public concern reasonably implies false and defamatory facts regarding public figures or officials, those individuals must show that such statements were made with knowledge of their false implications or with reckless disregard of their truth. Similarly, where such a statement involves a private figure on a matter of public concern, a plaintiff must show that the false connotations were made with some level of fault as required by *Gertz.* [T]he enhanced appellate review required by *Bose Corp.* [§ 10–8.1] provides assurance that the foregoing determinations will be made in a manner so as not to "constitute a forbidden intrusion of the field of free expression."

Brennan, J., joined by Marshall, J., filed a dissenting opinion. In their view, the statements at issue in this case "cannot reasonably be interpreted as stating or implying defamatory facts about petitioner" because, read in context, the columnist's assumption that the petitioner lied at the court hearing is "patently conjecture."

10–8.2 *Privacy*

COX BROADCASTING CORP. v. COHN
420 U.S. 469, 95 S.Ct. 1029, 43 L.Ed.2d 328 (1975).

M<small>R</small>. J<small>USTICE</small> W<small>HITE</small> delivered the opinion of the Court.

The issue before us in this case is whether, consistently with the First and Fourteenth Amendments, a State may extend a cause of action for damages for invasion of privacy caused by the publication of the name of a deceased rape victim which was publicly revealed in connection with the prosecution of the crime.

In August 1971, appellee's 17–year–old daughter was the victim of a rape and did not survive the incident. Six youths were soon indicted for murder and rape. Although there was substantial press coverage of the crime and of subsequent developments, the identity of the victim was not disclosed pending trial, perhaps because of Ga.Code Ann. § 26–9901 (1972), which makes it a misdemeanor to publish or broadcast the name or identity of a rape victim. In April 1972, some eight months later, the six defendants appeared in court. Five pleaded guilty to rape or attempted rape, the charge of murder having been dropped. The guilty pleas were accepted by the court, and the trial of the defendant pleading not guilty was set for a later date.

In the course of the proceedings that day, appellant Wassell, a reporter covering the incident for his employer, learned the name of the victim from an examination of the indictments which were made available for his inspection in the courtroom. That the name of the victim appears in the indictments and that the indictments were public records available for inspection are not disputed. Later that day, Wassell broadcast ... a news report concerning the court proceedings. The report named the victim of the crime and was repeated the following day.

In May 1972, appellee brought an action for money damages against appellants, relying on § 26–9901 and claiming that his right to privacy had been invaded by the television broadcasts giving the name of his deceased daughter. Appellants admitted the broadcasts but claimed that they were privileged under both state law and the First and Fourteenth Amendments. [The Georgia trial and supreme courts rejected appellants' constitutional claims.] ...

Georgia stoutly defends both § 26–9901 and the State's common-law privacy action challenged here. Its claims are not without force, for powerful arguments can be made, and have been made, that however it may be ultimately defined, there *is* a zone of privacy surrounding every individual, a zone within which the State may protect him from intrusion by the press, with all its attendant publicity. Indeed, the central thesis of the root article by Warren and Brandeis, The Right to Privacy, 4 Harv.L.Rev. 193, 196 (1890), was that the press was overstepping its prerogatives by publishing essentially private information and that there should be a remedy for the alleged abuses. . . .

These are impressive credentials for a right of privacy, but we should recognize that we do not have at issue here an action for the invasion of privacy involving the appropriation of one's name or photograph, a physical or other tangible intrusion into a private area, or a publication of otherwise private information that is also false although perhaps not defamatory. The version of the privacy tort now before us—termed in Georgia "the tort of public disclosure,"—is that in which the plaintiff claims the right to be free from unwanted publicity about his private affairs, which, although wholly true, would be offensive to a person of ordinary sensibilities. Because the gravamen of the claimed injury is the publication of information, whether true or not, the dissemination of which is embarrassing or otherwise painful to an individual, it is here that claims of privacy most directly confront the constitutional freedoms of speech and press. The face-off is apparent, and the appellants urge upon us the broad holding that the press may not be made criminally or civilly liable for publishing information that is neither false nor misleading but absolutely accurate, however damaging it may be to reputation or individual sensibilities.

It is true that in defamation actions where the protected interest is personal reputation, the prevailing view is that truth is a defense; and the message of *New York Times Co. v. Sullivan,* and like cases is that the defense of truth is constitutionally required where the subject of the publication is a public official or public figure. . . . Rather than address the broader question whether truthful publications may ever be subjected to civil or criminal liability consistently with the First and Fourteenth Amendments, or to put it another way, whether the State may ever define and protect an area of privacy free from unwanted publicity in the press, it is appropriate to focus on the narrower interface between press and privacy that this case presents, namely, whether the State may impose sanctions on the accurate publication of the name of a rape victim obtained from public records—more specifically, from judicial records which are maintained in connection with a public prosecution and which themselves are open to public inspection. We are convinced that the State may not do so.

In the first place, in a society in which each individual has but limited time and resources with which to observe at first hand the operations of his government, he relies necessarily upon the press to bring to him in convenient form the facts of those operations. . . .

Appellee has claimed in this litigation that the efforts of the press have infringed his right to privacy by broadcasting to the world the fact that his daughter was a rape victim. The commission of crime, prosecutions resulting from it, and judicial proceedings arising from the prosecutions, however, are without question events of legitimate concern to the public and consequently fall within the responsibility of the press to report the operations of government. The special protected nature of accurate reports of judicial proceedings has repeatedly been recognized. This Court, in an opinion written by Mr. Justice Douglas, has said: "A trial is a public event.... *Those who see and hear what transpired can report it with impunity....* " *Craig v. Harney,* 331 U.S. 367, 374, 67 S.Ct. 1249, 1254, 91 L.Ed. 1546 (1947)(emphasis added).

[E]ven the prevailing law of invasion of privacy generally recognizes that the interests in privacy fade when the information involved already appears on the public record. The conclusion is compelling when viewed in terms of the First and Fourteenth Amendments and in light of the public interest in a vigorous press.... By placing the information in the public domain on official court records, the State must be presumed to have concluded that the public interest was thereby being served. Public records by their very nature are of interest to those concerned with the administration of government, and a public benefit is performed by the reporting of the true contents of the records by the media. The freedom of the press to publish that information appears to us to be of critical importance to our type of government in which the citizenry is the final judge of the proper conduct of public business. In preserving that form of government the First and Fourteenth Amendments command nothing less than that the States may not impose sanctions on the publication of truthful information contained in official court records open to public inspection.

We are reluctant to embark on a course that would make public records generally available to the media but forbid their publication if offensive to the sensibilities of the supposed reasonable man. Such a rule would make it very difficult for the media to inform citizens about the public business and yet stay within the law.... At the very least, the First and Fourteenth Amendments will not allow exposing the press to liability for truthfully publishing information released to the public in official court records. If there are privacy interests to be protected in judicial proceedings, the States must respond by means which avoid public documentation or other exposure of private information.

Appellant Wassell based his televised report upon notes taken during the court proceedings and obtained the name of the victim from the indictments handed to him at his request during a recess in the hearing. Appellee has not contended that the name was obtained in an improper fashion or that it was not on an official court document open to public inspection. Under these circumstances, the protection of freedom of the press provided by the First and Fourteenth Amendments bars the State of Georgia from making appellants' broadcast the basis of civil liability.

Reversed.

MR. CHIEF JUSTICE BURGER concurs in the judgment.

[The opinions of POWELL, J., concurring, of DOUGLAS, J., concurring in the judgment, and of REHNQUIST, J., dissenting for want of jurisdiction, are omitted.]

Notes

In *Florida Star v. B.J.F.*, 491 U.S. 524, 109 S.Ct. 2603, 105 L.Ed.2d 443 (1989), Marshall, J., for the Court, held that a Florida statute (§ 794.03) could not constitutionally make a newspaper civilly liable for publishing the name of a rape victim obtained from a publicly released police report. The Florida Star mistakenly violated its own internal policy of not publishing the names of sexual offense victims. The victim then sued the newspaper for negligently violating the statute, and was awarded $75,000 in compensatory damages and $25,000 in punitive damages. The Court distinguished *Cox Broadcasting* as a case where the name of the rape victim "was obtained from courthouse records open to public inspection." The Court acknowledged that the press plays an important role in subjecting trials to public scrutiny, but here the newspaper was not reporting from a judicial proceeding but from a police report. However, the Court still reversed, though it did not accept appellant's invitation to hold broadly that truthful publication may never be punished consistent with the First Amendment. "Our cases have carefully eschewed reaching this ultimate question, mindful that the future may bring scenarios which prudence counsels our not resolving anticipatorily." The Court concluded that it was only holding that "where a newspaper publishes truthful information which it has lawfully obtained, punishment may lawfully be imposed, if at all, only when narrowly tailored to a state interest of the highest order, and that no such interest is satisfactorily served by imposing liability under § 794.03 to appellant under the facts of this case."

Scalia, J., concurring in part and concurring in the judgment, said:

I think it sufficient to decide this case to rely upon the third ground set forth in the Court's opinion, that a law cannot be regarded as protecting an interest "of the highest order," *Smith v. Daily Mail Publishing Co.*, [§ 10–2] and thus as justifying a restriction upon truthful speech, when it leaves appreciable damage to that supposedly vital interest unprohibited. In the present case, I would anticipate that the rape victim's discomfort at the dissemination of news of her misfortune among friends and acquaintances would be at least as great as her discomfort at its publication by the media to people to whom she is only a name. Yet the law in question does not prohibit the former in either oral or written form. Nor is it at all clear, as I think it must be to validate this statute, that Florida's general privacy law would prohibit such gossip. Nor, finally, is it credible that the interest meant to be served by the statute is the protection of the victim against a rapist still at large—an interest that arguably would extend only to mass publication. There would be little reason to limit a statute with that objective to rape alone; or to extend it to all rapes, whether or not the felon has been apprehended and confined. In any case, the instructions here did not require the jury to find that the rapist was at large. This law has every appearance of a prohibition that society is prepared to impose upon the press but not upon itself. Such a prohibition does not protect an interest "of the highest order."

White, J., joined by Rehnquist, C.J., & O'Connor, J., dissented. A week after the rape—

> while her assailant was still at large, an account of this assault—identifying by name B.J.F. as the victim—was published by The Florida Star. As a result, B.J.F. received harassing phone calls, required mental health counseling, was forced to move from her home, and was even threatened with being raped again. Yet today, the Court holds that a jury award of $75,000 to compensate B.J.F. for the harm she suffered due to the Star's negligence is at odds with the First Amendment.

Should Florida be able to impose greater restrictions on the institutional press than on other speech? The "free press" is not preferred over "free speech," but can it be treated worse?

ZACCHINI v. SCRIPPS–HOWARD BROADCASTING CO.

433 U.S. 562, 97 S.Ct. 2849, 53 L.Ed.2d 965 (1977).

MR. JUSTICE WHITE delivered the opinion of the Court.

Petitioner, Hugo Zacchini, is an entertainer. He performs a "human cannonball" act in which he is shot from a cannon into a net some 200 feet away. Each performance occupies some 15 seconds. In August and September 1972, petitioner was engaged to perform his act on a regular basis at the Geauga County Fair in Burton, Ohio.... On August 30, a freelance reporter for Scripps–Howard Broadcasting Co., the operator of a television broadcasting station and respondent in this case, attended the fair. He carried a small movie camera. Petitioner noticed the reporter and asked him not to film the performance. The reporter did not do so on that day; but on the instructions of the producer of respondent's daily newscast, he returned the following day and videotaped the entire act. This film clip, approximately 15 seconds in length, was shown on the 11 o'clock news program that night, together with favorable commentary.

Petitioner then brought this action for damages, alleging that he is "engaged in the entertainment business," that the act he performs is one "invented by his father and ... performed only by his family for the last fifty years," that respondent "showed and commercialized the film of his act without his consent," and that such conduct was an "unlawful appropriation of plaintiff's professional property." Respondent answered and moved for summary judgment, which was granted by the trial court.

[P]etitioner is not contending that his appearance at the fair and his performance could not be reported by the press as newsworthy items. His complaint is that respondent filmed his entire act and displayed that film on television for the public to see and enjoy. This, he claimed, was an appropriation of his professional property. The Ohio Supreme Court agreed that petitioner had "a right of publicity" that gave him "personal control over commercial display and exploitation of his personality and the exercise of his talents." This right of "exclusive control over the publicity given to his performances" was said to be such a "valuable part of the benefit which may be attained by his talents and efforts" that it was entitled to legal protection. It was also observed, or at least expressly assumed, that petitioner had not abandoned his rights by performing under the circumstances present at the Geauga County Fair Grounds.

The Ohio Supreme Court nevertheless held that the challenged invasion was privileged, saying that the press "must be accorded broad latitude in its choice of how much it presents of each story or incident, and of the emphasis to be given to such presentation. No fixed standard which would bar the press from reporting or depicting either an entire occurrence or an entire discrete part of a public performance can be formulated which would not unduly restrict the 'breathing room' in reporting which freedom of the press requires." Under this view, respondent was thus constitutionally free to film and display petitioner's entire act.

The Ohio Supreme Court relied heavily on *Time, Inc. v. Hill*, 385 U.S. 374, 87 S.Ct. 534, 17 L.Ed.2d 456 (1967), but that case does not mandate a media privilege to televise a performer's entire act without his consent. Involved in *Time, Inc. v. Hill* was a claim under the New York "Right of Privacy" statute that Life Magazine, in the course of reviewing a new play, had connected the play with a long-past incident involving petitioner and his family and had falsely described their experience and conduct at that time. The complaint sought damages for humiliation and suffering flowing from these nondefamatory falsehoods that allegedly invaded Hill's privacy. The Court held, however, that the opening of a new play linked to an actual incident was a matter of public interest and that Hill could not recover without showing that the Life report was knowingly false or was published with reckless disregard for the truth—the same rigorous standard that had been applied in *New York Times Co. v. Sullivan*.

Time, Inc. v. Hill, which was hotly contested and decided by a divided Court, involved an entirely different tort from the "right of publicity" recognized by the Ohio Supreme Court. As the opinion reveals in *Time, Inc. v. Hill,* the Court was steeped in the literature of privacy law and was aware of the developing distinctions and nuances in this branch of the law. The Court, for example, cited W. Prosser, Law of Torts 831–832 (3d ed. 1964), and the same author's well-known article, Privacy, 48 Calif.L.Rev. 383 (1960), both of which divided privacy into four distinct branches.* The Court was aware that it was adjudicating a

---

* "The law of privacy comprises four distinct kinds of invasion of four different interests of the plaintiff, which are tied together by the common name, but otherwise have almost nothing in common except that each represents an interference with the right of the plaintiff ... 'to be let alone.' " Prosser, Privacy, 48 Calif.L.Rev., at 389.

Thus, according to Prosser, some courts had recognized a cause of action for "intrusion" upon the plaintiff's seclusion or solitude; public disclosure of "private facts" about the plaintiff's personal life; publicity that places the plaintiff in a "false light" in the public eye; and "appropriation" of the plaintiff's name or likeness for commercial

"false light" privacy case involving a matter of public interest, not a case involving "intrusion," "appropriation" of a name or likeness for the purposes of trade, or "private details" about a non-newsworthy person or event. It is also abundantly clear that *Time, Inc. v. Hill* did not involve a performer, a person with a name having commercial value, or any claim to a "right of publicity." This discrete kind of "appropriation" case was plainly identified in the literature cited by the Court and had been adjudicated in the reported cases.

The differences between these two torts are important. First, the State's interests in providing a cause of action in each instance are different. "The interest protected" in permitting recovery for placing the plaintiff in a false light "is clearly that of reputation, with the same overtones of mental distress as in defamation." Prosser, supra. By contrast, the State's interest in permitting a "right of publicity" is in protecting the proprietary interest of the individual in his act in part to encourage such entertainment. As we later note, the State's interest is closely analogous to the goals of patent and copyright law, focusing on the right of the individual to reap the reward of his endeavors and having little to do with protecting feelings or reputation. Second, the two torts differ in the degree to which they intrude on dissemination of information to the public. In "false light" cases the only way to protect the interests involved is to attempt to minimize publication of the damaging matter, while in "right of publicity" cases the only question is who gets to do the publishing. An entertainer such as petitioner usually has no objection to the widespread publication of his act as long as he gets the commercial benefit of such publication. Indeed, in the present case petitioner did not seek to enjoin the broadcast of his act; he simply sought compensation for the broadcast in the form of damages.

Nor does it appear that our later cases, such as *Rosenbloom v. Metromedia, Inc.,* 403 U.S. 29, 91 S.Ct. 1811, 29 L.Ed.2d 296 (1971); *Gertz v. Robert Welch, Inc.;* and *Time, Inc. v. Firestone,* require or furnish substantial support for the Ohio court's privilege ruling. These cases, like *New York Times* emphasize the protection extended to the press by the First Amendment in defamation cases, particularly when suit is brought by a public official or a public figure. None of them involve an alleged appropriation by the press of a right of publicity existing under state law.

Moreover, *Time, Inc. v. Hill, New York Times, Metromedia, Gertz,* and *Firestone* all involved the reporting of events; in none of them was there an attempt to broadcast or publish an entire act for which the performer ordinarily gets paid. [P]etitioner's state-law right of publicity would not serve to prevent respondent from reporting the newsworthy facts about petitioner's act. Wherever the line in particular situations is to be drawn between media reports that are protected and those that are

purposes. One may be liable for "appropria-
tion" if he "pirate[s] the plaintiff's identity   for some advantage of his own."

not, we are quite sure that the First and Fourteenth Amendments do not immunize the media when they broadcast a performer's entire act without his consent. The Constitution no more prevents a State from requiring respondent to compensate petitioner for broadcasting his act on television than it would privilege respondent to film and broadcast a copyrighted dramatic work without liability to the copyright owner; or to film and broadcast a prize fight; or a baseball game, where the promoters or the participants had other plans for publicizing the event. There are ample reasons for reaching this conclusion.

The broadcast of a film of petitioner's entire act poses a substantial threat to the economic value of that performance. As the Ohio court recognized, this act is the product of petitioner's own talents and energy, the end result of much time, effort, and expense. Much of its economic value lies in the "right of exclusive control over the publicity given to his performance"; if the public can see the act free on television, it will be less willing to pay to see it at the fair.* The effect of a public broadcast of the performance is similar to preventing petitioner from charging an admission fee. "The rationale for [protecting the right of publicity] is the straight-forward one of preventing unjust enrichment by the theft of good will. No social purpose is served by having the defendant get free some aspect of the plaintiff that would have market value and for which he would normally pay." Moreover, the broadcast of petitioner's entire performance, unlike the unauthorized use of another's name for purposes of trade or the incidental use of a name or picture by the press, goes to the heart of petitioner's ability to earn a living as an entertainer. Thus, in this case, Ohio has recognized what may be the strongest case for a "right of publicity"—involving, not the appropriation of an entertainer's reputation to enhance the attractiveness of a commercial product, but the appropriation of the very activity by which the entertainer acquired his reputation in the first place.

Of course, Ohio's decision to protect petitioner's right of publicity here rests on more than a desire to compensate the performer for the time and effort invested in his act; the protection provides an economic incentive for him to make the investment required to produce a performance of interest to the public. This same consideration underlies the patent and copyright laws long enforced by this Court.... The Constitution does not prevent Ohio from making a similar choice here in deciding to protect the entertainer's incentive in order to encourage the production of this type of work.**

---

* It is possible, of course, that respondent's news broadcast increased the value of petitioner's performance by stimulating the public's interest in seeing act live. In these circumstances, petitioner would not be able to prove damages and thus would not recover....

** ... Federal District Courts have rejected First Amendment challenges to the federal copyright law on the ground that

"no restraint [has been] placed on the use of an idea or concept." *United States v. Bodin*, 375 F.Supp. 1265, 1267 (W.D.Okl. 1974).... Of course, this case does not involve a claim that respondent would be prevented by petitioner's "right of publicity" from staging or filming its own "human cannonball" act....

There is no doubt that entertainment, as well as news, enjoys First Amendment protection. It is also true that entertainment itself can be important news. But it is important to note that neither the public nor respondent will be deprived of the benefit of petitioner's performance as long as his commercial stake in his act is appropriately recognized. Petitioner does not seek to enjoin the broadcast of his performance; he simply wants to be paid for it. Nor do we think that a state-law damages remedy against respondent would represent a species of liability without fault contrary to the letter or spirit of *Gertz v. Robert Welch, Inc.* Respondent knew that petitioner objected to televising his act but nevertheless displayed the entire film.

We conclude that although the State of Ohio may as a matter of its own law privilege the press in the circumstances of this case, the First and Fourteenth Amendments do not require it to do so.

Reversed.

Mr. Justice Powell, with whom Mr. Justice Brennan and Mr. Justice Marshall join, dissenting.

Disclaiming any attempt to do more than decide the narrow case before us, the Court reverses the decision of the Supreme Court of Ohio based on repeated incantation of a single formula: "a performer's entire act." The holding today is summed up in one sentence: "Wherever the line in particular situations is to be drawn between media reports that are protected and those that are not, we are quite sure that the First and Fourteenth Amendments do not immunize the media when they broadcast a performer's entire act without his consent." I doubt that this formula provides a standard clear enough even for resolution of this case.* In any event, I am not persuaded that the Court's opinion is appropriately sensitive to the First Amendment values at stake, and I therefore dissent.

Although the Court would draw no distinction, I do not view respondent's action as comparable to unauthorized commercial broadcasts of sporting events, theatrical performances, and the like where the broadcaster keeps the profits. There is no suggestion here that respondent made any such use of the film. Instead, it simply reported on what petitioner concedes to be a newsworthy event, in a way hardly surprising for a television station—by means of film coverage. The report was part of an ordinary daily news program, consuming a total of 15 seconds. It is

---

* Although the record is not explicit, it is unlikely that the "act" commenced abruptly with the explosion that launched petitioner on his way, ending with the landing in the net a few seconds later. One may assume that the actual firing was preceded by some fanfare, possibly stretching over several minutes, to heighten the audience's anticipation: introduction of the performer, description of the uniqueness and danger, last-minute checking of the apparatus, and entry into the cannon, all accompanied by suitably ominous commentary from the master of ceremonies. If this is found to be the case on remand, then respondent could not be said to have appropriated the "entire act" in its 15–second newsclip—and the Court's opinion then would afford no guidance for resolution of the case. Moreover, in future cases involving different performances, similar difficulties in determining just what constitutes the "entire act" are inevitable.

a routine example of the press' fulfilling the informing function so vital to our system.

The Court's holding that the station's ordinary news report may give rise to substantial liability has disturbing implications, for the decision could lead to a degree of media self-censorship. Hereafter, whenever a television news editor is unsure whether certain film footage received from a camera crew might be held to portray an "entire act,"*** he may decline coverage—even of clearly newsworthy events—or confine the broadcast to watered-down verbal reporting, perhaps with an occasional still picture. The public is then the loser. This is hardly the kind of news reportage that the First Amendment is meant to foster.

In my view the First Amendment commands a different analytical starting point from the one selected by the Court. Rather than begin with a quantitative analysis of the performer's behavior—is this or is this not his entire act?—we should direct initial attention to the actions of the news media: what use did the station make of the film footage? When a film is used, as here, for a routine portion of a regular news program, I would hold that the First Amendment protects the station from a "right of publicity" or "appropriation" suit, absent a strong showing by the plaintiff that the news broadcast was a subterfuge or cover for private or commercial exploitation.

I emphasize that this is a "reappropriation" suit rather than one of the other varieties of "right of privacy" tort suits identified by Dean Prosser in his classic article. In those other causes of action the competing interests are considerably different. The plaintiff generally seeks to avoid any sort of public exposure, and the existence of constitutional privilege is therefore less likely to turn on whether the publication occurred in a news broadcast or in some other fashion. In a suit like the one before us, however, the plaintiff does not complain about the fact of exposure to the public, but rather about its timing or manner. He welcomes some publicity, but seeks to retain control over means and manner as a way to maximize for himself the monetary benefits that flow from such publication. But having made the matter public—having chosen, in essence, to make it newsworthy—he cannot, consistent with the First Amendment, complain of routine news reportage.

Since the film clip here was undeniably treated as news and since there is no claim that the use was subterfuge, respondent's actions were constitutionally privileged. I would affirm.

[The dissenting opinion of Stevens, J., is omitted.]

Notes

1. *Harper & Row Publishers, Inc. v. Nation Enterprises*, 471 U.S. 539, 105 S.Ct. 2218, 85 L.Ed.2d 588 (1985). The Court held that *The Nation*

*** Such doubts are especially likely to arise when the editor receives film footage of an event at a local fair, a circus, a sports competition of limited duration (e.g., the winning effort in a ski-jump competition), or a dramatic production made up of short skits, to offer only a few examples.

Magazine violated the copyright laws when it published, without permission, extensive quotations from a purloined copy of former President Ford's then unpublished memoirs, "A Time to Heal." *The Nation* excerpt, which focused on Ford's pardon of former President Nixon, was designed to scoop an article based on Ford's memoirs that *Time* Magazine had earlier contracted to publish. Because of *The Nation's* publication, *Time* canceled its plans to publish its own article.

The Nation's generous verbatim excerpts were, under the circumstances, a copyright infringement not sanctioned as a "fair use" under the Copyright Act. The Court rejected the argument that the first amendment required a different standard simply because the information conveyed is of high public concern:

> [C]opyright assures those who write and publish factual narratives such as "A Time to Heal" that they may at least enjoy the right to market the original expression contained therein as just compensation for their investment. "[T]o propose that fair use be imposed whenever the 'social value [of dissemination] ... outweighs any detriment to the artist,' would be to propose depriving copyright owners of their right in the property precisely when they encounter those users who could afford to pay for it." ... In view of the First Amendment protections already embodied in the Copyright Act's distinction between copyrightable expression and uncopyrightable facts and ideas, and the latitude for scholarship and comment traditionally afforded by fair use, we see no warrant for expanding the doctrine of fair use to create what amounts to a public figure exception to copyright.

Justice Brennan, joined by White and Marshall, JJ., dissented.

2. *San Francisco Arts & Athletics, Inc. v. United States Olympic Committee, Inter–National Olympic Committee*, 483 U.S. 522, 107 S.Ct. 2971, 97 L.Ed.2d 427 (1987). Section 110 of the Amateur Sports Act of 1978 authorized the United States Olympic Committee (USOC) to prohibit any person from using the word "Olympic" for the "purpose of trade, to induce the sale of any goods or services, or to promote any theatrical exhibition, athletic performance, or competition." San Francisco Arts & Athletics, Inc. (SFAA), a nonprofit corporation, sought to promote the "Gay Olympic Games" in 1982 and every four years thereafter. The Gay Games were touted as opening with a ceremony that "will rival the traditional Olympic Games." Over 2000 relay runners starting from New York would carry the "Gay Olympic Torch" and light the "Gay Olympic Flame." The winners of the various contests would receive gold, silver, and bronze medals. The SFAA proposed to sell T-shirts, buttons and other items, all showing the title "Gay Olympic Games." At the request of the USOC, the district court enjoined the use of the word "Olympic" in the description of the planned games (which were then held under the name "Gay Games I," in 1982, and "Gay Games II" in 1986). The Supreme Court, per Powell, J., affirmed.

Powell concluded that Congress intended to provide the USOC with protection broader than normal trademark protection, and that the USOC has "exclusive control of the use of the word 'Olympic' without regard to whether an unauthorized use of the word tends to cause confusion." (In addition, an unauthorized user would not have the normal statutory trademark defenses). Also, because the SFAA sought to sell T-shirts, bumper stickers, etc., all emblazoned with "Gay Olympic Games", the "possibility of confusion as to sponsorship is obvious." The Court said: "Under § 110, the USOC may prohibit purely promotional uses of the word *only* when the promotion relates to an athletic or theatrical event. The USOC created the value of the word by using it in connection with an athletic event." (emphasis added). The Court said that there was no need to decide whether Congress could ever grant a private entity exclusive use of a generic word, because "Olympic" was not generic.

The Court also declared: "Nor is it clear that § 110 restricts purely expressive uses of the word 'Olympic' "(At this point the Court cited a lower court decision, *Stop the Olympic Prison v. USOC,* 489 F.Supp. 1112, 1118–21 (S.D.N.Y.1980), which upheld the use of the Olympic logo of five interacting rings and the Olympic torch on a poster opposing the planned conversion of the Olympic Village at Lake Placid. The lower court "found that the use of the symbols did not fit the commercial or promotional definition of uses in § 110.").

Brennan, J., joined by Marshall, J., dissented and argued that § 110 violated free speech. It was overbroad because it was susceptible of applying to a substantial amount of noncommercial speech, and because it discriminated on the basis of content. Brennan noted that over 200 organizations listed in just the Los Angeles and Manhattan telephone directories start with the word "Olympic."

10–9.   THE RIGHT OF ASSOCIATION

10–9.1 Inquiries into Associations

NATIONAL ASSOCIATION FOR THE ADVANCEMENT OF COLORED PEOPLE v. ALABAMA EX REL. PATTERSON
357 U.S. 449, 78 S.Ct. 1163, 2 L.Ed.2d 1488 (1958).

Mr. Justice Harlan delivered the opinion of the Court.

We review from the standpoint of its validity under the Federal Constitution a judgment of civil contempt entered against petitioner, the National Association for the Advancement of Colored People, in the courts of Alabama. The question presented is whether Alabama, consistently with the Due Process Clause of the Fourteenth Amendment, can compel petitioner to reveal to the State's Attorney General the names and addresses of all its Alabama members and agents, without regard to their positions or functions in the Association. The judgment of contempt was based upon petitioner's refusal to comply fully with a court order requiring in part the production of membership lists. Petitioner's claim is that the order, in the circumstances shown by this record, violated rights assured to petitioner and its members under the Constitution....

The Association both urges that it is constitutionally entitled to resist official inquiry into its membership lists, and that it may assert, on behalf of its members, a right personal to them to be protected from compelled disclosure by the State of their affiliation with the Association as revealed by the membership lists. We think that petitioner argues more appropriately the rights of its members, and that its nexus with them is sufficient to permit that it act as their representative before this Court. In so concluding, we reject respondent's argument that the Association lacks standing to assert here constitutional rights pertaining to the members, who are not of course parties to the litigation. . . .

We thus reach petitioner's claim that the production order in the state litigation trespasses upon fundamental freedoms protected by the Due Process Clause of the Fourteenth Amendment. Petitioner argues that in view of the facts and circumstances shown in the record, the effect of compelled disclosure of the membership lists will be to abridge the rights of its rank-and-file members to engage in lawful association in support of their common beliefs. It contends that governmental action which, although not directly suppressing association, nevertheless carries this consequence, can be justified only upon some overriding valid interest of the State.

Effective advocacy of both public and private points of view, particularly controversial ones, is undeniably enhanced by group association, as this Court has more than once recognized by remarking upon the close nexus between the freedoms of speech and assembly. It is beyond debate that freedom to engage in association for the advancement of beliefs and ideas is an inseparable aspect of the "liberty" assured by the Due Process Clause of the Fourteenth Amendment, which embraces freedom of speech. . . . The fact that Alabama, so far as is relevant to the validity of the contempt judgment presently under review, has taken no direct action to restrict the right of petitioner's members to associate freely, does not end inquiry into the effect of the production order. In the domain of these indispensable liberties, whether of speech, press, or association, the decisions of this Court recognize that abridgment of such rights, even though unintended, may inevitably follow from varied forms of governmental action. . . .

It is hardly a novel perception that compelled disclosure of affiliation with groups engaged in advocacy may constitute [an] effective restraint on freedom of association. . . . This Court has recognized the vital relationship between freedom to associate and privacy in one's associations. When referring to the varied forms of governmental action which might interfere with freedom of assembly, it said in *American Communications Assn. v. Douds,* [339 U.S. 382 at 402, 70 S.Ct. 674, at 686, 94 L.Ed. 925]: "A requirement that adherents of particular religious faiths or political parties wear identifying arm-bands, for example, is obviously of this nature." Compelled disclosure of membership in an organization engaged in advocacy of particular beliefs is of the same order. Inviolability of privacy in group association may in many circumstances be indispensable to preservation of freedom of association, particularly where a group espouses dissident beliefs.

We think that the production order, in the respects here drawn in question, must be regarded as entailing the likelihood of a substantial restraint upon the exercise by petitioner's members of their right to freedom of association. Petitioner has made an uncontroverted showing that on past occasions revelation of the identity of its rank-and-file members has exposed these members to economic reprisal, loss of employment, threat of physical coercion, and other manifestations of public hostility. Under these circumstances, we think it apparent that compelled disclosure of petitioner's Alabama membership is likely to affect adversely the ability of petitioner and its members to pursue their collective effort to foster beliefs which they admittedly have the right to advocate, in that it may induce members to withdraw from the Association and dissuade others from joining it because of fear of exposure of their beliefs shown through their associations and of the consequences of this exposure.

It is not sufficient to answer, as the State does here, that whatever repressive effect compulsory disclosure of names of petitioner's members may have upon participation by Alabama citizens in petitioner's activities follows not from *State* action but from *private* community pressures. The crucial factor is the interplay of governmental and private action, for it is only after the initial exertion of state power represented by the production order that private action takes hold.

We turn to the final question whether Alabama has demonstrated an interest in obtaining the disclosures it seeks from petitioner which is sufficient to justify the deterrent effect which we have concluded these disclosures may well have on the free exercise by petitioner's members of their constitutionally protected right of association. . . .

It is important to bear in mind that petitioner asserts no right to absolute immunity from state investigation, and no right to disregard Alabama's laws. [P]etitioner does not deny Alabama's right to obtain from it such information as the State desires concerning the purposes of the Association and its activities within the State. Petitioner has not objected to divulging the identity of its members who are employed by or hold official positions with it. It has urged the rights solely of its ordinary rank-and-file members. This is therefore not analogous to a case involving the interest of a State in protecting its citizens in their dealings with paid solicitors or agents of foreign corporations by requiring identification.

. . . The exclusive purpose was to determine whether petitioner was conducting intrastate business in violation of the Alabama foreign corporation registration statute, and the membership lists were expected to help resolve this question. [But the NAACP has now admitted its presence in the state and offered to comply with the state registration statute, although still claiming that the statute does not apply to it.] . . .

From what has already been said, we think it apparent that *New York ex rel. Bryant v. Zimmerman*, 278 U.S. 63, 49 S.Ct. 61, 73 L.Ed. 184, cannot be relied on in support of the State's position, for that case involved markedly different considerations in terms of the interest of the State in obtaining disclosure. There, this Court upheld, as applied to a member of a local chapter of the Ku Klux Klan, a New York statute requiring any unincorporated association which demanded an oath as a condition to membership to file with state officials copies of its " . . . constitution, bylaws, rules, regulations and oath of membership, together with a roster of its membership and a list of its officers for the current year." In its opinion, the Court took care to emphasize the nature of the organization which New York sought to regulate. The decision was based on the particular character of the Klan's activities, involving acts of unlawful intimidation and violence, which the Court assumed was before the state legislature when it enacted the statute, and of which the Court itself took judicial notice. Furthermore, the situation before us is significantly different from that in *Bryant,* because the organization there had made no effort to comply with any of the requirements of New York's statute but rather had refused to furnish the State with *any* information as to its local activities.

We hold that the immunity from state scrutiny of membership lists which the Association claims on behalf of its members is here so related to the right of the members to pursue their lawful private interests privately and to associate freely with others in so doing as to come within the protection of the Fourteenth Amendment. And we conclude that Alabama has fallen short of showing a controlling justification for the deterrent effect on the free enjoyment of the right to associate which disclosure of membership lists is likely to have. Accordingly, the judgment of civil contempt and the $100,000 fine which resulted from petitioner's refusal to comply with the production order in this respect must fall. . . .

Notes

1. ADMINISTRATIVE AND LEGISLATIVE INVESTIGATIONS. *Barenblatt v. United States,* 360 U.S. 109, 79 S.Ct. 1081, 3 L.Ed.2d 1115 (1959) upheld the power of a congressional subcommittee to compel a witness to answer questions about his "participation in or knowledge of alleged Communist Party activities at educational institutions in this country." The Communist Party is not "an ordinary political party" for there is a "close nexus between the Communist Party and violent overthrow of government." Petitioner argued that the investigation was really aimed at the theoretical classroom discussion of communism, not its revolutionary aspects. But Harlan, J., for the Court, disagreed. "An investigation of advocacy of or preparation for overthrow certainly embraces the right to identify a witness as a member of the Communist Party and to inquire into the various manifestations of the Party's tenets."

In *Gibson v. Florida Legislative Investigation Committee,* 372 U.S. 539, 83 S.Ct. 889, 9 L.Ed.2d 929 (1963), the Court, per Goldberg, J., prohibited an attempt of a state legislative committee to secure the contents of the membership lists of the Miami branch of the NAACP. The committee was investigating communist infiltration of various organizations including the NAACP and wanted to know if certain alleged communists were also members of the NAACP. The local NAACP president volunteered to answer membership questions based on his personal knowledge but would not bring the membership lists to the hearing. The NAACP had adopted resolutions every year since 1950 barring Communists from membership. The legislative committee was not seeking information as to whether anyone was a Communist but rather whether certain persons were members of the NAACP, a "concededly legitimate and nonsubversive organization." Such a request was different from requesting Communist Party membership. Moreover, to say that it is permissible to inquire into Communist infiltration of an organization "does not mean that it is permissible to demand or require from such other groups disclosure of their membership by inquiry into their records when such disclosure will seriously inhibit or impair the exercise of constitutional rights and has not itself been demonstrated to bear a crucial relation to a proper governmental interest or to be essential to fulfillment of a proper government purpose." The state had failed to show a "substantial connection" between the NAACP branch and Communist activities. Evidence that 14 people were alleged to be Communists and had attended or were members of the NAACP branch was indirect, equivocal, and mostly hearsay.

DeGregory v. Attorney General, 383 U.S. 825, 86 S.Ct. 1148, 16 L.Ed.2d 292 (1966) upheld a witness' refusal to answer questions by the New Hampshire Attorney General concerning Communist activities prior to 1957. In that year the state enacted a statute authorizing the Attorney General to conduct such investigations. A 1955 report had connected the appellant with the Communist Party in 1953, over 10 years prior to the investigation. The Court, per Douglas, J., emphasized that the staleness of the basis for the investigation, and the subject matter, made "indefensible such exposure of one's associational and political past—exposure which is objectionable and damaging in the extreme to one whose associations and political views do not command majority approval."

2. ADMISSION TO THE BAR. In several cases the Supreme Court attempted to outline the limits on state inquiries that are precedent to admission to the bar. *Konigsberg v. State Bar (Konigsberg I),* 353 U.S. 252, 77 S.Ct. 722, 1 L.Ed.2d 810 (1957) held that mere membership in the Communist Party does not support an inference that the applicant lacked good moral character. See also, *Schware v. Board of Bar Examiners,* 353 U.S. 232, 77 S.Ct. 752, 1 L.Ed.2d 796 (1957). *Konigsberg v. State Bar (Konigsberg II),* 366 U.S. 36, 81 S.Ct. 997, 6 L.Ed.2d 105 (1961) held that the applicant could be denied admission because he refused to answer questions about his possible membership in the Communist Party. Although he could not be refused admission merely because of his past membership, the refusal to answer obstructed the investigation because it deprived the committee of the opportunity of investigating further to determine if the applicant was an active member with knowledge of the Communist Party's illegal goals and with a specific intent to aid in the implementation of those goals.

In 1971 the Supreme Court decided three cases on admission to the bar, only one of which produced a majority opinion. That case was *Law Students Civil Rights Research Council, Inc. v. Wadmond,* 401 U.S. 154, 91 S.Ct. 720, 27 L.Ed.2d 749 (1971). The bar asked the applicant if he was knowingly a member of any group advocating or teaching the overthrow of the Government by force or violence or other unlawful means. If the answer was yes, the next question was whether the applicant had specific intent to further the aims of that organization by force or violence. The Court, per Stewart, J., held that the use of such a bifurcated inquiry was valid. In *Baird v. State Bar,* 401 U.S. 1, 91 S.Ct. 702, 27 L.Ed.2d 639 (1971), the Court, with no majority opinion, invalidated an attempt to make an applicant state whether she had ever been a member of the Communist Party or any organization that advocates overthrow of the Government by force or violence. Black, J., for a plurality of four Justices argued that the question was an invalid attempt to inquire about a person's views or associations. Stewart, J., concurring, found that the question was deficient because it was not confined to "knowing" membership, i.e., that the person knew that the organization was a Communist or Communist front group. *In re Stolar,* 401 U.S. 23, 91 S.Ct. 713, 27 L.Ed.2d 657 (1971) invalidated a similar question. It also invalidated two questions requiring the applicant to list all the organizations to which he had belonged since registering as a law student and all those of which he had ever been a member. Again Black, J., for a plurality, and Stewart, J., separately, found the questions overbroad and placed pressures on a student to avoid controversial organizations.

3. CIVIL LIABILITY OF ASSOCIATIONS FOR CONDUCT OF MEMBERS. *NAACP v. Claiborne Hardware Co.,* 458 U.S. 886, 102 S.Ct. 3409, 73 L.Ed.2d 1215 (1982) overturned, with no dissent, a Mississippi State Court judgment against the NAACP and certain individuals for business losses suffered by several white merchants because of an economic boycott against them. On October 31, 1969, several hundred blacks at a local NAACP meeting voted to boycott white merchants in Claiborne County, after failure to achieve their demands regarding racial equality. Although some boycott supporters engaged in acts of violence, most of the practices used to encourage support for the boycott were peaceful, and protected by the First Amendment. The Supreme Court held that the State cannot award damages for the consequences of protected activity, but only for losses "proximately caused by unlawful conduct...." Nor may it impose civil liability on an individual just because he belonged to a group and some of the members of that group committed acts of violence. "Mere association" with a group "absent a specific intent to further an unlawful aim embraced by that group" cannot make one liable. Only those persons who actually engaged in violence or threats of violence can be held liable. Nor can the NAACP be liable unless it "authorized—either actually or apparently—or ratified unlawful conduct...."

Contrast, *FTC v. Superior Court Trial Lawyers Association,* 493 U.S. 411, 110 S.Ct. 768, 107 L.Ed.2d 851 (1990). Various individual lawyers (not employees of any employer) in Washington, D.C. agreed not to represent indigent criminal defendants in the Superior Court unless the District increased their compensation, which eventually occurred. Later, the Federal Trade Commission ruled that the lawyers' conduct violated § 5 of the FTC Act, and issued a cease-and-desist order against future boycotts. The Supreme Court ruled that *Claiborne Hardware* did not immunize this boycott from the antitrust laws. In *Claiborne,* the boycott supporters sought no special advantage for themselves; that case does not apply to a boycott conducted by business competitors who "stand to profit financially from a lessening of competition in the boycotted market."

10–9.2 Loyalty Oaths

COLE v. RICHARDSON

405 U.S. 676, 92 S.Ct. 1332, 31 L.Ed.2d 593 (1972).

MR. CHIEF JUSTICE BURGER delivered the opinion of the Court.

In this appeal we review the decision of the three-judge District Court holding a Massachusetts loyalty oath unconstitutional.

The appellee, Richardson, was hired as a research sociologist by the Boston State Hospital. Appellant Cole is superintendent of the hospital. Soon after she entered on duty Mrs. Richardson was asked to subscribe to the oath required of all public employees in Massachusetts. The oath is as follows:

> I do solemnly swear (or affirm) that I will uphold and defend the Constitution of the United States of America and the Constitution of the Commonwealth of Massachusetts and that I will oppose the overthrow of the government of the United States of America or of this Commonwealth by force, violence or by any illegal or unconstitutional method.

Mrs. Richardson informed the hospital's personnel department that she could not take the oath as ordered because of her belief that it was in violation of the United States Constitution. [Thus she was terminated. She then brought this suit.] . . .

A review of the oath cases in this Court will put the instant oath into context. We have made clear that neither federal nor state government may condition employment on taking oaths that impinge on rights guaranteed by the First and Fourteenth Amendments respectively, as for example those relating to political beliefs. Nor may employment be conditioned on an oath that one has not engaged, or will not engage, in protected speech activities such as the following: criticizing institutions of government; discussing political doctrine that approves the overthrow of certain forms of government; and supporting candidates for political office. Employment may not be conditioned on an oath denying past, or abjuring future, associational activities within constitutional protection; such protected activities include membership in organizations having illegal purposes unless one knows of the purpose and shares a specific intent to promote the illegal purpose. . . . And, finally, an oath may not be so vague that " 'men of common intelligence must necessarily guess at its meaning and differ as to its application, [because such an oath] violates the first essential of due process of law.' " Concern for vagueness in the oath cases has been especially great because uncertainty as to an oath's meaning may deter individuals from engaging in constitutionally protected activity conceivably within the scope of the oath.

An underlying, seldom articulated concern running throughout these cases is that the oaths under consideration often required individuals to reach back into their past to recall minor, sometimes innocent, activities. They put the government into "the censorial business of investigating, scrutinizing, interpreting, and then penalizing or approving the political viewpoints" and past activities of individuals. *Law Students Civil Rights Research Council v. Wadmond,* 401 U.S., at 192, 91 S.Ct., at 740 (Marshall, J., dissenting).

Several cases recently decided by the Court stand out among our oath cases because they have upheld the constitutionality of oaths, addressed to the future, promising constitutional support in broad terms. These cases have begun with a recognition that the Constitution itself prescribes comparable oaths in two articles. Article II, § 1, cl. 8, provides that the President shall swear that he will "faithfully execute the Office ... and will to the best of [his] Ability, preserve, protect and defend the Constitution of the United States." Article VI, cl. 3, provides that all state and federal officers shall be bound by an oath "to support this Constitution." The oath taken by attorneys as a condition of admission to the Bar of this Court identically provides in part "that I will support the Constitution of the United States"; it also requires the attorney to state that he will "conduct [himself] uprightly, and according to law." ... Thus in *Ohlson v. Phillips,* 397 U.S. 317, 90 S.Ct. 1124, 25 L.Ed.2d 337 (1970), we sustained the constitutionality of a state requirement that teachers swear to "uphold" the Constitution. The District Court had concluded that the oath was simply a " 'recognition that ours is a government of laws and not of men,' "and that the oath involved an affirmation of "organic law" and rejection of "the use of force to overthrow the government."

The District Court in the instant case properly recognized that the first clause of the Massachusetts oath, in which the individual swears to "uphold and defend" the Constitutions of the United States and the Commonwealth, is indistinguishable from the oaths this Court has recently approved. Yet the District Court applied a highly literalistic approach to the second clause to strike it down. We view the second clause of the oath as essentially the same as the first.

The second clause of the oath contains a promise to "oppose the overthrow of the government of the United States of America or of this Commonwealth by force, violence or by any illegal or unconstitutional method." The District Court sought to give a dictionary meaning to this language and found "oppose" to raise the specter of vague, undefinable responsibilities actively to combat a potential overthrow of the government. That reading of the oath understandably troubled the court because of what it saw as vagueness in terms of what threats would constitute sufficient danger of overthrow to require the oath giver to actively oppose overthrow, and exactly what actions he would have to take in that respect.

But such a literal approach to the second clause is inconsistent with the Court's approach to the "support" oaths. One could make a literal argument that "support" involves nebulous, undefined responsibilities for action in some hypothetical situations.... We have rejected such rigidly literal notions and recognized that the purpose leading legislatures to enact such oaths, just as the purpose leading the Framers of our Constitution to include the two explicit constitutional oaths, was not to create specific responsibilities but to assure that those in positions of public trust were willing to commit themselves to live by the constitutional processes of our system.... Here the second clause does not require specific action in some hypothetical or actual situation. Plainly "force, violence or ... any illegal or unconstitutional method" modifies "overthrow" and does not commit the oath taker to meet force with force. Just as the connotatively active word "support" has been interpreted to mean simply a commitment to abide by our constitutional system, the second clause of this oath is merely oriented to the negative implication of this notion; it is a commitment not to use illegal and constitutionally unprotected force to change the constitutional system. The second clause does not expand the obligation of the first; it simply makes clear the application of the first clause to a particular issue. Such repetition, whether for emphasis or cadence, seems to be the wont of authors of oaths. That the second clause may be redundant is no ground to strike it down; we are not charged with correcting grammar but with enforcing a constitution.

The purpose of the oath is clear on its face. We cannot presume that the Massachusetts Legislature intended by its use of such general terms as "uphold," "defend," and "oppose" to impose obligations of specific, positive action on oath takers. Any such construction would raise serious questions whether the oath was so vague as to amount to a denial of due process.

Nor is the oath as interpreted void for vagueness.... It is punishable only by a prosecution for perjury and, since perjury is a knowing and willful falsehood, the constitutional vice of punishment without fair warning cannot occur here. Nor here is there any problem of the punishment inflicted by mere prosecution. There has been no prosecution under this statute since its 1948 enactment, and there is no indication that prosecutions have been planned or begun. The oath "triggered no serious possibility of prosecution" by the Commonwealth. Were we confronted with a record of actual prosecutions or harassment through threatened prosecutions, we might be faced with a different question. Those who view the Massachusetts oath in terms of an endless "parade of horribles" would do well to bear in mind that many of the hazards of human existence that can be imagined are circumscribed by the classic observation of Mr. Justice Holmes, when confronted with the prophecy of dire consequences of certain judicial action, that it would not occur "while this Court sits." *Panhandle Oil Co. v. State of Miss. ex rel. Knox,* 277 U.S. 218, at 223, 48 S.Ct. 451, at 453, 72 L.Ed. 857 (dissenting)....

The judgment of the District Court is reversed and the case is remanded for further proceedings consistent with this opinion.

MR. JUSTICE POWELL and MR. JUSTICE REHNQUIST took no part in the consideration or decision of this case.

MR. JUSTICE MARSHALL, with whom MR. JUSTICE BRENNAN joins, dissenting.

. . . In my opinion, the second half of the oath is not only vague, but also overbroad. . . . It is vague because "men of common intelligence [must] speculate at their peril on its meaning." . . . The most striking problem with the oath is that it is not clear whether the last prepositional phrase modified the verb "oppose" or the noun "overthrow." Thus, an affiant cannot be certain whether he is swearing that he will "oppose" governmental overthrow by utilizing every means at his disposal, including those specifically prohibited by the laws or constitutions he has sworn to support, or whether he has merely accepted the responsibility of opposing illegal or unconstitutional overthrows. [T]he affiant is left with little guidance as to the responsibilities he has assumed in taking the oath. In what form, for example, must he manifest his opposition to an overthrow? . . . Vagueness is also inherent in the use of the word "overthrow." When does an affiant's undefined responsibility under the oath require action: When an overthrow is threatened? When an overthrow is likely to be threatened? When a threatened overthrow has some chance of success? . . .

The Court's prior decisions represent a judgment that simple affirmative oaths of support are less suspect and less evil than negative oaths requiring a disaffirmance of political ties, group affiliations, or beliefs. Yet, I think that it is plain that affirmative oaths of loyalty, no less than negative ones, have odious connotations and that they present dangers. . . .

Loyalty oaths do not have a very pleasant history in this country. Whereas they may be developed initially as a means of fostering power and confidence in government, there is a danger that they will swell "into an instrument of thought control and a means of enforcing complete political conformity." Within the limits of the Constitution it is, of course, for the legislators to weigh the utility of the oaths and their potential dangers and to strike a balance. But, as a people, we should always keep in mind the words of MR. JUSTICE BLACK, concurring in *Speiser v. Randall,* 357 U.S., at 532, 78 S.Ct., at 1354:

> Loyalty oaths, as well as other contemporary "security measures," tend to stifle all forms of unorthodox or unpopular thinking or expression—the kind of thought and expression which has played such a vital and beneficial role in the history of this Nation. The result is a stultifying conformity which in the end may well turn out to be more destructive to our free society than foreign agents could ever hope to be. . . . I am certain that loyalty to the United States can never be secured by the endless proliferation of "loyalty" oaths; loyalty must arise spontaneously from the hearts of people who love their country and respect their government.

Accordingly, I would affirm the decision of the District Court.

[The concurring opinion of STEWART & WHITE, JJ., and the dissenting opinion of DOUGLAS, J., are omitted.]

10–9.3 Patronage Dismissals

BRANTI v. FINKEL
445 U.S. 507, 100 S.Ct. 1287, 63 L.Ed.2d 574 (1980).

MR. JUSTICE STEVENS delivered the opinion of the Court.

The question presented is whether the First and Fourteenth Amendments to the Constitution protect an assistant public defender who is satisfactorily performing his job from discharge solely because of his political beliefs. . . .

The critical facts can be summarized briefly. The Rockland County Public Defender is appointed by the County Legislature for a term of six years. He in turn appoints nine assistants who serve at his pleasure. The two respondents have served as assistants since their respective appointments in March 1971 and September 1975; they are both Republicans.

Petitioner Branti's predecessor, a Republican, was appointed in 1972 by a Republican-dominated County Legislature. By 1977, control of the legislature had shifted to the Democrats and petitioner, also a Democrat, was appointed to replace the incumbent when his term expired. As soon as petitioner was formally appointed on January 3, 1978, he began executing termination notices for six of the nine assistants then in office. Respondents were among those who were to be terminated. With one possible exception, the nine who were to be appointed or retained were all Democrats and were all selected by Democratic legislators or Democratic town chairmen on a basis that had been determined by the Democratic caucus. The District Court found that Finkel and Tabakman had been selected for termination solely because they were Republicans and thus did not have the necessary Democratic sponsors. . . .

In *Elrod v. Burns,* [427 U.S. 347, 96 S.Ct. 2673, 49 L.Ed.2d 547 (1976)], the Court held that the newly elected Democratic sheriff of Cook County, Ill., had violated the constitutional rights of certain non-civil service employees by discharging them "because they did not support and were not members of the Democratic Party and had failed to obtain the sponsorship of one of its leaders." That holding was supported by two separate opinions.

Writing for the plurality, Mr. Justice Brennan identified two separate but interrelated reasons supporting the conclusion that the discharges were prohibited by the First and Fourteenth Amendments. First, he analyzed the impact of a political patronage system* on freedom of belief and association. Noting that in order to retain their jobs, the

---

* Mr. Justice Brennan noted that many other practices are included within the definition of a patronage system, including placing supporters in government jobs not made available by political discharges, granting supporters lucrative government contracts, and giving favored wards improved public services. In that case, as in this, however, the only practice at issue was the dismissal of public employees for partisan reasons. In light of the limited nature of the question presented, we have no occasion to address petitioner's argument that there is a compelling governmental interest in maintaining a political sponsorship system for filling vacancies in the public defender's office.

sheriff's employees were required to pledge their allegiance to the Democratic party, work for or contribute to the party's candidates, or obtain a Democratic sponsor, he concluded that the inevitable tendency of such a system was to coerce employees into compromising their true beliefs. That conclusion, in his opinion, brought the practice within the rule of cases like *Board of Education v. Barnette,* 319 U.S. 624, 63 S.Ct. 1178, 87 L.Ed. 1628 [(1943)], condemning the use of governmental power to prescribe what the citizenry must accept as orthodox opinion.

Second, apart from the potential impact of patronage dismissals on the formation and expression of opinion Mr. Justice Brennan also stated that the practice had the effect of imposing an unconstitutional condition on the receipt of a public benefit and therefore came within the rule of cases like *Perry v. Sindermann,* [§ 6–3.1, supra]. In support of the holding in *Perry* that even an employee with no contractual right to retain his job cannot be dismissed for engaging in constitutionally protected speech, the Court had stated:

> For at least a quarter-century, this Court has made clear that even though a person has no "right" to a valuable governmental benefit and even though the government may deny him the benefit for any number of reasons, there are some reasons upon which the government may not rely. It may not deny a benefit to a person on a basis that infringes his constitutionally protected interests—especially, his interest in freedom of speech. For if the government could deny a benefit to a person because of his constitutionally protected speech or associations, his exercise of those freedoms would in effect be penalized and inhibited. This would allow the government to "produce a result which [it] could not command directly." ...

If the First Amendment protects a public employee from discharge based on what he has said, it must also protect him from discharge based on what he believes. Under this line of analysis, unless the Government can demonstrate "an overriding interest," "of vital importance," requiring that a person's private beliefs conform to those of the hiring authority, his beliefs cannot be the sole basis for depriving him of continued public employment.

Mr. Justice Stewart's concurring opinion avoided comment on the first branch of Mr. Justice Brennan's analysis, but expressly relied on the same passage from *Perry v. Sindermann* that is quoted above.

Petitioner argues that *Elrod v. Burns* should be read to prohibit only dismissals resulting from an employee's failure to capitulate to political coercion. Thus, he argues that, so long as an employee is not asked to change his political affiliation or to contribute to or work for the party's candidates, he may be dismissed with impunity. [P]etitioner's interpretation would require the Court to repudiate entirely the conclusion of both Mr. Justice Brennan and Mr. Justice Stewart that the First Amendment prohibits the dismissal of a public employee solely because of his private political beliefs....

Both opinions in *Elrod* recognize that party affiliation may be an acceptable requirement for some types of government employment. Thus, if an employee's private political beliefs would interfere with the discharge of his public duties, his First Amendment rights may be required to yield to the State's vital interest in maintaining governmental effectiveness and efficiency. In *Elrod,* it was clear that the duties of the employees—the chief deputy of the process division of the sheriff's office, a process server and another employee in that office, and a bailiff and security guard at the Juvenile Court of Cook County—were not of that character, for they were, as Mr. Justice Stewart stated, "nonpolicymaking, nonconfidential" employees.**

As Mr. Justice Brennan noted in *Elrod,* it is not always easy to determine whether a position is one in which political affiliation is a legitimate factor to be considered. Under some circumstances, a position may be appropriately considered political even though it is neither confidential nor policymaking in character. As one obvious example, if a State's election laws require that precincts be supervised by two election judges of different parties, a Republican judge could be legitimately discharged solely for changing his party registration. That conclusion would not depend on any finding that the job involved participation in policy decisions or access to confidential information. Rather, it would simply rest on the fact that party membership was essential to the discharge of the employee's governmental responsibilities.

It is equally clear that party affiliation is not necessarily relevant to every policymaking or confidential position. The coach of a state university's football team formulates policy, but no one could seriously claim that Republicans make better coaches than Democrats, or vice versa, no matter which party is in control of the state government. On the other hand, it is equally clear that the governor of a state may appropriately believe that the official duties of various assistants who help him write speeches, explain his views to the press, or communicate with the legislature cannot be performed effectively unless those persons share his political beliefs and party commitments. In sum, the ultimate inquiry is not whether the label "policymaker" or "confidential" fits a particular position; rather, the question is whether the hiring authority can demonstrate that party affiliation is an appropriate requirement for the effective performance of the public office involved.

Having thus framed the issue, it is manifest that the continued employment of an assistant public defender cannot properly be conditioned upon his allegiance to the political party in control of the county government. The primary, if not the only, responsibility of an assistant public defender is to represent individual citizens in controversy with the State.*** [W]hatever policymaking occurs in the public defender's office

---

** The plurality emphasized that patronage dismissals could be justified only if they advanced a governmental, rather than a partisan, interest. . . .

*** This is in contrast to the broader public responsibilities of an official such as a prosecutor. We express no opinion as to whether the deputy of such an official could

must relate to the needs of individual clients and not to any partisan political interests. Similarly, although an assistant is bound to obtain access to confidential information arising out of various attorney-client relationships, that information has no bearing whatsoever on partisan political concerns. Under these circumstances, it would undermine, rather than promote, the effective performance of an assistant public defender's office to make his tenure dependent on his allegiance to the dominant political party.

Accordingly, the entry of an injunction against termination of respondents' employment on purely political grounds was appropriate and the judgment of the Court of Appeals is

Affirmed.

MR. JUSTICE POWELL with whom MR. JUSTICE REHNQUIST joins, and with whom MR. JUSTICE STEWART joins as to Part I, dissenting. . . .

I. The Court contends that its holding is compelled by the First Amendment. In reaching this conclusion, the Court largely ignores the substantial governmental interests served by patronage. Patronage is a long-accepted practice that never has been eliminated totally by civil service laws and regulations. The flaw in the Court's opinion lies not only in its application of First Amendment principles, but also in its promulgation of a new, and substantially expanded, standard for determining which governmental employees may be retained or dismissed on the basis of political affiliation. . . . The Court gives three examples to illustrate the standard. Election judges and certain executive assistants may be chosen on the basis of political affiliation; college football coaches may not.* . . .

One example at the national level illustrates the nature and magnitude of the problem created by today's holding. The President customarily has considered political affiliation in removing and appointing United States Attorneys. Given the critical role that these key law enforcement officials play in the administration of the Department of Justice, both Democratic and Republican Attorneys General have concluded, not surprisingly, that they must have the confidence and support of the United States Attorneys. And political affiliation has been used as one indicator of loyalty.

Yet, it would be difficult to say, under the Court's standard, that "partisan" concerns properly are relevant to the performance of the

be dismissed on grounds of political party affiliation or loyalty.

* The rationale for the Court's conclusion that election judges may be partisan appointments is not readily apparent. The Court states that "if a State's election laws require that precincts be supervised by two election judges of different parties, a Republican judge could be legitimately discharged solely for changing his party registration." If the mere presence of a state law mandat-

ing political affiliation as a requirement for public employment were sufficient, then the legislature of Rockland County could reverse the result of this case merely by passing a law mandating that political affiliation be considered when a Public Defender chooses his assistants. Moreover, it is not apparent that a State could demonstrate, under the standard approved today, that only a political partisan is qualified to be an impartial election judge.

duties of a United States Attorney. This Court has noted that "[t]he office of public prosecutor is one which must be administered with courage and independence." Nevertheless, I believe that the President must have the right to consider political affiliation when he selects top ranking Department of Justice officials. The President and his Attorney General, not this Court, are charged with the responsibility for enforcing the laws and administering the Department of Justice. The Court's vague, overbroad decision may cast serious doubt on the propriety of dismissing United States Attorneys, as well as thousands of other policymaking employees at all levels of government, because of their membership in a national political party.

A constitutional standard that is both uncertain in its application and impervious to legislative change will now control selection and removal of key governmental personnel. Federal judges will now be the final arbiters as to who federal, state and local governments may employ. . . .

II. The Court errs not only in its selection of a standard, but more fundamentally in its conclusion that the First Amendment prohibits the use of membership in a national political party as a criterion for the dismissal of public employees. . . . No constitutional violation exists if patronage practices further sufficiently important interests to justify tangential burdening of First Amendment rights. . . .

III. Patronage appointments help build stable political parties by offering rewards to persons who assume the tasks necessary to the continued functioning of political organizations. . . . Political parties, dependent in many ways upon patronage, serve a variety of substantial governmental interests. A party organization allows political candidates to muster donations of time and money necessary to capture the attention of the electorate. . . . Patronage—the right to select key personnel and to reward the party "faithful"—serves the public interest by facilitating the implementation of policies endorsed by the electorate. [T]he effect of the Court's decision will be to decrease the accountability and denigrate the role of our national political parties. . . .

IV. . . . The voters of Rockland County are free to elect their Public Defender and assistant public defenders instead of delegating their selection to elected and appointed officials. Certainly the Court's holding today would not preclude the voters, the ultimate "hiring authority," from choosing both Public Defenders and their assistants by party membership. The voters' choice of public officials on the basis of political affiliation is not yet viewed as an inhibition of speech; it is democracy. . . .

Although the voters of Rockland County could have elected both the Public Defender and his assistants, they have given their legislators a representative proxy to appoint the Public Defender. And they have delegated to the Public Defender the power to choose his assistants. Presumably the voters have adopted this course in order to facilitate more effective representative government. Of course, the voters could have instituted a civil service system that would preclude the selection of either the Public Defender or his assistants on the basis of political affiliation. But the continuation of the present system reflects the electorate's decision to select certain public employees on the basis of political affiliation. . . .

V. [T]he First Amendment does not incorporate a national civil service system. I would reverse the judgment of the Court of Appeals.

MR. JUSTICE STEWART, dissenting.

I joined the judgment of the Court in *Elrod v. Burns*, because it is my view that, under the First and Fourteenth Amendments, "a nonpolicymaking, nonconfidential government employee can[not] be discharged . . . from a job that he is satisfactorily performing upon the sole ground of his political beliefs." That judgment in my opinion does not control the present case for the simple reason that the respondents here clearly are not "nonconfidential" employees.

The employees in the *Elrod* case were three process servers and a juvenile court bailiff and security guard. The respondents in the present case are lawyers, and the employment positions involved are those of assistants in the office of the Rockland County Public Defender. The analogy to a firm of lawyers in the private sector is a close one, and I can think of few occupational relationships more instinct with the necessity of mutual confidence and trust than that kind of professional association. . . .

Notes

1. *United States Civil Service Commission v. National Association of Letter Carriers,* 413 U.S. 548, 93 S.Ct. 2880, 37 L.Ed.2d 796 (1973), considered the Hatch Act, which prohibited federal employees from taking "an active part in political management or in political campaigns." That section, the Court said, is not unconstitutional on its face. Congress has the power to prevent its employees from holding party office, working at the polls, and acting as party paymaster for other party workers, actively managing a partisan campaign for elective office, serving as a delegate to a party convention, and similar activities. The Act "specifically provides that the employee retains the right to vote as he chooses and to express his opinion on political subjects and campaigns." The judgment of Congress is that "partisan political activities by federal employees must be limited if the Government is to operate effectively and fairly, elections are to play their proper part in representative government, and employees themselves are to be sufficiently free from improper influences. The restrictions so far imposed on federal employees are not aimed at particular parties, groups, or points of view, but apply equally to all partisan activities of the type described." They neither discriminate against racial, ethnic, or religious minorities, nor seek to control political opinions or beliefs, nor interfere with or influence anyone's vote at the polls. The employees must not only avoid "practicing political justice, but it is also critical that they appear to the public to be avoiding it." A judgment of the Hatch Act is that the Government work force should not be built into "a powerful, invincible, and perhaps corrupt political machine." Not only are these interests important, but "[n]either the right to associate nor the right to participate in political activities is absolute in any event." Accord, *United Public Workers v. Mitchell,* 330 U.S. 75, 67 S.Ct. 556, 91 L.Ed. 754 (1947).

2. With *Branti* contrast *Connick v. Myers,* 461 U.S. 138, 103 S.Ct. 1684, 75 L.Ed.2d 708 (1983), holding (5 to 4) that free speech guarantees do not prevent the discharge of a state employee for circulating a questionnaire concerning internal office affairs. This questionnaire by Myers (an assistant district attorney who was objecting to a transfer) solicited the views of fellow staffers regarding office transfer policy, office morale, the level of confidence in supervisors, and whether employees felt pressured to work in political campaigns. The district attorney fired her for insubordination. Myers claimed that her employment had been improperly terminated because of her exercise of free speech.

As to all the questions (except the last one regarding pressure to work on political campaigns) the Court held that the public employee spoke not as a citizen "upon matters of public concern" but rather as an employee on matters "only of personal interest" and therefore "absent the most unusual circumstances" a federal court should not intervene in the wisdom of such personnel decisions. The last question did involve a matter of public concern, but the "limited First Amendment interest involved here does not require that Connick tolerate action which he reasonably believed would disrupt the office, undermine his authority, and destroy close working relationships. Myers' discharge therefore did not offend the First Amendment."

3. *Rankin v. McPherson,* 483 U.S. 378, 107 S.Ct. 2891, 97 L.Ed.2d 315 (1987) held (5 to 4) that it was unconstitutional for a constable to fire a data-entry employee for privately remarking to a co-worker (who was her boy-friend), after hearing of an attempt on President Reagan's life, "If they go for him again, I hope they get him." The Court, per Marshall, J., held that the statement constituted "a matter of public concern" and was protected free speech. (In contrast, an actual threat to kill the President would not be protected, the Court said.) It is irrelevant that the statement made was inappropriate and controversial. In this case the constable did not demonstrate that the state's interest justified firing the data-entry employee. She had purely clerical duties, no law enforcement duties, and made the statement privately, in a room not readily accessible to the public. There was no evidence that the employee's statement had discredited her office or interfered with its efficient functioning.

4. *Rutan v. Republican Party of Illinois,* 497 U.S. 62, 110 S.Ct. 2729, 111 L.Ed.2d 52 (1990). The Court (5 to 4), per Brennan, J., extended *Branti.* Not only does discharging public employees on the basis of their political affiliation violate the First Amendment, but related patronage practices "involving low-level public employees"—regarding hiring, promotion, transfer, and recall after layoff—may not constitutionally be based on party affiliation and support. "Unless these patronage practices are narrowly tailored to further vital government interests, we must conclude that they impermissibly encroach on First Amendment freedoms." In footnote 8 the Court said that the First Amendment "protects state employees not only from patronage dismissals but 'even an act of retaliation as trivial as failing to hold a birthday party for a public employee ... when intending to punish her for exercising her free speech rights.' "

The Government's interest in having effective employees "can be met by discharging, demoting or transferring staffmembers whose work is deficient." And the Government's interest "in securing employees who will loyally implement its policies can be adequately served by choosing or dismissing certain high-level employees on the basis of their political views."

Scalia, J., joined by Rehnquist, C.J., Kennedy, J., & (in part), O'Connor, J., dissented:

> Today the Court establishes that the constitutional principle that party membership is not a permissible factor in the dispensation of government jobs, except those jobs for the performance of which party affiliation is an "appropriate requirement." [I]f there is any category of jobs for whose performance party affiliation is not an appropriate requirement, it is the job of being a judge, where partnership is not only unneeded but positively undesirable. It is, however, rare that a federal administration of one party will appoint a judge from another party. ...Thus, the new principle that the Court today announces will be enforced by a corps of judges (the Members of this Court included) who overwhelming owe their office to its violation. Something must be wrong here, and I suggest it is the Court.

He added: "Every ethnic group that has achieved political power in American cities has used the bureaucracy to provide jobs in return for political support. It's only when Blacks begin to play the same game that the rules get changed." Finally, Scalia argued that *Branti* should be overruled:

> A few examples will illustrate the shambles *Branti* has produced. A city cannot fire a deputy sheriff because of his political affiliation, but then again perhaps it can, especially if he is called the "police captain." A county cannot fire on that basis its attorney for the department of social services, nor its assistant attorney for family court, but a city can fire its solicitor and his assistants, or its assistant city attorney, or its assistant state's attorney, or its corporation counsel. A city cannot discharge its deputy court clerk for his political affiliation, but it can fire its legal assistant to the clerk on that basis. Firing a juvenile court bailiff seems impermissible, but it may be permissible if he is assigned permanently to a single judge. [footnotes, citing lower court cases, omitted.]

5. *O'Hare Truck Service, Inc. v. City of Northlake,* 518 U.S. 712, 116 S.Ct. 2353, 135 L.Ed.2d 874 (1996). O'Hare Truck Service was on a rotation list of companies available to perform towing services at the request of the city. It was removed from the list after its owner (John Gratzianna), refused to contribute to the respondent mayor's reelection campaign. Allegedly, the removal was in retaliation for this refusal. The Seventh Circuit dismissed the claim, arguing that *Branti* and *Elrod* do not apply to independent contractors. Kennedy, J., for the Court, reversed. This is not a case where O'Hare Trucking was "part of a constituency that must take its chance of being favored or ignored in the larger political process—for example, by residing or doing business in a region the government rewards or spurns in the construction of public works. Gratzianna instead was targeted with a specific demand for political support. When Gratzianna refused, the city terminated a relationship that, based on longstanding practice, he had reason to believe would continue." The "inevitable" case-by-case adjudication will allow the courts to consider the necessity of allowing government the "discretion inherent" in awarding contracts. There is no First Amendment violation if the government terminates its affiliation with the contractor for reasons unrelated to free speech (e.g., the provider is unreliable) if this justification is not a pretext, or if the contractor's affiliation "is an appropriate requirement for the effective performance" of the job.

Board of County Commissioners v. Umbehr, 518 U.S. 668, 116 S.Ct. 2342, 135 L.Ed.2d 843 (1996), decided the same day as *O'Hare Truck,* involved Umbehr, a trash hauler and outspoken critic of the Board of County Commissioners. Umbehr alleged that the Commissioners voted to terminate or prevent the automatic renewal of his at-will contract to haul trash for the County, because of his criticism of them. O'Connor, for the Court, held that the First Amendment protects independent contractors for termination of at-will government contracts in retaliation for their exercise of free speech. "To prevail, Umbehr must show that the termination of his contract was motivated by his speech on a matter of public concern," which requires him to prove "more than the mere fact that he criticized the Board members before they terminated him." If he shows that, the Board will win if it can show, by a preponderance of the evidence, that, in light of their knowledge at the time of the termination, the Board members would have terminated the contract regardless of the speech, or if the Board proves that "the County's legitimate interests as contractor, deferentially viewed, outweigh the free speech interests at stake." Evidence that the Board members discovered facts after termination that would have led to a later termination anyway, and evidence of mitigation of Umbehr's loss by means of subsequent contracts with the cities, would be relevant in accessing the appropriate remedy. The Court emphasized "the limited nature" of its decision. This case concerns the termination of a "pre-existing commercial relationship with the government," so "we need not address the possibility of suits by bidders or applicants for new government contracts who cannot rely on such a relationship."

Scalia, J., joined by Thomas, J., dissented in both *Umbehr* and *O'Hare Truck:* "The Democratic mayor gives the city's municipal bond business to what is known to be a solid Democratic law firm—taking it away from the solid Republican law firm that had the business during the previous, Republican, administration. What else is new? Or he declines to give the construction contract for the new municipal stadium to the company that opposed the bond issue for its construction, and that in fact tried to get the stadium built across the river in the next State." Such favoritism is common, and "no one has ever thought it violated—of all things—the First Amendment."

10–9.4 *Regulating the Membership of Associations*

ROBERTS v. UNITED STATES JAYCEES

468 U.S. 609, 104 S.Ct. 3244, 82 L.Ed.2d 462 (1984).

JUSTICE BRENNAN delivered the opinion of the Court.

This case requires us to address a conflict between a State's efforts to eliminate gender-based discrimination against its citizens and the constitutional freedom of association asserted by members of a private organization. In the decision under review, the Court of Appeals for the Eighth Circuit concluded that, by requiring the United States Jaycees to admit women as full voting members, the Minnesota Human Rights Act violates the First and Fourteenth Amendment rights of the organization's members. We noted probable jurisdiction, and now reverse.

The United States Jaycees (Jaycees), founded in 1920 as the Junior Chamber of Commerce, is a nonprofit membership corporation, incorporated in Missouri with national headquarters in Tulsa, Oklahoma. The objective of the Jaycees, as set out in its bylaws, is to pursue

> such educational and charitable purposes as will promote and foster the growth and development of young men's civic organizations in the United States, designed to inculcate in the individual membership of such organization a spirit of genuine Americanism and civic interest, and as a supplementary education institution to provide them with opportunity for personal development and achievement and an avenue for intelligent participation by young men in the affairs of their community, state and nation, and to develop true friendship and understanding among young men of all nations.

The organization's bylaws establish seven classes of membership, including individual or regular members, associate individual members, and local chapters. Regular membership is limited to young men between the ages of 18 and 35, while associate membership is available to individuals or groups ineligible for regular membership, principally women and older men. An associate member, whose dues are somewhat lower than those charged regular members, may not vote, hold local or national office, or participate in certain leadership training and awards programs. . . .

In 1974 and 1975, respectively, the Minneapolis and St. Paul chapters of the Jaycees began admitting women as regular members. [T]he two chapters have been in violation of the national organization's bylaws for about 10 years. . . . In December 1978, the president of the national organization advised both chapters that a motion to revoke their charters would be considered at a forthcoming meeting of the national board of directors in Tulsa. Shortly after receiving this notification, members of both chapters filed charges of discrimination with the Minnesota Department of Human Rights. The complaints alleged that the exclusion of women from full membership required by the national organization's bylaws violated the Minnesota Human Rights Act (Act), which provides in part:

It is an unfair discriminatory practice:

To deny any person the full and equal enjoyment of the goods, services, facilities, privileges, advantages, and accommodations of a place of public accommodation because of race, color, creed, religion, disability, national origin or sex. Minn.Stat. § 363.03, subd. 3 (1982).

[In response to a question certified to it by the federal district court, the Minnesota Supreme Court held] that the statute is applicable to any "public business facility." [And] the Jaycees organization (a) is a "business" in that it sells goods and extends privileges in exchange for annual membership dues; (b) is a "public" business in that it solicits and recruits dues-paying members based on unselective criteria; and (c) is a public business "facility" in that it conducts its activities at fixed and mobile sites within the State of Minnesota. . . .

Our decisions have referred to constitutionally protected "freedom of association" in two distinct senses. In one line of decisions, the Court has concluded that choices to enter into and maintain certain intimate human relationships must be secured against undue intrusion by the State because of the role of such relationships in safeguarding the individual freedom that is central to our constitutional scheme. In this respect, freedom of association receives protection as a fundamental element of personal liberty. In another set of decisions, the Court has recognized a right to associate for the purpose of engaging in those activities protected by the First Amendment—speech, assembly, petition for the redress of grievances, and the exercise of religion. The Constitution guarantees freedom of association of this kind as an indispensable means of preserving other individual liberties.

[T]he nature and degree of constitutional protection afforded freedom of association may vary depending on the extent to which one or the other aspect of the constitutionally protected liberty is at stake in a given case. We therefore find it useful to consider separately the effect of applying the Minnesota statute to the Jaycees on what could be called its members' freedom of intimate association and their freedom of expressive association.

A. The Court has long recognized that, because the Bill of Rights is designed to secure individual liberty, it must afford the formation and preservation of certain kinds of highly personal relationships a substantial measure of sanctuary from unjustified interference by the State. The personal affiliations that exemplify these considerations, and that therefore suggest some relevant limitations on the relationships that might be entitled to this sort of constitutional protection, are those that attend the creation and sustenance of a family—marriage, childbirth, the raising and education of children, and cohabitation with one's relatives. Family relationships, by their nature, involve deep attachments and commitments to the necessarily few other individuals with whom one shares not only a special community of thoughts, experiences, and beliefs but also distinctively personal aspects of one's life. Among other things, therefore, they are distinguished by such attributes as relative smallness, a high degree of selectivity in decisions to begin and maintain the affiliation, and seclusion from others in critical aspects of the relationship. As a general matter, only relationships with these sorts of qualities are likely to reflect the considerations that have led to an understanding of freedom of association as an intrinsic element of personal liberty. Conversely, an association lacking these qualities—such as a large business enterprise—seems remote from the concerns giving rise to this constitutional protection. Accordingly, the Constitution undoubtedly imposes constraints on the State's power to control the selection of one's spouse that would not apply to regulations affecting the choice of one's fellow employees.

Between these poles, of course, lies a broad range of human relationships that may make greater or lesser claims to constitutional protection from particular incursions by the State. Determining the limits of state authority over an individual's freedom to enter into a particular association therefore unavoidably entails a careful assessment of where that relationship's objective characteristics locate it on a spectrum from the most intimate to the most attenuated of personal attachments. We need not mark the potentially significant points on this terrain with any precision. We note only that factors that may be relevant include size, purpose, policies, selectivity, congeniality, and other characteristics that in a particular case may be pertinent. In this case, however, several features of the Jaycees clearly place the organization outside of the category of relationships worthy of this kind of constitutional protection.

The undisputed facts reveal that the local chapters of the Jaycees are large and basically unselective groups. At the time of the state administrative hearing, the Minneapolis chapter had approximately 430 members, while the St. Paul chapter had about 400. Apart from age and sex, neither the national organization nor the local chapters employs any criteria for judging applicants for membership, and new members are routinely recruited and admitted with no inquiry into their backgrounds. In fact, a local officer testified that he could recall no instance in which an applicant had been denied membership on any basis other than age or sex. Furthermore, despite their inability to vote, hold office, or receive certain awards, women affiliated with the Jaycees attend various meetings, participate in selected projects, and engage in many of the organization's social functions. Indeed, numerous non-members of both genders regularly participate in a substantial portion of activities central to the decision of many members to associate with one another, including many of the organization's various community programs, awards ceremonies, and recruitment meetings.

In short, the local chapters of the Jaycees are neither small nor selective. Moreover, much of the activity central to the formation and maintenance of the association involves the participation of strangers to that relationship. Accordingly, we conclude that the Jaycees chapters lack the distinctive characteristics that might afford constitutional protection to the decision of its members to exclude women. We turn therefore to consider the extent to which application of the Minnesota statute to compel the Jaycees to accept women infringes the group's freedom of expressive association.

B. An individual's freedom to speak, to worship, and to petition the Government for the redress of grievances could not be vigorously protected from interference by the State unless a correlative freedom to engage in group effort toward those ends were not also guaranteed. According protection to collective effort on behalf of shared goals is especially important in preserving political and cultural diversity and in shielding dissident expression from suppression by the majority.... In view of the various protected activities in which the Jaycees engage, that right is plainly implicated in this case. Government actions that may unconstitutionally infringe upon this freedom can take a number of forms. Among other things, government may seek to impose penalties or withhold benefits from individuals because of their membership in a disfavored group; it may attempt to require disclosure of the fact of membership in a group seeking anonymity; and it may try to interfere with the internal organization or affairs of the group. By requiring the Jaycees to admit women as full voting members, the Minnesota Act works an infringement of the last type. There can be no clearer example of an intrusion into the internal structure or affairs of an association than a regulation that forces the group to accept members it does not desire. Such a regulation may impair the ability of the original members to express only those views that brought them together. Freedom of association therefore plainly presupposes a freedom not to associate.

The right to associate for expressive purposes is not, however, absolute. Infringements on that right may be justified by regulations adopted to serve compelling state interests, unrelated to the suppression of ideas, that cannot be achieved through means significantly less restrictive of associational freedoms. We are persuaded that Minnesota's compelling interest in eradicating discrimination against its female citizens justifies the impact that application of the statute to the Jaycees may have on the male members' associational freedoms.

On its face, the Minnesota Act does not aim at the suppression of speech, does not distinguish between prohibited and permitted activity on the basis of viewpoint, and does not license enforcement authorities to administer the statute on the basis of such constitutionally impermissible criteria. Nor do the Jaycees contend that the Act has been applied in this case for the purpose of hampering the organization's ability to express its views. Instead, as the Minnesota Supreme Court explained, the Act reflects the State's strong historical commitment to eliminating discrimination and assuring its citizens equal access to publicly available goods and services. That goal, which is unrelated to the suppression of expression, plainly serves compelling state interests of the highest order....

By prohibiting gender discrimination in places of public accommodation, the Minnesota Act protects the State's citizenry from a number of serious social and personal harms. [Gender discrimination] deprives persons of their individual dignity and denies society the benefits of wide participation in political, economic, and cultural life. [T]he Minnesota court noted the various commercial programs and benefits offered to members and stated that, "[l]eadership skills are 'goods,' [and] business contacts and employment promotions are 'privileges' and 'advantages'. . . . " Assuring women equal access to such goods, privileges, and advantages clearly furthers compelling state interests.

In applying the Act to the Jaycees, the State has advanced those interests through the least restrictive means of achieving its ends. Indeed, the Jaycees have failed to demonstrate that the Act imposes any serious burdens on the male members' freedom of expressive association. . . . The Act requires no change in the Jaycees' creed of promoting the interests of young men, and it imposes no restrictions on the organization's ability to exclude individuals with ideologies or philosophies different from those of its existing members. Moreover, the Jaycees already invite women to share the group's views and philosophy and to participate in much of its training and community activities. Accordingly, any claim that admission of women as full voting members will impair a symbolic message conveyed by the very fact that women are not permitted to vote is attenuated at best. . . . In claiming that women might have a different attitude about such issues as the federal budget, school prayer, voting rights, and foreign relations, or that the organization's public positions would have a different effect if the group were not "a purely young men's association," the Jaycees rely solely on unsupported generalizations about the relative interests and perspectives of men and women. [W]e have repeatedly condemned legal decision-making that relies uncritically on such assumptions. In the absence of a showing far more substantial than that attempted by the Jaycees, we decline to indulge in the sexual stereotyping that underlies appellee's contention that, by allowing women to vote, application of the Minnesota Act will change the content or impact of the organization's speech.

In any event, even if enforcement of the Act causes some incidental abridgement of the Jaycees' protected speech, that effect is no greater than is necessary to accomplish the State's legitimate purposes. As we have explained, acts of invidious discrimination in the distribution of publicly available goods, services, and other advantages cause unique evils that government has a compelling interest to prevent—wholly apart from the point of view such conduct may transmit. Accordingly, like violence or other types of potentially expressive activities that produce special harms distinct from their communicative impact, such practices are entitled to no constitutional protection. . . .

We turn finally to appellee's contentions that the Minnesota Act, as interpreted by the State's highest court, is unconstitutionally vague and overbroad. . . . In deciding that the Act reaches the Jaycees, the Minnesota Supreme Court used a number of specific and objective criteria—regarding the organization's size, selectivity, commercial nature, and use of public facilities—typically employed in determining the applicability of state and federal anti-discrimination statutes to the membership policies of assertedly private clubs. The Court of Appeals ... concluded that the Minnesota court introduced a constitutionally fatal element of uncertainty into the statute by suggesting that the Kiwanis Club might be sufficiently "private" to be outside the scope of the Act. Like the dissenting judge in the Court of Appeals, however, we read the illustrative reference to the Kiwanis Club, which the record indicates has a formal procedure for choosing members on the basis of specific and selective criteria, as simply providing a further refinement of the standards used to determine whether an organization is "public" or "private." By offering this counter-example, the Minnesota Supreme Court's opinion provided the statute with more, rather than less, definite content.

The contrast between the Jaycees and the Kiwanis Club drawn by the Minnesota court also disposes of appellee's contention that the Act is unconstitutionally overbroad. [T]he Minnesota Supreme Court expressly rejected the contention that the Jaycees should "be viewed analogously to private organizations such as the Kiwanis International Organization." The state court's articulated willingness to adopt limiting constructions that would exclude private groups from the statute's reach, together with the commonly used and sufficiently precise standards it employed to determine that the Jaycees is not such a group, establish that the Act, as currently construed, does not create an unacceptable risk of application to a substantial amount of protected conduct....

JUSTICE REHNQUIST concurs in the judgment.

THE CHIEF JUSTICE [BURGER] and JUSTICE BLACKMUN took no part in the decision of this case.

JUSTICE O'CONNOR, concurring in part and concurring in the judgment....

The Court analyzes Minnesota's attempt to regulate the Jaycees' membership using a test that I find both over-protective of activities undeserving of constitutional shelter and under-protective of important First Amendment concerns. The Court declares that the Jaycees' right of association depends on the organization's making a "substantial" showing that the admission of unwelcome members "will change the message communicated by the group's speech." [T]he focus on such a connection is objectionable.... Whether an association is or is not constitutionally protected in the selection of its membership should not depend on what the association says or why its members say it....

On the one hand, an association engaged exclusively in protected expression enjoys First Amendment protection of both the content of its message and the choice of its members. Protection of the message itself is judged by the same standards as protection of speech by an individual. Protection of the association's right to define its membership derives from the recognition that the formation of an expressive association is the creation of a voice, and the selection of members is the definition of that voice.... On the other hand, there is only minimal constitutional protection of the freedom of *commercial* association. There are, of course, some constitutional protections of commercial speech—speech intended and used to promote a commercial transaction with the speaker. But the State is free to impose any rational regulation on the commercial transaction itself. . . .

Many associations cannot readily be described as purely expressive or purely commercial. No association is likely ever to be exclusively engaged in expressive activities, if only because it will collect dues from its members or purchase printing materials or rent lecture halls or serve coffee and cakes at its meetings. [A]n association should be characterized as commercial, and therefore subject to rationally related state regulation of its membership and other associational activities, when, and only when, the association's activities are not predominantly of the type protected by the First Amendment. It is only when the association is predominantly engaged in protected expression that state regulation of its membership will necessarily affect, change, dilute, or silence one collective voice that would otherwise be heard. An association must choose its market. Once it enters the marketplace of commerce in any substantial degree it loses the complete control over its membership that it would otherwise enjoy if it confined its affairs to the marketplace of ideas.

Determining whether an association's activity is predominantly protected expression will often be difficult, if only because a broad range of activities can be expressive. It is easy enough to identify expressive words or conduct that are strident, contentious, or divisive, but protected expression may also take the form of quiet persuasion, inculcation of traditional values, instruction of the young, and community service. . . .

Minnesota's attempt to regulate the membership of the Jaycees chapters operating in that State presents a relatively easy case for application of the expressive-commercial dichotomy. . . . Notwithstanding its protected expressive activities, the Jaycees—otherwise known as the Junior Chamber of Commerce—is, first and foremost, an organization that, at both the national and local levels, promotes and practices the art of solicitation and management. The organization claims that the training it offers its members gives them an advantage in business, and business firms do indeed sometimes pay the dues of individual memberships for their employees. Jaycees members hone their solicitation and management skills, under the direction and supervision of the organization, primarily through their active recruitment of new members. "One of the major activities of the Jaycees is the sale of memberships in the organization. It encourages continuous recruitment of members with the expressed goal of increasing membership. . . . The Jaycees itself refers to its members as customers and membership as a product it is selling." . . .

Notes

1. In *Tashjian v. Republican Party of Connecticut,* 479 U.S. 208, 107 S.Ct. 544, 93 L.Ed.2d 514 (1986), the Court (5 to 4) invalidated a state law to the extent that it conflicted with a Connecticut Republican Party rule that permitted independent voters to vote in Republican primaries for federal and state-wide offices. State law provided that any previously unaffiliated voter could become eligible to vote in the Party's primary by enrolling as a Party member as late as noon on the last business day preceding the primary. The Court never cited *Roberts v. United States Jaycees* but said that the Connecticut law violated freedom of association.

In 1976 a three judge court had upheld the Connecticut law when an independent voter sought a declaratory judgment that he had a right to vote in the Republican primary; the Court summarily affirmed. *Nader v. Schaffer,* 429 U.S. 989, 97 S.Ct. 516, 50 L.Ed.2d 602 (1976). Several years later the Republican state convention adopted new rules allowing independents to vote in the Republican Party so long as their ballots were limited to federal and state-wide offices (but not other offices, such as mayor, or state representative).* The State of Connecticut refused to change its primary laws, so the Party sued.

Tashjian specifically approved of *Nader v. Schaffer* upholding the closed primary, but Marshall, J., for the Court distinguished it because it had been brought by independent voters, not the Republican Party itself: in the *Nader* case "the nonmember's desire to participate in the party's affairs is overborne by the countervailing and legitimate right of the party to determine its own membership." Now, the Republican Party itself objected to the law, contending it impermissibly burdened the rights of the members to determine for themselves with whom they will associate in their quest for political success. This attempt to broaden the base of public participation "is conduct undeniably central to the exercise of the right of association." The state statute it did not advance any compelling State interests. For example, it did not prevent raiding of the Republican Party, because a raid on the Republican Party primary by independent voters is a "curious concept," and if such a raid were to occur, the State law could not prevent independents from registering as Republicans on the business day before the primary. The Court added a narrowing footnote:

> "Our holding today does not establish that state regulation of primary voting qualifications may never withstand challenge by a political party or its membership. A party seeking, for example, to open its primary to all voters, including members of other parties, would raise a different combination of considerations. [Then], the effect of one party's broadening of participation would threaten other parties with the disorganization effects which the statutes were designed to prevent. [A] State may adopt a 'policy of confining each voter to a single nominating act,' a policy decision which is not involved in the present case. The analysis of these situations derives much from the particular facts involved.... "

---

* The motivation behind this change was that U.S. Senator Weicker from Connecticut, in a reelection bid, was concerned that he could not win a primary without an influx of non-Republican voters. (Plaintiffs' admissions, in Joint Appendix at 124–127.) Other Republican candidates did not want independents voting in their primary, and so a compromise was reached with independents limited to voting for state-wide offices. Mr. Weicker, in 1988, lost his reelection bid to the U.S. Senate and subsequently was elected Governor, running as an independent.

Scalia, J., joined by Rehnquist, C.J., & O'Connor, J., dissented: "Appellees only complaint is that the Party cannot leave the selection of its candidates to persons who are *not* members of the Party, and are unwilling to become members. It seems to me fanciful to refer to this as an interest in freedom of association between the members of the Republican Party and the putative independent voters." (emphasis in original). Even if the Party wanted its candidates to be determined by outsiders, there is no reason why the State is bound to honor that desire, any more than it should honor a party's desire that its candidates "be selected by convention rather than by primary, or by the party's executive committee in a smoke-filled room."**

Eu v. San Francisco County Democratic Central Committee, 489 U.S. 214, 109 S.Ct. 1013, 103 L.Ed.2d 271 (1989) unanimously invalidated provisions of the California Election Code that prohibited official governing bodies of political parties from endorsing candidates in party primaries, and dictated the organization and composition of political parties. Relying on *Tashjian* the Court said, if "the challenged law burdens the rights of political parties and their members, it can survive constitutional scrutiny only if the State shows that it advances a compelling state interest, and is narrowly tailored to serve that interest." The California law burdened associational rights of the political parties and their members. The endorsement prohibition, for example, frustrated the ability of the party to spread its message. The statutory restrictions on organization prevented the parties from governing themselves as they think best and interfered with the parties' choice of leaders. The "State has not shown that its regulation of internal party governance is necessary to the integrity of the electoral process." Stevens, J., concurring, warned that phrases such as "compelling state interest" and "least restrictive means" are "really not very helpful for constitutional analysis. They are too convenient and result oriented, and I must endeavor to disassociate myself from them."

Timmons v. Twin Cities Area New Party, 520 U.S. 351, 117 S.Ct. 1364, 137 L.Ed.2d 589 (1997) upheld anti-fusion laws. "Fusion" is the nomination by two or more political parties of the same candidate for the same office. While New York State allows fusion candidates, most states now ban them, claiming that they increase ballot manipulation and confusion. Major parties also do not want to give to third parties power to shift support to a major party candidate. In this case, Andy Dawkins, a state representative was running as the Democratic–Farmer–Labor Party candidate and the New Party wanted to list him as their candidate too. Neither Dawkins nor the DFL Party objected to the dual ballot listing, but the law prohibited it.

** The majority also held that the implementation of Party rules—which established qualifications for voting for congressional elections that differed from the voting qualifications in elections for the more numerous house of the state legislature—did not violate the Qualifications Clause, Art. I, § 2, cl. 1, and the Seventeenth Amendment. Primaries are subject to these clauses, but their purposes are satisfied "if all those qualified to participate in the selection of members of the more numerous branch of the state legislature are also qualified to participate in the election of Senators and Members of the House of Representatives." There is no need for "perfect symmetry." Stevens, J., joined by Scalia, J., dissented because the Court "separates the federal qualifications from their state counterparts, inexplicably treating the mandatory 'shall have' language of the clauses as though it means only that the federal voters 'may but need not have' the qualifications of state voters."

Fusion would allow the New Party to use the ballot to communicate to the public that it supports Dawkins, and Dawkins would know (because each party's votes are counted separately) about the make-up of his constituency.

Rehnquist, C.J., for the Court, upheld Minnesota's anti-fusion laws. First, he offered this test:

> When deciding whether a state election law violates First and Fourteenth Amendment associational rights, we weigh the "character and magnitude" of the burden the State's rule imposes on those rights against the interests the State contends justify that burden, and consider the extent to which the State's concerns make the burden necessary. Regulations imposing severe burdens on plaintiffs' rights must be narrowly tailored and advance a compelling state interest. Lesser burdens, however, trigger less exacting review, and a State's "important regulatory interests" will usually be enough to justify "reasonable, nondiscriminatory restrictions." No bright line separates permissible election-related regulation from unconstitutional infringements on First Amendment freedoms.

The anti-fusion law was a "lesser burden" that triggered a "less exacting review." *Tashjian* and *Eu* involved regulation of political parties' internal affairs and core associational activities, but Minnesota's fusion ban does not. The ban applies to major and minor parties alike, and "simply precludes one party's candidate from appearing on the ballot, as that party's candidate, if already nominated by another party. Respondent is free to try to convince Representative Dawkins to be the New Party's, not the DFL's, candidate." The lower court, which had invalidated the fusion ban, noted that minor parties need fusion-based alliances to thrive. The Court responded that, even if true, the "supposed benefits of fusion to minor parties does not require that Minnesota permit it." States have a "strong interest" in the "stability of their political systems." While states may not "completely insulate" the two major parties from third-party competition, states may "enact reasonable election regulations that may, in practice, favor the traditional two-party system, and that temper the destabilizing effects of party-splintering and excessive factionalism. "

Stevens, J., joined by Ginsburg, J. (and by Souter, J., in part) dissented. Fusion allows voters with viewpoints not adequately represented by the platforms of the two major parties to "indicate to a particular candidate that—in addition to his support for the major party views—he should be responsive to the views of the minor party whose support for him was demonstrated where political parties demonstrate support—on the ballot." Souter, J., also filed a dissenting opinion.

2. *New York State Club Association, Inc. v. City of New York,* 487 U.S. 1, 108 S.Ct. 2225, 101 L.Ed.2d 1 (1988), without dissent, rejected the facial constitutional challenge to a city law that forbade discrimination on the basis of race, creed, color, national origin or sex of any private club, defined as "any institution, club or place of accommodation [that] has more than four hundred members, provides regular meal service and regularly receives payment for dues, fees, use of space, facilities, services, meals or beverages directly or indirectly from or on behalf of nonmembers for the furtherance of trade or business." The purpose of the law was to offer all persons "a fair

and equal opportunity to participate in the business and professional life of the city.... " The law exempted "benevolent orders" (e.g., the Loyal Order of Moose, the Nobles of the Mystic Shrine, etc.) and religious corporations. These exceptions did not violate equal protection because it was rational for the city to conclude that the exempted organizations were different: "small clubs, benevolent orders and religious corporations have not been identified as places where business activity is prevalent.... "

3. *Keller v. State Bar of California,* 496 U.S. 1, 110 S.Ct. 2228, 110 L.Ed.2d 1 (1990). The Court, speaking through Chief Justice Rehnquist, unanimously held that the State Bar of California (an "integrated" or "unified" bar, that is, an association created by state law, to which lawyers must join and pay dues as a condition of practicing law), may not constitutionally use compulsory dues to finance political and ideological causes. The State Bar may only use compulsory dues to finance regulation of the legal profession or to improve the quality of legal services (e.g., bar dues may be used to propose ethical codes or discipline Bar members). The unified bar may not use mandated dues to promote political or ideological activities (e.g., to endorse gun control or nuclear freeze initiatives). "Government officials are expected as a part of the democratic process to represent and to espouse the views of a majority of their constituents." But the State Bar of California, which is not part of the general government of California, is more analogous to labor unions representing public and private employees, and that, therefore, should be subject to the same constitutional rule in order to protect free speech and free association interests.

HURLEY v. IRISH–AMERICAN GAY, LESBIAN AND BISEXUAL GROUP OF BOSTON

515 U.S. 557, 115 S.Ct. 2338, 132 L.Ed.2d 487 (1995).

JUSTICE SOUTER delivered the opinion for a unanimous Court.

The issue in this case is whether Massachusetts may require private citizens who organize a parade to include among the marchers a group imparting a message the organizers do not wish to convey. We hold that such a mandate violates the First Amendment.

March 17 is set aside for two celebrations in South Boston. As early as 1737, some people in Boston observed the feast of the apostle to Ireland, and since 1776 the day has marked the evacuation of royal troops and Loyalists from the city.... The tradition of formal sponsorship by the city came to an end in 1947, however, when Mayor James Michael Curley himself granted authority to organize and conduct the St. Patrick's Day–Evacuation Day Parade to the petitioner South Boston Allied War Veterans Council, an unincorporated association of individuals elected from various South Boston veterans groups. Every year since that time, the Council has applied for and received a permit for the parade, which at times has included as many as 20,000 marchers and drawn up to 1 million watchers. No other applicant has ever applied for that permit. Through 1992, the city allowed the Council to use the city's official seal, and provided printing services as well as direct funding.

1992 was the year that a number of gay, lesbian, and bisexual descendants of the Irish immigrants joined together with other supporters to form the respondent organization, GLIB, to march in the parade as a way to express pride in their Irish heritage as openly gay, lesbian, and bisexual individuals.... Although the Council denied GLIB's application to take part in the 1992 parade, GLIB obtained a state-court order to include its contingent, which marched "uneventfully" among that year's 10,000 participants and 750,000 spectators.

In 1993, after the Council had again refused to admit GLIB to the upcoming parade, the organization and some of its members filed this suit ... alleging violations of the State and Federal Constitutions and of the state public accommodations law, which prohibits "any distinction, discrimination or restriction on account of ... sexual orientation ... relative to the admission of any person to, or treatment in any place of public accommodation, resort or amusement." Mass.Gen.Laws § 272:98. [T]he state trial court ruled that the parade fell within the statutory definition of a public accommodation, which includes "any place ... which is open to and accepts or solicits the patronage of the general public and, without limiting the generality of this definition, whether or not it be ... (6) a boardwalk or other public highway [or] ... (8) a place of public amusement, recreation, sport, exercise or entertainment," The court found that the Council had no written criteria and employed no particular procedures for admission, voted on new applications in batches, had occasionally admitted groups who simply showed up at the parade without having submitted an application, and did "not generally inquire into the specific messages or views of each applicant." The court consequently rejected the Council's contention that the parade was "private" (in the sense of being exclusive), holding instead that "the lack of genuine selectivity in choosing participants and sponsors demonstrates that the Parade is a public event." It found the parade to be "eclectic," containing a wide variety of "patriotic, commercial, political, moral, artistic, religious, athletic, public service, trade union, and eleemosynary themes," as well as conflicting messages. While noting that the Council had indeed excluded the Ku Klux Klan and ROAR (an antibusing group), it attributed little significance to these facts, concluding ultimately that "[t]he only common theme among the participants and sponsors is their public involvement in the Parade."

The court ... found the Council's "final position [to be] that GLIB would be excluded because of its values and its message, *i.e.,* its members' sexual orientation." This position, in the court's view, was not only violative of the public accommodations law but "paradoxical" as well, since "a proper celebration of St. Patrick's and Evacuation Day requires diversity and inclusiveness." ... The court held that because the statute did not mandate inclusion of GLIB but only prohibited discrimination based on sexual orientation, any infringement on the Council's right to expressive association was only "incidental" and "no greater than necessary to accomplish the statute's legitimate purpose" of eradicating discrimination. *Id.* citing *Roberts v. United States Jaycees.* Accordingly, it ruled that "GLIB is entitled to participate in the Parade on the same terms and conditions as other participants." The Supreme Judicial Court of Massachusetts affirmed.... We granted certiorari to determine whether the requirement to admit a parade contingent expressing a message not of the private organizers' own choosing violates the First Amendment. We hold that it does and reverse.

[O]ur obligation is to " 'make an independent examination of the whole record,' ... so as to assure ourselves that th[is] judgment does not constitute a forbidden intrusion on the field of free expression."

[W]e use the word "parade" to indicate marchers who are making some sort of collective point, not just to each other but to bystanders along the way. Indeed a parade's dependence on watchers is so extreme that ... "if a parade or demonstration receives no media coverage, it may as well not have happened." Parades are thus a form of expression, not just motion, and the inherent expressiveness of marching to make a point explains our cases involving protest marches.... Accord, *Shuttlesworth v. Birmingham* (1969).

The protected expression that inheres in a parade is not limited to its banners and songs, however, for the Constitution looks beyond written or spoken words as mediums of expression. [A] narrow, succinctly articulable message is not a condition of constitutional protection, which if confined to expressions conveying a "particularized message," would never reach the unquestionably shielded painting of Jackson Pollock, music of Arnold Schönberg, or Jabberwocky verse of Lewis Carroll.

Not many marches, then, are beyond the realm of expressive parades, and the South Boston celebration is not one of them. Spectators line the streets; people march in costumes and uniforms, carrying flags and banners with all sorts of messages (*e.g.,* "England get out of Ireland," "Say no to drugs"); marching bands and pipers play, floats are pulled along, and the whole show is broadcast over Boston television. [T]he Council is rather lenient in admitting participants. But a private speaker does not forfeit constitutional protection simply by combining multifarious voices, or by failing to edit their themes to isolate an exact message as the exclusive subject matter of the speech. Nor, under our precedent, does First Amendment protection require a speaker to generate, as an original matter, each item featured in the communication. [T]he presentation of an edited compilation of speech generated by other persons is a staple of most newspapers' opinion pages, which, of course, fall squarely within the core of First Amendment security, as does even the simple selection of a paid noncommercial advertisement for inclusion in a daily paper, see *New York Times [v. Sullivan]*. The selection of contingents to make a parade is entitled to similar protection. Respondents' participation as a unit in the parade was equally expressive....

The Massachusetts public accommodations law under which respondents brought suit ... has been applied in a peculiar way. ...The petitioners disclaim any intent to exclude homosexuals as such, and no individual member of GLIB claims to have been excluded from parading as a member of any group that the Council has approved to march. Instead, the disagreement goes to the admission of GLIB as its own parade unit carrying its own banner. Since every participating unit affects the message conveyed by the private organizers, the state courts' application of the statute produced an order essentially requiring petitioners to alter the expressive content of their parade. [T]he state courts' application of the statute had the effect of declaring the sponsors' speech itself to be the public accommodation. Under this approach any contingent of protected individuals with a message would have the right to participate in petitioners' speech, so that the communication produced by the private organizers would be shaped by all those protected by the law who wished to join in with some expressive demonstration of their own. But this use of the State's power violates the fundamental rule of protection under the First Amendment, that a speaker has the autonomy to choose the content of his own message.

"Since *all* speech inherently involves choices of what to say and what to leave unsaid," one important manifestation of the principle of free speech is that one who chooses to speak may also decide "what not to say." Although the State may at times "prescribe what shall be orthodox in commercial advertising" by requiring the dissemination of "purely factual and uncontroversial information," *Zauderer v. Office of Disciplinary Counsel of Supreme Court of Ohio* (1985), outside that context it may not compel affirmance of a belief with which the speaker disagrees. Indeed this general rule, that the speaker has the right to tailor the speech, applies not only to expressions of value, opinion, or endorsement, but equally to statements of fact the speaker would rather avoid, subject, perhaps, to the permissive law of defamation. Nor is the rule's benefit restricted to the press, being enjoyed by business corporations generally and by ordinary people engaged in unsophisticated expression as well as by professional publishers. Its point is simply the point of all speech protection, which is to shield just those choices of content that in someone's eyes are misguided, or even hurtful.

[T]he Council clearly decided to exclude a message it did not like from the communication it chose to make, and that is enough to invoke its right as a private speaker to shape its expression by speaking on one subject while remaining silent on another. The message it disfavored is not difficult to identify. ... The parade's organizers ... may object to unqualified social acceptance of gays and lesbians or have some other reason for wishing to keep GLIB's message out of the parade. But whatever the reason, it boils down to the choice of a speaker not to propound a particular point of view, and that choice is presumed to lie beyond the government's power to control.

Respondents argue that any tension between this rule and the Massachusetts law falls short of unconstitutionality, citing the most recent of our cases on the general subject of compelled access for expressive purposes, *Turner Broadcasting* (1994) [§ 10–5]. There we reviewed regulations requiring cable operators to set aside channels for designated broadcast signals, and applied only intermediate scrutiny. Respondents contend on this authority that admission of GLIB to the parade would not threaten the core principle of speaker's autonomy because the Council, like a cable operator, is merely "a conduit" for the speech of participants in the parade "rather than itself a speaker." But this metaphor is not apt here, because GLIB's participation would likely be perceived as having resulted from the Council's customary determination about a unit admitted to the parade, that its message was worthy of presentation and quite possibly of support as well. A newspaper, similarly, "is more than a passive receptacle or conduit for news, comment, and advertising".....

In *Turner Broadcasting,* we found this problem absent in the cable context, because "[g]iven cable's long history of serving as a conduit for broadcast signals, there appears little risk that cable viewers would assume that the broadcast stations carried on a cable system convey ideas or messages endorsed by the cable operator." ... Parades and demonstrations, in contrast, are not understood to be so neutrally presented or selectively viewed. [D]isclaimers would be quite curious in a moving parade. Without deciding on the precise significance of the likelihood of misattribution, it nonetheless becomes clear that in the context of an expressive parade, as with a protest march, the parade's overall message is distilled from the individual presentations along the way, and each unit's expression is perceived by spectators as part of the whole.

[Also, a] cable is not only a conduit for speech produced by others and selected by cable operators for transmission, but a franchised channel giving monopolistic opportunity to shut out some speakers. This power gives rise to the government's interest in limiting monopolistic autonomy in order to allow for the survival of broadcasters who might otherwise be silenced and consequently destroyed. The government's interest in *Turner Broadcasting* was not the alteration of speech, but the survival of speakers.... Considering that GLIB presumably would have had a fair shot (under neutral criteria developed by the city) at obtaining a parade permit of its own, respondents have not shown that petitioners enjoy the capacity to "silence the voice of competing speakers," as cable operators do with respect to program providers who wish to reach subscribers. Nor has any other legitimate interest been identified in support of applying the Massachusetts statute in this way to expressive activity like the parade.

The ... object of [Mass.Gen.Laws § 272:98] is to ensure by statute for gays and lesbians desiring to make use of public accommodations what the old common law promised to any member of the public wanting a meal at the inn, that accepting the usual terms of service, they will not be turned away merely on the proprietor's exercise of personal preference. When the law is applied to expressive activity in the way it was done here, its apparent object is simply ... to allow exactly what the general rule of speaker's autonomy forbids.

It might, of course, have been argued that a broader objective is apparent: that the ultimate point of forbidding acts of discrimination toward certain classes is to produce a society free of the corresponding biases. Requiring access to a speaker's message would thus be not an end in itself, but a means to produce speakers free of the biases, whose expressive conduct would be at least neutral toward the particular classes, obviating any future need for correction. But if this indeed is the point of applying the state law to expressive conduct, it is a decidedly fatal objective.... Our tradition of free speech commands that a speaker who takes to the street corner to express his views in this way should be free from interference by the State based on the content of what he says. The very idea that a noncommercial speech restriction be used to produce thoughts and statements acceptable to some groups or, indeed, all people, grates on the First Amendment, for it amounts to nothing less than a proposal to limit speech in the service of orthodox expression. The Speech Clause has no more certain antithesis. While the law is free to promote all sorts of conduct in place of harmful behavior, it is not free to interfere with speech for no better reason than promoting an approved message or discouraging a disfavored one, however enlightened either purpose may strike the government.

New York State Club Association [*v. City of New York*] is also instructive by the contrast it provides. There, we turned back a facial challenge to a state antidiscrimination statute on the assumption that the expressive associational character of a dining club with over 400 members could be sufficiently attenuated to permit application of the law even to such a private organization, but we also recognized that the State did not prohibit exclusion of those whose views were at odds with positions espoused by the general club memberships. See also *Roberts* [*v. United States Jaycees*]. In other words, although the association provided public benefits to which a State could ensure equal access, it was also engaged in expressive activity; compelled access to the benefit, which was upheld, did not trespass on the organization's message itself. If we were to analyze this case strictly along those lines, GLIB would lose. Assuming the parade to be large enough and a source of benefits (apart from its expression) that would generally justify a mandated access provision, GLIB could nonetheless be refused admission as an expressive contingent with its own message just as readily as a private club could exclude an applicant whose manifest views were at odds with a position taken by the club's existing members.

Our holding today rests not on any particular view about the Council's message but on the Nation's commitment to protect freedom of speech. Disapproval of a private speaker's statement does not legitimize use of the Commonwealth's power to compel the speaker to alter the message by including one more acceptable to others. Accordingly, the judgment of the Supreme Judicial Court is reversed and the case remanded for proceedings not inconsistent with this opinion.

It is so ordered.

10–10. SYMBOLIC SPEECH

UNITED STATES v. O'BRIEN
391 U.S. 367, 88 S.Ct. 1673, 20 L.Ed.2d 672 (1968).

MR. CHIEF JUSTICE WARREN delivered the opinion of the Court.

On the morning of March 31, 1966, David Paul O'Brien and three companions burned their Selective Service registration certificates on the steps of the South Boston Courthouse.... For this act, O'Brien was indicted, tried, convicted, and sentenced in the United States District Court for the District of Massachusetts. He did not contest the fact that he had burned the certificate. He stated in argument to the jury that he burned the certificate publicly to influence others to adopt his antiwar beliefs, as he put it, "so that other people would reevaluate their positions with Selective Service, with the armed forces, and reevaluate their place in the culture of today, to hopefully consider my position."
...

Section 462(b), [which O'Brien was charged with violating] is part of the Universal Military Training and Service Act of 1948. Section 462(b)(3), one of six numbered subdivisions of § 462(b), was amended by Congress in 1965, (adding the words italicized below), so that at the time O'Brien burned his certificate an offense was committed by any person, "who forges, alters, *knowingly destroys, knowingly mutilates, or* in any manner changes any such certificate.... " (Italics supplied.) In the District Court, O'Brien argued that the 1965 Amendment prohibiting the knowing destruction or mutilation of certificates was unconstitutional because it was enacted to abridge free speech, and because it served no legitimate legislative purpose.... We hold that the 1965 Amendment is constitutional both as enacted and as applied....

O'Brien first argues that the 1965 Amendment is unconstitutional as applied to him because his act of burning his registration certificate was protected "symbolic speech" within the First Amendment. His argument is that the freedom of expression which the First Amendment guarantees includes all modes of "communication of ideas by conduct," and that his conduct is within this definition because he did it in "demonstration against the war and against the draft."

We cannot accept the view that an apparently limitless variety of conduct can be labeled "speech" whenever the person engaging in the conduct intends thereby to express an idea. However, even on the assumption that the alleged communicative element in O'Brien's conduct is sufficient to bring into play the First Amendment, it does not necessarily follow that the destruction of a registration certificate is constitutionally protected activity. This Court has held that when "speech" and "nonspeech" elements are combined in the same course of conduct, a sufficiently important governmental interest in regulating the nonspeech element can justify incidental limitations on First Amendment freedoms. To characterize the quality of the governmental interest which must appear, the Court has employed a variety of descriptive terms: compelling; substantial; subordinating; paramount; cogent; strong. Whatever imprecision inheres in these terms, we think it clear that a government regulation is sufficiently justified if it is within the constitutional power of the Government; if it furthers an important or substantial governmental interest; if the governmental interest is unrelated to the suppression of free expression; and if the incidental restriction on alleged First Amendment freedoms is no greater than is essential to the furtherance of that interest. We find that the 1965 Amendment to § 12(b)(3) of the Universal Military Training and Service Act meets all of these requirements, and consequently that O'Brien can be constitutionally convicted for violating it.

The constitutional power of Congress to raise and support armies and to make all laws necessary and proper to that end is broad and sweeping. The power of Congress to classify and conscript manpower for military service is "beyond question." Pursuant to this power, Congress may establish a system of registration for individuals liable for training and service, and may require such individuals within reason to cooperate in the registration system. The issuance of certificates indicating the registration and eligibility classification of individuals is a legitimate and substantial administrative aid in the functioning of this system. And legislation to insure the continuing availability of issued certificates serves a legitimate and substantial purpose in the system's administration. . . .

The registration certificate serves as proof that the individual described thereon has registered for the draft. The classification certificate shows the eligibility classification of a named but undescribed individual. Voluntarily displaying the two certificates is an easy and painless way for a young man to dispel a question as to whether he might be delinquent in his Selective Service obligations. [S]ince both certificates are in the nature of "receipts" attesting that the registrant has done what the law requires, it is in the interest of the just and efficient administration of the system that they be continually available, in the event, for example, of a mix-up in the registrant's file. . . . The information supplied on the certificates facilitates communication between registrants and local boards, simplifying the system and benefiting all concerned. To begin with, each certificate bears the address of the registrant's local board, an item unlikely to be committed to memory. Further, each card bears the registrant's Selective Service number, and a registrant who has his number readily available so that he can communicate it to his local board when he supplies or requests information can make simpler the board's task in locating his file. . . . The many functions performed by Selective Service certificates establish beyond doubt that Congress has a legitimate and substantial interest in preventing their wanton and unrestrained destruction and assuring their continuing availability by punishing people who knowingly and wilfully destroy or mutilate them. . . .

It is equally clear that the 1965 Amendment specifically protects this substantial governmental interest. We perceive no alternative means that would more precisely and narrowly assure the continuing availability of issued Selective Service certificates than a law which prohibits their wilful mutilation or destruction. The 1965 Amendment prohibits such conduct and does nothing more. In other words, both the governmental interest and the operation of the 1965 Amendment are limited to the noncommunicative aspect of O'Brien's conduct. The governmental interest and the scope of the 1965 Amendment are limited to preventing harm to the smooth and efficient functioning of the Selective Service System. When O'Brien deliberately rendered unavailable his registration certificate, he wilfully frustrated this governmental interest. For this noncommunicative impact of his conduct, and for nothing else, he was convicted.

The case at bar is therefore unlike one where the alleged governmental interest in regulating conduct arises in some measure because the communication allegedly integral to the conduct is itself thought to be harmful. In *Stromberg v. People of State of California,* 283 U.S. 359, 51 S.Ct. 532, 75 L.Ed. 1117 (1931), for example, this Court struck down a statutory phrase which punished people who expressed their "opposition to organized government" by displaying "any flag, badge, banner, or device." Since the statute there was aimed at suppressing communication it could not be sustained as a regulation of noncommunicative conduct.

In conclusion, we find that because of the Government's substantial interest in assuring the continuing availability of issued Selective Service certificates, because amended § 462(b) is an appropriately narrow means of protecting this interest and condemns only the independent noncommunicative impact of conduct within its reach, and because the noncommunicative impact of O'Brien's act of burning his registration certificate frustrated the Government's interest, a sufficient governmental interest has been shown to justify O'Brien's conviction.

O'Brien finally argues that the 1965 Amendment is unconstitutional as enacted because what he calls the "purpose" of Congress was "to suppress freedom of speech." We reject this argument because under settled principles the purpose of Congress, as O'Brien uses that term, is not a basis for declaring this legislation unconstitutional.

It is a familiar principle of constitutional law that this Court will not strike down an otherwise constitutional statute on the basis of an alleged illicit legislative motive. . . . Inquiries into congressional motives or purposes are a hazardous matter. When the issue is simply the interpretation of legislation, the Court will look to statements by legislators for guidance as to the purpose of the legislature, because the benefit to sound decision-making in this circumstance is thought sufficient to risk the possibility of misreading Congress' purpose. It is entirely a different matter when we are asked to void a statute that is, under well-settled criteria, constitutional on its face, on the basis of what fewer than a handful of Congressmen said about it. What motivates one legislator to make a speech about a statute is not necessarily what motivates scores of others to enact it, and the stakes are sufficiently high for us to eschew guesswork. We decline to void essentially on the ground that it is unwise legislation which Congress had the undoubted power to enact and which could be reenacted in its exact form if the same or another legislator made a "wiser" speech about it.

[Only three Congressmen, in the floor debates, commented on this legislation.] It is principally on the basis of the statements by these three Congressmen that O'Brien makes his congressional-"purpose" argument. We note that if we were to examine legislative purpose in the instant case, we would be obliged to consider not only these statements but also the more authoritative reports of the Senate and House Armed Services Committees.... While both reports make clear a concern with the "defiant" destruction of so-called "draft cards" and with "open" encouragement to others to destroy their cards, both reports also indicate that this concern stemmed from an apprehension that unrestrained destruction of cards would disrupt the smooth functioning of the Selective Service System....

[The concurring opinion of HARLAN, J., and the dissenting opinion of DOUGLAS, J., are omitted.]

TINKER v. DES MOINES INDEPENDENT COMMUNITY SCHOOL DISTRICT

393 U.S. 503, 89 S.Ct. 733, 21 L.Ed.2d 731 (1969).

MR. JUSTICE FORTAS delivered the opinion of the Court.

Petitioner John F. Tinker, 15 years old, and petitioner Christopher Eckhardt, 16 years old, attended high schools in Des Moines, Iowa. Petitioner Mary Beth Tinker, John's sister, was a 13–year–old student in junior high school. In December 1965, a group of adults and students in Des Moines held a meeting at the Eckhardt home. The group determined to publicize their objections to the hostilities in Vietnam and their support for a truce by wearing black armbands during the holiday season and by fasting on December 16 and New Year's Eve. Petitioners and their parents had previously engaged in similar activities, and they decided to participate in the program.

The principals of the Des Moines schools became aware of the plan to wear armbands. On December 14, 1965, they met and adopted a policy that any student wearing an armband to school would be asked to remove it, and if he refused he would be suspended until he returned without the armband. Petitioners were aware of the regulation that the school authorities adopted.

On December 16, Mary Beth and Christopher wore black armbands to their schools. John Tinker wore his armband the next day. They were all sent home and suspended from school until they would come back without their armbands. They did not return to school until after the planned period for wearing armbands had expired—that is, until after New Year's Day. . . .

First Amendment rights, applied in light of the special characteristics of the school environment, are available to teachers and students. It can hardly be argued that either students or teachers shed their constitutional rights to freedom of speech or expression at the schoolhouse gate. . . .

The problem posed by the present case does not relate to regulation of the length of skirts or the type of clothing, to hair style, or deportment. It does not concern aggressive, disruptive action or even group demonstrations. Our problem involves direct, primary First Amendment rights akin to "pure speech." The school officials banned and sought to punish petitioners for a silent, passive expression of opinion, unaccompanied by any disorder or disturbance on the part of petitioners. There is here no evidence whatever of petitioners' interference, actual or nascent, with the schools' work or of collision with the rights of other students to be secure and to be let alone. Accordingly, this case does not concern speech or action that intrudes upon the work of the schools or the rights of other students. . . . There is no indication that the work of the schools or any class was disrupted. Outside the classrooms, a few students made hostile remarks to the children wearing armbands, but there were no threats or acts of violence on school premises.

The District Court concluded that the action of the school authorities was reasonable because it was based upon their fear of a disturbance from the wearing of the armbands. But, in our system, undifferentiated fear or apprehension of disturbance is not enough to overcome the right to freedom of expression. Any departure from absolute regimentation may cause trouble. Any variation from the majority's opinion may inspire fear. Any word spoken, in class, in the lunchroom, or on the campus, that deviates from the views of another person may start an argument or cause a disturbance. But our Constitution says we must take this risk; and our history says that it is this sort of hazardous freedom—this kind of openness—that is the basis of our national strength and of the independence and vigor of Americans who grow up and live in this relatively permissive, often disputatious, society.

In order for the State in the person of school officials to justify prohibition of a particular expression of opinion, it must be able to show that its action was caused by something more than a mere desire to avoid the discomfort and unpleasantness that always accompany an unpopular viewpoint. Certainly where there is no finding and no showing that engaging in the forbidden conduct would "materially and substantially interfere with the requirements of appropriate discipline in the operation of the school," the prohibition cannot be sustained.

In the present case, the District Court made no such finding, and our independent examination of the record fails to yield evidence that the school authorities had reason to anticipate that the wearing of the armbands would substantially interfere with the work of the school or impinge upon the rights of other students. . . . On the contrary, the action of the school authorities appears to have been based upon an urgent wish to avoid the controversy which might result from the expression, even by the silent symbol of armbands, of opposition to this Nation's part in the conflagration in Vietnam. . . .

It is also relevant that the school authorities did not purport to prohibit the wearing of all symbols of political or controversial significance. The record shows that students in some of the schools wore buttons relating to national political campaigns, and some even wore the Iron Cross, traditionally a symbol of Nazism. The order prohibiting the wearing of armbands did not extend to these. Instead, a particular symbol—black armbands worn to exhibit opposition to this Nation's involvement in Vietnam—was singled out for prohibition. Clearly, the prohibition of expression of one particular opinion, at least without evidence that it is necessary to avoid material and substantial interference with school work or discipline, is not constitutionally permissible. . . .

If a regulation were adopted by school officials forbidding discussion of the Vietnam conflict, or the expression by any student of opposition to it anywhere on school property except as part of a prescribed classroom exercise, it would be obvious that the regulation would violate the constitutional rights of students, at least if it could not be justified by a showing that the students' activities would materially and substantially disrupt the work and discipline of the school. . . . In the circumstances of the present case, the prohibition of the silent, passive "witness of the armbands," as one of the children called it, is no less offensive to the Constitution's guarantees. . . .

We express no opinion as to the form of relief which should be granted, this being a matter for the lower courts to determine. We reverse and remand for further proceedings consistent with this opinion.

Reversed and remanded.

Mr. Justice Black, dissenting. . . .

Assuming that the Court is correct in holding that the conduct of wearing armbands for the purpose of conveying political ideas is protected by the First Amendment, the crucial remaining questions are whether students and teachers may use the schools at their whim as a platform for the exercise of free speech—"symbolic" or "pure"—and whether the courts will allocate to themselves the function of deciding how the pupils' school day will be spent. While . . . neither the State nor the Federal Government has any authority to regulate or censor the content of speech, I have never believed that any person has a right to give speeches or engage in demonstrations where he pleases and when he pleases. . . . While the absence of obscene remarks or boisterous and loud disorder perhaps justifies the Court's statement that the few armband students did not actually "disrupt" the classwork, I think the record overwhelmingly shows that the armbands did exactly what the elected school officials and principals foresaw they would, that is, took the students' minds off their classwork and diverted them to thoughts about the highly emotional subject of the Vietnam war. [I]f the time has come when pupils of state-supported schools, kindergartens, grammar schools, or high schools, can defy and flout orders of school officials to keep their minds on their own schoolwork, it is the beginning of a new revolutionary era of permissiveness in this country fostered by the judiciary....

[The concurring opinions of STEWART, J., and WHITE, J., and the dissenting opinion of HARLAN, J., are omitted.]

Notes

1. In *Board of Education v. Pico,* 457 U.S. 853, 102 S.Ct. 2799, 73 L.Ed.2d 435 (1982) the issue was whether the First Amendment restricted the decision of a local School Board to remove certain books from high school and junior high school libraries. The books were not obscene in a constitutional sense but the Board concluded that the books were "anti-American, anti-Christian, anti-Semitic, and just plain filthy." The Court could produce no majority opinion and returned the case to the lower courts for a trial on the merits.

Brennan, J., joined by Marshall & Stevens, JJ., and in part by Blackmun, J., emphasized that the case did not involve any required reading or judicial intrusion on the Board's discretion to prescribe curricula. "[T]he only books at issue are *library* books, books that by their nature are optional rather than required reading." (emphasis in original). Students have a "right to receive ideas." While free speech rights must be interpreted in light of the special characteristics of the school environment under *Tinker*, the school library is a special locus of free speech. Thus—

Petitioners rightly possess significant discretion to determine the content of their school libraries. But that discretion may not be exercised in a narrowly partisan or political manner. If a Democratic school board, motivated by party affiliation, ordered the removal of all books written by or in favor of Republicans, few would doubt that the order violated the constitutional rights of the students denied access to those books.... Our Constitution does not permit the official suppression of *ideas*. Thus whether petitioners' removal of books from their school libraries denied respondents their First Amendment rights depends upon the motivation behind petitioners' actions. If petitioners *intended* by their removal decision to deny respondents access to ideas with which petitioners disagreed, and if this intent was the decisive factor in petitioners' decision, then petitioners have exercised their discretion in violation of the Constitution. [R]espondents implicitly concede that an unconstitutional motivation would *not* be demonstrated if it were shown that petitioners had decided to remove the books at issue because those books were pervasively vulgar. And again, respondents concede that if it were demonstrated that the removal decision was based solely upon the "educational suitability" of the books in question, then their removal would be "perfectly permissible." [N]othing in our decision today affects in any way the discretion of a local school board to choose books to *add* to the libraries of their schools. Because we are concerned in this case with the suppression of ideas, our holding today affects only the discretion to *remove* books.

Blackmun, J., concurred in part and in the judgment, argued that "removing a learned treatise criticizing American foreign policy from an elementary school library because the students would not understand it is an action unrelated to the *purpose* of suppressing ideas. [R]emoving the same treatise because it is 'anti-American' raises a far more difficult issue." White, J., concurring in the judgment, would abstain from issuing advice on the Constitutional issues involved until after a full trial as to why the Board removed the books.

Burger, C.J., joined by Powell, Rehnquist, & O'Connor, JJ., dissented because the Board placed no speech restraints on the students: they could read the books, available from public libraries, bookstores, or elsewhere; they could discuss the books in class. There is no " 'right' to have the government provide continuing access to certain books." The plurality's test, allowing the books to be withdrawn if "educationally unsuitable," is standardless. Why must a book be "pervasively vulgar" before it is offensive; would not "random" vulgarity be enough to make the book inappropriate? The Burger dissent also found no justification in the plurality's distinction between "*removing* unwanted books and *acquiring* books." (emphasis in original). Books do not have any constitutional tenure.

Rehnquist's dissent, joined by Burger, C.J., & Powell, J., agreed with the plurality that a Democratic school board could not order the removal of all books written by Republicans, but "would save for another day" such extreme examples because the books here were removed because of their vulgarity and profanity. Moreover, if Brennan "truly has found a 'right to receive ideas,' " his "distinction between acquisition and removal makes little sense."

2. *Clark v. Community for Creative Non–Violence*, 468 U.S. 288, 104 S.Ct. 3065, 82 L.Ed.2d 221 (1984) upheld a National Park Service regulation prohibiting camping in certain parks. The regulation prohibited demonstrators from sleeping in two Washington, D.C. parks—Lafayette Park and the Mall—in connection with a demonstration intended to call attention to the plight of the homeless. The regulation is proper, whether is a time, place, or manner restriction, or a regulation of symbolic conduct.

3. *Wayte v. United States*, 470 U.S. 598, 105 S.Ct. 1524, 84 L.Ed.2d 547 (1985). The Government adopted a passive enforcement policy for the Selective Service Act—under which the Government only prosecuted those who reported themselves as having violated the law by refusing to register with the Selective Service System (or were reported by others) and then still refused to register after being warned by the Government. The petitioner claimed that this selective enforcement impermissibly targeted vocal nonregistrants for prosecution on the basis of their exercise of First Amendment rights. The Court held that policy did not violate the First or Fifth Amendments.

First, there was no violation of Fifth Amendment equal protection because the petitioner could not demonstrate that the enforcement policy selected nonregistrants for prosecution on the basis of their speech: the

Government did not prosecute those who protested registration but did not report themselves or were not reported by others, while it did prosecute those who reported themselves or were reported by others even though they did not publicly protest. Even if the passive enforcement policy had a discriminatory effect on vocal protestors, there was no proof of discriminatory purpose, "that the Government prosecuted him *because of* his protest activities." (emphasis in original).

Secondly, the Government enforcement plan did not violate the *O'Brien* test. The passive enforcement policy promoted prosecutorial efficiency; the nonregistrant's letters provided "strong, perhaps conclusive evidence" of an intent not to register; and the prosecution of visible nonregistrants promoted general deterrence. There was "no more limitation on speech than was necessary to ensure registration for the national defense."

TEXAS v. JOHNSON
491 U.S. 397, 109 S.Ct. 2533, 105 L.Ed.2d 342 (1989).

JUSTICE BRENNAN delivered the opinion of the Court.

After publicly burning an American flag as a means of political protest, Gregory Lee Johnson was convicted of desecrating a flag in violation of Texas law. This case presents the question whether his conviction is consistent with the First Amendment. We hold that it is not.

While the Republican National Convention was taking place in Dallas in 1984, respondent Johnson participated in a political demonstration dubbed the "Republican War Chest Tour." [T]he purpose of this event was to protest the policies of the Reagan administration and of certain Dallas-based corporations. The demonstrators ... spray-painted the walls of buildings and overturned potted plants, but Johnson himself took no part in such activities. He did, however, accept an American flag handed to him by a fellow protestor who had taken it from a flag pole outside one of the targeted buildings.

The demonstration ended in front of Dallas City Hall, where Johnson unfurled the American flag, doused it with kerosene, and set it on fire. While the flag burned, the protestors chanted, "America, the red, white, and blue, we spit on you." After the demonstrators dispersed, a witness to the flag-burning collected the flag's remains and buried them in his backyard. No one was physically injured or threatened with injury, though several witnesses testified that they had been seriously offended by the flag-burning.

Of the approximately 100 demonstrators, Johnson alone was charged with a crime. The only criminal offense with which he was charged was the desecration of a venerated object in violation of Tex.Penal Code Ann. § 42.09(a)(3) (1989).* After a trial, he was convicted,

---

* Tex.Penal Code Ann. § 42.09 (1989) provides in full: "§ 42.09. Desecration of Venerated Object

sentenced to one year in prison, and fined $2,000. The Court of Appeals for the Fifth District of Texas at Dallas affirmed Johnson's conviction, but the Texas Court of Criminal Appeals reversed, holding that the State could not, consistent with the First Amendment, punish Johnson for burning the flag in these circumstances....

Johnson was convicted of flag desecration for burning the flag rather than for uttering insulting words.... We must first determine whether Johnson's burning of the flag constituted expressive conduct, permitting him to invoke the First Amendment in challenging his conviction. If his conduct was expressive, we next decide whether the State's regulation is related to the suppression of free expression. See, e.g., *United States v. O'Brien*. If the State's regulation is not related to expression, then the less stringent standard we announced in *United States v. O'Brien* for regulations of noncommunicative conduct controls. If it is, then we are outside of *O'Brien*'s test, and we must ask whether this interest justified Johnson's conviction under a more demanding standard.*** A third possibility is that the State's asserted interest is simply not implicated on these facts, and in that event the interest drops out of the picture.

... The State of Texas conceded for purposes of its oral argument in this case that Johnson's conduct was expressive conduct, and this concession seems to us [to be] prudent.... Johnson burned an American flag as part—indeed, as the culmination—of a political demonstration that coincided with the convening of the Republican Party and its renomination of Ronald Reagan for President. The expressive, overtly political nature of this conduct was both intentional and overwhelmingly apparent. At his trial, Johnson explained his reasons for burning the flag as follows: "The American Flag was burned as Ronald Reagan was being

"(a) A person commits an offense if he intentionally or knowingly desecrates:

"(1) a public monument; (2) a place of worship or burial; or (3) a state or national flag.

"(b) For purposes of this section, 'desecrate' means deface, damage, or otherwise physically mistreat in a way that the actor knows will seriously offend one or more persons likely to observe or discover his action.

"(c) An offense under this section is a Class A misdemeanor."

*** Although Johnson has raised a facial challenge to Texas' flag-desecration statute, we choose to resolve this case on the basis of his claim that the statute as applied to him violates the First Amendment. Section 42.09 regulates only physical conduct with respect to the flag, not the written or spoken word, and although one violates the statute only if one "knows" that one's physical treatment of the flag "will serious-

ly offend one or more persons likely to observe or discover his action," this fact does not necessarily mean that the statute applies only to *expressive* conduct protected by the First Amendment. *Cf. Smith v. Goguen*, 415 U.S. 566, 588, 94 S.Ct. 1242, 1254, 39 L.Ed.2d 605 (1974)(White, J., concurring in judgment)(statute prohibiting "contemptuous" treatment of flag encompasses only expressive conduct). A tired person might, for example, drag a flag through the mud, knowing that this conduct is likely to offend others, and yet have no thought of expressing any idea; neither the language nor the Texas courts' interpretations of the statute precludes the possibility that such a person would be prosecuted for flag desecration. Because the prosecution of a person who had not engaged in expressive conduct would pose a different case, and because we are capable of disposing of this case on narrower grounds, we address only Johnson's claim that § 42.09 as applied to political expression like his violates the First Amendment.

renominated as President. And a more powerful statement of symbolic speech, whether you agree with it or not, couldn't have been made at that time. It's quite a just position [juxtaposition]. We had new patriotism and no patriotism." In these circumstances, Johnson's burning of the flag was conduct "sufficiently imbued with elements of communication," to implicate the First Amendment.

The Government generally has a freer hand in restricting expressive conduct than it has in restricting the written or spoken word. See *O'Brien*. It may not, however, proscribe particular conduct *because* it has expressive elements. [A]lthough we have recognized that where " 'speech' and 'nonspeech' elements are combined in the same course of conduct, a sufficiently important governmental interest in regulating the nonspeech element can justify incidental limitations on First Amendment freedoms," we have limited the applicability of *O'Brien*'s relatively lenient standard to those cases in which "the governmental interest is unrelated to the suppression of free expression." In stating, moreover, that *O'Brien*'s test "in the last analysis is little, if any, different from the standard applied to time, place, or manner restrictions," we have highlighted the requirement that the governmental interest in question be unconnected to expression in order to come under *O'Brien*'s less demanding rule.

. . . The State offers two separate interests to justify this conviction: preventing breaches of the peace, and preserving the flag as a symbol of nationhood and national unity. We hold that the first interest is not implicated on this record and that the second is related to the suppression of expression.

Texas claims that its interest in preventing breaches of the peace justifies Johnson's conviction for flag desecration. However, no disturbance of the peace actually occurred or threatened to occur because of Johnson's burning of the flag. . . . The State's emphasis on the protestors' disorderly actions prior to arriving at City Hall is not only somewhat surprising given that no charges were brought on the basis of this conduct, but it also fails to show that a disturbance of the peace was a likely reaction to *Johnson*'s conduct. . . .

The State's position, therefore, amounts to a claim that an audience that takes serious offense at particular expression is necessarily likely to disturb the peace and that the expression may be prohibited on this basis. Our precedents do not countenance such a presumption. On the contrary, they recognize that a principal "function of free speech under our system of government is to invite dispute. It may indeed best serve its high purpose when it induces a condition of unrest, creates dissatisfaction with conditions as they are, or even stirs people to anger." Thus, we have . . . required careful consideration of the actual circumstances surrounding such expression, asking whether the expression "is directed to inciting or producing imminent lawless action and is likely to incite or produce such action." *Brandenburg v. Ohio* . . . .

Nor does Johnson's expressive conduct fall within that small class of "fighting words" that are "likely to provoke the average person to retaliation, and thereby cause a breach of the peace." No reasonable onlooker would have regarded Johnson's generalized expression of dissatisfaction with the policies of the Federal Government as a direct personal insult or an invitation to exchange fisticuffs.... We do not suggest that the First Amendment forbids a State to prevent "imminent lawless action." *Brandenburg*. And, in fact, Texas already has a statute specifically prohibiting breaches of the peace, which tends to confirm that Texas need not punish this flag desecration in order to keep the peace.

The State also asserts an interest in preserving the flag as a symbol of nationhood and national unity. [T]his interest is related to expression in the case of Johnson's burning of the flag.... We are thus outside of *O'Brien*'s test altogether.

It remains to consider whether the State's interest in preserving the flag as a symbol of nationhood and national unity justifies Johnson's conviction.... Johnson was not, we add, prosecuted for the expression of just any idea; he was prosecuted for his expression of dissatisfaction with the policies of this country, expression situated at the core of our First Amendment values.

Moreover, Johnson was prosecuted because he knew that his politically charged expression would cause "serious offense." If he had burned the flag as a means of disposing of it because it was dirty or torn, he would not have been convicted of flag desecration under this Texas law: federal law designates burning as the preferred means of disposing of a flag "when it is in such condition that it is no longer a fitting emblem for display." 36 U.S.C. § 176(k), and Texas has no quarrel with this means of disposal. Brief for Petitioner 45. The Texas law is thus not aimed at protecting the physical integrity of the flag in all circumstances, but is designed instead to protect it only against impairments that would cause serious offense to others. Texas concedes as much: "Section 42.09(b) reaches only ... intentional or knowing abuse, that is, the kind of mistreatment that is not innocent, but rather is intentionally designed to seriously offend other individuals." *Id*.

Whether Johnson's treatment of the flag violated Texas law thus depended on the likely communicative impact of his expressive conduct. [T]his restriction on Johnson's expression is content-based.... We must therefore subject the State's asserted interest in preserving the special symbolic character of the flag to "the most exacting scrutiny."*

---

* Our inquiry is, of course, bounded by the particular facts of this case and by the statute under which Johnson was convicted. There was no evidence that Johnson himself stole the flag he burned, nor did the prosecution or the arguments urged in support of it depend on the theory that the flag was stolen. Thus, our analysis does not rely on the way in which the flag was acquired, and nothing in our opinion should be taken to suggest that one is free to steal a flag so long as one later uses it to communicate an idea. We also emphasize that Johnson was prosecuted *only* for flag desecration—not for trespass, disorderly conduct, or arson.

Texas argues that its interest in preserving the flag as a symbol of nationhood and national unity survives this close analysis. Quoting extensively from the writings of this Court chronicling the flag's historic and symbolic role in our society, the State emphasizes the " 'special place' reserved for the flag in our Nation.... " If there is a bedrock principle underlying the First Amendment, it is that the Government may not prohibit the expression of an idea simply because society finds the idea itself offensive or disagreeable.... We have not recognized an exception to this principle even where our flag has been involved. In *Street v. New York,* 394 U.S. 576, 89 S.Ct. 1354, 22 L.Ed.2d 572 (1969), we held that a State may not criminally punish a person for uttering words critical of the flag.

[N]othing in our precedents suggests that a state may foster its own view of the flag by prohibiting expressive conduct relating to it.*

Texas' focus on the precise nature of Johnson's expression, moreover, misses the point of our prior decisions: their enduring lesson, that the Government may not prohibit expression simply because it disagrees with its message, is not dependent on the particular mode in which one chooses to express an idea.* If we were to hold that a State may forbid flag-burning wherever it is likely to endanger the flag's symbolic role, but allow it whenever burning a flag promotes that role—as where, for example, a person ceremoniously burns a dirty flag—we would be saying that when it comes to impairing the flag's physical integrity, the flag itself may be used as a symbol—as a substitute for the written or spoken word or a "short cut from mind to mind"—only in one direction. We would be permitting a State to "prescribe what shall be orthodox" by saying that one may burn the flag to convey one's attitude toward it and its referents only if one does not endanger the flag's representation of nationhood and national unity.

We never before have held that the Government may ensure that a symbol be used to express only one view of that symbol or its referents.

---

* Our decision in *Halter v. Nebraska,* 205 U.S. 34, 27 S.Ct. 419, 51 L.Ed. 696 (1907), addressing the validity of a state law prohibiting certain commercial uses of the flag, is not to the contrary. That case was decided "nearly 20 years before the Court concluded that the First Amendment applies to the States by virtue of the Fourteenth Amendment." More important, as we continually emphasized in *Halter* itself, that case involved purely commercial rather than political speech. Nor does *San Francisco Arts & Athletics v. Olympic Committee,* [§ 10–2] 2971, 2973, 97 L.Ed.2d 427 (1987), addressing the validity of Congress' decision to "authoriz[e] the United States Olympic Committee to prohibit certain commercial and promotional uses of the word 'Olympic,' "relied upon by the dissent, even begin to tell us whether the Government may criminally punish physical conduct towards the flag engaged in as a means of political protest.

* The dissent appears to believe that Johnson's conduct may be prohibited and, indeed, criminally sanctioned, because "his act ... conveyed nothing that could not have been conveyed and was not conveyed just as forcefully in a dozen different ways." Not only does this assertion sit uneasily next to the dissent's quite correct reminder that the flag occupies a unique position in our society—which demonstrates that messages conveyed without use of the flag are not "just as forcefu[l]" as those conveyed with it—but it also ignores the fact that, in *Spence* [*v. Washington,* 418 U.S. 405, 411 n. 4, 94 S.Ct. 2727, 2731 n. 4, 41 L.Ed.2d 842 (1974)], we "rejected summarily" this very claim.

Indeed, in *Schacht v. United States,* [398 U.S. 58, 90 S.Ct. 1555, 26 L.Ed.2d 44 (1970)] we invalidated a federal statute permitting an actor portraying a member of one of our armed forces to " 'wear the uniform of that armed force if the portrayal does not tend to discredit that armed force.' " This proviso, we held, "which leaves Americans free to praise the war in Vietnam but can send persons like Schacht to prison for opposing it, cannot survive in a country which has the First Amendment."

We perceive no basis on which to hold that the principle underlying our decision in *Schacht* does not apply to this case. To conclude that the Government may permit designated symbols to be used to communicate only a limited set of messages would be to enter territory having no discernible or defensible boundaries. Could the Government, on this theory, prohibit the burning of state flags? Of copies of the Presidential seal? Of the Constitution? In evaluating these choices under the First Amendment, how would we decide which symbols were sufficiently special to warrant this unique status? To do so, we would be forced to consult our own political preferences, and impose them on the citizenry, in the very way that the First Amendment forbids us to do. There is, moreover, no indication—either in the text of the Constitution or in our cases interpreting it—that a separate juridical category exists for the American flag alone. . . .

[O]ur toleration of criticism such as Johnson's is a sign and source of our strength. Indeed, one of the proudest images of our flag, the one immortalized in our own national anthem, is of the bombardment it survived at Fort McHenry. It is the Nation's resilience, not its rigidity, that Texas sees reflected in the flag—and it is that resilience that we reassert today.

The way to preserve the flag's special role is not to punish those who feel differently about these matters. It is to persuade them that they are wrong. [P]recisely because it is our flag that is involved, one's response to the flag-burner may exploit the uniquely persuasive power of the flag itself. We can imagine no more appropriate response to burning a flag than waving one's own, no better way to counter a flag-burner's message than by saluting the flag that burns, no surer means of preserving the dignity even of the flag that burned than by—as one witness here did—according its remains a respectful burial. We do not consecrate the flag by punishing its desecration, for in doing so we dilute the freedom that this cherished emblem represents.

Johnson was convicted for engaging in expressive conduct. The State's interest in preventing breaches of the peace does not support his conviction because Johnson's conduct did not threaten to disturb the peace. Nor does the State's interest in preserving the flag as a symbol of nationhood and national unity justify his criminal conviction for engaging in political expression. The judgment of the Texas Court of Criminal Appeals is therefore affirmed.

Justice Kennedy, concurring.

[S]ometimes we must make decisions we do not like. We make them because they are right, right in the sense that the law and the Constitution, as we see them, compel the result.... It is poignant but fundamental that the flag protects those who hold it in contempt....

CHIEF JUSTICE REHNQUIST, with whom JUSTICE WHITE and JUSTICE O'CONNOR, join, dissenting.

In holding this Texas statute unconstitutional, the Court ignores Justice Holmes' familiar aphorism that "a page of history is worth a volume of logic." For more than 200 years, the American flag has occupied a unique position as the symbol of our Nation, a uniqueness that justifies a governmental prohibition against flag burning in the way respondent Johnson did here. [Chief Justice Rehnquist then followed with a thorough discussion of the history of the American flag, and quoted references to the flag in "The Star Spangled Banner" and Ralph Waldo Emerson's "Concord Hymn". He also reprinted John Greenleaf Whittier's poem, "Barbara Frietchie" (including the famous lines: " 'Shoot if you must, this old grey head,/But spare your country's flag,' she said.")]

Both Congress and the States have enacted numerous laws regulating misuse of the American flag. Until 1967, Congress left the regulation of misuse of the flag up to the States.... With the exception of Alaska and Wyoming, all of the States now have statutes prohibiting the burning of the flag. Most of the state statutes are patterned after the Uniform Flag Act of 1917, which in § 3 provides: "No person shall publicly mutilate, deface, defile, defy, trample upon, or by word or act cast contempt upon any such flag, standard, color, ensign or shield." Most were passed by the States at about the time of World War I.

The American flag, then, throughout more than 200 years of our history, has come to be the visible symbol embodying our Nation.... The flag is not simply another "idea" or "point of view" competing for recognition in the marketplace of ideas. Millions and millions of Americans regard it with an almost mystical reverence regardless of what sort of social, political, or philosophical beliefs they may have....

Here it may equally well be said that the public burning of the American flag by Johnson was no essential part of any exposition of ideas, and at the same time it had a tendency to incite a breach of the peace. Johnson was free to make any verbal denunciation of the flag that he wished; indeed, he was free to burn the flag in private. He could publicly burn other symbols of the Government or effigies of political leaders....

The result of the Texas statute is obviously to deny one in Johnson's frame of mind one of many means of "symbolic speech." Far from being a case of "one picture being worth a thousand words," flag burning is the equivalent of an inarticulate grunt or roar that, it seems fair to say, is most likely to be indulged in not to express any particular idea, but to antagonize others.... It was Johnson's use of this particular symbol, and not the idea that he sought to convey by it or by his many other expressions, for which he was punished.

Our prior cases dealing with flag desecration statutes have left open the question that the Court resolves today. In *Street v. New York,* the defendant burned a flag in the street, shouting "We don't need no damned flag" . . . The Court ruled that since the defendant might have been convicted solely on the basis of his words, the conviction could not stand, but it expressly reserved the question of whether a defendant could constitutionally be convicted for burning the flag.

Chief Justice Warren, in dissent, stated: "I believe that the States and Federal Government do have the power to protect the flag from acts of desecration and disgrace. . . . " Justices Black and Fortas also expressed their personal view that a prohibition on flag burning did not violate the Constitution. See *id.,* (Black, J., dissenting)("It passes my belief that anything in the Federal Constitution bars a State from making the deliberate burning of the American Flag an offense"); *id.* (Fortas, J., dissenting)("[T]he States and the Federal Government have the power to protect the flag from acts of desecration committed in public. . . . A person may 'own' a flag, but ownership is subject to special burdens and responsibilities. A flag may be property, in a sense; but it is property burdened with peculiar obligations and restrictions. . . . "). . . .

The Court concludes its opinion with a regrettably patronizing civics lecture, presumably addressed to the Members of both Houses of Congress, the members of the 48 state legislatures that enacted prohibitions against flag burning, and the troops fighting under that flag in Vietnam who objected to its being burned: "The way to preserve the flag's special role is not to punish those who feel differently about these matters. It is to persuade them that they are wrong." [O]ne of the high purposes of a democratic society is to legislate against conduct that is regarded as evil and profoundly offensive to the majority of people—whether it be murder, embezzlement, pollution, or flag burning. . . .

JUSTICE STEVENS, dissenting.

. . . The concept of "desecration" does not turn on the substance of the message the actor intends to convey, but rather on whether those who view the *act* will take serious offense. Accordingly, one intending to convey a message of respect for the flag by burning it in a public square might nonetheless be guilty of desecration if he knows that others—perhaps simply because they misperceive the intended message—will be seriously offended. Indeed, even if the actor knows that all possible witnesses will understand that he intends to send a message of respect, he might still be guilty of desecration if he also knows that this understanding does not lessen the offense taken by some of those witnesses. . . .

The Court is therefore quite wrong in blandly asserting that respondent "was prosecuted for his expression of dissatisfaction with the policies of this country, expression situated at the core of our First Amendment values." Respondent was prosecuted because of the method he chose to express his dissatisfaction with those policies. Had he chosen to spray paint—or perhaps convey with a motion picture projector—his message of dissatisfaction on the facade of the Lincoln Memorial, there would be no question about the power of the Government to prohibit his means of expression. The prohibition would be supported by the legitimate interest in preserving the quality of an important national asset. Though the asset at stake in this case is intangible, given its unique value, the same interest supports a prohibition on the desecration of the American flag.* . . .

Notes

1. On April 8, 1989, the Presidium of the USSR Supreme Soviet adopted legislation making it a criminal offense to "discredit" a public official. Soviet reformers immediately attacked this legislation. In defense of the legislation, the Soviet old guard published an article in *Nedelya,* the Sunday supplement to *Izvestia,* with a circulation of millions. (*Nedelya,* 1989, No. 15, p. 19). This article listed dozens of foreign laws punishing disrespect for public officials or public symbols. In particular it listed 18 U.S.C.A. § 700, punishing "Desecration of the Flag of the United States" and 24 Penn. Code § 1104, punishing desecration of state and local flags.

Andrei Sakharov, speaking to the Congress of People's Deputies (see, *Izvestia,* May 29, 1989, p. 6) attacked the April 8, 1989 legislation as limiting free speech:

> The Edict of the Presidium of the Supreme Soviet of the USSR [was] adopted on April 8. [It] contradicts the principles of democracy. There is a most important principle, which is formulated in the Universal Declaration of Human Rights, adopted in 1948, and by such an international organization as "Amnesty International." This is the principle that no actions connected with persuasion, unless they are connected with violence or with a call to violence, can be the subject of criminal prosecution. This is a key principle lying at the base of a democratic political system. And this key word "violence" is lacking in the language of the Edict of April 8. . . . A law should not be capable of ambiguous interpretation; this is fraught with huge dangers.

On June 8, 1989, the Congress responded to the criticism of the legislation by Sakharov and other Soviet reformers by repealing the edict.

2. When this flag burning case was publicly announced, Justice Brennan took the uncommon step of reading excerpts for more than 10 minutes, rather than giving the more usual two minute summaries. Justice Stevens also read equally lengthy portions of his dissent. President Bush announced that he would seek a constitutional amendment to prohibit the burning of

---

* The Court suggests that a prohibition against flag desecration is not content-neutral because this form of symbolic speech is only used by persons who are critical of the flag or the ideas it represents. [A] prohibition against the desecration of a gravesite is content-neutral even if it denies some protesters the right to make a symbolic statement by extinguishing the flame in Arlington Cemetery where John F. Kennedy is buried while permitting others to salute the flame by bowing their heads. Few would doubt that a protester who extinguishes the flame has desecrated the gravesite, regardless of whether he prefaces that act with a speech explaining that his purpose is to express deep admiration or unmitigated scorn for the late President. . . .

the American Flag. Bipartisan Congressional support greeted this proposal. Contemporaneous public opinion polls indicated that the flag decision was very unpopular. Congress did not propose an amendment but did enact a new statute prohibiting flag burning. That statute was promptly challenged, and two lower federal courts invalidated it. The Supreme Court also invalidated that new statute, in the following case.

UNITED STATES v. EICHMAN
496 U.S. 310, 110 S.Ct. 2404, 110 L.Ed.2d 287 (1990).

JUSTICE BRENNAN delivered the opinion of the Court.

In these consolidated appeals, we consider whether appellees' prosecution for burning a United States flag in violation of the Flag Protection Act of 1989 is consistent with the First Amendment. Applying our recent decision in *Texas v. Johnson*, the District Courts held that the Act cannot constitutionally be applied to appellees. We affirm.*

After our decision in *Johnson*, Congress passed the Flag Protection Act of 1989. The Act provides in relevant part:

"(a)(1) Whoever knowingly mutilates, defaces, physically defiles, burns, maintains on the floor or ground, or tramples upon any flag of the United States shall be fined under this title or imprisoned for not more than one year, or both.

"(2) This subsection does not prohibit any conduct consisting of the disposal of a flag when it has become worn or soiled.

"(b) As used in this section, the term 'flag of the United States' means any flag of the United States, or any part thereof, made of any substance, of any size, in a form that is commonly displayed." 18 U.S.C.A. § 700.

The Government ... invites us to reconsider our rejection in *Johnson* of the claim that flag-burning as a mode of expression, like obscenity or "fighting words," does not enjoy the full protection of the First Amendment. Cf. *Chaplinsky v. New Hampshire*. This we decline to do.* The only remaining question is whether the Flag Protection Act is sufficiently distinct from the Texas statute that it may constitutionally be applied to proscribe appellees' expressive conduct.

The Government contends that the Flag Protection Act is constitutional because, unlike the statute addressed in *Johnson*, the Act does not target expressive conduct on the basis of the content of its message. The Government asserts an interest in "protect[ing] the physical integrity of the flag under all circumstances" in order to safeguard the flag's identity

---

* The Seattle appellees were also charged with causing willful injury to federal property in violation of 18 U.S.C.A. §§ 1361 and 1362. This charge remains pending before the District Court, and nothing in today's decision affects the constitutionality of this prosecution. [footnote repositioned].

* We deal here with concededly political speech and have no occasion to pass on the validity of laws regulating commercial exploitation of the image of the United States flag. See *Texas v. Johnson,* 491 U.S. 397, 415–416, n. 10 (1989); cf. *Halter v. Nebraska,* 205 U.S. 34 (1907).

" 'as the unique and unalloyed symbol of the Nation.' ''The Act proscribes conduct (other than disposal) that damages or mistreats a flag, without regard to the actor's motive, his intended message, or the likely effects of his conduct on onlookers....

Although the Flag Protection Act contains no explicit content-based limitation on the scope of prohibited conduct, it is nevertheless clear that the Government's asserted *interest* is "related 'to the suppression of free expression,' ''and concerned with the content of such expression. The Government's interest in protecting the "physical integrity" of a privately owned flag** rests upon a perceived need to preserve the flag's status as a symbol of our Nation and certain national ideals. But the mere destruction or disfigurement of a particular physical manifestation of the symbol, without more, does not diminish or otherwise affect the symbol itself in any way. For example, the secret destruction of a flag in one's own basement would not threaten the flag's recognized meaning. Rather, the Government's desire to preserve the flag as a symbol for certain national ideals is implicated "only when a person's treatment of the flag communicates [a] message" to others that is inconsistent with those ideals.

... The Act criminalizes the conduct of anyone who "knowingly mutilates, defaces, physically defiles, burns, maintains on the floor or ground, or tramples upon any flag." 18 U.S.C.A. § 700(a)(1). Each of the specified terms—with the possible exception of "burns"—unmistakably connotes disrespectful treatment of the flag and suggests a focus on those acts likely to damage the flag's symbolic value. And the explicit exemption in § 700(a)(2) for disposal of "worn or soiled" flags protects certain acts traditionally associated with patriotic respect for the flag....

Affirmed.

JUSTICE STEVENS, with whom THE CHIEF JUSTICE, JUSTICE WHITE and JUSTICE O'CONNOR join, dissenting.

[T]he integrity of the symbol has been compromised by those leaders who seem to advocate compulsory worship of the flag even by individuals whom it offends, or who seem to manipulate the symbol of national purpose into a pretext for partisan disputes about meaner ends. [But] I remain persuaded that the considerations identified in my opinion in *Texas v. Johnson* are of controlling importance in this case as well. Accordingly, I respectfully dissent.

Notes

1. In *Halter v. Nebraska,* 205 U.S. 34, 27 S.Ct. 419, 51 L.Ed. 696 (1907), cited in *Eichman* at note 4, Harlan, J., for the Court, upheld a Nebraska statute that made it a misdemeanor to sell merchandise that had printed, for purposes of advertisement, a representation of the flag of the United States. The state law expressly excluded any newspaper, periodical,

---

** Today's decision does not affect the extent to which the Government's interest in protecting publicly owned flags might justify special measures on their behalf.

or book on which there was a representation of a flag "disconnected from any advertisement." The defendants had offered for sale a bottle of beer on which, for purposes of advertisement, there was printed a representation of the American flag. Only Peckham, J., dissented, without opinion.

2. After *Eichman,* a proposed constitutional amendment to prohibit flag-burning again failed to achieve the necessary votes in Congress. If *Eichman* had gone the other way, would it be legal to explode fireworks depicting the flag, or to place the flag design on a birthday cake that is then cut and eaten, or to burn a newspaper that included a photograph of the flag, or to make a movie where actors, portraying war protestors, burn the flag?

10–11. CAMPAIGN FINANCING

BUCKLEY v. VALEO
424 U.S. 1, 96 S.Ct. 612, 46 L.Ed.2d 659 (1976).

PER CURIAM.*

These appeals present constitutional challenges to the key provisions of the Federal Election Campaign Act of 1971 (Act), and related provisions of the Internal Revenue Code of 1954, all as amended in 1974.

The Court of Appeals, in sustaining the legislation in large part against various constitutional challenges, viewed it as "by far the most comprehensive reform legislation [ever] passed by Congress concerning the election of the President, Vice–President, and members of Congress." The statutes at issue summarized in broad terms, contain the following provisions: (a) individual political contributions are limited to $1,000 to any single candidate per election, with an overall annual limitation of $25,000 by any contributor; independent expenditures by individuals and groups "relative to a clearly identified candidate" are limited to $1,000 a year; campaign spending by candidates for various federal offices and spending for national conventions by political parties are subject to prescribed limits; (b) contributions and expenditures above certain threshold levels must be reported and publicly disclosed; (c) a system for public funding of Presidential campaign activities is established by Subtitle H of the Internal Revenue Code; and (d) a Federal Election Commission is established to administer and enforce the legislation. . . .

I.   CONTRIBUTION AND EXPENDITURE LIMITATIONS . . .

The constitutional power of Congress to regulate federal elections is well established and is not questioned by any of the parties in this case. Thus, the critical constitutional questions presented here go not to the basic power of Congress to legislate in this area, but to whether the specific legislation that Congress has enacted interferes with First

---

* The per curiam and other opinions in this case total 294 pages in the U.S. Reports. Only a small portion of the 234 page per curiam opinion (including a 94 page appendix) and portions of two separate opinions are excerpted here.

Amendment freedoms or invidiously discriminates against nonincumbent candidates and minor parties in contravention of the Fifth Amendment.

A. General Principles

... Appellees contend that what the Act regulates is conduct, and that its effect on speech and association is incidental at most. Appellants respond that contributions and expenditures are at the very core of political speech, and that the Act's limitations thus constitute restraints on First Amendment liberty that are both gross and direct.

In upholding the constitutional validity of the Act's contribution and expenditure provisions on the ground that those provisions should be viewed as regulating conduct, not speech, the Court of Appeals relied upon *United States v. O'Brien,* [§ 10–10, supra].... We cannot share the view that the present Act's contribution and expenditure limitations are comparable to the restrictions on conduct upheld in *O'Brien.* [T]his Court has never suggested that the dependence of a communication on the expenditure of money operates itself to introduce a nonspeech element or to reduce the exacting scrutiny required by the First Amendment....

Even if the categorization of the expenditure of money as conduct were accepted, the limitations challenged here would not meet the *O'Brien* test because the governmental interests advanced in support of the Act involve "suppressing communication." The interests served by the Act include restricting the voices of people and interest groups who have money to spend and reducing the overall scope of federal election campaigns. Although the Act does not focus on the ideas expressed by persons or groups subject to its regulations, it is aimed in part at equalizing the relative ability of all voters to affect electoral outcomes by placing a ceiling on expenditures for political expression by citizens and groups. Unlike *O'Brien,* where the Selective Service System's administrative interest in the preservation of draft cards was wholly unrelated to their use as a means of communication, it is beyond dispute that the interest in regulating the alleged "conduct" of giving or spending money "arises in some measure because the communication allegedly integral to the conduct is itself thought to be harmful."

Nor can the Act's contribution and expenditure limitations be sustained, as some of the parties suggest, by reference to the ... proposition that the government may adopt reasonable time, place, and manner regulations, which do not discriminate among speakers or ideas, in order to further an important governmental interest unrelated to the restriction of communication.... The critical difference between this case and those time, place, and manner cases is that the present Act's contribution and expenditure limitations impose direct quantity restrictions on political communication and association by persons, groups, candidates, and political parties in addition to any reasonable time, place, and manner regulations otherwise imposed.

A restriction on the amount of money a person or group can spend on political communication during a campaign necessarily reduces the quantity of expression by restricting the number of issues discussed, the depth of their exploration, and the size of the audience reached. This is because virtually every means of communicating ideas in today's mass society requires the expenditure of money....

By contrast with a limitation upon expenditures for political expression, a limitation upon the amount that any one person or group may contribute to a candidate or political committee entails only a marginal restriction upon the contributor's ability to engage in free communication. A contribution serves as a general expression of support for the candidate and his views, but does not communicate the underlying basis for the support. The quantity of communication by the contributor does not increase perceptibly with the size of his contribution, since the expression rests solely on the undifferentiated, symbolic act of contributing. At most, the size of the contribution provides a very rough index of the intensity of the contributor's support for the candidate. A limitation on the amount of money a person may give to a candidate or campaign organization thus involves little direct restraint on his political communication, for it permits the symbolic expression of support evidenced by a contribution but does not in any way infringe the contributor's freedom to discuss candidates and issues. While contributions may result in political expression if spent by a candidate or an association to present views to the voters, the transformation of contributions into political debate involves speech by someone other than the contributor.

... The overall effect of the Act's contribution ceilings is merely to require candidates and political committees to raise funds from a greater number of persons and to compel people who would otherwise contribute amounts greater than the statutory limits to expend such funds on direct political expression, rather than to reduce the total amount of money potentially available to promote political expression....

In sum, although the Act's contribution and expenditure limitations both implicate fundamental First Amendment interests, its expenditure ceilings impose significantly more severe restrictions on protected freedoms of political expression and association than do its limitations on financial contributions.

B. Contribution Limitations

1. The $1,000 Limitation on Contributions by Individuals and Groups to Candidates and Authorized Campaign Committees. Section 608(b) provides, with certain limited exceptions, that "no person shall make contributions to any candidate with respect to any election for Federal office which, in the aggregate, exceed $1,000." ...

Appellees argue that the Act's restrictions on large campaign contributions are justified by three governmental interests. [T]he primary interest served by the limitations and, indeed, by the Act as a whole, is the prevention of corruption and the appearance of corruption spawned by the real or imagined coercive influence of large financial contributions on candidates' positions and on their actions if elected to office. Two "ancillary" interests underlying the Act are also allegedly furthered by the $1,000 limits on contributions. First, the limits serve to mute the voices of affluent persons and groups in the election process and thereby to equalize the relative ability of all citizens to affect the outcome of elections. Second, it is argued, the ceilings may to some extent act as a brake on the skyrocketing cost of political campaigns and thereby serve to open the political system more widely to candidates without access to sources of large amounts of money.

It is unnecessary to look beyond the Act's primary purpose—to limit the actuality and appearance of corruption resulting from large individual financial contributions—in order to find a constitutionally sufficient justification for the $1,000 contribution limitation.... To the extent that large contributions are given to secure a political *quid pro quo* from current and potential office holders, the integrity of our system of representative democracy is undermined....

Appellants contend that the contribution limitations must be invalidated because bribery laws and narrowly drawn disclosure requirements constitute a less restrictive means of dealing with "proven and suspected *quid pro quo* arrangements." But laws making criminal the giving and taking of bribes deal with only the most blatant and specific attempts of those with money to influence governmental action. And ... Congress was surely entitled to conclude that disclosure was only a partial measure, and that contribution ceilings were a necessary legislative concomitant to deal with the reality or appearance of corruption inherent in a system permitting unlimited financial contributions, even when the identities of the contributors and the amounts of their contributions are fully disclosed....

We find that, under the rigorous standard of review established by our prior decisions, the weighty interests served by restricting the size of financial contributions to political candidates are sufficient to justify the limited effect upon First Amendment freedoms caused by the $1,000 contribution ceiling....

Apart from these First Amendment concerns, appellants argue that the contribution limitations work such an invidious discrimination between incumbents and challengers that the statutory provisions must be declared unconstitutional on their face.... Absent record evidence of invidious discrimination against challengers as a class, a court should generally be hesitant to invalidate legislation which on its face imposes evenhanded restrictions....

The charge of discrimination against minor-party and independent candidates is more troubling, but the record provides no basis for concluding that the Act invidiously disadvantages such candidates. [Using a similar analysis the Court upheld sections of the Act providing for a $5000 limit on contributions by political committees, limitations on volunteers' incidental expenses, and a $25,000 limit on an individual's total contributions during any calendar year.]

C. Expenditure Limitations

The Act's expenditure ceilings impose direct and substantial restraints on the quantity of political speech. The most drastic of the limitations restricts individuals and groups, including political parties that fail to place a candidate on the ballot, to an expenditure of $1,000 "relative to a clearly identified candidate during a calendar year." § 608(e)(1). Other expenditure ceilings limit spending by candidates, § 608(a), their campaigns, § 608(c), and political parties in connection with election campaigns, § 608(f). It is clear that a primary effect of these expenditure limitations is to restrict the quantity of campaign speech by individuals, groups, and candidates. The restrictions, while neutral as to the ideas expressed, limit political expression "at the core of our electoral process and of the First Amendment freedoms."

1. The $1,000 Limitation on Expenditures "Relative to a Clearly Identified Candidate". Section 608(e)(1) provides that "[n]o person may make any expenditure ... relative to a clearly identified candidate during a calendar year which, when added to all other expenditures made by such person during the year advocating the election or defeat of such candidate, exceeds $1,000." The plain effect of § 608(e)(1) is to prohibit all individuals, who are neither candidates nor owners of institutional press facilities, and all groups, except political parties and campaign organizations, from voicing their views "relative to a clearly identified candidate" through means that entail aggregate expenditures of more than $1,000 during a calendar year. The provision, for example, would make it a federal criminal offense for a person or association to place a single one-quarter page advertisement "relative to a clearly identified candidate" in a major metropolitan newspaper....

We find that the governmental interest in preventing corruption and the appearance of corruption is inadequate to justify § 608(e)(1)'s ceiling on independent expenditures.... So long as persons and groups eschew expenditures that in express terms advocate the election or defeat of a clearly identified candidate, they are free to spend as much as they want to promote the candidate and his views. ... § 608(e)(1) limits expenditures for express advocacy of candidates made totally independently of the candidate and his campaign. Unlike contributions, such independent expenditures may well provide little assistance to the candidate's campaign and indeed may prove counterproductive. The absence of prearrangement and coordination of an expenditure with the candidate or his agent not only undermines the value of the expenditure to the candidate, but also alleviates the danger that expenditures will be given as a *quid pro quo* for improper commitments from the candidate. Rather than preventing circumvention of the contribution limitations, § 608(e)(1) severely restricts all independent advocacy despite its substantially diminished potential for abuse.

While the independent expenditure ceiling thus fails to serve any substantial governmental interest in stemming the reality or appearance of corruption in the electoral process, it heavily burdens core First

Amendment expression.... Advocacy of the election or defeat of candidates for federal office is no less entitled to protection under the First Amendment than the discussion of political policy generally or advocacy of the passage or defeat of legislation.

It is argued, however, that the ancillary governmental interest in equalizing the relative ability of individuals and groups to influence the outcome of elections serves to justify the limitation on express advocacy of the election or defeat of candidates imposed by § 608(e)(1)'s expenditure ceiling. But the concept that government may restrict the speech of some elements of our society in order to enhance the relative voice of others is wholly foreign to the First Amendment....

For the reasons stated, we conclude that § 608(e)(1)'s independent expenditure limitation is unconstitutional under the First Amendment.

2. Limitation on Expenditures by Candidates from Personal or Family Resources. The Act also sets limits on expenditures by a candidate "from his personal funds, or the personal funds of his immediate family, in connection with his campaigns during any calendar year." § 608(a)(1). These ceilings vary from $50,000 for Presidential or Vice Presidential candidates to $35,000 for senatorial candidates, and $25,000 for most candidates for the House of Representatives.

The ceiling on personal expenditures by candidates on their own behalf, like the limitations on independent expenditures contained in § 608(e)(1), imposes a substantial restraint on the ability of persons to engage in protected First Amendment expression. The candidate, no less than any other person, has a First Amendment right to engage in the discussion of public issues and vigorously and tirelessly to advocate his own election and the election of other candidates. Indeed, it is of particular importance that candidates have the unfettered opportunity to make their views known so that the electorate may intelligently evaluate the candidates' personal qualities and their positions on vital public issues before choosing among them on election day....

The primary governmental interest served by the Act—the prevention of actual and apparent corruption of the political process—does not support the limitation on the candidate's expenditure of his own personal funds.... We therefore hold that § 608(a)'s restriction on a candidate's personal expenditures is unconstitutional.

3. Limitations on Campaign Expenditures. Section 608(c) places limitations on overall campaign expenditures by candidates seeking nomination for election and election to federal office. Presidential candidates may spend $10,000,000 in seeking nomination for office and an additional $20,000,000 in the general election campaign. §§ 608(c)(1)(A), (B). The ceiling on senatorial campaigns is pegged to the size of the voting-age population of the State with minimum dollar amounts applicable to campaigns in States with small populations....

No governmental interest that has been suggested is sufficient to justify the restriction on the quantity of political expression imposed by

§ 608(c)'s campaign expenditure limitations. The major evil associated with rapidly increasing campaign expenditures is the danger of candidate dependence on large contributions. The interest in alleviating the corrupting influence of large contributions is served by the Act's contribution limitations and disclosure provisions rather than by § 608(c)'s campaign expenditure ceilings....

The interest in equalizing the financial resources of candidates competing for federal office is no more convincing a justification for restricting the scope of federal election campaigns. Given the limitation on the size of outside contributions, the financial resources available to a candidate's campaign, like the number of volunteers recruited, will normally vary with the size and intensity of the candidate's support. There is nothing invidious, improper, or unhealthy in permitting such funds to be spent to carry the candidate's message to the electorate. Moreover, the equalization of permissible campaign expenditures might serve not to equalize the opportunities of all candidates, but to handicap a candidate who lacked substantial name recognition or exposure of his views before the start of the campaign.... The First Amendment denies government the power to determine that spending to promote one's political views is wasteful, excessive, or unwise.... For these reasons we hold that § 608(c) is constitutionally invalid.

In sum, the provisions of the Act that impose a $1,000 limitation on contributions to a single candidate, § 608(b)(1), a $5,000 limitation on contributions by a political committee to a single candidate, § 608(b)(2), and a $25,000 limitation on total contributions by an individual during any calendar year, § 608(b)(3), are constitutionally valid. These limitations, along with the disclosure provisions, constitute the Act's primary weapons against the reality or appearance of improper influence stemming from the dependence of candidates on large campaign contributions. The contribution ceilings thus serve the basic governmental interest in safeguarding the integrity of the electoral process without directly impinging upon the rights of individual citizens and candidates to engage in political debate and discussion. By contrast, the First Amendment requires the invalidation of the Act's independent expenditure ceiling, § 608(e)(1), its limitation on a candidate's expenditures from his own personal funds, § 608(a), and its ceilings on overall campaign expenditures, § 608(c). These provisions place substantial and direct restrictions on the ability of candidates, citizens, and associations to engage in protected political expression, restrictions that the First Amendment cannot tolerate.

II.   REPORTING AND DISCLOSURE REQUIREMENTS ...

A.   *General Principles*

Unlike the overall limitations on contributions and expenditures, the disclosure requirements impose no ceiling on campaign-related activities. But we have repeatedly found that compelled disclosure, in itself, can seriously infringe on privacy of association and belief guaranteed by the First Amendment.

[S]ignificant encroachments on First Amendment rights of the sort that compelled disclosure imposes cannot be justified by a mere showing of some legitimate governmental interest. Since *NAACP v. Alabama* [§ 10–9.1, supra] we have required that the subordinating interests of the State must survive exacting scrutiny.... The governmental interests sought to be vindicated by the disclosure requirements are of this magnitude. They fall into three categories. First, disclosure provides the electorate with information "as to where political campaign money comes from and how it is spent by the candidate" in order to aid the voters in evaluating those who seek federal office.... Second, disclosure requirements deter actual corruption and avoid the appearance of corruption by exposing large contributions and expenditures to the light of publicity.... Third, and not least significant, recordkeeping, reporting, and disclosure requirements are an essential means of gathering the data necessary to detect violations of the contribution limitations described above....

B. Application to Minor Parties and Independents

Appellants contend that the Act's requirements are overbroad insofar as they apply to contributions to minor parties and independent candidates because the governmental interest in this information is minimal and the danger of significant infringement on First Amendment rights is greatly increased....

It is true that the governmental interest in disclosure is diminished when the contribution in question is made to a minor party with little chance of winning an election.... But no appellant in this case has tendered record evidence of the sort proffered in *NAACP v. Alabama*.... On this record, the substantial public interest in disclosure identified by the legislative history of this Act outweighs the harm generally alleged.... Where it exists the type of chill and harassment identified in *NAACP v. Alabama* can be shown. We cannot assume that courts will be insensitive to similar showings when made in future cases. We therefore conclude that a blanket exemption is not required....

III. Public Financing of Presidential Election Campaigns

... Section 9006 [of the Internal Revenue Code] establishes a Presidential Election Campaign Fund (Fund), financed from general revenues in the aggregate amount designated by individual taxpayers, under § 6096, who on their income tax returns may authorize payment to the Fund of one dollar of their tax liability in the case of an individual return or two dollars in the case of a joint return. The Fund consists of three separate accounts to finance (1) party nominating conventions, (2) general election campaigns, and (3) primary campaigns.

Chapter 95 of Title 26, which concerns financing of party nominating conventions and general election campaigns, distinguishes among "major," "minor," and "new" parties. A major party is defined as a party whose candidate for President in the most recent election received 25% or more of the popular vote. A minor party is defined as a party whose candidate received at least 5% but less than 25% of the vote at the most recent election. All other parties are new parties, including both newly created parties and those receiving less than 5% of the vote in the last election.

Major parties are entitled to $2,000,000 to defray their national committee Presidential nominating convention expenses [and] must limit total expenditures to that amount.... A minor party receives a portion of the major-party entitlement determined by the ratio of the votes received by the party's candidate in the last election to the average of the votes received by the major parties' candidates.... No financing is provided for new parties, nor is there any express provision for financing independent candidates or parties not holding a convention....

Appellants insist that Chapter 95 falls short of the constitutional requirement in that its provisions supply larger, and equal, sums to candidates of major parties, use prior vote levels as the sole criterion for pre-election funding, limit new-party candidates to post-election funds, and deny any funds to candidates of parties receiving less than 5% of the vote. These provisions, it is argued, are fatal to the validity of the scheme, because they work invidious discrimination against minor and new parties in violation of the Fifth Amendment. We disagree.

As conceded by appellants, the Constitution does not require Congress to treat all declared candidates the same for public financing purposes. [A]ppellants have made no showing that the election funding plan disadvantages nonmajor parties by operating to reduce their strength below that attained without any public financing. First, such parties are free to raise money from private sources, and by our holding today new parties are freed from any expenditure limits, although admittedly those limits may be a largely academic matter to them. But since any major-party candidate accepting public financing of a campaign voluntarily assents to a spending ceiling, other candidates will be able to spend more in relation to the major-party candidates. The relative position of minor parties that do qualify to receive some public funds because they received 5% of the vote in the previous Presidential election is also enhanced. Public funding for candidates of major parties is intended as a substitute for private contributions; but for minor-party candidates such assistance may be viewed as a supplement to private contributions since these candidates may continue to solicit private funds up to the applicable spending limit. [T]he general election funding system does not work an invidious discrimination against candidates of nonmajor parties. [The Court also upheld the federal financing of the nominating convention and the primary elections.] ...

CONCLUSION

In summary, we sustain the individual contribution limits, the disclosure and reporting provisions, and the public financing scheme. We conclude, however, that the limitations on campaign expenditures, on independent expenditures by individuals and groups, and on expenditures by a candidate from his personal funds are constitutionally infirm....

MR. CHIEF JUSTICE BURGER, concurring in part and dissenting in part. . . .

The Court's attempt to distinguish the communication inherent in political *contributions* from the speech aspects of political *expenditures* simply "will not wash." We do little but engage in word games unless we recognize that people—candidates and contributors—spend money on political activity because they wish to communicate ideas, and their constitutional interest in doing so is precisely the same whether they or someone else utters the words. . . . In striking down the limitations on campaign expenditures, the Court relies in part on its conclusion that other means—namely, disclosure and contribution ceilings—will adequately serve the statute's aim. It is not clear why the same analysis is not also appropriate in weighing the need for contribution ceilings in addition to disclosure requirements. Congress may well be entitled to conclude that disclosure was a "partial measure," but I had not thought until today that Congress could enact its conclusions in the First Amendment area into laws immune from the most searching review by this Court. . . .

I [also] dissent from Part III sustaining the constitutionality of the public financing provisions of Subtitle H. . . . The public monies at issue here are not being employed simply to police the integrity of the electoral process or to provide a forum for the use of all participants in the political dialogue, as would, for example, be the case if free broadcast time were granted. Rather, we are confronted with the Government's actual financing, out of general revenues, a segment of the political debate itself. As Senator Howard Baker remarked during the debate on this legislation:

> [T]here is something politically incestuous about the Government financing and, I believe, inevitably then regulating, the day-to-day procedures by which the Government is selected. [I]t is extraordinarily important that the Government not control the machinery by which the public expresses the range of its desires, demands, and dissent.

[T]he inappropriateness of subsidizing, from general revenues, the actual political dialogue of the people—the process which begets the Government itself—is as basic to our national tradition as the separation of church and state also deriving from the First Amendment. . . .

MR. JUSTICE WHITE, concurring in part and dissenting in part. . . .

It would make little sense to me, and apparently made none to Congress, to limit the amounts an individual may give to a candidate or spend with his approval but fail to limit the amounts that could be spent on his behalf. Yet the Court permits the former while striking down the latter limitation. . . . Let us suppose that each of two brothers spends $1 million on TV spot announcements that he has individually prepared and in which he appears, urging the election of the same named candidate in identical words. One brother has sought and obtained the approval of the candidate; the other has not. The former may validly be prosecuted under § 608(e); under the Court's view, the latter may not, even though the candidate could scarcely help knowing about and appreciating the expensive favor. [L]imiting independent expenditures is essential to prevent transparent and widespread evasion of the contribution limits. . . .

[The separate opinions of MARSHALL, BLACKMUN, & REHNQUIST, JJ., each concurring in part and dissenting in part, are omitted.]

Notes

1. *Citizens Against Rent Control/Coalition for Fair Housing v. City of Berkeley,* 454 U.S. 290, 102 S.Ct. 434, 70 L.Ed.2d 492 (1981). The Court, per Burger, C.J., invalidated a Berkeley ordinance setting a $250 limitation on contributions to committees formed to support or oppose ballot measures. *First Nat'l Bank v. Bellotti,* § 10–7, supra, had held that the state could not prohibit corporations from making contributions or expenditures advocating views on ballot measures, just as it could not prohibit individuals from so doing. The Berkeley ordinance did not apply to expenditures by an individual, but it did apply when contributions were made in concert with one or more others in the exercise of the right of association. "To place a spartan limit—or indeed any limit—on individuals wishing to band together to advance their views on a ballot measure, while placing none on individuals acting alone, is clearly a restraint of association."

Buckley v. Valeo, said the Court, justified limits on political contributions because of "the perception of undue influence of large contributors to a *candidate.*" (emphasis in original). The *Buckley* rationale supports limits on contributions to candidates or their committees, but "does not support limitations on contributions to committees formed to favor or oppose *ballot measures.*" (emphasis in original). To the extent that the state wishes to protect the integrity of the political system by making known the identity of supporters and opponents of ballot measures it could outlaw anonymous contributions and require that contributors reveal their identities and the amounts of their contributions.

White, J., dissented, arguing that the ordinance was tailored to fit *Buckley* and *Bellotti* because it regulated contributions but not expenditures and did not prohibit corporate spending.

Contrast *California Medical Association v. Federal Election Commission,* 453 U.S. 182, 101 S.Ct. 2712, 69 L.Ed.2d 567 (1981), where a fragmented Court upheld provisions of the Federal Election Campaign Act of 1971, which prohibited individuals and unincorporated associations from contributing more than $5000 per year to any *multi*candidate political action committee. Political action committees were similarly prohibited from knowingly accepting contributions in excess of this limit. Multicandidate political action committees, like political parties, advocate the views and candidacies of a number of candidates.

In *Federal Election Commission v. National Conservative Political Action Committee (NCPAC),* 470 U.S. 480, 105 S.Ct. 1459, 84 L.Ed.2d 455 (1985), a divided Court invalidated a provision of the Presidential Election Campaign Fund Act that made it a crime for independent "political committees" to spend more than $1,000 to further a candidate's election. The political committees in this case raised money by general and specific direct mail solicitations. Their political expenditures were "independent" in that they were not made at the request of, or in coordination with, the candidate's official campaign committee or any of its agents.

Justice Rehnquist, for the Court, recognized that the "PACs in this case, of course, are not lone pamphleteers or street corner orators in the Tom Paine mold," but nonetheless, in a nationwide Presidential election, "allowing the presentation of views while forbidding the expenditure of more than $1,000 to present them is much like allowing a speaker in a public hall to express his views while denying him the use of an amplifying system." The FEC argued that the contributions to the independent PACs were not individual speech but "speech by proxy." The Court responded: "To say that their collective action in pooling their resources to amplify their voices is not entitled to full First Amendment protection would subordinate the voices of those of modest means as opposed to those sufficiently wealthy to be able to buy expensive media ads with their own resources." Unlike *California Medical Association* the present case involves "limitations on expenditures by PACs, not on the contributions they receive.... " In addition, "these contributions are predominantly small and thus do not raise the same concerns as the sizeable contributions involved in *California Medical Association.*"

The Court then distinguished an earlier decision, *FEC v. National Right to Work Committee (NRWC),* 459 U.S. 197, 103 S.Ct. 552, 74 L.Ed.2d 364 (1982), "We held in *NRWC* that a rather intricate provision of the Federal Election Campaign Act dealing with the prohibition of corporate campaign contributions to political candidates did not violate the First Amendment." The limitation in *NRWC* on the solicitation of contributions was constitutional "in view of the well-established constitutional validity of legislative regulation of corporate contributions to candidates for public office." *NRWC,* said the Court, "turned on the special treatment historically accorded corporations." The state confers "special advantages" on the corporate form, and, in return, "individuals acting jointly through corporations forgo some of the rights they have as individuals."

The PACs in this case, *NCPAC,* happen to be incorporated but "this is not a 'corporations' case" because the challenged statute applies to any organization whether or not incorporated. Independent expenditures, uncoordinated with the candidate or his or her campaign, are unlikely to have even the appearance of corruption because the absence of coordination undermines the value of the expenditure and "thereby alleviates the danger that the expenditures will be given as a *quid pro quo* for improper commitments from the candidate." Finally, the groups and associations in *NCPAC* were designed expressly to participate in political debate, and hence are "quite different from the traditional corporations organized for economic gain."

The Court reaffirmed that a corporation's constitutional right to spend funds "to propagate its views on issues of general public interest," *First National Bank v. Bellotti,* § 10–7, has different constitutional stature than corporate contributions to candidates. The Court noted that *Bellotti* did not reach nor "do we need to reach in this case, the question whether a corporation can constitutionally be restricted in making independent expenditures to influence elections for public office." The Court considered that issue in *Austin v. Michigan Chamber of Commerce,* (1990), excerpted below.

Justice White's dissent registered his continued belief that *Buckley* was wrongly decided. Justice Marshall's dissent also announced: "I am now unpersuaded by the distinction [between contributions and expenditures] established in *Buckley.* "

In *Federal Election Commission v. Massachusetts Citizens for Life, Inc.,* 479 U.S. 238, 107 S.Ct. 616, 93 L.Ed.2d 539 (1986), the Court invalidated § 316 of the Federal Election Campaign Act, 2 U.S.C.A. § 441b, as applied. That section prohibited a corporation from using treasury funds to make any expenditure "in connection with any election to any public office." Such expenditures must be financed, instead, by voluntary contributions to a separate segregated fund. The Massachusetts Citizens for Life, Inc. (MCFL), a nonprofit, nonstock corporation dedicated to fostering respect for human life, "born and unborn," raised money through garage sales, raffles, donations, etc., but did not accept contributions from business corporations or unions.

The Federal Election Commission claimed that the MCFL violated § 441b when it used its corporate funds to widely distribute a "Special Election Edition" newsletter distributed prior to the September 1978 primary elections. This newsletter urged people to support pro-life candidates and listed the candidates' views on MCFL legislation.

Justice Brennan, for the Court, explained that direct "corporate spending on political activity raises the prospect that resources amassed in the economic marketplace may be used to provide an unfair advantage in the political marketplace." While the relative availability of funds is a rough barometer of support, the resources of a business corporation "are not an indication of popular support for the corporation's political ideas." Thus, § 441b required that the corporation establish political committees in order to engage in campaign spending. "Groups such as MCFL, however, do not pose that danger of corruption. MCFL was formed to disseminate political ideas, not to amass capital."

MCFL had three features "essential" to the Court's holding that it may not constitutionally be bound by § 441b. First, it was formed for the express purpose of promoting political ideas and cannot engage in business activities. Second, it had no shareholders who have a claim to its assets. Third, MCFL was not established by a business corporation or labor union and accepted no contributions from such entities so it could not be their conduit.

2. The Kentucky Corrupt Practices Act prohibited a candidate from making an expenditure, loan, or promise as to action to be taken when elected, in consideration for a vote or support of any person. Carl Brown, a candidate for the office of County Commissioner, promised the voters in a press conference that if elected he would lower his salary $3,000 per year. Because the salary had been "fixed by law" the Kentucky Court of Appeals held that the Corrupt Practices Act prohibited Brown's promise. Since Brown had been elected the state court declared the election void and found that Free Speech guarantees were inapplicable.

The U.S. Supreme Court disagreed and explored the distinction between this case and permissible laws prohibiting bribery in political campaigns, in *Brown v. Hartlage,* 456 U.S. 45, 102 S.Ct. 1523, 71 L.Ed.2d 732 (1982). The Court concurred that the state could prohibit bribes to buy votes. While there might be some borderline cases between corrupt arrangements and normal, open, candidate promises (e.g., to lower taxes, to provide some group with public services), this case was far from that border. Brown's promise was not a private, politically corrupt arrangement. His "generalized" commitment "was conditioned not on any particular vote or votes, but entirely on the *majority's* vote."

3. *Brown v. Socialist Workers '74 Campaign Committee,* 459 U.S. 87, 103 S.Ct. 416, 74 L.Ed.2d 250 (1982) applied *Buckley* and invalidated certain disclosure requirements of the Ohio Campaign Expense Reporting Law, to the extent that the law was applied to the Socialist Workers Party, "a minor political party which historically has been the object of harassment by government officials and private parties." The test to judge the validity of compelled disclosure is whether there is "a reasonable probability that the compelled disclosure of a party's contributors' names will subject them to threats of harassment, or reprisals from either Government officials or private parties." The record demonstrated such harassment, e.g., threatening phone calls, hate mail, burning of Socialist Workers Party literature, destruction of the members' property, the firing of shots at a Party office. There was also government harassment, including a "massive" FBI surveillance of the Party and the use of informants.

4. *Meyer v. Grant,* 486 U.S. 414, 108 S.Ct. 1886, 100 L.Ed.2d 425 (1988) unanimously invalidated, as a violation of the first amendment right of political speech, a Colorado statute that made it a crime to pay persons to circulate initiative petitions. Colorado argued that because the initiative is a state-created right, the state could place any restrictions on that right. The state's argument relied on *Posadas de Puerto Rico Associates v. Tourism Co.,* § 10.7. The Court said that the argument in *Posadas* (that the greater power to ban casino gambling included the lesser power to ban advertising of casino gambling) was limited to "commercial speech" cases.

AUSTIN v. MICHIGAN CHAMBER OF COMMERCE
494 U.S. 652, 110 S.Ct. 1391, 108 L.Ed.2d 652 (1990).

JUSTICE MARSHALL delivered the opinion of the Court.

In this appeal, we must determine whether § 54(1) of the Michigan Campaign Finance Act violates either the First or the Fourteenth Amendment to the Constitution. Section 54(1) prohibits corporations from using corporate treasury funds for independent expenditures in support of or in opposition to any candidate in elections for state office. Corporations are allowed, however, to make such expenditures from segregated funds used solely for political purposes. In response to a challenge brought by the Michigan State Chamber of Commerce, the Sixth Circuit held that § 54(1) could not be applied to the Chamber, a Michigan nonprofit corporation, without violating the First Amendment. Although we agree that expressive rights are implicated in this case, we hold that application of § 54(1) to the Chamber is constitutional because the provision is narrowly tailored to serve a compelling state interest. Accordingly, we reverse the judgment of the Court of Appeals.

Section 54(1) of the Michigan Campaign Finance Act prohibits corporations from making contributions and independent expenditures in connection with state candidate elections.* The issue before us is only the constitutionality of the State's ban on independent expenditures....

The State contends that the unique legal and economic characteristics of corporations necessitate some regulation of their political expenditures to avoid corruption or the appearance of corruption. State law grants corporations special advantages—such as limited liability, perpetual life, and favorable treatment of the accumulation and distribution of assets—that enhance their ability to attract capital and to deploy their resources in ways that maximize the return on their shareholders' investments. These state-created advantages not only allow corporations to play a dominant role in the nation's economy, but also permit them to use "resources amassed in the economic marketplace" to obtain "an unfair advantage in the political marketplace." [*FEC v. Massachusetts Citizens for Life (MCFL)*] "[T]he compelling governmental interest in preventing corruption support[s] the restriction of the influence of political war chests funneled through the corporate form." *FEC v. National Conservative Political Action Committee.*

... We emphasize that the mere fact that corporations may accumulate large amounts of wealth is not the justification for § 54; rather, the unique state-conferred corporate structure that facilitates the amassing of large treasuries warrants the limit on independent expenditures. Corporate wealth can unfairly influence elections when it is deployed in the form of independent expenditures, just as it can when it assumes the guise of political contributions. We therefore hold that the State has articulated a sufficiently compelling rationale to support its restriction on independent expenditures by corporations.

We next turn to the question whether the Act is sufficiently narrowly tailored to achieve its goal. We find that the Act is precisely targeted to eliminate the distortion caused by corporate spending while also allowing corporations to express their political views. Contrary to the dissents' critical assumptions, the Act does not impose an *absolute* ban on all forms of corporate political spending but permits corporations to make independent political expenditures through separate segregated funds. Because persons contributing to such funds understand that their money will be used solely for political purposes, the speech generated accurately reflects contributors' support for the corporation's political views.

The Chamber contends that even if the Campaign Finance Act is constitutional with respect to for-profit corporations, it nonetheless

---

* Section 54(1) is modeled on a provision of the Federal Election Campaign Act of 1971, that requires corporations and labor unions to use segregated funds to finance independent expenditures made in federal elections.

cannot be applied to a nonprofit ideological corporation like a chamber of commerce. In MCFL, we held that the nonprofit organization there had "features more akin to voluntary political associations than business firms, and therefore should not have to bear burdens on independent spending solely because of [its] incorporated status." ...

The first characteristic of Massachusetts Citizens for Life, Inc., that distinguished it from ordinary business corporations was that the organization "was formed for the express purpose of promoting political ideas, and cannot engage in business activities." ... In contrast, the Chamber's bylaws set forth more varied purposes, several of which are not inherently political. For instance, the Chamber compiles and disseminates information relating to social, civic, and economic conditions, trains and educates its members, and promotes ethical business practices....

We described the second feature of MCFL as the absence of "shareholders or other persons affiliated so as to have a claim on its assets or earnings. This ensures that persons connected with the organization will have no economic disincentive for disassociating with it if they disagree with its political activity." Although the Chamber also lacks shareholders, many of its members may be similarly reluctant to withdraw as members even if they disagree with the Chamber's political expression, because they wish to benefit from the Chamber's nonpolitical programs and to establish contacts with other members of the business community.... Thus, we are persuaded that the Chamber's members are more similar to shareholders of a business corporation than to the members of MCFL in this respect.

The final characteristic upon which we relied in MCFL was the organization's independence from the influence of business corporations. On this score, the Chamber differs most greatly from the Massachusetts organization. MCFL was not established by, and had a policy of not accepting contributions from, business corporations. [But] more than three-quarters of the Chamber's members are business corporations, whose political contributions and expenditures can constitutionally be regulated by the State....

The Chamber also attacks § 54(1) as underinclusive because it does not regulate the independent expenditures of unincorporated labor unions.* Whereas unincorporated unions, and indeed individuals, may be able to amass large treasuries, they do so without the significant state-conferred advantages of the corporate structure....

Because we hold that § 54(1) does not violate the First Amendment, we must address the Chamber's contention that the provision infringes its rights under the Fourteenth Amendment. The Chamber argues that the statute treats similarly situated entities unequally. Specifically, it contends that the State should also restrict the independent expendi-

---

* The Federal Election Campaign Act restricts the independent expenditures of labor organizations as well as those of corporations. 2 U.S.C. § 441b(a).

tures of unincorporated associations with the ability to accumulate large treasuries and of corporations engaged in the media business.

Because the right to engage in political expression is fundamental to our constitutional system, statutory classifications impinging upon that right must be narrowly tailored to serve a compelling governmental interest. We find that, even under such strict scrutiny, the statute's classifications pass muster under the Equal Protection Clause. [T]he State's decision to regulate only corporations is precisely tailored to serve the compelling state interest of eliminating from the political process the corrosive effect of political "war chests" amassed with the aid of the legal advantages given to corporations.

Similarly, we find that the Act's exemption of media corporations from the expenditure restrictions does not render the statute unconstitutional. The "media exception" excludes from the definition of "expenditure" any "expenditure by a broadcasting station, newspaper, magazine, or other periodical or publication for any news story, commentary, or editorial in support of or opposition to a candidate for elective office . . . in the regular course of publication or broadcasting." . . .

Although all corporations enjoy the same state-conferred benefits inherent in the corporate form, media corporations differ significantly from other corporations in that their resources are devoted to the collection of information and its dissemination to the public. . . .

It is so ordered.

JUSTICE BRENNAN, concurring.

[T]he Michigan law protects dissenting shareholders of business corporations that are members of the Chamber to the extent that such shareholders oppose the use of their money, paid as dues to the Chamber out of general corporate treasury funds, for political campaigns. . . .

JUSTICE SCALIA, dissenting.

"Attention all citizens. To assure the fairness of elections by preventing disproportionate expression of the views of any single powerful group, your Government has decided that the following associations of persons shall be prohibited from speaking or writing in support of any candidate: _____" In permitting Michigan to make private corporations the first object of this Orwellian announcement, the Court today endorses the principle that too much speech is an evil that the democratic majority can proscribe. I dissent because that principle is contrary to our case law and incompatible with the absolutely central truth of the First Amendment: that government cannot be trusted to assure, through censorship, the "fairness" of political debate.

The Court's opinion says that political speech of corporations can be regulated because "[s]tate law grants [them] special advantages," and because this "unique state-conferred corporate structure . . . facilitates the amassing of large treasuries." This analysis seeks to create one good argument by combining two bad ones. Those individuals who form that type of voluntary association known as a corporation are, to be sure, given special advantages—notably, the immunization of their personal fortunes from liability for the actions of the association—that the State is under no obligation to confer. But so are other associations and private individuals given all sorts of special advantages that the State need not confer, ranging from tax breaks to contract awards to public employment to outright cash subsidies. It is rudimentary that the State cannot exact as the price of those special advantages the forfeiture of First Amendment rights. The categorical suspension of the right of any person, or of any association of persons, to speak out on political matters must be justified by a compelling state need. Which is why the Court puts forward its second bad argument, the fact that corporations "amas[s] large treasuries." But that alone is also not sufficient justification for the suppression of political speech, unless one thinks it would be lawful to prohibit men and women whose net worth is above a certain figure from endorsing political candidates. Neither of these two flawed arguments is improved by combining them....

Justice Brennan's concurrence would have us believe that the prohibition adopted by Michigan and approved by the Court is a paternalistic measure to protect the corporate shareholder of America. [S]uch solicitude is a most implausible explanation for the Michigan statute, inasmuch as it permits corporations to take as many ideological and political positions as they please, so long as they are not "in assistance of, or in opposition to, the nomination or election of a candidate." Mich.Comp. Laws § 169.206(1) (1979). That is indeed the Court's sole basis for distinguishing *First National Bank of Boston v. Bellotti,* which invalidated restriction of a corporation's general political speech. The Michigan law appears to be designed, in other words, neither to protect shareholders, nor even (impermissibly) to "balance" general political debate, but to protect political candidates.

[E]ven if the object of the prohibition could plausibly be portrayed as the protection of shareholders (which the Court's opinion, at least, does not even assert), that would not suffice as a "compelling need" to support this blatant restriction upon core political speech. A person becomes a member of that form of association known as a for-profit corporation in order to pursue economic objectives, *i.e.,* to make money. [T]he shareholder knows that management may take any action that is ultimately in accord with what the majority (or a specified supermajority) of the shareholders wishes, so long as that action is designed to make a profit. That is the deal. The corporate actions to which the shareholder exposes himself, therefore, include many things that he may find politically or ideologically uncongenial: investment in South Africa, operation of an abortion clinic, publication of a pornographic magazine, or even publication of a newspaper that adopts absurd political views and makes catastrophic political endorsements. His only protections against such assaults upon his ideological commitments are (1) his ability to persuade a majority (or the requisite minority) of his fellow shareholders that the action should not be taken, and ultimately (2) his ability to sell his stock. . . .

Finally, a few words are in order concerning the Court's approval of the Michigan law's exception for "media corporations." This is all right, we are told, because of "the unique role that the press plays in 'informing and educating the public, offering criticism, and providing a forum for discussion and debate.' "But if one believes in the Court's rationale of "compelling state need" to prevent amassed corporate wealth from skewing the political debate, surely that "unique role" of the press does not give Michigan justification for *excluding* media corporations from coverage, but provides especially strong reason to *include* them. Amassed corporate wealth that regularly sits astride the ordinary channels of information is much more likely to produce the New Corruption (too much of one point of view) than amassed corporate wealth that is generally busy making money elsewhere. . . .

Members of the institutional press, despite the Court's approval of their illogical exemption from the Michigan law, will find little reason for comfort in today's decision. The theory of New Corruption it espouses is a dagger at their throat. The Court today holds merely that media corporations *may* be excluded from the Michigan law, not that they *must* be. We have consistently rejected the proposition that the institutional press has any constitutional privilege beyond that of other speakers. . . . One must hope, I suppose, that Michigan will continue to provide this generous and voluntary exemption. . . .

Perhaps the Michigan law before us here has an unqualifiedly noble objective—to "equalize" the political debate by preventing disproportionate expression of corporations' points of view. . . . The incumbent politician who says he welcomes full and fair debate is no more to be believed than the entrenched monopolist who says he welcomes full and fair competition. Perhaps the Michigan legislature was genuinely trying to assure a "balanced" presentation of political views; on the other hand, perhaps it was trying to give unincorporated unions (a not insubstantial force in Michigan) political advantage over major employers. Or perhaps it was trying to assure a "balanced" presentation because it knows that with evenly balanced speech incumbent officeholders generally win. The fundamental approach of the First Amendment, I had always thought, was to assume the worst, and to rule the regulation of political speech "for fairness' sake" simply out of bounds. . . .

JUSTICE KENNEDY, with whom JUSTICE O'CONNOR and JUSTICE SCALIA join, dissenting.

The majority opinion validates not one censorship of speech but two. One is Michigan's content-based law which decrees it a crime for a nonprofit corporate speaker to endorse or oppose candidates for Michigan public office. By permitting the statute to stand, the Court upholds a direct restriction on the independent expenditure of funds for political speech for the first time in its history.

The other censorship scheme, I most regret to say, is of our own creation. It is value-laden, content-based speech suppression that permits some nonprofit corporate groups but not others to engage in political speech. After failing to disguise its animosity and distrust for the particular kind of political speech here at issue—the qualifications of a candidate to understand economic matters—the Court adopts a rule that allows Michigan to stifle the voices of some of the most respected groups in public life, on subjects central to the integrity of our democratic system. Each of these schemes is repugnant to the First Amendment and contradicts its central guarantee, the freedom to speak in the electoral process. . . .

[The separate opinion of Stevens, J., concurring, is omitted.]

Notes

Colorado Republican Federal Campaign Committee v. Federal Election Commission, 518 U.S. 604, 116 S.Ct. 2309, 135 L.Ed.2d 795 (1996). The Colorado Republican Party (before it had selected its Senate candidate) bought radio advertisements attacking the Democratic Party's likely candidate for Senate. The Federal Election Commission claimed that this "expenditure" exceeded the dollar limits that the Federal Election Campaign Act (FECA), § 441a(d)(3), imposed on a political party's expenditure in connection with the general election campaign. The Court, with no majority opinion, ruled that the First Amendment prohibited applying § 441a(d)(3) to this expenditure, because the political party had made expended funds "independently," without coordination with any candidate. Breyer, J., announced the judgment of the Court, and delivered an opinion joined by O'Connor & Souter, JJ. They refused to consider the broader question whether, in the special case of political parties, the First Amendment also forbids congressional efforts to limit coordinated expenditures.

Kennedy, J., joined by Rehnquist, C.J., & Scalia, J., filed an opinion concurring in the judgment and dissenting in part. They concluded that the FECA, on its face, violates the First Amendment when it restricts spending by a political party in cooperation, consultation, or concert with a candidate. Thomas, J., joined by Rehnquist, C.J. & Scalia, J., also filed an opinion concurring in the judgment and dissenting in part, concluding that § 441a(d)(3) is unconstitutional on its face. Thomas said: "in the specific context of campaign funding by political parties, the anti-corruption rationale loses its force. What could it mean for a party to 'corrupt' its candidate or to exercise 'coercive' influence over him? The very aim of a political party is to influence the candidate's stance on issues and, if the candidate takes office or is reelected, his votes." In a portion of his opinion not joined by any other Justice, Thomas argued that the Court should reject *Buckley v. Valeo* because there is no constitutionally significant difference between campaign contributions and expenditures. Bribery laws and disclosure laws offer less restrictive means of preventing corruption.

10–12. OBSCENITY

10–12.1 Defining Obscenity

ROTH v. UNITED STATES

354 U.S. 476, 77 S.Ct. 1304, 1 L.Ed.2d 1498 (1957).*

MR. JUSTICE BRENNAN delivered the opinion of the Court.

The constitutionality of a criminal obscenity statute is the question in each of these cases. In *Roth,* the primary constitutional question is whether the federal obscenity statute violates the provision of the First Amendment that "Congress shall make no law ... abridging the freedom of speech, or of the press...." In *Alberts,* the primary constitutional question is whether the obscenity provisions of the California Penal Code invade the freedoms of speech and press as they may be incorporated in the liberty protected from state action by the Due Process Clause of the Fourteenth Amendment....

The dispositive question is whether obscenity is utterance within the area of protected speech and press.* Although this is the first time the question has been squarely presented to this Court, either under the First Amendment or under the Fourteenth Amendment, expressions found in numerous opinions indicate that this Court has always assumed that obscenity is not protected by the freedoms of speech and press. The guaranties of freedom of expression in effect in 10 of the 14 States which by 1792 had ratified the Constitution, gave no absolute protection for every utterance. Thirteen of the 14 States provided for the prosecution of libel, and all of those States made either blasphemy or profanity, or both, statutory crimes....

All ideas having even the slightest redeeming social importance— unorthodox ideas, controversial ideas, even ideas hateful to the prevailing climate of opinion—have the full protection of the guaranties, unless excludable because they encroach upon the limited area of more important interests. But implicit in the history of the First Amendment is the rejection of obscenity as utterly without redeeming social importance. This rejection for that reason is mirrored in the universal judgment that obscenity should be restrained, reflected in the international agreement of over 50 nations, in the obscenity laws of all of the 48 States, and in the 20 obscenity laws enacted by the Congress from 1842 to 1956.... We hold that obscenity is not within the area of constitutionally protected speech or press.

It is strenuously urged that these obscenity statutes offend the constitutional guaranties because they punish incitation to impure sexual *thoughts,* not shown to be related to any overt antisocial conduct which is or may be incited in the persons stimulated to such

---

* Together with *Alberts v. California.*

* No issue is presented in either case concerning the obscenity of the material involved.

thoughts.... It is insisted that the constitutional guaranties are violated because convictions may be had without proof either that obscene material will perceptibly create a clear and present danger of antisocial conduct, or will probably induce its recipients to such conduct. But, in light of our holding that obscenity is not protected speech, [it is unnecessary to consider such issues.] ...

However, sex and obscenity are not synonymous. Obscene material is material which deals with sex in a manner appealing to prurient interest.** The portrayal of sex, e.g., in art, literature and scientific works, is not itself sufficient reason to deny material the constitutional protection of freedom of speech and press. Sex, a great and mysterious motive force in human life, has indisputably been a subject of absorbing interest to mankind through the ages; it is one of the vital problems of human interest and public concern.... It is therefore vital that the standards for judging obscenity safeguard the protection of freedom of speech and press for material which does not treat sex in a manner appealing to prurient interest.

The early leading standard of obscenity allowed material to be judged merely by the effect of an isolated excerpt upon particularly susceptible persons. *Regina v. Hicklin,* [1868] L.R. 3 Q.B. 360. Some American courts adopted this standard but later decisions have rejected it and substituted this test: whether to the average person, applying contemporary community standards, the dominant theme of the material taken as a whole appeals to prurient interest. The *Hicklin* test, judging obscenity by the effect of isolated passages upon the most susceptible persons, might well encompass material legitimately treating with sex, and so it must be rejected as unconstitutionally restrictive of the freedoms of speech and press. On the other hand, the substituted standard provides safeguards adequate to withstand the charge of constitutional infirmity. Both trial courts below sufficiently followed the proper standard....

It is argued that the statutes do not provide reasonably ascertainable standards of guilt and therefore violate the constitutional requirements of due process.... The thrust of the argument is that these words ["obscene," "lewd," "filthy," "lascivious," "indecent"] are not sufficiently precise because they do not mean the same thing to all people, all the time, everywhere.

Many decisions have recognized that these terms of obscenity statutes are not precise. This Court, however, has consistently held that lack of precision is not itself offensive to the requirements of due process. [A]ll that is required is that the language "conveys sufficiently definite

---

** I.e., material having a tendency to excite lustful thoughts.... We perceive no significant difference between the meaning of obscenity developed in the case law and the definition of the A.L.I., Model Penal Code, § 207.10(2) (Tent.Draft No. 6, 1957), viz.:

" ... A thing is obscene if, considered as a whole, its predominant appeal is to prurient interest, i.e., a shameful or morbid interest in nudity, sex, or excretion, and if it goes substantially beyond customary limits of candor in description or representation of such matters.... "

warning as to the proscribed conduct when measured by common understanding and practices.... " These words, applied according to the proper standard for judging obscenity, already discussed, give adequate warning of the conduct proscribed and mark "... boundaries sufficiently distinct for judges and juries fairly to administer the law.... That there may be marginal cases in which it is difficult to determine the side of the line on which a particular fact situation falls is no sufficient reason to hold the language too ambiguous to define a criminal offense.... "

In summary, then, we hold that these statutes, applied according to the proper standard for judging obscenity, do not offend constitutional safeguards against convictions based upon protected material, or fail to give men in acting adequate notice of what is prohibited....

MR. CHIEF JUSTICE WARREN, concurring in the result.

... The history of the application of laws designed to suppress the obscene demonstrates convincingly that the power of government can be invoked under them against great art or literature, scientific treatises, or works exciting social controversy. Mistakes of the past prove that there is a strong countervailing interest to be considered in the freedoms guaranteed by the First and Fourteenth Amendments.

... It is not the book that is on trial; it is a person.... The personal element in these cases is seen most strongly in the requirement of *scienter*. Under the California law, the prohibited activity must be done "wilfully and lewdly." The federal statute limits the crime to acts done "knowingly." In his charge to the jury, the district judge stated that the matter must be "calculated" to corrupt or debauch. The defendants in both these cases were engaged in the business of purveying textual or graphic matter openly advertised to appeal to the erotic interest of their customers. They were plainly engaged in the commercial exploitation of the morbid and shameful craving for materials with prurient effect. I believe that the State and Federal Governments can constitutionally punish such conduct. That is all that these cases present to us, and that is all we need to decide....

MR. JUSTICE HARLAN, concurring in the result in No. 61, and dissenting in No. 582....

I do not think that reviewing courts can escape [their] responsibility by saying that the trier of the facts, be it a jury or a judge, has labeled the questioned matter as "obscene," for, if "obscenity" is to be suppressed, the question whether a particular work is of that character involves not really an issue of fact but a question of constitutional *judgment* of the most sensitive and delicate kind. Many juries might find that Joyce's "Ulysses" or Boccaccio's "Decameron" was obscene, and yet the conviction of a defendant for selling either book would raise, for me, the gravest constitutional problems, for no such verdict could convince me, without more, that these books are "utterly without redeeming social importance." In short, I do not understand how the Court can resolve the constitutional problems now before it without making its own independent judgment upon the character of the material upon which these convictions were based....

I concur in the judgment of the Court in No. 61, *Alberts v. California*.... In judging the constitutionality of this conviction, we should remember that our function in reviewing state judgments under the Fourteenth Amendment is a narrow one. We do not decide whether the policy of the State is wise, or whether it is based on assumptions scientifically substantiated. We can inquire only whether the state action so subverts the fundamental liberties implicit in the Due Process Clause that it cannot be sustained as a rational exercise of power.... Clearly the state legislature has made the judgment that printed words *can* "deprave or corrupt" the reader—that words can incite to antisocial or immoral action. The assumption seems to be that the distribution of certain types of literature will induce criminal or immoral sexual conduct. It is well known, of course, that the validity of this assumption is a matter of dispute among critics, sociologists, psychiatrists, and penologists.... Nothing in the Constitution requires California to accept as truth the most advanced and sophisticated psychiatric opinion. It seems to me clear that it is not irrational, in our present state of knowledge, to consider that pornography can induce a type of sexual conduct which a State may deem obnoxious to the moral fabric of society. In fact the very division of opinion on the subject counsels us to respect the choice made by the State....

What has been said, however, does not dispose of the case. It still remains for us to decide whether the state court's determination that this material should be suppressed is consistent with the Fourteenth Amendment; and that, of course, presents a federal question as to which we, and not the state court, have the ultimate responsibility. And so, in the final analysis, I concur in the judgment because, upon an independent perusal of the material involved, and in light of the considerations discussed above, I cannot say that its suppression would so interfere with the communication of "ideas" in any proper sense of that term that it would offend the Due Process Clause. I therefore agree with the Court that appellant's conviction must be affirmed.

I dissent in No. 582, *Roth v. United States,*.... I do not think it follows that state and federal powers in this area are the same, and that just because the State may suppress a particular utterance, it is automatically permissible for the Federal Government to do the same. [T]he interests which obscenity statutes purportedly protect are primarily entrusted to the care, not of the Federal Government, but of the States. Congress has no substantive power over sexual morality. Such powers as the Federal Government has in this field are but incidental to its other powers, here the postal power, and are not of the same nature as those possessed by the States, which bear direct responsibility for the protection of the local moral fabric....

I judge this case, then, in view of what I think is the attenuated federal interest in this field, in view of the very real danger of a deadening uniformity which can result from nation-wide federal censorship, and in view of the fact that the constitutionality of this conviction must be weighed against the First and not the Fourteenth Amendment. So viewed, I do not think that this conviction can be upheld....

MR. JUSTICE DOUGLAS, with whom MR. JUSTICE BLACK concurs, dissenting.

. . . The tests by which these convictions were obtained require only the arousing of sexual thoughts. Yet the arousing of sexual thoughts and desires happens every day in normal life in dozens of ways. Nearly 30 years ago a questionnaire sent to college and normal school women graduates asked what things were most stimulating sexually. Of 409 replies, 9 said "music"; 18 said "pictures"; 29 said "dancing"; 40 said "drama"; 95 said "books"; and 218 said "man." . . .

Any test that turns on what is offensive to the community's standards is too loose, too capricious, too destructive of freedom of expression to be squared with the First Amendment. Under that test, juries can censor, suppress, and punish what they don't like, provided the matter relates to "sexual impurity" or has a tendency "to excite lustful thoughts." This is community censorship in one of its worst forms. It creates a regime where, in the battle between the literati and the Philistines, the Philistines are certain to win. If experience in this field teaches anything, it is that "censorship of obscenity has almost always been both irrational and indiscriminate." Lockhart & McClure, [Literature, The Law of Obscenity, and the Constitution, 38 Minn.L.Rev. 295,] at 371. The test adopted here accentuates that trend.

[T]here is no special historical evidence that literature dealing with sex was intended to be treated in a special manner by those who drafted the First Amendment. In fact, the first reported court decision in this country involving obscene literature was in 1821. I reject, too, the implication that problems of freedom of speech and of the press are to be resolved by weighing against the values of free expression, the judgment of the Court that a particular form of that expression has "no redeeming social importance." The First Amendment, its prohibition in terms absolute, was designed to preclude courts as well as legislatures from weighing the values of speech against silence. The First Amendment puts free speech in the preferred position.

Freedom of expression can be suppressed if, and to the extent that, it is so closely brigaded with illegal action as to be an inseparable part of it. As a people, we cannot afford to relax that standard. For the test that suppresses a cheap tract today can suppress a literary gem tomorrow. All it need do is to incite a lascivious thought or arouse a lustful desire. The list of books that judges or juries can place in that category is endless.

I would give the broad sweep of the First Amendment full support. I have the same confidence in the ability of our people to reject noxious literature as I have in their capacity to sort out the true from the false in theology, economics, politics, or any other field.

Notes

1. FURTHER ATTEMPTS AT DEFINITION. In *Jacobellis v. Ohio,* 378 U.S. 184, 84 S.Ct. 1676, 12 L.Ed.2d 793 (1964), Brennan, J.'s plurality opinion, joined by Goldberg, J., emphasized that the Court in obscenity cases must make "an independent constitutional judgment on the facts of the case as to whether the material involved is constitutionally protected." The standard of review is not "sufficient evidence;" rather, the Court must exercise *de novo* review of the work. The reference in *Roth* to "contemporary community standards" was not to state or local communities but to "society at large," "the public or people in general." This national standard meant that the definition of obscenity might vary because of the passage of time, but not because of a change in location. Warren, C.J., joined by Clark, J., dissenting, argued that local community standards should govern.

Justice Stewart's concurrence stated simply:

It is possible to read the Court's opinion in *Roth v. United States* and *Alberts v. California,* in a variety of ways. In saying this, I imply no criticism of the Court, which in those cases was faced with the task of trying to define what may be indefinable. I have reached the conclusion, which I think is confirmed at least by negative implication in the Court's decisions since *Roth* and *Alberts,* that under the First and Fourteenth Amendments criminal laws in this area are constitutionally limited to hard-core pornography. I shall not today attempt further to define the kinds of material I understand to be embraced within that shorthand description; and perhaps I could never succeed in intelligibly doing so. But I know it when I see it, and the motion picture involved in this case is not that.

In *A Book Named "John Cleland's Memoirs of a Woman of Pleasure" v. Attorney Gen. of Massachusetts,* 383 U.S. 413, 86 S.Ct. 975, 16 L.Ed.2d 1 (1966), the Court, again with no majority opinion, reversed a decision that a book, "Memoirs of a Woman of Pleasure," was obscene. The book, commonly called "Fanny Hill," was written about 1750. A Massachusetts law allowed the Attorney General to put on trial the book itself rather than its publisher or distributor in order to seek a declaration of obscenity. Justice Brennan's plurality opinion explained:

We defined obscenity in *Roth* in the following terms: [W]hether to the average person, applying contemporary community standards, the dominant theme of the material taken as a whole appeals to prurient interest. Under this definition, as elaborated in subsequent cases, three elements must coalesce: it must be established that (a) the dominant theme of the material taken as a whole appeals to a prurient interest in sex; (b) the material is patently offensive because it affronts contemporary community standards relating to the description or representation of sexual matters; and (c) the material is utterly without redeeming social value. . . .

The Supreme Judicial Court erred in holding that a book need not be "unqualifiedly worthless before it can be deemed obscene." A book cannot be proscribed unless it is found to be *utterly* without redeeming social value. This is so even though the book is found to possess the requisite prurient appeal and to be patently offensive. Each of the three federal constitutional criteria is to be applied independently; the social value of the book can neither be weighed against nor canceled by its prurient appeal or patent offensiveness.

In other cases some Justices believed that "pandering" should be probative of obscenity in close cases, see *Ginzburg v. United States,* infra, and that the Government should be able to employ a different definition of obscenity to protect juveniles, see *Ginsberg v. New York,* infra. Brennan explained: "In the face of this divergence of opinion the Court began the practice in *Redrup v. New York,* 386 U.S. 767, 87 S.Ct. 1414, 18 L.Ed.2d 515 (1967), of per curiam reversals of convictions for the dissemination of material that at least five members of the Court, applying their separate tests, deemed not to be obscene." He added, "No fewer than 31 cases have been disposed of in this fashion."*

2. PANDERING. Brennan's majority opinion in *Ginzburg v. United States,* 383 U.S. 463, 86 S.Ct. 942, 16 L.Ed.2d 31 (1966) assumed that the three publications involved in that case, standing alone, might not be obscene, but nonetheless upheld the conviction because of their pandering, a "background of commercial exploitation of erotica solely for the sake of their prurient appeal." The trial court found that the publisher, because of the salacious appeal of such names, sought mailing privileges from Intercourse and Blue Ball, Pennsylvania, and eventually settled on Middlesex, New Jersey. The advertising circulars emphasized the sexual candor of the materials and guaranteed full refunds if they "failed to reach you because of U.S. Post Office censorship interference."

The Court argued: "The deliberate representation of petitioners' publications as erotically arousing, for example, stimulated the reader to accept them as prurient; he looks for titillation, not for saving intellectual content." Also "the brazenness of such an appeal heightens the offensiveness of the publication to those who are offended by such material." If the "purveyor's sole emphasis is on the sexually provocative aspects of his publications, that fact may be decisive in the determination of obscenity."

Black, Douglas, Harlan, & Stewart, JJ., each dissented in separate opinions. Harlan noted that the majority's "curious result is reached through the elaboration of a theory of obscenity entirely unrelated to the language, purposes, or history of the federal statute now being applied, and certainly different from the test used by the trial court to convict the defendants."

Splawn v. California, 431 U.S. 595, 97 S.Ct. 1987, 52 L.Ed.2d 606 (1977) agreed as to the relevance of pandering: "There is no doubt that as a matter of First Amendment obscenity law, evidence of pandering to prurient interests in the creation, promotion, or dissemination of material is relevant to determining whether the material is obscene." Stevens, J., joined by Brennan (who wrote the majority in *Ginzburg*), Stewart, & Marshall, JJ., dissented: "[I]f they were not otherwise obscene, I cannot understand how these films lost their protected status by being truthfully described. . . . Only an accurate description can enable a potential viewer to decide whether or not he wants to see them."

---

* *Paris Adult Theatre I v. Slaton,* 413 U.S. 49, 82 & n. 8, 93 S.Ct. 2628, 2646 & n. 8, 37 L.Ed.2d 446 (1973)(Brennan, J., dissenting). This case is excerpted below.

3. PROTECTION OF JUVENILES. Justice Brennan, for the Court in *Ginsberg v. New York,* 390 U.S. 629, 88 S.Ct. 1274, 20 L.Ed.2d 195 (1968), explained that this case presented "the question of the constitutionality on its face of a New York criminal obscenity statute which prohibits the sale to minors under 17 years of age of material defined to be obscene on the basis of its appeal to them whether or not it would be obscene to adults." The Court upheld the law even though the " 'girlie' picture magazines involved in the sales are not obscene for adults." Such variable obscenity is within the power of the state, for the state's power over children is broader than its power over adults. The law supports the parents' claim of authority to direct the rearing of their children. If the parents want their children to see such materials, nothing in the law prohibits them from purchasing the magazines for their children. Second, the "State has an independent interest in the well-being of its youth." Justice Stewart concurred on the basis that "in some precisely delineated areas, a child—like someone in a captive audience—is not possessed of that full capacity for individual choice which is the presupposition of First Amendment guarantees."

4. PRIVATE POSSESSION. *Stanley v. Georgia,* 394 U.S. 557, 89 S.Ct. 1243, 22 L.Ed.2d 542 (1969), per Marshall, J., reversed an obscenity conviction because "the mere private possession of obscene matter cannot constitutionally be made a crime." The right of speech protects also the right to receive. In the home, this right takes on an "added dimension" because of the fundamental right to be free, "except in very limited circumstances, from unwanted governmental intrusions into one's privacy." The defendant had a right "to satisfy his intellectual and emotional needs in the privacy of his own home." While the state contended that viewing such obscenity could lead to deviant criminal behavior, there "appears to be little empirical basis for that assertion."

Though the Court stated that *Roth* was not impaired by its holding, some lower courts and commentators thought otherwise. Their predictions did not bear fruit. In *United States v. Reidel,* 402 U.S. 351, 91 S.Ct. 1410, 28 L.Ed.2d 813 (1971) the Court, per White, J., held that a federal obscenity statute was constitutional as applied to the distribution of obscene materials to willing adult recipients. The focus of *Stanley* "was on freedom of mind and thought and on the privacy of one's home. It does not require that we fashion or recognize a constitutional right in people like Reidel to distribute or sell obscene materials." Thus the state may prohibit an individual from transporting obscene materials for private use. *United States v. Orito,* 413 U.S. 139, 93 S.Ct. 2674, 37 L.Ed.2d 513 (1973). See also, *United States v. 12 200–Ft. Reels of Super 8mm. Film,* 413 U.S. 123, 93 S.Ct. 2665, 37 L.Ed.2d 500 (1973), holding (5 to 4) that Congress may prohibit the importation of obscene matter even though the material was only for the importer's private, personal use and possession. To hold otherwise "would be not unlike compelling the Government to permit importation of prohibited or controlled drugs for private consumption as long as such drugs are not for public distribution or sale."

MILLER v. CALIFORNIA

413 U.S. 15, 93 S.Ct. 2607, 37 L.Ed.2d 419 (1973).

MR. CHIEF JUSTICE BURGER delivered the opinion of the Court.

This is one of a group of "obscenity-pornography" cases being reviewed by the Court in a re-examination of standards enunciated in earlier cases involving what Mr. Justice Harlan called "the intractable obscenity problem." . . . This case involves the application of a State's criminal obscenity statute to a situation in which sexually explicit materials have been thrust by aggressive sales action upon unwilling recipients who had in no way indicated any desire to receive such materials. . . .

Apart from the initial formulation in the *Roth* case, no majority of the Court has at any given time been able to agree on a standard to determine what constitutes obscene, pornographic material subject to regulation under the States' police power. We have seen "a variety of views among the members of the Court unmatched in any other course of constitutional adjudication." . . .

The case we now review was tried on the theory that the California Penal Code § 311 approximately incorporates the three-stage *Memoirs* test, supra. But now the *Memoirs* test has been abandoned as unworkable by its author,* and no Member of the Court today supports the *Memoirs* formulation.

This much has been categorically settled by the Court, that obscene material is unprotected by the First Amendment. . . . We acknowledge, however, the inherent dangers of undertaking to regulate any form of expression. State statutes designed to regulate obscene materials must be carefully limited. As a result, we now confine the permissible scope of such regulation to works which depict or describe sexual conduct. That conduct must be specifically defined by the applicable state law, as written or authoritatively construed. A state offense must also be limited to works which, taken as a whole, appeal to the prurient interest in sex, which portray sexual conduct in a patently offensive way, and which, taken as a whole, do not have serious literary, artistic, political, or scientific value.

The basic guidelines for the trier of fact must be: (a) whether "the average person, applying contemporary community standards" would find that the work, taken as a whole, appeals to the prurient interest; (b) whether the work depicts or describes, in a patently offensive way, sexual conduct specifically defined by the applicable state law; and (c) whether the work, taken as a whole, lacks serious literary, artistic, political, or scientific value. We do not adopt as a constitutional standard the "*utterly* without redeeming social value" test of *Memoirs v. Massa-*

---

* See the dissenting opinion of Mr. Justice Brennan in *Paris Adult Theatre I v. Slaton.*

chusetts, that concept has never commanded the adherence of more than three Justices at one time. If a state law that regulates obscene material is thus limited, as written or construed, the First Amendment values applicable to the States through the Fourteenth Amendment are adequately protected by the ultimate power of appellate courts to conduct an independent review of constitutional claims when necessary.

We emphasize that it is not our function to propose regulatory schemes for the States. That must await their concrete legislative efforts. It is possible, however, to give a few plain examples of what a state statute could define for regulation under part (b) of the standard announced in this opinion, supra:

(a) Patently offensive representations or descriptions of ultimate sexual acts, normal or perverted, actual or simulated.

(b) Patently offensive representations or descriptions of masturbation, excretory functions, and lewd exhibition of the genitals.

Sex and nudity may not be exploited without limit by films or pictures exhibited or sold in places of public accommodation any more than live sex and nudity can be exhibited or sold without limit in such public places. At a minimum, prurient, patently offensive depiction or description of sexual conduct must have serious literary, artistic, political, or scientific value to merit First Amendment protection. For example, medical books for the education of physicians and related personnel necessarily use graphic illustrations and descriptions of human anatomy. In resolving the inevitably sensitive questions of fact and law, we must continue to rely on the jury system, accompanied by the safeguards that judges, rules of evidence, presumption of innocence, and other protective features provide, as we do with rape, murder, and a host of other offenses against society and its individual members.

Mr. Justice Brennan, author of the opinions of the Court, or the plurality opinions, [in many previous obscenity cases], has abandoned his former position and now maintains that no formulation of this Court, the Congress, or the States can adequately distinguish obscene material unprotected by the First Amendment from protected expression, *Paris Adult Theatre I v. Slaton,* (Brennan, J., dissenting). Paradoxically, Mr. Justice Brennan indicates that suppression of unprotected obscene material is permissible to avoid exposure to unconsenting adults, as in this case, and to juveniles, although he gives no indication of how the division between protected and nonprotected materials may be drawn with greater precision for these purposes than for regulation of commercial exposure to consenting adults only. Nor does he indicate where in the Constitution he finds the authority to distinguish between a willing "adult" one month past the state law age of majority and a willing "juvenile" one month younger.

Under the holdings announced today, no one will be subject to prosecution for the sale or exposure of obscene materials unless these materials depict or describe patently offensive "hard core" sexual conduct specifically defined by the regulating state law, as written or construed. We are satisfied that these specific prerequisites will provide fair notice to a dealer in such materials that his public and commercial activities may bring prosecution. . . .

It is certainly true that the absence, since *Roth,* of a single majority view of this Court as to proper standards for testing obscenity has placed a strain on both state and federal courts. But today, for the first time since *Roth* was decided in 1957, a majority of this Court has agreed on concrete guidelines to isolate "hard core" pornography from expression protected by the First Amendment. . . .

Under a National Constitution, fundamental First Amendment limitations on the powers of the States do not vary from community to community, but this does not mean that there are, or should or can be, fixed, uniform national standards of precisely what appeals to the "prurient interest" or is "patently offensive." These are essentially questions of fact, and our Nation is simply too big and too diverse for this Court to reasonably expect that such standards could be articulated for all 50 States in a single formulation, even assuming the prerequisite consensus exists. When triers of fact are asked to decide whether "the average person, applying contemporary community standards" would consider certain materials "prurient," it would be unrealistic to require that the answer be based on some abstract formulation. The adversary system, with lay jurors as the usual ultimate factfinders in criminal prosecutions, has historically permitted triers of fact to draw on the standards of their community, guided always by limiting instructions on the law. To require a State to structure obscenity proceedings around evidence of a *national* "community standard" would be an exercise in futility. . . .

We conclude that neither the State's alleged failure to offer evidence of "national standards," nor the trial court's charge that the jury consider state community standards, were constitutional errors. Nothing in the First Amendment requires that a jury must consider hypothetical and unascertainable "national standards" attempting to determine whether certain materials are obscene as a matter of fact. . . . It is neither realistic nor constitutionally sound to read the First Amendment as requiring that the people of Maine or Mississippi accept public depiction of conduct found tolerable in Las Vegas, or New York City. . . .

In sum, we (a) reaffirm the *Roth* holding that obscene material is not protected by the First Amendment; (b) hold that such material can be regulated by the States, subject to the specific safeguards enunciated above, without a showing that the material is *"utterly* without redeeming social value"; and (c) hold that obscenity is to be determined by applying "contemporary community standards," not "national standards." The judgment of the Appellate Department of the Superior Court, Orange County, California, is vacated and the case remanded to that court for further proceedings not inconsistent with the First Amendment standards established by this opinion.

Vacated and remanded.

[The dissenting opinion of Douglas, J., and the dissenting opinion of Brennan, J., joined by Stewart and Marshall, JJ., are omitted.]

PARIS ADULT THEATRE I v. SLATON
413 U.S. 49, 93 S.Ct. 2628, 37 L.Ed.2d 446 (1973).

Mr. Chief Justice Burger delivered the opinion of the Court.

[W]e do not undertake to tell the States what they must do, but rather to define the area in which they may chart their own course in dealing with obscene material. . . . Here, Georgia imposed no restraint on the exhibition of the films involved in this case until after a full adversary proceeding by the Georgia Supreme Court that the materials were constitutionally unprotected. . . . Nor was it error to fail to require "expert" affirmative evidence that the materials were obscene when the materials themselves were actually placed in evidence. . . .

[W]e hold that there are legitimate state interests at stake in stemming the tide of commercialized obscenity, even assuming it is feasible to enforce effective safeguards against exposure to juveniles and to passersby. Rights and interests "other than those of the advocates are involved." These include the interest of the public in the quality of life and the total community environment, the tone of commerce in the great city centers, and, possibly, the public safety itself. The Hill–Link Minority Report of the Commission on Obscenity and Pornography indicates that there is at least an arguable correlation between obscene material and crime. . . . It is not for us to resolve empirical uncertainties underlying state legislation, save in the exceptional case where that legislation plainly impinges upon rights protected by the Constitution itself. . . .

From the beginning of civilized societies, legislators and judges have acted on various unprovable assumptions. Such assumptions underlie much lawful state regulation of commercial and business affairs. The same is true of the federal securities and antitrust laws and a host of federal regulations. On the basis of these assumptions both Congress and state legislatures have, for example, drastically restricted associational rights by adopting antitrust laws, and have strictly regulated public expression by issuers of and dealers in securities, profit sharing "coupons," and "trading stamps," commanding what they must and must not publish and announce. Understandably those who entertain an absolutist view of the First Amendment find it uncomfortable to explain why rights of association, speech, and press should be severely restrained in the marketplace of goods and money, but not in the marketplace of pornography. . . . The sum of experience, including that of the past two decades, affords an ample basis for legislatures to conclude that a sensitive, key relationship of human existence, central to family life, community welfare, and the development of human personality, can be debased and distorted by crass commercial exploitation of sex. Nothing in the Constitution prohibits a State from reaching such a conclusion and acting on it legislatively simply because there is no conclusive evidence or empirical data.

... States are told by some that they must await a "laissez-faire" market solution to the obscenity-pornography problem, paradoxically "by people who have never otherwise had a kind word to say for laissez-faire," particularly in solving urban, commercial, and environmental pollution problems. The States, of course, may follow such a "laissez-faire" policy and drop all controls on commercialized obscenity, if that is what they prefer, just as they can ignore consumer protection in the marketplace, but nothing in the Constitution *compels* the States to do so with regard to matters falling within state jurisdiction....

Finally, petitioners argue that conduct which directly involves "consenting adults" only has, for that sole reason, a special claim to constitutional protection. Our Constitution establishes a broad range of conditions on the exercise of power by the States, but for us to say that our Constitution incorporates the proposition that conduct involving consenting adults only is always beyond state regulation, is a step we are unable to take.* ...

... The judgment is vacated and the case remanded to the Georgia Supreme Court for further proceedings not inconsistent with this opinion and *Miller v. California.*

MR. JUSTICE BRENNAN, with whom MR. JUSTICE STEWART and MR. JUSTICE MARSHALL join, dissenting....

Our experience with the *Roth* approach has certainly taught us that the outright suppression of obscenity cannot be reconciled with the fundamental principles of the First and Fourteenth Amendments.... Any effort to draw a constitutionally acceptable boundary on state power must resort to such indefinite concepts as "prurient interest," "patent offensiveness," "serious literary value," and the like. [W]e are manifestly unable to describe it in advance except by reference to concepts so elusive that they fail to distinguish clearly between protected and unprotected speech. [N]o one definition, no matter how precisely or narrowly drawn, can possibly suffice for all situations, or carve out fully suppressible expression from all media without also creating a substantial risk of encroachment upon the guarantees of the Due Process Clause and the First Amendment....

Our experience since *Roth* requires us not only to abandon the effort to pick out obscene materials on a case-by-case basis, but also to reconsider a fundamental postulate of *Roth:* that there exists a definable class of sexually oriented expression that may be totally suppressed by the Federal and State Governments. Assuming that such a class of

---

* The state statute books are replete with constitutionally unchallenged laws against prostitution, suicide, voluntary self-mutilation, brutalizing "bare fist" prize fights, and duels, although these crimes may only directly involve "consenting adults." Statutes making bigamy a crime surely cut into an individual's freedom to associate, but few today seriously claim such statutes violate the First Amendment or any other constitutional provision.... As Professor Irving Kristol has observed: "Bearbaiting and cockfighting are prohibited only in part out of compassion for the suffering animals; the main reason they were abolished was because it was felt that they debased and brutalized the citizenry who flocked to witness such spectacles." On the Democratic Idea in America 33 (1972).

expression does in fact exist, I am forced to conclude that the concept of "obscenity" cannot be defined with sufficient specificity and clarity to provide fair notice to persons who create and distribute sexually oriented materials, to prevent substantial erosion of protected speech as a byproduct of the attempt to suppress unprotected speech, and to avoid very costly institutional harms....

[T]he state interests in protecting children and in protecting unconsenting adults may stand on a different footing from the other asserted state interests. It may well be, as one commentator has argued, that "exposure to [erotic material] is for some persons an intense emotional experience. A communication of this nature, imposed upon a person contrary to his wishes, has all the characteristics of a physical assault.... [And it] constitutes an invasion of his privacy.... " But cf. *Cohen v. California,* [§ 10–4, supra]. Similarly, if children are "not possessed of that full capacity for individual choice which is the presupposition of the First Amendment guarantees," *Ginsberg v. New York,* (Stewart, J., concurring), then the State may have a substantial interest in precluding the flow of obscene materials even to consenting juveniles.

But, whatever the strength of the state interests in protecting juveniles and unconsenting adults from exposure to sexually oriented materials, those interests cannot be asserted in defense of the holding of the Georgia Supreme Court in this case. That court assumed for the purposes of its decision that the films in issue were exhibited only to persons over the age of 21 who viewed them willingly and with prior knowledge of the nature of their contents. And on that assumption the state court held that the films could still be suppressed. The justification for the suppression must be found, therefore, in some independent interest in regulating the reading and viewing habits of consenting adults....

In short, while I cannot say that the interests of the State—apart from the question of juveniles and unconsenting adults—are trivial or nonexistent, I am compelled to conclude that these interests cannot justify the substantial damage to constitutional rights and to this Nation's judicial machinery that inevitably results from state efforts to bar the distribution even of unprotected material to consenting adults. I would hold, therefore, that at least in the absence of distribution to juveniles or obtrusive exposure to unconsenting adults, the First and Fourteenth Amendments prohibit the State and Federal Governments from attempting wholly to suppress sexually oriented materials on the basis of their allegedly "obscene" contents. Nothing in this approach precludes those governments from taking action to serve what may be strong and legitimate interests through regulation of the manner of distribution of sexually oriented material....

[The dissenting opinion of Douglas, J., is omitted.]

Notes

1. *Hamling v. United States,* 418 U.S. 87, 94 S.Ct. 2887, 41 L.Ed.2d 590 (1974). The Court, speaking through Justice Rehnquist, elaborated on

the community standards test. *Miller* had rejected the requirement of a uniform nationwide standard but "did not require as a constitutional matter the substitution of some smaller geographical area into the same sort of formula." The federal obscenity statute also should not be interpreted as requiring proof of uniform national standards. The federal law permits the juror to draw on the knowledge of the community or vicinage, from which he or she comes. Because the jurors in this case came from the Southern District of California, "it would be the standards of that 'community' upon which the jurors would draw. But this is not to say that a district court would not be at liberty to admit evidence of standards existing in some place outside of this particular district, if it felt such evidence would assist the jurors in the resolution of the issues which they were to decide." The fact that "distributors of allegedly obscene materials may be subjected to varying community standards in the various federal districts into which they transmit the materials does not render a federal statute unconstitutional because of the failure of application of uniform national standards of obscenity."

The Court reaffirmed the rule that the Government must show scienter, i.e., "that a defendant had knowledge of the contents of the materials he distributed and that he knew the character and nature of the materials." But the Government need not show that the defendant knew of the legal status of the materials. To require such proof "would permit the defendant to avoid prosecution by simply claiming that he had not brushed up on the law."

That same day the Court decided *Jenkins v. Georgia,* 418 U.S. 153, 94 S.Ct. 2750, 41 L.Ed.2d 642 (1974). The Court, again speaking through Justice Rehnquist, reversed the obscenity conviction of defendant, who was charged with showing the film "Carnal Knowledge" in a theatre. The movie (released in 1971) had appeared on several "Ten Best" lists for the year. The Court explained that *Miller* did not mandate that the jurors be instructed to apply a hypothetical statewide community standard. *Miller* only made clear that "state juries need not be instructed to apply 'national standards.' " The Court also approved of the trial instruction to apply "community standards" even though the court did not specify the community.

The Court then turned to the film itself. "Our own viewing of the film satisfies us that 'Carnal Knowledge' could not be found under the *Miller* standard to depict sexual conduct in a patently offensive way." The nudity alone did not make the film obscene, and "it would be a serious misreading of *Miller* to conclude that the juries have unbridled discretion in determining what is 'patently offensive.' "

Justice Brennan, joined by Stewart and Marshall, JJ., concurred in the result: "After the Court's decision today, there can be no doubt that *Miller* requires appellate courts—including this Court—to review independently the constitutional fact of obscenity." Thus "one cannot say with certainty that material is obscene until at least five members of this Court, applying inevitably obscure standards, have pronounced it so."

2. *Kaplan v. California,* 413 U.S. 115, 93 S.Ct. 2680, 37 L.Ed.2d 492 (1973), decided the same day as *Miller,* held that books containing no pictures but only words may be constitutionally obscene, even though, the

Court acknowledged, books "have a different and preferred place in our hierarchy of values. . . . "

3. *Pope v. Illinois,* 481 U.S. 497, 107 S.Ct. 1918, 95 L.Ed.2d 439 (1987) held that the "value" of an allegedly obscene work (the third prong of the *Miller* test) is not to be determined by the jury being instructed to decide whether "a reasonable person would find [serious literary, artistic, political, or scientific] value in the material taken as a whole." While the "community standards" test applies to the first and second prongs of *Miller,* the danger of applying it to the third prong is that a juror "could consider himself bound to follow prevailing local views on value without considering whether a reasonable person would arrive at a different conclusion." The value of a work does not vary from community to community based on the degree of local acceptance it has won.

Justice Scalia, concurring, urged reexamination of *Miller*: "in my view it is quite impossible to come to an objective assessment of (at least) literary or artistic value, there being many accomplished people who have found literature in Dada and art in the replication of a soup can." Justice Stevens, joined by Marshall, J., dissented and argued that a state may not criminalize the "mere possession or sale of obscene literature, absent some connection to minors, or obtrusive display to unconsenting adults." In footnote 11, this dissent noted that the "insurmountable vagueness problems involved in criminalization are not in my view, implicated with respect to civil regulation of sexually explicit material, an area in which the States retain substantial leeway." Justice Brennan joined all but footnote 11 of the Stevens' dissent.

4. *Sable Communications of California, Inc. v. FCC,* 492 U.S. 115, 109 S.Ct. 2829, 106 L.Ed.2d 93 (1989) held that § 223(b) of the Communications Act of 1934, as amended in 1988, can constitutionally impose an outright ban on "obscene" interstate, pre-recorded, commercial telephone messages ("dial-a-porn"). White, J., for the Court noted that the Court has "repeatedly held that the protection of the First Amendment does not extend to obscene speech." The Court, however, invalidated the portion of the statute that imposed an outright ban, regardless of age, on "indecent" dial-a-porn messages. "Sexual expression which is indecent but not obscene is protected by the First Amendment; and the government does not submit that the sale of such materials to adults could be criminalized solely because they are indecent." The Government does have a compelling interest in protecting the "physical and psychological well-being of minors," including protecting them from "literature that is not obscene by adult standards." But the means used here—a total legislative ban—are not narrowly tailored to serve that purpose. "The FCC, after lengthy proceedings, determined that its credit card, access code, and scrambling rules were a satisfactory solution to the problem of keeping indecent dial-a-porn messages out of the reach of minors." The Court rejected (as unpersuasive and not supported by the evidence) the Government's argument that an outright ban was appropriate because some enterprising youngsters could evade the rules. And the Court distinguished *FCC v. Pacifica,* § 10.5 as "an emphatically narrow holding;" it did not involve a total ban, for the FCC sought to channel the indecent material to a time of day when children were thought to be less likely to listen. *Pacifica* also relied on the "unique" attributes of broadcasting, not

involved in this case. In the present case there is also no "captive audience" or unwilling listener problem as there was in *Pacifica*.

Brennan, J., joined by Marshall and Stevens, JJ., concurred in part and dissented in part, stating: "I have long been convinced that the exaction of criminal penalties for the distribution of obscene materials to consenting adults is constitutionally intolerable."

NEW YORK v. FERBER

458 U.S. 747, 102 S.Ct. 3348, 73 L.Ed.2d 1113 (1982).

JUSTICE WHITE delivered the opinion of the Court.

At issue in this case is the constitutionality of a New York criminal statute [§ 263.15] which prohibits persons from knowingly promoting sexual performances by children under the age of 16 by distributing material which depicts such performances.... A a"sexual performance is defined as 'any performance or part thereof which includes sexual conduct by a child less than sixteen years of age,'" § 263.1. "Sexual conduct" is in turn defined in § 263.3: "'Sexual conduct' means actual or simulated sexual intercourse, deviate sexual intercourse, sexual bestiality, masturbation, sado-masochistic abuse, or lewd exhibition of the genitals." A performance is defined as "any play, motion picture, photograph or dance" or "any other visual presentation exhibited before an audience." § 263.4 ... A companion provision bans only the knowing dissemination of obscene material. § 263.10.

This case arose when Paul Ferber, the proprietor of a Manhattan bookstore specializing in sexually oriented products, sold two films to an undercover police officer. The films are devoted almost exclusively to depicting young boys masturbating. Ferber was indicted on two counts of § 263.10 and two counts of § 263.15, the two New York laws controlling dissemination of child pornography. After a jury trial, Ferber was acquitted of the two counts of promoting an obscene sexual performance, but found guilty of the two counts under § 263.15, which did not require proof that the films were obscene....

... Like obscenity statutes, laws directed at the dissemination of child pornography run the risk of suppressing protected expression by allowing the hand of the censor to become unduly heavy. For the following reasons, however, we are persuaded that the States are entitled to greater leeway in the regulation of pornographic depictions of children.

First. [A] state's interest in "safeguarding the physical and psychological well being of a minor" is "compelling." ... We shall not second-guess this legislative judgment. [V]irtually all of the States and the United States have passed legislation proscribing the production of or otherwise combatting "child pornography." The legislative judgment, as well as the judgment found in the relevant literature, is that the use of children as subjects of pornographic materials is harmful to the physiological, emotional, and mental health of the child. That judgment, we think, easily passes muster under the First Amendment.

Second. The distribution of photographs and films depicting sexual activity by juveniles is intrinsically related to the sexual abuse of children in at least two ways. First, the materials produced are a permanent record of the children's participation and the harm to the child is exacerbated by their circulation. Second, the distribution network for child pornography must be closed if the production of material which requires the sexual exploitation of children is to be effectively controlled. [T]he question under the *Miller* test of whether a work, taken as a whole, appeals to the prurient interest of the average person bears no connection to the issue of whether a child has been physically or psychologically harmed in the production of the work....

Third. The advertising and selling of child pornography provides an economic motive for and is thus an integral part of the production of such materials, an activity illegal throughout the nation....

Fourth. The value of permitting live performances and photographic reproductions of children engaged in lewd sexual conduct is exceedingly modest, if not *de minimis.* We consider it unlikely that visual depictions of children performing sexual acts or lewdly exhibiting their genitals would often constitute an important and necessary part of a literary performance or scientific or educational work. If it were necessary for literary or artistic value, a person over the statutory age who perhaps looked younger could be utilized. Simulation outside of the prohibition of the statute could provide another alternative. Nor is there any question here of censoring a particular literary theme or portrayal of sexual activity. The First Amendment interest is limited to that of rendering the portrayal somewhat more "realistic" by utilizing or photographing children.

Fifth. Recognizing and classifying child pornography as a category of material outside the protection of the First Amendment is not incompatible with our earlier decisions.... There are, of course, limits on the category of child pornography which, like obscenity, is unprotected by the First Amendment. As with all legislation in this sensitive area, the conduct to be prohibited must be adequately defined by the applicable state law, as written or authoritatively construed. Here the nature of the harm to be combatted requires that the state offense be limited to works that *visually* depict sexual conduct by children below a specified age. The category of "sexual conduct" proscribed must also be suitably limited and described.

The test for child pornography is separate from the obscenity standard enunciated in *Miller,* but may be compared to it for purpose of clarity. The *Miller* formulation is adjusted in the following respects: A trier of fact need not find that the material appeals to the prurient interest of the average person; it is not required that sexual conduct portrayed be done so in a patently offensive manner; and the material at issue need not be considered as a whole. We note that the distribution of descriptions or other depictions of sexual conduct, not otherwise obscene, which do not involve live performance or photographic or other visual reproduction of live performances, retains First Amendment protection. As with obscenity laws, criminal responsibility may not be imposed without some element of scienter on the part of the defendant.

Section 263.15's prohibition incorporates a definition of sexual conduct that comports with the above-stated principles. The forbidden acts to be depicted are listed with sufficient precision and represent the kind of conduct that, if it were the theme of a work, could render it legally obscene: "actual or simulated sexual intercourse, deviate sexual intercourse, sexual bestiality, masturbation, sadomasochistic abuse, or lewd exhibition of the genitals." § 263.3. The term "lewd exhibition of the genitals" is not unknown in this area and, indeed, was given in *Miller* as an example of a permissible regulation. A performance is defined only to include live or visual depictions: "any play, motion picture, photograph or dance . . . or other visual representation before an audience." § 263.4. Section 263.15 expressly includes a scienter agreement.

We hold that § 263.15 sufficiently describes a category of material the production and distribution of which is not entitled to First Amendment protection. [T]here is nothing unconstitutionally "underinclusive" about a statute that singles out this category of material for proscription. It also follows that the State is not barred by the First Amendment from prohibiting the distribution of unprotected materials produced outside the State.

It remains to address the claim that the New York statute is unconstitutionally overbroad because it would forbid the distribution of material with serious literary, scientific or educational value or material which does not threaten the harms sought to be combatted by the State. . . . While the reach of the statute is directed at the hard core of child pornography, the Court of Appeals was understandably concerned that some protected expression, ranging from medical textbooks to pictorials in National Geographic would fall prey to the statute. How often, if ever, it may be necessary to employ children to engage in conduct clearly within the reach of the § 263.15 in order to produce educational, medical or artistic works cannot be known with certainty. Yet we seriously doubt, and it has not been suggested, that these arguably impermissible applications of the statute amount to more than a tiny fraction of the materials within the statute's reach. Nor will we assume that the New York courts will widen the possibly invalid reach of the statute by giving an expansive construction to the proscription on "lewd exhibition[s] of the genitals." Under these circumstances, § 263.15 is "not substantially overbroad and whatever overbreadth exists should be cured through case-by-case analysis of the fact situations to which its sanctions, assertedly, may not be applied."

Because § 263.15 is not substantially overbroad, it is unnecessary to consider its application to material that does not depict sexual conduct of a type that New York may restrict consistent with the First Amendment.

As applied to Paul Ferber and to others who distribute similar material, the statute does not violate the First Amendment as applied to the States through the Fourteenth. The decision of the New York Court of Appeals is reversed and the case is remanded to that Court for further proceedings not inconsistent with this opinion.

So ordered.

JUSTICE O'CONNOR, concurring.

Although I join the Court's opinion, I write separately to stress that the Court does not hold that New York must except "material with serious literary, scientific or educational value," from its statute. The Court merely holds that, even if the First Amendment shelters such material, New York's current statute is not sufficiently overbroad to support respondent's facial attack. The compelling interests identified in today's opinion suggest that the Constitution might in fact permit New York to ban knowing distribution of works depicting minors engaged in explicit sexual conduct, regardless of the social value of the depictions. For example, a 12–year–old child photographed while masturbating surely suffers the same psychological harm whether the community labels the photograph "edifying" or "tasteless." The audience's appreciation of the depiction is simply irrelevant to New York's asserted interest in protecting children from psychological, emotional, and mental harm.

[I]t is quite possible that New York's statute is overbroad because it bans depictions that do not actually threaten the harms identified by the Court. For example, clinical pictures of adolescent sexuality, such as those that might appear in medical textbooks, might not involve the type of sexual exploitation and abuse targeted by New York's statute. Nor might such depictions feed the poisonous "kiddie porn" market that New York and other States have attempted to regulate. Similarly, pictures of children engaged in rites widely approved by their cultures, such as those that might appear in issues of *National Geographic,* might not trigger the compelling interests identified by the Court. It is not necessary to address these possibilities further today, however, because this potential overbreadth is not sufficiently substantial to warrant facial invalidation of New York's statute.

JUSTICE BRENNAN, with whom JUSTICE MARSHALL joins, concurring in the judgment.

[I]n my view application of § 263.15 or any similar statute to depictions of children that in themselves do have serious literary, artistic, scientific or medical value, would violate the First Amendment. As the Court recognizes, the limited classes of speech, the suppression of which does not raise serious First Amendment concerns, have two attributes. They are of exceedingly "slight social value," and the State has a compelling interest in their regulation. The First Amendment value of depictions of children that are in themselves serious contributions to art, literature or science, is, by definition, simply not *"de minimis."* At the same time, the State's interest in suppression of such materials is likely to be far less compelling. For the Court's assumption of harm to the child resulting from the "permanent record" and "circulation" of the child's "participation," lacks much of its force where the depiction is a serious contribution to art or science. The production of materials of serious value is not the "low-profile clandestine industry" that according to the Court produces purely pornographic materials. In short, it is inconceivable how a depiction of a child that is itself a serious contribution to the world of art or literature or science can be deemed "material outside the protection of the First Amendment." . . .

[STEVENS, J., concurred in the judgment; BLACKMUN, J., concurred in the result without opinion.]

Notes

Osborne v. Ohio, 495 U.S. 103, 110 S.Ct. 1691, 109 L.Ed.2d 98 (1990), held that the state may constitutionally prohibit the possession and viewing of child pornography at home. The distinction with *Stanley v. Georgia,* § 10–12.1, is "obvious: the State does not rely on a paternalistic interest in regulating Osborne's mind." Rather, the purpose of the law is "to protect the victims of child pornography; it hopes to destroy a market for the exploitative use of children." The Court went on to conclude that the statute was not overbroad. The law prohibited any person from possessing or viewing any material or performance showing a minor who is not his child or ward in a state of nudity unless (a) the material or performance is presented for a bona fide purpose by or to a person having a proper interest therein, or (b) the possessor knows that the minor's parents or guardian has consented in writing to such photographing or use of the minor. As construed by the Ohio Supreme Court, the law required proof of scienter and is limited to depictions of nudity that involve lewd exhibition or involve graphic focus of the minor's genitals. Brennan, J., joined by Marshall & Stevens, JJ., dissented, arguing that "our decision in *Stanley v. Georgia* prevents the State from criminalizing appellant's possession of the photographs at issue in this case."

10–12.2 Zoning

YOUNG v. AMERICAN MINI THEATRES, INC.
427 U.S. 50, 96 S.Ct. 2440, 49 L.Ed.2d 310 (1976).

MR. JUSTICE STEVENS delivered the opinion of the Court.*

Zoning ordinances adopted by the city of Detroit differentiate between motion picture theaters which exhibit sexually explicit "adult" movies and those which do not. The principal question presented by this case is whether that statutory classification is unconstitutional because it is based on the content of communication protected by the First Amendment. . . . Instead of concentrating "adult" theaters in limited zones, these ordinances require that such theaters be dispersed. Specifi-

---

* Part III of this opinion is joined by only The Chief Justice [Burger], Mr. Justice White, and Mr. Justice Rehnquist.

cally, an adult theater may not be located within 1,000 feet of any two other "regulated uses" or within 500 feet of a residential area. The term "regulated uses" includes 10 different kinds of establishments in addition to adult theaters. The classification of a theater as "adult" is expressly predicated on the character of the motion pictures which it exhibits. If the theater is used to present "material distinguished or characterized by an emphasis on matter depicting, describing or relating to 'Specified Sexual Activities' or 'Specified Anatomical Areas,' "** it is an adult establishment.

[T]he Detroit Common Council made a finding that some uses of property are especially injurious to a neighborhood when they are concentrated in limited areas. The decision to add adult motion picture theaters and adult book stores to the list of businesses which, apart from a special waiver, could not be located within 1,000 feet of two other "regulated uses," was, in part, a response to the significant growth in the number of such establishments. In the opinion of urban planners and real estate experts who supported the ordinances, the location of several such businesses in the same neighborhood tends to attract an undesirable quantity and quality of transients, adversely affects property values, causes an increase in crime, especially prostitution, and encourages residents and businesses to move elsewhere.

Respondents are the operators of two adult motion picture theaters. One, the Nortown, was an established theater which began to exhibit adult films in March 1973. The other, the Pussy Cat, was a corner gas station which was converted into a "mini theater," but denied a certificate of occupancy because of its plan to exhibit adult films. Both theaters were located within 1,000 feet of two other regulated uses and the Pussy Cat was less than 500 feet from a residential area. The respondents brought two separate actions against appropriate city officials, seeking a declaratory judgment that the ordinances were unconstitutional and an injunction against their enforcement. . . .

I. There are two parts to respondents' claim that the ordinances are too vague. They do not attack the specificity of the definition of "Specified Sexual Activities" or "Specified Anatomical Areas." They argue, however, that they cannot determine how much of the described activity may be permissible before the exhibition is "characterized by an emphasis" on such matter. In addition, they argue that the ordinances

---

** These terms are defined as follows:

"For the purpose of this Section, 'Specified Sexual Activities' is defined as:

"1. Human Genitals in a state of sexual stimulation or arousal;

"2. Acts of human masturbation, sexual intercourse or sodomy;

"3. Fondling or other erotic touching of human genitals, pubic region, buttock or female breast.

"And 'Specified Anatomical Areas' is defined as:

"1. Less than completely and opaquely covered: (a) human genitals, pubic region, (b) buttock, and (c) female breast below a point immediately above the top of the areola; and

"2. Human male genitals in a discernibly turgid state, even if completely and opaquely covered."

are vague because they do not specify adequate procedures or standards for obtaining a waiver of the 1,000–foot restriction.

We find it unnecessary to consider the validity of either of these arguments in the abstract. For even if there may be some uncertainty about the effect of the ordinances on other litigants, they are unquestionably applicable to these respondents. The record indicates that both theaters propose to offer adult fare on a regular basis. Neither respondent has alleged any basis for claiming or anticipating any waiver of the restriction as applied to its theater. It is clear, therefore, that any element of vagueness in these ordinances has not affected these respondents. . . . Since there is surely a less vital interest in the uninhibited exhibition of material that is on the borderline between pornography and artistic expression than in the free dissemination of ideas of social and political significance, and since the limited amount of uncertainty in the ordinances is easily susceptible of a narrowing construction, we think this is an inappropriate case in which to adjudicate the hypothetical claims of persons not before the Court.

The only area of protected communication that may be deterred by these ordinances comprises films containing material falling within the specific definitions of "Specified Sexual Activities" or "Specified Anatomical Areas." The fact that the First Amendment protects some, though not necessarily all, of that material from total suppression does not warrant the further conclusion that an exhibitor's doubts as to whether a borderline film may be shown in his theater, as well as in theaters licensed for adult presentations, involves the kind of threat to the free market in ideas and expression that justifies [judicial intervention].

II. Petitioners acknowledge that the ordinances prohibit theaters which are not licensed as "adult motion picture theaters" from exhibiting films which are protected by the First Amendment. Respondents argue that the ordinances are therefore invalid as prior restraints on free speech.

The ordinances are not challenged on the ground that they impose a limit on the total number of adult theaters which may operate in the city of Detroit. There is no claim that distributors or exhibitors of adult films are denied access to the market or, conversely, that the viewing public is unable to satisfy its appetite for sexually explicit fare. Viewed as an entity, the market for this commodity is essentially unrestrained.

It is true, however, that adult films may only be exhibited commercially in licensed theaters. But that is also true of all motion pictures. The city's general zoning laws require all motion picture theaters to satisfy certain locational as well as other requirements; we have no doubt that the municipality may control the location of theaters as well as the location of other commercial establishments, either by confining them to certain specified commercial zones or by requiring that they be dispersed throughout the city. . . .

Putting to one side for the moment the fact that adult motion picture theaters must satisfy a locational restriction not applicable to other theaters, we are also persuaded that the 1,000–foot restriction does not, in itself, create an impermissible restraint on protected communication. The city's interest in planning and regulating the use of property for commercial purposes is clearly adequate to support that kind of restriction applicable to all theaters within the city limits. . . .

III. [Statements in earlier cases] read literally and without regard for the facts of the case in which it was made, would absolutely preclude any regulation of expressive activity predicated in whole or in part on the content of the communication. But we learned long ago that broad statements of principle, no matter how correct in the context in which they are made, are sometimes qualified by contrary decisions before the absolute limit of the stated principle is reached. . . .

The question whether speech is, or is not, protected by the First Amendment often depends on the content of the speech. Thus, the line between permissible advocacy and impermissible incitation to crime or violence depends, not merely on the setting in which the speech occurs, but also on exactly what the speaker had to say. . . .

Even within the area of protected speech, a difference in content may require a different governmental response. In *New York Times Co. v. Sullivan*, [§ 10–8.1, supra], we recognized that the First Amendment places limitations on the States' power to enforce their libel laws. [A]lthough the content of a story must be examined to decide whether it involves a public figure or a public issue, the Court's application of the relevant rule may not depend on its favorable or unfavorable appraisal of that figure or that issue. [Similarly,] the regulation of the places where sexually explicit films may be exhibited is unaffected by whatever social, political, or philosophical message a film may be intended to communicate; whether a motion picture ridicules or characterizes one point of view or another, the effect of the ordinances is exactly the same.

Moreover, even though we recognize that the First Amendment will not tolerate the total suppression of erotic materials that have some arguably artistic value, it is manifest that society's interest in protecting this type of expression is of a wholly different, and lesser, magnitude than the interest in untrammeled political debate that inspired Voltaire's immortal comment. ["I disapprove of what you say, but I will defend to the death your right to say it."] Whether political oratory or philosophical discussion moves us to applaud or to despise what is said, every school child can understand why our duty to defend the right to speak remains the same. But few of us would march our sons and daughters off to war to preserve the citizen's right to see "Specified Sexual Activities" exhibited in the theaters of our choice. Even though the First Amendment protects communication in this area from total suppression, we hold that the State may legitimately use the content of these materials as the basis for placing them in a different classification from other motion pictures.

The remaining question is whether the line drawn by these ordinances is justified by the city's interest in preserving the character of its neighborhoods.... The record discloses a factual basis for the Common Council's conclusion that this kind of restriction will have the desired effect.*** It is not our function to appraise the wisdom of its decision to require adult theaters to be separated rather than concentrated in the same areas....

Since what is ultimately at stake is nothing more than a limitation on the place where adult films may be exhibited, even though the determination of whether a particular film fits that characterization turns on the nature of its content, we conclude that the city's interest in the present and future character of its neighborhoods adequately supports its classification of motion pictures....

The judgment of the Court of Appeals is

Reversed.

MR. JUSTICE POWELL, concurring.

Although I agree with much of what is said in the Court's opinion, and concur in Parts I and II, my approach to the resolution of this case is sufficiently different to prompt me to write separately.* I view the case as presenting an example of innovative land-use regulation, implicating First Amendment concerns only incidentally and to a limited extent....

The inquiry for First Amendment purposes is not concerned with economic impact; rather, it looks only to the effect of this ordinance upon freedom of expression. This prompts essentially two inquiries: (I) Does the ordinance impose any content limitation on the creators of adult movies or their ability to make them available to whom they desire, and (ii) does it restrict in any significant way the viewing of these movies by those who desire to see them? On the record in this case, these inquiries must be answered in the negative. At most the impact of the ordinance on these interests is incidental and minimal. Detroit has silenced no message, has invoked no censorship, and has imposed no limitation upon those who wish to view them. The ordinance is addressed only to the places at which this type of expression may be presented, a restriction that does not interfere with content....

MR. JUSTICE STEWART, with whom MR. JUSTICE BRENNAN, MR. JUSTICE MARSHALL, and MR. JUSTICE BLACKMUN join, dissenting.

***The Common Council's determination was that a concentration of "adult" movie theaters causes the area to deteriorate and become a focus of crime, effects which are not attributable to theaters showing other types of films. It is this secondary effect which these zoning ordinances attempt to avoid, not the dissemination of "offensive" speech....

* I do not think we need reach, nor am I inclined to agree with, the holding in Part III (and supporting discussion) that nonobscene, erotic materials may be treated differently under First Amendment principles from other forms of protected expression. I do not consider the conclusions in Part I of the opinion to depend on distinctions between protected speech.

The Court today holds that the First and Fourteenth Amendments do not prevent the city of Detroit from using a system of prior restraints and criminal sanctions to enforce content-based restrictions on the geographic location of motion picture theaters that exhibit nonobscene but sexually oriented films. I dissent from this drastic departure from established principles of First Amendment law....

The fact that the "offensive" speech here may not address "important" topics—"ideas of social and political significance," in the Court's terminology,—does not mean that it is less worthy of constitutional protection. [I]n the absence of a judicial determination of obscenity, it is by no means clear that the speech is not "important" even on the Court's terms....

I can only interpret today's decision as an aberration. The Court is undoubtedly sympathetic, as am I, to the well-intentioned efforts of Detroit to "clean up" its streets and prevent the proliferation of "skid rows." But it is in those instances where protected speech grates most unpleasantly against the sensibilities that judicial vigilance must be at its height....

MR. JUSTICE BLACKMUN, with whom MR. JUSTICE BRENNAN, MR. JUSTICE STEWART, and MR. JUSTICE MARSHALL join, dissenting.

[A]n independent ground on which, for me, the challenged ordinance is unconstitutional ... is vagueness.

We should put ourselves for a moment in the shoes of the motion picture exhibitor. Let us suppose that, having previously offered only a more innocuous fare, he decides to vary it by exhibiting on certain days films from a series which occasionally deals explicitly with sex. The exhibitor must determine whether this places his theater into the "adult" class prescribed by the challenged ordinance. If the theater is within that class, it must be licensed, and it may be entirely prohibited, depending on its location.

"Adult" status *vel non* depends on whether the theater is "used for presenting" films that are "distinguished or characterized by an emphasis on" certain specified activities, including sexual intercourse, or specified anatomical areas. It will be simple enough, as the operator screens films, to tell when one of these areas or activities is being depicted, but if the depiction represents only a part of the films' subject matter, I am at a loss to know how he will tell whether they are "distinguished or characterized by an emphasis" on those areas and activities. The ordinance gives him no guidance. Neither does it instruct him on how to tell whether, assuming the films in question are thus "distinguished or characterized," his theater is being "used for presenting" such films. That phrase could mean *ever* used, *often* used, or *predominantly* used, to name a few possibilities.... The exhibitor's compounded task of applying the statutory definitions to himself and his neighbors, furthermore, is an ongoing one. At any moment he could become a violator of the ordinance because some neighbor has slipped into a "regulated use" classification.... Lest he let down his guard, he should remember that if he miscalculates on any of these issues, he may pay a fine or go to jail. . . .

[T]his ordinance prohibits the showing of certain films in certain places, imposing criminal sanctions for violation of the ban. And however distasteful we may suspect the films to be, we cannot approve their suppression without any judicial finding that they are obscene under this Court's carefully delineated and considered standards.

Notes

1. *Schad v. Borough of Mount Ephraim*, 452 U.S. 61, 101 S.Ct. 2176, 68 L.Ed.2d 671 (1981). An adult book store in a commercial zone introduced a coin-operated mechanism that permitted a customer to watch a live dancer, usually nude, performing behind a glass panel. This action violated a local ordinance that prohibited all live entertainment (e.g., plays, dance, concerts) in the commercial zone. White, J., for the Court, overturned the appellants' convictions under the First and Fourteenth Amendments on the grounds that the appellee failed to justify the exclusion of live entertainment from the broad range of commercial uses that were permitted (e.g., motels, banks, retail stores, etc.). The Court said that *Young v. American Mini Theatres* "did not purport to approve the total exclusion from the city of theaters showing adult, but not obscene, materials." Here, "there is no evidence in this record to support the proposition that the kind of entertainment appellants wish to provide is available in reasonably nearby areas." Burger, C.J., joined by Rehnquist, J., dissented, arguing that "Mount Ephraim did nothing more than employ traditional police power to provide a setting of tranquility."

2. *City of Renton v. Playtime Theatres, Inc.*, 475 U.S. 41, 106 S.Ct. 925, 89 L.Ed.2d 29 (1986). Justice Rehnquist for the Court (with only Brennan and Marshall dissenting) upheld a zoning ordinance that prohibited "adult" motion picture theaters from locating within 1,000 feet of any residential zone, single-or multiple-family dwelling, church, park, or school. The district court found that the city council's "'*predominate* concerns' were with the secondary effects of adult theatres [e.g., to prevent crime, protect the city's retail trade, maintain property values, and preserve the quality of life], and not with the content of adult films themselves." (emphasis in original). This finding was "more than adequate to establish that the city's pursuit of its zoning interests here was unrelated to the suppression of free expression." The ordinance was a "content-neutral" speech regulation because it was "*justified* without reference to the content of the regulated speech." (emphasis in original). Renton was also entitled to rely on the experiences of Seattle and other cities. "The First Amendment does not require a city, before enacting such an ordinance, to conduct new studies or produce evidence independent of that already generated by other cities, so long as whatever evidence the city relies upon is reasonably believed to be relevant to the problem that the city addresses." The Court upheld the ordinance because it served a substantial governmental interest (preserving the quality of life), and allowed reasonable alternative avenues of communication: more than five percent of the entire land area of Renton was allowed to be used by adult theatres. "Cities may regulate adult theatres by dispersing them, as in

Detroit [in *American Mini Theatres*], or by effectively concentrating them, as in Renton." Unlike *Schad,* the Renton ordinance was "narrowly tailored" to those theatres producing the unwanted secondary effects.

10–12.3 The Internet

RENO v. AMERICAN CIVIL LIBERTIES UNION
521 U.S. 844, 117 S.Ct. 2329, 138 L.Ed.2d 874 (1997).

JUSTICE STEVENS delivered the opinion of the Court.

At issue is the constitutionality of two statutory provisions enacted to protect minors from "indecent" and "patently offensive" communications on the Internet. Notwithstanding the legitimacy and importance of the congressional goal of protecting children from harmful materials, we agree with the three-judge District Court that the statute abridges "the freedom of speech" protected by the First Amendment.

I. The District Court made extensive findings of fact [that] describe the character and the dimensions of the Internet, the availability of sexually explicit material in that medium, and the problems confronting age verification for recipients of Internet communications. Because those findings provide the underpinnings for the legal issues, we begin with a summary of the undisputed facts.

THE INTERNET The Internet is an international network of interconnected computers. ... The number of "host" computers—those that store information and relay communications—increased from about 300 in 1981 to approximately 9,400,000 by the time of the trial in 1996. Roughly 60% of these hosts are located in the United States. About 40 million people used the Internet at the time of trial, a number that is expected to mushroom to 200 million by 1999. ...

Navigating the [World Wide] Web is relatively straightforward. A user may either type the address of a known page or enter one or more keywords into a commercial "search engine" in an effort to locate sites on a subject of interest. ... Access to most Web pages is freely available, but some allow access only to those who have purchased the right from a commercial provider. The Web is thus comparable, from the readers' viewpoint, to both a vast library including millions of readily available and indexed publications and a sprawling mall offering goods and services.

From the publishers' point of view, it constitutes a vast platform from which to address and hear from a world-wide audience of millions of readers, viewers, researchers, and buyers. Any person or organization with a computer connected to the Internet can "publish" information. Publishers include government agencies, educational institutions, commercial entities, advocacy groups, and individuals. Publishers may either make their material available to the entire pool of Internet users, or confine access to a selected group, such as those willing to pay for the privilege. "No single organization controls any membership in the Web, nor is there any centralized point from which individual Web sites or services can be blocked from the Web.''

SEXUALLY EXPLICIT MATERIAL Sexually explicit material on the Internet includes text, pictures, and chat and ''extends from the modestly titillating to the hardest-core.'' These files are created, named, and posted in the same manner as material that is not sexually explicit, and may be accessed either deliberately or unintentionally during the course of an imprecise search. ''Once a provider posts its content on the Internet, it cannot prevent that content from entering any community.'' . . .

Though such material is widely available, users seldom encounter such content accidentally. ''A document's title or a description of the document will usually appear before the document itself . . . and in many cases the user will receive detailed information about a site's content before he or she need take the step to access the document. Almost all sexually explicit images are preceded by warnings as to the content.'' For that reason, the ''odds are slim'' that a user would enter a sexually explicit site by accident. Unlike communications received by radio or television, ''the receipt of information on the Internet requires a series of affirmative steps more deliberate and directed than merely turning a dial. A child requires some sophistication and some ability to read to retrieve material and thereby to use the Internet unattended.''

Systems have been developed to help parents control the material that may be available on a home computer with Internet access. A system may either limit a computer's access to an approved list of sources that have been identified as containing no adult material, it may block designated inappropriate sites, or it may attempt to block messages containing identifiable objectionable features. [But parental control software] cannot now screen for sexually explicit images. Nevertheless, the evidence indicates that ''a reasonably effective method by which parents can prevent their children from accessing sexually explicit and other material which parents may believe is inappropriate for their children will soon be available.''

AGE VERIFICATION The problem of age verification differs for different uses of the Internet. The District Court categorically determined that there ''is no effective way to determine the identity or the age of a user who is accessing material through e-mail, mail exploders, newsgroups or chat rooms.'' [E]ven if it were technologically feasible to block minors' access to newsgroups and chat rooms containing discussions of art, politics or other subjects that potentially elicit ''indecent'' or ''patently offensive'' contributions, it would not be possible to block their access to that material and ''still allow them access to the remaining content, even if the overwhelming majority of that content was not indecent.''

Technology exists by which an operator of a Web site may condition access on the verification of requested information such as a credit card number or an adult password. Credit card verification is only feasible, however, either in connection with a commercial transaction in which the card is used, or by payment to a verification agency. Using credit card possession as a surrogate for proof of age would impose costs on non-commercial Web sites that would require many of them to shut down. For that reason, at the time of the trial, credit card verification was "effectively unavailable to a substantial number of Internet content providers." Moreover, the imposition of such a requirement "would completely bar adults who do not have a credit card and lack the resources to obtain one from accessing any blocked material."

Commercial pornographic sites that charge their users for access have assigned them passwords as a method of age verification. The record does not contain any evidence concerning the reliability of these technologies. Even if passwords are effective for commercial purveyors of indecent material, the District Court found that an adult password requirement would impose significant burdens on noncommercial sites, both because they would discourage users from accessing their sites and because the cost of creating and maintaining such screening systems would be "beyond their reach." . . .

II. The Telecommunications Act of 1996, was [designed] to reduce regulation and encourage "the rapid deployment of new telecommunications technologies." . . . The Act includes seven Titles, six of which are the product of extensive committee hearings and the subject of discussion in Reports prepared by Committees of the Senate and the House of Representatives. By contrast, Title V—known as the "Communications Decency Act of 1996" (CDA)—contains provisions that were either added in executive committee after the hearings were concluded or as amendments offered during floor debate on the legislation. An amendment offered in the Senate was the source of the two statutory provisions challenged in this case. They are informally described as the "indecent transmission" provision and the "patently offensive display" provision. The first, 47 U.S.C.A. § 223(a), prohibits the knowing transmission of obscene or indecent messages to any recipient under 18 years of age. It provides in pertinent part:

"(a) Whoever—

"(**1**) in interstate or foreign communications . . .

"(B) by means of a telecommunications device knowingly—

"(I) makes, creates, or solicits, and

"(ii) initiates the transmission of,

"any comment, request, suggestion, proposal, image, or other communication which is obscene or indecent, knowing that the recipient of the communication is under 18 years of age, regardless of whether the maker of such communication placed the call or initiated the communication; . . .

"(**2**) knowingly permits any telecommunications facility under his control to be used for any activity prohibited by paragraph (1) with the intent that it be used for such activity, "shall be fined under Title 18, or imprisoned not more than two years, or both."

The second provision, § 223(d), prohibits the knowing sending or displaying of patently offensive messages in a manner that is available to a person under 18 years of age. It provides:

"(d) Whoever—

"(**1**) in interstate or foreign communications knowingly—

"(A) uses an interactive computer service to send to a specific person or persons under 18 years of age, or

"(B) uses any interactive computer service to display in a manner available to a person under 18 years of age,

"any comment, request, suggestion, proposal, image, or other communication that, in context, depicts or describes, in terms patently offensive as measured by contemporary community standards, sexual or excretory activities or organs, regardless of whether the user of such service placed the call or initiated the communication; or

"(**2**) knowingly permits any telecommunications facility under such person's control to be used for an activity prohibited by paragraph (1) with the intent that it be used for such activity,

"shall be fined under Title 18, or imprisoned not more than two years, or both."

The breadth of these prohibitions is qualified by two affirmative defenses. See One covers those who take "good faith, reasonable, effective, and appropriate actions" to restrict access by minors to the prohibited communications. § 223(e)(5)(A). The other covers those who restrict access to covered material by requiring certain designated forms of age proof, such as a verified credit card or an adult identification number or code. § 223(e)(5)(B).

III. [A]fter the President signed the statute, [two suits were brought and consolidated.] After an evidentiary hearing, [a three-judge court unanimously enjoined] the Government from enforcing the prohibitions in § 223(a)(1)(B) insofar as they relate to "indecent" communications, but expressly preserve[d] the Government's right to investigate and prosecute the obscenity or child pornography activities prohibited therein. The injunction against enforcement of §§ 223(d)(1) and (2) is unqualified because those provisions contain no separate reference to obscenity or child pornography.

The Government ... argues that the District Court erred in holding that the CDA violated both the First Amendment because it is overbroad and the Fifth Amendment because it is vague. While we discuss the vagueness of the CDA because of its relevance to the First Amendment overbreadth inquiry, we conclude that the judgment should be affirmed without reaching the Fifth Amendment issue. ...

IV. In arguing for reversal, the Government contends that the CDA is plainly constitutional under three of our prior decisions: (1)

Ginsberg v. New York (1968) [§ 10–12.1]; (2) *FCC v. Pacifica Foundation* (1978) [§ 10–5]; and (3) *Renton v. Playtime Theatres, Inc.* (1986) [§ 10–2.2]. A close look at these cases, however, raises—rather than relieves—doubts concerning the constitutionality of the CDA.

In *Ginsberg,* we upheld the constitutionality of a New York statute that prohibited selling to minors under 17 years of age material that was considered obscene as to them even if not obscene as to adults.... In four important respects, the statute upheld in *Ginsberg* was narrower than the CDA. First, we noted in *Ginsberg* that "the prohibition against sales to minors does not bar parents who so desire from purchasing the magazines for their children." Under the CDA, by contrast, neither the parents' consent—nor even their participation—in the communication would avoid the application of the statute.[32] Second, the New York statute applied only to commercial transactions, whereas the CDA contains no such limitation. Third, the New York statute cabined its definition of material that is harmful to minors with the requirement that it be "utterly without redeeming social importance for minors." The CDA fails to provide us with any definition of the term "indecent" as used in § 223(a)(1) and, importantly, omits any requirement that the "patently offensive" material covered by § 223(d) lack serious literary, artistic, political, or scientific value. Fourth, the New York statute defined a minor as a person under the age of 17, whereas the CDA, in applying to all those under 18 years, includes an additional year of those nearest majority.

In *Pacifica,* we upheld a declaratory order of the Federal Communications Commission, holding that the broadcast of a recording of a 12–minute monologue entitled "Filthy Words" that had previously been delivered to a live audience "could have been the subject of administrative sanctions." The Commission had found that the repetitive use of certain words referring to excretory or sexual activities or organs "in an afternoon broadcast when children are in the audience was patently offensive" and concluded that the monologue was indecent "as broadcast." ... First, the order in *Pacifica,* issued by an agency that had been regulating radio stations for decades, targeted a specific broadcast that represented a rather dramatic departure from traditional program content in order to designate when—rather than whether—it would be permissible to air such a program in that particular medium. The CDA's broad categorical prohibitions are not limited to particular times and are not dependent on any evaluation by an agency familiar with the unique characteristics of the Internet. Second, unlike the CDA, the Commission's declaratory order was not punitive; we expressly refused to decide whether the indecent broadcast "would justify a criminal prosecution." Finally, the Commission's order applied to a medium which as a matter of history had "received the most limited First Amendment protection,"

---

32. Given the likelihood that many E-mail transmissions from an adult to a minor are conversations between family members, it is therefore incorrect for the dissent to suggest that the provisions of the CDA, even in this narrow area, "are no different from the law we sustained in *Ginsberg.*"

in large part because warnings could not adequately protect the listener from unexpected program content. The Internet, however, has no comparable history. Moreover, the District Court found that the risk of encountering indecent material by accident is remote because a series of affirmative steps is required to access specific material.

In *Renton,* we upheld a zoning ordinance that kept adult movie theatres out of residential neighborhoods. The ordinance was aimed, not at the content of the films shown in the theaters, but rather at the "secondary effects"—such as crime and deteriorating property values—that these theaters fostered.... According to the Government, the CDA is constitutional because it constitutes a sort of "cyberzoning" on the Internet. But the CDA applies broadly to the entire universe of cyberspace. And the purpose of the CDA is to protect children from the primary effects of "indecent" and "patently offensive" speech, rather than any "secondary" effect of such speech. Thus, the CDA is a content-based blanket restriction on speech, and, as such, cannot be "properly analyzed as a form of time, place, and manner regulation."

These precedents, then, surely do not require us to uphold the CDA and are fully consistent with the application of the most stringent review of its provisions.

V. [S]ome of our cases have recognized special justifications for regulation of the broadcast media that are not applicable to other speakers, see *Red Lion Broadcasting Co. v. FCC* (1969) [§ 10–5]; *FCC v. Pacifica Foundation* (1978)[§ 10–5]. In these cases, the Court relied on the history of extensive government regulation of the broadcast medium; the scarcity of available frequencies at its inception; and its "invasive" nature.

Those factors are not present in cyberspace. Neither before nor after the enactment of the CDA have the vast democratic fora of the Internet been subject to the type of government supervision and regulation that has attended the broadcast industry. Moreover, the Internet is not as "invasive" as radio or television. The District Court specifically found that "[c]ommunications over the Internet do not 'invade' an individual's home or appear on one's computer screen unbidden. Users seldom encounter content 'by accident.' "It also found that "[a]llmost all sexually explicit images are preceded by warnings as to the content," and cited testimony that " 'odds are slim' that a user would come across a sexually explicit sight by accident." ...

Finally, unlike the conditions that prevailed when Congress first authorized regulation of the broadcast spectrum, the Internet can hardly be considered a "scarce" expressive commodity. ...

VI. Regardless of whether the CDA is so vague that it violates the Fifth Amendment, the many ambiguities concerning the scope of its coverage render it problematic for purposes of the First Amendment. For instance, each of the two parts of the CDA uses a different linguistic form. The first uses the word "indecent," 47 U.S.C.A. § 223(a), while the second speaks of material that "in context, depicts or describes, in terms patently offensive as measured by contemporary community standards, sexual or excretory activities or organs," § 223(d). Given the absence of a definition of either term, this difference in language will provoke uncertainty among speakers about how the two standards relate to each other and just what they mean. Could a speaker confidently assume that a serious discussion about birth control practices, homosexuality, the First Amendment issues raised by the Appendix to our *Pacifica* opinion, or the consequences of prison rape would not violate the CDA? This uncertainty undermines the likelihood that the CDA has been carefully tailored to the congressional goal of protecting minors from potentially harmful materials.

The vagueness of the CDA is a matter of special concern for two reasons. First, the CDA is a content-based regulation of speech. The vagueness of such a regulation raises special First Amendment concerns because of its obvious chilling effect on free speech. Second, the CDA is a criminal statute. . . .

The Government argues that the statute is no more vague than the obscenity standard this Court established in *Miller v. California* (1973). But that is not so. In *Miller,* this Court reviewed a criminal conviction against a commercial vendor who mailed brochures containing pictures of sexually explicit activities to individuals who had not requested such materials. Having struggled for some time to establish a definition of obscenity, we set forth in *Miller* the test for obscenity that controls to this day:

> "(a) whether the average person, applying contemporary community standards would find that the work, taken as a whole, appeals to the prurient interest; (b) whether the work depicts or describes, in a patently offensive way, sexual conduct specifically defined by the applicable state law; and (c) whether the work, taken as a whole, lacks serious literary, artistic, political, or scientific value."

Because the CDA's "patently offensive" standard (and, we assume *arguendo,* its synonymous "indecent" standard) is one part of the three-prong *Miller* test, the Government reasons, it cannot be unconstitutionally vague.

The Government's assertion is incorrect as a matter of fact. The second prong of the *Miller* test—the purportedly analogous standard—contains a critical requirement that is omitted from the CDA: that the proscribed material be "specifically defined by the applicable state law." This requirement reduces the vagueness inherent in the open-ended term "patently offensive" as used in the CDA. Moreover, the *Miller* definition is limited to "sexual conduct," whereas the CDA extends also to include (1) "excretory activities" as well as (2) "organs" of both a sexual and excretory nature.

The Government's reasoning is also flawed. Just because a definition including three limitations is not vague, it does not follow that one

of those limitations, standing by itself, is not vague.[38] Each of *Miller*'s additional two prongs—(1) that, taken as a whole, the material appeal to the "prurient" interest, and (2) that it "lac[k] serious literary, artistic, political, or scientific value"—critically limits the uncertain sweep of the obscenity definition. The second requirement is particularly important because, unlike the "patently offensive" and "prurient interest" criteria, it is not judged by contemporary community standards. This "societal value" requirement, absent in the CDA, allows appellate courts to impose some limitations and regularity on the definition by setting, as a matter of law, a national floor for socially redeeming value. The Government's contention that courts will be able to give such legal limitations to the CDA's standards is belied by *Miller*'s own rationale for having juries determine whether material is "patently offensive" according to community standards: that such questions are essentially ones of *fact*.
. . .

VII. We are persuaded that the CDA lacks the precision that the First Amendment requires when a statute regulates the content of speech. In order to deny minors access to potentially harmful speech, the CDA effectively suppresses a large amount of speech that adults have a constitutional right to receive and to address to one another. That burden on adult speech is unacceptable if less restrictive alternatives would be at least as effective in achieving the legitimate purpose that the statute was enacted to serve. [T]he Government may not "reduc[e] the adult population . . . to . . . only what is fit for children." . . .

In arguing that the CDA does not so diminish adult communication, the Government relies on the incorrect factual premise that prohibiting a transmission whenever it is known that one of its recipients is a minor would not interfere with adult-to-adult communication. The findings of the District Court make clear that this premise is untenable. Given the size of the potential audience for most messages, in the absence of a viable age verification process, the sender must be charged with knowing that one or more minors will likely view it. Knowledge that, for instance, one or more members of a 100–person chat group will be minor—and therefore that it would be a crime to send the group an indecent message—would surely burden communication among adults.

. . . By contrast, the District Court found that "[d]espite its limitations, currently available *user-based* software suggests that a reasonably effective method by which *parents* can prevent their children from accessing sexually explicit and other material which *parents* may believe is inappropriate for their children will soon be widely available." (emphases added).

The breadth of the CDA's coverage is wholly unprecedented. Unlike the regulations upheld in *Ginsberg* and *Pacifica*, the scope of the CDA is not limited to commercial speech or commercial entities. Its open-ended

---

38. Even though the word "trunk," standing alone, might refer to luggage, a swimming suit, the base of a tree, or the long nose of an animal, its meaning is clear when it is one prong of a three-part description of a species of gray animals.

prohibitions embrace all nonprofit entities and individuals posting indecent messages or displaying them on their own computers in the presence of minors. The general, undefined terms "indecent" and "patently offensive" cover large amounts of nonpornographic material with serious educational or other value.[44] Moreover, the "community standards" criterion as applied to the Internet means that any communication available to a nation-wide audience will be judged by the standards of the community most likely to be offended by the message. The regulated subject matter includes any of the seven "dirty words" used in the Pacifica monologue, the use of which the Government's expert acknowledged could constitute a felony. It may also extend to discussions about prison rape or safe sexual practices, artistic images that include nude subjects, and arguably the card catalogue of the Carnegie Library. . . .

The breadth of this content-based restriction of speech imposes an especially heavy burden on the Government to explain why a less restrictive provision would not be as effective as the CDA. It has not done so. . . . Particularly in the light of the absence of any detailed findings by the Congress, or even hearings addressing the special problems of the CDA, we are persuaded that the CDA is not narrowly tailored if that requirement has any meaning at all.

VIII. In an attempt to curtail the CDA's facial overbreadth, the Government advances three additional arguments. . . .

The Government first contends that, even though the CDA effectively censors discourse on many of the Internet's modalities—such as chat groups, newsgroups, and mail exploders—it is nonetheless constitutional because it provides a "reasonable opportunity" for speakers to engage in the restricted speech on the World Wide Web. This argument is unpersuasive because the CDA regulates speech on the basis of its content. A "time, place, and manner" analysis is therefore inapplicable. . . .

The Government also asserts that the "knowledge" requirement of both §§ 223(a) and (d), especially when coupled with the "specific child" element found in § 223(d), saves the CDA from overbreadth. Because both sections prohibit the dissemination of indecent messages only to persons known to be under 18, the Government argues, it does not require transmitters to "refrain from communicating indecent material to adults; they need only refrain from disseminating such materials to persons they know to be under 18." This argument ignores the fact that most Internet fora—including chat rooms, newsgroups, mail exploders, and the Web—are open to all comers. . . . Even the strongest reading of the "specific person" requirement of § 223(d) cannot save the statute. It would confer broad powers of censorship, in the form of a "heckler's

---

44. Transmitting obscenity and child pornography, whether via the Internet or other means, is already illegal under federal law for both adults and juveniles. See 18 U.S.C.A. §§ 1464–1465 (criminalizing obscenity); § 2251 (criminalizing child pornography). In fact, when Congress was considering the CDA, the Government expressed its view that the law was unnecessary because existing laws already authorized its ongoing efforts to prosecute obscenity, child pornography, and child solicitation.

veto,'' upon any opponent of indecent speech who might simply log on and inform the would-be discoursers that his 17–year-old child—a "specific person . . . under 18 years of age"—would be present.

Finally, we find no textual support for the Government's submission that material having scientific, educational, or other redeeming social value will necessarily fall outside the CDA's "patently offensive" and "indecent" prohibitions.

IX. The Government's three remaining arguments focus on the defenses provided in § 223(e)(5). First, relying on the "good faith, reasonable, effective, and appropriate actions" provision, the Government suggests that "tagging" provides a defense that saves the constitutionality of the Act. The suggestion assumes that transmitters may encode their indecent communications in a way that would indicate their contents, thus permitting recipients to block their reception with appropriate software. [But this] proposed screening software does not currently exist. Even if it did, there is no way to know whether a potential recipient will actually block the encoded material. Without the impossible knowledge that every guardian in America is screening for the "tag," the transmitter could not reasonably rely on its action to be "effective."

For its second and third arguments concerning defenses—which we can consider together—the Government relies on the latter half of § 223(e)(5), which applies when the transmitter has restricted access by requiring use of a verified credit card or adult identification. . . . Under the findings of the District Court, however, it is not economically feasible for most noncommercial speakers to employ such verification. Accordingly, this defense would not significantly narrow the statute's burden on noncommercial speech. Even with respect to the commercial pornographers that would be protected by the defense, the Government failed to adduce any evidence that these verification techniques actually preclude minors from posing as adults. . . .

X. At oral argument, the Government relied heavily on its ultimate fall-back position: If this Court should conclude that the CDA is insufficiently tailored, it urged, we should save the statute's constitutionality by honoring the severability clause, and construing nonseverable terms narrowly. In only one respect is this argument acceptable.

A severability clause requires textual provisions that can be severed. We will follow § 608's guidance by leaving constitutional textual elements of the statute intact in the one place where they are, in fact, severable. The "indecency" provision, § 223(a), applies to "any comment, request, suggestion, proposal, image, or other communication which is *obscene or indecent*." (Emphasis added.) Appellees do not challenge the application of the statute to obscene speech, which, they acknowledge, can be banned totally because it enjoys no First Amendment protection. As set forth by the statute, the restriction of "obscene" material enjoys a textual manifestation separate from that for "indecent" material, which we have held unconstitutional. Therefore, we will sever the term "or indecent" from the statute, leaving the rest of

§ 223(a) standing. In no other respect, however, can § 223(a) or § 223(d) be saved by such a textual surgery.

The Government also draws on an additional, less traditional aspect of the CDA's severability clause, which asks any reviewing court that holds the statute facially unconstitutional not to invalidate the CDA in application to "other persons or circumstances" that might be constitutionally permissible. [However, in] considering a facial challenge, this Court may impose a limiting construction on a statute only if it is "readily susceptible" to such a construction. The open-ended character of the CDA provides no guidance whatever for limiting its coverage.

This case is therefore unlike those in which we have construed a statute narrowly because the text or other source of congressional intent identified a clear line that this Court could draw.... This Court "will not rewrite a ... law to conform it to constitutional requirements."[50]

XI. In this Court, though not in the District Court, the Government asserts that—in addition to its interest in protecting children—its "[e]qually significant" interest in fostering the growth of the Internet provides an independent basis for upholding the constitutionality of the CDA [However,] we presume that governmental regulation of the content of speech is more likely to interfere with the free exchange of ideas than to encourage it. The interest in encouraging freedom of expression in a democratic society outweighs any theoretical but unproven benefit of censorship.

For the foregoing reasons, the judgment of the district court is affirmed.

It is so ordered.

JUSTICE O'CONNOR, with whom THE CHIEF JUSTICE joins, concurring in the judgment in part and dissenting in part.

I write separately to explain why I view the Communications Decency Act of 1996 (CDA) as little more than an attempt by Congress to create "adult zones" on the Internet. [T]he creation of such zones can be constitutionally sound. Despite the soundness of its purpose, however, portions of the CDA are unconstitutional because they stray from the blueprint our prior cases have developed for constructing a "zoning law" that passes constitutional muster.

[A] zoning law is valid if (I) it does not unduly restrict adult access to the material; and (ii) minors have no First Amendment right to read or view the banned material. As applied to the Internet as it exists in 1997, the "display" provision and some applications of the "indecency transmission" and "specific person" provisions fail to adhere to the first of these limiting principles by restricting adults' access to protected materials in certain circumstances. Unlike the Court, however, I would invalidate the provisions only in those circumstances.

---

50. [The] judicial rewriting of statutes would derogate Congress's "incentive to draft a narrowly tailored law in the first place".

I. ... Given the present state of cyberspace, I agree with the Court that the "display" provision cannot pass muster. Until gateway technology is available throughout cyberspace, and it is not in 1997, a speaker cannot be reasonably assured that the speech he displays will reach only adults because it is impossible to confine speech to an "adult zone." Thus, the only way for a speaker to avoid liability under the CDA is to refrain completely from using indecent speech. But this forced silence impinges on the First Amendment right of adults to make and obtain this speech....

The "indecency transmission" and "specific person" provisions present a closer issue, for they are not unconstitutional in all of their applications. [T]he "indecency transmission" provision makes it a crime to transmit knowingly an indecent message to a person the sender knows is under 18 years of age. § 223(a)(1)(B). The "specific person" provision proscribes the same conduct, although it does not as explicitly require the sender to know that the intended recipient of his indecent message is a minor. § 223(d)(1)(A). Appellant urges the Court to construe the provision to impose such a knowledge requirement, and I would do so.

So construed, both provisions are constitutional as applied to a conversation involving only an adult and one or more minors—*e.g.*, when an adult speaker sends an e-mail knowing the addressee is a minor, or when an adult and minor converse by themselves or with other minors in a chat room. In this context, these provisions are no different from the law we sustained in *Ginsberg*....

The analogy to *Ginsberg* breaks down, however, when more than one adult is a party to the conversation. If a minor enters a chat room otherwise occupied by adults, the CDA effectively requires the adults in the room to stop using indecent speech ..... The CDA is therefore akin to a law that makes it a crime for a bookstore owner to sell pornographic magazines to anyone once a minor enters his store. Even assuming such a law might be constitutional in the physical world as a reasonable alternative to excluding minors completely from the store, the absence of any means of excluding minors from chat rooms in cyberspace restricts the rights of adults to engage in indecent speech in those rooms. The "indecency transmission" and "specific person" provisions share this defect.

But these two provisions do not infringe on adults' speech in *all* situations.... I would therefore sustain the "indecency transmission" and "specific person" provisions to the extent they apply to the transmission of Internet communications where the party initiating the communication knows that all of the recipients are minors.

II. Whether the CDA substantially interferes with the First Amendment rights of minors, and thereby runs afoul of the second characteristic of valid zoning laws, presents a closer question. [A]ppellees have not carried their burden [to show "substantial" overbreadth in this facial challenge]. [T]he universe of speech constitutionally protected as to minors but banned by the CDA—*i.e.*, the universe of material that is "patently offensive," but which nonetheless has some redeeming value for minors or does not appeal to their prurient interest—is a very small one. . . . While discussions about prison rape or nude art, may have some redeeming education value for *adults*, they do not necessarily have any such value for *minors*, and under *Ginsberg*, minors only have a First Amendment right to obtain patently offensive material that has "redeeming social importance *for minors*." (emphasis added). There is also no evidence in the record to support the contention that "many [e]-mail transmissions from an adult to a minor are conversations between family members," *ante*, n. 32, and no support for the legal proposition that such speech is absolutely immune from regulation. Accordingly, in my view, the CDA does not burden a substantial amount of minors' constitutionally protected speech.

. . . Because the rights of adults are infringed only by the "display" provision and by the "indecency transmission" and "specific person" provisions as applied to communications involving more than one adult, I would invalidate the CDA only to that extent. Insofar as the "indecency transmission" and "specific person" provisions prohibit the use of indecent speech in communications between an adult and one or more minors, however, they can and should be sustained. The Court reaches a contrary conclusion, and from that holding that I respectfully dissent.

10–12.4 Public Indecency

BARNES v. GLEN THEATRE, INC.
501 U.S. 560, 111 S.Ct. 2456, 115 L.Ed.2d 504 (1991).

CHIEF JUSTICE REHNQUIST announced the judgment of the Court and delivered an opinion in which JUSTICES O'CONNOR and KENNEDY joined.

. . . The Kitty Kat Lounge, Inc. (Kitty Kat) is located in the city of South Bend. It sells alcoholic beverages and presents "go-go dancing." Its proprietor desires to present "totally nude dancing," but an applicable Indiana statute regulating public nudity requires that the dancers wear "pasties" and a "G-string" when they dance. . . . Respondent Glen Theatre, Inc., is an Indiana corporation with a place of business in South Bend. Its primary business is supplying so-called adult entertainment through written and printed materials, movie showings, and live entertainment at an enclosed "bookstore." The live entertainment at the "bookstore" consists of nude and seminude performances and showings of the female body through glass panels. Customers sit in a booth and insert coins into a timing mechanism that permits them to observe the live nude and seminude dancers for a period of time. [We] now hold that the Indiana statutory requirement that the dancers in the establishments involved in this case must wear pasties and a G-string does not violate the First Amendment.[1]

---

1. The Indiana Supreme Court [in prior　　litigation] appeared to give the public inde-

Several of our cases contain language suggesting that nude dancing of the kind involved here is expressive conduct protected by the First Amendment.... In *Schad v. Borough of Mount Ephraim,* [§ 10–12.2] we said that "[f]urthermore, as the state courts in this case recognized, nude dancing is not without its First Amendment protections from official regulation" (citations omitted). These statements support the conclusion of the Court of Appeals that nude dancing of the kind sought to be performed here is expressive conduct within the outer perimeters of the First Amendment, though we view it as only marginally so. This, of course, does not end our inquiry. We must determine the level of protection to be afforded to the expressive conduct at issue, and must determine whether the Indiana statute is an impermissible infringement of that protected activity.

Indiana, of course, has not banned nude dancing as such, but has proscribed public nudity across the board. The Supreme Court of Indiana has construed the Indiana statute to preclude nudity in what are essentially places of public accommodation such as the Glen Theatre and the Kitty Kat Lounge. [M]inors are excluded and there are no nonconsenting viewers. Respondents contend that while the state may license establishments such as the ones involved here, and limit the geographical area in which they do business, it may not in any way limit the performance of the dances within them without violating the First Amendment. The petitioner contends, on the other hand, that Indiana's restriction on nude dancing is a valid "time, place or manner" restriction....

The "time, place, or manner" test was developed for evaluating restrictions on expression taking place on public property which had been dedicated as a "public forum," although we have on at least one occasion applied it to conduct occurring on private property. See *Renton v. Playtime Theatres, Inc.,* [§ 10–12.2]. [T]his test has been interpreted to embody much the same standards as those set forth in *United States v. O'Brien,* [§ 10–10], and we turn, therefore, to the rule enunciated in *O'Brien.*

Applying the four-part *O'Brien* test ... , we find that Indiana's public indecency statute is justified despite its incidental limitations on some expressive activity. The public indecency statute is clearly within

---

cency statute a limiting construction to save it from a facial overbreadth attack:

"There is no right to appear nude in public. Rather, it *may* be constitutionally required to tolerate or to allow some nudity as a part of some larger form of expression meriting protection, when the communication of ideas is involved." *State v. Baysinger,* 272 Ind. 236, 247, 397 N.E.2d 580, 587 (1979)(emphasis added) appeals dism'd *sub nom. Clark v. Indiana,* 446 U.S. 931, and *Dove v. Indiana,* 449 U.S. 806 (1980).

Five years after *Baysinger,* however, the Indiana Supreme Court reversed a decision

of the Indiana Court of Appeals holding that the statute did "not apply to activity such as the theatrical appearances involved herein, which may not be prohibited absent a finding of obscenity," in a case involving a partially nude dance in the "Miss Erotica of Fort Wayne" contest. *Erhardt v. State,* 468 N.E.2d 224 (Ind.1984). The Indiana Supreme Court did not discuss the constitutional issues beyond a cursory comment that the statute had been upheld against constitutional attack in *Baysinger,* and Erhardt's conduct fell within the statutory prohibition.... [footnote repositioned] the constitutional power of the State and furthers substantial governmental interests. [T]he statute's purpose of protecting societal order and morality is clear from its text and history. Public indecency statutes of this sort are of ancient origin, and presently exist in at least 47 States. Public indecency, including nudity, was a criminal offense at common law.... Public nudity was considered an act *malum en se.* Public indecency statutes such as the one before us reflect moral disapproval of people appearing in the nude among strangers in public places. This public indecency[2] ... statute follows a long line of earlier Indiana statutes banning all public nudity....

This interest is unrelated to the suppression of free expression. Some may view restricting nudity on moral grounds as necessarily related to expression. We disagree. It can be argued, of course, that almost limitless types of conduct—including appearing in the nude in public—are "expressive," and in one sense of the word this is true. People who go about in the nude in public may be expressing something about themselves by so doing. But the court rejected this expansive notion of "expressive conduct" in *O'Brien*....

Respondents contend that even though prohibiting nudity in public generally may not be related to suppressing expression, prohibiting the performance of nude dancing is related to expression because the state seeks to prevent its erotic message. [W]e do not think that when Indiana applies its statute to the nude dancing in these nightclubs it is proscribing nudity because of the erotic message conveyed by the dancers. Presumably numerous other erotic performances are presented at these establishments and similar clubs without any interference from the state, so long as the performers wear a scant amount of clothing. Likewise, the requirement that the dancers don pasties and a G-string does not deprive the dance of whatever erotic message it conveys; it simply makes the message slightly less graphic. The perceived evil that Indiana seeks to address is not erotic dancing, but public nudity. The appearance of people of all shapes, sizes and ages in the nude at a beach, for example, would convey little if any erotic message, yet the state still seeks to prevent it. Public nudity is the evil the state seeks to prevent, whether or not it is combined with expressive activity. [W]hile the dancing to which [the Indiana statute] was applied had a communicative element, it was not the dancing that was prohibited, but simply its being done in the nude.

2. Indiana Code § 35–45–4–1 (1988) provides:

"Public Indecency

"Sec. 1. (a) A person who knowingly or intentionally, in a public place:

"(1) engages in sexual intercourse; (2) engages in deviate sexual conduct; (3) appears in a state of nudity; or (4) fondles the genitals of himself or another person;

commits public indecency, a Class A misdemeanor.

"(b) 'Nudity' means the showing of the human male or female genitals, pubic area, or buttocks with less than a fully opaque covering, the showing of the female breast with less than a fully opaque covering of any part of the nipple, or the showing of the covered male genitals in a discernibly turgid state." [footnote repositioned]

The fourth part of the *O'Brien* test requires that the incidental restriction on First Amendment freedom be no greater than is essential to the furtherance of the governmental interest. As indicated in the discussion above, the governmental interest served by the text of the prohibition is societal disapproval of nudity in public places and among strangers. The statutory prohibition is not a means to some greater end, but an end in itself. It is without cavil that the public indecency statute is "narrowly tailored;" Indiana's requirement that the dancers wear at least pasties and a G-string is modest, and the bare minimum necessary to achieve the state's purpose.

The judgment of the Court of Appeals accordingly is

Reversed.

JUSTICE SCALIA, concurring in the judgment.

I agree that the judgment of the Court of Appeals must be reversed. In my view, however, the challenged regulation must be upheld, not because it survives some lower level of First–Amendment scrutiny, but because, as a general law regulating conduct and not specifically directed at expression, it is not subject to First–Amendment scrutiny at all.... The intent to convey a "message of eroticism" (or any other message) is not a necessary element of the statutory offense of public indecency; nor does one commit that statutory offense by conveying the most explicit "message of eroticism," so long as he does not commit any of the four specified acts in the process.

. . . Were it the case that Indiana *in practice* targeted only expressive nudity, while turning a blind eye to nude beaches and unclothed purveyors of hot dogs and machine tools, it might be said that what posed as a regulation of conduct in general was in reality a regulation of only communicative conduct. Respondents have adduced no evidence of that. Indiana officials have brought many public indecency prosecutions for activities having no communicative element.[2]

The dissent confidently asserts, that the purpose of restricting nudity in public places in general is to protect nonconsenting parties from offense; and argues that since only consenting, admission-paying patrons see respondents dance, that purpose cannot apply and the only remaining purpose must relate to the communicative elements of the performance. Perhaps the dissenters believe that "offense to others" *ought* to be the only reason for restricting nudity in public places generally, but there is no basis for thinking that our society has ever shared that Thoreauvian "you-may-do-what-you-like-so-long-as-it-does-not-injure-someone-else" beau ideal—much less for thinking that it was written into the Constitution. The purpose of Indiana's nudity law would be violated, I think, if 60,000 fully consenting adults crowded into the

---

2. Respondents also contend that the statute, as interpreted, is not content-neutral in the expressive conduct to which it applies, since it allegedly does not apply to nudity in theatrical productions. I am not sure that theater versus non-theater represents a distinction based on content rather than format, but assuming that it does the argument nonetheless fails for the reason the plurality describes, *ante*, n. 1.

Hoosierdome to display their genitals to one another, even if there were not an offended innocent in the crowd. Our society prohibits, and all human societies have prohibited, certain activities not because they harm others but because they are considered, in the traditional phrase, *"contra bonos mores,"* *i.e.,* immoral. In American society, such prohibitions have included, for example, sadomasochism, cockfighting, bestiality, suicide, drug use, prostitution, and sodomy. While there may be great diversity of view on whether various of these prohibitions should exist (though I have found few ready to abandon, in principle, all of them) there is no doubt that, absent specific constitutional protection for the conduct involved, the Constitution does not prohibit them simply because they regulate "morality." See *Bowers v. Hardwick.* See also *Paris Adult Theatre I v. Slaton.* The purpose of the Indiana statute, as both its text and the manner of its enforcement demonstrate, is to enforce the traditional moral belief that people should not expose their private parts indiscriminately, regardless of whether those who see them are disedified. Since that is so, the dissent has no basis for positing that, where only thoroughly edified adults are present, the purpose must be repression of communication.[3]

Since the Indiana regulation is a general law not specifically targeted at expressive conduct, its application to such conduct does not in my view implicate the First Amendment. The First Amendment explicitly protects "the freedom of speech [and] of the press"—oral and written speech—not "expressive conduct." When any law restricts speech, even for a purpose that has nothing to do with the suppression of communication (for instance, to reduce noise, to regulate election campaigns, or to prevent littering), we insist that it meet the high, First–Amendment standard of justification. But virtually *every* law restricts conduct, and virtually *any* prohibited conduct can be performed for an expressive purpose—if only expressive of the fact that the actor disagrees with the prohibition. It cannot reasonably be demanded, therefore, that every restriction of expression incidentally produced by a general law regulating conduct pass normal First–Amendment scrutiny, or even—as some of our cases have suggested, see *e.g., United States v. O'Brien,*—that it be justified by an "important or substantial" government interest. [W]e have never invalidated the application of a general law simply because the conduct that it reached was being engaged in for expressive purposes and the government could not demonstrate a sufficiently important state interest.

---

3. The dissent, also misunderstands what is meant by the term "general law." I do not mean that the law restricts the targeted conduct in all places at all times. A law is "general" for the present purposes if it regulates conduct without regard to whether that conduct is expressive. Concededly, Indiana bans nudity in public places, but not within the privacy of the home. (That is not surprising, since the common law offense, and the traditional moral prohibition, runs against *public* nudity, not against all nudity.) But that confirms, rather than refutes, the general nature of the law: one may not go nude in public, whether or not one intends thereby to convey a message, and similarly one *may* go nude in private, again whether or not that nudity is expressive.

This is not to say that the First Amendment affords no protection to expressive conduct. Where the government prohibits conduct *precisely because of its communicative attributes,* we hold the regulation unconstitutional. See, *e.g., United States v. Eichman,* (burning flag); *Texas v. Johnson,* (same).[4] In each of the foregoing cases, we explicitly found that suppressing communication was the object of the regulation of conduct. Where that has not been the case, however—where suppression of communicative use of the conduct was merely the incidental effect of forbidding the conduct for other reasons—we have allowed the regulation to stand. *O'Brien,* (law banning destruction of draft card upheld in application against cardburning to protest war).

All our holdings (though admittedly not some of our discussion) support the conclusion that "the only First Amendment analysis applicable to laws that do not directly or indirectly impede speech is the threshold inquiry of whether the purpose of the law is to suppress communication. If not, that is the end of the matter so far as First Amendment guarantees are concerned; if so, the court then proceeds to determine whether there is substantial justification for the proscription." Such a regime ensures that the government does not act to suppress communication, without requiring that all conduct-restricting regulation (which means in effect all regulation) survive an enhanced level of scrutiny....

JUSTICE SOUTER, concurring in the judgment.

[I] rest my concurrence in the judgment, not on the possible sufficiency of society's moral views to justify the limitations at issue, but on the State's substantial interest in combating the secondary effects of adult entertainment establishments of the sort typified by respondents' establishments. It is, of course, true that this justification has not been articulated by Indiana's legislature or by its courts. ... Our appropriate focus is not an empirical enquiry into the actual intent of the enacting legislature, but rather the existence or not of a current governmental interest in the service of which the challenged application of the statute may be constitutional.... The type of entertainment respondents seek to provide is plainly of the same character as that at issue in *Renton* [and] *American Mini Theatres,* [§ 10–12.2]. ... I do not believe that a State is required affirmatively to undertake to litigate this issue repeatedly in every case....

JUSTICE WHITE, with whom JUSTICE MARSHALL, JUSTICE BLACKMUN, & JUSTICE STEVENS join, dissenting.

4. It is easy to conclude that conduct has been forbidden because of its communicative attributes when the conduct in question is what the Court has called "inherently expressive," and what I would prefer to call "conventionally expressive"—such as flying a red flag. I mean by that phrase (as I assume the Court means by "inherently expressive") conduct that is normally engaged in for the purpose of communicating an idea, or perhaps an emotion, to someone else. [E]ven if [dancing fits this description], this law is directed against nudity, not dancing. Nudity is *not* normally engaged in for the purpose of communicating an idea or an emotion.

The Court's analysis is erroneous in several respects. Both the Court and Justice Scalia in his concurring opinion overlook a fundamental and critical aspect of our cases upholding the States' exercise of their police powers. None of the cases they rely upon, including *O'Brien* and *Bowers v. Hardwick,* involved anything less than truly *general* proscriptions on individual conduct. In *O'Brien,* for example, individuals were prohibited from destroying their draft cards at any time and in any place, even in completely private places such as the home. Likewise, in *Bowers,* the State prohibited sodomy, regardless of where the conduct might occur, including the home as was true in that case.... By contrast, in this case Indiana does not suggest that its statute applies to, or could be applied to, nudity wherever it occurs, including the home. We do not understand the Court or Justice Scalia to be suggesting that Indiana could constitutionally enact such an intrusive prohibition, nor do we think such a suggestion would be tenable....

We are told by the Attorney General of Indiana that, in *State v. Baysinger,* 272 Ind. 236, 397 N.E.2d 580 (1979), the Indiana Supreme Court held that the statute at issue here cannot and does not prohibit nudity as a part of some larger form of expression meriting protection when the communication of ideas is involved. Petitioners also state that the evils sought to be avoided by applying the statute in this case would not obtain in the case of theatrical productions, such as *Salome* or *Hair.* Neither is there any evidence that the State has attempted to apply the statute to nudity in performances such as plays, ballets or operas. "No arrests have ever been made for nudity as part of a play or ballet." App. 19 (affidavit of Sgt. Timothy Corbett).

Thus, the Indiana statute is not a *general* prohibition of the type we have upheld in prior cases. As a result, the Court's and Justice Scalia's simple references to the State's general interest in promoting societal order and morality is not sufficient justification for a statute which concededly reaches a significant amount of protected expressive activity. Instead, in applying the *O'Brien* test, we are obligated to carefully examine the reasons the State has chosen to regulate this expressive conduct in a less than general statute. In other words, when the State enacts a law which draws a line between expressive conduct which is regulated and nonexpressive conduct of the same type which is not regulated, *O'Brien* places the burden on the State to justify the distinctions it has made. Closer inquiry as to the purpose of the statute is surely appropriate.

... The purpose of forbidding people from appearing nude in parks, beaches, hot dog stands, and like public places is to protect others from offense. But that could not possibly be the purpose of preventing nude dancing in theaters and barrooms since the viewers are exclusively consenting adults who pay money to see these dances. The purpose of the proscription in these contexts is to protect the viewers from what the State believes is the harmful message that nude dancing communicates.

[T]he Court concedes that nude dancing conveys an erotic message and concedes that the message would be muted if the dancers wore pasties and G-strings. Indeed, the emotional or erotic impact of the dance is intensified by the nudity of the performers.... The nudity is itself an expressive component of the dance, not merely incidental "conduct." We have previously pointed out that " '[n]udity alone' does not place otherwise protected material outside the mantle of the First Amendment." *Schad v. Mt. Ephraim.*

This being the case, it cannot be that the statutory prohibition is unrelated to expressive conduct. Since the State permits the dancers to perform if they wear pasties and G-strings but forbids nude dancing, it is precisely because of the distinctive, expressive content of the nude dancing performances at issue in this case that the State seeks to apply the statutory prohibition. It is only because nude dancing performances may generate emotions and feelings of eroticism and sensuality among the spectators that the State seeks to regulate such expressive activity, apparently on the assumption that creating or emphasizing such thoughts and ideas in the minds of the spectators may lead to increased prostitution and the degradation of women. But generating thoughts, ideas, and emotions is the essence of communication. The nudity element of nude dancing performances cannot be neatly pigeonholed as mere "conduct" independent of any expressive component of the dance....

Justice Scalia's views are similar to those of the Court and suffer from the same defects. [T]he premise for the Justice's position—that the statute is a *general* law of the type our cases contemplate—is nonexistent in this case. Reference to Justice Scalia's own hypothetical makes this clear. We agree with Justice Scalia that the Indiana statute would not permit 60,000 consenting Hoosiers to expose themselves to each other in the Hoosierdome. No one can doubt, however, that those same 60,000 Hoosiers would be perfectly free to drive to their respective homes all across Indiana and, once there, to parade around, cavort, and revel in the nude for hours in front of relatives and friends. It is difficult to see why the State's interest in morality is any less in that situation, especially if, as Justice Scalia seems to suggest, nudity is inherently evil, but clearly the statute does not reach such activity. As we pointed out earlier, the State's failure to enact a truly general proscription requires closer scrutiny of the reasons for the distinctions the State has drawn....

Notes

California v. LaRue, 409 U.S. 109, 93 S.Ct. 390, 34 L.Ed.2d 342 (1972) upheld the facial constitutionality of a statute prohibiting acts of "gross sexuality," including the display of the genitals and live or filmed performances of sexual acts, in establishments licensed by the State to serve liquor. The Court assumed that not all of the prohibited acts might be obscene, but argued that the statute was within the State's broad power under the Twenty-first Amendment to regulate the sale of liquor. Later, *New*

York State Liquor Authority v. Bellanca, 452 U.S. 714, 101 S.Ct. 2599, 69 L.Ed.2d 357 (1981)(per curiam), held (again relying on the Twenty-first Amendment) that it was constitutional for the state to forbid topless dancing in an establishment licensed to serve liquor. In *44 Liquormart, Inc. v. Rhode Island*, 517 U.S. 484, 116 S.Ct. 1495, 134 L.Ed.2d 711 (1996) the Court invalidated a state law that banned accurate retail liquor advertisements except at the point of sale. Stevens, J., joined by Scalia, Kennedy, Souter, & Ginsburg, JJ., referred to *Bellanca* and *California v. LaRue* and said that the result would have been "precisely the same" even if there had been no reliance on the Twenty-first Amendment: "Without questioning the holding in *LaRue*, we now disavow its reasoning insofar as it relied on the Twenty-first Amendment. [W]e now hold that the Twenty-first Amendment does not qualify the constitutional prohibition against laws abridging the freedom of speech embodied in the First Amendment."

10–12.5 *Prior Restraint*

FREEDMAN v. MARYLAND

380 U.S. 51, 85 S.Ct. 734, 13 L.Ed.2d 649 (1965).

MR. JUSTICE BRENNAN delivered the opinion of the Court.

Appellant sought to challenge the constitutionality of the Maryland motion picture censorship statute, and exhibited the film "Revenge at Daybreak" at his Baltimore theatre without first submitting the picture to the State Board of Censors as required by § 2 thereof. The State concedes that the picture does not violate the statutory standards and would have received a license if properly submitted, but the appellant was convicted of a § 2 violation despite his contention that the statute in its entirety unconstitutionally impaired freedom of expression. We reverse.

In *Times Film Corp. v. City of Chicago*, 365 U.S. 43, 81 S.Ct. 391, 5 L.Ed.2d 403 [1961], we considered and upheld a requirement of submission of motion pictures in advance of exhibition [but we only held that a prior restraint was not necessarily unconstitutional under all circumstances.] [A]ccepting the rule in *Times Film*, [petitioner here] argues that § 2 constitutes an invalid prior restraint because, in the context of the remainder of the statute, it presents a danger of unduly suppressing protected expression. He focuses particularly on the procedure for an initial decision by the censorship board, which, without any judicial participation, effectively bars exhibition of any disapproved film, unless and until the exhibitor undertakes a time-consuming appeal to the Maryland courts and succeeds in having the Board's decision reversed.

. . . The administration of a censorship system for motion pictures presents peculiar dangers to constitutionally protected speech. Unlike a prosecution for obscenity, a censorship proceeding puts the initial burden on the exhibitor or distributor. Because the censor's business is to censor, there inheres the danger that he may well be less responsive than a court—part of an independent branch of government—to the constitutionally protected interest in free expression. And if it is made unduly onerous, by reason of delay or otherwise, to seek judicial review, the censor's determination may in practice be final.

Applying the settled rule of our cases, we hold that a noncriminal process which requires the prior submission of a film to a censor avoids constitutional infirmity only if it takes place under procedural safeguards designed to obviate the dangers of a censorship system. First, the burden of proving that the film is unprotected expression must rest on the censor. . . . Second, while the State may require advance submission of all films, in order to proceed effectively to bar all showings of unprotected films, the requirement cannot be administered in a manner which would lend an effect of finality to the censor's determination whether a film constitutes protected expression. [B]ecause only a judicial determination in an adversary proceeding ensures the necessary sensitivity to freedom of expression, only a procedure requiring a judicial determination suffices to impose a valid final restraint. To this end, the exhibitor must be assured, by statute or authoritative judicial construction, that the censor will, within a specified brief period, either issue a license or go to court to restrain showing the film. Any restraint imposed in advance of a final judicial determination on the merits must similarly be limited to preservation of the status quo for the shortest fixed period compatible with sound judicial resolution. Moreover, we are well aware that, even after expiration of a temporary restraint, an administrative refusal to license, signifying the censor's view that the film is unprotected, may have a discouraging effect on the exhibitor. Therefore, the procedure must also assure a prompt final judicial decision, to minimize the deterrent effect of an interim and possibly erroneous denial of a license.

Without these safeguards, it may prove too burdensome to seek review of the censor's determination. Particularly in the case of motion pictures, it may take very little to deter exhibition in a given locality. The exhibitor's stake in any one picture may be insufficient to warrant a protracted and onerous course of litigation. The distributor, on the other hand, may be equally unwilling to accept the burdens and delays of litigation in a particular area when, without such difficulties, he can freely exhibit his film in most of the rest of the country; for we are told that only four States and a handful of municipalities have active censorship laws.

It is readily apparent that the Maryland procedural scheme does not satisfy these criteria. First, once the censor disapproves the film, the exhibitor must assume the burden of instituting judicial proceedings and of persuading the courts that the film is protected expression. Second, once the Board has acted against a film, exhibition is prohibited pending judicial review, however protracted. Under the statute, appellant could have been convicted if he had shown the film after unsuccessfully seeking a license, even though no court had ever ruled on the obscenity of the film. Third, it is abundantly clear that the Maryland statute provides no assurance of prompt judicial determination. We hold, therefore, that appellant's conviction must be reversed. The Maryland scheme fails to provide adequate safeguards against undue inhibition of protected expression, and this renders the § 2 requirement of prior submission of films to the Board an invalid previous restraint. . . .

MR. JUSTICE DOUGLAS, whom MR. JUSTICE BLACK joins, concurring.

On several occasions I have indicated my view that movies are entitled to the same degree and kind of protection under the First Amendment as other forms of expression. For the reasons there stated, I do not believe any form of censorship—no matter how speedy or prolonged it may be—is permissible. . . .

Notes

Alexander v. United States, 509 U.S. 544, 113 S.Ct. 2766, 125 L.Ed.2d 441 (1993). Defendant was convicted of violating federal obscenity laws, based on a finding that 7 items (4 magazines and 3 videotapes) sold at several of defendant's stores were constitutionally obscene. These obscenity convictions were also the predicates for his three RICO (Racketeer Influenced and Corrupt Organizations Act) convictions. The trial court imposed a prison term of 6 years, fined defendant $100,000, ordered him to pay the costs of prosecution, incarceration, and supervised release, and—pursuant to his RICO conviction—ordered him to forfeit his wholesale and retail businesses, and all their assets, and almost $9 million acquired through racketeering activity. (The Government destroyed these materials, after deciding that it did not want to go into the business of selling indecent materials to the public, even if they were not legally "obscene.")

Defendant argued that the RICO forfeiture provisions were a prior restraint on speech and overbroad. Rehnquist, C.J., for the Court, rejected that argument. First, the forfeiture was not a prior restraint on speech but a permissible criminal punishment. There was no legal restraint on defendant's ability to engage in any expressive activity. The forfeiture only prevented him from financing his expressive activities with assets derived from *prior* racketeering offenses. This is not a case where the Government seized materials because it suspected them to be obscene, without a prior judicial determination as to obscenity. Rather, defendant's RICO convictions caused his assets to be forfeited because they were directly related to his *past* racketeering violations. The forfeit, in short, was a punishment for past conduct, not a restraint on future speech. This result is no more chilling than the threat of a prison term or a large fine, which are clearly constitutional. The Court then remanded for the lower courts to determine whether the forfeiture, on top of his prison term and fine, is an "excessive" fine under the Eighth Amendment.

Kennedy, J., joined by Blackmun & Stevens, JJ., and in part by Souter, J., dissented. Souter, J., concurred in the judgment in part and dissented in part, arguing that the First Amendment forbids the forfeiture of defendant's expressive materials "in the absence of an adjudication that it is obscene or otherwise of unprotected character. . . . "

Chapter 11

RELIGION

11–1. FINANCIAL ASSISTANCE TO RELIGION

11–1.1 Tax Exemption to Churches

WALZ v. TAX COMMISSION OF CITY OF NEW YORK
397 U.S. 664, 90 S.Ct. 1409, 25 L.Ed.2d 697 (1970).

Mr. Chief Justice Burger delivered the opinion of the Court.

Appellant, owner of real estate in Richmond County, New York, sought an injunction in the New York courts to prevent the New York City Tax Commission from granting property tax exemptions to religious organizations for religious properties used solely for religious worship. The exemption from state taxes is authorized by Art. 16, § 1, of the New York Constitution.... The essence of appellant's contention was that the New York City Tax Commission's grant of an exemption to church property indirectly requires the appellant to make a contribution to religious bodies and thereby violates provisions prohibiting establishment of religion under the First Amendment which under the Fourteenth Amendment is binding on the States....

The Establishment and Free Exercise Clauses of the First Amendment are not the most precisely drawn portions of the Constitution. The sweep of the absolute prohibitions in the Religion Clauses may have been calculated; but the purpose was to state an objective, not to write a statute. In attempting to articulate the scope of the two Religion Clauses, the Court's opinions reflect the limitations inherent in formulating general principles on a case-by-case basis. The considerable internal inconsistency in the opinions of the Court derives from what, in retrospect, may have been too sweeping utterances on aspects of these clauses that seemed clear in relation to the particular cases but have limited meaning as general principles.

The Court has struggled to find a neutral course between the two Religion Clauses, both of which are cast in absolute terms, and either of which, if expanded to a logical extreme, would tend to clash with the other.... The general principle deducible from the First Amendment and all that has been said by the Court is this: that we will not tolerate either governmentally established religion or governmental interference with religion. Short of those expressly proscribed governmental acts there is room for play in the joints productive of a benevolent neutrality which will permit religious exercise to exist without sponsorship and without interference....

The legislative purpose of the property tax exemption is neither the advancement nor the inhibition of religion; it is neither sponsorship nor hostility. New York, in common with the other States, has determined that certain entities that exist in a harmonious relationship to the community at large, and that foster its "moral or mental improvement," should not be inhibited in their activities by property taxation or the hazard of loss of those properties for nonpayment of taxes. It has not singled out one particular church or religious group or even churches as such; rather, it has granted exemption to all houses of religious worship within a broad class of property owned by nonprofit, quasi-public corporations which include hospitals, libraries, playgrounds, scientific, professional, historical, and patriotic groups. The State has an affirmative policy that considers these groups as beneficial and stabilizing influences in community life and finds this classification useful, desirable, and in the public interest. Qualification for tax exemption is not perpetual or immutable; some tax-exempt groups lose that status when their activities take them outside the classification and new entities can come into being and qualify for exemption.

Governments have not always been tolerant of religious activity, and hostility toward religion has taken many shapes and forms—economic, political, and sometimes harshly oppressive. Grants of exemption historically reflect the concern of authors of constitutions and statutes as to the latent dangers inherent in the imposition of property taxes; exemption constitutes a reasonable and balanced attempt to guard against those dangers. The limits of permissible state accommodation to religion are by no means co-extensive with the noninterference mandated by the Free Exercise Clause. To equate the two would be to deny a national heritage with roots in the Revolution itself. We cannot read New York's statute as attempting to establish religion; it is simply sparing the exercise of religion from the burden of property taxation levied on private profit institutions.

We find it unnecessary to justify the tax exemption on the social welfare services or "good works" that some churches perform for parishioners and others—family counseling, aid to the elderly and the infirm, and to children. Churches vary substantially in the scope of such services; [t]o give emphasis to so variable an aspect of the work of religious bodies would introduce an element of governmental evaluation and standards as to the worth of particular social welfare programs, thus producing a kind of continuing day-to-day relationship which the policy of neutrality seeks to minimize....

Determining that the legislative purpose of tax exemption is not aimed at establishing, sponsoring, or supporting religion does not end the inquiry, however. We must also be sure that the end result—the effect—is not an excessive government entanglement with religion. The test is inescapably one of degree. Either course, taxation of churches or exemption, occasions some degree of involvement with religion. Elimination of exemption would tend to expand the involvement of government by giving rise to tax valuation of church property, tax liens, tax foreclosures, and the direct confrontations and conflicts that follow in the train of those legal processes.

Granting tax exemptions to churches necessarily operates to afford an indirect economic benefit and also gives rise to some, but yet a lesser, involvement than taxing them. In analyzing either alternative the questions are whether the involvement is excessive, and whether it is a continuing one calling for official and continuing surveillance leading to an impermissible degree of entanglement. Obviously a direct money subsidy would be a relationship pregnant with involvement and, as with most governmental grant programs, could encompass sustained and detailed administrative relationships for enforcement of statutory or administrative standards, but that is not this case. The hazards of churches supporting government are hardly less in their potential than the hazards of government supporting churches; each relationship carries some involvement rather than the desired insulation and separation. We cannot ignore the instances in history when church support of government led to the kind of involvement we seek to avoid.

The grant of a tax exemption is not sponsorship since the government does not transfer part of its revenue to churches but simply abstains from demanding that the church support the state. No one has ever suggested that tax exemption has converted libraries, art galleries, or hospitals into arms of the state or put employees "on the public payroll." There is no genuine nexus between tax exemption and establishment of religion. As Mr. Justice Holmes commented in a related context "a page of history is worth a volume of logic." The exemption creates only a minimal and remote involvement between church and state and far less than taxation of churches. It restricts the fiscal relationship between church and state, and tends to complement and reinforce the desired separation insulating each from the other.

Separation in this context cannot mean absence of all contact; the complexities of modern life inevitably produce some contact and the fire and police protection received by houses of religious worship are no more than incidental benefits accorded all persons or institutions within a State's boundaries, along with many other exempt organizations. The appellant has not established even an arguable quantitative correlation between the payment of an ad valorem property tax and the receipt of these municipal benefits.

[A]n unbroken practice of according the exemption to churches, openly and by affirmative state action, not covertly or by state inaction, is not something to be lightly cast aside.... If tax exemption can be seen as this first step toward "establishment" of religion, as Mr. Justice Douglas fears, the second step has been long in coming. Any move that realistically "establishes" a church or tends to do so can be dealt with "while this Court sits." ...

MR. JUSTICE DOUGLAS, dissenting....

Churches perform some functions that a State would constitutionally be empowered to perform. I refer to nonsectarian social welfare operations such as the care of orphaned children and the destitute and people who are sick. A tax exemption to agencies performing those functions would therefore be as constitutionally proper as the grant of direct subsidies to them. Under the First Amendment a State may not, however, provide worship if private groups fail to do so....

That is a major difference between churches on the one hand and the rest of the nonprofit organizations on the other. Government could provide or finance operas, hospitals, historical societies, and all the rest because they represent social welfare programs within the reach of the police power. In contrast, government may not provide or finance worship because of the Establishment Clause any more than it may single out "atheistic" or "agnostic" centers or groups and create or finance them....

The exemptions provided here insofar as welfare projects are concerned may have the ring of neutrality. But subsidies either through direct grant or tax exemption for sectarian causes, whether carried on by church *qua* church or by church *qua* welfare agency, must be treated differently, lest we in time allow the church *qua* church to be on the public payroll, which, I fear, is imminent....

[The concurring opinion of BRENNAN, J., and the opinion of HARLAN, J., are omitted.]

Notes

Texas Monthly, Inc. v. Bullock, 489 U.S. 1, 109 S.Ct. 890, 103 L.Ed.2d 1 (1989) invalidated—6 to 3, with no majority opinion—a Texas statute that exempted from its sales tax periodicals "published or distributed by a religious faith and that consist wholly of writings promulgating the teaching of the faith and books that consist wholly of writings sacred to a religious faith." Brennan, J., announced the judgment of the Court and delivered an opinion joined by Marshall & Stevens, JJ. He argued that the law violates the Establishment Clause because the exemption was "confined exclusively to publications advancing the tenets of a religious faith." The "breadth of New York's property tax exemption was essential to our holding" in *Walz.* "If the State chose to subsidize, by means of a tax exemption, all groups that contributed to the community's cultural, intellectual, and moral betterment, then the exemption for religious publications could be retained, provided that the exemption swept as widely as the property tax exemption we upheld in *Walz.*"

White, J., concurring in the judgment, argued that the law violated the press clause of the first amendment because Texas discriminates on the basis of the content of the publications (periodicals "that consist wholly of writings promulgating the teachings of the faith") in determining whether to grant the exemption. Blackmun, J., joined by O'Connor, J., concurred in the judgment: "a tax exemption *limited to* the sale of religious literature by religious organizations violates the Establishment Clause." (emphasis in original). Texas engaged in "preferential support for the communication of religious messages."

Scalia, J., joined by Rehnquist, C.J. & Kennedy, J., dissented. The opinions of Brennan and Blackmun, JJ., he said, are based on the bold assertion that "government may not 'convey a message of endorsement of religion,' "an assertion that is unsupported given such realities as the text of the Declaration of Independence, the inscriptions on our coins, and the invocation with which sessions of our Court are opened. *Walz,* Scalia said, rested "upon the more direct proposition that 'exemption constitutes a reasonable and balanced attempt to guard against' the 'latent dangers' of governmental hostility towards religion 'inherent in the imposition of property taxes.' " *Walz* had specifically found "it unnecessary to justify the tax exemption on the social welfare services or 'good works' that some churches perform for parishioners and others. . . . "

Jimmy Swaggart Ministries v. Board of Equalization, 493 U.S. 378, 110 S.Ct. 688, 107 L.Ed.2d 796 (1990) unanimously held that the religion clauses do not prevent a state from imposing generally applicable sales and use taxes to sales of books, tapes, and other religious and nonreligious merchandise by religious organizations. Such sales and use taxes are to be distinguished from flat license taxes: because license taxes are fixed in amount and unrelated to the scope of the activities or to revenues received, they operate as preconditions or prior restraints on the exercise of religious freedom.

11–1.2 Elementary and Secondary Schools

ZORACH v. CLAUSON

343 U.S. 306, 72 S.Ct. 679, 96 L.Ed. 954 (1952).

Mr. Justice Douglas delivered the opinion of the Court.

New York City has a program which permits its public schools to release students during the school day so that they may leave the school buildings and school grounds and go to religious centers for religious instruction or devotional exercises. A student is released on written request of his parents. Those not released stay in the classrooms. The churches make weekly reports to the schools, sending a list of children who have been released from public school but who have not reported for religious instruction.

This "released time" program involves neither religious instruction in public school classrooms nor the expenditure of public funds. All costs, including the application blanks are paid by the religious organizations. The case is therefore unlike *McCollum v. Board of Education,* 333 U.S.

203, 68 S.Ct. 461, 92 L.Ed. 649, which involved a "released time" program from Illinois. In that case the [public school] classrooms were turned over to religious instructors. We accordingly held that the program violated the First Amendment which (by reason of the Fourteenth Amendment) prohibits the states from establishing religion or prohibiting its free exercise.

Appellants, who are taxpayers and residents of New York City and whose children attend its public schools,[4] challenge the present law, contending it is in essence not different from the one involved in the *McCollum* case. Their argument, stated elaborately in various ways, reduces itself to this: the weight and influence of the school is put behind a program for religious instruction; public school teachers police it, keeping tab on students who are released; the classroom activities come to a halt while the students who are released for religious instruction are on leave; the school is a crutch on which the churches are leaning for support in their religious training; without the cooperation of the schools this "released time" program, like the one in the *McCollum* case, would be futile and ineffective. . . .

It takes obtuse reasoning to inject any issue of the "free exercise" of religion into the present case. No one is forced to go to the religious classroom and no religious exercise or instruction is brought to the classrooms of the public schools. . . . If in fact coercion were used, if it were established that any one or more teachers were using their office to persuade or force students to take the religious instruction, a wholly different case would be presented. Hence we put aside that claim of coercion both as respects the "free exercise" of religion and "an establishment of religion" within the meaning of the First Amendment.

Moreover, apart from that claim of coercion, we do not see how New York by this type of "released time" program has made a law respecting an establishment of religion within the meaning of the First Amendment. There is much talk of the separation of Church and State in the history of the Bill of Rights and in the decisions clustering around the First Amendment. There cannot be the slightest doubt that the First Amendment reflects the philosophy that Church and State should be separated. And so far as interference with the "free exercise" of religion and an "establishment" of religion are concerned, the separation must be complete and unequivocal. The First Amendment within the scope of its coverage permits no exception; the prohibition is absolute. The First Amendment, however, does not say that in every and all respects there shall be a separation of Church and State. Rather, it studiously defines the manner, the specific ways, in which there shall be no concert or union or dependency one on the other. That is the common sense of the matter. Otherwise the state and religion would be aliens to each other— hostile, suspicious, and even unfriendly. Churches could not be required

---

4. No problem of this Court's jurisdiction is posed in this case since, unlike the appellants in *Doremus v. Board of Education*, 342 U.S. 429, 475, 72 S.Ct. 394, 96 L.Ed. 475, appellants here are parents of children currently attending schools subject to the released time program.

to pay even property taxes. Municipalities would not be permitted to render police or fire protection to religious groups. Policemen who help parishioners into their places of worship would violate the Constitution. Prayers in our legislative halls; the appeals to the Almighty in the messages of the Chief Executive; the proclamations making Thanksgiving Day a holiday; "so help me God" in our courtroom oaths—these and all other references to the Almighty that run through our laws, our public rituals, our ceremonies would be flouting the First Amendment. A fastidious atheist or agnostic could even object to the supplication with which the Court opens each session: "God save the United States and this Honorable Court."

We would have to press the concept of separation of Church and State to these extremes to condemn the present law on constitutional grounds. The nullification of this law would have wide and profound effects. A Catholic student applies to his teacher for permission to leave the school during hours on a Holy Day of Obligation to attend a mass. A Jewish student asks his teacher for permission to be excused for Yom Kippur. A Protestant wants the afternoon off for a family baptismal ceremony. In each case the teacher requires parental consent in writing. In each case the teacher, in order to make sure the student is not a truant, goes further and requires a report from the priest, the rabbi, or the minister. The teacher in other words cooperates in a religious program to the extent of making it possible for her students to participate in it. . . .

We are a religious people whose institutions presuppose a Supreme Being. We guarantee the freedom to worship as one chooses. We make room for as wide a variety of beliefs and creeds as the spiritual needs of man deem necessary. We sponsor an attitude on the part of government that shows no partiality to any one group and that lets each flourish according to the zeal of its adherents and the appeal of its dogma. When the state encourages religious instruction or cooperates with religious authorities by adjusting the schedule of public events to sectarian needs, it follows the best of our traditions. For it then respects the religious nature of our people and accommodates the public service to their spiritual needs. To hold that it may not would be to find in the Constitution a requirement that the government show a callous indifference to religious groups. That would be preferring those who believe in no religion over those who do believe. [W]e find no constitutional requirement which makes it necessary for government to be hostile to religion and to throw its weight against efforts to widen the effective scope of religious influence. The government must be neutral when it comes to competition between sects. It may not thrust any sect on any person. It may not make a religious observance compulsory. It may not coerce anyone to attend church, to observe a religious holiday, or to take religious instruction. But it can close its doors or suspend its operations as to those who want to repair to their religious sanctuary for worship or instruction. No more than that is undertaken here. . . .

In the *McCollum* case the classrooms were used for religious instruction and the force of the public school was used to promote that instruction. Here, as we have said, the public schools do no more than accommodate their schedules to a program of outside religious instruction. We follow the *McCollum* case. But we cannot expand it to cover the present released time program unless separation of Church and State means that public institutions can make no adjustments of their schedules to accommodate the religious needs of the people. We cannot read into the Bill of Rights such a philosophy of hostility to religion.

Affirmed.

MR. JUSTICE BLACK, dissenting.

Illinois ex rel. McCollum v. Board of Education held invalid as an "establishment of religion" an Illinois system under which school children, compelled by law to go to public schools, were freed from some hours of required school work on condition that they attend special religious classes held in the school buildings.... I see no significant difference between the invalid Illinois system and that of New York here sustained. Except for the use of the school buildings in Illinois, there is no difference between the systems which I consider even worthy of mention. In the New York program, as in that of Illinois, the school authorities release some of the children on the condition that they attend the religious classes, get reports on whether they attend, and hold the other children in the school building until the religious hour is over.... Difficulty of decision in the hypothetical situations mentioned by the Court, but not now before us, should not confuse the issues in this case. Here the sole question is whether New York can use its compulsory education laws to help religious sects get attendants presumably too unenthusiastic to go unless moved to do so by the pressure of this state machinery.

MR. JUSTICE JACKSON, dissenting.

... Here schooling is more or less suspended during the "released time" so the nonreligious attendants will not forge ahead of the churchgoing absentees. But it serves as a temporary jail for a pupil who will not go to Church. It takes more subtlety of mind than I possess to deny that this is governmental constraint in support of religion. It is as unconstitutional, in my view, when exerted by indirection as when exercised forthrightly. As one whose children, as a matter of free choice, have been sent to privately supported Church schools, I may challenge the Court's suggestion that opposition to this plan can only be antireligious, atheistic, or agnostic. My evangelistic brethren confuse an objection to compulsion with an objection to religion. It is possible to hold a faith with enough confidence to believe that what should be rendered to God does not need to be decided and collected by Caesar....

[The dissenting opinion of FRANKFURTER, J., is omitted.]

COMMITTEE FOR PUBLIC EDUC. AND RELIGIOUS LIBERTY v. REGAN

444 U.S. 646, 100 S.Ct. 840, 63 L.Ed.2d 94 (1980).

Mr. Justice White delivered the opinion of the Court.

The issue in this case is the constitutionality under the First and Fourteenth Amendments of the United States Constitution of a New York statute authorizing the use of public funds to reimburse church-sponsored and secular nonpublic schools for performing various testing and reporting services mandated by state law. . . .

In 1970 the New York Legislature appropriated public funds to reimburse both church-sponsored and secular nonpublic schools for performing various services mandated by the State. The most expensive of these services was the "administration, grading and the compiling and reporting of the results of tests and examinations." Covered tests included both state-prepared examinations and the more common and traditional teacher-prepared tests. . . . In *Levitt v. Committee for Public Education,* 413 U.S. 472, 93 S.Ct. 2814, 37 L.Ed.2d 736 (1973)(*Levitt I*), the Court struck down this enactment as violative of the Establishment Clause. The majority focused its concern on the statute's reimbursement of funds spent by schools on traditional teacher-prepared tests. The Court was troubled that, "despite the obviously integral role of such testing in the total teaching process, no attempt is made under the statute, and no means are available, to assure that internally prepared tests are free of religious instruction." . . .

The Court distinguished its earlier holdings in *Everson v. Board of Education,* 330 U.S. 1, 67 S.Ct. 504, 91 L.Ed. 711 (1947), and *Board of Education v. Allen,* 392 U.S. 236, 88 S.Ct. 1923, 20 L.Ed.2d 1060 (1968), on grounds that the state aid upheld in those cases, in the form of bus rides and loaned secular textbooks for sectarian schoolchildren, was "of a substantially different character" from that presented in *Levitt I.* . . . The crucial feature that distinguished tests, according to the Court, was that, " '[i]n terms of potential for involving some aspect of faith or morals in secular subjects, a textbook's content is ascertainable, but a teacher's handling of a subject is not.' "Thus, the inherent teacher discretion in devising, presenting, and grading traditional tests, together with the failure of the legislature to provide for a method of auditing to ensure that public funds would be spent exclusively on secular services, disabled the enactment from withstanding constitutional scrutiny.

Almost immediately the New York Legislature attempted to eliminate these defects from its statutory scheme. A new statute was enacted in 1974, and it directed New York's Commissioner of Education to apportion and to pay to nonpublic schools the actual costs incurred as a result of compliance with certain state-mandated requirements, including

the requirements of the state's pupil evaluation program, the basic educational data system, regents examinations, the statewide evaluation plan, the uniform procedure for pupil attendance reporting, and other similar state prepared examinations and reporting procedures. 1974 N.Y.Laws, ch. 507, § 3.

Of single interest and importance in light of *Levitt I,* the new scheme does not reimburse nonpublic schools for the preparation, administration, or grading of teacher-prepared tests. Further, the 1974 statute, unlike the 1970 version struck down in *Levitt I,* provides a means by which payments of state funds are audited, thus ensuring that only the actual costs incurred in providing the covered secular services are reimbursed out of state funds.

Although the new statutory scheme was tailored to comport with the reasoning in *Levitt I,* the District Court invalidated the enactment with respect to both the tests and the reporting procedure. The District Court understood the decision in *Meek v. Pittenger,* 421 U.S. 349, 95 S.Ct. 1753, 44 L.Ed.2d 217 (1975), to require this result. In *Meek,* decided after *Levitt I,* this Court held unconstitutional two Pennsylvania statutes insofar as they provided auxiliary services and instructional material and equipment apart from textbooks to nonpublic schools in the State, most of which were sectarian. The Court ruled that in "religion-pervasive" institutions, secular and religious education are so "inextricably intertwined" that "[s]ubstantial aid to the educational function of such schools ... necessarily results in aid to the sectarian school enterprise as a whole" and hence amounts to a forbidden establishment of religion.

Levitt II was appealed to this Court. We vacated the District Court's judgment and remanded the case in light of our decision in *Wolman v. Walter,* 433 U.S. 229, 97 S.Ct. 2593, 53 L.Ed.2d 714 (1977). On remand the District Court ruled that under *Wolman* "state aid may be extended to [a sectarian] school's educational activities if it can be shown with a high degree of certainty that the aid will only have secular value of legitimate interest to the State and does not present any appreciable risk of being used to aid transmission of religious views." Applying this "more flexible concept," the District Court concluded that New York's statutory scheme of reimbursement did not violate the Establishment Clause....

Under the precedents of this Court a legislative enactment does not contravene the Establishment Clause [1] if it has a secular legislative purpose, [2] if its principal or primary effect neither advances or inhibits religion, and [3] if it does not foster an excessive government entanglement with religion. See *Roemer v. Maryland Public Works Bd.,* 426 U.S. 736, 748, 96 S.Ct. 2337, 2348, 49 L.Ed.2d 179 (1976); *Committee for Public Education v. Nyquist,* 413 U.S. 756, 772–773, 93 S.Ct. 2955, 2965, 37 L.Ed.2d 948 (1973); *Lemon v. Kurtzman,* 403 U.S., at 612–613, 91 S.Ct., at 2111.

In *Wolman v. Walter,* supra, this Court reviewed and sustained in relevant part an Ohio statutory scheme that authorized, *inter alia,* the expenditure of state funds "[t]o supply for use by pupils attending nonpublic schools within the district such standardized tests and scoring services as are in use in the public schools of the state."

We held that this provision, which was aimed at providing the young with an adequate secular education, reflected a secular state purpose. As the opinion of Mr. Justice Blackmun stated, "[t]he State may require that schools that are utilized to fulfill the State's compulsory-education requirement meet certain standards of instruction, ... and may examine both teachers and pupils to ensure that the State's legitimate interest is being fulfilled." Mr. Justice Blackmun further explained that under the Ohio provision the nonpublic school did not control the content of the test or its result. This "serves to prevent the use of the test as a part of religious teaching, and thus avoids that kind of direct aid to religion found present in *Levitt [I]*." The provision of testing services hence did not have the primary effect of aiding religion. It was also decided that "the inability of the school to control the test eliminates the need for the supervision that gives rise to excessive entanglement." We thus concluded that the Ohio statute, insofar as it concerned examinations, passed our Establishment Clause tests.

We agree with the District Court that *Wolman v. Walter* controls this case. Although the Ohio statute under review in *Wolman* and the New York statute before us here are not identical, the differences are not of constitutional dimension. [L]ike the Ohio statute, the New York plan calls for tests that are prepared by the State and administered on the premises by nonpublic school personnel. The nonpublic school thus has no control whatsoever over the content of the tests. The Ohio tests, however, were graded by the State; here there are three types of tests involved, one graded by the State and the other two by nonpublic school personnel, with the costs of the grading service, as well as the cost of administering all three tests, being reimbursed by the State. In view of the nature of the tests, the District Court found that the grading of the examinations by nonpublic school employees afforded no control to the school over the outcome of any of the tests.

The District Court explained that the State-prepared tests are primarily of three types: pupil evaluation program (PEP) tests, comprehensive ("end-of-the-course") achievement tests, and Regents Scholarship and College Qualifications Tests (RSCQT). Each of the tests addresses a secular academic subject; none deals with religious subject matter. The RSCQT examinations are graded by State Education Department personnel, and the District Court correctly concluded that "the risk of [RSCQT examinations] being used for religious purposes through grading is non-existent." The PEP tests, administered universally in grades three and six and optionally in grade nine, are graded by nonpublic school employees, but they "consist entirely of objective, multiple-choice questions, which can be graded by machine and, even if graded by hand, afford the schools no more control over the results than if the tests were graded by the State." The comprehensive tests, based on state courses of study for use in grades nine through twelve, are also graded on the premises by school employees, but "consist largely or entirely of objective questions with multiple-choice answers." Even though some of the comprehensive tests may include an essay question or two, the District Court found that the chance that grading the answers to state-drafted questions in secular subjects could or would be used to gauge a student's grasp of religious ideas was "minimal," especially in light of the "complete" state procedures designed to guard against serious inconsistencies in grading and any misuse of essay questions. These procedures include the submission of completed and graded comprehensive tests to the State Department of Education for review off the school premises. . . .

The District Court was also correct in its characterization of the record-keeping and reporting services for which the State reimburses the nonpublic school. Under the New York law, "[e]ach year, private schools must submit to the State a Basic Educational Data System (BEDS) report. This report contains information regarding the student body, faculty, support staff, physical facilities, and curriculum of each school. Schools are also required to submit annually a report showing the attendance record of each minor who is a student at the school." Although recordkeeping is related to the educational program, the District Court characterized it and the reporting function as "ministerial [and] lacking in ideological content or use." These tasks are not part of the teaching process and cannot "be used to foster an ideological outlook." Reimbursement for the costs of so complying with state law, therefore, has primarily a secular, rather than a religious, purpose and effect.

The New York statute, unlike the Ohio statute at issue in *Wolman*, provides for direct cash reimbursement to the nonpublic school for administering the state-prescribed examinations and for grading two of them. We agree with the District Court that such reimbursement does not invalidate the New York statute. . . . A contrary view would insist on drawing a constitutional distinction between paying the nonpublic school to do the grading and paying state employees or some independent service to perform that task, even though the grading function is the same regardless of who performs it and would not have the primary effect of aiding religion whether or not performed by nonpublic school personnel. In either event, the nonpublic school is being relieved of the cost of grading state-required, state-furnished examinations. We decline to embrace a formalistic dichotomy that bears so little relationship either to common sense or to the realities of school finance. None of our cases requires us to invalidate these reimbursements simply because they involve payments in cash. The Court "has not accepted the recurrent argument that all aid is forbidden because aid to one aspect of an institution frees it to spend its other resources on religious ends."[6]

---

6. As Mr. Justice Blackmun wrote in *Roemer v. Maryland Works Bd.*, (footnote omitted), "The Court has not been blind to the fact that in aiding a religious institution to perform a secular task, the State frees the institution's resources to be put to sectarian ends. If this were impermissible, however, a church could not be protected by the police and fire departments, or have its public sidewalk kept in repair. The Court

We agree with the District Court that "[t]he services for which the private schools would be reimbursed are discrete and clearly identifiable." The reimbursement process, furthermore, is straightforward and susceptible to the routinization that characterizes most reimbursement schemes. On its face, therefore, the New York plan suggests no excessive entanglement, and we are not prepared to read into the plan as an inevitability the bad faith upon which any future excessive entanglement would be predicated.

This is not to say that this case, any more than past cases, will furnish a litmus-paper test to distinguish permissible from impermissible aid to religiously oriented schools. [O]ur decisions have tended to avoid categorical imperatives and absolutist approaches at either end of the range of possible outcomes. This course sacrifices clarity and predictability for flexibility, but this promises to be the case until the continuing interaction between the courts and the States—the former charged with interpreting and upholding the Constitution and the latter seeking to provide education for their youth—produces a single, more encompassing construction of the Establishment Clause.

The judgment of the District Court is

Affirmed.

MR. JUSTICE BLACKMUN, with whom MR. JUSTICE BRENNAN and MR. JUSTICE MARSHALL join, dissenting.

The Court in this case, I fear, takes a long step backwards in the inevitable controversy that emerges when a state legislature continues to insist on providing public aid to parochial schools. I thought that the Court's judgments in *Meek v. Pittenger,* and in *Wolman v. Walter,* (which the Court concedes is the controlling authority here), at last had fixed the line between that which is constitutionally appropriate public aid and that which is not. The line necessarily was not a straight one. It could not be, when this Court, on the one hand, in *Everson v. Board of Education,* by a 5–4 vote, decided that there was no barrier under the First and Fourteenth Amendments to parental reimbursement of the cost of fares for the transportation of children attending parochial schools, and in *Board of Education v. Allen,* by a 6–3 vote, ruled that New York's lending of approved textbooks to students in private secondary schools was not violative of those Amendments, and yet, on the other hand, in *Lemon v. Kurtzman,* struck down, as violative of the Religion Clauses, statutes that, respectively, would have supplemented nonpublic school teachers' salaries and would have authorized the "purchase" of certain "secular educational services" from nonpublic schools, and also in *Levitt v. Committee for Public Education, (Levitt I),* struck down New York's previous attempt to reimburse nonpublic schools for the expenses of tests and examinations. See also *Committee for Public Education v. Nyquist,* where the Court nullified New York's financial aid programs for "maintenance and repair" of facilities and equipment, a tuition reim-

never has held that religious activities must   be discriminated against in this way." . . .

bursement plan, and tax relief for parents who did not qualify for tuition reimbursement, and *Sloan v. Lemon,* 413 U.S. 825, 93 S.Ct. 2982, 37 L.Ed.2d 939 (1973), where the Court ruled invalid a state plan for parental reimbursement of a portion of nonpublic school tuition expenses. . . .

. . . The District Court found that $8–10 million annually would be expended under Chapter 507, with the great majority of these funds going to sectarian schools to pay for personnel costs associated with attendance reporting. The court found that such payments would amount to from 1% to 5.4% of the personnel budget of an individual religious school receiving assistance under Chapter 507. Moreover, Chapter 507 provides direct cash payments by the State of New York to religious schools, as opposed to providing services or providing cash payments to third parties who have rendered services. And the money paid sectarian schools under Chapter 507 is designated to reimburse costs that are incurred by religious schools in order to meet basic state testing and reporting requirements, costs that would have been incurred regardless of the availability of reimbursement from the State. . . .

MR. JUSTICE STEVENS, dissenting. . . .

In groping for a rationale to support today's decision, the Court has taken a position that could equally be used to support a subsidy to pay for staff time attributable to conducting fire drills or even for constructing and maintaining fireproof premises in which to conduct classes. Though such subsidies might represent expedient fiscal policy, I firmly believe they would violate the Establishment Clause of the First Amendment. . . .

MUELLER v. ALLEN
463 U.S. 388, 103 S.Ct. 3062, 77 L.Ed.2d 721 (1983).

JUSTICE REHNQUIST delivered the opinion of the Court.

Minnesota allows taxpayers, in computing their state income tax, to deduct certain expenses incurred in providing for the education of their children. Minn.Stat. § 290.09(22). The United States Court of Appeals for the Eighth Circuit held that the Establishment Clause of the First and Fourteenth Amendments was not offended by this arrangement. . . .

Minnesota, like every other state, provides its citizens with free elementary and secondary schooling. It seems to be agreed that about 820,000 students attended this school system in the most recent school year. During the same year, approximately 91,000 elementary and secondary students attended some 500 privately supported schools located in Minnesota, and about 95% of these students attended schools considering themselves to be sectarian.

Minnesota, by a law originally enacted in 1955 and revised in 1976 and again in 1978, permits state taxpayers to claim a deduction from gross income for certain expenses incurred in educating their children. The deduction is limited to actual expenses incurred for the "tuition, textbooks and transportation'' of dependents attending elementary or secondary schools. A deduction may not exceed $500 per dependent in grades K through six and $700 per dependent in grades seven through twelve.

... Petitioners place particular reliance on our decision in *Committee for Public Education v. Nyquist,* [413 U.S. 756, 93 S.Ct. 2955, 37 L.Ed.2d 948 (1973)], where we held invalid a New York statute providing public funds for the maintenance and repair of the physical facilities of private schools and granting thinly disguised ''tax benefits,'' actually amounting to tuition grants [i.e., tax credits], to the parents of children attending private schools. As explained below, we conclude that § 290.09(22) bears less resemblance to the arrangement struck down in *Nyquist* than it does to assistance programs upheld in our prior decisions and those discussed with approval in *Nyquist.*

The general nature of our inquiry in this area has been guided, since the decision in *Lemon v. Kurtzman,* 403 U.S. 602, [91 S.Ct. 2105, 29 L.Ed.2d 745] (1971), by the ''three-part'' test laid down in that case: ''First, the statute must have a secular legislative purpose; second, its principal or primary effect must be one that neither advances nor inhibits religion ... ; finally, the statute must not foster 'an excessive government entanglement with religion.' '' ...

Little time need be spent on the question of whether the Minnesota tax deduction has a secular purpose.... A state's decision to defray the cost of educational expenses incurred by parents—regardless of the type of schools their children attend—evidences a purpose that is both secular and understandable. An educated populace is essential to the political and economic health of any community.... Similarly, Minnesota, like other states, could conclude that there is a strong public interest in assuring the continued financial health of private schools, both sectarian and non-sectarian. By educating a substantial number of students such schools relieve public schools of a correspondingly great burden—to the benefit of all taxpayers. In addition, private schools may serve as a benchmark for public schools, in a manner analogous to the ''TVA yardstick'' for private power companies....

We turn therefore to the more difficult but related question whether the Minnesota statute has ''the primary effect of advancing the sectarian aims of the nonpublic schools.'' In concluding that it does not, we find several features of the Minnesota tax deduction particularly significant. First, an essential feature of Minnesota's arrangement is the fact that § 290.09(22) is only one among many deductions—such as those for medical expenses, and charitable contributions—available under the Minnesota tax laws.... Under our prior decisions, the Minnesota legislature's judgment that a deduction for educational expenses fairly equalizes the tax burden of its citizens and encourages desirable expenditures for educational purposes is entitled to substantial deference.[6]

6. Our decision in *Nyquist* is not to the   contrary on this point. We expressed con-

Other characteristics of § 290.09(22) argue equally strongly for the provision's constitutionality. Most importantly, the deduction is available for educational expenses incurred by *all* parents, including those whose children attend public schools and those whose children attend non-sectarian private schools or sectarian private schools.... In this respect, as well as others, this case is vitally different from the scheme struck down in *Nyquist*. There, public assistance amounting to tuition grants, was provided only to parents of children in *nonpublic* schools....

We also agree with the Court of Appeals that, by channeling whatever assistance it may provide to parochial schools through individual parents, Minnesota has reduced the Establishment Clause objections to which its action is subject. It is true, of course, that financial assistance provided to parents ultimately has an economic effect comparable to that of aid given directly to the schools attended by their children. It is also true, however, that under Minnesota's arrangement public funds become available only as a result of numerous, private choices of individual parents of school-age children. For these reasons, we recognized in *Nyquist* that the means by which state assistance flows to private schools is of some importance: we said that "the fact that aid is disbursed to parents rather than to ... schools" is a material consideration in Establishment Clause analysis, albeit "only one among many to be considered." It is noteworthy that all but one of our recent cases invalidating state aid to parochial schools have involved the direct transmission of assistance from the state to the schools themselves. The exception, of course, was *Nyquist,* which, as discussed previously is distinguishable from this case on other grounds. Where, as here, aid to parochial schools is available only as a result of decisions of individual parents no "imprimatur of State approval," can be deemed to have been conferred on any particular religion, or on religion generally....

Petitioners argue that, notwithstanding the facial neutrality of § 290.09(22), in application the statute primarily benefits religious institutions. Petitioners rely, as they did below, on a statistical analysis of the type of persons claiming the tax deduction. They contend that most parents of public school children incur no tuition expenses, see Minn. Stat. § 120.06, and that other expenses deductible under § 290.09(22) are negligible in value; moreover, they claim that 96% of the children in private schools in 1978–1979 attended religiously-affiliated institutions. Because of all this, they reason, the bulk of deductions taken under § 290.09(22) will be claimed by parents of children in sectarian schools. Respondents reply that petitioners have failed to consider the impact of

siderable doubt there that the "tax benefits" provided by New York law properly could be regarded as parts of a genuine system of tax laws. Plainly, the outright grants to low-income parents did not take the form of ordinary tax benefits.... While the economic consequences of the program in *Nyquist* and that in this case may be difficult to distinguish, we have recognized on other occasions that "the form of the [state's assistance to parochial schools must be examined] for the light that it casts on the substance." The fact that the Minnesota plan embodies a "genuine tax deduction" is thus of some relevance, especially given the traditional rule of deference accorded legislative classifications in tax statutes.

deductions for items such as transportation, summer school tuition, tuition paid by parents whose children attended schools outside the school districts in which they resided, rental or purchase costs for a variety of equipment, and tuition for certain types of instruction not ordinarily provided in public schools.

We need not consider these contentions in detail. We would be loath to adopt a rule grounding the constitutionality of a facially neutral law on annual reports reciting the extent to which various classes of private citizens claimed benefits under the law. Such an approach would scarcely provide the certainty that this field stands in need of, nor can we perceive principled standards by which such statistical evidence might be evaluated. Moreover, the fact that private persons fail in a particular year to claim the tax relief to which they are entitled—under a facially neutral statute—should be of little importance in determining the constitutionality of the statute permitting such relief.

[W]e believe it wiser to decline to engage in the type of empirical inquiry into those persons benefited by state law which petitioners urge.[10] Thus, we hold that the Minnesota tax deduction for educational expenses satisfies the primary effect inquiry of our Establishment Clause cases.

Turning to the third part of the *Lemon* inquiry, we have no difficulty in concluding that the Minnesota statute does not "excessively entangle" the state in religion. The only plausible source of the "comprehensive, discriminating, and continuing state surveillance," necessary to run afoul of this standard would lie in the fact that state officials must determine whether particular textbooks qualify for a deduction. In making this decision, state officials must disallow deductions taken from "instructional books and materials used in the teaching of religious tenets, doctrines or worship." Minn.Stat. § 290.09(22). Making decisions such as this does not differ substantially from making the types of decisions approved in earlier opinions of this Court. In *Board of Education v. Allen,* for example, the Court upheld the loan of secular textbooks to parents or children attending nonpublic schools; though state officials were required to determine whether particular books were or were not secular, the system was held not to violate the Establish-

---

10. Our conclusion is unaffected by the fact that § 290.09(22) permits deductions for amounts spent for textbooks and transportation as well as tuition. In *Everson v. Board of Education,* 330 U.S. 1, 67 S.Ct. 504, 91 L.Ed. 711 (1947), we approved a statute reimbursing parents of *all* schoolchildren for the costs of transporting their children to school. Doing so by means of a deduction, rather than a direct grant, only serves to make the state's action less objectionable. Likewise, in *Board of Education v. Allen,* 392 U.S. 236, 88 S.Ct. 1923, 20 L.Ed.2d 1060 (1968), we approved state loans of textbooks to *all* schoolchildren; although we disapproved, in *Meek v. Pittenger* and *Wolman v. Walter* direct loans of instructional materials to sectarian schools, we do not find those cases controlling. First, they involved assistance provided to the schools themselves, rather than tax benefits directed to individual parents. [Also] state assistance for the rental of calculators, ice skates, tennis shoes, and the like, scarcely poses the type of dangers against which the Establishment Clause was intended to guard.

ment Clause. The same result follows in this case.[11]

For the foregoing reasons, the judgment of the Court of Appeals is

Affirmed.

JUSTICE MARSHALL, with whom JUSTICE BRENNAN, JUSTICE BLACKMUN and JUSTICE STEVENS join, dissenting.

The Establishment Clause of the First Amendment prohibits a State from subsidizing religious education, whether it does so directly or indirectly. In my view, this principle of neutrality forbids not only the tax benefits struck down in *Committee for Public Education v. Nyquist,* 413 U.S. 756, 93 S.Ct. 2955, 37 L.Ed.2d 948 (1973), but any tax benefit, including the tax deduction at issue here, which subsidizes tuition payments to sectarian schools. I also believe that the Establishment Clause prohibits the tax deductions that Minnesota authorizes for the cost of books and other instructional materials used for sectarian purposes. . . .

That the Minnesota statute makes some small benefit available to all parents cannot alter the fact that the most substantial benefit provided by the statute is available only to those parents who send their children to schools that charge tuition. It is simply undeniable that the single largest expense that may be deducted under the Minnesota statute is tuition. The statute is little more than a subsidy of tuition masquerading as a subsidy of general educational expenses. The other deductible expenses are *de minimis* in comparison to tuition expenses.

. . . Of the total number of taxpayers who are eligible for the tuition deduction, approximately 96% send their children to religious schools. Parents who send their children to free public schools are simply ineligible to obtain the full benefit of the deduction except in the unlikely event that they buy $700 worth of pencils, notebooks, and bus rides for their school-age children. [A]ny generally available financial assistance for elementary and secondary school tuition expenses mainly will further religious education because the majority of the schools which charge tuition are sectarian. . . .

The majority also asserts that the Minnesota statute is distinguishable from the statute struck down in *Nyquist* in another respect: the tax benefit available under Minnesota law is a "genuine tax deduction," whereas the New York law provided a benefit which, while nominally a deduction, also had features of a "tax credit." Ante, at n. 6. . . .

11. No party to this litigation has urged that the Minnesota plan is invalid because it runs afoul of the rather elusive inquiry, subsumed under the third part of the *Lemon* test, whether the Minnesota statute partakes of the "divisive political potential" condemned in *Lemon* . . . . The Court's language in *Lemon I* respecting political divisiveness was made in the context of Pennsylvania and Rhode Island statutes which provided for either direct payments of, or reimbursement of, a proportion of teachers' salaries in parochial schools. [T]he language must be regarded as confined to cases where direct financial subsidies are paid to parochial schools or to teachers in parochial schools.

There is no reason to treat Minnesota's tax deduction for textbooks any differently. Secular textbooks, like other secular instructional materials, contribute to the religious mission of the parochial schools that use those books. Although this Court upheld the loan of secular textbooks to religious schools in *Board of Education v. Allen,* supra, [t]his basis for distinguishing secular instructional materials and secular textbooks is simply untenable, and is inconsistent with many of our more recent decisions concerning state aid to parochial schools. In any event, the Court's assumption in *Allen* that the textbooks at issue there might be used only for secular education was based on the fact that those very books had been chosen by the State for use in the public schools. In contrast, the Minnesota statute does not limit the tax deduction to those books which the State has approved for use in public schools. Rather, it permits a deduction for books that are chosen by the parochial schools themselves. Indeed, under the Minnesota statutory scheme, textbooks chosen by parochial schools but not used by public schools are likely to be precisely the ones purchased by parents for their children's use....

Notes

School District of the City of Grand Rapids v. Ball, 473 U.S. 373, 105 S.Ct. 3216, 87 L.Ed.2d 267 (1985). A public School District adopted two programs that financed classes for nonpublic school students. These classes were taught by public school teachers but were conducted in classrooms located in, and leased from, the nonpublic schools. Under the Shared Time Program, the full time public school employees taught courses during the regular school day. These courses, such as remedial reading, were intended to supplement the "core curriculum" courses required by the state. Under the Community Education Program, part-time public school employees offered voluntary courses (such as Chess, Spanish, or Nature Appreciation), which began at the end of the regular school day. These voluntary courses were also offered in the public schools. Of the 41 private schools participating in these programs, 40 were religious schools. "Each room used in the program has to be free of any crucifix, religious symbol, or artifact, although such religious symbols can be present in the adjoining hallways, corridors, and other facilities used in connection with the program."

The Court, in an opinion by Brennan, J., invalidated the programs as having the "primary or principal" effect of promoting religion. The state-paid teachers might be influenced by the pervasively sectarian nature of the religious schools where they work, and might "subtly (or overtly) conform their instruction to the environment in which they teach." Most of these part-time public school employees were also full-time nonpublic school employees, teaching in the same nonpublic schools in which the Community Education Program classes were held. Inherent in state-supported public instruction in religious schools is a symbolic union that threatens to convey to students and the general public a message of state support for religion. Also, the programs subsidized religious functions of the religious schools by relieving them of their responsibility for secular subjects. The Court explained:

McCollum v. Board of Education held that a public school may not permit part-time religious instruction on its premises as a part of the school program, even if participation in that instruction is entirely voluntary and even if the instruction itself is conducted only by nonpublic-school personnel. Yet in *Zorach v. Clauson,* the Court held that a similar program conducted off the premises of the public school passed constitutional muster. The difference in symbolic impact helps to explain the difference between the cases. The symbolic connection of church and state in the *McCollum* program ... was conspicuously absent in the *Zorach* program.

Burger, C.J., & O'Connor, J., each concurred in the judgment and dissented in part. They would have upheld the Shared Time (but not the Community Education) Program. White, J., & Rehnquist, J., filed dissenting opinions.

The same day, in *Aguilar v. Felton,* 473 U.S. 402, 105 S.Ct. 3232, 87 L.Ed.2d 290 (1985), Brennan, J., for the Court (5 to 4) invalidated another program. New York used federal funds from to hire public school employees to teach in New York City nonpublic schools to help educationally deprived children from low income families. The City made the teacher assignments and used field personnel to supervise the teachers and monitor the classes. The main difference with the *Grand Rapids* case was that New York City had adopted a pervasive monitoring system to assure that the program would not be used either intentionally or unwittingly to inculcate religious beliefs in the students. However, the majority held that such monitoring would "inevitably" result in excessive entanglement of Church and State.

The Court later overruled *Aguilar* and *Ball* in part in, *Agostini v. Felton* (1997), excerpted below.

Zobrest v. Catalina Foothills School District, 509 U.S. 1, 113 S.Ct. 2462, 125 L.Ed.2d 1 (1993). Plaintiff Zobrest, a ninth grader, was deaf from birth. He attended his first five grades in a school for the deaf, and the next three at a public school with a sign-language interpreter. He chose to attend a Catholic High School and requested that the public school district provide a sign-language interpreter, pursuant to the federal Individual with Disabilities Act and its state-law counterpart.

Rehnquist, C.J., for the Court, held that the Establishment Clause did not prevent the school district from supplying the interpreter because there is no Establishment Clause violation if a government program neutrally provides benefits to a broad class of citizens, defined without reference to religion, even though religious institutions may also receive an attenuated financial benefit. Because parents are free to choose where their child will attend school, the government-paid interpreter will be in a religiously affiliated school only because of the parents' private decision. The statute created no financial incentive for the parents to chose a sectarian school, and there was no state decision-making that is responsible for the interpreter's presence in a sectarian school.

The Court distinguished *School District of Grand Rapids v. Ball* because here the child is the primary beneficiary. An interpreter (unlike a teacher or guidance counselor) does not add or subtract from the school's environment, but merely interprets to the deaf student whatever material is presented to the class as a whole. The statute "creates a neutral government program" that did not dispense aid to schools but to individual handicapped children. A flat, absolute bar to placing a public employee in a sectarian school would be "smack[] of antiquated notions of 'taint,' " and "exalt form over substance." Even the respondents admitted that there would be no Establishment Clause problem if the Act provided for the government funds to go directly to the parents, who in turn would hire the interpreter.

Blackmun, J., joined by Souter, J., dissented and argued: "This distinction between the provision of funds and the provision of a human being is not merely one of form."

Board of Education of Kiryas Joel Village School District v. Grumet, 512 U.S. 687, 114 S.Ct. 2481, 129 L.Ed.2d 546 (1994). Believers of Satmar Hasidim, a strict form of Judaism, purchased land in the 1970's in the town of Monroe, and began assembling the community that became the Village of Kiryas Joel. Pursuant to New York's generally applicable village incorporation law, the boundaries of the Village of Kiryas Joel were drawn to include just the 320 acres owned and inhabited entirely by Satmars. The village fell within the Monroe–Woodbury Central School District until 1989, when a special state statute ("special statute") carved out a separate school district following village lines. Children in this village attended private religious schools, which did not offer any distinctive services to handicapped children (e.g., the deaf, the mentally retarded), although state and federal law entitled these handicapped children to special education services even when enrolled in private schools. Starting in 1984 the Monroe–Woodbury Central School District (a public school) provided such services for the children of Kiryas Joel at an annex to Bais Rochel (a private school), but a year later ended that arrangement in response to *Aguilar v. Felton,* and *School District of Grand Rapids v. Ball.* The handicapped children from Kiryas Joel were then forced to attend public schools outside the village, but many parents withdrew their children from the secular schools, because of "the panic, fear and trauma [they] suffered in leaving their own community and being with people whose ways were so different." New York then passed the special statute, constituting the Village of Kiryas Joel as "a separate school district [that] shall have and enjoy all the powers and duties of a union free school district.... " This school board ran only a special education program for handicapped children; the other village children attended private religious schools, which did not offer special educational services. If any Kiryas Joel child without handicap wanted a public-school education, the district would pay tuition to send the child into Monroe–Woodbury or another nearby school district. Neighboring districts also sent their handicapped Hasidic children to Kiryas Joel.

A fragmented Court concluded that the special statute creating the separate school district violated the Establishment Clause. Souter, J. (joined by Blackmun, Stevens, & Ginsburg, JJ.) for the plurality, concluded that "this unusual act is tantamount to an allocation of political power" based on a "religious criterion" and thus violates the establishment clause. In a footnote, Souter noted that this district is "distinguishable from one whose boundaries are derived according to neutral historical and geographic criteria, but whose population happens to comprise coreligionists."

Kennedy, J., concurred in the judgment, said that the establishment clause was violated because the state drew political boundaries on the basis of religion. Blackmun, J.'s, concurring opinion argued that this case signaled no retreat from *Lemon v. Kurtzman,* because New York's law had the primary effect of advancing religion and involved "entanglement" with religion. Stevens, J., joined by Blackmun & Ginsburg, JJ., filed a concurring opinion arguing that New York's solution "affirmatively supports a religious sect's interest in segregating itself and preventing its children from associating with their neighbors." O'Connor, J., concurred in part and in the judgment, objecting to New York's favoritism towards one religion.

Scalia, J., joined by Rehnquist, C.J. & Thomas, J., dissented. "Justice Souter's position boils down to the quite novel proposition that any group of citizens (say, the residents of Kiryas Joel) can be invested with political power, but not if they all belong to the same religion. Of course such *disfavoring* of religion is positively antagonistic to the purposes of the Religion Clauses, and we have rejected it before." (emphasis in original). The Founding Fathers would be "astonished" to find the establishment clause employed to prohibit "characteristically and admirably American accommodation of the religious practices (or more precisely, cultural peculiarities) of a tiny minority sect."

AGOSTINI v. FELTON
521 U.S. 203, 117 S.Ct. 1997, 138 L.Ed.2d 391 (1997).

JUSTICE O'CONNOR delivered the opinion of the Court.

In *Aguilar v. Felton* (1985), this Court held that the Establishment Clause of the First Amendment barred the city of New York from sending public school teachers into parochial schools to provide remedial education to disadvantaged children pursuant to a congressionally mandated program. [A permanent injunction was entered, and now], petitioners—the parties bound by that injunction—seek relief from its operation. Petitioners maintain that *Aguilar* cannot be squared with our intervening Establishment Clause jurisprudence and ask that we explicitly recognize what our more recent cases already dictate: *Aguilar* is no longer good law. We agree with petitioners that *Aguilar* is not consistent with our subsequent Establishment Clause decisions and further conclude that, on the facts presented here, petitioners are entitled under Federal Rule of Civil Procedure 60(b)(5) to relief from the operation of the District Court's prospective injunction.

In 1965, Congress enacted Title I of the Elementary and Secondary Education Act of 1965 to "provid[e] full educational opportunity to every child regardless of economic background." S. Rep. No. 146, 89th Cong., 1st Sess. 5 (1965) (hereinafter Title I). Toward that end, Title I channels federal funds, through the States, to "local educational agencies" (LEA's). The LEA's spend these funds to provide remedial education, guidance, and job counseling to eligible students. An eligible student is one (i) who resides within the attendance boundaries of a public school located in a low-income area, and (ii) who is failing, or is at risk of failing, the State's student performance standards. Title I funds must be made available to *all* eligible children, regardless of whether they attend public schools, and the services provided to children attending private schools must be "equitable in comparison to services and other benefits for public school children."

An LEA providing services to children enrolled in private schools is subject to a number of constraints that are not imposed when it provides aid to public schools. Title I services may be provided only to those private school students eligible for aid, and cannot be used to provide services on a "school-wide" basis. In addition, the LEA must retain complete control over Title I funds; retain title to all materials used to provide Title I services; and provide those services through public employees or other persons independent of the private school and any religious institution. The Title I services themselves must be "secular, neutral, and nonideological," and must "supplement, and in no case supplant, the level of services" already provided by the private school.

[The New York City Board of Education], an LEA, first applied for Title I funds in 1966 and has grappled ever since with how to provide Title I services to the private school students within its jurisdiction. Approximately 10% of the total number of students eligible for Title I services are private school students. Recognizing that more than 90% of the private schools within the Board's jurisdiction are sectarian, the Board initially arranged to transport children to public schools for after-school Title I instruction. But [a]ttendance was poor, teachers and children were tired, and parents were concerned for the safety of their children. The Board then moved the after-school instruction onto private school campuses, as Congress had contemplated when it enacted Title I. After this program also yielded mixed results, the Board implemented the plan we evaluated in *Aguilar v. Felton.*

That plan called for the provision of Title I services on private school premises during school hours. Under the plan, only public employees could serve as Title I instructors and counselors. Assignments to private schools were made on a voluntary basis and without regard to the religious affiliation of the employee or the wishes of the private school. [A] large majority of Title I teachers worked in nonpublic schools with religious affiliations different from their own. The vast majority of Title I teachers also moved among the private schools, spending fewer than five days a week at the same school.

Before any public employee could provide Title I instruction at a private school, she would be given a detailed set of written and oral instructions emphasizing the secular purpose of Title I and setting out the rules to be followed to ensure that this purpose was not compromised.... All religious symbols were to be removed from classrooms used for Title I services. The rules acknowledged that it might be necessary for Title I teachers to consult with a student's regular classroom teacher to assess the student's particular needs and progress, but admonished instructors to limit those consultations to mutual professional concerns regarding the student's education. To ensure compliance with these rules, a publicly employed field supervisor was to attempt to make at least one unannounced visit to each teacher's classroom every month.

In 1978, six federal taxpayers—respondents here—sued the Board [seeking] declaratory and injunctive relief, claiming that the Board's Title I program violated the Establishment Clause.... While noting that the Board's Title I program had "done so much good and little, if any, detectable harm," the Court of Appeals nevertheless held that *Meek v. Pittenger* (1975), and *Wolman v. Walter* (1977), compelled it to declare the program unconstitutional. In a 5–4 decision, this Court affirmed on the ground that the Board's Title I program necessitated an "excessive entanglement of church and state in the administration of [Title I] benefits." ...

[T]he Board reverted to its prior practice of providing instruction at public school sites, at leased sites, and in mobile instructional units (essentially vans converted into classrooms) parked near the sectarian school. The Board also offered computer-aided instruction, which could be provided "on premises" because it did not require public employees to be physically present on the premises of a religious school.

It is not disputed that the additional costs of complying with *Aguilar*'s mandate are significant. Since the 1986–1987 school year, the Board has spent over $100 million providing computer-aided instruction, leasing sites and mobile instructional units, and transporting students to those sites. ...

The question we must answer is a simple one: Are petitioners entitled to relief from the District Court's permanent injunction under Rule 60(b)? Rule 60(b)(5), the subsection under which petitioners proceeded below, states:

> "On motion and upon such terms as are just, the court may relieve a party ... from a final judgment [or] order ... [when] it is no longer equitable that the judgment should have prospective application."

[I]t is appropriate to grant a Rule 60(b)(5) motion when the party seeking relief from an injunction or consent decree can show "a significant change either in factual conditions or in law." ...

In order to evaluate whether *Aguilar* has been eroded by our subsequent Establishment Clause cases, it is necessary to understand the rationale upon which *Aguilar*, as well as its companion case, *School Dist. of Grand Rapids v. Ball* (1985) [Casebook, p. 1061], rested. ...

Distilled to essentials, the Court's conclusion that the Shared Time program in *Ball* had the impermissible effect of advancing religion rested on three assumptions: (i) any public employee who works on the premises of a religious school is presumed to inculcate religion in her work; (ii) the presence of public employees on private school premises creates a symbolic union between church and state; and (iii) any and all public aid that directly aids the educational function of religious schools impermissibly finances religious indoctrination, even if the aid reaches such schools as a consequence of private decisionmaking. Additionally, in *Aguilar* there was a fourth assumption: that New York City's Title I program necessitated an excessive government entanglement with religion because public employees who teach on the premises of religious schools must be closely monitored to ensure that they do not inculcate religion.

Our more recent cases have undermined the assumptions upon which *Ball* and *Aguilar* relied. To be sure, the general principles we use to evaluate whether government aid violates the Establishment Clause have not changed since *Aguilar* was decided. For example, we continue to ask whether the government acted with the purpose of advancing or inhibiting religion, and the nature of that inquiry has remained largely unchanged. Likewise, we continue to explore whether the aid has the "effect" of advancing or inhibiting religion. What has changed since we decided *Ball* and *Aguilar* is our understanding of the criteria used to assess whether aid to religion has an impermissible effect.

As we have repeatedly recognized, government inculcation of religious beliefs has the impermissible effect of advancing religion. Our cases subsequent to *Aguilar* have, however, modified in two significant respects the approach we use to assess indoctrination. First, we have abandoned the presumption erected in *Meek* and *Ball* that the placement of public employees on parochial school grounds inevitably results in the impermissible effect of state-sponsored indoctrination or constitutes a symbolic union between government and religion. In *Zobrest v. Catalina Foothills School Dist.* we examined whether the IDEA, 20 U.S.C.A. § 1400 *et seq.*, was constitutional as applied to a deaf student who sought to bring his state-employed sign-language interpreter with him to his Roman Catholic high school. We held that this was permissible, expressly disavowing the notion that "the Establishment Clause [laid] down [an] absolute bar to the placing of a public employee in a sectarian school." ... In the absence of evidence to the contrary, we assumed instead that the interpreter would dutifully discharge her responsibilities as a full-time public employee and comply with the ethical guidelines of her profession by accurately translating what was said. Because the only *government* aid in *Zobrest* was the interpreter, who was herself not inculcating any religious messages, no *government* indoctrination took place and we were able to conclude that "the provision of such assistance [was] not barred by the Establishment Clause." *Zobrest* therefore expressly rejected the notion—relied on in *Ball* and *Aguilar*—that, solely because of her presence on private school property, a public employee will be presumed to inculcate religion in the students. *Zobrest* also implicitly repudiated another assumption on which *Ball* and *Aguilar* turned: that the presence of a public employee on private school property creates an impermissible "symbolic link" between government and religion.

Justice Souter contends that *Zobrest* did not undermine the "presumption of inculcation" erected in *Ball* and *Aguilar*, and that our conclusion to the contrary rests on a "mistaken reading" of *Zobrest*. In his view, *Zobrest* held that the Establishment Clause tolerates the presence of public employees in sectarian schools "only in ... limited circumstances"—*i.e.,* when the employee "simply translates for one student the material presented to the class for the benefit of all students." ...

In *Zobrest*, however, we did not expressly or implicitly rely upon the basis Justice Souter now advances for distinguishing *Ball* and *Aguilar*. If we had thought that signers had no "opportunity to inject religious content" into their translations, we would have had no reason to consult the record for evidence of inaccurate translations. The signer in *Zobrest* had the same opportunity to inculcate religion in the performance of her duties as do Title I employees, and there is no genuine basis upon which to confine *Zobrest*'s underlying rationale—that public employees will not be presumed to inculcate religion—to sign-language interpreters. Indeed, even the *Zobrest* dissenters acknowledged the shift *Zobrest* effected in our Establishment Clause law when they criticized the majority for "stray[ing] ... from the course set by nearly five decades of Establishment Clause jurisprudence." (Blackmun, J., dissenting). ...

Second, we have departed from the rule relied on in *Ball* that all government aid that directly aids the educational function of religious schools is invalid. In *Witters v. Washington Dept. of Servs. for Blind* (1986), we held that the Establishment Clause did not bar a State from issuing a vocational tuition grant to a blind person who wished to use the grant to attend a Christian college and become a pastor, missionary, or youth director. [T]he tuition grants were " 'made available generally without regard to the sectarian-nonsectarian, or public-nonpublic nature of the institution benefited.' "The grants were disbursed directly to students, who then used the money to pay for tuition at the educational institution of their choice. In our view, this transaction was no different from a State's issuing a paycheck to one of its employees, knowing that the employee would donate part or all of the check to a religious institution. In both situations, any money that ultimately went to religious institutions did so "only as a result of the genuinely independent and private choices of" individuals. The same logic applied in *Zobrest*, where we allowed the State to provide an interpreter, even though she would be a mouthpiece for religious instruction, because the IDEA's neutral eligibility criteria ensured that the interpreter's presence in a sectarian school was a "result of the private decision of individual parents" and "[could] not be attributed to *state* decisionmaking." (emphasis added). Because the private school would not have provided an interpreter on its own, we also concluded that the aid in *Zobrest* did not indirectly finance religious education by "reliev[ing] the sectarian schoo[l] of costs [it] otherwise would have borne in educating [its] students."

Zobrest and *Witters* make clear that, under current law, the Shared Time program in *Ball* and New York City's Title I program in *Aguilar* will not, as a matter of law, be deemed to have the effect of advancing religion through indoctrination. Indeed, each of the premises upon which we relied in *Ball* to reach a contrary conclusion is no longer valid. First, there is no reason to presume that, simply because she enters a parochial school classroom, a full-time public employee such as a Title I teacher will depart from her assigned duties and instructions and embark on religious indoctrination, any more than there was a reason in *Zobrest* to think an interpreter would inculcate religion by altering her translation of classroom lectures. [We] reject respondents' remarkable argument that we must presume Title I instructors to be "uncontrollable and sometimes very unprofessional."

As discussed above, *Zobrest* also repudiates *Ball*'s assumption that the presence of Title I teachers in parochial school classrooms will, without more, create the impression of a "symbolic union" between church and state. [But] Justice Souter does not disavow the notion, uniformly adopted by lower courts, that Title I services may be provided to sectarian school students in off-campus locations, even though that notion necessarily presupposes that the danger of "symbolic union" evaporates once the services are provided off-campus. Taking this view, the only difference between a constitutional program and an unconstitutional one is the location of the classroom, since the degree of cooperation between Title I instructors and parochial school faculty is the same no matter where the services are provided. We do not see any perceptible (let alone dispositive) difference in the degree of symbolic union between a student receiving remedial instruction in a classroom on his sectarian school's campus and one receiving instruction in a van parked just at the school's curbside. To draw this line based solely on the location of the public employee is neither "sensible" nor "sound," and the Court in *Zobrest* rejected it.

Nor under current law can we conclude that a program placing full-time public employees on parochial campuses to provide Title I instruction would impermissibly finance religious indoctrination. In all relevant respects, the provision of instructional services under Title I is indistinguishable from the provision of sign-language interpreters under the IDEA. Both programs make aid available only to eligible recipients. That aid is provided to students at whatever school they choose to attend. Although Title I instruction is provided to several students at once, whereas an interpreter provides translation to a single student, this distinction is not constitutionally significant. Moreover, as in *Zobrest*, Title I services are by law supplemental to the regular curricula. These services do not, therefore, "reliev[e] sectarian schools of costs they otherwise would have borne in educating their students." *Zobrest*.

Justice Souter . . . points to three differences he perceives between the programs: (i) Title I services are distributed by LEA's "directly to the religious schools" instead of to individual students pursuant to a formal application process; (ii) Title I services "necessarily reliev[e] a religious school of 'an expense that it otherwise would have assumed' "; and (iii) Title I provides services to more students than did the programs in *Witters* and *Zobrest*. None of these distinctions is meaningful. While

... individual students may not directly apply for Title I services, it does not follow from this premise that those services are distributed "directly to the religious schools." In fact, they are not. No Title I funds ever reach the coffers of religious schools, and Title I services may not be provided to religious schools on a school-wide basis. Title I funds are instead distributed to a *public* agency (an LEA) that dispenses services directly to the eligible students within its boundaries, no matter where they choose to attend school. Moreover, we fail to see how providing Title I services directly to eligible students results in a greater financing of religious indoctrination simply because those students are not first required to submit a formal application.

We are also not persuaded that Title I services supplant the remedial instruction and guidance counseling already provided in New York City's sectarian schools. Although Justice Souter maintains that the sectarian schools provide such services and that those schools reduce those services once their students begin to receive Title I instruction, his claims rest on speculation about the impossibility of drawing any line between supplemental and general education, and not on any evidence in the record that the Board is in fact violating Title I regulations by providing services that supplant those offered in the sectarian schools. . . .

What is most fatal to the argument that New York City's Title I program directly subsidizes religion is that it applies with equal force when those services are provided off-campus, and *Aguilar* implied that providing the services off-campus is entirely consistent with the Establishment Clause. [C]ontrary to our conclusion in *Aguilar*, placing full-time employees on parochial school campuses does not as a matter of law have the impermissible effect of advancing religion through indoctrination.

[The next question is whether the criteria by which an aid program identifies its beneficiaries] might themselves have the effect of advancing religion by creating a financial incentive to undertake religious indoctrination. Cf. *Witters* (upholding neutrally available program because it did not "create a financial incentive for students to undertake sectarian education"). This incentive is not present, however, where the aid is allocated on the basis of neutral, secular criteria that neither favor nor disfavor religion, and is made available to both religious and secular beneficiaries on a nondiscriminatory basis. Under such circumstances, the aid is less likely to have the effect of advancing religion.

In *Ball* and *Aguilar*, the Court gave this consideration no weight. Before and since those decisions, we have sustained programs that provided aid to *all* eligible children regardless of where they attended school. See, *e.g., Everson v. Board of Ed. of Ewing* (1947) (sustaining local ordinance authorizing all parents to deduct from their state tax returns the costs of transporting their children to school on public buses); *Board of Ed. v. Allen* (1968) (sustaining New York law loaning secular textbooks to all children); *Mueller v. Allen* (1983) (sustaining

Minnesota statute allowing all parents to deduct actual costs of tuition, textbooks, and transportation from state tax returns); *Witters* (sustaining Washington law granting all eligible blind persons vocational assistance); *Zobrest* (sustaining section of IDEA providing all "disabled" children with necessary aid).

Applying this reasoning to New York City's Title I program, it is clear that Title I services are allocated on the basis of criteria that neither favor nor disfavor religion. The services are available to all children who meet the Act's eligibility requirements, no matter what their religious beliefs or where they go to school. The Board's program does not, therefore, give aid recipients any incentive to modify their religious beliefs or practices in order to obtain those services.

We turn now to *Aguilar*'s conclusion that New York City's Title I program resulted in an excessive entanglement between church and state. . . . Not all entanglements, of course, have the effect of advancing or inhibiting religion. Interaction between church and state is inevitable, and we have always tolerated some level of involvement between the two. Entanglement must be "excessive" before it runs afoul of the Establishment Clause.

[T]he Court's finding of "excessive" entanglement in *Aguilar* rested on three grounds: (i) the program would require "pervasive monitoring by public authorities" to ensure that Title I employees did not inculcate religion; (ii) the program required "administrative cooperation" between the Board and parochial schools; and (iii) the program might increase the dangers of "political divisiveness." Under our current understanding of the Establishment Clause, the last two considerations are insufficient by themselves to create an "excessive" entanglement. They are present no matter where Title I services are offered, and no court has held that Title I services cannot be offered off-campus. Further, the assumption underlying the first consideration has been undermined. In *Aguilar*, the Court presumed that full-time public employees on parochial school grounds would be tempted to inculcate religion, despite the ethical standards they were required to uphold. Because of this risk *pervasive* monitoring would be required. But after *Zobrest* we no longer presume that public employees will inculcate religion simply because they happen to be in a sectarian environment. Since we have abandoned the assumption that properly instructed public employees will fail to discharge their duties faithfully, we must also discard the assumption that *pervasive* monitoring of Title I teachers is required. There is no suggestion in the record before us that unannounced monthly visits of public supervisors are insufficient to prevent or to detect inculcation of religion by public employees. . . .

To summarize, New York City's Title I program does not run afoul of any of three primary criteria we currently use to evaluate whether government aid has the effect of advancing religion: it does not result in governmental indoctrination; define its recipients by reference to religion; or create an excessive entanglement. We therefore hold that a federally funded program providing supplemental, remedial instruction to disadvantaged children on a neutral basis is not invalid under the Establishment Clause when such instruction is given on the premises of sectarian schools by government employees pursuant to a program containing safeguards such as those present here. The same considerations that justify this holding require us to conclude that this carefully constrained program also cannot reasonably be viewed as an endorsement of religion. Accordingly, we must acknowledge that *Aguilar*, as well as the portion of *Ball* addressing Grand Rapids' Shared Time program, are no longer good law.

The doctrine of *stare decisis* does not preclude us from recognizing the change in our law and overruling *Aguilar* and those portions of *Ball* inconsistent with our more recent decisions. . . .We therefore overrule *Ball* and *Aguilar* to the extent those decisions are inconsistent with our current understanding of the Establishment Clause. [O]ur Establishment Clause law has "significant[ly] change[d]" since we decided *Aguilar*. We are only left to decide whether this change in law entitles petitioners to relief under Rule 60(b)(5). We conclude that it does. Our general practice is to apply the rule of law we announce in a case to the parties before us. . . .

For these reasons, we reverse the judgment of the Court of Appeals and remand to the District Court with instructions to vacate its September 26, 1985, order.

It is so ordered.

JUSTICE SOUTER, with whom JUSTICE STEVENS and JUSTICE GINSBURG join, and with whom JUSTICE BREYER joins as to Part II, dissenting. . . .

I. [What] was significant in *Aguilar* and *Ball* about the placement of state-paid teachers into the physical and social settings of the religious schools was not only the consequent temptation of some of those teachers to reflect the schools' religious missions in the rhetoric of their instruction, with a resulting need for monitoring and the certainty of entanglement. See *Aguilar* (monitoring); *Ball* (risk of indoctrination). What was so remarkable was that the schemes in issue assumed a teaching responsibility indistinguishable from the responsibility of the schools themselves. The obligation of primary and secondary schools to teach reading necessarily extends to teaching those who are having a hard time at it, and the same is true of math. Calling some classes remedial does not distinguish their subjects from the schools' basic subjects, however inadequately the schools may have been addressing them.

What was true of the Title I scheme as struck down in *Aguilar* will be just as true when New York reverts to the old practices with the Court's approval after today. There is simply no line that can be drawn between the instruction paid for at taxpayers' expense and the instruction in any subject that is not identified as formally religious. While it would be an obvious sham, say, to channel cash to religious schools to be credited only against the expense of "secular" instruction, the line between "supplemental" and general education is likewise impossible to draw. If a State may constitutionally enter the schools to teach in the manner in question, it must in constitutional principle be free to assume, or assume payment for, the entire cost of instruction provided in any ostensibly secular subject in any religious school. [T]here was no stopping place in principle once the public teacher entered the religious schools to teach their secular subjects.

It may be objected that there is some subsidy in remedial education even when it takes place off the religious premises, some subsidy, that is, even in the way New York City has administered the Title I program after *Aguilar*. [But] the difference in the degree of reasonably perceptible endorsement is substantial. Sharing the teaching responsibilities within a school having religious objectives is far more likely to telegraph approval of the school's mission than keeping the State's distance would do. [I]f a line is to be drawn short of barring all state aid to religious schools for teaching standard subjects, the *Aguilar–Ball* line was a sensible one capable of principled adherence. . . .

II.   . . . *Zobrest v. Catalina Foothills School Dist.* held that the Establishment Clause does not prevent a school district from providing a sign-language interpreter to a deaf student enrolled in a sectarian school. . . . In *Zobrest* the Court did indeed recognize that the Establishment Clause lays down no absolute bar to placing public employees in a sectarian school, but the rejection of such a *per se* rule was hinged expressly on the nature of the employee's job, sign-language interpretation (or signing) and the circumscribed role of the signer. . . . The signer could thus be seen as more like a hearing aid than a teacher, and the signing could not be understood as an opportunity to inject religious content in what was supposed to be secular instruction. *Zobrest* accordingly holds only that in these limited circumstances where a public employee simply translates for one student the material presented to the class for the benefit of all students, the employee's presence in the sectarian school does not violate the Establishment Clause. . . .

The Court notes that aid programs providing benefits solely to religious groups may be constitutionally suspect, while aid allocated under neutral, secular criteria is less likely to have the effect of advancing religion. The opinion then says that *Ball* and *Aguilar* "gave this consideration no weight," and accordingly conflict with a number of decisions. [However,] evenhandedness is a necessary but not a sufficient condition for an aid program to satisfy constitutional scrutiny. Title I services are available to all eligible children regardless whether they go to religious or public schools, but . . . that fact does not define the reach of the Establishment Clause. If a scheme of government aid results in support for religion in some substantial degree, or in endorsement of its value, the formal neutrality of the scheme does not render the Establishment Clause helpless or the holdings in *Aguilar* and *Ball* inapposite.

[The dissenting opinion of GINSBURG, J., joined by STEVENS, SOUTER, and BREYER, JJ. is omitted.]

11–1.3 Higher Education

ROEMER v. BOARD OF PUBLIC
WORKS OF MARYLAND

426 U.S. 736, 96 S.Ct. 2337, 49 L.Ed.2d 179 (1976).

Mr. Justice Blackmun announced the judgment of the Court and delivered an opinion in which The Chief Justice [Burger] and Mr. Justice Powell joined.

We are asked once again to police the constitutional boundary between church and state. Maryland, this time, is the alleged trespasser.... The challenged grant program ... provides funding for [any accredited private institution of higher learning in Maryland, subject to various exceptions]. The aid is in the form of an annual fiscal year subsidy to qualifying colleges and universities. The formula by which each institution's entitlement is computed ... now provides for a qualifying institution to receive, for each full-time student (excluding students enrolled in seminarian or theological academic programs), an amount equal to 15% of the State's per-full-time-pupil appropriation for a student in the state college system. [A] recipient institution may put [the grants] to whatever use it prefers, with but one exception.... "None of the moneys payable under this subtitle shall be utilized by the institutions for sectarian purposes." ...

After carefully assessing the role that the Catholic Church plays in the lives of these institutions [receiving the challenged aid], the District Court ruled that the amended statute was constitutional.... The court considered the original, unamended statute to have been unconstitutional under *Lemon I,* [403 U.S. 602, 91 S.Ct. 2105, 29 L.Ed.2d 745 (1971)] but it refused to order a refund of amounts theretofore paid out, reasoning that any refund was barred by the decision in *Lemon v. Kurtzman,* 411 U.S. 192, 93 S.Ct. 1463, 36 L.Ed.2d 151 (1973)(*Lemon II*).[11] ...

A system of government that makes itself felt as pervasively as ours could hardly be expected never to cross paths with the church.... It long has been established, for example, that the State may send a cleric, indeed even a clerical order, to perform a wholly secular task. In *Bradfield v. Roberts,* 175 U.S. 291, 20 S.Ct. 121, 44 L.Ed. 168 (1899), the Court upheld the extension of public aid to a corporation which, although composed entirely of members of a Roman Catholic sisterhood

---

11. *Lemon II* posed the question of the appropriate relief to be ordered in light of *Lemon I's* invalidation of the Pennsylvania private school aid statute. Future payments under that statute were enjoined, and there was no claim that the Constitution required the refunding to the State of amounts already paid out. The statute's challengers, however, did seek to enjoin the payment of funds intended to reimburse aided schools for expenses incurred in reliance on the statute prior to its invalidation in *Lemon I.* This Court affirmed the denial of the injunction, reasoning that the payments would not substantially undermine constitutional interests, and that there had been reasonable reliance by the schools on receipt of the funds, especially since the challengers, although they had filed suit before the expenses were incurred, had dropped an attempt to enjoin payments pending the outcome of the litigation.

acting "under the auspices of said church," was limited by its corporate charter to the secular purpose of operating a charitable hospital.... In *Tilton v. Richardson,* 403 U.S. 672, 91 S.Ct. 2091, 29 L.Ed.2d 790 (1971), a companion case to *Lemon I,* [the challenged aid] was in the form of federal grants for the construction of academic facilities at private colleges, some of them church related, with the restriction that the facilities not be used for any sectarian purpose.[17] Applying *Lemon I's* three-part test, the Court found the purpose of the federal aid program there under consideration to be secular. Its primary effect was not the advancement of religion, for sectarian use of the facilities was prohibited. Enforcement of this prohibition was made possible by the fact that religion did not so permeate the defendant colleges that their religious and secular functions were inseparable. On the contrary, there was no evidence that religious activities took place in the funded facilities. Courses at the colleges were "taught according to the academic requirements intrinsic to the subject matter," and "an atmosphere of academic freedom rather than religious indoctrination" was maintained.

Turning to the problem of excessive entanglement, the Court first stressed the character of the aided institutions. It pointed to several general differences between college and precollege education: College students are less susceptible to religious indoctrination; college courses tend to entail an internal discipline that inherently limits the opportunities for sectarian influence; and a high degree of academic freedom tends to prevail at the college level. It found no evidence that the colleges in *Tilton* varied from this pattern. Though controlled and largely populated by Roman Catholics, the colleges were not restricted to adherents of that faith. No religious services were required to be attended. Theology courses were mandatory, but they were taught in an academic fashion, and with treatment of beliefs other than Roman Catholicism. There were no attempts to proselytize among students, and principles of academic freedom prevailed. With colleges of this character, there was little risk that religion would seep into the teaching of secular subjects, and the state surveillance necessary to separate the two, therefore, was diminished. The Court next looked to the type of aid provided, and found it to be neutral or non-ideological in nature. [P]hysical facilities were capable of being restricted to secular purposes. Moreover, the construction grant was a one-shot affair, not involving annual audits and appropriations.

As for political divisiveness, no "continuing religious aggravation" over the program had been shown, and the Court reasoned that this might be because of the lack of continuity in the church-state relationship, the character and diversity of the colleges, and the fact that they served a dispersed student constituency rather than a local one. "[C]umulatively," all these considerations persuaded the Court that church-state entanglement was not excessive.

---

17. The restriction, as imposed, was to remain in effect for 20 years following construction. Since the Court could not ap-prove the facilities' sectarian use even after a 20-year period, it excised that time limitation from the statute.

In *Hunt v. McNair,* 413 U.S. 734, 93 S.Ct. 2868, 37 L.Ed.2d 923 (1973), the challenged aid was also for the construction of secular college facilities, the state plan being one to finance the construction by revenue bonds issued through the medium of a state authority. In effect, the college serviced and repaid the bonds, but at the lower cost resulting from the tax-free status of the interest payments. The Court upheld the program on reasoning analogous to that in *Tilton.* In applying the second of the *Lemon I's* three-part test, that concerning "primary effect," the following refinement was added:

> Aid normally may be thought to have a primary effect of advancing religion when it flows to an institution in which religion is so pervasive that a substantial portion of its functions are subsumed in the religious mission or when it funds a specifically religious activity in an otherwise substantially secular setting.

Although the college which *Hunt* concerned was subject to substantial control by its sponsoring Baptist Church, it was found to be similar to the colleges in *Tilton* and not "pervasively sectarian." *As* in *Tilton,* state aid went to secular facilities only, and thus not to any "specifically religious activity." . . .

The first part of *Lemon I's* three-part test is not in issue; appellants do not challenge the District Court's finding that the purpose of Maryland's aid program is the secular one of supporting private higher education generally, as an economic alternative to a wholly public system. . . .

While entanglement is essentially a procedural problem, the primary-effect question is the substantive one of what private educational activities, by whatever procedure, may be supported by state funds. *Hunt* requires (1) that no state aid at all go to institutions that are so "pervasively sectarian" that secular activities cannot be separated from sectarian ones, and (2) that if secular activities *can* be separated out, they alone may be funded.

(1) The District Court's finding in this case was that the appellee colleges are not "pervasively sectarian." This conclusion it supported with a number of subsidiary findings concerning the role of religion on these campuses: (a) Despite their formal affiliation with the Roman Catholic Church, the colleges are "characterized by a high degree of institutional autonomy." . . . (b) The colleges employ Roman Catholic chaplains and hold Roman Catholic religious exercises on campus. Attendance at such is not required; the encouragement of spiritual development is only "one secondary objective" of each college; and "at none of these institutions does this encouragement go beyond providing the opportunities or occasions for religious experience." (c) Mandatory religion or theology courses are taught at each of the colleges, primarily by Roman Catholic clerics, but these only supplement a curriculum covering "the spectrum of a liberal arts program." Nontheology courses are taught in an "atmosphere of intellectual freedom" and without "religious pressures." Each college subscribes to, and abides by, the 1940

Statement of Principles on Academic Freedom of the American Association of University Professors. (d) Some classes are begun with prayer.... There is no "actual college policy" of encouraging the practice. "It is treated as a facet of the instructor's academic freedom." Classroom prayers were therefore regarded by the District Court as "peripheral to the subject of religious permeation," as were the facts that some instructors wear clerical garb and some classrooms have religious symbols.... (e) The District Court found that, apart from the theology departments, faculty hiring decisions are not made on a religious basis.... (f) The great majority of students at each of the colleges are Roman Catholic, but ... the student bodies "are chosen without regard to religion."

... The general picture that the District Court has painted of the appellee institutions is similar in almost all respects to that of the church-affiliated colleges considered in *Tilton* and *Hunt*.[21] We find no constitutionally significant distinction between them, at least for purposes of the "pervasive sectarianism" test.

(2) Having found that the appellee institutions are not "so permeated by religion that the secular side cannot be separated from the sectarian," the District Court proceeded to the next question posed by *Hunt:* whether aid in fact was extended only to "the secular side." This requirement the court regarded as satisfied by the statutory prohibition against sectarian use, and by the administrative enforcement of that prohibition through the Council for Higher Education. We agree....

If the foregoing answer to the "primary effect" question seems easy, it serves to make the "excessive entanglement" problem more difficult. The statute itself clearly denies the use of public funds for "sectarian purposes." It seeks to avert such use, however, through a process of annual interchange—proposal and approval, expenditure and review—between the colleges and the Council. In answering the question whether this will be an "excessively entangling" relationship, we must consider the several relevant factors identified in prior decisions: First is the character of the aided institutions. This has been fully described above. As the District Court found, the colleges perform "essentially secular educational functions," that are distinct and separable from religious activity.... We agree with the District Court that "excessive entanglement" does not necessarily result from the fact that the subsidy is an annual one. It is true that the Court favored the "one-time, single-purpose" construction grants in *Tilton* because they entailed "no continuing financial relationships or dependencies, no annual audits, and no government analysis of an institution's expenditures." ... The present statute contemplates annual decisions by the Council as to what is a "sectarian purpose," but, as we have noted, the secular and sectarian

21. [T]he District Court was unable to find, as was stipulated in *Tilton,* that mandatory theology or religion courses are taught without taint of religious indoctrination. This is not inconsistent, however, with the District Court's finding of a lack of pervasive sectarianism. The latter condition would exist only if, because of the institution's general character, courses other than religion or theology courses could not be funded without fear of religious indoctrination....

activities of the colleges are easily separated. Occasional audits are possible here, but we must accept the District Court's finding that they would be "quick and non-judgmental." They and the other contacts between the Council and the colleges are not likely to be any more entangling than the inspections and audits incident to the normal process of the colleges' accreditations by the State . . . .

There is no exact science in gauging the entanglement of church and state. The wording of the test, which speaks of "*excessive* entanglement," itself makes that clear. [T]he District Court gave dominant importance to the character of the aided institutions and to its finding that they are capable of separating secular and religious functions. For the reasons stated above, we cannot say that the emphasis was misplaced or the finding erroneous. The judgment of the District Court is affirmed.

It is so ordered.

MR. JUSTICE WHITE, with whom MR. JUSTICE REHNQUIST joins, concurring in the judgment.

. . . No one in this case challenges the District Court's finding that the purpose of the legislation here is secular. And I do not disagree with the plurality that the primary effect of the aid program is not advancement of religion. That is enough in my view to sustain the aid programs against constitutional challenge, and I would say no more.

MR. JUSTICE BRENNAN, with whom MR. JUSTICE MARSHALL joins, dissenting.

[T]he Act provides for payment of general subsidies to religious institutions from public funds and I have heretofore expressed my view that "[g]eneral subsidies of religious activities would, of course, constitute impermissible state involvement with religion." . . .

MR. JUSTICE STEWART, dissenting.

[T]he decisive differences between this case and *Tilton v. Richardson,* 403 U.S. 672, lie in the nature of the theology courses that are a compulsory part of the curriculum at each of the appellee institutions and the type of governmental assistance provided to these church-affiliated colleges. In *Tilton* the Court emphasized that the theology courses were taught as academic subjects. ". . . The schools introduced evidence that they made no attempt to indoctrinate students or to proselytize. Indeed, some of the required theology courses at Albertus Magnus and Sacred Heart are taught by rabbis." Here, by contrast, the District Court was unable to find that the compulsory religion courses were taught as an academic discipline.

... All five defendants staff their religion or theology departments chiefly with clerics of the affiliated church. At two defendants, Western Maryland and Mt. St. Mary's, *all* members of the religion or theology faculty are clerics. The problem presented by the make-up of these departments is obvious. Recognition of the academic freedom of these instructors does not necessarily lead to a conclusion that courses in the religion or theology departments at the five defendants have no overtones of indoctrination....

[The dissenting opinion of STEVENS, J., is omitted.]

Notes

1.   In *Witters v. Washington Department of Services for the Blind*, 474 U.S. 481, 106 S.Ct. 748, 88 L.Ed.2d 846 (1986), Justice Marshall for the Court held that nothing in the First Amendment prevented a state from extending financial assistance under a state vocational rehabilitation assistance program to a blind person who was attending a private Christian college and studying to become a pastor, missionary, or youth director. "Any aid provided under Washington's program that ultimately flows to religious institutions does so only as a result of the genuinely independent and private choices of aid recipients." The program "creates no financial incentive for students to undertake sectarian education," and the "mere circumstance that petitioner has chosen to use neutrally available state aid to help pay for his religious education [does not] confer any message of state endorsement of religion." There were no dissents.

2.   The Adolescent Family Life Act of 1981 (AFLA) authorized federal grants to both public and private organizations to provide services in the area of premarital adolescent sexual relations and pregnancy. The Act required the grantees to furnish counseling and education relating to these subjects, but forbade the use of funds for family planning and promotion of abortion. The Act said that the complexity of the problem required the involvement of religious and charitable organizations. Some of the federal grant money went to organizations connected with religious denominations. *Bowen v. Kendrick*, 487 U.S. 589, 108 S.Ct. 2562, 101 L.Ed.2d 520 (1988) refused (5 to 4) to invalidate the law on its face, but remanded the case to determine whether any of the grants made violated the Establishment Clause.

Rehnquist, C.J., for the Court, ruled, first, that under the *Lemon v. Kurtzman* test, the Act was motivated "primarily, if not entirely," by a valid secular purpose—eliminating or reducing the problems caused by adolescent sexuality, pregnancy, and parenthood. Second, the Act does not have the primary effect of advancing religion because it only allows, but does not require, that grantees to be affiliated with a religious organization, and the services provided (e.g., adoption counseling, education) are not inherently religious in nature. Congress wanted "broad-based community involvement" and thought that religious organizations can aid in solving the problem. Finally, on its face the Act passes the third part of the *Lemon* test: "Most of the cases in which the Court has divided over the 'entanglement' part of the *Lemon* test have involved aid to parochial schools [which the Court found to be] 'pervasively sectarian'.... Here, by contrast, there is no reason to assume that the religious organizations which may receive grants are 'pervasively sectarian' in the same sense.... " The Court then remanded so that the trial judge could determine if any of the grantees are "pervasively sectarian" like parochial schools, or if the grants are used to fund specific religious activities and, if they are, to devise a remedy to insure that the grants awarded comply with the statute and the Constitution.

Blackmun, J., joined by Brennan, Marshall, and Stevens, JJ., dissented, because this law "encouraged the use of public funds for such [religious] instruction, by giving religious groups a central pedagogical and counseling role without imposing any restraints on the sectarian quality of the participation"—e.g., one prospective grantee described a method of family planning in the grant application as "not only a method of birth regulation but also a philosophy of procreation," with the method promoted as helping spouses "to make themselves better instruments in God's plan."

11–2. NONFINANCIAL ASSISTANCE TO RELIGION

11–2.1 Prayers, Symbols, and Curriculum

SCHOOL DISTRICT OF ABINGTON TOWNSHIP v. SCHEMPP

374 U.S. 203, 83 S.Ct. 1560, 10 L.Ed.2d 844 (1963).

MR. JUSTICE CLARK delivered the opinion of the Court. . . .

The Facts in Each Case: No. 142. The Commonwealth of Pennsylvania by law, requires that "At least ten verses from the Holy Bible shall be read, without comment, at the opening of each public school on each school day. Any child shall be excused from such Bible reading, or attending such Bible reading, upon the written request of his parent or guardian." The Schempp family, husband and wife and two of the three children, brought suit to enjoin enforcement of the statute. . . .

No. 119. In 1905 the Board of School Commissioners of Baltimore City adopted a rule [providing] for the holding of opening exercises in the schools of the city, consisting primarily of the "reading, without comment, of a chapter in the Holy Bible and/or the use of the Lord's Prayer." The petitioners, Mrs. Madalyn Murray and her son, William J. Murray III, are both professed atheists. Following unsuccessful attempts to have the respondent school board rescind the rule, this suit was filed for mandamus to compel its rescission and cancellation. It was alleged that William was a student in a public school of the city and Mrs. Murray, his mother, was a taxpayer therein. . . .

First, this Court has decisively settled that the First Amendment's mandate that "Congress shall make no law respecting an establishment of religion, or prohibiting the free exercise thereof" has been made wholly applicable to the States by the Fourteenth Amendment. Second, this Court has rejected unequivocally the contention that the Establishment Clause forbids only governmental preference of one religion over another. Almost 20 years ago in *Everson,* [*v. Board of Educ.,* 330 U.S. 1, 15, 67 S.Ct. 504, 91 L.Ed. 711 (1947)], the Court said that "[neither a state nor the Federal Government can set up a church. Neither can pass laws which aid one religion, aid all religions, or prefer one religion over another." . . .

The interrelationship of the Establishment and the Free Exercise Clauses was first touched upon by Mr. Justice Roberts for the Court in

Cantwell v. Connecticut, 310 U.S. 296 [1940], at 303–304, where it was said that their "inhibition of legislation" had

> a double aspect. On the one hand, it forestalls compulsion by law of the acceptance of any creed or the practice of any form of worship. Freedom of conscience and freedom to adhere to such religious organization or form of worship as the individual may choose cannot be restricted by law. On the other hand, it safeguards the free exercise of the chosen form of religion. Thus the Amendment embraces two concepts,—freedom to believe and freedom to act. The first is absolute but, in the nature of things, the second cannot be.

[I]n *Engel v. Vitale,* [370 U.S. 421, 82 S.Ct. 1261, 8 L.Ed.2d 601 (1962)], only last year, these principles were so universally recognized that the Court, without the citation of a single case and over the sole dissent of Mr. Justice Stewart, reaffirmed them. The Court found the 22–word prayer used in "New York's program of daily classroom invocation of God's blessings as prescribed in the Regents' prayer ... [to be] a religious activity." It held that "it is no part of the business of government to compose official prayers for any group of the American people to recite as a part of a religious program carried on by government."

[T]o withstand the strictures of the Establishment Clause there must be a secular legislative purpose and a primary effect that neither advances nor inhibits religion. The Free Exercise Clause, likewise considered many times here, withdraws from legislative power, state and federal, the exertion of any restraint on the free exercise of religion. Its purpose is to secure religious liberty in the individual by prohibiting any invasions thereof by civil authority. Hence it is necessary in a free exercise case for one to show the coercive effect of the enactment as it operates against him in the practice of his religion. The distinction between the two clauses is apparent—a violation of the Free Exercise Clause is predicated on coercion while the Establishment Clause violation need not be so attended.

Applying the Establishment Clause principles to the cases at bar we find that the States are requiring the selection and reading at the opening of the school day of verses from the Holy Bible and the recitation of the Lord's Prayer by the students in unison. These exercises are prescribed as part of the curricular activities of students who are required by law to attend school. They are held in the school buildings under the supervision and with the participation of teachers employed in those schools.... We agree with the trial court's finding as to the religious character of the exercises. Given that finding, the exercises and the law requiring them are in violation of the Establishment Clause.

There is no such specific finding as to the religious character of the exercises in No. 119, and the State contends (as does the State in No. 142) that the program is an effort to extend its benefits to all public school children without regard to their religious belief. Included within its secular purposes, it says, are the promotion of moral values, the contradiction to the materialistic trends of our times, the perpetuation of our institutions and the teaching of literature. The case came up on demurrer, of course, to a petition which alleged that the uniform practice under the rule had been to read from the King James version of the Bible and that the exercise was sectarian. The short answer, therefore, is that the religious character of the exercise was admitted by the State. But even if its purpose is not strictly religious, it is sought to be accomplished through readings, without comment, from the Bible. Surely the place of the Bible as an instrument of religion cannot be gainsaid, and the State's recognition of the pervading religious character of the ceremony is evident from the rule's specific permission of the alternative use of the Catholic Douay version as well as the recent amendment permitting nonattendance at the exercises. None of these factors is consistent with the contention that the Bible is here used either as an instrument for nonreligious moral inspiration or as a reference for the teaching of secular subjects.

The conclusion follows that in both cases the laws require religious exercises and such exercises are being conducted in direct violation of the rights of the appellees and petitioners.[9] Nor are these required exercises mitigated by the fact that individual students may absent themselves upon parental request, for the fact furnishes no defense to a claim of unconstitutionality under the Establishment Clause. Further, it is no defense to urge that the religious practices here may be relatively minor encroachments on the First Amendment. The breach of neutrality that is today a trickling stream may all too soon become a raging torrent and, in the words of Madison, "it is proper to take alarm at the first experiment on our liberties."

It is insisted that unless these religious exercises are permitted a "religion of secularism" is established in the schools. We agree of course that the State may not establish a "religion of secularism" in the sense of affirmatively opposing or showing hostility to religion, thus "preferring those who believe in no religion over those who do believe." *Zorach v. Clauson,* supra. We do not agree, however, that this decision in any sense has that effect. In addition, it might well be said that one's education is not complete without a study of comparative religion or the history of religion and its relationship to the advancement of civilization. It certainly may be said that the Bible is worthy of study for its literary and historic qualities. Nothing we have said here indicates that such study of the Bible or of religion, when presented objectively as part of a secular program of education, may not be effected consistently with the First Amendment. But the exercises here do not fall into those categories. They are religious exercises, required by the States in violation of

9. It goes without saying that the laws and practices involved here can be challenged only by persons having standing to complain. But the requirements for standing to challenge state action under the Establishment Clause, unlike those relating to the Free Exercise Clause, do not include proof that particular religious freedoms are infringed. The parties here are school children and their parents, who are directly affected by the laws and practices against which their complaints are directed. These interests surely suffice to give the parties standing to complain. . . .

the command of the First Amendment that the Government maintain strict neutrality, neither aiding nor opposing religion.

Finally, we cannot accept that the concept of neutrality, which does not permit a State to require a religious exercise even with the consent of the majority of those affected, collides with the majority's right to free exercise of religion.[10] While the Free Exercise Clause clearly prohibits the use of state action to deny the rights of free exercise to *anyone,* it has never meant that a majority could use the machinery of the State to practice its beliefs....

Mr. Justice Brennan, concurring.

[A]n awareness of history and an appreciation of the aims of the Founding Fathers do not always resolve concrete problems.... It may be that Jefferson and Madison would have held such exercises to be permissible.... But I doubt that their view, even if perfectly clear one way or the other, would supply a dispositive answer to the question presented by these cases. A more fruitful inquiry, it seems to me, is whether the practices here challenged threaten those consequences which the Framers deeply feared; whether, in short, they tend to promote that type of interdependence between religion and state which the First Amendment was designed to prevent....

The saying of invocational prayers in legislative chambers, state or federal, and the appointment of legislative chaplains, might well represent no involvements of the kind prohibited by the Establishment Clause. Legislators, federal and state, are mature adults who may presumably absent themselves from such public and ceremonial exercises without incurring any penalty, direct or indirect. It may also be significant that, at least in the case of the Congress, Art. I, § 5, of the Constitution makes each House the monitor of the "Rules of its Proceedings" so that it is at least arguable whether such matters present "political questions" the resolution of which is exclusively confided to Congress. See *Baker v. Carr,* [§ 1–2.4, supra]. Finally, there is the difficult question of who may be heard to challenge such practices.

The holding of the Court today plainly does not foreclose teaching *about* the Holy Scriptures or about the differences between religious sects in classes in literature or history. Indeed, whether or not the Bible is involved, it would be impossible to teach meaningfully many subjects in the social sciences or the humanities without some mention of religion.

[T]he use of the motto "In God We Trust" on currency, or documents and public buildings and the like may not offend the clause. It is not that the use of those four words can be dismissed as "de minimis"— for I suspect there would be intense opposition to the abandonment of

---

10. We are not of course presented with and therefore do not pass upon a situation such as military service, where the Government regulates the temporal and geographic environment of individuals to a point that, unless it permits voluntary religious services to be conducted with the use of government facilities, military personnel would be unable to engage in the practice of their faiths.

that motto. The truth is that we have simply interwoven the motto so deeply into the fabric of our civil polity that its present use may well not present that type of involvement which the First Amendment prohibits.

This general principle might also serve to insulate the various patriotic exercises and activities used in the public schools and elsewhere which, whatever may have been their origins, no longer have a religious purpose or meaning. The reference to divinity in the revised pledge of allegiance, for example, may merely recognize the historical fact that our Nation was believed to have been founded "under God." Thus reciting the pledge may be no more of a religious exercise than the reading aloud of Lincoln's Gettysburg Address, which contains an allusion to the same historical fact.

MR. JUSTICE STEWART, dissenting.

[I]t seems to me clear that certain types of exercises would present situations in which no possibility of coercion on the part of secular officials could be claimed to exist. Thus, if such exercises were held either before or after the official school day, or if the school schedule were such that participation were merely one among a number of desirable alternatives, it could hardly be contended that the exercises did anything more than to provide an opportunity for the voluntary expression of religious belief. . . .

[The concurring opinion of DOUGLAS, J., & of GOLDBERG, J., joined by HARLAN, J., are omitted].

Notes

1.   In *Minersville School District v. Gobitis,* 310 U.S. 586, 60 S.Ct. 1010, 84 L.Ed. 1375 (1940), Justice Frankfurter for the Court, upheld a Pennsylvania regulation requiring school children and their teachers to salute the national flag as part of a daily school exercise. The Gobitis children, members of the Jehovah's Witnesses, refused on the grounds that showing such respect for the flag is forbidden by the Scriptural prohibition against worshiping false gods and making graven images. Therefore the school authorities expelled them and they entered private school. Chief Justice Hughes and Justices Stone, Roberts, Black, Reed, Douglas, and Murphy all joined Frankfurter's opinion. Justice McReynolds concurred in the judgment, without opinion. Justice Stone was the sole dissenter.

Gobitis received widespread publicity. It appeared to endorse the salute, and "its implied rebuke of the Witnesses, aggravated the already charged situation."

The most spectacular manifestation of anti-Witness hostility was a sharp outbreak of violence. In June, 1940, several hundred incidents occurred in which force was directed against Jehovah's Witnesses; violent incidents continued at a rate of almost a hundred a month through most of 1940, all following a fixed pattern. Hundreds of street fights broke out. A Jehovah's Witness, distributing tracts on a street corner, was approached by several toughs carrying an American flag. When he refused their command to salute the flag, they beat him and destroyed his literature. Where the approach was made to a group of Witnesses, the affair turned into a full-scale brawl.

Often the violence transcended mere street-fighting, especially in the period immediately following the *Gobitis* decision. On June 9, 1940, an angry mob sacked and burned a Witness "Kingdom Hall" at Kennebunk, Maine. On June 22 a Witness was tarred and feathered in Parco, Wyoming. On June 27 a mob of veterans forcibly deported a large number of Witnesses from Jackson, Mississippi, eventually dropping them off at Dallas, Texas. In August a Nebraska Witness was abducted from his home and partially castrated. While the frequency of violent incidents tapered off after 1940, nasty cases continued to occur.[1]

In *West Virginia State Board of Education v. Barnette,* 319 U.S. 624, 63 S.Ct. 1178, 87 L.Ed. 1628 (1943), Justice Jackson for the Court (6 to 3), overruled *Gobitis.* Justices Roberts and Reed dissented, without opinion, and referred to the majority's opinion in *Gobitis.* Justice Frankfurter wrote a strong dissent.[2]

Jackson explained the issue before the Court did not really "turn on one's possession of particular religious views or the sincerity with which they are held. While religion supplies appellees' motive for enduring the discomforts of making the issue in this case, many citizens who do not share these religious views hold such a compulsory rite to infringe constitutional liberty of the individual. It is not necessary to inquire whether non-conformist beliefs will exempt from the duty to salute unless we first find power to make the salute a legal duty." The *Barnette* Court noted that *Gobitis* had assumed the existence of the power and then rejected a claim of immunity based on religious beliefs. *Barnette* found no such power.

If there is any fixed star in our constitutional constellation, it is that no official, high or petty, can prescribe what shall be orthodox in politics, nationalism, religion, or other matters of opinion or force citizens to confess by word or act their faith therein. [T]he action of the local authorities in compelling the flag salute and pledge transcends constitutional limitations on their power and invades the sphere of intellect and spirit which it is the purpose of the First Amendment of our Constitution to reserve from all official control.

Barnette then affirmed the lower court judgment enjoining enforcement of the flag salute law against Jehovah's Witnesses.

Note that *Barnette,*—unlike *Schempp* and other school prayer cases—did not strike down the flag salute all together, but only required that all those

---

1. Manwaring, The Flag–Salute Case, at 27–28, in The Third Branch of Government: 8 Cases in Constitutional Politics (C. Pritchett & A. Westin, eds. 1963).

2. In dissent Frankfurter wrote: "One who belongs to the most vilified and persecuted minority in history is not likely to be insensible to the freedoms guaranteed in our Constitution. Were my purely personal attitude relevant, I should wholeheartedly associate myself with the general libertarian views in the Court's opinion, [but] I

cannot bring my mind to believe that the 'liberty' secured by the Due Process Clause gives this Court authority to deny to the State of West Virginia the attainment of that which we all recognize as a legitimate legislative end, namely, the promotion of good citizenship, by employment of the means here chosen."

Jackson was appointed to the Court in 1941. His opinion was joined by Stone (now Chief Justice) and Justices Black, Douglas, Murphy, and Rutledge (appointed in 1943).

objecting to the salute be excused. *Schempp,* at the end of the majority opinion, cited and quoted *Barnette* with approval. Are the two cases consistent?

2. After *School District of Abington Township v. Schempp,* would it be constitutional for a grade school class to learn and sing religious Christmas carols—e.g., "Silent Night, Holy Night"—as the school year approached Christmas? Could a school district arrange its school calendar so that school vacations always included the Christmas season? The Easter season? (Easter is a movable holiday).

3. *Stone v. Graham,* 449 U.S. 39, 101 S.Ct. 192, 66 L.Ed.2d 199 (1980)(per curiam). A Kentucky statute required that on the wall of each public classroom there be posted a copy of the Ten Commandments, purchased with private funds. At the bottom of each display there was the following notation: "The secular application of the Ten Commandments is clearly seen in its adoption as the fundamental legal code of Western Civilization and the Common Law of the United States." The Supreme Court found no secular purpose and hence a violation of the Establishment Clause. The Commandments are a "sacred text" that do not confine themselves "to arguably secular matters, such as honoring one's parents, killing or murder" but also concern religious duties such as avoiding idolatry. "This is not a case in which the Ten Commandments are integrated into the school curriculum, where the Bible may constitutionally be used in an appropriate study of history, civilization, ethics, comparative religion, or the like.... If the posted copies of the Ten Commandments are to have any effect at all, it will be to induce the school children to read, meditate upon, perhaps to venerate and obey, the Commandments."

Contrast *Marsh v. Chambers,* 463 U.S. 783, 103 S.Ct. 3330, 77 L.Ed.2d 1019 (1983), where the Court, per Burger, C.J., held that there is no violation of the Establishment Clause when the Nebraska legislature begins each of its sessions with a prayer, in the Judaeo–Christian tradition, by a chaplain paid by the state with the legislature's approval. A member of the Nebraska legislature objected to this practice. A Presbyterian minister had served as chaplain since 1965, receiving nearly $320 per month for each month while the legislature was in session. The Court upheld the Nebraska practice, after weighing the historical background:

> The opening of sessions of legislative and other deliberative public bodies with prayer is deeply embedded in the history and tradition of this country. From colonial times through the founding of the Republic and ever since, the practice of legislative prayer has coexisted with the principles of disestablishment and religious freedom. In the very courtrooms in which the United States District Judge and later three Circuit Judges heard and decided this case, the proceedings opened with an announcement that concluded, "God save the United States and this Honorable Court." The same invocation occurs at all sessions of this Court.

> [T]he First Congress, as one of its early items of business, adopted the policy of selecting a chaplain to open each session with prayer. [The] delegates [to the first Congress] did not consider opening prayers as a proselytizing activity or as symbolically placing the government's "offi-

cial seal of approval on one religious view". [Moreover, here] the individual claiming injury by the practice is an adult, presumably not readily susceptible to "religious indoctrination," or peer pressure.

In light of the unambiguous and unbroken history of more than 200 years, there can be no doubt that the practice of opening legislative sessions with prayer has become part of the fabric of our society. To invoke Divine guidance on a public body entrusted with making the laws is not, in these circumstances, an "establishment" of religion or a step toward establishment; it is simply a tolerable acknowledgment of beliefs widely held among the people of this country.... The content of the prayer is not of concern to judges where, as here, there is no indication that the prayer opportunity has been exploited to proselytize or advance any one, or to disparage any other, faith or belief.

Brennan, J., joined by Marshall, J., dissented. Brennan recalled his concurring opinion in *Schempp*, but stated:

[A]fter much reflection, I have come to the conclusion that I was wrong then and that the Court is wrong today. I now believe that the practice of official invocational prayer, as it exists in Nebraska and most other State Legislatures, is unconstitutional. It is contrary to the doctrine as well the underlying purposes of the Establishment Clause, and it is not saved either by its history or by any of the other considerations suggested in the Court's opinion....

Lee v. Weisman, 505 U.S. 577, 112 S.Ct. 2649, 120 L.Ed.2d 467 (1992) held (5 to 4) that it violated the Establishment Clause for a public secondary school to invite a member of the clergy to deliver a nonsectarian benediction or prayer at official graduation ceremonies. Kennedy, J., joined by Blackmun, Stevens, O'Connor, & Souter, JJ., refused to reconsider *Lemon v. Kurtzman* and concluded that the state may not subject "primary and secondary school children" to the dilemma of either participating in the graduation ceremony "with all that implies," or of protesting. The Court said that it was not addressing the constitutionality of such actions as applied to "mature adults," but as to children the "[r]esearch in psychology" supports the view that there is "subtle and indirect" coercion because there is "public pressure, as well as peer pressure, on attending students to stand as a group or, at least, maintain respectful silence through the Invocation and Benediction."

Blackmun, J., concurring, joined by Stevens & O'Connor, JJ., argued that "proof of government coercion is not necessary to prove an Establishment Clause violation...." Souter, J., joined by Stevens & O'Connor, JJ., also filed a concurring opinion emphasizing that there is a violation of the Establishment Clause even without coercion.

Scalia, J., joined by Rehnquist, C.J., & White & Thomas, JJ., dissented, objecting to the majority's lack of reference to history: there is a "longstanding American tradition of nonsectarian prayer to God at public celebrations generally." The Declaration of Independence appealed "to the Supreme Judge of the world;" George Washington "deliberately made a prayer a part of his first official act as President" when he delivered his inaugural, as did other Presidents. The majority's reference to "psychological coercion" is "psychology practice by amateurs." The majority's argument that—

1340 RELIGION Ch. 11

a student who simply *sits* in "respectful silence" during the invocation and benediction (when all others are standing) has somehow joined—or would somehow be perceived as having joined—in the prayers is nothing short of ludicrous. We indeed live in a vulgar age. But surely "our social conventions" have not coarsened to the point that anyone who does not stand on the chair and shout obscenities can reasonably be deemed to have assented to everything said in his presence. (emphasis in original.)

4. *Larkin v. Grendel's Den, Inc.*, 459 U.S. 116, 103 S.Ct. 505, 74 L.Ed.2d 297 (1982). A Massachusetts statute said: "Premises . . . located within a radius of five hundred feet of a church or school shall not be licensed for the sale of alcoholic beverages if the governing body of such church or school files written objection thereto." This statute, said the Court, has a valid secular purpose, to protect "spiritual, cultural, and educational centers from the 'hurly-burly' associated with liquor outlets." But these objectives could have been met if the state either had an "absolute legislative ban on liquor outlets within reasonable prescribed distances from churches, schools, hospitals and like institutions, or by ensuring a hearing for the views of affected institutions at the licensing proceedings where, without question, such views would be entitled to substantial weight." What the state could not do was give to a church veto power over a governmental licensing authority. This statute "provides a significant symbolic benefit to religion in the minds of some [and] enmeshes churches in the exercise of substantial governmental powers. . . . " The law violated the establishment clause.

Rehnquist, J., was the sole dissenter. The state statute had originally been a flat ban on liquor licenses within 500 feet of a church or school:

The flat ban, which the majority concedes is valid, is more protective of churches and more restrictive of liquor sales than the present § 16C. . . . If a particular church or a particular school located within the 500 foot radius chooses not to object, the state has quite sensibly concluded that there is no reason to prohibit the issuance of the license. Nothing in the Court's opinion persuades me why the more rigid prohibition would be constitutional, but the more flexible not. . . . Section 16C does not sponsor or subsidize any religious group or activity. It does not encourage, much less compel, anyone to participate in religious activities or to support religious institutions. To say that it "advances" religion is to strain at the meaning of that word.

5. *The Church of Jesus Christ of Latter–day Saints v. Amos*, 483 U.S. 327, 107 S.Ct. 2862, 97 L.Ed.2d 273 (1987). Religious entities associated with the Church of Jesus Christ of Latter–Day Saints ran a nonprofit facility open to the public. The facility terminated an employee because he was not a member of the Church. He alleged religious discrimination in violation of Title VII of the Civil Rights Act of 1964, and the Church responded that § 702 of Title VII exempted from its provisions religious discrimination by religious employers even if the hiring is for a nonreligious job. The Court, with no dissent, held that the § 702 exemption was constitutional and did not constitute an Establishment.

The Establishment Clause allows ample room for the Government to offer benevolent neutrality, the Court said. The exemption reduced significant governmental interference with the ability of religious organizations to define and implement their religious missions. Section 702 did not entangle church and state but effected a more complete separation between the two. Although § 702 gives employees of religious employers fewer rights than employees of secular employers, there is no violation of equal protection because the statute, neutral on its face, does not discriminate among religions and is motivated by the desire to limit governmental interference with free exercise. This classification rationally furthers this legitimate goal. In such cases the Court will not apply strict scrutiny.

EPPERSON v. ARKANSAS
393 U.S. 97, 89 S.Ct. 266, 21 L.Ed.2d 228 (1968).

MR. JUSTICE FORTAS delivered the opinion of the Court.

This appeal challenges the constitutionality of the "anti-evolution" statute which the State of Arkansas adopted in 1928 to prohibit the teaching in its public schools and universities of the theory that man evolved from other species of life.... The Arkansas statute was an adaptation of the famous Tennessee "monkey law" which that State adopted in 1925. The constitutionality of the Tennessee law was upheld by the Tennessee Supreme Court in the celebrated *Scopes* case in 1927....

Susan Epperson, a young woman who graduated from Arkansas' school system and then obtained her master's degree in zoology at the University of Illinois, was employed by the Little Rock school system in the fall of 1964 to teach 10th grade biology at Central High School. At the start of the next academic year, 1965, she was confronted by [a] new textbook [that included a section on the Darwinian theory] (which one surmises from the record was not unwelcome to her). She faced at least a literal dilemma because she was supposed to use the new textbook for classroom instruction and presumably to teach the statutorily condemned chapter; but to do so would be a criminal offense and subject her to dismissal.

She instituted the present action in the Chancery Court of the State, seeking a declaration that the Arkansas statute is void and enjoining the State and the defendant officials of the Little Rock school system from dismissing her for violation of the statute's provisions. H.H. Blanchard, a parent of children attending the public schools, intervened in support of the action. On appeal, the Supreme Court of Arkansas reversed [the Chancery Court]. Its two-sentence opinion is set forth in the margin.[7] It sustained the statute as an exercise of the State's power to specify the

---

7. "Per Curiam. Upon the principal issue, that of constitutionality, the court holds that Initiated Measure No. 1 of 1928, Ark.Stat.Ann. § 80–1627 and § 80–1628 (Repl.1960), is a valid exercise of the state's power to specify the curriculum, in its public schools. The court expresses no opinion on the question whether the Act prohibits any explanation of the theory of evolution or merely prohibits teaching that the theory is true; the answer not being necessary to a decision in the case, and the issue not having been raised."

curriculum in public schools. It did not address itself to the competing constitutional considerations.

"The decree is reversed and the cause dismissed.

"Ward, J., concurs. Brown, J., dissents. "Paul Ward, Justice, concurring. I agree with the first sentence in the majority opinion.

"To my mind, the rest of the opinion beclouds the clear announcement made in the first sentence."

[C]ounsel for the State, in oral argument in this Court, candidly stated that, despite the State Supreme Court's equivocation, Arkansas would interpret the statute "to mean that to make a student aware of the theory . . . just to teach that there was such a theory" would be grounds for dismissal and for prosecution under the statute; and he said "that the Supreme Court of Arkansas' opinion should be interpreted in that manner." He said: "If Mrs. Epperson would tell her students that 'Here is Darwin's theory, that man ascended or descended from a lower form of being,' then I think she would be under this statute liable for prosecution."

In any event, we do not rest our decision upon the asserted vagueness of the statute. . . . Under either interpretation, the law must be stricken because of its conflict with the constitutional prohibition of state laws respecting an establishment of religion or prohibiting the free exercise thereof. The overriding fact is that Arkansas' law selects from the body of knowledge a particular segment which it prescribes for the sole reason that it is deemed to conflict with a particular religious doctrine; that is, with a particular interpretation of the Book of Genesis by a particular religious group. . . . The State's undoubted right to prescribe the curriculum for its public schools does not carry with it the right to prohibit, on pain of criminal penalty, the teaching of a scientific theory or doctrine where that prohibition is based upon reasons that violate the First Amendment. It is much too late to argue that the State may impose upon the teachers in its schools any conditions that it chooses, however restrictive they may be of constitutional guarantees.

In the present case, there can be no doubt that Arkansas has sought to prevent its teachers from discussing the theory of evolution because it is contrary to the belief of some that the Book of Genesis must be the exclusive source of doctrine as to the origin of man. No suggestion has been made that Arkansas' law may be justified by considerations of state policy other than the religious views of some of its citizens. It is clear that fundamentalist sectarian conviction was and is the law's reason for existence.[16] Its antecedent, Tennessee's "monkey law," candidly stated its purpose: to make it unlawful "to teach any theory that denies the story of the Divine Creation of man as taught in the Bible, and to teach instead that man has descended from a lower order of animals." Perhaps the sensational publicity attendant upon the *Scopes* trial induced Arkan-

---

16. The following advertisement is typical of the public appeal which was used in the campaign to secure adoption of the statute:

sas to adopt less explicit language. It eliminated Tennessee's reference to "the story of the Divine Creation of man" as taught in the Bible, but there is no doubt that the motivation for the law was the same: to suppress the teaching of a theory which, it was thought, "denied" the divine creation of man.

"THE BIBLE OR ATHEISM, WHICH?

"All atheists favor evolution. If you agree with atheism vote against Act No. 1. If you agree with the Bible vote for Act No. 1.... Shall conscientious church members be forced to pay taxes to support teachers to teach evolution which will undermine the faith of their children? The Gazette said Russian Bolshevists laughed at Tennessee. True, and that sort will laugh at Arkansas. Who cares? Vote FOR ACT No. 1." The Arkansas Gazette, Little Rock, Nov. 4, 1928, p. 12, cols. 4–5.

Letters from the public expressed the fear that teaching of evolution would be "subversive of Christianity," id., Oct. 24, 1928, p. 7, col. 2; see also id., Nov. 4, 1928, p. 19, col. 4; and that it would cause school children "to disrespect the Bible," id., Oct. 27, 1928, p. 15, col. 5. ...

Arkansas' law cannot be defended as an act of religious neutrality. Arkansas did not seek to excise from the curricula of its schools and universities all discussion of the origin of man. The law's effort was confined to an attempt to blot out a particular theory because of its supposed conflict with the Biblical account, literally read. Plainly, the law is contrary to the mandate of the First, and in violation of the Fourteenth, Amendment to the Constitution.

The judgment of the Supreme Court of Arkansas is

Reversed.

MR. JUSTICE BLACK, concurring.

I am by no means sure that this case presents a genuinely justiciable case or controversy. Although Arkansas Initiated Act No. 1, the statute alleged to be unconstitutional, was passed by the voters of Arkansas in 1928, we are informed that there has never been even a single attempt by the State to enforce it. And the pallid, unenthusiastic, even apologetic defense of the Act presented by the State in this Court indicates that the State would make no attempt to enforce the law should it remain on the books for the next century. Now, nearly 40 years after the law has slumbered on the books as though dead, a teacher alleging fear that the State might arouse from its lethargy and try to punish her has asked for a declaratory judgment holding the law unconstitutional. She was subsequently joined by a parent who alleged his interest in seeing that his two then school-age sons "be informed of all scientific theories and hypotheses...." But whether this Arkansas teacher is still a teacher, fearful of punishment under the Act, we do not know. It may be, as has been published in the daily press, that she has long since given up her job as a teacher and moved to a distant city, thereby escaping the dangers she had imagined might befall her under this lifeless Arkansas Act. And there is not one iota of concrete evidence to show that the parent-intervenor's sons have not been or will not be taught about evolution. The textbook adopted for use in biology classes in Little Rock includes an entire chapter dealing with evolution. There is no evidence that this chapter is not being freely taught in the schools that use the textbook and no evidence that the intervenor's sons, who were 15 and 17 years old when this suit was brought three years ago, are still in high school or yet to take biology. Unfortunately, however, the State's languid interest in the case has not prompted it to keep this Court informed concerning facts that might easily justify dismissal of this alleged lawsuit as moot or as lacking the qualities of genuine case or controversy.

... It is plain that a state law prohibiting all teaching of human development or biology is constitutionally quite different from a law that compels a teacher to teach as true only one theory of a given doctrine. It would be difficult to make a First Amendment case out of a state law eliminating the subject of higher mathematics, or astronomy, or biology from its curriculum. And, for all the Supreme Court of Arkansas has said, this particular Act may prohibit that and nothing else. This Court, however, treats the Arkansas Act as though it made it a misdemeanor to teach or to use a book that teaches that evolution is true. But it is not for this Court to arrogate to itself the power to determine the scope of Arkansas statutes. Since the highest court of Arkansas has deliberately refused to give its statute that meaning, we should not presume to do so.

It seems to me that in this situation the statute is too vague for us to strike it down on any ground but that: vagueness. Under this statute as construed by the Arkansas Supreme Court, a teacher cannot know whether he is forbidden to mention Darwin's theory at all or only free to discuss it as long as he refrains from contending that it is true. It is an established rule that a statute which leaves an ordinary man so doubtful about its meaning that he cannot know when he has violated it denies him the first essential of due process. ...

The Court, not content to strike down this Arkansas Act on the unchallengeable ground of its plain vagueness, chooses rather to invalidate it as a violation of the Establishment of Religion Clause of the First Amendment. I would not decide this case on such a sweeping ground for the following reasons, among others.

1. In the first place I find it difficult to agree with the Court's statement that "there can be no doubt that Arkansas has sought to prevent its teachers from discussing the theory of evolution because it is contrary to the belief of some that the Book of Genesis must be the exclusive source of doctrine as to the origin of man." It may be instead that the people's motive was merely that it would be best to remove this controversial subject from its schools; there is no reason I can imagine why a State is without power to withdraw from its curriculum any subject deemed too emotional and controversial for its public schools. And this Court has consistently held that it is not for us to invalidate a statute because of our views that the "motives" behind its passage were

improper; it is simply too difficult to determine what those motives were. See, e.g., *United States v. O'Brien,* [§ 10–10, *supra*].

2.   A second question that arises for me is whether this Court's decision forbidding a State to exclude the subject of evolution from its schools infringes the religious freedom of those who consider evolution an anti-religious doctrine. If the theory is considered anti-religious, as the Court indicates, how can the State be bound by the Federal Constitution to permit its teachers to advocate such an "anti-religious" doctrine to school children? The very cases cited by the Court as supporting its conclusion hold that the State must be neutral, not favoring one religious or anti-religious view over another.... Since there is no indication that the literal Biblical doctrine of the origin of man is included in the curriculum of Arkansas schools, does not the removal of the subject of evolution leave the State in a neutral position toward these supposedly competing religious and anti-religious doctrines? Unless this Court is prepared simply to write off as pure nonsense the views of those who consider evolution an anti-religious doctrine, then this issue presents problems under the Establishment Clause far more troublesome than are discussed in the Court's opinion.

3.   I am also not ready to hold that a person hired to teach schoolchildren takes with him into the classroom a constitutional right to teach sociological, economic, political, or religious subjects that the school's managers do not want discussed.... I question whether it is absolutely certain, as the Court's opinion indicates, that "academic freedom" permits a teacher to breach his contractual agreement to teach only the subjects designated by the school authorities who hired him.

Certainly the Darwinian theory, precisely like the Genesis story of the creation of man, is not above challenge. In fact the Darwinian theory has not merely been criticized by religionists but by scientists, and perhaps no scientist would be willing to take an oath and swear that everything announced in the Darwinian theory is unquestionably true....

I would either strike down the Arkansas Act as too vague to enforce, or remand to the State Supreme Court for clarification of its holding and opinion.

[The separate concurring opinions of HARLAN, J. & STEWART, J., are omitted.]

Notes

1.   In *Poe v. Ullman,* 367 U.S. 497, 81 S.Ct. 1752, 6 L.Ed.2d 989 (1961) plaintiffs sued for declaratory judgments that Connecticut statutes prohibiting the use of contraceptive devices were unconstitutional. Justice Frankfurter, for the plurality, noted that the Connecticut law had been on the books since 1879; that only once was a prosecution initiated (in 1940), which was dismissed after the Supreme Court of Errors sustained the legislation; and that contraceptives "are commonly and notoriously sold in Connecticut drugstores" without any prosecution. "It is clear that the mere existence of

a state penal statute would constitute insufficient grounds to support a federal court's adjudication of its constitutionality in proceedings brought against the State's prosecuting officials if real threat of enforcement is wanting." Justiciability is "not a legal concept with a fixed content or susceptible of scientific verification. Its utilization is the result of many subtle pressures, including the appropriateness of the issues for decision by this Court and the actual hardship to the litigations of denying them the relief sought. Both of these factors justify withholding adjudication of the constitutional issue raised under the circumstances and in the manner in which they are now before the Court."

Is the *Epperson* Court's willingness to decide the issue on the merits consistent with Justice Frankfurter's refusal to do so in *Poe?* In light of *Epperson,* was the Court's refusal to reach the merits in *Poe* constitutionally compelled?

2. *Harris v. McRae,* 448 U.S. 297, 100 S.Ct. 2671, 65 L.Ed.2d 784 (1980) upheld the constitutionality of the Hyde Amendment, which restricted federal funding of abortions. One of the arguments of those attacking the Hyde Amendment was that it "violates the Establishment Clause because it incorporates into law the doctrines of the Roman Catholic Church concerning the sinfulness of abortion and the time at which life commences." The Court majority, speaking through Justice Stewart, disagreed: "[I]t does not follow that a statute violates the Establishment Clause because it 'happens to coincide or harmonize with the tenets of some or all religions.' That the Judaeo–Christian religions oppose stealing does not mean that a State or the Federal Government may not, consistent with the Establishment Clause, enact laws prohibiting larceny. The Hyde Amendment, as the District Court noted, is as much a reflection of 'traditionalist' values towards abortion, as it is an embodiment of the views of a particular religion. In sum, we are convinced that the fact that the funding restrictions in the Hyde Amendment may coincide with the religious tenets of the Roman Catholic Church does not, without more, contravene the Establishment Clause."

3. SCIENTIFIC CREATIONISM. Some teachers present to their students both the Darwinian theory and the theory of the "scientific creationists." A Cleveland lawyer who works for the creationists claims that, unlike the earlier laws invalidated by the Supreme Court, today's proposed laws "seek to teach 'the Creation as revealed by science.'" Some "creationists don't think their viewpoint is getting a fair shake.... 'It's the Scopes trial reversed,' says Ronald Lee, a creationist who heads the Iowa State University chapter of Students for Origins Research. 'Before, they restricted evolution,' he says. 'Now they're restricting Creation.'" Some creationists claim, for example, that the fossil records demonstrate that there "was a great catastrophe," with parallels to the Biblical flood, and that the evolutionists' methods of radioactive dating are faulty. "[T]he scientific evidence for Creation is overwhelming, says David Menton, a creationist who is associate professor of anatomy at Washington University at St. Louis. 'More and more reasonable scientists are speaking out against this silly theory of evolution,' he says." An evolutionist at Ball State University countered: " 'People, and

especially undergraduate students, are willing to accept just about any crackpot scheme these days.' "[1]

Could a state legislature draft a constitutional bill requiring state teachers to teach the creation theory (not to teach it as the "truth," but simply to teach it as a theory)? Without the benefit of any state law on the subject, could a grade or high school teacher give equal time to the creationist view?

Edwards v. Aguillard, 482 U.S. 578, 107 S.Ct. 2573, 96 L.Ed.2d 510 (1987) invalidated, on its face (7 to 2), Louisiana's "Balanced Treatment for Creation–Science and Evolution–Science in Public School Instruction" Act. The Act defined the theory of creation science as "the scientific evidences for creation and inferences from those scientific evidences." The law forbade the teaching of evolution in public schools unless accompanied by teaching in creation science. The law violated the Establishment Clause, the Court said, because the law's purpose was to promote a particular religious belief. The law had "no clear secular purpose." The Act's stated purpose was to promote academic freedom, yet it "is clear from the legislative history that the purpose of the legislative sponsor, Senator Bill Keith, was to narrow the science curriculum.... The Act does not grant teachers a flexibility that they did not already possess to supplant the present science curriculum with the presentation of theories, besides evolution, about the origin of life." Nor does the Act further the goal of "fairness; teaching all of the evidence," because of its discriminatory preference for creation science. For example, the law supplies research services for creation science but not for evolution, and it forbids discrimination against those who teach creationism but not evolution.

As in *Epperson v. Arkansas,* the "preeminent purpose of the Louisiana legislature was clearly to advance the religious viewpoint that a supernatural being created humankind." Indeed, Senator Keith's expert on creation science testified at the legislative hearings that "the theory of creation science included belief in the existence of a supernatural creator." Justice Brennan, for the Court, said:

> "We do not imply that a legislature could never require that scientific critiques of prevailing scientific theories be taught. [T]eaching a variety of scientific theories about the origins of humankind to schoolchildren might be validly done with the clear secular intent of enhancing the effectiveness of science instruction. But because the primary purpose of the Creationism Act is to endorse a particular religious doctrine, the Act furthers religion in violation of the Establishment Clause."

Justice Scalia, joined by Rehnquist, C.J., dissented. Even assuming that the Establishment Clause "on the basis of motivation alone, without regard to its effects" could invalidate a law, this law was still proper. The statute itself defined creation science as " 'the *scientific evidences* for creation and inferences from those scientific evidences.' (emphasis added)." The dissent discussed the evidence and concluded that, from the little evidence available on the motives of those who supported the law, the motive was not bad. Senator Keith, for example, "stressed that 'to ... teach religion and disguise

1. Rout, "Modern Creationists Seeking Equal Time in U.S. Classrooms," Wall St. Jrl., June 15, 1979, at 1, col. 4, and 23, cols. 1–4 (midwest ed.).

it as creationism ... is not my intent. My intent is to see to it that our textbooks are not censored.'" The law, the dissent argued, had a valid secular purpose: *"students'* freedom from *indoctrination.* The legislature wanted to ensure that students would be free to decide for themselves how life began, based upon a fair and balanced presentation of the scientific evidence...." (emphasis in original).

4. Private Law 92–60 (Dec. 15, 1971) provided that the book, *Science and Health With Key to the Scriptures*, by Mary Baker Eddy, and all editions thereof, "was granted copyright for a term of 75 years from the enactment of the law, or from the publication of any later editions, 'whichever is later.'" In effect the copyright could exist in perpetuity. Leaving aside for the moment the clause in the Constitution providing that Congress shall have the power to establish copyrights "for limited Times," (Art. 1, § 8, cl. 8), is the grant of such a copyright to the Christian Science Church invalid under *Epperson?*

5. PREFERENCE AMONG RELIGIONS. *Larson v. Valente,* 456 U.S. 228, 102 S.Ct. 1673, 72 L.Ed.2d 33 (1982) held that a Minnesota statute imposing certain reporting and registration requirements only on those religious organizations that solicit more than 50% of their funds from nonmembers violated the Establishment Clause. The plaintiffs were members of the Holy Spirit Association for the Unification of World Christianity (the Unification Church, or "Moonies"). The three-part test of *Lemon v. Kurtzman,* 403 U.S. 602, 91 S.Ct. 2105, 29 L.Ed.2d 745 (1971)—that the law have a secular purpose, that its primary effect neither advance nor inhibit religion, and that it not foster excessive governmental entanglement with religion—is inapplicable, said the Court, because it only applies to laws affording a uniform benefit to all religions. The Minnesota 50% rule discriminated among religions—well-established churches who have "achieved strong but not total financial support from their members" versus "churches which are new and lacking in a constituency, or which, as a matter of policy, may favor public solicitation over general reliance on financial support from members." Such laws must pass strict scrutiny:

> The clearest command of the Establishment Clause is that one religious denomination cannot be officially preferred over another.... Free exercise thus can be guaranteed only when legislators and voters are required to accord to their own religions the very same treatment given to small, new, or unpopular denominations. [W]hen we are presented with a state law granting a denominational preference, our precedents demand that we treat the law as suspect and we apply strict scrutiny in adjudging its constitutionality. The fifty percent rule ... must be invalidated unless it is justified by a compelling governmental interest, and unless it is closely fitted to further that interest.

The Minnesota statute was not "closely fitted" to further the state goal of protecting citizens from abusive practices in the solicitation of charitable funds. The legislative history showed "that the provision was drafted with the explicit intention of including particular religious denominations and excluding others." For example, one senator said, "I'm not sure why we're so hot to regulate Moonies anyway."

LYNCH v. DONNELLY

465 U.S. 668, 104 S.Ct. 1355, 79 L.Ed.2d 604 (1984).

THE CHIEF JUSTICE [BURGER] delivered the opinion of the Court.

We granted certiorari to decide whether the Establishment Clause of the First Amendment prohibits a municipality from including a crèche, or Nativity scene, in its annual Christmas display.

Each year, in cooperation with the downtown retail merchants' association, the City of Pawtucket, Rhode Island, erects a Christmas display as part of its observance of the Christmas holiday season. The display is situated in a park owned by a nonprofit organization and located in the heart of the shopping district. The display is essentially like those to be found in hundreds of towns or cities across the Nation— often on public grounds—during the Christmas season. The Pawtucket display comprises many of the figures and decorations traditionally associated with Christmas, including, among other things, a Santa Claus house, reindeer pulling Santa's sleigh, candy-striped poles, a Christmas tree, carolers, cutout figures representing such characters as a clown, an elephant, and a teddy bear, hundreds of colored lights, a large banner that reads "SEASONS GREETINGS," and the crèche at issue here. All components of this display are owned by the City.

The crèche, which has been included in the display for 40 or more years, consists of the traditional figures, including the Infant Jesus, Mary and Joseph, angels, shepherds, kings, and animals, all ranging in height from 5″ to 5′. In 1973, when the present crèche was acquired, it cost the City $1365; it now is valued at $200. The erection and dismantling of the crèche costs the City about $20 per year; nominal expenses are incurred in lighting the crèche. No money has been expended on its maintenance for the past 10 years.

Respondents, Pawtucket residents and individual members of the Rhode Island affiliate of the American Civil Liberties Union, and the affiliate itself, brought this action in the United States District Court for Rhode Island, challenging the City's inclusion of the crèche in the annual display. The District Court held that the City's inclusion of the crèche in the display violates the Establishment Clause, which is binding on the states through the Fourteenth Amendment. [W]e reverse.

[T]he metaphor [of a "wall" between Church and State] is not a wholly accurate description of the practical aspects of the relationship that in fact exists between church and state. [T]he Constitution [does not] require complete separation of church and state; it affirmatively mandates accommodation, not merely tolerance, of all religions, and forbids hostility toward any. . . .

The Court's interpretation of the Establishment Clause has comported with what history reveals was the contemporaneous understanding of its guarantees. . . . Our history is replete with official references to the value and invocation of Divine guidance in deliberations and pronouncements of the Founding Fathers and contemporary leaders. Beginning in the early colonial period long before Independence, a day of Thanksgiving was celebrated as a religious holiday to give thanks for the bounties of Nature as gifts from God. President Washington and his successors proclaimed Thanksgiving, with all its religious overtones, a day of national celebration[2] and Congress made it a National Holiday more than a century ago. That holiday has not lost its theme of expressing thanks for Divine aid any more than has Christmas lost its religious significance.

Executive Orders and other official announcements of Presidents and of the Congress have proclaimed both Christmas and Thanksgiving National Holidays in religious terms. And, by Acts of Congress, it has long been the practice that federal employees are released from duties on these National Holidays, while being paid from the same public revenues that provide the compensation of the Chaplains of the Senate and the House and the military services. Thus, it is clear that Government has long recognized—indeed it has subsidized—holidays with religious significance.

Other examples of reference to our religious heritage are found in the statutorily prescribed national motto "In God We Trust," which Congress and the President mandated for our currency, and in the language "One nation under God," as part of the Pledge of Allegiance to the American flag.... The very chamber in which oral arguments on this case were heard is decorated with a notable and permanent—not seasonal—symbol of religion: Moses with Ten Commandments. Congress has long provided chapels in the Capitol for religious worship and meditation.... Presidential Proclamations and messages have also issued to commemorate Jewish Heritage Week, and the Jewish High Holy Days.

... We have refused "to construe the Religion Clauses with a literalness that would undermine the ultimate constitutional objective *as illuminated by history.*" ... Rather than mechanically invalidating all governmental conduct or statutes that confer benefits or give special recognition to religion in general or to one faith—as an absolutist approach would dictate—the Court has scrutinized challenged legislation or official conduct to determine whether, in reality, it establishes a religion or religious faith, or tends to do so....

In the line-drawing process we have often found it useful to inquire whether the challenged law or conduct has a secular purpose, whether its principal or primary effect is to advance or inhibit religion, and whether it creates an excessive entanglement of government with religion. *Lemon [v. Kurtzman,* 403 U.S. 602, 91 S.Ct. 2105, 29 L.Ed.2d 745

---

2. The day after the First Amendment was proposed, Congress urged President Washington to proclaim "a day of public thanksgiving and prayer, to be observed by acknowledging with grateful hearts the many and signal favours of Almighty God."
...

(1971)]. But, we have repeatedly emphasized our unwillingness to be confined to any single test or criterion in this sensitive area....

In this case, the focus of our inquiry must be on the crèche in the context of the Christmas season.... The District Court inferred from the religious nature of the crèche that the City has no secular purpose for the display. In so doing, it rejected the City's claim that its reasons for including the crèche are essentially the same as its reasons for sponsoring the display as a whole. The District Court plainly erred by focusing almost exclusively on the crèche. When viewed in the proper context of the Christmas Holiday season, it is apparent that, on this record, there is insufficient evidence to establish that the inclusion of the crèche is a purposeful or surreptitious effort to express some kind of subtle governmental advocacy of a particular religious message. In a pluralistic society a variety of motives and purposes are implicated. The City, like the Congresses and Presidents, however, has principally taken note of a significant historical religious event long celebrated in the Western World. The crèche in the display depicts the historical origins of this traditional event long recognized as a National Holiday.

The narrow question is whether there is a secular purpose for Pawtucket's display of the crèche. The display is sponsored by the City to celebrate the Holiday and to depict the origins of that Holiday. These are legitimate secular purposes.[6] The District Court's inference, drawn from the religious nature of the crèche, that the City has no secular purpose was, on this record, clearly erroneous.[7]

The District Court found that the primary effect of including the crèche is to confer a substantial and impermissible benefit on religion in general and on the Christian faith in particular. [T]o conclude that the primary effect of including the crèche is to advance religion in violation of the Establishment Clause would require that we view it as more beneficial to and more an endorsement of religion, for example, than ... the release time program for religious training in *Zorach,* supra; and the legislative prayers upheld in *Marsh* [*v. Chambers,* supra]. Here, whatever benefit to one faith or religion or to all religions, is indirect, remote and incidental; display of the crèche is no more an advancement or endorsement of religion than the Congressional and Executive recognition of the origins of the Holiday itself as "Christ's Mass," or the exhibition of literally hundreds of religious paintings in governmentally supported museums....

Entanglement is a question of kind and degree. In this case, however, there is no reason to disturb the District Court's finding on the

6. The City contends that the purposes of the display are "exclusively secular." We hold only that Pawtucket has a secular purpose for its display, which is all that *Lemon* requires. Were the test that the government must have "exclusively secular" objectives, much of the conduct and legislation this Court has approved in the past would have been invalidated.

7. Justice Brennan argues that the City's objectives could have been achieved without including the crèche in the display. True or not, that is irrelevant. The question is whether the display of the crèche violates the Establishment Clause.

absence of administrative entanglement. There is no evidence of contact with church authorities concerning the content or design of the exhibit prior to or since Pawtucket's purchase of the crèche. No expenditures for maintenance of the crèche have been necessary; and since the City owns the crèche, now valued at $200, the tangible material it contributes is *de minimis*.

The Court of Appeals correctly observed that this Court has not held that political divisiveness alone can serve to invalidate otherwise permissible conduct. And we decline to so hold today. This case does not involve a direct subsidy to church-sponsored schools or colleges, or other religious institutions, and hence no inquiry into potential political divisiveness is even called for. In any event, apart from this litigation there is no evidence of political friction or divisiveness over the crèche in the 40–year history of Pawtucket's Christmas celebration....

We are satisfied that the City has a secular purpose for including the crèche, that the City has not impermissibly advanced religion, and that including the crèche does not create excessive entanglement between religion and government.

Justice Brennan describes the crèche as a "re-creation of an event that lies at the heart of Christian faith." ... To forbid the use of this one passive symbol—the crèche—at the very time people are taking note of the season with Christmas hymns and carols in public schools and other public places, and while the Congress and Legislatures open sessions with prayers by paid chaplains would be a stilted overreaction contrary to our history and to our holdings. If the presence of the crèche in this display violates the Establishment Clause, a host of other forms of taking official note of Christmas, and of our religious heritage, are equally offensive to the Constitution....

JUSTICE O'CONNOR, concurring.

[P]olitical divisiveness along religious lines should not be an independent test of constitutionality.... Guessing the potential for political divisiveness inherent in a government practice is simply too speculative an enterprise, in part because the existence of the litigation, as this case illustrates, itself may affect the political response to the government practice....

JUSTICE BRENNAN, with whom JUSTICE MARSHALL, JUSTICE BLACKMUN and JUSTICE STEVENS join, dissenting.

... Applying [the *Lemon v. Kurtzman*] test to this case, the Court reaches an essentially narrow result which turns largely upon the particular holiday context in which the City of Pawtucket's nativity scene appeared. The Court's decision implicitly leaves open questions concerning the constitutionality of the public display on public property of a crèche standing alone, or the public display of other distinctively religious symbols such as a cross.[1] Despite the narrow contours of the

---

1. For instance, nothing in the Court's opinion suggests that the Court of Appeals

Court's opinion, our precedents in my view compel the holding that Pawtucket's inclusion of a life-sized display depicting the biblical description of the birth of Christ as part of its annual Christmas celebration is unconstitutional. Nothing in the history of such practices or the setting in which the City's crèche is presented obscures or diminishes the plain fact that Pawtucket's action amounts to an impermissible governmental endorsement of a particular faith.

[A]ll of Pawtucket's "valid secular objectives can be readily accomplished by other means." Plainly, the City's interest in celebrating the holiday and in promoting both retail sales and goodwill are fully served by the elaborate display of Santa Claus, reindeer, and wishing wells that are already a part of Pawtucket's annual Christmas display.... To be found constitutional, Pawtucket's seasonal celebration must at least be non-denominational and not serve to promote religion. The inclusion of a distinctively religious element like the crèche, however, demonstrates that a narrower sectarian purpose lay behind the decision to include a nativity scene....

Finally, it is evident that Pawtucket's inclusion of a crèche as part of its annual Christmas display does pose a significant threat of fostering "excessive entanglement." As the Court notes, the District Court found no administrative entanglement in this case, primarily because the City had been able to administer the annual display without extensive consultation with religious officials. Of course, there is no reason to disturb that finding, but it is worth noting that after today's decision, administrative entanglements may well develop. Jews and other non-Christian groups, prompted perhaps by the Mayor's remark that he will include a Menorah in future displays, can be expected to press government for inclusion of their symbols, and faced with such requests, government will have to become involved in accommodating the various demands. More importantly, although no political divisiveness was apparent in Pawtucket prior to the filing of respondents' lawsuit, that act, as the District Court found, unleashed powerful emotional reactions which divided the City along religious lines....

[The dissenting opinion of BLACKMUN, J., joined by STEVENS, J., is omitted.]

Notes

In *Allegheny County v. ACLU, Greater Pittsburgh Chapter,* 492 U.S. 573, 109 S.Ct. 3086, 106 L.Ed.2d 472 (1989), the Court ruled (5 to 4) that the for the Third Circuit erred when it found that a city-financed platform and cross used by Pope John Paul II to celebrate mass and deliver a sermon during his 1979 visit to Philadelphia was an unconstitutional expenditure of city funds. *Gilfillan v. City of Philadelphia,* 637 F.2d 924 (C.A.3 1980).... And given the Court's focus upon the otherwise secular setting of the Pawtucket crèche, it remains uncertain whether absent such secular symbols as Santa Claus' house, a talking wishing well, and cut-out clowns and bears, a similar nativity scene would pass muster under the Court's standard. Cf. *McCreary v. Stone,* 575 F.Supp. 1112 (S.D.N.Y.1983)(holding that village did not violate Establishment Clause by refusing to permit a private group to erect a crèche in a public park).

middle prong of the three-part *Lemon v. Kurtzman* test was violated when the county government allowed a Christmas nativity scene to be placed on the Grand Staircase of the Allegheny County Courthouse. The Holy Name Society (a Roman Catholic group) donated this crèche, which bore a sign to that effect. At the crest of the manger was a statute of an angel holding a banner that said, "Gloria in Excelsis Deo" (Glory to God in the Highest). "This praise to God in Christian terms is indisputably religious—indeed sectarian—just as it is when said in the Gospel or in a church service," said Blackmun, J., for the Court.[1] Unlike *Lynch,* nothing in the courthouse display detracts from the Christian message glorifying God for the birth of Jesus. The Court concluded: "*Lynch* teaches that government may celebrate Christmas in some manner and form, but not in a way that endorses Christian doctrine. Here, Allegheny County has transgressed this line."

Justice Blackmun and five other justices[2] also concluded (6 to 3) that the display of the Chanukah (or Hanukkah) menorah in front of the City County Building was constitutional. This display featured a 46–foot Christmas tree, a sign bearing the Mayor's name and entitled "Salute to Liberty."[3] and an 18–foot menorah (candelabrum).

Blackmun, J. explained that Chanukah (an annual Jewish holiday that falls closest to Christmas) celebrates the Maccabees' rededication of the Temple of Jerusalem after recapturing it from the Seleucid Empire. During the rededication of the Temple, the Maccabees had only enough oil for the menorah to burn one day, but the oil miraculously lasted for eight days (until new oil was obtained). His opinion on the menorah—which no other Justice joined—argued: "Because government may celebrate Christmas as a secular holiday, it follows that government may also acknowledge Chanukah as a secular holiday." Blackmun claimed that the "Christmas tree, unlike the menorah, is not itself a religious symbol." And this tree, he asserted, "is clearly the predominate element in the city's display." Also, the Mayor's sign saluting liberty "further diminishes the possibility that the tree and the menorah will be interpreted as a dual endorsement of Christianity and Judaism." Blackmun argued that the display of the menorah does not have the effect of promoting or endorsing religious beliefs "given its 'particular physical setting.' "To emphasize the fact-bound nature of this case, the Appendix included photographs of the nativity scene and the menorah display; Blackmun noted that on remand the lower court could consider whether the menorah violated the "purpose" or "entanglement" prongs of the *Lemon* test; and the last footnote his opinion emphasized that "on other facts a menorah display could constitute an impermissible endorsement of

---

1. On the question of whether this crèche scene was prohibited, Blackmun, J. was joined by Brennan, Marshall, Stevens, & O'Connor, JJ.

2. O'Connor, J., in a separate opinion, agreed that "Pittsburgh's combined holiday display of a Chanukah menorah, a Christmas tree, and a sign saluting liberty does not have the effect of conveying an endorsement of religion." Kennedy, J. (joined Rehnquist, C.J. & White & Scalia, JJ.), also did not join in Blackmun's reasoning but agreed that the menorah display was consti-

tutional. Marshall, Brennan & Stevens, JJ., dissented from the ruling that the menorah display does not have the prohibited effect of endorsing religion.

3. The sign below the "Salute to Liberty" title stated:

"During this holiday season, the City of Pittsburgh salutes liberty. Let these festive lights remind us that we are the keepers of the flame of liberty and our legacy of freedom."

religion." Blackmun admitted that the "rationale of the majority opinion in *Lynch* is none too clear. . . . "

Kennedy, J., joined by Rehnquist, C.J., & White and Scalia, JJ., concurred in the judgment in part and dissented in part. Kennedy reasoned that the displays of the crèche and menorah on government property "do no more than 'celebrate the season,' "and acknowledge the historical background and the religious and secular nature of the Chanukah and Christmas holidays. "This interest falls well within the tradition of government accommodation and acknowledgment of religion that has marked our history from the beginning." This dissent also noted that it was "content for present purposes to remain within the *Lemon* framework, but do not wish to be seen as advocating, let alone adopting, that test as our primary guide in this difficult area."

WALLACE v. JAFFREE
472 U.S. 38, 105 S.Ct. 2479, 86 L.Ed.2d 29 (1985).

JUSTICE STEVENS delivered the opinion of the Court.

At an early stage of this litigation, the constitutionality of three Alabama statutes was questioned: (1) § 16–1–20, enacted in 1978, which authorized a one-minute period of silence in all public schools "for meditation";[1] (2) § 16–1–20.1, enacted in 1981, which authorized a period of silence "for meditation or voluntary prayer";[2] and (3) § 16–1–20.2, enacted in 1982, which authorized teachers to lead "willing students" in a prescribed prayer to "Almighty God . . . the Creator and Supreme Judge of the world."

At the preliminary-injunction stage of this case, the District Court distinguished § 16–1–20 from the other two statutes. It then held that there was "nothing wrong" with § 16–1–20, but that §§ 16–1–20.1 and 16–1–20.2 were both invalid because the sole purpose of both was "an effort on the part of the State of Alabama to encourage a religious activity." . . . The Court of Appeals agreed with the District Court's initial interpretation of the purpose of both §§ 16–1–20.1 and 16–1–20.2, and held them both unconstitutional. We have already affirmed the Court of Appeals' holding with respect to § 16–1–20.2. Moreover, appellees have not questioned the holding that § 16–1–20 is valid. Thus, the narrow question for decision is whether § 16–1–20.1 which authorizes a

---

1. Alabama Code § 16–1–20 (Supp. 1984), reads as follows:

"At the commencement of the first class each day in the first through the sixth grades in all public schools, the teacher in charge of the room in which each such class is held shall announce that a period of silence, not to exceed one minute in duration, shall be observed for meditation, and during any such period silence shall be maintained and no activities engaged in."

Appellees have abandoned any claim that § 16–1–20 is unconstitutional.

2. Alabama Code § 16–1–20.1 (Supp. 1984) provides:

"At the commencement of the first class of each day in all grades in all public schools the teacher in charge of the room in which each class is held may announce that a period of silence not to exceed one minute in duration shall be observed for meditation or voluntary prayer, and during any such period no other activities shall be engaged in."

period of silence for "meditation or voluntary prayer," is a law respecting the establishment of religion within the meaning of the First Amendment. . . .

Just as the right to speak and the right to refrain from speaking are complimentary components of a broader concept of individual freedom of mind, so also the individual's freedom to choose his own creed is the counterpart of his right to refrain from accepting the creed established by the majority. At one time it was thought that this right merely proscribed the preference of one Christian sect over another, but would not require equal respect for the conscience of the infidel, the atheist, or the adherent of a non-Christian faith such as Mohammedism or Judaism.[36] But when the underlying principle has been examined in the crucible of litigation, the Court has unambiguously concluded that the individual freedom of conscience protected by the First Amendment embraces the right to select any religious faith or none at all. . . .

[T]he First Amendment requires that a statute must be invalidated if it is entirely motivated by a purpose to advance religion. In applying the purpose test, it is appropriate to ask "whether government's actual purpose is to endorse or disapprove of religion." In this case, the answer to that question is dispositive. For the record not only provides us with an unambiguous affirmative answer, but it also reveals that the enactment of § 16–1–20.1 was not motivated by any clearly secular purpose—indeed, the statute had *no* secular purpose.

The sponsor of the bill that became § 16–1–20.1, Senator Donald Holmes, inserted into the legislative record—apparently without dissent—a statement indicating that the legislation was an "effort to return voluntary prayer" to the public schools. Later Senator Holmes confirmed this purpose before the District Court. In response to the question whether he had any purpose for the legislation other than returning voluntary prayer to public schools, he stated, "No, I did not have no [sic] other purpose in mind." The State did not present evidence of *any* secular purpose.[45] . . .

The legislative intent to return prayer to the public schools is, of course, quite different from merely protecting every student's right to engage in voluntary prayer during an appropriate moment of silence

---

36. Thus Joseph Story wrote:

"Probably at the time of the adoption of the constitution, and of the amendment to it, now under consideration [First Amendment], the general, if not the universal sentiment in America was, that Christianity ought to receive encouragement from the state, so far as was not incompatible with the private rights of conscience, and the freedom of religious worship. An attempt to level all religions, and to make it a matter of state policy to hold all in utter indifference, would have created universal disapprobation, if not universal indignation." 2 J. Story, Commentaries on the Constitution

of the United States § 1874, p. 593 (1851)(footnote omitted).

45. Appellant Governor George C. Wallace now argues that § 16–1–20.1 "is best understood as a permissible accommodation of religion" [B]ut it is undisputed that at the time of the enactment of § 16–1–20.1 there was no governmental practice impeding students from silently praying for one minute at the beginning of each school day; thus, there was no need to "accommodate" or to exempt individuals from any general governmental requirement because of the dictates of our cases interpreting the Free Exercise Clause. . . .

during the school day. The 1978 statute already protected that right, containing nothing that prevented any student from engaging in voluntary prayer during a silent minute of meditation. Appellants have not identified any secular purpose that was not fully served by § 16–1–20 before the enactment of § 16–1–20.1. Thus, only two conclusions are consistent with the text of § 16–1–20.1: (1) the statute was enacted to convey a message of State endorsement and promotion of prayer; or (2) the statute was enacted for no purpose. No one suggests that the statute was nothing but a meaningless or irrational act.... The Legislature enacted § 16–1–20.1 despite the existence of § 16–1–20 for the sole purpose of expressing the State's endorsement of prayer activities for one minute at the beginning of each school day. The addition of ''or voluntary prayer'' indicates that the State intended to characterize prayer as a favored practice. Such an endorsement is not consistent with the established principle that the Government must pursue a course of complete neutrality toward religion....

The judgment of the Court of Appeals is affirmed.

It is so ordered.

CHIEF JUSTICE BURGER, dissenting.

... To suggest that a moment-of-silence statute that includes the word ''prayer'' unconstitutionally endorses religion, while one that simply provides for a moment of silence does not, manifests not neutrality but hostility toward religion. For decades our opinions have stated that hostility toward any religion or toward all religions is as much forbidden by the Constitution as is an official establishment of religion. The Alabama legislature has no more ''endorsed'' religion than a state or the Congress does when it provides for legislative chaplains, or than this Court does when it opens each session with an invocation to God....

Curiously, the opinions do not mention that *all* of the sponsor's statements relied upon—including the statement ''inserted'' into the Senate Journal—were made *after* the legislature had passed the statute; indeed, the testimony that the Court finds critical was given well over a year after the statute was enacted. As even the appellees concede, see Brief for Appellees 18, there is not a shred of evidence that the legislature as a whole shared the sponsor's motive or that a majority in either house was even aware of the sponsor's view of the bill when it was passed. The sole relevance of the sponsor's statements, therefore, is that they reflect the personal, subjective motives of a single legislator. No case in the 195–year history of this Court supports the disconcerting idea that post-enactment statements by individual legislators are relevant in determining the constitutionality of legislation.

Even if an individual legislator's after-the-fact statements could rationally be considered relevant, all of the opinions fail to mention that the sponsor also testified that one of his purposes in drafting and sponsoring the moment-of-silence bill was to clear up a widespread misunderstanding that a schoolchild is legally *prohibited* from engaging in silent, individual prayer once he steps inside a public school building.

See App. 53–54. That testimony is at least as important as the statements the Court relies upon, and surely that testimony manifests a permissible purpose. . . .

. . . Congress amended the statutory Pledge of Allegiance 31 years ago to add the words "under God." Act of June 14, 1954, Pub.L. 396, 68 Stat. 249. Do the several opinions in support of the judgment today render the Pledge unconstitutional? That would be the consequence of their method of focusing on the difference between § 16–1–20.1 and its predecessor statute rather than examining § 16–1–20.1 as a whole. Any such holding would of course make a mockery of our decisionmaking in Establishment Clause cases. . . .

JUSTICE WHITE, dissenting.

. . . As I read the filed opinions, a majority of the Court would approve statutes that provided for a moment of silence but did not mention prayer. But if a student asked whether he could pray during that moment, it is difficult to believe that the teacher could not answer in the affirmative. If that is the case, I would not invalidate a statute that at the outset provided the legislative answer to the question "May I pray?" This is so even if the Alabama statute is infirm, which I do not believe it is, because of its peculiar legislative history. . . .

JUSTICE REHNQUIST, dissenting.

Thirty-eight years ago this Court, in *Everson v. Board of Education,* 330 U.S. 1, 16, 67 S.Ct. 504, 512, 91 L.Ed. 711 (1947) summarized its exegesis of Establishment Clause doctrine thus:

> In the words of Jefferson, the clause against establishment of religion by law was intended to erect "a wall of separation between church and State." *Reynolds v. United States,* [98 U.S. 145, 164, 25 L.Ed. 244 (1879)].

This language from *Reynolds,* a case involving the Free Exercise Clause of the First Amendment rather than the Establishment Clause, quoted from Thomas Jefferson's letter to the Danbury Baptist Association the phrase "I contemplate with sovereign reverence that act of the whole American people which declare that their legislature should 'make no law respecting an establishment of religion, or prohibiting the free exercise thereof,' thus building a wall of separation between church and State."[1]

It is impossible to build sound constitutional doctrine upon a mistaken understanding of constitutional history, but unfortunately the Establishment Clause has been expressly freighted with Jefferson's misleading metaphor for nearly forty years. Thomas Jefferson was of course in France at the time the constitutional amendments known as the Bill of Rights were passed by Congress and ratified by the states. His letter to the Danbury Baptist Association was a short note of courtesy,

---

1. *Reynolds* is the only authority cited as direct precedent for the "wall of separation theory." *Reynolds* is truly inapt; it dealt with a Mormon's Free Exercise Clause challenge to a federal polygamy law.

written fourteen years after the amendments were passed by Congress. He would seem to any detached observer as a less than ideal source of contemporary history as to the meaning of the Religion Clauses of the First Amendment.

Jefferson's fellow Virginian James Madison, with whom he was joined in the battle for the enactment of the Virginia Statute of Religious Liberty of 1786, did play as large a part as anyone in the drafting of the Bill of Rights. He had two advantages over Jefferson in this regard: he was present in the United States, and he was a leading member of the First Congress. [He] was undoubtedly the most important architect among the members of the House of the amendments which became the Bill of Rights.... His original language "nor shall any national religion be established" obviously does not conform to the "wall of separation" between church and State idea which latter day commentators have ascribed to him. His explanation on the floor of the meaning of his language—"that Congress should not establish a religion, and enforce the legal observation of it by law" is of the same ilk. When he replied to Huntington in the debate over the proposal which came from the Select Committee of the House, he urged that the language "no religion shall be established by law" should be amended by inserting the word "national" in front of the word "religion." ...

The actions of the First Congress, which re-enacted the Northwest Ordinance for the governance of the Northwest Territory in 1789, confirm the view that Congress did not mean that the Government should be neutral between religion and irreligion. The House of Representatives took up the Northwest Ordinance on the same day as Madison introduced his proposed amendments which became the Bill of Rights; [i]t seems highly unlikely that the House of Representatives would simultaneously consider proposed amendments to the Constitution and enact an important piece of territorial legislation which conflicted with the intent of those proposals. The Northwest Ordinance, 1 Stat. 50, reenacted the Northwest Ordinance of 1787 and provided that "[r]eligion, morality, and knowledge, being necessary to good government and the happiness of mankind, schools and the means of education shall forever be encouraged." Land grants for schools in the Northwest Territory were not limited to public schools. It was not until 1845 that Congress limited land grants in the new States and Territories to nonsectarian schools....

The Court strikes down the Alabama statute because the State wished to "endorse prayer as a favored practice." ... George Washington himself, at the request of the very Congress which passed the Bill of Rights, proclaimed a day of "public thanksgiving and prayer, to be observed by acknowledging with grateful hearts the many and signal favors of Almighty God." History must judge whether it was the father of his country in 1789, or a majority of the Court today, which has strayed from the meaning of the Establishment Clause....

[The concurring opinion of POWELL, J., & the opinion of O'CONNOR, J., concurring in the judgment, are omitted.]

11–2.2 *The Public Forum and the Establishment Clause*

Introductory Notes

1. *Widmar v. Vincent,* 454 U.S. 263, 102 S.Ct. 269, 70 L.Ed.2d 440 (1981). The University of Missouri at Kansas City made its facilities generally available for the activities of registered student groups, but a University regulation prohibited the use by groups "for purposes of religious worship or religious teaching." The University justified its regulation as maintaining strict separation between Church and State, but the Court held that the regulation violated the free exercise and free speech clauses. The establishment clause did not compel the regulation because an open-forum policy "including nondiscrimination against religious speech, would have a secular purpose [to provide a forum in which students could exchange views] and would avoid entanglement with religion." In fact, to enforce an exclusion of religious speech would require monitoring of meetings, risking greater entanglement. Thus, the University's interest in discriminating against speech on the basis of content is not sufficiently compelling.

2. *Board of Education of Westside Community Schools v. Mergens,* 496 U.S. 226, 110 S.Ct. 2356, 110 L.Ed.2d 191 (1990). In 1984, Congress enacted the Equal Access Act, 20 U.S.C.A. §§ 4071–4074, which provided that public secondary schools receiving federal financial assistance and maintaining a "limited open forum" were prohibited from denying (on the basis of the content of the speech at such meeting) "equal access" to students who wish to meet within the forum. The Act said that a "limited open forum" exists whenever a public secondary school "grants an offering to or opportunity for one or more noncurriculum related student groups to meet on school premises during noninstructional time." If a school covered by the Act allowed even one noncurriculum related student group to meet, the school could not deny other clubs, on the basis of the content of their speech, equal access to meet on school premises during noninstructional time. The school refused to recognize a Christian Club, where members planned to read, discuss the Bible, have fellowship, and to pray together.

O'Connor, delivering the opinion of the Court (except for Part III), ruled that the Act was constitutional, and required the school to recognize the Christian Club. She explained that a "noncurriculum related student group" is any student group that does not "*directly* relate to the body of courses offered by the school." (emphasis in original) The school in this case, for example, recognized the "Subsufers" (a club for students interested in scuba diving, a subject not taught or soon to be taught in any regularly offered course), and a Chess Club (although chess was not part of the curriculum). In contrast, a French Club (if French is taught or soon to be added to the curriculum) would be curriculum related. In Part III, O'Connor, J. (joined by Rehnquist, C.J., & White & Blackmun, JJ.) concluded that the Act did not violate the Establishment Clause because, under the Act, the school would not lead or direct a religious club but would merely permit a student-initiated and student-led club to meet after school, just as it permits other clubs to do. Also, for the school to grant permission to the Christian Club does not convey a message of state approval or endorsement of the particular religion. Kennedy, J., joined by Scalia, J., rejected this "endorsement test" because it was too vague and might result in hostility to religion. It is enough that the government does not give "direct benefits" to religion to the degree that it establishes a religion, and that the government does not coerce any student to participate. Marshall, J., joined by Brennan, J., concurred in the judgment. Stevens, J., dissented to the majority's interpretation of the Act.

3. *Lamb's Chapel v. Center Moriches Union Free School District*, 508 U.S. 384, 113 S.Ct. 2141, 124 L.Ed.2d 352 (1993), without dissent, invalidated New York regulations used to deny access to school premises to a church that wished to exhibit for public viewing and for religious purposes a film on family and child-rearing issues. The school rule allowed after-hours use of school property for social, civic, and recreational uses but not for religious purposes. White, J., for the Court, agreed that the school had created only a limited public forum, but then it denied access to this nonpublic forum based on the viewpoint of the speaker: the rules permitted school property to be used for the presentation of all views about family planning and child-rearing except those dealing with the subject from a religious viewpoint. There was no Establishment Clause violation under the three-part test of *Lemon v. Kurtzman*, because the film would not be shown during school hours, the school was not sponsoring the test, and it was not realistic to think that the general public would think that the school was endorsing religion or any particular creed. Any benefit to religion or to the particular church was incidental.

Scalia, J., joined by Thomas, J., concurred in the judgment, and objected to the majority's invocation of *Lemon*:

> "Like some ghoul in a late-night horror movie that repeatedly sits up in its grave and shuffles abroad, after being repeatedly killed and buried, *Lemon* stalks out Establishment Clause jurisprudence once again, frightening the little children and school attorneys of Center Moriches Union Free School District.... Over the years, however, no fewer than five of the currently sitting Justices have, in their own opinions, personally driven pencils through the creature's heart (the author of today's opinion repeatedly), and the sixth has joined an opinion doing so.... What a strange notion, that a Constitution which *itself* gives 'religion in general' preferential treatment (I refer to the Free Exercise Clause) forbids endorsement of religion in general."

Kennedy, J., concurring in part and in the judgment, agreed "that the Court's citation of *Lemon v. Kurtzman* is unsettling and unnecessary."

CAPITOL SQUARE REVIEW AND ADVISORY BOARD v. PINETTE
515 U.S. 753, 115 S.Ct. 2440, 132 L.Ed.2d 650 (1995).

JUSTICE SCALIA announced the judgment of the Court and delivered the opinion of the Court with respect to Parts I, II, and III, and an opinion with respect to Part IV, in which the CHIEF JUSTICE, JUSTICE KENNEDY and JUSTICE THOMAS join.

[The issue is whether] a State violates the Establishment Clause when, pursuant to a religiously neutral state policy, it permits a private party to display an unattended religious symbol in a traditional public forum located next to its seat of government.

I. Capitol Square is a 10–acre, state-owned plaza surrounding the Statehouse in Columbus, Ohio. For over a century the square has been used for public speeches, gatherings, and festivals advocating and celebrating a variety of causes, both secular and religious. Ohio Admin.Code Ann. § 128–4–02(A) (1994) makes the square available "for use by the public . . . for free discussion of public questions, or for activities of a broad public purpose," and Ohio Rev.Code Ann. § 105.41 (1994), gives the Capitol Square Review and Advisory Board responsibility for regulating public access. To use the square, a group must simply fill out an official application form and meet several criteria, which concern primarily safety, sanitation, and non-interference with other uses of the square, and which are neutral as to the speech content of the proposed event.

It has been the Board's policy "to allow a broad range of speakers and other gatherings of people to conduct events on the Capitol Square." Such diverse groups as homosexual rights organizations, the Ku Klux Klan and the United Way have held rallies. The Board has also permitted a variety of unattended displays on Capitol Square: a State-sponsored lighted tree during the Christmas season, a privately-sponsored menorah during Chanukah, a display showing the progress of a United Way fundraising campaign, and booths and exhibits during an arts festival. . . .

In November 1993, . . . the Board granted a rabbi's application to erect a menorah. That same day, the Board received an application from respondent Donnie Carr, an officer of the Ohio Ku Klux Klan, to place a cross on the square from December 8, 1993, to December 24, 1993. The Board denied that application on December 3, informing the Klan by letter that the decision to deny "was made upon the advice of counsel, in a good faith attempt to comply with the Ohio and United States Constitutions, as they have been interpreted in relevant decisions by the Federal and State Courts."

[T]he Ohio Klan, through its leader Vincent Pinette, filed the present suit . . . seeking an injunction requiring the Board to issue the requested permit. The Board defended on the ground that the permit would violate the Establishment Clause. The District Court determined that Capitol Square was a traditional public forum open to all without any policy against free-standing displays; that the Klan's cross was entirely private expression entitled to full First Amendment protection; and that the Board had failed to show that the display of the cross could reasonably be construed as endorsement of Christianity by the State. The District Court issued the injunction. . . .

II. First, a preliminary matter: Respondents contend that we should treat this as a case in which freedom of speech (the Klan's right to present the message of the cross display) was denied because of the

State's disagreement with that message's political content, rather than because of the State's desire to distance itself from sectarian religion. [However], the case was not presented and decided that way. The record facts before us and the opinions below address only the Establishment Clause issue; that is the question upon which we granted certiorari; and that is the sole question before us to decide.

Respondents' religious display in Capitol Square was private expression. Our precedent establishes that private religious speech, far from being a First Amendment orphan, is as fully protected under the Free Speech Clause as secular private expression. *Lamb's Chapel v. Center Moriches Union Free School Dist.* (1993); *Board of Ed. of Westside Community Schools (Dist. 66) v. Mergens,* (1990); *Widmar v. Vincent,* (1981); *Heffron v. International Soc. for Krishna Consciousness, Inc.* (1981) [§ 10–3.3]. Indeed, in Anglo–American history, at least, government suppression of speech has so commonly been directed *precisely* at religious speech that a free-speech clause without religion would be *Hamlet* without the prince. Accordingly, we have not excluded from free-speech protections religious proselytizing, *Heffron,* or even acts of worship, *Widmar.* Petitioners do not dispute that respondents, in displaying their cross, were engaging in constitutionally protected expression. They do contend that the constitutional protection does not extend to the length of permitting that expression to be made on Capitol Square.

It is undeniable, of course, that speech which is constitutionally protected against state suppression is not thereby accorded a guaranteed forum on all property owned by the State. *Perry Ed. Assn. v. Perry Local Educators' Assn.* (1983) [§ 10–3.3]. The right to use government property for one's private expression depends upon whether the property has by law or tradition been given the status of a public forum, or rather has been reserved for specific official uses. If the former, a State's right to limit protected expressive activity is sharply circumscribed: it may impose reasonable, content-neutral time, place and manner restrictions (a ban on all unattended displays, which did not exist here, might be one such), but it may regulate expressive *content* only if such a restriction is necessary, and narrowly drawn, to serve a compelling state interest. These strict standards apply here, since the District Court and the Court of Appeals found that Capitol Square was a traditional public forum. . . .

III. There is no doubt that compliance with the Establishment Clause is a state interest sufficiently compelling to justify content-based restrictions on speech. See *Lamb's Chapel; Widmar.* Whether that interest is implicated here, however, is a different question. And we do not write on a blank slate in answering it. We have twice previously addressed the combination of private religious expression, a forum available for public use, content-based regulation, and a State's interest in complying with the Establishment Clause. Both times, we have struck down the restriction on religious content. *Lamb's Chapel, supra; Widmar, supra.*

In *Lamb's Chapel*, a school district allowed private groups to use school facilities during off-hours for a variety of civic, social and recreational purposes, excluding, however, religious purposes. We held that even if school property during off-hours was not a public forum, the school district violated an applicant's free-speech rights by denying it use of the facilities solely because of the religious viewpoint of the program it wished to present. ... The *Lamb's Chapel* reasoning applies *a fortiori* here, where the property at issue is not a school but a full-fledged public forum.

Lamb's Chapel followed naturally from our decision in *Widmar*, in which we examined a public university's exclusion of student religious groups from facilities available to other student groups. ...We stated categorically that "an open forum in a public university does not confer any imprimatur of state approval on religious sects or practices."

Quite obviously, the factors that we considered determinative in *Lamb's Chapel* and *Widmar* exist here as well. The State did not sponsor respondents' expression, the expression was made on government property that had been opened to the public for speech, and permission was requested through the same application process and on the same terms required of other private groups.

IV. Petitioners argue that one feature of the present case distinguishes it from *Lamb's Chapel* and *Widmar*: the forum's proximity to the seat of government, which, they contend, may produce the perception that the cross bears the State's approval. They urge us to apply the so-called "endorsement test," see, *e.g., Allegheny County v. American Civil Liberties Union, Greater Pittsburgh Chapter; Lynch v. Donnelly* (1984), and to find that, because an observer might mistake private expression for officially endorsed religious expression, the State's content-based restriction is constitutional.

... "Endorsement" connotes an expression or demonstration of approval or support. Our cases have accordingly equated "endorsement" with "promotion" or "favoritism." *Allegheny County.* We find it peculiar to say that government "promotes" or "favors" a religious display by giving it the same access to a public forum that all other displays enjoy. And as a matter of Establishment Clause jurisprudence, we have consistently held that it is no violation for government to enact neutral policies that happen to benefit religion. See, *e.g., Bowen v. Kendrick* (1988); *Witters v. Washington Dept. of Services for Blind* (1986); *Mueller v. Allen* (1983); *McGowan v. Maryland* (1961). Where we have tested for endorsement of religion, the subject of the test was either expression *by the government itself, Lynch, supra,* or else government action alleged to *discriminate in favor* of private religious expression or activity, *Board of Ed. of Kiryas Joel Village School Dist. v. Grumet* (1994), *Allegheny County, supra.* The test petitioners propose, which would attribute to a neutrally behaving government *private* religious expression, has no antecedent in our jurisprudence, and would better be called a "transferred endorsement" test.

Petitioners rely heavily on *Allegheny County* and *Lynch,* but each is easily distinguished. In *Allegheny County* we held that the display of a privately-sponsored crèche on the "Grand Staircase" of the Allegheny County Courthouse violated the Establishment Clause. That staircase was not, however, open to all on an equal basis, so the County was *favoring* sectarian religious expression. Id. at n. 50 ("[t]he Grand Staircase does not appear to be the kind of location in which all were free to place their displays"). We expressly distinguished that site from the kind of public forum at issue here, and made clear that if the staircase were available to all on the same terms, "the presence of the crèche in that location for over six weeks would then *not* serve to associate the government with the crèche." (emphasis added). In *Lynch* we held that a city's display of a crèche did not violate the Establishment Clause because, in context, the display did not endorse religion. [T]he case neither holds nor even remotely assumes that the government's neutral treatment of *private* religious expression can be unconstitutional.

Petitioners argue that absence of perceived endorsement was material in *Lamb's Chapel* and *Widmar.* We did state in *Lamb's Chapel* that there was "no realistic danger that the community would think that the District was endorsing religion or any particular creed." But that conclusion was not the result of empirical investigation; it followed directly, we thought, from the fact that the forum was open and the religious activity privately sponsored. It is significant that we referred only to what would be thought by "the community"—not by outsiders or individual members of the community uninformed about the school's practice. Surely some of the latter, hearing of religious ceremonies on school premises, and not knowing of the premises' availability and use for all sorts of other private activities, *might* leap to the erroneous conclusion of state endorsement. But, we in effect said, given an open forum and private sponsorship, erroneous conclusions do not count. So also in *Widmar.* Once we determined that the benefit to religious groups from the public forum was incidental and shared by other groups, we categorically rejected the State's Establishment Clause defense.

What distinguishes *Allegheny County* and the dictum in *Lynch* from *Widmar* and *Lamb's Chapel* is the difference between government speech and private speech. "[T]here is a crucial difference between *government* speech endorsing religion, which the Establishment Clause forbids, and *private* speech endorsing religion, which the Free Speech and Free Exercise Clauses protect." *Mergens* (O'Connor, J., concurring).[2] Petitioners assert, in effect, that that distinction disappears when the private speech is conducted too close to the symbols of government. But

---

2. This statement in Justice O'Connor's *Mergens* concurrence is followed by the observation: "We think that secondary school students are mature enough and are likely to understand that a school does not endorse or support student speech that it merely permits on a nondiscriminatory basis." Justice O'Connor today says this ob-servation means that, even when we recognize private speech to be at issue, we must apply the endorsement test. But that would cause the second sentence to contradict the first, saying in effect that the "difference between *government* speech . . . and *private* speech" is *not* "crucial."

that, of course, must be merely a subpart of a more general principle: that the distinction disappears whenever private speech can be mistaken for government speech. That proposition cannot be accepted, at least where, as here, the government has not fostered or encouraged the mistake.

Of course, giving sectarian religious speech preferential access to a forum close to the seat of government (or anywhere else for that matter) would violate the Establishment Clause (as well as the Free Speech Clause, since it would involve content discrimination). And one can conceive of a case in which a governmental entity manipulates its administration of a public forum close to the seat of government (or within a government building) in such a manner that only certain religious groups take advantage of it, creating an impression of endorsement *that is in fact accurate.* But those situations, which involve governmental *favoritism,* do not exist here. Capitol Square is a genuinely public forum, is known to be a public forum, and has been widely used as a public forum for many, many years. Private religious speech cannot be subject to veto by those who see favoritism where there is none.

The contrary view, most strongly espoused by Justice Stevens, but endorsed by Justice Souter and Justice O'Connor as well, exiles private religious speech to a realm of less-protected expression heretofore inhabited only by sexually explicit displays and commercial speech. It will be a sad day when this Court casts piety in with pornography, and finds the First Amendment more hospitable to private expletives, see *Cohen v. California* (1971), than to private prayers. This would be merely bizarre were religious speech simply *as* protected by the Constitution as other forms of private speech; but it is outright perverse when one considers that private religious expression receives *preferential* treatment under the Free Exercise Clause. It is no answer to say that the Establishment Clause tempers religious speech. By its terms that Clause applies only to the words and acts of *government.* It was never meant, and has never been read by this Court, to serve as an impediment to purely *private* religious speech connected to the State only through its occurrence in a public forum.

Since petitioners' "transferred endorsement" principle cannot possibly be restricted to squares in front of state capitols, the Establishment Clause regime that it would usher in is most unappealing. To require (and permit) access by a religious group in *Lamb's Chapel,* it was sufficient that the group's activity was not in fact government sponsored, that the event was open to the public, and that the benefit of the facilities was shared by various organizations. Petitioners' rule would require school districts adopting similar policies in the future to guess whether some undetermined critical mass of the community might nonetheless perceive the district to be advocating a religious viewpoint. ...Policy makers would find themselves in a vise between the Establishment Clause on one side and the Free Speech and Free Exercise Clauses on the other. Every proposed act of private, religious expression in a public forum would force officials to weigh a host of imponderables. How close to government is too close? What kind of building, and in what context, symbolizes state authority? If the State guessed wrong in one direction, it would be guilty of an Establishment Clause violation; if in the other, it would be liable for suppressing free exercise or free speech (a risk not run when the State restrains only its *own* expression).

The "transferred endorsement" test would also disrupt the settled principle that policies providing incidental benefits to religion do not contravene the Establishment Clause. That principle is the basis for the constitutionality of a broad range of laws, not merely those that implicate free-speech issues. It has radical implications for our public policy to suggest that neutral laws are invalid whenever hypothetical observers may—*even reasonably*—confuse an incidental benefit to religion with state endorsement.[3]

If Ohio is concerned about misperceptions, nothing prevents it from requiring all private displays in the Square to be identified as such. That would be a content-neutral "manner" restriction which is assuredly constitutional. But the State may not, on the claim of misperception of official endorsement, ban all private religious speech from the public square, or discriminate against it by requiring religious speech alone to disclaim public sponsorship.[4]

Religious expression cannot violate the Establishment Clause where it (1) is purely private and (2) occurs in a traditional or designated public forum, publicly announced and open to all on equal terms. Those conditions are satisfied here, and therefore the State may not bar respondents' cross from Capitol Square.

The judgment of the Court of Appeals is *affirmed*.

Justice O'Connor, with whom Justice Souter and Justice Breyer join, concurring in part and concurring in the judgment.

---

3. [T]he endorsement test does not supply an appropriate standard for the inquiry before us. It supplies no standard whatsoever. The lower federal courts that the concurrence identifies as having "applied the endorsement test in precisely the context before us today," have reached precisely *differing* results—which is what led the Court to take this case. And if further proof of the invited chaos is required, one need only follow the debate between the concurrence and Justice Stevens' dissent as to whether the hypothetical beholder who will be the determinant of "endorsement" should be *any* beholder (no matter how unknowledgeable), or the *average* beholder, or (what Justice Stevens accuses the concurrence of favoring) the "ultra-reasonable" beholder. And of course even when one achieves agreement upon that question, it will be unrealistic to expect different judges (or should it be juries?) to reach consistent answers as to what any beholder, the average beholder, or the ultra-reasonable beholder (as the case may be) would think. It is irresponsible to make the Nation's legislators walk this minefield.

4. [W]e do not inquire into the adequacy of the identification which was attached to the cross ultimately erected in this case. The difficulties posed by such an inquiry, however, are yet another reason to reject the principle of "transferred endorsement." The only principled line for adequacy of identification would be identification that is legible at whatever distance the cross is visible. Otherwise, the uninformed viewer who does not have time or inclination to come closer to read the sign might be misled, just as (under current law) the uninformed viewer who does not have time or inclination to inquire whether speech in Capitol Square is publicly endorsed speech might be misled. Needless to say, such a rule would place considerable constraint upon religious speech, not to mention that it would be ridiculous. But if one rejects that criterion, courts would have to decide (on what basis we cannot imagine) how large an identifying sign is large enough. Our Religion Clause jurisprudence is complex enough without the addition of this highly litigable feature.

.... I see no necessity to carve out, as the plurality opinion would today, an exception to the endorsement test for the public forum context. [O]n the facts of this case that there is "no realistic danger that the community would think that the [State] was endorsing religion or any particular creed," by granting respondents a permit to erect their temporary cross on Capitol Square. I write separately, however, to emphasize that ... the endorsement test necessarily focuses upon the perception of a reasonable, informed observer....

To the plurality's consideration of the open nature of the forum and the private ownership of the display, however, I would add the presence of a sign disclaiming government sponsorship or endorsement on the Klan cross, which would make the State's role clear to the community. This factor is important because, as Justice Souter makes clear, certain aspects of the cross display in this case arguably intimate government approval of respondents' private religious message—particularly that the cross is an especially potent sectarian symbol which stood unattended in close proximity to official government buildings. In context, a disclaimer helps remove doubt about State approval of respondents' religious message....

Our agreement as to the outcome of this case, however, cannot mask the fact that I part company with the plurality on a fundamental point: I disagree that "[i]t has radical implications for our public policy to suggest that neutral laws are invalid whenever hypothetical observers may—*even reasonably*—confuse an incidental benefit to religion with State endorsement." On the contrary, when the reasonable observer would view a government practice as endorsing religion, I believe that it is our *duty* to hold the practice invalid. [The Establishment] Clause is more than a negative prohibition against certain narrowly defined forms of government favoritism; it also imposes affirmative obligations that may require a State, in some situations, to take steps to avoid being perceived as supporting or endorsing a private religious message. That is, the Establishment Clause forbids a State from hiding behind the application of formally neutral criteria and remaining studiously oblivious to the effects of its actions. Governmental intent cannot control, and not all state policies are permissible under the Religion Clauses simply because they are neutral in form....

[T]he Establishment Clause inquiry cannot be distilled into a fixed, *per se* rule ... Our fundamental point of departure, [from Justice Stevens is that, in] my view, proper application of the endorsement test requires that the reasonable observer be deemed more informed than the casual passerby postulated by the dissent.

[T]he reasonable observer in the endorsement inquiry must be deemed aware of the history and context of the community and forum in which the religious display appears.... Nor can the knowledge attributed to the reasonable observer be limited to the information gleaned simply from viewing the challenged display. ... An informed member of the community will know how the public space in question has been used in the past—and it is that fact, not that the space may meet the legal definition of a public forum, which is relevant to the endorsement inquiry.... The reasonable observer would recognize the distinction between speech the government supports and speech that it merely allows in a place that traditionally has been open to a range of private speakers accompanied, if necessary, by an appropriate disclaimer....

JUSTICE SOUTER, with whom JUSTICE O'CONNOR and JUSTICE BREYER join, concurring in part and concurring in the judgment.

[I]n some circumstances an intelligent observer may mistake private, unattended religious displays in a public forum for government speech endorsing religion.... When an individual speaks in a public forum, it is reasonable for an observer to attribute the speech, first and foremost, to the speaker, while an unattended display (and any message it conveys) can naturally be viewed as belonging to the owner of the land on which it stands.

[Petitioners] could have granted the application subject to the condition that the Klan attach a disclaimer sufficiently large and clear to preclude any reasonable inference that the cross was there to "demonstrat[e] the government's allegiance to, or endorsement of, Christian faith."[2] In the alternative, the Board could have instituted a policy of restricting all private, unattended displays to one area of the square, with a permanent sign marking the area as a forum for private speech carrying no endorsement from the State....

JUSTICE STEVENS, dissenting.

The Establishment Clause should be construed to create a strong presumption against the installation of unattended religious symbols on public property. ... The very fact that a sign is installed on public property implies official recognition and reinforcement of its message. That implication is especially strong when the sign stands in front of the seat of the government itself. The "reasonable observer" of any symbol placed unattended in front of any capitol in the world will normally assume that the sovereign—which is not only the owner of that parcel of real estate but also the lawgiver for the surrounding territory—has sponsored and facilitated its message....

Because structures on government property—and, in particular, in front of buildings plainly identified with the state—imply state approval of their message, the Government must have considerable leeway, outside of the religious arena, to choose what kinds of displays it will allow and what kinds it will not. [O]ur "public forum" cases do not foreclose public entities from enforcing prohibitions against all unattended displays in public parks, or possibly even limiting the use of such displays to the communication of non-controversial messages. [T]he Establishment Clause prohibits government from allowing, and thus endorsing, unattended displays that take a position on a religious issue. If the State

---

2. Of course the presence of a disclaimer does not always remove the possibility that a private religious display "convey[s] or attempt[s] to convey a message that religion or a particular religious belief is favored or preferred," when other indicia of endorsement (*e.g.*, objective indications that the government in fact invited the display or otherwise intended to further a religious purpose) outweigh the mitigating effect of the disclaimer, or when the disclaimer itself does not sufficiently disclaim government support. In this case, however, there is no reason to presume that an adequate disclaimer could not have been drafted.

allows such stationary displays in front of its seat of government, viewers will reasonably assume that it approves of them.... [13]

JUSTICE GINSBURG, dissenting.

... If the aim of the Establishment Clause is genuinely to uncouple government from church, a State may not permit, and a court may not order, a display of this character....

[The concurring opinion of THOMAS, J. is omitted.]

Notes

1. Justice Souter expressed particular concern with unattended, stationary displays, *if* they are religious ("observer may mistake private, unattended religious displays"). Stevens also applied his opinion to "the installation of unattended religious symbols on public property." Both Justices apparently would allow an unattended, stationary display on a public forum, if it was political. Suppose that the KKK applied for a permit to display, on Capitol Square, a giant hooded sheet. May the state prohibit that non-religious display? What if a reasonable observer would think that the state endorsed the Klan's message? Assume the Klan displayed (for political purposes) a burning cross (which is a typical KKK political symbol). Should that be allowed? What about a burning bush? (Or, is that symbol, from the Book of Exodus, religious?)

2. The cross in *Pinette* is pictured here. Given the size of the cross, if a sign must dissociate the cross from the State Capitol, how large must that sign be in the view of Justices O'Connor or Souter?

13. Indeed, I do not think *any* disclaimer could dispel the message of endorsement in this case....

ROSENBERGER v. RECTOR AND VISITORS OF THE UNIVERSITY OF VIRGINIA

515 U.S. 819, 115 S.Ct. 2510, 132 L.Ed.2d 700 (1995).

JUSTICE KENNEDY delivered the opinion of the Court.

The University of Virginia, an instrumentality of the Commonwealth for which it is named and thus bound by the First and Fourteenth Amendments, authorizes the payment of outside contractors for the printing costs of a variety of student publications. It withheld any authorization for payments on behalf of petitioners for the sole reason that their student paper "primarily promotes or manifests a particular belie[f] in or about a deity or an ultimate reality." That the paper did promote or manifest views within the defined exclusion seems plain enough. The challenge is to the University's regulation and its denial of authorization, the case raising issues under the Speech and Establishment Clauses of the First Amendment....

Before a student group is eligible to submit bills from its outside contractors for payment by the fund described below, it must become a "Contracted Independent Organization" (CIO). CIO status is available to any group the majority of whose members are students, whose managing officers are full-time students, and that complies with certain procedural requirements. A CIO must file its constitution with the University; must pledge not to discriminate in its membership; and must include in dealings with third parties and in all written materials a disclaimer, stating that the CIO is independent of the University and that the University is not responsible for the CIO. CIOs enjoy access to University facilities, including meeting rooms and computer terminals. A standard agreement signed between each CIO and the University provides that the benefits and opportunities afforded to CIOs "should not be misinterpreted as meaning that those organizations are part of or controlled by the University, that the University is responsible for the organizations' contracts or other acts or omissions, or that the University approves of the organizations' goals or activities."

All CIOs may exist and operate at the University, but some are also entitled to apply for funds from the Student Activities Fund (SAF). Established and governed by University Guidelines, the purpose of the SAF is to support a broad range of extracurricular student activities that "are related to the educational purpose of the University." ... The SAF receives its money from a mandatory fee of $14 per semester assessed to each full-time student. The Student Council, elected by the students, has the initial authority to disburse the funds, but its actions are subject to review by a faculty body chaired by a designee of the Vice President for Student Affairs.

Some, but not all, CIOs may submit disbursement requests to the SAF. The Guidelines recognize 11 categories of student groups that may seek payment to third-party contractors because they "are related to the educational purpose of the University of Virginia." One of these is "student news, information, opinion, entertainment, or academic communications media groups." [However,] student activities which are excluded from SAF support are religious activities, philanthropic contributions and activities, political activities, activities that would jeopardize the University's tax exempt status, those which involve payment of honoraria or similar fees, or social entertainment or related expenses. The prohibition on "political activities" is defined so that it is limited to electioneering and lobbying. The Guidelines provide that "[t]hese restrictions on funding political activities are not intended to preclude funding of any otherwise eligible student organization which ... espouses particular positions or ideological viewpoints, including those that may be unpopular or are not generally accepted." A "religious activity," by contrast, is defined as any activity that "primarily promotes or manifests a particular belie[f] in or about a deity or an ultimate reality."

... If an organization seeks SAF support, it must submit its bills to the Student Council, which pays the organization's creditors upon determining that the expenses are appropriate. No direct payments are made to the student groups. During the 1990–1991 academic year, [f]ifteen of the groups were funded as "student news, information, opinion, entertainment, or academic communications media groups."

Petitioners' organization, Wide Awake Productions (WAP), qualified as a CIO. Formed by petitioner Ronald Rosenberger and other undergraduates in 1990, WAP ... publishes *Wide Awake: A Christian Perspective* at the University of Virginia. The paper's Christian viewpoint was evident from the first issue, in which its editors wrote that the journal "offers a Christian perspective on both personal and community issues, especially those relevant to college students at the University of Virginia." The editors committed the paper to a two-fold mission: "to challenge Christians to live, in word and deed, according to the faith they proclaim and to encourage students to consider what a personal relationship with Jesus Christ means." The first issue had articles about racism, crisis pregnancy, stress, prayer, C.S. Lewis' ideas about evil and free will, and reviews of religious music.... By June 1992, WAP had distributed about 5,000 copies of Wide Awake to University students, free of charge.

WAP had acquired CIO status soon after it was organized. This is an important consideration in this case, for had it been a "religious organization," WAP would not have been accorded CIO status. As defined by the Guidelines, a "religious organization" is "an organization whose purpose is to practice a devotion to an acknowledged ultimate reality or deity." At no stage in this controversy has the University contended that WAP is such an organization.

A few months after being given CIO status, WAP requested the SAF to pay its printer $5,862 for the costs of printing its newspaper. The

Appropriations Committee of the Student Council denied WAP's request on the ground that Wide Awake was a "religious activity" within the meaning of the Guidelines, *i.e.*, that the newspaper "promote[d] or manifest[ed] a particular belie[f] in or about a deity or an ultimate reality." It made its determination after examining the first issue. WAP [sued, alleging] that refusal to authorize payment of the printing costs of the publication, solely on the basis of its religious editorial viewpoint, violated their rights to freedom of speech and press, to the free exercise of religion, and to equal protection of the law....

It is axiomatic that the government may not regulate speech based on its substantive content or the message it conveys. Other principles follow from this precept. In the realm of private speech or expression, government regulation may not favor one speaker over another. Discrimination against speech because of its message is presumed to be unconstitutional. These rules informed our determination that the government offends the First Amendment when it imposes financial burdens on certain speakers based on the content of their expression. *Simon & Schuster, Inc. v. Members of N.Y. State Crime Victims Bd.* (1991). When the government targets not subject matter but particular views taken by speakers on a subject, the violation of the First Amendment is all the more blatant. Viewpoint discrimination is thus an egregious form of content discrimination. The government must abstain from regulating speech when the specific motivating ideology or the opinion or perspective of the speaker is the rationale for the restriction. See *Perry Ed. Assn. v. Perry Local Educators' Assn.* (1983).

These principles provide the framework forbidding the State from exercising viewpoint discrimination, even when the limited public forum is one of its own creation.... Once it has opened a limited forum, [t]he State may not exclude speech where its distinction is not "reasonable in light of the purpose served by the forum," nor may it discriminate against speech on the basis of its viewpoint. Thus, in determining whether the State is acting to preserve the limits of the forum it has created so that the exclusion of a class of speech is legitimate, we have observed a distinction between, on the one hand, content discrimination, which may be permissible if it preserves the purposes of that limited forum, and, on the other hand, viewpoint discrimination, which is presumed impermissible when directed against speech otherwise within the forum's limitations.

The SAF is a forum more in a metaphysical than in a spatial or geographic sense, but the same principles are applicable. See, *e.g., Perry Ed. Assn.* (forum analysis of a school mail system). The most recent and most apposite case is our decision in *Lamb's Chapel v. Center Moriches Union Free School Dist.* (1993), ... Our conclusion was unanimous: "[I]t discriminates on the basis of viewpoint to permit school property to be used for the presentation of all views about family issues and child-rearing except those dealing with the subject matter from a religious standpoint."

[I]t must be acknowledged, the distinction [between content and viewpoint discrimination] is not a precise one. [N]onetheless, that here, as in *Lamb's Chapel,* viewpoint discrimination is the proper way to interpret the University's objections to Wide Awake. By the very terms of the SAF prohibition, the University does not exclude religion as a subject matter but selects for disfavored treatment those student journalistic efforts with religious editorial viewpoints. Religion may be a vast area of inquiry, but it also provides, as it did here, a specific premise, a perspective, a standpoint from which a variety of subjects may be discussed and considered. The prohibited perspective, not the general subject matter, resulted in the refusal to make third-party payments, for the subjects discussed were otherwise within the approved category of publications.

The dissent's assertion that no viewpoint discrimination occurs because the Guidelines discriminate against an entire class of viewpoints reflects an insupportable assumption that all debate is bipolar and that anti-religious speech is the only response to religious speech. Our understanding of the complex and multifaceted nature of public discourse has not embraced such a contrived description of the marketplace of ideas.... It is as objectionable to exclude both a theistic and an atheistic perspective on the debate as it is to exclude one, the other, or yet another political, economic, or social viewpoint. The dissent's declaration that debate is not skewed so long as multiple voices are silenced is simply wrong; the debate is skewed in multiple ways.

[J]ust as the school district in *Lamb's Chapel* pointed to nothing but the religious views of the group as the rationale for excluding its message, so in this case the University justifies its denial of SAF participation to WAP on the ground that the contents of Wide Awake reveal an avowed religious perspective .....

The University tries to escape the consequences of our holding in *Lamb's Chapel* by urging that this case involves the provision of funds rather than access to facilities. [W]e have permitted the government to regulate the content of what is or is not expressed when it is the speaker or when it enlists private entities to convey its own message. In the same vein, in *Rust v. Sullivan,* we upheld the government's prohibition on abortion-related advice applicable to recipients of federal funds for family planning counseling. There, the government did not create a program to encourage private speech but instead used private speakers to transmit specific information pertaining to its own program. We recognized that when the government appropriates public funds to promote a particular policy of its own it is entitled to say what it wishes. When the government disburses public funds to private entities to convey a governmental message, it may take legitimate and appropriate steps to ensure that its message is neither garbled nor distorted by the grantee.

It does not follow, however, and we did not suggest in *Widmar*, that viewpoint-based restrictions are proper when the University does not itself speak or subsidize transmittal of a message it favors but instead expends funds to encourage a diversity of views from private speakers. A holding that the University may not discriminate based on the viewpoint of private persons whose speech it facilitates does not restrict the University's own speech, which is controlled by different principles. For that reason, the University's reliance on *Regan v. Taxation with Representation of Wash.* (1983) is inapposite as well. *Regan* involved a challenge to Congress' choice to grant tax deductions for contributions made to veterans' groups engaged in lobbying, while denying that favorable status to other charities which pursued lobbying efforts. [That case] reaffirmed the requirement of viewpoint neutrality in the Government's provision of financial benefits by observing that "[t]he case would be different if Congress were to discriminate invidiously in its subsidies in such a way as to 'ai[m] at the suppression of dangerous ideas.' " *Regan* relied on a distinction based on preferential treatment of certain speakers—veterans organizations—and not a distinction based on the content or messages of those groups' speech. The University's regulation now before us, however, has a speech-based restriction as its sole rationale and operative principle.

The distinction between the University's own favored message and the private speech of students is evident in the case before us. The University itself has taken steps to ensure the distinction in the agreement each CIO must sign. The University declares that the student groups eligible for SAF support are not the University's agents, are not subject to its control, and are not its responsibility. Having offered to pay the third-party contractors on behalf of private speakers who convey their own messages, the University may not silence the expression of selected viewpoints.

The University urges that, from a constitutional standpoint, funding of speech differs from provision of access to facilities because money is scarce and physical facilities are not. [T]he underlying premise that the University could discriminate based on viewpoint if demand for space exceeded its availability is wrong. . . . Had the meeting rooms in *Lamb's Chapel* been scarce, had the demand been greater than the supply, our decision would have been no different. It would have been incumbent on the State, of course, to ration or allocate the scarce resources on some acceptable neutral principle; but nothing in our decision indicated that scarcity would give the State the right to exercise viewpoint discrimination that is otherwise impermissible.

Vital First Amendment speech principles are at stake here. The first danger to liberty lies in granting the State the power to examine publications to determine whether or not they are based on some ultimate idea and if so for the State to classify them. The second, and corollary, danger is to speech from the chilling of individual thought and expression. That danger is especially real in the University setting, [with] a background and tradition of thought and experiment that is at the center of our intellectual and philosophic tradition. . . .

The Guideline invoked by the University to deny third-party contractor payments on behalf of WAP effects a sweeping restriction on student thought and student inquiry in the context of University sponsored publications. The prohibition on funding on behalf of publications that "primarily promot[e] or manifes[t] a particular belie[f] in or about a deity or an ultimate reality," in its ordinary and commonsense meaning, has a vast potential reach. . . . Were the prohibition applied with much vigor at all, it would bar funding of essays by hypothetical student contributors named Plato, Spinoza, and Descartes. And if the regulation covers, as the University says it does, those student journalistic efforts which primarily manifest or promote a belief that there is no deity and no ultimate reality, then undergraduates named Karl Marx, Bertrand Russell, and Jean–Paul Sartre would likewise have some of their major essays excluded from student publications. . . .

Based on the principles we have discussed, we hold that the regulation invoked to deny SAF support, both in its terms and in its application to these petitioners, is a denial of their right of free speech guaranteed by the First Amendment. It remains to be considered whether the violation following from the University's action is excused by the necessity of complying with the Constitution's prohibition against state establishment of religion. . . .

The Court of Appeals ruled that withholding SAF support from Wide Awake contravened the Speech Clause of the First Amendment, but proceeded to hold that the University's action was justified by the necessity of avoiding a violation of the Establishment Clause, an interest it found compelling. [T]he Fourth Circuit asserted that direct monetary subsidization of religious organizations and projects is "a beast of an entirely different color." The court declared that the Establishment Clause would not permit the use of public funds to support " 'a specifically religious activity in an otherwise substantially secular setting.' " [T]he University's provision of SAF funds for its publication would "send an unmistakably clear signal that the University of Virginia supports Christian values and wishes to promote the wide promulgation of such values." . . .

A central lesson of our decisions is that a significant factor in upholding governmental programs in the face of Establishment Clause attack is their neutrality towards religion. [T]he guarantee of neutrality is respected, not offended, when the government, following neutral criteria and evenhanded policies, extends benefits to recipients whose ideologies and viewpoints, including religious ones, are broad and diverse. *Witters v. Washington Dept. of Services for Blind* (1986); *Mueller v. Allen* (1983); *Widmar.* More than once have we rejected the position that the Establishment Clause even justifies, much less requires, a refusal to extend free speech rights to religious speakers who participate in broad-reaching government programs neutral in design. See *Lamb's Chapel; Mergens; Widmar.*

The governmental program here is neutral toward religion. There is no suggestion that the University created it to advance religion or adopted some ingenious device with the purpose of aiding a religious cause. ...WAP did not seek a subsidy because of its Christian editorial viewpoint; it sought funding as a student journal, which it was. The neutrality of the program distinguishes the student fees from a tax levied for the direct support of a church or group of churches.... Our decision, then, cannot be read as addressing an expenditure from a general tax fund. Here, the disbursements from the fund go to private contractors for the cost of printing that which is protected under the Speech Clause of the First Amendment. This is a far cry from a general public assessment designed and effected to provide financial support for a church.

Government neutrality is apparent in the State's overall scheme in a further meaningful respect. The program respects the critical difference "between *government* speech endorsing religion, which the Establishment Clause forbids, and *private* speech endorsing religion, which the Free Speech and Free Exercise Clauses protect." In this case, "the government has not willfully fostered or encouraged" any mistaken impression that the student newspapers speak for the University. *Capital Square Review and Advisory Bd. v. Pinette.* The University has taken pains to disassociate itself from the private speech involved in this case. The Court of Appeals' apparent concern that Wide Awake's religious orientation would be attributed to the University is not a plausible fear, and there is no real likelihood that the speech in question is being either endorsed or coerced by the State.

The Court of Appeals (and the dissent) are correct to extract from our decisions the principle that we have recognized special Establishment Clause dangers where the government makes direct money payments to sectarian institutions, [but we] do not confront a case where, even under a neutral program that includes nonsectarian recipients, the government is making direct money payments to an institution or group that is engaged in religious activity. Neither the Court of Appeals nor the dissent, we believe, takes sufficient cognizance of the undisputed fact that no public funds flow directly to WAP's coffers.

It does not violate the Establishment Clause for a public university to grant access to its facilities on a religion-neutral basis to a wide spectrum of student groups, including groups which use meeting rooms for sectarian activities, accompanied by some devotional exercises. See *Widmar; Mergens.* This is so even where the upkeep, maintenance, and repair of the facilities attributed to those uses is paid from a student activities fund to which students are required to contribute. The government usually acts by spending money. Even the provision of a meeting room, as in *Mergens* and *Widmar,* involved governmental expenditure, if only in the form of electricity and heating or cooling costs. The error made by the Court of Appeals, as well as by the dissent, lies in focusing on the money that is undoubtedly expended by the government, rather than on the nature of the benefit received by the recipient. If the expenditure of governmental funds is prohibited whenever those funds pay for a service that is, pursuant to a religion-neutral program, used by a group for sectarian purposes, then *Widmar, Mergens,* and *Lamb's Chapel* would have to be overruled. Given our holdings in these cases, it follows that a public university may maintain its own computer facility and give student groups access to that facility, including the use of the printers, on a religion neutral, say first-come-first-served, basis. If a religious student organization obtained access on that religion-neutral basis and used a computer to compose or a printer or copy machine to print speech with a religious content or viewpoint, the State's action in providing the group with access would no more violate the Establishment Clause than would giving those groups access to an assembly hall. There is no difference in logic or principle, and no difference of constitutional significance, between a school using its funds to operate a facility to which students have access, and a school paying a third-party contractor to operate the facility on its behalf. The latter occurs here. The University provides printing services to a broad spectrum of student newspapers. . . . Any benefit to religion is incidental to the government's provision of secular services for secular purposes on a religion-neutral basis. Printing is a routine, secular, and recurring attribute of student life.

By paying outside printers, the University in fact attains a further degree of separation from the student publication, for it avoids the duties of supervision, escapes the costs of upkeep, repair, and replacement attributable to student use, and has a clear record of costs. . . . It would be formalistic for us to say that the University must forfeit these advantages and provide the services itself in order to comply with the Establishment Clause. It is, of course, true that if the State pays a church's bills it is subsidizing it, and we must guard against this abuse. That is not a danger here, based on the considerations we have advanced and for the additional reason that the student publication is not a religious institution, at least in the usual sense of that term as used in our case law, and it is not a religious organization as used in the University's own regulations. It is instead a publication involved in a pure forum for the expression of ideas, ideas that would be both incomplete and chilled were the Constitution to be interpreted to require that state officials and courts scan the publication to ferret out views that principally manifest a belief in a divine being.

Were the dissent's view to become law, it would require the University, in order to avoid a constitutional violation, to scrutinize the content of student speech, lest the expression in question—speech otherwise protected by the Constitution—contain too great a religious content. The dissent, in fact, anticipates such censorship as "crucial" in distinguishing between "works characterized by the evangelism of Wide Awake and writing that merely happens to express views that a given religion might approve." That eventuality raises the specter of governmental censorship, to ensure that all student writings and publications meet some baseline standard of secular orthodoxy....

To obey the Establishment Clause, it was not necessary for the University to deny eligibility to student publications because of their viewpoint. The neutrality commanded of the State by the separate Clauses of the First Amendment was compromised by the University's course of action. The viewpoint discrimination inherent in the University's regulation required public officials to scan and interpret student publications to discern their underlying philosophic assumptions respecting religious theory and belief. That course of action was a denial of the right of free speech and would risk fostering a pervasive bias or hostility to religion, which could undermine the very neutrality the Establishment Clause requires. There is no Establishment Clause violation in the University's honoring its duties under the Free Speech Clause.

The judgment of the Court of Appeals must be, and is, reversed.

It is so ordered.

JUSTICE O'CONNOR, concurring.

[C]ertain considerations specific to the program at issue lead me to conclude that by providing the same assistance to Wide Awake that it does to other publications, the University would not be endorsing the magazine's religious perspective. First, the student organizations, at the University's insistence, remain strictly independent of the University.... Second, financial assistance is distributed in a manner that ensures its use only for permissible purposes.... Third, assistance is provided to the religious publication in a context that makes improbable any perception of government endorsement of the religious message. Wide Awake does not exist in a vacuum. It competes with 15 other magazines and newspapers for advertising and readership.... Finally, although the question is not presented here, I note the possibility that the student fee is susceptible to a Free Speech Clause challenge by an objecting student that she should not be compelled to pay for speech with which she disagrees....

JUSTICE THOMAS, concurring....

Even assuming that the Virginia debate on the so-called "Assessment Controversy" was indicative of the principles embodied in the Establishment Clause, this incident hardly compels the dissent's conclusion that government must actively discriminate against religion. The dissent's historical discussion glosses over the fundamental characteristic of the Virginia assessment bill that sparked the controversy: The assessment was to be imposed for the support of clergy in the performance of their function of teaching religion.... According to Madison, the Virginia assessment was flawed because it "violate[d] that equality which ought to be the basis of every law." Madison's Remonstrance ¶ 4. The assessment violated the "equality" principle not because it allowed religious groups to participate in a generally available government program, but because the bill singled out religious entities for special benefits. . . .

Stripped of its flawed historical premise, the dissent's argument is reduced to the claim that our Establishment Clause jurisprudence permits neutrality in the context of access to government *facilities* but requires discrimination in access to government *funds*. [The Establishment] Clause does not compel the exclusion of religious groups from government benefits programs that are generally available to a broad class of participants. Under the dissent's view, however, the University of Virginia may provide neutral access to the University's own printing press, but it may not provide the same service when the press is owned by a third party. Not surprisingly, the dissent offers no logical justification for this conclusion, and none is evident in the text or original meaning of the First Amendment. . . .

JUSTICE SOUTER, with whom JUSTICE STEVENS, JUSTICE GINSBURG and JUSTICE BREYER join, dissenting.

The Court today, for the first time, approves direct funding of core religious activities by an arm of the State. . . . Using public funds for the direct subsidization of preaching the word is categorically forbidden under the Establishment Clause, and if the Clause was meant to accomplish nothing else, it was meant to bar this use of public money. Evidence on the subject antedates even the Bill of Rights itself, as may be seen in the writings of Madison, whose authority on questions about the meaning of the Establishment Clause is well settled. Four years before the First Congress proposed the First Amendment, Madison gave his opinion on the legitimacy of using public funds for religious purposes[:]

> "Who does not see that . . . the same authority which can force a citizen to contribute three pence only of his property for the support of any one establishment, may force him to conform to any other establishment in all cases whatsoever?" James Madison, Memorial and Remonstrance Against Religious Assessments ¶ 3

. . . . There is no viewpoint discrimination in the University's application of its Guidelines to deny funding to Wide Awake. Under those Guidelines, a "religious activit[y]," which is not eligible for funding, is "an activity which primarily promotes or manifests a particular belief(s) in or about a deity or an ultimate reality." It is clear that this is the basis on which Wide Awake Productions was denied funding. . . . If the Guidelines were written or applied so as to limit only such Christian advocacy and no other evangelical efforts that might compete with it, the discrimination would be based on viewpoint. But [the regulation] applies to Muslim and Jewish and Buddhist advocacy as well as to Christian. And since it limits funding to activities promoting or manifesting a particular belief not only "in" but "about" a deity or ultimate reality, it applies to agnostics and atheists as well as it does to deists and theists.

[The Guidelines] deny funding for the entire subject matter of religious apologetics. . . .

11-3. RELIGIOUSLY BASED EXCEPTIONS TO STATE IMPOSED DUTIES

McGOWAN v. MARYLAND
366 U.S. 420, 81 S.Ct. 1101, 6 L.Ed.2d 393 (1961).

MR. CHIEF JUSTICE WARREN delivered the opinion of the Court. . . .

Appellants are seven employees of a large discount department store located on a highway in Anne Arundel County, Maryland. They were indicted for the Sunday sale of a three-ring loose-leaf binder, a can of floor wax, a stapler and staples, and a toy submarine in violation of Md.Ann.Code, Art. 27, § 521. Generally, this section prohibited, throughout the State, the Sunday sale of all merchandise except the retail sale of tobacco products, confectioneries, milk, bread, fruits, gasoline, oils, greases, drugs and medicines, and newspapers and periodicals. [A]ppellants contend that the statutes violate the guarantee of separation of church and state in that the statutes are laws respecting an establishment of religion . . .

The essence of appellants' "establishment" argument is that Sunday is the Sabbath day of the predominant Christian sects; that the purpose of the enforced stoppage of labor on that day is to facilitate and encourage church attendance. . . . There is no dispute that the original laws which dealt with Sunday labor were motivated by religious forces. But what we must decide is whether present Sunday legislation, having undergone extensive changes from the earliest forms, still retains its religious character.

. . . The title of the major series of sections of the Maryland Code dealing with Sunday closing—Art. 27, §§ 492–534C—is "Sabbath Breaking"; § 492 proscribes work or bodily labor on the "Lord's day," and forbids persons to "profane the Lord's day" by gaming, fishing et cetera; § 522 refers to Sunday as the "Sabbath day." [M]any of the exempted Sunday activities in the various localities of the State may only be conducted during the afternoon and late evening; most Christian church services, of course, are held on Sunday morning and early Sunday evening. [And] certain localities do not permit the allowed Sunday activities to be carried on within one hundred yards of any church where religious services are being held. This is the totality of the evidence of religious purpose which may be gleaned from the face of the present statute and from its operative effect. . . .

The existing Maryland Sunday laws are not simply verbatim re-enactments of their religiously oriented antecedents. Only § 492 retains the appellation of "Lord's day" and even that section no longer makes recitation of religious purpose. It does talk in terms of "profan[ing] the Lord's day," but other sections permit the activities previously thought to be profane. Prior denunciation of Sunday drunkenness is now gone. Contemporary concern with these statutes is evidenced by the dozen changes made in 1959 and by the recent enactment of a majority of the exceptions.... After engaging in the close scrutiny demanded of us when First Amendment liberties are at issue, we accept the State Supreme Court's determination that the statutes' present purpose and effect is not to aid religion but to set aside a day of rest and recreation.

... It is true that if the State's interest were simply to provide for its citizens a periodic respite from work, a regulation demanding that everyone rest one day in seven, leaving the choice of the day to the individual, would suffice. However, the State's purpose is not merely to provide a one-day-in-seven work stoppage. In addition to this, the State seeks to set one day apart from all others as a day of rest, repose, recreation and tranquility—a day which all members of the family and community have the opportunity to spend and enjoy together, a day on which there exists relative quiet and disassociation from the everyday intensity of commercial activities, a day on which people may visit friends and relatives who are not available during working days.

Accordingly, the decision is

Affirmed.

Separate Opinion of MR. JUSTICE FRANKFURTER, whom MR. JUSTICE HARLAN joins.[1] ...

To ask what interest, what objective, legislation serves, of course, is not to psychoanalyze its legislators, but to examine the necessary effects of what they have enacted. If the primary end achieved by a form of regulation is the affirmation or promotion of religious doctrine—primary, in the sense that all secular ends which it purportedly serves are derivative from, not wholly independent of, the advancement of religion—the regulation is beyond the power of the state.... Or if a statute furthers both secular and religious ends by means unnecessary to the effectuation of the secular ends alone—where the same secular ends could equally be attained by means which do not have consequences for promotion of religion—the statute cannot stand. A State may not endow a church although that church might inculcate in its parishioners moral concepts deemed to make them better citizens, because the very *raison d'etre* of a church, as opposed to any other school of civilly serviceable morals, is the predication of religious doctrine. However, inasmuch as individuals are free, if they will, to build their own churches and worship in them, the State may guard its people's safety by extending fire and police protection to the churches so built. [T]he private and unformulated influences which may work upon legislation are not open to judicial probing. "The decisions of this court from the beginning lend no support whatever to the assumption that the judiciary may restrain the exercise of lawful power on the assumption that a wrongful purpose or motive has caused the power to be exerted." *McCray v. United States,* 195 U.S.

---

1. This opinion also applies to *Braunfeld v. Brown,* excerpted infra, and other opinions dealing with Sunday Closing Laws, all decided the same day.

27, 56, 24 S.Ct. 769, 49 L.Ed. 78. "Inquiry into the hidden motives which may move [a legislature] to exercise a power constitutionally conferred upon it is beyond the competency of courts." *Sonzinsky v. United States,* 300 U.S. 506, 513–514, 57 S.Ct. 554, 81 L.Ed. 772. . . .

MR. JUSTICE DOUGLAS, dissenting.[2]

. . . The "establishment" clause protects citizens also against any law which selects any religious custom, practice, or ritual, puts the force of government behind it, and fines, imprisons, or otherwise penalizes a person for not observing it. The Government plainly could not join forces with one religious group and decree a universal and symbolic circumcision. Nor could it require all children to be baptized or give tax exemptions only to those whose children were baptized. Could it require a fast from sunrise to sunset throughout the Moslem month of Ramadan? I should think not. Yet why then can it make criminal the doing of other acts, as innocent as eating, during the day that Christians revere? Sunday is a word heavily overlaid with connotations and traditions deriving from the Christian roots of our civilization that color all judgments concerning it. . . .

BRAUNFELD v. BROWN
366 U.S. 599, 81 S.Ct. 1144, 6 L.Ed.2d 563 (1961).

MR. CHIEF JUSTICE WARREN announced the judgment of the Court and an opinion in which MR. JUSTICE BLACK, MR. JUSTICE CLARK, and MR. JUSTICE WHITTAKER concur.

This case concerns the constitutional validity of the application to appellants of the Pennsylvania criminal statute, enacted in 1959, which proscribes the Sunday retail sale of certain enumerated commodities. [T]he only question for consideration is whether the statute interferes with the free exercise of appellants' religion. Appellants are merchants in Philadelphia who engage in the retail sale of clothing and home furnishings within the proscription of the statute in issue. Each of the appellants is a member of the Orthodox Jewish faith, which requires the closing of their places of business and a total abstention from all manner of work from nightfall each Friday until nightfall each Saturday. . . . Appellants contend that the enforcement against them of the Pennsylvania statute will prohibit the free exercise of their religion because, due to the statute's compulsion to close on Sunday, appellants will suffer substantial economic loss, to the benefit of their non-Sabbatarian competitors, if appellants also continue their Sabbath observance by closing their businesses on Saturday. . . .

Certain aspects of religious exercise cannot, in any way, be restricted or burdened by either federal or state legislation. Compulsion by law of the acceptance of any creed or the practice of any form of worship is strictly forbidden. The freedom to hold religious beliefs and opinions is

---

2. This opinion also applies to *Braunfeld v. Brown,* excerpted infra, and other opinions dealing with Sunday Closing Laws, all decided the same day.

absolute. Thus, in *West Virginia State Board of Education v. Barnette*, this Court held that state action compelling school children to salute the flag, on pain of expulsion from public school, was contrary to the First and Fourteenth Amendments when applied to those students whose religious beliefs forbade saluting a flag. But this is not the case at bar; the statute before us does not make criminal the holding of any religious belief or opinion, nor does it force anyone to embrace any religious belief or to say or believe anything in conflict with his religious tenets.

However, the freedom to act, even when the action is in accord with one's religious convictions, is not totally free from legislative restrictions.... Thus, in *Reynolds v. United States,* this Court upheld the polygamy conviction of a member of the Mormon faith despite the fact that an accepted doctrine of his church then imposed upon its male members the *duty* to practice polygamy. And, in *Prince v. Massachusetts,* 321 U.S. 158, 64 S.Ct. 438, 88 L.Ed. 645, this Court upheld a statute making it a crime for a girl under eighteen years of age to sell any newspapers, periodicals or merchandise in public places despite the fact that a child of the Jehovah's Witnesses faith believed that it was her religious *duty* to perform this work.

It is to be noted that, in the two cases just mentioned, the religious practices themselves conflicted with the public interest. In such cases, to make accommodation between the religious action and an exercise of state authority is a particularly delicate task, because resolution in favor of the State results in the choice to the individual of either abandoning his religious principle or facing criminal prosecution. But, again, this is not the case before us because the statute at bar does not make unlawful any religious practices of appellants; the Sunday law simply regulates a secular activity and, as applied to appellants, operates so as to make the practice of their religious beliefs more expensive. Furthermore, the law's effect does not inconvenience all members of the Orthodox Jewish faith but only those who believe it necessary to work on Sunday. And even these are not faced with as serious a choice as forsaking their religious practices or subjecting themselves to criminal prosecution....

To strike down, without the most critical scrutiny, legislation which imposes only an indirect burden on the exercise of religion, i.e., legislation which does not make unlawful the religious practice itself, would radically restrict the operating latitude of the legislature. Statutes which tax income and limit the amount which may be deducted for religious contributions impose an indirect economic burden on the observance of the religion of the citizen whose religion requires him to donate a greater amount to his church; statutes which require the courts to be closed on Saturday and Sunday impose a similar indirect burden on the observance of the religion of the trial lawyer whose religion requires him to rest on a weekday. The list of legislation of this nature is nearly limitless....

Of course, to hold unassailable all legislation regulating conduct which imposes solely an indirect burden on the observance of religion would be a gross oversimplification. If the purpose or effect of a law is to impede the observance of one or all religions or is to discriminate invidiously between religions, that law is constitutionally invalid even though the burden may be characterized as being only indirect. But if the State regulates conduct by enacting a general law within its power, the purpose and effect of which is to advance the State's secular goals, the statute is valid despite its indirect burden on religious observance unless the State may accomplish its purpose by means which do not impose such a burden. . . .

[Appellants] contend that the State should cut an exception from the Sunday labor proscription for those people who, because of religious conviction, observe a day of rest other than Sunday. By such regulation, appellants contend, the economic disadvantages imposed by the present system would be removed and the State's interest in having all people rest one day would be satisfied. A number of States provide such an exemption, and this may well be the wiser solution to the problem. But our concern is not with the wisdom of legislation but with its constitutional limitation. Thus, reason and experience teach that to permit the exemption might well undermine the State's goal of providing a day that, as best possible, eliminates the atmosphere of commercial noise and activity. Although not dispositive of the issue, enforcement problems would be more difficult since there would be two or more days to police rather than one and it would be more difficult to observe whether violations were occurring.

Additional problems might also be presented by a regulation of this sort. To allow only people who rest on a day other than Sunday to keep their businesses open on that day might well provide these people with an economic advantage over their competitors who must remain closed on that day; this might cause the Sunday-observers to complain that their religions are being discriminated against. With this competitive advantage existing, there could well be the temptation for some, in order to keep their businesses open on Sunday, to assert that they have religious convictions which compel them to close their businesses on what had formerly been their least profitable day. This might make necessary a state-conducted inquiry into the sincerity of the individual's religious beliefs, a practice which a State might believe would itself run afoul of the spirit of constitutionally protected religious guarantees. Finally, in order to keep the disruption of the day at a minimum, exempted employers would probably have to hire employees who themselves qualified for the exemption because of their own religious beliefs, a practice which a State might feel to be opposed to its general policy prohibiting religious discrimination in hiring. For all of these reasons, we cannot say that the Pennsylvania statute before us is invalid, either on its face or as applied.

Mr. Justice Harlan concurs in the judgment. Mr. Justice Brennan and Mr. Justice Stewart concur in our disposition of appellants' claims under the Establishment Clause and the Equal Protection Clause. Mr.

Justice Frankfurter and Mr. Justice Harlan have rejected appellants' claim under the Free Exercise Clause in a separate opinion.

Accordingly, the decision is

Affirmed.

Mr. Justice Brennan, concurring and dissenting . . .

In fine, the Court, in my view, has exalted administrative convenience to a constitutional level high enough to justify making one religion economically disadvantageous. The Court would justify this result on the ground that the effect on religion, though substantial, is indirect. The Court forgets, I think, a warning uttered during the congressional discussion of the First Amendment itself: " . . . the rights of conscience are, in their nature, of peculiar delicacy, and will little bear the gentlest touch of governmental hand. . . . " I would reverse this judgment and remand for a trial of appellants' allegations, limited to the free-exercise-of-religion issue.

[The dissenting opinion of Stewart, J., is omitted].

SHERBERT v. VERNER
374 U.S. 398, 83 S.Ct. 1790, 10 L.Ed.2d 965 (1963).

Mr. Justice Brennan delivered the opinion of the Court.

Appellant, a member of the Seventh-day Adventist Church, was discharged by her South Carolina employer because she would not work on Saturday, the Sabbath Day of her faith. When she was unable to obtain other employment because from conscientious scruples she would not take Saturday work, she filed a claim for unemployment compensation benefits under the South Carolina Unemployment Compensation Act. . . . The appellee Employment Security Commission, in administrative proceedings under the statute, found that appellant's restriction upon her availability for Saturday work brought her within the provision disqualifying for benefits insured workers who fail, without good cause, to accept "suitable work when offered . . . by the employment office or the employer . . ." The Commission's finding was sustained by the [state courts]. . . .

We turn first to the question whether the disqualification for benefits imposes any burden on the free exercise of appellant's religion. We think it is clear that it does. In a sense the consequences of such a disqualification to religious principles and practices may be only an indirect result of welfare legislation within the State's general competence to enact; it is true that no criminal sanctions directly compel appellant to work a six-day week. But this is only the beginning, not the end, of our inquiry. For "[i]f the purpose or effect of a law is to impede the observance of one or all religions or is to discriminate invidiously between religions, that law is constitutionally invalid even though the burden may be characterized as being only indirect." *Braunfeld v. Brown.* Here not only is it apparent that appellant's declared ineligibility for benefits derives solely from the practice of her religion, but the pressure upon her to forego that practice is unmistakable. The ruling forces her to choose between following the precepts of her religion and forfeiting benefits, on the one hand, and abandoning one of the precepts of her religion in order to accept work, on the other hand. Governmental imposition of such a choice puts the same kind of burden upon the free exercise of religion as would a fine imposed against appellant for her Saturday worship. Nor may the South Carolina court's construction of the statute be saved from constitutional infirmity on the ground that unemployment compensation benefits are not appellant's "right" but merely a "privilege." It is too late in the day to doubt that the liberties of religion and expression may be infringed by the denial of or placing of conditions upon a benefit or privilege.... Significantly South Carolina expressly saves the Sunday worshipper from having to make the kind of choice which we here hold infringes the Sabbatarian's religious liberty.... The unconstitutionality of the disqualification of the Sabbatarian is thus compounded by the religious discrimination which South Carolina's general statutory scheme necessarily effects.

We must next consider whether some compelling state interest enforced in the eligibility provisions of the South Carolina statute justifies the substantial infringement of appellant's First Amendment right.... No such abuse or danger has been advanced in the present case. The appellees suggest no more than a possibility that the filing of fraudulent claims by unscrupulous claimants feigning religious objections to Saturday work might not only dilute the unemployment compensation fund but also hinder the scheduling by employers of necessary Saturday work.... Even if consideration of such evidence is not foreclosed by the prohibition against judicial inquiry into the truth or falsity of religious beliefs, *United States v. Ballard*, 322 U.S. 78, 64 S.Ct. 882, 88 L.Ed. 1148—a question as to which we intimate no view since it is not before us—it is highly doubtful whether such evidence would be sufficient to warrant a substantial infringement of religious liberties. For even if the possibility of spurious claims did threaten to dilute the fund and disrupt the scheduling of work, it would plainly be incumbent upon the appellees to demonstrate that no alternative forms of regulation would combat such abuses without infringing First Amendment rights.

In these respects, then, the state interest asserted in the present case is wholly dissimilar to the interests which were found to justify the less direct burden upon religious practices in *Braunfeld v. Brown*. The Court recognized that the Sunday closing law which that decision sustained undoubtedly served "to make the practice of [the Orthodox Jewish merchants'] ... religious beliefs more expensive." But the statute was nevertheless saved by a countervailing factor which finds no equivalent in the instant case—a strong state interest in providing one uniform day of rest for all workers. That secular objective could be achieved, the Court found, only by declaring Sunday to be that day of rest. Requiring exemptions for Sabbatarians, while theoretically possible, appeared to present an administrative problem of such magnitude, or to afford the exempted class so great a competitive advantage, that such a requirement would have rendered the entire statutory scheme unworkable. In the present case no such justifications underlie the determination of the state court that appellant's religion makes her ineligible to receive benefits.

In holding as we do, plainly we are not fostering the "establishment" of the Seventh-day Adventist religion in South Carolina, for the extension of unemployment benefits to Sabbatarians in common with Sunday worshippers reflects nothing more than the governmental obligation of neutrality in the face of religious differences, and does not represent that involvement of religious with secular institutions which it is the object of the Establishment Clause to forestall. Nor does the recognition of the appellant's right to unemployment benefits under the state statute serve to abridge any other person's religious liberties. Nor do we, by our decision today, declare the existence of a constitutional right to unemployment benefits on the part of all persons whose religious convictions are the cause of their unemployment. This is not a case in which an employee's religious convictions serve to make him a nonproductive member of society. Finally, nothing we say today constrains the States to adopt any particular form or scheme of unemployment compensation. Our holding today is only that South Carolina may not constitutionally apply the eligibility provisions so as to constrain a worker to abandon his religious convictions respecting the day of rest....

Mr. Justice Harlan, whom Mr. Justice White joins, dissenting.

... What the Court is holding is that if the State chooses to condition unemployment compensation on the applicant's availability for work, it is constitutionally compelled to *carve out an exception*—and to provide benefits—for those whose unavailability is due to their religious convictions. Such a holding has particular significance in two respects. *First,* despite the Court's protestations to the contrary, the decision necessarily overrules *Braunfeld v. Brown* .... The secular purpose of the statute before us today is even clearer than that involved in *Braunfeld.* And just as in *Braunfeld*—where exceptions to the Sunday closing laws for Sabbatarians would have been inconsistent with the purpose to achieve a uniform day of rest and would have required case-by-case inquiry into religious beliefs—so here, an exception to the rules of eligibility based on religious convictions would necessitate judicial examination of those convictions and would be at odds with the limited purpose of the statute to smooth out the economy during periods of industrial instability. Finally, the indirect financial burden of the present law is far less than that involved in *Braunfeld.* Forcing a store owner to close his business on Sunday may well have the effect of depriving him of a satisfactory livelihood if his religious convictions require him to close on Saturday as well. Here we are dealing only with temporary benefits, amounting to a fraction of regular weekly wages and running for not more than 22 weeks. Clearly, any differences between this case and *Braunfeld* cut against the present appellant.

[U]nder the circumstances of this case it would be a permissible accommodation of religion for the State if it *chose* to do so, to create an exception to its eligibility requirements for persons like the appellant. The constitutional obligation of "neutrality," see *School District of Abington Township v. Schempp,* is not so narrow a channel that the slightest deviation from an absolutely straight course leads to condemnation.... For very much the same reasons, however, I cannot subscribe to the conclusion that the State is constitutionally *compelled* to carve out an exception to its general rule of eligibility in the present case....

[The opinion of STEWART, J., concurring in the result, and the concurring opinion of DOUGLAS, J., are omitted.]

WISCONSIN v. YODER
406 U.S. 205, 92 S.Ct. 1526, 32 L.Ed.2d 15 (1972).

MR. CHIEF JUSTICE BURGER delivered the opinion of the Court....

Respondents Jonas Yoder and Wallace Miller are members of the Old Order Amish religion, and respondent Adin Yutzy is a member of the Conservative Amish Mennonite Church. They and their families are residents of Green County, Wisconsin. Wisconsin's compulsory school-attendance law required them to cause their children to attend public or private school until reaching age 16 but the respondents declined to send their children, ages 14 and 15, to public school after they completed the eighth grade. The children were not enrolled in any private school, or within any recognized exception to the compulsory-attendance law, and they are conceded to be subject to the Wisconsin statute.

On complaint of the school district administrator for the public schools, respondents were charged, tried, and convicted of violating the compulsory-attendance law in Green County Court and were fined the sum of $5 each. Respondents defended on the ground that the application of the compulsory-attendance law violated their rights under the First and Fourteenth Amendments. The trial testimony showed that respondents believed, in accordance with the tenets of Old Order Amish communities generally, that their children's attendance at high school, public or private, was contrary to the Amish religion and way of life. They believed that by sending their children to high school, they would not only expose themselves to the danger of the censure of the church community, but, as found by the county court, also endanger their own salvation and that of their children. The State stipulated that respondents' religious beliefs were sincere.

... Old Order Amish communities today are characterized by a fundamental belief that salvation requires life in a church community separate and apart from the world and worldly influence.... Formal high school education beyond the eighth grade is contrary to Amish beliefs, not only because it places Amish children in an environment hostile to Amish beliefs with increasing emphasis on competition in class work and sports and with pressure to conform to the styles, manners, and ways of the peer group, but also because it takes them away from their community, physically and emotionally, during the crucial and formative adolescent period of life.

[I]n order for Wisconsin to compel school attendance beyond the eighth grade against a claim that such attendance interferes with the practice of a legitimate religious belief, it must appear either that the State does not deny the free exercise of religious belief by its requirement, or that there is a state interest of sufficient magnitude to override the interest claiming protection under the Free Exercise Clause.

... A way of life, however virtuous and admirable, may not be interposed as a barrier to reasonable state regulation of education if it is based on purely secular considerations; to have the protection of the Religion Clauses, the claims must be rooted in religious belief. Although a determination of what is a "religious" belief or practice entitled to constitutional protection may present a most delicate question,[6] the very concept of ordered liberty precludes allowing every person to make his own standards on matters of conduct in which society as a whole has important interests. Thus, if the Amish asserted their claims because of their subjective evaluation and rejection of the contemporary secular values accepted by the majority, much as Thoreau rejected the social values of his time and isolated himself at Walden Pond, their claims would not rest on a religious basis. Thoreau's choice was philosophical and personal rather than religious, and such belief does not rise to the demands of the Religion Clauses. Giving no weight to such secular considerations, however, we see that the record in this case abundantly supports the claim that the traditional way of life of the Amish is not merely a matter of personal preference, but one of deep religious conviction, shared by an organized group, and intimately related to daily living....

The impact of the compulsory-attendance law on respondents' practice of the Amish religion is not only severe, but inescapable, for the Wisconsin law affirmatively compels them, under threat of criminal sanction, to perform acts undeniably at odds with fundamental tenets of their religious beliefs. See *Braunfeld v. Brown*....

We turn, then, to the State's broader contention that its interest in its system of compulsory education is so compelling that even the established religious practices of the Amish must give way....

The State advances two primary arguments in support of its system of compulsory education. It notes, as Thomas Jefferson pointed out early in our history, that some degree of education is necessary to prepare citizens to participate effectively and intelligently in our open political system if we are to preserve freedom and independence. Further, education prepares individuals to be self-reliant and self-sufficient participants in society. We accept these propositions. However, the evidence adduced by the Amish in this case is persuasively to the effect that an

---

6. See U.S. v. Ballard, 322 U.S. 78, 64   S.Ct. 882, 88 L.Ed. 1148 (1944).

additional one or two years of formal high school for Amish children in place of their long-established program of informal vocational education would do little to serve those interests.... It is one thing to say that compulsory education for a year or two beyond the eighth grade may be necessary when its goal is the preparation of the child for life in modern society as the majority live, but it is quite another if the goal of education be viewed as the preparation of the child for life in the separated agrarian community that is the keystone of the Amish faith.

The State attacks respondents' position as one fostering "ignorance" from which the child must be protected by the State. No one can question the State's duty to protect children from ignorance but this argument does not square with the facts disclosed in the record. Whatever their idiosyncrasies as seen by the majority, this record strongly shows that the Amish community has been a highly successful social unit within our society, even if apart from the conventional "mainstream." Its members are productive and very law-abiding members of society; they reject public welfare in any of its usual modern forms....

The State, however, supports its interest in providing an additional one or two years of compulsory high school education to Amish children because of the possibility that some such children will choose to leave the Amish community, and that if this occurs they will be ill-equipped for life.... There is nothing in this record to suggest that the Amish qualities of reliability, self-reliance, and dedication to work would fail to find ready markets in today's society. Absent some contrary evidence supporting the State's position, we are unwilling to assume that persons possessing such valuable vocational skills and habits are doomed to become burdens on society should they determine to leave the Amish faith, nor is there any basis in the record to warrant a finding that an additional one or two years of formal school education beyond the eighth grade would serve to eliminate any such problem that might exist....

Contrary to the suggestion of the dissenting opinion of Mr. Justice Douglas, our holding today in no degree depends on the assertion of the religious interest of the child as contrasted with that of the parents. It is the parents who are subject to prosecution here for failing to cause their children to attend school, and it is their right of free exercise, not that of their children, that must determine Wisconsin's power to impose criminal penalties on the parent. The dissent argues that a child who expresses a desire to attend public high school in conflict with the wishes of his parents should not be prevented from doing so. There is no reason for the Court to consider that point since it is not an issue in the case. The children are not parties to this litigation....

Our holding in no way determines the proper resolution of possible competing interests of parents, children, and the State in an appropriate state court proceeding in which the power of the State is asserted on the theory that Amish parents are preventing their minor children from attending high school despite their expressed desires to the contrary. Recognition of the claim of the State in such a proceeding would, of course, call into question traditional concepts of parental control over the religious upbringing and education of their minor children recognized in this Court's past decisions. It is clear that such an intrusion by a State into family decisions in the area of religious training would give rise to grave questions of religious freedom comparable to those raised here. . . .

For the reasons stated we hold, with the Supreme Court of Wisconsin, that the First and Fourteenth Amendments prevent the State from compelling respondents to cause their children to attend formal high school to age 16. Our disposition of this case, however, in no way alters our recognition of the obvious fact that courts are not school boards or legislatures, and are ill-equipped to determine the "necessity" of discrete aspects of a State's program of compulsory education. [C]ourts must move with great circumspection in performing the sensitive and delicate task of weighing a State's legitimate social concern when faced with religious claims for exemption from generally applicable educational requirements. It cannot be overemphasized that we are not dealing with a way of life and mode of education by a group claiming to have recently discovered some "progressive" or more enlightened process for rearing children for modern life. . . .

Mr. Justice Douglas, dissenting in part.

. . . If the parents in this case are allowed a religious exemption, the inevitable effect is to impose the parents' notions of religious duty upon their children. Where the child is mature enough to express potentially conflicting desires, it would be an invasion of the child's rights to permit such an imposition without canvassing his views. [I]t is an imposition resulting from this very litigation. As the child has no other effective forum, it is in this litigation that his rights should be considered. And, if an Amish child desires to attend high school, and is mature enough to have that desire respected, the State may well be able to override the parents' religiously motivated objections. [The child] may want to be a pianist or an astronaut or an oceanographer. To do so he will have to break from the Amish tradition. It is the future of the student, not the future of the parents, that is imperiled by today's decision. If a parent keeps his child out of school beyond the grade school, then the child will be forever barred from entry into the new and amazing world of diversity that we have today. . . .

I think the emphasis of the Court on the "law and order" record of this Amish group of people is quite irrelevant. A religion is a religion irrespective of what the misdemeanor or felony records of its members might be. I am not at all sure how the Catholics, Episcopalians, the Baptists, Jehovah's Witnesses, the Unitarians, and my own Presbyterians would make out if subjected to such a test. It is, of course, true that if a group or society was organized to perpetuate crime and if that is its motive, we would have rather startling problems akin to those that were raised when some years back a particular sect was challenged here as operating on a fraudulent basis. *United States v. Ballard,* 322 U.S. 78, 64

S.Ct. 882, 88 L.Ed. 1148. But no such factors are present here, and the Amish, whether with a high or low criminal record, certainly qualify by all historic standards as a religion within the meaning of the First Amendment....

[The concurring opinion of STEWART, J., joined by BRENNAN, J., and the concurring opinion of WHITE, J., joined by BRENNAN and STEWART, JJ., are omitted. POWELL and REHNQUIST, JJ., took no part in the consideration or decision of this case.]

ESTATE OF THORNTON v. CALDOR, INC.
472 U.S. 703, 105 S.Ct. 2914, 86 L.Ed.2d 557 (1985).

CHIEF JUSTICE BURGER delivered the opinion of the Court.

We granted certiorari to decide whether a state statute that provides employees with the absolute right not to work on their chosen Sabbath violates the Establishment Clause of the First Amendment.

In early 1975, petitioner's decedent Donald E. Thornton began working for respondent Caldor, Inc., a chain of New England retail stores; he managed the men's and boys' clothing department in respondent's Waterbury, Connecticut, store....

In 1977, following the state legislature's revision of the Sunday-closing laws, respondent opened its Connecticut stores for Sunday business. In order to handle the expanded store hours, respondent required its managerial employees to work every third or fourth Sunday. Thornton, a Presbyterian who observed Sunday as his Sabbath, initially complied with respondent's demand.... In November 1979, however, Thornton informed respondent that he would no longer work on Sundays because he observed that day as his Sabbath; he invoked the protection of Conn.Gen.Stat. § 53–303e(b)(Supp.1962–1984), which provides: "No person who states that a particular day of the week is observed as his Sabbath may be required by his employer to work on such day. An employee's refusal to work on his Sabbath shall not constitute grounds for his dismissal."

Thornton rejected respondent's offer either to transfer him to a management job in a Massachusetts store that was closed on Sundays, or to transfer him to a nonsupervisory position in the Torrington store at a lower salary. In March 1980, respondent transferred Thornton to a clerical position in the Torrington store; Thornton resigned two days later and filed a grievance with the State Board of Mediation and Arbitration alleging that he was discharged from his manager's position in violation of Conn.Gen.Stat. § 53–303e(b).... After holding an evidentiary hearing the Board evaluated the sincerity of Thornton's claim and concluded it was based on a sincere religious conviction; it ... ordered respondent to reinstate Thornton with backpay and compensation for lost fringe benefits.

[T]he Court has frequently relied on our holding in *Lemon [v. Kurtzman*, 403 U.S. 602, 91 S.Ct. 2105, 29 L.Ed.2d 745 (1971)] for guidance [in Establishment Clause cases], and we do so here. To pass constitutional muster under *Lemon* a statute must not only have a secular purpose and not foster excessive entanglement of government with religion, its primary effect must not advance or inhibit religion.

The Connecticut statute challenged here guarantees every employee, who "states that a particular day of the week is observed as his Sabbath," the right not to work on his chosen day. Conn.Gen.Stat. § 53–303e(b). The State has thus decreed that those who observe a Sabbath any day of the week as a matter of religious conviction must be relieved of the duty to work on that day, no matter what burden or inconvenience this imposes on the employer or fellow workers. The statute arms Sabbath observers with an absolute and unqualified right not to work on whatever day they designate as their Sabbath. . . .

There is no exception under the statute for special circumstances, such as the Friday Sabbath observer employed in an occupation with a Monday through Friday schedule—a school teacher, for example; the statute provides for no special consideration if a high percentage of an employer's workforce asserts rights to the same Sabbath. Moreover, there is no exception when honoring the dictates of Sabbath observers would cause the employer substantial economic burdens or when the employer's compliance would require the imposition of significant burdens on other employees required to work in place of the Sabbath observers. Finally, the statute allows for no consideration as to whether the employer has made reasonable accommodation proposals.

This unyielding weighting in favor of Sabbath observers over all other interests contravenes a fundamental principle of the Religion Clauses, so well articulated by Judge Learned Hand:

> The First Amendment . . . gives no one the right to insist that in pursuit of their own interests others must conform their conduct to his own religious necessities. *Otten v. Baltimore & Ohio R. Co.,* 205 F.2d 58, 61 (C.A.2 1953).

As such, the statute goes beyond having an incidental or remote effect of advancing religion. The statute has a primary effect that impermissibly advances a particular religious practice.

We hold that the Connecticut statute, which provides Sabbath observers with an absolute and unqualified right not to work on their Sabbath, violates the Establishment Clause of the First Amendment. Accordingly, the judgment of the Supreme Court of Connecticut is affirmed.

Affirmed.

Justice Rehnquist dissents.

Justice O'Connor, with whom Justice Marshall joins, concurring.

. . . I do not read the Court's opinion as suggesting that the religious accommodation provisions of Title VII of the Civil Rights Act are similarly invalid. These provisions preclude employment discrimination based on a person's religion and require private employers to reasonably accommodate the religious practices of employees unless to do so would cause undue hardship to the employer's business. 42 U.S.C.A. §§ 2000e(j) and 2000e–2(a)(1). Like the Connecticut Sabbath law, Title VII attempts to lift a burden on religious practice that is imposed by *private* employers, and hence it is not the sort of accommodation statute specifically contemplated by the Free Exercise Clause. The provisions of Title VII must therefore manifest a valid secular purpose and effect to be valid under the Establishment Clause. In my view, a statute outlawing employment discrimination based on race, color, religion, sex, or national origin has the valid secular purpose of assuring employment opportunity to all groups in our pluralistic society. Since Title VII calls for reasonable rather than absolute accommodation and extends that requirement to all religious beliefs and practices rather than protecting only the Sabbath observance, I believe an objective observer would perceive it as an anti-discrimination law rather than an endorsement of religion or a particular religious practice.

Notes

1. SINCERITY OF RELIGIOUS BELIEFS. Note that in *Yoder* the state had stipulated to the sincerity of the respondents' religious beliefs and that both the majority opinion (at footnote 6) and Justice Douglas, at the end of his excerpted dissent, cited *United States v. Ballard,* 322 U.S. 78, 64 S.Ct. 882, 88 L.Ed. 1148 (1944), (*Ballard I*) an opinion authored by Justice Douglas. In *Ballard* respondents were convicted of using the mails to defraud in that they had fraudulently solicited funds and membership in the "I Am" movement. For example, defendants represented "that Guy W. Ballard, now deceased, alias Saint Germain, Jesus, George Washington, and Godfre Ray King, had been selected and thereby designated by the alleged 'ascertained masters,' Saint Germain, as a divine messenger" who would transmit to mankind the words of Saint Germain; and that Guy Ballard and Edna Ballard and Donald Ballard "did falsely represent to persons intended to be defrauded that [they] had the ability to cure persons of those diseases" normally classified as incurable, and that respondents "well knew" that all of these representations were "false and untrue."

The trial court instructed the jury that "the religious beliefs of these defendants cannot be an issue in this court" but the jury should determine if "these defendants honestly and in good faith believe those things." After conviction, the circuit court reversed, holding that the restriction of the issue to the question of good faith was error; it remanded for a new trial. The Supreme Court reversed:

> Heresy trials are foreign to our Constitution. Men may believe what they cannot prove. They may not be put to the proof of their religious doctrines or beliefs. Religious experiences which are as real as life to some may be incomprehensible to others.... The religious views espoused by respondents might seem incredible, if not preposterous, to most people. But if those doctrines are subject to trial before a jury charged with finding their truth or falsity, then the same can be done

with the religious beliefs of any sect. When the triers of fact undertake that task, they enter a forbidden domain.

The Supreme Court never decided whether the trial court was correct in allowing the jury to examine the defendants' good faith. The Court remanded so that the circuit court could consider other issues that had been raised. Later the Court reversed the convictions based on one of these issues, the exclusion of women from the jury. *Ballard v. United States,* 329 U.S. 187, 67 S.Ct. 261, 91 L.Ed. 181 (1946)(*Ballard II*).

Justice Jackson dissented in *Ballard I* and would have completely dismissed the indictment. "I do not see how we can separate an issue as to what is believed from considerations as to what is believable. The most convincing proof that one believes his statements is to show that they have been true in his experience. Likewise, that one knowingly falsified is best proved by showing that what he said happened never did happen."[1]

In *Thomas v. Review Board,* 450 U.S. 707, 101 S.Ct. 1425, 67 L.Ed.2d 624 (1981), the Court, per Burger, C.J., held that under *Sherbert v. Verner* it was unconstitutional for Indiana to deny unemployment benefits to a Jehovah's Witness who quit his job when he was transferred to a department that produced turrets for military tanks. He said that his religious beliefs forbade participation in the production of armaments:

> The Indiana court also appears to have given significant weight to the fact that another Jehovah's Witness had no scruples about working on tank turrets; for that other Witness, at least, such work was "scripturally" acceptable. Intrafaith differences of that kind are not uncommon among followers of a particular creed, and the judicial process is singularly ill equipped to resolve such differences in relation to the Religion Clauses. One can, of course, imagine an asserted claim so bizarre, so clearly nonreligious in motivation, as not to be entitled to protection under the Free Exercise Clause; but that is not limited to beliefs which are shared by all of the members of a religious sect.... Courts are not arbiters of scriptural interpretation. The narrow function of a reviewing court in this context is to determine whether there was an appropriate finding that petitioner terminated his work because of an honest conviction that such work was forbidden by his religion.

Frazee v. Illinois Department of Employment Security, 489 U.S. 829, 109 S.Ct. 1514, 103 L.Ed.2d 914 (1989). The state agency disqualified Frazee from receiving unemployment benefits because he refused to work on Sunday as part of his "personal professed religious belief." Frazee said that he was a Christian, but the state denied the applicability of *Sherbert* and *Thomas* because Frazee was not a member of an established religious sect nor did his refusal result from a "tenet, belief or teaching of an established religious body." The state conceded Frazee's sincerity. Justice White, for a unanimous Court, reversed. "Our judgments in [*Sherbert* and *Thomas*] rested on the fact that each of the claimants had a sincere belief that religion

---

1. Stone, C.J., joined by Roberts & Frankfurter, JJ., dissented in *Ballard I,* and would have reinstated the district court's conviction. They argued that "none of the respondents' constitutional rights are violated if they are prosecuted for the fraudulent procurement of money by false representations as to their beliefs, religious or otherwise."

required him or her to refrain from the work in question. Never did we suggest that unless a claimant belongs to a sect that forbids what his job requires, his belief, however sincere, must be deemed a purely personal preference rather than a religious belief."

Goldman v. Weinberger, 475 U.S. 503, 106 S.Ct. 1310, 89 L.Ed.2d 478 (1986) upheld the power of the Air Force to forbid one of its personnel from wearing a yarmulke while in uniform. The petitioner was an Orthodox Jew and ordained Rabbi who served as a clinical psychologist at a mental health clinic on base. Rehnquist, J., for the Court emphasized the "great deference" the judiciary should give to the military concerning the military's judgment that standardized uniforms encouraged subordination of personal preferences in favor of the overall group mission and hierarchical unity. The Court accepted this "considered military judgment" rather than expert testimony claiming that religious exceptions are desirable and increase morale. "The Air Force has drawn the line essentially between religious apparel which is visible and that which is not, and we hold that those portions of the regulations challenged here reasonably and evenhandedly regulated dress in the interest of the military's perceived need for uniformity."

Brennan, J., joined by Marshall, J., rejected the Government's argument that a ruling favoring Dr. Goldman would raise the specter of a "rag-tag band of soldiers," with a Jew wearing a yarmulke, a Sikh wearing a turban, a Satchidananda Ashram–Integral Yogi wearing a saffron robe, and a Rastafarian wearing dreadlocks. "[T]urbans, saffron robes, and dreadlocks are not before us in this case and must each be evaluated against the reasons a service branch offers for prohibiting personnel from wearing them while in uniform . . . . " The military would have to provide "a *reasoned* basis" for its decision, such as "functional utility, health and safety considerations, and the goal of a polished, professional appearance" (emphasis in original). Brennan accused the majority of adopting a "subrational-basis standard" for review of military decisions.

Blackmun's dissent disagreed with Brennan's suggestion that noncombat personnel could wear yarmulkes but not turbans or dreadlocks because the latter are "less 'polished,' "but he would allow denials of religious requests on neutral grounds such as safety. He said that the Air Force did not show that any significant number of personnel would request religious exemptions. O'Connor's dissent, also joined by Marshall, argued that the Air Force presented no proof in this case that granting an exception would do substantial harm to military discipline.

Congress responded to *Goldman* by enacting 10 U.S.C.A. § 774, *"Religious apparel: wearing while in uniform."* This law allows a member of the armed forces to wear religious apparel (defined as "apparel the wearing of which is part of the observance of the religious faith practiced by the member") while in uniform, unless the Secretary of Defense determines that wearing the item "would interfere with the performance of the member's military duties" or the Secretary determines "that the item of apparel is not neat and conservative."

2. CONSCIENTIOUS OBJECTION TO MILITARY SERVICE. *United States v. Seeger,* 380 U.S. 163, 185, 85 S.Ct. 850, 863–864, 13 L.Ed.2d 733 (1965) held that individuals were entitled, under the statute, to exemption from combatant

service in the armed forces because they were, by reason of their religious training and belief (and not because of essentially political, sociological, or philosophical views), conscientiously opposed to participation in war in any form. Such persons must have a "sincere and meaningful belief which occupies in the life of its possessor a place parallel to that filled by" God. The Court reaffirmed *Ballard* and held that the draft boards were "not free to reject beliefs because they consider them 'incomprehensible.' Their task is to decide whether the beliefs professed by a registrant are sincerely held and whether they are, in his own scheme of things, religious. But we hasten to emphasize that while the 'truth' of a belief is not open to question, there remains the significant question of whether it is 'truly held.' This is the threshold question of sincerity which must be resolved in every case. It is, of course, a question of fact—a prime consideration to the validity of every claim for exemption as a conscientious objector."

Gillette v. United States, 401 U.S. 437, 91 S.Ct. 828, 28 L.Ed.2d 168 (1971) upheld the constitutionality of a federal law exempting from military service those who conscientiously object to all wars but not those who conscientiously object only to unjust wars. The statute "does not discriminate on the basis of religious affiliation or belief, apart of course from beliefs concerning war." Although the objection must be grounded in religious training and belief, the statute does not require any particular sectarian affiliation or theological position. The Court found valid secular purposes to granting some exemption, both pragmatically (the difficulty of converting a sincere objector into an effective fighting man) and philosophically: "Quite apart from the question whether the Free Exercise Clause might require some sort of exemption, it is hardly impermissible for Congress to try to accommodate free exercise values, in line with 'our happy tradition' of 'avoiding unnecessary clashes with the dictates of conscience.' "

In addition, "valid neutral reasons exist for limiting the exemption to objectors to all war, and the section therefore cannot be said to reflect a religious preference." The claim to objection to a particular war "would involve a real danger of erratic or even discriminatory decisionmaking in administrative practice." Nor did the Free Exercise Clause require exemption for such objectors. The Court concluded: "it is supportable for Congress to have decided that the objector to all war—to all killing in war—has a claim that is distinct enough and intense enough to justify special status, while the objector to a particular war does not. Of course, we do not suggest that Congress would have acted irrationally or unreasonably had it decided to exempt those who object to particular wars."

3. APPLYING TAX REQUIREMENTS. *United States v. Lee,* 455 U.S. 252, 102 S.Ct. 1051, 71 L.Ed.2d 127 (1982) upheld the imposition of social security taxes as applied to persons who object on religious grounds to receipt of public insurance benefits and to payment of taxes to support public insurance funds. "Not all burdens on religion are unconstitutional. The state may justify a limitation on religious liberty by showing that it is essential to accomplish an overriding governmental interest." The Court therefore ruled against Lee, a member of the Old Order Amish:

> Unlike the situation presented in *Wisconsin v. Yoder* it would be difficult to accommodate the comprehensive social security system with

myriad exceptions flowing from a wide variety of religious beliefs. The obligation to pay the social security tax initially is not fundamentally different from the obligation to pay income taxes.... The tax system could not function if denominations were allowed to challenge the tax system because tax payments were spent in a manner that violates their religious belief. Because the broad public interest in maintaining a sound tax system is of such a high order, religious belief in conflict with the payment of taxes affords no basis for resisting the tax.

Bob Jones University v. United States, 461 U.S. 574, 103 S.Ct. 2017, 76 L.Ed.2d 157 (1983) upheld the statutory authority of the Internal Revenue Service to deny tax-exempt status to religious, charitable, and educational institutions that engage in racial discrimination. Bob Jones University permitted unmarried blacks to enroll but denied admission to applicants in an interracial marriage or those who "espouse" interracial marriage or dating. The other petitioner, Goldsboro Christian Schools, Inc., had a racially discriminatory admissions policy and normally accepted only whites, but had, on occasion, accepted children from racially mixed marriages where one of the parents is white. Both schools based their policy on their interpretations of the Bible.

The I.R.S. position did not violate the free exercise rights of these schools because of the overriding governmental interest involved:

Denial of tax benefits will inevitably have a substantial impact on the operation of private religious schools, but will not prevent those schools from observing their religious tenets. The governmental interest at stake here is compelling. [T]he Government has a fundamental, overriding interest in eradicating racial discrimination in education—discrimination that prevailed, with official approval, for the first 165 years of this Nation's history. That governmental interest substantially outweighs whatever burden denial of tax benefits places on petitioners' exercise of their religious beliefs. The interests asserted by petitioners cannot be accommodated with that compelling governmental interest, and no "less restrictive means" are available to achieve the governmental-interest.

Bowen v. Roy, 476 U.S. 693, 106 S.Ct. 2147, 90 L.Ed.2d 735 (1986). Appellant Roy claimed that the free exercise clause required the Government to accommodate his religiously-based objection to the statutory requirement: (1) that a social security number be provided by an applicant seeking certain welfare benefits, and (2) that the states use these numbers in administering the benefit programs. Appellees claimed that obtaining a social security number for their two year old daughter, Little Bird of the Snow, would violate their recently acquired Native American religious beliefs. Roy testified that the uniqueness of the social security number as an identifier "will serve to 'rob the spirit' of his daughter." He emphasized that the evil flowed "simply from *obtaining* a number." (emphasis in original) On the last day of the trial, however, it came out that Little Bird of the Snow in fact had a social security number from birth. Roy was recalled to the stand and testified that his daughter's spirit "would be robbed only by 'use' of the number."

Burger, C.J., for every member of the Court except White, J., rejected the claim that the Government's use of the social security number raised a free exercise claim. "The Free Exercise Clause simply cannot be understood to require the Government to conduct its own internal affairs in ways that comport with the religious beliefs of particular citizens.... Roy may no more prevail on his religious objection to the Government's use of a social security number for his daughter than he could on a sincere religious objection to the size or color of the Government's filing cabinets. The Free Exercise Clause affords an individual protection from certain forms of governmental compulsion; it does not afford an individual a right to dictate the conduct of the Government's internal procedures."

Burger turned to Roy's objection that, as a condition of eligibility, each applicant for welfare aid furnish his or her social security number to the Government. Only Powell and Rehnquist joined this portion of the opinion. Burger concluded that the requirement is constitutional, relying in part on *United States v. Lee.* "The test applied in cases like *Wisconsin v. Yoder* is not appropriate in this setting. In the enforcement of a facially neutral and uniformly applicable requirement for the administration of welfare programs reaching many millions of people, the Government is entitled to a wide latitude." Nor are *Sherbert v. Verner,* or *Thomas v. Review Board,* applicable because in those cases the statutes denied unemployment compensation for those who "without good cause" quit work or refused to work. "The 'good cause' standard created a mechanism for individualized exemptions. If a state creates such a mechanism, its refusal to extend an exemption to an instance of religious hardship suggests a discriminatory intent." It is not necessary to show that the Social Security requirement is the least restrictive means of accomplishing a compelling state interest. The "Government meets its burden when it demonstrates that a challenged requirement for governmental benefits, neutral and uniform in its application, is a reasonable means of promoting a legitimate public interest."

O'Connor, J., joined by Brennan & Marshall, JJ., dissented from this portion of Burger's opinion, and would hold that "the Government must accommodate a legitimate free exercise claim unless pursuing an especially important interest by narrowly tailored means." She would rule for Roy because "granting an exemption to Little Bird of the Snow, and to the handful of others who can be expected to make a similar religious objection to providing the social security number in conjunction with the receipt of welfare benefits will not demonstrably diminish the Government's ability to combat welfare fraud."

Does that mean that religions with few believers have more rights than religions with many adherents?

White, J., dissented entirely, simply citing *Thomas v. Review Board* and *Sherbert v. Verner.* Stevens, J., concurred in part and in the result. Blackmun, J., concurred in part.

Lyng v. Northwest Indian Cemetery Protective Association, 485 U.S. 439, 108 S.Ct. 1319, 99 L.Ed.2d 534 (1988). O'Connor, J., for the Court, held that the free exercise clause did not prohibit the Federal Government from permitting timber harvesting and the construction of a road through a portion of a National Forest, which was traditionally used for religious purposes by members of three American Indian tribes. O'Connor concluded that this case could not be meaningfully distinguished from *Bowen v. Roy.* The respondents argued that the Government action in *Lyng* was different because it would physically destroy "the environmental conditions and privacy without which the [religious] practices cannot be conducted." But the Government action here did not coerce any persons into acting contrary to their religious beliefs, and the "crucial word in the constitutional text is 'prohibit.'" A contrary ruling would give the Indians *de facto* beneficial ownership of large tracts of land owned by the Government.

In *Hernandez v. Commissioner of Internal Revenue,* 490 U.S. 680, 109 S.Ct. 2136, 104 L.Ed.2d 766 (1989), the Court, per Justice Marshall, held that taxpayers may not deduct, as charitable contributions, payments made to the Church of Scientology for "auditing" and "training" sessions, for which the Church charges a "fixed donation" (also known as a "price"), that is set forth in schedules with prices varying depending on the session's length and sophistication. At training sessions people learn how to become auditors. At auditing sessions the auditor seeks to identify the participant's areas of spiritual difficulty. Although the auditor has a one-to-one encounter with a participant, the content of each session is not individually tailored. These mandatory fixed charges are based on a central belief of Scientology, the "doctrine of exchange," that provides that when someone receives something he must pay something back.

Justice Marshall held that the mandatory payments do not qualify as a tax deductible "gift" or "contribution" because they are part of a "quintessential *quid pro quo*" in which the taxpayers received, in exchange for their money, auditing and training sessions. He rejected the argument that the benefits that the taxpayers received were purely religious in nature, and the claim that "payments made for the right to participate in a religious service should be automatically deductible under § 170" of the Internal Revenue Code.

Justice Marshall also rejected the taxpayers' Free Exercise claim. Section 170 was facially neutral and did not distinguish among sects. There is no prohibited entanglement when the IRS, in determining whether a payment is part of a *quid pro quo,* ascertains from the institution the prices of its services and commodities, the regularity with which such payments are waived, and other pertinent information, none of which requires any inquiry into religious doctrine. If there is a claim that a portion of a payment was a contribution, that does not force the Government to place a monetary value on a religious benefit, for if there is no comparable good or service sold in the market place, the IRS can inquire into the cost (if any) to the donee of providing the goods or service. The argument that the loss of the charitable deduction results in a marginally larger tax burden has no limitation. "In any event, we need not decide whether the burden of disallowing the § 170 deduction is substantial, for our decision in [*United States v.*] *Lee* establishes that even a substantial burden would be justified by the 'broad public interest in maintaining a sound tax system,' free of 'myriad exceptions flowing from a wide variety of religious beliefs.'"

The taxpayers also argued that the IRS was inconsistent in allowing, for example, deductions for pew rents, building fund assessments, and periodic dues paid to a church. The Court's response:

> The IRS' application of the "contribution or gift" standard may be right or wrong with respect to these other faiths, or it may be right with respect to some religious practices and wrong with respect to others.... Only upon a proper factual record could we make these determinations. Absent such a record, we must reject petitioner's administrative consistency argument.

O'Connor, J., joined by Scalia, J., dissented.[3] Given the IRS' trial stipulation that Scientology is a "religion" and that each Scientology branch is a "church," within the meaning of the tax laws, the IRS cannot treat this religion less favorably than others:

> In exchange for their payment of pew rents, Christians receive particular seats during worship services. Similarly, in some synagogues attendance at the worship services for Jewish High Holy Days is often predicated upon the purchase of a general admission ticket or a reserved seat ticket. Religious honors such as publicly reading from Scripture are purchased or auctioned periodically in some synagogues of Jews from Morocco and Syria. Mormons must tithe ten percent of their income as a necessary but not sufficient condition to obtaining a "temple recommend," i.e., a right to be admitted into the temple. A Mass stipend—a fixed payment given to a Catholic priest, in consideration of which he is obliged to apply the fruits of the Mass for the intention of the donor—has similar overtones of exchange.... There is no indication whatever that the IRS has explicitly and affirmatively reevaluated its longstanding interpretation of § 170 and decided to analyze *all* fixed religious contributions under a *quid pro quo* standard. There is no indication whatever that the IRS has abandoned its 70-year practice with respect to payments made by those other than Scientologists. [Here we have] the differential application of a standard based on constitutionally impermissible differences drawn by the Government among religions.

4. APPLICATION OF LABOR REQUIREMENTS. In *Tony and Susan Alamo Foundation v. Secretary of Labor,* 471 U.S. 290, 105 S.Ct. 1953, 85 L.Ed.2d 278 (1985) a unanimous Court upheld the minimum wage, overtime, and recordkeeping requirements of the Fair Labor Standards Act to workers staffing the commercial activities of a religious foundation. Most of these workers were drug addicts, derelicts, or criminals before their rehabilitation by the Foundation. The workers received no cash but the Foundation provided them with food, clothing, and shelter. The petitioners claimed that the receipt of "wages" would violate the religious convictions of the workers, called "associates". Yet the federal law does not require the payment of cash wages; the Foundation could continue to pay the associates in the form of benefits, as long as it paid the statutory amount. Even if the Foundation paid the statutory amount due the workers in cash, "there is nothing in the Act to prevent the associates from returning the amounts to the Foundation,

3. Brennan & Kennedy, JJ., took no part in the consideration or decision of this case.

provided that they did so voluntarily. We therefore fail to perceive how application of the Act would interfere with the associates' right to freely exercise their religious beliefs." Nor would recordkeeping requirements of "commercial activities" undertaken with a "business purpose" inhibit religious activity or entangle the government with religion.

5. PRISONS *O'Lone v. Estate of Shabazz,* 482 U.S. 342, 107 S.Ct. 2400, 96 L.Ed.2d 282 (1987) found (5 to 4) no violation of the free exercise clause in prison regulations that inhibited certain prisoners who were members of the Islamic faith in exercising their religious beliefs. The prisoners wanted to attend Jumu'ah, a Friday Muslim congregational service held on the prison grounds, but prison rules, in order to relieve overcrowding, required that all prisoners in the category of "gang minimum" be assigned work outside the main prison building where the Muslim services were held. The prison officials presented evidence showing that the return of the prisoners to the prison during the work day resulted in security risks and administrative burdens. For example, because only one guard supervised each detail of prisoners (8–15 prisoners) the whole detail was forced to return to the main gate whenever one prisoner wanted to return to the facility. If the prison placed all the Muslim inmates in one or two details, the prison officials feared that "affinity groups" would flourish and threaten prison security. Thus, all inmates assigned to outside work details could not return except for an emergency. This prohibition on return prevented those Muslims assigned to outside work from attending Jumu'ah.

The Court majority, per Rehnquist, C.J., said that the test to determine if the regulation is valid is whether "it is reasonably related to legitimate penological interests." This test is "less restrictive than that ordinarily applied to alleged infringements of fundamental Constitutional rights." The majority then upheld the regulations. It noted that in other respects the prison accommodated Muslim beliefs. The "right to congregate for prayer or discussion is 'virtually unlimited except during working hours,' and the state-provided imam has free access to the prison." Muslim prisoners are also given different meals whenever pork is served in the prison cafeteria.

Justice Brennan, joined by Marshall, Blackmun, and Stevens, JJ., dissented. They would require the prison officials to demonstrate that "the restrictions they have imposed are necessary to further an important government interest, and that these restrictions are no greater than necessary to achieve prison objectives."

EMPLOYMENT DIVISION, DEPARTMENT OF HUMAN RESOURCES v. SMITH
494 U.S. 872, 110 S.Ct. 1595, 108 L.Ed.2d 876 (1990).

JUSTICE SCALIA delivered the opinion of the Court.

This case requires us to decide whether the Free Exercise Clause of the First Amendment permits the State of Oregon to include religiously inspired peyote use within the reach of its general criminal prohibition on use of that drug, and thus permits the State to deny unemployment benefits to persons dismissed from their jobs because of such religiously inspired use. . . .

Respondents, Alfred Smith and Galen Black were fired from their jobs with a private drug rehabilitation organization because they ingested peyote for sacramental purposes at a ceremony of the Native American Church, of which both are members. When respondents applied to petitioner Employment Division for unemployment compensation, they were determined to be ineligible for benefits because they had been discharged for work-related "misconduct". The Oregon Court of Appeals reversed that determination, holding that the denial of benefits violated respondents' free exercise rights under the First Amendment. . . .

Respondents' claim for relief rests on our decisions in *Sherbert v. Verner*, [and] *Thomas v. Review Board, Indiana Employment Security Div.*, in which we held that a State could not condition the availability of unemployment insurance on an individual's willingness to forgo conduct required by his religion. [H]owever, the conduct at issue in those cases was not prohibited by law.

[Respondents assert] that their religious motivation for using peyote places them beyond the reach of a criminal law that is not specifically directed at their religious practice, and that is concededly constitutional as applied to those who use the drug for other reasons. As a textual matter, we do not think the words must be given that meaning. It is no more necessary to regard the collection of a general tax, for example, as "prohibiting the free exercise [of religion]" by those citizens who believe support of organized government to be sinful, than it is to regard the same tax as "abridging the freedom . . . of the press" of those publishing companies that must pay the tax as a condition of staying in business. It is a permissible reading of the text, in the one case as in the other, to say that if prohibiting the exercise of religion (or burdening the activity of printing) is not the object of the tax but merely the incidental effect of a generally applicable and otherwise valid provision, the First Amendment has not been offended. Compare *Citizen Publishing Co. v. United States,* 394 U.S. 131, 139, 89 S.Ct. 927, 931–32, 22 L.Ed.2d 148 (1969)(upholding application of antitrust laws to press), with *Grosjean v. American Press Co.,* 297 U.S. 233, 250–251, 56 S.Ct. 444, 449, 80 L.Ed. 660 (1936)(striking down license tax applied only to newspapers with weekly circulation above a specified level).

Our decisions reveal that the latter reading is the correct one. We have never held that an individual's religious beliefs excuse him from compliance with an otherwise valid law prohibiting conduct that the State is free to regulate. . . . We first had occasion to assert that principle in *Reynolds v. United States,* 98 U.S. 145, 25 L.Ed. 244 (1879), where we rejected the claim that criminal laws against polygamy could not be constitutionally applied to those whose religion commanded the practice. "Laws," we said, "are made for the government of actions, and while they cannot interfere with mere religious belief and opinions, they may with practices. . . . Can a man excuse his practices to the contrary because of his religious belief? To permit this would be to make the professed doctrines of religious belief superior to the law of the land, and in effect to permit every citizen to become a law unto himself.'' . . .

The only decisions in which we have held that the First Amendment bars application of a neutral, generally applicable law to religiously motivated action have involved not the Free Exercise Clause alone, but the Free Exercise Clause in conjunction with other constitutional protections, such as freedom of speech and of the press, see *Cantwell v. Connecticut,* 310 U.S., at 304–307, 60 S.Ct., at 903–905 (invalidating a licensing system for religious and charitable solicitations under which the administrator had discretion to deny a license to any cause he deemed nonreligious); *Murdock v. Pennsylvania,* 319 U.S. 105, 63 S.Ct. 870, 87 L.Ed. 1292 (1943)(invalidating a flat tax on solicitation as applied to the dissemination of religious ideas); *Follett v. McCormick,* 321 U.S. 573, 64 S.Ct. 717, 88 L.Ed. 938 (1944)(same), or the right of parents, acknowledged in *Pierce v. Society of Sisters,* 268 U.S. 510, 45 S.Ct. 571, 69 L.Ed. 1070 (1925), to direct the education of their children, see *Wisconsin v. Yoder,* 406 U.S. 205, 92 S.Ct. 1526, 32 L.Ed.2d 15 (1972)(invalidating compulsory school-attendance laws as applied to Amish parents who refused on religious grounds to send their children to school) . . . .

The present case does not present such a hybrid situation, but a free exercise claim unconnected with any communicative activity or parental right. Respondents urge us to hold, quite simply, that when otherwise prohibitable conduct is accompanied by religious convictions, not only the convictions but the conduct itself must be free from governmental regulation. We have never held that, and decline to do so now. . . .

Respondents argue that even though exemption from generally applicable criminal laws need not automatically be extended to religiously motivated actors, at least the claim for a religious exemption must be evaluated under the balancing test set forth in *Sherbert v. Verner.* Under the *Sherbert* test, governmental actions that substantially burden a religious practice must be justified by a compelling governmental interest. . . . We have never invalidated any governmental action on the basis of the *Sherbert* test except the denial of unemployment compensation. Although we have sometimes purported to apply the *Sherbert* test in contexts other than that, we have always found the test satisfied. . . .

Even if we were inclined to breathe into *Sherbert* some life beyond the unemployment compensation field, we would not apply it to require exemptions from a generally applicable criminal law. The *Sherbert* test, it must be recalled, was developed in a context that lent itself to individualized governmental assessment of the reasons for the relevant conduct. [O]ur decisions in the unemployment cases stand for the proposition that where the State has in place a system of individual exemptions, it may not refuse to extend that system to cases of ''religious hardship'' without compelling reason.

Whether or not the decisions are that limited, they at least have nothing to do with an across-the-board criminal prohibition on a particular form of conduct. [T]he sounder approach, and the approach in accord with the vast majority of our precedents, is to hold the test inapplicable to such challenges. The government's ability to enforce generally applicable prohibitions of socially harmful conduct, like its ability to carry out other aspects of public policy, "cannot depend on measuring the effects of a governmental action on a religious objector's spiritual development." To make an individual's obligation to obey such a law contingent upon the law's coincidence with his religious beliefs, except where the State's interest is "compelling"—permitting him, by virtue of his beliefs, "to become a law unto himself," *Reynolds v. United States,*—contradicts both constitutional tradition and common sense.

The "compelling government interest" requirement seems benign, because it is familiar from other fields. But using it as the standard that must be met before the government may accord different treatment on the basis of race, or before the government may regulate the content of speech, is not remotely comparable to using it for the purpose asserted here. What it produces in those other fields—equality of treatment, and an unrestricted flow of contending speech—are constitutional norms; what it would produce here—a private right to ignore generally applicable laws—is a constitutional anomaly.[3] . . .

If the "compelling interest" test is to be applied at all, then, it must be applied across the board, to all actions thought to be religiously commanded. Moreover, if "compelling interest" really means what it says (and watering it down here would subvert its rigor in the other fields where it is applied), many laws will not meet the test. Any society adopting such a system would be courting anarchy, but that danger increases in direct proportion to the society's diversity of religious beliefs, and its determination to coerce or suppress none of them. [P]recisely because we value and protect that religious divergence, we cannot afford the luxury of deeming *presumptively invalid,* as applied to the religious objector, every regulation of conduct that does not protect an interest of the highest order . . . .

3. Justice O'Connor suggests that "[t]here is nothing talismanic about neutral laws of general applicability," and that all laws burdening religious practices should be subject to compelling-interest scrutiny because "the First Amendment unequivocally makes freedom of religion, like freedom from race discrimination and freedom of speech, a 'constitutional norm,' not an 'anomaly.'" (O'Connor, J., concurring). But this comparison with other fields supports, rather than undermines, the conclusion we draw today. Just as we subject to the most exacting scrutiny laws that make classifications based on race, or on the content of speech, so too we strictly scrutinize governmental classifications based on religion. But we have held that race-neutral laws that have the *effect* of disproportionately disad-vantaging a particular racial group do not thereby become subject to compelling-interest analysis under the Equal Protection Clause, see *Washington v. Davis,* [§ 8–2.13] (police employment examination); and we have held that generally applicable laws unconcerned with regulating speech that have the *effect* of interfering with speech do not thereby become subject to compelling-interest analysis under the First Amendment, see *Citizen Publishing Co. v. United States,* 394 U.S. 131, 139, 89 S.Ct. 927, 22 L.Ed.2d 148 (1969)(antitrust laws). Our conclusion that generally applicable, religion-neutral laws that have the effect of burdening a particular religious practice need not be justified by a compelling governmental interest is the only approach compatible with these precedents.

Values that are protected against government interference through enshrinement in the Bill of Rights are not thereby banished from the political process. Just as a society that believes in the negative protection accorded to the press by the First Amendment is likely to enact laws that affirmatively foster the dissemination of the printed word, so also a society that believes in the negative protection accorded to religious belief can be expected to be solicitous of that value in its legislation as well. It is therefore not surprising that a number of States have made an exception to their drug laws for sacramental peyote use. But to say that a nondiscriminatory religious-practice exemption is permitted, or even that it is desirable, is not to say that it is constitutionally required, and that the appropriate occasions for its creation can be discerned by the courts. It may fairly be said that leaving accommodation to the political process will place at a relative disadvantage those religious practices that are not widely engaged in; but that unavoidable consequence of democratic government must be preferred to a system in which each conscience is a law unto itself or in which judges weigh the social importance of all laws against the centrality of all religious beliefs.

Because respondents' ingestion of peyote was prohibited under Oregon law, and because that prohibition is constitutional, Oregon may, consistent with the Free Exercise Clause, deny respondents unemployment compensation when their dismissal results from use of the drug. The decision of the Oregon Supreme Court is accordingly reversed.

It is so ordered.

JUSTICE O'CONNOR, with whom JUSTICE BRENNAN, JUSTICE MARSHALL, and JUSTICE BLACKMUN join as to Parts I and II, concurring in the judgment.[1] . . .

I. . . . I agree with the Court's implicit determination that the constitutional question upon which we granted review—whether the Free Exercise Clause protects a person's religiously motivated use of peyote from the reach of a State's general criminal law prohibition—is properly presented in this case. . . .

II. [T]he freedom to act, unlike the freedom to believe, cannot be absolute. [T]he Government [must] justify any substantial burden on religiously motivated conduct by a compelling state interest and by means narrowly tailored to achieve that interest. . . . Even if, as an empirical matter, a government's criminal laws might usually serve a compelling interest in health, safety, or public order, the First Amendment at least requires a case-by-case determination of the question, sensitive to the facts of each particular claim. [W]e cannot assume, merely because a law carries criminal sanctions and is generally applicable, that the First Amendment never requires the State to grant a limited exemption for religiously motivated conduct. . . .

---

1. Although Justice Brennan, Justice Marshall, and Justice Blackmun join Parts I and II of this opinion, they do not concur in the judgment.

III. . . . In light of our recent decisions holding that the governmental interests in the collection of income tax, *Hernandez* [*v. Commissioner of Internal Revenue*], a comprehensive social security system, see [*United States v.*] *Lee,* and military conscription, see *Gillette* [*v. United States*], are compelling, respondents do not seriously dispute that Oregon has a compelling interest in prohibiting the possession of peyote by its citizens. [T]he critical question in this case is whether exempting respondents from the State's general criminal prohibition "will unduly interfere with fulfillment of the governmental interest." . . . Because the health effects caused by the use of controlled substances exist regardless of the motivation of the user, the use of such substances, even for religious purposes, violates the very purpose of the laws that prohibit them. Cf. *State v. Massey,* 229 N.C. 734, 51 S.E.2d 179 (denying religious exemption to municipal ordinance prohibiting handling of poisonous reptiles), appeal dism'd *sub nom. Bunn v. North Carolina,* 336 U.S. 942, 69 S.Ct. 813, 93 L.Ed. 1099 (1949). Moreover, in view of the societal interest in preventing trafficking in controlled substances, uniform application of the criminal prohibition at issue is essential to the effectiveness of Oregon's stated interest in preventing any possession of peyote.

For these reasons, I believe that granting a selective exemption in this case would seriously impair Oregon's compelling interest in prohibiting possession of peyote by its citizens. Under such circumstances, the Free Exercise Clause does not require the State to accommodate respondents' religiously motivated conduct. . . .

JUSTICE BLACKMUN, with whom JUSTICE BRENNAN and JUSTICE MARSHALL join, dissenting.

[I]t is important to articulate in precise terms the state interest involved. It is not the State's broad interest in fighting the critical "war on drugs" that must be weighed against respondents' claim, but the State's narrow interest in refusing to make an exception for the religious, ceremonial use of peyote. . . . The State proclaims an interest in protecting the health and safety of its citizens from the dangers of unlawful drugs. It offers, however, no evidence that the religious use of peyote has ever harmed anyone. The factual findings of other courts cast doubt on the State's assumption that religious use of peyote is harmful. . . .

The State's apprehension of a flood of other religious claims is purely speculative. Almost half the States, and the Federal Government, have maintained an exemption for religious peyote use for many years, and apparently have not found themselves overwhelmed by claims to other religious exemptions. Allowing an exemption for religious peyote use would not necessarily oblige the State to grant a similar exemption to other religious groups. The unusual circumstances that make the religious use of peyote compatible with the State's interests in health and safety and in preventing drug trafficking would not apply to other religious claims. Some religions, for example, might not restrict drug use to a limited ceremonial context, as does the Native American Church.

See, *e.g.*, *Olsen,* 279 U.S.App.D.C., at 7, 878 F.2d, at 1464 ("the Ethiopian Zion Coptic Church ... teaches that marijuana is properly smoked 'continually all day' "). Some religious claims, involve drugs such as marijuana and heroin, in which there is significant illegal traffic, with its attendant greed and violence, so that it would be difficult to grant a religious exemption without seriously compromising law enforcement efforts. That the State might grant an exemption for religious peyote use, but deny other religious claims arising in different circumstances, would not violate the Establishment Clause. Though the State must treat all religions equally, and not favor one over another, this obligation is fulfilled by the uniform application of the "compelling interest" *test* to all free exercise claims, not by reaching uniform *results* as to all claims. A showing that religious peyote use does not unduly interfere with the State's interests is "one that probably few other religious groups or sects could make," *Yoder*....

Notes

1. *Church of Lukumi Babalu Aye, Inc. v. City of Hialeah,* 508 U.S. 520, 113 S.Ct. 2217, 124 L.Ed.2d 472 (1993). Santeria is a combination of tradition African religion and Roman Catholicism. Adherents include thousands of people, typically Cuban–Americans, who live in South Florida. A principal form of devotion is ritual sacrifice of animals such as goats, turtles, doves, and sheep. The animals are killed by cutting their carotid arteries in the neck, after which the congregation usually (but not always) eats the cooked remains. When a Santeria church planned to establish a house of worship in the city of Hialeah, the city council passed several overlapping ordinances specifically designed to forbid animal sacrifice. One law made it illegal to "sacrifice" any animal in the city limits, and defined "sacrifice" as the "unnecessary" killing of an animal in a public or private ritual "not for the primary purpose of food consumption." The law created an exception for slaughtering by "licensed establishments" and for "small numbers of hogs and/or cattle per week in accordance with an exemption provided by state law."

Kennedy, J., for the Court, invalidated the various ordinances. *Smith*'s requirements that the law be neutral and of general applicability are "interrelated," and thus failure to satisfy one requirement is "a likely indication that the other has not been satisfied." These ordinances did not meet either requirement. Under *Smith,* if the object of a law is to restrict practices because of their religious motivation, then "the law is not neutral." The object of the Hialeah ordinances was to infringe on Santeria practices. Additional evidence of "religious gerrymandering" is that the law defines "sacrifice" to exclude almost all killing of animals *except* for killing for religious reasons. The law even exempted Kosher slaughter of animals. "Careful drafting" of the laws "ensured that, although Santeria sacrifice is prohibited, killings that are no more necessary or humane in almost all other circumstances are unpunished." Under *Smith,* if the state grants individualized exemptions from general requirements, the state "may not refuse to extend that system of cases of 'religious hardship' without compelling reason."

If the city is concerned about improper disposal of animal remains, it could have imposed general rules governing disposal of organic garbage. If the city were really concerned about how animals are treated while in confinement, it could regulate that, regardless of the motivation for confining the animal. Instead, the city chose to prohibit possession of animals only if the purpose was sacrifice. The city stated that it wanted to prevent cruelty to animals, but it allowed many types of animal deaths for nonreligious reasons, such as fishing, extermination of mice in the home, and the infliction of pain "in the interest of medical science." The law allowed the use of live rabbits to train greyhounds. This non-neutral law was not of general applicability, could not be justified on the grounds that it advanced "interests of the highest order," and was not narrowly drawn to meet such interests.

Souter, J., concurred in part and in the judgment, stating, "I have doubts about whether the *Smith* rule merits adherence." Blackmun, J., joined by O'Connor, J., concurred in the judgment stating that they "continue to believe that *Smith* was wrongly decided. . . ."

2. Congress responded to *Smith* by enacting the Religious Freedom Restoration Act of 1993 (RFRA), 42 U.S.C.A. §§ 2000bb, et seq. Section 2000bb–1 provides: "Government shall not substantially burden a person's exercise of religion even if the burden results from a rule of general applicability," unless the Government shows that the burden is "in furtherance of a compelling governmental interest," and is "the least restrictive means of furthering" that interest. RFRA has spawned a great deal of litigation in the lower courts. One court, for example, upheld an injunction that orders an elementary school to make an exception to its "no weapons policy," and allow Sikh children as young as 7 years old to carry a kirpan (a 7–inch knife), which their religion requires them to wear at all times. The trial court had concluded that the knives were dangerous, and the children's faith allows or requires them to use the knives "in propagation of 'God's justice.'" *Cheema v. Thompson*, 67 F.3d 883, 887 (9th Cir.1995)(Wiggins, J., dissenting).

3. In *City of Boerne v. Flores*, 521 U.S. 507, 117 S.Ct. 2157, 138 L.Ed.2d 624 (1997), Kennedy, J., for the Court (5 to 4) [excerpted in § 9–1], invalidated RFRA, as not within Congressional power under the Fourteenth Amendment, § 5. The Catholic Archbishop of San Antonio had been denied a building permit to enlarge a church that had become too small for its worshipers because zoning authorities determined that it was in an historic preservation district.

O'Connor, J., filed a dissent. In the portion joined by Breyer, J., she argued that *Smith* was incorrectly decided and should be overruled. *Smith* has—

"harmed religious liberty. For example, a Federal District Court, in reliance on *Smith*, ruled that the Free Exercise Clause was not implicated where Hmong natives objected on religious grounds to their son's autopsy, conducted pursuant to a generally applicable state law. *Yang v. Sturner*, 750 F.Supp. 558, 559 (D.R.I.1990). The Court of Appeals for the Eighth Circuit held that application of a city's zoning laws to prevent a church from conducting services in an area zoned for commercial uses raised no free exercise concerns, even though the city permitted secular not-for-profit organizations in that area. *Cornerstone Bible Church v. Hastings,* 948 F.2d 464 (C.A.8 1991); *State v. Hershberger,* 462 N.W.2d 393 (Minn.1990) (Free Exercise Clause provided no basis for exempting an Amish farmer from displaying a bright orange triangle on his buggy, to which the farmer objected on religious grounds, even though the evidence showed that some other material would have served the State's purpose equally well). [L]ower courts applying *Smith* no longer find necessary a searching judicial inquiry into the possibility of reasonably accommodating religious practice."

Scalia, J., joined by Stevens, J., concurred in part, and disputed O'Connor's claim that history supported her position in *Smith*.

Should the law provide for exceptions for autopsies when family members object on religious grounds? Autopsies are usually performed to determine the cause of death (*e.g.,* foul play). Should family members be able to stop them for religious reasons? What if Satanists objected for religious reasons to an autopsy of an alleged human sacrifice? Under *Smith,* is it constitutional for a state to forbid a church from operating in an area when it allows secular nonprofit organizations?

Chapter 12

THE PROCEDURAL CONTEXT OF CONSTITUTIONAL LITIGATION

12–1. RIPENESS

INTERNATIONAL LONGSHOREMEN'S AND WAREHOUSEMEN'S UNION, LOCAL 37 v. BOYD

347 U.S. 222, 74 S.Ct. 447, 98 L.Ed. 650 (1954).

MR. JUSTICE FRANKFURTER delivered the opinion of the Court.

This is an action by Local 37 of the International Longshoremen's and Warehousemen's Union and several of its alien members to enjoin the District Director of Immigration and Naturalization at Seattle from so construing § 212(d)(7) of the Immigration and Nationality Act of 1952 as to treat aliens domiciled in the continental United States returning from temporary work in Alaska as if they were aliens entering the United States for the first time. Declaratory relief to the same effect is also sought. [P]etitioners asserted in the alternative that such a construction of the challenged statute would be unconstitutional. [T]he union has over three thousand members who work every summer in the herring and salmon canneries of Alaska, that some of these are aliens, and that if alien workers going to Alaska for the 1953 canning season were excluded on their return, their "contract and property rights [would] be jeopardized and forfeited." The District Court entertained the suit but dismissed it on the merits. In our order of October 12, 1953, we postponed the question of jurisdiction to the hearing on the merits.

On this appeal, appellee contends that the District Court should not have reached the statutory and constitutional questions—that it should have dismissed the suit for want of a "case or controversy," for lack of standing on the union's part to bring this action, because the Attorney General was an indispensable party, and because habeas corpus is the

1412

exclusive method for judicial inquiry in deportation cases. Since the first objection is conclusive, there is an end of the matter.

Appellants in effect asked the District Court to rule that a statute the sanctions of which had not been set in motion against individuals on whose behalf relief was sought, because an occasion for doing so had not arisen, would not be applied to them if in the future such a contingency should arise. That is not a lawsuit to enforce a right; it is an endeavor to obtain a court's assurance that a statute does not govern hypothetical situations that may or may not make the challenged statute applicable. Determination of the scope and constitutionality of legislation in advance of its immediate adverse effect in the context of a concrete case involves too remote and abstract an inquiry for the proper exercise of the judicial function. *Muskrat v. United States,* [§ 1–2.3, supra]. Since we do not have on the record before us a controversy appropriate for adjudication, the judgment of the District Court must be vacated, with directions to dismiss the complaint.

It is so ordered.

MR. JUSTICE BLACK, with whom MR. JUSTICE DOUGLAS concurs, dissenting.

This looks to me like the very kind of "case or controversy" courts should decide. [A]s I read the record it shows that judicial action is absolutely essential to save a large group of wage earners on whose behalf this action is brought from irreparable harm due to alleged lawless enforcement of a federal statute. My view makes it necessary for me to set out the facts with a little more detail than they appear in the Court's opinion.

Every summer members of the appellant union go from the west coast of continental United States to Alaska to work in salmon and herring canneries under collective-bargaining agreements. As the 1953 canning season approached the union and its members looked forward to this Alaska employment. A troublesome question arose, however, on account of the Immigration and Nationality Act of 1952. Section 212(d)(7) of this new Act has language that given one construction provides that all aliens seeking admission to continental United States from Alaska, even those previously accepted as permanent United States residents, shall be examined as if entering from a foreign country with a view to excluding them on any of the many grounds applicable to aliens generally. This new law created an acute problem for the union and its numerous members who were lawful alien residents, since aliens generally can be excluded from this country for many reasons which would not justify deporting aliens lawfully residing here. The union and its members insisted on another construction. They denied that Congress intended to require alien workers to forfeit their right to live in this country for no reason at all except that they went to Alaska, territory of the United States, to engage in lawful work under a lawfully authorized collective-bargaining contract. The defendant immigration officer announced that the union's interpretation was wrong and that workers going to Alaska would be subject to examination and exclusion. This is the controversy.

It was to test the right of the immigration officer to apply § 212(d)(7) to make these workers subject to exclusion that this suit was filed by the union and two of its officers on behalf of themselves and all union members who are aliens and permanent residents. True, the action was begun before the union members went to Alaska for the 1953 canning season. But it is not only admitted that the immigration official intended to enforce § 212(d)(7) as the union and these workers feared. It is admitted here that he has since done precisely that. All 1953 alien cannery workers have actually been subjected to the wearisome routine of immigration procedure as though they had never lived here. And some of the union members are evidently about to be denied the right ever to return to their homes on grounds that could not have been legally applied to them had they stayed in California or Washington instead of going to Alaska to work for an important American industry.

Thus the threatened injury which the Court dismisses as "remote" and "hypothetical" has come about. For going to Alaska to engage in honest employment many of these workers may lose the home this country once afforded them. This is a strange penalty to put on productive work. Maybe this is what Congress meant by passing § 212(d)(7). And maybe in these times such a law would be held constitutional. But even so, can it be that a challenge to this law on behalf of those whom it hits the hardest is so frivolous that it should be dismissed for want of a controversy that courts should decide? Workers threatened with irreparable damages, like others, should have their cases tried.

Notes

1. "The basic rationale of the ripeness doctrine 'is to prevent the courts, through avoidance of premature adjudication, from entangling themselves in abstract disagreements over administrative policies, and also to protect the agencies from judicial interference until an administrative decision has been formalized and its effects felt in a concrete way by the challenging parties.' [T]he question of ripeness turns on 'the fitness of the issues for judicial decision' and 'the hardship to the parties of withholding court consideration.'" *Pacific Gas & Electric Co. v. State Energy Resources Conservation & Development Commission*, 461 U.S. 190, 103 S.Ct. 1713, 75 L.Ed.2d 752 (1983). Which of these policies, if any, apply to the facts in the *International Longshoremen's* case?

If you were plaintiff's lawyer in this case, what if anything could you have done, in fashioning your complaint, to make the case appear more ripe?

Is the result in the *International Longshoremen's* case required by Article III?

2. *Steffel v. Thompson*, 415 U.S. 452, 94 S.Ct. 1209, 39 L.Ed.2d 505 (1974). Petitioner, who was distributing handbills on the exterior sidewalk of a shopping center protesting the Vietnam War, refused to leave when asked. Then, a summoned police officer threatened to arrest him if he did not leave. He left and sued for a declaratory judgment and an injunction that the state

law was being applied unconstitutionally. The Court held that the case was ripe remanded for further proceedings:

> [P]etitioner has alleged threats of prosecution that cannot be characterized as "imaginary or speculative." He has twice been warned to stop handbilling that he claims is constitutionally protected and has been told by the police that if he again handbills at the shopping center and disobeys a warning to stop he will likely be prosecuted. The prosecution of petitioner's handbilling companion is ample demonstration that petitioner's concern with arrest has not been "chimerical." In these circumstances, it is not necessary that petitioner first expose himself to actual arrest or prosecution to be entitled to challenge a statute that he claims deters the exercise of his constitutional rights. Moreover, petitioner's challenge is to those specific provisions of state law which have provided the basis for threats of criminal prosecution against him.

If one need not actually be prosecuted under a statute in order to contest its constitutionality, at what point is the challenge insufficiently ripe?

3. *Williamson County Regional Planning Commission v. Hamilton Bank*, 473 U.S. 172, 105 S.Ct. 3108, 87 L.Ed.2d 126 (1985). A land developer sued the Planning Commission alleging that its application of zoning laws to its property amounted to a "taking" of property for which just compensation was due. The jury awarded $350,000 but the Supreme Court reversed: "a claim that the application of government regulations effects a taking of property interest is not ripe until the government entity charged with implementing the regulations has reached a final decision regarding the application of the regulation to the property at issue." The developer did not seek variances that would have allowed it to develop the property as it had planned. In addition, if there were a "taking," the developer did not seek compensation from the already established state procedures. If a state provides adequate procedures for seeking just compensation, "the property owner cannot claim a violation of the Just Compensation Clause until it has used the procedure and been denied just compensation." All that is required is that a "reasonable, certain and adequate provision for obtaining compensation" exist at the time of the "taking."

Contrast, *Lucas v. South Carolina Coastal Council*, 505 U.S. 1003, 112 S.Ct. 2886, 120 L.Ed.2d 798 (1992). Lucas challenged a state statute regulating his property after he purchased it but before he built on it. He alleged that the new law amounted to a regulatory "taking" of property requiring just compensation. While the case was pending in the state court system, South Carolina enacted an amendment that might allow Lucas to secure a special permit allowing him to build on his property. This new state law did not mean that Lucas' taking claim was unripe. Because the state supreme court reached the merits of the controversy (and decided against Lucas), Lucas has a claim for a preamendment deprivation of property; he properly alleged injury-in-fact with respect to this preamendment deprivation of property. This new state-created amendment did not restore to him his preamendment deprivation of property.

12–2. MOOTNESS

DEFUNIS v. ODEGAARD
416 U.S. 312, 94 S.Ct. 1704, 40 L.Ed.2d 164 (1974).

PER CURIAM.

In 1971 the petitioner Marco DeFunis, Jr., applied for admission as a first-year student at the University of Washington Law School, a state-operated institution. The size of the incoming first-year class was to be limited to 150 persons, and the Law School received some 1,600 applications for these 150 places. DeFunis was eventually notified that he had been denied admission. He thereupon commenced this suit in a Washington trial court, contending that the procedures and criteria employed by the Law School Admissions Committee invidiously discriminated against him on account of his race in violation of the Equal Protection Clause of the Fourteenth Amendment to the United States Constitution.

DeFunis brought the suit on behalf of himself alone, and not as the representative of any class, against the various respondents, who are officers, faculty members, and members of the Board of Regents of the University of Washington. He asked the trial court to issue a mandatory injunction commanding the respondents to admit him as a member of the first-year class entering in September 1971, on the ground that the Law School admissions policy had resulted in the unconstitutional denial of his application for admission. The trial court agreed with his claim and granted the requested relief. DeFunis was, accordingly, admitted to the Law School and began his legal studies there in the fall of 1971. On appeal, the Washington Supreme Court reversed the judgment of the trial court and held that the Law School admissions policy did not violate the Constitution. By this time DeFunis was in his second year at the Law School.

He then petitioned this Court for a writ of certiorari, and Mr. Justice Douglas, as Circuit Justice, stayed the judgment of the Washington Supreme Court pending the "final disposition of the case by this Court." By virtue of this stay, DeFunis has remained in law school, and was in the first term of his third and final year when this Court first considered his certiorari petition in the fall of 1973. Because of our concern that DeFunis' third-year standing in the Law School might have rendered this case moot, we requested the parties to brief the question of mootness before we acted on the petition. In response, both sides contended that the case was not moot. The respondents indicated that, if the decision of the Washington Supreme Court were permitted to stand, the petitioner could complete the term for which he was then enrolled but would have to apply to the faculty for permission to continue in the school before he could register for another term. We granted the petition for certiorari on November 19, 1973 [and the case was orally argued on February 26, 1974].

In response to questions raised from the bench during the oral argument, counsel for the petitioner has informed the Court that De-Funis has now registered "for his final quarter in law school." Counsel for the respondents have made clear that the Law School will not in any way seek to abrogate this registration. In light of DeFunis' recent registration for the last quarter of his final law school year, and the Law School's assurance that his registration is fully effective, the insistent question again arises whether this case is not moot, and to that question we now turn.

The starting point for analysis is the familiar proposition that "federal courts are without power to decide questions that cannot affect the rights of litigants in the case before them." The inability of the federal judiciary "to review moot cases derives from the requirement of Art. III of the Constitution under which the exercise of judicial power depends upon the existence of a case or controversy." Although as a matter of Washington state law it appears that this case would be saved from mootness by "the great public interest in the continuing issues raised by this appeal," the fact remains that under Art. III "[e]ven in cases arising in the state courts, the question of mootness is a federal one which a federal court must resolve before it assumes jurisdiction."

[A]ll parties agree that DeFunis is now entitled to complete his legal studies at the University of Washington and to receive his degree from that institution. A determination by this Court of the legal issues tendered by the parties is no longer necessary to compel that result, and could not serve to prevent it. DeFunis did not cast his suit as a class action, and the only remedy he requested was an injunction commanding his admission to the Law School. He was not only accorded that remedy, but he now has also been irrevocably admitted to the final term of the final year of the Law School course. The controversy between the parties has thus clearly ceased to be "definite and concrete" and no longer "touch[es] the legal relations of parties having adverse legal interests." It matters not that these circumstances partially stem from a policy decision on the part of the respondent Law School authorities. . . .

There is a line of decisions in this Court standing for the proposition that the "voluntary cessation of allegedly illegal conduct does not deprive the tribunal of power to hear and determine the case, i.e., does not make the case moot." These decisions and the doctrine they reflect would be quite relevant if the question of mootness here had arisen by reason of a unilateral change in the *admissions procedures* of the Law School. For it was the admissions procedures that were the target of this litigation, and a voluntary cessation of the admissions practices complained of could make this case moot only if it could be said with assurance "that 'there is no reasonable expectation that the wrong will be repeated.' " Otherwise, "[t]he defendant is free to return to his old ways," and this fact would be enough to prevent mootness because of the "public interest in having the legality of the practices settled." But mootness in the present case depends not at all upon a "voluntary cessation" of the admissions practices that were the subject of this litigation. It depends, instead, upon the simple fact that DeFunis is now in the final quarter of the final year of his course of study, and the settled and unchallenged policy of the Law School to permit him to complete the term for which he is now enrolled.

It might also be suggested that this case presents a question that is "capable of repetition, yet evading review," *Southern Pacific Terminal Co. v. ICC,* 219 U.S. 498, 515, 31 S.Ct. 279, 283, 55 L.Ed. 310 (1911), and is thus amenable to federal adjudication even though it might otherwise be considered moot. But DeFunis will never again be required to run the gauntlet of the Law School's admission process, and so the question is certainly not "capable of repetition" so far as he is concerned. Moreover, just because this particular case did not reach the Court until the eve of the petitioner's graduation from law school, it hardly follows that the issue he raises will in the future evade review. If the admissions procedures of the Law School remain unchanged, there is no reason to suppose that a subsequent case attacking those procedures will not come with relative speed to this Court, now that the Supreme Court of Washington has spoken. This case, therefore, in no way presents the exceptional situation in which the *Southern Pacific Terminal* doctrine might permit a departure from "[t]he usual rule in federal cases ... that an actual controversy must exist at stages of appellate or certiorari review, and not simply at the date the action is initiated."

Because the petitioner will complete his law school studies at the end of the term for which he has now registered regardless of any decision this Court might reach on the merits of this litigation, we conclude that the Court cannot, consistently with the limitations of Art. III of the Constitution, consider the substantive constitutional issues tendered by the parties.[5] Accordingly, the judgment of the Supreme Court of Washington is vacated, and the cause is remanded for such proceedings as by that court may be deemed appropriate.

It is so ordered.

Mr. Justice Brennan, with whom Mr. Justice Douglas, Mr. Justice White, and Mr. Justice Marshall concur, dissenting.

I respectfully dissent. Many weeks of the school term remain, and petitioner may not receive his degree despite respondents' assurances that petitioner will be allowed to complete this term's schooling regardless of our decision. Any number of unexpected events—illness, economic necessity, even academic failure—might prevent his graduation at the end of the term. Were that misfortune to befall, and were petitioner required to register for yet another term, the prospect that he would again face the hurdle of the admissions policy is real, not fanciful; for respondents warn that "Mr. DeFunis would have to take some appropri-

---

5. It is suggested in dissent that "[a]ny number of unexpected events—illness, economic necessity, even academic failure—might prevent his graduation at the end of the term." "But such speculative contin-gencies afford no basis for our passing on the substantive issues [the petitioner] would have us decide," in the absence of "evidence that this is a prospect of 'immediacy and reality.' "

ate action to request continued admission for the remainder of his law school education, and *some discretionary action by the University on such request would have to be taken.*" Respondents' Memorandum on the Question of Mootness 3–4 (emphasis supplied). Thus, respondents' assurances have not dissipated the possibility that petitioner might once again have to run the gauntlet of the University's allegedly unlawful admissions policy.... Since respondents' voluntary representation to this Court is only that they will permit petitioner to complete this term's studies, respondents have not borne the "heavy burden," of demonstrating that there was not even a "mere possibility" that petitioner would once again be subject to the challenged admissions policy. On the contrary, respondents have positioned themselves so as to be "free to return to [their] old ways."

I can thus find no justification for the Court's straining to rid itself of this dispute. [T]here is no want of an adversary contest in this case. ...Moreover, in endeavoring to dispose of this case as moot, the Court clearly disserves the public interest. The constitutional issues which are avoided today concern vast numbers of people, organizations, and colleges and universities, as evidenced by the filing of twenty-six *amicus curiae* briefs. Few constitutional questions in recent history have stirred as much debate, and they will not disappear. They must inevitably return to the federal courts and ultimately again to this Court. Because avoidance of repetitious litigation serves the public interest, that inevitability counsels against mootness determinations, as here, not compelled by the record. [W]e should not transform principles of avoidance of constitutional decisions into devices for sidestepping resolution of difficult cases....

[A separate dissenting opinion of DOUGLAS, J., is omitted.]

Notes

1. *Super Tire Engineering Co. v. McCorkle,* 416 U.S. 115, 94 S.Ct. 1694, 40 L.Ed.2d 1 (1974), was decided the same day as *DeFunis,* though neither case cited the other. In *Super Tire,* employers whose plants were struck sued for injunctive and declaratory relief against the state welfare administration, which had applied state regulations allowing workers engaged in an economic strike to be eligible for public assistance through state welfare programs. By the time the Supreme Court heard the case the strike was over, but Blackmun, J., for the Court (5 to 4), held that the claim was not moot, because the issue was capable of repetition yet evading review. The government action complained of "directly affect[ed] and continu[es] to affect, the behavior of citizens in our society." Many strikes do not last long enough to allow for complete judicial review. "A strike that lasts six weeks, as this one did, may seem long, but its termination, like pregnancy at nine months and elections spaced at year-long or biennial intervals, should not preclude challenge to state policies that have had their impact and continue in force, unabated and unreviewed. The judiciary may not close the door to the resolution of the important questions these concrete disputes present." Stewart, J., joined by Burger, C.J., Powell, & Rehnquist, JJ., dissented.

Given *Super Tire,* was *DeFunis* compelled by Article III? If not compelled, can you still justify the majority's invoking the mootness doctrine?

2. *DeFunis* came from a state court. Does the federal decision on mootness bind the Washington state supreme court? May the state court on remand reinstitute its prior order? If *Super Tire* had been brought in a state court and that court had held that the case was moot under state constitutional requirements, would that decision prevent the U.S. Supreme Court from hearing the appeal?

3. Class Actions. If DeFunis had instituted a class action would the case still be moot simply because it is moot as to the named plaintiff, DeFunis? In *Sosna v. Iowa,* 419 U.S. 393, 95 S.Ct. 553, 42 L.Ed.2d 532 (1975) plaintiff attacked the constitutionality of Iowa's durational residency requirement for invoking that state's divorce jurisdiction. When the lower federal court rendered its judgment the case was not moot, but, by the time her case had reached the Supreme Court, plaintiff had long since satisfied the state residency requirement. "If appellant had sued only on her own behalf, both the fact that she now satisfies the one-year residency requirement and the fact that she has obtained a divorce elsewhere would make this case moot.... But appellant brought this suit as a class action and sought to litigate ... in a representative capacity." Thus the controversy was alive as to the class of persons she had been certified to represent. When "the issue sought to be litigated escapes full appellate review at the behest of any single challenger [then it] does not inexorably become moot by the intervening resolution of the controversy as to the named plaintiffs. [T]he same exigency that justifies this doctrine serves to identify its limits. In cases in which the alleged harm would not dissipate during the normal time required for resolution of the controversy, the general principles of Art. III jurisdiction require that the plaintiff's personal stake in the litigation continue throughout the entirety of the litigation." The Court then upheld the Iowa statute.

Contrast *Hall v. Beals,* 396 U.S. 45, 90 S.Ct. 200, 24 L.Ed.2d 214 (1969)(per curiam). Appellants moved to Colorado in June, 1968, but could not to register to vote in the November election, because they would not have satisfied the six month residency requirement by election day. They filed a class action, lost in the trial level (and thus could not vote in the 1968 election), and appealed to the U.S. Supreme Court. Colorado then amended its election laws to reduce the residency requirement to two months. The case was now moot, because the Court should "review the judgment below in light of the Colorado statute as it now stands, not as it once did." The "appellants object now to the two-month residency requirement, [but] so far as they are concerned nothing in the Colorado legislative scheme as now written adversely affects either their present interests, or their interest at the time this litigation was commenced. Nor does the result differ because the appellants denominated their suit a class action on behalf of disenfranchised voters. The appellants 'cannot represent a class of [which] they are not a part,'—that is, the class of voters disqualified in Colorado by virtue of the new two-month requirement, a class of which the appellants have never been members."

United States Parole Commission v. Geraghty, 445 U.S. 388, 100 S.Ct. 1202, 63 L.Ed.2d 479 (1980) held (5 to 4) that the plaintiff, who brought a class action challenging the validity of certain parole guidelines, could continue his appeal of a lower court ruling denying certification even though he had been released from prison while the appeal was pending. If the class had been certified, the mootness of Geraghty's personal claim would not have rendered the controversy moot under *Sosna.* Hence the erroneous denial of a class certification should not lead to the opposite result. The certification, if granted, may be treated as relating back to the original erroneous denial. Given the "flexible character of the Art. III mootness doctrine," the right of the named plaintiff to class certification is analogous "to the private attorney general concept." Powell, J., joined by Burger, C.J., & Stewart & Rehnquist, JJ., dissented and objected to the flexibility evidenced in the majority opinion. "Art. III contains no exception for class actions."

Compare *Deposit Guaranty National Bank v. Roper,* 445 U.S. 326, 100 S.Ct. 1166, 63 L.Ed.2d 427 (1980), decided the same day. Respondents were holders of bank credit cards who instituted a class action claiming usurious finance charges. The Court held that neither the defendant's tender to the individual plaintiffs of the maximum amount that they could have recovered, nor the district court's entry of judgment in favor of plaintiffs over their objections mooted their case, so that they could appeal the adverse class certification ruling, because plaintiffs retained "a continuing individual interest in the resolution of the class certification question in their desire to shift part of the cost of litigation to those who will share in its benefits if the class is certified and ultimately prevails."

Given this line of cases, would you have advised DeFunis' lawyer to file a class action? Would it still have been better tactically to file an individual action? Would it be wise for a law school, in order to protect its affirmative action program from judicial attack, to have a policy of mooting all cases brought by individual plaintiffs like DeFunis?

4.   Assume that a criminal defendant appeals a state conviction on the grounds that it was secured by using evidence unconstitutionally seized. By the time the case reaches the U.S. Supreme Court the defendant has served his six month sentence and has been released. Is the case moot? Is it relevant that state law provides that the defendant's conviction may be used to impeach his character if he should put it in issue at any future criminal trial? See *Sibron v. New York,* 392 U.S. 40, 88 S.Ct. 1889, 20 L.Ed.2d 917 (1968).

Assume that a state law provides that a voter must enroll in the party of his choice at least 30 days before the general election in order to be eligible to vote in the next party primary. Petitioners were disenfranchised from voting in the June, 1972 primary because they had not enrolled in a party at least 30 days before the previous general election (November, 1971). By the time the petitioners reached the Supreme Court, the June, 1972 primary had passed. The case is not a class action. Is it moot? See *Rosario v. Rockefeller,* 410 U.S. 752, 756, n. 5, 93 S.Ct. 1245, 1249, n. 5, 36 L.Ed.2d 1 (1973).

5.   *Church of Scientology v. United States,* 506 U.S. 9, 113 S.Ct. 447, 121 L.Ed.2d 313 (1992). The IRS subpoenaed a state court Clerk to produce two tapes, in the Clerk's custody, recording conversations between officials of the Church of Scientology and their attorneys. The Church opposed the

subpoena and unsuccessfully requested a stay of its enforcement. Pursuant to a federal district court order, the Clerk turned over the tapes to the IRS. The court of appeals then ruled the appeal moot, claiming that it was impossible to grant the Church effectual relief. A unanimous Court reversed. Although "there is nothing a court can do to withdraw all knowledge or information that IRS agents may have acquired by examination of the tapes—a court can fashion *some* form of meaningful relief. . . . " (emphasis in original). The court, for example, can order the Government to destroy or return any and all copies in its possession.

Arizonans for Official English v. Arizona, 520 U.S. 43, 117 S.Ct. 1055, 137 L.Ed.2d 170 (1997). The voters of Arizona approved a State constitutional amendment that made English "the official language of the State," required the State to "act in English and in no other language," and authorized State residents and businesses to sue in State court to enforce this law. Maria–Kelly Yniguez, a State employee, sued in federal court claiming that the Arizona constitutional provision violated her free speech because she feared discharge or other discipline if she spoke Spanish while serving the State. The federal district court held that the English-only law violated the First Amendment. The Governor (whom the trial court ruled was the only proper defendant) announced that she would not appeal, and the federal court denied the State Attorney General's motion to intervene to contest the ruling on appeal.

Yniguez then resigned her State job. The Ninth Circuit allowed the Arizonians for Official English Committee (AOE) and its Chairman Park (who had sponsored the constitutional amendment) to intervene to support the law's constitutionality; the Ninth Circuit also ruled that the Attorney General could not intervene as a party but could make an argument. The Ninth Circuit affirmed after ruling that Yniguez's resignation did not moot the case because she had asked for injunctive and declaratory relief and for "all other relief that the Court deems just and proper," which the Ninth Circuit interpreted to include a request for nominal damages.

Ginsburg, J., for the unanimous Court, reversed on grounds of mootness. Assuming, without deciding, that AOE and Park had standing, the case was moot because Yniguez had quit her State job and could no longer be affected by the English-only provision that applied to State employees. The controversy must exist at all stages of review, not only when the complaint was filed. Even if Yniguez had asked for nominal damages, she was suing under a federal statute [42 U.S.C.A. § 1983] that creates no damage remedy against a State. While Arizona had waived its Eleventh Amendment immunity, that was not the barrier. "The stopper was that § 1983 creates no remedy against the State." Moreover, the Ninth Circuit did not explain how the State Attorney General, an "intervenor the court had designated a nonparty could be subject, nevertheless, to an obligation to pay damages."

6. *Northeastern Florida Chapter of Associated General Contractors of America v. City of Jacksonville,* 508 U.S. 656, 113 S.Ct. 2297, 124 L.Ed.2d 586 (1993). Petitioner sought declaratory and injunctive relief against a city ordinance that required that 10% of the money spent on city contracts be set aside for minority businesses. Most of petitioner's members did not qualify as minority businesses. Thomas, J., for the Court, held that the case was not

moot even though the city had repealed the ordinance after certiorari was granted, and then replaced it with another that still set aside certain contracts, but with various variations; this time the set aside only applied to black minorities and to females, and the 10% set aside was changed to a flexible 5% to 16% "participation goal." This voluntary cessation of a challenged practice does not make a case moot because the defendant is free to reinstate the challenged practice. Moreover, in this case, such a risk is not merely theoretical because the city's new ordinance (like the old one) also accords preferential treatment when city contracts are awarded.

O'Connor, J., joined by Blackmun, J., dissented on the mootness issue; they conceded that the case is not moot merely because the law is altered "in some insignificant respect," but argued that the Court should treat a controversy as moot if the government replaces the challenged statute with "more narrowly drawn legislation pending our review, and the plaintiff seeks only prospective relief," not damages. In a footnote, the Court rejected the dissent's position, and its view that the law in question had been "sufficiently altered."

12–3. TAXPAYER STANDING

MASSACHUSETTS v. MELLON
FROTHINGHAM v. MELLON
262 U.S. 447, 43 S.Ct. 597, 67 L.Ed. 1078 (1923).

MR. JUSTICE SUTHERLAND delivered the opinion of the Court.

These [two] cases ... challenge the constitutionality of the Act of November 23, 1921, commonly called the Maternity Act. Briefly, it provides for an initial appropriation and thereafter annual appropriations for a period of five years, to be apportioned among such of the several States as shall accept and comply with its provisions, for the purpose of cooperating with them to reduce maternal and infant mortality and protect the health of mothers and infants. It creates a bureau to administer the act in cooperation with state agencies, which are required to make such reports concerning their operations and expenditures as may be prescribed by the federal bureau. Whenever that bureau shall determine that funds have not been properly expended in respect of any State, payments may be withheld.

It is asserted that these appropriations are for purposes not national, but local to the States, and together with numerous similar appropriations constitute an effective means of inducing the States to yield a portion of their sovereign rights.... In the *Massachusetts* case it is alleged that the plaintiff's rights and powers as a sovereign State and the rights of its citizens have been invaded and usurped by these expenditures and acts; and that, although the State has not accepted the act, its constitutional rights are infringed by the passage thereof and the imposition upon the State of an illegal and unconstitutional option either to yield to the Federal Government a part of its reserved rights or lose the share which it would otherwise be entitled to receive of the moneys appropriated. In the *Frothingham* case plaintiff alleges that the effect of the statute will be to take her property, under the guise of taxation, without due process of law.

We have reached the conclusion that the cases must be disposed of for want of jurisdiction without considering the merits of the constitutional questions. [T]he State of Massachusetts presents no justiciable controversy either in its own behalf or as the representative of its citizens. The appellant in the second suit has no such interest in the subject-matter, nor is any such injury inflicted or threatened, as will enable her to sue.

First. The State of Massachusetts in its own behalf, in effect, complains that the act in question invades the local concerns of the State, and is a usurpation of power, viz: the power of local self government reserved to the States.

Probably, it would be sufficient to point out that the powers of the State are not invaded, since the statute imposes no obligation but simply extends an option which the State is free to accept or reject. But we do not rest here. Under Article III, § 2, of the Constitution, the judicial power of this Court extends "to controversies ... between a State and citizens of another State" and the Court has original jurisdiction "in all cases ... in which a State shall be party." The effect of this is not to confer jurisdiction upon the Court merely because a State is a party, but only where it is a party to a proceeding of judicial cognizance. Proceedings not of a justiciable character are outside the contemplation of the constitutional grant....

What, then, is the nature of the right of the State here asserted and how is it affected by this statute? [W]hat burden is imposed upon the States, unequally or otherwise? Certainly there is none, unless it be the burden of taxation, and that falls upon their inhabitants, who are within the taxing power of Congress as well as that of the States where they reside. Nor does the statute require the States to do or to yield anything. If Congress enacted it with the ulterior purpose of tempting them to yield, that purpose may be effectively frustrated by the simple expedient of not yielding.

In the last analysis, the complaint of the plaintiff State is brought to the naked contention that Congress has usurped the reserved powers of the several States by the mere enactment of the statute, though nothing has been done and nothing is to be done without their consent; and it is plain that that question, as it is thus presented, is political and not judicial in character, and therefore is not a matter which admits of the exercise of the judicial power.... [I]n so far as the case depends upon the assertion of a right on the part of the State to sue in its own behalf we are without jurisdiction. In that aspect of the case we are called upon to adjudicate, not rights of person or property, not rights of dominion over physical domain, not quasi-sovereign rights actually invaded or threatened, but abstract questions of political power, of sovereignty, of government....

We come next to consider whether the suit may be maintained by the State as the representative of its citizens. To this the answer is not doubtful. We need not go so far as to say that a State may never intervene by suit to protect its citizens against any form of enforcement of unconstitutional acts of Congress; but we are clear that the right to do so does not arise here. Ordinarily, at least, the only way in which a State may afford protection to its citizens in such cases is through the enforcement of its own criminal statutes, where that is appropriate, or by opening its courts to the injured persons for the maintenance of civil suits or actions. But the citizens of Massachusetts are also citizens of the United States. It cannot be conceded that a State, as *parens patriae,* may institute judicial proceedings to protect citizens of the United States from the operation of the statutes thereof. While the State, under some circumstances, may sue in that capacity for the protection of its citizens (*Missouri v. Illinois and Chicago District,* 180 U.S. 208, 241, 21 S.Ct. 331, 45 L.Ed. 497), it is no part of its duty or power to enforce their rights in respect of their relations with the Federal Government. In that field it is the United States, and not the State, which represents them as *parens patriae,* when such representation becomes appropriate; and to the former, and not to the latter, they must look for such protective measures as flow from that status.

Second. The attack upon the statute in the *Frothingham* case is, generally, the same, but this plaintiff alleges in addition that she is a taxpayer of the United States; and her contention, though not clear, seems to be that the effect of the appropriations complained of will be to increase the burden of future taxation and thereby take her property without due process of law. The right of a taxpayer to enjoin the execution of a federal appropriation act, on the ground that it is invalid and will result in taxation for illegal purposes, has never been passed upon by this Court.... The interest of a taxpayer of a municipality in the application of its moneys is direct and immediate and the remedy by injunction to prevent their misuse is not inappropriate. It is upheld by a large number of state cases and is the rule of this Court. *Crampton v. Zabriskie,* 101 U.S. 601, 609, 25 L.Ed. 1070. Nevertheless, there are decisions to the contrary. See, for example, *Miller v. Grandy,* 13 Mich. 540, 550. The reasons which support the extension of the equitable remedy to a single taxpayer in such cases are based upon the peculiar relation of the corporate taxpayer to the corporation, which is not without some resemblance to that subsisting between stockholder and private corporation. But the relation of a taxpayer of the United States to the Federal Government is very different. His interest in the moneys of the Treasury—partly realized from taxation and partly from other sources—is shared with millions of others; is comparatively minute and indeterminable; and the effect upon future taxation, of any payment out of the funds, so remote, fluctuating and uncertain, that no basis is afforded for an appeal to the preventive powers of a court of equity.

The administration of any statute, likely to produce additional taxation to be imposed upon a vast number of taxpayers, the extent of whose several liability is indefinite and constantly changing, is essentially a matter of public and not of individual concern. If one taxpayer may champion and litigate such a cause, then every other taxpayer may do the same, not only in respect of the statute here under review but also in respect of every other appropriation act and statute whose administration requires the outlay of public money, and whose validity may be questioned. The bare suggestion of such a result, with its attendant inconveniences, goes far to sustain the conclusion which we have reached, that a suit of this character cannot be maintained. It is of much significance that no precedent sustaining the right to maintain suits like this has been called to our attention, although, since the formation of the government, as an examination of the acts of Congress will disclose, a large number of statutes appropriating or involving the expenditure of moneys for non-federal purposes have been enacted and carried into effect.... Looking through forms of words to the substance of their complaint, it is merely that officials of the executive department of the government are executing and will execute an act of Congress asserted to be unconstitutional; and this we are asked to prevent. To do so would be not to decide a judicial controversy, but to assume a position of authority over the governmental acts of another and co-equal department, an authority which plainly we do not possess.

No. 24, Original, dismissed. No. 962 affirmed.

Notes

1. Are the conclusions in *Massachusetts* and *Frothingham* required by Article III or simply a product of judicial self-restraint? How might you develop arguments to support either view?

2. If Congress enacted a law providing funds to build a church and the Executive Branch proceeded to implement that law, who might have standing to claim a violation of the establishment of religion clause of the First Amendment?

3. *Wyoming v. Oklahoma,* 502 U.S. 437, 112 S.Ct. 789, 117 L.Ed.2d 1 (1992) ruled that Wyoming had standing to challenge Oklahoma legislation that required Oklahoma coal-fired electric generating plants (including privately owned plants) producing power for sale in Oklahoma to run a mixture of coal containing at least 10% Oklahoma-mined coal. Wyoming challenged the Oklahoma rule as a violation of the dormant Commerce Clause. Although Wyoming did not itself sell coal, it imposed severance taxes on the extraction of coal within its boundaries, and Oklahoma law deprived Wyoming of tax revenues by causing a decline in the amount of coal mined in Wyoming. Wyoming does not claim merely a loss in general tax revenues; rather it has lost specific tax revenues, which are directly traceable to the Oklahoma law. The Court then found that the Oklahoma law violated the dormant commerce clause.

4. Various cases both before and after *Massachusetts* have allowed the state to sue as *parens patriae* when the defendant was not the United States. See, e.g., *Missouri v. Illinois,* 180 U.S. 208, 21 S.Ct. 331, 45 L.Ed. 497 (1901), permitting Missouri, on behalf of its citizens, to sue Illinois and a Chicago

sanitation district to enjoin the discharge of sewage into the Mississippi River. A state may also sue as *parens patriae* to enjoin antitrust violations but cannot, in that capacity, sue for damages because there would be duplicative recoveries by the actually injured citizens and by the state as well. *Hawaii v. Standard Oil Co.,* 405 U.S. 251, 92 S.Ct. 885, 31 L.Ed.2d 184 (1972). A state, however, may sue for damages to its proprietary interests. See, *Georgia v. Evans,* 316 U.S. 159, 62 S.Ct. 972, 86 L.Ed. 1346 (1942), holding that a state is a "person" for purposes of section 7 of the Sherman Act and therefore is entitled to sue for treble damages when, as a purchaser of asphalt, it is injured by antitrust violations.

In actions by states against the United States, consider these two cases. First, *Missouri v. Holland,* 252 U.S. 416, 40 S.Ct. 382, 64 L.Ed. 641 (1920) excerpted at § 5–2, supra, allowed Missouri to sue to enjoin a U.S. game warden from attempting to enforce the Migratory Bird Treaty Act of 1918 and accompanying regulations. The state alleged that the acts of the defendant contravened state law. The Court said that the state's bill in equity "is a reasonable and proper means to assert the alleged quasi sovereign rights of a State."

In *Oklahoma v. United States Civil Service Commission,* 330 U.S. 127, 67 S.Ct. 544, 91 L.Ed. 794 (1947) the Court heard Oklahoma's challenge to the constitutionality of the Hatch Act. The U.S. Civil Service Commission notified Oklahoma that one of its employees in the state highway department had engaged in improper political activities in violation of section 12 of the federal Hatch Act. The Commission ordered that the offending employee be removed or the appropriate federal agency would withhold highway grants to Oklahoma equal to two years compensation. Oklahoma sought review of the federal administrative order. The federal government relied in part on *Massachusetts v. Mellon* to argue that the state suffered no injury that it may legally protect from withdrawal by the United States of a grant-in-aid. The Court held:

> The issue is whether Oklahoma can challenge the constitutionality of § 12 on statutory review of a Commission order. Subsection (c) gives to any party aggrieved a judicial review of the Commission order. The review is on the entire record and extends to questions of fact and questions of law. . . . We think the challenge can be made in these review proceedings to the constitutionality of the law upon which the order under review is predicated.

The Court then upheld the constitutionality of the Commission's order.

Can you fashion a consistent rule to explain these cases?

FLAST v. COHEN
392 U.S. 83, 88 S.Ct. 1942, 20 L.Ed.2d 947 (1968).

Mr. Chief Justice Warren delivered the opinion of the Court. . . .

In this case, we must decide whether the *Frothingham* barrier should be lowered when a taxpayer attacks a federal statute on the ground that it violates the Establishment and Free Exercise Clauses of the First Amendment.

Appellants filed suit in the United States District Court for the Southern District of New York to enjoin the allegedly unconstitutional expenditure of federal funds under Titles I and II of the Elementary and Secondary Education Act of 1965. [T]he appellants were resting their standing to maintain the action solely on their status as federal taxpayers. The appellees, who are charged by Congress with administering the Elementary and Secondary Education Act of 1965, were sued in their official capacities.

The gravamen of the appellants' complaint was that federal funds appropriated under the Act were being used to finance instruction in reading, arithmetic, and other subjects in religious schools, and to purchase textbooks and other instructional materials for use in such schools. Such expenditures were alleged to be in contravention of the Establishment and Free Exercise Clauses of the First Amendment....

Although the barrier *Frothingham* erected against federal taxpayer suits has never been breached, the decision has been the source of some confusion and the object of considerable criticism. The confusion has developed as commentators have tried to determine whether *Frothingham* establishes a constitutional bar to taxpayer suits or whether the Court was simply imposing a rule of self-restraint which was not constitutionally compelled.... The opinion delivered in *Frothingham* can be read to support either position.

[T]he judicial power of federal courts is constitutionally restricted to "cases" and "controversies." As is so often the situation in constitutional adjudication, those two words have an iceberg quality, containing beneath their surface simplicity submerged complexities which go to the very heart of our constitutional form of government. Embodied in the words "cases" and "controversies" are two complementary but somewhat different limitations. In part those words limit the business of federal courts to questions presented in an adversary context and in a form historically viewed as capable of resolution through the judicial process. And in part those words define the role assigned to the judiciary in a tripartite allocation of power to assure that the federal courts will not intrude into areas committed to the other branches of government. Justiciability is the term of art employed to give expression to this dual limitation placed upon federal courts by the case-and-controversy doctrine.... "[It] is ... not a legal concept with a fixed content or susceptible of scientific verification. Its utilization is the resultant of many subtle pressures.... "

Part of the difficulty in giving precise meaning and form to the concept of justiciability stems from the uncertain historical antecedents of the case-and-controversy doctrine. For example, Mr. Justice Frankfurter twice suggested that historical meaning could be imparted to the concepts of justiciability and case and controversy by reference to the practices of the courts of Westminster when the Constitution was adopted. *Joint Anti–Fascist Committee v. McGrath,* 341 U.S. 123, 150, 71 S.Ct. 624, 95 L.Ed. 817 (1951)(concurring opinion); *Coleman v. Miller,*

307 U.S. 433, 460, 59 S.Ct. 972, 985, 83 L.Ed. 1385 (1939)(separate opinion). However, the power of English judges to deliver advisory opinions was well established at the time the Constitution was drafted. . . .

Additional uncertainty exists in the doctrine of justiciability because that doctrine has become a blend of constitutional requirements and policy considerations. And a policy limitation is "not always clearly distinguished from the constitutional limitation." . . .

. . . The Government views [taxpayer] suits as involving no more than the mere disagreement by the taxpayer "with the uses to which tax money is put." According to the Government, the resolution of such disagreements is committed to other branches of the Federal Government and not to the judiciary. Consequently, the Government contends that, under no circumstances, should standing be conferred on federal taxpayers to challenge a federal taxing or spending program. An analysis of the function served by standing limitations compels a rejection of the Government's position.

. . . The "gist of the question of standing" is whether the party seeking relief has "alleged such a personal stake in the outcome of the controversy as to assure that concrete adverseness which sharpens the presentation of issues upon which the court so largely depends for illumination of difficult constitutional questions." *Baker v. Carr,* 369 U.S. 186, 204, 82 S.Ct. 691, 703, 7 L.Ed.2d 663 (1962). In other words, when standing is placed in issue in a case, the question is whether the person whose standing is challenged is a proper party to request an adjudication of a particular issue and not whether the issue itself is justiciable. . . .

When the emphasis in the standing problem is placed on whether the person invoking a federal court's jurisdiction is a proper party to maintain the action, the weakness of the Government's argument in this case becomes apparent. The question whether a particular person is a proper party to maintain the action does not, by its own force, raise separation of powers problems related to improper judicial interference in areas committed to other branches of the Federal Government. Such problems arise, if at all, only from the substantive issues the individual seeks to have adjudicated. Thus, in terms of Article III limitations on federal court jurisdiction, the question of standing is related only to whether the dispute sought to be adjudicated will be presented in an adversary context and in a form historically viewed as capable of judicial resolution. A taxpayer may or may not have the requisite personal stake in the outcome, depending upon the circumstances of the particular case. Therefore, we find no absolute bar in Article III to suits by federal taxpayers challenging allegedly unconstitutional federal taxing and spending programs. There remains, however, the problem of determining the circumstances under which a federal taxpayer will be deemed to have the personal stake and interest that impart the necessary concrete adverseness to such litigation so that standing can be conferred on the taxpayer *qua* taxpayer consistent with the constitutional limitations of Article III.

[I]n ruling on standing, it is both appropriate and necessary to look to the substantive issues for another purpose, namely, to determine whether there is a logical nexus between the status asserted and the claim sought to be adjudicated....

The nexus demanded of federal taxpayers has two aspects to it. First, the taxpayer must establish a logical link between that status and the type of legislative enactment attacked. Thus, a taxpayer will be a proper party to allege the unconstitutionality only of exercises of congressional power under the taxing and spending clause of Art. I, § 8, of the Constitution. It will not be sufficient to allege an incidental expenditure of tax funds in the administration of an essentially regulatory statute. This requirement is consistent with the limitation imposed upon state-taxpayer standing in federal courts in *Doremus v. Board of Education,* 342 U.S. 429, 72 S.Ct. 394, 96 L.Ed. 475 (1952). Secondly, the taxpayer must establish a nexus between that status and the precise nature of the constitutional infringement alleged. Under this requirement, the taxpayer must show that the challenged enactment exceeds specific constitutional limitations imposed upon the exercise of the congressional taxing and spending power and not simply that the enactment is generally beyond the powers delegated to Congress by Art. I, § 8. When both nexuses are established, the litigant will have shown a taxpayer's stake in the outcome of the controversy and will be a proper and appropriate party to invoke a federal court's jurisdiction.

The taxpayer-appellants in this case have satisfied both nexuses to support their claim of standing under the test we announce today. Their constitutional challenge is made to an exercise by Congress of its power under Art. I, § 8, to spend for the general welfare, and the challenged program involves a substantial expenditure of federal tax funds.[23] In addition, appellants have alleged that the challenged expenditures violate the Establishment and Free Exercise Clauses of the First Amendment. Our history vividly illustrates that one of the specific evils feared by those who drafted the Establishment Clause and fought for its adoption was that the taxing and spending power would be used to favor one religion over another or to support religion in general. James Madison, who is generally recognized as the leading architect of the religion clauses of the First Amendment, observed in his famous Memorial and Remonstrance Against Religious Assessments that "the same authority which can force a citizen to contribute three pence only of his property for the support of any one establishment, may force him to conform to any other establishment in all cases whatsoever." The concern of Madison and his supporters was quite clearly that religious liberty ultimately would be the victim if government could employ its

---

23. Almost $1,000,000,000 was appropriated to implement the Elementary and Secondary Education Act in 1965.

taxing and spending powers to aid one religion over another or to aid religion in general. The Establishment Clause was designed as a specific bulwark against such potential abuses of governmental power, and that clause of the First Amendment[25] operates as a specific constitutional limitation upon the exercise by Congress of the taxing and spending power conferred by Art. I, § 8.

The allegations of the taxpayer in *Frothingham v. Mellon,* supra, were quite different from those made in this case, and the result in *Frothingham* is consistent with the test of taxpayer standing announced today. The taxpayer in *Frothingham* attacked a federal spending program and she, therefore, established the first nexus required. However, she lacked standing because her constitutional attack was not based on an allegation that Congress, in enacting the Maternity Act of 1921, had breached a specific limitation upon its taxing and spending power. [T]he Due Process Clause of the Fifth Amendment does not protect taxpayers against increases in tax liability, and the taxpayer in *Frothingham* failed to make any additional claim that the harm she alleged resulted from a breach by Congress of the specific constitutional limitations imposed upon an exercise of the taxing and spending power. In essence, Mrs. Frothingham was attempting to assert the States' interest in their legislative prerogatives and not a federal taxpayer's interest in being free of taxing and spending in contravention of specific constitutional limitations imposed upon Congress' taxing and spending power.

We have noted that the Establishment Clause of the First Amendment does specifically limit the taxing and spending power conferred by Art. I, § 8. Whether the Constitution contains other specific limitations can be determined only in the context of future cases. However, whenever such specific limitations are found, we believe a taxpayer will have a clear stake as a taxpayer in assuring that they are not breached by Congress. Consequently, we hold that a taxpayer will have standing consistent with Article III to invoke federal judicial power when he alleges that congressional action under the taxing and spending clause is in derogation of those constitutional provisions which operate to restrict the exercise of the taxing and spending power. The taxpayer's allegation in such cases would be that his tax money is being extracted and spent in violation of specific constitutional protections against such abuses of legislative power. Such an injury is appropriate for judicial redress, and the taxpayer has established the necessary nexus between his status and

---

25. Appellants have also alleged that the Elementary and Secondary Education Act of 1965 violates the Free Exercise Clause of the First Amendment. This Court has recognized that the taxing power can be used to infringe the free exercise of religion. *Murdock v. Commonwealth of Pennsylvania,* 319 U.S. 105, 63 S.Ct. 870, 87 L.Ed. 1292 (1943). Since we hold that appellants' Establishment Clause claim is sufficient to establish the nexus between their status and the precise nature of the constitutional infringement alleged, we need not decide whether the Free Exercise claim, standing alone, would be adequate to confer standing in this case. We do note, however, that the challenged tax in *Murdock* operated upon a particular class of taxpayers. When such exercises of the taxing power are challenged, the proper party emphasis in the federal standing doctrine would require that standing be limited to the taxpayers within the affected class.

the nature of the allegedly unconstitutional action to support his claim of standing to secure judicial review. Under such circumstances, we feel confident that the questions will be framed with the necessary specificity, that the issues will be contested with the necessary adverseness and that the litigation will be pursued with the necessary vigor to assure that the constitutional challenge will be made in a form traditionally thought to be capable of judicial resolution. We lack that confidence in cases such as *Frothingham* where a taxpayer seeks to employ a federal court as a forum in which to air his generalized grievances about the conduct of government or the allocation of power in the Federal System.

While we express no view at all on the merits of appellants' claims in this case, their complaint contains sufficient allegations under the criteria we have outlined to give them standing to invoke a federal court's jurisdiction for an adjudication on the merits.

Reversed.

MR. JUSTICE DOUGLAS, concurring.

While I have joined the opinion of the Court, I do not think that the test it lays down is a durable one for the reasons stated by my Brother Harlan. I think, therefore, that it will suffer erosion and in time result in the demise of *Frothingham v. Mellon,* 262 U.S. 447, 43 S.Ct. 597, 67 L.Ed. 1078. It would therefore be the part of wisdom, as I see the problem, to be rid of *Frothingham* here and now.

I do not view with alarm, as does my Brother Harlan, the consequences of that course. *Frothingham,* decided in 1923, was in the heyday of substantive due process, when courts were sitting in judgment on the wisdom or reasonableness of legislation. [W]e no longer undertake to exercise that kind of power. Today's problem is in a different setting. Most laws passed by Congress do not contain even a ghost of a constitutional question. The "political" decisions, as distinguished from the "justiciable" ones, occupy most of the spectrum of congressional action. . . .

There has long been a school of thought here that the less the judiciary does, the better. It is often said that judicial intrusion should be infrequent, since it is "always attended with a serious evil, namely, that the correction of legislative mistakes comes from the outside, and the people thus lose the political experience, and the moral education and stimulus that come from fighting the question out in the ordinary way, and correcting their own errors"; that the effect of a participation by the judiciary in these processes is "to dwarf the political capacity of the people, and to deaden its sense of moral responsibility." J. Thayer, John Marshall 106, 107 (1901).

The late Edmond Cahn, who opposed that view, stated my philosophy. He emphasized the importance of the role that the federal judiciary was designed to play in guarding basic rights against majoritarian control. He chided the view expressed by my Brother Harlan: "we are entitled to reproach the majoritarian justices of the Supreme Court ... with straining to be reasonable when they ought to be adamant." ...

MR. JUSTICE FORTAS, concurring.

... The status of taxpayer should not be accepted as a launching pad for an attack upon any target other than legislation affecting the Establishment Clause.

MR. JUSTICE HARLAN, dissenting.

The problems presented by this case are narrow and relatively abstract, but the principles by which they must be resolved involve nothing less than the proper functioning of the federal courts, and so run to the roots of our constitutional system. The nub of my view is that the end result of *Frothingham v. Mellon,* was correct, even though, like others, I do not subscribe to all of its reasoning and premises. Although I therefore agree with certain of the conclusions reached today by the Court, I cannot accept the standing doctrine that it substitutes for *Frothingham,* for it seems to me that his new doctrine rests on premises that do not withstand analysis. Accordingly, I respectfully dissent.

... An action brought to contest the validity of tax liabilities assessed to the plaintiff is designed to vindicate interests that are personal and proprietary.... I take it that the Court, although it does not pause to examine the question, believes that the interests of those who as taxpayers challenge the constitutionality of public expenditures may, at least in certain circumstances, be similar. Yet this assumption is surely mistaken.

The complaint in this case, unlike that in *Frothingham,* contains no allegation that the contested expenditures will in any fashion affect the amount of these taxpayers' own existing or foreseeable tax obligations.... Nor are taxpayers' interests in the expenditure of public funds differentiated from those of the general public by any special rights retained by them in their tax payments. The simple fact is that no such rights can sensibly be said to exist. Taxes are ordinarily levied by the United States without limitations of purpose; absent such a limitation, payments received by the Treasury in satisfaction of tax obligations lawfully created become part of the Government's general funds. The national legislature is required by the Constitution to exercise its spending powers to "provide for the common Defence and general Welfare." Art. I, § 8, cl. 1. Whatever other implications there may be to that sweeping phrase, it surely means that the United States holds its general funds, not as stakeholder or trustee for those who have paid its imposts, but as surrogate for the population at large....

Surely it is plain that the rights and interests of taxpayers who contest the constitutionality of public expenditures are markedly different from those of "Hohfeldian" plaintiffs,[5] including those taxpayer-

---

5. The phrase is Professor Jaffe's, adopted, of course, from W. Hohfeld, Fundamental Legal Conceptions (1923). I have here employed the phrases "Hohfeldian" and "non-Hohfeldian" plaintiffs to mark the distinction between the personal and

plaintiffs who challenge the validity of their own tax liabilities. We must recognize that these non-Hohfeldian plaintiffs complain, just as the petitioner in *Frothingham* sought to complain, not as taxpayers, but as "private attorneys-general." The interests they represent, and the rights they espouse, are bereft of any personal or proprietary coloration. They are, as litigants, indistinguishable from any group selected at random from among the general population, taxpayers and nontaxpayers alike. These are and must be, to adopt Professor Jaffe's useful phrase, "public actions" brought to vindicate public rights.

[N]on–Hohfeldian plaintiffs as such are not *constitutionally* excluded from the federal courts. The problem ultimately presented by this case is, in my view, therefore to determine in what circumstances, consonant with the character and proper functioning of the federal courts, such suits should be permitted. With this preface, I shall examine the position adopted by the Court. . . .

The Court's analysis consists principally of the observation that the requirements of standing are met if a taxpayer has the "requisite personal stake in the outcome" of his suit. This does not, of course, resolve the standing problem; it merely restates it. The Court implements this standard with the declaration that taxpayers will be "deemed" to have the necessary personal interest if their suits satisfy two criteria: *first,* the challenged expenditure must form part of a federal spending program, and not merely be "incidental" to a regulatory program; and *second,* the constitutional provision under which the plaintiff claims must be a "specific limitation" upon Congress' spending powers. The difficulties with these criteria are many and severe, but it is enough for the moment to emphasize that they are not in any sense a measurement of any plaintiff's interest in the outcome of any suit. . . .

It is surely clear that a plaintiff's interest in the outcome of a suit in which he challenges the constitutionality of a federal expenditure is not made greater or smaller by the unconnected fact that the expenditure is, or is not, "incidental" to an "essentially regulatory" program. . . . His interest as taxpayer arises, if at all, from the fact of an unlawful expenditure, and not as a consequence of the expenditure's form. Apparently the Court has repudiated the emphasis in *Frothingham* upon the amount of the plaintiff's tax bill, only to substitute an equally irrelevant emphasis upon the form of the challenged expenditure.

The Court's second criterion is similarly unrelated to its standard for the determination of standing. The intensity of a plaintiff's interest in a suit is not measured, even obliquely, by the fact that the constitutional provision under which he claims is, or is not, a "specific limitation" upon Congress' spending powers. Thus, among the claims in *Frothingham* was the assertion that the Maternity Act deprived the

proprietary interests of the traditional plaintiff, and the representative and public interests of the plaintiff in a public action. I am aware that we are confronted here by a spectrum of interests of varying intensities, but the distinction is sufficiently accurate, and convenient, to warrant its use at least for purposes of discussion.

petitioner of property without due process of law. The Court has evidently concluded that this claim did not confer standing because the Due Process Clause of the Fifth Amendment is not a specific limitation upon the spending powers.[11] Disregarding for the moment the formidable obscurity of the Court's categories, how can it be said that Mrs. Frothingham's interests in her suit were, as a consequence of her choice of a constitutional claim, necessarily less intense than those, for example, of the present appellants?

. . . If this case involved a tax specifically designed for the support of religion, as was the Virginia tax opposed by Madison in his Memorial and Remonstrance, I would agree that taxpayers have rights under the religious clauses of the First Amendment that would permit them standing to challenge the tax's validity in the federal courts. But this is not such a case, and appellants challenge an expenditure, not a tax. . . .

It seems to me clear that public actions, whatever the constitutional provisions on which they are premised, may involve important hazards for the continued effectiveness of the federal judiciary. Although I believe such actions to be within the jurisdiction conferred upon the federal courts by Article III of the Constitution, there surely can be little doubt that they strain the judicial function and press to the limit judicial authority. There is every reason to fear that unrestricted public actions might well alter the allocation of authority among the three branches of the Federal Government. [S]uch actions would, even without conscious abuse, go far toward the final transformation of this Court into the Council of Revision which, despite Madison's support, was rejected by the Constitutional Convention. I do not doubt that there must be "some effectual power in the government to restrain or correct the infractions" of the Constitution's several commands, but neither can I suppose that such power resides only in the federal courts.

[T]here is available a resolution of this problem that entirely satisfies the demands of the principle of separation of powers. This Court has previously held that individual litigants have standing to represent the public interest, despite their lack of economic or other personal interests, if Congress has appropriately authorized such suits. I would adhere to that principle. Any hazards to the proper allocation of authority among the three branches of the Government would be substantially diminished if public actions had been pertinently authorized by Congress and the President. . . .

[The concurring opinion of Stewart, J., is omitted.]

Notes

1. What does *Frothingham* mean after *Flast?* Is it fair to say that all of the Justices in *Flast* agreed that plaintiffs were not barred from bringing

---

11. It should be emphasized that the Court finds it unnecessary to examine the history of the Due Process Clause to determine whether it was intended as a "specific limitation" upon Congress' spending and taxing powers. Nor does the Court pause to examine the purposes of the Tenth Amendment, another of the premises of the constitutional claims in *Frothingham*.

their taxpayer suit by Article III? If so, what is the real nature of the disagreement between Douglas on the one hand and Fortas on the other? Between Douglas and Harlan? Between Harlan and the other Justices?

2. Are there any constitutional limits to the extent to which Congress, by statute, can either expand or contract standing? After *Flast* could Congress provide by law that standing in such circumstances does not exist? Before *Flast* could Congress provide that *Flast*-type standing does exist?

3. If plaintiffs win their suit on the merits, will it result in any reduction in their tax burden, even an infinitesimal reduction? Assume that Congress enacts a tax earmarked for religious purposes, e.g., a .01% payroll tax to finance the building of a church. If plaintiffs win their suit on the merits, will it result in a reduction of their taxes? Would Harlan find standing in such a case?

4. The majority makes the point, at n. 23, that the challenged Congress appropriated nearly $1 billion to implement the challenged law. What if Congress had only appropriated "three pence"? Would plaintiffs still have standing?

Assume that the U.S. Post Office plans to issue a special postage stamp to celebrate Easter. Assume further that the Post Office is not completely self-supporting and still relies on tax dollars to make up its budget deficit. Would a taxpayer have standing to challenge, as a violation of the establishment clause, the decision to issue an Easter stamp? What if the stamp increases Post Office revenue? What if the stamp reproduces a medieval painting (already displayed in a federal museum) of the resurrection of Christ?

5. As the Court indicated in n. 25, it found taxpayer standing under the establishment clause but reserved the question of such standing under the free exercise clause. Is there any meaningful way to distinguish between these two clauses under the *Flast* test?

6. In *Doremus v. Board of Education*, 342 U.S. 429, 72 S.Ct. 394, 96 L.Ed. 475 (1952) plaintiffs sought a declaratory judgment in state court that a state statute was unconstitutional. That statute required that public school teachers read, without comment, five verses of the Old Testament at the opening of each public school day. The state supreme court held that the law was constitutional. On appeal, the U.S. Supreme Court noted that there were two types of plaintiffs, and neither had standing. One appellant was the parent of a 17 year old daughter in a high school that followed the state Bible reading statute. Her complaint did not allege that she was injured or offended in any way by the Bible reading. Moreover, "this child had graduated from the public schools before this appeal was taken to this Court." As to those parties suing in their capacity as taxpayers, there was no allegation that the Bible reading in the public schools "is supported by any separate tax or paid for from any particular appropriation or that it adds any sum whatever to the cost of conducting the school." Nor was there any allegation that the Bible reading "increases any tax they do pay or that as taxpayers they are, will, or possibly can be out of pocket because of it."

The Supreme Court found no standing and dismissed the appeal without reaching the merits. Is *Doremus* still good law after *Flast?*

Contrast *ASARCO Inc. v. Kadish,* 490 U.S. 605, 109 S.Ct. 2037, 104 L.Ed.2d 696 (1989). State taxpayers and a state teacher's association brought suit in Arizona state court arguing that a state statute governing mineral leases was unconstitutional because it was inconsistent with the federal laws that originally granted those lands to Arizona. The state supreme court ruled for plaintiffs. The Court was evenly divided on the question whether the plaintiffs met the federal requirement for standing if they had sued in a federal court.[1] Nonetheless, Kennedy, J., for the Court, joined by Brennan, White, Marshall, Blackmun, & Stevens, JJ., concluded that the U.S. Supreme Court could review the decision below. State courts are not bound by federal standing requirements because they are not Article III courts. The issue, therefore, is "whether a judgment rendered by the state courts in these circumstances can support jurisdiction in this Court to review the case." The majority argued that "the decision to be reviewed poses a serious and immediate threat to the continuing validity of those leases by virtue of its holding that they were granted under improper procedures and an invalid law." However, if the Supreme Court vacated the state court judgment on the grounds of lack of standing, it would be imposing federal standing requirements on state courts. Therefore:

> When a state court has issued a judgment in a case where plaintiffs in the original action had no standing to sue under the principles governing the federal courts, we may exercise our jurisdiction on certiorari if the judgment of the state court causes direct, specific, and concrete injury to the parties who petition for our review, where the requisites of a case or controversy are also met.
>
> We are not unmindful of the paradox that would result if respondents (plaintiffs below) prevail on the merits, for then they will have succeeded in obtaining a federal determination here that was unavailable if the action had been filed initially in federal court. Nonetheless, although federal standing "often turns on the nature and source of the claim asserted," it "in no way depends on the merits of the [claim]." The rule we adopt is necessary in deference to the States and in response to the petitioning parties who seek this forum to redress a real and current injury stemming from the application of federal law. We therefore conclude that we may properly decide this case.

The Court then affirmed the Arizona Supreme Court decision holding that the state statute governing mineral leases was in conflict with federal law and thus unconstitutional.

Rehnquist, C.J., joined by Scalia, J., concurred in part and dissented in part:

1. The plaintiffs argued that the state law deprived the school trust fund of millions of dollars, thereby resulting in higher taxes. But it was pure speculation, said Kennedy, J. (joined by Rehnquist, C.J. & Stevens & Scalia, JJ.) that the invalidation of the state law would result in any tax relief for the taxpayers, or increased money for state education: because state education is not financed solely from the school trust fund, an increase in those revenues could just as well result in the state reducing its supplement from general revenues.

Brennan, J. (joined by White, Marshall, & Blackmun, JJ.) objected both to the decision to reach the standing issue and also to the conclusion on this issue. O'Connor, J., took no part in the consideration or decision of this case.

In *Doremus,* we dismissed an appeal from state court by taxpayers because they lacked standing. The Court now says that although the *Doremus* case is good law for plaintiffs who lack standing but lost in the state court on the merits of their federal claim, it is not good law for such plaintiffs who prevailed on the merits of their federal question in the state courts. The fact that such a rule has a very one-sided application does not necessarily mean it is wrong, but it should at least require a very persuasive justification—a more persuasive one than the Court provides in its opinion.

The Court justifies the result it reaches by saying that the state court judgment adverse to petitioners is itself a form of "injury" which supplies Article III standing. The difficulty with this explanation is that petitioners—mineral lessees and defendants in the courts below—have always been able to show that a judgment adverse to their position would "injure" them in a very real sense. The defect in the state court proceedings, so far as Article III standing is concerned, was not that the proceedings did not threaten to injure the petitioners but that the operation and enforcement of the challenged statute did not injure plaintiffs-respondents. The subsequent proceedings in the state court have obviously not cured this defect....

The Court is concerned with the fact that if it applies *Doremus* as sauce for the goose as well as for the gander state courts will remain free to decide important questions of federal statutory and constitutional law without the possibility of review in this Court. This is true, but I think it a rather unremarkable proposition. Some state courts render advisory decisions on federal law of no binding force even within the State. See, e.g., Mass. Const., Art. LXXXV (amending the Massachusetts Constitution to provide that: "Each branch of the legislature, as well as the governor or the council, shall have authority to require the opinions of the justices of the supreme judicial court, upon important questions of law, and upon solemn occasions"). [T]he interpretation of federal law may affect the governance of the State and thereby make some people better off and some worse off. Yet none of these decisions of federal law are reviewable in this or any other federal court. I see no reason to fear that our dismissal of the present appeal would lead to a legal landscape in which we would no longer have the opportunity to review many important decisions on questions of federal law. Therefore I see no reason why this Court should bend its Article III jurisprudence out of shape to avoid a largely imaginary problem.

7. Since *Flast* the Court has not found that any other clause of the Constitution meets the *Flast* test. *United States v. Richardson,* 418 U.S. 166, 94 S.Ct. 2940, 41 L.Ed.2d 678 (1974) held (5 to 4) that a federal taxpayer has no standing to bring an action alleging that certain provisions concerning public reporting of expenditures under the Central Intelligence Agency Act violates Article I, § 9, cl. 7, requiring the public reporting of public moneys. The plaintiff "asks the courts to compel the Government to give him information on precisely how the CIA spends its funds. Thus there is no 'logical nexus' between the asserted status of taxpayer and the claimed failure of the Congress to require the Executive to supply a more detailed report of the expenditures of that agency."

Schlesinger v. Reservists Committee to Stop the War, 418 U.S. 208, 94 S.Ct. 2925, 41 L.Ed.2d 706 (1974) held (6 to 3) that a federal taxpayer has no standing to bring an action alleging that Article I, § 6, cl. 2—requiring that no Senator or Representative may hold any other office under the United States—made Congressmen ineligible to hold simultaneously a commission in the Armed Forces Reserve. The majority also denied standing to those who sued in their capacity as "citizens," because generalized citizen interest is not a sufficient basis for standing.

Valley Forge Christian College v. Americans United for Separation of Church and State, Inc., 454 U.S. 464, 102 S.Ct. 752, 70 L.Ed.2d 700 (1982) held (5 to 4) held that a taxpayers' organization dedicated to the separation of Church and State was without standing to challenge a transfer of surplus United States property to a religious education institution given at no cost to that religious institution. The Secretary of Defense closed a military hospital; then the General Services Administration, pursuant to statute, declared it to be "surplus property." The Department of Health, Education and Welfare then conveyed it (a 77 acre tract) to the Valley Forge Christian College. At the time of conveyance the property had an appraised value of $577,500, but the Secretary of HEW discounted that value to zero because of the Secretary's computation of a 100% public benefit allowance. The Valley Forge Christian College, a nonprofit educational school under the supervision of the Assemblies of God, has a self-described purpose is to train men and women for Christian service as either ministers or lay people. Faculty members must be "baptized in the Holy Spirit and be living consistent Christian lives."

Plaintiff sued, claiming that the transfer of property violated the Establishment Clause. The Court found no standing as taxpayers:

> First, the source of their complaint is not a congressional action, but a decision by HEW to transfer a parcel of federal property. *Flast* limited taxpayer standing to challenges directed "only [at] exercises of congressional power." Second, and perhaps redundantly, the property transfer about which respondents complain was not an exercise of authority conferred by the Taxing and Spending Clause of Art. I, § 8. The authorizing legislation, the Federal Property and Administrative Services Act of 1949, was an evident exercise of Congress' power under Art. IV, § 3, cl. 2.

The majority found no other basis for standing and explicitly noted that "the assumption that if respondents have no standing to sue, no one would have standing, is not a reason to find standing." Brennan, J., joined by Marshall & Blackmun, JJ., dissented, and said that the majority opinion "utterly fails, except by the sheerest form of *ipse dixit,* to explain why this case is unlike *Flast....* " Stevens also wrote a dissenting opinion.

Does *Valley Forge* apply to personal property? If the Federal Government gives surplus *textbooks* to parochial schools, would anyone have standing to object?

12–4. NONTAXPAYER STANDING

Persons (or associations) sue to vindicate their constitutional or statutory rights not only in their capacity as taxpayers but also in their personal capacity. Sometimes they sue (or defend) on a claim and seek to vindicate the rights of third parties. The first series of cases will explore primarily the minimum Article III requirements of standing. Then we will turn to problems of third party standing and Congressional standing. Finally, we will focus on an issue that permeates all standing cases: the extent to which the Court should erect standing barriers that are not required by Article III but are justified by policy grounds and prudential concerns.

In considering these three problem areas, seek to determine whether the Article III standing requirement is set too high or too low; whether the restrictions on third party standing should be reduced or increased; and whether the prudential limitations are principled. Finally, think about whether the standing doctrine should be discretionary or based on non-discretionary neutral principles.

12–4.1 The Requirement of "Injury in Fact" and "Causal Connection"

DUKE POWER CO. v. CAROLINA ENVIRONMENTAL STUDY GROUP, INC.
438 U.S. 59, 98 S.Ct. 2620, 57 L.Ed.2d 595 (1978).

Mr. Chief Justice Burger delivered the opinion of the Court.

These appeals present the question of whether Congress may, consistent with the Constitution, impose a limitation on liability for nuclear accidents resulting from the operation of private nuclear power plants licensed by [the Nuclear Regulatory Commission of] the Federal Government.

[Because] it [is] impossible totally to rule out the risk of a major nuclear accident Congress responded in 1957 by passing the Price–Anderson Act. The Act had the dual purpose of "protect[ing] the public and . . . encourag[ing] the development of the atomic energy industry." 42 U.S.C.A. § 2012(I). In its original form, the Act limited the aggregate liability for a single nuclear incident to $500 million plus the amount of liability insurance available on the private market—some $60 million in 1957. [T]he actual ceiling on liability was the amount of private insurance coverage plus the Government's indemnification obligation which totaled $560 million. . . .

Duke Power Co. is an investor-owned public utility which is constructing one nuclear power plant in North Carolina and one in South Carolina. Duke Power, along with the NRC, was sued by appellees, two organizations—Carolina Environmental Study Group and the Catawba Central Labor Union—and 40 individuals who live within close proximity to the planned facilities. The action was commenced in 1973, and sought, among other relief, a declaration that the Price–Anderson Act is unconstitutional. [The district] court determined that appellees had standing and . . . went on to hold that the Price–Anderson Act was unconstitutional in two respects: (a) it violated the Due Process Clause of the Fifth Amendment because it allowed injuries to occur without assuring adequate compensation to the victims; (b) the Act offended the equal protection component of the Fifth Amendment by forcing the victims of nuclear incidents to bear the burden of injury, whereas society as a whole benefits from the existence and development of nuclear power. . . .

The essence of the standing inquiry is whether the parties seeking to invoke the court's jurisdiction have "alleged such a personal stake in the outcome of the controversy as to assure that concrete adverseness which sharpens the presentation of issues upon which the court so largely depends for illumination of difficult constitutional questions." *Baker v. Carr,* [§ 1–2.4]. [T]his requirement of a "personal stake" has come to be understood to require not only a "distinct and palpable injury," to the plaintiff, but also a "fairly traceable" causal connection between the claimed injury and the challenged conduct. Application of these constitutional standards to the factual findings of the District Court persuades us that the Art. III requisites for standing are satisfied by appellees.

We turn first to consider the kinds of injuries the District Court found the appellees suffered. It discerned two categories of effects which resulted from the operation of nuclear power plants in potentially dangerous proximity to appellees' living and working environment. The immediate effects included: (a) the production of small quantities of non-natural radiation which would invade the air and water; (b) a "sharp increase" in the temperature of two lakes presently used for recreational purposes resulting from the use of the lake waters to produce steam and to cool the reactor; (c) interference with the normal use of the waters of the Catawba River; (d) threatened reduction in property values of land neighboring the power plants; (e) "objectively reasonable" present fear and apprehension regarding the "effect of the increased radioactivity in air, land and water upon [appellees] and their property, and the genetic effects upon their descendants"; and (f) the continual threat of "an accident resulting in uncontrolled release of large or even small quantities of radioactive material" with no assurance of adequate compensation for the resultant damage. Into a second category of potential effects were placed the damages "which may result from a core melt or other major accident in the operation of a reactor. . . . "

[W]e need not determine whether all the putative injuries identified by the District Court, particularly those based on the possibility of a nuclear accident and the present apprehension generated by this future uncertainty, are sufficiently concrete to satisfy constitutional requirements. It is enough that several of the "immediate" adverse effects were found to harm appellees. Certainly the environmental and aesthetic consequences of the thermal pollution of the two lakes in the vicinity of the disputed power plants is the type of harmful effect which has been deemed adequate in prior cases to satisfy the "injury in fact" standard. And the emission of non-natural radiation into appellees' environment would also seem a direct and present injury, given our generalized concern about exposure to radiation and the apprehension flowing from the uncertainty about the health and genetic consequences of even small emissions like those concededly emitted by nuclear power plants.

The more difficult step in the standing inquiry is establishing that these injuries "fairly can be traced to the challenged action of the defendant," *Simon v. Eastern Ky. Welfare Rights Org.*, 426 U.S. 26, 41, 96 S.Ct. 1917, 1926, 48 L.Ed.2d 450 (1976), or put otherwise, that the exercise of the Court's remedial powers would redress the claimed injuries. The District Court discerned a "but for" causal connection between the Price–Anderson Act, which appellees challenged as unconstitutional, "and the construction of the nuclear plants which the [appellees] view as a threat to them." Particularizing that causal link to the facts of the instant case, the District Court concluded that "there is a substantial likelihood that Duke would not be able to complete the construction and maintain the operation of the McGuire and Catawba Nuclear Plants but for the protection provided by the Price–Anderson Act."

These findings, which, if accepted, would likely satisfy the second prong of the constitutional test for standing as elaborated in *Simon*,[20] are challenged on two grounds. First, it is argued that the evidence presented at the hearing, contrary to the conclusion reached by the District Court, indicated that the McGuire and Catawba nuclear plants would be completed and operated without the Price–Anderson Act's limitation on liability....

The District Court's finding of a "substantial likelihood" that the McGuire and Catawba nuclear plants would be neither completed nor operated absent the Price–Anderson Act rested in major part on the testimony of corporate officials before the Joint Committee on Atomic Energy (JCAE) in 1956–1957 when the Price–Anderson Act was first considered and again in 1975 when a second renewal was discussed. [I]ndustry spokesmen for the utilities and the producers of the various component parts of the power plants expressed a categorical unwillingness to participate in the development of nuclear power absent guarantees of a limitation on their liability.... Considering the documentary evidence and the testimony in the record, we cannot say we are left with "the definite and firm conviction that" the finding by the trial court of a substantial likelihood that the McGuire and Catawba nuclear power plants would be neither completed nor operated absent the Price–Anderson Act is clearly erroneous; and hence, we are bound to accept it.

The second attack on the District Court's finding of a causal link warrants only brief attention. Essentially the argument is, as we understand it, that Price–Anderson is not a "but for" cause of the injuries appellees claim since, if Price–Anderson had not been passed, the Gov-

---

20. Our recent cases have required no more than a showing that there is a "substantial likelihood" that the relief requested will redress the injury claimed to satisfy the second prong of the constitutional standing requirement.

ernment would have undertaken development of nuclear power on its own and the same injuries would likely have accrued to appellees from such Government-operated plants as from privately operated ones. Whatever the ultimate accuracy of this speculation, it is not responsive to the simple proposition that private power companies now do in fact operate the nuclear-powered generating plants injuring appellees, and that their participation would not have occurred but for the enactment and implementation of the Price–Anderson Act. Nothing in our prior cases requires a party seeking to invoke federal jurisdiction to negate the kind of speculative and hypothetical possibilities suggested in order to demonstrate the likely effectiveness of judicial relief.

It is further contended that in addition to proof of injury and of a causal link between such injury and the challenged conduct, appellees must demonstrate a connection between the injuries they claim and the constitutional rights being asserted. This nexus requirement is said to find its origin in *Flast v. Cohen,* where the general question of taxpayer standing was considered:

> The nexus demanded of federal taxpayers has two aspects to it. First, the taxpayer must establish a logical link between that status and the type of legislative enactment attacked. . . . Secondly, the taxpayer must establish a nexus between that status and the precise nature of the constitutional infringement alleged.

Since the environmental and health injuries claimed by appellees are not directly related to the constitutional attack on the Price–Anderson Act, such injuries, the argument continues, cannot supply a predicate for standing.[23] We decline to accept this argument. [I]t implicitly assumes that the nexus requirement formulated in the context of taxpayer suits has general applicability in suits of all other types brought in the federal courts. No cases have been cited outside the context of taxpayer suits where we have demanded this type of subject-matter nexus between the right asserted and the injury alleged, and we are aware of none. Instead, in *Schlesinger v. Reservists Comm. to Stop the War,* [§ 12–3, supra], we explicitly rejected such a broad compass for the *Flast* nexus requirement:

> Looking "to the substantive issues" which *Flast* stated to be both "appropriate and necessary" in relation to taxpayer standing was for the express purpose of determining "whether there is a logical nexus between the [taxpayer] status asserted and the claim sought to be adjudicated." This step is not appropriate on a claim of citizen standing since the *Flast* nexus test is not applicable where the taxing and spending power is not challenged. . . .

We continue to be of the same view and cannot accept the contention that, outside the context of taxpayers' suits, a litigant must demonstrate anything more than injury in fact and a substantial likelihood that the

---

23. The only injury that would possess the required subject-matter nexus to the due process challenge is the injury that would result from a nuclear accident causing damages in excess of the liability limitation provisions of the Price–Anderson Act.

judicial relief requested will prevent or redress the claimed injury to satisfy the "case or controversy" requirement of Art. III.[25]

Our prior cases have, however, acknowledged "other limits on the class of persons who may invoke the courts' decisional and remedial powers," which derive from general prudential concerns "about the proper—and properly limited—role of the courts in a democratic society." Thus, we have declined to grant standing where the harm asserted amounts only to a generalized grievance shared by a large number of citizens in a substantially equal measure. See *United States v. Richardson,* supra. We have also narrowly limited the circumstances in which one party will be given standing to assert the legal rights of another....

There are good and sufficient reasons for this prudential limitation on standing when rights of third parties are implicated—the avoidance of the adjudication of rights which those not before the Court may not wish to assert, and the assurance that the most effective advocate of the rights at issue is present to champion them. We do not, however, find these reasons a satisfactory predicate for applying this limitation or a similar nexus requirement to all cases as a matter of course. Where a party champions his own rights, and where the injury alleged is a concrete and particularized one which will be prevented or redressed by the relief requested, the basic practical and prudential concerns underlying the standing doctrine are generally satisfied when the constitutional requisites are met.

We conclude that appellees have standing to challenge the constitutionality of the Price–Anderson Act.

The question of the ripeness of the constitutional challenges raised by appellees need not long detain us. To the extent that "issues of ripeness involve, at least in part, the existence of a live 'Case or Controversy,'" our conclusion that appellees will sustain immediate injury from the operation of the disputed power plants and that such injury would be redressed by the relief requested would appear to satisfy this requirement.

The prudential considerations embodied in the ripeness doctrine also argue strongly for a prompt resolution of the claims presented. Although it is true that no nuclear accident has yet occurred and that such an occurrence would eliminate much of the existing scientific uncertainty surrounding this subject, it would not, in our view, significantly advance our ability to deal with the legal issues presented nor aid us in their resolution. However, delayed resolution of these issues would foreclose any relief from the present injury suffered by appellees—relief that would be forthcoming if they were to prevail in their various challenges to the Act. Similarly, delayed resolution would frustrate one of the key purposes of the Price–Anderson Act—the elimination of

---

25. Both at the time of its formulation, see *Flast v. Cohen* (Harlan, J., dissenting), and more recently, see *United States v. Richardson* (Powell, J., concurring), there have been questions as to whether the nexus requirement, even in the context of taxpayers' suits, is constitutionally mandated or is instead simply a prudential limitation.

doubts concerning the scope of private liability in the event of major nuclear accident. In short, all parties would be adversely affected by a decision to defer definitive resolution of the constitutional validity *vel non* of the Price–Anderson Act. Since we are persuaded that "we will be in no better position later than we are now" to decide this question, we hold that it is presently ripe for adjudication. . . .

[The Court went on to find no violation of due process or equal protection.]

MR. JUSTICE STEVENS, concurring in the judgment.

The string of contingencies that supposedly holds this litigation together is too delicate for me. We are told that but for the Price–Anderson Act there would be no financing of nuclear power plants, no development of those plants by private parties, and hence no present injury to persons such as appellees; we are then asked to remedy an alleged due process violation that may possibly occur at some uncertain time in the future, and may possibly injure the appellees in a way that has no significant connection with any present injury. It is remarkable that such a series of speculations is considered sufficient either to make this litigation ripe for decision or to establish appellees' standing.[1] . . .

The Court's opinion will serve the national interest in removing doubts concerning the constitutionality of the Price–Anderson Act. I cannot, therefore, criticize the statesmanship of the Court's decision to provide the country with an advisory opinion on an important subject. [But we] are not statesmen; we are judges. When it is necessary to resolve a constitutional issue in the adjudication of an actual case or controversy, it is our duty to do so. But whenever we are persuaded by reasons of expediency to engage in the business of giving legal advice, we chip away a part of the foundation of our independence and our strength. . . .

[The concurring opinion of REHNQUIST, J. & the opinion concurring in the result of STEWART J., are omitted.]

Notes

1. In *Association of Data Processing Service Organizations, Inc. v. Camp*, 397 U.S. 150, 90 S.Ct. 827, 25 L.Ed.2d 184 (1970), sellers of data processing services to businesses sued the Comptroller of the Currency because he had issued a ruling allowing national banks to make data processing services available to other banks and bank customers. Douglas, J., for the Court, found standing and fashioned a new two-pronged test. "The first question is whether the plaintiff alleges that the challenged action has caused him injury in fact, economic or otherwise." Petitioners met this test because the Comptroller's ruling, by allowing the bank competition, might

---

1. With respect to whether appellees' claim of present injury is sufficient to establish standing, it should be noted that some sort of financing is essential to almost all projects, public or private. Statutes that facilitate and may be essential to the financing abound—from tax statutes to statutes prohibiting fraudulent securities transactions. One would not assume, however, that mere neighbors have standing to litigate the legality of a utility's financing.

entail some future loss of profits. Second, it must be determined "whether the interest sought to be protected by the complainant is arguably within the zone of interests to be protected or regulated by the statute or constitutional guarantee in question." Without deciding the merits, the Court held that the relevant section of the act *arguably* brought a competitor within the zone of interests protected by it. Further supporting the finding of standing was the fact that a statute was involved. "Where statutes are concerned, the trend is toward enlargement of the class of people who may protest administrative action." And there was no evidence that Congress sought to preclude judicial review in favor of administrative discretion.

That same day, in *Barlow v. Collins,* 397 U.S. 159, 90 S.Ct. 832, 25 L.Ed.2d 192 (1970), the Court, again through Justice Douglas, held that tenant farmers eligible for payments under a cotton program enacted as part of the Food and Agriculture Act have standing to challenge the validity of an amended regulation. The farmers had a personal stake in the amended regulation, which caused them injury in fact, and they were arguably within the zone of interests protected by the Act, which does not preclude judicial review.

Brennan, J., joined by White, J., concurred in the result but dissented to the reasoning. In their view Douglas' two step analysis was unnecessary. It should only be necessary for plaintiff to allege injury in fact.

In *Sierra Club v. Morton,* 405 U.S. 727, 92 S.Ct. 1361, 31 L.Ed.2d 636 (1972), the Court (4 to 3) held that the Sierra Club did not have standing to contest a proposed development in the Mineral King Valley. The allegation that the proposed road through the National Park "would destroy or otherwise adversely affect the scenery, natural and historic objects and wildlife in the park and impair the enjoyment of the park for future generations" amounts to injury in fact. But the flaw in the Sierra Club complaint was that the Sierra Club did not allege that it or its members would be affected in any of their aesthetic or environmental activities by the development. The Sierra Club on remand could amend its complaint to make the necessary allegations.

Three Justices dissented and would have allowed standing. Douglas' dissent argued that the Court should allow "environmental issues to be litigated before federal agencies or federal courts in the name of the inanimate object about to be despoiled . . . and where injury is the subject of public outrage."

In *United States v. Students Challenging Regulatory Agency Procedures (SCRAP),* 412 U.S. 669, 93 S.Ct. 2405, 37 L.Ed.2d 254 (1973), SCRAP (an unincorporated association of five law students) sued to enjoin the ICC from allowing the railroads to collect a 2½% surcharge. SCRAP alleged that each of its members "suffered economic, recreational and aesthetic harm directly as a result of the adverse environmental impact of the railroad freight structure, as modified by the Commission's actions. . . . " Among other things, the air that SCRAP members breath, it was alleged, suffered increased pollution caused by the modified rate structure. The majority explained that "standing is not to be denied simply because many people suffer the same injury." Even though there is an "attenuated line of causation to the eventual injury of which the appellees complained," there was at least an "identifiable trifle" that justified the standing. Plaintiff at trial still had to prove its allegations and chain of events, but the allegations were enough for standing. "Of course, pleadings must be something more than an ingenious academic exercise in the conceivable."

2.   In finding standing in *Duke Power,* did the majority use the two prong test of *Association of Data Processing Serv. Organizations v. Camp,* or is it using some other test?

After *United States v. SCRAP* was the finding of standing in *Duke Power* inevitable, or could you distinguish the cases?

3.   Do you find the majority or concurring opinions in *Duke Power* more persuasive? If the Court had invalidated the statutory limitation on liability for a nuclear accident, could Duke Power Co. nonetheless go ahead and, consistently with the Court's decision, construct the nuclear reactor? Would the environmental and aesthetic consequences of the nuclear reactor exist, notwithstanding the invalidity of the federal statute? Was it necessary for Duke Power Co. to even be a defendant party to this action?

4.   Assume a state law provides that men cannot purchase liquor until they reach 21 but women can purchase it at 18. A man who is 18 sues, claiming that the statutory classification violates the equal protection guarantees of the Fourteenth Amendment. Do not consider whether he is right on the merits, but only the issue of standing. The state argues that if the law is invalidated the legislature could raise the age for both males and females to 21, and then the male plaintiff would be no better off. Does the male have standing? Cf. *Craig v. Boren,* § 8–2.41.

Assume a male challenges a state statute requiring husbands (but not wives) to pay alimony to needy former spouses. The male plaintiff presently is forced to pay alimony to his needy former wife. If the plaintiff's claim were upheld, the state could force spouses to pay alimony to their needy former spouses without regard to sex and the male plaintiff would still have to pay alimony. So he would be no better off. Does he have standing? See *Orr v. Orr,* 440 U.S. 268, 99 S.Ct. 1102, 59 L.Ed.2d 306 (1979).

12–4.2 Third Party Standing

SINGLETON v. WULFF
428 U.S. 106, 96 S.Ct. 2868, 49 L.Ed.2d 826 (1976).

MR. JUSTICE BLACKMUN delivered the opinion of the Court (Parts I, II–A, and III) together with an opinion (Part II–B) in which MR. JUSTICE BRENNAN, MR. JUSTICE WHITE, and MR. JUSTICE MARSHALL joined.

[T]his case involves a claim of a State's unconstitutional interference with the decision to terminate pregnancy. The particular object of the challenge is a Missouri statute excluding abortions that are not "medically indicated" from the purposes for which Medicaid benefits are available to needy persons. In its present posture, however, the case presents two issues not going to the merits of this dispute. The first is whether the plaintiff-appellees, as physicians who perform nonmedically indicated abortions, have standing to maintain the suit, to which we answer that they do. The second is whether the Court of Appeals, exercising jurisdiction because the suit had been dismissed in the District Court for lack of standing, properly proceeded to a determination of the merits, to which we answer that it did not. . . .

II

Although we are not certain that they have been clearly separated in the District Court's and Court of Appeals' opinions, two distinct standing questions are presented. We have distinguished them in prior cases, and they are these: First, whether the plaintiff-respondents allege "injury in fact," that is, a sufficiently concrete interest in the outcome of their suit to make it a case or controversy subject to a federal court's Art. III jurisdiction, and, second, whether, as a prudential matter, the plaintiff-respondents are proper proponents of the particular legal rights on which they base their suit.

A. The first of these questions needs little comment, [because] the respondent-physicians suffer concrete injury from the operation of the challenged statute. . . . If the physicians prevail in their suit to remove this limitation, they will benefit, for they will then receive payment for the abortions. The State (and Federal Government) will be out of pocket by the amount of the payments. The relationship between the parties is classically adverse, and there clearly exists between them a case or controversy in the constitutional sense.

B. The question of what rights the doctors may assert in seeking to resolve that controversy is more difficult. The Court of Appeals adverted to what it perceived to be the doctor's own "constitutional rights to practice medicine." We have no occasion to decide whether such rights exist. Assuming that they do, the doctors, of course, can assert them. It appears, however, that the Court of Appeals also accorded the doctors standing to assert, and indeed granted them relief based partly upon, the rights of their patients. We must decide whether this assertion of *jus tertii* was a proper one.

Federal courts must hesitate before resolving a controversy, even one within their constitutional power to resolve, on the basis of the rights of third persons not parties to the litigation. The reasons are two. First, the courts should not adjudicate such rights unnecessarily, and it may be that in fact the holders of those rights either do not wish to assert them, or will be able to enjoy them regardless of whether the in-court litigant is successful or not. See *Ashwander v. TVA,* 297 U.S. 288, 345–348, 56 S.Ct. 466, 482–83, 80 L.Ed. 688 (1936)(Brandeis, J., concurring)(offering the standing requirement as one means by which courts avoid unnecessary constitutional adjudications). Second, third parties themselves usually will be the best proponents of their own rights. The courts depend on effective advocacy, and therefore should prefer to construe legal rights only when the most effective advocates of those rights are before them. The holders of the rights may have a like preference, to the extent they will be bound by the courts' decisions under the doctrine of *stare decisis.* These two considerations underlie the

Court's general rule: "Ordinarily, one may not claim standing in this Court to vindicate the constitutional rights of some third party." *Barrows v. Jackson,* 346 U.S., at 255, 73 S.Ct. at 1034.

Like any general rule, however, this one should not be applied where its underlying justifications are absent. With this in mind, the Court has looked primarily to two factual elements to determine whether the rule should apply in a particular case. The first is the relationship of the litigant to the person whose right he seeks to assert. If the enjoyment of the right is inextricably bound up with the activity the litigant wishes to pursue, the court at least can be sure that its construction of the right is not unnecessary in the sense that the right's enjoyment will be unaffected by the outcome of the suit. Furthermore, the relationship between the litigant and the third party may be such that the former is fully, or very nearly, as effective a proponent of the right as the latter. Thus in *Griswold v. Connecticut,* [§ 8–3.42, supra], where two persons had been convicted of giving advice on contraception, the Court permitted the defendants, one of whom was a licensed physician, to assert the privacy rights of the married persons whom they advised. The Court pointed to the "confidential" nature of the relationship between the defendants and the married persons, and reasoned that the rights of the latter were "likely to be diluted or adversely affected" if they could not be asserted in such a case. See also *Barrows v. Jackson* (owner of real estate subject to racial covenant granted standing to challenge such covenant in part because she was "the one in whose charge and keeping repose[d] the power to continue to use her property to discriminate or to discontinue such use"). A doctor-patient relationship similar to that in *Griswold* existed in *Doe v. Bolton,* where the Court also permitted physicians to assert the rights of their patients. 410 U.S., at 188–189. Indeed, since that right was the right to an abortion, *Doe* would flatly control the instant case were it not for the fact that there the physicians were seeking protection from possible criminal prosecution.

The other factual element to which the Court has looked is the ability of the third party to assert his own right. Even where the relationship is close, the reasons for requiring persons to assert their own rights will generally still apply. If there is some genuine obstacle to such assertion, however, the third party's absence from court loses its tendency to suggest that his right is not truly at stake, or truly important to him, and the party who is in court becomes by default the right's best available proponent. Thus, in *NAACP v. Alabama,* 357 U.S. 449, 78 S.Ct. 1163, 2 L.Ed.2d 1488 (1958), the Court held that the National Association for the Advancement of Colored People, in resisting a court order that it divulge the names of its members, could assert the First and Fourteenth Amendment rights of those members to remain anonymous. The Court reasoned that "[t]o require that [the right] be claimed by the members themselves would result in nullification of the right at the very moment of its assertion."[6]

6. Mr. Justice Powell objects that such   an obstacle is not enough, that our prior

Application of these principles to the present case quickly yields its proper result. The closeness of the relationship is patent, as it was in *Griswold* and in *Doe* . . . . Aside from the woman herself, therefore, the physician is uniquely qualified to litigate the constitutionality of the State's interference with, or discrimination against, [the abortion] decision.

As to the woman's assertion of her own rights, there are several obstacles. For one thing, she may be chilled from such assertion by a desire to protect the very privacy of her decision from the publicity of a court suit. A second obstacle is the imminent mootness, at least in the technical sense, of any individual woman's claim. . . . It is true that these obstacles are not insurmountable. Suit may be brought under a pseudonym, as so frequently has been done. A woman who is no longer pregnant may nonetheless retain the right to litigate the point because it is " 'capable of repetition yet evading review.' "And it may be that a class could be assembled, whose fluid membership always included some women with live claims. But if the assertion of the right is to be "representative" to such an extent anyway, there seems little loss in terms of effective advocacy from allowing its assertion by a physician.

For these reasons, we conclude that it generally is appropriate to allow a physician to assert the rights of women patients as against governmental interference with the abortion decision . . .

III

On this record, we do not agree, however, with the action of the Court of Appeals in proceeding beyond the issue of standing to a resolution of the merits of the case. [T]he case is remanded with directions that it be returned to the District Court so that petitioner may file an answer to the complaint and the litigation proceed accordingly.

It is so ordered.

Mr. Justice Stevens, concurring in part.

In this case (1) the plaintiff-physicians have a financial stake in the outcome of the litigation, and (2) they claim that the statute impairs their own constitutional rights. They therefore clearly have standing to bring this action. . . . Because I am not sure whether the analysis in Part II–B would, or should, sustain the doctors' standing, apart from those two facts, I join only Parts I, II–A, and III of the Court's opinion.

Mr. Justice Powell, with whom The Chief Justice [Burger], Mr. Justice Stewart, and Mr. Justice Rehnquist join, concurring in part and dissenting in part. . . .

cases allow assertion of third-party rights only when such assertion by the third parties themselves would be "in all practicable terms impossible." Carefully analyzed, our cases do not go that far. The Negro real-estate purchaser in *Barrows,* if he could prove that the racial covenant alone stood in the way of his purchase (as presumably he could easily have done, given the amicable posture of the seller in that case), could surely have sought a declaration of its invalidity or an injunction against its enforcement. The Association members in *NAACP v. Alabama* could have obtained a similar declaration or injunction, suing anonymously by the use of pseudonyms. . . .

As the Court notes, respondents by complaint and affidavit established their Art. III standing [because they] have performed abortions for which Missouri's Medicaid system would compensate them directly if the challenged statutory scheme did not preclude it. . . . Beyond this question, however, lies the further and less easily defined inquiry of whether it is prudent to proceed to decision on particular issues even at the instance of a party whose Art. III standing is clear. This inquiry has taken various forms, including the one presented by this case: whether, in defending against or anticipatorily attacking state action, a party may argue that it contravenes someone else's constitutional rights.

This second inquiry is a matter of "judicial self-governance." The usual—and wise—stance of the federal courts when policing their own exercise of power in this manner is one of cautious reserve. This caution has given rise to the general rule that a party may not defend against or attack governmental action on the ground that it infringes the rights of some third party, and to the corollary that any exception must rest on specific factors outweighing the policies behind the rule itself.

The plurality acknowledges this general rule, but identifies "two factual elements"—thought to be derived from prior cases—that justify the adjudication of the asserted third-party rights: (I) obstacles to the assertion by the third party of her own rights, and (ii) the existence of some "relationship" such as the one between physician and patient. In my view these factors do not justify allowing these physicians to assert their patients' rights. . . .

The plurality purports to derive from [our prior] cases the principle that a party may assert another's rights if there is "some genuine obstacle" to the third party's own litigation. But this understates the teaching of those cases: On their facts they indicate that such an assertion is proper, not when there is merely some "obstacle" to the rightholder's own litigation but when such litigation is in all practicable terms impossible. Thus, in its framing of this principle, the plurality has gone far beyond our major precedents.

Moreover, on the plurality's own statement of this principle and on its own discussion of the facts, the litigation of third-party rights cannot be justified in this case. The plurality virtually concedes, as it must, that the two alleged "obstacles" to the women's assertion of their rights are chimerical. Our docket regularly contains cases in which women, using pseudonyms, challenge statutes that allegedly infringe their right to exercise the abortion decision. Nor is there basis for the "obstacle" of incipient mootness when the plurality itself [admits] no such obstacle exists. In short, in light of experience which we share regularly in reviewing appeals and petitions for certiorari the "obstacles" identified by the plurality as justifying departure from the general rule simply are not significant. . . .

The plurality places primary reliance on a second element, the existence of a "confidential relationship" between the rightholder and the party seeking to assert her rights. . . .

With all respect, I do not read [our prior] cases as merging the physician and his patient for constitutional purposes. The principle they support turns not upon the confidential nature of a physician-patient relationship but upon the nature of the State's impact upon that relationship. In each instance the State directly interdicted the normal functioning of the physician-patient relationship by criminalizing certain procedures. In the circumstances of direct interference, I agree that one party to the relationship should be permitted to assert the constitutional rights of the other, for a judicial rule of self-restraint should not preclude an attack on a State's proscription of constitutionally protected activity. But Missouri has not directly interfered with the abortion decision—neither the physicians nor their patients are forbidden to engage in the procedure. The only impact of § 208.152(12) is that, because of the way Missouri chose to structure its Medicaid payments, it causes these doctors financial detriment. This affords them Art. III standing because they aver injury in fact, but it does not justify abandonment of the salutary rule against assertion of third-party rights.

The physicians have offered no special reason for allowing them to assert their patients' rights in an attack on this welfare statute, and I can think of none. Moreover, there are persuasive reasons not to permit them to do so. It seems wholly inappropriate, as a matter of judicial self-governance, for a court to reach unnecessarily to decide a difficult constitutional issue in a case in which nothing more is at stake than remuneration for professional services. And second, this case may well set a precedent that will prove difficult to cabin. No reason immediately comes to mind, after today's holding, why any provider of services should be denied standing to assert his client's or customer's constitutional rights, if any, in an attack on a welfare statute that excludes from coverage his particular transaction.[7] . . .

Notes

1. Does the dissent argue that allowing third party standing is inconsistent with the requirements of Article III? Wherein lies the disagreement? Which of the opinions in *Singleton* do you find the most persuasive?

2. Assume that a state imposes a six-month residency requirement as a prerequisite for an indigent to obtain a state financed abortion under the state welfare laws. Should a pregnant woman (not an indigent and not a resident for the prior six months) have standing to claim that the law is unconstitutional? Should the husband of an indigent pregnant woman who has not been resident for six months have standing to claim that the law is unconstitutional?

3. *Broadrick v. Oklahoma*, 413 U.S. 601, 93 S.Ct. 2908, 37 L.Ed.2d 830 (1973) upheld the constitutionality of a state law that prohibited partisan

---

7. . . . The ease with which the plurality would allow assertion of such standing in this case—based on nothing more substantial than a professional (or perhaps only an abortion-clinic) relationship and dimly perceived "obstacles" to the rightholder's own litigation—suggests that "the proper result" usually will be third-party standing. . . .

political activities by the state's classified civil servants. The appellants were charged with "patent violations" of the state law in that they actively participated in the reelection of their superior and asked for similar assistance from the other employees. Such conduct was obviously prohibited by section 818 of the statute and was not constitutionally protected under the First Amendment. But appellants claimed that the statute is overbroad—

> and must therefore be struck down on its face and held to be incapable of any constitutional application. We do not believe that the overbreadth doctrine may appropriately be invoked in this manner here....
>
> It has long been recognized that the First Amendment needs breathing space and that statutes attempting to restrict or burden the exercise of First Amendment rights must be narrowly drawn and represent a considered legislative judgment that a particular mode of expression has to give way to other compelling needs of society. As a corollary, the Court has altered its traditional rules of standing to permit—in the First Amendment area—"attacks on overly broad statutes with no requirement that the person making the attack demonstrate that his own conduct could not be regulated by a statute drawn with the requisite narrow specificity." Litigants, therefore, are permitted to challenge a statute not because their own rights of free expression are violated, but because of a judicial prediction or assumption that the statute's very existence may cause others not before the court to refrain from constitutionally protected speech or expression.... Application of the overbreadth doctrine in this manner is, manifestly, strong medicine. It has been employed by the Court sparingly and only as a last resort. Facial overbreadth has not been invoked when a limiting construction has been or could be placed on the challenged statute. [T]he plain import of our cases is, at the very least, that facial overbreadth adjudication is an exception to our traditional rules of practice and that its function, a limited one at the outset, attenuates as the otherwise unprotected behavior that it forbids the State to sanction moves from "pure speech" toward conduct and that conduct—even if expressive— falls within the scope of otherwise valid criminal laws that reflect legitimate state interests in maintaining comprehensive controls over harmful, constitutionally unprotected conduct. Although such laws, if too broadly worded, may deter protected speech to some unknown extent, there comes a point where that effect—at best a prediction— cannot, with confidence, justify invalidating a statute on its face and so prohibiting a State from enforcing the statute against conduct that is admittedly within its power to proscribe. To put the matter another way, particularly where conduct and not merely speech is involved, we believe that the overbreadth of a statute must not only be real, but substantial as well, judged in relation to the statute's plainly legitimate sweep. It is our view that § 818 is not substantially overbroad and that whatever overbreadth may exist should be cured through case-by-case analysis of the fact situations to which its sanctions, assertedly, may not be applied.

Lewis v. City of New Orleans, 415 U.S. 130, 94 S.Ct. 970, 39 L.Ed.2d 214 (1974), invalidated a Louisiana statute that provided: "It shall be unlawful and a breach of the peace for any person wantonly to curse or revile or to use obscene or opprobrious language toward or with reference to any member of the city police while in the actual performance of his duty." The statute was unconstitutional on its face because, as construed by the state court, it could apply to speech that, although vulgar or offensive, is protected free speech. "In that circumstance it is immaterial whether the words appellant used might be punishable under a properly limited statute or construction." *City of Houston v. Hill,* 482 U.S. 451, 107 S.Ct. 2502, 96 L.Ed.2d 398 (1987), invalidated, as overbroad, a municipal ordinance making it a crime "to interrupt any policeman in the execution of his duty." The ordinance punished only spoken words and was not limited to "fighting words" (see § 10–4), or even obscene or opprobrious language. The law had been used to arrest people for "yelling," "refusing to remain silent," "cursing," etc. But the "freedom of individuals verbally to oppose or challenge police action without thereby risking arrest is one of the principal characteristics by which we distinguish a free nation from a police state." The ordinance's "plain language" is "admittedly violated scores of times daily, yet only some individuals—those chosen by the police in their unguided discretion—are arrested."

12–4.3 *Congressional Standing*

RAINES v. BYRD
521 U.S. 811, 117 S.Ct. 2312, 138 L.Ed.2d 849 (1997)

CHIEF JUSTICE REHNQUIST delivered the opinion of the Court.*

The District Court for the District of Columbia declared the Line Item Veto Act unconstitutional. On this direct appeal, we hold that appellees lack standing to bring this suit, and therefore direct that the judgment of the District Court be vacated and the complaint dismissed.

The appellees are six Members of Congress, four of whom served as Senators and two of whom served as Congressmen in the 104th Congress (1995–1996). [They all voted "nay" when both Houses passed the Line Item Veto Act.] On April 4, 1996, the President signed the Line Item Veto Act (Act) into law [and it] went into effect on January 1, 1997. The next day, appellees [sued] the Secretary of the Treasury and the Director of the Office of Management and Budget, alleging that the Act was unconstitutional. [The provisions of this law, which do not use the term "veto," authorize the President to "cancel" certain spending and tax benefit measures after he has signed them into law. Then, Congress may consider the President's "disapproved" bills and take action to render his cancellation "null and void."]

The Act provides that "[a]ny Member of Congress or any individual adversely affected by [this Act] may bring an action, in the United States District Court for the District of Columbia, for declaratory judgment and injunctive relief on the ground that any provision of this part violates the Constitution." Appellees [claim] that the Act "unconstitutionally expands the President's power," and "violates the requirements of

---

* Justice GINSBURG joins this opinion.

bicameral passage and presentment by granting to the President, acting alone, the authority to 'cancel' and thus repeal provisions of federal law.'' They alleged that the Act injured them ''directly and concretely . . . in their official capacities'' in three ways:

> ''The Act . . . (a) alter[s] the legal and practical effect of all votes they may cast on bills containing such separately vetoable items, (b) divest[s] the [appellees] of their constitutional role in the repeal of legislation, and (c) alter[s] the constitutional balance of powers between the Legislative and Executive Branches, both with respect to measures containing separately vetoable items and with respect to other matters coming before Congress.''

[T]he District Court (i) denied appellants' motion to dismiss, holding that appellees had standing to bring this suit and that their claim was ripe, and (ii) granted appellees' summary judgment motion, holding that the Act is unconstitutional. As to standing, the court noted that the Court of Appeals for the District of Columbia ''has repeatedly recognized Members' standing to challenge measures that affect their constitutionally prescribed lawmaking powers.'' . . . We now hold that appellees have no standing to bring this suit, and therefore direct that the judgment of the District Court be vacated and the complaint dismissed.

Under Article III, § 2 of the Constitution, the federal courts have jurisdiction over this dispute between appellants and appellees only if it is a ''case'' or ''controversy.'' This is a ''bedrock requirement.'' . . .

One element of the case-or-controversy requirement is that appellees, based on their complaint, must establish that they have standing to sue . . . . . To meet the standing requirements of Article III, ''[a] plaintiff must allege *personal injury* fairly traceable to the defendant's allegedly unlawful conduct and likely to be redressed by the requested relief.'' For our purposes, the italicized words in this quotation . . . are the key ones. We have consistently stressed that a plaintiff's complaint must establish that he has a ''personal stake'' in the alleged dispute, and that the alleged injury suffered is particularized as to him. . . .

We have always insisted on strict compliance with this jurisdictional standing requirement. See, *e.g, Muskrat v. United States* (1911)[Casebook, § 1–2.3]. And our standing inquiry has been especially rigorous when reaching the merits of the dispute would force us to decide whether an action taken by one of the other two branches of the Federal Government was unconstitutional. [The] ''law of Art. III standing is built on a single basic idea—the idea of separation of powers.'' In the light of this overriding and time-honored concern about keeping the Judiciary's power within its proper constitutional sphere,[3] we must put

---

3. It is settled that Congress cannot erase Article III's standing requirements by statutorily granting the right to sue to a plaintiff who would not otherwise have standing. *Gladstone, Realtors v. Village of Bellwood* (1979). We acknowledge, though, that Congress' decision to grant a particular plaintiff the right to challenge an act's constitutionality eliminates any prudential standing limitations and significantly lessens the risk of unwanted conflict with the

aside the natural urge to proceed directly to the merits of this important dispute and to "settle" it for the sake of convenience and efficiency. Instead, we must carefully inquire as to whether appellees have met their burden of establishing that their claimed injury is personal, particularized, concrete, and otherwise judicially cognizable.

We have never had occasion to rule on the question of legislative standing presented here. In *Powell v. McCormack* (1969) [Casebook, § 1–2.4], we held that a Member of Congress' constitutional challenge to his exclusion from the House of Representatives (and his consequent loss of salary) presented an Article III case or controversy. But *Powell* does not help appellees. First, appellees have not been singled out for specially unfavorable treatment as opposed to other Members of their respective bodies. Their claim is that the Act causes a type of institutional injury (the diminution of legislative power), which necessarily damages all Members of Congress and both Houses of Congress equally. See n. 7, *infra*. Second, appellees do not claim that they have been deprived of something to which they *personally* are entitled—such as their seats as Members of Congress after their constituents had elected *them*. Rather, appellees' claim of standing is based on a loss of political power, not loss of any private right, which would make the injury more concrete. Unlike the injury claimed by Congressman Adam Clayton Powell, the injury claimed by the Members of Congress here is not claimed in any private capacity but solely because they are Members of Congress. If one of the Members were to retire tomorrow, he would no longer have a claim; the claim would be possessed by his successor instead. The claimed injury thus runs (in a sense) with the Member's seat, a seat which the Member holds (it may quite arguably be said) as trustee for his constituents, not as a prerogative of personal power.

The one case in which we have upheld standing for legislators (albeit *state* legislators) claiming an institutional injury is *Coleman v. Miller* (1939) [Casebook, § 1–2.4]. Appellees, relying heavily on this case, claim that they, like the state legislators in *Coleman*, "have a plain, direct and adequate interest in maintaining the effectiveness of their votes," sufficient to establish standing. In *Coleman*, 20 of Kansas' 40 State Senators voted not to ratify the proposed "Child Labor Amendment" to the Federal Constitution. With the vote deadlocked 20–20, the amendment ordinarily would not have been ratified. However, the State's Lieutenant Governor, the presiding officer of the State Senate, cast a deciding vote in favor of the amendment, and it was deemed ratified (after the State House of Representatives voted to ratify it). The 20 State Senators who had voted against the amendment, joined by a 21st State Senator and three State House Members, filed an action in the Kansas Supreme Court seeking a writ of mandamus that would compel the appropriate state officials to recognize that the legislature had not in fact ratified the amendment. That court held that the members of the legislature had

Legislative Branch when that plaintiff   brings suit.

standing to bring their mandamus action, but ruled against them on the merits.

This Court affirmed. By a vote of 5–4, we held that the members of the legislature had standing.[5] In explaining our holding, we repeatedly emphasized that if these legislators (who were suing as a bloc) were correct on the merits, then their votes not to ratify the amendment were deprived of all validity. . . .

It should be equally obvious that appellees' claim does not fall within our holding in *Coleman*, as thus understood. They have not alleged that they voted for a specific bill, that there were sufficient votes to pass the bill, and that the bill was nonetheless deemed defeated. In the vote on the Line Item Veto Act, their votes were given full effect. They simply lost that vote.[7] Nor can they allege that the Act will nullify their votes in the future in the same way that the votes of the *Coleman* legislators had been nullified. In the future, a majority of Senators and Congressman can pass or reject appropriations bills; the Act has no effect on this process. In addition, a majority of Senators and Congressman can vote to repeal the Act, or to exempt a given appropriations bill (or a given provision in an appropriations bill) from the Act; again, the Act has no effect on this process. *Coleman* thus provides little meaningful precedent for appellees' argument.[8]

Nevertheless, appellees rely heavily on our statement in *Coleman* that the Kansas senators had "a plain, direct, and adequate interest in

---

5. Chief Justice Hughes wrote an opinion styled "the opinion of the Court." Four Justices concurred in the judgment, partially on the ground that the legislators lacked standing. See (opinion of Black, J., joined by Roberts, Frankfurter, and Douglas, JJ.); (opinion of Frankfurter, J., joined by Roberts, Black, and Douglas, JJ.). Two justices dissented on the merits. See (opinion of Butler, J., joined by McReynolds, J.). Thus, even though there were only two Justices who joined Chief Justice Hughes's opinion on the merits, it is apparent that the two dissenting Justices joined his opinion as to the standing discussion. Otherwise, Justice Frankfurter's opinion denying standing would have been the controlling opinion.

It is obvious, then, that our holding in *Coleman* stands for the proposition that legislators whose votes would have been sufficient to defeat (or enact) a specific legislative act have standing to sue if that legislative action goes into effect (or does not go into effect), on the ground that their votes have been completely nullified.

7. Just as appellees cannot show that their vote was denied or nullified as in *Coleman* (in the sense that a bill they voted for would have become law if their vote had not been stripped of its validity), so are they unable to show that their vote was denied or nullified in a discriminatory manner (in

the sense that their vote was denied its full validity in relation to the votes of their colleagues). Thus, the various hypotheticals offered by appellees in their briefs and discussed during oral argument have no applicability to this case. See Reply Brief for Appellees 6 (positing hypothetical law in which "first-term Members were not allowed to vote on appropriations bills," or in which "*every* Member was disqualified on grounds of partiality from voting on major federal projects in his or her own district").

8. Since we hold that *Coleman* may be distinguished from the instant case on this ground, we need not decide whether *Coleman* may also be distinguished in other ways. For instance, appellants have argued that *Coleman* has no applicability to a similar suit brought in federal court, since that decision depended on the fact that the Kansas Supreme Court "treated" the senators' interest in their votes "as a basis for entertaining and deciding the federal questions." They have also argued that *Coleman* has no applicability to a similar suit brought by federal legislators, since the separation-of-powers concerns present in such a suit were not present in *Coleman,* and since any federalism concerns were eliminated by the Kansas Supreme Court's decision to take jurisdiction over the case.

maintaining the effectiveness of their votes." Appellees claim that this statement applies to them because their votes on future appropriations bills (assuming a majority of Congress does not decide to exempt those bills from the Act) will be less "effective" than before, and that the "meaning" and "integrity" of their vote has changed. The argument goes as follows. Before the Act, Members of Congress could be sure that when they voted for, and Congress passed, an appropriations bill that included funds for Project X, one of two things would happen: (i) the bill would become law and all of the projects listed in the bill would go into effect, or (ii) the bill would not become law and none of the projects listed in the bill would go into effect. Either way, a vote for the appropriations bill meant a vote for a package of projects that were inextricably linked. After the Act, however, a vote for an appropriations bill that includes Project X means something different. Now, in addition to the two possibilities listed above, there is a third option: the bill will become law and then the President will "cancel" Project X.

Even taking appellees at their word about the change in the "meaning" and "effectiveness" of their vote for appropriations bills which are subject to the Act, we think their argument pulls *Coleman* too far from its moorings. Appellees' use of the word "effectiveness" to link their argument to *Coleman* stretches the word far beyond the sense in which the *Coleman* opinion used it. There is a vast difference between the level of vote nullification at issue in *Coleman* and the abstract dilution of institutional legislative power that is alleged here. To uphold standing here would require a drastic extension of *Coleman*. We are unwilling to take that step. . . .

In sum, appellees have alleged no injury to themselves as individuals (contra *Powell*), the institutional injury they allege is wholly abstract and widely dispersed (contra *Coleman*), and their attempt to litigate this dispute at this time and in this form is contrary to historical experience. We attach some importance to the fact that appellees have not been authorized to represent their respective Houses of Congress in this action, and indeed both Houses actively oppose their suit. We also note that our conclusion neither deprives Members of Congress of an adequate remedy (since they may repeal the Act or exempt appropriations bills from its reach), nor forecloses the Act from constitutional challenge (by someone who suffers judicially cognizable injury as a result of the Act). Whether the case would be different if any of these circumstances were different we need not now decide.

We therefore hold that these individual members of Congress do not have a sufficient "personal stake" in this dispute and have not alleged a sufficiently concrete injury to have established Article III standing.[11] The judgment of the District Court is vacated, and the case is remanded with instructions to dismiss the complaint for lack of jurisdiction.

---

11. In addition, it is far from clear that this injury is "fairly traceable" to appellants, as our precedents require, since the alleged cause of appellees's injury is not appellants' exercise of legislative power but the actions of their own colleagues in Congress in passing the Act.

It is so ordered.

Justice Souter, concurring in the judgment, with whom Justice Ginsburg joins, concurring.

... Although the contest here is not formally between the political branches (since Congress passed the bill augmenting Presidential power and the President signed it), it is in substance an interbranch controversy about calibrating the legislative and executive powers, as well as an intrabranch dispute between segments of Congress itself. Intervention in such a controversy would risk damaging the public confidence that is vital to the functioning of the Judicial Branch, by embroiling the federal courts in a power contest nearly at the height of its political tension.

While it is true that a suit challenging the constitutionality of this Act brought by a party from outside the Federal Government would also involve the Court in resolving the dispute over the allocation of power between the political branches, it would expose the Judicial Branch to a lesser risk. Deciding a suit to vindicate an interest outside the Government raises no specter of judicial readiness to enlist on one side of a political tug-of-war, since "the propriety of such action by a federal court has been recognized since *Marbury v. Madison* (1803)." And just as the presence of a party beyond the Government places the Judiciary at some remove from the political forces, the need to await injury to such a plaintiff allows the courts some greater separation in the time between the political resolution and the judicial review....

Justice Stevens, dissenting.

[B]ecause the impairment of that constitutional right has an immediate impact on their official powers, in my judgment [the Members of Congress] need not wait until after the President has exercised his cancellation authority to bring suit. Finally, the same reason that the respondents have standing provides a sufficient basis for concluding that the statute is unconstitutional....

Justice Breyer, dissenting.

[T]he dispute before us, when compared to *Coleman*, presents a much stronger claim, not a weaker claim, for constitutional justiciability. The lawmakers in *Coleman* complained of a lawmaking procedure that, at worst, improperly counted Kansas as having ratified one proposed constitutional amendment, which had been ratified by only 5 other States, and rejected by 26, making it unlikely that it would ever become law. The lawmakers in this case complain of a lawmaking procedure that threatens the validity of many laws (for example, all appropriations laws) that Congress regularly and frequently enacts.... I do not believe that the Court can find this case nonjusticiable without overruling *Coleman*. [But] because the majority has decided that this dispute is not now justiciable and has expressed no view on the merits of the appeal, I shall not discuss the merits either, but reserve them for future argument.

Notes

In *Clinton v. City of New York*, 524 U.S. 417 118 S.Ct. 2091, 141 L.Ed.2d 393 (1998), excerpted in § 5–9, the City of New York and others sued President Clinton, et al., claiming that they had been injured by his decision to "cancel" a portion of a federal statute that waived the Federal Government's right to recoup certain funds from New York. Separately, owners of certain food refiners and processors sued, claiming that they had been injured by President Clinton's "cancellation" of a provision of a law that allowed them to defer recognition of capital gains. The Court held that these appellees had standing. President Clinton's exercise of his cancellation authority removed any issue about the ripeness of the dispute, and the parties alleged a "personal stake" in an actual injury rather than an "institutional injury" that was "abstract and widely dispersed." Stevens, J., for the Court, then held that the Line Item Veto Act violated the Presentment Clause. Scalia, joined by O'Connor, and by Breyer, J., in part, would have denied standing to some of the appellees and would have upheld the Line Item Veto statute as to those who had standing. Breyer, J., joined by O'Connor & Scalia, JJ. in part, found standing but would have upheld the constitutionality of the Line Item Veto.

12–4.4 Prudential Limitations

WARTH v. SELDIN
422 U.S. 490, 95 S.Ct. 2197, 45 L.Ed.2d 343 (1975).

MR. JUSTICE POWELL delivered the opinion of the Court.

Petitioners, various organizations and individuals resident in the Rochester, N.Y., metropolitan area, brought this action in the District Court for the Western District of New York against the town of Penfield, an incorporated municipality adjacent to Rochester, and against members of Penfield's Zoning, Planning, and Town Boards. Petitioners claimed that the town's zoning ordinance, by its terms and as enforced by the defendant board members, respondents here, effectively excluded persons of low and moderate income from living in the town, in contravention of petitioners' First, Ninth, and Fourteenth Amendment rights and in violation of 42 U.S.C.A. §§ 1981, 1982, and 1983.... The Court of Appeals [held] that none of the plaintiffs, and neither Housing Council nor Home Builders Association, had standing to prosecute the action. [W]e affirm.

I. ... Petitioners' complaint alleged that Penfield's zoning ordinance, adopted in 1962, has the purpose and effect of excluding persons of low and moderate income from residing in the town. In particular, the ordinance allocates 98% of the town's vacant land to single-family detached housing, and allegedly by imposing unreasonable requirements relating to lot size, setback, floor area, and habitable space, the ordinance increases the cost of single-family detached housing beyond the means of persons of low and moderate income. Moreover, according to petitioners, only 0.3% of the land available for residential construction is allocated to multifamily structures (apartments, townhouses, and the like), and even on this limited space, housing for low-and moderate-income persons is not economically feasible because of low density and other requirements.... To relieve these various harms, petitioners asked the District Court to declare the Penfield ordinance unconstitutional, to enjoin the defendants from enforcing the ordinance, to order the defendants to enact and administer a new ordinance designed to alleviate the effects of their past actions, and to award $750,000 in actual and exemplary damages....

II. We address first the principles of standing relevant to the claims asserted by the several categories of petitioners in this case. In essence the question of standing is whether the litigant is entitled to have the court decide the merits of the dispute or of particular issues. This inquiry involves both constitutional limitations on federal-court jurisdiction and prudential limitations on its exercise. In both dimensions it is founded in concern about the proper—and properly limited—role of the courts in a democratic society....

Although standing in no way depends on the merits of the plaintiff's contention that particular conduct is illegal, it often turns on the nature and source of the claim asserted. [Thus] Congress may grant an express right of action to persons who otherwise would be barred by prudential standing rules. Of course, Art. III's requirement remains: the plaintiff still must allege a distinct and palpable injury to himself, even if it is an injury shared by a large class of other possible litigants. But so long as this requirement is satisfied, persons to whom Congress has granted a right of action, either expressly or by clear implication, may have standing to seek relief on the basis of the legal rights and interests of others, and, indeed, may invoke the general public interest in support of their claim....

III. With these general considerations in mind, we turn first to the claims of petitioners Ortiz, Reyes, Sinkler, and Broadnax, each of whom asserts standing as a person of low or moderate income and, coincidentally, as a member of a minority racial or ethnic group. We must assume, taking the allegations of the complaint as true, that Penfield's zoning ordinance and the pattern of enforcement by respondent officials have had the purpose and effect of excluding persons of low and moderate income, many of whom are members of racial or ethnic minority groups. We also assume, for purposes here, that such intentional exclusionary practices, if proved in a proper case, would be adjudged violative of the constitutional and statutory rights of the persons excluded....

In their complaint, petitioners Ortiz, Reyes, Sinkler, and Broadnax alleged in conclusory terms that they are among the persons excluded by respondents' actions. None of them has ever resided in Penfield; each claims at least implicitly that he desires, or has desired, to do so. Each asserts, moreover, that he made some effort, at some time, to locate housing in Penfield that was at once within his means and adequate for his family's needs. Each claims that his efforts proved fruitless. We may assume, as petitioners allege, that respondents' actions have contributed, perhaps substantially, to the cost of housing in Penfield. But there remains the question whether petitioners' inability to locate suitable housing in Penfield reasonably can be said to have resulted, in any concretely demonstrable way, from respondents' alleged constitutional and statutory infractions. Petitioners must allege facts from which it reasonably could be inferred that, absent the respondents' restrictive zoning practices, there is a substantial probability that they would have been able to purchase or lease in Penfield and that, if the court affords the relief requested, the asserted inability of petitioners will be removed.

We find the record devoid of the necessary allegations. As the Court of Appeals noted, none of these petitioners has a present interest in any Penfield property; none is himself subject to the ordinance's strictures; and none has ever been denied a variance or permit by respondent officials. Instead, petitioners claim that respondents' enforcement of the ordinance against third parties—developers, builders, and the like—has had the consequence of precluding the construction of housing suitable to their needs at prices they might be able to afford. The fact that the harm to petitioners may have resulted indirectly does not in itself preclude standing. When a governmental prohibition or restriction imposed on one party causes specific harm to a third party, harm that a constitutional provision or statute was intended to prevent, the indirectness of the injury does not necessarily deprive the person harmed of standing to vindicate his rights. But it may make it substantially more difficult to meet the minimum requirement of Art. III: to establish that, in fact, the asserted injury was the consequence of the defendants' actions, or that prospective relief will remove the harm.

Here, by their own admission, realization of petitioners' desire to live in Penfield always has depended on the efforts and willingness of third parties to build low-and moderate-cost housing. The record specifically refers to only two such efforts ... But the record is devoid of any indication that these projects, or other like projects, would have satisfied petitioners' needs at prices they could afford, or that, were the court to remove the obstructions attributable to respondents, such relief would benefit petitioners. Indeed, petitioners' descriptions of their individual financial situations and housing needs suggest precisely the contrary— that their inability to reside in Penfield is the consequence of the economics of the area housing market, rather than of respondents' assertedly illegal acts. In short, the facts alleged fail to support an actionable causal relationship between Penfield's zoning practices and petitioners' asserted injury....

We hold only that a plaintiff who seeks to challenge exclusionary zoning practices must allege specific, concrete facts demonstrating that the challenged practices harm *him,* and that he personally would benefit in a tangible way from the court's intervention.[18] ...

---

18. This is not to say that the plaintiff who challenges a zoning ordinance or zoning practices must have a present contrac- tual interest in a particular project. A par- ticularized personal interest may be shown in various ways, which we need not under-

IV. The petitioners who assert standing on the basis of their status as taxpayers of the city of Rochester present a different set of problems.... Their argument, in brief, is that Penfield's persistent refusal to allow or to facilitate construction of low-and moderate-cost housing forces the city of Rochester to provide more such housing than it otherwise would do; that to provide such housing, Rochester must allow certain tax abatements; and that as the amount of tax-abated property increases, Rochester taxpayers are forced to assume an increased tax burden in order to finance essential public services.

"Of course, pleadings must be something more than an ingenious academic exercise in the conceivable." *United States v. SCRAP*. We think the complaint of the taxpayer-petitioners is little more than such an exercise. Apart from the conjectural nature of the asserted injury, the line of causation between Penfield's actions and such injury is not apparent from the complaint. Whatever may occur in Penfield, the injury complained of—increases in taxation—results only from decisions made by the appropriate Rochester authorities, who are not parties to this case.

But even if we assume that the taxpayer-petitioners could establish that Penfield's zoning practices harm them, their complaint nonetheless was properly dismissed. Petitioners do not, even if they could, assert any personal right under the Constitution or any statute to be free of action by a neighboring municipality that may have some incidental adverse effect on Rochester. On the contrary, the only basis of the taxpayer-petitioners' claim is that Penfield's zoning ordinance and practices violate the constitutional and statutory rights of third parties, namely, persons of low and moderate income who are said to be excluded from Penfield. In short the claim of these petitioners falls squarely within the prudential standing rule that normally bars litigants from asserting the rights or legal interests of others in order to obtain relief from injury to themselves. As we have observed above, this rule of judicial self-governance is subject to exceptions, the most prominent of which is that Congress may remove it by statute. Here, however, no statute expressly or by clear implication grants a right of action, and thus standing to seek relief, to persons in petitioners' position. In several cases, this Court has allowed standing to litigate the rights of third parties when enforcement of the challenged restriction against the litigant would result indirectly in the violation of third parties' rights. But the taxpayer-petitioners are not themselves subject to Penfield's zoning practices. Nor do they allege that the challenged zoning ordinance and practices preclude or otherwise adversely affect a relationship existing between them and the persons whose rights assertedly are violated. No relationship, other than an incidental congruity of interest, is alleged to exist between the Rochester

take to identify in the abstract. But usually the initial focus should be on a particular project. We also note that zoning laws and their provisions, long considered essential to effective urban planning, are peculiarly within the province of state and local legislative authorities. They are, of course, subject to judicial review in a proper case. But citizens dissatisfied with provisions of such laws need not overlook the availability of the normal democratic process.

taxpayers and persons who have been precluded from living in Penfield. Nor do the taxpayer-petitioners show that their prosecution of the suit is necessary to insure protection of the rights asserted, as there is no indication that persons who in fact have been excluded from Penfield are disabled from asserting their own right in a proper case. In sum, we discern no justification for recognizing in the Rochester taxpayers a right of action on the asserted claim.

V. We turn next to the standing problems presented by the petitioner associations—Metro–Act of Rochester, Inc., one of the original plaintiffs; Housing Council in the Monroe County Area, Inc., which the original plaintiffs sought to join as a party-plaintiff; and Rochester Home Builders Association, Inc., which moved in the District Court for leave to intervene as plaintiff. There is no question that an association may have standing in its own right to seek judicial relief from injury to itself and to vindicate whatever rights and immunities the association itself may enjoy. Moreover, in attempting to secure relief from injury to itself the association may assert the rights of its members, at least so long as the challenged infractions adversely affect its members' associational ties. With the limited exception of Metro–Act, however, none of the associational petitioners here has asserted injury to itself.

Even in the absence of injury to itself, an association may have standing solely as the representative of its members. The possibility of such representational standing, however, does not eliminate or attenuate the constitutional requirement of a case or controversy. The association must allege that its members, or any one of them, are suffering immediate or threatened injury as a result of the challenged action of the sort that would make out a justiciable case had the members themselves brought suit. So long as this can be established, and so long as the nature of the claim and of the relief sought does not make the individual participation of each injured party indispensable to proper resolution of the cause, the association may be an appropriate representative of its members, entitled to invoke the court's jurisdiction.

A

Petitioner Metro–Act's claims to standing on its own behalf as a Rochester taxpayer, and on behalf of its members who are Rochester taxpayers or persons of low or moderate income, are precluded by our holdings in Parts III and IV, supra, as to the individual petitioners, and require no further discussion. Metro–Act also alleges, however, that 9% of its membership is composed of present residents of Penfield. It claims that, as a result of the persistent pattern of exclusionary zoning practiced by respondents and the consequent exclusion of persons of low and moderate income, those of its members who are Penfield residents are deprived of the benefits of living in a racially and ethnically integrated community. Referring to our decision in *Trafficante v. Metropolitan Life Ins. Co.,* 409 U.S. 205, 93 S.Ct. 364, 34 L.Ed.2d 415 (1972), Metro–Act argues that such deprivation is a sufficiently palpable injury to satisfy the Art. III case-or-controversy requirement, and that it has standing as the representative of its members to seek redress.

We agree with the Court of Appeals that *Trafficante* is not controlling here. In that case, two residents of an apartment complex alleged that the owner had discriminated against rental applicants on the basis of race, in violation of § 804 of the Civil Rights Act of 1968. They claimed that, as a result of such discrimination, "they had been injured in that (1) they had lost the social benefits of living in an integrated community; (2) they had missed business and professional advantages which would have accrued if they had lived with members of minority groups; (3) they had suffered embarrassment and economic damage in social, business, and professional activities from being 'stigmatized' as residents of a 'white ghetto.' "In light of the clear congressional purpose in enacting the 1968 Act, and the broad definition of "person aggrieved" in § 810(a), we held that petitioners, as "person[s] who claim[ed] to have been injured by a discriminatory housing practice," had standing to litigate violations of the Act. We concluded that Congress had given residents of housing facilities covered by the statute an actionable right to be free from the adverse consequences to them of racially discriminatory practices directed at and immediately harmful to others.

Metro–Act does not assert on behalf of its members any right of action under the 1968 Civil Rights Act, nor can the complaint fairly be read to make out any such claim. In this, we think, lies the critical distinction between *Trafficante* and the situation here. . . .

Even if we assume, *arguendo,* that apart from any statutorily created right the asserted harm to Metro–Act's Penfield members is sufficiently direct and personal to satisfy the case-or-controversy requirement of Art. III, prudential considerations strongly counsel against according them or Metro–Act standing to prosecute this action. We do not understand Metro–Act to argue that Penfield residents themselves have been denied any constitutional rights, affording them a cause of action under 42 U.S.C.A. § 1983. Instead, their complaint is that they have been harmed indirectly by the exclusion of others. This is an attempt to raise putative rights of third parties, and none of the exceptions that allow such claims is present here. In these circumstances, we conclude that it is inappropriate to allow Metro–Act to invoke the judicial process.

B

Petitioner Home Builders, in its intervenor-complaint, asserted standing to represent its member firms engaged in the development and construction of residential housing in the Rochester area, including Penfield. Home Builders alleged that the Penfield zoning restrictions, together with refusals by the town officials to grant variances and permits for the construction of low-and moderate-cost housing, had deprived some of its members of "substantial business opportunities and profits." Home Builders claimed damages of $750,000 and also joined in the original plaintiffs' prayer for declaratory and injunctive relief.

As noted above, to justify any relief the association must show that it has suffered harm, or that one or more of its members are injured. E.g., *Sierra Club v. Morton,* [§ 12–4.1, *supra*]. But, apart from this, whether an association has standing to invoke the court's remedial powers on behalf of its members depends in substantial measure on the nature of the relief sought. If in a proper case the association seeks a declaration, injunction, or some other form of prospective relief, it can reasonably be supposed that the remedy, if granted, will inure to the benefit of those members of the association actually injured. Indeed, in all cases in which we have expressly recognized standing in associations to represent their members, the relief sought has been of this kind.

The present case, however, differs significantly as here an association seeks relief in damages for alleged injuries to its members. Home Builders alleges no monetary injury to itself, nor any assignment of the damages claims of its members. No award therefore can be made to the association as such. Moreover, in the circumstances of this case, the damages claims are not common to the entire membership, nor shared by all in equal degree. To the contrary, whatever injury may have been suffered is peculiar to the individual member concerned, and both the fact and extent of injury would require individualized proof. Thus, to obtain relief in damages, each member of Home Builders who claims injury as a result of respondents' practices must be a party to the suit, and Home Builders has no standing to claim damages on his behalf.

Home Builders' prayer for prospective relief fails for a different reason. It can have standing as the representative of its members only if it has alleged facts sufficient to make out a case or controversy had the members themselves brought suit. No such allegations were made. The complaint refers to no specific project of any of its members that is currently precluded either by the ordinance or by respondents' action in enforcing it . . . .

A like problem is presented with respect to petitioner Housing Council. The affidavit accompanying the motion to join it as plaintiff states that the Council includes in its membership "at least seventeen" groups that have been, are, or will be involved in the development of low-and moderate-cost housing. But, with one exception, the complaint does not suggest that any of these groups has focused its efforts on Penfield or has any specific plan to do so. Again with the same exception, neither the complaint nor any materials of record indicate that any member of Housing Council has taken any step toward building housing in Penfield, or has had dealings of any nature with respondents. The exception is the Penfield Better Homes Corp. As we have observed above, it applied to respondents in late 1969 for a zoning variance to allow construction of a housing project designed for persons of moderate income. . . . It is therefore possible that in 1969, or within a reasonable time thereafter, Better Homes itself and possibly Housing Council as its representative would have had standing to seek review of respondents' action. The complaint, however, does not allege that the Penfield Better Homes project remained viable in 1972 when this complaint was filed, or that respondents' actions continued to block a then-current construction project. In short, neither the complaint nor the record supplies any basis from which to infer that the controversy between respondents and Better Homes, however vigorous it may once have been, remained a live, concrete dispute when this complaint was filed.

VI. ... We agree with the District Court and the Court of Appeals that none of the petitioners here has met this threshold requirement [of standing]. Accordingly, the judgment of the Court of Appeals is

Affirmed.

Mr. Justice Douglas, dissenting.

[T]he Court reads the complaint and the record with antagonistic eyes.... I would let the case go to trial and have all the facts brought out. Indeed, it would be better practice to decide the question of standing only when the merits have been developed. I would reverse the Court of Appeals.

Mr. Justice Brennan, with whom Mr. Justice White and Mr. Justice Marshall join, dissenting.

... While the Court gives lip service to the principle, oft repeated in recent years, that "standing in no way depends on the merits of the plaintiff's contention that particular conduct is illegal," in fact the opinion, which tosses out of court almost every conceivable kind of plaintiff who could be injured by the activity claimed to be unconstitutional, can be explained only by an indefensible hostility to the claim on the merits. I can appreciate the Court's reluctance to adjudicate the complex and difficult legal questions involved in determining the constitutionality of practices which assertedly limit residence in a particular municipality to those who are white and relatively well off, and I also understand that the merits of this case could involve grave sociological and political ramifications. But courts cannot refuse to hear a case on the merits merely because they would prefer not to. [T]he very fact that, as the Court stresses, these petitioners' claim rests in part upon proving the intentions and capabilities of third parties to build in Penfield suitable housing which they can afford ... makes it particularly inappropriate to assume that these petitioners' lack of specificity reflects a fatal weakness in their theory of causation.... This Court has not required such unachievable specificity in standing cases in the past, see *SCRAP,* supra....

Two of the petitioners are organizations among whose members are building concerns.... In particular, one member, Penfield Better Homes, "*is* and has been actively attempting to develop moderate income housing in ... Penfield" (emphasis supplied), [App.], at 174, but has been unable to secure the necessary approvals. Ibid.

The Court finds that these two organizations lack standing to seek prospective relief for basically the same reasons: none of their members is, as far as the allegations show, *currently* involved in developing a *particular* project. [However] the merits of the exclusion of this or that project is not at the heart of the complaint; the claim is that respondents will not approve *any* project which will provide residences for low-and moderate-income people.

When this sort of pattern-and-practice claim is at the heart of the controversy, allegations of past injury, which members of both of these organizations have clearly made, and of a future intent, if the barriers are cleared, again to develop suitable housing for Penfield, should be more than sufficient....

Notes

1. Does *United States v. SCRAP,* § 12–4.1, survive *Warth?* Does *Warth* survive *Duke Power,* § 12–4.1?

2. Note that in section V(A) of the majority opinion in *Warth,* Justice Powell denied standing to an organization, some of whose members were Penfield residents alleging that Penfield's intentional exclusionary zoning practices denied them their constitutional and statutory rights to reside in a racially integrated Penfield. Powell also wrote the majority opinion in *Gladstone, Realtors v. Village of Bellwood,* 441 U.S. 91, 99 S.Ct. 1601, 60 L.Ed.2d 66 (1979), which found standing on the part of the Village of Bellwood and individual homeowners (one black and four whites) and residents of Bellwood who sued realtors for alleged racial steering, i.e., directing prospective home buyers interested in equivalent properties to different areas according to their race:

> The gist of Bellwood's complaint is that petitioners' racial steering effectively manipulates the housing market in the described area of the Village.... Although the complaints are more conclusory and abbreviated than good pleading would suggest, construed favorably to Bellwood they allege that this conduct is affecting the Village's racial composition.... If, as alleged, petitioners' sales practices actually have begun to rob Bellwood of its racial balance and stability, the Village has standing to challenge the legality of that conduct. [The] individual respondents [who] actually reside within the target area of Bellwood ... claim that the transformation of their neighborhood from an integrated to a predominantly Negro community is depriving them of "the social and professional benefits of living in an integrated society." [This injury is] sufficient to satisfy the constitutional standing requirement of actual or threatened harm.

The Court also held that the respondents had standing under § 812 of Title VIII of the Civil Rights Act of 1968, which the Court construed to provide for standing as broadly as Article III permits.[1]

1. *Havens Realty Corp. v. Coleman,* 455 U.S. 363, 102 S.Ct. 1114, 71 L.Ed.2d 214 (1982)(per Brennan, J.) held that, under this same Act construed in *Bellwood,* "testers" have standing to sue. "Testers" are persons who pose as renters or purchasers for the purposes of gathering information of illegal racial steering. Under *Bellwood* the sole requirement for standing under § 812 is the Article III minima of injury-in-fact: under the federal law a tester has suffered this legal injury if he has been told inaccurate information regarding the sale or rental of a dwelling because of his race. Powell, J., joined opinion of the Court and wrote a separate concurring opinion.

Is Powell's opinion in *Warth* consistent with Powell's opinion in *Bellwood?*

3.   In section III of *Warth,* Powell denied standing to racial minorities who were nonresidents of Penfield and who had alleged that Penfield's zoning practices excluded members of racial minorities. In *Village of Bellwood,* Powell said: "Although we intimate no view as to whether persons residing outside of the target neighborhood have standing to sue under § 812 of Title VIII, we do not foreclose consideration of this question if, on remand, the District Court permits [such persons] to amend their complaints to include allegations of actual harm."

Could Powell, consistent with *Warth,* find standing as to these nonresidents? What facts would they have to allege to show actual harm, economic or otherwise?

4.   In section V(B) of *Warth,* Powell denied standing to an organization representing builders of low and moderate cost housing who claimed loss of profits because they were not able to build in Penfield. Cf. *Village of Arlington Heights v. Metropolitan Housing Development Corp.,* 429 U.S. 252, 97 S.Ct. 555, 50 L.Ed.2d 450 (1977). Powell again wrote the majority opinion. In that case a nonprofit developer contracted to purchase a tract of land in the Village to build racially integrated low and moderate cost housing. The contract was contingent upon obtaining a rezoning and receiving federal assistance. After the Village refused to rezone, the developer sued, claiming a violation of the equal protection clause and the federal Fair Housing Act. The Court found standing for both the developer (MHDC) and a black who probably would move into the housing project if it were completed. Powell said:

> Here there can be little doubt that MHDC meets the constitutional standing requirements. The challenged action of the petitioners stands as an absolute barrier to constructing the housing that MHDC contracted to place on the Viatorian site. If MHDC secures the injunctive relief it seeks, that barrier will be removed. An injunction would not, of course, guarantee that Lincoln Green will be built. MHDC would still have to secure financing, qualify for federal subsidies, and carry through with construction. But all housing developments are subject to some extent to similar uncertainties. When a project is as detailed and specific as Lincoln Green, a court is not required to engage in undue speculation as a predicate for finding that the plaintiff has the requisite personal stake in the controversy. MHDC has shown injury to itself that is "likely to be redressed by a favorable decision."

Is Powell's refusal to speculate in *Warth* consistent with his refusal to engage in "undue speculation" in *Arlington Heights?*

International Union, United Automobile, Aerospace, and Agricultural Implement Workers of America v. Brock, 477 U.S. 274, 106 S.Ct. 2523, 91 L.Ed.2d 228 (1986) upheld the standing of a union to sue on behalf of its members to challenge the Secretary of Labor's interpretation of a federal law's unemployment eligibility requirements. The union met the three part test to determine if an association has standing. First, there were some union members who would have standing to sue in their own right; second, the interests that the union sought to protect were germane to the organization's purpose; and third, neither the claim asserted nor the relief requested required the participation of individual members in the lawsuit. Unlike *Warth,* where the association could not seek damages for the profits and losses of its members, because that would require individualized proof, the association's suit raises a "pure question" of law: whether the Secretary properly interpreted certain eligibility provisions. The relief requested was simply an order to the Secretary to notify all state agencies of the proper construction of the Act, and to direct those agencies to apply the proper eligibility standards. Four members of the Court dissented, but only one of them (Justice Powell) on the standing issue. Powell thought that there was a danger of inadequate representation;, and would not find "—on the basis of the record before us—that the UAW had standing based on an amorphous and unenumerated group of injured parties."

5. *Lujan v. Defenders of Wildlife,* 504 U.S. 555, 112 S.Ct. 2130, 119 L.Ed.2d 351 (1992) held that respondents had no standing to challenge a rule promulgated by the Secretary of Interior that interpreted the Endangered Species Act to apply only to actions that federal agencies take in the United States or on the high seas. The Respondents wanted the Secretary to apply the law to any action funded by federal agencies, even actions in foreign nations. Scalia, J., announced the judgment of the Court and delivered the opinion of the Court except as to part III–B, which only Rehnquist, C.J. & White & Thomas, JJ., joined.

Assuming that activities funded abroad threatened certain species, there still was no "injury in fact" merely because two members of the plaintiff filed affidavits stating that they had traveled to Egypt in the past, before a particular project began, in order to observe the endangered Nile crocodile. That does not show the need for present injunctive relief. These two people also stated that they intend to return some time in the future, where they will presumably be deprived of the opportunity to observe certain species, but that is "simply not enough," because there is no "description of concrete plans." The Court also rejected, as "beyond all reason," the plaintiffs' argument that "anyone who goes to see Asian elephants in the Bronx Zoo" has standing to challenge a development project in Sri Lanka funded in part by any federal agency.

In Part III–B, the plurality opinion, Scalia, J. argued that the plaintiffs did not demonstrate that a victory in this case would redress plaintiffs' concerns because "the agencies funding the projects are not parties to the case." Also, federal agencies usually provide only a small portion of the funding for foreign projects, and plaintiffs did not show that withdrawing such funding would cause the projects to be suspended or cause less harm to endangered species.

In Part IV the Court held that a "citizen-suit" provision in the Endangered Species Act did not provide standing. The injury-in-fact requirement is not satisfied "by congressional conferral upon all persons of an abstract, self-contained, noninstrumental 'right' to have the Executive observe the procedures required by law." For example, Congress did not provide a "cash bounty for the victorious plaintiff."

If a plaintiff raises only a general grievance about government and seeks relief that provides no more tangible benefit to him than the public at large, that "does not state an Article III case or controversy." Congress does not have the power to "convert the undifferentiated public interest in executive officers' compliance with the law into an 'individual right'" vindicated in the courts. This principle does not contradict the principle in *Warth v. Sedlin* that the injury may exist solely by virtue of "statutes creating legal rights, the invasion of which creates standing," because the statutory broadening of "the categories of injury that may be alleged in support of standing is a different matter from abandoning the requirement that the party seeking review must himself have suffered [a concrete] injury."

Compare *Federal Election Commission v. Akins,* 524 U.S. 11, 118 S.Ct. 1777, 141 L.Ed.2d 10 (1998). The Federal Election Campaign Act of 1971 ("FECA") imposes extensive record keeping and disclosure requirements on "political committees," defined in the statute as "any committee" or "other group of persons" receiving more in $1000 in contributions or making more than $1000 in expenditures in a given year "for the purpose of influencing any election for Federal office." Respondents [voters with views often opposed to those of the American Israel Public Affairs Committee ("AIPAC")] petitioned the Federal Election Commission ("FEC") to treat the AIPAC as a "political committee." Breyer, J., for the Court (6 to 3) ruled that the Respondent-voters have standing to challenge the FEC's decision not to bring an enforcement action against the AIPAC. The Court then remanded so that the lower court could determine if the AIPAC is a "political committee" in light of the new FEC regulations.

The respondents have standing because, first, the FECA specifically provides that "[a]ny person" who believes that the FECA has been violated may file a complaint with the FEC, and "[a]ny party aggrieved" by an FEC order dismissing such a complaint may seek district court review of the dismissal. Use of the term "aggrieved" indicates congressional intent "to cast the standing net broadly—beyond the common-law interests and substantive statutory rights upon which 'prudential' standing traditionally rested." Respondents' claim (their failure to obtain information that would have had to be disclosed if the FEC treated the AIPAC as a political committee) is injury that FECA seeks to redress. It is an "injury in fact," because, although it is widely shared, it is concrete and particular. The "informational injury" is "directly related to voting, the most basic of political rights" and is "fairly traceable" to the FEC decision to which the respondents complain. The courts can "redress" that injury, even though the FEC might then exercise its discretionary powers to reach the same result (*i.e.,* nonenforcement) for a different reason. While an agency's decision not to undertake an enforcement action is usually not subject to judicial review, "[w]e deal here with a statute that explicitly indicates the contrary."

Scalia, J., joined by O'Connor & Thomas, JJ., dissented, arguing, first, that the statute should not be interpreted to allow a private party to bring an executive agency into court to compel its enforcement of the law against a third party. Second, if the statute means that, it is unconstitutional because it transfers from the Executive to the courts the responsibility to "take Care that the Laws be faithfully executed."

6. *Northeastern Florida Chapter of Associated General Contractors of America v. City of Jacksonville*, 508 U.S. 656, 113 S.Ct. 2297, 124 L.Ed.2d 586 (1993). A construction contractors' association sought to invalidate a city ordinance that required the city to set aside a certain percentage of city contracts for minority owned and female owned businesses. The trial court entered summary judgment for the contractors' association, but the Eleventh Circuit vacated the ruling, claiming that the contractor's association lacked standing because it had not demonstrated that, "but for" the challenged ordinance, any member of the association would have bid successfully for a contract. Thomas, J., for the Court reversed and remanded for further proceedings:

> When the government erects a barrier that makes it more difficult for members of one group to obtain a benefit than it is for members of another group, a member of the former group seeking to challenge the barrier need not allege that he would have obtained the benefit but for the barrier in order to establish standing. The "injury in fact" in an equal protection case of this variety is the denial of equal treatment resulting from the imposition of the barrier, not the ultimate inability to obtain the benefit.

Justice Thomas explained that *Warth* did not involve a claim that any discriminatory classification prevented the plaintiffs from *applying* on an equal footing with other contenders for a state benefit. The *Warth* plaintiffs complained that the town officials refused to grant variances and permits. Their grievance "was not that they could not compete equally; it was that they did not win."

The Mexican–American Legal Defense and Education Fund, the American Civil Liberties Union, and other civil rights groups files amicus curiae briefs supporting the petitioner. Are you surprised that they supported the petitioner, which opposed the minority set-asides?

7. Should the Court be more willing to find no standing if the substantive constitutional issues are difficult and any alleged constitutional violation is unclear? Is that any different than the Court's refusal to take a difficult case by denying certiorari? Should the Court feel more (or less) free to find standing when constitutional (as opposed to merely statutory) issues are involved? Consider Justice Rutledge's comments for the Court in *Rescue Army v. Municipal Court of City of Los Angeles*, 331 U.S. 549, 67 S.Ct. 1409, 91 L.Ed. 1666 (1947):

> [T]his Court has followed a policy of strict necessity in disposing of constitutional issues. The earliest exemplifications, too well known for repeating the history here, arose in the Court's refusal to render advisory opinions and in applications of the related jurisdictional policy drawn from the case and controversy limitation. . . .

> The policy, however, has not been limited to jurisdictional determinations. For, in addition, "the Court [has] developed, for its own governance in the cases confessedly within its jurisdiction, a series of rules under which it has avoided passing upon a large part of all the constitutional questions pressed upon it for decision."[31] Thus, as those

---

31. Brandeis, J., with whom Stone, Rob-   erts & Cardozo, JJ., concurred, in *Ashwan-*

rules were listed in support of the statement quoted, constitutional issues affecting legislation will not be determined in friendly, nonadversary proceedings; in advance of the necessity of deciding them; in broader terms than are required by the precise facts to which the ruling is to be applied; if the record presents some other ground upon which the case may be disposed of; at the instance of one who fails to show that he is injured by the statute's operation, or who has availed himself of its benefits; or if a construction of the statute is fairly possible by which the question may be avoided.

Some, if not indeed all, of these rules have found "most varied applications." And every application has been an instance of reluctance, indeed of refusal, to undertake the most important and the most delicate of the Court's functions, notwithstanding conceded jurisdiction, until necessity compels it in the performance of constitutional duty. [I]t is not altogether speculative that a contrary policy, of accelerated decision, might do equal or greater harm for the security of private rights, without attaining any of the benefits of tolerance and harmony for the functioning of the various authorities in our scheme. For premature and relatively abstract decision, which such a policy would be most likely to promote, have their part too in rendering rights uncertain and insecure.

As with the case and controversy limitation, however, the choice has been made long since. Time and experience have given it sanction. They also have verified for both that the choice was wisely made. Any other indeed might have put an end to or seriously impaired the distinctively American institution of judicial review.[38] And on the whole, in spite of inevitable exceptions, the policy has worked not only for finding the appropriate place and function of the judicial institution in our governmental system, but also for the preservation of individual rights.

der v. Tennessee Valley Authority, 297 U.S. 288, concurring opinion at 346, 56 S.Ct. 466, 482, 80 L.Ed. 688.

38. It is not without significance for the policy's validity that the periods when the power has been exercised most readily and broadly have been the ones in which this Court and the institution of judicial review have had their stormiest experiences. See e.g., Brant, Storm Over the Constitution (1936).

Index

References are to Pages

0—314—24652—5